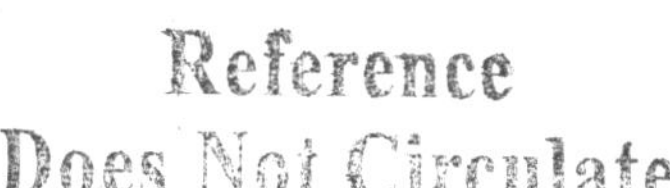

# Oxford Dictionary of National Biography

*Volume 24*

# Oxford Dictionary of National Biography

IN ASSOCIATION WITH

The British Academy

*From the earliest times to the year 2000*

*Edited by*
H. C. G. Matthew
*and*
Brian Harrison

*Volume 24*

Grigg–Hanboys

Great Clarendon Street, Oxford OX2 6DP

Oxford University Press is a department of the University of Oxford.
It furthers the University's objective of excellence in research, scholarship,
and education by publishing worldwide in

Oxford New York

Auckland Bangkok Buenos Aires Cape Town
Chennai Dar es Salaam Delhi Hong Kong Istanbul Karachi
Kolkata Kuala Lumpur Madrid Melbourne Mexico City Mumbai Nairobi
São Paulo Shanghai Taipei Tokyo Toronto

Oxford is a registered trade mark of Oxford University Press
in the UK and in certain other countries

Published in the United States
by Oxford University Press Inc., New York



First published 2004



British Library Cataloguing in Publication Data
Data available

Library of Congress Cataloging in Publication Data
Data available: for details see volume 1, p. iv

ISBN 0-19-861374-1 (this volume)
ISBN 0-19-861411-X (set of sixty volumes)

Text captured by Alliance Phototypesetters, Pondicherry
Illustrations reproduced and archived by
Alliance Graphics Ltd, UK
Typeset in OUP Swift by Interactive Sciences Limited, Gloucester
Printed in Great Britain on acid-free paper by
Butler and Tanner Ltd,
Frome, Somerset

# LIST OF ABBREVIATIONS

## 1 *General abbreviations*

| | |
|---|---|
| AB | bachelor of arts |
| ABC | Australian Broadcasting Corporation |
| ABC TV | ABC Television |
| *act.* | active |
| A$ | Australian dollar |
| AD | *anno domini* |
| AFC | Air Force Cross |
| AIDS | acquired immune deficiency syndrome |
| AK | Alaska |
| AL | Alabama |
| A level | advanced level [examination] |
| ALS | associate of the Linnean Society |
| AM | master of arts |
| AMICE | associate member of the Institution of Civil Engineers |
| ANZAC | Australian and New Zealand Army Corps |
| appx *pl.* appxs | appendix(es) |
| AR | Arkansas |
| ARA | associate of the Royal Academy |
| ARCA | associate of the Royal College of Art |
| ARCM | associate of the Royal College of Music |
| ARCO | associate of the Royal College of Organists |
| ARIBA | associate of the Royal Institute of British Architects |
| ARP | air-raid precautions |
| ARRC | associate of the Royal Red Cross |
| ARSA | associate of the Royal Scottish Academy |
| art. | article / item |
| ASC | Army Service Corps |
| Asch | Austrian Schilling |
| ASDIC | Antisubmarine Detection Investigation Committee |
| ATS | Auxiliary Territorial Service |
| ATV | Associated Television |
| Aug | August |
| AZ | Arizona |
| *b.* | born |
| BA | bachelor of arts |
| BA (Admin.) | bachelor of arts (administration) |
| BAFTA | British Academy of Film and Television Arts |
| BAO | bachelor of arts in obstetrics |
| *bap.* | baptized |
| BBC | British Broadcasting Corporation / Company |
| BC | before Christ |
| BCE | before the common (*or* Christian) era |
| BCE | bachelor of civil engineering |
| BCG | bacillus of Calmette and Guérin [inoculation against tuberculosis] |
| BCh | bachelor of surgery |
| BChir | bachelor of surgery |
| BCL | bachelor of civil law |
| BCnL | bachelor of canon law |
| BCom | bachelor of commerce |
| BD | bachelor of divinity |
| BEd | bachelor of education |
| BEng | bachelor of engineering |
| bk *pl.* bks | book(s) |
| BL | bachelor of law / letters / literature |
| BLitt | bachelor of letters |
| BM | bachelor of medicine |
| BMus | bachelor of music |
| BP | before present |
| BP | British Petroleum |
| Bros. | Brothers |
| BS | (1) bachelor of science; (2) bachelor of surgery; (3) British standard |
| BSc | bachelor of science |
| BSc (Econ.) | bachelor of science (economics) |
| BSc (Eng.) | bachelor of science (engineering) |
| bt | baronet |
| BTh | bachelor of theology |
| *bur.* | buried |
| C. | command [identifier for published parliamentary papers] |
| *c.* | *circa* |
| c. | *capitulum pl. capitula*: chapter(s) |
| CA | California |
| Cantab. | Cantabrigiensis |
| cap. | *capitulum pl. capitula*: chapter(s) |
| CB | companion of the Bath |
| CBE | commander of the Order of the British Empire |
| CBS | Columbia Broadcasting System |
| cc | cubic centimetres |
| C$ | Canadian dollar |
| CD | compact disc |
| Cd | command [identifier for published parliamentary papers] |
| CE | Common (*or* Christian) Era |
| cent. | century |
| cf. | compare |
| CH | Companion of Honour |
| chap. | chapter |
| ChB | bachelor of surgery |
| CI | Imperial Order of the Crown of India |
| CIA | Central Intelligence Agency |
| CID | Criminal Investigation Department |
| CIE | companion of the Order of the Indian Empire |
| Cie | Compagnie |
| CLit | companion of literature |
| CM | master of surgery |
| cm | centimetre(s) |

| | |
|---|---|
| Cmd | command [identifier for published parliamentary papers] |
| CMG | companion of the Order of St Michael and St George |
| Cmnd | command [identifier for published parliamentary papers] |
| CO | Colorado |
| Co. | company |
| co. | county |
| col. *pl.* cols. | column(s) |
| Corp. | corporation |
| CSE | certificate of secondary education |
| CSI | companion of the Order of the Star of India |
| CT | Connecticut |
| CVO | commander of the Royal Victorian Order |
| cwt | hundredweight |
| $ | (American) dollar |
| *d.* | (1) penny (pence); (2) died |
| DBE | dame commander of the Order of the British Empire |
| DCH | diploma in child health |
| DCh | doctor of surgery |
| DCL | doctor of civil law |
| DCnL | doctor of canon law |
| DCVO | dame commander of the Royal Victorian Order |
| DD | doctor of divinity |
| DE | Delaware |
| Dec | December |
| dem. | demolished |
| DEng | doctor of engineering |
| des. | destroyed |
| DFC | Distinguished Flying Cross |
| DipEd | diploma in education |
| DipPsych | diploma in psychiatry |
| diss. | dissertation |
| DL | deputy lieutenant |
| DLitt | doctor of letters |
| DLittCelt | doctor of Celtic letters |
| DM | (1) Deutschmark; (2) doctor of medicine; (3) doctor of musical arts |
| DMus | doctor of music |
| DNA | dioxyribonucleic acid |
| doc. | document |
| DOL | doctor of oriental learning |
| DPH | diploma in public health |
| DPhil | doctor of philosophy |
| DPM | diploma in psychological medicine |
| DSC | Distinguished Service Cross |
| DSc | doctor of science |
| DSc (Econ.) | doctor of science (economics) |
| DSc (Eng.) | doctor of science (engineering) |
| DSM | Distinguished Service Medal |
| DSO | companion of the Distinguished Service Order |
| DSocSc | doctor of social science |
| DTech | doctor of technology |
| DTh | doctor of theology |
| DTM | diploma in tropical medicine |
| DTMH | diploma in tropical medicine and hygiene |
| DU | doctor of the university |
| DUniv | doctor of the university |
| dwt | pennyweight |
| EC | European Community |
| ed. *pl.* eds. | edited / edited by / editor(s) |
| Edin. | Edinburgh |
| edn | edition |
| EEC | European Economic Community |
| EFTA | European Free Trade Association |
| EICS | East India Company Service |
| EMI | Electrical and Musical Industries (Ltd) |
| Eng. | English |
| enl. | enlarged |
| ENSA | Entertainments National Service Association |
| ep. *pl.* epp. | *epistola(e)* |
| ESP | extra-sensory perception |
| esp. | especially |
| esq. | esquire |
| est. | estimate / estimated |
| EU | European Union |
| ex | sold by (*lit.* out of) |
| excl. | excludes / excluding |
| exh. | exhibited |
| exh. cat. | exhibition catalogue |
| f. *pl.* ff. | following [pages] |
| FA | Football Association |
| FACP | fellow of the American College of Physicians |
| facs. | facsimile |
| FANY | First Aid Nursing Yeomanry |
| FBA | fellow of the British Academy |
| FBI | Federation of British Industries |
| FCS | fellow of the Chemical Society |
| Feb | February |
| FEng | fellow of the Fellowship of Engineering |
| FFCM | fellow of the Faculty of Community Medicine |
| FGS | fellow of the Geological Society |
| fig. | figure |
| FIMechE | fellow of the Institution of Mechanical Engineers |
| FL | Florida |
| *fl.* | *floruit* |
| FLS | fellow of the Linnean Society |
| FM | frequency modulation |
| fol. *pl.* fols. | folio(s) |
| Fr | French francs |
| Fr. | French |
| FRAeS | fellow of the Royal Aeronautical Society |
| FRAI | fellow of the Royal Anthropological Institute |
| FRAM | fellow of the Royal Academy of Music |
| FRAS | (1) fellow of the Royal Asiatic Society; (2) fellow of the Royal Astronomical Society |
| FRCM | fellow of the Royal College of Music |
| FRCO | fellow of the Royal College of Organists |
| FRCOG | fellow of the Royal College of Obstetricians and Gynaecologists |
| FRCP(C) | fellow of the Royal College of Physicians of Canada |
| FRCP (Edin.) | fellow of the Royal College of Physicians of Edinburgh |
| FRCP (Lond.) | fellow of the Royal College of Physicians of London |
| FRCPath | fellow of the Royal College of Pathologists |
| FRCPsych | fellow of the Royal College of Psychiatrists |
| FRCS | fellow of the Royal College of Surgeons |
| FRGS | fellow of the Royal Geographical Society |
| FRIBA | fellow of the Royal Institute of British Architects |
| FRICS | fellow of the Royal Institute of Chartered Surveyors |
| FRS | fellow of the Royal Society |
| FRSA | fellow of the Royal Society of Arts |

| | |
|---|---|
| FRSCM | fellow of the Royal School of Church Music |
| FRSE | fellow of the Royal Society of Edinburgh |
| FRSL | fellow of the Royal Society of Literature |
| FSA | fellow of the Society of Antiquaries |
| ft | foot *pl.* feet |
| FTCL | fellow of Trinity College of Music, London |
| ft-lb per min. | foot-pounds per minute [unit of horsepower] |
| FZS | fellow of the Zoological Society |
| GA | Georgia |
| GBE | knight or dame grand cross of the Order of the British Empire |
| GCB | knight grand cross of the Order of the Bath |
| GCE | general certificate of education |
| GCH | knight grand cross of the Royal Guelphic Order |
| GCHQ | government communications headquarters |
| GCIE | knight grand commander of the Order of the Indian Empire |
| GCMG | knight or dame grand cross of the Order of St Michael and St George |
| GCSE | general certificate of secondary education |
| GCSI | knight grand commander of the Order of the Star of India |
| GCStJ | bailiff or dame grand cross of the order of St John of Jerusalem |
| GCVO | knight or dame grand cross of the Royal Victorian Order |
| GEC | General Electric Company |
| Ger. | German |
| GI | government (*or* general) issue |
| GMT | Greenwich mean time |
| GP | general practitioner |
| GPU | [Soviet special police unit] |
| GSO | general staff officer |
| Heb. | Hebrew |
| HEICS | Honourable East India Company Service |
| HI | Hawaii |
| HIV | human immunodeficiency virus |
| HK$ | Hong Kong dollar |
| HM | his / her majesty('s) |
| HMAS | his / her majesty's Australian ship |
| HMNZS | his / her majesty's New Zealand ship |
| HMS | his / her majesty's ship |
| HMSO | His / Her Majesty's Stationery Office |
| HMV | His Master's Voice |
| Hon. | Honourable |
| hp | horsepower |
| hr | hour(s) |
| HRH | his / her royal highness |
| HTV | Harlech Television |
| IA | Iowa |
| ibid. | *ibidem*: in the same place |
| ICI | Imperial Chemical Industries (Ltd) |
| ID | Idaho |
| IL | Illinois |
| illus. | illustration |
| illustr. | illustrated |
| IN | Indiana |
| in. | inch(es) |
| Inc. | Incorporated |
| incl. | includes / including |
| IOU | I owe you |
| IQ | intelligence quotient |
| Ir£ | Irish pound |
| IRA | Irish Republican Army |
| ISO | companion of the Imperial Service Order |
| It. | Italian |
| ITA | Independent Television Authority |
| ITV | Independent Television |
| Jan | January |
| JP | justice of the peace |
| jun. | junior |
| KB | knight of the Order of the Bath |
| KBE | knight commander of the Order of the British Empire |
| KC | king's counsel |
| kcal | kilocalorie |
| KCB | knight commander of the Order of the Bath |
| KCH | knight commander of the Royal Guelphic Order |
| KCIE | knight commander of the Order of the Indian Empire |
| KCMG | knight commander of the Order of St Michael and St George |
| KCSI | knight commander of the Order of the Star of India |
| KCVO | knight commander of the Royal Victorian Order |
| keV | kilo-electron-volt |
| KG | knight of the Order of the Garter |
| KGB | [Soviet committee of state security] |
| KH | knight of the Royal Guelphic Order |
| KLM | Koninklijke Luchtvaart Maatschappij (Royal Dutch Air Lines) |
| km | kilometre(s) |
| KP | knight of the Order of St Patrick |
| KS | Kansas |
| KT | knight of the Order of the Thistle |
| kt | knight |
| KY | Kentucky |
| £ | pound(s) sterling |
| £E | Egyptian pound |
| L | lira *pl.* lire |
| l. *pl.* ll. | line(s) |
| LA | Lousiana |
| LAA | light anti-aircraft |
| LAH | licentiate of the Apothecaries' Hall, Dublin |
| Lat. | Latin |
| lb | pound(s), unit of weight |
| LDS | licence in dental surgery |
| *lit.* | literally |
| LittB | bachelor of letters |
| LittD | doctor of letters |
| LKQCPI | licentiate of the King and Queen's College of Physicians, Ireland |
| LLA | lady literate in arts |
| LLB | bachelor of laws |
| LLD | doctor of laws |
| LLM | master of laws |
| LM | licentiate in midwifery |
| LP | long-playing record |
| LRAM | licentiate of the Royal Academy of Music |
| LRCP | licentiate of the Royal College of Physicians |
| LRCPS (Glasgow) | licentiate of the Royal College of Physicians and Surgeons of Glasgow |
| LRCS | licentiate of the Royal College of Surgeons |
| LSA | licentiate of the Society of Apothecaries |
| LSD | lysergic acid diethylamide |
| LVO | lieutenant of the Royal Victorian Order |
| M. *pl.* MM. | Monsieur *pl.* Messieurs |
| m | metre(s) |

| | |
|---|---|
| m. *pl.* mm. | membrane(s) |
| MA | (1) Massachusetts; (2) master of arts |
| MAI | master of engineering |
| MB | bachelor of medicine |
| MBA | master of business administration |
| MBE | member of the Order of the British Empire |
| MC | Military Cross |
| MCC | Marylebone Cricket Club |
| MCh | master of surgery |
| MChir | master of surgery |
| MCom | master of commerce |
| MD | (1) doctor of medicine; (2) Maryland |
| MDMA | methylenedioxymethamphetamine |
| ME | Maine |
| MEd | master of education |
| MEng | master of engineering |
| MEP | member of the European parliament |
| MG | Morris Garages |
| MGM | Metro-Goldwyn-Mayer |
| Mgr | Monsignor |
| MI | (1) Michigan; (2) military intelligence |
| MI1c | [secret intelligence department] |
| MI5 | [military intelligence department] |
| MI6 | [secret intelligence department] |
| MI9 | [secret escape service] |
| MICE | member of the Institution of Civil Engineers |
| MIEE | member of the Institution of Electrical Engineers |
| min. | minute(s) |
| Mk | mark |
| ML | (1) licentiate of medicine; (2) master of laws |
| MLitt | master of letters |
| Mlle | Mademoiselle |
| mm | millimetre(s) |
| Mme | Madame |
| MN | Minnesota |
| MO | Missouri |
| MOH | medical officer of health |
| MP | member of parliament |
| m.p.h. | miles per hour |
| MPhil | master of philosophy |
| MRCP | member of the Royal College of Physicians |
| MRCS | member of the Royal College of Surgeons |
| MRCVS | member of the Royal College of Veterinary Surgeons |
| MRIA | member of the Royal Irish Academy |
| MS | (1) master of science; (2) Mississippi |
| MS *pl.* MSS | manuscript(s) |
| MSc | master of science |
| MSc (Econ.) | master of science (economics) |
| MT | Montana |
| MusB | bachelor of music |
| MusBac | bachelor of music |
| MusD | doctor of music |
| MV | motor vessel |
| MVO | member of the Royal Victorian Order |
| n. *pl.* nn. | note(s) |
| NAAFI | Navy, Army, and Air Force Institutes |
| NASA | National Aeronautics and Space Administration |
| NATO | North Atlantic Treaty Organization |
| NBC | National Broadcasting Corporation |
| NC | North Carolina |
| NCO | non-commissioned officer |
| ND | North Dakota |
| n.d. | no date |
| NE | Nebraska |
| *nem. con.* | *nemine contradicente*: unanimously |
| new ser. | new series |
| NH | New Hampshire |
| NHS | National Health Service |
| NJ | New Jersey |
| NKVD | [Soviet people's commissariat for internal affairs] |
| NM | New Mexico |
| nm | nanometre(s) |
| no. *pl.* nos. | number(s) |
| Nov | November |
| n.p. | no place [of publication] |
| NS | new style |
| NV | Nevada |
| NY | New York |
| NZBS | New Zealand Broadcasting Service |
| OBE | officer of the Order of the British Empire |
| obit. | obituary |
| Oct | October |
| OCTU | officer cadets training unit |
| OECD | Organization for Economic Co-operation and Development |
| OEEC | Organization for European Economic Co-operation |
| OFM | order of Friars Minor [Franciscans] |
| OFMCap | Ordine Frati Minori Cappucini: member of the Capuchin order |
| OH | Ohio |
| OK | Oklahoma |
| O level | ordinary level [examination] |
| OM | Order of Merit |
| OP | order of Preachers [Dominicans] |
| op. *pl.* opp. | opus *pl.* opera |
| OPEC | Organization of Petroleum Exporting Countries |
| OR | Oregon |
| orig. | original |
| OS | old style |
| OSB | Order of St Benedict |
| OTC | Officers' Training Corps |
| OWS | Old Watercolour Society |
| Oxon. | Oxoniensis |
| p. *pl.* pp. | page(s) |
| PA | Pennsylvania |
| p.a. | per annum |
| para. | paragraph |
| PAYE | pay as you earn |
| pbk *pl.* pbks | paperback(s) |
| *per.* | [during the] period |
| PhD | doctor of philosophy |
| pl. | (1) plate(s); (2) plural |
| priv. coll. | private collection |
| pt *pl.* pts | part(s) |
| pubd | published |
| PVC | polyvinyl chloride |
| q. *pl.* qq. | (1) question(s); (2) quire(s) |
| QC | queen's counsel |
| R | rand |
| R. | Rex / Regina |
| *r* | recto |
| *r.* | reigned / ruled |
| RA | Royal Academy / Royal Academician |

| | |
|---|---|
| RAC | Royal Automobile Club |
| RAF | Royal Air Force |
| RAFVR | Royal Air Force Volunteer Reserve |
| RAM | [member of the] Royal Academy of Music |
| RAMC | Royal Army Medical Corps |
| RCA | Royal College of Art |
| RCNC | Royal Corps of Naval Constructors |
| RCOG | Royal College of Obstetricians and Gynaecologists |
| RDI | royal designer for industry |
| RE | Royal Engineers |
| repr. *pl.* reprs. | reprint(s) / reprinted |
| repro. | reproduced |
| rev. | revised / revised by / reviser / revision |
| Revd | Reverend |
| RHA | Royal Hibernian Academy |
| RI | (1) Rhode Island; (2) Royal Institute of Painters in Water-Colours |
| RIBA | Royal Institute of British Architects |
| RIN | Royal Indian Navy |
| RM | Reichsmark |
| RMS | Royal Mail steamer |
| RN | Royal Navy |
| RNA | ribonucleic acid |
| RNAS | Royal Naval Air Service |
| RNR | Royal Naval Reserve |
| RNVR | Royal Naval Volunteer Reserve |
| RO | Record Office |
| r.p.m. | revolutions per minute |
| RRS | royal research ship |
| Rs | rupees |
| RSA | (1) Royal Scottish Academician; (2) Royal Society of Arts |
| RSPCA | Royal Society for the Prevention of Cruelty to Animals |
| Rt Hon. | Right Honourable |
| Rt Revd | Right Reverend |
| RUC | Royal Ulster Constabulary |
| Russ. | Russian |
| RWS | Royal Watercolour Society |
| S4C | Sianel Pedwar Cymru |
| *s.* | shilling(s) |
| s.a. | *sub anno*: under the year |
| SABC | South African Broadcasting Corporation |
| SAS | Special Air Service |
| SC | South Carolina |
| ScD | doctor of science |
| S$ | Singapore dollar |
| SD | South Dakota |
| sec. | second(s) |
| sel. | selected |
| sen. | senior |
| Sept | September |
| ser. | series |
| SHAPE | supreme headquarters allied powers, Europe |
| SIDRO | Société Internationale d'Énergie Hydro-Électrique |
| sig. *pl.* sigs. | signature(s) |
| sing. | singular |
| SIS | Secret Intelligence Service |
| SJ | Society of Jesus |
| Skr | Swedish krona |
| Span. | Spanish |
| SPCK | Society for Promoting Christian Knowledge |
| SS | (1) Santissimi; (2) Schutzstaffel; (3) steam ship |
| STB | bachelor of theology |
| STD | doctor of theology |
| STM | master of theology |
| STP | doctor of theology |
| *supp.* | supposedly |
| suppl. *pl.* suppls. | supplement(s) |
| s.v. | *sub verbo* / *sub voce*: under the word / heading |
| SY | steam yacht |
| TA | Territorial Army |
| TASS | [Soviet news agency] |
| TB | tuberculosis (*lit.* tubercle bacillus) |
| TD | (1) *teachtaí dála* (member of the Dáil); (2) territorial decoration |
| TN | Tennessee |
| TNT | trinitrotoluene |
| trans. | translated / translated by / translation / translator |
| TT | tourist trophy |
| TUC | Trades Union Congress |
| TX | Texas |
| U-boat | *Unterseeboot*: submarine |
| Ufa | Universum-Film AG |
| UMIST | University of Manchester Institute of Science and Technology |
| UN | United Nations |
| UNESCO | United Nations Educational, Scientific, and Cultural Organization |
| UNICEF | United Nations International Children's Emergency Fund |
| unpubd | unpublished |
| USS | United States ship |
| UT | Utah |
| *v* | verso |
| v. | versus |
| VA | Virginia |
| VAD | Voluntary Aid Detachment |
| VC | Victoria Cross |
| VE-day | victory in Europe day |
| Ven. | Venerable |
| VJ-day | victory over Japan day |
| vol. *pl.* vols. | volume(s) |
| VT | Vermont |
| WA | Washington [state] |
| WAAC | Women's Auxiliary Army Corps |
| WAAF | Women's Auxiliary Air Force |
| WEA | Workers' Educational Association |
| WHO | World Health Organization |
| WI | Wisconsin |
| WRAF | Women's Royal Air Force |
| WRNS | Women's Royal Naval Service |
| WV | West Virginia |
| WVS | Women's Voluntary Service |
| WY | Wyoming |
| ¥ | yen |
| YMCA | Young Men's Christian Association |
| YWCA | Young Women's Christian Association |

## 2 *Institution abbreviations*

| | |
|---|---|
| All Souls Oxf. | All Souls College, Oxford |
| AM Oxf. | Ashmolean Museum, Oxford |
| Balliol Oxf. | Balliol College, Oxford |
| BBC WAC | BBC Written Archives Centre, Reading |
| Beds. & Luton ARS | Bedfordshire and Luton Archives and Record Service, Bedford |
| Berks. RO | Berkshire Record Office, Reading |
| BFI | British Film Institute, London |
| BFI NFTVA | British Film Institute, London, National Film and Television Archive |
| BGS | British Geological Survey, Keyworth, Nottingham |
| Birm. CA | Birmingham Central Library, Birmingham City Archives |
| Birm. CL | Birmingham Central Library |
| BL | British Library, London |
| BL NSA | British Library, London, National Sound Archive |
| BL OIOC | British Library, London, Oriental and India Office Collections |
| BLPES | London School of Economics and Political Science, British Library of Political and Economic Science |
| BM | British Museum, London |
| Bodl. Oxf. | Bodleian Library, Oxford |
| Bodl. RH | Bodleian Library of Commonwealth and African Studies at Rhodes House, Oxford |
| Borth. Inst. | Borthwick Institute of Historical Research, University of York |
| Boston PL | Boston Public Library, Massachusetts |
| Bristol RO | Bristol Record Office |
| Bucks. RLSS | Buckinghamshire Records and Local Studies Service, Aylesbury |
| CAC Cam. | Churchill College, Cambridge, Churchill Archives Centre |
| Cambs. AS | Cambridgeshire Archive Service |
| CCC Cam. | Corpus Christi College, Cambridge |
| CCC Oxf. | Corpus Christi College, Oxford |
| Ches. & Chester ALSS | Cheshire and Chester Archives and Local Studies Service |
| Christ Church Oxf. | Christ Church, Oxford |
| Christies | Christies, London |
| City Westm. AC | City of Westminster Archives Centre, London |
| CKS | Centre for Kentish Studies, Maidstone |
| CLRO | Corporation of London Records Office |
| Coll. Arms | College of Arms, London |
| Col. U. | Columbia University, New York |
| Cornwall RO | Cornwall Record Office, Truro |
| Courtauld Inst. | Courtauld Institute of Art, London |
| CUL | Cambridge University Library |
| Cumbria AS | Cumbria Archive Service |
| Derbys. RO | Derbyshire Record Office, Matlock |
| Devon RO | Devon Record Office, Exeter |
| Dorset RO | Dorset Record Office, Dorchester |
| Duke U. | Duke University, Durham, North Carolina |
| Duke U., Perkins L. | Duke University, Durham, North Carolina, William R. Perkins Library |
| Durham Cath. CL | Durham Cathedral, chapter library |
| Durham RO | Durham Record Office |
| DWL | Dr Williams's Library, London |
| Essex RO | Essex Record Office |
| E. Sussex RO | East Sussex Record Office, Lewes |
| Eton | Eton College, Berkshire |
| FM Cam. | Fitzwilliam Museum, Cambridge |
| Folger | Folger Shakespeare Library, Washington, DC |
| Garr. Club | Garrick Club, London |
| Girton Cam. | Girton College, Cambridge |
| GL | Guildhall Library, London |
| Glos. RO | Gloucestershire Record Office, Gloucester |
| Gon. & Caius Cam. | Gonville and Caius College, Cambridge |
| Gov. Art Coll. | Government Art Collection |
| GS Lond. | Geological Society of London |
| Hants. RO | Hampshire Record Office, Winchester |
| Harris Man. Oxf. | Harris Manchester College, Oxford |
| Harvard TC | Harvard Theatre Collection, Harvard University, Cambridge, Massachusetts, Nathan Marsh Pusey Library |
| Harvard U. | Harvard University, Cambridge, Massachusetts |
| Harvard U., Houghton L. | Harvard University, Cambridge, Massachusetts, Houghton Library |
| Herefs. RO | Herefordshire Record Office, Hereford |
| Herts. ALS | Hertfordshire Archives and Local Studies, Hertford |
| Hist. Soc. Penn. | Historical Society of Pennsylvania, Philadelphia |
| HLRO | House of Lords Record Office, London |
| Hult. Arch. | Hulton Archive, London and New York |
| Hunt. L. | Huntington Library, San Marino, California |
| ICL | Imperial College, London |
| Inst. CE | Institution of Civil Engineers, London |
| Inst. EE | Institution of Electrical Engineers, London |
| IWM | Imperial War Museum, London |
| IWM FVA | Imperial War Museum, London, Film and Video Archive |
| IWM SA | Imperial War Museum, London, Sound Archive |
| JRL | John Rylands University Library of Manchester |
| King's AC Cam. | King's College Archives Centre, Cambridge |
| King's Cam. | King's College, Cambridge |
| King's Lond. | King's College, London |
| King's Lond., Liddell Hart C. | King's College, London, Liddell Hart Centre for Military Archives |
| Lancs. RO | Lancashire Record Office, Preston |
| L. Cong. | Library of Congress, Washington, DC |
| Leics. RO | Leicestershire, Leicester, and Rutland Record Office, Leicester |
| Lincs. Arch. | Lincolnshire Archives, Lincoln |
| Linn. Soc. | Linnean Society of London |
| LMA | London Metropolitan Archives |
| LPL | Lambeth Palace, London |
| Lpool RO | Liverpool Record Office and Local Studies Service |
| LUL | London University Library |
| Magd. Cam. | Magdalene College, Cambridge |
| Magd. Oxf. | Magdalen College, Oxford |
| Man. City Gall. | Manchester City Galleries |
| Man. CL | Manchester Central Library |
| Mass. Hist. Soc. | Massachusetts Historical Society, Boston |
| Merton Oxf. | Merton College, Oxford |
| MHS Oxf. | Museum of the History of Science, Oxford |
| Mitchell L., Glas. | Mitchell Library, Glasgow |
| Mitchell L., NSW | State Library of New South Wales, Sydney, Mitchell Library |
| Morgan L. | Pierpont Morgan Library, New York |
| NA Canada | National Archives of Canada, Ottawa |
| NA Ire. | National Archives of Ireland, Dublin |
| NAM | National Army Museum, London |
| NA Scot. | National Archives of Scotland, Edinburgh |
| News Int. RO | News International Record Office, London |
| NG Ire. | National Gallery of Ireland, Dublin |

| | |
|---|---|
| NG Scot. | National Gallery of Scotland, Edinburgh |
| NHM | Natural History Museum, London |
| NL Aus. | National Library of Australia, Canberra |
| NL Ire. | National Library of Ireland, Dublin |
| NL NZ | National Library of New Zealand, Wellington |
| NL NZ, Turnbull L. | National Library of New Zealand, Wellington, Alexander Turnbull Library |
| NL Scot. | National Library of Scotland, Edinburgh |
| NL Wales | National Library of Wales, Aberystwyth |
| NMG Wales | National Museum and Gallery of Wales, Cardiff |
| NMM | National Maritime Museum, London |
| Norfolk RO | Norfolk Record Office, Norwich |
| Northants. RO | Northamptonshire Record Office, Northampton |
| Northumbd RO | Northumberland Record Office |
| Notts. Arch. | Nottinghamshire Archives, Nottingham |
| NPG | National Portrait Gallery, London |
| NRA | National Archives, London, Historical Manuscripts Commission, National Register of Archives |
| Nuffield Oxf. | Nuffield College, Oxford |
| N. Yorks. CRO | North Yorkshire County Record Office, Northallerton |
| NYPL | New York Public Library |
| Oxf. UA | Oxford University Archives |
| Oxf. U. Mus. NH | Oxford University Museum of Natural History |
| Oxon. RO | Oxfordshire Record Office, Oxford |
| Pembroke Cam. | Pembroke College, Cambridge |
| PRO | National Archives, London, Public Record Office |
| PRO NIre. | Public Record Office for Northern Ireland, Belfast |
| Pusey Oxf. | Pusey House, Oxford |
| RA | Royal Academy of Arts, London |
| Ransom HRC | Harry Ransom Humanities Research Center, University of Texas, Austin |
| RAS | Royal Astronomical Society, London |
| RBG Kew | Royal Botanic Gardens, Kew, London |
| RCP Lond. | Royal College of Physicians of London |
| RCS Eng. | Royal College of Surgeons of England, London |
| RGS | Royal Geographical Society, London |
| RIBA | Royal Institute of British Architects, London |
| RIBA BAL | Royal Institute of British Architects, London, British Architectural Library |
| Royal Arch. | Royal Archives, Windsor Castle, Berkshire [by gracious permission of her majesty the queen] |
| Royal Irish Acad. | Royal Irish Academy, Dublin |
| Royal Scot. Acad. | Royal Scottish Academy, Edinburgh |
| RS | Royal Society, London |
| RSA | Royal Society of Arts, London |
| RS Friends, Lond. | Religious Society of Friends, London |
| St Ant. Oxf. | St Antony's College, Oxford |
| St John Cam. | St John's College, Cambridge |
| S. Antiquaries, Lond. | Society of Antiquaries of London |
| Sci. Mus. | Science Museum, London |
| Scot. NPG | Scottish National Portrait Gallery, Edinburgh |
| Scott Polar RI | University of Cambridge, Scott Polar Research Institute |
| Sheff. Arch. | Sheffield Archives |
| Shrops. RRC | Shropshire Records and Research Centre, Shrewsbury |
| SOAS | School of Oriental and African Studies, London |
| Som. ARS | Somerset Archive and Record Service, Taunton |
| Staffs. RO | Staffordshire Record Office, Stafford |
| Suffolk RO | Suffolk Record Office |
| Surrey HC | Surrey History Centre, Woking |
| TCD | Trinity College, Dublin |
| Trinity Cam. | Trinity College, Cambridge |
| U. Aberdeen | University of Aberdeen |
| U. Birm. | University of Birmingham |
| U. Birm. L. | University of Birmingham Library |
| U. Cal. | University of California |
| U. Cam. | University of Cambridge |
| UCL | University College, London |
| U. Durham | University of Durham |
| U. Durham L. | University of Durham Library |
| U. Edin. | University of Edinburgh |
| U. Edin., New Coll. | University of Edinburgh, New College |
| U. Edin., New Coll. L. | University of Edinburgh, New College Library |
| U. Edin. L. | University of Edinburgh Library |
| U. Glas. | University of Glasgow |
| U. Glas. L. | University of Glasgow Library |
| U. Hull | University of Hull |
| U. Hull, Brynmor Jones L. | University of Hull, Brynmor Jones Library |
| U. Leeds | University of Leeds |
| U. Leeds, Brotherton L. | University of Leeds, Brotherton Library |
| U. Lond. | University of London |
| U. Lpool | University of Liverpool |
| U. Lpool L. | University of Liverpool Library |
| U. Mich. | University of Michigan, Ann Arbor |
| U. Mich., Clements L. | University of Michigan, Ann Arbor, William L. Clements Library |
| U. Newcastle | University of Newcastle upon Tyne |
| U. Newcastle, Robinson L. | University of Newcastle upon Tyne, Robinson Library |
| U. Nott. | University of Nottingham |
| U. Nott. L. | University of Nottingham Library |
| U. Oxf. | University of Oxford |
| U. Reading | University of Reading |
| U. Reading L. | University of Reading Library |
| U. St Andr. | University of St Andrews |
| U. St Andr. L. | University of St Andrews Library |
| U. Southampton | University of Southampton |
| U. Southampton L. | University of Southampton Library |
| U. Sussex | University of Sussex, Brighton |
| U. Texas | University of Texas, Austin |
| U. Wales | University of Wales |
| U. Warwick Mod. RC | University of Warwick, Coventry, Modern Records Centre |
| V&A | Victoria and Albert Museum, London |
| V&A NAL | Victoria and Albert Museum, London, National Art Library |
| Warks. CRO | Warwickshire County Record Office, Warwick |
| Wellcome L. | Wellcome Library for the History and Understanding of Medicine, London |
| Westm. DA | Westminster Diocesan Archives, London |
| Wilts. & Swindon RO | Wiltshire and Swindon Record Office, Trowbridge |
| Worcs. RO | Worcestershire Record Office, Worcester |
| W. Sussex RO | West Sussex Record Office, Chichester |
| W. Yorks. AS | West Yorkshire Archive Service |
| Yale U. | Yale University, New Haven, Connecticut |
| Yale U., Beinecke L. | Yale University, New Haven, Connecticut, Beinecke Rare Book and Manuscript Library |
| Yale U. CBA | Yale University, New Haven, Connecticut, Yale Center for British Art |

# 3 *Bibliographic abbreviations*

| | |
|---|---|
| Adams, *Drama* | W. D. Adams, *A dictionary of the drama*, 1: *A–G* (1904); 2: *H–Z* (1956) [vol. 2 microfilm only] |
| *AFM* | J O'Donovan, ed. and trans., *Annala rioghachta Eireann / Annals of the kingdom of Ireland by the four masters*, 7 vols. (1848–51); 2nd edn (1856); 3rd edn (1990) |
| Allibone, *Dict.* | S. A. Allibone, *A critical dictionary of English literature and British and American authors*, 3 vols. (1859–71); suppl. by J. F. Kirk, 2 vols. (1891) |
| *ANB* | J. A. Garraty and M. C. Carnes, eds., *American national biography*, 24 vols. (1999) |
| Anderson, *Scot. nat.* | W. Anderson, *The Scottish nation, or, The surnames, families, literature, honours, and biographical history of the people of Scotland*, 3 vols. (1859–63) |
| *Ann. mon.* | H. R. Luard, ed., *Annales monastici*, 5 vols., Rolls Series, 36 (1864–9) |
| *Ann. Ulster* | S. Mac Airt and G. Mac Niocaill, eds., *Annals of Ulster (to AD 1131)* (1983) |
| *APC* | *Acts of the privy council of England*, new ser., 46 vols. (1890–1964) |
| *APS* | *The acts of the parliaments of Scotland*, 12 vols. in 13 (1814–75) |
| Arber, *Regs. Stationers* | F. Arber, ed., *A transcript of the registers of the Company of Stationers of London, 1554–1640 AD*, 5 vols. (1875–94) |
| *ArchR* | *Architectural Review* |
| *ASC* | D. Whitelock, D. C. Douglas, and S. I. Tucker, ed. and trans., *The Anglo-Saxon Chronicle: a revised translation* (1961) |
| *AS chart.* | P. H. Sawyer, *Anglo-Saxon charters: an annotated list and bibliography*, Royal Historical Society Guides and Handbooks (1968) |
| *AusDB* | D. Pike and others, eds., *Australian dictionary of biography*, 16 vols. (1966–2002) |
| Baker, *Serjeants* | J. H. Baker, *The order of serjeants at law*, SeldS, suppl. ser., 5 (1984) |
| Bale, *Cat.* | J. Bale, *Scriptorum illustrium Maioris Brytannie, quam nunc Angliam et Scotiam vocant: catalogus*, 2 vols. in 1 (Basel, 1557–9); facs. edn (1971) |
| Bale, *Index* | J. Bale, *Index Britanniae scriptorum*, ed. R. L. Poole and M. Bateson (1902); facs. edn (1990) |
| *BBCS* | *Bulletin of the Board of Celtic Studies* |
| *BDMBR* | J. O. Baylen and N. J. Gossman, eds., *Biographical dictionary of modern British radicals*, 3 vols. in 4 (1979–88) |
| Bede, *Hist. eccl.* | *Bede's Ecclesiastical history of the English people*, ed. and trans. B. Colgrave and R. A. B. Mynors, OMT (1969); repr. (1991) |
| Bénézit, *Dict.* | E. Bénézit, *Dictionnaire critique et documentaire des peintres, sculpteurs, dessinateurs et graveurs*, 3 vols. (Paris, 1911–23); new edn, 8 vols. (1948–66), repr. (1966); 3rd edn, rev. and enl., 10 vols. (1976); 4th edn, 14 vols. (1999) |
| *BIHR* | *Bulletin of the Institute of Historical Research* |
| Birch, *Seals* | W. de Birch, *Catalogue of seals in the department of manuscripts in the British Museum*, 6 vols. (1887–1900) |
| *Bishop Burnet's History* | *Bishop Burnet's History of his own time*, ed. M. J. Routh, 2nd edn, 6 vols. (1833) |
| *Blackwood* | *Blackwood's [Edinburgh] Magazine*, 328 vols. (1817–1980) |
| Blain, Clements & Grundy, *Feminist comp.* | V. Blain, P. Clements, and I. Grundy, eds., *The feminist companion to literature in English* (1990) |
| *BL cat.* | *The British Library general catalogue of printed books* [in 360 vols. with suppls., also CD-ROM and online] |
| *BMJ* | *British Medical Journal* |
| Boase & Courtney, *Bibl. Corn.* | G. C. Boase and W. P. Courtney, *Bibliotheca Cornubiensis: a catalogue of the writings … of Cornishmen*, 3 vols. (1874–82) |
| Boase, *Mod. Eng. biog.* | F. Boase, *Modern English biography: containing many thousand concise memoirs of persons who have died since the year 1850*, 6 vols. (privately printed, Truro, 1892–1921); repr. (1965) |
| Boswell, *Life* | *Boswell's Life of Johnson: together with Journal of a tour to the Hebrides and Johnson's Diary of a journey into north Wales*, ed. G. B. Hill, enl. edn, rev. L. F. Powell, 6 vols. (1934–50); 2nd edn (1964); repr. (1971) |
| Brown & Stratton, *Brit. mus.* | J. D. Brown and S. S. Stratton, *British musical biography* (1897) |
| Bryan, *Painters* | M. Bryan, *A biographical and critical dictionary of painters and engravers*, 2 vols. (1816); new edn, ed. G. Stanley (1849); new edn, ed. R. E. Graves and W. Armstrong, 2 vols. (1886–9); [4th edn], ed. G. C. Williamson, 5 vols. (1903–5) [various reprs.] |
| Burke, *Gen. GB* | J. Burke, *A genealogical and heraldic history of the commoners of Great Britain and Ireland*, 4 vols. (1833–8); new edn as *A genealogical and heraldic dictionary of the landed gentry of Great Britain and Ireland*, 3 vols. [1843–9] [many later edns] |
| Burke, *Gen. Ire.* | J. B. Burke, *A genealogical and heraldic history of the landed gentry of Ireland* (1899); 2nd edn (1904); 3rd edn (1912); 4th edn (1958); 5th edn as *Burke's Irish family records* (1976) |
| Burke, *Peerage* | J. Burke, *A general* [later edns *A genealogical*] *and heraldic dictionary of the peerage and baronetage of the United Kingdom* [later edns *the British empire*] (1829–) |
| Burney, *Hist. mus.* | C. Burney, *A general history of music, from the earliest ages to the present period*, 4 vols. (1776–89) |
| Burtchaell & Sadleir, *Alum. Dubl.* | G. D. Burtchaell and T. U. Sadleir, *Alumni Dublinenses: a register of the students, graduates, and provosts of Trinity College* (1924); [2nd edn], with suppl., in 2 pts (1935) |
| *Calamy rev.* | A. G. Matthews, *Calamy revised* (1934); repr. (1988) |
| *CCI* | *Calendar of confirmations and inventories granted and given up in the several commissariots of Scotland* (1876–) |
| *CCIR* | *Calendar of the close rolls preserved in the Public Record Office*, 47 vols. (1892–1963) |
| *CDS* | J. Bain, ed., *Calendar of documents relating to Scotland*, 4 vols., PRO (1881–8); suppl. vol. 5, ed. G. G. Simpson and J. D. Galbraith [1986] |
| *CEPR letters* | W. H. Bliss, C. Johnson, and J. Twemlow, eds., *Calendar of entries in the papal registers relating to Great Britain and Ireland: papal letters* (1893–) |
| *CGPLA* | *Calendars of the grants of probate and letters of administration* [in 4 ser.: England & Wales, Northern Ireland, Ireland, and Éire] |
| Chambers, *Scots.* | R. Chambers, ed., *A biographical dictionary of eminent Scotsmen*, 4 vols. (1832–5) |
| *Chancery records* | chancery records pubd by the PRO |
| *Chancery records* (RC) | chancery records pubd by the Record Commissions |

| | |
|---|---|
| *CIPM* | *Calendar of inquisitions post mortem*, [20 vols.], PRO (1904–); also *Henry VII*, 3 vols. (1898–1955) |
| Clarendon, *Hist. rebellion* | E. Hyde, earl of Clarendon, *The history of the rebellion and civil wars in England*, 6 vols. (1888); repr. (1958) and (1992) |
| Cobbett, *Parl. hist.* | W. Cobbett and J. Wright, eds., *Cobbett's Parliamentary history of England*, 36 vols. (1806–1820) |
| Colvin, *Archs.* | H. Colvin, *A biographical dictionary of British architects, 1600–1840*, 3rd edn (1995) |
| Cooper, *Ath. Cantab.* | C. H. Cooper and T. Cooper, *Athenae Cantabrigienses*, 3 vols. (1858–1913); repr. (1967) |
| *CPR* | *Calendar of the patent rolls preserved in the Public Record Office* (1891–) |
| Crockford | *Crockford's Clerical Directory* |
| CS | Camden Society |
| *CSP* | *Calendar of state papers* [in 11 ser.: *domestic, Scotland, Scottish series, Ireland, colonial, Commonwealth, foreign, Spain* [at Simancas], *Rome, Milan*, and *Venice*] |
| CYS | Canterbury and York Society |
| *DAB* | *Dictionary of American biography*, 21 vols. (1928–36), repr. in 11 vols. (1964); 10 suppls. (1944–96) |
| *DBB* | D. J. Jeremy, ed., *Dictionary of business biography*, 5 vols. (1984–6) |
| *DCB* | G. W. Brown and others, *Dictionary of Canadian biography*, [14 vols.] (1966–) |
| *Debrett's Peerage* | *Debrett's Peerage* (1803–) [sometimes *Debrett's Illustrated peerage*] |
| Desmond, *Botanists* | R. Desmond, *Dictionary of British and Irish botanists and horticulturists* (1977); rev. edn (1994) |
| *Dir. Brit. archs.* | A. Felstead, J. Franklin, and L. Pinfield, eds., *Directory of British architects, 1834–1900* (1993); 2nd edn, ed. A. Brodie and others, 2 vols. (2001) |
| *DLB* | J. M. Bellamy and J. Saville, eds., *Dictionary of labour biography*, [10 vols.] (1972–) |
| DLitB | Dictionary of Literary Biography |
| *DNB* | *Dictionary of national biography*, 63 vols. (1885–1900), suppl., 3 vols. (1901); repr. in 22 vols. (1908–9); 10 further suppls. (1912–96); *Missing persons* (1993) |
| *DNZB* | W. H. Oliver and C. Orange, eds., *The dictionary of New Zealand biography*, 5 vols. (1990–2000) |
| *DSAB* | W. J. de Kock and others, eds., *Dictionary of South African biography*, 5 vols. (1968–87) |
| *DSB* | C. C. Gillispie and F. L. Holmes, eds., *Dictionary of scientific biography*, 16 vols. (1970–80); repr. in 8 vols. (1981); 2 vol. suppl. (1990) |
| *DSBB* | A. Slaven and S. Checkland, eds., *Dictionary of Scottish business biography, 1860–1960*, 2 vols. (1986–90) |
| *DSCHT* | N. M. de S. Cameron and others, eds., *Dictionary of Scottish church history and theology* (1993) |
| Dugdale, *Monasticon* | W. Dugdale, *Monasticon Anglicanum*, 3 vols. (1655–72); 2nd edn, 3 vols. (1661–82); new edn, ed. J. Caley, J. Ellis, and B. Bandinel, 6 vols. in 8 pts (1817–30); repr. (1846) and (1970) |
| *DWB* | J. E. Lloyd and others, eds., *Dictionary of Welsh biography down to 1940* (1959) [Eng. trans. of *Y bywgraffiadur Cymreig hyd 1940*, 2nd edn (1954)] |
| *EdinR* | *Edinburgh Review, or, Critical Journal* |
| EETS | Early English Text Society |
| Emden, *Cam.* | A. B. Emden, *A biographical register of the University of Cambridge to 1500* (1963) |
| Emden, *Oxf.* | A. B. Emden, *A biographical register of the University of Oxford to AD 1500*, 3 vols. (1957–9); also *A biographical register of the University of Oxford, AD 1501 to 1540* (1974) |
| *EngHR* | *English Historical Review* |
| *Engraved Brit. ports.* | F. M. O'Donoghue and H. M. Hake, *Catalogue of engraved British portraits preserved in the department of prints and drawings in the British Museum*, 6 vols. (1908–25) |
| ER | The English Reports, 178 vols. (1900–32) |
| *ESTC* | *English short title catalogue, 1475–1800* [CD-ROM and online] |
| Evelyn, *Diary* | *The diary of John Evelyn*, ed. E. S. De Beer, 6 vols. (1955); repr. (2000) |
| Farington, *Diary* | *The diary of Joseph Farington*, ed. K. Garlick and others, 17 vols. (1978–98) |
| *Fasti Angl.* (Hardy) | J. Le Neve, *Fasti ecclesiae Anglicanae*, ed. T. D. Hardy, 3 vols. (1854) |
| *Fasti Angl., 1066–1300* | [J. Le Neve], *Fasti ecclesiae Anglicanae, 1066–1300*, ed. D. E. Greenway and J. S. Barrow, [8 vols.] (1968–) |
| *Fasti Angl., 1300–1541* | [J. Le Neve], *Fasti ecclesiae Anglicanae, 1300–1541*, 12 vols. (1962–7) |
| *Fasti Angl., 1541–1857* | [J. Le Neve], *Fasti ecclesiae Anglicanae, 1541–1857*, ed. J. M. Horn, D. M. Smith, and D. S. Bailey, [9 vols.] (1969–) |
| *Fasti Scot.* | H. Scott, *Fasti ecclesiae Scoticanae*, 3 vols. in 6 (1871); new edn, [11 vols.] (1915–) |
| *FO List* | *Foreign Office List* |
| Fortescue, *Brit. army* | J. W. Fortescue, *A history of the British army*, 13 vols. (1899–1930) |
| Foss, *Judges* | E. Foss, *The judges of England*, 9 vols. (1848–64); repr. (1966) |
| Foster, *Alum. Oxon.* | J. Foster, ed., *Alumni Oxonienses: the members of the University of Oxford, 1715–1886*, 4 vols. (1887–8); later edn (1891); also *Alumni Oxonienses … 1500–1714*, 4 vols. (1891–2); 8 vol. repr. (1968) and (2000) |
| Fuller, *Worthies* | T. Fuller, *The history of the worthies of England*, 4 pts (1662); new edn, 2 vols., ed. J. Nichols (1811); new edn, 3 vols., ed. P. A. Nuttall (1840); repr. (1965) |
| GEC, *Baronetage* | G. E. Cokayne, *Complete baronetage*, 6 vols. (1900–09); repr. (1983) [microprint] |
| GEC, *Peerage* | G. E. C. [G. E. Cokayne], *The complete peerage of England, Scotland, Ireland, Great Britain, and the United Kingdom*, 8 vols. (1887–98); new edn, ed. V. Gibbs and others, 14 vols. in 15 (1910–98); microprint repr. (1982) and (1987) |
| Genest, *Eng. stage* | J. Genest, *Some account of the English stage from the Restoration in 1660 to 1830*, 10 vols. (1832); repr. [New York, 1965] |
| Gillow, *Lit. biog. hist.* | J. Gillow, *A literary and biographical history or bibliographical dictionary of the English Catholics, from the breach with Rome, in 1534, to the present time*, 5 vols. [1885–1902]; repr. (1961); repr. with preface by C. Gillow (1999) |
| *Gir. Camb. opera* | *Giraldi Cambrensis opera*, ed. J. S. Brewer, J. F. Dimock, and G. F. Warner, 8 vols., Rolls Series, 21 (1861–91) |
| *GJ* | *Geographical Journal* |

Gladstone, *Diaries* — *The Gladstone diaries: with cabinet minutes and prime-ministerial correspondence*, ed. M. R. D. Foot and H. C. G. Matthew, 14 vols. (1968–94)

*GM* — *Gentleman's Magazine*

Graves, *Artists* — A. Graves, ed., *A dictionary of artists who have exhibited works in the principal London exhibitions of oil paintings from 1760 to 1880* (1884); new edn (1895); 3rd edn (1901); facs. edn (1969); repr. [1970], (1973), and (1984)

Graves, *Brit. Inst.* — A. Graves, *The British Institution, 1806–1867: a complete dictionary of contributors and their work from the foundation of the institution* (1875); facs. edn (1908); repr. (1969)

Graves, *RA exhibitors* — A. Graves, *The Royal Academy of Arts: a complete dictionary of contributors and their work from its foundation in 1769 to 1904*, 8 vols. (1905–6); repr. in 4 vols. (1970) and (1972)

Graves, *Soc. Artists* — A. Graves, *The Society of Artists of Great Britain, 1760–1791, the Free Society of Artists, 1761–1783: a complete dictionary* (1907); facs. edn (1969)

Greaves & Zaller, *BDBR* — R. L. Greaves and R. Zaller, eds., *Biographical dictionary of British radicals in the seventeenth century*, 3 vols. (1982–4)

Grove, *Dict. mus.* — G. Grove, ed., *A dictionary of music and musicians*, 5 vols. (1878–90); 2nd edn, ed. J. A. Fuller Maitland (1904–10); 3rd edn, ed. H. C. Colles (1927); 4th edn with suppl. (1940); 5th edn, ed. E. Blom, 9 vols. (1954); suppl. (1961) [see also *New Grove*]

Hall, *Dramatic ports.* — L. A. Hall, *Catalogue of dramatic portraits in the theatre collection of the Harvard College library*, 4 vols. (1930–34)

*Hansard* — *Hansard's parliamentary debates*, ser. 1–5 (1803–)

Highfill, Burnim & Langhans, *BDA* — P. H. Highfill, K. A. Burnim, and E. A. Langhans, *A biographical dictionary of actors, actresses, musicians, dancers, managers, and other stage personnel in London, 1660–1800*, 16 vols. (1973–93)

*Hist. U. Oxf.* — T. H. Aston, ed., *The history of the University of Oxford*, 8 vols. (1984–2000) [1: *The early Oxford schools*, ed. J. I. Catto (1984); 2: *Late medieval Oxford*, ed. J. I. Catto and R. Evans (1992); 3: *The collegiate university*, ed. J. McConica (1986); 4: *Seventeenth-century Oxford*, ed. N. Tyacke (1997); 5: *The eighteenth century*, ed. L. S. Sutherland and L. G. Mitchell (1986); 6–7: *Nineteenth-century Oxford*, ed. M. G. Brock and M. C. Curthoys (1997–2000); 8: *The twentieth century*, ed. B. Harrison (2000)]

*HJ* — *Historical Journal*

HMC — Historical Manuscripts Commission

Holdsworth, *Eng. law* — W. S. Holdsworth, *A history of English law*, ed. A. L. Goodhart and H. L. Hanbury, 17 vols. (1903–72)

HoP, *Commons* — *The history of parliament: the House of Commons* [*1386–1421*, ed. J. S. Roskell, L. Clark, and C. Rawcliffe, 4 vols. (1992); *1509–1558*, ed. S. T. Bindoff, 3 vols. (1982); *1558–1603*, ed. P. W. Hasler, 3 vols. (1981); *1660–1690*, ed. B. D. Henning, 3 vols. (1983); *1690–1715*, ed. D. W. Hayton, E. Cruickshanks, and S. Handley, 5 vols. (2002); *1715–1754*, ed. R. Sedgwick, 2 vols. (1970); *1754–1790*, ed. L. Namier and J. Brooke, 3 vols. (1964), repr. (1985); *1790–1820*, ed. R. G. Thorne, 5 vols. (1986); in draft (used with permission): *1422–1504*, *1604–1629*, *1640–1660*, and *1820–1832*]

*IGI* — *International Genealogical Index*, Church of Jesus Christ of the Latterday Saints

*ILN* — *Illustrated London News*

IMC — Irish Manuscripts Commission

Irving, *Scots.* — J. Irving, ed., *The book of Scotsmen eminent for achievements in arms and arts, church and state, law, legislation and literature, commerce, science, travel and philanthropy* (1881)

*JCS* — *Journal of the Chemical Society*

*JHC* — *Journals of the House of Commons*

*JHL* — *Journals of the House of Lords*

John of Worcester, *Chron.* — *The chronicle of John of Worcester*, ed. R. R. Darlington and P. McGurk, trans. J. Bray and P. McGurk, 3 vols., OMT (1995–) [vol. 1 forthcoming]

Keeler, *Long Parliament* — M. F. Keeler, *The Long Parliament, 1640–1641: a biographical study of its members* (1954)

Kelly, *Handbk* — *The upper ten thousand: an alphabetical list of all members of noble families*, 3 vols. (1875–7); continued as *Kelly's handbook of the upper ten thousand for 1878* [1879], 2 vols. (1878–9); continued as *Kelly's handbook to the titled, landed and official classes*, 94 vols. (1880–1973)

*LondG* — *London Gazette*

*LP Henry VIII* — J. S. Brewer, J. Gairdner, and R. H. Brodie, eds., *Letters and papers, foreign and domestic, of the reign of Henry VIII*, 23 vols. in 38 (1862–1932); repr. (1965)

Mallalieu, *Watercolour artists* — H. L. Mallalieu, *The dictionary of British watercolour artists up to 1820*, 3 vols. (1976–90); vol. 1, 2nd edn (1986)

*Memoirs FRS* — *Biographical Memoirs of Fellows of the Royal Society*

MGH — Monumenta Germaniae Historica

*MT* — *Musical Times*

Munk, *Roll* — W. Munk, *The roll of the Royal College of Physicians of London*, 2 vols. (1861); 2nd edn, 3 vols. (1878)

*N&Q* — *Notes and Queries*

*New Grove* — S. Sadie, ed., *The new Grove dictionary of music and musicians*, 20 vols. (1980); 2nd edn, 29 vols. (2001) [also online edn; see also Grove, *Dict. mus.*]

Nichols, *Illustrations* — J. Nichols and J. B. Nichols, *Illustrations of the literary history of the eighteenth century*, 8 vols. (1817–58)

Nichols, *Lit. anecdotes* — J. Nichols, *Literary anecdotes of the eighteenth century*, 9 vols. (1812–16); facs. edn (1966)

*Obits. FRS* — *Obituary Notices of Fellows of the Royal Society*

O'Byrne, *Naval biog. dict.* — W. R. O'Byrne, *A naval biographical dictionary* (1849); repr. (1990); [2nd edn], 2 vols. (1861)

OHS — Oxford Historical Society

*Old Westminsters* — *The record of Old Westminsters*, 1–2, ed. G. F. R. Barker and A. H. Stenning (1928); suppl. 1, ed. J. B. Whitmore and G. R. Y. Radcliffe [1938]; 3, ed. J. B. Whitmore, G. R. Y. Radcliffe, and D. C. Simpson (1963); suppl. 2, ed. F. E. Pagan (1978); 4, ed. F. E. Pagan and H. E. Pagan (1992)

OMT — Oxford Medieval Texts

Ordericus Vitalis, *Eccl. hist.* — *The ecclesiastical history of Orderic Vitalis*, ed. and trans. M. Chibnall, 6 vols., OMT (1969–80); repr. (1990)

Paris, *Chron.* — *Matthaei Parisiensis, monachi sancti Albani, chronica majora*, ed. H. R. Luard, Rolls Series, 7 vols. (1872–83)

*Parl. papers* — *Parliamentary papers* (1801–)

*PBA* — *Proceedings of the British Academy*

| | |
|---|---|
| Pepys, *Diary* | *The diary of Samuel Pepys*, ed. R. Latham and W. Matthews, 11 vols. (1970–83); repr. (1995) and (2000) |
| Pevsner | N. Pevsner and others, Buildings of England series |
| *PICE* | *Proceedings of the Institution of Civil Engineers* |
| *Pipe rolls* | *The great roll of the pipe for …*, PRSoc. (1884–) |
| PRO | Public Record Office |
| *PRS* | *Proceedings of the Royal Society of London* |
| PRSoc. | Pipe Roll Society |
| *PTRS* | *Philosophical Transactions of the Royal Society* |
| *QR* | *Quarterly Review* |
| RC | Record Commissions |
| Redgrave, *Artists* | S. Redgrave, *A dictionary of artists of the English school* (1874); rev. edn (1878); repr. (1970) |
| *Reg. Oxf.* | C. W. Boase and A. Clark, eds., *Register of the University of Oxford*, 5 vols., OHS, 1, 10–12, 14 (1885–9) |
| *Reg. PCS* | J. H. Burton and others, eds., *The register of the privy council of Scotland*, 1st ser., 14 vols. (1877–98); 2nd ser., 8 vols. (1899–1908); 3rd ser., [16 vols.] (1908–70) |
| *Reg. RAN* | H. W. C. Davis and others, eds., *Regesta regum Anglo-Normannorum, 1066–1154*, 4 vols. (1913–69) |
| *RIBA Journal* | *Journal of the Royal Institute of British Architects* [later *RIBA Journal*] |
| *RotP* | J. Strachey, ed., *Rotuli parliamentorum ut et petitiones, et placita in parliamento*, 6 vols. (1767–77) |
| *RotS* | D. Macpherson, J. Caley, and W. Illingworth, eds., *Rotuli Scotiae in Turri Londinensi et in domo capitulari Westmonasteriensi asservati*, 2 vols., RC, 14 (1814–19) |
| RS | Record(s) Society |
| Rymer, *Foedera* | T. Rymer and R. Sanderson, eds., *Foedera, conventiones, literae et cuiuscunque generis acta publica inter reges Angliae et alios quosvis imperatores, reges, pontifices, principes, vel communitates*, 20 vols. (1704–35); 2nd edn, 20 vols. (1726–35); 3rd edn, 10 vols. (1739–45), facs. edn (1967); new edn, ed. A. Clarke, J. Caley, and F. Holbrooke, 4 vols., RC, 50 (1816–30) |
| Sainty, *Judges* | J. Sainty, ed., *The judges of England, 1272–1990*, SeldS, suppl. ser., 10 (1993) |
| Sainty, *King's counsel* | J. Sainty, ed., *A list of English law officers and king's counsel*, SeldS, suppl. ser., 7 (1987) |
| SCH | Studies in Church History |
| *Scots peerage* | J. B. Paul, ed. *The Scots peerage, founded on Wood's edition of Sir Robert Douglas's Peerage of Scotland, containing an historical and genealogical account of the nobility of that kingdom*, 9 vols. (1904–14) |
| SeldS | Selden Society |
| *SHR* | *Scottish Historical Review* |
| *State trials* | T. B. Howell and T. J. Howell, eds., *Cobbett's Complete collection of state trials*, 34 vols. (1809–28) |
| *STC, 1475–1640* | A. W. Pollard, G. R. Redgrave, and others, eds., *A short-title catalogue of … English books … 1475–1640* (1926); 2nd edn, ed. W. A. Jackson, F. S. Ferguson, and K. F. Pantzer, 3 vols. (1976–91) [see also Wing, *STC*] |
| STS | Scottish Text Society |
| SurtS | Surtees Society |
| Symeon of Durham, *Opera* | *Symeonis monachi opera omnia*, ed. T. Arnold, 2 vols., Rolls Series, 75 (1882–5); repr. (1965) |
| Tanner, *Bibl. Brit.-Hib.* | T. Tanner, *Bibliotheca Britannico-Hibernica*, ed. D. Wilkins (1748); repr. (1963) |
| Thieme & Becker, *Allgemeines Lexikon* | U. Thieme, F. Becker, and H. Vollmer, eds., *Allgemeines Lexikon der bildenden Künstler von der Antike bis zur Gegenwart*, 37 vols. (Leipzig, 1907–50); repr. (1961–5), (1983), and (1992) |
| Thurloe, *State papers* | *A collection of the state papers of John Thurloe*, ed. T. Birch, 7 vols. (1742) |
| *TLS* | *Times Literary Supplement* |
| Tout, *Admin. hist.* | T. F. Tout, *Chapters in the administrative history of mediaeval England: the wardrobe, the chamber, and the small seals*, 6 vols. (1920–33); repr. (1967) |
| TRHS | *Transactions of the Royal Historical Society* |
| *VCH* | H. A. Doubleday and others, eds., *The Victoria history of the counties of England*, [88 vols.] (1900–) |
| Venn, *Alum. Cant.* | J. Venn and J. A. Venn, *Alumni Cantabrigienses: a biographical list of all known students, graduates, and holders of office at the University of Cambridge, from the earliest times to 1900*, 10 vols. (1922–54); repr. in 2 vols. (1974–8) |
| Vertue, *Note books* | [G. Vertue], *Note books*, ed. K. Esdaile, earl of Ilchester, and H. M. Hake, 6 vols., Walpole Society, 18, 20, 22, 24, 26, 30 (1930–55) |
| *VF* | *Vanity Fair* |
| Walford, *County families* | E. Walford, *The county families of the United Kingdom, or, Royal manual of the titled and untitled aristocracy of Great Britain and Ireland* (1860) |
| *Walker rev.* | A. G. Matthews, *Walker revised: being a revision of John Walker's Sufferings of the clergy during the grand rebellion, 1642–60* (1948); repr. (1988) |
| Walpole, *Corr.* | *The Yale edition of Horace Walpole's correspondence*, ed. W. S. Lewis, 48 vols. (1937–83) |
| Ward, *Men of the reign* | T. H. Ward, ed., *Men of the reign: a biographical dictionary of eminent persons of British and colonial birth who have died during the reign of Queen Victoria* (1885); repr. (Graz, 1968) |
| Waterhouse, *18c painters* | E. Waterhouse, *The dictionary of 18th century painters in oils and crayons* (1981); repr. as *British 18th century painters in oils and crayons* (1991), vol. 2 of *Dictionary of British art* |
| Watt, *Bibl. Brit.* | R. Watt, *Bibliotheca Britannica, or, A general index to British and foreign literature*, 4 vols. (1824) [many reprs.] |
| *Wellesley index* | W. E. Houghton, ed., *The Wellesley index to Victorian periodicals, 1824–1900*, 5 vols. (1966–89); new edn (1999) [CD-ROM] |
| Wing, *STC* | D. Wing, ed., *Short-title catalogue of … English books … 1641–1700*, 3 vols. (1945–51); 2nd edn (1972–88); rev. and enl. edn, ed. J. J. Morrison, C. W. Nelson, and M. Seccombe, 4 vols. (1994–8) [see also *STC, 1475–1640*] |
| *Wisden* | *John Wisden's Cricketer's Almanack* |
| Wood, *Ath. Oxon.* | A. Wood, *Athenae Oxonienses … to which are added the Fasti*, 2 vols. (1691–2); 2nd edn (1721); new edn, 4 vols., ed. P. Bliss (1813–20); repr. (1967) and (1969) |
| Wood, *Vic. painters* | C. Wood, *Dictionary of Victorian painters* (1971); 2nd edn (1978); 3rd edn as *Victorian painters*, 2 vols. (1995), vol. 4 of *Dictionary of British art* |
| *WW* | *Who's who* (1849–) |
| *WWBMP* | M. Stenton and S. Lees, eds., *Who's who of British members of parliament*, 4 vols. (1976–81) |
| *WWW* | *Who was who* (1929–) |

**Grigg, Edward William Macleay**, **first Baron Altrincham** (**1879–1955**), colonial administrator and politician, was born on 8 September 1879 in Madras, the only son of Henry Bidewell Grigg (*d.* 1894) of the Indian Civil Service and his wife, Elizabeth Louisa (*d.* 1920), eldest daughter of Sir Edward Deas Thomson, colonial secretary of New South Wales (1837–56). A scholar of both Winchester College and New College, Oxford, he obtained a second class in classical moderations (1900) and a third in *literae humaniores* (1902). In 1902 he won the Gaisford Greek verse prize.

Journalism was Grigg's first calling. In 1903 he joined the staff of *The Times* as secretary to G. E. Buckle, the editor, then moved to *The Outlook* as assistant editor (1905–6) to J. L. Garvin. In 1908, after two years of widespread and intensive travel, he returned to *The Times* as head of its colonial department. His family background, his personal knowledge of imperial affairs, and his reverence for Joseph Chamberlain and Lord Milner well fitted him for this post. At no time in its history, Grigg was later proud to recall, did that newspaper exercise a more salutary and decisive influence upon national policy than in the years immediately before the First World War. He resigned in 1913 to become joint editor of the *Round Table*.

Grigg was thirty-four at the outbreak of war in 1914. Scorning the posts of dignified safety which could have been his for the asking, he joined the Grenadier Guards as an ensign and was sent out to the 2nd battalion in France. The Scribe, as he was affectionately called in the brigade, showed outstanding qualities of gallantry and leadership throughout the heavy fighting in which the guards division was engaged. Winston Churchill, then a major in the Oxfordshire yeomanry, was for a short time attached to Grigg's company to gain experience of trench warfare. Early in 1916 Grigg was transferred to the staff. By the end of the war he had risen to be lieutenant-colonel and GSO1 of the guards division. He was awarded the MC in 1917 and the DSO in 1918, created CMG in 1919, and mentioned in dispatches.

It was during his years in the grenadiers that Grigg first met the prince of Wales, whom he accompanied on tours of Canada in 1919 and of Australia and New Zealand in 1920 as military secretary and special adviser. For these services, not always free from anxiety, he was appointed successively CVO (1919) and KCVO (1920). On his return he joined the staff of the prime minister, Lloyd George, as a private secretary. To the traditional loyalties of the post he added an intense personal admiration for his mercurial chief which blinded him to all criticism, however well founded. He served his master with memorable fidelity throughout some difficult political situations. At Cannes in January 1922 he took part in the historic game of golf which caused the downfall of Aristide Briand. When Lloyd George himself fell from power later that year Grigg was offered a choice of senior appointments in the civil service. He preferred instead to enter the House of Commons, representing Oldham (1922–5) as a Lloyd George Liberal. As secretary to the Rhodes Trust from 1923 to 1925 he was also able to maintain a close interest in imperial affairs.

**Edward William Macleay Grigg, first Baron Altrincham (1879–1955)**, by Walter Stoneman, 1931

In 1925 Grigg was appointed governor of Kenya. In 1923 he had married Joan Alice Katherine Dickson-Poynder [*see* Grigg, Joan Alice Katherine, Lady Altrincham (1897–1987)], only child of John Poynder Dickson-Poynder, Lord Islington. They had one daughter and two sons. His wife's instinctive sympathy for all races, expressed particularly in her patronage of nursing and maternity services, enhanced the distinction of her husband's administration. The task with which Grigg had been charged was to unite the three east African territories of Kenya, Uganda, and Tanganyika. Largely owing to the opposition of Sir Donald Cameron, governor of Tanganyika, and to lukewarm support from the British government, this mission failed. But there was much else in his programme which brought lasting economic benefit to the colony and created stable conditions most likely to attract European capital. Agriculture and forestry, communications and schools, town planning and security of land tenure were all improved during his energetic and sometimes exacting rule. Believing that the civilization of an age is reflected in its buildings, he dignified Kenya with two splendid government houses—at Nairobi and Mombasa—and with the law courts in Nairobi, all designed by Sir Herbert Baker, but was unable to realize an ambitious project for central government offices. He was appointed KCMG in 1928.

Appreciation of his governorship has since been tempered by belittlement of Grigg's trust in tribal self-government and provincial autonomy. He rejected the later fashion of thought that Kenya should progress through the multiracial state towards a common citizenship. This, he believed, could lead only to the ultimate extinction of the white settler and to an overwhelming African ascendancy: a prospect he deplored, not because he felt that Africans as such were unfitted to govern themselves, but because he feared that they would be required to administer an alien system of Western government without the necessary education and experience. To the end of his days he set his face against so abrupt an abdication of what he held to be Great Britain's imperial mission.

On returning to England in 1930 Grigg was offered a choice of Indian governorships. Neither he nor his wife, however, was in robust health and he refused them all. It was the fatal turning point of his life. Whatever his opinion of African incapacity for self-rule, it did not extend to the peoples of India. As a boy he had seen his parents' house thronged with Indian visitors and developed a sympathetic understanding of their aspirations. He might have been one of the greatest of Indian administrators; instead he determined to remain at home and to plunge once more into the world of politics. Lacking the instincts of political manoeuvre and self-advancement, and further handicapped by his known allegiance to Lloyd George, Grigg was doomed to fail in this venture.

In the general election of 1931, although already adopted as National Conservative candidate for Leeds Central, Grigg stood down with characteristic unselfishness in favour of the former Labour member who proposed to stand as a 'national' candidate. Two years later, having in the meantime served as chairman of the milk reorganization commission, he returned to the House of Commons as member for Altrincham. It is to his credit that he recognized the menace of Nazi Germany before most of his colleagues. In two eloquent works, *The Faith of an Englishman* (1936) and *Britain Looks at Germany* (1938), he pleaded for a stern policy of defence. Yet he continued to believe that such a course of action was not incompatible with wholehearted support for the administrations of Stanley Baldwin and Neville Chamberlain. Too loyal to be a rebel, he would plead with his leaders in private but recoiled from criticizing them in public. His name is not to be found among those Conservatives who abstained in the 'Munich' division.

Denied office until the outbreak of the Second World War, Grigg was appointed parliamentary secretary to the Ministry of Information in its opening days. In April 1940 he became financial secretary, and in May joint parliamentary under-secretary, at the War Office. He held the latter post until March 1942, having earlier refused Churchill's offer of promotion as first commissioner of works since it depended upon his acceptance of a peerage. Thereafter he was inadequately employed for a man of his talents, but in November 1944 returned to office as minister resident in the Middle East in succession to Lord Moyne and was sworn of the privy council. The defeat of the Churchill government in July 1945 put an end to both his political ambitions and his active political life, although he was to assume the editorship of the *National Review* in 1948. He was created Baron Altrincham in 1945 and died at his house at Tormarton, in Gloucestershire, on 1 December 1955, after a long illness. His last reserves of strength were drained in the completion of *Kenya's Opportunity* (1955), a final tribute to the land which was so much a part of his life. His elder son, John Edward Poynder (1924–2001), succeeded to the title but disclaimed it in 1963. Altrincham was survived by his wife.

Ned Grigg was a handsome man, well above middle height and with the complexion of a countryman. Yet his soldierly bearing concealed a nervous system ill suited to the hubbub of politics. Opposition to his impulsive enthusiasms evoked bursts of impatience, even of rage. Then the clouds would lift: in his family circle or when entertaining a few close friends—drawn mostly from the Milner 'kindergarten'—he would both show and inspire deep affection. He was half a poet. Few other colonial governors would have written: 'The very thought of Kenya is like sunlight to me, sunlight crisp as mountain air in the high places of the earth.' He found perennial solace in the plays of Shakespeare and in listening to music.

KENNETH ROSE, *rev.*

**Sources** *The Times* (2 Dec 1955) • *WWW* • personal knowledge (1971) • private information (1971) • *WWBMP*, vol. 3 • Burke, *Peerage* (1980) • E. W. M. Grigg, *Kenya's opportunity: memories, hopes and ideas* (1955) • *CGPLA Eng. & Wales* (1956)

**Archives** Bodl. Oxf., corresp. and papers; memoranda relating to reform of House of Lords • Bodl. RH, corresp. and papers relating to Kenya • News Int. RO, papers as imperial editor of *The Times* | Bodl. Oxf., corresp. with Lionel Curtis • Bodl. Oxf., letters to Lady Milner • Bodl. Oxf., corresp. with Sir Alfred Zimmern • CAC Cam., corresp. with Sir E. L. Spears • HLRO, letters to Lord Beaverbrook • NA Scot., corresp. with Lord Lothian • NL Aus., corresp. with Viscount Novar • U. Leeds, Brotherton L., corresp. with Henry Drummond-Wolff, etc. | FILM BFI NFTVA, news footage

**Likenesses** W. Stoneman, three photographs, 1921–41, NPG [*see illus.*] • R. Nester, pencil drawing, priv. coll.

**Wealth at death** £8823 5*s*. 5*d*.: probate, 18 April 1956, *CGPLA Eng. & Wales*

**Grigg, Sir (Percy) James (1890–1964)**, public servant, was born at 4 Danby Terrace, Withycombe Raleigh, Exmouth, Devon, on 16 December 1890, the eldest of the three sons of Frank Alfred Grigg, a journeyman carpenter, and his wife, Jane Elizabeth Crocker; she was the daughter of a tailor and had been a children's nurse. Shortly after their son was born the Griggs moved to Bournemouth, and P. J., as he subsequently became widely known in Whitehall, was educated at an elementary school from which he gained a scholarship to Bournemouth secondary school; in 1909 he entered St John's College, Cambridge, as a senior scholar. He graduated with first-class honours in both parts one (1910) and two (1912) of the mathematical tripos, and in 1913 was placed first in the examination for entrance to the administrative class of the civil service and appointed to the Treasury.

In June 1915 Grigg was permitted to apply for a commission in the army, but was rejected on account of short

Sir (Percy) James Grigg (1890–1964), by Walter Stoneman, 1934

sight; a few months later he tried again, and this time was accepted. He joined the Royal Garrison Artillery as a second lieutenant, and served in eastern Europe until 1918 when he was transferred to the office of external ballistics where he worked until the war ended. One of his colleagues there was Gertrude Charlotte, daughter of the Revd George Frederick Hough, and a niece of the bishop-suffragan of Woolwich. They married in July 1919 after Grigg had returned to the Treasury. The marriage was childless.

Sir Warren Fisher, permanent secretary to the Treasury, speedily recognized Grigg's ability, and in 1921, when Sir Robert Horne became chancellor of the exchequer, Fisher persuaded him to appoint Grigg as his principal private secretary. P. J. remained in this post for almost ten years, in which time he served five chancellors including Stanley Baldwin, Neville Chamberlain, Philip Snowden, and Winston Churchill, with whom Grigg worked for nearly five years from 1924 to 1929.

The decade between 1921 and 1930 was a period of momentous developments in the economic and financial policies of the governments led by Lloyd George, Bonar Law, Stanley Baldwin, and Ramsay MacDonald, and Grigg saw many changes of direction and gained invaluable experience as an administrator. He accompanied Baldwin and Montagu Norman, governor of the Bank of England, to Washington for the negotiations leading in 1923 to the settlement of British war debts to the United States; he was working with Churchill when in 1925 it was decided that the pound sterling should return to the gold standard at its pre-war parity. He saw the development of the crisis in the coal industry and the general strike of 1926, and supported the chancellor of the exchequer in dealing with some of the financial problems that faced the Labour government in 1930 and 1931 leading to Snowden's decision to abandon the gold standard and to the formation of the National Government.

Snowden was still chancellor when Grigg ceased to be his principal private secretary and became chairman of the board of customs and excise. After a month he was transferred as chairman of the Board of Inland Revenue. Grigg himself wrote that 'it was known that the Inland Revenue would have to produce a scheme for taxing Land Values against the Budget of 1931, and the Chancellor wanted to have somebody at the head of it whom he knew and who knew him and how his mind worked' (Grigg, 238). His uneventful tenure of this post did not last long. At the end of 1933 Sir Samuel Hoare asked him to go to India to succeed Sir George Schuster as finance member of the viceroy's executive council. For the next five years Grigg applied his mind, with its respect for order and efficiency, to the intractable problems of the subcontinent in which the Government of India Act of 1935 extended quasi self-government to the provinces and the Congress Party grew steadily in power. He sought to improve communications and create better conditions in the rural areas, but his efforts were unpopular with Congress, and all his five budgets were rejected in the assembly and had to be enacted by the viceroy's certificate.

When he returned to London in 1939 Grigg expected to succeed Sir Warren Fisher as permanent secretary to the Treasury, but he was disappointed and was offered instead the Colonial Office or the War Office. He chose the War Office. Grigg wrote that, at the outbreak of war in 1939, the impression of the War Office left on his mind was 'one of considerable confusion'. He set out at once to improve this situation. In 1940 he became chairman of the standing committee on army administration set up to increase efficiency in organization and to simplify procedure, and when, in November 1941, Sir Alan Brooke became chief of the Imperial General Staff the two worked closely together in the necessary reorganization of the army. Their co-operation became even more effective when, in February 1942, Churchill took the unusual step of appointing Grigg to be secretary of state for war when he dismissed H. D. R. Margesson, following the fall of Singapore. Brooke confided to his diary,

> Thus started a long association with P. J. Grigg for which I thank heaven. I received nothing but assistance and support during the whole of our time together and could not have asked for anyone better to work with. One of the quickest and ablest brains I have ever met. A slightly suspicious nature at times until one had gained his confidence. A heart of gold! (Bryant, 317–18)

For three years, from the military and naval disasters of 1942 to the victories of 1945, Brooke and Grigg collaborated in the arduous task of creating the British military organization and the efficient, well-trained armies that fought successfully in north Africa and Europe until Hitler was defeated. Throughout this time Grigg was nationalist MP for East Cardiff, and when the 1945 election brought about the downfall of Churchill's government Grigg lost his seat and ceased to be secretary of state for war.

It was fortunate for the British war effort that Grigg and Brooke, two men who were never afraid to speak their minds with brutal frankness, should have had complete confidence in each other's ability and absolute trust in each other's integrity. From his early years as a principal private secretary Grigg, with his passion for efficiency, had often been regarded as intolerant and arrogant. John C. C. Davidson, parliamentary private secretary to Baldwin when he was president of the Board of Trade, was critical of Grigg as a colleague. 'P. J. wasn't a really attractive person', he said, 'because he lacked human sympathy and was intolerant' (James, 10). Years later, Herbert Morrison described Grigg in unflattering terms:

> Grigg had a considerable flair for frank speech, aggravated by a hot temper. I recall a day at No. 10 when we were all waiting to enter the Cabinet Room. I was chatting to Sir James and we began mildly to disagree. In a matter of a moment or two he was denouncing me and being extremely rude. I mildly enquired who was having a row with whom. Sir John Anderson, another civil servant turned minister, who was present on this occasion, said 'It's all right, Herbert. You need not be upset. It's just James's way of talking. He can't help it'. (Morrison, 207)

Grigg undoubtedly prized competence and precision above tact and diplomacy, but he was able to win the confidence of statesmen as widely different in outlook as Philip Snowden and Winston Churchill. The former described him as a civil servant of exceptional merit, and the latter, while he was chancellor of the exchequer, expressed the greatest admiration for his gifts and character. R. M. Barrington-Ward, editor of *The Times*, referred in his diary (on 18 February 1941) to a dinner with the permanent secretary at the War Office in which they talked together about Churchill. 'Much talk of Winston,' he wrote, 'whom he knows better than most people both in his strong and his weak points', and added, 'He has a fine intelligence and courage. I have a great regard for him and respect for his common sense' (McLachlan, 188). The fact that Churchill selected Grigg to be secretary of state for war in a time of grave crisis shows clearly enough that the prime minister had no doubts about his capacity as an administrator.

After his defeat in the general election of 1945 Grigg found himself, at the age of fifty-four, without employment. In 1946, however, he became the first British executive director of the International Bank for Reconstruction and Development, and in 1947 he was appointed financial adviser and then director of the Imperial Tobacco Company. He also held directorships of the Prudential Assurance Company and the National Provincial Bank. In 1948 he published his autobiography, *Prejudice and Judgment*. He was appointed chairman of the Bass, Ratcliff and Gretton Company in 1959, and on its merger with Mitchells and Butlers, Birmingham, in 1961, became chairman of the new group. In 1954, in consequence of the recommendations of a committee on departmental records of which Grigg was chairman, responsibility for the Public Record Office was transferred from the master of the rolls to the lord chancellor. Grigg was chairman of an advisory committee on recruitment to the forces which, in 1958, recommended improved pensions and allowances for the armed forces.

Grigg was appointed KCB in 1932 and KCSI in 1936; he was sworn of the privy council in 1942, became an honorary fellow of St John's College, Cambridge, in 1943, honorary LLD of Bristol University in 1946, and honorary bencher of the Middle Temple in 1954. He died at Beaumont House, Beaumont Street, London, on 5 May 1964.

H. F. OXBURY, *rev.*

**Sources** *The Times* (7 May 1964) • P. J. Grigg, *Prejudice and judgment* (1948) • A. Bryant, *The turn of the tide, 1939–1943: a study based on the diaries and autobiographical notes of Field Marshal the Viscount Alanbrooke* (1957) • H. S. Morrison, *Herbert Morrison: an autobiography* [1960] • P. Snowden, *An autobiography*, 2 vols. (1934) • H. M. Hyde, *Baldwin: the unexpected prime minister* (1973) • *Memoirs of a Conservative: J. C. C. Davidson's memoirs and papers, 1910–37*, ed. R. R. James (1969) • D. McLachlan, *In the chair: Barrington-Ward of* The Times, *1927–1948* (1971) • b. cert. • *CGPLA Eng. & Wales* (1964)

**Archives** CAC Cam., corresp. and MSS | BL OIOC, corresp. with Sir Findlater Stewart, MSS EUR D 714 • King's Lond., Liddell Hart C., corresp. with Sir B. H. Liddell Hart • NL Wales, corresp. with Thomas Jones | FILM BFI NFTVA, news footage

**Likenesses** W. Stoneman, photograph, 1934, NPG [*see illus.*] • W. Stoneman, photograph, 1942, NPG

**Wealth at death** £49,466: probate, 15 June 1964, *CGPLA Eng. & Wales*

**Grigg** [*née* Dickson-Poynder], **Joan Alice Katherine**, **Lady Altrincham** (1897–1987), organizer of maternity and nursing services in Africa, was born at Hartham Park, near Corsham, Wiltshire, on 11 September 1897, the only child of John Poynder Dickson-*Poynder, Baron Islington (1866–1936), and his wife, Anne Beauclerk Dundas (*d.* 1958). Joan's father, a landowner, sat as a Conservative MP until 1905 when he joined the Liberal Party, and in 1910 was raised to the peerage on his appointment as governor-general of New Zealand.

Known as Joanie, Joan Dickson-Poynder was educated mainly by a governess from Alsace and spoke French and German fluently. She was a great beauty: when John Sargent drew her in charcoal at the age of thirteen he was so taken by his subject that he offered to paint a full-length oil portrait as a gift (the offer was declined on the grounds that it would interrupt her studies). Since her father was chairman of the Royal Northern Hospital, and her mother founded day nurseries for poor children in London's East End, she was brought up to regard public service as a duty. During the First World War, aged nineteen, she volunteered as a nurse in the voluntary aid detachment. She worked first at a military hospital in Canterbury and was then transferred in 1917 to a Red Cross hospital at Rouen in France. By the end of the war she was working with the French army.

On 31 January 1923 Joan married Sir Edward William Macleay *Grigg (1879–1955), a Liberal MP. Seventeen years her senior, he was an idealist like her, with a particular interest in imperial affairs. They had two sons and one daughter. Two years after the marriage and a year after the birth of their first child, her husband was appointed governor of Kenya, at that time a British crown colony. The Griggs moved to Nairobi, where they lived between 1925 and 1930. Apart from her friendship with Karen Blixen, the Danish novelist, Joan found the social side of life at Government House 'sometimes terribly trying' (Lady Grigg to Lord and Lady Islington, 8 Dec 1925, quoted in Williams, 89). She longed to use her role as governor's wife to do some good for the Kenyan people, especially the very poor. Her days, she wrote in a letter to her parents, 'simply bristle with all the problems you put so much of your life's work into' (Lady Grigg to Lord and Lady Islington, quoted ibid., 91).

In 1926 Joan Grigg created the Lady Grigg Welfare League as a way of providing nursing and maternity services for women and children of all races. It was supported by energetic fund-raising efforts in Kenya and in Britain. The first branch of the league, which opened in 1926, was a child welfare home for Arabs and Africans in Mombasa. The second branch, which opened the following year, was the African Maternity and Child Welfare Hospital and Training Centre at Pumwani, Nairobi. The league quickly developed into three combined enterprises: maternity hospitals and training schools for Africans in Nairobi and Mombasa; a maternity hospital, school for midwives, and infant welfare clinic for Indians; and a hostel in Nairobi for training nurses to serve the European community. Midwifery training was regarded by the league as a priority, and the first probationers passed their examination in 1929. Without these efforts, virtually nothing would have been done by the British administration for Kenyan mothers.

The separate sections of the league reflected the racial divisions in Kenya. However, Lady Grigg was especially concerned to help African women and children and did not accept the view, which was widely held in Britain, that 'native' women gave birth without difficulty. She believed that their need was in fact greater because of their poverty and also because of female circumcision, which was practised by many Kenyan tribes and which could make childbirth dangerous and sometimes fatal. On a visit to Britain in 1927, she wrote a fund-raising letter to *The Times* (11 June 1927) which emphasized the particular needs of African mothers and the importance of training African midwives. She was delighted with a donation from Queen Mary, but disappointed that nearly all the money from donors was earmarked for the European nurses' association and maternity home. Joan Grigg's views on race were unorthodox for her time and for her social class. She did not believe there was any future in Kenya for large-scale white settlement. This was one of the few issues on which she disagreed with her husband.

After the Griggs's return to Britain from Kenya in 1930, they lived at Tormarton Court, near Badminton in Gloucestershire. In 1933 Sir Edward became a Conservative MP, and in 1944 he was made minister resident in the Middle East. The Griggs moved to Cairo, Egypt, where Joan hoped to embark on the same kind of work for women's health as that which she had started in Kenya; however, a change of government in Britain brought them home in less than a year. She then devoted herself to family life and her local community. In 1945 she started an East African Women's Society as a multiracial alternative to the East African Women's League, which was for white people only.

In 1945 Joan Grigg became Lady Altrincham when her husband went to the House of Lords as first Baron Altrincham. On the latter's death in 1955 their elder son, the writer and historian John Edward Poynder Grigg (1924–2001), inherited the title, but in 1963 he disclaimed his peerage for life.

Joan Grigg died at Tormarton Court on 10 August 1987. Her work in Kenya laid the foundation of a maternity service that not only served the needs of women in Nairobi and Mombasa, but also trained midwives to care for mothers in outlying areas. The Pumwani Hospital in Nairobi, which developed out of the Pumwani Centre first set up by the Lady Grigg Welfare League, is one of the largest maternity hospitals in Africa: the original building still exists and is the school of midwifery at the centre of the hospital. The Coast Province General Hospital in Mombasa still has a maternity ward called the Lady Grigg.

SUSAN WILLIAMS

**Sources** A. S. Williams, *Ladies of influence* (2000) • *Annual Report of the Lady Grigg Welfare League: African Section* (1929–31) • *Annual Report of the Lady Grigg Welfare League: Indian Section* (1929) • *Annual Report of the Lady Grigg Welfare League: European Branch* (1932) • *The Times* (11 June 1927) • *Annual Report of the Kenya Colony and Protectorate Native Affairs Department* (1931–4) • private information, 2004 [British Red Cross, family] • Burke, *Peerage* (1967)
**Archives** priv. coll., private papers
**Wealth at death** £1,048,308: probate, 16 March 1988, *CGPLA Eng. & Wales*

**Griggs, Frederick Landseer Maur** (1876–1938), etcher, illustrator, and architect, was born on 30 October 1876 at 21 High Street, Hitchin, Hertfordshire, the eldest of four children of Frederick Griggs (1849–1926) and his wife, Jemima Elizabeth (Mimie; 1852–1900), daughter of Thomas Bailey, hatter. His parents were Baptists; his father, a baker and confectioner, was a deacon of the church, while his mother gave Bible classes, and taught in a local school for adult education. The neo-Gothic architecture of the newly built chapel they attended had a lifelong effect on Griggs's artistic vision. Griggs attended several schools in Hitchin; he also took drawing lessons, and in the mechanics' institute library discovered the work of Samuel Palmer, a seminal influence. In 1892 he began work as an architectural draughtsman under Walter Millard, moving in 1895 to the offices of C. E. Mallows. In 1897 he set up a studio in Hitchin, and exhibited his first work, an architectural perspective, at the Royal Academy.

In 1900 Macmillan & Co. commissioned drawings from Griggs for the Hertfordshire book in their series Highways and Byways. This became his most substantial achievement: over nearly forty years he illustrated twelve volumes of the series, books which demonstrate his technical virtuosity as well as his visionary talents. The volume on Cambridgeshire (1909) is particularly fine. His preliminary drawings also provided inspiration for his imaginative compositions.

In 1903 Griggs arrived at Chipping Campden in the Cotswolds, where C. R. Ashbee had established his Guild and School of Handicraft the previous year. The guild's dedication to the preservation of traditional skills and ideals of craftsmanship impressed Griggs; he took lodgings in the guild hostel in 1904, before moving to Dover's House in the High Street. Here he lived until 1930, when he built his own New Dover's House close by. He quickly made a name as an illustrator, while developing the imaginative compositions which became his hallmark. *Sutton* (1912, two variant states) moves the subject for the first time beyond architectural topography to express the spirit and history of the place. In 1916 he was elected associate member of the Royal Society of Painter-Etchers and Engravers; two years later he became a fellow, elected to the council in 1920.

Griggs was received into the Catholic church in 1912, taking the baptismal name Maur. To mark the occasion he designed a bell, named Maurus, for the local church of St Catherine's, and in 1913 produced the striking plate *Maur's Farm* (1913–22, five variant states).

As an architect Griggs worked principally on small-scale projects for Campden friends. His major architectural achievement lay in the war memorials he designed during 1919. These works, done without payment, continue to adorn the Gloucestershire countryside at Broadway, Snowshill, Painswick, and Upton St Leonards, as well as his own Chipping Campden; each was designed to be appropriate to its setting and the history of the site.

Griggs was now producing his most ambitious designs, towering compositions of Gothic spires and turrets, deliberately archaic, expressing his sense of the symbolic and emotional grandeur of the past contrasted to the present. *Anglia perdita* (1921, five variant states) is typical in its evocation of a lost, timeless world of spiritual beauty, visions which attracted a disillusioned post-war society. From 1921 he established his own press to prove his plates, facilitating his habit of revising past works. The progress of his skies is especially interesting, the blankness of early plates being later elaborated to richer meteorological effects. His assistant was Nina Blanche Muir (1900–1988), whom he married at Brompton Oratory on 9 January 1922. Their son, John Coelfrid (1922–1944), was followed by five daughters: Mary (*b.* 1923), Millicent (*b.* 1926), Hilda (*b.* 1931), Barbara (*b.* 1932), and Agnes (1937–1939). This large family added to the strain of the financial insecurity of the fluctuating print market; from 1926 plans for his new home caused further anxiety. New Dover's House was a characteristic Griggs creation: a modern medieval manor house in the finest Cotswold tradition. Once installed, Griggs enlarged his printing works to produce finished etchings. A painstaking craftsman, he selected handmade papers to complement individual subjects, and designed several typefaces, notably the Leysbourne (renamed Littleworth), for the Shakespeare Head Press.

Of middle height, lean and intense, Griggs impressed acquaintances with his grave, quiet manner. His health was never robust, and in public he was diffident, disliking display, although he was a fluent lecturer and speaker. Nor was he always serious—he had infectious enthusiasm, a gift for friendship, and an ability to extemporize on the piano which made him a valued party guest. He also took an interest in younger artists: Graham Sutherland was only one who owed his beginnings as an etcher to the encouragement of Fred Griggs.

In 1922 Griggs became one of the few etcher associates of the Royal Academy. He was elected Royal Academician in 1931; his diploma work was the large etching *Lanterns of Sarras* (1932, four variant states). With its great bell-towers, divided bridge, and mysterious figures, bathed in light from a delicately etched sky, *Sarras* epitomizes Griggs's combination of technical skill and visionary conviction. In 1933 he served on the academy selection committee, and the following year held the mastership of the Art-Workers' Guild. In August 1937, despite increasing frailty, Griggs undertook the *Highways and Byways of Essex*. He died at his home with the work unfinished, on 7 June 1938, and was buried in St Catherine's Church, Chipping Campden, on 10 June. JUSTINE HOPKINS

**Sources** J. N. Moore, *F. L. Griggs: the architecture of dreams* (1999) • F. A. Comstock, *A Gothic vision: F. L. Griggs and his work* (1966) • M. Gullick, *The watercolour record of F. L. Griggs* (1977) • H. J. Wright, *The etched work of F. L. Griggs* (1941) • F. C. Brown, 'The architectural renderings of F. L. Griggs', *Architectural Review* [New York], new ser., 2 (1913) • R. G. Alexander, *The engraved work of F. L. Griggs, ARA, RE: etchings and drypoints, 1912–28* (1928) • T. A. Clark, *Silences of noons: the work of F. L. Griggs* (1988) [exhibition catalogue, Cheltenham Art Gallery, 5 Nov – 31 Dec 1988] • M. C. Salaman, ed., *F. L. Griggs* (1926), vol. 12 of *Modern masters of etching* (1924–32) • M. C. Salaman, *Modern book illustrators and their work* (1922) • R. Lister, 'F. L. Griggs: an appreciation', *The best of Mr Frederick Landseer Maur Griggs* (1974) • R. L. Hine, 'The life and art-work of F. L. Griggs RA', *Relics of an un-common attorney*, ed. [F. L. Hine and M. M. Bozman] (1951) • G. Powell, 'Frederick Griggs, RA and Chipping Campden', *Gloucestershire History*, 3 (1989), 11–15

**Archives** AM Oxf., corresp. • BL, letters to Macmillan & Co., MS 55228 • U. Glas., Wright MSS, letters | Cheltenham Art Gallery and Museum, letters to W. Millard

**Likenesses** H. Payne, drawing, 1921 • H. Wrightson, photograph, 1921, repro. in Moore, *F. L. Griggs*

**Wealth at death** £7471 6s.: administration, 3 Aug 1938, *CGPLA Eng. & Wales* • art of unstable value; owed £500 on building of Chipping Campden house, auctioned after death

**Griggs, John** (1551/2–1598), carpenter, was the son of Simon Griggs, citizen and butcher of London, and his wife, Elizabeth, who lived in Pudding Lane in the parish of St Margaret, New Fish Street. Simon Griggs died in 1570, leaving the lease on his house to his wife and the rest of his goods to his wife and children. On 1 November 1573 John Griggs (said to be twenty-one years old) was apprenticed for seven years to a carpenter, Richard Smith the elder, and on 22 October 1574 he transferred to another, Richard Holgates, who lived in Griggs's parish. Griggs became free of the Carpenters more than two years early, on 8 July 1578, by managing to transfer to the Carpenters his patrimonial right to be free of the Butchers. He did not, however, take an apprentice carpenter until 1 November 1580, when his seven years were up.

Griggs is remembered mainly for his associations with the theatrical world. He built the Rose Playhouse for Philip Henslowe in 1587. In the spring of 1592 he supplied materials towards its enlargement and then contributed to building a house for Edward Alleyn, the celebrated actor who had married Henslowe's stepdaughter. On 29 July (giving his age, curiously, as forty-three) he took Margaret Brayne's side in her dispute with James Burbage about the ownership of The Theatre in Shoreditch. In a deposition, Griggs said that he knew all the parties to the dispute and was 'familierlie acquainted' with Burbage 'long before' 1576, when the playhouse was built, 'and ever syns' (Wallace, 134). He knew the motives of Burbage and John Brayne in building the playhouse and how they had financed its building, but he did not know details of what had happened thereafter. In March he was one of two 'welbeloued and trustye frendes' whom Holgates chose to be overseers of his will (GL, MS 9171/17).

Griggs and his wife, Anne, became close friends of both Henslowe and Alleyn. On 5 July and 28 September 1593 Henslowe told Alleyn in letters that Griggs and his wife had 'comendations vnto you', and on 1 August Alleyn asked his wife in a letter to convey his 'harty comend[ations] to m$^{r}$ grigs his wife and all his houshould' (*Henslowe's Diary*, 275, 276, 281). In 1595 Henslowe paid Griggs £5 to take Mary Henslowe, Henslowe's niece, as an apprentice so that she might learn needlework with Griggs's wife.

At various times Griggs called himself either a carpenter or a citizen and butcher of London. He was living in Pudding Lane (where he must have spent a great part of his life) in 1592 and was expensively buried in the parish church in 1598, as was his wife in 1600 or 1601. They were survived by a daughter, Mary, who had married an actor at the Rose, Robert Shaa, in May 1598. Shaa paid for his mother-in-law's burial place, and, on 15 September 1601, Mary Shaa claimed the administration of her mother's goods. HERBERT BERRY

**Sources** B. Marsh, J. Ainsworth, and A. M. Millard, eds., *Records of the Worshipful Company of Carpenters*, 7 vols. (1913–68), vols. 5–7 · *Henslowe's diary*, ed. R. A. Foakes and R. T. Rickert (1961) · M. Edmond, 'The builder of the Rose Theatre', *Theatre Notebook*, 44 (1990), 50–54 · C. W. Wallace, *The first London theatre* (1913) · GL, MS 9171/15, fol. 363 · GL, MS 9171/17, fol. 428*v* · GL, MS 9168/15, fol. 185*v* · GL, MS 11761

**Griggs, William** (1832–1911), inventor of a photolithographic process, was the son of a gate-keeper to the duke of Bedford at Woburn, Bedfordshire, where he was born on 4 October 1832. After the death of his father Griggs started working life as an apprentice carpenter at the age of twelve. When he was eighteen he moved to London to work in the Indian court of the Great Exhibition of 1851, and the same year he married Elizabeth Jane Gill (*d*. 1903). Griggs took the opportunity to improve his scanty education at evening classes, notably at King's College. In 1855 he was selected to be technical assistant to the reporter on Indian products and director of the Indian Museum, then in the India House, Leadenhall Street.

Griggs's artistic tastes and keen interest in photography and lithography were encouraged by Dr John Forbes Watson, who became his chief in 1858. At Watson's instance Griggs was installed at Fife House, Whitehall, pending completion of the India Office, in a studio and workshops for photolithographic work. Like many contemporary photographers he took a keen interest in the process of photozincography, details of which were published in pamphlets by the director-general of the Ordnance Survey, General Sir Henry James, and his assistant, Captain A. De Courtenay Scott. By careful experiment Griggs found that the use of cold, instead of hot, water in developing the transfer left the gelatine in the whites of the transfer, thus giving firmer adhesion to the stone and serving as a support to the fine lines. He also devised a practicable colour photolithographic process, by first printing from a photolithographic transfer a faint impression on the paper to serve as a 'key', separating the colours on duplicate negatives by varnishes, then photolithographing the dissected portions on stones, and finally registering and printing each in its position and particular colour, with the texture, light, and shade of the original.

Griggs greatly reduced the cost of producing colour work by a simplified form of this innovation, namely by a photolithographic transfer from a negative of the original to stone, printed as a 'key' in a suitable colour, superimposing thereon, in exact register, transparent tints in harmony with the original. Opaque colours, when necessary, were printed first. So far from keeping secret or patenting these improvements, on 14 April 1868 Griggs described and gave practical demonstrations of them to the London Photographic Society, showing examples prepared for the Indian Museum which, according to one of his audience, showed 'all the glowing colours of the Eastern designs'. His pioneering work in the wide diffusion of colour printing led a contemporary to claim that, but for his 'brilliant and painstaking work, chromolithography as a means of illustrating books would be almost a lost art, like that of coloured aquatint' (Hardie, 255–6).

In 1868 Griggs established photolithographic works at his Peckham residence, Elm House, just off Rye Lane. This was soon after the publication of his first notable achievement—the beautiful plates illustrating Dr Forbes Watson's *Textile Manufactures and Customs of the People of India* (1866)—which was followed by illustrations to *Tree and Serpent Worship in India* (1868), by James Fergusson. Griggs also reproduced some of the prince consort's drawings for Queen Victoria, and was thereafter chromolithographer to the queen and subsequently to Edward VII. Griggs continued to work at the India Office after the contents of the Indian Museum were dispersed to South Kensington and other sites in 1878. He finally left in 1885 to concentrate on his business, but retained his contacts with the India Office, which remained one of his most valued customers.

Griggs was as successful in bringing down the price of reproducing old manuscripts and letterpress texts as he had been in reducing costs in chromolithography. His production of fifty copies of the *Mahabhasya* (the standard authority on Sanskrit grammar), consisting of 4674 pages (1871), was carried out for £6000 less than the estimate for a tracing of the original manuscript by hand, an enormous sum at the time. More widely known were his Shakespeare quartos, with critical introductions by Frederick James Furnivall and others, in forty-three volumes (1881–91); hand-traced facsimiles of the same works by E. W. Ashbee, superintended by James Orchard Halliwell-Phillipps, had been sold at more than eight times the price.

Sir George Birdwood was a great admirer of Griggs's work and gave him constant encouragement. It was on Birdwood's initiative in 1881 that Griggs secured the patronage of the committee of council on education for a series of shilling Portfolios of Industrial Art, chiefly selected from the Chinese, Persian, Arabian, Sicilian, Italian, Russian, and Spanish specimens at the South Kensington Museum. At the time of Griggs's death 200 of these had been issued. Under an arrangement with the government of India, also negotiated at Birdwood's instance, Griggs issued, from January 1884, the quarterly *Journal of Indian Art and Industry*, in imperial quarto at 2s., a venture which was continued by his successors in business. A notable work in the same field, edited by Colonel T. H. Hendley, was his *Asian Carpet Designs* (1905) of 150 coloured plates, sold at £18 a copy. Griggs was equally successful in illustrating such works as: Dr James Burgess's reports on the archaeology of western India over many years, and his *Ancient Monuments of India* (1897 to 1911); Hendley's many works on the art and history of Rajputana; facsimiles of illuminated manuscripts at the British Museum (1889–1903), and other works for the trustees; Sir Richard Temple's work on spirit worship in Burma, *The Thirty-Seven Nats* (1906); and many scientific works, such as Dr M. C. Cooke's *Illustrations of British Fungi* (2nd edn, 6 vols., 1884–8) and his *Handbook* thereof (2nd edn, 1887). The fullest, though by no means a complete, list of Griggs's works appeared in the *Journal of Indian Art* in January 1912.

In his later years Griggs was assisted in business by his two sons, Charles and Walter. The business originally traded at Elm House, Peckham, in Griggs's name, but for a few years in the 1870s the postal address showed only the names of his two sons. For a time another company held a controlling interest in the business but the interest was reacquired by Griggs; on 20 December 1906 the firm of W. Griggs & Sons was formed into a public company. Griggs was for a time managing director, but following an accident and his suffering the early stages of Parkinson's disease he resigned from the company in January 1910. Griggs died at Jaipur, Madeira Avenue, Worthing, on 7 December 1911, and was buried in the Forest Hill cemetery, only a few miles from the Peckham works where he spent so many years of his working life. His second son, Walter, continued the business on his father's lines for a few years only.

As well as being a British pioneer of colour photolithography, Griggs was a leading exponent of the art for the last quarter of the nineteenth century. He was one of the first to practise halftone block making and collotype and helped to bring about rapid printing using cylinder presses. He was also a more than competent photographer. Griggs was always enthusiastic about his work, and keen to pass on his skills. On Saturday afternoons it was not unusual for him to entertain at his works parties of students from the London County Council School of Engraving. Other Saturdays and holidays he would spend at the British Museum or the South Kensington Museum taking photographs which he would later work up into colour prints from memory. In a professional journal published shortly after his death Griggs was affectionately described as 'that venerable craft father of ours', a measure of the high esteem in which he was held by his peers.

F. H. Brown, *rev.* John Ward

**Sources** G. Birdwood, introduction, in W. Griggs, G. Birdwood, and W. Foster, *The relics of the honorable East India Company* (1909), i–xiv • W. Griggs, *Photo-chrom-lithography: electric and daylight studio* (1882) • *British Journal of Photography* (24 April 1868) • *Photographic News* (24 April 1868) • *Journal of the Photographic Society of London*, 13 (1868–9), 21–4 • G. Wakemen, *Victorian book illustration* (1973) • *Journal of Indian Art* (Jan 1912) • *The Times* (8 Dec 1911) • *British Printer*, 144 (Dec 1911–March 1912) • *Printers Register* (8 Jan 1912) • *The Times* (25 Sept 1912) • M. Hardie, *English coloured books* (1906), 255–6 • d. cert.

**Wealth at death** £4669 18s. 6d.: probate, 29 Jan 1912, *CGPLA Eng. & Wales*

**Grignion, Charles** (*bap.* **1721**, *d.* **1810**), engraver and draughtsman, was born at the King's Arms and Dial in Russell Street, Covent Garden, the son of the Huguenot watchmaker Daniel Grignion (1684–1763) and his wife, Eleonor, and baptized at the French church, Savoy, Westminster, in October 1721. He studied in Paris for a few months under J. P. Le Bas and then at Gravelot's drawing school in Covent Garden, alongside Thomas Gainsborough. Gravelot's influence is shown in Grignion's 1737 drawing of his elder brother Thomas (1717–1784), now in the British Museum. His engraved frontispiece, after Gravelot, published by J. Rocque as *Views of the Adjacent Villages in the County of Middx* (Bibliothèque Nationale, Paris), must predate Gravelot's departure for France in 1745.

Grignion developed a career as a historical engraver and book illustrator. In 1746 he engraved Hogarth's portrait of David Garrick as Richard III, and later he worked on the second plate of Hogarth's 1754 Election series. The 1747 subscription ticket to the Westminster French Charity School (Banks Collection, British Museum) demonstrates Grignion's loyalty to the London Huguenot community.

The earliest record of a cricket match was promoted by the *General Advertiser* in July 1748: 'A Print of a Match of Cricket from a Picture painted by Mr. Hayman, and Engraved by Mr Grignion … at Five Shillings' (priv. coll.). Other topographical views included Grignion's engraving of Ranelagh Gardens, London, after Canaletto, published by Robert Sayer in Fleet Street in 1751 and Henry Overton of Newgate in 1752 and later pirated by Henry Bowles. Among his portraits was one of Admiral Anson, after Arthur Pond, for which he was paid 16 guineas. His architectural work involved plates for William Chambers's *Designs for Chinese Buildings* (1757) and James Stuart and Nicholas Revett's *Antiquities of Athens* (1762). In 1765 he was elected to the committee of the Society of Artists.

Grignion's mature drawing style is shown in the portrait (*c.*1770) of Chit Qua, the Chinese modeller (Ashmolean Museum, Oxford). He continued working until he was in his late eighties. Two years before his death his nephew wrote that the Italian artists Cipriani and Bartolozzi believed that Grignion was the 'Father and Founder of the English school of Engraving'. Afflicted by failing eyesight, he died in poverty on 1 November 1810 in Kentish Town and was buried in the church of St John the Baptist there.

Grignion's lengthy obituary in the *Gentleman's Magazine* claimed that he possessed that rare talent, 'the power of giving a free and faithful translation of a picture, the quality and cast of his productions were bold and original' (*GM*, 1st ser., 80, 1810, 499–500). His mature works had a 'happy carelessness of execution' (ibid.)—a reference to his light draughtsmanlike style in the French tradition.

**Reynolds Grignion** (*d.* 1787), engraver, was probably a relative of Charles Grignion. He was employed by booksellers and was a member of the Goldsmith's Society in Little St Martin's Lane. While resident in Lichfield Street, Westminster, Grignion married Jane Guiot on 28 October 1742; his daughters Jane and Mary and sons Claudius and Isaac were probably from this first marriage. He married his second wife, Magdalen, on 15 September 1782; she had a grown-up son from her own earlier marriage. Grignion settled his stock-in-trade to the value of over £700 on his sons and at his death cancelled the outstanding debt on this sum. In later years he and his wife lived in King's Road, Chelsea, where he died on 14 October 1787. The *Gentleman's Magazine* noted the death of 'the celebrated engraver' (*GM*, 1st ser., 57, 1787, 937). Judging from the bequests in his will, Grignion's craft brought him reasonable prosperity. TESSA MURDOCH

**Sources** R. Godfrey, *Printmaking in Britain* (1978) • T. Clayton, *The English print, 1688–1802* (1997) • T. Murdoch, ed., *The quiet conquest: the Huguenots, 1685–1985* (1985) [exhibition catalogue, Museum of London, 15 May – 31 Oct 1985] • T. Murdoch, 'Huguenot artists, designers and craftsmen in Great Britain and Ireland, 1680–1760', PhD diss., U. Lond., 1982 • J. Sunderland, 'John Hamilton Mortimer: his life and works', *Walpole Society*, 52 (1986), esp. 142, 179–180, 218 [whole issue] • letter from Thomas Grignion to George Cumberland, 31 Dec 1808, BL, Add. MS 36501 • BM, department of prints and drawings, Whitley papers • *Monthly Magazine* (1805), 539 • *Monthly Magazine* (1808) • *GM*, 1st ser., 80 (1810), 499–500 • *GM*, 1st ser., 57 (1787), 937 • will of Reynolds Grignion, PRO, PROB 11/1158, sig. 450
**Archives** BM, Whitley papers
**Likenesses** C. Grignion, self-portrait; Christies, 12 Nov 1968, lot 72 • T. Unwins, pencil drawing (aged ninety-two), BM
**Wealth at death** died in poverty: *GM* (1810)

**Grignion, Charles** (*bap.* **1753**, *d.* **1804**), history and portrait painter, was baptized on 30 December 1753, the son of Thomas Grignion (*d.* 1784) of Great Russell Street, Covent Garden, an acclaimed watchmaker of Huguenot descent, and his wife, Mary; he was the nephew of the engraver Charles *Grignion (*d.* 1810). He won prizes at the Society of Arts for drawing (1764 and 1768) and in 1769 enrolled as a student of painting at the Royal Academy. He was also a pupil of Giovanni Battista Cipriani: in 1770 he exhibited *A Head in Oils* at the academy, giving his address in the catalogue as 'At Mr Cipriani's'. During the following decade he exhibited portraits and subject pictures frequently at the academy, now giving his address as 'At Mr Grignions, Russell St'. In 1776 he won the academy's gold medal for his painting *The Choice of Hercules*, making him eligible for a travel grant for three years' study in Rome, which he won with a great majority of votes in April 1781. He arrived in the city in December with his travelling companion, the painter Robert Fagan. An obligation accompanying the grant was to produce a picture for the exhibition. This, *Captain Cook Attacked by the Natives*, was finally sent to London in 1783 and exhibited at the academy the following year. Reporting the dispatch of the painting in a letter to Sir William Chambers of 3 September 1783, Grignion said he was 'always employed'. Although the £30 allowed to him for return travel at the expiry of the grant was paid in full in February 1785, he remained in Italy for the rest of his life.

In 1787 Grignion was living with the Italian sculptor Bartolomeo Cavaceppi in the strada Laurina. In that year Charles Long, for whom Grignion acted as a guide, described him as 'a sensible fellow who falls a little short in the execution of his painting' (BL, Add. MS 36495, fol. 201). None the less, Grignion received commissions, notably in 1787, for Edward, second Baron Clive, for a large painting, *Prometheus*, which was never completed, and two Roman genre scenes in watercolour for the same patron (1790; Powis Castle, Montgomeryshire; also engraved). Large-scale drawings of antiquities were commissioned by John Penn in 1791, and a further large-scale painting, *Homer Reading his Poems*, for Thomas Noel, second Baron Berwick, in 1792. He also painted portraits of the Hon. Charlotte Clive (1787; Powis Castle) and Sir Corbet Corbet (1793). Grignion was also an active art dealer and guide for grand tourists; the diary of the widow Sarah Bentham for December 1793 records their activities together. Grignion, who remained unmarried, was a well-liked and prominent member of the British art community in Rome. He was associated with Fagan (who took over as Bentham's guide in January 1794), the sculptor John Deare, who was said to have died in his arms in 1798, and the painters Hugh Robinson and James Durno.

Grignion's greatest coup in art dealing was securing, with Fagan, the purchase of the Altieri Claudes (Anglesey Abbey, Cambridgeshire). These were shipped to England in 1799, under armed escort arranged by Nelson, whom Grignion had met and sketched earlier that year (a drawn portrait is at the Royal United Services Institution). The French invasion of Rome in 1798 made life there perilous, and Grignion left in August 1799 for Leghorn, where he seems to have turned to landscape painting. He died of fever at Leghorn on 4 November 1804 and was buried there, later that year. His personal possessions were sent back to his brother, Thomas Grignion, in London. The sale of Grignion's art collection (Sothebys 24–5 July 1821) contained many drawings and paintings by him, including *Death of Captain Cook*, in a 'gilt frame', and his pictures *Cephalus and Procris*, *Leucotha Aiding Ulysses*, and *The Death of*

*Polynicus*, as well as drawings by Robinson and Deare, testifying to the close working relations between these artists. Although his more ambitious subject pictures are untraced, and contemporaries were doubtful of his abilities, Grignion was an important figure in the Anglo-Roman art world of the 1790s. MARTIN MYRONE

**Sources** G. Cumberland, 'Biography of Charles Grignion', *Monthly Magazine*, 27 (Jan 1809) • J. Ingamells, ed., *A dictionary of British and Irish travellers in Italy, 1701–1800* (1997) • Farington, *Diary* • S. Bentham, grand tour journal, 1793–4, PRO, 30/9/43 • council minutes, RA • *A catalogue of the collection of Thomas Grignion* [sale catalogue, Sothebys, 24–5 July 1821] • C. Grignion, letter, catalogue (1973), 315 [sale catalogue, Sothebys, London, 5–6 Feb 1973] • *The exhibition of the Royal Academy* (1770–81); (1784) [exhibition catalogues] • A. Wilton and I. Bignamini, eds., *Grand tour: the lure of Italy in the eighteenth century* (1996) [exhibition catalogue, Tate Gallery, London, Oct 1996 – Jan 1997 and Palazzo delle Esposizioni, Rome, Feb–Apr 1997] • R. Trevelyan, 'Robert Fagan, an Irish bohemian in Italy', *Apollo*, 96 (1972), 298–311 • Cumberland letters, BL, Add. MS 36495 • *IGI*

**Grignion, Reynolds** (*d.* 1787). *See under* Grignion, Charles (*bap.* 1721, *d.* 1810).

**Grigor, James** (*c.*1811–1848), nurseryman and botanist, lived and worked in Old Lakenham, Norwich, Norfolk. He was the author of the *Eastern Arboretum, or, Register of Remarkable Trees, Seats, Gardens … in the County of Norfolk* (1841), illustrated with fifty etched plates, issued in fifteen numbers. In the preface Grigor states that he had devoted 'twenty years to practical botanical pursuits', and his work was highly praised by J. C. Loudon. He won a gold medal for his 'Report on Trimingham and Runton plantations in the county of Norfolk, belonging to Sir Edward North Buxton, Bart.', published in the *Transactions of the Highland and Agricultural Society of Scotland* (new ser., 10, 1848, 557–74). Grigor died of tuberculosis, at Norwich, on 22 April 1848.

B. D. JACKSON, *rev.* ANNE PIMLOTT BAKER

**Sources** Desmond, *Botanists* • *N&Q*, 7th ser., 7 (1889), 257 • d. cert.

**Grigson, Geoffrey Edward Harvey** (1905–1985), poet and writer, was born on 2 March 1905 at Pelynt, Cornwall, the seventh and last son (there were no daughters) of Canon William Shuckforth Grigson, vicar of Pelynt, and his wife, Mary Beatrice, daughter of John Simon Boldero, vicar of Amblecote, near Stourbridge, Staffordshire. At the time his father was fifty-nine years old and his mother forty-two. His childhood and adolescence, as described in his vivid, impressionistic autobiography *The Crest on the Silver* (1950), were deeply unhappy. He was sent as a boarder to a preparatory school at the age of five, then to a minor public school in Leatherhead which he detested. This was succeeded by what he called a profitless sojourn at St Edmund Hall, Oxford, where he gained a third class in English in 1927. These years were marked also by grief at the death of three of his brothers during the First World War, including one whom he particularly loved. Three more were to die during the Second World War, so that by the end of it this seventh son was the only survivor of his parents' large family.

Grigson came down from Oxford an awkward, reticent young man, loving Cornwall and the countryside, knowing little of London, where he was to spend much of his future career. On 1 July 1929 he married Frances Franklin Galt (1906/7–1937), the daughter of Thomas Franklin Galt, an American attorney. They had one daughter. After the death of his first wife, he married Berta Emma Beatrix (*b.* 1915/16), the daughter of Otto Kunert, an Austrian major, on 8 October 1938. They had a son and a daughter. Meanwhile, Grigson had worked on the *Yorkshire Post*, then the *Morning Post*, where he became literary editor. He founded *New Verse* (1933–9), a 'malignant egg' as he later called it, the most influential British poetry magazine of the 1930s. In *New Verse* he printed the finest poets of the W. H. Auden generation, but the magazine was almost equally known for his own criticism of his contemporaries, always unsparing and at times ferocious. He later regretted what he called such savage use of the billhook, but he still employed it often, in hundreds of reviews written for *The Observer*, the *Manchester Guardian*, the *New Statesman*, and other papers. Some of the best and sharpest of them were gathered together in *The Contrary View* (1974) and *Blessings, Kicks and Curses* (1982).

*New Verse* was the beginning of a literary career which embraced art criticism, anthologies of verse and prose, guides to the countryside and its flora, and the writing of poems. Grigson spent the war years in the BBC at Evesham and Bristol, but thereafter was a freelance, making his home at the farmhouse he had found in Wiltshire, living mostly by literary journalism, but never relaxing his standards. The results were remarkable, in both quality and variety. The finest of his essays on art are to be found in *The Harp of Aeolus* (1947), which includes appreciations of artists as diverse as George Stubbs, Francis Danby, and de Chirico, and along with this book should be put *Samuel Palmer: the Visionary Years* (1947), which prompted a revised view of Palmer's genius. *The Romantics* (1943) and *Before the Romantics* (1946), two of the first among many anthologies, mark the immense scope of his reading, his endless curiosity about the relationship of man and nature, and his concern with the shape and sound of language. He had a quite separate fame as author of *The Englishman's Flora* (1955), *The Shell Country Book* (1962), and other works about the English countryside.

And last, and to Grigson most importantly, he was a poet. His first book, *Several Observations* (1939), fulfilled his own requirements of 'taking notice, for ends not purely individual, of the universe of objects and events'. All his poems do this, whether they are lyrical, satirical, or views of scenes and people. Genuine feeling and observation, and a refusal of rhetorical gestures, are the hallmarks of his poetry. *Collected Poems* appeared in 1963, and a further volume covering the years up to 1980 in 1982. In the same year he published *The Private Art*, a 'poetry notebook' of comments and quotations that emphasized again the generosity and tough delicacy of his mind. *Grigson at Eighty*, edited by R. M. Healey, a collection of tributes from friends and admirers, appeared in the year of his death.

In person Grigson was tall, handsome, and enthusiastic, with an attractive blend of sophistication and innocence.

The fierceness of his writing was belied by a gentle, sometimes elaborately polite manner. He distrusted all official bodies dealing with the arts, and served on no committees. When, in 1972, he received the Duff Cooper memorial prize for a volume of poems, his short speech made clear his uneasiness on such large formal occasions.

Grigson's second marriage had ended in divorce, and he married Jane (1928–1990), daughter of George Shipley McIntire CBE, town clerk of Sunderland. Jane *Grigson became a celebrated cookery expert; they had one daughter. Grigson died on 28 November 1985 at Broad Town Farm, near Swindon, his Wiltshire home, and was buried in the churchyard of Christ Church, Broad Town.

JULIAN SYMONS, *rev.*

**Sources** R. M. Healey, ed., *Grigson at eighty* (1985) · G. Grigson, *The crest on the silver* (1950) · personal knowledge (1990) · private information (1990) · *Sunday Times* (1 Dec 1985) · *The Observer* (1 Dec 1985) · *The Times* (30 Nov 1985) · *The Times* (14 Dec 1985)

**Archives** BL, notebook, Add. MS 53787 · Ransom HRC, corresp. and literary MSS · State University of New York, Buffalo, corresp. and literary MSS · U. Birm. L., notebook | U. Leeds, Brotherton L., letters to *London Magazine* · U. Reading L., corresp. with Paul Ferris

**Likenesses** F. Godwin, bromide print, 1970, NPG

**Wealth at death** under £40,000: probate, 20 Feb 1986, *CGPLA Eng. & Wales*

**Grigson** [*née* McIntire], **(Heather Mabel) Jane** (**1928–1990**), writer on cookery, was born on 13 March 1928 in Gloucester, the elder daughter (there were no sons) of George Shipley McIntire (*d.* 1990), deputy town clerk of Gloucester, and his wife, Doris Mabel Frampton Berkley, artist. When she was four her father became town clerk of Sunderland, and he bequeathed quietly left-wing politics to his daughters. It was the good fresh fish and the straightforwardness of north country food that first delighted Jane in her lifetime's study. In 1939 Wearside was a target for German bombing, and she and her sister were sent to Casterton School (originally for clergy daughters) in Westmorland, where Jane encountered the outstanding English teaching of a Miss Bevis. In 1946 she went to Cambridge, where she attended Newnham College. She obtained a third class in part one of the English tripos (1948) and a second (division two) in part two (1949).

Jane McIntire's first job was at Heffer's Art Gallery in Cambridge. In 1952 she went to work for the publisher Thames and Hudson, who recommended her as research assistant to Geoffrey Edward Harvey *Grigson (1905–1985) for his series of separate books *People, Places, Things, and Ideas* (4 vols., 1954). She had bought his anthology *Visionary Poems and Passages, or, The Poet's Eye* (1944) when she was fifteen. Grigson was the son of William Shuckforth Grigson, vicar of Pelynt, Cornwall. He was twenty-three years older than Jane, had been married twice before, and had three grown-up or adolescent children. They lived together and in the mid-1950s she changed her name by deed poll to Grigson; twenty years later they were able to marry. They had one daughter, Sophie, who also became a cookery expert. They lived partly at Broad Town Farm House, Broad Town, near Wootton Bassett in Wiltshire, and partly in France, at Troo, in the Loir valley. In both places they absorbed the landscape and history, and gave news of them in different literary forms.

Jane Grigson's first published writing was for the *Sunderland Echo*, a piece on Bede. She made a new translation (1959) of Carlo Collodi's *Pinocchio*, and one of Cesare Beccaria's *Dei delitti e delle pene* (as *Of Crimes and Punishments*, 1963), for which she jointly won the John Florio prize. She found her true vocation when a reader of Geoffrey Grigson's book *Painted Caves* (1957) wrote to him from Troo, asking if he knew of that semi-troglodyte village. They went to see, and soon bought their own habitable cave. Jane Grigson had started as Geoffrey's amanuensis, but in Troo she emerged as her own writer. The variety and excellence of the local raw materials, the skills of their neighbours, and her own developing conviction that because cooking is a central part of life it should be as carefully written about as any other art form, led to the first of her many books: *Charcuterie and French Pork Cookery* (1967). This was a breakthrough into a new literacy about cooking, and she was immediately recognized as a serious writer. Later landmark books were *Fish Cookery* (1973, enlarged as *Jane Grigson's Fish Book*, 1993), which restored fish cookery to its rightful place, and *English Food* (1974). The tiny *Cooking of Normandy* (1987), written for sale at Sainsbury's, raised that often footling genre to a new level.

From 1968 until the week of her death Jane Grigson wrote for the *Observer Magazine*, to which Elizabeth David had recommended her. Several of her books were collections of articles. She campaigned against the bad as well as for the good, denouncing the degradation and sometimes danger inflicted on eaters by food adulterators in general. Elizabeth David awoke post-war Britain from its devotion to oversized and overcooked food, and Jane Grigson carried the awakening forward by opening the whole wide history and context of foods, dishes, utensils, and methods. Above all she sought to, and did, convey the reliable pleasures of knowledgeable cooking and eating. She herself put it:

> Cooking something delicious is really much more satisfactory than painting pictures or throwing pots. Food has the tact to disappear, leaving the room and opportunity for masterpieces to come. The mistakes don't hang on the walls or stand on the shelves to reproach you for ever.

Jane Grigson was generous, scholarly, and deeply cheerful, combining outgoingness with equanimity; she was also smoothly and unobtrusively beautiful, with wavy fair hair and green eyes. When already terminally ill, she spoke and raised funds to fight off threats from developers to the great neolithic monument at Avebury near her Wiltshire home. She died of cancer at Broad Town on 12 March 1990 and was buried in Christ Church churchyard there beside her husband, who had died in 1985. Her collection of cookery books became the core of the Jane Grigson Library at the Guildhall Library in the City of London.

WAYLAND KENNET, *rev.*

**Sources** *The Times* (14 March 1990) · personal knowledge (1996) · private information (1996)

**Archives** GL

**Wealth at death** £407,868: probate, 3 Oct 1990, *CGPLA Eng. & Wales*

**Grim, Edward** (*fl.* **1170–*c*.1186**), biographer, was a clerk, born in Cambridge, who had acquired the title of master before December 1170, when he visited Thomas *Becket, then archbishop, at Canterbury. He is perhaps to be identified with the Master Evrardus, or Errardus, who had been ejected from the rectory of Saltwood during Becket's exile, and was recommended for compensation by Bishop Arnulf of Lisieux following the peace of Fréteval in July 1170. Grim was present in Canterbury Cathedral on 29 December 1170, when the four knights attacked and murdered the archbishop, and his courageous action in attempting to defend Becket from William de Tracy's blow, in which his own arm was nearly severed, earned him a place in Herbert of Bosham's register of the *eruditi sancti Thomae* ('St Thomas's learned men'), even though he had not been a member of the archbishop's household. His later career is unknown, but he was dead by the time that Herbert compiled his list (*c*.1186). His *Vita sancti Thomae* was the first major life of Becket to be written, *c*.1171–2 in its first recension. Its manuscript survival suggests a moderate success. It was a principal source for the metrical French life composed by Guernes de Pont-Ste-Maxence in 1172–4, and excerpts were interpolated into the second recension of William fitz Stephen's *Vita sancti Thomae*, the so-called 'first' *Quadrilogus*, and some later adaptations of the 'second' *Quadrilogus* in the early thirteenth century. A widely disseminated twelfth-century *Passio beati Thomae* claims him as its author, but the attribution is highly dubious. A. J. Duggan

**Sources** J. C. Robertson and J. B. Sheppard, eds., *Materials for the history of Thomas Becket, archbishop of Canterbury*, 7 vols., Rolls Series, 67 (1875–85) • A. Duggan, *Thomas Becket: a textual history of his letters* (1980), 176–82, 271 • A. J. Duggan, 'The Salem FitzStephen: Heidelberg Universitäts-Bibliothek Cod. Salem ix.30', *Mediaevalia Christiana, XIe–XIIIe siècles: hommage à Raymonde Foreville*, ed. C. E. Viola (Paris and Tournai, 1989), 51–86 • A. J. Duggan, 'The Lyell version of the *Quadrilogus* life of St Thomas of Canterbury', *Analecta Bollandiana*, 112 (1994), 105–38 • *Vita sancti Thomae Cantuariensis archiepiscopi et martyris*, ed. J. A. Giles, 2 vols., Patres Ecclesiae Anglicanae (1845) • E. Walberg, *La tradition hagiographique de Saint Thomas Becket avant la fin du XIIe siècle* (Paris, 1929) • F. Barlow, *Thomas Becket* (1986), 4, 89 • *The letters of Arnulf of Lisieux*, ed. F. Barlow, CS, 3rd ser., 61 (1939)

**Archives** BL, Arundel MS 27, fols. 1ra–48va • BL, Cotton MS Vespasian E.x, fols. 200*r*–261*r* | BL, Add. MS 16607, fols. 1*r*–16*v* [fragment] • BL, Cotton MS Julius D.xi, fols. 94*r*–98*r* [fragment] • BL, Cotton MS Vitellius C.xii, fols. 254vb–280rb

**Grimald, Nicholas** (*b.* **1519/20**, *d.* in or before **1562**), poet, was once assumed to have been the son of John Baptista Grimaldi, a henchman of Henry VII's notorious tax collectors Sir Richard Empson and Edmund Dudley. But no contemporary documents support this elevated connection. In 'A Funerall Song, upon the Death of Annes his Moother' Grimald stated that his family home was at the village of 'Brownshold' (now Leighton Bromswold), north-west of Huntingdon, from which area variants of the family name are traceable in legal records as far back as the mid-fifteenth century. From the same source it can be inferred that he was born in 1519 or 1520.

**Education and early career** Descended from this yeoman stock, Grimald depicts himself in 'A Funerall Song' as the only son among several daughters of a happy rural family. While his father tended his sheep ('What gayn the wooll, what gayn the wed had braught, / It was his meed, that me there dayly taught'), his mother determined on a brilliant academic future for her son ('You mee streightway did too the Muses send, / Ne suffered long a loyteryng lyfe to spend'; from 'A Funerall Song, upon the Death of Annes his Moother', reprinted in Rollins, 1.112). Probably under the guidance of Gilbert Smith, prebendary of Leighton Bromswold from 1507 until 1549 and founder of a free school there, Grimald progressed in 1536 to Christ's College, Cambridge, whence he graduated BA in 1539–40. He transferred to Oxford in the following year on Smith's advice, from whom he also received funds for his books and maintenance. For his first few months at Oxford, Grimald lodged at Brasenose College, again probably through the influence of Smith, a relative of the college's first principal, Matthew Smith. During the bitter winter of 1541–2 Grimald composed a Latin resurrection play, *Christus redivivus* (1543), probably for performance in college during the following Easter. In April 1542 his BA degree was incorporated at Oxford, so that he could enter Merton College as a probationer fellow on 5 May 1542, from where he was awarded the degree of MA in 1544. (Grimald should not be confused during the 1540s with another student of Christ's College, Nicholas Grenewell.)

Grimald almost certainly stayed in Oxford after 1544 since a copy of another Latin tragedy on the life and death of John the Baptist, *Archipropheta* (1548), was submitted in support of his application for a fellowship to Dr Richard Cox, the new dean of Christ Church, who presided over the refoundation (November 1546) and reopening (January 1547) of the college. An autograph manuscript of this play (BL, Royal MS 12 A XLVI, perhaps the copy submitted to Cox) is dated from Exeter College, where Grimald may have then been resident. According to Anthony Wood, Grimald's application was successful and he was employed as 'a senior or theologist' with responsibilities to 'read lectures on rhetoric in the refectory there' (Bodl. Oxf., MS Wood C. 8, fol. 1*v*; a receipt for Grimald's college salary, dated 3 Oct 1550, with a note in his own hand, is in Bodl. Oxf., MS Tanner 106, fol. 43). John Bale collected a long list in Latin (*Scriptorum … catalogus*, 1557, based upon his manuscript notebook, 'Index Britanniae scriptorum') of what he considered to be Grimald's writings and if this information is reliable, then some of the translations and commentaries on the classics mentioned below may have been compiled by Grimald for these lectures. Grimald and Bale seem to have developed a close academic friendship, as is suggested by Bale's probable involvement in the publication of two of Grimald's Latin dramas (see below) and by the inclusion in Bale's *Index* of Grimald's (now lost) 'Epistolas quasdam ad Baleum'.

Grimald's distinction as a scholar and lecturer led to a licence being granted (2 January 1552) by Richard Sampson, bishop of Lichfield, for him to preach at Eccles, near

Manchester. In the following year he was appointed chaplain to Nicholas Ridley, bishop of London, who recommended him for preferment and commended him for his 'eloquence in both English and Latin' in a letter of 18 November 1552 to Sir John Gates and Sir William Cecil (*Works*, 361). Ridley publicly confirmed his high opinion of Grimald by choosing him to deliver a Latin address in April 1553, *Oratio ad pontifices* (printed 1583), before the assembled bishops at synod on the urgent need to address problems with absentee clergymen. Grimald's tract *Vox populi* (listed in Bale's *Index*) tackled a similar topic, namely, 'those rectors, vicars, archdeacons, deans, prebendaries, etc., who spend their lives far from their flocks, or do not perform their sacred duties' (Merrill, *Life and Poems of Nicholas Grimald*, 27). Anthony Wood claimed to have seen a 1549 printed edition of *Vox populi* and it seems likely that Grimald's *Oratio ad pontifices* was a reworked Latin version of this tract.

As early as 1549 Grimald was also involved in compiling moralizing condemnations of the easy lifestyles of Oxford-educated clerics. In a Latin letter (BL, Lansdowne MS 2, fols. 77–8, 12 May 1549; Merrill, *Life and Poems of Nicholas Grimald*, 38–43), to Sir William Cecil (then the duke of Somerset's master of the court of requests), Grimald described the high levels of idleness or absenteeism of the fellows of Christ Church and other colleges. This letter also reveals that Grimald was effectively operating as a spy for Cecil on Roman Catholics at Oxford and that he was ready and willing to supply Cecil with lists of nonconformists.

**Possible apostasy under Mary I** On 18 November 1552 Ridley successfully recommended Grimald for the chantership of St Paul's Cathedral (*Works*, 337). The accession of Queen Mary, however, led to Ridley's imprisonment first at London and then in the Bocardo gaol at Oxford. From there Ridley wrote to Austin Bernhere, one of Latimer's most loyal servants, confirming that he still held Grimald in high regard, despite Bernhere's clear suspicions of his loyalty ('at your last being here you cast cold water upon mine affection towards Grimbold'; Merrill, *Life and Poems of Nicholas Grimald*, 44). Ridley also suggested in the same letter that Grimald could be asked to translate Laurentius Valla's *De falso credita et ementita Constantini Donatione declamatio* (1439), which denounced the pope's claims to temporal dominion; and Aeneas Sylvius's (that is, Pope Pius II) *De gestis Basiliensis Concilii*, which upheld the supremacy of the Council of Basel over that of the papacy. Ridley's brother-in-law, George Shipside, was entrusted with sending copies of Ridley's theological writings done while in prison to Grimald. Others were soon of the opinion that Grimald had betrayed the recently arrested and imprisoned Shipside in this activity, although Ridley still clung to a belief in the loyalty of his protégé: 'it will not sink into my head to think that Grimbold would ever play me such a Judas's part'. But in a later letter Ridley seemed finally to acknowledge the general doubts over Grimald's loyalty (*Works*, 361, 537).

Even if he was a covert informer, Grimald himself eventually fell under the suspicions of the Catholic authorities. In a letter of January 1558 to the protestant martyr John Bradford, Ridley noted that Grimald had been in the Bocardo and mentioned that he had even been under threat of being 'hanged, drawn and quartered' before being removed to the Marshalsea and ultimately freed (*Works*, 371, 379). It is certainly possible that Grimald became an apostate to Catholicism in order to save his own life. Even Ridley suspected that he 'escaped not without some becking and bowing (alas) of his knee unto Baal' (ibid., 388). John Bradford confirmed this suspicion when he noted that Grimald's prison conversion had been held up to him by the Catholic interrogator, Dr Weston, as a means of saving his own life (*Writings of John Bradford*, 548). John Foxe recounted in his *Actes and Monuments* how another protestant martyr, Laurence Sanders, met Grimald, 'a man who had more store of good gifts than of great constancy', at St Albans on his way to the stake at Coventry. Sanders is said to have given Grimald 'a lesson meet for his lightness', which he received with 'shrugging and shrinking' (*Acts and Monuments*, 6.627). Merrill firmly condemned Grimald as 'a timeserver, shifting from the Roman Catholic faith, and then back again, recanting secretly, and betraying his friends, as was necessary to save his life' (Merrill, *Life and Poems of Nicholas Grimald*, 50)—a view supported by a contemporary Latin satire, 'Carmen in laudem Grimmoaldi', which denounced Grimald as a 'deceiver' and a 'detractor' who had branded many 'with infamy' (Bodl. Oxf., MS Duke Humfrey b. 1, fol. 186). Other scholars have remained resistant to the idea of Grimald's apostasy (see C. R. Baskervill in *Modern Philology*, 23, 1926; and A. W. Reed in *Review of English Studies*, 2, 1926). J. N. King has also assumed that Grimald's 'later reputation as an apostate must have been based on hearsay' because of Bale's praise for his Christian faith in his *Catalogus* (King, 243). Whatever the truth of the matter, there is no evidence that Grimald gained any public or academic preferment after 1558. In fact, he seems to disappear entirely from written records after his probable involvement in the publication of Richard Tottel's *Songes and Sonettes* (1557).

**Grimald's writings** Grimald is a prime example of a writer in both Latin and English who was highly regarded as a humanist scholar in his own day but is now generally neglected except for occasional consideration in scholarly studies of Tudor poetic miscellanies, academic Latin drama, and translations from the classics. But, apart from Sir Thomas Wyatt (ninety-six poems) and Henry Howard, earl of Surrey (forty poems), Grimald's verses were the most prominent in the first edition of Tottel's *Songes and Sonettes* (published on 5 June 1557 and surviving in a unique copy at the Bodleian Library), which contained forty poems attributed to Grimald. Grimald was perhaps even the editor of this first edition of the volume (Byrom, 'The case for Nicholas Grimald'; but disputed by Rollins, 2.93); and he had certainly had business dealings with Tottel, who in the previous year published his translation of Cicero's *De officiis* (as *Thre Bokes of Duties*). A second edition appeared on 31 July but only nine of Grimald's poems were retained: it has been suggested that this was either through Grimald's own modesty as an editor or because Tottel feared that Grimald's name, on account of his religious recantation, would harm the sale of the volume. Someone, most probably Tottel himself, may have removed all of Grimald's poems which contained any personal allusions (such as the elegy on his mother) and substituted initials for his name.

Some ten of Grimald's contributions to the *Songes and Sonettes* were literal translations or adaptations from Theodore Beza, while others were also derived from neo-Latin sources (perhaps the *Carmina et epigrammata* and *Cantiones rythmicae* listed by Bale). Two of Grimald's poems in the *Songes and Sonettes*, 'The Death of Zoroas' (based on a Latin poem from the *Alexandreis* of Phillipus Gaultherus de Châtillon) and 'Marcus Tullius Ciceroes Death' (from Beza), were among the earliest published examples of English blank verse and were perhaps compiled by Grimald in imitation of the earl of Surrey's blank-verse translation of the second and fourth books of the *Aeneid*. Grimald also deserves credit as a neo-classical pioneer of the English heroic couplet, the measure used most frequently in his contributions to the first edition of *Songes and Sonettes*. Grimald was an editor (or private annotator) of Wyatt's autograph manuscript, BL, Egerton MS 2711, which bears his emendations (largely to spellings and punctuation) on some ten poems at the beginning of the manuscript (fols. 4–11) and the addition of a complete stanza, 'O restfull place: reneewer of my smart', in his hand.

It is probable that only a small amount of Grimald's own English and Latin verses has survived (see Hughey, 'Harington manuscript', 428–9). Bale refers to Grimald's 'Restitutio psalmorum Thome Viati' and also notes in his *Index* that Grimald wrote in English 'Psalmi Davidis aliquot rythmis explicati', citing his source 'from his [Grimald's] own study'. This literary interest was supported by Grimald's textual and theological work on the biblical Psalms, as indicated by Bale's reference to his now lost 'Explicationes psalmorum'. Bale also lists either the composition or editorship of a volume of 155 panegyrical poems, 'Congratulatorium carmen', on Protector Somerset's release from the Tower of London on 16 February 1550. Five of Grimald's poems in Tottel's *Songes and Sonnettes* were intended as new year gifts to Somerset's daughters. Grimald also offers in this collection two epitaphs (one certainly adapted from Beza) on Sir James Wilford, an ally of Somerset, and another on Somerset's aunt, Lady Anne Wentworth. Bale's list refers to other lost poetical works, including two volumes of 'Carmina et epigrammata', 'Cantiones rythmicae', and a planned edition or translation of Joseph of Exeter's Latin epic poem, 'De Bello Trojano'. Grimald also contributed three Latin and one English commendatory poems to *A Preservative of Triacle Agaynst the Poyson of Pelagius* (1551) by William Turner; and two Latin poems to Thomas Cooper's edition of Sir Thomas Eliot's Latin dictionary, *Bibliotheca Eliotae* (1552). Grimald's interests as a collector of earlier English poetry is demonstrated by a manuscript in the Bodleian Library (MS Greaves 60), a unique and fragmentary text of the fourteenth-century alliterative poem, 'Alexander A' (or *Alisaunder of Macedoine*), which is copied out entirely in Grimald's own hand.

In addition to his work as a collector and editor of English poetry, Grimald is also notable for his interests in Latin drama. His resurrection play, *Christus redivivus: comoedia tragica sacra* (1543), was also performed and printed in a pirated edition at Augsburg in 1556. In its 'Epistola nuncupatoria' to Gilbert Smith, Grimald defended his dramatic preferences for tragicomedy, witty variations in diction for high and low characters (including four swaggering soldiers), and a flexible approach to the three unities. Its influence in Germany remained strong and it provided the major source for the third of twelve dramas included in Sebastian Wild's *Schöner Comedien und Tragedien swölff* (1566). Wild's version of Grimald's play is itself one of the two identified sources for the earliest surviving text (1662) of the passion play presented each year at Oberammergau. Bale also mentions Grimald's 'Christus nascens', a comedy probably intended either as a companion to *Christus redivivus* or as a nativity play for performance by Oxford students at Christmas time.

Both *Christus redivivus* and Grimald's Latin tragedy on the life and death of John the Baptist, *Archipropheta* (1548), were published by Martin Gymnicus, probably through the influence of John Bale who was in Germany between 1540 and 1547 and also had Gymnicus as his printer. This latter drama, dedicated to Richard Cox, dean of Christ Church, deserves some notice as the 'first published tragedy to be written in England' (Norland, 333). Compiled some fifteen years before the earliest English tragedy, *Gorboduc* (performed 1561), and based upon both the Bible and Josephus's *Antiquities of the Jews*, it offered a 'subtle fusion of classical form and biblical content' (King, 297) and a deliberate 'emphasis upon presentation rather than narration' (Norland, 323). Grimald's lyrical speeches and choruses were firmly focused upon the characterization and interaction of his protagonists, producing a 'human tragedy, not a political statement or a religious lesson' (ibid., 326). *Archipropheta* also included the antics of a court fool as a counterpoint to the main biblical tragedy and it seems that the dramatic interaction of tragedy and comedy appealed strongly to Grimald. Bale ascribed to him a tragicomedy called 'Famae comedia'; two comedies on 'Troilus ex Chaucero' and 'De puerorum in musicis institutione'; and an interest in Terence's *Andria*.

Grimald's surviving translations into English include that from Cicero entitled *Thre Bokes of Duties* (1556), printed by Tottel and dedicated to Thomas Thirleby, bishop of Ely. Grimald also compiled a Latin paraphrase of four books of Virgil's *Georgics* (printed 1591) which was warmly commended by Barnabe Googe in his 'Epytaphe of Maister Thomas Phayre' (Googe, 73–4). In the *Short-Title Catalogue* Grimald is identified as the translator of *A True Description of the Antichrist* (1592), from a work by Georg Sohn; but since Sohn was only eleven years old when Grimald died this attribution is clearly wrong. There is also no evidence to support the identification of Grimald as the English translator of Laurence Humphrey's *The Nobles, or, Of Nobilitye* (1563) or as the author of the anonymous *The Institucion of a Gentleman* (1555). Of works which have not survived, Bale mentions Grimald's abstract, paraphrase, and commentary on Virgil's *Eclogues*; various translations of Cicero's letters and his *Partitiones* (on the divisions of oratory); two volumes of either a translation of or commentary on Horace's *Epistles*; eight volumes of Xenophon's *Cyropaedia*; two volumes of Hesiod of Ascraea's *Works and Days*; Plato's *Crito*; his emendations of Matthew of Vendôme's *Tobias*; and his study of rhetoric, *Rhetorica in usum Britannorum* (Bodl. Oxf., MS Greaves 60, fol. 1*r*, contains the title only of his 'schoole of Rhetorik').

Although the exact cause, date, and location of Grimbald's death are unknown, in his *Eglogs, Epytaphes, and Sonettes* (1563) Barnabe Googe included 'An Epytaphe on the Death of Nicholas Grimaold', which was presumably penned before Googe's own departure abroad in May 1562. There is no evidence that Grimald ever married or had children, although some of his verses (derived from originals by Beza) in Tottel's *Songes and Sonettes* refer to his love for 'Carie Day' and Mistress Damascene Awdley (probably a relative of John, Lord Audley), and offer a debate on the efficacy of marriage.

MICHAEL G. BRENNAN

**Sources** L. R. Merrill, *The life and poems of Nicholas Grimald* (1925) [see also reviews by C. R. Baskervill, *Modern Philology*, 23 (1926), 37–8, and A. W. Reed, *Review of English Studies*, 2 (1926), 483–5] • Bale, *Cat.* • Bale, *Index* • R. Hughey, ed., *The Arundel Harington manuscript of Tudor poetry*, 2 vols. (1960) • H. R. Rollins, ed., *Tottel's miscellany (1557–1587)*, 2 vols. (1929); rev. edn (1965) • F. S. Boas, *University drama in the Tudor age* (1914) • N. Grimald, *Christus redivivus: archipropheta*, ed. K. T. von Rosador (Hildesheim, 1981) • J. W. Binns, *Intellectual culture in Elizabethan and Jacobean England: the Latin writings of the age* (1990) • T. Turville-Petre, 'Nicholas Grimald and *Alexander A*', *English Literary Renaissance*, 6 (1976), 180–86 • H. J. Byrom, 'The case for Nicholas Grimald as editor of *Tottel's miscellany*', *Modern Language Review*, 27 (1932), 125–43 • R. Hughey, 'The Harington manuscript at Arundel Castle and related documents', *The Library*, 4th ser., 15 (1934–5), 388–444 • J. M. Hart, 'Nicholas Grimald's *Christus redivivus*', *Publications of the Modern Language Association of America*, 14 (1899), 369–448 • H. B. Norland, *Drama in early Tudor Britain, 1485–1558* (1995) • H. H. Hudson, 'Grimald's translations from Beza', *Modern Language Notes*, 39 (1924), 388–94 • J. N. King, *English Reformation literature: the Tudor origins of the protestant tradition* (1982) • L. R. Merrill, 'Nicholas Grimald, the Judas of the Reformation', *Publications of the Modern Language Association of America*, 37 (1922), 216–27 • G. W. Pigman III, *Grief and English Renaissance elegy* (1985) • G. P. Shannon, 'Nicholas Grimald's heroic couplet and the Latin elegiac distich', *Publications of the Modern Language Association of America*, 45 (1930), 532–42 • G. P. Shannon, 'Nicholas Grimald's list of the muses', *Modern Language Quarterly*, 8 (1947), 43–5 • J. Strype, *Ecclesiastical memorials*, 7 vols. (1816), vol. 4, pt 2, p. 269 • G. C. Taylor, 'The *Christus redivivus* of Nicholas Grimald and the Hegge resurrection plays', *Publications of the Modern Language Association of America*, 41 (1926), 84–9 • Venn, *Alum. Cant.*, 1/1–4 • Foster, *Alum. Oxon.*, *1500–1714* • Bodl. Oxf., MS Wood C. 8 • Bodl. Oxf., MS Tanner 106 • Bodl. Oxf., MS Duke Humphrey b. 1 • *The writings of John Bradford*, ed. A. Townsend, 1 vol. in 2 pts, Parker Society, 31 (1848–53) • BL, Lansdowne MS 2 • A. Clark, *Lincoln diocese documents, 1450–1544* (1914) • B. Googe, *Eglogs, epytaphes, and sonettes*, ed. E. Arber (1871) • *The acts and monuments of John Foxe*, ed. S. R. Cattley, 8 vols. (1837–41) [vol. 6] • *The works of Nicholas Ridley*, ed. H. Christmas, Parker Society, 1 (1841)

**Archives** Bodl. Oxf., autograph notebook, Greaves MS 60

**Grimaldi, Joseph** [Giuseppe] (**1709x16?–1788**), dancer and dentist, was probably born between 1709 and 1716, perhaps in Malta, the son of the dancer John Baptist Grimaldi (*fl.* 1709–1741) and his wife, Catherine (*d.* 1773). Many details of his life and circumstances are based on hearsay, conjecture, and fragmentary information. He was one of a family of Italian entertainers who performed throughout western Europe, 'where he spent the first forty years of his life' (Findlater, 33). His father, also known as Nicolini, was the first to use Grimaldi's byname of Gamba di Ferro, or Iron Legs. Grimaldi may have appropriated his father's stage name to bolster his status and career in England, or confusion in later accounts of his life may be responsible for an erroneous conflation of the father's achievements with those of his son.

When Grimaldi first settled in England is uncertain. He appeared as a dancer at the King's Theatre on 10 January 1758 and may have continued to perform there during the rest of the season. He performed at Drury Lane during the 1759–60 season and in every following season (apart from 1777–8) for the next twenty-six years. As a dancer he excelled in the role of Pantaloon in numerous harlequinades; as a ballet master he both choreographed and performed in dances which were presented either as set pieces in a longer stage play or as separate items in the programme. He also acted as *maître de ballet* during the summer months at Sadler's Wells Theatre from 1763 onwards and at the Royal Circus in 1782. Following in the footsteps of his paternal grandfather, also John Baptist Grimaldi (who appears to have spent some time in England and whose will, dated 11 March 1760, can be found in the Public Record Office), he practised dentistry alongside his career in dance, advertising himself as a 'Surgeon-Dentist, who has had the Honour of attending her MAJESTY, the Prince of Wales, and the Prince and Princess of Brunswic' (Highfill, Burnim & Langhans, *BDA*).

On 13 April 1762, when he was in his late forties or early fifties, Grimaldi married a sixteen-year-old dancer, Mary Blagden (1745/6–1781). There were four children from this first marriage: Mary, baptized at St Paul's, Covent Garden, on 19 January 1763; Isabella Louisa, baptized at St Paul's on 14 October 1764; Margaret Charlotta, born in 1765; and Catherine, born in 1767. During the 1760s Grimaldi had a number of affairs with young dancers and entertainers. He had contracted syphilis by 1767 and infected his wife with the disease, insisting on having sexual relations with her while she was carrying their fourth daughter. Grimaldi and Mary stopped living together in 1775, and in 1779 Mary—two years before her death—began divorce proceedings on the grounds of severe cruelty and abuse. About 1775 Grimaldi began a relationship with Rebecca Brooker (*d.* 1819), a young dancer at Drury Lane, by whom he had two, or possibly three, illegitimate children: Joseph *Grimaldi, the future clown Joey, born on 18 December 1778, baptized at St Clement Danes on 28

December; and John Baptist, born some time in 1780. William, mentioned in Grimaldi's will, may have been a third son by Rebecca (being one of the three young Grimaldis who performed alongside her in the Drury Lane season 1789–90). However, he may have been the result of a parallel relationship, for, in the same month and year as Joseph was born, another illegitimate child, Henrietta Marguerite, was born to Ann Perry, with whom Grimaldi was having an affair. Ann later adopted the name Grimaldi and lived with Grimaldi at 125 High Holborn, while Grimaldi continued to maintain a household with Rebecca Brooker and their children at Theatre Court, Lambeth. Old Grim had a reputation as a coarse humorist and an obscene practical joker, a harsh and cruel teacher, an accomplished dancer and pantomimist, and a violent and melancholic human being whose obsession with death is recorded in numerous contemporary anecdotes, in Charles Dickens's *Memoirs of Joseph Grimaldi*, and in the bizarre details of the will he made on 25 February 1786. He requested that, on the day that he was buried, his eldest child, Mary, should sever his head from his body. Grimaldi died of dropsy two years later, on 14 March 1788, perhaps at Theatre Court, Lambeth, and Mary employed a surgeon to carry out the beheading. She touched the knife as he did so. Grimaldi also stipulated that Mary, Joseph, John Baptist, and William should share his estate equally and that Margaret and Catherine should receive nothing; no mention was made of his other children or of Rebecca Brooker or Ann Perry. He was buried at the Northampton Chapel in Exmouth Street, Clerkenwell, on 23 March 1788.

LESLIE DU S. READ

**Sources** R. Findlater, *Joe Grimaldi: his life and theatre*, 2nd edn (1978) · C. Dickens, *Memoirs of Joseph Grimaldi*, ed. R. Findlater, rev. edn (1968) · Highfill, Burnim & Langhans, *BDA* · M. Wilson Dissher, *Clowns and pantomimes* (1925)

**Likenesses** print, 1788, BM

**Wealth at death** see conjectures detailed in Highfill, Burnim & Langhans, *BDA*, 396

**Grimaldi, Joseph** [Joe] (**1778–1837**), actor and pantomimist, was born on 18 December 1778 in Stanhope Street, Clare Market, London, into a family of dancers and clowns (he claimed, it appears falsely, to have been born a year later). His paternal grandfather, Giovanni Battista 'Iron Legs' Grimaldi, was known in Italy and France, and his father, Joseph (Giuseppe) *Grimaldi (*d*. 1788), a dancer and Pantaloon, first appeared in London, possibly as a balletmaster, at the King's Theatre in the Haymarket. In 1758–9 Giuseppe Grimaldi was engaged by Garrick to play in pantomimes at Drury Lane; later he also performed at Sadler's Wells. He was notorious for his grotesque and indelicate humour and for his practical jokes. Grimaldi's mother, Rebecca Brooker, danced and played utility parts at Drury Lane and Sadler's Wells. Joe Grimaldi's first appearance, as a child dancer, was at Sadler's Wells on 16 April 1781, when he played one of the Evils which emerged from the box in a pantomime entitled *Pandora's Box*. He also took part in a Drury Lane pantomime in 1781 or 1782. For some years, between the end of the Christmas

**Joseph Grimaldi (1778–1837)**, by Samuel De Wilde, *c*.1807 [as Clown in *Harlequin and Mother Goose, or, The Golden Egg*]

pantomime season at Drury Lane and the opening of Sadler's Wells, he attended Mr Ford's academy, a boarding-school at Putney. When the Drury Lane and Sadler's Wells seasons overlapped in early summer and again in early autumn, he regularly acted at Drury Lane and Sadler's Wells on the same night, taking a hackney coach, or occasionally running, from one to another.

At Sadler's Wells, Grimaldi played the dwarf in *Valentine and Orson* (1794) as well as evil sans-culotte characters and French prisoners of war in the revolutionary dramas then drawing large crowds to the theatre. In 1796 he took the part of an evil witch in Charles Dibdin's pantomime *The Talisman, or, Harlequin Made Happy*. In 1799 he married Maria Hughes, the eldest daughter of Richard Hughes, one of the Sadler's Wells proprietors. To his enormous sadness, she died a year later in childbirth. Three years later, in 1802, Grimaldi married Mary Bristow, an actress at Drury Lane. Their only son, **Joseph Samuel William Grimaldi** (1802–1832), was born on 21 November 1802.

In 1799 Grimaldi played a series of legitimate parts at Drury Lane, including a countryman in Sheridan's *A Trip to Scarborough* (a bowdlerized version of Vanbrugh's *The Relapse*) and a maid in *Rule a Wife and Have a Wife*. As

Camazin, a Tartar chief in J. P. Kemble's *Lodoiska*, he displayed his skill in acrobatic swordsmanship to some acclaim. His crawling fight in this play was said to have provided the inspiration for Kean's final combat in *Richard III*. The following year he also performed the part of the Second Gravedigger in *Hamlet* at Drury Lane.

Grimaldi's first appearance as a clown took place at Sadler's Wells in 1800, when he played Guzzle the Drinking Clown in an innovative pantomime called *Peter Wilkins, or, Harlequin in the Flying World*. The pantomime had been written by Charles Dibdin and the scene painter Robert Andrews. Rather than featuring only one clown, as was customary, *Peter Wilkins* included two: Grimaldi, and the leading London clown, John Baptist Dubois, who took the part of Gobble the Eating Clown. *Peter Wilkins* also introduced innovations of costume and make-up for the two clowns, who were dressed in extravagant, particoloured costumes, and appeared with white faces ornamented by two red half-moons on the cheek rather than with the conventional ruddy complexions of eighteenth-century clowns.

In the summer of 1801 Dubois and Grimaldi dramatized their comic rivalry as Sadler's Wells clowns in the form of a scene disputing who could make the ugliest face. At the end of the 1801 season Dubois left Sadler's Wells and Grimaldi rapidly began to be celebrated as the unchallenged king of clowns. In the years that followed he began to perform in the provinces on short trips and also to play assorted comic parts, usually associated with skulduggery. These included one of the leading desperadoes in Dibdin's serio-comic pantomine *The Great Devil* and Rufo the Robber in *Red Riding Hood* (Sadler's Wells, 1803). Grimaldi also performed a number of 'noble savage' parts, some of them in 'blackface'. Among these were Friday in *Robinson Crusoe*, Kanto in *La Pérouse*, and the Indian Ravin in *Ko and Zoa* (Sadler's Wells, 1802).

In 1805, having quarrelled with the Drury Lane management, Grimaldi spent time in Dublin performing at Astley's Theatre and at Crow Street. On his return he made his Covent Garden début in October 1806, performing the role of the gentle 'savage' Orson (a part originally played by Dubois) in Thomas Dibdin's melodrama *Valentine and Orson*. But the most famous of his 'savage' roles was that of the Wild Man in Charles Dibdin's aquadrama *The Wild Man, or, Water Pageant* (Sadler's Wells, 1809), written especially for him. Dibdin introduced into this piece a scene, accompanied by a lute, which depicted the influence of music on the 'savage' mind. The scene soon became famous in its own right and, billed as 'The Power of Music', was performed all over London and in the provinces.

Grimaldi's fame, however, derived from his performances as clown in many pantomimes, both at Sadler's Wells and at Covent Garden, throughout his career. As Charles Dibdin remarked in his *Memoirs*, Grimaldi 'in every respect, founded a *New School* for Clowns'. Together with the pantomime arrangers Charles and Thomas Dibdin and Charles Farley, Grimaldi transformed the clown from a rustic booby into the star of metropolitan pantomime. Exuberant, mischievous, larcenous, and amoral, Grimaldi's clown epitomized the retributive desires of the Regency period. He attacked watchmen, tripped up old women, and stole incessantly, whether sausages, fruit, letters, loaves, or tablecloths. Grimaldi's clown possessed no respect for property, propriety, or authority. The clown also satirized aspects of contemporary British society, as in his ridicule of the Regency dandy and in his comic mockery of absurdities in female dress. In addition Grimaldi was renowned for his transformations, in which, in a parody of the ingenious gadgets produced during this period, he assembled models of living creatures from miscellaneous props such as household objects and vegetables and created absurd stagecoaches from brooms and large cheeses.

One of Grimaldi's greatest successes was his performance in *Harlequin and Mother Goose, or, The Golden Egg*, the Christmas pantomime written by Thomas Dibdin and performed at Covent Garden in 1806. The piece became the most successful pantomime ever staged at Covent Garden; fashionable and influential people, including Byron and Lord Eldon, flocked from all over London to see it. 'Never did I see a leg of mutton stolen with such superhumanly sublime impudence as by that man', Lord Eldon would later remember. Among other memorable productions were *Harlequin and Asmodeus, or, Cupid on Crutches* (Covent Garden, 1810) in which Grimaldi created a Vegetable Man out of assorted vegetables, including turnip hands and carrot fingers, from the market at Covent Garden. The following year, in *Harlequin and Padmanaba, or, The Golden Fish*, Grimaldi invented a burlesque coach—from four cheeses, a fender, and a cradle—in imitation of the ostentatious curricle-riding eccentric Romeo Coates. *Harlequin and the Red Dwarf* (Covent Garden, 1812) included a notorious burlesque of the hussars in which, to the delight of the audience, Grimaldi dressed himself in two black varnished coal scuttles for boots and a white bearskin for a pelisse.

Critics often remarked on the possessed, almost demonic quality of Grimaldi's mime and the expressiveness of his face and gestures. His performances of comic songs, interspersed with his inimitable patter, were celebrated. The most notable of these were 'A Typitywitchet, or, Pantomimical Paroxysms', first sung at Sadler's Wells in Charles Dibdin's pantomime *Bang up, or, Harlequin Prime* (1811), 'A Man Ran away with the Monument', from *London, or, Harlequin and Time* (Sadler's Wells, 1813), and, most famous of all, 'Hot Codlins', sung in *The Talking Bird, or, Perizade Columbine* (Covent Garden, 1819).

Grimaldi made pantomime respectable and also fashionable. He acquired fame and large sums of money, but improvidence, together with an extravagant lifestyle, meant that he rarely kept the money for long. Among his admirers was Lord Byron, who subscribed to Grimaldi's benefit performances at Covent Garden. Grimaldi later met him in 1812 at Berkeley Castle, and, when he left England in 1816, Byron presented the performer with a silver snuff-box. Grimaldi was also much admired by the theatre critic William Hazlitt, and his memoirs were edited by Charles Dickens.

After a disagreement over his salary, Grimaldi left Sadler's Wells in 1816 and went on a very profitable tour in the provinces. Having bought an eighth share in the theatre, he returned to Sadler's Wells in 1818. A year later he became stage manager in succession to Charles Dibdin, who had left after a dispute with the partners. But Grimaldi's health had been declining for some time. In 1822 he played Tycobroc, slave to the Enchanter of Uxi, in an Easter piece called *The Vision of the Sun*, but in 1823 he handed the part over to his son, who, following his 1814 début in *Robinson Crusoe*, had appeared with great success as Clown in *Harlequin and Poor Robin, or, The House that Jack Built* at Covent Garden. By now almost completely disabled, Grimaldi was engaged at Sadler's Wells to oversee the pantomime and coach the clowns. His last appearance in public took place at Drury Lane in June 1825. Grimaldi's son, who had seemed to be full of promise, had become wild and uncontrollable, and drank himself to an early death on 11 December 1832.

Grimaldi died on 31 May 1837 at 33 Southampton Street, Pentonville, London. He was buried in the graveyard at St James's Street Chapel, Pentonville Hill, next to his friend Charles Dibdin. JANE MOODY

**Sources** R. Findlater, *Grimaldi, king of clowns* (1955) · *Memoirs of Joseph Grimaldi*, ed. C. Dickens (1884) · *Professional and literary memoirs of Charles Dibdin the younger*, ed. G. Speaight (1956) · D. Mayer, *Harlequin in his element: the English pantomime, 1806–1836* (1969) · *Leigh Hunt's dramatic criticism, 1808–1831*, ed. C. Houtchens and L. Houtchens (1949) · H. D. Miles, *The life of Joseph Grimaldi* (1838) · M. W. Disher, *Clowns and pantomimes* (1925) · *Oxberry's Dramatic Biography*, new ser., 1/7 (1827), 108–22 · *DNB* · *IGI* · M. W. Disher, 'Grimaldi, Joseph', *The Oxford companion to the theatre*, ed. P. Hartnoll, 3rd edn (1967) · *GM*, 1st ser., 102/2 (1832), 581

**Likenesses** S. De Wilde, etching, pubd 1807, BM, NPG · S. De Wilde, watercolour, *c.*1807 (as Clown in *Harlequin and Mother Goose, or, The golden egg*), Garr. Club [*see illus.*] · J. E. T. Robinson, watercolour, 1819, Garr. Club · T. Blood, stipple, pubd 1820 (after T. Wageman), BM, NPG · W. Greatbach, engraving, 1846 (after drawing by T. Raven), repro. in Dickens, ed., *Memoirs*, frontispiece · J. Cawse, oils, NPG · oils, Garr. Club · prints, BM, NPG · prints (after J. E. T. Robinson), Harvard TC · prints and pottery, Theatre Museum, London, Harry Beard collection

**Grimaldi, Joseph Samuel William** (1802–1832). *See under* Grimaldi, Joseph (1778–1837).

**Grimaldi, Stacey, Marquess Grimaldi in the Genoese nobility (1790–1863)**, antiquary and genealogist, was born in the parish of St James, Westminster, on 18 October 1790. He was the second son of William *Grimaldi, Marquess Grimaldi (1751–1830), miniature painter, of Albemarle Street, London, and his wife, Frances (*d.* 1813), daughter of Louis Barker of Rochester. For over forty years Grimaldi practised as a solicitor in the City of London. He was eminent as a record lawyer and was engaged in several important record trials and peerage cases. In 1825 he married Mary Ann (1803–1877), daughter of Thomas George Knapp of Haberdashers' Hall and Norwood, Surrey. They had six sons and three daughters.

Grimaldi's great-grandfather, whose own father had been doge of Genoa in 1671, left that city after its bombardment by Louis XIV in 1684 and settled in Britain; the family laid claim to the principality of Monaco. In 1834 Stacey Grimaldi published *The Genealogy of the Family of Grimaldi of Genoa*. A copy, with manuscript additions by the author, in the British Library has the note:

> The principality of Monaco is now (1834) claimed from the reigning Prince of Monaco by the Marquess Luigi Grimaldi della Pierta, on the ground that it is a male fief, and ought not to have descended to heirs female, and this pedigree has been compiled to show at Genoa and Turin that the Grimaldis of England are the oldest branch, and have prior claims.

Upon the death of Stacey's elder brother in the following year the family claims were vested in him. His youngest son, the Revd Alexander Beaufort Grimaldi, deposited at the Manchester City Library a collection of manuscripts relating to the history of the Grimaldi family, and the Society of Antiquaries MS B34WZ also contains information on the family history.

Grimaldi was, stated the *Gentleman's Magazine*, 'an excellent herald and genealogist, and his extensive library contained many rare works on these subjects' (*GM*, 14, 1863, 661). His library consisted of about 2800 volumes, valued at approximately £1000; he transferred about 475 of these volumes, with forty-one tracts or pamphlets, in 1862 to the Incorporated Law Society for a modest sum. The society (now the Law Society) has a manuscript list of books, *Bibliotheca heraldica etc Grimaldiana* (1843), that he wished to see in its library. He was generous in lending books, sharing genealogical information, and making searches for others among the records; he corresponded with a wide range of fellow antiquaries and genealogists (BL Add. MSS 34188–34189). Grimaldi took part in the events leading to the passing of the Public Records Act in 1838; with W. H. Black, he had drafted a bill in 1837 aimed at improving conditions for users of the public records, which was not, however, enacted.

Grimaldi's substantial writings included forty-one articles submitted to the *Gentleman's Magazine* during the period 1813–61. In 1835 he published a copy of *Grimaldi's Roll of Arms*, then in his ownership and now in the Rylands Library. His youngest son published a revised and extended edition of *The Synopsis of English History* (1870) and his *Miscellaneous Writings*, in four parts (1874–81). *Origines genealogicae* (1828), Grimaldi's most substantial work, was based on his extensive working knowledge of the records and was 'Published expressly for the assistance of Claimants to Hereditary Titles, Honours, or Estates' (title-page). 'No work of the kind', he wrote in the prospectus, 'has been hitherto attempted' (BL, Add. MS 24188, fol. 39). In 1824 he was elected a fellow of the Society of Antiquaries. He was appointed to lecture on the public records at the Incorporated Law Society in 1834; he subsequently published his lecture notes, and in 1853 was appointed auditor of that society.

Late in 1828 Grimaldi moved with his family to Maze Hill, Greenwich, and about 1861 he moved to Herndon House, Eastry, in Kent, where he died on 28 March 1863; he was buried on 4 April 1863 at St Mary the Virgin, Eastry. His wife and all of their nine children survived him.

COLIN LEE

**Sources** *GM*, 1st ser., 100/2 (1830), 197, 300 · *GM*, 1st ser., 102/1 (1832), 26 · *GM*, 1st ser., 102/2 (1832), 508 · *GM*, 2nd ser., 2 (1834), 430 · *GM*, 3rd ser., 14 (1863), 661 · S. Antiquaries, Lond., MS B34WZ · *Herald and Genealogist*, 1 (1863), 545, 548–9 · S. Grimaldi, corresp., BL, Add. MSS 34188–34189 · A. R. Wagner, *A catalogue of English mediaeval rolls of arms*, Harleian Society, 100 (1950), 62 · *Proceedings of the Society of Antiquaries of London*, 2nd ser., 2 (1861–4), 254–5 · J. D. Cantwell, *The Public Record Office, 1838–1958* (1991), 6, 59 · T. D. Tremlett, H. Stanford London, and A. Wagner, eds., *Rolls of arms, Henry III*, Harleian Society, 113–14 (1967), 90 · Venn, *Alum. Cant.* · *DNB* · *CGPLA Eng. & Wales* (1863) · parish register, St Mary the Virgin, Eastry, Kent, 4 April 1863 [burial]

**Archives** Man. CL, MSS · S. Antiquaries, Lond., materials relating to family history, MS B34WZ

**Wealth at death** under £1500: probate, 6 June 1863, *CGPLA Eng. & Wales*

**Grimaldi, William, Marquess Grimaldi in the Genoese nobility (1751–1830)**, miniature painter, was born in Christopher's Alley, Shoreditch, London, on 26 August 1751 and baptized at home on 22 September, the fourth but eldest surviving son of Alexander Grimaldi, Marquess Grimaldi (1724–1800), of Christopher's Alley, Shoreditch, and his second wife, Esther Barton (*d.* 1774) of Gloucester. He was the grandson of Alessandro Maria Grimaldi, Marquess Grimaldi (1659–1732), a Genoese nobleman and artist who had settled in England after the bombardment of Genoa in 1684. In 1764 William Grimaldi was bound as an apprentice to his uncle Thomas *Worlidge (1700–1766), a miniature and portrait painter. After his initial training he began to practise independently as a miniature painter and exhibited his work for the first time at the Free Society of Artists in 1768. He travelled extensively throughout the country in search of custom during the 1770s, visiting Gosport and Portsmouth in 1772, Southampton, Gloucester, Worcester, and Shrewsbury in 1773, Chester in 1774, Southampton and Newport in 1775, and Portsmouth and Southampton in 1776, exhibiting in the meanwhile at the Free Society of Artists until 1770 and at the Society of Artists in 1772. He worked in Paris from 1777 to 1783, imbuing his miniatures with a distinctly continental flavour from then on, and he was later erroneously to style himself a member of the Académie Royale.

In 1783 Grimaldi married Frances Barker (1750–1813), the daughter of Lewis Barker and Frances Willis of Rochester, Kent. After having returned to London, he began to work in enamel as well as in watercolour, honing his technique by copying the paintings of Hoppner, Beechey, Reynolds, and others. It may have been through Reynolds that Grimaldi was introduced to the royal family, and he was subsequently appointed miniature painter to the duke and duchess of York (1791), and to George IV when prince of Wales (1806) and king (1824). Several of the miniatures which he painted in this capacity remain in the Royal Collection and others are in the Victoria and Albert Museum and the Wallace Collection, London. His successful practice was conducted from studios at 2 Albemarle Street and then at 16 Hunter Street, London, and he exhibited at the Royal Academy almost continuously from 1786 until his death, which occurred at his home, 16 Upper Ebury Street, Chelsea, London, on 27 May 1830. He was buried in the City burial-ground.

Grimaldi and his wife had four children: Louisa Frances (1785–1873), William (1786–1835), Henry (1792–1806), and Stacey *Grimaldi (1790–1863), who, as Marquess Grimaldi, succeeded to the title which his brother William had inherited but never used. Louisa Frances Grimaldi (later Mrs John Edmeads) also painted miniatures, but William Grimaldi is not known to have had any other pupils. His reputation has only ever been marred by the inconsistency of his work, which, at its best, is 'of outstanding merit' (Foskett, 552). V. Remington

**Sources** *GM*, 1st ser., 100/1 (1830), 566 · A. B. Grimaldi, *A catalogue … of paintings, drawings and engravings by and after William Grimaldi* (privately printed, London, 1873) · G. Reynolds, *English portrait miniatures* (1952); rev. edn (1988), 145–6 · D. Foskett, *Miniatures: dictionary and guide* (1987), 298–9, 552 · B. S. Long, *British miniaturists* (1929), 180–81 · L. R. Schidlof, *The miniature in Europe in the 16th, 17th, 18th, and 19th centuries*, 2 (1964), 312–13 · Graves, *RA exhibitors* · R. Walker, *The eighteenth and early nineteenth century miniatures in the collection of her majesty the queen* (1992), 324–36 · *DNB* · P. J. Noon, *English portrait drawings and miniatures* (New Haven, CT, 1979), 88–9 [exhibition catalogue, Yale U. CBA, 5 Dec 1979 – 17 Feb 1980] · parish register, 22 Sept 1751, London, Shoreditch, St Leonard [baptism]

**Likenesses** M. Grimaldi, pencil drawing (after L. Edwards), NPG

**Grimbald** [St Grimbald] (*d.* **901?**), Benedictine monk, assisted King Alfred in his literary work and is regarded traditionally as the co-founder of the New Minster (later Hyde Abbey) at Winchester. What is known of the life of Grimbald of St Bertin is a mixture of fact and confusion, out of which a certain amount of coherence may be extracted. Traditionally said to have been born at Thérouanne, about 30 miles east of Boulogne, he was sent at an early age to the nearby abbey of St Bertin at St Omer, where he became a monk and eventually a priest. There is virtually no record of his life there. He comes to light only in the years 883–6, when Archbishop Fulco of Rheims, in a well-known letter to Alfred the Great, agrees that Grimbald (who was possibly about to become a prominent figure in the archbishop's circle) should, under certain conditions, go to England in order to help Alfred in his struggle against cultural as well as political barbarism. In England by 887, Grimbald seems to have spent the rest of his life there, based (again according to tradition) in a *monasteriolum* (cell or small monastery) at Winchester.

Grimbald's primary role seems to have been as adviser and assistant to Alfred, as the king tried to implement his programme of having translated into Old English certain Latin works he regarded as basic. Alfred acknowledged this help in his celebrated prose preface to the *Regula pastoralis* of Gregory the Great, where he names four assistants, one being 'Grimbald my mass-priest'. Already by 893, Asser's contemporary life of Alfred (completed in that year, though Alfred lived until 899) speaks of Grimbald's skill at chanting and his scriptural learning.

That Grimbald was brought from Flanders simply to help Alfred with his literary endeavours, however, seems unlikely, especially in view of Fulco's letter, which made it plain that he expected his protégé quickly to become a bishop in England. Reasons why this did not happen range from possible linguistic difficulties for Grimbald (a matter connected with the vexed question of whether his native vernacular was basically Germanic or Romance) to his humility: tradition here supplies the detail that on the death of Archbishop Æthelred of Canterbury in 888, Grimbald declined Alfred's proffer of the see and instead recommended Plegemund, another of the king's literary helpers, who did in fact become the next archbishop.

It is almost certain that Grimbald died in 901 (not 902 or 903, as is frequently stated), probably on 8 July and most likely at Winchester. His *monasteriolum* is thought to have been connected in some way with the foundation by Edward the Elder, Alfred's son and successor, of a religious house there, probably staffed by secular canons. This house, originally called the New Minster to distinguish it from the adjacent Old Minster (the cathedral), soon came to regard Grimbald as in some sense its co-founder, along with the king, or even as its first abbot, though he died before it was dedicated in 903. In any case, he was buried there, and a cult quickly came into being, abetted by the popularity of relics of St Judoc (alias Josse), which he was supposed to have obtained from Picardy, and, probably soon after the dedication, by the translation of the body of his patron, King Alfred. About 964 the New Minster was reorganized, in the wake of widespread monastic reform, to be a true Benedictine abbey; and in 1110, partly as a consequence of the monastic overcrowding in the city itself, it moved outside the walls of Winchester and took the name of Hyde. By at least that time it was dedicated to St Peter and St Grimbald.

The Hyde connection is particularly important because a breviary from that abbey, of *c.*1300, is the sole means of preservation of the most extensive, and perhaps reliable, medieval source for Grimbald's life, the *Vita prima* (to distinguish it from two or three later lives), excerpts from which are preserved in the lessons for St Grimbald's day, 8 July. Although the conventions and fabrications of hagiography are much in evidence (for example, in the detail that the four-year-old Alfred, on his way to Rome in 853, stopped at St Bertin and there singled out Grimbald for future notice), the more sober parts of what has been referred to here as tradition come largely from this source. Much less reputable are stories, found in the intensive interpolations in manuscripts of Asser's life, which involve Grimbald in controversies at a mythically extant University of Oxford.

Grimbald's cult spread fairly rapidly in tenth- and eleventh-century England, generally as a consequence of some connection with the New Minster. After the Norman conquest it is less prominent, except at Hyde. Further significance can be posited for him as the importer of, or at least means of transmission for, certain continental manuscripts which, because of either their contents or their handwriting, played vital roles in the revival of English culture in the tenth century. In so far as this may be true, Grimbald can be seen as a key figure, not only in that Alfredian programme of translations by which notable segments of the Latin Christian past were put into the English vernacular, but also in the passing of the high literary and artistic culture of the Carolingian world into the England of Alfred's successors. RICHARD W. PFAFF

**Sources** *Acta sanctorum: Julius*, 2 (Antwerp, 1721), 651–8 • J. B. L. Tolhurst, ed., *The monastic breviary of Hyde Abbey, Winchester*, 4, HBS, 78 (1939), fols. 288*r*–290*v* • D. Whitelock, M. Brett, and C. N. L. Brooke, eds., *Councils and synods with other documents relating to the English church, 871–1204*, 2 (1981) [letter of Fulk to Alfred] • *English historical documents*, 1, ed. D. Whitelock (1955) • *Asser's Life of King Alfred: together with the 'Annals of Saint Neots' erroneously ascribed to Asser*, ed. W. H. Stevenson (1904); repr. with a supplementary article by D. Whitelock (1959) • *Alfred the Great: Asser's Life of King Alfred and other contemporary sources*, ed. and trans. S. Keynes and M. Lapidge (1983) • P. Grierson, 'Grimbald of St Bertin's', *EngHR*, 55 (1940), 529–61 • J. Bately, 'Grimbald of St Bertin's', *Medium Aevum*, 35 (1966), 1–10 • M. Biddle, 'Felix urbs Winthonia: Winchester in the age of monastic reform', *Tenth-century studies*, ed. D. Parsons (1975), 123–40 • M. B. Parkes, 'The palaeography of the Parker manuscript of the *Chronicle*, laws, and Sedulius, and historiography at Winchester in the late ninth and tenth centuries', *Anglo-Saxon England*, 5 (1976), 148–71 • J. Pycke, 'Grimbald', *Dictionnaire d'histoire et de géographie ecclésiastiques*, ed. A. Baudrillart and others, 22 (Paris, 1988), 266–9

**Grimble, Sir Arthur Francis** (1888–1956), colonial governor and ethnographer, was born in Hong Kong on 11 June 1888, the son of Frank Grimble, a partner in the Admiralty contractors Caird and Rayner, and his wife, Blanche Ann Arthur. He was educated at Chigwell School, Essex, from 1898 to 1907, and Magdalene College, Cambridge, from 1907 to 1910, where he read law, and then spent over three years on the continent, acquiring fluency in both French and German. He joined the colonial administrative service in 1914 and was posted to the Gilbert and Ellice Islands, where he rose to be resident commissioner, before transfer in 1933 as administrator of St Vincent. In 1936 he was appointed governor of the Seychelles and in 1942 governor of the Windward Islands. He married Olivia Mary Jarvis of Sharnbrook, Bedfordshire, in 1914; they had four daughters.

After his retirement in 1948 Grimble became one of the best-known of all colonial administrators and, through him, the Gilbert Islands better known than most dependencies. His delightful broadcast tales of his Pacific experiences, so well narrated by himself, were an immediate success. Published in 1952 under the title *A Pattern of Islands*, the book became a General Certificate of Education text, introducing several generations to an empire already largely dismantled. Published in the United States as *We Chose the Islands*, it was translated into many languages and made into a rather bad film, *Pacific Destiny*, in 1957. More atoll stories were told in the *Return to the Islands*, published posthumously in 1957. Both books drew upon Grimble's scholarly knowledge of Micronesian ethnology, an interest originally encouraged by W. H. R. Rivers, whom he knew at Cambridge and whose research in Melanesia had determined Grimble to apply for the cadetship in the western Pacific. Early in his career Grimble published papers in the journals of the Royal Anthropological Institute and the Polynesian Society and was invited to apply for the new chair of anthropology at the University of Sydney. Papers recording his fieldwork, deposited in the Pacific Manuscripts Bureau, have been edited by H. E. Maude as *Tungaru Traditions: Writings on the Atoll Culture of the Gilbert Islands* (1989). Maude commented that 'the fact that the gist of what he recorded still stands as valid to-day as when he first penned it is a remarkable tribute to the scrupulous care with which he conducted his field research over sixty years ago' (Maude, xxvi). Some of his earlier papers have also been arranged and beautifully illustrated by his daughter Rosemary as *Migrations, Myth and Magic from the Gilbert Islands* (1972).

Grimble was more than fluent in Gilbertese, he was master of classical Gilbertese, no longer spoken and scarcely remembered. This linguistic skill enabled him to entice from elders, who remembered atoll life before significant Western contact, knowledge of traditional custom and values already being ridiculed by the younger, mission-educated generation. Maude, who served under him, described Grimble as a 'courteous disciple and rapporteur' (Maude, xxiii), but the research which led to his deep understanding and enjoyment of the people he called 'princes in laughter and friendship, poetry and love' (Grimble, *Pattern of Islands*, 12) was partly an antidote to what he referred to as exile; the loneliness of long tours spent in the extremely limited atoll environment, separated from his family. In ten years he was with them for only nine months. He was frequently ill with amoebic dysentery and colitis. By the time of his transfer to the Caribbean he was exhausted after nearly twenty years in one of the smallest and remotest of colonies, desperate for a change and the opportunity to demonstrate his worth in a bigger, more important arena as well as the chance to enjoy normal family life.

That at least Grimble achieved in the West Indies but his career was to remain confined to islands and at its peak was subject to the constraints of wartime. He retired in 1948. Remembered as a courteous, kindly administrator, insatiably curious about people, Grimble was a paternalist who favoured slow evolution. Criticized for his regulations for good order and cleanliness, his purpose was to sustain custom in the face of mission attempts to destroy it, just as he wrote a spirited defence of the dancing which the London Missionary Society had sought to have forbidden. His greatest contribution as an administrator, was, perhaps, as the first lands commissioner in the land-hungry Gilbert and Ellice Islands where there were more land disputes than people. His fluency and understanding of custom enabled him to establish an effective system of land registration and courts which has stood the test of time.

The image gained from Grimble's books of a benign, mild tempered, and just if omniscient administrator was sadly tarnished twenty years after his death during one of the longest ever actions in the Chancery Division of the High Court. The administrative headquarters of the Gilbert and Ellice Islands in Grimble's day was Ocean Island, more correctly called Banaba. Only 2½ square miles in all, it was, like its neighbour Nauru, phosphate-rich and mined by the British phosphate commissioners, agents of the British, Australian, and New Zealand governments. The actions, brought by Rotan Tito on behalf of the Banaban landowners, against the phosphate commissioners and the attorney-general, as representing the British government, concerned physical claims relating to failure to meet contractual obligations and to the unauthorized mining of land, and financial claims relating to royalties. By the time of the actions most of the island had been mined and the Banabans had long been resettled in Fiji. The claims, which went back virtually to the discovery of phosphate, were in the main dismissed, some as unmeritorious, but the vice-chancellor called attention to grave breaches of governmental obligations and was critical of the role Grimble had played as resident commissioner. After his failure, during negotiations for additional mining land, to persuade the Banabans to accept a realistic price Grimble had written a letter to them, in a style which they would have expected and appreciated but which, translated into modern idiom forty years later caused the vice-chancellor to comment that 'it could only be read with a sense of outrage' (*Law Reports*, Chancery Division, 1977, 235–7). Grimble saw himself as defender of the Banabans—as his letter said as their father—and did his utmost to negotiate a better deal for them. At the same time he knew the British phosphate commissioners and phosphate revenue provided the only hope for their future, so his letter spoke of the choice between life and death. When the land was eventually acquired compulsorily it was Grimble, as resident commissioner, who was legally required to fix the royalty.

The legal complexities of the actions were unlikely press material, but Grimble's name was well known to the public. In innumerable articles and a BBC television programme, entitled *Go Tell It to the Judge* (first broadcast on 6 January 1977), Grimble was cast as fallen idol. There was little understanding of the culture of the time, of the jack of all trades role of any colonial administrator in an isolated and remote place, or of the difficult task of trying to be fair to both landowners and miners. Ironically, had Grimble not written so engagingly about the people he so greatly liked and admired and for whom he fought so hard, the court actions would have attracted far less attention.

Grimble was appointed CMG in 1930 and promoted to KCMG in 1938. He died in the Watlington Hospital, Dorchester, Oxfordshire, on 12 December 1956, his wife surviving him. J. H. SMITH

**Sources** A. F. Grimble, *A pattern of islands* (1952) • A. F. Grimble, *Return to the islands* (1957) • H. E. Maude, ed., *Tungaru traditions: writings on the Atoll culture of the Gilbert Islands* (1989) • B. MacDonald, *Guderallas of the empire* (1982) • B. MacDonald, *'Grimble of the Gilbert Islands: myth and man', More Pacific portraits*, ed. D. Scarr (1979), 211–29 • M. Williams and B. MacDonald, *The phosphateers* (1985) • M. G. Silverman, *Disconcerting issue* (1971) • *'Tito and others v. Waddell and others', Law reports: chancery division* (1973) [R. no. 2013] • *'Tito and others v. Attorney-General', Law reports: chancery division* (1971) [R. no. 3670] • R. Grimble, *Migrations, myth and magic from the Gilbert Islands* (1972) • *The Times* (13 Dec 1956) • *CGPLA Eng. & Wales* (1957) • *Go tell it to the judge*, BBC television programme, 6 Jan 1977 • *DNB*

**Archives** Australian National University, Canberra, Pacific Manuscripts Bureau • PRO, western Pacific high commission archives | FILM BBC TV programme on the Gilbert Islands, *Go tell it to the judge*, first broadcast on 6 Jan 1977
**Likenesses** photograph, BBC Picture Archive, London
**Wealth at death** £9074 0s. 5d.: probate, 31 Jan 1957, *CGPLA Eng. & Wales*

**Grimes, Mary Katharine** (1861–1921), promoter of emigration, was born on 26 September 1861 in Funchal, Madeira, the eldest of three daughters of John Ralph Grimes and his wife, Mary Ann, eldest daughter of George Lund MD of Edinburgh, Scarborough, and Madeira. She was educated at home. Her early life is obscure, but by her early twenties she was living in London and had become involved in voluntary work as honorary secretary and librarian of Battersea parochial library. She was subsequently a poor-law infirmary visitor and visitor for the Metropolitan Association for Befriending Young Servants, first in Wandsworth and Battersea (1885–94), and subsequently in Lambeth between 1897 and 1901. She served as honorary secretary of the Clapham and East Battersea committee of the Charity Organization Society (COS) between 1884 and 1897, and was representative at council of the Brixton committee of the COS in 1898 and 1899.

It is probable that, in the course of her voluntary work, Grimes became familiar with the arguments favouring emigration of the disadvantaged in society, and about 1901 she became honorary secretary of the Church Emigration Society (which became the Church of England Council for Empire Settlement). She was also, from 1904, a member of the emigration committee of the Church of England Waifs and Strays Society (later known as the Children's Society). The Church Emigration Society was formed mainly for the purpose of establishing an efficient system of commendation of emigrants by the clergy in England to the clergy in the colonies, and in her capacity as secretary she entered into extensive correspondence with the clergy in Canada, South Africa, Australia, and New Zealand, and kept in touch with emigrants supported by the society. She represented the society at the emigration conference convened by the Royal Colonial Institute, of which she was an associate, in May 1910, and gave evidence on the work of the society to the dominions royal commission in October 1912. She was appointed visitor to the Ministry of Pensions in 1918.

Mary Grimes epitomized the type of female charity worker described in *Our Waifs and Strays* (May 1885, 5), the magazine of the Church of England Waifs and Strays Society. 'The best secretaries, as a rule,' it suggested, 'are middle-aged unmarried ladies … Ladies are better than gentlemen, as they are more persevering beggars, and go more into details.' Her membership of the moderate Conservative and Unionist Women's Franchise Association and National Union of Women's Suffrage Societies suggests she felt that women deserved a greater role in the political life of the country, though she does not appear to have been active in the suffrage movement. She was interested in music, photography, and travel. She visited Vancouver Island and British Columbia, Canada, in 1905, and made a trip to South Africa in 1914. She also had an interest in gardening and was elected a fellow of the Royal Horticultural Society in 1912.

Mary Grimes was in South Africa at the beginning of a tour on Church Emigration Society business that was to take in Australia and New Zealand when she contracted gastric influenza. She died in Cape Town on 10 January 1921, and was buried at Maitland No. 1 cemetery the following day. JUDY COLLINGWOOD

**Sources** *WWW* • *Church Times* (28 Jan 1921) • *Cape Times* (11 Jan 1921) • *Our Waifs and Strays* (Feb 1921), 20
**Wealth at death** £1890 12s. 9d.: PRO

**Grimes, William Francis** (1905–1988), archaeologist, was born on 31 October 1905 at Glyn House, Woodbine Terrace, Pembroke, the eldest son of four children of Thomas George Grimes, a draughtsman who worked for the Pembroke Docks Board, and his wife, Edith May Williams. His parents were both Welsh. Grimes was educated at Pembroke county school—where apparently his love for archaeology was first kindled by a teacher—and, after his father moved to Bedford to work on airships, subsequently at Bedford modern school.

Grimes returned to Wales to read Latin at the University College of Wales, Cardiff, graduating in 1926 with first-class honours. Characteristically he went straight from his graduation ceremony to the National Museum of Wales, where he took up office as assistant keeper of archaeology. He worked under the newly appointed keeper of archaeology, V. E. Nash-Williams, who had himself just replaced Cyril Fox, who had been appointed director to succeed Mortimer Wheeler after his move to the London Museum. At the National Museum Grimes studied the material from the Roman pottery works at Holt, Denbighshire. For this work he was awarded the degree of MA by the University of Wales in 1930; it was published as *Holt, Denbighshire: the Works Depot of the Twentieth Legion at Castle Lyons* (1930). In spite of this research, stemming in part from his classical training, Grimes's main interest was in the prehistory of Wales and he regularly published on this topic in *Archaeologia Cambrensis* and the *Bulletin of the Board of Celtic Studies*; he also provided summaries for the *Proceedings of the Prehistoric Society*.

In recognition of this work Grimes was elected a fellow of the Society of Antiquaries on St David's day 1934, and was admitted the following week when he travelled to London to hear the Wheelers give a lecture on their excavations at Verulamium. In 1939 the National Museum of Wales published Grimes's *Guide to the Collection Illustrating the Prehistory of Wales*. In 1949 this was to win him the G. T. Clark prize, awarded for research on the archaeology of Wales and the marches; Professor V. Gordon Childe was the assessor for the prehistory section. This work was republished in 1951, with a second edition in 1959, as *The Prehistory of Wales*.

In 1928 Grimes married Barbara Lilian Morgan (1905–*c*.1961), whom he had known in his boyhood in Pembroke. There were two children, Rosemary and Roger. In 1935, to celebrate the centenary of the Royal Institution of South Wales in Swansea, Grimes helped to mount a special exhibition in the antiquities department. It was during these visits that he met his future wife, Mrs Audrey Williams (1902–1978), who had read English at Somerville College in Oxford, and who was then honorary assistant and later honorary secretary and curator of the Royal Institution. Audrey, who was active in excavating a number of prehistoric sites on the Gower peninsula, was to become a close family friend, and she was to work with Grimes on a number of excavations including those at the Dan-yr-Ogof caves at the head of the Swansea valley. Grimes always acknowledged Audrey as the better excavator.

It was Grimes's skill as an excavator that led to his appointment as an assistant archaeology officer to the Ordnance Survey in Southampton. He took up the position in October 1938, and was to work alongside O. G. S. Crawford. Grimes edited a collection of essays, *Aspects of Archaeology in Britain and Beyond*, in Crawford's honour (1951). Both Crawford and Grimes responded to the call for help when the Sutton Hoo ship burial was discovered in Suffolk in the early summer of 1939. A contemporary report noted that Grimes's 'work in dissecting and removing the majority of the buried deposits was invaluable' (*Antiquaries Journal*, 20, 1940, 192).

With the outbreak of war, Grimes was seconded to the Ministry of Works to excavate in advance of the construction of defence sites. Audrey Williams was one of his colleagues through the war years. This 'rescue' archaeological fieldwork took Grimes round Britain, and it was noted that he was 'continuously in the field without more than one week free at any time between excavations' (B. H. St J. O'Neil, 'War and archaeology in Britain', *Antiquaries Journal*, 28, 1948, 23). One of these wartime excavations was at Heathrow, where he uncovered an Iron Age religious site.

Grimes had a strong vision of the role of museums in post-war Britain, presenting his views in *Antiquity* (1944). In 1945 he was appointed director of the London Museum, succeeding Mortimer Wheeler. The blitz had wrought considerable damage to the heart of the capital, and in 1946 Grimes was appointed honorary director of excavations for the Roman and Medieval London excavation council. As a result of this work, Grimes was granted freedom of the City of London in 1952, and was made a CBE in 1955. The excavation which captured the public's imagination was the discovery of a Roman temple of Mithras at Walbrook in 1954. This work had been conducted with Audrey Williams, who had joined the staff of the Verulamium Museum after the war. Grimes also excavated on the site of a number of City churches including St Bride's, Fleet Street.

In 1956 Grimes was appointed director of the Institute of Archaeology and professor of archaeology in the University of London as successor to V. Gordon Childe. Childe vacated the chair early to allow his successor to oversee the move of the institute to Gordon Square; he had in fact revealed to Grimes his intention to commit suicide. In 1959 Grimes's marriage was dissolved, and he married Audrey Williams, who had in the mean time remarried and become divorced.

In spite of his move to London, Grimes retained strong links with Wales, serving as president of the Cambrian Archaeological Association in 1963–4. In 1961 he was awarded an honorary degree of DLitt from the University of Wales, based on a portfolio of published work on the archaeology of Wales with special reference to prehistoric burial monuments. Further recognition was made by his appointment as an honorary professorial fellow of the University College of Swansea (1975), and his election as fellow of the University College of Cardiff (1981). Grimes was a member of the royal commissions on the ancient monuments in Wales and Monmouthshire (1948–78), and on historical monuments (England) (1964–78). He was also actively involved with numerous national archaeological societies and organizations, such as the Society of Antiquaries, the Royal Archaeological Institute, and the Council for British Archaeology. On Grimes's retirement, Lord Fletcher commented, 'it has become almost trite to observe that no committee on an archaeological subject is complete unless graced with the presence of Professor Grimes' (D. E. Strong, ed., *Archaeological Theory and Practice: Essays Presented to Professor William Francis Grimes*, 1973, x). This was especially true of his commitment to amateur local societies; particular mention should be made of his work with the field studies centre at Dale in Pembrokeshire.

Grimes was a skilled artist and draughtsman. He was an accomplished violinist as a student at Cardiff, although he ceased to play upon graduation in case it distracted him from his archaeology. He was known by his nickname, Peter, which had been applied to him by Audrey. As a young man he had flaming red hair, and in later life he invariably sported a red carnation in the lapel of his jacket. Ralph Merrifield remembered Grimes as 'single-minded and conscientious in his pursuit of truth, with a preference for solving problems by orderly, logical steps, and a distrust of hypotheses that had not been thoroughly tested' (Merrifield, 278).

Grimes retired in 1973 to Swansea, living in Audrey's house in Brynmill. Audrey died in Aberystwyth in 1978, immediately prior to the presentation to Grimes on his retirement from the royal commission. In 1980 Grimes married his third wife, Mrs Molly Waverley Sholto Douglas (*b.* 1926), a friend since his retirement to Swansea. In the final two years of his life he became increasingly disabled by Parkinson's disease, dying at his home, 29 Bryn Road, Brynmill, Swansea, on Christmas day 1988. He was cremated and his ashes were scattered, like those of his beloved Audrey's, at Pwlldu Bay at the foot of the Bishopston valley on the Gower peninsula. DAVID GILL

**Sources** R. Merrifield, 'William Francis Grimes, 1905–1988', *London Topographical Record*, 26 (1990), 271–93 [incl. bibliography compiled by Ortrun Peyn] • J. Hall and J. Macdonald, 'W. F. Grimes (1905–1988)', *Transactions of the London and Middlesex Archaeological Society*, 39 (1988), xi–xv • *The Times* (28 Dec 1988) • D. Miles, 'Professor W. F. Grimes', *Archaeologia Cambrensis*, 138 (1989), 115–16 • *Antiquaries Journal*, 69 (1989), 410–11 • *British Archaeological Newsletter*, 4/2 (March 1989), 22 • *Annual Report of the National Museum of Wales* (1988–9), 9–10 • private information (2004)

**Archives** Museum of London, London Archaeological Archive and Study Centre, Grimes London archive · National Monuments Record of Wales, Aberystwyth, corresp.; drawings; MSS; photographs · NMG Wales, general archive · S. Antiquaries, Lond., corresp. and papers relating to Beaker culture, MS 897 | Bodl. Oxf., corresp. with O. G. S. Crawford
**Likenesses** photograph, repro. in Hall and Macdonald, 'W. F. Grimes'
**Wealth at death** under £70,000: probate, 21 April 1989, *CGPLA Eng. & Wales*

**Grimm, Samuel Hieronymus** (*bap.* 1733, *d.* 1794), watercolour painter, was baptized on 18 January 1733 at Burgdorf, in the canton of Bern, Switzerland, the youngest of three children of Johann Jakob Grimm (*d.* 1749), notary. In the 1750s he was a pupil in Bern of the painter Johann L. Aberli. His first known professional works are views of glaciers in the Bernese Oberland, prepared in 1758 for G. S. Gruner's *Die Eisgebirge des Schweizerlandes* (1760). The associated tour gave rise to a long narrative poem, which Grimm published with other poems in 1762; a poetic eulogy to Frederick the Great of Prussia had been published in Berlin in 1758. This was the extent of his own published literary efforts, and Grimm subsequently concentrated on illustrating those of other people, working mainly for the Bern publisher B. L. Walthard from 1764 until 1775.

In or soon after August 1765 Grimm moved to Paris where he joined the circle of J. G. Wille, a leading engraver, whose studio was a place of cheerful comradeship. With other artists he made excursions in the vicinity of Paris and in 1766—in the company of Philipp Hackert and Nicolas Pérignon—took a walking tour to sketch in Normandy. The surviving pictures are in watercolour, for by this date Grimm had ceased to work in oils. France was only a staging post: in February 1768 he left Paris for London. There he took lodgings with Mrs Susanna Sledge, a printseller at 1 Henrietta Street, St Paul's, Covent Garden, London, where (or near by) he remained for the rest of his life; he never married. He was soon absorbed into London artistic circles, probably mixing with other Swiss immigrants. He exhibited at the Society of Artists within months of arriving in London, and at the Royal Academy from the following year continuously until 1781, and again in 1783–4 and 1793. Elected to the Society of Arts in November 1773, he was an active member on its committee of polite arts until 1777.

Grimm's artistic output in England fell into three categories. First, there were designs for commercial engravings. He continued to work for Swiss publishers, and in London six satirical mezzotints drawn by him appeared in 1771–4, as well as, for example, prefatory illustrations to Francis Grose's *Antiquities of England and Wales*, volume 1 (1773). Second, various watercolours of Shakespearian, classical, and genre scenes, and also topographical views around London, may have been made speculatively in hope of attracting publishers or orders for copies from private collectors. Third, and most important, were commissioned watercolours of antiquities, historic buildings, and landscapes.

In this last field Grimm was well established from 1773. Some commissions were very specific. The Society of Antiquaries retained him on four occasions between 1779 and 1791 to copy Tudor paintings. Two clients wanted illustrations for their books, Gilbert White for his celebrated *Natural History and Antiquities of Selborne* (1789)—this was a month's work, including small assignments for several neighbours, in 1776—and Henry Penruddocke Wyndham, with whom Grimm travelled for three months in 1777, for the second edition of *A Gentleman's Tour through Monmouthshire and Wales* (1781). Lord Scarbrough evidently commissioned views of his Yorkshire estates in 1781. But of longer standing were the three 'worthy friends and employers' whom Grimm named in his will. Cornelius Heathcote Rodes (1755–1825) of Barlborough Hall, Derbyshire, knew Grimm in 1773 and employed him at least in 1781 and again for several months in 1785, to sketch in the Chesterfield area. Sir William Burrell (1732–1796) retained him for the fortnight from Whitsun each year between 1780 and 1791 (except 1786) to work in Sussex: in some twenty-two weeks Grimm undertook the studies from nature for nearly 900 finished watercolours, now in the British Library. But most significant of the three was Sir Richard Kaye (1736–1809), who, as the king's sub-almoner, commissioned pictures of the Maundy ceremony in 1773 and gave Grimm frequent employment for the rest of his life. Kaye's collection, now in the British Library, runs to some 2500 finished pictures. The counties most represented reflect Kaye's succession of ecclesiastical preferments, in Nottinghamshire, the north-east, and Lincolnshire; and tours they made during Kaye's summer sojourns at west country health resorts from 1788 to 1790.

In recommending Grimm to Sir Richard Worsley in 1777, Francis Grose wrote that 'he is nearly the best draughtsman in London. His expenses will be very moderate … This Grim is a very modest, well behaved man and will do as he is bid and not give himself those impertinent airs frequently assumed by artists much his inferiors in abilities' (Isle of Wight RO, JER/WA/39/5/135). Gilbert White described Grimm's technique:

> He first of all sketches his scapes with a lead-pencil; then he pens them all over, as he calls it, with indian ink, rubbing out the superfluous pencil-strokes; then he gives a charming shading with a brush dipped in indian ink; and last he throws a light tinge of water-colours over the whole. (Holt-White, 1.326)

Trained by a Swiss miniaturist and drawing directly from nature, Grimm worked best in a free, exact, but lively style with careful detailing. But as a journeyman artist he had to satisfy a variety of clients, and some wanted the highly finished English stained topographical drawing. Grimm's studio work could not compete with that of contemporaries such as Paul Sandby and Michael Angelo Rooker.

Grimm died on 14 April 1794, at the house of William Wellings, engraver, in Tavistock Street, St Paul's, Covent Garden, London, and was buried on 18 April at the parish church there, Kaye conducting the funeral. His intense modesty was reflected in his instruction for his papers to be destroyed. An engraving reputedly of him in the Witt Library, Courtauld Institute of Art, London, shows a thick-necked man with fleshy features and wavy hair.

JOHN H. FARRANT

**Sources** R. M. Clay, *Samuel Hieronymus Grimm of Burgdorf in Switzerland* (1941) • P. Joyner, *Samuel Hieronymus Grimm: views in Wales* (1983) • J. H. Farrant, *Sussex depicted: views and descriptions, 1600–1800*, Sussex RS, 85 (2001), 45–50 • R. Holt-White, *The life and letters of Gilbert White of Selborne*, 2 vols. (1901) • *GM*, 1st ser., 64 (1794), 576 • PRO, PROB 11/1247/322 [printed in Farrant, 137–8] • Isle of Wight RO, JER/WA/39/5/135

**Likenesses** engraving (after photograph of an engraving in Witt Library; of S. H. Grimm ?), repro. in Joyner, *Samuel Hieronymus Grimm*, pl. 1

**Wealth at death** £306; plus sale of his drawings and personal possessions: will, PRO, PROB 11/1247/322

**Grimond, Joseph** [Jo], **Baron Grimond** (**1913–1993**), politician, was born on 29 July 1913 at 8 Abbotsford Crescent, St Andrews, Fife, the youngest of the three children of Joseph Bowman Grimond (1876–1929), jute manufacturer, and his wife, Helen Lydia (1875–1953), daughter of Alexander Richardson of Birkenhead. The Grimond family originated from Perthshire. In the mid-nineteenth century Joseph Grimond, great-grandfather of Jo Grimond, left the family farm near Blairgowrie to learn the trades of spinning and weaving in Lancashire. He returned to Dundee where at Bowbridge he established one of the largest jute mills in Europe. The family firm of J. and A. D. Grimond prospered and the Grimonds became leading members of the Dundee jutocracy. Thanks to the family's considerable wealth Jo Grimond, as he was almost invariably called from a young age, had a comfortable and stimulating childhood; there were annual visits to France in the winter, and frequent fishing parties and sojourns in country houses belonging to distant relatives in the summer.

**Education, marriage, and early career** Grimond's schooldays were initially rather less idyllic. The first of the family to be educated outside Scotland, he was sent at the age of eight to board at Evelyns, a preparatory school in Hillingdon, Middlesex, which he hated. Eton College, to which he progressed at the age of thirteen, came as a great relief, and strongly influenced both the nature and direction of his political ambitions. While his parents were both Liberals, there was no tradition of active political involvement in the family. He later attributed his commitment to Liberalism to the influence of his teachers at Eton, particularly Sir Robert Birley. In what was perhaps the first indication of his radical sympathies, he invited Mahatma Gandhi to address the college's Political Society (of which he was president). Much to his surprise, the Indian statesman accepted the invitation. Endowed with considerable physical strength, and standing well over 6 feet tall, Grimond excelled on the games field at Eton and attracted a wide circle of friends through the charm and affability that were to stand him in good stead throughout his political career. He also achieved considerable academic success, notably in history.

From Eton, Grimond won a Brackenbury scholarship to Balliol College, Oxford, where he read philosophy, politics, and economics, and obtained first-class honours in

**Joseph Grimond, Baron Grimond (1913–1993)**, by Walter Bird, 1961

1935. The atmosphere and traditions of Balliol further shaped his Liberalism, which remained throughout his political life first and foremost a broad, humane, intellectual creed rooted in the idealist philosophy of G. E. Moore and T. H. Green. Grimond held that the ultimate purpose of politics was to enable people to delight in the pleasures of social intercourse and enjoy the beautiful things of life. Although he was not remotely precious or affected, there was something of the aesthete in his make-up, reflected in a love of books and paintings. His studies at Oxford were also probably primarily responsible for imparting a strong moral dimension to his Liberalism. He believed passionately that both parliament and the universities existed to promote a sense of civic moral purpose and engage in a moral critique of the life of the nation. This high-minded exercise was for him rooted in a combination of classical humanism and Christianity filtered through the lens of the Enlightenment. This rather donnish and whiggish stance informed his political life, and those who took a less lofty approach to the business of politics complained that his approach was too detached and his speeches too sermonic in tone. Eton and Oxford certainly left him unashamedly élitist; he held that 'a country requires an informed and educated minority to guard and extend its best traditions and bring criticism to bear on the conduct of its affairs' (Grimond, *Memoirs*, 58). It was at Oxford that Grimond decided to be a Liberal politician. His first experience of electioneering was in 1935 when he helped Arthur Irvine, Liberal candidate for Kincardine and West Aberdeenshire. Having decided that the law provided the most suitable preparatory career for an aspiring politician, he won a Harmsworth law scholarship and was called to the bar by the Middle Temple in 1937. He practised at the criminal bar until the outbreak of the Second World War.

Grimond's wife, the Hon. **Laura Miranda Grimond**, Lady Grimond (1918–1994), whom he married on 31 May 1938, was born in London on 13 October 1918, the younger daughter and second of the four children of Sir Maurice Bonham Carter (1880–1960), public servant, and his wife, (Helen) Violet Bonham *Carter, Baroness Asquith of Yarnbury (1887–1969), politician, daughter of Herbert Henry *Asquith, first earl of Oxford and Asquith. She was educated privately in London, France, and Austria. As the granddaughter of a Liberal prime minister and daughter of a lifelong Liberal who served as president of both the Liberal Party Organization and the Women's Liberal Federation, she had politics in her blood, and might well have pursued a political career herself had she not chosen to devote much of her energy to supporting her husband and bringing up their four children, Andrew (1939–1966), Grizelda Jane (*b.* 1942), John Jasper (*b.* 1946), and Thomas Magnus (*b.* 1959). As well as being a particularly happy union, marriage into the Asquith clan brought Jo Grimond into the heart of the old Liberal establishment and opened many doors which were to be useful in his subsequent political career.

Three days before the Second World War began in September 1939 Grimond joined the Fife and Forfar yeomanry. He spent virtually the entire war as a staff officer in the United Kingdom. His only excursion abroad was in June 1945 when he went to Normandy a fortnight after D-day as deputy assistant adjutant-general of the 53rd (Welsh) division. Despite the impressive title he had little to do and saw no real action as the division moved across Belgium in the wake of the retreating German troops. He ended the war as a major. Meanwhile his wife, Laura, spent the war years largely on her own, bringing up their two eldest children.

**MP for Orkney and Shetland** In 1940 Grimond was selected as Liberal candidate for Orkney and Shetland. This had been a Liberal seat until the general election of 1935, but was then won by a Conservative, Colonel Basil Neven-Spence, with a majority of 2226. Grimond threw himself with gusto into the July 1945 general election campaign and, much to his surprise, came within 329 votes of victory. So began a love affair with the sturdy, independent electorate of the United Kingdom's most northerly constituency and with the rigours of electioneering via boat and plane among its scattered islands.

Thanks largely to the good offices of the Bonham Carters, at the end of the war Grimond was offered the post of director of personnel in the European office of the UN Relief and Rehabilitation Administration. Although not a natural administrator he remained in this post for two years before finding a more congenial billet in his beloved native land as secretary of the National Trust for Scotland, where he spent three happy years. His colleagues were exasperated by his habit of floating ideas but failing to come to any decision; his family connections with the jute barons, however, secured for the trust the gardens at Threave House in Kirkcudbrightshire and the Hill of Tarvit mansion house in north-east Fife.

Somewhat characteristically, Grimond was in two minds about fighting the general election of February 1950. He had just been taken on by the Glasgow publishers Collins, and nearly abandoned his candidacy. In the event, however, he not only fought but won Orkney and Shetland, with a majority of 2956. He was to represent the northern isles in the House of Commons for the next thirty-three years. It would be hard to think of a better match between a constituency and its representative. Grimond loved and idealized the islanders' independent-mindedness, sturdy self-reliance, and strong sense of community born of their long crofting traditions and high educational standards. For their part the islanders took the radical orator with his striking good looks and patrician charm to their hearts. He revelled in the adventures of being stranded on remote islands for days at a time and having to be carried on piggy back through rapidly advancing tides. He even cheerfully put up with the cramped seats in the tiny aeroplanes which flew him between London and his constituency and in which he travelled 75,000 miles or so each year. He delighted in pointing out to mainland MPs that it was as far from the south of Orkney to the north of Shetland as from London to York. For Grimond, Orkney and Shetland provided a paradigm of the tolerant, resourceful, civilized society imbued with community values which he wanted Britain to be. As applied to the depressed industrial heartlands of central Scotland and northern England, or the self-satisfied suburbia of the south, it was a hopelessly unrealistic vision, but it was to exercise a strong appeal to the youthful idealism of many of those whom Grimond attracted to the Liberal cause through his speeches and writings.

The parliamentary Liberal Party which Grimond joined was tiny: only nine MPs had been returned in the 1950 election. He was appointed party whip within three days of taking his seat in the House of Commons. He took several years to make much impact at Westminster, but his rousing oratorical powers quickly made him a commanding figure at the annual Liberal assemblies. A speech which he made at the 1956 assembly in Folkestone was particularly well received; when next day the party leader, Clement Davies, announced his resignation there was little doubt in anyone's mind that the obvious successor was the 43-year-old whip.

**Leader of the Liberal Party** The party of which Grimond became leader on 5 November 1956 had just six MPs, reduced to five in the Carmarthen by-election in February 1957, and was arguably at its lowest ebb since the First World War—uncertain of what it stood for, unappealing to the electorate, and seemingly destined to be wiped out as a force in British politics. Grimond rapidly rallied the party and showed himself to be the most attractive and popular leader of the Liberals since Lloyd George. His greatest success lay in attracting both young people and an impressive coterie of intellectuals into the Liberal fold on the basis of its appeal as a fresh, forward-looking, and radical force, without either the ideological baggage or the class consciousness of the Conservatives and Labour. He brought back into Liberalism the intellectual ferment that it had last known in the early days of Beveridge and Keynes.

Grimond gave an early earnest of his radicalism over the Suez crisis. The parliamentary Liberal Party was split over the wisdom of the government's military intervention. The new leader came out strongly against the government's policy, winning the plaudits of the party's left-wingers and pacifists. He was the first British party leader to come out positively in favour of Britain entering the new European Economic Community, and he vigorously championed the causes of industrial co-partnership and electoral reform. Grimond's speeches to the party faithful were marked by a similar sense of energy and dynamism. At his first assembly as leader (in Southport, in September 1957) he told the cheering delegates, 'In the next ten years, it is a question of get on or get out' (Joyce, 153).

Under Grimond's leadership the Liberals achieved a succession of spectacular by-election results. In February 1958 his old friend Ludovic Kennedy came within 4500 votes of winning Rochdale; in March the same year his brother-in-law, Mark Bonham *Carter, won Torrington from the Conservatives. In the general election of October 1959 the Liberal Party won only six seats, although its share of the vote more than doubled (from 2.7 per cent in May 1955 to 5.9 per cent). Nevertheless, a sensational victory by Eric Lubbock in Orpington in March 1962 seemed to herald a new dawn for the party after nearly fifty years in the wilderness. Indeed, a National Opinion Poll published in its aftermath showed the Liberals briefly to be the most popular party in the country. For this electoral success Grimond could claim much of the credit. He was easily the most telegenic of the three party leaders, and was sufficiently patrician in manner and style to make the Liberals an attractive alternative for Conservatives disaffected with the long years of tory government under Harold Macmillan. In a series of books and pamphlets, notably *The Liberal Future* (1959) and *The Liberal Challenge* (1963), he presented the Liberals as a dynamic, classless party committed to reducing income tax and seizing the benefits of new technology. He also floated, although characteristically never fully developed, the idea of a realignment on the left in British politics; he envisaged a liberal social democratic party committed to Europe and free from Labour's commitment to nationalization and the trade unions, emerging as the main opposition to the Conservatives, with a small Marxist socialist party on the fringe. At the September 1963 party assembly, in Brighton, he likened himself to a military commander leading his troops 'towards the sound of gunfire' (Joyce, 154).

Although the October 1964 general election showed the Liberals gaining ground, with nine seats and 11.2 per cent of the popular vote, it marked the beginning of the end for Grimond's vision of a realignment on the left. While this had seemed at least a remote possibility during the long years of Conservative government, and while Hugh Gaitskell, to whom Grimond felt close, was Labour leader, Labour's victory in 1964 under its new leader, Harold Wilson, changed the landscape. Despite having a tiny majority Wilson had no interest in joining with the Liberals, and was much more committed than Gaitskell had been to Labour's trade union base. Grimond also found that many Liberals were unenthusiastic about realignment involving closer relations with Labour, and there was considerable unease within the party when he indicated in a newspaper interview that he would be prepared to contemplate some kind of merger with Labour if there could be agreement on long-term policies and aims.

By 1965 Grimond had had enough of being party leader, although one would hardly have guessed it from the rousing peroration of his address at that year party's assembly in Scarborough, telling Liberals that at last they had their 'teeth in the red meat of power' (Joyce, 155). He had become tired of the punishing and tedious tasks involved in leading a small party. He was disappointed at the party's reaction to his suggestion that Liberals should be prepared to co-operate with a Labour government, and he responded somewhat petulantly by not turning up for important meetings and becoming rather distant in manner. Undoubtedly his own temperament—with its easy-going vagueness, lack of sticking power, and preference for alighting butterfly-like briefly on one idea and then moving on to the next—was not conducive to the long haul and persistent grind required of party leaders. He was persuaded by close confidants to stay on and lead the Liberals into the March 1966 election, which he did, on a manifesto of defence cuts, entry into Europe, and a new approach to industrial relations based on partnership rather than confrontation. Although the party's vote went down (to 8.5 per cent), it increased its representation at Westminster to twelve MPs. The most important result of the election for the Liberals, however, was Labour's comfortable majority of nearly a hundred seats, which finally ditched any residual hopes of realignment or Liberal–Labour co-operation.

**Elder statesman** Grimond announced his resignation in January 1967 and was succeeded, as he had hoped, by Jeremy Thorpe. In many ways Grimond's post-1967 role as the party's elder statesman suited him more than his period as leader. He served from 1967 to 1983 as a trustee of the Manchester Guardian and Evening News Ltd and continued an active involvement in university affairs which had begun when he was elected to a three-year term as rector of Edinburgh University in 1960. The students of Aberdeen chose him as their rector in 1969 and in 1970 he was elected as chancellor of the University of Kent. The following year he chaired a committee of inquiry into the administration of Birmingham University.

In many ways academic life might well have suited Grimond in his later years, but he continued in politics, still relishing his representation of Orkney and Shetland, and writing increasingly idiosyncratic articles for the daily and weekly press. He took little active role in either policy or strategy making during the Liberals' period of considerable electoral success in the early 1970s. However, he found himself unexpectedly called back to be leader when Jeremy Thorpe resigned in May 1976 amid allegations of criminal activity. Seen as the one person around whom the party could unite at a time of considerable difficulty and frenzied media attention, Grimond was originally approached by David Steel, the party's chief whip, to take on the leadership for an extended period. He refused and with some reluctance agreed only to act as caretaker until new rules were drawn up for electing the next leader. In the event, he assumed the role for less than three months before his protégé, David Steel, took over as the new leader in July.

Grimond became an increasingly maverick and even mischievous figure during his last years in parliament. His long-standing commitment to Scottish self-government, the subject on which he had made his maiden speech, led him to flirt with the Scottish nationalists and on more than one occasion he came close to joining them. At the same time he found himself intellectually attracted by many of the libertarian free-market ideas taken up by Conservatives after 1974. In 1977 he joined his old friend Robert Oakshott to establish Job Ownership Ltd as a kind of merchant bank to support worker co-operatives, and he became a strong champion of the Mondragon co-operative movement in northern Spain. The promotion of industrial co-operatives and local community-based initiatives in the field of social welfare was a major theme of his book *The Common Welfare* (1978). Its main target, however, was the growth of bureaucracy and the bureaucratic temperament, which became something of an obsession in his later years. For him the Labour Party was wedded to centralist statism and he was uneasy about the Lib–Lab pact forged by David Steel and James Callaghan in 1977 despite the fact that it was in many ways what he himself had advocated fifteen years earlier.

The breakaway from the Labour Party of leading pro-Europeans to form the new Social Democratic Party in March 1981 might have been expected to delight Grimond; it was, after all, the first major step towards the realignment of the left of which he had dreamed for so long. Yet he had equivocal feelings about the Social Democrats, many of whom he felt were Fabian bureaucratic centralists at heart. He did, however, agree to appear on the platform along with Roy Jenkins and Shirley Williams at a fringe meeting on the eve of the Liberal Party assembly at Llandudno in September 1981. His presence there and his speech welcoming the formation of the new party helped to reassure rank-and-file Liberals who were uneasy about being bounced by David Steel into a close relationship with the Social Democrats, and helped to produce a huge majority for an electoral pact between the two parties when the matter was debated in the assembly. In 1983 he published a characteristically idiosyncratic *Personal Manifesto*, which continued to hammer the bureaucratic mentality. He quit the Commons at the election of June the same year, bequeathing his Orkney and Shetland constituency to a Liberal successor, Jim Wallace, a feat which had not been achieved by any other Liberal MP in the post-war period. He was created a life peer and took the title Baron Grimond of Firth from his Orkney home, the old manse of the parish of Firth.

Afflicted by increasing deafness, Grimond was a somewhat remote figure in his last years. He gave the impression of becoming increasingly reactionary, and looked back fondly to the old ways and values of his childhood days in his delightful book *The St Andrews of Jo Grimond* (1992). He died in Orkney on 24 October 1993, following a stroke, and was buried in the churchyard of the parish of Firth on 29 October. He was survived by his wife, daughter, and two of his three sons.

Like her husband Laura Grimond developed a love for Orkney and Shetland and when he was elected as the islands' MP in 1950, she determined that as far as possible Orkney should be the family home. (Through necessity, they also kept a house in London, where she served as a magistrate until 1960.) During his time as Liberal Party leader, she took the burden of constituency work on her shoulders, tirelessly trekking round remote village halls and visiting isolated crofts. She stood as Liberal candidate for West Aberdeen in 1970 and worked for over twenty years for the Women's Liberal Federation, serving as president from 1983 to 1985. She was a member of the SDP/Liberal Alliance's defence commission from 1984 to 1986, where she was remembered for her robust opposition to unilateralism. She had a deep affection for Scotland, and particularly for its archaeological and natural heritage. She sat on the Scottish Ancient Monuments Board from 1974 to 1980, was a councillor for the parishes of Firth and Harray, chaired the housing committee of the Orkney Islands council, and founded the Orkney Heritage Society. She suffered a stroke in December 1992 and never fully recovered. She died in London on 15 February 1994 and was buried next to her husband on 21 February 1994 in the churchyard of the parish of Firth in Orkney. A memorial service was held for both Jo and Laura Grimond at St James's, Piccadilly, on 10 May 1994. IAN BRADLEY

**Sources** J. Grimond, *Memoirs* (1979) • J. Grimond, *The St Andrews of Jo Grimond* (1992) • C. Cook, *A short history of the liberal party*, 4th edn (1993) • P. Bartram, *David Steel: his life and politics* (1981) • I. Crewe and A. King, *The birth, life and death of the social democratic party* (1995) • I. Bradley, 'Jo Grimond: an essentially liberal message', *The Times* (4 Sept 1978) • *The Times* (26 Oct 1993) • *The Times* (30 Oct 1993) • *The Times* (17 Feb 1994) • *The Times* (11 May 1994) • *The Independent* (26 Oct 1993) • *The Independent* (17 Feb 1994) • *WWW* • D. Brack and M. Baines, eds., *Dictionary of liberal biography* (1998) • I. Elliott, ed., *The Balliol College register, 1900–1950*, 3rd edn (privately printed, Oxford, 1953) • personal knowledge (2004) • private information (2004) • Burke, *Peerage* • P. Joyce, 'Laura Grimond', *Dictionary of liberal biography*, ed. D. Brack and M. Baines (1998), 155–6 • *Debrett's Peerage*

**Archives** NL Scot., constituency papers • NL Scot., corresp. and papers | JRL, letters to Sir Leonard Behrens; letters to the *Manchester Guardian* • King's Lond., Liddell Hart C., corresp. with Sir B. H. Liddell Hart • NL Wales, letters to Emlyn Hooson and Rhys Gerran Lloyd • Orkney Library, Kirkwall, Orkney, corresp. with E. W. Marwick; corresp. relating to Orkney seal culling

**Likenesses** W. Bird, photograph, 1961, NPG [*see illus.*] • S. Heydinger, photograph, *c*.1963, Hult. Arch. • R. Speller, photograph,

Sept 1964, Hult. Arch. • photographs, 1964–75, Hult. Arch. • D. Sim, group portrait, photograph, Feb 1966, Hult. Arch. • D. N. Smith, photograph, 27 April 1966, Hult. Arch. • double portrait, photograph, 1967 (with Jeremy Thorpe), Hult. Arch. • J. Hodder, double portrait, photograph, Sept 1981 (with David Steel), Hult. Arch. • N. Sinclair, photograph, 1992, NPG • M. Cole, cartoon, repro. in *The Times* (4 Sept 1978) • P. Heron, oils, Scot. NPG • D. Low, cartoon, NPG • I. MacInnes, oils, priv. coll. • photograph, repro. in *The Times* (26 Oct 1993) • photograph, repro. in *The Independent* (26 Oct 1993) • photograph (Laura Grimond), repro. in *The Times* (17 Feb 1994) • photograph (Laura Grimond), repro. in *The Independent* (17 Feb 1994)

**Wealth at death** £690,896: probate, 11 May 1994, *CGPLA Eng. & Wales* • £748,988—Laura Grimond: probate, 1994, *CGPLA Eng. & Wales*

**Grimond, Laura Miranda**, **Lady Grimond** (**1918–1994**). *See under* Grimond, Joseph, Baron Grimond (1913–1993).

**Grimshaw,** (**John**) **Atkinson** (**1836–1893**), landscape painter, was born on 6 September 1836 at 9 Back Park Street, Leeds, the third son of six children of David Grimshaw (*b.* 1811), a policeman, and his wife, Mary Atkinson. In 1842 the family moved to Norwich, where Grimshaw briefly attended the grammar school. In 1848 the Grimshaws moved back to Leeds, where David Grimshaw obtained a job on the railways; the family also kept a grocer's shop in Brunswick Row. By 1852 Grimshaw had obtained a position as a clerk with the Great Northern Railway Company. He had begun to paint by the late 1850s and does not seem to have received any formal training as an artist. Family tradition relates that his mother disapproved of this activity, threw his paints on the fire, and even turned off the gas in his room.

On 24 October 1856 Grimshaw married his cousin, Frances Theodosia (1835–1917), daughter of James Dibdin Hubbard, editor of the *Wakefield Journal*. The couple first lived in Wallace Street, New Wortley, Leeds. In 1861 Grimshaw gave up his railway job to paint full time. His early paintings were small in scale and consisted of still-life studies of birds' nests, fruit and flowers, and woodland scenes. His few attempts at figure painting were extremely tentative and hesitant. In emulation of Millais, Grimshaw signed his earliest pictures with a Gothic-style monogram *JAG*, then changed to using *J. A. Grimshaw* and then *John Atkinson Grimshaw*. By the late 1860s, however, he had decided on the form *Atkinson Grimshaw* as his preferred name which was how he was usually known.

Grimshaw's early paintings were influenced by the work of the Pre-Raphaelites. The Leeds stockbroker Thomas Plint owned a significant collection of modern paintings, including works by Millais, Holman Hunt, and D. G. Rossetti. Plint lent some of these works to the Leeds Philosophical and Literary Society, of which Grimshaw's father was a member. Another important influence was the Leeds-based painter of Pre-Raphaelite landscapes John William Inchbold (1830–1888), a friend of John Ruskin. Grimshaw was attracted to Ruskin's rallying call from *Modern Painters* to 'go to nature in all singleness of heart' (Ruskin, 416), and for a brief period in the mid-1860s Grimshaw painted in minute detail in vivid colours on a white ground, emulating Inchbold and other Pre-Raphaelite artists. These were mainly views of the Lake District, for example *The Bowder Stone* (Tate Collection), which followed a visit to the area in 1863. He also used photographs as an *aide-mémoire* for these lakeland views, and throughout his life may have relied on photography as a basis for some of his paintings. However, by the late 1860s Grimshaw had turned to the depiction of moonlight, which was to become his trademark.

In 1870, after moving around Leeds, the Grimshaw family settled at Old Hall, Knostrop (dem. 1960), a seventeenth-century stone-built manor house 2 miles east of Leeds town centre. The setting would have had tremendous appeal to Grimshaw, whose Romanticism manifested itself in the titles of his paintings, often related to the works of Romantic poets, including Keats and Longfellow, and also in the names of his children. Old Hall remained the Grimshaw family's main home for the next twenty-three years; of the couple's fifteen children only six survived to adulthood.

The 1870s were Grimshaw's most successful decade artistically and financially. He was represented by Thomas Agnew & Sons of Bond Street, London, who bought his paintings between 1871 and 1880 and showed his work at their London and provincial galleries. During this time the main elements of Grimshaw's most frequent subject matter and customary style emerged: damp, autumnal lanes featuring a lonely house and single figure, often illuminated by moonlight, seen through a trellis of bare branches. In 1874 the Royal Academy accepted *The Lady of the Lea*, a painting in this mode, for its annual exhibition. Grimshaw was to show there again in 1880, 1885, and 1886. Scenes of Liverpool, Hull, and Glasgow docks were another important subject, providing the artist with an endlessly varied compositional motif. Typically these works utilized a formula of converging buildings and dock-side shipping, a wet road reflecting passers-by and the lights from the shop windows, for example *The Old Custom House, Liverpool, Looking North* (Walker Art Gallery, Liverpool).

For a period from the mid-1870s until 1886 Grimshaw was also attracted to the style and technique of Lawrence Alma-Tadema and J. J. Tissot, producing similar pictures of fashionable ladies in settings from ancient Rome and in domestic interiors replete with a wealth of detail, for example *Fiametta* (Cartwright Hall, Bradford) and *Summer* (priv. coll.). In 1885, Grimshaw also exhibited at the recently established Grosvenor Gallery, London, a painting entitled *A Vestal* (priv. coll.). Recognition encouraged the artist to rent a second home in Scarborough on the Yorkshire coast, overlooking North Bay. The town was to become Grimshaw's favourite subject, for example *Lights in the Harbour* (Crescent Art Gallery, Scarborough), and he painted its streets and bay more often than any other locality.

In the midst of this prosperity came disaster when Grimshaw was forced to guarantee a bill for a friend who defaulted. The details are unclear but family history dates the years of struggle and 'mass production' of paintings from about the beginning of the 1880s. The bill was probably taken over by the Harrogate solicitor Walter Battle, whose art collection included many Grimshaws. These may have been acquired as part payment of the debt. It must be supposed that the greatly increased output of paintings from the early 1880s was in response to the financial crisis.

Grimshaw also painted a series of great views of London and the Thames, for example *Reflections on the Thames, Westminster* (Leeds City Art Gallery). Such paintings are majestic in concept and realization; most have a blaze of light on the river and an all-enveloping film of colour. When Grimshaw needed to show human activity, figures were taken from engravings after Frank Holl and Gustave Doré. Family tradition also relates an artistic connection between Grimshaw and Whistler, who became acquainted when Grimshaw took a studio in Manresa Road, Chelsea, about 1885. Whistler supposedly remarked that he thought he had invented the nocturne until he saw Grimshaw's moonlights.

In the last years of his life Grimshaw moved towards a simpler tonal arrangement in a series of river estuary paintings and two beach scenes, as well as some snow scenes painted in the last winter of his life, such as *Snow and Mist: Caprice in Yellow Minor* (Leeds City Art Gallery). Grimshaw's paintings of Victorian streets and river life resonated with the influence of the poets Grimshaw loved: Keats, Tennyson, Longfellow. He died on 31 October 1893 at Old Hall, Knostrop, Leeds, and was buried on 4 November at Woodhouse cemetery, Leeds.

ALEXANDER ROBERTSON

**Sources** A. Robertson, *Atkinson Grimshaw* (1988) • recollections of Elaine Grimshaw, *c.*1970, priv. coll. [daughter] • D. Bromfield, 'The art of Atkinson Grimshaw', in A. Robertson, *Atkinson Grimshaw, 1836–1893* (1979), 5–21 [exhibition catalogue, Leeds City Art Gallery, 13 Oct – 10 Nov 1979, Southampton Art Gallery, 24 Nov – 29 Dec 1979, and Walker Art Gallery, Liverpool, 12 Jan – 9 Feb 1980] • J. Ruskin, *Modern painters*, 3rd edn, 1 (1846), 416 • M. Bartram, *The Pre-Raphaelite camera* (1985) • P. McEvansoneya, 'Atkinson Grimshaw, Frank Holl and fallen women', *Leeds Art Calendar*, 112 (1993), 3–6 • S. K. Payne, *Atkinson Grimshaw: knight's errand* (1987) • private information (2004) [Guy Ragland Phillips, grandson] • m. cert. • d. cert.
**Archives** priv. coll., recollections of Elaine Grimshaw and her son Guy Ragland Phillips
**Likenesses** F. Scrimshaw, photograph, *c.*1857, Leeds Museums and Galleries • C. A. Duval & Co., photographs, *c.*1870
**Wealth at death** £973 18*s.* 7*d.*: administration, 10 Jan 1894, *CGPLA Eng. & Wales*

**Grimshaw, Mortimer** (1824/5–1869), cotton weaver and labour leader, was born into a working-class family in or near Great Harwood in north-east Lancashire. Little is known about his family background, but his father is said to have had a reputation as a radical orator. Grimshaw worked intermittently as a cotton weaver, and achieved local—briefly, national—fame as a strike leader and political activist in the mid-1850s.

Grimshaw rose to prominence in the 'Jacobin' village of Royton, outside Oldham, as a factory reformer, and claimed to have been blacklisted by the cotton manufacturers for his political campaigning. This included support for the not always consistent aims of the tory-radical enemies of free trade, led by William Busfeild Ferrand MP, and for the rump of the Chartist movement, which was controlled by Ernest Jones (1819–1869); in 1854 Grimshaw was involved in Jones's ill-fated labour parliament. He was a forthright opponent of *laissez-faire* and a vigorous advocate of political democracy. Grimshaw was motivated by a burning hatred of unrestricted competition and a deep fear of the mill owners' class power, and his uneasy combination of traditional plebeian radicalism, proto-socialism, and populist tory protectionism was characteristic of many in the mid-century labour movement in Lancashire.

When, in 1853, the Preston cotton workers struck for a 10 per cent increase in wages, Grimshaw was an ever present figure at their mass meetings, wearing a white hat after the fashion of Orator Hunt and William Cobbett, his fist in the air, defending the 'factory slaves' against the despotism of their masters and the tyranny of the Manchester school of political economy. When opponents of the strike tried to convince the weavers of the immutable force of the supposedly natural laws of wages, Grimshaw pointed scornfully to the establishment of an employers' association as proof that they were all protectionists. Together with the more restrained George Cowell, a Preston man, Grimshaw was the acknowledged leader of the seven-month strike.

A large, swarthy man with a somewhat vulpine appearance and a face much marked by smallpox, Grimshaw was noted for the power of his lungs, which earned him the nickname 'the Thunderer of Lancashire' during the strike. The cotton employers feared his influence over their operatives, and he was frequently denounced in the middle-class press. Charles Dickens caricatured him as a brash, insensitive, and unscrupulous demagogue: Grimshaw is the 'Gruffshaw' of Dickens's article 'On strike', the Slackbridge of his novel *Hard Times*. A more sympathetic viewpoint was that he was an enthusiast, whose judgement was sometimes overpowered by the warmth of his feelings and whose oratory appealed especially to women workers. If the steadier Cowell was the Richard Cobden of the Preston strike, Grimshaw was its John Bright. He resisted all attempts to 'padlock his mouth', speaking at sixty or more public meetings during the strike, several times urging the construction of co-operative mills as a long-term challenge to the power of capital.

When the strike ended in defeat, there was no further role for Grimshaw. He would have made a poor trade union secretary, even had there been a stable union with the resources to employ him. The final years of his life were a sad anticlimax. He attempted to intervene, with very little success, in several subsequent strikes, and then made an abortive attempt to raise funds allowing him to emigrate. He was finally reduced to hawking his services to the employers as a freelance industrial mediator and anti-union agitator, and revealed his growing tory sympathies by speaking in support of the Confederacy during the American Civil War. Grimshaw died in obscurity in Rishton of phthisis on 22 December 1869. He was described on his death certificate simply as a power-loom weaver. He had long since ceased to be a figure of any importance in the labour movement. J. E. KING

**Sources** H. I. Dutton and J. E. King, *Ten per cent and no surrender* (1981) • E. M. Jones, 'Deference and the Blackburn working class', MA diss., University of Warwick, 1984 • *Blackburn Standard* (29 Dec 1869)

**Likenesses** etching, repro. in *People's Paper* (4 Feb 1854)

**Grimshaw, William** (1708–1763), Church of England clergyman, was born at Brindle, near Preston, Lancashire, on 3 September 1708, the eldest son of William Grimshaw (1674–1754), a small farmer or husbandman, and his wife, Ann Firth. After attending Blackburn grammar school and Hesketh Free School, he was admitted sizar at Christ's College, Cambridge, in 1726 and graduated BA in 1730. He was ordained by Bishop Peploe of Chester as deacon on 4 April 1731, and as priest on 10 September 1732. He held the curacy of St Mary's Chapel, Todmorden, from 1731 until 1742, when he was appointed perpetual curate of Haworth, a chapelry of ease in the parish of Bradford. In 1735 he married Sarah Sutcliffe (*b*. 1710), a widow, with whom he had two children, John (1736–1766) and Jane (1737–1750). After her death in 1739 he married Elizabeth Cockcroft in 1741; she died in 1746. Grimshaw remained at Haworth until his death.

In childhood Grimshaw had felt alarming pangs of conscience. At Todmorden in the winter of 1733–4 he experienced a spiritual awakening which deepened in 1738 (when he made the first of several solemn covenants with God), and was intensified after the death of his first wife, Sarah, in 1739, which plunged him into a torment of doubt and sexual temptation. A turning point came when the reflection of light from a pewter plate on a friend's shelf guided his eye to a treatise on justification by the puritan John Owen. Soon afterwards he read a tract by Robert Seagrave and began tentatively to preach salvation by faith. Up to this point he had no direct contact with the Methodist movement.

Grimshaw's preaching at Haworth set off a noisy revival, drawing such numbers that he had to address crowds in the churchyard. He launched out on monthly 'visitations' through his moorland parish, conducting cottage services and preaching at a dozen centres. On 2 September 1744, after collapsing in church, he fell into a trance and had a vision of the crucified Christ which deeply affected his ministry. At first Grimshaw kept clear of Methodism, now burgeoning near him, but soon linked up with it. In 1744 his parish was visited by the Scots pedlar-preacher William Darney, loosely allied to Methodism, who seems to have deepened his understanding of the assurance of salvation: it was local gossip that 'Mad Grimshaw is turned Scotch Will's clerk' (Myles, 18). He welcomed other evangelical leaders: in 1746 Charles Wesley visited Haworth and, in 1747, John Wesley, followed later by George Whitefield, William Romaine, Henry Venn, and John Newton. Grimshaw overcame his hesitation about preaching beyond his own parish and set out as an evangelist, tending societies on an itinerant 'Round', usually within a radius of some 15 miles of Haworth,

William Grimshaw (1708–1763), by J. Thomson, pubd 1821

though he made excursions much further afield. Yet he did not neglect his own parish, continually touring its moorland settlements so that nobody should have an excuse for not hearing his message.

Grimshaw was an alarming preacher and a moral disciplinarian: his parishioners were said to be more afraid of their parson than of a justice of the peace. He opposed wakes, horse races, hunting, and card playing, and enforced sabbath observance, allegedly driving absentees into church during the singing of the psalm. A visitor saw people on a Sunday morning leaping from the windows of a public house and jumping over a wall because they saw him coming. But if fierce, Grimshaw was not harsh, and as a pastor he blended authoritarianism with humility, bluntness with tenderness, solemnity with humour. His church was packed and had to be enlarged. In his sermons he used homely metaphor and dialect terms ('market language') and would name communicants affectionately at the altar, sometimes touching one by the ear. He held a high view of the sacraments, and could administer the eucharist in a state of near ecstasy. On arriving at Haworth he found a dozen communicants, but he soon had 300 to 500 in winter and more than 1000 in summer on great occasions: when Whitefield assisted him in 1753, the congregation consumed thirty-five bottles of wine. In appearance Grimshaw was heavy-featured, with a pockmarked face. Robust and compact, he drove himself hard on his Pennine journeys, preaching in alternate weeks through two circuits, in one twenty-four to thirty times, and in the other (his 'idle' week) twelve to fourteen. In 1749 he published *Answer to a Sermon Lately Published Against the Methodists by the Rev. Mr. George White*, a local opponent who organized anti-Methodist mobbing. He left several devotional and autobiographical papers.

Grimshaw is a specimen of the 'half-regular' clergymen who linked early Methodism with the later evangelical school in the church. He had close relations with John Wesley, overseeing Methodist societies and taking part in quarterly meetings and preachers' conferences. In 1758 he built a chapel in his parish (partly with funding from a successful lottery ticket) to maintain 'gospel' preaching should he be succeeded by a non-evangelical minister. In the Methodist Connexion he held an honoured position after John and Charles Wesley, with the right to appoint the preachers should the brothers predecease him. Yet his loyalty to Methodism was qualified. While accepting a Wesleyan position on assurance, he did not share the Wesleys' 'Arminianism', but was an eirenic, undogmatic Calvinist. In his last years he was disturbed at the drift of Methodism away from the church, exemplified in pressure for the lay administration of the sacraments and for the protective registration of Methodist preaching-houses as dissenting meeting-houses under the Toleration Act. Though not greatly dismayed when converts slipped away into dissent or became nonconformist ministers (as at least five of them did), he was saddened when one opened a Baptist chapel in Haworth parish.

On 7 April 1763 Grimshaw died, aged fifty-four, at his home at Sowdens, Haworth, of 'putrid fever' (probably typhus), caught by visiting sick parishioners. He was buried at St Mary's Church, Luddendon, Yorkshire, two days later. With typical humility he said that his last words ought to be 'here goes—*an unprofitable servant*' (Middleton, 4.413). Unsurprisingly, Grimshaw became a figure of local legend, and echoes of his words can be found in the Brontë novels. JOHN WALSH

**Sources** F. Baker, *William Grimshaw, 1708–1763* (1963) · W. Grimshaw, *An answer to a sermon lately published against the Methodists, by the Rev. Mr George White* (1749) · R. S. Hardy, *William Grimshaw, incumbent of Haworth 1742–63* (1860) · W. Myles, *Life and writings of the late Revd. William Grimshaw*, 2nd edn (1813) · J. Newton, *Memoirs of the life of the late Revd. William Grimshaw* (1799) · J. W. Laycock, *Methodist heroes in the great Haworth round, 1734–84* (1909) · JRL, Methodist Archives and Research Centre, PLP 47.15.5, 47.15.13; DDWes 2/57–60, 4/92, 6/7, 7/45, 9/13, 9/34 · E. Middleton, ed., *Biographia evangelica*, 4 vols. (privately printed, London, 1779–86)

**Archives** JRL, Methodist Archives and Research Centre, corresp., diary, and papers; papers | Wesley College, Bristol, letters to Mrs Gallatin

**Likenesses** J. Thomson, stipple, NPG; repro. in *Methodist Magazine*, 44 (1821) [*see illus.*]

**Grimshawe, Thomas Shuttleworth** (1777/8–1850), biographer, the son of John Grimshawe, solicitor and five times mayor of Preston, and his wife, Penelope, was born at Preston. He entered Brasenose College, Oxford, in 1794, and graduated BA in 1798 and MA in 1800. He was vicar of Biddenham, Bedfordshire, from 1808 to 1850, and with this living held the rectory of Burton Latimer, Northamptonshire, from 1809 to 1843. In 1822 he wrote a pamphlet, *The Wrongs of the Clergy of the Diocese of Peterborough*, which was reviewed by Sydney Smith in the *Edinburgh Review* (November 1822). His *Memoir of the Rev. Legh Richmond* was first published in 1828, and had reached an eleventh edition by 1846. His best book is the *Life and Works of William Cowper* (8 vols., 1835), republished several times. Grimshawe was much distinguished by his zeal and activity in the Jewish and church missionary cause, and in his seventies travelled up the Nile and on to Jerusalem and other parts of the Holy Land. He was married to Charlotte Anne, daughter of George Livius of Caldwell Priory, Bedfordshire. He died on 17 February 1850, and was buried in the chancel of Biddenham church, where there is a monument to his memory. One of his sons, Charles Livius, was high sheriff of Bedfordshire in 1866; the other, John Barham, died in Trinity College, Cambridge, in 1835. One of his daughters was married to Legh Richmond.

C. W. SUTTON, *rev.* SARAH BROLLY

**Sources** Allibone, *Dict.* · *N&Q*, 2nd ser., 12 (1861), 86 · J. Foster, ed., *Pedigrees of the county families of England*, 1: *Lancashire* (1873) · J. F. Waller, ed., *The imperial dictionary of universal biography*, 3 vols. (1857–63) · *DNB*

**Archives** Beds. & Luton ARS, bills and accounts

**Grimston, Edward** (*d.* 1478), administrator and diplomat, was the son of Robert Grimston, and of his wife, a daughter (name unknown) of Sir Anthony Spelman or Spilman. His place and date of birth are not known. His father, the second son of an old Holderness family, was established in Ipswich by Henry V's reign. Grimston's career, with its close dependence on the de la Pole family, earls, later dukes, of Suffolk, suggests that his father served the de la Poles, and like them moved from Holderness to Suffolk. No dates are known for his parents' deaths.

Grimston may have been brought up in the Suffolk household, and was certainly there by 1437; a royal grant noted his good service in Suffolk's company during Henry VI's minority. He accompanied Dr Stephen Wilton on embassy to the duchess of Burgundy in 1441. In 1446–7 he was involved at Calais in lengthy negotiations about Netherlands trade. In February 1449 he was sent on an important mission to Charles VII of France, followed immediately by another mission to the duchess of Burgundy. He was awarded the reversion to the captaincy of Valognes in 1445, but to no effect, since the incumbent, Sir John Robsart, outlived the town's capture by the French. More significant was Grimston's appointment as treasurer of the chamber and keeper of the king's jewels, on 9 March 1448, jointly with John Merston, the previous holder. He was involved in what seem to have been dubious financial dealings in the company of London merchants; one of his victims, John Wilkins, chapman of Stratford upon Avon, was in 1452 to attempt to raise a rebellion in Kent.

The loss of Normandy, and the fall of the duke of Suffolk, in 1449–50 ended Grimston's public career. He was indicted in London on 4 July 1450 at the instigation of Cade's rebels, implausibly accused of plotting the overthrow of the king and his replacement by Suffolk's son. In November 1450 parliament obtained his removal from office and from the king's presence, as part of the wholesale purge of Suffolk's following. Ignoring two commissions for his trial, Grimston went to ground for 'drede of persones that bene hasty and hote' (*Verulam MSS*, 8). Probably by 1452, however, he was wanting to clear his name. The accusations centred on his mission to France in 1449.

**Edward Grimston** (*d.* **1478**), by Petrus Christus, 1446

This had unfortunately coincided with the English capture of the Breton castle of Fougères, which in turn precipitated the French conquest of Normandy. Grimston was accused of taking bribes from Charles VII and from the duke of Somerset, and of concealing what he had learned at the French court—in effect, of colluding in the French conquest. He denied these accusations, citing the honour of his name and arms, borne, he claimed, for 400 years. Thereafter he held no further office until his brief appointment to the Suffolk bench during Henry VI's readeption in 1470–71.

Grimston's first wife was one Alice, recorded on her tomb as 'brought up from infancy with … Alice, first duchess of Suffolk', the wife of his patron. Alice Grimston became a gentlewoman to Queen Margaret. The date of the marriage is unknown, as is Alice's parentage. She died in 1456. He married in 1459 Mary, daughter of Sir William Drury, and, through her mother, a great-granddaughter of Katherine Swynford [*see* Katherine, duchess of Lancaster], and as such kin to the duchess of Suffolk. With her he had five sons and three daughters (the preservation of the hours as well of the dates of their births suggesting a fashionable interest in astronomy), including Edward, second son and eventual heir. Described as still young and beautiful, she died on 6 March 1470. On 20 August 1471 Grimston married (in the presence of the then duke and duchess of Suffolk) Philippa, daughter of John, first Lord Tiptoft, and sister to John Tiptoft, earl of Worcester. She was the widow successively of Thomas, Lord Ros (executed in 1464), and of Sir Thomas Wingfield (who had died by January 1469). Grimston petitioned Edward IV for the confirmation of the lands, valued at 400 marks, granted her by the king after Ros's attainder; she claimed kinship to the king through her mother, of Mortimer descent. Grimston died on 23 September 1478, described as of Rishangles Lodge, and was buried at nearby Thorndon in Suffolk, in a tomb depicting him in full armour. His widow, with whom he had no children, was living in January 1487.

Grimston is not only commemorated by his tomb effigy, for his portrait was painted in 1446 by Petrus Christus, then active in Bruges. He is depicted as a young man, negligently fingering a collar of SS, in a domestic interior. The portrait is in oil on wood. It includes the Grimston arms; on the back is inscribed 'Petrvs Xri me fecit Ao. 1446'. After the Van Eyck portrait of a cardinal, now widely regarded as Cardinal Henry Beaufort, it is the earliest surviving painting of a non-royal English person, as opposed to a likeness within a larger composition, and the first English family portrait. It remains the property of the Grimston family, now earls of Verulam, on long-term loan to the National Gallery, London. C. S. L. DAVIES

**Sources** *Report on the manuscripts of the earl of Verulam*, HMC, 64 (1906) · W. J. Thoms, A. W. Franks, and G. Scharf, 'Instructions given by King Henry VI to Edward Grimston and others', *Archaeologia*, 40 (1866), 451–82 · W. Hervey, *The visitation of Suffolk, 1561*, ed. J. Corder, 2 vols., Harleian Society, new ser., 2–3 (1981–4) · *Chancery records* · *RotP*, vol. 5 · I. M. W. Harvey, *Jack Cade's rebellion of 1450* (1991) · J. Upton, *Petrus Christus* (1990) · J. Ferguson, *English diplomacy, 1422–1461* (1972) · N. H. Nicolas, ed., *Proceedings and ordinances of the privy council of England*, 7 vols., RC, 26 (1834–7), vol. 5 · H. Ellis, ed., *Original letters illustrative of English history*, 2nd ser., 1 (1827) · R. Virgoe, ed., 'Some ancient indictments', *Kent Records*, ed. F. R. H. Du Boulay, Kent Record Society, 18 (1964), 214–65 · D. MacCulloch, ed., *The chorography of Suffolk*, Suffolk RS, 19 (1976)

**Archives** priv. coll.

**Likenesses** P. Christus, oils on wood, 1446, National Gallery, London [*see illus.*] · tomb effigy, *c.*1478, Thorndon, Suffolk

**Grimston, Edward** (**1507/8–1600**), soldier and administrator, was born between February 1507 and February 1508, probably at Thorndon, Suffolk, or at Ipswich, elder son (at his father's death he had a brother and two sisters) of Edward Grimston (1462–1520), gentleman, of Thorndon (probably Rishangles Lodge), and his wife, Anne, daughter of John Garneys or Garnish of Kenton, Suffolk. Edward *Grimston (*d.* 1478) was his paternal grandfather. His father left all his property, including a lordship in Yorkshire, to Anne, with reversion to Edward. She was alive in 1524, when the Suffolk subsidy return enters her as liable only on 'goods' worth £20.

Grimston senior's will provided for school education for the children. The younger Edward Grimston evidently entered the service of Charles Brandon, duke of Suffolk, his father's master. He first appears as a 'gentleman' carrying the coffin at the funeral of the duchess, Mary Tudor, queen of France, in 1533. He became a king's spear in 1539, and a foundation member of the gentleman pensioners in 1540, presumably through Suffolk's patronage. He began his active military career in 1543 as a cavalryman with the band sent to help Charles V on the French–Flemish border, and then took part in the Boulogne campaign

**Edward Grimston (1507/8–1600)**, attrib. Robert Peake the elder, 1590

of 1544. In 1545 he was arranging the shipping of supplies from Dover. He was considered for command of 2000 men, but Suffolk advised against this, preferring the lord chamberlain, Paulet. But from November 1545 to March 1546 Grimston was acting captain of Portsmouth. In December 1549 he was granted former chantry lands in Ipswich worth some £11 p.a., allegedly a gift intended by Henry VIII; presumably he had supported John Dudley, later duke of Northumberland, in the October coup. He was paymaster to foreign mercenary troops in England between August 1549 and June 1550, and paid funds for the suppressing of the 1549 rebellion in Norfolk when foreign troops were diverted there. Then he became a 'chief captain' at Calais. It is possible that he sat in the parliament of March 1553 for the Cornish seat of Bossiney. He tried, unsuccessfully, to persuade Ipswich to elect William Honing, clerk of the signet, to the same parliament. Grimston probably had a house in Ipswich, since his eldest son, who must have been born by about 1540, mentioned the parish of St Stephen there as his birthplace.

In March 1553 Grimston was appointed comptroller of Calais, backdated to the death of his predecessor the previous September, a post officially worth some £200 p.a. He was clearly in high favour with the Northumberland government. His protestantism had been indicated as early as 1537 when he defended John Bale from allegations made about him at Thorndon. In 1549 Richard Argentyne, schoolmaster at Ipswich, dedicated to him his translation of Zwingli's *Certayne Preceptes*. Grimston served at Calais in Queen Mary's reign under a fellow protestant and Suffolk neighbour, Thomas, Lord Wentworth, lord deputy. He employed as tutor to his children there a distinguished French poet, one Nicolas Denisot, who had earlier been tutor in the family of Protector Somerset. Unfortunately Denisot was a French spy who took advantage of his post with Grimston to gather intelligence on the sorry state of the Calais fortifications; although discovered and arrested, he escaped to report personally to Henri II. This no doubt added to the suspicion with which the Calais authorities were regarded by the Marian government.

When the town of Calais fell in January 1558 Grimston, with Wentworth and other officials, was charged with treason for supposedly colluding in the French conquest. He had, however, been taken prisoner, and from February 1558 was lodged in the Paris Bastille, unable to pay the ransom of 10,000 crowns demanded, and, by his own account, resisting attempts to recruit him into French service. He escaped in October 1559, cutting his way through the bars with a file smuggled in by the English ambassador, Sir Nicholas Throckmorton, and passing himself off in Paris as a Scot. His vivid memoir of his adventures, written in 1594, is substantiated by Throckmorton's contemporary report. Back in England he was imprisoned briefly in the Tower before being released to house arrest under the aegis of his friend Sir John Mason. He stood trial on the treason charge at the Guildhall on 1 December 1559 and was acquitted by the jury, in spite of a vehement prosecution by the attorney-general. Grimston claimed that the queen herself was 'fully resolved to pardon me' had he been found guilty. Two of his colleagues were in fact found guilty and pardoned shortly after, and Grimston remembered that he 'did sweat like a hot summer's day' at the thought of the charges against him.

Grimston resumed his military career as muster master with the army in the north, based at Berwick, from August 1560 to November 1562, and again briefly in September 1565. He became MP for Ipswich in 1563, and again in 1571 and 1572. He was sworn as a free burgess of the borough in December 1563. In 1574 he had a house in the parish of St Mary Tower there. Allegations of sharp practice about the financing of a projected new gaol may have put him at odds with the town authorities. He sat for Eye in the parliament of 1589, for Orford in that of 1593, at which 'Old Grimston told an old tale' about Dover in 1545, and was an active committee member. He was JP for Suffolk in 1552–3, in 1557–8, and from 1566 until his death, and sat on many local commissions, in Suffolk and in eastern England more generally. Rather remarkably, given his protestantism, he was among the East Anglian gentry who paid their respects to the duke of Norfolk on his flight to Keninghall in September 1569. Farming the collection of the aulnage, a privilege first granted him in 1553, and his many commissions—for instance those for the discovery of concealed lands—would have been profitable. Although he lost some goods and lands with the fall of Calais, he had purchased the manor of Rishangles in 1557. Grimston evidently rose to the upper layers of the Suffolk gentry. Unfortunately his will does not survive, but he had substantially increased his standing in Suffolk.

Heraldic visitations record that Grimston was twice

married. His first wife was a daughter to an Ipswich merchant called Sturrup, and widow to one Hall. The second wife was a daughter of one Banks. No first name is given for any of these persons, nor dates for the marriages, though his wife Elizabeth was granted custody of his lands during his imprisonment in 1558; given the likely ages of his children, she was probably the second wife. Both marriages produced children. There were five sons living in 1563, and there are records of at least two daughters.

Printed accounts confuse various Edward Grimstons. The Edward Grimston who entered Gray's Inn in 1559, keeping lodgings there for the rest of his life, and was a friend of Nathaniel Bacon was Grimston's son and heir. He was associated with his father in various commissions. He may also have been the Edward Grimston who matriculated at Gonville Hall in 1554, and the one who became a master in chancery in 1601. He married an heiress, Joan Risby of Lavenham, bought himself an estate at Bradfield in Essex (and hence he, not his father, would be the Essex JP of 1591), and died in 1610. He was the father of Harbottle Grimston (1578–1648), and grandfather of Sir Harbottle *Grimston (1603–1685), from whom descend the earls of Verulam. Another of Grimston's sons was also named Edward; he is recorded as serjeant-at-arms to James I and Charles I. The Edward Grimston who appears voluminously in the state papers as diplomatic agent and spy in France in 1582–92 was too junior in both years and status to be either our Grimston or his heir, though he could conceivably be the younger son of that name.

Edward Grimston died at Ipswich in February or March 1600, aged ninety-two, and was buried at Rishangles parish church; his tomb had an epitaph praising his service to four monarchs and his faithfulness to one religion.

C. S. L. Davies

**Sources** *Report on the manuscripts of the earl of Verulam*, HMC, 64 (1906) [Grimston MSS, incl. Edward Grimston's autobiographical account, pp. 13–22] • HoP, *Commons, 1558–1603* • S. J. Gunn, *Charles Brandon, duke of Suffolk, c.1484–1545* (1988) • D. MacCulloch, *Suffolk and the Tudors: politics and religion in an English county, 1500–1600* (1986) • *Chancery records* • C. Jugé, *Nicolas Denisot du Mans (1515–1559): essai sur sa vie et ses œuvres* (Paris, 1907) • N. Bacon, *The annalls of Ipswche*, ed. W. H. Richardson (1884) • J. Webb, *Poor relief in Elizabethan Ipswich*, Suffolk RS, 9 (1966) • T. E. Hartley, ed., *Proceedings in the parliaments of Elizabeth I*, 3 vols. (1981–95) • W. A. Copinger, *The manors of Suffolk*, 7 vols. (1905–11) • W. Hervey, *The visitation of Suffolk, 1561*, ed. J. Corder, 2 vols., Harleian Society, new ser., 2–3 (1981–4) • W. C. Metcalfe, ed., *The visitations of Essex*, 2 vols., Harleian Society, 13–14 (1878–9) • *LP Henry VIII*, 18/1, no. 832; 19/1, no. 275; 20/2, nos. 61, 800; 21/1, no. 303 • *CPR, 1549–51*, 114; *1553*, 41 • J. Strype, *Ecclesiastical memorials*, 3 vols. (1822), vol. 2 • PRO, PROB 11/116 [will of Edward Grimston, son and heir of this Edward Grimston] • W. C. Richardson, ed., *Report of the royal commission of 1552* (1974) • *CSP for., 1559–60*, nos. 133–7 • *CSP dom., addenda, 1547–65*, 502–3 • *Report of the Deputy Keeper of the Public Records*, 4 (1843), appx 2, pp. 261–2 • *The papers of Nathaniel Bacon of Stiffkey*, ed. A. H. Smith, G. M. Baker, and R. W. Kenny, 1: *1556–1577*, Norfolk RS, 46 (1979) • PRO, E 101/531/39 [Grimston's account for payment of mercenaries, 1549/50]

**Archives** Herts. ALS, narrative of his escape from the Bastille

**Likenesses** attrib. R. Peake the elder, oils, 1590, Gorhambury, Hertfordshire [*see illus.*]

**Grimston, Elizabeth**. *See* Grymeston, Elizabeth (*b.* in or before 1563, *d.* 1601x4).

**Grimston, Sir Harbottle**, **second baronet** (1603–1685), barrister and politician, was the second son of Sir Harbottle Grimston, first baronet (*d.* 1648), of Bradfield Hall, Essex, and his wife, Elizabeth, daughter of Ralph Coppinger of Stoke, Kent. Born on 27 January 1603 at his grandfather's house at Rishangles, near Thorndon, Suffolk, he matriculated at Emmanuel College, Cambridge, in 1619. After leaving without a degree he entered Lincoln's Inn in 1621.

**Marriage and early career** The two most important early influences on Grimston were his father and his father-in-law, Sir George Croke. The son and heir of Edward Grimston, MP and master in chancery, Sir Harbottle senior was knighted in 1604 and created a baronet in 1611. For the next forty years he was active in Essex politics, serving as a justice of the peace, frequently sitting in parliament, and being closely associated with the towns of Harwich and Colchester. In 1621 he was called before the council for not being willing to lend money to the king, and although he was made a commissioner for collecting the forced loan of 1626 he was imprisoned for refusing, explaining in a petition to the king that his conscience obliged him to respect the numerous historical precedents, including Magna Carta, that clearly made it unlawful for such an obligation to be pressed on the subjects without their consent. Meanwhile, following the death of his elder brother, Edward, in 1624, Harbottle junior became heir to his father's estates in Essex and Suffolk, and was thinking of abandoning the law for the life of a country squire when he fell in love with Mary Croke (*d.* 1649), whose father had recently been appointed a judge and who would later become well known for ruling against the crown in the case of ship money. Croke evidently made it a condition of his approval of the marriage that Harbottle should take his legal career seriously. While the two events may or may not have been directly connected Grimston was called to the bar in 1628, and the couple married in April 1629. The wedding was followed by a lavish banquet provided by Grimston's father at Bradfield. About the same time he also engaged in professional socializing with other young lawyers, including Edward Hyde, Challoner Chute, and Bulstrode Whitelocke.

Grimston was returned to parliament by Harwich in October 1628 but apparently played no part in the proceedings in 1629. In July 1631 he acted as an adviser to the mayor and aldermen of the town in connection with a petition they addressed to the privy council about the misdemeanours of a local clergyman, William Innes, who was allegedly vexing inhabitants with suits in the ecclesiastical courts. In response the council appointed commissioners, including the earl of Warwick and Sir Harbottle senior, to report on the case, but the court of high commission considered the report so unreasonably hostile to Innes that Sir Harbottle and the others were obliged to acknowledge their fault and beg a pardon. Nevertheless,

**Sir Harbottle Grimston, second baronet (1603–1685)**, by unknown artist, 1660s

Harbottle junior became recorder of Harwich in 1634 and recorder of Colchester in 1638, positions he held until he resigned them in 1648 and 1649; he also sat on the commissions of the peace for Middlesex from 1634, and on that for Essex between 1638 and 1648.

**Long parliament and civil war** Judging from their surviving papers the family kept a keen eye on the important political developments of the 1630s. When parliament was called again in 1640 Sir Harbottle senior sat for Harwich; he was subsequently active in the eastern association and two years before his death in 1648 became a presbyterian elder at Bradfield. Returned for Colchester, Harbottle junior was one of the first speakers in both the Short and Long Parliaments to call for a redress of grievances. Clarendon noted that he vigorously attacked financial expedients such as ship money. Although he was later among those who argued successfully that the record of Sir George Croke made him an exception, Grimston lashed out at judges who had overthrown the law and bishops who had done the same to religion. On 9 November he was appointed to a committee charged with drawing a remonstrance on the deplorable estate of the kingdom, and he was also a member of the committee that investigated the part played by Archbishop William Laud in framing the canons of 1640. In a speech subsequently published, on 18 December Grimston argued with great vehemence in favour of a motion to impeach Laud, denouncing him as the source of all current discontents, civil as well as ecclesiastical. He was 'the stye of all Pestilent filth, that hath infected the State, and Government of the Church and Common-wealth' (*Mr Grymstons Speech in Parliament*).

Although he disliked clerical pretensions and the excessive use of ecclesiastical power to deprive ministers, it is not clear how far Grimston opposed episcopacy as an institution. Like many others he may have looked towards a more moderate course of parliamentary action in the wake of the execution of Strafford and the resolution of legal grievances during the course of 1641, but the unsuccessful attempt by Charles I to arrest the five members in January 1642 apparently galvanized his allegiance to parliament. His speech defending the privileges of the House of Commons, which was published, claimed that the existence of the high court of parliament cheered and comforted 'the drooping Spirits of men groaning under the burthen of tyrannicall oppression inflicted on them unjustly and maliciously by unmercifull and wicked men that have usurped to themselves places and offices of power and authority both in State and Church' (*Mr Grimston his Speech, at the Committee Sitting in Guildhall*). According to Bulstrode Whitelocke, Grimston was among a group of lawyers who thought it lawful to accept parliamentary appointments of lord lieutenants, and in turn the commissions which they subsequently issued to their deputies, but in June he accepted the position of deputy lieutenant of Essex only on the condition that it was not intended to make war on the king. Aware that cloth workers in Essex had frequently been on the verge of discontent during the 1630s, Grimston, along with Sir Thomas Barrington, was sent home to Essex late in August 1642 to restore order following attacks on property and papists in the Stour valley. They arrested the causes of the local discontent, Sir John Lucas and his wife, and reported back to the house that the troubles had subsided once it had been made clear that parliament did not condone the pillaging and disorder.

Giving up his residence in Colchester early in 1643 Grimston was apparently increasingly alarmed by the spread of religious nonconformity there. Deeply concerned also about the consequences of the war on his locality as well as on the nation as a whole he was none the less active during the spring and summer in raising money to support the military activities of the eastern association. Although his name is listed by Rushworth as one of those who took the covenant in September 1643, Grimston told Gilbert Burnet, who served as his chaplain for many years after the Restoration, that he had refused to do so, and that he had been unwilling to support the parliamentary alliance with Scotland. In any event, he may have drifted into the background for the next few years before reappearing in 1647, when he served on the parliamentary committee for plundered ministers and on that for hearing appeals from the visitors of Oxford University. He was also appointed a commissioner for disbanding the army, and in November chaired a committee investigating the escape of the king from Hampton Court. In June 1648 his house, Bradfield Hall, was occupied in his absence by a party of troops belonging to the parliamentary army of the earl of Warwick, who plundered it and turned out his wife. In August 1648 he was involved in negotiations over the treaty of Newport, begging the king to make up his mind about the offer as quickly as possible before all chance of reaching an accommodation had disappeared. A few weeks before his death Grimston told Burnet that in 1647 or 1648 he had presented the House of Commons with evidence that Oliver Cromwell and the army were planning to use force against parliament, but that Cromwell escaped unscathed by falling down on his knees and giving a long speech attesting to his innocence and that of the rest of the officers. Although the story is unsubstantiated, Grimston was one of the members purged by Colonel Pride on 6 December 1648, and he was thought of sufficient importance to be imprisoned by the army until the end of January 1649, when he gave an engagement not to do any disservice to parliament or army. After signing a remonstrance against the acts of the Rump, he retired into private life, resigning the recordership of Colchester (6 July 1649), and devoting his leisure to the education of his children, with whom he travelled on the continent for a time.

**Retirement and Restoration** Grimston's wife, Mary—with whom he had two daughters and six sons of whom only the sixth, Samuel *Grimston, survived—died herself in June 1649. On 10 April 1651 he married Anne, the daughter and heir of Sir Nathaniel Bacon of Culford, Suffolk, and a niece of Lord Chancellor Francis Bacon. The widow of Sir Thomas Meutys, she had a life interest in the manor of Gorhambury in Hertfordshire, which Grimston then made his principal seat, and to which he subsequently purchased the reversion. During this same period he also began to devote much of his time to publishing an edition of the law reports of Sir George Croke. In one of the prefaces Grimston notes that owing to the times he was obliged to undertake a translation of the material from law French into English; evidently fearing that pirated editions might be published from manuscript copies of the original, he was successful in getting parliamentary recognition of his copyright to the authoritative texts which had been left to him in Croke's will. The first volume, which covered cases from the reign of Charles I, when Croke himself was a judge, appeared along with some biographical notes on the author in 1657, and contained a certificate of approval signed by nine Cromwellian judges. Apart from the fact that the reports were in themselves of considerable technical value, there were many interests within the legal community at this time who sought to share in Croke's reputation as the acceptable face of traditional English common law. A second volume, containing cases from the reign of James I, was published in 1658 and that for Elizabeth I in 1661; there were two further editions of the whole set before 1685.

Although Grimston spent much of the 1650s away from the political stage he was almost certainly active behind the scenes. Having become a bencher at Lincoln's Inn in 1648 he assumed the position of keeper of the black book in 1653 and became treasurer in 1658. He was returned as MP for Essex in 1656, but was not permitted to take his seat; along with ninety-seven others he signed a remonstrance and appeal against the exclusion. On the collapse of the Cromwellian protectorate in April 1658 Grimston was named to a committee for overseeing the summonsing of a new parliament. When the secluded members of the Long Parliament were readmitted in February 1659 he was elected to the council of state. When the Convention Parliament assembled in April 1660 Grimston, sitting once again for Colchester, was quickly elected speaker, enjoying the support of members of the 'presbyterian party' (*Autobiography*, 116–17); these included a number of other lawyers who were known to favour an accommodation with Charles II, and who began the proceedings by denouncing Cromwell as a tyrant and usurper. In his capacity as speaker he signed the letter inviting Charles to return from exile, went to Breda to accompany him on his voyage, and gave a speech at the Banqueting House in Whitehall which welcomed the 'restitution of your Majesty to the exercise of Your just and most indubitable Native Right of Soveraignty, and the deliverance of your people from Bondage and Slavery'. Charles had, he said, 'overcome and conquered the Hearts and Affections of all Your people in Three great Nations, the Hearts and Affections of all that are worthy the name of good Christians or reasonable men' (*The Speech of Sir Harbottle Grimston*, 3, 4–5).

**Master of the rolls** Having served on the commission that tried the regicides in October 1660 Grimston was rewarded with a life patent to the mastership of the rolls. In addition to putting him in charge of the care of the public records this post made him the judicial deputy to the lord chancellor in the court of chancery. Burnet described him as a patient and impartial judge, and he appears to have enjoyed good relations with Lord Chancellor Clarendon and later on with Nottingham. In 1664 one Nathanial Bacon, a disgruntled litigant, was fined and imprisoned for attempting to procure Grimston's assassination, but Sir Harbottle was much more disconcerted by the attempts in 1666 of Lord Thomas Fanshawe, MP for Hertfordshire, to resurrect the past by disinterring the civil war records of those, including Grimston, who had escaped prosecution at the time of the Restoration.

Though no longer speaker Grimston was returned again as MP for Colchester to the Cavalier Parliament of 1661, and he was appointed chief steward of the borough of St Albans by the charter granted to the town in 1664. During the course of the 1660s he was listed as supporting the court party, and was named to several committees, but took little part in debates. By the mid-1670s, however, he again became a critic of court policies. In 1675 he spoke in favour of a bill to prevent illegal financial impositions by the crown, and called for election of a new parliament, noting that 'A standing Parliament is as inconvenient as a standing army'. In 1677 he advocated the 'old Parliament way' of having supply and redress of grievances go 'hand in hand … We must strengthen people's hearts before we can lighten their purses' (HoP, *Commons, 1660–90*, 447). In 1678 he supported the first article of impeachment against Danby, and later spoke against the power of the king to grant him a pardon, claiming that it would completely undermine the power of parliament to complain about ministers. Returned again for Colchester for both elections in 1679, Grimston was listed by Shaftesbury as a likely supporter of the whigs, and he was appointed to seven committees and made several speeches. Citing his age and ill health Grimston asked to stand down for the election in February 1681, but the mayor of Colchester successfully persuaded him not to. He appears to have taken little part in the proceedings, but voted to exclude the future James II from the throne. Although Grimston advised the mayor and corporation in July 1683 to declare their unanimous 'abhorrency of the late anti-monarchical conspiracy' (*Verulam MSS*, 84) to destroy the sacred person of the king, Burnet may have accurately summed up his position by declaring:

> His principal was that allegiance and protection were mutual obligations and that the one went for the other. He thought the law was the measure of both and that when a legal protection was denied to one that paid a legal allegiance, the subject had a right to defend himself. (Burnet, 253)

Vehemently anti-popish, he also disliked the *jure divino* pretensions of the Anglican bishops; though sympathetic to dissenters he appears always to have been a conformist himself. He died of apoplexy on 2 January 1685 and was buried in the chancel of St Michael's Church, St Albans. His contemporary Sir Henry Chauncy ascribed to him 'a nimble fancy, a quick apprehension, memory, an eloquent tongue, and a sound judgment'. He was 'of free access, sociable in company, sincere to his friends, hospitable in his house, charitable to the poor, and an excellent master to his servants' (Chauncy, 465).

CHRISTOPHER W. BROOKS

**Sources** HoP, *Commons, 1660–90* · 'Grimston', HoP, *Commons, 1604–29* [draft] · *The diary of Bulstrode Whitelocke, 1605–1675*, ed. R. Spalding, British Academy, Records of Social and Economic History, new ser., 13 (1990) · G. Burnet, *History of his own time*, new edn, 2 (1883) · *Report on the manuscripts of the earl of Verulam*, HMC, 64 (1906) · *The journal of Sir Simonds D'Ewes from the beginning of the Long Parliament to the opening of the trial of the earl of Strafford*, ed. W. Notestein (1923) · *The autobiography of Sir John Bramston*, ed. [Lord Braybrooke], CS, 32 (1845) · Clarendon, *Hist. rebellion* · E. Wells, 'Common law reporting in England, 1550–1650', DPhil diss., U. Oxf., 1994 · J. Walter, *Understanding popular violence in the English revolution: the Colchester plunderers* (1999) · *Mr Grymstons speech in parliament upon the accusation and impeachment of William Laud, arch-bishop of Canterbury, upon high treason. Declaring his wicked proceedings, and exhorbitant power, both in church and Commonwealth* (1641) · *Mr Grimston his speech, at the committee sitting in Guildhall on Thursday the 6 of January 1641. Concerning the breaches of the priviledges of parliament; by breaking open the chambers, studies, and trunks of the Lord Kimbolton, and the rest of the members of the House of Commons accused by his majesty of high treason* (1642) · *The speech of Sir Harbottle Grimston, baronet, speaker of the honourable House of Commons, to the kings most excellent majesty. Delivered in the Banquetting-House at Whitehal, 29 May 1660* (1660) · will, PRO, PROB 11/379, sig. 5 · H. Chauncy, *The historical antiquities of Hertfordshire* (1700)

**Archives** Herts. ALS, corresp. and papers · Herts. ALS, Gorhambury MSS | BL, letters to Sir Thomas Barrington, Egerton MSS 2646–2648

**Likenesses** oils, *c.*1650, Gorhambury, near St Albans, Hertfordshire · oils, 1660, NPG · oils, second version, 1660–69, Palace of Westminster, London [*see illus.*] · M. Beale, portrait, Gorhambury, near St Albans, Hertfordshire · P. Lely, portrait, NPG · portraits, Gorhambury, near St Albans, Hertfordshire

**Wealth at death** £10,000 bequeathed as marriage portion for granddaughter; very wealthy: will, PRO, PROB 11/379, sig. 5

**Grimston, James Brabazon** [*known as* James Forrester], **fifth earl of Verulam (1910–1960)**, businessman, was born on 11 October 1910 at 4 South Eaton Place, Belgravia, London. Styled Baron Forrester from birth, and Viscount Grimston from 1924, he was the eldest of the four sons of James Walter Grimston, fourth earl of Verulam (1880–1949), electrical engineer and founder of Enfield Cables Ltd, and his wife, Lady Violet Constance Maitland Brabazon (1886–1936), younger daughter of Reginald Brabazon, twelfth earl of Meath. His two youngest brothers were killed in action in the Second World War. From Eton College, where he won the Jelf Latin verse prize four times and rowed in the school eight, he went up to Christ Church, Oxford, in 1929, where he was awarded a second in zoology in 1932. As an undergraduate he was already interested in business and made a number of factory visits, especially to those concerned with industrial welfare, such as the Bourneville factory and garden city in Birmingham. He spent much of the winter of 1932–3 working in a zinc rolling mill in Austria, and in 1933 set up Enfield Zinc Products Ltd in Tottenham, where he was managing director until 1938. He was also made a director of Enfield Cables Ltd in 1936.

In July 1931 Grimston spent three weeks in Bryn-mawr, Brecknockshire, at the first work camp organized by the newly formed British branch of the Service Civil International (SCI), a peace movement aimed at creating worldwide friendship through voluntary service, founded in 1921 by the Swiss Pierre Ceresole. A group of Quakers had been living in Bryn-mawr for three years, experimenting in involving the local community in reconstruction, and the international volunteers joined their project to turn an old rubbish dump into public swimming baths and gardens, working alongside local unemployed men to clear the site. After this experience Grimston wrote a pamphlet, *Ars laborandi: some Notes of the Art of Navvying* (1932), under the name James (Jim) Forrester, as he always called himself in Wales. In 1932 he became secretary of the southern branch of the British committee of the SCI and spent a month at an SCI work camp at Safien, in Switzerland, helping to clear away debris caused by a landslide.

In 1934 the organizations working at Bryn-mawr split, with the International Voluntary Service for Peace (the former SCI) continuing to run international work camps, while Peter Scott, a Quaker who had been working on the Bryn-mawr experiment since 1928, founded the Subsistence Production Society (SPS) in 1935. Scott was one of the Order of Friends; although not formally part of the Society of Friends this had grown out of the group of Quakers working at Bryn-mawr, who believed in the need for radical change in the social and economic system and thought that this could be achieved through experiment. The immediate task was to organize older unemployed men to produce essential goods for their personal consumption, and to own their means of production. Grimston became a member of the order, and from May 1935 until 1939 spent two out of every three weeks in south

Wales, working at Tottenham for the third week. Early in 1936 Forrester was made area organizer of the SPS of the eastern valleys of Monmouthshire, and with financial help from Lord Nuffield and the commissioner for the special areas he began to turn the Old Brewery at Cwmafon into workshops—for tailoring, boot repairing, and knitting, among other things—and a bakery and butchery, while a dairy farm was started. In return for thirty hours' unpaid work a week the men were able to buy what they needed for their families at cost price. Later in 1936 the Bryn-mawr SPS was started on the same lines, and from 1936 to 1939 Forrester organized the recruitment of volunteers for international summer work camps in the eastern valleys and in Bryn-mawr. To gain publicity for the work of the SPS he arranged a royal tour of the eastern valleys project on 13 November 1936, the last public engagement of Edward VIII, and helped to organize the filming of *Eastern Valley* in 1937. He also started Brynmawr Furniture Makers Ltd, which had a London showroom, and in July 1939 toured factories in Hungary and Austria, looking for ideas to improve the quality of the Bryn-mawr furniture. With the approach of war many of the unemployed were absorbed into the new munitions factories, and the SPS activities were closed down at the end of 1939. Grimston remained deeply concerned about the problems of south Wales, and when in 1940 he helped to found the Association for Planning and Regional Reconstruction, which was concerned with post-war reconstruction, the first papers dealt with reconstruction in south Wales. He was also responsible for building a rubber factory at Brynmawr, which opened in 1951.

Grimston became assistant to his father at Enfield Cables Ltd in 1938, and managing director from 1943 to 1953. He remained a director until 1954, and from 1949 he was chairman of Enfield Rolling Mills Ltd, founded by the third earl, which took over Enfield Cables in 1959. After the war he made long business trips every year, and it was during a visit to Portugal in 1947 that he fell down the side of a dam while studying an electrification scheme and fractured his skull. Though unconscious for six days he made a complete recovery. He became interested in power, and at Enfield Cables, in collaboration with the De Havilland Aircraft Company and the English Electric Company, he was involved in the first trials of wind power, and mounted an exhibition, 'Energy from the Wind', in the grounds of Gorhambury, his home in St Albans.

Grimston succeeded to the earldom in 1949, and although at Enfield he continued to be known as Mr Forrester he used his title in his various public activities. He was involved in an extraordinarily wide range of activities; interested in industrial welfare, health, education, and children, he lectured frequently and seemed to collect committees. At the end of his life he was chairman of the British Institute of Management, president of the St Mary's Hospital medical school, chairman of the governors of Bryanston School, chairman of the National Baby Welfare Council, treasurer of the British Pestalozzi Children's Village Trust, president of the English Folk Dance and Song Society, chairman of the Ancient Monuments Society, and a member of the North Thames Gas Board. He was also president of the Cremation Society from 1955 to 1958.

In addition Grimston was closely involved in local activities in St Albans. Elected president of the St Albans and mid-Herts Hospital in 1938, he helped to draw up the plans for a new hospital in 1947; he edited *St Albans by the People of the City* (1940); he was churchwarden of St Michael's; and he served as mayor of St Albans in 1956–7. He also wrote the official guidebook to Gorhambury, a Palladian house built between 1777 and 1784, with part of the site of Roman Verulamium in the grounds, arranged for the cataloguing of its collection of portraits, and undertook extensive repairs.

To manage all these activities as well as his business career Grimston was extremely well organized. Driven by the determination to do what he thought was important, he displayed single-mindedness and an ability to switch off and turn to something else. An excellent chairman and fund-raiser, he paid meticulous attention to detail. He also liked to write poetry, which he often included in his speeches. He died, of cancer, on 13 October 1960 at Gorhambury; he was cremated, following a funeral service at St Michael's, in St Albans, on 18 October. Never having married, he was succeeded to the title by his brother, John Grimston. ANNE PIMLOTT BAKER

**Sources** Gorhambury, St Albans, archives • private information (2004) [Gorhambury archivist] • E. Best and B. Pike, eds., *International Voluntary Service for Peace, 1920–1946* (1948) • H. Jennings, *Brynmawr: a study of a distressed area* (1934) • *The Times* (15 Oct 1960); (17 Oct 1960); (19 Oct 1960) • *Bryanston School Magazine* (1961) • *WW* • Burke, *Peerage* • b. cert. • *CGPLA Eng. & Wales* (1960)

**Archives** Old Gorhambury House, Hertfordshire, archives | FILM BFI NFTVA, *Eastern valley*, 1937

**Likenesses** photograph, 1960 (*Mother and child*) • portrait (posthumous), Gorhambury, Hertfordshire

**Wealth at death** £17,398 1*s*. 6*d*.: probate, 19 Dec 1960, *CGPLA Eng. & Wales*

**Grimston, Robert** (1816–1884), cricketer and promoter of telegraphy, fourth son of James Walter Grimston, first earl of Verulam (1775–1845), and his wife, Charlotte (1783–1863), second daughter of Charles *Jenkinson, first earl of Liverpool, was born at 42 Grosvenor Square, London, on 18 September 1816. He was a descendant of William Luckyn Grimston and the nephew of Robert Banks Jenkinson, second earl of Liverpool and prime minister at the time of his birth. Grimston's early years were spent at Gorhambury, Hertfordshire, the family seat, and as a boy he was distinguished for his love of field sports. After attending a preparatory school at Hatfield, Hertfordshire, he was at Harrow School (1828–34). It was said that at the age of fifteen he hired a post-chaise and pursued a burglar from Gorhambury to London, securing his arrest and transportation.

In 1834 Grimston was entered as a commoner at Christ Church, Oxford. John Ruskin, who was a fellow undergraduate, described him as 'a man of gentle birth and amiable manners, and of herculean strength, whose love of dogs and horses, and especially of boxing, was stupendous'. He was a bold rider, an excellent judge of horses, and rode in steeplechases. He broke his leg on one occasion while hunting with Baron de Rothschild's hounds. He was carried off on a gate, and, a train having stopped at a signal, he was put into the guard's van and by his own request taken to St George's Hospital, London.

As a cricketer Grimston was in the Harrow side in 1834, though only as twelfth man, in the match against Eton at Lord's. He won a blue for cricket at Oxford in 1838, opening the batting against Cambridge in what became the first of a sequence of matches broken only by the two world wars. His three brothers also all played first-class cricket. Only his eldest brother, James (1809–1895), failed to get a blue, as Oxford did not play Cambridge during his time. Robert made occasional appearances for Middlesex and was one of the founder members of the wandering club I Zingari. As a player he was most effective against fast bowling. It was alleged that when facing Kent's Alfred Mynn he took two bats to the wicket—the heavier one with which to play Mynn's bowling. He was an opponent of change, resenting both the growth of professionalism in cricket and the introduction of mowing machines at Lord's.

After leaving Oxford in 1838, Grimston entered Lincoln's Inn; he practised at the bar (1843–52) before joining the boards of various electric telegraph companies. He succeeded Robert Stephenson in 1859 as chairman of the International Telegraph Company and, in 1868, became chairman of the Indo-European Telegraph Company, which opened up the telegraph route to India.

Grimston preserved his interest in cricket until his death. In 1846 he assisted in the formation of Surrey County Cricket Club, which began playing in Kennington Oval, then a market garden. He was a member of the Marylebone Cricket Club and was elected president in 1883, becoming the first (and only) president to die in office. On 7 April 1884, while at Gorhambury, he was found dead in his chair. He was buried five days later in the family vault at St Michael's Church, St Albans. Grimston, who was unmarried, was a man averse to change of all kinds, and was tenacious of his opinions, but made full allowance for the conscientious dissent of others. The MCC report on his death called him a 'true friend and thorough sportsman'. He was charitable towards the distressed and severely condemned betting and gambling. A memorial to him at Harrow School pays tribute to him as a coach who taught cricket, manliness, and honour.

GERALD M. D. HOWAT

**Sources** [A. Haygarth], *Frederick Lillywhite's cricket scores and biographies*, 2 (1862) • A. Haygarth, *Arthur Haygarth's cricket scores and biographies*, 14 (1895) • F. Gale, *Life of the hon. Robert Grimston* (1885) • Lord Harris and F. S. Ashley-Cooper, *Lord's and the MCC* (1914) • P. Bailey, P. Thorn, and P. Wynne-Thomas, *Who's who of cricketers* (1984)

**Likenesses** Dickinson, photograph, *c.*1870, Marylebone Cricket Club, Lord's, London • photograph, *c.*1870, repro. in *Fores's Sporting Notes and Sketches* (July 1884) • photograph, *c.*1870, repro. in *Cricket* (17 April 1884) • Barraud, photograph, NPG

**Wealth at death** £112,586 17*s.* 0*d.*: probate, 13 May 1884, *CGPLA Eng. & Wales*

**Grimston, Sir Samuel, third baronet** (1644–1700), politician, was born on 7 January 1644, the sixth but only surviving son of Sir Harbottle *Grimston, second baronet (1603–1685), and his first wife, Mary (*d.* 1649), daughter of Sir George *Croke. He was educated at home by his father and entered Clare College, Cambridge, on 27 May 1663. He was admitted to Lincoln's Inn on 4 January 1668, and was called to the bar on 5 August 1670 at the request of John Churchill, reader of the inn. By that date he was already in parliament, the Gorhambury estate purchased by his father providing Grimston with the opportunity to enter the House of Commons for nearby St Albans at a by-election on 15 May 1668. On 14 February 1670 Grimston married Elizabeth (*d.* 1672), daughter of Heneage *Finch, the solicitor-general and later first earl of Nottingham. Their only daughter, Elizabeth, married William *Savile [*see under* Savile, George, first marquess of Halifax], son and heir to the first marquess of Halifax in 1687, and died in 1694. After the death of his first wife from smallpox Grimston married, on 17 April 1673, Lady Anne (1654–1713), daughter of John Tufton, second earl of Thanet. They had a son and a daughter who both died young.

Grimston was generally perceived as a court supporter in his first decade in parliament, in company with his father, but by 1677 the opposition leader, the earl of Shaftesbury, could account him 'worthy'. Grimston lost his seat in the election of February 1679, but was returned in both August 1679 and February 1681, although he was inactive in both these parliaments. Having succeeded his father he failed to win a seat at the 1685 general election. Grimston was returned to the Convention of 1689 and retained his St Albans seat for the rest of his life. He was classed as a tory by the marquess of Carmarthen in 1690, but seems to have been more of a country whig than anything else. He was forecast as likely to vote on the country side of several questions, but he signed the Association of 1696 and did not vote on the contentious question of the Fenwick attainder bill later that year.

Grimston died on 17 October 1700. He was buried on 29 October after an elaborate funeral. With no surviving children he left an estate of about £8000 per annum to his great-nephew, William Luckyn, provided that he changed his name to Grimston and paid his granddaughter, Lady Anne Savile, £30,000 over a period of twenty-three years. Grimston's wife, by all accounts a large woman unable to climb a narrow winding stairway to her husband's retreat known for that reason as 'Mount Pleasant', survived him until 22 November 1713.

STUART HANDLEY

**Sources** HoP, *Commons*, *1660–90* • HoP, *Commons*, *1690–1715* [draft] • Venn, *Alum. Cant.* • W. P. Baildon, ed., *The records of the Honorable Society of Lincoln's Inn: the black books*, 3 (1899), 69 • N. Luttrell, *A brief historical relation of state affairs from September 1678 to April 1714*, 1 (1857), 324; 4 (1857), 686, 699 • G. C. Williamson, *Lady Anne Clifford* (1922), 479–81 • *CSP dom.*, *1671–2*, 128 • *Report on the manuscripts of the earl of Verulam*, HMC, 64 (1906), 112–13 • M. M. Verney, ed., *Verney letters of the eighteenth century*, 2 vols. (1930), vol. 1, pp. 86–8 • will, PRO, PROB 11/460 • R. Clutterbuck, ed., *The history and antiquities of the county of Hertford*, 1 (1815)

**Likenesses** attrib. G. Kneller, oils, Gorhambury, Hertfordshire

**Wealth at death** very wealthy; his heir received £8000 p.a.; granddaughter received £30,000: will, PRO, PROB 11/460

**Grimston, William Luckyn, first Viscount Grimston** (**1683–1756**), politician, was the second son of Sir William Luckyn, third baronet, MP for Little Walton, Essex, and his wife, Mary, the daughter of William Sherrington. Having been adopted as heir by his great-uncle Sir Samuel *Grimston, he succeeded to the Grimston estates and assumed the surname on Sir Samuel's death in 1700. On 14 August 1706 he married Jane (Jean), the daughter of James Cooke of London. The marriage lasted fifty years and produced nineteen children.

In 1710 Grimston was returned as whig member of parliament for St Albans, the seat formerly held by Sir Samuel Grimston. With the support of the duke and duchess of Marlborough, he held the seat at elections in 1713 and 1715. A loyal if unremarkable government supporter, he was, on 29 May 1719, created a peer of Ireland, with the titles Baron Dunboyne and Viscount Grimston. He lost his seat in 1722, having offended Sarah, duchess of Marlborough, with what she considered his 'insolent' suggestion that they should join forces at the election. He was returned five years later, but then fell foul of the duchess once more, this time by refusing to support the political aspirations of her grandson John Spencer. Without the support of either the duchess or the corporation, Grimston was again defeated at the 1734 election.

According to Samuel Johnson, the duchess continued to ridicule Grimston by republishing a play, *The Lawyer's Fortune, or, Love in a Hollow Tree* (1705), which he had written, reissued, and then attempted to remove from circulation by buying all extant copies. The work had been mocked by Swift in his verses 'On Poetry, a Rhapsody' (1733) and in Pope's 'Imitations of Horace, Satire II' (1734), in which Grimston was identified as a 'booby Lord'. This theme was carried on in the 1736 edition of Grimston's play, which, although anonymous, was embellished by a dedication to 'The Right Sensible, the Lord Flame', a frontispiece showing an ass wearing a coronet, and a headpiece depicting an elephant on a tightrope. There has been some debate over the validity of Johnson's story. In contrast to the *Dictionary of National Biography*, which was doubtful as to the duchess's involvement, more recent studies regard her as responsible for the play's publication as revenge for Grimston's having opposed her interests at the 1734 election. In the year after the play's republication Grimston became fourth baronet, of Luckyn (4 February 1737. The feud with the duchess continued, with both parties supporting rival candidates for the St Albans seat in 1741 and 1743. Grimston finally saw his son, a supporter of the duke of Newcastle, returned in 1754.

Grimston died on 15 October 1756, aged seventy-three, and was buried on 28 October 1756 at St Michael's Church, St Albans. His wife died on 12 March 1765; his title and estate were inherited by their second son, James (1711–1773).

Philip Carter

**Sources** GEC, *Peerage*, new edn • R. R. Sedgwick, 'Grimston, William', HoP, *Commons* • *DNB* • F. Harris, *A passion for government: the life of Sarah, duchess of Marlborough* (1991) • *The poems of Alexander Pope*, ed. J. Butt, 11 vols. (1961–9) • *The poems of Jonathan Swift*, ed. H. Williams, 3 vols. (1963) • J. Boswell, *The life of Samuel Johnson*, 2 vols. (1791)

**Likenesses** M. Dahl, oils, Old Gorhambury House, Hertfordshire • oils, Old Gorhambury House, Hertfordshire

**Grimstone, Mary Leman**. *See* Gillies, Mary Leman (*b*. *c*.1800, *d*. in or after 1851).

**Grimthorpe**. For this title name *see* Beckett, Edmund, first Baron Grimthorpe (1816–1905).

**Grindal, Edmund** (1516x20–1583), archbishop of York and of Canterbury, was sixty-three years of age at his death in July 1583 according to his funerary monument, although there is contrary evidence that he died aged sixty-six, which would mean that he was born in 1516 or 1517.

**Origins and formation** Grindal came from the west of Cumberland, which he described as a 'little angle', the most ignorant in religion and oppressed by covetous landlords of any part of the realm. It is a remarkable fact that the archbishops of Canterbury and York at the very centre of Elizabeth's reign, Grindal and Edwin Sandys, knew each other 'as brothers' in St Bees, a coastal village dominated by an ancient Benedictine priory which Grindal replaced with the grammar school which still flourishes. An old question whether Grindal was born in St Bees itself, or in the outlying hamlet of Hensingham, now a suburb of Whitehaven, has been resolved by archaeological evidence. The birthplace is Cross Hill, St Bees, nowadays 19 Finkle Street. Grindal would refer to 'the house wherein I was born', with the lands attached to it worth under 20*s*. in rent, but 'well builded at the charges of my father and brother' (Nicholson, 321–2). Modern research has established that in 1560 the rent was in fact only 8*s*. 2*d*. and that the holding was of about 30 acres. And yet the birthplace was a substantial house of stone, complete with lofty hall, parlour, and solar. Were the 'statesmen' of early modern Cumberland better housed, and better off, than has been supposed? Or did Grindal's father, William, have some additional source of wealth? The family's gentry connections are perhaps significant.

The property was inherited by Grindal's elder brother Robert, who with his wife and only son, Edmund, died in 1569. A surviving daughter married into the gentry clan of the Dacres, taking with her the house which to this day is decorated with wall paintings of the Dacre device of sable-beaked griffins. Grindal retained a lifelong interest in the township and in his kindred, purchasing the impropriated parochial tithes for their benefit from the diplomat Sir Thomas Challoner, who had acquired the lands, coal mines, and salt pans of the dissolved priory, and negotiating for his brother the purchase of one of the new fifty-year leases which Challoner had substituted for his former customary tenancy. Later the terms of Grindal's grammar school foundation made it possible to secure for the St Bees farmers generous leases to run at fixed rents for a thousand years.

**Edmund Grindal** (1516x20–1583), by unknown artist, 1580

For generations, talented boys had escaped their impoverished northern environment by climbing an educational ladder into an ecclesiastical career in the more prosperous south, a route taken by more than one Grindal, including William Grindal, one of the future Queen Elizabeth's tutors. After a schooling of which nothing is known, Grindal began his Cambridge career at Magdalene (then known as Buckingham) College, moving on to Pembroke College at some point in the later 1530s. He proceeded BA in 1538, was elected to a fellowship, and in 1540 took his MA and was junior treasurer of his college. In 1549 he proceeded BTh and in the same year became president of Pembroke, acting as head in the absence of the master, Bishop Nicholas Ridley. He served as senior proctor in 1548–9 and was Lady Margaret preacher in 1550; but unlike Sandys, who was by then master of St Catharine's College, a DTh, and, in 1552, vice-chancellor, this was as far as Grindal proceeded in the academic *cursus honorum*. Already his sights were set beyond academe, in a church now flung into the turmoil of the Edwardian Reformation. It was much later, as a public figure and a bishop, that Pembroke elected him its absentee master in 1559, a position he resigned after three years, and that the university made him, in 1564, a doctor of theology.

**The Edwardian apprenticeship** Grindal was ordained deacon by John Bird, bishop of Chester, in 1544. According to common practice in the northern province, ordination to the priesthood would have followed almost immediately, but it seems to have gone unrecorded. More than twenty years later, Grindal would tell a group of puritan separatists in London: 'I have said mass; I am sorry for it' (*A Parte of a Register*, 32). His rejection of the mass had occurred as Henry VIII's reign neared its end when, having passed a Lutheran phase, Heinrich Bullinger's tract *De origine erroris* won him over to something close to the Zwinglian position on the eucharist. Later he defended the reformed doctrine of the sacrament in his only (and hardly successful) attempt at popular theology, included by John Foxe in *Acts and Monuments* as 'A Fruitful Dialogue' between Custom and Verity.

The chronology of Grindal's perhaps politically opportune conversion parallels what happened at much the same time to Archbishop Thomas Cranmer, encouraged by Ridley. Pembroke College was a nest for a precocious clutch of protestant reformers and publicists who included John Rogers, the biblical translator and protomartyr of Mary's reign, John Bradford, Thomas Sampson, and the pioneering naturalist, William Turner, not to speak of Ridley, now a protestant bishop. According to Turner, Grindal became Ridley's 'fidus Achates', which implies a special intimacy.

An equally strong influence was Martin Bucer, the German reformer who was regius professor of divinity in Edwardian Cambridge. Grindal was no doubt welcome in Bucer's model protestant household, and it is known from Sampson that he was one of his 'familiars', addressed as 'doctissime et carissime Grindalle' (whereas Matthew Parker, who preached Bucer's funeral sermon, was 'clarissimus' rather than 'carissimus') (Collinson, *Grindal*, 50). After spending much of Mary's reign in Bucer's Strasbourg, Grindal returned to see to the retrieval of his host's English writings. As archbishop of Canterbury he would receive the dedication of *Scripta Anglicana*, while his annotated copy of Bucer's English masterpiece, *De regno Christi*, is evidence that this vision of Christian discipline and pastoral care was the model for Grindal's episcopal style and conduct.

Grindal first attracted public attention in June 1549, when he took part in a disputation on transubstantiation laid on as part of a royal visitation of the university, the visitors including Ridley, Sir Thomas Smith, and Sir John Cheke. Two years later, more private debates on the eucharist held in London, partly in the house of William Cecil, further exposed him to men who counted, and Cecil would become, as Grindal acknowledged in the last months of his life, 'the principal procurer' of all his preferments (Nicholson, 402).

Ridley became bishop of London in April 1550, and as vacancies in the chapter of St Paul's fell vacant proceeded to install a kind of general staff consisting of his own collegians, Bradford, Rogers, and Grindal, men fit 'both with life and learning to set forth God's word in London and in the whole diocese of the same' (*Works of Nicholas Ridley*, 331–4). This was achieved only after a fight with entrenched and conservative interests, and at court. But on 24 August 1551 Grindal was made precentor of St Paul's, a living worth £46. Ridley was by nature an episcopal martinet, but when 'dearly beloved brother Grindal' escaped the Marian persecution by going into exile, he would be humbly content with Rogers and Bradford 'to make up the trinity out of Paul's church' to go to the stake (*Writings of John Bradford*, 2.192).

Before that, and as religious revolution proceeded on its reckless course, Grindal was appointed one of six 'chaplains ordinary' of the king, who were to divide their time between preaching at court and in the country. He was given a prebend in Westminster Abbey and drew an income of more than £100 a year. In October 1552 he took part in a review of the forty-two articles of religion. Grindal was now poised for high office, Ridley reporting that he was 'or shall be named to be a bishop in the north parts' (*Works of Nicholas Ridley*, 336). The see in question was Newcastle, an invention to be carved out of the wealthy bishopric of Durham as a devious ecclesiastical stratagem of the duke of Northumberland. But then Northumberland reshuffled the cards. Ridley was to return to the north, to be replaced in London by Grindal. Before any of this could happen, the young king died. With Mary's successful coup and the collapse of the Edwardian experiment, Grindal was one of those who denounced Northumberland's cynical manipulation of religion, and not only with the benefit of hindsight. According to John Knox, a sermon preached by Grindal at court in Lent 1553 plainly foretold the king's death and blamed his ministers for their 'railing' against the preachers of God's word.

**A Germanical nature** Grindal was not dangerously compromised by the events accompanying and following Mary's accession. Nevertheless, there seems to have been a strategic decision taken that he should go into exile. He resigned the precentorship of St Paul's by 28 April 1554 and his Westminster prebend two weeks later. Although Foxe does not say so in his account of Sandys's departure in May, Grindal was probably in the same party, together with Richard Cox, the future bishop of Ely, and Thomas Sampson. The destination was Strasbourg, where Grindal arrived no later than August 1554, and where there is evidence of his presence through most of the four years of exile which followed. But between May 1555 and May 1556 his whereabouts are unrecorded, and it must have been then that, in Foxe's words, he 'went into the country to learn the Dutch tongue' (*Acts and Monuments*, 8.598). There is evidence that these language studies took place at Wasselheim, where Grindal lodged with the pastor, Jakob Heldelin, and he also spent some time in Speyer. Back in Elizabethan England, Sandys wished that Archbishop Parker, who had not shared in the Marian exile, would be more tolerant of 'Germanical natures' (Bruce and Perowne, 125). Grindal's was the most Germanical nature of all. He retained a reading knowledge of the language, as bishop of London employed as his secretary the son of a German minister, and took a well-informed interest in German theological controversies, and politics.

Bucer's secretary Conrad Hubert thought that Grindal had no expectation of ever returning to England and was looking for employment in Germany. That may have been so, but the exile community in Strasbourg had some of the character of a government in only temporary exile. As a public figure, this was where Grindal belonged, and although the theologian Pietro Martire Vermigli (known as Peter Martyr), who had returned from his chair in Edwardian Oxford to lecture in Strasbourg, called him 'my most dear friend in England' (LPL, MS 2010, fol. 114), Grindal, unlike the scholars Sandys and John Jewel, did not follow him when he withdrew to the more congenial theological climate of Zürich. Strasbourg was responsible for the future. That involved bringing to heel a rival group in Frankfurt which in its bid for leadership of the English diaspora, and potentially for the future direction of English protestantism, proposed to jettison English ways in favour of the example of 'the best reformed churches'. It fell to Grindal to travel to Frankfurt to persuade John Knox and the other leaders to retain at least 'the effect and substance' of the Edwardian book, only to be told that his journey 'for the establishment of ceremonies' was a waste of time (Collinson, *Grindal*, 76). Richard Cox then resorted to the dubious tactics which provoked the 'Troubles at Frankfort', splitting the congregation in two and sending Knox and his party on their travels to Geneva, with momentous consequences for the churches in both England and Scotland. Grindal was part of the plot, telling Ridley that the Frankfurt church was 'well quieted by the prudence of Master Cox' (*Works of Nicholas Ridley*, 533–5, 386–8).

John Foxe was on the opposite side in this quarrel, but he worked in partnership with Grindal in an enterprise which would lead to *Acts and Monuments*, a book destined to be hugely formative in the fashioning of a specifically English protestant consciousness. Grindal played a key role in acquiring through the protestant underground such 'monuments' of the Marian persecution as the last writings and trial records of Ridley and Cranmer. He assumed that 'the history of the martyrs', and he was perhaps the first to use the phrase, would be a collective enterprise. But Foxe picked up this ball and ran with it. It was against Grindal's advice that in August 1559 he published in Basel *Rerum in ecclesia gestarum*, an early version of what was to become 'Foxe's book of martyrs'—and no one else's.

By then Grindal was back in England. No sooner did the news reach Strasbourg of the death of Mary than, 'compelled by the urgency of my friends' (Collinson, *Grindal*, 82), he met up with Sandys and after a difficult winter journey arrived in London on the very day that Queen Elizabeth was crowned, 15 January 1559.

**The Elizabethan settlement** The making of the new parliamentary settlement of religion is poorly documented, and its day-to-day politics will never be known. Consequently, when Sandys wrote of 'tossings and griefs, alterations and mutations' (Bruce and Perowne, 68), it is not clear whether he referred only to difficulties with the Marian bishops and other Catholics, or to those, perhaps the queen included but not to be named, who wished to curb the advanced protestant aspirations of returned exiles like himself. For the émigré protestant divines were simultaneously agents and critics of the settlement. Grindal preached at court in Lent 1559 and played a leading role with other exiles in the set-piece disputation against the bishops in Westminster Abbey. He was close to the man of the hour, Sir William Cecil, and it must have been an assumption that his 1553 nomination for the bishopric of London would now take effect. This duly happened on 22 June 1559, after Bishop Edmund Bonner had been forced out of office. On 14 May, Whitsunday, the Act of Uniformity had come into force, and it was Grindal who had been put up at Paul's Cross to proclaim 'the restoring of the book of King Edward' (Churton, 392–8). In the summer of 1559, as his friends and colleagues fanned out across the country to conduct a royal visitation of the church, Grindal and Matthew Parker, nominated archbishop of Canterbury, were the first to be appointed to the new and permanent ecclesiastical commission which was to oversee the church at large from its political centre in London.

Yet the more than twenty years of episcopal office which lay ahead are full of evidence that the Elizabethan religious settlement, with its concessions to traditional religious practice, was for Grindal a second best which he had not only to endure but to enforce. When the first confrontation with nonconformity occurred, he told Bullinger in Zürich: 'We who are now bishops, on our first return, and before we entered on our ministry, contended long and earnestly for the removal of those things that have occasioned the present dispute'. But they were 'unable to prevail' (Robinson, *Zurich Letters*, 1.169). Abortive attempts to perfect the settlement in the first convocation held under the new dispensation in 1563 were the work not of a 'puritan' opposition but of the bishops themselves, and Grindal was prominently involved.

The first year was one of make or break, and Grindal himself is on record as saying that he and others only consented to become bishops in order to prevent the preferment of 'semi-papists' and other time-servers. (However, his eighteenth-century biographer John Strype wholly misrepresented Grindal and exaggerated any thoughts of *nolo episcopari* which he may have entertained by attributing to him a series of neurotic letters to Peter Martyr which were in fact written by Thomas Sampson, who indeed never became a bishop.) It was not until 21 December 1559 that Grindal was consecrated, and it was as late as 21 March 1560 that he took possession of the temporalities of the see. In the intervening months several battles had been fought, one of them over legislation enforcing an unfavourable bargain whereby the crown acquired much episcopal real estate in exchange for assets of an only nominally equivalent value, such as impropriate parochial tithes and other spiritual revenues, a challenge to episcopal consciences as well as revenues. This was very nearly a resigning matter. But the diocese of London escaped comparatively lightly, thanks perhaps to Grindal's friendship with the principal architect of the scheme, Cecil.

The unworldly and unmarried Grindal was more concerned with two other sticking points: crosses and altars. The royal injunctions had required the destruction of all 'monuments of superstition' and the visitors had interpreted this liberally, removing altars and making a holocaust of crosses ('roods') and rood imagery. Initially Elizabeth may have intended to order the reinstatement of both. But a deal was struck by which she retained the cross in her own royal chapel, in the face of sustained criticism, and sanctioned an order which recognized the *fait accompli* of the destruction of altars and provided an orderly procedure for their replacement by holy tables. Grindal was the draftsman of two statements which may have been instrumental in bringing about this compromise: 'Reasons against images in churches', a peroration deriving from something written by Ridley in Edward's reign, but with an added appeal 'not to strain us any further' and to accept 'this our plainness and liberty' (Corpus Christi College, Cambridge, MS 105, art. 11, 201–15); and a denunciation of altars, as incompatible with the legacy of Cranmer, Ridley, and the other martyrs.

**London** In much Anglican historiography Grindal appears as a feeble and incompetent bishop. If his London episcopate had been better documented, and even more his critically important role in the ecclesiastical commission, for which there is almost no surviving archive, it might well have been otherwise. In the absence of much formal documentation, the ninety-eight letters which survive from Grindal to Cecil, sixty-eight of them written in his ten years as bishop of London, speak volumes for his standing within the early Elizabethan regime.

The greatest initial problem which Grindal faced as a bishop with jurisdiction over 92 parishes in the city of London, and 480 in the rest of his large diocese, extending over Essex, Middlesex, and part of Hertfordshire, was manpower. The church was depleted by death, deprivation, and lack of confidence in its future. In his first two years, Grindal was obliged to ordain 294 clergy, almost as many as in the next eight. A high proportion were nongraduates and more than half were over the age of thirty. But when Parker wrote to Grindal as dean of his province to comment critically on the opening of the floodgates to shoddy goods he was not singling out the bishop of London for particular criticism. In Parker's own diocese there were 233 ordinations in eight months, 150 of them on a single day. Nor was Grindal's policy indiscriminate. As many as a tenth of his ordinands were returned exiles (including John Foxe), and several of them were 'gospellers' from an artisan background. Evidently Grindal was partly looking to the needs of a kind of protestant church within the larger ecclesiastical structure. But the fusion of a church of martyrs and exiles with the establishment was proceeding, especially in Grindal's senior appointments. All but one of his archdeacons and his first chancellor and vicar-general were returned exiles. Grindal's first visitation of his diocese, in 1561, witnessed an energetic effort to cleanse the Augean stables of his cathedral church, and a tour of the country which may have done more to reveal the scale of pastoral neglect than to cure it. But the rare survival of a register of disciplinary cases shows that Grindal, self-consciously adopting the model of the 'primitive' and pastoral bishop, took personal charge of very many cases involving erring and recalcitrant clergy, holding court in his house at St Paul's or in his country manors at Fulham and Hadham.

The years 1561 and 1563 witnessed two major disasters. On 4 June 1561 St Paul's was struck by lightning, starting a fire which destroyed the steeple and most of the roof. Much of Grindal's time was now spent, in co-operation with the civil power, and especially Cecil, in finding the huge sums of money and the materials needed for rebuilding. An early Elizabethan historian, Sir John Hayward, thought that the rescue of St Paul's was Grindal's abiding claim to fame. Two years later London was hit by one of the gravest visitations of bubonic plague in its history. Grindal was busy, with Parker, in preparing special orders of prayer and fasting, but he was characteristically practical in limiting their use to 'moderate assemblies' in parish churches rather than in mass gatherings.

For as long as he was bishop of London, Grindal had a distinct role, and almost a separate existence, in respect of the so-called stranger churches, the London congregations of French, Dutch, Italian, and, intermittently, Spanish protestant asylum seekers. Under the terms of a generous charter granted by Edward VI, these people constituted a self-governing 'corpus corporatum et politicum', with church premises in which to assemble, including the large church of Austin Friars, which became the Dutch church, and, for the French, St Anthony's Chapel, Threadneedle Street. Loosely confederated in a *coetus*, the congregations chose their own officers and determined their forms of worship and discipline, but their constitution empowered a quasi-episcopal superintendent, representing the authority of the crown. The first superintendent, the Polish nobleman John à Lasco, was himself a stranger, but under Elizabeth the office was vested in the bishop of London, *ex officio*.

Here was a permeable membrane between the emergent world of presbyterian Calvinism and the royally and episcopally ordered Church of England. In the perception of more 'forward' English protestants, the stranger churches were model churches, an example which it was hoped all England might follow. Conversely, the superimposition of an episcopal superintendent was intended to bring them into conformity with the Church of England. According to the privy council, they were to use no religious forms 'contrary to our law'. But Grindal chose to exercise his powers within the spiritual economy of the churches, not as an alien intruder into their affairs. It was typical that he should order his parish churches not to admit to communion foreigners who had withdrawn from the discipline of their own churches, which the clerk of the French congregation called 'acte de levesque remarquable' (Johnston, 97).

Grindal's excellent relations with the churches were cemented by a firm alliance with John Calvin, whose action in dispatching to London as pastor of the French church one of his principal lieutenants, Nicolas des Gallars, is indicative of some anxiety about the way things were going in England. For his part, Grindal assured Calvin that des Gallars had been of great assistance to himself 'and our churches' (Collinson, *Grindal*, 134). But the little world of the stranger churches was no bed of roses. Des Gallars brought Genevan discipline, but he met with resistance and there were rivals for his office, including, embarrassingly, Grindal's Strasbourg landlord, Pierre Alexandre, a distinguished but prickly man. Grindal was forced to intervene repeatedly, to uphold the authority of des Gallars, but also to effect a series of reconciliations between the factions. There was also a prolonged *cause célèbre* in the Dutch church, which centred on the alleged heterodoxy of the martyrologist Adriaan van Haemstede, whom Grindal was obliged to excommunicate, twice; and further troubles surrounding two Spanish evangelical scholars, first Casiodoro de Reina and then Antonio del Corro. For the most part, Grindal was on the side of the 'discipline' against dissidence, but he was not always comfortable with the heresy hunting associated with international Calvinism. He respected de Reina's scholarship and made possible the publication of his Spanish Bible. A copy in Grindal's library is inscribed by the translator with a reference to the bishop's action in rescuing his manuscripts 'ex hostium manibus'. And Grindal turned a partially sighted eye to Corro's heresies. This was Calvinism with a human or perhaps an Anglican face.

**Puritanism** In 1566 Grindal was thrown into the second of the crises which were to dramatize the difficulty of combining leadership of the progressive protestant cause with episcopal responsibilities. In January 1565 it was decided—whether by the queen herself, or Cecil, or Parker is far from clear—to clamp down on nonconformity, especially in respect of ecclesiastical vestments and other items of prescribed clerical costume, principally the surplice and the square or cornered cap, 'the pope's attire' according to those who denounced these concessions to unreconstructed religious conservatism. A year later, in March 1566, thirty-seven London clergy who refused conformity were suspended and threatened with deprivation. It was just before Easter, ecclesiastically the busiest season of the year. Those suspended included some of Grindal's choicest ordinands, men who had dominated the most prominent London pulpits and some of the only ministers who were acceptable to London's godly protestants. The fragile coalition of followers of the old and the new which was the Elizabethan church threatened to split asunder. In the midst of this crisis, which involved demonstrations and the first use of the printing press by those now to be nicknamed puritans, Parker made this exasperated comment:

> And now my lord of London by experience feeleth and seeth the marks and bounds of these good sprights which, but for his tolerations etc., had been suppressed for five or six years ago, and had prevented all this unquietness now taken, and both his reputation better saved and my poor honesty not so foully traduced. (Bruce and Perowne, 284)

This was only partly justified, since Grindal had been far from inactive in the promotion of clerical conformity. But he had never concealed his own distaste for the disputed ceremonies, and in some special circumstances he had condoned their abandonment. He told a group of radical puritan laymen (if the puritan laymen are to be believed): 'You see me wear a cope or a surplice in Paul's. I had rather minister without these things, but for order's sake and obedience to the prince' (*A Parte of a Register*, 32). But Grindal was not alone in having his doubts about the wisdom, and even the legality, of the new hardline policy. He and Parker were given no support at all by the politicians, and even the queen failed to back with her own authority the orders the archbishop was trying to enforce, so that they appeared under the feeble title of 'Advertisements'. And it was always Grindal's instinct to be pastoral rather than punitive. His patience was remarkable, even when he was hooted at by demonstrating housewives with cries of 'ware horns' and told by one radical spirit that he was 'a man accused before God' (Collinson, *Grindal*, 177).

But two years of grappling with the incorrigibles who were prepared to cut loose from their parish churches, the first separatists, turned Grindal into one of the most resolute opponents of 'people fanatical and incurable'. Their schism was an insult to 'the whole state of the Church reformed in King Edward's days', and to the Marian martyrs (Collinson, *Grindal*, 181–2). He was no less hostile to the new presbyterian tendency which was announced in the Cambridge lectures of Thomas Cartwright and in the radical pamphlet *An Admonition to the Parliament* (1572). Cartwright, he said, had 'a busy head, stuffed full of singularities' (Nicholson, 304–5). Yet Grindal would remain accessible and sympathetic to genuinely scrupulous consciences, 'godly brethren which do wish that such things as are amiss were reformed', although one of these brethren, his old friend Sampson, wondered how the bishop could touch pitch and not be himself defiled (Inner Temple Library, MS Petyt 538/47, no. 188, fols. 336–7).

**York** In 1570 Grindal became archbishop of York. It may look as if he was being kicked upstairs to a remote province where a bishop soft on puritanism could do less harm. And it is true that Parker already had his eye on John Aylmer as 'a good, fast, earnest servitor' for London (Aylmer would have to wait another seven years, and it was Sandys who succeeded Grindal) whereas he thought Grindal 'fit for York' (Bruce and Perowne, 359–60). It would be Aylmer's own preferred solution to the problem of puritanism to let the puritans loose on the Catholics of the north. But it would be absurd to suggest that in the immediate aftermath of the northern rising Cecil was getting rid of Grindal by sending him to York. His promotion was of a piece with the appointment, two years later, of Henry Hastings, third earl of Huntingdon, as president of the council in the north. There was need for the smack of firm government, and for protestant government. It was only now that the Reformation in the sense of the effective protestantization of the region happened, and Grindal was its principal agent.

There was a slow and discouraging start. The legal formalities went smoothly and Grindal was installed in York Minster on 9 June. But this was by proxy, and it would be the best part of a year before he would see the minster for himself. First he had to go to Canterbury to be inducted, the occasion for one of Parker's big parties, then he had to sort out a scandal in the affairs of a charitable foundation, the London hospital of the Savoy, and when he finally set out for York in August illness interrupted his journey. He had a cool reception as he entered Yorkshire, with only a dozen members of the local gentry turning out to welcome him on behalf of the government. Arriving at Cawood Castle he found it dank and unwholesome. But no sooner had he decided to make his home at Bishopthorpe than his health collapsed, leaving him cooped up at Cawood for the winter. It was not until March 1571 that Grindal entered York and took his presiding seat in the ecclesiastical commission for the northern province. After that his grip was rarely relaxed, and for the next five years he seems to have been continuously resident except for absence at the parliament held in the early summer of 1572.

During his months of enforced inactivity, many of Grindal's functions were performed by Richard Barnes, suffragan bishop of Nottingham before his appointment to Carlisle in July 1570. But Grindal later suspected Barnes of corruption and opposed his promotion to Durham in 1577, which made him an enemy on the episcopal bench. Barnes's departure from Nottingham left the coast clear for his ally the archdeacon, John Lowth, a venal pluralist with ambitions to be independent of York, another enemy who provoked Grindal to uncharacteristic vindictiveness.

Writing to Cecil on his first arrival in the north, Grindal conveyed a sense of culture shock. So much of the old religion was still alive and well ('they offer money, eggs etc. at the burial of their dead: they pray on beads') that it was as if this was another church altogether (Nicholson, 325–6). He addressed the problem of what has been called 'survivalism' in his primary visitation, which began in May 1571, and which in its attack, for example, on altars and crosses was the equivalent for the north of the royal visitation of 1559. (But plenty of 'survivalism' survived to be detected in later visitations.) This was also a watershed for York Minster, where, with the full co-operation of the dean, the zealous Matthew Hutton, Grindal introduced a new culture of sermons under orders which would survive without alteration until 1685.

Grindal was a new broom mostly in his own diocese, leaving to Barnes the primary metropolitical visitation of the vast diocese of Chester, as well as of Carlisle. Although archival losses make this a matter of conjecture, it seems likely that Grindal's ongoing policy, so far as routine ecclesiastical justice was concerned, was one of devolution, following a practice long established in the south of strengthening the role of archdeacons' courts. Of this trend nearly independent Nottingham was an extreme example.

Grindal's own preferred court, counting for much more than his regular court of audience, was the York ecclesiastical commission, a mixed clerical and lay tribunal appointed under letters patent, with powers to fine and imprison. This was to be the principal weapon against Catholicism in the years before new penal legislation made the secular courts competent in this area. In four and a half years, Grindal presided over the commission on 157 days, 55 of them between March and December 1571. He seems to have been under the benign illusion that to haul prominent Catholics before him and to ask them to discuss their 'doubts' in civilized conference would solve the problem, and he later reported to the queen that he had achieved the 'most assured, dutiful obedience of your subjects in those parts' (Nicholson, 381). In fact mass recusancy was growing under his very nose, leaving his successor, Sandys, and Huntingdon to apply harsher countermeasures to hundreds of cases. But to be fair to Grindal, he knew that the most realistic remedy for Catholicism was to inflict swingeing fines, not merely for absence from church, for Catholics often attended church, but for failure to receive communion, and in the parliament of 1572, and again in 1576 as archbishop of Canterbury, he headed efforts to bring in legislation to that effect. Although these were unsuccessful, this fed in to the legislation of 1581 which raised the penalty for recusancy to £20 a month—but removed from the front line of the battle the bishops who, sitting as ecclesiastical commissioners, were most likely to have won it.

Protestantization of the north depended, in the long term, on importing a new kind of clergyman. Grindal could not hope to change things overnight. Hundreds of beneficed clergy enjoyed their freeholds, and it was not possible to refuse institution to all the unsuitable men legally presented to livings by patrons. But much as he had done in London, Grindal operated a two-stream ordination policy: 'ordines generales', for the parishes had to be supplied, and 'ordines speciales', often involving a single hand-picked individual. Protestant graduates already in orders, with the potential to become evangelists, were imported from the south. By such means, as Grindal later boasted to the queen, he had procured 'above forty learned preachers and graduates, within less than six years, to be placed within the diocese of York' (Nicholson, 380–81). Market towns were targeted. It was thanks to arrangements which Grindal made with the corporation of Hull that a preacher called Melchior Smith was able to convert the town to a militant protestant future. But the remote Pennine uplands were also reached. In August 1572 Grindal ordained a Pembroke man, Christopher Shute, and licensed him to preach throughout the province. As vicar of Giggleswick for more than fifty years, Shute was one of the founders of a radical protestant tradition in Craven which in the seventeenth century tended to Quakerism.

**Canterbury** Although it was by no means in the natural order of events for an archbishop of York to be translated to Canterbury, Grindal's promotion was not the anomaly which some Anglican historians have supposed it to be, following the eighteenth-century lead of a notorious sermon by Dr Sacheverell. No bishop was more respected, and Grindal's reputation was one of *gravitas* and firmness. But to understand the circumstances of the promotion, it is necessary to see some way into the innerness of Elizabethan high politics, which often involved an adversarial relationship between the queen and leading figures in her court and privy council, especially where matters of religion, together with related policy choices, were concerned.

With Parker's breath scarcely out of his body, Cecil, now Lord Burghley, told Sir Francis Walsingham that Grindal was the 'meetest man to succeed'. 'Take my proxy for my poor voice' (PRO, SP 12/103/48). That was in May 1575. Yet it was not until six months later that he could tell Grindal that the queen 'will have your Grace come to the province of Canterbury' (Inner Temple Library, MS Petyt 538/47, no. 267, fol. 502), arousing in the archbishop 'many conflicts with myself about that matter' (BL, Lansdowne MS 20, no. 69, fol. 168). Only on Christmas eve did Elizabeth sign the *congé d'élire*. That there had been something of a conspiracy to secure that signature is suggested by a letter to Grindal from an unnamed courtier (possibly Sir Walter Mildmay), assuring him that his appointment was 'greatly hoped for by the godly and well-affected of this realm', and indicating some of the areas which required his reforming hand. 'I know it will be hard for you to do that good that you and your brethren desire. Yet (things discreetly ordered) somewhat there may be done'. These things would be better discussed by word of mouth than committed to paper (PRO, SP 59/19, fol. 248*v*).

The sense of urgency conveyed in this anonymous missive was prompted by the imminent recall of parliament which it was widely hoped, and not merely by 'puritans', would stiffen the laws against Catholics and tackle abuses in ecclesiastical discipline and the scandal of the unlearned ministry. But Grindal's journey south was delayed by illness and he arrived in London only a matter of days before the parliamentary session began. At his installation and enthronement in Canterbury Cathedral he was represented by proxy, and it cannot be proved that he ever visited Canterbury as archbishop.

Meanwhile the 'somewhat' to which Grindal's anonymous correspondent referred was at least attempted. The archbishop headed a committee of lay and spiritual lords which urged the queen to give passage to a bill increasing the fines for recusancy and enforcing participation in the communion: but without success. As for the programme for reform of the church's ministry and discipline, which was initiated in the House of Commons, further high-level negotiations persuaded the queen to refer the entire matter to convocation, 'considering that reformation hereof is to be principally sought in the clergy'. Although in the same message (conveyed to the Commons by Mildmay) Elizabeth declared her commitment 'to the reformation of abuses in the Church' (Neale, 352), this looks like a cynically diversionary move. The canons which emerged from convocation, and which were perhaps all that the queen could tolerate, watered down the parliamentary reform programme, so that even Mildmay would later describe them as 'little or nothing to the purpose' (Collinson, *Elizabethan Puritan Movement*, 163). Trouble was stored up for the parliaments which would follow in 1581 and 1584, with Grindal no longer present to help promote reforms which might have halted the emergent puritan movement in its tracks. But in the months after the prorogation of parliament, the archbishop negotiated with the privy council a radical reform of his court of faculties, a machine for the legalized evasion of church discipline to which Mildmay or another had in the anonymous letter drawn particular attention. And he initiated a review of the state of his other spiritual courts which elicited from his chancellor a report which began: 'In your Grace's Court of Audience, as in all other your courts, so things be out of order that few things be as they should be' (Strype, 307).

**The queen, the archbishop, and the prophesyings** At this point a cloud the size of a man's hand appeared on the horizon, the first sign of the storm which would destroy Grindal's archiepiscopate. In early June 1576 Grindal received letters from the earl of Leicester, Lord Burghley, and Sir Francis Walsingham, all warning him that news had reached court of certain 'disorders' involving preachers in the midlands. The reports concerned what were known as 'exercises of prophesying', a form of scriptural preaching conference borrowed from the Swiss Reformation and adapted as a means of in-house training to convert the pig's ear of the unlearned clergy into the silk purse of a godly preaching ministry; and as a powerhouse of provincial protestantism. The exercises were mostly authorized by the bishops, but not by the queen, who ordered their suppression whenever she heard of them. In the past her orders had been quietly evaded, but Grindal was being warned that now the matter was taken more seriously, and on 12 June, when he went to court, Elizabeth confronted her archbishop with an order to act.

It took two to make the tragedy which was now to happen. Grindal was not one to take evasive action. Instead, he wrote to all his bishops calling for factual and evaluative reports on the exercises. Of the fifteen bishops whose replies are known, only four were hostile, while eight were warmly favourable. Grindal sat down with his chaplains to compose a learned treatise in defence of the prophesyings, but also a set of orders for their tighter regulation. But when a fully briefed Grindal returned to court (and it was now December) he was not heard by a queen who was so incensed against the exercises that 'down she would have them' (Northants. RO, MS F.(M).P.70.c), ordering Grindal by his own authority not only to suppress the prophesyings but to 'abridge' the number of preachers, having expressed the opinion that three or four were enough for a shire.

Instead, Grindal went home to write the famous 6000-word letter, his 'book to the queen', which explained why he could do no such thing. He could not believe that such a strange opinion could enter her head as that it could be good to have few preachers. Preaching was not only the ordinary means of salvation but the best guarantee of order and obedience. As for the exercises, he could not with a safe conscience give his assent to their suppression, still less order it. 'Bear with me, I beseech you, Madam, if I choose rather to offend your earthly Majesty than to offend the heavenly majesty of God'. Grindal's model was some of the epistles of St Ambrose to the emperor Theodosius, which lured him into sentiments more appropriate to the fourth than the sixteenth century. Ambrose had written that palaces belong to emperors, churches to bishops, and had asked what would happen if a bishop was to be taught by a lay person. Elizabeth should leave matters of religion to those who knew about such things, and should not 'use to pronounce so resolutely and peremptorily' as she might do in civil matters: 'Remember, Madam, that you are a mortal creature.' But although this was to borrow from the oration which Ambrose made when he excommunicated Theodosius, there was no question of Grindal excommunicating his sovereign. Rather he offered to surrender the office to which she had appointed him (Nicholson, 376–90). It was an offer which she was strongly inclined to accept.

Quoting Ambrose, Grindal claimed to have written with his own hand, for the queen's eyes only. But whereas no holograph of the letter is known to exist, there are several surviving copies in an identical secretary hand, which suggests that it was in the hands of privy councillors, who may have prevented the queen seeing it for several days (the near fortnight between 8 and 20 December), using the time to propose as a compromise the exclusion of a popular auditory from the exercises: a deal which Grindal refused. After this nothing happened for five months, while Grindal stayed away from court and Burghley and Leicester continued to do their best to save him. But on 7 May the queen herself wrote in the most peremptory terms to the bishops, ordering the suppression of the assemblies called exercises, 'for that the same are not nor have been appointed or warranted by us or our laws' (Nicholson, 467–9). Her order was duly obeyed in Grindal's own diocese, further evidence of the limits on his propensity for defiance. But before the end of the month Grindal was sequestered and confined to Lambeth House, after appearing before the council and refusing to back down: 'a second offence of disobedience, greater than the first' (BL, Harley MS 5176, fol. 95). All the ordinary business of his office was now conducted by the ecclesiastical lawyers. But Elizabeth intended much worse: deprivation, something for which, as Burghley pointed out, there was no obvious precedent.

**Enforced retirement and death** More than legal difficulties troubled Burghley and his colleagues. The Grindal affair happened at a crossroads of Elizabethan policy and at a critical moment for the protestant cause, not only in England but across the North Sea. And it had ramifications. It was a rumour picked up by Elizabeth's early historians that the real cause of the archbishop's troubles was a machination by Dr Julio Borgarucci, physician to both the queen and Leicester, who was also implicated in the plot. Unless Leicester was wholly duplicitous, that was partly false, but perhaps only partly, since Burghley did complain that Dr Julio knew more about what was to happen to Grindal than he did. Borgarucci, whose marital problems required corrupt ecclesiastical justice, may stand for other conservative interests for whom Grindal was bad news. Conversely the archbishop's disgrace sent signals which were utterly discouraging to zealous protestants.

Burghley wrote darkly that to deprive Grindal would mean 'peril'. 'These proceedings cannot but irritate our merciful God' (BL, Add. MS 5935, fol. 68). Another councillor, Sir Francis Knollys, linked Grindal's fate with dangerous developments in the Low Countries and Scotland and the growing threat of Catholicism at home. If he were to be deprived, 'then up starts the pride and practice of the papists' and the political triumph of what he called 'King Richard the Second's men' (BL, Harley MS 6992, fol. 89).

Grindal lived on hope and was soon free to leave Lambeth for his manor at Croydon. But in November things took a turn for the worse. He was to appear before the council in Star Chamber and either to declare his fault or 'receive his deprivation', apparently without further ado or due legal process. The manoeuvres undertaken by the council to prevent this alarming dénouement provide an instructive insight into the complexities of Elizabethan politics. With Grindal refusing to yield so much as an inch, his poor health was eventually the only card left to play with. He repeatedly failed to appear in Star Chamber and even the queen was reluctant to deprive him in his absence. So she had to be content with a propaganda exercise in which Sir Nicholas Bacon addressed an empty chair with a rehearsal of the enormity of Grindal's offence. But of course Elizabeth was not content. Two months later, she made clear her displeasure at the 'daring' of the council in its dealings with Grindal, and Mildmay, of all people, was busy composing a memorandum intended to justify deprivation. But soon the talk turned to resignation, and then, thanks to the helpful intervention of the rising star at court, Sir Christopher Hatton, there was even hope of the archbishop being forgiven. But fresh rumours of puritan disorders in the north, spread by that old enemy Bishop Barnes, provoked another upset, and in the summer of 1578 Grindal was only at the beginning of his long Kafkaesque ordeal.

The intermittent efforts made by Grindal himself and others on his behalf to obtain a royal pardon came to a head in the convocation of Canterbury, meeting in conjunction with the parliament of 1581, a session in which John Whitgift, who was to succeed Grindal, made his mark. The lower house pleaded with the bishops for an initiative through the fluent rhetoric of Toby Mathew, and the bishops themselves addressed the queen on the shame and injury ('detrimentum') caused by the continued incapacity of their metropolitan. All to no avail. Strype's suggestion that Grindal's sequestration was lifted, perhaps early in 1582, is without foundation. The Church of England was bereft of normal metropolitan leadership for the full six years which elapsed between his suspension and his death.

Not that this was reflected in the archbishop's register, since the vicar-general and other officers would have dealt with the routine business in any case, although the metropolitan visitation on which Grindal was embarked at the time of his sequestration was reduced to a formality. Nor were the archbishop's spiritual functions impeded. For example, he continued to participate in the consecration of bishops. And the privy council frequently instructed him to act on a variety of matters 'nothwithstanding your present sequestration' (LPL, Grindal's register, fol. 234*v*). But in many less tangible respects, the archbishop's lack of authority and 'credit' was crippling, and 'reform' was halted in its tracks. By 1581 he was seriously ill and nearly blind. It was this which made the solution of retirement practical politics, although legally this was hardly more straightforward than deprivation. The details, including Grindal's pension, which Burghley thought should be set at £700 or £800, were under discussion through the spring of 1583, and the archbishop even composed a draft of the formal act of resignation. But negotiations were still incomplete when Grindal died on 6 July at Croydon; he was buried there on 1 August. The story told by Whitgift's secretary and first biographer, Sir George Paule, that his master 'utterly refused' to accept the archbishopric on Grindal's resignation, and that the queen declared that 'as she had made him an archbishop, so he should die an archbishop' (Paule, 34–6) is probably an invention.

Grindal's greatest concern in his final days was to place on a secure legal basis the modest educational endowments by which he would wish to be remembered: principally his grammar school at St Bees, and scholarships and fellowships at Pembroke College and Queen's College, Oxford, linked with St Bees. A large portion of his library also went to Queen's, where some eighty volumes, bearing printed labels inserted at the time of the bequest, are still to be found. There were numerous other legacies to servants and relations. But the surprising thing is that this bachelor bishop died worth so little. His total receipts from his three sees in twenty-three years have been roughly calculated at £40,000, whereas his residual estate was probably not worth as much as £4000, less than a single year's income from the see of Canterbury. This contrasts with the fortunes of Grindal's boyhood friend Sandys whose twenty-eight years as a bishop served to establish six of his seven sons (not to speak of his daughters) in the ranks of the gentry, three of them with knighthoods.

**Grindal and posterity** 'Such bishops would have prevented our contentions and wars' was Richard Baxter's verdict on Grindal, two generations on, in the preface to his *Gildas Salvianus* (1656). Others who praised him in the seventeenth century included John Milton, who had little time for the Elizabethan bishops but thought Grindal 'the best of them' (Milton, 15), and William Prynne, who denounced Parker and Whitgift but thought Grindal 'a grave and pious man' (Prynne, 147–9). This is evidence that in this afterlife Grindal had been recruited by the puritans and nonconformists. Daniel Neal in his *History of the Puritans* would call him 'the good old archbishop', 'upon the whole … one of the best of Queen Elizabeth's bishops' (Neal, 1.346–7). Consequently he was to be demonized by the opposite tendency of high Anglicanism as a renegade bishop who had defiled and betrayed the ark of the covenant. In his notorious sermon of 5 November 1709, *The Perils of False Brethren, both in Church and State*, the high-flyer Henry Sacheverell launched a veiled attack on Archbishop Thomas Tenison, not to speak of the ministry of the day, in the character of the original 'false brother' Grindal, 'that false son of the Church', 'a perfidious prelate' by whom Queen Elizabeth had been deluded into granting a toleration for the 'Genevian Discipline' (Collinson, *Grindal*, 18).

Sacheverell was the immediate provocation for the publication, in 1710, of a full-scale life by John Strype, which indeed would probably never have seen the light of day but for a subscription list which included many prominent whig politicians and churchmen. Ralph Thoresby, who was not a whig, conceded that the 'hasting' of Strype's *Life of Grindal* was 'the best effect that Dr Sacheverell's heat has produced' (Hunter, 2.257). Strype's intention was to recover the Grindal who was a son of the Church of England as well as of the Reformation, the very type of 'the good temper and spirit of the true Church of England' (Collinson, *Grindal*, 18).

But for any such purpose, his biography, if it can be called that, was a failure. Strype's way of writing history was merely to stitch together paraphrases of his sources, so that an anonymous critic, who may have been Sacheverell himself, not unfairly called his *Grindal* 'a compendious trifle', written by 'our modern appendix-monger' (*Memorials of Archbishop Grindal*). In the late nineteenth and early twentieth centuries, with a modernized and liberalized kind of high Anglicanism in the intellectual and historiographical ascendancy, it was a version of Sacheverell's Grindal, not Strype's, which stuck, his identifying characteristic, 'weakness'. According to Sir Sidney Lee he 'feebly temporised with dissent' (Acton and others, 3.304). Bishop Mandell Creighton in the *Dictionary of National Biography* found him 'infirm of purpose'. W. H. Frere, another bishop, charged Grindal with a 'natural incapacity for government' (Frere, *English Church*, 192), a phrase echoed by W. P. M. Kennedy, who continued Frere's edition of episcopal visitation articles and injunctions, as 'a constitutional incapacity for administration', Grindal's 'outstanding weakness' (Kennedy, 260). It hardly needs to be said that these judgements rested on no serious investigation of the records of Grindal's administration. But consequently it became a problem to explain how the 'mistake' (Welsby, 1) of appointing such a man should have been made. H. M. Gwatkin had in 1917 attributed it to 'some passing turn of policy' (Gwatkin, 255).

The purpose of Patrick Collinson's *Archbishop Grindal*, published in 1979, was not to 'rehabilitate' the archbishop, which arguably is not the historian's role, but rather to restore a sense of how Grindal was perceived by his contemporaries, which emphatically was not as a weak or incompetent administrator. As for the affair of the prophesyings, the cause of Grindal's downfall and the principal basis of Sacheverell's indictment and of all subsequent negative assessments by Anglican historians, it is now known that the 'exercises' were warmly endorsed by a majority of Grindal's suffragans; that they were not, as such, a piece of 'puritanism'; and that they, rather than Queen Elizabeth's prohibition, pointed forward to the character and tone of the Church of England in the early seventeenth century. That is as much as to say that Grindal had previously been judged by the standards of an Anglicanism which had yet to be invented. So much is clear from the important study by Kenneth Fincham, *Prelate as Pastor: the Episcopate of James I* (1990), although, in a significant correction of Collinson, Fincham points out that Jewel, not Grindal, was the model for the pastoral, evangelical Jacobean episcopate, thanks largely to the influence of Laurence Humphrey's life of Jewel, published in 1573.

PATRICK COLLINSON

**Sources** P. Collinson, *Archbishop Grindal, 1519–1583: the struggle for a reformed church* (1979) · J. Strype, *The history of the life and acts of … Edmund Grindal* (1710); new edn (1821) · W. Nicholson, ed., *The remains of Edmund Grindal*, Parker Society, 9 (1843) · P. Collinson, *Godly people: essays on English protestantism and puritanism* (1983), 19–44, 109–34, 213–44, 245–72, 371–98 · Archbishop Edwin Sandys, memorandum, PRO, SP 15/12/92 · *The works of Nicholas Ridley*, ed. H. Christmas, Parker Society, 1 (1841) · H. Robinson, ed. and trans., *Original letters relative to the English Reformation*, 1 vol. in 2, Parker Society, [26] (1846–7) · [W. Whittingham?], *A brieff discours off the troubles begonne at Franckford* (1575); repr. with introduction by [J. Petherham] as *A brief discourse of the troubles begun at Frankfort* (1846) · H. Robinson, ed. and trans., *The Zurich letters, comprising the correspondence of several English bishops and others with some of the Helvetian reformers, during the early part of the reign of Queen Elizabeth*, 2 vols., Parker Society, 7–8 (1842–5) · *The acts and monuments of John Foxe*, ed. S. R. Cattley, 8 vols. (1837–41) · *Correspondence of Matthew Parker*, ed. J. Bruce and T. T. Perowne, Parker Society, 42 (1853) · D. J. Crankshaw, 'Preparations for the Canterbury provincial convocation of 1562–63: a question of attribution', *Belief and practice in Reformation England: a tribute to Patrick Collinson from his students*, ed. S. Wabuda and C. Litzenberger (1998), 60–93 · CCC Cam., MS 105, art. 11, pp. 201–15 · register of Bishop Edmund Grindal of London, GL, MS 9531/13 · *Registrum Matthei Parker, diocesis Cantuariensis, AD 1559–1575*, ed. W. H. Frere and E. M. Thompson, 1, CYS, 35 (1928) · Vicar General Book 'Huick', LMA · GL, MS 9537/2 · J. H. Hessells, ed., *Ecclesiae Londino-Batavae archivum*, 3 vols. in 4 (1887–97) · F. de Schickler, *Les églises du réfuge en Angleterre*, 3 vols. (Paris, 1892) · J. Hayward, *Annals of the first four years of the reign of Queen Elizabeth*, ed. J. Bruce, CS, 7 (1840) · *A parte of a register* [1593] · W. J. Sheils, ed., *Archbishop Grindal's visitation, 1575: comperta and detecta book* (1977) · act books of the ecclesiastical commission for the province of York, Borth. Inst., HC. AB 5–8 · P. Tyler, *The ecclesiastical commission and Catholicism in the north, 1562–1577* (1960) · P. Collinson, *The Elizabethan puritan movement* (1967); pbk edn (1990) · J. E. Neale, *Elizabeth I and her parliaments*, 1: *1559–1581* (1953) · PRO, state papers Scotland, border papers, SP 59/19, fol. 248v · register of Archbishop Edmund Grindal, LPL · Inner Temple Library, London, MS Petyt 538/54 · LPL, MS 2003 · S. E. Lehmberg, 'Archbishop Grindal and the prophesyings', *Historical Magazine of the Protestant Episcopal Church*, 34 (1965), 87–145 · W. Mildmay, 'The occasion whereupon the displeasure grew from the queen's Majesty to the archbishop of Canterbury', Northants. RO, MS F.(M).P.70.c · BL, Harley MS 5176 · 'Archbishop Grindal's last will and testament', *The remains of Edmund Grindal*, ed. W. Nicholson, Parker Society, 9 (1843), 458–63 · 'Things prepared at the funeral of Edmund Grindal archbishop of Canterbury who died on Saturday 6 July 1583', PRO, state papers domestic, James I, SP 14/89/6 · W. Jackson, 'Archbishop Grindal and his grammar school of St Bees', *Papers and pedigrees mainly relating to Cumberland*, 2, Cumberland and Westmorland Antiquarian and Archaeological Society, extra ser., 6 (1892) · E. Johnston, ed., *Actes du consistoire de l'église française de Threadneedle Street*, Huguenot Society of London, 38 (1937) · G. Paule, *The life of the most reverend and religious prelate John Whitgift* (1698) · BL, Add. MS 5935 · BL, Harley MS 6992 · PRO, state papers domestic, Elizabeth I, SP 12/103/48 · R. Churton, *The life of Alexander Nowell, dean of St Paul's* (1809) · *The writings of John Bradford*, ed. A. Townsend, 1 vol. in 2 pts, Parker Society, 31 (1848–53) · R. Baxter, *Gildas Salvianus* (1656) ·

J. Milton, *Of reformation, touching church discipline in England* (1641) • W. Prynne, *The antipathie of the English lordly prelacie*, 2 vols. (1641) • D. Neal, *The history of the puritans or protestant nonconformists*, ed. J. Toulmin, 5 vols. (1793–7) • H. Sacheverell, *The perils of false brethren, both in church, and state* (1709) • [J. Hunter], ed., *Letters of eminent men, addressed to Ralph Thoresby*, 2 vols. (1832) • *Memorials of Archbishop Grindal* (1710) • J. E. E. D. Acton and others, eds., *The Cambridge modern history*, 14 vols. (1902–12), vol. 3 • W. H. Frere, *The English church in the reigns of Elizabeth and James I* (1904) • W. P. M. Kennedy, *Studies in Tudor history* (1916) • P. A. Welsby, *George Abbot, the unwanted archbishop* (1962) • H. M. Gwatkin, *Church and state in England to the death of Queen Anne* (1917) • K. Fincham, *Prelate as pastor: the episcopate of James I* (1990)

**Archives** BL, corresp. and papers, Harley MSS • Inner Temple, London, corresp. and papers • LPL, corresp. and papers

**Likenesses** oils, *c*.1580, LPL • portrait, versions, 1580, the Deanery, Canterbury [*see illus.*] • Passe, line engraving, BM, NPG; repro. in H. H. [H Holland], *Herōologia Anglica* (1620) • portrait, third version, Old Schools, Cambridge

**Wealth at death** approx. £4000: will

**Grindal, William** (*d.* 1548), royal tutor, was educated at Cambridge University, probably at St John's College, where he graduated BA in 1541/2. Nothing is known about his earlier life, but it is possible that he was related to Edmund Grindal, the future archbishop of Canterbury. During the year 1542/3 he took up a fellowship at St John's College. An excellent Greek scholar, he developed a close friendship with his tutor, Roger Ascham, Greek lecturer there. It was Ascham who, in the summer of 1544, proposed his pupil for a post of Greek reader at St John's, but the fellows voted against him. The disappointed Ascham attributed this to jealousy and spite, and the close relationship between them does seem to have aroused resentment, but it is possible that the tutor's insistent advocacy and conservative northern religious background may each have had a bearing on the rejection of his protégé.

Grindal was finding it difficult to subsist on his fellowship, and Ascham was for a time unable to find a position for him. However, in July 1544 John Cheke, then regius professor in Greek at St John's, left the college to become tutor to Prince Edward; Grindal may also have played a part in the prince's education. Towards the end of 1546, and following representations from Ascham, Cheke was able to secure for Grindal the post of tutor to Princess Elizabeth at Enfield. Grindal, thus elevated, was able to introduce his former tutor to Lady Jane Grey and to Ann Parr, younger sister of Queen Katherine. It seems that Grindal was a good tutor to Elizabeth. Ascham wondered 'to what degree of skill in Latin and Greek she might arrive, if she shall proceed in that course of study wherein she hath begun by the guidance of Grindal', and was uncertain 'whether to admire more the wit of her who learned, or the diligence of him who taught' (Strype, 4–5). But Grindal's career was cut tragically short. He died, unmarried, of the plague in January 1548. Ascham recalled that the loss of William Grindal affected him as keenly as that of his parents. STEPHEN WRIGHT

**Sources** L. V. Ryan, *Roger Ascham* (1963) • Venn, *Alum. Cant.* • Cooper, *Ath. Cantab.* • J. Strype, *The history of the life and acts of the most reverend father in God Edmund Grindal*, new edn (1821) • *The whole works of Roger Ascham*, ed. J. Giles, Lives of Old Authors (1865), vols. 1 and 2 • T. Baker, *History of the college of St John the Evangelist, Cambridge*, ed. J. E. B. Mayor, 2 vols. (1869) • J. Loach, *Edward VI*, ed. G. Bernard and P. Williams (1999), 12

**Likenesses** line engraving, BM, NPG; repro. in T. Fuller, *Abel Redevivus* (1651)

**Grinfield, Edward William** (1785–1864), biblical scholar, was the son of Thomas Grinfield, Moravian minister, and his wife, Anna Joanna, *née* Barham, the daughter of Joseph Foster Barham of Bedford. Thomas *Grinfield (1788–1870) was his brother. He went to school at Wingfield, Wiltshire, where Thomas De Quincey, author of *Confessions of an Opium Eater*, was a schoolmate. He matriculated at Lincoln College, Oxford, on 26 May 1802, and graduated BA in 1806 and MA in 1808. He was ordained a priest in 1808 by the bishop of Lincoln.

After studying at Lincoln's Inn and the Inner Temple, Grinfield became minister of Laura Chapel, Bath. Later he moved to London, where he sometimes preached at Kensington, and where he wrote many theologically conservative pamphlets, articles, and reviews. Among his early works were *Reflections on the Connection of the British Government with the Protestant Religion* (1807), *The Crisis of Religion* (1811), and *Connection of Natural and Revealed Theology* (1818). A staunch defender of the established church and of protestantism, his *Christian Sentiments Suggested by the Present Crisis, or, Civil Liberties Founded upon Self-Restraint* (1831), *Reflections after a Visit to the University of Oxford* (on the Hampden case, 1836), *Sermon on Paley's Exposition of the Law of Honour* (1824), and *The Doctrinal Harmony of the New Testament* all bore witness to his theological and political conservatism, and to his mistrust of modern biblical scholarship and religious pluralism.

Grinfield was particularly alarmed by the spread of dangerous opinions, which he hoped to stem through pamphlets such as *Reflections upon the Influence of Infidelity and Profaneness on Public Liberty, with a Plan for National Circulating Libraries* (1817), *Strictures on Mr. Lancaster's System of Popular Education* (1812), and *Thoughts on Lord Brougham's Education Bill* (1821). His scholarship was mainly in the controversial field of the Septuagint, and included his polemical *Expostulatory Letter to the Right Rev. Bishop Wiseman on the Interpolated Curse in the Vatican Septuagint* (1850) and *An Apology for the Septuagint* (1850). This was followed by *The Jesuits: an Historical Sketch* (1851, 1853) and *The Christian Cosmos: the Son of God, the Revealed Creator* (1856).

In 1859 Grinfield founded and endowed a lectureship on the Septuagint at the University of Oxford. He died at his home, 6 Lower Brunswick Place, Brighton, on 9 July 1864, and was buried in the churchyard at Hove, Sussex. He is presumed to have been married, as letters survive from a son-in-law. N. D. F. PEARCE, *rev.* SINÉAD AGNEW

**Sources** Boase, *Mod. Eng. biog.* • Foster, *Alum. Oxon.* • R. Eden, *The history of preaching* (1880), i–iii • A. H. Japp [H. A. Page], *Thomas de Quincey: his life and writings*, new edn (1890), 16, 81, 260, 261, 451, 512 • *Men of the time* (1862) • Allibone, *Dict.* • Watt, *Bibl. Brit.*

**Wealth at death** under £16,000: probate, 15 Aug 1864, *CGPLA Eng. & Wales*

**Grinfield, Thomas** (1788–1870), Church of England clergyman and hymn writer, son of Thomas Grinfield, a Moravian minister in Bristol, and Anna Joanna Barham, was born at Bath on 27 September 1788, the brother of Edward William *Grinfield. Educated at St Paul's Cray, Kent, and at Trinity College, Cambridge, he proceeded BA in 1812 and MA in 1815, and was ordained deacon in 1813. He married his first cousin, Mildred Foster Barham, and became curate at St Sidwells, Exeter, then rector of Shirland, Derbyshire, from 1827 until his death. Later he lived at Clifton, and was for twenty-three years in charge of St Mary-le-Port, Bristol (from 1847 until his death). He died at his home, 25 Richmond Terrace, Clifton, on 8 April 1870, and was buried in the cemetery at Weston-super-Mare. Studious and contemplative, he was an accomplished scholar and poet. His works included *Epistles and Miscellaneous Poems* (1815), on the themes of fancy, memory, and the beauty of nature, and *The History of Preaching*, edited posthumously (1880), as well as numerous other works on religious themes and several hymns, popular in their day. Besides this, he published a multitude of short poems and lectures. He left several unpublished manuscripts, including a series of theological lectures.

N. D. F. PEARCE, *rev.* SARAH BROLLY

**Sources** Boase, *Mod. Eng. biog.* • Venn, *Alum. Cant.* • J. Julian, ed., *A dictionary of hymnology*, rev. edn (1907) • Crockford (1870) • *CGPLA Eng. & Wales* (1870)

**Wealth at death** under £16,000: resworn probate, Jan 1872, *CGPLA Eng. & Wales* (1870)

**Grisaunt, William** (*supp. fl.* 1350). *See under* English, William (*fl.* 1219–1231).

**Grisewood, Frederick Henry** [Freddie] (1888–1972), broadcaster, was born on 11 April 1888 at Daylesford, Worcestershire, the eldest of three children of the Revd Arthur George Grisewood, rector of Daylesford, and his wife, Lilian Lockwood. He was educated at Radley College and Magdalen College, Oxford (where he gained a pass degree in Greek and Latin moderations in 1908), before studying singing in London, Paris, and Munich. He sang the bass solo part in the first performance in England of I. G. Henschel's Requiem in 1913. Later he gave singing lessons to, among others, Robert Boothby and John Cyril Maude. In 1915 Grisewood married at Writtle (a village which was to play a major role in the early history of broadcasting) Gladys Elizabeth (Betty), the eldest daughter of William Thomas Roffey, a City merchant, of Chelmsford, Essex; they had one daughter.

Grisewood's career was transformed first as a result of war service with the Oxford and Buckinghamshire light infantry—he was invalided out in 1918—and second by the development of broadcasting. It was not until 1923 that he recovered from his war disabilities; it was not until 1929, when he had already broadcast on several occasions as a singer, that he joined the still young British Broadcasting Corporation. Freddie, as he was always known, continued his association with it until the eve of his death, becoming what *The Times* called in his obituary notice 'a well-loved broadcaster'. Grisewood was one of the BBC's best-known personalities, and in 1959 he published *My Story of the BBC*, a popular book on its history. It was interspersed with pictures, many of himself at the microphone.

Frederick Henry Grisewood (1888–1972), by Lenare, 1940

Grisewood applied for a job in the BBC without being interviewed by Sir John Reith, whom he subsequently came greatly to admire. He began his work as an announcer (a versatile occupation at a time when within the BBC there was an unusual blend of formality and improvisation) at Savoy Hill. It was the unexpected, he recalled, that made life worth living; there was much that was unexpected even in *Children's Hour*, in which he was expected to take part. His voice was well known to a growing listening public by the time that he ceased to be an announcer in 1937. Indeed, before then he had taken part in 1931 (as the narrator) in Leslie Bailey's first *Scrapbook*. From announcing Grisewood moved into outside broadcasting, making a new reputation with *The World Goes By* and savouring an entirely new experience as one of the commentators at George VI's coronation. He was technically a freelance, though a very professional one, as he was to be again after 1945. During the Second World War he worked full time first as an announcer in the overseas service and then as the regular speaker in *The Kitchen Front*, a programme originally devised by the Ministry of Food. His voice became as well known at this time as those of J. B. Priestley and Charles Hill. Like theirs, his was distinctive, beautifully modulated, and full of warmth. He also revealed during these war years the sense of humour and the unfailing courtesy that characterized his broadcasting after 1945.

The ability to make people laugh, he maintained, was a priceless asset.

Although Grisewood's sports commentaries were much appreciated and revealed the knowledge and love of sport that he had demonstrated at Radley and Oxford, it was through his role as question-master, an occupation created during the war, that he excelled. The programme series that is most remembered is *Any Questions*, devised in Bristol and first broadcast from Winchester in September 1949. The wartime *The Brains Trust* was one of its begetters, but very soon it established an identity of its own. Grisewood was the perfect chairman, keeping politicians, including the most awkward, in their place, prompting and at the same time cosseting artists, writers, and academics, and always making the newcomer feel at home. The programme series moved after his death out of the west region and into other parts of the country, but under Grisewood's deeply appreciated chairmanship there was a strong rapport between chairman and local west country audiences.

Grisewood was crippled by arthritis in his last years and walked with a stick, but he always seemed cheerful and in the most difficult circumstances even-tempered. Indeed, as he explained in his autobiography, his optimism was profound: 'Good is always coming, though few have at all times the simplicity and courage to believe it' (Grisewood, 256). He was appointed OBE in 1959. After his first marriage was dissolved, he married in 1941 Aileen Croft, sister of one of England's most successful women tennis players and daughter of Edgar Clarkson Scriven, merchantman, of Leeds. Grisewood died on 15 November 1972 in a nursing home in Grayshott, Hampshire. Asa Briggs, *rev.*

**Sources** *The Times* (16 Nov 1972) • *The Times* (20 Nov 1972) • *The Times* (22 Nov 1972) • *Ariel* (24 Nov 1972) • F. H. Grisewood, *The world goes by* (1952) [autobiography] • personal knowledge (1986) • *CGPLA Eng. & Wales* (1973) • A. Briggs, *The history of broadcasting in the United Kingdom*, 4 vols. (1961–79)

**Archives** BBC WAC | FILM BFI NFTVA, documentary footage • BFI NFTVA, performance footage • IWM FVA, actuality footage | SOUND BL NSA, current affairs recording • BL NSA, oral history interview

**Likenesses** Lenare, photograph, 1940, NPG [*see illus.*]

**Wealth at death** £2818: probate, 16 Feb 1973, *CGPLA Eng. & Wales*

**Grisewood, Harman Joseph Gerard** (1906–1997), broadcaster and broadcasting executive, was born on 8 February 1906 at Wormleybury, Broxbourne, Hertfordshire, one of four children of Lieutenant-Colonel Harman Joseph Grisewood of the 4th hussars, who had been secretary of the Anti-Socialist Union, and his wife, Lucille Geneviève, *née* Cardozo. From both sides of the family he inherited 'mixed blood—French, Greek, English, Italian' (Grisewood, 53), a breadth of background which helped spawn a passionate Europeanism. His main childhood home was a thirteenth-century mansion in Thame, Oxfordshire, which suited his parents' devout Roman Catholicism in that it had its own resident priest and chapel, whose bell was rung each day. Once stoned in Thame with his siblings by angry townspeople who hated 'Romish paraphernalia' (ibid., 8), he remained a lifelong Catholic, though his faith co-existed with a broadly liberal outlook. As one of the BBC's most senior mandarins, he argued in 1952 that the BBC had a duty to the 'world of disbelief and doubt and the world of reason as opposed to faith' (Wolfe, 428).

Grisewood went to Ampleforth College, where he grappled with Euclid and went beagling, and Worcester College, Oxford, where he read history and was a keen actor with the Oxford University Dramatic Society (OUDS). He left in 1927 with a pass degree in English literature. His first job consisted of writing the labels for plums in kirsch at Fortnum and Mason, but he was invited by Alan Howland (who had also been at Worcester and prominent in OUDS) to visit him at the BBC in Savoy Hill, where Howland ran *Children's Hour*. Then and there Grisewood was asked to read some of *Ivanhoe* on the air, did so, liked it, and joined the BBC. From 1929 to 1933 he acted on radio, his roles ranging from Tweedledum to Edward II. He was then made an announcer—like his elder cousin Freddie Grisewood of *Any Questions?* fame—before moving on to programme organizing and planning.

In 1941 (when he declined the role of Jesus in Dorothy L. Sayers's ground-breaking *The Man Born to be King*) Grisewood was appointed assistant controller of the European service, a new division based at Bush House and partly run by the shadowy political warfare executive from Woburn Abbey. In 1946 he returned to Broadcasting House and a job in the talks department, where the Soviet spy Guy Burgess had worked for five years, but he resigned in July 1947. This may have been due in part to dislike of certain colleagues, 'so far to the Left as to be real Communists' (Carpenter, 67), and in part to domestic matters: 1947 was the year in which he and his wife, (Clotilde) Margaret Bailey (*b.* *c.*1915), whom he had married on 14 September 1940, produced their only child, Sabina.

Two months after quitting, however, Grisewood returned to the BBC as planner of the Third Programme, which was less than a year old. In 1948 he became its second controller. He spent a total of five happy years at the Third, where his wide-ranging cultural interests were able at last to blossom. Under him the network covered the Festival of Britain and Goethe's bicentenary; carried influential talks by Fred Hoyle, Iris Murdoch, and Gilbert Ryle; broadcast Cecil Day Lewis's new translation of the *Aeneid* and the première of T. S. Eliot's *The Cocktail Party*; and launched *Record Review*, which was still going strong more than fifty years later under the slightly updated title *CD Review*. But like all his successors he tried to 'broaden the appeal of the Third without sacrificing quality' (Carpenter, 85–6), the equivalent of squaring the circle. His series on light music, for example, was supported by Sir Thomas Beecham but sternly opposed by E. M. Forster.

In 1952 Grisewood was promoted to director of the spoken word, responsible for talks, religion, news, and education. The BBC's internal structure eventually made the post 'damned awkward' (Grisewood, 192) and in 1955 it was abolished. Made chief assistant to the director-general in that year, he found himself at the centre of the 1956 Suez row between the government and the BBC. In his autobiography he controversially claimed that William Clark, Eden's press secretary, had told him that 'the

Prime Minister had instructed the Lord Chancellor to prepare an instrument which would take over the BBC altogether and subject it wholly to the will of the government' (ibid., 199). However, this statement 'lacks any independent confirmation, inside or outside the BBC' (Briggs, 95) and Leonard Miall, a former BBC executive, claimed that Clark admitted to him later that he had 'exaggerated the specific plans afoot' (*The Independent*, 10 Jan 1997). Throughout Suez, during which he did much to maintain the BBC's political independence (the director-general, Sir Ian Jacob, being absent at a Commonwealth broadcasting conference in Australia), Grisewood was hobbling about with a stick, laid low by rheumatoid arthritis. He was appointed CBE in 1960.

Grisewood left the BBC in 1964 and briefly joined *The Times* in 1966 under the editorship of his former BBC chief Sir William Haley. He was persuaded to start a diary in the paper, did not take to it, and left after six months. He served on several official bodies, including the Younger committee on privacy and the lord chancellor's committee on defamation. He was the author of several books, including an autobiography, *One Thing at a Time* (1968), and two novels, *The Recess* (1963) and *The Last Cab on the Rank* (1964). He also edited a number of works by his friend the Welsh poet and painter David Michael Jones. He spent his last years living at the Old School House, Castle Hill, Eye, Suffolk, where he died of heart failure on 8 January 1997. He was survived by his wife, Margaret, from whom he was separated, and by their daughter. PAUL DONOVAN

**Sources** H. Grisewood, *One thing at a time: an autobiography* (1968) • H. Carpenter, *The envy of the world: fifty years of the BBC Third Programme and Radio 3, 1946–1996* (1996) • K. M. Wolfe, *The churches and the BBC, 1922–1956* (1984) • A. Briggs, *The history of broadcasting in the United Kingdom*, rev. edn, 5 (1995) • *The Times* (11 Jan 1997) • *The Independent* (10 Jan 1997) • *The Independent* (20 Jan 1997) • *WWW* [forthcoming] • b. cert. • m. cert. • d. cert.

**Archives** BBC WAC | Bodl. Oxf., corresp. with William Clark • Georgetown University, Washington, corresp. with David Jones, Rene Hague, and Christopher Sykes; letters to Christopher Sykes • Yale U., Beinecke L., corresp. with David Jones | SOUND BBC, oral history project

**Likenesses** D. Jones, portrait, 1932, NMG Wales; repro. in *The Independent* (10 Jan 1997) • photograph, repro. in *The Times* • photograph, repro. in *The Independent* (10 Jan 1997) • photographs, repro. in Grisewood, *One thing at a time*

**Wealth at death** under £180,000: probate, 14 Feb 1997, *CGPLA Eng. & Wales*

**Grisi, Giulia** (1810?–1869), singer, was born in Milan, probably on 22 May 1810, the daughter of Gaetano Grisi, a surveyor officer in Napoleon's army, and his wife, Giovanna Grassini. Her aunt and sister were famous opera singers. After convent schooling at Gorizia she undertook vocal studies in Bologna, where she made her début in the autumn of 1828 in a minor part in Rossini's *Zelmira*. Under a six-year contract with the impresario Alessandro Lanari she sang in Florence, Pisa, and Milan, becoming known for the extraordinary beauty of voice and person. In 1832 she fled to Paris. This breach debarred her from ever again singing opera in Italy; the Lanari contract, though disadvantageous, had been renegotiable at intervals. However, she went on to launch a great career in Paris, where she made her début in October 1832, and in London, from March 1834. She appeared each year in both cities, missing London in 1842 and dropping regular Paris appearances after 1848. Italian opera meant a largely imported repertory: the only well-remembered new parts she created after Adalgisa in Bellini's *Norma* (Milan, 1831; he thought her 'cold') were Elvira in his *I puritani* (1835), which established her, Rubini, Tamburini, and Lablache as a matchless quartet, and Norina in Donizetti's *Don Pasquale* (1843). Her acting ability developed slowly; as Norma she struck some as too violent.

**Giulia Grisi** (1810?–1869), by François Bouchot, 1840

Grisi's marriage on 24 April 1836 to Auguste Gérard de Melcy failed. In 1838 he wounded in a duel her lover Viscount Castlereagh (later marquess of Londonderry) (1805–1872), with whom she had a son, George Frederick Ormsby; a legal separation, probably in 1844, gave Gérard a lifelong share of her earnings. In 1841, however, she had formed a relationship with the tenor Mario (G. B. de Candia; 1810–1883). Ostensibly married, the couple had six daughters, three of whom died young. They often appeared together, famously in *Lucrezia Borgia*, *Les Huguenots*, and *Il trovatore*. In 1847 they led the secession from Her Majesty's to establish the Royal Italian Opera at Covent Garden.

Grisi dominated London opera until her first retirement (1854). Though matronly and worn of voice, she remained handsome; after an American tour she returned to Covent Garden, retired again in 1861, then, because she and Mario had overspent, made a last provincial tour and an unsuccessful London appearance in 1866. She died at the Hôtel du Nord in Berlin of pneumonia on 29 November 1869, and was buried on 2 December in the Père Lachaise cemetery, Paris. The renowned *Times* critic J. W. Davison commented that 'no foreign singer ever kept so firm a hold on the affections of the English public' (*Mendelssohn to Wagner*, 474–5). JOHN ROSSELLI

**Sources** E. Forbes, *Mario and Grisi* (1985) • W. Beale, *The light of other days*, 2 vols. (1890) • H. S. Edwards, *The prima donna*, 2 vols. (1888) • H. F. Chorley, *Thirty years' musical recollections*, 2 vols. (1862) • *From Mendelssohn to Wagner: being the memoirs of J. W. Davison, forty years the music critic of The Times*, ed. H. Davison (1912) • A. Soubies, *Le Théâtre-Italien de 1801 à 1913* (1913) • L. Arditi, *My reminiscences*, ed. Baroness von Zedlitz, 2nd edn (1896) • H. Rosenthal, *Two centuries of opera at Covent Garden* (1958) • M. De Angelis, ed., *Le cifre del melodramma*, 2 vols. (1982) • Mrs G. Pearse and F. Hird, *The romance of a great singer* (1910) • *The Times* (30 Nov 1869)
**Archives** Museo Teatrale alla Scala, Milan • Royal Opera House, London | Archives Nationales, Paris, archives du Théâtre National de l'Opéra, papers of the Édouard Robert-Carlo Severini management of the Théâtre-Italien • Biblioteca Nazionale Centrale, Florence, Fondo Lanari, papers of Alessandro Lanari • Biblioteca Nazionale Centrale, Florence, corresp. and papers of Alessandro Lanari
**Likenesses** R. J. Lane, lithograph, pubd 1836 (after A. E. Chalon), BM, NPG • F. Bouchot, portrait, 1840, Royal Academy of Music, London [*see illus.*] • C. F. Fuller, marble bust, 1858, Royal College of Music • J. C. Armytage, engraving (after photograph after Barsan), repro. in E. C. Clayton, *Queens of song*, 2 vols. (1863), vol. 2, frontispiece • Caldesi, photograph, priv. coll. • Princess Victoria, drawing, Royal Arch. • E. Walker, engraving (after oil portrait), repro. in Pearse and Hird, *Romance of a great singer* • oils, repro. in Mrs G. Pearse, *The enchanted past* (1926) • print (after drawing after Lord Leighton), repro. in Forbes, *Mario and Grisi* (1985), 50–51 • print, repro. in Forbes, *Mario and Grisi*
**Wealth at death** earned large sum but lived expensively; houses and staff in three countries; Paris house sold just before death (1868)

**Grisoni, Giuseppe** (1699–1769). *See under* Venetian painters in Britain (*act.* 1708–*c.*1750).

**Grissell, Thomas** (1801–1874), public works contractor, was born on 4 October 1801 at Stockwell, Surrey, the eldest of the nine children of Thomas De la Garde Grissell (1778–1847) of the East India Company's service, and his wife, Ann (*d.* 1847), daughter of James Peto of Godalming, Surrey. He was educated at St Paul's School, London, with the intention of his entering the medical profession, but in 1815 Grissell was articled to his uncle Henry Peto, perhaps at that time the country's principal public works contractor (his partner having died the previous year). Ten years later, when the collapse of part of his work on the London custom house discredited Peto, Grissell was admitted partner. On his uncle's death in 1830 he succeeded to a half share in the business and estate, together with his cousin Samuel Morton *Peto, who married Grissell's sister Mary. In the highly competitive building world of the 1830s their business rapidly secured a position as the leading public works contractor. Grissell's business ethos was summed up in his motto 'Press forward'.

Grissell and Peto ran a vertically integrated business, controlling all operations from stone quarrying to the provision of fittings for their buildings, and employing a highly disciplined workforce under capable foremen; this enabled them to exploit the advantages of the system of lump-sum contracting then coming into vogue. Grissell claimed to have introduced important innovations in building technique also, such as the use of the 'whole timber' scaffolding, braced and bolted, that could support a travelling crane powered by a steam engine. The partners obtained the commission for Charles Barry's Birmingham grammar school (1833–5), and then in London that for Hungerford market at £42,400, which proved very remunerative. Nelson's Column, the Reform, Conservative, and Oxford and Cambridge clubs, and Clerkenwell Prison followed, as well as a number of churches. They built the Lyceum Theatre in sixteen weeks, and the St James's in ten. The large breweries and fire offices provided regular work, and the partners netted an average £11,000–£12,000 per annum on a capital of £50,000.

They also engaged in the new field of railway construction, undertaking part of the Great Western Railway, including the Hanwell Viaduct, much of the South Eastern Railway, and extensive works under Robert Stephenson, as well as improvements in the Severn navigation under the civil engineer William Cubitt. However, according to Peto, Grissell 'did not like the risks involved in the large railway undertakings, which needed large capital', so when the partnership was dissolved on 2 March 1846 he took over 'the building business, saw-mills, and premises', and the Severn contract, a stock-in-trade and plant that Peto calculated at £150,000, 'including houses built and building for the firm' (presumably on a speculative basis), 'and, besides, he will have a large and *abundant* capital in money' (Peto, 13, 16).

Most notably, however, the firm had won successive contracts for the new Houses of Parliament between 1839 and 1850, work supervised entirely by Grissell, and from 1846 in his sole name. The first two contracts, for the river front, were lump-sum, but subsequently the architect, Charles Barry, recommended that further contracts should be based on a schedule of prices. Grissell leased quarries for Cornish granite and for the Anston stone employed for the facing, and successfully contended with a serious masons' strike in 1841, caused by the relentless regime of his foreman. But in 1845, with more than a thousand of his men on site, he sought to terminate his contract for woodwork because it was financially unsatisfactory: Barry calculated that an upward revision of prices would still yield only eight or nine per cent profit. Signature of the revised contract was to be long delayed because Grissell was unwilling to accept responsibility for fire risk—a serious consideration since work was being pressed on by candlelight—and objected to the architect's attempt to control the subcontracting habitual in the traditional craft organization of the industry. (Even Grissell's highly integrated building service could not embrace trades of which he seldom had need, ironwork in particular being subcontracted to his nephew at the Regent's Canal ironworks.) By the end of 1851, Grissell found his prices barely remunerative for the 'most unusual and elaborate work', with its 'extraordinary quality of the workmanship' (PRO Work 11/6/5, fol. 91), but the office of works none the less believed it might be executed more cheaply (and secured a 30 per cent reduction from a new contractor), so that to Grissell's disappointment he was unable to complete the Houses of Parliament. As associate of the Institution of Civil Engineers from 1843 (when he was also elected fellow of the Society of Antiquaries), Grissell served on its council in 1845, and in 1846 constructed at cost a lecture room for the institution to T. H. Wyatt's designs.

Few of the architects who employed him could live on the scale achieved by Grissell. From about 1847 he lived at 19 Kensington Palace Gardens, one of a pair of mansions designed in Barry's office and built by Grissell's own firm using surplus stone from the Houses of Parliament; he employed a domestic staff of nine, including two footmen. In 1850 he bought Norbury Park, a Georgian estate in Surrey (which he was to entail on his descendants), and commenced life as a country gentleman and county magistrate, becoming high sheriff in 1854. He also held a directorate of the Western Life Office.

Grissell's first wife, Sarah Bensley, whom he married on 8 May 1825, died in childbirth in 1829, leaving two sons surviving; two years later, on 2 April 1831, he married Eliza (1798–1863), daughter of John Marklow and widow of John Sheen, with whom he had four more sons, two of whom died young: Hartwell (1839–1907) became a Roman Catholic and chamberlain of honour to the Pope. Grissell, a keen upholder of his family connections, bequeathed as heirlooms for Norbury Park a number of paintings and sculptures by Italian and English masters, including his own portrait by Henry William Pickersgill. In his last years he altered bequests to some of his children in no fewer than eight codicils to his will. He died at Norbury Park on 26 May 1874 and was buried in Mickleham, Surrey. Among his legacies were £5000 to his nephew Henry Peto (son of his late partner), £1000 for a new Anglican church nearby at West Humble and £250 to the Institute of British Architects to fund a medal for the best set of drawings in constructive architecture by a young architect.

M. H. PORT

**Sources** *PICE*, 39 (1874–5), 289–90 • T. Grissell, 'Account of the scaffolding used in erecting the "Nelson Column", Trafalgar Square', *PICE*, 3 (1844), 203–17 • M. H. Port, ed., *The Houses of Parliament* (1976) • Burke, *Gen. GB* (1937) • will of Thomas Grissell, PR, 25 June 1874, Principal Registry of the Family Division, London • census returns for London, 1851, 1861, 1871 • H. Peto, *Sir Morton Peto: a memorial sketch* (1893) • *CGPLA Eng. & Wales* (1874) • d. cert. • Work 11/6/5, PRO, fols. 12, 91

**Likenesses** H. W. Pickersgill, portrait; bequeathed to Norbury Park, Surrey • Wyon, bust; bequeathed to Norbury Park, Surrey

**Wealth at death** under £200,000: double probate, April 1875, *CGPLA Eng. & Wales*

**Grocyn, William** (1449?–1519), cleric and Greek scholar, was son of a tenant of Winchester College at Colerne, Wiltshire, and lived as a boy in the parish of St Nicholas, Bristol. Scholar of Winchester College on 26 September 1463, he took the statutory oath there on 17 January 1465. Admitted scholar of New College, Oxford, on 7 September 1465 and elected fellow in 1467, he was tutor to William Warham, later archbishop of Canterbury and Grocyn's patron. Grocyn was MA by 1474; he may have been scribe to the university in 1476 and may have taught for Lincoln College, by whom he was paid 40s. in 1477. In June 1491 he was admitted BTh.

In March 1481 Grocyn resigned his fellowship, having been presented on 19 February to the New College living of Newton Longville, Buckinghamshire, which he had vacated by December 1504: a commemorative brass was placed in the church by New College in the late nineteenth century. He was canon of Lincoln and prebendary of South Scarle from 7 October 1485 (vacated by May 1514); rector of Debden, Essex (9 December 1492; vacated by May 1493); rector of Shepperton, Middlesex (5 December 1504; vacated by April 1513); and rector of East Peckham, Kent (20 December 1511; vacated by December 1517). His most important preferments were to the living of St Lawrence Jewry in London (26 December 1496; resigned 28 May 1517); and to the mastership of the College of All Saints, Maidstone, Kent (from 17 April 1506 until his death).

Grocyn was divinity reader at Magdalen College in 1483. As respondent to Master John Taylor in a theological disputation before Richard III and Bishop Waynflete in the college hall, on 25 July, he received a gift of money and a buck. In March 1488 he vacated this readership and left Oxford for Italy, to improve his Latin and the Greek he had probably begun to learn. Little is certain about Grocyn's early knowledge of Greek except that he would have had the opportunity to learn it from the 1460s onwards, that he signed his name in Greek characters in the university letter-book in 1476, and that the *Dictionary of National Biography*'s statement that he could have learned it from Cornelio Vitelli from 1475 is unfounded. Vitelli may have been in Oxford in 1482–6, and is first securely documented in England in 1489–90. William Latimer and Erasmus in 1517 as well as George Lily, son of Grocyn's godson William Lily, in 1548 indicate that Grocyn knew at least the rudiments before departure. He studied in Florence with Angelo Poliziano and Demetrius Chalcondyles, for at least two years according to Latimer who, with Thomas Linacre, was his fellow student. Through the Florentine humanists he knew Girolamo Aleandro and Aldus Manutius; the German humanist and Hebraist Johann Reuchlin is said to have been his friend and Erasmus's great Basel printer Johann Froben sent him greetings. A letter to Aldus, dated from London on 27 August, prefacing Linacre's Latin translation of Pseudo-Proclus's *De sphaera*, in *Astronomici veteres* (Venice, October 1499) is Grocyn's only published work, though Fuller's *Worthies* in 1662 records the Latin epigram on Julia, who threw a snowball at her lover, first attributed to him by John Bale (Riese, 706). Aldus praises Grocyn's Latin and Greek learning; Grocyn's letter thanks Aldus for kindness to Linacre, Aldus's helper with his Aristotle (1495–8); he congratulates Aldus on leaving the flighty Plato (*polymythe* [*sic*]) aside in favour of the learned philosopher (*polymathe* [*sic*]).

Grocyn returned to Oxford by 2 June 1491, rented a room

in Exeter College from Hilary term 1491 to Trinity term 1493, and gave the first Greek public lectures to the university. Erasmus, visiting England for the first time in 1499, found him associated with John Colet, Thomas Linacre, and Thomas More; he was amazed at the intellectual level of this outpost of learning and Grocyn's universal scholarship. Colet had then been lecturing in Oxford on the Pauline epistles and studying the works attributed to Paul's convert Dionysius, with whom Grocyn also occupied himself. A letter from London by Thomas More relates that More's preceptor Grocyn, who was also, he wrote in 1504, the sole guide of his life in Colet's absence, began a well-attended lecture series in St Paul's Cathedral on the Dionysian *Celestial Hierarchy*. This letter is datable by its reference to the 'recent' ceremonial entry into London of Katherine of Aragon (12 November 1501). More says nothing of Lorenzo Valla's demonstration that the author of the *Celestial Hierarchy* and the *Ecclesiastical Hierarchy* was not St Paul's convert of Acts 17: 31. Knowledge of this was not current in northern Europe until Erasmus, finding in 1504 a manuscript of Valla's *Collatio novi testamenti* as Valla had revised it in the 1450s, had it printed in 1505. In 1516 Erasmus aroused clerical indignation by citing Valla in his *Annotations* on the New Testament; and in his second edition of 1519 he added the extra authority of Grocyn, who had 'many years ago' begun to lecture on the *Celestial Hierarchy* at St Paul's, and been won in mid-course to the revisionist opinion (that is, of Valla and Erasmus). In his *Supputatio calumniarum natalis Bedae* of 1526 Erasmus repeated this testimony, and in his *Declarationes ad censuras Lutetiae vulgatas* of 1532, asserted that Grocyn had followed Valla 'thirty years ago'. Erasmus's references have been conflated to make Grocyn a sceptic about the apostolicity of Pseudo-Dionysius, and the lectures given at Colet's invitation. Colet, however, was not dean until 1504–5 and there is no evidence that he acted for the incumbent before 1503. About Dionysius he seems to have remained a traditionalist. Grocyn may have accepted the up-to-date view; there is no evidence beyond Erasmus's statements, much later, that he did so before Erasmus's discovery, or that Colet invited Grocyn to preach in St Paul's at any time.

By 1501 Grocyn must have been established in London, though the exact date of his removal there is uncertain. Erasmus wrote to Germain de Brie (Brixius) in 1520 that Thomas More learned Greek from Grocyn and Linacre; More himself mentions Linacre only. In Oxford Grocyn may have known and taught William Lily, his godson whom he remembered in his will, and Richard Croke, his 'pupil-servant'; he may also later have introduced Erasmus's pupil-servant Henry Bullock to him. Erasmus lodged with Grocyn gratis during his visit in 1506, when Grocyn introduced him to Warham at Lambeth. On Grocyn's advice Erasmus dedicated to Warham his translation of Euripides' *Hecuba*, and Warham paid him for it. When Grocyn asked Erasmus how much, Erasmus teased and nettled him into a retort ungracious enough to make Erasmus offer Warham the dedication of his *Iphigenia* also and to tell the story nearly twenty years later. During 1509–11 Erasmus may have been Grocyn's guest; in 1511, when he departed for Cambridge, he took with him on loan Grocyn's copy of St Basil on Isaiah. He was embarrassed at being able to make no return for such hospitality.

Like many Tudor humanists Grocyn owed much of his European reputation to Erasmus. In his own right he had the respect and affection of his learned English contemporaries and juniors. His name, with those of Colet, More, Cuthbert Tunstal, Hugh Oldham, John Yonge, and others, is recorded in the admissions book of Doctors' Commons in London, though he never signed. His death is recorded there. Praises of the breadth and almost pedantic depth of his learning, his Latinity, his theology, his goodness, and generosity recur in letters by Erasmus to Aldus, Germain de Brie, Guillaume Budé (Budaeus), Colet, John and Robert Fisher, Latimer, Linacre, Richard Pace, Joost Vroye (Gaverius), and Roger Wentford, who obtained for Erasmus in 1518 some New Testament notes of Grocyn. Beatus Rhenanus echoes these praises. Letters to Erasmus from Latimer and More mention him, and More cites him in his *Letter to a Monk* as a guarantor of Erasmus's worth (1519). In 1517 Erasmus warns Latimer by Grocyn's example of excessive scholarly modesty; in 1528 he makes Grocyn a laconic but polished Ciceronian, who had preferred not to ruin already defective eyesight by writing. He was much gratified in 1500 because the trustworthy Grocyn had agreed to distribute in England 100 copies of his *Adagia*. To Aldus in 1506 he values Grocyn's approbation of his Euripides translations and in 1524 calls the now dead Grocyn to witness that these were indeed his own work. Grocyn's disablement by paralysis late in life grieved him, as he wrote to Warham, John Fisher, Colet, and Pace, adding that their relations had not always been all they might.

After his appointment to the College of All Saints Grocyn spent much time in Maidstone, where he apparently was when he suffered his stroke in 1518. He died there in 1519, between 2 June, when he made his will (proved by his executor and residuary legatee Linacre on 20 July 1522), and October. In 1516 the will of Dr John Yonge, master of the rolls, restored to him 'without any manner of redemption' his plate, which he had given in security for a loan. While master of All Saints' he brought suit against Sir Thomas Kempe, concerning Tremworth Manor and the advowson of Crundale, Kent. He was buried in All Saints', Maidstone.

In religion and philosophy Grocyn was conservative. His forward-looking Greek and Latin attainments, if eclipsed by the succeeding generation, and his remarkable library of manuscripts and printed books, recoverable partly from an inventory written by Linacre after his death, make him with Linacre the most significant of the earliest Tudor humanists. Among the many classical authors he owned are those newly discovered in the fifteenth century; there are many fathers, some scholastic philosophy, and canon law. The notable Latin humanist leaven is almost entirely Italian: Petrarch's *Rerum memorandarum libri*, Valla's annotations on the New Testament and the

Psalms and his *Elegantiae*, Francesco Filelfo, Aeneas Sylvius Piccolomini, Ermolao Barbaro, Marsilio Ficino, Pietro Crinito, Nicolò Perotti's and Calepino's dictionaries. Erasmus's printed bilingual New Testament and *Adagia* both figure, as does Robert Gaguin's *De gestis Francorum*. Grocyn's Greek library, mostly manuscript, was the best in Britain. Over thirty books are now in Corpus Christi College, Oxford, some having been bought by the college at the prompting of John Claymond, its first president, others received by bequest from him: Plato, Pseudo-Dionysius (also in Latin) and other Neoplatonists, Aristotle (including the Aldine edition), Julius Pollux and the *Suda*, Demosthenes, Thucydides, Euclid, Ptolemy, Origen, St Basil, much St John Chrysostom, and Theophylact. Some have an Italian provenance; some were written between 1499 and 1500, perhaps for Grocyn, in Reading by the Greek scribe Joannes Serbopoulos. Two others of Grocyn's Greek books are in New College, and one in Liverpool. J. B. TRAPP

**Sources** Emden, *Oxf.* • will, 20 July 1522, PRO, PROB 11/19/30 • A. M. Burrows, 'Linacre's catalogue of Grocyn's books, followed by a memoir of Grocyn', *Collectanea: second series*, ed. A. M. Burrows, OHS, 16 (1890), 319–24 • *The correspondence of Erasmus*, ed. and trans. R. A. B. Mynors and others, 22 vols. (1974–94) • *Erasmus's annotations on the New Testament: Acts, Romans, I and II Corinthians*, ed. A. Reeve (1990) • *Desiderii Erasmis Roterodami opera omnia*, ed. J. Leclerc, 9 (Leiden, 1706), 446D, 676A–B, 917B–C • D. Erasmus, 'Dialogus Ciceronianus', ed. P. Mesnard, in *Opera omnia Desiderii Erasmi Roterodami*, 1/2 (Amsterdam, 1971), 581–710, esp. 676 • D. Erasmus, '"The Ciceronianus": a dialogue on the ideal Latin style: *Dialogus Ciceronius*', trans. B. I. Knott, *Literary and educational writings*, 6, ed. A. H. T. Levi (1986), vol. 28 of *Collected works of Erasmus*, ed. W. K. Ferguson and others (1974–), 323–448 • *The correspondence of Sir Thomas More*, ed. E. F. Rogers (1947), letters 2, 3, 15, 67, 83 • T. More, *In defense of humanism*, ed. D. Kinney (1986), 15, 102–3, 208–9 • LPL, MS S. R. 136, fol. 11 • F. Maddison, M. Pelling, and C. Webster, eds., *Essays on the life and works of Thomas Linacre, c.1460–1524* (1977) [index s.v. Grocin] • R. Weiss, *Humanism in England during the fifteenth century*, 3rd edn (1967) • J. K. McConica, *English humanists and Reformation politics under Henry VIII and Edward VI* (1965) • P. O. Kristeller, *Iter Italicum*, 7 vols. (1963–97), vol. 4, no. 51a • P. G. Bietenholz and T. B. Deutscher, eds., *Contemporaries of Erasmus: a biographical register*, 2 (1986), 135–6 • J. I. Catto, 'Scholars and studies in Renaissance Oxford', *Hist. U. Oxf.* 2: *Late med. Oxf.*, 769–84, esp. 780–81 • N. R. Ker, 'The provision of books', *Hist. U. Oxf.* 3: *Colleg. univ.*, 441–77, esp. 458–9, pl. XIVB • J. B. Trapp, *Erasmus, Colet and More: the early Tudor humanists and their books* (1991), 103–13 • A. Riese, ed., *Anthologia latina, sive, Poesis latinae supplementum: pars prior, carmina in codicibus scripta*, 2 (Leipzig, 1906)

**Wealth at death** see will, 20 July 1522, PRO, PROB 11/19/30

**Groenevelt, Joannes** (*bap.* **1648**, *d.* **1715/16**), physician and surgeon, was baptized on 14 May 1648 in the Reformed church of Deventer in the Dutch province of Overijssel; he was the only surviving son of Frans Groenevelt and Goedekin ter Klocken. In mid-January 1666 he matriculated into the well-regarded local 'Illustre School'; in September 1667 he matriculated in medicine at the University of Leiden. Apparently because of the epidemic that occurred in Leiden at the end of the summer of 1669, which forced the university to close for a time, Groenevelt migrated to Utrecht to complete his medical studies, defending his thesis, 'De calculo vesicae', and taking his degree, on 18 March 1670. Perhaps after a visit to France, Groenevelt moved to Amsterdam, where he joined the Collegium Medicum and married Cristina de Ruijter (*c*.1650–1713) on 4 March 1672. He also entered into a joint practice with the Amsterdam city surgeon Henricus Velthuys, who had an especially good reputation for surgically removing bladder stones. When Velthuys died in May 1674 he left his instruments to Groenevelt, and urged him to take up surgical practice himself.

Groenevelt may have served as physician to the newly liberated Dutch garrison at Grave in October 1674. Then, late in the year, or early in 1675, he and his wife arrived in London. On 5 May 1675 their first child, Franciscus, was baptized at the Dutch church at Austin Friars, and on 24 June Groenevelt obtained his papers of denization from the English crown. Another son, Elias, was baptized at Austin Friars on 4 November 1677, and a daughter, Christina, on 2 April 1679. The family resided in Throgmorton Street, just around the corner from the church. Groenevelt published a version of his medical thesis as *Lithologia: a Treatise of the Stone and Gravel* (1677). In the spring of 1682 he helped the Royal Society to publish an important work by one of his old friends from Deventer, Willem ten Rhijne. He joined the Royal College of Physicians, London, on 2 April 1683 as a licentiate, and in 1684 published his *Dissertatio lithologica*, which became well regarded in England and on the continent, with a second edition in 1687. In 1686 he signed a contract with John Browne, surgeon to St Thomas's Hospital, London, to train him in removing bladder stones using his methods (although Browne brought suit in 1687 for breach of contract, with Groenevelt counter-suing). On 12 August 1687 Groenevelt joined with four other licentiates of the college in the 'repository', a group practice in King's Street, where they took turns seeing patients and selling medications from a large stock they collected and compounded on site; each also took it in turn to visit the sick in their homes for one week. To bring in custom, the group published *The Oracle for the Sick* (1687), which contained a series of medical questions mimicking the questions that a doctor would ask on seeing a patient, which could be filled out and sent to the repository through the penny post system; remedies and instructions on use would be sent in return. The members of the Repository practice drew censures from the Royal College of Physicians, but they seem to have prospered. Groenevelt also published *Arthritology, or, A Discourse of the Gout* (1691), in which he claimed to have found a new and better way of treating gout and the many other diseases caused by faults in the juices of the blood.

It may have been hearing of Groenevelt's new remedy that caused Suzanna Withall to seek his assistance in the summer of 1693; but on 27 July 1694 she and supporting witnesses complained to the censors of the Royal College of Physicians that his pills had left her an invalid. The censors found him guilty of malpractice for giving cantharides internally, but one of the censors, Edward Tyson, prevented them from exacting a penalty. Further internal troubles in the college caused delays, but in April 1697 the censors fined Groenevelt £20 and sent him to Newgate prison. Groenevelt obtained release on habeas corpus, and permanent freedom because of the general pardon of William III after the death of Queen Mary. Supported by the London apothecaries and surgeons, he fought the censors by charging them in court with not having taken the necessary oaths, sued them for false imprisonment, and engaged in a publicity battle with them via pamphlets and the newspapers. The censors in turn helped Mrs Withall bring a civil suit against Groenevelt for £2000, although the jury found him not guilty at the conclusion of a six-hour trial on 7 December 1697. Groenevelt then sought further vindication by publishing *De tuto cantharidum in medicina usu interno* (1698). The case he had lodged against the censors became an issue in the House of Lords in the spring of 1698; his suit for false imprisonment failed in king's bench in June 1700, but created important precedent by placing courts such as the college's under the supervision of the courts of common law. Even though he was found not guilty, Groenevelt's practice declined, and in 1703 he also became deeply embroiled on the losing side of a bitter dispute within the church of Austin Friars. By 1710 he was rumoured to be going blind and to have shaking hands; he could no longer pay his dues to the college, and in December he became an object of its charity. His children had all died, and his wife apparently returned to Amsterdam, where she was buried in December 1713. Groenevelt tried to restore his reputation with *A Compleat Treatise of the Stone and Gravel* (1710), and wrote a medical textbook, *Fundamenta medicinae scriptoribus* in 1714, apparently for money. In 1714 he moved to St John's Priory, where he died, being buried outside the church of St James's, Clerkenwell on 15 January 1716.

HAROLD J. COOK

**Sources** letters of Groenevelt, BL, Sloane collection, 2729, various folios • L. Celer, *The late censors deservedly censured; and their spurious litter of libels against Dr Greenfield, and others, justly expos'd to contempt* (1698) [Lysiponius Celer may be Groenevelt's pseudonym] • *The oath taken by the censors, who are the examiners of the college, before the president and the college, upon the day of their admission into their office* [n.d., 1700?] • *Reasons humbly offered to the right honourable, the Lords spiritual and temporal in parliament, assembled, why Dr Thomas Burwell, Dr Richard Torlesse, Dr William Dawes, and Dr Thomas Gill…should not be excused from the penalty of the act 25 Car. II* [1700] • *A reply to the reasons against the censors of the college of physicians; for not qualifying themselves according to the statute of 25 Car. II* [n.d., 1698?] • *A reply to the remarks upon the reasons, why the late censors should not be excus'd from the penalty of the 25 Car. II vindicating the reasons, and shewing the fallacy of the remarks* [n.d., 1697?] • H. J. Cook, *Trials of an ordinary doctor: Joannes Groenevelt in 17th-century London* (1994)

**Archives** BL, letters • CL • Gemeente archief, Amsterdam • Gemeente archief, Deventer • Gemeente archief, Zutphen • Guildhall, London • LMA • PRO • RCP Lond.

**Grogan, Cornelius** (1738–1798), Irish nationalist, was probably born in Johnstown, Wexford, Ireland, the third child and eldest surviving son of John Grogan (1716–1783), landowner, of Johnstown Castle, Wexford, and his wife, Catherine Knox (*b.* 1720), daughter and heir of Major Andrew Knox of Rathmacknee Castle. A member of the established Church of Ireland, he succeeded to the family estates on the death of his father in 1783. He was high sheriff of co. Wexford and from 1783 to 1790 he represented Enniscorthy in the Irish parliament. A wealthy and enterprising landlord, he was a major shareholder in the first Wexford Bridge, a toll bridge built by the American Lemuel Cox in 1795. In July 1786 *Walker's Hibernian Magazine* reported his marriage to Rebecca Frost of co. Wexford, who was probably his housekeeper. They had at least one child.

Grogan was a popular and prominent figure of outspoken liberal views who, in common with other co. Wexford landlords, such as the Colcloughs, the Harveys of Bargy Commons, and the Hattons of Clonard House, was well respected by his Catholic tenants. From as early as 1779 he and Beauchamp Bagenal Harvey supported William Hatton and others of the liberal protestant faction who welcomed co-operation with the Catholic population over the formation of the volunteers. He was sympathetic to the cause of the Catholic convention and was one of 'the virtuous and independent forty-five' who voted against the protestant ascendancy's intransigence over Catholic relief at the meeting of the grand jury in Wexford on 22 September 1792. He joined the Society of United Irishmen, of which his peers in co. Wexford, like Harvey, John Colclough, John Boxwell, and Henry Hughes, were early adherents. In 1794 the society veered sharply towards armed revolution as the only means of achieving its political aims. Grogan was nervous of revolution and on 20 September 1797 he voted to proclaim disturbed areas of Wexford. He none the less continued to attend meetings, at which the plans of the United Irishmen were openly discussed, at the Colclough house in George Street, Wexford.

Following the outbreak of hostilities on 26 May 1798, and the capture of Wexford port by the United Irish insurgents on 30 May, Grogan became involved in the civilian wing of the United Irishmen and was appointed commissary-general, or head of the committees responsible for supplying the insurgent army with provisions, by his friend the elected commander-in-chief of the United Irish Army, Beauchamp Bagenal Harvey. He set up a procedure for transporting grain and livestock into town and secured a guard on every home in the neighbourhood that stood in danger of being attacked or plundered. Initially the insurgents had remarkable success in the south-east of Ireland until they were overwhelmed militarily towards the end of June.

After the recapture of Wexford port by the crown forces under General Gerard Lake, Grogan, painfully ill from gout, was arrested in his home, Johnstown Castle, to which he had returned. He was taken to Wexford on 23 June, court-martialled, and sentenced to death, although the court was illegally constituted. He was hanged on the bridge of which he was a shareholder by sailors of the Royal Navy on 28 June 1798. His friends John Colclough and Beauchamp Bagenal Harvey suffered with him. Their heads were severed and placed upon the spikes of the nearby court house. Their bodies were thrown into the Slaney River. Grogan's body was later grappled, brought ashore, and interred in the family burial-ground in Rathaspeck churchyard, which adjoined the Johnstown Castle estate, on 29 June 1798. His head was later recovered by an old family servant named Devereux and buried with the body.

While awaiting his court martial in Wexford gaol Grogan made a will, in which he left his personal effects to Rebecca Frost. He may have been only a 'tenant for life' in Johnstown, thus facilitating the return of the property to his younger brother, John Grogan, following the payment of a heavy fine. Another brother, Thomas Grogan Knox, was killed at the battle of Arklow on 9 June 1798 while an officer in the Castletown yeoman cavalry of the crown forces. NICHOLAS FURLONG

**Sources** NL Ire., Grogan MSS • R. J. Hayes, ed., *Manuscript sources for the history of Irish civilisation*, 11 vols. (1965) • E. Hay, *Insurrection of the county of Wexford* (1803) • T. A. Ogle, *The Irish militia officer* (1873) • E. Culleton, N. Furlong, and P. Sills, eds., *By Bishops Rath and Noman Fort* (1994) • D. Gahan, *The people's rising: Wexford, 1798* (1995) • K. Whelan, ed., *Wexford history and society* (1987) • L. Swords, ed., *Protestant Catholic and dissenter* (1997) • E. Barrett, *Reluctant rebel: the story of Cornelius Grogan* (1998) • D. Keogh and N. Furlong, eds., *The mighty wave: the 1798 rebellion in Wexford* (1996) • Burke, *Peerage* • *DNB* • H. Grattan, *Memoirs of the life and times of the Rt Hon. Henry Grattan*, 5 vols. (1839–46) • J. A. Froude, *The English in Ireland in the eighteenth century*, 3 vols. (1872–4) • *Correspondence of Charles, first Marquis Cornwallis*, ed. C. Ross, 3 vols. (1859) • *IGI* • parish records, Rathaspeck, Wexford, Ireland • private information (2004) [A. Grogan]
**Archives** NL Ire., family papers
**Likenesses** K. Kearns, artist's impression (after death mask), repro. in Barrett, *Reluctant rebel*, cover • death mask, NL Ire.; repro. in Keogh and Furlong, eds., *Mighty wave*, 63
**Wealth at death** estate valued at £8000 p.a. (minimum): T. Packenham, *The year of liberty* (1969); Barrett, *Reluctant rebel*

**Grogan, Ewart Scott** (1874–1967), settler in Kenya, was born on 12 December 1874 at 61 Eaton Square, Belgravia, son of William *Grogan (1824–1891), a fashionable house and estate agent, and his second wife, Jane Sams, *née* Scott (1846–1895), a widow. He was the eldest of eight children of this marriage, but William Grogan's sixth son and fourteenth child. His father had professional dealings (1854–90) with Gladstone, from whom the boy got his forename. After schooling at Boxgrove School, Guildford (1881–7), and Winchester College (1888–91) he read law at Jesus College, Cambridge (1893), but was sent down for rowdyism (1895). He studied briefly at the Slade School of Art before volunteering in the second Matabele (Ndebele) campaign (1896). In fulfilment of a boyhood dream he was the first white man to traverse Africa (1898–1900). His journey on foot from the Cape to Cairo required valour and fortitude. He mapped districts, and earned the scorn of topographers by naming four peaks east of Kivu mounts Dorothy, Margaret, Hilda, and Sybil, after his sisters and his fiancée's cousin (later Viscountess Monsell). His record of this adventure, *From Cape to Cairo* (1900), dedicated to Rhodes, is written with vivid power but often strident or vulgar: he used the term 'nigger' to denote black Africans throughout.

After obtaining a forestry concession of 132,000 acres in British East Africa (1904) Grogan became with Hugh Cholmondeley, third Baron Delamere, the most successful leader of the East Africa Protectorate pioneers. Richard Meinertzhagen wrote on 23 May 1904, 'he has great charm, a brain as clear as crystal and a strong character. He not only means what he says but says what he thinks' (Meinertzhagen, 165). Lord Cranworth found him 'good-looking, with a fine physique and an impelling eye; he had a presence in full keeping with his reputation' (Cranworth, 25). Though Grogan appeared impulsive, his stunts were calculated. He proved an astute speculator, buying large land tracts in and around Nairobi. From 1905 until the 1930s he published many influential letters in *The Times*. Elected first president of the Colonists' Association (1907), he repeatedly clashed with colonial officialdom. He talked fierily about settlers' rights, and among other provocations went out at midnight to peg a claim encircling Nairobi which was found to be legal. In the gravest incident he was convicted of flogging in front of Nairobi court house three Kikuyu servants who had jolted his sister and other white women in a rickshaw (1907). Grogan considered 'the nigger the most hideous of God's creations' and despised 'any disciple of the poor-dear-black-man, down-with-the-Maxim, Africa-for-the-African Creed' (*From Cape to Cairo*, 78, 168–9). The flogging was condemned by the colonial secretary Elgin and by Winston Churchill, who called Grogan a 'ruffian' (Hyam, 412). Sentenced to one month's imprisonment he became a bogeyman to officials and was not nominated to the legislative council until 1922. Instead he was elected first chairman of the Convention of Associations, known as the Settlers' Parliament (1911). In the legislative council he represented a succession of constituencies (with an interval in 1931–6) until 1956. His firebrand speeches were sometimes insolent. His racial antagonism to Indian immigration was strenuously articulated in speeches and writings (Grogan, 'Kenya: the logic of facts').

In the British general election of 1910 Grogan unsuccessfully contested Newcastle under Lyme as a Liberal Unionist. As a campaign preliminary he published his protectionist tract *The Economic Calculus* (1909). Grogan joined the protectorate's war council (1914) and his oratory was crucial to rousing settlers to war mobilization (1915). He undertook intelligence work with the east African force and was a liaison officer in the Belgian Congo. Blackwater fever contracted in wartime, financial worries, and domestic unhappiness changed him at this time; he became cruel and sarcastic at home, though to friends he remained charming. Having attended the Paris peace conference as adviser to Lord Milner on African frontiers, he took a lead in currency and economic issues affecting Kenya (as the colony was named) during the 1920s. In 1922 he opened Mombasa's first deep-water pier with railway wharves. He next bought 100,000 acres (1928–30) for the cultivation of sisal and citrus fruits, and eventually amassed 500,000 acres. Torr's Hotel in Nairobi was built by him (1928). He was the first passenger to fly across Africa from Cairo to Cape (1932).

Grogan married on 11 October 1900 Gertrude Edith (1876–1943), daughter of James Watt, New Zealand sheep rancher. To his enduring disappointment they had four daughters. After the First World War he conducted a succession of discreet affairs. In 1919 he fathered a daughter with Doris Tate-Smith (1890–1993), a nurse who was an architect's widow. He fathered another daughter in 1929 with Doreen Wright (*b.* 1900), the wife of a political colleague. Latterly he was increasingly isolated by a possessive Irish consort-housekeeper, Camilla Towers. After selling his business interests (1957–62) he endured a miserable decline into deafness and blindness before dying on 16 August 1967 at Rondebosch, Cape Province, South Africa. He was buried the following day in Maitland cemetery there. RICHARD DAVENPORT-HINES

**Sources** E. Paice, *Lost lion of empire* (2001) • N. Wymer, *The man from the Cape* (1959) • L. Farrant, *The legendary Grogan* (1981) • R. Meinertzhagen, *Kenya diary, 1902–1906* (1957) • Lord Cranworth, *Kenya chronicles* (1939) • E. S. Grogan and A. H. Sharp, *From Cape to Cairo: the first traverse of Africa from south to north* (1900) • [E. S. Grogan], 'Kenya: the settlers' case', *Round Table*, 26 (1935), 82–97 • E. S. Grogan, 'Kenya: the logic of facts', *National Review*, 81 (1923), 239–44 • R. Hyam, *Elgin and Churchill at the colonial office, 1905–1908* (1968), 411–12 • G. H. Mungeam, *British rule in Kenya, 1895–1912: the establishment of administration in the East Africa Protectorate* (1966) • E. Trzebinski, *The Kenya pioneers* (1985) • *The Times* (25 April 1905) • *The Times* (28 April 1905) • *The Times* (5 May 1905) • *The Times* (16 May 1905) • *The Times* (1 May 1907) • *The Times* (29 May 1907) • *The Times* (28 Dec 1907) • *The Times* (26 June 1908) • *The Times* (4 Aug 1908) • *The Times* (22 Aug 1908) • *The Times* (4 Feb 1909) • *The Times* (18 Jan 1911) • *The Times* (1 Feb 1911) • *The Times* (24 July 1911) • *The Times* (9 Feb 1920) • *The Times* (13 Feb 1920) • *The Times* (16 Feb 1920) • *The Times* (6 March 1920) • F. Brittain, 'E. S. Grogan', *Jesus College Annual Report* (1968) • b. cert. • m. cert.

**Archives** Kenya National Archives, Nairobi | Bodl. Oxf., papers of Viscount Milner • Bodl. RH, papers of Lord Chandos • Bodl. RH, papers of Sir Robert Coryndon • Bodl. RH, papers of Elspeth Huxley • Bodl. RH, papers of Sir William McMillan • Bodl. RH, papers of Richard Meinertzhagen • Bodl. RH, papers of Lady Moore • CAC Cam., papers of Sir Winston Churchill • CAC Cam., papers of Lord Lloyd • priv. coll., Walter George family papers • priv. coll., Crawford family papers • priv. coll., Hunter family papers • priv. coll., Dorothy Slater family papers • U. Cam., Royal Commonwealth Society collection, Arnold Paice papers

**Likenesses** photographs, 1876–1932, repro. in Farrant, *Legendary Grogan* (1980), 180–1 • photograph, 1900, repro. in Grogan and Sharp, *From Cape to Cairo*, frontispiece • photograph, *c.*1950, repro. in Wymer, *Man from the Cape*, frontispiece

**Wealth at death** made trusts for his legitimate and illegitimate families, 1962: Farrant, *Legendary Grogan*, 236

**Grogan, Nathaniel** (1739/40–1807), painter and etcher, was born in Cork, the son of a wood-turner and block maker to whom he was initially apprenticed. As an artist he was encouraged by John Butts (who also helped the painter James Barry) but was largely self-taught through copying engravings after Dutch masters. A surviving drawing after Egbert Heemskerk (priv. coll.) shows his competence as a draughtsman. Owing to his father's disapproval of his artistic efforts Grogan enlisted and served in the army during the American War of Independence. On 31 December 1777 he advertised himself in the *Pennsylvania Ledger* for 'sign and ornamental painting, with pencil work in general'.

Grogan returned to Cork after the war and, though he continued to work as a draughtsman, watercolourist, etcher, and mezzotint scraper he became known as an oil painter of landscapes and genre subjects of which the *Itinerant Preacher* and *The Wake* are best known today. Pasquin, who probably knew him, noted that 'his forte consists in an apt delineation of humorous subjects; in which he correctly represents the manners and customs of the Irish peasantry' (Pasquin, 53). Both of the above-mentioned oils confirm Pasquin's comments and they are very important social documents as well as paintings. Many of his genre subjects are set in landscapes, for instance, in his watercolour of *The Old Bridge and Blarney Castle, Co. Cork* (on loan to Limerick Museum), the peasants dancing and chatting are as important as the architecture. His masterpiece *Boats on the River Lee in Front of Tivoli* (National Gallery of Ireland, Dublin) again shows his excellence in dealing with figures. Grogan's engraved series of twelve views of the environs of Cork were advertised in the *New Cork Evening Post* in 1796. His topographical watercolours for these and other subjects are among his best works. He exhibited four landscapes at the Free Society of Artists in London in 1792 and may have visited London at that time.

Grogan painted murals for Sir Henry Hayes at his house, Vernon Mount, Cork. The drawing-room ceiling depicts Minerva throwing away the spears of war and encouraging the arts of painting, music, and architecture. In the upstairs lobby he painted, in simulated niches, grisaille gods alternating with urns. Grogan died in 1807, aged sixty-seven, and was buried in St Fin Barre's Cathedral, Cork. He left two sons, Nathaniel and Joseph, both artists of mediocre quality who taught art and continued to paint in their father's style.

L. H. CUST, *rev.* ANNE CROOKSHANK

**Sources** W. G. Strickland, *A dictionary of Irish artists*, 2 vols. (1913) • P. Murray, *Illustrated summary catalogue of the Crawford Municipal Art Gallery* (Cork, 1991), 173–4, 70 • A. Pasquin [J. Williams], *An authentic history of the professors of painting, sculpture, and architecture who have practiced in Ireland … to which are added, Memoirs of the royal academicians* [1796]; facs. edn as *An authentic history of painting in Ireland* with introduction by R. W. Lightbown (1970), 53 • 'Gleanings on old Cork artists [pt 1]', *Journal of the Cork Historical and Archaeological Society*, 2nd ser., 6 (1900), 104–11, esp. 106–8 • A. Crookshank and the Knight of Glin [D. Fitzgerald], *The painters of Ireland, c.1660–1920* (1978), 70 • A. Crookshank and the Knight of Glin [D. Fitzgerald], *The watercolours of Ireland: works on paper in pencil, pastel and paint, c.1600–1914* (1994), 78–80

**Grogan, William** (1824–1891), estate agent, was born on 3 August 1824 in Pollen Street, Westminster, the son of Nicholas Grogan (*d. c.*1845), tea dealer and wine merchant, and his wife, Sarah Bean. He may have been the William Grogan who was briefly in partnership about 1848–9 with John Scott, a hosier and outfitter at 88 Strand, but by mid-1850 he was engaged in the newly flourishing trade of estate agent at 33 Conduit Street, Bond Street, handling property as far afield as Windsor. By 1853 he had moved to superior premises at 66 Park Street, where he remained for at least ten years, handling high-class property; he is also recorded at 103 Harley Street throughout the 1860s, and later at 125 Piccadilly, where in the 1880s he formed a partnership with Jermyn Boyd; the firm of Grogan and Boyd, surveyors and auctioneers, survived until the early 1960s.

The partnership had a number of influential clients. As early as 1855 Grogan was in frequent communication with W. E. Gladstone, evidently over the politician's move to no. 11 Carlton House Terrace, and Gladstone again employed him in 1874 to sell that house and its contents. Grogan found him a smaller one nearby for the season, and eventually negotiated a thirty-year lease of 73 Harley Street for him. He remained in contact with Gladstone for the rest of his life.

On 29 June 1847 at St Giles-in-the-Fields Grogan married Mary A. Adams, daughter of Thomas Adams, landed proprietor; they had one son and eight daughters. Living at first modestly at Brentford and then about 1858–61 at Melville House, North End Road, Fulham, Grogan was enabled by his success in business to move his home to Phillimore Gardens, Kensington. His wife died at some point after 1867, and on 14 August 1874 he married Jane Sams, widow, of Piccadilly, daughter of John Ward Scott, gentleman, and born in Exeter about 1845. Grogan and his second wife had five sons (of whom the second, Ewart Scott *Grogan, made the first traverse of Africa from south to north) and three daughters. After his second marriage he moved to Eaton Square, and about 1878 to Queen's Gate, South Kensington, where his steadily increasing family was supported by a butler and six female servants.

Grogan died at 6 First Avenue, his house in Brighton, on 19 June 1891. His share in the business carried on at 125 Piccadilly (together with the lease and furniture) was bequeathed to the two eldest of his sons by his second wife. Grogan's freehold at Brighton and his leasehold houses at 16 Belgrave Square and 4 Belgrave Place he left in trust for his widow. M. H. PORT

**Sources** *Boyle's Court Guide* · *Royal blue book* [annuals] · *The Post Office directory* (1828–1964) · will, proved, 24 July 1891 · parish registers (births and baptisms), St George, Hanover Square, Westminster, London, Aug 1824 · census returns, 1861, PRO, RG 9/27 fol. 26; 1881, RG 11/48, fols. 70–73; 1891, RG 12/32, fol. 90 · parish register (marriages), St Giles-in-the-Fields, London, 1847 · parish register (marriages), St George, Hanover Square, Westminster, London, 1874 · Venn, *Alum. Cant.* · *The Times* (25 July 1850) · Gladstone, *Diaries* · *CGPLA Eng. & Wales* (1891)

**Wealth at death** £109,472 16*s*. 1*d*.: probate, 24 July 1891, *CGPLA Eng. & Wales*

**Gronniosaw, Ukawsaw** [*pseud.* James Albert] (*b.* **1710x14**, *d.* after **1772**), freed slave and autobiographer, was probably born in Bornu (now north-eastern Nigeria), the youngest of the six children of the eldest daughter of the king of Bournou (Bornu). Spiritually dissatisfied with the animist faith in which he was brought up, he soon alienated himself from his friends and relatives by his constant questions challenging their faith in physical objects, as well as by his growing belief in the existence of an uncreated creator. Increasingly 'dejected and melancholy' (*Narrative*, 11), the adolescent Gronniosaw seized the opportunity offered him by a trading African merchant from the Gold Coast to accompany the merchant to his home, more than 1000 miles away, where Gronniosaw could play with boys his own age, and 'see houses with wings to them walk upon the water, and should also see the white folks' (ibid.). When he arrived at the Gold Coast, however, the local king thought him a spy, and decided to behead him. Affected by Gronniosaw's obvious courage in the face of death, the king relented, choosing to sell him into slavery rather than kill him.

Rejected by a French slave trader because he was so small, Gronniosaw successfully implored a Dutch captain to buy him. On the voyage to Barbados, in a scene imitated in later slave narratives, he watched his new master reading, and, thinking the book talked to the Dutchman, held his ear close to it, hoping it would speak to him as well. He blamed his complexion for the book's silence. In Barbados he was purchased by a man named Vanhorn, who took him to New York city, where he was soon sold as a domestic slave to Theodorus Jacobus Frelinghuysen, a wealthy Dutch Reformed clergyman in New Jersey, and a friend of the English evangelist George Whitefield. Introduced to Christianity by Frelinghuysen, and to reading by his schoolmaster Peter Van Arsdalen, Gronniosaw soon experienced despair when he became convinced that his own sins were too great to deserve salvation.

About 1747, after reading the spiritual writings of John Bunyan and Richard Baxter, an attempt at suicide, and a three-day illness, Gronniosaw experienced his own spiritual rebirth when he recalled the words from the Bible 'Behold the lamb of God'. His new-found happiness was quickly ended by the death of his master, who freed him in his will, and by recurrent spiritual doubts. As a free man, Gronniosaw worked for various members of the Frelinghuysen family, all of whom, however, died within four years of the minister's death.

Having lost his friends in America, Gronniosaw decided to go to England and above all to Kidderminster, the birthplace of Baxter, because his reading and experience in meeting Whitefield in New Jersey had convinced him that the English 'people must be all *Righteous*' (*Narrative*, 28). Because of debts he had to work his way across the Atlantic during the Seven Years' War, first as a cook on a privateer, and later as an enlistee in the 28th regiment of foot. His lack of interest in money caused him to be cheated repeatedly. Landing at Portsmouth, England, near the end of 1762 brought Gronniosaw further disappointment when he discovered the English to be no more pious than the Americans. Disillusioned, he went to London, where Whitefield found him housing. There he fell in love at first sight with an English weaver named Betty, who introduced him to the preaching of the eminent Baptist Dr Andrew Gifford.

After about three weeks in London, Gronniosaw (who by now had adopted the name James Albert) agreed to go to the Netherlands at the request of some friends of his late master to be examined about his experiences by several Calvinist ministers. While there he was hired as a butler in the household of a very rich Amsterdam merchant, who treated him more as a friend than as a servant, and whose wife wanted him to marry her maid, an attractive young woman who had saved a good deal of money. But Gronniosaw chose to return to London after a year to be baptized by Gifford and to wed Betty, despite the objections of his English friends to his marrying a poor widow. Although Betty normally earned a good living as a weaver, Gronniosaw and his wife and growing family soon fell on hard times because of the post-war economic depression. Through a series of Quaker contacts, he was able to find employment outside of London, first in Colchester, then in Norwich, and later in Kidderminster. Unfortunately, much of his work was seasonal, leading to long periods of deprivation and near-starvation during the winters, with the brief exception of the time spent in Norwich, where Betty was also able to find employment before their children contracted smallpox. They experienced both the generosity of benefactors such as Henry Gurney, a Quaker worsted manufacturer and banker in Norwich, and the cruelty of the unnamed Baptist minister, Quakers, and Anglican minister, all of whom refused to give a proper burial to one of Gronniosaw's daughters, who had died of fever in Norwich. His *Narrative* closes with the 'very poor Pilgrims' living in abject poverty in Kidderminster, their faith in God still intact (*Narrative*, 48).

Dedicated to Selina Hastings, countess of Huntingdon, *A narrative of the most remarkable particulars in the life of James Albert Ukawsaw Gronniosaw, an African prince, as related by himself*, published in Bath in 1772, 'was taken from his own Mouth, and committed to Paper by the elegant Pen of a young LADY of the Town of LEOMINSTER', according to its preface, written by the countess's cousin Walter Shirley (*Narrative*, 3). In 1809 the 'young LADY' was identified, probably incorrectly, as Hannah More. By 1800 the *Narrative* had appeared in at least ten editions in England and America, as well as in a Welsh translation (1779) and as a serial in the *American Moral and Sentimental Magazine* in New York (1797). Its initial publication in 1772 marked the beginning of the modern Anglophone tradition of autobiographies written or dictated by former slaves of African descent. VINCENT CARRETTA

**Sources** *A narrative of the most remarkable particulars in the life of James Albert Ukawsaw Gronniosaw, an African prince, as related by himself* (1772)

**Gronow, Rees Howell** (1794–1865), writer, was the eldest son of William Gronow, a prosperous Welsh landowner of Court Herbert, Glamorgan, and his wife, Anne, only daughter of Rees Howell of Gwryd. He was born on 7 May 1794 and educated at Eton College when John Keate was headmaster and P. B. Shelley was a fellow pupil. On 24 December 1812 he received a commission as an ensign in the 1st foot guards, and after mounting guard at St James's Palace for a few months was sent with a detachment of his regiment to Spain. In 1813 he took part in the final encounters of the Peninsular War, and in the following year returned with his battalion to London. Here he became one of the dandies of the town, and was among the very few officers who were admitted to Almack's assembly rooms, where he witnessed the introduction of quadrilles and waltzes in place of the old reels and country dances.

In need of money to equip himself for further services abroad, Gronow obtained an advance of £200 from his agents, Cox and Greenwood; he went with this money to a gambling-house in St James's Square and won £600, with which he bought two horses at Tattersall's and other necessaries. Then, without troubling to obtain permission, he crossed the channel and, grudgingly allowed to remain with his regiment which was already engaged with the enemy when he arrived at Quatre Bras, he was able to witness the battle of Waterloo, and provided one of the best first-hand accounts of it that has survived. He entered Paris on 25 June 1815 and three days later was promoted lieutenant. He remained in the army for a further six years, obtaining no higher rank than captain in a regiment in which majorities and colonelcies were sold for extremely high sums. These, extravagant as he was, he could not afford. In June 1823 he became insolvent and was briefly imprisoned under the Insolvent Debtors Act. In 1830 his father died, and the next year—his finances consequently in a far more healthy condition—he was established in a house in Mayfair which had once belonged to Beau Brummell. He was now able to enter upon a political career. After unsuccessfully contesting Grimsby in 1831, he was returned for Stafford the following year by means of extensive bribery. In 1835, however, he was defeated by F. L. Holyoake Goodricke who distributed bribes on a scale described as 'profligate'. Abandoning hope of a further political career, Gronow devoted the next thirty years to a life of idleness and fashionable pursuits in London and, later, in Paris, where he was present during the *coup d'état* of 1–2 December 1851.

**Rees Howell Gronow (1794–1865)**, by James Charles Armytage (after Pauline Bossange)

Gronow's name is chiefly remembered in connection with the four volumes of his reminiscences. The first, entitled *Reminiscences of Captain Gronow, formerly of the Grenadier Guards and member of parliament for Stafford, being anecdotes of the camp, the court, and the clubs, at the close of the last war with France, related by himself*, was published in 1861.

A second revised edition appeared the following year. In 1863 he published *Recollections and Anecdotes, being a Second Series of Reminiscences by Captain R. H. Gronow*, and in 1865, the year of his death, appeared *Celebrities of London and Paris, being a Third Series of Reminiscences and Anecdotes*. This was followed in 1866 by *Captain Gronow's last recollections, being the fourth and final series of his reminiscences and anecdotes*. In 1889 a new edition of the above volumes was published under the title *The reminiscences and recollections of Captain Gronow with illustrations from contemporary sources by Joseph Grego*. When Gronow relates his personal experiences, as in his account of the state of Paris in 1815, the condition of society in London in his own time, and the doings of the court of Napoleon III, his testimony is to be relied on, but his second-hand stories and anecdotes of persons whom he did not know, while almost unfailingly entertaining, are *ben trovato* rather than historically accurate.

Gronow was a handsome man, always faultlessly dressed and well liked in society. An engraving of a portrait by J. C. Armytage appears in the *Reminiscences* (1889). With the exception of one Captain Ross he was said to have been the best pistol-shot of his day, and in early life took part in several duels. He married first, in 1825, Antoinine Didier of the Paris Opera, with whom he had a daughter, Mathilde. His second wife was a Mlle de St Pol, with whom he had four more children, who were said to have been left by their impoverished father 'wholly unprovided for' following his death in Paris on 20 November 1865. CHRISTOPHER HIBBERT

**Sources** R. H. Gronow, *The reminiscences of Captain Gronow*, 4 vols. (1861–6) · *Captain Gronow: his reminiscences of Regency and Victorian life*, ed. C. Hibbert (1991), vii–xvii · A. H. Guernsey, 'Last of the dandies', *Harper's New Monthly Magazine*, 25 (1862), 745–53 · *GM*, 4th ser., 1 (1866), 148 · H. de Villemessant, *Mémoires d'un journaliste: souvenirs de jeunesse* (Paris, 1867), chap. 9 · Walford, *County families* · *DNB*
**Likenesses** J. C. Armytage, stipple (after P. Bossange), NPG [*see illus.*] · P. Bossange, miniature; Christies, 25 Nov 1980, lot 24 · G. Hayter, group portrait, oils (*The House of Commons, 1833*), NPG

**Gronwy Ddu**. *See* Owen, Goronwy (1723–1769).

**Groom, Charles Ottley** (1839–1894), impostor, was born on 14 May 1839 at Merchiston, Tobago, the posthumous son of Charles Edward Groom (1815–1838), sugar planter, and his wife, Ann (1815–1895), daughter of Archibald Napier. His childhood was mainly spent in Sussex with a highly protective mother, with whom he lived until his death. He was a sickly child with precocious interests in natural history, science, and antiquarianism: 'My intellectual activity and vivid imagination was doubtless the cause of my delicacy. My mind was full of gigantic schemes, which were little influenced by my capacity for their execution' (Napier, *Tommy Try*, 57). His earliest works were ornithological. In 1873 his testimony to a House of Commons select committee assisted the enactment of the Wild Birds Protection Bill.

Among Groom's publications, *Tommy Try, or, What he did in Science* (1869) is a charming if arch memoir of his boyhood. In *The Book of Nature and the Book of Man* (1870) Groom vividly argued that humankind represented the microcosm of creation which all lower forms of life imitated. Its preface (ascribed to the dead Lord Brougham and Vaux) boasted that 'the author has strode the gulf between Physics and Metaphysics, Mind and Matter, Instinct and Reason, God and Man'. Groom in 1875 read a paper before the British Association promoting his vegetarian cure for alcoholism, and issued several vegetarian tracts. His book *Lakes and Rivers* (1879) was published under the auspices of the Society for Promoting Christian Knowledge. In his *Prospectus* (1886), issued to attract subscribers for a complete edition of his works, Groom published testimonials to the greatness of his *Book of Nature* from celebrities who were no longer living and who could not repudiate the grotesqueries foisted on them: he claimed that Victor Hugo attributed his deathbed Christian conversion to Groom's treatise and that he confessed, 'I never wished so much to steal a book as this' (*Prospectus*, v).

Groom's chief impostures were genealogical. They began with his change of surname to Napier (1865), although until the late 1870s he was usually known as C. O. Groom Napier (of Merchiston). He then adopted the title of prince of Mantua and Montferrat, and elaborated a pedigree tracing his descent from many great historical figures, most notably King David of Israel. It was on this basis that he described himself as prince of the house of David, in which title he claimed to have been certified by Sir George Jessel. He and his mother assumed the princely surname of Gonzaga. The prince also bore subsidiary titles, including prince of Ferrera, Nevers, Rethel, and Alençon; Baron de Tobago; and master of Lennox, Kilmahew, and Merchiston. On 24 March 1879 he held a banquet for 7000 guests in a specially constructed pavilion at Greenwich, the walls of which were hung with 700 illuminated leaves of vellum illustrating his pedigree. He was too unwell to attend the festivities, which were conducted on strict vegetarian and teetotal principles, with outlandish salads and sucking pigs modelled in piecrust and containing fruit and vegetable jellies. A beverage of his devising, curry champagne, concocted from curry powder and ginger beer, was served. The dipsomaniacs whom he had rescued by his vegetarian cure wore on their backs pieces of yellow silk embroidered with broken bottles.

In 1882 the prince announced the Mantua and Montferrat Medal Fund, founded by a fourteenth-century Gonzaga ancestor to confer recognition upon eminent artists and scientists. His family, so he pretended, had awarded gold medals to Raphael, Michelangelo, Dante, Galileo, Columbus, Cervantes, Lope de Vega, Erasmus, Milton, Molière, and Rubens; Shakespeare was so grateful for the award in 1614 that he intended to write a play about the family. Mantua medals were issued widely: if Froude, Gladstone, Huxley, and Shaftesbury were suspicious, Ruskin, Tennyson, Manning, and Leighton seem to have been duped. One recipient was Sir Richard Owen, whose medal is in the British Museum; Groom was later 'warned off the BM' (Sherborn, 61). In 1883 he announced that an eighteenth-century duke of Mantua and Montferrat had left money for educational purposes which, by accumulation, amounted to £750,000. A great meeting was held at Exeter Hall (15 June) to allot this sum for the establishment of a Welsh university. The prince read a long, rambling speech together with much implausible family correspondence, including a letter from Dante (July 1317) to his ancestor: 'Your medal cheers me from a melancholy deep as hell itself' (*The Times*, 16 June 1883). This fiasco exploded most of his pretensions. He also issued in 1883 a vague but grandiloquent listing of the contents of his private museum, including natural history specimens, ancestral portraits by great masters, antiquities, and relics—almost all probably bogus.

The prince having become a director of the City of Genoa Waterworks Company (registered 1886), some bondholders sued him on grounds of misrepresentations in the prospectus. He settled with them in 1888, but one creditor petitioned for his bankruptcy over a debt of £1016 (December 1889). He obtained his discharge from bankruptcy in March 1890.

The prince's manners were courtly, benevolent, and melancholic. He was characterized as 'a notorious rogue and thief', who 'sold false nuggets to Ruskin' and tried to kill the mineralogist Thomas Davies by dropping a boulder on him from a high ladder in the Strand (Sherborn, 62–3). He died of long-standing cardiac disease on 17 January 1894 at 18 Elgin Avenue, Maida Vale, his death being registered as that of Charles de Bourbon d'Este Paleologues Gonzaga, prince of Mantua and Montferrat. His mother (who was dying of stomach cancer) arranged for the posthumous publication of *Visions of the Interior of the Earth, and of Past, Present and Future Events* (1894), an account of his trances under the charge of the Archangel Gabriel, patron saint of the house of Gonzaga.

RICHARD DAVENPORT-HINES

**Sources** C. O. G. Napier, *Tommy Try, or, What he did in science* (1869) • C. O. Groom Napier, *Works of H. R. and M. S. H. the prince of Mantua, prince of Ferrara, Nevers, Rethel and Alençon, with an introduction by the late Charles Reade and M. Victor Hugo* (1886) • *Memorandum on the contents of the private museum collected by HMSH the prince of Mantua and Montferrat* (1883) • C. C. Osborne, 'A London Munchausen', *Cornhill Magazine*, [3rd] ser., 33 (1912), 337–57 • C. D. Sherborn, *Where is the — collection?* (1940), 61–3 • *The Times* (6 March 1865) • *The Times* (1 Oct 1873) • *The Times* (15 Oct 1873) • *The Times* (17 Nov 1873) • *The Times* (22 Nov 1873) • *The Times* (16 June 1883) • *The Times* (17 Dec 1889) • *The Times* (18 Jan 1890) • *The Times* (1 Feb 1890) • *The Times* (15 March 1893) • *The Athenaeum* (18 May 1895), 626 • *Report of the British Association for the Advancement of Science*, 34 (1864), 95 • *Report of the British Association for the Advancement of Science* (1875), 217–18 • d. cert. • C. O. Groom, *Vegetarianism and temperance* (1880)

**Likenesses** pen-and-ink sketch, 1855 (of Groom?), repro. in Napier, *Tommy Try*, 301

**Groom, John Alfred** (1845–1919), founder of the John Grooms charity for disabled children, was born at 6 North Street, Clerkenwell, London, on 15 August 1845, the son of George Paul Groom, a copperplate printer, and his wife, Sarah Maria, *née* Wigton. His father died about 1855, leaving a family of five boys and one girl to be brought up by their mother. Although not the eldest, John became the effective leader and he left school to earn what money he could as an errand-boy. He was later apprenticed in an engine-turning business, where he learned the trade of silver engraving. At twenty-one he finished his apprenticeship and set up his own engraving business, with a machine shop in a glass-fronted shed in the garden of his house in Sekforde Street, Clerkenwell. The Grooms were regular churchgoers, and from the age of sixteen John taught at a Sunday school. With a friend who was a City of London commissioner he visited homes in the slum districts, an experience which intensified his determination to help those most in need.

Soon after setting up his own business Groom was asked to become superintendent of a nearby mission hall. This voluntary post gave full scope to his philanthropic instincts, and while his brothers helped to run the engraving business he put much of his energy and money into the mission work. The mission hall enabled him to help the blind and disabled girls whom he saw every day on the streets of the capital selling flowers and watercress to passers-by. Their work was both seasonal and dependent upon good weather, as fewer flowers were sold on dull days. If they did not make enough money they would often sleep out at night, fearful of returning home. Calling on family and friends to help, Groom hired a large meeting room near Covent Garden. There he founded, in 1866, the Watercress and Flower Girls' Christian Mission, commonly known in its early days as 'John Groom's Crippleage'.

The mission became a centre where the girls could get a free mug of cocoa early in the mornings. Twice weekly there was a hot dinner, for which they paid a nominal halfpenny. They were encouraged to wash, make themselves tidy, and mend their clothes, while Groom read Bible stories. He also encouraged them to attend one of the three Sunday schools which he had started in different parts of the capital. The mission was given a powerful boost when the earl of Shaftesbury offered to become its president and to use his many contacts to help raise funds. Shaftesbury had spotted Groom going about his work in the poorer districts, where he was a familiar figure in his top hat and frock coat, and they became close friends.

Groom married, on 5 March 1868, Sarah (*b.* 1849/50), the daughter of George John Farrington, a coachman. They had three sons and a daughter. His wife, 'a very practical Christian' (Martin, 8), helped in the mission work. He seems to have married a second time for at his death he left a widow, Ada Margaret.

Groom wanted above all else to give the blind and disabled girls a degree of independence, but while some were found work in domestic service most remained on the street. He saw a long-term solution in the manufacture of handmade flowers, which were then becoming popular. The mission hall was converted into a daytime factory, and a flower-making business was begun. Groom was a 'practical man with no use for slipshod amateurism', and he mastered the trade himself (*The Times*, 21 Feb 1966). Under his guidance the venture soon took off and he turned his attention full-time to flower making. His brothers also helped to work the machines that stamped the petals out of stiffened 'sateen': they were then coloured and shaped by the girls, and worked around stems made of wire wrapped in green paper. The girls became highly skilled at all kinds of flower, even orchids.

In 1894 the mission moved to larger premises at Woodbridge Chapel, close to Sekforde Street, and the flowers were by now sold wholesale to private houses and businesses. There were exhibitions in town halls of flowers and flower making, and in 1906 the girls were invited to decorate the Guildhall for the lord mayor's banquet, a highly praised piece of work. They later produced 30,000 blooms for a banquet in honour of the king and queen of Norway. Queen Alexandra also supported the mission, and in 1912 she ordered thousands of roses which were sold on the inaugural Queen Alexandra rose day, 26 June 1912, when nearly £18,000 was collected for charitable causes.

From the beginning the girls were paid a wage and given accommodation in houses in Sekforde Street, close to their work, which were rented with funds raised by an appeal. House-mothers were employed to look after them, and in this way the first 'John Grooms home' was established—an early step towards the provision of specialist housing for the disabled. In 1890 Groom got the backing of the mission committee and launched an appeal for funds with which to open an orphanage in Clacton-on-Sea, Essex. Soon there were six homes—each named after a flower—housing 100 blind and disabled girls from the age of two to twelve. When old enough the girls went to local schools and then into domestic service, or else joined the flower making in London. By 1913 there were nearly 260 girls involved in the flower making, all of them blind or disabled, and earning between 10*s.* and 15*s.* a week.

Groom managed to balance the demands of his charity with a happy family life. He was a keen supporter of Chelsea Football Club and went to home games, when he would swap his trademark top hat for a flat cap. He continued as superintendent and secretary of the mission until the year before his death, when he retired in failing health. In his last year he lived at the orphanage in Clacton, where he died on 27 December 1919. He was buried in Highgate cemetery. His eldest son, Alfred, took over the mission work, and in 1932 the flower making occupied a large site at Edgware, with specialist homes around a purpose-built factory. As the demand for artificial flowers declined the range of activities increased, and disabled boys as well as girls were admitted, but the emphasis remained on their attaining a degree of independence. More than a century after its foundation the 'John Grooms charity' was still providing employment and homes for disabled people. MARK POTTLE

**Sources** N. Martin, *A man with a vision: the story of John Groom* (1983) · *The Times* (19 Dec 1911), 9a · *The Times* (6 June 1911) · *The Times* (4 July 1912) · *The Times* (20 Dec 1912), 13f · *The Times* (30 Dec 1912), 9a · *The Times* (7 Jan 1913), 8f · *The Times* (28 Sept 1963), 10c · *The Times* (21 Feb 1966), 13e · *Annual Register* (1912) · census returns, 1881 · b. cert. · m. cert. · d. cert. · will, 20 Dec 1916

**Likenesses** photograph, repro. in Martin, *A man with a vision*, facing p. 6

**Wealth at death** £3386 14*s.* 11*d.*: probate, 31 March 1920, *CGPLA Eng. & Wales*

**Groombridge, Stephen** (1755–1832), astronomer, was born at Goudhurst, Kent, on 7 January 1755, the sixth of the seven children, and the only one to reach adulthood, of Thomas Groombridge (*d.* 1797), who was in commerce, and his wife, Mary (*d.* 1793). About 1776 he succeeded to the business of a linen draper to whom he had been apprenticed. On 24 January 1793 he married Lavinia Martha Treacher (*c.*1769–1832), the niece of Sir John Treacher of Oxford. An income from retailing, supplemented by West Indian trading, enabled him to retire in 1815.

As a youth Groombridge was keenly interested in and taught himself astronomy, and then had a small observatory at Goudhurst. After moving in 1802 to 6 Eliot Place, Blackheath, less than a mile from the Royal Observatory, Greenwich, he converted a stable adjacent to his dining-room into an observatory. Boldly, since it would be a new and expensive venture, he persuaded Edward Troughton to make him a large transit circle to overcome the known deficiencies of Francis Wollaston's design for the first English transit circle made by William Cary in 1793. In 1806 Troughton delivered a reversible instrument of 3.5 inches aperture and 5 feet focal length. It was the only one made by Troughton, the first really successful one anywhere, and equal or superior to any meridian instrument in Europe. With it the observer could simultaneously obtain the two co-ordinates of right ascension and declination at a single observation. The instrument was sold to Sir James South in 1823, and later came into the ownership of the Science Museum, London.

Groombridge set himself to catalogue all stars brighter than magnitude 8.5 between the north celestial pole and declination +38 degrees. Commencing at the age of fifty-one, he worked alone on an extremely difficult task which required great care, skill, and constant labour. He presented to the Royal Society in 1810 and 1814 the results of about 1000 preliminary observations of fifty stars to determine the correction for atmospheric refraction. It is remarkable that, although he did not retire until 1815, between 1806 and 1816 he made some 50,000 observations of more than 4000 stars. Indefatigable and dexterous, he often left the table or friends temporarily to step into his observatory and make an observation. Among those he recorded, in 1842 Argelander discovered that star number 1830 had the large proper motion across the sky of 7 seconds of arc a year, hence known as the 'Runaway star', or 'Groombridge's star'; it has been much studied since.

From 1817 Groombridge spent ten years applying the corrections for refraction, instrument, and clock errors to all the observations, then reducing the apparent to mean or actual positions for about one-third of the stars. His work was stopped in 1827 when he was partially paralysed by a stroke, from which he never fully recovered. The board of longitude had the catalogue completed by Henry Taylor, an assistant at the Royal Observatory, and it was printed in 1832. However, fraudulent mistakes by Taylor were detected, and the astronomer royal, George Airy, had it suppressed. Revised and corrected under Airy's supervision, the catalogue of 4243 circumpolar stars for epoch 1810 was published in 1838.

While Groombridge had no special interest in higher mathematics, he was a skilled observer. Although he had only two microscopes to read his settings, his work was credited with greater accuracy than contemporary work at the Madras, Radcliffe, and Armagh observatories. Apart from practical use, because his catalogue recorded fainter stars than any other—about 1000 fainter than magnitude 8—it laid the foundation for determining their proper motions by later comparison, and hence something of the dynamics of our galaxy. The Radcliffe observer Manuel J. Johnson dedicated himself to reobserving the catalogue between 1839 and 1859. Greenwich reobserved the stars again at the end of the century, and in 1905 also published a revised reduction of the original catalogue.

Groombridge was elected a fellow of the Royal Society in 1812, and in 1820 was a founder and until 1827 served as a council member of the Astronomical Society of London, later the Royal Astronomical Society. Among twelve papers on astronomical subjects published between 1808 and 1826 in various journals, including the *Philosophical Magazine*, *Quarterly Journal of Science*, and *Philosophical Transactions of the Royal Society of Edinburgh*, six submitted to the Astronomical Society included 'Universal tables for the reduction of the fixed stars' (1820), 'Observations of the planets' (1822), and a report of the annular eclipse of 1820 (*Memoirs of the Royal Astronomical Society*, 1.135). He reported the partial eclipse of 1816 to the Royal Society, and his observations from 1807 to 1823 of four minor planets discovered elsewhere between 1800 and 1807 were published in issues of the *Berlin Ephemeris*.

Appreciated for his talents, integrity, and kindness by contemporaries as shrewd as Richard Sheepshanks, Groombridge died at Blackheath on 30 March 1832. A memorial tablet in the church declared him to have been 'full of Christian faith and hope'. He was buried on 6 April in Goudhurst churchyard, it is believed in a vault with a now illegible inscription, surrounded by the graves of his family. His wife, Lavinia, survived him exactly five months. They had lost their only son, Stephen Paris, as an infant; their only daughter, Mary, who had married a vicar in Northumberland, also predeceased them.

ROGER HUTCHINS

**Sources** B. J. W. Brown, 'Stephen Groombridge, FRS (1755–1832)', *Journal of the British Astronomical Association*, 42 (1931–2), 212–14 • H. C. King, *The history of the telescope* (1955); repr. (1979), 234–6 • [R. Sheepshanks], 'Stephen Groombridge', *Monthly Notices of the Astronomical Society of London*, 2 (1831–3), 145–7 • J. Ashbrook, 'The story of Groombridge, 1830', *The astronomical scrapbook: skywatchers, pioneers, and seekers in astronomy*, ed. L. J. Robinson (1984), 352–9 • *DNB* • F. Addey, remarks on 'Stephen Groombridge', *Journal of the British Astronomical Association*, 42 (1931–2), 199–200 • L. Boss, 'The new reduction of the meridian observations of Groombridge', *Journal of the British Astronomical Association*, 17 (1906–7), 53 • *History of the Royal Astronomical Society*, [1]: *1820–1920*, ed. J. L. E. Dreyer and H. H. Turner (1923); repr. (1987), 65 • A. McConnell, *Instrument makers to the world: a history of Cooke, Troughton & Simms* (1992), 11, 31 • *Catalogue of scientific papers*, Royal Society, 3 (1869), 27 • S. Groombridge, 'Observations on atmospheric refraction as it affects astronomical observations', *PTRS*, 100 (1810), 190–203 • *GM*, 1st ser., 63 (1793), 89

**Archives** RAS, observing notebooks, 18/11, 18/12

**Likenesses** portrait, repro. in F. W. Dyson and W. G. Thackeray, *New reduction of Groombridge's circumpolar catalogue for the epoch 1810.0* (1905) • portrait, repro. in Ashbrook, 'The story of Groombridge', 353

**Groombridge, William** (1748–1811), miniature and landscape painter, was born near Tunbridge Wells, Kent (possibly at Goudhurst); he may have been the William Groombridge, son of Henry and Philadelphia, who was baptized at Tonbridge, Kent, on 12 December 1750. He was probably a pupil of a local watercolourist, the elder James Lambert of Lewes. Working in both oil and watercolour, he exhibited at the Royal Academy from 1770 to 1790, at first from addresses in Goudhurst and in Bromley. He moved to London about 1776 but appears to have returned to Kent in 1786, exhibiting from Canterbury. Groombridge published a volume of sonnets in 1789, and—perhaps after periods in Paris, a debtors' prison, and Jamaica—settled in the United States about 1794. There his wife, Catherine (*c*.1760–1837), an amateur watercolourist, whom he had married about 1792, ran girls' schools, which financed them both; she, not he, features in the trade directories.

Despite his industry—some 123 paintings and drawings are recorded—Groombridge was no more successful in the New World than the Old. He was a founder of the Philadelphia Columbianum, or 'American Academy', in 1795, lived for a period of time in New York, and finally settled in Baltimore in 1804. Here he acquired an uncomfortable champion in Eliza Anderson (known as Beatrice Ironsides), the vitriolic publisher and editor of the Baltimore *Observer*. She preferred him to his fellow immigrant Francis Guy, proclaiming that 'to produce paintings really fine, he needs only to meet with persons sufficiently generous and discerning, to indemnify him for the time and expence [*sic*] the necessary studies would cost him' (*The Observer*, 20 June 1807). He died at his wife's school, at 16 Calvert Street, Baltimore, Maryland, on 24 May 1811. He was survived by his wife. Examples of his work are in the collections of the Baltimore Museum of Art and the Maryland and Pennsylvania historical societies.

HUON MALLALIEU

**Sources** J. H. Pleasants, *Four late eighteenth century Anglo-American landscape painters* (1943) • *The Observer* [Baltimore, MD] (20 June 1807) • *Federal Gazette and Baltimore Daily Advertiser* (Nov 1807) • *Federal Gazette and Baltimore Daily Advertiser* (26 May 1811) • *IGI*

**Wealth at death** $2359: *The Observer*; Pleasants, *Four late … landscape painters*

**Groome, Francis Hindes** (1851–1902), scholar of Gypsy life and writer, was born at the rectory of Monk Soham, Suffolk, on 30 August 1851, the second son of Robert Hindes *Groome (1810–1889), archdeacon of Suffolk, and Mary Jackson, daughter of the rector of Swanage. Through his father's mother there was a family connection with East Dereham, and, there is some ground for believing, blood relationship with the traveller and linguist George Borrow, whom he was later to meet. In 1861 he was at school at Wyke Regis, near Weymouth. From 1865 to 1869 he was at Ipswich grammar school under H. A. Holden, where he distinguished himself both in Latin prose and in Latin verse. There too he won several cups for rowing, and helped to found and edit a school magazine. He read for a year with Francis de Winton at Bochrwyd on the Wye in Radnorshire and went up to Corpus Christi College, Oxford, matriculating in October 1870; in 1871 he was elected a postmaster of Merton College. Even in early boyhood Gypsy life seen in glimpses had exercised a singular fascination over him, and an assistant master, Mr Sanderson, at Ipswich shared his interest in Romani and Gypsy lore. At Oxford he came to know Gypsies intimately, a fact which gave a new turn to his life. He left Oxford without taking a degree, spent some time in 1873 at Göttingen, a centre of Gypsy studies, and for years lived much with Gypsies at home and abroad; he travelled on the Puszta with Hungarian Gypsies, and elsewhere with Romanian and Roumelian companies. In 1875 he eloped to Germany with an English Gypsy and singer, Esmeralda Lock (1854–1939), who at the time was still the wife of Hubert Smith. After the divorce Groome married her in 1876, and the two lived together in Edinburgh. This marriage effectively ended in 1899.

In 1876 Groome settled down to regular literary work in Edinburgh. He was soon one of the most valued workers on the staff of the *Globe Encyclopaedia* (6 vols., 1876–9). In 1877 he began jointly to edit 'Suffolk notes and queries' in the *Ipswich Journal*. He edited the *Ordnance Gazetteer of Scotland* (6 vols., 1882–5; 2nd edn, 1893–5), which became a standard work of reference. In 1885 he joined the literary staff of Messrs W. and R. Chambers, and as sub-editor and copious contributor gave invaluable assistance in preparing the new edition of *Chambers's Encyclopaedia* (10 vols., 1888–92). He had a large share in a gazetteer (1895), and was joint editor of a biographical dictionary, both published by the same house. Meanwhile he was an occasional contributor to *Blackwood's Magazine*, *The Bookman*, and other periodicals, wrote many articles for the *Dictionary of National Biography*, and did much systematic reviewing for *The Athenaeum*. *A Short Border History* was issued in 1887. The delightful sketches of his father and his father's friend, Edward FitzGerald, published as *Two Suffolk Friends* in 1895, were expanded from two articles in *Blackwood's Magazine* in 1889 and 1891.

At the same time Groome wrote much on Gypsies. His article 'Gipsies', contributed to the ninth edition of the *Encyclopaedia Britannica*, made him known to the world as a Gypsyologist. *In Gipsy Tents* (1880; 2nd edn, 1881) recorded much of his own experience. He was joint editor of the first series of the *Journal of the Gypsy Lore Society* (1888–92; revived in 1907), and a paper by him, 'The influence of the Gypsies on the superstitions of the English folk', was printed in 1891 in the *Transactions of the International Folk-Lore Congress*. His hypothesis was that Gypsies had probably disseminated many European folk beliefs and tales, some of which had originated in India. Walter Watts-Dunton said that in Groome's remarkable Gypsy novel, with the oddly irrelevant title *Kriegspiel* (1896), 'there was more substance than in five ordinary stories', the Gypsy chapters, with autobiographical elements, being 'absolutely perfect'. *Gypsy Folk Tales* (1899) contains over seventy tales with variants from many lands, and the elaborate introduction is a monument of erudition and ripe scholarship, reiterating his 1891 paper. He attributed to the Gypsies the introduction to Europe of playing cards and puppetry, among other skills. He produced also an edition of George Borrow's *Lavengro* (1901), with notes and a valuable introduction. When his working powers failed him, Groome was assisting in the preparation of a new edition of *Chambers's Cyclopaedia of English Literature* (3 vols., 1901–3), and for more than a year he was a confirmed invalid. He died in London on 24 January 1902, and was buried beside his father and mother in Monk Soham churchyard, Suffolk.

Nothing in Groome's life is more remarkable than that he should have passed so swiftly and cheerfully from a bohemian life into the bondage of systematic labour, and have worked in the new conditions with a rare efficiency. A singularly alert, swift, and eager intellect, he was unwearied in research, impatient of anything less than precision, a frank and fearless critic, and a man of strong convictions. Thoroughly at home in wide fields of historical and philological research, and in some of them a master, he had a knowledge of the romantic side of Scottish history such as few Scotsmen possessed, notably of Jacobite literature in all its ramifications native and foreign. His vivacious style showed a marked individuality. He was a close friend of Swinburne and the writer Walter Watts-Dunton, and he maintained a correspondence with eminent scholars of Gypsy lore all over Europe, including August Friedrich Pott and Franz von Miklosich; some of his many letters to C. G. Leland are quoted in Elizabeth Pennell's biography of Leland (1906).

DAVID PATRICK, *rev.* D. S. KENRICK

**Sources** T. Watts-Dunton, 'The Tarno Rye', *The Athenaeum* (22 Feb 1902), 243–6 · M. O. Jones, 'Frances Hindes Groome: "scholar Gypsy and Gypsy scholar"', *Journal of American Folklore*, 80 (1967), 71–80 · 'Esmeralda Groome: an appreciation by her Romani pen', *Journal of the Gypsy Lore Society*, 3rd ser., 18 (1939), 153–8 · *The Scotsman* (25 Jan 1902)

**Archives** Boston Athenaeum, Boston, corresp., notebooks, and papers · NL Scot., 'Jacobite index' [compiled by Groome] · U. Lpool L. | BL, corresp. with G. C. Leyland, Add. MSS 37173–37174

**Likenesses** photograph (aged twenty-five), repro. in 'Esmeralda Groome: an appreciation', facing p. 156 · photographs, U. Lpool L., Gypsy Lore Society collection

**Groome, John** (1678/9–1760), Church of England clergyman and benefactor, was the son of John Groome of Norwich. After attending Norwich grammar school he entered Magdalene College, Cambridge, as a sizar on 14 October 1695, and graduated BA in 1699. In July 1709 he was presented to the vicarage of Childerditch, Essex, and became also chaplain to Robert, earl of Holdernesse. Groome married Mary Moor of the parish of St James, Westminster, at Gray's Inn chapel on 28 June 1718. The couple did not have any children.

Groome was the author of several devotional works. *The Golden Cordial* (1705) provided prayers for every day of the week. *The Sinner Convicted* (1705) was an attack on atheism. In addition, grieved at what he saw as unjust reflections cast upon the clergy, Groome wrote *The Dignity and Honour of the Clergy Represented in an Historical Collection* (1710). This aimed to show the significant contribution which the clergy made to the nation 'by their universal learning, acts of charity, and the administration of civil offices'.

Groome died in the parish of St Mary, Whitechapel, on 31 July 1760, and was buried at Childerditch. By his will he bequeathed property for founding exhibitions at Magdalene College, preference to be given to clergymen's sons from Essex. He provided for the payment of £6 a year to the succeeding vicars of Childerditch for ever, that they might go to the college on St Mary Magdalen's day, 22 July, 'when the publick benefactions are read over' to see that his exhibitions were filled in, the profits of such as were vacant to go to the vicar. Groome also gave his library to Magdalene College.

GORDON GOODWIN, *rev.* ROBERT BROWN

**Sources** Venn, *Alum. Cant.* • P. Morant, *The history and antiquities of the county of Essex*, 2 vols. (1768) • *GM*, 1st ser., 30 (1760), 394 • will, PRO, PROB 11/858, sig. 324

**Wealth at death** left property for funding exhibitions at Magdalene College, Cambridge: will, PRO, PROB 11/858, sig. 324; *DNB*

**Groome, Robert Hindes** (1810–1889), Church of England clergyman, was born at Framlingham on 18 January 1810, the second son of the Revd John Hindes Groome (1776–1845), rector of Earl Soham and Monk Soham in Suffolk, and his wife, Mary (*c.*1784–*c.*1867), daughter of William Burcham of London and his wife, Rebecca Keer of Framlingham. His grandfather Robinson Groome had been a merchant and mariner of Aldeburgh. Educated at Norwich School under Edward Valpy and Howes, Groome entered Gonville and Caius College, Cambridge, as a pensioner in 1828, graduating BA in 1832 and MA in 1836. He made some lifelong friends, including Edward FitzGerald (1809–1883), the poet and translator, through the musical society, in which he played the cello and Fitz the piano. Groome was ordained deacon in 1833 and priest in 1834. After two years as curate of Tannington-with-Brundish he travelled in Germany from 1835 to 1838 as tutor to Rafael Mendizabal, son of the Spanish financier and ambassador. He was curate of Corfe Castle for six years, and for a year mayor. On 1 February 1843 he married Mary (1815–1893), the youngest daughter of the rector of Swanage, the Revd James Leonard Jackson, and his wife, Louisa Decima Hyde Wollaston. Four sons and two daughters of his eight children outlived him. On his father's death in 1845 Groome succeeded at Monk Soham, his elder brother taking over Earl Soham and both advowsons. For his straggling parish of 1600 acres, its population of 500 declining, Groome built a village school and rectory, and restored the church, providing an organ and hanging the bells. He was appointed an honorary canon of Norwich in 1858, and for five years from 1861 he edited the *Christian Advocate and Review*. In 1869 Bishop J. T. Pelham made him archdeacon of Suffolk, an office which failing eyesight compelled him to resign in 1887; nearly 200 of the clergy he had served subscribed to a presentation portrait.

It was among his own literary circle, mostly Cambridge men—W. B. Donne, William Airy, W. H. Thompson (master of Trinity), and Bradshaw (the university librarian), as well as FitzGerald and Charles Keene—that this warm and sturdily humorous countryman came into his own. Well and widely read, Groome wrote little and published less, but his second son, Francis Hindes *Groome (1851–1902), preserved his father's most memorable anecdotes, and the Suffolk dialect folk tales which he usually signed John Dutfen, in *Two Suffolk Friends* (1895); 'The Only Darter' and 'Master Charley' are the finest. Robert encouraged and assisted Francis to edit a series of 'Suffolk notes and queries' for the *Ipswich Journal* in 1877–8; they wrote most of the content themselves.

Groome and FitzGerald, the two Suffolk friends of Francis Groome's title, meant a great deal to each other. Woodbridge, FitzGerald's home, was only fourteen miles from Soham, so visits and notes were exchanged rather than letters: in fact, in *The Letters of Edward FitzGerald* there are only four short letters to Groome, although he is often mentioned in others to mutual friends. In 1876 FitzGerald told John Allen, archdeacon of Shropshire, that 'Groome has been up to London about his Eyes, … He has good Daughters who will do for him as Milton's did for their Father' (FitzGerald to Allen, 9 Dec 1876; *Letters of Edward FitzGerald*, 3.726). FitzGerald and Groome worked together for members of their circle: in 1867, eager to help Edward Byles Cowell obtain the new chair of Sanskrit at Cambridge, they agreed that Groome should write to Thompson at Trinity, and the application met with success. They shared to the full their love of music, but in religion FitzGerald was unorthodox, although not an atheist; he gave up church attendance in 1852, but that only made Groome more important to him. He told Donne in a letter that his friend had preached at Woodbridge: 'I did not venture into the sacred Edifice: but I looked through a Glass Door in the Porch and saw RG and heard his Voice (*not* the Words) ascending and descending in a rather dramatic way' (FitzGerald to Donne, 3 Dec 1862; *Letters of Edward FitzGerald*, 2.469). The friendship ended only with FitzGerald's death in 1883.

In photographs Groome appears tall and spare, with a slight stoop, his eyes dim: it is moving to find the imposing chair in which he sat for the camera in the church today. Groome died on 19 March 1889 at his rectory and was buried four days later in Monk Soham churchyard. His wife lived a further four years at the Manor House, Pakenham, before joining him in the churchyard, where four yews presented by FitzGerald still grow by the gate over a century later.

J. M. BLATCHLY

**Sources** F. H. Groome, *Two Suffolk friends* (1895) • *The letters of Edward FitzGerald*, ed. A. M. Terhune and A. B. Terhune, 4 vols. (1980) • d. cert. • m. cert. • Venn, *Alum. Cant.* • *DNB*

**Likenesses** W. R. Symonds, oils, *c.*1887, Christchurch Mansion, Ipswich • photographs, repro. in Groome, *Two Suffolk friends*, frontispiece, facing p. 20 • photographs, priv. coll.

**Wealth at death** £4035 5*s.* 7*d.*: probate, 10 April 1889, *CGPLA Eng. & Wales*

**Grosart, Alexander Balloch** (1827–1899), literary scholar and theologian, was born at Stirling on 18 June 1827, the son of William Grosart, builder and contractor, and his wife, Mary Balloch. He was educated privately and at the parish school of Falkirk, and, according to Smeaton, 'Young Grosart was not fifteen when he entered the University of Edinburgh', for 'In those days the fashion prevailed of sending youths to college at a much earlier age than now' (Smeaton, 528). This would put his admission to the university in 1842, not in 1848 as has been proposed elsewhere. He had intended to prepare for the ministry, but he had early acquired a love for literary and antiquarian studies, and although he failed to take a degree, his studies prepared him for the special work to which he later devoted his life. In 1851 he published an edition of the works of Robert Fergusson with a preface, a list of editions, a life of the poet, a critical essay, and a glossary. The edition of Fergusson, with its scholarly paraphernalia, was to be a prototype of much of his later work.

Grosart entered the theological hall of the United Presbyterian Church in Edinburgh that same year and in due course was licensed by the presbytery of Edinburgh in January 1856. He received a call from the First Congregation of Kinross and was ordained there on 29 October 1856. He soon won a reputation as a preacher in this large and influential church and also became well known as an author of religious manuals, as well as a literary antiquary. He declined a call to Woolwich in January 1862 but three years later accepted one from the newly formed congregation of Princes Park, Liverpool. Between 1862 and 1865 he married the daughter of David McDowall JP, a builder and contractor of Dublin. He was translated to Mount Street Presbyterian Church, Blackburn, Lancashire, on 4 March 1868, shortly after which he moved with most of the congregation to a new church, St George's, in Preston New Road. During his ministry the membership of this church was nearly tripled. When the church was free from debt, a new church was started in the Whalley Range district of Blackburn in 1884. Notwithstanding his literary occupations, Grosart was a popular, diligent, and sympathetic performer of his pastoral duties.

Grosart's reputation was as a great Elizabethan and Jacobean scholar. He reprinted thirty-nine volumes under the general title of the Fuller Worthies Library (1868–76), including authors such as Donne, Herbert, and Crashaw. This was followed by eighteen volumes of another series entitled Occasional Issues of Unique and very Rare Books (1875–83), which was privately printed. This series, like the others, included a list of the subscribers to each volume, alphabetically and democratically arranged, and found among these lists were such well-known names as Edmund Gosse, George Saintsbury, A. C. Swinburne, H. H. Furness, F. S. Palgrave, and Henry Morley. No pains were spared to ensure that the editions were limited; an assurance to this effect printed under the list of subscribers was reinforced by the statement that 'Proof-sheets and waste pages have been destroyed'. All the volumes featured a biographical and bibliographical introduction, ranging in length from a few pages, to that for *Alba: the Month's Minde of a Melancholy Lover*, which ran to sixty-nine pages. The style of the introductions is arch, with various injunctions to the reader to turn to such and such a poem or passage or to mark the felicity of some turn of phrase. All have appended notes and illustrations. A third series, with fourteen volumes, was entitled the Chertsey Worthies Library (1876–81), named after the home of Abraham Cowley, one of the poets making part of that series. A fourth series of reprints, the Huth Library (1881–6), named after the great book collector, ran to twenty-nine volumes, with a number of promised volumes abandoned, presumably because of Grosart's advanced age and uncertain health. Among the authors in this collection were Robert Greene, Thomas Nashe, Gabriel Harvey, and Thomas Dekker.

In addition to the four named series of reprints, with their emphasis on lay literature, Grosart had early reprinted a number of volumes by puritan divines, including *The Complete Works of Richard Sibbes* (7 vols., 1862–4); *The Works of Thomas Brooks* (6 vols., 1866–7); Herbert Palmer's *Memorials of Godliness* (1865); Michael Bruce's *Poems* (1865); and Richard Gilpin's *Demonologia sacra* (1867). In two pamphlets he set himself to solve two problems of authorship. The title of the first, *Lord Bacon not the Author of 'Christian Paradoxes'* (1865), as indeed he was not, needs no further explanation. The second, *Who Wrote 'Brittain's Ida'* (1869), concerned the poem previously ascribed to Edmund Spenser but which Grosart correctly claimed for Phineas Fletcher. It was not, however, until 1920 that he was proved right.

Grosart reprinted and edited volumes for the Chetham Society, for the Roxburghe Club, and for the Camden Society, in addition to a number of volumes not associated with any series or society. One estimate puts the total number of volumes he reprinted and/or edited at 300. He also added to his editions of the works of the puritan divines a small number of religious publications. And he was himself the author of hymns and religious poems which were collected and published in 1890 under the title *Songs of the Day and Night, or, Three Centuries of Original Hymns*. Possibly his proudest moment was when he was thanked by Tennyson for his dedication to the poet of his edition of Spenser (*Letters of … Tennyson*, 3.298, 301–3).

Grosart was not, however, without his critics. Smeaton wrote (albeit disapprovingly of her), that 'Mrs. Humphrey Ward … has said that "*all* the work he did will have to be done over again"' (Smeaton, 531). Grosart's friend, Edward Dowden, often assisted him in reading his proofs, and Grosart had earlier acknowledged Dowden's help in his edition of the uncollected prose writings of Wordsworth, three volumes (1876). Dowden also wrote one of the critical essays accompanying Grosart's edition of the works of Spenser (10 vols., 1880–88). Yet Dowden was not entirely happy with Grosart's scholarship, pointing out 'a passage in Drayton's "Owl" which throws light on that poem about which Grosart has been manufacturing a mare's nest, "The Phoenix and the Turtle"' (*Letters of Edward Dowden*, 133). And five years after Grosart's death, Dowden harked back to the Spenser edition for which Grosart had provided a biographical memoir, writing, 'I have Grosart's wild wilderness of a Life, which of course contains some valuable things' (ibid., 330), damning with faint praise. Even Smeaton, while lauding Grosart's textual and editorial labours, was prepared to admit that his critical work left much to be desired (Smeaton, 531). But even more severe was Charles Eliot Norton on Grosart's edition of Donne's poetry, which, he wrote:

> while containing much that is of value as affording means for ascertaining the correct readings of doubtful passages, does not itself provide a satisfactory text. It is, in truth, disfigured by pedantry in following the spelling of ill-written manuscripts, and by blunders proceeding from carelessness and lack of intelligence. (C. E. Norton, 'The text of Donne's poems', *Studies and Notes in Philosophy and Literature*, 5, 1896)

Norton gives a number of examples in a footnote (ibid., 3–4), ignoring Grosart's justification for his editorial methods, found in the preface to the edition:

> I do not hide from myself that it needs courage (though I do not claim praise for its exercise) to edit and print the Poetry of DR. JOHN DONNE in our day. Nor would I call it literary prudery that shrinks from giving publicity to such sensuous things (to say the least) as indubitably are found therein … I deplore that Poetry, in every way almost so memorable …, should be stained even to uncleanliness in sorrowfully too many places.

As an ordained minister he had, of necessity, to explain why he had elected to edit poetry of the kind written by Donne.

Grosart travelled to the great libraries of France, Germany, Italy, and Russia, as well as to those of England, Scotland, and Ireland. Once he came upon the rare volumes he sought, it was he who made all the arrangements for their reprinting, their subscription lists, and their prices. In August 1877 he was honoured by the University of Edinburgh, where he had not earned a degree, with the honorary degree of LLD. The University of St Andrews conferred on him the degree of DD. He resigned his position as minister at Blackburn in November 1892 for health reasons. Grosart retired to Dublin in 1892, where he died at Bank Villa on 16 March 1899 and was buried in Mount Jerome cemetery. He was survived by four sons. An obituary notice in an Irish newspaper noted that:

> He managed to make a great reputation both as a preacher and as a man of letters, a combination extremely rare, but in his case so striking as to be unique. At one time he was spoken of in England as if there were two Dr. Grosarts. (Smeaton, 534)

It is perhaps fitting to close the saga of Grosart's efforts with Smeaton's statement that at the time of Grosart's death 'In company with Mr. Keith Leask and myself he had been planning a monumental "History of Scottish Literature" in twelve volumes, which he had regarded as his *magnum opus*' (ibid., 537). ARTHUR SHERBO

**Sources** W. H. O. Smeaton, 'A great Elizabethan scholar: the late A. B. Grosart, D.D., LLD.', *Westminster Review*, 151 (1899), 527–37 · *DNB* · *Letters of Edward Dowden and his correspondents*, ed. E. D. Dowden and H. M. Dowden (1914) · *The letters of Alfred Lord Tennyson*, ed. C. Y. Lang and E. F. Shannon, 3: *1871–1892* (1990)

**Archives** Blackburn Central District Library, notebook · CUL, letters, notes, and receipts · NL Wales, letters · TCD, sermons and letters | BL, letters to Gladstone, Add. MSS 44405–44526 · BL, letters to W. C. Hazlitt, Add. MSS 38900–38913, *passim* · Bodl. Oxf., letters to George Bell & Sons; letters to W. T. Brooke; corresp. with Sir Henry Taylor; corresp. with H. H. Vaughan · JRL, letters to W. E. A. Axon · NL Scot., letters to William Blackwood & Sons · TCD, letters to Edward Dowden; letters to W. E. H. Lecky · U. Aberdeen L., letters to Peter Buchan · U. Edin. L., letters to J. Halliwell-Phillipps; letters to D. Laing · U. Reading L., letters to George Bell & Sons

**Grose, Francis** (*bap.* 1731, *d.* 1791), antiquary, was born in his father's house in Broad Street, St Peter-le-Poer, London, the eldest of seven children of Francis Jacob Grose (*d.* 1769), an immigrant Swiss jeweller, and his wife, Anne (*d.* 1773), daughter of Thomas Bennett of Greenford, Middlesex; he was baptized on 11 June 1731 in the parish of St Peter-le-Poer. His later scholarship suggests he received a classical education, but in early 1747 he was in Flanders with Howard's (later 19th) regiment of foot, probably a volunteer in search of a commission. This he gained in December 1748 as a cornet in Cobham's (later 10th) regiment of dragoons. While deployed against smugglers in Kent he married, at Harbledown in May 1750, Catherine (1733?–1774), daughter of William Jordan, vintner of Canterbury. They had ten children, of whom two sons and four daughters survived to adulthood.

With a young family, and his regiment ordered to Scotland, Grose retired from the army in October 1751. His father bought for him in 1755 the place of Richmond herald, but Grose showed no great taste for heraldry and sold it in February 1763. As early as 1749, though, he was sketching medieval buildings in Kent, and in the mid-1750s attended William Shipley's drawing school in London. The embodiment of the militia enabled him to don uniform again while avoiding distant postings. In November 1759 he was commissioned as a lieutenant in the Surrey regiment and appointed adjutant and paymaster of the 2nd (western) battalion. Its movements provided ample opportunities for drawing. The battalion was disembodied in December 1762, but as adjutant Grose continued to receive salary in peacetime. Promotion to captain in 1765 gave him the title by which he was commonly to be known.

Now living in Wandsworth, Surrey, Grose sketched in the vicinity and on social visits to relatives. In London, though only an indifferent draughtsman, he mixed with professional and amateur artists, and exhibited at the Society of Artists in 1767–8 and at the Royal Academy in the nine years following. His first published pictures were etchings in the second edition of *A Voyage to the East Indies* (1766) by his brother John Henry *Grose (*b.* 1732, *d.* in or after 1774) writer on India. His militia salary, together with inheritances from his parents and on his wife's death in 1774, gave him the means to maintain his family in comfort, with prudent management.

Hope of profit, therefore, may not have prompted the publication of Grose's *The Antiquities of England and Wales*. This work published engravings, much smaller than, but similar in character to, the Bucks' *Views* (1726–42), generally panoramas of medieval structures intended to convey the maximum information, rather than interesting compositions or illustrations of details. Grose's novelty was to

Francis Grose (*bap.* 1731, *d.* 1791), by Nathaniel Dance, 1787

publish text with the views. His purpose, stated in the introduction, was popular, 'for the use of such as are desirous of having, without much trouble, a general knowledge of the subjects treated in this publication', and a similar motive guided his contributions to the periodical *Antiquarian Repertory* (1775–86). The first part of the *Antiquities* appeared in February or March 1772, with each view and its descriptive text on a separate page. Periodically a title-page and introduction were issued to signal completion of a volume.

From 1772 Grose was touring to make sketches which were engraved and published within a few months, and was borrowing pictures from friends, particularly John Inigo Richards, Paul Sandby, and, from 1774, Moses Griffiths. Sometimes the accompanying text came almost entirely (with acknowledgement) from published books, or from fellow antiquaries; in other cases Grose was in correspondence to collect material from which he could draft. Part 60, issued in June 1776, closed the fourth volume and, with a set of thirty-three plans, the project, but only until he started publishing the supplement a year later. This reached three parts before a lengthy interruption.

The cause was the militia's embodiment, from March 1778 to February 1783. Grose did not enjoy this active service. First, the Surrey militia functioned as a single battalion, so increasing his responsibilities. Most of the summers—the prime time for antiquarian tours—were spent in camp with other corps for training. Secondly, his easy relationship with the previous commanding officer, George Onslow, was lacking with Jeremiah Hodges, who was the target of some biting satire by Grose in *Advice to the Officers of the British Army*, published anonymously in 1782. Thirdly, his haphazard management of the regiment's finances landed him in substantial debt to his fellow officers: so much so as to shape the rest of his life.

Grose gave up the large house in Wandsworth for lodgings at Clement's Inn, just west of the City of London (first taken in 1771), and then nearby with his publisher Samuel Hooper, now being a regular and genial participant in the Society of Antiquaries, to which he had been elected in 1757. The sympathetic sketch by Nathaniel Dance engraved in 1787 shows the stocky, corpulent figure which Grose himself caricatured. From 1783 he published in a torrent to make a living. The *Supplement to the Antiquities* was resumed, with a greater proportion of views from other artists, particularly S. H. Grimm, and was completed with 309 plates in 1787. This and the main series were reissued in a cheaper edition in 1783–7. *A Classical Dictionary of the Vulgar Tongue* (1785) and *A Provincial Glossary, with a Collection of Local Proverbs, and Popular Superstitions* (1787) were at the time the largest assemblage of 'non-standard' words or meanings, about 9000, omitted from Samuel Johnson's *Dictionary*; they drew on his fieldwork as far back as the 1750s. The first parts of two other pioneering works appeared in 1786: *Military Antiquities* and *A Treatise on Ancient Armour*. Both relied mainly on his specialist library and the armouries at the Tower of London, but also included observations on military music from the 1740s. Of more popular appeal was *Rules for Drawing Caricaturas: with an Essay on Comic Painting* (1788).

By now Grose must have exhausted for publication the stock of sketches and notes which he had accumulated over forty years. He returned to viewing monuments of antiquity, even though (as he said in a volume of satirical essays, *The Grumbler*, 1791) he was too fat to ride a horse and too poor to keep a carriage. *The Antiquities of Scotland* was compiled with tours in 1788, 1789, and 1790 and publication was completed in April 1791. On his second tour, in summer 1789, he met Robert Burns and the two became firm friends. He became the subject of some witty verses by Burns, who was inspired by Grose to write 'Tam o' Shanter' to accompany a drawing of Alloway kirk printed in *The Antiquities of Scotland*. Work began on *The Antiquities of Ireland* in 1790, but on his next visit, on 12 May 1791, he died suddenly of an apoplectic fit at Horace Hone's house in Dame Street, Dublin, and was buried on 18 May 1791 at Drumcondra church, co. Meath. His nephew Daniel and Dr Edward Ledwich completed the project in 1796. His library and drawings were dispersed at auction.

Undecided what profession to follow, Francis Grose in his early years had the makings of the dilettante antiquary. At the age of forty, however, he was inspired to respond to widening interest in British antiquities and to make the remains of the past more intelligible and accessible to his lay readers. Financial necessity later drove him harder. While he may not have advanced the scholarly projects of the Society of Antiquaries' leading figures—who may not always have been amused by his wit and caricatures—he had an uncommon breadth of conception of what antiquarian studies should embrace. Burns had 'never seen a man of more original observation, anecdote and remark' (*The Letters of Robert Burns*, ed. J. de L. Ferguson and G. R. Roy, 3 vols., 1985, 1.423), and, well equipped by an amiable personality, Grose was as able to collect dialect among the rank and file of the army as to examine the curios of the gentry. By doing so he contributed significantly to the study of slang and folklore and of military antiquities, as well as to popular appreciation of the medieval monuments of Britain. JOHN H. FARRANT

**Sources** J. H. Farrant, 'The travels and travails of Francis Grose, FSA', *The Antiquaries' Journal*, 75 (1995), 365–80 • *DNB* • *GM*, 1st ser., 39 (1769), 608 • *GM*, 1st ser., 61 (1791), 493 • parish register (baptism), London, St Peter-le-Poer, 11 June 1731 • Canterbury Cathedral Archives, DCb/MB 1750/1 [marriage licence] • 'Memoir of Francis Grose, esq., FAS', *Dublin Chronicle* (31 May 1791)

**Archives** BL, notes and drawings, MS tour, Add. MS 17398; Add. MS 21550; Eg MS 1843 • Bodl. Oxf., correspondence, notes, drawings and other MSS • S. Antiquaries, Lond., Grose pictures | S. Antiquaries, Lond., Snelgrove MSS, notes and copies, c.1960–90, on Grose by Dudley Snelgrove, MS 964

**Likenesses** N. Dance, portrait, chalk, 1787, Scot. NPG [*see illus.*]

**Grose, Francis** (1758?–1814). *See under* New South Wales Corps (*act.* 1789–1810).

**Grose, John** (*bap.* **1758**, *d.* **1821**), Church of England clergyman, was baptized on 26 February 1758 in Richmond, Surrey, the eldest son of John Henry *Grose (*b.* 1732, *d.* in or after 1774) of Richmond, writer on India, and Sarah Smalley (*bap.* 1733, *d.* 1788/9), daughter of John Browning, wool stapler, of Barnaby Street, Southwark, Surrey. Grose was elected FSA on 4 May 1780, with his uncles Francis and Daniel Grose among his sponsors. In 1782 he published by subscription a volume of thirty essays which had already appeared in periodicals, as *Ethics, Rational and Theological, with Cursory Reflections on the General Principles of Deism*. The *Reflections*, observed the reviewer in the *Gentleman's Magazine*, showed Grose 'to be a rational as well as scriptural believer' (*GM*, 1st ser., 52, 1782, 442). Only later did he enter university, matriculating from St Mary Hall, Oxford, on 29 May 1783. His graduation is unrecorded but in later years he described himself as MA.

Grose took Anglican orders and held several small preferments in or close to the City of London. His first wife, Ann Meriton, with whom he had a son, died in 1787 and within a year Grose married Anna Carter Eugenia Hillyard, the widow of an officer in 1st foot guards. They had a son and a daughter. For periods at least as long as those shown, Grose was minister of the Tower (1787–94); lecturer of St Olave, Southwark (1794–1816); curate of the united parishes of St Margaret Pattens and St Gabriel Fenchurch (1800–2), and then of St Margaret Pattens alone (1804–16); Wednesday evening lecturer of St Antholin, Budge Row (1804); and lecturer of St Benet Gracechurch (1808–16). He was also chaplain to the countess dowager of Mexborough (1800–16). In 1805 the patronage of the rectory of Netteswell, Essex, fell to the crown, as the previous incumbent was a lunatic, and Grose was presented to it.

Grose published by subscription 74 of his sermons in six collections between 1800 and 1816. He died, probably at the rectory in Little Tower Street, St Margaret Pattens, London, before 14 March 1821, and was survived by his second wife, Anna.

GORDON GOODWIN, *rev.* JOHN H. FARRANT

**Sources** J. Grose, *Twelve sermons*, 6 vols. (1800–16) • J. Grose, *Sermons on various subjects*, 5 vols. (1802–16) • *DNB* • J. C. C. Smith, ed., *The parish registers of Richmond, Surrey*, 2 vols. (1903–5) • minute book XVII: 1780, 2 March, 4 May, 11 May, Society of Antiquaries • Foster, *Alum. Oxon.* • *VCH Essex*, 8.211 • *GM*, 1st ser., 57 (1787), 837 • PRO, PROB 6/197, fol. 224 • *IGI*

**Wealth at death** under £200: administration, 1821, PRO, PROB 6/197, fol. 224

**Grose, John Henry** (*b.* **1732**, *d.* in or after **1774**), East India Company servant and writer on India, was born on 24 August 1732 in St Peter-le-Poer, City of London, probably at his father's house in Broad Street. He was the second of seven children of Francis Jacob Grose (*d.* 1769), an immigrant Swiss jeweller, and his wife, Anne (*d.* 1773), daughter of Thomas Bennett of Greenford, Middlesex. After taking a course in writing and merchants' accounts at J. Bland's academy in Bishopsgate, Grose was elected a writer in the East India Company in November 1749 and arrived to serve in the Bombay presidency in August 1750. He was advanced to deputy secretary early in 1753, but his career ended soon after, when he was dismissed the service and sent home, 'having been deprived of his senses for some months past, and there being no hope of his recovery' (Bombay public consultations, 14 Dec 1753, BL OIOC, P/341/19, p. 414).

On 11 December 1755 he married Sarah Smalley (*bap.* 1733, *d.* 1788/9), daughter of John Browning, woolstapler of Barnaby Street, Southwark, Surrey, with whom he had two sons. His elder son, John *Grose, was an Anglican clergyman. They lived in Richmond, Surrey, to which his father had retired. He fell into serious debt. By paying off debts and forgiving loans, his father in his lifetime gave him his entire inheritance and it may have been his death which forced Grose in 1770 to escape his creditors by going to France. He lived at Dieppe and Rouen, latterly teaching languages. Perhaps because his mother's death brought another inheritance (though vested in two of his brothers), he returned to England in 1774, but only after being imprisoned for attempting to travel without a passport and badly injuring one of those arresting him. No later reference to him has been found.

In 1757 was published over his name *A Voyage to the East-Indies, with Observations on Various Parts there*. In 400 pages the book describes his outward voyage, Bombay and its governance by the East India Company, Surat, the recent history of the Mughal empire, local religions and the progress of the Catholic missions, and a miscellany of social practices. The French translation of 1758 stated that he had been helped by the observations of 'M. Cl.'—possibly John Cleland, who, having served at Bombay in 1728–40, edited notes which Grose had made. In the second edition of 1766 were added a derivative account of the Seven Years' War and six etchings probably by his brother the antiquary Francis *Grose. In the third edition of 1772 the anonymous editor included Charmichael's *Journey from Aleppo to Busserah* in 1771. The book was an early, popular account of India based on first-hand observation, but was soon superseded by the more scholarly work of the early orientalists. JOHN H. FARRANT

**Sources** J. H. Grose, *A voyage to the East Indies*, new edn, 2 vols. (1772) • writers' petitions, BL OIOC, J/1/1 • Bombay public consultations, BL OIOC, P/341/18–19 • wills, PRO, PROB 11/953/414 and 11/991/391 [Francis Jacob Grose and Anne Grose] • Richmond land tax, Surrey HC, QS 6/7 • PRO, SP 78/292, fols. 98–100, 212–4 • Bigland pedigrees, Coll. Arms, XI, fol. 56; XXI, fol. 230 • parish register, London, St Peter-le-Poer (transcript), GL • *IGI* • deeds of Jacob Grose's property, Hants. RO, Appleshaw deeds, 59M74, E/T 34–81

**Grose, Sir Nash** (1740–1814), judge, was the son of Edward Grose, of the City of London. Educated at Tonbridge School, he went on to Trinity Hall, Cambridge, in June 1757. He later graduated LLB (1768) and was fellow of his college (1776–9). Groomed for the legal profession, he was admitted to Lincoln's Inn in Trinity term 1756, and called to the bar on 26 November 1766. He married a Miss Dennett (*d*. 1794) of the Isle of Wight, and they had at least one son, Edward Grose (*d*. 1815), who served as an officer under Wellington.

Grose joined in weekly gatherings of rising young barristers at a villa at Putney taken by Lloyd Kenyon, later chief justice of king's bench for a majority of the years Grose served on that court. Others at the weekly gatherings included Alexander Wedderburn (later Lord Loughborough), Beaumont Hotham, James Mansfield, James Wallace, John Skynner, Pepper Arden, and John Scott (later Lord Eldon). Well suited for the law, Grose became proficient in special pleading, while at the same time exhibiting enough eloquence in the courtroom to ensure his success at *nisi prius*. A biographer writing just three years after Grose became a judge observed: 'Professional ability, we believe, *alone*, raised Mr. Grose to the Bench, who, in the course of twenty years practice, established a professional Character equally eminent and amiable;—his share of business was, consequently, extensive' (Rede, 68).

Grose's extensive practice was mainly in common pleas, where he became the leader of the bar after the death in 1779 of Serjeant John Glynn. He also appeared not infrequently in king's bench. As counsel for defendant in the king's bench case of *Kingston* v. *Preston* he successfully appealed to Lord Mansfield's business acumen in what would become a milestone decision in contract law. Later, when Grose was himself a judge on king's bench and a similar case came before the court (*Glazebrook* v. *Woodrow*, 1799), he strongly commended the Kingston decision, helping to establish it as a leading case for centuries to follow. A retired barrister, inclined to be critical, described Grose as having a sour complexion and a sour-looking face; but mentioned his toughness and an instinct for rooting out perjury, pettifogging, and fraud (Espinasse).

Grose was designated a serjeant-at-law on 28 April 1774. On the death of Sir Edward Willes, Grose was named a judge of king's bench and was knighted. He took his seat on the court on 9 February 1787, and served faithfully and capably until infirmities caused him to resign in Easter vacation 1813. By Lord Campbell's eyewitness account, Grose's appearance 'was very foolish' (Campbell, 3.58), but Campbell acknowledged Grose's ability as a judge, quoting the following epigram by Erskine: 'Grose *justice*, with his *lantern* jaws, Throws *light* upon the English laws' (ibid.). According to Sir William Holdsworth, Grose was 'perhaps the least remarkable' of the puisne judges on king's bench in the late eighteenth century, but was nevertheless 'a sound lawyer who … expressed his opinions shortly and clearly', exhibiting a mind that 'had a strain of legal conservatism' (Holdsworth, *Eng. law*, 12.485).

Grose died on 31 May 1814 at Petersfield, Hampshire, and was buried at The Priory, his country estate on the Isle of Wight. His wife had died in 1794 at the judge's house in Bloomsbury Square, London. JAMES OLDHAM

**Sources** *Strictures on the lives and characters of the most eminent lawyers of the present day* (1790) • John, Lord Campbell, *The lives of the chief justices of England*, 3 vols. (1849–57) • Holdsworth, *Eng. law* • W. P. Baildon and R. Roxburgh, eds., *The records of the Honorable Society of Lincoln's Inn: the black books*, 5 vols. (1897–1968) • Foss, *Judges* • J. Haydn, *The book of dignities: containing lists of the official personages of the British empire*, ed. H. Ockerby, 3rd edn (1894) • G. T. Kenyon, *Life of Lloyd, first Lord Kenyon* (1873) • *LondG* (6–10 Feb 1787) • *GM*, 1st ser., 84/1 (1814), 629–30 • J. Oldham, 'Detecting non-fiction: sleuthing among manuscript case reports for what was really said', *Law reporting in England*, ed. C. Stebbings (1995) • W. C. Townsend, *The lives of twelve eminent judges*, 2 vols. (1846) • [J. Watkins and F. Shoberl], *A biographical dictionary of the living authors of Great Britain and Ireland* (1816) • *Public characters*, 10 vols. (1799–1809) • [I. Espinasse], 'My contemporaries: from the notebooks of a retired barrister', *Fraser's Magazine*, 6 (1832), 224–8

**Archives** Isle of Wight RO, Newport, corresp. and papers; letters and wills

**Likenesses** J. Kay, caricature, etching, 1800, NPG

**Grose, Thomas Hodge** (1845–1906), college teacher and university administrator, born at Redruth in Cornwall on 9 November 1845, was the fourth son of James Grose, a Wesleyan minister. An elder brother, James, went to India in 1860 in the civil service, and died a member of council at Madras on 7 June 1898. Educated at Manchester grammar school, under the strenuous high-mastership of Frederick William Walker, Grose was elected to a scholarship at Balliol College, Oxford, in 1864. He was one of the few to obtain four first classes, two in moderations and two again in the final schools (classics and mathematics). He graduated BA in 1868, proceeding MA in 1871. He entered as a student at Lincoln's Inn, but his plans changed and he did not go to the bar.

In 1870 Grose was elected to a fellowship at Queen's College, Oxford, being appointed tutor in the following year, and there the rest of his life was spent. In 1872 he was ordained deacon, but his clerical work was confined to the duties of college chaplain and sermons in the chapel. In

1887 he was elected to the hebdomadal council, and in 1897 to the office of university registrar, which he held until his death. In 1871 he had been president of the Oxford Union, and in 1887, when the finances of the society were in low water, he was appointed to the new office of senior treasurer, which likewise he continued to hold until his death. Between 1876 and 1898 he served as examiner in the school of *literae humaniores* no fewer than a dozen times. He was also president of the Association for the Education of Women and of the Women's Suffrage Society, and latterly a member of the education committee of Nottinghamshire county council. Like others of his generation, he felt no impulse to undertake original research; his only contribution to literature was to assist Thomas Hill Green in editing *The Philosophical Works of David Hume* (1874–5).

Grose's best work was done in his rooms at Queen's. Shy and reserved in manner, with gestures that were awkward and a voice that was gruff, he won the respect and affection of many generations of undergraduates. Himself unmarried, he devoted his time and his money to fatherly relations among an ever expanding circle of those who were to him in the place of sons. He followed closely every stage of his pupils' future life, however far removed they might be from Oxford. In his early years he had been a keen fives player and an alpine climber. He was a member of the Alpine Club from 1900 until his death. Latterly his chief outdoor pursuit was field botany. Almost to the last he travelled much abroad, his interest being divided between natural scenery and art museums. In 1894 he paid a nine months' visit to India. His rooms ultimately became a storehouse of artistic objects and photographs brought back from foreign lands. He died in college, after a long and painful illness, on 11 February 1906, and was buried at Holywell cemetery, Oxford. His principal legacy was to establish in his college a tradition of close personal relations between tutors and undergraduates.

J. S. COTTON, *rev.* M. C. CURTHOYS

**Sources** personal knowledge (1912) • G. S. Gillett, *T. H. Grose: a memory* (1907) • *Thomas Hodge Grose: obituary notices* (1906) • R. H. Hodgkin, *Six centuries of an Oxford college: a history of the Queen's College, 1340–1940* (1949) • J. Foster, *Oxford men and their colleges* (1893)
**Likenesses** R. E. Morrison, oils, 1903, Queen's College, Oxford
**Wealth at death** £2255 19*s.* 11*d.*: probate, 14 March 1906, *CGPLA Eng. & Wales*

**Groser, St John Beverley** (1890–1966), Church of England clergyman and Christian socialist, was born on 23 June 1890 at Beverley, Western Australia, the youngest son of Thomas Eaton Groser and his wife, Phoebe Wainwright. His parents were missionaries and Groser was sent to school in England at Ellesmere College in Shropshire, a Woodard foundation, and high Anglican in ethos. After studying at the College of the Resurrection, Mirfield, he was ordained deacon and priest in the Church of England. He became a socialist while a curate in Newcastle during the First World War. After a wartime chaplaincy in France, he undertook a further curacy in Cornwall. In December 1917 he married Mary Agnes (*d.* 1970), the daughter of the priest of that parish, the Revd M. A. Bucknall. In 1922 Groser became curate of St Michael's, Poplar, east London. These were troubled years, and in 1927 he was dismissed, along with his colleague and brother-in-law Jack Bucknall, from his curacy. His involvement with Conrad Noel and the Catholic Crusade was a key element in his dismissal, though his role in the general strike (when he was beaten by police batons) did not help his relations with the hierarchy. His licence to officiate was removed for some time in this period.

In 1928 Groser became priest-in-charge of Christ Church, Watney Street, Stepney, where he built up a lively, socially involved community. During these years rent strikes occurred, and the battle of Cable Street (when the British Union of Fascists was prevented from marching through the Jewish area of Whitechapel) took place in October 1936. Groser played a major role both in the housing conflicts, as chair of Stepney Tenants' Defence League, and in the resistance to fascism. He opposed means testing and the use of police powers over 'loitering with intent' against unemployed people. He was a member of the London county council's committee on poor relief applications and chair of the local public assistance committee. In 1941 Christ Church was destroyed, and he and his congregation moved to St George-in-the-East, where he remained until 1948.

Groser was profoundly influenced by Noel and the Catholic Crusade, and the Stepney chapter of the crusade was based at Watney Street. Like Noel, he saw the importance of festivity, of colour, music, and dancing, in the creation of a Christian social consciousness. The Watney Street church was an urban representation of what Thaxted was struggling to manifest in the countryside, with joyful festivals, folk-dancing, and processions. Here too was a democratic Christian community, and a strong sense of the liturgy as a sacramental prefiguring of a liberated world.

In 1948 Groser became warden, and later master, of the Royal Foundation of St Katherine, a community of medieval origin, newly located at the Limehouse end of Cable Street, and it was there that he spent the last years of his active life. Supported by colleagues such as Ethel Upton and Dorothy Halsall, he made St Katherine's a centre for Christian discourse, and a power-house of debate and discussion about the future of east London. Here dockers and trade unionists, Christians and Jews, elderly people, and a wide range of social and political groups would meet, making the centre a kind of early 'think-tank' and centre of commitment to the health and welfare of the East End. He was a key figure in the founding of Stepney Old People's Welfare Association and Stepney Coloured People's Association. He retained some outside commitments, playing the part of Becket in the film *Murder in the Cathedral* in 1951.

Politically Groser was one of the first generation of clergy to take Marxism and class-struggle politics seriously. He saw the racial dimensions of Mussolini's fascism at an early stage. Some claimed that he never came to terms with the post-war political settlement in Britain and was more at home amid struggle. Certainly it is his work in the 1930s and 1940s which is most remembered. Theologically, Groser was a traditional Catholic Christian. He saw God, and orthodox faith in God, as subversive. In a sermon at St Paul's Cathedral in 1934 he claimed that 'nothing but the religion of the Incarnation fearlessly taught and worked out in practice in a new social ethic can save the situation' (Halsall). His commitment was to a 'rebel church'. Yet one of the best summaries of his significance came from the former chief rabbi Sir Israel Brodie. Groser, he said, 'embodied the characteristics of the saint', with his 'Amos-like indignation at the grinding of the faces of the poor and his desire for radical social change' (Brill, 102). Groser was undoubtedly one of the most significant Christian socialist figures in twentieth-century Britain. Hannan Swaffer, writing in the *Daily Herald* in 1936, said that he was the best-known priest in the East End of London (19 Oct 1936). Yet he figures hardly at all in the histories of Christian socialism, with the exception of the recent studies by Chris Bryant and Alan Wilkinson, and he is ignored in lives of George Lansbury and other political figures in East London on whom he had an important influence. He wrote only one book. Yet the impact of Groser, not only on the Church of England and the labour movement, but also, through the Student Christian Movement and numerous student missions, on the wider Christian community, and, locally, on struggles around housing, fascism, and the care of the elderly, was enormous. He died on 19 March 1966 at the Churchill Hospital, Oxford, and was buried in the churchyard at Watlington on 25 March. KENNETH LEECH

**Sources** D. Halsall, 'Record of talks, sermons, and writings of St John Beverley Groser, 1926–1961', LPL [also in LPL] • 'Black Sunday tension in the East End', *The Star* (2 Oct 1936) • J. Boggis, 'John Groser: some memories', *Cosmos* (summer 1966), 7–10 • D. Barker, 'Father Groser probes East End's unrest', *Evening Standard* (3 Nov 1936) • K. Brill, ed., *John Groser, East London priest* (1971) • K. Brill and M. 'Espinasse, 'Groser, St John Beverley', *DLB*, vol. 6 • C. Bryant, *Possible dreams: a personal history of the British Christian socialists* (1996) • St J. B. Groser, *Politics and persons* (1949) • St J. B. Groser, 'Loitering with intent', *Daily Herald* (13 March 1935) • St J. B. Groser, 'The Church of England and politics', *Mirfield Gazette*, 13 (Dec 1926), 5–8 • St J. B. Groser, *Does socialism need religion?* (1951) • H. Swaffer, 'Here is a bold priest', *Daily Herald* (3 April 1936) • H. Swaffer, 'East End in fear', *Daily Herald* (19 Oct 1936) • A. Wilkinson, *Christian socialism: Scott Holland to Tony Blair* (1998) • *The Times* (26 March 1966) • *CGPLA Eng. & Wales* (1966) • d. cert.

**Archives** Bancroft Road Library, Tower Hamlets, London, collection of sermons, talks, etc.; working papers relating to life of Dorothy Halsall • LPL, corresp. and MSS | FILM BFI NFTVA, documentary footage

**Wealth at death** £999: probate, 23 May 1966, *CGPLA Eng. & Wales*

**Gross, (Imre) Anthony Sandor** (1905–1984), painter and etcher, was born in Dulwich, London, on 19 March 1905, the elder child and only son of Alexander Gross, formerly Grosz (1880–1958), a naturalized British subject of Hungarian origin who had settled in the London area as a map publisher, and his wife, Isabelle Crowley (1886–1937), who was a playwright and suffragette. Phyllis Isobel *Pearsall, map publisher, was his younger sister.

**(Imre) Anthony Sandor Gross (1905–1984)**, self-portrait, *c.*1925 [*Self-Portrait in a Fez*]

In 1923, after general education at Repton School, Derbyshire, where his first attempts at etching were encouraged, Gross began full-time art training in London, studying painting at the Slade School of Fine Art and etching, in the evenings, at the Central School of Arts and Crafts. Later that year he moved to Paris, continuing with these subjects respectively at the Académie Julian and the École des Beaux-Arts. In April 1924 he went on to Madrid, where he enrolled in the engraving class of the Real Academia de Bellas Artes de San Fernando. Thence, with the aid of a donkey, he spent the summer roaming the countryside, his sketchbook always at the ready. In October 1925, the year of his first one-man exhibition in London, he went back for six months to the Académie Julian. In subsequent years he visited Andalusia, Morocco and Algeria, as well as Italy, Belgium, and France. Thus he not only experienced considerable variety in his formal training but also gained first-hand knowledge of these places and their peoples, even taking part in some bull-fighting. In 1930 he married the painter Marcelle Marguerite (Daisy; 1899–1988), a fashion artist, whose father, Henri Florenty, owned an artificial flower factory and shop. They had one son, Jean-Pierre Anthony (Pete), a historian, and one daughter, Mary (later Mary West), who was her father's printer from 1973.

Gross made friends with many artists in France, not least the engravers S. W. Hayter and Joseph Hecht. He was at first best-known for his topographical works but his series of paintings and prints entitled Sortie d'Usine (completed 1930–31) had as their subject-matter the workers from the local factories and these pictures, so vital and subtle in line, together with those called La Zone, named after a Parisian shanty suburb, reveal his understanding of their life. In contrasting mood and in collaboration with the American Hector Hoppin, he then set about producing thousands of drawings for the cartoon film *La joie de vivre* (1933), followed by (in London, for Alexander Korda) *Fox Hunt* (1936), meanwhile illustrating Jean Cocteau's *Les enfants terribles* for a special edition.

Gross stayed in London from 1934 to 1937 and returned to England again at the outbreak of the Second World War, first of all recording the routine activities at various training depots and then, in 1941, being appointed an official war artist. He went via South Africa to Cairo, and for most of 1942 travelled extensively in Egypt (where he met fellow war artists Edward Ardizzone and Edward Bawden), Palestine, Lebanon, Syria, Iraq, and Persia, producing work in all these countries. Recalled to Cairo, he was posted to India, and then Burma, where he traversed mountainous jungle terrain to paint near the Japanese lines. Back in Europe in 1944, he crossed to Normandy on D-day, wading ashore with his watercolour paper held high above his head. He was present at the liberation of Paris and accompanied the allied armies into Germany. The Imperial War Museum in London possesses more than 300 examples of the resulting work.

Soon after the war Gross produced illustrations for editions of Emily Brontë's *Wuthering Heights* (in 1947) and John Galsworthy's *The Forsyte Saga* (in 1950) and colour lithographs for Lyons restaurants. He also taught at the Central School from 1948 to 1954. In 1955 he bought a house at Le Boulvé, not far from his wife's home town of Villeneuve-sur-Lot (hence the large etchings Le Boulvé Suite, 1956) and thereafter spent the summer months there each year and the winters working in London. He was head of the etching and engraving department of the Slade School from 1955 to 1971 and his authoritative book *Etching, Engraving and Intaglio Printing* was published in 1970. Writing of his work he said, 'I have always held an unfashionable view that drawing is the prime factor in pictorial art—the understanding of how things are constructed, the shape of everything, be it flower or factory girl, landscape or insect', and there can be no better example of this than in the text and illustrations for *The Very Rich Hours of Le Boulvé* (1980).

Gross was a prolific artist (among other things producing over 360 copperplate etchings and engravings), inventive in his methods, full of energy and working seven days a week, an optimist who enjoyed good company, walking, fishing, and cooking. He was a member of the London Group from 1948 to 1971, was made honorary member of the Royal Society of Painter–Etchers and Engravers and an associate of the Royal Academy in 1979, becoming Royal Academician in 1980 (his oil painting *Les causses* won the Wollaston award that year), and was appointed CBE in 1982. Anthony Gross died at Le Boulvé on 8 September 1984 and was buried on 11 September in Villeneuve-sur-Lot. He was survived by his wife.

S. C. HUTCHISON, *rev.* ROBIN HERDMAN

**Sources** M. Gross and P. Gross, eds., *Anthony Gross* (1992) • R. Herdman, *The prints of Anthony Gross* (1991) • A. Weight, 'Anthony Gross, R.A., C.B.E.: a war artist's diary', *Imperial War Museum Review*, 11 (1997), 18–26 • J. D. Potter, *No time for breakfast* (1951) • personal knowledge (1990, 2004) • private information (2004) [family, friends] • *The Times* (12 Sept 1984) • *CGPLA Eng. & Wales* (1984)

**Archives** IWM, war artists archive, GP/55/34 | FILM BFI, London

**Likenesses** Swaine, photograph, 1924, repro. in Herdman, *Prints of Anthony Gross* • A. Gross, self-portrait, drawing, *c.*1925, unknown collection; copyprint, NPG [*see illus.*] • A. Everett Orr, oils, 1926, repro. in Gross and Gross, eds., *Anthony Gross* • P. F. Millard, drawing, 1926, priv. coll.; repro. in Gross and Gross, eds., *Anthony Gross* • three photographs, 1942–73, repro. in Gross and Gross, eds., *Anthony Gross* • B. Hardy, photographs, 1948, Hult. Arch. • B. Herdman, photograph, 1984, repro. in Herdman, *Prints of Anthony Gross*

**Wealth at death** £142,091: probate, 13 Nov 1984, *CGPLA Eng. & Wales*

**Gross, William Mayer-** (1889–1961), psychiatrist, was born on 15 January 1889 in Bingen-am-Rhein, Germany, the son of Max Mayer, trader, and Mathilde Gross; his forename at birth was Willy. He was educated at a local preparatory school, then at the *Gymnasium* in Worms, and studied medicine at Heidelberg, Kiel, and Munich. He qualified in medicine at Heidelberg University in 1912 and presented his doctoral thesis in the following year, having become an assistant in the Heidelberg Psychiatric Clinic. In 1914, he was called up and served for a year on the western front during the First World War before being transferred to a base hospital for psychiatric casualties at Heidelberg.

Mayer-Gross married in 1919 and had one son. After the war, he was one of a group of younger psychiatrists who studied the phenomenology of mental illness by observation and interview, leading to improvement in clinical methods, the delimitation of syndromes, and better understanding of the interaction between personality and the pathological process. This 'Heidelberg school' became influential, but also controversial, since it departed from the previous emphasis of trying to discover the causes of psychosis by physical investigation. Mayer-Gross was co-founder of the journal *Nervenarzt* in 1928 and was appointed professor *extraordinarius* in 1929. He also contributed an extensive and important section on clinical aspects of schizophrenia to Oswald Bumke's *Lehrbuch der Geisteskrankheiten* (1924). This presentation of the symptoms, cause, and diagnosis of the disorder has been described as 'a triumph of knowledge and sustained effort' (Lewis).

After the Nazi seizure of power Mayer-Gross was able to come to England in 1933, with the help of the Commonwealth Fund, which provided a clinical fellowship at the Maudsley Hospital, London. This was continued by the Rockefeller Foundation, who also brought over Eric Guttman and Alfred Meyer. These immigrants contributed greatly to the academic, clinical, and research activities of the Maudsley, which was then the only university postgraduate psychiatric centre in England. They showed how rigorous methods could be applied to clinical research, and they provided a conceptual framework more suitable for research than anything which could be derived from Meyerian psychobiology, which had strongly influenced the institution up to then. In 1939 Mayer-Gross was appointed director of research at Crichton Royal Hospital, Dumfries; he requalified in medicine at the Scottish royal colleges and became a naturalized British subject, changing his first name to William. Although without any university affiliation, the hospital was well endowed and its facilities were of an exceptionally high standard. Mayer-Gross pursued an active programme of research, which had been fragmentary up to then, and his work had a stimulating effect on psychiatry throughout Scotland. He also wrote the first modern British postgraduate textbook of psychiatry, together with Eliot Slater and Martin Roth; *Clinical Psychiatry* was published in 1954.

Mayer-Gross retired as a consultant in 1955 and became senior fellow in a new department of experimental psychiatry in Birmingham, which up to then had had no academic or research activities in psychiatry. Not long afterwards the head of the department moved to the United States and Mayer-Gross took over its direction. He also headed research at the Uffculme Clinic, which he had helped to found; this was one of the first units in Britain focused on psychotherapeutic treatment. For two periods, he represented the World Health Organization in India, where he helped to establish a teaching and research centre at Bangalore. He was also guest professor at Munich and Hamburg. Mayer-Gross was elected FRCP in 1951 and president of the section of psychiatry of the Royal Society of Medicine in 1954. His nature was generous and direct and entirely free from rancour. He had both immense energies for remarkable productivity and unflagging interest, enthusiasm, and industry. Without ever having held a university teaching post in Britain, he was more influential on younger psychiatrists than any other teacher of his time. Mayer-Gross died in Dudley Road Hospital, Birmingham, on 15 February 1961, shortly after Heidelberg University had invited him to return and direct a new psychopharmacological laboratory.

HUGH FREEMAN

**Sources** A. Lewis, 'William Mayer-Gross: an appreciation', *Psychological Medicine*, 7, 11–18 • Munk, *Roll* • d. cert. • *CGPLA Eng. & Wales* (1961)

**Wealth at death** £4967 1*s*. 0*d*.: administration with will, 11 Sept 1961, *CGPLA Eng. & Wales*

**Grosse, Alexander** (1595/6–1654), Church of England clergyman, was the son of William Grosse, a husbandman of Christow, Devon. After attending Exeter School for five years under 'Mr Periman', on 26 July 1618, aged twenty-two, he was admitted sizar of Gonville and Caius College, Cambridge, but it was from Trinity Hall that he graduated BA in 1622. About this time he married a woman named Pascow. Their son Alexander was born in 1622 or 1623. Before 19 August 1631 Grosse was preacher at Plympton St Mary, Devon, but he was in Plymouth on that day to preach the funeral sermon of Matthias Nicols, lecturer of the town. In an address published as *Deaths Deliverance and Eliah's Fiery Charet* (1632) Grosse bid his hearers consider carefully the choice of successor to Nicols. This was good advice, for a complex struggle was in progress over the positions of vicar and lecturer, in which the town, having acquired the rights of presentation, sought to appoint puritan clergymen against opposition from the king and the bishop of Exeter.

In 1632 Grosse returned to university, this time at Oxford, where he was enrolled as a sojourner in Exeter College in order (according to Anthony Wood) to attend the lectures of John Prideaux, regius professor of divinity. He was incorporated MA about January 1633 and graduated BD on 23 February. Meanwhile on 12 September 1632 a general meeting of the common council of Plymouth had elected Grosse to be the next vicar of St Andrew (still the town's only parish) on the death or vacation of Henry Wallis, and on 27 May following the records mention a covenant between Grosse and the town, which seems to suggest that Grosse was by then actually employed as lecturer. On the same day Charles I wrote to Bishop Joseph Hall that the vicar 'has been troubled by refractory persons endeavouring to maintain a lecturer there contrary to the approbation of the incumbent'. Hall was instructed to settle 'Thomas Bedford … in the place of the lecturer, and not to permit him to be disquieted by—Grosse' (*CSP dom.*, *1633–4*, 73), and this seems to have been implemented. However, the town's governors were not finished. When Wallis died in January 1634 they offered the vicarage not to Bedford, but to Grosse. Grosse was promptly refused institution by Bishop Hall, and Aaron Wilson was imposed instead: this inaugurated a rancorous struggle involving a suit in Star Chamber and the vicar's imprisonment in 1642 at the instance of the town.

Grosse evaded these hostilities. On 16 January 1639 he was presented by the crown to the rectory of Bridford, Devon, from where he published *The Happiness of Enjoying and Making a True and Speedie Use of Christ* (1640) and probably a catechism, *A Fiery Pillar of Heavenly Truth* (1641). In *Sweet and Soule-Perswading Inducements Leading unto Christ* (1642) he denounced 'time-serving politicians and carnall neutralizing middle men' as 'spiritual harlots' (A3*v*). He supported parliament in the civil war, during which, John Walker was told, he contested with William Garnet for the vicarage of Dunsford, success depending on the military situation. This was still unfavourable when on 29 March 1645 Grosse was at Plymouth, preaching *Christ the Christian's Choice* (1645) at the funeral of one John Caws, one of the town magistrates, though he is given in that work, published by mid-June, as pastor of Bridford. On 9 December 1647 Grosse was nominated to the rich vicarage of Ashburton, Devon, and in 1648, before 27 June, he signed from there *The Joint-Testimony of the Ministers of Devon*, which strongly suggests that Wood was right to label him a presbyterian. Among Grosse's long devotional works was *The Buddings and Blossomings of Old Truths* (1656) where in his epistle John Welden, of Ermington, Devon, describes the author as 'a skilful, powerful dispenser of the word'. Grosse died in 1654 and was buried at Ashburton on 10 April. The administration of his property was granted on 5 May 1654 to his widow.

STEPHEN WRIGHT

**Sources** R. N. Worth, *Calendar of the Plymouth municipal records* (1893) · M. Stoyle, *Loyalty and locality: popular allegiance in Devon* (1994) · J. Venn and others, eds., *Biographical history of Gonville and Caius College*, 1: *1349–1713* (1897) · Venn, *Alum. Cant.* · *Walker rev.* · *Calamy rev.* · Wood, *Ath. Oxon.*, new edn, vol. 3 · Wood, *Ath. Oxon.: Fasti* (1815) · J. Rowe, *The ecclesiastical history of old Plymouth* (1876) · *CSP dom.*, *1633–4*; *1638–9* · W. A. Shaw, *A history of the English church during the civil wars and under the Commonwealth, 1640–1660*, 2 vols. (1900) · *The joint-testimony of the ministers of Devon* (1648)

**Grosseteste, Robert** (*c.*1170–1253), scientist, theologian, and bishop of Lincoln, combined a very humble origin with torrential energy, great ability, and a rarely paralleled breadth of intellectual interests. His career followed no ordinary pattern, and can be divided into five distinct periods.

**Origins, early studies, and first employment, c.1170–1195** It is hard to disentangle fact from legend during Grosseteste's early years. It is certain that he came from a very poor family in Suffolk, and it is probable that he was born in one of the three places called Stow in that county, and it is also likely—though this is known only from much later testimony, which may, however, have earlier sources now lost—that in his youth he was supported at school in Lincoln by the generosity of Adam of Wigford, a man well known for his philanthropic activities, who was the first mayor of the town. According to the late medieval source (Richard of Bardney) which supplies information about Grosseteste's early years at school in Lincoln, he went from Lincoln to Cambridge, where schools for higher studies were beginning to flourish in the 1180s. Apart from this dubious ray of light, all is darkness until he appears as the last, and presumably most junior, witness of a charter of Hugh, bishop of Lincoln, of about 1190.

Grosseteste evidently had no assured position in the bishop's household, for in 1196 or thereabouts he joined the household of William de Vere, bishop of Hereford. This move was possibly the result of a warm testimonial from Gerald of Wales, who had recently come from Hereford and was studying at Lincoln. Gerald's letter testifies to Grosseteste's wide knowledge of the liberal arts, medicine, and law, but provides no further details.

**In the diocese of Hereford; scientific writings, 1196–1220** Whether or not as a result of Gerald's testimonial, Grosseteste is next found from 1196 to 1198 witnessing several charters of Bishop William. But William died unexpectedly, in December 1198, before he had given Grosseteste a benefice, which would have been the normal reward for a substantial period of service; and it seems that the new bishop of Hereford, Giles de Briouze, brought his own household with him. At all events, he did not employ Grosseteste. Nevertheless it seems likely that Grosseteste continued to be employed in the Hereford diocese by Hugh Foliot, who was archdeacon of Shropshire from about 1195 until he became bishop of Hereford in 1219. The evidence is scanty but it is consistent. First, Hugh

Robert Grosseteste (*c.*1170–1253), illuminated initial

Foliot and Grosseteste are recorded as being joint papal judge-delegates at some time between 1214 and 1216 in a case concerning a parish in the diocese of Hereford. Then, when Hugh Foliot himself became bishop of Hereford, there is evidence that Grosseteste was still a member of his staff. Further, in 1220, Grosseteste was accused by royal justices of hearing a case in an ecclesiastical court in Shropshire that should have been heard in the royal court.

Scanty though this evidence is, it all points in the same direction, and indicates that these central years of Grosseteste's life from the age of about twenty-five to fifty were spent in administrative work in the diocese of Hereford. Further, this location is consistent with his intellectual history during these years, for Hereford was the most active centre of scientific studies in England, and Grosseteste's learned works during these years—except for one general survey of the liberal arts—are all scientific: *On the Calendar*, *On the Movements of the Planets*, *On the Origin of Sounds*; as well as some astronomical calculations contained in Bodl. Oxf., MS Savile 21, which seem to be in his very unusual handwriting, relating to the period of King John's death, which took place on 19 October 1216. Chronology, astrology, astronomy, and comets were subjects common to several scholars in the cathedral ambiance of Hereford, and Grosseteste wrote something on all of them. More broadly, all his written works from 1200 to 1220 belong to, and extend, the tradition of English astronomical and computational studies established by a long series of scholars from Walcher of Malvern, Petrus Alfonsi, and Adelard of Bath in the early years of the twelfth century, and continued by Daniel of Morley, Robert of Ketton, Robert of Chester, Roger Infans of Hereford, and Alfred of Shareshill in the late twelfth and early thirteenth centuries.

Although Grosseteste's works during these years can all

be associated with this local tradition of scientific work, he showed his superiority to his environment by turning his mind to the principles of the natural sciences, and he wrote the first of all medieval Latin commentaries on Aristotle's *Posterior Analytics*, with its account of the principles of scientific knowledge. This is the more remarkable because, although this work of Aristotle's had been translated into Latin in the mid-twelfth century, no scholar in western Europe before Grosseteste had undertaken to study and comment on it in detail, still less had any of the scientific scholars in the tradition to which Grosseteste belonged shown any theoretical understanding of the relationship between the methods of observation and calculation in the sciences with which Grosseteste and other English scientists were familiar, and the principles of demonstration, which are discussed in Aristotle's *Posterior Analytics*.

Thus Grosseteste's commentary, completed probably about 1220, not only brought the early scientific period of his life to a close, but also displayed a level of philosophical maturity quite beyond the scope of any earlier medieval scientists. So, although Grosseteste's scientific work has several characteristics which he shared with his colleagues at Hereford, and though like them he had no academic position and only a relatively humble place in ecclesiastical society, he alone showed a capacity to transcend the limitations of his local circumstances. Even if he had died before writing his commentary on the *Posterior Analytics*, his works would have sufficed to give Grosseteste a distinctive place in the history of scientific thought; but it is this commentary that provides the first evidence of his having greater intellectual powers and a wider range and more lively awareness of the general principles of scientific thought than any of his contemporaries.

Before leaving this period of his life, however, it must also be noted that ecclesiastical administration was considerably disrupted throughout England during the interdict from 1208 to 1214, and it is certain that Grosseteste, like many other ecclesiastical officials whose administrative work was interrupted, spent some time in France during these years. Looking back on his life as he lay on his deathbed, he recalled that he had heard a team of preachers, which included Stephen Langton, preaching in France against the heretical Cahorsins about 1212. This incident would probably have been in southern France where the Cahorsins were numerous; but there is also some evidence of Parisian influence in Grosseteste's work on the calendar. So it seems likely that he visited or passed through Paris at least on this occasion, though there is nothing to suggest that he taught or studied in the Parisian schools.

**Years of transition, c.1220–1225** The five years between about 1220 and 1225 continue the very sparsely documented period of Grosseteste's life. His first biographer, Richard of Bardney, writing in the early sixteenth century but probably drawing on earlier material, relates that he came into contact with the royal household, and was in some way associated with the complicated negotiations between Pope Honorius III and the government of the young Henry III between 1222 and 1224. These negotiations led to the papal declaration that Henry III, though still technically a minor, was capable of undertaking the work of government. According to this account it was the young king who urged Grosseteste to turn his attention to theology. No contemporary evidence has been found to support this connection, but in whatever circumstances and under whatever influences the change in his interests took place, it is certain that during these years new studies and opportunities make their appearance in Grosseteste's development.

The most important new elements in his intellectual life following the completion of his commentary on Aristotle's *Posterior Analytics* were, first, that he enlarged his Aristotelian programme by beginning a commentary on Aristotle's *Physics*, which he completed gradually over the following ten years; second, that he undertook a very extensive course of reading in the fundamental sources of both Latin and Greek theology; and third that he began to acquire a working knowledge of Greek, which had been very elementary when he wrote his commentary on the *Posterior Analytics*. Further, at about this time, he began reading and annotating (using a code of symbols of his own devising) the Latin fathers, in particular Augustine, Gregory the Great, and Anselm's *Cur Deus homo*; and several manuscripts have survived which show his system of annotation in use.

So there are several converging lines of evidence pointing to new influences and new opportunities coming into Grosseteste's life at this time. The Hereford-based scientific studies of the years from about 1196 to 1220, having culminated in his commentary of the *Posterior Analytics* and in his beginning a commentary on Aristotle's *Physics*, were augmented—though never wholly replaced—by new developments, which were predominantly theological, along lines that show a marked originality of approach. These initiatives could all have sprung from Grosseteste's own mind with its widely ranging search for knowledge; but there were probably also outside influences at work which are at present obscure but may have arisen from an association with the royal court in the last years of Henry III's minority.

**Teaching in the University of Oxford, 1225–1231** It is important to recognize that the years 1225–35, though centred in Oxford and showing a continuous intellectual development, represent two distinct periods in Grosseteste's religious life, running from 1225 to 1231 and 1231 to 1235. The year 1225 marked the definitive end of the period of Grosseteste's life associated with the diocese of Hereford, and brought him back to the diocese of Lincoln where his adult life had started. The first symptom of this change is found in the episcopal register of Hugh of Wells, bishop of Lincoln (*d.* 1235), which records that on 25 April 1225 the bishop gave Master Robert Grosseteste, who was still only in deacon's orders, conditional succession to the rectory of Abbotsley, Huntingdonshire. This preferment was subject to the non-appearance of any lawful claimant before 6

May 1225. No other claimant having appeared, Grosseteste received his first assured position in the ecclesiastical hierarchy as rector of a small village midway between Oxford and Cambridge.

Moreover, and almost certainly in association with this move, Grosseteste began at about this time to lecture in the Oxford schools, and a record of his lectures on the Psalms has survived in a small group of manuscripts of which one (Durham Cathedral, MS A. III. 12) can be dated about 1230. This manuscript is particularly important in providing evidence of Grosseteste's continuing development in three distinct areas while giving this course of lectures: first, in using a growing range of sources; second, in his increasing command of the works of Greek theologians; and, third, in the widening range and depth of his discussion of theological problems.

Grosseteste began his course very simply in dealing with the analysis of the nature of things mentioned by the Psalmist such as leaves, sap, mountains, and air; tears, eyes, heart, lungs, and blood; and in finding symbolic meanings of these images as referring to such subjects as human pride, humility, or justice. Then gradually he spoke at increasing length on theological and pastoral problems and quoted an ever extending body of both Latin and Greek texts. So the record of these lectures provides the most valuable evidence there is of Grosseteste's continuing theological and linguistic development during these years.

Then further, in 1229, while still continuing his lectures, Grosseteste was appointed archdeacon of Leicester; and, probably at about this same date, an incident occurred which shows that he had become a dominant figure in the university. To understand what happened it must be recalled that the constitution of the university had been laid down by the papal legate who in 1214 drew up the terms on which the schools of Oxford would reopen after their long closure, which had become complete in 1210 and lasted until the end of the interdict in 1214. Among other measures, the legate had laid down that the masters of Oxford, on returning from their exile, should have a chancellor appointed annually by the bishop of Lincoln.

Naturally (as had happened slightly earlier in Paris) the Oxford masters soon began, and long continued, to seek to have a voice in the appointment of their chancellor. One of the earliest symptoms of this was that, at a date that cannot be precisely determined, but which was probably about 1228–30, the masters, or a faction among them, chose Grosseteste as their chancellor without waiting for an episcopal nomination or perhaps even (so far as is known) for Grosseteste's consent. The bishop naturally rejected this infringement by the rebellious masters of his right of appointment, but he evidently felt sufficient respect for Grosseteste to allow him to perform the duties of chancellor for a year, with the reduced title of master of the schools.

This incident is known only because, as late as 1295, when the masters made a similar bid to nominate their chancellor, the bishop of Lincoln, Oliver Sutton, recalled Grosseteste's illicit nomination under his predecessor, Hugh of Wells, and ordered the record of it to be entered in his register as confirmation of his right to choose annually the chancellor of the university.

**Lector to the Oxford Franciscans, 1231–1235** Despite these varied symptoms of success Grosseteste was contemplating a substantial change of direction which marked a new revolution in his personal life. This showed itself in 1231–2 in his divesting himself of his university position and his other marks of worldly success. In 1231 he gave up his archdeaconry of Leicester and his other sources of income including his parish of Abbotsley, and became lector to the recently founded community of Franciscan friars outside the Oxford city wall. Later writers were to see this move simply as a side-step from one kind of academic work to another, for the Franciscans soon became an integral, and even a leading, part of the university. But this was not the situation in 1231, and Grosseteste's move was a complicated act of self-denial which put him firmly in the category of supporters of a new way of life.

Indeed it is very likely that the precise influence and the date that led to this change of life can be determined. On 11 November 1229 the Dominican preacher Brother Jordan of Saxony visited Oxford and preached a sermon to the masters of the university attacking academic pride and calling for a renewal of pastoral commitment. Grosseteste was much moved by this sermon, for he later wrote to Brother Jordan recalling the conversations they had had during his visit to Oxford, and he kept a copy of the sermon in the manuscript, now at Durham, in which he wrote his lectures. Methodically he began divesting himself of his various offices and sources of income. This process took several months, but he did not, as some other masters did, renounce everything and become a Franciscan; and this was not for him a case of half measures, for, as he bluntly told his Franciscan listeners, he considered that working for one's living—ideally as the new Beguines of the Rhineland worked for their scanty earnings—represented a higher way of life than that of the Franciscans, who chose to beg. Nevertheless, though his own renunciation was carefully limited, his move to the friars represented a real self-denial and established him firmly as their friend.

Grosseteste held his position as lector for about four years from 1231 until 1235, and during these years he wrote four small but remarkably original theological works: *De decem mandatis* ('On the ten commandments'), *De cessatione legalium* ('On the end of the Old Testament law'), *Hexaëmeron* ('On the six days of creation'), and commentary on the epistle to the Galatians. He also continued his scientific works with a treatise *On Light*, placing special emphasis on the concept and place of light in the created order of the universe, and completed his commentary on Aristotle's *Physics*. Besides all this, he had by now obtained a sufficient command of Greek to contemplate making a new translation of the *Hierarchies* attributed to Dionysius. So, while his transfer from the university to the Franciscans inaugurated a new phase in his personal life, it also brought the culmination of his theological studies and initiated a new stage in his work as a translator. But he was also on the brink of a new expansion of his horizon.

**Election as bishop of Lincoln, 1235** Hugh of Wells, who had been bishop of Lincoln since 1213, died on 7 February 1235. The cathedral canons had long altercations about his successor; then quite unexpectedly and unanimously they chose Grosseteste on 25 March. Three weeks later their choice was approved by Henry III, the temporalities being restored on 16 April, and the new bishop was consecrated by the archbishop of Canterbury on 17 June 1235. So he became the episcopal ruler of the largest diocese in England, stretching from the Humber to the Thames, with eight archdeaconries and nearly two thousand parishes.

Grosseteste brought to this task the same independence and indefatigable energy that he had shown in his intellectual enquiries. Indeed, far from diminishing the range of these enquiries, his new position provided him with ample resources for employing helpers in his translations from Greek and seeking Greek manuscripts in foreign libraries. He had several episcopal residences scattered throughout his diocese; and he seems to have used his small manor house at Liddington in Rutland for study, retirement, and probably for housing his group of translators of ancient Greek texts, while making his larger residence at Buckden in Huntingdonshire his main administrative headquarters.

From this point on, sources of information on Grosseteste become exceptionally abundant, and the central thread running through his very diversified activities of the next eighteen years is a passionate, though often frustrated, regard for the pastoral care of the parishes and religious communities in his diocese. He spoke to all, high and low alike, with the same independence and vigour that was evident in all he did. As an extension of his central pastoral concern, he also found time for very active interventions in the political affairs of the kingdom and in relations between the papacy and the local churches, while still continuing, and enlarging, his learned enterprises. These different aspects of his life as bishop of Lincoln will each require separate treatment, but—by way of introduction—an incident in his work as archdeacon of Leicester may be recalled, for it exhibits the intransigence and rejection of compromises which are the hallmark of his work as a bishop.

**The Jews of Leicester** Grosseteste had become archdeacon of Leicester in 1229, and in 1231 Simon de Montfort (*d.* 1265) acquired the lordship of the town. One of the first things he did—evidently with Grosseteste's approval—was to expel the town's flourishing Jewish community, which thereupon went to Winchester, where there was already a large Jewish population. Here the new arrivals were given a friendly reception by Margaret de Quincy, countess of Winchester, who had formerly been countess of Lincoln. Although the whole business had passed beyond his jurisdiction, Grosseteste wrote her a long and vehement letter arguing against her reception of the Jews, and urging that they should be subjected to every deprivation short of death, and particularly deprived of their sole trade of usury. It is a letter of peculiarly unattractive violence, and shows the lengths to which he was prepared to go in guarding the Christian population from the 'moneylenders', and forbidding their rulers to draw any profit from the only livelihood open to the Jews scattered throughout the towns of western Europe. In Grosseteste's view they were to be given over to slavery, to earn their living by the sweat of their brows; and he described rulers who received any benefit from the usury of the Jews as drinking the blood of victims whom it was their duty to protect. There is no need for further elaboration, but the letter deserves mention as the first expression of the extremism that is evident in Grosseteste's approach to all practical problems, of which there will be several examples in his administration of his diocese.

**Grosseteste's mission in his diocese** In an account of his ministry that Grosseteste wrote for the pope in 1250, this is how he described his first year as bishop:

> I began to perambulate my bishopric, archdeaconry by archdeaconry, and rural deanery by rural deanery, requiring the clergy of each deanery to bring their people to have their children confirmed, to hear the word of God, and to make their confessions. (Gieben, 375–6)

This sums up the central theme of his life as bishop from beginning to end: his concern for the religious life of the whole population of his diocese and the persistent organized effort that he devoted to this task.

To assist him in this work Grosseteste was accompanied in all his regular visitations of his diocese by a small group of Franciscan and Dominican friars, whom he selected with special regard to their suitability as confessors for all the people summoned to come to him during his perambulations. Pastoral concern was at the centre of all that he did, and in his first months as bishop he refused to institute to benefices at least three nominees of important men on the ground of insufficient learning. Then, besides his concern for the pastoral care of the whole diocesan population, he was no less active in regulating the discipline of all the monastic houses in his diocese that were not exempt from his jurisdiction. Acting on this principle he deposed seven abbots and four priors as a result of the first visitation of the monasteries in his diocese, made during the first six months of his episcopate. His insistence on his rights of visitation also brought Grosseteste into a dispute with the canons of Lincoln Cathedral which lasted for at least six years.

Of course Grosseteste was not alone among contemporary bishops in these pastoral activities. The thirteenth century was unique in the energy displayed by bishops in holding councils and making visitations, in which they repeated and enforced the rules of conduct and faith as defined especially in the general councils of 1123, 1179, and 1215; but Grosseteste was outstanding in the range, promptitude, and systematic rigour of his measures, bringing to this work an unquenchable energy and down-to-earth concentration on details, such as condemning the celebration of the Feast of Fools, to which few other bishops would stoop. But, on the other hand, it was recorded of him that he would never pass a dead body in a ditch (and it seems they were a not unfamiliar sight) without stopping to give it burial with the full rites in consecrated ground, even though this meticulous procedure would make him late for the meeting of the royal court that was the cause of this journey.

**Pastoral activity and the kingdom of England** Grosseteste approached national affairs, in which he now as a bishop had a central role, with the same meticulous concern for the full execution of his responsibilities without regard for expediency. This soon involved him in a difference of opinion with the general body of bishops on the subject of a distinction between canon law and secular law with regard to succession to landed estates. In secular law, children who had been born before the marriage of their parents were not eligible to succeed to hereditary parental estates: that right belonged to the eldest son born after the marriage of the parents. But, in canon law, as most explicitly interpreted by Pope Alexander III (*r.* 1159–81), the marriage of the parents entirely legitimatized their premarital children.

The consequences of this conflict of laws had been discussed by barons and bishops in 1234. A change of the law on this matter, besides altering expectations of succession for the future, would open the way to disputes about succession going back far into the past, and in view of these complications, the bishops had agreed on a formula for evading the issue: in future, when an ecclesiastical court was required to make a declaration as to the status of a claimant to property on the death of a landholder, it would make no judgment about 'legitimacy' or 'illegitimacy', but simply state that the parents of the claimant had been married on such and such a date, and the claimant to the property had been born on such and such a date, leaving the question of succession to property to be settled by the secular court. The practical effect of this would of course be that, without any explicit rejection of the principle as expressed in canon law, the old secular rule of succession would continue to be effective.

This seemed to satisfy everybody—but not Grosseteste. Within months of his becoming a bishop he was refusing to co-operate in this evasion, and insisted on stating explicitly that a claimant born to parents who were married after his birth was 'legitimate', without further qualification. In defence of his position he wrote a twenty-page letter to William of Raleigh, one of the king's intimate legal counsellors, explaining with a vast array of quotations and arguments that the suggested compromise, whereby children born before their parents' marriage would continue to be excluded from succession to their parental estates, was contrary to the Bible (eight pages), to reason (three pages), to nature (two pages), and to canon law, civil law, and ancient custom (one and a half pages between them).

William of Raleigh replied to Grosseteste's thunderbolt in a somewhat jocular fashion; and to this letter Grosseteste sent a further, and by no means jocular, answer defending his position. But clearly his impassioned plea was looked on by others besides William of Raleigh as an eccentricity, and new adjustments in the procedure were devised that allowed the law to continue to operate as before. When the issue was raised again, at Merton in 1236, the barons made sure of this with their famous declaration: 'Non volumus leges Angliae mutari' ('We do not want the laws of England to be changed').

This was only one example of the superabundance of energy and (as many thought) perverse arguments with which Grosseteste approached every issue. He saw it as the duty of all those in places of authority to ensure that the part of the transitory world for which they were responsible reflected the eternal will of God as closely as possible. He did this to the best of his ability on every issue; but, so far as the issue of succession was concerned, in the end his objection was quietly ignored by men who wanted no unnecessary changes. He met a similar reaction, though one much more damaging to himself, when his principle of pastoral care *à outrance* was applied to the actions of the papacy, and this will require separate treatment.

**Diocesan affairs in relation to the papacy** Grosseteste had the highest possible view both of the nature and role of the papacy in the church as a whole, and of the pastoral responsibilities of bishops in their respective dioceses. In principle of course there was no conflict between these two; but when a pope used papal powers over local churches for family enrichment or the promotion of unworthy relatives, or even (and this was much more widely prevalent) for the administrative needs of the papacy, to the detriment of the pastoral care of ordinary people, then—in Grosseteste's view—the pope betrayed his office and lost his authority as pope. So, from Grosseteste's very exalted view of the papacy, there followed the need to oppose the pope.

It is unlikely that he ever envisaged a situation of such fundamental papal corruption as would justify an anti-papal movement at large. This was what John Wyclif would read into his words a hundred years later, when he pointed to Grosseteste as the founding father of anti-papal doctrine and activity. But Grosseteste's opposition to Innocent IV was based on the narrower ground of the pope's betrayal of his pastoral office in the interests of family or administrative expediency. In detail, what he vehemently objected to was that pope, king, or any other ecclesiastical or lay authority should use their rights of presentation, however acquired, to give parishes to men who had no interest in, or capacity for, meeting the pastoral needs of ordinary people. This problem consumed more of his energies and brought him into conflict with a wide range of owners of rights of parochial appointment: in the first place his own chapter; then the king and royal officials; and eventually the pope. It was the final stage that clouded his last years.

**Grosseteste and the papacy** Grosseteste paid two visits to the papal curia, and on both occasions he used his visit as an opportunity for raising this fundamental problem. The first occasion was in 1245, when he went to Lyons at the time of the general council under Innocent IV, determined to get papal support for imposing limits on the power of members of his chapter to give benefices to members of their families or friends without regard to their aptitude for performing their parochial duties. The sharp and cynical eye of the St Albans chronicler, Matthew Paris, described him as going 'like Ishmael a stranger to peace' to get at great cost a papal letter curtailing the freedom of his chapter in this matter (Paris, *Chron.*, 5.186). He did not get much, but at least he got something, though exactly what it amounted to in practice is not easy, or perhaps possible, to say.

Grosseteste's second visit to the pope in 1250 was more serious. In preparation he wrote a whole dossier of documents dealing with various aspects of the venality of the papal curia in conferring benefices on relatives, or members of the curia, who did not, or could not, or would not, perform the pastoral duties attached to their benefices, and who were thus, in Grosseteste's last reported words on his deathbed, guilty of slaying souls by defrauding them of pastoral care, and were therefore 'heretics' in the true sense of the word.

The reading of Grosseteste's statements to members of the papal curia, in which he unburdened his soul by denouncing false pastors in the church, must have taken several sessions over a period of two or three days. Those whom he described as antichrists and limbs of Satan masquerading as angels of light and endowed with the persona of Jesus Christ were, he declared, to be found throughout the church; but above all they were to be found in the papal curia, the *fons et origo*—as he believed—of all the evil in the church.

It is to be noticed that in these very fiery speeches Grosseteste indicted not the pope himself but the curia, which increasingly provided the driving force in the church and spoke in the name of the pope in a daily flow of letters. Matthew Paris, who greatly admired Grosseteste in some ways, and whose admiration grew after his death, clearly thought him unbalanced, and no doubt others thought the same. But in these passionate utterances, as in all Grosseteste's efforts as bishop, there was a determined, unremitting, concern for pastoral care. This (as he saw it) was everywhere being thrust aside by the needs of administration or family endowment or personal ease; and this was the theme that Grosseteste presented at the papal curia in 1250 in a series of theses that are certainly the greatest survey of the state of Christendom, in its internal failings and in its relationship to the outside world, in the thirteenth century. They are all the more impressive because, though they savagely attacked papal actions, they were written by a devoted papalist, who elaborated his message in person at the papal court at the height of its medieval development.

There were several apocalyptic predictions of doom current at this time, chiefly those associated with Joachim di Fiore, and Grosseteste was certainly aware of them. But his own analysis of the situation, though pessimistic, was not visionary. It belonged to the world of practical reality, which could (he believed) be repaired if the pope would concentrate on pastoral care rather than on the mundane interests of the church. Grosseteste had grasped a truth about the smallness and vulnerability of Christendom which was gradually becoming clear from the reports of travellers. But above all he had come to think that there was a fatal weakness at the heart of Christendom caused by the papal misuse of spiritual offices for private and family, or for administrative, ends.

Innocent IV's reaction to Grosseteste's elaborations of his criticisms of the curia in 1250 seems to have been (in effect) to suspend him by sending his instructions about presentations in the diocese of Lincoln to his own agent and to the archdeacon of Canterbury. Of course, from Grosseteste's point of view, this simply embodied the flaw at the centre of the papal position; and was a further assault on the episcopal office. Consequently the last years of his life were ravaged by a deep sense of failure, summed up in the hostility of the papal curia and his sense of the impending failure of Christendom, which he expressed most movingly on his deathbed.

**Grosseteste's deathbed** Grosseteste's final words on his deathbed were reported to Matthew Paris by the Franciscan physician who attended him, and by the archdeacon of Bedford, John of Crakehall, who was also present, and they are the greatest set piece in his *Chronica majora*. According to this report, Grosseteste asked his physician to give him a definition of heresy, and when he hesitated he himself supplied it in words which may be summarized thus:

> Heresy is an opinion [*sententia*] chosen by human sense, contrary to Scripture, openly declared, and pertinaciously defended; and to defy the gospel by giving the care of souls to those who are inadequate either in learning or in commitment is heresy in action. Many defy the gospel in this way, the pope most of all; and it is the duty of all faithful persons, and more particularly the Franciscans and Dominicans, to oppose such a person. (Paris, *Chron.*, 5.401–2)

Exhausted by these and other similarly horrific reflections, Grosseteste died at Buckden during the night of the feast of St Denis (to Grosseteste, as to all his contemporaries, identifiable with Dionysius the Areopagite), on 9 October 1253, and the air was filled with strange sounds of bells and perturbations of nature. These events almost at once provoked local veneration at Grosseteste's tomb in Lincoln Cathedral, and stimulated five successive attempts by the bishop and chapter between 1254 and 1307 to procure Grosseteste's canonization by the Holy See. They were all unsuccessful.

**Grosseteste's many-sided character and personal characteristics** Although his theses of 1250 were his final words on the whole problem of Christendom, there were several other sides to Grosseteste's character. Physically impressive—when his tomb was opened in 1782 he was found to have been slightly over 6 feet tall—he was dignified, sociable, and at ease with people at every level of society. He amazed his aristocratic contemporaries, who all knew of his humble origin, by his exquisite courtesy and the easy confidence with which he moved in the society of the great and managed the wealth that had come into his hands. The greatest magnates recognized the charm of his personality and the good manners that prevailed in his household, and they were glad to send their sons to him to learn the rules of courtesy. Moreover he loved music, kept a private harpist, and wrote a long poem in French, *Le château d'amour*, designed to provide a lay audience with an outline of Christian theology, in the metre and rhyming couplets that were to be used by Walter Scott in his *Lay of the Last Minstrel*. Then too, amid all his episcopal duties and learned enterprises, he wrote a set of *Rules* for the management of his episcopal estates, which he revised for the use of the Countess Margaret of Lincoln, descending to such details as the need to take care that the straw after threshing should bring half as much as the corn. So here, in the details of his episcopal duties, and as in his earlier observations on tides, eclipses, and comets, nothing was too small to escape his notice.

As for Grosseteste's learning Greek and the use that he made of his knowledge, it is not known what inspired this great extension of his interests rather late in life, but the moment was certainly propitious on several grounds. First, after the Latin capture of Constantinople in 1204 contacts between western European and Greek scholars were closer than they had been for several hundred years; second, the time was ripe for completing the absorption of ancient Greek learning through direct contact with the original sources; and, third, the stream of scientific work by scholars outside the great schools was increasingly impinging on the main stream of theological questions.

It was in this atmosphere that Grosseteste began learning Greek and turning his attention to theology in the 1220s, and that one scholar, John of Basingstoke, who had spent several years in Athens, brought some Greek books back to England. He may have been Grosseteste's earliest teacher of Greek, for within a few months of becoming bishop of Lincoln Grosseteste made him archdeacon of Leicester. He was clearly on the lookout for further scholars with a knowledge of Greek, and masters Robert the Greek and Nicholas the Greek (or Sicilian) soon also joined his household. Grosseteste now had money to spend on seeking Greek manuscripts, and some of the books on which he spent it are recorded.

It might seem that this avid search for knowledge about every aspect of the created universe somewhat contradicted Grosseteste's strong emphasis on the primacy of pastoral care in the work of all who held the endowments of the church in trust. But he clearly regarded everything that led to a better understanding of creation and redemption in all their aspects as contributing to the pastoral office. In this light the resources which the bishopric put into his hands were never better employed than in the scholarly work which contributed towards making the Greek masterpieces of the past available to the Latin West.

One discovery which he greatly prized, and which he caused to be translated into Latin, was the original Greek of *The Testament of the Twelve Patriarchs*, which John of Basingstoke, who had heard of the existence of the work in Athens, brought to his attention, and which Grosseteste translated with the help of Nicholas the Greek. It has turned out to be a forgery, but this is one of the hazards of scholarship, and Grosseteste's use of his resources for promoting scholarly work must be accounted one of his most solid claims to fame. Nor is it to be looked on as an afterthought for which the revenues of his bishopric provided the necessary money, for the broadening of his horizons went back at least fifteen years before he became a bishop, and it continued until the end of his life with new translations and commentaries on the *Hierarchies* of Dionysius and Aristotle's *De caelo* and *Nicomachean Ethics*. They were all part of his general aim of extending knowledge of the divine act of creation, and they all had a place in his conception of a pastoral ministry.

When these varied aspects of his life are taken into account, Grosseteste deserves to be recognized as a man of outstanding power in four main areas: as one of the most forceful and original interpreters of the Christian universe in the light of the Greek and Arabic science; as a theologian who had formed his mind on a wide reading of the main Latin and Greek fathers; as a man of action in attempting to give practical realization to an ideal of pastoral care; and as a man of the people at a time when it was almost impossible for such a man to get either the education or the promotion necessary for achieving real distinction either as a scholar or as a man of action. He overcame every obstacle in achieving these ends. The violence of his opinions on practical matters, which has been illustrated in his advice about the treatment of the Jews, was balanced, indeed prompted, by a deep concern for the souls of ordinary people; and the remarkable urbanity of his relationships with king and barons had a similar foundation.

**Posthumous influence** In the context of the massive intellectual constructions of the schools which were approaching the height of their systematic development during Grosseteste's lifetime, his own learned works—powerful, many-sided, and original though they are as examples of what could be achieved by an independent intellect—were too far removed from the main stream of scholastic thought to make a profound impression on the intellectual development of his time. A few of Grosseteste's works—in particular his commentary on Aristotle's *Posterior Analytics*—achieved a permanent place among scholastic texts. But it was only in the late fourteenth and early fifteenth centuries, in the first place with Wyclif and his followers, that he became a symbol for a kind of reforming zeal with which he would himself have had little sympathy. He had no quarrel with the principles of scholastic thought or with papal government. What he wanted was to extend the range of texts available for scholastic study, and to bring papal power back to the simple aim of pastoral care; and this meant that popes, bishops, and clergy alike should concentrate all their efforts on the promotion of truth, justice, and the salvation of souls.

Although Grosseteste displayed throughout his long life very remarkable powers of mind, will, and physical energy, he did not have the influence either on the events of his time or on the development of contemporary learning that he might have had in a period of greater upheaval. For this he had to wait until the late fourteenth century, when Wyclif and his followers eagerly sought out and read the drafts and completed works that he had bequeathed to the library of the Oxford Franciscans. Here they thought they had found a reformer like themselves. They did not see that Grosseteste's violence was very different from theirs in being directed, not against the system, but against the use of power for ends other than pastoral care. Consequently when he was read by men of conservative instincts—as for instance Dr Thomas Gascoigne (*d.* 1458) in the early fifteenth century—they found him very different from the man imagined and praised by Wyclif: Gascoigne saw him as a man of old-fashioned principles, and thought him better than Thomas Aquinas, and close to Augustine.

Later reformers in the sixteenth century do not seem to have had much interest in Grosseteste's works, but in the late seventeenth century some of his *dicta* were published by E. Brown in 1690, and his late medieval life by Richard of Bardney was published by Henry Wharton in 1691. Scholarly editions of Grosseteste began with the publication of his letters by H. R. Luard in the Rolls Series in 1861 and of his short scientific treatises by Ludwig Baur in 1912. But the study of his work in its contemporary context began with the surveys of S. Harrison Thomson (1940) and A. C. Crombie (1953), followed by the volume of studies edited by D. A. Callus (1955). During the last forty years the flow has been very considerable. The best survey of the books owned by Grosseteste is by R. W. Hunt in Callus (1955), and the best survey of Grosseteste's thought as a whole down to the date of its publication is by J. McEvoy (1982). More recently, the study by R. W. Southern (1986, 2nd edn 1992) has radically revised perceptions of the structure of Grosseteste's career, while placing him in his wider European context. The continuing process whereby Grosseteste's writings are made available in modern critical editions can only enhance his reputation. It seems likely that when that process is complete, he will take his place in the first rank of medieval Englishmen.

R. W. SOUTHERN

**Sources** WORKS: TEXTS AND SURVEYS L. Baur, *Die Philosophischen Werke des Robert Grosseteste, Bishofs von Lincoln, Beitrage zur Geschichte der Philosophie des Mittelalters*, 9 (1912) • R. Grosseteste, *Commentarius in Posteriorum analyticorum libros*, ed. P. Rossi (Florence, 1981) • R. Grosseteste, *Hexaëmeron*, ed. R. C. Dales and S. Gieben (1982) • R. Grosseteste, *De cessatione legalium*, ed. R. C. Dales and E. B. King (1986) • R. Grosseteste, *Commentarius in VIII libros physicorum Aristotelis*, ed. R. C. Dales (Boulder, CO, 1963) • R. Grosseteste, *De decem mandatis*, ed. R. C. Dales and E. B. King (1987) • *Roberti Grosseteste episcopi quondam Lincolniensis epistolae*, ed. H. R. Luard, Rolls Series, 25 (1861) • R. Grosseteste, *Le château d'amour*, ed. J. Murray (1918) • *Walter of Henley's Husbandry together with Robert Grosseteste's Rules*, ed. and trans. E. Lamond (1890) • *Walter of Henley, and other treatises on estate management and accounting*, ed. D. Oschinsky (1971), 388–415 • E. Brown, ed., *Fasciculus rerum expetendarum ac fugiendarum* (1690), 2.244–307 [sel. of Grosseteste's *dicta*] • S. Gieben, 'Robert Grosseteste at the papal court, Lyons, 1250, edition of the documents', *Collectanea Franciscana*, 41 (1971), 340–93 • R. W. Hunt, 'The library of Robert Grosseteste', *Robert Grosseteste, scholar and bishop*, ed. D. A. Callus (1955), 121–49 • R. Barbour, 'A MS of Ps-Denys copied for Robert Grosseteste', *Bodleian Quarterly Review*, 6 (1958), 401–15 • A. C. Dionisotti, 'On the Greek studies of Robert Grosseteste', *The uses of Greek and Latin: historical essays* (1988), 19–39 • S. Harrison Thomson, *The writings of Robert Grosseteste* (Colorado, 1963)

HISTORICAL SOURCES *Ann. mon.*, vols. 1–5, esp. vols. 1, 3 • *Gir. Camb. opera*, 1.93, 249 • D. Whitelock, M. Brett, and C. N. L. Brooke, eds., *Councils and synods with other documents relating to the English church, 871–1204*, 1 (1981), 201–7, 261–78, 479–81 • Paris, *Chron.*, vols. 3–6 • J. Stevenson, ed., *Chronicon de Lanercost, 1201–1346*, Bannatyne Club, 65 (1839), 43–6, 50, 58, 72, 187–8 • Richardo monacho Bardeniensi, 'Life of Robert Grosthed', in [H. Wharton], *Anglia sacra*, 2 (1691), 325–41 [see also J. C. Russell, *Medievalia et Humanistica*, 2 (1943), 45–55] • F. Hill, *Medieval Lincoln* (1948), 194–5 • *Hist. U. Oxf.* 1: *Early Oxf. schools*, 29–36 • *Fratris Thomae vulgo dicti de Eccleston tractatus de adventu Fratrum Minorum in Angliam*, ed. A. G. Little (1951), 99

RECORD SOURCES cartulary of St Guthlac, Balliol Oxf., MS 271 • U. Rees, ed., *The cartulary of Haughmond Abbey* (1985), 69 • R. R. Darlington, ed., *The cartulary of Worcester Cathedral Priory (register I)*, PRSoc., 76, new ser., 38 (1968), 72–3 • *Curia regis rolls preserved in the Public Record Office* (1922–), vol. 9 • F. N. Davis and others, eds., *Rotuli Hugonis de Welles, episcopi Lincolniensis*, CYS, 3 (1908), 48 • F. N. Davis, ed., *Rotuli Roberti Grosseteste*, Lincoln RS, 11 (1914) • R. M. T. Hill, ed., *The rolls and register of Bishop Oliver Sutton*, 5, Lincoln RS, 60 (1965), 59–61

MODERN STUDIES AND INTERPRETATIONS D. A. Callus, ed., *Robert Grosseteste, scholar and bishop* (1955) • A. C. Crombie, *Robert Grosseteste and the origins of experimental science, 1100–1700* (1953) • J. McEvoy, *The philosophy of Robert Grosseteste* (1982) [incl. extensive bibliography] • R. W. Southern, *Robert Grosseteste: the growth of an English mind in medieval Europe*, 2nd edn (1992) • J. McEvoy, ed., 'Robert Grosseteste: new perspectives on his thought and scholarship', *Instrumenta Patristica* [special issue], 27 (1995) • D. Owen, ed., *A history of Lincoln Minster* (1994)

LATER INFLUENCE R. Thomson, *The Latin writings of John Wyclif* (Toronto, 1983) • T. Gascoigne, *Loci e libro veritatum*, ed. J. E. Thorold Rogers (1881)

**Likenesses** drawing, BL, MS Harley 3860, fol. 48 • episcopal seal, BL; Birch, *Seals*, 1605 • illuminated initial, BL, Royal MS 6 E.v, fol. 6 [*see illus.*]

**Grossmith, George** (1847–1912), entertainer and author, was born in London on 9 December 1847, the eldest of the three children of the journalist and entertainer, George Grossmith (1820–1880) and his wife, Louisa Emmeline Grossmith, *née* Weedon (*d.* 1882). While his father was alive he was referred to outside the family as George Grossmith junior. Within the family the two were sometimes called, respectively, George the First and George the Second. Later, when he became well known, Grossmith acquired the nickname 'Gee-Gee'.

George Grossmith (and his younger brother Weedon [*see below*]) had a lively, happy childhood both at home and at school. He was educated first at Massingham House, a preparatory school in Hampstead, then at North London Collegiate School in Camden Town. Among his youthful enthusiasms were cycling, pugilism, and photography. His father worked as chief reporter for *The Times* and other newspapers at Bow Street police court; and one day in 1865, when not available to be in court himself, he got George junior to take the time off school and deputize as reporter in his stead. The experiment was a success, and the following year, when the latter left school, he learned

George Grossmith (1847–1912), by Lock & Whitfield

more fully what the job required and became chief stand-in reporter in his own right. Among the profusion of cases of which he was to write reports was that of the Clerkenwell bombing by the Fenians in 1867.

As the years went by Grossmith's father spent less and less time at Bow Street and more and more time following a second profession, that of solo entertainer (the working life of Grossmith himself was to develop along much the same lines). Grossmith's own career as a public entertainer began when he took part as an amateur in local 'penny readings'. His first professional engagement came in November 1870 with a nightly spot at the Royal Polytechnic Institution in Regent Street, and during the next few years he gave countless entertainments at literary institutes and public halls, to church groups and to branches of the YMCA up and down the country. By the middle of the 1870s he was also giving them at smart 'society' parties. (He was to call his first volume of reminiscences *A Society Clown*, 1888.) On top of all this he undertook two or three joint entertainment tours with his father and participated on various occasions in an entertainment run by the energetic duo Mr and Mrs Howard Paul. In 1876–7 he toured similarly with the actress and singer Florence Marryat.

Grossmith's performances as an entertainer consisted primarily of what he called 'sketches'. These were made up of anecdotes, mildly satirical comment, ad lib chat, and comic songs, and may best be described as a light-hearted sending up of various aspects of contemporary life and manners. Nearly all his material he wrote and composed himself. His work was consistently amusing, while as a composer he had an attractive gift of tunefulness. Both these attributes come across particularly clearly in a short play with songs which he wrote for himself and Florence Marryat, *Cups and Saucers* (1876). A lively tune is also the basis of his one song still occasionally heard a century later: 'See me dance the polka' (1886). Equally to the point, he was the complete performer. Skill as a pianist (he performed for the most part sitting at a piano), skill as a raconteur, skill as a mimic, facial expression, timing—he had it all. A short, dapper figure, he turned his lack of inches to positive advantage, and audiences took to him everywhere.

On 14 May 1873 Grossmith married Emmeline Rosa Noyce (*d.* 1905), the daughter of a north London doctor; it was a happy marriage from the first. In all, the couple had four children: George *Grossmith (*b.* 1874), Sylvia (*b.* 1875), Lawrence (*b.* 1877), and Cordelia (*b.* 1880). The family lived initially in Blandford Square, Marylebone, before moving in or about 1885 to 28 Dorset Square nearby, the house most closely associated with their name.

During their occupancy it was a house that bubbled with life and laughter. Except for short periods when he tried, ultimately unsuccessfully, to act the stern Victorian paterfamilias, Grossmith was as genial a personality in private life as he was on the entertainment platform. Though he claimed to resent being asked to play the clown or the humorist when, for example, invited out to dinner ('any hostess who asked me to her residence in the expectation that I should gratuitously amuse her guests would find me particularly prosaic', he wrote in *A Society Clown*), he had a love of fun and practical joking that was never stilled for long.

Meanwhile, in 1877 the direction of Grossmith's professional life had unexpectedly changed. That autumn Arthur Sullivan offered him a part in a new comic opera which he (Sullivan) had written in conjunction with the librettist W. S. Gilbert. This was *The Sorcerer*, their third collaboration, and the first full-length work the pair had produced for the impresario Richard D'Oyly Carte. It was an offer which Grossmith thought about long and hard before accepting, but accept it in the end he did. The part Gilbert and Sullivan wanted him to play was the sorcerer himself, John Wellington Wells, the opera's chief comic character. In that part Grossmith made an immediate hit, and in consequence of this Gilbert and Sullivan gave him the chief comic part in each of the operas they produced for D'Oyly Carte over the twelve years that followed. These parts were Sir Joseph Porter, the 'ruler of the queen's navee', in *HMS Pinafore*; Major-General Stanley in *The Pirates of Penzance*; Reginald Bunthorne, the 'fleshly poet' in *Patience*; the Lord Chancellor in *Iolanthe*; King Gama in *Princess Ida*; Ko-Ko, the 'lord high executioner', in *The Mikado*; Robin Oakapple in *Ruddigore*; and Jack Point, the 'strolling jester' in *The Yeomen of the Guard*. In addition he played the Learned Judge in a revival of the one-act piece *Trial by Jury*.

As a performer of Gilbert and Sullivan, Grossmith had

just one weakness: the lack of a true operatic voice. His was a pleasant light baritone, no more. But it was a weakness he skilfully minimized. 'His admirable singing with no voice' (as one critic put it of his performance as the Lord Chancellor) was 'a feat at once astonishing and delightful to all who have any care for phrasing and intonation'. Intonation, indeed, in the sense of exact, incisive diction, was one of his greatest strengths. It was for him that most of the operas' famous patter songs were written. Another of his strengths was agility on his feet, and thus most of the occasional bursts of comic dancing which the works contain were allotted to him too.

Throughout this period Grossmith continued to give his 'society' and other entertainments; and in August 1889, towards the end of the *Yeomen* run, he left the D'Oyly Carte Company to resume one-man entertaining on a full-time basis. Over the next decade and more, with only a few gaps, he toured the British Isles (and on five occasions America and Canada) for eight or nine months at a stretch, presenting his 'humorous and musical recitals', as he now called his performances, in a seemingly endless series of one- and two-night stands. By this time he had become without question the most popular solo entertainer of the day, not to mention the most successful financially. Week in, week out his tours earned him far more than he had earned—or was ever likely to have earned—with D'Oyly Carte. According to various reports he netted £10,000 in his first seven months alone.

During these years Grossmith continued to write and compose all his own material. In the 1880s he also composed the music for four short stage pieces by the playwright Arthur Law. In 1892 he did the same for a full-length piece by Gilbert, *Haste to the Wedding*. He contributed on several occasions to the magazine *Punch*, including (1884) a series of ten skits inspired by his Bow Street experiences, which he called *Very Trying*.

And it was also in these years that, in conjunction with his brother Weedon, Grossmith produced the work by which he is most obviously remembered today: the comic novel *The Diary of a Nobody*. *The Diary of a Nobody* first appeared as a serial in *Punch* in 1888–9 and was published (in considerably expanded form) as a book by J. W. Arrowsmith of Bristol in June 1892. It was at once recognized as one of the most amusing novels in the English language. Similarly the 'nobody' of the title—Charles Pooter of The Laurels, Brickfield Terrace, Holloway—was immediately recognized as one of the great English comic characters. The book was also a sharp analysis of social insecurity.

Up to 1900 and for the three years or so following, Grossmith's life was, overall, one of success and happiness. But, by contrast, his final years were marked by sadness and periodic despair. On 28 February 1905, after a long illness, his wife died. He found her death hard to bear, and at much the same time his own health began to break up. The strain of constant performing—and, even more, the strain of all the travelling that went with it—had worn him out. Against his better judgement he was persuaded to carry on giving his entertainments for a few years more. His final appearance was at Brighton in November 1908.

The following year Grossmith retired to Folkestone, where he wrote a second volume of reminiscences, *Piano and I* (1910), and where, on 1 March 1912, he died at his home, 32 Manor Road. He was buried at Kensal Green cemetery, London, on 5 March.

Grossmith's younger brother, **(Walter) Weedon Grossmith** (1854–1919), artist and actor, always known simply as Weedon or 'Wee-Gee', was born on 9 June 1854. Having been educated at, in turn, Massingham House, North London Collegiate, and Simpson's School, a local private establishment, he went on to study at the West London School of Art and the Royal Academy. His ambition was to become a fashionable portrait painter, and he had portraits and other pictures hung at the academy and elsewhere. But his success as an artist was not as great as he had hoped, and in 1885 he turned to the stage.

After a period of mixed fortunes, this second career took off in May 1888 when Grossmith played opposite Henry Irving at the Lyceum Theatre in Charles Selby's *Robert Macaire*. Thereafter he made his name as a comedy character actor. 'I am almost invariably cast for cowards, cads and snobs,' he once wrote, and he was particularly good at portraying harassed, misunderstood *little* men (for, like George, he was physically small). He appeared in plays by, among others, Henry Arthur Jones, A. W. Pinero, and Jerome K. Jerome. He wrote a number of plays himself, the most successful of which was *The Night of the Party* (1901). He also made various excursions into theatrical management.

But nothing Grossmith achieved in the theatrical field brought him the lasting fame that he and George achieved with *The Diary of a Nobody*, his main contribution to the novel in its finished form being the illustrations. In their precise and careful detail these illustrations (thirty-three black and white line drawings) reinforce the text to perfection. They have been included in all but two or three editions of the book published since his time.

In 1895 Grossmith married an actress, May Lever Palfrey. They had one child, a daughter, Nancy. He died in London on 14 June 1919. TONY JOSEPH

**Sources** G. Grossmith, *A society clown: reminiscences* (1888) · G. Grossmith, *Piano and I: further reminiscences* (1910) · G. Grossmith, *'Gee-Gee'* (1933) · W. Grossmith, *From studio to stage* (1913) · T. Joseph, *George Grossmith: biography of a Savoyard* (1982) · P. Fitzgerald, *Chronicles of Bow Street police-office*, 2 vols. (1888) · R. Allen, *The first night Gilbert and Sullivan* (1976) · *Punch*, 86 (1884), 13–192 · 'Diary of a nobody', *Punch*, 94–6 (1888–9) · *Saturday Review*, 54 (1882), 764–5 · private information (2004) · d. cert. · d. cert. [Weedon Grossmith] · *The Times* (6 March 1912) · *The Times* (20 June 1919)

**Archives** BL, Add. MSS 42578, 56719, 57045b · Theatre Museum, London, corresp. | BL, corresp. with W. S. Gilbert, Add. MS 49332 · Durham RO, letters to Lord Londonderry · Richmond Local Studies Library, London, Sladen MSS

**Likenesses** W. Grossmith, portrait, 1887, repro. in Grossmith, *Piano and I* · Barraud, woodburytype photograph, BM, NPG; repro. in *The Theatre*, 4th ser., 5 (1885), 284 · Ellis & Walery, two postcards, NPG · H. Furniss, two caricatures, pen-and-ink sketches, NPG · Jack, chromolithograph, NPG; repro. in *Society* (6 Jan 1883) · J. W. Kent, lithograph, Harvard TC · Lock & Whitfield, woodburytype photograph, NPG [*see illus.*] • Spy [L. Ward], caricature, chromolithograph, NPG; repro. in *VF* (21 Jan 1888)

**Wealth at death** £19,628 19*s*. 6*d*.: probate, 3 May 1912, *CGPLA Eng. & Wales* • £8474 14*s*. 10*d*.—(Walter) Weedon Grossmith: probate, 1 Sept 1919, *CGPLA Eng. & Wales*

**Grossmith, George** (1874–1935), actor-manager and playwright, was born at 15 Maitland Park Villas, Haverstock Hill, London, on 11 May 1874, the first son of George *Grossmith (1847–1912), the celebrated slightly singing comedian of the Savoy Theatre company, and his wife, Emmeline Rosa, *née* Noyce. He was educated at University College School, London, and in Paris, and aimed hopefully by his parents at a career in the army, but at the age of eighteen he ventured on to the stage in a small comic role in his father's musical *Haste to the Wedding*. After the indifferent run of that piece he moved on to a series of similar parts in similar shows, making his first notable success as the foppish Sir Percy Pimpleton in the variety musical *Morocco Bound* (1893). He worked up his originally supporting part in this show throughout the run with extra sight and word gags until his performance became one of the most prominent and popular features of the entertainment. In 1894 he was cast in a similar 'dude' role, Bertie Boyd, in the Gaiety Theatre's musical comedy *The Shop Girl* and he scored a star-sized hit as 'beautiful, bountiful Bertie' in both London and New York, establishing himself thereby as the stage 'Johnnie' *par excellence* of the *fin de siècle* musical theatre. He married on 23 September 1895 Elizabeth Gertrude Rudge (1873–1951), known during her career in supporting roles in musical comedy and burlesque as Adelaide Astor; her father, Henry Rudge, of Edgbaston, was a brass founder. They had a son and two daughters, the elder of whom, Ena Grossmith (1896–1944), also made a career in the theatre.

In the years that followed his appearance as Bertie Boyd, Grossmith mixed appearances in comedy with parts in a brace of short-lived musical pieces (*Great Caesar*, *The Gay Pretenders*) of his own making, but success of the *Shop Girl* kind returned only when he rejoined George Edwardes's stable of stars, appearing for the popular producer on the road (*Kitty Grey*), in London (*The Toreador*, 1901) and in America before settling down to become a favourite fixture at Edwardes's flagship Gaiety Theatre. Between 1903 and 1913 Grossmith provided light comedy and lively songs in a series of 'dude-y' roles in *The Orchid* (Bedelia), *The Spring Chicken*, *The New Aladdin*, *The Girls of Gottenburg*, *Our Miss Gibbs* (Yip-I-Addy-I-Ay), *Peggy*, *The Sunshine Girl*, and *The Girl on the Film*, becoming in the process one of the most popular stage stars of the Edwardesian era.

At the same time Grossmith continued to venture, with more success than previously, into stage authorship, and the librettos of four of the internationally played Gaiety musicals of this period (*The Spring Chicken*, *The Girls of Gottenburg*, *Havana*, and *Peggy*) came at least partly from his pen. He also had a hand in the construction of some of London's earliest twentieth-century revues (*Rogues and Vagabonds*, *Venus*, *Oh! Indeed*, *Hullo … London!*, *Everybody's doing it*, *Kill That Fly!*, *Eightpence a Mile*, *Not Likely*, *The Bing Boys are Here*, and so on), and in the years that followed his name appeared regularly in a libretto credit on his shows as well as a performing one, and sometimes even a directing one.

In 1914, with the Gaiety and George Edwardes both ailing, Grossmith turned producer as well, allying himself with Dutch cinema magnate Edward Laurillard in an attempt to carry on with the kind of comedy and light music based shows which the Gaiety had mounted in its most effective years. The team scored a veritable hit with their first effort, a musicalized *Dominos roses* called *Tonight's the Night*, on Broadway and at the Gaiety, and won another long run at the same house with a second made-over French comedy, *Theodore and Co.*, but after Edwardes's death they were bested by the growingly ambitious Alfred Butt in the battle for the control of the Gaiety and ousted. The partners nevertheless went on to further London hits with *Mr Manhattan*, *Arlette*, and *Yes, Uncle!* (and a flop with their first transatlantic show, *Oh, Boy!*) in other houses until their own new theatre, the Winter Garden, built on the site of the famous old Middlesex Music Hall (a site today housing the New London Theatre) was ready to open in May 1919. Grossmith's performing career had meanwhile been interrupted by war service in the Royal Naval Volunteer Reserve, into which he was commissioned in 1916.

Grossmith starred alongside Leslie Henson in the Winter Garden's initial productions, *Kissing Time* (1919) and *A Night Out* (1920), as the theatre quickly established itself as a major West End musical venue. The partnership with Laurillard self-destructed amicably in 1921, after the pair had made an attempt to expand, Edwardes-fashion, beyond their own theatre. Grossmith teamed thereafter with Edwardes's former chief lieutenant Pat Malone to mount a series of mostly imported shows between 1920 and 1926 at the Winter Garden (*Sally*, *The Cabaret Girl*, *The Beauty Prize*, a revival of *Tonight's the Night*, *Primrose*, *Tell me More*, and *Kid Boots*). *Sally* was a grand hit and *The Cabaret Girl* did fairly, but the later shows proved losers, and ultimately Grossmith and Malone went out of business.

During the Winter Garden years, Grossmith played less frequently in his own shows, and he scored his most singular hit in years when, while his producing venture was failing in Drury Lane, he introduced the role of Billy Early in the original British production of *No, No, Nanette* (1925) at the Palace Theatre. After the end of the Winter Garden venture he limited himself to performing, appearing in musical comedy in Britain (*Lady Mary*, *The Five O'Clock Girl*) and America (*Princess Charming*, *Meet my Sister*) until 1931, and also in several films. He was subsequently briefly (1931–2) and not very happily in charge at the Theatre Royal, Drury Lane (*The Land of Smiles*, *Cavalcade*) and also headed for a short time London Film Productions Ltd. He died at Beaumont House, 3 Beaumont Street, London, on 6 June 1935.

Tall and gangling, with a 'face hardly less extraordinary than his curious legs and a humour as unctuous as his father's at his best' (Hicks, *Seymour Hicks: Twenty-Four Years of an Actor's Life* 1910, 188), and a physique ready made for the kind of comedy in which he excelled, Grossmith nevertheless harboured a lifelong weakness for playing romantic roles. His dashing dressing led to such nicknames as the Hope Brothers Beau and the Schoolgirls' Dream, but his attempts to angle his parts in the direction of herodom proved unwise, and it was as the vacuous and cheerful 'Johnnie', with his twinking feet and half-a-voice, that he won his greatest successes as a performer. As a producer his greatest achievement was with his largely self-adapted and always strongly backed series of from-the-French shows (*Tonight's the Night*, *Theodore and Co.*, *Yes, Uncle!*, *Kissing Time*, *A Night Out*), a series which brought British musical comedy on from its mostly fairly plotless existence under Edwardes's regime to a peak of genuine musical comedy worthy of both parts of its name.

KURT GÄNZL

**Sources** K. Gänzl, *The encyclopedia of the musical theatre*, 2 vols. (1994); 2nd edn 3 vols. (2001) · K. Gänzl, *The British musical theatre*, 2 vols. (1986) · *The Era* · G. Grossmith, *G. G.* (1933) [autobiography] · b. cert. · *DNB* · d. cert.

**Archives** BL, corresp. with Society of Authors, Add. MS 56719

**Likenesses** caricature, 1893, repro. in Grossmith, *G. G.*, 8 · M. Beerbohm, watercolour and ink caricature, 1910, V&A · W. Grossmith, portrait, 1917 · J. Russell & Sons, photograph, *c*.1917, NPG · E. Kapp, drawing, 1919, Barber Institute of Fine Arts, Birmingham · H. Coster, photographs, 1933, NPG · Ellis & Walery, photographs, NPG · Lock & Whitfield, photographs, NPG · R. S. Sherriffs, ink caricature, NPG · photographs, repro. in Grossmith, *G. G.*

**Wealth at death** £14,945 16*s*. 5*d*.: administration with will, 29 July 1935, *CGPLA Eng. & Wales*

**Grossmith, (Walter) Weedon** (1854–1919). *See under* Grossmith, George (1847–1912).

**Grosvenor** [*formerly* Gravener], **Benjamin** (1676–1758), Presbyterian minister, was born Benjamin Gravener in London, probably in Watling Street, on 1 January 1676, the son of Charles Gravener (*b*. 1652, *d*. after 1700), a prosperous City upholsterer. He was convinced of the Christian message as a child when he happened to hear an unknown Baptist preacher.

> When he was about ten years old his tender mind was so impressed with an awful view of the evil of sin, and the dreadful consequences of offending his Maker, that, for some considerable time, his life was quite a burden to him. (*Protestant Dissenter's Magazine*, 201)

He was baptized at the age of fourteen by Benjamin Keach and became a member of the Particular Baptist chapel at Goat Yard Passage, Horslydown.

Gravener entered Timothy Jollie's academy at Attercliffe, Yorkshire, in 1693 to prepare for the ministry, where he probably renewed his youthful contact with William Harris, later a fellow minister and lifelong friend. While at the academy Gravener altered his views on baptism and became a Presbyterian. Having returned to London in 1695, where he studied under private tutors, he was dismissed from membership of his Baptist church. While he was debating whether to withdraw from his plan to become a minister, he was encouraged by the London Presbyterians and became assistant to Joshua Oldfield at Maid Lane, Southwark, in 1699. Early recognized as an able preacher he was made a lecturer at Old Jewry in 1702.

Benjamin Grosvenor (1676–1758), by unknown artist

He resigned after his appointment as pastor of the large congregation at Crosby Square in 1704, an office which he retained until 1749. His popularity as a preacher increased the congregation to one of the largest and richest in London. He added the lectureship at Weigh House to his responsibilities in 1707. On 15 July 1703 he married Mary South (*d*. November 1707), daughter of Captain South of Bethnal Green. It was about this time that his father got into financial difficulties which required his son's continued support. This may have led Benjamin to change his name to Gravenor in 1710, and finally to adopt the name of Grosvenor in 1716, when he became the Tuesday morning lecturer at Salters' Hall. On 31 May 1712 he married his second wife, Elizabeth Prince, who also predeceased him.

Grosvenor's fame rested on his preaching, controversial lecturing, and writing. He published nearly thirty works, mainly sermons, of which a collected edition appeared in 1809. His contribution in 1716, entitled 'Bigotry', to the influential *Occasional Papers* (known as the Bagwell papers) had a marked effect in forming the ideas of dissenters on the subject of religious liberty, and 'to its influence may be largely ascribed the action of the non-subscribing majority at Salters' Hall in 1719' (*DNB*). Grosvenor is said to have drawn up the *Authentick Account* (1719) of the Salters' Hall proceedings, which was the first of many pamphlets issued by the non-subscribers and listed the non-subscribers' names. His best-known work, *The Mourner* (1731), a religious treatise on consolation, had gone to eighteen editions by 1804 and 'consoled many a mind under the deepest affliction' (*Protestant Dissenter's Magazine*, 205). He believed in mutual toleration in relation to religious differences; his own theology was that of a moderate Calvinist.

> His judgement and faith, in the doctrines of the christian religion, were steady and unshaken. And though I know not that his sentiments ever much altered, on any point of controversy, yet he detested censoriousness, and abounded in candour and moderation. (Barker, 36)

However, his lectures against popery in 1735 brought him wide attention at a time when the question of the Young Pretender was in the public mind. He wrote further pieces on political and controversial matters that were published anonymously. In 1730 the University of Edinburgh made him DD.

It is claimed Grosvenor spoke softly and could not be heard by some.

> His voice though small was sweet and melodious, especially until 1726 when in a painful operation his Uvula was cut out of his mouth … which ever afterwards occasioned an impediment in his pronunciation. … He delivered serious truths from the pulpit with uncommon freedom and energy … it should be allowed, that occasionally some of his lively turns needed an apology. (Barker, 35–6)

He continued in his ministry too long for the health of the congregation. 'Dr Grosvenor retained his pulpit longer than prudence dictated, for when he relinquished the duties of active life the church had lost its former prosperity. The efforts of Dr Hodge, who succeeded, to revive the dwindling interest were unavailing' (Pike, 93). His response to an over-zealous enquirer, who deserved something sharper, reflects his ready wit.

> At Isaac Watts' funeral (1748), a friend exclaimed, 'Well, Dr Grosvenor, you have seen the last of Dr Watts, and you will soon follow; what think you of death?' 'Think of it? Why, when death comes I shall smile upon death if God smile upon me'. (Pike, 93)

Grosvenor died after a long illness on 27 August 1758 at his home in Hoxton Square, Shoreditch, and was buried in Bunhill Fields in the family grave of his first wife. Of his five sons and one daughter, only the youngest son was alive at his death—'his children, inheriting neither their father's prudence or piety, occasioned him very heavy affliction' (Barker, 34). In his will he left a bequest to the Presbyterian Fund and his library to the Warrington Academy.

Grosvenor was held in such regard that Thomas Gibbon published a long poem in 1759 in his memory, *The Tears of Friendship, an Elegiac Ode on the Death of Benjamin Grosvenor.* Stanza xxx sums up its florid, but heartfelt, style:

> But Grosvenor's gone: no more my joyful Eye
> Shall see his Face majestically sweet,
> Where, with the Prophet's awful Dignity,
> Each soft attractive Grace had fix'd its Seat.

Alan Ruston

**Sources** *Protestant Dissenter's Magazine*, 4 (1797), 201–5 • G. H. Pike, *Ancient meeting-houses, or, Memorial pictures of nonconformity in old London* (1870), 90–93 • *DNB* • J. Barker, *A sermon, occasioned by the death of the Revd Benjamin Grosvenor* (1758) • C. Surman, index, DWL • will, PRO, PROB 11/840, sig. 263 • *IGI* • W. Wilson, *The history and antiquities of the dissenting churches and meeting houses in London, Westminster and Southwark*, 4 vols. (1808–14), vol. 1, pp. 344–6 • W. D. Jeremy, *The Presbyterian Fund and Dr Daniel Williams's Trust* (1885), 25, 124 • T. Gibbon, *The tears of friendship, an elegiac ode* (1759), stanza xxx • J. A. Jones, ed., *Bunhill memorials* (1849), 71–2 • T. G. Crippen, 'The Attercliffe Academy', *Transactions of the Congregational Historical Society*, 4 (1909–10), 338

**Archives** DWL, MSS

**Likenesses** van der Gucht, engraving, *c.*1731, DWL • Hopwood, stipple, pubd 1808, NPG • portrait, DWL [*see illus.*]

**Wealth at death** several thousand pounds: will, PRO, PROB 11/840 fols. 144*v*–146*r*

**Grosvenor, Hugh Lupus, first duke of Westminster (1825–1899)**, landowner, racehorse owner, and politician, was born on 13 October 1825 at Eaton Hall, Cheshire, the second but first surviving son, and fifth of the thirteen children, of Richard *Grosvenor, second marquess of Westminster (1795–1869), and his wife, Elizabeth Mary (1797–1891), younger daughter of George Granville Leveson-Gower, second marquess of Stafford and later first duke of Sutherland.

**Politics, marriage, and dukedom** Educated at Eton College from 1839 to 1843 and at Balliol College, Oxford, from 1843 to 1847, Grosvenor left Oxford without taking a degree because it suited the family's interests that he should enter parliament for the Grosvenor borough of Chester in January 1847, as soon as his uncle Lord Robert Grosvenor decided to leave that seat in favour of an unopposed return for one of the two Middlesex seats. Earl Grosvenor, as Hugh Lupus was styled, remained one of Chester's MPs until he went to the Lords as the third marquess of Westminster on his father's death in October 1869, but at least until 1866 the Commons did not take up much of his time. True, his maiden speech in 1851 was quite a success, but that was wholly fortuitous since he stumbled into a debate on the suppression of disorders in Ceylon three days after his return from an extensive tour of India and Ceylon, so that he had an unchallenged claim to be the only member of the house with up-to-date, firsthand knowledge of conditions in the island. In the course of this tour, made in palanquins with two first cousins, Hugh visited Katmandu and became one of the first Englishmen to set eyes on and describe a Pekinese, which he called 'a curious little chinese dog with longish chestnut hair and curled up tail, no nose at all, a little black mouth and a tongue sticking out. There are only four of these dogs in Nepal' (Huxley, 51). This kind of thing, and shooting and stalking in the highlands, interested him a great deal more than parliament, where he was a reliable and silent whig-Liberal.

On 28 April 1852 Grosvenor married his first cousin, Lady Constance Sutherland-Leveson-Gower (1834–1880), fourth daughter of the second duke of Sutherland and his wife, Harriet Howard. The duchess of Sutherland was a close friend of Queen Victoria, mistress of the robes from 1837 to 1841 (and in subsequent whig-Liberal administrations) and thus one of the foremost whig ladies in the 1839 'bedchamber' crisis, and Constance also became a Victorian favourite. She stayed several times at Osborne before her marriage, and Victoria was so taken with her that in 1850 she commissioned Winterhalter to paint her portrait; it is in Windsor Castle. Victoria and Albert attended the wedding, in the Chapel Royal, St James's Palace, the

**Hugh Lupus Grosvenor, first duke of Westminster (1825–1899)**, by Sir John Everett Millais, 1872

most dazzling event of the season. Hugh and Constance, as Earl and Countess Grosvenor, were launched on an active and fashionable social life. Their first child, a son, was born in 1853 and Victoria became his godmother; others followed rapidly, and between 1853 and 1874 Constance had eleven children, of whom eight survived infancy—five boys and three girls.

In 1866 Grosvenor the socialite and back-bencher transformed himself into a serious politician with his moderate but unyielding opposition to Gladstone's Reform Bill. He became bracketed with Lowe and Horsman as an Adullamite, although his stand, unlike theirs, was not against extending the franchise but in favour of a comprehensive measure of reform which should include proposals for franchise extension and redistribution of seats in one bill. This might have been only a tactical argument, anticipating the line taken by Salisbury in 1884, but it was probably decisive in leading to Gladstone's defeat and resignation, and to the Derby government and the second Reform Act, in whose passage Grosvenor voted with Disraeli on most clauses. Estrangement from Gladstone did not last long, the two being quite friendly neighbours in the country, seeing more of each other particularly after Gladstone inherited Hawarden in 1874. Already in 1871 Gladstone asked the new marquess to move the address in the Lords, and the next year offered him office as under-secretary at the War Office, which was declined. Nevertheless, when Grosvenor was made duke of Westminster in Gladstone's resignation honours in February 1874 it was not in recognition of any particular political or national services. This, the only dukedom in the UK peerage created in Victoria's reign apart from those bestowed on members of the royal family (Abercorn's dukedom of 1868 was in the Irish peerage), and the last new non-royal dukedom of modern times, appears to have been conferred chiefly on the grounds of Westminster's immense wealth and high social position. The one clue on motivation is unhelpful. Hugh Lupus's cousin Lord Granville wrote to Gladstone a week before the announcement, asking 'has it ever crossed you [*sic*] to make your Cheshire neighbour a Duke', to which the reply was 'your suggestion about Westminster has often crossed my mind and I have every disposition to recommend it' (Gladstone and Granville, nos. 976–7). The dukedom was certainly very pleasing to Victoria, because of her fondness for Constance, the new duchess, and may have been an inexpensive way for Gladstone to improve relations with the queen. It also served to signal Gladstone's continuing friendship with the whig aristocracy, much to the disgust of Hugh's mother, who had become very reactionary in her views and feared and loathed Gladstone as a dangerous demagogic maniac.

This political alignment was demonstrated by the new duke later in the 1870s, when he strongly supported Gladstone in the campaigns against the Bulgarian atrocities and the jingoism of Disraeli's anti-Russian posturing. When Gladstone returned to power in 1880 the duke supported the ministry by serving as master of the horse, an appropriately equine but not an actively political office. In 1886 he fell out with Gladstone over home rule, which brought reconciliation with his mother in her declining years (she died in 1891), and a sharp rebuke from Gladstone for striking 'a fresh blow at the aristocracy' (Huxley, 165). The estrangement was acute, leading the duke to take down the portrait of Gladstone by Sir John Millais (1879) which hung at Eaton, and sell it; it found its way to the National Portrait Gallery after being owned by Sir Charles Tennant. Eventually the Eastern question once again brought the two men together, the duke applauding and publicly supporting Gladstone's denunciations of the Armenian massacres in 1896, so that when Gladstone died in 1898 it was not at all surprising that the duke launched and presided over a Gladstone National Memorial committee, which met in Grosvenor House, and commissioned statues for London, Edinburgh, and Dublin (the last refused to accept the statue, which was erected at Hawarden instead), and rebuilt the St Deiniol's Library, also at Hawarden.

**Landed inheritance and the turf** Hugh Lupus appreciated statues, and one of his first acts on inheriting the family estates was to commission G. F. Watts (Sir Edwin Landseer having turned down the commission on grounds of age) to execute a grand equestrian statue of his namesake, Hugh Lupus the Norman earl of Chester. 'All the Americans on landing in Liverpool go to see Eaton', he wrote, 'and I should like to show them … something good on arrival on our shores' (Huxley, 94). Good it may have been as sculpture, but Hugh Lupus had not previously appreciated how well the Norman earl had earned the nickname Wolf; he harried the Welsh cruelly, he was gluttonous and greedy, and he fathered numerous bastards. Learning this, the Victorian Lupus had doubts, but in the end went ahead and the huge statue was placed to look down a 2 mile avenue to the Welsh hills in the west. This was an ornamental and symbolic part of the great rebuilding of Eaton, to the designs of Alfred Waterhouse, which was put in hand in 1870 and completed ten years later, at a cost of nearly £600,000. A vast, cheerless, Gothic structure with lavish use of cast iron, it was redeemed by a comfortable family wing that was in effect a separate house. Guests were not greatly amused by the carillon of twenty-eight bells in the great clock tower, playing twenty-eight different tunes, and remorselessly sounding every quarter hour throughout the night. Hugh Lupus inherited one of the richest estates in the country, worth at least £152,000 a year in 1869, but his father, as not infrequently happens with the very rich, imagined that he was always about to run out of money and was thrifty to the point of meanness, so that Lupus was kept on a tight rein, claiming that it was quite impossible to live on the £8000 a year which he was allowed in the 1850s. His father's answer to pleas for more money was simple: 'I believe that every-day-clean-shirt system at Eton did your temperament much harm … Your habits are expensive and you live in an expensive society' (Huxley, 73).

Hugh Lupus greeted the financial liberation of his father's death not exactly with an orgy of self-indulgence, for he remained abstemious in his habits, but with that kind of liberal spending which he regarded as virtually a public duty incumbent upon his rank. Alongside the great rebuilding of Eaton, where a private light railway was constructed to bring in supplies, and visitors, from Balderton, there was expenditure on Grosvenor House in Mayfair, on Cliveden, which had come to him on the death of his mother-in-law, and on building several shooting lodges on the large sporting estates in Sutherland which he rented from his cousin the duke. Deer stalking, and shooting both in the highlands and in Cheshire, were prime interests which he pursued into his final years, shooting a record number of snipe on the marshes near Eaton four months before he died. He spent some money in adding to the Grosvenor art collection, which had been effectively founded by his grandfather in 1806, but his genuinely ducal extravagance was to aspire to become king of the turf.

In 1875 Westminster started his racing stable at Eaton, a stud which grew to employ thirty grooms and boys, with two or three stallions and up to a score of brood mares, and the pick of their progeny, under the stud manager. The duke did not regard this as any kind of extravagance, but as the performance of an aristocratic duty to support racing and improve the quality of racehorses, not entirely hypocritically since he refused to gamble and never placed a bet even on one of his own horses. One of his horses won the Derby in 1880—this was Bend 'Or, named after the original Grosvenor coat of arms, which began racing in 1879 with a blaze of wins, in the year when the duke's grandson and eventual heir Hugh Richard, who was himself known as Bend 'Or, was born—and he had further Derby winners in 1882, 1886, and 1899. In the twenty-five years of his career as a breeder and owner, Westminster's horses won hundreds of races with a total take in prize money of about £300,000; together with receipts from sales of horses for racing or for stud it is possible that the enterprise was nearly self-financing.

The duke was an extremely popular racing figure, his yellow and black colours had crowds of devoted followers, and his obituaries gave as much space to his racing career as to all the rest of his life. Strangely, as *The Times* observed:

> The nonconformist conscience which was so much disturbed by Lord Rosebery's racing successes, never, so far as we know, resented those of the Duke of Westminster. He seemed to stand out of the reach of the censorious attacks of the large class which loves to call in question the conduct of those in high places. … He could pass from a racecourse to take the chair at a missionary meeting [the notice went on] without incurring the censure of the strictest. (*The Times*, 23 Dec 1899, 6)

It helped that he was not a betting man. But he was such a large-scale and important philanthropist that it would, in any case, have been expedient to overlook any lapses from 'respectable' behaviour. He supported a large number of charities, and in his time was president or chairman of five London hospitals, the Royal Society for the Prevention of Cruelty to Animals, the Metropolitan Drinking Fountains and Cattle Troughs Association, the Gardeners' Royal Beneficent Institution, the Hampstead Heath Protection Society, the Early Closing Association, the United Committee for the Prevention of Demoralization of Native Races by the Liquor Traffic, and a member of the council for the promotion of cremation. Cremation, deeply unpopular with the church, he regarded as an inexpensive remedy for the crippling debts often incurred by ordinary families because of unnecessarily lavish funerals; and he had been a firm temperance man since his twenty-year old younger brother Gilbert became an alcoholic and died at sea in 1854.

**London estate owner and town planner** The money to sustain Westminster's philanthropy and ducal style came mainly from the ground rents of Mayfair and Belgravia, which grew from about £115,000 a year to some £250,000 a year between 1870 and 1899. The main lines of residential and commercial development had already been laid down before he succeeded his father, but he took seriously his role as chairman of the Grosvenor estate board, which managed the estate, and frequently attended its meetings and influenced its decisions. He was an autocratic, paternalistic, and generally benevolent landlord. There was an immense amount of rebuilding in Mayfair in his time, as the original leases fell in, and the duke personally composed the list of approved architects for employment in these works, favouring Norman Shaw, Aston Webb, Alfred Waterhouse, and a few others. In contrast to the Italianate stucco stipulated by his father, the duke supported Queen Anne revival and South Kensington red brick and terracotta, commenting on new buildings in Duke Street 'the more red brick the better' (Sheppard, 39.53). He liked stucco to be painted bright orange, and railings either chocolate or red, and it behoved lessees to humour him. He objected to any building works going on during the season, strongly opposed proposals to erect telegraph poles and wires in the district, and pressed for Oxford Street to be paved with wooden blocks. Three new churches, two schools, a library, a new vestry office, and a dozen blocks of artisan dwellings were built with his encouragement and financial help, and he waged a vigorous campaign against the demon drink, reducing the number of pubs and beerhouses on the Mayfair estate from forty-seven in 1869 to eight in 1891. He 'was most anxious for a great many more urinals being erected in the Parish and in London generally' and was especially keen on providing urinals in mews for the outdoor servants, but when Lord Manners's coachman complained that the urinal in Reeves Mews could be seen from his upper windows he had it moved. When the duchess of Marlborough complained that a dentist in Grosvenor Street was visible from her house opposite, the dentist was asked 'to put up a muslin curtain to prevent his dentistry patients being seen' (ibid., 63). And he overruled a clause in one of his own leases, which prohibited a butcher in Mount Street from publicly exposing carcases, personally visiting the shop and ruling that 'Butcher Green's exhibition of prominent carcases of sheep may be permitted as an ornament to the street' (ibid., 65). In short he was a one-man planning and enforcement officer, sometimes arbitrary or capricious in his rulings, but generally liked by the wealthy and fashionable for whose comfort and convenience Mayfair and Belgravia were regulated. The family lawyer and chief agent, Boodle, told the select committee on town holdings in 1887 that the duke ran the property in a public-spirited way regardless of his own pecuniary interests. The duke's aim, Boodle said, was:

> to have wide thoroughfares instead of narrow, to set back houses in rebuilding so as to obtain broad areas and a good basement for servants … He also wishes to have effective architecture, to insist upon good sanitary arrangements in houses, to promote churches, chapels, and schools, and open spaces for recreation. ('Select committee on town holdings', q. 6118)

He did this 'chiefly because he desires better houses, and he is a great lover of architecture and likes a handsome town, and he would sacrifice enormously to carry that out on his estate' (ibid.). This was aristocratic enlightened self-interest, planning and managing for a long-term family future, rather than self-sacrifice.

**Second marriage and death** The duke was the inevitable choice as the first lord lieutenant of the county of London when the London county council was created in 1888, just as he had been the natural successor to Lord Egerton in the lord lieutenancy of Cheshire in 1883, while his presidency of the Royal Agricultural Society in 1892 reflected an acquaintance with farming which went beyond conventional landlord concerns into up-to-date knowledge of fertilizers and silage. The success story was interrupted in 1880 when his much-loved wife Constance—perhaps too much loved, as she was notoriously unfaithful—died of Bright's disease after a summer when daily medical bulletins issued from Grosvenor House, in the manner of royal illnesses. Two years later the duke went to Latimer, Buckinghamshire, to attend the funeral of his daughter Beatrice's father-in-law, and promptly fell in love with Beatrice's young sister-in-law Katherine Caroline (1857–1941), third daughter of William George Cavendish, second Baron Chesham, and his wife, Henrietta Frances Lascelles. She was then aged twenty-four; they married a month later, in June 1882. Not only was the new duchess, Katie, younger than the duke's eldest son, Victor, and two of his daughters, Elizabeth and Beatrice, and confusingly both aunt and step-grandmother to Beatrice's four children, but also her own four children, two sons and two daughters born between 1883 and 1892, were younger than eight of her thirteen step-grandchildren. Katie, who lived until 1941, handled this curious family situation with great tact and won the warm affection of most of the varied brood. The duke, clearly still most active and steering his Seats for Shop Assistants Bill through its second reading in July 1899 (part of the early closing campaign), went to visit his newly married granddaughter Constance Sibell ('Cuckoo'), countess of Shaftesbury, at St Giles House in Cranborne, Dorset, where he developed bronchitis and died on 22 December 1899. As a supporter of cremation and subscriber to the Woking crematorium he was cremated there on 24 December and his ashes were buried in Eccleston churchyard, Cheshire, on 28 December. His eldest son Victor having died in 1884, he was succeeded by his grandson, Bend 'Or, as second duke.

F. M. L. Thompson

**Sources** G. Huxley, *Victorian duke: the life of Hugh Lupus Grosvenor, first duke of Westminster* (1967) • F. H. W. Sheppard, ed., *The Grosvenor estate in Mayfair*, 1: *General history*, Survey of London, 39 (1977) • *The Times* (23 Dec 1899) • *DNB* • GEC, *Peerage* • *The political correspondence of Mr Gladstone and Lord Granville, 1868–1876*, ed. A. Ramm, 2 vols., CS, 3rd ser., 81–2 (1952) • 'Select committee on town holdings', *Parl. papers* (1887), 13.41, no. 260 • M. Girouard, *The Victorian country house*, rev. edn (1979) • *CGPLA Eng. & Wales* (1900)

**Archives** priv. coll., corresp. and papers | BL, corresp. with W. E. Gladstone, Add. MS 44337 • BL, letters to Mrs W. E. Gladstone, Add. MSS 46228–46229 • Bodl. Oxf., letters to Sir Robert Morier • NL Scot., corresp. incl. with Lord Rosebery • U. Lpool L., Sydney Jones Library, letters to William Rathbone

**Likenesses** G. Richmond, crayon, 1856, Grosvenor House, London • J. E. Millais, oils, 1872, Eaton Hall, Cheshire [*see illus.*] • J. E. Millais, oils, 1872, Ragley Hall, Warwickshire • Downey, photograph, *c.*1880, NPG • photograph, *c.*1895, repro. in Huxley, *Victorian duke* • C. J. Blomfield, monument, 1900–02, Chester Cathedral • W. Carter, portrait, exh. RA 1901, Westminster City Library, London • Ape [C. Pellegrini], caricature, chromolithograph, NPG; repro. in *VF* (16 July 1870) • Ape [C. Pellegrini], lithograph, repro. in *VF* (6 Dec 1887) • T. O. Barlow, engraving (after J. E. Millais), BM, NPG • J. Brown, stipple (after photograph by Southwell), BM;

repro. in *Baily's Magazine* (1864) • Caldesi, Blanford & Co., carte-de-visite, NPG • W. & D. Downey, woodburytype, NPG; repro. in W. Downey and D. Downey, *The cabinet portrait gallery*, 1 (1890) • W. Holl, stipple (after G. Richmond; *Grillion's Club* series), BM • G. Pilotell, dry point, BM • D. J. Pound, line engraving (after photograph by J. and C. Watkins), NPG • H. T. Wells, group portrait, oils (*Wimbledon, 1864*), Althorp House, Northamptonshire • bas-relief on bronze tablet, Chesham Buildings, London • oils, Chester town hall • portrait, repro. in *ILN* (18 Feb 1871), 159 • portrait, repro. in *ILN* (25 June 1892), 791 • portrait, repro. in *ILN* (15 Dec 1894), 739 • portrait, repro. in *Baily's Magazine*, 9 (1865), 55 • prints, NPG

**Wealth at death** £594,229 1s. 0d.: probate, 14 Feb 1900, *CGPLA Eng. & Wales* • Reputedly the wealthiest man in Britain, with real estate worth about £6,000,000.

**Grosvenor, John** (1742–1823), surgeon and journal editor, was born in Oxford in 1742, the son of Stephen Grosvenor, sub-treasurer of Christ Church, and his wife, Sarah, daughter of the Revd Tottie, vicar of Ecclesall, Yorkshire. Grosvenor trained under a Mr Russell of Worcester, and was possibly apprenticed to William Grosvenor of Bewdley, Worcestershire, before walking the wards in the London hospitals. He was soon appointed surgeon to the Lock Hospital but returned to Oxford in 1768 on the invitation of his uncle Dr Tottie, canon of Christ Church, to become anatomical surgeon to John Parsons (1742–1785), Dr Lee's reader in anatomy. He was admitted to the privileges of the university on 24 February 1768. Grosvenor was considered a skilled surgeon who possessed almost 'magical dexterity' (*GM*, 1823, 276) of the hand, and, following the death of Sir Charles Nourse, found himself with an immense practice in Oxford and the surrounding area. He was especially successful in his treatment of stiff and diseased joints by friction, a treatment he first used with success on his own diseased knee. Grosvenor became quite affluent and was eventually able to resign from his position as anatomical surgeon and reduce his own practice.

Grosvenor could be reserved and taciturn, especially with men, but enjoyed the company of women, in which he 'indulged in an easy raillery and playful badinage which never failed to delight highly the younger part of his fair auditors' (*GM*, 1823, 277). He married twice. On 17 March 1791 he married Anne, daughter of Mr Hough of the East India Company and widow of his former colleague John Parsons. His second wife was Charlotte, daughter of Charles Marsack of Caversham Park, Oxford. There were no children from either marriage. Grosvenor had some literary talent and it was rumoured that he had once published a series of letters that ridiculed various Oxford worthies. In 1795, following the death of William Jackson, the university printer, Grosvenor became chief proprietor and editor of the *Oxford Journal*. Editing the newspaper was obviously not an onerous task for Grosvenor, as it is said he was able to complete it while taking breakfast. Grosvenor died in Oxford on 30 June 1823.

MICHAEL BEVAN

**Sources** *DNB* • P. J. Wallis and R. V. Wallis, *Eighteenth century medics*, 2nd edn (1988) • *GM*, 1st ser., 61 (1791), 380 • *GM*, 1st ser., 93/2 (1823), 276–8

**Likenesses** R. Dighton, caricature, coloured etching, pubd 1808, BM, Wellcome L. • C. Turner, mezzotint (after T. Leeming, 1812), Wellcome L.

**Grosvenor, Sir Richard, first baronet** (1585–1645), magistrate and politician, was born at Eaton Hall, near Chester, Cheshire, on 9 January 1585, the eldest surviving son and the third of seventeen children of Richard Grosvenor, esquire (1562–1619), of Eaton, Cheshire, and his wife, Christian (*d.* 1610), daughter of Sir Richard Brooke of Norton, Cheshire. He was educated in the puritan household of John Bruen, esquire, of Stapleford in Cheshire, and at Queen's College, Oxford, where he matriculated on 26 October 1599 and graduated BA on 30 June 1602. Meanwhile, he had married in 1600 Lettice, daughter of Sir Hugh *Cholmondeley of Cholmondeley, Cheshire. They had one son and three daughters before Lettice's death on 20 January 1612. Two years later, in 1614, he married Elizabeth, daughter of Sir Thomas Wilbraham of Woodhey, Cheshire, and after her death, he married Elizabeth (*d.* 1627), daughter of Sir Peter *Warburton of Grafton, Cheshire. Grosvenor was knighted on 24 August 1617 and made a baronet on 23 February 1622.

Grosvenor made his principal mark in local affairs. He succeeded his father as a JP for Cheshire in 1619 and he served on the bench until his removal, as part of a purge by George Villiers, first duke of Buckingham, on 26 October 1626. He was also sheriff of Cheshire in 1623–4 and of Flintshire in 1624–5. Although not one of the foremost Cheshire gentry in terms of wealth or landholdings, Grosvenor became the most influential local governor in the area of his main estate, immediately to the south of Chester. This was because of his industry and his abilities as a man of affairs, and also because of his reputation as a supporter of puritan ministers. William Hinde, who had probably been his tutor at Queen's College, described him as a paragon of the godly gentleman, and another leading Cheshire puritan preacher, Nathaniel Lancaster, hailed him in 1628 as 'a father of the country' (Lancaster, sig. A2).

Grosvenor represented Cheshire in the parliaments of 1621, 1626, and 1628–9. He was not in the front rank of Commons spokesmen, but he was an effective, if rather long-winded, public speaker and a diligent attender of committees. Most of his interventions in parliament were concerned either with the welfare of his Cheshire constituents or with the defence of the Calvinist religion. In 1621 he spoke out against the patentee Sir Giles Mompesson, and the popish threat to the palatinate, and in 1629 he delivered a notable attack on the influence of the king's Arminian advisers. He was also a meticulous parliamentary diarist, providing the fullest known account of debates in 1626, 1628, and 1629.

Grosvenor's third and last wife died on 12 March 1627. Between 1629 and 1638 he was imprisoned in the Fleet, having become liable for the debts of his brother-in-law, Peter Daniel, esquire. Although he was not restored to the bench after his return to the county, he remained an influential figure in local politics. In May 1640 he arbitrated a dispute over the parliamentary election for Chester, and in July 1642 he played a leading role in organizing, and probably also drafting, the Cheshire remonstrance, a petition containing over 8000 signatures, which called on the king and parliament to settle their differences and avoid civil war. During the war Grosvenor remained neutral; he is not to be confused with his eldest son, Richard Grosvenor esq., who played a prominent part in the royalist defence of Chester.

Grosvenor's speeches and writings make it possible to reconstruct his political views in considerable detail. He was a firm believer in the divine right of kingship and in patriarchal authority, but at the same time he staunchly defended the liberties of the subject and of parliament's role as 'the representative of the people'. Above all, he was concerned to root out the evil of popery and to overcome the influence of 'evil counsellors' close to the king. In many respects he was the archetype of the 'patriots' and 'public men' who played a crucial political role as spokesmen for their localities and 'the country' in the years preceding the civil war. Grosvenor died at Eaton Hall on 14 September 1645 and was buried in Eccleston church, Cheshire. RICHARD CUST

**Sources** *The papers of Sir Richard Grosvenor, 1st bart, 1585–1645*, ed. R. Cust, Lancashire and Cheshire RS, 134 (1996) · R. Cust and P. G. Lake, 'Sir Richard Grosvenor and the rhetoric of magistracy', *BIHR*, 54 (1981), 40–53 · Eaton Hall, Chester, Grosvenor MSS · N. Lancaster, *The proofe of profession: Tabitha's funerall* (1628) [copy in Cheshire RO, H 25.2] · W. Hinde, *A faithfull remonstrance of the holy life and happy death of John Bruen* (1641) · G. Ormerod, *The history of the county palatine and city of Chester*, 2nd edn, ed. T. Helsby, 3 vols. (1882) · G. P. Higgins, 'County government and society in Cheshire, c.1590–1640', MA diss., U. Lpool, 1974 · J. T. Hopkins, '"Such a twin likeness there was in the pair": an investigation into the painting of the Cholmondeley sisters', *Transactions of the Historic Society of Lancashire and Cheshire*, 141 (1991), 1–37 · J. S. Morrill, *Cheshire, 1630–1660: county government and society during the English revolution* (1974)

**Archives** Eaton Hall, near Chester, MSS · University of Kansas, Lawrence, Kenneth Spencer Research Library, MSS

**Grosvenor, Richard**, first Earl Grosvenor (1731–1802), politician and landowner, was born on 18 June 1731 at Eaton Hall, Cheshire, the elder son of Sir Robert Grosvenor, sixth baronet (1695–1755), MP for Chester from 1733 to 1755, and Jane (1704/5–1791), daughter of Thomas Warre of Shepton Beauchamp and Swell Court, Somerset. He was educated at Oriel College, Oxford, from 1748, and took the degrees of MA in 1751 and DCL in 1754. On the death on 1 August 1755 of his father, whom he had joined in the Commons as a member for Chester at the general election of 1754, he succeeded as seventh baronet and thereafter exercised the electoral patronage of Chester, which he represented until 1761. He consolidated his Cheshire estates, for instance by purchasing the hamlet of Belgrave and the manor of Eccleston in 1758, and established close connections with Chester, where he served as mayor in 1759 and paid for the erection of the east gate in 1769.

In politics, Grosvenor at first followed the tory predilections of his father, but came to ally himself with William Pitt the elder. On 23 November 1758 he seconded the address and spoke in favour of the Pitt–Newcastle coalition. It was through Pitt that he was created Baron Grosvenor on 8 April 1761, and he took his seat in the Lords on 3 November that year. But he did not follow Pitt into opposition, instead supporting the ministry of the earl of Bute,

**Richard Grosvenor, first Earl Grosvenor (1731–1802)**, by Sir Joshua Reynolds, 1760

whose peace preliminaries he seconded in the Lords on 9 December 1762. He prepared some 'hints respecting our acquisitions in America' and other papers (dated 2 February 1763) (BL, Add. MS 38335, fols. 1–5, 14–33). In May 1765 he expressed to Bute's successor, George Grenville, his 'great concern [at] a report of your being to quit' office (BL, Add. MS 57825, fol. 30), and he opposed the ensuing Rockingham administration's American policy, protesting against the repeal of the Stamp Act (11 and 17 March 1766). He subsequently sided again with the earl of Chatham (as Pitt had become) on his return to power in late 1766.

On 19 July 1764 Grosvenor had married Henrietta (*bap.* 1745, *d.* 1828), daughter of Henry Vernon of Hilton Park, Staffordshire, former MP for Lichfield and Newcastle under Lyme, with whom he had four sons. She attracted the attentions of George III's brother, Henry Frederick, duke of Cumberland, and embarked on an affair, which was brought to a sordid end by their discovery *in flagrante delicto* in November 1769. Grosvenor brought an action for criminal conversation against the prince, whose correspondence with his mistress was published with an account of the trial, and in July 1770 Grosvenor was awarded damages of £10,000. Satirized as 'the Cheshire Cornuto', he was also known to be guilty of adultery and therefore could not sue for divorce, but he separated from his wife, upon whom he settled £1200 a year. Lady Grosvenor later married (1 September 1802) George Porter, who inherited the title of Baron de Hochepied in the Hungarian nobility in 1819; they died within three months of each other in early 1828.

With his wife effectively pensioned off Grosvenor was

free to return to a lifestyle that combined the rakish pursuits of horse-racing and womanizing with political influence. He was made a fellow of the Royal Society in 1771. During the 1770s he supported the North ministry's policy during the American War of Independence. Although he was disappointed never to have been appointed lord lieutenant of Cheshire, he thereafter usually aligned himself with ministers. Having voted against Fox's India Bill on 17 December 1783, on the recommendation of William Pitt the younger he was rewarded with the title of Earl Grosvenor on 5 July 1784. In later life he increasingly delegated the exercise of the family's political influence to his son Robert *Grosvenor, Viscount Belgrave, later second Earl Grosvenor and first marquess of Westminster (1767–1845).

Grosvenor was the principal patron of the satirist and journalist William Gifford and contributed to the Grosvenor family's extensive art collection. Grosvenor commissioned Richard Dalton, keeper of the king's pictures and antiquary to George III, to acquire works in Italy for the collection, and also purchased paintings from Benjamin West—including the original of *The Death of Wolfe*—Thomas Gainsborough, Richard Wilson, and George Stubbs. The collection would be expanded dramatically by his son. Under his auspices, the literary pieces composed at a gathering at Eaton in 1788 were published in Chester in 1789 as *The Eaton Chronicle, or, The Salt-Box*. He died at Earls Court, Kensington, on 5 August 1802, and was buried in the family vault at Eccleston, Cheshire, on 15 August. According to the artist Joseph Farington, who in 1793 had described him as one of the 'most profligate men, of his age, in what relates to women' (Farington, *Diary*, 1.5), he

> had been in a bad state of health owing to a surgical complaint two years before he died. It was a *stricture* owing to injections while he was a free liver and for temporary relief an aperture was made *as a passage*, which ever remained an open wound. He declined gradually and bore his illness with much patience. (ibid., 6.2098)

Grosvenor, who had always been 'a *dupe* to the turf' (ibid.) and had had to make economies by selling his stock-breeding stables in 1796, left debts of at least £150,000. Ironically, given their Mayfair estates in London, the family's fortunes were potentially vast, and would indeed increase dramatically under the second earl.

S. M. Farrell

**Sources** *GM*, 1st ser., 72 (1802), 789 • J. Croston, *County families of Lancashire and Cheshire* (1887), 334–5 • BL, Add. MS 38335, fols. 1–5, 14–33 • BL, Add. MS 57825, fol. 30 • *The genuine copies of letters which passed between his royal highness the duke of Cumberland and Lady Grosvenor, to which is annexed, a clear and circumstantial account of the trial*, 5th edn (1770) • J. Chandos, 'Marriage (and one or two other social institutions) Georgian style', *Horizon* [New York], 16/4 (1974), 96–101 • *The Eaton Chronicle, or, The salt-box* (1789) • J. V. Beckett, *The aristocracy in England, 1660–1914*, pbk edn (1988) • Farington, *Diary* • F. H. W. Sheppard, ed., *The Grosvenor estate in Mayfair*, 1: *General history*, Survey of London, 39 (1977) • J. Young, *A catalogue of the pictures at Grosvenor House, London* (1820) • *IGI* • G. Ormerod, *The history of the county palatine and city of Chester*, 2nd edn, ed. T. Helsby, 2 (1882), 843

**Archives** priv. coll., letters and papers

**Likenesses** J. Reynolds, oils, 1760, priv. coll. [*see illus.*] • H. R. Cook, stipple, pubd 1808 (after J. Reynolds), BM, NPG • T. L. Atkinson, mezzotint (after T. Gainsborough), BM, NPG • W. Dickinson, mezzotint (in robes of mayor of Chester; after B. West), BM • T. Gainsborough, portrait, Chester • portrait, repro. in Chandos, 'Marriage … Georgian style' • portrait (after J. Reynolds)

**Wealth at death** personalty sworn under £70,000, but debts of over £100,000: PRO, death duty records, IR 26/66, no. 80; Beckett, *Aristocracy in England*, 304; Farington, *Diary*, 6.2098

**Grosvenor, Richard**, **second marquess of Westminster (1795–1869)**, aristocrat, was born on 27 January 1795 at Millbank House, Westminster, the eldest of the three sons of Robert *Grosvenor, second Earl Grosvenor and first marquess of Westminster (1767–1845), and Lady Eleanor Egerton (1770–1846). Known as Viscount Belgrave from 1802 to 1831, and as Earl Grosvenor from then until 1845, he was educated at Westminster School and Christ Church, Oxford, where he graduated MA in 1818. On 16 September 1819 he married Lady Elizabeth Mary Leveson-Gower (1797–1891), second daughter of the first duke of Sutherland. The marriage sealed the connections between the Grosvenors and the 'whig cousinhood'. The couple had nine daughters, five of whom married peers, and four sons, one of whom died in infancy. The marchioness, a celebrated beauty, published two accounts of the European travels on which she accompanied her husband. Their youngest daughter, Theodora *Guest, was also an author and benefactor.

Grosvenor was whig MP for Chester from 1818 to 1830, for Cheshire from 1830 to 1832, and for South Cheshire from 1832 to 1834. He patronized the turf, winning the St Leger with Touchstone in 1834. He succeeded his father as second marquess on 17 February 1845. He seldom spoke in the House of Lords, and devoted himself chiefly to the improvement of his London property. From 1845 to 1867 he was lord lieutenant of Cheshire, and from 1850 to 1852 lord steward of the household. He received the Order of the Garter on 6 July 1857. After a short illness he died at Fonthill Gifford, Wiltshire, on Sunday 31 October 1869, and was buried at Eccleston, Cheshire. *The Times* stated that 'he administered his vast estate with a combination of intelligence and generosity not often witnessed'. Of reserved habits and inexpensive tastes, despite his huge wealth, he disliked any kind of ostentation and extravagance. He gave generously to charitable causes and built and restored many churches and schools, principally in Cheshire and Chester. He was succeeded by his second son, Hugh Lupus *Grosvenor, first duke of Westminster.

H. R. Tedder, *rev.* K. D. Reynolds

**Sources** GEC, *Peerage* • HoP, *Commons* • G. Huxley, *Lady Elizabeth and the Grosvenors* (1965) • *The Times* (2 Nov 1869) • *Chester Chronicle* (6 Nov 1869)

**Archives** BL, corresp. with W. E. Gladstone, Add. MSS 44364–44410, *passim* • BL, corresp. with Sir Robert Peel, Add. MSS 40560–40581, *passim* • JRL, letters to Edward D. Davenport • Keele University Library, letters to Ralph Sneyd • priv. coll., corresp. and political papers • W. Sussex RO, letters to duke of Richmond

**Likenesses** C. Turner, mezzotint, pubd 1833 (after W. Jones), BM, NPG • T. Thornycroft, statue, 1869, Grosvenor Park, Chester • T. Uwins, watercolour and pencil, BM • portrait, Royal Collection

**Wealth at death** under £800,000: probate, 20 Dec 1869, *CGPLA Eng. & Wales*

**Grosvenor, Richard de Aquila, first Baron Stalbridge** (**1837–1912**), railway administrator and politician, the fourth son of Richard *Grosvenor, second marquess of Westminster (1795–1869), and his wife, Lady Elizabeth Mary Leveson-Gower, the second daughter of George Granville Leveson-*Gower, first duke of Sutherland, was born at Motcombe House, Motcombe, Dorset, on 28 January 1837. He was educated at Westminster School and at Trinity College, Cambridge, where he matriculated in 1855, and graduated MA three years later. He became member of parliament for Flintshire as a Liberal as early as 1861, and retained his seat until 1886. He was sworn of the privy council in 1872, and was vice-chamberlain of the royal household from 1872 to 1874.

Grosvenor was chief whip for the whole of Gladstone's eventful second administration (1880–85) and proved quite a competent party organizer on a day-to-day basis, though offering little of help in the longer-term development of the party. His chief asset was his ability to keep the whigs from defecting. He made clear his opposition to home rule in the autumn of 1885 and in 1886 he was not offered a post in the new government but was created Baron Stalbridge. He was subsequently a staunch and influential member of the Liberal Unionist organization. He told Gladstone that '*every* Irishman, without exception always jobs' (Matthew, *Gladstone*, 205).

Stalbridge's chief work was done in connection with the London and North-Western Railway Company, of which he was a director for more than forty years and for half that period the chairman. He became a director in 1870; he was elected chairman in succession to Sir Richard Moon in 1891, and held the office until 1911. Throughout that period he took an active interest in the progress and development of railways. He made himself conversant with the design and construction of the successive types of locomotive which were brought into use; and it was said that no railway director had ridden more miles upon the footplate than Lord Richard Grosvenor during the early years of his directorship. He was also actively concerned with many schemes for helping the employees of his company, by such means as the improvement of their savings bank, their superannuation fund, and the fund for their widows and orphans. From 1897 he presided over the meetings of their ambulance centre, established in connection with the St John Ambulance Association. Stalbridge's interest in railway matters was not, however, limited to the affairs of the London and North-Western. The Universal Exhibition held at Paris in 1867 had given a great impulse to plans for bringing nations into closer contact by improving their communications. Grosvenor became the head of an Anglo-French company formed to promote a channel tunnel, and he continued throughout his life to advocate linking up the English and continental railway systems by a submarine tunnel.

Grosvenor married twice. His first wife, whom he married in 1874, was the Hon. Beatrice Charlotte Elizabeth Vesey (1845–1876), daughter of Thomas, third Viscount De Vesci; they had one daughter. In 1879 he married Eleanor Frances Beatrice Hamilton (*d.* 1911), daughter of Robert Hamilton Stubber, of Moyne, Queen's county; they had three sons and two daughters. As a sportsman he was extremely fond of hunting, an enthusiastic deerstalker, and a member of the Royal Yacht Squadron. He died, after a prolonged illness, on 18 May 1912 at his house, 22 Sussex Square, London, and was buried at Motcombe.

A. C. Bell, *rev.* H. C. G. Matthew

**Sources** *The Times* (20 May 1912) · *Daily Telegraph* (20 May 1912) · Gladstone, *Diaries* · H. C. G. Matthew, *Gladstone, 1875–1898* (1995) · Venn, *Alum. Cant.*

**Archives** BL, corresp. with W. E. Gladstone, Add. MSS 44315–44316 · BL, letters to Sir E. W. Hamilton, Add. MSS 48622–48625 · Bodl. Oxf., corresp. with Lord Kimberley

**Likenesses** Caldesi, Blanford & Co., carte-de-visite, NPG · wood-engraving, NPG; repro. in *ILN* (13 Feb 1864)

**Wealth at death** £5863 10*s.* 2*d.*: probate, 2 July 1912, *CGPLA Eng. & Wales*

**Grosvenor, Sir Robert** (*d.* 1396), soldier, of Hulme, Cheshire, is known primarily as the defendant in the heraldic case of *Scrope* v. *Grosvenor*. The earliest known Grosvenor, Robert (*fl.* 1162–1173), received a grant of Budworth, Cheshire, from Hugh, earl of Chester (*d.* 1181). A junior line was established at Hulme from *c.*1233 by Ranulph Grossum Venator (Ranulph the Fat Hunter), from whom Sir Robert was descended. The house comprised a hall, knight's chamber and chapel, kitchen, buttery, larder, and wine cellar.

In 1385 Sir Robert Grosvenor was engaged in the expedition against Scotland, and was there challenged by Sir Richard *Scrope as to his right to bear the arms 'azure, a bend or'. A trial was held immediately at Newcastle on 20 August, and adjourned to meet at Westminster on 12 October. On 16 May 1386, Thomas of Woodstock, duke of Gloucester, as constable of England, ordered both parties to appear with their proofs on 21 January 1387, and appointed commissioners to collect evidence. The rest of the year was occupied with hearings in London, the north, and the midlands. Great numbers of witnesses were summoned on either side. More than 207 knights and gentlemen of Lancashire and Cheshire had testified to the use of the bend or by Grosvenor and by his ancestors, although others appeared for Scrope and several declined to testify. The poet Geoffrey Chaucer recalled that he had first seen Grosvenor's arms hanging outside an inn in Friday Street, London.

A spurious lineage history circulated among many of the Grosvenor witnesses, in which the family claimed a direct male descent through nine generations from an autochthonous Gilbert Grosvenor, nephew of Hugh d'Avranches, earl of Chester (*d.* 1101), in the time of William I. Of their own experiences many reported that Grosvenor's military career had begun during the collapse of English lordship in Gascony. In 1369 he was with Sir James Audley at the capture of La Roche-sur-Yon; he appears as a man-at-arms, with one companion, on the muster roll for the expedition but returned to England without licence. The following year he was in the service of Edward, the Black Prince, at the siege of Limoges, and in 1372 he joined Edward III's abortive French expedition. During all these campaigns Grosvenor is stated to have used the disputed arms. His father, Ralph, was reported to have died before he could bear the arms in Picardy, although Robert's guardian, Sir John Danyers, who married his ward to his daughter *c*.1359, is said to have challenged another claimant, a Cornish squire named Thomas Carminow, on the River Marne during Edward III's final campaign in France, in 1359–60.

On 12 May 1389 the constable gave judgment against Grosvenor, who was condemned with costs, and assigned to him the same arms 'with a plain bordure, argent'. Grosvenor at once appealed against this decision, also later alleging that Scrope had obtained commissioners in the appeal by fraud. The summons to the parties in the suit to appear before the king was repeated on 15 May, commissioners were appointed to hear the case, and the trial commenced on 30 May 1389; the royal decision was given on 27 May 1390, when the judgment of the constable was confirmed, but the award of differenced arms was annulled. The king complained at the duration of the case. Grosvenor and his descendants adopted the arms 'azure, a garbe or' in allusion to their feigned kinship to the earls of Chester.

On 28 November 1390 letters patent were issued directing that Grosvenor was to be held liable for the costs, which amounted to £466 13*s*. 4*d*., and on 3 October 1391 a further fine of 50 marks was imposed for his contumacy. Amity was only restored in November 1391 when Grosvenor was challenged in parliament by Scrope and pleaded poverty. In return for remission of the costs he was compelled to withdraw all charges of falsehood which, he said, had only been spoken on the advice of his lawyers, and agreed to the enrolment of a final memorandum which, since he had little French, was read to him in English by John of Gaunt, duke of Lancaster.

Grosvenor was appointed sheriff of Cheshire, 'during pleasure', on 1 January 1389, and was again sheriff in 1394. He died at Hulme Hall on 22 April 1396. With his first wife he had no children; with a second, Joan (*d*. *c*.1396), daughter of Sir Robert Pulford, whom he married *c*.1378, he had a son, Sir Thomas Grosvenor of Hulme, from whom the dukes of Westminster descended. PHILIP MORGAN

**Sources** N. H. Nicolas, ed., *The Scrope and Grosvenor controversy*, 2 vols. (privately printed, London, 1832) • Ches. & Chester ALSS, Shakerley of Hulme and Somerford, DSS deeds (unlisted) • Palatinate of Chester, inquisitions post mortem, PRO, CHES 3/15 (9) • *CClR, 1389–92*, 517–19 • Rymer, *Foedera*, 1st edn, 7.676–8 • W. H. B. Bird, 'The Grosvenor myth', *The Ancestor*, 1 (1902), 166–88 • W. H. B. Bird, 'Lostock and the Grosvenors', *The Ancestor*, 2 (1902), 148–55 • H. F. Burke, 'Some Cheshire deeds', *The Ancestor*, 2 (1902), 129–47 • H. F. Burke, 'Some Cheshire deeds', *The Ancestor*, 6 (1903), 19–45 • R. Stewart-Brown, 'The Scrope and Grosvenor controversy, 1385–91', *Transactions of the Historic Society of Lancashire and Cheshire*, 89 (1937), 1–22 • G. Barraclough, ed., *The charters of the Anglo-Norman earls of Chester, c.1071–1237*, Lancashire and Cheshire RS, 126 (1988), 163 • G. Ormerod, *The history of the county palatine and city of Chester*, 2nd edn, ed. T. Helsby, 3 (1882), 144–8 • exchequer, king's remembrancer, accounts various, PRO, E101/29/24 • Palatinate of Chester, indictment rolls, PRO, CHES 25/4 m. 22

**Archives** Ches. & Chester ALSS, Shakerley of Hulme and Somerford, DSS deeds

**Wealth at death** £44 13*s*. 4*d*. p.a.; owed arrears of £208 18*s*. 10*d*.: inquisition post mortem, PRO, C 3/15

**Grosvenor, Robert, first marquess of Westminster (1767–1845)**, politician, was the third son and only surviving child of Richard *Grosvenor, first Earl Grosvenor (1731–1802). He was born in the parish of St George, Hanover Square, London, on 22 March 1767, and was educated at Westminster School and then Harrow School, and afterwards at Trinity College, Cambridge, taking his degree of MA in 1786. His father had made a home at Eaton for William Gifford, who acted as tutor to the son, then Viscount Belgrave, and travelled with him on two continental tours. Gifford speaks warmly of his 'most amiable' and 'accomplished' pupil ('Mr. Gifford's autobiographical memoir', in Nichols, *Illustrations*, 6.14–28).

From 1788 to 1790 Lord Belgrave was MP for the governmental seat of East Looe, and on 15 August 1789 was appointed a lord of the Admiralty, an office which he held until 25 June 1791. Peter Pindar styled him 'the Lord of Greek' for having upon his first entrance in parliament shocked the House of Commons with a quotation from Demosthenes (Mathias, 144). At the general election in 1790 Lord Belgrave was elected MP for Chester, and continued to represent the city until 1802. Between 1793 and 1801 he was a commissioner of the Board of Control, latterly supporting Addington's ministry.

Lord Belgrave married, on 28 April 1794, Eleanor (1770–1846), daughter and sole heir of the first earl of Wilton and his wife, Eleanor, the Egerton estates thus coming to the Grosvenor family. They had three sons, including the politician Robert *Grosvenor, and a daughter. About 1795 he printed for private circulation a quarto volume, containing 'Charlotte', an elegy, and other poems in English and Latin. During the war with France he raised a regiment of volunteers in the city of Westminster, and was appointed major-commandant on 21 July 1798. On the death of his father he became second Earl Grosvenor on 5 August 1802 and an extremely wealthy man. In 1803 he began to rebuild Eaton Hall on a very extensive scale. He extended his Cheshire property and bought extensively at Shaftesbury and Stockbridge. In 1826 he obtained special powers by act of parliament, and set to work with the help of William Cubitt to lay out in roads, streets, and squares that part of his London estate which came to be called Belgravia. Pimlico was soon after also built over. This urban development was to make the Grosvenors one of the richest families in Britain.

At the coronation of William IV, Grosvenor was created marquess of Westminster on 13 September 1831. On this occasion the arms of the city of Westminster were granted to him as a coat of augmentation. He received the Garter on 11 March 1841.

Grosvenor was a man of taste, and largely increased the famous Grosvenor gallery of pictures, adding to it several collections. A *Catalogue of the pictures at Grosvenor House, London, with etchings from the whole collection, and historical notices* (1821), was compiled by John Young. He took an active part in public affairs. On Pitt's death, he attached himself to the whigs, his family remaining prominent in whig politics until 1886. He voted for the Reform Bill and contributed to the Anti-Corn Law League. Among the many

**Robert Grosvenor, first marquess of Westminster (1767–1845),** by Thomas Gainsborough, 1785–8

improvements that he made in Chester (of which he was mayor 1807–8) was the north gate, erected from the designs of Thomas Harrison in 1810. Some of the most famous racehorses of the day were owned by him, and he left a large stud. Westminster died at Eaton Hall on 17 February 1845 and was buried at Eccleston. Lady Westminster died in 1846, aged seventy-six.

H. R. TEDDER, *rev.* H. C. G. MATTHEW

**Sources** GEC, *Peerage* · *GM*, 2nd ser., 23 (1845), 666 [abstract of will] · *Cheshire Chronicle* (21 Feb 1845) · HoP, *Commons* · Nichols, *Illustrations* · T. J. Mathias, *The pursuits of literature: a satirical poem in four dialogues*, 16th edn (1812)
**Archives** City Westm. AC, corresp. · priv. coll., papers
**Likenesses** T. Gainsborough, portrait, 1785–8, Eaton Hall, Cheshire [*see illus.*] · F. Chantrey, bust, AM Oxf. · F. Chantrey, pencil sketches, NPG · G. Hayter, group portrait, oils (*The trial of Queen Caroline, 1820*), NPG · H. Meyer, stipple (after J. Hoppner), BM, NPG; repro. in T. Cadell and W. Davies, *The British gallery of contemporary portraits* (1811) · P. C. Wonder, group portrait, study (*Patrons and lovers of art, 1826*), NPG · J. Young, mezzotint (after Hoppner)

**Grosvenor, Robert, first Baron Ebury** (1801–1893), politician, was the third son of Robert *Grosvenor, first marquess of Westminster (1767–1845), and his wife, Eleanor (1770–1846), daughter and later sole heir of Thomas Egerton, earl of Wilton. He was born at Millbank House, Westminster, on 24 April 1801. His elder brothers were Richard *Grosvenor, second marquess of Westminster, and Thomas Grosvenor, second earl of Wilton. Hugh Lupus Grosvenor, first duke of Westminster, was his nephew. Styled the Hon. Robert Grosvenor from 1801 to 1831 and Lord Robert Grosvenor from 1831, when his father became marquess, he was educated at Westminster School from 1810 to 1816, and then at Christ Church, Oxford, where he matriculated in 1818 and graduated BA with third-class honours in classics in 1821. Admitted a student of Lincoln's Inn, in 1821, he was elected member of parliament for Shaftesbury as a whig in April 1822. During this period he was attracted to the whig circle of the sixth duke of Devonshire. For seven parliaments, from June 1826 to January 1847, he represented Chester, where his father exercised great political influence.

In 1830 Grosvenor visited the northern African states; on his return he published *Extracts from the journal of Lord Robert Grosvenor: being an account of his visit to the Barbary regencies in the spring of 1830* (1831). (In 1852 he also published, anonymously, extracts from his journal during travels in Germany during the summer of 1851.) He married on 17 May 1831 Charlotte Arbuthnot (1808–1891), eldest daughter of Henry *Wellesley, Baron Cowley, with whom he had five sons and two daughters. When the whigs gained power in 1830, he was sworn of the privy council on 1 December and was appointed comptroller of the royal household, a post he held until 1834. When Lord John Russell returned to power in 1846, Grosvenor was for a few months treasurer of the household and groom of the stole to the prince consort.

Grosvenor, whose seat was at Moor Park, Rickmansworth, represented the large constituency of Middlesex as a whig-Liberal from June 1847 to August 1857. Not a particularly active figure in party politics, he carried measures to reduce corruption in elections, although he had opposed the ballot in 1839. As an evangelical, he had a strong interest in social reform, supporting Lord Ashley's Ten Hours Bill in 1847 and measures to improve public health, and serving as a member of the royal commission on the health of the metropolis from 1847 to 1850. He was chairman of the Metropolitan Sanitary Association (1850) and vice-patron of the Incorporated Society for Improving the Condition of the Labouring Classes. In 1854 he carried a bill to provide county industrial schools, which were aimed at young delinquents. His most controversial measure was his Sunday Trading Bill, introduced in 1855, forbidding most shops in London to open on Sundays. Popular hostility to the measure, which was attacked as a hypocritical aristocratic attempt to impose sabbatarianism on the poor, led to a riot in Hyde Park on 1 July 1855. Grosvenor, who was obliged to leave London for fear of the mob, withdrew his bill.

On Lord Palmerston's recommendation Grosvenor was elevated to the peerage on 15 September 1857 as Baron Ebury of Ebury Manor, Middlesex. In the House of Lords Ebury engaged mainly in religious and philanthropic causes. He belonged to the later evangelicals, numerous within the church but now facing the Tractarians. He wished to reform the existing ecclesiastical laws and suppress such practices as ritualism and confession and also to abolish obsolete liturgical forms and services. He insisted that parliament alone had the right to legislate for the church without consulting the convocations. His main opponent was Samuel Wilberforce, bishop of Oxford, who denounced his 'really troublesome demands by legislation'.

In 1859 Ebury obtained the removal from the prayer book of the state services for King Charles the martyr, for the restoration of Charles II, and for Guy Fawkes Day. During the 1860s he joined with Lord Westmeath and Lord Shaftesbury in raising the ritual question, but he was the most persistent, introducing several motions concerning it but failing to secure any legislation. He was not, however, occupied with ritualism alone. His main efforts from 1857 to 1866 concerned the burial service. For four successive years he appealed for a royal commission 'to obviate the evil complained of as arising from the present compulsory and indiscriminate use of the burial service'. This aroused intense controversy. He made passionate speeches insisting that the clergy should not have to read 'in sure and certain hope of eternal life' over persons for whom they might have no such hope; but the bishops opposed his proposal because nonconformists wished to make it an opportunity for their ministers to hold their own funeral services in churchyards.

Eventually Ebury moved the appointment of a commission in 1867, but by then the subject had become connected with ritualism, and the commission, of which he was a member, dealt with both matters. Parliament eventually passed some changes in the prayer book, including a revised lectionary, which Ebury had long urged, in 1871, and the Burial Laws Amendment Act in 1880, but by then Ebury wanted more extensive prayer book reform. In 1854 he had founded and in 1859 become president of the Prayer Book Revision Society, which sought to revise the Anglican liturgy, partly with a view to encouraging union between the established church and nonconformists. In 1874 the society produced a revised prayer book 'to cut away the supports, apparent or real, of a Romanizing system'. He failed in 1879 with a bill for amending the prayer book, and in 1889 he resigned from the presidency of the society. He was disappointed that the bishops would not support him in what he considered a vital church matter. His evangelical concern to promote knowledge of the Bible led him to establish the Scripture Readers' Association.

Another cause for which Ebury contended at this time was the modification of the form of clerical subscription, which since 1604 had required clergymen at ordination and on accepting ecclesiastical preferment to assent to every word in the Thirty-Nine Articles and the prayer book. He insisted that many conscientious men were deterred from entering the ministry as a result. Annually he petitioned the Lords to consider this. A. C. Tait, then bishop of London, supported him, and following the report of a royal commission on the subject, to which Ebury belonged, he secured the passing of the Clerical Subscription Act of 1865, which required the clergy merely to accept the articles and prayer book as 'agreeable to the Word of God'. As most bishops had forecast, there was no increase in the number of men seeking ordination.

Ebury, though always whig in outlook, was an independent member of the Lords, which deprived him of party support for his reforms. In 1864 he presided at a banquet in honour of Garibaldi, who was visiting Britain. Later Ebury was a Liberal Unionist and voted against Gladstone's Home Rule Bill in September 1893, being by many years the oldest peer to participate in the division.

Ebury died at his London house, 35 Park Street, on 18 November 1893 and was buried four days later in the graveyard of Holy Trinity parish church of Northwood, Middlesex, towards the building of which he had subscribed nearly all the money needed. His letters and speeches were collected in E. V. Bligh's *Lord Ebury as a Church Reformer* (1891). LEONARD W. COWIE

**Sources** E. V. Bligh, *Lord Ebury as a church reformer* (1891) · *The Times* (20 Nov 1893) · *The Times* (23 Nov 1893) · GEC, *Peerage* · Boase, *Mod. Eng. biog.* · *Men of the time* (1875) · B. Harrison, 'The Sunday trading riots of 1855', *HJ*, 8 (1965), 219–45 · M. A. Crowther, *Church embattled: religious controversy in mid-Victorian England* (1970) · S. Meacham, *Lord Bishop: the life of Samuel Wilberforce* (1970) · W. Benham and R. T. Davidson, *Life of Archibald Campbell Tait*, 2 vols. (1891) · H. P. Liddon, *The life of Edward Bouverie Pusey*, ed. J. O. Johnston and others, 4 vols. (1893–7) · P. Mandler, *Aristocratic government in the age of reform: whigs and liberals, 1830–1852* (1990)

**Archives** Bodl. Oxf., journal and corresp. · NRA, priv. coll., corresp. and papers · Yale U., Beinecke L., journal | BL, corresp. with W. E. Gladstone, Add. MSS 44358–44446, *passim* · Ches. & Chester ALSS, journals of his tutor James Lyons · LPL, corresp. with A. C. Tait · PRO, corresp. with Lord John Russell, PRO 30/22 · U. Southampton L., letters to first duke of Wellington · UCL, corresp. with Edwin Chadwick

**Likenesses** Ape [C. Pellegrini], caricature, chromolithograph, NPG; repro. in *VF* (15 April 1871) · G. Hayter, group portrait, oils (*The House of Commons, 1833*), NPG · Hills & Saunders, photograph, repro. in *ILN* (25 Nov 1893), 662 · F. C. Lewis, stipple (after J. Slater; *Grillion's Club* series), BM, NPG · D. J. Pound, line print (after photograph by Mayall), BM, NPG · J. & C. Watkins, carte-de-visite, NPG · portrait, repro. in D. J. Pound, *Drawing room portrait gallery of eminent personages*, 2nd ser. (1859)

**Wealth at death** £147,048 7s.: probate, 1 March 1894, *CGPLA Eng. & Wales*

**Grosvenor, Sir Thomas, third baronet (1655–1700)**, politician, was born on 20 November 1655, the eldest son of Roger Grosvenor (1629–1661), of Eaton, Cheshire, and his wife, Christian (*b.* 1629, *d.* in or before 1673), daughter of Sir Thomas Myddelton, of Chirk, Denbighshire. Following the death of his father in a duel, Grosvenor became the heir of his grandfather, Sir Richard Grosvenor, second baronet, whom he succeeded on 31 January 1664. On 7 April 1670 Grosvenor was granted a pass to travel abroad for 'his education and experience' (Gatty, 1.215), together with John Edisbury (presumably his stepfather), and a tutor, one Gaillard. For the next three years he travelled in France, Italy, and the Levant. In summer 1677 he was granted the freedom of Chester and in September he became an alderman. On 10 October 1677 he married Mary (1665–1730), daughter and heir of Alexander Davies, a scrivener, of Ebury, Middlesex. She brought Grosvenor the estates which would become the cornerstone of the family's later wealth, being Ebury farm, east of Chelsea, and a large holding between Tyburn Brook and Park Lane, then well into London's rural surroundings. They had five sons—Thomas and Roger, who died young; Richard (1689–1732), subsequently fourth baronet; Thomas (1693–1733),

**Sir Thomas Grosvenor, third baronet** (1655–1700), by Sir Peter Lely, 1678

afterwards fifth baronet; and Robert (1695–1755), eventually sixth baronet—and three daughters, Elizabeth and Mary, who also died young, and Anne (1700–1731), born posthumously, who married William, second son of John Leveson-Gower, first Baron Gower.

In February 1679 Grosvenor was able to assert his family's traditional influence in Chester, and he was returned to parliament for the borough. In April he risked the wrath of his fellow MPs by espousing the interest of Chester in the import of Irish cattle, remarking that he would always prefer the good of the city before his own interest. Grosvenor was evidently regarded as a member of the opposition, for Anthony Ashley Cooper, first earl of Shaftesbury, marked him as 'worthy', although he did not vote on the Exclusion Bill. Grosvenor was returned to parliament again in September 1679, but he was now probably opposed to exclusion as he was given local office as a justice of the peace for the county. He did not stand at the election of February 1681. However, Grosvenor was very active in the tory cause in Chester. Following the tory mayoral victory in September 1682 Grosvenor supported the attempt to force the surrender of the borough's charter by seeking a writ of *quo warranto* from the government. With the success of this strategy Grosvenor was able to negotiate with the ministry on the contents of the charter. When the new charter was finally issued on 4 March 1685, Grosvenor was named as mayor and most of his whig opponents had been omitted from the corporation. Meanwhile, Grosvenor was foreman of the grand jury which in September 1683 presented Charles Gerard, first earl of Macclesfield, as dangerous to the kingdom because of his suspected complicity in the Rye House plot. Macclesfield's riposte, a suit of *scandalum magnatum*, saw Grosvenor first ensure in April 1684 that he was allowed 'common' bail for appearing to answer the writ, and then secure the dismissal of the charge by the exchequer.

The outbreak of Monmouth's rebellion in 1685 saw Grosvenor raise an independent horse troop, which was subsequently merged into the earl of Shrewsbury's cuirassiers. During the early part of James II's reign, Grosvenor's wife decided to become a Catholic. This caused a considerable degree of marital conflict, with Bishop Thomas Cartwright of Chester being called upon to mediate in January 1687, and with Lady Grosvenor threatening to enter a convent if 'he did not alter speedily and consult her reputation and his own better than he did' (*Diary of Thomas Cartwright*, 23). In April 1687 Grosvenor 'delivered up his commission' in the army after being closeted by the king in favour of repeal of the laws against Catholics, subsequently telling Bishop Cartwright that 'he thought the King expected the taking off all penal laws' (ibid., 43). Grosvenor was purged from Chester corporation in August 1688 in preparation for the elections which James II hoped would produce a parliament willing to repeal the Test and penal laws.

Despite being returned to office in Chester, Grosvenor was defeated in the elections to the convention. However, he served as sheriff of Cheshire from 8 November 1688 to 18 March 1689. The use of his house at Eaton as a meeting place for Catholics led to some disquiet, but this did not prevent Grosvenor being returned to parliament at the 1690 election. He was classed as a tory, and had to face accusations of Jacobitism in the Commons on 26 April 1690 from Cheshire whigs keen to discredit him. Grosvenor was able to assert that the accusation was malicious and that the government, in the form of Charles Talbot, twelfth earl of Shrewsbury, secretary of state, had rejected the charges. Grosvenor ceased to be an alderman of Chester in 1693, but he was re-elected to parliament for the city in 1695. Grosvenor refused the voluntary association in February 1696 and voted against the attainder of Sir John Fenwick in November 1696. Nevertheless, he was returned again at the 1698 election.

Grosvenor made his will on 21 June 1700 when 'weak of body' (will, PRO, PROB 11/457, fol. 106*v*) and he died at the end of the month, being buried at Eccleston, Cheshire, on 2 July 1700. His will left his children under the guardianship of Sir Richard Myddelton, third baronet, and Thomas and Francis Cholmondeley. His widow travelled abroad and married Edward Fenwick, the brother of her Catholic chaplain, Lodowick Fenwick, in June 1701. This marriage had considerable financial implications, as Grosvenor and others had begun to develop her substantial estates in St James's and Chelsea, Middlesex. The marriage was annulled by the court of delegates in February 1705 because Lady Grosvenor was not '*compos mentis*' (*Portland MSS*, vol. 4, p. 166) at the time of the marriage. She was subsequently declared a lunatic, and died on 12 January 1730.

STUART HANDLEY

**Sources** G. Hampson and B. D. Henning, 'Grosvenor, Sir Thomas, 3rd bt', HoP, *Commons, 1660–90* · HoP, *Commons, 1690–1715* [draft] · GEC, *Baronetage* · C. T. Gatty, *Mary Davies and the manor of Ebury*, 2 vols. (1921) · *The diary of Thomas Cartwright, bishop of Chester*, ed. J. Hunter, CS, 22 (1843) · will, PRO, PROB 11/457, fols. 106v–107v · P. D. Halliday, *Dismembering the body politic: partisan politics in England's towns, 1650–1730* (1998), 232–5, 280–8 · *The manuscripts of his grace the duke of Portland*, 10 vols., HMC, 29 (1891–1931), vol. 2, p. 156; vol. 4, pp. 166–7 · C. Dalton, ed., *English army lists and commission registers, 1661–1714*, 2 (1894), 15 · *IGI* · *CSP dom.*, 1683–4, 391 · H. T. Dutton, 'The Stuart kings and Chester corporation', *Journal of the Chester and North Wales Archaeological and Historic Society*, new ser., 28 (1928–9), 180–210

**Archives** priv. coll., personal, political, and family papers

**Likenesses** P. Lely, oils, 1678, priv. coll. [*see illus.*] · J. Young, etching (after P. Lely), BM; repro. in J. Young, *Grosvenor Gallery* (1821)

**Grosvenor, Thomas** (1764–1851), army officer, third son of Thomas Grosvenor (1734–1795) of Swell Court, Somerset, and his wife, Deborah, daughter and coheir of Stephen Skynner of Walthamstow, Essex, was born on 30 May 1764. His father, MP for Chester, was the only brother of Richard Grosvenor, first Earl Grosvenor (1731–1802). Like his father Grosvenor was educated at Westminster School (admitted November 1773). On 1 October 1779 he was appointed ensign, 1st foot guards; he became lieutenant and captain in 1784, and captain and lieutenant-colonel on 25 April 1793. As a subaltern he commanded the Bank of England picket during the 1780 Gordon riots. He served with his battalion in Flanders in 1793, and again in Holland and in the retreat to Bremen in 1794–5, and in the expedition to The Helder in 1799. He was promoted brevet colonel in 1796 and major-general on 29 April 1802, and he held brigade commands in the west of England and in the London district during the invasion alarms of 1803–5.

Grosvenor commanded a brigade in the 1807 Copenhagen expedition, and in the disastrous 1809 Walcheren expedition, when he was second in command of Sir Eyre Coote's division. He was appointed colonel of the 97th Queen's German foot in 1807, and in February 1814 was transferred to the 65th foot, with which he remained until his death. He became lieutenant-general in April 1808, and general in August 1819.

The Grosvenor family had great influence with the corporation and guilds of the freeman-franchise city of Chester, for which Grosvenor's father was an MP from 1755 to 1795. Following the latter's death Grosvenor was MP for the city from 1795 to 1825. A whig, he began by supporting Pitt's ministry but later he supported the opposition. In May 1802 he opposed the suppression of bull-baiting. In 1825 he vacated the seat in favour of the Hon. (afterwards Lord) Robert Grosvenor, and was returned instead for the venal scot and lot borough of Stockbridge, Hampshire. He retired from parliament at the 1830 general election.

Grosvenor was for many years a keen supporter of horse-racing, and won the Oakes in 1807 and 1825. He married first, on 6 April 1797, Elizabeth (*d.* 26 July 1830), daughter of Sir Gilbert Heathcote, third baronet, of Normanton, Rutland, and second, on 15 October 1831, Anne, youngest daughter of George Wilbraham of Delamere Lodge, Cheshire, at one time MP for Cheshire. There were no surviving children from either marriage. On 9 November 1846 (birthday of the young prince of Wales) Grosvenor and Sir George Nugent, the two senior generals in the army, and the marquess of Anglesey, their junior, were created field marshals. Grosvenor died at his residence, Mount Ararat, Richmond Hill, Richmond, Surrey, on 20 January 1851. After his death his widow kept a school in a cottage in the grounds; Mount Ararat was demolished about 1897. H. M. CHICHESTER, *rev.* ROGER T. STEARN

**Sources** *GM*, 2nd ser., 35 (1851), 313 · M. H. Port, 'Grosvenor, Thomas II', HoP, *Commons* · *Old Westminsters*, vol. 1 · N. B. Leslie, *The succession of colonels of the British army from 1660 to the present day* (1974) · Boase, *Mod. Eng. biog.* · private information (2004)

**Archives** BL, journal of Copenhagen expedition, Add. MS 49059 · priv. coll., papers | NL Wales, letters to Louisa Lloyd · priv. coll., corresp. with Drummond family

**Likenesses** J. Young, etching, 1821 (after J. Hoppner), BM; repro. in J. Young, *Grosvenor House, London* (1821) · R. Seymour, print, BM; repro. in Wildrake [George Tattersall], ed., *Cracks of the day* (1841) · oils, NPG

**Grote, Arthur** (1814–1886), administrator in India and entomologist, son of George Grote, a banker of Beckenham, Kent, and his wife, Selina Mary, was born on 29 November 1814. George *Grote the historian was his eldest brother. He was educated at the East India Company's college at Haileybury, where he won prizes in classics, Persian, Hindustani, Bengali, and Arabic. He arrived in Calcutta in 1833 and rose steadily through a range of judicial and revenue postings in the Lower Provinces of Bengal to become in 1857 commissioner of Nadia. In 1863, backed by almost thirty years' experience of district administration, he was made a member of the board of revenue in Calcutta. He retained this position until his retirement in 1868. He married firstly, at Calcutta in 1834, Helen Anne Mackenzie (1818/19–1838), and secondly, at Midnapore in 1840, Mary Anne Howell. A daughter, Selina Mary, was born in 1837, and a son, Arthur George, in 1842.

Grote was a keen student of zoology and natural history and published a number of papers in the transactions of the Linnean Society and the Zoological Society, of which latter organization he also served as president. He contributed the introduction to *Descriptions of new Indian lepidopterous insects from the collection of the late Mr. W. S. Atkinson* (1879). In India he was president of the Asiatic Society of Bengal from 1859 until 1862 and again in 1865 and a member of the Horticultural Society of India. To mark his departure from India each of these societies commissioned a portrait of him from John Prescott Knight RA. He was a fellow of the Royal Society and a council member of both University College and University College Hospital. He died at his home in London, 42 Ovington Square, on 4 December 1886. KATHERINE PRIOR

**Sources** *ILN* (18 Dec 1886), 659 · H. T. Prinsep and R. Doss, eds., *A general register of the Hon'ble East India Company's civil servants of the Bengal establishment from 1790 to 1842* (1844) · F. C. Danvers and others, *Memorials of old Haileybury College* (1894) · E. Kilmurray, *Dictionary of British portraiture*, 3 (1981) · ecclesiastical records, East India Company, BL OIOC · BL OIOC, Haileybury MSS · *The Bengal obituary, or, A record to perpetuate the memory of departed worth*, Holmes & Co. (1848) · *CGPLA Eng. & Wales* (1886)

**Likenesses** J. P. Knight, oils, exh. RA 1869, Asiatic Society, Calcutta, India · J. P. Knight, oils, exh. RA 1870, Horticultural Society of India • R. T., wood-engraving (after photograph by Fradelle and Young), NPG; repro. in *ILN* (18 Dec 1886), 657

**Wealth at death** £2990 0s. 5*d*.: probate, 31 Dec 1886, *CGPLA Eng. & Wales*

**Grote, George** (1794–1871), historian and politician, was born on 17 November 1794 at Clay Hill, near Beckenham, Kent, the eldest of the eleven children of George Grote (1762–1830), banker, and Selina Mary Peckwell (1774–1845), daughter of the Revd Henry *Peckwell and his wife, Bella Blosset. He was of Dutch origin, his paternal grandfather having immigrated in 1731.

**Education and early years** George Grote's formal education began at Sevenoaks grammar school when he was five. In 1804, at the age of nine, he entered Charterhouse, where his father had been a student. The curriculum was almost entirely classical, and he emerged six years later thoroughly trained in Latin and Greek and with two lifelong friends, George Waddington (1793–1869), later dean of Durham, and Connop Thirlwall (1797–1875), later bishop of St David's and also a historian of ancient Greece. His formal education now ended, for, instead of proceeding to university, he was placed by his father, at the age of fifteen, in the family bank, Prescott and Grote, in Threadneedle Street, London, where he worked for the next thirty-three years, becoming a partner at the age of twenty-one.

Grote found banking wearisome and complained that it 'stupifies the mind' and 'is dull and wretched … to a mind which has a glimpse of a nobler sphere of action' (Grote, *Personal Life*, 13). Yet in spite of being actively engaged in the bank's business, he also made time to pursue his true calling—study and scholarship—by rising early and reading widely in the literature of Greece and Rome, philosophy, and political economy. He also became fluent in French and German and taught himself some Italian. Noting that his wide learning was the fruit of self-education, Henry Reeve observed, 'the natural bent of his mind to philosophy and letters must have been irresistible' (Reeve, 221).

Grote's bookishness provided a refuge from his uncongenial family. His exacting father discouraged intellectual interests, and Grote's resentment of his father's insistence that he sacrifice a university education for a career in banking never left him. His deeply religious mother was equally unsympathetic, for her rigorous moralism made her intolerant of innocent amusements and even boyish high spirits. Life at home was disciplined, dreary, and vapid.

In 1815, at the age of twenty-one, Grote found another refuge from home in the company of Harriet Lewin (1792–1878) [*see* Grote, Harriet], to whom he was introduced by his friend George Warde Norman. She lived 6 miles from Grote's home, and they met at a dance that followed a Sunday cricket match in which Grote took part. She was lively and attractive, and they soon discovered a shared interest in music, and he was pleased by her welcoming his didacticism, as he shared with her his views about political economy, politics, and theology. Their mutual passion and Grote's wish to get married, however, were frowned

George Grote (1794–1871), by Herbert Watkins, 1857

upon by his father, on whom he was financially dependent, and only after a lapse of three years did the father agree to an engagement, providing the marriage be delayed for another two years. Before this time elapsed, however, the young couple took matters into their own hands and they were secretly married on 5 March 1820. Eleven months later they suffered misfortune when a prematurely born son died after a week, and this was followed by a threat to Harriet's life from puerperal fever. The marriage remained childless, and Harriet adopted the role of companionate wife, sharing her husband's interests and helping him achieve his political and intellectual ambitions.

**Radicalism** During the engagement there was a momentous change that focused Grote's intellectual interests and drew him to practical politics. In spring 1819, while visiting David Ricardo, he met James Mill. Like Ricardo before him, Grote found in Mill a powerful catalyst to systematic study and practical action. Mill's theorizing was compelling, for he provided closely reasoned and far-reaching explanations which Grote eagerly accepted. Mill was especially persuasive in discussions which resembled Platonic dialogues. 'Conversation with him', Grote recalled, 'was not merely instructive, but provocative to the dormant intelligence', and this gave him 'powerful intellectual ascendancy over younger minds' (Bain, *Minor Works*, 284). Before meeting Mill, Grote had read widely, but after exposure to the spell of Mill's conversation, he organized his understanding of all subjects in terms adopted from Mill. He became a utilitarian in philosophy, an associationist in psychology, an advocate of democratic reform in his politics, and a confirmed atheist. His wife recalled that after a year or so, 'there existed but little difference, in point of opinion, between master and pupil'. Mill's influence on Grote was so great that (again in Harriet Grote's words) he 'may be said to have inspired and directed many of the important actions of his life' (Grote, *Personal Life*, 22–3).

The impact of Mill's political teaching was evident in Grote's first publication, *Statement of the Question of Parliamentary Reform* (1821), a long pamphlet in which many of Mill's arguments were used to refute an article critical of universal suffrage by Sir James Mackintosh. Claiming that his analysis had a scientific basis, Grote explained political conduct in terms of self-interest, arguing that in the absence of democratic institutions, governments inevitably will abuse power in the interest of the few and to the detriment of the 'numerous classes'. To guarantee that government will serve the entire populace, Grote insisted that the electorate must be large enough to have an interest similar to that of the community, which meant there should be universal, or at least a greatly extended, suffrage. Grote also urged the need for secret ballot and frequent elections, and thus defended the main parts of the radical programme formulated by James Mill and Jeremy Bentham.

Grote was soon put in touch with Bentham, the mentor and patron of utilitarian radicalism. Grote studied Bentham's writings on law and politics and became a frequent visitor to his house, and this led to literary co-operation. They agreed about religion: both were atheists and both were convinced that religious belief caused greater harm than benefits. Bentham had a vast accumulation of notes bearing on this theme, and Grote agreed to use them in writing a book laying out the worldly consequences of religious belief, especially of belief in an afterlife. Using the pseudonym Philip Beauchamp, in *Analysis of the Influence of Natural Religion on the Temporal Happiness of Mankind* (1822), Grote argued that for most persons anticipations of posthumous rewards and punishments and religious belief generally led to worldly misery. He pointed to the demands of religion for self-denial and asceticism—fasting, celibacy, and abstinence from social enjoyments and mirth; the spoiling of pleasure by preliminary scruples and subsequent guilt; religious enmities; and the corruption of judgement that prevents proper consideration of empirical evidence when it contradicts religious claims. The apparent effectiveness of religious belief in shaping conduct, Grote argued, can be explained as the effect of public opinion and not religion. While he claimed that his analysis focused only on natural religion, its arguments were also applicable to revealed religion. This claim, like the use of a pseudonym, reflected the authors' conviction that they could be prosecuted for heretical opinions. This book should be considered a jointly authored work, and Grote's role in assembling the evidence and composing the arguments reveals the extent of his distance from conventional religious opinions.

Grote found most of his friends during the 1820s among the coterie surrounding James Mill and Bentham: they included John Stuart Mill, Charles Buller, Charles Austin, John Austin, Sarah Austin, Charles Hay Cameron, John Romilly, John Black, and John Roebuck. Some of these joined together to form a small reading group for discussion of works on political economy, law, and philosophy. Their meetings took place in Grote's house in Threadneedle Street, and Grote took part when philosophic subjects were discussed.

With the great increase of public support for parliamentary reform during the period 1830–32, Grote's hopes, like those of the other Benthamite radicals, were raised, and in 1831 he published *Essentials of Parliamentary Reform*, in which he again proposed a greatly extended suffrage, secret ballot, and frequent, preferably annual, elections to parliament. The arguments were not much different from those in the pamphlet published a decade earlier, though they were a shade more radical. He added the bold suggestion that public feeling made the situation in 1831 comparable to the years immediately preceding the revolution in France in 1789, and he affirmed his radical identity by doubting whether genuine reform could be expected from the new whig government. In arguing for a democratic electorate, he acknowledged that it should be introduced in stages to allow time for the education of new voters and to avoid alarming the middle classes.

During this period Grote was drawn into the extra-parliamentary agitation for reform, though less actively than his fellow radicals, partly from temperamental reticence but also because his position in the City made restraint appropriate. Whereas the others, led by James Mill, and his friends Francis Place and Joseph Parkes, were eager to represent public feeling as posing a threat to the government, Grote was reluctant to encourage manifestations of disorder. Thus when he organized and addressed a public meeting after the Lords rejected the second Reform Bill, he put aside his distrust of the whig government and expressed confidence it would persist in promoting parliamentary reform, a stance that disappointed Place, who had urged him to adopt a bolder position. Grote also declined Place's invitation to become a member of the council of the National Political Union, an organization that sought to mobilize public opinion and represent it as angry, demanding, and potentially violent. Grote's refusal to go along with aggressive radical tactics became most evident in May 1832 when Place tried to organize a run on the banks as a way of preventing the government from falling into the hands of the duke of Wellington and the tory party. Association with these tactics would have undermined Grote's position in the City; he also opposed them as a matter of conviction, and he publicly repudiated Place's activities.

**Parliamentary years** With passage of the Reform Bill in 1832, there was a prospect for further reform, and this led Grote, along with other Benthamite radicals, to seek a seat in parliament. Popular enthusiasm for reform allowed him to head the poll, and he became member of parliament for the City of London in the first reformed parliament. Along with other radicals, Grote sat not on the government side but on the opposition benches. This position was adopted in spite of the fact that the whigs had carried the Reform Bill, for, in the Benthamite or philosophic radical perspective, the whigs were regarded as representing aristocratic interests and therefore as adversaries of those representing popular, democratic interests. Grote was widely regarded as leader of the radicals in parliament, this by virtue of his position in the City, his gravitas, and his being somewhat older than many of his fellow radicals: his wife proudly called him 'a chief of opposition' (Lewin, 1.329).

In this position, Grote was at the centre of debates about tactics that divided moderate and more determined radicals and reformers. As the size of the government's majority diminished during the 1830s, the government became increasingly dependent on support from the more radical reformers, and this created an opportunity for the radicals to demand concessions in exchange for their votes. Many of the philosophic radicals favoured hard bargaining, even if their withholding support were to cause the fall of the government and accession to office by the tories; whereas others were prepared to give grudging support to the government, settling for whatever less than radical reforms the government might concede. Grote wavered but tended to reject the aggressive tactics, in spite of his wife's disagreement with his moderate position. Many who agreed with her thought him inadequate as a leader. John Stuart Mill called him faint-hearted, and Parkes said he 'wants devil' (Parkes to Durham, 26 Jan 1835, Lambton MSS, Lambton Park). These judgements were given credence by his speeches, for though they were intellectually substantial, in style he was somewhat stiff and lacking in warmth and vigour. His position at the fulcrum of this debate about tactics was acknowledged in a pamphlet that attempted to tilt the balance against those who would allow the whig government to fall, *Shall we overturn the coach? or, What ought the radicals to do? discussed in a letter to George Grote, esq., MP from a radical member of the House of Commons* (1839).

During his years in the Commons Grote was closely associated with the ballot question. In his maiden speech and on five other occasions he introduced motions proposing secret voting in parliamentary elections, and he even constructed a model ballot box, which he displayed in the House of Commons and throughout the country. The secret ballot was defended as a way of countering bribery and intimidation of voters, therefore making election results an authentic reflection of the electorate's wishes. He regarded it as the most important part of the radical programme, for he assumed a great deal of latent radical sentiment among the public, and secret voting would allow it to become evident. Although his motions proposing a secret ballot were not successful, the size of the votes supporting him increased (except in 1836) throughout the decade.

Grote's morale suffered as radical prospects diminished. It became evident that the radical programme enjoyed scant support and that the government would make few concessions to radical demands. Grote complained about the 'profound slumber' (Grote, *Personal Life*, 130) of politics, and as the radicals more and more took on the appearance of a small and ineffective faction, Macaulay scathingly said the radical party was reduced to Grote and his wife. Grote's standing with his constituents also suffered, and in the elections of 1835 and 1837 his once substantial majority fell, in 1837 to only six votes. Facing another election in 1841, he decided to withdraw. The lure of scholarship overcame his sense of public duty, especially as the quest for radical political change appeared to be futile.

**History of Greece** The twelve volumes of Grote's *History of Greece* provide ample evidence of his devotion to scholarship, his vast erudition, and the political and philosophical views he valued, which clearly affected his historical judgements. Claims for the honour of having suggested the subject have been made both by Grote's wife and by John Stuart Mill on behalf of his father, but Grote, who was described by Alexander Bain as 'a Greece-intoxicated man' (Bain, *John Stuart Mill*, 94), hardly needed any encouragement. Work began in 1823 and received strong impetus from his indignation about William Mitford's *History of Greece* (1784–1810), which was then regarded as authoritative. Grote believed Mitford neglected important sources and was insufficiently critical of those he did use, and worse, he defended monarchy, and, as the next best kind of rule, oligarchy, and heaped 'hatred and contempt … [on] the democratical communities' of ancient Greece. This made him 'eminently agreeable to the reigning interests in England' ('Institutions of Ancient Greece', *Westminster Review*, 5 April 1826, 284, 331). Countering Mitford's bias became Grote's mission, but work was interrupted in 1830 by reform politics and resumed only after retirement from the House of Commons in 1841; and with full retirement from the bank in 1843 (after more than three decades), his time was entirely devoted to it. The first two volumes were published in March 1846, and the final volume appeared only ten years later.

The scope of the *History* is vast. Grote begins with a description of myths and legends, even though he regarded surviving accounts of them as unreliable and therefore beyond the jurisdiction of history. His historical analysis begins with the early eighth century BC, a period for which there is sufficient evidence, and it continues until the period of Macedonian domination late in the fourth century BC.

Although he describes all Greek communities, including those in Asia and in the western Mediterranean and Gaul, Grote's focus is on Athens, especially in the fifth century BC, and his work is a celebration of Periclean Athens for being a republic, for its autonomy, its large measure of tolerance, creative genius, and cultural accomplishments, even its imperial achievements, and above all its democracy. Periclean Athens had all the qualities of Grote's ideal regime. Since it replaced oligarchical government, he could regard it as being ruled by the many rather than the few, and this characterization gave it some affinity with the kind of democracy advocated by the Benthamite radicals. His defence of Periclean democracy, however, included arguments that were not part of the Benthamite rationale. It produced self-disciplined citizens who volunteered services to the regime and even sacrificed for it, and this resulted from its capacity to generate 'an earnest and unanimous attachment to the constitution in the bosoms of the citizens' and from 'an energy of public and private action, such as could never be obtained under an oligarchy'. This kind of citizenship, he claimed, could only be based on 'the personal character of the people … [and] individual virtue' (*History*, chap. 31). These observations show that, along with his Benthamism, Grote was also influenced by civic republican ideas.

Another feature of Athenian democracy was the special quality of the attachment of its citizens to the regime. Their allegiance was not to a person or a class but to constitutional forms that defined the powers of government and the rights of citizens. This Grote called 'constitutional morality' (*History*, chaps. 31, 62), and it allowed liberty, including freedom to criticize government, and restrained majorities. The assumption that majorities would accept constitutional limitations on their power allowed Grote to defend his ideal of democracy against Mitford and many contemporaries who believed a democratic majority would be driven by resentment and greed to despoil the rich. Citizens who submitted to constitutional morality, Grote held, would do no such thing. Athenian democracy was unique in the extent to which it developed this sense of constitutional morality.

Democracy was also upheld by Grote as the source of the flowering of Greek genius in the fifth century BC. As a result of 'democratical fervor', Athenians discovered in themselves new resources, aspirations, and abilities. 'The democracy was the first creative cause of that astonishingly personal and many-sided energy which marked the Athenian character' (*History*, chap. 31), and this led to great oratory, splendid art and architecture, drama and poetry, and philosophy. The proliferation of discasteries (or jury courts) that required argument and rhetoric especially contributed to speculation and philosophy. Thus Grote's rationale for Athenian democracy was intellectual and cultural as well as political.

Grote's praise of Athenian democracy led him to elevate Pericles to heroic status. Pericles was called a constitutional innovator for expanding the democratic institutions introduced by Cleisthenes. He also was praised for instilling a new sense of power among poorer citizens; for promoting the arts; for construction of the long walls, which enhanced security; and for expanding trade; and he was exonerated from charges of corrupt use of public money and of responsibility for starting the Peloponnesian War.

The value of the *History* arises from Grote's mastery of ancient sources and his sceptical approach to claims not sustained by evidence. Thus he discounted much of what he called legendary Greece as being beyond the scope of history. He did not hesitate to disagree with Plutarch, for example, about Lycurgus or Pericles, or with Thucydides about Cleon, or with contemporary German scholars, with whose work he was familiar. Grote's independent judgement came into play in challenges to the scholarly consensus; for example, he defended the Sophists and the demagogue Cleon and justified ostracism, which he explained as a way of removing from a regime a political figure who threatened its stability and which therefore was a safeguard of democracy. Grote's work also had the merit of focusing on social structure, which he analysed in terms of occupation, family, kinds of property, and class. As for his writing style, while it is difficult to be lively throughout twelve volumes, there are many passages that reflect the author's enthusiasms and moral seriousness, and the work is always clear and never dull.

Particular judgements can be shown to be incorrect, partly because new evidence, some of it from excavations, has been discovered since Grote wrote. If the *History* falls short of contemporary standards, however, it is for his exaggerated praise of democratic Athens, which was not as stable, nor as tolerant, as he suggested. Grote, for example, goes far to exonerate democratic Athens for Socrates's condemnation and death, holding Socrates himself responsible, pointing to his belief in his divine mission, his willingness to die before the decay of old age set in, and his wish to die a martyr to a noble cause. Liberty of speech was the first of Athenian privileges, and therefore one should focus on the 'long toleration' (*History*, chap. 68) of Socrates and not on the outcome of his trial which he brought upon himself. Thus Grote, like Mitford, allowed his political perspective to shape his historical judgements, and this occurred in spite of his awareness of the risks, for he warned about a powerful idea becoming dominant and leading one 'to make a place for it among the realities of the past' (*History*, chap. 6).

Grote can also be criticized for interpreting Greek developments in terms of parallels with English history and for using nineteenth-century language to describe events in fifth-century Athens. Thus he described the struggle between the Many and the Few and the march of democracy in Athens; and Pericles was called head of the party of movement and as being like both a prime minister and president of a democracy.

The *History of Greece* was well received and a commercial success; it was used at English universities, went through several editions, and became the standard work in English for the next half century; it was also translated into German and French. Profits from the book paid for the building of a new residence at East Burnham, Buckinghamshire, in 1853, which was named History Hut. The main gratification for Grote, however, was living a scholarly life, and in spite of the endless hours devoted to the book, he observed, 'My day is always too short' (Clarke, 79). Fascinated as he was by Greece, when invited to join John Stuart Mill on a journey to that country, he declined.

**Philosophical writings** Grote's interest in philosophy had begun early. During the 1820s he carefully read most of the works of Kant and Plato. He encouraged his friend Sir William Molesworth to edit Thomas Hobbes's English and Latin works, and the sixteen-volume edition was dedicated to Grote, who published a long 'Notice of Sir William Molesworth's edition of the works of Hobbes' in the *Spectator* in 1839. Several papers on philosophical subjects were later published posthumously in *Minor Works* (1873) and *Fragments on Ethical Subjects* (1876). His wife reported that nothing delighted him more than philosophical conversations with his friends Alexander Bain (1818–1903) or John Stuart Mill. He was a spokesman for empiricism against intuitionism and, on ethical questions, he defended utilitarianism. He faced a critic on these matters in a younger brother, John *Grote (1813–1866), who was a clergyman and professor of moral philosophy at Cambridge.

After completing the *History*, Grote turned to Greek philosophy, and after nine years published in three formidable volumes *Plato, and the other Companions of Sokrates* (1865). Next, he turned to Aristotle but the work was incomplete when he died, and it was left to Alexander Bain and George Croom Robertson (1842–1892) to edit the surviving manuscripts for the posthumous *Aristotle* (1872). Grote thought of the books on Greek philosophy as continuations of the *History* and the three works together as a trilogy.

In the work on Plato, Grote provided detailed accounts of the arguments of each dialogue without, however, offering an interpretation of Platonic philosophy generally, for he discerned two quite different aspects of Plato's outlook, one open, enquiring and critical, which he approved, and another positive and dogmatic, which was unacceptable. The former, a product of the elenchus or dialogic method, was found in what Grote called the dialogues of search, and he valued it for fostering scepticism, stimulating enquiry, undermining customary authorities, and for being the condition of existence for philosophy or reasoned truth. The other part of Plato's philosophy appeared in the dialogues of exposition, and he associated it with orthodoxy and coercion. These two perspectives were evident in Plato's two representations of Socrates. The freethinking enquirer who asks questions but has no answers, who acknowledges his own ignorance, and is an isolated dissenter among people falsely persuaded of their own knowledge—this character appears in many of the dialogues and is the real Socrates. But in the *Republic* he reverses roles, taking the part of King Nomos, an authority on all matters, spiritual and temporal, from whom all public sentiment emanates and by whom orthodoxy is determined. This character created a regime in which Socrates as the practitioner of elenchus could not exist.

**Later years** During the last two decades of his life, Grote took an active part in the governance of leading institutions concerned with scholarly enquiry and public education. From 1859 he was a trustee of the British Museum, and in 1849 he resumed serving University College, London, having been one of its founders and a member of its council from 1827 to 1830. He continued as a member of the council from 1849 to 1871; and he became a member of the senate in 1850, treasurer in 1860, and president of the council in 1868. From 1862 to 1871 he was vice-chancellor of the University of London. He took an active part and had considerable influence on the operation and policies of each of these bodies.

Having a firm belief in non-sectarian education, in 1866, as a member of the council of University College, London, Grote took a leading part in a notable controversy over an appointment to the chair of logic and mental philosophy. He had been dissatisfied with the previous occupant, who had been an ineffective teacher and, a more serious objection, a clergyman. Grote's resignation from the council in 1829 (effective from 1830) was in response to this professor's appointment at a meeting from which Grote was absent. In 1866 when the Revd James Martineau, a distinguished Unitarian theologian and publicist, was recommended to the council, Grote strongly objected on the ground that such an appointment was inconsistent with the religious neutrality appropriate for such a chair. The disagreement within the council was discussed in the newspapers, and after impassioned debates and intense struggle, Grote prevailed and gained the appointment of George Croom Robertson, whose secular outlook Grote represented as a gain for inductive and scientific philosophy. His position in this controversy was in keeping with his conception of philosophy, modelled on Socrates in the elenchus, as searching for truth without being hampered by prior commitments or unexamined assumptions. It also was an outgrowth of his own rejection of all theistic positions.

Grote's religious opinions developed early and did not change much throughout his life. He leaned to scepticism even before encountering James Mill, who led him to even more radical conclusions. Since he advocated free enquiry and insisted that all belief should be sustained by empirical evidence, it is not surprising that he rejected theological claims. His rejection of revealed religion went beyond the more modest argument in the *Analysis of … Natural Religion* (1822), and his atheism is evident in letters in which he tried to persuade his fiancée and one of her sisters that their religious beliefs lacked foundation. His religious opinions, however, were revealed to only a few persons, Alexander Bain and John Stuart Mill among them, for he was convinced that in all societies, including democratic Athens and liberal England, there existed a powerful inclination to persecute. He discussed this in his *Plato* (notably in the analysis of *Gorgias*) and in his 1866 review of Mill's *Examination of Sir William Hamilton's Philosophy*, in which he asserted that if a man renounced the deity, 'proclaiming openly that he does so—he must count upon such treatment as will go far to spoil the value of the present life to him'. Consequently, such a person 'purchases an undisturbed life only by being content with that "semi-liberty under silence and concealment", for which Cicero was thankful under the dictatorship of Julius Caesar' (Bain, *Minor Works*, 300, 301). Evidently Grote considered himself to be such a person.

Grote retained his early political opinions, and he continued to call himself a radical, and in 1866 he expressed gratitude for James Mill's early guidance. As time passed, however, his early opinions were held with less enthusiasm and less confidence. Although he remained a republican, he acknowledged there could be abuse of power in a popular government. By 1867 he was no longer sure that the secret ballot was essential, and he lost confidence that constitutional change would certainly bring improvement. However, he did not become an apostate, as shown by his irritation with John Stuart Mill for criticizing the secret ballot, leaning to socialism, and adopting some Comtean ideas.

After more than forty years of affectionate marital companionship, during the early 1860s the Grotes' marriage faced a crisis. Susan *Durant (1827–1873), a sculptor, was commissioned to create a portrait medallion of Grote, and within two years, according to his wife, he 'made an old fool of himself' (B. and P. Russell, eds., *Amberley Papers*, 1937, 1.477). The infatuation lasted three years. The only evidence about this episode comes from Harriet Grote, who told close friends of her anger and her threat to separate, and this was followed by an end of the connection with Durant. Her pride in her husband survived these uncomfortable years; she continued to refer to him as the Historian, and, as if to assert her proprietary claim on him, at this time, in 1866, she began work on her *Personal Life of George Grote* (1873), which, she explained, was about 'our two lives [which] ran in one channel' (Grote, *Personal Life*, v).

Among the many honours awarded to Grote, he received honorary doctorates from Oxford University in 1853 and Cambridge in 1861. He was made a foreign member of the Institut de France in 1864, replacing Macaulay; and he became a fellow of the Royal Society. In 1869 Gladstone invited him to accept a peerage, which he declined on the ground that he could not assume new public duties, though one may suspect that he also was asserting republican sentiments and his long-standing aversion to aristocracy.

Grote's interests were quite varied. He loved music and attended opera and ballet. He shared his wife's interests in the arts and befriended Felix Mendelsohn, the singer Jenny Lind, and the ballerina Fanny Elssler. He read French and German literature, impressing Theodor Gomperz by knowing by heart most of Goethe's *Faust*, part one. As a young man he enjoyed riding and later he relaxed by taking long walks and by playing whist and billiards. He travelled to the continent quite frequently and was especially fond of visiting Germany, Paris, and Rome. His friendships later in life were formed with those who shared his intellectual interests, such as George Cornewall Lewis (1806–1863), William Smith (1813–1893), Bain, and Mill. He also enjoyed convivial dinners at 'the Club'—the one made famous by Dr Johnson.

Grote was above average height and had a spacious brow, which many associated with his intellectualism. Others were struck by his manners and temperament more than by physical appearance. Unfailingly he was described as modest, gentle, courteous, considerate, perhaps somewhat formal, and gentlemanly. He showed no asperity towards those who disagreed; was careful to avoid giving pain; and appeared open and free from prejudice. Yet several friends described him as gloomy, prone to depression, and (in Mill's words) as having 'constitutionally low spirits' (Clarke, 173).

Grote was moderately wealthy, almost always, after his father's death in 1830, owning houses in both town and country, as well as an estate in Lincolnshire, an interest in the bank, and £40,000 in personal property. But he never played the part of the rich man, nor was he eager to take part in the social world in which wealth mattered. He provided financial help to those supporting good causes: to John Chapman for the *Westminster Review*, Auguste Comte after he was forced out of the Ecole Polytechnique, and French liberals after the revolution of 1830, to whom he sent £500. He also left £6000 to University College, London, to endow the chair of logic and mental philosophy.

Grote enjoyed good health through most of his life, showing signs of decline only during his last three years. In 1868 he suffered tremors in his hands and had the gait of an old man. Early in 1871 he contracted kidney disease, and this led to his death on 18 June 1871 at his home, 12 Savile Row, London. Quite remarkably, in view of his atheism, he was buried in Westminster Abbey on 24 June. At least a couple of those who took the initiative to arrange this—Henry Reeve and John Romilly—must have known about Grote's religious opinions. Mill, who shared those opinions, was a pall bearer but recognized how unsuitable it was, and he probably realized that Grote would not have chosen the abbey as a place of burial.

JOSEPH HAMBURGER

**Sources** H. Grote, *The personal life of George Grote* (1873) • M. L. Clarke, *George Grote: a biography* (1962) • T. H. Lewin, ed., *The Lewin letters … 1756–1884*, 2 vols. (1909) • A. Bain, 'Critical estimate of character and writings', in *The minor works of George Grote*, ed. A. Bain (1873) • F. M. Turner, *The Greek heritage in Victorian Britain* (1981) • H. H. Bellot, *University College, London, 1826–1926* (1929) • H. Grote, *The philosophical radicals of 1832: comprising the life of Sir William Molesworth, and some incidents connected with the reform movement from 1832 to 1842* (1866) • G. Grote, *Posthumous papers*, ed. Mrs Grote [H. Grote] (1874) • W. Thomas, *The philosophic radicals: nine studies in theory and practice, 1817–1841* (1979) • A. Bain, *John Stuart Mill: a criticism: with personal recollections* (1882) • J. S. Mill, *Autobiography* (1873) • H. Reeve, 'Personal memoir of Mr Grote', *EdinR*, 138 (1873), 218–45 • H. G. Hewlett, ed., *Henry Fothergill Chorley: autobiography, memoir, and letters*, 2 vols. (1873) • I. Guest, *Fanny Elssler* (1970) • *CGPLA Eng. & Wales* (1871)

**Archives** BL, corresp. and papers, Add. MSS 46691, 29513–29532 • Bodl. Oxf., essays, notes, and papers; letters and papers • CUL, historical notes and papers for history of Greece • Dulwich College, corresp. on property • LUL, Senate House Library, essays and notes • Trinity Cam., corresp. and papers • UCL, corresp.; diaries; letters; part of MS of history of Greece | BL, letters to A. Panizzi, Add. MSS 36717–36726, *passim* • BL, corresp. with F. Place, Add. MSS 35144–35151, *passim* • CKS, letters to G. W. Norman • John Murray, London, archives • Maison d'Auguste Comte, Paris, letters to Auguste Comte • NL Scot., corresp. with Edward Ellice • NL Wales, letters to Sir George Cornewall Lewis • Trinity Cam., Houghton MSS • U. Birm. L., special collections department, letters to Harriet Martineau • UCL, corresp. with Alex Bain and G. C. Robertson • UCL, letters to Sir William Smith

**Likenesses** J. Brown, engraving, 1805 (after miniature portrait by unknown artist), repro. in A. Bain, ed., *Minor works of George Grote* • T. Stewardson, oils, 1824, NPG • pen-and-ink, 1824 (after T. Stewardson), NPG • S. P. Denning, portrait, 1834; formerly at Provincial Bank, London, 1962 • stipple, pubd 1838, BM • J. Doyle, chalk caricature, 1839, BM • photograph, *c.*1844 (with Harriet Grote), Haydn

Museum, Eisenstadt · G. F. Watts?, crayon drawing, 1844–5, John Murray, publisher, London · W. Behnes, marble bust, 1852, UCL · H. Watkins, albumen print, 1857, NPG [*see illus.*] · S. Durant, marble medallion, 1862, UCL · J. E. Millais, oils, 1870, U. Lond., Senate House · C. Bacon, marble bust, 1872, Westminster Abbey, London · L. Dickinson, lithograph (after G. F. Watts; aged fifty), BM, NPG · G. Hayter, group portrait, oils (*The House of Commons, 1833*), NPG · Maull & Co., carte-de-visite, NPG · Maull & Polyblank, carte-de-visite, NPG · H. Robinson, stipple, BM, NPG; repro. in J. Saunders, *Saunders' portraits and memoirs of eminent living political reformers* (1840) · photograph, NPG

**Wealth at death** under £120,000: probate, 14 July 1871, *CGPLA Eng. & Wales*

**Grote** [*née* Lewin], **Harriet** (**1792–1878**), woman of letters, was born on 1 July 1792 at Ridgeway, near Southampton, Hampshire, the fifth of twelve children of Thomas Lewin (1753–1843), retired employee of the East India Company, and Mary Hale (1768–1837). She had four sisters and seven brothers.

The Lewins were comfortably off, as Harriet's father had made a modest fortune in Madras. Her education was left to a succession of governesses, but her father, who had a fine voice and was proficient at several instruments, stimulated her lifelong love of music, and Harriet became an accomplished pianist and also mastered the cello. She was on the tall side, striking in appearance, athletic, high-spirited, unconventional in ambition, attitudes, and dress, and her personality was so dominant that within the family she was referred to as The Empress.

Harriet Lewin's interests changed dramatically during her courtship by George *Grote (1794–1871), the radical politician and historian of Greece. He was obliged to work in his father's bank, but he was dedicated to scholarship and had strong opinions about politics. Expecting his future wife to share his interests and eager to set her on the right path, he guided her through classic texts of political economy and philosophy. She was an apt student and adopted his opinions about utilitarian ethics, radical politics of the Benthamite variety, Malthusianism, political economy, and atheism, and the direction of her thinking was set for the remainder of her life. She never ceased to be eagerly interested in politics and books, which led Cobden to call her 'a remarkable woman, desperately blue in the stocking' (R. Cobden to K. Cobden, 26 Jan 1846, BL, Add. MS 50748, fols. 198–201).

After being acquainted for five years and engaged for two, Harriet Lewin and George Grote eloped and married on 5 March 1820, since Grote's father refused to agree to a date for their marriage. Initially they resided at Stoke Newington, with another dwelling at the bank in Threadneedle Street in the City. There was one child, a son, born prematurely in 1820, who survived for only a week.

Now Harriet was introduced to Grote's circle of radical and intellectual friends, notably Jeremy Bentham, David Ricardo, James Mill, Francis Place, John Stuart Mill, John Austin, Sarah Austin, and Joseph Parkes, and their influence moved her further towards political radicalism. In 1832 Grote was elected to parliament for the City of London, and the decade that followed was perhaps the most exhilarating and memorable of Harriet's life. Her husband now became the leading spokesman for the philosophic radicals, a parliamentary faction advocating democratizing constitutional reforms, especially a greatly extended suffrage, frequent parliaments, and a secret ballot; in the press there were references to the 'Grote conclave' (*The Examiner*, 28 Jan 1838, 65–6). Since the philosophic radicals regarded the whig government as a major obstacle to the adoption of their programme they sat on the opposite side of the house, allowing Harriet to claim that her husband was 'chief of opposition' (Lewin, 1.329). Since the government throughout the 1830s had only a small majority, the radicals hoped they might extract concessions in exchange for radical votes. This required that they threaten to bring down the government. They disagreed about these tactics, and Harriet was not reticent about taking part in the deliberations, and, in contrast to her more cautious husband, she advocated the bold position; this led one disapproving observer to declare her 'more of a man, but not a better man than her husband' (Albany Fonblanque to Durham, 2 Jan 1837, Lambton MSS).

**Harriet Grote (1792–1878)**, by unknown artist

When in the later 1830s it became evident that the whig government would not yield to philosophic radical pressure, the small section led by Grote became demoralized and soon disbanded. The tactics advocated by Harriet had failed, but, as many acknowledged, she had been a significant player. The editor of *The Examiner*, Albany Fonblanque, referred to 'Mrs. Grote's little party' (Fonblanque to Durham, 2 Jan 1837, Lambton MSS), and Macaulay observed that the radical party was reduced to Grote and his wife. Her friend Sydney Smith called her 'queen of the radicals', and her old associate Francis Place, who agreed with her about tactics, claimed 'she *was* the philosophic radicals' (Wilson, 254). Perhaps the highest accolade came from Cobden: 'Had she been a man, she would have been the leader of a party' (J. Buckley, *Joseph Parkes*, 1926, 151). It is understandable that in her later writing she often focused on this period and looked back on the 1830s as 'a pregnant decade, if ever there was one' (Harriet Grote to Harriet Martineau, 2 Feb 1867, Martineau MSS).

Harriet's active involvement in politics came to an end after Grote's refusal to seek re-election in 1841. She now renewed her interest in the arts and intensified her patronage of the Viennese danseuse Fanny Elssler and also braved respectable opinion by serving for four years as surrogate mother to Elssler's illegitimate daughter. In 1845 she found a new object for her patronage—the Swedish singer Jenny Lind. During this period she also indulged her love of travel, especially to Paris, where she had many friends, including Tocqueville, Faucher, Comte, Cousin, Guizot, Scheffer, and Triqueti. In England she was on easy terms with men of letters and politicians. On one occasion, looking forward to a weekend at Bowood that was to include Ellice, Lowe, and Senior, she asked, 'who is to do the listening?' (Harriet Grote to Edward Ellice, 7 Jan 1860, Canadian Public Archives, A10). This assumption of equality with men did not go unnoticed, however, and some thought her manly. Sydney Smith announced he was going to call on the two Mr Grotes, and Cobden described her haranguing a family party 'like a regular politician in breeches' (R. Cobden to K. Cobden, 26 Jan 1846, BL, Add. MS 50748, fols. 198–201).

Harriet sympathized with the organized feminist movement as it emerged during the 1850s and 1860s. For all her independence and assertiveness, she bridled when recalling the barriers she had faced and concluded that life made 'every woman's lot a penn' worth' and she was left 'lamenting that I ever was born a woman' (Lewin, 2.151). Meanwhile she supported reform of the married woman's property law and extension of the suffrage to women, helped found the Society of Female Artists (1857), and regretted not being thirty years younger and leader of the women's movement.

When in her seventies and taking stock of her life, Harriet gained consolation by recalling the intellectually great men she had known. Her husband was placed high on her list, along with Bentham, James Mill, Tocqueville, John Austin, Charles Austin, and John Stuart Mill. Among the fifty-seven names, she also included Henry Thomas Buckle, Étienne Dumont, Henry Hallam, Benjamin Jowett, Thomas Babington Macaulay, Sir James Mackintosh, Felix Mendelsohn, Henry Reeve, John Romilly, J. B. Say, Nassau Senior, Sydney Smith, and William Whewell. These friendships generated her most enduring legacy—her lively, opinionated, gossipy, humorous letters, which apparently resembled her conversation, filled with original and pungent expressions. In contrast, her published articles, biographies, and memoirs seem pale and pedestrian.

Harriet's discontents turned to bitterness in 1864, when, after forty-four years of marriage, there was an 'earthquake'—the discovery that her husband was romantically attached to Susan Durant, the sculptor who created the marble medallion of Grote that now hangs in University College, London (Harriet Grote to Helen Taylor, 29 Nov 1868, Mill-Taylor MSS, BLPES). The episode came to an end only after she threatened separation. Although she complained to close friends about this disloyalty, she made no allusion to it in her *Personal Life of George Grote*, which she wrote after his death in 1871. Her last years were devoted to writing the *Life* (1873) and arranging her husband's posthumous publications. Earlier she published some of her contributions to periodicals in *Collected Papers, in Prose and Verse, 1842–1862* (1862), a *Memoir of the Life of Ary Scheffer* (1860), and *The philosophical radicals of 1832: comprising the life of Sir William Molesworth, and some incidents connected with the reform movement from 1832 to 1842* (1866). Harriet Grote died in her house, Ridgeway, at Shere, Surrey, on 29 December 1878. She was buried at Shere.

JOSEPH HAMBURGER

**Sources** T. H. Lewin, ed., *The Lewin letters … 1756–1884*, 2 vols. (1909) • UCL, Grote MSS • M. L. Clarke, *George Grote* (1962) • H. Grote, *The personal life of George Grote* (1873) • J. Hamburger, *Intellectuals in politics: John Stuart Mill and the philosophic radicals* (1965) • H. Grote, *The philosophic radicals of 1832* (1866) • Lady Eastlake [E. Rigby], *Mrs. Grote* (1880) • G. Grote, *Posthumous papers*, ed. Mrs Grote [H. Grote] (1874) • U. Birm., Martineau MSS • Canadian Public Archives, Ellice MSS • Cobden MSS, BL • M. Wilson, *Jane Austen and some contemporaries* (1938) • Lambton Castle, co. Durham, Lambton MSS • J. Soden and C. Baile de Laperrière, eds., *The Society of Women Artists exhibitors, 1855–1996*, 4 vols. (1996)

**Archives** UCL, corresp., diaries, and papers; letters | BL, letters to Charles Babbage, Add. MSS 37187–37200, *passim* • BL, corresp. with Lord Broughton, Add. MS 47229 • BL, corresp. with W. E. Gladstone, Add. MSS 44441–44458, *passim* • BL, letters to Lady Holland, Add. MS 52117 • BL, letters to Sir A. H. Layard, Add. MSS 38983–39021, 39103, *passim* • BL, corresp. with Francis Place, Add. MSS 35144–35151, *passim* • BLPES, Mill-Taylor collection • CKS, letters to G. W. Norman • John Murray, London, John Murray MSS • NL Wales, letters to Sir George Cornwall Lewis • NL Wales, corresp. with Nassau Senior • Riksarkivet, Stockholm, Francis Lewin and Nils Koch MSS • Trinity Cam., Houghton MSS • U. Birm. L., letters to Harriet Martineau • U. Durham L., letters to third Earl Grey

**Likenesses** drawing, 1806, repro. in Lewin, ed., *The Lewin letters*, vol. 1, facing p. 144 • H. Tomlin, portrait, *c.*1820–1829 (after sketch by E. Landseer), repro. in Lewin, ed., *The Lewin letters*, vol. 1, facing p. 290 • photograph, *c.*1844, Haydn Museum, Eisenstadt • C. Lewis, lithograph (after C. Landseer), BM • photograph, repro. in Lewin, ed., *The Lewin letters*, vol. 2, facing p. 309 • photograph (in old age), repro. in Clarke, *George Grote*, 176 • portrait, Royal Bank of Scotland Group Art Collection [*see illus.*]

**Wealth at death** under £70,000: probate, 11 Jan 1879, *CGPLA Eng. & Wales*

**Grote, John** (1813–1866), philosopher, Grotius to his friends, was born on 5 May 1813 at Clay Hills, Beckenham, Kent, the ninth of eleven children of George Grote (1762–1830), merchant banker, and his wife, Selina Mary, daughter of Henry Peckwell, evangelical clergyman, and Bella

Blosset. John's eldest brother, George *Grote, Greek historian and influential member of the philosophical radical movement, assumed control of the family bank in Threadneedle Street, London. In 1831, after his father's death, John, who had been educated privately, entered Trinity College, Cambridge, where he excelled in both mathematics and classics triposes in 1835. Encultured in the Trinity network around William Whewell and elected fellow in 1837, Grote thrived on the conversations with, and the friendships around, the mathematician and editor of *Bacon's Works*, Robert Leslie Ellis. Resisting his mother's evangelicalism, he evolved an independent religious position which approximated most to the broad church. He was ordained deacon in 1842, priest in 1844, and obtained the college living of Trumpington, near Cambridge, in 1847. A collection of *Sermons* was published in 1872. A confirmed bachelor, he enjoyed family life and hosted 'Groteries', and *c.*1848 he became guardian to and fostered his orphaned niece Alexandrina (Allie) Jessie Grote (1831–1927), who later married the philosopher Joseph Bickersteth Mayor.

Grote became an active liberal reforming member of his college and university and, after an unsuccessful candidature for the chair of modern history at Cambridge in 1849, he succeeded Whewell as Knightbridge professor of moral philosophy in 1855. A weak physical condition associated with lung disorders, a nervous and fidgety disposition, and feared periods of melancholy and indolence did not prevent Grote presenting comprehensive lectures, especially on the syllabuses for the revised moral sciences tripos he pioneered in 1860. His greatest service was to establish a philosophical debating society, the Grote Club, and after his death the Grote Society, a precursor of the Moral Sciences Society, was established. Papers were read after dinner in Trumpington by members, including the moral philosopher Henry Sidgwick, whom Grote influenced profoundly, the logician John Venn, Joseph Bickersteth Mayor, the Hegelian and mathematician John Rickards Mozley (1840–1931), and subsequently, under the guidance of F. D. Maurice, successor to the Knightbridge chair, the economist Alfred Marshall and the philosopher William K. Clifford.

Upright in stature and nature, fastidious yet kindly and encouraging in manner, ingenious and provocative in debate, Grote elaborated the analytic, ordinary language and conversational style that were to mark both his writings and the spirit of later Cambridge philosophy. On most philosophical issues he took an independent and eclectic position, but of the rival interpretations of his corpus his chosen identification with nascent British idealism, identified by him in the writings of James Frederick Ferrier and confirmed later by Bernard Bosanquet, must be prioritized. His idealism emerged from efforts to adjudicate between the indigenous philosophies of time. In *Exploratio philosophica: Rough Notes on Modern Intellectual Science, Part 1* (1865) he analyses critically and constructively the 'three kinds of philosophy' then dominant: the sense-data phenomenalism of Locke, Hume, and Mill; the 'true and real philosophy' of idealism identified in Kant, Whewell, Hamilton, and Ferrier; and the flawed attempt to apply science to the mind and philosophy in psychophysiology, materialism, and positivism. He sought to unravel the conflations of distinct languages and disciplines, especially science, history, philosophy, and religion, first exemplified in 'Old studies and new', in *Cambridge Essays* (1856).

Grote's unique metaphysics is elaborated in book 2 of *Exploratio philosophica, Part 2* (1900), on 'Immediateness and reflection', where he unpacks a Hegelian-style phenomenology in which the original coherence of feeling and being in immediateness, the 'given', is disrupted by knowledge, reflection, and judgement, especially the recognition of 'wants'. He coins, contrasts, and synchronizes 'knowledge of acquaintance and judgement' to explain this. The resulting 'doubleness' in which we separate wants and ideals, self and other, subject and object, mind and matter, is and ought, past and future, provides the 'resistance' that hampers philosophy and practical life and which thought and action are intended to overcome. Book 5, entitled 'Idealism and positivism', exposes the partial character of positivism, which fails to recognize 'the universe, as exhibiting mind and involving purpose, mind such as we exercise in ordering and arranging things, and purpose such as induces us to construct or make things' (J. Grote, *Exploratio philosophica, Part 2*, 1900, 293).

Grote's *Treatise on the Moral Ideals*, written *c.*1864 and published in 1876, explores with great precision and clarity the plurality of independently valued moral and political purposes that our 'wants' call forth to make life more satisfactory. That these ideals cohere and that there is something at stake in moral argument, he considers to be reflexive presumptions or beliefs all of us 'instinctively and intuitively have'. While all ideals entail an imperative, an ought to be, all can be known by ordinary thinking and talking and all achieved by ordinary human conduct. Happiness is only one goal of human conduct, a more coherent science of which, eudaemonics, he proposes as a replacement for utilitarianism. Aretaics, the science of virtue, and our active nature which encompasses deontics, deals with what ought not to be done, not what is unpleasant, with 'what I should do', rather than 'what we desire'.

Grote's *c.*1863 *Examination of the Utilitarian Philosophy* (1870), described as the most 'meticulous philosophical scrutiny' (Schneewind, *Mill*, xiv) and the 'best hostile criticism' of Mill (Bain, 115), informed most later critiques of Mill's *Utilitarianism*. Like Sidgwick and Moore, Grote insists that the ideal of happiness requires an intuitive grounding and that questions of duty, justice, and virtue should be answered on the basis of particular social relationships, not deduced from general abstract moral principles. As a prolegomena to the whole corpus, Grote produced a profoundly significant philosophy of language, published in parts as 'On glossology' in the *Journal of Philology* (1872–4), and 'Thought versus learning', in *Good Words* (1871). The pursuit of knowledge and judgement should be directed not to thinking but to language, and especially the meaning of words. Thinking is language unspoken; words carry meanings as well as signifying things. He proposes that as words mean what they are used to mean by the users in everyday conversation, we should study divergent and changing usage and the ever changing play of the sound word (phonem) and the thought word (noem or meaning). For this innovation, for his methods and style of patient clarification of issues and language, for his faith in conversation, ordinary language, and usages as philosophical tools, for his common-sense approach and avoidance of philosophical allegiances, doctrines, sectarianism, for his rebuttal of positivism, phenomenalism, and utilitarianism, we can concur with the claim that 'Grote's philosophy is in manner an early, perhaps the first, example of that Cambridge spirit …, which was to reach its culmination in the work of G. E. Moore' (Passmore, *A Hundred Years of Philosophy*, 1968, 54), but should perhaps develop the claim to include B. Russell, L. Wittgenstein, and M. Oakeshott (Gibbins, 'John Grote and modern Cambridge philosophy').

Rival interpretations identify Grote as a religious philosopher, a moralist, a 'Cambridge moralist' (Schneewind, *Sidgwick's Ethics*, 117–21), an intuitionist and a personalist idealist. His reputation was never high outside mid-century Cambridge, but it underwent a small revival between 1900 and 1930 in Oxford, Scotland, and America, and in the 1960s, led by Jerome B. Schneewind, Anthony Quinton, and Lauchlin D. MacDonald. All underestimated his minor works, the significance of his ideas on language, and his use of the comparative historical method and relational social theory. Grote's death on 21 August 1866, at the vicarage, Trumpington, Cambridge, from exhaustion and respiratory failure, probably induced by bronchiectasis, robbed philosophy of a unique and fertile mind which new scholarship and close study of the modern Cambridge tradition could and should revive. He was buried on 23 August in the churchyard of St Mary and St Michael, Trumpington. JOHN R. GIBBINS

**Sources** J. R. Gibbins, 'John Grote, Cambridge University and the development of Victorian ideas', PhD diss., U. Newcastle, 1988 • J. R. Gibbons, 'John Grote and modern Cambridge philosophy', *Philosophy* (1998), 73, 453–77 • Trinity Cam. • Trinity Cam., Mayor MSS • J. B. Schneewind, *Sidgwick's ethics and Victorian moral philosophy* (1977) • J. Passmore, *A hundred years of philosophy*, 2nd edn (1966); repr. (1968) • C. E. Whitmore, 'The significance of John Grote', *Philosophical Review*, 36 (1927), 307–37 • L. D. MacDonald, *John Grote: a critical estimate of his writings* (1966) • G. W. Cunningham, *The idealistic argument in recent British and American philosophy* (1933) • B. Bosanquet, 'Review of *Exploratio philosophica*, part 2', *Archiv für Systematische Philosophie*, 8 (1902), 128–30 • T. T. Segerstedt, *The problem of knowledge in Scottish philosophy: Reid — Stewart — Hamilton — Ferrier* (1934) • A. Quinton, *Utilitarian ethics* (1973) • J. B. Schneewind, ed., *Mill: a collection of critical essays* (1968) • A. Bain, *John Stuart Mill: a criticism with personal recollections* (1882) • T. M. Forsyth, *English philosophy: a study of its method and general development* (1910)

**Archives** Trinity Cam., corresp. and papers | Trinity Cam., Ellis MSS; Mayor MSS; Whewell MSS

**Likenesses** cabinet photograph, 1862, Trinity Cam. • engraving (aged fifty; after photograph), repro. in J. Grote, *Exploratio philosophica: rough notes on modern intellectual science* (1900), part 2 • three photographs, priv. coll.

**Wealth at death** under £7000: probate, 10 Sept 1866, *CGPLA Eng. & Wales*

**Grove, Eleanor** (1826–1905), educationist, was the youngest of a large and distinguished family. She was born in Clapham, Surrey, daughter of Thomas Grove, a businessman and a devout Congregationalist, and his wife, Mary Blades. It was an educated and musical home, influenced by the ethos of the evangelical Clapham Sect. Through her elder brother George *Grove, subsequently editor of *Grove's Dictionary of Music and Musicians*, and her other sisters and brothers and their spouses, Eleanor Grove came into contact with many distinguished circles. The private income which she inherited from her parents left her freer to choose her sphere of life than many of her contemporaries.

Little is known of Eleanor Grove's formal education, but it is clear that she was a person of considerable culture. In her twenties she went to Germany as governess to Marie von Arnim, a niece of Bismarck, of whom she was always an admirer. Later she moved to Vienna, where she lived with a Jewish family, and translated Ebers's *An Egyptian Princess* and Goethe's *Wilhelm Meister's Apprenticeship* for Tauchnitz's *Collection of German Authors*, first published in 1867.

It was her brother George who told Eleanor Grove of the vacancy for an assistant secretary at Queen's College, Harley Street, in 1872, and who actually substituted for her at the interview, owing to a delay in the transmission of a telegram. Her references and her contacts were such that she was appointed. In 1875 she was promoted to the post of Lady Resident with responsibility for discipline, for superintending the college servants, and for giving guidance to the students in their studies. She enjoyed the contacts she made there, and formed a lifelong friendship with Rosa Morison, the assistant Lady Resident. At the same time she was frustrated by the college's failure to take advantage of the new opportunities open to women through London University, and in effect its refusal to develop into a college for higher education; she roused the ire of the more conservative members of the college council on more than one occasion. In 1881 she resigned, protesting against what she regarded as poor management and lack of vision.

After a short period of travel in Germany together, Eleanor Grove and Rosa Morison offered their services to the first hall of residence for women attending University College, London (College Hall). Again the Grove family connections proved useful for Eleanor was able to arrange the lease of a house in Byng Place through the good offices of a brother-in-law, the Revd Joshua Harrison, a Congregational minister and secretary to the Coward Trustees, who owned the house. In 1882 she was officially appointed principal. Despite an old-fashioned appearance, resplendent in lace cap and tea-gown, she was youthful in spirit, and entered sympathetically into the aspirations of her students. She cared deeply about the status of women in society, and publicly supported both the women's suffrage movement and the movement for women's participation in local government. She was a witty conversationalist and a good correspondent. Ill health forced her to retire in 1890, though she continued to live near University College, at 15 Tavistock Square. After some years as an invalid, suffering from asthma and bronchitis, she died at home, of heart failure on 22 November 1905. Her funeral was held in St Pancras Church, London, and she was buried in Norwood cemetery on the 27th. ELAINE KAYE

**Sources** L. McDonald, 'Miss Grove', typescript, UCL • A. M. Copping, *The story of College Hall* (1974) • H. H. Bellot, *University College, London, 1826–1926* (1929) • C. L. Graves, *The life and letters of Sir George Grove* (1903) • E. Kaye, *A history of Queen's College, London, 1848–1972* (1972) • *UCL Union Magazine* (1904–6) [UCL Archive] • *University College London Gazette* (1901) [UCL Archive] • *The Times* (27 Nov 1905) • *Englishwoman's Review*, 38 (1906), 67–8 • d. cert. • probate • *IGI* • *The Times* (24 Nov 1905)

**Wealth at death** £8661 5*s*. 9*d*.: probate, 21 Dec 1905, *CGPLA Eng. & Wales*

**Grove, Sir George** (1820–1900), writer on music and lexicographer, was born on 13 August 1820 at Thurlow Lodge, 74 Thurlow Terrace, Clapham, Surrey, the eighth of the eleven children of Thomas Grove (1774–1852), fishmonger and venison dealer, and his wife, Mary (1784–1856), *née* Blades. Having learned the basics of literacy from his elder sister Bithiah, he went as a weekly boarder to a school in Clapham. From 1834 to 1836 he was a pupil of Charles Pritchard, a distinguished mathematician, at Clapham grammar school. A regular worshipper at the parish church, he was able to hear the music of J. S. Bach played by the organist there, John Blackburn. At the age of sixteen—competent in classics and mathematics—he was apprenticed to Alexander Gordon, a well-known civil engineer. Before long he was assisting his employer in building the Birmingham to London railway. He also heard as much music as he could and in the British Museum Library copied significant sections from otherwise unavailable sources. His transcriptions show a keen musical-analytical sense.

In 1839 Grove qualified as a graduate of the Institute of Civil Engineering, after which he spent two years in Napier's Foundry, Broomielaw, Glasgow. This was followed by a voyage to Jamaica to supervise the erection of the first lighthouse on the island. A similar duty in Bermuda—through faulty planning in London—obliged Grove to stay there for three years. During his long absence from London he read voraciously. One night on the sea shore, feeling a particular empathy with S. T. Coleridge, he noted mystically, 'a great star, *slanting down* to the sea line, [making] an impression of *eternity* on me' (Young, 38). Grove's next engineering duties were his last: he joined Robert Stephenson's team, working first on the new railway station in Chester and then the Britannia Bridge at the Menai Strait. In Chester he took every opportunity to hear music in the cathedral, while both there and in Bangor his interest in Welsh music was stimulated by the composer John Owen ('Owain Alaw').

In 1850, with the bridge nearing completion, Grove began to consider his future. Fortuitously, the committee of the Society of Arts in London—planning for the Great Exhibition of 1851—was seeking a new secretary. After a short trial period, the post was offered to Grove. On 23 December 1851 he married Harriet (*d*. 1914), the sister of

**Sir George Grove** (1820–1900), by Robert Jefferson Bingham, 1863

his schoolfriend George Bradley. In 1852, after a brief period in rooms provided by the society, the Groves took a house in Sydenham. Grove's management of the affairs of the exhibition led to his appointment as secretary to the Crystal Palace. Rebuilt in Sydenham, this was to become a centre for educational, cultural, and recreational activity. A liberal idealist, Grove proposed the acquisition of all the published works of J. S. Bach by the British Museum and the popularization of music in the Crystal Palace. Here he hired a wind band with Heinrich Schallehn as conductor. After the first of the Saturday concerts, on 22 September 1855, Schallehn was displaced by August Manns. Under him the band developed into a disciplined orchestra, attracting audiences with programmes judiciously chosen by Grove and Manns until the end of the century.

On 26 January 1856 Grove provided programme notes for a bicentenary concert of Mozart's music, and he continued to write such notes for Crystal Palace audiences for forty years. He had, however, another string to his literary bow. He was a fluent writer, whether about engineering or any other subject in which he had interest. His invaluable editing of *Sinai and Palestine* (1856) by Arthur Stanley—later dean of Westminster—led to the assistant editorship of William Smith's *Bible Dictionary*. With characteristic thoroughness, Grove involved himself deeply in the history, geography, and religion of the Holy Land, which he visited in 1858 and 1861. Four years later he was honorary secretary to the Palestine Exploration Fund. All this activity is reflected in many scholarly essays in the *Bible Dictionary* and elsewhere. In 1860 the Groves moved into their last home, conveniently near to the Crystal Palace. In 1866 Grove became assistant editor of *Macmillan's Magazine*, but music was rarely out of mind. Next year, with Arthur Sullivan, he went to Vienna. The time spent there was profitable: Grove and Sullivan were able to find the parts of Schubert's *Rosamunde* music, thought to have been lost. In the following March it was played for the first time at the Crystal Palace. By this time Grove was deeply immersed also in the music of Beethoven, Mendelssohn, and Schumann. In 1873, while retaining interest in the concerts, he gave up his secretarial position at the Crystal Palace to become a general editor for Macmillan, continuing as editor of their *Magazine*. Politically radical and in religion a modernist, he exercised considerable authority.

In 1874 Grove's experience of lexicography, his knowledge of music and musicians, and his talent for finding capable writers led to a contract from Macmillan to edit a new, two-volume dictionary of music. For contributors he turned to experienced musical writers, occasional gifted amateurs, a few European scholars, and pioneers in the discipline of musicology, including C. H. H. Parry and W. Barclay Squire. In 1878 the first of the four volumes of the *Dictionary of Music and Musicians*—always to be known as 'Grove'—was issued (subsequent volumes appeared in 1880, 1883, and 1889). Throughout 1882 Grove led a fund-raising campaign, the success of which ensured the official opening of the new Royal College of Music by the prince of Wales on 7 May 1883. He received a knighthood that year. The teaching staff, appointed by Grove as first director, and led by Parry and Stanford, carried the college with distinction into the twentieth century. Grove retired in 1894, by which time a new building was under construction. In 1896 Grove's *Beethoven and his Nine Symphonies*, modestly 'addressed to the amateurs of this country', appeared.

Among Victorians Grove was alone in ability to combine technology and art on the highest level. His character was complex. A vivid sense of humour could at times run into 'convulsions of mirth'. Indifference to 'athleticism and field sports' distanced him from male students. Parry disliked Grove's sentimentality and his habit of calling his students his 'children'. His family comprised three sons and two daughters—the elder of whom predeceased him. Never mentioned during his lifetime was the birth of his son (registered as George Grove), on 2 March 1842, to Elizabeth Blackwell in the union workhouse, Stratford upon Avon. Grove both worked and entertained intensively, in part, at least, to escape from reality. To one of his first students, Edith Oldham, from Dublin, Grove became intensely attached. The letters which he wrote to her until the last days of his life are the truest index to the depths of his character. The bleakness of his marriage was thus described on 12 February 1891: 'All through my C. Palace work, my Bible Dictionary work … musical Dictionary, College—all the countless things I have tried—to everything she has been absolutely cold'. In January 1899 Grove suffered a minor stroke, after which his health gradually but inexorably deteriorated. He died at his home in Lower Sydenham, London, on 28 May 1900. The funeral service, at St Bartholomew's Church, Sydenham, was conducted by George Granville Bradley, dean of Westminster, and Grove was buried in Ladywood cemetery, Lewisham, on 31 May. PERCY M. YOUNG

**Sources** P. M. Young, *George Grove, 1820–1900: a biography* (1980) · 'Royal College of Music', *MT*, 31 (1890), 475 · *MT*, 38 (1897), 657–64 · *Catalogue of the principal instrumental and vocal works performed at the Saturday concerts from 1855 to 1882*, Crystal Palace · third report of Clapham grammar school, 1838 · Mozart bicentenary concert, 1856 · Beethoven commemoration, 17 Dec 1870 · *Young Woman*, 4 (1895–6), 227–30 · C. L. Graves, 'Sir George Grove, centenary study', *Music and Letters*, 1 (1920), 330–33 · J. Bennett, *Forty years of music, 1865–1905* (1908) · H. S. Wyndham, *August Manns and the Saturday concerts: a memoir and a retrospect* (1909) · J. Dibble, *C. Hubert H. Parry: his life and music* (1992), chap. 8

**Archives** Bodl. Oxf., letters · Royal College of Music, London, corresp. | BL, letters to F. G. Edwards, Egerton MSS 3091, 3097B · BL, letters to Mary Gladstone, Add. MS 46521 · BL, letters to Sir A. H. Layard, Add. MSS 38991–39119, *passim* · BL, corresp. with Macmillans, Dean Stanley, etc., Add. MSS 35222–35227, 39679, 50852, 54793 · BL, letters to E. Speyer, Add. MS 42233 · CAC Cam., letters to Oscar Browning · FM Cam., letters to W. B. Squire · Palestine Exploration Fund, London, corresp. relating to Palestine Exploration Fund · University of British Columbia Library, letters to H. R. Haweis

**Likenesses** H. Phillips, oils, 1861 · R. J. Bingham, photograph, 1863, NPG [*see illus.*] · Mayall & Newman, photograph, *c.*1891, Brighton · Spy [L. Ward], watercolour caricature, 1891, Royal College of Music, London; repro. in 'Music', *Chronicles in cartoon* (1906–7), 7 · H. A. Olivier, oils, *c.*1894, Athenaeum, London · C. W. Furse, oils, 1895, Royal College of Music, London · A. Gilbert, bronze bust, 1895, Royal College of Music, London · Braun & Cie., *c.*1896, repro. in *Young Woman*, 279 · Adèle of Vienna, photograph, repro. in *Young Woman*, 227 · J. Caswall Smith, photograph, repro. in *MT* (1897) · F. S. Mosuklos, portrait

**Wealth at death** £31,744 14*s.* 9*d.*: probate, 13 Aug 1900, *CGPLA Eng. & Wales*

**Grove, (Agnes) Geraldine** [*née* (Agnes) Geraldine Lane Fox; *later* (Agnes) Geraldine Fox-Pitt], **Lady Grove (1863–1926)**, essayist, was born on 25 July 1863, the seventh of nine children of General Augustus Henry Lane Fox (later Pitt-Rivers; 1827–1900) [*see* Rivers, Augustus Henry Lane Fox Pitt-], and Alice Margaret Stanley (*d.* 1910), daughter of the second Baron Stanley of Alderly. Known as Geraldine she was a boarder at Oxford high school until 19 December 1879. In 1880 her father, Lane, a key figure in British archaeology and first inspector of ancient monuments, inherited Rushmore, a 29,000 acre estate in Dorset, from his great-uncle George Pitt, second Lord Rivers. He duly added, by royal licence, Pitt-Rivers to his name as well as to that of his eldest son, Alexander Edward. The rest of the children became Fox-Pitt. In 1881 Geraldine met Walter John Grove (1852–1932), son of Thomas Fraser Grove, first baronet (1823–1897), of Ferne, and Katherine Grace (*d.* 1879), daughter of the Hon. Walter O'Grady. They married on 20 July 1882 and had five children. On his father's death in 1897 Walter Grove succeeded to the baronetcy and inherited numerous family properties.

Geraldine Lane Fox kept diaries from 1879 until her death. Largely a form of recording the day's events and often written in shorthand code, the diaries provide insight into the life and preoccupations of a woman involved in reform causes of the 1890s. From 1892 she became active in the women's suffrage movement, using her talents as an essayist to write pieces on the issue for periodicals that included the *Cornhill Magazine* and the *Fortnightly Review*. She also used her position as a married aristocrat to speak publicly at suffrage meetings.

Lady Grove's role as both guest and hostess brought her in contact with a variety of literary and political figures. In 1894 she met Rudyard Kipling and his wife, and in 1895 she met Thomas Hardy at her parents' estate, Rushmore. She corresponded with Hardy from 1895 to 1901, during which time they formed a pupil–mentor relationship; she engaged him to help her select topics for periodical publications and get her works published, as she seems to have sought a broader audience for her social and political essays. In 1896, for example, he suggested that she address how children are educated; an essay, 'What should children be told?', appeared in two parts in the *Free Review*, for July–August 1896. In surviving letters Hardy admires the 'vigour' of her prose and the power of her persuasive pieces, referring to her affectionately as his 'good little pupil'.

In 1899 Lady Grove was active in the anti-vivisection movement and was a member of the Society for the Protection of Children, involved in adoption reform among other activities. Her first book, *71 Days Camping in Morocco*, was published in 1902; in this illustrated work she critiqued Robert B. Cunninghame-Graham's popular *Mogreb-el-Acksa* (1898; repr. 1997) for what she perceived as pro-Eastern sentiments. In 1903 she accepted 10 guineas a month to write essays on popular themes for the *New Review*. The success of *The Social Fetich* (1907), which was dedicated to Hardy, led to more offers from editors to write for their publications. *The Human Woman* (1908) contains her speech on women and citizenship delivered at the International Congress of Women in Paris in 1900; *On Fads* (1910) was equally successful. Both these collections provide lively and informed treatments of such topics as why women's newspapers lacked intellectual content, who controlled the theatres, and what women's roles in public life should be.

While travelling in Germany in 1906 Lady Grove became ill and tuberculosis was diagnosed. She died on 7 December 1926 at her home, Sedgehill Manor, Wiltshire, and was buried at Berwick St John, Wiltshire. On her death she was eulogized by Hardy in his poem 'Concerning Agnes'. She was survived by her husband.

Beverly E. Schneller

**Sources** *Collected letters of Thomas Hardy*, ed. R. W. Purdy and M. Millgate (1980), vol. 2 • *The Grove diaries*, ed. D. Hawkins (1995) • A. Grove, *71 days camping in Morocco* (1902) • A. Grove, *The human woman* (1908) • D. Hawkins, *Concerning Agnes* (1982) • A. Grove, *On fads* (1910) • A. Grove, *The social fetich*, 2nd edn (1908) • R. B. Cunninghame-Graham, *Mogreb-el-Acksa*, repr. (1997) • Burke, *Peerage*

**Archives** priv. coll., family papers and photographs • Wilts. & Swindon RO, diaries and letters

**Likenesses** F. Beaumont, double portrait, 1892 (with her son Terence), repro. in Hawkins, *Concerning Agnes* • S. Queensbury, bust, 1894 • H. W. Barnett, photogravure, repro. in Grove, *71 days camping*, frontispiece • K. Collings, studio portrait, repro. in Grove, *Social fetich* • double portrait (with Oenone), repro. in Hawkins, ed., *Grove diaries* • photographs, priv. coll. • portraits, repro. in Hawkins, *Concerning Agnes*

**Wealth at death** £808 14s. 0d.: probate, 1927, *CGPLA Eng. & Wales*

**Grove, Henry** (1684–1738), Presbyterian minister and tutor, was born on 4 January 1684 at Taunton, the youngest of the fourteen children of Thomas Grove (*c.*1632–*c.*1712), apothecary, and his second wife, Elizabeth, daughter of John and Susannah Rowe of Crediton. Elizabeth's brother, John Rowe (1626–1677), was ejected from a lectureship at Westminster Abbey in 1660. Of the children of Thomas and Elizabeth, only Henry and Anne survived childhood. Anne married John Amory, a Taunton grocer, and their son, Thomas, was Grove's successor. Grove's grandfather, Edward Grove, vicar of Pinhoe, Devon, was ejected in 1662.

Grove was taught classics at Taunton grammar school, and at fourteen entered Taunton Academy. Here he studied and prepared for the ministry under Matthew Warren, who was also the minister of Pauls Meeting with Emmanuel Harford. In 1703 Grove left for London to study at Newington Green Academy under his cousin, Thomas Rowe (1656/7–1705), son of his uncle, John Rowe, and remained there for almost two years, reading philosophy, learning Hebrew, and listening to the leading preachers. Here he became a lifelong friend of Isaac Watts, although they often differed on the issues of the day.

Towards the end of 1704 Grove returned to Taunton and on 28 December 1704 married Elizabeth Marshall (*d.* 1736), daughter of Nicholas Marshall and Elizabeth Smith. He preached in and around Taunton but on 14 June 1706 Warren died, followed by Harford on 4 August 1706. Edmund Batson succeeded them as minister of Pauls Meeting, and the Presbyterian ministers of Somerset met to decide the future of Taunton Academy. The meeting appointed Grove, aged twenty-two, as tutor in ethics and pneumatology, Robert Darch, minister at Bishops Hull, as tutor in physics and mathematics, and Stephen James, minister of Fulwood, as tutor in divinity. In September 1706 James asked the Exeter Assembly, which supervised ministerial training, grants, and ordinations, to approve the methods of the new management of the academy, which it did, wishing them 'all good success' (Brockett, 62). The academy flourished, educating well over 100 young men for both secular and religious careers. The academy did close down before the passing of the Schism Act that would have barred dissenters from teaching. However, Queen Anne died on the day that the act was due to come into force, 1 August 1714, and so it was ignored and the academy revived. Darch became unwilling to continue in the academy, and Grove took responsibility for his subjects. James died in 1725, which left Grove in sole charge, and Amory was brought in as assistant lecturer. Grove sought to inspire in his pupils a love of truth, virtue, liberty, and genuine religion, although he was not determined

**Henry Grove** (1684–1738), by or after John Wollaston

enough to control those students who needed a very firm hand. He devised systems for teaching his subjects, his favourite being ethics, but like Warren he thought that the scriptures were the basis of all teaching. The writings of Newton and Locke appealed to him, but he was not an uncritical reader of their works.

On Grove's return to Taunton his preaching attracted notice. In addition to his duties in the academy he preached for Darch at Bishops Hull and for James Strong at West Hatch. He preached on alternate Sundays for more than eighteen years but barely received £20 a year. He received even less for his teaching, but he did inherit his father's estate about 1712. Despite his relative poverty he was generous in his charity. When James died Grove succeeded him at Fulwood, and Amory replaced Grove at Bishops Hull and West Hatch. Grove belonged to a tightly knit community of dissenters centred upon Pauls Meeting where, on retirement from Bishops Hull, Darch and his wife rented a pew. Soon after James's death Batson married his widow, Joan, on 13 May 1725. Grove's brother-in-law, John Amory, was an executor of Harford's will and also a trustee of Pauls Meeting, as were Grove's father and his father-in-law, Nicholas Marshall. When Thomas Amory was ordained at Pauls Meeting on 7 October 1730 as assistant to Batson, Grove preached the sermon. Although he received invitations from churches in Exeter, London, and elsewhere, Grove refused to leave the community.

Grove's aim in preaching was not to encourage party factions but to stimulate love of God, of Jesus, and of mankind. Ethics were always central to his sermons. He believed in natural religion but also in revealed religion expressed in the mediation of Christ and in divine assistance. He preached funeral sermons for James and Darch, and also for members of the Welman family who worshipped at Fulwood and who were described by Philip Doddridge as 'the glory of the dissenters in these parts' (*Calendar*, ed. Nuttall, 151, no. 775). During his wife's illness Grove preached several sermons on 1 Thessalonians 5:18, and after the death of one of their children he preached from Genesis 42:36, and entitled his sermon 'The mourning parent'. In his preaching he preferred to appeal to reason rather than to the emotions. He disliked factions and withdrew from the debates of his time. Strong, in his sermon at Grove's funeral, quoted him as saying 'The older I grow, the less inclined I am to quarrel with men of different opinions' (Strong, 26). The principal controversy was concerning Arianism and Amory's heterodoxy and Grove was criticized for not making a stand for orthodoxy, particularly when Amory, in 1732, left Pauls Meeting over a financial dispute with Batson to found the New Meeting at Tancred Street, nominally Presbyterian but where the congregation held Arian beliefs.

In 1714 Grove published four essays in volume 8 of *The Spectator*, one of which drew a comment from Samuel Johnson, 'One of the finest pieces in the English language is the paper on Novelty, yet we do not hear it talked of. It was written by Grove, a dissenting *teacher*' (*Boswell's Life of Johnson*, ed. R. W. Chapman, new edn, 1980, 740). In 1722 he wrote five letters to *St James's Journal*, the first was 'A defence of Presbyterians'. In 1730 he was involved in an exchange of essays with Joseph Hallett (1691–1744) concerning 'The proof of a future state from reason' but his most popular publication, running to eight editions, was *A Discourse Concerning the Nature and Design of the Lord's Supper* (1732). Some of Grove's poems were published, as were several of his hymns. These appeared in the hymnbooks of the day but, as with his poetry, their popularity has not lasted. A relative by marriage, the poet Elizabeth Rowe, dedicated one of her poems to him and he returned the courtesy in two of his own. When he died he was writing her biography.

Grove and his wife had thirteen children, but only five survived their parents. Elizabeth suffered for a long time from a nervous disorder and died, insane, in 1736. Grove had a weak constitution that was made worse by the strain of preaching and teaching. Every spring he developed a fever, and in 1718 he nearly died. He preached at Taunton on Sunday 19 February 1738 and felt inspired but soon developed a headache, for him the usual preliminary to a fever. He was taken ill and died at about 7 a.m. on 27 February. He was buried on 3 March at Pauls Meeting; Thomas Amory paid for his grave. Inside Pauls Meeting is Grove's memorial in Latin, composed by John Ward of Gresham College. Amory became head of Taunton Academy, and edited and published all Grove's writings. Fulwood Chapel is now a private house and Pauls Meeting became Taunton United Reformed Church in 1972.

BRIAN W. KIRK

**Sources** T. Amory, preface, in H. Grove, *Sermons and tracts*, 1 (1740) · 'The life of Henry Grove', Somerset Archaeological and Natural History Society library · J. Strong, *The suddenness of Christ's coming* (1738) · H. McLachlan, *English education under the Test Acts:*

*being the history of the nonconformist academies, 1662–1820* (1931) • DWL, New College collection, L54-4-63; L54-4-64 • J. Manning, 'Memorial of dissenting academies in the west of England', *Monthly Repository*, 13 (1818), 89–90 • A. Brockett, ed., *The Exeter assembly: the minutes of the assemblies of the United Brethren of Devon and Cornwall, 1691–1717*, Devon and Cornwall RS, new ser., 6 (1963) • E. Green, *Bibliotheca Somersetensis* (1902) • *Calendar of the correspondence of Philip Doddridge*, ed. G. F. Nuttall, HMC, JP 26 (1979) • *DNB*

**Archives** Harris Man. Oxf., lecture notes

**Likenesses** G. Vertue, line engraving (after J. Wollaston), BM, NPG; repro. in Grove, *Sermons and tracts*, vol. 1, frontispiece • by or after J. Wollaston, oils, DWL [*see illus.*]

**Grove, Joseph** (*d.* 1764), biographer, says in his account of William, third duke of Devonshire, that his parents lived in Chipping Norton, Oxfordshire, where the family had resided above a century and a half, and that his mother, who had been married to his father above fifty-three years, died on 22 January 1739, aged seventy-three, and his father on 22 March 1740, aged eighty-three.

Grove practised as an attorney and amassed considerable wealth. Besides property in various counties, he possessed a 'pleasant little seat in Richmond, Surrey, called the Belvidere'. In or before 1709 he married Rebecca, daughter of Joseph Willmott, citizen and haberdasher of London; she died in 1745 leaving no surviving children. Thereafter when Grove visited London he lodged in the parish of St Clement Danes, at the house of a Mrs Mary Parr, to whom he left an annuity of £14 and all his effects in her possession. After his retirement from the practice of the law Grove wrote a number of historical works which made little impact either on contemporaries or on subsequent historians. He had a passion for 'adorning' his books with copperplates, which from their unintentional comicality serve to relieve the heaviness of the text. His principal work was *The History of the Life and Times of Cardinal Wolsey* (1742). This was followed by several further essays on Wolsey and a biography of the Cavendish family, *The Lives of All the Earls and Dukes of Devonshire* (1764). A proposed biography of Henry VIII remained unfinished at the time of Grove's death at Mrs Parr's residence in London on 27 March 1764. He was buried on 2 April in Richmond church.

GORDON GOODWIN, *rev.* ADAM I. P. SMITH

**Sources** W. T. Lowndes, *The bibliographer's manual of English literature*, 4 vols. (1834) • J. Grove, *The lives of all the earls and dukes of Devonshire* (1764) • D. E. Baker, *Biographia dramatica, or, A companion to the playhouse*, rev. I. Reed, new edn, rev. S. Jones, 3 vols. in 4 (1812)

**Grove, Matthew** (*fl. c.*1583), poet, is known only for *The Most Famous and Tragicall Historie of Pelops and Hippodamia*, published in 1587.

A 'Matthew Grove of Staple Inn' entered Gray's Inn in 1570. Eccles identifies him with the poet, and notes his involvement in numerous lawsuits. However, this litigious Matthew Grove (*b.* 1552) was born too early to match the self-description in 'The Authors Epistle' of *Pelops* of the poet's 'tender quill'. Although the book's publisher, Richard Smith, states in his odd verse dedication that he'd kept Grove's 'pamphlet' after rescuing it from 'water cleere' for 'Foure yeere and more' before issuing it at his own cost in 1587, this would make the poet a youth *c.*1583, and so too young in 1570 to have progressed from Staple Inn. R. Smith's verse dedication, claiming

> The aucthor sure I doe not know,
> Ne whether he be high or low,
> Or now alive, or els be dead,

may outline all that is known biographically.

*Pelops* is dedicated both in verse by R. Smith and in self-effacing prose by Grove to Sir Henry Compton (*d.* 1589). The dedications imply that Smith, but not Grove, hoped for financial reward. The title poem recounts the legend behind the curse on Pelops's sons Atreus and Thyestes and on his grandson Agamemnon, stressing superstitious credulity in the culture of King Onomaus.

Most of the following eighty-eight 'Epigrams and Sonets', from two lines to several pages long, are patriotic, moralistic, proverbial, sententious, jesting, or else portray lovers' wrangling. B. J. SOKOL

**Sources** M. Eccles, *Brief lives: Tudor and Stuart authors* (1982) • J. Foster, *The register of admissions to Gray's Inn, 1521–1889, together with the register of marriages in Gray's Inn chapel, 1695–1754* (privately printed, London, 1889) • *The poems of Matthew Grove (1587)*, ed. A. B. Grosart (1878) • L. R. Zocca, *Elizabethan narrative poetry* (1970)

**Grove, Robert** (*c.*1634–1696), bishop of Chichester and religious controversialist, was born in London, the son of William Grove of Morden, Dorset. He may well be the Robert, son of William Grove, baptized in St Giles Cripplegate on 29 September 1634. He attended Winchester College in 1645 and was admitted as a pensioner to St John's College, Cambridge, in 1652. He was elected a scholar in 1653, graduated BA in 1657, and became a fellow in 1659. He proceeded MA in 1660 and BD in 1667, and was created DD in 1681. In 1667 he became chaplain to the bishop of London and was presented to the rectory of Wennington in Essex, which was in the bishop's gift. In 1669 he was granted the rectory of Langham in Essex by Charles II. Within a month he was also collated to the rectory of Aldham by the bishop of London. But he resigned both of these livings in 1670 when he was presented, again by the bishop of London, to the wealthy living of St Andrew Undershaft, London. He was prebendary of Willesden in St Paul's Cathedral from 1679 to 1691, when he was elevated to the see of Chichester.

Grove's fame derived in no small part from his literary sparring with dissenters. In 1676 William Jenkins preached a funeral sermon at the burial of the nonconformist minister Lazarus Seaman. Jenkins took the occasion to cast many aspersions on the conforming clergy. The sermon obviously gained some notoriety, because Grove felt compelled to answer the accusations in his *Vindication of the Conforming Clergy from the Unjust Aspersions of Heresie* (1676). Grove objected to the intemperate language Jenkins used when he lambasted Anglican divines. It was, he maintained, precisely because the conforming clergy were so moderate and temperate that Jenkins could insinuate that they were heretics; the only reason he could call them Socinians (those who held a 'heresy' that

**Robert Grove** (*c.*1634–1696), by unknown artist

entailed the idea that Christ was not fully divine) was 'because they are able to confute them without running into an unseemly passion'. Jenkins also charged that Anglican priests were papists, but, Grove said, he could do this only 'because, though possibly they believe it, yet they do not make it a fundamental Article, that the pope is Antichrist' (Grove, *Vindication*, 2nd edn, 1680, 12). The controversy died down for a few years, but was fanned back to life when Jenkins, with the assistance of others, issued a Latin tome, *Celeusma* (1679), in which he attempted to catalogue the errors and 'heresies' of the Anglican clergy. Grove was not deterred by this new attack: he answered with his own Latin treatise, *Responsio ad nuperum libellum qui inscribitur celeusma seu clamor ad theologos hierarchiae Anglicanae* (1680). William Nicholls, who wrote the popular *Defence of the Doctrine and Discipline of the Church of England* in the early eighteenth century, maintained that Grove's arguments and, indeed, his Latin grammar were far superior to those of Jenkins. In fact, it was largely this exchange that established Grove's reputation, because, as Nicholls noted, 'Mr. Jenkins rather encreased the fame of this excellent Person [Grove], than injured it' (Nicholls, 86). In the wake of this dispute Grove wrote *A Perswasive to Communion with the Church of England* (1682/3), which remained popular among Anglican clergymen for generations.

Grove's religious and political activity is also noteworthy. He sided with the tories during the exclusion crisis, and after James was safely on the throne in 1685 he preached a sermon (*Seasonable Advice to the Citizens, Burgesses, and Free-Holders of England*, 1685), in which he used Filmeresque arguments to allay fears about James's Catholicism. He urged his hearers not to elect MPs who had voted for exclusion, or who would not be wholly loyal to the king. 'I am sure', he averred, 'that it is far beyond the ordinary rate of a Moral impossibility' that James would try to rule arbitrarily and impose popery (Grove, *Seasonable Advice*, 24). Yet three years later Grove reportedly played a significant role in drawing up the petition in protest of James's declaration of indulgence, and soon thereafter he became chaplain to William III. He advanced further in September 1690, when he was collated archdeacon of Middlesex, and again in August 1691 when he was installed as bishop of Chichester. There are indications, though, that Grove did not wholeheartedly support the Williamite regime: in a general election in Sussex in 1695, he threw his support to the opposition candidate, Robert Orme, who was reportedly tainted by Jacobitism.

Grove was married to Elizabeth Cole of Dover. The parish registers of St Andrew Undershaft record the baptisms of five children to Robert and Elizabeth Grove between December 1671 and August 1679 and there may have been others born. Elizabeth Grove proved his will, which charged her with the care of their children. Grove died, aged sixty-two, in a bizarre accident in 1696: he was riding in a coach in rough terrain when the horses went 'mad' and became uncontrollable. He jumped from the coach and broke both of his legs severely. The surgeons could not agree how best to treat him. Eventually they amputated his legs, but it was too late: the infection had spread and he died. Upon his death, an anonymous writer commented:

> the Jacobites will censure it as a just judgment of God upon one that forsook his Loyalty; the Dissenters will some of them say, this is the end of their peevish adversary; But others of them acknowledge that he was almost the only man that grew better by a Bishoprick: his preferments made him kinder to them. (Add. MS 4460, fol. 53b)

His untimely death resulted in a difficult situation for his family, since he had not provided adequately for them (Lansdowne MS 987, vol. 84, fol. 120*v*). Grove was buried in Chichester Cathedral. J. S. CHAMBERLAIN

**Sources** R. Grove, *Seasonable advice to the citizens, burgesses, and freeholders of England* (1685) · R. Grove, *A perswasive to communion with the Church of England* (1683) · R. Grove, *An answer to Mr. Lowth's letter to Dr. Stillingfleet* (1687) · R. Grove, *A sermon preached before the king and queen at Whitehall* (1690) · R. Grove, *A short defence of the church and clergy of England* (1681) · R. Grove, *A vindication of the conforming clergy from the unjust aspersions of heresie, &c. In answer to some parts of Mr. Jenkyn's funeral sermon upon Dr. Seaman*, 2nd edn (1680) · W. Nicholls, *A defence of the doctrine and discipline of the Church of England*, 3rd edn (1730) · R. A. Beddard, 'The Sussex general election of 1695: a contemporary account by Robert Middleton, vicar of Cuckfield', *Sussex Archaeological Collections*, 106 (1968), 145–57 · account of Grove's death, BL, Add. MS 4460, fol. 53b · J. Spurr, *The Restoration Church of England, 1646–1689* (1991), 95, 125, 331 · J. S. Chamberlain, 'Portrait of a high church clerical dynasty in Georgian England: the Frewens and their world', *The Church of England, c.1689–c.1833*, ed. J. Walsh and others (1993), 299–316, esp. 301 · Venn, *Alum. Cant.*, 1/2.271 · PRO, PROB 11/434, fol. 332*v* · Bishop Kennet's biographical record of Grove, BL, Lansdowne MS 987, vol. 84, fol. 120 · *DNB* · *IGI* [parish registers, St Giles Cripplegate and St Andrew Undershaft, London] · *Fasti Angl., 1541–1857*, [St Paul's, London], 11, 65

**Likenesses** oils, St John Cam. [*see illus.*]

**Grove, Sir William Robert** (1811–1896), natural philosopher and judge, was born in Swansea on 11 July 1811, the only son of John Grove, a magistrate and deputy lieutenant of Glamorgan and his wife, Anne Bevan. Educated by a succession of private tutors, he entered Brasenose College, Oxford, where he studied classics, matriculating on 6 February 1829 and graduating BA in 1832. Following his university career he went to London to prepare for a legal career. There is some suggestion that Grove's father had originally intended that he should join the clergy, but that religious scruples would not allow him to take such a step. Grove was admitted as a student at Lincoln's Inn on 11 November 1831 and he was called to the bar on 23 November 1835.

The origins of Grove's interest in natural philosophy and electricity are unclear. One early biographical notice relates the presumably apocryphal story that the young Grove constructed his own electrical machine and air pump from household oddments but that his experiments caused so much damage that his father refused to allow their continuation. There was also certainly at least some natural philosophical activity and interest among the Grove family's acquaintances in the Swansea area. There is some suggestion as well that Grove's tutor at Oxford was the mathematician and natural philosopher Baden Powell. It is certainly the case that he joined the Royal Institution in 1835 and that in June of the same year he was one of eleven founder members of the Swansea Literary and Philosophical Society. This society later developed into the Royal Institution of South Wales and Grove maintained active links with it for at least the next decade.

On 27 May 1837 Grove married Emma Maria (*d.* 1879), daughter of John Diston Powles of Summit House, Middlesex, a fellow member of the Royal Institution. They had at least one son, Coleridge. Following his marriage Grove embarked on a tour of the continent to improve his health. It was during this period that he seriously took up the study and practice of experimental natural philosophy. Grove's first natural philosophical publication appeared at about this period in a letter to the editors of the *Philosophical Magazine* on 'New voltaic combinations'.

Grove's letter set out some suggestions concerning the construction of electric batteries, with a view to improving their performance. This was a matter of crucial importance to electricians during the 1830s since the current from most designs of battery decayed rapidly as the metal poles polarized. The only extant solution to this problem, the cell invented by the chemist John Frederic Daniell, was comparatively expensive. Grove continued this theme in subsequent publications in the *Philosophical Magazine* and elsewhere. This work culminated in 1839 when, during a visit to Paris, a paper was read out to the Académie des Sciences on his behalf describing his new 'Pile voltaique d'une grande energie électro-chimique'. This was the nitric acid battery that was to make Grove's

**Sir William Robert Grove** (1811–1896), by Maull & Polyblank, 1850s

initial reputation as a natural philosopher. Back in England during the summer of 1839 he gave an account of the new battery at the annual gathering of the British Association for the Advancement of Science in Birmingham. His performance came to the attention of Michael Faraday who invited the young philosopher to demonstrate his discovery at one of the Royal Institution's prestigious Friday evening discourses on 13 March 1840.

Grove's discourse at the Royal Institution was widely reported and the power of his battery earned him widespread recognition. By the end of 1840 he had been elected a fellow of the Royal Society. The list of his proposers, which included such names as William Thomas Brande, William Snow Harris, and Charles Wheatstone, indicates that he was by now well established among the higher echelons of London's natural philosophical community. Throughout 1840 Grove was making every effort to secure an institutional base for his work. Such a base was essential since as a struggling young barrister he lacked the necessary resources to finance his experimental interests. The fact that many of his early contributions to the *Philosophical Magazine* were dated from Swansea suggests that he was having difficulty in even finding space for his experimental work in the metropolis. His efforts attracted the attention of John Peter Gassiot, a fellow electrician who, as one of the managers of the London Institution, was on the committee appointed to establish that institution's first permanent professorial post. Early in 1841

Grove took up the position of professor of experimental philosophy at the London Institution.

The London Institution was in several respects a highly appropriate forum for Grove, having been founded in 1805 by a group of prominent City men in an explicit effort to bring together the natural philosopher and the man of commerce. Grove's own inaugural lecture at the institution, 'On the progress of physical science since the opening of the London Institution', delivered on 19 January 1842, emphasized exactly these themes of the relationships between natural philosophy and commercial, industrial expansion and progress. The lecture also contained the first hint of the doctrine which was to seal Grove's philosophical reputation, the correlation of physical forces. In 1842 Grove also announced his invention of the gas battery (the origin of the modern fuel cell). He enthusiastically described this new instrument as a beautiful instance of the correlation of natural forces. Indeed much of his experimental work during his tenure at the London Institution, including the research described in his 1846 Bakerian lecture before the Royal Society 'On certain phenomena of voltaic ignition and the decomposition of water into its constituent gases by heat', can be understood as instantiations of the new doctrine of correlation.

Despite his rising reputation as an experimentalist and his position at the London Institution, Grove's relationship with the Royal Society during the early 1840s was clearly somewhat fraught. In an angry letter to Faraday he complained of the difficulties of getting his work published in the prestigious *Philosophical Transactions* unless he first 'made interest' with some influential fellow. In an anonymous contribution to *Blackwood's Magazine* on 'Physical science in England' he lambasted both the Royal Society and the increasingly influential specialist scientific societies for their nepotism and corruption, calling for full-scale reform of England's scientific institutions.

In 1844 Grove was appointed a vice-president of the Royal Institution. In 1846 he resigned his position as professor at the London Institution, citing the increasing financial difficulties of bringing up a growing young family on a meagre salary and his consequent increasing legal professional commitments. Grove's resignation coincided with both his election to the council of the Royal Society and the publication of his influential essay *On the Correlation of Physical Forces*, based on his lectures at the London Institution during his tenure there. The essay went through six expanding editions, the last being in 1874.

In this essay, regarded by many as being a precursor to the theory of the conservation of energy, Grove argued that all physical forces such as electricity, heat, light, magnetism, and so forth, should be regarded as being correlated, or mutually inter-related. Any one of these forces could be used to produce any of the others such that no particular force could be said to be the particular cause of another. Under particular circumstances any one of them might be the cause and any of the others the effect. In many ways, the essay was an argument against traditional notions of causality. Grove advanced a large number of experimental examples from the various branches of the physical sciences to substantiate his claims. He suggested that the main task of the natural philosopher was to demonstrate how this principle of correlation operated universally.

Grove's appointment to the Royal Society's council coincided with the culmination of long-standing efforts to reform the society's charter. A charter committee had been established to examine such a possibility and Grove was soon appointed as one of its members. For Grove and his fellow campaigners, particularly Leonard Horner and Edward Sabine, the crucial reform required was to limit the number of fellows elected annually to the society and to alter the mode of election such that the council, rather than the fellowship as a whole, had the power of nomination. After a long and often acrimonious campaign the Royal Society's statutes were revised in 1847 to limit the number of fellows elected annually to a list of fifteen to be recommended to the fellowship as a whole by the council. Shortly afterwards the marquess of Northampton, then the Royal Society's president, and Peter Mark Roget, the senior secretary, both of whom had vigorously opposed the reforms, announced their resignations. The reforms gave Grove and his fellow reformers, who now dominated the society's council, control over the fellowship's future constitution and its direction as a whole. In celebration they founded a new dining club, the Philosophical Club, composed of forty-seven selected members of the society.

The Philosophical Club's membership was instrumental in appointing the earl of Rosse as the next president of the Royal Society, though they failed in their efforts to have Grove himself elected as secretary to replace Roget. For the next decade they and Grove played a key role in campaigning for greater state support for science and particularly for the housing of all the specialist scientific bodies under the same roof as the Royal Society at Burlington House. In this way Grove had a major role to play in the increasing institutionalization and professionalization of British science during the nineteenth century.

Following his resignation from the professorship at the London Institution, Grove's experimental output decreased markedly. He was awarded the Royal Society's royal medal in 1847 for his work on the gas battery and worked during the 1850s on electrical conduction through vacuum. He delivered a second Bakerian lecture before the Royal Society in 1852 on 'The electro-chemical polarity of gases'. He no longer had the laboratory facilities to sustain his experimental work and was in any case increasingly preoccupied by his legal work. He had become a QC on the south Wales and Chester circuits in 1853. In 1855 Grove briefly considered applying for the recently vacated chair of chemistry at Oxford, which would have provided him with an opportunity to resume his natural philosophical pursuits, but he was ultimately unwilling to face a contested election.

In 1866 Grove was appointed president of the British

Association for the Advancement of Science for its annual meeting, held that year at Nottingham. His presidential address at that gathering again took up the theme of correlation. He was the first president of the British Association publicly to announce his support for Charles Darwin's theory of evolution by natural selection. In 1872 he gave evidence before the royal commission on scientific instruction and the advancement of science (the Devonshire commission).

Grove was appointed a judge to the court of common pleas in 1871 and knighted in 1872. In 1880 he was appointed to the queen's bench. Following his retirement from his judgeship in 1887 he became a member of the privy council. He died at his home, 115 Harley Street, London, on 1 August 1896 after a long illness and was buried at Highgate cemetery. IWAN RHYS MORUS

**Sources** M. L. Cooper and V. M. D. Hall, 'William Robert Grove and the London Institution, 1841–1845', *Annals of Science*, 39 (1982), 229–54 • I. R. Morus, 'Correlation and control: William Robert Grove and the construction of a new philosophy of scientific reform', *Studies in the History and Philosophy of Science*, 22 (1991), 589–621 • E. Edwards, *Portraits of men of eminence in literature, science and the arts, with biographical memoirs*, ed. L. Reeve and E. Walford, 6 vols. (1863–7) • election certificate, RS • *DNB* • d. cert.

**Archives** Royal Institution of Great Britain, London, corresp. and papers

**Likenesses** Bosley, lithograph, pubd 1849 (after daguerreotype by Claudet), BM • Shappen, group portrait, lithograph, pubd 1850 (after daguerreotypes by Mayall), BM • Maull & Polyblank, photograph, 1850–59, NPG [*see illus.*] • group portrait, *c.*1860 (*Faraday refusing the presidency of the Royal Society*), RS • J. Durham, marble bust, *c.*1876, Royal Institution of Great Britain, London • Lock & Whitfield, woodburytype, 1877, NPG; repro. in T. Cooper, *Men of mark: a gallery of contemporary portraits*, 2 (1877) • Bassano, photograph, NPG • H. Donald-Smith, oils (posthumous), NPG • London Stereoscopic Co., carte-de-visite, NPG • Spy [L. Ward], caricature, watercolour study, NPG; repro. in *VF* (8 Oct 1887) • photograph, repro. in *Portraits of men of eminence*, 3 (1865)

**Wealth at death** £216,734 11s. 4d.: probate, 17 Nov 1896, *CGPLA Eng. & Wales*

**Grover, Henry Montague** (1791–1866), writer, born at Watford, Hertfordshire, was the eldest son of Harry Grover, solicitor, of Hemel Hempstead, and Sybilla, daughter of George Phillip Ehret. He was educated at the local school and at St Albans grammar school. By 1816 he had established himself in practice as a solicitor in Bedford Row, London. He retired from business in 1824, and proceeded to Peterhouse, Cambridge, where he graduated LLB in 1830. He was ordained deacon in 1828, and presented in 1833 to the rectory of Hitcham, Buckinghamshire.

Grover wrote poetical works including *Anne Boleyn, a Tragedy* (1826) and *Socrates, a Dramatic Poem* (1828). His theological works included *The History of the Resurrection Authenticated* (1841), *Analogy and Prophecy, Keys of the Church* (1846), and *A Catechism for Sophs*. His interest in astronomy was evidenced in *Soundings of antiquity: a new method of applying the astronomical evidences to the events of history* (1862), and he also wrote a political pamphlet entitled *Corn and Cattle Against Cotton and Calico* (n.d.). Because of ill health Grover lived a secluded life; he died at the rectory, Hitcham, on 20 August 1866, leaving at least one son, John William *Grover. GORDON GOODWIN, *rev.* MARI G. ELLIS

**Sources** Venn, *Alum. Cant.* • Crockford (1865) • *Clergy List* (1847) • *GM*, 4th ser., 2 (1866), 553

**Wealth at death** under £2000: probate, 19 Sept 1866, *CGPLA Eng. & Wales*

**Grover, John William** (1836–1892), civil engineer, was born on 20 April 1836, the only son of the Revd Henry Montague *Grover (1791–1866) of Boveney Court, Burnham, Buckinghamshire, and rector of Hitcham, Buckinghamshire. He was educated at Marlborough College and in Germany, and then became a pupil of Sir Charles Fox, at that time partner in Fox Henderson, a leading ironwork contractor; at the close of his pupillage he worked for John Fowler, carrying out preliminary surveys for the Great Northern Railway in Portugal. He was next appointed a draughtsman in the office of works of the government Department of Science and Art, and soon became head of the engineering and constructive branch. Among the works he superintended were the north and south courts of the South Kensington Museum, and the conservatory of the Royal Horticultural Society. He also designed the domes for the 1862 Exhibition building.

In January 1862 Grover set up in business as a consulting engineer in Westminster, and during the next eleven years he practised largely as a railway engineer, working on lines in England and Wales, and surveying in continental Europe and Mexico. He designed several outstanding structures at this time, including an iron seaside pier at Clevedon, Somersetshire with R. J. Ward, and the Kingsland Bridge, a 200 ft iron structure over the Severn. Such were his reputation and expertise that he can be regarded as one of the first consulting structural engineers. This is perhaps best exhibited in his assistance to Major-General Henry Y. D. Scott in the design of the Royal Albert Hall. At this time he wrote several books illustrating typical railway structures, based on his own work and that of I. K. Brunel and R. J. Ward.

In 1873 Grover visited Venezuela to make surveys for the mountain railway line from La Guaira to Caracas, and he also made a hydrographical survey of the coast near La Guaira for the proposed harbour works. On his return to England he gave up railway work and turned his attention to waterworks. At home he designed a scheme for Bridgend, and overseas he reported on water supply in the West Indies, Egypt, Austria, Denmark, Italy, and Switzerland. He designed and was responsible for several systems in the chalk districts round London, a subject in which he became an expert, and on which he was regularly consulted. His paper to the Institution of Civil Engineers in 1887, entitled 'Chalk water springs in the London basin' (*Proc. Inst. Civil Engineers*, 90.1), was based on his experience with the supply to Newbury, Wokingham, Leatherhead, and Rickmansworth.

Of the patents taken out by Grover the most important was that for his so-called 'spring washer', used to prevent the slackening of permanent-way fish bolts on railway lines; these washers were extensively used in all parts of the world.

Grover was elected a member of the Institution of Civil Engineers in 1867 and contributed papers and to discussions. He was also a fellow of the Society of Antiquaries and a vice-president of the British Archaeological Association. In connection with his antiquarian pursuits he was instrumental in the recovery and restoration of the Clapham marbles in St Paul's Church, Clapham. He died at his home, Chase Lodge, 27 North Side, Clapham Common on 23 August 1892.

T. H. BEARE, *rev.* MIKE CHRIMES

**Sources** *PICE*, 112 (1892–3), 347–9 • *The Times* (31 Aug 1892) • *The Engineer* (2 Sept 1892), 204 • *Engineering* (2 Sept 1892)
**Archives** PRO, RAIL/Manchester and Milford railway • PRO, PRAIL/SER, Westerham Valley branch • V&A
**Wealth at death** £40,955 13*s*. 2*d*.: probate, 10 Sept 1892, *CGPLA Eng. & Wales*

**Groves, Anthony Norris** (1795–1853), missionary and a founder of the (Plymouth) Brethren, was born at Newton, Hampshire, on 1 February 1795. His staunchly Anglican parents had lost their savings in speculations, but they were able to send him to a school at Lymington, and then to Dr Ray at Fulham, Middlesex. Groves next studied chemistry in London under Savory and Moore; he also availed himself of the offer of his uncle, James Thompson, a well-known dentist practising in Hanover Square, to study dentistry, and at the same time he acquired a knowledge of surgery in the London hospitals. Groves became so skilful a dentist that by the age of eighteen he was able to support himself, and he took up residence at Plymouth in 1814, where he also devoted himself to many scientific pursuits. He was a leading member of the Athenaeum, and early on became a friend and patron of John Kitto of Plymouth. In 1816 he married his cousin, Mary Bethia Thompson (*d.* 1831), and in 1818 moved from Plymouth to Exeter.

Groves had for some time been deeply impressed with a sense of his religious duties, and in 1825 he was instrumental in the conversion to Christianity of Michael Solomon Alexander, later bishop of Jerusalem. While studying at Trinity College, Dublin, with the intention of seeking ordination in the Church of England, in 1828 Groves associated with John Nelson Darby and other early founders of the (Plymouth) Brethren, and stated his views respecting Christians meeting together in brotherhood with no other tenets than faith in Christ. Already in 1825 he had taken charge of a small independent congregation at Poltimore, near Exeter, and he was influenced by members of the Society of Friends. While preparing for ordination he discovered that his objection to article 37 of the Church of England, which declared war lawful for Christians, barred his way. He soon concluded, however, that ordination was not required by scripture in order to preach the gospel.

By 1829 Groves had saved a considerable sum of money from the exercise of his profession; his wife during the same period had inherited £10,000 on the death of her father, and they therefore determined to devote themselves and their wealth to missionary work. Although he had corresponded with the (Anglican) Church Missionary Society about a connection, he now found himself unwilling to accept their regulations, which allowed only ordained missionaries to celebrate communion. In a decisive break with the Church of England and existing missionary organizations, he decided to become a missionary unconnected with any missionary society.

On 12 June 1829 Groves, accompanied by his wife and family, John Kitto, and others, sailed for St Petersburg. He then travelled overland, and on 6 December entered Baghdad, where he took up residence as a teacher of Christianity. Working with Karl Gottlieb Pfander, the pietist missionary scholar, he helped the poor with his surgical knowledge, established an Arabic school, and made attempts at the conversion of the Jewish residents. In 1831, his second year in Baghdad, the plague appeared; half of the population died within two months, including Mary Groves, who died on 14 May, and their baby daughter. In June, Baghdad was besieged by the pasha of Mosul, and Groves, already ill with typhus fever, was now in danger from the soldiers of losing his life. In April 1833 he left Baghdad for Bombay and western India, and visited the major missionary stations. During a spell at Tinnevelly, in the far south of India, he became embroiled in a controversy over church order between the Revd Charles T. E. Rhenius and the Church Missionary Society that led eventually to a schism in the Indian church.

Groves returned to England in December 1834, and on 25 April 1835 at Malvern he married Harriet Baynes, third daughter of General Edward Baynes of Sidmouth. In 1836 he sailed to India, to spend a year in Madras, practising his profession as a dentist. In 1837 he moved inland from Madras to Chittoor, where he devoted himself to building up a self-supporting mission free of the bureaucratic shackles of the established missionary societies. Amid much criticism he continued his support for Rhenius and encouraged an independent mission established in Tinnevelly by an Indian Christian, J. C. Aroolappen. Groves visited England in 1848, and in the following year returned to India for the last time. By 1852 his health had failed, and he finally came home, landing at Southampton on 25 September. Groves's sons, Henry and Edward, continued in India, and ran a sugar factory at Seringapatam, near Mysore. Groves himself died at 21 Paul Street, Bristol, the residence of his brother-in-law George Müller, on 20 May 1853, and was buried in Arnos Vale cemetery. His second wife survived him.

An engaging conversationalist of unfailing courtesy, Groves met with controversy throughout his life as a result of his conviction that Christians should worship together irrespective of sectarian distinctions. An exchange of letters in 1834, when he was in India, led to a parting of ways with J. N. Darby and his followers, the Exclusive Brethren, who withdrew from communion with all other denominations. Groves became a respected leader of the less exclusive Open Brethren. His mission work was sustained not by a regular salary from a missionary society but by irregular support from friends, a practice later emulated on a larger scale by missionaries in China and Africa as well as India.

G. C. BOASE, *rev.* JEFFREY COX

**Sources** [H. Groves], *Memoir of the late Anthony Norris Groves … by his widow* (1856) • F. R. Coad, *A history of the Brethren movement* (1968) • F. A. Tatford, *A. N. Groves, the father of faith missions* (1979) • S. Neill, *A history of Christianity in India, 1707–1858* (1985) • G. H. Lang, *Anthony Norris Groves, saint and pioneer* (1939) • T. Stunt, *From awakening to secession: radical evangelicals in Switzerland and Britain, 1815–1835* (2000)

**Groves, Sir Charles Barnard** (1915–1992), conductor, was born on 10 March 1915 at 52 Park Hall Road, London, the only child of Frederick Groves and his wife, Annie, *née* Whitehead. His father, who had been invalided out of the trenches during the First World War, died when Groves was only six. His mother died four years later, and Groves was made a ward of court. His musical education began when he was sent to St Paul's Cathedral choir school as a chorister. Later he attended Sutton Valence School in Kent. He showed exceptional promise and entered the Royal College of Music (of which he was to become a fellow), where he studied piano and organ. In 1937, at the age of twenty-two, he accompanied the choral rehearsals for Toscanini's broadcast performance of Brahms's Requiem, an achievement which led to his appointment as chorus master of the BBC opera unit. He then graduated via the BBC Theatre Orchestra and the BBC Revue Orchestra to the conductorship of the Manchester-based BBC Northern (later Philharmonic) Orchestra, a post he held from 1944 until 1951. During this period, because he was in charge of a broadcasting orchestra, he began to acquire an exceptionally large repertory. It was in Manchester, in 1948, that he met and married a BBC colleague, Hilary Barchard. There were three children, Sally, Mary and Jonathan, the first and last of whom were to pursue careers in music.

Success with the BBC Northern Orchestra brought Groves an invitation from Bournemouth corporation to become their director of music and conductor of the municipal orchestra. He made the move in 1951, and the orchestra was renamed the Bournemouth Symphony Orchestra in 1954. During nearly ten years he greatly enhanced the standards and standing of the orchestra, and he played a large part in saving the orchestra from disbandment following the corporation's withdrawal of its grant. He moved in 1961 to Cardiff, where he took up the post of resident music director of the Welsh National Opera. Once again he contributed to the strong development of a company with high ideals and ever-expanding achievement. His own versatility was apparent in fine performances of *Figaro*, *William Tell*, and *Lohengrin*.

Groves was now formidably well equipped, and it was not surprising that he was engaged by the Royal Liverpool Philharmonic Orchestra, whose music director and resident conductor he was from 1963 to 1977. This period was the apex of his career. He made his home in Liverpool and

Sir Charles Barnard Groves (1915–1992), by unknown photographer

committed himself wholeheartedly to the city's orchestra. It was a time when funding—never lavish—was at least adequate. As a consequence he was able to undertake grandiose projects—a complete Mahler cycle, Messiaen's *Turangalîla-symphonie*, and Berlioz's Te Deum (complete with twelve harps) at the opening of Liverpool's Metropolitan Cathedral. He was a generous champion of living British composers, performing works by more than twenty of them, and he found space for some of the international figures, including Lutosławski, Henze, and Berio. Among a number of his innovations was a series of seminars for young conductors in which Andrew Davis, Mark Elder, and John Eliot Gardiner took part. On one such occasion Groves noted the presence in his orchestra, as an extra percussion player, of a young teenager named Simon Rattle. When he left Liverpool in 1977 he bequeathed to his successor an orchestra of character and quality; it had some important recordings—Delius, Elgar, and Walton in particular—to its credit. But the invitation, from Lord Harewood, to join the English National Opera as music director was one he should perhaps have declined: he was over sixty, and he found the stress of combining administration with conducting too much for him. He resigned after two seasons.

Groves was in constant demand on the concert platform. In 1975 he had toured Japan with Pierre Boulez and the BBC Symphony Orchestra and, as a result of this, he was regularly invited to Tokyo, to which city he introduced Delius's *A Mass of Life*, one of his very finest interpretations. He toured extensively in Australasia and Latin America as well as Europe, invariably presenting British music. At home, in 1984, he joined the English Sinfonia as president and artistic adviser, later also becoming principal conductor of the Guildford Philharmonic (1987) and music director of the Leeds Philharmonic Society (1988).

A respected figure in the music profession, Groves was generous with his time and experience where honorary commitments were concerned. He was president of the Incorporated Society of Musicians in 1972 and again in 1982, president of the National Federation of Music Societies from 1972 to 1980, and president of the National Youth Orchestra from 1977 to 1992, and was elected an honorary member of the Royal Philharmonic Society in 1990. He was honoured by the conservatoires: as companion of the Royal Northern College of Music (whose council he chaired from 1973 to 1990), as fellow of the Royal College of Music, Guildhall School of Music and Drama, Trinity College of Music, and London College of Music, and as an honorary member of the Royal Academy of Music. Passionately concerned with the welfare of musicians, he was prominent on the picket line outside Broadcasting House during the musicians' strike against the BBC in 1980. When it was over he gallantly agreed to 'mind' the BBC Scottish Symphony Orchestra until permanent arrangements could be agreed. Appointed OBE in 1958 and CBE in 1968, he was knighted in 1973. He received doctorates from Liverpool, Salford, and Surrey universities, as well as from the Open University, and he was a fellow of the polytechnics of Liverpool and Manchester. He was made a freeman of the City of London in 1976.

Despite his status, his experience, and the respect which he commanded, despite also his firm Christian faith, Groves remained, privately, a man who constantly questioned his own standards. Fastidious in his preparation of even the most undemanding of concerts and a superb accompanist, he often suffered from a fear that he might let his colleagues down. It was a needless fear, but a real one, and there were indeed times when overwork, or nervousness, or some absence of the fire of conviction resulted in lacklustre performances. But when he was completely confident his work was compelling and authoritative. In the mould of Wood or Boult, rather than Beecham or Barbirolli, he shared with the first two a profound sense of duty towards British, and particularly living British, composers. Overseas he performed music by Elgar, Vaughan Williams, Holst, Delius, Britten, Walton, Tippett, Goehr, and Musgrave. His premières included works by Lennox Berkeley, David Blake, Gordon Crosse, Jonathan Harvey, Robin Holloway, Daniel Jones, John McCabe, Edmund Rubbra, Edwin Roxburgh, Giles Swayne, Priaulx Rainier, and Hugh Wood. He recorded music by Arnold, Butterworth, Bliss, Bridge, Maxwell Davies, Hoddinott, Mathias, Grace Williams, and Williamson, among others. He was an admirable ambassador for British music.

In person Groves was a reassuring figure: his straight back, firm bearded chin, and stocky build inspired confidence, despite his own self-doubts. His marriage was exceptionally happy and his Anglican faith was a constant source of strength. He was working when he suffered a heart attack early in 1992, and he died in London on 20 June 1992. There is a memorial stone to his memory in the crypt of St Paul's Cathedral. ROBERT PONSONBY

**Sources** *New Grove* · *The Independent* (22 June 1992) · *The Times* (22 June 1992) · private information (2004) · personal knowledge (2004)

**Archives** NL Wales, corresp. and papers | SOUND BL NSA, performance recordings

**Likenesses** photograph, repro. in *The Times* · photograph, repro. in *The Independent* · photograph, News International Syndication, London [*see illus.*]

**Wealth at death** £284,139: probate, 7 Sept 1992, *CGPLA Eng. & Wales*

**Groves, John Thomas** (*c*.1761–1811), architect, was the son of John Groves or Grove, master builder, to whom he was apprenticed in 1775. Although referred to in 1794 as a builder, he had exhibited views of Westminster at the Royal Academy in 1778 and 1780, before spending a period in Italy; on returning to Westminster, he exhibited in 1791 a view of the Sybil's Temple, Tivoli. In August 1793 he was one of twelve architects nominated in an abortive project for obtaining designs for new houses of parliament. He was elected to the Florentine Academy and to the Society of Antiquaries in 1794, having been appointed that June to the clerkship of the office of works for St James's, Westminster, and Whitehall after the resignation of John Soane, who was said to have been 'the means of obtaining it' for him (Farington, *Diary*, 1.254).

None the less, Groves proved to be a creature of Soane's rival James Wyatt, surveyor-general of the king's works from 1796, whose controversial election to the Society of Antiquaries Groves actively supported in 1797. As clerk of works he carried out minor works on official buildings, including 10 Downing Street. He proved one of the worst officers of the slothful Wyatt regime, executing works without proper authority, failing to present accounts on time, seriously exceeding estimates, and malingering. Fraudulent as well as inefficient, he co-operated with contractors to enable them to pay allowances to officials. Malicious towards a difficult colleague, towards a subordinate who crossed him he was positively malevolent. As surveyor to the commissioners for the improvement of Westminster from 1807, Groves superintended Wyatt's mediocre Gothic designs for refronting the House of Lords. He also at that time obtained the surveyorship to the General Post Office and to the Ordnance office, in succession to Wyatt. He served as master of the Tylers' and Bricklayers' Company in 1810–11.

Groves also conducted a private practice, designing in the Wyatt manner. Broomfield Lodge, Clapham Common (1797), was illustrated in the first volume of George Richardson's *New Vitruvius Britannicus*, published in 1810. Groves rebuilt Tewin Water, Hertfordshire (*c*.1798; much altered), for Henry Cowper, clerk of the House of Lords. A house at Morden, Surrey (*c*.1800; dem.), and the stuccoed bathhouse at Tunbridge Wells are also by Groves. In addition he repaired the bishop's palace at Ely (1795), worked with James Wyatt on the west front of the cathedral (1800–02), designed a marble pulpit there in the Norman style, and drew out a west tower for Wyatt's Gothic East Grinstead church (1811; executed by his friends H. W. Inwood and W. Inwood after his death). In 1807 he designed a monument to Lord Nelson on Portsdown Hill, Hampshire, paid for by naval subscriptions. A memorial obelisk to the second Lord Clancarty, at Garbally, Ireland, is described by Howard Colvin as 'his most original work' (Colvin, *Archs.*, 433). After recovering from one paralytic stroke, he suffered a second as he descended the steps of the Treasury, and died the following day, 24 August 1811, in his official house in Great Scotland Yard. He left a widow, Jane Sarah, whom he probably married in 1799, and a young son and three young daughters. In addition to his personal wealth he also left leasehold houses in College Street, Westminster, and a freehold estate at Great Marlow, Buckinghamshire. M. H. PORT

**Sources** Colvin, *Archs.* • J. M. Crook and M. H. Port, eds., *The history of the king's works*, 6 (1973) • *GM*, 1st ser., 81/2 (1811), 287, 494 • will, PRO, PROB. 10/4008 • Farington, *Diary*, 1.254; 3.845, 864, 935–6; 8.2938, 3061 • Graves, *RA exhibitors* • J. Ingamells, *British and Irish travellers in Italy, 1701–1800* (1997), 436

**Likenesses** F. Wheatley, oils, exh. RA 1790

**Wealth at death** under £3500—personalty: will, PRO, PROB 10/4008

**Grozer, Joseph** (*c.*1755–1798), mezzotint engraver, is stated to have been born about 1755, but nothing is known of his parentage, origins or training. He was an able engraver in mezzotint, and executed many plates after Sir Joshua Reynolds, George Romney, and others. Among his earliest known engravings were *The Young Shepherdess* (1784) and *The Theory of Design* (1785), both after Reynolds. Grozer published some of his own prints from his residence at 8 Castle Street, Leicester Square. His later mezzotint engravings include *Master Braddyll, Frederick, Viscount Duncannon, Henrietta, Viscountess Duncannon, Hon. Frances Harris (with a Dog)*, and *Lord Loughborough*, after Reynolds; *James, Earl of Cardigan* and *Abraham Newland*, after Romney; *Morning, or, The Benevolent Sportsman* and *Evening, or, The Sportsman's Return*, after George Morland; *The Duke and Duchess of York*, after Henry Singleton; and *Euhun Sang Lum Akao*, a Chinese, after H. Danloux. Grozer worked occasionally in stipple, among these engravings being *The Age of Innocence* and *Sophia, Lady St Asaph*, after Reynolds, and *Sergeant Daniel McLeod*, after W. R. Bigg.

Grozer had earlier lived with Sarah Cooper, but they had parted company on account of her violence towards him. At the time of writing his will, on 26 April 1798, he was living with a spinster, Jane Moore, who had a son, Frederick. Their intention to marry was prevented by Grozer's death shortly afterwards. Grozer's will, proved on 15 May 1798, instructed his executors, Paul Colnaghi, printseller of Pall Mall, and Bennett, a local apothecary, to continue the business if they considered it worth while; however, they chose to close it down and dispose of his plates. ANITA MCCONNELL

**Sources** J. C. Smith, *British mezzotinto portraits*, 4 vols. in 5 (1878–84) • T. Dodd, 'Memoirs of English engravers', BL, Add. MS 33401 • E. Hamilton, *Catalogue raisonné of the engraved works of Sir Joshua Reynolds* (1874)

**Likenesses** group portrait, line engraving, pubd 1798 (after P. Sanby), BM

**Grub, George** (1812–1892), ecclesiastical historian, born at Old Aberdeen on 4 April 1812, was the only child of George Grub, convenor of the trades at Old Aberdeen, and his wife, Christian Volum. He entered King's College, Aberdeen, at the age of thirteen and a half, and then joined the law office of Alexander Allan, under whom he served his apprenticeship. After qualifying in 1836, he was in 1841 appointed librarian to the Aberdeen Society of Advocates, a post he held until his death. In 1843 he became lecturer on Scottish law in Marischal College, Aberdeen, and after the union of King's and Marischal colleges (1860) he substituted for Professor Patrick Davidson, who never lectured. On Davidson's death in 1881, he became professor of law in the university. He was a careful rather than a brilliant teacher, but deeply loved and respected by his students. In 1856 he graduated AM at Aberdeen, and in 1864 he received the degree of LLD from his university. He resigned his chair in 1891.

By birth an inheritor of the Scottish non-juring tradition, Grub was himself an accomplished theologian; he followed the course of the Oxford Movement with sympathetic interest and in the congregation to which he belonged (St John's Episcopal Church, Aberdeen) he supported the incumbent, Patrick Cheyne, throughout a prosecution occasioned by the latter's teaching of the doctrine of the real presence, which led to the indictment of the bishop of Brechin, Alexander Penrose Forbes, and the intervention of Pusey and Keble in the bishop's defence. It took some time to heal the sores occasioned by the controversy.

At Aberdeen in the early 1830s, Grub was one of a group of young episcopalian lawyers dedicated to history and antiquities—John Hill Burton (1809–1881), Joseph Robertson (1810–1866), and John Stuart (1813–1877). With them he was a co-founder in 1839 of the Spalding Club, for which he edited, in conjunction with Joseph Robertson, Gordon's *History of Scots Affairs* (1840–42). His edition of Thomas Innes's *History of Scotland, Civil and Ecclesiastical* (1853) included a life of Innes. The work by which he is best known, *An ecclesiastical history of Scotland from the introduction of Christianity to the present time* (4 vols., 1861) established him as the foremost church historian in Scotland. Clear and unaffected in style, the work is learned and exact, but without the liveliness and wit that characterized the author as a conversationalist. As a historian he was scrupulously fair, although he did not conceal his enthusiastic toryism and profound attachment to the episcopal church. He also contributed articles on Scottish church history and antiquities to Chambers's *Encyclopaedia* and to the Aberdeen Philosophical Society.

Grub's legal practice was never extensive, and until the last ten years of his life his salary was modest, though sufficient for his wants. In spite of his preoccupation with religion and study, he enjoyed society, and his wit and store of anecdote made him a delightful companion. In appearance, he was of about middle height; he was rendered lame in early life by the ossification of his right knee. He was married to Ann Lyall, who died many years before him, leaving him with a daughter and two sons, George and Charles, both of whom became clergymen. Grub died at his home, 153 Crown Street, Aberdeen on 23 September 1892, and was buried in the cathedral churchyard at Old Aberdeen.

James Cooper, *rev.* G. Martin Murphy

**Sources** W. Walker, *Three churchmen* (1893), 193–276 • P. J. A. [P. J. Anderson], ed., *Aurora borealis academica: Aberdeen University appreciations, 1860–1889* (1899), 205–11 • *CCI* (1892)
**Archives** University of Dundee, archives, corresp. with Alexander Forbes
**Likenesses** G. Reid, oils, 1892, U. Aberdeen, Marischal College • G. Reid, oils, Advocates Hall, Aberdeen
**Wealth at death** £7226 12*s.* 10*d.*: confirmation, 30 Nov 1892, *CCI*

**Grubb, Edward** (1854–1939), pacifist and social reformer, was born on 19 October 1854 at Sudbury, Suffolk, the fourth of five children of Jonathan Grubb (1808–1894), banker and Quaker minister, and his second wife, Elizabeth Burlingham (1813–1893). The father was of Irish descent but lived his adult life in England.

Grubb was educated at home until 1865, when he entered Sidcot School in Somerset, the first of three Quaker institutions he attended. After three years at Bootham School in York, he determined to follow a teaching career and enrolled at Flounders Institute, Ackworth, the training ground for Quaker teachers. Grubb's conventional Quaker education gave him sufficient confidence to undertake studies in philosophy and political economy at University College, London, from where he graduated BA in 1876 and MA in 1880, but the biblically based evangelicalism of his parents' generation provided an inadequate shield to protect his faith from the influences of the materialistic philosophers he encountered in his studies. By the time he had completed his formal education Grubb had drifted into a slough of spiritual despond. Unable to find solace within the confines of evangelical Quakerism, he recalled feeling 'utterly alone,' fearing a final slide into 'bleak Agnosticism' (Grubb, 301).

During the following decade, however, Grubb drew comfort from his marriage, in 1877, to Emma Maria Horsnaill (1857–1939), joy from their growing family (the first of five surviving children was born in 1878), and stability from secure tenure at Quaker schools in York and Scarborough. Gradually recovering his faith, partly through intensive reading of T. H. Green and other neo-Hegelian philosophers and partly through the inspiration of the American Quaker poet John Greenleaf Whittier, Grubb subsequently joined other liberal Friends in their efforts to make Quakerism a viable, relevant faith. Central to the work of these makers of the 'Quaker renaissance' was restoration of the egalitarian principle of the inner light, abandoned by evangelical Friends, to its central position in Quaker belief and practice. Recorded as a minister by Scarborough meeting in 1894, Grubb spread his vision of Quakerism through both his ministry and his published work. In a series of articles and books, including *Social Aspects of the Quaker Faith* (1899) and *Authority and the Light Within* (1908), Grubb sought to make his fellow Quakers aware of modern religious and scientific ideas while pioneering a new social outlook which eschewed traditional philanthropy for a systematic, progressive approach to the ills of industrial society.

In 1901 Grubb left teaching and moved to the London area, becoming proprietor–editor of the *British Friend*, a Quaker monthly which served as a forum for disseminating his progressive views. In that same year Grubb was appointed secretary to the Howard Association for Prison Reform. In this capacity he undertook a three-month fact-finding tour of American prisons, conducting a series of interviews with people who ranged from Theodore Roosevelt in the White House to Jane Addams at Hull House and Booker T. Washington at Tuskegee Institute. Grubb resigned from his position with the Howard Association in 1905 but continued to edit the *British Friend* until its demise in 1913.

Until the outbreak of the Second South African War, Grubb's acceptance of Friends' traditional peace testimony was *pro forma*, but when a number of prominent Quakers supported the British cause in South Africa, Grubb concluded: 'If *that* war could be condoned by so-called pacifists … *any* war could be' (Grubb, 307), and he embraced absolute, uncompromising pacifism. He also made the *British Friend* an implacable foe of the National Service League's efforts to impose compulsory military training on British youth. When, in 1909, J. St Loe Strachey, editor of *The Spectator*, published *A New Way of Life*, representing compulsory service as the means for halting creeping moral degeneracy, Grubb responded with *The True Way of Life*, attacking popular militarism as a throwback to barbarism and gaining considerable attention within the peace movement. Grubb was also instrumental in securing Quaker approval of a definitive declaration of pacifism as 'an organic outgrowth of our Faith' (*Minutes and Proceedings of the Yearly Meeting of Friends*, 1912, 114).

The outbreak of the First World War was a shattering blow to Grubb, but he recovered by throwing himself into the anti-war movement, playing a key role in the formation of the Fellowship of Reconciliation and, from July 1915, acting as treasurer of the No-Conscription Fellowship (NCF), Britain's largest anti-war, anti-conscription organization. Within the NCF, Grubb was chief fund-raiser, drawing upon the resources of wealthy Quakers to support the fellowship's struggle. In May 1916 Grubb was among NCF leaders, mainly socialists and agnostics, prosecuted for publishing an allegedly seditious pamphlet. His demeanour on the witness stand moved a co-defendant, Bertrand Russell, to remember Grubb as someone he admired 'very greatly' (Russell, 39). Grubb was convicted with the others, but allowed his fine to be paid so that he could continue to keep the NCF solvent.

After the war ended, Grubb became increasingly absorbed in Quaker religious thought. During the last twenty years of his life he produced a dozen books and numerous articles on Quaker theology and practice, the final legacy to his beloved Religious Society before he died at his home, 9 Sollershott, Letchworth, on 23 January 1939. He was buried on 26 January at the Friends' meeting-house in Hitchin. THOMAS C. KENNEDY

**Sources** J. Dudley, *The life of Edward Grubb, 1854–1939* (1946) • 'Dictionary of Quaker biography', RS Friends, Lond. [card index] • E. Grubb, 'Some personal experiences', *Friends' Quarterly Examiner*, 72 (1938), 296–311 • R. A. Rempel, 'Edward Grubb and the Quaker renaissance in Britain, 1880–1914', unpublished paper, 1978, RS Friends, Lond. • T. C. Kennedy, 'The ubiquitous friend: Edward Grubb and the modern British peace movement', *Peace Research*, 17/2 (May 1985), 1–10 • W. J. McGuire, 'A friend to the prisoner: Edward Grubb's American tour of 1904 and Quaker social action', PhD diss., University of Arkansas, 1992 • *Minutes and proceedings of the yearly meeting of Friends, 1912* (1912) • B. Russell, *The autobiography of Bertrand Russell*, 2 (1968) • *CGPLA Eng. & Wales* (1939)

**Archives** RS Friends, Lond., corresp. and autobiography; minutes, records of work, and documents | U. Warwick Mod. RC, papers on prison reform • University of South Carolina, Columbia, Lord Allen of Hurtwood MSS

**Likenesses** two photographs, 1901–14, RS Friends, Lond.

**Wealth at death** £8248 6*s*. 6*d*.: probate, 27 March 1939, *CGPLA Eng. & Wales*

**Grubb, Sir Howard** (1844–1931). *See under* Grubb, Thomas (1800–1878).

**Grubb, Sir Kenneth George** (1900–1980), missionary and public servant, was born on 9 September 1900 in Oxton, Nottinghamshire, the youngest in the family of three sons and one daughter of the rector of the village, Harry Percy Grubb, and his wife, Margaret Adelaide Crichton-Stuart. His father was an Irishman of evangelical leanings and his mother counted Henry Labouchere, who defended 'free thought' against W. E. Gladstone, as a great-uncle. He won a foundation scholarship to Marlborough College but towards the end of the First World War absconded to join the Royal Navy by misrepresenting his age. His failure to enter upon a university education when peace came remained for him a source of lifelong dissatisfaction.

Grubb was moved instead to a clear religious commitment at this time and enlisted with the Worldwide Evangelization Crusade to study the Indian dialects of the Amazon basin, where the crusade intended to start work. His five years of lonely exploration of the upper Amazon revealed his capacity to make contact with suspicious indigenous tribes, and to master 200 dialects—his linguistic survey being published in 1927. Then, shaking himself free of a too narrow and fractious employer, he joined the Survey Application Trust and devoted ten more years to the production of a series of surveys of the missionary situation in all of Latin America from the Rio Grande to Cape Horn—models of factual analysis allied to shrewd judgement—followed by further surveys in other parts of the world.

As the war with Hitler loomed Grubb was recruited to the group planning the proposed Ministry of Information, and subsequently appointed head of section for Latin America. In 1941 he was promoted on merit to be overseas controller of publicity, covering the whole world except the USA, a position that brought him into touch with the highest level of debate on foreign policy and war aims,

Sir Kenneth George Grubb (1900–1980), by Elliott & Fry, 1953

and made him familiar with civil service procedures and the ways of the Foreign Office. When the end of the war was in sight Archbishop William Temple and others perceived the contribution a layman of such experience could make in the ecumenical enterprise of rebuilding and renewal facing the church worldwide.

He became president of the Church Missionary Society in 1944, and for a quarter of a century guided the strategy of its operations across the world through the period of decolonization and the emergence of indigenous and independent churches in Asia and Africa. At the same time he was recruited as a participant in a new ecumenical experiment in post-war peacemaking, under the initial chairmanship of John Foster Dulles, later to be named the Commission of the Churches on International Affairs, jointly sponsored by the World Council of Churches and the International Missionary Council. For the first twenty-three years of its life Grubb chaired this commission, composed of laymen prominent in foreign affairs and churchmen of every church except the Roman Catholic, which brought a new level of professionalism to its task and a wider international representation to bear than ever before. His enigmatic and formal manner was matched by an intuitive sensitivity and a relentless practicality that gave the commission a unique style in ecclesiastical circles, and a weighty authority. Meanwhile, maintaining his business interests, he organized in 1946 the Hispanic Council and the Luzo Brazilian Council in response to the needs of Anglo-Latin American business groups in Britain. He was a distinguished member of the Royal Institute of

International Affairs, and was a founder member and first chairman of council of the Institute for Strategic Studies.

Grubb edited successive editions of the *World Christian Handbook* for twenty years, and among his own writings were *Amazon and Andes* (1930), *Parables from South America* (1932), and his autobiography, which was published in 1971 by Hodder and Stoughton under the title *Crypts of Power*. He was appointed CMG in 1942 for his services in the Ministry of Information and was advanced to KCMG in 1970 'for services to the Church of England'. He had been knighted in 1953.

Grubb married in 1926 Eileen Sylvia, daughter of Alfred Knight, assayer of metals; they had two sons. She accompanied him on one of his long journeys into the interior of Brazil, but died in childbirth in Almada, Portugal, in 1932. In 1935 he married Nancy Mary, daughter of Charles Ernest Arundel, a company secretary; they had a son and a daughter.

Grubb was a man of lonely and melancholy disposition, apparently remote except to a small circle of intimate friends to whom he revealed unexpected affection and merriment. A linguist, he was an exacting artist in the use of words, a master of English literature, a skilful committee chairman, a demanding employer, and an unwavering friend to the strangely varied circle of his closest associates. To them he also disclosed the depth of his central religious devotion, as well as the burden he bore as a lifelong sufferer from petit mal. Grubb died at Salisbury, Wiltshire, on 3 June 1980. ALAN BOOTH, *rev.*

**Sources** K. Grubb, *Crypts of power: an autobiography* (1971) • private information (1986) • personal knowledge (1986) • *The Times* (5 June 1980) • *CGPLA Eng. & Wales* (1980)
**Archives** HLRO, corresp. with Lord Davidson
**Likenesses** Elliott & Fry, photograph, 1953, NPG [*see illus.*]
**Wealth at death** £66,215: probate, 20 Oct 1980, *CGPLA Eng. & Wales*

**Grubb** [*née* Pim], **Sarah** (1746–1832), miller and benefactor, was born on 11 December 1746 at Mountrath, Queen's county, the eldest of the fifteen children of John Pim (1718–1797), a rich Dublin wool merchant, and his wife, Sarah Clibborn (1724–1812) of Moate Castle, co. Westmeath; she was related through both parents to most of the prominent Quaker families in Ireland. Educated by her mother, she grew up in Dublin and Ballitore, co. Kildare, where she formed lasting friendships with the schoolmaster Richard Shackleton and his daughter Deborah. She moved to Middlesex with her family in 1771 and settled at a house called Tanner's End, Tottenham, where she mixed in fashionable Quaker society in and around London, describing her experiences to Deborah Shackleton with characteristic openness and liveliness. The English Quakers, she noted, loved finery whereas the Irish retained the 'plain' dress but entertained lavishly. Throughout her life she kept up a wide correspondence.

On 8 April 1778 Sarah married John Grubb (1737–1784), a flour miller of Anner Mills, Clonmel, co. Tipperary, the second son of Joseph Grubb (1709–1782) and his wife, Sarah Greer (1717–1788), and thus she entered the circle of wealthy Quaker families who controlled Clonmel's milling industry in its golden age. Although some in this circle lived 'like princes of the earth' (*Journal of William Savery*, 267), the Grubbs chose to live plainly and their comfortable home, Anner Mills, for years provided hospitality to numerous travelling Quaker ministers, ranging from Catherine Phillips and William Savery, to Thomas Shillitoe and Elizabeth Fry. This extremely happy marriage ended prematurely with John Grubb's death from overwork in 1784.

Sarah chose to take her husband's place and run the mills herself, with the support of her brother Joshua, a prominent Dublin banker. She entrusted her five small daughters to Sarah Lynes (later Grubb), who came from London in 1787 and later became a leading Quaker travelling minister. Her sister Elizabeth Pim took over the Anner Mills household. Sarah Grubb found that business, and contact with the country people, raised her spirits. The mills had ten pairs of stones and three water wheels, and with David Malcomson as her first manager, followed by John Barclay Clibborn (a cousin who married her daughter Elizabeth) she was independently successful as 'Sarah Grubb, Miller and Corn Dealer' (*Directory of Clonmel*, 1787). This success was largely due to her strict integrity, and a policy of always using cash when buying in, and selling at low rates rather than giving credit.

Possessed of great clearness of mind and a powerful character, Sarah Grubb was also a person of warm human sympathy and benevolence. She did what she could to alleviate widespread local misery caused by poverty and drunkenness, and she was quick to send aid to those afflicted by the 1798 rising. She was a great encourager of the education of the young, and a supporter of Quaker building projects, helping to fund Newtown School, Waterford (established 1798), and Garryroan meeting-house, co. Tipperary (1789). Further afield she supported the fight against slavery and helped German refugees in London. The combination of success in business and social beneficence won her the nickname the Queen of the South.

Her spiritual life was characterized by thanksgiving and a desire to come close to God, and 'her countenance often strikingly indicated the near access and sweet communion she was favoured to enjoy' (*Annual Monitor*, 1834, 27). As an elder for over forty years, she strongly maintained the old Quaker testimonies, lovingly admonishing young and old alike, be it for playing music or straying into unorthodoxy.

Sarah Grubb's business acumen and philanthropic instincts resurfaced in at least two of her grandchildren, John Grubb Richardson (1813–1890) who in 1845 used Anner Mills money to build the model industrial village of Bessbrook, co. Armagh, and Lydia Goodbody (1810–1886), active in the pioneering jute industry at Clara, King's county.

Sarah Grubb considered herself 'over bulky' in appearance (Sarah Grubb to Eliza Greer, August 1785, MS, Dublin Friends' Historical Library), she enjoyed a green old age, and was described by Joseph John Gurney in 1827 as 'a veteran of the good cause, strong in her intellectual and lively in her spiritual faculties' (*Memoirs of … Gurney*, 1.350). She was lampooned by Sarah D. Greer in *Quakerism, or, The Story of my Life* (first published in London in 1851, and published in Dublin in 1852) as Sarah Mills, a clever, wilful and dominating woman; however, the attack was part of a general attempt to defame Quakerism, and is probably unrepresentative of her character. She died, leaving a fortune estimated at over £100,000, at her home, Anner Mills, on 31 October 1832, and her body was interred on 2 November in the Quaker burial-ground at Clonmel.

PETER LAMB

**Sources** Dublin Friends' Historical Library, Grubb Collection and Selina Fennell Collection, MSS • *Annual Monitor* (1834), 24–8 • O. C. Goodbody, *Guide to Irish Quaker records, 1654–1860* (1967) • R. S. Harrison, *A biographical dictionary of Irish Quakers* (1997) • W. P. Burke, *History of Clonmel* (1907) • G. Watkins-Grubb, *The Grubbs of Tipperary: studies in heredity and character* (1972) • Burke, *Gen. Ire.* (1976) • *A journal of William Savery*, ed. J. Evans (1844) • F. R. Taylor, *Life of William Savery of Philadelphia, 1750–1804* (1925), chaps. 22–3 • *Memoirs of the life of Catherine Phillips* (1797) • *Journal of Thomas Shillitoe* (1839) • *Memoirs of Joseph John Gurney*, 2 vols. (1854) • *Annual Monitor* (1887), 91–8 [obit. of Lydia Goodbody] • *Annual Monitor* (1891), 99–122 [obit. of John Grubb Richardson] • *Bessbrook, the model village, 1845–1945*, rev. enlarged edn (1995) • F. B. Pim, 'A Pim genealogy', typescript, [n.d., c.1965] • mill books, NA Ire.

**Archives** Religious Society of Friends, Dublin, corresp., MSS

**Likenesses** silhouette (in old age), Religious Society of Friends, Dublin

**Wealth at death** over £100,000; owned Anner Mills, Anner House, and lands; est. several thousand pounds p.a. income

**Grubb** [*née* Tuke], **Sarah** (1756–1790), Quaker minister and author, was born on 20 June 1756 in York, the second of the five children of William *Tuke (1732–1822), philanthropist and founder of the York Retreat, and his first wife, Elizabeth (1729–1760), daughter of John Hoyland of Woodhouse, Yorkshire. One of her brothers, Henry *Tuke (1755–1814), also became a prominent Quaker minister. Following her mother's death, her father married Esther Maud (1727–1794). Sarah and her siblings were grateful to Esther for her tenderness and care for them and for the fact that they were treated no differently from their stepmother's own children. Aged sixteen, Sarah helped Esther care for the American Quaker John Woolman during his last illness. His example of resignation and faith made a great impression on her mind and she long remembered his words to her: 'My child, thou seems very kind to me, a poor creature. The Lord will reward you for it' (*Some Account*, 3). Sarah first appeared in the ministry, after much hesitation and agonizing, in 1779 at the age of twenty-three. As she describes it, 'I ventured on my knees, and in a manner I believe scarcely intelligible, poured out a few petitions' (ibid., 13). Sarah at once embarked on local journeys in the ministry with her stepmother and other relations. In time these travels became extensive and a dominant part of her religious life.

In 1782 Sarah married Robert Grubb (1743–1797) of Clonmel, co. Tipperary, who had lived for some time in York, and they settled at the village of Foston, 10 miles away. However, almost at once Sarah left on a visit to Scotland with Mary Proud, which she found 'a painful exercising time'. On her return she settled into a domestic life which involved frequent travel, sometimes with her husband, but also with female companions. In 1786 Sarah accompanied Rebecca Jones of Philadelphia on a visit to Wales, and in the following year went to Ireland, again with Rebecca Jones.

Grubb also found time to act as clerk of the women's yearly meeting in London in both 1786 and 1787. During this period Sarah felt called to leave the security of York and her family, and in 1787 she and Robert moved to Ireland and settled near Clonmel. A year later they went with other Friends, including George and Sarah Dillwyn of America, to the Netherlands, Germany, and France. Although she had no children of her own, Sarah had decided views on education. She believed that children needed both discipline and respect and should be taught useful skills. In York in 1784 she had helped her stepmother to establish a school for girls, and when they moved to Ireland she and Robert founded Suir Island Girls' School at their home on the same principles.

In 1790 Grubb, together with her husband and the Dillwyns, again travelled in the ministry on the continent. When Sarah returned she was physically exhausted and ill but, pausing only to visit her family in York for a few days, she went straight to Dublin for the Ireland half-yearly meeting to report on her travels to Friends. On returning home still weak and unwell she stayed only two weeks before travelling to Cork to attend the quarterly meeting. Here she collapsed and, after ten days' illness, died on 8 December 1790 at the age of thirty-four. She was buried four days later. Her journal, *Some Account of the Life and Religious Labours of Sarah Grubb*, was published in 1792 along with writings on religion and education, including *Some Remarks on Christian Discipline* (1795) and *A Serious Meditation* (n.d.). A collection of her correspondence appeared in 1848. Although she experienced spiritual struggles in her youth, once she had dedicated her life to the service of God, Sarah Grubb never spared herself, while remaining modest about her efforts. 'We have done little,' she told Irish friends at the end of her life, 'but the Lord is doing much' (Bevan, 58).

GIL SKIDMORE

**Sources** *Some account of the life and religious labours of Sarah Grubb*, ed. L. Murray (1792) • J. G. Bevan, *Piety promoted … the tenth part* (1810); 3rd edn (1838) • 'Dictionary of Quaker biography', RS Friends, Lond. [card index] • W. K. Sessions and M. Sessions, *The Tukes of York in the seventeenth, eighteenth and nineteenth centuries* (1971)

**Grubb** [*née* Lynes], **Sarah** [Sally] (**1773–1842**), Quaker travelling minister, was born on 13 April 1773 at Wapping Wall, Lower Shadwell, London, the eighth of the eleven children (four of whom died in infancy) of Mason Lynes (1738?–1781) and Hannah Lynes. After education at the Quaker school in Islington Road, London, Sally (as she was known), at the age of fourteen, went to Ireland. For ten years she looked after the five children of Sarah (Pim) Grubb (1746–1832), who in her widowhood was running a successful milling business at Anner Mills, Clonmel, co. Tipperary. It was not long before Sally felt called to the vocal ministry. Her gift was acknowledged by the co. Tipperary monthly meeting in 1794, calling her 'into a path much untrodden, having to go into markets, and to declare the truth in the streets' (*Selection*, 4). There followed what, but for the forbearance of her mistress, could have been a time of strained relationships, for Sally's extended 'travels in the ministry' throughout Ireland undoubtedly conflicted with her responsibilities as an employee.

In 1797 Sally returned to London, but came back to Clonmel in 1803 on her marriage, on 8 September, to John Grubb (1766–1841), first cousin of Sarah (Pim) Grubb's husband, who, with his brother Joseph, ran a grocery business in the town. They had four children. There was considerable opposition from the extended family when Sally announced that a sense of religious duty necessitated the family moving to England. In 1818 they went to Bury St Edmunds, in 1823 to Chelmsford, in 1829 to Stoke Newington, and finally settled in 1835 in Sudbury, Suffolk. Both John (who had been acknowledged as a minister in 1796) and Sally were uneasy at the growth of Quaker evangelical theology and the philanthropic preoccupations connected with it. Eighteenth-century Friends had stressed the 'light within', the insufficiency of reason, and the dangers of 'creaturely activity'—activity, that is, undertaken without the compelling drive of the holy spirit. Whatever leanings Sally may already have had to uphold these views, they were reinforced by her meeting in Ireland in 1793 with the saintly Rhode Island Quaker Job Scott (1751–1793).

As evangelicalism increased among British Quakers in the 1820s and 1830s, Sarah (Lynes) Grubb became one of the recognized leaders of the conservatives. Her opposition was not only to out-and-out evangelicals but also to those, like Joseph John Gurney, who took a middle course. Indeed, she was first among those conservative Friends who in 1837 voiced their opposition to his visit to America. To a schoolgirl at Stoke Newington in the 1830s Sarah Grubb appeared 'like some weird prophetess, very forbidding and gaunt, who even eschewed a white lining to her Friends' bonnet' (*J. Friends Hist. Soc.* 17, 1920, 115). She was lively in manner and her sense of humour, of which there is no hint in her published letters, was fondly remembered. In mid-January 1842, feeling 'more unwell than usual' (*Selection*, 448), Sarah retired to her room, where she remained until her death on 16 March 1842; her body was interred in Sudbury Friends' burial-ground.

EDWARD H. MILLIGAN

**Sources** *A selection from the letters of the late Sarah Grubb* (1848) • *A testimony of the quarterly meeting of Munster concerning Sarah Grubb* (1843) • *Annual Monitor* (1844), 37–47 • 'Dictionary of Quaker biography', RS Friends, Lond. [card index] • 'Notes on the life of Emma Marshall', *Journal of the Friends' Historical Society*, 17 (1920), 115 • London and Middlesex Quarterly Meeting births digest, RS Friends, Lond. • digest of deaths, 1837–1961, RS Friends, Lond.
**Archives** Friends Historical Library, Dublin • RS Friends, Lond.
**Likenesses** silhouette, *c*.1830, RS Friends, Lond. • S. Lucas, oils, RS Friends, Lond.; repro. in *A monthly meeting at Earith, 1836*

**Grubb, Thomas** (1800–1878), engineer and telescope builder, was born on 4 August 1800 at Waterford, son of William Grubb, draper, of Capel Street, Dublin, and his second wife, Eleanor Fayle, both members of the Society of Friends. Thomas was the great-great-grandson of Ishmael Grubb who had emigrated to Ireland from Northamptonshire in 1656. He disowned the Society of Friends on his marriage to Sarah Purser on 12 September 1826. They had nine children.

The nature of Grubb's education and training is unknown, but by about 1830 he was in business in Dublin as a mechanical engineer. His first telescopes were modest instruments for his own use. He soon made contact with the then substantial Irish astronomical community, and in particular with the Revd Thomas Romney Robinson (1793–1882), director of Armagh observatory. Robinson appreciated his skill and inventiveness, and had a knowledge of optics which complemented Grubb's understanding of the mechanical problems of mounting large telescopes. Through Robinson, Grubb was asked to mount a 13.3 inch lens by Cauchoix of Paris for E. J. Cooper of Markree, co. Sligo. As a preparation for working on this instrument he made a full-scale model which was transformed into a 15 inch reflector for the Armagh observatory. The metal mirror of this telescope was supported by a system of triangular levers designed by Grubb, which greatly reduced the flexure of the mirror under its own weight. This system was used by the third earl of Rosse in mounting the mirror of his 6 foot telescope at Parsonstown, King's county, which he completed in 1845. Grubb also made various minor optical components for him.

Grubb's mastery of mounting large telescopes led to other commissions, including the 'Sheepshanks telescope' for the Royal Observatory, Greenwich (1838), a 22 inch reflecting telescope for the University of Glasgow (1853), and a 12 inch refractor for Trinity College's observatory at Dunsink, co. Dublin, in 1868. Grubb did not make the object glasses or primary mirrors for these instruments.

Grubb's business was not confined to astronomy. He carried out a variety of scientific work for Trinity College, Dublin, and in 1839 made about twenty sets of magnetometers for Professor Humphrey Lloyd, who was establishing a network of magnetic observatories in the British colonies: Lloyd preferred to have them made in Dublin rather than London so that he could oversee the work. From 1840 until his death Grubb was engineer to the Bank of Ireland, responsible for designing and constructing machines for engraving, printing, and numbering banknotes.

The success of Rosse's 6 foot telescope in revealing that some nebulae had a spiral structure, and in greatly increasing the number of nebulae known, prompted Robinson to argue that a comparable telescope built by Grubb should be sent to the southern hemisphere to review the southern skies. Robinson's requests for funding were rejected by the government in 1850 and 1853, but in 1862 the colony of Victoria offered to pay for an instrument. After indecision and disagreement about the nature of the most suitable telescope, Grubb signed a contract in 1866 for the construction of a Cassegrain reflector with two interchangeable 4 foot metal mirrors. It was made in

1866–7 in specially built premises in Rathmines, on the south side of Dublin, and installed at Melbourne in 1869. Hailed before its erection as a technical triumph, it was such an expensive and embarrassing failure that its defects were never analysed dispassionately, but the principal one was probably the inability of the astronomers in Melbourne to repolish the mirrors in the way that the earl of Rosse had regularly reworked his at Parsonstown. The choice of metal at a time when silvered glass mirrors were being made in increasingly good quality was unfortunate. Thomas Grubb was elected FRS in 1864 and died at his house, 141 Leinster Road, Rathmines, on 19 September 1878. He was buried at Mount Jerome cemetery, Dublin.

**Sir Howard Grubb** (1844–1931), maker of scientific instruments, was the fifth and youngest son of Thomas Grubb. He was born in Dublin and read civil engineering at Trinity College, Dublin. He joined his father in business in 1865 and took control of the firm in 1868: he remained in charge for fifty-seven years. He made most of the large telescopes required by Britain and the colonies during his lifetime, including five instruments for the Royal Observatory, Greenwich, in 1890–97; on one of these, a 30 inch Cassegrain reflector, P. J. Melotte discovered the eighth satellite of Jupiter in 1908. Grubb also had significant sales elsewhere, from the 27 inch refractor for the University of Vienna in 1881, which was for a short time the largest refractor in the world, to the 40 inch reflector for Simeiz observatory in the Crimea, which was delivered after he retired. The majority of his largest instruments were refractors. Around 1890 he delivered seven of the thirteen photographic instruments for the worldwide *Carte du ciel* project. It was with one of these telescopes, at a solar eclipse in 1919, that Sir Arthur Eddington provided the first experimental verification of Einstein's theory of relativity by showing that the apparent position of a star was altered when its light passed close to the sun. Grubb also made smaller telescopes but did not sell them under his own name.

In the second half of the nineteenth century astronomical research required larger telescopes which could be used to photograph increasingly faint objects: these instruments required very steady mountings and smooth driving mechanisms. From the 1860s spectroscopy developed rapidly; the spectroscope was at the centre of the new science of astrophysics, and Howard Grubb was a leader in the improvement of instruments to meet these demands. In 1870 he built a 15 inch refractor which was bought by the Royal Society and used by William and Mary Huggins in their pioneering work on photographing stellar spectra. Grubb was more of a scientist than his father and was able to master a succession of technical challenges, though in the optical design of some of his largest instruments he was aided by another Irishman, Sir George Gabriel Stokes, Lucasian professor of mathematics at Cambridge. Sir David Gill, after his retirement from his post in South Africa, gave Grubb advice on designing his largest telescopes. In 1871 Grubb married Mary Hester Walker (*d.* 1931), daughter of a physician from Louisiana: they had four sons and three daughters. He was elected a fellow of the Royal Society in 1883, and was knighted in 1887.

At the beginning of the twentieth century Grubb became interested in the military use of optical instruments, and designed rangefinders and gunsights. He constructed the first submarine periscope. During the First World War his firm became heavily involved in the war effort, and because of unrest in Ireland it was moved by the government to St Albans in 1916–18. Grubb sold the firm to Sir Charles Algernon Parsons in 1925, when it was transferred to Tyneside. Grubb retired to Ireland. He died at 13 Longford Terrace, Monkstown, co. Dublin, on 16 September 1931. JOHN BURNETT

**Sources** J. E. Burnett and A. D. Morrison-Low, *Vulgar and mechanick: the scientific instrument trade in Ireland, 1650–1921* (1989), 94–117 • J. A. Bennett, *Church, state, and astronomy in Ireland: 200 years of Armagh observatory* (1990), 81–3, 131–4 • P. A. Wayman, *Dunsink observatory, 1785–1985: a bicentennial history* (1987) • Grubb family pedigree, Religious Society of Friends, Dublin, library • I. S. Glass, *Victorian telescope makers: the lives and letters of Thomas and Howard Grubb* (1997) • H. C. King, *The history of the telescope* (1955), 264–7, 299–301, 306 • *The Observatory*, 2 (1879), 203 • *Proceedings of the Royal Irish Academy*, 2nd ser., 3: Science (1877–83), 70 • *PRS*, 135A (1932), iv–ix [obit. of Howard Grubb] • *Monthly Notices of the Royal Astronomical Society*, 92 (1931–2), 253–5 [Howard Grubb] • probate (Mary Hester Walker), NA Ire.

**Archives** NMM, Greenwich Observatory • RAS, letters | CUL, letters to Sir George Stokes, Add. 7342, 7656 • priv. coll., letters to third and fourth earls of Rosse

**Likenesses** photograph, *c.*1870, repro. in Glass, *Victorian telescope makers*, ii • Werner & Son, photograph, 1894 (Howard Grubb), repro. in *British Journal of Photography* (8 June 1894), supplement • photograph, *c.*1900 (Howard Grubb), repro. in King, *History of the telescope*, 301

**Gruffudd**. *See also* Griffith, Griffiths, Gryffyth.

**Gruffudd ab Ednyfed** (*fl.* 1246–1256). *See under* Tudor family, forebears of (*per. c.*1215–1404).

**Gruffudd ab Ieuan ap Llywelyn Fychan** (*c.*1485–1553), poet, was born close to Newmarket in Flintshire, the son of Ieuan ap Llywelyn Fychan, a member of a landed family who leased estates at Llannerch, near St Asaph, from the crown, and his wife, Annes, daughter of Rhys ap Cynwrig of Tegeingl. Little is known of Gruffudd ab Ieuan's early life, until he became distinguished as a poet during the 1520s. He succeeded to the family estates, renewing his father's grant in 1522, 1529, and 1544. In 1523 he approached the architect of the nearby church of St George's in a poetic epistle, desiring him to rebuild his 'high-crested, too long-sided, soot-accumulating old ornament of ancient workmanship from time immemorial' at Llannerch (NL Wales, MS 3029B).

By 1523 Gruffudd ab Ieuan had attained such distinction as a poet that together with his friend Tudur Aled he was appointed as an adviser to the commissioners for holding the important eisteddfod at Caerwys in Flintshire, the supposed site of Gruffudd ap Cynan's great eisteddfod of 1100; a poem by Gruffudd on the art of poetry probably belongs to this period. The three commissioners were members of the leading local landed families, and the two poets were employed to give professional advice on the judging of the work of bards and musicians. Upwards of a hundred poems attributed to Gruffudd ab Ieuan survive, generally in manuscript collections of *barddoniaeth* (poetic art) by various hands collected between the sixteenth and nineteenth centuries, but rigorous screening would reduce this number considerably. His favoured literary form was the *cywydd*, a composition in rhyming couplets following complex rules of consonance. Since he composed poetry for his own pleasure, some of his poems are for his friends, others are love poems or meditations on religious themes. Unhappily, his most famous *cywydd*, an early protestant attack on images, is almost certainly not by him. He was, however, an interesting and accomplished poet.

Gruffudd ab Ieuan married twice. His first wife, Jonet, was the daughter of Richard ap Hywel of Mostyn, one of the commissioners at the Caerwys eisteddfod. The youngest of their four children, Alice, became distinguished in her own right as a poet, as did her sister Catrin. His second wife, Alice, the daughter of John Owen of Llansanffraid, was also a member of a landowning family. Five children were born to this marriage. The eldest son, Edward, succeeded to Llannerch on his father's death, but died without issue in 1601, bequeathing the estate to Peter Mutton. The second son, Thomas, became the founder of the noted north Wales family of Griffiths of Garn and Plasnewydd.

Gruffudd ab Ieuan possessed a noted library which apparently included a copy of the Middle Welsh translation of Peter of Poitiers's *Promptuarium bibliae*. Many of his manuscripts passed ultimately through his descendants the Davies family of Llannerch into the hands of the Davies-Cookes of Gwasaney, and thence to the National Library of Wales. In 1543 and 1544 Gruffudd ab Ieuan was included on the list of names for pricking as high sheriff of Denbighshire, and he was a commissioner of array for the county in 1544. In the same year he was granted his lands for life. He died between 11 March and 3 May 1553 at Lleweni Isaf, and is traditionally believed to have been buried at Henllan in Denbighshire.

MARTIN E. SPEIGHT

**Sources** *DWB* • T. A. Glenn, *The family of Griffith of Garn and Plasnewydd* (1934) • J. C. Morrice, *Detholiad o waith Gruffudd ab Ieuan ab Llewelyn Vychan* (1910) • Ll. N. V. L. Mostyn and T. A. Glenn, *History of the family of Mostyn of Mostyn* (1925) • W. J. Gruffudd, *Llenyddiaeth Cymru* (1926) • P. C. Bartrum, ed., *Welsh genealogies*, AD *1400–1500*, 18 vols. (1983), 542 • J. Jones, '"Pump Llyfr moysen yn Gymraeg" a'r "Beibyl ynghmraec"', *BBCS*, 9 (1937–9), 215–19 • W. A. Bebb, 'Dyddiadau Gruffud ab Ieuan ap Llewelyn Vychan', *BBCS*, 10 (1939–41), 116–20 • T. Roberts, 'Dyddiadau Gruffudd ab Ieuan ap Llewelyn Vychan', *BBCS*, 10 (1939–41), 233–9 • T. Roberts, 'Gruffud ab Ieuan ap Llewelyn Vychan (?–1553)', *BBCS*, 16 (1954–6), 253–4

**Gruffudd ab Ifor** (*d.* 1210). *See under* Ifor ap Meurig (*fl.* 1158).

**Gruffudd ap Cynan** (1054/5–1137), king of Gwynedd, was born in Dublin, the son of Cynan, son of Iago, king of Gwynedd, and Ragnhildr, daughter of *Olaf (Amlaíb) Sihtricson (*d.* 981), king of Dublin. **Iago ab Idwal ap Meurig** (*d.* 1039), Gruffudd's paternal grandfather, succeeded Llywelyn ap Seisyll as king of Gwynedd on the latter's death in 1023 and was killed, perhaps by Gruffudd ap Llywelyn, in 1039; nothing else is known of his reign. Iago's wife is named in later medieval pedigrees as Afandreg daughter of Gwair; their son, Cynan, may well have been the 'son of Iago' who killed Gruffudd ap Llywelyn in 1063.

Gruffudd is the only medieval Welsh secular ruler for whom a near contemporary biography survives, namely *Historia Gruffud vab Kenan*, a text written in Welsh in the early thirteenth century based on a Latin work, now lost, probably composed during the reign of Gruffudd's son and successor, *Owain Gwynedd (*d.* 1170). The *Historia* provides the fullest account of Gruffudd's family background and life and, while some of its information and especially interpretations are incorrect or misleading, it is an invaluable source for its subject.

According to the *Historia*, Gruffudd had not only inherited the right to rule Gwynedd by virtue of his paternal descent from Rhodri Mawr (*fl.* 844–878) but had inherited royal status from his mother, who was related both to Scandinavian kings and to several Irish dynasties. Fostered at the monastery of Swords, near Dublin, Gruffudd is said to have been informed of his entitlement to rule Gwynedd by his mother and sought assistance from an Irish king—probably Muirchertach Ó Brián (*d.* 1119), ruler of Dublin under his father, Toirrdelbach, from 1075 to 1086—to recover his patrimonial kingdom. Thus began twenty-five years of struggle to achieve mastery in Gwynedd against other Welsh dynasties and, above all, the Normans.

In 1075 Gruffudd—described as 'the grandson of Iago' in Welsh annalistic sources, presumably reflecting the obscurity of his father, Cynan—sailed from Dublin to Anglesey in a bid to seize Gwynedd from Trahaearn ap Caradog (*d.* 1081) and his ally Cynwrig ap Rhiwallon. Supported by the men of Anglesey, the Norman Robert of Rhuddlan, and the leading nobles of the western peninsula of Llŷn, Gruffudd led a force that defeated and killed Cynwrig near Clynnog Fawr; it then marched south to Meirionydd, where, at a place called Gwaederw, it defeated Trahaearn, who fled to his native region of Arwystli in central Wales. These successes were followed, according to the *Historia*, by a raid on Gruffudd's erstwhile Norman ally, Robert, at Rhuddlan. However, Gruffudd soon faced a revolt in Llŷn and was then defeated by Trahaearn at the battle of Bron-yr-erw, above Clynnog Fawr, and forced to flee to Anglesey and thence to Wexford.

Although Gruffudd harassed him from the sea, Trahaearn remained in control of Gwynedd until 1081. However, in that year Gruffudd sailed to Porth Glais near St David's with Hiberno-Scandinavian forces from Waterford and, in alliance with Rhys ap Tewdwr of Deheubarth (*d.* 1093), defeated and killed Trahaearn (along with his allies Meilyr ap Rhiwallon ap Cynfyn and Caradog ap Gruffudd) at Mynydd Carn. Gruffudd advanced north, ravaging Arwystli and Powys *en route*, and established himself in Gwynedd. Again, though, his ascendancy was only brief, for Hugh, earl of Chester, and his Norman associates, clearly aware of the threat he posed to their ambitions to conquer the region, inveigled him to Rug in Edeirnion where he was captured (by Robert of Rhuddlan, according to Orderic Vitalis) and taken to the earl's prison in Chester. There Gruffudd remained, it seems, for at least the next twelve years. The *Historia* provides a colourful account of his escape and subsequent wanderings in Wales and Ireland; his unsuccessful attempt, with the help of Godred, king of Man, to dislodge the Normans from the castle of Aberlleiniog on Anglesey; and his capture of the Norman castle of Nefyn in Llŷn. These last events appear to be related to the Welsh revolt of 1094, but the extent of Gruffudd's involvement in that is uncertain; the only leader mentioned in the Welsh chronicles is Cadwgan ap Bleddyn (*d.* 1111). Orderic Vitalis names a 'Gruffudd king of the Welsh' as the leader of the raid that led to the death of Robert of Rhuddlan on the Great Orme, almost certainly in 1093, but the identification is open to question, for the event is not mentioned in the *Historia*, which would surely have trumpeted its hero's part in such a significant blow to Norman power in north Wales (Ordericus Vitalis, *Eccl. hist.*, 4, 140).

The Norman hold on Gwynedd was only finally broken in 1098. In the summer of that year the earls of Chester and Shrewsbury mounted a campaign to recover the region. This compelled Cadwgan ap Bleddyn and Gruffudd ap Cynan to withdraw, with all their people, to Anglesey, which they sought to defend with the aid of a Hiberno-Scandinavian fleet. The latter was suborned by the Normans, however, and both Welsh leaders fled to Ireland. But the killing of Hugh de Montgomery, earl of Shrewsbury, by Magnus Bareleg, king of Norway, who suddenly appeared with a fleet off Anglesey, led to the Normans' abandoning their attempt to conquer the island, and the following year the Welsh leaders returned from Ireland and Anglesey was granted to Gruffudd, possibly under the overlordship of the earl of Chester.

After 1099 Gruffudd gradually built up his power in north Wales, first over Gwynedd west of the River Conwy, and then over territories to the east and south. Surviving details of this achievement are few: the bulk of the *Historia* focuses on the turbulent years in which Gruffudd sought to establish his authority in his patrimonial kingdom, and references to the king in Welsh chronicles and other sources are scanty. Yet there can be little doubt that the initial phase of consolidation owed much to the minority in the earldom of Chester from 1101 to 1114 together with the goodwill of Henry I, who, according to the *Historia*, granted Gruffudd Llŷn, Eifionydd, Ardudwy, and Arllechwedd. However, by 1114 Gruffudd's power was such that Henry I felt it necessary to lead a major campaign against him, which compelled the latter to submit to the king and pay a large tribute. Thereafter Gruffudd was careful not to provoke Henry, refusing shelter to the fugitive Gruffudd ap Rhys of Deheubarth (*d.* 1137) in 1115 and to Maredudd ap Bleddyn of Powys (*d.* 1132) in 1121. Within north Wales, however, Gruffudd's power grew apace. He was able to keep the see of Bangor vacant following the translation to Ely in 1109 of the Norman appointee, Hervey, and then to secure the consecration as bishop of his nominee, David the Scot (*d.* 1139), in 1120. From the 1120s Gruffudd embarked on a policy of territorial expansion, providing a channel for the ambitions of his sons, who led the campaigns and whom he set over the annexed lands. Thus in 1124 Cadwallon and Owain were sent into Meirionydd, over which they appear to have established control by 1136; in 1125 Cadwallon killed his three maternal uncles, rulers of Dyffryn Clwyd, thereby exterminating the only powerful dynasty in north-east Wales, and himself perished near Llangollen in 1132 while attacking Powys; and in 1136 Owain and his younger brother, Cadwaladr, led attacks against the Normans in Ceredigion.

Gruffudd was afflicted by blindness in his last years. He died, aged eighty-two, in 1137 and was buried in Bangor Cathedral. His passing was mourned in an elegy by the court poet, Meilyr Brydydd, who praised the king's ferocity in war. Among those present at Gruffudd's death, according to the *Historia*, was his wife, Angharad (*d.* 1162), daughter of *Owain ab Edwin of Dyffryn Clwyd, whom he had married *c.*1095. She was the mother of Gruffudd's sons Cadwallon, Owain Gwynedd, and *Cadwaladr [*see under* Owain Gwynedd] and his daughters Gwenllian, who married Gruffudd ap Rhys (*d.* 1137), Marared, Rainillt, Annest, and Susanna, who married Madog ap Maredudd (*d.* 1160). In addition, later medieval pedigrees state that Gruffudd had five sons and three daughters with at least three other partners. These conventional sexual mores were matched by conventional piety. Gruffudd was present on Bardsey Island at the first stage of the translation to Llandaff of the relics of St Dyfrig and the hermit Elgar in 1120, and made deathbed bequests of money to major churches in Ireland and Wales as well as to the Benedictine priories of Chester and Shrewsbury; furthermore, he apparently consented to the translation to the latter church of the relics of St Gwenfrewi (Winifred) from Gwytherin.

The *Historia* also relates that the king 'built large churches in his own major courts' in a passage praising the peace and prosperity which resulted from his rule 'with an iron rod' (Evans, *A Mediaeval Prince of Wales*, 81, 82). Notwithstanding its rhetorical exaggeration, the passage reflects a view shared by modern scholars that from 1099 Gruffudd brought stability, and with it economic recovery and advance, to Gwynedd after the disruptions—caused principally by Norman attempts at conquest—of the later eleventh century. Above all, he succeeded in re-establishing the dynasty of Rhodri Mawr, excluded from power in north Wales since 1039, as rulers of Gwynedd, a position maintained by his successors until the extinction of native rule in 1283. HUW PRYCE

**Sources** *Historia Gruffud vab Kenan / Gyda rhagymadrodd a nodiadau gan*, ed. D. S. Evans (1977) · D. S. Evans, ed. and trans., *A mediaeval prince of Wales: the life of Gruffudd ap Cynan* (1990) [Eng. trans. of *Historia Gruffud vab Kenan*, with orig. Welsh text] · T. Jones, ed. and trans., *Brut y tywysogyon, or, The chronicle of the princes: Peniarth MS 20*

(1952) • T. Jones, ed. and trans., *Brut y tywysogyon, or, The chronicle of the princes: Red Book of Hergest* (1955) • T. Jones, ed. and trans., *Brenhinedd y Saesson, or, The kings of the Saxons* (1971) [another version of *Brut y tywysogyon*] • J. Williams ab Ithel, ed., *Annales Cambriae*, Rolls Series, 20 (1860) • Ordericus Vitalis, *Eccl. hist.*, vol. 4 • *Gwaith Meilyr Brydydd a'i ddisgynyddion*, ed. J. E. C. Williams (1994) • J. E. Lloyd, *A history of Wales from the earliest times to the Edwardian conquest*, 3rd edn, 2 vols. (1939); repr. (1988) • R. R. Davies, *Conquest, coexistence, and change: Wales, 1063–1415*, History of Wales, 2 (1987) • K. L. Maund, ed., *Gruffudd ap Cynan: a collaborative biography* (1996) • K. L. Maund, *Ireland, Wales, and England in the eleventh century* (1991) • S. Duffy, 'Ostmen, Irish, and Welsh in the eleventh century', *Peritia*, 9 (1995), 378–96 • B. T. Hudson, 'The destruction of Gruffudd ap Llywelyn', *Welsh History Review / Cylchgrawn Hanes Cymru*, 15 (1990–91), 331–50

**Wealth at death** exact sum unknown; some bequests: Evans, ed., *Historia Gruffud vab Kenan*

**Gruffudd ap Gwenwynwyn** (*d.* 1286), baron in Wales, was lord of Cyfeiliog, Upper Powys, or, as it was called from his father, Powys Wenwynwyn. He was the son of *Gwenwynwyn, the son of *Owain Cyfeiliog, and Margaret Corbet. The expulsion of his father from his dominions by Llywelyn ab Iorwerth led to Gruffudd's being brought up in England, where in 1216 his father died. He was supported by a charge on the revenues of his estates, which remained in Llywelyn's hands, by the dower of his mother's English estates, and by occasional grants from the exchequer, as for example in 1224, when he received half a mark because he was sick. Llywelyn kept Powys Wenwynwyn in his hands until his death in 1240, though after 1233 Gruffudd and his followers seem to have frequented the king's border castles. In 1241 Gruffudd paid a fine of 300 marks to the king and obtained the seisin of all his father's estates, doing homage for them to Henry alone, so that he held as a baron of the king, and was independent of the princes of Gwynedd. In the same year he acted as a surety for Senena, wife of Gruffudd ap Llywelyn, in her agreement with Henry III for the release of her husband.

In 1244 Gruffudd was one of the three Welsh magnates who alone remained faithful to the king when Dafydd ap Llywelyn went to war. He was besieged in his castle of Tafolwern, and though steadfast himself was much afraid that his followers would desert to Prince Dafydd. In 1247, after Dafydd's death, Gruffudd was one of the leaders of a south Welsh army which ravaged Gwynedd.

Gruffudd's fidelity to the English king involved him similarly in conflicts with Llywelyn ap Gruffudd, and brought him more privileges and grants from the crown. After the Lord Edward's officers had enraged the people of north-east Wales by their insensitive rule, Llywelyn marched against Gruffudd, and in 1257 deprived him of nearly all his lands. Later the same year he lost his territories altogether, and took refuge in England, where in 1260 he was summoned, doubtless for his English estates, to serve against Llywelyn. But the English connection had done Gruffudd very little good, and since 1255 he had also been involved in a long and troublesome dispute with his kinsman Thomas Corbet of Caus, for the possession of Gorddwr. In 1263 he made his peace with Llywelyn and on bended knee did homage to him as prince of Wales, receiving in return some additional grants of territory. He at once attacked and destroyed Corbet's castle of Gwyddgrug at Forden near Montgomery in the interest of his new lord. In 1267, when the treaty of Montgomery recognized Llywelyn as prince of Wales, Gruffudd was recognized by Henry III as a vassal of the prince, but was not required to restore any land which he had held when with the king.

Gruffudd was not long contented as a vassal of the prince of Wales. In 1274 he plotted with Llywelyn's brother and heir Dafydd to assassinate the prince. Dafydd would become prince and one of his daughters would marry Gruffudd's eldest son Owain, while Gruffudd himself would receive the adjacent territories of Ceri and Cedewain. The plot failed and Gruffudd had to seek pardon and hand over Owain as a hostage. Owain made a full confession to the bishop of Bangor and Llywelyn sent a delegation to Gruffudd, who received them well at Pool Castle (Welshpool), his chief residence. But Gruffudd then imprisoned them and fled to join Dafydd in England. Llywelyn now overran Powys; but the king's campaign in 1276–7 compelled him to relinquish his conquests, and Gruffudd was again restored. Henceforth he remained faithful to King Edward. A prolonged territorial dispute with Llywelyn over the cantref of Arwystli was still unresolved when war again broke out in 1282. The fall of Llywelyn left him no longer any temptation to do more than play the part of an English baron; in the Arwystli dispute he had demanded that the action be tried in the king's court by the common law because he was a baron of the march. The weekly market at his town of Welshpool, which in 1279 had been suppressed as likely to injure the king's town of Montgomery, was restored in 1282. In 1283 he was summoned to the council which tried and sentenced his former ally, Dafydd, at Shrewsbury.

Gruffudd died some time between 17 February 1286 and the summer of that year. His career as well as that of his father illustrates very remarkably the process of transition by which a Welsh prince could become an English baron and a Welsh kingdom a marcher lordship. As ruler of Powys he had sought to add to his territory, as may be seen in his dispute with Corbet and in his annexation of most of Mechain after 1277.

Gruffudd had married Hawise, daughter of John (III) *Lestrange of Knockin, some time before 1242. They had a numerous family, among whom he distributed his estates by a deed preserved on the Welsh roll of 6 Edward I. Owain the eldest had Cyfeiliog and Arwystli. Lesser portions were provided for his other sons, Llywelyn, Ieuan, Gwilym, Dafydd, and Gruffudd to be held of Owain. He also left a daughter, Margaret, who married Fulk Fitzwarine of Whittington. Hawise, his wife, died in 1310. His heir, Owain de la Pole, as he was generally called, died in 1293, leaving his son and heir, Gruffudd, only two years old. On the latter's death in 1309 Powys went to his sister, Hawise Gadarn, who in the same year married John Charlton, first Baron Charlton of Powys. T. F. Tout, *rev.* A. D. Carr

**Sources** T. Jones, ed. and trans., *Brut y tywysogyon, or, The chronicle of the princes: Peniarth MS 20* (1952) • J. Williams ab Ithel, ed., *Annales Cambriae*, Rolls Series, 20 (1860) • J. G. Edwards, *Calendar of ancient*

*correspondence concerning Wales* (1935) • *Littere Wallie*, ed. J. G. Edwards (1940) • J. C. Davies, ed., *The Welsh assize roll, 1277–1284* (1940) • J. B. Smith, *Llywelyn ap Gruffudd, tywysog Cymru* (1986) • R. Morgan, 'The barony of Powys, 1275–1360', *Welsh History Review / Cylchgrawn Hanes Cymru*, 10 (1980–81), 1–42 • J. E. Lloyd, *A history of Wales from the earliest times to the Edwardian conquest*, 3rd edn, 2 vols. (1939); repr. (1988) • G. T. O. Bridgeman, 'The princes of upper Powys', *Montgomeryshire Collections*, 1 (1867–8), 1–103

**Gruffudd ap Llywelyn** (*d.* **1063**), king of Gwynedd and of Deheubarth, was an aggressive and powerful ruler of Gwynedd from 1039 to 1063 and, after a series of attempts to secure the south, he ruled Deheubarth from 1055 until his death.

Gruffudd's father, **Llywelyn ap Seisyll** (*d.* 1023), was a man of obscure parentage. While Seisyll cannot be linked with any known lineage, later genealogies suggest that Llywelyn's mother was Prawst, a descendant of Rhodri Mawr of Gwynedd (844–878). Llywelyn himself married into the ruling dynasty of Deheubarth; his wife, Angharad, was the daughter of *Maredudd ab Owain (*r.* 986–99). The brief record of his career shows him to have been active in north and south Wales. In the north, in 1017 or 1018, he defeated and killed Aeddan ap Blegywryd, who has been identified as a usurper seeking to rule Gwynedd, or (since his name does not occur in any royal genealogy) as a powerful local figure who had to be won over or subdued by any legitimate claimant. From 1018 Llywelyn was ruler of Gwynedd. In south Wales an Irish adventurer, Rhain, claiming to be a son of Maredudd ab Owain, seemed likely to establish himself as the ruling prince until Llywelyn defeated him in battle at Abergwili in 1022. The sources do not establish whether Llywelyn was then acting as a representative of the southern dynasty of Hywel Dda, or as an aggressive ruler of the northern kingdom pursuing ambitions in Deheubarth. In what was clearly a year of crisis, each version of the *Brut y tywysogyon* records a flattering encomium of his quality.

His death in 1023, which was noted without further comment, marked a temporary eclipse of his dynasty. In that year the old line of Gwynedd was re-established when Iago ab Idwal became ruler. He held power until he was killed and replaced by Gruffudd ap Llywelyn in 1039. Writing many years later, in the 1180s, Walter Map drew on border traditions and presented Gruffudd growing up as a spineless youth, lacking in confidence and drive. His sister, seeking to urge him to action, reproached him, as the only son and heir of his father, for his lack of purpose. By 1039 that phase had passed. Gruffudd may have been, as the *Brenhinedd y Saesson* claims, responsible for the death of Iago. Certainly, as soon as he became king of Gwynedd, Gruffudd was involved in battle with the men of Mercia whom he defeated at Rhyd-y-groes on the Severn. Whether he or the Mercians took the initiative in seeking that encounter is not known. For the next sixteen years his main objective was to make himself master of Deheubarth, but he was thwarted by the resilience and resistance of the two princes ruling south Wales, Hywel ab Edwin, between 1039 and 1044, and Gruffudd ap Rhydderch, between 1044 and 1055. Twice, in 1039 and 1041, he defeated Hywel but failed to take his kingdom. In 1041, after the battle of Pencader, he captured Hywel's wife and 'took her as his own' (*Brut: Peniarth MS 20*, 13). He was himself captured by a Scandinavian force in 1042. Hywel made alliance with the Scandinavians—the Ostmen—based in Ireland, but, as the *Brut* makes clear, Gruffudd overcame them and finally defeated and killed Hywel in 1044. He could not prevent Gruffudd ap Rhydderch from establishing himself as king in Hywel's place.

There was heavy fighting between the northern king and Gruffudd ap Rhydderch and his brother, Rhys, in 1045. In the following year Gruffudd ap Llywelyn allied with an English earl, Swein son of Godwine, and they campaigned together in Wales. It is generally assumed that this alliance was an attempt to dislodge his rival in the south. The struggle for power was checked by a crisis, little short of a disaster, within Wales. The men of Ystrad Tywi attacked Gruffudd ap Llywelyn's bodyguard—his *teulu*—and about 140 of them were killed. It was a great loss: Gruffudd had the strength to seek revenge in Ystrad Tywi, but not to renew hostilities on a large scale, and the southern prince was left undisturbed for a number of years. A raid on Herefordshire in 1052, extending as far as Leominster, was attributed to him by John of Worcester; it remains inherently unlikely, though John's claim cannot lightly be put aside. With the deaths of Rhys ap Rhydderch in 1053 and of Gruffudd ap Rhydderch in 1055, the southern kingdom could not produce a strong candidate, and Gruffudd ap Llywelyn could establish himself as ruler of Wales.

From 1055 to 1063 Gruffudd was primarily concerned with relations with England. His policy was, in part, a continuation of the aggressive policy pursued on the English frontier by Gruffudd ap Rhydderch and, in part, a reaction to political events in England. In 1055 Ælfgar, son of Leofric, earl of Mercia, was forced into exile in the course of a power struggle between the earls of Wessex and Mercia. Ælfgar countered by recruiting a fleet from the Scandinavians settled in Ireland and by forming an alliance with Gruffudd ap Llywelyn, who was the most prominent leader of the combined force. The defence of the southern frontier had been entrusted to Ralph de Mantes, earl of Hereford, who relied on castles and knights, on the continental pattern. When the attack came the English defence collapsed and Ralph's army suffered heavy casualties. Hereford was taken; the town and its cathedral were destroyed by fire, and Gruffudd returned to Wales with substantial plunder. Reinforcements were brought from all over England under Harold, earl of Wessex, but he was content to refortify Hereford, and to negotiate at Billingsley peace terms which, all too soon, were compromised. Leofgar, the new bishop of Hereford, one of Harold's clerical followers, was secular and belligerent in outlook. In June, 1056, he led an army against Gruffudd, and was soundly defeated, again with heavy losses.

His action put Earl Harold's integrity at risk, and peace was restored only by calling on Earl Leofric and Ealdred, bishop of Worcester, and ultimately on King Edward. Despite his military dominance, Gruffudd accepted by a formal oath that he would be a faithful under-king, perhaps content with recognition by the English of his territorial and other acquisitions. Walter Map recorded an anecdote which demonstrates a generous trait in Gruffudd's character. The two rulers faced each other on opposite banks of the Severn, waiting for the other to make the first move. When Edward the Confessor set out from Aust in a small boat, Gruffudd leapt into the river to meet him and carried him on his shoulders to the shore. The Mercian–Welsh alliance was strengthened by a marriage between Gruffudd and Edith [*see* Ealdgyth], daughter of Earl Ælfgar. It was called into action again in 1058, when Ælfgar and Gruffudd were once more linked with a Norwegian fleet, but the Anglo-Saxon Chronicle does not make explicit the cause or the development of this obscure episode.

Nor are the events of 1062 wholly clear. Earl Ælfgar was the recipient of a royal writ late in the summer of 1062, and apparently died soon afterwards. At Christmas, Earl Harold was sent on a surprise attack on Gruffudd's court at Rhuddlan, but the prince escaped by sea. A campaign and blockade mounted in the summer of 1063 by Earl Harold and Earl Tostig left him with less hope of survival. He moved inland, and was killed in August by enemies in Wales. His head was taken to Earl Harold, and ultimately delivered to Edward the Confessor. Gwynedd and Powys were given to his half-brothers, Bleddyn and Rhiwallon, who ruled as client kings, and in the south the old dynasty of Deheubarth was restored.

Of his family little is known. He had a liaison with the wife of Hywel ab Edwin, taken as part of the spoils of war in 1041. He married *Ealdgyth, daughter of Earl Ælfgar, and they had a daughter, later the wife of Osbern fitz Richard; their daughter married another marcher lord, Bernard de Neufmarché. Walter Map wrote of a wife of great beauty whom Gruffudd loved; that may be a reference to Ealdgyth, noted for her beauty. No sons were recorded in any genealogy, but two sons are named in chronicle sources, Maredudd and Ithel (*recte* Idwal), both of whom died in 1069. An Owain ap Gruffudd who died ten years earlier may have been a third son.

Gruffudd's reign was important for Wales. Territorial gains which he had made along the northern frontier as far as Bistre, (Bishopstree, near Mold), and which he and Gruffudd ap Rhydderch had made in the south, extended Welsh rule eastwards. He had a court poet, Berddig, who was given three rills, with five plough teams in Gwent. There were substantial losses after his final defeat and death. His alliance with Mercia gave him greater influence in English affairs than any other Welsh ruler of the eleventh century. In terms of English domestic politics it also made him a dangerous figure in the eyes of the earls of Wessex and Northumbria, and for that he eventually paid a heavy price. He gave Wales unity for a brief eight years. When the writer of the *Brut* praised him as 'the head and shield of the Britons' (*Brut: Peniarth MS 20*, 15), he was looking at the past. At no point in Gruffudd's reign could the possibility of the succession of a Norman king in England be identified as a future problem for Welsh princes. He disappeared from the scene before the Norman invasion of England in 1066 produced new and potentially dangerous problems for Wales. When that threat emerged, the country had returned once more to its traditional pattern of multiple kingship and disruptive rivalries.

David Walker

**Sources** T. Jones, ed. and trans., *Brut y tywysogyon, or, The chronicle of the princes: Peniarth MS 20* (1952) • T. Jones, ed. and trans., *Brenhinedd y Saesson, or, The kings of the Saxons* (1971) [another version of *Brut y tywysogyon*] • *ASC*, s.a. 1055, 1056, 1063, 1065 [texts C, D] • *The chronicle of John of Worcester, 1118–1140*, ed. J. R. H. Weaver (1908) • W. Map, *De nugis curialium / Courtiers' trifles*, ed. and trans. M. R. James, rev. C. N. L. Brooke and R. A. B. Mynors, OMT (1983) • K. L. Maund, *Ireland, Wales, and England in the eleventh century* (1991) • K. L. Maund, 'The Welsh alliances of Earl Ælfgar of Mercia and his family in the mid-eleventh century', *Anglo-Norman Studies*, 11 (1988), 181–90 • D. G. Walker, 'A note on Gruffudd ap Llywelyn (1039–1063)', *Welsh History Review / Cylchgrawn Hanes Cymru*, 1 (1960–63), 83–94 • D. Walker, *Medieval Wales* (1990)

**Wealth at death** presumably wealthy

**Gruffudd ap Llywelyn** (*d.* 1244), ruler in Wales, was the son of *Llywelyn ab Iorwerth (*d.* 1240) and Tangwystl, daughter of Llywarch Goch. Between 1211 and 1215 he was a hostage in England. In 1220 he was excluded from the succession in favour of his half-brother Dafydd on account of his illegitimacy. Dafydd was the son of Llywelyn and Joan, King John's illegitimate daughter. By 1221 Gruffudd held the cantref of Meirionnydd and the commote of Ardudwy but he lost them when he quarrelled with his father, and war was averted only by clerical mediation. In 1223 Gruffudd was entrusted by Llywelyn with an army to oppose William (II) Marshal, earl of Pembroke, who had returned from Ireland to south Wales, and had taken Cardigan and Carmarthen from Llywelyn. An inconclusive battle was fought near Carmarthen, but lack of provisions immediately afterwards obliged Gruffudd to return to Gwynedd. A little later Gruffudd again took up arms and intercepted the earl in Carnwyllion. He had held the whole of southern Powys since at least 1226, as well as the cantref of Llŷn. Afterwards, however, he seems to have quarrelled with his father again, and underwent six years' imprisonment at Deganwy. He was released in 1234. According to Matthew Paris he again went to war against his father in 1237 and Llywelyn was compelled to submit himself to the English. The last years of Llywelyn's reign seem to have seen a struggle between Gruffudd and his half-brother Dafydd. In 1238 Dafydd received the fealty of the Welsh barons, and took all Gruffudd's dominions away from him except Llŷn. *Brut y tywysogyon* and *Annales Cambriae* state that in 1239 Gruffudd was entrapped into a conference with Dafydd, and imprisoned with his eldest son Owain, at Cricieth, but Matthew Paris places this event after Llywelyn's death in April 1240.

The bishop of Bangor excommunicated Dafydd in 1241 and went to England, where he persuaded King Henry to take up the cause of Gruffudd, whose supporters promised a heavy tribute to the king. On 12 August 1241 Senena, Gruffudd's wife, made a convention with Henry at Shrewsbury, agreeing to pay 600 marks for the release of her husband and son. Many of the Welsh magnates favoured his cause. Henry invaded north Wales and Dafydd was compelled to submit, on 29 August 1241 in the treaty of Gwern Eigron. He now handed over Gruffudd and Owain to Henry's custody, warning him that if Gruffudd were released there would be more troubles in Wales. The question of Gruffudd's claims was to be submitted to the king's judgement.

Gruffudd was now sent to London under the care of John of Lexinton, and confined in the Tower, along with his son Owain and some other Welsh captives. He was, however, honourably treated. The king allowed half a mark a day for his support, and his wife, Senena, was allowed to visit him. He tried, however, to escape, on the night of 1 March 1244, having made a rope from his linen, and broke his neck in the attempt, as he was a very tall and heavy man. In 1248 his body was brought back to Wales and buried in the abbey of Aberconwy. He had four sons, Owain Goch, *Llywelyn (ap Gruffudd), *Dafydd (ap Gruffudd), and Rhodri. T. F. Tout, *rev.* A. D. Carr

**Sources** Paris, *Chron.* • T. Jones, ed. and trans., *Brut y tywysogyon, or, The chronicle of the princes: Peniarth MS 20* (1952) • G. A. Williams, 'The succession to Gwynedd, 1238–47', *BBCS*, 20 (1962–4), 393–413 • J. B. Smith, *Llywelyn ap Gruffudd, tywysog Cymru* (1986) • J. E. Lloyd, *A history of Wales from the earliest times to the Edwardian conquest*, 3rd edn, 2 vols. (1939); repr. (1988) • J. Williams ab Ithel, ed., *Annales Cambriae*, Rolls Series, 20 (1860)

**Likenesses** M. Paris, manuscript drawing, in or before 1259 (Gruffudd and Dafydd at their father's deathbed), CCC Cam., MS 16, fol. 132*r* • M. Paris, manuscript drawing, in or before 1259 (death of Gruffudd), CCC Cam., MS 16, fol. 169

**Gruffudd ap Madog** (*d.* 1269). *See under* Madog ap Gruffudd Maelor (*d.* 1236).

**Gruffudd ap Maredudd** (*d.* in or before 1319). *See under* Gruffudd ap Rhys (*d.* 1201).

**Gruffudd ap Nicolas** (*b. c.*1390, *d.* in or after 1460), landowner and administrator, was the son of Nicolas ap Philip ap Syr Elidyr Ddu and Jenet, daughter of Gruffudd ap Llywelyn Foethus; both families came from the Tywi valley (Carmarthenshire), which Gruffudd dominated in Henry VI's reign. Tradition says that his father and mother lived at Crug, near Llandeilo, and that Nicolas died just before Gruffudd was born. By *c.*1415 Gruffudd was a minor official in the lordship of Kidwelly, where his father's family lived and, like other Welshmen after Glyn Dŵr's revolt, he shouldered further responsibilities in the 1420s—as bailiff itinerant of Kidwelly and deputy steward of Carnwyllion (November 1424). From 1425 he acquired office in his mother's country, west of the Tywi, notably as sheriff of Carmarthenshire (1426) and deputy constable of Dinefwr Castle (1428). His property and wealth increased too, partly through the favour of the steward of Kidwelly, Sir John Scudamore. During these years he seems to have resided at or near Crug and acquired property near the towns of Llandeilo, Newton, and Dinefwr.

After Edmund Beaufort, count of Mortain, became steward of Kidwelly in 1433, he too used Gruffudd as his deputy, and about March 1437 Gruffudd was made a denizen to whom Henry IV's penal legislation against Welshmen no longer applied. Later that year he deputized for the absentee justiciar of south Wales, Lord Audley. Indeed, Gruffudd owed his position to Henry VI's appointment of nobles to senior office in south Wales and Kidwelly—nobles who surrendered effective authority to local men like Gruffudd. He acquired estates in Cardiganshire (1437) and in 1439 a sixty-year lease of the castle of Dinefwr and the town of Newton where his family came to reside. By the 1440s he dominated west Wales, and his attachment to Humphrey, duke of Gloucester, the justiciar (1440–47), was illustrated when Gruffudd and other Welshmen accompanied the duke to Bury St Edmunds, where Humphrey suddenly died (1447). Gruffudd's career was unaffected.

Gruffudd was well placed to exploit the crown's rights and was useful to the duke of York in his lordship of Narberth (Pembrokeshire) in 1449 and to the bishop of St David's. His son Thomas had forcibly extended his father's interests in Cardiganshire (1439–42). The seventeenth-century life of his grandson, Rhys ap Thomas, relates how Gruffudd's retainers overawed royal commissioners and sent them back to Westminster in his livery. The behaviour of his son Owain was just as lawless in Carmarthenshire and Pembrokeshire, but by this stage (1452) Gruffudd's dominance was complete and the receiver of Pembroke was his brother-in-law, John Perrot. Gruffudd's marriage into gentry families like his own extended his influence: Mabli was the daughter of Maredudd ap Henry Dwnn of Kidwelly; Margaret was the daughter of Sir Thomas Perrot of Pembrokeshire; and Jane was the daughter of Jankyn ap Rhys ap Dafydd of Cardiganshire. His son Thomas married Elizabeth, daughter of Sir John Gruffudd of Abermarlais (Carmarthenshire).

The Wars of the Roses created even greater opportunities for Gruffudd, but also a dilemma. In the 1450s he sustained Henry VI's regime because he owed his position to Henry's ineffectual rule; he oppressed his neighbours and spurned royal and parliamentary complaint, but when his and the king's interests coincided he could be a vigorous governor, declaring his loyalty in 1450 and offering aid against the duke of York. The creation of Jasper Tudor as earl of Pembroke in November 1452, and the grant to the earl of estates held by Gruffudd, were a challenge. When York became protector of England in 1454–5, an effort was made to remove Gruffudd and his family from office, but attempts to arrest him failed and he and Thomas ap Gruffudd continued as deputy chamberlains of south Wales. He regarded Carmarthen Castle as his own and fortified it. In 1455–6 Gruffudd faced a new dilemma after York's victory at St Albans (22 May 1455), for the duke became constable of Aberystwyth and Carmarthen castles and at Kidwelly the new steward was Edward Bourchier, York's kinsman. Gruffudd and his sons were accordingly deprived of office and summoned before the council on pain of treason. The Act of Resumption of 1456 deprived him of Dinefwr Castle, which was granted to York's councillor, William Herbert of Raglan in Gwent. The arrival of Edmund Tudor, earl of Richmond, in south Wales by May 1456, and his seizure of Carmarthen Castle, may not have been welcomed by Gruffudd, with whom he clashed in Kidwelly. But the invasion of York's retainers in August was worse:

they took Carmarthen and Aberystwyth castles and proceeded to rule in York's name. Gruffudd resolved to come to terms with the royalists, especially after Richmond died (November 1456). Gruffudd and his sons, Thomas and Owain, were pardoned on 26 October. Jasper Tudor replaced York at Aberystwyth, Carmarthen, and Carreg Cennen castles in April 1457 and Gruffudd was associated with him; he was mayor of Carmarthen in 1456–7.

Gruffudd was still alive on 29 February 1460, when he bequeathed York's former castle and lordship of Narberth to his son Owain; he probably died soon after. The later story that he fought at Mortimer's Cross with Edward, earl of March, is mistaken. Rather did his sons hold Carreg Cennen against the Yorkists until 1462. Gruffudd was admired by Welsh poets whom he patronized, not least at the important eisteddfod he organized at Carmarthen (or Newton) *c*.1451. The seventeenth-century description of him seems apt:

> a man of a hott, firie, and cholerrick spiritt; one whos counsells weare all 'in turbido', and therefore naturallie fitlie composed and framed for the times; verie wise he was, and infinitlie subtile and craftie, ambitiouse beyond measure, of a busie stirring braine … (Griffiths, *Sir Rhys ap Thomas*, 161)

R. A. Griffiths

**Sources** R. A. Griffiths, 'Gruffydd ap Nicholas and the rise of the house of Dinefwr', *National Library of Wales Journal*, 13 (1963–4), 256–68 • R. A. Griffiths, 'Gruffydd ap Nicholas and the fall of the house of Lancaster', *Welsh History Review / Cylchgrawn Hanes Cymru*, 2 (1964–5), 213–31 • R. A. Griffiths, 'A tale of two towns: Llandeilo Fawr and Dinefwr in the Middle Ages', *Sir Gâr: studies in Carmarthenshire history*, ed. H. James (1991), 205–26 • R. A. Griffiths, *Sir Rhys ap Thomas and his family: a study in the Wars of the Roses and early Tudor politics* (1993) • *Chancery records* • PRO • NL Wales, Badminton papers • NL Wales, Dynevor papers • NL Wales, Slebech papers • 'A short view of the long life of … Rice ap Thomas', *Cambrian Register*, 1 (1796), 49–144 • R. A. Griffiths and R. S. Thomas, *The principality of Wales in the later middle ages: the structure and personnel of government*, 1: *South Wales, 1277–1536* (1972) • P. C. Bartrum, ed., *Welsh genealogies, AD 1400–1500*, 18 vols. (1983) • D. J. Bowen, 'Dafydd ab Edmwnt ac Eisteddfod Caerfyrddin', *Barn*, 133–55 (1973–5), 441–8

**Gruffudd ap Rhydderch** (*d.* **1055**). *See under* Caradog ap Gruffudd ap Rhydderch (*d.* 1081).

**Gruffudd ap Rhys** (*d.* **1137**), ruler in south Wales, was brought up in Ireland, where in his childhood he had fled with his kinsfolk after the defeat and death of his father, *Rhys ap Tewdwr (*d.* 1093), at the hands of Bernard of Neufmarché in 1093. On that fatal day nearly all Rhys's old kingdom was seized by Norman adventurers. *Nest, Rhys's daughter, became the bride of Gerald of Windsor, steward of Pembroke.

When Gruffudd had grown up to manhood he became weary of exile and about 1113 he returned to Dyfed. For two years he wandered about the country, staying sometimes with his brother-in-law, Gerald of Windsor, sometimes with his own kinsmen. His return seems to have inspired the conquered Welsh with the hope of regaining their liberty under his rule. 'At last', says the Welsh chronicle, *Brut y tywysogyon*, 'he was accused before the king, and it was alleged that the minds of all the Britons [that is, the Welsh] were with him, scorning the royal power of King Henry'. His request for a part of his father's lands was refused.

Gruffudd now escaped to Gwynedd in north Wales and sought refuge with its king, Gruffudd ap Cynan. His brother Hywel ap Rhys, who had escaped maimed from the prison of Arnulf de Montgomery, went with him. Gruffudd ap Cynan treated them well at first, but was persuaded by Henry I to give up the fugitives. Gruffudd ap Rhys discovered his treachery, and managed to escape to the sanctuary of the church of Aberdaron in Llŷn, whence he returned to the south and went to Ystrad Tywi. For the rest of 1115 he led fierce attacks on the French and Flemish settlers in his father's realm. In the spring of 1116 he burnt Narberth Castle, and soon after attacked the castle of Llandovery, but he succeeded only in burning the outworks. Soon afterwards he failed equally at 'a castle that was situated near Swansea'. Then he was joined, in the words of *Brut y tywysogyon*, by 'many young imbeciles from all sides, lured by desire for booty or by an urge to restore and renew the Britannic kingdom' and 'made great depredations round and about him'. Gruffudd subsequently became so formidable that William of London abandoned his castle of Ogmore. Gruffudd was thence invited by his kinsmen into Ceredigion and, after defeating the Flemings, destroyed the castle of Ralph (or Razo), the steward of Earl Gilbert, at Peithyll, and marched against Aberystwyth. Owain ap Cadwgan was now inspired by Henry I to put down 'the petty thief Gruffudd', but he was slain by the Flemings. This failure seems to have secured Gruffudd a position in Deheubarth.

The chroniclers make no further mention of Gruffudd for several years. By 1127 he was in possession of a portion of land which the king had given him. According to Gerald of Wales, who was the grandson of Gruffudd's sister, in the days of Henry I, Gruffudd was 'lord of a single commote, that of Caeo in Cantref Mawr'. Gruffudd abated nothing of his wider claims to Deheubarth, and Gerald tells how even the wildfowl of Llan-gors Lake testified that he was the rightful prince of south Wales.

In 1127 Gruffudd was expelled even from his modest estate and fled to Ireland, but seems soon to have returned, and was probably in the dense forests of Cantref Mawr when the death of Henry I and the weak rule of King Stephen inspired the Welsh to make a great attempt to recover their freedom. Gruffudd was now again in close alliance with Gruffudd ap Cynan and his sons, and had married as his second wife Gwenllian, eldest daughter of the northern Welsh king. In January 1136 a great Welsh host attacked Gower. Gerald of Wales relates that Gruffudd hurried to Gwynedd to obtain the assistance of his brothers-in-law, while his wife Gwenllian, 'like an Amazon and a second Penthesilea', commanded his followers in the south. She was slain in battle near Kidwelly by Maurice of London, lord of Kidwelly; Morgan, one of her and Gruffudd's four sons, perished with her, and a second, Maelgwn, was taken prisoner. But Owain and Cadwaladr, sons of Gruffudd ap Cynan, now came down from the north, destroyed Aberystwyth Castle, and on a second expedition in the second week of October they fought along with Gruffudd ap Rhys a great battle at Crug Mawr near Cardigan, in which they won a decisive victory over Stephen, constable of Cardigan, 'all the Flemings, all the knights and all the French from the estuary of the Neath to the estuary of the Dyfi' (*Brut y tywysogyon*). No help came to the vanquished from England.

In 1137 Gruffudd led an expedition against the cantref of Rhos in Dyfed. He died soon afterwards—according to John of Worcester, 'through the treachery of his wife' (whom he had presumably married after the death of Gwenllian). His place of burial is unknown. He was, says *Brut y tywysogyon*, 'the light and strength and excellence of the men of the south'. In recording his death the monks of the Glamorgan abbey of Margam describe him as 'king of the men of Dyfed'. His sons Cadell (*d.* 1175) and Anarawd (*d.* 1143) (from his first marriage) and Maredudd (*d.* 1155), and the Lord *Rhys ap Gruffudd (*d.* 1197) (the two surviving sons from his marriage to Gwenllian) each sought in turn to maintain and expand his power.

T. F. Tout, *rev.* Huw Pryce

**Sources** T. Jones, ed. and trans., *Brut y tywysogyon, or, The chronicle of the princes: Red Book of Hergest*, 2nd edn (1973) · T. Jones, ed. and trans., *Brenhinedd y Saesson, or, The kings of the Saxons* (1971) [another version of *Brut y tywysogyon*] · T. Jones, ed. and trans., *Brut y tywysogyon, or, The chronicle of the princes: Peniarth MS 20* (1952) · J. Williams ab Ithel, ed., *Annales Cambriae*, Rolls Series, 20 (1860) · *The chronicle of John of Worcester, 1118–1140*, ed. J. R. H. Weaver (1908) · *Florentii Wigorniensis monachi chronicon ex chronicis*, ed. B. Thorpe, 2 vols., EHS, 10 (1848–9) · *Gir. Camb. opera* · J. E. Lloyd, *A history of Wales from the earliest times to the Edwardian conquest*, 3rd edn, 2 vols. (1939); repr. (1988) · R. R. Davies, *Conquest, coexistence, and change: Wales, 1063–1415*, History of Wales, 2 (1987) · R. S. Babcock, 'Imbeciles and Normans: the ynfydion of Gruffudd ap Rhys reconsidered', *Haskins Society Journal*, 4 (1992), 1–9 · R. R. Davies, 'Henry I and Wales', *Studies in medieval history presented to R. H. C. Davis*, ed. H. Mayr-Harting and R. I. Moore (1985), 133–47 · *An inventory of the ancient monuments in Glamorgan, 3/1a: The early castles, from the Norman conquest to 1217*, Royal Commission on Ancient and Historical Monuments in Wales and Monmouthshire (1991)

**Gruffudd ap Rhys** (*d.* 1201), prince of Deheubarth, was the son of *Rhys ap Gruffudd (the Lord Rhys) (1131/2–1197). Gruffudd was the ancestor of a lineage that shared lordship over the patrimony of Rhys ap Gruffudd until the virtual extinction of the dynasty during Edward I's conquest of Wales.

**Gruffudd ap Rhys** Gruffudd, a son of Rhys and his wife, Gwenllian, daughter of Madog ap Maredudd (*d.* 1160) of Powys, was the eldest of Rhys's legitimate sons. He appears to have been the designated heir to the patrimony and he was married to Matilda (*d.* 1210), daughter of William (III) de Briouze (*d.* 1211), the most powerful of the marcher lords of the late twelfth century. The impending succession had led to conflict within the family as early as 1189 when Rhys is known to have encountered resistance from his eldest but illegitimate son, **Maelgwn ap Rhys** (*d.* 1231), who was to found a second important lineage. Rhys placed Maelgwn in Briouze's prison but he escaped in 1192 and joined his father at the siege of the castle of Swansea, an offensive that occasioned the summoning of a large English army. Maelgwn's presence was still troublesome and, during the continuing internecine conflict, Rhys ap Gruffudd was himself incarcerated by Maelgwn and another son in 1194. Promptly upon Rhys's death in 1197 Gruffudd went to Richard I to secure recognition of his succession and he made his peace with the bishop of St David's, consenting to be scourged as penance for an outrage upon the bishop with which his father had been charged. Gruffudd immediately faced strenuous conflict with Maelgwn who, forming an alliance with Gwenwynwyn ab Owain (*fl.* 1186–1216) of Powys, wrested possession of Ceredigion from him. Gruffudd was captured and placed first in Gwenwynwyn's prison and then transferred to the king's custody in Corfe Castle. Released in 1198, he scored considerable success in asserting his authority in Ceredigion, and Maelgwn incurred the Welsh annalist's censure when, in 1199, he sold Cardigan Castle to the English so as to deny it to his brother. Gruffudd was also engaged to good purpose in Ystrad Tywi, taking the castle of Llandovery and Cantref Bychan. He had done much to secure his patrimony when he died on 25 July 1201. The annalist's encomium of Gruffudd, who was buried at the Cistercian abbey of Strata Florida, reflects his highly favourable estimation of the son of Rhys ap Gruffudd who was by Welsh right a true prince and heir, and conveys his critical regard for Maelgwn who, though once extolled for his valour, had recently incurred much adverse comment.

**The sons of Gruffudd ap Rhys** Gruffudd's young sons, Rhys (*d.* 1222) and **Owain ap Gruffudd** (*d.* 1235), maintained the struggle for the inheritance with the other two main contenders, Maelgwn ap Rhys and **Rhys Gryg** (*d.* 1233), another son of Rhys ap Gruffudd, who founded a third important lineage. In the early years of the thirteenth century, with the benefit of the support of Llywelyn ab Iorwerth (*d.* 1240), prince of Gwynedd, Rhys and Owain vigorously contested possession of Ceredigion and deprived their adversaries of the key castles of Dinefwr and Llandovery in Ystrad Tywi. They shared Llywelyn's discomfiture following John's invasion of Gwynedd in 1211 and were forced to yield their territory in Ceredigion, where Falkes de Bréauté fortified the castle of Aberystwyth for the king. When, during the next year, Maelgwn ap Rhys and Rhys Gryg joined Llywelyn in fierce resistance to John, Rhys and Owain found themselves dependent upon the king's support. This proved to be of little avail and the successes of the previous years were placed in jeopardy. It was only in 1215 that the contenders for supremacy in Deheubarth were reconciled when, for the first time, all the surviving descendants of Rhys ap Gruffudd were allied with Llywelyn against John. At a gathering at Aberdyfi the next year Deheubarth was partitioned. The sons of Gruffudd ap Rhys secured the greater part of Ceredigion, Rhys Gryg won the main part of Ystrad Tywi, including the castle of Dinefwr, and Maelgwn received lands in Dyfed and the remaining parts of Ceredigion and Ystrad Tywi. Adjustments were made in 1222, upon the death of Rhys ap Gruffudd, and again in 1225. Rhys Gryg held the whole of Ystrad Tywi, which after his death came to be shared between his sons Rhys Mechyll and *Maredudd ap Rhys

Gryg (*d.* 1271). In Ceredigion the distribution which initially gave Maelgwn the southern portion and Owain the northern portion came to be much changed. Ultimately the descendants of Owain secured an extensive estate in the southern and middle commotes (Is Coed, Gwynionydd, Caerwedros, Mabwynion, Pennardd, Anhuniog, and Mefenydd), while those of Maelgwn were confined to a much smaller estate in the north (Creuddyn, Perfedd, and Genau'r-glyn). Their fortunes, and particularly their relations with the successive princes of Gwynedd, Llywelyn ab Iorwerth, Dafydd ap Llywelyn (*d.* 1246), and Llywelyn ap Gruffudd (*d.* 1282), are recorded by successive annalists at Strata Florida.

**The lineage of Maelgwn ap Rhys** Maelgwn ap Rhys was succeeded in 1231 by his son **Maelgwn Fychan** (*d.* 1257), who had to struggle to safeguard the interests of his house in the vicissitudes of the period following the death of Llywelyn ab Iorwerth in 1240. His difficulties were particularly acute during the conflicts of 1244–6 when royal officers were able to exploit differences among the princes to further their purposes. Maelgwn was forced to flee to Gwynedd where he joined its princes in a defiant resistance in the mountains which was likened by the annalist to the valour of the Maccabees. He returned to an estate further diminished by the crown's annexation of the commote of Perfedd. Predeceased by his son Rhys ap Maelgwn (*d.* 1255), Maelgwn Fychan was succeeded by his grandson **Rhys Fychan ap Rhys ap Maelgwn** (*d.* 1302). A sworn man of Llywelyn ap Gruffudd, Rhys Fychan was confronted in 1277 with the advance of a powerful royal army into his lands. Following his submission in early May he was among the lords of Deheubarth sent to the king to do homage, but his troubles were not ended. Shortly afterwards, with a royal castle being built at Llanbadarn Fawr and his authority destroyed, he, like his grandfather before him, took refuge in Gwynedd. Under the terms of the treaty of Aberconwy in November, Rhys Fychan became one of five lords whose homage Llywelyn ap Gruffudd was allowed to retain, but he remained exiled from his estates in Ceredigion. He participated in the war of 1282–3 in the alliance of Welsh princes against Edward I and briefly endeavoured to reassert his position in northern Ceredigion. He withdrew to Gwynedd once more, but then submitted to the king and served in his forces. As late as May 1283 he received a grant of the cantref of Penweddig (the three commotes of northern Ceredigion) from Dafydd ap Gruffudd, but, with the king's forces already well entrenched there, the charter was of no practical significance and was probably made in an attempt to wean Rhys from the king's alliance. He broke with the king yet again, but by August 1283 he had been captured and dispatched for perpetual imprisonment. On his death in 1302 he was accorded the honour of a burial in Windsor at the king's expense.

**The lineage of Owain ap Gruffudd** The lineage of Owain ap Gruffudd (*d.* 1235) was represented in the middle years of the century by **Maredudd ab Owain** (*d.* 1265), a substantial figure who, at his death, was commemorated by the poet Y Prydydd Bychan (*fl.* 1222–1268) and described by the Welsh annalist as 'defender of all Deheubarth and counsellor of all Wales' (*Brut: Peniarth MS 20*, 114). In the period following the death of Llywelyn ab Iorwerth his allegiance was sought by Dafydd ap Llywelyn and the crown. Maredudd's importance can be gauged by the attempts that were made by the king's commanders in south-west Wales to wean him from his attachment to Dafydd ap Llywelyn in 1244–6. They were conscious that 'it is not easy to control the Welsh except through one of their own nation [*lingua*]' (Edwards, *Calendar*, 48), and urged that terms be agreed with Maredudd that would bring him into the king's allegiance. He was enticed with the prospect that he might benefit from Maelgwn Fychan's disinheritance. His adherence to Llywelyn ap Gruffudd upon his advance into Deheubarth at the end of 1256 ensured the prince's supremacy in Ceredigion. He was among the prince's leading magnates, sharing in his military achievements and participating in his councils. Married to a daughter of Gilbert de Vall of Dale in the earldom of Pembroke, for whom he made dower provision much in accord with English practice, Maredudd ruled a substantial and stable barony. At his death, however, his lands were divided among his sons. Owain ap Maredudd died in 1275, leaving as his heir **Llywelyn ab Owain** (*fl.* 1275–1283), whose young age enabled him to survive the tumultuous years which saw his kinsmen's lordship erased. **Cynan ap Maredudd** (*fl.* 1277–1297) and **Gruffudd ap Maredudd** (*d.* in or before 1319) submitted to the king's commander in May 1277 and were sent to Edward I to do homage. They were reinstated in their lands but, finding the extension of royal authority in Ceredigion irksome, they were among the princes in rebellion in 1282. In their statement to Archbishop Pecham they alleged that Robert de Tibetot (*d.* 1298), justice of west Wales from 1280, had undermined their jurisdiction over their patrimony. Whereas, they insisted, all Christian men enjoyed their laws and customs in their lands, they had been denied the laws of Wales, which had remained inviolate until the imposition of royal authority after the war of 1277. At the start of renewed conflict in March 1282 Gruffudd ap Maredudd and his third cousin, Rhys Fychan ap Rhys ap Maelgwn, attacked the castle of Llanbadarn Fawr. They maintained their resistance and forced the king's commanders to send a contingent to take their castle of Trefilan in September. Gruffudd remained in arms, a member of the small cohort of princes allied with Dafydd ap Gruffudd until, in June 1283, he and his nephew Llywelyn ab Owain surrendered. Cynan and Rhys Fychan were serving with the king's forces in the spring but later resumed an active resistance which they maintained until their surrender in August. Gruffudd, Cynan, and Rhys Fychan were detained at various English castles, including Bridgnorth, Nottingham, Bamburgh, and Newcastle, Northumberland. They were in time allowed to be counted among the 'king's Welshmen' in the royal household, and Gruffudd and Cynan served in the Flanders campaign in 1297. Gruffudd, who was dead by 1319, and Cynan were allowed an income from the manor of Edwinstowe, Nottinghamshire, but they never returned to the lands of their forebears.

**The family's legacy** By the end of the conflict the only territory allowed to any member of the lineages of Gruffudd ap Rhys and Maelgwn ap Rhys was the estate in Is Coed and Mabwynion held by Llywelyn ab Owain. In the mid-fourteenth century this was divided between his granddaughters, one of whom, Elen, was the mother of Owain *Glyn Dŵr. He came to her share of the estate and through his mother he was thus linked with the princes who had once ruled Deheubarth in its entirety.

*Brut y tywysogyon*, containing numerous references to the activities of members of the lineages and notices of their burial in the chapter house, reflects the close association between the Cistercian convent of Strata Florida and those who exercised lordship in Ceredigion. Secular patronage is indicated in charters of Maelgwn ap Rhys and Maelgwn Fychan, Rhys ap Gruffudd, and Cynan ap Maredudd, which refer to gifts by other members of their family. Literary associations are illustrated in poetry addressed by Phylip Brydydd to Rhys ap Gruffudd and by Y Prydydd Bychan's estimation of the valour and generosity of Owain ap Gruffudd, Rhys ap Gruffudd, and Maredudd ab Owain. The later years of the thirteenth century bring evidence of lay interest in prose works. Madog ap Selyf, a cleric or possibly a monk, translated the legendary chronicle of Turpin from Latin into Welsh at the request of Gruffudd ap Maredudd. Brother Gruffudd Bola translated the Athanasian creed into Welsh at the request of **Efa ferch Maredudd** (*fl.* 1300), daughter of Maredudd ab Owain, a task he undertook out of love for her and in her honour. She was one of the first Welsh women whose ability to read is documented, and her descendants were patrons of devotional treatises in Welsh in the fourteenth century. Brother Gruffudd and Madog ap Selyf may have been members of the convent at Strata Florida where, late in the century, a major corpus of court poetry of the period of the princes, the Hendregadredd manuscript, was written. No surviving manuscript of *Brut y tywysogyon* can be shown to have been written in the abbey scriptorium, but both the lost Latin text on which the surviving Welsh versions were based, and one of the Welsh texts, may well have been composed there. J. B. SMITH

**Sources** PRO · *Chancery records* · J. E. Lloyd, *A history of Wales from the earliest times to the Edwardian conquest*, 2 vols. (1911) · J. B. Smith, *Llywelyn ap Gruffudd, tywysog Cymru* (1986) · J. B. Smith, *Llywelyn ap Gruffudd, prince of Wales* (1998) · R. R. Davies, *Conquest, coexistence, and change: Wales, 1063–1415*, History of Wales, 2 (1987) · J. B. Smith, 'The *Cronica de Wallia* and the dynasty of Dinefwr', *BBCS*, 20 (1962–4), 261–82 · R. A. Griffiths, *Conquerers and conquered in medieval Wales* (1994) · *Littere Wallie*, ed. J. G. Edwards (1940) · T. Jones, ed. and trans., *Brut y tywysogyon, or, The chronicle of the princes: Red Book of Hergest* (1955) · *Gwaith Bleddyn Fardd ac eraill o feirdd ail hanner y drydedd ganrif ar ddeg*, ed. R. Andrews and others (1996) · J. B. Smith, 'Dynastic succession in medieval Wales', *BBCS*, 33 (1986), 199–232 · T. Jones, ed. and trans., *Brut y tywysogyon, or, The chronicle of the princes: Peniarth MS 20* (1952) · J. G. Edwards, *Calendar of ancient correspondence concerning Wales* (1935) · *Registrum epistolarum fratris Johannis Peckham, archiepiscopi Cantuariensis*, ed. C. T. Martin, 2, Rolls Series, 77 (1884) · J. Morris-Jones and T. H. Parry-Williams, eds., *Llawysgrif Hendregadredd* (1933)

**Gruffudd ap Rhys** (*fl.* 1256–1267). *See under* Ifor ap Meurig (*fl.* 1158).

**Gruffudd, Sir, ap Rhys** (1479–1521). *See under* Rice family (*per. c.*1500–1651).

**Gruffudd ap Rhys**. *See* Rice, Gruffudd (*c.*1526–1592), *under* Rice family (*per. c.*1500–1651).

**Gruffudd Fychan** (*d.* 1289). *See under* Madog ap Gruffudd Maelor (*d.* 1236).

**Gruffudd Gryg** (*fl. c.*1340–1380), poet, was the son of Cynfrig ap Gruffudd of Tregwehelyth, Llantrisant, Anglesey, apparently a substantial freeholder. Since Gruffudd styles himself *pencerdd* (chief poet) in one poem, refers to his pupils in another, and is bold enough to challenge Dafydd ap Gwilym to poetic debate, it may be assumed that he received a proper education as a professional poet. He apparently remained a man of substance and was *rhingyll* (sergeant) of the commote of Malltraeth in 1357–8. His epithet Gryg may be translated as 'the Hoarse' or 'the Stammerer'.

Seventeen of Gruffudd's poems have survived, together with a few *englynion*. Of these poems, only one is an *awdl*; the rest are *cywyddau*. The *awdl* and one of the *cywyddau* are religious in theme, while a second *cywydd* laments the degenerate state of the world. Two more *cywyddau* are skilful love poems of the kind made popular by Dafydd ap Gwilym. A pilgrimage to Santiago de Compostela provided matter for three *cywyddau*: a rebuke to the moon for causing foul weather at sea, a plea to the wave to act as love messenger, and a loving description, composed in Navarre, of his native Anglesey. A further three *cywyddau* were for local magnates: Einion ap Gruffudd of Chwilog in Caernarvonshire (he was sheriff, 1352–5); the seven sons of Iorwerth ap Gruffudd of the commote of Llifon in Anglesey, whom the poet had somehow offended; and a mock elegy for Rhys ap Gruffudd ap Tudur of the Penmynydd family. Four *cywyddau* from Gruffudd's side of the debate with Dafydd ap Gwilym have survived; the point of substance at issue was the legitimacy of the new love poetry [*see* Cywyddwyr (*act. c.*1330–*c.*1650)]. When it was concluded, Gruffudd and Dafydd wrote mock elegies for each other, but Gruffudd's fine *cywydd* to the yew tree above Dafydd's grave at Strata Florida Abbey appears to be genuine. R. GERAINT GRUFFYDD

**Sources** *Cywyddau Dafydd ap Gwilym a'i gyfoeswyr*, ed. I. Williams and T. Roberts, 2nd edn (1935), 131–52 · D. Johnston, ed., *Blodeugerdd Barddas o'r bedwaredd ganrif ar ddeg* (1989), 83–90 · *Gwaith Dafydd ap Gwilym*, ed. T. Parry (1952), 56–9, 388–412, 427–30 · J. G. Evans, ed., *The poetry in the Red Book of Hergest* (1911), col. 1297 · G. A. Williams, 'Cywydd Gruffudd Gryg i Dir Môn', *Ysgrifau beirniadol*, 13 (1985), 146–54 · E. D. Jones, 'Cartre Gruffudd Gryg', *National Library of Wales Journal*, 10 (1957–8), 230–31 · D. W. Wiliam, 'Y traddodiad barddol ym Mhlwyf Bodedern, Môn', *Transactions of the Anglesey Antiquarian Society and Field Club* (1969), 39–74, esp. 47–53 · A. T. E. Matonis, 'Later medieval poetics and some Welsh bardic debates', *BBCS*, 29 (1980–82), 635–65 · A. D. Carr, *Medieval Anglesey* (1982), 80, 222–3

**Gruffudd Hiraethog** (*d*. 1564), poet and herald, was born in Llangollen, the son of Mathew, the son of Mawd y Glyn and Owain Cyfeiliog. He married Catrin, the daughter of Edward ap Robert ab Ieuan ab Owain Glyndŵr. The warrant granted to Gruffudd in 1545/1546 on graduating as *disgybl pencerddaidd* (senior pupil) has survived, and in it Lewis Morgannwg is named as his teacher. Later on he graduated as *pencerdd*, and became *athro* (teacher) for the three bardic provinces of Aberffraw, Dinefwr, and Mathrafal. As herald he was deputy over Wales under Garter, Norroy, and Clarenceux, the first known holder of the office. A copy of the instructions issued to him by the College of Arms is extant. Among his pupils were the notable *Cywyddwyr (strict-metre poets) Lewis ab Edward, 'Sir' Owain ap Gwilym, Owain Gwynedd, Siôn Phylip, Siôn Tudur, Wiliam Cynwal, and Wiliam Llŷn, and on account of this alone he would have secured himself a significant place in the history of bardism in Wales.

Of Gruffudd Hiraethog's poems, 125 compositions in the form of *awdlau* (10) and *cywyddau* (115) have been preserved in manuscripts, as well as *englynion* (stanzas). They are typical of the strict-metre poetry of 1300–1650, and consist of eulogies, elegies, satires, and begging and debate poems. They are well crafted, as expected, but for the most part are not particularly memorable. Their period is *c*.1535–1564, and in the main they celebrate the generosity of patrons throughout north Wales. Only two poems to patrons living in south Wales have survived.

Gruffudd accomplished immense work as a genealogist and herald, and his collections contain material for both north and south Wales, and beyond. He was a careful and discerning chronicler, and his contributions in these fields are well regarded.

The miscellany consisting of proverbs, prose, and poetry compiled by Gruffudd Hiraethog to entertain expatriate Welshmen and to preserve the language in their midst is known as *Lloegr drigiant ddifyrrwch Brytanaidd Gymro* ('Entertainment for the Britannic Welshman residing in England'), and is deserving of special notice. The work was dedicated to Rhisiart Mostyn of Bodysgallen (near Llandudno), himself living in exile at the time. It was never published, and perhaps was only meant to be circulated in manuscript copies.

Gruffudd is also significant on account of his friendship with the great Renaissance scholar William Salesbury. Among the first books printed in Welsh was Salesbury's *Oll synnwyr pen Kembero ygyd* (1547), a collection of proverbs copied from one of Hiraethog's manuscripts, and in the preface he pays a generous tribute to the poet's achievements to date. Salesbury's 'Llyfr rhetoreg' (1552) ('Book of rhetoric') is dedicated to Gruffudd Hiraethog 'and others of his craft'. This work was not intended for publication, but rather to acquaint the Welsh poets with the art of rhetoric. Here he refers to Gruffudd as 'my chief companion in such matters'.

Gruffudd died in Llangollen in May 1564, and was buried there. The elegy for him by his pupil William Llŷn is deservedly well known. D. J. Bowen

**Sources** D. J. Bowen, *Gwaith Gruffudd Hiraethog* (1990) · M. P. Siddons, *The development of Welsh heraldry*, vols. 1–3 (1991–3)

**Gruffudd Llwyd, Sir** [Gruffudd ap Rhys] (*d*. 1335), soldier and administrator, was the son of Rhys ap Gruffudd (*d*. 1284) and a great-grandson of Ednyfed Fychan (*d*. 1246), seneschal to Llywelyn ab Iorwerth, called Llywelyn the Great (*d*. 1240). Gruffudd's forebears had ties of service with the thirteenth-century princes, but his father had served Edward I in the wars of 1277 and 1282–3. Rhys died in 1284, leaving his estates, including Tregarnedd, Anglesey, and Dinorwig, Caernarfon, and his share of lands at Llanrhystud, Cardigan, and Llansadwrn, Carmarthen, to his son. Gruffudd joined Queen Isabella's household and, a yeoman of the king's household by 1283, he soon began a long but not unbroken association with the crown as its leading servant in north Wales. In 1294–5 he served in the forces engaged in suppressing the rebellion of Madog ap Llywelyn but before the end of 1295, 'by the malice of his enemies' according to his own account (Edwards, 'Sir Gruffydd Llwyd', 600), he began an imprisonment lasting six months. Whatever the reason for his detention, service in Flanders in 1297, when he led an infantry force from north Wales, was a means of earning renewed royal confidence in his fidelity. Thereafter he frequently served as a commissioner of array in north Wales, raising forces for Scotland, and he is found in attendance on the prince of Wales during the campaigns of 1301 and 1306. Knighted by 1301, he served terms as sheriff of each of the counties of Anglesey, Caernarfon, and Merioneth.

Gruffudd Llwyd played an important role in the difficult situation which confronted Edward II in 1315–16. An army under Edward Bruce waged a forceful and destructive campaign in Ireland, and the Scots' emphasis on their kinship with the Irish raised fears that the Welsh, too, might be involved in a broad challenge to English authority. Commissioners sent to Wales to provide for the defence of the land were instructed to communicate with influential members of the Welsh community and were specially urged to consult Gruffudd Llwyd. He subsequently took part in discussions with the king's council at Clipstone, Nottinghamshire, 'concerning the state of the land of Wales' (Smith, 'Gruffydd Llwyd', 465), and these formed the basis of ordinances issued at the Lincoln parliament early in 1316 to meet Welsh discontent. Their promulgation was prompted by rebellion in Glamorgan, but it was feared in council that insurrection, fomented perhaps by intervention on the part of the Scots, might spread to other parts of Wales. Forces from north Wales raised for service in Scotland under Gruffudd Llwyd's leadership were turned back at Chester, on information transmitted by his chaplain, because they might be needed at home in the event of attack from Ireland.

Gruffudd appears to be one upon whose judgement and influence the king's council relied, but even at this time of conspicuous service he endured a long imprisonment which probably began with his detention at Rhuddlan in December 1316. In a petition of 1318 he asked that he might know the charges against him, on account of which he had already been incarcerated for eighteen months.

The reasons for his detention are never stated, and the problem is made more intriguing by the existence of letters by Edward Bruce and Gruffudd Llwyd, derived from the papers of the seventeenth-century antiquary Robert Vaughan. Bruce made an appeal, based on the common ancestry of the Scots and the Welsh, for a combined endeavour by which the two peoples would be released from English oppression. While his incentive to extend the armed struggle to Wales is evident, Gruffudd's reply, promising a Welsh response to a Scots intervention, is difficult to understand. Whether he was inveigled into a positive reply, possibly by adversaries bent on discrediting him, or whether this was a serious aberration on his part is impossible to determine. Gruffudd's letter was written swiftly after Roger Mortimer of Chirk (*d.* 1326) resumed the office of justice of Wales, and an animosity engendered during Mortimer's first period in office, and intensified upon his return to Wales, may explain his action.

Their antagonism was undoubtedly an influence which mattered greatly during Edward II's conflict with his baronial opponents in 1321–2. Mortimer and those associated with him won support among the Welsh communities of the marcher areas, but his alienation of the leaders of native society in the crown lands, where he had exercised authority as justice, remained a decisive influence. Between November 1321 and February 1322 Gruffudd Llwyd launched vigorous assaults on the marchers' positions and thereby contributed much to the king's triumph over his adversaries. He may well have been exacting retribution for earlier injustices.

Gruffudd was prominent in royal service in the period 1322–6, and he was one to whom Edward turned for aid upon Roger Mortimer of Wigmore's return to the realm, with Queen Isabella, in September 1326. The king's capture in the Welsh march enabled Mortimer to establish a hold on the administration of the crown lands. Writs were issued summoning Welsh representatives to the parliament at which Edward would be deposed, but they met with a resistance that was particularly pronounced in Merioneth, where Gruffudd Llwyd was sheriff. There was a Welsh conspiracy to release Edward from Berkeley Castle, and Gruffudd Llwyd was one of thirteen imprisoned at Caernarfon on account of their reaction to the king's deposition. In 1331 with Gruffudd's support a close associate, Hywel ap Gruffudd, brought an action in the king's bench against William Shalford, alleging Shalford's complicity in the murder of Edward II. Gruffudd is not known to have been active thereafter, and when summoned for service in Scotland in 1335 he was excused, possibly on grounds of ill-health. He was dead by 12 July 1335. Gruffudd Llwyd married Gwenllian and had two sons: Gruffudd, who died in 1322 while serving in a force led to Scotland by his father; and Ieuan, a cleric, later archdeacon of Anglesey, who succeeded to Gruffudd Llwyd's estates. According to the genealogies he also had seven daughters.

Older accounts, on the basis of a mistaken impression of the events of 1321–2, depict Gruffudd Llwyd as a Welsh patriot in resolute opposition to English authority. Even so, the poet Gwilym Ddu, in two poems composed during Gruffudd's imprisonment in 1316–18, one of them indicating confinement at Rhuddlan, expressed his grief at the injustice inflicted upon his patron by the English. Casnodyn, in a poem to Gwenllian, prayed God's help to secure her husband's release from iron fetters.

J. B. SMITH

**Sources** PRO · *Chancery records* · J. G. Edwards, 'Sir Gruffydd Llwyd', *EngHR*, 30 (1915), 589–601 · J. B. Smith, 'Gruffydd Llwyd and the Celtic alliance, 1315–1318', *BBCS*, 26 (1974–6), 463–78 · J. B. Smith, 'Edward II and the allegiance of Wales', *Welsh History Review / Cylchgrawn Hanes Cymru*, 8 (1976–7), 139–71 · R. Frame, 'The Bruces in Ireland, 1315–18', *Irish Historical Studies*, 19 (1974–5), 3–37 · D. R. Johnson and others, eds., *Gwaith Gruffudd ap Tudur Gwilym Ddu o Arfon et al.* (1995) · J. G. Edwards, *Calendar of ancient correspondence concerning Wales* (1935) · A. A. M. Duncan, *The acts of Robert I, king of Scots, 1306–1329* (1988) · R. R. Davies, *Conquest, coexistence, and change: Wales, 1063–1415*, History of Wales, 2 (1987)

**Gruffudd Llwyd** (*fl.* **1380–1420**), poet, was the son of Dafydd ab Einion Lygliw and nephew to the poet Hywel ab Einion Lygliw. He was a native of the parish of Llangadfan in Powys, and most of his patrons were noblemen of mid-Wales. A number of learned references and a smattering of Latin in his poems suggest that he had some ecclesiastical education. He was also learned in traditional Welsh lore, and took pride in his bardic status, declaring that he was not one of the 'vain minstrels'. The poet Rhys Goch Eryri was one of his bardic pupils and composed an elegy on his death. Fewer than twenty of Gruffudd's poems have survived, and although he lived through the Glyn Dŵr rebellion there is no mention of it in his work. However, one of the two poems he addressed to Glyn Dŵr does express a sense of resentment at the oppression of the Welsh, and the sombreness of his work in general can be seen to reflect the mood of the years leading up to the rebellion. DAFYDD JOHNSTON

**Sources** *Cywyddau Iolo Goch ac eraill*, ed. H. Lewis, T. Roberts, and I. Williams, new edn (1937) · *Gwaith Gruffudd Llwyd a'r Llygliwiaid eraill*, ed. R. Ifans (2000)

**Gruffudd of Bromfield**. *See* Gruffudd ap Madog (*d.* 1269) *under* Madog ap Gruffudd Maelor (*d.* 1236).

**Gruffudd, Elis** (*b. c.*1490, *d.* in or after **1556**), copyist and chronicler, was born at Gronant Uchaf, Gwesbyr, Llanasa, Flintshire. He himself is the source for almost all that is known of his life and career, though a few details are supplied or confirmed by external references. His genealogy has not been recorded, but he appears to have inherited a small estate which became the subject of legal wrangling, and he probably had wide family and social connections as one of the minor gentry in Flintshire, which would have facilitated his entry into service with English nobility, as one of the many Welshmen who joined the retinues of English noblemen in the period. He served in several campaigns, probably from about the age of twenty: Venlo (1511), Cadiz (1511), Fuenterrabia (1512), and Tournai (1514 onwards).

Gruffudd entered the service of Sir Robert Wingfield in 1518 and accompanied him to Calais, where Wingfield was deputy in 1520. He was an avid observer of the meeting at the Field of Cloth of Gold in 1521, and he fought in the army of the duke of Suffolk in the campaign in France in the last months of 1523. He spent the next years, 1524–9, as a member of the Wingfield household in London, describing himself as overseer of the mansion. Whatever his duties may have been, he found enough time to enjoy and to describe vividly many aspects of the life of London, and he also had leisure to compile, about 1527, a large compendium (Cardiff Central Library, MS 3.4) of fourteenth- and fifteenth-century gentry poetry, popular religious, historical, and astronomical treatises and lists, and a version of *The Seven Sages of Rome*, all typical of the native gentry culture of the time.

Gruffudd is best known, however, by his preferred self-description as 'a soldier of Calais'. He enlisted in the garrison in January 1530 and spent the rest of his active life there. He married Elizabeth Manfield in Calais, acquired land, set up house, and had two children. He describes many of his duties as a soldier, and he clearly enjoyed the ceremonial aspect of military life, especially the opportunities afforded him to observe the comings and goings of leading figures. He was tipstaff about 1546.

Gruffudd continued his literary activities in Calais. During a period of ill health about 1548 he put together a collection of his translations of English medical books (NL Wales, Cwrtmawr MS 1). His most important work was an extensive chronicle of the six ages of the world from the creation to his own time, a two-volume manuscript (NL Wales, MS 5276 and Mostyn MS 158), which he arranged should be sent to a friend, probably a kinsman, at Pant-y-llondy, Gwesbyr, for safe keeping soon after its completion about 1552–3 (the last date in the chronicle is 1552). Gruffudd was probably inspired to write his world chronicle by his knowledge of similar works in English and French. He was able to bring together in Calais a number of familiar histories. He names Ranulf Higden's *Polychronicon* and John Trevisa's translation, Edmund Hall, John Rastell, and Jean Froissart, but for the most part he refers merely to 'French books', 'English books', 'English chronicle', 'my copy' as sources. He rarely quotes directly from his sources but paraphrases and gives the gist of what he reads.

More remarkably Gruffudd had access to 'Welsh writings', unfortunately unnamed, and he also relied on oral sources ('a credible person', 'old folk', 'some … others', 'the opinion of the people') from his own cultural inheritance, acquired from what must have been a rich oral and literary culture in the north-east Wales of his early years. His chronicle is well structured, and as it progresses it becomes increasingly focused on Wales, regarded here as part of English history. He has a sound grasp of Welsh legendary history so that he is able to include at the appropriate points some folk tales, the first full version of the Taliesin prose-verse tale, and an extended Arthurian section together with other material.

Throughout his chronicle Gruffudd comments critically on the value of his sources, literary and oral. He appears to have received little training as a scribe and he has a personal idiosyncratic literary style underlying which is a strong aural sense. He is, nevertheless, an intelligent and able writer with consciously developed literary skills. He has a fine eye for dramatic situations, both contemporary and historical, and he can write effective dialogue. His extended anecdotes are narratives carefully constructed to achieve his desired literary effects or to make an implicit comment. Though Gwenogvryn Evans may have claimed too much for him as the author of some of 'the most readable prose in the Welsh language after the Mabinogion' (*Welsh Language MSS*, viii), he is now recognized as a master of narrative and a serious and effective writer.

Always interested in life around him, Gruffudd is a keen observer of people and commentator on events so that, drawing on personal experience, recollections, and possibly notes taken during his long career, he can describe graphically what he sees and hears. His account of numerous closely observed contemporary events and his own well-judged comments on situations and conditions make him a valuable 'unofficial' contemporary witness, but in Welsh historiography he represents the last stages of the declining traditional Welsh gentry culture recorded by one who represents the sociological changes which were transforming that class in the sixteenth century.

Both Gruffudd and his wife were alive in 1556, but nothing more is heard of him after that. It is not known where or when he died. BRYNLEY F. ROBERTS

**Sources** T. Jones, 'A Welsh chronicler in Tudor England', *Welsh History Review / Cylchgrawn Hanes Cymru*, 1 (1960–63), 1–17 · P. Morgan, 'Elis Gruffudd of Gronant: Tudor chronicler extraordinary', *Flintshire Historical Society Journal*, 25 (1971–2), 9–20 · P. Morgan, 'Elis Gruffudd yng Nghalais', *BBCS*, 21 (1964–6), 214–18 · C. Lloyd-Morgan, 'Elis Gruffydd a thraddodiad Cymraeg Calais a Chlwyd', *Cof Cenedl*, 11 (1996), 31–58 · J. Hunter, *Soffistri'r Saeson* (2000) · *Report on manuscripts in the Welsh language*, 2 vols. in 7, HMC, 48 (1898–1910), vol. 1/1, pp. i–xii, 214–21 · M. Tibbott, *Castell yr iechyd gan Elis Gruffydd* (1969)

**Archives** NL Wales

**Gruffydd, Owen** (*c*.1643–1730), Welsh-language poet and genealogist, was born in the parish of Llanystumdwy, Caernarvonshire, where he remained throughout his life. He was a weaver by trade and is said to have been the unacknowledged son of a priest, Gruffydd Owen. Certainly his poetry is that of a convinced churchman. He wrote angrily against Cromwell and the parliamentarians, 'the enemies of light'. Humphrey Humphreys (1648–1712), the enlightened bishop of Bangor, shared his poetic and antiquarian interests and was his friend and patron. When Humphreys moved in 1701 to become bishop of Hereford, Gruffydd wrote poems bemoaning the loss to religion and culture of an eminently generous and learned leader.

Owen Gruffydd was the last of the traditional poets of the commote of Eifionydd—and, indeed, of Wales in general. He was a tireless chronicler of pedigrees and wrote dozens of pedigree poems, mainly in the *cywydd* metre, lauding the virtues and tracing the noble antecedents of the ancient families and gentry of Eifionydd, Arfon, Llŷn, and Meirionnydd. Following the poets of the middle ages he journeyed on circuit to the homes of these landed families, soliciting their patronage and returning eulogy and elegy in time-honoured payment. This won him a reputation as a scholar-poet and antiquarian firmly in the tradition of the medieval bards. While he had mastered the style of the earlier poets of the nobility, these pedigree poems make heavy reading. In his elegy to his friend Siôn Dafydd Las or Laes (John Davies; *c.*1665–1695), the household bard of the Nannau family, genuine feeling struggles for expression, but such examples are rare.

Like most poets of the seventeenth and eighteenth centuries Gruffydd also produced a considerable body of verse in the free metres. These were songs set to be sung to Welsh and borrowed English tunes, carols and poems in the popular *tri thrawiad* metre and other alliterative metres. They were invariably written on religious, cautionary, and moralistic subjects such as 'The Day of Judgement', 'Old Age and Youth', 'The Creation of Man, his Fall and Deliverance', 'A Song of Praise', praise for salvation. O. M. Edwards called him the poet of old age, the grave, and the judgement to come. During his last years he lost his sight and depended on William Elias and other friends to preserve his poems. He was buried in Llanystumdwy on 6 December 1730. He was unmarried.

Some of Owen Gruffydd's poems appeared in *Carolau a Dyriau Duwiol* (1696, 1720, 1729) before his death and more in *Blodeu-gerdd Cymry* (1759). The greater part of his verse remains in manuscript (in collections in the British Library, Cardiff Public Library, and National Library of Wales, Cwrt-Mawr MSS). The elegies written by his bardic pupils Michael Pritchard (*c.*1709–1733) and particularly William Elias (1708–1787) show that Gruffydd, while not a fully professional poet, was an important link in the interregnum between the demise of the poetic tradition and the neo-classical revival of the mid-eighteenth century.

E. G. MILLWARD

**Sources** *Gwaith Owen Gruffydd o Lanystumdwy* (1904) · *Y Traethodydd*, 1 (1845), 372–6 · *Y Llenor*, 2 (1895), 50–66 · *Cymru*, 3 (1892), 132 · *Cell meudwy, sef, Gweithiau barddonol a rhyddieithol Ellis Owen*, ed. R. I. Jones (1877), 58–60 · W. Rowland, *Gwŷr Eifionydd* (1953), 45–52
**Likenesses** cartoon, repro. in *Y Llenor*, 2

**Gruffydd, Thomas** (1815–1887), harpist, was born at Llangynidr, Brecknockshire, Wales. His maternal grandfather was the rector of the parish, in which his ancestors were yeomen. When he was three he lost one eye through falling on a hatchet, and when a schoolboy almost lost the other by a blow. He was already musical, and after these accidents devoted all his energies to music and particularly to playing the harp. He was a pupil of John Wood Jones, the resident harpist to the Gwynne family of Glan Brân, near Llandovery. He subsequently held a similar position at Llanofer, where he also kept a small-holding. He had a high reputation as a harpist in south-east Wales and became a popular penillion singer. In 1843 he accompanied Jones to Buckingham Palace to play Welsh airs before the queen and Prince Albert. The influential Welsh historian and antiquary Thomas Price (Carnhuanawc) was present at the time and was asked by the prince to explain the peculiarities of the Welsh triple harp. Gruffydd was also invited alone to give recitals at Marlborough House.

Gruffydd won the triple harp competition at the Abergavenny eisteddfod in 1836 and at numerous other eisteddfods. In 1867 he visited Brittany, accompanied by his daughter, spending most of the time as a guest of the Comte de la Villemarqué, who presented him on leaving with a gold ring bearing the inscription 'Keltied bro C'hall da Gruffydd, Llanover' ('From the Celts of the districts of the Gauls to Gruffydd of Llanofer'). He was made harpist to the prince of Wales, before whom he played when the prince visited Raglan and Chepstow castles. He was for many years recognized as the greatest Welsh harpist of his age. One of his songs, 'Gwlad y beirdd' ('The land of the bards'), was published. He died at his home, Tŷ Eglwys, Llanofer, Abergavenny, on 30 August 1887 and was buried in Llanofer churchyard beside his parents.

R. M. J. JONES, *rev.* TREVOR HERBERT

**Sources** *DWB* · Gwynionydd, '"Gruffydd," y Telynor Cymreig, drwy Bennodiad Neilltuol i'w Uchelder Breninol Tywysog Cymru', *Y Geninen*, 6 (1888), 189–90 · d. cert.

**Gruffydd, William John** (1881–1954), writer and university teacher, was born in Gorffwysfa, Bethel, in the parish of Llanddeiniolen, Caernarvonshire, on 14 February 1881, the eldest child in the family of two sons and two daughters of John Griffith (1852–1929), quarryman, and his wife, Jane Elizabeth Gruffydd (1859–*c.*1927), daughter of Thomas Gruffydd. He received his early education at Bethel primary school and Caernarfon county school. Caernarvonshire always exerted a strong influence on Gruffydd: 'To me it would seem that *no* Welshman has ever been more conscious than I have of his roots' (Gruffydd, trans. Lloyd, 58). He rebelled early in his career against the constricting standards of his culture, and while still in his teens began to take a passionate interest in Welsh poetry. From 1899 to 1903 he was an exhibitioner at Jesus College, Oxford, taking a third class in classical honour moderations (1901) and graduating with a second in English (1903). In 1900 he published with R. Silyn Roberts a book of lyrical verse entitled *Telynegion*. He taught for a year in Scarborough (an unhappy experience), and for two years at Beaumaris grammar school before being appointed in 1906 to an assistant lectureship in the department of Celtic at what became University College, Cardiff.

In the same year Gruffydd published his second volume of poetry, *Caneuon a cherddi*. His early poetry was suffused with an Englishness and a romanticism which was lacking from his later work. On 16 August 1909 he married Gwenda Evans (*b.* 1883/4), daughter of Thomas Evans, the Calvinistic Methodist minister of Aber-carn; they had one son, and settled in Tongwynlais, Glamorgan (Gwenda later published translations from French literature). In 1910 Gruffydd won the crown poem competition at the national eisteddfod on the subject of Lord Rhys: in its control of poetic structure in the Welsh language it is judged one of his primary literary achievements.

After 1910 Gruffydd's poetic output was spasmodic due to the demands of scholarship. A subtle and discerning critic and anthologist, he produced an edition of Goronwy

Owen's *Cywyddau* (1907) and in 1909 *Y flodeugerdd newydd* ('The new anthology'), a selection of medieval poetry intended for college use. (A later anthology, *Flodeugerdd Gymraeg*, was published in 1931). In 1907–8 Gruffydd published landmark papers in the *Transactions of the Guild of Graduates* on the connections between Welsh and continental literature in the fourteenth and fifteenth centuries, and in 1912–13 in the *Transactions of the Honourable Society of Cymmrodorion*.

In the same period he also wrote a play, *Beddau'r proffwydi* ('The graves of the prophets'), first produced by the students' Welsh Drama Society in March 1913. This and another play, *Dyrchafiad arall i Gymro* (1914), were significant contributions to a new naturalistic movement in Welsh drama.

From 1915 to 1918 Gruffydd served as an officer in the Royal Naval Volunteer Reserve, predominantly in the Persian Gulf, and by the time he was released he had been appointed professor of Celtic (a title later changed to Welsh) at Cardiff, a post he held until his retirement in 1946. Among his important contributions to scholarship *Llenyddiaeth Cymru, 1460–1600* (1922) and *Llenyddiaeth Cymru, 1540–1660* (1926), a history of Welsh literature, are significant.

From 1922 until it ceased publication in 1951 Gruffydd edited *Y Llenor*, the highly successful Welsh quarterly journal, to which many of the leading Welsh writers of the period frequently contributed. The editorial notes, which commented, often with scorching indignation, on many aspects of life in Wales, including support for the Welsh language, aroused considerable interest and feeling and contributed greatly to the character and impact of the journal. Gruffydd contributed autobiographical pieces as well as poetry.

The collection *Ynys yr hud a chaneuon eraill* (1923) is considered to be Gruffydd's first mature work—here he returned to the working community of his childhood in a tauter style and more sombre tone than the effusions of his earlier verse. *Caniadau* (1932), a selection which he himself made of his poetry down to 1931, which excludes much of his early poetry, is a useful edition of his later work.

Prose became Gruffydd's main medium of literary expression in his later years, and among his more important works are the autobiographical *Hen atgofion* (1936), his biography of Owen Morgan Edwards (1937), both of which are classics of Welsh prose literature, and *Y tro Olaf* (1939). From 1950 onwards he made Welsh translations of *Antigone* and *King Lear* for broadcast.

Gruffydd's major contributions to Welsh scholarship were the numerous studies he published of the intricate structure of the four branches of the Mabinogi and of aspects of the Arthurian legend, a field in which his interest had been aroused by the work of Sir John Rhŷs. Outstanding among those contributions are his *Math vab Mathonwy* (1928) and *Rhiannon* (1953) which, in spite of some evident shortcomings, particularly a failure on the author's part to make sufficient use of the comparative method, testify to Gruffydd's originality of mind, his general perceptiveness, and his clarity of exposition. The validity of his basic hypothesis has not been seriously challenged.

Gruffydd's lifelong adherence to the principles of tolerance and freedom of thought, as well as his strong aversion to dogma and to any formalized critical doctrine, stemmed partly from his nonconformist upbringing and beliefs. Temperamental, moody, and irascible, he appeared to many of his critics to be culpably inconsistent in the attitudes he took to some of the contentious issues of his day. His shifting standpoints, however, were invariably based on genuine conviction. In 1943 he fought a famous by-election for the University of Wales seat when he stood as the official Liberal candidate against Saunders Lewis of Plaid Cymru. He held the seat until it was abolished in 1950. He was elected president of the council of the national eisteddfod (1945), and was awarded the gold medal of the Honourable Society of Cymmrodorion (1946) and honorary doctorates by the universities of Rennes (1946) and Wales (1947).

During the Second World War and after Gruffydd suffered periods of ill health. He began to find editing *Y Llenor* troublesome and he retired from the Welsh chair in 1946. He moved then to Chertsey to concentrate on politics but, beleaguered by further illness, he returned to Caernarvonshire. He died at his home in Bangor Road, Caernarfon, on 29 September 1954, and was buried at Llanddeiniolen graveyard, not far from the yew tree which is the subject of one of his most celebrated poems.

Gruffydd was one of the most important literary figures writing in Welsh between the wars: his poems about working communities contributed to the development of Welsh poetry away from romanticism and lyricism.

C. W. Lewis, *rev.* Clare L. Taylor

**Sources** W. J. Gruffydd, *The years of the locust*, trans. D. M. Lloyd (1976), trans. as *The year of the locust* [Welsh orig., *Hen atgofion: blynyddoedd y locust*] · T. J. Morgan, *W. J. Gruffydd* (1970) · D. Johnston, ed., *A guide to Welsh literature*, 6: *c.*1900–1996 (1998) · M. Stephens, ed., *The Oxford companion to the literature of Wales* (1986) · T. R. Chapman, *W. J. Gruffydd* (1993) · b. cert. · m. cert. · d. cert. · *CGPLA Eng. & Wales* (1955)

**Archives** NL Wales, corresp. and papers | NL Wales, corresp. with E. T. John · NL Wales, letters to Sir Thomas Parry-Williams

**Wealth at death** £3747 0s. 4d.: probate, 17 Feb 1955, *CGPLA Eng. & Wales*

**Grumbold, Robert** (*bap.* 1639, *d.* 1720), mason and architect, was baptized in June 1639 at Raunds, Northamptonshire, the son of Edward and Mary Grumbold, and was a member of a family of masons originating at the quarry villages of Raunds and Weldon which was active in the Northamptonshire area over several generations. It is not known where he learned his trade, but if it was not in Raunds it could have been in Cambridge, where a Thomas Grumbold (*d.* 1657) had settled; and it was in Cambridge that he established himself, perhaps succeeding to Thomas Grumbold's business. In the course of a long career he became the leading locally based figure in the architecture of the town during the later seventeenth century and the beginning of the eighteenth, and was involved in many of the collegiate building projects of the period.

Like many other master masons, Grumbold worked as an executant of both his own and others' designs. His first recorded project in Cambridge was the building of the west range of Clare College (1669–76), where Thomas Grumbold had worked previously and where the design was probably the joint work of Grumbold, a 'surveyor' called Jackson, and the college authorities. Subsequent works designed by him include the north range at Clare (1682–6) and probably the rebuilding of St Catharine's College (1674–1704). The most important project on which he acted as contracting mason only was the building of the library at Trinity College (1676–84) to the design of Sir Christopher Wren, and he was also associated with the latter over some work at Ely Cathedral (1699). The contact with Wren is of particular interest in that it provided an influence on Grumbold's own architectural style, to be seen, for example, in the Clare north range; but otherwise his designs display a pleasant artisan manner rather than a full understanding of the grammar of classical architecture.

Grumbold's will indicates that he accumulated considerable wealth, acquiring a substantial amount of leasehold property in Cambridge. He appears to have had one son and one daughter living at the time of his death, which occurred in Cambridge on 7 December 1720.

Peter Leach

**Sources** Colvin, *Archs.* • D. Knoop and G. P. Jones, 'The rise of the mason contractor', *RIBA Journal*, 43 (1935–6), 1061–71, esp. 1069–70 • G. F. Webb, 'Robert Grumbold and the architecture of the Renaissance in Cambridge', *Burlington Magazine*, 47 (1925), 314–19; 48 (1926), 36–41 • R. Willis, *The architectural history of the University of Cambridge, and of the colleges of Cambridge and Eton*, ed. J. W. Clark, 3 (1886)

**Wealth at death** £938 10s. 0d.—in goods: will, 23 Dec 1720, Cambs. AS

**Grundy, John** (*bap.* **1719**, *d.* **1783**), civil engineer, baptized at Congerstone, Leicestershire, on 1 July 1719, was the elder son of John Grundy senior (*c.*1696–1748), land surveyor and civil engineer, and his wife, Elizabeth Dalton. About 1738 the family moved to Spalding in Lincolnshire, where in 1743 Grundy married Lydia Knipe (1721–1764). They had two daughters. Mary, the elder, married William Thompson, to whom Grundy bequeathed the greater part of his estate, the younger, unmarried, daughter having predeceased him. In 1766, two years after his wife's death, Grundy married Mrs Ann Maud, widow of the vicar of St Neots. There were no children of this second marriage.

In the early 1740s Grundy worked as assistant to his father who, starting as a land surveyor in Leicestershire, had been called in 1731 to survey land belonging to the duke of Buccleuch around Spalding. This gave the elder Grundy an opportunity to study fen drainage and flow of water in open channels which, complemented by his ability in mathematics, made him an authority on the subject. Between 1734 and 1736 he reported on South Holland Fen, improvements of the River Dee, and the drainage of Deeping Fen. In 1738 he and Humphrey Smith were jointly appointed 'surveyors and agents' (engineers) of this large tract of fenland in Lincolnshire. In 1742 he became sole agent and held this post, with freedom to undertake some outside work, until a year before his death in 1748. These other works included repairs to sea defences on the Norfolk coast and a report on the River Witham published in 1744 with his son as joint author.

The younger John Grundy's independent career began in 1745 with a series of works at Grimsthorpe (near Grantham) for the duke of Ancaster, one of which was an earth dam with a compacted clay core for the Great Water Lake completed in 1748. In that year he succeeded his father as engineer of Deeping Fen, and retained this position until 1764; one of several works by him was the rebuild of Six Doors sluice on the River Welland. Meanwhile his practice as a consultant was growing: at least ten reports appeared in the 1750s followed by a very important one on the Witham in 1761 by Grundy, as senior author, John Smeaton, and Langley Edwards. Works based on this report, carried out 1763–7 under the direction of Edwards, included a new 9 mile channel for the river and the Grand Sluice at Boston.

When Grundy retired as engineer of Deeping Fen in 1764 Thomas Hogard took his place. Grundy, retained as a consultant, was free to direct the construction, and also produce the designs, of works elsewhere, with a resident engineer on each. The largest of these was Holderness drainage (1765–7), involving the greatly improved drainage of 11,000 acres of low ground north of Hull. Others were the Louth Navigation (1765–7), Driffield Navigation (1767–70), on both of which the locks could accommodate Yorkshire keels of 14 ft beam, and Laneham drainage (1770–72) in Nottinghamshire. Also in this period he acted as engineer in charge of the Adlingfleet drainage (1767–9), an area of 5000 acres adjacent to the lower reaches of the Trent, the planning of which had been carried out by Smeaton in 1764.

In 1771 Grundy became a founder member of the Society of Civil Engineers, along with Thomas Yeoman (president), Smeaton, Robert Mylne, John Golborne, Robert Whitworth, and a few others who formed the core of the profession in its early days.

The last phase of Grundy's career included two major projects—the Hull Dock, for which he produced the plan and designs in 1774 (constructed 1775–8 under Henry Berry of Liverpool), and the Market Weighton Drainage and Navigation. The latter secured the drainage of 16,000 acres by a 6 mile cut from an outfall sluice (with an adjacent navigation lock) on the Humber, and 40 miles of secondary drains. Grundy's report and plan are dated 1772. He directed the main works from 1772 to 1775, when the resident engineer, Samuel Allam, took charge until completion in 1780.

Between 1750 and 1778 Grundy produced more than fifty reports, thirteen of which were printed. All of these he or his clerk copied into 'report books' together with estimates, observations, drawings, and letters, a total of some five thousand quarto pages. The books passed to his son-in-law William Thompson and were purchased by Sir

Joseph Banks in 1793. Grundy died on 15 June 1783 at Spalding, Lincolnshire, and is buried in Spalding parish church. A. W. Skempton

**Sources** A. W. Skempton, 'The engineering works of John Grundy (1719–1783)', *Lincolnshire History and Archaeology*, 19 (1984), 65–82 • N. R. Wright, *John Grundy of Spalding, engineer, 1719–1783* (1983) • O. S. Pickering, 'The re-emergence of the engineering reports of John Grundy of Spalding', *Transactions* [Newcomen Society], 60 (1988–9), 137–43 • A. W. Skempton, *British civil engineering, 1640–1840: a bibliography of contemporary printed reports, plans, and books* (1987)
**Archives** Inst. CE, papers and drawings | priv. coll. • U. Leeds, Brotherton L.
**Likenesses** two portraits, *c.*1743–*c.*1765, priv. coll.

**Grundy, John** (1782–1843), Unitarian minister, was born on 7 February 1782 at Hinckley, Leicestershire, the eldest son and second of the four children of Thomas Grundy, a hosier, and his wife, Elizabeth Estlin. He was baptized on 12 May 1783 by Thomas Belsham (1750–1829). Educated at Bristol by his uncle, John Prior *Estlin (1747–1817), he entered Manchester Academy in September 1797, with an exhibition from the Presbyterian Fund, but returned to Bristol the following year to complete his studies for the ministry under Estlin's direction. His first settlement, in 1804, was at Churchgate Street Chapel, Bury St Edmunds, Suffolk, where two preceding ministries had ended in strained circumstances probably accounted for, to judge from delphic exchanges of letters, by disagreement over unitarian doctrines. The invitation to Grundy and his letter of acceptance are both ringing declarations of the right of ministers to preach freely without dictation and of the correlative limitation that a minister cannot impose his views on the congregation, a theme to which Grundy returned in 1824 in *The Reciprocal Duties of Ministers and Congregations*.

Grundy's pastorate at Bury St Edmunds was brief but satisfactory, as is suggested by expressions of mutual esteem exchanged at the end of 1806, when he left to join James Tayler (1765–1831) in the pastorate at High Pavement Chapel, Nottingham. In January 1811 he became minister at Cross Street Chapel, Manchester, where he was joined later that year by John Gooch Robberds as co-pastor. At Cross Street, Grundy's controversial preaching alienated some older members of the congregation, who had much of 'primitive puritanism' among them. His doctrinal lectures created an unusual degree of religious ferment: 'Grundy and no devil for ever' was chalked on the walls of his meeting-house.

In 1810 Grundy married Anne (1779–1855), daughter of John Hancock of Nottingham. They had four sons and four daughters. One son, Francis Henry (*d.* 1889), was the author of *Pictures of the Past* (1879), which records some reminiscences of Branwell Brontë. The eldest daughter, Maria Anne (*d.* 1871), married Swinton Boult (1809–1876).

In 1811 Grundy published *Christianity: an Intellectual and Individual Religion*, a sermon preached on the afternoon of 20 October at the opening of a new chapel in Renshaw Street, Liverpool, where, again, some members of the congregation, accustomed to the Arian minister Robert Lewin (1739–1825), were scandalized by the open unitarianism; oddly enough, that morning Lewin had preached on the mutual obligations of ministers and congregations. A note added to the published version of Grundy's sermon, on the growth of unitarian opinion in Boston, Massachusetts, led to a correspondence with Francis Parkman (1788–1852), minister of New North Church in Boston and father of the historian of the same name.

In 1824 Grundy accepted an invitation to succeed John Yates (1755–1826) and Pendlebury Houghton (1758–1824) as sole minister at Paradise Street Chapel, Liverpool, where in 1832 he was joined in the pastorate by James Martineau. Before leaving Manchester in September 1824, Grundy was presented with a silver tea service at a public farewell dinner on 12 August. A speech by George Harris (1794–1859), a fiery Unitarian preacher from Bolton, who acknowledged that a sermon by Grundy in London in 1811 had determined him on a ministerial career, led to a long and acrimonious discussion in the newspapers (in which Grundy took no part), known as the Manchester Socinian controversy. With that title, the papers were reprinted under evangelical auspices in 1825. The publication's contemptuous introduction and the appended list of chapels and funds which Unitarians had allegedly perverted from the intentions of orthodox donors fuelled an agitation that culminated in a decision of the House of Lords in 1842 adverse to Unitarians, largely reversed in the Dissenters' Chapels Act of 1844.

In 1835, because of failing health, Grundy retired to Chideock, near Bridport, Dorset, where he died of 'debility attended by paralysis' on 9 May 1843. He was buried in the graveyard of the Unitarian chapel, Bridport.

R. K. Webb

**Sources** *DNB* • Registers, Great Meeting House, Hinckley • Congregational records, Churchgate Street Chapel, Bury St Edmunds • J. Birt, ed., *The Manchester Socinian controversy* (1825) • d. cert. • *Monthly Repository*, 19/574 (Sept 1824) • *IGI*
**Likenesses** S. W. Reynolds, mezzotint, pubd 1825 (after H. Wyatt), BM, NPG • engraving, repro. in T. Baker, *Memorials of a dissenting chapel* (1884), 51

**Grundy, John Clowes** (1806–1867), printseller, publisher, and art patron, was born in Bolton-le-Moors on 3 August 1806. He was the eldest son of John Grundy, a cotton spinner, and his wife, Elizabeth Leeming, who raised their family in accordance with the recently established Swedenborgian doctrines of spirituality and family values. Indeed, the Grundys seem to have been a particularly close-knit family. Although there is no evidence that the parents were artistic, all four of John and Elizabeth Grundy's sons followed careers in the arts. In the case of the engraver Thomas Leeming Grundy [*see below*] and his brother Joseph Leeming Grundy (1812–1902), a watercolourist, they were practising artists; John Clowes Grundy, a picture dealer in Manchester, and Robert Hindmarsh Grundy (1816–1865), a Liverpool printseller, were both on the commercial side of the art world.

Little is known of the early life of any of the Grundy brothers, except for **Thomas Leeming Grundy** (1808–1841), printmaker, who was born in Bolton on 6 January 1808. By about 1822 he was apprenticed to a Manchester writing engraver but soon showed promise beyond the requirements of that sort of 'business engraving' (*Art Union*). Aspiring to work as a line engraver, he moved to London in 1828 and began engraving plates for the annuals, after images by the likes of Henry Liverseege or Clarkson Stanfield. He obviously recognized the possibilities that further training would generate so, in 1830, he became assistant and pupil to the 'celebrated engraver' (*Art Union*) G. T. Doo. Next he worked for Eliza Goodall, a landscape engraver, before setting up on his own. After this point Grundy had no shortage of work; he continued to engrave for the annuals but also executed many large plates in a variety of printmaking techniques, including line engraving. Notable among these is an etched portrait of the duke of Wellington, and several Scottish landscapes after D. O. Hill for *The Land of Burns* (1840), as well as some separate plates such as *The Keepsake* (1837) after Stanfield. He was talented and widely admired; his obituary in the *Art Union* lamented 'had he lived, there is little doubt he would have taken a high rank in his profession' (*Art Union*). Leaving a widow and a child, he died in Camden on 10 March 1841 and was buried in St Pancras old churchyard.

Ironically, it was not until the 1840s that the separate fortunes of his brothers Robert and John really began to flourish. From some letters of David Cox which were sent to 'Mr. Grundy, *the younger*, Printseller, near the Exchange, Manchester' (Roe, 54) we know that Robert was based in Manchester at the start of his career. The Exchange was, however, the address more usually associated with the business of John Clowes Grundy. From his posthumous sale catalogue, which included the furnishings and 'marbles' from 'Exchange Street', we see that Grundy intended his showroom to be a fashionable and dignified gathering place. As a connoisseur and avid collector of a wide variety of painted, engraved, and applied arts he undoubtedly mixed easily with connoisseurs and customers. Also, in keeping with the contemporary fashion, people probably gathered at his Manchester showroom to discuss and view contemporary art. They may also have come to subscribe for copies of publishing projects such as David Roberts's lavish six-volume *The Holy Land*, with coloured lithographs by Louis Haghe, which Grundy helped Sir Francis Moon to publish in 1842.

It is indicative that John Clowes Grundy's brief *Gentleman's Magazine* obituary praised him as a 'senior member of the print establishment' (*GM*), as this description indicates the many aspects of the northern and national art world in which he was involved. He was both friend and patron to many contemporary artists such as David Cox, whose skill he had been quick to spot. He also made special efforts to advance the work of some favourites. In 1835 he had collaborated in publishing the complete mezzotint works of Henry Liverseege and, in 1848, Samuel Prout acknowledged how useful he was as provincial representative. Grundy was not only concerned with the well-being of individual artists but held views on the status of printmaking in general. In 1847, along with his brother Robert, he was one of the founder members of the Printsellers' Association, which was established to protect the rights of printmakers and to ensure the quality and authenticity of prints in the market place. In addition to his enthusiastic involvement in contemporary art production, he amassed a large number of antiques, curiosities, and old master engravings at his house, The Cliff, Higher Broughton. John Clowes Grundy died at the British Hotel, Cockspur Street, Charing Cross, on 19 May 1867, while visiting London, and was survived by at least two sons who continued their father's business. LUCY PELTZ

**Sources** G. W. Friend, ed., *An alphabetical list of engravings declared at the office of the Printsellers' Association, London*, 2 vols. (1892) · *Art Union*, 3 (1841), 134 [T. L. Grundy] · *Catalogue of extensive and valuable stock of modern pictures and drawings and ancient and modern engravings* (1867) · D. Bank and A. Esposito, eds., *British biographical archive*, 2nd series (1991) [microfiche] · B. Hunnisett, *A dictionary of British steel engravers* (1980) · R. Lockett, *Samuel Prout, 1783–1852* (1985) · *GM*, 4th ser., 4 (1867), 116 · F. G. Roe, *David Cox* (1925) · N. N. Solly, *Memoir of the life of David Cox* (1873); facs. edn (1973) · *CGPLA Eng. & Wales* (1867)

**Wealth at death** under £20,000: probate, 13 Aug 1867, *CGPLA Eng. & Wales*

**Grundy, Thomas Leeming** (1808–1841). *See under* Grundy, John Clowes (1806–1867).

**Gruneisen, Charles Lewis** (1806–1879), journalist and music critic, was born on 2 November 1806 in Bloomsbury, London, the son of Charles Gruneisen of Stuttgart, Germany, who had been naturalized in 1796. He was educated at home by a private tutor, then at a school in Pentonville, and went on to study in the Netherlands before turning to journalism. Sub-editor of the Conservative *Guardian* from 1832, he was editor of the *British Traveller and Commercial and Law Gazette* in 1833 for a few months before his appointment as foreign editor of the *Morning Post*.

In London, Gruneisen had met supporters of Don Carlos of Spain, who had refused to recognize the regency of Queen Maria Christina for her young daughter, Isabella, who had succeeded to the Spanish throne in 1833. In 1837 he was sent to Spain by the *Morning Post* as war correspondent. Despite British official support for the regency—a British legion had been sent to help Queen Isabella—Gruneisen attached himself to the Carlist army, and for over five months marched with the army to Madrid, retreating with it until its defeat at the battle of Retuerta. Gruneisen was imprisoned on his way home by supporters of the regency, narrowly escaped being shot as a spy, and was released only after Palmerston had intervened. Don Carlos decorated him with the cross of the order of Charles III, and a cross to commemorate the victory at Los Navarros. He was one of the most important of the early Victorian war correspondents.

Gruneisen returned to London at the beginning of 1838, and in January 1839 married Emma Jane Moore. They went to live in Paris, where from 1839 to 1844 he was Paris correspondent of the *Morning Post*. While there he started sending music reviews back to London, which helped to make European composers and performers better known in England. He organized a pigeon post to carry his dispatches. On his return to London he became editor of a new paper, the *Great Gun*, as well as contributing music reviews to several newspapers. He is mentioned by Beethoven's biographer and former secretary, Anton Schindler, as representing the *Britannia* in Bonn in 1845, when several journalists interviewed him about the correct tempi of Beethoven's piano sonatas.

It was as music critic of the *Morning Chronicle* that Gruneisen campaigned in 1846 for the establishment of a second Italian opera company in London, to rival the Italian Opera at Her Majesty's Theatre in the Haymarket, which had been the scene of quarrels between the singers and the management since the late 1830s, to the detriment of musical standards. He was the moving spirit behind the composer Giuseppe Persiani's purchase of the lease of the Covent Garden Theatre, in order to convert it into an opera house. Michael Costa, a close friend, had resigned as conductor at Her Majesty's Theatre in January 1846, and he was persuaded to become musical director and conductor at Covent Garden, bringing the principal singers, and most of the orchestra, with him. Frederick Beale, of the music publishers Cramer, Beale & Co., was appointed general manager, and the new Royal Italian Opera opened in 1847 with a performance of Rossini's *Semiramide*. In 1848 Meyerbeer's *Les Huguenots*, sung in Italian, was performed in the presence of Queen Victoria—the first state visit to the Royal Italian Opera. The queen had selected *Les Huguenots* from a list of possible works after Gruneisen had advised that it be put at the top of the list, in the hope that she would choose it. It was also Gruneisen's idea that all performances at Covent Garden should be sung in Italian, with any non-Italian operas translated into Italian. While in Paris, Gruneisen had met Meyerbeer, who later entrusted him with a score of his new opera, *Le prophète*. First performed in Paris in April 1849, it had been so enthusiastically received that theatres all over Europe were competing to stage it. Through Gruneisen *Le prophète* had its first London performance at Covent Garden on 24 July 1849, with Pauline Viardot García repeating her Paris success. Gruneisen continued to support Covent Garden until 1869, when he attacked Frederick Gye, manager since 1850, in *The Standard*, comparing Gye's management of Covent Garden to Benjamin Lumley's mismanagement of Her Majesty's Theatre in the 1840s.

Gruneisen continued to work as a music critic, enjoying controversy, and he was one of the first to write positively about the music of Wagner. In 1870 he became music critic of *The Athenaeum*, succeeding Cowden Clarke, who had taken over from H. F. Chorley in 1868. He continued to write such damning reviews of performances at Covent Garden that Frederick Gye published a pamphlet, *The Royal Italian Opera and the 'Athenaeum' Newspaper* (1875), in protest. Gruneisen also wrote a column of musical gossip for the *Queen* newspaper. He published a *Memoir of Meyerbeer* (1848), *The Opera and the Press* (1869), and *Sketches of Spain and the Spaniards during the Carlist Civil War* (1874), and he contributed additional notes to the *Life of F. Mendelssohn Bartholdy* (1876) by W. A. Lampadius.

A lifelong Conservative, Gruneisen was involved in the foundation in 1852 of the Conservative Land Society, formed as a counter to the National Land Society organized by Cobden and Bright to enfranchise radical voters. He was a member of the original committee, and served as secretary from 1853 to 1872. He died on 1 November 1879 at his home, 16 Surrey Street, Strand, London, and he was buried in Highgate cemetery on the 7th. His wife survived him. ANNE PIMLOTT BAKER

**Sources** R. T. Bledsoe, *Henry Fothergill Chorley* (1998) • L. Langley, 'Italian opera and the English press, 1836–1856', *Periodica Musica*, 6 (1988), 3–10 • H. Rosenthal, *Two centuries of opera at Covent Garden* (1958) • S. Sadie, ed., *The new Grove dictionary of opera*, 4 vols. (1992) • A. Saint and others, *A history of the Royal Opera House, Covent Garden, 1732–1982* (1982) • J. Diprose, *Some account of the parish of Saint Clement Danes*, [1] (1868), 184–5 • *The Times* (4 Nov 1879) • *The Athenaeum* (8 Nov 1879), 603 • R. J. Wilkinson-Latham, *From our special correspondent* (1979) • *IGI* • *CGPLA Eng. & Wales* (1879)

**Wealth at death** under £1000: probate, 3 Dec 1879, *CGPLA Eng. & Wales*

**Grunfeld, Henry** [*formerly* Heinrich Grünfeld] (**1904–1999**), banker, was born on 1 June 1904 in Breslau, Germany, the elder son and second of the three children of Max Grünfeld (1863–1939), steel manufacturer, and his wife, Rosa, *née* Haendler (1879–1961). Both his parents' families were prominent in the steel and chemical industries in Upper Silesia. The Grünfeld family moved to Berlin in 1910, where young Heinrich attended local schools until the First World War, when his parents moved to a suburban villa. Returning to Berlin after the war, he witnessed the violence attending the Kapp putsch of 1920. After education at the Kaiserin-Augusta Gymnasium and finishing secondary schooling in 1922 at the Staatliche Wilhelms-Gymnasium, he started working in the Berlin office of his father's firm, A. Niederstetter & Co., a leading supplier to German industry of steel tubes and related products. He combined long office hours with studying law and political science at the University of Berlin, but also enjoyed the rich cultural life of the capital in the evenings, when he and friends regularly attended concerts, theatre, and cabaret. He completed his doctorate in law in 1926 at the University of Breslau, where he wrote a thesis on the participation of worker representatives in German corporate governance. Before then, when he was not yet twenty-one, he took over management of his father's firm in Breslau. He very soon had to confront critical problems posed by the great inflation, industrial unrest, and the world depression following the Wall Street crash of 1929. From his beginnings as a manager he acquired a reputation in the steel industry for courageous sang-froid, sagacity, and natural authority far beyond his years.

On 21 December 1931 Grünfeld married (Berta) Lotte Oliven (1906–1993), and they departed as planned for their honeymoon, despite urgent pleas for him to join a committee of steel cartel executives who were meeting the Reich chancellor to discuss the financial crisis. In March 1933, two months after Hitler seized power, Grünfeld and his father were summoned to a Berlin hotel to meet their company lawyer; to their surprise he appeared in SA uniform and told them they could no longer continue in the management of their Berlin office. Grünfeld was, however, able for a time to carry on in Breslau, where his position as chairman of the regional steel cartel and acting Spanish consul conferred temporary immunity from Nazi persecution. That ended abruptly on 20 April 1934 when he was arrested at his office by the Gestapo, without warrant or any charge, forbidden to contact his wife or a lawyer, and imprisoned—for the first twenty-four hours without food or drink. Released after three days, he soon left for London, in order to canvass emigration and employment possibilities. After a six-week stay he returned to Breslau, where he and his father came under increasing pressure to sell their firm. They were eventually compelled to accept a price based on the book value of the enterprise in 1898, taking no account of its increase in size and value between then and 1934. From this derisory sum, 25 per cent was deducted for the so-called Reich flight tax, and the proceeds were then denominated in blocked marks, which in 1935 fetched only some 10 per cent of their nominal value. In order to collect even the resulting paltry amount, Grünfeld had to surmount endless bureaucratic obstacles. After further deductions and commissions, he was left with some £4000 with which to start life in England.

On the introduction of mutual business acquaintances, Grünfeld (who Anglicized his name to Henry Grunfeld shortly after arriving in England) met Siegmund Warburg for the first time on 17 March 1935 in The Hague, where they discussed the possibility of collaboration. That initially took the form of Warburg's New Trading Company, established earlier in London, taking a 10 per cent participation in the capital of Grunfeld's own company, incorporated in 1935 as Portman Hill & Co. The two men shared modest City offices and gradually built up financing business, Portman Hill largely in factoring and New Trading in the more traditional range of merchant banking, with helpful backing from N. M. Rothschild & Sons. Both men later recalled that they started in London with empty desks, aiming initially only to cover expenses, but ambitious to recoup the standing and fortunes of which they had been stripped by the Nazis. After some eighteen months' collaboration, Grunfeld and Warburg resolved to work together; within two years, Grunfeld sold his shares in Portman Hill to New Trading Company, and officially joined Warburg in that enterprise.

At the outbreak of war Grunfeld was still a German national, and expected to be among those in his position who were being interned, some deported to Australia or Canada. Noting that the police usually came to arrest aliens between eight and nine in the morning, he left his home daily at seven o'clock and walked about the London parks until the danger period had passed. His position was eventually regularized, and he volunteered for fire-watching duties. He became a British subject in May 1946. In the same year New Trading Company adopted the name S. G. Warburg & Co. Ltd; at that time it had capital and reserves of some £290,000, and continued gradually to build its business. By the mid-1950s it had acquired a stock-exchange listing through a holding company named Mercury Securities. Buying Seligman Brothers in 1957, S. G. Warburg & Co., still with only some eighty staff, gained access to the Accepting Houses Committee, and thus to the top rank of London merchant banks.

Despite these and other successes, including a growing list of corporate and other clients, Warburgs was the butt of some condescending City amusement for its austere business-focused lunches, unusually long working hours, and Teutonic attention to detail. Condescension ended in 1958 after Warburgs successfully advised an Anglo-American group in its takeover of British Aluminium, against bitter opposition from much of the City establishment. This contested takeover bid marked a revolution in City practice and traditional relations among shareholders and corporate managers. Warburgs became a prominent name and a stream of clients now came to the firm, whose international expertise was especially valued in rapidly developing global markets.

It was widely recognized that the Warburgs corporate culture, based on open communication, collegial as well as individual responsibility, and perfectionism in every aspect of business, gave the firm unique competitive advantages. While Siegmund Warburg was the indubitable leader, with his star quality and notable diplomatic brio, it was Grunfeld who was the reliably brilliant executant of firm policy. By choice remaining mostly in the background, Grunfeld was none the less crucially involved in every significant piece of business, often deploying formidable negotiating skills to bring transactions to a successful conclusion. He assumed primary responsibility for the firm's profitable metals-trading subsidiary, Brandeis Goldschmidt & Co., and played a leading role as financial adviser to the British television company ATV and the Thomson Organisation, among others. The Warburg–Grunfeld collaboration, refined through years of shared experience, was so seamless that it became difficult to distinguish their respective contributions; when Siegmund Warburg famously said, 'I could not have done it without you and you could not have done it without me', Grunfeld is reported to have replied, 'You are probably right' (private information). Grunfeld also shared with Warburg thoroughly assimilated German Jewish origins. Although neither ever observed Jewish rituals, both were very much attached to their heritage with its emphasis on ethical teachings and on general culture, and having suffered the quintessential Jewish experience of persecution and exile were steadfast in successfully defending their firm when it was attacked in the late 1960s in the context of the Arab anti-Israel boycott.

After pioneering the Eurobond revolution, S. G. Warburg & Co. expanded in size and became very much part of the City establishment, a change in scale and character that evoked dismay rather than self-congratulation on Grunfeld's part. By the 1970s Warburgs was widely perceived as the most distinguished merchant bank in London, though the firm never realized its ambition to play a truly important global role, largely owing to disappointments in North America, where successive strategic alliances failed to cohere. Siegmund Warburg—nominally retired in 1964, though active in the firm until his death in 1982—relinquished the chairmanship of Mercury Securities to Grunfeld, who carried on until 1974, when he in turn retired, aged seventy, as chairman of both Mercury and S. G. Warburg & Co. Grunfeld's retirement, too, was purely nominal: he continued to go to his office daily until just a day before his death, available to colleagues for advice, encouragement, and warnings that were not invariably heeded, especially as American styles in business-getting and executive compensation forced Warburgs into competitive emulation that Grunfeld deplored. When Swiss Bank Corporation acquired the S. G. Warburg Group in 1994, Grunfeld—then non-executive president of the group—was named senior adviser, a position he retained as the firm mutated, first into SBC Warburg, then into Warburg Dillon Read.

Tall, invariably dressed with sober elegance, Grunfeld had a penetrating gaze behind clear-framed spectacles. He was reserved, despite his eminence quite reticent, and he could be intimidating, though friends and colleagues were allowed a glimpse of his understated wry sense of humour. He had witnessed much human folly and evil, and had no illusions, but he was neither cynical nor pessimistic. He lived resolutely in the present, meticulously planning for the future. Stoic in most things, he suffered uncomplainingly from arthritis until both knees were replaced when he was well into his nineties; even then he would dismiss his wheelchair at the threshold and walk unaided into meetings. Although living in England for the larger part of his life, and a polished stylist in written English, he never lost his German accent nor his continental formality. Nor did he ever permit relaxation of the awesome standard he set for himself and others; perfectionism was evident in all he undertook. Those who saw him outside the City, in his country house in Surrey, knew another aspect of Grunfeld: his devotion to home and family, his garden, music, books, and the ceramics that he collected with discernment. He died at the London Clinic, 20 Devonshire Place, London, on 10 June 1999, of mesenteric thrombosis, leaving an estate valued at more than £34 million. He was survived by his son, Thomas, and numerous grandchildren, his daughter Louisa having predeceased him in 1985 and his wife, Lotte, in 1993. Obituaries paid tribute to his exceptional qualities of mind and leadership, his integrity and independence, and his contributions to the City, as a living link to pre-war *haute banque* traditions. A. J. SHERMAN

**Sources** *The Independent* (12 June 1999) • *The Times* (14 June 1999) • *The Guardian* (22 June 1999) • H. Grünfeld, 'Betriebsratsmitglieder im Aufsichtsrat, und in der Generalversammlung der Aktiengesellschaft', doctorate of law diss., University of Breslau, 1926, title-page • *Frankfurter Allgemeine Zeitung* (27 May 1994) • *S. G. Warburg Group Newsletter*, 88 (May/June 1994) • programme, ninetieth-birthday dinner, 6 June 1994, Claridges, London [privately printed, London, 1994] • Haendler–Grunfeld family tree, priv. coll. • *WWW* • personal knowledge (2004) • private information (2004) [Thomas Grunfeld, Oscar H. Lewisohn, family; Lord Roll, P. J. R. Spira, George S. Warburg, colleagues] • d. cert.

**Archives** S. G. Warburg & Co., London | FILM priv. coll., video interview

**Likenesses** photograph, repro. in *The Independent* • photograph, repro. in *The Times* • photograph, repro. in *The Guardian*

**Wealth at death** £34,385,837—gross; £34,092,815—net: probate, 9 Sept 1999, *CGPLA Eng. & Wales*

**Grunfeld, Isidor** (1900–1975), rabbi, was born on 27 October 1900 in Tauberettersheim, near Würzburg, Bavaria, the eldest son of wealthy cattle drover and agricultural merchant Joseph Grunfeld and his second wife, Carolina Fromm. Both his parents claimed family connections with important rabbis. Joseph was a descendant of Rabbi Meir of Rothenberg, and Carolina was related to Rabbi Isaac Dov (Seligman Baer) Bamberger of Würzburg, as well as being a cousin of the psychoanalyst Eric Fromm. Joseph Grunfeld's first wife had died during or just after the First World War, leaving four young children, two boys and two girls. Carolina bore seven more children; the combined family, which was brought up as a single unit, consisted of six boys and five girls.

Isidor Grunfeld was educated privately by a Lithuanian rabbi who taught him the Talmud in Yiddish. From 1920 to 1925 he studied law and philosophy at Frankfurt and Heidelberg universities, gaining a doctorate in comparative Roman and Talmudic law. While pursuing a secular education, Grunfeld continued at *yeshivot* (Talmudic colleges) in these towns and, something of a student activist at a time of rising nationalist tensions, was knifed in an incident at Marburg. He was for a short time senior master in mathematics and Talmud at the Jewish secondary school in Hamburg. He then pursued a legal career. He was called to the bar at the county court of Würzburg and acted as assessor of the juvenile court.

Grunfeld's father had been a supporter of the Hovevei Tsion ('Lovers of Zion'), a proto-Zionist society which advocated agricultural colonization in Palestine. Isidor Grunfeld joined the German Zionist Federation and afterwards the *Mizrakhi* religious Zionist organization. Grunfeld married Dr Judith Rosenbaum, a schoolteacher [*see* Grunfeld, Judith (1902–1998)], in Würzburg on 22 November 1932; they had five children, two daughters followed by three sons. When Hitler came to power in 1933 Grunfeld left Germany for Palestine, where he became articled to Mordechai Eliash, later first Israeli ambassador to Britain.

Late in 1933 Grunfeld travelled to London to read for the English bar with a view to returning to Palestine on qualifying. His plans were overtaken by the urgent need to rescue his family from Germany. On the strength of affidavits that he provided, the whole family arrived in England in 1938. He enrolled at Jews' College and qualified for the rabbinate in 1938. He served as minister of the Finsbury Park District (United) Synagogue between 1936 and 1938 and took up permanent residence in Green Lanes, north London. However, his rare combination of legal and rabbinical training was quickly put to more direct use. Chief Rabbi J. H. Hertz recruited Grunfeld as the first registrar to the London *bet din* (Jewish ecclesiastical court), in 1939 he was promoted *dayan* (judge), and in 1951 senior *dayan*, as successor to Rabbi Yehezkel Abramsky. During the Second World War, Grunfeld narrowly escaped when the offices of the *bet din* in Mulberry Street, off Commercial Road, east London, were bombed. In 1952, together with Rabbi Alexander Altmann of the Manchester *bet din*, Grunfeld assumed the temporary role of acting chief rabbi, while Israel Brodie was away on a pastoral tour of Australia. He retired from the *bet din* in 1965 after a serious heart attack the previous year. At this time he was privately unhappy at the harsh treatment meted out to Rabbi Louis Jacobs, one of the most gifted religious thinkers produced by Anglo-Jewry, whose outspoken unorthodox views may have cost him the chief rabbinate.

In January 1946 Chief Rabbi Hertz asked Grunfeld to take his place as the first witness called to testify before the Anglo-American commission of inquiry into Palestine, being held in London. Indeed, throughout the late 1930s and during the Second World War, Grunfeld evinced deep personal interest in the plight of the Jews of Europe. In 1940 he was acting chairman of the chief rabbi's Religious Emergency Council, set up to aid refugees from Nazism. In this capacity he went to Cyprus to report on conditions in the internment camps. He organized welfare provision for some 5000 Jewish refugees and lobbied for their entry into Palestine. He was also chairman of the commission on the status of Jewish war orphans in Europe, dedicated after the war to retrieving Jewish children who had been sheltered in Christian homes and restoring them to the Jewish community. He made an emotional appeal to the Human Rights Commission on this issue. He served as chairman of the Anglo-Jewish Association and the Central British Fund for World Jewish Relief. He was active in Amnesty International and spoke out in favour of world peace.

Grunfeld was a prolific writer in English on Jewish religious themes, and published several popular titles as well as articles in the general press. He wrote a two-volume study of the Jewish dietary laws and another about the will and testament in Jewish law. He devoted his retirement to editing and annotating English translations of the writings of Rabbi Samson Raphael Hirsch, the German founder of neo-Orthodoxy. Hirsch's philosophy, which combined strict adherence to Jewish tradition and interaction with the modern secular world, greatly influenced Grunfeld's own life. Aged seventy-five, Isidor Grunfeld died in the Royal Northern Hospital, Holloway, London, of a heart attack on 8 September 1975 and was buried the same day in the Har Menuhot cemetery in Jerusalem.

SHARMAN KADISH

**Sources** *The Times* (10 Sept 1975) · *The Times* (15 Sept 1975) · *Jewish Chronicle* (12 Sept 1975) · *Jewish Chronicle* (28 Oct 1960) · J. Carlebach, 'The impact of German Jews on Anglo-Jewry: Orthodoxy, 1850–1950', *Second chance: two centuries of German-speaking Jews in the United Kingdom*, ed. W. E. Mosse (1991), 405–23, esp. 418–19 · *CGPLA Eng. & Wales* (1976) · private information (2004) [Anne Ruth Cohn, daughter] · *Jewish Year Book* · C. Roth, ed., *Encyclopaedia Judaica*, 7 (Jersualem, 1971), 949

**Archives** LMA, archives of London Beth Din

**Wealth at death** £27,015: probate, 25 June 1976, *CGPLA Eng. & Wales*

**Grunfeld** [*née* Rosenbaum], **Judith** (**1902–1998**), headmistress, was born in Budapest, Hungary, on 18 December 1902, the youngest of four children, two boys and two girls, of Sandor Rosenbaum, a highly regarded scholar of Talmud, and his wife, Sarah Bamberger. She was descended from rabbis on both sides, from the Würzburger rav, Rabbi Bamberger, who was her mother's grandfather. The Rosenbaums were directly descended from the sixteenth-century rabbi Maharal (Judah Löw ben Bezalel), the creator, according to legend, of the Prague *golem*.

Judith grew up in Frankfurt and was educated at the city's Hirsch Real Schule, where she studied both religious and secular subjects. From there she went on to Frankfurt University, at a time when it was highly unusual for an Orthodox Jewish woman to receive a higher education. She studied psychology, philosophy, and natural science, obtaining her doctorate in the latter as well as a teaching diploma.

Judith toyed with the idea of settling in Palestine but instead, on the recommendation of Rabbi Jacob Rosenheim of Agudat Yisrael, she went to work for the fledgeling Beis Ya'akov ('house of Jacob') Jewish girls' school movement, which had been founded by the former seamstress Sarah Schenierer in Cracow, Poland, in 1917. The schools were officially taken under the wing of the strictly Orthodox non-Zionist Aguda once Rosenheim assumed the presidency in 1929. From 1924 to 1932 Judith helped to develop the Beis Ya'akov teachers' training seminary in Cracow, in the capacity of both teacher and fundraiser. For the first time girls from traditional Jewish backgrounds were encouraged to learn and to pursue a career in teaching. The Beis Ya'akov network expanded to some 230 schools, creating new opportunities for women in the Jewish world of eastern Europe, although not without opposition from some rabbis who feared that the education of women would undermine family life and the woman's primary role as wife and mother.

On 22 November 1932 Judith married Isidor *Grunfeld (1900–1975), later a rabbi, in Germany before they emigrated to England. In London the following year she joined the staff of the girls' Jewish secondary school, later renamed the Avigdor after its founder, another central European immigrant, Rabbi Avigdor (Victor) Schonfeld. She became headmistress in 1934. The school had been started in September 1929 in Alexandra Villas, Seven Sisters Road, Finsbury Park, poorly equipped with twenty pupils on the roll. In 1936 Board of Education inspectors refused to recognize the school. Under Grunfeld's direction standards rapidly rose and more suitable premises were secured, for the boys at Aberglaslyn, Amhurst Park, and for the girls (from 1935 housed separately) at Northfield, 111 Stamford Hill. The schools expanded in size especially with the influx of child refugees from central Europe in 1938–9. In 1939 there were about 450 pupils.

On 1 September 1939, three days before the outbreak of war, the schools were evacuated to Shefford, Bedfordshire, where they remained until 1945, growing to some 600 pupils and 25 staff. Grunfeld worked in conjunction with Abraham Levene, who became headmaster of the boys' school. She later wrote a memoir (1980), *Shefford*, about her experience there, perhaps the most fulfilling of her life. She sought and largely succeeded in providing a substitute family life in a traditional Jewish atmosphere for her many orphaned charges in a peaceful haven of rural England during those war-torn years. The schools now won praise from the government inspectors. An appreciative former pupil wrote an affectionate biography of the headmistress, who was nicknamed by the children 'the Queen'.

Back in London after the war, the school opened a preparatory department in August 1945 to which Grunfeld transferred her headship. She retired in 1955 to care for her husband, who had fallen seriously ill and entered into twenty years of declining health. She retained a public profile until herself succumbing to ill health in her nineties, giving lectures and classes to Jewish audiences and former pupils in Britain, North America, and Israel.

Judith Grunfeld was a pioneer of Jewish education for Orthodox Jewish girls, and in her own person presented a rare role model for her pupils. She managed successfully to combine the demands of traditional Jewish family life with pursuit of a professional career. Her own children, five in all, were all former pupils of the Avigdor schools. She died on 14 May 1998, aged ninety-five, in the Homerton Hospital, Hackney, London, and was buried next to her husband in the Har Menuhot cemetery in Jerusalem.

SHARMAN KADISH

**Sources** *Jewish Chronicle* (29 May 1998) • *Jewish Tribune* (21 May 1998) • M. Dansky, *Rebbetzen Grunfeld* (1994) • J. Grunfeld, *Shefford: the story of a Jewish school community in evacuation, 1939–45* (1980) • J. Carlebach, 'The impact of German Jews on Anglo-Jewry: Orthodoxy, 1850–1950', *Second chance: two centuries of German-speaking Jews in the United Kingdom*, ed. W. E. Mosse (1991), 405–23 • J. Grunfeld-Rosenbaum, 'Sara Schenierer: the story of a great movement', *Jewish leaders*, ed. L. Jung (1953), 407–32 • *Jewish Year Book* • *CGPLA Eng. & Wales* (1998) • d. cert. • private information (2004) [Anne Ruth Cohn, daughter] • C. Roth, ed., *Encyclopaedia Judaica*, 7 (Jersualem, 1971), 949

**Likenesses** photograph, repro. in *Jewish Chronicle*

**Wealth at death** under £200,000: probate, 4 Jan 1999, *CGPLA Eng. & Wales*

**Grünhut, Max** (1893–1964), criminologist, was born on 7 July 1893 in Magdeburg, Germany, the son of Leo Grünhut and his wife, Betty Eppstein. His father was professor and chief analytical chemist at the German research institute founded in Munich during the First World War. After attending the *Gymnasium* in Wiesbaden, Grünhut studied law at the universities of Heidelberg, Munich, and Kiel between 1912 and 1914. During the First World War he volunteered as a nurse in a military ambulance and was seriously wounded in a Russian air raid. In 1922 he married Elisabeth Braun (*d.* 1964), the daughter of a Lutheran minister.

After gaining the doctorate of law at the new University of Hamburg in 1922 Grünhut was appointed *Privatdozent* in the seminar for criminal law and criminal policy, and was greatly influenced by its director, Moritz Liepmann, a follower of Franz von Liszt, the leader of the progressive International Association of Criminal Law. He was attracted by its emphasis on the social implications of criminal law, particularly as regards prison discipline, juvenile delinquency, and the prevention of crime. In 1923, after publishing his notable dissertation on the topic of 'Anselm von Feuerbach and the problem of criminal responsibility', he was appointed assistant professor and, two years later, full professor at the University of Jena, where he collaborated with the Municipal School of Social Work. In 1928 he was called to the chair of criminal law at the University of Bonn.

Grünhut's reputation flourished. In 1926 he published *Begriffsbildung und Rechtsanwendung im Strafrecht* ('Legal concepts in criminal cases'), followed a year later by a collaborative text (with L. Frede, an official in the Thuringian ministry of justice) on the reform of the penal system. This was followed by *Strafrechtswissenschaft und Strafrechtspraxis* ('Criminal cases and jurisprudence') (1932) and, after Liepmann's death, he helped dutifully to complete his teacher's important study *Krieg und Kriminalität in Deutschland* ('War and delinquency in Germany') (1930). His breadth of learning was revealed in a stream of articles on criminal law, jurisprudence, and penology, including 'Probation and parole' and 'Capital punishment', of which he was a staunch opponent. He also became an editor of the leading criminal policy journal *Zeitschrift für die gesamte Strafrechtswissenschaft*.

In 1933, at the age of forty, this distinguished career was shattered. The University of Bonn dismissed Grünhut from his chair without compensation, under the Nazi anti-Jewish 'Aryan clause' introduced into the German civil service law. He was forced to exist on a temporary grant. A patriotic Lutheran, he found this hard to bear. Soon after his dismissal, his circumstances were reported to the Academic Assistance Council in London (from 1937 known as the Society for the Protection of Science and Learning) which had been set up 'to help scholars displaced from university teaching or research positions for reasons of racial origin, political or religious opinion'. Grünhut proved to be a very difficult person to help. At first he did not want to leave Germany, hoping that the situation might improve. More importantly, criminology was unknown at that time as an academic discipline in England. The London School of Economics, which invited him to lecture in 1934, was the only place to show an interest but it was already committed to taking the distinguished German criminologist Hermann Mannheim.

The situation in Bonn became intolerable. Grünhut was becoming mentally exhausted, his grant had run out, his wife was sick, and they were socially isolated. In 1937, after another fruitless visit to England, the society wrote to the warden of All Souls College, Oxford. After initial hesitation, the college, which was already helping three other German refugee scholars, decided to offer him a place at an annual salary of £300. His visa was granted just in time—in January 1939. After release from internment in October 1940, a new career began. Grünhut was a member of common room, not a fellow of All Souls, and by 1947 the college was anxious about his future. He had, like other displaced scholars, been invited to return to his post in Bonn, but because of his wife's delicate health and nervous state, he decided not to do so. However, from 1950 onwards he often lectured in Bonn in the summer months, and in 1954 the University of Bonn made him professor emeritus.

After so many anxious years, events suddenly took a turn for the better. In October 1947 Grünhut was appointed the first lecturer in criminology at Oxford. This was a just reward for the efforts he had made to introduce the subject through conscientiously prepared lectures—slowly and emphatically delivered in a thick guttural accent—at the delegacy for social training at Barnett House. More importantly, perhaps, his merits as a thorough scholar had been revealed in his major work, a historical and comparative study entitled *Penal Reform* published by Oxford University Press in 1948. It was a document of its time and has now become rather dated. In 1950 he was reappointed for a further five years and within a year advanced to reader in criminology, a post he held with distinction until his retirement in 1960.

Grünhut took advantage of the clause in the Criminal Justice Act of 1948 which allowed the Home Office to make grants to further criminological research. They were at first very modest—£250 in 1949 and £400 in 1950–51—but from his research base, a small room in the New Bodleian Library, and with the help of research assistants, notably Sarah McCabe, he produced a stream of research reports. His best works were *Juvenile Offenders before the Courts* (1956), *Probation and Mental Treatment* (1963), and two articles on detention centres, published in the *British Journal of Criminology* in 1954 and 1960. He concluded prophetically that, though short punitive detention might have been appropriate for a small number of young men, it would, with widespread use, degenerate into another name for short prison sentences.

Grünhut was a progressive humanist who did not believe that criminology could be a wholly scientific, let alone a statistically calibrated, endeavour. He gave an enlightening lecture, 'Statistics in criminology', to the Royal Statistical Society, published in its *Journal* in 1951. He was far too aware of what he called the infinite variety and complexities of human nature, the difficulty of understanding it, the limitations of all penal methods, and the need to respect the human rights and dignity of the offender.

During the war years Grünhut helped the Foreign Office and the Royal Institute of International Affairs with legal work and similarly assisted the Supreme Headquarters Allied Expeditionary Force in 1944–5, which undoubtedly helped to speed up his naturalization in 1947. He was a member of the Home Office Probation Advisory and Training Board, of the executive committee of the Howard League for Penal Reform, and of the Lutheran Council of Great Britain. He served the United Nations by producing a valuable report on the *Practical Results and Financial Aspects of Adult Probation in Selected Countries* (1954). In Oxford he founded and presided over the undergraduate group Crime-a-Challenge, which still continues fifty years later as the Oxford Crime Forum.

Grünhut was renowned for his modesty and conscientiousness. His students and colleagues found beneath his reserve a person of warmth, gentleness, and charm. 'Goodness' was a word his *Times* obituarist rightly applied. He never forgot those who made possible the transformation of his existence in a new country and the opportunity to be an influential pioneer in a new subject. His achievement was acknowledged by appointment as an OBE in 1961. He died on 6 February 1964 at St Luke's Home, 20 Linton Road, Oxford, aged seventy, and was cremated at Oxford crematorium. He was followed fifteen days later by his wife, Elisabeth. They had no children. Grünhut was honoured by the University of Bonn law faculty in 1965 with a memorial volume, which contained an appreciation of his career and character by E. Friesenhahn and of his scholarship by H. von Weber. ROGER HOOD

**Sources** *The Times* (8 Feb 1964) · *The Times* (17 Feb 1964) · Bodl. Oxf., Society for the Protection of Science and Learning · *British Journal of Criminology*, 4 (1963–4), 313–15 · personal knowledge (2004) · *CGPLA Eng. & Wales* (1964) · H. Kaufmann, E. Schwinge, and H. Welzel, eds., *Erinnerungsgabe für Max Grünhut (1893–1964)* (1965) · d. cert.

**Wealth at death** £20,783: administration with will, 17 April 1964, *CGPLA Eng. & Wales*

**Gryffyth, Jaspar** (*d.* 1614), antiquary and Church of England clergyman, was born in Guilsfield, Montgomeryshire, the son of Hugh Gryffyth (*c.*1540–*c.*1586) and Lowri Gwynn. He first appears in historical records in a pedigree of 1586 recording his marriage to Mary, the daughter of John Roberts, a wealthy Welsh merchant based in London, with whom he was later to have at least four children. His education is shrouded in mystery; the 1586 pedigree describes him as a 'bachlor off art' (Cardiff, MS 2.36, fol. 65), but this may be an error. On 24 July 1592 he was ordained deacon and priest in the diocese of St Asaph by Hugh Bellot, bishop of Bangor, and he was appointed rector of Longston in Montgomeryshire in 1595, which he held in plurality from 1599 when he became the warden of Ruthin Hospital in Denbighshire. His most important preferment was to take him out of Wales, to Hinckley in Leicestershire (1600–14), a living which he held in plurality with that of Llansannan, Montgomeryshire (1605–14). A suggestion that he was at one time chaplain to Archbishop Bancroft is wholly unsupported in fact.

The progress of Gryffyth's career owed much to his relationship with Gabriel Goodman, dean of Westminster, who also patronized Gryffyth's brother Robert. Goodman was closely associated with Ruthin, and it was to him that Gryffyth owed his preferment to the hospital there and to the living at Hinckley, which was in the gift of the dean of Westminster. It is also likely that it was through his association with Goodman that Gryffyth came into contact with circles of Welsh and English intellectuals and antiquaries who gravitated to Westminster in the 1580s and 1590s, owing to the dean's patronage, the presence of parliament, and the records stored in the abbey. The copy of William Morgan's translation of the Bible into Welsh which Morgan gave to Westminster Abbey in 1588 has an inscription in Gryffyth's hand witnessing the gift. The most prominent of these antiquaries was Sir Robert Cotton, with whom Gryffyth was certainly acquainted, as he wrote to Cotton in 1613 sending details of forty manuscripts from which he hoped Cotton would choose items for borrowing, in return for the loan of a manuscript of Nennius. The evidence of this list, together with another list of early writers in his hand in an edition of John Bale's *Illustrium maioris Britanniae scriptorum … summarium* (1548), and the evidence from the twenty-nine surviving books and manuscripts which he is known to have owned or borrowed, indicates that Gryffyth was more than just an educated cleric: he had a profound interest in the Welsh medieval past, owning some of the most significant manuscripts of medieval Welsh law, in both Latin and Welsh versions. Similarly he owned the most important manuscripts of medieval Welsh poetry, including the Black Book of Carmarthen and the Llyfr Gwyn Rhydderch. Other writers—Welsh and otherwise—present in his collections included Geoffrey of Monmouth, Gildas, Ponticus Virunius, Caradoc of Lancarfan, and David Powel. The annotations in his copy of Bale show that Gryffyth was also familiar with the work of a range of early writers, at this date only known from a few manuscripts, chiefly in the collections of Sir Robert Cotton.

The circles in which Gryffyth moved included other significant antiquaries, but Cotton was the source of many key texts. From the 1613 letter we learn that Gryffyth was keen to borrow a copy of Nennius from Cotton, whose loan lists record several other manuscripts loaned to him, and also a famous Anglo-Saxon coin, the gold mancus by the moneyer Pendraed, who worked for Offa and Cenwulf. In return Gryffyth also gave books to Cotton, including an important manuscript of the medieval Welsh laws. Cotton may well have introduced Gryffyth to other members of the Society of Antiquaries, including the lawyer Francis Tate, John Stow, and William Fleetwood. Gryffyth thus had access to a key generation of antiquaries and collectors of manuscripts from the British medieval collections, by then widely dispersed. In London he would also have had access to the book trade, through which such items could also be acquired, but either way he owned volumes which had been in libraries at Canterbury, Winchester, Carmarthen, Brecon, and Haughmond.

The exact date of Gryffyth's death is not known, but on 18 May 1614 he drew up a will which was proved ten days later. He was buried in Hinckley parish church. He was survived by his wife, Mary, his son, and three daughters.

RICHARD OVENDEN

**Sources** R. Ovenden, 'Jaspar Gryffyth and his books', *British Library Journal*, 20 (1994), 107–34 • E. D. Jones, 'Jaspar Griffith (Gryffyth), warden of Ruthin (d. 1614)', *National Library of Wales Journal*, 1 (1939–40), 168–70 • C. E. Wright, *Fontes Harleiani* (1972), 173 • South Glamorgan Central Library, Cardiff, MS 2.36, fol. 65 • *Heraldic visitations of Wales and part of the marches … by Lewys Dwnn*, ed. S. R. Meyrick, 2 vols. (1846) • B. F. Roberts, ed., *Brut y brenhinedd* (Dublin, 1971) • H. D. Emanuel, *Latin texts of the Welsh laws* (1967) • will, Leicester district probate registry, 1614/25

**Wealth at death** £157 17*s*. 4*d*.: will, Leicester district probate registry, 1614/25

**Gryg, Gruffydd**. *See* Gruffudd Gryg (*fl. c.*1340–1380).

**Grymeston** [Grimston; *née* Bernye], **Elizabeth** (*b*. in or before **1563**, *d*. **1601x4**), author, was the daughter of a substantial landowner, Martin Bernye, and his wife, Margaret Flynte, of Gunton, Norfolk. By 1584 Elizabeth had married Christopher Grymeston (*b*. 1563/4), fellow of Gonville and Caius College, Cambridge, youngest son of Thomas Grymeston and Dorothy Thwaytes of Smeeton in Yorkshire. College regulations forbade the marriage of fellows, yet Christopher even served in 1588 as bursar of the college. This implies that the marriage must have been concealed, despite the births of several children, at least until 1592. In that year Christopher left Caius and on 31 January 1593 was admitted to Gray's Inn. Christopher's separation from Caius probably resulted from discovery of the marriage; alternatively, it may have resulted from his and Elizabeth's apparently recusant leanings, sympathies like those of some members of their families; an Elizabeth Grymeston of Nidd (Yorkshire), possibly the author, was fined as a recusant in 1592 or 1593. Thomas Legge, master of Caius at this period, was unusually tolerant of recusants.

Only one further incident in the story of Elizabeth and Christopher Grymeston is known until 1604, the year in which the first edition of her posthumously printed advice book, *Miscelanea: Meditations, Memoratives*, appeared. In 1595 Martin Bernye rewrote his will, appointing his wife and his son-in-law as executors, leaving a life interest in his estate to his wife, and devolving his estate on Elizabeth, Christopher, and their heirs. This arrangement may explain Elizabeth's allusion, in her introductory letter to *Miscelanea*, to her mother's 'undeserved wrath'. Another allusion there, to 'eight severall sinister assaults' on Christopher which have left her 'doubtfull' of his life, is puzzling (*Miscelanea*, 3rd edn, sig. A2*v*).

Elizabeth was still alive in 1601, since she quotes poems that were unpublished until that year. By 1604, according to a prefatory poem by Simon Grahame in the *Miscelanea*, she had died. She herself had written that a 'languishing consumption', occasioned, she states, by her mother's enmity, apparently impelled her to compose her book of advice as a legacy, a 'veni mecum' (3rd edn, sig. A2*v*), for her son, Bernye, the only surviving child of 'nine … which God did lend me' (3rd edn, sig. A4*v*). The first edition consists of fourteen chapters; the second (1606?), third (1608?), and fourth (1618?), which are '[a]ugmented with addition of other hir Meditations' (2nd edn, title-page), are entitled *Miscellanea: Prayers, Meditations, Memoratives*, and consist of twenty chapters, six additional ones being inserted after chapter 12 of the first edition, so that chapters 13 and 14 are renumbered 19 and 20 in the later editions.

Grymeston's advice book is the earliest of a number of seventeenth-century exemplars of a new sub-genre, the mother's advice book. It is perhaps the most learned and polished of these tracts of pious advice addressed by a mother to her child. Christian humanists such as Thomas More and Juan Luis Vives, and protestant reformers such as Thomas Becon, Matthew Griffeth, and William Gouge, encouraged women to train their children in religion.

This gave women an authority to compose advice books in an age which taught them to eschew public speech. Like a number of other women affected by these novel theories which recognized the importance of the mother's influence on her children, Grymeston penned instructions to her child because she feared she would not live to provide him with guidance later in life. Unlike advice books by fathers, her tract is deeply permeated by religiosity and highly apologetic for the author's temerity in writing. In this respect it is similar to works by Dorothy Leigh, Elizabeth Clinton, and Elizabeth Joceline. Grymeston's tract is outstanding for its richness of paraphrase, including English poetry culled from Robert Allott's *Englands Parnassus* (1600). Although Grymeston does not express overtly Roman Catholic positions, her text often seems to have a Roman Catholic cast. It engages in frequent and lengthy paraphrases of patristic sources, the Vulgate, Catholic martyrs, and two Catholic poets, Richard Rowlands (or Verstegan), and her kinsman, Robert Southwell. Although none of the poetry she includes is original, her paraphrases create of her borrowings a moving amalgam that, she tells Bernye, is 'the true portrature of thy mothers minde' (*Miscelanea*, 3rd edn, sig. A2*v*).

BETTY S. TRAVITSKY

**Sources** R. Hughey and P. Hereford, 'Elizabeth Grymeston and her *Miscelanea*', *The Library*, 4th ser., 15 (1934–5), 61–91 • B. Y. Fletcher and C. Sizemore, 'Elizabeth Grymeston's *Miscelanea: meditations, memoratives*: introduction and selected text', *University of Pennsylvania Library Chronicle*, 45, nos. 1–2 (1981), 53–83 • C. Sizemore, 'Early seventeenth-century advice books: the female viewpoint', *South Atlantic Bulletin*, 41 (1976), 41–8 • B. S. Travitsky, 'The new mother of the English Renaissance: her writings on motherhood', *The lost tradition: mothers and daughters in literature*, ed. C. N. Davidson and E. M. Broner (1979), 33–43 • V. Wayne, 'Advice for women from mothers and patriarchs', *Women and literature in Britain, 1500–1700*, ed. H. Wilcox (1996), 56–79 • E. V. Beilin, *Redeeming Eve: women writers of the English Renaissance* (1987) • B. S. Travitsky, 'The new mother of the English Renaissance (1489–1659): a descriptive catalogue', *Bulletin of Research in the Humanities*, 82 (1979), 63–89 • M. R. Mahl and H. Koon, 'Elizabeth Grymeston, d. 1603', *The female spectator: English women writers before 1800*, ed. M. R. Mahl and H. Koon (1977), 52–61 • P. Crawford, 'The construction and experience of maternity in seventeenth-century England', *Women as mothers in pre-industrial England*, ed. V. Fildes (1990), 3–38 • B. S. Travitsky, 'Elizabeth Grymeston', *Sixteenth-century British nondramatic writers: second series*, ed. D. A. Richardson, DLitB, 136 (1994), 164–7 • M. B. Rose, 'Where are the mothers in Shakespeare? Options for gender representation in the English Renaissance', *Shakespeare Quarterly*, 42 (1991), 291–314 • *Mother's advice books*, ed. B. S. Travitsky (1998) • Venn, *Alum. Cant.*

**Gryn, Hugo Gabriel** (1930–1996), rabbi and broadcaster, was born in Berehovo, Czechoslovakia, on 25 June 1930, in a home filled with great learning and warmth. His father, Géza Gryn (1900–1945), was a timber merchant; his mother was Bella Neufeld (1908–1964) of Silce. The Gryns were among the 10,000 Jews confined to the Berehovo ghetto in April 1944, and Hugo and his family (parents, grandparents, and ten-year-old brother, Gaby) were sent to Auschwitz on the last transport from Berehovo on 28 May 1944, arriving there on 31 May. Hugo, aged thirteen, was advised to say he was nineteen, a carpenter and joiner. He and his father were sent to work; his brother and

**Hugo Gabriel Gryn (1930–1996)**, by Mark Gerson, 1993

grandfather were sent to the gas chambers. His Orthodox father found ways to celebrate the Jewish festivals, even in Auschwitz. In 1945, with the allies approaching, Gryn and his father were among the 1600 Jews sent on the death march from the Lieberose camp to Sachsenhausen near Berlin, and on to Mauthausen in upper Austria, and then to Gunskirchen. Fewer than a thousand survived the march. Hugo and his father were liberated at Gunskirchen on 4/5 May 1945 by the Americans, but Géza Gryn died a few days later from typhus and exhaustion. Hugo's mother, Bella, also survived the camps.

In February 1946 Gryn was among the last group of boys to leave Prague for Great Britain, flown out in a Lancaster bomber arranged by the Central British Fund. He arrived at Prestwick, near Manchester, and was sent to Lasswade, Scotland, to the Polton House farm school. Later that year he won a scholarship to study mathematics and biochemistry at King's College, Cambridge, and completed the two-year course in the summer of 1948. He then volunteered to serve in the Israeli army to defend that country in its war of independence, and returned to London having contracted jaundice. In London, where he worked briefly as a biochemist and then as a teacher, he came under the influence of Rabbi Leo Baeck, the leader of German Judaism and Reform rabbi, who had survived the Theresienstadt (Terezin) ghetto. Baeck became his guide and mentor, as in a different way did Lily Montagu, the leader of British Liberal Judaism, who gave him insights into a different way of religious life. Both guided him towards the rabbinate, and in 1950 he went to the Hebrew

Union College in Cincinnati, a seminary for Reform rabbis, where he earned his bachelor of Hebrew letters degree, and subsequently his master's degree and doctorate as well. He was ordained there in 1957.

On 1 January 1957 Gryn married Jacqueline Selby in London. He was then sent to Bombay by the World Union for Progressive Judaism, which had sponsored his studies. He served the Jewish Religious Union there until 1960; his eldest daughter was born there. He then became executive director of the World Union for Progressive Judaism, working from its New York offices; three more children were born in New York. Gryn travelled extensively, particularly in Europe. In 1962 he accepted a position as a senior executive of the American Jewish Joint Distribution Committee (a welfare organization working with Jewish refugees), taking on difficult assignments in Prague and Budapest.

In 1964 Gryn became first the associate and then the senior rabbi of the West London Synagogue. It was the most prestigious post in British Progressive Judaism, and he held it until his death. In due course he became the central figure in British Reform Judaism; its organization, the Reform Synagogues of Great Britain, elected him its president in 1990 in recognition of his work. When the rabbis of the Union of Liberal and Progressive Judaism created an umbrella organization for all Progressive rabbis, the Council of Reform and Liberal Rabbis, Gryn served as chairman. Gryn was closely associated with the Leo Baeck College (founded in 1957); it shared the buildings of the West London Synagogue, and he served as the college's bursar, lecturer, and vice-president until his death. His teaching of practical rabbinics became essential to the more than 100 rabbis ordained during his association with the college. Education and interfaith activities were major concerns for him, and he served as chairman of the standing committee of interfaith dialogue in education in 1972. From 1991 he was also a governor of the World College of the Atlantic. From 1975 he was co-chairman of the London Rainbow Group, founded by the Revd Peter Schneider, which met alternately at Westminster Abbey and the West London Synagogue. Gryn was co-founder (with Bishop Jim Thompson) of the Interfaith Networth (UK) and its first joint chairman (1987–94), and he remained its guiding spirit.

The centre of Gryn's life continued to be his work as a rabbi. He was not an orator, but his quiet, sometimes stuttering style demanded attention because of its content, which displayed a deep spirituality and a love for his community. He had a congregation of close to 3000 families, most of whom felt they had a special relationship with their rabbi, and his pastoral work was phenomenal. It seemed that he had time for everyone, including itinerants and non-Jews, who brought him their problems. He was a 'rabbi's rabbi', a good colleague who gave sound advice. His common sense and practical experience were informed by a rabbinical tradition of knowledge of the text and an instinctive understanding of human problems. Some of his theological reflections were recorded in *Chasing Shadows* (2000), written with his daughter Naomi Gryn. In one of his many television appearances, on the BBC's *Light of Experience* in January 1978, he said that he had become aware of the need to act as a witness to the Holocaust experience. In 1986, when the *Terezin Kaddish* by Ronald Senator and Albert Friedlander was first presented in Canterbury Cathedral, Gryn was the narrator, and blew the shofar in a moving performance. It was part of his continuing task as a witness; his was always the calm voice of reconciliation.

As a religious thinker, he helped to influence the development of the British Reform movement: he chaired the group which wrote their standard prayer book, *Forms of Prayer* (1977), and the later liturgy, *Forms of Prayer 3: Prayers for the High Holydays* (1985), shows his influence in remembering the Holocaust within the liturgy. He had many links in the wider Jewish community, including close friendships with the two chief rabbis of his time, Lord Jakobovits and Rabbi Jonathan Sacks. This provided a bridge between the traditional and progressive communities: both chief rabbis held private and confidential meetings with the leaders of Progressive Judaism, and Gryn chaired many of the meetings. Conflicts and adverse publicity were avoided. Christian leaders also attended, and solid achievements within interfaith dialogue were achieved, not least through Gryn's skill in handling the discussions.

Gryn's role in Anglo-Jewish life grew out of the complexities of a community aware of its minority status. The traditional Jewish community has rigid organizational structures with a centralized 'government', in which the chief rabbi has much authority. The Progressive movement gives far more power to the laity, as every congregation is independent and its board of management employs the rabbi under the terms of a fixed contract. Rabbi Harold Reinhart ruled the West London Synagogue for decades, but was in the end retired against his will. He had, however, created a place for refugee rabbis, and was succeeded by Rabbi Van der Zyl from Germany. Gryn was more than a refugee: he was a concentration camp survivor who had to deal with the grandees of Anglo-Jewry. At the West London Synagogue he was surrounded by a capable staff and his charm and pastoral skills established him with the most influential members of the community. It may be argued that the expanding role he played in national public life was a key element in overcoming the resistance he encountered within his own congregation. His relationship with the archbishop of Canterbury and his work for interfaith harmony were even more instructive to his community than his sermons.

Hugo Gryn became one of the great friends of the British public through his regular television appearances and radio broadcasts, on *Pause for Thought* and *Thought for the Day*, the 'god slots' on Radio 2 and Radio 4, and on Radio 4's ethical discussion programme *The Moral Maze*. He was central to the popularity of the programmes, in which the studio team chaired by Michael Buerk quizzed witnesses about ethical issues of the day. Gryn offered sympathy and tolerance to witnesses, and summarized conclusions with great openness and honesty.

In 1989 Gryn and his daughter Naomi returned to his home town to film *Chasing Shadows*. It gave him a chance to deal with the past and future of the Jewish people, and showed 'his disposition to dwell on gladness as well as grief, and to express hope rather than despair' (*Daily Telegraph*). The film was broadcast on Channel 4 in 1991. Gryn was often interviewed on television when issues of concern to the Jewish community were discussed. He was an eloquent spokesman for the religious vision of the late twentieth century. The closing words of his posthumously published book, *Chasing Shadows*, summed up his view:

> Time is short and the task is urgent. Evil is real. So is good. There is a choice. And we are not so much chosen as choosers. Life is holy. All life. Mine and yours. And that of those who came before us and the life of those after us.

Hugo Gryn died from cancer at 27 Circus Road, Westminster, on 18 August 1996 at the age of sixty-six. His memorial service, on 20 February 1997, was the cause of an acrimonious dispute over the attendance of the Orthodox chief rabbi, Jonathan Sacks, which was opposed by many Orthodox Jews. ALBERT FRIEDLANDER

**Sources** H. Gryn and N. Gryn, *Chasing shadows* (2000) • *The Times* (20 Aug 1996) • *Daily Telegraph* (20 Aug 1996) • *The Independent* (20 Aug 1996) • *WWW* • personal knowledge (2004) • private information (2004) • m. cert. • d. cert.

**Likenesses** M. Gerson, photograph, 1993, NPG [*see illus.*] • photograph, 1994, repro. in *The Independent* • photograph, repro. in *The Times* • photograph, repro. in *Daily Telegraph*

**Wealth at death** £48,695: probate, 1997

**Guader, Ralph**. *See* Ralph, earl (*d.* 1097x9).

**Guala** [Guala Bicchieri] (*c.***1150–1227**), papal official, was a native of Vercelli in Lombardy. First recorded in 1187, he appears to have been trained in theology and law, possibly in France as well as Italy. Made cardinal-deacon of Santa Maria in Portico by Innocent III in 1205, Guala was papal legate successively in north Italy (1206–7) and France (1208–9), and was promoted to be cardinal-priest of San Martino in Montibus in 1211. Following the Fourth Lateran Council, at a date after 14 January 1216, he was appointed papal legate to England, possibly at the request of King John himself. Guala's experience particularly suited him to hold this legation, and his reconstructed *acta* help to throw light on the last year of John's reign and the early years of Henry III's. The importance of Guala's role was enhanced by the absence from England of the exiled Stephen Langton, archbishop of Canterbury, between September 1215 and May 1218. The new legate's involvement in English affairs extended back to the Evesham Abbey case of 1206. From 1213 he was enjoying an annual pension of 20 marks from England, and he is known to have been well informed on the activities of Nicolò of Tusculum, his predecessor there as papal legate (1213–14). The terms of Guala's commission from Innocent III are not recorded but, judging by their confirmation by Honorius III, they included the power to reform and to excommunicate, the preaching of the crusade, and the forging of a peace, or at least a truce, between England and France.

Soon after 24 February 1216 Guala set out from Rome for England. He took with him a commission from Innocent III to be presented at the Council of Melun (24–25 April 1216), instructing Philip Augustus and Prince Louis that the latter should not accept the rebels' offer of the English crown. On pain of excommunication the legate forbade in the strongest terms, either Louis to invade England in pursuit of his claim, or Philip to support such an invasion. None the less, on 21 May, Louis and his men landed in England. Guala was delayed by French denial of safe passage across the channel, but his first action on eventually reaching England via Germany was to implement his threat by convening a clerical council at Winchester on 29 May 1216. There he issued a solemn sentence of excommunication against Louis.

The importance in political terms of Guala's legation was greatly increased not only by Langton's absence but also by the death on 19 October 1216 of King John. He had entrusted his young son, Henry III, to Guala, who was one of the executors of his will, as the representative of the Holy See. As the boy was a papal vassal and ward, the legate acted as his protector and supervised his coronation on 28 October at Gloucester. This was an essential first step in overcoming those rebels who had called on Louis of France.

Although the principal English rebels had been excommunicated before his arrival, Guala was instrumental in offering plenary indulgence to all those who fought in the king's cause, thus elevating the venture to the status of a crusade. Honorius III, in letters of 17 January 1217, allowed Guala to dispense crusaders from their vows to the Holy Land if they were fighting for the king and against the rebels. So it was that at the battle of Lincoln, on 20 May 1217, the king's supporters wore white crosses over their armour. After the French fleet was destroyed in a naval battle off Sandwich on 24 August 1217, Louis was believed to have been brought to abandon the struggle by his fear that Guala would win over the city of London, the last stronghold of the rebels. The treaty of Kingston (or Lambeth) was negotiated between 11 and 20 September 1217. Guala administered absolution, imposed penance, and bound Louis and the French to the payment of a subsidy for the recovery of the Holy Land. The treaty excluded the clergy of both countries. The French clergy who had accompanied Louis into England were to perform penance while the English clergy who supported Louis were to be deprived of benefices and subjected to punishment. Several were forced to go to Rome to seek absolution.

His position as legate made Guala nominally the king's leading counsellor. His involvement in secular government, and the restoration of order in England, was by no means limited; thus he set his seal to reissues of Magna Carta and the charter of the forest in 1216 and 1217, negotiated with Llywelyn of Wales and Alexander II, king of Scots, sanctioned the measure of February 1218 to call in arrears of scutage, and was the first witness to regulations issued in November 1218 for the use of Henry III's new seal. But in such matters he acted with William (I) Marshal and others, and contemporaries were probably more impressed by his measures against rebel clerics and infringers of the interdict. He may, indeed, have been unduly zealous, depriving some one hundred clerks of their benefices, and purging the chapter of St Paul's, London. Pandulf, who succeeded him as legate, released thirteen ecclesiastics from the imprisonment to which Guala had condemned them, and may have restored some of those he had deprived. Among those who benefited from the vacancies so created were a number of Italians, some of them Guala's kinsmen or members of his household. He was himself alleged, perhaps correctly, to have profited financially from his legation, and he certainly took advantage of his position to secure the advowson of Chesterton, Cambridgeshire, for the Augustinian priory he was in process of founding at Vercelli. Yet the grant was justified by reference to Guala's having 'laboured long and hard for the king's peace and the peace of the realm' (Vincent, 15), and his labours, which also included introducing and implementing the decrees of the Fourth Lateran Council, and the preaching of the fifth crusade, had indeed been considerable. They were still remembered nearly fifty years later, in 1264, when another papal legate, Guy Foulquois, was trying to end another English civil war.

Guala's legation was terminated by papal letters of 12 September 1218. He appears to have relinquished his office at Reading in mid-November, and to have left England shortly afterwards. On his way back to Rome, in February and March 1219, he had the satisfaction of seeing the foundation of the priory of San Andrea in Vercelli. Guala's remaining years in the curia were active ones, and he retained his contacts with England, continuing to receive his pension until 1222. In 1225 he was appointed as one of two legates to southern Italy, negotiating the treaty of San Germano by which Frederick II agreed to undertake a crusade. Guala outlived Honorius III by two months. He made his will on 29 May 1227, and died in Rome on 31 May; he was probably buried in the church of St John Lateran there. BRENDA M. BOLTON

**Sources** *The letters and charters of Cardinal Guala Bicchieri, papal legate in England, 1216–1218*, ed. N. Vincent, CYS, 83 (1996) · F. M. Powicke and C. R. Cheney, eds., *Councils and synods with other documents relating to the English church, 1205–1313*, 1 (1964), 49–51 · A. P. Bagliani, *I testamenti dei cardinali del duecento*, Miscellanea della Società Romana di Storia Patria, 25 (1980), 110–20 · H. G. Richardson, 'Letters of the legate Guala', *EngHR*, 48 (1933), 250–59 · W. Maleczek, *Papst und Kardinalskolleg von 1191 bis 1216* (1984), 141–6 · A. Theiner, *Vetera monumenta Slavorum meridionalium historiam illustrantia*, 1 (Rome, 1863), 63 n. 6 · C. D. Fonseca, 'Bicchieri, Guala', *Dizionario biografico degli Italiani*, ed. A. M. Ghisalberti, 10 (Rome, 1968) · R. Aubert, 'Guala de Bicchieri (Jacques)', *Dictionnaire d'histoire et de géographie ecclésiastiques*, 22 (Paris, 1988), 492–5 · F. Cazel, 'The legates Guala and Pandulf', *Thirteenth century England: proceedings of the Newcastle upon Tyne conference* [Newcastle upon Tyne 1987], ed. P. R. Coss and S. D. Lloyd, 2 (1988), 15–21 · D. A. Carpenter, *The minority of Henry III* (1990)

**Wealth at death** quite wealthy: Bagliani, *I testamenti*; Vincent, ed., *Letters and charters*, xliv–xlv

**Guasacht maccu Buáin** (*fl.* late 5th cent.). *See under* Meath, saints of (*act. c.*400–*c.*900).

**Gubbins, Sir Colin McVean** (1896–1976), army officer and intelligence officer, was born in Tokyo on 2 July 1896, the younger son and third child in the family of two sons and three daughters of John Harington Gubbins (1852–1929), who was oriental secretary at the British legation, and his wife, Helen Brodie (*d.* 1922), daughter of Colin Alexander McVean JP of Mull. Educated at Cheltenham College and at the Royal Military Academy, Woolwich, he was commissioned in 1914 into the Royal Field Artillery.

**Sir Colin McVean Gubbins** (1896–1976), by Elliott & Fry

In the First World War, Gubbins served as a battery officer on the western front, was wounded, and was awarded the MC. He married Norah Creina (*b.* 1894/5), daughter of Surgeon-Commander Philip Somerville Warren RN of Cork on 22 October 1919; the couple had two sons, the elder of whom was killed at Anzio in 1944. Also in 1919 he joined the staff of W. E. Ironside in north Russia. It was the Bolshevik revolution no less than his subsequent experience in Ireland in 1920–22 that stimulated his lifelong interest in irregular warfare.

After special employment on signals intelligence at general headquarters India, Gubbins graduated at the Staff College at Quetta in 1928, and was appointed GSO3 in the Russian section of the War Office in 1931. Having been promoted brevet major, in 1935 he joined MT 1, the policy making branch of the military training directorate. In October 1938, in the aftermath of the Munich agreement, he was sent to the Sudetenland as a military member of the international commission—an experience which left him with a lasting sympathy for the Czechs. Promoted brevet lieutenant-colonel, he joined G(R)—later known as MI(R)—in April 1939. In this obscure branch of the War

Office he prepared training manuals on irregular warfare, translations of which were later to be dropped in thousands over occupied Europe; he also made a rapid visit to Warsaw to exchange views on sabotage and subversion with the Polish general staff.

On mobilization in August 1939 Gubbins was appointed chief of staff to the military mission to Poland, led by Adrian Carton de Wiart. Among the first to report on the effectiveness of the German Panzer tactics, Gubbins had no illusions about the Polish capacity to resist. Yet the campaign left him with an enduring sense of obligation to the Poles, whose chivalrous and romantic nature was somewhat akin to his own.

In October 1939, having returned to England, he was sent to Paris as head of a military mission to the Czech and Polish forces under French command. The mission was viewed with suspicion by the French since its main purpose was to keep the War Office in touch with the burgeoning Czech and Polish resistance movements. Gubbins was recalled from France in March 1940 to raise the 'independent companies'—forerunners of the commandos—which he later commanded in Norway. Although criticized in some quarters for having asked too much of untried troops, he showed himself to be a bold and resourceful commander, and was appointed to the DSO (1940). Back in England, he was charged by general headquarters home forces with forming a civilian force to operate behind the German lines if Britain were invaded. Stout-hearted but utterly inexperienced, these so-called auxiliary units could not have survived for long; but their secret recruitment, training, and equipment in the summer of 1940 was a remarkable feat of improvisation and personal leadership.

In November 1940 Gubbins became acting brigadier and, at the request of Hugh Dalton, the minister of economic warfare, was seconded to the Special Operations Executive (SOE) which had recently been established 'to co-ordinate all action by way of sabotage and subversion against the enemy overseas'. Besides maintaining his connections with the Poles and Czechs, he was initially given three tasks for which he was admirably qualified: to set up training facilities, to devise operating procedures acceptable to the Admiralty and Air Ministry, and to establish close working relations with the joint planning staff. Inevitably he bore the brunt of the suspicion and disfavour which SOE provoked in Whitehall—partly because of the nature of its operations and partly because of the excessive secrecy which surrounded them. However, Gubbins had no doubt it was his duty to identify with SOE notwithstanding all the risk of misrepresentation of his motives that this entailed.

Despite frustrations and disappointments—and there were many, due mainly to the shortage of aircraft—he persevered with training organizers and dispatching them to the field. The first liaison flight to Poland took place in February 1941, and during 1942 and 1943 European resistance movements patronized by SOE scored notable successes, including the raid on the heavy water installation in Norway which aborted Hitler's efforts to produce an atom bomb.

At this stage Gubbins had no direct responsibility for SOE's subsidiary headquarters in Cairo whose activities in Yugoslavia and Greece had for some time been raising awkward issues of foreign policy. However, in September 1943 these issues came to a head; Sir Charles Hambro resigned as executive head of SOE and Gubbins, now a major-general, was appointed his replacement. He immediately faced a concerted attack on SOE's autonomy, mounted by the Foreign Office, general headquarters Middle East, and the joint intelligence committee (JIC). As always, he had the steadfast support of his minister, the third earl of Selborne, but it was not until a meeting on 30 September, presided over by the prime minister, that a *modus operandi* was agreed. Nevertheless Gubbins's position remained precarious and in January 1944 there was a further attempt to dismantle SOE. This followed the disclosure that SOE's operations in the Netherlands had been penetrated by the Germans, for which Gubbins characteristically took the blame. Undaunted he set about co-ordinating the activities of the various resistance movements, now supported worldwide by SOE, with the operational requirements of individual commanders-in-chief. Although control was decentralized wherever possible, harnessing the force of resistance to the conventional war effort proved delicate and controversial, often politically as well as militarily. It involved consultation at the highest level, not only with the Foreign Office and the chiefs of staff, but also with representatives of the patriot organizations, the governments-in-exile, and other allied agencies—in particular the United States office of strategic services (OSS). In the event the organized resistance was more effective than Whitehall had expected. In north-west Europe, where SOE's activities remained under Gubbins's personal control, General Eisenhower later estimated that the contribution of the French Resistance alone had been worth six divisions.

When SOE was wound up in 1946 the War Office could offer Gubbins no suitable employment, and on retirement from the army he became managing director of a large firm of carpet and textile manufacturers. However, he kept in touch with the leading personalities in many of the countries he had helped to liberate. Invited by Prince Bernhard of the Netherlands, he joined the Bilderberg group; and he was an enthusiastic supporter of the special forces club, of which he was a co-founder.

Gubbins's first marriage ended in divorce in 1944; but on 25 September 1950 he married Anna Elise (*b.* 1914/15), widow of Lieutenant R. T. Tradin of the Royal Norwegian Air Force, and daughter of Hans Didrik Jensen of Tromsø, Norway. There were no children from the second marriage. A keen shot and fisherman, Gubbins spent his last years at his home in the Hebrides, Obbe Leverburgh, on the Isle of Harris. He was appointed CMG in 1944, advanced to KCMG in 1946, and appointed deputy lieutenant of the islands area of the Western Isles in 1976. He held fourteen foreign decorations. Gubbins died at Stornoway in the Hebrides on 11 February 1976.

Gubbins's creative spirit made him a natural leader of the young; and he delegated generously to those whom he trusted, both men and women. Above all, he was a dedicated professional soldier. With his quick brain, the imagination and energy necessary to transform ideas into action, and his force of will, he might have held high command in the field had his abilities not been confined to special operations. As it was, he left his mark on the history of almost every country which suffered enemy occupation in the Second World War.

PETER WILKINSON, *rev.*

**Sources** P. Wilkinson and J. B. Astley, *Gubbins and SOE* (1993) • W. J. M. Mackenzie, *The secret history of SOE* (2000) • *The Times* (12 Feb 1976) • *The Times* (17 Feb 1976) • *The Times* (19 Feb 1976) • personal knowledge (1986) • private information (1986) • *CGPLA Eng. & Wales* (1976) • *WWW* • m. cert. [Norah Creina Somerville Warren] • m. cert. [Anna Elise Tradin]
**Archives** Bodl. Oxf., corresp. with third earl of Selborne and others | SOUND BL NSA, oral history interview • IWM SA, oral history interview
**Likenesses** I. S. Bendle, portrait, priv. coll. • Elliott & Fry, photograph, NPG [*see illus.*]
**Wealth at death** £27,114: probate, 1 June 1976, *CGPLA Eng. & Wales*

**Gubbins, John Russell** (1838–1906), racehorse owner and breeder, was born on 16 December 1838 at the family home, Kilfrush, co. Limerick, the fourth son of Joseph Gubbins and his wife, Maria, daughter of Thomas Wise of Cork. He had three surviving brothers and five sisters. After being educated privately, Gubbins settled at Bruree House, Bruree, co. Limerick, in 1868. In 1879 he inherited some property in Knockany from his brother Stamer after the latter's death following an accident while schooling a horse. He also inherited a fortune from an uncle, Francis Wise of Cork. This enabled him to spend about £40,000 in building kennels and stables at Bruree, and buying horses and hounds. He hunted the Limerick countryside with both stag- and foxhounds, and was an active angler until forced to stop by the operations of the Land League in 1882.

From an early age Gubbins took a keen interest in horse-racing. At first his attention was mainly confined to steeplechasers, and he rode many winners at Punchestown and elsewhere in Ireland. He was the owner of Seaman when that horse won the grand hurdle race at Autheuil, but had sold him to Lord Manners before he won the Grand National at Liverpool in 1882. Buying the stallions Kendal and St Florian, he bred, from the mare Morganette, Galtee More by the former and Ard Patrick by the latter. Galtee More won the Two Thousand Guineas and the St Leger as well as the Derby in 1897, and was afterwards sold to the Russian government for £21,000. Ard Patrick was also sold for £21,000, to the Prussian government, which had purchased Galtee More from his Russian owners. A few days after the sale Ard Patrick won the Eclipse Stakes. The export of these outstanding horses did not endear Gubbins to the British breeding fraternity. Elsewhere, however, he gained a reputation as a kind and indulgent landlord and employer. He was high sheriff of co. Limerick in 1886.

In 1889 Gubbins married Edith Mabel (*d.* 1896), daughter of Charles Legh, of Adlington Hall, Cheshire. He headed the list of winning owners in 1897 with a total of £22,739, and was third in the list in 1903. Thereafter he was rarely seen on a racecourse, owing to failing health, and in 1904 he sold his horses in training. Gubbins died at his home, Bruree House, Bruree, on 20 March 1906, and was buried in the private burial-ground at Kilfrush. His marriage had been childless and his estates passed to his nephew John Norris Browning, a retired naval surgeon.

EDWARD MOORHOUSE, *rev.* WRAY VAMPLEW

**Sources** R. Mortimer, R. Onslow, and P. Willett, *Biographical encyclopedia of British flat racing* (1978) • *The Sportsman* (21 March 1906) • Burke, *Gen. GB* • H. S., *Baily's Magazine*, 85 (1906), 362–6
**Likenesses** Walery of Regent Street, photograph, repro. in H. S., 'The late Mr. John R. Gubbins', 364
**Wealth at death** £105,392 6*s*.: Irish probate sealed in London, 9 July 1906, *CGPLA Eng. & Wales*

**Gubbins, Martin Richard** (1812–1863), administrator in India, was the third of the four sons of Major-General Joseph Gubbins (*d.* 1832) of Kilfrush, co. Limerick, and Charlotte Bathoe (*d.* 1824). All four brothers served in India; the youngest of Martin's three sisters married the ninth duke of St Albans as his second wife. Educated at the East India College, Haileybury, from 1828 to 1830, Gubbins began his civil service career in India as a writer in 1830, and became assistant to the chief commissioner and resident at Delhi in 1831. After other postings, he went to Oudh on its annexation by Lord Dalhousie in 1856 as the financial commissioner. During the cold season of 1856–7 he made a tour as financial commissioner through the whole of Oudh to test the recent summary settlement of the land revenue. The settlement followed the pattern set by Robert Merttins Bird in 1833, but on this occasion it triggered a revolt of the talukdars. Gubbins attempted to redress the grievances of the landowners, a task made more difficult by disagreements with Coverley Jackson, the chief commissioner, who wished to deal harshly with the talukdars. He also clashed with Jackson's replacement, Henry Lawrence, who described the combative Gubbins as a 'troublesome co-adjutant', over the garrisoning of the residency. As head of intelligence, Gubbins was mistrustful of the Sepoys, and successfully recommended using European rather than Indian troops in the residency. From the beginning of the mutiny in 1857, he urged Lawrence to disarm the Sepoy regiments in the area, but his advice was not taken. On 30 May 1857 most of the troops rose in revolt. On 9 June, Gubbins was appointed head of a provisional government, during the absence of Lawrence through ill health. In this position he proceeded to disarm the remaining Sepoys, an order which was countermanded on Lawrence's return a few days later.

Gubbins strongly advised an attack on the rebel troops in the neighbourhood of Lucknow; but when Lawrence consented, the attack was made without proper preparation. The result was the disaster at Chinhat on 30 June, which led to the siege of Lucknow. Early in the siege, Lawrence was killed, leaving Gubbins as the senior official. During the siege he wrote *An Account of the Mutinies in Oudh*, which, after its publication in 1858, became one of the most famous accounts of the mutiny; but his criticisms of Lawrence were challenged by George Hutchinson's 1859 account, which was commissioned by Lawrence's successor, Sir James Outram. After the relief of Lucknow, Gubbins accompanied the army of Sir Colin Campbell to Cawnpore, and was then forced by ill health to return to England.

Gubbins was back in India at the end of 1858, and became judge of the supreme court of Agra. He resigned through ill health, and returned to England in January 1863. After his return he suffered from depression, and he committed suicide at his brother's home, Somerset House, Clarendon Place, Leamington Spa, on 6 May 1863. He was survived by his wife, Harriet Louisa, *née* Nepean.

E. J. RAPSON, *rev.* PETER PENNER

**Sources** P. Penner, *The patronage bureaucracy in north India* (1986), esp. 316–17 [references and notes] • C. Hibbert, *The great mutiny, India, 1857* (1978) • M. Edwardes, *A season in hell: the defence of the Lucknow residency* (1973) • M. Edwardes, *The necessary hell: John and Henry Lawrence and the Indian Empire* (1958) • M. R. Gubbins, *An account of the mutinies in Oudh* (1858) • *Lahore Chronicle* (19 Jan 1859) • *Lahore Chronicle* (9 April 1859) • *Lahore Chronicle* (2 July 1859) • J. W. Kaye and G. B. Malleson, *Kaye's and Malleson's History of the Indian mutiny of 1857–8*, new edn, 6 vols. (1897–8) • B. Smith, *John, Lord Lawrence* (1883) • S. N. Sen, *Eighteen fifty-seven* (1957) • F. C. Danvers and others, *Memorials of old Haileybury College* (1894), 395, 600 • *Royal Leamington Spa Courier* (9 May 1863), 10 • Burke, *Gen. GB* (1879)

**Wealth at death** under £5000: probate, 15 July 1863, *CGPLA Eng. & Wales*

**Gubbins, Norman Hector Leifchild** [*pseud.* Nathaniel Gubbins] (**1893–1976**), journalist and humorist, was born on 31 May 1893 at 4 Somerset Road, Ealing, Middlesex, the only surviving son (there were also three older daughters, of whom the younger two were twins) of William Gubbins, commercial traveller, formerly an Oxfordshire farmworker who had run away to London at the age of twelve to sell groceries, and his wife, Marie Cecile, *née* Richards. His father died when he was two. Gubbins was educated at Battersea Polytechnic, but left at sixteen, after the headmaster told his mother that educating him had proved a hopeless task. He began work at 10*s.* a week in the *Daily Express* library where, by his own testimony, he spent many miserable years filing cuttings in the wrong envelopes and losing reference books.

Gubbins served in the First World War as a private from August 1914 to February 1919; it was, he later said, an equally unhappy experience, but he was invalided home early, which may well have saved his life. On 4 February 1922 he married Phyllis Magdalen Hughes (*b.* 1894/5), fashion editor for the *Daily Mirror*. She was the daughter of Francis George Hughes, a furnishing company's representative. They had two daughters, Felicity Anne, who died at the age of thirty-eight, and Stephanie, who married Leo Halmsley, the writer. Gubbins's professional career continued to stall, however, as more years of miscasting as a reporter followed before the editor of the *Sunday Express*, John Rutherford Gordon, decided he needed a humorous column. Gubbins got the job, he later claimed, because there was no one else in the office at the time. His first column, under the generic strap-line 'Sitting on the fence', appeared on 30 November 1930 on page 3—a star position—and under his new byline, Nathaniel Gubbins, which was to remain with him for life.

The first few weeks were shaky; Gubbins seemed uncertain whether he could pull it off. But he soon got into his stride, and began to develop a whole bestiary of characters who were to delight millions of readers for the next twenty-three years. There was the Worm, apotheosis of the suburban man for whom Gubbins wrote. There was the Sparrow, vehicle for his most sustained and ferocious satire on the sex war (Sparrow dallied with the Other Sparrow at the Tree Tops Club). There was Sally the Cat, his archetypal female, and the Ginger Cat, a tom with all the foibles of its gender. His daughter Stephanie was the acknowledged basis for The Awful Child, forever asking awkward questions. Gubbins also produced a series of brilliant dialogues with his own stomach, which acquired a separate, living, suffering identity as Tum, his gastric *Doppelgänger*. (Gubbins suffered from chronic dyspepsia, smoked fifty cigarettes a day, and confessed he found the world intolerable without a glass in his hand.)

Gubbins was at his finest during the Second World War (he mocked his Home Guard service but in truth was an artillery officer at a secret Home Guard site). He was a hero to the Eighth Army, the darling of W. M. Aitken, first Baron Beaverbrook, and the subject of two *Times* leaders.

The BBC ran a series of Thursday evening programmes based on his characters in 1944. In 1953 Beaverbrook decided the column had lost its appeal and Gubbins was sacked; he moved to the *Sunday Dispatch*, but the transplant did not take. The last twenty years of his life were spent in retirement; indeed, in 1963 he had to write to the *Sunday Times* to point out that he was not, as they had reported, dead. Some thirteen years later, Gubbins succumbed to cancer and heart disease, and died on 3 February 1976 at Victoria Hospital in Deal.

GODFREY SMITH, *rev.*

**Sources** G. Smith, ed., *The best of Nathaniel Gubbins* (1978) • private information (1993) • b. cert. • m. cert. • d. cert. • *The Times* (5 Feb 1976)

**Wealth at death** £28,318: probate, 8 March 1976, *CGPLA Eng. & Wales*

**Gubiun** [Gibuin], **Ralph** (*d.* **1151**), abbot of St Albans, was probably born towards the end of the eleventh century. According to Matthew Paris he was an Englishman, although his name would suggest Norman origins (*Gesta abbatum*, 106). Two contradictory versions of Gubiun's early career are given in the *Gesta abbatum*. According to the first he joined the community as a youth, and distinguished himself in the production of books in the scriptorium before entering the service of Alexander, bishop of Lincoln (*d.* 1148), where he remained until becoming abbot. In the second and more plausible account he entered the bishop's service as a secular and rose to the position of chamberlain and bishop's chaplain before leaving to begin life as a monk at St Albans, at the bishop's suggestion. At Lincoln he studied the Bible under an Italian, Master Wodo; his experiences of intellectual life and book production there may explain both the close relationship between the abbey and the see, and the appearance of several Italian scholars at St Albans in the 1150s.

Gubiun probably entered St Albans in the 1130s. He rose quickly to prominence (though not perhaps as a copyist), and was elected abbot in 1146. Although he made several notable improvements during his short abbacy, expanding the abbey buildings, increasing the community's wealth, and securing the confirmation of the abbey's privileges from Pope Eugenius III (*r.* 1145–1153), he attracted bitter criticism, probably for his close association with, and apparent subjection to, Lincoln. He was also held responsible for the loss of some of the monks' most precious vestments, and for the degradation of the shrine of St Alban, which was robbed of costly gold decorations added by the previous abbot, Geoffrey. Matthew Paris also suggests that he became drawn into a conflict with the prior, Alcuin, who was driven as a result to join Westminster Abbey.

In his fourth or fifth year as abbot Gubiun fell sick and resigned the abbacy in favour of Robert of Gorham, the nephew of his predecessor Geoffrey. He died on 6 July 1151, and was buried at the entrance to the chapter house of St Albans Abbey. His remains were exhumed in 1979 and reburied, together with those of other twelfth-century abbots including Geoffrey, at the west end of the nave.

Matthew Paris describes Gubiun as a 'lover of books', and he was probably the author of, among other works, a history of Alexander the Great. Compiled from the work of a wide range of classical authors, including Solinus and Pompeius Trogus, the text includes as much topographical as historical detail. Two copies of his history survive, both perhaps transcribed at St Albans in the late twelfth or early thirteenth century. The text was used in the fourteenth century by the chronicler Ranulf Higden (*d.* 1364), and by the St Albans historian Thomas Walsingham (*d.* 1422) for his own *Historia Alexandri magni.*

James G. Clark

**Sources** *Gesta abbatum monasterii Sancti Albani, a Thoma Walsingham*, ed. H. T. Riley, 3 vols., pt 4 of *Chronica monasterii S. Albani*, Rolls Series, 28 (1867–9), vol. 1, pp. 106–10 • R. M. Thomson, *Manuscripts from St Albans Abbey, 1066–1235*, 1 (1982), 22–3 • Bale, *Cat.*, 1.193–4 • G. Cary, *The medieval Alexander* (1956), 68–9 • D. J. A. Ross, *Alexander historiatus* (1963), 75 • R. McKitterick and L. L. Cardozo, eds., *Lasting letters* (1992)

**Archives** BL, Cotton MS Claudius E.iv; MS 62777 • CCC Cam., MS 219 [copies] • Gon. & Caius Cam., MS 154

**Likenesses** probably A. Strayler, portrait, 1350–99, Cotton MS, Catalogus benefactorum, Nero D. vii

**Gudwal** [St Gudwal, Gurval, Goal, Gouezgal] (*supp. fl.* **7th cent.**), bishop of St Malo, is honoured at various places in Brittany, mainly in the dioceses of Vannes and St Malo, and chiefly at Locoal-Mendon, west of Auray on the south coast. There is no definite dating for his life but in the tenth century his relics were removed from Locoal-Mendon to Ghent, via Montreuil, near Boulogne (where they rested for some time); they are said to have reached Ghent (the abbey of St Peter and St Paul at Blandinberg) in 959. In England, St Gudwal was known in the tenth century from imported Breton litanies; relics of him were claimed by Exeter Cathedral in the eleventh century as a gift from Æthelstan; and there were later two dedications to him in Worcester diocese: a chapel in the city, and another at Finstall in the parish of Stoke Prior. The Ghent life was also known in England in the fourteenth century.

The Ghent life of St Gudwal was written in the twelfth century, based partly on older material from Brittany. It is very unclear in its geography; it claims that Gudwal was born in 'Britannia' (probably Britain) of noble parentage. He is portrayed as having been a successful bishop, in an unnamed see; finding his duties in that role a hindrance to the holy life, he resigned and retired, first to a monastery and then to a nearby island, where he was joined by disciples. Later he removed with his disciples, in seven ships, to a place where they built a fresh monastery, near to 'Cornuvia' (the Breton Cornouaille): the island of Locoal (literally, the church of Goal, or Gudwal) in Brittany, in the estuary of the River Etel, is intended. The older Breton material appears to have recounted mainly St Gudwal's efficacy in preventing the sea from inundating parts of the land around his monastery, and his dealings with a lord called Mevor, ruling some distance away in 'Cornuvia'. After his death his body was buried in the village of Le Plec, on a peninsula in the same estuary. Various cures are also recounted, and visions and miracles attendant upon his funeral. Some posthumous miracles in Ghent are recounted.

St Gudwal's cult is attested in litanies from Brittany and France from the tenth century onwards. Some ten chapels in his honour exist in various parts of south and west Brittany, under the local names of Goal and Gouezgal, and, in St Malo diocese, Gurval. In the latter diocese he was turned into a different person, and St Gurval was claimed as a former bishop of the diocese, St Malo's chosen successor in the see of Alet. It was there claimed that he was born in Britain, served under the Irish St Brendan, and came to Brittany when sent for by St Malo. However, Gurval is a possible dialectal variant of Gudwal, and the identity of their feast days (6 June) and the complementary distribution of the two cults make it almost certain that they are the same saint.

In Cornwall there is a church near Penzance dedicated to **St Gulval** (*fl.* before 1000). This saint was considered to be female; there is no record of her feast day, and she is consistently recorded, from the eleventh century onwards, as St Welvela or Gwelvela, always with 'l' and not 'd' in the first syllable. It seems unlikely that this is the Breton St Gudwal, first because of the consistency of the feminine gender, and second because Cornish 'l' should not represent Breton 'd'. However, nothing is known about the Cornish saint, and if these two objections could be overcome the Cornish church might represent a dedication to the Breton saint. There was a famous holy well at Gulval until the eighteenth century, but it has since been destroyed.

O. J. Padel

**Sources** G. H. Doble, *Saint Gulval or Gurval, bishop and confessor*, Cornish Saints, 30 (1933) • *Acta sanctorum: Junius*, 1 (Antwerp, 1695),

727–48 · M. Lapidge, ed., *Anglo-Saxon litanies of the saints* (1991), 261, 292 · T. D. Hardy, *Descriptive catalogue of materials relating to the history of Great Britain and Ireland*, 1, Rolls Series, 26 (1862), 371–3 [nos. 871–5] · A. de la Borderie, *Histoire de Bretagne*, 6 vols. (1896–1914), 1.492–6 · J.-M. le Mené, *Histoire du diocèse de Vannes* (1888), 1.60–2 · F. E. Warren, ed., *The Leofric missal* (1883), 4b · C. Horstman, ed., *Nova legenda Anglie, as collected by John of Tynemouth, J. Capgrave, and others*, 1 (1901), 501–4

**Guedalla, Philip** (1889–1944), historian and essayist, was born on 12 March 1889 in Elgin Avenue, Maida Vale, London, the only son of David Guedalla, an almond broker in Mincing Lane, who came from a Spanish-Jewish family, and his wife, Louise Soman. Guedalla's talents developed early, and at Rugby School, where he became head boy, the epigrammatic irreverence of his editorials in the school magazine, *The Meteor*, was a startling and popular innovation. This was a vein which he exploited with zest to the end of his life and never more successfully than during his brilliant career at Balliol College, Oxford. His bons mots as president of the Oxford Union (1911) went the rounds of the university; he figured as a much discussed Mark Antony in the Oxford University Dramatic Society production of *Julius Caesar*, and despite these distractions obtained first classes in classical moderations (1910) and modern history (1912).

Before he left Oxford, Guedalla had published two collections of light verse, *Ignes fatui* and *Metri gratia*, the former of which went to a second edition. But at this time his ambitions were not primarily literary; he confidently hoped to enter politics by way of the bar, to which he was called by the Inner Temple in 1913, and to become a Liberal cabinet minister, preferably as secretary of state for war. In this high ambition he was disappointed, and in public life at least the promise of Oxford never materialized. During the First World War he served as legal adviser to the contracts department of the War Office and Ministry of Munitions, and from 1917 to 1920 organized and acted as secretary to the Flax Control Board. In 1919 he married Nellie Maude, daughter of Albert Reitlinger, a banker. There were no children.

Guedalla, who was a founder in 1921 of the Liberal summer school, stood for parliament five times as a Liberal candidate (North Hackney, 1922; North-East Derbyshire, 1923, 1924; Rusholme, 1929; Withington, 1931), but he was always defeated; and unlike so many of his Liberal contemporaries he steadily refused to transfer his allegiance to the Labour Party. Working-class audiences, moreover, were sometimes mystified by speeches which retained all the epigrammatic glitter of his Oxford Union days.

Since Guedalla's first ambitious work, *Supers and Supermen* (1920), was marked by both verbal fireworks and lack of reverence for established reputations, it was inevitable that he should be hailed as a disciple of Lytton Strachey, whose *Eminent Victorians* had appeared in 1918. But although he may have relished the new fashion of denigration, Guedalla had set his literary course, and indeed formed the essentials of his literary style, before he left Oxford. And although as a writer he lacked Strachey's urbane subtlety, he was a more conscientious historical scholar. A historical work, he believed, should be good

**Philip Guedalla (1889–1944)**, by Sir William Rothenstein

entertainment, but it should be based upon sound research, and he sometimes complained that critics of his writings were too apt to be distracted from the research by the entertainment.

Guedalla was always more interested in men than movements, and *The Second Empire* (1922) was a study of the emperor rather than of the empire. In *A Gallery* (1924) and *Independence Day* (1926) he presented further collections of historical sketches in lighter vein, but in *Palmerston* (1926) he first displayed his full powers. Here, as in *Gladstone and Palmerston* (1928), *The Queen and Mr. Gladstone* (1933), and most conspicuously perhaps *The Duke* (1931), a full-length study of Wellington, there was depth as well as brilliance; Guedalla was now not only entertaining a considerable audience, but making solid contributions to knowledge. *The Hundred Days* (1934) was followed by *The Hundred Years* (1936) which anticipated the centenary of Queen Victoria's accession. In this last work, and notably in his study of Winston Churchill (1941) and in *The Two Marshals* (1943), a comparison of Bazaine and Pétain, his interest in the contemporary scene began to transfer itself, now that he had abandoned politics himself, to his writings. He died in St Mary's Hospital, Paddington, London, on 16 December 1944, of an illness contracted during the journeys which, as a temporary squadron leader in the Royal Air Force, he had devoted to preparing his last work, *Middle East, 1940–1942: a Study in Air Power* (1944). He was buried in Golders Green Jewish cemetery; his wife survived him.

Despite the cynical note which he occasionally sounded, Guedalla was a man of simple and kindly nature; and the persistence of his taste for epigram was evidence that he had remained young at heart. The opening sentences of his essay 'Ministers of state' provide a memorable example of his lively style: 'Any stigma, as the old saying is, will serve to beat a dogma. The unpopularity of received opinions renders it almost cowardly to disprove them, and one hates to hit a platitude when it is down' (Guedalla, *Collected Essays*, 3.15). As well as his writing he established a well-deserved reputation as a speaker and lecturer. ELTON, *rev.* MARK POTTLE

**Sources** *The Times* (18–19 Dec 1944) • P. Guedalla, *Collected essays* (1927) • P. Guedalla, *Mary Arnold* (1928) • personal knowledge (1959) • private information (1959) • M. Freeden, *Liberalism divided: a study in British political thought, 1914–1939* (1986) • I. Elliott, ed., *The Balliol College register, 1833–1933*, 2nd edn (privately printed, Oxford, 1934)

**Archives** Bodl. Oxf., literary MSS, corresp. and papers • Central Zionist Archives, Jerusalem, corresp. and literary papers • University of British Columbia, literary MSS and drawings | CAC Cam., corresp. with Sir E. Millington Drake and related papers • HLRO, letters to David Lloyd George • U. Southampton L., corresp. with Cecil Roth | SOUND BL NSA, current affairs footage

**Likenesses** M. Beerbohm, caricature, 1929, National Gallery of Victoria, Melbourne • H. Coster, photographs, 1930, NPG • M. Beerbohm, two cartoons, 1959, priv. coll. • J. Collier, portrait, 1959, priv. coll. • W. Rothenstein, chalk drawing, NPG [*see illus.*] • photograph, repro. in *The Times* (18 Dec 1944)

**Wealth at death** £21,368 14*s.* 7*d.*: probate, 31 Aug 1945, *CGPLA Eng. & Wales*

**Guercy, Balthasar** (*d.* 1557), surgeon and physician, was an Italian (de Guercis), born in Il Boscho in the duchy of Milan, though nothing is known of his parentage or birth. A belief that he was 'once of Canterbury' (Strype) is unconfirmed, and Guercy is noticed in England first about 1515, when, paid in advance, he was accused of failing to cure a bishop's servant of syphilis. On 7 November 1519 he obtained an injunction against Thomas Roos, a London surgeon, who had sought to bar him from the profession. (Seemingly, Guercy had already graduated at some foreign university.) A surgeon to Queen Katherine of Aragon, Guercy obtained denization, as a native of Italy, on 16 March 1522. John Skelton's ribald poem *Why Come ye Not to Court?*, from a few years later, alleged that 'Balthasor' had not cured Domingo Lomelino's nose, and that his promised treatment of 'our Cardinals [Wolsey's] eye' would result in its loss, and render him lame. About 1530 Guercy obtained a Cambridge MB. In 1532, as 'surgeon to the queen consort' *de facto* (Anne Boleyn), he was granted the income from lands in Edmonton, Middlesex; and in the following year Archbishop Cranmer wrote thanking him for his care in treating one of his chaplains for a 'disease … within his knee' (Cox, 248). On 20 August 1534 Guercy obtained licence to leave for Italy, presumably to further his medical studies, with three servants, five horses, and 200 crowns (the French *escu sol*, worth about 4*s.*).

On 11 December 1543 Eustace Chapuys, the Holy Roman emperor's ambassador in London, wrote telling the sieur de Granvelle that about six days previously Guercy, 'a singularly clever surgeon and able physician', had been sent to the Tower of London for upholding papal authority. Fearing that his friend—born within the empire—would be executed, Chapuys hoped that Charles V might ask Henry VIII to save him. Dismissing a warning that persecution of Guercy could rebound on English protestants overseas, the privy council observed that Guercy, living here for over twenty years, had obtained denization, and had married an Englishwoman. On 2 February 1544 Chapuys wrote to inform Charles V that Henry had had Guercy released, 'for the Emperor's sake'. Following '16 years of study and practice' (Emden, *Oxf.*), Guercy was granted his MD degree by special grace at Cambridge, and, in the same year (1546), he and his wife, Joan, purchased the cottage in which they lived in St Mary Street, St Mary Axe parish, London, from Anthony Bonvisi. Later Guercy removed to a large messuage within the close of the former St Helen's Priory, in Bishopsgate.

For his Catholic sentiments Guercy fled from England without permission in early 1551, to find sanctuary overseas. Excluded by name from Edward VI's general act of pardon (1553), he was back in England by 14 January 1554, when he was pardoned by Queen Mary. He was made fellow of the College of Physicians in 1556.

By a will dated 14 December 1556 Guercy left his residence in the close and four other properties in St Helen's, Bishopsgate, and ten other messuages in the parishes of St Mary Axe and St Andrew Undershaft, with properties (not specified) in Walthamstow and elsewhere in Waltham Forest, Essex, distributed among his sons, Benedict and Richard, and daughter Frances. Seemingly, his wife had died.

On 7 January 1557 Guercy, 'aged and weak of body and diseased', made his will (*recte* testament). One daughter, Frances, widow of Thomas Polsted, was to have £30 a year, and the other, Mary Polley, £200. Christ's Hospital, the Black Friars, Friars Observant, Sheen Priory, and Syon Abbey were each left £10, with £40 among the poor in Todmarton (Oxfordshire), St Helen's, Bishopsgate, and 'Sandye Acre' prebend. Small bequests were made to friends—including Drs John Fryer and (John) Clement—and to servants. He left black gowns to Andrew Guercy (relationship, if any, unknown), who witnessed the will, and his wife. The executors were to be Benedict Guercy, John Fryer, Richard Haywood, and Benedict Browne; William Rastell and Ranulph Cholmley, recorder of London, were to be overseers. A codicil added that day stipulated that John Baptist Affaitadi's company in Antwerp was to retain and use Guercy's 'stock of money' for six years, after which principal and interest were to be divided between his sons Benedict and Richard. Guercy died on 7 January 1557, and is said to have been buried at St Helen's, Bishopsgate, on 10 January, probate being granted eight days later.

Guercy's son and heir, Benedict, who graduated BCL at St Edmund Hall, Oxford, in 1538, was aged forty by 13 February 1557. JOHN BENNELL

**Sources** *CSP Spain, March 1541 – Dec 1543*, no. 267; 1544, no.7 • PRO, PROB 11/39, q.2 • G. S. Fry, ed., *Abstracts of inquisitiones post mortem relating to the City of London*, 1: 1485–1561, British RS, 15 (1896), 144–6 • Munk, *Roll* • *The poetical works of John Skelton*, ed. A. Dyce, 2 (1843), 63, 373 • *Miscellaneous writings and letters of Thomas Cranmer*, ed. J. E.

Cox, Parker Society, [18] (1846), 248 • *LP Henry VIII*, 3/2, appx 5 (p. 1562), no. 2108; 7, no. 1122(10); 19/1, nos. 6, 84; 21/1, no. 1383(10) • Emden, *Oxf.*, 4.22 • *CPR, 1550–53*, 78; *1553–4*, 425; *1555–7*, 434–6 • C. H. Talbot and E. A. Hammond, *The medical practitioners in medieval England: a biographical register* (1965), 21, 355 • J. Strype, *Ecclesiastical memorials*, 2/2 (1822), 68 • Cooper, *Ath. Cantab.*, 1.173

**Guerden, Aaron** (*c.*1602–1676?), physician and master of the mint, was the son of Michel Guerden (*c.*1560–1640), royal seneschal of Jersey, and his wife, Marie (*d.* 1620), daughter of Aaron Stocall, constable of St Saviour's, and the grandson of a Swiss minister who had settled in Jersey. He was educated at Cambridge, where he matriculated from Pembroke College in 1619 and graduated BA in 1622/3 and MA in 1627. He was a fellow of Queens' College (1628–31) and took his MD degree at Rheims in 1634. He seems to have practised as a physician in London illegally in the later 1630s and was cited before the court of physicians in 1640 for not having a licence. He remained active as a physician throughout his life, being ordered by the Rump Parliament in 1653 to examine and report on 220 sick soldiers, and being elected an honorary fellow of the College of Physicians in 1664. (His brother Denis was physician in charge of Ely House, the bishop's London residence converted into a hospital for maimed soldiers in the early 1650s.) It is not clear how he supported himself throughout the 1640s, except that he was based in London.

In 1645 William Prynne sought to defend the royalist governor of Jersey, Sir Philippe De Carteret, from charges of corruption and false religion brought against him by a group of Jersey exiles, among whom Guerden and his brother were named. To Prynne these men were Anabaptists, who 'promise themselves all the Offices and government of the Island when reduced and to set up their religion there *cum privilegio*' (Prynne). The charge of Anabaptism was strongly denied at the time, but the fact that all Denis's children were baptized as adults lends some support to Prynne's claim. Furthermore the fact that a royalist mint was set up in Aaron's (sequestered) house in Jersey, and that William Prynne accused both Guerden brothers of lobbying parliament on behalf of convicted Jersey coiners and counterfeiters (the leader of whom, Maximilian Messervy, was almost certainly related to them), suggests some earlier contact with minting coin, and may help to explain why Aaron was suddenly appointed master of the mint in May 1649. This followed Sir Robert Harley's resignation as master worker of the mint because he refused to 'coyne with the new stamp' (that is, one bearing the emblems of the Commonwealth), and it followed the Rump's decision not to accept the nomination of Sir John Wollaston 'that he might not be esteemed a monopoliser of the best places of honour, trust and profit in the nation'. Instead they determined 'to bestow that place on Doctor Aaron Gourdian' (*The Moderate*, 15/22 May 1649, 508).

There are regular references to Guerden as master worker in the newspapers and council papers throughout the 1650s. The evidence however suggests that his lack of knowledge and background caused both inefficiency and financial loss to the mint, to its warden (Oliver St John) and to Guerden, who was still pursuing claims for several hundred pounds in 1664. A correspondent in Amsterdam in 1652 wrote that although the 'Warden is a very ingenious Mints-Man … he is matched with such ignorant wilfull men … that almost all things goe contrary to his minde and he cannot doe that good in the Mint as he would' (T. Violet, *The Answer of the Corporation of Moniers*, 1653). On 11 April 1651 Guerden was appointed a member of the council of trade and on 25 June 1653 one of the commissioners for governing the affairs of Somers Island, and he remained active in this until at least 1656. In 1655 Cromwell invited him to return to Jersey as one of the eleven jurats but he declined, preferring to remain at the mint. At the Restoration, 'he made his peace, but lost his job, under Charles II' (Challis, 326). It is not known whether Guerden was ever married and the date of his death is recorded as 1676 but on uncertain authority.

In 1649 Guerden's name appeared on a remarkable pamphlet entitled *A Most Learned, Conscientious and Devout Exercise*, which purports to be an account of a speech made by Cromwell at Sir Peter Temple's house in Lincoln's Inn Fields, on the eve of his departure for Ireland, to those independents who had broken from him at the time of the regicide. In it, Cromwell pleaded with them to come back to parliament to assist him defeat the Irish rising. Much of the pamphlet is a burlesque but it also contains a penetrating analysis of the political situation in Ireland, and some sensational claims about how the independents had tried to persuade Fairfax on 29 January 1649 to overrule Cromwell and prevent the regicide. Cromwell is alleged to have

> gone to [Fairfax] at Queen-Street, attended with two Troops of my own Regiment, to remove the scruples he made upon that Rascally Priest's [Obadiah Sedgwick's] letter, or to secure him by force in case he had contracted more, and would not be satisfied. But he (good man) gave me thanks for my pains and told me I fully resolved him. (*A most Learned, Conscientious and Devout Exercise*, 12)

This pamphlet may be a distorted and hostile rendering of a very important actual event, and is worthy of serious study. JOHN MORRILL

**Sources** C. E. Challis, ed., *A new history of the royal mint* (1992) • *A most learned, conscientious and devout exercise held forth at Sir Peter Temple's in Lincoln's Inn Fields by Lieut. General Cromwell as it was faithfully taken down in characters by Aaron Guerden* (1649) • Venn, *Alum. Cant.* • J. A. Messervy, 'La famille Guerdain', *Annual Bulletin* [Société Jersiaise], 4 (1897–1901), 65–7 • R. Brenner, *Merchants and revolution: commercial change, political conflict, and London's overseas traders, 1550–1653* (1993) • G. R. Balleine, *A biographical dictionary of Jersey*, [1] [1948] • J. Twigg, *A history of Queens' College, Cambridge, 1448–1986* (1987) • G. E. Aylmer, *The state's servants: the civil service of the English republic, 1649–1660* (1973) • *The Moderate* (May 1649) • *CSP dom.*, 1651; 1653; 1656 • *CSP col.*, 1653 • *JHC*, 6 (1648–51) • W. Prynne, *The lyar confounded, or, A brief refutation of John Lilburne's miserably mis-stated case, mistaken law, seditious calumnies and most malicious lies* (1645) • *Pseudo-Mastix* (1645) [a reply by the gentlemen of Jersey to *The lyar confounded*]

**Guersye, Balthasar**. *See* Guercy, Balthasar (*d.* 1557).

**Guest, Lady Charlotte Elizabeth**. *See* Schreiber, Lady Charlotte Elizabeth (1812–1895).

**Guest, Christopher William Graham**, Baron Guest (**1901–1984**), judge, was born on 7 November 1901 at 5 Church Hill, Edinburgh, the son of Edward Graham Guest (1868–1962), a director of McVitties Guest & Co. Ltd, a well-known firm of bakers and confectioners in Edinburgh, and his wife, Mary Catherine (*d.* 1928), daughter of William Thompson of Walton Grange, Stone, Staffordshire. He was educated at Merchiston Castle School, Edinburgh, Clare College, Cambridge (MA), and Edinburgh University (LLB). He was admitted to the Faculty of Advocates in Scotland in 1925 and immediately commenced practice. He was also called to the bar in England (Inner Temple) in 1929 but his practice was entirely within the Scottish legal system as an advocate. He married on 3 September 1927 Constance Jessie, younger daughter of Finlay Ramage of Edinburgh. This marriage was dissolved in 1940 and on 28 June 1941 he married Catherine Geraldine (*b.* 1915), youngest daughter of John Beaumont Hotham of Milne Graden, Berwickshire, a clerk of the House of Lords. With his first wife Guest had a son. There were three sons and a daughter from his second marriage.

In 1930 Guest published *Guest on Valuation*, a textbook on the law of valuation in Scotland, which was revised by two junior advocates in 1954 to take account of changes in the law. From 1939 to 1945 he served in the army, first as a second lieutenant in the Royal Artillery and from 1942 to 1945 as a major and deputy judge-advocate in the War Office. In the general election of 1945 he stood as a Unionist in Kirkcaldy and was appointed KC in the same year. He had been appointed an advocate depute during the spring of 1945 but demitted office later in the year when the Labour government took office. A tall, commanding figure with a well-modulated voice, Guest quickly developed a large practice at the senior bar, where his services were much in demand. After being grilled by Guest, a witness was once audibly heard to whisper: 'How did I do, under cross examination by that Socratic icicle?' (private information).

Guest served as president for Scotland of the transport tribunal from 1947 to 1955, as sheriff of Ayr and Bute from 1952 to 1954, and of Perth and Angus from 1954 to 1955. He resigned the latter office on his election as dean of the Faculty of Advocates, an election which reflected the high esteem in which he was held by his professional colleagues. In 1957 he was appointed a senator of the college of justice in Scotland, with the judicial title of Lord Guest, and adorned the bench as a dignified and imposing figure. On 20 January 1961 he was created a life peer on appointment as a lord of appeal in ordinary, taking the title Baron Guest, of Graden in the county of Berwick, and sworn of the privy council, an office he held until his retirement in 1971. He had in 1961 become bencher of the Inner Temple.

Between 1945 and his retirement Guest held a number of other appointments. He was a trustee of the National Library of Scotland from 1952 to 1957 and served as chairman of a number of other bodies: these included the building legislative committee from 1954 to 1957, the Scottish Agricultural Wages Board from 1955 to 1961, and the committee of inquiry into the Scottish licensing laws from 1959 to 1963. In 1973 Dundee University conferred the honorary degree of LLD. Guest lived in Edinburgh for most of his life and died there on 25 September 1984 at his home, 22 Lennox Street. His second wife survived him.

LORD JAUNCEY OF TULLICHETTLE

**Sources** personal knowledge (2004) • private information (2004) [Lord Mackay of Clashfern] • Burke, *Peerage* (1967) • records of the Faculty of Advocates • *WWW* • *The Times* (27 Sept 1984) • b. cert. • d. cert.

**Wealth at death** £369,746.25: confirmation, 17 Dec 1984, NA Scot., SC 70/1/3956/236–245

**Guest, (Thomas) Douglas** (*b.* **1779/80**, *d.* in or after **1839**), history and portrait painter, was the son of a man who settled in Salisbury and, according to Joseph Farington, practised both as a portrait painter and a watchmaker (Farington, *Diary*, 8.2947, 10.3726). His father may have been the Thomas Guest recorded in the council minutes of the Royal Academy Schools, 31 March 1777 (Foskett, *Miniatures: Dictionary and Guide*, 553). Guest entered the Royal Academy Schools on 23 December 1801, 'aged twenty-one' (Hutchison, 161) and began exhibiting there in 1803 when he submitted a portrait of his tutor, the sculptor Joseph Wilton RA. In 1805 he was awarded the gold medal for historical painting, for his *Bearing the Dead Body of Patroclus to the Camp, Achilles's Grief* (exh. British Institution, 1807; ex Sothebys, 16 September 1986, lot 249). In the following year he made copies from old master paintings on display at the British Institution, working alongside Benjamin West, president of the Royal Academy, and Henry Howard RA. Joseph Farington makes reference to his conduct at this time, Guest's overbearing behaviour at a British Institution dinner in November 1807 causing Farington to note him as 'a character likely to be troublesome in the profession' (*Diary*, 8.3153). His efforts to win first prize at the British Institution that year were unsuccessful, as was his candidacy for associate at the Royal Academy. Further attempts by Guest at election in 1811 and 1812 proved to be similarly disappointing. In the intervening period between 1808 and 1811 he painted the large picture *The Transfiguration* (1809), which he presented as an altar piece to St Thomas's Church, Salisbury.

His output consisted more and more of historical and mythological subjects with the occasional portrait undertaken, as with those of the pugilists Tom Cribb and Tom Molineux following their famous encounter on 28 September 1811 (ex Sothebys, 27 June 1973, lot 108 as a pair). Guest's reputation as an outspoken and headstrong figure was clearly illustrated by his dispute with the countess of Berkeley in March 1813. The countess had commissioned Guest to paint *A Ship in Distress*, for 100 guineas, the subject being drawn from her return journey from Madeira. Communications between the two parties became hostile over Guest's questionable activities regarding the fate of a related portrait study and oil sketch. The countess appealed to the Royal Academy to intercede on her behalf, which they did.

In 1816 Guest exhibited *The Battle of Waterloo* at the

British Institution, his (unsuccessful) entry for their competition for works to commemorate the end of the Napoleonic wars. His *Inquiry into the Causes of the Decline of Historical Painting* was published in 1829 and comprises a meditation on the dearth of public patronage for historical subjects. A commentary, published by the *Polytechnic Journal* in 1840, on the respective merits of Joseph Wilton RA and Henry Fuseli RA is thought to have been penned by Guest. He last exhibited at the British Institution in 1839; the date of his death remains unknown. He may have been the T. Guest jun. who exhibited miniatures at the Royal Academy in 1801. TINA FISKE

**Sources** T. D. Guest, 'An inquiry into the causes of the decline of historical painting', 1829, BL, D-7858.9.17 • Farington, *Diary* • J. Turner, ed., *The dictionary of art*, 34 vols. (1996) • S. C. Hutchison, 'The Royal Academy Schools, 1768–1830', *Walpole Society*, 38 (1960–62), 123–91, esp. 161 • W. T. Whitley, *Art in England, 1800–1820* (1928) • B. Stewart and M. Cutten, *The dictionary of portrait painters in Britain up to 1920* (1997) • Graves, *RA exhibitors* • Graves, *Brit. Inst.* • Waterhouse, *18c painters* • D. Foskett, *A dictionary of British miniature painters*, 2 vols. (1972) • L. Binyon, *Catalogue of drawings by British artists and artists of foreign origin working in Great Britain*, 4 vols. (1898–1907) • artist's file, archive material, Courtauld Inst., Witt Library • D. Foskett, *Miniatures: dictionary and guide* (1987) • *DNB*
**Archives** NRA, family and professional papers
**Likenesses** A. E. Chalon, group portrait, Indian ink and watercolour (*Students at the British Institution*), BM

**Guest, Edmund** (1514–1577), bishop of Salisbury, was born at Northallerton, Yorkshire, the son of Thomas Geste from Rough Heath in the parish of King's Norton, Worcestershire. Educated at York grammar school and Eton College, in 1536 he was elected a scholar of King's College, Cambridge. A fellow from 1539, he graduated BA in 1541 and proceeded MA in 1544, the same year that he became vice-provost of the college. In 1548 he published *A Treatise Against the Privy Mass*, dedicated to the newly elected provost John Cheke, in which he argued that the Catholic doctrine of the mass was 'directly repugnaunt agaynst gods wrytten truth' (Dugdale, 87). Other works attributed to him by Bale, on the eucharist and on free will, are not otherwise recorded. In 1549 Guest spoke against transubstantiation in the debates held in Cambridge. His public commitment to the protestant cause may have prompted the grant of a licence to preach in 1551, the year in which he proceeded BTh. He continued to take part in university disputations, notably in 1552 in a controversy with Christopher Carlile over Christ's descent into hell.

Guest remained in England during Mary's reign, frequently changing his place of residence, presumably to avoid arrest. He was closely associated at this time with Nicholas Bullingham, later bishop of Lincoln, and may also have been in contact with Matthew Parker, whose domestic chaplain he became in 1559. In the debates on the future of the church in England which began in Westminster Abbey in March 1559 he was the only non-exile to be selected to speak on the reformers' side, and he also took an active part in the revision of the 1552 service book. He is said to have taken the revised book to Sir William Cecil, with a letter of his own explaining the alterations, but doubt has been cast on the ascription of the letter. After these exertions he looked for promotion, in August 1559 seeking unsuccessfully to be appointed dean of Worcester. On 7 November 1559, however, he was presented by the crown to the archdeaconry of Canterbury, a position that he held *in commendam* with another Kentish living after he was consecrated bishop of Rochester on 24 March 1560.

In October 1560 Parker suggested to Cecil that Guest, as a northerner, might be translated to Durham, but the proposal came to nothing. He was, however, appointed lord almoner to the queen in 1560, and was made chancellor of the Order of the Garter about the same time. He is known to have preached before Elizabeth in 1560 on repentance and faith, and as one of the Lent preachers in 1564. He preached at Rochester on the real presence in the eucharist in the early 1560s, and took part in discussions of the drafting of the twenty-ninth of the Thirty-Nine Articles: controversialists both of his own time and of nineteenth-century eucharistic debates cited his opinions in justification of their claims.

As one of the ecclesiastical commissioners who sat regularly in London, Guest was perhaps Parker's most constant supporter in his drive for ritual conformity in the mid-1560s. He was one of the four bishops who helped the archbishop to draw up the Book of Advertisements in early 1565, and appears to have been unsympathetic to attempts by more moderate churchmen to escape the consequences of its provisions. In March that year he and Parker were the only two commissioners who withheld their consent to a petition from an influential group of reformers, headed by Miles Coverdale, Laurence Humphrey, and Thomas Sampson, that they be exempted from using the canonical vestments. In May 1565 Guest and Parker headed a quorum of five commissioners who sanctioned the deprivation of Guest's former household chaplain, Edward Brocklesby, for refusing the surplice.

Guest was one of those who superintended the production of the Bishops' Bible, published in 1568, and was entrusted with oversight of the revised translation of the psalms, corresponding with Parker about it. On 24 December 1571 he was translated to Salisbury in succession to John Jewel, resigning the archdeaconry of Canterbury and his court post of lord almoner. In 1576 he was one of the few bishops who expressed outright hostility to the 'prophesyings', the clerical religious exercises that Edmund Grindal, Parker's successor as archbishop of Canterbury, was determined to defend and Elizabeth determined to suppress. Otherwise the diocesan records of Rochester and Salisbury yield almost nothing about his pastoral activities as bishop. He was, however, apparently active in defending the privileges of his various offices. In 1563 he was in dispute with the sheriffs of London, asserting his right as lord almoner to the goods of suicides, and as bishop of Salisbury he resisted the crown's attempt to extract from the see a lease of the manor of Sherborne.

Guest remained unmarried, perhaps one of the keys to the favour he received from the queen. He died at Salisbury on 28 February 1577, leaving gold rings to William Cecil, now Lord Burghley, to Sir Christopher Hatton, and to Sir Nicholas Bacon. He bequeathed £20 to the city of Salisbury, and all his books to the library of his cathedral, which he described as now decayed. A number of his own writings survive in manuscript, mostly in the library of Corpus Christi College, Cambridge; several of them were printed by Dugdale. They show Guest to have been a man of considerable learning. A sermon preached in 1560 as bishop of Rochester on Mark 1: 15 includes references to the Bible, St Augustine, the fifth-century church history of Socrates Scholasticus, such classical authors as Plato and Seneca, more recent ones like Erasmus and Sir Thomas More, and an edict of Henry V against swearing. As he instructed, Guest was buried in the cathedral choir; his gravestone was later moved to the north-east transept. A memorial brass shows a round-faced man, with short hair, a beard, and a moustache, robed, and carrying books and a staff. JANE FREEMAN

**Sources** H. G. Dugdale, *Life and character of Edmund Geste, the principal compiler of the liturgy of the Church of England* (1840) • J. Strype, *Annals of the Reformation and establishment of religion … during Queen Elizabeth's happy reign*, new edn, 4 vols. (1824) • J. Strype, *The life and acts of Matthew Parker*, new edn, 3 vols. (1821) • J. Strype, *The history of the life and acts of the most reverend father in God Edmund Grindal*, new edn (1821) • J. Strype, *Ecclesiastical memorials*, 3 vols. (1822) • *APC*, 1558–77 • *CSP dom.*, 1547–80; 1601–3, with additions 1547–65; *addenda*, 1566–79 • *Fasti Angl.*, 1541–1857, [Salisbury] • *Fasti Angl.*, 1541–1857, [Canterbury] • [E. Guest], *The Denison case: the letter of Geste, bishop of Rochester, who penned art. XXVIII, to Cecil, secretary to Queen Elizabeth etc.* (Joseph Masters and Co., London, [n.d.]) • W. Goode, *A supplement to his work on the eucharist* (1858) • G. F. Hodges, *Bishop Guest: articles twenty eight and twenty nine* (1894) • G. J. Cuming, *History of the Anglican liturgy* (1969) • B. Usher, 'The deanery of Bocking and the demise of the vestiarian controversy', *Journal of Ecclesiastical History* (July 2001), 434–55

**Archives** CKS, register • Wilts. & Swindon RO, register

**Likenesses** brass and monumental inscription, Salisbury Cathedral

**Wealth at death** bequests totalling £130; plus library: will, cited Dugdale, *Life and character*

**Guest, Edwin** (1800–1880), historian and philologist, descended from a family settled at King's Norton, Worcestershire, was born on 10 September 1800, the only surviving son of Benjamin Guest (*d.* 1843), a prosperous merchant in Birmingham, and his wife, Sarah (*d.* 1807), who belonged to the Scottish family of Rio. His mother died when Guest was a child and his only sister died unmarried in 1837. He was educated locally at King Edward's School and, being left largely to his own devices in the last year there, was able to lay the foundations of a wider knowledge than was to be had from the curriculum. His training with David Cox the painter was useful when he came to illustrate his archaeological papers.

Guest entered Gonville and Caius College, Cambridge, in 1819, won several prizes, was eleventh wrangler and BA in 1824, and was elected fellow in that year. He then travelled abroad and spent a year at Weimar, where he attracted Goethe's notice by the promptness with which he obtained for him Shelley's free translation of scenes from *Faust*. By his own testimony he became an intimate of Goethe's circle, and in later life often spoke of him. Guest had been admitted to Lincoln's Inn in 1822 and, after

**Edwin Guest** (1800–1880), by Sir John Watson-Gordon, 1860

pupillage with John Campbell, was called to the bar in June 1828. He practised for some years and was on the midland circuit, but abandoned the law for literary and historical researches. He was elected FRS in 1839 and honorary FSA in 1852, and proceeded LLD in 1853. Crabb Robinson, who met him in 1848, found he 'talked with great intelligence on German matters … Evidently an able man; he has the outward marks of a superior person' (E. J. Morley, ed., *Henry Crabb Robinson on Books and their Writers*, 2, 1938, 679). In 1852 after a disputed election, on the grounds that he was not a Norfolk man as the founder's statutes required, Guest became master of Caius and was not unseated by a series of protests. His mastership was uneventful, except for a vast scheme of college rebuilding; Longfellow remembered the 'amiable and excellent Master … who had a mania for building' (Brooke, 214). After a term as vice-chancellor he took no prominent part in university affairs, though he was known to be firmly Conservative in politics and evangelical in his churchmanship. On 28 September 1859 he married Anne (1823–1900), daughter of Joseph Ferguson, sometime member of parliament for Carlisle, and widow of Robert Murray Banner, a major in the 93rd highlanders. They had no children.

The only complete book Guest ever published was his *History of English Rhythms* (1838), probably the most important work of the century—for good and ill—on English prosody. He brought to the subject patient investigation, vast reading in medieval literature of which much was still in manuscript or unfamiliar publications, and a fresh interest in phonetics and dialect. But the work was badly flawed. The first volume was printed before the second (in which some of his ideas changed) was written, the arrangement was awkward, and the printing poor. The main principles of his system, in particular the one that the laws of Old English must and should govern later verse, soon came to be seen as untenable. Nevertheless the *History* was a thesaurus to which others resorted for their illustrations, and it was reprinted and tidied up by Walter Skeat in 1882. Even Saintsbury, who finally demolished the substance of Guest's prosodic theories, wrote respectfully of his merits as an acute and learned scholar, and long after his death described the work as 'by far the best book existing on the subject' (Saintsbury, 1.3). Guest helped to found the Philological Society in 1842, acted as its secretary, and contributed more than a score of articles to its *Proceedings*: they are enumerated by Skeat.

Guest also wrote a dozen papers, notable for their erudition, on the early settlement of Britain. Some were originally delivered as lectures before the Archaeological Institute, of which he was a prominent member. Indeed he almost created the academic study of Romano-British history, especially in its topographical aspect. He tramped many miles inspecting boundaries, dykes, and coasts. He made a close study of Julius Caesar's invasion of Britain, surveying both sides of the channel, and in 1863 was applied to for his views on behalf of Napoleon III, who was then engaged on a biography of the great commander. Guest gave Napoleon's librarian, Alfred Maury, a personal interview and expounded his conclusions carefully and at length. 'It won't suit the emperor', was the laconic reply. Guest's articles were almost all collected in the second volume of his *Origines Celticae*, edited by William Stubbs and C. Deedes after the author's death. The *Origines* itself is a fragmentary, lengthy, and largely unread treatise on a deeply perplexing theme. Guest's friend E. A. Freeman, who ranked him with J. M. Kemble and Sir Francis Palgrave as a historian, observed in his obituary that Guest was not known to the educated public as he deserved to be; his method of publishing was no doubt much to blame, as was his reluctance to venture an opinion unsupported by what he considered full evidence.

Guest bought Sandford Park, an estate at Sandford St Martin, Oxfordshire, about 1850, and divided his time between there and Cambridge. He never quite recovered from an attack of paralysis in 1873, and resigned the mastership a month before his death on 23 November 1880 at Sandford, where he was buried on 30 November; his wife survived him. JOHN D. PICKLES

**Sources** E. Guest, *Origines Celticae*, ed. W. Stubbs and C. Deedes, 2 vols. (1883) · J. Venn and others, eds., *Biographical history of Gonville and Caius College*, 3: *Biographies of the successive masters* (1901), 140–46, 173, 292 · E. A. Freeman, *The Spectator* (4 Dec 1880) · *The Athenaeum* (4 Dec 1880), 744–5 · E. Marshall, *Cambridge Independent Press* (4 Dec 1880) [incl. paragraph by Rev. Edward Marshall repr. from *Oxford Journal*, with reference to Guest's sister (1802–37)] · C. N. L. Brooke, *A history of Gonville and Caius College* (1985), 213–15 · G. E. B. Saintsbury, *A history of English prosody* (1923), 1.3; 3.275–92 · E. Guest, *A history of English rhythms*, ed. W. W. Skeat (1882) · parish register, St Martin's, Birmingham, 17 Jan 1803 · *Aris's Birmingham Gazette* (6 July 1807)

**Archives** CUL | JRL, letters to E. A. Freeman

**Likenesses** J. Watson-Gordon, oils, 1860, Gon. & Caius Cam. [*see illus.*] · Elliott & Fry, photograph, CUL · G. J. Stodart, engraving (after pencil sketch), repro. in Guest, *Origines Celticae* · oils, Gon. & Caius Cam.

**Wealth at death** £30,000: resworn probate, Dec 1900, *CGPLA Eng. & Wales* (1881)

**Guest, Frederick Edward** (1875–1937), politician and promoter of aviation, was born in London on 14 June 1875, the third son in the family of five sons and four daughters of Ivor Bertie Guest, first Baron Wimborne (1835–1914), and his wife, Lady Cornelia Henrietta Maria (1847–1927), eldest daughter of John Winston Spencer *Churchill, seventh duke of Marlborough, and sister of Lord Randolph *Churchill. Ivor Churchill *Guest, first Viscount Wimborne, was his elder brother.

Guest was educated at Winchester College before becoming an army officer. In 1894 he obtained a commission in the East Surrey regiment and in 1897 joined the first Life Guards, serving in the White Nile in 1899–1900 and then in the Second South African War, for which he received the queen's medal with five clasps. For the rest of his life it was as Captain Guest that he was invariably known.

On 28 June 1905 Guest married Amy (*d.* 1959), a wealthy heiress, daughter of Henry Phipps, a Pittsburgh ironmaster. It may have been the resulting improvement in his financial circumstances which then encouraged him to embark on a political career. He had recently left the Conservatives for the Liberal Party in support of free trade, along with other members of his family, notably his cousin and near contemporary, Winston Churchill, to whom he remained politically and personally close throughout his life. Between 1907 and 1910 he acted as Churchill's private secretary. In January 1910, after three abortive attempts to enter the Commons, he was returned for East Dorset, where his father had his country residence. However, four months later he was unseated for exceeding the maximum expenditure permitted during an election campaign, following a court hearing which also provided strong circumstantial evidence of the intimidation of tenants and dependants. This set-back did not stop him from regaining the seat at the next election, in December 1910. In 1911 he was appointed a lord of the Treasury and in 1912 a treasurer of the royal household.

On the outbreak of war Guest promptly offered himself for service, and was appointed an extra aide-de-camp to Lord French, before going on to fight in east Africa in 1916–17. He was made DSO in 1917, CBE in 1919, and was also made chevalier of the Légion d'honneur. Politically he made an even bigger mark on wartime public life. As early as 1915 he had come out in support of national service, and he was later associated with the Liberal war committee, a group of 'ginger Liberals' who looked to Lloyd George for a patriotic lead. In March 1917, soon after Lloyd George became prime minister, he was made Coalition Liberal chief whip, with responsibility for organization and fund-raising, as well as for disciplining the parliamentary party.

Guest was initially reluctant to formalize the growing division between the followers of Lloyd George and Asquith, but it nevertheless fell to him in the summer of 1918 to negotiate an electoral pact with Conservative central office. In the December 1918 election this deal led to the issuing of the 'coupon' to 159 favoured pro-Lloyd George Liberals, who were thus sheltered from Conservative attack; but, inevitably, it also led to a damaging schism within the Liberal Party.

From his early days Guest had shared with Churchill a strong belief in the desirability of 'national politics', and after 1918 he saw a priceless opportunity to make coalition government a permanent part of the British political scene. He therefore warmly supported the attempt at a fusion of the Liberal and Conservative parties under Lloyd George's leadership in the spring of 1920. This venture failed, but spectacular success attended Guest's efforts to make Lloyd George financially independent by exploiting to the hilt the government's powers of patronage. By the time the premier went out of office, there was probably some £3 million in the so-called Lloyd George Fund. However, to such reckless lengths did Guest take his honours trafficking—for example, employing honours touts such as Maundy Gregory [*see* Gregory, Arthur John Peter Michael Maundy] as middlemen—that he provoked protests from Conservative central office which feared, with good reason, that the entire honours system was being brought into disrepute. Conservatives also complained about the way in which Freddie was poaching in what had traditionally been their own territory. These resentments contributed to the honours scandal of 1922, which permanently damaged Lloyd George's reputation and weakened his ailing government.

As chief whip Guest regularly bombarded the prime minister with letters of banal political advice, whose contents would have confirmed other Coalition Liberals such as Edwin Montagu in their view of him as a 'half wit'. However, Lloyd George knew that he owed much to Guest's activities as a cunning backroom fixer, and rewarded him with the grant of a privy councillorship in 1920 before promoting him in April 1921 to the office of secretary of state for the air, albeit outside the cabinet. A keen aviator, Guest here played a minor part in the desperate struggle to maintain the air force's institutional independence in the face of hostile attacks from the War Office and the Admiralty. He also took the important initiative of appointing Sir William Sefton Brancker as director of civil aviation.

In the general election which followed the fall of the coalition government in October 1922 Guest suffered defeat at East Dorset at the hands of an independent Conservative backed by Lord Beaverbrook, an old friend with whom he had recently quarrelled. In 1923 he returned to parliament, this time as MP for Stroud, after winning a triangular contest dominated by the issue of free trade, the defence of which was by now the only cause still keeping him within the Liberal fold—for a hostility to any legislative measure savouring of 'socialism' had become his obsession, far outweighing his loyalty to the precariously reunited Liberal Party. Thus during the Labour minority government of 1924, and subsequently, he acted as the informal leader of a group of right-wing Liberals who constantly defied their own front bench by voting with the Conservatives. At constituency level, too, he pursued an independently 'anti-socialist' strategy, being returned in the 1924 general election for Bristol North in a straight fight with Labour after negotiating a pact with the local Conservatives. Such co-operation with the old enemy exasperated not only the Asquithians, who never forgave him for his earlier role as architect of the 1918 coupon arrangement, but eventually proved too much even for Lloyd George, who ran an official candidate against him in the 1929 general election, so handing the seat over to Labour.

In 1930 Guest finally did what he had for so long been threatening, and followed his illustrious cousin into the Conservative Party. A delighted Churchill suggested to Baldwin that this act of apostasy should be rewarded with a peerage. Baldwin thought otherwise. However, in the 1931 general election Guest was elected as the Conservative member for Plymouth Drake, a safe seat which he held until his death.

After 1931, as chairman of the private members' air committee of the House of Commons, Guest joined forces with Churchill in protests against Britain's inadequate air defences. Indeed it was aviation matters which increasingly absorbed his attention. For example, when in 1930 Brancker was killed in the accident to the airship R 101, Guest succeeded him as deputy master of the newly established Guild of Air Pilots and Air Navigators, a position for which he was qualified through his possession of a pilot's licence. On his death in 1937 the guild organized a memorial service in his honour at St George's, Hanover Square.

Guest's political career was highly controversial. From his days as Coalition Liberal whip he was the man who knew where all the bodies were buried, and as a trustee of the Lloyd George Fund he may possibly have had some kind of hold over Lloyd George himself—if Lloyd George's private remarks are to be taken at face value. Orthodox Liberals saw him as a rogue and a 'wrong 'un', who had done a grave disservice both to Liberalism and to the traditional decencies of public life.

All the same, Freddie's geniality and hospitality made him generally popular in the Commons. Unfriendly critics may have called him a playboy and a snob, but most saw him as that well-loved type, the aristocratic sportsman—a role to which Guest conformed by engaging in big-game hunting and by indulging his passion for polo well into middle age. Moreover, everyone could admire the cool courage with which he confronted not only his adversaries in battle and on the polo field, but also the incurable cancer which was to cut short his life. Guest died in his sleep on 28 April 1937, at his country home, Ivy House, French Street, Sunbury-on-Thames, Middlesex. Two days later he was cremated at Golders Green. His wife, with whom he had two sons and a daughter, lived on until 1959. Both sons later moved permanently to the United

States and took up American citizenship, further strengthening the Guest family's already strong transatlantic connections. G. R. SEARLE

**Sources** *DNB* • K. O. Morgan, 'Lloyd George's stage army: the coalition liberals, 1918–22', *Lloyd George: twelve essays*, ed. A. J. P. Taylor (1971), 225–54 • M. E. Montgomery, *Gilded prostitution: status, money and transatlantic marriages, 1870–1914* (1989) • M. Gilbert, *Winston S. Churchill*, 5: *1922–1939* (1976) • J. Turner, *British politics and the Great War: coalition and conflict, 1915–1918* (1992) • G. R. Searle, *Corruption in British politics, 1895–1930* (1987) • D. M. Cregier, 'Lloyd George's lucre: the national liberal fund', *Chiefs without Indians* (1982), 113–47 • H. M. Hyde, *British air policy between the wars, 1918–1939* (1976) • T. Cullen, *Maundy Gregory, purveyor of honours* (1974) • *The Times* (29 April 1937) • Burke, *Peerage* (1967) • *CGPLA Eng. & Wales* (1937)

**Archives** BL OIOC, letters to Lord Reading, MSS Eur. E 238, F 118 • CAC Cam., corresp. with Churchill • HLRO, corresp. with Lord Beaverbrook • HLRO, corresp. with David Lloyd George, etc.

**Likenesses** W. Stoneman, photograph, 1921, NPG • Press Association Ltd, photograph (with Churchill), repro. in Gilbert, *Winston S. Churchill*, vol. 4, following p. 464 • photograph, repro. in *The Times* • photograph, Hult. Arch.; repro. in Cullen, *Maundy Gregory*, facing p. 89

**Wealth at death** £89,998 18*s*. 9*d*.: probate, 23 June 1937, *CGPLA Eng. & Wales*

**Guest, George** (1771–1831), organist, was born on 1 May 1771 at Bury St Edmunds, the son of the organist **Ralph Guest** (1742–1830). His father was born at Broseley in Shropshire, where he trained as a chorister before moving to London at the age of twenty-one and attending Portland Chapel. He finally settled at Bury St Edmunds in 1768, and was organist of St Mary's Church there from 1805 to 1822; he also instructed private pupils on the organ. He published various glees and songs, as well as *The Psalms of David*, to which he later added a supplement entitled *Hymns and Psalms*. He died at Bury St Edmunds in June 1830.

George Guest was chorister of the Chapel Royal, and the 'Master Guest' who was one of the principal treble singers (in *Messiah* and miscellaneous concerts) for the Hereford music festival of 1783 and the Handel commemoration of 1784. He was organist at Eye, Suffolk, in 1787, and at St Peter's, Wisbech, Cambridgeshire, from 1789 to 1831. Among his compositions were four fugues and sixteen voluntaries for the organ, the cantatas *The Afflicted African* and *The Dying Christian*, three quartets for flute and strings, three duets for two cellos, pieces for military bands, hymns, glees, and songs. He died at Wisbech at the age of sixty, after a long and severe illness, on 10 or 11 September 1831. It is probable that John Guest (*fl.* 1795), a music master of Bury, and Jane Mary Guest [*see* Miles, Jane Mary (*c.*1762–1846)], a pianist, composer, and instructor of Princess Charlotte of Wales, were relatives.

L. M. MIDDLETON, *rev.* NILANJANA BANERJI

**Sources** *New Grove* • [J. S. Sainsbury], ed., *A dictionary of musicians*, 2 vols. (1824) • Brown & Stratton, *Brit. mus.* • J. D. Brown, *Biographical dictionary of musicians: with a bibliography of English writings on music* (1886) • D. Lysons and J. Arnott, *Origin and progress of the meeting of the three choirs of Gloucester, Worcester and Hereford* (1865) • *Bury and Norwich Post* (June 1830) • *Bury and Norwich Post* (Sept 1831) • [Clarke], *The Georgian era: memoirs of the most eminent persons*, 4 (1834), 54 • C. F. Pohl, *Mozart und Haydn in London*, 2 vols. (Vienna, 1867), 15, 275 • *The early diary of Frances Burney, 1768–1778*, ed. A. R. Ellis, 1 (1889), 342

**Guest, Ivor Churchill, first Viscount Wimborne** (1873–1939), politician, was born at Wimborne House, Arlington Street, London, on 16 January 1873, the eldest of five sons of Ivor Bertie Guest, first Baron Wimborne (1835–1914), whose wealth derived from the Dowlais ironworks, and his wife, Lady Cornelia Henrietta Maria Spencer Churchill (1847–1927), daughter of John Winston Spencer *Churchill, seventh duke of Marlborough. Frederick Edward *Guest was his younger brother. He was educated at Eton College, and at Trinity College, Cambridge, where he read history and showed an early interest in politics. He unsuccessfully contested Plymouth as a Unionist in January 1898, but was elected unopposed at a by-election in February 1900. At the 1900 general election he held one of the two Plymouth seats along with Henry Duke, later his chief secretary for Ireland. Meanwhile he had served as a captain in the Dorsetshire imperial yeomanry in South Africa, winning the queen's medal. On 10 February 1902 he married the Hon. Alice Katherine Sibell Grosvenor (1880–1948), daughter of Robert Wellesley Grosvenor, the second Baron Ebury; they had a son and a daughter.

As a Unionist backbencher Guest soon became involved in the controversy of free trade versus tariff reform that was dividing the party. He had earlier (February 1903) been among the twenty-five Unionist MPs, led by his cousin Winston Churchill, who had attacked the Unionist government's army reforms. In February 1904 he warned in the House of Commons that the Unionist leader, A. J. Balfour, must decide 'whether the next Administration … was to be a free-trade or protectionist Administration'. He declared himself a free trader, but he demanded that the government have the courage 'to take one side or the other' (*Hansard 4*, 129.1410–1413). After voting for the opposition free trade amendment he realized that it was futile to try to pursue a political career in an amorphous group between the Unionist and Liberal parties. Like his cousin he decided to cross the floor of the Commons, and on 7 April 1904 he announced in *The Times* that he would contest Cardiff district of boroughs as a Liberal, Winston Churchill having interceded with the Liberal whip, Herbert Gladstone, to secure the constituency for him. He was returned for Cardiff in the general election of 1906 with a large majority.

After 1906 Guest's main political interests were army reform, which he now supported, and women's suffrage, which he strongly opposed. Lloyd George, president of the Board of Trade, had in 1906 appointed him chairman of the royal commission on coast erosion and afforestation, which reported in 1909. He did not seek re-election for Cardiff at the January 1910 general election, but accepted Asquith's offer of a peerage to help strengthen the government's representation in the House of Lords. He was created a peer in his father's lifetime, and entered the Lords in March 1910 as Baron Ashby St Ledgers. He was sworn of the privy council in the same week, joining the government as paymaster-general (until 1912). In 1913 he was appointed lord-in-waiting to George V. Owing to his change of party allegiance, he remained an unpopular figure in political and social circles, where the rhyme

> One must suppose that God knew best
> When He created Ivor Guest
> (*Letters to Venetia Stanley*, 162)

was current. Following his father's death in February 1914 he succeeded as second Baron Wimborne.

When war broke out in 1914 Wimborne volunteered his services, and was appointed to the staff of Sir Bryan Mahon at the Curragh Camp, Ireland, recently the scene of the celebrated (or notorious) Curragh mutiny when certain British officers declared that they would resign their commissions rather than accept orders to move against the protestant and Unionist Ulster Volunteer Force. Winston Churchill continued to press his cousin's claims for office until, towards the end of 1914, Asquith asked Wimborne to become lord lieutenant of Ireland on the expiry of Lord Aberdeen's term of office in February 1915. Wimborne accepted and held the post until May 1918.

Wimborne was in many respects an appropriate choice for the lord lieutenancy. Whatever weight might be attached to *The Times* obituarist's comment that his love of sport and horses 'assured him of a warm welcome by a horse-loving race' (15 June 1939), Wimborne certainly set out to get to grips with the Dublin Castle administration, and he quickly established good relations with the Irish home rule leader, John Redmond, who like himself was anxious about the fall in recruiting in Ireland in 1915. In public Wimborne defended the Irish recruiting figures, pointing out that, given the number of men of military service age, and the number engaged in agriculture, and those unfit, 'it would be surprising if, after all these deductions were made the balance of men available exceeded 100,000' (Dungan, 36). But, like all Irish officials at this time, he was governed by the fact that the sole purpose of the castle was to keep the British government satisfied that Ireland was quiet, rather than follow any innovative policies. Moreover, Dublin Castle had watched throughout 1912 to 1914 as law and order were threatened by the presence of political armies, the Ulster Volunteer Force, and the Irish Volunteers. Now there was a perceived danger of renewed sedition and the possibility of German intervention to foment trouble. Wimborne was alert to this, but was frustrated by the refusal of the under-secretary, Sir Matthew Nathan, to let him see any papers or take part in administration. In the event, this was a piece of luck. When the Easter rising broke out in April 1916 Wimborne, together with his chief secretary, Sir Augustine Birrell, duly resigned, but while Birrell's career was over, Wimborne was exonerated by an official inquiry, and reinstated as lord lieutenant on 9 August 1916, to 'assuage the feelings of our Nationalist friends' (O'Halpin, 124).

However, in another sense this was bad luck, for over the next two years Wimborne presided over a deteriorating Irish political situation. He found himself shoring up a collapsing administration, but at least his new chief secretary, H. E. Duke, worked out a procedure whereby the lord lieutenant would have a greater say in affairs, see the appropriate papers, and minute them 'if and when he sees fit', and, if a difference of opinion were to arise on matters of policy, Wimborne's views were to be put separately to the cabinet. He was to have a fair say in the exercise of patronage, and his position with regard to the army and police was to be defined 'with a view to the better utilization and efficient direction of and regulation of the services' (O'Halpin).

Wimborne's influence on Irish policy, though now more clearly indicated, remained slight. His disposition was for conciliation, and he made efforts to revive the home rule negotiations towards the end of 1916, but he was anxious to suppress the rising Sinn Féin movement, and in July 1917 he wanted to take strong measures following the victory of Eamon De Valera, a survivor of the Easter rising, in the East Clare by-election. On the broader political front he revived the idea of a 'delimitation' of Ulster which would give the Unionists a potentially homogeneous bloc (but including co. Tyrone). The Irish nationalist leaders, already anxious about their damaged political fortunes, showed no enthusiasm for the idea.

The crisis that was approaching the Irish administration came to a head in 1918, when the question of applying conscription to Ireland could not be avoided any longer because of the German offensive on the western front in March 1918. Wimborne was far from optimistic about the prospects of enforcing conscription. An Irish convention, initiated in July 1917 to try to get Irish politicians to solve their own problems (or at least stop diverting British attention from the war), was reaching the final stages of its deliberations, and Wimborne feared that if conscription were enforced before it reported there would be an 'explosion'. His appreciation of the position was that, if the nationalists were promised home rule followed by conscription, they would not accept it; if the Unionists were asked to accept conscription followed by home rule, they would be equally hostile; if conscription and home rule were introduced simultaneously, opposition would be general. On the whole Wimborne favoured bringing in the two measures at the same time. Bonar Law, the Unionist leader, agreed with him, but was unwilling to stir up trouble in Unionist Ulster. The government resolved to implement home rule and conscription, while denying that the two were interdependent, which proved disastrous; but by then Wimborne had been replaced as lord lieutenant by Lord French whose military presence, it was assumed, would better enforce the government's policy.

Wimborne, created a viscount in June 1918, was now free to pursue his other abiding interests, sport and art collecting, though in truth he had never wholly neglected these: he had inherited a fine collection of *objets d'art*, particularly French decorative art and furniture, from his father and grandmother. He was a fine polo player and captain of the 'Quidnuncs'; in 1914 he organized and financed a successful cup-winning team, which played in America. However, he maintained a political interest, and was sympathetic to the emerging Labour Party; in 1931 he at first supported the National Government in the economic crisis, and became first president of the National

Liberal Party, an office which he vacated only because of poor health. His sporting prowess declined with increasing years, but in his day he was a good tennis player, golfer, and fencer. He rode to hounds, and remained a well-known figure in the Pytchley hunt. He experienced the joy of seeing the winner of the 1939 Derby, Fancy Free, in his colours.

It is easy to see Wimborne as a *grand seigneur*, even as a kind of amateur in politics; but he was sincere in his attempts to settle Ireland in volatile and trying circumstances that were not of his making. He played little part in day-to-day administration, and his lord lieutenancy was marked by a rapid descent into lawlessness, but this must be seen in the light of the pre-war history of Ireland, which soon reasserted itself after the false dawn of August–September 1914, when Ireland, in the words of Sir Edward Grey, appeared to be the 'one bright spot'. The most formidable political personality would probably have found it hard to manage, let alone settle, Ireland. Wimborne at least meant well.

Wimborne died at his London home, Wimborne House, Arlington Street, on 14 June 1939, and was buried at Ashby St Ledgers, Northamptonshire, on 19 June. His wife survived him. His son, Ivor Guest (1903–1967), National Conservative MP for Brecon and Radnor from 1935 to 1939, succeeded him to the title. D. George Boyce

**Sources** *The Times* (15 June 1939) · E. O'Halpin, *The decline of the union: British government in Ireland, 1892–1920* (1987) · R. B. MacDowell, *The Irish convention* (1970) · T. W. Moody and others, eds., *A new history of Ireland, 6: Ireland under the Union, 1870–1921* (1996) · M. Dungan, *They shall grow not old: Irish soldiers and the Great War* (1997) · *Inside Asquith's cabinet: from the diaries of Charles Hobhouse*, ed. E. David (1977) · J. Turner, *Lloyd George's secretariat* (1980) · R. A. Rempel, *Unionists divided: Arthur Balfour, Joseph Chamberlain, and the unionist free traders* (1972) · S. Gwynn, *John Redmond's last years* (1919) · *H. H. Asquith: letters to Venetia Stanley*, ed. M. Brock and E. Brock (1982) · P. Addison, *Churchill on the home front, 1900–1955* (1992)

**Archives** Bodl. Oxf., corresp. with Herbert Asquith · Bodl. Oxf., letters to Sir Matthew Nathan · HLRO, letters to David Lloyd George · priv. coll., Merrivale MSS · PRO, Cabinet MSS | FILM BFI NFTVA, 'Ireland's new viceroy: amidst enthusiastic manifestations of goodwill, Lord Wimborne makes his state entry into Dublin as lord lieutenant of Ireland', 15 April 1915 · BFI NFTVA, news footage

**Likenesses** W. Stoneman, photograph, 1921, NPG · O. Edis, photograph, 1931, NPG · W. Orpen, portrait; known to be in family possession in 1949 · photograph, repro. in *The Times*

**Wealth at death** £408,398 1s. 7d.: probate, 26 Feb 1940, *CGPLA Eng. & Wales*

**Guest, Sir (Josiah) John, first baronet (1785–1852)**, ironmaster, was born at Dowlais, near Merthyr Tudful, on 2 February 1785, the eldest child of Thomas Guest, manager and part owner of the Dowlais ironworks, and Jemima Revel Phillips of Shifnal in Shropshire. He had one brother and three sisters. His grandfather John Guest had moved from Shropshire to south Wales, where he helped to start a furnace at Merthyr Tudful in the 1760s; he then became manager at Dowlais, which was transformed over successive decades by the Napoleonic Wars and the international development of the railway from a modest venture into the largest ironworks in the world. In turn Guest

**Sir (Josiah) John Guest, first baronet (1785–1852)**, by William Walker, pubd 1852 (after Richard Buckner)

followed his father into management of the Dowlais Iron Company in 1807, having gained a valuable informal apprenticeship in the works after attending Bridgnorth grammar school. By 1830 Wales and Monmouthshire accounted for nearly 45 per cent of Britain's total pig iron production, much of it concentrated at Dowlais and the other three major ironworks clustered (and competing) in the Merthyr area.

From the mid-1830s to the late 1840s the Dowlais works were in their heyday. By 1845 they boasted eighteen blast furnaces (the average number for ironworks was three), each producing over a hundred tons weekly. The site covered 40 acres and the workforce numbered more than seven thousand. A second works, the Ifor works (the Welsh spelling of Guest's eldest son's name), had been erected in 1839 at a cost of £47,000. As the railway network expanded at home and abroad so the Dowlais Iron Company seized opportunities for new contracts both within Britain and further afield, notably in Germany, Russia, and America. In 1844, for example, an order was placed for an unprecedented 50,000 tons of rails for Russia.

Guest was forward thinking, engaging with key figures in scientific and technological development. He was elected a fellow of the Geological Society in 1818 and of the Royal Society in 1830. In 1834 he became an associate of the Institution of Civil Engineers. His business interests included coal mines in the Forest of Dean and he was the first chairman of the Taff Vale Railway Company.

Guest's first wife, Maria Elizabeth (*née* Ranken), whom he married on 11 March 1817, was Irish, the third daughter of William Ranken. She died in January 1818, less than a year after their marriage, aged only twenty-three. There were no children. On 29 July 1833 Guest married into the English aristocracy: Lady Charlotte Elizabeth Bertie (1812–1895) was the eldest child of the late ninth earl of Lindsey; she was twenty-one and remarkably gifted. They had ten children. Surviving her husband, Lady Charlotte Guest [*see* Schreiber, Lady Charlotte Elizabeth] became an important figure in Welsh culture and art.

The Guests lived in Dowlais House in the 1830s and 1840s; in 1846 they also purchased Canford Manor near Wimborne in Dorset for over £350,000. With the help of the architect Sir Charles Barry they turned Canford into their main home (although Dowlais House was retained), and in the 1851 census the ironmaster, in residence at Canford, was described as a landed proprietor. Guest was made a baronet on 14 August 1838 but his eldest son, Sir Ivor Bertie Guest, was elevated to the peerage, becoming the first Baron Wimborne in 1880; his eldest son, Ivor Churchill Guest, became a viscount in 1918.

Guest was also a politician. Between 1826 and 1831 he represented Honiton, Devon, initially supporting the Canningite tories but then becoming increasingly independent and in favour of parliamentary reform. During the reform crisis he lost his seat but he was returned in the new reformed parliament of 1832 as a whig, the first member of parliament for Merthyr Tudful. He retained his seat until his death twenty years later. He won some support from the non-voters as well as from the small electorate, adopting a fairly progressive stance on a number of issues. He had helped to mediate during the Merthyr rising of 1831. He attempted to deflect movements such as Chartism through the exercise of employer paternalism, encouraging rational recreation and incrementalist change through education. The educational system (for both sexes) promoted by the Guests was forward looking and their works schools renowned.

Guest owned the Newton Nottage estate in the south of the county of Glamorgan (where he also had a seaside home, Sully House). The Dowlais Iron Company did not, however, own the land on which the Dowlais works stood. In the 1840s its proprietor, the tory marquess of Bute, prevaricated over the renewal of the lease, endangering the livelihoods of about 12,000 families now dependent on the Dowlais works. Annual profits were consistently high from the mid-1830s until 1848—in 1847 they exceeded £170,000—but fears over whether the lease would be renewed in 1848 resulted in the deliberate running down of operations. By the end of the decade profits had plummeted and for 1849 amounted to less than £16,000. When the dispute was settled in 1848 the Guests were greeted in Dowlais like triumphal feudal lords returning from battle.

Yet further quibbles meant that the new lease was not actually signed until just after Sir John died in 1852. The previous year he had bought the shares held by his nephew Edward Hutchins and finally become the sole owner of the company. Although the iron trade was past its height, the production of steel and mergers with other firms would ultimately ensure the survival of the family business name and fortune in the form of Guest, Keen, and Nettlefold.

In his last years severe kidney problems forced Sir John to rely increasingly on his wife's business skills and on the management structure he had evolved. When he died on 26 November 1852 an estimated 20,000 gathered for the funeral in Dowlais and *The Times* attributed to his foresight much of the wealth and prosperity of mid-nineteenth century Britain. ANGELA V. JOHN

**Sources** E. Jones, *A history of GKN*, 1: *Innovation and enterprise, 1759–1918* (1987) · R. Guest and A. V. John, *Lady Charlotte: a biography of the nineteenth century* (1989) · Glamorgan RO, Cardiff, Dowlais Iron Company MSS · priv. coll., Lady Charlotte Guest, MS journals · C. Evans, *The labyrinth of flames: work and social conflict in early industrial Merthyr Tydfil* (1993) · J. A. Owen, *The history of the Dowlais iron works, 1759–1970* (1977) · *Merthyr Historian*, 1 (1976) · G. A. Williams, *The Merthyr rising* (1978) · L. W. Evans, 'Sir John and Lady Charlotte Guest's educational scheme at Dowlais in the mid-nineteenth century', *National Library of Wales Journal*, 9 (1955–6), 265–86 · *GM*, 2nd ser., 39 (1853), 91–2 · *The Times* (9 Dec 1852) · C. L. Gillham, 'The politics of Sir John Guest, 1825–1852', MA diss., U. Wales, 1972

**Archives** Glamorgan RO, Cardiff, corresp.; notebooks · priv. coll. | LUL, corresp. with J. U. Rastrick

**Likenesses** R. J. Lane, lithograph, pubd 1839 (after J. Thompson), BM, NPG · W. Walker, mezzotint, pubd 1852 (after painting by R. Buckner), Glamorgan RO, Cardiff, BM, NPG [*see illus.*] · J. Edwards, bust, Cyfarthfa Castle Museum, Merthyr Tudful · J. Edwards, marble bust, Cyfarthfa Castle Museum, Merthyr Tudful · G. Hayter, group portrait, oils (*The House of Commons, 1833*), NPG · oils, NMG Wales · portrait, Guest, Keen & Nettlefold plc Head Office · portrait (after engraving by R. J. Lane; after a painting by J. Thompson), NMG Wales

**Wealth at death** £500,000: will, Dowlais Iron Company MSS

**Guest, Joshua** (1660–1747), army officer, was born in humble circumstances, probably in Halifax, Yorkshire; his mother, Mary Guest (1640–1729), was apparently not married at the time of his birth. Joshua Guest began life as an ostler at The Angel inn in Halifax, but he enlisted into Charles Seymour, sixth duke of Somerset's regiment of dragoons during James Scott, duke of Monmouth's rising in 1685. Guest saw service with his regiment under William III in Ireland and in Flanders, and took part in the expedition of James Butler, second duke of Ormond, to Cadiz in 1702 during the War of the Spanish Succession (1702–13).

Having served in the ranks until 1704, Guest was appointed cornet in Captain Henry Hunt's troop of Carpenter's dragoons (later the 3rd Queen's Own hussars) on 24 February that year. He served with the regiment in Spain under Peterborough, and was present at the disastrous battle of Almanza (1707). Joshua Guest is noted as a captain when claiming expenses incurred in bringing to England dispatches from Spain in July 1708. He subsequently became lieutenant-colonel and commanded his regiment, and on 5 June 1713 he was awarded a brevet colonelcy.

Following the 1715 Jacobite rising, Guest led his dragoons in the pursuit of fugitives after the re-occupation of Perth in January 1716. He was stationed in Staffordshire and Warwickshire, an area of known Jacobite sympathies, during the 1719 'little rising'. He reputedly received a letter from George I authorizing him to 'burn, shoot, or destroy without asking questions' (*DNB*). Guest behaved with great restraint, discreetly letting the local gentry know the manner of orders he carried. This course of action was entirely successful and the district remained calm.

Guest was one of the commissioners appointed to inquire into the causes of unrest in Glasgow during 1725. He became brigadier-general on 24 November 1735, and major-general on 2 July 1739. In 1745 Guest was barrack-master for north Britain and he went into half pay retirement, under an arrangement with the next senior officers in the regiment (now Bland's dragoons) who drew reduced pay while he lived. He was appointed lieutenant-general and governor of Edinburgh District at the time of the 1745 Jacobite rising. During the occupation of Edinburgh by the rebels, Guest robustly defended the castle, threatening to bombard the town if a blockade was attempted. Although he was undoubtedly in communication with the Jacobite Lord George Murray, he rejected an offered bribe to surrender the place. There was friction between Guest and the governor of Edinburgh Castle, Lieutenant-General George Preston, who at eighty-six was even older than Guest, but suggestions that Guest would have surrendered the castle after the government defeat at Prestonpans (1745) are unconvincing. Following the battle of Culloden (1746) Guest had the castle guns fired in celebration, to counter rumours that Cumberland had suffered a defeat. He returned to London to receive the grateful thanks of George II, but Preston was virtually ignored.

On 14 October 1747 Joshua Guest died at his lodgings in Brook Street, London; he was buried in Westminster Abbey. His widow, Sarah, erected a monument to his memory in the abbey, and she was buried near him after she died on 17 July 1751. The couple apparently had no children and the property they had accumulated in Yorkshire passed to Guest's nephew Sammy Smith.

Joshua Guest progressed from inn servant to lieutenant-general, moving through the ranks of the army in a manner that would be extraordinary in any age. The veteran general never forgot his labours when a common soldier, and it was reported that Guest would send plates of food to the sentry at his door with the remark 'I remember when I stood sentinel I often had abundant cause to envy those at dinner inside' (*DNB*). JAMES FALKNER

**Sources** *DNB* • C. Dalton, ed., *English army lists and commission registers, 1661–1714*, 6 vols. (1892–1904) • *Colburn's United Service Magazine*, 1 (1868) • W. Wheater, 'Memoir of Lieutenant-General Guest', *Colburn's United Service Magazine*, 3 (1868), 73–9 • H. Bolitho, *The galloping third* (1968) • N. B. Leslie, *The succession of colonels of the British army from 1660 to the present day* (1974) • W. A. Speck, *The Butcher: the duke of Cumberland and the suppression of the 45* (1981) • B. Lenman, *The Jacobite risings in Britain, 1689–1746* (1980) • NAM, Ogilby Trust files, 3rd Hussars box • tombstone, Westminster Abbey, London • F. Maclean, *Bonnie Prince Charlie* (1988), 73

**Archives** Highland Council Archive, corresp. with Kennedy • NL Scot., corresp., mainly with fourth marquess of Tweeddale

**Likenesses** R. Taylor, bust, 1752, Westminster Abbey

**Guest, Ralph** (1742–1830). *See under* Guest, George (1771–1831).

**Guest** [*née* Grosvenor], **Lady Theodora** (1840–1924), author and benefactor, was born at 15 Grosvenor Square, London, on 7 July 1840, the youngest of the thirteen children of Richard *Grosvenor, second marquess of Westminster (1795–1869), and his wife, *née* Lady Elizabeth Mary Leveson-Gower (1797–1891), younger daughter of George Granville Leveson-*Gower, first duke of Sutherland, and his wife, Elizabeth Leveson-*Gower, nineteenth countess of Sutherland in her own right. Lady Theodora spent most of her early life at Motcombe House, near Shaftesbury, in Dorset, where she was educated privately by governesses and tutors. Her parents, especially her father, gave her a strict moral upbringing, endeavouring—with great success—to instil the principle of 'noblesse oblige'. Between 1865 and 1868 she contributed several articles and poems to *Once a Week* and the *Gentleman's Magazine*. Her fondness for her Dorset home and the surrounding countryside led her to write her first book, *Motcombe Past and Present* (1867). Two further editions followed in 1868 and 1873. A devout, low-church Anglican, she demonstrated her biblical knowledge and evangelical zeal in her second book, *Simple Thoughts on Bible Truths* (1873).

When Lady Theodora's father died in 1869 Lady Westminster inherited his Dorset and Wiltshire estates for her lifetime. Lady Theodora then became a constant companion and support to her mother, undertaking many duties on her behalf and assisting in the management of the estates. She gave much personal attention to the village schools and to the night school at Motcombe where she taught. She rode regularly to hounds and was an enthusiastic supporter of hunting throughout her life. It was owing to her that the Hunt Servants Benefit Society was founded in 1872.

In 1874 Lady Westminster purchased Barcote, an estate near Faringdon, Berkshire, and built a large house there for her daughter. But before its completion Lady Theodora became engaged to Thomas Merthyr Guest (1838–1904), second son of Sir Josiah John *Guest and his wife, subsequently Lady Charlotte *Schreiber. They were married in Motcombe church on 8 March 1877. Their only child, Elizabeth Augusta, was born in 1879. In that year Inwood House at Henstridge, Somerset, became their home. The Guests travelled extensively and a tour of North America prompted Lady Theodora to write *A Round Trip in North America* (1895), illustrated by her own sketches.

Lady Theodora was well known in the south-west for her charitable works and her generous support for many good causes. Her biggest single philanthropic act was building and equipping a cottage hospital, in memory of her husband, at Templecombe, near her home, which she ran for several years at her own expense. She was a staunch Conservative, actively campaigning on behalf of the party, particularly at election times, when she spoke from the platform. In 1908 she declined an invitation to join the suffragette organization the Women's Social and Political

Union, and published her reasons for doing so. She then aligned herself with the Anti-Suffrage League.

Like her mother-in-law, Lady Theodora was a collector and connoisseur of porcelain and Battersea enamels. A keen gardener, her gardens and conservatories at Inwood contained many varieties of tropical plants and fruit, for which they were well known.

Even after the rural aristocracy had lost much of their power and influence in the twentieth century, Lady Theodora remained a representative of the old order. She was a great personality, 'a *grande Dame* of the old school' (*The Times*, 26 March 1924), and a link with Victorian society. She died at Inwood on 24 March 1924 and was buried in Henstridge churchyard on 28 March.

LAURENCE CLARK

**Sources** Lady Theodora Guest's journals and letters, priv. coll. • L. Clark, 'The Right Honourable Lady Theodora Guest, grande dame of the old school', *Dorset Year Book* (1995), 9–16 • *Western Gazette* (28 March 1924) • *The Times* (26 March 1924) • G. Huxley, *Lady Elizabeth and the Grosvenors* (1965) • d. cert.

**Archives** priv. coll.

**Likenesses** F. G. Cotman, oils, 1881 (*Where is your master?*), priv. coll. • F. G. Cotman, oils, 1882 (*Dummy whist*), priv. coll.

**Wealth at death** £315,272 16*s*. 11*d*.: probate, 16 July 1924, *CGPLA Eng. & Wales*

**Guevara, Álvaro Ladrón de** (1894–1951), artist and boxer, was born on 13 July 1894 at Cerro Alegre, Valparaiso, Chile, the tenth of the twelve children of Luis Ladrón de Guevara (1840?–1912), a prosperous woollen exporter, and his wife, Ida Juana María Reimers Bode (1857–1943). Luis Guevara, though he knew only a few words of English, was passionately Anglophile and sent his children to the best English schools in Chile. His wife, whom he married when she was just sixteen, came from a wealthy Danish family, her own mother was German, and their daughters all married men of different nationalities; thus the young Álvaro Guevara grew up in cosmopolitan surroundings. His childhood was spent between two homes—the ostentatiously decorated house embellished everywhere with gold leaf, which his father had built overlooking Valparaiso harbour, where he maintained a large staff and a menagerie of animals, and which was destroyed by an earthquake in 1906; and the farmhouse beside a volcano on their *fundo* (country estate) at Curileo in Arauco. Guevara took an energetic part in the family routine of tennis tournaments, riding expeditions, musical entertainments, and parties; he also showed a precocious talent for both painting and boxing.

In 1910, at the suggestion of his elder brother Lucho, who was running the family's business interests in Yorkshire, Guevara and his two youngest sisters were sent to England; their parents followed shortly afterwards and moved into the Majestic Hotel at Harrogate. Guevara entered Bradford Technical College, where he was miserable and homesick: he had no inclination to train for the wool trade and left without any qualifications. However, encouraged by his brother's friends William and Albert Rothenstein, he secretly attended evening classes at the local art school; and in 1912 he applied to, and was awarded a scholarship at, the Slade School of Fine Art in London.

Guevara joined the Slade at one of its most brilliant periods. His fellow pupils included David Bomberg, Mark Gertler, Paul and John Nash, and Stanley and Gilbert Spencer. These, and the female students—among whom were Dora Carrington, Iris Tree, and Lady Diana Manners (later Diana Cooper)—were intrigued by the exuberant but conscientious South American, though they soon took to him and dubbed him Chile, the nickname by which he was afterwards always known. During his four years at the Slade (1912–16) Guevara picked up a handful of prizes. More importantly, he caught the eye of former students such as C. R. W. Nevinson and of three older and eminent figures: Augustus John, whose table at the Café Royal or Tour Eiffel restaurant he often joined; Walter Sickert, who introduced him to the Marylebone swimming-baths, where he painted a series of scenes in the manner of Matisse; and Roger Fry, whose two post-impressionist exhibitions he had seen and who invited him to exhibit at the Omega workshops in 1916. The interiors of theatres and cafés were often the subjects of Guevara's paintings: they were executed in the bright, simplified idiom of the modern movement and brought him quick recognition. He first exhibited at the New English Art Club in 1915 (he was elected a member in 1920), was given a one-man show at the Chenil Galleries in 1917, and was a regular contributor to exhibitions of the National Portrait Society and the International Society.

Guevara also enjoyed a heady social success in the worlds of bohemia and the beau monde, to which the portraits he painted at this time are testament. These were perhaps his most notable achievements: he succeeded in relating his sitters closely to their environment and realizing a precise but rich harmony of colour and design, as well as a telling revelation of character. Among his best-known images are *Mrs Lewis of the Cavendish* (1915, exh. New English Art Club 1922; priv. coll.), a portrait of the hotel owner Rosa Lewis; *Ronald Firbank* (1919, exh. Tate Gallery, London, 1921; untraced); and *Nancy Cunard* (1919, National Gallery of Victoria, Melbourne). Guevara was bewitched by Nancy Cunard and obsessively in love with her for several years. At the same time, Edith Sitwell had fallen for him; he painted a celebrated portrait of her, *The Editor of 'Wheels'* (*c*.1916, Tate collection), and, though her passion was unrequited, they remained close allies. The poetry he was then writing was an important bond between Guevara and both women. The Sitwells were one of several artistic groupings in London whose encouragement and patronage he enjoyed; and Edith's brother Osbert wrote the introduction to his exhibition at the Leicester Galleries in 1926, held after a period of a few years during which he lived in Chile.

In 1927 Guevara moved to Paris, where he was prominent in the society that gathered at the atelier of Gertrude Stein and Alice B. Toklas. He was given an exhibition at the Galerie Van Leer in November 1928 and on its last day there he met the painter Meraud Michael Guinness (1904–1993), daughter of Sir Benjamin and Lady Guinness, whose first show followed his. She had previously tried to elope with the artist Christopher Wood and had then become the pupil and mistress of another, Francis Picabia. Guevara's encounter with her ended his long search for a wife. He and Meraud were married in London in 1929 and their daughter Bridget (known as Nini) was born in Paris in 1931. Less than a year later, however, they parted, and Guevara sank into a long despondency, during which he often preferred to write rather than paint.

As the citizen of a neutral country, Guevara remained in Paris after the German invasion in 1940. But the following year he was taken hostage by the Nazis and incarcerated in the notoriously brutal Cherche-Midi prison. After being diagnosed as paranoid, he was repatriated to Chile. At the war's end he was appointed Chilean honorary consul in London; a year later he was transferred to Bern as cultural attaché. In 1948 Meraud Guinness persuaded him to move to Aix-en-Provence, and he made a studio in the grounds of La Tour de César, the estate where she and her coterie of gypsies and hangers-on had settled, and where he was reunited with his daughter.

Through his last years in Provence, when he was slowly dying, Guevara displayed the dignity which was the essential aspect of his character. He was always immaculately groomed, and dressed in a dark suit and white silk shirt even when painting; his voice was gentle, foreign, and friendly. His exotic good looks—his height, olive skin, and glossy blue-black hair—were immediately attractive, and he had several affairs with people of both sexes. In all his various vocations, including boxing (for which he won the gold belt as champion of all weights in South America in 1924), he maintained an air of supreme cultivation.

Guevara died of cancer of the liver and lungs at La Tour de César on 11 October 1951; the funeral took place on 15 October and his body was later interred locally in St Marc's cemetery. One of his few surviving writings, his *Dictionnaire intuitif*, unfinished at his death, was privately printed in 1954 at Meraud Guinness's instigation. In the early 1970s—just before publication of Diana Holman-Hunt's entertaining biography—a discovery was made of more than forty of his works, including some of his most important post-impressionist paintings, which were thought to have been destroyed in London during the blitz. Their subsequent exhibition confirmed his early distinction and secured his posthumous reputation.

James Beechey

**Sources** D. Holman-Hunt, *Latin among lions: Alvaro Guevara* (1974) · J. Rothenstein, introduction, *Alvaro Guevara, 1894–1951: a Chilean painter in London and Paris* (1974) [exhibition catalogue, P. & D. Colnaghi & Co. Ltd, London, 3 Dec 1974 – 10 Jan 1975] · private information (2004) · *The Times* (3 June 1993)

**Archives** Tate collection, corresp. and papers relating to work | Tate collection, Meraud Guiness MSS

**Likenesses** G. Beresford, photograph, 1920, NPG · A. Guevara, self-portrait, oils, 1921, repro. in Holman-Hunt, *Latin among lions*; priv. coll.

**Guggenheim, Edward Armand** (1901–1970), physical chemist, physicist, and statistician, was born on 11 August 1901 in Manchester, the elder son of the family of three children of Armand Guggenheim, a senior partner in E. Spinner & Co., importers of cotton and exporters of cotton cloth, and his wife, Marguerite Bertha Simon. Originally of Swiss nationality, his father became a naturalized British subject in 1906 and was the Swiss consul in Manchester from 1917 to 1923. Guggenheim was educated at Terra Nova School, Birkdale, Southport, and, from the age of fourteen and with a junior scholarship, at Charterhouse School. In 1917 he gained a senior scholarship and was head of house in his last year, when he won another scholarship, to Gonville and Caius College, Cambridge. There he obtained a first class both in the mathematical tripos, part one (1921), and in chemistry in the natural sciences tripos, part two (1923).

Guggenheim spent the next two years doing research under the supervision of Ralph H. Fowler, who inspired his lifelong interest in statistical mechanics. Despite his excellent academic record, however, he failed to obtain a fellowship at Gonville and Caius; so great was his disappointment that it was only the persuasion of the eminent lawyer, A. D. McNair, which prevented him from giving up science and reading for the bar. Instead, he continued his scientific studies in Denmark, first with Professor J. N. Brønsted and then with Professor N. Bjerrum at the Royal Agricultural College in Copenhagen. (Subsequently he was greatly gratified by his election in 1951 as a foreign member of the Danish Academy of Sciences, and by the invitation to deliver the Bjerrum memorial lecture nine years later.)

Guggenheim returned to England in 1931, accepting the hospitality of Professor F. G. Donnan (himself a renowned thermodynamicist) at University College, London, and wrote his first book, *Modern Thermodynamics by the Methods of W. Gibbs* (1933). Its outstanding display of scholarship, elegant presentation, and maturity of thought established his reputation and revolutionized the teaching of the subject. Nevertheless, his search for a senior university post over the next few years was surprisingly unsuccessful. After a year as visiting professor of chemistry at Stanford University, California (1932–3), he was a temporary lecturer at Reading University (1933–5), an assistant lecturer at University College, London, and, following promotion to a full lecturership, a reader in the chemical engineering department at Imperial College. During this period he produced a series of important scientific papers which gained for him a Cambridge ScD. In 1934 Guggenheim married Simone, the daughter of August Ganzin, of Toulon; this happy marriage ended twenty years later, in 1954, with her death in tragic circumstances. His second marriage, to Ruth Helen (Peggy), *née* Clarke, widow of Major Charles Fleming Aitken, took place in 1955. There were no children of either marriage.

At the outbreak of war in 1939, Guggenheim's services were quickly enlisted by the navy and later by the Montreal Laboratory of Atomic Energy (1944–6). His greatest satisfaction was associated with the neutralization of German magnetic mines which initially wrought such devastation on allied supply ships. One possible mode of defence was to set up an applied magnetic field to simulate the magnetism of ships, thus activating the trigger mechanism and destroying the mine. This idea was in danger of being abandoned on the recommendation of Professor F. A. Lindemann, adviser to the Admiralty, but calculations by Guggenheim clearly showed that the method would be successful, a conclusion which was confirmed by experimental trials on the canoe lake at Portsmouth.

In 1946 Guggenheim returned to his pre-war post at Imperial College and was elected a fellow of the Royal Society. In the same year he was appointed professor of chemistry and head of department at Reading University, a post which he held until his retirement in 1966. Of more than a hundred papers and eleven books, over half appeared during his professorship.

In the post-war years Guggenheim was chairman of the publications committee of the Faraday Society and in 1967 was elected an honorary life member, a distinction limited to ten persons, for his outstanding contributions to physical chemistry and to the society. As a member of the commission on symbols and units of both the International Union of Pure and Applied Physics and the International Union of Pure and Applied Chemistry and of the symbols committee of the Royal Society, his personal contribution was widely praised.

Guggenheim was a man of great culture, being keenly interested in music, literature, and the theatre, and was a master of five languages, besides being an accomplished chess player. One of his greatest pleasures was his beautifully maintained garden of 4 acres in Caversham, containing a swimming pool and tennis court for his relaxation. A severe illness during 1963–4, from which he only partially recovered, greatly restricted his activities until his death in Reading on 9 August 1970. F. C. Tompkins, *rev.*

**Sources** F. C. Tompkins and C. F. Goodeve, *Memoirs FRS*, 17 (1971), 303–26 • *The Times* (11 Aug 1970) • *CGPLA Eng. & Wales* (1970)
**Likenesses** W. Stoneman, photograph, 1946, RS • photograph, repro. in Tompkins and Goodeve, *Memoirs FRS*, facing p. 303
**Wealth at death** £206,406: probate, 1 Dec 1970, *CGPLA Eng. & Wales*

**Guggisberg, Sir (Frederick) Gordon** [*pseud.* Ubique] (**1869–1930**), army officer and colonial governor, was born in Toronto on 20 July 1869, eldest son of Frederick Guggisberg (*d.* 1873), a retail dry-goods merchant, of Galt, Ontario, and his wife, the American Dora Louise Willson. The long-held belief that the family name was adopted by a Jewish ancestor who had fled from Poland to avoid conscription into the Russian army and settled in the Swiss village of Guggisberg has been discounted. The Guggisbergs were an established protestant Bern family, though Lady Guggisberg maintained they came from Stuttgart.

On his father's death in 1873 Guggisberg's mother moved to Toronto and married an English admiral, Ramsey Dennis. Gordon was taken to England and sent to Burney's academy at Gosport (*c.*1879) and then, in 1886, to the Royal Military Academy (RMA), Woolwich. Here he developed his love of cricket. Having been commissioned into the Royal Engineers in 1889, he was posted to Singapore in 1893, where he fell in love with Ethel Emily Hamilton, daughter of his commanding officer, Colonel Way. They eloped and were married in Trichinopoly, south India, on 20 September 1895. They had three daughters. On returning to England in 1896 Guggisberg became instructor in fortification at Woolwich. He published an enthusiastic if somewhat juvenile history of the RMA in 1900, *The Shop*, followed by a semi-fictional study, *Modern Warfare* (1903), under the pseudonym Ubique. He was gazetted captain in 1900 after completing his term at the RMA, and in 1902 he was seconded to the Colonial Office as assistant director of a survey of the Gold Coast. His lifetime commitment to west Africa had started.

Before taking up the substantive appointment of director of surveys in Accra in 1905, Guggisberg, whose first wife had left him in 1902, married, on 15 August 1905, the musical comedy actress Decima *Moore (1871–1964), divorced wife of Cecil Ainslie Walker-Leigh. Together they sailed to the Gold Coast and together they published an account, *We Two in West Africa* (1909). Returning to England in 1908, Guggisberg assumed regimental duties at Chatham, now promoted major. Two years later he was back in west Africa, this time as director of surveys in Southern Nigeria. Here he found full scope for his energy and organizational skill, compiling a *Handbook of the Southern Nigerian Survey and Textbook of Topographical Survey in West Africa* (1911), which earned Colonial Office commendation as a model text. When the plan to amalgamate Southern and Northern Nigeria was approved in 1912, Guggisberg was made acting surveyor-general. His appointment as director of public works in Accra was overtaken by the outbreak of war. He resumed military duties, serving with the Royal Engineers on the Somme and commanding an infantry brigade, and ending up as a deputy inspector-general of training. Guggisberg was promoted brigadier-general, awarded the DSO, and mentioned in dispatches five times. Lady Guggisberg, too, had a good war. She was appointed CBE for her work in Paris organizing a leave club for British officers and, after the armistice, a British empire leave club in Cologne.

In 1919 Guggisberg was made governor of the Gold Coast. Here he established such a reputation that his tenure was extended. Long after the Gold Coast's independence in 1957, he was still remembered for such major achievements as developing the railways and the deep-water harbour at Takoradi; planning the Prince of Wales College at Achimota, opened in 1927, and the premier higher education institution in west Africa before the war; initiating a long-term scheme for the accelerated Africanization of the predominantly European civil service; and completing the magnificent Korle Bu Hospital. Throughout, his governorship was motivated by a positive faith in the capabilities of Africans, an attitude not always discernible among colonial administrators of the period. It was, as *The Times* obituarist was subsequently to note, always Guggisberg's endeavour 'to give the natives a sporting chance to place themselves alongside Europeans in any sphere of life' (22 April 1930).

With no other governorship vacant, Guggisberg spent 1927 on Colonial Office conferences and committees and, at the invitation of Jesse Jones of the Phelps–Stokes Fund, visited the USA. The outcome of this visit (he also included a return to the family home in southern Ontario) was the booklet written with A. G. Fraser, founding principal of Achimota, *The Future of the Negro* (1929). It complemented Guggisberg's pamphlet on an educational philosophy for Africa, *The Keystone* (1924), and was the only publication he cared to list in *Who's Who*. Despite his increasing ill health, which encouraged him to hope for an appointment to the temperate Newfoundland, he accepted the trying climate and lesser governorship of British Guiana in 1928. There he was scandalized by the wretched educational system. He was now fifty-eight and, having come late into the colonial service, was desperate to accumulate ten years' service and so qualify for a pension. Within eight months, his health was broken. After being carried to the Georgetown dockside in an ambulance, he sailed home and retired. The contrast to his success in the Gold Coast was sharp: in his biographer's words, 'his very reputation was perhaps his greatest handicap' (Wraith, *Guggisberg*). Guggisberg died in a boarding house, 27 Cantelupe Road, Bexhill, on 21 April 1930, and was buried in the municipal cemetery, Bexhill, on April 30. In a relatively lengthy obituary carried by *The Times* headed 'An able colonial governor', the writer placed Guggisberg's early survey work in west Africa above both his governorships. A headstone was erected in the cemetery, on the initiative of Paramount Chief Nana Sir Ofori Atta, in 1934.

Tall, athletic, and distinguished, Guggisberg's dignified appearance rendered him a classic colonial governor. Yet that was the one thing he was not. His background and his education, abetted by the assumption within the colonial service of Jewish ancestry, meant that he was—despite his cricket—outside the middle-class, public-school, mould of his service colleagues. Indeed his applications to transfer to the colonial administrative service, in 1912 and again in 1918, had been turned down—until he came in at the top. His shipboard snub by the aristocratic Sir Hugh Clifford, his predecessor in Government House, Accra, became part of colonial service lore. So, too, did other stories, engagingly of how he asked the Colonial Office to include in the next batch of administrative cadets for Accra one slow left-arm bowler, and, less happily, of his fury when his wife, with the stage in her blood, broke protocol by stepping forward ahead of the king's representative to greet Princess Marie Louise on her visit to Accra in 1925.

Besides receiving the DSO, Guggisberg was appointed CMG in 1908 and KCMG in 1922. He was a chevalier of the Légion d'honneur (1917). It is rare to find a colonial governor honoured after independence, but a statue of Guggisberg sculpted by Saka Acquaye was erected outside the Korle Bu Hospital in 1975. A. H. M. KIRK-GREENE

**Sources** R. E. Wraith, *Guggisberg* (1967) • *DNB* • G. G. W., 'Brigadier-General Sir Frederick Gordon Guggisberg', *Royal Engineers Journal*, new ser., 45 (1931), 135–40 • R. E. Wraith, 'Frederick Gordon Guggisberg: myth and mystery', *African Affairs*, 80 (1981), 116–22 • H. Goodall, *Beloved imperialist* (1998) • *The Times* (22 April 1930) • D. Kimble, *A political history of Ghana, 1850–1928* (1965) • F. M. Bourret, *Ghana: the road to independence, 1919–1957* (1960) • D. Moore and F. G. Guggisberg, *We two in west Africa* (1909) • m. cert. • d. cert.

**Archives** Bodl. RH, biographical notes on family; order of memorial service at Holy Trinity Church, Accra, and at Achimota, MS Afr. s. 1957; MS Afr. s. 1563 | Bodl. RH, R. E. Wraith, material collected for biography

**Likenesses** S. Acquaye, statue, Korle Bu Hospital, Ghana • Swaine of New Bond Street, photograph, repro. in Wraith, 'Frederick Gordon Guggisberg', facing p. 114; priv. coll. • photographs, Bodl. RH

**Wealth at death** £2640 5s.: probate, 30 Aug 1930, *CGPLA Eng. & Wales*

**Gui** (*c.*1014–1074/5), bishop of Amiens, was the second of four known sons of Enguerrand (I), count of Ponthieu, a small principality in Picardy, situated round the mouth of the River Somme. Adelvie, widow of Baudouin, count of Boulogne, seems to have been his stepmother. His grandfather, Hugues (I), a knight of Hugues Capet, king of France (*r.* 987–96), had been rewarded with the castellany of Abbeville, the advocacy of the nearby abbey of St Riquier, and his lord's daughter in marriage. He was to keep the Normans at bay; and his descendants remained faithful to the Capetian monarchy. Two of Gui's nephews (Count Enguerrand (II) in 1053 and Waleran in 1054) were killed, and another (Count Gui (I) in 1054) was captured when campaigning against the Normans. On the other hand, another of these brothers, Hugues, 'the noble heir of Ponthieu' (*Carmen de Hastingae proelio*, l. 537), was in the Norman army at Hastings and took a prominent part in the killing of King Harold. But they were not all soldiers. Enguerrand (I) put his second and third sons, Gui and Foulques, to be educated at St Riquier under Abbot Enguerrand, a pupil of the famous scholar Fulbert of Chartres. Gui became a canon of the cathedral church of Amiens, probably under Bishop Foulques (II) (1030–58), a son of Drogo, count of the Vexin, and Godgifu, sister of Edward the Confessor. He was promoted archdeacon, probably of Ponthieu, about 1045, became Foulques's trusted agent, and succeeded him in 1058. On 23 May 1059 Gui, together with his brother Foulques, by then abbot of Forêt-l'Abbaye, and his nephew, Count Gui (I), attended the coronation at Rheims of Henri I's son, the infant Philippe I; and thereafter he seems regularly to have visited the French royal court. He did, however, have some contacts with England. In 1056, when archdeacon, he witnessed a charter of Baudouin of Flanders together with Earl Harold, the future king. He acquired a valuable vestment given by Queen Edith to Abbot Gervin (I) of St Riquier, and Orderic Vitalis seems to have thought that in May 1068 he accompanied the Duchess Matilda to her coronation at Westminster. However that may be, no extant Norman ducal or English royal charter is witnessed by the bishop. Hariulf, monk of St Riquier, whose *Chronicon centulense* provides most of what is known of Ponthieu at this time, regarded Gui as among Abbot Enguerrand's most distinguished pupils and thereafter a benefactor of the house. And, notwithstanding Gui's disputes with the neighbouring abbey of Corbie, he would seem to have been, by the standards of his time, a respectable prelate in the traditional aristocratic mould. A cadet member of a comital family renowned for its martial exploits, he may have been no less addicted to hunting and hawking than his even nobler predecessor. He died on 22 December 1074 or 1075, when he would have been about sixty.

The one literary composition indisputably attributed to Gui is a short epitaph on his master, Abbot Enguerrand, transmitted by Hariulf. But Orderic Vitalis (*d.* 1142) believed that the bishop had written a poem on the battle of Hastings. And when G. H. Pertz in 1826 discovered such a poem, untitled, unattributed, and incomplete, but with a prologue addressed by 'W.' to 'L.', this appeared to be the lost work. The abbreviated text was interpreted as Gui (Wido) addressing Lanfranc (*d.* 1089), abbot of Caen and later archbishop of Canterbury, and no persuasive alternatives have ever been found. The poem of at least 836 lines (the manuscript is defective) is written in elegiac couplets after a preface in hexameters. Its declared purpose is to commemorate William's achievements in the west; and it describes the Conqueror's invasion of England from the arrival of his fleet at St Valéry-sur-Somme until its successful conclusion with the duke's coronation as king, a period of little more than three months. Its attribution to Gui has, however, never been uncontested, largely because its tone and some of its detail differ from the long-established version of events based on the interrelated narratives of the Norman writers William of Jumièges, William of Poitiers, and their twelfth-century successors. In the poem the Normans and their leader are not the only heroes. Eustace of Boulogne, who, though he fought at Hastings, had earlier been hostile to the Normans, is featured prominently; and the death of Harold, which clinches the victory at Hastings, is attributed to the combined efforts of the duke, Eustace, Hugues of Ponthieu, and Gilfard (probably either Walter Giffard of Longueville-sur-Scie or the French baron Robert fitz Gilfard). In contrast, and significantly, neither of the two Williams tells how Harold died. The crux is the relationship between the poem and the relevant narrative in William of Poitiers's much more fulsome eulogy of the Conqueror. One is undoubtedly dependent on the other. If the poet was the borrower, he could not, because of the date of the prose account, have been Gui. But it would seem more likely that William of Poitiers used what he could of the poem and modified or discarded whatever he found objectionable or unsuited to his purpose. Indeed, the poem, a rhetorical exercise slightly anti-Norman in tone and stressing the contributions of the princes of Picardy to the campaign, suits Gui well. If so, the poem, written perhaps in 1067, is the earliest surviving account of the Norman invasion and the one uncanonical version. Therefore, although it may be no more trustworthy than the other accounts, it has to be taken seriously.

FRANK BARLOW

**Sources** *The Carmen de Hastingae proelio of Guy, bishop of Amiens*, ed. and trans. F. Barlow, OMT, [2nd edn] (1999) • Hariulf, *'Chronicon centulense: chronique de l'abbaye de Saint-Riquier*, ed. F. Lot (1894) • Ordericus Vitalis, *Eccl. hist.*, vol. 2 • M. Prou, ed., *Recueil des actes de Philippe Ier, roi de France* (1909) • F. Barlow, 'The *Carmen de Hastingae proelio*', *Studies in international history: essays presented to W. Norton Medlicott*, ed. K. Bourne and D. C. Watt (1967), 35–67; repr. in *The Norman conquest and beyond* (1983), 189–222 • R. H. C. Davis, 'The *Carmen de Hastingae proelio*', *EngHR*, 93 (1978), 241–61 • E. M. C. van Houts, 'Latin poetry and the Anglo-Norman court, 1066–1135: the *Carmen de Hastingae proelio*', *Journal of Medieval History*, 15 (1989), 39–62

**Guidott, Thomas** (1638?–1706), physician and writer, was probably born at Lymington, Hampshire, in September 1638, and was the eldest son of Francis Guidott, a descendant of Antonio Guidotti, a Florentine. He apparently went to school at Dorchester and entered Wadham College, Oxford, in 1656, paying his caution money as a commoner on 19 December 1656. He was awarded a BA on 16 January 1660 and an MA on 16 October 1662. He gained an MB on 14 July 1666 and apparently performed his exercise for MD in Oxford in 1671, but never took the degree.

In 1667 Guidott settled in Bath, where he received support from long-established physicians in the city, notably John Maplet and Samuel Bave, and built up a practice. He clearly sought to establish a national reputation for himself and for his adopted city, for in 1669 he published the third edition of Edward Jorden's 1632 *A Discourse of Natural Bathes* to which he attached his own *Appendix Concerning Bathe*. Guidott followed this between 1673 and 1676 with several publications about the properties of the Bath waters, about the antiquity of Bath as a place of therapy, and about the lives of physicians who had practised there during the seventeenth century.

When writing the biographies of his fellow physicians Guidott particularly commended learning and scholarship (especially in Latin and Greek) as well as their personal qualities. He took care to note, and often to print, any verses which they might have written in Latin or in English and to record any verses which were composed on their deaths or which were placed on their memorials in Bath Abbey (Guidott, 152 (182*r*) ff., 195). This interest reflected his own literary pretensions and he included satirical verses that he had written on the death of Mr Somerschall, a chemical doctor in Bath who apparently died in poverty. Such verses, which led Thomas Hearne to describe him as 'vain, conceited [and] whimsical' (*Remarks*, 1.123) and Wood to write of his 'impudence, lampooning, and libelling' (Wood, *Ath. Oxon.*, 4.734), apparently damaged his reputation in the city and he left for London in 1679, subsequently dividing his medical practice and residence between London and Bath. He did not, however, abandon his versifying, for in 1684 he published a verse satire entitled *Gideon's Fleece* replying to Gideon Harvey's attack on the Royal College of Physicians, and ten years later seems to have published satirical verses on the deaths of Dr Charles Conquest and of William Gould (*An Epitaph on Don Quicksot; by a Quaker* and *Don Quicksilver*).

As his defence of the traditionalists in the College of Physicians against Gideon Harvey suggests, Guidott aligned himself with learned physic and was hostile to any who attacked the authority of physicians. This is not to suggest that he opposed the new philosophy. Anthony Wood (who knew, corresponded with, and received gifts of books from him) recorded that he was well acquainted with anatomy from his years in Oxford, and was invited in

1664 to go and study further with the Danish anatomist Thomas Bartholin. He further noted that Guidott's reputation was sufficient for him to be offered positions as professor at Venice and Leiden, but that he declined the offers. Guidott's own publications on Bath waters reveal that he was also up to date in the use of chemical analysis, contradicting the opinion of his Oxford friend John Mayow that the Bath waters contained no nitre, and carefully recording the weight of the water from different springs in different atmospheric conditions. When his *De thermis Britannicis*, an account of the mineral water baths of Britain, was published in 1691 after more than five years of negotiations with printers, the subscribers included many of the most eminent physicians in the land.

Guidott's contemporary reputation was based as much on his antiquarian erudition as on his therapeutic efficacy. He edited and published a manuscript of Theophilus's work on urines, *Theofilou peri ouron biblion: Theophili de urinis* (1703), although Hearne complained that he did not present a copy to the Bodleian Library as he should have done, and composed a manuscript history of Aesculapius (BL, Sloane MS 2038). He collected and printed inscriptions in Bath Abbey and sent his notes on the antiquities of Bath to Edmund Gibson for inclusion in his revision of Camden's *Britannica* (Bodl. Oxf., MS Eng. b 2043, fols. 272, 280; E. Gibson, *Camden's Britannica, Newly Translated into English*, 1695, 79–82). Guidott also corresponded with antiquarians such as Gibson, Peter Le Neve, and Anthony Wood, while William Petyt took transcriptions from medieval manuscripts in his possession (Bodl. Oxf., MS Rawl. D 867, fols. 65, 67; Bodl. Oxf., MS Tanner 24, fol. 147; *Life and Times of Anthony Wood*, 2.503, 4.229; J. Conway Davies, ed., *Catalogue of Manuscripts in the Library of the … Inner Temple*, 1972, 290, 346).

Guidott's final publication, a critique of Sir John Floyer's advocacy of cold bathing and a characteristic defence of the utility of hot baths like those of Bath, appeared in 1705, but he died the following spring and was buried in Bath Abbey on 18 March 1706. He does not seem to have married or left direct descendants, for in 1716 'a great Collection of Antiquities belonging to Bath' which he had accumulated over the course of his life were noted as being in the possession of a cousin in Hampshire (Bodl. Oxf., MS Ballard 24, fol. 133). However, their present location is unknown. Wood's *Athenae Oxonienses* (1828), 4.735 lists at least some of his manuscripts.

MARK S. R. JENNER

**Sources** Wood, *Ath. Oxon.*, new edn, 4.734–5 · J. W. Clay, ed., *The registers of St Paul's Cathedral*, Harleian Society, register section, 26 (1899) · *The life and times of Anthony Wood*, ed. A. Clark, 5 vols., OHS, 19, 21, 26, 30, 40 (1891–1900) · *Remarks and collections of Thomas Hearne*, ed. C. E. Doble and others, 11 vols., OHS, 2, 7, 13, 34, 42–3, 48, 50, 65, 67, 72 (1885–1921) · T. Guidott, *A century of observations* (1676) · R. B. Gardiner, ed., *The registers of Wadham College, Oxford*, 2 vols. (1889–95) · Bodl. Oxf., MS Tanner 24, fol. 147 · Bodl. Oxf., MS Ballard 24, fol. 133 · Bodl. Oxf., MS Wood F 42, fols. 116–18, 122–122r · BL, Sloane MS 2038 · BL, Add. MS 37474, fol. 169 · Bodl. Oxf., MS Rawl. D. 867, fols. 65, 67 · Bodl. Oxf., MS Eng. b 2043 · *DNB*
**Archives** BL, Sloane MS 2038

**Guidotti, Sir Antonio** (1492–1555), merchant and diplomat, was born on 27 May 1492 in Florence, the son of Andrea di Zanobi Guidotti (1457–1520) and Lucretia d'Antonio Gondi. The evidence suggests he received legal training in Italy before he arrived in Southampton in the 1510s to join his brother Pier Francesco; a third brother, Giovanbattista, appears in later records. Antonio received letters of denizenship on 8 February 1533. The brothers Guidotti established a flourishing merchant business, specializing in importing wine and luxury goods and exporting English wool. It was Antonio, however, who most successfully established himself among the civic leaders through his marriage *c*.1520 to Dorothy Huttoft (*d*. in or after 1557), daughter of Henry Huttoft, twice mayor of Southampton and a friend of Thomas Cromwell. Huttoft included Guidotti in many business dealings, and together they were among the most eminent wine importers in England. Through Huttoft, Guidotti was introduced to members of the English court, including Arthur Plantagenet, Viscount Lisle, and John Dudley, earl of Warwick and later duke of Northumberland.

In the mid-1530s Guidotti began to suffer massive business failures, which also resulted in severe financial difficulties for many of his Southampton associates, including his father-in-law, Huttoft. In June 1535 he owed £1341. 0s. 6d. to the English crown alone, and, unable to pay his debts, he left his family and obligations and fled to the continent. He had certainly over extended his credit, and may well have been unduly ambitious in his undertakings. It was probably characteristic of him that in March 1537 he should have written to Cromwell with a plan for restoring the flagging Southampton economy by transplanting silk weavers from Messina to the Hampshire port town. The death in 1540 of Henry Huttoft, who had stood surety for his son-in-law's debts, brought Guidotti back to England. He spent more than a year in a debtors' prison and was released in March 1542.

Recognizing that his merchant career was in ruins, Guidotti reinvented himself as a professional diplomat, capitalizing on his contacts at the English court as well as his family and mercantile contacts abroad (his maternal uncle Antonio Gondi was an influential figure in France). Although there had been mediators between France and England before Guidotti, it was he who successfully brought the two countries together in 1549–50 to treat for peace and arrange for the restoration to the French of the English-held town of Boulogne. Upon his return to England, Edward VI rewarded him for his efforts with a gold chain worth £48, a knighthood, and a pension for his son Giovanni, who had been a junior member of the delegation. Guidotti was also a member of the embassy to France of 1551 headed by William Parr, marquess of Northampton, to present Henri II with the Order of the Garter and also to press for a marriage between Edward VI and Mary Stewart, who was then living in France. If the proposed union was rebuffed, the English delegation had ancillary orders to pursue a match between Edward and Henri II's daughter, Elisabeth, and a preliminary marriage treaty to this effect was signed in July 1551.

Guidotti's actions during the Boulogne negotiations suggested to many that he had loyalties to the French as well as the English; the Welsh chronicler Elis Gruffydd denounced him as a 'false snake' and one who was 'pulling two faces under the same hood' (Davies, 76). How far he was acting in the interests of France can only be surmised, but Guidotti was sending information about the Boulogne talks not only to England but also to his native Florence and its ruler, Duke Cosimo (I) de' Medici. During these negotiations, he worked to unite England and Florence through a marriage between the young Princess Elizabeth and Francesco, the eldest son and heir of Cosimo. Guidotti's own enthusiasm for the match, however, was no match for the tepid interest displayed by the English, who questioned the prudence of allying with a state closely associated with the Spanish Habsburgs while simultaneously negotiating a complex peace with the French Valois. Discussion of the Tudor–Medici union ceased at the conclusion of the Boulogne affair.

Having accomplished much in England and France, Guidotti asked his Florentine ruler for leave to return home, and was granted a formal entry into Florence in mid-1553. In that same year he became a Florentine senator, the first and only member of his house to do so. He held numerous civic offices and died as commissioner of the Tuscan hill town of Volterra on 27 November 1555. His three sons, Giovanni, Pier Francesco, and Andrea, petitioned for their father's removal from the cathedral crypt there and reburial in the main Florentine cathedral, Santa Maria del Fiore. In 1560 Duke Cosimo ordered Guidotti's remains to be reinterred instead in the church of San Marco in Florence, where a memorial plaque, said to be the work of the son of the political theorist Niccolò Machiavelli, commemorates him. Guidotti's widow married John Harman, a gentleman usher in Anne of Cleves's household, in December 1557. L. E. Hunt

**Sources** L. E. Hunt, 'Tudor politics, Tuscan ambition: a Florentine diplomat and intelligencer in sixteenth-century Europe', PhD diss., University of Toronto, 2000 • A. A. Ruddock, 'Antonio Guidotti', *Hampshire Field Club and Archaeological Society Papers and Proceedings*, 15 (1941–3), 34–42 • C. Platt, *Medieval Southampton: the port and trading community, AD 1000–1600* (1973) • D. L. Potter, 'The treaty of Boulogne and European diplomacy, 1549–50', *BIHR*, 55 (1982), 50–65 • A. A. Ruddock, *Italian merchants and shipping in Southampton, 1270–1600*, Southampton RS (1951) • *N&Q*, 2nd ser., 4 (1857), 392, 438 • 'Genealogia dell'antica e nobile famiglia dei signori conti Rustichelli, già fiorentina ora veneziana', *Delizie degli Eruditi Toscani*, ed. P. I. de S. Luigi, 14 (1770–89) • G. Schanz, *Englische Handelspolitik gegen Ende des Mittelalters mit besonderer Berücksichtigung des Zeitalters der beiden ersten Tudors, Heinrich VII und Heinrich VIII*, 2 vols. (Leipzig, 1881) • M. Bryn Davies, 'Boulogne and Calais from 1545–1550', *Bulletin of the Faculty of Arts of Fouad I University, Cairo*, 12/1 (1950), 1–90 • *Literary remains of King Edward the Sixth*, ed. J. G. Nichols, 2 vols., Roxburghe Club, 75 (1857); repr. [1963] • *LP Henry VIII*, 6.196; 8.878

**Archives** Archivio del Stato, Florence, medicieo del principato • PRO, state papers • Southampton City RO, Southampton Corporation Records

**Guild, Jean** (*bap.* 1573, *d.* 1667), philanthropist, was baptized Janet in Aberdeen on 27 December 1573, one of three surviving daughters of Matthew Guild, a wealthy and influential armourer in Old Aberdeen, and his wife, Marjorie Donaldson; her brother was William *Guild (1586–1657). She married David Anderson (*d.* 1629), a wealthy merchant of New Aberdeen, who because of his mechanical and engineering skills went by the contemporary nickname of Davie Do A'thing. His commercial success allowed him to buy the estate of Finzeauch (or Finshaugh), in the parish of Keig, presbytery of Alford, Aberdeenshire. He died on 9 October 1629, leaving his wife, five daughters, and a son, David. David studied mathematics at Paris, where his father's cousin Alexander Anderson was a professor; his sister Janet, who in 1621 had married the Revd John Gregory, was the mother of James *Gregory (1638–1675).

In 1649 Jean Guild, with others in her family who had inherited from her late husband, gifted land in Aberdeen and 4700 Scots merks for the maintenance and education of ten poor orphans in the burgh. As was conventional the friends and relatives of the benefactors were to have first call on the orphans' places. The most interesting aspect of the benefaction is the distinction it makes between male and female orphans; while boys were to be supported until the age of eighteen girls were to have the benefit only until they reached fifteen, or until such time as they were able to support themselves through some lawful calling. As well as being influenced by the wishes of her late husband Jean Guild may also have been motivated by the writings and preaching of her brother, who was a great advocate of philanthropy, and by the virtues of a fitting education. She died on 9 January 1667, 'a good sober woman' ('Diary of John Row', 100), and was buried probably near her husband in St Nicholas's kirkyard, Aberdeen. Shona MacLean Vance

**Sources** Aberdeen City Library, MS OPR 168 A/1 • J. Shirrefs, *An inquiry into the life, writings and character of the Reverend Doctor William Guild … with some strictures upon Spalding's account of him* (1799) • J. A. Henderson, *Aberdeenshire epitaphs and inscriptions: with historical, biographical, genealogical and antiquarian notes* (1907) • P. D. Lawrence, 'The Gregory family: a biographical and bibliographical study', PhD diss., U. Aberdeen, 1971 • Aberdeen City Archive, council register, vol. 53/1 • *Mortifications under the charge of the provost, magistrates, and town council of Aberdeen* (1849) • mortification accounts, Aberdeen City Archive, vol. 1 • 'Diary of John Row, principal of King's College, etc.', *Scottish Notes and Queries*, 7 (1893–4), 38–40, 52–4, 70–71, 84–5, 98–100, 122–3, 152–3, 164–5

**Wealth at death** comfortable; large benefaction to orphans in Aberdeen

**Guild, William** (1586–1657), Church of Scotland minister and benefactor, was born in Aberdeen, the son of Matthew Guild, an armourer and member of the Corporation of Hammermen; he had three sisters, Jean *Guild, Christian, and Margaret. An early student at Marischal College, Aberdeen, William entered between 1598 and 1605 and developed a keen interest in theology there. His first charge, in 1608, was at Kinneddar, or King-Edward, in the presbytery of Turriff in the synod of Aberdeen. In the same year he published his first works, *The New Sacrifice of Christian Incense* and *The Only Way to Salvation*, exhibiting what was to be a characteristic rejection of free will and of transubstantiation, and a largely Calvinist flavour. He married

Katharine Rowen in 1610, a marriage which lasted for the rest of his life, though it produced no children. In 1617 Guild was one of the ministers who signed the protestation to James VI against royal control and innovations in the church, and in 1618 he published *Moses Unveiled*. In 1623 he donated a house, Trinity Friars, to the burgh of Aberdeen, and endowed it as a hospital.

After over two productive decades at Kinneddar, Guild was translated to the second charge of St Nicholas, Aberdeen, in 1631, and in the same year was appointed the king's chaplain. In 1633 he funded the glazing of Greyfriars church, Aberdeen, with contributions from Alexander Stewart, a merchant. That same year he gave the Trade Hall to the corporations of Aberdeen as a hospital for indigent artisans. About 1634 he received the degree of doctor of divinity, though at that time the non-academic use of that degree was disputed in Scotland. In 1635 he was one of the several Aberdonian divines to speak at the funeral of their late bishop, Patrick Forbes of Corse.

Guild's attachment to Charles I may have been what led him to be numbered among the 'Aberdeen Doctors' (with John Forbes of Corse, Alexander Scrogie, William Leslie, Robert Baron, James Sibbald, and Alexander Ross) in their opposition to the covenant in 1638, but after the first round of the 'paper debate' between the ministers and academics of Aberdeen and the covenant's representatives there Guild was won over to the side of the covenant. He signed that same year, with three reservations: he refused to condemn episcopacy; he promised to disregard, rather than condemn, the Perth articles; and he swore loyalty to Charles I. Although the rival commission of James Sibbald and Robert Baron was stronger, Guild was one of the accepted commissioners to the general assembly of 1638, but when he returned home he did not implement the acts excommunicating the bishops, possibly fearing the reputed sympathy for episcopacy in Aberdeen. At about this time he published *A Friendly and Faithful Advice to the Nobility, Gentry and Others*, an appeal for moderation and peace between the factions of the day, partly so that protestants could show a common front against Catholics and avoid accusations of schism. Although his anti-Catholicism was clearly demonstrated in works such as *Papists Glorying in Antiquity, Turned to their Shame* (1626) and *An Antidote Against Popery* (Aberdeen, 1639), he was seen by others as theologically and politically malleable. When asked to subscribe the covenant unconditionally he is said to have fled for the Low Countries, but as he was the rector of King's College, Aberdeen, from 1639 through to 1644, it is unlikely that he was away from Aberdeen for very long. His appointment to this post by the covenanters can be seen as a moderate move, particularly considering Guild's reservations when signing the covenant.

In 1640 Guild replaced William Leslie, who had been deposed for failing to subscribe the covenant, as principal of King's College, Aberdeen. In 1641 Charles I granted Guild the house and garden formerly belonging to the bishop of Aberdeen, which Guild gave to the poor of the burgh. It was in that same year that Guild preached his last sermon in New Aberdeen, with John Row taking up the second charge of St Nicholas, and Guild focusing on his newly acquired academic role. After General Monck's 1651 visitation of King's College, Aberdeen, Guild was deposed and replaced, again by John Row. The synod of Aberdeen declared this move illegal, but they protested to no avail. Guild applied for Row's previous position as minister of the second charge of St Nicholas, Aberdeen, but was unsuccessful.

Guild continued to write in his retirement. Six of his twenty-two works were published after he was deposed, with two of those published posthumously. He died in Aberdeen in 1657 at the age of seventy-one. His will provided 7000 merks Scots (£4667 13*s*. 4*d*. Scots or approximately £389 sterling) to the town council and kirk session of Aberdeen for the care of orphans. His biographers make no mention of provision in the will for members of his family. R. P. WELLS

**Sources** J. Shirrefs, *An inquiry into the life, writings and character of the Reverend Doctor William Guild … with some strictures upon Spalding's account of him* (1799) • *Fasti Scot.*, new edn, 6. 2, 265 • J. Gordon, *History of Scots affairs from 1637–1641*, ed. J. Robertson and G. Grub, 3 vols., Spalding Club, 1, 3, 5 (1841) • J. Row, *The history of the Kirk of Scotland, from the year 1558 to August 1637*, ed. D. Laing, Wodrow Society, 4 (1842), 491, 495–6, 506 • J. Stuart, ed., *Selections from the records of the kirk session, presbytery, and synod of Aberdeen*, Spalding Club, 15 (1846), 112–13, 218, 221, 232, 259 • J. Stuart, ed., *Extracts from the council register of the burgh of Aberdeen, 1625–1747*, 2, Scottish Burgh RS, 9 (1872), 22, 52, 66, 114, 242–3 • Chambers, *Scots.*, rev. T. Thomson (1875), 1. 182–3 • Anderson, *Scot. nat.*, 384 • P. J. Anderson, ed., *Officers and graduates of University and King's College, Aberdeen, MVD–MDCCCLX*, New Spalding Club, 11 (1893), 9–11, 20, 117, 315 • *Fasti academiae Mariscallanae Aberdonensis: selections from the records of the Marischal College and University, MDXCIII–MDCCCLX*, 2, ed. P. J. Anderson, New Spalding Club, 18 (1898), 11, 187, 201 • J. Spalding, *Memorialls of the trubles in Scotland and in England, AD 1624 – AD 1645*, ed. J. Stuart, 2 vols., Spalding Club, [21, 23] (1850–51) • *The historical works of Sir James Balfour*, ed. J. Haig, 3 (1824), 77

**Wealth at death** 7000 merks Scots [£389 sterling]: Shirrefs, *Inquiry into … William Guild*; Chambers, *Scots.*

**Guildford, Sir Edward** (*c*.1479–1534), administrator, was the eldest son of Sir Richard *Guildford (*c*.1450–1506) and his first wife, Anne, daughter of John Pympe of Kent. His career was intertwined with that of his half-brother Sir Henry *Guildford, born of Sir Richard's second marriage, to Joan, daughter of Sir William Vaux of Harrowden; both were intimate friends of Henry VIII and active in royal service.

From 1493 to 1506 Edward Guildford and his father were joint masters of the royal armoury. Upon his father's death in 1506 Edward succeeded to his properties at Halden and Hemsted, Kent, and became sole master of the armoury, a position he was to hold for the rest of his life. He was a JP for Kent (1503–34) and in 1503 was named bailiff of Winchelsea, where he subsequently oversaw the construction of a new bridge and tower. As a squire of the body Guildford received an allowance of cloth for livery at the funeral of Henry VII, and with his brother joined Henry VIII in feasting and celebrating the new king's coronation and marriage. In November 1509 he was granted a pardon and release of debts owed to the crown as administrator of his father's estate. When Edmund Dudley was attainted and executed in 1510, Guildford was given four of his manors in Lincolnshire and named guardian of his son John Dudley, the future duke of Northumberland. It was in response to Guildford's petition that John Dudley was restored in blood by the parliament of 1512. By 1526 Guildford had married his daughter, Jane, to his ward, who had earlier accompanied him on campaign in France.

As master of the armoury Guildford was deeply involved in the preparations for Henry VIII's French campaign of 1513. He purchased nearly 13,000 harnesses for footmen from Italian merchants, including members of the Frescobaldi, Cavalcanti, and Portinari families, as well as a few 'hoisting harnesses' for horsemen and an engraved and gilt harness for the king himself. In addition he helped arrange for the jousts and tournaments held in October at Tournai, where he was knighted on 25 September.

In the following years Guildford continued to handle royal business in France. In 1514 he was in Guisnes. In 1515 he undertook a mission to Margaret of Savoy. He was sent to France again in 1516 and in May 1519 was appointed marshal of Calais. This may have been the result of manoeuvrings at the English court; as master of the armoury Guildford was a prominent figure, organizing jousts and taking the role of marshal, as, for instance, at the joust arranged for the foreign ambassadors on 7 July 1517. When, under pressure from Wolsey, Henry's young 'minions' were temporarily forbidden the court in spring 1519, Guildford (although hardly young) was believed at the French court to have been among the courtiers thus relegated. He was still at Calais in 1520, where he arranged the elaborate lodgings for the meeting between Henry VIII and François I at the Field of Cloth of Gold in June. His accounts reflect the cost of purchasing swords and horses for ceremonial jousts, including horses from Spain and Italy. He also helped prepare for Emperor Charles V's visit to Calais a month later. In 1521 he became constable of Dover Castle and lord warden of the Cinque Ports, in accordance with a reversion he had been granted ten years earlier. In 1522 he took part in raids into northern France, while late in 1523 he played a significant role in the campaign led by Charles Brandon, duke of Suffolk, who was also an old friend—Guildford had attended Brandon's first, secret, marriage, and was a godfather to his daughter. On 14 November he captured the castle of Bohen or Boghan, which was thought to be impregnable.

Guildford resigned his office at Calais in 1524 and subsequently remained in England, managing his lands in Kent and acting as keeper of North Frith Park, an office he was given upon the attainder of the third duke of Buckingham in 1521. He was involved in presenting charges of treason and illegal retaining against Buckingham's son-in-law George Neville, third Baron Bergavenny; Bergavenny was found guilty but pardoned in March 1522. Old rivalries probably lay behind Guildford's involvement in proceedings against Bergavenny, he and his father having been at odds with George Neville since Henry VII's reign. He may have been a member of the parliament of 1523, returns for which do not survive, for an undated letter which twentieth-century scholarship assigns to that year asks a neighbour to set aside the revenue from his timber sales 'against the day of choosing knights of the shire' (*LP Henry VIII*, addenda, vol. 1, pt 1, no. 375). As lord warden of the Cinque Ports his membership might well be expected. It may be, however, that this attempt to influence the election dates from 1529, when both Sir Edward and his brother Sir Henry sat for Kent in the Reformation Parliament.

Guildford did not live to see the end of that parliament, for he died at Leeds Castle, of which he was constable, on 4 June 1534. He left no will. He had married twice. He and his first wife, Eleanor, daughter of Thomas *West, eighth Baron West and ninth Baron de la Warr, whom he married in or before 1496, had a son and a daughter; his second marriage, to Joan, daughter of Stephen Pitlesden, was childless. Guildford's son had predeceased him leaving no children, so the inheritance was disputed between Guildford's daughter, Jane *Dudley [*see under* Dudley, John, duke of Northumberland], married to John *Dudley, and his nephew John Guildford, the closest male heir. In 1534 John Dudley, who also prevailed in the inheritance dispute, was returned to Guildford's seat in the Commons. Despite his several offices Guildford did not have great wealth. His father had died in debt and Sir Edward himself was obliged to sell some of his lands in order to pay his debts to the king. STANFORD LEHMBERG

**Sources** *LP Henry VIII*, vols. 1–7, addenda • HoP, *Commons, 1509–58*, 2.262–3 • J. J. Scarisbrick, *Henry VIII* (1968) • C. G. Cruickshank, *The English occupation of Tournai, 1513–1519* (1971) • J. G. Russell, *The Field of Cloth of Gold* (1969) • S. Anglo, *Spectacle, pageantry and early Tudor policy* (1969) • S. E. Lehmberg, *The Reformation Parliament, 1529–1536* (1970) • D. Loades, *John Dudley, duke of Northumberland, 1504–1553* (1996)

**Archives** PRO, official account books

**Wealth at death** in debt to crown, 1521; sold lands: *LP Henry VIII*

**Guildford, Sir Henry** (1489–1532), courtier, was the third son of Sir Richard *Guildford and his second wife, Joan, daughter of Sir William Vaux of Harrowden.

**Master of the revels** Like his father, who had served Henry VII as master of the ordnance and controller of the household, young Henry Guildford opted for a career at the royal court; indeed, he probably had little choice since, as a younger son whose father was considerably in debt when he died in 1506, he inherited little land and an annuity of only £10. Even before Henry VIII succeeded to the throne in April 1509, he had become a close companion of the future king: only about two years older than the Tudor prince and, like him, physically well-built (as is evident from a drawing made by Hans Holbein in 1527), Guildford shared both his love of jousting and delight in courtly entertainments. When in April 1512 he married Margaret, daughter of Sir Thomas Bryan of Ashridge, the wedding was attended by both the king and his sister Princess Mary. As an esquire of the body and master of the revels by 1513, Guildford soon attracted the attention of contemporaries, while the Tudor chronicler Edward Hall recorded several of his exploits. During the new year festivities in

**Sir Henry Guildford** (1489–1532), by Hans Holbein the younger, 1527

January 1510, for instance, he and his half-brother Sir Edward *Guildford formed two of a small company headed by the king who, one morning, burst into Queen Katherine of Aragon's chamber dressed as Robin Hood and his men 'in short coats of Kentish kendal' and proceeded to entertain her with their dancing and boisterous exuberance; a year later, for twelfth night, he designed a moving stage in the form of a mountain which, approaching the king, suddenly opened and revealed a troupe of morris dancers; and, when describing one of the early tournaments of the reign, Hall particularly highlighted the presence of the young Henry Guildford:

> hym selfe and his horse in russet cloth of golde and clothe of silver, closed in a device, or a pageant made lyke a Castell or a Turret, wrought of Russet sercenet florence, wrought, and set out in golde with hys worde or posye, and all his men in Russet satyn and white, with hosen to thesame, and their bonettes of lyke colors. (*Hall's Chronicle*, 518)

Although it is not known just how often, or for how long, Guildford took on the mantle of master of the revels, he certainly acted before the king in the autumn of 1513 during an entertainment to celebrate the capture of Tournai and he was partly responsible for at least one theatrical performance devised for Cardinal Wolsey. He may also have played a pivotal role in promoting the compilation of a volume of songs which contains several lyrics penned by the king himself (BL, Add. MS 31922). But when the council complained to Henry VIII in May 1519 about the unsuitability of several young men of his privy chamber—they were unduly 'familier or homely' with the king, reported Hall, and 'played such lighte touches' in his presence that 'they forgat themselfes' (*Hall's Chronicle*, 598)—Guildford was one of a number of courtiers to be temporarily purged.

**The king's companion in arms** Not only did Sir Henry Guildford share Henry VIII's taste for war games during the king's early years, he also experienced real military campaigning as his master sought to make his mark in western Europe. When in May 1511 a force was dispatched to Spain under Thomas, Lord Darcy, to join Ferdinand of Aragon's 'crusade' against the Moors of north Africa, Guildford accompanied it as provost marshal. In the event Darcy's men were not required, and indeed they thoroughly disgraced themselves by getting drunk and running amok in Cadiz. Guildford remained in Spain for several months, however, and on 15 September was knighted by Ferdinand at Burgos, his arms being augmented by a pale pomegranate on a white shield. Thereafter he travelled home overland and, shortly after his return, received the honour of knighthood again, this time at the hands of his own king at Westminster on 30 March 1512. Later in the year, in August 1512, Guildford took part in a disastrous naval engagement off Brest, as joint captain with fellow courtier Sir Charles Brandon of sixty yeomen of the guard aboard the *Sovereign*. In 1513 Henry VIII himself, anxious for personal glory and yearning to cut a dash as a warlord, mounted an invasion of France. Guildford embarked from Southampton, commanding a hundred men of the king's ward. At the siege of Thérouanne in August 1513, and presumably at the so-called battle of the Spurs fought in the middle of the month, he carried the royal standard. Soon afterwards, after the capture of Tournai, he was created a knight-banneret before returning to England. In May 1514 he journeyed to Calais on an expedition led by John Bourchier, Lord Berners, and, five months later, after peace had been concluded with France, he went there again, *en route* for the coronation of Henry VIII's sister Mary as the new queen of Louis XII of France.

**Master of the horse and controller of the household** After several summers spent campaigning abroad, Sir Henry Guildford now returned to a more settled life in England, particularly at court where he soon gained new responsibilities. On 6 November 1515 he was appointed master of the horse with a salary of £40 a year, and in 1516 was made a royal councillor. Nevertheless he remained, first and foremost, a personal servant of the king: in September 1521, indeed, he was peremptorily recalled from Calais when Henry VIII found himself short of attendants in his privy chamber, and in January 1526, as a royal confidant sanctioned to deal with petitions of grievance presented to the king personally, he was one of the few men assigned lodgings in the royal house under the Eltham ordinances. His attendance at council meetings was rare, his presence being recorded on only six occasions in the decade after 1516; but as a royal councillor he did from time to time put his name to diplomatic documents (such as the protocol of the treaty of London on 2 October 1518 and the treaty of marriage between Princess Mary and the French dauphin two days later). As master of the horse he accompanied Henry VIII to meet François I at the spectacular Field of Cloth of Gold in June 1520: he is recorded as leading his master's spare mount on to the field, both he and the horse richly adorned. Soon afterwards he was also present when Henry VIII met the emperor Charles V at Gravelines.

Two years later, in 1522, having surrendered his post as master of the horse to Sir Nicholas Carew, Guildford became controller of the royal household. Among his duties, seemingly, was the auditing of accounts of banquets and revels, while as chamberlain of the receipt of the exchequer from 1525 he also superintended the cutting of tallies, as well as becoming custodian of original treaties and similarly valuable documents. Thus there is record of Cardinal Wolsey requesting Guildford to send him the book containing the Eltham ordinances (recently signed by the king) in 1526, while in June 1527 he delivered out of the exchequer to Stephen Gardiner, the cardinal's secretary, several boxes containing international treaties and associated papers. His position as a trusted intimate of Henry VIII is further demonstrated by the fact that in June 1525 he witnessed the grant of the earldom of Nottingham to the king's bastard son Henry Fitzroy, while in May 1526 he himself became a knight of the Garter. He had already been twice named for a stall by all the other knights, but passed over by the king, who in this context appears to have preferred members of the nobility. His position as a highly favoured courtier and royal official over many years enabled Guildford to build up a wide circle of friends and acquaintances beyond the purely political sphere: in 1519, for instance, he received two letters from Erasmus praising Henry VIII's court; he became an associate of the English humanist John Colet; he and the poet Sir Thomas Wyatt were jointly responsible, in 1526, for the construction of a banqueting house at Greenwich; and, when the painter Hans Holbein the younger paid his first visit to England in 1527, he found early subjects in Sir Henry Guildford and his second wife. It is a further sign of the range of Guildford's interests that Holbein should have portrayed him with a hat-badge decorated with a clock and surveying instruments, the so-called 'typus geometricus'.

**Cardinal Wolsey, Anne Boleyn, and the king's Great Matter** For most of Guildford's court career, no royal minister enjoyed greater prestige and power than Cardinal Thomas Wolsey. No doubt their paths frequently crossed and, on occasion, the minister drew the courtier into the world of diplomacy. In the autumn of 1521, for instance, Guildford accompanied Wolsey on a diplomatic mission to Calais; he journeyed with him to Dover in May 1522 to meet the emperor Charles V and escort him to Windsor; and, in the summer of 1527, he once more travelled to Calais in the cardinal's entourage, progressed through France with him, and was even saluted as an ambassador by François I at Amiens. By 1529, however, Wolsey's evident failure to secure an annulment of Henry VIII's marriage to Katherine of Aragon had seriously undermined his position and Guildford, elected knight of the shire for Kent in the Reformation Parliament which first met in November of that year, inevitably became embroiled. When, during the very first parliamentary session, the Commons complained of excessive fees demanded by clergy for proving wills, Guildford's declaration that as executor of Sir William Crompton he had paid 1000 marks to Wolsey and Archbishop William Warham of Canterbury may well have sparked off the protest. Shortly afterwards, on 1 December 1529, he signed the forty-four articles of complaint against Wolsey prepared by a committee of both houses for presentation to the king, perhaps because the cardinal had earlier advised Henry that his annuity of £100 might be revoked and some of his offices be redistributed if he became captain of Guînes.

Acting on Thomas Cromwell's recommendation, Wolsey now made a determined effort to placate those whose friendship he deemed worth having: for Guildford he spoke of securing an additional annuity of £40, and perhaps the courtier did in return make cautious, if futile, representations to the king on the cardinal's behalf. Meanwhile Guildford had become involved, both as a member of parliament and personally, in the matter of Henry VIII's divorce. At the end of September 1528, when Cardinal Lorenzo Campeggi visited England as papal legate assigned to deal with the king's marital affairs, Guildford, as controller of the household, was much occupied with preparations for his reception, and met him on his arrival in Kent. In 1529 he was one of the witnesses called upon to confirm the consummation of the marriage between the king's elder brother, Arthur, and Katherine of Aragon: however, as he attested, he was unable to do so since he had been a mere boy at the time. On 13 July 1530 he was one of the 'milites et doctores in parliamento' who signed a letter to Pope Clement VII urging him to accede to the king's desire for an annulment of his marriage. Clearly, Guildford remained in high favour with the king and, on 8 December 1529, he had witnessed at Westminster the charter which created Anne Boleyn's father earl of Wiltshire. But, although he was a member of the abortive delegation that endeavoured to persuade Katherine of Aragon to 'be sensible' in May 1531, he none the less spoke out in council in favour of the queen. He was also heard to remark that all lawyers and theologians arguing the king's case at this time should be put in a cart, shipped to Rome, and there exposed for the charlatans they were.

According to the imperial ambassador Eustace Chapuys, Anne Boleyn, already enjoying considerable political influence as the king's mistress and well aware of Guildford's dislike of her, in June 1531 threatened him with the loss of the controllership when she became queen. He replied that he would save her the trouble and immediately went to the king to tender his resignation. Henry VIII would have none of it, however, declaring that he should simply ignore 'women's talk' and insisting he remain in office. Moreover, although Guildford did retire to his home in Kent for a while to cool off, he was back at court by November 1531 at the latest when, as one of the king's councillors, he took part in negotiations at Greenwich with a special envoy from Charles V; on 1 January 1532 he not only received a new year gift from Henry VIII but also presented the king with a gold tablet; and he remained controller of the household until his death a few months later.

**Economic fortunes and provincial interests** As a virtually penniless younger son, Sir Henry Guildford's fortunes depended largely on royal favour. Early in Henry VIII's reign, on 29 March 1510, he was granted the wardship of Anne, daughter and heir of Sir John Langford; on 6 June 1512, shortly after his first marriage, the king granted Guildford and his wife the manors of Hampton in Arden, Warwickshire, and Bicker, Lincolnshire; and on 3 December 1512 he became bailiff of the manor of Sutton Coldfield in Warwickshire and keeper of Sutton Park. Once he had been appointed constable of Leeds Castle in Kent and keeper of the parks of Leeds and Langley on 12 December 1512 the castle probably became his chief residence: in 1520 he seems to have entertained Charles V there, and when in the later 1520s Thomas Cromwell came as Wolsey's agent to suppress minor religious houses in Kent, Guildford invited him to visit the castle.

Guildford's position in that county was consolidated when on 12 February 1521 he was granted custody of the manor of Leeds and the lordship of Langley for forty years at an annual rent of £27 15*s.* 8*d.* Other property and responsibilities in Kent also came his way: on 24 April 1522, for instance, he obtained the manor of Hadlow, and on 1 September following, a forty-year lease of the manor of Eltham, with a house called Corby Hall and the stewardship of the manor of Lee near Lewisham; while on 15 July 1524 he was granted North Frith Park. Also in 1524 he became chief steward of the archbishop of Canterbury's castles and manors. From the end of 1514 until his death he served as a JP in Kent; between 1514 and 1524 he was four times a subsidy commissioner in the county; in 1529 he and his half-brother Sir Edward Guildford were elected knights of the shire for Kent. Sir Henry's financial rewards included an annuity of 50 marks in November 1515, later raised to £100.

The fact that he was assessed for subsidy at £300 in February 1524 and £520 in May 1526 would seem to indicate a rapid advance in Guildford's fortunes; yet in March 1513 and at other times he received advances of money from the king to enable him to repay loans, while at his death his debts were said to have far exceeded the value of his goods in Leeds Castle and his London home. Much of his plate was later given by Henry VIII to Anne Boleyn. In his will, made on 18 May 1532, Guildford requested that if he died within 40 miles of London he should be buried in the church of the Blackfriars (where he had already ordered his tomb). He appointed his wife his executor and charged her with the payment of his debts. He was dead by 27 May and was buried where he had wished. His first wife had died some time before 1525, when he married Mary, daughter of Sir Robert Wotton of Boughton Malherbe, Kent. There were no children of either marriage. His widow subsequently married as her second husband Sir Gawain Carew of Devon. KEITH DOCKRAY

**Sources** *LP Henry VIII*, vols. 1–6 • *Hall's chronicle*, ed. H. Ellis (1809) • H. Miller, 'Guildford, Sir Henry', HoP, *Commons, 1509–58*, 2.263–5 • *DNB* • J. J. Scarisbrick, *Henry VIII* (1968) • D. Starkey, *The reign of Henry VIII: personalities and politics* (1985) • R. B. Wernham, *Before the Armada: the growth of English foreign policy, 1485–1588* (1966) • J. G. Russell, *The Field of Cloth of Gold: men and manners in 1520* (1969) • E. W. Ives, *Anne Boleyn* (1986) • P. W. Fleming, 'The Hautes and their "circle": culture and the English gentry', *England in the fifteenth century* [Harlaxton 1986], ed. D. Williams (1987), 85–102 • D. Starkey, ed., *Henry VIII: a European court in England* (1991) • S. J. Gunn, *Charles Brandon, duke of Suffolk, c.1484–1545* (1988)

**Likenesses** H. Holbein, chalk drawing, 1527, Royal Collection; repro. in Starkey, *Reign of Henry VIII*, p. 45 • H. Holbein the younger, oils, 1527, Royal Collection [*see illus.*] • W. Hollar, print (after H. Holbein the younger), NPG

**Wealth at death** debts allegedly far exceeded value of goods in Leeds Castle and London home: Miller, 'Guildford, Sir Henry', 2.264

**Guildford, Nicholas of** (*fl.* **13th cent.**), supposed poet, occurs three times in the Middle English debate poem *The Owl and the Nightingale*, in two manuscripts (BL, Cotton MS Caligula A.ix, and Oxford, Jesus College, MS 29), both dated palaeographically as of the later thirteenth century, as Maister Nichole of Guldeforde, variously spelt. 'Master' conveys academic status. J. Stevenson, in the introduction to the first edition (Frenchifying 'of' to 'de') suggests, 'There seems reason to believe that in the Master Nicholas de Guilford of Portesham … we may recognize the author of the Owl and the Nightingale' (*The Owl and the Nightingale*, ed. Stevenson, vii), echoing the note (in Thomas Wilkins's late seventeenth-century hand, imitating the medieval hand of the manuscript) on the folio preceding the debate, that quotes a quatrain in which 'Mayster Iohan … of Guldeuorde' is named, 'whereby the Author may bee gues't at'. Nothing is known about John of Guildford except for that quatrain, which, on stylistic grounds, is unlikely to be by the poet of the debate. In style and prosody it is like the preceding poem, 'La passyun Ihesu Crist en engleys', at the end of which Wilkins copied it.

In early scholarly consideration of the manuscripts, John of Guildford plays some role. The *Catalogi librorum manuscriptorum Angliae et Hiberniae* of 1687 regards him as the author of the unhomogeneous group of poems from 'La passyun' and the debate to 'Hwi ne serue we Crist?' (fols. 144–187*v*). Thomas Warton in 1774 ascribes Wilkins's note to 'the veary learned Edward Lhuyd', and believes John of Guildford to be the author of 'La passyun'. He states that the birds' debate is to be 'left to the judgment of one John de Guldevord', not Nicholas. Joseph Ritson's *Bibliographia poetica* (1802) indicated that in the Cotton manuscript 'one Nichole of Guldeforde is twice named … not indeed as the poet, but as a … fit judge of their controversy' and that probably Nicholas was brother of John de Guldevord (Ritson, 5–6).

Thomas Wright's edition (1843) agrees with Stevenson in the presumption of Nicholas's authorship. In Wright's *Biographia Britannica literaria* (1846), he writes that the name occurs 'in a way which would lead any one acquainted with the manner in which writers of the middle ages name themselves to believe him to be the author'. He takes John of Guildford to be the author of 'La passyun', 'and he has been supposed to have been the brother or a near relation of Nicholas' (Wright, 438, 439).

The presumption is based on two exchanges about Nicholas between the birds. The first concerns who is to judge between them. The disputants agree. The Nightingale knows that Nicholas's wisdom and sense of justice make him a fit judge, and the Owl adds that, though in his youth he had shown an inclination towards well-born and slender creatures, he is no longer frivolous. In the second exchange the Wren, of authority in the avian world, joins in the praise. Some facts can be gleaned about him. Nicholas has only one place of abode, Portesham, Dorset—a parish (its church has Norman traces) closely connected with the abbey of Abbotsbury. That he is not preferred and able to enjoy plurality is a great shame to his unscrupulous bishops. Things are better as far as Scotland through what Nicholas says and writes, presumably the Wren's hyperbole, but it has been used in an attempt to identify him with a known jurist.

Nicholas of Guildford exists only as a person praised in *The Owl and the Nightingale*, and thought its author by some. John of Guildford exists only in Wilkins's transcript of a lost 'broken leaf' attached to a religious poem in one of the two manuscripts in which the debate has survived. There is no evidence for establishing any relationship between them. E. G. STANLEY

**Sources** *The Owl and the Nightingale reproduced in facsimile*, ed. N. R. Ker, EETS, old ser., 251 (1963) • *The Owl and the Nightingale*, ed. J. Stevenson, Roxburghe Club (1838), vii • *The Owl and the Nightingale*, ed. T. Wright, Percy Society, 39 (1843), vii • *The Owl and the Nightingale*, ed. J. W. H. Atkins (1922), xxxviii–xlvi, 148–50 • *The Owl and the Nightingale*, ed. E. G. Stanley (1960), 19–22 • E. Bernard, ed., *Catalogi librorum manuscriptorum Angliae et Hiberniae*, 2 vols. in 1 (1697), pt 2, p. 69 • T. Warton, *The history of English poetry*, 4 vols. (1774–81), vol. 1, pp. 25–6 • J. Ritson, *Bibliographia poetica* (1802), 5–6 • T. Wright, *Biographia Britannica literaria*, 2: *Anglo-Norman period* (1846), 438–9 • C. L. Wrenn, 'Curiosities in a medieval manuscript', *Essays and Studies by Members of the English Association*, 25 (1939), 101–15 • C. Sisam, 'The broken leaf in MS. Jesus College, Oxford, 29', *Review of English Studies*, new ser., 5 (1954), 337–43 • F. L. Utley, 'Dialogues, debates, and catechisms', *A manual of the writings in Middle English, 1050–1500*, ed. A. E. Hartung, 3 (1972), 716–20, 874–82

**Archives** BL, Cotton MS Caligula A.ix • Jesus College, Oxford, MS 29

**Guildford, Sir Richard** (*c.*1450–1506), administrator, was born at Cranbrook, near Rolvenden, Kent, the son of Sir John Guildford of Rolvenden (1430–1493) and his first wife, Alice Waller. Richard Guildford's first marriage (before 1479) to Anne, daughter of John Pympe, an important Kentish landowner, brought him into contact with servants of the Beauforts in the south-east, and, together with links to Sir Reginald Bray, the receiver-general to Lady Margaret Beaufort, helped in 1483 to bring him into the network of conspirators on behalf of Henry Tudor. Both Richard Guildford and his father were attainted following the abortive rebellion against Richard III in October 1483. Richard escaped to join Henry Tudor in exile, and landed with him at Milford Haven in August 1485, where he was knighted. Guildford's later service as master of the ordnance probably indicates that he was prominent in organizing Tudor's campaign to Bosworth, but his presence at the battle is not recorded.

After Bosworth, Guildford's earlier associations and services brought him rapid promotion. He quickly became master of the ordnance and armoury in the Tower of London (an appointment renewed in 1493), a chamberlain of the exchequer, and keeper of Kennington in Surrey, where Henry VII stayed before his coronation. He was master of horse and a privy councillor by 1487, a knight of the king's body by 1488, and he also received wardships and other lands in reward. Guildford's links to the crown were underlined by Henry VII's presence at his second marriage, to Joan Vaux, which had occurred by 1489. By 1494 Guildford was controller of the household. He was present in 1494 when the king's second son, Henry, was created duke of York, and shortly afterwards was one of six commissioners appointed to arrange the marriage of Prince Arthur and Katherine of Aragon. He was sheriff of Kent in 1494–5, and was sent to thank the commons of Kent for resisting Perkin Warbeck's landing at Deal in 1495. Guildford was MP for Kent in the parliament held that year, and probably also in the other parliaments of the reign. In 1496 he became steward of the lands of Cecily, duchess of York, in the south-east, and was made a banneret after the defeat of the Cornish rising at Blackheath in 1497. He accompanied Henry VII to his meeting with Archduke Philip outside Calais in 1500, and was elected a knight of the Garter that same year. In 1501 he was involved in the preparations for Katherine of Aragon's arrival in England.

Although he fulfilled the normal role of a royal councillor (arbitrating in regional disputes, obtaining royal favour for associates, and enforcing royal prerogative rights), Guildford also displayed more unusual skills. He had a major role in the organization of security within Henry VII's regime. In 1487 a grant of the manor of Higham in Sussex required him to construct a defensive tower at Camber, and in 1497 he secured licences to recover further coastal marsh in Sussex; an area still known as the Guildford Level. By 1503, and perhaps earlier, Guildford was organizing spying missions to infiltrate followers of the exiled earl of Suffolk, the Yorkist claimant Edmund de la Pole. As master of the ordnance Guildford had particular responsibilities for military logistics, and he supplied arms and equipment for various campaigns, including the Breton expeditions of 1489–91, and the invasion of France in 1492. As an engineer Guildford was given £100 in 1486 for ship construction—perhaps that of the *Mary Gylford*—and at Easter 1487 he was building other vessels, including the *Regent*.

Indebtedness, however, dogged Guildford for much of his career. In 1486 he was pressed for a debt outstanding since 1482, and financial irregularities, which King Henry intended to investigate personally, probably forced the surrender of his exchequer post in May 1487. Guildford secured an act in 1495 to release land in Kent from the restrictions of gavelkind tenure, so that it could be put up for sale on the open market, but by 1503 he was in arrears for the farm of Winchelsea, and owed money for wardships, for official duties, and to private individuals. In November 1503 management of his debts was transferred to the abbot of Battle, who was still paying related obligations in 1505.

In June 1505 Guildford was arrested for a debt under statute staple to John Nailer, a servant of George Neville, Lord Bergavenny, and in July he was investigated for non-return of accounts as master of the ordnance and armoury between 1486 and 1492. He was imprisoned in the Fleet, but released under bond to appear before the king. A pardon on 4 April 1506, of all debts arising from his offices, did not deter his creditors, and many of his former duties were assigned to others, including his son Edward *Guildford.

Even after the intervention of Bray and the king, Guildford's financial preoccupations meant that he was unable to maintain his role within the Kentish royal affinity. After 1503 Lord Bergavenny exploited Sir Richard's difficulties, and began to recruit Guildford associates into his own retinue. Ill feeling may have developed from 1500, when Bergavenny was granted the keepership of Southfrith Park, an estate previously under Guildford's control. That Guildford retaliated is suggested by his inclusion among those Kentishmen targeted by an anti-retaining proclamation in 1502. Open hostility between the two had broken out by 1503, when a riot between Guildford's youngest son, George, and Bergavenny's leading servants disrupted Aylesford manor court. This feuding continued after Sir Richard's death, despite Bergavenny's prosecution for illegal retaining in 1506.

The combination of Guildford's insolvency and his feud with Bergavenny probably forced Henry VII to acquiesce in Guildford's removal from office, which was perhaps engineered by the king's financial agents, Sir Richard Empson and Edmund Dudley. Sir Richard probably avoided prosecution by electing to travel in pilgrimage to Jerusalem in April 1506, which effectively marked his retirement from high office. However, his death in Jerusalem on 6 September 1506 (probably from fever), avoided the complication of his rehabilitation into the Kentish élite. He was buried on Mount Syon in Jerusalem the following day. In his will, dated 8 April 1506 (the day before his departure), he deposited goods and books with the black friars in London, and willed that 'above all thinges' his debts should be settled, instructing feoffees to divert profits from his lands towards the same (PRO, PROB 11/17, fol. 225*v*). Guildford was survived by his second wife, and by children from both his marriages, including his son Henry *Guildford who opted, like his father, for a career at the royal court. SEAN CUNNINGHAM

**Sources** *Chancery records* • J. C. Wedgwood and A. D. Holt, *History of parliament*, 1: *Biographies of the members of the Commons house, 1439–1509* (1936) • BL, Add. MS 21480 • W. Campbell, ed., *Materials for a history of the reign of Henry VII*, 2 vols., Rolls Series, 60 (1873–7) • M. Mercer, 'Kent and national politics, 1437–1534', PhD diss., U. Lond., 1995 • will, 1506, PRO, PROB 11/17, fol. 225*v* • H. Ellis, ed., *The pylgrymage of Sir Richard Guylforde to the Holy Land, AD 1506*, CS, 51 (1851) • exchequer, queen's remembrancer, memoranda rolls, PRO, E 159/284, mm. 36, 36d • I. S. Leadham, 'An unknown conspiracy against King Henry VII', *TRHS*, new ser., 16 (1902), 133–58 • *RotP*, vol. 6 • court of king's bench, ancient indictments, PRO, KB 9/430, mm 48–69 • J. Anstis, ed., *The register of the most noble order of the Garter*, 2 vols. (1724)

**Wealth at death** see will, 1506, PRO, PROB 11/17, fol. 225*v*

**Guilford**. For this title name *see* North, Francis, first Baron Guilford (1637–1685); North, Francis, first earl of Guilford (1704–1790); North, Frederick, second earl of Guilford (1732–1792); North, George Augustus, third earl of Guilford (1757–1802) [*see under* North, Frederick, second earl of Guilford (1732–1792)]; North, Francis, fourth earl of Guilford (1761–1817) [*see under* North, Frederick, second earl of Guilford (1732–1792)]; North, Frederick, fifth earl of Guilford (1766–1827).

**Guillamore**. For this title name *see* O'Grady, Standish, first Viscount Guillamore (1766–1840); O'Grady, Standish, second Viscount Guillamore (1792–1848) [*see under* O'Grady, Standish, first Viscount Guillamore (1766–1840)].

**Guillemard, William Henry** (1815–1887), Church of England clergyman, was born at Hackney on 23 November 1815, the son of Daniel Guillemard, a Spitalfields silk merchant, and Susan, daughter of Henry Venn of Payhembury, Devon. His father's family was of Huguenot descent. After education at Christ's Hospital he entered Pembroke College, Cambridge, in December 1833 and graduated BA in 1838. In the same year he gained the Crosse divinity scholarship and became a fellow of Pembroke, proceeding MA in 1841, BD in 1849, and DD in 1870. He was classical lecturer of his college, but declined the tutorship on grounds of poor health. He was ordained deacon in 1841, and priest in 1844.

At Cambridge, Guillemard helped to promote the Oxford Movement, and was an energetic member of the Cambridge Camden Society (later the Ecclesiological Society), established in 1839 to promote church restoration and the revival of ritual. Guillemard married, on 12 July 1849, Elizabeth Susanna, the daughter of W. H. Turner of Birmingham; she predeceased him by a few months. They had one son, Laurence Nunns Guillemard (later high commissioner for the Malay states), and five daughters.

From 1848 to 1869 Guillemard was headmaster of the Royal College at Armagh. His tenure of the post was not altogether a success, since his pronounced, though moderate, high-churchmanship roused the suspicion of the local protestants. He enjoyed, however, the confidence of Lord John Beresford, the primate. In 1869 he was appointed vicar of Little St Mary's, Cambridge. During the seventeen years of his incumbency he made the church a centre of spiritual renewal, and organized the first retreats and Lenten conferences to be held at Cambridge. He also raised a fund to endow a chaplaincy at Addenbrooke's Hospital.

Weak health led Guillemard to resign his living a few months before his death, which took place at Waterbeach on 2 September 1887. He was buried in the Cambridge cemetery. His main contribution to scholarship, besides occasional pamphlets and sermons, was an unfinished work, *Hebraisms of the Greek Testament* (1879).

EDMUND VENABLES, *rev.* G. MARTIN MURPHY

**Sources** Venn, *Alum. Cant.* · *The Guardian* (7 Sept 1887) · *The Guardian* (14 Sept 1887) · Boase, *Mod. Eng. biog.* · personal knowledge (1890) · private information (1890)
**Archives** CUL, letters to Sir George Stokes
**Wealth at death** £18,462: probate, 26 Sept 1887, *CGPLA Eng. & Wales*

**Guillim, John** (1550–1621), herald, the elder of two sons and one of six children of John Agullim or Gwillim (*d.* 1581) of Westbury-on-Severn, subsequently of Minsterworth, both in Gloucestershire, and his wife, Margaret, daughter of Nicholas Woodhouse of London, pewterer, and his wife, Catherine, daughter and sole heir of Eustace Hatheway of Minsterworth. Guillim was reputedly educated at Oxford and one of his manuscript volumes of collectanea in the Bodleian Library (Rawlinson, B. 102) reveals a mastery of French and Latin. Guillim was exposed to heraldry from an early age. His father was of Welsh extraction, being a descendant in the male line of Bleddyn ap Maenyrch (*d.* 1093), the ancestor of many Brecknockshire families, and received some time between 1557 and 1567 a confirmation of quartered arms and the grant of a crest from William Hervy, Clarenceux king of arms.

In an office copy of the 1569 heralds' visitation of Gloucestershire (College of Arms, MS D. 12, 129b) is a pedigree dated 1572 entered by Guillim's father; his son John was then aged twenty-two and unmarried. By 1575 he had married Frances, daughter of Richard Dennys of Siston, Gloucestershire, and his wife, Anne, daughter of Sir John St John of Bletsoe, Bedfordshire, and their son St John Guillim had been born, to be joined later by a daughter, Margaret. A funeral certificate reveals that Guillim's father, then described as 'The Worshipful John Gwillim, Lord of the Manor of Hatheweys in the parish of Minsterworth', died a widower at his manor house on 23 March 1581 (Coll. Arms, MS letter I, 10, 162). Guillim gave his father a heraldic funeral at Minsterworth on 19 April.

Guillim began writing his one work, and the reason for his subsequent deserved fame, *A Display of Heraldrie*, at the age of forty-four in 1595. In 1604 he was created Portsmouth pursuivant-extraordinary and in 1607 he was the owner of a now lost roll of arms of about 1300, named Guillim's roll after him, which contained 148 shields and was copied in that year by Nicholas Charles, Lancaster herald, who noted that it was 'in the custody of Mr. John Guiliams Portesmouth who lent me the originall' (A. R. Wagner, *A Catalogue of English Medieval Rolls of Arms*, 1950, 26). In 1611 Guillim's *Display of Heraldrie* was published with a colophon dated 1610. It contained 283 folio pages and more than 500 woodcuts of shields in the text, illustrating the arms of named families and early seventeenth-century office-holders. On 12 May 1612 he sold a manuscript heraldic notebook (now BL, Harley MS 1386) to John Withie, the herald painter. As Portsmouth pursuivant Guillim attended the funeral of Henry, prince of Wales, on 7 December 1612 and on 10 December 1613 was created Rouge Croix pursuivant, though the patent backdating his salary to Michaelmas 1613 was dated only on 26 February 1618. As Rouge Croix he attended the funeral in July 1617 of the queen, Anne of Denmark, and was one of the two officers of arms who organized the funeral of Sir John Herbert at Cardiff on 23 September 1617. He also attended the funeral of Sir Rowland Lytton at Knebworth on 23 June 1619. He died on 7 May 1621 and was buried on 9 May at St Benet Paul's Wharf.

Guillim's *Display of Heraldrie*, of which there were further posthumous enlarged editions, was to remain the standard textbook on English heraldry until the second half of the eighteenth century, and it is still regularly used by working heralds in the twenty-first century.

The *Display*, which quotes earlier English and continental writers, is divided into six sections of which the first commences with the origins of heraldry, the second contains the basic divisions of the shield, the third and largest describes natural as compared to man-made charges, which are in the fourth section, the fifth has patterned coats without a predominant tincture, and the sixth deals with marshalling of arms. Sir William Dugdale told Anthony Wood that the work was that of John Barkham, dean of Bocking in Essex, who considered it too frivolous a subject to publish under his own name and gave it to Guillim. This is refuted in Philip Bliss's edition of Wood's *Athenae Oxonienses* (1815) by quoting a letter from George Ballard to Dr Rawlinson which refers to the original manuscript of 438 pages written in one hand begun, as the author notes on the title-page, in the year 1595 when he was aged forty-four, which does not coincide with Barkham's age; it does, however, fit with Guillim's age of twenty-two in 1572. The arms of more than twenty Gloucestershire families are noted, which suggests Guillim's, not Barkham's, authorship, as are the arms of Guillim's paternal grandmother's family of Deane which he quartered and the arms of his maternal grandmother Hatheway which are impaled with Guillim in the section on marshalling. On the other hand the arms of Oxford University (p. 197) and its colleges Corpus Christi (p. 162) and Magdalen (p. 247) occur and Barkham, a fellow of Corpus Christi, may have sent material to Guillim. The text (pp. 174 and 178) mentions two coats in the window of New Inn Hall in London, one of the inns of chancery, perhaps implying that the author had some link with it, and the methodical logical arrangement could suggest a legal training. Thomas Moule's *Bibliotheca heraldica* (1822), p. 73, adds in support of Guillim's authorship that the highly complimentary verses prefixed to the volume by his seniors in office can hardly be supposed to have been written with an intention to sanction a fiction. It is these verses which give the only indication of Guillim's character.

Sir William Segar, Garter, describes Guillim as 'kinde friend and fellow' and John Speed, the historian and cartographer who was helped by John Barkham, dedicates his verses 'to his worthy and well-deserving friend'. St John Guillim survived his father and was a widower of

Clerkenwell, Middlesex, in April 1622, aged forty-seven, when he obtained a licence to remarry. St John's son Robert recorded a pedigree at the heralds' visitation of Lincolnshire in 1634. THOMAS WOODCOCK

**Sources** W. H. Godfrey, A. Wagner, and H. Stanford London, *The College of Arms, Queen Victoria Street* (1963), 214 · Wood, *Ath. Oxon.*, new edn, 2.288–9 · funeral certificate of John Gwillim, Coll. Arms, MS letter 1, 10/162 · pedigree of Agullims, 1572, in office copy of 'Heralds' visitation of Gloucestershire', Coll. Arms, MS D12 129b · T. Moule, *Bibliotheca heraldica Magnae Britanniae* (privately printed, London, 1822), 72–4, 116, 121, 151–2, 205, 319–20 · M. P. Siddons, *The development of Welsh heraldry*, 2 (1993), 200 · A. R. Wagner, *A catalogue of English mediaeval rolls of arms*, Harleian Society, 100 (1950), 26 · J. Dallaway, *Origin and progress of the science of heraldry in England* (1793), 245–8 · parish register, London, St Benet Paul's Wharf, 9 May 1621, GL [burial] · W. Musgrave, *Obituary prior to 1800*, ed. G. J. Armytage, 3, Harleian Society, 46 (1900), 103 · 'Heralds' visitation of Lincolnshire', pedigree, 1634, Coll. Arms, MS I, C 23, 88b

**Archives** BL, Harley MSS 1386, 6067 | Bodl. Oxf., MS Rawl. B. 102

**Wealth at death** £10: administration, 18 May 1621

**Guilpin, Everard** (*b. c.*1572), poet and satirist, was the eldest child of John Guilpin and Thomasin Everard, who had been married in Gillingham, Norfolk, on 27 February 1571. John Guilpin served as clerk of the pleas in the court of exchequer; he was buried on 11 March 1591. On 29 June 1592 Thomasin married William Guarsi, uncle of the satirist John Marston, and the family home was thereafter at Bungay in Suffolk.

Guilpin attended Highgate grammar school, and was entered at Emmanuel College, Cambridge, in 1588 and at Gray's Inn in 1591. According to the register of St Mary's, Bungay, on 3 February 1607 he married Sarah Guarsi of that town, and she was almost certainly the daughter of William, his stepfather, by a previous marriage. Nothing is known of his later life.

Guilpin was one of a number of clever young men who consciously modelled themselves on the Roman poets Martial, Juvenal, and Persius. Joseph Hall, who survived to become a bishop, was for a long time considered the most representative of these Elizabethan satirists. Donne is by far the best of them, but Marston, still an underrated figure, produced some savage swingeing stuff in his *Scourge of Villainie*, while Guilpin can fairly be described as a lesser Marston. The two men were associates: 'Satyra nova', added to the 1599 edition of *The Scourge*, is addressed by Marston to his 'very friend, Maister E. G.', and *The Whipper of the Satyr, his Pennance* (1601), ascribed to Guilpin, is a defence of Marston's satire. Guilpin's reputation depends, however, on *Skialetheia, or, A Shadowe of Truth* (1598). The following year it was called in by Archbishop Whitgift and burnt, along with Marston's *Scourge* and other books deemed to be subversive.

Guilpin's strength lay in invective, and *Skialetheia* is full of it. Its seven satires respectively decry poetry, hypocrisy, painted women, inconstancy, jealousy, vanity, and the tyranny of opinion. Satire V gives a lively notion of the hubbub in city streets:

There squeaks a cart-wheele, here a tumbrel rumbles;
Heere scolds an old Bawd, there a Porter grumbles.
Heere two tough Car-men combat for the way,
There two for looks begin a coward fray,
Two swaggering knaves here brable for a whore,
There braules an Ale-knight for his fat-grown score.

This is written in an equivalent of the Latin distich, a sprung version of the heroic couplet in which these poets chose to satirize what they took to be the follies of the age. At a time which we are accustomed to regard as the high point of English civilization, what Marston and Guilpin could see was dirt, disease, and malpractice.

PHILIP HOBSBAUM

**Sources** E. Gilpin, *Skialetheia, or, The shadow of truth*, ed. D. A. Carroll (1974) · R. E. Brettie, 'Everard Guilpin and John Marston 1576–1634', *Review of English Studies*, new ser., 16 (1965), 396–9 · *The poems of John Marston*, ed. A. Davenport (1961) · J. Peter, *Complaint and satire in early English literature* (1956) · [J. Weever, N. Breton, and E. Guilpin], *The whipper pamphlets: (1601)*, ed. A. Davenport (1951)

**Guînes**. For this title name *see* Vere, Aubrey (III) de, count of Guînes and earl of Oxford (*d.* 1194).

**Guingand, Sir Francis Wilfred** [Freddie] **de** (**1900–1979**), army officer, was born on 28 February 1900 at Acton, Middlesex, the second of the four children and eldest of the three sons of Francis Julius de Guingand, a manufacturer of briar-root pipes, and his wife, Mary Monica (*née* Priestman). He was educated at Ampleforth College (1913?–18) and the Royal Military College, Sandhurst (1918–19), before being commissioned into the West Yorkshire regiment (the Prince of Wales's Own) in December 1919. Two years later his regiment was serving in the 17th infantry brigade at Cork in Ireland. The brigade-major was Captain (brevet major) Bernard Montgomery (later Field Marshal Viscount Montgomery of Alamein). It was as chief of staff to Montgomery, when he commanded the Eighth Army and Twenty-First Army group in the Second World War, that de Guingand gained prominence.

Their paths crossed again when Freddie, as de Guingand was universally known, was at his regimental depot at York in 1922. Montgomery, on the staff of the 49th Territorial Army division, lived in the same officers' mess, and they struck up a friendship. Their paths then diverged. De Guingand, bored with regimental soldiering in England and keen to increase his income—he had expensive tastes: gambling, card-playing, and racing, as well as shooting and fishing—volunteered in 1926 to serve with the King's African rifles in Nyasaland. He stayed there for five years, acquiring a lifelong affection for Africa. In 1932 he returned to his regiment as adjutant of its 1st battalion in Egypt, where Montgomery was commanding the 1st battalion of the Royal Warwickshire regiment. On an important exercise Montgomery was made to act as brigade commander, with de Guingand as his brigade-major. It was the first of several occasions on which, later in life, de Guingand was to claim that his cooler judgement saved Montgomery from the consequences of his own impetuousness. Montgomery was certainly impressed with his ability, and persuaded him to attempt the Staff College examination, rather than return to Nyasaland. De Guingand had left it late; but in 1934, when he was in India, pressure from Montgomery obtained a nomination for

**Sir Francis Wilfred de Guingand (1900–1979)**, by Walter Stoneman, 1944

him to the Staff College at Camberley. On graduation in 1936 he was appointed brigade-major to the small arms school at Netheravon, and he was still there in June 1939, when he was posted as military assistant to the secretary of state for war, Leslie Hore-Belisha. This appointment gave him an insight both into the conduct of military affairs at the highest level and into its political aspects. His judgement in these matters was to prove sounder than Montgomery's.

When Hore-Belisha was dismissed in January 1940, de Guingand, at his own request, left also, being posted as an instructor, now in the rank of lieutenant-colonel, to the newly formed Middle East Staff College at Haifa, moving on from there at the end of the year to become the army member of the joint planning staff in Cairo. He became highly critical of his commander-in-chief, accusing General Sir Archibald Wavell of taking an over-optimistic view of the prospects of British intervention in Greece in May 1941. He therefore welcomed Wavell's supersession by Sir Claude Auchinleck, whom he warmly admired. The admiration was mutual, Auchinleck appointing him as the director of military intelligence in February 1942, and subsequently, when Auchinleck had assumed direct command of the Eighth Army from Lieutenant-General Neil Ritchie and halted Rommel on the Alamein line in July of that year, as brigadier general staff at Eighth Army headquarters. De Guingand himself felt that he lacked experience for both these appointments; but his clarity and speed of mind, his sense of the possible, his ability to analyse a problem and draw together the different characters at work on it, made him the perfect staff officer.

It was therefore a fortunate chance which brought de Guingand at 7.30 a.m. on 13 August 1942 to the point near Alexandria where the road from Cairo joined the coastal road which led to El Alamein and eventually to Tunis. There he met the newly arrived Montgomery. De Guingand expressed his disquiet at the general malaise of the Eighth Army. This was music to Monty's ears, and the dramatic results have been fully recorded. Montgomery announced that de Guingand was to be accepted as his chief of staff with full authority over all branches, logistic as well as operational. It was therefore something of a shock to be warned by his master a few days later that he had asked the War Office to replace him by Brigadier Frank Simpson, his principal staff officer in a succession of commands. Fortunately for both de Guingand and Montgomery, Sir Alan Brooke, the Chief of the Imperial General Staff, refused: Freddie stayed with Monty to the war's end.

But then the intimate relationship, which had been established and which lasted until VE-day, began to fall apart on the issue of where the credit lay for the decisions on which Montgomery's claim to fame rested. De Guingand never ceased to express the highest admiration for Montgomery, while acknowledging that he had defects of judgement and character which led him into error from time to time. In later years de Guingand claimed credit for the important change of plan in the later stages of the battle of El Alamein, which led to the final breakthrough; for the change of plan at Mareth to switch the main effort far out to the left and for devising with Harry Broadhurst, the commander of the desert air force, the exceptional air support for it; for recognizing that the initial plans for the landings both in Sicily and in Normandy were unsound, and recommending the changes on which Montgomery insisted. All these decisions Montgomery made much of as his own: neither in their lifetimes was able to reveal the extent to which they were based on intelligence from ULTRA decryptions. While fully supporting Montgomery against the criticism levelled at him, by Sir Arthur Tedder and others, over the Normandy campaign, de Guingand never concealed his disagreement with his chief in the protracted argument with Eisenhower over the subsequent strategy and the need for an overall land force commander. De Guingand admitted failing to appreciate the importance of an early clearance of the Scheldt estuary in order to open Antwerp as the allies' main supply port, but accepted no responsibility for Arnhem, as he was away sick at the time.

Sickness, in the form of stomach trouble, which long after the war was diagnosed as due to a gallstone, removed de Guingand from the scene at several crucial periods, the first being after El Alamein. If the doctors then had had their way, his period as chief of staff to Montgomery would have been short; but Montgomery overruled them, and de Guingand used the opportunity to marry, on 17 December 1942, Arlie Roebuck Stewart, the beautiful Australian widow of a brother officer, Major H. D. Stewart, and daughter of Charles Woodhead, a company director of Brisbane. They had one daughter, and the marriage was dissolved in 1957.

The disagreement between Montgomery and Eisenhower festered throughout the last winter of the war, and came to a head as a result of the former's tactless briefing of the press during the Ardennes battle. His remarks were taken as an insult to the American generals, Bradley and Patton, and Eisenhower had drafted a signal to General Marshall protesting that he could stand it no longer. Fortunately his chief of staff, Bedell Smith, was on excellent terms with de Guingand whom he alerted. In very hazardous weather, the latter flew to see Eisenhower and flew back to persuade Montgomery to dispatch an apologetic signal. Eisenhower tore up his draft. De Guingand believed that he had saved his master from dismissal, and resented Montgomery's pretence in his memoirs that he had himself taken the initiative to send de Guingand to see Eisenhower. De Guingand never forgave his chief for that and three other actions. The first was the brusque refusal to let de Guingand be present at the formal surrender of the Germans on Lüneburg Heath; the second, the failure to allot him any part in the victory parade in London; and the final blow, the abandonment of Montgomery's pledge to make de Guingand vice-chief of the Imperial General Staff, when he became the chief. The last blow was especially hard, not only because Simpson received the post, but because Montgomery announced the decision to him in an offhand manner, and de Guingand, against medical advice and his own wishes, had taken up the post of director of military intelligence at the War Office in 1945 to prepare himself for it. He never knew that it was Brooke who had insisted that Montgomery could not import his favourites from Twenty-First Army group into all the important posts in the War Office. He left the army in 1946 in the permanent rank of major-general.

This bitter blow was almost certainly a blessing in disguise, since it forced him to turn his hand to business, at which, through the influence of friends and his own natural ability, he was successful, gaining an income which allowed him to indulge in his favourite activities, as a bon viveur, gambler, and sportsman. His first venture was in Southern Rhodesia at the end of 1946 and he moved later to Johannesburg, where he became deputy chairman of Tube Investments Ltd. He left in 1960 to join the tobacco firm Rothmans, as chairman of their subsidiary group in Britain. His first book, *Operation Victory*, published in 1947, was one of the earliest authoritative accounts of the war and ran into seven editions in hardback and three impressions in paperback. His other publications, *African Assignment* (1953), *Generals at War* (1964), and *Brass Hat to Bowler Hat* (1979) were not of the same standard. In addition to his clear and agile mind and his grasp of detail, one of his principal gifts was his ability to bring people of different views and interests together. He himself had an open mind and by nature was inclined to welcome strangers. All who worked with him regarded him with admiration and affection in equal proportions. He was the perfect foil to Montgomery. His imaginative and widely ranging mind, fertile with ideas, was subjected to his master's passion for simplification and concentration on one fundamental issue. He was to Montgomery as Berthier was to Napoleon, and perhaps more.

De Guingand was appointed OBE in 1942, CBE in 1943, KBE in 1944, and CB in 1943. He was awarded the DSO in 1942. He died in Cannes on 29 June 1979.

MICHAEL CARVER

**Sources** N. Hamilton, *Monty*, [1]: *The making of a general, 1887–1942* (1981) • N. Hamilton, *Monty*, [2]: *Master of the battlefield, 1942–1944* (1983) • N. Hamilton, *Monty*, [3]: *The Field Marshal, 1944–1976* (1986) • F. W. de Guingand, *Operation victory* (1947) • F. W. de Guingand, *African assignment* (1953) • F. W. de Guingand, *Generals at War* (1964) • F. W. de Guingand, *Brass hat to bowler hat* (1979) • *The Times* (19 Nov 1979) • private information (2004) • personal knowledge (2004) • b. cert. • Burke, *Peerage* • *WW*

**Archives** King's Lond., Liddell Hart C., military papers | King's Lond., Liddell Hart C., corresp. with Sir B. H. Liddell Hart | FILM IWM FVA, documentary footage • IWM FVA, home footage

**Likenesses** S. Morse-Brown, pencil, 1943, IWM • W. Stoneman, photograph, 1944, NPG [*see illus.*] • J. Pannett, chalk, 1968, NPG

**Guinness, Aileen Sibell Mary**. *See* Plunket, Aileen Sibell Mary (1904–1999).

**Guinness, Sir Alec** (1914–2000), actor, was born at 155 Lauderdale Mansions, Paddington, London, on 2 April 1914, the son of Agnes Cuffe (or de Cuffe, *b.* 1886/7), daughter of Edward Charles Cuffe RN. When Alec was five his mother married David Daniel Stiven (*b.* 1880/81), a lieutenant in the Royal Army Service Corps. He was known as Alec Stiven until he was fourteen, when he was told casually that his real name was Guinness.

There has been much speculation about the identity of Guinness's father, with strenuous efforts made to link him with the brewing Guinness family, but the name of his father has never been established. There is no doubt that Guinness's somewhat shadowy background contributed a certain opacity to many of the roles he subsequently played during his career as an actor, on the stage, in films, and on television.

Guinness was educated at Pembroke Lodge, Southbourne, and at Roborough in Eastbourne. His headmaster pulled a few strings and Guinness was taken on as a copywriter at Ark's Publicity, an advertising agency in Lincoln's Inn Fields, London. 'I was paid a pound a week, later rising to thirty shillings, for generally making a hash of my job.' And, once a week, Guinness went to the theatre, usually to the Old Vic, where one could get in for sixpence. He had had his first real taste of the theatre in Bournemouth in 1930, seeing Sybil Thorndike and her husband, Lewis Casson, in a melodrama called *The Squall* and in Ibsen's *Ghosts*.

With surprising bravado, Guinness telephoned John Gielgud, whom he had never met, and asked his advice. Gielgud, possibly thinking that his young caller was indeed a member of the brewing family, suggested he try

Sir Alec Guinness (1914–2000), by Anthony Buckley, 1948

Martita Hunt, as she needed the money. After an agonizing interview Hunt agreed to coach him at a pound an hour. She suggested that he should apply to the Royal Academy of Dramatic Art for a scholarship, but as one was not available that year he enrolled at the Fay Compton School. Guinness's first stage appearance was in *Libel!* at the Playhouse Theatre. However, it was Gielgud who gave him his first real part, as Osric in *Hamlet* at the New Theatre in 1934 (something of an improvement after playing a Chinese coolie, a French pirate, and an English sailor in Noel Langley's *Queer Cargo*).

In the following year Guinness appeared in André Obey's *Noah*, under the direction of Michel Saint-Denis, and in Gielgud's production of *Romeo and Juliet*; in 1936 he appeared in Chekhov's *The Seagull*, directed by Komisarjevsky. The last three years before the outbreak of the Second World War saw Guinness establish himself in a string of classic plays, mainly at the Old Vic and the Queen's Theatre. His directors included Saint-Denis, Gielgud, and, most significantly, Tyrone Guthrie. Parts in *Love's Labour's Lost*, *As You Like It*, *The Witch of Edmonton*, *Hamlet* (Osric again), *Twelfth Night*, *Henry V*, *Richard II*, *The School for Scandal* (Snake), *The Three Sisters*, *The Merchant of Venice*, *The Doctor's Dilemma* (Louis Dubedat), *Trelawny of the 'Wells'*, and *The Rivals* (Bob Acres) followed in rapid succession. The culminating point was his Hamlet in Guthrie's famous—some would say notorious—modern-dress production at the Old Vic in 1938. The critic James Agate wrote that Guinness's portrayal 'had a value of its own' (*The Guardian*).

On 20 June 1938, Guinness married the artist Merula Sylvia Salaman (1914–2000), whom he had met when they were both playing in *Noah* (he was a wolf, she a tiger). She was born on 16 October 1914, the daughter of Major Michael Hewitt Salaman, of the Royal North Devon hussars yeomanry, and his wife, Chattie, daughter of Colonel Edward Baldwin Wake of the 21st hussars, and a descendant of Hereward the Wake. Both of her parents had been at the Slade School of Art (with Augustus John) and her brother Michael exhibited alongside Picasso, Braque, Bonnard, and Dufy. Merula Guinness's own career as an artist began to flourish after the Second World War. In the meantime she toured with her husband. In 1940 their son Matthew was born.

In 1939 Guinness appeared in W. H. Auden's and Christopher Isherwood's *The Ascent of F6* at the Old Vic and played Herbert Pocket in his own adaptation of Dickens's *Great Expectations*, performed at the Rudolf Steiner Hall (his other adaptation was of Dostoievsky's *The Brothers Karamazov*). Guinness joined the Royal Navy as a rating in 1941, and was commissioned in the following year. He later commanded a landing craft taking supplies to Yugoslav partisans. During the war the Admiralty temporarily released Guinness in 1942 so that he could appear on Broadway in Terence Rattigan's *Flare Path*. His account of his naval career, in *Blessings in Disguise*, was entitled 'Damage to the Allied Cause', but action mainly in the Mediterranean was not without its moments of drama and even bravery.

Between 1946 and 1948 Guinness was at the New Theatre, playing the Fool in Laurence Olivier's production of *King Lear*, Eric Birling in J. B. Priestley's *An Inspector Calls*, De Guiche in Tyrone Guthrie's production of *Cyrano de Bergerac*, Abel Drugger in Ben Jonson's *The Alchemist*, Richard II under Ralph Richardson's direction, the Dauphin in Shaw's *Saint Joan*, and roles in *The Government Inspector* and *Coriolanus*; he himself directed *Twelfth Night*.

**First film roles** The year 1946 also saw a major departure in Guinness's career. David Lean cast him as Herbert Pocket in his hugely successful film of *Great Expectations* with John Mills as Pip. This was followed by one of Guinness's greatest roles, that of Fagin in *Oliver Twist* (1948), also directed by Lean. In later years Guinness's portrayal was much criticized as an example of antisemitic stage Jewishness. Many years afterwards he received similar criticism for his role as Professor Godbole in *A Passage to India* (1984), a film which Guinness hated so much that he had to leave the première in America to be physically sick. Guinness's next role—or rather roles—on celluloid brooked no criticism. In Robert Hamer's *Kind Hearts and Coronets* (1949) Guinness was able to exhibit his talent for characterization by playing all eight members of the d'Ascoyne family who, one by one, are killed off by the murderous Dennis Price. The phrase *tour de force* is almost a cliché, but here it was entirely deserved. *Kind Hearts and Coronets* is one of the classics of film comedy.

The 1950s were a golden age for Ealing comedies and for Alec Guinness. Roles in *The Lavender Hill Mob* (1951), the rather surreal *Man in the White Suit* (1951), and *The Ladykillers* (1955) followed over the next five years. Despite these successes, Guinness remained an enigma. According to one obituarist, 'A reluctance to expose himself, an almost neurotic discretion, was famously the mark of both his professional and his personal style' (*The Guardian*). Another considered that 'even in his more extrovert roles, he seemed to preserve the marrow of his anonymity' (*The Independent*). Guinness did not neglect the stage. He appeared in T. S. Eliot's *The Cocktail Party*, in the title role of another *Hamlet*, in more Shakespeare at Tyrone Guthrie's festival at Stratford, Ontario, in Bridget Boland's powerful *The Cardinal* and Feydeau's *Hotel Paradiso*, and perhaps most memorably in Terence Rattigan's *Ross*, with Guinness as another enigma, T. E. Lawrence. But the cinema took up more and more of Guinness's time. There were a few comedies, *Father Brown* (1954), *The Swan* (1956), *Barnacle Bill* (1957); a war film, *Malta Story* (1953); a melodrama, *The Scapegoat*, from Daphne du Maurier's novel. But there were also three outstanding performances: as Gulley Jimson, the anarchic painter in *The Horse's Mouth* (1958), adapted by Guinness himself from Joyce Cary's novel; as Wormald, the innocent salesman dragged into a world of spies and counter-spies in Graham Greene's *Our Man in Havana* (1960); and as Colonel Nicholson in *The Bridge on the River Kwai* (1957). Guinness's portrayal of a brave, stiff-necked, perverse army officer in Japanese hands during the Second World War was another *tour de force*, and it won him the Oscar for best actor.

Then, almost as if to show a completely different side to the military psyche, Guinness took the part, in *Tunes of Glory* (1960), of a heavy-drinking, loud-mouthed, risen-from-the-ranks officer, in perfect juxtaposition to John Mills's well-meaning, humourless, ultimately tragic incomer. Other films of this period were less satisfactory: the overblown *Doctor Zhivago* (1965), a (brilliant) cameo role in *Lawrence of Arabia* (1962), a dignified Charles I in *Cromwell* (1970), the rather feeble *Comedians* (1967) from another Graham Greene novel, Marcus Aurelius in *The Fall of the Roman Empire* (1964), Marley's Ghost in *Scrooge* (1970). Of considerably more substance were his appearances on the stage in Arthur Miller's *Incident at Vichy* in 1966, John Mortimer's *A Voyage Round my Father* in 1969, and Simon Gray's *Wise Child* (1967), in which Guinness appeared, greatly to his fans' amazement, as the transvestite criminal Mrs Artminster. There was a disastrous Macbeth (with Simone Signoret as a very Gallic Lady Macbeth), at the Royal Court Theatre, London, in 1966.

**Popular success** 1973 brought the first of Guinness's collaborations with Alan Bennett. *Habeas Corpus* revealed Guinness in another unexpected guise, playing a randy dentist and doing a very neat dance in grey top hat and morning coat. But it was the film *Star Wars* (1977) that made Guinness an international star, and which also, through a shrewd contractual clause, bolstered his finances until his death. At first reluctant to take on the role of Obi-Wan Kenobi, he was won over by the director–producer George Lucas. Guinness was now seen by millions who had never heard of *Kind Hearts and Coronets* or *The Bridge on the River Kwai*, and he forbade any mention of the film by his friends. Once, famously, he was asked for his autograph by an eager mother and her small son. Eventually Guinness agreed to sign—but on one condition: the boy should never see *Star Wars* again. Inevitably there were floods of tears. Guinness nevertheless appeared in the sequels *The Empire Strikes Back* (1980) and *The Return of the Jedi* (1983).

On the stage Guinness appeared in another Alan Bennett play, *The Old Country* (1977), playing a retired spy; and in Julian Mitchell's adaptation of Ivy Compton-Burnett's *A Family and a Fortune*. In 1979 he found yet another vast audience, this time through his immensely subtle performance as the inscrutable George Smiley in the television adaptation of John le Carré's *Tinker, Tailor, Soldier, Spy*, which was followed in 1981 by *Smiley's People*.

With Alan Strachan, Guinness devised a not entirely successful one-man show as Dean Swift, *Yahoo* (1976); there was a final Shakespeare role, Shylock at Chichester; a superb piece of acting as old Mr Dorrit; and a sinister cameo role as the appalling Mr Todd in Evelyn Waugh's *A Handful of Dust*. His last appearance was for television, in Jack Rosenthal's *Eskimo Day* in 1996.

Alec Guinness displayed his other talent, as a writer. In a highly selective memoir, *Blessings in Disguise* (1985), he showed that he was a master of the anecdote, and equally a master of disguise. In a series of episodes and pen portraits, who was out was often more remarkable than who was in: Gielgud and Richardson were included, of course, but not Laurence Olivier. One chapter, about a lunch with the travel writer Freya Stark in Asolo, had to be omitted because of his contention that she had tried to poison him with snake venom (it was restored in a later edition once the presumed poisoner was safely dead). The book was a bestseller, as were *My Name Escapes Me* (1997) and *A Positively Final Appearance* (1999), both of which were culled from the diaries he kept. A final work, *A Commonplace Book*, was published in 2001.

Religious faith was a vital element in Guinness's life. He was received into the Roman Catholic church in 1956, and his wife, Merula, followed him soon afterwards. She had long abandoned her theatrical career, but had developed her remarkable talent as an artist. She specialized in naive paintings, often creating wonderfully simple, colourful images in the form of miniature tapestries. Animals, favoured saints such as St Jerome, and nature were her most frequent subjects. She showed mainly at the Crane Kalman Gallery in Knightsbridge, but in 1997 her pictures were included in a Salaman family exhibition at Gallery 27 in Cork Street. She hated London, rarely accompanying her husband on his frequent forays in search of entertainment, books, friends, and a bit of luxury at the Connaught Hotel. She preferred to remain at their house near Petersfield in Hampshire, tending her goats and dogs.

**Death and assessment** Guinness died from cancer in The King Edward VII Hospital, Easebourne, near Midhurst, Sussex, on 5 August 2000, and was buried in Petersfield, Hampshire; his wife, Merula, died only a few months later on 18 October. He had been knighted in 1959, appointed CBE in 1955, and made a Companion of Honour in 1994. As an actor on the stage he was the equal of Laurence Olivier,

John Gielgud, Ralph Richardson, Michael Redgrave, and Paul Scofield. But it was as an actor in films and on television that Guinness soared. His range was extraordinary, and his ability to absorb himself in his roles, so that they became him rather than the reverse, was unsurpassed. In *Blessings in Disguise*, he wrote:

> It would be impossible to define in what way, exactly, I have been influenced by John Gielgud, for instance, or Guthrie, Komisarjevsky, Basil Dean, Michel Saint-Denis or a host of others. They have all left an indelible mark and I count myself lucky in having crossed their paths. Perhaps Edith Evans, Leon Quartermain, Ernest Milton and Ralph Richardson were the performers to whose lightest word, professionally, I paid most attention.

And in another passage he revealed an innate modesty and self-awareness:

> He is well aware that he is not in the same class as Olivier, Richardson, Gielgud or the other Greats. His pleasure is in putting little bits of things together, as if playing with a jigsaw puzzle.

It was, though, a more complex jigsaw puzzle than met the eye. Like all great actors, Guinness was a mixture—of the vulnerable and the self-assertive, of the public and the intensely private. He was a stickler for punctuality and for good service in restaurants, of which he was a connoisseur. He was a wonderful host, but a nervous guest. He combined touches of flamboyance with a fervent desire for anonymity. He hated cant, change (which in his opinion was almost always for the worse), and assaults on the English language, particularly on the BBC. He had extraordinary courtesy but could be very sharp with people who offended him. The layers and subtleties of his complex personality contributed immensely to his unique qualities as an actor. Indeed, his skill as an actor was such that it becomes difficult to know just who was the 'real' Alec Guinness. CHRISTOPHER SINCLAIR-STEVENSON

**Sources** A. Guinness, *Blessings in disguise* (1985) • J. R. Taylor, *Alec Guinness: a celebration* (1994) • *Alec: a birthday present for Alec Guinness* (1994) • A. Guinness, *My name escapes me: the diary of a retiring actor* (1997) • A. Guinness, *A positively final appearance: a journal, 1996–98* (1999) • A. Guinness, *A commonplace book* (2001) • *WW* • b. cert. • m. cert. • d. cert. • m. cert. [Agnes Cuffe, mother] • *The Guardian* (8 Aug 2000) • *The Independent* (8 Aug 2000) • *The Times* (8 Aug 2000) • *Daily Telegraph* (8 Aug 2000) • private information (2004) [family]

**Archives** priv. coll. | BL, corresp. with Sir Sydney Cockerell, Add. MS 52717 • Georgetown University, Lauinger Library, letters to Elizabeth Jennings | FILM BFI NFTVA, 'Parkinson: the interviews', BBC 1, 10 Oct 1997 • BFI NFTVA, Legends, ITV, 14 Aug 2001 | SOUND BL NSA, performance recordings

**Likenesses** A. Buckley, photograph, 1948, NPG [*see illus.*] • A. Newman, bromide print, 1978, NPG • E. Frink, bronze bust, 1984, NPG • D. Hill, oils, NPG • photographs, Hult. Arch.

**Guinness, Arthur** (1725–1803). *See under* Guinness, Arthur (1768–1855).

**Guinness, Arthur** (1768–1855), brewer and banker, was born on 12 March 1768 in Dublin, the second son of the surviving six sons and four daughters of the twenty-one children born to **Arthur Guinness** (1725–1803), brewer, and his wife, Olivia (*d.* 1814), the well-connected daughter and coheir of William Whitmore of Dublin. Arthur Guinness senior was the son of Richard Guinness, agent and receiver of Dr Arthur Price (*d.* 1752), archbishop of Cashel, and his wife, Elizabeth Read (1698–1742). He received a legacy of £100 from Dr Price's estate, and this helped him start up in brewing; by 1755 he was running a small brewery in Leixlip, near Dublin. Four years later he obtained a lease on a long established brewery in James's Gate (or St James's Gate), Dublin, which, with his name, was to become famous worldwide. Although the brewery was not large and had been out of production for several years, Guinness quickly turned around its affairs. Within four years he had been elected warden of the Dublin Corporation of Brewers (he was master in 1768); in 1764 he bought a country house at Beaumont, on the northern shore of Dublin Bay.

Brewers in Dublin faced many difficult years between 1772 and 1795, but when the beer duty was removed in 1795 and the Irish pound devalued two years later, the large inputs of English beer began to contract sharply. By the late 1790s Guinness's had an output of some 12,000 barrels a year which generated generous profits of some £6000 a year. In addition, Arthur Guinness senior had invested in a flourishing flour-milling business at Kilmainham. Like generations of later Guinnesses, his interests were not narrowly focused on the brewery. As an evangelical Christian he was involved in charitable effort: he was governor of Meath Hospital; he began the firm's long association with St Patrick's Cathedral, Dublin (his eldest son, Hosea, was its chancellor); and he opened the first Sunday school in Ireland in 1786. His last years were spent at Beaumont, and the firm and his family's wealth (he left some £25,000) were well established on his death on 23 January 1803.

Of his six sons, three were active in the brewery: Arthur, Benjamin (1777–1826), and William Lunell (1779–1842). Arthur was the key figure, 'shrewd, forthright and immensely able' (Lynch and Vaizey, 104). He was as prominent in Irish banking circles as he was in brewing. Director of the Bank of Ireland in 1808, he served as governor from 1820, giving evidence as an exponent of the currency school to the House of Lords committee into the state and value of promissory notes in Scotland and Ireland (1826). The firm suffered a rough decade after 1815, partly as a result of Arthur's preoccupation with banking matters, but more as a consequence of the post-1815 recession. Certainly, Guinness's sales contracted by almost 60 per cent between 1815 and the low point of 1823 when only 27,185 barrels were sold. Thereafter, as a result above all of exploiting sales of extra-stout in the English market by a network of pushing, independent agents in major ports and cities (especially London, Liverpool, and Bristol), sales took off. By the early 1840s when Arthur had handed over the day-to-day management at James's Gate to his third son, Benjamin Lee *Guinness, they were averaging around 73,000 barrels. By the time of Arthur's death in 1855, sales had exceeded well over 100,000 barrels for the previous five years. With over half their sales in England and Scotland, Guinness was largely unaffected by the great famine. Arthur Guinness junior was undoubtedly the firm's chief architect, turning it by 1840 into the biggest business enterprise in Ireland. Much more able than his brothers, he basically brewed two types of stout of superb quality and vigorously marketed them in the Dublin region and in England.

Guinness was twice married. His first wife, whom he married on 7 May 1793, was Anne, eldest daughter and coheir of Benjamin Lee of Merrion, co. Dublin; they had three sons and six daughters. She died on 21 February 1817 and four years later he married Maria Barker, who predeceased him in 1837. Guinness's eldest son, William Smythe Lee Grattan Guinness (1795–1864), like many of his family, became a clerk in holy orders. His second son, Arthur Lee (1797–1863), was a bachelor with artistic leanings who withdrew from the brewery partnership in 1838 in some financial disarray. His pro-Catholic politics and associates proved to be too extreme for his younger brother, Benjamin Lee Guinness, and his father, a deeply pious evangelical member of the Church of Ireland, for whom religion was a central feature of life.

As paterfamilias of the Guinness clan, with over forty nieces and nephews, Arthur Guinness held a large and somewhat feckless family together, providing affection and counsel, financial and spiritual advice in equal quantities. Politically a liberal, advocating Catholic emancipation and parliamentary reform, he stopped well short of supporting Daniel O'Connell's moves in the late 1830s to repeal the union. He was a man of wide interests, prominent in the charitable and business life of Dublin (but uninterested in its social whirl). A member of the Farming Society of Ireland, he bought large estates in Wicklow and Wexford. He never sought election to parliament and discouraged his son, Benjamin Lee, from doing so. He died in Dublin on 9 June 1855. R. G. Wilson

**Sources** P. Lynch and J. Vaizey, *Guinness's brewery in the Irish economy, 1759–1876* (1960) • M. Guinness, *The Guinness legend* (1989) • GEC, *Peerage* • Burke, *Gen. GB* (1937)

**Likenesses** J. C. Miles, portrait, repro. in Lynch and Vaizey, *Guinness's brewery*, frontispiece • G. Sanders, mezzotint (after F. W. Burton), NG Ire. • portrait, repro. in Lynch and Vaizey, *Guinness's brewery*, facing p. 70

**Wealth at death** £150,000: Lynch and Vaizey, *Guinness's brewery*, 147 • approx. £25,000; Arthur Guinness: Lynch and Vaizey, *Guinness's brewery*, 147

**Guinness, Arthur Edward**, Baron Ardilaun (1840–1915), politician and philanthropist, was the eldest son of Sir Benjamin Lee *Guinness, first baronet (1798–1868), MP, and his wife, Elizabeth (*d.* 1865), daughter of Edward Guinness, of Dublin. He was born at St Anne's, Clontarf, co. Dublin, on 1 November 1840 and was educated at Eton and at Trinity College, Dublin, where he graduated in 1862. Upon the death of his father in 1868 he succeeded as second baronet and became the head of the famous brewery at St James's Gate, Dublin, founded by his grandfather. He lacked interest in industrial management, however, and took advantage of a new deed drawn up in 1876 to retire in favour of his brother Edward Cecil *Guinness (later earl of Iveagh).

Guinness was returned unopposed as Conservative MP for Dublin city in his father's place in May 1868. In 1869 he lost the seat after a petition. Guinness's political campaigns were known for the marshalling of brewery workers at the polls, and for extravagant expenditure. He re-entered parliament for Dublin city at the general election in 1874 and held the seat until defeated in 1880, when he was raised to the peerage as Baron Ardilaun, of Ashford, co. Galway. On 16 February 1871 he married Lady Olivia Charlotte White (1850–1925), daughter of the third earl of Bantry.

Guinness's devotion to the interests of the city of Dublin was conspicuous from the beginning of his public life. In 1872, with his brother, he originated, and took financial responsibility for, the Dublin Exhibition of Arts and Science. He completed the restoration, begun by his father, of Archbishop Marsh's Library. In 1877 he rebuilt the Coombe Lying-in Hospital, and the building by the government of the Science and Art Museum in Dublin was due to his advocacy in the House of Commons. He took a practical interest in the improvement of working-class housing and was president of the artisans' dwellings company, the first company inaugurated in Dublin for this purpose. It was, however, alleged by the crown solicitor in 1872 that his chairmanship of the first Dublin sewerage company was motivated by personal financial interest.

It was entirely due to Guinness that the beautiful public park of some 22 acres known as St Stephen's Green was acquired, laid out, and handed over under a special act of parliament for the use of the citizens of Dublin. In 1899 he purchased the Muckross estate, co. Kerry, which adjoins the lakes of Killarney, in order to save it and the lakes from falling into the hands of a commercial syndicate.

Lord Ardilaun was a generous supporter of the Church of Ireland. At the time of its disestablishment he contributed largely to its capital funds, and up to his death he bore half the expense of the choir of St Patrick's Cathedral. From 1897 to 1913 he was president of the Royal Dublin Society; the publication of the society's history was due to his initiative and liberality. In 1900 Ardilaun became the proprietor of the *Dublin Daily Express* and the *Dublin Evening Mail*, which were fervently Unionist in tone. He was so staunch a Conservative that in 1898 he declined to accept the lieutenancy of county Dublin, because it was offered to him by a Conservative lord lieutenant of Ireland (Earl Cadogan) at a moment when the loyalists of Ireland felt bitterly that their cause had been betrayed by Lord Salisbury's government. In 1900 he financed and helped organize an electoral revolt against the constructive Unionist MP Horace Plunkett and the government's conciliation policy. The consequence was the loss of the last two Unionist Dublin seats to the nationalists.

Ardilaun's principal seat was at St Anne's, Clontarf, where he and Lady Ardilaun entertained generously and received in 1900 a visit from Queen Victoria. A large part of each year he spent on his Galway estate at Ashford, where he used the income derived from industrial profits to give employment on a large scale, in making roads and planting trees. He also maintained for many years a steamer on Lough Corrib between Cong and Galway for the benefit of his tenants and the neighbourhood.

Lord Ardilaun died, childless, on 20 January 1915 at St Anne's, Clontarf, and was buried in the mortuary chapel attached to the church of All Saints, which he had built on his co. Dublin estate. The barony became extinct, and he was succeeded as third baronet by his nephew Sir Algernon Arthur St Lawence Lee Guinness (1883–1954).

B. J. PLUNKET, *rev.* PETER GRAY

**Sources** P. Lynch and J. Vaizey, *Guinness's brewery in the Irish economy, 1759–1876* (1960) • A. Gailey, *Ireland and the death of kindness: the experience of constructive unionism, 1890–1905* (1987) • K. T. Hoppen, *Elections, politics, and society in Ireland, 1832–1885* (1984) • M. E. Daly, *Dublin: the deposed capital—a social and economic history, 1860–1914* (1984) • *Annual Register* (1915) • *The Times* (21 Jan 1915) • H. S. Guinness and B. Guinness, *The Guinness family*, 3 vols. (1953–69) • GEC, *Peerage* • Burke, *Peerage* (1939)
**Archives** Business Archive Council, London
**Likenesses** T. Farrell, bronze statue, 1891, St Stephen's Green, Dublin • W. Orpen, portrait, *c.*1913, Royal Dublin Society • lithograph, NPG
**Wealth at death** £495,638 2*s.* 9*d.*: probate, 7 April 1915, *CGPLA Ire.*

**Guinness, (Arthur Francis) Benjamin, third earl of Iveagh (1937–1992)**, brewing company chairman, was born on 20 May 1937 at Elveden Hall, Suffolk, the only son of Arthur Onslow Edward Guinness, Viscount Elveden (1912–1945) and Lady Elizabeth Cecilia Hare, younger sister of William, fifth earl of Listowel, a prominent Labour peer. On 8 February 1945 Arthur Guinness, serving with the allied forces at Nijmegen, was killed by a stray German V2 rocket. Benjamin, as he was always called, was then only seven, and became heir presumptive to a title, an immense fortune, large estates in England and Ireland, and the management of a major international commercial enterprise. He lacked the qualities necessary for shouldering such a burden.

Benjamin Guinness's grandfather, Rupert Edward Cecil Lee *Guinness, second earl of Iveagh and head of the dynasty, had lost a brother and two sons in tragic circumstances. He was determined that Benjamin should be groomed to undertake all the responsibilities that family tradition demanded, even though there were other male members of the extensive clan who could have shared these duties. As well as being chairman of the brewery, an active member of the House of Lords, and a prominent philanthropist, Rupert was a leading agricultural reformer. Thus at Eton, and later at Trinity College, Cambridge, the almost pathologically shy Benjamin, who had a passion for history and art, was steered into scientific studies.

As soon as he was twenty-one he was taken onto the brewery board. In 1960 he was appointed assistant managing director of the parent company and two years later his 88-year-old grandfather yielded the chairmanship into his hands. On 12 March 1963 he married Miranda Daphne Jane, daughter of Major Michael Smiley of Castle Fraser, Aberdeenshire. They had two sons and two daughters. In 1967 Benjamin inherited the earldom. It was his misfortune to be thrust into commercial prominence at a time when a new, aggressive, acquisitive spirit was spreading throughout the world of international corporate business. Take-overs and mergers were the order of the day. The era of family concerns run by benevolent proprietors as personal fiefdoms was passing rapidly. Over the next decade Arthur Guinness, Son & Co. diversified and expanded into new markets in its efforts to maintain a lead role among the multinationals, but by the 1980s it was obvious that the company needed to recruit leaders from among the new-style dynamic and ruthless managers who understood the changed rules of the game.

Lord Iveagh had already distanced himself from the brewery and his other English responsibilities. After 1974 he lived permanently on his estate of Farmleigh, near Dublin, for tax reasons, and he subsequently took out Irish citizenship. He was from 1973 to 1977 a member of the Irish senate, thus enjoying the rare distinction of being a member of both the British and the Irish legislature. In 1984 he sold (for £5.7 million) the contents of Elveden Hall, the Suffolk mansion where he had been brought up and where his grandfather and great-grandfather had regularly entertained the leaders of society. At Farmleigh he was able to escape the pressures of big business and enjoy those pastimes close to his heart—racing, farming, and collecting antiquarian books. However, these panaceas could not preserve his health. He had been diagnosed as suffering from diverticulitis, and over the years underwent thirteen operations.

In 1981 Lord Iveagh appointed Edward Saunders as chief executive of the Guinness conglomerate and was content to leave management entirely in the hands of this resourceful, go-getting entrepreneur. The new man restructured the company and dramatically revived Guinness fortunes. At the height of his power he masterminded a management reorganization which elevated himself to the position of chairman and Benjamin to the newly created post of president, effectively shorn of the last vestiges of real power. Within weeks the baroque edifice began to crumble. Saunders's major coup had been the takeover of the Distillers Co. Ltd, but soon afterwards a Department of Trade and Industry enquiry produced evidence of alleged financial misconduct. This led, in 1990, to one of the most sensational and acrimonious trials in British commercial history. It would be over-dramatic to claim that this was the last straw for Lord Iveagh. He was already a broken man. He had taken to heavy drinking and smoking and now succumbed to cancer of the throat. The Iveaghs' marriage had collapsed in 1984, but his former wife nursed Benjamin through the final stages of his illness. Death came on 18 June 1992, in London, three weeks after he had resigned from the Guinness board, the last member of the family to be associated with a company founded by his great-great-great-great-grandfather in 1759.

DEREK WILSON

**Sources** private information (2004) [the earl of Iveagh; C. E. Guinness] • D. Donaldson and I. Watt, *Guinness plc: investigation under sections 432(2) and 442 of the Companies Act, 1985* (1997) • D. Wilson, *Dark and light: the story of the Guinness family* (1998) • *The Times* (20 June 1992) • *The Independent* (4 July 1992) • *The Independent* (3 Aug 1992)
**Likenesses** oils, Park Royal Brewery, London

**Wealth at death** £13,946,423: probate, 10 Dec 1992, *CGPLA Eng. & Wales*

**Guinness, Sir Benjamin Lee, first baronet (1798–1868),** brewer, was born in Dublin on 1 November 1798, the third son of Arthur *Guinness (1768–1855), brewer, and his wife, Anne, eldest daughter and coheir of Benjamin Lee of Merrion, co. Dublin. He began his apprenticeship in the brewery at the age of sixteen and was admitted to a partnership six years later. Although his father survived for another thirty-five years and was in the words of the firm's historians 'the main architect of the firm' (Lynch and Vaizey, 248), Benjamin Lee also played a leading part. He was astute and competent and, although shy, essentially a more sociable animal than his father and grandfather, and if religion appeared to remain the cornerstone of his life, with prayers said at home twice daily, he was a less committed Christian than other members of his family. He has been described as the first Guinness to achieve 'a serene equipoise between God and Mammon which has ever since been the hallmark of his family' (Guinness, 61).

Effectively taking over the management of Arthur Guinness & Sons about 1840 and ably assisted by his partners John Purser junior and John Tertius Purser, Benjamin Lee Guinness saw the firm's output burgeon in the next quarter of a century, so that on his death he was reckoned to be Ireland's richest inhabitant. Certainly, sales of Guinness grew almost fivefold from an annual average of 72,877 barrels in the years 1840–44 to 341,572 in 1865–9. Expansion was on all fronts: in Dublin, in Britain, and, above all, across Ireland after 1850. Here beer was distributed by the new railways through an expanding network of agencies and stores. The firm, with fewer than ten tied houses in Dublin, offered only tiny discounts (unlike its British counterparts) and undertook the most minimal advertising (it adopted Brian Bóruma's harp as its famous trademark in 1862). Basically it relied on the fame and excellence of its two main beers, single and double stout, and its salesmen, agents, and bottlers.

Benjamin Lee Guinness achieved a new level of prominence for the Guinness family in Ireland. In 1851 he was elected the first lord mayor of Dublin under the reformed corporation, carrying out his duties with great state. Late in 1861 he began, at his own expense, the complete restoration of St Patrick's Cathedral, Dublin, one of Ireland's national monuments which was then in a near derelict state. He supervised the work himself, spending a colossal £150,000 on its repair. When it was reopened with a great service on 24 February 1865 Lord Wodehouse, the lord lieutenant of Ireland, said that:

> work which was too great for the knights of St Patrick, or for the Ecclesiastical Commissioners, or the Bench of Bishops, which the Irish Parliament refused to undertake and which the British Parliament never entertained the thought of executing has been accomplished within four years by a single merchant. (Lynch and Vaizey, 181)

Guinness's stock in Dublin stood high.

In 1866 Guinness was given an honorary doctorate of

**Sir Benjamin Lee Guinness, first baronet (1798–1868),** by Isaac Parkes

law by the University of Dublin, and in April 1867 was created a baronet. Two years earlier he had been elected member of parliament for Dublin in the Conservative interest, and continued to represent the city until his death. The citizens of Dublin and the dean and chapter of St Patrick's presented him with addresses (afterwards exhibited at the Paris Exhibition) on 31 December 1865 expressive of gratitude for what he had done for the city. He was one of the ecclesiastical commissioners for Ireland, a governor of Simpson's Hospital, and vice-chairman of the Dublin Exhibition Palace. At the time of his death Sir Benjamin was engaged in the restoration of Archbishop Marsh's Public Library, a building adjoining St Patrick's Cathedral. He demonstrated his practical interest in Irish archaeology by carefully preserving the antiquarian remains existing on his estates in co. Galway. He was generous both to charity and to his own large extended family.

In 1837 Guinness married his first cousin Elizabeth (*d.* 1865), third daughter of Edward Guinness (1772–1833) whom the family biographer categorized as the first of a long line of Guinness black sheep (Guinness, 11). Extremely devout and frequently ailing, Benjamin was devoted to Bessie, as his wife was known. They had a daughter, Ann, who married the fourth Lord Plunket, archbishop of Dublin, and three sons: Arthur Edward *Guinness who succeeded as second baronet, and was created Lord Ardilaun in 1880; (Benjamin) Lee who never went into the business and like his elder siblings married into the Irish aristocracy; and Edward Cecil *Guinness, first earl of Iveagh.

Sir Benjamin Lee Guinness died at his London residence, 27 Norfolk Street, Park Lane, on 19 May 1868 and was buried in the family vault in Mount Jerome cemetery, Dublin, on 27 May. The direction of the great firm passed to his eldest and youngest sons. The eldest, Arthur Lee, succeeded to the family estates in co. Galway and co. Mayo which Benjamin had acquired (30,858 acres in 1883), the youngest, Edward Cecil, to the great Guinness town house in Dublin, 80 St Stephen's Green. On his death, the firm was on the eve of its most notable period of expansion, his family, with its vast wealth, about to be catapulted into the Anglo-Irish aristocracy. No other family or firm, except perhaps the Rothschilds, better illustrates the place of the plutocracy of new money in late Victorian and Edwardian Britain than the Guinnesses.

G. C. Boase, *rev.* R. G. Wilson

**Sources** P. Lynch and J. Vaizey, *Guinness's brewery in the Irish economy, 1759–1876* (1960) • T. R. Gourvish and R. G. Wilson, *The British brewing industry, 1830–1980* (1994) • M. Guinness, *The Guinness legend* (1989) • GEC, *Peerage* [Ardilaun; Iveagh] • *Dod's Peerage* (1917) • *DNB* • *CGPLA Eng. & Wales* (1868)

**Archives** Arthur Guinness, Son & Co. Ltd, London

**Likenesses** J. H. Foley, bronze statue, *c*.1875, St Patrick's Cathedral churchyard, Dublin • I. Parkes, bronze medallion, National Museum of Ireland, Dublin [*see illus.*] • photograph, repro. in Lynch and Vaizey, *Guinness's brewery*, 178 • wood-engraving, NPG; repro. in *ILN* (1865)

**Wealth at death** under £60,000 in England: Irish probate resworn in England, June 1869, *CGPLA Eng. & Wales* • under £1,100,000: *DNB*; Lynch and Vaizey, *Guinness's brewery*

**Guinness, Bryan Walter**, second Baron Moyne (1905–1992), poet and novelist, was born on 27 October 1905 at 11 Grosvenor Place, London, the eldest of three children of Walter Edward *Guinness (1880–1944), MP, later first Baron Moyne of Bury St Edmunds, and his wife, Lady Evelyn Hilda Stuart, *née* Erskine (1883–1939), daughter of the fourteenth earl of Buchan.

A sensitive boy, Guinness loathed his preparatory school. Perhaps the most effective scene in his novels is the passage in *Landscape with Figures* (1934) which describes the torments of his dormitory. At Eton, one morning at chapel, he suddenly found he was unable to get off his knees; this was the start of an attack of polio which set him back academically and made participation in games impossible. The late diagnosis of the disease—the fault of his Eton dame who thought he was malingering—meant that he never grew to his full height. His father, who was tiny, good-looking, and perfectly proportioned, was known as 'the pocket Adonis'. Bryan Guinness inherited his father's piercing blue eyes and handsome features but not his proportions: his feet and hands were too big and he should have been a few inches taller. He was nevertheless a graceful dancer, and when he waltzed with his mother the whole ballroom would stop to watch. Oxford he enjoyed; he belonged to the 'Brideshead generation' with Evelyn Waugh, Brian Howard, and Harold Acton. However, he worried his mother because he underspent his allowance, a worry uncommon for most parents of an undergraduate. It was an early sign of his shrinking dread of ostentation.

After leaving Christ Church with a degree in French and German, Guinness read for the bar. He also went to dances, at one of which, in 1928, he met the eighteen-year-old Diana Freeman-Mitford (1910–2003), daughter of David Bertram Ogilvy Freeman-Mitford, second Baron Redesdale (1878–1958). They married on 30 January 1929 and had two sons. Diana, freed from the countrified parents that her sister Nancy was to immortalize in her novels, longed for society. Guinness, it became clear, wanted to settle down to enjoy just such a quiet rural life as she had escaped. His poem 'The Cocktail Party' starts:

> Here friendship founders in a sea of 'friends',
> And harsh-lipp'd *bubbly* cannot make amends.

In 1931, discouraged by a colleague who told him that he was unlikely to be given briefs because of his wealth, he left the bar and bought Biddesden House in Wiltshire. In 1932 Diana fell in love with Sir Oswald Mosley, soon to become leader of the British Union of Fascists. She divorced Guinness in 1934. On 21 September 1936, Guinness married Elisabeth Nelson (1912–1999) from Argyll. Her tastes, unlike Diana's, corresponded with his and together they built up the farm and Arabian horse stud at Biddesden. Their happy marriage produced four sons and five daughters.

Guinness had already published his first novel, *Singing out of Tune* (1933), and followed it with *A Week by the Sea* (1936). *Lady Crushwell's Companion* (1938) reflected his increasing interest in farming. The style was graceful and the reviewers were polite, but the novels did not really catch on. Where he did receive some recognition was as a poet, particularly for his collection *Under the Eyelid* (1935). He produced a further six volumes of poetry.

The first of several children's books, *The Story of Johnny and Jemima*, appeared in 1936. Some regard this as Guinness's best work, in which good triumphs over evil with just enough violence to please a child. Illustrated by Roland Pym, it was the start of a fruitful collaboration. Guinness's play, *The Fragrant Concubine*, was performed in the West End in 1938. During the war Guinness was part of the Spears mission and served as liaison officer with the French in Syria. He was in the region when his father, as minister resident in the Middle East, was assassinated by Jewish terrorists. He inherited Knockmaroon, a house overlooking the Liffey near Dublin, and from then on divided his time between Ireland and England, with many journeys abroad. He became vice-chairman of Arthur Guinness, Son & Co. in 1949.

After the war Guinness also produced six more children's books, including *The Children in the Desert* (1946), five novels, and five plays. *A Riverside Charade* was performed at the Abbey Theatre, Dublin, in 1954. His novella, *A Fugue of Cinderellas* (1956), records the gently competing sensibilities of a group of well-meaning people. His *Collected Poems, 1927–1955* was published in 1956. There were also two collections of short stories and three volumes of autobiography, *Dairy not Kept* (1975), *Potpourri from the Thirties* (1982), and *Personal Patchwork* (1986).

One of Guinness's salient characteristics was a real reverence for the arts. He was a governor of the National Gallery of Ireland from 1955 and a member of the Irish Academy of Letters. As Lord Moyne, he was quite assiduous in the House of Lords, although making speeches did not come easily to him. He would be better known as a writer, perhaps, had he managed to suppress his natural kindliness and delicacy and admitted more of the ruthlessness of life into his writing.

Bryan Guinness died at Biddesden House on 6 July 1992; his ashes were buried in Ludgershall churchyard, Wiltshire, on 30 July. *On a Ledge*, his final collection of poems, was published posthumously in 1992.

CHARLOTTE MOSLEY

**Sources** private information (2004) · B. Guinness, *Dairy not kept* (1975) · B. Guinness, *Potpourri from the thirties* (1982) · B. Guinness, *Personal patchwork, 1939–1945* (1986)
**Archives** NRA, priv. coll., corresp. and literary papers
**Likenesses** H. Lamb, group portrait, oils, 1930 (with his family), priv. coll. · H. Lamb, oils, 1955, priv. coll. · R. Pym, group portrait, oils, 1957 (with his family), priv. coll.
**Wealth at death** £12,963: probate, 7 Dec 1992, *CGPLA Eng. & Wales*

**Guinness, Edward Cecil, first earl of Iveagh** (1847–1927), brewer and philanthropist, was born at St Anne's, Clontarf, co. Dublin, on 10 November 1847, the youngest of the three sons of Sir Benjamin Lee *Guinness (1798–1868), brewer, and his wife, Elizabeth (*d.* 1865), third daughter of Edward Guinness of Dublin. Unlike his two elder brothers who went to Eton College, Edward Cecil was taught by tutors in the strict, protestant atmosphere of St Anne's and 80 St Stephen's Green, the great Dublin town house his father bought in 1856. At the age of fifteen he entered the family's St James's Gate brewery and he seems to have acted as Sir Benjamin's secretary. He also attended, part-time, Trinity College, Dublin, where he took his degree with special merit in 1870.

**Early career in brewing** The apple of his father's eye, Edward Guinness was intelligent, serious, and good-looking. He was also, at twenty, immensely rich. Sir Benjamin's fortune, the biggest then recorded in Ireland, was shared after his death principally between Edward and his elder brother Arthur (1840–1915), later first Baron Ardilaun. Together they inherited a brewery producing 350,000 barrels a year (placing it among the largest half-dozen in the United Kingdom); they shared profits of £120,000; and they inherited private fortunes of at least £0.25 million apiece. Arthur was left the family's landed estates in co. Galway while Edward was left to rattle in 80 St Stephen's Green. Very few men have enjoyed greater success in business than Edward Guinness, even fewer have enjoyed affluence on this scale so soon. Great riches did not turn his head. It is clear that his father had picked him out to run the brewery because he was remarkably like himself, 'possessing a capacity for quick decision, a flair for business and an intuitive understanding of men's characters' (Lynch and Vaizey, 236). In fact there was already an effective management system in place at St James's Gate headed by the able and experienced general manager, John Tertius Purser (1809–1893), whose family had been involved in running the brewery for three generations since 1799. Nevertheless, Edward, joint proprietor of the brewery with his brother, was drawn centrally into its affairs. No decision was taken without his approbation.

**Edward Cecil Guinness, first earl of Iveagh** (1847–1927), by Werner & Son, pubd 1903

The late 1860s and early 1870s were wonderful years for brewers. Consumption of beer in Britain and Ireland leapt ahead. The fortunes of the leading firms, Bass, Allsopp, and Guinness grew at an undreamed pace. Guinness's sales soared from 350,000 barrels in 1868 to 779,000 barrels in 1876 (123 per cent), profits from £102,000 to £302,000 (196 per cent). The brewery was extended in 1870 and again in 1876, the old site enlarged by the purchase of land between St James's Street and the River Liffey. Much of the growth came from porter or single stout sales in an Ireland at last enjoying a modest prosperity following the great famine, but also from the sales of double or extra-stout to Britain (about two-fifths of total sales in 1876), promoted by independent agencies and bottlers operating under an exclusive dealing clause.

The Guinness brothers enjoyed their prosperity to the full. Arthur, a fierce unionist, became deeply involved in politics (he was MP for the city of Dublin, 1868–9 and 1874–80), philanthropy, and, later, newspaper proprietorship. In 1871 he married into the Irish aristocracy. Lady Olivia White, daughter of the third earl of Bantry, disliked trade as much as she disapproved of Irish home rule. Certainly after his marriage Arthur's interest in the brewery declined. Increasingly, he seems to have seen the brewery principally as a source of income, extracting no less than £450,000 between 1868 and 1875 (Edward took £345,000). Arthur, hitherto restricted by the terms of his father's will which laid down that if either of his sons withdrew from the firm they should be allowed to extract only a negligible amount of capital from it, allowed Edward to buy him out from the business at the expiration of their first partnership deed. A new valuation of the brewery was made, recognizing its great advance in the past seven years. Arthur, willing to go, was paid the massive sum of £680,000 over four years.

**Marriage and unionist politics** Edward Guinness was now sole proprietor of the second largest brewery in the world; but it by no means confined his horizons. On 20 May 1873 he married a distant cousin three years his senior, Adelaide Maria (*d*. 1916), daughter of Richard *Guinness (1797–1857) of Deepwell, co. Dublin, a well-connected barrister, bankrupt, and one-time MP for Kinsale and Barnstaple. They had three sons. Adelaide was cultured and a great socialite, and together the Guinnesses, sticklers as they were for the social proprieties, threw themselves into the élite whirl of Dublin and London with great zest. Edward already possessed a London house in Berkeley Square; in 1874 he bought Farmleigh on the edge of Phoenix Park, Dublin. By the mid-1870s they were enjoying an annual income of £150,000 and they settled into the routine of the aristocratic super-rich: Dublin and London during their respective seasons, yachting at Cowes, shooting in Scotland, and jaunts to the continent. Somehow Guinness fitted the careful digestion of daily reports from the brewery into this punishing schedule and made precise notes in his pocket books. He was consulted on everything; he was obsessive about detail and little escaped his attention.

Although an unwavering unionist, Edward Guinness was less involved in politics than Arthur, created Baron Ardilaun in 1880 and the first member of the 'beerage'. He too had ambitions for a peerage, however. He was publicly dutiful in Dublin, largely underwriting with Arthur for instance the great Irish Exhibition held in the city in 1872. He was sheriff in 1876 and high sheriff of the county in 1885, and following the success of the visit by the prince of Wales to Dublin that year he was created a baronet. He would have liked to have represented County Dublin in parliament, and it was with some reluctance—perhaps sensing his defeat—that he stood for the St Stephen's Green constituency later the same year. After pumping at least £30,000 into Conservative Party funds in the 1880s, he received his reward in 1891 when he was admitted to the United Kingdom peerage as first Baron Iveagh. He was invested a knight of St Patrick in 1895.

**Brewing and philanthropy** In October 1886 Guinness became a public company. Sales and profits during the previous decade had grown, if not as spectacularly as in the period between 1868 and 1876, nevertheless buoyantly, especially in comparison with some of the leading English brewers. The prospectus disclosed that sales had averaged 1,138,000 barrels and net profits £452,000 over the previous four years. Edward, retaining a third of the equity, convinced Baring Brothers (who on their first venture into company flotation managed the subscription somewhat ineptly) that the firm, even without owning any public houses, was worth £6 million. Shares were oversubscribed twenty times, prices rising to a 60 per cent premium on the first day of trading. The spectacular success of Guinness's sale released an avalanche of brewery company conversions. Sir Edward, who continued to buy further shares in the late 1880s, agreed to stay on for three years as managing director and chairman as a guarantee of his involvement in the company's affairs. Anxious to step down from both offices in 1890, he calculated that by 1900, if he spent no more than £100,000 a year, he would have a fortune of £15 million.

What should Guinness do with his vast riches? The firm had long had a leading reputation for its social welfare especially in workers' housing, pensions, and medical provision. Indeed, by 1900 the brewery was operating a system of social security for its 5000 employees which in its range and liberality was probably unequalled in the British Isles. By 1907 the firm's welfare schemes were costing it £40,000 a year, over a fifth of its wages bill. Sir Edward, seeing the logic of a healthy and loyal workforce, again was centrally involved. He gave evidence before the royal commission on the housing of the working classes in 1886 and about the hundreds of tenements his firm had built. In 1890 he set up the Guinness Trust with £250,000 for housing the poor in London and Dublin and a decade later gave £230,000 to the Iveagh Trust to clear the infamous Bull Alley slums in Dublin. He provided a further £100,000 to erect a new Iveagh market in the city, as well as funds to build the Iveagh Play Centre. In addition he donated £250,000 in 1900 to the Lister Institute of Preventive Medicine. He made large and regular gifts to Trinity College, Dublin (he was elected chancellor of the university in 1908), St Patrick's Cathedral, and the Dublin hospitals. He gave a further £50,000 to the hospitals on the occasion of the state visits to Dublin of Edward VII and George V. In 1909 the nationalist corporation of the city held a special meeting to present him with an address of thanks for his great benefactions and the interest he had always shown in its prosperity and affairs. When in the following year there was a move to elect him lord mayor, however, he declined with great tact.

**Houses and sport** What really distinguished Lord Iveagh (who enjoyed four titles in his lifetime, being advanced to a viscountcy in 1905 and an earldom in 1919), however, was the fact that he combined immense business skills and a keen interest in social welfare with a vigorous social life. His annual migratory passage and Lady Iveagh's predilection for formal entertainment on the grand scale have already been noted. He became famed for his shoots, in an era when the steam yacht and the *grande battue* were the status symbols of both super-rich landed aristocrats and new commercial and industrial plutocrats alike. In 1894, after protracted wrangling, he bought Maharaja Duleep Singh's 17,000 acre Breckland estate in west Suffolk for £160,000. Its soils were so marginal that, given the low agriculture prices of the late nineteenth century, it was little use for farming purposes. With the purchase of a further 6000 acres, Lord Iveagh turned it into the best shoot in England.

Elvedon Hall, already eccentrically rebuilt to reflect the maharaja's tastes, was trebled in size. What was a sizeable house was converted by a team of 150 men working for 4 years at a cost of £115,000 effectively into a *grand luxe* private hotel. Perhaps no room in England was more redolent of Edwardian high society's passion for luxury than its marble Indian Hall. The Victorian gossip Augustus Hare found the house 'almost appallingly luxurious, such masses of orchids, electric light everywhere etc.' (*My Solitary Life*, 1953 edn, 270). In 1914 the estate was staffed by almost 400 workers, with 76 men in the game department alone. Invitations to shoot were highly prized. Edward VII and George V were regular visitors (Lord Iveagh received the GCVO in 1910 for his services to the sovereign). By 1900 annual bags of over 100,000 head of game were being recorded. In 1912 five guns, including George V, shot 3248 head of game in a single day, an unsurpassed national record. Providing superbly organized entertainment on this scale, often for the king or his heir, was as time-consuming as keeping the world's largest brewery on course.

In addition to Elvedon, the Iveaghs had a house in Cowes, as well as living in great state at 5 Grosvenor Place, London, and Farmleigh and 80 St Stephen's Green in Dublin. All their residences were furnished to provide the same opulent comfort. In the course of only four years, between 1887 and 1891, Lord Iveagh acquired a large picture collection, buying principally from the dealers Thomas Agnew & Sons, and spending over £530,000 on 200 pictures. These included good Dutch paintings (later the glory of the Kenwood collection), but the core of the collection gratified contemporary taste for portraits by Reynolds, Romney, and Gainsborough. Already good examples of these were costing in excess of £10,000 apiece. Their purchase must have helped replenish the coffers of many a landowner distressed by the course of agricultural depression. The cascade of brewing profits indeed fell amply.

**Further progress in brewing** Remarkably, the brewery went from strength to strength. Many English breweries, including the largest, marked time after 1900, hit by a decline in beer consumption and, after 1906, the depredations of an increasingly hostile Liberal government and, perhaps above all, from the costs of acquiring tied-house estates at insane prices in the boom of the late 1890s. At least from the latter phenomenon Guinness escaped entirely. Lord Iveagh had four abiding principles in guiding the brewery: that it should own no public houses; that it should provide a consistently good premium product; that the independent bottlers and brewers who bottled and sold Guinness through their retail outlets should fix their own prices for it; that discounts and advertising should be kept to a minimum. The recipe worked wonderfully well, at least until 1920. No other brewery could match its stouts, which with pale ale constituted one of the two great beers of the Victorian and Edwardian era. Moreover, uniquely, the brewery produced only three variations of a single beer type: porter or single stout (sold entirely in Ireland), double or extra, and foreign stout for export (never more than 5 per cent of sales). Sales burgeoned by some 3 per cent per annum between 1888 and 1914, and without the interest charges on the purchase of public houses which other brewers faced, but with continuing low raw material prices, profits soared. After 1903 these were never less than £1 million each year; between 1886 and 1914 they netted a total of £25 million. By the outbreak of the First World War, Guinness produced 2,652,000 barrels a year (more than twice its nearest rival, Bass) to supply 10.3 per cent of the United Kingdom beer market. Given that they were achieved solely from a Dublin base, without amalgamation, and without the support of a tied-house network, these are astonishing figures.

Although Lord Iveagh was not even a director of the firm between 1890 and 1897, he was, as principal shareholder, consulted on every matter. He advised, exhorted, approved. In 1886 he had admitted two of his wife's brothers into directorships of the firm. The younger of the two, Cecil Guinness, managing director after 1886, was able, but naturally turned to his brother-in-law. Fortunately, his deputy Christopher La Touche, who succeeded him in 1902, was progressive in his outlook and became an increasingly dominant figure in the brewery. In 1902 Lord Iveagh resumed his chairmanship of Arthur Guinness, a post he held until his death. Certainly, Lord Iveagh vigorously supported the two big new departures in company policy after the 1890s: the recruitment of Oxbridge science graduates to the ranks of the dozen brewers the company employed, and the famed researches, headed by the brilliant experimental chemist, Alexander Forbes Watson, on barley, yeast, and secondary fermentation.

**Later years and death** Slim and below medium height, Lord Iveagh seemed almost physically frail in his last years. Although contemporaries noted his good manners and natural dignity, others remarked upon a vanity and natural reserve. And although he did not interfere in his sons' lives, he remained a distant, forbidding figure to them. He and Lady Iveagh (who died in 1916) came to seem increasingly old-fashioned and aloof. In the last decade of his life he appeared a somewhat lonely figure. The First World War changed the world around him; Ireland descended into civil war; Lloyd George menaced the beer industry, brewers, and their wealth.

Lord Iveagh's capacity for business finance and administration and his good judgement about men and affairs did not desert him, however. He came to rely increasingly on his secretary, C. H. Bland, and his financial assistant, Colonel G. W. Addison. Members of the Dublin board who ran the firm were frequently summoned to attend meetings at 5 Grosvenor Place as he came to spend less time in Ireland. And perhaps the disposition of his wealth began to obsess him more. By any standards it was prodigious, far out-distancing that of the old aristocracy which had dominated society and politics in his youth. In 1910 he reckoned his income from all sources was in the region of £650,000 a year. Of this he spent no more than a third, and he was able to set up ample trusts for his three sons (all three had married into the English aristocracy in 1903, Lord Iveagh supposedly cleaning up the market for antique silver candlesticks to shower upon them) and their descendants. In 1911–12, thoroughly alarmed by Lloyd George's taxation proposals to soak the rich, he began to buy property and securities in America on a large scale.

Although the profitability of the brewery kept up well after 1920, because raw material prices remained low (dividends increased to 32 per cent in 1925–6), sales of Guinness contracted sharply. Of course it was a feature all brewers shared during the deep post-war depression which set in during 1921. Guinness's Irish sales fell by more than a quarter between 1920–21 and 1923–4, those in Britain by as much as 28 per cent between 1921 and 1926 (double the rate most British breweries experienced). The price of Guinness was too high and with the lower gravities enforced by the war it was a less stable brew than in the past. The firm was living on its name and reputation; the old pre-1914 formula needed fundamental revision. With a managing director hesitant to change anything, the brewery for the first time faltered. Lord Iveagh, still totally engaged, encouraged wide-ranging enquiries into the problem, but recommendations about improving trade management, higher gravities, pricing, and above all more advertising were not put in place before he died.

In 1925 Lord Iveagh made his last big imaginative benefaction. Kenwood House, the great house designed by Robert Adam for the earls of Mansfield at Hampstead, fell on bad times during the war. There were proposals to sell it to a building syndicate. Some of the land was acquired and eventually handed to the London county council, but the fate of the house and of its immediate surrounding policies was still insecure in 1925. Lord Iveagh bought the house for £108,000, filled it with some of his furniture and pictures, spent five nights in it, and then set up a trust, with a capital sum of £50,000, to maintain the house and its collection as an art gallery open to the public. Few gifts have been more splendid or more widely appreciated.

Lord Iveagh died on 7 October 1927, at 5 Grosvenor Place, London, a month before his eightieth birthday and was buried on the 12th beside his wife in Elvedon church. He was survived by his three sons: Rupert Edward Cecil Lee *Guinness, the second earl; the Hon. Ernest Guinness, vice-chairman of the company from 1913 to 1949; and the Hon. Walter *Guinness, first Baron Moyne. His estate of £11 million was one of the largest then recorded in Britain. R. G. Wilson

**Sources** G. Martelli, *Man of his time: a life of the first earl of Iveagh* (privately printed, 1957) • P. Lynch and J. Vaizey, *Guinness's brewery in the Irish economy, 1759–1876* (1960) • P. Brendon, *Head of Guinness: the life and times of Rupert Guinness, 2nd earl of Iveagh* (privately printed, 1979) • S. R. Dennison and O. MacDonagh, *Guinness, 1886–1939: from incorporation to the Second World War* (1998) • GEC, *Peerage* • *DNB* • *Brewing Trade Review* (Nov 1927) • T. R. Gourvish and R. G. Wilson, *The British brewing industry, 1830–1980* (1994) • T. Corran, 'Guinness, Edward Cecil', *DBB* • *CGPLA Eng. & Wales* (1927) • *The Times* (8 Oct 1927)

**Archives** Arthur Guinness, Son & Co. Ltd, London

**Likenesses** W. L. Collis, photogravure, 1903 (after Wermer & Son), NPG • Werner & Son, photogravure, pubd 1903, NPG [*see illus.*] • W. Orpen, oils, 1904, Guinness & Co. Ltd, London • H. M. Paget, portrait, *c.*1912 (after A. S. Cope, *c.*1912), Kenwood House, London • W. L. Collis, photogravure, photograph, *c.*1926, NPG • W. Stoneman, photograph, 1926, NPG • Spy [L. Ward], caricature, chromolithograph, NPG; repro. in *VF* (11 July 1891) • photographs, repro. in Martelli, *Man of his time* [privately printed]

**Wealth at death** £11,000,000: probate, 2 Nov 1927, *CGPLA Eng. & Wales*

**Guinness, Fanny Emma** (1831–1898). *See under* Guinness, Henry Grattan (1835–1910).

**Guinness** [*née* Onslow], **Gwendolen Florence Mary, countess of Iveagh** (1881–1966), politician, was born at 7 Richmond Terrace, Whitehall, London, on 22 July 1881, the elder daughter of William Hillier *Onslow, fourth earl of Onslow (1853–1911), and his wife, the Hon. Florence Coulston Gardner (1853–1934). She grew up in a family steeped in traditions of public service. As a child she acted as secretary to her father when he served as governor-general of New Zealand (1889–92). Throughout her life she carried out her public role with 'an engaging mixture of firmness and gaiety' (*The Times*, 17 Feb 1966). Her route into public life was, however, very conventional. She married on 8 October 1903 the brewer Rupert Edward Cecil Lee *Guinness (1874–1967), styled Viscount Elveden (1919–27), who became second earl of Iveagh in 1927. They had five children: two sons (the first of whom died shortly after his birth in 1906) and three daughters. She subsequently assisted her husband in nine election campaigns in the Guinness family seat at Southend-on-Sea. She also took part in philanthropic work, and during the First World War organized relief efforts for prisoners of war, for which she was appointed CBE in 1920.

This practical experience combined with her social standing led to Lady Iveagh's appointment as chairman of the Conservative Party's women's advisory committee from 1925 to 1933, a period in which the party built up a female membership of 1 million. She also served as chairman of the National Union of Conservative and Unionist Associations in 1930. In spite of this, Lady Iveagh was no feminist. In 1928 she wrote that sex privileges were becoming as obsolete as class privileges (*Time and Tide*, 22 June 1928); and as a parliamentary candidate in 1927 she pointedly refused to answer the questions put to her by the National Union of Societies for Equal Citizenship, which was keen to promote her election. Only the accident of her husband's elevation to the peerage in 1927 led her to enter parliament by stepping into his Southend seat at a by-election in November of that year. In a safe Conservative constituency she always polled over half the votes, and in 1931 reached 85 per cent; the following year she was granted the freedom of Southend.

Between 1929 and 1935 Lady Iveagh remained an inconspicuous back-bencher who gave loyal support to Stanley Baldwin as party leader. MPs were said to crowd into the chamber for her rare appearances, partly to view her fashionable clothes. In the 1931–2 session of parliament she remained wholly silent; she made but a single speech in 1928–9, 1932–3, and 1933–4. In her maiden speech on the prayer book measure of 1927 Lady Iveagh endeavoured to come to the rescue of the government by defending the proposals, partly on the grounds that they would reduce the existing confusion within the Church of England, and on the grounds that the 1662 prayer book had lost much of its meaning. Similarly when Baldwin's 1928 Representation of the People Bill, which granted women the vote at the age of twenty-one, was under attack from the *Daily Mail* and some right-wing tories, including the duchess of Atholl, she defended the policy; the 1918 reform had been illogical, she claimed, for though in part the result of women's wartime work, it had excluded those women who had filled the gaps in the labour force. She also suggested that as no evidence had emerged of a political division between the sexes, the fact that women would comprise a majority of the electorate posed no dangers.

Outside parliament and the Conservative Party, Lady Iveagh involved herself, encouraged by a visit to Canada, in the Overseas Training School, whose object was to prepare young women who planned to settle in the colonies by teaching them cookery, preserving, dairying, and poultry-rearing. These agricultural interests were also reflected in her efforts in conjunction with her husband to raise the productivity of the Elveden estate in Suffolk; they helped to pioneer the consumption of pure milk by forming the Association of Certified Pure Milk Producers. In 1956 Lady Iveagh presented her Surrey childhood home, Clandon Park, to the National Trust. She died at home at Pyrford Court, Pyrford, Surrey, on 16 February 1966 and was buried at Elveden. Her eldest daughter, Honor Dorothy Mary, married Sir Henry *Channon; her second daughter, Patricia Florence Susan, married Alan Tindal Lennox-*Boyd, first Viscount Boyd of Merton.

MARTIN PUGH

**Sources** *The Times* (17 Feb 1966) · *Hansard* · M. Pugh, *Women and the women's movement in Britain, 1914–1959* (1992) · B. Harrison, 'Women in a men's house: the women MPs, 1919–45', *HJ*, 29 (1986), 623–54 · GEC, *Peerage* · b. cert. · m. cert.

**Wealth at death** £337,318: probate, 4 May 1966, *CGPLA Eng. & Wales*

**Guinness, Henry Grattan** (1835–1910), evangelist and trainer of missionaries, was born on 11 August 1835 at Montpelier House, near Kingstown, Ireland, the eldest son in the family of one daughter and three sons of John Grattan Guinness (1783–1850), captain in the army, who saw service in India; his mother was Jane Lucretia, daughter of William Cramer (an accomplished violinist and composer, and son of Johann Baptist *Cramer, musical composer), and also the widow of Captain J. N. D'Esterre, who was killed by Daniel O'Connell in a duel in February 1815. Henry's grandfather, Arthur *Guinness (1768–1855) of Beaumont, co. Dublin, established the first Sunday school in Ireland, in Dublin in 1786. During their father's lifetime the family lived variously at Dublin, Liverpool, Clifton, and Cheltenham. After education at private schools at Clevedon and Exeter, Guinness at the age of seventeen went to sea, and travelled to Mexico and the West Indies.

After returning to England in March 1854 Guinness experienced an evangelical conversion. In January 1856 he entered New College, St John's Wood, London, to train for the Congregational ministry; he did not complete his course. While at New College he supplied the pulpit for

Henry Grattan Guinness (1835–1910), by Robinson

three months at Moorfields Tabernacle, with such success that he was invited to become the pastor. Guinness declined, but was instead 'ordained' at the tabernacle on 29 July 1857 to the work of an itinerant interdenominational evangelist. To this work Guinness now devoted his life at home and abroad, and there followed preaching tours on the continent in January 1858, in Ireland in 1858 and 1859, and in America from November 1859 to May 1860.

On 2 October 1860, at the Friends' meeting-house in Princes Street, Bath, Guinness married Fanny Emma [**Fanny Emma Guinness** (1831–1898)], third child of Major Edward Marlborough Fitzgerald and Mabel Stopford, daughter of Admiral Sir Robert Stopford (1768–1847). Since the age of eight Fanny Fitzgerald had been brought up by a pious Quaker couple, Arthur and Mary West, who were members of the Tottenham meeting of the Society of Friends. The Wests, along with other members of the Tottenham meeting, became associated with the early Christian (Plymouth) Brethren movement, and as a result Fanny acquired strong links with the Brethren, though remaining formally affiliated to the Society of Friends at the time of her marriage. Through her Brethren acquaintances Henry Grattan Guinness was introduced to the Brethren movement, and he acquired from the Brethren a fascination with the topic of biblical prophecy which remained with him for the rest of his life. The Guinnesses moved widely in Brethren circles throughout their marriage, though Guinness never wholly severed his connections with the Congregationalists and in his final years worshipped regularly in the Church of England.

After their marriage the Guinnesses travelled continuously for twelve years. They visited Canada in 1861 and Egypt and Palestine in 1862. Guinness then held a short pastorate at Liverpool, and afterwards worked in Ireland. Towards the close of 1865 he took a house at 31 Baggot Street, Dublin, with a view to forming a training home for evangelists and missionaries. In 1866 he also conducted in Dublin the Merrion Hall Mission, and there he had an important influence on the young Thomas John Barnardo (1845–1905). In 1867 the Guinnesses left Dublin for Bath. Work in France occupied much of their time from 1868 to 1872. In 1873 Guinness founded the East London Institute for Home and Foreign Missions, for the training of young men and women for home and foreign missionary work. He directed the institute until his death, and his wife Fanny served as secretary, and was responsible for the budget. The institute was first located at 29 Stepney Green, and subsequently at Harley House, Bow. Barnardo was a co-director. In its first year there were thirty-two students, and after three years other branches were formed in London, and one was installed at Cliff College, Curbar, Derbyshire. Accommodation was provided for 100 men and women; over 1400 men and women were trained in the period up to 1914, when the institute closed.

With the opening up of the Congo and the publication of H. M. Stanley's letters at the end of 1877, Guinness and his wife resolved to concentrate on foreign missions. A monthly magazine, *The Regions Beyond*, edited by Fanny Guinness, was started in 1878. Through the initiative of Alfred Tilly of Cardiff, the Livingstone Inland Mission was formed in the Congo in 1878, and in 1880 it became a branch of the institute, with the Guinnesses as director and secretary. It was transferred to the control of the American Baptist Missionary Union in 1884. A new mission to the interior of Africa, the Congo Balolo Mission, was founded in 1889, and others followed in South America—in Peru in 1897, and Argentina in 1899. The organizations were combined in 1899 to form the Regions Beyond Missionary Union, an interdenominational body whose activities were further extended to India by the formation of the Bihar mission in the Bengal presidency in 1901.

Although Guinness did not himself visit central Africa, he travelled in the interest of his missions to Algeria in 1879, to America in 1889 (where he inspired the creation in Boston and Minneapolis of training institutions similar to his own), to India and Burma in November 1896, and to China and Japan in 1897. A visit to Egypt in 1899–1900 led indirectly to the formation in 1904 of the Sudan United Mission, as a result of the marriage in Cairo in February 1900 of the Guinnesses' second daughter, Lucy Evangeline (1865–1906), to the German missionary pioneer Karl Kumm (1874–1930). The Guinnesses had five daughters, of whom three died in infancy, and two sons. All the surviving children engaged in their parents' missionary efforts. The elder son, Dr Harry Grattan Guinness (1861–1915), also became a director of the mission at Harley House, and took a prominent part in the agitation against the Belgian rubber atrocities in the Congo. The eldest daughter, Mary Geraldine (1862–1949), later became celebrated with her husband, Dr Howard Taylor, as the biographer of James Hudson Taylor (1832–1905), founder of the China Inland Mission. Lucy edited *The Regions Beyond* for several years after her mother's death in 1898; she also published books on South America and India, and was a writer of religious verse. Her father published a memoir of her in 1907. The younger son, Gershom Whitfield (1869–1927), became a missionary doctor in Henan with the China Inland Mission.

Henry and Fanny Guinness jointly published several works on biblical prophecy. The most important, *The Approaching End of the Age in the Light of History, Prophecy, and Science*, first published in 1878, went through fourteen editions by 1918. Both also published works as individual authors, of which the best known were Fanny Guinness's *The First Christian Mission on the Congo*, which appeared about 1880, and *The New World of Central Africa* (1890). For the last seven years of her life Fanny Guinness was paralysed; she died at Cliff College, Curbar, Derbyshire, on 3 November 1898, and was buried in Baslow churchyard.

On 7 July 1903, Henry Grattan Guinness married Grace Alexandra, hospital nurse, youngest of the seven children of Charles Russell Hurditch, a leading figure among the Christian Brethren. She was forty years his junior. After their wedding Guinness took his young bride on a five-year world tour, which included visits to Switzerland (1903), America and Canada (1904), Japan and China (1905), and Australia and New Zealand (1906). He concluded the tour with a visit to South Africa, where he preached to racially mixed congregations. It was 1908 before they returned to England. They had two sons, John Christopher and Paul Grattan.

Henry Grattan Guinness received an honorary DD degree from Brown University, Providence, USA, in 1889. He was also elected a fellow of the Royal Astronomical Society in recognition of his astronomical work, which was sparked off by his interest in prophecy. He spent his last two years in Bath, where he died at his home, Lynton Lodge, Oldfield Park, of pleurisy and pericarditis on 21 June 1910. He was buried in the cemetery at Bath Abbey, survived by his second wife.

W. B. Owen, *rev.* Brian Stanley

**Sources** M. Guinness, *The Guinness legend* (1989) · *The Regions Beyond*, 31 (1911), 3–64 · D. Lagergren, *Mission and state in the Congo* (1970) · Mrs H. Taylor [M. G. Guinness], *Guinness of Honan* (1930) · S. Neill, G. H. Anderson, and J. Goodwin, eds., *Concise dictionary of the Christian world mission* (1970), 238 · m. certs. · *CGPLA Eng. & Wales* (1910)

**Archives** Regions Beyond Missionary Union archives · SOAS, Overseas Missionary Fellowship archives · U. Edin., Centre for the Study of Christianity in the Non-Western World | BLPES, corresp. with E. D. Morel

**Likenesses** O. Edis, photograph, *c.*1910, NPG · Robinson, photograph, NPG [*see illus.*]

**Wealth at death** £4699 2*s.* 11*d.*: probate, 19 Aug 1910, *CGPLA Eng. & Wales*

**Guinness, Maureen Constance** (1907–1998). *See under* Plunket, Aileen Sibell Mary (1904–1999).

**Guinness, Oonagh** (1910–1995). *See under* Plunket, Aileen Sibell Mary (1904–1999).

**Guinness, Richard Samuel** (1797–1857), land agent and politician, was born in Dublin on 17 June 1797, the second son of Richard Guinness (1755–1829), barrister, and Mary, elder daughter of George Darley of The Scalp, co. Wicklow, and great-nephew of Arthur Guinness, founder of the St James's Gate Brewery. Educated at Trinity College, Dublin, where he graduated in 1818, Guinness was called to the bar in Ireland three years later. From 1822 he served as a receiver under the court of chancery in Ireland, acting as auditor of several large estates. In partnership with his brother, Robert Rundall (1789–1857), Guinness also founded a small land agency and banking firm, R. S. Guinness & Co., at 5 Kildare Street, Dublin. In 1834 the bank was appointed the first Dublin agent for the leading provincial bank, the Agricultural and Commercial Bank. The business flourished until 1836 when Robert, who had raised the initial capital for the venture, withdrew from the partnership. The following year, Robert entered into a new agreement with one of his former apprentices, John Ross Mahon, and established the well-known banking firm Guinness Mahon.

The brothers' relationship may well have been strained by the financial crisis of 1836 when the Agricultural and Commercial Bank was forced to suspend payments. The main reason, however, was the extravagant lifestyle adopted by Richard after his marriage on 25 November 1833 to Katherine Frances (*d.* 1881), second daughter of Sir Charles Jenkinson, tenth baronet, a relative of Robert Banks Jenkinson, second earl of Liverpool, prime minister. Katherine was determined to maintain the standards she had always enjoyed and had no intention of being eclipsed by her younger sister, Eleanor, who in 1830 had married the second duc de Montebello. Her ambitions were far beyond her husband's resources, and in July 1849 R. S. Guinness & Co. collapsed, leaving Richard bankrupt.

A protestant and tory, Guinness served as member of parliament for Kinsale from 1847 to 1848, and subsequently overcame his financial difficulties sufficiently to allow him to sit for Barnstaple, Devon from 1854 to 1857. (He was unable to take his seat between August and December 1854 because of a discrepancy in the return made by the mayor to the clerk of the court.) His rare contributions to debates were confined to Irish issues: compensation for tenants' improvements and the administration of chancery estates. He was best known for the high collars he favoured which forced up his chin giving him the air of a pelican, and earning him the nickname Old Pel. Guinness died on 28 August 1857. Of his eight children, Arthur Cecil shared his mother's extravagant tastes and died in penury. Others inherited the Guinness drive, and their father's bankruptcy was no bar to their progress in Ireland's leading firm, Arthur Guinness, Son & Co. Sir Reginald Robert (1842–1895) served as chairman of the company from 1890 to 1902; the youngest son, Claude (1852–1895), was managing director from 1890 to 1893. Presumably their progress was aided by the marriage of Adelaide, the fourth daughter, to her cousin, Edward Cecil Guinness, the first earl of Iveagh, the head of the firm: she certainly proved her husband's equal as a brilliant socialite. CHRISTINE CLARK

**Sources** M. Guinness, *The Guinness legend* (1989) • *WWBMP*, vol. 1 • *Hansard 3* (1847), vol. 95; (1855), vol. 139 • Burke, *Peerage* (1963) • G. L. Barrow, *The emergence of the Irish banking system, 1820–1845* (1975) • Burke, *Gen. Ire.* (1958)

**Wealth at death** £100: administration, 1860, Ireland

**Guinness, Rupert Edward Cecil Lee, second earl of Iveagh** (1874–1967), brewer and agricultural improver, was born in Berkeley Square, London, on 29 March 1874, the eldest of the three sons of Edward Cecil *Guinness (1847–1927), who was created earl of Iveagh in 1919, and his wife, Adelaide Maria, the daughter of Richard Samuel Guinness MP, of Deepwell, co. Dublin, a distant cousin of her husband. The politician Walter *Guinness was his brother. He was born heir to great family wealth and also to the heavy responsibilities carried by his father, who in 1876 became the sole proprietor of the St James's Gate brewery in Dublin and in 1886, when Guinness became a public company, its first chairman.

**Early years** Guinness's childhood was not easy. His immensely able father was, at least with his family, a forbidding figure, reserved and unemotional. At St George's preparatory school in Ascot and later at Eton College (1888–93) his progress, because he suffered from serious dyslexia (then quite unrecognized), was painfully slow in all academic subjects except science. The latter was an interest he developed most successfully throughout a long and full life. But an inability to express himself orally or on paper always remained. Mercifully, he was tall, powerfully built, and good at sport and possessed, according to his housemaster at Eton, a superb disposition: 'I think that his character is one of the most perfect I have ever met with in a boy here' (Brendon, 39–40). These and other encomiums must have been music to the ears of his father, troubled by the lack of academic progress of his eldest son. Moreover, behind the genial exterior and equable temperament there was a burning determination to succeed. His prowess at rowing was impressive testimony to his ambition. Besides rowing in the Eton eight which won the ladies' plate at Henley in 1893, he won the diamond sculls in 1895, and in the following year, by winning both the diamond and the Wingfield sculls, he became the undisputed British amateur rowing champion. Sadly it was to be the end of his rowing career, for his father, on unfounded medical advice, believing Rupert had an enlarged heart condition, told him to give up the sport. It was ironic that he survived in first-rate health into his nineties. His chest expansion was the largest his doctor had ever encountered in an octogenarian. He went up to Trinity College, Cambridge, for three terms in October 1896; he coached boats and achieved little else.

Water, however, continued to exercise an attraction for Guinness. In 1901 his 90 foot racing yawl, the *Leander*, won the king's cup at Cowes and the Vasco Da Gama challenge cup in Portugal. He was later asked by the Admiralty to

**Rupert Edward Cecil Lee Guinness, second earl of Iveagh** (1874–1967), by Howard Coster, 1931

raise and command the naval force that became the London division of the Royal Naval Volunteer Reserve, a task which he undertook during the decade preceding the outbreak of the First World War.

**Political involvement** In 1899, with little or no experience of the brewery, Guinness became a director of Arthur Guinness, Son & Co. Ltd. Indeed, he had little opportunity to become much involved with the company's affairs because of the outbreak of the Second South African War, and in 1900 he was in South Africa working with the mobile Irish hospital, donated to the war effort by his father, as aide to its commander, Sir William Thomson. He was appointed CMG in 1901 for his services in South Africa. Following his return to England, he began to interest himself seriously in politics and, after becoming a member of the London school board, was adopted in 1903 as Conservative candidate for the Haggerston division of Shoreditch in the East End of London. He was a member of the London county council (1904–10) and chairman of the London education committee (1911–13). On 8 October 1903 he married Gwendolen Onslow (1881–1966) [*see* Guinness, Gwendolen Florence Mary], the elder daughter of the fourth earl of Onslow and his wife, Florence Coulston, the daughter of the third and last Baron Gardner. They had a son and three daughters. Between 1919 and 1927 Guinness had the title of Viscount Elveden.

As a couple the Guinnesses got on superbly well, and Gwendolen made her first public speech during their engagement. She was energetic and a good businesswoman, and she helped her husband with his letters, speeches, and manifestos. He was good-humoured and a bedrock of common sense and stability. She later had a distinguished career herself in politics and her first experience of them, shared with her husband, was the seven years of hard political labour in their east London constituency. Indeed in 1903 they acquired a home there (266 Kingsland Road, Haggerston), where they lived for several weeks each year and reputedly visited every house in the constituency. Through their tireless political and charitable work they acquired a good knowledge of the working classes and social reform.

In 1908 Guinness was returned as a Conservative MP for the Haggerston division of Shoreditch, which seat he held until January 1910, when he was narrowly defeated at the general election; he stood again there unsuccessfully in December 1910. After this setback Rupert and Gwendolen Guinness, both enthusiastic supporters of Joseph Chamberlain's imperialist ideals, visited Canada and were immensely struck by the opportunities in this new country for enterprising emigrants from home. Guinness determined to establish an organization in which emigrants could be effectively prepared for the very different conditions of life in Canada. He bought Woking Park farm with 500 acres, close to his own estate at Pyrford (which he had bought from his father-in-law and where he built a large country house to his own design in 1906), and set up a training establishment. By 1914 it had produced more than 200 well-instructed emigrants. Gwendolen Guinness sought to establish a similar organization for women in Canada, but war prevented its development.

Guinness was appointed CB in 1911. In 1912 he was elected member for the south-eastern division of Essex, a constituency which later became the borough of Southend. He continued his uninterrupted representation of the borough until he succeeded in 1927, on his father's death, to the earldom of Iveagh. A biographer has commented that 'Rupert was no politician' (Brendon, 138), but he was a hard-working and popular member (though he seldom spoke in the Commons), well liked in his constituency, and extremely generous to a host of causes in Southend. His wife stood at the by-election caused by this event and was elected. She in her turn continued to represent the borough with great success and an increasing majority at each election until she retired from politics in 1935 after eight years in the House of Commons. After 1935 the constituency returned as members Sir Henry *Channon and his son Sir Paul, the son-in-law and grandson of the Iveaghs. It is the most remarkable record of continuous family representation in a twentieth-century British constituency.

**Scientific research** Guinness's interest in science and the practical applications of scientific research was stronger at this period in his life than his concern with politics, and he was particularly fascinated by the techniques and potentialities of preventive medicine. He was fortunate in being able to combine his interest with the material means to support research and ensure that results were carried through. He involved himself deeply in the running of the Lister Institute of Preventive Medicine, endowed by his father, of which he was a governor for many years. He took a close interest in the work of Almroth Wright and Alexander Fleming, both of whom became his lifelong friends, and this resulted in the setting up of what eventually became the Wright–Fleming Institute of Microbiology at St Mary's Hospital, Paddington. It made many contributions to medical knowledge in the fields of allergy control, antibiotics, and preventive medicine techniques. Guinness was chairman and a generous benefactor for the greater part of the institute's life.

Guinness's scientific interest was also strongly directed towards agricultural questions, and particularly the problems of dairy farming. He was convinced of the possibility of reducing the incidence of bovine tuberculosis in children by producing clean milk. Before 1914 he had designed and made bottling and sterilizing equipment for use with his dairy herd at Pyrford. He stimulated and financed practical and successful research at the Rothamsted Experimental Station in Harpenden (later the Institute of Arable Crops Research) with E. John Russell, the director, and Dr Hanneford Richards, into the best ways of making and storing farmyard manure. His intense practical and scientific preoccupation in farming questions was further developed in response to the acute shortages of foodstuffs towards the end of the First World War.

The outbreak of war found Guinness commanding the London division of the Royal Naval Volunteer Reserve (RNVR) and anxious to find the right employment in the war effort for the thousand men collected and trained largely by his own efforts in the preceding years. To his and their dismay they found themselves limited to military activities on land only. It was hard to accept after so many years of patient preparation. Guinness's efforts were then directed to the carrying out of recruiting drives throughout the country, which were vigorous and successful. In 1916 he was promoted to acting captain and made aide-de-camp to the king, the first RNVR officer to be so honoured.

Their large London house, 11 St James's Square, given to Guinness by his father in 1905, had been turned by Gwendolen Guinness into an office for the organization of relief measures for prisoners of war. Gwendolen was appointed a member of the National Prisoners of War Fund and in 1920 was appointed CBE for the extensive work which she did in this field. In 1916 the Guinnesses both went again to Canada, his mission this time being to find volunteers to serve in the Royal Navy. This was a difficult and frustrating assignment and was only partially successful. Finally Guinness was demobilized to do what he was perhaps best qualified to do for the war effort, namely, grow and produce more food at home.

**Agricultural research** Work undertaken with Rothamsted on clean milk and on the use of manure and its manufacture from straw by chemical treatment was carried out at Guinness's Pyrford farm. One discovery from this work led to the establishment of the Agricultural Developments Company to produce and put on the market ADCO, a compost accelerator, which remained in wide use for many years. Tuberculin-tested milk was also being produced from the Pyrford herd. In 1920 Elveden, as Guinness had become, was one of the founders and the first chairman of the Tuberculin Tested Milk Producers Association, with offices in St James's Square. His important active pioneer work in the campaign for clean milk eventually led to universal acceptance of the principles involved and a big reduction in the incidence of bovine tuberculosis in children.

Elveden had been working closely also with the Research Institute in Dairying of University College, Reading, with its first director, Professor Stenhouse Williams, and later with his successor, Professor H. D. Kay, and by contributing substantial material help to the institute enabled it to set up its own experimental farm, Shinfield Manor, near Reading. The major part he played in the development of the institute was publicly recognized in the conferment of the degree of honorary DSc by the University College of Reading. Lady Elveden was closely involved in this pioneer agricultural work at Pyrford. Her interest was acknowledged when she was asked to open the new National Institute for Research in Dairying in 1924. Another of the agricultural organizations to which they both gave help was the Chadacre Agricultural Institute, founded by Elveden's father, near Bury St Edmunds in 1921. He was a long-serving chairman of the institute and each year offered a job on his Elveden farms to the best student to pass out of the college.

In 1926 the Elvedens paid a six-month visit to India, at the time when Lady Elveden's brother-in-law, Lord Irwin (afterwards the first earl of Halifax), was viceroy. On 7 October the following year the first earl of Iveagh died and Lord Elveden inherited the title and the great 23,000 acre Elveden estate. The house, trebled in size by his father, was vast, and the estate provided the finest shooting in England. The upkeep of both on the Edwardian scale (together they employed 397 people in 1914) would have been a colossal and probably impossible task, physically and financially. Lord Iveagh had very many other responsibilities, his chairmanship of the Guinness company, his many charitable, scientific, and agricultural commitments, his other houses and estates in England, Ireland, and Italy. Lady Iveagh was an active member of parliament and prominent in public life.

**Estate management** The idea of running and managing Elveden in the pre-1914 style was itself daunting even for a man of Lord Iveagh's great wealth. For one year, however, it was maintained on the old scale for the visit to Elveden in 1928 of King George V and Queen Mary. From then on, however, the emphasis in management changed, and Iveagh started the enormous task of converting Elveden into an efficient and economic farming unit. He created the most outstanding farming enterprise in Britain in the twentieth century, contemporaries comparing his endeavours with those of Thomas William Coke of Holkham, the most celebrated agricultural improver of the classic agricultural revolution.

The Breckland estate of Elveden bought by the first Lord Iveagh in 1894 was highly marginal land in the driest corner of Britain and was largely overrun by rabbits. It consisted of poor arable, of worse pasture, and, principally, of heath and warren. During the first earl's ownership (1894–1927), years which coincided with a period of almost continuous agricultural depression, the estate was run as an unrivalled shoot. The second earl, less keen on shooting than his father, set about demonstrating that the light land estate could be used efficiently for food production and that the heaths could be reclaimed for effective farming. The project was on an immense scale. Initially beginning with 5000 acres, the enterprise by the reclamation of heaths (largely after 1945) had almost doubled in size by the 1960s. The venture, commenced in the teeth of agricultural depression in the late 1920s and requiring large-scale investment in capital and labour, was a daunting one: a staggering 30 miles of fencing against the myriads of rabbits was erected in the 1930s. The key to Iveagh's success was to increase soil fertility by heavy stocking with tuberculin-free dairy and beef herds, and by growing vast acreages, for grazing and silage, of deep-rooting lucerne, a crop to which the bone-dry brecks were ideally suited. By the late 1950s Elveden was the largest mixed farm in England, growing 4500 acres of lucerne and clover and 3000 acres of barley and stocked with more than 2000 head of cattle. In 1962 the dairy farms produced over half a million gallons of milk. In addition there were 7000 acres of forest. All were beautifully maintained and managed by an army of 260 workers. The Elveden experiment succeeded largely because of Iveagh's driving persistence and determination to carry it through, but also because he had the means to experiment on so large a scale and the resources to be able to accept losses on the farms in the depressed 1930s before the enterprise became fully efficient and, after the early 1940s, eventually profitable.

The entire Elveden establishment could not be kept going after 1931, but during the 1930s Lady Iveagh maintained and used the new wing of the house. She was deeply engaged in politics and entertained political friends there. Lord Iveagh also took on many duties in public life. He was a lieutenant of the City of London and deputy lieutenant of Suffolk and Essex. He received honorary degrees from universities in Britain and Ireland in recognition of his agricultural work. In both countries he supported a great many causes covering scientific, medical, agricultural, and direct charitable endeavours and took an active part in the direction of as many of them as possible. He was a particularly involved chairman in directing and expanding the Guinness Trust in England and the Iveagh Trust in Dublin, housing charities established originally by the first Lord Iveagh.

**Guinness** In 1927 Lord Iveagh succeeded his father as chairman of Guinness. During the 1920s, although still highly profitable (because of rock-bottom raw material costs) with huge reserves, the company's affairs had faltered. The early 1920s were not good for brewers generally, and Guinness's progress was particularly troubled by the nervous relations existing between the new Irish Free State and Britain. There was an inherent tension in that Guinness stout was brewed in Dublin and consumed chiefly in Britain. As early as 1913, when affairs began to deteriorate sharply in Ireland, there were plans to build a new Guinness brewery by the Manchester Ship Canal. Indeed, land was acquired there for this purpose; but the war and the troubles halted any further realization of the scheme, although it was never entirely abandoned in the 1920s. It was in this uneasy situation for the company that Iveagh succeeded to the chairmanship. With little working knowledge of the brewery (his second brother, Ernest, had been far more active in its affairs), he was largely content to devolve decisions to his executive directors and managers.

Iveagh was no cipher as a businessman, however, and he was highly supportive of two major switches in company policy in the 1930s. First, he was prominent in mounting the best-known advertising campaign of the 1930s, Guinness's path-creating venture into this field, with its slogan 'Guinness is good for you'. He possibly coined the phrase, and his was perhaps the smiling face which appeared in the Guinness glass. Certainly the advertising campaign turned sales round after 1930. Secondly, amid great secrecy, a new brewery was built in 1934–6 at Park Royal in west London. It was the 'economic war' of tariffs after 1931 between Ireland and the United Kingdom which led to the revival of the old 1913 plans, but now, with British sales further concentrated in the south-east, the decision was taken to find a site near London. After delicate diplomatic exchanges with both the Irish and British governments, and careful publicity about intentions and the fact that the new brewery was capable of producing a near-identical product to that so famously brewed in Dublin since 1759, Park Royal was opened in 1936. Soon it was producing a quarter of the firm's output and supplying half of the British market for Guinness. Park Royal was a sensible venture. During the Second World War the company was able to keep production going in both countries and maintain supplies throughout Great Britain. Shortly before the outbreak of the war Iveagh presented the great Guinness Dublin town house in St Stephen's Green, which he had inherited from his father, to the Republic of Ireland and, named Iveagh House, it became the department for foreign affairs of the Irish government.

Throughout the Second World War the concentration at Elveden was on increasing production of food, and the successes achieved resulted in wide acclaim. But just as the war was ending Lord and Lady Iveagh suffered the shattering blow of the death on active service in the Netherlands of their only son, Arthur, Lord Elveden, a major in the 55th Suffolk and Norfolk yeomanry. In 1936 he had married Lady Elizabeth Hare, the younger daughter of the fourth earl of Listowel, and left three children, the eldest of whom, (Arthur Francis) Benjamin, was to succeed Lord Iveagh. Two months before Lord Elveden's death, Iveagh's younger brother, the first Baron Moyne, minister in residence in the Middle East, had been assassinated in Cairo.

Recognition of Iveagh's great achievements came in full measure in later life. In 1955 he was appointed a knight of the Order of the Garter. When he was presented with the first landowners' gold medal at the Royal Agricultural Society in 1958, the nonagenarian Viscount Bledisloe handed it over to the 85-year-old Lord Iveagh with the words, 'it is so nice to give it to an up and coming young man'. He also added that, through the transformation of his Suffolk breckland acres, his imaginative dairying projects and his enthusiasm in the field of veterinary research had become a legend in the annals of British agriculture. In 1964 Iveagh was made a fellow of the Royal Society, an accolade which pleased him enormously. His response to these great honours was modest and, like many old men, he grew more reactionary; he disliked bureaucracy (he won a celebrated victory against the Forestry Commission in the early 1950s), but always he was friendly and humorous and devoted to his grandchildren.

**Final years** The Guinness company moved after the war into a new phase of growth and diversification. Again, Iveagh gave his managing director, Sir Hugh Beaver, his head. In 1950, when it produced a record 3,185,000 barrels, the company began an extensive modernization programme. Its sales abroad, especially in west Africa and Malaya, flourished, and it diversified in a number of directions—confectionery, pharmaceuticals, the publication of the immensely successful *Guinness Book of Records*, and the production, in partnership with other breweries, of Harp lager. Well into his old age, Iveagh remained engaged in Guinness's affairs, not resigning the chairmanship until he was eighty-eight. He was a force in preserving Guinness's brewing traditions, but he was determined the firm should make use of commercial television for advertising. He was also determined to pass on family succession: in 1959 to his son-in-law Alan Lennox-Boyd, Viscount Boyd of Merton, a former cabinet minister, as managing director, and in 1962 to his grandson Benjamin Guinness, Viscount Elveden, as chairman. During the thirty-five years in which he presided over Guinness, the firm grew from a private company into a multinational concern with worldwide interests and activities. Iveagh also presided over the massive celebrations of the bicentenary of the Guinness company in 1959.

During the late 1950s Iveagh began to relinquish some of the many offices he still held, including the chairmanship of the Wright-Fleming Institute in 1957. He and Lady Iveagh gave up their regular prize-giving visits to Chadacre. In 1963 he resigned from the chancellorship of Trinity College, Dublin, an office he had held since 1927, and in which role he had conferred honorary degrees on many eminent people, including Eamon De Valera. In 1963 he handed his Elveden farms over to his grandson. Lady Iveagh died at Pyrford on 16 February 1966 and he, soon after, also at Pyrford, on 14 September 1967, as a result of a heart attack. They were both buried at Elveden churchyard in Suffolk. R. G. Wilson

**Sources** P. Brendon, *Head of Guinness: the life and times of Rupert Guinness, 2nd earl of Iveagh* (privately printed, 1979) · G. Martelli, *The Elveden enterprise: a story of the second agricultural revolution* (1952) · G. Martelli, *The Elveden estate, 1953–1963* (privately printed, [n.d.]) · G. Martelli, *Man of his time: a life of the first earl of Iveagh* (privately printed, 1957) · H. D. Kay, *Memoirs FRS*, 14 (1968), 287–307 · S. R. Dennison and O. MacDonagh, *Guinness, 1886–1939: from incorporation to the Second World War* (1998) · *CGPLA Eng. & Wales* (1968) · *The Times* (14 Feb 1966) · *The Times* (15 Sept 1967) · Burke, *Peerage* · *DNB*

**Archives** Bodl. Oxf., corresp. with Viscount Addison relating to agricultural matters

**Likenesses** W. Stoneman, photograph, 1921, NPG · H. Coster, photograph, 1931, NPG [*see illus.*] · W. Stoneman, portrait, 1948, NPG · J. Gilray, double portrait (with Lady Iveagh), Iveagh House, St James's Square, London · H. Oliver, portrait, Iveagh House, St James's Square, London · double portraits (with Lady Iveagh), Guinness plc, London

**Wealth at death** £262,149 effects in England: probate, 15 July 1968, *CGPLA Eng. & Wales*

**Guinness, Walter Edward, first Baron Moyne** (1880–1944), politician and traveller, was born in Dublin on 29 March 1880 in the house, 80 St Stephen's Green, which was afterwards presented to the Irish nation by his brother in 1939 and housed the Irish department of external affairs. He was the third son of the brewer and philanthropist Edward Cecil *Guinness, later the first earl of Iveagh (1847–1927), and his wife, Adelaide Maria Guinness (1844–1916). Like his brothers he was educated at Eton College, where he rowed for three years in the eight and in due course became captain of the boats. Under him as president the Eton Society was reformed so as to admit intellectual as well as athletic representatives, and its debates were revived. Moreover, at Eton he developed a particular and enduring interest in biology, but instead of pursuing this bent at Oxford, as he had intended, he volunteered for service in the Second South African War with the Suffolk yeomanry (Loyal Suffolk hussars). He was wounded, mentioned in dispatches, and awarded the queen's medal with four clasps. On 24 June 1903 he married Lady Evelyn Hilda Stuart Erskine (1883–1939), daughter of the fourteenth earl of Buchan. They had two sons and one daughter.

While Walter Guinness was growing up the family spent an increasing amount of time in England, and in the early 1890s his father bought a famous sporting estate at Elveden in Suffolk, a circumstance which made it appropriate that Walter Guinness should stand as Conservative candidate for the Stowmarket division. Although defeated at the general election of 1906, he was returned at a by-election in 1907 for Bury St Edmunds which, as a division of Suffolk, he continued to represent until 1931. He was a member of the London county council from 1907 to 1910. From the First World War Guinness retired as lieutenant-colonel, having served first in Gallipoli and Egypt as a major with the Suffolk yeomanry and afterwards with the 10th battalion of the London regiment. He had been three times mentioned in dispatches, and was appointed DSO in 1917 with bar in 1918.

Guinness's high public spirit and wide interests led him to pursue an extremely full life in which politics, scientific travel, and a share in the direction of his father's benefactions in England and Ireland, as well as of the Guinness breweries, were intertwined. Before the war he had made his house at Grosvenor Place in London into 'an imposing private "annexe" of the Carlton Club, where the King's (Tory) ministers could discuss affairs of state' in the most pleasant social surroundings (Mullally, 4). He was appointed under-secretary of state for war in 1922, followed by the financial secretaryship of the Treasury in 1923, and again in 1924–5 under Winston Churchill as chancellor of the exchequer. He became personally close to Churchill, who later described him as 'a most agreeable, intelligent and unusual friend' (Guinness, 298). He was sworn of the privy council in 1924 and entered the cabinet in November 1925 as minister of agriculture. During his tenure of the office he introduced the system of the national mark for eggs, and it was largely owing to his efforts that the sugar beet industry was built up. With the defeat of the Conservatives in 1929 he retired from office, and in January 1932 he was raised to the peerage as Baron Moyne of Bury St Edmunds in the county of Suffolk.

Out of office Moyne was able increasingly to combine his public service with that eagerness for travel which he had always displayed. As early as 1902 he had gone on the first of many big-game hunting expeditions—later in life he grew less inclined towards shooting except as necessary for food—and before 1914 he had travelled extensively on map-making expeditions in Asia Minor and become conversant with the plight of the Armenians and other minorities, for whom he then saw hope in Turkish reform rather than in foreign intervention. (It was during one of his absences in Asia Minor that the *Outlook*, of which he had become the proprietor, published without his knowledge a series of articles on the Marconi affair in 1912. On his return home he gave evidence in support of the editor before the select committee of inquiry.)

After being raised to the peerage Moyne not only acted as chairman of the departmental committee on housing in 1933, of the royal commission on the University of Durham in 1934, and of the departmental committee on British films in 1936, but he was also financial commissioner to Kenya in 1932 and chairman of the West Indies royal commission in 1938 and 1939, placing his yacht *Rosaura* at the disposal of the members for residence and for transport. This yacht was a sister ship to another named *Roussalka* which was wrecked in 1933 off the west coast of Ireland, and both were used by Moyne to enable him to travel to distant places in search of biological specimens and archaeological material. In 1934 he travelled to the island of Komodo, near New Guinea, and brought back living specimens of Komodo dragons for the gardens of the London Zoological Society. His subsequent journey to New Guinea in 1935 he described in his book *Walkabout* (1936), and a later journey to Greenland and to the little known Bay Islands off the coast of Honduras in *Atlantic Circle* (1938).

On the outbreak of war in 1939 Moyne undertook to act as chairman of the Polish Relief Fund and lent for its offices part of his London house at 10 and 11 Grosvenor Place. Although he had served as minister of agriculture, he agreed to serve as joint parliamentary secretary to the minister on the formation of the Churchill government in 1940. The next year Moyne succeeded Lord Lloyd as secretary of state for the colonies and leader of the House of Lords. In August 1942 he was appointed deputy minister of state in Cairo, and in January 1944 he succeeded Richard Gardiner Casey as minister resident in the Middle East.

Moyne had previously declared his support for the establishment of an Arab federation. In the emotional atmosphere of the Jewish fight for a homeland he was regarded with suspicion by some Zionist groups. He had also been accused of making an 'anti-semitic and anti-Zionist' speech in the House of Lords in June 1942 (Heller, 106), and 'as an amateur anthropologist' of making 'certain remarks regarding racial characteristics' (Guinness, 299). It was clear that, as Heller admits, 'Moyne was no worse than other British decision-makers. He supported partition and the establishment of a Jewish state' (Heller, 324). But he also received the blame for the deaths, in December 1941, of hundreds of Jews on the steamship *Struma*. Its sinking followed the refusal of visas to its passengers to enter Palestine, a decision which had been made when Moyne was colonial secretary. He had also opposed the establishment of specifically Jewish army units in the Middle East, partly to avoid offending Arab sensibilities. As a result he had long been part of the 'rogues gallery' (Heller, 123) of radical Zionist groups.

On 6 November 1944 Moyne was assassinated in Cairo by two members of the Fighters for Israel's Freedom (previously the Stern gang). This act proved largely counterproductive. For Churchill, who had previously been sympathetic to the Zionist cause, his friend's death was 'a real turning-point' (Rose, 164). In early 1944 the 'creation of a sovereign Jewish state … was back on the agenda' in Britain. After the assassination Churchill 'postponed implementation indefinitely' (Kolinsky, 205). He refused to meet again with Chaim Weizmann, president of the World Zionist Organisation, although he was 'a very old friend' (Gilbert, 1052). The killing was condemned by Jewish leaders and newspapers in Britain and Palestine, but significant damage had been done to the Zionist cause.

Moyne was cremated at Golders Green, Middlesex, on 17 November 1944, after his body had been flown back to Britain. He was succeeded by his eldest son, Bryan Walter *Guinness. MOYNE, *rev.* MARC BRODIE

**Sources** *The Times* (7 Nov 1944) · *The Times* (17 Nov 1944) · personal knowledge (1959) · private information (1959) · Burke, *Peerage* (1999) · F. Mullally, *The silver salver: the story of the Guinness family* (1981) · M. Guinness, *The Guinness legend* (1989) · J. Heller, *The Stern gang: ideology, politics and terror, 1940–1949* (1995) · N. Rose, 'Churchill and Zionism', *Churchill*, ed. R. Blake and W. R. Louis (1996) · M. Kolinsky, *Britain's war in the Middle East: strategy and diplomacy, 1936–42* (1999) · I. Black, 'Assassins', *Guardian Weekend* (5 Nov 1994), 39–43 · M. Gilbert, *Winston S. Churchill*, 7: *Road to victory, 1941–1945* (1986) · *WWW* · *CGPLA Eng. & Wales* (1944)

**Archives** Bodl. Oxf., corresp. with Lord Monckton · Bodl. RH, corresp. with Lord Lugard · TCD, corresp. with Thomas Bodkin · U. Lond., Institute of Commonwealth Studies, MSS relating to royal commission on the West Indies | FILM BFI NFTVA, news footage | SOUND IWM SA, recorded talk

**Likenesses** W. Stoneman, four photographs, 1919–41, NPG · group photograph, 1926, Hult. Arch. · photograph, 1930, Hult. Arch. · T. Cottrell, cigarette card, NPG · photograph, repro. in Heller, *Stern gang* · photograph, repro. in *The Times* (7 Nov 1944) · photograph, repro. in *The Guardian* (5 Nov 1994)
**Wealth at death** £2,000,000: probate, 2 Dec 1944, *CGPLA Eng. & Wales*

**Guirey** [*née* Obolensky], **Princess Sylvia** (**1931–1997**), artist and art patron, was born on 18 May 1931 in Austria, the daughter of Princess Alice Obolensky (1902–1956), daughter of John Jacob Astor IV, a member of the American branch of the Astor family. Beautiful, rich, and unhappy, at the time of Sylvia's birth Alice was married to her first husband, Prince Serge Obolensky, a former tsarist officer, but her daughter's father was Raimund von Hofmannsthal, an Austrian writer and son of the poet Hugo von Hofmannsthal. The Obolenskys divorced in 1932, and Alice married Hofmannsthal; Sylvia remained known as Sylvia Obolensky. Her mother divorced Hofmannsthal in 1940 and went on to marry and divorce twice more: in 1940 she married Philip Harding, an English journalist, and in 1946 David Pleydell-Bouverie, an American architect. Sylvia had one elder brother and two sisters (officially half-sisters, although the elder was the daughter of Alice's second marriage). She spent her childhood constantly on the move between homes at Rheinbeck, on the Astor estate overlooking the Hudson River in New York; Hanover Lodge, in Regent's Park, London; and Schloss Kammer, on the Attersee, in Austria, and her mother entertained lavishly wherever she went. During the Second World War Alice stayed in London but her children were shipped back to the United States with their Irish nurse to live in the St Regis Hotel, owned by Alice's brother Vincent, and later in Obolensky's apartment in New York, while he was serving in the US Army. Sylvia was educated by a governess and went on to the Brearly School, in New York, and the Art Students League. Her mother had returned to New York in 1946 but continued to spend much of the year in London. Alice had a passion for art and ballet, and her homes became centres for artists, dancers, and writers, including Osbert and Edith Sitwell, Aldous Huxley, and Frederick Ashton, and, in America, Gore Vidal and Tennessee Williams. She was an important patron of the Sadler's Wells Ballet Company from its founding in 1931 and paid for its first visit to the United States, in 1949; she later became a benefactress of the New York City Ballet. Sylvia grew up amid all this artistic activity.

Alice had always been eccentric; Joyce Grenfell, a niece of Nancy Astor, described her turning up to one of Nancy Astor's parties looking like a Chinese pagoda: 'very attractive and queer but definitely oriental' (J. Grenfell, *Darling Ma*, 1988, 119). After her final divorce she became increasingly strange. She had been one of the first four people to enter the tomb of Tutankhamun in 1922, and had helped herself to a fabulous necklace; she now became obsessed with Egyptology and the death cults of the pharaohs. Living most of the time at Rheinbeck, she learned to read hieroglyphics so that she could read messages from the past, and became convinced that she was the reincarnation of an Egyptian princess who had been forced to renounce the religion of the sun. When she died, in 1956, there were rumours that she had taken an overdose. But despite her eccentricity she was a powerful influence on Sylvia's early life.

In 1950 Sylvia married Jean Louis Ganshof van der Meersch (1927–1982), a Belgian financier, whom she divorced in 1957. She became very interested in stage design, working in New York with the Russian painter and stage designer Eugene Berman (1899–1972) on several productions, including a new production of *Don Giovanni* at the Metropolitan Opera in 1957. In that year she married Prince Azamat Kadir Sultan Guirey (1924–2001), who claimed to be descended from Genghis Khan: they had two sons and one daughter, and divorced in 1963. They moved to London in the late 1950s, and Sylvia became an excellent cook, reputedly serving the best food in London. Having inherited a share of her grandmother's large fortune, in 1958, she began to collect contemporary art, and became interested in pop art in the 1960s, buying mainly from the Robert Fraser Gallery, an important London exhibitor; in the 1970s she supported young conceptual artists, entertaining artists and dealers at her house in Elm Place, off the Fulham Road. She took a studio in Gloucester Road and began to paint seriously in the late 1960s. After her first exhibition, at the Situation Gallery in London, in 1972, she showed at the Sao Paolo Biennale in 1973, and in 1976 her work was included in the 'New Talent' show at the Betty Parsons Gallery, in New York, and the Arts Council Serpentine Show, in London. She continued to exhibit regularly at the Hester van Royen Gallery and the Benjamin Rhodes Gallery in London and at the Betty Parsons Gallery.

Sylvia Guirey died on 27 June 1997 at her home, 241 New Kings Road, Fulham, London. ANNE PIMLOTT BAKER

**Sources** D. Wilson, *The Astors* (1993) · L. Kavaler, *The Astors: a family chronicle* (1966), 254–66 · *Daily Telegraph* (22 July 1997) · d. cert.
**Likenesses** photograph, 1961, repro. in *Daily Telegraph*
**Wealth at death** £1,465,876: probate, 5 Feb 1998, *CGPLA Eng. & Wales*

**Guisborough** [Hemingford, Hemingburgh], **Walter of** (*fl.* *c.***1290**–*c.***1305**), chronicler and Augustinian canon, was a member of the priory of St Mary at Guisborough. According to his latest editor, Harry Rothwell, the correct version of his name is likely to be Walter of Guisborough. That name occurs in the best manuscripts of his work, and is mentioned in the earliest medieval source that quotes his chronicle. Of the names used by previous editors, Walter of Hemingford is found only in late marginal additions, while the name Walter of Hemingburgh occurs solely in the colophon of one manuscript, BL, Lansdowne MS 239. A Walter of Hemingburgh was, however, sub-prior of Guisborough Priory in the early fourteenth century. In view of this circumstance that name cannot be entirely discounted. None the less the manuscript evidence suggests that the most probable name of the author of the Guisborough account was Walter of Guisborough.

Apart from the fact that he wrote his chronicle *c.*1305,

little is known about Walter of Guisborough. Guisborough itself was never a centre of chronicle writing, and Walter of Guisborough is the only author of a chronicle that is known to survive from that house. Although it has been suggested that parts of a missing Guisborough chronicle may lie behind the fourteenth-century section of the Anonimalle chronicle, this appears unlikely. Guisborough's chronicle itself extends from the time of the Norman conquest to 1305, and is indebted in its opening section to northern sources like the chronicle of William of Newburgh and the Durham compilation known as the *Historia post Bedam*. For the thirteenth century Guisborough used the work of Martinus Polonus. After 1290 his chronicle is supposedly an original source, although even here there are similarities between parts of his work and other northern accounts. The inclusion in this section of his chronicle of a number of documents suggests a system of record keeping at Guisborough which was to add significantly to the value of his work.

For the middle years of the thirteenth century Guisborough's narrative is relatively brief. The main interest of his chronicle has traditionally been seen to lie in its account of Edward I's reign, and in particular in its account of Edward's later years. Recent research suggests, however, that as a detailed guide to events in the south of England during Edward's reign the chronicle is not reliable. An analysis of the well-known part, which describes the attitude of the opposition party during the crisis of 1296–7, reveals many errors. Although Guisborough had the ability to dramatize and to depict clearly the issues that divided contemporaries, his love of a good story often conflicted with the accuracy of his reporting. Certain of the speeches that he includes in his text, such as the earl marshal's reply to Edward I in 1297, may well be literary inventions. But for northern history, and Anglo-Scottish relations in particular, Guisborough's narrative is more firmly based. The close links existing between the priory of Guisborough and northern families such as the Bruces provided him with important sources of information. The documents that he quotes on Anglo-Scottish history, including the Latin form of Roger Brabazon's statement at Norham in 1291, add considerably to the value of his work. His chronicle also affords some insight into northern opinion at a time when important events were happening in the north.

Guisborough's chronicle survives in some ten manuscripts. Considerable portions of his text were worked into Knighton's chronicle at Leicester, and into the Osney–Abingdon compilations made in the south later. Guisborough appears to have ended his account in 1305. An addition to the chronicle covering the years from 1305 to 1312 was the work of a continuator possibly from Durham. A further continuation, extending from 1327 to 1347, and known traditionally as the Continuation of Hemingburgh, is found together with the full text of Guisborough's chronicle only in one sixteenth-century transcript. It has no intrinsic connection with Guisborough's work, and is a version of the *Historia aurea* for these years. JOHN TAYLOR

**Sources** *The chronicle of Walter of Guisborough*, ed. H. Rothwell, CS, 3rd ser., 89 (1957) • A. Gransden, *Historical writing in England*, 1 (1974), 470–76

**Guise, John** (1682/3–1765), army officer and art collector, was the son of William *Guise (*bap.* 1652, *d.* 1683) of Ablode Court, Sandhurst, Gloucestershire (where John was born), professor of oriental languages at Oxford, and his wife, Frances, the daughter and coheir of George Southcote, of Buckland All Saints, Devon. He entered Gloucester Hall at Oxford in July 1697 and then Merton College, from where he matriculated in July 1698, aged fifteen. He was admitted a gentleman commoner at Christ Church on 18 October 1700 and graduated BA on 20 March 1702, having been admitted a student of the Middle Temple in May 1700. Later in 1702 he sought election as a fellow of All Souls, but his candidacy was rejected by the visitor, Archbishop Thomas Tenison. In 1704 he abandoned his academic ambitions and left Oxford.

On 9 April 1706 Guise was appointed captain in the 1st regiment of foot guards, with which he served during Marlborough's campaigns in Flanders, including Oudenarde (1708), down to the peace of Utrecht. His commission was renewed upon the accession of George I in 1714, and in 1719 he commanded the battalion of seven companies of the 1st guards (415 strong) sent on the Vigo expedition. On 23 October 1723 he married Mary Ann Ursula, the eldest daughter of Philibert D'Hervart, of Bern, Switzerland. They had one son, William Guise, (*c.*1728–1751). In 1724 he was promoted second major, in 1727 regimental major, and in July 1735 lieutenant-colonel.

Thirty years' service with the 1st guards ended in 1738, when Guise was made honorary colonel of the 6th (Warwickshire) regiment of foot. In July 1739 he was promoted brigadier-general, in which capacity he served in the expedition to Cartagena (1740–41). In this ill-fated and poorly led campaign Guise was one of the few to return with his reputation intact. He distinguished himself by his bravery when in command of the assault on the castle at San Lazar; after carrying the enemy's outworks and withstanding a most disastrous fire for several hours, the attack was withdrawn with the loss of 600 killed and wounded out of a force of 1200. The 6th foot were sent as reinforcements to Jamaica in early 1742. Guise fell ill and returned to England soon after they arrived, having been promoted to the rank of major-general in February 1742.

Guise's reputation for an all too ready wit and somewhat outlandish bravery (but not rodomontade) was established for posterity by Horace Walpole, who wrote to Sir Horace Mann on 7 July 1742:

> Your relation Guise is arrived from Carthagena, madder than ever. As he was marching up to one of the forts, all his men deserted him; his lieutenant advised him to retire; he replied, 'He never had turned his back yet, and would not now,' and stood all the fire. When the pelicans [artillery balls of 6 lb weight] were flying over his head, he cried out, 'What would brave Chloe [the duke of Newcastle's French cook] give for some of these to make a pelican pie!' When he is brave enough to perform such actions really as are almost incredible, what pity it is that he should for ever persist in saying things that are totally so! (Walpole, *Corr.*, 17.485)

**John Guise** (1682/3–1765), by Sir Joshua Reynolds, 1755–6

Recalling the incident twelve years later (8 November 1754), Walpole again wrote to Mann:

> what a pity it is, that a man who can deal in hyperboles at the mouth of a cannon, should be fond of them with a glass of wine in his hand! I have heard Guise affirm that the colliers at Newcastle feed their children with fire shovels!
> (ibid., 20.450)

Decimated by disease, Guise's regiment was shipped back home from Cartagena with the remnants of the expedition in July 1743, and after being restored to strength was marched to Scotland in February 1744 to counter the growing risk of rebellion. Guise was made lieutenant-general in 1745, but it is not clear that he served with his regiment during the Jacobite rising, in which the 6th foot was detailed to garrison the line of forts running between Fort William and Inverness. Two companies served at the battle of Prestonpans in September: nearly all were killed or taken prisoner. After the final defeat of the rising the regiment was brought together at Berwick and returned to Scotland until 1751. Guise was made governor of Berwick in 1753 and full general in 1762. He died in London on 12 June 1765.

By his will of 24 April 1760 Guise bequeathed a substantial collection of paintings to his old college Christ Church, Oxford. He was known to the celebrated antiquary George Vertue (1684–1756) as a lover of painting and a connoisseur who specialized in old Italian masters and contemporary copies. About 1720 he became a patron of Jacob Christofel Le Blon, a painter who had devised a process for manufacturing colour mezzotints. Guise was chairman of the company set up to exploit the invention, the Picture Office, but the concern was bankrupt by 1723, losing Guise, by his own estimate, between £600 and £700. In the 1730s he was giving private viewings of his collection to London society, and during the 1740s he became an adviser on artistic matters to Frederick, prince of Wales. He apparently acquired this love of painting from General Wade, with whom he served on the Vigo expedition in 1719, and later the duke of Cumberland. Most of the best paintings were collected advantageously during several long visits to the continent, certainly to Paris and probably also to Florence and Rome. Well over a hundred were obtained during the last five years of his life, and these became the subject of a lawsuit brought by the college against Guise's executor Mr Barrow, who interpreted the bequest to mean only those paintings collected up to the date of the will (1760) and not the later ones. The college's action for recovery was successful, and all 257 paintings were reunited in 1767. As a peace offering, two were returned to the family, including a portrait of Guise by Gavin Hamilton, painted at Rome about 1753. Between 1770 and 1773 the college employed the German restorer Richard Bonus to restore the collection, during which time it suffered severe maltreatment which led to further neglect. Not all the collection was spoilt, however. According to the cataloguer, James Byam Shaw, there remain two fine Tintorettos, a Veronese, four works by Annibale Carracci, and three Van Dycks, as well as examples of Lotto, Giralomo de Treviso, and others. JONATHAN SPAIN

**Sources** J. Byam Shaw, *Drawings by old masters at Christ Church, Oxford* (1976) · J. Byam Shaw, *Paintings by old masters at Christ Church, Oxford* (1967) · J. Byam Shaw, *Old master drawings from Christ Church, Oxford* (1972) · J. Maclean, 'Elmore and the family of Guise', *Transactions of the Bristol and Gloucestershire Archaeological Society*, 3 (1878–9), 49–78 · R. Cannon, ed., *Historical record of the sixth, or royal first Warwickshire regiment of foot* (1839) · C. L. Kingsford, *The story of the Royal Warwickshire regiment, formerly the sixth foot* (1921) · C. Dalton, ed., *English army lists and commission registers, 1661–1714*, 6 vols. (1892–1904) · F. W. Hamilton, *The origin and history of the first or grenadier guards*, 3 vols. (1874) · Fortescue, *Brit. army* · K. Tomasson and F. Buist, *Battles of the '45* (1962); repr. (1978) · *Manuscripts of the earl of Egmont: diary of Viscount Percival, afterwards first earl of Egmont*, 3 vols., HMC, 63 (1920–23) · Foster, *Alum. Oxon.* · Walpole, *Corr.*, vols. 17, 20 · *GM*, 1st ser., 35 (1765), 299 · J. Turner, ed., *The dictionary of art*, 34 vols. (1996), vol. 13, p. 837

**Likenesses** G. Hamilton, portrait, *c.*1753 · J. Reynolds, oils, 1755–6, Christ Church Oxf. [*see illus.*] · J. Bacon senior, marble bust, *c.*1770 (after J. Reynolds), Christ Church Oxf. · A. Pesne, portrait

**Guise, Sir John Wright, third baronet** (1777–1865), army officer, born at Highnam Court, Highnam, Gloucestershire, on 20 July 1777, was the second son of Sir John Guise (1733–1794) of Highnam Court, who was created a baronet in December 1783 (the family baronetcy of the first creation had become extinct in 1773). His mother, Elizabeth, was the daughter and heir of Thomas Wright. He was appointed ensign, 70th foot, on 4 November 1794, and was transferred in 1795 to the 3rd foot guards, in which he became lieutenant and captain in 1798, captain and lieutenant-colonel in 1805, and major in 1814. He served with them at Ferrol, Vigo, and Cadiz in 1800, in Egypt in 1801, in Hanover during 1805–6, and in Portugal in 1809.

He was present at Busaco, and commanded the light companies of the guards, with some companies of the 95th rifles attached, at Fuentes de Oñoro. He commanded the 1st battalion, 3rd guards in the Peninsular campaigns of 1812–14, including the battle of Salamanca, the capture of Madrid, the siege of Burgos, the battle of Vitoria, the passage of the Bidassoa, the battle of the Nive, the battle of the Adour, and the investment of Bayonne, where he took command of the 2nd brigade of guards after Major-General Edward Stopford was wounded.

Guise received the Peninsular War medal and gold cross. He became a major-general in 1819, was made KCB in September 1831, became a lieutenant-general in 1841, colonel 85th foot from June 1847, general in November 1851, and GCB in November 1862. On 12 August 1815 he married Charlotte Diana (*d.* February 1835), daughter of John Vernon of Clontarf Castle, co. Dublin; they had several children, including William Vernon, fourth baronet. Guise succeeded to the baronetcy on the death of his brother, Berkeley William, second baronet, on 23 July 1834. Guise was senior general in the *Army List* at the time of his death, which occurred at his home, Elmore Court, Elmore, Gloucestershire, on 1 April 1865.

H. M. Chichester, *rev.* David Gates

**Sources** *GM*, 3rd ser., 18 (1865), 666 • Boase, *Mod. Eng. biog.* • *The dispatches of … the duke of Wellington … from 1799 to 1818*, ed. J. Gurwood, 4: *Peninsula, 1790–1813* (1835), 776 • *Army List* (1791–1838) • *Army List* (1865) • Burke, *Peerage* (1959) • A. B. Rodger, *The war of the second coalition: 1798–1801, a strategic commentary* (1964) • D. Gates, *The Spanish ulcer: a history of the Peninsular War* (1986) • *CGPLA Eng. & Wales* (1865)

**Archives** Glos. RO • priv. coll., journals and commonplace books

**Wealth at death** under £30,000: probate, 30 June 1865, *CGPLA Eng. & Wales*

**Guise, William** (*bap.* **1652**, *d.* **1683**), orientalist, was baptized on 30 September 1652 in the parish of Elmore on the River Severn, south-west of Gloucester. The eldest son of John Guise and his wife, Hester, daughter of Major Stratford, he came from a distinguished family of landowners. His father, who inherited Ablode Court a couple of miles north of Gloucester in the parish of Sandhurst, was described as 'a gentleman of an estate of £500 a year' (*Letters of Humphrey Prideaux*, 44), while his father's elder brother, Christopher, was created a baronet by Charles II and inherited the family seat of Elmore Court.

On 21 May 1669 Guise matriculated as a commoner at Oriel College, Oxford. On 9 November 1670 he was also admitted to Lincoln's Inn. At Oxford he must have benefited from the teaching of Edward Pococke, professor of Hebrew and Arabic, and in 1671 was already able to contribute a poem in Syriac to *Epicedia universitatis Oxoniensis*, the university's volume commemorating the death of the duchess of York. He graduated BA as a fellow of All Souls College on 4 April 1674 and proceeded MA on 16 October 1677.

Guise, who was ordained, resigned his fellowship in 1680 to marry Frances, the learned daughter of George Southcote of Devon and, judging from Humphrey Prideaux's references to Guise in 1681 as 'my kinsman', a relative of the Prideaux family. They were to have two daughters, Frances (1681) and Mary (1683), and a son, John *Guise (1682/3–1765). Enjoying an annual income of some £500 from the family estate (which Prideaux regarded as particularly impressive), Guise continued to reside in Oxford in the parish of St Michael and leased a property in Berkeley from the first earl.

Guise's reputation as a scholar was immense. In 1675 Prideaux had referred to him as 'the greatest miracle in the knowledge of [Arabic] that I ever heard of' (*Letters of Humphrey Prideaux*, 44). Six years later he called him 'an ornament to the University' and commended his learning and piety (ibid., 110)—praise which was subsequently echoed by Guise's friend Edward Bernard. Besides being a linguist of genius, Guise was accomplished in mathematics, theology, philosophy, and law, and Prideaux only failed to have him appointed a justice of the peace late in 1681 because his MA degree was considered too junior. The fragment of an attack on Thomas Hobbes's *Leviathan* remains a testimonial of his orthodoxy (Bodl. Oxf., MS Marsh 253, fol. 58*r*).

To Arabic, Hebrew, Syriac, and Aramaic, Guise added numerous other languages including Turkish, Samaritan, Persian, Ethiopic, and Armenian. He used them for biblical scholarship, studying the Armenian version of the Septuagint and making notes on the Arabic Pentateuch which were published over a century later by Joseph White in his *Letter to the … Bishop of London, Suggesting a Plan for a New Edition of the LXX* (1779). Guise's most important work, however, was his translation of, and commentary on, *Zeraim*, a tract of the Mishnah, the great collection of Jewish law. His edition, printed after Pococke's translation of Maimonides' preface to the Mishnah, was published posthumously by Bernard in 1690, and was part of an increasingly informed examination of Judaism and rabbinic texts which had got under way in England earlier in the century. Guise's contribution has justly been called 'the high point of Hebrew studies at Oxford' (Feingold, 465).

Even if Guise brought much of his learning to bear on the study of the Bible and Judaism he also had an exceptional interest in Islamic texts. By 1673 he had copied out the first seventy-eight suras of the Koran, collating the text from three manuscripts procured for him by Bernard from the library of St John's College (Bodl. Oxf., MS Marsh 533). Besides having access to the various Oxford libraries, both public and private, he also appears to have had a collection of his own, and when Abraham Hinckelmann published his Arabic edition of the Koran in Hamburg in 1694 he collated it with a manuscript that had belonged to Guise. One of the most remarkable features of his commentary on *Zeraim* is the breadth of Guise's Arabic sources—lexicographical, medical, zoological, geographical, and, most striking of all, poetic: he seems to have been the first European Arabist to quote both the eighth-century poet Dhu'l-Rumma and the seventh-century ʿAbd Allah ben Rawaha. When he died he was preparing an edition of Abu'l-Fida's *Geography* (Oxford, All Souls College, MS 287). He had completed his transcription of the Arabic, and had hoped to add notes and a Latin translation. He also compiled an English–Turkish vocabulary (Bodl. Oxf., MS Marsh 253) and added to the interleaved copy of Francesco Rivola's Armenian–Latin lexicon lent to him by Thomas Marshall (Bodl. Oxf., MS Marshall 30).

Prideaux thought Guise would be a worthy successor of Pococke and indeed, all that we know of Guise suggests the greatest promise. By 23 August 1683, however, he had been stricken by smallpox, and drew up his will, 'sick in body'. He died on 3 September and was buried on the same day in the chancel of St Michael's Church. His younger brother John, who had joined him at Oriel in 1671 and received his BA and MA degrees at Corpus Christi, had been appointed chaplain to the Levant Company in Aleppo on 6 September 1681 and was to die in 1687.

ALASTAIR HAMILTON

**Sources** G. J. Toomer, *Eastern wisedome and learning: the study of Arabic in seventeenth-century England* (1996) • M. Feingold, 'Oriental studies', *Hist. U. Oxf.* 4: *17th-cent. Oxf.*, 449–503 • *Letters of Humphrey Prideaux … to John Ellis*, ed. E. M. Thompson, CS, new ser., 15 (1875) • Wood, *Ath. Oxon.*, new edn, 4.114–15 • Foster, *Alum. Oxon.* • W. Guise, *Misnae pars: ordinis primi Zeraim Tituli septem*, ed. E. Bernard (1690) • [J. Guise], *Autobiography of Thomas Raymond, and Memoirs of the family of Guise of Elmore, Gloucestershire*, ed. G. Davies, CS, 3rd ser., 28 (1917), 83–184 • J. B. Pearson, *A biographical sketch of the chaplains to the Levant Company, maintained at Constantinople, Aleppo and Smyrna, 1611–1706* (1883) • J. Burke and J. B. Burke, *A genealogical and heraldic history of the extinct and dormant baronetcies of England, Ireland and Scotland*, 2nd edn (1841); repr. (1844) • *DNB* • W. P. Baildon, ed., *The records of the Honorable Society of Lincoln's Inn: admissions*, 1 (1896) • J. White, *A letter to the … bishop of London, suggesting a plan for a new edition of the LXX* (1779), 30–55 • will, PRO, PROB 11/374, fols. 183v–184r • parish register, Oxford, St Michael, Oxon. RO [burial] • parish register, Elmore, Glos. RO [birth]

**Archives** All Souls Oxf., transcription of the Arabic text of Abu 'l-Fida's *Geography*, MS 287 • Bodl. Oxf., transcription of first 78 suras of Koran, Marsh MS 533 • Bodl. Oxf., notes and texts in Syriac and Arabic, Marsh MS 88 • Bodl. Oxf., English–Turkish vocabulary and notes, incl. attack on Hobbes, Marsh MS 253

**Wealth at death** 'an estate of his own about £500 per annum': Prideaux, *Letters*; will, PRO, PROB 11/374, fols. 183v–184r

**Gulbenkian, Calouste Sarkis** (1869–1955), oil industrialist and benefactor, was born in Scutari, adjacent to Constantinople, in Turkey, on 23 March 1869, one of three sons of Sarkis Gulbenkian (*d.* 1894), a trader in kerosene and a provincial banker. Although he respected his family, Calouste does not seem to have had close relations with his brothers throughout his life.

**Early life and marriage** Armenian by birth and tradition, Gulbenkian was initially educated locally and gained admission to Robert's College, Constantinople. He then attended the École Supérieure, Marseilles, before being admitted to King's College, London, in 1884, where he was elected an associate in 1887, having been awarded prizes and commendations in physics and mechanics. In that year he returned home to Constantinople, where his linguistic proficiency and technical training provided the essential elements for his subsequent career.

Gulbenkian was soon representing his father's interests, gaining experience of commercial affairs, and acquainting himself with the Ottoman corridors of political power. In particular, he impressed the Ottoman authorities with his understanding of the political and

**Calouste Sarkis Gulbenkian (1869–1955)**, by Charles Joseph Watelet, 1912

economic issues involved with the nascent oil industry; and he was soon consulted about oil concessions and the prospects for oil in Turkish territories. His ambitions were aroused. He was a good-looking, elegant young man of medium stature, with dark eyebrows and bright eyes and with a well-trimmed moustache and beard. In later life his domed, balding forehead and bushy eyebrows were prominent, and a tendency to plumpness was noticeable.

Gulbenkian courted and eventually married in London in 1892 Nevarte Esseyan (*d.* 1952), whose father, Ohannes, was a substantial man of business in Constantinople. Their honeymoon was spent in Paris where their host was César Ritz, a lifelong friend. The couple settled in London at 36 Hyde Park Gardens, living there from 1900 to 1925. They had a son, Nubar Sarkis (*b.* 1896), and a daughter, Rita. Nevarte was more outgoing than her husband—humorous and charming, entertaining with warmth and a real social flair. He was dutiful and patriarchal, insisting on obedience and respect rather than exhibiting affection, but he was devoted to her. Proud of his strong-willed son's ability, he was disappointed at his undue attitude of independence and regretted what he regarded as his ostentatious manner. Nubar feared rather than loved his father, but admitted his father's indulgence towards him, though he resented his tight financial control.

**Career in oil** Well established at the turn of the century, Gulbenkian gradually extended the scope and scale of his commercial operations in London and Constantinople, with frequent visits to Paris, where he based himself at the Ritz Hotel. He and his family had survived the worst excesses of the Armenian massacres of 1896; and out of those misfortunes he came to know and befriend the Mantachev family, who had widespread petroleum interests in Russia; he became acquainted with Nubar Pasha, a prominent Egyptian politician and a relative of his wife. Such distinguished figures were important contacts and Gulbenkian's affairs prospered at a time when oil, as a result of new discoveries and the impact of new technology, was playing an increasing role in world trade. Although Russian and American production dominated the opening years of the twentieth century, Dutch and British interests were beginning to become important and prospects for oil in the Middle East brightened with the commencement of oil production in Persia in 1908.

Gulbenkian was at the heart of these developments, though he strangely failed to recognize the significance of the Persian oil find and its adverse repercussions on his own interests. He was more concerned with the potential for discovering oil in the Ottoman empire, and especially in Mesopotamia, which potential he pursued with 'unusual foresight and persistence' (*The Times*, 21 July 1955). However, Gulbenkian was aware of the interplay of the respective strengths of the main international oil companies; and he was closely involved with Henri Deterding and Marcus Samuel of Royal Dutch Shell, and with Shell's entry into the US market in 1912.

There was fierce international competition to obtain the concession to explore for oil in Mesopotamia, and Gulbenkian played an important role in the consortium of rival interests that was eventually formed. In 1912 he was one of the partners involved in the formation of a company for the eventual exploitation of the assumed oil reserves of Mesopotamia. This was the Turkish Petroleum Company (TPC), later renamed the Iraq Petroleum Company (IPC), in 1929. This became Gulbenkian's principal concern; he originally held a 15 per cent interest in the company, and then 5 per cent. He derived from it not only immense wealth, but also the sobriquet of 'Mr Five Per Cent'.

**Developing interests** Despite the political and economic gyrations in those years just before and after the First World War, especially in the Middle East, Gulbenkian managed to protect his own interests in Mesopotamia as the pace of exploration accelerated. In 1925 a new concession was signed with the government of Iraq. In 1928 oil was discovered at Baba Gurgur and in the same year a new constitution for the company was agreed. This confirmed the shareholdings of the Anglo-Persian Oil Company (later BP) and Royal Dutch Shell, and provided for the inclusion of French instead of German interests, as well as allowing for American participation and Gulbenkian's 5 per cent share. However, there were self-denying clauses in the agreement which prevented the partners in IPC from taking concessions elsewhere in the Ottoman empire. Gulbenkian's interests by this time were held by a Canadian company and were registered in Canada. With the discovery of oil in Kirkuk in 1934 and the completion of the first pipeline, Iraq became a major oil-producing region.

Although Iraq remained the main focus for his oil interests, Gulbenkian had also become involved in the formulation of French oil policy, especially during the First World War when he became a confidant of Senateur Henri Bérenger, the minister in charge of oil affairs. He also at this time acted as the representative of Royal Dutch Shell in France.

In the early 1920s Gulbenkian extended his oil interests to the emerging areas of production in Venezuela, in the course of which an unfortunate quarrel with Henri Deterding came to a head. Both men were strong-minded and opinionated. Gulbenkian felt that Deterding had treated some of the shareholders in Venezuelan Oil Concessions Ltd with scant regard, including himself. Deterding denied the accusations: compromise proved impossible and the break was absolute. Unfortunately it blighted the career of Gulbenkian's son, Nubar, who was Deterding's personal assistant and thought by some to be the right person to become his successor. Calouste, however, was adamant that his son leave Shell, which he did, to concentrate on family affairs. In 1927 Gulbenkian acquired a new residence in Paris, at 51 avenue d'Iena, a large and imposing house which he made into a home and a gallery for his greatly respected collection of art.

During the negotiations following the cancellation of the Anglo-Persian Oil Company's concession in 1932, Gulbenkian acted as adviser to the Persian government, though he played very little part in the final settlement of the dispute. The 1930s were a rewarding time for him, as oil from Iraq began to flow, and he enjoyed the company of a wide range of friends drawn not only from business and politics but from the cultural world, including Upham Pope, the American historian of Persian art, and Sir Kenneth Clark, director of the National Gallery.

**Later years and death** The onset of the Second World War not only shattered the international scene, it changed Gulbenkian's life. He had retained his British nationality (granted in 1902), but he also held an Iranian diplomatic passport. After the surrender of France in 1940 he remained in Vichy France with the Iranian diplomatic mission. It was then claimed that his British nationality brought him within the provisions of the Trading with the Enemy Act and prevented him, like the Compagnie Française des Petroles (CFP), from participating in the business of the IPC. The custodian of enemy property was empowered to vest in himself 'enemy' property and act as if he owned it. By agreement with the custodian a vesting order was made in relation to Gulbenkian's IPC shares, and the custodian then appointed an associate of Gulbenkian and his lawyer in England to represent the custodian at IPC meetings. When diplomatic relations between Iran and France were severed in 1942, Gulbenkian, persuaded by Nubar, found refuge in Portugal rather than Switzerland and he installed himself at the Aviz Hotel in Lisbon. Soon after he arrived, the vesting order was revoked and the IPC shares were returned to him; he remained in Lisbon for the rest of his life.

The war caused fundamental changes in the balances of political and commercial power. The United States rejected past isolationism and responded to the challenge of the cold war, adopting an interventionist policy in respect of Arab-Israeli differences. By 1943 the Middle East had become the recognized dominant oil region of the world, and Saudi Arabia became the focus of American attention. Efforts were made by the American companies in IPC to free themselves from the agreement not to take concessions elsewhere in the former Ottoman empire. The American companies claimed that the discontinuity in IPC affairs, caused by the wartime 'enemy' status of Gulbenkian and the French company CFP, meant that the 1928 agreement had been frustrated and that they should be permitted to participate in Saudi Arabian concessions. This was challenged legally but after lengthy and complicated negotiations a settlement was ultimately reached out of court in 1948. By then Gulbenkian was in declining health and his affairs were being handled by a group of his closest advisers, including his son, Nubar, his son-in-law, Kevork Loris Esseyan, and his nephew Roberto Gulbenkian. Predeceased by his wife in 1952, Gulbenkian, who confidently expected to live to an advanced age, died on 20 July 1955 in Lisbon. He was cremated in Switzerland and his remains were committed to the care of the church of St Sarkis, in London, with full Armenian rites.

During a successful and fulfilling life of business enterprise, Gulbenkian's determination of character, adaptability of manner, shrewdness in negotiation, integrity in business, hard-working attention to detail, and cosmopolitan outlook were always apparent. With little or no organization behind him he largely managed his enterprises himself, with only a small staff in the later years of his life. He had little use for formal office routine and relied upon personal contact.

**The Gulbenkian legacy** During his lifetime Gulbenkian had one indulgence, his caring concern for his art treasures—his 'children', as he termed them. They formed the core of one of the finest individual private collections in the world. The story is told that as a boy his father had rewarded him for some school success and that with the money he had gone to the bazaar and purchased one antique coin, rather than saving it, as his father had expected. After the Russian Revolution he succeeded in acquiring some fine items there including Jean Antoine Houdon's *Diana*, *Hélène Fourment* by Peter Paul Rubens, and *Pallas Athene* by Rembrandt, as well as fine gold and silver ware by François Thomas Germain.

Gulbenkian's collection was based on his personal choice and owed nothing to extravagance or fashion. Every piece was in the finest condition and he took the best advice available. His range was wide: books, manuscripts, paintings, statuary, textiles, coins, carpets, and various *objets d'art*. Knowledgeable himself, he was respected by dealers and art historians alike. While he felt more at home with art of the past he had some choice modern examples and appreciated the artistic virtuosity of René Lalique and Auguste Rodin. He was on good terms with curators and directors of national galleries, such as Sir Kenneth Clark in London and John Walker in Washington, and in middle life he lent generously to the National Gallery and the National Gallery of Art. He was a generous benefactor to the Armenian church and founded and endowed the church of St Sarkis in London, in memory of his parents. He contributed to the Armenian patriarchy of Jerusalem and was a frequent contributor to philanthropic good causes and reliefs without seeking public acknowledgement. It was in keeping with the private nature of his character.

Gulbenkian did not travel a great deal but he was enthusiastic about the delights of architecture and was particularly moved by the charms of the Alhambra. In Egypt he was impressed with the sense of great antiquity. Not only was he deeply appreciative of the beauty and grace of art, especially of the feminine figure, but he was also very sensible of the natural and scenic beauty occasioned by sunrises and sunsets. In 1937 he purchased a romantic park with beautiful trees, Les Enclos, near Deauville, a favourite haunt, where he often spent part of the summer.

Gulbenkian had already begun in 1938 to refer to his intention to establish a permanent home for his art treasures, without deciding on anything very practical except some ideas for a gallery in London. Plans became more definite in a will drawn up on 6 May 1950 and more precise in his will of 18 June 1953. Controversy subsequently attended the creation and organization of the Calouste Gulbenkian Foundation for charitable, artistic, educational, and scientific purposes: Nubar stated that it failed to represent the objectives of his father; and Lord Radcliffe, closest confidant, legal adviser, and first choice of Gulbenkian to be the initial chairman, declined the honour. In the event Dr José de Azeredo Perdigão, Gulbenkian's Portuguese lawyer, succeeded, and he successfully guided the foundation on its way for more than thirty-five years.

After Gulbenkian's death a long and appreciative obituary in *The Times* carried the apt headline, 'Great wealth amassed and well spent'. It mentioned that his 'entrenched 5 per cent gave Gulbenkian a unique position in industrial democracy' (ibid.), and described how when negotiations affecting his interests were undertaken, he ranked on a par with governments. Gulbenkian, it argued, was one of those, like Cecil Rhodes and Ferdinand de Lesseps, whose commercial kingdoms gave them an international standing in their own right (*The Times*, 21 July 1955). R. W. FERRIER

**Sources** R. Hewins, *Mr Five Per Cent* (1957) • N. Gulbenkian, *Pantaraxia* (1965) • J. Lodwick and D. H. Young, *Gulbenkian: an interpretation of Calouste Sarkis Gulbenkian* (1958) • J. A. Perdigão, *Calouste Gulbenkian, collector*, trans. A. L. Marques (1969) • R. W. Ferrier, *The history of the British Petroleum Company*, 1: *The developing years, 1901–1932* (1982) • S. H. Longrigg, *Oil in the Middle East*, 3rd edn (1968) • M. Kent, *Oil and empire: British policy and Mesopotamian oil, 1900–1920* (1976) • B. Shwadran, *The Middle East, oil and the great powers* (1956) • E. Penrose and E. F. Penrose, *Iraq, international relations and national development*, pts 1–3 (1978) • H. Bérenger, *La pétrole et la France* (1921) •

H. Bérenger, *La politique de pétrole* (1920) • R. W. Ferrier, 'French oil policy, 1917–30', *Enterprise and history: essays in honour of Charles Wilson*, ed. D. C. Coleman and P. Mathias (1984), 237–62 • A. D. Miller, *Saudi Arabian oil and American foreign policy, 1939–1949* (1980) • I. H. Anderson, *ARAMCO, the United States and Saudi Arabia, 1933–1950* (1981) • *WWW* • *The Times* (21 July 1955) • *The Times* (30 July 1958)

**Archives** Calouste Gulbenkian Foundation, Lisbon

**Likenesses** C. J. Watelet, oils, 1912, Calouste Gulbenkian Foundation [*see illus.*] • photograph, 1934, repro. in Perdigão, *Calouste Gulbenkian* (1969), facing p. 62

**Wealth at death** £196,508 18*s*. 0*d*.: administration with will, 26 June 1956, *CGPLA Eng. & Wales* • approx. £300,000,000: *The Times*, 30 July 1955

**Gull, Cyril Arthur Edward Ranger** [*pseud.* Guy Thorne] (**1875–1923**), journalist and novelist, was born Arthur Edward Ranger Gull on 18 November 1875 at St John's Parsonage, Little Hulton, Lancashire, the first of two sons of the Revd Joseph Edward Gull (*b*. 1851), curate of Little Hulton and later vicar of Pendleton and of Rainhill, Lancashire, and his wife, Jessie Ranger (*b*. 1855). Having been educated at Manchester grammar school and at Denstone College he matriculated at Oxford University in 1894, as a non-collegiate student, but left without completing his first year.

Gull began his literary career as a journalist in London (which seems to be when he started to use the name Cyril), initially as a staff member of the *Saturday Review*, then as a writer for *The Echo*, *The Bookman*, *The Academy*, and *London Life*, and finally on the staff of the *Daily Mail* and of the satirical and gossip weekly *Society*. As a serious drinker and convivial man about town Gull was popular on Fleet Street and the Strand, and made a number of friends among the circle of bohemian artists and writers encouraged by the publisher Leonard Smithers; these included the illustrator Aubrey Beardsley, the watercolourist Scotson Clarke, the writers George Reginald Bacchus, Hannaford Bennett, and Sydney Cooper, and the poets Cotsford Dick and Ernest Dowson. With this group Gull regularly frequented such 'decadent' pubs and nightclubs as the Café Royal, the Bodega, and Gatti's, and enjoyed lavish dinner parties at Smithers's home in Bedford Square, and later in Maida Vale. During frequent visits to Cornwall, Gull was equally flamboyant; his friend Compton Mackenzie remembered that he 'made a habit of concealing bottles of whisky all over the moors so that on country walks he could boast he was never more than a quarter of a mile from refreshment' (Mackenzie, 12).

Gull's literary interests, however, turned increasingly from journalism to fiction and in 1898 he published his first novel, *The Hypocrite*. On 12 December 1898 he married Frances Beatrice (*b*. 1876), daughter of Major General George Alfred Wilson, but by 1912 he was married to Helena, the daughter of Augustus Hands. His public life, however, remained defined almost entirely by a male coterie.

Having adopted the pseudonym Guy Thorne in 1903, Gull published *When it was Dark: the Story of a Great Conspiracy*, which became an Edwardian best-seller and achieved a sale of over half a million copies. It was read and praised throughout the English-reading world and translated into several European languages. The simple plot features a Jewish villain, Constantine Schaube, who persuades an acquaintance at the British Museum to manufacture false archaeological evidence to prove that Christ never rose from the dead. Once Christianity has been perceived as a fraud, social order is destroyed; mayhem and violence, including financial panic and rape, sweep through the Western world. At the end of the novel, and just before all hope for humankind is lost, Schaube's evil plot is exposed by the novel's hero, the gentlemanly English curate Basil Gortre, and the world slowly returns to Christianity, prosperity, and calm.

Gull's novel was read both as a Christian tract and as a shocking and irreverent book that challenged the premises of faith and social conventions. Apparently Gull assumed his pseudonym in this work for at least a double purpose: to mask, for a wide readership, the racy young cynic that indeed he was, and simultaneously to give him the freedom to explore conservative Christian ideas rooted in his vicarage upbringing. Throughout the rest of his career he published more than fifty books, some (such as *The Harvest of Love*, 1905, and *The Air Pirate*, 1919) under his own name, others (such as *Made in his Image*, 1907, and *Love and the Freemason*, 1915) as Guy Thorne.

Gull's often sentimental and over-written prose earned him a wide audience who apparently did not object to unlikely coincidences, simple plots, flat characters, or statements that might or might not be satiric, such as 'June with her magic flutes had come to the duchy' or 'He staggered into the glare, among the tawny bastions, and then fell back in overwhelming awe' (C. Ranger-Gull, *Portalone*, 54, 284).

Throughout his career as a novelist Gull was interested also in autobiographical fiction (often much embellished) and in *romans à clef*, and figured as a thinly disguised character in his own work, such as *Portalone* (1908), set in Cornwall and featuring many of the local people and places that he came to know during visits to St Ives. He is also identifiable as a character in fiction by his friends, for example R. G. Bacchus's multi-volume erotic novel *The Confessions of Nemesis Hunt* (1902–6).

An ardent traveller, Gull made frequent trips to the continent, especially to France and as far afield as the Greek islands and north Africa. He was widely read in French as well as English literature, and passionate about country life and sports, especially shooting, serving for a time as vice-president of the Wild Fowlers' Association of Great Britain and Ireland. One of his neighbours, Richard Aldington, described meeting him in the drawing-room of Gull's country house in Kent about 1909, and found him 'a pale plump man who thought very highly of his abilities … He was an industrious writer … an amiable cynic and practised journalist'. From 'the strong moral line he took in print' the young Aldington had expected a more serious figure, but found instead 'a tubby little *bon vivant* who never refused a double whisky' (Aldington, 41–2). Indeed Gull was a contradiction: churning out what the public wanted, he was lively, intelligent, charming, and accomplished, a satirist capable in even his most pedestrian and conventional fiction of clever caricature and sharp wit.

After a bout of influenza, complicated by bronchitis and chronic diabetes, he died at his home—14 Maresfield Gardens, Hampstead, London—on 9 January 1923.

CAROLINE ZILBOORG

**Sources** R. Aldington, *Life for life's sake* (1968) · J. G. Nelson, *Publisher to the decadents: Leonard Smithers in the careers of Beardsley, Wilde, Dowson* (Pennsylvania, 2000) · C. Holmes and G. Mitchell, 'When it was dark: Jews in the literature of Guy Thorne', *Exploring stereotyped images in Victorian and twentieth-century literature and society*, ed. J. Morris (New York, 1993), 231–45 · *WWW, 1916–28* · *Cox's county who's who series: Norfolk, Suffolk, and Cambridgeshire* (1912) · Oxf. UA · b. cert. · m. cert. · d. cert. · G. Thorne, 'The Strand of twenty years ago: some personal reminiscences', *J. P.'s Weekly* (11 July 1913), 37 · M. Whybrow, *St Ives, 1883–1993: portrait of an art colony* (1994) · C. Mackenzie, *My life and times: octave three, 1900–1907* (1965) · C. Ranger-Gull, *Portalone* (1908) · R. G. Bacchus, *The confessions of Nemesis Hunt* (privately printed, London, 1902–6)

**Likenesses** photographs, repro. in Nelson, *Publisher to the decadents*

**Gull, Sir William Withey, first baronet (1816–1890)**, physician, was born at Colchester on 31 December 1816 and baptized there on 9 February 1817, eighth of ten children of John Gull (1778–1827), a barge owner and wharfinger of Thorpe-le-Soken, Essex, and his wife, Elizabeth Cooper (*b.* 1773) of Capel St Mary, Suffolk. His parents were independent and industrious and a friend's offer of a scholarship at Christ's Hospital for the eldest son was indignantly turned down, being seen as charity. John died of cholera in London in 1827, leaving William's mother a single parent. An earnest churchwoman, William's mother brought the children up to be self-reliant. Initially William went to a school kept by two elderly women and was then sent to another run by the Revd Seaman. He was a day boy there until the age of fifteen, when he became a boarder, staying until he was seventeen. Finally he was placed with Mr Abbott at Lewes for two years, living with the family, helping in the school, and teaching himself Greek. While there he met the noted botanist Joseph Woods and spent a great deal of time with him studying the local flora and fauna. In 1835 he returned home. He wanted to go to sea, but his mother refused her permission.

Gull was then befriended by a rector from neighbouring Beaumont, one of several local parishes which formed part of the Guy's Hospital estate. He was the nephew of Benjamin Harrison, the Guy's treasurer, and helped Gull with his classical studies. At his request Harrison offered Gull a position as a clerk in the Guy's counting house. In September 1837 he started as a medical apprentice with two rooms and £50 p.a. at Harrison's expense. In 1838 he matriculated at London University, and was offered free entry to Guy's medical school. Gull studied hard and repeatedly won prizes. In 1841 he graduated MB from London University with honours in physiology, comparative anatomy, medicine, and surgery, and was given the post of medical tutor at Guy's. In 1842 he was appointed to teach materia medica, and Harrison gave him a small house with a salary of £100. In 1843 he was appointed medical superintendent of the ward for lunatics, where he effected several changes. He was lecturer on natural philosophy at Guy's from 1843 to 1847, and on physiology and comparative anatomy from 1846 to 1856. In 1848 he took his MD and, on 18 April married in Guernsey, Susan Anne, (1819/20–1894), daughter of Colonel Lacey of Carlisle; they had several children, of whom a son and a daughter survived their father. Also in 1848 he became an FRCP, and in 1847–9 was Fullerian professor of physiology at the Royal Institution. In 1851 he was appointed assistant physician at Guy's and in 1856 full physician, a post he held until 1865, when he resigned owing to the demands of private practice. Gull remained consulting physician until his death, later becoming a governor, and he acted as medical referee for the Professional Life Assurance Company. From 1856 to 1889 he served on the senate of London University, the first graduate to do so. He was a member of the General Medical Council from 1871 to 1883 and in 1886–7. Gull came to public notice in 1871 when he attended the prince of Wales during his severe illness with typhoid fever. He was knighted in January 1872 and was created a baronet in February of the same year.

Gull was an exact clinical physician, whose success was based on acute observation, a retentive memory, minute scrutiny of all the facts, and an immense capacity for work. A great strength was his willingness to admit that he did not have the answer. In 1848, for example, he reported with William Baly to the cholera committee on a replication study which illustrated that the work of two Bristol doctors on microscopic evidence for bacteriology was not proven. Gull was a great one for aphorisms and always had a ready quotation to illustrate his point. He was an early exponent of the iatrogenic effect of medication, aiming to introduce as little medicine as possible. He hated, 'drenching people with nauseous drugs', but used them willingly where he considered their efficacy proven.

Gull never published a book. His academic reputation was founded on a stream of journal papers, many of which were joint publications. He was an early advocate of collaborative research and in 1884 attended the Medical Congress at Copenhagen as the representative of the International Society for the Collective Investigation of Disease. He argued that contributions from different nationalities with different methodologies would advance medical knowledge. He was one of the chief promoters of the Association for the Advancement of Medicine by Research. Gull also took an active part in the vivisection controversy, supporting it for the sake of medical progress. His paper on anorexia broke new ground, he was one of the first to recognize that fevers had a natural course which he illustrated with graphs, and he first described myxoedema. In 1877 he also gave evidence to a peers' select committee on intemperance.

Gull's abiding passion was the study of nature in which he saw the hand of God. He was a great walker, frequently visiting his highland home. His parents were high-church, but William was heavily influenced by the Guy's chaplain, the Christian socialist Frederick Denison Maurice. He described himself as a Christian agnostic. A deeply spiritual man, he observed the ordinances of the church, but essentially disliked dogma and ceremony. He loved detail, and would pore over a book for hours, studying the same volume for a year. Gull had a powerful physique and bore a strong resemblance to Napoleon I. He was beloved of his patients, but his imperious, often sarcastic manner, and dogmatism alienated many colleagues. He was never made president of the Royal College.

In the autumn of 1887 Gull was paralysed while on holiday in Scotland, which caused his retirement; a third attack caused his death on 29 January 1890 at his home, 74 Brook Street, Grosvenor Square, London. He was buried at Thorpe-le-Soken. His son, Sir William Cameron Gull (1860–1922) succeeded him as second baronet.

NICK HERVEY

**Sources** *A collection of the published writings of William Withey Gull Bart MD FRS, physician to Guy's Hospital*, ed. T. D. Acland, New Sydenham Society (1896) • Boase, *Mod. Eng. biog.*, 1.1256–7 • *BMJ* (1 Feb 1890), 256–63 • *The Lancet* (2 July 1870), 1–6 • S. Wilks and G. T. Bettany, *A biographical history of Guy's Hospital* (1892) • *IGI* • *GM*, 2nd ser., 29 (1848), 540 • *CGPLA Eng. & Wales* (1890)

**Archives** Wellcome L., lecture notes and MSS | Bodl. Oxf., letters to H. W. Acland and S. A. Acland • LMA, corresp. relating to Guy's Hospital • Wellcome L., MSS relating to the treatment of the prince of Wales for typhoid, MS 5873

**Likenesses** Ape [C. Pellegrini], caricature, watercolour study, NPG; repro. in *VF* (18 Dec 1875) • Lock & Whitfield, woodburytype, NPG; repro. in T. Cooper, *Men of mark: a gallery of contemporary portraits* (1878) • drawing, Guy's Hospital, London • lithograph, NPG • portrait, repro. in *ILN* (1 Feb 1890), 131 • portrait, repro. in *Midland Medical Miscellany*, 3 (1884), 97–8 • wood-engraving, NPG; repro. in *ILN*, lix (23 Dec 1871), 612

**Wealth at death** £344,022 19*s*. 7*d*.: probate, 17 March 1890, *CGPLA Eng. & Wales*

**Gulliford, Ronald** (1920–1997), educationist, was born on 8 December 1920 in Manchester, the second son of Frederick George Gulliford, blacksmith, originally of Somerset mining stock, and his wife, Lily, *née* Latchem. When he was four years old his family moved to Gloucester, where his father worked in the railway workshops. His earliest influences came in part from his father, a radical-thinking autodidact, and from his Methodist upbringing. Together these gave him a deep concern for the sanctity and rights of the individual, which later deeply influenced his educational thinking. He attended Carton Road junior school, Gloucester, from 1926 to 1932, when he won a scholarship to the Crypt School, Gloucester. He went up the school on the science side. In the sixth form he played for both the first eleven and the first fifteen. He founded a short-lived communist group and became a member of the Peace Pledge Union. Although he was a strong candidate for a scholarship to either Oxford or Cambridge university, family financial constraints dictated otherwise. He went to Saltley Training College, Birmingham, in 1938, after passing his higher schools certificate, with a loan from the Gloucester education committee. As a conscientious objector he was then directed into teaching. Over the next few years he held posts in St Albans and Maidstone and, at his own expense, he obtained first a degree in psychology as a part-time student of Birkbeck College, London, and then a diploma in educational psychology at the University of Birmingham. With all his debts paid he married, on 27 May 1950, Alison Barbara Dawe (1925/6–1971), a teacher in an infants' school, and daughter of Kenneth Dawe. They had four children.

In 1951 Gulliford joined the University of Birmingham as a lecturer in special education at a time of rapid change in educational practice and thought. Growing parental pressure and expectations, and advances in medical science and in educational techniques, helped to fuel the realization that children previously deemed ineducable would benefit from full-time education. In 1971, the year after the passing of the Education (Handicapped Children) Act, Gulliford published his seminal *Special Educational Needs*, in which he argued that the practice of categorizing a child according to a particular disability, usually a medical one, was simplistic. He gave a comprehensive analysis of the learning difficulties experienced by the individual child and of the ways in which help could be provided in special as well as mainstream schools. In 1973 the government appointed a committee under the chairmanship of Mary Warnock to 'review educational provision … for children and young people handicapped by disabilities of body or mind', to which Gulliford was co-opted. As a generalist among specialists he was influential in moving the committee to think not in terms of handicap, based on the traditional medical habit of concentrating on what was wrong with a child, but about the broader concept of an educational need or needs. He also played an important role in encouraging the committee to abandon the previous practice of seeing only some 2 per cent of children as in need of special education, but to think more widely in terms of 20 per cent who would at some time in their school lives need some form of remedial help in ordinary schools. The title of the committee's report, *Special Educational Needs* (1978), was testimony to his influence, as was the content of the legislation of 1981.

When Gulliford was appointed to a personal chair of special education in 1976 there were only two other professors of special education in the British education system. Despite the death of his wife in 1971, following an accident while ice skating, and having to cope with four young children single-handed, he wrote extensively, acted as a member of the editorial boards of several learned journals, and published a wide range of books, articles, and educational material for children with special needs. Two years before his retirement in 1986 he was made CBE for his services to education. In his later years he developed Alzheimer's disease. He died at his home, 53 Billesley Lane, Birmingham, on 30 November 1997 and was cremated at Robin Hill crematorium, Solihull, on 4 December. He was survived by his two sons, one in medicine, the other a research chemist, and two daughters, both of whom became psychologists.

J. S. HURT

**Sources** *The Independent* (23 Dec 1997) • *The Guardian* (26 Jan 1998) • *British Journal of Special Education*, 25 (1998), 7–9 • *The Cryptian* (1998), 89–90 • J. S. Hurt, *Outside the mainstream: a history of special education* (1988) • private information (2004) [A. Gulliford and others] • personal knowledge (2004) • m. cert. • *CGPLA Eng. & Wales* (1998)

**Archives** priv. coll.

**Likenesses** photograph, repro. in *The Independent* • photograph, repro. in *The Guardian*

**Wealth at death** £331,458: probate, 1998, *CGPLA Eng. & Wales*

**Gulliver, George** (1804–1882), anatomist and physiologist, was born at Banbury, Oxfordshire, on 4 June 1804, and after an apprenticeship with Jones and Wise, surgeons of Banbury, he entered St Bartholomew's Hospital, London, where he became prosector to John Abernethy and dresser to William Lawrence. Becoming MRCS in June 1826 he was gazetted hospital assistant to the forces in May 1827, and became assistant surgeon to the forces in June 1828. In June 1829 he was made assistant surgeon to the 71st Highland light infantry and later served for three years as staff assistant surgeon, during which time he had charge of the museum at Fort Pitt, Chatham, where he also had responsibility for the surgical division. He became assistant surgeon to the Royal Horse Guards (Blues) in June 1843 and was later promoted to surgeon. He retired from the army in 1853.

Gulliver was elected fellow of the Royal Society in 1838, of the Royal College of Surgeons in 1843, and in 1852 member of the council of the latter body. In 1861 he was Hunterian professor of comparative anatomy and physiology, and in 1863 delivered the Hunterian oration, in which he strongly put forward the neglected claims of William Hewson and John Quekett as discoverers.

Gulliver wrote no systematic work, although he edited an English translation of F. Gerber's *Elements of the General and Minute Anatomy of Man and the Mammalia* in 1842, adding, besides numerous notes, an appendix giving an account of his own researches on the blood, chyle, and lymph. In 1846 he edited for the Sydenham Society *The Works of William Hewson, F.R.S*, with copious notes and a biography of Hewson. He also supplied notes to Rudolph Wagner's *Elements of Physiology*, translated by Robert Willis (1844). His Hunterian lectures, 'Blood, lymph, and chyle of vertebrates', were published in the *Medical Times and Gazette* from 2 August 1862 to 13 June 1863. Most of his work is scattered through various periodicals; a list of them is given in the Royal Society's *Catalogue of Scientific Papers*. He was the first to give extensive tables of measurements and full observations on the shape and structure of the red blood corpuscles in man and many vertebrates, resulting in several interesting discoveries. In some points he corrected the prevailing views adopted from John Hunter as to the coagulation of the blood, at the same time confirming other views of Hunter; he noted the fibrillar form of clot fibrin, the so-called molecular base of chyle, the prevalence of naked nuclei in chyle and lymph, and the intimate connection of the thymus gland with the lymphatic system. His work in connection with the formation and repair of bone had considerable significance. To pathology he rendered important services, showing the prevalence of cholesterine and fatty degeneration in several organs and morbid products, the significance of the softening of clots of fibrin, and some of the characteristics of tubercle. In botany also Gulliver did original work, proving the important varieties of character in raphides, pollen, and some tissues, and their taxonomic value.

Gulliver was knowledgeable about literature, art, and ecclesiastical architecture, and enjoyed angling on the property of his friend Lord Henry Bentinck. According to an obituarist Gulliver's 'calm and sober judgement kept all his observations strictly within the range of facts. He never wandered into the bewildering region of speculation, and entertained a profound reverence for the Almighty, both in His works and Word' (*Edinburgh Medical Journal*, 671). He died at his home, 27 Old Dover Road, Canterbury, on 17 November 1882, leaving a wife, Anne, and a son, George (1852–91), who became assistant physician to St Thomas's Hospital, London. Gulliver was buried in Nackington cemetery, near Canterbury.

G. T. BETTANY, *rev.* MICHAEL BEVAN

**Sources** *Edinburgh Medical Journal*, 28 (1882–3), 668–72 • V. G. Plarr, *Plarr's Lives of the fellows of the Royal College of Surgeons of England*, rev. D'A. Power, 2 vols. (1930) • *CGPLA Eng. & Wales* (1882)

**Wealth at death** £23,289 11*s*. 0*d*.: probate, 23 Dec 1882, *CGPLA Eng. & Wales*

**Gulliver, James Gerald** (1930–1996), businessman, was born on 17 August 1930 at 18 Smith Drive, Campbeltown, Argyll, the youngest child and only son of William Frederick Gulliver, master grocer, and his wife, Mary Lafferty. His father ran a successful business, and as a child Gulliver delivered groceries on the traditional errand boy's bicycle to his father's customers. He was dux (head boy) of Campbeltown grammar school and gained a first-class honours degree in mathematics and engineering at Glasgow University. He was awarded a Fulbright scholarship and finished his education at Georgia Institute of Technology. Subsequently he completed a short service commission in the Royal Navy (1956–9) before joining the management consultancy Urwick, Orr, & Partners in 1961. On 22 November 1958 he married Margaret Joan Cormack (*b*. 1930/31), a state registered nurse and daughter of John Godfrey Cormack, a medical practitioner. They had three sons and two daughters.

Gulliver's abilities were first recognized by Garfield Weston, chairman of Associated British Foods. During the 1960s Weston sought to parallel in Britain his success in Canada with the development of a diversified food manufacturing and retailing group. Associated British Foods had created through acquisition the Fine Fare group of food stores and, in order to control Fine Fare's store development programme Weston also owned a building company, Headway. Gulliver was recruited to manage Headway and he did so with such effect that Weston, in a typically bold move, appointed him in 1965 managing director of Fine Fare. At that time Fine Fare was struggling to compete with Tesco and Sainsbury's, then a strong southern regional company.

With great concentration and energy Gulliver became directly responsible for every aspect of Fine Fare's activities. He quickly grasped that a retail company had two prime constituents—the customer and the supplier. He engaged at a high level with the key food manufacturers to convince them that Fine Fare would become a major and countervailing force in food retailing. Despite Weston's misgivings, Gulliver cancelled Fine Fare's contract with Pink Stamps and invested the savings in sharper pricing and heavier advertising. Gulliver's success at Fine

Fare prompted Weston to invite him to tackle the problems faced by Loblaws stores in Canada. During 1972 Gulliver contributed strongly to Loblaws' revival but increasingly felt that his future should be as an entrepreneur (a word which became his leitmotif).

In late 1972 Gulliver left Fine Fare, and he and two close associates, Alistair Grant and David Webster, acquired an investment in Oriel Foods, a small quoted food company with interests in edible oil refining and food wholesaling. Swiftly Gulliver then acquired cash and carry, retailing, and wholesaling businesses during 1973. To his surprise he was approached by the Radio Corporation of America (RCA), the large US conglomerate, which was interested in purchasing Oriel. In January 1974 Gulliver sold Oriel to RCA and became a comparatively wealthy man. For three years he and his team continued to run Oriel, with one important new acquisition, Morris and David Jones, which doubled Oriel's scale and profitability.

In 1977 Gulliver left Oriel and set up James Gulliver Associates, which later became Argyll Group plc and eventually Safeway plc. From a small capital base Gulliver acquired significant financial interests in and effective management control of four small quoted companies: Alpine Holdings, Morgan Edwards, Louis C. Edwards, and Amalgamated Distilled Products. Each was used as the core of a discrete sectoral development programme. Alpine was sold in 1983 for a substantial profit. Morgan Edwards and Louis C. Edwards were merged in 1981, and soon afterwards Gulliver re-acquired Oriel Foods from RCA and swiftly concluded his most important deal, the acquisition of James Goldsmith's Allied Suppliers, a large supermarket business making profits of only £11 million from sales of £940 million. Allied Suppliers provided Gulliver and his team with the scale which enabled him to exploit the lessons learned at Fine Fare. Over a three-year period net margins were tripled and within five years pre-tax profits rose to £70 million.

Modelling his ambitions on his mentor Garfield Weston, Gulliver saw that while food retailing provided an excellent business in the UK, if he wished to become a large international group the preferred strategy would be to acquire a branded consumer product business, where sales expansion would not be dependent upon real estate. He and his team decided that Scotland's premier company Distillers was grossly under-exploiting the array of liquor brands within its portfolio. As a Scot, Gulliver—supported by his two Scottish associates Grant and Webster—reasoned that although Distillers was considered impregnable to a hostile bid from outside Scotland, Argyll could perhaps finesse its acquisition by stressing the need for Distillers to be truly directed from Scotland rather than from its palatial St James's Square headquarters. He also reasoned that the model for the development of Distillers was cognac, which earned 40 per cent of the profit earned by Scotch whisky from 10 per cent of its sales volume, through skilful marketing and exploitation of its heritage. To give Amalgamated Distilled Products the required scale and muscle, Gulliver created the Argyll Group, by using James Gulliver Associates as the vehicle for the merger of the now substantial food interests with the rather smaller drinks business.

In August 1985 Gulliver discussed the feasibility of acquiring Distillers through the medium of a friendly journalist. The resulting press speculation forced Gulliver, with advice from the city, to state that he had no immediate intention of making an offer. The Takeover Panel ruled that Argyll would be precluded from making a move for at least three months. Alerted, Distillers began to prepare its defence; and, more importantly, Guinness, under Ernest Saunders, realized that if Gulliver made a move, Distillers would be in play and might prefer a white knight with a 200-year-old pedigree to an aggressive Scottish predator. Argyll's formal offer for Distillers, launched on 2 December 1985, was the signal for Guinness to present itself as a preferred suitor, even persuading Distillers to finance its bid costs. After a series of manoeuvres, some underhand and some illegal, Guinness captured Distillers in April 1986. Gulliver, at that time unaware of the Guinness 'dirty tricks' campaign, wrote to Saunders wishing him success.

During 1986 Gulliver once again decided to pursue a range of private business interests and became non-executive chairman of Argyll, retiring from the board two years later after the acquisition of Safeway from its US owners. He made his home in Scotland and gained great enjoyment from farming his land in Fife and decorating his town house in Heriot Row. His wide range of interests included serving as vice-president of Manchester United Football Club, trustee of the duke of Edinburgh's award scheme, and visiting professor at Glasgow University, which awarded him an honorary doctorate in 1989. He was an enthusiastic and adventurous skier and a keen yachtsman. He was *Guardian* young businessman of the year in 1972, and was created CVO in 1996.

Gulliver's first three marriages ended in divorce. His second marriage, on 12 March 1977, was to Joanne Sims (*b.* 1946/7), secretary, daughter of Rufus Graham Sims, sales manager. His third marriage, on 3 April 1985, was to Marjorie Hazel Henderson, *née* Moncrieff (*b.* 1955/6), secretary and restaurateur, daughter of John Moncrieff, farmer. His fourth marriage, on 24 July 1993, was to Melanie Crossley (*b.* 1963), chartered accountant, daughter of John Crossley, carpet retailer. He died at the Royal Infirmary, Edinburgh, on 12 September 1996, and was survived by his wife Melanie and the five children of his first marriage.

Alistair Grant

**Sources** *Daily Telegraph* (13 Sept 1996) • *The Times* (14 Sept 1996) • *The Independent* (23 Sept 1996) • *WWW* • personal knowledge (2004) • private information (2004) • b. cert. • m. cert. [Marjorie Hazel Moncrieff] • m. cert. [Margaret Joan Cormack] • m. cert. [Joanne Sims] • m. cert. [Melanie Crossley] • d. cert.

**Likenesses** photograph, repro. in *Daily Telegraph* • photograph, repro. in *The Times* • photograph, repro. in *The Independent*

**Gully, James Manby** (1808–1883), physician and hydropath, was born on 14 March 1808 in Kingston, Jamaica, the son of Daniel Gully, a coffee planter of Irish descent. The family moved to Liverpool in 1814, where

Gully was sent to study with a Dr Pulford; he then went on to the Collège de Sainte-Barbe in Paris. In 1825 he entered Edinburgh University as a medical undergraduate and spent his fourth year as an 'externe' pupil and dresser back in Paris at the Hotel Dieu under Dupuytren. In 1829 he qualified MD at Edinburgh and became a licentiate of the Royal College of Surgeons of Edinburgh. For a year he enjoyed the lively literary milieu of the city, meeting many of the writers and friends who were to feature later in one of the first successes of his career, his *Lectures on the Moral and Physical Attributes of Men of Genius and Talent* (1836). But in 1830 a series of blows fell when his father, mother, and fiancée died in quick succession, and the family fortune collapsed owing to the Emancipation Act, which freed plantation slave workers.

Forced to make a living Gully moved to London and set up a practice in Leicester Square, Soho. In 1831 he married a family friend, Fanny Court (*d.* 1838); between 1832 and 1837 they had four children (two boys and two girls) and to supplement his income Gully also established his journalistic career, as co-editor of the *London Medical and Surgical Journal* and the *Liverpool Medical Gazette*. In the former he published in 1834–5 a condensed account of Broussais's 'Lectures on general pathology', and in the latter F. Magendie's 'The rationale of morbid symptoms'; both were well received, as had been his 1834 translation, with teaching notes, of Tiedemann's *Physiologie des Menschen*. About this time Gully was also elected a fellow of the Royal Medical and Chirurgical Society of London, and a fellow of the Royal Physical Society of Edinburgh.

In 1836 Gully moved his practice west to Sackville Street in Piccadilly, where he became a neighbour to his future collaborator, Dr James Wilson, with whom he shared the radical medical view that much of current medical practice was 'effete, inefficient, if not positively harmful' (Gully). Gully was a moderate Liberal in his politics. In 1838 family tragedy struck again when his wife, Fanny, died of smallpox; Gully managed to continue to write and socialize and his adaptation of Dumas's *The Lady of Bellisle* opened at the Drury Lane Theatre on 4 December 1839. But in 1840 his youngest daughter, also named Fanny, died of croup, and shortly afterwards, on 14 October 1840, Gully married a widow, Frances Kibble, who was seventeen years older than himself. The marriage was a failure from the start since Frances refused to undertake care of the children, and they separated shortly afterwards. During this period Gully was still active in the medical field, producing a tract on nervous diseases in 1837, and his first exploratory work on physiology, *The Simple Treatment of Disease Deduced from the Methods of Expectancy and Revulsion*, in 1842.

That same year James Wilson came back from Graefenburg in Austria, 'filled to the brim' (Gully) with the hydropathic water cures practised by Vincent Priessnitz and determined to introduce them into England. The two friends joined forces, and finding Malvern, Worcestershire, an 'appropriate locality for the practice of hydropathy' (ibid.) Wilson at once settled there, followed a few months afterwards by Gully and his family. Malvern was a small old spa town, and Wilson was able to purchase a bankrupt hotel while Gully took on two large houses in Wells Road. Wilson's book *The Water Cure* (1842–3), published immediately on his return, brought the first patients in, and from then on both practices flourished, bringing a new 'health industry' to Malvern. Acting as both partners and rivals, Gully and Wilson were quickly able to re-equip their houses as 'sanatoriums' with all the requisite indoor and outdoor baths and douches. The outdoor regime was strict and invigorating, but not gruelling (donkey rides were a speciality), and throughout the 1840s and 1850s Malvern attracted a stream of celebrated visitors, including royalty. Gully wrote his most popular work, *The Water Cure in Chronic Disease*, in 1846, and from 1847 onwards he treated, among others, Alfred Tennyson, Thomas Carlyle, Bishop Wilberforce, and Charles Darwin. He became editor of the *Water Cure Journal* in 1848. Gully continued to be intellectually radical in his therapeutics, and later developed an interest in mesmerism and homoeopathy; he also wrote a popular *Guide to Domestic Hydrotherapeia* in 1863. Wilson's was the larger hydro, but Gully was more involved in the development of the town. Between 1856 and 1866 he was chairman of the Malvern Improvement Commissioners, he started the *Malvern News*, and he supervised the building of a new railway station, a luxury hotel, gas works, and a new school, Malvern College—not without some resistance from local inhabitants. For relaxation, Gully spent three months of each year on the continent, and in later life he became a fervent believer in spiritualism, acting as the friend and protector to the spiritualist medium Daniel Dunglas Home and his family. He also edited *Drawings Descriptive of Spirit Life and Progress. By a Child Twelve Years of Age* (1874).

In 1867 James Wilson died and, though he had been estranged from Gully for many years, it was the end of an era. Five years later in 1872 Gully resigned his practice to his partner Dr W. T. Fernie, with full public honours. His retirement was blighted, however, after 1876, when his name was linked intimately with a woman friend, Mrs Charles Bravo, who was accused of murdering her husband. The Bravo case caused a popular sensation and ruined Gully's professional reputation. After the inquiry his name was removed from all the medical societies and journals of the day. He withdrew from public life, and died on 27 March 1883 at Orwell Lodge, Bedford Hill Road, Balham, London. His last work, *A Monograph on Fever and its Treatment by Hydrotherapeutic Means*, was edited posthumously in 1885 by his son, a future speaker of the House of Commons, William Court *Gully. VIRGINIA SMITH

**Sources** P. G. Mann, *Collections for a life and background of James Manby Gully* (1983) · J. Morris, *Dr Gully of Malvern* (1872) · *The Times* (5 April 1883), 5 · J. M. Gully, *Malvern News* (19 Jan 1867) [obit. of James Wilson] · L. R. Croft, *The life and death of Charles Darwin* (1989) · *Three weeks in wet streets, being the diary and doings of a moist visitor to Malvern* (1851) · m. cert. [second marriage to Frances Kibble]

**Likenesses** Spy [L. Ward], watercolour, 1876, Wellcome L. · Spy [L. Ward], caricature, chromolithograph, NPG, Wellcome L.; repro. in *VF* (5 Aug 1876) · portrait, Malvern Council offices · wood-engraving, Wellcome L.

**Wealth at death** £29,823 12*s*. 4*d*.: probate, 1 May 1883, *CGPLA Eng. & Wales*

**Gully, John** (1783–1863), prize-fighter, racehorse owner, and politician, was born on 21 August 1783 at The Crown inn, Wick, near Bristol, where his father was the landlord. During Gully's boyhood, the family moved to Bath, where his father became a butcher, and he was brought up to his father's trade. After his father's death the business gradually declined, and at the age of twenty-one Gully became an inmate of the kings' bench prison, London. He had for some time taken an interest in prize-fighting matches, and this led in 1805 to his receiving a visit from an acquaintance, Henry Pearce, the 'Bristol Game-Chicken', the champion of England. The two men had a 'set-to' which so impressed the onlookers that a number of prize-fight promoters paid Gully's debts, and took him to Virginia Water, where he was trained for a more serious fight with Pearce. The contest took place at Hailsham in Sussex on 8 October 1805, before a huge crowd, among whom was the duke of Clarence (afterwards William IV). After a fight of seventy-seven minutes, during which there were sixty-four rounds, Gully, who was nearly blinded, gave in.

Ill health forced the 'Bristol Game-Chicken' to retire in December 1805 and Gully was regarded as his legitimate successor, although he was never formally nominated champion. No challenger for his title came forward for two years. At length he was matched to meet Bob Gregson, the Lancashire heavyweight, for 200 guineas a side. His opponent measured 6 feet 2 inches in height, and was famously strong, while Gully himself was 6 feet tall. The fight took place on 14 October 1807, at Six Mile Bottom, on the Newmarket road. This encounter was remarkable for its brutality; both men became quite exhausted, but in the thirty-sixth round Gully landed a blow which prevented Gregson from continuing. Captain Barclay took the winner off the ground in his carriage, and the next day drove him in triumph on to the Newmarket racecourse. Gregson, not being satisfied, again challenged his opponent. This match, which was for £250 a side, took place in Sir John Sebright's park, near Market Street, Hertfordshire, on 10 May 1808, the combatants being watched by about a hundred noblemen and gentlemen on horseback and in carriages. The crowd was so great that it was rumoured the French had landed, and the volunteers were called out. The two men fought in white breeches and silk stockings, without shoes. After the twenty-seventh round Gregson was too exhausted to continue. In this contest which lasted an hour and a quarter, Gully, who had commenced with his left arm in a partially disabled condition, showed a complete knowledge of prize-fighting and a remarkable quickness of hitting.

In June 1808, with Tom Cribb, Gully took a joint benefit at the Tennis Court in London, when he formally retired from the ring. By this time he had become the landlord of The Plough inn, 23 Carey Street, Lincoln's Inn Fields, London. He began devoting himself to the business of a betting man, and became in 1812 the owner of horses of his

**John Gully** (1783–1863), by Samuel Drummond, 1805–8

own, Cardenio being his first. He moved around this time to Newmarket, and became more seriously involved in racing in 1827, when he gave Lord Jersey 4000 guineas for his Epsom Derby winner Mameluke. He backed his purchase for the St Leger that year, but James Robinson on Matilda took the race, and Gully lost £40,000. In 1830 he became a betting partner with Robert Ridsale, when their horse Little Red Rover ran second to Priam for the Derby. Their best year, however, was 1832, when they won the Derby with St Giles, and Gully took the St Leger with Margrave, making £50,000 on the former and £35,000 on the latter race. However, having fallen out with Ridsale in the hunting-field, he horsewhipped him, which led to his having to pay £500 damages for assault. In partnership with John Day, Gully won the Two Thousand Guineas in 1844 with Ugly Buck, and in 1846 he took both the Derby and the Oaks (with Pyrrhus the First and Mendicant), an event previously accomplished only once, when Sir Charles Bunbury's Eleanor carried off both prizes in 1801. Gully was again the winner of the Two Thousand Guineas with Hermit in 1854, and in the same year he won the Derby with Andover, having the bookmaker Henry Padwick for his partner in the latter horse. During this period as a racehorse owner and gambler Gully purchased Upper Hare Park, near Newmarket, from Lord Rivers, but he subsequently sold it to Sir Mark Wood. He then bought Ackworth Park, near Pontefract, Yorkshire, becoming MP for that pocket borough from 10 December 1832 to 17 July 1837. Politically, he described himself as a reformer, supporting the ballot and shorter parliaments. In 1835 he brought a legal action against the editor of *The Age* for a slander in connection with the Pontefract election. He unsuccessfully contested the seat again in June 1841. Having amassed a considerable fortune from his racing interests, he also acquired a degree of respectability. In 1836 he was presented at court. He married twice, and had twelve children with each wife. His first wife was the daughter of a London publican; his second, Mary, survived him.

Having sold Ackworth Park to Kenny Hill, Gully took up his residence at Marwell Hall, near Winchester. He had, however, invested his winnings in coalworks in the north and in land. He purchased a number of shares in the new Hetton colliery, which he held until they had risen to a high premium. About 1838 he was involved in setting up the Thornley collieries, and he also had a share in the Trindon collieries. In 1862 he became sole proprietor of the Wingate Grange estate and collieries. By this time he had moved to Cocken Hall, near Durham. He died at the North Bailey in Durham on 9 March 1863, and was buried at Ackworth, near Pontefract, five days later.

G. C. BOASE, *rev.* EMMA EADIE

**Sources** B. Darwin, *John Gully and his times* (1935) · 'John Gully, pugilist and legislator', *Monthly Chronicle of North Country Lore and Legend*, 2/12 (Feb 1888), 74–7 · *Sporting Review*, 49 (1863), 274–6, 306–10 · *The Greville memoirs, 1814–1860*, ed. L. Strachey and R. Fulford, 8 vols. (1938), vol. 2, pp. 334–5 · C. Lane, *Harry Hall's classic winners* (1990) · W. Day, *Reminiscences of the turf*, 2nd edn (1886), 53–70 · J. Rice, *History of the British turf*, 1 (1879), 172–3, 288–93 · P. Egan, *Boxiana, or, Sketches of ancient and modern pugilism*, 1 (1812) · *New Sporting Magazine*, 8 (Nov 1834), 59, 60, 279 · *The Fancy*, 2 (1826), 365–72 · *WWBMP*

**Likenesses** S. Drummond, oils, 1805–8, NPG [*see illus.*] · H. Hall, oils, *c.*1830, repro. in Lane, *Harry Hall's classic winners*; priv. coll. · J. B. Hunt, stipple, pubd 1863 (after A. Cooper), NPG · G. Hayter, group portrait, oils (*The House of Commons, 1833*), NPG · R. Seymour, lithograph, BM; repro. in Wildrake [G. Tattersall], *Cracks of the day* (1841) · mezzotint, BM · portrait, repro. in H. D. Miles, *Pugilistica: the history of British boxing*, 1 (1880) · portrait, repro. in *New Sporting Magazine* · portrait, repro. in *Sporting Review* · portrait, repro. in *Baily's Magazine*, 2 (1861)

**Wealth at death** under £70,000: probate, 27 May 1863, *CGPLA Eng. & Wales*

**Gully, William Court**, **first Viscount Selby** (1835–1909), speaker of the House of Commons, born in London on 29 August 1835, was the second son of Dr James Manby *Gully (1808–1883), physician in Great Malvern, and his wife, Fanny (*d.* 1838), daughter of Thomas Court. He was educated privately, and at the early age of sixteen went to Trinity College, Cambridge. Gully was president of the Cambridge Union in 1855 and in 1856 he graduated BA with a first class in the moral sciences tripos; he proceeded MA in 1859. On 26 January 1860 he was called to the bar at the Inner Temple, and joined the northern circuit. He shared the usual struggles of a junior barrister, and considered giving up the law; he and his friends Charles Russell (later lord chief justice) and Farrer Herschell (later lord chancellor) are said to have considered trying their fortunes in the Indian or colonial courts. In time Gully established a good legal practice, especially in commercial cases at Liverpool. He had a fine presence in court and a sound legal knowledge. While working in the north, he

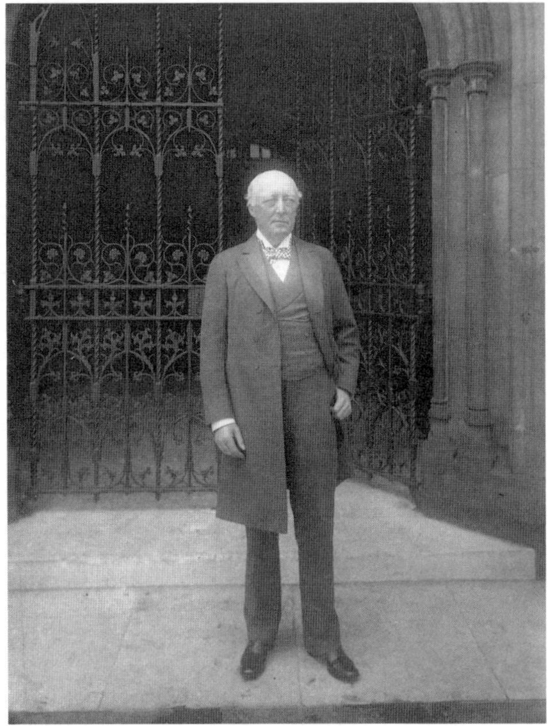

**William Court Gully, first Viscount Selby (1835–1909)**, by Sir Benjamin Stone, 1898

married, on 15 April 1865, Elizabeth Anne Walford (*d.* 1906), daughter of Thomas Selby of Whitley and Wimbish, Essex; they had two sons and four daughters.

In 1880 Gully entered politics, standing as a Liberal for Whitehaven, where he was defeated by 182 votes by George Cavendish-Bentinck, who was supported by the Lowther interest. He failed again there against the same opponent in 1885. In 1886 at Carlisle he defeated F. A. Cavendish-Bentinck and entered the Commons as a Liberal; he held the seat until he was created a peer. Initially, he rarely attended the Commons and made little impact; he secured his income by becoming recorder of Wigan in 1892.

Gully's moment came in the spring of 1895. In February A. W. Peel announced his intention to resign the speakership of the Commons. Rosebery's Liberal government was weak and the Unionist opposition announced their intention of running a candidate, Sir Matthew White Ridley. The Liberals cast about for a candidate: L. H. Courtney, a Liberal Unionist, was considered; Sir Henry Campbell-Bannerman wanted the post but could not be spared by the cabinet; Henry Labouchere noticed Gully's inoffensive competence and suggested his name. On 4 April the Liberal cabinet decided to support Gully and on 8 April 1895, in the first contested election for the speakership since 1839, he was elected in a vote of 285 to 274, the sixth Liberal speaker in a row. The angry Unionists decided, against convention, to oppose Gully at the general election in July 1895, but he held his seat, and when the Commons met in

August 1895 the Unionists, impressed by Gully's performance in the brief time thus far available to him, did not oppose his re-election as speaker. He retained the office in 1900 and retired in March 1905. Although a Liberal, his speakership was thus almost wholly served in a Commons with a large Unionist majority.

Gully was sandwiched chronologically between two very strong speakers, A. W. Peel and J. W. Lowther. He was fortunate that no major constitutional question came his way and, with his younger son, Edward Walter Karslake Gully (1870–1931), acting as his secretary, he established a reputation for competence. He was 'handsome, dignified, courteous, impartial' (*DNB*). He tidied up the putting of supplementary questions at question time. He was sometimes seen as over-legalistic and pedantic and was sometimes accused of bending over too far towards the Unionist government. He was usually quick and effective in procedural questions, but he lost the confidence of the Irish nationalists in an incident on 5 March 1901 when he called the police to clear the house when about a dozen home-rule MPs refused to leave their seats for a division called by J. W. Lowther as chairman of the committee of supply. Gully was correct according to the rule then in force (but subsequently repealed) but his action was felt to have made the house look foolish. The Irish never forgave him and often provoked him with shouts of 'Send for the police!' when he rose in the speaker's chair. The episode dented Gully's authority and shook his self-confidence.

In March 1905 Gully's poor health and the serious illness of his wife (to whom he was devoted, and who died on 15 November 1906) caused him to resign, thus allowing the tottering Unionist majority the election of his successor, J. W. Lowther. Gully was created Viscount Selby (his wife's family name) and given the customary pension of £4000 p.a. (despite J. Keir Hardie's challenge to the relevant legislation on 21 June 1905 to reduce the pension to £1000 p.a.). His seat was at Sutton Place, Seaford. Gully's health quickly revived and he became a regular attender at debates in the Lords and continued to participate in public life. He was chairman of the royal commission on motor cars, and also of the commission on vaccination; and was chairman of the Board of Trade arbitration committee in 1908, and a member of the permanent arbitration court at The Hague. He was also chairman of the executive committee of the Franco-British exhibition of 1908. Gully was made an honorary LLD of Cambridge University in 1900, and an honorary DCL of Oxford University in 1904, and received the freedom of the City of London on his resignation of the office of speaker. He was taken seriously ill while staying at Menaggio, on Lake Como, in September 1909. He returned to Britain, where he made a temporary recovery, but he died on 6 November of that year at his London home, 3 Buckingham Gate; he was buried at Brookwood cemetery. His first son, James William Herschell Gully (1867–1923), succeeded to the title.

H. C. G. MATTHEW

**Sources** *The Times* (8–11 Nov 1909) • *Carlisle Express and Examiner* (13 Nov 1909) • A. I. Dasent, *The speakers of the House of Commons* (1911) • P. Stansky, *Ambitions and strategies* (1964) • H. W. Lucy, *Later peeps at parliament* (1905) • *DNB* • P. Laundy, *The office of speaker in the parliaments of the Commonwealth* (1984)

**Archives** CUL, department of manuscripts and university archives, corresp. and papers, travel journal | Bodl. Oxf., letters to Sir William Harcourt and Lewis Harcourt

**Likenesses** J. Collier, oils, 1898, Inner Temple, London • B. Stone, photograph, 1898, NPG [*see illus.*] • Bassano, cabinet photograph, NPG • G. Reid, oils, Palace of Westminster, London • Spy [L. Ward], caricature, chromolithograph, NPG; repro. in *VF* (17 Sept 1896) • B. Stone, photographs, NPG

**Wealth at death** £61,294: administration with will, 6 Dec 1909, *CGPLA Eng. & Wales*

**Gulston, Joseph** (1744/5–1786), book and art collector and connoisseur, was the eldest son of Joseph Gulston (1693/4–1766), a successful loan contractor with mercantile interests in Lisbon, and his wife, Mericas Sylva (1714/15–1799), the daughter of a Portuguese merchant. His father became MP in turn for Tregony (1737) and Poole (1741). His parents, who had secretly married, fearing the disapproval of his father's elder sister Anne, lived separately and did not acknowledge their marriage until some fifteen years later. Thus for the first few years of his life Joseph, with his elder sister, Elizabeth, was brought up by his mother in a house in Greenwich; these difficult yet romantic circumstances formed the basis of Clementina Black's novel *Mericas* (1880).

Gulston, a beautiful but sickly child, was 'spoiled intolerably' by his mother (Nichols, *Illustrations*, 5.22) and at the age of six was sent to school at Worcester. Six years later, in 1756, he moved to Eton with his younger brother John, and on 18 February 1763 he matriculated from Christ Church, Oxford. Sent to Hamburg to learn business so that he could succeed his father, he devoted his time there to music instead. Even the sudden death of his brother in 1764 failed to make Gulston shake off his customary indolence, and his narrow election as MP for Poole in May 1765 owed much more to his elderly father's exertions than to his own. During his three years in parliament he was a government supporter, yet he never voted nor spoke in the house. Defeated with Thomas Calcraft at Poole in 1768 he withdrew his name from the by-election in 1769, and retreated from politics until 1780.

His father's death on 16 August 1766 brought Gulston a town house in Soho, the family home at Ealing Grove in Middlesex, an estate in Hertfordshire worth £1500 p.a., and a fortune of £250,000 in funds. On 24 June the following year he married Elizabeth Bridgetta (1749/50–1780), the second daughter of Sir Thomas Stepney, sixth baronet, and his wife, Elizabeth Lloyd. A celebrated beauty, Elizabeth was a skilful artist and etched portraits of her husband and of Dr Pierre-François Le Courayer; she was also an amateur astronomer and poet. Fond of extravagance, Gulston and his wife rapidly dissipated his father's fortune. Their house at Ealing Grove was transformed into an Italianate villa, at the cost of £30,000, and Gulston spent vast amounts indulging his principal passion in life, collecting books and prints. A fellow of the Society of Antiquaries, he amassed an unrivalled collection of prints, which included 18,000 foreign and 23,500 British portraits, 11,000 British satirical and political prints, and

14,500 topographical prints. James Granger was a frequent visitor to Ealing Grove and compiled much of his *Biographical History of England* from Gulston's collection of portrait prints. Horace Walpole was less than happy at Gulston's rapacious approach to collecting, which had greatly inflated prices in the print market; he complained to William Cole in November 1772 that Gulston had taken advantage of his generosity and had cherry-picked his own collection of portrait prints, carrying off 187 of his favourite and rarest items.

Gulston's money soon ran out and by 1775 he was forced to sell Ealing Grove, which was bought for £12,000 by the duke of Marlborough. He and his wife and their children, Polly and Joseph, moved to Smedmore on the Isle of Purbeck; three years later they moved to a cottage in Wimborne Minster and discharged their servants. His wife died on 9 March 1780, aged only thirty, and was buried in Ealing church. Gulston once more was elected MP for Poole in 1780 but lost his seat in 1784 by five votes, by failing to get out of bed until too late in the day to solicit the votes of five Quaker constituents. Gulston's belated attempts at financial retrenchment failed, and in June 1784 he sold his books at auction. His entire collection of prints was sold over thirty-eight days from 16 January to 15 March 1786, but yielded only £7000. Overwhelmed with family cares—his son had opposed his wishes and embarked for Quebec as an ensign—and facing financial ruin, Gulston moved to his mother's house, where he fell ill. He died at Bryanston Street, London, on 16 July 1786, aged forty-one, and was buried in Ealing church. He left in manuscript an unfinished biographical dictionary of foreign visitors to England, which was intended as a supplement to Granger's *Biographical History*; though bought by a bookseller, probably Edward Jeffery of Pall Mall, it was never published and is now in the British Library. His son died at Lausanne on 18 December 1790, aged twenty-two, after a short and troubled career. RICHARD GARNETT, *rev.* S. J. SKEDD

**Sources** Nichols, *Illustrations*, 5.1–60 • *GM*, 1st ser., 56 (1786), 622 • L. B. Namier, 'Gulston, Joseph (*c*.1694–1766)', 'Gulston, Joseph (?1744–86)', HoP, *Commons, 1754–90* • Walpole, *Corr.*
**Archives** BL, collections relating to foreign visitors to Britain and MS biographical dictionary of foreigners, Add. MSS 24353–24356, 34280–34285 • Bodl. Oxf., list of engraved portraits illustrative of English history, together with notes relating to foreigners • Lewis Walpole Library, commonplace book • Norfolk RO, Norwich, memoir
**Likenesses** F. Cotes, double portrait, pastel drawing, 1754 (with his brother), J. Paul Getty Museum, California • V. Green, mezzotint, pubd 1771 (after F. Cotes), BM • J. Watson, mezzotint, 1776 (after H. D. Hamilton), BM, NPG • E. B. Gulston, engraving (after H. D. Hamilton) • H. D. Hamilton, portrait

**Gulval,** St (*fl.* before **1000**). *See under* Gudwal (*supp. fl.* 7th cent.).

**Gumble, Thomas** (*bap.* **1626**, *d.* **1676**), Church of England clergyman and biographer, was baptized on 22 November 1626 at St Stephen, Norwich, a younger son of John Gumble of that parish. Having attended Norwich School, he was admitted as a sizar to Gonville and Caius College, Cambridge, on 14 February 1643. He graduated BA early in 1647, proceeded MA in 1650, and became vicar of Chipping Wycombe, Buckinghamshire. Favoured by the protectorate government, he was appointed, in late 1655, as one of the two clergymen licensed to preach before the new council for Scotland. Soon afterwards he made the acquaintance of George Monck, and after the fall of Richard Cromwell in April 1659 he began to serve as the general's private chaplain. He initially welcomed the re-establishment of the Rump Parliament, but his deep sense of social conservatism and increasingly ill-disguised royalism led him to advocate a return to monarchy 'frankly and boldly … to the General' (Price, 20–21). As a man who enjoyed good relations with the officers of the garrison at Edinburgh, and who possessed an 'excellent dexterity at spiriting a cause', Gumble was invaluable to Monck in gauging the likely reactions of both soldiers and politicians to the possible entry of the parliamentary army of Scotland into the sphere of English politics (Price, 48–9).

It is possible, though hotly contested, that by 21 August 1659 Gumble had drafted for Monck a manifesto that supported the Cheshire rising of Sir George Booth. Only the spectacular collapse of the rebellion, so Gumble later claimed, prevented the document from becoming public. Accompanying the army on its decisive march south in January 1660, Gumble was at the crossing of the River Coldstream, on 2 January, and recorded that 'the poor redcoats wad[ed] through the Snow knee-deep, and through the Ice and Waters' (Gumble, 187–96). He, however, was quick to secure comfortable lodgings for himself and, on the morning of 4 January, was observed to have 'stragled out of his Quarters [on the road between Wooler and Morpeth], and found Christmasse-Pie and strong Beer at a Gentleman's House' (Price, 77). Later that day he was sent on ahead of the army in order to carry Monck's letters to parliament and the City of London. He arrived in the capital on 12 January and distributed the general's address to the MPs and was questioned by them. Though little is known of the replies he made to them, he seems to have been well received and was granted £100 as a reward for his services. Having been charged 'with many particulars about which he was to negotiate' and being left 'to his Judgment upon the place, to proceed in what he should think fit', Gumble also sought to appear before the council of state later that evening (Gumble, 202, 214). However, after being kept waiting until after midnight he returned to his lodgings and subsequently embarked on a policy of courting individual MPs at meetings hastily arranged at the home of the speaker of the House of Commons.

After three days of canvassing in London, Gumble rejoined Monck and the army at Mansfield, Nottinghamshire, and reported favourably on the mood of parliament and the general's friends in the City. Known as a confidant of Monck's, he found that his star was in the ascendant, and rewards were not slow in coming. On 26 January 1660 parliament recommended that he should be elected as a fellow at Eton College as soon as there was a vacancy, and at the Restoration he took rooms in the Cockpit of Whitehall Palace as an important permanent member of

General Monck's household. Having been ordained deacon and priest at Lincoln on 19 December 1660, by the mandate of Bishop George Morley he was installed as a canon of Winchester Cathedral on 17 July 1661, and he was made DD by royal appointment in the same year. Appointed to be the vicar of East Lavant, Sussex, on 21 May 1663, Gumble proved to be an absentee incumbent, and it took an appeal by the king to quieten both Bishop Morley and the rumblings of displeasure in his own diocese, pointing out that his 'attendance on the Duke of Albemarle and others in and about London prevents his residence at Winchester, as bound by statute' (*CSP dom., 1663–4*, 57 and 146; *1664–5*, 554). Gumble even chose to remain with his master at Whitehall during the worst ravages of the plague of 1665, though he could hardly 'write of it without terrour and trembling … [as] Death … rode triumphant [through] every street' (Gumble, 413–14). Once Monck gained command of the battle fleet in 1666, Gumble had been expected to accompany him to sea as chaplain of the *Royal Charles*. However, he appealed that he might be exempted from service on account of his ill health and 'languishing sickness' (*CSP dom., 1665–6*, 262; Gumble, xv). Samuel Pepys, fortunately, accepted his excuses and the position was offered instead, on Gumble's recommendation, to an experienced naval chaplain.

In the knowledge that Monck himself was sickening, in the closing days of 1669 Gumble accompanied Gilbert Sheldon, the archbishop of Canterbury, to his chambers with the express hope that the old soldier would endow a hospital, to be run by the Church of England for the benefit of former servicemen. The general testily pointed out that he had already made a will and, despite Gumble's protests, sent both his protégé and the archbishop away empty-handed. Monck's death, on 2 January 1670, dealt Gumble's considerable ambitions a heavy blow and deprived him of his most influential patron. Having attended the dying general and then his magnificent funeral at Westminster Abbey, Gumble wrote angrily to Lord Arlington's secretary complaining 'that several stationers are endeavouring to scribble out some imperfect pieces of the life of the late Duke of Albemarle' and urging him to prevent their publication (*CSP dom., 1670*, 21). Determined to frustrate their plans, by May 1670 he completed his own *Life of General Monck, Duke of Albemarle* (1671). Though his only literary work, this biography provided a seminal account of the general's rise to power and was translated into French by Guy Miege, for an edition published as *La vie du General Monck* in Rouen in the following year. The themes of the rightful return of a king; the restoration of 'traditional' élites in both church and state; and the evils brought about by the usurpation of power, were—in later years—clearly comforting and appealing fictions which were eagerly taken up by the Jacobite movement. In 1712 a new title-page was added at Cologne to some copies of Miege's edition, and the repackaged work was sold in order to raise funds for James Stuart's flagging cause.

With royal patronage unforthcoming and with his sickness still persisting, Gumble appears to have withdrawn from court circles. He died, unmarried, on 9 September 1676, probably at Winchester, and left his estate to be administered by his brothers, Stephen and John; he was buried in Winchester Cathedral, where a small inscription records both his death and his burial. Gifted as a writer, negotiator, and propagandist, Gumble clearly cherished the memory of his patron and hero, while also genuinely concerning himself with the subsequent fate of those 'poor disbanded cold-streamers' who had 'served the General with Faithfulness and gallantry' (Gumble, vii, 485–6).

John Callow

**Sources** Venn, *Alum. Cant.* • T. Gumble, *The life of General Monck, duke of Albemarle* (1671) • J. Price, *The mystery and method of his majesty's happy restauration* (1680) • *Fasti Angl., 1541–1857*, [Canterbury] • *Fasti Angl.* (Hardy), vol. 3 • *CSP dom., 1659–60; 1663–70* • M. Ashley, *General Monck* (1977) • G. Davies, *The restoration of Charles II, 1658–1660* (1955) • T. R. Jamison, *George Monk and the Restoration: victor without bloodshed* (Fort Worth, Texas, 1975) • R. Hutton, *The Restoration: a political and religious history of England and Wales, 1658–1667* (1985) • *IGI* [St Stephen, Norwich, parish register] • A. Laurence, *Parliamentary army chaplains, 1642–1651*, Royal Historical Society Studies in History, 59 (1990) • 'Winchester Cathedral memorials' (typescript), 1937–8, Winchester Cathedral Library • administration, PRO, PROB 6/52, fol. 41*r*.

**Archives** Winchester Cathedral, ledger book XV, pp. 36–7 • Winchester Cathedral Library, 'Winchester Cathedral memorials' (typescript), 1937; rev. 1952, p. 128 | Hants. RO, Bishop George Morley's papers, A/1/33, fol. 63

**Wealth at death** see administration, PRO, PROB 6/52, fol. 41*r*

**Gundeville, Hugh de** (*d.* 1181?), administrator, appears to have come from Somerset or Gloucestershire. He is first recorded in 1147, when, styled constable, he witnessed a charter of Robert, earl of Gloucester (*d.* 1147); shortly afterwards, with the same designation, he was one of the hostages for the observance of the treaty between Robert's son, Earl William (*d.* 1183), and Roger, earl of Hereford (*d.* 1155). In 1166 he was said to hold two fees of William de Mohun, lord of Dunster in Somerset, and also to have been enfeoffed with land on Earl William's demesne. In 1153 or 1154 he attested a charter of Duke Henry for St Augustine's, Bristol, and became an important royal servant when the duke became king as Henry II. In 1155/6 he had the custody of lands at Langport and Curry Rivel in Somerset, and from 1157/8 he accounted for the royal manor of King's Somborne, Hampshire. Ten years later he had custody of the honour of Basing, also in Hampshire, accounting for the aid due from its knights towards the marriage in 1168 of the king's daughter Matilda (*d.* 1189).

Gundeville frequently witnessed charters of Henry II and undertook a variety of duties for him, including maintenance for the royal family, purchase of horses for the king's use, and works in Winchester. In 1164 he was one of the envoys sent to the pope to put Henry II's case against Thomas Becket. In 1170 he acted for the king on Becket's return to England, and was one of the 'tutors' of Henry, the Young King, with whom those wishing to approach the latter on Becket's behalf had to negotiate. In the following year he accompanied Henry II to Ireland, and was one of the men to whom the king entrusted the custody of Waterford, but he had left Ireland by the end of 1172, and attended the king's Christmas court at Caen.

From Easter 1170 Gundeville had been sheriff of Hampshire, an office he held until Michaelmas 1179. He was also sheriff of Northamptonshire from Michaelmas 1174 to Easter 1177, and of Devon from Easter 1177 to Michaelmas 1179. In 1176 and 1177 he was a justice itinerant in the midlands, and sat in the exchequer afterwards to settle business arising from the eyre. He was rewarded with pardons of scutage in Gloucestershire, Sussex, Devon, Dorset, and Somerset. He held the honour of Arundel apparently through his wife, Agnes de Falaise, with whom he was a benefactor of Boxgrove Priory, Sussex. He also gave revenues in Winchester to Goring Priory, Oxfordshire. He probably died about Easter 1181, because he ceased to hold lands entrusted to him by the king half way through the financial year 1180–81. He appears to have been disposing of his estates before his death, since at Michaelmas 1181 his nephews Hamelin and Robert de Gundeville were proffering to have seisin of lands at Ham in Somerset and Tarrant Gunville in Dorset, as they had had it before the death of their uncle Hugh. JULIA BOORMAN

**Sources** *Pipe rolls* • W. Farrer, *Honors and knights' fees … from the eleventh to the fourteenth century*, 2 (1924), 53; 3 (1925), 41–6 • R. B. Patterson, ed., *Earldom of Gloucester charters* (1973) • R. W. Eyton, *Court, household, and itinerary of King Henry II* (1878) • *Radulfi de Diceto … opera historica*, ed. W. Stubbs, 1: *1148–79*, Rolls Series, 68 (1876), 315 • *The historical works of Gervase of Canterbury*, ed. W. Stubbs, 1: *The chronicle of the reigns of Stephen, Henry II, and Richard I*, Rolls Series, 73 (1879), 190 • *Gir. Camb. opera*, 5. 286 • D. M. Stenton, ed., *Pleas before the king or his justices, 1198–1212*, 3, SeldS, 83 (1967), appx 1 • L. Fleming, ed. and trans., *The chartulary of Boxgrove Priory*, Sussex RS, 59 (1960), no. 104 • H. Hall, ed., *The Red Book of the Exchequer*, 3 vols., Rolls Series, 99 (1896), vol. 1, pp. 226, 291 • *VCH Somerset*, 3.22 • *VCH Sussex*, 4.17, 145 • T. R. Gambier-Parry, ed., *A collection of charters relating to Goring, Streatley and the neighbourhood, 1181–1546*, 1, Oxfordshire RS, 13 (1931) • M. T. Flanagan, *Irish society, Anglo-Norman settlers, Angevin kingship: interactions in Ireland in the late twelfth century* (1989)

**Gundrada de Warenne**. *See* Warenne, Gundrada de (*d.* 1085).

**Gundry, Nathaniel** (*bap.* **1701**, *d.* **1754**), judge and politician, baptized on 2 April 1701, was the only son of Nathaniel Gundry (*d.* 1736), merchant and twice mayor of Lyme Regis, Dorset, and his wife, Elizabeth, daughter and heir of Thomas Warren of Maidenhayne, Musbury, near Axminster, Devon. Admitted to the Middle Temple in 1720, he was called to the bar in November 1725, and migrated to Lincoln's Inn in 1729. In 1741 he was elected member of parliament for Dorchester, and served until 1750.

Gundry married Mary Kelloway (1717/18–1791), and they had a son and a daughter. Although a whig, he sided with the opposition which defeated Sir Robert Walpole in 1742, and the silk gown which he obtained in that year may have been in some measure a political reward. Sir Charles Hanbury Williams wrote: 'That his majesty might not want good and able counsellors learned in the law, lo! Murray the orator and Nathaniel Gundry were appointed King's counsel' (*Works of Sir C. H. Williams*, 3.37). It is at this time that his reports of cases, begun as a student in 1721, came to an end; the series, filling fourteen notebooks, survives in Lincoln's Inn, where Gundry became a bencher the year after taking silk. His professional standing justified his being regarded as a candidate for the office of solicitor-general on Sir John Strange's resignation in 1742, but he was passed by, possibly because, as the satirists alleged, he was considered stiff and unbending in politics. As the author of the satirical poem *The Causidicade* wrote of him in 1743, 'The Man who is stiff, like an Oak, seldom Rises' (p. 18).

As it turned out, Gundry opposed the new administration as well, and told Henry Pelham he detested the tories. In due course both Pelham and Hardwicke felt able to propose him for a judgeship, as 'thoroughly well affected' to the government, and he was appointed a puisne justice of the common pleas in June 1750 in the vacancy created by the death of Sir Thomas Abney. Lord Egmont described him to the prince of Wales as of good character, but not very able. He sat as a judge for less than four years, and died on 23 March 1754 from gaol fever contracted on the Lent circuit at Launceston, Cornwall. He was buried at Musbury, where he had resided in the maternal house of Maidenhayne, leased from Lady Drake. His son, Nathaniel, inherited the mansion which the judge had built at Chalbury, Dorset. J. H. BAKER

**Sources** R. S. Lea, 'Gundry, Nathaniel', HoP, *Commons*, 1715–54, 2.91–2 • Sainty, *King's counsel* • Sainty, *Judges* • Foss, *Judges* • *GM*, 1st ser., 24 (1754), 191 • *GM*, 1st ser., 61 (1791), 1159 • H. A. C. Sturgess, ed., *Register of admissions to the Honourable Society of the Middle Temple, from the fifteenth century to the year 1944*, 3 vols. (1949) • W. P. Baildon and R. Roxburgh, eds., *The records of the Honorable Society of Lincoln's Inn: the black books*, 5 vols. (1897–1968) • PRO, E403/1956 • W. Musgrave, *Obituary prior to 1800*, ed. G. J. Armytage, 1, Harleian Society, 44 (1899) • J. Hutchins, *The history and antiquities of the county of Dorset*, 2 vols. (1774) • *The works of … Sir Chas. Hanbury Williams*, ed. H. Walpole and E. Jeffrey, 3 vols. (1822) • 'Morgan a Barrister', *The causidicade: a panegyri-serio-comic dramatical poem* (1743)

**Archives** Lincoln's Inn, London, law reports, MSS Misc 31–45

**Gundulf** (**1023/4–1108**), bishop of Rochester, was born in the Norman Vexin to Hatheuin and Adelisa in 1023 or 1024. No text mentions any other relatives, so he may well have been of modest birth, but his parents seem to have destined him for a clerical career from early in his life.

**Early career** After elementary education nearer home, Gundulf went to study grammar at Rouen and became a member of the cathedral clergy there. Archdeacon William, himself a later archbishop, introduced him to the favour and friendship of Archbishop Maurilius (1055–67), but this period can only have been brief. Late in 1057 a substantial party set out on pilgrimage to Jerusalem; it included Thierry, lately abbot of St Evroult, one of his monks, Archdeacon William, Gundulf, and at least one layman of rank. The journey was extremely arduous; Abbot Thierry died on the road in August 1058 and Gundulf was at one point left, apparently dying. During a severe storm at sea on their way back, both William and Gundulf vowed to enter religion if they survived.

Gundulf hastened to fulfil his vow by entering the abbey of Le Bec, founded some twenty years earlier and now celebrated for the presence of Prior Lanfranc. It appears that this was in 1059, for on the list of Le Bec professions Gundulf stands sixty-second, immediately before

Anselm, the later abbot and archbishop of Canterbury, who was to become his closest friend for the rest of his long life. The warmth of Anselm's regard for him, to which the life of Gundulf constantly refers, is also attested by a number of letters, though none survive from Gundulf in return. His rise to office was rapid; his earnest prayer, marked by frequent tears, was a much admired aspect of his devotion, as was his devotion to the Virgin. Several years later Anselm was to send him his prayer to her, undertaken at another's request but with Gundulf in mind as its reader. More practical gifts also marked Gundulf out, for he soon became sacrist. In 1063 Prior Lanfranc left to become first abbot of the ducal foundation at St Étienne of Caen and took Gundulf with him. At about this time Gundulf arranged for his mother to become a nun at the twin foundation of La Trinité. It is not explicitly stated that he was prior of St Étienne, but he may well have been. According to a later tale, while he and two fellow monks at Caen were taking the *sortes biblicae* (that is, seeking prophecy by turning the pages of the Bible at random) Gundulf came upon 'Fidelis seruus et prudens, quem constituit Dominus suus super familiam suam' ('who then is a faithful and wise servant, whom his lord hath made ruler over his household'; Matthew 24:45). Lanfranc interpreted this as a sign that Gundulf was to become a bishop; but he took more immediate steps to put the omen into effect by taking him with him to Canterbury on his appointment as archbishop in 1070 and appointing him head of his household there. The only specific task known from these years was Gundulf's care for the poor, particularly during a severe famine in London. His presence at the elevation of the relics of St Dunstan in the new church at Christ Church was to be only the first of many such recorded occasions he attended.

**Reform of the diocese of Rochester** The bishopric of Rochester had fallen on evil days by the time of the conquest. When Siward, the last Saxon bishop, died between 1072 and 1075 the community had been reduced to four or five impoverished canons. Although Lanfranc may have begun the process of recovering the lost estates of the church, the see was still barely in existence. The archbishop appointed Ernost, another monk of Caen, as bishop, but he died in July 1076, after barely six months in office. Lanfranc now turned to Gundulf. He sent him to the king in Normandy for approval and on his return consecrated him at Canterbury on 19 March 1077. The gospel text (in fact, a paraphrase) read over him was 'And he shall be as one of the prophets' (Cambridge, Trinity College MS R.7.5, fol. 250*v*). At Rochester, where the new bishop was soon received in procession and enthroned, he certainly played a decisive role. Over the next ten years archbishop and bishop together were to transform the fortunes of the diocese.

The conventional date for the transformation of the impoverished community of cathedral clerks into a monastic community of twenty-two monks is given as 1083, the same year as that in which Durham was similarly changed. However, the process must have been slow and may well have begun very shortly after Gundulf arrived. Within a few years the community had been installed in a new church (of which only the crypt now survives) and provision had been made for their support out of the endowments of the church, in part recovered from others, in part increased by a mass of individually small but cumulatively valuable gifts of tithes, lands, and churches, granted by both Norman incomers and Englishmen of varying rank. At every turn Lanfranc was involved: he paid for the splendid feretory to which Paulinus, the only saint among the earlier bishops, was translated; he intervened to secure the valuable gifts of estates at Lambeth, Surrey, and Haddenham, Buckinghamshire; he gave the church precious plate and vestments. By the time Gundulf died the new community had risen to sixty monks. There was a price to be paid. The earlier loose dependence of Rochester on Canterbury, imperfectly visible in the record, gave way to a more precise subordination. The bishop became the archbishop's formal deputy in all those acts of order which the archbishop's wide estates and responsibilities impeded; Rochester was made a see formally, as well as effectively, in the archbishop's gift; the estates of Rochester, uniquely in the Conqueror's England, were held of Canterbury and not of the crown.

Gundulf too had tasks beyond the diocese. He became something of an expert in the translation of saints. He attended the elevation of St Eadburh *c.*1085, viewed the body of Edward the Confessor at Westminster in 1102, and presided, after Lanfranc's death, at perhaps the most solemn of all, the translation of St Augustine to his shrine in the new church of St Augustine's Abbey, Canterbury, in September 1091. He was celebrated too for his skill at building; he played a major part in the king's new stone keep, the White Tower at London, where he stayed with a prosperous burgess, Edmer 'ænhande', a benefactor of Rochester. At Rochester itself, besides the church and some conventual buildings of which no trace remains after two later fires, he was responsible for the outer walls of the castle. His direct contribution to these works remains uncertain, if its importance does not. At West Malling he established a house of nuns some time before 1100. He built them a church, of which some fragments may survive, recruited experienced sisters from several houses, and watched over the rapid development of a settlement around the hitherto deserted site.

**Secular and ecclesiastical politics, 1087–1107** Although devoted to Lanfranc and to Anselm, his successor at Canterbury, Gundulf was plainly skilled at retaining the confidence of their opponents. In the crisis after the accession of William II, Rochester was seized by the supporters of Duke Robert, among whom Odo of Bayeux, the new king's half-uncle, played a leading part. Odo was already himself a friend of the cathedral priory. Gundulf succeeded in mitigating the ill effects of the war and secured compensation later for such damage as was done. After the death of Lanfranc, Gundulf took charge of the archbishopric for the four-year vacancy. Among his tasks was the resolution of a crisis at the abbey of St Augustine in Canterbury. The monks had resisted the imposition of a new abbot by Lanfranc earlier; and once the archbishop was dead they expelled Abbot Wido by force. Gundulf and Walkelin, bishop of Winchester, were among those sent by the king to enforce order. The community was expelled, and replaced, at least for a while, by monks from Christ Church, while the citizens who had joined in the riot were blinded. In 1093 King William, on his deathbed, as he supposed, appointed Anselm, abbot of Le Bec, the new archbishop. Gundulf received the appointment with delight and escorted the archbishop-elect around the Canterbury manors until his consecration at Canterbury on 4 December 1093. On 11 February bishop and archbishop joined the king at the consecration of Battle Abbey. Relations between the new archbishop and the king were soon strained to breaking point and at Rockingham in February 1095 they came to a head. Gundulf alone stood by his archbishop. In the brief period of partial reconciliation that followed he assisted at the consecration of the bishops of Worcester and Hereford at St Paul's in June and of Malchus of Waterford at Canterbury in December 1096. In the autumn of 1097 Anselm went into exile and Gundulf again took care of the affairs of Canterbury, as he was to do later, in Anselm's second exile from 1103 to 1106. A series of charters for his church show that Gundulf retained King William's confidence, for all his loyalty to Anselm. On 15 July 1100 he participated in the dedication of the rebuilt abbey at Gloucester. Two weeks later King William died in the New Forest and his younger brother Henry seized the treasury at Winchester before hastening to Westminster for a hurried coronation. Gundulf was one of the three bishops who seem to have attended. Subsequently he enjoyed the friendship of both Henry and his queen, who asked him to baptize her son. He played an active part in composing the dispute between the king and Robert, his older brother, who invaded England in 1101, soon after Anselm's return from exile, and he attended the royal court at Windsor in September which sealed their reconciliation. In September 1102 Gundulf was at Westminster for Anselm's council, the first of its kind since the death of Lanfranc. On 6 March 1103 he was at Canterbury when the king pursued further his quarrel with Anselm over investitures and he seized his moment to secure a large general confirmation of the rights of his church; the original of this still survives, with the only extant impression of Gundulf's seal along with those of Anselm and the king.

**Death and reputation** By 1107 Gundulf was becoming very infirm. Undeterred by his weakness he continued to circulate his diocese in a litter and redoubled his generosity to the poor. As his end approached, he received absolution from his old friend Anselm and had himself carried into the cathedral church. There, at last, he appointed an abbess to the nunnery of Malling. The act in which this is recorded reports the presence of Ralph, the exiled abbot of Sées, whom he prophesied correctly would become his successor, as well as Ralph, his former prior, now abbot of Battle. On 8 March 1108 Gundulf died at Rochester Cathedral priory, in about his eighty-fifth year, and was buried in the cathedral by Anselm.

Gundulf was later remembered by his monks for his fervent piety, his love for the poor, his gift for retaining the friendship of people of every condition, and, above all, for his devotion to his cathedral priory. It is one of the more inconvenient consequences of this regard for his memory that later monks were to produce a string of forgeries in his name, regulating the division of estates and rights between bishop and priory. Behind this screen of fabrications his work at Rochester remains clear and remarkable. It was to shape the diocese until the Reformation.

MARTIN BRETT

**Sources** R. Thomson, ed., *The life of Gundulf bishop of Rochester* (1977) · P. Sawyer, ed., *Textus Roffensis: Rochester Cathedral Library manuscript A.3.5*, 2 vols. (1957–62) · *S. Anselmi Cantuariensis archiepiscopi opera omnia*, ed. F. S. Schmitt, 6 vols. (1938–61) · Ordericus Vitalis, *Eccl. hist.* · H. R. Luard, ed., *Flores historiarum*, 3 vols., Rolls Series, 95 (1890) · *Eadmeri Historia novorum in Anglia*, ed. M. Rule, Rolls Series, 81 (1884) · Eadmer, *The life of St Anselm, archbishop of Canterbury*, ed. and trans. R. W. Southern, 2nd edn, OMT (1972) · D. C. Douglas, ed., *The Domesday Monachorum of Christ Church, Canterbury* (1944) · *Reg. RAN*, vols. 1–2 · J. Thorpe, ed., *Registrum Roffense, or, A collection of antient records, charters and instruments … illustrating the ecclesiastical history and antiquities of the diocese and cathedral church of Rochester* (1769) · A. A. Porée, *Histoire de l'abbaye du Bec*, 2 vols. (1901) · *Willelmi Malmesbiriensis monachi de gestis pontificum Anglorum libri quinque*, ed. N. E. S. A. Hamilton, Rolls Series, 52 (1870) · William of Malmesbury, *Gesta regum Anglorum / The history of the English kings*, ed. and trans. R. A. B. Mynors, R. M. Thomson, and M. Winterbottom, 2 vols., OMT (1998–9) · 'Acta Lanfranci', *MS A*, ed. J. M. Bateley (1986), vol. 3 of *The Anglo-Saxon chronicle: a collaborative edition*, ed. D. Dumville and M. Lapidge, 83–9 · D. Whitelock, M. Brett, and C. N. L. Brooke, eds., *Councils and synods with other documents relating to the English church, 871–1204*, 2 (1981) · John of Worcester, *Chron.* · E. Searle, ed., *The chronicle of Battle Abbey*, OMT (1980), 96 · M. L. Colker, 'A hagiographic polemic', *Mediaeval Studies*, 39 (1977), 60–108 · 'La vie de S. Édouard le Confesseur par Osbert de Clare', ed. M. Bloch, *Analecta Bollandiana*, 41 (1923), 5–131, esp. 121 · W. Stubbs, ed., *Memorials of St Dunstan, archbishop of Canterbury*, Rolls Series, 63 (1874), 413 · M. Brett, 'Forgery at Rochester', *Fälschungen im Mittelalter*, MGH Schriften, 33/4 (Hanover, 1988), 397–412 · W. Fröhlich, 'Die bischöflichen Kollegen des hl. Erzbischofs Anselm von Canterbury', *Analecta Anselmania*, 1 (1969), 223–67, esp. 241–4 · R. W. Southern, *Saint Anselm and his biographer: a study of monastic life and thought, 1059–c.1130* (1963) · R. W. Southern, *Saint Anselm: a portrait in a landscape* (1990) · R. Eales and R. Sharpe, eds., *Canterbury and the Norman conquest: churches, saints and scholars, 1066–1109* (1995) · N. Yates and P. A. Welsby, eds., *Faith and fabric: a history of Rochester cathedral, 604–1994* (1996) · R. A. L. Smith, 'The place of Gundulf in the Anglo-Norman church', *EngHR*, 58 (1943), 257–72 · M. Brett, *The English church under Henry I* (1975) · R. Brown, H. M. Colvin, and A. J. Taylor, eds., *The history of the king's works*, 1–2 (1963) · M. R. James, *The western manuscripts in the library of Trinity College, Cambridge: a descriptive catalogue*, 4 vols. (1900–04), vols. 1–2 · J. Le Patourel, 'The reports of the trial on Penenden Heath', *Studies in medieval history presented to Frederick Maurice Powicke*, ed. R. W. Hunt and others (1948), 15–26 · *Fasti Angl., 1066–1300*, [Monastic cathedrals] · D. Bates, ed., *Regesta regum Anglo-Normannorum: the Acta of William I, 1066–1087* (1998) · C. W. Hollister, *Henry I* (2001) · M. Brett and J. Gribbin, eds., *Canterbury, 1070–1136*, English Episcopal Acta [forthcoming]

**Archives** CKS, Rochester episcopal archives · Medway Archives and Local Studies Centre, Strood, near Rochester, Kent, Rochester priory materials | BL, Cotton MSS

**Likenesses** seal, Medway Archives and Local Studies Centre, Strood, near Rochester, Kent

**Gunn, Barnabas** [Barnaby] (*d.* **1753**), organist and composer, subscribed in 1728 to J. E. Galliard's *Hymn of Adam and Eve*, and may at that time have been organist of St Philip's Church, Birmingham. From 1730 to 1739 he was organist of Gloucester Cathedral; eight infants (two sons and six daughters), children of Barnaby or Barnabas and Anne Gunn, were baptized in Gloucester between 1732 and 1739. Two further daughters of the same parents were baptized at St Philip's, Birmingham, in 1749 and 1753: Gunn was organist of that church, and of St Martin's, Birmingham, from 1740 until his death in 1753. He was also postmaster of Birmingham. He appears additionally to have been organist of Chelsea Hospital, Middlesex, with a deputy performing the duties of the office. In the summers from 1748 to 1753 he organized concerts at Duddeston (later Vauxhall) Gardens, Birmingham.

Gunn's compositions, principally songs, but also works for violin and harpsichord, were subjected to ridicule by William Hayes in *The Art of Composing Music by a Method Entirely New, Suited to the Meanest Capacity* (1751), who suggested they were produced by a machine, a 'Spruzzarino', randomly squirting ink at music paper. Gunn's *Twelve English Songs … by the New-Invented Method of Composing with the Spruzzarino* (*c.*1751) indicates that he had a sense of humour; the inclusion of Handel's name among the 464 subscribers to his *Two Cantatas and Six Songs* (1736) suggests his work was not entirely without merit. He died in Birmingham on 6 February 1753.

L. M. MIDDLETON, *rev.* K. D. REYNOLDS

**Sources** W. Shaw, 'Gunn, Barnabas', *New Grove* · 'Gunn, Barnabas', Grove, *Dict. mus.* (1927) · *IGI*

**Gunn, Battiscombe George** (**1883–1950**), Egyptologist, was born on 30 June 1883 in London, the elder son of George Gunn, of the London stock exchange, and his wife, Julia Alice, second daughter of John Moore Philp (1819–1899), London newspaper editor. After being educated in the late 1890s at Bedales School, at Westminster School, and finally at Allhallows School, Honiton, he went to a tutor in Wiesbaden until, when he was eighteen, a family financial crisis necessitated his return to England. Gunn had already become interested in Egyptology at school, but his father discouraged this as unpractical, and directed him towards a business career. Accordingly he tried working in a City bank, and then training as an engineer, but although he had a good head for figures and was competent at the work he could not enjoy it, for his tastes and talents were literary and artistic. He continued with Egyptology as much as he could, teaching himself enough about hieroglyphs to publish his first book, *The Instruction of Ptah-hotep*, in 1906. It contained translations of ancient Egyptian wisdom literature and proved very popular. Gunn found more congenial employment in 1908–11, as private secretary to Arthur Pinero, and then went to Paris, where he was for a short time sub-editor of the *Continental Daily Mail*.

Gunn never lost sight of Egyptology, however, and won the attention of such leading Egyptologists as W. M. Flinders Petrie and Alan Gardiner. It was as one of Petrie's staff that he first visited Egypt in 1913–14, working at Haraga, near al-Lahun, with Reginald Engelbach for the British School of Archaeology in Egypt, his own responsibility being the epigraphy.

When war broke out in 1914 Gunn enlisted immediately, but was invalided out of the army in 1915. He then returned to London to work as Gardiner's assistant in his study of ancient Egyptian onomastica, progressing gradually from pupil to highly valued collaborator. During this period he married his first wife, Lillian Florence, widow of Howard Hughes and daughter of Charles Stephen Meacham, director, of Godstone Green, Surrey; the couple had one son. He went back to Egypt in 1921 to take part, with Leonard Woolley and T. E. Peet, in the excavation (1921–2) of Tell al-Amarna (the ancient Akhetaten) for the Egypt Exploration Society, and was given a post in the Egyptian Antiquities Service, for which he excavated with Cecil Mallaby Firth around the Teti pyramid at Saqqara (1924–7). During these years he spent most of his summers on the continent, mainly in Vienna. In 1928 he was made assistant conservator in the Egyptian Museum, Cairo, where he remained until his appointment, in 1931, as curator of the Egyptian section of the University Museum, Philadelphia. In 1934 he returned to England as professor of Egyptology and fellow of the Queen's College, Oxford, and was awarded an honorary MA; one of his most important tasks as professor was to supervise the creation of the new Griffith Institute (1937–9) endowed by F. Ll. Griffith as an international centre for Egyptology. From September 1935 to December 1939 he edited the *Journal of Egyptian Archaeology*. He was elected FBA in 1943. His first marriage was eventually dissolved, and on 7 July 1948 he married Constance Anna, daughter of Peter Rogers, civil servant, of Edinburgh. He died on 27 February 1950 at the Acland Nursing Home in Oxford, after a long illness, and was survived by his wife. His remains were cremated at Oxford on 2 March.

Despite his archaeological activities Gunn was primarily a philologist. His most important work was *Studies in Egyptian Syntax* (1924), which significantly advanced the understanding of the verbal system; drawing as it does on examples from the whole of classical Egyptian literature, it illustrates his vast knowledge of the material as well as the perceptiveness which allowed him to notice points overlooked by other scholars. The reputation it brought him was so great that he was appointed Oxford professor even though he had no degree. After his appointment he spent most of his time and energy on teaching, at which he proved gifted, and his own research suffered accordingly. He demanded the highest standard of accuracy both from himself and from others, but spared himself no trouble in helping both pupils and colleagues, who frequently turned to him. For these reasons his published output was relatively small—a full bibliography is given in *Proceedings of the British Academy*, 36 (1950), 236–9—but it was always of the highest quality; his detailed reviews were considered particularly useful. As well as Egyptian, he knew Latin, Greek, Hebrew, and Arabic, and spoke several modern languages fluently, especially French. He was a charming and generous man, remembered with affection and respect by friends and pupils alike.

R. S. SIMPSON

**Sources** *DNB* • W. R. Dawson, 'Battiscombe George Gunn, 1883–1950', *PBA*, 36 (1950), 229–39 • *Journal of Egyptian Archaeology*, 36 (1950), 104–5 • A. H. G., *Oxford Magazine* (27 April 1950), 404–6 • *The Times* (2 March 1950), 9 • *The Times* (3 March 1950), 7 • *Annales du Service des Antiquités de l'Égypte*, 50 (1950), 421–7 • C. Bax, *Inland far: a book of thoughts and impressions* (1925), 257–89, 308 • W. R. Dawson and E. P. Uphill, *Who was who in Egyptology*, 3rd edn, rev. M. L. Bierbrier (1995), 183–4 • *WWW, 1941–50* • B. L. Gimson, ed., *Bedales school roll* (1952) • *Old Westminsters*, vol. 3 • A. H. Gardiner, *My working years* (privately printed, London, 1963), 31–3

**Archives** AM Oxf., papers incl. notebooks, notes, photographs, squeezes, tracings, and indexes • U. Durham L. | AM Oxf., corresp. with Jaroslav Cerny; papers and letters to Sir A. H. Gardiner • Egypt Exploration Society, corresp. with the society

**Likenesses** D. Morris, charcoal?, repro. in Bax, *Inland far*, facing p. 258 • photograph, repro. in Dawson, 'Battiscombe George Gunn', pl. 1 • photograph, U. Oxf., Griffith Institute

**Wealth at death** £4125 14*s*. 6*d*.: probate, 24 June 1950, *CGPLA Eng. & Wales*

**Gunn, Daniel** (1773–1848), Congregational minister, was born at Wick, in Caithness, Scotland. He was educated at the high school in Edinburgh, and trained for the ministry under Greville Ewing at Glasgow. After being an itinerant minister in Ireland for six years, in 1810 he became pastor of a small congregation at Ilfracombe in Devon. In 1813 he moved to Bishop's Hull, Somerset, in 1814 to Chard, Somerset, and in 1816 to Christchurch, Hampshire.

At Christchurch Gunn found a small congregation, partly consisting of Baptists. He preached a sermon which, as he afterwards said, 'converted all the sensible baptists in the place', and his congregation soon grew to 1000 souls. Yet he strongly opposed any manifestation of religious feeling, and his preaching was unemotional; no one was allowed to preach emotional religion in his pulpit, and the laymen whom he sent into the neighbouring villages were strictly forbidden to add anything to the printed sermons he gave them.

Gunn was chiefly known for his Sunday school, which attracted visitors from all parts of the country, and from America. He insisted that all the children in his congregation should belong to the Sunday school, and there were usually about 400 members. He also founded a day school.

Gunn married three times and lived like a country gentleman at Burton, near Christchurch. He died at Burton on 17 June 1848.

EDWIN CANNAN, *rev.* ANNE PIMLOTT BAKER

**Sources** S. Newth, *The Congregationalist*, 10 (1881), 111–23 • private information (1890)

**Gunn, Herbert Smith** [Bert] (1903–1962), newspaper editor, was born on 3 April 1903 at 225 Old Road, West Gravesend, Kent, the younger son of Herbert Gunn, merchant seaman and marine engineer, and his wife, Alice Eliza Smith. Nothing is known about his education. In 1920 Bert Gunn began his training as a reporter on the *Kent Messenger* but, only twenty-one years old, he headed for the Far East, getting a job as a sub-editor on the *Straits Times* in Singapore. A year later he returned to England to join the *Manchester Evening News*. He followed this with sub-editing stints on the London *Evening News* (1929) and the London *Evening Standard* (1931). On 12 September 1925 he married Annie Charlotte (*b.* 1903/4), daughter of Alexander Thomson, a farmer. The couple had two sons.

Gunn's abilities soon attracted the attention of Arthur Christiansen, editor of the *Daily Express*, and as a result in 1936 he became its first northern editor in Manchester. He later transferred to London as assistant editor and then between 1943 and 1944 was managing editor of the *Daily Express*. It was there that he created the headline referring to Hitler as 'It's that man again', which afterwards became the title for Tommy Handley's long-running radio show *ITMA*. His first marriage having ended in divorce, on 29 January 1944 Gunn married Margaret Olive Melville Edwards (*b.* 1912/13), who was a reporter on the *Daily Mail*. She was the daughter of James Alexander Melville Brown, a company director, and the divorced wife of Philip Osbert Clifford Edwards. The couple had two sons.

In 1944 Lord Beaverbrook appointed Gunn editor of the *Evening Standard* in succession to Michael Foot, but it eventually became apparent there was a fundamental clash between them on editorial strategy. Gunn wanted to edit a popular paper, Beaverbrook wanted it to appeal mainly to the City and West End audiences. Their differences came to a head when, in 1950, with the Labour government returned for a second term, Beaverbrook suggested a malicious diary paragraph about John Strachey, secretary of state for war, indicating that his communist past made his loyalty questionable. Unfortunately Gunn promoted this to a front-page splash which emphasized the scurrility of the piece and led to a further clash with Beaverbook.

Gunn was also in trouble when a Labour MP said in an article in the trade press that newspapers were paying MPs for information about private meetings of the Labour Party. The committee of privileges investigated the matter and under pressure from the attorney-general Bert Gunn revealed that the MP who wrote the article, Garry Allighan, was himself the source of stories paid for by the *Evening Standard*. This led to Allighan's enforced resignation from the house.

In 1952, no longer wishing to continue battling with Beaverbrook, Gunn resigned from the *Evening Standard* and was quickly recruited by the second Lord Rothermere to join Associated Newspapers. A year later Rothermere appointed him editor of the ailing *Daily Sketch*, and within six years Bert Gunn had doubled its circulation. One of his most significant appointments then was that of David English as features editor. Vere Harmsworth was the managing director of the *Daily Sketch* at the time, and thus Bert Gunn was instrumental in launching the highly successful friendship and collaboration of David English and Vere Harmsworth who, between them, were eventually to transform the fortunes of Associated Newspapers.

In December 1959 Bert Gunn was appointed editor of the *Sunday Dispatch* but when, for commercial reasons, it was merged with the *Sunday Express* in 1961 he was very upset. By this time his health was failing, and the merger triggered his early resignation from the Associated Newspaper Group in 1962.

Herbert Gunn was a superb newspaper craftsman whose technical abilities were not always matched by editorial judgement. A newspaperman through and through, held in high regard by his colleagues, he was brilliant at turning a news story into an eye-catching page layout. Though professionally tough, personally Gunn was the kindest of men, giving particular encouragement to the younger members of his staff. Tall, silver-haired, with a prematurely lined face and immaculate clothes, he was more like a visiting diplomat than a newspaperman. He smoked too much, drank too much, slept very little, yet had amazing energy.

As a one-time president of the Institute of Journalists, Gunn went on record as a staunch upholder of the freedom of the press. He none the less had an uneasy relationship with the Press Council, which criticized him over a number of breaches of good taste and good manners. For example, he ignored a request from Princess Marina to regard the party for the coming of age of her son as a private occasion. As a result, after censure from the Press Council, he had to apologize to both the queen and Princess Marina. However, in every case where he was criticized he published the Press Council findings in a prominent position in the *Daily Sketch*.

During his retirement Gunn helped his wife launch a women's magazine, but this folded after very few issues. Theirs was a particularly happy marriage which lasted until his death from cancer on 2 March 1962 at his London home, the Coach House, 32 Somerset Road, Wimbledon. One of the sons from his first marriage was Thom Gunn, the poet. CHARLES WINTOUR

**Sources** personal knowledge (2004) • private information (2004) [family] • *WWW* • *The Times* (5 March 1962) • *CGPLA Eng. & Wales* (1962) • b. cert. • m. certs. • d. cert.

**Archives** HLRO, corresp. with Lord Beaverbrook

**Wealth at death** £24,454 13*s*. 0*d*.: probate, 12 April 1962, *CGPLA Eng. & Wales*

**Gunn** [*née* Fubister]**, Isabel** [*alias* John Fubister] (**1780–1861**), sailor and cross-dresser, was born in Orkney, on 1 August 1780, the daughter of John Fubister and Girzal Allan, and was baptized Isabel Fubister on 7 August in St Andrew's parish, Orkney. Few details are known about her life until she signed on with David Geddes, an agent for the Hudson's Bay Company (HBC) at Stromness in June 1806, disguised as John Fubister. The name was probably borrowed from her brother John, who was baptized on 20 March 1783. She set sail aboard the *Prince of Wales* on 29 June to begin the six-week journey of 3000 miles across the north Atlantic. The crew arrived at Fort Albany, on James Bay, after a five-day journey travelling south in a shallop (a three-masted boat with lug sails) from Moose Factory on 27 August 1806. Fubister undertook several journeys canoeing up river to deliver supplies to the company's fur trading outposts. On 22 June 1807 the new governor, James Hodgson, set off for Martin's Fall with a crew that included one Fubbister and another Orcadian, John Scarth (*b*. 1770), for a 1800-mile journey up river as part of a larger brigade destined for Pembina Post on the Red River.

Fubister was abruptly forced to give up 'his' disguise when, during Christmas 1807, he was among a group of HBC men celebrating at the home of a Northwest Company officer, Alexander Henry. Fubister, feeling unwell, asked to lie down and Henry made the following entry in his journal of 29 December:

> I was surprised at the fellow's demand; however, I told him to sit down and warm himself. I returned to my own room, where I had not been long before he sent one of my people, requesting the favour of speaking with me. Accordingly, I stepped down to him and was much surprised to find him extended on the hearth, uttering dreadful lamentations; he stretched out his hands towards me, and in piteous tones begged me to be kind to a poor, helpless, abandoned wretch, who was not the sex I had supposed but an unfortunate Orkney girl, pregnant and actually in childbirth. … In about an hour she was safely delivered of a fine boy. (*New Light*)

After this spectacular disclosure Fubister returned to her former identity (although she inexplicably took the surname Gunn) and returned to Fort Albany in May 1808, travelling with Hugh Heney's party. Since she was the first European woman ever to travel this far west (the HBC refused to allow their employees to bring their wives or families) news about her extraordinary journey travelled quickly. On 24 May fur trapper Peter Fidler noted in his 'Journal of a journey from Swan to the Red River' that

> the woman Mary Fubbester [*sic*] who was delivered of a Boy 5th Jany last is also gone out—she hired with Mr. Geddes in Stromness as a man, in men's clothing 1806—remained at Albany one winter and her sex was not known till delivery except to one John Scart [*sic*] her parmour on whose account she came out—she worked at anything and well like the rest of the men.

Back at Albany Fort, Isabel was put to work washing for her former colleagues and minding the eleven children of the HBC's officers. A letter sent home to Orkney by schoolteacher William Harper suggests that she resented this new form of employment. He wrote that his compatriot was living 'with her child and her chief employment is washing for all hands which indeed she is no witch at as far as I think she has been washing for me … she seems not inclined to go home' (Harper to W. Watt, 5 Sept 1808, Ernest Marwich MSS). But she managed to stay an additional year and sailed home with her son, James Scarth, on 20 September 1809.

Isabel Gunn never married but retired to Stromness with her son, where she became known as a local witch who sold love potions and charms to the young. Despite her extraordinary adventure she died a pauper, alone, at South End, Main Street, Stromness, Orkney, on 7 November 1861. JULIE WHEELWRIGHT

**Sources** *New light on the early history of the greater northwest: the manuscript journals of Alexander Henry and of David Thompson, … 1799–1814*, ed. E. Coues, 3 vols. (1897); repr. (1965) • Provincial Archives of Manitoba, Winnipeg, Manitoba, Hudson's Bay Company Archives • Orkney Parish Archives, Kirkwall, Orkney, Ernest Marwick MSS • bap. reg. Scot., 1 Aug 1780, St Andrew's, Kirkwall, Orkney • bap. reg. Scot., 7 Aug 1780, St Andrew's, Kirkwall, Orkney • C. N. Bell, *Transcripts of the Historical and Scientific Society of Manitoba*, 37

(1889) • C. N. Bell, 'First white woman in Western Canada', *Winnipeg Free Press* (23 June 1934) • J. Wheelwright, *Amazons and military maids*, new edn (1994) • P. Fidler, 'Journal of a journey from Swan to the Red River', Provincial Archives of Manitoba, Winnipeg, Manitoba, Hudson's Bay Company Archives, 3/3, fol. 58 • b. cert. • Register of deaths, 1861–1965, Stromness, Orkney

**Wealth at death** pauper

**Gunn, Sir (Herbert) James** (1893–1964), painter, was born at 56 Wilton Street, Glasgow, on 30 June 1893, the ninth of ten children of Richard Gunn (*d.* 1918), tailor, and his wife, Thomasina Munro. When he was five years old he was taken every Saturday for drawing lessons at the studio of a family friend, A. Brownlie Docharty. He was educated at Glasgow high school from 1902 to 1908 and went on to the Glasgow School of Art the following year. There he soon fell out with Maurice Greiffenhagen, the school's director, and spent the rest of the year in commercial work, designing lids for biscuit tins. In 1910 he enrolled at the Edinburgh College of Art under Morley Fletcher and in 1911 went on to the Académie Julian in Paris, where he worked under Jean-Paul Laurens.

It was from this time and travels in Spain, undertaken at the instigation of the London dealer W. B. Paterson, that Gunn's painting took its shape. The French virtues of paint applied bluntly and freshly, a broad tonal design, and colours close together, stood Gunn in good stead for the rest of his life, not only in his portraits but also in the hundreds of Lavery-like landscape sketches, of which he used to speak in his later years but never showed. His life as a painter was interrupted by the First World War, in which he lost two brothers, and he enlisted with the Artists' Rifles in 1915 and was commissioned into the 10th (Scottish) rifles in 1917. On 9 January 1919 he married a widow, (Mary) Gwendoline Charlotte Thorne, daughter of Captain H. E. Hillman RN; they had three daughters. He and his first wife divorced in 1927 and on 22 August 1929 he married (Marie) Pauline Miller (*d.* 1950), daughter of A. P. Miller; they had one son and one daughter. Pauline was the model of some of the best-known of Gunn's paintings.

In 1929 Gunn made a conscious decision to devote himself to portraiture, and the lessons of Velázquez came to fruition in the late twenties with a portrait of his friend William Hutchison (The Fine Art Society, London, in 1994), and three portraits of the artist James Ferrier Pryde (1931; one on loan to the Scottish National Portrait Gallery, Edinburgh). It is not only the shadows cast by the figures which make them so substantial but also the pattern of tone which gives the men the look of being cut out by the action of the light. The conversation piece depicting Hilaire Belloc, G. K. Chesterton, and Maurice Baring (1932), and the portrait of Lord Crawford (1939), both of which are in the National Portrait Gallery, London, were also painted in colours sombre but never muddy; in these works the paint was more thinly applied—a technique which foreshadowed his later pictures, such as the famous portrait of his second wife, *Pauline in the Yellow Dress* (1944, Harris Museum and Art Gallery, Preston), and the portrait, undertaken on his own initiative, of Delius (1933, Bradford Art Galleries and Museums), in which the blind composer (who had lost his sight and the use of his limbs by 1928) sits listening, his attenuated and useless hands laid on a rug.

**Sir (Herbert) James Gunn (1893–1964)**, self-portrait, 1925

Portraits of prime ministers, field marshals, judges, dons, bankers, and even the actress and singer Gracie Fields (commissioned by public subscription in 1938 for the Art Gallery, Rochdale) were among the many which Gunn executed with close attention to design and to the texture of clothes. A later success was *Conversation Piece at Royal Lodge, Windsor*, a portrait of George VI and his family commissioned for the National Portrait Gallery in 1950 and painted with what, at the time, seemed 'a degree of needless scrupulosity'. Gunn had already painted the king in 1944 and in 1946 was commissioned to paint Queen Elizabeth for the Middle Temple, London. His portrait of Elizabeth II, painted for the Royal Artillery regiment, was voted 'painting of the year' at the Royal Academy in 1953, though the state portrait painted in 1956 was, however, generally considered to be a disappointment. In boardrooms and college halls the visitor is often stopped by one of Gunn's portraits, severe and even bitter in expression, painted with scrupulous distinction, with nothing evaded, neither the wrinkled hands nor the pin-stripe suit. The gravity of the man is met by the honesty of the painter, but it is an honesty which does not boast of exposure or disrespect. Neither sitter nor artist doubts the place that each has in society. For that reason, as well as for the precision of the workmanship, and the pleasure in catching a likeness (perhaps his greatest pleasure at the end of his life), Gunn's portraits seem destined to sustain their power.

Gunn suffered long from official indifference and saw

his work rejected by the Royal Academy, even as late as 1942. After thirty years he was made an ARA, in 1953, and in the same year he became president of the Royal Society of Portrait Painters, where he had exhibited since 1926. He became an RA in 1961 and was knighted in 1963. He received honorary degrees from Manchester (1945) and Glasgow (1963). His sombre and elegant figure, and his kindly, handsome face, seemed to carry with them a weight not only of dignity but of a sense of neglect which would have been erased if he could have heard the enthusiasm of young artists who saw for the first time four of his best portraits in his memorial display at the summer exhibition at the Royal Academy in 1965. James Gunn died in the King Edward VII Hospital for Officers, London, on 30 December 1964. A major exhibition of his work was mounted by the Scottish National Portrait Gallery in 1994. PETER GREENHAM, *rev.* ROBIN GIBSON

**Sources** [J. Holloway], *Sir James Gunn, 1893–1964* (1994) [exhibition catalogue, Edinburgh, London, and Preston, 3 Dec 1994 – 1 July 1995] • *CGPLA Eng. & Wales* (1965) • *The Times* (1 Jan 1965)
**Archives** Bodl. Oxf., corresp. with Lord Woolton • NL Scot., letters to Katherine Kay
**Likenesses** H. J. Gunn, five self-portraits, oils, 1910–45, priv. colls. [*see illus.*] • W. O. Hutchison, oils, 1911, Scot. NPG • T. & R. Annan, photograph, *c.*1923, priv. coll. • W. O. Hutchison, portrait, oils, *c.*1928, Royal Scot. Acad. • D. Wilding, photograph, *c.*1930, priv. coll. • W. Dring, drawings, 1954, priv. coll. • C. Sabatini, bronze bust, exh. RA 1955, priv. coll. • G. H. Paulin, bronze bust, exh. RA 1959, priv. coll. • W. Bird, photograph, 1963, NPG
**Wealth at death** £24,588: probate, 8 Feb 1965, *CGPLA Eng. & Wales*

**Gunn, John** (*c.*1765–*c.*1824), writer on music, was born in Edinburgh. He taught the cello and the flute in Cambridge before moving to London about 1790. While continuing to teach he translated A. D. R. Borghese's *New and General System of Music* from the Italian, and also wrote *The Theory and Practice of Fingering for the Violoncello* (1793), *Forty Scotch Airs, Arranged as Trios for Flute, Violin, and Violoncello* (1793), and other works on instrumental playing.

In 1795 Gunn returned to Edinburgh, and in 1802 married Anne Young (*d.* 1826), a pianist and the author of *An Introduction to Music … Illustrated by the Musical Games and Apparatus* (*c.*1803). In 1801 Gunn published an *Essay … on the application of the principles of harmony, thorough bass, and modulation to the violoncello*, explaining how to harmonize a bass line on the cello. His most important work, *An Historical Enquiry Respecting the Performance on the Harp in the Highlands of Scotland*, was published in 1807.

Gunn, a fellow of the Antiquarian Society of Edinburgh, died in Edinburgh about 1824. ANNE PIMLOTT BAKER

**Sources** *New Grove* • Highfill, Burnim & Langhans, *BDA* • D. Baptie, ed., *Musical Scotland, past and present: being a dictionary of Scottish musicians from about 1400 till the present time* (1894), 72 • J. C. Dalyell, *Musical memoirs of Scotland* (1849), 235–6 • W. Matheson, ed., *The blind harper / An clarsair dall*, Scottish Gaelic Texts Society, 12 (1970)

**Gunn, Muriel Amy**. *See* Cornell, Muriel Amy (1906–1996).

**Gunn, Neil Miller** (1891–1973), novelist, was born on 8 November 1891 at Dunbeath, Caithness, the seventh of

Neil Miller Gunn (1891–1973), by unknown photographer, 1920s

the nine children of James Gunn (1847–1916), fishing boat skipper, and his second wife, Isabella Miller (1855–1926?).

**Education and early years** He was educated at Dunbeath School, where he excelled in English and mathematics but disappointed in history. In his final term a prose piece, 'The Sea Storm', won particular praise, prophesying Gunn's hallmark powers of description of life in northern Scotland. That year, 1904, he flitted to the other end of Scotland, St John's Town of Dalry, Kirkcudbrightshire, where he lived with his married elder sister Mary and her husband, a Dr Keiller. There Gunn received private tuition in Latin from the local headmaster, and tuition in poetry, art, and French from an elderly private tutor, J. G. Carter, once an assistant to John Blackie, the nationalist and classical scholar. Carter imparted to Gunn a love of nineteenth-century poets from Shelley to Tennyson, and of Fitzgerald's Omar Khayyam, and he encouraged an interest in native flora and fauna. By Gunn's reckoning, Carter could not keep pace with his pupil's self-taught mathematics.

In the spring of 1907 Gunn took an exam in Edinburgh for entrance to the civil service. He passed easily. By the summer he was in London, not yet sixteen, working as a clerk in Shepherd's Bush Post Office Savings Bank. His elder brother James, in his mid-twenties, was already a civil servant in the capital, and though Gunn also made friends with Londoners, he became part of an informal but supportive network of young Scottish émigrés. In London the spirit of intellectual enquiry which had been gently awakened in him in Dalry was found again listening to debate at speaker's-corner, and reading Wells and T. H. Huxley. It was in London that he began to think of himself as a socialist. Intellectual life, though, had its limits. In Scotland Gunn had enjoyed athletics, curling, and shinty, and poaching salmon in his much-loved local river, Dunbeath Water. In England he played football for his civil service team in west London and occasionally visited the music-hall and opera in town.

In 1909 Gunn transferred to Edinburgh where he worked for a further two years as a clerk at a tax office. After another successful exam and six weeks' training, on 21 December 1911 he was appointed an officer of the customs and excise. He was based at Inverness where for the next decade he specialized in pensions. This required his covering long distances across northern Scotland. Though later, when he was about forty, he suffered an injury which left him blind in one eye (the accident's cause is to this day obscure), a photograph of Gunn from these earlier days shows him tall (6 feet 1 inch), cigarette on lip, goggles on forehead, and sitting commandingly astride a 500 cc Rudge Multi motorbike, staring determinedly to camera. His job involved assessing claimants by interview, latent material perhaps for the sinister Questioner in his dystopian novel *The Green Isle of the Great Deep* (1944). He was also required to act as a locum for excise officers attached to distilleries. It was through this that in 1914 he met Maurice Walsh, an exciseman at Forres, Moray, and later author of *The Quiet Man*. They became close friends and encouraged each other to write.

At the outbreak of the First World War Gunn's employers did not pressure him into enlisting. Instead, he was stationed at Kinlochleven in Argyll, where, apart from his customs and excise duties, he assisted the Admiralty in issuing mine-evading instructions to ships. Here he began tentatively to write poetry and short fiction, gaining his first publication in a London magazine, *The Apple-Tree*, in May 1918. Gunn's mother, having seen four of her sons sign up, had been keen for him to stay at home. The Home Office also preferred that he remained working for the government in Scotland. Two of Gunn's elder brothers were killed in the war, a third died of heart disease while in the army, and one of Gunn's younger brothers, John, was gassed, though he later recovered. His father died in 1916. Nevertheless, Gunn finally signed up in 1918, days before the armistice. He was not required to serve.

By 1920 Gunn was in love with Jessie (Daisy) Dallas Frew (1887/8–1963), the daughter of John Rose Frew, a jeweller. Daisy then worked at her father's shop in Dingwall. With a precipitate stationing to Lancashire in 1921, Gunn married Daisy on 24 March of that year at Wigan register office, but by the end of 1922 they had been relocated and were back in Scotland, at Lybster, Caithness. Finally, in 1923, Gunn became the distillery officer at Glen Mhor distillery, Inverness, where he worked for the next fourteen years. From 1926 they lived in a bungalow they had had built, Larachan. With the stability the job gave him, with its relatively gentle workload and his new house, Gunn was able to write in earnest.

**First writings** In 1923 his short stories had been championed by C. M. Grieve (Hugh MacDiarmid), who published his work in *Scottish Nation* and *Northern Review* and encouraged Gunn to see his work as part of the modern 'Scottish Renaissance'. Gunn's stories also found publication in the *Cornhill*: even at this stage his work appealed both to the intelligentsia and to readers humbly in search of a good yarn. By the end of the decade J. B. Salmond's *Scots Magazine* was Gunn's most consistent publisher of his work, taking short stories, one-act plays, and serializing two novels. His first book, *The Grey Coast*, was published by Cape in 1926 and, as a tale of emotional claustrophobia at the edge of an agoraphobic landscape, is typical of his fiction of the 1920s. In these stories (many in the short story form) the fey Celticism of Fiona Macleod is both an influence and a subject of interrogation; key characters are intensely introspective to the extent of self-defeat; highland harbours and crofts are in decline. The only releases are a Lawrentian eroticism and glimpses of a delighting sensuality.

Drama was of perennial interest to Gunn. After Maurice Walsh and his wife, Toshon, returned to Ireland in 1922 he would stay with them at least annually, taking advantage of his visits to see performances at the Abbey Theatre in Dublin. He was inspired in his fiction by the outpouring of Irish writing from Pearse to Joyce, and Irish drama was an impetus for his plays. Though never an unqualified success, these were performed over the next twenty-five years at every level of Scottish drama, first on BBC radio in 1929, by the Scottish National Players at Glasgow's Lyric Theatre the same year, by amateur actors in the community theatre movement of the 1930s, on wartime radio, and at the Edinburgh festival in 1952. Through drama Gunn became a close friend of the playwright O. H. Mavor, (James Bridie).

After *The Grey Coast* Gunn found it difficult to publish a second novel, though a collection of short stories, *Hidden Doors*, was issued in 1929 by the Edinburgh independent Porpoise Press. Cape regarded him as a one-novel novelist. After other rejections and the shelving of the allegedly anti-English *The Lost Glen*, eventually published in 1932, Gunn returned to Porpoise for the publication of *Morning Tide* (1931). With a trading agreement linking it to Faber, Porpoise now had editorial back-up, an entrée to the London reviews, and, through Faber's links with Harcourt Brace, better access to America. *Morning Tide*, a Book Society choice, was an expansion of an earlier short story about fishermen avoiding disaster at sea with heroism and panache. As so much of Gunn's fiction reworks earlier ideas with new perspectives, it recalls the subject of his prize-winning school essay, written in the first years of the new century. It seems also to offer an alternative to Synge's tragic play *Riders to the Sea* (1904), and introduces another characteristic of much of Gunn's succeeding fiction: at the heart of often elegiac stories there is usually an earned optimism, a confidence in the continuity of human stoicism, of ingenuity and affection.

**Political activities and personal relationships** Gunn had joined the National Party of Scotland in 1929, and the next five years were spent as a political activist in nationalist politics. Though on the left, he helped negotiate the merger of the NPS with the more right-wing Scottish Party, forming the Scottish National Party in 1934. Grieve was expelled from the new organization as an extremist. This aggravated a breakdown in their friendship which had begun two years earlier. In letters to Gunn, Grieve had argued for the supremacy of poetry as an art form, dismissing the novel in general and Gunn's novels in particular. After fitful correspondence that lasted until the outbreak of the Second World War meaningful communication between them went dead. Gunn's entry into artistic and political life following the success of *Morning Tide* and the emergence of the SNP brought him new friends and influential acquaintances. T. S. Eliot visited him in Inverness three times before the war, and Gunn counted as friends or friendly correspondents the writers Catherine Carswell, Naomi Mitchison, Edwin Muir, Nan Shepherd, and the artist Keith Henderson. In the summer of 1934 he also began a secret, lifelong affair with Margaret MacEwen (*b.* 1913), daughter of the nationalist Sir Alexander MacEwen, and during the war a communist.

Though both Gunn and Daisy came from large families, they were unable to have children. Daisy had successive miscarriages and, fifty years later, in the delirium of the last hours of his life, Gunn mourned a stillborn son. Despite or because of this, one of his achievements in *Morning Tide* and several later novels is the sensitive portrayal of a boy's growing up, a theme to which his spare but well-observed dialogue and acute appreciation of the sensual world seem well suited.

**Later novels** Perhaps remembering his poor performance in history at school, lessons which he later suggested were obsessed with dates and English heroes, Gunn published two historical novels in succession. *Sun Circle* (1933) is a novel about a viking raid, and *Butcher's Broom* (1934) describes the highland clearances. The latter, in its mixing of social history, polemic, and the recreation of an isolated 'primitive' society, suggests that it is not only for his descriptions of fishing communities that Gunn has been compared to Herman Melville. It was not until *Highland River* (1937), however, that a more self-conscious novelist emerged. Reorientating flashbacks, the protagonist in philosophical free fall, a subtly ironic portrayal of an intellectual exiled from his community, and a unique use of the third person with past and present tenses, offer this novel as a case study of a human's development from childhood to mature self-consciousness, and reveal a novel of technical virtuosity engaging with large themes. Add to this the novel's meditation on growing up, on the effects of the First World War, and on the very nature of being itself, and *Highland River* stands as a substantial contribution to later modernism.

Other, less assured, novels followed. After *Highland River*'s success Gunn had resigned his excise job, had already withdrawn from behind-the-scenes politics, bought a boat to sail round the Hebrides—(recounted in *Off in a Boat* (1938))—sold Larachan, and in late 1938 settled with Daisy in rented accommodation, Braefarm House near Dingwall. He was now writing for a living, supplementing his income from fiction by journalism on local and national issues, from the fishing industry to Scottish independence. Porpoise had folded, Gunn had been taken on by Faber, and though *Wild Geese Overhead* (1939), a novel based largely in Glasgow, and *Second Sight* (1940), set in a hunting lodge, were not failures in terms of sales or contemporary reviews, they seem now awkward responses to the author's sense of a general moral disintegration for which metropolitan life was (he seems to have felt) partly to blame. The defensiveness of these, returned to with equally unsatisfying results in *The Drinking Well* (1947), *The Shadow* (1948), and *The Lost Chart* (1949), is not to be found in *The Silver Darlings* (1941). This novel describes an infant, Finn, growing up in a Caithness fishing community immediately after the Napoleonic wars. Its synthesis of folklore, folksong, historical detail, episodes of high adventure, acute psychological observation, and symphonic recurrences of intense, almost supernatural experiences, make it a third high point in Gunn's *œuvre*.

After *The Silver Darlings*, *Young Art and Old Hector* (1942) adopts a more prosaic aesthetic: the conversations and experiences of the eponymous child and old man are set out in affectionate homage to the wit and warmth of Highland life. In the Scottish tradition of literature evoking children's views of the world, *Young Art* looks back to Stevenson's *A Child's Garden of Verses* and forward to the earlier poetry of Ian Hamilton Finlay. It was followed immediately by *The Serpent* (1943), the story of an atheist's intense relationship with his family and community, and then by the only sequel Gunn ever wrote, *The Green Isle of the Great Deep* (1944). In this dystopia Young Art and Old Hector enter, by way of nearly drowning, a Celtic heaven with a difference: it has been organized on ultra-rationalist lines. Controlled by a bureaucracy armed with sophisticated forms of psychological torture, heaven's people are superficial, dutiful, and humourless (this is five years before *Nineteen Eighty-Four*). Art and Hector, with the help of one of the few vibrant citizens in this eerie Tir-nan-Og, Mary, finally manage to bring the government of heaven down and help reinstate a fairer one. The allegory finishes deftly with man and boy safely returned to the riverside in real time.

The novel's spirit of reconstruction is paralleled in Gunn's own work on the post-war hospital committee in Scotland, whose report in 1943 is said to have contributed to the formation of the National Health Service. Gunn would later be called upon for other public duty work including the commission of inquiry into crofting conditions, which resulted in the establishment of the Crofters' Commission. In 1948 he was made an honorary doctor of letters by Edinburgh University.

After *The Green Isle* Gunn returned to *Highland River*'s interest in the relationship between academics and intellectuals and the communities they attempt to describe or relate to. *The Key of the Chest* (1946), *The Silver Bough* (1948), and *The Well at the World's End* (1951) gently satirize teacherly romanticism while affirming both the individual's and any given community's ability to survive and even triumph in the face of tragedy. Although these philosophical books were received at the time with some bemusement (Edwin Muir's voice being a notable exception), in the last quarter of the twentieth century they began to have a more positive critical reception. In particular, their playfulness and sophisticated sense of irony found better recognition. Gunn's elegiac optimism is also present in his last novels, the suspenseful *Bloodhunt* (1952), and the enigmatic *The Other Landscape* (1954), both taking as a starting point a tragic death (respectively, murder and death in childbirth) and then envisaging the painful but certain reconstruction of the lives of the survivors. *The Other Landscape* was, however, a substantial departure for Gunn. Its interest in the limits of language and human knowledge and, for example, their analogue in the sea, while recalling his youthful fascination with mathematical systems, has some affinity with W. S. Graham's *The Nightfishing* (1955).

Gunn's last book was *The Atom of Delight* (1956), an essay recounting and analysing incidents in the first two decades of his life. Its comparisons of Western and Far Eastern ideas of self, familiar to a later generation brought up on *Zen and the Art of Motorcycle Maintenance*, and its openness to a hyper-material interpretation of consciousness, found it new readers in the 1980s, when it went through two new editions. At the time, however, it had a puzzled reception and this, as well as Gunn's failing energies and increasing ill health, discouraged him from writing further books.

Daisy died in 1963, and Gunn, of cancer, on 15 January 1973 at the Royal Infirmary, Inverness. They were buried in Dingwall cemetery. On a road on the hills above Dingwall, near Braefarm House, there is a memorial to Gunn.

RICHARD PRICE

**Sources** N. M. Gunn, *The atom of delight* (1956) • F. R. Hart and J. B. Pick, *Neil M. Gunn: a highland life* (1981) • N. M. Gunn, *Selected letters*, ed. J. B. Pick (1987) • R. P. Gunn, *Neil M. Gunn and Dunbeath* (1986) • m. cert. • d. cert.

**Archives** NL Scot., corresp., literary MSS, notebooks • Ransom HRC, MSS and literary papers | NL Scot., letters to Francis Hart [copies] • NL Scot., letters to Hector MacIver • NL Scot., letters to Alexander Reid • NL Scot., letters to Nan Shepherd • North Highland Archive, letters to Fred Robertson | FILM BBC Scotland archives, Glasgow • Scottish Film Archive, Glasgow

**Likenesses** photograph, 1920–29, NL Scot. [*see illus.*] • S. Cursiter, group portrait, 1950 (*Authors in session*), Glasgow Art Gallery • E. Coia, group portrait, ink, chalk, and pencil, 1957, Scot. NPG • G. Sutherland, portrait, *c.*1961 (commissioned by Caithness city council as a gift for the author) • J. M. Bain, oils, Scottish Arts Council, Edinburgh; on loan to department of psychology, U. Edin. • photographs, repro. in Hart and Pick, *Neil M. Gunn* • photographs, repro. in A. Scott and P. Gifford, eds., *Neil M. Gunn: the man and the writer* (1973)

**Wealth at death** £125,107.84: confirmation, 9 March 1973, *CCI*

**Gunn, Ronald Campbell** (1808–1881), naturalist and colonial official, was born in Cape Town on 4 April 1808, the son of an army officer, William Gunn (*d.* 1826), and his wife, Margaret, *née* Wilson (*d.* 1812). After a period spent as a child on Réunion, and education at Aberdeen, he joined his father in Barbados and later became a clerk with the Royal Engineers in Antigua. At the suggestion of his brother William (1800–1868), Gunn went to Van Diemen's Land in 1830 and became assistant overseer of the prisoners' barracks in Hobart Town. He held many official and private managerial roles until, in 1876, ill health forced his retirement from his final posts as deputy commissioner of crown lands and deputy recorder of titles.

**Ronald Campbell Gunn (1808–1881)**, by unknown artist

In the early 1830s Gunn met William Hooker's correspondent and collector in Van Diemen's Land, Robert Lawrence, and soon 'acquired a passionate taste for … Botany' (Lawrence to Hooker, 2 April 1832, RBG Kew, Directors' correspondence). After Lawrence's death in October 1833 Gunn became Hooker's main correspondent in Van Diemen's Land and a point of contact for visiting naturalists. These included, in 1840, Joseph Hooker, who continued to receive Gunn specimens while preparing *Flora Tasmaniae*, in the compilation of which he was largely indebted to Gunn's labours, for there 'are few Tasmanian plants that [he] has not … collected with singular tact and judgement' (J. Hooker, *Flora Tasmaniae*, 1860, cxxv).

Gunn, who was regarded by contemporaries as an excellent botanist, became a fellow of the Linnean Society in 1850, and of the Royal Society in 1854. He played a major part in the continuity of scientific life of the Tasmanian colony during the years when successive societies were founded (and foundered on social tensions), finally becoming a member of the Royal Society of Tasmania in 1848. He maintained a scientific correspondence with other colonies, published in local journals, and supplied specimens and opinions to many. Gunn was married twice. His first wife, Eliza Ireland, died during childbirth in 1836, in Dublin. His second marriage, in 1841, was to Margaret Legrand (1817–1895), daughter of David Jamieson of Glen Leith, near New Norfolk, Tasmania. The couple had five children. Gunn died on 13 March 1881 at his home, Newstead House, near Launceston, Tasmania and was buried at the Presbyterian cemetery at Launceston on 16 March. His wife died in 1895. Gunn is commemorated by the genera *Gunnia* and *Gunniopsis*, and over a hundred species. A. M. Lucas

**Sources** directors' correspondence, Royal Collection • Gunn correspondence, Mitchell L., NSW • *Launceston Examiner* (14 March 1881) • *Launceston Examiner* (16 March 1881) • *Launceston Examiner* (17 March 1881) • correspondence, 1829, PRO, CO 280/23 • C. Finney, *Paradise revealed: natural history in nineteenth-century Australia* (1993), 28–9 • Linnean Society election certificate, Linn. Soc. • election certificate, RS • A. D. Chapman, *Australian plant name index*, 4 vols. (Canberra, 1991) • T. E. Burns and J. R. Skemp, 'Gunn, Ronald Campbell', *AusDB*, vol. 1

**Archives** Mitchell L., NSW • NL NZ, Turnbull L., corresp. • Royal Horticultural Society, London, botanical papers | RBG Kew, directors' corresp.

**Likenesses** crayon drawing, RBG Kew [*see illus.*]

**Wealth at death** £1611 16*s*. 8*d*.: administration with will, 27 Jan 1882, *CGPLA Eng. & Wales*

**Gunn, William** (1750–1841), antiquary and Church of England clergyman, was born on 7 April 1750 at Guildford, Surrey, the son of Alexander Gunn of Irstead, Norfolk. He was educated at Fletcher's private school at Kingston for six years, and matriculated at Gonville and Caius College, Cambridge, as a sizar at Easter 1784. He obtained the degree of BD as a ten-year man in 1795, holding a scholarship over this eleven-year period.

Gunn was ordained deacon at Norwich on 12 June 1774, and priest on 11 June 1775, and acted as curate of Irstead from 1774. Within a few years he received his own benefices in Norfolk. He became vicar of Felmingham in 1779 and curate of Hoveton St John with St Peter in 1780, holding both until 1786. In 1784 he received additionally from Lord Orford the rectory of Sloley, Norfolk, and in 1786 Bishop Bagot of Norwich preferred him to the consolidated livings of Barton Turf and Irstead. In 1789 Gunn married Anne Mack (1768–1828), daughter of John Mack of Sloley, and continued to live as a Norfolk scholar-parson, amateur architect, and justice of the peace (appointed 1802), while always insisting that 'My own family and a very few friends excepted, the country affords me little pleasure, nor did it ever; the amusements of it, strictly so called, were ever lost upon me' (W. Gunn to Mrs Flaxman, 22 Jan 1820, BL, Add. MS 39781, fol. 498).

Once Gunn was provided with three comfortable livings, he devoted his time to antiquarian pursuits and made his first visit to Italy in 1785. He travelled via Nice, Genoa, and Pisa, and reached Rome in time for the 'splendid Pantomimes' (Riviere, 358) of Holy Week and reception by Pius VI. Unperturbed by the outbreak of war in Europe, he journeyed to Italy again in 1792 with his young wife and small daughter, Marianne, spending the winter of 1792–3 in Rome and striking up an acquaintance with George III's son, Prince Augustus. On 4 April 1793 Gunn married the prince to Lady Augusta Murray in breach of the Royal Marriages Act (making him technically a felon), with all three swearing to keep it a secret. The prince, after being created duke of Sussex, appointed Gunn his senior chaplain from gratitude. While in Rome, Gunn was elected to the Society of the Arcadians, and formed a lasting friendship with John Flaxman and his family. The Gunns were back in England by October 1793.

Away from Roman society, most of Gunn's time was spent in research in the Vatican and other Roman libraries, producing 'extracts' from sixteenth-century state papers relating to England, which he published privately in 1803. They described the ancient manner of placing the country under military array and various modes of defence deployed in times of danger. In the Vatican he discovered a tenth-century manuscript of the *Historia Brittonum*, commonly ascribed to Nennius, which Gunn printed in 1819 with an English version, facsimile of the original, notes, and illustrations. His *Inquiry into the Origin and Influence of Gothic Architecture* appeared in London in 1819. He did not expect the book to commend itself to modern devotees of the style, telling Mrs Flaxman, 'should it be deemed of sufficient importance to excite attention I don't expect the Goths will let me come off with whole bones' (W. Gunn to Mrs Flaxman, Dec 1817?, BL, Add. MS 39781, fol. 491). His most important work was *Cartonensia, or, An historical and critical account of the tapestries in the palace of the Vatican; copied from the designs of Raphael, etc., to which are subjoined remarks on the causes which retard the progress of the higher departments of the art of painting in this country* (1831). Gunn's linguistic talents and scholarship won him plaudits in Italy and he was admitted into the Accademia della Crusca under the name of Filistor.

Gunn's concern with the social dislocation caused by pauperism led him in 1834 to recommend several remedial measures to guard against agricultural distress. Following his wife's death in 1828, he resigned Irstead and Barton Turf in 1829 in favour of his son, John Gunn, on receiving the vicarage of Gorleston (with Southtown), Suffolk, from Mrs Browne, widow of Dr Browne, the previous incumbent and master of Christ's College, Cambridge. Gunn died at Smallburgh Grange, near Norwich, Norfolk (the main family home since 1809), on 11 April 1841, and was buried at Sloley. Nigel Aston

**Sources** *GM*, 2nd ser., 16 (1841), 548–9 • J. Venn and others, eds., *Biographical history of Gonville and Caius College*, 2: *1713–1897* (1898), 109 • Venn, *Alum. Cant.* • D. Turner, *List of Norfolk benefices* (1847), 62, 63, 64 • W. C. Hall, *A short history of Barton Turf parish church* (1934) • W. C. Hall, *Notes on St Michael's church, Irstead, Norfolk* (1934) • C. L. S. Linnell, *St Bartholomew's church, Sloley* (1960) • J. Quinton, ed., *Bibliotheca Norfolciensis: a catalogue of the writings of Norfolk men and of works relating to the county of Norfolk in the library of Mr J. J. Colman, at Carrow Abbey Norwich* (1896) • M. Riviere, 'The Rev. William Gunn, BD: a Norfolk parson on the grand tour', *Norfolk Archaeology*, 33 (1962–5), 351–98 • A. W. Moore, *Norfolk and the grand tour: eighteenth-century travellers abroad and their souvenirs* (1985), 160–62 [exhibition catalogue, Norwich Castle Museum, 5 Oct – 24 Nov 1985] • J. Ingamells, ed., *A dictionary of British and Irish travellers in Italy, 1701–1800* (1997), 437–8 • *DNB* • *IGI* • BL, Add. MS 39781, fols. 491, 498

**Archives** Norfolk RO, corresp. | BL, corresp. Flaxman family, Add. MS 39781, fols. 154, 167, 169, 181, 431, 439, 449, 488, 490, 491, 496, 498, 506; Add. MS 39782, fols. 203, 221, 295; Add. MS 39783, fols. 142, 203, 210, 212; Add. MS 39790, fols. 16b–51

**Likenesses** Mrs. D. Turner, etching, 1821 (after portrait by E. Turner), BM • R. J. Lane, lithograph, 1841? (after drawing by J. Flaxman), BM, NPG; repro. in F. Johnson, *Norfolk and Norwich portraits* (1911), 79

**Gunnell, Richard** (*d.* 1634), actor and impresario, began his career as an actor in Prince Henry's company, playing at the Fortune Theatre under the management of Edward Alleyn. He was one of the fourteen names in the company's patent when it became the Lord Palsgrave's Men, in 1613. His fellows included Sam Rowley, a celebrated clown, and John Shank, a famous jig-dancer. Evidently a good friend of Alleyn, whose diary names him and his family dining with the Alleyns on a number of occasions, Gunnell moved gradually from acting into management with the Palsgrave's. When in 1618 Alleyn set up a deal with his tenants the Palsgrave's company at the Fortune, Gunnell was one of the four to take a part share. The deal was designed to imitate the King's Men's part ownership of their theatres, by which the company's leading players, the theatre's tenants, took out shares in the ownership of the building. Gunnell took a full one-eighth share.

A Catholic, like his rival and model Christopher Beeston, Gunnell first appears in the London records on 27 March 1612, when he was accused by a haberdasher of a breach of the peace. He was bailed out by Thomas Downton and another fellow actor on an unusually high-priced bond. Actors commonly bought their fellows out of gaol, since their services were needed on stage every day. The conflict may have related to buying clothes for the company. He was married by this time, since two daughters were baptized in the parish of St Giles Cripplegate (in January 1614 and September 1615). His wife, Elizabeth (*d.* 1641?), was later to have a legal struggle over his properties after he died intestate. Gunnell wrote verses for his 'verie good friend' John Smith's *Description of New England* in 1616, and after a fire at the Fortune in 1621 he wrote at least two plays, *The Hungarian Lion* (1623) and *The Way to Content All Women, or, How a Man may Please his Wife* (1624). None of the plays that he and his fellows wrote for the company at this time got into print. Through this period—certainly from 1618 when he bought his share in the Fortune—he appears to have served as company manager. He appears as the Fortune's representative in the records of the master of the revels for the Palsgrave's and for payments for other performances (including a tightrope walker) at the Fortune.

The years from 1621 were hard for Gunnell and the company. Unlike the burning of the Globe, which happened in an afternoon during a performance, the Fortune's fire happened at midnight, and in the absence of people to help rescue the company's valuables, as they did at the Globe, all of its plays and costumes were lost. Gunnell and the other leading players also lost their investment in the playhouse, and had to help pay for its reconstruction. The company in fact never recovered. On 30 April 1624 Gunnell had to take out a bond with six of the actors, including the clown Andrew Cane and William Cartwright, to hold them in the Palsgrave's. The company dissolved during the long closure of the playhouses through the dreadful plague epidemic that erupted shortly after James died in 1625. Gunnell then created a new company, merging elements from two former groups of James's time, his own Palsgrave's (now the King of Bohemia), with the Lady Elizabeth's (now the Queen of Bohemia).

From 1626, when playing re-started, for the next three years the King and Queen of Bohemia's Men continued to use the Fortune, with Gunnell as their landlord, as their London base. But a new pattern was emerging in London playgoing, and soon Gunnell launched a copy of it by building a small indoor playhouse, the Salisbury Court, in association with William Blagrave of the revels office. Since 1609 the King's Men had used an amphitheatre for summer playing and a roofed hall for the winter. In 1616 Christopher Beeston built a second hall theatre, the Cockpit, and ran it along with the Red Bull amphitheatre, one company in each, to his considerable profit. In 1629 Gunnell followed suit, adding the smallest of London's three hall playhouses to his open-air Fortune. The Salisbury Court Theatre was built in Whitefriars, a London suburb south of Fleet Street, near the river and his customers from the inns of court.

The hall playhouses catered to the gentry, especially to students and lawyers, rather than to the London citizenry, and charged higher prices accordingly. Gunnell set up a new company for it, chiefly of 'youths'—boy players whose playing carried a better social cachet than the companies of adult players. Among the plays he commissioned and staged at the new playhouse were George Chapman's *Sir Giles Goosecap*, Henry Glapthorne's *The Lady Mother*, Nathanael Richards's *Messallina*, Thomas Rawlins's *The Rebellion*, a play which had an almost unprecedented initial nine-day run, and equally notably *The Muses' Looking Glass*, the promising Thomas Randolph's earliest attempt at theatre writing. His *Amyntas* soon followed. With the young William Heminges's first play, in March 1633, *The Madcap, or, The Coursing of the Hare* (now lost), these plays show how ready Gunnell was to try his hand and his new company's with young writers. Shakerley Marmion wrote two plays for Gunnell there. It was a smaller theatre than the other two halls, and King Charles intervened at one point to ban gallants from using stools to sit on its stage, as they usually did at the other two, the Blackfriars and the Cockpit. However, partly because of its smaller capacity, it never quite secured the status of the other two halls that dominated playwriting in the 1630s. One of Marmion's plays, his *Holland's Leaguer*, has a prologue where he claimed to be almost but not quite overawed by the 'two great Lawrels' that 'over-top us'.

In July 1634, during another plague epidemic, an Oxford man, Samuel Crosfield, wrote a diary listing the playing companies then in the university town. His account names:

> The Company of Salisbury Court at the further end of fleet street against the Conduit: The cheife whereof are 1. Mr. Gunnell a Papist. 2. Mr. John Yongue. 3. Edward Gibbs a

fencer. 4. Timothy Reed. 5. Christofer Goad. 6. Sam. Thompson. 7. Mr. Staffeild. 8. John Robinson. 9. Courteous Grevill. these are the cheife whereof 7 are called sharers i.e. such as pay wages to the servants & equally share in the overplus. (Crosfield, 72)

Reed was the Salisbury Court's star, a famous clown, Robinson was a promising young actor who later married Gunnell's widow, Elizabeth. Gunnell never became exclusively an impresario.

Gunnell died early in October 1634, and was buried at St Bride's in Fleet Street on the 7th. The register described him as of Salisbury Court, where he had a dwelling house. He had been back there from July, when the King's Revels returned to perform at the hall playhouse. Some time before his death he appears to have passed on the management of the newer of his two playhouses, and its company, to a new man. The ambitions of the man who took over his role as impresario at Salisbury Court, Richard Heton, may have been a factor behind that. Heton, who was never an actor, proved less congenial as a theatre manager than Gunnell, both for the companies he managed and for the playwrights from whom he commissioned plays.

In 1637 Thomas Jordan published an elegy written for '*his Inestimable friend, Mr.* Richard Gunnell, *Gent.*', in which he writes of 'his neglected ashes' (Bentley, 2.457).

Andrew Gurr

**Sources** E. A. J. Honigmann and S. Brock, eds., *Playhouse wills, 1558–1642: an edition of wills by Shakespeare and his contemporaries in the London theatre* (1993), 233 · G. E. Bentley, *The Jacobean and Caroline stage*, 7 vols. (1941–68), vol. 2, pp. 454–8; vol. 4, pp. 516–18 · M. Eccles, 'Elizabethan actors, II: E–J', *N&Q*, 236 (1991), 454–61, esp. 457 · S. Marmion, 'Prologue', *Holland's leaguer* (1632) · *The diary of Thomas Crosfield*, ed. F. S. Boas (1935)

**Gunning, Elizabeth**. *See* Campbell, Elizabeth, duchess of Argyll and *suo jure* Baroness Hamilton of Hameldon (*bap.* 1733, *d.* 1790).

**Gunning** [*married name* Plunkett]**, Elizabeth (1769–1823)**, novelist, was the only child of John Gunning (1742–1797) of Castle Coote in Ireland, who was then deputy adjutant-general in north Britain, and his wife, Susannah *Gunning, *née* Minifie (1739/40–1800), a clergyman's daughter and novelist. Elizabeth had for aunts the beautiful Gunning sisters: Maria, countess of Coventry, who died before Elizabeth was born, and Elizabeth, duchess of Argyll. (The latter was mother to another novelist, Lady Charlotte Bury, *née* Campbell.) Elizabeth Gunning grew up in Edinburgh, spending several years without her father during the war in America. On his return the Gunnings lived for about four years at Langford Court in Somerset, before moving to London in June 1788. They rented a house in St James's Place and another in Twickenham. Elizabeth was already rumoured to be engaged to her cousin the marquess of Lorne, heir to the duke of Argyll.

By summer 1790 rumours were rife of an even grander suitor for Elizabeth: the marquess of Blandford, heir to the duke of Marlborough. In November doubts were cast on this story; letters from Blandford were produced, denied, then identified as forgeries. Either Elizabeth or her mother was generally supposed to have committed this grave (indeed, capital) offence in pursuit of a brilliant marriage like those of the earlier Miss Gunnings. Horace Walpole was an assiduous reporter (often in a spirit of fantasy) of the public accusations and counter-accusations. In February 1791 John Gunning, apparently in righteous anger, turned his wife and daughter out of his house; they were taken in by Blandford's grandmother, the highly respectable duchess of Bedford. Susannah Gunning published an emotional but unspecific defence of her daughter and attack on her husband and his cousin Captain Essex Bowen, in the form of a letter to the duke of Argyll (as notional head of the family). Bowen retaliated in print. Elizabeth Gunning's narrative of her side of the story remained unpublished; she reportedly told her father she would never see him again until he acknowledged her innocence.

A year later John Gunning was sued for damages by the husband of his mistress, for whom he had been running a faro bank. Susannah continued her public relations campaign in two works of 1792. In *Virginius and Virginia*, a long poem about ancient Rome, Virginius kills his daughter to prevent her marriage. In the novel *Anecdotes of the Delborough Family* a father turns his daughter out when she claims the right to choose a husband. A preface says this was written years before the recent events; disbelief in this claim gave the novel a success unprecedented in Susannah Gunning's career, but equalled by *Memoirs of Mary* (1793), which is even more clearly based in fact. Contemporary opinion blamed one or other of the Gunning women for trying to ensnare Blandford by duplicity; John Gunning, whose financial problems were desperate, looks at least as likely a candidate today.

In 1794 'Miss Gunning' published her own first novel, *The Packet*. In it Elizabeth does not write directly of herself, although marriage into the nobility was a favourite motif with her as with her mother. *The Packet* opens by acknowledging that fashionable people will read it only for Elizabeth Gunning's name. She went on to publish nine novels (including *The Heir Apparent* (1802), which her mother left unfinished at her death), a collection of fairy tales for children, and two plays (not staged). She translated five works from French, all from obscure authors except for *Conversations on the Plurality of Worlds* (1803) from the original by Fontenelle, which had also been translated by Aphra Behn.

Elizabeth Gunning's early novels are, like her mother's, sentimental, with heavy-footed humour, trite moralizing, a self-consciously elaborate style, and intense class-consciousness. Each woman wrote more interestingly, with more criticism of society, later in life. Elizabeth skilfully wooed a public and constructed a career. She published about half her works before her marriage in 1803 to Major J. Plunkett from Kinnaird in co. Roscommon, with whom she had several children.

In 1815 Elizabeth Gunning published her last novel, *The Man of Fashion, a Tale of Modern Times*, whose protagonist loses his position as heir to an earldom, and finds that of his children only the illegitimate one is dutiful. She died at Melford House, Long Melford, Suffolk, on 20 July 1823.

ISOBEL GRUNDY

**Sources** Blain, Clements & Grundy, *Feminist comp.* • I. Gantz, *The pastel portrait: the Gunnings of Castle Coote and Howards of Hampstead* (1963) • *GM*, 1st ser., 38 (1768), 398 • *GM*, 1st ser., 70 (1800), 904, 1000 • *GM*, 1st ser., 73 (1803), 1251 • *GM*, 1st ser., 93/2 (1823), 190 • S. Gunning, *A letter from Mrs. Gunning, addressed to his grace the duke of Argyll* … (1791) • E. Bowen, *A statement of facts, in answer to Mrs. Gunning's letter*… (1791) • Foster, *Alum. Oxon.* • *The letters of Horace Walpole, fourth earl of Orford*, ed. P. Toynbee, 16 vols. (1903–5); suppl., 3 vols. (1918–25) • P. Perkins, 'The fictional identities of Elizabeth Gunning', *Tulsa Studies in Women's Literature*, 15/1 (spring 1996), 83–98
**Likenesses** F. Bartolozzi, stipple, 1796 (after R. Saunders), BM; repro. in *Memoirs of Madame de Barneveldt* (1796)

**Gunning, Henry** (1768–1854), university bedell and author, was born at Newton, Cambridgeshire, on 13 February 1768. His father, Francis Gunning, who was vicar of Newton and also of the adjacent parishes of Thriplow and Hauxton, was the grandson of William Gunning, the first cousin and secretary of Peter Gunning, successively bishop of Chichester and Ely. Henry was educated first at Ely, in a school kept by Jeffrey Bentham, a minor canon of the cathedral, and brother of James Bentham, and afterwards in the endowed school of Sleaford, Lincolnshire, under the Revd Edward Waterson. He entered Christ's College, Cambridge, as a sizar in October 1784, where he gained a scholarship, and graduated BA as fifth wrangler in 1788 (MA, 1791). In 1794 he married a Miss Bertram, who predeceased him.

On 13 October 1789 Gunning was elected one of the esquire bedells of the university, whose main function was to attend the vice-chancellor during university ceremonies. He became senior esquire bedell in 1827. In that capacity he received gold chains from three successive chancellors of the university: the marquess of Camden, 1834, the duke of Northumberland, 1844, and Prince Albert, 1847.

An advanced whig in politics Gunning took an active part in local politics, was a strenuous supporter of the cause of parliamentary reform, and after the passing of the Municipal Corporations Act was from 1835 to 1841 a member of the town council of Cambridge. In 1847 he fell, by slipping on an orange peel, which left him incurably lame. His official connection with the university continued for more than sixty-five years. He was highly regarded for his courtesy, gentlemanly bearing, and readiness to communicate his extensive knowledge respecting academic ceremonies and privileges. He died at Brighton on 4 January 1854. His eldest son—and the only one who survived him—was Henry Bertram Gunning (*d.* 1888) of Little Shelford, Cambridgeshire, formerly a charity commissioner and an assistant tithe commissioner for East Anglia. Another son, Francis John Gunning (*d.* 1846), was a solicitor and town clerk of Cambridge from 1836 to 1840; and a third son, Frederick Gunning (*d.* 1850), was a barrister in extensive practice on the Norfolk circuit, and the author of *A Practical Treatise on the Law of Tolls* (1833).

Gunning is chiefly remembered for his *Reminiscences of the University, Town, and County of Cambridge from the Year 1780* (to 1820) (2 vols., 1854). Although he did not begin these entertaining sketches until he was more than eighty years old, they betray few marks of senility. The anecdotes of his contemporaries are highly amusing, and his facts are generally accurate, though his judgments of individuals are sometimes coloured by personal animosity. Notice of its impending publication was viewed with disquiet by the heads of the Cambridge colleges, only one of whom was prepared to become a subscriber. The work was published posthumously; it had been dictated to an amanuensis, Mary Beart, who prepared it for publication. Gunning also prepared a new edition of Adam Wall's *Ceremonies Observed in the Senate House of the University of Cambridge* (1828) and wrote a pamphlet *Compositions for Degrees* (1850). As esquire bedell, he was responsible for publishing the votes taken at elections to university offices, including the two university members of parliament.

THOMPSON COOPER, *rev.* M. C. CURTHOYS

**Sources** *GM*, 2nd ser., 42 (1854), 207, 342 • D. A. Winstanley, introduction, in H. Gunning, *Reminiscences of Cambridge: a selection*, ed. D. A. Winstanley (1932), vii–xvi • A. T. Bartholomew, ed., *Gunning's last years: nine letters from Miss Mary Beart to Professor Adam Sedgwick* (1912) • Venn, *Alum. Cant.* • H. P. Stokes, *The esquire bedells of the University of Cambridge* (1911) • Boase, *Mod. Eng. biog.* • P. Searby, *A history of the University of Cambridge*, 3: 1750–1870, ed. C. N. L. Brooke and others (1997)
**Likenesses** Davy & Son, lithograph, repro. in Gunning, *Reminiscences*, vol. 1 • J. T. Woodhouse, oils, Christ's College, Cambridge

**Gunning, John** (*d.* 1798), surgeon, was assistant surgeon to St George's Hospital, London, from 21 January 1760 to 4 January 1765, and full surgeon from that date until his death. In 1773 he was elected steward of anatomy by the Company of Surgeons, but paid the fine rather than serve. Having been elected to the court of assistants in 1784, in 1789 he was elected examiner on the death of Percivall Pott, and in the same year he was chosen master of the company, and spent his year in office trying to reform the company's administration and reorganize its work. His attack upon the expensive system of dinners of the courts of assistants and of examiners and his philippic on retiring from office on 1 July 1790 show that he could be fearlessly outspoken. 'Your theatre', he said in his last address,

> is without lectures, your library-room without books is converted into an office for your clerk, and your committee-room is become his eating-parlour … If, gentlemen, you make no better use of the hall than what you have already done, you had better sell it, and apply the money for the good of the company in some other way. (Cope, 14)

The court of assistants appointed a committee to consider the question, and some reforms were effected. Gunning had also recommended that the company should offer a series of fifteen lectures in surgery, and in 1790 he was elected the first professor of surgery; he refused the honour on the grounds that it occupied too much of his time, and no new appointment was made.

Gunning was in general antagonistic towards his colleague at St George's, John Hunter, who was frequently overbearing to his professional colleagues, who in turn considered that Hunter neglected the proper business of a surgeon for unpractical pursuits. The quarrel rose to its height during the election of a surgeon in succession to Charles Hawkins. Thomas Keate was supported by Gunning, and Everard Home by Hunter, and after a sharp contest Keate was elected. A dispute ensued about fees for surgical lectures, which led to controversy between Gunning, senior surgeon, supported by two of his colleagues, and Hunter. It ended in John Hunter's dramatically sudden death on 16 October 1793.

In 1796 it was decided to sell the Surgeons' Hall on account of the cost of repairs, but on 7 July Gunning, on behalf of the committee, reported that as no one had bid within £200 of the price set upon it, it had been bought in. At the same court Henry Cline was elected a member of the court of assistants, in the absence of a governor (one having just died, and the other being blind and paralysed in Warwickshire). This voided the charter. A bill brought into parliament in 1797 to indemnify the company, and to give it greater power over the profession, after passing the Commons was lost in the House of Lords through the influence of Edward Thurlow, owing, it is said, to his grudge against Gunning. Thurlow having said 'There's no more science in surgery than in butchery', Gunning had retorted 'Then, my lord, I heartily pray that your lordship may break your leg, and have only a butcher to set it'.

Gunning had been appointed surgeon-general of the army in 1793, on the death of John Hunter; he was also senior surgeon-extraordinary to the king. Gunning was elected a fellow of the Royal Society in 1782. He died at Bath on 14 February 1798. His nephew John Gunning served as surgeon with the army in Flanders in 1793–4, throughout the Peninsular War, and at Waterloo. Between 1806 and 1808 he lectured in surgery at 43 Conduit Street, Hanover Square, London. He was nominally surgeon to St George's from 1800 to 1823, but soon after the peace he settled in Paris, where he died in 1863 in his ninetieth year.

G. T. Bettany, *rev.* Michael Bevan

**Sources** S. C. Lawrence, *Charitable knowledge: hospital pupils and practitioners in eighteenth-century London* (1996) · D. Ottley, *The life of John Hunter* (1839) · J. F. South, *Memorials of the craft of surgery in England* (1886) · *GM*, 1st ser., 63 (1793), 1062 · *GM*, 1st ser., 68 (1798), 177 · W. E. Page, 'Account of St George's Hospital', *St George's Hospital Reports*, 1 (1866) · Z. Cope, *The Royal College of Surgeons of England: a history* (1959) · *The record of the Royal Society of London*, 4th edn (1940)

**Gunning, Maria**. *See* Coventry, Maria, countess of Coventry (*bap.* 1732, *d.* 1760).

**Gunning, Peter** (1614–1684), bishop of Ely and theologian, was born at the vicarage, Hoo, Kent, on 11 January 1614 and baptized at Lower Hoo church five days later, the son of Peter Gunning, the vicar there, and his wife, Ellen. His uncle Richard Gunning settled in Ireland and was the ancestor of the eighteenth-century diplomat Sir Robert Gunning. After education at King's School, Canterbury, Gunning matriculated in 1629 at Clare College, Cambridge, where he graduated top of the list as BA in 1633. Awarded a probationary fellowship at Clare in that year,

Peter Gunning (1614–1684), by unknown artist, *c.*1675–80

he proceeded to a full fellowship two years later, when he proceeded MA. Gunning was clearly a man of promise; a letter from Barnabas Oley to the earl of Exeter in 1640 commends him as a possible personal chaplain, but Gunning remained at Clare until 1644, when he was ejected by the parliamentary commissioners. One of his successors in the fellowship was John Tillotson, the future archbishop of Canterbury, who was appointed in 1651, and whom Gunning insisted should be ejected at the Restoration in 1660 in order to allow his return; Gunning's theological position was more traditional—and less accommodating than Tillotson's. Gunning preached a sermon in Little St Mary's (where he also served as a curate after his ordination) in May 1643 condemning the covenant, thereby nailing his colours firmly to the royalist mast: such a public act would have brought his views to the attention of the authorities in no uncertain way. On leaving Cambridge he moved to Oxford, where the royal court was based; he was appointed chaplain of New College in July 1644, and also curate at the nearby village of Cassington. His preaching drew him to royal attention and on 23 July 1646, the day before the surrender to the parliamentarian forces, Gunning and certain other Cambridge notables were awarded the degree of BD.

Gunning spent the years from then until the Restoration among royalists. He served as tutor in the households of Lord Hatton and Sir Francis Compton, and then became chaplain to Sir Robert Shirley. Upon the latter's death in the Tower of London in 1656, Gunning began to officiate at the chapel of Exeter House on the Strand. Here he could use the Book of Common Prayer services; they were officially proscribed but by this time such a practice was tolerated. The eucharist was celebrated each month, a frequency that was to be advocated at the Restoration. Indeed, such was the popularity of the ministry of Jeremy Taylor and Gunning at Exeter House that the congregation was nicknamed the Grand Assembly. John Evelyn mentions Gunning many times. On 3 December 1657: 'Mr Gunning preached on: 3.John.3 against the Anabaptists, shewing the effect & necessity of the Sacrament of Baptisme' (Evelyn, 3.202). Evelyn was also present when troops under colonels Edward Whalley and William Goffe interrupted the Christmas day communion service that Gunning conducted that year:

> These wretched miscreants held their muskets against us as we came up to receive the Sacred Elements, as if they would have shot us at the Altar, but yet suffering us to finish the Office of Communion, as perhaps not in their Instructions what they should do in case they found us in that Action. (ibid., 3.204)

In 1658 Gunning brought out his first publication, *A Contention for Truth, in Two Public Disputations upon Infant Baptism*, which had taken place between himself and Henry Denne in the church of St Clement Danes. Baptism was much disputed at the time: Baptists like Denne contended that only 'believers' should be baptized, extreme puritans held that only the children of believing parents should, whereas prayer book conformists believed in the necessity of baptism, godparents making the promises in the name of the church. Gunning's style is thus that of the controversialist, unlike more moderate figures such as Simon Patrick, who in the same year published a work on baptism, *Aqua genitalis*, which made the same points but in a more conciliatory manner. 1658 also saw the publication by the Catholic protagonists of *Scisme Unmask't*, an account of a disputation which had occurred the previous year between Gunning and John Pearson on the one part and two Catholic priests on the other, as to whether it was the church of England or of Rome which was schismatical.

At the beginning of 1660 Gunning was still preaching at Exeter House: on 1 January both Evelyn and Samuel Pepys heard him preach. With the return of the monarchy his career flourished. He was restored to his fellowship by royal command on 20 June, and was the next day created DD, the speed of which indicated royal favour to a loyal servant. Further honours followed. He was made Lady Margaret professor of divinity in 1660 and was appointed master of Corpus Christi College, Cambridge, in February 1661. In June 1661 he relinquished these posts to take up the regius chair of divinity and the more prestigious mastership of St John's College, Cambridge. He also acquired other preferments: he was made a prebendary of Canterbury Cathedral in July 1660 and later that year was instituted to the rectories of Cottesmore in Rutland and Stoke Bruerne in Northamptonshire. The chapter of Canterbury elected him a proctor in the Canterbury convocation, as did the clergy of Peterborough diocese in which Stoke Bruerne was situated. These Restoration preferments brought him into the limelight as a tough-minded and dedicated churchman: 'the fittest man', Anthony Wood recalled, '... to settle the university right in their principles again, after many corruptions had crept in there by means of the rebellion' (Wood, *Ath. Oxon.*, 3rd edn, 1813–20, 4.142).

When in 1661 Charles II decreed by letters patent that a conference should be held at the chapel of the Savoy in the hope of reaching some measure of agreement between the episcopalian and the presbyterian parties, Gunning was among those deputed as an alternate to the designated bishops. Richard Baxter attended as a presbyterian. The atmosphere was hardly conducive to the kind of rapprochement in view—the presbyterian nominee Anthony Tuckney was forced to resign the mastership of St John's and the regius professorship in favour of Gunning while the conference was actually in progress. When after some stalemate sessions it was agreed that a small group of three from each side should meet in order to take the disputes as far as they could, Gunning and Baxter emerged as the two main contenders in a debate which centred on kneeling at communion; this was a topic dear to Gunning's heart, in view of the fact that he had administered the bread in St Margaret's, Westminster, the previous May when the House of Commons was required to attend the prayer book rite. But whereas Baxter is credited with the tone of a mediator, Gunning demonstrated a thorough knowledge of history and a passionate style in argument; as Baxter himself wrote:

> Dr. Gunning was their forwardest and greatest speaker, understanding well what belonged to a disputant; a man of greater study and industry than any of them; well-read in fathers and Councils; and of a ready tongue; (and I hear and believe, of a very temperate life, as to all carnal excesses whatsoever); but so vehement for his high, imposing principles, and so over-zealous for Arminianism, and formality and church pomp, and so very eager and fervent in his discourse, that I conceive his prejudice and passion much perverted his judgement, and I am sure they made him lamentably over-run himself in his discourses. (*Reliquiae Baxterianae*, 1.2.364)

Gilbert Burnet betrays a similar view, describing Baxter and Gunning as 'a couple of fencers engaged in disputes, that could never be brought to an end' (*Bishop Burnet's History*, 1.329).

The Savoy conference could not succeed in the task of uniting the two sides. When the revision of the prayer book came before convocation Gunning took his part in the proceedings. He argued strongly about the age of confirmation; he helped to draft the declaration on kneeling at communion; and when it came to the form for consecrating bishops, he was responsible—along with another Savoy conference nominee, John Pearson—for an insertion which made explicit that bishops were a separate order from priests. This view, held by many at the time, is consistent with a sermon Evelyn heard Gunning preach fifteen years later in 1676. The famous 'Prayer for all sorts and conditions of men' has sometimes been attributed to Gunning, even with the suggestion that it was composed for use at St John's College, Cambridge, during his mastership, and that the reference to those who profess and call themselves Christians may be a veiled Gunning-style dart aimed at puritans. However, liturgical scholars tend to regard the prayer as more likely the work of Edward Reynolds, who was at the Savoy conference as a presbyterian, perhaps with some editorial work by Robert Sanderson.

Gunning relinquished his Cambridge posts and his livings just prior to his consecration as bishop of Chichester in March 1670. He was translated to Ely in March 1675, where he remained until his death, in the bishop's palace, nine years later on 6 July 1684; he was buried in the south aisle of the presbytery in Ely Cathedral, where a fine monument with an effigy in marble was subsequently erected. He was a great benefactor in his lifetime, relieving the poor, supporting scholars at the university, and contributing endowments to the poor clergy of both the dioceses he served as bishop. Such generosity was reflected in his will, which also bequeathed his considerable library to his old college, Clare, and £300 towards building a chapel there. As a bishop he was known to be hard on nonconformity. In 1678 he defended the Test Act against charges that it implied that Roman Catholics were idolatrous. He is credited with having planted what is now the second largest plane tree in England, at the Old Palace in Ely.

Opinions among his contemporaries differ on Gunning, which is hardly surprising in view of the position he took up at a time of division and ferment in church and state. Evelyn said with admiring candour that 'he can do nothing but what is well'; Margaret Godolphin regarded it as a privilege that she was brought by her mother to be confirmed by him; Peter Barwick admired him greatly; his brother, John Barwick, dean of St Paul's, sent for Gunning in his last hours to minister the sacrament to him on 22 October 1664; and Denis Grenville, dean of Durham, regarded him as his spiritual adviser, made his confession to him, and recorded with obvious warmth that on 9 November 1679 he was able to receive the sacrament from Gunning's own hands at his chapel in London. There can be no doubt that Gunning touched the lives of many people, not just the prominent who met him in person and who left attestations of his diligence as a pastor. Portraits of him—two at St John's College, Cambridge, the third at Bishop's House, Ely—depict a man both formidable and learned. But the clue to his theological personality perhaps lies in the character of his literary output. His writing career began in 1658 with a work on baptism written in a controversial style. His longest known work is an expanded version of a sermon on fasting which was preached before Charles II, and which was dedicated to him. The fast—in Lent or at any other time—was not the most significant religious theme of the seventeenth century, but it was a topic frequently touched upon by its preachers, Lancelot Andrewes included. It appears to have been a feature of the spiritual armoury that was dear to Gunning's heart, for Evelyn recorded that Gunning helped to organize a private fast in October 1659 on behalf of the nation as an act of prayerful penitence. Gunning's published sermon is a lengthy and carefully annotated work of historical scholarship, which shows features observed by Baxter at the Savoy conference—a grasp of the writings of the early fathers, a conviction in the tradition of the church, and an austere lifestyle; and the various appendices betray yet more information about the meaning of Lent, and about fasting. Gunning believed in tradition, and that—in its prayer book rather than its puritan form—people would benefit from being fed by it, as the end of his discourse on fasting shows:

> That this precious new wine, even for the more precious old wine's sake, may not be poured out, spilt, or lost; for that cause I have made this profusion of sand and labour: that no vessels old or new may perish, is my heart's desire and prayer. (Gunning, 179)

KENNETH W. STEVENSON

**Sources** W. J. Harrison, *Notes on the masters, fellows, scholars, and exhibitioners of Clare College* (1953) • J. R. Wardale, ed., *Clare College: letters and documents* (1903) • J. R. Wardale, *Clare College* (1899) • J. Bentham, *The history and antiquities of the conventual and cathedral church of Ely*, ed. J. Bentham, 2nd edn (1812) • *Clare College, 1326–1926* (1928), vol. 1 • G. J. Cuming, *A history of Anglican liturgy*, 2nd edn (1982) • J. Spurr, *The Restoration Church of England, 1646–1689* (1991) • Evelyn, *Diary*, vols. 3–4 • *Reliquiae Baxterianae, or, Mr Richard Baxter's narrative of the most memorable passages of his life and times*, ed. M. Sylvester, 1 vol. in 3 pts (1696) • P. Gunning, *The Paschal or Lent fast*, Library of Anglo-Catholic Theology (1845) • E. Cardwell, *A history of conferences and other proceedings connected with the revision of the Book of Common Prayer* (1840) • will, PRO, PROB 11/376, sig. 89 • Clare College, Cambridge, archives • *Fasti Angl., 1541–1857*, [Ely] • *Fasti Angl., 1541–1857*, [Chichester] • *Fasti Angl., 1541–1857*, [Canterbury] • Pepys, *Diary*, vols. 1–2 • J. Gascoigne, *Cambridge in the age of the Enlightenment* (1989) • H. I. Longden, *Northamptonshire and Rutland clergy from 1500*, ed. P. I. King and others, 16 vols. in 6, Northamptonshire RS (1938–52), vol. 6, p. 91

**Likenesses** oils, *c.*1675–1680, St John Cam. [*see illus.*] • oils, 1680, bishop's house, Ely • D. Loggan, line engraving, BM, NPG • engraving (after D. Loggan), St John Cam. • engraving, St John Cam. • oils, St John Cam. • oils, St John Cam. • oils (other versions of portrait, *c.*1675–1680), bishop's house, Ely, Old Schools, Cambridge

**Wealth at death** will includes generous bequests to church of his baptism, Clare College, St John's College, poor clergy of Ely's diocese: will, PRO, PROB 11/376, sig. 89

**Gunning, Sir Robert, first baronet** (1731–1816), diplomatist, was born on 8 June 1731, the eldest son of Robert Gunning (*d.* 1750) and Catherine (*d.* 1782), daughter of John Edwards. He was descended from Richard Gunning, an uncle of Peter Gunning, bishop of Ely, who settled in Ireland in the time of James I. On 27 March 1752 he married Elizabeth, daughter of John Harrison of Grantham, who died only a few weeks later, on 14 April 1752. He subsequently married, on St Valentine's day 1757, Anne (*d.* 1770), only daughter of Robert Sutton of Scofton, Nottinghamshire, and Anne Throckmorton. They had three children, George William, Charlotte Margaret, and Barbara Evelyn Isabella.

Gunning entered the diplomatic service, and on 23 November 1765 was appointed minister-resident at Copenhagen, where he arrived in early March 1766. His instructions were to assist the envoy-extraordinary and minister-plenipotentiary, Walter Titley, and on Titley's death (27 February 1768) Gunning succeeded to his post. On 13 April 1771 he was appointed envoy-extraordinary to the court of Prussia, but he never took up the position in Berlin.

Gunning finally left Copenhagen in June 1771 and in

May 1772 was appointed envoy-extraordinary and minister-plenipotentiary to the court of Russia, where he arrived on 18 June. His brief was to offer the services of the British government as mediator between Russia and the Porte, with a view to effecting a peace treaty, and to support Catherine the Great's policies in Poland, but to attempt to secure toleration for the Greek church and other dissident religious bodies. He proved to be a favourite of the empress, who frequently admitted him to private audiences, and on one occasion ordered through him four copies of Kennicott's edition of the Old Testament in Hebrew. The tact, zeal, and discretion with which he discharged his duties were highly appreciated by George III, who, unsolicited, nominated him a knight of the Bath on 2 June 1773, and requested the empress to invest him with the insignia of the order. She consented, and selected 9 July, the anniversary of her own accession, for the ceremony, and when it was over gave him the gold-hilted sword set with diamonds with which she had knighted him.

In the summer of 1775 Gunning was instructed to sound the Russian foreign minister, Panin, as to the possibility of obtaining Russian troops for service in North America. Gunning received encouraging replies from Panin, and afterwards from the empress herself, and negotiations were opened for a contingent of 20,000 fully equipped (except for field pieces) Russian infantry to be placed under the command of a British general, and transported in British ships to Canada. A pretext for rupturing the negotiations was found in the demand of the British government that the principal officers of the Russian contingent should take the oath of allegiance to the British crown, but Gunning's conduct in the affair was much praised by Lord Suffolk, secretary of state for the north. In the following November Gunning sought and obtained his recall on account of ill health, and had left St Petersburg by February 1776. He was rewarded with a baronetcy on 3 September 1778, and was installed knight of the Bath on 19 May 1779. He died at his seat at Horton, near Northampton, on 22 September 1816.

J. M. Rigg, *rev.* R. D. E. Eagles

**Sources** D. B. Horn, ed., *British diplomatic representatives, 1689–1789*, CS, 3rd ser., 46 (1932) · GEC, *Peerage* · GEC, *Baronetage* · N. H. Nicolas, *History of the orders of knighthood of the British empire*, 3 (1842) · *GM*, 1st ser., 22 (1752), 143 · *GM*, 1st ser., 27 (1757), 141 · *GM*, 1st ser., 35 (1765), 539 · *GM*, 1st ser., 41 (1771), 572 · *GM*, 1st ser., 60 (1790), 83 · *GM*, 1st ser., 86/2 (1816), 465–6 · Nichols, *Illustrations*, 6.153

**Archives** BL, corresp. and MSS, Egerton MSS 2680–2706 · HMC, Parc. MSS, X report, 400 | BL, letters to Sir Robert Murray Keith, Add. MSS 35504–35508, *passim* · HMC, III report, 250 · NRA priv. coll., letters to Lord Cathcart

**Likenesses** G. Romney, oils, Montreal Museum of Fine Arts, Canada

**Gunning** [*née* Minifie], **Susannah** (1739/40–1800), novelist, was one of at least two daughters of James Minifie, a clergyman of Staplegrove, Somerset. She published two novels written with her sister Margaret, *The History of Lady Frances S. and Lady Caroline S* (1763) and *The Picture* (1766), and four more on her own by the end of the 1760s. These books achieved both a mild degree of popularity and a certain amount of ridicule for their excessively sentimental plots: a contemporary coined the adjective 'minific' to describe breathlessly hyperbolic prose. On 8 August 1768 Susannah married John Gunning (*d.* 1797), the only son of John Gunning of Castle Coote, Ireland, and his wife, Bridget, daughter of the sixth Viscount Bourke of Mayo. While the younger John Gunning had a moderately successful military career (he served in the British army during the American War of Independence and eventually became a lieutenant-general), he was better known for being the brother of Maria and Elizabeth Gunning, the famous society beauties who became, respectively, the countess of Coventry and the duchess of Hamilton and Argyll.

Susannah Gunning probably did not publish any more fiction for over two decades after her marriage. *The Count de Poland* (1780), which at the time was said to be by her, is almost certainly by Margaret Minifie; according to Blain, so is *Coombe Wood* (1783), which has also been attributed to Susannah Gunning. Her literary career was reanimated in the 1790s after a major scandal in the winter and spring of 1791 involving her only child, Elizabeth [*see* Gunning, Elizabeth], who had apparently let it be known among her friends that she was engaged to the marquess of Blandford. Blandford and his parents, the duke and duchess of Marlborough, hastily denied this as soon as rumours, and what was quickly proved to be a forged letter from Marlborough, started circulating. Matters were further complicated by a letter, possibly a forgery, in which Elizabeth confessed to a Mrs Bowen, a distant relative, that she was actually in love with her cousin the marquess of Lorne. This letter was sent to General Gunning, who responded by turning his wife and daughter out of his house. (In another bizarre twist, it was Blandford's maternal grandmother, the duchess of Bedford, who then helped them find accommodation.) Susannah Gunning promptly launched a pamphlet war with an appeal to the duke of Argyll, Lorne's father, to help her clear her daughter's name, and writers ranging from Horace Walpole (in his letters) to anonymous pamphleteers and newspaper columnists gleefully contributed to what Walpole called the 'Gunningiad'.

Gunning's pamphlet, which is at least as melodramatic as any of her novels, portrays Elizabeth as the victim of nefarious plots by her father, who was determined to blacken her name so that he could justify himself in casting her off and refusing any dowry or any further financial support for either his wife or his daughter. Gunning does not seem to have succeeded in convincing many readers to believe her version of the case. David Rivers, writing in 1798, thought the pamphlet 'deform[ed]' by 'foolish and simple anecdotes', and that 'it abounds infinitely more in invective than argument' (Rivers, 1.230). The *London Chronicle*, going even further, decided that the scheme of using false love-letters to destroy the reputation of an innocent girl had to be 'the offspring of a female imagination', and pointed out that Gunning herself, 'who is perfectly conversant in Novels and consquently fertile in the contrivance of new incidents and unexpected situations', was an obvious suspect (*London Chronicle*, 181). A later pamphlet, supposedly the confessions of General Gunning (though its authenticity has been doubted), claims as well that Susannah Gunning was behind the whole affair. The pamphlet alleged that her attempt to win a marquess for her daughter went badly askew when she could not decide whether to settle on Lorne or Blandford as her future son-in-law; General Gunning, who had known her plans all along, was then obliged to abandon his wife to salvage his own reputation. What in fact happened has never been determined, but the story of a matchmaking scheme gone wrong is probably the most plausible of the explanations offered.

With no support forthcoming from their powerful relatives, Susannah and Elizabeth Gunning retreated to France until gossip died down, but they subsequently used their notoriety to help their literary careers. Susannah Gunning's next novels, *Anecdotes of the Delborough Family* (1792) and *Memoirs of Mary* (1793), contain thinly disguised references to her daughter's story, with the latter focusing on a virtuous heroine who has two lovers—one of them a distant cousin—turned against her by forged letters. *Virginius and Virginia*, Gunning's 1792 poem, even brings allusions to the Gunning family problems into a story drawn from Roman history. Elizabeth Gunning, who began her own career as a novelist in 1794 with *The Packet*, also includes numerous references to the scandal in her book. Susannah Gunning's marriage did not recover from the rupture in 1791, and the following year John Gunning caused another major scandal when he eloped to Naples with his mistress in order to avoid paying the £5000 damages awarded to her husband in a trial for criminal conversation. He remained there and remained estranged from his wife and daughter until his death on 2 September 1797. According to the *Gentleman's Magazine*, he did, however, change his will at the last minute to include a legacy of both money and property for his wife.

In her later fiction, as in her earlier work, Gunning consistently endorses sentimental virtue and domestic propriety, values which seem decidedly at odds with events of the melodramatic and scandal-ridden final decade of her life. Indeed, the picture of her presented by an anonymous friend in the foreword of her last novel, *The Heir Apparent* (1802), which was left unfinished at her death and completed by her daughter, is extremely difficult to reconcile with the combative, vigorously outspoken, and apparently unembarrassable Gunning of 1791. According to that friend, Gunning's 'name [is] ever attended by the recollection of her virtues', and '[h]er life, from her cradle to her grave, was a life of holiness' ('Foreword', Gunning, *Heir*). Her literary reputation was summed up in a less partial obituary in the *Gentleman's Magazine*, which described her as 'a lady well known, if not highly celebrated, in the republick of letters' and placed her work 'among the middling class of novels' (*GM*, 70, 1000). Susannah Gunning died at Down Street, London, of an unidentified but—again, according to her anonymous friend—painfully debilitating disease on 28 August 1800, aged sixty. She was buried in Westminster Abbey. PAM PERKINS

**Sources** *GM*, 1st ser., 70 (1800), 1000 · 'Foreword', S. Gunning, *The heir apparent* (1802) · Blain, Clements & Grundy, *Feminist comp.* · [D. Rivers], *Literary memoirs of living authors of Great Britain*, 2 vols. (1798) · *London Chronicle* (19–22 Feb 1791), 181 · *DNB* · J. Todd, ed., *A dictionary of British and American women writers, 1660–1800* (1984) · *GM*, 1st ser., 67 (1797), 892 · S. Gunning, *Memoirs of Mary* (1793) · S. Minifie and M. Minifie, *The history of Lady Frances S. and Lady Caroline S.* (1763) · [M. Minifie], *The union* (1803)

**Gunnis, Rupert Forbes** (1899–1965), historian of British sculpture, was born on 11 March 1899 at 79 Cadogan Square, London, the second of the three sons of Francis George Gunnis (*d.* 1932), a sugar merchant, and his wife, Ivy Marion (1869–1960), daughter of Lieutenant-Colonel Henry Dorrien Streatfeild of Chiddingstone Castle in Kent. Rupert Gunnis was educated at Eton College until 1916, and in 1923, after a spell as secretary to the last commissioner of the British South Africa Company, he entered the colonial service. He served successively as private secretary to the governors of Uganda (1923–6) and Cyprus (1926–32). From 1932 to 1935 he acted as an inspector of antiquities for the Cyprus Museum and his guidebook, *Historic Cyprus: a Guide to its Towns and Villages, Monasteries and Castles* (1936), the fruit of his extensive researches into the history and archaeology of the island, has become a classic of its kind. Gunnis returned to England in 1939. During the Second World War he inherited the fortune of his paternal aunt, the widow of General Sir Francis Lloyd, which enabled him to purchase Hungershall Lodge, a large house in Tunbridge Wells, Kent. Here Gunnis established himself in some style, attended by his Cypriot manservant, Namuk Kemal, and devoted his time to antiquarian pursuits, particularly the study of British monumental sculpture.

Gunnis had been interested in church monuments since boyhood, but from about 1942 he began distilling the notes made on visits to churches, libraries, and muniment rooms all over Britain into an index of information about monumental sculptors and statuaries. Initially the index appears to have been destined for inclusion in Katherine Esdaile's projected 'Dictionary of British sculptors in England', and it may have been she who encouraged Gunnis to widen his researches to include all sculptors from the time of the Reformation to the opening of the Great Exhibition. On Esdaile's death in 1950, he was the natural heir to her unrealized project. His *Dictionary of British Sculptors, 1660–1851* appeared in 1953.

Gunnis's dictionary revolutionized the study of British sculpture, providing the foundation for all later studies on the subject. A new revised edition appeared in 1968, with a second preface by Gunnis, written in 1964, in which he stated that he had collected 'a great deal more information' on British sculptors, but noted that 'it is quite impossible to add all this information, for had I done so the book would have been more than twice its original size' (Gunnis, 2nd edn, 9). The long-awaited third revision of Gunnis's dictionary was scheduled for publication in

2004. Gunnis published little else, apart from several minor articles on church monuments. He also collaborated with Margaret Whinney on a catalogue, *The Collection of Models at University College by John Flaxman* (1967).

With his independent means, bookish habits, and delight in the curious, Gunnis can be seen as one of the last gentleman antiquaries. He was a thickset man, with a moustache and owlish, black-framed spectacles, and had a mischievous sense of humour. He died, unmarried, of a heart attack on 31 July 1965, while staying at Stratfield Saye House, near Reading, and was buried in the Streatfeild Mausoleum in Chiddingstone churchyard, Kent. A brass plaque in the church at Chiddingstone describes him as an 'Author, Antiquary, Lover of the Arts'. Gunnis formed a notable collection of eighteenth- and nineteenth-century English sculpture, most of which he bequeathed to the Victoria and Albert Museum in London. His principal memorial, however, is his dictionary which remains an essential work of reference for the study of British sculpture. TIM KNOX

**Sources** R. Gunnis, *Dictionary of British sculptors, 1660–1851* (1953); new edn (1968) · T. Knox, 'Portrait of a collector: Rupert Gunnis at Hungershall Lodge and his bequest to the Victoria and Albert Museum', *Sculpture Journal*, 2 (1998), 85–96 · D. Symons, 'Rupert Gunnis, 1899–1965', *Cahier: Centre D'Études Chypriotes*, 7 (1987), 3–9 · J. Harris, *No voice from the hall* (1998), 86–92 · R. Storrs, *Orientations* (1937), 577–8, 596 · *Kent and East Sussex Courier* (Aug 1965) · *The Times* (3 Aug 1965) · *The Times* (5 Aug 1965) · b. cert. · d. cert.

**Archives** Courtauld Inst. · Henry Moore Institute, Leeds · Sussex Archaeological Society, Lewes, corresp. and MSS · V&A · Yale U. CBA, corresp. and papers

**Likenesses** K. Mann, oils, *c*.1916, priv. coll.; repro. in Knox, 'Portrait', fig. 8 · B. Bailey, photograph, 1963, Courtauld Inst., Conway Library; repro. in Knox, 'Portrait', fig. 1 · B. Bailey, photograph, *c*.1964, Courtauld Inst., Conway Library

**Wealth at death** £132,279: probate, 8 Sept 1965, *CGPLA Eng. & Wales*

**Gunter, Anne** (*bap.* 1584), demoniac, was baptized at Hungerford on 10 May 1584, the fifth and youngest child of Brian Gunter (*c*.1540–1628) and Anne Gunter (*d.* 1617). She enjoyed a brief period of fame in the summer and autumn of 1605 when James VI and I interested himself in her supposedly bewitched condition.

The Gunters were an extensive gentry clan which had originated in Abergavenny, and which by the time of Anne's birth was firmly established in Berkshire. About 1588 Anne's family moved to North Moreton in that county when her father inherited the village's rectory on the death of a brother. Brian Gunter was a contentious, litigious, and violent man, this last quality being demonstrated in May 1598 when he inflicted fatal injuries on John and Richard Gregory, members of a local yeoman family, in the course of a brawl at a village football match.

In summer 1604 Anne Gunter briefly fell ill; her sickness at this stage was attributed to 'the mother', or hysteria. She rapidly recovered, but fell ill again in October of that year. This time the symptoms persisted, and, when the numerous doctors who were called to examine her failed to diagnose a natural disease, it was decided that she was bewitched. By this point, indeed, she was showing the classic symptoms of what might be described as possession by witchcraft, including going into fits and comas and vomiting pins, and was naming three village women as her tormentors. The chief of these was Elizabeth Gregory, who had married into the family upon two of whose members Brian Gunter had inflicted fatal injuries in 1598.

As was common in such cases Anne Gunter's sufferings attracted a large audience, among which, remarkably, were a number of figures from Oxford University. Anne's elder sister Susan was married to Thomas Holland, regius professor of divinity at Oxford, and at one point Anne was lodged in his apartments at Exeter College, where he was rector, while her father obviously enjoyed a wide social circle at the university. Among those who witnessed her sufferings were Bartholomew Warner, regius professor of medicine, and a man who was subsequently to achieve considerable eminence at Oxford, John Prideaux.

Elizabeth Gregory and another of the suspected women were tried for witchcraft at the Abingdon assizes on 1 March 1605, and acquitted. Matters should have ended there, but Gunter's afflictions persisted. She was taken into custody for observation by Henry Cotton, bishop of Salisbury; most of those who examined her at this stage were convinced she was simulating being bewitched or possessed. Brian Gunter, however, was anxious to demonstrate the genuine nature of his daughter's afflictions, and took her to meet James VI and I when the king visited Oxford University in August 1605.

James was sceptical, and passed Gunter's case on to Richard Bancroft, the archbishop of Canterbury, who in turn delegated investigating her to Samuel Harsnett. Bancroft and Harsnett had been involved in investigating a number of incidents of possession, witchcraft, and exorcism (notably those involving John Darrell) and had developed a thoroughly sceptical position, while the physician Edward Jorden, another proven sceptic, was brought in to examine Anne. The net effect of their efforts was that by 10 October 1605 James was able to write a letter to the earl of Salisbury stating that Anne had confessed that she had simulated her sufferings at her father's instigation.

Early in 1606 Star Chamber proceedings were initiated against Brian and Anne Gunter for false accusations: Harsnett and Richard Neile were heavily involved in orchestrating these proceedings, which were probably initiated by Bancroft. More than fifty witnesses gave evidence, their depositions covering hundreds of foolscap pages, making this among the best documented English witchcraft cases. The Gunter case showed many remarkable features, but is perhaps chiefly significant for demonstrating how witchcraft accusations, begun in the context of personal grudges and village conflicts, might emerge in the context of national ecclesiastical politics. The scepticism of those leading clerics who brought the Gunters to trial was part and parcel of their hostility to the pretensions to powers of exorcism made by certain godly ministers, a hostility which was but one strand in an anti-puritanism which involved conflicting visions of the church.

Gaps in documentation mean that the outcome of the

Star Chamber proceedings cannot be established, while we have no sure evidence of Anne Gunter's later fate. James's letter of 10 October 1605 mentions that Anne had fallen in love with one of Bancroft's servants, surnamed Asheley, and that a marriage was being arranged with royal support, and a number of other sources support this story, but no record of such a marriage, or of any other indication of what later happened to Anne, has yet been found. Brian Gunter died at Oxford, and was buried at St Mary the Virgin on 17 November 1628.

JAMES SHARPE

**Sources** J. Sharpe, *The bewitching of Anne Gunter: a horrible and true story of deception, witchcraft, murder and the king* (1999) • PRO, STAC 8/4/10 • parish register, Hungerford, 10 May 1584, Berks. RO, MF 136 [baptism] • BL, Add. MS 12497 [letter of James I to earl of Salisbury, 10 Oct 1605], fols. 197–8 • R. Johnstone, *Historia rerum Britannicarum … ab anno 1572, ad annum 1628* (1655), 401 • parish register, Oxford, St Mary the Virgin [burial], 17 Nov 1628 • parish register, North Moreton, Berkshire [burial], 11 April 1617

**Gunter, Edmund** (1581–1626), mathematician, was born in Herefordshire, the son of a Welshman from Gunterstown, Brecknockshire. He was a queen's scholar at Westminster School from where he entered Christ Church, Oxford, matriculating on 25 January 1600. During his time at Oxford his interest in mathematics (already manifested in a fascination with sundials) flourished, and he began to devise his own mathematical instruments. He gained his BA on 12 December 1603 and his MA on 2 July 1606. At about this time he wrote a Latin manuscript on his sector, developed from the earlier instrument of Thomas Hood.

Gunter took holy orders in 1615, being awarded his BD on 23 November. He was established in that year as rector of both St Mary Magdalen, Oxford, and St George's, Southwark. He began to spend time in Gresham College where his friend Henry Briggs was professor of geometry. Briggs had suggested Gunter as the successor to the first Gresham professor of astronomy, but the post was granted to Thomas Williams. Gunter in fact became the third astronomy professor on the resignation of Williams in 1620, and was appointed on 6 March of that year.

The same year Gunter was interviewed by Sir Henry Savile for the new Savilean chair of geometry at Oxford, but was rejected in favour of Henry Briggs. According to Aubrey's account of the event, Gunter appeared to have been turned down for being over-interested in the use of instruments in mathematics (*Brief Lives*, under 'Sir Henry Savile'). He remained as a Gresham professor until his death.

At Gresham, Gunter devoted most of his time to the development of instruments and to the investigation of the newly discovered logarithms. He devised the first table of logarithms of trigonometrical functions, dubbing them 'artificial sines and tangents'. These were published as *Canon triangulorum, or, Table of Artificial Sines and Tangents* (1620), in which he also introduced the terms 'cosine' and 'cotangent'. He lectured on much of his logarithmic work at Gresham, where he also considered the use of mathematical instruments in astronomy and navigation.

In 1622 Gunter's investigations at Limehouse, Deptford, of the magnetic variation of the compass needle produced results differing from William Borough's, obtained more than forty years earlier. He assumed an error in Borough's measurements, but this was in fact the first observation of temporal change in magnetic variation, a contribution acknowledged by his successor, Henry Gellibrand, who discovered the phenomenon. In the same year Gunter engraved a new sundial at Whitehall, which carried many different dial plates and supplied a wealth of astronomical data. Prompted by Prince Charles, he wrote an explanation of the dials, published as *The Description and Use of his Majesties Dials in White-Hall Garden* (1624). The sundial was demolished in 1697.

Easily the most substantial of Gunter's works was *The Description and Use of the Sector, the Crosse-Staffe and other such Instruments* (1623) which explained instruments which he had designed. Apart from the two mentioned in the title it also included an astronomical quadrant and a 'cross-bow'—an alternative to the backstaff used by sailors for solar altitude measurements. Although this instrument did not become popular the others all did, in one form or another. The Gunter sector was a much more complex instrument than Thomas Hood's. It allowed calculations involving square and cubic proportions, and carried various trigonometrical scales. Moreover it had a scale for use with Mercator's new projection of the sphere, making this projection more manageable for navigators who were only partially mathematically literate. The sector was sold as a navigational instrument throughout the seventeenth century and survived in cases of drawing instruments for nearly three hundred years. The most striking feature of the cross-staff, distancing it from other forms of this instrument, was the inclusion of logarithmic scales. This was the first version of a logarithmic rule, and it was from Gunter's work that logarithmic slide rules were developed, instruments that remained in use until the late twentieth century.

Gunter also invented a surveying chain and is credited by De Morgan (*Arithmetical Books*, xxv) with introducing the decimal separator. He died on 10 December 1626 at Gresham College and was buried the following day at St Peter-le-Poer, Old Broad Street. Gunter was a firm advocate of the use of instruments in mathematics for easing the work of various mathematical practitioners, notably surveyors and navigators. His instruments were designed with these aims in mind. In particular his work on logarithms, their applications to trigonometry, and their inclusion on instruments greatly simplified the processes of mathematical calculation. His books were popular for many years after his death: an edition of all his works was produced by Samuel Foster in 1636 and this had three more editions, the last in 1680, which had additions by Foster, Henry Bond, and William Leybourn.

H. K. HIGTON

**Sources** E. G. R. Taylor, *The mathematical practitioners of Tudor and Stuart England* (1954) • Wood, *Ath. Oxon.* • Foster, *Alum. Oxon.* • E. Gunter, *The description and use of the sector, the crosse-staffe and other such instruments* (1623) • J. Welch, *A list of scholars of St Peter's College,*

*Westminster* (1788) • J. Ward, *The lives of the professors of Gresham College* (1740) • B. Martin, *Biographia philosophica* (1764) • A. De Morgan, *Arithmetical books from the invention of printing to the present time* (1847) • *Aubrey's Brief lives*, ed. O. L. Dick (1949)

**Gunter, James** (1731–1819), confectioner, was born on 25 July 1731 in the parish of St Marylebone, Middlesex, the third child and first son of James Gunter and his wife, Hannah Greenough. The precise circumstances of Gunter's education are unknown, but he was probably apprenticed to Domenico Negri, his brother-in-law, who operated a confectionery business at 7 Berkeley Square from 1757. Gunter married Mary Masson (1752?–1827) at St George's, Hanover Square, on 26 October 1776. They had seven children: James, who died in infancy, Robert, William, Anne, Caroline, Elizabeth (later Negri), and Charlotte.

In 1777 Negri made Gunter a partner in the business, a relationship confirmed in a 1784 trade card bearing the two names. Gunter may also have operated a second shop in New Bond Street between 1787 and 1796. From 1802 Gunter was the sole trader at the Berkeley Square shop and from 1817 until his death in 1819 the business was known as James and Robert Gunter, or Gunter & Son. As a confectioner, Gunter created and sold sweetmeats, dessert biscuits, dried and candied fruits, and other delicacies. Gunter's renown as a supplier of confectionery to members of the royal family and aristocracy was enhanced by his catering for balls and receptions, and the Gunter name was synonymous with such lavish entertainments well into the twentieth century.

Before 1799 Gunter probably lived on his Berkeley Square shop premises; he served as a captain in the parochial St George's volunteer corps. From 1797 he began purchasing property in Earls Court and Old Brompton villages, then still on the fringes of west London development. By 1815 he owned over 60 acres in the area, devoted to market gardens and fruit-growing hothouses. His property interests were not merely horticultural. Between 1797 and 1799 he acquired Earls Court Lodge (demolished 1973), in which he and his family lived for nearly sixty years. Gunter owned the lease of Earls Court House, previously the home of the surgeon John Hunter, and also of the land on which William Cobbett set up his nursery between 1821 and 1827. From as early as 1805 he oversaw the development of villa residences in the area, and at his death, he also owned property in Marylebone, Paddington, and Grosvenor Square.

Gunter died on 19 September 1819 of a fit of apoplexy which seized him while he was staying with his family in Worthing, Sussex. He was buried in the family vault in the churchyard of St Mary Abbots, Kensington, on 27 September. In his fifty-page will dated 11 September 1819, Gunter left £20,000 in trust to provide for his three unmarried daughters, while the remainder of the personal and real estate was left to his surviving son, Robert, and formed the basis for extensive mid-nineteenth-century residential developments in Earls Court. A successful tradesman who converted his profits into impressive real estate investments, Gunter was nevertheless celebrated in obituaries as a man of unostentatious philanthropy, while Guglielmo Jarrin, a confectioner in the Gunters' employ, eulogized his late master in 1820 for his 'fostering care and … his unceasing desire for the perfection of his art—his encouragement of emulation—and just appreciation of industry' (Jarrin, dedication).

Gunter's surviving son, **Robert Gunter** (1783–1852), was born on 31 March 1783 in the parish of St George, Hanover Square, London. He also entered the confectionery trade, and in 1815 was sent by his father to study the subject in Paris. After his father's death, Robert assumed sole control of the Berkeley Square business, which flourished under his management, and in July 1821 he was granted a royal warrant as purveyor extraordinary to the royal household. From 1837, Gunter took on his cousin John (son of William Gunter, brother to James) as his business partner, and from 1841 withdrew from an active role in the shop.

Gunter was undoubtedly busy elsewhere. He developed the Earls Court market gardens and nurseries, which were considered to be the second largest such concern in London in the 1820s. He continued to sell building leases on properties in west London and served as a director of the ill-fated Birmingham, Bristol, and Thames Junction Railway Company (incorporated 1836). He married twice. His first wife was Fanny (1808?–1835), daughter of William Thompson of Durham, whom he married on 8 February 1831; and they had two sons, Robert (1831–1905) and James (1833–1908). Gunter's second marriage, to Jane (*d.* 1897), daughter of William Maude of Blackburn, Lancashire, took place on 6 June 1838. They had two daughters, Edith Maude (1841–1846) and Hilda Maude (*b.* 1849).

Robert Gunter died aged sixty-nine at Earls Court, Middlesex, on 16 October 1852. He was an extremely wealthy man at the time of his death, due to his careful management of the Earls Court and other London properties he and his father had accumulated. However, Gunter's legacies emphasized his desire to distance the Gunter name from the confectionery trade, and his sons' military, political, and real estate achievements exemplify the success of his wishes. S. M. Pennell

**Sources** E. David, *Harvest of the cold months: the social history of ice and ices* (1994), 310–72 • H. Hobhouse, ed., *Southern Kensington: Kensington Square to Earl's Court*, Survey of London, 42 (1986), 196–203, 324, 344–7 • will, 11 Sept 1816, PRO, PROB 11/6123, sig. 573 • parish register (baptism), St George, Hanover Square, Westminster, 7 April 1783 • parish register (marriage), St George, Hanover Square, Westminster, 26 Oct 1776 • parish register (baptism), London, St Marylebone, 15 Aug 1731 • St George, Hanover Square, parochial rate books, 1774–87, City Westm. AC • parish register (burial), Kensington, London, St Mary Abbots • A. Heal, 'Gunter of Berkeley Square', *N&Q*, 159 (1930), 99 • *The epicure's almanack, or, Calendar of good living* (1815) • G. A. Jarrin, *The Italian confectioner, or, Complete economy of desserts … by G. A. Jarrin, ornamental confectioner at Messrs. Gunters* (1820) • *The Times* (24 Sept 1819), 3 • *Kent's London and Westminster directories* (1774–1815) • *Kent's original London directory* (1816) • *The Post Office directory* (1802–20) • *Morning Chronicle* (24 Sept 1819) • will of Robert Gunter, 31 July 1846, PRO, PROB 11/6163, sig. 916 • Burke, *Peerage* • Liber Warrant, 1784–1821, PRO, LS 13/267, fol. 93 (p. 195) • *GM*, 2nd ser., 38 (1852), 657 [Robert Gunter] • W. Schupbach, 'Earl's Court House from John Hunter to Robert Gardiner Hill', *Medical History*, 30 (1986), 351–6 • T. Faulkner, *History and antiquities of Kensington* (1820) • A. Adburgham, *Silver fork society* (1983), 216–17

**Archives** priv. coll.
**Wealth at death** over £20,000: will, 1816, PRO, PROB 11/6123, sig. 573 • over £25,000—Robert Gunter: will, 1846, PRO, PROB 11/6163, sig. 916

**Gunter** [*née* Cresswell], **Mary** (**1586–1622**), convert to protestantism, was the daughter of Thomas Cresswell, gentleman, and a kinswoman of Sir Christopher Blount, third husband of Lettice Dudley, dowager countess of Leicester and Essex. Her parents having died in her infancy Mary was raised by an elderly Catholic lady. After her guardian's death, when Mary was fourteen, she moved into Blount's household and, following his execution in 1601, continued to live with his widow at Drayton Basset, Staffordshire. Upon discovering that Mary was planning to join a Catholic nunnery abroad the countess confiscated her rosary and devotional books and, with the assistance of her chaplain, John Wilson, converted her ward to protestantism. Subsequently, according to her husband's later account of her spiritual pilgrimage, Mary overcame a period of temptation when she doubted her conversion's validity and even God's existence. From 1607, besides attending public and private religious services, she read the scriptures daily and fasted six days a year. In 1617 she began to keep a catalogue of her sins and, recalling that some of the old lady's servants had bribed her to steal money from their mistress, Mary gave part of the marriage portion bestowed upon her by the countess to the old lady's heir.

Mary resided in the countess's household until 1621 and, some time before her departure, she married Humphrey Gunter, a servant of the countess and probably a member of the Berkshire gentry of that name. Their only son was no longer an infant when Mary died, on 6 February 1622, after an illness of ten weeks. She was buried at St Mary's, Reading, where her husband erected to her memory a brass plate which displayed the arms of Gunter impaling Cresswell and depicted Mary kneeling at a prayer desk with her son kneeling behind her; the last line of the verse honouring her read, 'Till then farewell sweet saynt my halfe my hart'. The funeral sermon preached by the puritan preacher of Reading, Thomas Taylor, was published in 1622 as *Pilgrim's Profession*, with an appended life by her husband. Dedicated to the countess of Leicester and Essex this volume is significant because it was one of only about two dozen commemorative sermons for women that were published between 1601 and 1630; in addition only one similar publication in this period, that honouring Katherine Brettergh in 1601, contained so lengthy an appended statement. Although it proved less popular than that of Brettergh it still appealed to purchasers who longed to know about the trials of an extremely religious woman who had been snatched from Catholicism. Reprinted three times by 1633, it was included by Samuel Clarke in *The Lives of Sundry Eminent Persons in this Later Age* (1683).

Retha M. Warnicke

**Sources** H. T. Morley, *Monumental brasses of Berkshire, 14th to 17th century* (1924) • S. Clark [S. Clarke], *The lives of sundry eminent persons in this later age* (1683) • *VCH Berkshire*, vol. 4 • *Pilgrim's profession, or, A sermon preached at the funeral of Mrs Mary Gunter by Mr Thomas Taylor* (1622) • J. Wilson, *Some helpes to faith* (1625) • *The pilgrim's profession* (1625) *by Thomas Taylor* (1995) [with introduction by B. A. Doebler and R. M. Warnicke]
**Likenesses** brass plate, 1622, St Mary's, Reading; repro. in Morley, *Monumental brasses*

**Gunter, Raymond Jones** (**1909–1977**), trade unionist and politician, was born at High Street, Llanhilleth, Abertillery, Monmouthshire, on 30 August 1909, the son of Miles Gunter, a fruiterer and later a colliery pumpsman, and his wife, Clara Adeline Jones. After attending Abertillery and Newbridge secondary schools, he became, at the age of fourteen, a booking clerk with the Great Western Railway. When he was sixteen, he joined the Railway Clerks' Association (later the Transport Salaried Staffs' Association) and the Labour Party. He became active in both. On 4 August 1934, at the Methodist church at Newbridge, he married Elsie (*d.* 1971), an elementary school teacher, daughter of James Elkins (a coalminer), with whom he had one son. During the Second World War Gunter enlisted in the Royal Engineers in 1941 and was promoted to staff captain in 1943, overseeing the transport of arms from Iraq to the USSR.

Gunter returned to Britain in 1945 to contest Essex South-East in the general election and, to his surprise, won the seat. He was then narrowly elected for Doncaster in 1950 and equally narrowly defeated in 1951. He unsuccessfully contested Doncaster again in 1955 but eventually found a safe haven in Southwark, for which he sat from 1959 to 1972.

While out of the House of Commons, Gunter became president of the Transport Salaried Staffs' Association in 1956, having previously been its treasurer, and he held the post until 1964. Emphatically anti-Bevanite, he was a member of the national executive committee of the Labour Party from 1955 to 1966 and, as head of the party's organization committee, took a tough line against left-wing critics during the early 1960s. He was a steadying and unifying influence during the clash over unilateral disarmament during and after the 1960 party conference, and for a brief moment he was seen as a future leader of the party. He became opposition spokesman on power in 1960 and then served as shadow minister of labour from 1961 until the 1964 general election. He was also chairman of the Labour Party from 1964 to 1965.

On 17 October 1964 Harold Wilson included Gunter in his new cabinet as minister of labour. Gunter called his new post 'a bed of nails' (Wigham, 'Much more a unionist'). Under any administration of the period, mediating between employers and workers was an exacting and unenviable task, but in 1964 the Ministry of Labour was expected to construct the coherent and genuine labour market policy that seemed an essential prerequisite to union participation in a voluntary incomes policy. It thus formed a pivot around which the government hoped to turn its social and economic policies.

Gunter's performance as minister of labour was mixed. He piloted through parliament the Redundancy Payments Act and successfully set up the industrial training boards required by the Industrial Training Act of January 1964.

However, in both instances the spadework had already been done by the previous Conservative government. His Trade Disputes Act (1965) overturned the *Rookes* v. *Barnard* judicial decision of 1964 that threatened the unions' legal immunity in respect of strikes. The achievement which probably gave him greatest satisfaction was paving the way to ending casual dock working by setting up the Devlin committee.

In other respects, Gunter's achievements were less satisfactory. His creation of the Donovan commission (the royal commission on trade unions and employers' associations) in April 1965 soured his relations with the unions. During the seamen's strike of May 1966 his ministerial status was undermined when the handling of the dispute was taken over by Wilson. The strike helped to precipitate an economic crisis in July 1966, but Gunter in cabinet was unable to resist either the imposition of the pay freeze or the subsequent prolongation of statutory control of collective bargaining.

In April 1968 Wilson moved Gunter to the Ministry of Power. Gunter bitterly resented this, not least because he loathed his successor, Barbara Castle, and resented Wilson's expansion of the now renamed Department of Employment and Productivity. Two months later, on 28 June, he resigned from the cabinet. Had he chosen to go in April his motives would have been clear, but as it was they were obscure. For this reason, his resignation is remembered as an example of how not to resign (Kaufman, 168–9). But his comment that he would be forgotten within ten years (Wigham, 'Much more a unionist') proved correct.

Ray Gunter was a rotund and smilingly self-confident figure, who employed an emotional, rumbustious, and sometimes demagogic oratory in the service of the Labour right. After meeting him in May 1968, Richard Crossman, who 'never trusted him a yard', described him as 'a huge, squat bullfrog of a man, with a great Welsh voice and the less attractive qualities of the Welsh as well' (Crossman, *Diaries*, 3.50). He was pro-European long before this became common in the Labour Party and was a firm believer in co-operation between management and workers. In a sense he was more a trade unionist than a politician, though his white-collar connections disadvantaged him within the TUC general council, where some referred to him dismissively as 'the ticket collector' (Jenkins, 7). Within the cabinet he was unpopular among some of his colleagues for leaking information to the press (*Castle Diaries, 1964–70*, 304). His appointment and dismissal as minister of labour mirror the changing attitude of Wilson's government to the unions. Gunter campaigned relentlessly against traditions and practices that were dear to many Unionists but that he perceived to be hampering change; in a speech to the Scottish council of labour he remarked, 'I do wish so many of the comrades would stop equating profits with incest or lechery', adding that profitable industry meant further investment and more jobs (*Sunday Times*, 20 Aug 1967). For this he was bitterly resented by the left, and when he returned to the back benches he had few political reserves on which to draw. His Europeanism was a major factor in his decision to resign the Labour whip in February 1972, when he insisted 'our country has a new role in Europe, not only on economic grounds' (*The Times*, 17 Feb 1972). He also cited his resentment at the dominant role of intellectuals, whom he thought out of touch with the interests of ordinary people, among a Labour leadership lacking the working-class ballast which he, Frank Cousins, and George Brown had provided. He died at his cottage, Y Bwthyn Bach, Launceston Close, Old Town, St Mary's, on the Isles of Scilly on 11 April 1977. HUGH PEMBERTON

**Sources** *The Times* (16 April 1977) · E. Wigham, 'Much more a unionist than a politician', *The Times* (1 July 1968), 9 · E. Wigham, *Strikes and the government, 1893–1974* (1976) · E. Shaw, *Discipline and discord in the labour party: the politics of managerial control in the labour party, 1951–87* (1988) · A. Watkins, 'The consequences of Mr Gunter', *New Statesman* (5 July 1968), 2 · 'Correspondence with George Brown about the importance of a genuine labour market policy to incomes policy', PRO, LAB 43/424 · D. Howell, *British social democracy: a study in development and decay* (1976) · H. Pelling, *A history of British trade unionism*, 4th edn (1987) · R. H. S. Crossman, *The diaries of a cabinet minister*, 3 vols. (1975–7) · *The Castle diaries, 1964–1970* (1984) · L. Minkin, *The labour party conference: a study in the politics of intra-party democracy* (1978) · G. Kaufman, *How to be a minister* (1997) · E. Heffer, *The class struggle in parliament: a socialist view of industrial relations* (1973) · E. Short, *Whip to Wilson* (1989) · H. Wilson, *The labour government, 1964–1970: a personal record* (1971) · P. Jenkins, *The battle of Downing Street* (1970) · *CGPLA Eng. & Wales* (1977) · b. cert. · m. cert. · d. cert.

**Archives** FILM BFI NFTVA, party political footage · BFI NFTVA, propaganda film footage (government)

**Likenesses** F. Topolski, portrait, NPG · photograph, repro. in *The Times*

**Wealth at death** £34,985: probate, 20 July 1977, *CGPLA Eng. & Wales*

**Gunter, Robert** (1783–1852). *See under* Gunter, James (1731–1819).

**Günther** [Gunther], **Albert Charles Lewis Gotthilf** [*formerly* Albert Karl Ludwig Gotthilf] (**1830–1914**), ichthyologist and museum administrator, was born at Esslingen in the state of Württemberg, south Germany, on 3 October 1830, the elder son of Friedrich Gotthilf Günther (1800–1835), *Stiftungs-kommissar* of estates in Möhringen, and his wife, (Eleonore) Louise (1806–1899), the daughter of Ludwig Friedrich Nagel, the Lutheran pastor at Vaihingen. At an early age he developed an interest in natural history and pursued this at the Stuttgart Museum and with the Württemberg Natural History Society.

Gunther's education was dependent on grants and scholarships. He attended the Eberhard-Ludwig Gymnasium in Stuttgart from the age of seven. In 1847, following family tradition, he entered the Höheres Evangelisches-Theologisches Stift, University of Tübingen, to study for the Lutheran ministry, but later considered these years of theological study (1847–51) 'as a loss of time from his life' (Gunther, *Century of Zoology*, 227).

During 1848 Gunther decided to give himself up 'almost entirely to systematic zoological study' (Gunther, *Century of Zoology*, 223) and attended the classes in physiology and anatomy, as well as using the collections in the Königliches Naturalien-Kabinet and the local zoo. By passing his theological examination in 1851, he obtained a grant that allowed him to continue such studies officially. His tutor, Professor Wilhelm von Rapp, encouraged him to undertake a thesis on the fishes of the River Neckar with which he gained MA and DPhil degrees (1853). Gunther then studied medicine, initially at the University of Berlin and later at Bonn University. At this time, financial difficulties forced him to seek employment as a private tutor. With the assistance of one employer, Charles Milner, he returned to Tübingen for the final two years of his medical degree. Shortly after graduating in 1857, he published the *Handbuch der Medicinischen Zoologie* (1858).

Gunther's mother had travelled to England in 1854 in order to help the family's financial situation; she became a language teacher at Brighton. While visiting her in July of that year, Gunther was able to make his first sea-shore observations, and to travel to London where he met Richard Owen and J. E. Gray. With few opportunities in Germany, he returned to Brighton in the summer of 1857, intending to widen his medical experience by working in local hospitals, as well as continuing to study marine invertebrate faunas. Hoping for a position at the British Museum, Gunther wrote to J. E. Gray. Gray engaged him to list the snake specimens in the museum's spirit collection for a fee of £75, work published as a *Catalogue of Colubrine Snakes* (1858). Although working in the cellars, Gunther later recalled: 'That [first] year was one of the happiest of my life. Unhampered by any other worry or interest I gave myself entirely up to the task' (Gunther, *Century of Zoology*, 261). Later he wrote: 'I could not have come to England at a better time' (ibid., 273).

Gunther now became engrossed in scientific work. At a salary of £200 per annum, he began the great eight-volume *Catalogue of Fishes in the British Museum* (1859–70) which secured his reputation as, in Newton's words, 'immeasurably the greatest ichthyologist of the age' (Gunther, *Century of Zoology*, 285). However, the work had its defects, since Gunther was unaware at the time of the necessity for any preparatory study, and had no precise view of the classification of fishes. He also completed a *Catalogue of Batrachia salientia in the British Museum* (1860) that listed the museum's collection of frogs and the innovative *Geographical Distribution of Reptiles* (1858).

Deciding to remain in England, Gunther severed his obligation to the ecclesiastical authorities to return to Württemberg by obtaining the king's dispensation in 1861. During 1862, with influential support, he was appointed to fill the vacancy for an assistant in the department of zoology, and at the age of thirty-two finally acquired the 'official status' that allowed him to devote his time exclusively to research and cataloguing.

A monograph on *The Reptiles of British India* (1864) followed from his need to study these animals in order to name material in the museum's collection and was produced within three years during his 'spare time'. That same year he initiated the *Record of Zoological Literature* which is seen as one of Gunther's outstanding contributions to natural history because of its influence in raising the standards of zoological taxonomy. It listed all current literature and aimed to provide an assessment of each work. Gunther himself was very critical of undisciplined nomenclature and the methods used by other zoologists. Such criticism, apart from the ill feeling it caused, earned Gunther the enmity of several ichthyologists (Gunther, *Century of Zoology*, 291–3). Commenting on two of his reviews, a friend, Alfred Newton, wrote: 'You bite one as if you were a viperian snake and roll up the other to squash as if you were a boa constrictor' (Newton to Gunther, 31 July 1871, box 16, Gunther archive). Gunther also realized the problem and had previously written to Newton: 'it worries me too much; I am not organised to take things calmly; I feel easily annoyed … and a disappointment in the morning … sours my temper for the whole day' (Gunther, *Century of Zoology*, 293). The claim on his time and the effect on his health (shown earlier by a breakdown in March 1866 which had required two months' rest) led to his resignation as editor in 1870.

Two years earlier, on 16 November 1868, Gunther had married Roberta M'Intosh, a natural history artist, whom he had met when attending the British Association meeting at Dundee in 1867. She died on 2 September 1869 shortly after giving birth to their son, Robert William Theodore *Gunther. After J. E. Gray had a stroke in 1869, Gunther assisted in running the museum's zoology department and when George Gray the assistant keeper died in 1872, Gunther succeeded him. Soon after, in 1874, he became naturalized. In February 1875, after J. E. Gray's retirement, Gunther was (automatically) appointed keeper of zoology. One of his first administrative tasks, between 1882 and 1883, was organizing for the removal of the natural history collections from the British Museum to the new building at South Kensington. He also had to establish separate and safe storage for the spirit collections and adapt the galleries to accommodate the principal collections. Further, in addition to agitating for a general library, Gunther ensured that the zoology department had its own reference library by 'spending hours up ladders' searching in Quaritch's bookshop (Gunther, *Century of Zoology*, 358). He also gradually increased the number of scientific staff and released them from menial duties by encouraging the senior attendants to undertake such work. Gunther was responsible for the popular exhibit of British nesting birds in the new museum galleries. Later, in 1912, he published a general history of the department of zoology between 1856 and 1895 as an appendix to the *History of the Collections*.

Throughout his career at the museum, Gunther acquired many major collections and encouraged travellers and collectors to make further additions to the national collection. Between 1868 and his retirement in 1895 the number of specimens in the department increased from one million to two and a quarter million. Mary Kingsley recorded in *Travels in West Africa* (1897):

> his courtesy and attention gave me the thing a worker in any [field] most wants—the sense that the work was worth doing … with the knowledge that if these things interest a man like him, it was more than sufficient reason … to go on collecting. (p. 7)

Gunther became a fellow of the Zoological Society of

London in 1862; he served on council from 1868 to 1905 and as vice-president for various periods between 1874 and 1905. In 1867 he was elected a fellow of the Royal Society of London and was a member of council from 1874 to 1876 and a vice-president in 1875–6. He did not become a fellow of the Linnean Society of London until 1877, then served on its council from 1878 to 1905 and as president from 1896 to 1900. He sat on several government commissions and other bodies concerned with pollution.

Gunther was an experienced field naturalist, an expert angler, a skilful shot, had a great fondness for pets of all kinds, and successfully reared various species of birds in his aviaries at home—winning a bronze medal from the Avicultural Society in 1904. His publications and wide knowledge of animal life assisted many of his contemporaries; Darwin acknowledged that parts of his *Descent of Man* owed much to Gunther's work. Gunther himself adopted an attitude of neutrality to the concept of evolution: influenced by the older ideas of his teachers and his religious upbringing, he restricted himself to observation or description and analysis of the data. On the other hand he was a pioneer in the field of the geographical distribution of animals.

Gunther's *Catalogue of Fishes*, although criticized, has been cited as the 'foundation of modern ichthyology' (D. S. Jordan, 1922) and regarded as one of the pioneer contributions to systematic taxonomy. The *Introduction to the Study of Fishes* (1880) became very popular despite criticism for its failure to adopt the revised classification of others. In *Shore Fishes* (1879) and *Deep-Sea Fishes of the Challenger Expedition* (1887) Gunther distinguished the chief bathymetrical zones of the ocean and described the characteristics of the deep-sea fishes. His last contribution to systematic zoology was to complete the ninth volume of *Fische der Südsee* (1873–81) in 1909. Gunther also had another significant role through his many publications on herpetology, while his most notable individual discovery was the recognition that the New Zealand *Tuatara* was not a true lizard, but an archaic lizard-like reptile.

Gunther has been described as tall, somewhat lightly built with a wiry physique, and fair hair and blue eyes. 'A man of strong character, he kept everybody up to the mark' (letter from Lord Walsingham to director of British Museum, 4 Feb 1914, Gunther, *Century of Zoology*, 451). Sherborn (Norman, 123) revealed that he never lost his accent. Abrupt in speech, somewhat conservative, he maintained an official demeanour within the museum according to his position, but outside he became very cordial. Following the death of his first wife, in 1879 he married Theodora Dowlish Drake whom he had met while on holiday at Fowey, Cornwall, in 1875.

For most of his life Gunther enjoyed perfect health, but in 1907 he succumbed to an attack of double pneumonia and his eyesight began to fail. After an unsuccessful operation for abdominal pains in the autumn of 1913, he continued to decline and died on 1 February 1914 at his home, 2 Lichfield Road, Kew Gardens, Surrey. He was buried on 4 February in Old Richmond cemetery. R. J. Cleevely

**Sources** A. E. Gunther, *A century of zoology at the British Museum through the lives of two keepers, 1815–1914* (1975), 211–475, 496–513 · A. E. Gunther, *The founders of science at the British Museum, 1753–1900* (1980), ix, 219 · R. T. Gunther, 'Bibliography of the works of Albert Günther', *Annals and Magazine of Natural History*, 10th ser., 6 (1930), suppl., 32a, pp. 233–86 · J. R. Norman, *Squire: memories of Charles Davies Sherborn* (1944) · A. Alcock, 'Dr Albert Karl Ludwig Gotthilf Günther', *Proceedings of the Linnean Society of London*, 126th session (1913–14), 48–52 · W. C. M'Intosh, *Proceedings of the Royal Society of Edinburgh*, 34 (1913–14), 269–77 · W. C. M. [W. C. M'Intosh], *PRS*, 88B (1914–15), xi–xxvi [incl. portrait] · 'Dr Albert Günther', *Nature*, 92 (1913–14), 664–66 · W. T. Stearn, *The Natural History Museum at South Kensington: a history of the British Museum (Natural History), 1753–1980* (1981), 167–9 · H. Dolezal, 'Günther, Albert Charles Lewis Gotthilf', *Neue deutsche Biographie*, ed. Otto, Graf zu Stolberg-Wernigerode (Berlin, 1953–) · *Geological Magazine*, new ser., 6th decade, 1 (1914), 141–2 · *The Times* (2 Feb 1914) · *Richmond and Twickenham Times* (7 Feb 1914) · A. C. L. Gunther, 'Catalogue of the Swainson correspondence in the possession of the Linnean Society', *Proceedings of the Linnean Society of London* (1900), 14–61 · D. S. Jordan, *The days of a man*, 2 vols. (1922), 2.270–71 · *The correspondence of Charles Darwin*, ed. F. Burkhardt and S. Smith, [13 vols.] (1985–)

**Archives** BL, corresp. and diary, Add. MSS 54488–54491 · Bodl. Oxf., papers · Humboldt University, Berlin, Museum für Naturkunde, corresp. · Linn. Soc., papers · MHS Oxf., corresp. and papers · Musee Lab. Zool. Anatom, Portugal, corresp. · NHM, corresp. and papers; notes and papers relating to RS's expedition to Rodriguez Island · Oxf. U. Mus. NH, corresp. · Rijksmuseum van Natuurlijke Historie, Leiden, corresp. | CUL, letters to Charles Darwin · Elgin Museum, letters to George Gordon · MHS Oxf., corresp. with his son R. W. T. Gunther · NHM, corresp. with Richard Owen and William Clift · Oxf. U. Mus. NH, corresp., mainly letters to Sir E. B. Poulton · U. Birm. L., special collections department, letters to T. C. Eyton and Rose M. Eyton · U. Cam., department of zoology, Alfred Newton letters

**Likenesses** photograph, 1867, repro. in Gunther, *Century of zoology*, facing p. 338 · two group portraits, photographs, 1885–95, NHM, department of zoology; repro. in Gunther, *Century of zoology* (1975), facing pp. 408, 409 · two photographs, 1886, NHM; repro. in Stearn, *Natural history museum*, fig. 19 · L. Gee, drawing, 1900, NPG · L. Gee, watercolour, 1900, NPG; repro. in D. S. Jordan, *A guide to the study of fishes*, 2 vols. (1905) · watercolour, 1900, repro. in Alcock, 'Dr Albert Karl Ludwig Gotthilf Günther' · T. Gunther, drawing, *c.*1905, repro. in Gunther, *Founders of science*, 132 · F. Bowcher, bronze plaques, 1912, BM, Linn. Soc.

**Wealth at death** £2522 10*s.* 1*d.*: probate, 3 March 1914, *CGPLA Eng. & Wales*

**Gunther, Robert William Theodore** (1869–1940), zoologist and antiquary, was born on 23 August 1869 at St James's Road, Surbiton, Surrey. He was the only child of the zoologist Albert Charles Lewis Gotthilf *Günther (1830–1914), who from Württemberg, then Tübingen, came to England to seek scientific employment, and his first wife, Roberta (*d.* 1869), the sixth and youngest daughter of baillie John M'Intosh of St Andrews. She was a gifted zoological painter, and sister of William Carmichael M'Intosh (1838–1931), also a zoologist.

Gunther's mother died ten days after his birth. He was cared for by his talented and artistic grandmother Louisa, and his father, for ten years, until his father remarried after becoming keeper of the zoological department at the British Museum in 1875. As a child Gunther was inattentive to the schooling of a governess, and to the teachers at a dame-school, but entered University College School in 1878. However, he absorbed his family's consummate involvement in medicine, natural history, and

**Robert William Theodore Gunther (1869–1940)**, by Elliott & Fry, *c.*1925

the museum. His childhood was characterized by a number of collecting and practical hobbies; he was stimulated by walks with his father during which they collected specimens. After 1883, when the family moved to Kew, he had the run of the gardens and developed a deep interest in botany. At the age of sixteen he won prizes in natural philosophy and practical chemistry, and in 1886 left school to attend Ray Lankester's biology lectures at University College, London. In 1887 he successfully sought election to a demyship at Magdalen College, Oxford, because it had its own laboratory. A second year at University College enabled him to pass the classical responsions, and in 1888 he took up his four-year demyship. These were happy years, encouraged by the president, Herbert Warren, and by his tutor, Edward Chapman, and Gunther developed a lifelong love for Oxford. He became prominent in the university's Junior Scientific Club. He attended the inventor Frederick Jervis-Smith's lectures on mechanics and physics. Gunther became a craftsman with the lathe. He discovered role models in the scientific technician Robert Hooke (1635–1703) and the antiquary and museum curator Robert Plot (1640–1696). He learned practical astronomy from Professor Charles Pritchard. Gunther thrived at Oxford, and graduated in 1892 with a first in morphology (later termed zoology). An extension of his demyship, and the university's biological scholarship, enabled him to study for two years at the Marine Zoological Research Laboratory in Naples. There he studied marine and freshwater *medusae*, and after 1901 undertook multidisciplinary research based on a study of the relative movements of the land and sea. His book *Pausilypon* (1913) presented superb fieldwork, pioneering underwater archaeology on the imperial villa at that site. Extensive travel between 1897 and 1914 enabled him to study a salt lake in Persia, extinct volcanoes, and to survey the Italian coast. Magdalen appointed him lecturer in natural science (1894), then tutor and fellow, 1896–1920, then a research fellow of the college until 1928. Gunther was elected a fellow of the Linnean Society in 1900, and in December he married Amy (1868–1964), the elder daughter of Eustace Neville-Rolfe (*d.* 1908) of Heacham, Norfolk, the consul for southern Italy. She retired in the late 1920s to the Heacham family home, but Gunther remained in their home on Folly Bridge, Oxford.

Gunther's first career was academic, and devoted to Magdalen College. As natural science tutor he had supervision of all Magdalen's science students, and from 1894 of the Daubeny Laboratory (which served a wider clientele within the university). He also lectured in comparative anatomy (biology) from 1900 to 1918, was librarian, 1920–23, published various works relating to Magdalen's history, and was a curator of the adjacent botanic garden, 1914–20. His duties left him ample time for vacation research, and for his extensive interests in Oxford. In 1902 he persuaded Magdalen to build an extension to the laboratory. He had assimilated his tutor Edward Chapman's veneration for the memory of Charles Daubeny, and this increasingly deflected Gunther from the present to the past, from nature to artefacts, from laboratory to museum collection. An addicted antiquary, he published the history of the Daubeny Laboratory (1904), then registers of those who had worked there. To the university's eighteenth-century chemical apparatus, which Daubeny had transferred to the laboratory, by 1916 Gunther was gradually adding instruments and books. However, by 1908 he was at loggerheads with the classicists who dominated the tutorial board and who, in Gunther's opinion, would not fund the laboratory research adequately. When as part of a rationalization of the science facilities within the university, the college allocated the laboratory to the botany department, they emptied his rooms while he was on vacation in 1923. He railed against the fellows for destroying his researches in natural science, but in fact apart from one visit in 1922 he had not returned to Italy since 1907, and was now preoccupied with his vision for a museum. In 1927 the college did not renew his fellowship. This strengthened his determination to fight to establish a unique museum in Oxford.

In 1917 Gunther had conceived the idea of restoring the Old Ashmolean building to a museum, and his enduring legacy is his foundation there in 1924 of the Museum of the History of Science. In 1915 he had begun cataloguing and photographing old or early scientific instruments and specimens which remained, frequently neglected, in college and university departments. This enabled him in 1919 to mount a temporary loan exhibition of early scientific instruments. Inspired by this exhibition, in 1924 Lewis Evans presented his valuable collection of scientific instruments and books to the university as a core around which the university's own material could be gathered for permanent display in the Old Ashmolean building. Gunther was appointed first curator of the Lewis Evans Collection, and so at the age of fifty-five he began a new career. The collection opened to the public in May 1925, with financial assistance from the Goldsmiths and other city companies interested in fine craftsmanship. He began a battle to house and develop that core collection. He won some space in the Old Ashmolean building of 1683, above its basement chemical laboratory. Remorseless campaigning against the bitter opposition of a few individuals in key positions eventually consolidated his achievement of 1924; in 1935 the museum was formally created which 'bridged the gap between antiquarianism and science' (Simcock, 51), and which after Gunther's death came to occupy the whole splendid building. However, despite his having been appointed Oxford's first reader in the history of science in 1934, he retained it without stipend, and in 1938 he resigned in protest. In 1936 he was invited to stage an exhibition in Cambridge, similar to his venture in Oxford. This, along with his survey of the sister university's scientific instruments and memorabilia published as *Early Science in Cambridge* (1937), sowed the seed which became the Whipple Museum of the History of Science.

Between 1920 and 1937 Gunther published prolifically, largely at his own expense. This included his cornucopia *Early Science in Oxford* (14 volumes, 1920–45). His need to work alone exposed him to criticisms that could have been avoided by consultation. He was 'far too quick, and too impatient' (Gunther, 300) to be an outstanding scholar, but he deployed an archaeological enthusiasm for and knowledge of many sciences and architecture. He gave numerous lectures to, and was well known in, the British Association, Royal Geographical Society, Linnean Society, Ray Society, Zoological Society, and Oxford Architectural and Historical Society. His *Oxford Gardens* (1912) and more particularly *Early British Botanists and their Gardens* (1922) established him as one of the great historians of botany. *The Astrolabes of the World* (1932), a lavishly illustrated catalogue and the first study of its kind in the field of scientific instruments, was completed after an immense correspondence. For all their shortcomings his works are primary sourcebooks full of unique material, and remain an indispensable starting point for scholars. Meanwhile, his biographies rescued men such as architect Sir Roger Pratt, botanist John Goodyear, and medieval plant painter Apuleius Barbarus from oblivion.

Gunther was tall, slim, nervously energetic, and afflicted by gastric disorders. He was learned, aloof, single-minded, and an indomitable polemicist. His quest for knowledge was active and practical. He was often a deft persuader, but with no time for pretentious subtleties was impatient of the complacency of academic Oxford. His preferred style of written communications with the world was often 'blunt to the point of folly' but he never avoided his antagonists 'with whom he was always calm and courteous' (Simcock, 48). By mid-life he had developed a consuming concern for preservation; anyone who fell short of giving that priority was a 'vandal'. Made an honorary LLD of St Andrews University in 1925, he was vice-president of the Linnean Society in 1927–8. Gunther emerged from within science. He rediscovered Oxford's earlier greatness in science, and at considerable self-sacrifice did unique historical work to realize his vision. This was not only to establish a museum for the preservation and study of scientific apparatus, but to anchor Oxford's scientific heritage within the resurrected Old Ashmolean building. Gunther was a pioneer of the new subject of history of science but, true to form, stayed aloof from its mainstream (which was textual and philosophical). He concentrated instead on the 'archaeology of science', which was in practice the history of scientific instruments. He is undoubtedly the principal founder of this specialism as a serious academic discipline.

After a week in hospital with gastric disorder Gunther died of heart disease while asleep at a friend's house, the Corner House, South Stoke, Oxfordshire, on 9 March 1940. He was cremated and the ashes were interred at his wife's home at Heacham, Norfolk. They had two sons, of whom the elder, Eustace Rolfe, an oceanographer, died in a flying accident on active service in May 1940. The other son, Albert Everard (1904–1998), a geologist, explorer, and mountaineer, became an important benefactor of his father's museum, and his biographer (1967).

ROGER HUTCHINS

**Sources** A. E. Gunther, *Early science in Oxford*, 15: *Robert T. Gunther: a pioneer in the history of science* (1967) · A. V. Simcock, ed., *Robert T. Gunther and the Old Ashmolean* (1985) · G. D. H. Carpenter and T. G. B. Osborn, 'R. T. Gunther', *Proceedings of the Linnean Society of London*, 152nd session (1939–40), pl. iv, 366–8 · A. S. Russell, 'Dr R. T. Gunther', *Nature*, 145 (1940), 541–2 · [R. V. M. Benecke], ed., *The Magdalen College register* (1934), 107–8 · *The Times* (11 March 1940), 10d · *DNB* · MHS Oxf., Gunther papers · Magd. Oxf., Gunther MSS · J. Morrell, *Science at Oxford, 1914–1939: transforming an arts university* (1997) · b. cert. · d. cert.

**Archives** Bodl. Oxf., corresp. and papers · Linn. Soc., lecture notes · Magd. Oxf., corresp. and MSS · MHS Oxf., collections incl. some of his own corresp. and papers · MHS Oxf., corresp. and MSS · NHM, corresp. and papers · RIBA BAL, MS and transcripts of Sir Roger Pratt's notebooks | MHS Oxf., corresp. with G. H. Gabb · Norfolk RO, genealogical notes and corresp. mainly between him and his wife

**Likenesses** photograph, *c.*1900, Magd. Oxf. · Elliott & Fry, photograph, *c.*1925, NPG [*see illus.*]

**Wealth at death** £16,562 12*s.* 7*d.*: probate, 11 Sept 1940, *CGPLA Eng. & Wales*

**Gunthorpe, John** (*d.* **1498**), dean of Wells and administrator, probably took his name from Gunthorpe in Lincolnshire, where he possessed lands. He was probably a student at Cambridge, where, already in holy orders, he was a master of arts of the university by 1452, and served as junior proctor in 1454–5. However, he only obtained grace for admission to the degree of BTh as late as 1469, taking it by 1472 (Leland's claim that he first studied at

Oxford, glossed by Anthony Wood, who assigned him to Balliol College, appears unfounded). In August 1460, probably through the patronage of Bishop William Grey of Ely (*d.* 1478), he was attending Guarino da Verona's lectures on rhetoric at the studium of Ferrara, and also studying Greek under him, as he had been for some time; his colophon to his transcript of Seneca's *Tragedies* (BL, Harley MS 2485) dated August 1460 shows that he had been reading 'poetry', presumably within the context of the *Studia humanitatis*. At Ferrara he also became acquainted with John Free, a compatriot who had been resident in Ferrara for some years from 1456 at Grey's expense. After Guarino's death in December 1460 Gunthorpe followed Free to Rome, where, after examination, he became minor penitentiary for the English nation and papal chaplain on 28 January 1462, taking his oath of office on 1 February. (On 25 March 1469, after four years' absence by Gunthorpe, the post was reallocated.) Free died in Rome on 30 October 1465, and Gunthorpe left for England in possession of part of his late friend's library. By 7 January 1466 he was rector (with disputed title) of Ditcheat, Somerset, and the following month rector of Cley next the Sea, Norfolk, held simultaneously through a papal dispensation dated 26 February; these were the first of a number of English preferments, usually held briefly.

Pre-eminence in Latin rhetoric was appreciated by Edward IV's circle as vital for a diplomat; Gunthorpe's studies and connections at the papal court paved the way for royal patronage and further ecclesiastical advancement. Perhaps by early 1466 he was secretary and chaplain to the queen (a post he held until 1477), possibly through the support of Grey, who was a distant relative of the queen's first husband. By 6 August 1466, when he was appointed an envoy to Enrique IV of Castile, Gunthorpe was already one of the king's chaplains; in March 1470 he went on a second mission to Castile. On 30 September 1467, possibly likewise through Grey's influence, he was appointed warden of the King's Hall, Cambridge, an office he vacated in December 1473. In the summer of 1468 he attended Margaret, the king's sister, on her marriage to Charles, duke of Burgundy, giving two orations. In December 1468 he was appointed king's almoner, in which capacity he was to accompany the king on his invasion of France in 1475, and on 21 June 1471 clerk of the parliament. He vacated this office at Michaelmas 1483. On 18 December 1472 he was elected dean of Wells, an office he retained until his death.

Gunthorpe was dean of the Chapel Royal by January 1478, when he assisted at the wedding of Richard, duke of York, to Anne Mowbray, and remained dean when early in 1483 Edward reorganized it under the new title of 'royal free chapel of the Household' (he was finally replaced about 14 May 1483); briefly, in the early months of 1483, he was also dean of the newly established king's free chapel of St Peter-within-the-Tower. Already by 1482 a king's councillor, he was made keeper of the privy seal by Richard of Gloucester, as protector, on 10 May 1483, and confirmed by him, as king, on 27 June. He was one of the commission appointed to treat with the Scots at Nottingham in September 1484, and in late February 1485 was sent to extend the truce with the duke of Brittany. He obtained a general pardon from Henry VII on 12 February 1486, and in mid-December following he was sent to Maximilian, king of the Romans, to renew the latter's treaty with Edward IV; in Spain in March 1488, and again a year later, he was instrumental in concluding the treaty of Medina del Campo with the 'Catholic monarchs'.

The remnants of Gunthorpe's library (twenty-three manuscripts and nine incunables) reflect the Latin curriculum of the *Studia humanitatis*; of particular interest is his Latin vocabulary, compiled doubtlessly under Guarino's tutelage as a personal aid for rhetoric, while the margins of his Louvain-printed *Elegantoliae* by Agostino Dati, itself a guide to eloquence, have phrases marked by him presumably deemed most apt for orations; his notes on Guarino's lectures on Seneca's *Tragedies* are in the margins of his manuscript of that work. Extant are five of Gunthorpe's orations, and two incomplete treatises—*Dialectica* (part 1 only is known) and *Rhetorica*—are attributed to him. Gunthorpe conformed to contemporary Italian taste when in 1480 he sponsored the rebuilding of the deanery at Wells, where a prominent decorative feature is his own device: guns—playing on his own name—and lions' heads, with the motto 'Mais pour le mieulx'. He died at Wells on 25 June 1498, and his tomb is, as he requested, in St Katherine's Chapel, against the south wall of the south-east transept of the cathedral; his will was proved the following 26 August. He had already given the cathedral a silver-gilt image of Our Lady, and also the manor of Alverton, Somerset, to provide for a daily 'low' mass. He had previously donated manuscripts to Jesus College, Cambridge, perhaps on its foundation two years before his death. CECIL H. CLOUGH

**Sources** Emden, *Cam.*, 275–7 · A. B. Cobban, *The King's Hall within the University of Cambridge in the later middle ages*, Cambridge Studies in Medieval Life and Thought, 3rd ser., 1 (1969), 287 · A. F. Pollard, 'Fifteenth-century clerks of parliament', *BIHR*, 15 (1937–8), 137–61, esp. 152–5 · R. Horrox and P. W. Hammond, eds., *British Library Harleian manuscript 433*, 4 vols. (1979–83) · J. Gairdner, *History of the life and reign of Richard the Third*, rev. edn (1898), 339 · G. Buck, *The history of King Richard the Third*, ed. A. N. Kincaid (1979); repr. with corrections (1982), 57 · R. Fox, *Letters, 1486–1527*, ed. P. A. Allen and H. M. Allen (1929), 12–13 · R. Weiss, *Humanism in England during the fifteenth century*, 3rd edn (1967) · R. J. Mitchell, *John Free: from Bristol to Rome in the fifteenth century* (1955) · M. Lowry, 'The arrival and use of continental printed books in Yorkist England', *Le livre dans l'Europe de la Renaissance* [Tours 1985], ed. P. Aquilon, H.-J. Martin, and others (Paris, 1988), 450–59 · C. L. Scofield, *The life and reign of Edward the Fourth*, 2 (1923), 205 · P. Chaplais, *English medieval diplomatic practice*, 1, PRO (1982), nos. 138–40 · C. Woodforde, *Stained glass in Somerset* (1946), 132 48 · D. E. Rhodes, *A catalogue of the incunabula in all the Oxford libraries outside the Bodleian* (1982)

**Gunton, George** (*bap.* **1801**, *d.* **1890**), brickmaker, was born within the parish of Costessey, 4 miles west of Norwich, and baptized on 8 July 1801 in the Roman Catholic chapel attached to Costessey Hall, the son of John Gunton, and his wife, Elizabeth, *née* Spaul. His father was from the extended family of Norfolk Guntons, which documents of the eighteenth and nineteenth centuries link to various branches of the brick trade.

Gunton, brought up as a brickmaker, might possibly have remained a journeyman brickmaker had not his work with moulded ware come to the notice of Sir George William Jerningham, lord of the manor and patron of the local Catholic congregation. From the late 1820s Jerningham began to transform the modest Tudor manor house which was then Costessey Hall into the towered and castellated mansion which was to be called Costessey Park, in celebration of his elevation, following earlier claims, to the barony of Stafford. The architect for the rebuilding, John Chessel Buckler, passed on to Gunton designs for windows, corbel-tables, pinnacles, and chimneys, taken not only from Norfolk mansions of the fifteenth to seventeenth centuries but also from some properties of the Jerningham family elsewhere, notably from Thornbury Castle in Gloucestershire.

Gunton's success in reproducing these designs led, by degrees, to his building up of a repertoire of Gothic and Tudor mouldings so that when, in the 1840s, the demand for special wares at Costessey Park fell back as the building work there came nearer to completion, he was able to undertake orders for other clients and architects who were, it can be supposed, familiar with his work at Costessey. This was the case with the architect Anthony Salvin, who made drawings of the Costessey chimneys and who commissioned Gunton to supply decorative brickwork for Flixton Hall in Suffolk, raised in the years following 1844. Country-house projects were occasional and it was from this time that Gunton advertised his 'Norman and Elizabethan' red-brick and white-brick wares in the Norwich press. Parsonage houses being rebuilt in this period took large quantities of what became known as Cosseyware, to embellish gables, windows, and chimneys: the same were used to embellish village schools. But the larger market was in the towns, and it was house building within the expanding suburbs of the city of Norwich which provided Gunton with the bulk of his orders. Gunton would work to designs provided by his clients or he would supply from stock.

Gunton retired from the business in 1868 and the further expansion of the enterprise at Costessey was the achievement of his sons, George Gunton (1829–1899) and William Gunton (1847–1944), in whose period of management the firm penetrated the national market, sending Cosseyware as far as Cheshire and Brighton. Cosseyware was used, notably, for town halls, theatres, libraries, nonconformist chapels, and hotels. What made national distribution possible was the growing rail network, to which Norwich itself had been connected since 1845, and the publicity for Cosseyware, made by the firm itself in a series of detailed brochures. Those which survive, dating from the Edwardian period, describe, illustrate, and price almost 300 items in a variety of styles.

In achieving widespread distribution of its wares the firm benefited from the support provided by prominent Norwich architects with practices extending to other parts of the country. Edward Boardman looked to the continent for his inspiration and for his rebuilding of the Princes Street Congregational Chapel (1869), the Castle Chambers (1877), and the Royal Hotel (1896–7), all in Norwich; he commissioned from the Gunton Brothers a range of Italian Renaissance and Franco-Flemish late Gothic mouldings which contrasted markedly with the previous range of Cosseyware. George John Skipper matched Boardman's eclecticism and shared some of his preferences, and to achieve the French and Flemish Renaissance character of the three hotels planned by himself for the seaside resort of Cromer he placed further demands on the skill and versatility of the Costessey mouldmakers. The *tour de force* of both Skipper and Guntons was Skipper's office (1896) at 7 London Street, Norwich, a Renaissance-inspired composition of superimposed arches and panelwork with depictions, in the panels, of the architect, a client, and various building craftsmen.

To meet the growing demand for Cosseyware, George Gunton and his sons had to find ways to expand their production. The tithe apportionment for Costessey shows George Gunton's brickyard, rented from the Costessey Hall estate, to have been contained within a 2 acre site in 1839 and to have been furnished with a single brick-kiln. By 1882, when the parish had been freshly mapped by the Ordnance Survey, the brickyard took in three times the original area and included two kilns, some ten or so drying hacks, a drying shed, and two moulding sheds. Some forty men and boys were working in the brickyard at this time. The increased capacity afforded by extended premises and plant was not sufficient, and between 1892 and 1903 Gunton Brothers purchased brickyards in other parts of Norfolk: at Barney, near Fakenham; at West Runton, near Cromer; and at Little Plumstead, to the east of Norwich.

The high point in the production of Cosseyware occurred in the late Victorian and early Edwardian era. Thereafter, architectural taste began to change, although for Tudor and early Jacobean halls, such as Oxburgh and Blickling, replica parts were still required. Demonstrations of this change were provided by Guntons' own supporters, Boardman and Skipper, who began to design buildings in a more vernacular style, with decorative features provided not by specially made parts but by the use of common materials intermixed or set out in patterns. Production at the Gunton yards was in decline before the outbreak of war in 1914, and William Gunton closed the Costessey brickyard in 1915. The Gunton brickyards elsewhere remained in operation and at Little Plumstead William Gunton's son, William Herbert Gunton (*c.*1877–1964), continued with the production of ornamental ware until the outbreak of war in 1939 put an end to all Gunton brickmaking.

An appreciation of the work of George Gunton and his successors at Costessey must start with the realization that the ornamental brickwork they produced was a necessary accompaniment to the florid styles of brick architecture in favour in the Victorian and Edwardian period. Notwithstanding the high levels of skill achieved, they operated within the limits of their craft, working within existing processes and methods of production. While the firm made use of contemporary brickyard innovations, such as tramways to transport the clay, mechanical apparatus to prepare the clay for moulding, and drying sheds for all-year-round production, increased output was achieved, essentially, by the multiplication of kilns and the increased application of labour. The business remained, as it had started, a family concern. George Gunton himself made the brick moulds, although he was later assisted by William Hastings, a carpenter living next to the brickyard. Mouldmaking was later assumed, in succession, by William Gunton and William's son, Frederick George Gunton (*c*.1886–1942).

The success of the Gunton enterprise can be seen to have depended on a number of fortuitous factors: the rebuilding of Costessey Hall, the proximity of the city of Norwich, the development of the railway network, and access to publicity. However, George Gunton and his successors had the ability and determination to take advantage of the opportunities presented to them. Their enterprise made little fortune for themselves. The yard at Costessey was rented. What wealth was gained was distributed through large families. Eleven children (seven sons and four daughters) were born to George Gunton and his wife, Eleanor, *née* Newton (1805?–1892). In Costessey itself there remain a dozen houses in West End embellished with decorative elements from the Costessey brickyard, including the houses built for themselves by George Gunton and his son George. Unfortunately, the great halls carrying their work at Costessey and Flixton have been demolished, as have two of the Cromer hotels. The Roman Catholic church of St Walstan in Costessey, raised (1841) in red brick in a plain Early English style and incorporating moulded bricks from the Costessey brickyard, stands above the churchyard where, as is indicated by an upright tombstone, George Gunton was buried together with his wife, Eleanor, following their deaths respectively, on 18 November 1890 and 18 January 1892 at their home in West End, Costessey. ROBIN LUCAS

**Sources** *Gunton Bros.: moulded and ornamental brickworks—Costessey, Barney, West Runton, Little Plumstead* (1903) • R. Lucas, 'Neo-Gothic, Neo-Tudor, Neo-Renaissance: the Costessey brickyard', *Victorian Society Journal* (1997), 25–37 • H. E. Gunton, 'Costessey brickworks', *Transactions* [Newcomen Society], 41 (1968–9), 165–8 • tithe apportionment for the parish of Costessey, 1838–9, Norfolk RO, TA 555 • ordnance survey sheet, 25 inches-to-the-mile, 62.4, 1882–1907 • registers of the Roman Catholic congregation, Costessey, Norfolk, 1785–1890, Norfolk RO, MF/RO 571 • census returns, 1841, 1851, 1861, 1871, 1881, 1891 • tombstone inscriptions in the churchyards of Saint Walstan's (RC), Costessey; Saint Edmund's, Costessey; Saint Protase and Saint Gervase's, Little Plumstead [all near Norwich] • *Norwich Mercury* (29 June 1844) [advertisements] • *Norwich Mercury* (5 April 1851) [advertisements] • *The Builder*, 6 (1848), 412, 587 [notices] • *Mineral statistics of the United Kingdom*, pt 2 (1858), 55 • C. L. Eastlake, *A history of the Gothic revival* (1872), 110

**Likenesses** group photograph, *c*.1895, priv. coll.

**Wealth at death** £1015 11*s*. 6*d*.: probate, 10 March 1891, *CGPLA Eng. & Wales*

**Gunton, Simon** (*bap*. 1609, *d*. 1676), Church of England clergyman and antiquary, was baptized on 30 December 1609 at St John the Baptist, Peterborough, the son of William Gunton (*fl*. 1609–1620) and his wife, Ellen. William subsequently became diocesan registrar at Peterborough and Simon's scholarly interests were stimulated by the cathedral building, whose monumental inscriptions he listed, and the records in his father's care. He matriculated from Magdalene College, Cambridge, in the Lent term of 1627, graduating BA in 1631 and proceeding MA in 1634. In 1636 Gunton married Susan Dickenson of Peterborough; they had two sons and four daughters. He was ordained priest at Peterborough on 4 June 1637, being appointed to the vicarage of Pytcheley the following October. He was appointed a minor canon of Peterborough in 1643 and first prebend and sub-treasurer there in 1646, although this did not come into effect due to the civil war. He remained at Peterborough for most of the 1640s but at some point joined the household of James Stuart, duke of Lennox. He had his living at Pytcheley sequestered in 1650, though he appears to have been appointed to the vicarage at Leighton Bromswold, Huntingdonshire, about 1651.

In 1650 Gunton published anonymously a pamphlet, *Ortholatreia, or, A Brief Discourse Concerning Bodily Worship*, in which he defended prayer book worship, and which was subsequently reissued under his name in 1661. His views on the necessity for order and decency in worship were given a further airing in 1657 in a book entitled *God's house, with the nature and use thereof, as it ought to be understood and respected by Christians under the gospel*, which he dedicated to the son of his patron, the young Esme Stuart, duke of Lennox.

Gunton was described as vicar of St John, Peterborough, in 1658 and he took formal possession of the living on 24 September 1660, at which time he was also restored to his cathedral post. He remained at St John's until 1667, staying firmly at his post during the ravages of the plague in the town in 1665, but resigned soon after being appointed to the rectory of Fiskerton, Lincolnshire, which was in the gift of the dean and chapter at Peterborough. He remained at Fiskerton, which he retained with his cathedral post, for the rest of his life. He played a large part in restoring worship to his beloved cathedral after the Restoration, and his lifelong antiquarian enthusiasms were a natural corollary to his churchmanship.

Gunton died in May 1676, and was buried on 17 May in Fiskerton church. He left a substantial manuscript collection of notes which were published in revised form by Simon Patrick, dean of Peterborough, in 1686, as *The history of the church of Peterburgh, wherein the most remarkable things concerning that place, from the first foundation of … are represented*. The title adequately describes the scope of the work, which was illustrated with engravings, and following the loss of many of the cathedral archives and the defacing of its monuments during the wars, the text and the appendices of charters which were annexed became a standard source for diocesan and county historians, including the bishop, White Kennett, and a number of annotated copies survive. WILLIAM JOSEPH SHEILS

**Sources** H. I. Longden, *Northamptonshire and Rutland clergy from 1500*, ed. P. I. King and others, 16 vols. in 6, Northamptonshire RS (1938–52) • *Walker rev.* • S. Gunton, *The history of the church of Peterburgh*, ed. S. Patrick (1686) • Venn, *Alum. Cant.*

**Archives** U. Durham L., corresp. and papers

**Guntrip, Henry James Samuel** [Harry] (1901–1975), psychotherapist and Congregational minister, the son of Henry Richard Guntrip (*d.* *c.*1923) and his wife, Harriet Louise Jessop (*d.* 1953), was born at 103 Dulwich Road, London, on 29 May 1901. His father, a commercial clerk, was the youngest of seven children. Before his marriage he was lively and enjoyed cricket. A Methodist lay preacher, he was founder of a breakaway evangelical movement, The Ranters. His liveliness declined after his marriage to Harriet Jessop, a harsh, dominating, and unmaternal woman whose own childhood had left her embittered. Because of her own mother's incapacity she had cared for many younger siblings. In marriage she had no more time for babies; she wanted to be a businesswoman, and was a shopkeeper. Harry was the first child; a brother, Percy, was born two years later. At sixteen months Percy died, when Harry was three and a half, and this trauma and his own and his mother's responses to it were central to his childhood illness. After Percy's death he became seriously ill but recovered by being sent away from his mother, who was incapable of keeping him emotionally alive. She dressed him as a girl and had him circumcised when he was five. Between three and a half and five he developed psychosomatic illnesses, later understood as attempts to gain his mother's love and attention.

Guntrip's fight for independence began by joining the Salvation Army at the age of eight. From 1913 he attended Alleyn's School, Dulwich, where he was a vigorous athlete, particularly enjoying cricket. He was an enthusiastic member of the Salvation Army but, after two years of training to become an officer he left and in 1921 went to London University where he took a degree in philosophy and psychology; a degree in divinity at the Congregational New College followed in 1924. In his theological and philosophical training he was influenced by the personal relationship philosophy of John MacMurray and the philosophy of Martin Buber; he later found resonances of these in his psychoanalytic work. Guntrip entered the Congregational ministry, first at St John's Church, Ipswich, then at Salem Congregational Church, Leeds, where he spent the rest of his life. He was an energetic minister, a powerful orator, and a good communicator; he strove to integrate religion and psychoanalysis, seeing both of them as dedicated vocations to bring God's love and understanding. His marriage in the early 1920s to Bertha Kind, a shorthand typist and then nurse, whom he had met in the Salvation Army, was an invaluable support throughout his life.

Guntrip's journey into psychotherapy began when he sought help for his own distress, insomnia, and psychosomatic symptoms. He began therapy with two Freudian-inclined therapists, Hugh Crichton-Miller and Clifford Allen, both of whom stuck to rigid Oedipal-level interpretations. He was not much helped by this therapy and it was a great relief when he was introduced to the object relations theory of Ronald Fairbairn. By now Guntrip had become a therapist himself in Leeds with patients referred both by Leeds University and by general practitioners.

Fairbairn, a philosophically trained psychoanalyst, evolved a radical revision of psychoanalytic theory, replacing Freud's drive theory, that biological forces seek tension relief, with the relational theory, that human infants seek and need loving and caring responsiveness. Failing to get these, if the mother is not able to be appropriately loving, they turn inwards, feeling that their own love is bad and dangerous and that this is why they have been rejected. Living primarily within inner worlds with internal objects they are not able to experience full loving relationships. From 1949 to 1960 Guntrip worked with Fairbairn, travelling from Leeds to Edinburgh for his eleven hundred sessions, constantly overworking to make up for lost time at his ministry. In addition, he was treating many patients and lecturing in the university. Using his photographic memory Guntrip began his psychoanalytical autobiography, recording all his dreams and all his sessions. His analysis with Fairbairn enabled him to explore his relationship with his mother, not approached in his previous therapy, and the consequences of Percy's death. His mother, increasingly paranoid, insisted on living with him and Bertha for the last nine years of her life, which compounded his psychological difficulties.

In Guntrip's account he was not only Fairbairn's patient, he became his collaborator in his revision of psychoanalytic theory and in the early 1960s began to write his own psychoanalytic papers. In 1960 Guntrip felt that his work with him had reached its limits as Fairbairn aged and had recurrent illnesses. In 1962 Guntrip began analysis with Donald Winnicott in London, who, he felt, would understand and cope with his needs to regress to very early stages of infantile dependence and helplessness; according to Guntrip's account he found what he needed. His healing relationship with Winnicott released him from his closed inner world. The analysis ended in 1969; Winnicott, in fragile health, died in 1971.

In the years following this analysis Guntrip wrote the papers and books that made his international reputation and led to invitations to the United States. The first visit, in 1968, to New York and Washington came through the interest aroused by his papers on the schizoid personality, the books *Personality Structure and Human Interaction* (1961), *Schizoid Phenomena, Object-Relations and the Self* (1968), and the growing interest in America about British contributions to psychoanalysis. Though not a member of the British Psychoanalytic Society, Guntrip's importance was eventually conceded and he was invited to speak to the society, which greatly pleased him.

Guntrip was a fluent, clear writer, able to articulate emotional conflicts and issues, to clarify psychoanalytic theory, and to insist on the need for continuing theoretical and technical developments. He saw the problem of schizoid isolation as the core of neurosis, the withdrawal from full relationships through fear and terror, the false belief that one's own love is bad and destructive. The only release from this is through a psychoanalysis in which these fears are understood, where the real loving attitude of the therapist to the patient gradually allows fears to surface and the patient can take the risk of entering into a fuller relationship with the therapist. Guntrip's writings have been influential and have made psychoanalysis, in particular object relations theory, more accessible. They are the writings of a man with a mission to communicate and to convert, and represent his own integration of religion and psychodynamic science.

As well as Guntrip's rich legacy of papers and books there is a fascinating (unpublished) psychoanalytic autobiography, a record of his dreams of over thirty years and of his analyses with Fairbairn and Winnicott, subject of a famous paper (Guntrip, 'My experience'). Valuable as this legacy is, it has to be treated with reserve: we have only Guntrip's account, and the very fact of his writing accounts of all his analytic sessions indicates compulsive overactivity, a feature of his psychopathology. We do not know how much his accounts of Fairbairn's and Winnicott's interpretations represent what they actually were. With this reservation, this is a unique record of deep psychoanalytic experiences.

Guntrip died in the General Infirmary, Leeds, from carcinomatosis on 18 February 1975. His wife survived him. MALCOLM PINES

**Sources** *Personal relations therapy: the collected papers of H. J. S. Guntrip*, ed. J. Hazel (1994) • J. Hazel and H. J. S. Guntrip, *A psychoanalytical biography* (1996) • H. J. S. Guntrip, 'My experience of analysis with Fairbairn and Winnicott: how complete a result does psychoanalytic therapy achieve?', *International Review of Psychoanalysis*, 2 (1975), 145–56 • 'Guntrip's psychoanalytic autobiography', Menninger Foundation, Topeka, Kansas • b. cert. • d. cert.

**Archives** Menninger Foundation, Topeka, Kansas

**Wealth at death** £16,776: probate, 27 March 1975, *CGPLA Eng. & Wales*

**(Agnes) Elisabeth Guppy (1838–1917),** by Frederick Augustus Hudson, 1872 [right, with Mrs Tebb (left), Miss Georgiana Houghton (seated), and a manifestation]

**Guppy** [*formerly* Nicholl; *other married name* Guppy-Volckman], **(Agnes) Elisabeth (1838–1917)**, medium, was born Agnes Elisabeth White at 1 Gloucester Crescent, Regent's Park, London, the daughter of Charles Taylor White. Her parents died when she was eleven months old and she was raised by her maternal grandfather, the London sculptor William Ginsell Nicholl (1796–1871), who taught her sculpting and photography. She took her grandfather's name, and was known from an early age as Elisabeth Nicholl (or Nichol). From the age of nine she had visions of spirit figures, which persisted despite exercise and the water cure. In the early 1860s her photographic skills attracted Fanny Sims, an amateur photographer and sister of the naturalist Alfred Russel Wallace. Sims convinced her of her spiritual powers, and in December 1866 Miss Nicholl held her first séances in the Wallace household. Her powers caused tables to rap messages and nearby objects to levitate. Later that month she first produced the apports for which she became celebrated: fresh flowers materialized out of the darkness and fell onto participants' laps. During this period she became a professional mesmeric healer, which enabled her to finance private evening séances. Her mediumship was strengthened through collaboration with mediums such as Mrs Makdougall Gregory, Georgiana Houghton (*d.* 1887), and Catherine Berry (1813–1891): her apports now included fruit and small animals, she began producing spirit drawings, and during one séance with Wallace she levitated herself onto a table.

On 10 December 1867 Miss Nicholl married Samuel Guppy (1790?–1875), a rich and elderly spiritualist and amateur photographer. The newly wedded couple subsequently toured Europe and enthralled nobility and literati with séance apports. Elisabeth's first child, Thomas, was born in Naples during September 1869. On returning to England in July 1870 the couple lived in Highbury, where Mrs Guppy gave private séances and taught mediums such as Frank Herne and Charles Williams. Her most celebrated achievement occurred on 3 June 1871, when she was allegedly transported 3 miles from Highbury to a joint Herne–Williams séance in Holborn. A séance participant had jokingly asked the invisible spirits to bring her there—considered an impossible feat, as she was an enormous woman. Minutes later an entranced Mrs Guppy appeared above the séance table, unaware of her new surroundings.

In January 1872 Mrs Guppy became the first British

medium to materialize spirit hands and faces. In the following March the London photographer Frederick Hudson used her mediumship to produce some of the first British spirit photographs. However, Mrs Guppy's stardom was soon threatened by the sensational young medium Florence Cook (1856–1904), who could materialize a fully formed spirit called Katie King. By late 1873 Mrs Guppy had grown so jealous that she devised plots to expose Cook as a fraud. Although she attracted attention for her own fully formed materializations, Mrs Guppy's subsequent sharp decline in popularity suggests that these plots tarnished her reputation. Investigators' opinion of Mrs Guppy was not always favourable: Lord Rayleigh, having attended several of her séances in mid-1874, decided he could not stand her 'even in the cause of science and philosophy'; in 1886 Eleanor Sidgwick supported her sister's suspicions that Mrs Guppy's materializations were caused by devices concealed inside her voluminous gown.

Samuel Guppy died in April 1875 and Elisabeth later married William Volckman, a lawyer whom she had used to expose Cook in December 1873. From the late 1870s a protracted illness forced her to discontinue regular séances and take the water cure. By 1897 she had recovered and was once again producing apports and fully formed materializations in private séances. Elisabeth Guppy-Volckman died at 3 Norfolk Square, Brighton, on 9 December 1917. RICHARD NOAKES

**Sources** 'Mrs. Guppy's Mediumship', *The Spiritualist* (15 Sept 1870) • F. Podmore, *Modern spiritualism*, 2 (1902) • A. R. Wallace, *My life: a record of events and opinions*, 2 vols. (1905), vol. 2 • C. Berry, *Experiences in spiritualism* (1876) • G. Houghton, *Evenings at home in spiritual séance* (1881) • G. Houghton, *Chronicles of the photographs of spiritual beings* (1882) • R. Pearsall, *The table-rappers* (1972) • R. G. Medhurst and K. M. Goldney, 'William Crookes and the physical phenomena of mediumship', *Proceedings of the Society for Psychical Research*, 54 (1963–6), 25–157 • A. Wallace, 'The transit of Mrs. Guppy', *Light*, 38 (1918), 259 • R. J. Strutt, *Life of John William Strutt, third Baron Rayleigh* (1924) • E. Sidgwick, 'Results of a personal investigation into the physical phenomena of spiritualism', *Proceedings of the Society for Psychical Research*, 4 (1886–7), 45–74 • Memento, 'The mediumship of Madame Guppy Volckman', *Light*, 17 (1897), 255–6
**Archives** BL, Alfred Russel Wallace MSS
**Likenesses** photograph, 1860–1869?, Mary Evans Picture Library, London • photograph, 1870?, repro. in R. Stemman, *Spirits and spirit worlds* (1975), 41 • F. A. Hudson, group photograph, 1872, repro. in Houghton, *Chronicles*, pl. 4 [*see illus.*]
**Wealth at death** £13,098 4*s*. 5*d*.: probate, 2 May 1918, *CGPLA Eng. & Wales*

**Gurdon, Sir Adam de**. *See* Gurdun, Sir Adam (*c*.1220–1305).

**Gurdon, Brampton** (*c*.1672–1741), theologian, was born in Letton, Norfolk, one of three sons of Brampton Gurdon (*d*. 1691), Church of England clergyman, and Elizabeth Thornhagh of Skeffington, Leicestershire, daughter of Colonel Francis Thornhagh of Fenton, Nottinghamshire. His elder brother was the antiquary Thornhagh *Gurdon. After schooling in Wymondham, Norfolk, he matriculated at Gonville and Caius College, Cambridge, in 1688, graduating BA in 1692 and MA in 1695. He was ordained deacon on 19 September 1697 and priest on 25 September of the following year. In 1695 he was elected fellow of his college, a post he resigned in 1721. In 1717 he was curate of St Vedast in London. His Boyle lectures of 1721–2 were published as *The Pretended Difficulties in Natural or Reveal'd Religion No Excuse for Infidelity* (1723) and were reprinted in the third volume of S. Letsome and I. Nicholl's *Religion* (1739). They also appeared in abridged form, edited by Gilbert Burnet, vicar of Coggeshall, Essex, in 1737. Gurdon also wrote *Probabile est animam non semper cogitare* in verse (1696), and several sermons and tracts defending the truth of the gospels.

Gurdon was a favourite of Lord Chancellor Macclesfield, who made him his chaplain and gave him the rectory of Stapleford Abbots, Essex, on 17 March 1720, a living he resigned on 3 November 1724, at about which time he became rector of St Nicholas, London and St Edmund, King and Martyr, Lombard Street, London. On 16 March 1727 he was collated to the archdeaconry of Sudbury and was installed by proxy the following day. He became rector of Denham, Buckinghamshire, on 17 October 1730, and held these preferments until his death, in the parish of St Giles-in-the-Fields, London, on 20 November 1741. He had no wife or children. ADAM JACOB LEVIN

**Sources** Venn, *Alum. Cant.* • J. L. Chester and J. Foster, eds., *London marriage licences, 1521–1869* (1887), 598 • P. Morant, *The history and antiquities of the county of Essex*, 1 (1768), 178 • *Fasti Angl., 1541–1857*, [Ely], 50 • G. Lipscomb, *The history and antiquities of the county of Buckingham*, 4 vols. (1831–47), vol. 4, p. 448 • *GM*, 1st ser., 11 (1741), 609 • *DNB*
**Wealth at death** see administration, Dec 1741, PRO, PROB 6/117, fol. 208

**Gurdon, John** (1595–1679), politician, was born on 3 July 1595, the eldest of nine children of Brampton Gurdon (*d*. 1649), of Assington, Suffolk, and Letton, Norfolk, and his first wife, Elizabeth, daughter of Edward Barrett of Belhowse, Alveley, Essex. He was admitted as a pensioner to the puritan seminary of Emmanuel College, Cambridge, on 13 April 1611, matriculating the same year, and entered Gray's Inn on 16 November 1614. He married Anne (*d*. 1681), daughter of Sir Calthorpe Parker of Erwarton, Suffolk; they had five sons and three daughters.

Gurdon belonged to the wealthier gentry and was left a substantial estate, including lands in Suffolk and Essex, by his grandfather; in 1655 his landed income was estimated at £1400 per annum. He was elected to the House of Commons in 1640, representing Ipswich in both the Short and Long parliaments, and strongly supported the parliamentarian cause on the outbreak of civil war. Unlike his younger half-brother, Brampton, John was not a soldier, but was active in the Commons as a staunch ally of John Pym and soon earned a reputation as a radical. Indeed, he was one of the more prominent members of the war party between 1643 and 1645, and according to Clement Walker, Gurdon was 'a man hot enough for his zeal to set a kingdom on fire' (Brown, 34). In 1644 he played a prominent role in the radicals' attempt to discredit the earl of Essex and was a member of the Commons committee which investigated officers under the earl who were suspected of being unreliable. Locally, Gurdon's wartime services were appreciated and on 5 December 1643 £100 was voted to him by the town of Ipswich. He was an active member of the eastern association during the initial years of fighting, and later served on numerous parliamentarian committees during the second civil war and the interregnum.

Contrary to popular belief, Gurdon was not a regicide in 1649. Though appointed one of the commissioners of the high court of justice for the trial of Charles I, he refused to serve and absented himself between late December and the king's execution. However, he was sufficiently in tune with the new regime to be appointed a member of the council of state on 20 February 1650 and was re-elected on two subsequent occasions. Gurdon was frequently appointed to committees of the Rump Parliament and was elected for Suffolk as a member of the first protectorate parliament in 1654. His final activity on the national stage was in 1660 when he sat for Sudbury as an inactive member of the Convention Parliament. At its dissolution he retired from public life to Assington.

In religion Gurdon was a moderate puritan. In 1630 he was engaged in puritan colonization schemes, being a member of the Providence Island Company, alongside such puritan notables as the earl of Warwick, Lord Saye and Sele, and John Pym. He was also friendly with John Winthrop, first governor of Massachusetts and a sincere puritan, and in 1635 he presented the puritan cleric Thomas Walker to the living of Assington. When in November 1645 parliament nominated members of the classical presbyteries in Suffolk, Gurdon appeared among the lay elders. Later he was described as 'an honest religious Gentleman, but a Presbyterian throughout' (Fiennes, 138). Indeed, under the Commonwealth he was one of the Rump's foremost advocates of Presbyterianism, though he was tolerant of those holding other views. After the Restoration Gurdon's vicar, Thomas Walker, was ejected from his living for refusing to assent to the prayer book, but in 1672 Gurdon obtained a licence authorizing Walker to hold Presbyterian meetings at Assington Hall. John Gurdon died at his home, Assington Hall, on 9 September 1679.

GORDON BLACKWOOD

**Sources** M. Brown, 'Gurdon, John', Greaves & Zaller, *BDBR*, 2.34 • Keeler, *Long Parliament*, 199–200 • D. Brunton and D. H. Pennington, *Members of the Long Parliament* (1954), 78, 233 • J. T. Cliffe, *Puritans in conflict* (1988), 21, 37–8, 71, 101, 146–7, 154–5, 195 • J. T. Cliffe, *The puritan gentry: the great puritan families of early Stuart England* (1984), 94–5, 203–4 • J. T. Cliffe, *The puritan gentry besieged, 1650–1700* (1993), 4, 31, 44, 116, 215 • papers of David Elisha Davy, BL, Add. MS 19077, fol. 72 • records of the council of state, draft order books, PRO, SP 25/76A/30 • N. Bacon, *The annalls of Ipswche*, ed. W. H. Richardson (1884), 522 n. (b) • [N. Fiennes], *Vindiciae veritatis, or, An answer to a discourse entitled 'Truth it's manifest'* (1654), 138 • *CSP dom.*, 1650, 5 • D. Underdown, *Pride's Purge: politics in the puritan revolution* (1971), 64, 275, 375 • B. Worden, *The Rump Parliament, 1648–1653* (1974), 64, 126–7, 197 • A. M. Everitt, *Suffolk and the Great Rebellion, 1640–1660*, Suffolk Records Society, 3 (1960), 116 n. 3 • C. Holmes, *The eastern association in the English civil war* (1974), 50, 251 n. 78 • Venn, *Alum. Cant.*, 1/2.275 • J. Foster, *The register of admissions to Gray's Inn, 1521–1889, together with the register of marriages in Gray's Inn chapel, 1695–1754* (privately printed, London, 1889), 136 • G. Yule, *Puritans in politics* (1981), 252, 260 • *DNB* • M. W. Helms and P. Watson, 'Gurdon, John', HoP, *Commons, 1660–90*, 2.452–3

**Archives** BL, papers relating to landed income, Add. MS 19077, fol. 72 • PRO, draft order books relating to appointees to Suffolk military commission, SP 25/76A/30

**Gurdon, Thornhagh** (1663–1733), antiquary, was born at Letton, Norfolk, on 28 July 1663, the eldest son of Brampton Gurdon (*d.* 1691), Church of England clergyman, and Elizabeth Thornhagh; he was the elder brother of John Gurdon and Brampton *Gurdon, theologian. After schooling at Wymondham and Earl Stonham schools, he was admitted as a commoner to Gonville and Caius College, Cambridge, on 23 April 1681, from where he matriculated in 1681 and received the degree of MA *comitiis regiis* in 1682. In April 1698 he married Elizabeth Cooke (*d.* 1745), daughter and coheir of Sir William Cooke, bt, of Brome, Suffolk. They had two sons and three daughters. Early in the eighteenth century Gurdon was appointed receiver-general of Norfolk. He lived mostly at Norwich, where in 1728 he published anonymously an *Essay on the antiquity of the castel of Norwich, its founders and governors from the kings of the East Angles down to modern times*. In 1731 he published his *History of the High Court of Parliament* in two volumes. He was elected a fellow of the Society of Antiquaries in 1718.

Gurdon died on 19 November 1733 and was buried in the church of Cranworth-with-Letton, Norfolk. He appears erroneously as 'Brampton Gourdon esq.' in Gough's *Chronological and Alphabetical Lists* (1798).

GORDON GOODWIN, *rev.* J. A. MARCHAND

**Sources** Venn, *Alum. Cant.* • will, PRO, PROB 11/664, sig. 61 • F. Blomefield and C. Parkin, *An essay towards a topographical history of the county of Norfolk*, [2nd edn], 11 vols. (1805–10), vol. 3, p. 92 • [J. Chambers], *A general history of the county of Norfolk*, 2 (1829), 1018 • GEC, *Baronetage* • R. G. [R. Gough], *British topography*, [new edn], 2 (1780), 11 • *IGI* • *Norfolk Archaeology*, 2 (1849), 370n.

**Wealth at death** £1000 left to each of three daughters; £800 to son: will, PRO, PROB 11/664, sig. 61

**Gurdon, Sir William Brampton** (1840–1910), civil servant and politician, was born in London on 5 September 1840, the younger son of Brampton Gurdon (*d.* 1881) of Letton Hall, Norfolk, and his wife, Henrietta Susannah, daughter of Nicholas William Ridley-Colborne, Baron Colborne. Robert Thornhagh Gurdon, first Baron Cranworth of Letton (1829–1902), was his brother. He was educated at Eton and at Trinity College, Cambridge. He joined the Treasury as a clerk in 1863 and quickly became private secretary to W. E. Gladstone—first, in 1865–6, when he was chancellor of the exchequer and then, from 1868 to 1874, when prime minister. Gurdon ran the prime minister's office at 10 Downing Street efficiently and unobtrusively, but without making much of a mark. After 1874 he returned to the Treasury and served on various commissions, such as Leon Say's monetary commission (1878) and the Transvaal inquiry commission (1881). Gurdon retired from the Treasury in 1885 to begin a political career. He stood unsuccessfully as a Liberal in South West Norfolk (December 1885), Rotherhithe (July 1886), and Colchester (at a by-election in 1888), before being returned for North Norfolk at a by-election in 1899, holding the seat until he retired in January 1910 (his brother had a little earlier held

Mid Norfolk for the Unionists). In 1906–10 he was chairman of the Commons' selection committee. He was knighted in 1882 and sworn of the privy council in 1907.

On 20 September 1888 Gurdon married Lady Eveline Camilla (*d.* 13 Sept 1894), daughter of Isaac Newton Wallop, fifth earl of Portsmouth, and his wife, Lady Eveline Alicia Juliana, *née* Herbert. They had no children. In 1869 Gurdon had bought Assington Hall and 3000 acres in Suffolk from a relative; he was a member of Suffolk county council and was lord lieutenant of the county from 1907. He died in Liverpool on 31 May 1910 on landing there from Tenerife. Gurdon was a sturdy landed Liberal in a predominantly tory county. His experience at the heart of politics in a great Liberal administration gave him an opportunity of which he was able to take only partial advantage, and he made more impact on the local than the national scene. H. C. G. MATTHEW

**Sources** Venn, *Alum. Cant.* • C. R. Dod, *The peerage, baronetage and knightage of Great Britain and Ireland* • Gladstone, *Diaries* • *The Times* (2 June 1910) • Burke, *Peerage* • Burke, *Gen. GB*

**Archives** Suffolk RO, Ipswich, political and other corresp. and papers | BL, corresp. with W. E. Gladstone, Add. MS 44182 • Bodl. Oxf., corresp. with Lord Kimberley • Bodl. RH, corresp. with Sir Godfrey Lagden

**Wealth at death** £75,341 11*s.* 6*d.*: resworn probate, 21 July 1910, *CGPLA Eng. & Wales*

**Gurdun** [Gurdon], **Sir Adam** (*c.*1220–1305), soldier and rebel, was the son of Adam Gurdun, a minor landowner and tenant by serjeanty in Hampshire, and his wife, Amiria. A minor when his father died, about 1231, Adam had probably come of age by 1241. In the following year he went with Henry III's army to Poitou, and he went on to serve the king in Gascony in 1253–4, and in Wales in 1257. In 1255, after obtaining a papal dispensation (which referred to him as a knight), he married Constance, daughter of John le Venuz and widow of Robert de Pont de l'Arche, a marriage which brought him estates in Hampshire, Dorset, and probably Gloucestershire, and the grant for life from his father-in-law of the keepership of Aliceholt and Woolmer forests in Wiltshire. In the civil war which broke out in 1264 Gurdun was an active supporter of Simon de Montfort. He had once been a member of the household of William (III) de Cantilupe, and this may have brought him into contact with Montfort, who was a chief mourner at Cantilupe's funeral in 1254. No doubt his military experience led to Gurdun being given the command of Lundy island off Devon and Dunster Castle in Somerset. He built up a considerable following in the south-west, and in 1265 beat off a seaborne attack from Wales upon Minehead in Somerset. After the battle of Evesham, Gurdun continued to resist the king's forces in southern England, and especially in his home county of Hampshire, where with his followers he infested the pass of Alton on the road from London to Winchester, to such effect that the Lord Edward himself resolved to dislodge him. Guided by a traitor, on the evening of 20 May 1266 Edward stormed the rebel fort, and engaged in hand-to-hand combat with Gurdun, whose courage and skill in arms so impressed him that he spared his life, though his followers are said to have been hanged on trees.

In the earliest chronicle accounts Gurdun was then thrown into prison in Windsor Castle, and record evidence shows that he was handed over to Edward's mother, Eleanor of Provence, to whom he would have paid the ransom for his lands which had led to their being restored to him by 1270. But the story was elaborated as time passed, with Edward being said to have had Gurdun's wounds bound up, 'not considering him an enemy but taking him with him as a guest' (*Flores historiarum*, 3.10), and to have treated him as a friend ever afterwards. In fact there is no evidence for personal friendship, but Gurdun, who lived for nearly forty years more, gave useful service to Henry III and his son in various capacities, especially in the royal forests. He was a forest justice in Berkshire, Wiltshire, and Gloucestershire in 1280–81, while in 1295, though he must by then have been in his seventies, he was appointed to guard the south coast of England against threatened French attacks. Following the death of his wife, Constance, perhaps before 1271, he married again; his new wife was named Agnes. He had a bastard son called John, but when he died, shortly before 8 April 1305, his sole legitimate heir was his daughter Joan, by then the widow of Robert Achard. There was no issue of her marriage. But if he had no physical descendants, the story of Adam Gurdun, the bold rebel leader who fought man to man with the future king, and prompted him to magnanimity by his fearless demeanour, may have contributed to the growth of the legend of Robin Hood.

HENRY SUMMERSON

**Sources** *Chancery records* • *Ann. mon.*, vols. 3, 4 • H. R. Luard, ed., *Flores historiarum*, 3 vols., Rolls Series, 95 (1890), vol. 3 • H. C. M. Lyte and others, eds., *Liber feodorum: the book of fees*, 3 vols. (1920–31) • *VCH Hampshire and the Isle of Wight*, vols. 3–4 • *CEPR letters*, vol. 1 • W. D. Macray, ed., *Calendar of charters and documents relating to Selborne and its priory*, 2 vols., Hampshire RS, 4, 9 (1891–4) • F. M. Powicke, 'King Edward I in fact and fiction', *Fritz Saxl, 1890–1948: a volume of memorial essays*, ed. D. J. Gordon (1957), 120–35 • J. Bain, 'Sir Adam Gurdun of Selborne', *The Genealogist*, new ser., 4 (1887), 1–4 • J. R. Maddicott, *Simon de Montfort* (1994)

**Wealth at death** lands worth £266 13*s.* 4*d.*, later disposed of by daughters; goods and chattels worth £294, later disposed of by daughters: Macray, ed., *Calendar*, 83, 84, 87

**Gurle** [Garrle], **Leonard** (*c.*1621–1685), gardener and nurseryman, had one of the earliest general nursery gardens in London from the early 1640s, when he moved from Southwark to a 12 acre site in east London between Brick Lane and Greatorex Street, north of Old Montagu Street. During the 1660s and 1670s his nursery was the largest in London, and he was famous as a supplier of fruit trees in particular, though he sold ornamental trees and shrubs and seeds as well. Leonard Meager in *The English Gardener* (1670) printed 'a Catalogue of divers sorts of Fruit, which I had of my very Loving friend Captain Garrle', containing over 300 varieties, many of them from France (Meager, 82). By 1661 Gurle had raised the hardy nectarine 'Elruge' and given it his own name reversed, with an extra 'e' for euphony.

In 1672 Gurle sold pear and other fruit trees, cypresses,

spruces, and other forest trees, jasmine, and honeysuckles, with a box of seeds, to Sir Roger Pratt, for his garden at Ryston Hall, near Downham, Norfolk. Late in 1674 he supplied fruit trees to Sir Richard Temple at Stowe, and to William Russell, first duke of Bedford, at Woburn Abbey. The Woburn order included dwarf plums and cherries, French pears, an Elruge nectarine, and other fruit, with more young trees 'to make good those that died last year' in accordance with Gurle's guarantee to supply 'the best of every sort in case any fail or die' (Thomson, 251). After the death of John Rose in 1677, Gurle succeeded him as the king's gardener at St James's Palace, with £320 a year to maintain the garden and another £240 a year as his own salary. There he had an official residence, but he continued to run his Whitechapel nursery, with another in London Fields.

Gurle died in the spring of 1685, before 2 April, and was buried in Woodham Walter, near Maldon, Essex, which may have been his place of birth. His widow, Joyce, was his second wife, whom he had married in 1676, and a son, William, was given the power to administer his estate. Two other sons, Martin and Joseph, baptized in 1641 and 1644, and three daughters, Rebecca, Margaret, and Jane, survived their father. The area occupied by the nursery was called Gurle's Ground for some time after Gurle's death; in 1719 part of it was still occupied by a Martin Girle, possibly the nurseryman's eldest son or a grandson.

SANDRA RAPHAEL, *rev.*

**Sources** J. Harvey, *Early nurserymen* (1974), 4–5, 45–6 • J. H. Harvey, 'Leonard Gurle's nurseries and some others', *Garden History*, 3/3 (1975), 42–9 • G. S. Thomson, *Life in a noble household, 1641–1700* (1937), 248–51 • L. Meager, *The English gardener* (1670)

**Gurnall, William** (*bap.* **1616**, *d.* **1679**), Church of England clergyman, was born in St Margaret's parish, King's Lynn, and baptized on 17 November 1616 at St Margaret's Church. He was the second son of Gregory Gurnall (*c.*1582–1631), linen draper, mayor of Lynn in 1624, and his wife, Catherine Dressyt. After Lynn grammar school William entered Emmanuel College, Cambridge, in March 1632; he graduated BA in 1635 and proceeded MA four years later. He may have begun his ministry in Sudbury, Suffolk, but was certainly curate to Ambrose Copinger at Lavenham in the same county, probably living with a brother or cousin James Gurnall there until Copinger died and he succeeded him. His contemporary, the clergyman and antiquary Matthias Candler, reported that the patron, Sir Simonds D'Ewes 'freely and very willingly gave the Rectory unto [Gurnall], although to him then unknown, at the request of the Parish, which hath been muche for the benefit of the Towne many waies' (BL, Add. MS 15520, fol. 59*v*). Gurnall helped his learned patron to know him better by writing regularly in Latin. Further evidence that Gurnall was not episcopally ordained comes from his description of D'Ewes as 'my Patron, Ordainer and Instituter' (letter of 24 Nov 1644, McKeon, 8); the following 16 December parliament ratified his presentation to the rectory for life. He entered family events in the parish register as 'pastor and preacher of God's word'.

At Stoke by Nayland, Suffolk, on 11 February 1646, Gurnall married Sarah, only child of Thomas Mott and Sarah (*née* Brand), his wife. Mott was vicar there, until he was ejected at the Restoration, and also lord of the manor of Wissington near by. Between 1647 and 1669 Sarah and William had at least eight sons and six daughters, six of whom survived their parents. Never himself in robust health, Gurnall was excused, on D'Ewes's intervention, when ordered to preach before parliament in November 1648. When D'Ewes died in 1650 the advowson passed to Sir William Bowes, of Great Bromley, Essex, who re-presented Gurnall to the rectory the day after his ordination by Edward Reynolds, bishop of Norwich, on 22 August 1662. His new conformity was attacked in *Covenant-Renouncers, Desperate Apostates* (1665), in which it was alleged that he was not 'alone in these horrible defilements, hateful to the Soul of God and his Saints' (*Covenant-Renouncers*, 6).

In 1662 the third and final part of Gurnall's treatise *The Christian in Compleat Armour* was published, the first and second parts having appeared in 1655 and 1658. The first part was dedicated to his flock at Lavenham; the third to the aged patroness of the godly, Mary, Lady Vere, of Kirby Hall, to whose care two of the royal children had been entrusted by the parliamentarian authorities in the civil war. Gurnall preached her funeral sermon at Hedingham, Essex, where she died, aged ninety, in December 1671. Its publication in 1672 was Gurnall's last. After a ministry of thirty-five years, he died on 12 October 1679, the day after he made his will, and was buried in Lavenham church or churchyard. He left property in the Marshland Walpoles of Norfolk (parishes near King's Lynn) and his books to his son John (*d.* 1700), later curate of Brockley near Bury St Edmunds. Gurnall's funeral sermon, preached by William Burkitt, rector of Milden near Lavenham, was published in 1680. When his widow, Sarah, was buried at Lavenham on 7 September 1698 her executor was their attorney son Joseph. Gurnall's only memorial is a line on a granddaughter's ledger slab of 1741 in Lavenham chancel.

Gurnall's main publication, however, had a significant impact both in his own lifetime and long after his death as a work of spiritual consolation and exhortation. In 1657 the puritan gentlewoman Katherine Gell told her spiritual mentor Richard Baxter how she was 'much recovered of that melancholy distemper that I used to complain of' by reading 'Mr Gurnalls *Ch[ristian] Ar[mour]*' (N. Keeble and G. F. Nuttall, eds., *Calendar of the Correspondence of Richard Baxter*, 2 vols., 1991, 1.273). The book was reprinted many times into the nineteenth and indeed the twentieth centuries and the translation into Welsh alone was reprinted four times between 1775 and 1809.

J. M. BLATCHLY

**Sources** H. McKeon, *An inquiry into the birth-place … life and writings of William Gurnall* (1830) • BL, Candler's Suffolk collections, Add. MS 15520 • will, Suffolk RO, Bury St Edmunds, IC 500/1/133 • will, Suffolk RO, Bury St Edmunds, IC 500/1/154 [John Gurnall] • administration, Suffolk RO, Bury St Edmunds, J 576/3–8 [Sarah Gurnall] • W. Burkitt, *The peoples zeal provok't to a holy emulation* (1680) • W. Gurnall, *The Christian in compleat armour*, 3 vols. (1655–62) •

*Covenant-renouncers, desperate apostates* (1665) • parish register, Lavenham, 12 Oct 1679, Suffolk RO, 12 Oct 1679 [burial]
**Archives** BL, letter to Simonds D'Ewes, Harley MS 374, fols. 138, 142, 146; 376, fols. 41–4
**Wealth at death** estates in Marshland, Norfolk: will, Suffolk RO, Bury St Edmunds, IC 500/1/133

**Gurnay** [Gurney], **Edmund** (1578–1648), Church of England clergyman, was born on 15 February 1578, one of the thirteen children of **Henry Gurnay** (1549–1616), gentleman, of Great Ellingham, Norfolk. Henry, born on 21 January 1549, was himself the son of Francis Gurnay (1521–1552x5) and Helen (*b.* 1528), daughter of Robert Holdiche of Ranworth, Norfolk; his mother married as her second husband in January 1560 or 1561 John Jernegan or Jerningham. In 1556 Henry inherited from his grandfather Anthony Gurnay manors and estates in various west and south Norfolk settlements, especially Great Ellingham, Irstead, and West Barsham (Suffolk). Having probably been a student at Christ's College, Cambridge, in 1564, on 10 June 1571 he married Ellen or Helen (*b.* 1547/8), daughter of John Blennerhasset of Barsham, Suffolk. Three years later they settled at Great Ellingham, where Gurnay significantly extended the manor house begun by his grandfather. They had seven sons and six daughters, of whom two sons and a daughter died young. Gurnay's commonplace book shows him to have been an affectionate father, his estates somewhat strained by the need to provide for so many children. It also shows that he was personally devout, and this is borne out by his will, which attests to his charitable commitment to the poor of his parish, and by the records of his library. Religious books predominated among nearly a hundred volumes, and included works both by church fathers and by contemporary theologians. He owned Walter Travers's book advocating a presbyterian church discipline, writings by defenders of the episcopal order like John Jewel and Adrian Saravia, and William Perkins's classic of puritan casuistry, *Cases of Conscience*.

Hatred of Rome bulked large in Henry Gurnay's religious thinking, inspiring him to compose a 320-stanza 'Anatomy of popery'. The orthodoxy of his protestantism appears in a remarkable proviso to his will: if his two unmarried daughters died young the money so released should be equally divided between his younger sons, 'so that none hould any fantasticall opinions, so adjudged by our Bishop or Civill Lawes' (will of Henry Gurnay, Norfolk RO). There is nothing to suggest which of his four younger sons he had in mind, but it is tempting to believe that he was thinking of Edmund, by this time a clergyman, if only for a certain eccentricity of thought noted in the latter by contemporaries. He died on 23 February 1616.

The choice of godparents for the infant Edmund reflected the family's elevated connections in the gentry world of west Norfolk: his father's brother Thomas and uncle Richard Stubbe of Sedgeford, and Elizabeth, wife of Henry Gawdy of Gawdy Hall. Edmund Gurnay was admitted to Queens' College, Cambridge, on 30 October 1594 and matriculated pensioner the following year. Having graduated in 1599, in 1601 he was elected a fellow of Corpus Christi College, where he proceeded MA in 1602 and BD in 1609. In 1599 he provided a laudatory—and shamelessly punning—verse preface to John Weever's *Epigrammes in the Oldest Cut, Newest Fashion*. In 1607 his fellowship was declared void following a reinterpretation of the college statutes, but he was reinstated following an appeal. Two years later, however, he was unanimously reprimanded by the college body after he had protested against the encroaching garden and double stipend of the master, Thomas Jegon.

In 1614 Gurnay was ordained priest by Bishop John Jegon of Norwich (the brother of Thomas) and was presented to Edgefield rectory by his godfather Stubbe. Early in the following year he resigned his fellowship upon his marriage to a woman named Ann (surname unknown). In 1620 he exchanged Edgefield for Harpley, also in Norfolk, to which he was presented by Stubbe's son-in-law Sir William Yelverton. By then he had started to publish. Like his father Gurnay was bitterly hostile to Catholicism. His earliest book, *Corpus Christi* (1619), was an attack on transubstantiation. *The Demonstration of Antichrist* (which survives only in its second edition of 1631) is dedicated to the prince of Wales, and since it acclaims the latter as sent by God's providence to give 'intelligence toward the discovering this Antichrist' (sig. d2v), was probably written following the return of Charles and Buckingham from Spain in 1623. It was followed by *The Romish Chain* (1624), which opens with an exhortation to the parliament then eager for war with Spain, urging it to stand firm in the maintenance of the royal supremacy before setting out to expose the chain of false claims and premises upon which the papacy staked its claim to universal monarchy. Gurnay's antipathy to Catholicism was also more privately expressed. On 2 June 1623 he and his wife baptized their daughter with the name Protestant. She died when only two weeks old, and was buried with an epitaph combining parental grief with godly militancy:

> Protestant [Gu]rnay here under I ly,
> Such name at first was I christned by …
> … should all fayle these stones should cry
> Perpetually we doe defye Roome's heresy; Idolotrye,
> Blood thirstness, and boundless soveraynty.
> (Gurney, 465–6)

Evidence of Gurnay's work as puritan pastor can be glimpsed in court records. Harpley was a poor village, and the living was valued at only £20 per annum in 1603. In 1621 he submitted a petition to the Norfolk bench appealing for the suppression of the town's alehouses. The magistrates complied, but a year later Gurnay presented another petition to the same end, claiming that more alehouses had now sprung up, which were impoverishing the town and encouraging social indiscipline and irreligion. Yet there were other, and more positive, dimensions to Gurnay's pastoral role besides that of social disciplinarian. Thus his kinsman Sir Nicholas L'Estrange recalled:

> Parson Edmond Gourny, inveighing against the common fault of the meaner sort of people, who are to prone to performe civill and outward respects, upon the coming of greater persons into the church, by rising, bowing, &c, sayes he: 'I like an holy-rowly-Powlinesse; for there sure, if

anywhere, we ought to be haile fellows well met'. (Thoms, 59)

Such a preference was at odds with the general reality of the seventeenth-century parish church, where the local social hierarchy was physically embodied in the seating arrangements.

L'Estrange's anecdote attests to a geniality in Gurnay which Thomas Fuller also noted. Fuller's pen portrait is both affectionate and somewhat defensive about his friend's eccentricity:

> An excellent scholar, who could be humorous, and would be serious, as he was himself disposed; his humours were never profane towards God, or injurious towards his neighbours; which premised, none have cause to be displeased, if in his fancies he pleased himself. (Fuller, *Worthies*, 2.463)

Local tradition claimed that when Gurnay was cited in the 1630s for not wearing his surplice in service time he responded to an order to wear it always by taking his instructions literally and riding home in it. Unsurprisingly he was hostile to Laudian innovations, and took up his pen again to attack them. In 1639 he published *Toward the Vindication of the Second Commandment*, in which he dealt in turn with every possible argument for the legitimacy of images in church, and in the process made it absolutely clear that he regarded Laudian policy on altars and ceremonies as rank idolatry. Two years later he published *An Appendix unto the Homily Against Images in Churches*, a title which underlines Gurnay's claim to uphold the traditions of the Church of England. Taking the opportunity of the time this book was more assertive than its predecessor, denouncing the setting up of images in English churches as a 'capitall scandall' which offered succour to recusants (p. 14). Both books were republished at the Restoration, the *Appendix* under the title *Gurnay Redivivus*.

Gurnay retained his living throughout the civil war. He died in 1648 and was buried on 14 May in St Peter Mancroft, Norwich, where his brother-in-law Thomas Osborne had been minister. His successor was instituted at Harpley the following day. Tim Wales

**Sources** D. Gurney, *The record of the house of Gournay*, 2 vols. (1848–58) • Fuller, *Worthies* (1840), 2.463 • *Masters' History of the college of Corpus Christi and the Blessed Virgin Mary in the University of Cambridge*, ed. J. Lamb (1831) • Venn, *Alum. Cant.* • W. J. Thoms, ed., *Anecdotes and traditions, illustrative of early English history and literature*, CS, 5 (1839), 6, 59 • Norfolk quarter sessions rolls, Norfolk RO, C/S3/23, 23A • K. Fincham, ed., *Visitation articles and injunctions of the early Stuart church*, 2 (1998) • parish registers, archdeaconry of Norwich (transcripts), 1623, Norfolk RO • will, 1623, Norfolk RO, diocese of Norwich consistory court [Henry Gurnay]

**Gurnay, Henry** (1549–1616). *See under* Gurnay, Edmund (1578–1648).

**Gurner, Stanley Ronald Kershaw** (1890–1939), headmaster and author, was born on 23 January 1890 at 12 Charterhouse Square, London, the second of the four children of Walter Gurner and his wife, Alice Mary Kershaw. His father, who was employed by a bank, left the family home and his wife provided for the education of their four children by running a small hotel. Gurner was profoundly affected by these unhappy circumstances. He was educated at the nearby Merchant Taylors' School and in 1908 followed his elder brother (who joined the Indian Civil Service in 1911) to Oxford, studying classics at St John's College and gaining a first in classical moderations (1910), although he was prevented from taking his final examinations by a mental breakdown and was awarded an *aegrotat* degree (1912). He then accepted temporary appointments as a teacher before joining the staff of Marlborough College in Wiltshire.

Shortly after the outbreak of the First World War Gurner gained a commission in the army cyclist corps and after being seriously wounded in France in 1917 was awarded the MC. Like so many of his contemporaries he was deeply marked by the horrors of that war, and published a volume of poetry in 1917. In 1918 he experienced some kind of religious conversion before returning to teach at Marlborough, where Cyril Norwood had meanwhile arrived as master. Gurner wrote a number of novels, which were moderately successful but never sold well; in all of them there is a strong autobiographical element. In *Pass Guard at Ypres* (1930) he argued that the loss of illusions was one of the sacrifices made by those who had fought in the war. He was uncomfortable in the world of the English boarding-school as he found it after the war, and as he characterized it in another novel, *Reconstruction* (1931). On 22 December 1919 he married Rosalie Leila Romer (*b.* 1894/5), with whom he adopted a son, Lionel (Leon).

In 1920, advised and helped by Norwood and never having been inside a state school, Gurner was appointed headmaster of the Strand School, a municipal grammar school in south London. The following six years were, by his own account, among the happiest of his life (*I Chose Teaching*, 1937). He sponsored the cause of the publicly funded grammar schools, urging that they were the true heirs of the best traditions of the English 'public' school. He shared the enthusiasms of many of his progressive contemporaries: Sir Ernest Barker, who was the chairman of governors at the Strand School, proclaimed in the preface to another of Gurner's novels that the grammar schools established under the Balfour Act of 1902 had taken thousands of boys and girls 'through the looking glass' into a world rich in opportunities hitherto confined to the privileged few (*The Day Boy*, 1924, 7). These themes were developed by Gurner in several articles and speeches, and repeated in *The Day Schools of England* (1930). The national system of public examinations introduced by H. A. L. Fisher in 1917 had narrowed the gap between independent and state schools, and for Gurner the important line of distinction now lay between boarding- and day schools, and not between independent and state schools. But it was of supreme importance to preserve the essential values enshrined in the traditional boarding-schools, which for Gurner as for Norwood were: religion, discipline, culture, team-spirit, and service. He believed in a sound secondary education for a carefully chosen minority of boys, selected without regard to the capacity of their parents to pay fees. His ideas reflected the presuppositions of his generation, and were not seriously challenged until the movement in the 1960s towards comprehensive forms of secondary education.

After a brief and stormy period as headmaster of King Edward VII School in Sheffield, whose leading citizens were harshly portrayed in *The Riven Pall* (1929), Gurner was appointed headmaster of Whitgift School: an independent day school in Croydon founded in the sixteenth century but then receiving government grants, and therefore embodying many of the ideals shared by Gurner and Norwood. Gurner was headmaster at the time when the school moved into new buildings but his tenure was flawed by his volatile temperament and frequent absences (Percy, 211). His financial problems became more severe, he drank heavily, and was involved in affairs of an uncertain nature with several women (Cecil, 233). The governors became aware that he was misusing school funds and on 17 May 1939, a few months before the outbreak of the Second World War, he committed suicide at 36 Sussex Gardens, Paddington, London. He was survived by his wife. H. G. JUDGE

**Sources** H. Cecil, *The flower of battle: British fiction writers of the First World War* (1995) • F. H. G. Percy, *Whitgift School: a history* (1991) • S. R. K. Gurner, *I chose teaching* (1937) • G. McCulloch, *Philosophers and kings: education and leadership in modern England* (1991) • V. Sillery, *St John's College biographical register, 1875–1919* (1981) • b. cert. • m. cert. • d. cert.

**Wealth at death** £2834 9*s*. 8*d*.: probate, 14 July 1939, *CGPLA Eng. & Wales*

**Gurney, Anna** (1795–1857), Old English scholar, was born on 31 December 1795, the youngest child of Richard Gurney (1742–1811), partner in Gurney's Bank, of Keswick, near Norwich, Norfolk, and his second wife, Rachel (*d.* 1825), second daughter of Osgood Hanbury of Holfield Grange, Essex, and half-sister of Hudson *Gurney. Her parents and most of her relatives were Quakers. When Gurney was only ten months old she was paralysed and lost the use of her legs. She passed through her busy, active, and happy life without ever being able to stand or move without mechanical aid. She was educated mainly by an elder sister, and then by a tutor, and at an early age she learnt Latin, Greek, Hebrew, and Old English. In 1819 she brought out anonymously, in a limited impression for private circulation, *A Literal Translation of the Saxon Chronicle: by a Lady in the Country*. The work went to a second edition, and was commended by James Ingram (*Saxon Chronicle with Translations*, 1823, 'Preface', 12).

In 1825, after the death of her mother, Gurney went to live at Northrepps Cottage, near Cromer, with her first cousin, Sarah Buxton, sister of Sir Thomas Fowell Buxton, and, when that lady died in 1839, continued to live there for the remainder of her life. There she bought at her own expense one of George William Manby's apparatuses for saving the lives of seamen wrecked on dangerous coasts, which fired a lifeline from a mortar to the shipwreck. In emergencies she had herself carried down to the beach, and directed the operations from her chair. She took a great interest in the emancipation of slaves, and closer to home she cared for the education and material welfare of poor children. She made a journey to Rome, and then visited Athens and Argos, and contemplated a voyage to the Baltic. In 1845 she became an associate of the British Archaeological Association; she was its first woman member and published two papers in the *Archaeologia*. In her later life Gurney studied Danish, Swedish, and Russian literature, and was an important translator of the works of Daniel Solander, botanist. After a short illness she died at Keswick Hall, near Norwich, the residence of her brother, Hudson Gurney (1775–1864), on 6 June 1857, and was buried in Overstrand church, near Cromer, on 11 June. 2000 people attended her funeral, and her coffin was borne by local fishermen. G. C. BOASE, *rev.* JOHN D. HAIGH

**Sources** *GM*, 3rd ser., 3 (1857), 226, 342–3 • *Journal of the British Archaeological Association*, 14 (1858), 187–9 • letters, *Archaeologia*, 32 (1847), 64–8; 34 (1852), 440–42 • E. Hoare, *The coming night, a sermon … on … the death of Miss Anna Gurney* (1857) • *The Times* (18 June 1857), 10 • Boase, *Mod. Eng. biog.* • V. Anderson, *The Northrepps grandchildren* (1968) • Burke, *Gen. GB* (1965–72), vol. 1

**Archives** Norfolk RO, corresp. and MSS | Bodl. RH, corresp. with Thomas Buxton, etc. • RS Friends, Lond., corresp. with Hudson Gurney, etc.

**Gurney, Archer Thompson** (1820–1887), Church of England clergyman and hymn writer, was born at Tregony in Cornwall on 15 July 1820. His father, **Richard Gurney** (1790–1843), was vice-warden of the stannaries of Devon. In 1830 he claimed to be elected member of parliament for Tregony in Cornwall, but did not succeed in obtaining the seat. He died at Bonn, Germany, in 1843.

Archer Gurney became a student of the Middle Temple on 29 April 1842, and was called to the bar on 8 May 1846. His career as a lawyer was short, as in 1849 he was ordained to the curacy of Holy Trinity, Exeter. In 1851 he took charge of St Mary's, Crown Street, Soho, where he remained until 1854, when he obtained the senior curacy of Buckingham. He was appointed chaplain to the Court Chapel, Paris, in 1858, and lived there until 1871. After his return to England he served as evening lecturer of Holy Trinity Church, Westminster (1872–4), curate of Holy Trinity Chapel, Brighton (1874–5), and curate-in-charge of St Andrew's, Hastings (1877–8). He assisted at St Katharine's Hospital, Regent's Park, London (1879–80), was curate in charge of Rhayader, Radnorshire (1880–81), and was curate in charge of Llangynidr, Brecknockshire (1882–3). His wife, Catherine Harriet, died in 1876, and in his last year he lived at 7 Keble Terrace, Oxford. Gurney died of disease of the kidneys at the Castle Hotel, 4 Northgate Street, Bath, on 21 March 1887, and was buried in Bath.

Gurney was a prolific pamphleteer and polemicist, but was most notable as a hymn writer, contributing 147 compositions to *A Book of Praise* (1862). Of these the most widely known was his Easter hymn 'Christ is risen, Christ is risen'. He also wrote plays, including *Turandot, Princess of China* (1836) and *Iphigenia at Delphi* (1855); dramatic poems, such as *King Charles the First* (1846); as well as songs and the words to Horsley's *Gideon, an Oratorio* (1859). His daughter-in-law, Dorothy Frances, *née* Blomfield (*b.* 1858), who was married to his son Gerald, was also a hymn writer.

G. C. BOASE, *rev.* LEON LITVACK

**Sources** J. Julian, ed., *A dictionary of hymnology*, rev. edn (1907); repr. in 2 vols. (1915) • *The Times* (29 March 1887) • *Guardian* (23

March 1887) · M. Frost, ed., *Historical companion to 'Hymns ancient and modern'* (1962) · J. Moffatt and M. Patrick, eds., *Handbook to the church hymnary, with supplement*, 2nd edn (1935)
**Archives** BL, letters to W. E. Gladstone, Add. MSS 44338–44453, *passim* · LPL, corresp. with A. C. Tait
**Wealth at death** £2129 6*s*. 2*d*.: probate, 5 May 1887, *CGPLA Eng. & Wales*

**Gurney, Daniel** (1791–1880), banker and antiquary, was born on 9 March 1791 at Earlham Hall, near Norwich, the youngest son (in a family of four boys and seven girls) of Quaker parents, John Gurney (1749–1809), banker, of Earlham, Norfolk, and his wife, Catherine Bell (1754–1792). He was the brother of the philanthropist Mrs Elizabeth *Fry and also of Joseph John *Gurney and Samuel *Gurney. He was directly descended from the ancient family of Gurney or Gournay, a younger branch of which held certain manors in Norfolk dating from the reign of Henry II.

In the history of English banking the Gurneys occupy a distinguished position as the founders of the most successful private bank in the provinces. As such, the family partnership, established in 1775 in Norwich, fulfilled a critical role in supporting the credit network outside London at a time of sustained economic expansion. The bank was an outgrowth from the family's long-established interests in the East Anglian woollen trade, a business in which they had habitually extended credit. In making the transition to full banking the Gurneys began to take deposits and extend loans. They also engaged in discounting, supplying their clients with bills on London and issuing banknotes convertible on sight into gold or Bank of England notes. In the matter of discounting the Gurneys developed a close working relationship with Richardson, Overend & Co., London's first true bill brokers, established in 1805. The business proved to be lucrative for both parties in so far as the Gurneys could invest surplus liquid funds at short term by discounting bills coming from the country's emergent industrial districts via the bill brokers.

The Gurneys' banking interests had a strong dynastic and kinship element from their inception. Intermarriage took place with other Quaker banking families such as the Backhouses, Peases, Birkbecks, and Barclays. Daniel Gurney himself entered the Lynn Bank as representative of the Norwich-based banking partnership, after completing his education in 1809. He married Lady Harriet Jemima Hay (*d.* 1837), the daughter of the fifteenth earl of Erroll, in 1822; they established their family home at North Runcton Hall, New Lynn, Norfolk, and had four sons.

Gurney managed the Lynn Bank in collaboration with a fellow Quaker, Henry Birkbeck, and on the latter's retirement in 1832 was appointed senior partner in Gurney & Co. of Norwich, a position which he held until the early 1860s. During that time three of his sons took positions in the bank—Francis Hay in 1847, and Charles Henry and Somerville Arthur in 1854. In 1896 the Gurneys merged their banking interests with the Backhouses of Darlington and Barclays of London to form a substantial joint-stock concern—Barclay & Co. of Lombard Street—destined to become one of the 'big five' clearing banks after the First World War. The merger was part of a general movement towards banking amalgamations in the late nineteenth century, a trend initiated in part by the Baring crisis in 1890 and a new-found awareness of the inadequacy of the cash reserves of private banks.

As the head of a highly successful bank, Gurney had much influence, both socially and politically. His amiability, courtesy, and generosity greatly endeared him to his contemporaries. He was mainly instrumental in establishing the West Norfolk and Lynn Hospital. One of his favourite pursuits was archaeology, and he was a prominent fellow of the Society of Antiquaries. He also took great interest in genealogy. In 1848 he printed, in two volumes for private circulation, an elaborate work entitled *The Record of the House of Gournay*, to which he afterwards (1858) added a supplement. This book was highly valued by contemporaries for its varied antiquarian information and research. In addition Gurney wrote several essays on banking which were printed for private consideration only. A Conservative in politics, he was a justice of the peace and deputy lieutenant for the county of Norfolk, and in 1853 filled the office of high sheriff.

Gurney died on 14 June 1880 at home at North Runcton Hall. M. W. Kirby

**Sources** P. W. Matthews, *History of Barclays Bank Limited*, ed. A. W. Tuke (1926) · V. Anderson, *Friends and relations: three centuries of Quaker families* (1980) · W. T. C. King, *History of the London discount market* (1936) · H. R. Fox Bourne, *English merchants: memoirs in illustration of the progress of British commerce*, 2 vols. (1866) · d. cert. · *CGPLA Eng. & Wales* (1880) · Boase, *Mod. Eng. biog.* · A. J. C. Hare, *The Gurneys of Earlham*, 2 vols. (1895) · Burke, *Gen. GB* (1965–72), vol. 1
**Archives** RS Friends, Lond. | BL, letters to J. Hunter, Add. MS 24864 · Bodl. Oxf., corresp. with Sir Thomas Phillipps · Norfolk RO, letters to Hudson Gurney
**Likenesses** portrait, repro. in Hare, *The Gurneys of Earlham*
**Wealth at death** under £4000: resworn probate, Jan 1881, *CGPLA Eng. & Wales* (1880)

**Gurney, Edmund** (1847–1888), psychical researcher and psychologist, was born on 23 March 1847 at Hersham, Surrey, the third son and fifth child of the Reverend John Hampden *Gurney (1802–1862) and his wife, Mary Grey (*d.* *c*.1857). He had eight brothers and sisters. From 1861 to 1863 he attended a private boarding-school at Blackheath, London, and thereafter was coached by a private tutor. Following the death of his father in 1862 he was placed under the guardianship of his uncle, Russell *Gurney. In 1866 Edmund went up to Trinity College, Cambridge. He shared the Porson prize in 1870 and was placed fourth in the classical tripos in 1871, taking his BA that year and his MA in 1874. He was elected a fellow of Trinity in 1872.

At this point it might have seemed that Gurney was destined for a famously successful career. His academic achievements were matched by his personal qualities. He was over 6 feet in height, thin and loosely built, but strong and athletic. William James described him as 'a magnificent Adonis … with an extremely handsome face, voice, and general air of distinction about him' (Epperson, 127), and wrote also of his 'tenderest heart' and 'mind of rare metaphysical power' (ibid.). George Eliot is said to have based the character of Daniel Deronda partly upon him.

**Edmund Gurney** (1847–1888), by unknown photographer

His deeply felt intellectual concerns were tempered by a wit, a humour, and a self-mockery that some mistook for ironic detachment. Conventional success, however, always eluded him. In part this may have been due to the manic-depressive tendencies which had already interrupted his undergraduate studies. Periods of immense energy and enthusiasm were succeeded by intervals of lassitude and deep despair. The deaths of his mother, when he was ten, and his father, when he was fifteen, may have exacerbated these problems, and his outlook was further darkened in 1875 when three of his sisters were drowned in a boating accident on the Nile.

Gurney's earliest and keenest ambition was to succeed as a performer and composer of music. His academic work was done almost in the intervals of practice on the piano. From 1872 to 1875 he studied intensively at Harrow under the famous music teacher John Farmer, but in vain. It seemed, as his close friend, F. W. H. Myers, remarked, as though '[n]ature had heaped upon him gifts which he did not care to use, only to deny him the one gift … which would have satisfied his inborn, ineradicable desire' (Myers, 360). In 1875 he moved to London, and took houses first in Clarges Street and then in Montpelier Square. Instead of struggling to acquire musical skills, he started to write about the psychology and philosophy of music.

Gurney resigned his college fellowship in 1877, and on 5 June the same year he married a clever and beautiful girl, Kate Sara Sibley; they had a daughter, Helen (*b.* 1881). Soon afterwards he took up the study of medicine, first at University College, London, and then at Cambridge. He may have felt the need for a settled career (although he had a sufficient private income, he was not rich) or he may have had an altruistic desire to help humanity. By 1880 he had passed the second part of his MB; but hospital training, at St George's, London, distressed him so much that in 1881 he abandoned medicine and turned to law.

Meanwhile Gurney was becoming increasingly well known in the intellectual world. In 1880 he had brought out a vast, though verbose, work on musical experience, *The Power of Sound*, which, astonishingly, was written while he was still a medical student. For Gurney melody was ideal motion, a moment by moment advance along a form which was apprehended as a whole through the very process of advance. Musical excellence was grasped by a special faculty of musical intuition, and gave rise to a unique kind of enjoyment not reducible to any other emotion. *The Power of Sound* had only a limited success, though it still finds admirers. After its publication Gurney's interests moved more and more into psychology and philosophy. He was one of a small but distinguished philosophical group, 'The Scratch Eight', which met regularly for dinner and discussion. He began to publish articles on philosophical and psychological themes in *Mind* and elsewhere. Early in 1882 he helped to found the Society for Psychical Research, and in 1883, abandoning his legal studies and with them all thoughts of a regular profession, he became the society's honorary secretary.

Gurney had already participated, during the period 1874–8, along with F. W. H. Myers and other Trinity friends, in investigations of spiritualistic phenomena. 'He sat', said Myers, 'in the *cénacles* of those happy believers, an alien, formidable figure, courteous indeed to all, but uncomprehended and incomprehensible by any' (Myers, 364). What he thought of the phenomena he did not make known. He held no settled religious beliefs, but, to judge from some of the essays reprinted in his *Tertium quid* (2 vols., 1887), he may have felt that, in a world filled with irremediable suffering, finding grounds, however tenuous, for hope of ultimate alleviation and recompense might lessen the sufferers' despair.

To psychical research Gurney brought a powerful analytic mind, a wide general knowledge of science, and a quite extraordinary capacity for sustained hard work. He experimented on thought transference, a phenomenon for which by 1886 he felt the evidence to be very strong. He conducted extensive experiments on hypnotism and believed he had established the occurrence of secondary or dissociated trains of consciousness in otherwise quite ordinary persons (the findings were published in *Mind* and in the *Proceedings of the Society for Psychical Research*). Above all he assembled, and had often personally investigated, many first-hand cases of apparent 'spontaneous' telepathy. These he classified and presented in the two volumes of *Phantasms of the Living* (1886), the main text of which was his own, even though F. W. H. Myers and Frank Podmore were named as co-authors. The principal focus of *Phantasms* is on cases of what Gurney termed 'telepathic hallucinations', that is, visual or auditory hallucinations of recognized persons, the occurrence of which coincides closely in time with the death of or an accident to the person recognized. He argued that the cases could not be dismissed as due to errors in testimony, and that the coincidences between deaths and hallucinations could not be set down to normal causes or to chance (he attempted to establish the hallucination rate among the population at large by a census of 5705 persons). *Phantasms* attracted a good deal of notice and a good deal of criticism, to which Gurney replied with calm good humour. It is still regarded as the great classic in its field.

Gurney was found dead on his bed at the Royal Albion Hotel, Brighton, Sussex, on 23 June 1888, his nose and mouth covered with a pad of cotton wool backed by a sponge bag. Friends who knew of his depressions and constant overwork feared that he might have taken his own life. The inquest, however, found that he had died from the use of chloroform probably to relieve facial neuralgia. Some doubts may remain, but the elaborate suicide theory propounded by T. H. Hall in *The Strange Case of Edmund Gurney* (1964) depends too heavily on supposition and oversight. Gurney was buried at Brighton extramural cemetery; his widow and daughter survived him.

ALAN GAULD

**Sources** G. Epperson, *The mind of Edmund Gurney* (1997) · F. W. H. Myers, 'The work of Edmund Gurney in experimental psychology', *Proceedings of the Society for Psychical Research*, 5 (1888–9), 359–73 · A. Gauld, *The founders of psychical research* (1968) · C. D. Broad, 'The life, work and death of Edmund Gurney', 1965, CUL, Society for Psychical Research archives · *DNB* · G. Epperson, *The musical symbol: a study of the philosophic theory of music* (1967); repr. with new preface as *The musical symbol: an exploration in aesthetics* (New York, 1990) · A. Lang, 'Gurney, Edmund', *Encyclopaedia Britannica*, 11th edn (1910–11) · *Mind*, 14 (1889), 630–31 · J. Oppenheim, *The other world: spiritualism and psychical research in England, 1850–1914* (1985) · *CGPLA Eng. & Wales* (1888) · m. cert.

**Archives** CUL, Society for Psychical Research archives · Harvard U., Houghton L., William James MSS · UCL, letters to James Sully

**Likenesses** W. B. Richmond, sketch, 1888, Society for Psychical Research, London · photograph, CUL, Society for Psychical Research archives · photograph, NPG [*see illus.*]

**Wealth at death** £17,782 14*s*.: resworn probate, Feb 1889, *CGPLA Eng. & Wales* (1888)

**Gurney** [*née* Batten], **Emelia Russell** (**1823–1896**), campaigner for women's higher education, was born on 26 July 1823, probably at Harrow, the elder daughter of the Revd Samuel Ellis Batten (1792–1830), assistant master at Harrow School, and his wife, Caroline, *née* Venn (1798–1870), daughter of John *Venn [*see under* Venn, Henry (1725–1797)]. Batten, 'whose gay and buoyant spirits made him the playfellow of his children' (*Letters*, 1), died in Emelia's seventh year, and her younger sister, Florence, died in adolescence. After Batten's death the family moved first to Pinner, in London, then to Hereford. They often travelled abroad and were in Italy when Florence died in 1842. As a result of these early losses, Caroline and Emelia became close friends, their intimacy barely disturbed by Emelia's marriage. Nevertheless, Emelia's memories were of a strict evangelical upbringing; she confessed that, for her, Christmas Day had always been 'a second Sunday in one week… when the worldly people (envied creatures!) amused themselves all the more, and without breaking one of the ten commandments either' (ibid., 62).

On 1 September 1852 Emelia Batten married Russell *Gurney (1804–1878), a QC nearly twenty years her senior who would later become recorder of London and Conservative MP. It was a successful match; the Gurneys were an affectionate couple with a strong intellectual affinity who shared reforming and religious interests. Shortly after their marriage they moved to 8 Kensington Palace Gardens, London, where they lived until Russell Gurney's death. The Gurneys had no children, but in 1862 they became guardians of the five children of Gurney's brother John Hampden *Gurney. They took a house for their wards which the family shared for three years. Although the ages of the children made it unnecessary for Russell and Emelia Gurney to live with them continuously, Emelia formed close ties of affection with them.

Emelia Gurney was one of the original members of the Kensington Society, a debating group for women, and she hosted parties where reformers and feminists could meet. She was known as a woman of great warmth and charm. In 1860, when she was chairing a committee formed by Elizabeth Blackwell to investigate the possibility of opening medical education to women, she was introduced to the young Elizabeth Garrett. The Gurneys helped Garrett take the first steps in her medical education and Emelia became a close friend, advising her on one occasion to use her feminine charms to overcome the hostility of male doctors.

Another friend from the Kensington Society, Emily Davies, who described her as 'heavenly', recruited Emelia to the campaign to admit women to local examinations, and she became one of the 'ladylike ladies' working for the cause (Stephen, 97, 152). She was involved in the establishment of Girton College from its earliest days, participating in the selection of its first site and the formulation of college rules. She approved of the recruitment of George Eliot to the campaign for a women's college, despite some supporters' misgivings about Eliot's personal morality. Emelia Gurney was one of the signatories of the college's articles of association (1872) and was a member of the college from 1872 until her death.

During this period the Gurneys travelled widely, including a trip to Jamaica in 1865, where Russell Gurney served as a commissioner investigating Governor Eyre's response to a recent uprising. She found the scenery beautiful and had some sympathy for the Jamaican people, yet it cannot be said that her appreciation of their culture transcended the prejudices of her time.

Caroline Batten died in 1870; Emelia grieved for her and consoled herself by furnishing a small cottage with mementoes of her mother. In 1871 the Gurneys travelled to Washington, DC, where they were to spend two winters while Russell Gurney acted as commissioner to arbitrate between British and American merchants.

Emelia Gurney's intense spirituality infused all of her work and, as she grew older, absorbed increasing amounts of her attention. In her youth she and her mother derived great spiritual refreshment from visits to Linlathen, home of the Scottish religious thinker Thomas Erskine. After her mother's death Emelia Gurney attended the series of spiritual conferences held at Broadlands, Hampshire, the home of her friends Mr and Mrs Cowper-Temple (later Lord and Lady Mount-Temple), between 1874 and 1888. She was eager to learn from religious teachers and once told her cousin, 'I have an intense pleasure in being converted' (*Letters*, 143). She became increasingly interested in the mystical aspects of Christian faith, linking it to her appreciation of beauty in nature and in art. Her family believed this freed her from 'the oppressive Calvinism of … her early youth' (ibid., 142).

Russell Gurney died suddenly in 1878. Emelia immediately moved to a small house in 3 Orme Square, Bayswater, which the Gurneys had established in 1875 as a convalescent home for women recently discharged from hospital. She desperately tried to fill the void with travel, visiting Palestine in 1883 and Sicily in 1889, by nursing both her convalescents and her friends, and with her religious faith.

About 1885 Emelia began reading Dante's *Divine Comedy* for spiritual nourishment and consolation, and in 1893, after a year of illness, she published *Dante's Pilgrim's Progress*. She had been negotiating for some time to buy a small piece of land on which to build a chapel in central London in memory of her husband. After many delays the Chapel of the Ascension, described by Cherry and Pevsner as 'chaste Italian Quattrocento', with paintings by the religious artist Frederic Shields, opened early in 1896 (Cherry and Pevsner, 673). At the opening of her long-awaited monument to her faith, Emelia Gurney contracted a chest infection, and, after lingering for seven months, died on 17 October 1896 at her home in Orme Square. The Chapel of the Ascension was little used and was demolished some time after 1950. ELIZABETH J. MORSE

**Sources** *Letters of Emelia Russell Gurney*, ed. E. M. Gurney (1902) • Boase, *Mod. Eng. biog.* • B. Stephen, *Emily Davies and Girton College* (1927) • L. Holcombe, *Wives and property: reform of married women's property law in nineteenth-century England* (1983) • F. Galton, *Memories of my life* (1908) • P. Levine, *Feminist lives in Victorian England* (1990) • D. W. Bebbington, *Evangelicalism in modern Britain: a history from the 1730s to the 1980s* (1989) • *The life and letters of Frederic Shields*, ed. E. Mills (1912) • F. Shields, *The Chapel of the Ascension: a descriptive handbook* (1897) • J. Manton, *Elizabeth Garrett Anderson* (1965) • W. B. Sloan, *These sixty years: the story of the Keswick Convention* (1935) • M. M. Hennell, *John Venn and the Clapham Sect* (1958) • *London: north-west*, Pevsner (1991) • d. cert.

**Likenesses** G. F. Watts, oils, 1866, repro. in Gurney, ed., *Letters*, frontispiece; known to be in family possession in 1908

**Wealth at death** £69,451 2s. 8d.: probate, 30 Nov 1896, *CGPLA Eng. & Wales*

**Gurney, Sir Goldsworthy** (1793–1875), surgeon and engineer, was born on 14 February 1793 at Treator, near Padstow, in Cornwall, the fourth son in the family of five sons and a daughter of John Gurney and his wife, Isabell, *née* Carter. He was named after his godmother, a daughter of General Goldsworthy. Educated at Truro grammar school, he spent holidays with a cousin, through whom he met Richard Trevithick, and witnessed some of Trevithick's earliest experiments with steam engines. He was placed with Dr Avery of Wadebridge as a medical student, which encouraged his curiosity in mechanics and chemistry, and before his twentieth birthday he succeeded to Avery's practice, retaining the confidence of Avery's patients. In March 1814 he married Elizabeth Symons, a lady of good family and ten years his senior. Their daughter, Anna Jane, was born the following year.

Sir Goldsworthy Gurney (1793–1875), by William Sharp, pubd 1829 (after Stephen Catterson Smith)

In 1820 Gurney moved his family to London, where he practised as a surgeon at 7 Argyle Street, Soho, supplementing his income by undertaking chemical analyses and giving scientific lectures. A son, John, was born in 1822; a promising child, he graduated from Trinity College, Cambridge, but died in 1847. Gurney soon gained a reputation among professional chemists and public alike as a competent and effective speaker, and in 1822 he was appointed lecturer in chemistry and natural philosophy at the Surrey Institution. These lectures, dealing chiefly with heat, electricity, and gases, were published as *The Elements of Science* in 1823. While preparing his course, Gurney had embarked on numerous experiments, which led him to important discoveries and inventions. For his oxy-hydrogen blowpipe, more powerful, yet safer, than the rather dangerous devices then available, he was awarded the gold Isis medal of the Royal Society of Arts in 1823. In addition, Gurney, whose musical talents had earlier led him to construct an organ, now devised and built an entirely novel instrument, resembling an upright piano, but producing notes by passing silk ribbons over glass. It was said to combine the softness of the musical glasses with the full and sustained tone of the organ, and to entrance all who listened to it; Gurney patented this instrument in 1825 and lent it to the Colosseum in Regent's Park, as one of the attractions. In his lecture on electricity, Gurney demonstrated how electric current passing through a wire placed over a magnetic needle caused the needle to deflect, an effect which in other hands became the basis of telegraphy. He also began the experiments on the steam jet, which came to dominate much of his life, and gave rise to his famous steam carriage.

Gurney's experiments on steam power for road vehicles had to overcome two handicaps which had hitherto retarded progress—the excessive weight of engine and boiler, and the tendency of the traction wheels to skid when power was applied. He began work at Argyle Street on a small model, powered by ammonia gas, which he was able to take up Kilburn Hill. He then rented a workshop in Oxford Street and built his first full-size carriage, which he tested on Windmill Hill, near Edgware. Having obtained a patent for his engine in 1825, and not finding anyone interested in exploiting it, he leased a former infirmary in Albany Street, Regent's Park, where he installed a manufactory, sent for his younger brother Samuel to assist him, and employed workmen to construct his carriages.

While the press reported on the increasingly successful performance of his vehicles, Gurney had to contend with opposition from those who saw their livelihoods threatened by the arrival of road vehicles travelling at 11 or 12 miles per hour, at a quarter the price of horse-drawn transport. He negotiated with several contractors eager to begin public services and, after a number of false starts and short trial runs, the Gurney steam carriage took Colonel Sir Charles Dance and other important figures to Melksham, near Bath, from where it was towed by horses into Bath, and there carried many passengers round the city, before returning under its own power to London. Although various regional services were then started up, Gurney met with increasing hostility, ranging from stone-throwing and the placing of obstacles on the highway ahead of his carriages to the imposition of prohibitive tolls on vehicles moved by machinery. A parliamentary committee was formed in 1831 to investigate the matter, but his hopes of the Toll Relief Bill's becoming law were dashed in 1834. Gurney's losses were considerable. He was obliged to repay contractors who could not afford to run his carriages; his four patents had cost £1200, and his expenditure on the manufactory and its workmen exceeded £25,000, debts which he cleared by the sale of his assets and with money advanced by friends. There was talk of a grant from the government, but nothing materialized.

Gurney retired to Cornwall in 1831, and resumed his interest in chemical lighting. When lecturing at the Surrey Institution he had discovered that both magnesia and lime, placed in the flame of his oxyhydrogen blowpipe, yielded a brilliant light. The lime light was used by Thomas Drummond, who had learned of it from Gurney in 1822, on trigonometrical surveys in Ireland in 1827, whence it became known as the Drummond light. During the period 1839–42 Gurney, in collaboration with others, was granted three patents for lights and burners. His 'Bude light' was generated by introducing oxygen into the hollow interior of an oil-lamp flame, where it combined with carbon and oil vapour to give an intense light. It was named after Gurney's Cornish residence where it had been developed. The Bude light and lime light were both tested by Michael Faraday at Trinity House as lighthouse burners. Another outcome of these experiments was an invitation to Gurney to design lighting for the House of Commons, replacing the 280 candles which added to the heat and stuffiness of the chamber. He arranged for a number of Bude lights to be installed above the chamber, separated by ground-glass plates so as to exclude all heat and fumes, the lights to be focused and reflected into the chamber.

An earlier interest in the lighting and ventilation of coal mines led to Gurney's being asked to deal with underground fires, some of which had burnt for many years, destroying potentially valuable coal and rendering parts of the mine inaccessible. Gurney found that he could smother these fires by passing air through a furnace to remove the oxygen and forcing this down into the depths by drawing up air from another shaft by means of his steam jet. Although Gurney's proposals had initially been scorned by the mine owners, the *Mining Journal* of 1851 paid tribute to the value of his work for the industry; he was also called to address parliamentary commissions on the subject. When the new houses of parliament were under construction in 1852 Gurney's advice was sought on their ventilation; his views were then disregarded, but in 1854 the members appointed a committee to investigate the unpleasant conditions in which they found themselves, and asked again for his assistance.

Gurney was then living in Cornwall. In 1845 he had purchased Hornacott Manor, near Launceston, which he was draining and improving; he was a magistrate for Devon and Cornwall, and was engaged in various agricultural experiments, so that his time was fully taken up, but he nevertheless responded to this appeal. He found that the objectionable smells resulted from the presence of so many people in the chamber, without the circulation of air which would remove body odours and stale breath. He proposed making all the windows to open, and installing a new design of furnace which could pass clean warm air through the building, the apparatus being adaptable in hot weather to cool the circulated air by means of cold water from a deep well. His trial installation was so successful that he was invited to take responsibility for lighting, warming, and ventilating the houses of parliament and, although reluctant to move from Cornwall, he finally accepted, undertaking these duties for £1000 per annum with the title of inspector of ventilation.

After the death of Gurney's first wife, he was married in November 1854 to Jane, the 25 year-old daughter of James Betty, a Devon sheep farmer. Gurney's daughter was forty by this time, which may have led to some conflict in the household. Another daughter, Elizabeth Jane, was born of the second marriage, but Jane and her child were not mentioned in Gurney's will, nor in any of his obituaries, though they both outlived him (Jane Gurney died at Exeter in 1911, and her daughter and son-in-law were at the funeral).

For all his contributions to industry and to the personal comfort of members of parliament, Gurney was meanly treated by those holding the purse-strings. In August 1863 his services were recognized with a knighthood, but the following October he was stricken with paralysis and obliged to resign his government appointment. He spent the rest of his life at Bude, cared for by his daughter Anna Jane, who had always taken a great interest in his discoveries and inventions and accompanied him on many of his formal duties in Cornwall. Gurney died at his home, Reeds, at Poughill, near Bude, on 28 February 1875, having been paralysed for eleven years. He was buried in the churchyard at Launcells. His estate was valued at under £300, possibly owing to his having made financial provision for the various members of his family, for in 1880 Anna Jane Gurney gave £500 towards the building of Truro Cathedral 'in memory of her father, Sir Goldsworthy Gurney, inventor of the steam jet, as a thank offering to almighty God for the benefit of high speed locomotion'. She also gave a turret clock to be installed at Poughill church, and donated a stained-glass window in St Margaret's, Westminster, unveiled in 1892, but destroyed during the Second World War, with its memorial tablet proclaiming Gurney's inventions.

G. B. SMITH, *rev.* ANITA MCCONNELL

**Sources** T. R. Harris, *Sir Goldsworthy Gurney, 1793–1875* (1975) • *The Engineer*, 39 (1875), 184 • *The Times* (26 Dec 1875) • *West Britain and Cornwall Advertiser* (18 March 1875) • *West Britain and Cornwall Advertiser* (8 April 1876) • G. Gurney, *Course of lectures on chemical science* (1823) • G. Gurney, *Observations on steam carriages on turnpike roads, with the report of the House of Commons* (1823) • G. Gurney, *Account of the invention of the steam-jet* (1859) • G. Gurney, *Observations … by which a seaman may identify lighthouses* (1864) • d. cert.

**Archives** Cornwall RO, papers

**Likenesses** W. Sharp, lithograph, pubd 1829 (after S. C. Smith), NPG [*see illus.*] • sketch, repro. in Harris, *Sir Goldsworthy Gurney*, cover

**Wealth at death** under £300: administration with will, 31 March 1875

**Gurney, Sir Henry Lovell Goldsworthy** (1898–1951), colonial administrator, was born at Poughill, Bude, in Cornwall, on 27 June 1898, the only son of Gregory Goldsworthy Henry Gurney, solicitor, and his wife, Florence Mary Lovell, daughter of Edwin Francis Chamier. Educated at Winchester College, he was commissioned into the King's Royal Rifle Corps in 1917 and was wounded shortly before the armistice.

After the war Gurney went as a scholar to University College, Oxford, winning a blue for golf. In 1921 he entered the colonial service, being appointed assistant district commissioner in Kenya. He later transferred to the secretariat, where he flourished. He married Isabel Lowther, daughter of T. Hamilton Weir of Bude, in 1924; they had two sons. In 1935 Gurney was promoted as assistant colonial secretary of Jamaica, but was soon transferred first to the Colonial Office and then back to Kenya in 1936. In 1938 he was appointed secretary to the east African governors' conference, whose role in co-ordinating the territories' defence and supplies grew in importance when Italy entered the Second World War in 1940. He effectively grappled with the complexities of liaising with various territorial, civil, and military authorities; his post was upgraded to chief secretary in 1941 and he was appointed CMG in 1942.

In 1944 Gurney was promoted to colonial secretary of the Gold Coast under Sir Alan Burns. Two years later he was transferred to the chief secretaryship of Palestine. He thereby missed the chance of promotion to a senior governorship in 1947, although he was rewarded with a knighthood. The Balfour declaration of 1917 had committed Britain to support the formation of a Jewish national home in Palestine without prejudicing the rights of non-Jewish (particularly Arab) communities. By 1946 these principles were irreconcilable and the British were the targets of the armed Jewish Irgun and Haganah forces and ran into opposition from international supporters of Zionism, especially in America. Rather than implement the UN resolution of November 1947 in favour of partition, the British decided to return the mandate to the UN and to withdraw by mid-May 1948. In doing so, they forfeited the respect of Arabs, provoked the hostility of Jews, and incurred considerable international opprobrium. Throughout these months Gurney's imperturbable even-handedness became legendary, winning him the loyalty of subordinates, and the respect of the military, but the hatred of some Jews.

Gurney was nearly fifty when he left Palestine and contemplated retiring, possibly to superintend the training of colonial service probationers at Oxford. Instead he was selected for Malaya, a valuable dependency which had been plunged into crisis in June 1948 with the outbreak of communist insurrection and the recall and subsequent death in an air crash of its high commissioner, Sir Edward Gent. Gurney was not keen on going to Malaya; having no knowledge of the country, he would have preferred another posting in Africa or the governorship of British Honduras, or Mauritius, or Cyprus. Moreover, European and local leaders in Malaya felt that the emergency called for someone with Malayan experience, or a senior colonial governor, or a major public figure. None the less, his calm temperament and clear thinking, his experience of liaising with the military, his administrative skills and proven ability to plan for the long term, together with the full endorsement of Sir Andrew Cunningham and Sir Alan Burns (Gurney's chiefs in Palestine and the Gold Coast respectively) made him the first choice of Arthur Creech Jones, secretary of state for the colonies. Acting once again for the public good, Gurney accepted.

Having to attend to family obligations in Britain, Gurney was not installed as high commissioner until early October 1948, three months after Gent's death. During the interregnum the federation of Malaya had been administered by Sir Alec Newboult in close collaboration with Malcolm MacDonald, commissioner-general in south-east Asia in 1948–55. Gurney swiftly set about investigating the causes of unrest and methods of countering it. He soon concluded that the heart of the problem lay in the alienated Chinese squatters on jungle fringes who, unlike the Malays, had little sense of belonging to Malaya and were easy prey for insurgents. Long before the notion of 'winning hearts and minds' was propagated during the Templer era, Gurney recognized that successful counter-insurgency would depend on gaining the confidence of Malaya's Chinese community. Although the British relied on Malay support, Gurney did all he could to promote good relations between Malays and Chinese lest insurgency and counter-insurgency transform the country into 'another Palestine'.

As high commissioner of Malaya in 1948–51, Gurney was frequently upstaged by Malcolm MacDonald and subsequently overshadowed by his successor, General Sir Gerald Templer (high commissioner, 1952–4). MacDonald exuded charm, and enjoyed company and conversation; he mingled easily with the new generation of Asians and also operated at a more elevated level of government than did the high commissioner. Wielding powers never enjoyed by Gurney, Templer has been credited with winning the emergency and setting Malaya on course for independence. By contrast, Gurney's civil service manner misled the less perceptive to underrate him: he was criticized by some for concentrating on a largely repressive campaign, yet by others for failing to invigorate that campaign. In fact his experiences in Palestine dissuaded him from martial law and encouraged him to focus on policing as the key to victory in what he believed was a civilian war. His assessment that insurgents depended upon food and information extracted from the rural Chinese resulted in the Briggs plan to isolate guerrilla fighters from vital supplies by compulsorily resettling half a million squatters in protected villages. In addition, looking beyond the emergency to an ultimately self-governing Malaya, Gurney introduced the quasi-ministerial member system, prepared more generous citizenship provisions for non-Malays, planned Malaya's first local elections, assisted at the birth of the Malayan Chinese Association (which would become a member of the post-colonial Alliance government), promoted the Rural and Industrial Development Authority in support of the economically disadvantaged Malay community, and set up the Employee Provident Fund, which helped sustain in old age Malayan workers of all races. Nevertheless, it was success in the emergency by which he was judged at the time, and in this he was hamstrung by the complexities of the federal constitution, disputes between the administrative, police, and military arms of government, and Chinese reluctance to side openly with the authorities. In 1951 counter-insurgency became bogged down and Gurney reached the end of his tether, proffering his resignation in April. The offer was declined, but ministers had begun to think that a new type of high commissioner was needed, a supremo who combined both civil and military power.

On 6 October 1951 Gurney's car was ambushed on its way from Kuala Lumpur to the hill station at Fraser's Hill. Courageous and composed to the last, Gurney got out of the car to draw the fire away from his wife and secretary. For the British, Gurney's death was the lowest point in the emergency, yet in many ways he had laid the foundations for their eventual success and Malayan independence, a contribution which was generously acknowledged by General Templer, the supremo whom Churchill appointed to succeed him in February 1952.

A. J. STOCKWELL

**Sources** *DNB* • A. J. Stockwell, ed., *Malaya*, 3 vols. (1995), ser. B/3 of *British documents on the end of empire* • A. Short, *The communist insurrection in Malaya, 1948–1960* (1975) • R. Stubbs, *Hearts and minds in guerrilla warfare: the Malayan emergency, 1948–1960* (1989) • A. J. Stockwell, 'British imperial policy and decolonization in Malaya, 1942–52', *Journal of Imperial and Commonwealth History*, 13 (1984–5), 68–87 • W. R. Louis, *Imperialism at bay, 1945–1951: the United States and the decolonization of the British empire* (1977) • R. Heussler, *Completing a stewardship* (1983) • N. Shepherd, *Ploughing sand: British rule in Palestine, 1917–1948* (1999) • *CGPLA Eng. & Wales* (1952) • *The Times* (8 Oct 1951)

**Archives** Bodl. RH, agricultural reports relating to Kenya • St Ant. Oxf., MSS | Bodl. RH, colonial records project; Heussler MSS • PRO, Colonial Office county series | FILM Granada TV, *End of Empire: Malaya* (1985)

**Likenesses** H. Speed, oils, legislative council chamber, Kuala Lumpur, Malaysia

**Wealth at death** £30,095 13*s*. 4*d*.: probate, 31 July 1952, *CGPLA Eng. & Wales*

**Gurney, Henry Palin** (1847–1904), educationist, was born on 7 September 1847 in London, the eldest son of Henry Gurney and his wife, Eleanor Palin. In 1856 he went to the City of London School, where he won the Beaufoy mathematical medal and was head of the school in science in 1865. He went up in 1866 to Clare College, Cambridge, where he read natural science and mathematics. He was a keen sportsman, running the mile for the university in 1868 and 1869, and rowing for his college. In 1870 he graduated fourth in the first class of the natural science tripos, and fourteenth wrangler in mathematics.

Gurney studied mineralogy and crystallography under William Hallowes Miller, whose highly mathematical and abstract approach had made it a branch of applied geometry, and for a time acted as his deputy. In 1875, his *Crystallography*, an elementary primer, was published by SPCK; it ran to several editions. He was one of the founders of the Crystallogical Society in 1876 and served on its first council. He also became a fellow of the Geological, Physical, and Mineralogical societies. In April 1870 he was elected to a fellowship in his college, which he held until 1883. In 1871 he was ordained, and he always took his clerical duties seriously. He was curate in the college living of Rotherhithe, and then (1876–86) at St Peter's, Bayswater.

In 1872 at Whitchurch, Herefordshire, Gurney married Louisa, daughter of the Revd E. Selby Hele of Grays, Essex. To support a wife and growing family, ultimately of nine daughters, among them Louisa *Gurney, he began teaching at Walter Wren's tutorial establishment, in Powis Square, Bayswater, London, a 'crammer' which prepared people for entrance examinations for the Indian and the home civil services, and the armed services. Gurney was exceptionally good at this work, where his mathematical background and teaching and administrative skills were helpful, and in 1877 he became managing partner of the firm, thereafter called Wren and Gurney. Many subsequently eminent men passed through it.

In 1894 Gurney was appointed principal of the Durham College of Science in Newcastle upon Tyne. William Charles Lake, dean of Durham and vice-chancellor, was keen to build up in Newcastle a college of science, affiliated to the University of Durham, as a genuine university college, teaching humanities as well as physical sciences and engineering. Dr William Garnett, Gurney's predecessor appointed in 1883, had promoted the scheme, a site had been bought in 1886, and work on the college begun the following year, though there was still some prejudice against university training for engineers, which had stifled earlier attempts to teach engineering in Durham. When Gurney arrived in 1894 the buildings were three-quarters completed, but the college was burdened by serious debt.

In post, Gurney took upon himself the chair of mathematics, and also lectured in mineralogy in addition to his administrative tasks. He also encouraged social and sporting activity among the students. Teaching of the arts began in connection with training teachers for secondary schools, by which Gurney set much store. In 1896 the University of Durham conferred upon him the degree of DCL. In 1901 further funds raised in memory of Lord Armstrong were devoted to the completion of the buildings, and the college, by now on a firmer footing, duly took Armstrong's name. Gurney also served on education committees and governing bodies of schools in the city of Newcastle, and acted as chaplain to the Rt Revd A. T. Lloyd, bishop of Newcastle, and also as warden of the diocesan house for fallen women. This trying and difficult work, as his bishop called it, took up his time at weekends.

Gurney's blend of what the bishop saw as high intellectual power and deep spirituality, as an ordained man of science, made him acceptable to both the Durham and Newcastle parts of the University of Durham. To a secular institution, just beginning to make its way, he brought the respectability and values associated with churchmen, and he left Armstrong College, Newcastle, in a strong position at his premature death. He was thus a participant in two of the major developments in education in nineteenth-century England: the coming of competitive examinations, and consequently of the crammers who prepared young gentlemen for them; and the rise of civic, 'red-brick', university colleges, later provincial universities.

On 13 August 1904, climbing alone on La Rousette at Arolla in Switzerland, Gurney fell 400 feet to his death. His body was found two days later, and brought home for burial at Ganerew, Herefordshire. He left a substantial estate. His wife survived him. DAVID KNIGHT

**Sources** A. T. Lloyd, *The Guardian* (24 Aug 1904) • *The Times* (16 Aug 1904) • *The Times* (23 Aug 1904) • *DNB* • C. E. Whiting, *The University of Durham, 1832–1932* (1932) • J. T. Fowler, *Durham University: earlier foundations and present colleges* (1904) • H. P. Gurney, 'A sketch of the history of the Durham college of science at Newcastle', *Memorials of William Charles Lake, dean of Durham, 1869–1894*, ed. K. Lake (1901), 330–32, appx • *CGPLA Eng. & Wales* (1904) • *DNB*

**Likenesses** A. H. Marsh, oils, 1906, U. Newcastle • C. Neuper, bust, U. Newcastle

**Wealth at death** £54,750 8*s*. 3*d*.: probate, 6 Oct 1904, *CGPLA Eng. & Wales*

**Gurney, Hudson** (1775–1864), antiquary and banker, was born in the Old Courthouse, Magdalen Street, Norwich, on 19 January 1775, the only son of Richard Gurney (1742–1811) and his first wife, Agatha Barclay (1753–1776). Both his parents were from Quaker families much involved in banking; his father was chief partner in the Gurney family's Norwich bank, and his mother was the daughter and heir of David *Barclay (1729–1809) of Youngsbury, Hertfordshire. The Anglo-Saxon scholar Anna *Gurney (1795–1857) was his half-sister.

Gurney was privately educated in the home of his maternal grandfather at Youngsbury, where he was joined (in 1787) by Thomas Young (1773–1829). Young had been intended as a fellow pupil and companion for Gurney but, following the failure of a tutor to turn up, ended up leading a small 'study-group' comprising himself, Gurney, and John Hodgkin (1766–1845).

In 1796 or 1797 Gurney became a partner in the Yarmouth branch of the family bank and in 1800, following the retirement of his kinsman Bartlett Gurney (1756–1803), he gained an interest in the main Norwich bank itself. During the peace of Amiens he spent some time in Paris and travelled to Rome in the company of his close friend George Gordon, fourth earl of Aberdeen (1784–1860), and George Whittington (*d.* 1807), a Cambridge ordinand. Gurney's experiences in Napoleonic France, which included a narrow escape from internment, led him, following the resumption of hostilities in 1803, to contribute to a military fund for the defence of Norfolk from invasion. As a result, he was disowned by the Quakers.

On 27 September 1809, at Marylebone church, Gurney married Margaret (Mag) Barclay Allardice (1779/80–1855), daughter of Robert Barclay Allardice (1732–1797), MP for Kincardineshire, and his wife, Sarah Anne Allardice. They had no children. In the same year David Barclay died and left Gurney the majority of his great wealth. Gurney inherited another fortune on the death of his father in 1811, and greatly enlarged both through investments in the brewery of Barclay, Perkins & Co. With his financial future secured his interest turned to politics and he became MP for Shaftesbury in 1812 (although he was unseated on petition the following year). He was returned to the Commons in 1816 as a paying guest of Sir Fitzwilliam Barrington for his nomination borough of Newtown, Isle of Wight, and held the seat until it was disenfranchised in 1832. Politically, Gurney was something of a gadfly, whose quirky independent stance led a radical commentator in 1831 to brand him 'a strange, unintelligible kind of person' (Carpenter, 271–2). He supported Catholic relief and opposed the Reform Act. Although not a forceful speaker, he gained a reputation as a pundit on fiscal matters. During the banking crisis of 1826 he led the delegation of bankers who forced a government climb-down over a proposed ban on the circulation of small notes, allegedly by threatening a run on the Bank of England. He had an ingrained distrust of theoreticians, notably Malthus, Ricardo, and especially Bentham, and was wary of legislative interference in general. Always averse to popular politics, he made no attempt to enter the reformed House of Commons.

Although he was a major partner in the family business from 1803 (when the firm was renamed Richard, John, Joseph, and Hudson Gurney) until his retirement in 1832, banking was never really to Gurney's taste. Indeed, it has since been said that his only real ambition was to 'write one good poem' (Anderson, opposite p. 161). His first publication, a privately printed *English History and Chronology in Rhyme*, was followed in 1799 by *Cupid and Psyche*, a verse 'translation' from Apuleius's comedy *The Golden Ass*. In 1814 he published *Heads of Ancient History from the Deluge to the Partition of Alexander's Empire*. *Observations on the Bayeux Tapestry* (1717) argued for the authenticity of the subject. In 1818 he was elected a fellow of the Society of Antiquaries, of which he was a vice-president from 1822 to 1846. For *Archaeologia* he wrote on English antiquities and the Bayeux tapestry, and in 1831 he printed a *Memoir of the Life of Thomas Young*, as an introduction to his former tutor's Egyptian dictionary. The antiquary Dawson Turner, who shared a Norfolk banking background, was a frequent correspondent and collaborator in antiquarian pursuits: they locked horns notably over Gurney's contention that Norwich had been the headquarters of the Iceni. He was a member of the British Archaeological Association (from 1843), and served as vice-president of the Norfolk and Norwich Archaeological Society. He was also elected FRS in 1818, but his interest in science seems to have been more academic than practical. However, he did materially support the researches of others, including the Gurneys' bank clerk Samuel Woodward (1790–1838). He later assisted Woodward's widow by organizing completion and publication of two of her husband's unfinished works. Gurney also employed Woodward's son, Samuel Pickforth Woodward (1821–1865), to catalogue his library of between ten and fifteen thousand volumes (of which he claimed to have read every one).

Following his retirement from business and politics in 1832, Gurney devoted much of his time to the building of a new and immensely grand Keswick Hall, near Norwich. However, he remained active in local affairs and served as high sheriff of Norfolk in 1835. He was a keen supporter of the Norwich Museum and Literary Institute, and a number of other local 'institutions of public utility … for religious, charitable … [and] sanitary purposes' (*GM*, new ser., 18, 109) also benefited from his generosity. He was considered liberal, kind, and hospitable, and his St James's residence, to which he moved in 1824, was 'for many years the resort of the *élite* of parliamentary and literary society' (ibid., 109–10). He was knowledgeable on a wide range of topics but, despite his affability, questioned everything and 'seemed never to agree with you' (*DNB*).

In 1843 Gurney had privately published a rendering, in English verse, of parts of Ludivico Ariosto's *Orlando Furioso*. From about this time, his health began to decline, though he lived another twenty years. He died at Keswick Hall on 9 November 1864, and was buried at Intwood churchyard, near Norwich, on 15 November. He left behind voluminous notes and diaries, a testament to grand literary aspirations that had fallen victim to his self-proclaimed indolence. For all that he died a millionaire; as he once observed, in all but revolutionary conditions, 'the banker holds the bag to those who have something to put in it' (Anderson, 283). PETER OSBORNE

**Sources** *DNB* • *GM*, 3rd ser., 18 (1865), 108–10 • V. Anderson, *Friends and relations: three centuries of Quaker families* (1980) • Burke, *Gen. GB* • P. Matthews, *History of Barclay's Bank, including the many private and joint stock banks amalgamated and affiliated with it* (1926) • *GM*, 1st ser., 79 (1809), 885 • [H. Gurney], *Memoir of the life of Thomas Young … with a catalogue of his works and essays* (1831) • private information (2004) [V. Anderson] • HoP, *Commons, 1820–32* [draft] • W. Carpenter, *The people's book: containing their chartered rights and practical wrongs* (1831) • d. cert.

**Archives** Norfolk RO, corresp. and papers • NRA, priv. coll., diary • Religious Society of Friends, Birmingham, corresp. and papers • S. Antiquaries, Lond., travel journal and verse translations | BL, letters to Lord Aberdeen, Add. MSS 43229–43255, *passim* • Bodl. Oxf., corresp. with Sir Thomas Phillips • RBG Kew, letters to Sir William Jackson Hooker • RS, corresp. with Sir J. F. W. Herschel • Trinity Cam., letters to Dawson Turner • Wellcome L., corresp. with Hodgkin family

**Likenesses** J. Cochran, stipple, 1823 (after A. Wivell), BM, NPG • Turner, etching (after J. Opie), BM, NPG

**Wealth at death** under £1,100,000 in England: probate, 12 Dec 1864, *CGPLA Eng. & Wales*

**Gurney, Ivor Bertie** (1890–1937), composer and poet, was born at 3 Queen Street, Gloucester, on 28 August 1890, the elder son and second in the family of two boys and two girls of David Gurney (1872–1919), proprietor of a small tailoring business, and his wife, Florence (1861–1945), daughter of William Lugg, house decorator. He was educated at the King's School as a chorister of Gloucester Cathedral, then as an articled pupil of the cathedral organist, A. Herbert Brewer, and finally, on winning a composition scholarship (1911), at the Royal College of Music under Sir Charles Stanford. During these formative years he owed much of his musical, literary, and intellectual development to his godfather, the Revd Alfred Hunter Cheesman (1865–1941), vicar of St Matthew's Church, Twigworth, near Gloucester. Cheesman, a philanthropic bachelor, made his large library available to the young Gurney and provided a stimulus and encouragement that was not available in his home and scarcely available at any of his official places of education.

Though rejected by the army in 1914 on grounds of defective eyesight, Gurney enlisted on 9 February 1915 while still a student and from 25 May 1916 served in France as a private with the 2nd/5th Gloucesters. He sustained a minor bullet wound on Good Friday 1917 and more serious gas injuries on or about 10 September 1917 during the third battle of Ypres (Passchendaele). He spent time in various war hospitals in England and, after showing signs of mental instability (including a suicide attempt on 19 June 1918), he was finally discharged in October 1918.

Gurney resumed his studies at the Royal College of Music, this time under Ralph Vaughan Williams, but could not concentrate. He returned to Gloucester and, failing to find permanent employment, had to live on a small

**Ivor Bertie Gurney** (1890–1937), by unknown photographer

disability pension and the charity of friends and family. Music now poured from him, but his behaviour (eccentric before the war) grew increasingly erratic. Further threats of suicide followed, and in September 1922 he was diagnosed as suffering from paranoid schizophrenia and was committed to Barnwood House Asylum, Gloucester. On 21 December 1922 he was transferred to the City of London Mental Hospital, near Dartford, Kent, where he remained until his death.

Opinions vary as to the origins of Gurney's mental problems. Although it would be unwise to dismiss his wartime experiences as a contributory factor, the source seems more likely to have been genetic and stemming from his mother's side of the family. Signs of instability were evident before the war, while the companionship of his fellow soldiers seems, by virtue of their shared suffering, to have afforded him a rare degree of stability. This evaporated as soon as he was granted his discharge and had to face the world alone. As a composer Gurney found his voice in 1913–14 with the composition of *Five Elizabethan Songs*. Although he wrote chamber and orchestral music, songs were his true vocation. Manuscripts of more than 300 are to be found in the Gurney archive at Gloucester Public Library. Poetry was a secondary interest that grew only when conditions in the trenches made composition almost impossible (he nevertheless did write several fine songs in the trenches). After the war he pursued both arts with equal fervour.

Gurney's songs began to find publishers from 1920 onwards. His two Housman cycles, *Ludlow and Teme* and *The Western Playland*, were included as part of the Carnegie Collection of British Music in 1923 and 1926 respectively. Both were scored for solo voice, piano, and string quartet and greatly enhanced his reputation as a composer of substance. However, it was not until the Oxford University Press issued two volumes of twenty songs in 1938 that his true stature could be appreciated. Further collections followed in 1952, 1959, and 1979, made possible by the faith and industry of Gurney's friend the musicologist Marion Scott (1877–1953), who had saved his manuscripts, and the editorial expertise of the composers Gerald Finzi and Howard Ferguson. His manuscripts pose great ethical and aesthetic problems because so much of his work is uneven, unpolished, and sometimes incoherent.

Similar considerations afflict his poetry, of which over 1700 items exist in the Gloucester archive. Two volumes were published during Gurney's lifetime: *Severn and Somme* (1917) and *War's Embers* (1919); and minor selections appeared in 1954 and 1973, edited by Edmund Blunden and Leonard Clark respectively. In 1982 the Oxford University Press issued a major selection of some 300 poems, edited by P. J. Kavanagh, and it was on the basis of this volume that his importance as a poet came to be recognized. Further evidence of the breadth of his literary abilities came with the publication in 1983 of his *War Letters*, and in 1991 of his *Collected Letters*, both edited by R. K. R. Thornton. In 1995 two volumes, *Best Poems* and *The Book of Five Makings*, which Gurney himself had planned and titled, were edited by R. K. R. Thornton and George Walter and issued under one cover by the Carcanet Press. A similar volume, *80 Poems or so*, from the same editors and publisher, followed in 1997. Since 1995 the establishment of an Ivor Gurney Society, which issues an annual journal (vol. 1, August 1995), has provided a focus for research into his life and work.

Gurney's poems celebrate his love of the Gloucestershire countryside with the same unsentimental vigour as they report on the realities of trench warfare and chart his gradual descent into madness. His songs are equally forceful and direct, covering a wide range of emotional expression and empathizing with poets of every period, particularly his contemporaries, the Georgians. In both fields he was an individualist, and in both his successes mark him out as an artist of power and originality.

Gurney died from tuberculosis on 26 December 1937 at the City of London Mental Hospital, Stone, near Dartford, Kent. He was buried on 31 December in St Matthew's churchyard at Twigworth, near Gloucester. He was unmarried. MICHAEL HURD

**Sources** M. Hurd, *The ordeal of Ivor Gurney* (1978) • *Collected letters: Ivor Gurney*, ed. R. K. R. Thornton (1991) • *Collected poems of Ivor Gurney*, ed. P. J. Kavanagh (1982) • A. Boden, *Stars in a dark night* (1986) • b. cert. • *CGPLA Eng. & Wales* (1938) • records of Dartford Mental Hospital, 21 Dec 1922–26 Dec 1937 • parish register, Gloucester, All Saints' Church, Lower Barton Street [baptism]

**Archives** Gloucester Public Library, corresp. and papers | SOUND BL NSA, 'Child of joy: an appreciation of Ivor Gurney', NP7138WRTR1 • BL NSA, documentary recordings • BL NSA, 'Ivor

Gurney: the poet and his songs', T2671BWBD1 · BL NSA, oral history interview · BL NSA, performance recordings
**Likenesses** R. Hall, portrait studies, *c*.1921, Gloucester Public Library, Gloucestershire collection · photograph, BL [*see illus.*] · photographs, Gloucester Public Library, Gloucestershire collection
**Wealth at death** £43 0s. 11*d*.: administration, 26 Feb 1938, *CGPLA Eng. & Wales*

**Gurney, John** (1688/9–1741), Quaker minister and wool stapler, was the son of John Gurney (1655–1721), a Quaker merchant of Norwich, who had been imprisoned from 1683 to 1685 for refusing the oath of allegiance and who brought up his family strictly in his own faith. With his wife, Elizabeth Swanton (*d.* 1728), the elder John Gurney had four sons. John, the eldest, was born in the parish of St Gregory, Norwich, on 16 July 1688 or 1689 and continued his father's business, thus becoming one 'of the wealthiest and principal merchants of Norwich' (Gurney, pt 3, 511). He married, on 9 August 1709, Elizabeth (*d.* 1757), daughter of Joseph Hadduck of Little Barningham, Norfolk. The marriage gave John Gurney the manor of Little Barningham. His two sons, John and Henry, were the founders of Gurney's Bank in Norwich in 1775; his descendants in the male line became extinct on the death of Bartlett Gurney of Cottishall in 1803; his brother Joseph was ancestor of the Gurneys of Keswick.

Having experienced a deepening of his faith in late youth Gurney was accepted as a Quaker minister at the age of about twenty-two. He won respect throughout the Society of Friends as a minister and as an active participant in the society's affairs and discipline, at both local and national levels. 'Great regard was paid to his judgement, not only in Monthly and Quarterly Meetings, but also in the Yearly Meeting at London' (*A Collection of Testimonies*, 134–7). At the yearly meeting in London in 1719, although personally satisfied in the matter, Gurney proposed a fresh approach to the government to secure a revised form of legal affirmation for those Quakers who could not conscientiously accept the existing words, and he played a leading part in securing this in 1721–2.

Norwich at that time was the centre of the East Anglian woollen industry, and in 1720 Gurney defended the interests of the woollen trade against the East India Company; in so doing he helped to secure an act which prohibited the wearing of calicoes. For this he won much popularity in Norwich and found himself called the Weavers' Advocate, or Friend. The legislation proved ineffective and inadvertently encouraged the domestic cotton industry in the long term. Gurney enjoyed the friendship of Sir Robert Walpole and his brother Horace but he declined Walpole's offer of a parliamentary seat for reasons of religious scruple as well as legal disability to accept.

A sermon which Gurney gave at Gracechurch Street meeting-house, London, in 1733, and which was taken down by Thomas Crowley, was printed in that year and again in 1785. A brief address on godliness, well grounded in scripture, it shows the practical character of Gurney's ministry, with a specific appeal to the young on that occasion. Verses in the *London Magazine* of 1736 celebrated the quality and integrity of Gurney's spoken contributions (Axon). He died at Norwich, after a long and painful illness, on 23 January 1741, aged fifty-two, and was mourned by the wider civic community as well as by Quakers.

H. F. Gregg

**Sources** D. Gurney, ed., *The record of the house of Gournay*, 4 vols. (1848–58) · digest registers of births, marriages, and burials, RS Friends, Lond. [Norfolk and Norwich quarterly meetings; microfilm, reel 6] · *A collection of testimonies* (1760) · W. E. A. Axon, 'Some Quaker teachers in 1736', *Journal of the Friends' Historical Society*, 5 (1908), 47 · R. Brown, *Society and economy in modern Britain, 1700–1850* (1991) · J. Smith, ed., *A descriptive catalogue of Friends' books*, 2 vols. (1867); suppl. (1893) · *A journal of the life of Thomas Story: containing an account of his remarkable convincement of, and embracing the principles of truth, as held by the people called Quakers*, ed. J. Wilson and J. Wilson (1747) · W. C. Braithwaite, *The second period of Quakerism*, ed. H. J. Cadbury, 2nd edn (1961) · J. K. Edwards, 'The Gurneys and the Norwich clothing trade in the eighteenth century', *Journal of the Friends' Historical Society*, 50 (1962–4), 134–5 · A. Raistrick, *Quakers in science and industry* (1950) · W. H. Bidwell, *Annals of an East Anglian bank* (1900) · A. J. C. Hare, *The Gurneys of Earlham*, 2 vols. (1895) · P. H. Emden, *Quakers in commerce: a record of business achievement* (1939) · Burke, *Gen. GB* (1965–72), vol. 1
**Likenesses** J. Basire (after ancient print), repro. in Gurney, *The record of the house of Gournay*, facing p. 552 · engraving, repro. in A. J. C. Hare, *The Gurneys of Earlham* (1895), vol. 1, p. 11

**Gurney, Sir John** (1768–1845), judge, was born in London on 14 February 1768, the son of Joseph *Gurney (1744–1815) of Walworth, legal and parliamentary stenographer [*see under* Gurney, Thomas], and his wife, who was the daughter of William Brodie of Mansfield. His grandfather, Thomas *Gurney, and his brother, William Brodie *Gurney, were also stenographers. He was educated partly at St Paul's School and partly by the Revd Mr Smith of Bottesdale, Suffolk. Through attending debating societies and accompanying his father in his duties in court he also received an informal grounding in the law and decided to become a lawyer. He was called to the bar at the Inner Temple on 3 May 1793. He married Maria, daughter of William Hawes MD; they had several children, including Russell *Gurney and John Hampden *Gurney.

Gurney applied himself to Old Bailey practice and joined the home circuit. He distinguished himself on 24 February 1794, during the absence of his leader, by successfully defending the bookseller Daniel Isaac Eaton in an action for libel. As a result, he was chosen junior counsel for the defence in the state trials of Thomas Hardy, John Horne Tooke, and John Thelwall in the same year, and in 1796 defended Robert Thomas Crossfield, who was charged with complicity in the Popgun Plot. In 1798 he appeared for Arthur O'Connor and others on the charge of high treason, and summed up their defence.

Being now leader of the Middlesex sessions, and having a good practice at Westminster Hall, Gurney applied for a patent of precedence as a king's counsel, but it was refused him. He did not obtain this status until in 1816 when he won it by his great skill in conducting the prosecution of Lord Cochrane and Cochrane Johnstone, accused of spreading false rumours of Bonaparte's death to make profit in the stock exchange. Against rivals as great as James Scarlett and John Copley he held the first place in the king's bench, and was also leader of the home circuit. In 1820 he conducted the prosecution of two of the Cato Street conspirators, and procured their conviction. On 13 February 1832 he was appointed a baron of the exchequer and knighted. In January 1845 he was compelled by failing health to retire. He died on 1 March 1845 at his house in Lincoln's Inn Fields. In both his private and public life Gurney was much esteemed. He was a good criminal lawyer, though not deeply learned, and was an independent and acute, but severe and somewhat harsh judge. In his early years he was a dissenter, but latterly he attended the services of the Church of England.

J. A. Hamilton, *rev.* Catherine Pease-Watkin

**Sources** Foss, *Judges* • *State trials*, 22.27; 30.711, 1341 • *Law Magazine*, 34 (1845), 278 • W. Ballantine, *Some experiences of a barrister's life*, 1 (1882), 262 • *Life of John, Lord Campbell, lord high chancellor of Great Britain*, ed. Mrs Hardcastle, 1 (1881), 221 • *Annual Register* (1845)
**Archives** Glamorgan RO, Cardiff, opinion on the criminal law consolidation bill
**Likenesses** W. Holl, stipple, pubd 1821 (after G. H. Harlow), BM, NPG • G. Richmond, group portrait, ink, pencil, and wash, *c.*1840–1845, NPG • J. Posselwhite, stipple (after G. Richmond), BM, NPG • lithograph, NPG • stipple, BM

**Gurney, John Hampden** (1802–1862), Church of England clergyman and writer, was the eldest son of the lawyer Sir John *Gurney (1768–1845) and his wife, Maria Hawes, daughter of William Hawes MD, chief founder of the Royal Humane Society. He was the brother of Russell *Gurney (1804–1878). Born at 12 Serjeants' Inn, Fleet Street, London, on 15 August 1802, Gurney was educated at Chobham School, Surrey, and at Trinity College, Cambridge, where he matriculated in 1819. He took a BA in 1824 and an MA in 1827. After studying law he decided to take holy orders, and was ordained deacon in 1827 and priest in 1829 by the bishop of Lincoln.

From 1827 to 1844 Gurney was curate of Lutterworth, Leicestershire—John Wyclif's last home—and from 1841 was chaplain to the Lutterworth poor-law union. Gurney's years at Lutterworth were crucial to his development as man and priest. On 20 December 1837 he preached a memorial sermon to Wyclif, whom he praised as the man who 'brought the book of God out of its hiding place and read it in the ears of all the people' (J. H. Gurney, *Sermon on Erecting a Memorial to John Wyclif*, 1838, 25). Gurney understood the power of music, and in 1838 produced a collection of hymns, followed in 1852 by *Psalms and Hymns for Public Worship, Selected for some of the Churches in Marylebone*. On 24 October 1839, in Edinburgh, Gurney married Mary Grey (*d.* 1857), eldest daughter of Henry *Grey (1778–1859), minister of St Mary's, Edinburgh; she shared her husband's love of music. The couple had three sons and six daughters, including Edmund *Gurney (1847–1888), the psychical researcher.

At Lutterworth, Gurney began lecturing to his parishioners in an attempt to raise rural standards of education for adults: 'what is school learning, after all,' he wrote, 'when children are turned out to be workers under twelve?' (J. H. Gurney, *Evening Recreations, or, Samples from the Lecture Room*, 1856, ix). He also supported educational and religious organizations, lecturing to mechanics' institutes, to the Young Men's Christian Association, and to the Society for Promoting Christian Knowledge. He was fascinated by history, which he embellished with Christian morals: in 'The fall of Mexico' he wrote that Cortes had 'a life adorned with brilliant achievements, and disgraced by some outrageous crimes' (ibid., 140). Perceiving the need for children's history books to bridge the gap between textbooks for younger children and multi-volumed scholarly histories, he later rewrote the lectures in a romantic and dramatic style, working in his holidays so as not to interfere with his parochial duties.

In 1844 Gurney left Lutterworth for London, where he became secretary to the Scripture Readers' Association and to the Royal Humane Society. His father died in 1845, leaving him his fortune. Soon afterwards, on 6 December 1847, Gurney was presented to the crown living of St Mary's, Bryanston Square, London, and he remained there until his death, becoming a popular preacher. His independent means relieved him of the necessity of seeking further preferment, and he became an important figure in the London religious world, offering generous assistance, as well as money, to local charities and to poorer priests in the East End. He wrote over twenty books of sermons, six books of hymns and psalms (which were constantly reprinted), seven volumes of *Historical Sketches*, and several pamphlets dealing with social problems. Unusually for a Church of England clergyman, he supported the repeal of the law forbidding marriage with a deceased wife's sister: 'If I were a Demagogue,' he wrote, 'wanting to rouse the passions of the working classes against the injustice of the rich man's legislation, I would not wish for a better topic' (W. W. Champneys and others, *Marriage with a Deceased Wife's Sister: Letters in Favour of a Repeal of the Law which prohibits Marriage with the Sister of a Deceased Wife*, 1849, 10).

Mrs Gurney died in 1857, the year in which Gurney was made a prebendary of St Pancras in St Paul's Cathedral, London. He continued to work at a headlong pace until he died suddenly of typhoid fever at his home, 63 Gloucester Place, Portman Square, London, on 8 March 1862. His brother, Russell Gurney, became guardian of his orphaned children. In a memorial sermon the Revd Brownlow Maitland described Gurney as 'a true, magnanimous and single-hearted man' (Maitland, 6).

Brenda Colloms

**Sources** *GM*, 3rd ser., 12 (1862), 783–4 • Venn, *Alum. Cant.* • B. Maitland, *Sermon on J. H. Gurney* (1862) • E. M. Goulburn, *Sermon on J. H. Gurney* (1862) • A. W. Thorold, *Sermon on J. H. Gurney* (1862) • T. H. Hall, *The strange case of Edmund Gurney* (1964) • Crockford (1860) • d. cert. • *DNB*
**Likenesses** photograph, repro. in *Church of England photographic portrait gallery* (1859), pl. xl
**Wealth at death** under £70,000: resworn probate, July 1862, *CGPLA Eng. & Wales*

**Gurney, Joseph** (1744–1815). *See under* Gurney, Thomas (1705–1770).

**Gurney, Joseph** (1804–1879), shorthand writer and biblical scholar, was the eldest son of William Brodie *Gurney (1777–1855), the philanthropist, and his wife, whose maiden name was Benham (*d.* 1830). He was born in London on 15 October 1804, a year after his parents' marriage, but details of his childhood and education are not known.

He acted as secretary to his first important committee of the House of Commons in 1822, and he continued to take notes until 1872. He was married twice: first to Emma (*d.* 1842), daughter of E. Rawlings, with whom he had several children, including the educationist Mary *Gurney, and then to Harriet, daughter of J. Tritton of Lombard Street, London. They had two sons, William Gurney and Joseph John Gurney.

On his father's resignation in 1849, Gurney was appointed shorthand writer to the houses of parliament. Like his father he was greatly interested in religious and philanthropic movements. He was for more than fifty years a member of the committee of the Religious Tract Society, and latterly its treasurer. He was also treasurer of the Baptist college in Regent's Park. He was well read in biblical scholarship and devoted much time to bringing out popular commentaries on the Bible. The best-known of these was *The annotated paragraph Bible, containing the Old and New testaments according to the Authorised Version, with explanatory notes, prefaces to the several books, and an entirely new selection of references to parallel and illustrative passages* (2 vols., 1850–60), published by the Religious Tract Society. It was highly popular and was well received on an academic level. The notes were prepared by able contemporaries under Gurney's supervision. Besides two or three other Bibles, he brought out the *Revised English Bible* (1877) on the same lines as, and closely resembling, the later official Revised Version. The profits of his literary works he gave to the Religious Tract Society. On his retirement from the office of shorthand writer to the houses of parliament in 1872, the office was given to his nephew, Mr William Henry Gurney Salter. Gurney died at his home, Tyndale Lodge, Wimbledon Common, Surrey, on 12 August 1879, and was buried at Norwood cemetery.

THOMPSON COOPER, *rev.* JOANNA HAWKE

**Sources** private information (1890) · *The Athenaeum* (23 Aug 1879), 241 · C. M. B., 'Joseph Gurney', *Sunday at Home* (20 Dec 1879), 810–14 · Boase, *Mod. Eng. biog.*
**Likenesses** portrait, repro. in C. M. B., 'Joseph Gurney', 810
**Wealth at death** under £60,000: resworn probate, Jan 1880, *CGPLA Eng. & Wales* (1879)

**Gurney, Joseph John** (1788–1847), banker and religious writer, was born on 2 August 1788 at Earlham Hall, Norwich, the eleventh of the twelve children of John Gurney (1749–1809) and Catherine Gurney, *née* Bell (1754–1792). The Gurneys, Quakers from the mid-seventeenth century, had developed a substantial wool-stapling business and were known for their social concern, evinced, for instance, in J. J. Gurney's great-great-uncle John Gurney (1688/9–1741), the Weaver's Friend. Informal banking led in 1770, when J. J. Gurney's grandfather died with an estate of £100,000, to the establishment of Gurney's Bank.

The Earlham Hall household was far from strict in its Quakerism and the Gurney children grew up in a whirl of social activity. About half J. J. Gurney's siblings, including Daniel *Gurney, Lousia [*see* Hoare, Louisa Gurney], and Hannah, who married Sir Thomas Fowell Buxton, became Anglicans; the other half remained Quaker—including

**Joseph John Gurney** (1788–1847), by Charles Edward Wagstaff (after George Richmond, 1836)

Samuel *Gurney (1786–1856) and Elizabeth [*see* Fry, Elizabeth], who married Joseph Fry. With her, J. J. Gurney was to remain particularly close.

In boyhood Gurney was sent with a cousin to Oxford to study under an Anglican tutor, though as dissenters they were precluded from admission to the university. It was at Oxford that, finding the small Quaker meeting uncongenial, he began to attend Church of England services. From his two years at Oxford he emerged at the age of seventeen with a good knowledge of the classics, Hebrew and New Testament Greek, and Italian.

Gurney now entered the family bank and in 1805 became a partner, a position he retained for the rest of his life. On the death of his father (whose business acumen he inherited) he became master of Earlham Hall, which was to be his home until his death. His investment policies enabled Gurney's Bank to weather the storm in the national financial crisis of 1825—and also, incidentally, enabled him to rescue Joseph Fry's London tea and banking business, though his brother-in-law's continued imprudence led to bankruptcy three years later.

In 1812 Gurney took the decisive step, which his sister Elizabeth had taken more than a decade earlier, of becoming a plain Friend, and was recognized by the Norfolk gentry as no longer joining in their social life. In 1818 his gift in the vocal ministry was acknowledged by his meeting, as Elizabeth Fry's had been in 1811. He agonized whether preoccupation with business and enjoyment of an affluent (though never ostentatious) lifestyle hindered his spiritual growth: his fellow Quakers, who often criticized him severely on both grounds, assumed a complacency which his journal shows to be unfounded. He was handsome and blessed with ease of manner, and to the young he was a magnet, yet his relationships with his fellow Quakers were often uneasy. It was, perhaps, not just his wealth and lifestyle which made him suspect in some eyes, but his suavity and air of sweet reasonableness.

Gurney was thrice married: on 10 September 1817 to Jane Birkbeck (1789–1822); on 18 July 1827 to Mary Fowler (1802–1835); and on 21 October 1841 to Eliza Paul Kirkbride (1801–1881). He had two children with his first wife.

Gurney was active in the fields of anti-slavery and prison reform, and with Elizabeth Fry visited many gaols, their visits resulting in such publications as *Notes on a Visit Made to some of the Prisons in Scotland and the North of England* (1819). But increasingly he saw his main task, both within the Society of Friends and outside it, as theological. In 1824 he published *Observations on the Religious Peculiarities of the Society of Friends*, a work which ran into many editions and was translated into German. The following year saw *Essays on the Evidences, Doctrines and Practical Operation of Christianity* and in 1830 appeared *Biblical Notes and Dissertations*, a work that stressed the doctrine of Christ's divinity.

Other works, shorter and longer, poured from Gurney's pen. As evangelicalism made headway among Quakers in Britain in the 1830s Gurney attempted to promote the evangelical cause in a manner consistent with the testimony of Friends. Thus, against the extreme evangelical Beaconites led by Isaac Crewdson, he maintained a belief in the universality of the inward light by asserting that the death of Christ led to a measure of the Spirit being bestowed on all humanity. He saw the scriptures not as 'the word of God', but still as 'unutterably stamped with the seal of divine authority' (J. J. Gurney, *Letter to Friends of the Monthly Meeting of Adrian, Michigan*, 1839, 4).

Yet Moses Brown, a prominent New England Friend, complained as early as 1833 that Gurney was 'too much of the new school' (J. Wilbur, *Journal of the Life of John Wilbur a Minister of the Gospel in the Society of Friends: with Selections from his Correspondence etc.*, 1859, 177), and a number of English Friends took a like view, protesting, indeed, in 1837 against his proposed religious travels to America. In that country he also found opposition: tension had already been building up between evangelicals and the conservatives, who perceived him as an exacerbating influence and a prime cause of later separations. The journeys of 1837–40 enabled him to see at first hand the effects of slavery and he prudently refrained from public utterance until he was sure of his facts. His *Free and Friendly Remarks on a Speech … by Henry Clay* (1839) was recognized as masterly and was followed by *A Winter in the West Indies* (1840), addressed to the same senator. He had talked during his extended visit with religious leaders, state governors, and Washington officials, as well as holding meetings with orthodox Friends, Hicksites, and the general public.

In the 1840s Gurney's visits to the continent of Europe provided opportunity to further his anti-slavery and prison reform preoccupations. Politically, he was against universal suffrage: this constitutional conservatism (though he was a whig) was supported by the experience of universal suffrage in Pennsylvania and New York, which he saw as working to the detriment of black people.

After the passing of the Reform Bill in 1832 Gurney had considered standing for parliament (Quakers then becoming eligible). He saw, but was not persuaded by, the argument that it was not consistent with his position as a ministering Friend, and as late as 1837 was still thinking it likely that he might feel called to serve 'for a specific purpose and a short time' (Swift, 104).

On 22 December 1846, as Gurney was riding home from Norwich, his horse stumbled and threw him to the ground with considerable force. He appeared to have suffered no injury, and attended the midweek meeting two days later and both meetings the following Sunday. Next day, however, he became seriously ill, dying at home on 4 January 1847. He was interred in the burial-ground of the Friends' meeting-house at Gildencroft, Norwich.

EDWARD H. MILLIGAN

**Sources** J. Smith, ed., *A descriptive catalogue of Friends' books*, 1 (1867), 881–95 • *Memoirs of Joseph John Gurney*, ed. J. B. Braithwaite, 2 vols. (1854) • D. E. Swift, *Joseph John Gurney: banker, reformer and Quaker* (1962) • S. Bright, 'Joseph John Gurney (1788–1847): a study in evangelical Quaker biography', MA diss., 1991 • J. J. Gurney, 'Autobiography, addressed to his nephew, 7mo 1837', RS Friends, Lond., MS vol. S 32 • *GM*, 2nd ser., 27 (1847), 313–16 • Norwich monthly meeting records • A. J. C. Hare, *The Gurneys of Earlham*, 2 vols. (1895) • P. H. Emden, *Quakers in commerce: a record of business achievement* (1939) • Burke, *Gen. GB* (1965–72), vol. 1

**Archives** Norfolk RO, diaries and corresp., notebooks • RS Friends, Lond., corresp. and journal letters | Bodl. RH, corresp. with Thomas Buxton • Edinburgh Central Reference Library, records of conversations with Thomas Chalmers • NL Scot., corresp. with Archibald Constable • U. Edin., New Coll. L., letters to Thomas Chalmers

**Likenesses** R. J. Lane, lithograph (after G. Richmond), BM • G. Richmond, portrait, priv. coll. • C. E. Wagstaff, mezzotint (after G. Richmond, 1836), BM, NPG [*see illus.*] • lithograph (after S. Debenham), NPG

**Gurney, Louisa Mary** (1873–1966), headmistress, was born at 16 Princes Street, Rotherhithe, London, on 11 June 1873, the daughter of Henry Palin *Gurney (1847–1904), a Church of England clergyman and mineralogist who became principal of the Durham College of Science (later Armstrong College), Newcastle upon Tyne, and his wife, Louisa, *née* Selby Hele. Her early years were spent in London, where she was educated privately before becoming a pupil at Notting Hill high school. She entered Girton College, Cambridge, in 1892, taking a second class in part one of the mathematical tripos (1895). She gained an honours BSc degree in mathematics (1898) and the secondary teachers' certificate (1899) at Durham University. As Cambridge degrees were not yet open to women, she took her MA from Trinity College, Dublin, in 1905. Like most of her fellow graduates she entered teaching: her first post was as temporary lady tutor at Durham College of Science, in 1896; she then became assistant mistress in mathematics at North London Collegiate School (to 1902).

In 1902 Gurney was appointed to the headship of Newcastle upon Tyne Church High School where she remained until she retired in 1936. She was already familiar with the school as two of her younger sisters had been pupils there, and she had earlier coached some of the girls in hockey. While she was head the school attained independence from the Church Schools Company (in 1925), and expanded. Determined to dedicate herself entirely to the school, she decided not to live at home for fear that she might be distracted by family life, so she settled at 16 Otterburn Terrace, near the school. Here from 1907 she took pupils as boarders, later moving to 5 Henshelwood Terrace. She was an advocate of the boarding system and wished to develop her school following the example of Cheltenham Ladies' College, believing that the Church of England character of the school could be more effectively diffused among boarders than among day pupils. Her vision for the future of the school, expounded in an essay presented to the governing body in 1918, was not endorsed by the governors and not implemented. Under her headship there was an early emphasis on science; Gurney deplored the importance attached to Latin and mathematics (although this was her own specialism) in the matriculation examinations, and she considered that a good school certificate 'in congenial subjects indicated a more useful type of girl than one drilled to the formal requirements of an exam board' (Scott and Wise, 51). She taught both scripture and mathematics throughout the school, her lively methods making the latter an absorbing subject.

Deeply interested in the development of each pupil as an individual, in their general health (a school doctor had been appointed in 1915), and in the problems of adolescence, Gurney distributed a copy of the pamphlet *The Health of Adolescent Girls*, published by the London Association of the Medical Women's Federation; it included three pages on menstruation, a subject not usually discussed openly at that time. Early in her time as headmistress she introduced prefects and the house system. A girl guide company was founded in 1917 and school visits began in 1925 with a trip to Paris.

Although Gurney took no part in professional associations, she was active in organizations in north-east England. She was the first woman appointed to the council of Armstrong College, a member of the local branch of the St John Ambulance Brigade, and a commandant of the voluntary aid detachment, receiving the Tyne garrison war medal in 1919. After her retirement in 1936, she lived with two friends at High Littleton House, near Bristol, where she was president of the local Women's Institute from 1937 to 1945. She maintained an interest in the school, opening Gurney House in 1947 and regularly attending meetings of the old girls' club. She moved to Oxford, where she died, unmarried, at Fairfield, 115 Banbury Road, on 17 February 1966 after suffering a stroke. A memorial service was held at the cathedral church of St Nicholas, Newcastle upon Tyne, in May 1966. J. B. GARRIOCK

**Sources** H. G. Scott and E. A. Wise, eds., *The centenary book of the Newcastle Church High School* (1985) • A. C. and F. M., eds., *The Newcastle upon Tyne Church High School, 1885–1935* (1935) • K. T. Butler and H. I. McMorran, eds., *Girton College register, 1869–1946* (1948) • E. M. Bell, *A history of the Church Schools Company, 1883–1958* (1958) • b. cert. • d. cert.

**Likenesses** photographs, 1916–35, repro. in Scott and Wise, eds., *Centenary book*, 50, 53, 55

**Wealth at death** £3108: probate, 4 May 1966, *CGPLA Eng. & Wales*

**Gurney, Mary** (1836–1917), educationist, was born at Denmark Hill, London, the elder daughter of Joseph *Gurney (1804–1879), parliamentary shorthand writer, and his first wife, Emma (*d.* 1842), daughter of E. Rawlings. In addition to her brother, William, and younger sister, Amelia, she had an unknown number of half-sisters, the daughters of her father's second marriage, to Harriet Tritton. Her upbringing following her mother's early death was presumably supervised by her father, a self-taught biblical scholar whose thirst for knowledge she certainly inherited. As a girl she taught herself Latin, Greek, and Italian, subjects unlikely to have been on offer at the school, Wincobank Hall, near Rotherham, Yorkshire, which she is said to have attended for 'a short period' (Magnus, *Mary Gurney*, 13); later, like her father, she used time spent on bus journeys to learn German, and later still acquired a working knowledge of Spanish. At home she took on, evidently with great verve, the early education of her half-sisters; many years later one of them, Catherine Gurney, recalled 'weeping miserably' when governesses came to take her place. Still living at home, she turned to voluntary work, becoming secretary of Wandsworth British Girls' School, an elementary school run by the British and Foreign School Society.

It cannot have been accidental that a school was the object of Mary Gurney's first endeavours: 'an educational enthusiasm', she declared not many years later, 'has always been part of myself' (Ridley, 123). In 1871 she made contact with fellow enthusiasts whose efforts were directed towards providing an affirmative answer to the question she asked in a paper delivered to the Social Science Congress at Leeds in September of that year: 'Are we to have education for our middle-class girls?' (reprinted in *The Education Papers: Women's Quest for Equality in Britain, 1850–1912*, ed. D. Spender, 1987). By 'middle-class' she meant 'the mass of girls between "the young ladies" whose parents pay £80 to £100, or even £200 or £300 per annum for instruction principally in so-called accomplishments, and girls trained in elementary schools on payment of 1d or 2d weekly'. In November, with encouragement from Frances Mary Buss, she joined the newly launched National Union for the Improvement of the Education of Women of All Classes, the brainchild of Maria Grey. She was promptly elected to its organizing committee and a year later to the council appointed to carry out the union's most urgent and most enduring project, the establishment of 'good and cheap day schools for girls'; these were to be financially self-supporting, although the initial capital would come from interest-bearing shares purchased by well-wishers. This scheme was put into practice through the formation of the Girls' Public Day School Company Ltd (GPDSC), launched in June 1872; the first school opened in Chelsea (it later migrated to Kensington) the following January.

Mary Gurney served on the council of the GPDSC (or GPDST as it became after reconstitution in 1905 as a trust) from 1872 until her death in 1917, and was an influential member of its small but powerful education committee, of which she was chair from 1897 to 1913. While her father was still alive she continued to live at home, which from about 1872 was Tyndale Lodge, near Wimbledon Common. But after his death in 1879, and apparently under no necessity to earn her own living, she set up house with her sister Amelia (neither of them married) in Kensington, within easy reach of the company's office in central London and a convenient starting point for countless journeys on the company's business. Having done much to promote the rapid proliferation of GPDSC high schools in London and its outskirts, but also countrywide—at one point in the mid-1890s there were more than thirty, divided almost equally between London and the provinces—she still contrived to devote personal attention to each, while keeping in view the interests and objectives of the operation as a whole. Recognizing the greater good, she did not vote against the closure of schools which proved unviable, but for sentimental reasons could never be persuaded to vote in favour. She fully supported the council's policy of maintaining a tight control over the schools and saw to it that weaknesses revealed by inspection reports, examination results, and returns of pupil numbers received immediate attention. In 1894, in tandem with the chairman of the GPDSC, W. H. Stone, she gave evidence to the royal commission on secondary education chaired by James Bryce, and in 1899 contributed to a volume of short essays, *What is Secondary Education?*, edited by Robert Pickett Scott.

Mary Gurney acted as mentor to a long succession of GPDSC headmistresses, in whose appointment she played a decisive part. Beneficiaries of her wisdom and sympathy, they usually accepted her occasional criticism in the professional spirit with which it was offered; she could, indeed, have been one of their number. She also served on the councils of the Maria Grey Training College, the Teachers' Training and Registration Society, and the London Society for the Extension of University Teaching; she was a governor of Cheltenham Ladies' College and of Princess Helena College. She was interested in the Froebel movement, joined the committee of the Froebel Society, and under the title *Kindergarten Practice* (1877) published her translation of a work by one of his followers, A. Koehler; she also translated scholarly articles from French, German, Spanish, and Italian, which appeared in journals such as *The Antiquary*. She signed the 1885 petition to the House of Lords in favour of the enfranchisement of women householders. In lending her support to the movement for the higher education of women she rejected the notion of a 'women's university' and in 1894 became a member of the governing body of Girton College, Cambridge, her cousin once removed, Russell Gurney, having been a supporter of Emily Davies, the founder of the college. With her sister, Amelia, she gave £1000 for extensions to the chemical laboratory, and their combined bequests to the college eventually amounted to almost £30,000. Privately, she gave financial help to promising scholars, whether at Girton or in the high schools; some doubtless fell into both categories.

Strong-minded, with a countenance to match, Mary Gurney was also tender-hearted and given to hospitality. She was an outstanding example of the cultivated single woman, continually developing her appreciation of music, painting, and architecture through travel and wide reading. She applied herself with equal diligence and success to the multiplication of seriously intentioned schools for girls at a time when few models were at hand and 'experience had often to be dearly bought' (Memorial leaflet, 1917, GPDST Archives). Her posthumous recognition as one of the four founders of the GPDST, the others being Maria Grey, Emily Shirreff, and Lady Stanley of Alderley, was no more than she deserved. Mary Gurney died at her home, 69 Ennismore Gardens, Kensington, on 8 October 1917 and was buried in Putney Vale cemetery. She bequeathed £500 to the GPDST to found a leaving scholarship. JANET SONDHEIMER

**Sources** L. Magnus, *Mary Gurney: an impression and a tribute* (1918) · L. Magnus, *The jubilee book of the Girls' Public Day School Trust, 1873–1923* (1923) · J. Kamm, *Indicative past: one hundred years of the Girls' Public Day School Trust* (1971) · M. Camillin, 'The "Active" Workers: the contribution of Mary Gurney and Penelope Lawrence to the development of female education in late 19th century England', MA diss., Institute of Education, London, 1993 · *The Times* (15 Oct 1917) · *Girton Review* (Easter 1918) · Girls' Public Day School Trust Archives, London · A. E. Ridley, *Frances Mary Buss and her work for education* (1895)

**Likenesses** photograph, Girls Public Day School Trust Archives, London

**Wealth at death** £21,918 7*s*. 3*d*.: probate, 9 June 1918, *CGPLA Eng. & Wales*

**Gurney, Priscilla Hannah** (1757–1828), Quaker minister, was born on 22 June 1757 at Norwich, Norfolk, the elder of the two daughters of Joseph Gurney (1729–1761), merchant, and Christiana Barclay (*c*.1739–1796). Though both her parents came from established Quaker families they had become lax in their observation of their faith, and in her autobiography Priscilla laments the worldliness in which she and her sister were brought up. Her father died when she was four, and when she was ten her mother married John Freame, her first cousin, and the family moved from Norfolk to Bush Hill, Enfield. In 1770 John Freame died and the family moved again, this time to Bath, which Priscilla saw as a 'vortex of dissipation' (Allen, 22). About two years later her mother married, as her third husband, William *Watson (1744–1824) [*see under* Watson, Sir William] of Bath, a physician, scientist, and non-Quaker.

In 1775, when she was eighteen, Priscilla went on an extended visit to her relatives in Norfolk and while there refused a marriage proposal from a young Quaker. This visit also brought into focus the spiritual dilemmas that she was facing. For several years afterwards she was torn between the influence of her Quaker relatives and her worldly friends in Bath, one of whom was zealous in urging her to convert to the Church of England. Eventually Priscilla, wanting to please her friend, was baptized into the established church and attended church services but she was still unsatisfied. Her Quaker relatives talked and wrote to her and gave her Quaker books to read. She tried to blot out the inward voice that she heard saying 'I must be a Quaker' by going to balls, concerts, and plays in Bath but the mental anguish of her spiritual struggle made her ill.

At last Priscilla decided to read some Quaker books and found to her surprise that she agreed with everything in Robert Barclay's *Apology*. She told her family that she was now a Quaker. Her mother asked her not to change her appearance and Priscilla tried to oblige but eventually she felt compelled to dress and speak as a 'plain Friend'. She was still struggling spiritually and felt more comfortable with other Quakers than with her family. When she was twenty-seven she refused another proposal from a young Quaker, who refused to accept her rejection. This emotional pressure made her ill and she took to her bed, where she was visited by several influential Friends. Among them was Mary Davis of Minehead, who befriended Priscilla, introduced her to Richard Reynolds and his wife, Rebecca, and took her to visit them at their home in Coalbrookdale. Mary and Priscilla planned to set up home together but Mary's death in 1791 put paid to this and Priscilla made her home instead with the Reynoldses, her 'parental friends' (Allen, 123), at Dale House, Coalbrookdale.

The close-knit Quaker circle of families at Coalbrookdale, enlivened by a constant stream of visitors, at last gave Priscilla a secure base in which she felt at home and to which she could contribute. She became a Quaker minister in 1792 and travelled both locally and as far afield as Scotland and the Isles of Scilly. Being 'small in person, beautiful in countenance, elegant in manner' (Hare, 302–3) she was the ideal person for her young cousin Elizabeth Gurney (later Fry) to be sent to visit in 1798, when she too was going through a spiritual struggle. Priscilla acted as a calm and sympathetic influence and introduced Elizabeth to Deborah Darby, who prophesied her future service. Elizabeth sat in cousin Prissy's little room and wrote in her journal, echoing her cousin's words, that she was 'never to forget this day while life is in my body. I know now what the mountain is I have to climb. *I am to be a quaker*' (J. Whitney, *Elizabeth Fry, Quaker Heroine*, 1937, 72).

In 1804 Richard Reynolds, following the death of his wife, decided to leave Coalbrookdale for Bristol, and Priscilla also moved away, back to Bath, where her sister still lived. She made a striking figure in her old-fashioned plain Quaker dress and black silk hood. Her friend Mary Ann Schimmelpenninck recalls that 'her dark intelligent eyes, her well-developed eye-bone and beautifully formed nose indicated at once strength and acuteness of intelligence and great delicacy of taste' (Hare, 303n.).

For the rest of her life Priscilla, in increasingly delicate health, lived in Bath and cultivated her talent for friendship. She was 'constant, ardent and faithful in attachment, earnestly persevering in the endeavour to serve her friends' (Allen, preface, ix). Eventually confined to her house by an extreme susceptibility of the lungs, she died in Bath on 17 November 1828, at the age of seventy-one. She was buried in Bath on 26 November.

Gil Skidmore

**Sources** S. Allen, ed., *Memoirs of the life and religious experience of Priscilla Hannah Gurney*, 2nd edn (1841) • A. J. C. Hare, *The Gurneys of Earlham*, 2 vols. (1895) • R. Labouchere, *Deborah Darby of Coalbrookdale, 1754–1810* (1993) • 'Dictionary of Quaker biography', RS Friends, Lond. [card index]

**Gurney, Sir Richard, baronet** (*bap.* **1578**, *d.* **1647**), mayor of London, was baptized in Surrey on 8 March 1578 at Croydon, the second son of Bryan Gurney or Gournard (*d.* 1602) of Croydon, a descendant of the Gurneys of Kendall, Westmorland, and his wife, Magdalen Hewet, whom he had married on 27 April 1567. Richard Gurney was married twice: his first wife was Elizabeth, daughter of Henry Sandford, esquire, of Birchington in the Isle of Thanet, Kent, with whom he had a son, Richard (who predeceased him), and two daughters; in October 1632 he married Elizabeth, widow of Robert South and daughter of Richard Gosson of Odiham, Hampshire, and London, a goldsmith; they had no children.

Gurney was bound apprentice to a relative in the Clothworkers' Company, John Colby, who was a prosperous Cheapside silk mercer. Having gained his freedom and entered the livery in 1604 and 1611 respectively, he became quarter warden of the Clothworkers in 1629, upper warden in 1631, and master in 1633. His rise to wealth was dramatic and in the best City of London tradition. In 1611 he inherited his former master's house and business, said to be worth £6000, and his first marriage was into a wealthy family. Some time was also spent travelling in France and Italy from which he gained important future trading contacts. He lived in great opulence, dividing his time between his City mansion house in Old Jewry and Pointer's Grove in Totteridge, Hertfordshire. Further properties and lands were also acquired in London, Middlesex, Wiltshire, Sussex, and Somerset. His civic career matched his rise to office to his wealth. Admitted a member of the Honourable Artillery Company in 1614, he served as sheriff in 1633–4 and alderman of Bishopsgate (in 1634–7) and of Dowgate (in 1637–42). His election as lord mayor in 1641, and as president of Christ's Hospital the same year, signified his arrival at the pinnacle of City power and authority.

Gurney's election as mayor, however, coming as it did at a time of political crisis and division in the City and nation, soon proved to be a poisoned chalice. In June 1639 he had been among the majority of aldermen who had refused the king's request for a loan, although their refusal may have been due more to anxieties over its future repayment than to exclusively political objections. In summer 1641 he had played a key role in the City's campaign against the immunity from arrest for debt enjoyed by members of parliament and their servants while parliament was sitting, which left their London creditors without any legal recourse. By the time of the mayoral election of 1641 his pro-court sympathies were well known and he was not accorded the smooth transition to power which was customarily given to an alderman with his seniority. There were rowdy scenes in the electoral body of common hall, where Thomas Soames was the favoured candidate, and only decisive action by the presiding sheriff ensured Gurney's eventual victory. His mayoralty was to be a continuous struggle: resisting radical initiatives, defending the City's constitution, and maintaining order on London streets.

One of Gurney's earliest actions as lord mayor was to respond enthusiastically to Secretary Nicholas's proposal that the City should entertain the king on his return from Scotland in November 1641. Gurney was said to have contributed a lavish £4000 towards the cost of this event and Charles took the opportunity to confer a knighthood upon his dutiful mayor. A baronetcy soon followed, earning Gurney the distinction of being the first lord mayor to be elevated to that rank during his term of office. Shortly after the king's return Gurney faced an increasingly urgent law and order problem in London as parliamentary and street politics rose in temperature and converged. Early in December he clashed with apprentices whose petition he had seized, and faced an angry demonstration at his very gate; mayoral precepts followed reminding masters of their duty to control their apprentices and servants. He did his utmost to oppose and obstruct the second London root and branch petition of 11 December, warning its supporters that it was a recipe for sedition. When Prophet Hunt was hauled before him for haranguing a City congregation on 19 December, Gurney promptly committed him to prison. In the aftermath of the violent demonstrations provoked by Thomas Lunsford's appointment to the lieutenancy of the Tower of London Gurney went to great lengths to restore order, spending the entire night of 27 December riding about the City to quell troublemakers and taking other highly exceptional measures. However, when Charles went into the City on 5 January in pursuit of the five members, he appears to have encountered a less compliant lord mayor. Gurney, speaking for the City, blamed the recent tumults on the lack of progress with religious reforms, fears of a return to popery, and the disruption of trade caused by political uncertainty. After he had accompanied the king out of the City later that day Gurney was reportedly set upon by citizens who accused him of being a traitor to the City and its liberties, and an armed escort was needed to convey him home.

As the political crisis deepened, Gurney assumed the role of a leading defender of constitutional tradition in both the City and the kingdom, and unsuccessfully sought to prevent control of London from falling into radical hands. During the early weeks of 1642 he struggled to resist changes both to the City's militia and to the mayoral and aldermanic veto over common council. The former saw Mayor Gurney and his senior aldermen deprived of their control over the militia, which was now vested in a London militia committee dominated by radical citizens. He served a crucial behind-the-scenes role in the petitioning campaign launched by George Benyon and other leading citizens to reverse the militia changes. Similarly, he did his best to obstruct the parliamentary leadership's assertion of control over the calling of common councils and the removal of the aldermanic veto over that assembly. He also intervened successfully in an aldermanic election for the ward of Vintry to outflank local radicals and ensure the choice of a suitably conservative figure. By the summer, with both sides moving towards war, his conservative constitutionalism was taking him into the royalist camp. On 9 June he furtively arranged for the royalist commission of array to be proclaimed in the City and a month later, on 9 July, he abruptly ended a meeting of common council to prevent its disposal of arms and ammunition recently arrived from Hull.

The parliamentary leadership and their radical allies in the City struck back. On 11 July Gurney was impeached for his role in the proclamation of the commission of array, his obstructiveness, and other evidence of partisanship. He was committed to the Tower, where, throughout his trial, he received a succession of distinguished City visitors. He was eventually removed from office on 11 August and was replaced subsequently as lord mayor by the parliamentarian radical Isaac Penington. Gurney spent the remainder of his life in the Tower, refusing to pay a fine of £5000 in March 1645 which might have secured his release, and suffering the sequestration of his estate. He died, perhaps in Old Jewry, on 6 October 1647 and was buried on 8 October in St Olave Jewry after a funeral service employing the outlawed Anglican liturgy. His will, made on 26 September 1647 and proved on 12 October, reveals the high price he paid for his royalism and recalcitrance, in terms of enforced land sales, and loss of credit and trade, amounting to many thousands of pounds. These losses may have totalled as much as £40,000. His two daughters by his first marriage—Elizabeth, who was married to Sir John Pettus, and Anne, the wife of Thomas Richardson of Hevingham, Norfolk (later baron of Cramond)—were coheirs and executors of his estate. His second wife survived him and was still living at Pointer's Grove, Totteridge, in 1652. KEITH LINDLEY

**Sources** K. Lindley, *Popular politics and religion in civil war London* (1997), 99–100, 102–4, 106, 108, 121–2, 145, 204, 207, 210–15 · will, PRO, PROB 11/201/201 · will of John Colby, PRO, PROB 11/117/10 · *Collectanea Topographica et Genealogica*, 4 (1837), 91 · GEC, *Baronetage*, 2.147, 460 · A. B. Beaven, ed., *The aldermen of the City of London, temp. Henry III–[1912]*, 2 (1913), 63, 180 · Clothworkers' Company records, Clothworkers' Hall, Dunster Court, London · V. Pearl, *London and the outbreak of the puritan revolution: city government and national politics, 1625–1643* (1961); repr. with corrections (1964), 98, 302–3 · *DNB* · M. A. E. Green, ed., *Calendar of the proceedings of the committee for advance of money, 1642–1656*, 1, PRO (1888), 158–61 · M. A. E. Green, ed., *Calendar of the proceedings of the committee for compounding … 1643–1660*, 2, PRO (1890), 858–62 · a return of the names of those who came to visit Mayor Gurney in the Tower, 12–19 July, 20 July 1642, HLRO, main papers collection · *IGI* · *The obituary of Richard Smyth … being a catalogue of all such persons as he knew in their life*, ed. H. Ellis, CS, 44 (1849), 24–5 · *The visitation of London, anno Domini 1633, 1634, and 1635, made by Sir Henry St George*, 1, ed. J. J. Howard and J. L. Chester, Harleian Society, 15 (1880), 336

**Wealth at death** manor in Sussex; lands in Somerset; mansion house and other property in London: will, PRO, PROB 11/201/201

**Gurney, Richard** (1790–1843). *See under* Gurney, Archer Thompson (1820–1887).

**Gurney, Russell** (1804–1878), judge and politician, was born at Norwood, Surrey, on 2 September 1804, the second son of Sir John *Gurney (1768–1845), baron of the exchequer, and his wife, Maria, daughter of William Hawes MD. Educated first at the boarding-school at Walthamstow run by the Congregationalist minister Eliezer Cogan, he was then taught by Henry Jowett, rector of Little Dunham, Norfolk, before entering Trinity College, Cambridge, in 1822. He graduated BA in 1826 and was called to the bar at the Inner Temple in 1828. In 1830 he was nominated common pleader in the City of London by his father's colleague Sir William Bolland. He had to pay a large sum for that office, which he held at the same time as enjoying a considerable practice in the courts. In 1845 he became a QC. Resigning the common pleadership, he turned down the offer of a larger sum for the office than he had paid for it so that the appointment could be thrown open to secure the fittest candidate. In 1850 the court of common council of the City of London appointed him judge of the sheriffs' court and the small debts court.

On 1 September 1852 Gurney married Emelia [*see* Gurney, Emelia Russell (1823–1896)], nearly twenty years his junior, the devout daughter of Samuel Ellis Batten, a master at Harrow School, and his wife, Caroline, youngest daughter of John Venn, rector of Clapham. Gurney's low-church Anglican sympathies commended him to his wife's Clapham sect family. After their marriage they set up house at 8 Kensington Palace Gardens, Emelia becoming a member of the Kensington Society. They shared reforming and philanthropic interests, and travelled widely. They had no children but became guardians to their nieces and nephews on the death of Gurney's elder brother, John Hampden *Gurney, in 1862.

In January 1856 Gurney became common serjeant of the City of London. He was elected recorder of London by the court of aldermen in December 1856. In this capacity he was legal adviser to the corporation, judge of the mayor's court, and a commissioner of the central criminal court, winning wide respect for his impartiality. Between 1862 and 1877 he was appointed by both Liberal and Conservative governments to serve on royal commissions on subjects including transportation and penal servitude, oaths, electoral boundaries, sanitary legislation, labour laws, extradition, endowed schools, and the constitution of Christ's Hospital. In December 1865 he was sent to Jamaica by the Liberal government as one of three commissioners (with Sir Henry Storks and J. B. Maule) to investigate Governor Eyre's handling of the insurrection on the island. He was sworn a privy councillor on his return. In 1871 he went to the USA as one of the commissioners appointed by the Gladstone administration to settle the claims of British and American merchants under article twelve of the treaty of Washington.

At the general election of 1865 Gurney was elected MP for Southampton as a Conservative, his party affiliation being largely determined by his support for the established church. In parliament he was recognized as one of a group of Conservative MPs who promoted, often with cross-party support, measures of legal, administrative, and social reform. His particular interest was in removing those aspects of the criminal law and its procedures which were considered to be unfavourable to the interests of the poor. In 1867 he carried a bill to remove defects in the administration of the criminal law, and his Larceny and Embezzlement Act (sometimes known as the Russell Gurney Act) in the following year removed a legal loophole which had threatened the security of trade union funds. He introduced a Public Prosecutors Bill (1871). With his cousin by marriage, James Fitzjames Stephen, he made an abortive attempt to codify the law relating to homicide.

Through his wife's connections with the campaigns of Elizabeth Blackwell and Emily Davies for the admission of women to the medical profession and to university examinations, Gurney became involved in the women's movement. At the Social Science Association in 1862 he read Emily Davies's paper entitled *Medicine as a Profession for Women* and in 1876 he carried a bill that permitted the medical licensing bodies to open their examinations to women (the act was known as Russell Gurney's Enabling Act). He was best known for his sponsorship of the Married Women's Property Bill, promoted by the Married Women's Property Committee and the Social Science Association, to end the hardship whereby the property of a married woman was treated by the law as the possession of her husband. Gurney's attempt to give married women rights of separate ownership was thwarted by a select committee of the House of Lords. Considerably watered down, his bill became law in 1870. A further act was needed, which was passed in 1882.

In 1874 Gurney successfully carried Archbishop Tait's Public Worship Regulation Bill through the House of Commons. It was an overtly protestant measure designed to repress the more extreme ritualists within the Anglo-Catholic wing of the Church of England. The founder with his wife of a convalescent home for women in Bayswater (1875), Gurney became in 1878 vice-president of the Charity Voting Reform Association set up to remove some of the abuses in charities where subscribers could select beneficiaries. He was by then in poor health, which forced him to resign the recordership in February 1878. He was elected FRS in 1875 and became prime warden of the Fishmongers' Company in 1876. Caroline Batten described him at the time of his marriage: 'He has quiet, easy, gentlemanly manners, is of middle height, has dark hair, dark intelligent eyes, an aquiline nose, and an air of *savoir faire* about him I much admire' (E. M. Gurney, ed., *Letters of Emelia Gurney*, 1902, 4). Gurney died of bronchitis at his home, 8 Kensington Palace Gardens, London, on 31 May 1878. He was survived by his wife. M. C. Curthoys

**Sources** *DNB* • Venn, *Alum. Cant.* • Boase, *Mod. Eng. biog.* • Ward, *Men of the reign* • *Law Times* (22 June 1878) • L. Holcombe, *Wives and property: reform of married women's property law in nineteenth-century England* (1983) • P. Smith, *Disraelian Conservatism and social reform*

(1967) • M. L. Shanley, *Feminism, marriage, and the law in Victorian England, 1850–1895* (1989) • P. Levine, *Feminist lives in Victorian England* (1990) • L. Goldman, *Science, reform, and politics in Victorian Britain: the Social Science Association, 1857–1886* (2002)

**Likenesses** G. F. Watts, oils, 1866, Montreal Museum of Fine Arts, Canada; repro. in E. M. Gurney, ed., *Letters of Emelia Russell Gurney* (1902), facing p. 173; study, Tate collection • W. W. Ouless, oils, 1875, Fishmongers' Hall, London • portrait, in or before 1878, repro. in *ILN*, 72 (1878), 589–90 • H. P. MacCarthy; copy, marble bust, Corporation of London • caricature, chromolithograph, NPG; repro. in *VF* (9 Sept 1871) • lithograph, NPG • stipple, NPG

**Wealth at death** under £70,000: probate, 29 July 1878, *CGPLA Eng. & Wales*

**Gurney, Samuel** (1786–1856), banker and philanthropist, was born at Earlham Hall, near Norwich, on 18 October 1786, the second son of John Gurney (1749–1809), Quaker banker, of Norwich, and his wife, Catherine (1754–1792), daughter of John Bell, merchant, of London. He was the brother of Joseph John *Gurney, Daniel *Gurney, Elizabeth *Fry, and Louisa Gurney *Hoare.

Samuel Gurney was educated at Wandsworth, Surrey, and at Hingham, Norfolk. At the age of fourteen he was placed in the counting-house of his brother-in-law and fellow Quaker, Joseph Fry, tea merchant and banker, of St Mildred's Court, Poultry, London. On 7 April 1808 he married his third cousin Elizabeth, daughter of James Sheppard of Ham House, Essex, a handsome residence, which the young couple inherited in 1812, and his wife, Sarah, fourth daughter of Henry Gurney of Norwich, founder of Gurney's Bank. Ham House was to be the Gurneys' place of residence during nearly the whole of their married life; they had nine children, including Samuel *Gurney who also became a philanthropist and banker. In 1874 their grandson John Gurney gave a large sum towards the City of London Corporation's purchase of Ham House and its grounds for a public space now known as West Ham Park. The wealth that came to Samuel Gurney from his father-in-law, as well as that bequeathed to him by his father, enabled him to negotiate a partnership with the bill-broking firm of Richardson and Overend in 1807. The firm's business grew rapidly, to the point where, by the early 1820s, it was the largest bill-broking concern in London, complementing the discounting of bills with the advance of credit on all kinds of securities.

In the panic of 1825 the firm, which had by then become Overend, Gurney & Co., were able to lend money to many houses to tide over their difficulties. Gurney henceforth became known as 'the bankers' banker', and many firms who had previously dealt with the Bank of England now commenced depositing their surplus cash in his hands. In 1856 it was calculated that his house held deposits amounting to £8 million. In his financial dealings Gurney was entirely representative of the developing network of credit which helped to propel British industrialization at a crucial phase. His financial standing was sustained by religious and kinship ties with fellow Quakers, and he conveyed a sense of trustworthiness and gained a reputation for unimpeachable integrity.

Gurney played a part in the efforts of J. J. Gurney, Fowell Buxton, and Elizabeth Fry for the improvement of prison discipline and the reform of the criminal code. He refused to prosecute a man who had forged his name, knowing well that death was the punishment for such an offence. He also promoted the Niger expedition, and in March 1841 entertained Captain H. D. Trotter (1802–1859), Commander W. Allen (1793–1864), and a large number of the officers of the expedition at a farewell dinner at Upton. In 1849 he undertook a tour of Ireland, where he made considerable gifts to poor people still suffering from the effects of the famine. He became treasurer of the British and Foreign School Society in 1843, and held that post until his death. Gurney was a generous patron of the infant colony of Liberia, kept up a correspondence with President Roberts, and for his many gifts was rewarded by his name being given to a town of Gallenas in 1851. In 1853 he accompanied a deputation sent to Napoleon III to express a desire for a long continuance of peace and amity between England and France.

Elizabeth Gurney died at Ham House on 14 February 1855; and in the autumn of that year, his own health having deteriorated, Samuel took up residence at Nice. Getting worse in the spring of 1856, he started back for England; but he got no further than Paris and died in a hotel in that city on 5 June 1856. He was buried in the Quaker burial-ground at Barking on 19 June, when an immense concourse of people attended the funeral. A 42 foot granite obelisk was erected in his memory in Stratford Broadway, London, in 1861. Gurney's eldest son, John Gurney of Earlham Hall, did not long survive him, dying on 23 September 1856.

It was fortunate that Gurney did not live to see the fate of Overend, Gurney & Co. Less than ten years after his death, in August 1865, a firm that was an exemplar of Quaker probity was reorganized as a joint-stock company; its failure on 10 May 1866, with liabilities of more than £11 million, was one of the great crashes in the history of the City of London in the nineteenth century.

G. C. Boase, *rev.* M. W. Kirby

**Sources** *Annual Monitor* (1856), 71–9 • *ILN* (5 July 1856), 16 • V. Anderson, *Friends and relations: three centuries of Quaker families* (1980) • A. Raistrick, *Quakers in science and industry* (1950); repr. (1968) • E. Isichei, *Victorian Quakers* (1970) • Mrs T. Geldart, *Memorials of Samuel Gurney* (1857) • W. F. Finlason, ed., *Report of the case of the Queen v. Gurney and others* (1870) • D. Kynaston, *The City of London*, 1 (1994) • A. J. C. Hare, *The Gurneys of Earlham* (1895) • P. H. Emden, *Quakers in commerce* (1939)

**Archives** RS Friends, Lond., corresp. | Bodl. RH, corresp. with Thomas Buxton

**Likenesses** R. Dighton, caricature, coloured etching, pubd 1820 (*They'll be done: we are obliged to thee*), BM, NPG • stipple and line print, pubd 1857, NPG • B. R. Haydon, group portrait, oils (*The Anti-Slavery Society Convention, 1840*), NPG • lithograph (after J. R. Dicksee), NPG • portrait, repro. in *ILN* • portrait, repro. in Geldart, *Memorials*

**Gurney, Samuel** (1816–1882), philanthropist and banker, was born on 3 February 1816, at Upton, Essex, the second of three sons of Samuel *Gurney (1786–1856), Quaker philanthropist and discount banker, and his wife, Elizabeth, *née* Sheppard (*d.* 1855). He had six sisters.

Educated at the Friends' school, Rochester, and at Grove House, Tottenham, Gurney married young in 1837. His wife was Ellen (1814–1892), daughter of William Foster Reynolds, of Carshalton House, Surrey. Gurney lived for many years at The Culvers, Carshalton, near the Reynolds property. He became a Surrey magistrate and was high sheriff of the county in 1861. Subsequently he moved to 20 Hanover Terrace, Regent's Park, and took a house at Brighton.

His father was a partner in Gurney's Bank of Norwich and in Overend, Gurney & Co., bill brokers of Lombard Street. When as a young man Gurney became a partner in the latter business it was already the leading discount house in the City of London. After his father's death in 1856 a new generation of partners made a series of bold and ill-judged investments before floating the business to the public in 1865. In the most notorious bankruptcy of the mid-Victorian period, Overend Gurney stopped payment on 10 May 1866, leaving debts of some £11 million. Other businesses were sunk in its wake and the limited liability company was temporarily discredited as a device. Samuel Gurney junior's reputation was less damaged by this fiasco than those of some colleagues: he remained on the board of companies interested in marine and life assurance, and in submarine telegraphy in the Mediterranean and elsewhere.

As befitted a Quaker, Gurney's chief contributions were public and philanthropic. The abolition of the slave trade in British colonies in 1833 had fissured the British anti-slavery movement. One new campaigning organization was the British and Foreign Anti-Slavery Society, formed in 1839 chiefly by whig radicals; Gurney joined its committee in 1846, and served as its president for eighteen years. Older generations of abolitionists considered that the society was antagonistic to anti-slavery's traditional religious and political ecumenicism. The society was riven by policy disputes. At its annual meeting in 1855, for example, Gurney left the chair in anger when speakers criticized Anthony Ashley Cooper, earl of Shaftesbury, and the Turkish Aid Mission Society of the USA for associating with slave owners. Gurney's relations with American merchants and financiers gave him a realistic sense of the prospects of American abolitionists. Like his father, Gurney was active in the peace movement, but felt alienated by the growing sectarian militancy of campaigners like Richard Cobden and John Bright.

From 1857 until 1865 Gurney was MP for the small borough of Penryn (which seat he represented jointly with the whig banker Thomas Baring, afterwards first earl of Northbrook). He was an independent Palmerstonian Liberal who supported religious liberty and the extension of free trade but made no parliamentary mark. He was one of a group of rich, influential Quakers nicknamed 'weighty Friends'.

Gurney served on committees for penal reform and for public amenities in London, and against the opium trade. He was a founder of the Metropolitan Drinking Fountain and Cattle Trough Association in 1859 which relieved alike the thirst of Londoners and the suffering of dumb beasts. The Linnean and Royal Geographic societies elected him to fellowships. Gurney died from diabetes at Bishop's Down, Grove Spa, Tunbridge Wells, on 4 April 1882. RICHARD DAVENPORT-HINES

**Sources** D. Turley, *The culture of English anti-slavery, 1780–1860* (1991) • A. Tyrrell, *Joseph Sturge and the 'moral radical party' in early Victorian Britain* (c.1987) • H. L. Malchow, *Gentlemen capitalists: the social and political world of the Victorian businessman* (1991) • P. Lubbock, *Earlham* (1922) • d. cert. • *CGPLA Eng. & Wales* (1882) • Boase, *Mod. Eng. biog.* • *ILN* (24 July 1859) • *DNB* • Burke, *Gen. GB* (1965–72) • P. Davies, *Troughs and drinking fountains* (1989)

**Archives** Norfolk RO, journal and scrapbook relating to Quaker visit to Metz

**Likenesses** portrait, repro. in *ILN*, 92, 94 • portrait, repro. in Davies, *Troughs and drinking fountains*

**Wealth at death** £10,260 14*s.* 1*d.*: probate, 14 June 1882, *CGPLA Eng. & Wales*

**Gurney, Thomas** (1705–1770), stenographer, was born at Woburn, Bedfordshire, on 7 March 1705, the son of John Gurney, a miller, and his wife, Hannah Young. The young Gurney, more interested in scholarly and mechanical arts than in agriculture, twice ran away from home. About 1720 he bid successfully at auction for a book on astrology. The lot also included a popular treatise on the art of shorthand, *La plume volante* (1707) by William Mason. Gurney mastered Mason's system and was soon adept at recording sermons. Gurney's fortuitous discovery of Mason was to have profound influence on the history of legal and government reporting in the eighteenth and nineteenth centuries.

For some years Gurney was a schoolmaster at Luton, Bedfordshire, and Newport Pagnell, Buckinghamshire. At Luton on 30 November 1730 he married Martha, daughter of Thomas Marsom (reputedly a friend of John Bunyan), with whom he had at least two children, Martha (*b.* 1733) and Joseph [*see below*]. Thomas Gurney may have had a later marriage, as his son Joseph named a half-sister Rebecca among the beneficiaries of his will.

Gurney went to London in 1737, and in 1749 he was a clockmaker in Bennett Street, near Christ Church, Southwark, and a shorthand teacher at the Last and Sugar-loaf, Water Lane, Blackfriars. It is likely that he recorded trials at the Old Bailey in an unofficial capacity for some years before he was appointed official shorthand writer for the court in 1748 (a claim of 1738 has not been substantiated). He also served in other law courts and the House of Commons.

Although Old Bailey trial records existed from the seventeenth century, one or more unknown shorthand reporters with remarkable literary talent inaugurated 'verbatim' reportage of some trials in December 1731, increasing the popularity of trial reports as a form of reading entertainment. The Old Bailey held eight sessions a year, each no longer than a week, between the December following the annual mayoral election and the next October. Each session was reported in two, sometimes three, pamphlets, commonly known as the *Old Bailey Sessions Papers*, which were hawked on the streets within days of the event. During his tenure, Gurney—presumably with the help of assistants (the names of two, Samuel Rudd and

Isaac Harman, are known)—recorded 10,437 cases for sessions between 1749 and 1769, including the celebrated trial of Elizabeth Canning in 1754. At this trial and another in 1756 Gurney was called upon to give testimony in court based on his shorthand notes. Shorthand had therefore advanced beyond the purpose of providing sensational literature for lay consumption and was recognized by the legal establishment.

On 16 October 1750 Gurney published *Brachygraphy, or, Short-Writing, Made Easy to the Meanest Capacity* (it went through seven editions, about 2500 copies, during his lifetime and had eleven more editions to 1884). This work was only a slightly modified version of Mason, whom Gurney acknowledged in his preface. Gurney made few changes to Mason's alphabet, though he eliminated many of Mason's arbitrary symbols, substituting his own. The *Old Bailey Sessions Papers* served as a convenient publicity vehicle, and *Brachygraphy* was 'incessantly advertised' (Langbein, 12). Gurney, moreover, signed and numbered each copy, a practice that conferred a quasi-copyright status to his book and was continued through the thirteenth edition (1803).

Gurney was not an innovator in the development of modern shorthand, and his system was by the mid-eighteenth century becoming antiquated. In 1763 the anonymous author of *The Alphabet of Reason* supposed Gurney's *Brachygraphy* 'to owe more of its reputation to his acquired manual dexterity than to the excellence of his scheme' (Butler, 77). Later critics shared his opinion (Lewis, 121; Pitman, 30). Gurney was none the less one of the most adept practitioners of any system, and it is doubtful that his own skill could be attained (as Gurney claimed) by those of the 'meanest capacity'. Erasmus Darwin, who never met Gurney, wrote a poem in praise of his system that Gurney published in the second edition of *Brachygraphy* (1752).

By contrast, the ordeal awaiting the new student of Gurney's method was chronicled by Charles Dickens in chapter 38 of *David Copperfield* (1850), where the young Copperfield is led to the 'confines of distraction' in his attempt to master the 'Egyptian Temple' of Gurney's alphabet. There follows 'a procession of new horrors, called arbitrary characters' in which 'a thing like the beginning of a cobweb, meant expectation' and 'a pen and ink skyrocket stood for disadvantageous'. While Copperfield's 'almost heart-breaking' experience mirrored something of the author's personal trials with Gurney's system, Dickens became a highly successful parliamentary reporter in the 1830s. Years later, in a letter to Wilkie Collins (6 June 1856, *Letters of Charles Dickens*), and in a dinner speech before the Newspaper Press Fund on 20 May 1865 (Kingston), he spoke nostalgically of this youthful occupation.

Gurney died on 22 June 1770 in the parish of Christ Church, Southwark. The second edition of a work entitled *Poems on Various Occasions* was published in 1790, its author 'Thomas Gurney, short-hand writer'. Only the initials T. G. appeared on the title-page of the first edition (1759). It is difficult to reconcile the fanatical anti-Methodism of the versifier with the apparent cosmopolitanism of Thomas Gurney, shorthand writer.

Thomas Gurney's son **Joseph Gurney** (1744–1815), stenographer and bookseller, succeeded his father as official reporter at the Old Bailey. At 54 Holborn he published and continued to sign and number editions of *Brachygraphy*, omitting from the ninth (1778) and subsequent editions his father's acknowledgement of indebtedness to William Mason. He married a daughter of William Brodie of Mansfield. About 1783 Gurney was appointed parliamentary shorthand reporter and served as government shorthand reporter at many state trials, including that of Warren Hastings. He published transcripts of at least forty trials in addition to speeches and sermons. By 1773 he published in partnership with his older sister Martha Gurney. From her premises at 34 Bell Yard, Temple Bar (later at 128 Holborn), she advertised, in addition to the highly popular trials, 'PECULIAR good pens … very superior to what are commonly offered to Sale' (*Old Bailey Sessions Papers*, December 1773, 20).

Gurney was an enterprising businessman, a keen defender of his shorthand system and his legal claim to publish transcripts of his notes in accordance with his status as official reporter. In 'J. Gurney's appeal to the public' (1771?), he defended the accuracy of his transcripts of George Whitefield's sermons against criticisms by Whitefield's trustees. A generation later, Gurney brought a successful copyright suit against the Longman publishing firm (*Gurney* v. *Longman and others*, 19 July 1806), in which the lord chancellor granted Gurney's request for an injunction order. It was noted that Gurney had paid a £100 annual licensing fee for the exclusive right to publish the *Old Bailey Sessions Papers*. A reference to the 'very inferior' Gurney shorthand system (*Eclectic Review*, 1805, 597) prompted a rebuttal by Gurney, who invited anyone to visit his home at Walworth, Surrey, to observe clerks accurately transcribing his shorthand notes.

Between 1802 and 1806 Gurney was joined by his son William Brodie Gurney, who then succeeded his father as official reporter to both houses of parliament. William Brodie Gurney continued to publish *Brachygraphy* but ceased to sign and number copies after the thirteenth edition (1803) which reached 6900 copies. In his will (26 October 1814) Joseph Gurney divided his estate among his children John, William, and Elizabeth. He bequeathed all copyrights, copper plates, unsold copies of published works, and shorthand notes to William; and an annuity to his sister Martha, who survived him, living to age eighty-four. He requested his burial be attended with 'as little Expense as may be consistent with dignity' and died at Walworth before 7 August 1815. The Gurney family, England's great stenographic dynasty, continued to play an important role in the English law courts and houses of parliament throughout the nineteenth century.

PAGE LIFE

**Sources** J. H. Langbein, 'Shaping the eighteenth-century criminal trial: a view from the Ryder sources', *University of Chicago Law Review*, 50 (1983), 1–136 • *DNB* • *ESTC* • *Annual Register* (1769) • *Eclectic Review*, 1 (1805), 597–8, 791–4 • *The Times* (18 July 1806), 3a • *The Times*

(21 July 1806), 3b–c · will, PRO, PROB 11/1571, sig. 437 [Joseph Gurney] · *The whole proceedings on the king's commission of the peace* (1769–70) [Old Bailey sessions papers, 30 May – 2 June, 11–18 July 1770]; (1773–4) [8–15 Dec 1773] · *GM*, 1st ser., 40 (1770), 280 · *GM*, 1st ser., 85/2 (1815), 476 · E. H. Butler, *The story of British shorthand* (1951) · A. Paterson, 'Some early shorthand systems: Thomas Gurney's brachygraphy', *Phonetic Journal*, 45 (1886), 285–6 · M. Levy, *The history of short-hand writing* (1862) · J. J. Gold, 'The battle of the shorthand books, 1635–1800', *Publishing History*, 15 (1984), 5–29 · J. H. Lewis, *An historical account of the rise and progress of short hand* (privately printed, London, c.1825) · I. Pitman, *A history of shorthand*, 3rd edn (1891) · J. E. Bailey, 'Gurney's shorthand', *N&Q*, 6th ser., 2 (1880), 81–2 · J. Westby-Gibson, *The bibliography of shorthand* (1887) · *The letters of Charles Dickens*, ed. M. House, G. Storey, and others, 8 (1995) · L. L. H., 'Gurney's "shorthand": Gurney family', *N&Q*, 6th ser., 4 (1881), 212 · T. Cooper, 'Mason's short-hand: Thomas Gurney', *N&Q*, 2nd ser., 3 (1857), 209 · W. J. Carlton, *Charles Dickens, shorthand writer: the 'prentice days of a master craftsman*, 1st edn (1926) · A. Kingston, 'Shorthand in literature: how Charles Dickens learnt shorthand', *Pitman's Shorthand Weekly*, 36 (1909), 240

**Archives** probably priv. coll., notebook using Mason's shorthand

**Likenesses** line engraving, 1752, repro. in Gold, 'The battle of the shorthand books, 1635–1800' · line engraving?, 1762?, priv. coll. · J. Collyer, line engraving, 1778? (after design by unknown artist), BM, NPG; repro. in Butler, *Story of British shorthand*, facing p. 103 · line engraving, BM, NPG

**Gurney, William Brodie** (1777–1855), shorthand writer and philanthropist, grandson of Thomas *Gurney (1705–1770) and brother of Sir John *Gurney (1768–1845), was the younger son of Joseph *Gurney (1744–1815) [*see under* Gurney, Thomas] and his wife, a daughter of William Brodie of Mansfield. Born at Stamford Hill, London, on 24 December 1777, he was taught by a Mr Burnside at Walworth, Surrey, in 1787, and afterwards by a Mr Freeman. He received adult baptism at Maze Pond Chapel, Southwark, on 1 August 1796.

Adopting the profession of his father and his grandfather, Gurney began practice as a shorthand writer in 1803, and between that date and 1844 he recorded many of the time's most important appeals, trials, courts martial, addresses, speeches, and libel cases, a number of which were printed as volumes from his notes. He reported the impeachment of Lord Melville in 1806, the proceedings against the duke of York in 1809, the trials of Lord Cochrane in 1814 and of Thistlewood in 1820, and the proceedings against Queen Caroline. In 1802, in conjunction with his father, he was appointed to take notes of evidence before the committees of the houses of Lords and Commons, and in May 1813 he was formally appointed shorthand writer to the houses of parliament. He is mentioned as a famous shorthand writer in Byron's *Don Juan* (1.189), and edited the fifteenth and sixteenth editions of his grandfather's *Brachygraphy* (1824, 1835).

Gurney and a friend, Joseph Fox, opened a Sunday school at Walworth in 1795, of which he in the following year became the secretary. In 1801 he founded the Maze Pond Sunday school, an establishment similar to a ragged school, and here he introduced the Scottish method of catechizing in the scriptures. In March 1803 he married Miss Benham, who died at Muswell Hill in 1830. One of their children was Joseph *Gurney (1804–1879). On 13 July 1803 Gurney was present at a public meeting in Surrey Chapel schoolroom, when the Sunday School Union was established. Of this society he became successively secretary, treasurer, and president, and at the jubilee meeting in 1853 was one of the three surviving original subscribers. In 1805, with other persons, he began *The Youth's Magazine*, a cheap popular periodical, devoted to religious subjects. It was the earliest publication of the kind. For ten years Gurney was a joint editor of this work, for thirty years its treasurer, and until his death an occasional contributor exercising some general supervision. A large profit made on it was devoted to educational and missionary institutions. He was also the author of a related work: *A lecture to children and youth on the history and characters of heathen idolatry, with some references to the effects of Christian missions* (1848).

Gurney was also a member of the first committee of the London Female Penitentiary, formed in 1807, and was one of the lay preachers who for many years took the Sunday services in that institution. In 1812, on the establishment of the Westminster auxiliary of the British and Foreign Bible Society, he was elected a member of the first committee, and soon after became secretary. In connection with the Baptist denomination he was treasurer of Stepney College from 1828, and of their foreign missions from 1835. Like his father he was warmly interested in the anti-slavery movement, and he contributed generously towards rebuilding chapels in Jamaica and sending additional ministers there, besides frequently receiving Baptist missionaries into his own house. He purchased a residence at Muswell Hill, Middlesex, in 1826, when the Revd Eustace Carey, who had recently returned from India, came to reside with him. The house was then licensed as a place of worship, and during four years Carey and other ministers held Sunday evening services in the drawing-room. Gurney died at Denmark Hill, Camberwell, London, on 25 March 1855.

G. C. Boase, *rev.* M. Clare Loughlin-Chow

**Sources** J. Angus, *Baptist Magazine*, 47 (1855), 529–32, 593–600 · W. H. Watson, *The first fifty years of the Sunday school* [1873], 69–75 · T. Anderson, *History of shorthand* (1882) · *Encyclopaedia Britannica*, 9th edn (1875–89), vol. 21, pp. 837, 841 · M. Levy, ed., *Taylor's system of shorthand writing* (1862) · Boase, *Mod. Eng. biog.*

**Likenesses** G. Hayter, group painting, oils, 1820 (*The trial of Queen Caroline, 1820*), NPG · T. Wright, stipple, 1821 (after A. Wivell), BM, NPG

**Gurwood, John** (1790–1845), army officer and editor of Wellington's dispatches, was the second son of one Gurwood; his widowed mother married H. Okey. He started work in an office, but after an unrequited love affair entered the army as ensign in the 52nd light infantry on 30 March 1808. Gurwood served with the 1st battalion, as ensign and lieutenant, in all the Peninsular engagements down to the storming of Ciudad Rodrigo on 19 January 1812, where he led the 'forlorn hope' of twenty-five who headed the 300 'stormers' of the 52nd. He was concussed in the breach from a head wound, but after regaining consciousness made his way to the citadel and took prisoner

**John Gurwood** (1790–1845), by William Salter, 1834–40

the governor, General Barrié, at dinner. The governor surrendered his sword, which Gurwood presented to Wellington. It was returned to him next day when Lord Fitzroy Somerset buckled it on Gurwood in the breach where he had been wounded. It was a light scimitar, which Gurwood was permitted to wear in place of the regulation pattern: it later passed to the museum of the Royal Green Jackets at Winchester. Gurwood was promoted to a company in the Royal African Corps, with which he never served, and was for a while aide-de-camp to Lord Edward Somerset, exchanging to the 9th light dragoons. He was brigade major of the Household Cavalry on its arrival in the Peninsula before transferring as brigade major of Lambert's brigade 6th division, of which particular mention was made in the dispatches at Nivelle, Nive, Orthez, and Toulouse.

After dismissal of the charges brought against Colonel Quentin of the 10th hussars by many of his officers at his court martial in October 1814, no fewer than twenty-five of the officers were posted to other regiments and were replaced by other officers posted in. Gurwood was one of them. He served as aide-de-camp to Sir Henry Clinton when the general was second in command under the prince of Orange in the Netherlands, and was for a short time deputy assistant quartermaster-general at the prince's headquarters. He was three times wounded in the Peninsula, and again severely wounded at Waterloo. He became a brevet major in 1817, was retired on half pay from the 1st West India regiment in 1822, obtained an attached lieutenant-colonelcy in 1827, and became brevet colonel in November 1841. He was one of the duke of Wellington's private secretaries, 1837–44, and was entrusted with the editing of the duke's general orders and selections from his dispatches.

The dispatches were published in two series. The first, *The Dispatches of Field Marshal the Duke of Wellington*, edited by Gurwood, comprised twelve volumes covering the years 1799–1815, and was published during the duke's lifetime in 1834–8; the second, or supplementary, series, was edited by the second duke between 1858 and 1872. Sir Charles Oman later criticized Gurwood's edition as tiresome to handle and incomplete. However, the duke was not always easy to work for: he refused, for example, to discuss details of Waterloo when Gurwood questioned him. The work occupied Gurwood for many years, and for his literary service he received a civil-list pension of £200 a year.

Gurwood and the duke were old friends, the duke taking care of Gurwood. He was made CB and in 1839 was appointed a deputy lieutenant of the Tower of London with a salary of £768 p.a., as well as a pension of £2000. However, Gurwood's closing years were clouded by ill health, partly as a result of his war wounds and partly because of the strain of editing the *Dispatches*. This resulted in a severe depressive illness, and on Christmas day 1845 Gurwood committed suicide in the lodgings in King's Road, Brighton, that he had temporarily taken for himself and his family. He was buried in the Tower of London, leaving a widow and three daughters.

Shortly after Gurwood's death the duke was horrified to be told that he had been collecting material with a view to publishing a life of Wellington. This the duke had forbidden. He wrote at once to Gurwood's widow requesting the return of all his papers, receiving in reply a most indignant letter from Mrs Gurwood denying the existence of any memoir, and saying her husband had burnt the duke's letters to him before he died. This received a thirteen-page letter of penitence and apology from the duke, after which the matter was closed.

H. M. Chichester, *rev.* James Lunt

**Sources** *Philippart's Roy. Mil. Cal.*, 336 (1820) · *GM*, 2nd ser., 25 (1846), 208–9 [preface to Gurwood's *Wellington's dispatches*] · *Oxfordshire Light Infantry Chronicle* (1896) · W. S. Moorsom, ed., *Historical record of the fifty-second regiment (Oxfordshire light infantry), from the year 1755 to the year 1858* (1860) · C. W. C. Oman, *Wellington's army, 1809–1814* (1912) · E. Longford [E. H. Pakenham, countess of Longford], *Wellington*, 2: *Pillar of state* (1972) · *The Times* (6 Jan 1846) · R. S. Liddell, *Memoirs of the Tenth Royal Hussars* (1891) · W. F. P. Napier, *History of the war in the Peninsula and in the south of France*, 6 vols. (1828–40)

**Archives** PRO, corresp. and papers relating to preparation of the Wellington dispatches, PRO 30/26/41–44 | BL, letters to earl of Liverpool, Add. MSS 38303, 38475, 38576 · BL, letters to third earl of Liverpool, loan 72 · BL, Napier MSS · U. Southampton L., corresp. with duke of Wellington · U. Southampton L., letters to duke of Wellington · W. Sussex RO, letters to duke of Richmond

**Likenesses** W. Salter, oil study, 1834–40 (for *Waterloo banquet at Apsley House*), NPG [*see illus.*] · S. Joseph, marble bust, 1840, Wellington Museum, London · Count D'Orsay, pencil drawing, 1845, Gov. Art Coll. · J. Hall, oils, Wellington Museum, Apsley House, London · A. Morton, double portrait, oils (with the duke of Wellington), Wallace Collection, London · W. Salter, group portrait, oils (*Waterloo banquet at Apsley House*), Wellington Museum, London

**Gutch, John** (1746–1831), antiquary and Church of England clergyman, was born at Wells on 10 January 1746, eldest son of John Gutch (1705–1772), town clerk of Wells, and Mary (*d.* 1765), daughter of Abraham Mathew of Shaftesbury. In 1765 he matriculated at Oxford University from All Souls College. In 1766 he began 'looking after the museum', and in the same year, on 7 November, was appointed a clerk of his college. He graduated BA in 1767, proceeded MA in 1771, and in 1768 was ordained and took charge as curate of Wellow and Foxcote, near Bath. In 1770 he was appointed chaplain of All Souls, a post which he held for over sixty years, combining it from 1771 with the librarianship of the college, from 1778 with chaplaincy of Corpus Christi College, and from 1795 with the rectory of St Clement's parish in the suburbs of Oxford. More briefly he held other cures, notably the rectories of Waterstock, Oxfordshire, and Kirkby Underwood, Lincolnshire. He became a notary public at Oxford in 1791, and registrar of the university in 1797, before retiring in 1824; he was also registrar of the chancellor's court and clerk of the Oxford market, a university appointment. He married in 1775 Elizabeth Weller (1753–1799), daughter of Richard Weller, sometime butler of Magdalen College. Through her he acquired his Oxford house, 8 Longwall Street, which survives much as he rebuilt it in 1793–4. They had six sons and six daughters; two of their sons were John Mathew *Gutch (1776–1861), journalist, and Robert *Gutch (*bap.* 1777, *d.* 1851), fellow of Queens' College, Cambridge. Elizabeth long predeceased him, dying in 1799.

An active man of business in his generation, Gutch is best-known to posterity by his books. In 1781, with the support of 750 subscribers, he published two volumes of *Collectanea curiosa*, miscellaneous tracts on historical and university matters taken chiefly from the manuscripts of Archbishop Sancroft in the Bodleian Library, together with selections from the archives of All Souls. The book caused a brief stir in Oxford because of its inclusion, albeit with reference to earlier times, of some anti-Jacobite material and a paper urging the limitation of fellowships to twenty years' tenure, to prevent dons becoming splenetic or 'sottish' (*Letters of Richard Radcliffe*, 190–91). His more lasting contribution was to edit Anthony Wood's English version of his history of Oxford University. Wood had been so displeased by the Latin version, bought from him by the university and altered and published by Dr John Fell in 1674, that he later translated and augmented the whole. From that version (now Bodl. Oxf., MSS Wood F. 1–2), with the encouragement of Thomas Wharton, Camden professor of ancient history, Gutch edited Wood's account of the colleges and halls (1786), with an appendix containing Wood's lists of university officials, the *Fasti* (1790), and finally the *History and Antiquities of the University of Oxford*, published in two volumes in 1792 and 1796. The *Fasti*, to which Gutch made additions up to his own time, were later re-edited and enlarged by Philip Bliss, his successor as university registrar; Gutch's summary of Wood's manuscripts in the *History and Antiquities* retained its value until replaced by Andrew Clark's work in the 1890s. Otherwise Gutch's edition, prepared 'on the whole with great faithfulness and completeness' (Wood, *History and Antiquities*), has never been superseded. His evident intention to publish a revised edition was not, however, fulfilled and his surviving papers (mostly in the Bodleian Library) suggest that he did little further historical research. E. F. Jacob's assessment of him as 'one of the finest antiquaries Oxford has produced' (Craster, 92) seems generous.

Gutch was a popular man, who lived a life of 'peculiar serenity and content' (*GM*, 203). He was small in stature, courteous and suave in manner, and of a gentle disposition, somewhat negligent in looking after his own money matters, and ever ready to help antiquaries. He was a friend of Richard Gough, who 'shewed great kindness' (Nichols, 5.555–6) to his family, and in his will left a third of the residue of his estate to Gutch. Gutch seldom quit home and left behind little correspondence. His diary reveals him in youth as an active sportsman, involved in shooting, skating, riding, and even hunting; his maturer years were dominated by antiquarian pursuits, university administration, and clerical work. He was a diligent college chaplain and All Souls showed its appreciation by presenting him with an engraved silver inkstand in 1819. The university granted him an annuity of £200 when he retired as registrar. As a parish priest his effort seems unremarkable, even before he grew old. His memorial in St Clement's Church credits him with the relocation and new building of that church in 1828, but much was owed to his energetic curate from 1824, John Henry Newman. It was Newman who inspired the subscription campaign, and Gutch's parishioners drew pointed contrast between their new 'proper minister' and the old man who 'preached very good doctrine but did not … visit the people at their houses' (*Letters and Correspondence*, 1.88).

Gutch died in Oxford of influenza on 1 July 1831, aged eighty-five, the oldest resident member of the university; he was buried on 7 July 1831 in the churchyard of St Peter-in-the-East. ALAN CROSSLEY

**Sources** *GM*, 1st ser., 101/2 (1831), 91, 201–3 • *Letters of Richard Radcliffe and John James of Queen's College, Oxford, 1755–83*, ed. M. Evans, OHS (1888), 47n., 190–91 • A. J. Jewers, ed., *Marriage licences in the diocese of Bath and Wells* (1909), 176n. [family genealogy] • parish registers (burial), Oxford, St Clement's • parish registers (deaths), Oxford, St Peter-in-the-East • private information (1890) • H. E. Salter, ed., *Oxford city properties*, OHS, 83 (1926), 66, 315 • H. H. E. Craster, *The history of All Souls College library*, ed. E. F. Jacob (1971), 83, 92 • *Letters and correspondence of John Henry Newman during his life in the English church*, ed. A. Mozley, 2 vols. (1891) • A. Wood, *The history and antiquities of the colleges and halls in the University of Oxford*, ed. J. Gutch (1786) [Gutch's annotated copy, Bodl. Oxf., G. A. Oxon. 4°74–9] • Gutch's surviving MSS, Bodl. Oxf., MSS Top. Oxon. c.34–7, c.125, d.45, f.2; MS Add. B 74 • Nichols, *Illustrations*, 5.555–6 • *The life and times of Anthony Wood*, ed. A. Clark, 4, OHS, 30 (1895), 228 ff. • Foster, *Alum. Oxon.* • parish register, St Cuthbert's, Wells, 27 Jan 1746 [baptism] • *DNB*

**Archives** All Souls Oxf., diary • Bodl. Oxf., historical collections, notes, and papers

**Likenesses** T. Wageman, engraving, repro. in A. Wood, *The history and antiquities of the University of Oxford*, 1 (1792) • T. Wageman, stipple, BM, NPG; repro. in A. Wood, *The history and antiquities of the colleges and halls in the University of Oxford*, ed. J. Gutch (1786), 1

**Gutch, John Mathew** (1776–1861), journalist and author, was born probably at Oxford, eldest son of John *Gutch

(1746–1831), antiquary and divine, and Elizabeth Weller (1753–1799), and brother of Robert *Gutch. He was educated at Christ's Hospital with Samuel Taylor Coleridge and Charles Lamb. Gutch entered business as a law stationer in Southampton Buildings, Chancery Lane, London, where Lamb lodged with him in 1800.

In 1803 Gutch moved to Bristol to become owner and printer of *Felix Farley's Bristol Journal*, with which he was connected for the rest of his life, although he sold his share of the paper in 1844. *Felix Farley* was one of several established newspapers in Bristol, with a circulation of about 1000 copies but a much higher readership. It was tory and, like much of the city establishment, sought a civic society that was cohesive and consensual. Gutch supported the unwritten agreement that one of Bristol's MPs was whig, the other tory, rejoicing in the appearance of unanimity given by uncontested elections, and on occasions of national celebration he portrayed Bristolians as happy, united, and loyal. He sought to play down the sharp political divisions exposed during the Queen Caroline affair in 1820, but found *Felix Farley* a rallying point for supporters of king and government. He himself became one of the loudest critics of the unreformed city corporation and associated Society of Merchant Venturers and Dock Company, which were closed bodies, eager to protect their privileges if necessary at the expense of the city at large. In the 1820s Gutch was at the centre of a carefully co-ordinated attack on the corporation by whig and tory newspapers and the Bristol chamber of commerce, which represented business interests other than those of the merchant venturers. His *Letters on the Impediments which Obstruct the Trade … of Bristol* (1823), which he had earlier published under the name of Cosmo in *Felix Farley*, attacked the corporation as the cause of the impediments, its ferocity earning him the name the Bristol Junius. Further criticism from *Felix Farley* was republished as *The Present Mode of Election of the … Common Council of Bristol* (1825). Latin verses in which his friend John Eagles, writing as Themaninthemoon, attacked the corporation were published by Gutch in *Felix Farley* and appeared in a translated and illustrated separate version in 1826. In the late 1820s, as the political composition of the corporation changed from whig to tory, and as opposition to it became increasingly radical, Gutch retreated and again sought to understate divisions in Bristol society while opposing radical reformers.

Some time before 1809 Gutch married Mary Wheeley, daughter of a coach maker of Birmingham. They had one son, John [*see below*], in 1809 while they were living in Bristol. Gutch was married again in 1823, this time to the daughter of a Mr Lavender, a banker from Worcester, to which city he moved to join his father-in-law in business, although he still went to Bristol each week to supervise the publication of *Felix Farley*. He had no children from his second marriage.

Having established his reputation as a journalist with *Felix Farley* and the Bristol *Country Constitutional Guardian* (1822–4), Gutch joined Robert Alexander to found the London *Morning Journal* on 6 October 1828. In the enterprise Gutch was sued for libelling George IV and Lord Lyndhurst in 1829. Gutch dissociated himself from the paper, but he was convicted and the paper suppressed in 1830. Further troubles awaited him in 1848 when his father-in-law's bank failed. Gutch's valuable library was sold in 1858 in London by Sotheby and Wilkinson for over £1800.

Gutch thought himself something of a scholar and patron of literature. While in Bristol he was active in the Philosophical and Literary Society, publishing in 1827 four papers he had read before them, and was a collector and seller of antiquarian books. In 1847 Gutch published *A Lytell Geste of Robin Hode* (2 vols.), which, despite its claim to be 'grounded on other documents than those made use of by his former biographer Mister Ritson', seems to have been largely based on Joseph Ritson's *Robin Hood* and much less commercially successful than it, though it was well received at the time. Gutch patronized John Eagles, publishing a collection of his verse in 1857, and was especially interested in George Wither, publishing his poems in 1820 (3 vols.), writing an unpublished life, and collecting his works. In addition he wrote several pamphlets on the history of Bristol and Warwickshire, following his father's antiquarian interests. He was a JP for Worcestershire, and a fellow of the Society of Antiquaries. He died at his home, Barbourne, near Worcester, on 20 September 1861, leaving an estate valued at under £20 after his losses.

His son, **John Wheeley Gough Gutch** (1809–1862), surgeon, was born in Bristol and educated as a surgeon at the Bristol Infirmary, a well-established voluntary hospital supported particularly by members of the Church of England and tories. He became a member of the Royal College of Surgeons and for a time practised in Florence. Afterwards he was appointed queen's messenger, from which post he retired on a pension shortly before his death. From 1842 to 1856 he edited the *Literary and Scientific Register*, an annual encyclopaedia. He was editor of the Meteorological Society's *Quarterly Journal* in 1843 and contributed to *Felix Farley*. He was a botanist and fellow of the Linnean Society from 1848. He died after a stroke at 38 Bloomsbury Square, London, on 30 April 1862, leaving a widow, Elizabeth Frances Gutch, but no children.

ELIZABETH BAIGENT

**Sources** M. Harrison, *Crowds and history* (1988) • *DNB* • Allibone, *Dict.* • R. B. Dobson and J. Taylor, *Rymes of Robyn Hood* (1976) • C. B. Perry, *The voluntary medical institutions of Bristol* (1984) • Boase, *Mod. Eng. biog.* • J. Britten and G. S. Boulger, eds., *A biographical index of British and Irish botanists* (1893) • *CGPLA Eng. & Wales* (1862)

**Archives** U. Edin. L., special collections division, letters to James Halliwell-Phillipps

**Likenesses** lithograph, BM

**Wealth at death** £20: administration, 29 Nov 1861, *CGPLA Eng. & Wales* • under £3000—John Wheeley Gough Gutch: probate, 3 June 1862, *CGPLA Eng. & Wales*

**Gutch, John Wheeley Gough** (1809–1862). *See under* Gutch, John Mathew (1776–1861).

**Gutch, Robert** (*bap.* **1777**, *d.* **1851**), Church of England clergyman, second son of the antiquary John *Gutch (1746–1831) and his wife, Elizabeth, *née* Weller (1753–1799), was baptized at St Peter-in-the-East, Oxford, on 25 August 1777. Educated at Christ's Hospital, London, he went up to Pembroke College, Cambridge, in 1797, migrated to Queens' College as a scholar two years later, and took his BA (as 7th wrangler) in 1801, and his MA in 1804. Elected to a Queens' fellowship in 1802, he had already taken a curacy under Jonathan Boucher at Epsom, Surrey. He helped with teaching as well as parochial duties, and probably took this over after Boucher's death in 1804. An Epsom sermon, *The Sword of the Lord and of Gideon* (1803), against the Napoleonic principles 'of usurpation, irreligion and anarchy' (p. 21), was his first excursion into print, to be followed by *The Lord's Debt Discharged* (1806), in aid of London hospitals.

Preferment in 1809 to the Queens' rectory of Seagrave, Leicestershire, provided security for his marriage on 18 June 1810 to Mary Anne James (*b.* 1785/6), daughter of John James, rector of Arthuret, Cumberland. Between then and 1826 they had six daughters—one of whom, Eleanor (*b.* 1818), married the historian E. A. Freeman, one of the pupils whom Gutch continued to take at Seagrave—and four sons, including Charles (1822–1896), who followed his father into Cambridge, the church, and the publication of sermons.

Gutch followed the anti-atheistic *Sword of the Lord* with *The Path of the Just* (1826) against over-strict predestinarians. Then came the anonymous satire *Special pleadings in the court of reason and conscience … at the trial of W. O. Woolfrey and others for conspiracy* (1836), decrying the attribution by a Leicestershire Roman Catholic priest of a young woman's recovery from an epileptic fit to the influence of a blessed medal. Gutch pointed to the natural progression of the fit, which had none the less been repeated since, and accused Woolfrey of 'mental reservations' in ever making the claim. Gutch published no more, but died at Seagrave on 8 October 1851 and was buried there. Gutch's wife outlived him. The *Gentleman's Magazine* regretted that:

> a disposition almost too modest and retiring prevented him from ever coming forth before the world, or giving himself any opportunity of obtaining that reputation to which his learning and ability were undoubtedly entitled … We believe he has left unpublished several valuable papers on biblical criticism and the Roman controversy. (*GM*, new ser., 36, 1851, 549–50)

Julian Lock

**Sources** *GM*, 2nd ser., 36 (1851), 549–50 • Venn, *Alum. Cant.* • 'Gutch, John', *DNB* • *IGI* • will, PRO, PROB 11/2145, sig. 31 • census returns for Seagrave, Leicestershire, 1851, PRO, HO 107/2087 (416/1), fol. 22 • parish register (baptisms), Oxford, St Peter-in-the-East, Oxfordshire Archives

**Archives** Bodl. Oxf., letters to John Nichols and/or John Bowyer Nichols, MS Eng. Lett. b 1., fols. 146–8

**Likenesses** stipple, BM

**Wealth at death** no value given: will, PRO, PROB 11/2145, sig. 31

**Guthfrith** (*b.* before **920**, *d.* **934**). *See under* Sihtric Cáech (*d.* 927).

**Guthlac** [St Guthlac] (**674–715**), hermit, was one of the most famous and influential holy men in the first 120 years of English Christianity, his fame owed in no small degree to the well-structured and vivid life of him written *c.*740 by the learned East Anglian monk, Felix. Guthlac was a member of the Mercian royal dynasty, a descendant of Icel; his father was Penwalh, his aristocratic mother, Tette. He was named after the tribe of Guthlacingas. The record of many such tribes, which contemporaries once recognized as distinct groups within the larger Anglo-Saxon settlements (for example, the Gumeningas, whose pagan sanctuary was at Harrow), survives only in names such as this. Guthlac was born in 674, one year later than Bede. From the age of fifteen he spent nine years as a warrior, leading a band of companions apparently as something of a freebooter, rather like the mythical Beowulf. Many of his military ventures, lucrative in booty so it was said, were doubtless directed against the hostile Welsh; but the feuds and infighting within the early Anglo-Saxon kingdoms probably also gave him plenty of opportunity. He experienced a conversion to a religious way of life and joined the double monastery at Repton (where surviving archaeological remains seemingly date from the eighth and even the seventh centuries). Guthlac spent two years at Repton under Abbess Ælfthryth, received the Roman tonsure, and learned the monastic way of life and worship. He then opted for solitude, made for the East Anglian fens, with 'black waters overhung by fog', and, being guided thither by one Tatwine, established his hermitage on the island of Crowland, where he remained for some fifteen years until his death in 715, probably on 3 April. The likely chronology of Guthlac, therefore (and there have been confusions about the dates), is that in 698 he joined Repton and in August 700 finally settled, after a previous inspection, at Crowland. He came to Crowland on St Bartholomew's day (24 August) and thereafter regarded this saint as an active force in his religious experience.

Guthlac's biographer drew on information from a priest called Wilfrid, said to be a frequent visitor to the saint, and one Cissa, Guthlac's successor in the Crowland hermitage; and he drew on several hagiographical models, such as Athanasius's life of Anthony, Gregory's *Dialogues*, the anonymous life of Fursa, and Jerome's life of Paul the Hermit, for his presentation of the material. Knowledge of Guthlac comes, therefore, shaped in Felix's cultural and learned mould. It might be doubted whether it is possible to get behind the tissue of received hagiographical motifs to the 'real' Guthlac. For instance, Felix follows the fourth-century bishop of Alexandria, Athanasius (whose Greek life of Anthony was known in the west from the sixth-century Latin translation of Evagrius), in recounting Guthlac's numbers of visitors as a hermit; but he also gives much circumstantial detail and names several names. Moreover, the very number of hagiographical models known to Felix obviously gave him flexibility to apply them to hard information which he was in a good position to obtain. In describing the general pattern of Guthlac the hermit's struggles with demons (and it is interesting for the population of East Anglia and perhaps for racial attitudes of the time that these demons spoke the British language rather than English) Felix follows the general lines of that of Athanasius's Anthony. Now they tempted him to despair, now to excess in fasting. One night they would come to his den (made in the side of an old barrow into which treasure-hunters had dug) as ghastly shrieking humans with wild faces, filthy beards, scabby thighs, and swollen ankles; another night they would assume the shapes of hostile beasts, roaring, hissing, or croaking (there is presumably a psychological reading beneath the literal one). In this respect the life approximates to a tract on how to master diabolical power and shows confidence that it could be thoroughly mastered. One should remember, however, that the life of Anthony was as likely to have been known to Guthlac (probably from his Repton days, though he was organized to read and write on Crowland), as it was to Felix. At the same time, in a long tradition of hagiography, Guthlac's obedience to God's commands is pointed up by the obedience of the animal world to him, illustrated, for instance, by his ability annually to direct the swallows where to nest.

The details concerning visitors to Guthlac's hermitage show his continuing connections with the highest echelons of lay and clerical society as well as, according to Felix, his attracting the poor and afflicted. The priest Wilfrid, long bound to Guthlac by the bonds of spiritual friendship, was a frequent visitor. Bishop Headda, who had been consecrated to Lichfield in 691 and became bishop of Leicester in 709, also visited, and with him his secretary (*librarius*) Wigfrith. Wigfrith had opined that having lived among the Irish he could tell a true hermit from a false one and would be able to do so in Guthlac's case; when the party sat down to a meal, Guthlac asked the astonished secretary what he now thought of the man whom he had promised to judge. A number of miracles had to do with the exercise of prophetic powers through similar insights into his visitors. Bishop Headda insisted on ordaining Guthlac a priest. There is a suggestion of reluctance in this on the part of Guthlac, who was now approaching the end of his life; possibly the bishop's object was not only to venerate the holy man's powers, but also to control them by drawing him more tightly into the organized hierarchy of the church. Other visitors were monks from Abbess Ecgburh, daughter of King Aldwulf of the East Angles, enquiring who would take over the hermitage after Guthlac's death. They received the answer that it was one who had not yet been baptized (Cissa might none the less have been an aristocrat). Altogether this aspect of the life particularly justifies the view, as does its dedication to King Ælfwald of the East Angles (*r.* *c.*713–749), that, though a monk himself, Felix had a lay audience as well as a clerical one in mind and that the work, like Bede's *Historia ecclesiastica*, was written for 'the public church'.

The most interesting and important of all Guthlac's visitors, however, was Æthelbald, king of the Mercians (*r.* 716–57), in the days before he was king. He was in exile from Mercia, being grandson of Penda's brother Eowa and hence seen as a rival to his second cousin Ceolred, who became king in 709. Guthlac prophetically told Æthelbald that he knew of his afflictions and that God had heard his prayers and would make him a ruler (*principem populorum*). After Guthlac's death, Æthelbald returned to Crowland, clearly at the crisis of the struggle for the Mercian kingship, stayed in the hut 'where he used to stay when Guthlac was alive' (Felix, 165), and received a vision of reassurance from the saint. Obviously this is written with a strong element of retrospect in the light of Æthelbald's known veneration for Guthlac (which does not invalidate it), for the king chose as his burial place Repton, where Guthlac had entered religion. Not only did Æthelbald embellish Guthlac's shrine at Crowland, but it has been plausibly argued that it was also he who was originally responsible for introducing the saint's cult, with relics, into Hereford, where by the tenth century a church was dedicated to Guthlac, which archaeology suggests goes back to the ninth or even the eighth century. Unfortunately Guthlac cannot be fitted into his place in the Mercian royal genealogy; but his staunch and doubtless morally effective support for Æthelbald, by no means a saint, must have owed less to bonds of spiritual friendship than to a sense of close relationship in their earthly lineage.

The prime mover of Guthlac's cult was his sister Pega, who opened the saint's grave after twelve months, found the body undecayed, and moved it to the shrine embellished by Æthelbald. This cult gathered new momentum in the late Anglo-Saxon period and in the twelfth century: several manuscripts of Felix's life date from this time; the eleventh-century Leofric missal contains a Guthlac mass; a Crowland calendar from the mid-eleventh century lists his translation as 30 August, and an Ely calendar of the eleventh century, attested by three manuscripts, has his commemoration as 26 August. The finest testimony to his cult is the Guthlac roll (BL, Harley Roll, Y.6), depicting the saint's life in eighteen roundels.

HENRY MAYR-HARTING

**Sources** Felix, *Life of Saint Guthlac*, ed. and trans. B. Colgrave (1956) • C. W. Jones, *Saints' lives and chronicles in early England* (1947) • H. Mayr-Harting, *The coming of Christianity to Anglo-Saxon England* (1972) • A. Thacker, 'Kings, saints and monasteries in pre-viking Mercia', *Midland History*, 10 (1985), 1–25 • J. Roberts, 'An inventory of early Guthlac materials', *Mediaeval Studies*, 32 (1970), 193–233 • D. W. Rollason, *Saints and relics in Anglo-Saxon England* (1989)

**Guthrie, Alexander** (*d.* **1582**), civic administrator and religious activist, is first recorded on 10 January 1549, when he was admitted burgess and guild brother of Edinburgh. Nothing is known of his parentage or education. He became a lawyer who also engaged in trade, and was appointed common clerk of Edinburgh, probably in 1553. Although his own activities among Edinburgh's growing circle of protestants in the 1550s are not recorded, his wife, Janet Henryson (or Henderson), was one of the group of wives of influential burgesses with whom John Knox corresponded while in exile in Geneva. She was addressed as his 'beloved sister' in a letter of March 1558 (*Knox's History*, 4.247).

In April 1559 Guthrie's career became embroiled in controversy, when he was arrested by the Catholic provost George, fifth Lord Seton. Later Guthrie was sent, along with the protestant minority group on the town council, to negotiate with the lords of congregation when they reached the capital in June 1559. Along with Adam Fullarton and Alexander Clark he became one of the most consistent of the 'better sort' who relied on the 'amity' with England. He was a regular informant for the English ambassador, Thomas Randolph, from at least October 1560 onwards. To his Roman Catholic enemies he was known as King Guthrie (Lynch, 24). As such he took a leading role alongside Knox in the consolidation of Edinburgh's reformation by the new regime, brought to power by a coup in 1559–60.

Guthrie's role in the government of the town increased through his continuous presence on the burgh council between 1561 and 1565. From 1562 he was also dean of guild, with responsibility for oversight of the burgh church of St Giles, for which Knox was first minister, and he was a member of the kirk session in 1561–2, the only year before the 1570s for which session records exist. Holding both burgh and political office simultaneously was unusual. It gave Guthrie a central place in the affairs of the capital in these years. He did not scruple to become involved in conspiracy and violence. He was one of the four 'captains' of protestant armed bands arrested for drilling in the royal park near the palace of Holyroodhouse in July 1565, shortly before the abortive coup led by James Stewart, earl of Moray. His connections with Edinburgh's legal establishment and with key protestant dissidents within the royal administration were demonstrated by the appearance in court as one of his sureties of Patrick Bellenden of Stenness, brother of the justice clerk John Bellenden of Auchnoull. In 1556 Guthrie had acted as godfather to one of the children of another influential legal family, the Bannatynes, which was in turn closely connected to the Bellendens.

In 1566 Guthrie was implicated in the murder of the queen's servant David Riccio. After fleeing with two prominent conspirators who both held high office, Bellenden of Auchnoull and James McGill, clerk register, Guthrie was outlawed and replaced as town clerk by a royal nominee, David Chalmers, despite a formal protest by the town council. The fact that he was among the last of the Riccio conspirators to be granted a remission, in December 1566, when he was also restored to office, confirms his prominence in the affair. His subsequent career was less colourful. He continued as town clerk until his death on 23 August 1582, though he had briefly been charged with treason for failing to leave the burgh for some six months after its occupation by the queen's party in April 1571; but he successfully denied presiding over meetings of the burgh court during that time. Although Guthrie again served on the council in 1576–8, his final years seem to have been spent largely in the burgh archives in his care; the earliest records of the burgh, dating from 1403, exist only as a partial transcript devised under his supervision in 1579–80. Guthrie was succeeded in office by his son, Alexander. His wife, who survived him, did not lose her radical opinions in her old age. She was exiled from the capital along with the wives of the burgh's exiled dissident ministers, in the autumn of 1584. She lived until 1600.

MICHAEL LYNCH

**Sources** M. Lynch, *Edinburgh and the Reformation* (1981), 260, 282, 331–2 [and the references therein] • J. D. Marwick, ed., *Extracts from the records of the burgh of Edinburgh, AD 1557–1571; 1573–1589*, [3–4], Scottish Burgh RS, 4–5 (1875–82) • T. van Heijnsbergen, 'The interaction between literature and history in Queen Mary's Edinburgh: the Bannatyne manuscript and its prosopographical context', *The Renaissance in Scotland: studies in literature, religion, history, and culture offered to John Durkan*, ed. A. A. MacDonald and others (1994), 183–225 • *John Knox's History of the Reformation in Scotland*, ed. W. C. Dickinson, 2 vols. (1949) • *The works of John Knox*, ed. D. Laing, 6 vols., Wodrow Society, 12 (1846–64), vol. 4 • R. Pitcairn, ed., *Ancient criminal trials in Scotland*, 7 pts in 3, Bannatyne Club, 42 (1833) • *CSP Scot.*, 1547–71 • Edinburgh testaments, 6 Dec 1583, General Register Office for Scotland, Edinburgh • Edinburgh testaments, 23 May 1600, General Register Office for Scotland, Edinburgh [Janet Henryson, wife]

**Guthrie, Sir David, of that ilk** (*d.* 1474), administrator, was the son of Master Alexander Guthrie (*d.* before 1455). Alexander's principal estate of Kincaldrum was in his native county of Angus, where he held both judicial and financial appointments, was sheriff-depute, and enjoyed the patronage of first the Ogilvys and then the Lindsay earls of Crawford. The date of David's birth is unknown, but in December 1443 he matriculated in arts at Cologne and on 20 May 1445 he was presented there for his bachelor's degree by another Scot who was to become prominent later in royal government as king's secretary, Archibald Whitelaw (*d.* 1495); Guthrie also incepted as master of arts at the University of Paris in 1447. He had succeeded to the estate of Kincaldrum by 1455, and first appears in a public role as sheriff-clerk and sheriff-depute of Forfar. Like that of his father, his career benefited from the patronage of the earls of Crawford. His first marriage was to a daughter of another Forfar family, the Maules of Panmure, but they had no children and it ended in annulment on grounds of consanguinity. His second marriage, to Janet, possibly a daughter of Dundas of that ilk, occurred before 1465.

Guthrie's career in royal administration began during the minority of James III, and may have been helped by the Crawford connection, since the fifth earl was prominent in the politics of the period. Guthrie was treasurer from 1461 to 1468, when he became lord clerk register, a post he held until 1473. He was also comptroller between 1466 and 1468. After the king's assumption of active control of government in 1469 Guthrie continued in office; he was comptroller again (1470–71) and justiciar south of Forth (1471–4). In 1467 and 1474, as one of the lords of the articles, he was responsible for preparing legislation. Further marks of the king's personal favour were the conferral of a knighthood and his appointment as captain of the royal guard in 1473. In 1466 he recovered the ancestral lands of Guthrie, Angus, which one of his forebears had sold, and in 1468 was given a royal licence to erect and fortify a tower there. His foundation of a collegiate church at Guthrie obtained papal confirmation in June 1479. The legal skills which Guthrie evidently possessed were not just placed at the disposal of the crown—in 1465 and 1466 he acted as forespeaker for William Douglas of Drumlanrig and Gilbert, Lord Kennedy, respectively, and in 1472 he received a grant from the earl of Erroll for his good counsel.

Guthrie's last appearance as a witness to royal documents in the register of the great seal occurs in June 1474, although an error in the printed version makes it seem that he was still active early in 1477. In fact he died between 7 and 14 July 1474; on 23 August 1474 Alexander Guthrie had an instrument of sasine for the lands of Guthrie as heir to the late David Guthrie.

HECTOR L. MACQUEEN

**Sources** J. M. Thomson and others, eds., *Registrum magni sigilli regum Scotorum / The register of the great seal of Scotland*, 11 vols. (1882–1914), vol. 2 · G. Burnett and others, eds., *The exchequer rolls of Scotland*, 7–8 (1884–5) · T. Dickson, ed., *Compota thesaurariorum regum Scotorum / Accounts of the lord high treasurer of Scotland*, 1 (1877) · H. Keussen, ed., *Die Matrikel der Universität Köln*, 1 (Bonn, 1928) · H. Denifle and A. Chatelain, eds., *Auctarium chartularii universitatis Parisiensis*, 2 (Paris, 1897) · N. Macdougall, *James III: a political study* (1982) · A. Borthwick and H. MacQueen, 'Three fifteenth-century cases', *Juridical Review*, new ser., 31 (1986), 123–51 · A. L. Murray, 'The lord clerk register', *SHR*, 53 (1974), 124–56 · R. J. Lyall, 'Scottish students and masters at the universities of Cologne and Louvain in the 15th century', *Innes Review*, 36 (1985), 55–73 · A. R. Borthwick, 'The king, council and councillors in Scotland, *c*.1430–1460', PhD diss., U. Edin., 1989 · A. R. Borthwick and H. L. MacQueen, '"Rare creatures for their age": Alexander and David Guthrie, graduate lairds and royal servants', *Church, chronicle and learning in medieval and early renaissance Scotland*, ed. B. E. Crawford (1999) · NA Scot., Guthrie of Guthrie MSS, GD 188/1 · NL Scot., Saltoun MSS, CH 14153, 14154 · NA Scot., Dunbar of Westfield titles, bundle 1/56 · Historisches Archiv der Stadt Köln, univ 479
**Archives** NA Scot., GD 188/1 | NL Scot., Saltoun MSS, CH 14153–14211

**Guthrie, Frederick** (1833–1886), chemist and physicist, was born on 15 October 1833 in Bayswater, London, youngest of the six children of Alexander Guthrie, a tailor. Francis Guthrie, who distinguished himself as a mathematician in South Africa, was an older brother. Guthrie's early interest in chemistry was stimulated by Henry Watts, his private tutor until he enrolled at University College School, London, in 1845. Four years later Guthrie matriculated at University College where he learned mathematics from Augustus De Morgan and made a special study of chemistry in the laboratories of Professor Williamson. Before his graduation in 1855, Guthrie followed the pattern of many British chemists in pursuing a doctorate in the Germanic states. After a spell with Bunsen at the University of Heidelberg, he investigated organic salts and acids with Kolbe at the University of Marburg, attaining his PhD *summa cum laude* in 1855. Parts of his thesis were published in Liebig's *Annalen* and in other international journals. These included Guthrie's findings on what later gained notoriety as mustard gas, and his more felicitous proposals on the therapeutic applications of amyl nitrite.

After returning to Britain, Guthrie accepted consecutive appointments as assistant in the laboratories of three distinguished chemistry professors: from 1856 he worked at Owens College, Manchester, with Edward Frankland, and then with his successor, Henry Roscoe, before taking up a post under Lyon Playfair at the University of Edinburgh in 1859. In that year his reputation in organic chemistry won Guthrie a fellowship of the Royal Society of Edinburgh, and a lectureship in chemistry and physics at the Royal College, Mauritius, which he commenced in May 1861; later that year, on 10 December, he and his wife, Agnes (*née* Bickell), had a son, Frederick Bickell Guthrie [*see below*]. One of Guthrie's colleagues in Mauritius was the novelist and writer Walter Besant, with whom Guthrie formed a lifelong friendship; indeed it was probably Besant's influence that led Guthrie, while in Mauritius, to express poetic ambitions in 'The Jew', published in 1863 under the pseudonym Frederick Cerny.

At this sparsely equipped outpost of the British empire Guthrie turned his chemical expertise to subjects immediately to hand such as the island's river-waters and its principal agricultural produce, sugar-cane. With similar resourcefulness he undertook an empirical investigation of fluid drops and bubbles in 1864–5, the results of which were published in the *Proceedings of the Royal Society*. However, as with many of his subsequent publications in physics, his non-mathematical conclusions were couched in his own idiosyncratic terminology. Two years later, in June 1867, both Besant and Guthrie left their posts after a major confrontation with the rector and at the height of a devastating fever epidemic.

On his return to London, Guthrie worked with John Tyndall (1820–1893) on the thermal resistance of liquids, the collaboration resulting in his sole publication in the Royal Society's *Philosophical Transactions*. After his six years of relative isolation from Europe, his more strictly chemical work was not so well received, however. 'Very bad' was the verdict of Herbert McLeod on a paper presented by Guthrie at the Chemical Society on 16 April 1868 (McLeod), and reviews of his chemistry textbooks were not always kinder. Guthrie's often precarious financial position improved somewhat in 1869 when, partly on Tyndall's recommendation, he took over Tyndall's lectureship in physics at the Department of Science and Art's School of Mines in Jermyn Street.

In this post Guthrie not only taught mining students, but shared with Thomas Henry Huxley the new task of giving summer practical courses to the schoolteachers from the Department of Science and Art. Both soon campaigned for working space to extend these classes into a full academic year, and upon removal in 1871–2 to the Science Schools (renamed the Normal School of Science in 1881) in South Kensington, Guthrie acquired a ground-floor suite of laboratories on Exhibition Road. Elevated to a professorship, Guthrie worked on an intensive yet frugal scheme to equip the department's teachers with the skills and apparatus to give practical instruction in physics. With the financial support of the department and the collaboration of London colleagues G. Carey Foster and William Barrett, and the later assistance of C. V. Boys, Guthrie's scheme enabled hundreds of teachers to give school demonstrations on light, heat, electricity, and magnetism. Gradually this programme transformed the papers of the 100,000 or so Department of Science and Art candidates in physics that Guthrie examined. His associated textbook *Magnetism and Electricity* (1873; 2nd edn, 1884) sold over 10,000 copies. In 1895, after his death, his 1877 text *Practical Physics* was translated into Japanese (rendered as Simple experiments in teaching physics, and some of his apparatus incorporated into Japanese classrooms.

Much scepticism had initially greeted Guthrie's Department of Science and Art-sponsored radical plan: 'Many told me that it could not succeed, many that it ought not to succeed' (Guthrie, 663). Given that it did succeed for many of his students, it is unfortunate that the most often cited source on Guthrie's instruction is the hostile testimony in H. G. Wells's autobiography. However, a few months after narrowly passing his last course in 1886, it was almost certainly Wells, as editor of *Science Schools Journal*, who described Guthrie as 'deservedly a favourite with all who have passed under his instruction' (Wells, 'Guthrie', 3). Guthrie's more distinguished scientific protégés Oliver Lodge, Silvanus Phillips Thompson, and John Ambrose Fleming certainly showed warm respect for 'old daddy', as they jokingly called him in the mid-1870s.

The successful launch of the Physical Society of London in March 1874 owed much to Guthrie's support among teachers of physics in English schools and colleges—especially in London. His reasons for founding it stemmed from his frustration at the Royal Society's publication of several innovative papers as abstracts in the society's *Proceedings* rather than in full in its more prestigious *Transactions*. It even took more than a year for Guthrie's account of 'approach caused by vibration' (1870) to appear in the *Proceedings*. He was none the less elected a fellow of the Royal Society in 1871 after Sir William Thomson took a keen interest in applying this paper's insights to his vortex model of the atom. In 1873, however, the Royal Society's referees were unconvinced by Guthrie's claims regarding a novel electrostatic phenomenon in hot metals, although this was subsequently interpreted by J. A. Fleming as the first observation of thermionic emission.

In the summer of 1873 Guthrie canvassed support for a new society to discuss 'incomplete' physical researches that could not find an audience among existing scientific institutions. From the first gathering in March 1874, Guthrie acted as demonstrator for the experimental illustrations that were a central feature of the Physical Society's fortnightly meetings. Many, if not all, papers were primarily about experimental matters: Alexander Graham Bell, for example, gave the London début of the telephone at a society meeting in 1877. Papers often related to lecture demonstration apparatus, reflecting the predominant presence of teachers in the society's membership. The *Proceedings of the Physical Society* were also a vehicle for Guthrie's own researches on eutectics and cryohydrates. Despite James Clerk Maxwell's refusal to join, almost every major physicist in England was a member of the society by the time of Guthrie's tenure as president in 1884–6.

Guthrie's wife, Agnes, predeceased him, as did two subsequent wives of whom nothing is known. Then, on 10 April 1882, he married Blanche Gertrude (*b.* 1861/2), daughter of Thomas Reynolds, professor of music. A genial, humorous, if eccentric character at the heart of London's physics community, Guthrie died from throat cancer four years later, on 21 October 1886. He was buried at Kensal Green cemetery on 26 October. The loyalty and affection which Guthrie inspired in his friends is palpable in the efforts to which Huxley and others went to secure a state pension for his widow and younger children.

**Frederick Bickell Guthrie** (1861–1927), agricultural chemist, was born on 10 December 1861 in Mauritius, the son of Frederick Guthrie and Agnes Bickell. He was educated at University College, London, and after receiving his PhD from the University of Marburg in 1882, he was successively demonstrator in chemistry at Queen's College, Cork (1882–88), the Royal College of Science, London (1888–90), and the University of Sydney (1890–91). On 15 November 1890 he married Ada Adams at Neutral Bay. The couple had two sons (both killed in the First World War) and a daughter.

Guthrie's main scientific research in Australia was undertaken as a chemist to the department of agriculture (1892–1924) where he collaboratively developed methods of analysing wheat flour and important new techniques in cross-breeding wheats to produce robust strains with good baking qualities. Author or co-author of 180 papers, he was, from 1903 to 1904, president of the Royal Society of New South Wales. He died at Moss Vale, New South Wales, on 7 February 1927. His name is commemorated in the Guthrie medal, awarded every three years by the Royal Australian Chemical Institute. GRAEME J. N. GOODAY

**Sources** G. C. Foster, 'Frederick Guthrie', *Nature*, 35 (1886–7), 8–10 • G. C. Foster, *Proceedings of the Physical Society*, 8 (1886–7), 9–13 • [H. G. Wells], 'The late Professor Guthrie', *Science Schools Journal*, 1 (1886), 3–4 • O. Lodge, *Past years: an autobiography* (1931) • J. A. Fleming, *Memories of a scientific life* (1934) • F. Guthrie, 'Cantor lectures [1–3]', *Journal of the Society of Arts*, 34 (1885–6), 629–41, 647–50, 659–63 • W. Besant, *Autobiography of Sir Walter Besant* (1902) • H. G. Wells, *Experiment in autobiography*, 1 (1934) • W. H. Brock and TeraKawa, 'The introduction of heurism into Japan', *History of Education*, 7 (1978), 35–44 • H. McLeod, 'Diary', Royal Institution of Great Britain, London • 'Guthrie, Frederick Bickell', *AusDB*, vol. 9 • *CGPLA Eng. & Wales* (1886)

**Archives** ICL, archives, Huxley MSS, corresp. with Blanche Guthrie • ICL, archives • RS, items concerning referees' reports for the Royal Society journals

**Likenesses** White of Littlehampton, photograph, repro. in T. Chambers, ed., *Register of associates, Royal College of Chemistry, Royal School of Mines* (1896), facing p. civ • portrait (after photograph by White), ICL • wood-engraving, NPG; repro. in *ILN* (13 Nov 1886)

**Wealth at death** £461 13*s*. 2*d*.: administration, 29 Nov 1886, *CGPLA Eng. & Wales*

**Guthrie, Frederick Bickell** (1861–1927). *See under* Guthrie, Frederick (1833–1886).

**Guthrie, George James** (1785–1856), surgeon, only son of Andrew Guthrie, of Lower James Street, Golden Square, London, a chiropodist, was born in London on 1 May 1785. Having been apprenticed to John Phillips, surgeon, in 1798, and after serving as assistant in the York Hospital,

London, Guthrie passed the examination for the membership of the Royal College of Surgeons on 5 February 1801, when not yet sixteen, in the year before an age limit of twenty-one was imposed.

In March 1801 Guthrie was appointed by Inspector-General Rush, a friend and a member of the army medical board, as assistant surgeon to the 29th regiment, with which he served in Canada from 1803 to 1808. He was then ordered to the Iberian peninsula, where he remained (except for an interval in 1810) from 1808 until 1814, taking principal charge of the wounded at many important battles, and gaining the duke of Wellington's special commendation. He was promoted staff surgeon in 1811. In his peninsular experiences, Guthrie often displayed the qualities of a soldier as well as of a surgeon; he captured a French gun single-handed from the retreating enemy at Oporto, and, after one battle, Albuera, where his assistant surgeon was killed at his side, he operated for eighteen hours a day for several days (Cantlie, 1.330–01). After the battle of Salamanca he introduced the practice of making long incisions through the skin to relieve diffused erysipelas, and in Lisbon he was among the first to employ a straight splint for fractured femurs. Guthrie is noted for reducing the number of amputations performed by army surgeons following gunshot wounds.

In 1814 Guthrie retired on half pay, and after returning to London he attended the surgical lectures of Charles Bell and Benjamin Brodie at the Great Windmill Street school of medicine, and of John Abernethy at St Bartholomew's Hospital. Guthrie's experiences during the Peninsular War enabled him to make considerable improvements in practical surgery. These included introducing the practice of ligaturing both ends of a divided artery, thus overturning standard surgical procedure. Guthrie made further surgical advances after Waterloo, when he successfully amputated a man's leg at the hip joint, divided the muscles of the calf to tie the main artery, and extracted a ball from a man's bladder. Each of these operations was new, and the cases excited great interest. After the war the patients were sent to the York Hospital, then situated where Eaton Square now stands, and Guthrie gave lectures and for two years took charge of two wards in which illustrative cases were treated and exhibited. He was also the first in England who used a lithotrite for crushing a stone in the bladder. At this time the duke of York offered him knighthood, which Guthrie declined owing to lack of means; he gave lectures on surgery at Little Windmill Street from October 1816 for nearly thirty years, and these were free to all the officers of the army, navy, and East India Company.

In December 1816 Guthrie founded an infirmary in London for diseases of the eye, afterwards the Royal Westminster Ophthalmic Hospital at Charing Cross, to which he was chief surgeon. An incautious remark that before a man could successfully remove cataracts he must have 'put out a hatful of eyes' in one of his lectures led to attacks upon him in *The Lancet*, which termed his hospital the 'blind manufactory' (Clarke, 259). Guthrie began an action for libel, which he afterwards withdrew when his partner in the hospital refused to support the practice. Thomas Wakley, the proprietor of *The Lancet*, subsequently apologized and became Guthrie's firm friend.

Guthrie was elected assistant surgeon to the Westminster Hospital in 1823, and full surgeon in 1827; he resigned in 1843 to make way for his son, Charles Guthrie, as assistant surgeon. In 1824 he became a member of the council of the Royal College of Surgeons, of which he was president in 1833, 1841, and 1854. He was professor of anatomy and surgery from 1828 to 1831, and lectured on the principal subjects in which he had made improvements. As a councillor he succeeded in carrying numerous reforms in college procedure and in its requirements from candidates for its diplomas; but he strongly opposed the new charter of 1843. He was elected a fellow of the Royal Society in 1827.

Guthrie was twice married. With his first wife, Margaret, daughter of Walter Patterson, lieutenant-governor of Prince Edward Island, he had two sons and one daughter; the elder son, the Revd Lowry Guthrie, died before him, and the younger, Charles Gardiner Guthrie, became a capable surgeon, but died in 1859, aged forty-two. Of his second wife little is known. Guthrie had keen, energetic features, with remarkably piercing black eyes. Clarke recalls him as 'shrewd, quick, active and robust, he was always in good spirits and most punctual in all his appointments' (Clarke, 258). His Hunterian oration in 1830, delivered without notes, hesitation, or mistake, was a notable success. His somewhat brusque military manner concealed a kind heart, and, though dreaded as an examiner, he never rejected a candidate by his unsupported vote. His lectures were very popular, being interspersed with anecdotes and illustrative cases, and caused an 'exhibition of jealousy among his colleagues' (Spicer, 102–3). As a surgeon his coolness and delicacy of hand were of the highest order.

Guthrie wrote numerous medical works, particularly on surgery and ophthalmology. His most celebrated work was that on gunshot wounds; published at the end of 1814, it dealt especially with wounds of the limbs requiring amputation and advocated immediate operation on the battlefield. The third edition, in 1827, was enlarged, and entitled *On Gunshot Wounds*; the work was translated into German in 1821. A compendium of his former works, with new comments, issued in 1853 as *Commentaries on the Surgery of the War, 1808–15*, reached a fifth edition; a sixth edition, with comments on the surgery of the Crimean War, appeared in 1855. These works are both interesting and graphic, and contain valuable comments on military arrangements.

Guthrie died at his home, 4 Berkeley Street, Berkeley Square, London, on 1 May 1856, and was buried at Kensal Green cemetery on 6 May.

G. T. Bettany, *rev.* Patrick Wallis

**Sources** 'Biographical sketch', *The Lancet* (15 June 1850), 726–38 • *The Lancet* (10 May 1856), 519–20 • J. F. Clarke, *Autobiographical recollections of the medical profession* (1874) • W. G. Spicer, *Westminster hospital: an outline of its history* (1924) • T. J. Pettigrew, *Medical portrait gallery: biographical memoirs of the most celebrated physicians, surgeons … who have contributed to the advancement of medical science*, 4 vols. in 2 [1838–40] • N. Cantlie, *A history of the army medical department*, 2 vols.

(1974) • J. H. Cole, 'Some observations of George James Guthrie on gunshot wounds', *Journal of the Royal Society of Medicine*, 84 (1991), 675–7 • P. J. Wallis and R. V. Wallis, *Eighteenth century medics*, 2nd edn (1988) • Boase, *Mod. Eng. biog.* • D. P. Henige, *Colonial governors from the fifteenth century to the present* (1970)

**Archives** RCS Eng., letters | W. Sussex RO, letters to duke of Richmond

**Likenesses** J. Cochran, 1840 (after H. Room), Wellcome L. • W. Walker, engraving, 1853? (after H. Room), RS • E. Davis, marble bust, 1857, RCS Eng. • Count D'Orsay, pencil drawing, RCP Lond. • R. Easton, miniature, NPG • H. Room, miniature, RCS Eng. • engraving (after sketch by H. Anelay), repro. in 'Biographical sketch', 727

**Guthrie, Sir Giles Connop McEachern, second baronet (1916–1979)**, airline administrator, was born in Westminster, London, on 21 March 1916, the son of Sir Connop Thirlwall Robert Guthrie, first baronet (1882–1945), a lieutenant in the Grenadier Guards, and his wife, Elia, *née* McEacharn. Educated at Eton College and at Cambridge, he began flying at university. In 1936, at the age of twenty, he partnered C. W. A. Scott in the Portsmouth to Johannesburg air race, theirs being the only team to complete the competition. After university Guthrie obtained his commercial pilot's licence and joined British Airways, a newly formed airline in competition with Imperial Airways. In 1939 he married Rhona, daughter of Frederic Stileman; they had three sons. He held the post of traffic officer with British Airways until the outbreak of war, when he joined the Fleet Air Arm as a fighter pilot. He was awarded the DSC in 1941 while serving on the aircraft-carrier HMS *Ark Royal*, and by 1943 had been promoted to the rank of lieutenant-commander.

With his father's death at the end of the war, Guthrie succeeded to the baronetcy. He remained in the Fleet Air Arm as a test pilot until 1946 and was appointed OBE. Returning to civilian life, he entered banking and became managing director of the merchant bank Brown, Shipley & Co., as well as holding positions on the boards of the Prudential Assurance Company and Radio Rentals. In 1959 he returned to civil aviation when he was appointed to the board of the state-owned British European Airways (BEA). He retained his membership of BEA for the next ten years, but at the beginning of 1964 he took on a more demanding assignment when he became chairman and chief executive of the British Overseas Airways Corporation (BOAC). At the time, BOAC was losing money and had an accumulated deficit of £80 million. His predecessors, the chairman Sir Matthew Slattery and the managing director Sir Basil Smallpiece, had requested government permission to write off the debt which had been incurred as part of the cost of introducing British aircraft to BOAC's fleet. However, the minister of aviation, Julian Amery, had preferred to await the findings of the confidential Corbett Report on BOAC's performance.

When Guthrie took up his position, he obtained not only the debt write-off which Slattery and Smallpiece had sought, but also a written undertaking from Amery that the airline would in future be run as a commercial enterprise, with any deviation from this policy—on grounds of national interest—requiring a specific directive from the minister. Under his chairmanship, BOAC was swiftly returned to profitability. It was an achievement aided by a general upturn in the airline industry after 1964, but performance was also raised by reducing the number of staff and closing unprofitable routes. At the heart of his plan to restore the corporation's finances was a deal negotiated with the government to reduce substantially the number of Super VC10 aircraft which had been ordered from Vickers some six years earlier.

A man of great personal charm, Guthrie brought a shrewd business mind and steady leadership to BOAC. He is chiefly remembered for restoring the profit motive to the management of the national-flag carrier at a time when it seemed to have lost its sense of purpose. To a certain extent his achievement was overshadowed by the implementation of the Edwards committee recommendations after 1969, and the subsequent merger of BOAC and BEA as the modern British Airways.

Guthrie retired as chairman of BOAC at the end of 1968. During the next two years he spent some time creating an airline self-insurance company, Air Transport Insurance, of which he was chairman. Otherwise he lived quietly in Jersey for the remainder of his life. He died of a malignant brain tumour on 31 December 1979. His eldest son, Malcolm Connop (*b.* 1942), succeeded to his title.

PETER J. LYTH

**Sources** *The Times* (3 Jan 1980) • *BOAC annual report and accounts* (1964–9) • W. Bray, *The history of BOAC, 1939–1974* (1973) • *The financial problems of the British Overseas Airway Corporation* (1963) • R. Higham, 'Guthrie, Sir Giles', *DBB*

**Guthrie [Guthry], Henry (1600?–1676)**, bishop of Dunkeld and historian, said to have been born in Coupar Angus, was the second son of Henry Guthrie (*d.* in or after 1633), minister of Bendochy, Forfarshire, who for a time had charge of Coupar Angus, and his wife, Elizabeth Small. He evidently gave 'proofs of his capacity and genius' early, making considerable progress with Greek and Latin at 'inferior schools' before progressing to the University of St Andrews (*Memoirs of Henry Guthry*, iv). After graduating on 16 July 1621 he studied theology, and served as a tutor in the earl of Mar's family for a time before being appointed minister of Guthrie (a church founded by his ancestors of the family of Guthrie of Guthrie) in 1625. He was presented to Stirling by Charles I in 1632, evidently on the recommendation of the earl of Mar, and in 1634 became a member of the Scottish court of high commission.

When opposition to the king's reforms in the worship and discipline of the Church of Scotland broke out in 1637, however, Guthrie joined in the agitation, signing the national covenant in 1638. Once the church was reformed on a presbyterian basis Guthrie's abilities led to his serving as moderator of the presbytery of Stirling and of the synod of Perth and Stirling, but he soon came into conflict with more radical presbyterian ministers over the question of private prayer meetings or conventicles. Guthrie believed these meetings were incompatible with presbyterianism and were likely to lead to independency, and suppressed them in Stirling. He attempted to get the general assembly to pass an act to ban them in 1639, but in spite of his 'verie loud complaints' (*Letters and Journals of Robert Baillie*, 1.249) agreement was reached only on measures to regulate them.

In 1640 Guthrie was chosen to preach before the general assembly in Aberdeen, but declined, evidently because he feared that that the provost of Aberdeen intended to use the occasion to request that he become minister there and he did not wish to leave Stirling. His opponents on the question of conventicles persuaded the assembly to rebuke him publicly for his presumption in refusing to preach, but this did not deter him from again raising the conventicles issue, and he found strong support (especially from northern Scotland) in condemning them. Again compromise was reached, but Guthrie had made himself many enemies, not only among those who supported conventicles but among men who feared that his insistence on raising such a divisive issue might prove disastrous. The covenanters were resisting Charles I's attempts to overthrow them in the bishops' wars, and many felt that if Guthrie had got his way in punishing those organizing conventicles this would have 'fyred our Church more than any other brand that Satan at this tyme, in all his witt, could have invented' (Gordon, 2.222).

The issue caused further bitter controversy in the 1641 assembly, and emerged again in 1643, when it debated the offers of the English parliamentarians to agree religious uniformity with Scotland in return for military help in their war against Charles I. Guthrie expressed suspicion, and demanded that the English be made to state explicitly that they would adopt presbyterianism, but he received no support, and instead 'all the zealots cried him down as a rotten malignant, and an enemy to the cause, conceiving that his pleading for Presbyterian government, flowed not from any love to it, but to baffle the work' (*Memoirs of Henry Guthry*, 137). In the end Guthrie, fearing discipline from the assembly for earlier expressions of dissent from church policy on intervention in England, 'made no dinne' and agreed that 'the necessitie of the tyme' (*Letters and Journals of Robert Baillie*, 1.291, 295) made it inexpedient to raise the issue of conventicles.

During the period of Scots intervention in the English war (1644–7) Guthrie continued to avoid involvement in controversy. But in 1648, when the church opposed a new intervention, this time to support Charles I under the terms of the engagement, Guthrie, 'a very bold man, but in this and the late [recent] Assemblies very quiet, gave in a petition against this course, but rather than to make dinn in vaine, took it up again', thus withdrawing it when it won no support (*Letters and Journals of Robert Baillie*, 3.55). After the overthrow of the engagers he was deposed from the ministry (14 November 1648), and it is said that he was 'forced to leave the Kingdome' for a time (Hunter, 1.176). However, in October 1655 the synod of Perth and Stirling declared him capable of being a minister, and in April 1656 he was admitted minister of Kilspindie.

Both before and after the restoration of the monarchy in 1660 Stirling made efforts to have him restored as minister there, but he refused on account of 'infirmity and weakness' (Hunter, 1.176). In July 1661 the Scottish parliament voted him £150 sterling for his sufferings, though this may never have been paid. Guthrie accepted the restoration of episcopacy, and from 1662 to 1665 he served as moderator of the presbytery of Perth. On 24 August 1665 he was consecrated bishop of Dunkeld, and from 1666 to 1672 was also the minister of Meigle in Perthshire.

The presbyterian experiment of the 1640s and 1650s had persuaded Guthrie that bishops were necessary to maintain orderly government of the church, but he was moderate in his claims for episcopacy, regarding it as expediency rather than ordained by God, and as a bishop he was reputed never to have 'carried his authority higher, than to be the settled president of his clergy' (*Memoirs of Henry Guthry*, xi). The zeal for suppressing potential schismatics that he had shown in the early 1640s faded with age and experience, and in July 1676 he refused to allow his clergy to read from their pulpits an act of the archbishop and synod of St Andrews denouncing schismatics.

In July 1674 Guthrie was described as 'an old, infirm man' (Hunter, 1.177). He died in 1676. There is no evidence that he ever married. Henry Guthrie's memoirs (originally called 'observations') of public events circulated widely in manuscript long before his death, though they were not published until 1702. They proved popular as a brief account of the troubles in Scotland, but their reliability is variable. They are valuable for events in the church in which Guthrie was himself involved, but though much of what he writes on politics was based on hearsay, it often preserves useful anecdotes. However, the work is, not surprisingly, also calculated to justify his own journey from episcopacy to presbyterianism and back again. Guthrie's hostility to the dukes of Hamilton, whom he (like many royalists) considered incompetent if not treacherous in their dealings with Charles I, provoked a furious response from the intemperate Sir James Turner, who compiled 'Bishop Guthry's observations of the late rebellion observed' designed to show that Guthrie was a man 'not to be trusted in what he writes' unless his words were supported 'by more faithfull authors' (Turner, 232). Turner accuses Guthrie of malicious lies, but it would probably be more accurate to condemn him for an over-readiness to believe rumours that supported his bias against the Hamiltons, and for a general tendency to present gossip as fact. DAVID STEVENSON

**Sources** J. Hunter, *The diocese and presbytery of Dunkeld, 1660–1689*, 2 vols. [1917] · *DNB* · *The memoirs of Henry Guthry, late bishop*, ed. G. Crawford, 2nd edn (1748) · J. Turner, *Memoirs of his own life and times, 1632–1670*, ed. T. Thomson, Bannatyne Club, 28 (1829) · *The letters and journals of Robert Baillie*, ed. D. Laing, 3 vols. (1841–2) · *Fasti Scot.*, new edn, vol. 7 · J. Gordon, *History of Scots affairs from 1637–1641*, ed. J. Robertson and G. Grub, 3 vols., Spalding Club, 1, 3, 5 (1841)

**Archives** Harvard U., Houghton L., memoirs, MS Eng 1078

**Guthrie, James** (*c.*1612–1661), Church of Scotland minister, was born about 1612, the son of the laird of Guthrie, a prominent Forfarshire landowner. He was educated at the University of St Andrews, where he graduated MA, and served as a regent of St Leonard's College; he was distinguished for his lectures on philosophy. Originally 'of the Episcopall way' (Wodrow, *Analecta*, 2.158), he seems to have harboured hopes of ecclesiastical preferment and even went so far as to court one of the archbishop's daughters, although in the event he married Jane Ramsay of Sheilhill. At some point during the 1630s, however, he became a zealous presbyterian, most likely through the influence of Samuel Rutherford, earning himself in time the nickname 'Sicker Foot'. Subsequently he aligned himself with what Stevenson termed the kirk's radical party, a group of presbyterian ministers who circumvented the religious policies of Charles I by keeping conventicles, or private prayer meetings, where the godly could assemble for religious instruction and mutual edification. In 1638 he signed the national covenant.

Ordained to Lauder, Berwickshire, in 1642, from 1643 onwards Guthrie was a regular member of both the general assembly and its powerful standing committee, the commission for the public affairs of the kirk. In 1646 he was chosen by the general assembly as part of a delegation to wait upon Charles I at Newcastle and press him to accept presbyterianism and the covenants. With the failure of the royalist engagement and the establishment of the theocratic kirk regime in 1648 he emerged as the natural leader of the radical party, succeeding the recently deceased George Gillespie as the chief architect of the assembly's acts and its commission's papers. He was no lover of the house of Stuart and, following the execution of Charles I on 30 January 1649, was 'passionate' against proclaiming Charles II king, 'till his qualification for government had first been tryed and allowed' (*Letters and Journals of Robert Baillie*, 114). He consequently opposed both the 1649 treaty of The Hague and the 1650 treaty of Breda.

Guthrie was translated to Stirling by order of the commission and admitted on 16 January 1650; he remained there until the Restoration. Following the Cromwellian invasion of Scotland in June 1650 he became an outspoken critic of the government. He denounced the king for his manifest insincerity in subscribing the covenants and called upon the committee of estates to purge the covenanting army of all known former engagers and royalist malignants. In the ensuing controversy between moderate and radical covenanters he was a leading proponent of the radicals' cause. On 24 October, at his insistence, the moderate controlled commission reluctantly passed an act excommunicating the royalist General John Middleton. The next Lord's day Guthrie pronounced the sentence from his Stirling pulpit, despite last-minute appeals by the king and estates. Middleton was outraged and never forgave the affront. In the same month Guthrie participated in the drafting of the western remonstrance, in which the radicals announced their intention to withhold support from Charles until he repented of his malignant associations. When the commission condemned the remonstrance on 28 November 1650 he and his radical colleagues engaged in a complete boycott of its meetings. He and David Bennet publicly denounced the first public resolution of 14 December 1650, in which the commission conceded to parliament that acts barring malignant royalists from military service might legally be lifted. For their efforts they were summoned to appear before the king and estates. The two complied but refused to acknowledge the jurisdiction of the crown in what they contended was a purely ecclesiastical matter. Undeterred Guthrie denounced the commission's second public resolution (24 May 1651), which paved the way for parliament's repeal of the 1646 and 1649 Acts of Classes, allowing malignants and former engagers back into public office.

At the July 1651 general assembly, which saw the national kirk irreparably divided between resolutioners and protesters, Guthrie joined the latter party in protesting the assembly's proceedings and declining its authority. The assembly subsequently deposed him and two other leading protesters from the ministry. He refused to accept the 'pretended' assembly's sentence and, soon after returning to Stirling, he and other local protesters formed a separate protesting presbytery of Stirling.

During the Cromwellian occupation of Scotland, Guthrie did not, contrary to what has often been reported, defend the office of the king. Rather, as the resolutioner Robert Baillie observed, he was one of those who had 'no scruple to lay aside the King, and to make the third article of our Covenant stand well enough with a freedome to change Monarchy with a Scottish Republick' (*Letters and Journals of Robert Baillie*, 176). He also rejected the Cromwellian vision of a united Christian Commonwealth and when the regime spurned the protesters' plea for Scottish independence in early 1652 he became one of its most outspoken critics, condemning its policy of religious toleration and its 'Erastian' encroachments into the kirk's sphere of authority. The next year he continued his public criticisms of the king and the resolutioners, recounting their numerous 'defections' from the covenants in his famous pamphlet *The Causes of the Lord's Wrath Against Scotland* (Edinburgh, 1653). In March 1653 he and his chief confidant, Lord Wariston, condemned the pro-English extremism of their colleague Patrick Gillespie and persuaded the national protesting party to adopt a policy of strict non-compliance with the Cromwellian authorities. The following year Guthrie denounced the new quasi-Independent ecclesiastical settlement commonly known as Gillespie's charter, 'wrote sharply against it', and refused to participate in its implementation (*Letters and Journals of Robert Baillie*, 283).

It is noteworthy, however, that, despite Guthrie's aversion to Erastianism, on at least two occasions, in June 1654 and July 1655, he used English civil and military authority to secure the installation of protesting ministers into disputed ecclesiastical vacancies. Such a seeming inconsistency did not escape the notice of his detractors, and prompted the resolutioner Robert Baillie to charge him with manifest hypocrisy. By late 1655, however, Guthrie's official stance on co-operation with the English had softened markedly. Incensed by the favouritism shown the resolutioners by the new Scottish council, he agreed to join his colleagues in petitioning the English council for the establishment of a protester-dominated commission to act as the nation's supreme religious authority. When the council rejected the petition and restored ecclesiastical authority to the kirk's ordinary courts he travelled to London with Wariston and Gillespie in January 1657 in order to petition the lord protector in person. While there he championed the protesters' cause before Cromwell in a series of debates with the resolutioner James Sharp.

After becoming thoroughly disillusioned with Wariston's increasing willingness to court English favour, however, Guthrie cut his stay short. Following his return to Scotland he resumed his former position of complete non-compliance with the English and, in October 1658, joined Samuel Rutherford and other protesters in issuing a public testimony against religious toleration. He also recommenced his polemic against the resolutioners and, in the pamphlet *Protesters No Subverters* (Edinburgh, 1658), charged them with imbibing an understanding of presbyterian church government which was 'popish, prelatical and tyrannical' (p. 10) in nature.

Following the Restoration, Guthrie and ten other leading protesters were arrested, on 23 August 1660, by order of the committee of estates while they were drafting a letter to the king congratulating him on his return and reminding him of his sworn obligation to uphold the covenants. Guthrie was imprisoned in Edinburgh Castle, transferred to Dundee on 20 October, and thence to Stirling, where he remained until his trial. On 19 September his pamphlet *The Causes of the Lord's Wrath* and Rutherford's *Lex rex* were proscribed and denounced as 'seditious and treasonable' (Wodrow, *History*, 1.75). Both titles were burned on 17 October by the public hangman at Edinburgh and St Andrews. On 20 February 1661 Guthrie was arraigned for high treason before the Scottish parliament, his nemesis Middleton presiding as commissioner. The indictment had six counts, including declining the king's authority in ecclesiastical matters and 'contriving' the western remonstrance and *The Causes of the Lord's Wrath*. By all accounts Guthrie defended himself brilliantly during his trial, surprising even his own lawyers with his knowledge of Scots law. His fate, however, had been predetermined and, on 25 May 1661, he was found guilty of treason and sentenced to death by hanging. He was executed at Edinburgh's Mercat Cross on 1 June. Legend has it that, at the last moment, he lifted the napkin from his face and uttered the prophetic cry which was long after the watchword of the persecuted conventiclers, 'The Covenants, the Covenants shall yet be Scotland's reviving' (Hewison, 92). His head was impaled for public viewing on the Nether Bow, where it remained for twenty-eight years, and his body was interred in the aisle of St Giles's Kirk. His wife, who survived him, died in March 1673.

K. D. HOLFELDER

**Sources** R. Wodrow, *Analecta, or, Materials for a history of remarkable providences, mostly relating to Scotch ministers and Christians*, ed. [M. Leishman], 4 vols., Maitland Club, 60 (1842–3), vol. 1, pp. 105–9; vol. 2, pp. 137–8, 158; vol. 3, pp. 92–104 • R. Wodrow, *The history of the sufferings of the Church of Scotland from the Restoration to the revolution*, ed. R. Burns, 1 (1828), 66–76, 84, 159–96 • *Fasti Scot.*, new edn, 4.318–19 • *The letters and journals of Robert Baillie*, ed. D. Laing, 3 (1842) • A. F. Mitchell and J. Christie, eds., *The records of the commissions of the general assemblies of the Church of Scotland*, 3 vols., Scottish History Society, 11, 25, 58 (1892–1909) • W. Stephen, ed., *Register of the consultations of the ministers of Edinburgh*, 2 vols., Scottish History Society, 3rd ser., 1, 16 (1921–30) • J. K. Hewison, *The covenanters: a history of the church in Scotland from the Reformation to the revolution*, 2 (1908), 92–3 • D. Stevenson, 'The radical party in the kirk, 1637–45', *Journal of Ecclesiastical History*, 25 (1974), 135–65 • J. Kilpatrick, 'James Guthrie, minister at Stirling, 1649–61', *Records of the Scottish Church History Society*, 11 (1951–3), 176–88 • T. Thomson, *Life of James Guthrie* (1846)

**Archives** NL Scot., corresp.

**Likenesses** S. Freeman, stipple, BM, NPG; repro. in Chambers, *Scots*.

**Guthrie, Sir James** (1859–1930), painter, was born on 10 June 1859 in Greenock, the youngest son of an Evangelical Union clergyman, the Revd John Guthrie DD (*d.* 1878), and his wife, Ann Orr. Guthrie initially attended Glasgow University, where he studied law. In 1877, under the influence of the academician John Drummond, he abandoned these studies and became a painter. He was chiefly self-taught, but having settled briefly in London following his father's death in 1878 he was given some encouragement by the painter John Pettie, who introduced him to fellow Scottish artists William Quiller Orchardson and Thomas Graham.

In the early 1880s Guthrie was active in Scotland and developing rapidly as an innovative and experimental painter. The years 1882–3 saw a radical shift in his painting as he moved from genre-based subjects and technique to a looser and high-keyed impressionism. In 1882 his painting *A Funeral Service in the Highlands* (Glasgow Art Gallery and Museum) extended the sentimental genre style of Victorian painting towards a more penetrating realism. By 1883, however, his loosely painted image of an artist working in the open air, *Hard at it* (Glasgow Art Gallery and Museum), showed clear evidence of the impressionist concern with the play of light on surface. His interest in impressionism developed from his introduction to the works of the French painter Jules Bastien-Lepage. Bastien-Lepage had exhibited at the Glasgow Institute in 1883 but it is probable that Guthrie had viewed his work earlier, in 1882, when he himself exhibited *A Funeral Service in the Highlands* at the Royal Academy and the Frenchman had several works on show in London galleries. The clearest indication of Bastien-Lepage's influence occurred in Guthrie's masterwork of 1883, *A Hind's Daughter* (National Gallery of Scotland, Edinburgh); this painting, of a young peasant girl cutting vegetables in a kitchen garden, utilized the characteristic pictorial devices of Bastien-Lepage in the full-length figure thrown to the front of the picture plane and balanced against a high horizon with vertical spines of vegetation. However, Guthrie eschews the mawkish sentiment of Bastien-Lepage's painting, and *A Hind's Daughter* is possibly the closest that any Scottish painter came to a critical realism that might rival the work of Gustave Courbet on the continent. Guthrie's work from 1882 to 1885 moved between the native genre tradition, a modest impressionism, and a significant realism. This restlessness marked him out as one of the most challenging artists of the period, and he became one of the leading lights among his Glasgow-based contemporaries.

During the 1880s and early 1890s Glasgow painting offered a real challenge to the dominance of the Royal Scottish Academy based in Edinburgh. This 'Glasgow school'—or the *Glasgow Boys, as that group of artists is sometimes known—challenged the romantic landscape painting and moral or literary subjects that permeated the academy by exploring new techniques and developing more contemporary themes. In this respect Glasgow-based painting focused on issues of labour, leisure, gender, and modern life. It is noteworthy, however, that no significant vision of the city itself was generated by these artists. In essence this was because the Glasgow school migrated from the city to the rural fringes of Scotland in the summer months; Guthrie and his circle worked in Berwickshire, Helensburgh, and the Trossachs, while his colleague and sometime rival for leadership of the group, William York Macgregor, painted chiefly in Crail and the east neuk of Fife. Guthrie had painted *A Hind's Daughter* while living in Cockburnspath, in Berwickshire, but it was in Helensburgh, to the west of Glasgow, that he completed his much admired *To Pastures New* (1883; Aberdeen Art Gallery) and his subsequent images of middle-class suburban life.

In 1885, following a period of despair in which he nearly abandoned painting, Guthrie was encouraged to turn to portraiture; his first commission in this field was a portrait of his uncle, *The Reverend Andrew Gardiner DD* (National Gallery of Scotland, Edinburgh). Portraiture became the basis of his subsequent career, and there can be no doubt that he flourished as a professional. During this time he worked from studios in both Glasgow and London. He also gained considerable recognition, being elected an associate of the Royal Scottish Academy in 1888, a full academician in 1892, and, eventually, president in 1902—a post that he held until 1919. In this period he moved to Edinburgh. His work became internationally recognized, particularly in Munich during 1890, where he was awarded a gold medal, and in Paris during 1891 he received a third-class medal from the official salon. It is generally agreed that he did much to put the Scottish academy's turbulent affairs in order, and he was knighted in 1903. From the time of his resignation as president of the Royal Scottish Academy until his death he continued to paint portraits. His last significant commission was a large group-portrait, *Statesmen of World War I*, completed for the National Portrait Gallery in London. Guthrie married Helen Newton Whitelaw (1859/1860–1912), daughter of Alexander Whitelaw, a soap manufacturer, on 7 September 1897; they had one son. Guthrie died on 6 September 1930 at Rowmore, Rhu, Dunbartonshire.

Guthrie was a talented painter who stood for a brief time at the forefront of radical experiments in the arts in Scotland. His late work was something of a compromise with these ambitions as the young innovator gave way to the competent professional. TOM NORMAND

**Sources** J. L. Caw, *Sir James Guthrie* (1937) • T. Normand, 'A realist view of a Victorian childhood: re-reading James Guthrie's *A hind's daughter*', *Scotland*, 4/2 (1997) • R. Billcliffe, *The Glasgow Boys: the Glasgow school of painting, 1875–1895* (1985) • *The Glasgow Boys*, Scottish Arts Council, 2 vols. (1968–71) • D. Macmillan, *Scottish art, 1460–2000* (2000) • m. cert. • d. cert.

**Archives** U. Glas., letters | NL Scot., letters to J. P. Mcgillivray

**Likenesses** J. Guthrie, self-portrait, oils, 1867, Scot. NPG • group photograph, 1883 (at Cockburnspath with E. A. Walton, J. Crawhall, G. Walton, and W. Hamilton), repro. in Billcliffe, *Glasgow Boys* • photographs, 1919, NPG • J. Guthrie, group portrait, self-portrait, ink caricature (with J. Crawhall and E. A. Walton), Scot. NPG • E. A. Walton, pencil drawing, Scot. NPG

**Wealth at death** £11,240 2*s.* 2*d.*: confirmation, 11 Feb 1931, *CCI*

**Guthrie, John** (*d.* 1649), bishop of Moray, was the eldest son of Patrick Guthrie, a goldsmith and one-time baillie of St Andrews, and Margaret Rait. He graduated MA at the University of St Andrews in 1597. That same year he became a reader at Arbroath and on 27 August 1599 he was presented by James VI to the ministry of Kinnel parish church in Perthshire. He then moved to Arbirlot, Forfarshire, in 1603.

Guthrie was a widely respected and conspicuous participant in the affairs of the higher church courts. He was one of the commissioners representing the presbytery of Arbroath at the famous Glasgow assembly of June 1610, and on 7 September was elected clerk of the synod of St Andrews. In 1617 he was transferred to the second charge in Perth. His loyalty to the episcopal regime and the king's cause was further manifest in his selection as a commissioner to, and a member of, the privy conference in the highly controversial Perth assembly of 1618. He was also a commissioner of the infamous court of high commission. Although initially reluctant to accept a move to St Giles, Edinburgh, royal pressure ensured that he was appointed to minister in the capital by 15 June 1621.

Guthrie's rise to prominence in the Scottish Jacobean church was effectively confirmed in August 1623 when he was made bishop of Moray in succession to Alexander Douglas. Although Row wrote that he 'instantlie removed from Edinburgh, went and made residence there in Moray' (Row, 336), in October he preached in St Giles, Edinburgh, a thanksgiving sermon for the safe return of Prince Charles from Spain and for the failure of the Spanish marriage project. Guthrie was part of a delegation sent by a convention of the church to court in the winter of 1626 to supplicate Charles I to make better provision for the ministry and to proceed against Roman Catholic recusants. In 1631 the bishop was appointed to a commission of inquiry into the origin of the fire which had destroyed the house of Frendraught. Guthrie was also a prominent participant in the solemnities surrounding Charles's Scottish coronation in June 1633, throwing specially commissioned silver coins in his capacity as lord eleemosynary, or alms-giver. To the consternation of many he preached before the king on 23 June wearing a surplice in a definitively Anglican service. On 3 October 1637 Guthrie commanded the ministers within the synod of Moray to purchase and conform to the practice of the new Scottish prayer book.

Guthrie was deposed from his bishopric by the Glasgow assembly on 11 December 1638 and finally excommunicated on 11 July 1639 for his obstinate refusal to sign or recognize the legality of the national covenant and for his unwillingness to conform to the reconstituted presbyterian ecclesiology. Guthrie was the only non-abjuring bishop to remain in Scotland. He continued to preach into March 1639 before seeking refuge in his episcopal residence at Spynie Palace, which he had provisioned with men, food, and ammunition for an expected siege. He held out until 16 July 1640, when he surrendered to Major-General Robert Munro of Foulis. From September he was incarcerated in the Tolbooth, Edinburgh. In November 1641 his petition to parliament for his liberation was granted on condition that he did not return to his former diocese.

After his release Guthrie settled at Guthrie, which he had purchased from his relative, Peter Guthrie, on 28 November 1636. He had married Nicolas Wood with whom he raised three sons and three daughters. Their eldest son, John (*d.* 1643), was minister of Keith and subsequently Duffus. Patrick became a burgess of Aberdeen, and Andrew, captured fighting for Charles I at Philiphaugh on 13 September 1645, was afterwards executed in St Andrews. Of their daughters, Bethia inherited Guthrie and married her cousin Francis Guthrie of Gaigie, Nicolas married Joseph Brodie, the minister of Forres, and Lucretia married David Collace, the minister of Kinneddar.

Notwithstanding some of the unsubstantiated claims of his presbyterian detractors, Guthrie had worked conscientiously and diligently to extirpate Roman Catholic recusancy, to reimpose ecclesiastical discipline, and to establish sufficient provision for the churches throughout his diocese. On reflection his claim that '[i]t was said by one and all (so far as ever I could learn) that I was a good Bishop, a good man and a good Countrey man' (Mullan, 193), while clearly biased, offers a relatively accurate summation of Guthrie's character and work. He died at Guthrie on 28 August 1649 and was buried in the aisle of Guthrie parish church beside his wife, who had died on 2 July 1645.

A. S. WAYNE PEARCE

**Sources** *Fasti Scot.*, new edn, 7.351 • D. G. Mullan, *Episcopacy in Scotland: the history of an idea, 1560–1608* (1986) • *The letters and journals of Robert Baillie*, ed. D. Laing, 1 (1841) • *The memoirs of Henry Guthry, late bishop*, 2nd edn (1747) • J. Spalding, *Memorialls of the trubles in Scotland and in England, AD 1624 – AD 1645*, ed. J. Stuart, 2 vols., Spalding Club, [21, 23] (1850–51) • J. Row, *The history of the Kirk of Scotland, from the year 1558 to August 1637*, ed. D. Laing, Wodrow Society, 4 (1842)
**Archives** NA Scot., diaries, sermons, letters, and papers, GD188

**Guthrie** [*née* Maltby; *other married name* Stephenson], **Kathleen Hilda (1906–1981)**, painter, was born on 26 February 1906, in Feltham, Middlesex, the second daughter of Ernest George William Maltby (1880?–1963), physician and surgeon, and his wife, Emily, *née* Worsfold (*d.* 1957), a talented amateur artist. When Kathleen was five the family moved to Brighton, where she was educated at St Michael's Hall School. In 1921 she enrolled as a student at the Slade School of Fine Art, London, under Henry Tonks and three years later won a five-year scholarship to the Royal Academy Schools. She met and fell in love with a former Slade prize-winning student, Robert Craig (Robin) Guthrie (1902?–1971), and on 5 May 1927 they married at Hampstead register office. The couple lived and worked in a semi-derelict old chapel in Parkhill Road, Hampstead, and Kathleen's painting became secondary to encouraging her partner to find portrait commissions and a source of income from teaching. (Robin Guthrie's portrait work is well represented in the National Portrait Gallery collection.) Her efforts were further interrupted by the birth of a son, David, in 1930. In the same year, Robin Guthrie and his friend Rodney Burn were recommended by Tonks to reorganize the Boston School of Fine Arts in the United States of America. The generous salary enabled Kathleen to hire a full-time nanny for her son and to paint in earnest. Her own show in Boston in 1932, which comprised mainly New England landscapes, was well received: the *Boston Herald* critic wrote 'seldom has such an original and delightfully fresh group of paintings been shown … built on a sound foundation of drawing and composition' (Eastaway, 3). These comments were to apply to most of her work.

The Guthries settled in Sussex in 1932, and tried to establish their reputations at home. Both relied on portraiture for an income. Many successful portraits of local worthies were completed by Kathleen, while Robin sought commissions among London society. Kathleen also developed at this time an individual simplified style of flower painting which became a distinguishing feature of her work. She painted mainly in gouache and oils, and later in acrylics. Her output was again reduced by the need to care for her son as well as by health problems. Protracted divorce proceedings which began in 1938 led to Kathleen Guthrie's severe mental breakdown.

In 1941 Kathleen Guthrie married (John) Cecil *Stephenson (1889–1965), an abstract artist and friend of Ben Nicholson and Barbara Hepworth. She came to live at 6 Mall Studios, collectively described by Herbert Read as 'a nest of gentle artists' (Guthrie, 71), where Stephenson had lived for many years. He proved to be a devoted husband and stepfather. During the war years Kathleen made many studies of the bombed city of London and became a member of the Artists' International Association. Her painting *A Bombed Hospital Ward* was bought by the Ministry of Information in 1941 and is now in the Imperial War Museum. Her 'Blitz notebook' was to influence some of her slightly macabre genre paintings such as *The Spy* (1942; priv. coll.) and *The Bicycle Ride* (1945; priv. coll.). Representational work, depicting stylized figure groups such as *The Tea-Party* and *The Piano-Player* (both priv. coll.), illustrate 'the delightful humorous undercurrent' in her work to which one critic referred (Eastaway, 3). Coming to live in Hampstead also fostered her love of the heath and the Highgate ponds which she painted repeatedly for the rest of her life; these paintings continue to be much sought after by Hampstead *aficionados*.

The first show of Kathleen Guthrie's work in England was arranged by Wolf Mankowitz at the Little Gallery in Piccadilly in 1947, and her work began to be purchased by discerning collectors, including Sir Kenneth Clark. After the war, there was a great resurgence of artistic activity in Hampstead centred on the Hampstead Artists' Council shows, in which both Kathleen and Cecil Stephenson exhibited regularly. She also served for many years as vice-chairman and on the selection committee of the Women's International Art Club, a necessary body during the years when it was often more difficult for women painters to exhibit their works. Financial difficulties in the 1950s had challenged Kathleen to seek other ways of making money. She tried, unsuccessfully, to become a textile designer for two or three years. A collection of her designs is in the archive of Marks and Spencer, London. She achieved more success with her silk-screen prints, especially simplified versions of her figure groups. Her interest in writing and illustrating children's books led to the publication of *The Magic Button* in 1959, followed by *The Magic Button to the Moon* in 1962.

In the 1950s Kathleen Guthrie had moved towards abstraction under the influence of her husband, who had acquired a reputation as an abstractionist. They both joined the Free Painters, painting hard-edged abstracts, and many of Kathleen's appeared in the exhibition devoted to her work at the New End Gallery in Hampstead in 1963. She held another exhibition of her work at the Drian Gallery, London, in 1966, which included eighteen abstracts. Reviewers commented favourably on her 'generous spacious pictures, full of atmosphere—[she] revels in the use of paint' and on her 'Delightful paintings of deliberately simplified and stylised figures' (Eastaway, 11), comments which give some indication of Kathleen Guthrie's status as an artist.

In 1960 Cecil Stephenson suffered the first of a series of strokes, and was nursed devotedly by his wife until his death in 1965. Financially secure she continued to paint with great vigour, moving on to less successful soft-edged abstracts, but still producing and selling landscapes and figurative works. Sketching trips to Scotland and Wales produced a series of semi-abstract landscapes translated from naturalistic sketches. Kathleen Guthrie died in the Royal Shrewsbury Hospital on 7 September 1981, while on a painting holiday in Shropshire with artist friends, and was cremated in Golders Green. Her work is held in private collections in America and France as well as at home; some of these are reproduced in *Studio International*, *The Listener*, and *Arts News*. MARJORIE GUTHRIE

**Sources** J. Eastaway [S. Guthrie], *A poet's eye* (1999) • S. Guthrie, *The life and art of John Cecil Stephenson: a Victorian painter's journey to abstract expressionism* (1997) • *CGPLA Eng. & Wales* (1981) • d. cert. • archives, Tate collection • IWM • *Ham and High* (11 Sept 1981) • D. Buckman, *Dictionary of artists in Britain since 1945* (1998)
**Archives** Tate collection, catalogues, press cuttings, papers
**Likenesses** Reprograph Studio, photograph, 1926, repro. in Eastaway, *Poet's eye*, 8/4 • R. Guthrie, oils, *c.*1928, priv. coll.
**Wealth at death** £71,934: probate, 15 Dec 1981, *CGPLA Eng. & Wales*

**Guthrie, (William) Keith Chambers** (1906–1981), classical scholar, was born in London on 1 August 1906, the younger child and only son of Charles Jameson Guthrie, who had moved from Scotland to London to work for the Westminster Bank, and his wife, Katharine Chambers, who was also of Scottish descent, her father, William, being an elder of the Presbyterian church. He was educated at Dulwich College whence he proceeded with an entrance scholarship to Trinity College, Cambridge, in 1925. He was placed in the first class in both parts of the classical tripos (1926 and 1928), with distinction in Greek philosophy in part two. He won the Browne university scholarship (1927), the university Craven studentship (1928), and the chancellor's medal (1929).

Guthrie took part between 1929 and 1932 in expeditions to Asia Minor with the American Society for Archaeological Research, though his interest was epigraphy, not archaeology. His work in this field was included in volume 4 of *Monumenta Asiae Minoris antiqua* (1933), edited by W. H. Buckler, W. M. Calder, and W. K. C. Guthrie. But his abiding interests were Greek religion and philosophy, and his first lectures were given in this field; he became a full university lecturer in 1935. In 1930 he was elected bye-fellow and in 1932 a full fellow of Peterhouse. In the course of his college teaching he supervised a Newnham undergraduate from Melbourne, Adele Marion, the daughter of Adam Loftus Ogilvie, civil servant. She obtained a first class in the tripos, and they married in 1933. It was a marriage of true minds, of shared interests (he pays tribute to her in *The Greeks and their Gods*), and of temperaments: both disliked fuss and falsity. They had two children—Robin, who was later director of the Joseph Rowntree Memorial Trust, and Anne, whose death in her twenties left Guthrie under the permanent shadow of a great sorrow.

During the Second World War Guthrie served in the intelligence corps, looking with his habitual neatness more like a soldier than his rather miscellaneous wartime colleagues. He reached the rank of temporary major. A posting to Istanbul made use of his knowledge of Turkish. Resuming his academic career after the war, he became successively Laurence reader in 1947 and then Laurence professor of ancient philosophy (1952–73). Always ready to take his share in administrative affairs, he was one of the university proctors in 1936–7, served on the council of the senate and the library syndicate, and was for eighteen years public orator (1939–57), presenting a succession of candidates for honorary degrees in felicitous Latin and meticulous detail.

In 1957 Guthrie was elected master of Downing College. His early years there with his wife as hostess were active and happy, but the end of his time was overshadowed by student unrest, and when the rewritten statutes of the college set fifteen years as the length of tenure of the mastership he took the opportunity to resign in 1972 and to devote himself to his main interest, Greek philosophy. He had already, in addition to his earlier *Orpheus and Greek Religion* (1935) and *The Greeks and their Gods* (1950), published work in this field: *The Greek Philosophers* (1950), two seminal articles on the development of Aristotle's thought (*Classical Quarterly*, 1933 and 1934), and his Messenger lectures at Cornell (*In the Beginning*, 1957).

In 1956 the officers of the Cambridge University Press invited Guthrie to undertake a comprehensive history of

Greek philosophy. The original plan was to cover in five volumes the whole field down to the Hellenistic philosophers, but to stop short at the Neoplatonists. When he died after the completion of the volume on Aristotle in 1981, the number was already six. The loss of the remainder was irreparable, but the achievement was great. The *History of Greek Philosophy* is meticulously comprehensive; anything omitted is of no importance, yet for all its thoroughness it never becomes tedious. There is a beautiful clarity in the treatment, and when the evidence has been reviewed the reader feels that, however difficult the process has been, the answer arrived at is right. The *History* is in fact one of the great works of scholarship of the twentieth century—of scholarship for, though it was a history of philosophy, he was a historian and not a philosopher, as he was himself the first to emphasize; though he could nod towards modern philosophy, fear of contamination made him keep it at a distance.

A man of slight physique, he was an elder of his church and a man of steady but unostentatious Christian faith, in whom a certain surface austerity would mellow into the warmth of friendship. He was elected a fellow of the British Academy in 1952 and became an honorary fellow of both Downing and Peterhouse. President of the Classical Association in 1967–8, he was made a Cambridge LittD (1959) and honorary DLitt of Melbourne (1957) and Sheffield (1967). In June 1980 he suffered a stroke which incapacitated him for further work and he died on 17 May 1981 in Cambridge. DESMOND LEE, *rev.*

**Sources** G. E. R. Lloyd, 'William Keith Chambers Guthrie, 1906–1981', *PBA*, 68 (1982), 561–7 · *The Times* (18 May 1981) · personal knowledge (1990)
**Archives** BL, corresp. with Sir Sydney Cockerell, Add. MS 52717
**Likenesses** B. Gaye, photograph, repro. in Lloyd, 'William Keith Chambers Guthrie', facing p. 561
**Wealth at death** £20,561: probate, 7 Jan 1982, *CGPLA Eng. & Wales* · £22,083: probate, 22 March 1982, *CGPLA Eng. & Wales*

**Guthrie, Matthew** (1743–1807), physician and natural philosopher, born on 24 March 1743, probably in Edinburgh, was the son of Hary Guthrie (1709–1794), an Edinburgh lawyer of known Jacobite sympathies, and his first wife, Rachel Milne (1719–1746). His grandfather was Gideon Guthrie (1663–1732), a well-known Scottish Episcopalian minister. The historian William Guthrie (1708?–1770) was his uncle. Matthew was the middle child, being flanked by an elder sister, Euphan, and a younger brother, William. Euphan's eldest daughter, Rachel (1759–1852?), married John Robison (1739–1805), who became professor of natural philosophy at Edinburgh, and it was with Robison, who was secretary to Admiral Sir Charles Knowles, that Guthrie arrived in St Petersburg in the late summer of 1769. Before this Guthrie had been apprenticed to an Edinburgh surgeon, William Inglis; after serving at sea in the employ of the East India Company he decided on his return to Scotland in 1764 to take a course in medicine at the University of Edinburgh. His name appears, under the date 24 December 1764, in the class-list for 'Anatomy, Chemistry and Theory and Practice of Medicine'. Among his teachers were John Hope, Robert Whytt, Alexander Monro secundus, William Cullen, and Joseph Black. Guthrie was also a friend of Andrew Duncan of the Medical Society of Edinburgh. It appears that he spent some time practising in London 'where his friends advisd him to goe to St Petersburgh where they hear there is great demand for people of his profession' (Cross, *By the Banks of the Neva*, 147). On his arrival in Russia, however, Guthrie was appointed only to the lowly level of lekar or surgeon, so he returned to Scotland to improve his qualifications and took the MA and MD degrees at St Andrews University on 16 April 1770, by virtue of testimonials signed by Thomas Young and Colin Drummond. This was a normal process for the time and Guthrie seems to have been a competent medical man.

Guthrie returned to Russia in 1770: his first appointment was to the admiralty (*admiralteystv-kollegiya*), and from there he was posted in 1772 as a surgeon to P. A. Rumyantsev's army corps in Moldavia and Wallachia, serving at the field marshal's headquarters at Jassy. He became involved with questions of quarantine and plague prevention, publishing a paper on the topic in *Medical and Philosophical Commentaries* (8, 1781). Until 1776 Guthrie travelled widely in the northern coastal territories of the Black Sea, a region in whose culture he developed a deep interest, as is manifested by his 'Noctes Rossicae' in the British Library, and by his supplement to his wife's travel diary, published in 1802. Guthrie then returned to St Petersburg and in March 1778 became chief physician to the imperial land cadet corps of nobles. He was also appointed councillor of state to Tsar Paul, in the suite of the Tsarina Catherine the Great, and later to Alexander I, thereby entering the ranks of the Russian hereditary nobility.

In 1781 Guthrie made an influential marriage to a French widow, Marie Dunant, *née* Romaud-Survesnes (*d.* 1800), acting director of the imperial convent for the education of noblewomen in Russia. Guthrie wrote an account of the institution for the use of John Howard, the Quaker reformer; it is preserved in the archives of the Royal Society (letters and papers, decade 7, no. 256). Guthrie and his wife had two daughters. The beautiful and vivacious Anastasia-Jessy (1782–1855) married Charles Gascoigne (1738–1806), then the most renowned iron-founder and engine builder in Russia. Guthrie's second daughter, Mary Elizabeth (1789–1850), married General Sir James Hay (1765–1837). Guthrie was variously described as 'the ubiquitous Dr. Matthew Guthrie' (John Howard); as 'pompous and pedantic' (William Coxe); as 'a gentleman of the most amiable manners, a philosopher and well known to the world for his various scientific and literary productions' (John Carr); and as 'a man of very clear ideas, perfectly acquainted with all the physical knowledge pursuing at present in England, a frequent correspondent with Priestley, Magellan and others of the English Philosophers and a man of inventive genius himself' (Samuel Bentham). Guthrie's house was a place of first resort for all English visitors with a taste for travel, science, medicine, natural history, and technology. He was also consulted by the Russian authorities on a variety of matters, including the copper-sheathing of the wooden hulls of the Russian navy, and the identification of foreigners who might be of use in Russia. He was elected to the Free Economic Society of St Petersburg in 1777. He was well known to Joseph Black, James Hutton, James Watt, Joseph Priestley, and, indeed, to most of the scientific literati of his time. Others of his acquaintance included the Portuguese industrial spy J. H. de Magellan; the Swiss F. X. Schwediaur and M. A. Pictet; the Scots engineer Charles Baird; and Sir John Sinclair. There is a delightful description of Guthrie's outdoor study in which he received several of these men in John Carr's *A Northern Summer* (1805, 326–7).

Guthrie was an unceasing communicator of things scientific. Several of his publications arose from letters, such as one to John Hope (*Medical and Philosophical Commentaries*, 4, 1776–7); another to Andrew Duncan on the use of *Rhododendron chrysanthemum* for the treatment of gout and rheumatism (ibid.); one to Joseph Priestley, 'On the antiseptic regimen of the natives of Russia' (Royal Society, London, letters and papers, decade 7, no. 8); and a communication to Richard Kirwan (ibid., decade 8, no. 68) on the freezing-point of mercury, a subject about which he also wrote to Joseph Black. From 1792 to 1794 Guthrie contributed fifty pieces to James Anderson's *The Bee, or, Literary Weekly Intelligencer*. Most of these pieces were edited or translated by Guthrie from other writers such as P. S. Pallas, M. V. Lomonosov, and even Catherine the Great herself. He may have been the translator of Catherine's story 'Khlor', translated as 'Ivan Czarowitz, or, The Rose without Prickles, that Stings not' in *The Bee* for 28 August and 11 September 1793; but he was certainly the translator of Catherine's opera *Oleg*, which he sent to his English publishers, Cadell and Davies, who decided not to publish it. In his correspondence with Joseph Black, Guthrie asked questions about the manufacture of steel. He also wrote letters to James Hutton, the great geologist, and exchanged mineral samples with him. Guthrie was a distinguished gemmologist, having a large collection of gems of his own and being well acquainted with the Russian royal collections, as well as other royal collections. Because of his links to Laxmann, he was able to give precise locations of Russian fossils and to provide contemporary Russian monetary values for gemstones.

Like other Scots doctors who preceded him in Russia, Guthrie disseminated rare plants and seeds, as well as common ones. Some of these were sent to John Hope, and to other collectors. Much of the stimulus to this work derived from P. S. Pallas and centred on medicinal plants, such as *Rhododendron chrysanthemum*, *Asafoetida*, and *Rheum palmatum*, but buckwheat and larch seed were also sent to Scotland from Russia. Besides these botanical matters Guthrie corresponded on textiles, animal husbandry, the prevention of scurvy, archaeology, geography, linguistics, ethnography, scientific instrumentation, and popular music, superstitions, and folklore. He collected specimens for geology, ornithology, ichthyology, entomology, and zoology.

Guthrie was elected a fellow of the Royal Society on 11 April 1782, was a member of the Edinburgh Philosophical Society, and a founder in November 1783 of the Royal Society of Edinburgh. He became a corresponding member on 25 June 1752 of the societies of antiquaries of London and Edinburgh, and of the Society for the Encouragement of Arts, Commerce, and Manufactures; and corresponded with the Manchester Literary and Philosophical Society. He also belonged to the New Music Society (Novoye Muzykalnoye Obshchestvo) of St Petersburg from its foundation in 1778 to its demise in 1792, and was a friend of Ivan Prach, the composer, and N. P. Yakhontov, the court musician. One of his last publications was his edition in 1802 of his wife's travel diaries, to which he added notes of his own. He died in St Petersburg on 7 August 1807 and was buried next to his wife in the city's Smolensk churchyard. ERIC H. ROBINSON

**Sources** *Selected writings on Russia by Matthew Guthrie, 1743–1807*, ed. K. A. Papmehl (1974) • K. A. Papmehl, 'Matthew Guthrie: the forgotten student of eighteenth-century Russia', *Canadian Slavonic papers*, 11 (1969), 167–81 • K. A. Papmehl, 'The quest for the nation's cultural roots in Russian historiography before Karamzin', *Russia and the world of the eighteenth century*, ed. R. P. Bartlett, A. G. Cross, and K. Rasmussen (1986), 22–35 • A. G. Cross, *By the banks of the Neva: chapters from the lives and careers of the British in eighteenth-century Russia* (1997) • A. G. Cross, 'Areticus and *The Bee*', *Oxford Slavonic Papers*, new ser., 2 (1969), 62–76 • A. Cross, ed., *Anglo-Russian relations in the eighteenth century* [1977] [exhibition catalogue, Library Concourse, University of East Anglia, Norwich, 5–29 July 1977] • A. G. Cross, 'A royal blue-stocking: Catherine the Great's early reputation in England as an authoress', *PMH Research Association*, 11, 85–99 • J. M. Sweet, 'Matthew Guthrie, 1743–1807: an eighteenth century gemmologist', *Annals of Science*, 20 (1964), 245–302 • J. H. Appleby, 'St Petersburg to Edinburgh: Matthew Guthrie's introduction of medicinal plants in the context of Scottish-Russian natural history exchange', *Archives of Natural History*, 14 (1987), 45–58 • P. Dukes and others, eds., *The Caledonian phalanx: Scots in Russia* (1987) • J. D. Comrie, *History of Scottish medicine to 1860* (1927) • bap. reg. Scot.

**Archives** BL, Add. MSS 14388, 14389, 33564 • U. Edin. L. • U. St Andr., muniments | BL, letters to Sir Joseph Banks, Add. MSS 8096–8099 • U. Edin., Black MSS

**Guthrie, Thomas** (1803–1873), Free Church of Scotland minister and philanthropist, was born at Brechin on 12 July 1803, the twelfth of thirteen children and the sixth son of David Guthrie (*d.* 1824) and Clementina Cay (1764–1841). His father was a merchant and banker who also served as provost of Brechin. His mother latterly attended the Secession church in Brechin, to which she often took Thomas. After attending school locally, he went to Edinburgh University at the age of twelve to study for the ministry of the Church of Scotland and finished his course two years before he was eligible for licence. He remained in Edinburgh to study medical and scientific subjects. He never gained academic distinction, but was better known for 'fun and fighting' (*Autobiography*, 40). Licensed by the presbytery of Brechin in February 1825, his refusal to align himself with the moderate party in the church denied him the influence required to find a charge quickly. He took the opportunity to continue his medical studies, and for that purpose attended the Sorbonne in Paris in the winter of 1826–7. Although engaged by his studies, he found little else in French life that appealed to him and much of which he disapproved. He had planned to spend the following winter at a German university but, in order

**Thomas Guthrie** (1803–1873), by David Octavius Hill and Robert Adamson, 1843

to keep the banking side of the family business afloat, for the next two years he stepped into the breach created by the death of his brother John.

Guthrie was ordained minister of Arbirlot, Forfarshire, in May 1830. On 6 October of that year he married Anne (1810–1899), daughter of the Revd James Burns of Brechin. The couple had four daughters and seven sons. He remained at Arbirlot for seven years, during which time he established a library and a savings bank. It was only with great reluctance that he left, but his growing reputation, founded in part on his participation in the controversies of the day, made a call to a city charge inevitable. He transferred to Old Greyfriars, Edinburgh, a collegiate charge, in September 1837. His understanding had been that he would be granted a parish of his own in which to prosecute an intensive territorial ministry and he was translated to the new parish of St John's in October 1840.

By this time events in the established church were moving closer to the Disruption of 1843. Guthrie belonged staunchly to the non-intrusion party and favoured the abolition of lay patronage from the outset of the controversy. He played a prominent role as a propagandist and defied the interdict of the court of session to preach in the presbytery of Strathbogie. After the Disruption he ministered to the congregation of Free St John's, only yards from his old church. His principal service to the Free Church was to gather money for the Manse Fund. In the year 1845–6 the self-styled 'Big Beggar Man' raised £116,370.

Guthrie next turned his attention to the plight of homeless and destitute children in Edinburgh. The idea of ragged schools was not his own, but his talent for publicity, through his pamphlet *Plea for Ragged Schools* (1847), soon established him as their main protagonist. In that year he established three schools in Edinburgh, in which children received food, education, and industrial training. The initiative was not free from controversy, a dispute arising over the nature of the religious instruction which Guthrie proposed, which some felt discriminated against Roman Catholic pupils. A rival institution, the United Industrial School, was set up.

These exertions took their toll, and in the autumn of 1847 a heart condition forced Guthrie to rest from his duties for nearly two years. In 1849 he was awarded the degree of DD from Edinburgh, the first Free Church minister to be so honoured since the Disruption. In November 1850 William Hanna became his colleague at Free St John's, lightening the pastoral burden. Guthrie's popularity as a preacher, however, was undiminished. The famous jostled with the humble at Free St John's for the privilege of hearing its legendary minister. He published his sermons with great success. *The Gospel in Ezekiel* (1856) was followed by *Christ and the Inheritance of the Saints* (1858) and *The Way to Life* (1862). The problem of drunkenness, which had struck him on his arrival in Edinburgh, helped to make him a total abstainer, a position latterly relinquished when, on medical advice, he resumed the consumption of wine. In 1850 he wrote the pamphlet *A Plea on Behalf of Drunkards, and Against Drunkenness*, and in 1857 his sermons on the subject were published as *The City: its Sins and Sorrows*.

In 1862 Guthrie served as moderator of the Free Church general assembly. Two years later his health forced his retirement from Free St John's, although he remained as minister emeritus. His congregation presented him with £5000 and a silver coffee and tea service in February 1865. Yet his capacity for work was not so much diminished as diverted by this latest reduction in his physical powers. He assumed the editorship of a periodical, the *Sunday Magazine*, on his retirement, having already been a contributor to a similar publication, *Good Words*. He also took a lively interest in numerous concerns, including union with the United Presbyterian church, the national provision of education, and the fortunes of the Waldensian church. He travelled widely on the continent and frequently retired to his highland retreat at Lochlee. In 1869 he was elected a fellow of the Royal Society of Edinburgh. Guthrie died on 24 February 1873 at St Leonards, Sussex. His funeral, attended by massive crowds, took place in Edinburgh on 28 February, when he was interred at the Grange cemetery. A statue of him was prominently placed in Princes Street, Edinburgh.

In appearance Guthrie was tall and large-boned, with long, lank hair and a sallow complexion. A high forehead was emphasized by receding hair and his lively grey eyes were set in an expressive face. One contemporary, unimpressed with his appearance, likened him to 'an Irish hedge-schoolmaster' (Smith, 343) with 'rusty black, hob-nailed shoes, between which and the bottom of his trousers a space of blue worsted stockings was developed, swinging a huge brown cotton umbrella over his shoulder'. Yet the same authority was quick to concede the difference between the man in the street and in the pulpit. In his day only Chalmers was thought a better preacher. His style was not informed by theological depth or intellectual accomplishment, but was underpinned by a thorough knowledge of human nature, a warm-heartedness, and an ability to speak vividly and in terms that all could understand. A. K. H. Boyd described him as 'equally master of humour and pathos' (A. K. H. Boyd, *Twenty-Five Years of St Andrews*, 1892, 1.103). His platform speaking was reckoned to be still more effective, since he was more inclined to indulge his humour on these occasions.

Although one of the greatest of Free Church leaders he was never narrowly sectarian, and one of his warmest friendships was with a minister of the established Church of Scotland, Norman Macleod. His contacts with Anglican and nonconformist churchmen were no less cordial, although his hostility to the Roman Catholic church never lessened. Guthrie cared little for any position in society or for any denominational loyalty in itself, but he would have been happy to be remembered as the Apostle of Ragged Schools. LIONEL ALEXANDER RITCHIE

**Sources** *Autobiography of Thomas Guthrie*, ed. D. K. Guthrie and C. J. Guthrie, another edn, 2 vols. in 1 (1877) • O. Smeaton, *Thomas Guthrie* (1900) • *Fasti Scot.* • J. Smith, *Our Scottish clergy*, 1st ser. (1848), 342–8 • B. W. Crombie and W. S. Douglas, *Modern Athenians: a series of original portraits of memorable citizens of Edinburgh* (1882), 83–7 • C. J. Guthrie, *Thomas Guthrie, preacher and philanthropist* (1899) • J. M. McBain, *Eminent Arbroathians* (1897), 285–302 • J. A. Wylie, *Disruption worthies: a memorial of 1843*, ed. J. B. Gillies, new edn (1881), 285–94

**Archives** NL Scot. | NA Scot., letters to Fox Maule • NA Scot., letters to Elizabeth Sprott • NL Scot., letters to duchess of Argyll • NL Scot., corresp. with A. Black and C. Black, notes • NL Scot., letters to J. S. Blackie • NL Scot., letters to Lady Emma Campbell • NRA Scotland, priv. coll., letters to Sir George Sinclair

**Likenesses** B. W. Crombie, coloured etching, 1841, NPG; repro. in Douglas, *Modern Athenians*, 88 • D. O. Hill and R. Adamson, photograph, 1843, NPG [*see illus.*] • D. O. Hill and R. Adamson, calotype, 1843–8, NPG • E. Burton, mezzotint, pubd 1852 (after J. W. Gordon), BM • G. Harvey, oils, 1855, Scot. NPG • J. Edgar, portrait, 1862, Scot. NPG • W. Brodie, bas-relief, St John's Free church, Edinburgh • Elliott & Fry, carte-de-visite, NPG • D. O. Hill and R. Adamson, photographs, NPG • J. le Conte, engraving (after J. Edgar), Scot. NPG • K. Macleay, watercolour, Scot. NPG • J. Magill, carte-de-visite, NPG • T. Rodger, carte-de-visite, NPG • J. Steell, bronze bust, Scot. NPG • lithograph, repro. in Wylie, *Disruption worthies*, facing p. 285 • oils, Scot. NPG • photograph, repro. in McBain, *Eminent Arbroathians*, facing p. 285 • portraits, repro. in Guthrie, *Thomas Guthrie* • prints, NPG • statue, Princes Street, Edinburgh

**Wealth at death** £5271 2*s*. 8*d*. in Scotland and England: inventory, 15 May 1873, NA Scot., SC 70/1/162/406 • £5854 0*s*. 3*d*.: additional inventory, 15 May 1889, NA Scot., SC 70/1/274/876

**Guthrie, Thomas Anstey** [*pseud.* F. Anstey] **(1856–1934)**, humorous writer, was born in London on 8 August 1856, probably at 7 St George's Terrace, Gloucester Road, the eldest of the three sons and one daughter of Thomas Anstey Guthrie (1822/3–1889), military tailor, of Cork Street, Burlington Gardens, and Augusta Amherst Austen (1827–1877), a professional pianist. The Guthries came from Forfarshire two or three generations back, and his mother came from Irish stock. Anstey was educated at a private school at Surbiton (the original of Crichton House in *Vice Versa*), at King's College School, and at Trinity Hall, Cambridge, where he read law. Anstey's literary endeavours, however, eclipsed law and he received a third class. While at Cambridge he contributed humorous pieces to the *Undergraduates' Journal* and other magazines such as *Mirth*, in the process of which he acquired the pseudonym F. Anstey because of a printing error (this name is sometimes mistakenly assumed to be a corruption of 'fantasy'). While at Cambridge he also embarked on 'Turned Tables'—the story of a father and son who magically exchange places, resulting in Mr Bultitude attending his son's school—which was inspired by his own encounters with his eccentric schoolmaster. It was serialized in the *Cambridge Tatler* and published as *Vice Versa* in 1882 following a hiatus after the death of his mother. He was called to the bar in 1881, but never practised, and eagerly took the chance of becoming a writer given him by the great success of *Vice Versa*. This first novel made him famous overnight and it is suggested that its humour precipitated Anthony Trollope's fatal stroke. It provided the model for other fantasies, including Mary Rogers's *Freaky Friday* (1972), which in some ways was the female version of the story which Anstey declined to write. *The Giant's Robe*, the story of a plagiarist, followed in 1883, but ironically charges of actual plagiarism blighted its success and Anstey's career as a serious novelist. In 1884 he collected his short stories in *The Black Poodle*, while *A Fallen Idol* (1886) demonstrated that Anstey was a competent horror writer.

In 1886 Anstey began a connection with *Punch*, and in 1887 was 'called to the Table' at the *Punch* office; he remained on the staff until 1930. With the series 'Voces populi', 'Mr. Punch's Young Reciter', 'Mr. Punch's Model Music-Hall Songs and Dramas', and 'Mr. Punch's Pocket Ibsen' (all of which were published in book form and remain of some socio-historical importance), Anstey developed a superior talent for burlesque and parody, for recording and subtly transmitting the day-to-day talk of Londoners. *The Man from Blankley's*, based on the *Punch* series, was later a successful play and film.

While working for *Punch* Anstey continued to write fiction. *The Pariah* (1889), another excursion into serious fiction, failed to restore his reputation in this genre. *Tourmalin's Time Cheques* (1891) has interest as one of the first literary experiments with the paradox of time travel, while the unsuccessful and anonymously published *The Statement of Stella Maberly* (1897) is an earnest treatment of schizophrenia. His children's book *Only Toys!* (1903) was moderately successful but has not been rediscovered by successive generations. *The Brass Bottle* (1900), based on the *Arabian Nights*, was, however, his most popular fantasy after *Vice Versa*, and in turn it influenced E. Nesbit's *Five Children and It* (1902). The dramatic qualities of his fiction resulted in *The Brass Bottle* being produced on stage in 1909 and on film in 1963. *Vice Versa* was produced as a Christmas play in 1910 (the most memorable film version starred Peter Ustinov in 1947).

During the First World War Anstey was a volunteer in the Inns of Court reserve corps and performed Home Guard duties. *In Brief Authority* (1915) was his last novel; its reliance on Germanic folklore sealed its unpopularity at the time of publication, although it has subsequently been critically acclaimed. In 1925 he issued the final volume of collected *Punch* sketches, *The Last Load*; it sold poorly. His later literary work was devoted largely to translating and adapting the plays of Molière for the English stage.

Anstey died of pneumonia at his home, 24 Holland Park Road, Kensington, on 10 March 1934. His ashes lie in the grave of his friend and brother-in-law George Millar in Blatchington churchyard in Sussex. He never married and had lived all his life in London, where he was recognized by his immaculate dress and prominent moustache, and respected by his wide circle of friends for his equable disposition.

In his autobiography, *The Long Retrospect* (1936), Anstey, with characteristic modesty, bears the decline of his reputation with clear-sightedness, dissecting his failures rather than exalting in his successes and grateful for his first flush of success and for his dwindling band of readers. He realized that he was out of favour in Britain in the 1930s (he had never enjoyed much popularity in America) and despite the enthusiasm of George Gordon, president of Magdalen College, Oxford, who propelled the publication of an omnibus edition of his popular fiction entitled *Humour and Fantasy* (1931), he was not surprised to learn that the public now found his reliance on the supernatural outmoded.

Anstey is finally, however, being recognized as one of the most popular and skilled of the late Victorian fantasists who used magic and humour to intersect with and unsettle the ordinary. Critics have remarked on his status as 'the best novelist of the tight space' (Lucas) and his ability to make plausible the most astonishing transformations. Some of his pieces have been reassessed as sophisticated satires of late nineteenth-century frailties (Harris-Fain), including his stories for children which can be considered as significant in the development of the form.

DOUGLAS WOODRUFF, *rev.* CLARE L. TAYLOR

**Sources** F. Anstey [T. A. Guthrie], *A long retrospect* (1936); repr. (1938) • D. Harris-Fain, ed., *British fantasy and science-fiction writers before World War I*, DLitB, 178 (1997) • L. M. Zaidman, ed., *British children's writers, 1880–1914*, DLitB, 141 (1994) • D. Pringle, ed., *St James guide to fantasy writers* (1996) • J. Stratford, 'F. Anstey', *British Museum Quarterly*, 33 (1968–9), 80–85 • E. V. Lucas, 'F. Anstey', *English Illustrated Magazine*, 29 (Aug 1903), 544–5 • E. F. Bleiler, *The guide to supernatural fiction* (1983) • S. J. Kunitz and H. Haycraft, eds., *Twentieth century authors: a biographical dictionary of modern literature* (1942) • personal knowledge (1949) • private information (1949) • d. cert. • *IGI*

**Archives** BL, corresp., journals, notebooks, and literary MSS, Add. MSS 54258–54312 • BL, diaries, Add. MSS 63551–63582 | BL, letters to William Archer, Add. MS 45291 • BL, corresp. with Society of Authors, incl. corresp. with his nephew, E. G. Millar, Add. MSS 56719, 63257–63259, 63304–63305 • Harvard U., Houghton L., letters

**Likenesses** Bassano, photograph, 1890–99, repro. in Anstey, *Long retrospect* • L. Campbell Taylor, oils, 1928–9, priv. coll. • Whitlock, photograph, 1930, repro. in Anstey, *Long retrospect* • L. A. Bell, chalk drawing, NPG • L. A. Bell, crayon drawing, priv. coll. • photograph, NPG

**Wealth at death** £38,293 16*s.* 1*d.*: probate, 10 May 1934, *CGPLA Eng. & Wales*

**Guthrie, Sir (William) Tyrone** (1900–1971), director and theatre designer, was born on 2 July 1900 at Tunbridge Wells, Kent, the elder child and only son of Thomas Clement Guthrie, doctor and surgeon, and his wife, Norah Emily Gorman Power. He had much theatrical blood in his veins, since his mother was the granddaughter of Tyrone Power, the first of a long line of popular actors, of whom Tyrone Power the film actor was Guthrie's cousin. He was educated at Wellington College, and won a history scholarship at St John's College, Oxford. He early showed that independence of spirit which later enabled him to transform the shape of theatre in Britain, Canada, and the United States by telling the authorities of St John's that if he won a scholarship he did not need the money, which he hoped would be given to a poorer man. It was not until he had done this that he told his father of the magnanimous gesture he had made on his behalf.

Guthrie went up to Oxford at the time of the armistice in a state of high exhilaration. He declared that 'certainly we are living in the most marvellous times since the Reformation—if not since Christ … For the young … it's an opportunity such as the world has never known before'. His Scots-Irish blood roused greater fires in him than were kindled by the gracious propriety of Tunbridge Wells. In 1923 he left university with a pass degree and immediately plunged into the society of those as yet unknown, but who were, with him, to become famous. He joined the company of J. B. Fagan at the Playhouse, Oxford, which in the early 1920s had in it such young players as John Gielgud, Richard Goolden, and Flora Robson. He was to see Flora Robson frequently in subsequent years, and proposed to her, but the proposal came to nothing because they could not agree whether to have children. Guthrie was further dashed by his great height and comparatively small head, and so gave up acting.

After working in radio in Belfast and then with the BBC, and at one or two other indeterminate occupations, Guthrie at last found his vocation by directing *The Anatomist* by James Bridie at the Westminster Theatre (1931), with Henry Ainley as Dr Knox and Flora Robson as the unfortunate prostitute, Mary Paterson, a part which she considered the finest performance she ever gave. Guthrie immediately recognized that he had a great gift, aided by his commanding height, his gentle voice, and inflexible determination, for controlling actors, and two years later Lilian Baylis appointed him as director of plays at the Old Vic and Sadler's Wells.

Guthrie's years at the Old Vic were a period of ambition, achievement, and frustration. He raised the standard of productions, but angered Lilian Baylis by bringing in outside stars such as Charles Laughton (whom she resented as

**Sir (William) Tyrone Guthrie (1900–1971)**, by Sir Cecil Beaton

too expensive), Flora Robson, and Athene Seyler. After Lilian Baylis's death in 1937 Guthrie was appointed administrator. When war came he was much criticized for evacuating the Old Vic to Burnley. He developed his conviction that the director was a more important element in a production than the actor, but when the Old Vic returned to London in 1944, reaching tremendous success in a temporary West End home at the New (later Albery) Theatre, Guthrie was overshadowed by the performances of Laurence Olivier, Ralph Richardson, and Sybil Thorndike, who had now joined the company. He felt rebuffed when knighthoods were conferred on Richardson and Olivier in 1947, and he himself was passed over. He ended the war very depressed, quite different from his mood of 1918, and resigned from the Old Vic. He travelled restlessly, and produced a fine *Oedipus Rex* for the Habimah company in Tel Aviv.

The turning point in his Guthrie's came in 1948, when he directed an adaptation of Sir David Lindsay's *Ane Satyre of the Three Estaits* in the Assembly Hall of the Church of Scotland at the second Edinburgh festival. Guthrie had long felt dissatisfied with the separation of audience and players by the conventional proscenium arch, and the thrust stage of the austere Assembly Hall, with the audience on three sides of it, enabled him to bring about a sense of participation between players and audience which became the keynote of the work by which he was to change the nature and shape of theatre in the Western world. Here he came into his kingdom, of which he felt he had been hitherto deprived. He suddenly saw the kind of theatre he wanted—a theatre of processions and banners and ritual, a theatre that was in itself a festival, an event, a celebration, in which the actor played an important but essentially subordinate part in the pageantry and splendour of the director's conception of the play, which he insisted was essentially subjective and need not conform with the author's. Inspired by this revelation, he established the Stratford Ontario Festival in 1952, in the second largest theatrical tent in the Western hemisphere, and in 1963 a theatre in Minneapolis based on the principles worked out at Edinburgh. Guthrie's theories have influenced the building of nearly all new theatres, and are particularly apparent in England in the construction of the Chichester Festival Theatre (1962) and the Olivier (1976). It was thus, rather than by individual productions, that Guthrie justified his conviction of 1918 that a new world was opening to those that could seize it.

Guthrie received many honours. He was knighted in 1961 and was chancellor of Queen's University, Belfast (1963–70). He was an honorary fellow of St John's College, Oxford (1964). He received honorary degrees from Queen's University, Trinity College, Dublin (1964), St Andrews (1956), Franklyn and Marshall University (Pennsylvania), Western Ontario (1954), Ripon College (Wisconsin), and Citadel Military College, Charleston.

On 31 August 1931 Guthrie married Judith, daughter of Gordon Bretherton, solicitor, and Nellie Lacheur, and, as he himself said, lived happily ever after. She died in 1972. There were no children of the marriage. He died on 15 May 1971 at his family estate, Annaghmakerrig, Doohat, near Newbliss, co. Monaghan, Éire. HAROLD HOBSON, *rev.*

**Sources** *The Times* (17 May 1971) · J. Forsyth, *Tyrone Guthrie: a biography* (1976) · T. Guthrie, *A life in the theatre* (1960) · personal knowledge (1986) · Burke, *Peerage* (1967) · *CGPLA Eng. & Wales* (1972)

**Archives** NRA, priv. coll., corresp. and literary papers · TCD, notebooks, sketchbooks, and corresp. | U. St Andr. L., letters to Cedric Thorpe Davie | FILM BFI NFTVA, documentary footage · BFI NFTVA, performance footage | SOUND BL NSA, 'A life in the theatre—commemorative portrait of Sir Tyrone Guthrie', 2 July 1972 · BL NSA, current affairs recording · BL NSA, documentary recordings · BL NSA, oral history interviews · BL NSA, performance recordings · BL NSA, recorded talks

**Likenesses** H. Coster, photograph, 1930–39, NPG · M. Austria, group portrait, photograph, 1948, NPG; *see illus. in* Crozier, Eric John (1914–1994) · C. Beaton, photograph, NPG [*see illus.*] · photographs, Theatre Museum, London · photographs, V&A

**Wealth at death** £52,183 in England and Wales: probate, 29 Sept 1972, *CGPLA Eng. & Wales*

**Guthrie, William** (1620–1665), Church of Scotland minister, was the eldest son of James Guthrie of Pitforthy, Forfarshire; the identity of his mother is unknown. He was educated at the University of St Andrews under his cousin, James Guthrie (*c*.1612–1661), regent of St Leonard's College and later minister of Stirling. William graduated MA on 5 June 1638, but continued his studies at St Andrews under Samuel Rutherford, professor of divinity. He was licensed to preach by the presbytery of St Andrews in August 1642. Shortly afterwards he accepted the post of tutor to James, eldest son of John Campbell, earl of Loudoun (1598–1662), a leading covenanter and chancellor of Scotland. On 7

November 1644 Guthrie was appointed minister of Fenwick, Ayrshire. The following August he married Agnes, daughter of David Campbell of Dalrymple, Ayrshire; they had two sons and four daughters.

A convinced adherent of the covenant Guthrie was present at the Mauchline rising against royalist forces in June 1648. As a consequence he was one of seven ministers 'summoned [by the general assembly] to answer as raisers of that tumult' in July, but emphatically denied that he had any part in 'persuad[ing] the people to meet there that day' (*Letters and Journals of Robert Baillie*, 3.53). The affair served only to reinforce his strict presbyterianism, and—as a commissioner to the general assembly of 1649—he supported the implementation of the Act of Classes, whereby all but the staunchest covenanters were to be excluded from public office. Thereafter Guthrie declined calls to more prestigious parishes in Stirling, Glasgow, and Edinburgh, preferring to continue his career as chaplain to the army. In this capacity he witnessed the rout of the covenanting army at Dunbar by Oliver Cromwell's forces on 3 September 1650.

As a consequence of this defeat Guthrie became embroiled in the bitter dispute between those resolved to rescind the Act of Classes (resolutioners), and those who wished to retain the act's exclusive policy (remonstrators). He argued—in 'tears, bot in vaine'—against separation over the issue (*Letters and Journals of Robert Baillie*, 3.193), but was one of twenty-eight ministers who signed a 'protestation and declinatour' against the constitution and decisions of the general assembly of 1651, at which the resolution was adopted (*Diary of Sir Archibald Johnston*, 93). Thereafter the two sides held separate councils, of which the minister was a regular member. He was appointed moderator of the separatist synod held at Edinburgh on 28 August 1654. Guthrie was a close friend and correspondent of Archibald Johnston of Wariston, co-author of the *National Covenant* and formerly clerk register of Scotland, from whom he sought advice regarding his 'personal formal soule covenanting' in the same year. Their discussions prompted Guthrie to produce a 'tractat' entitled *The Christian's Great Interest*, which the advocate greatly admired, and was much concerned to 'comunicate and presse on uthers' (ibid., 275, 280, 288). The work was published by popular demand at Edinburgh in 1659.

At the Restoration, however, public sympathy for Guthrie's particular brand of presbyterianism was driven underground. On 2 April 1661 the synod of Glasgow and Ayr refused their support to an eloquent petition written by Guthrie which called upon parliament to protect the liberties of the kirk. Its timing and nature, claimed the assembly, were 'inexpedient' (Hewison, 2.129). The truth of that statement was brought home to Guthrie when he attended the last hours of his cousin and former tutor, James Guthrie, executed for treason on 1 July. Nevertheless Guthrie remained 'a ringleader and a keeper-up of schism' in Ayrshire for some years (Anderson, *Scot. nat.*, 2.391), whose refusal to submit to episcopacy became a major embarrassment to Alexander Burnet, archbishop of Glasgow. In 1664 the *Sermon of Mr William Guthrie* was published at Edinburgh, and—despite the fact that the minister denied having a hand in its publication—the archbishop's patience snapped. Guthrie was deprived of his benefice on 24 July that year.

Although Guthrie's character was 'tempered with gravity as becometh a minister of Christ', his 'singular sallies of wit and innocent mirth' (Wodrow, *Select Biographies*, 2.65) earned him the appellation of 'the fool of Fenwick' which title reflects the fond regard in which the minister was held by his parishioners (*DNB*). He was a keen sportsman, but suffered frequent bouts of ill health and was often subject to attacks of the 'worme' (*Diary of Sir Archibald Johnston*, 275). Following the death of his brother in the summer of 1665 he returned to the family estate of Pitforthy, where he was 'seized with a complication of distempers', including an 'ulcer in his kidneys' (Howie, 333). Guthrie died on Wednesday 10 October 1665 in the house of his brother-in-law, Lewis Skinner, minister of Brechin, and was buried in Brechin church.

Guthrie's sermons and writings proved highly popular among later covenanters, leading to the publication of several of his sermons, including *Crumbs of Comfort*, which offered the same to like-minded presbyterians in 1681. As a consequence the house of Guthrie's widow was searched in 1682 and his papers carried off. A collection of his surviving works, entitled *Sermons Delivered in Times of Persecution in Scotland*, was published at Edinburgh in 1880. VAUGHAN T. WELLS

**Sources** W. K. Tweedie, ed., *Select biographies*, 2, Wodrow Society, 7/2 (1847) · R. Wodrow, *The history of the sufferings of the Church of Scotland, from the Restauration to the revolution*, 1 (1721) · *Diary of Sir Archibald Johnston of Wariston*, 2, ed. D. H. Fleming, Scottish History Society, 2nd ser., 18 (1919) · *The letters and journals of Robert Baillie*, ed. D. Laing, 3 (1842) · *Fasti Scot.*, new edn, vols. 3–4 · Wing, *STC* · W. H. Carslaw, preface, in J. Howie, *The Scots worthies*, ed. W. H. Carslaw, [new edn] (1870), ix–xv · J. K. Hewison, *The covenanters: a history of the church in Scotland from the Reformation to the revolution*, 2nd edn, 2 (1913) · Anderson, *Scot. nat.*, vol. 2 · *Letters of Samuel Rutherford*, ed. A. A. Bonar (1891); facs. repr. (1984) · J. Nicoll, *A diary of public transactions and other occurrences, chiefly in Scotland, from January 1650 to June 1667*, ed. D. Laing, Bannatyne Club, 52 (1836) · *DNB*
**Archives** NL Scot., sermon notes

**Guthrie, William** (1708?–1770), historian and political journalist, was born at Brechin, Forfarshire, the son of a Scottish Episcopal clergyman. He was reputedly educated at King's College, Aberdeen, though the published registers of matriculations and graduations do not contain his name. He left Scotland for London about 1730, intending to pursue a life as a man of letters.

Guthrie first emerged as a reporter of parliamentary business for the *Gentleman's Magazine*, a task in which he achieved real proficiency. But, writing under the pseudonym Jeffrey Broadbottom, he also produced rather more scurrilous material, including the infrequent periodical *Old England, or, The Constitutional Journal* (1743–6) and the blatantly scatological *Serious and Cleanly Meditations upon an House-of-Office (a Boghouse)* (1744). Guthrie was rewarded in 1745 with a government pension of £200 per annum from Henry Pelham. Although seemingly an ardent ally of the whig administrations, he was sufficiently influential—and unscrupulous—to receive a renewal of this payment under Lord Bute's administration in 1762.

Guthrie's scholarly interests having quickened through middle age, he had also begun work on a substantial project, the *History of England from the Invasion of Julius Caesar to 1688*. Published in four volumes in 1744–51, this benefited from his professional experience in that it made unprecedented use of parliamentary papers for the later period. Subsequently he produced several more works. His wider literary interests were also revealed in translations of Quintilian (1756) and Cicero (1744, 1745, 1755, 1758), in a sentimental history *The Friends* (1754), and in the critical work *Essay upon English Tragedy* (1757). But his finest work remained historical, Guthrie managing, like his compatriot Smollett, to bring considerable journalistic flair to the contemporary popularization of historiography. His *Complete List of the English Peerage* (1763) was useful in intent though not always accurate in its execution, containing numerous errors even in relation to George II's very recent reign. More competent and better received were a twelve-volume *General History of the World, from the Creation to the Present Time* (1764–7), published with collaborators, and a ten-volume *General History of Scotland* (1767). The latter was particularly intriguing for its exploration of early Scottish history which, in the immediate aftermath of Ossian's spectacular arrival on the literary stage, allowed Guthrie to tap into topical interest in his native country's Pictish and Gaelic past. John Pinkerton, who later made this his own particular specialism, reckoned Guthrie's the finest work on the subject hitherto written.

Guthrie's most successful work, however, was his *Geographical, Historical, and Commercial Grammar* (1770), in many ways built on the previous two works. It saw several later editions and eventually, in 1801, translation into French. In offering 'knowledge of the world, and of its inhabitants' (W. Guthrie, *Geographical, Historical, and Commercial Grammar*, 1770, 4), Guthrie developed a fluent simplification of Scottish Enlightenment historical and political analysis. Welcoming the 'rapid progress and general diffusion of learning and civility' which had granted him a privileged vantage point from which to survey the rest of history, he also viewed with great pride what he claimed had been the recent eradication of 'those illiberal prejudices, which not only cramp the genius, but sour the temper of man, and disturb all the agreeable intercourse of society' (ibid., 3). Guthrie's vision of progressive human evolution was also underpinned by the consuming faith in the ultimate triumph of commerce, cultivation, toleration, and liberty in modern Britain which his readers so often shared.

Guthrie's critical stock has subsequently fallen along with the credibility of the assumptions which once sustained it. Yet both Johnson and Boswell regarded him with affection, and he was reputed a serious scholar by his admiring contemporaries. He died in London on 9 March 1770 and was buried in Marylebone. DAVID ALLAN

**Sources** W. Anderson, *The Scottish biographical dictionary* (1845), 398–90 • Chambers, *Scots.* (1835), 2.186–8 • D. Allan, *Virtue, learning and the Scottish Enlightenment: ideas of scholarship in early modern history* (1993) • C. Kidd, *Subverting Scotland's past: Scottish whig historians and the creation of an Anglo-British identity, 1689–c.1830* (1993), 239 • Boswell, *Life*, 1.116–21; 2.52 • P. J. Anderson, ed., *Officers and graduates of University and King's College, Aberdeen, MVD–MDCCCLX*, New Spalding Club, 11 (1893) • *Officers of the Marischal College and University of Aberdeen, 1593–1860* (1897) • *DNB*

**Likenesses** I. Taylor, line engraving, BM, NPG; repro. in I. Taylor, *History of Scotland* (1767)

**Guthrie, William** (1835–1908), legal writer, born at Culhorn House, Stranraer, on 17 August 1835, was the eldest son of George Guthrie of Appleby, writer and factor to the earl of Stair, and his wife, Margaret, daughter of Robert McDonall. He was educated at Stranraer Academy and at the universities of Glasgow and Edinburgh. On 29 September 1858 he married Charlotte Carruthers (*d.* 1928), daughter of James Palmer of Edinburgh. They had four sons and two daughters. Guthrie was called to the Scottish bar on 4 June 1861. He acquired a substantial practice over the next thirteen years, during which time he was also editor of the *Journal of Jurisprudence*, from 1867 to 1874, and an official reporter of cases decided in the Court of Session, from 1871 to 1874. In 1871 he was appointed one of the commissioners under the Truck Act, in which capacity he reported on the fisheries and other industries of the Shetland Islands. In 1872 he was appointed registrar of friendly societies for Scotland.

In 1874 Guthrie replaced Gillespie Dickson as sheriff-substitute of Lanarkshire at Glasgow. He held this post for twenty-nine years, during which time he wrote prolifically on legal matters. Among his most important written work he edited Hunter's *Treatise on the Law of Landlord and Tenant* (1876), Erskine's *Principles of the Law of Scotland* (1870), and Bell's *Principles of the Law of Scotland* (1872); he translated the eighth volume of Savigny's *System of Modern Roman Law* and he wrote *The Law of Trades Unions in England and Scotland under the Trade Union Act of 1871* (1873), as well as various papers on the liability of trustees, with regard to the case concerning the City of Glasgow Bank.

In 1881 Guthrie received the honorary degree of LLD from Edinburgh University. Later he represented the Faculty of Advocates at a meeting of the International Law Association. In 1903 he was raised to the position of sheriff-principal of Lanarkshire at Glasgow, replacing Robert Berry. As a judge, he was said by *The Times* to be 'always courteous and urbane, if somewhat austere and dignified in his bearing'. He performed the tasks of his office effectively and took a prominent and useful part in public affairs: he was, for instance, one of the chief witnesses before the royal commission on the care of the feeble-minded.

Politically, Guthrie was a supporter of the Liberal Party. Like many others, however, he did not support Gladstone's Home Rule Bill, and he subsequently became a Liberal Unionist. He was also a strong churchman and held office in the Church of Scotland. He strenuously opposed the move for disestablishment, and published a pamphlet—*The Democratic View of the Church Question*—in support of a state church. Guthrie died in Glasgow, in the house of his son David, on 31 August 1908. He was buried in the Cathcart cemetery, Glasgow.

G. W. T. OMOND, *rev.* NATHAN WELLS

**Sources** *The Times* (2 Sept 1908) · F. J. Grant, ed., *The Faculty of Advocates in Scotland, 1532–1943*, Scottish RS, 145 (1944) · Irving, *Scots.* · *Men of the time* (1887) · *The Scotsman* (2 Sept 1908) · *Glasgow Herald* (2 Sept 1908) · *CCI* (1908)

**Wealth at death** £2320 11s. 10*d*.: confirmation, 16 Dec 1908, *CCI*

**Guthrum** (*d.* **890**), king of the East Angles, came from Denmark. Although no source names him as such, he was almost certainly a leader of the 'great summer army' which in April 871 joined the viking force then based at Reading. After fighting a series of engagements against the West Saxons, the combined army left Reading in the autumn of 871 and wintered in London. Coins bearing the name Hálfdan that were minted there indicate the identity of the army's most prominent leader at the time. From London, in the early autumn of 872, the army was drawn to Northumbria by a revolt against the Danish-appointed puppet king Ecgberht, before it settled for the winter in Mercia, at Torksey on the Trent. The vikings remained there for a year after the Mercians had bought peace from them, and late in 873 moved to Repton. They drove the Mercian king Burgred from his kingdom, establishing in his place Ceolwulf (*fl.* 874–879), who gave them hostages and swore oaths that Mercia should be at their disposal whenever they wanted it. In the following year the viking army divided into two. Hálfdan took one part of it north to a base on the Tyne from which he attacked the Picts and Strathclyde Britons. His army then settled in Northumbria from autumn 875, where they 'proceeded to plough and to support themselves' (*ASC*, s.a. 876).

It is as a leader of the other part of the army that Guthrum first appears in the historical record. The Anglo-Saxon Chronicle notes that in 874 he, together with the otherwise unknown Oscytel and Anund, took 'a great force' from Repton to Cambridge, where they stayed for a year. In the autumn of 875 the army boldly crossed Wessex, eluding the West Saxon *fyrd*, and entered Wareham. Perhaps because it was depleted after its division, the West Saxon king Alfred was able to treat with Guthrum's force on equal terms, giving it money, but also taking hostages—'the most important men next to their king in the army' (*ASC*, s.a. 876)—and extracting from them an oath that they would quickly leave Wessex, sworn on the vikings' holy ring: 'a thing which they would never do before for any nation' (ibid.). In the following year, however, Guthrum broke the oath and his entire army slipped out of Wareham by night and made for Exeter. Although Alfred gave chase the vikings were able to enter the fortress there. But Guthrum was compelled to make peace once again, perhaps because of the destruction of naval reinforcements off Swanage. He offered more hostages and, in the summer of 877, left Wessex for Gloucester in Mercia. The vikings then divided Mercia, sharing some of it out among themselves and leaving the remainder under the puppet king Ceolwulf.

Guthrum himself, however, was not yet ready to settle on the conquered land. In the second week of 878 he led an army from Gloucester to Chippenham, in Wessex. Probably in an attempt to enhance the significance of Alfred's later victory, the writer of the Anglo-Saxon Chronicle depicts this event as precipitating a viking occupation of Wessex: Alfred was forced to wander 'through the woods and fen-fastnesses with a small force' (*ASC*, s.a. 878). While it is true that Chippenham was a royal vill, there is no firm evidence that Alfred himself was there when Guthrum attacked. Nor was Wessex entirely at Guthrum's mercy, for it was at about this time that the ealdorman of Devon was able to defeat a viking landing at Countisbury, slaying its leader, an unnamed brother of Hálfdan and Ívarr. Furthermore, it was only some seven weeks after Guthrum had taken Chippenham that Alfred rallied the levies of Somerset, Wiltshire, and west Hampshire, and offered battle. His ensuing victory at Edington, in what is now Wiltshire, forced Guthrum back to Chippenham, where he was besieged for two weeks before submitting. Three weeks later an extended ceremony began at Aller, in modern Somerset, where Guthrum and thirty of his leading men were baptized. Alfred stood as godfather and Guthrum took the baptismal name of Æthelstan. The ceremony was completed at Wedmore, a few days later, when Alfred bestowed gifts on Guthrum and his companions. In the summer of 878 Guthrum took his army to Cirencester. Many may then have joined a recently arrived army camped at Fulham, which left for the continent in 879. That summer Guthrum took his remaining men back to East Anglia, where they settled.

It was probably at this time that a treaty, of which the text survives, was concluded between Guthrum and Alfred, formally recognizing and defining the boundary between Alfred's jurisdiction and that of Guthrum, and regulating relations between them. The boundary ran up the Thames to its confluence with the Lea, up the latter to its spring, in a straight line from there to Bedford, then along the Ouse to Watling Street. The establishment of the boundary was an important stage in Alfred's assumption of the leadership of all the English who were not under Scandinavian rule, reinforced by his taking decisive possession of London in 886. Although viking raiding parties crossed the boundary several times in the 880s, Guthrum himself is not again recorded as threatening the West Saxon kingdom. For more than a decade he ruled East Anglia as a Christian king: his coins bore his baptismal name of Æthelstan. Guthrum died in 890; the twelfth-century annals of St Neots claim that he was buried at the royal estate of Hadleigh in East Anglia.

MARIOS COSTAMBEYS

**Sources** *ASC*, s.a. 876, 878 · F. M. Stenton, *Anglo-Saxon England*, 3rd edn (1971) · *The chronicle of Æthelweard*, ed. and trans. A. Campbell (1962) · *Alfred the Great: Asser's Life of King Alfred and other contemporary sources*, ed. and trans. S. Keynes and M. Lapidge (1983) · D. Dumville and M. Lapidge, eds., *The annals of St Neots, with Vita prima sancti Neoti* (1985), vol. 17 of *The Anglo-Saxon Chronicle*, ed. D. Dumville and S. Keynes (1983–)

**Guto'r Glyn** (*fl.* *c.*1435–*c.*1493), poet, is probably identifiable with Guto ap Siancyn y Glyn, though scholarly opinion is divided on this matter. The 'Glyn' of his name may have been Glyn Ceiriog or Glyndyfrdwy (now both in Clwyd). According to the later poet Tudur Aled it was Guto of all Welsh poets who excelled in composing praise poems to noblemen: his work amply bears out this judgement, often boldly transcending poetic convention and delighting with its wit, vigour, and original imagery [*see also* Cywyddwyr (*act.* *c.*1330–*c.*1650)]. As a young man Guto saw service in France, probably in the retinue of Sir William ap Thomas of Raglan, and addressed spirited poems to fellow Welshmen Sir Richard Gethin and Matthew Gough. Guto was a faithful Yorkist who served in Edward IV's guard, hailing the king in a poem as 'the great bull descended from the Mortimers'. Among his more important patrons were the sons of Sir William ap Thomas, William Herbert, first earl of Pembroke, and Sir Richard Herbert. The brothers' execution after the battle of Banbury in 1469 moved Guto to compose a poignant and bitter elegy, blaming the tragedy on English treachery. As well as these leading figures Guto's patrons included numerous members of the minor gentry and ecclesiastics, and during a long poetic career he travelled extensively throughout Wales. He settled in Oswestry, becoming a burgess there, before retiring in old age to Valle Crucis Abbey, Llangollen, where he was succoured by his friend and patron Abbot Dafydd ab Ieuan ab Iorwerth. He died at the abbey and was buried there.

GRUFFYDD ALED WILLIAMS

**Sources** J. Ll. Williams and I. Williams, *Gwaith Guto'r Glyn* (1939) • J. Ll. Williams, 'Guto ap Siancyn, neu Guto'r Glyn', *Y Llenor*, 10 (1931), 152–60 • S. Lewis, 'Gyrfa filwrol Guto'r Glyn', *Ysgrifau Beirniadol*, 9 (1976), 80–99 • J. E. C. Williams, 'Guto'r Glyn', *A guide to Welsh literature*, ed. A. O. H. Jarman and G. R. Hughes, 2: *1282–c.1550* (1979), 218–42 • E. Roberts, *Y beirdd a'u Noddwyr ym Maelor* (1977)

**Gutteridge, Harold Cooke** (1876–1953), jurist, was born on 16 July 1876 at Naples, Italy, the second son of Michael Gutteridge, a pioneer of departmental stores in southern Italy, and his wife, Ada, daughter of Samuel Cooke, of Liversedge, Yorkshire. Until the age of twelve he was at a Swiss school in Naples where, in addition to Italian which was almost one of his native languages, he acquired much French and German. He then went to the Leys School and to King's College, Cambridge, where he took first-class honours in the historical (1898) and law (part one, 1899) triposes.

Gutteridge was called to the bar in 1900 by the Middle Temple (ultimately becoming a bencher) and took silk in 1930. He practised mainly in commercial matters until the outbreak of war in 1914, when he joined the Territorial Force. He served in the Army Ordnance Corps with the British Salonika force from 1916 to 1919, was mentioned in dispatches, and retired with the rank of captain. In 1905 he married Mary Louisa, daughter of Joseph Jackson; they had three children.

In 1919 Gutteridge was elected Sir Ernest Cassel professor of industrial and commercial law in the University of London. This post he held for eleven years (while maintaining a consultant practice); he played a very considerable part in developing the faculty of law from a body of part-time teachers into a mainly full-time faculty.

Although he was typically English in most respects, Gutteridge's knowledge of languages made him very popular with foreign colleagues and pupils. Possessing this equipment and the large knowledge of commercial and maritime law which he had acquired both in practice and as a teacher, he found his interests becoming more and more directed towards conflict of laws and comparative law. In 1930 the University of Cambridge created for him a readership in comparative law, which enabled him to concentrate on his chosen field. It was later converted into a chair, which he held until 1941. He was a fellow of Trinity Hall. His reputation attracted many foreign research students to Cambridge, and in some western European countries he was regarded as 'the apostle of the common law'.

Gutteridge was a member of many government commissions and committees—the royal commission on the manufacture of and traffic in arms (1935), the law revision committee (1933), the lord chancellor's committees on the enforcement of foreign judgments (1932) and on legal education (1933 and 1938), the shipping claims tribunal (1939), the Geneva conference on the unification of the law of bills of exchange and cheques (1931), and the Hague conference on private international law (1930). He was doctor of laws in the universities of London and Cambridge and received honorary doctorates from the universities of Lyon, Grenoble, Paris, and Salonika.

Gutteridge's principal publications were a notable thirteenth edition of *Smith's Mercantile Law* (1931), *Bankers' Commercial Credits* (1932, a book on a subject little known outside the circle of merchants and bankers and their legal advisers), and *Comparative Law*, published in 1946, followed by a second edition in 1949 and editions in French, Japanese, and Spanish. A bibliography of his publications, comprising more than fifty contributions to periodicals and joint works, was compiled by his successor at Cambridge, Professor C. J. Hamson, and printed in the July 1954 issue of the *International and Comparative Law Quarterly* together with three obituary notices. His first book was *Nelson and the Neapolitan Jacobins* (Navy Records Society, 1903), which was marked by his great admiration of Nelson and his enduring affection for Naples and for the sea.

Although comparative law had already occupied the attention of some distinguished lawyers in Great Britain and the Society of Comparative Legislation and its *Journal* had existed for half a century, Gutteridge's *Comparative Law* was the first systematic attempt to state the case for the recognition of what was almost a new subject in Great Britain both as a branch of legal studies and as a practical instrument of legal progress. Moreover, it is clear throughout the book that he regarded as one of the main functions of comparative law the promotion of a reciprocal basis of understanding among lawyers practising or teaching in widely differing legal systems, particularly the common law and the modern civil law of continental Europe. His achievement in this respect needed more than sound learning and good judgement; it was largely due to the influence of his personality and to his evident intellectual integrity.

In appearance Gutteridge was short, portly, and rubicund, suggesting, perhaps, a distinguished naval officer rather than a scholar. He had a most lovable character which won for him a host of friends. His daughter, Joyce Ada Cooke Gutteridge, became one of the legal advisers to the Foreign Office. His elder son, Michael, a lieutenant in the Royal Tank Corps, died in India in 1935; the other, Richard, became a chaplain in the Royal Air Force. Gutteridge died at his home, The Rydings, 4 Sylvester Road, Cambridge, on 30 December 1953. McNair, *rev.*

**Sources** *The Times* (31 Dec 1953) · *WWW* · *International and Comparative Law Quarterly*, 3/3 (July 1954), 373–92 · *Revue International de Droit Comparé*, 6 (1954), 77–85 · *Cambridge Law Journal*, [12] (1954), 197–200 · *American Journal of Comparative Law*, 3/3 (summer 1954), 474–6 · Venn, *Alum. Cant.* · personal knowledge (1971) · *CGPLA Eng. & Wales* (1954)

**Likenesses** photograph (as elderly man), Trinity Hall, Cambridge

**Wealth at death** £99,491 1s. 1d.: probate, 8 April 1954, *CGPLA Eng. & Wales*

**Gutteridge, Joseph** (1816–1899), silk weaver and naturalist, was born on 23 March 1816 in Coventry, the eldest of the three sons of Joseph Gutteridge, a recruiting sergeant, and his first wife, Sarah Shaw. Educated from 1821 in two schools, run by a Quaker woman and Wesleyan preacher respectively, he then went to Berkswell, where his uncle was a schoolmaster. There he made swift progress, particularly in natural science. After further study at Baker, Billing, and Crowe's charity school, where discipline was harsh, he was apprenticed to learn the craft of ribbon weaving about 1829. He found work at the Jacquard loom tiring, but continued to gain intense pleasure from observation of birds and plant life as well as geology and entomology. His invalid mother died and a tyrannical stepmother added to the misery of slumps in trade and riots against the introduction of steam power. However, by this time he was already known as a talented weaver who could also repair clocks and watches (he later made furniture, musical instruments, and even a microscope). He formed a botanical collection, classified according to Dr Withering (1776) and on Linnaean lines.

Still in indentures, Gutteridge married Sara Bate (*d.* 1855), a poor freethinker, on 5 January 1835 at St John the Baptist Church; they had five children. About this time Gutteridge acquired atheistical opinions from the discussions of the Coventry Mutual Improvement Class, and socialist principles from Robert Owen. During the slumps of 1838–45 his growing family suffered severe privations from unemployment and illness, but he was refused help from a local charity by a clergyman on the grounds of his unbelief. His pride and independence of judgement also alienated him from the trade-union movement. Kindly neighbours saved the family from the workhouse or starvation, and the Manchester Oddfellows helped him to bury his fourth child, who died from smallpox.

In spite of industrial injury and unorthodox views, Gutteridge made progress in his trade, becoming a foreman and then working at home on an *à la bar* loom. A visit to the Great Exhibition of 1851 revived his interest in the applied arts and in natural science, particularly foreign botanical specimens. His wife's death from tuberculosis in December 1855 drew him to spiritualism: on 17 May 1857 Gutteridge married his second wife, Mary Hendon, a Wesleyan, at Bedworth. With an employer he worked on improvements to the Jacquard loom for the manufacture of brocaded ribbons, but received no benefit from the patent. He took a minor but active part in the strike and lock-out of 1860–61 which followed the Cobden trade treaty: he hated the factory system which ensued, but soon adopted firm Liberal views.

Gutteridge was a pioneer of silk brocades in five colours for exhibition, and of portraits and views in silk. In September 1867 he was delegated as a working man to visit the Paris Exhibition and Switzerland for the Society of Arts, publishing an account in the society's *Reports of Artisans … Paris Universal Exhibition of 1867* (1867, 141–3). He then worked for Thomas Stevens, celebrated for bookmarks and pictures in silk, giving exhibitions of his craft in Yorkshire in August 1870. Gutteridge was held in respect and gave evidence during a legal dispute over the needle-loom patent in 1874.

Old age and a decline in the Coventry silk industry brought Gutteridge close to destitution by 1891, when John Cox of the *Coventry Herald* encouraged him to co-operate in a series of autobiographical articles, based on a diary which was also the source of his autobiography, *Lights and Shadows in the Life of an Artisan* (1893). A copy was presented to W. E. Gladstone, and there were favourable reviews. A gift from the royal bounty fund and the provision of an annuity by friends followed. Having regained his religious faith through a study of natural science, he presented his extensive and well-catalogued natural history collection to his native city in 1896.

Gutteridge died at his home, 18 Yardley Street, Coventry, on 4 November 1899, following a stroke. A memorial service in the Great Meeting-House stressed his example to the young. His autobiography remains an impressive source for the history of the silk industry, working-class life, and urban development during the industrial revolution. V. E. Chancellor

**Sources** J. Gutteridge, *Lights and shadows in the life of an artisan* (1893) · V. E. Chancellor, ed., *Master and artisan in Victorian England* (1969) · Society of Arts, *Reports of artisans selected by a committee appointed by the council of the Society of Arts to visit the Paris Universal Exhibition, 1867* (1867) · J. Dodge, *Silken weave, ribbon making in Coventry* (1988) · A. W. Coysh and R. K. Henrywood, *Bookmarkers* (1994) · review of *Lights and shadows in the life of an artisan*, *The Athenaeum* (5 Aug 1893), 184–5 · *Medium and Daybreak* (1 Sept 1893) · *Journal des Débats* (1893) · Gladstone, *Diaries*, vols. 12–13 · *Coventry Herald* (8 May–12 June 1891) · *Coventry Herald* (16 June 1893) · *Coventry Herald* (17 Nov 1899) · *Coventry Times* (Nov 1899) · W. Jolly, *John Duncan, weaver and botanist* (1883) · *IGI* · J. Prest, *The industrial revolution in Coventry* (1960)

**Archives** Herbert Art Gallery and Museum, Coventry, MSS and letters relating to autobiography

**Likenesses** group portrait, 1867, repro. in *Reports of artisans*, facing p. 188 • photograph (in later life), Herbert Art Gallery and Museum, Coventry; repro. in *Medium and Daybreak* • portrait, repro. in Gutteridge, *Lights and shadows*, frontispiece

**Gutteridge, William** (*fl.* **1813**). *See under* Gutteridge, William (1798–1872).

**Gutteridge, William** (**1798–1872**), violinist and organist, was born on 16 July 1798 in Chelmsford, Essex, and lived as a child at Tenterden in Kent, where he had lessons on the violin from a dancing-master. Further musical instruction was obtained in Brussels, where he stayed during the events of 1815 and led the band of the theatre in the park. On his return to England in around 1818, Gutteridge held a similar post at the Birmingham theatre, and somewhat later that of chorus master at the Surrey theatre. He became a member of George IV's band of seventy performers, under Franz Cramer, and afterwards of William IV's private band, and was occasional organist at the royal chapel of the Brighton Pavilion.

Gutteridge was very active in Brighton, where he resided from about 1823 until his death. He led the orchestra of the Brighton theatre, and was organist of St Peter's Church from its opening in 1828. In the same year he helped in the re-establishment of the Old Sacred Harmonic Society and became conductor, then leader, of the new society of that name. He opened a music warehouse in Castle Square for a short time, and was enterprising in introducing great performers to Brighton audiences, notably Paganini, Giuditta Pasta, and John Braham. Gutteridge's compositions include services, anthems, nocturnes, galops, rondos for piano, and numerous songs, but it is as a violinist and organist that he is chiefly remembered. His talent secured him the direct patronage of royalty, and he consequently took part in a quartet with George IV and the two princes who afterwards became king of the Belgians and king of Hanover. He also accompanied Queen Victoria (September 1837) in a song from Michael Costa's *Malek Adel* (judged at the time to have been sung 'in a pure, unaffected, correct, and charming manner') on the old pavilion organ, and counted the then duke of Cambridge among his pupils.

Gutteridge was greatly respected for his excellent personal qualities, and his reminiscences of an active life were said to have added interest to his conversation. An example of his adventures was his reputed elopement (from Margate to Gretna Green) with a lady with whom he afterwards had nineteen children, seven of whom survived their parents. Gutteridge died a widower on 23 September 1872, at 55 London Road, Brighton, and was buried in a vault in the old churchyard of St Nicholas.

Another **William Gutteridge** (*fl.* 1813), musician, was military music master and bandmaster of the 62nd regiment and published *The Art of Playing Gutteridge's Clarinet* in 1824. L. M. Middleton, *rev.* David J. Golby

**Sources** [J. S. Sainsbury], ed., *A dictionary of musicians*, 1 (1824), 310 • *The Harmonicon*, 1 (1823), 171 • Brown & Stratton, *Brit. mus.*
**Wealth at death** under £800: administration, 16 Dec 1872, *CGPLA Eng. & Wales*

**Guttmann, Sir Ludwig** (**1899–1980**), neurosurgeon, was born on 3 July 1899 in Tost, Upper Silesia, into a Jewish family, the first born, and the only son, among the four children of Bernhard Guttmann, an innkeeper and distiller, and his wife, Dorothea, daughter of Marcus Weissenburg, a farmer. In 1902 the family moved to Konigshütte, where Guttmann was educated. It was a coal-mining town which had the first accident hospital in the world, where he worked as a medical orderly in 1917–18. He started medical studies in Breslau and continued in Würzburg and Freiburg, where he experienced the antisemitism of a nationalistic student corps. He passed his final examination (MD, Freiburg) in 1924 and, rather by chance, obtained a post with Professor Otfrid Foerster in Breslau. Foerster, a neurologist and self-taught neurosurgeon, was an exacting master, and Guttmann worked eighteen hours a day for the next four years. In 1927 he married Else, daughter of Solomon Samuel, furniture dealer, of Mulhouse. They had a son, Dennis, who became a consultant physician, and a daughter, Eva.

In 1928 Guttmann went to Hamburg to run a neurosurgical service in a municipal psychiatric hospital with 3000 beds. Here he gained valuable experience, before returning to Breslau in 1929 as Foerster's first assistant and in 1930 as *Privatdozent*. Foerster was passionately interested in the pathophysiology of nervous disease, and the influence of his teaching and writing can clearly be seen in Guttmann's investigations and in his *Spinal Cord Injuries* (1973; 2nd edn, 1976). Unfortunately Foerster's neurosurgical technique was not good, and in this respect he and his pupils did not commend themselves to British neurosurgeons.

In 1933 the National Socialists came to power, and at once forced all Jewish doctors to leave Aryan hospitals. Guttmann became neurologist and neurosurgeon to the Jewish hospital in Breslau and in 1937 was elected its medical director. He wrote that he was neither 'mishandled' nor insulted personally. He witnessed the burning of the books of non-Aryan authors at the university in 1934, and the burning of the synagogue on 9 November 1938—the *Kristallnacht*—when he admitted to hospital any male person who presented himself. Next morning he had to justify to the Gestapo sixty-four admissions. By improvised diagnoses most patients were saved, but a few, and some doctors, were taken to concentration camps. In 1938 Guttmann was allowed to visit Lisbon, and the following year he and his family were granted visas to go to England, where he made contact with the Society for the Protection of Science and Learning and was invited to Oxford. The family was helped to settle into a new home, and schools for the children, by A. D. Lindsay, master of Balliol, and by the fellows, and Guttmann started work in the Nuffield department of neurosurgery in the Radcliffe Infirmary under Hugh Cairns. There Guttmann continued his research on the neuro-regulation of sweat glands, taught orthopaedic surgeons the diagnosis and treatment of nerve injuries, and took part in animal experimental work on nerve injuries. He was frustrated by the lack of responsible clinical work, and in 1943 accepted an offer from Brigadier George Riddoch to start a centre for paraplegics in the hutted hospital of the Emergency Medical Service at Stoke Mandeville. At this time paraplegics were regarded as hopeless cases who died within two years as there was no effective treatment.

The new centre opened on 1 March 1944. The only hope came from Dr D. Munro of Boston, who had started turning patients every two hours day and night to allow bedsores to heal, and had had some success in the treatment of urinary infections. Guttmann began with these measures and improved on them. He showed that all antiseptics retarded the healing of bedsores, which were finally mastered by excision of necrotic tissues, skin grafting, and the training of patients in constant vigilance. Penicillin and later streptomycin made the control of infections and especially urinary infections possible. Patients were encouraged to sit up, to walk with calipers, and after 1947 to take part in sports such as wheelchair basketball, archery, and table tennis. Sheltered workshops were a great success and were encouraged by the Ministry of Labour. During his retirement Guttmann greatly expanded the facilities for sport and wrote a *Textbook of Sport for the Disabled* (1976).

Medical staff from many countries came to Stoke Mandeville for training, and similar centres were named after Guttmann in Spain, West Germany, and Israel. His influence also spread through the journal *Paraplegia* and the International Society for Paraplegia which he founded. The Stoke Mandeville games and the Olympic games for the paralysed, which he started, have been successful and inspiring events. He was loved by his patients and his staff, but his conviction of the rightness of his decisions made him a difficult colleague on committees. His work totally changed the outlook for paraplegics, and many other disabilities are likely to be influenced by his programme of continuous personal care from the acute injury to discharge from hospital and long after.

Guttmann was naturalized in 1945. He was appointed OBE in 1950 and CBE in 1960, and was knighted in 1966. He became FRCS in 1961, FRCP in 1962 (MRCP, 1947), and FRS and honorary FRCP(C) in 1976, and was given honorary degrees by Durham (1961), Trinity College, Dublin (1969), and Liverpool (1971). He held many foreign honours. In 1971 the sports stadium was opened by the queen. In 1972 Else received a severe head injury in a road accident which left her unconscious for the last twenty-one months of her life. While his wife was in hospital, Guttmann moved into a bungalow, Menorah, Northumberland Avenue, Aylesbury, where he died on 18 March 1980.

D. Whitteridge, *rev.*

**Sources** D. Whitteridge, *Memoirs FRS*, 29 (1983), 227–44 · *Paraplegia*, 17 (May 1979) [issue in honour of Guttmann's eightieth birthday] · private information (1986) · personal knowledge (1986) · S. Goodman, *Spirit of Stoke Mandeville* (1986) · *CGPLA Eng. & Wales* (1980) · d. cert.

**Archives** Wellcome L., corresp. with Sir Ernst Chain

**Wealth at death** £152,283: probate, 31 July 1980, *CGPLA Eng. & Wales*

**Guttsman, William Leo** [Willi; *formerly* Wilhelm Leo Guttsmann] (**1920–1998**), librarian and political sociologist, was born in Berlin on 23 August 1920, one of two children of Walter Johann Guttsmann (1880–1941), a native of Berlin, and his wife, Helene, who was born on 5 August 1887 in Strehlen, Silesia. Walter Guttsmann was a leading engineer in the prominent electronics firm AEG. Both parents were patriotic bourgeois Jews, laid off by the Nazis and imagining themselves to be safe until they were forcibly taken eastwards, to be murdered in 1941, probably at Auschwitz. Willi himself endured a period in Buchenwald on the occasion of the *Kristallnacht* of 9–10 November 1938, before his parents managed to get him an emigration visa that enabled him to escape to England, with no money or relatives, in February 1939. As a nineteen-year-old he was given work picking potatoes on an isolated farm in Scotland, but when the war finally came he was classified as an enemy alien and deported to Australia. All this he endured quietly and with philosophical acceptance, but also with a tenacious resolve to survive his misfortunes.

The bureaucratic authorities would not reclassify Guttsman but returned him to Britain. From that point his life gradually turned from disaster to eccentric success. He came back to be united with his beloved Valerie Lichtigová, whom he had first met in Scotland, where she, a refugee from Czechoslovakia, was employed as a dairymaid and given a sleeping berth above the cows. They married on 11 July 1942 and worked for the rest of the war with a group of young Jews, he on a farm and she cultivating a market garden near St Albans. In 1942 Guttsman began a part-time degree course at Birkbeck College, and in 1946 went on to study for an MSc (Econ) at the London School of Economics and Political Science (LSE), an institution especially hospitable to refugees from fascist regimes, who included Karl Popper, Ilya Neustadt, and Claus Moser. In the early post-war years jobs in the social sciences in Britain were hard to come by; Guttsman, like Neustadt, found one at LSE as a library assistant, in fact as a lowly basement boy. He combined his duties as librarian with preparing, first, a thesis and, later, a book supervised by David Glass and other colleagues at LSE. The book, *The British Political Élite* (1963), became the most frequently cited work on this topic, widely admired for its combination of learned history and exact statistical analysis—a model of its kind.

Then came Guttsman's great career opportunity: the opening of the new Robbins universities of the 1960s. Among the first five foundations was the University of East Anglia, where the vice-chancellor, Frank Thistlethwaite, envisaged a central library with open access. The chief architect was Denys Lasdun. Thistlethwaite sought a founding librarian and approached LSE; Guttsman was appointed, fitting the job specification as a competent acquisitions librarian and a devotee of the arts. From the outset he treated his job at Norwich as a vocation, a way of life. Not only did he continue to write books himself, including *The German Social Democratic Party, 1875–1933* (1981) and ending with *Art for the Workers* (1997), but he also quickly assembled a teaching collection, organized exhibitions, and impressed both colleagues and students, as well as Denys Lasdun, with his meticulous and exacting discipline in the running of a highly efficient modern library.

Guttsman stayed at the University of East Anglia until he retired in 1985, as emeritus librarian. His wife was a psychiatric social worker, and they were both energetically and happily involved in the town and the university. Valerie Guttsman was lord mayor of Norwich in 1979–80 and was appointed OBE in 1991, for community service. Guttsman was proud of the achievements of his wife and of their daughter Janet, a journalist. He remained an eccentric individualist who never hid his socialist sympathies or his discriminating love for England. He very seldom spoke his mother tongue. He was modest but articulate, shy but determined. He was one among many Jewish continental refugees who contributed spectacularly to the cultural life of war-time and post-war Britain, its science, its drama, its art, its architecture, its music, and—perhaps, above all—its universities. Willi Guttsman died, of cancer, at his home, 9 Osborne Court, Lime Tree Road, Norwich, on 13 February 1998. He was survived by his wife and daughter. A. H. HALSEY

**Sources** R. J. Evans, 'W. L. Guttsman, 1920–1998', *German History*, 16/3 (1998) • P. Lasko, *The Independent* (25 March 1998) • *The Times* (28 Feb 1998) • V. Morgan, *The Guardian* (20 April 1998) • private information (2004) • personal knowledge (2004) • m. cert. • d. cert.

**Wealth at death** under £180,000: administration with will, 28 May 1998, *CGPLA Eng. & Wales*

**Gützlaff, Karl Friedrich August** [Charles Gutzlaff] (**1803–1851**), missionary and civil servant, son of Johann Jakob Gützlaff (1767–1825), a tailor, and Maria Elisabeth Gützlaff, *née* Behneken (1767–1807), was born in Pyritz, province of Pomerania, Prussia, on 8 July 1803. Having attended Pyritz municipal school from 1811 to 1816, he was apprenticed to a brazier in Stettin. However, finding foreign evangelistic work more attractive, he entered Jänicke's Missionary School in Berlin in 1821. After further training in Rotterdam, he was ordained in 1826 and sent to the Dutch East Indies as an agent of the Netherlands Missionary Society. After a brief spell in Batavia with William Henry Medhurst, Gützlaff set out on 8 April 1827 to convert the Chinese settlers in the Riau archipelago. A year later he embarked on independent missionary work among the Chinese of Bangkok, Siam. On 26 November 1829, during a visit to Malacca, Gützlaff married Maria Newell (*c.*1794–1831) of the London Missionary Society.

Being a restless spirit with seemingly boundless energy, Gützlaff next turned up on the China coast. As a result of his trip to Tientsin (Tianjin) in a Chinese junk in 1831, British traders began to make use of his extraordinary linguistic talents in their efforts to find new markets. Although he was later criticized for having associated with opium smugglers to propagate Christianity, Gützlaff regarded these trips as unique opportunities to preach and distribute Christian literature beyond the confines of Canton (Guangzhou). Moreover, his *Journal of Three Voyages Along the Coast of China in 1831, 1832, 1833* (1834) generated

**Karl Friedrich August Gützlaff (1803–1851)**, by Richard James Lane, 1835 (after George Chinnery, exh. RA 1835) [in the dress of a Fokien sailor]

considerable interest in China in Western political, commercial, and religious circles, as did his *Sketch of Chinese history, ancient and modern, comprising a retrospect of the foreign intercourse and trade with China* (1834) and the more controversial *China opened, or, A display of the topography, history, customs, manners, etc. of the Chinese empire* (1838). All three were written in English. At the same time, Gützlaff sought to create greater awareness among the Chinese of Western achievements through religious and secular publications such as his serial *Dong-Xi yang kao meiyue tongji zhuan* (the 'East-West monthly magazine'), which between 1833 and 1839 contained contributions on Western science, geography, government, and history. During these busy and adventurous years, he still found time on 6 May 1834 to marry the independent missionary Mary Wanstall (1799–1849) at Malacca.

In 1835 Gützlaff entered British government service as an assistant interpreter and Chinese secretary to the chief superintendent of trade in China. During the First Opium War (1839–42) he was appointed civil administrator at Tinghai (Dinghai; July 1840 – February 1841) at the time of the first British occupation of Chushan Island, and subsequently at Ningpo (Ningbo; October 1841 – May 1842). During the intervening military campaigns he was interpreter to the commander of the British expeditionary force and was present as indispensable interpreter–negotiator at the conclusion of the treaty of Nanking (Nanjing) on 29 August 1842. He spent a further eleven months (September 1842 – August 1843) as civil magistrate on Chushan Island during the second British occupation. Having failed to secure a consulship on account of his alien status, Gützlaff succeeded John Robert Morrison as first Chinese secretary to her majesty's government in Hong Kong in 1843.

Although a civil servant, Gützlaff did not neglect his missionary work. During the First Opium War he had come to realize that 'China can be evangelised only by the Chinese'. To this end, in 1844 he formed the controversial Chinese Union of indigenous colporteurs and evangelists to carry the gospel to all parts of the Chinese empire. Foreign missionaries, living in Chinese style, were to provide only initial training and guidance.

In September 1849 Gützlaff left for Europe to garner support for the Chinese Union. Yet while he was enthusiastically welcomed in several European countries, the fraudulent activities of his unscrupulous Chinese associates were exposed by less credulous Hong Kong missionaries. When Gützlaff returned to the colony in early 1851 his Chinese Union was on the point of collapse. Disappointed and worn out by overexertion, he died from dropsy on 9 August 1851 and was buried in Happy Valley cemetery, Hong Kong, leaving a widow, Dorothy Gabriel (1821–1888), whom he had married in Bristol on 17 September 1850.

History has not been kind to Karl Gützlaff. One scholar calls him 'a cross between parson and pirate, charlatan and genius, philanthropist and crook' (A. Waley, *The Opium War through Chinese Eyes*, 1958, 233). He was a missionary enthusiast with progressive ideas, yet also a poor judge of men and lacking in organizational skills. Still, his career of 'missionary-diplomat' has to be seen in its proper historical context. At a time when China remained a closed country, his role as cultural mediator between East and West was not without merit. Moreover, Gützlaff's vital government service during and after the First Opium War was fully recognized by the British authorities.

R. G. TIEDEMANN

**Sources** H. Schlyter, *Karl Gützlaff als Missionar in China* (1946) • A. Goslinga, *Dr Karl Gützlaff en het Nederlandsche Protestantisme in het midden der vorige eeuw* (1941) • J. G. Lutz, 'Karl F. A. Gützlaff: missionary entrepreneur', *Christianity in China: early protestant missionary writings*, ed. S. W. Barnett and J. K. Fairbank (1985), 61–87 • J. G. Lutz, 'The missionary-diplomat Karl Gützlaff and the Opium War', *Proceedings of the first international symposium on church and state in China*, ed. Li Ch'i-fang and others (1987), 215–38 • G. Hood, *Mission accomplished? The English Presbyterian mission in Lingtung, south China* (1986), 11–53 • J. G. Lutz, 'The grand illusion: Karl Gützlaff and popularization of China missions in the United States during the 1830s', *United States attitudes and policy towards China: the impact of American missionaries*, ed. P. Neils (1990), 46–77 • J. G. Lutz, 'The attitude of Karl Gützlaff towards Catholicism and Catholic missions in China: 1830s, 1840s', *Historiography of the Chinese Catholic Church: nineteenth and twentieth centuries*, ed. J. Heyndrickx (1994), 199–205 • H. Schlyter, *Der China-Missionar Karl Gützlaff und seine Heimatbasis* (Lund, 1976) • BL OIOC, N/1/24, fol. 299 • *Singapore Chronicle* (15 May 1834) • Bristol RO, FCP/StW/R/2(a)1 • parish register (marriage), 17 Sept 1850, Clifton parish church, Bristol • VEM, Wuppertal, Germany, Archives of the Rhenish Missionary Society

**Archives** U. Birm., Orchard Learning Resources Centre, corresp. and papers relating to missionary activity in China

**Likenesses** R. J. Lane, engraving, 1835 (after G. Chinnery, exh. RA 1835), NPG [*see illus.*] • photographs, repro. in H. Schlyter, *Theodor Hamberg: den förste svenske Kinamissionären* (Lund, 1952) • portrait, repro. in Schlyter, *Der China-Missionar Karl Gützlaff*, cover • portrait, London, Mansell Collection, London

**Wealth at death** Mexican $30,000: Archives of the Rhenish Missionary Society, VEM, Wuppertal, Germany • £30,000: *South China Morning Post* (18 July 1933), 15

**Guy of Warwick** (*supp. fl. c.*930), legendary hero, seems to have little or no basis in history. Possibly his name comes from the historical Wigod of Wallingford, cup-bearer of Edward the Confessor, and one or two other names recall pre-conquest traditions of battles against the vikings, but the bulk of his story is romantic fiction. Its essential elements are all to be found in the Anglo-Norman *Gui de Warewic*, one of the 'ancestral romances' which provided Norman families with an ancient ancestry. It was written *c.*1232–1242 possibly by a canon of Osney for Thomas, earl of Warwick (*d.* 1242), heir through his mother of the d'Oilly family, constables of Oxford, and patrons of the abbey. One of Wigod's daughters had married Robert (II) d'Oilly (*d.* 1142); Brian fitz Count, the husband of his other daughter, defended Wallingford in 1139, and may have provided hints for some of the hero's exploits. The Middle English versions (from *c.*1300) derive from the Anglo-Norman. In the Middle English romance Guy, the son of Syward of Wallingford, falls in love with Felice, the daughter of Rohaut, the earl of Warwick. When he is rejected, he goes overseas to prove himself in tournaments. Sent away yet again by his beloved, he wins glory in battle, and the emperor of Constantinople offers him his daughter in marriage, but he refuses. Guy helps Tirri of Gormoise recover his lady, and after seven years returns to England, where he kills a dragon and marries Felice. After only a fortnight he leaves his bride, who is now pregnant, and sets out on a pilgrimage to Jerusalem. He has suddenly been struck by the thought that he has never served God, who has done him much honour, in the way he has suffered hardship for the sake of his lady. Felice laments and gives him a gold ring. He kills a giant in Alexandria, and rescues Tirri, who has been falsely accused. Disguised as a palmer, he returns to England, and saves King Æthelstan from Anlaf and the Danes by overcoming the Danish giant Colbrand in an epic battle at Winchester (which in the later English tradition became the most popular incident in the story). He retires to Warwick, and lives as a hermit. On the point of death he reveals his identity to Felice by means of the ring. In grief she follows him to the grave. Meanwhile their son Reinbrun, who was born after his father left, has been carried off from Wallingford by pirates. He is brought up in Africa by the daughter of King Argus. Heraud, the faithful steward of Guy, sets out in search of him, and finds him (after fighting with him in ignorance of his true identity). After a series of further adventures they return home to England.

Chaucer made use of the romance in his parody in *Sir Thopas*. But for all its extravagances, it is not hard to see why its excitingly told adventures and its blend of love, chivalry, ascetic religion, and a high-minded celebration of loyalty made it immensely popular. The Anglo-Norman romance found its way into continental French, into prose, and into print in the sixteenth century. English versions were printed by Pynson, Wynkyn de Worde, and Copland, and lived on in chapbooks and other forms of popular literature until the nineteenth century—and as children's stories, even later. There were ballads, and a play by Dekker and Day. The battle with Colbrand was treated in a separate lay; there was a homiletic version in the *Speculum Gy de Warewyke* (in which Guy asks Alcuin for advice on how to escape the enticements of the world).

In the early fourteenth century the chronicler Peter Langtoft worked the story of the fight at Winchester into history. Anlaf, defeated at 'Brunnanburg sur Humbre', fled to Denmark, but returned with Colbrand to besiege Athelstan at Winchester (combining the two invasions of Olaf Sihtricson and Olaf Tryggvason). God sent him a dream, that an old palmer would appear and undertake the battle—this was really Guy of Warwick, whose 'book' tells how he killed Colbrand. A Latin prose account of the battle by one Gerard of Cornwall was influential. Lydgate based his version, made for Margaret, countess of Shrewsbury, the daughter of Richard Beauchamp, earl of Warwick (*d.* 1439), on part of this. Chroniclers such as Knighton, Hardyng, Rous, Fabyan, Holinshed, Stow, and Dugdale accepted the legend as an actual event occurring in the reign of Æthelstan, the victor of 'Brunanburh' (937). The Beauchamp family built Guy's Tower at Warwick, and the castle still contains supposed relics of the hero. Guy's Cliffe, near Warwick, is the legendary site of his hermitage. DOUGLAS GRAY

**Sources** A. Ewert, ed., *Gui de Warewic: roman du XIIIe siècle* (Paris, 1932–3) · J. Zupitza, ed., *The romance of Guy of Warwick*, 5 vols., EETS, extra ser., 25, 26, 42, 49, 59 (1875–91) · M. D. Legge, *Anglo-Norman literature and its background* (1963), 162–71 · M. J. Donovan and others, 'Romances', *A manual of the writings in Middle English, 1050–1500*, ed. J. B. Severs, 1 (1967), 27–31, 217–20 · R. S. Crane, 'The vogue of *Guy of Warwick* from the close of the middle ages to the Romantic revival', *Publications of the Modern Language Association of America*, 30 (1915), 125–94

**Guy, Henry** (*bap.* **1631**, *d.* **1711**), politician, was the only son of Henry Guy (*d.* 1640) of Tring, Hertfordshire, and his wife, Elizabeth (1603–1690), the daughter of Francis Wethered of Ashlyns, Great Berkhamsted, Hertfordshire, where Guy's baptism took place on 16 June 1631. He was admitted to Gray's Inn in 1648, and migrated to the Inner Temple in 1652. He also appears to have been at Christ Church, Oxford, and belatedly received the degree of MA in September 1663.

As a young man Guy became a close friend of Charles II during the king's exile in Holland. After the Restoration he began to make his mark in London as a rising man of enterprise, associating himself with property developers and financiers, most notably Sir William Pulteney who was probably a distant kinsman. In 1662 he became one of a three-man commission for cleaning the streets and the licensing of hackney coaches in London. Through early success in various money-making ventures, assisted by his contacts at court, he became a man of substantial means, so much so that by 1667 he was a joint partner, with his uncle Francis Wethered, in the excise farm for Yorkshire for which the quarterly rent exceeded £5000. This grant, which he held until 1671, was said to have been Guy's reward for 'pimping' for the king, and yielded him a profit of £50,000. Another joint rental, obtained in 1664, gave him a twenty-one-year share in the reliefs from Queen Henrietta Maria's jointure lands, and yet further opportunities to profiteer came with the commissionership for wine licences in London which he held between 1668 and 1671.

Already a familiar figure at court, Guy was appointed cup-bearer to Catherine of Braganza in 1669. In March the following year he became MP for Hedon, Yorkshire, having in the course of his revenue-raising activities established an interest there, and he was subsequently to retain the seat in every parliament until 1695. He naturally featured as a firm supporter of the court, and it was probably owing to his court contacts that he was invited in 1671 to join a syndicate to manage the customs farm, though the initiative had to be dropped upon the government's assumption of direct control of this branch of the revenue. By 1673–4, during the early years of Lord Danby's administration, he had entered the orbit of Robert Spencer, second earl of Sunderland, whose long career in high politics was just beginning, and whose devoted henchman Guy later became. In this initial phase of their long association, Guy's flair for financial business no doubt fixed him in the earl's reckoning as a potentially useful ally and man of business, while Sunderland supplied Guy's need for an ambitious aristocratic patron. Guy's career took a step further in 1675 when he was brought in to the king's household as a groom of the bedchamber with a salary of £500 a year, which office he held until 1679.

In 1679, on the fall of Danby, Guy was appointed secretary to the Treasury, quite probably on Sunderland's recommendation. He was already by this stage handling 'secret service' payments for the king outside of Treasury supervision, apparently under cover of his role as receiver-general of the fee farm arrears, to which he was appointed in 1677. In this capacity Guy merits an important place in the development of the Treasury. Over the next ten years, while Treasury chiefs came and went, Guy remained in place, thus breaking the traditional practice of replacing the secretary each time the Treasury commission was reshuffled. Not only did he turn the office into a position of considerable personal power and influence through his mastery over the administrative process, but he also continued to control the secret service accounts under the direct supervision of the king instead of the Treasury ministers. He made enormous gains in fees and perquisites, and his income, totalling some £3500 a year before 1685, and as much as £5000 afterwards, exceeded that of any Treasury commissioner. There were also of course the profits from shadier dealings; he was widely supposed, for example, to have made a fortune by taking advantage of his Treasury position to purchase exchequer tallies at discount and obtaining payment from them in full. While such activities drew scorn from some quarters, in others his friendship was much valued.

In politics Guy was naturally a high-church courtier, and

in the 1679 parliament he voted against the exclusion of the duke of York from the throne. Retained in office when the duke succeeded as James II, he assisted Sunderland, who now led the pro-Catholic faction at court, in undermining the earl of Rochester's ministerial supremacy. After Sunderland succeeded in supplanting Rochester as the king's chief minister in December 1686 Guy was Sunderland's chief henchman, although unlike Sunderland he did not convert to catholicism. Guy was also prominent during these years in his native county of Hertfordshire, holding various local offices including the mayoralty of St Albans during 1685–6. Upon James's flight in November 1688, he continued to run the Treasury office and gave valuable assistance to the incoming regime. He was dismissed from his Treasury post, however, in April 1689 following an inevitable attack in the Commons on his management of the secret service funds.

Nevertheless, Guy's connection with such senior figures as lords Godolphin and Sydney, given ministerial office after the revolution, helped to ensure his swift political comeback. In March 1690 he was made a customs commissioner, and in June William III dined with him at his country house at Tring. Subsequently, with his close associate Charles Duncombe, he was instrumental in smoothing Lord Sunderland's return to court. In 1691 Guy was reappointed Treasury secretary, largely through the efforts of Godolphin, who now headed the Treasury board. As Sunderland moved back to the centre of political activity at court, Guy's role as the earl's loyal lieutenant brought him once more into the limelight. He played a key part in assisting Sunderland with the formation of a new 'court party' to stem the tide of opposition in the Commons during the 1693–4 session, but stories of his behind-the-scenes bribery and liberal use of secret service money did him little credit. It was revealed that Guy had syphoned off government funds for the repair of the town hall in his constituency town of Hedon, and pamphleteers and squib-writers had a field day with inflated talk of his disposition of huge sums of 'hush-money' among MPs. The junto whigs Thomas Wharton and Charles Montagu were quick to exploit the situation in the Commons, and early in 1695 a series of inquiries was launched into areas of government corruption. In mid-February Guy was found to have accepted a bribe from a regimental agent and was committed to the Tower where he remained until May. Although he was implicated in further financial scandal involving the East India Company, no further action against him was taken. Having chosen to resign from his Treasury post in April, he was nevertheless allowed to name William Lowndes, his able chief clerk, as his successor, and also to enjoy a substantial share in the profits of the secretaryship, an indication that for the time being he was to have a continuing involvement in the running of Treasury business.

Guy did not seek re-election to parliament in the 1695 general election, but continued to assist in Sunderland's various political schemes in support of the king's government. He forged an important and enduring connection with Robert Harley which, during the later 1690s, served as a sometimes useful link between the government and Harley's country party. Guy returned to the Commons, as MP for Hedon, in 1702, but due to Sunderland's death in September 1702, and his own increasing infirmity, was no longer politically active, and he stood down at the next election in 1705.

During his final years Guy appears to have lived mainly in London. Although in his younger days he had kept a mistress, a woman called Kathy Priors who in 1691 left him to marry a son of Lord Grandison, he remained unmarried. In 1702 he sold his estate at Tring, of which the manor had been granted him in 1680, with its fine house designed for him by Wren and said to have been financed from Guy's Treasury pickings. Guy died on 23 February 1711 and was buried on 28 February at St James's, Piccadilly. He left most of his estate, valued at some £100,000, to William Pulteney, the grandson of his old friend and business partner Sir William, and who subsequently gained fame as Walpole's opponent. A. A. Hanham

**Sources** HoP, *Commons, 1660–90* · HoP, *Commons, 1690–1715* [draft] · S. B. Baxter, *The development of the treasury, 1660–1702* (1957)
**Archives** BL, corresp. with William Blathwayt and others, Add. MSS 38694, fol. 51; 38695, fol. 79; 38714, fols. 60–63, 73, 80 · U. Nott. L., letters to first earl of Portland · Yale U., Beinecke L., letters to William Blathwayt
**Wealth at death** approx. £100,000, also property at Stoke Newington, Hornsey, and Clerkenwell: will, PRO, PROB 11/520/66; N. Luttrell, *A brief historical relation of state affairs* (1857), vol. 6, p. 695

**Guy, Sir Henry Lewis** (1887–1956), mechanical engineer, was born at Penarth on 15 June 1887, the second son of Richard Guy, wholesale meat supplier, and his wife, Letitia, *née* Lewis. Railways intrigued him, and after education at the county (later grammar) school, Penarth, he became a pupil to the Taff Vale Railway. He studied at the University College of South Wales, gaining in 1909 the college diploma in both mechanical and electrical engineering and winning the Bayliss prize of the Institution of Civil Engineers, a national scholarship, and a Whitworth exhibition. He then joined the British Westinghouse Company and in 1915 became centrifugal pump and turbocompressor engineer. In 1914 he married Margaret Paton Williams, daughter of Samuel Benion Williams, coal merchant, of Holyhead. They had two daughters, both of whom married chartered mechanical engineers.

Guy was appointed chief engineer of the mechanical department of the Metropolitan-Vickers Electrical Company in 1918, a post which he retained until 1941, when he resigned to become secretary of the Institution of Mechanical Engineers (IME), of which he was then a vice-president. He retired from professional work in 1951.

During his years in industry Guy was responsible for inventions and researches directed to the improvement of steam power plant and he regularly published the results of his work, mostly in the *Proceedings* of the IME. Among them was his paper 'The economic value of increased steam pressure', which gained the Hawksley gold medal in 1927; in 1939 he delivered the Parsons memorial lecture and was awarded the Parsons memorial medal.

His ten years' work as secretary of the IME was pursued

with characteristic vigour through the difficult war and post-war years. During this period the institution increased considerably not only in size but also in national and international prestige. He made significant contributions to the formation of the Royal Corps of Electrical and Mechanical Engineers, and also to the method of distribution of the *Proceedings* of the IME, by selection, to an increasing membership. After his retirement, honorary membership of the institution was conferred upon him.

Elected a fellow of the Royal Society in 1936, Guy served on its council in 1938–9, was appointed chairman of the engineering sciences sectional committee in 1940, and in 1941 joined the executive committee of the National Physical Laboratory. Later he became chairman of the committee of the British Electrical and Allied Industries Research Association, which organized the research work on the properties of steam. He was subsequently appointed chairman of its power plant section, and member and chairman of several committees of the British Standards Institution.

Guy was a member of the Scientific Advisory Council of the Ministry of Supply from 1939, and during the war was chairman of various committees dealing with such national issues as gun design, armament development, static detonation, the work and staffing of the Royal Aircraft Establishment, the organization of aircraft armament research and development, and the technical organization of the army; in 1945–7 he was chairman of the Armaments Development Board. He also served from 1944 on the advisory council of the Department of Scientific and Industrial Research, and was chairman from 1947 of the department's mechanical engineering research board, serving on its fuel research board and scientific grants committee. He was a member from 1942 of the mechanical engineering advisory committee of the Ministry of Labour, and a trustee (1946–8) of the Imperial War Museum.

Guy received in 1939 the honorary DSc of the University of Wales and the honorary associateship of the Manchester College of Technology. He was appointed CBE in 1943, and knighted in 1949.

Broad-shouldered and stocky, Guy was endowed with great physical strength. A tireless worker, he quested unceasingly for plans which would enhance the future of engineering and of engineers. He could not suffer fools gladly, but took endless care to explain the details of his plans to those who were prepared to help. He had forthright respect for straight dealing, was completely unmoved by officialdom, and would tenaciously pursue a decided course even in the face of enlightened opposition. Unfortunately he overtaxed himself in later life by maintaining the pace and drive of his youth, and would have accomplished more, with less personal strain, had he learned to make full use of the initiative of those around him. He was devoted to graphs as aids to deductive planning. Once, when a colleague asked him if he even graphed the trends of his household expenses, he smiled and said, revealingly, 'No, that would take all the fun out of it.'

When ill health forced Guy to retire, he moved to Enniskerry, Ravine Road, Canford Cliffs, Dorset, spending much time painting in oils and listening to good music. He died there on 20 July 1956. B. G. Robbins, *rev.*

**Sources** *Institution of Mechanical Engineers: Proceedings*, 164 (1951), 31–2 • personal knowledge (1971) • private information (1971) • d. cert. • *Chartered Mechanical Engineer*, 3 (1956), 359 • *Engineer*, 202 (1956), 111 • *Engineering*, 182 (1956), 104 • *Nature*, 178 (1956), 346 • *The Times* (25 July 1956), 13c
**Archives** Institution of Mechanical Engineers, London, corresp. and papers
**Likenesses** portrait, repro. in *Engineer*, 202 (1956), p. 111
**Wealth at death** £44,933 3*s*. 4*d*.: probate, 13 Sept 1956, *CGPLA Eng. & Wales*

**Guy, John** (*c*.1575–1628), colonial governor, was born in Bristol, son of Thomas Guy, a shoemaker. When the New-Founde-Lande was claimed by John Cabot for Henry VII in 1497, Bristol and west country fishing interests had been harvesting cod from its waters for a generation. But although the benefits of a colony on the island were promoted in the Tudor period, and a colony proclaimed by Sir Humphrey Gilbert in St John's in 1583, the crown remained indifferent until Guy visited the island in 1608 and renewed the call in a pamphlet of that year, now lost. The context was favourable: the end of a generation of European wars in 1604 and the opening of new markets; the freeing up of men and resources that had sustained privateering; the chance to make the fishery a 'nursery for seamen' (James I c. 29); competition with Dutch and Danish fishing interests; and the strategic value of Newfoundland as a way-station to Virginia.

In 1610 the London and Bristol Company (consisting of forty-eight principals, ten of them from Bristol) obtained a royal charter for settlement there, 'confidant that it is habitable in winter … lying more to the Southward than any parte of England' (D. B. Quinn, A. M. Quinn, and S. Hillier, 4.131). In practice the company controlled only the coast between Cape Bonavista and St Mary's Bay and, crucially, it was denied management of the migratory fishery, which employed 200 English ships in summer 1620. The company's hopes rested on winning first choice of fishing grounds and exploiting them for the full season after the summer visitors had departed, and on trapping furs, selling land, mining iron ore, and trading salt, sarsaparilla, and naval stores. Guy, a well-known Bristol merchant, had a one-sixteenth share in the prisage, Bristol's wine importing cartel, and had served on the common council (1603) and as mayor (1605). A company shareholder and 'a man very industrious and of great experience' (Stow, 1019), he was appointed, with unlimited local authority, to head the colony.

That the initial share offerings at £25 appreciated by 1616 to £70 was due to Guy's administrative skills and leadership, and to the mild first winter enjoyed by the thirty-nine men and women who planted at Cuper's Cove (Cupids) in Conception Bay in August 1610. Colonists cleared land, planted crops, and during the winter built a 6 ton pinnace for exploring the coast, six fishing boats, and a forge, and began a larger house. They laid plans for three return trips to England the next season.

Guy continued to be optimistic: from 'husbandrie, fishinge, and trade … the Colonie wilbe soone able to supporte it selfe' (Guy to Sir Percival Willoughby, 6 Oct 1610, U. Nott. L., Middleton MS Mi X 1/2). But the well-intentioned fishery regulations which he issued in 1611 were derided and ignored by the migratory fishermen, and he lacked the men and ships to claim fishing berths before their arrival. He returned to England and was elected treasurer of the Bristol Society of Merchant Venturers. In 1612 he sailed back to Newfoundland with sixteen women settlers, but that summer began the settlement's long decline. The pirate Peter Easton terrorized the coast, freely impressing fishermen, and though Guy negotiated immunity, he had to suspend plans for a satellite colony at Renewse on the southern Avalon peninsula, and delay an expedition to Trinity Bay. The latter gave him contact with a party of Beothuks at Bull Arm and an exchange of goods, but did not lead to further trade. His final winter there destroyed earlier optimism: the weather was grim; all the livestock perished; scurvy was rampant; though one child was born, eight colonists among twenty-two ill in mid-February died. Supplies and new apprentices arrived in March 1613, but Guy left in April. Spirits were low and only thirty colonists remained to face the next winter.

Back in Bristol, Guy blamed the company and its permanent treasurer, London merchant John Slany, for failing 'to obtayne … what they in common honestie should of them selves have … done, as namlie payment of wadges [and] accomplishing theire woorde with me for the portion of land promised me'. He even considered taking them to court (Middleton MSS). By 1616 he had received his land, Seaforest, near Harbour Grace, but there is no evidence that he returned to Cupids. He resumed his political career in Bristol, serving again as mayor (1618), alderman (1619), and master of the Society of Merchant Venturers (1622). He sat for Bristol in the parliament of 1621 and was again returned on 20 October 1624. He argued against extraordinary crown prerogatives like ship money, against a free fishery as imperial policy, and in favour of further colonization.

Meanwhile, the company was racked by internal disputes and financial losses. It failed soon after 1628, as did most of the interests to which it had sold land. An exception was Bristol's Hope, probably founded by Guy loyalists who shared his disillusionment with the London managers. By 1631 a Nicholas Guy (father of the child born in 1613) claimed annual profits up to £100 from his plantation at Carbonear. John Guy had already died, and was buried on 23 February 1628. In his will, proved in 1629, he left Seaforest to his three youngest sons. John, the eldest son, Guy's widow, Anne, three daughters, and a daughter-in-law shared a substantial estate which included his Bristol house, several farms, the manor of Kingston Seymour, and his share in the wine prisage. Regarded as a benefactor of the poor for his advocacy of workhouses, he is commemorated at St Stephen's Church, Bristol. A Newfoundland stamp of 1910 offers an imagined likeness.

CHRISTOPHER ENGLISH

**Sources** U. Nott., Middleton MSS, Mi X 1/1–66 • G. T. Cell, *English enterprise in Newfoundland, 1577–1660* (1969) • G. T. Cell, ed., *Newfoundland discovered: English attempts at colonisation, 1610–1630*, Hakluyt Society, new ser., 160 (1982) • G. T. Cell, 'Guy, John', *DCB*, vol. 1 • G. T. Cell, 'The Cupids Cove settlement: a case study of the problems of early colonisation', *Early European settlement and exploitation in Atlantic Canada*, ed. G. M. Story (1982) • D. B. Quinn, A. M. Quinn, and S. Hillier, eds., *New American world: a documentary history of North America to 1612*, 4 (1979) • D. B. Quinn, *Explorers and colonies: America, 1500–1625* (1990) • J. Stow and E. Howes, *Annales, or, A generall chronicle of England … unto the end of this present yeere, 1631* (1631) • R. W. Guy, 'John Guy, Newfoundland's first legal settler and governor' (1972) • D. W. Prowse, *A history of Newfoundland from the English, colonial, and foreign records* (1895) • F. Madden and D. Fieldhouse, eds., *Select documents on the constitutional history of the British empire and commonwealth*, 1 (1985) • L. F. Stock, ed., *Proceedings and debates of the British parliaments respecting North America*, 1: *1542–1688* (1924) • P. McGrath, 'Bristol and America', *The Westward enterprise: English activities in Ireland, the Atlantic, and America, 1486–1650*, ed. K. R. Andrews, N. P. Canny, and P. E. H. Hair (1978), 81–102 • J. Latimer, *The history of the Society of Merchant Venturers of the city of Bristol* (1903) • R. G. Lounsbury, *The British fishery at Newfoundland, 1634–1763*, [another edn] (Hamden, CT, 1969) • W. Gilbert, '"*Divers Places*": the Beothuk Indians and John Guy's voyage into Trinity Bay in 1612', *Newfoundland Studies*, 6/2 (autumn 1990), 147–67 • memorial, St Stephen's Church, Bristol

**Archives** LPL, account of his twelve voyages, made for his daughter | U. Nott., Middleton MSS, Mi X 1/1–66

**Guy, Thomas** (1644/5?–1724), philanthropist and founder of Guy's Hospital, the eldest of three children of Thomas Guy (*d.* 1652x4), lighterman, coalmonger, and carpenter, and his wife, Anne Vaughton of Tamworth, Staffordshire, was born in London in Pritchard's Alley, Fair Street, Horsleydown, Southwark, in a large dissenting community. His father was an Anabaptist, which explains the absence of a birth record, and died when Thomas was eight, after which Anne returned to Tamworth, where she married again in 1661; her family were well known in the area, having furnished generations of parish officials. Guy was probably educated at Tamworth Free Grammar School, and on 3 September 1660 he was apprenticed to John Clarke, bookseller, in Mercers' Hall Porch, Cheapside, London. He lived through the great disasters of the Restoration, and on 7 October 1668 was admitted a freeman of the Stationers' Company. On 14 October 1668 he was made a freeman of the City of London, and on 6 October 1673 he was admitted into the livery of the Stationers' Company.

In 1668 Guy bought a newly built shop near the Stocks Market in the City, at the junction of Cornhill and Lombard Street, with a stock worth £200. As a protestant Guy wanted to offer bibles for sale, but this was the sole privilege of the king's printers, who were also members of the Stationers' Company. Their bibles were of inferior quality, and Guy joined other booksellers in illegally importing Dutch bibles—and becoming subjected to endless harassment and seizures. The Stationers' Company had had a monopoly since the reign of Elizabeth I to produce prayer books, primers, psalters, and almanacs, which formed the legal basis for what was known as the English Stock. However, not all its members shared in this monopoly. Oxford University also had the right to print bibles, but did not have the presses to do so. The Stationers' Company paid the university £200 a year not to produce bibles, but was not printing many itself. In 1679 Bishop Fell and a Dr Yates contracted with Guy and Peter Parker to become university printers at Oxford, and they set up a press which met the demand for cheap, mass-produced bibles. Guy and Parker were chosen as less senior members of the Stationers' Company who were willing to break ranks. In 1691 the company ousted them from this contract, after they had started to bind up psalms with their bibles, once again to meet a need that English Stock was failing to satisfy. This contract had established Guy in the trade and was the foundation of his success. In fourteen years he is said to have amassed £15,000, and he named his shop the Oxford Arms.

Although Guy later acquired a reputation as a miser, as early as 1678 he had founded an almshouse with a library in Tamworth for six poor women, which was enlarged in 1693 to accommodate fourteen men and women. Prior to this he had contributed funds to the grammar school, and in 1686 to Lord Weymouth's workhouse, where the poor were to be educated and employed. In 1701 he paid for a new town hall in Tamworth. Having campaigned unsuccessfully in 1690 to represent Tamworth in parliament, he was elected in November 1695 in the whig interest. He remained an MP until July 1708, when he failed to get re-elected. Guy was clearly very upset at being rejected, and threatened to pull down his town hall. He declined an invitation to stand again, and in his will specifically excluded the citizens of Tamworth from access to his almshouse, while including all the neighbouring parishes.

By 1708 Guy was an eminent figure among London booksellers; however, he eschewed all the pomp and expense of guild life. In 1694 he was elected sheriff of London but paid a £400 fine rather than take up office. It was this sort of behaviour which gained him a reputation for being tight-fisted. By the late 1670s Guy had money to invest. He dealt in seamen's pay-tickets (at a 30–50 per cent discount), a high-risk commodity at the time. This arrears of sailors' pay formed the beginnings of the national debt. Guy also lent money to the English Stock and made large private loans to landowners. Although Guy has been accused of being a stockjobber, he had already invested in sailors' tickets when in 1710 they were put into the South Sea Company. In 1720 Guy is said to have possessed £45,500 of the original expanded South Sea stock when the company took on three-fifths of the national debt. Guy began to sell out his £100 shares at £300, and had sold them all by the time they reached £600. It was this which made his vast fortune.

In 1704 Guy became a governor of St Thomas's Hospital, by which time he had left the management of his business to his partners Varnum and Osborne. He was greatly influenced by Dr Richard Mead, who prompted him to found a new hospital. In 1721 Guy bought some land from the St Thomas's governors, intending the new hospital to be part of the same foundation. When the building had reached a second storey, however, he decided on a separate administration. The building cost £18,793 and was roofed in just before his death.

A number of apocryphal stories exist concerning Guy, several emanating from a book by John Dunton, a fellow bookseller who in 1705 published *Life and Errors*, in which he praised Guy's charitable works. By 1728, however, Dunton was a failed businessman, and he wrote a jaundiced monograph, *An Essay on Death-Bed Charity*, in which he attacked Guy, who had refused to lend him money, saying he had 'liv'd undesir'd, and dyed unlamented' (Dunton, 1728). He accused Guy of stinting the poor in his lifetime, which was clearly untrue. More seriously he suggested that Guy paid his bookbinders starvation wages. This may well have been true and reflective of sharp business practice. Samuel Wilks, the hospital's historian, owned a copy of Guy's will, on which a memorandum noted that someone had removed his apprenticed son from Guy owing to his extreme parsimony. According to Nichols, Guy's habit as a single man and very penurious 'was to dine on his shop counter, with no other tablecloth than an old newspaper; he was also as little nice in regard to his apparel' (Nichols, *Lit. anecdotes*, 599). It is not clear whether Dunton expressed a wider view, but clearly the idea of Guy as miser has a much earlier date than Nichols's late Georgian account. In 1737 the Norwich-based German painter John Theodore Heins produced two paintings, *Thomas Guy Counting his Money* and *The Death of Thomas Guy*, which were widely distributed as prints. In the first Guy is depicted as a miser who has been interrupted by a clergyman asking for a donation. In the second Guy's fingers point towards a ring of keys, the gates to heaven, and a horned and tailed figure, which is seen leaving the scene top left. Modern apologists have preferred to see this as charity driving out the devil of greed, and taken as a pair the paintings appear to present a Hogarthian morality tale.

Guy remained unmarried, and the other famous story told of him is that he intended to marry a maidservant. However, after he had left exact instructions for the pavement outside his front door to be repaired, she presumed on her forthcoming status and gave the workmen permission to extend their work. On discovering this Guy became so angry he abandoned his wedding plans.

Guy died on 27 December 1724 at his home in London at the junction of Cornhill and Lombard Street. He was buried in St Thomas's parish church, Southwark, on 7 January 1725, with great pomp, after lying in state in Mercers' Chapel. His remains were reinterred in the crypt of Guy's Hospital chapel in 1778.

Guy left estate in Staffordshire, Warwickshire, and Derbyshire to more than 100 relatives and acquaintances, mostly in sums of £1000. He left £1000 to discharge poor debtors in London, Middlesex, and Surrey, in sums not exceeding £5 each (600 people were helped by this benefaction). To Christ's Hospital he left £400 annually for the board and education of four poor children, and money was left to his Tamworth almshouse. The bulk of his fortune, £200,000, founded Guy's Hospital, London. It was intended for 400 sick persons, deemed to be incurable and ineligible for treatment elsewhere. A ward for twenty incurable lunatics was also established. The executors and trustees were tasked with securing an act of parliament incorporating them with the governors of St Thomas's; they were to purchase lands, ground rents, and estates to maintain the hospital for the benefit of the sick poor. The act was obtained in 1725 and empowered the executors to set up a monument to Guy in the chapel, designed by John Bacon. In the centre of the square at the front of the hospital is a bronze statue by Scheemakers of Guy in his livery. On the west side, in bas-relief, is represented the parable of the Good Samaritan, and on the east side Christ healing the impotent man. In pictorial representations Guy appears long-faced, with a high forehead and a firm, self-possessed expression. NICK HERVEY

**Sources** S. Wilks and G. T. Bettany, *A biographical history of Guy's Hospital* (1892) · A. B. Shaw, 'Scenes from the life of Thomas Guy: the miser and the deathbed by John Theodore Heins (1697–1756)', *Guy's Hospital Gazette*, [3rd ser.], 99 (1985), 64–6 · H. C. Cameron, *Mr Guy's Hospital, 1726–1948* (1954) · C. Blagden, *The Stationers' Company: a history, 1403–1959* (1960) · H. Sharp, 'The will of Thomas Guy', *Family Tree Magazine*, 15/1 (Nov 1998), 3–5 · C. Knight, *Shadows of the old booksellers* (1865) · *Thomas Guy, friend of the poor* (1959) · J. Dunton, *An essay on death-bed charity, exemplified in the life of Mr Thomas Guy* (1728) · Nichols, *Lit. anecdotes* · *DNB*

**Archives** LMA, records of Guy's Hospital, London, incl. executor's ledger, H9/G4/E

**Likenesses** J. Vanderbank, oils, 1706, Guy's Hospital, London; repro. in *The Graphic* (14 May 1887) · P. Scheemakers, bronze statue, c.1734, Guy's Hospital, London · J. T. Heins, oils, 1737 (*Thomas Guy counting his money*), Norwich Castle Museum · J. T. Heins, oils, 1737 (*The death of Thomas Guy*), Norwich Castle Museum · Cook, line engraving, 1784 (after F. Bartolezzi; after J. Bacon sen., 1779), Wellcome L. · wood-engraving, 1834, Wellcome L. · F. Bartolezzi, line engraving (after J. Bacon sen., 1779), Wellcome L. · Beynon and Co., lithograph (*Past surgeons and physicians*), Wellcome L. · C. W. Cope, oils, Guy's Hospital, London · P. Grave, line engraving (after D. Heins), NPG, Wellcome L. · D. Le Marchand, relief bust on ivory tablet, V&A · M. H. Middleton, line engraving (after J. Bacon sen., 1779), Wellcome L. · line engraving (after P. Scheemakers, 1731), Wellcome L. · stipple (after wax model by F. le Pipre), Wellcome L.

**Wealth at death** over £300,000: will, PRO, PROB 11/601, sig. 7

**Guy, William Augustus** (*bap.* **1810**, *d.* **1885**), physician and statistician, the son of William and Margaret Guy, was baptized at St Peter the Less, Chichester, on 14 June 1810. He spent his early years with his grandfather and was educated at Christ's Hospital, and for five years at Guy's Hospital in London. He won the Fothergillian medal of the Medical Society of London in 1831 for the best essay on asthma, and the following year he entered Pembroke College, Cambridge, where, after further study for two years at Heidelberg and Paris, he took his MB degree, in 1837.

In 1838 Guy was appointed professor of forensic medicine at King's College, London; in 1842 he became assistant physician at King's College Hospital, and from 1846 to 1858 he was dean of the medical faculty. Early in his career

William Augustus Guy (*bap.* **1810**, *d.* **1885**), by Ernest Edwards, 1868

he directed his attention to statistics, and he was one of the honorary secretaries of the Statistical Society from 1843 to 1868. In 1844 he gave evidence before the commission on the health of towns, on the state of printing offices in London and on the consequent development of pulmonary consumption among printers. He took part in founding the Health of Towns Association, and frequently drew public attention to questions of sanitary reform through his statistical and medical investigations, lectures, and writings. In doing so he played a valuable part in the improvement of ventilation, the utilization of sewage, the health of bakers and soldiers, and the reduction of hospital mortality rates.

Guy edited the *Journal of the Statistical Society* from 1852 to 1856, and was vice-president of the society from 1869 to 1872 and president from 1873 to 1875. He was elected a fellow of the Royal College of Physicians in 1844, and was Croonian lecturer in 1861, Lumleian lecturer in 1868, and Harveian orator in 1875. He was frequently the college censor and examiner. He was appointed one of the royal commissioners on penal servitude in 1878, and on criminal lunatics in 1879. Elected a fellow of the Royal Society in 1866 he was vice-president in 1876–7.

Guy's *Principles of Forensic Medicine*, first published in 1844 and frequently re-edited, became a standard work, the fourth and later editions having been edited by David Ferrier. Although often consulted in medico-legal cases Guy would never give evidence publicly, partly from oversensitiveness and partly because he distrusted juries. He retired from medical practice many years before his death, retaining only his insurance work. He had broad political and religious sympathies. He died at his residence, 12 Gordon Street, Gordon Square, London, on 10 September 1885, leaving a widow, Georgina Lucinda.

As well as *Principles of Forensic Medicine*, for which he was best known, Guy wrote numerous other books and articles, largely on issues in forensic medicine; he also published works on sanitation and health in the workplace, as well as various statistical studies.

G. T. Bettany, *rev.* Richard Hankins

**Sources** *The Lancet* (19 Sept 1885) · *Journal of the Statistical Society*, 48 (1885), 505, 650, 651 · Venn, *Alum. Cant.* · Munk, *Roll* · *CGPLA Eng. & Wales* (1886) · *IGI*
**Likenesses** E. Edwards, photograph, 1868, Wellcome L. [*see illus.*]
**Wealth at death** £43,829 1s. 0d.: resworn probate, 1886, *CGPLA Eng. & Wales*

**Guyon, Richard Debaufre** (1813–1856), army officer, was third son of John Guyon, of the Royal Navy, who, after much service, retired with the rank of commander on 28 July 1829, and died at Richmond, Surrey, on 15 January 1844, and his wife, Elizabeth. Richard Guyon was born at Walcot, Bath, on 31 March 1813, and being intended for the army at an early age held a commission in the Surrey militia. He afterwards studied in the military academy in Vienna, and aged eighteen received an appointment in Prince Joseph's 2nd regiment of Hungarian hussars, where he attained the rank of captain. In November 1838 he married a daughter of Field Marshal Baron Spleny, commander of the Hungarian life guards. Soon after his marriage he left the Austrian service, and retired to an estate belonging to his wife near Pest, where he occupied himself in cultivating farms.

When the Hungarian revolutionary war broke out in 1848, the Magyars called on Guyon to take command of the *Landsturm* and the *honved Landwehr*. Although originally a cavalry officer, he soon mastered his new position, and at the battle of Sukoro, on 29 September 1848, he defeated Jellachich, the ban of Croatia, and his 50,000 men, and obliged them to retreat. On 30 October, at the battle of Schewechat, he led the advance guard of the right of the Hungarian army, where he three times repulsed the serezans of Jellachich, and after a desperate struggle drove the Austrians from the village of Mannsworth. For this he was made a colonel, and put in command of the 1st division, which formed the advance guard of the upper army, then led by Görgey. He again distinguished himself by storming the pass of Branitzko, which was defended by General Schlick, one of the ablest of the Austrian generals. This victory, which he achieved with only 10,000 men against 25,000, made the union of the upper forces and the Theiss army possible. For these services the Hungarian diet decreed that his name should be inscribed on a bronze pillar. He was present with his troops at battle of Kaplona, on 26 February 1849, where he covered Dembrinski's battered corps as they retired on the second day of the engagement. On his promotion as a general he was sent by Kossuth to make an entry into Komorn, then besieged, and to take the command of that place; this he successfully accomplished on 21 April, and three days afterwards was instrumental in raising the siege. Resigning the command of Komorn in June he joined the forces of Vetter, and on 14 July in a brilliant engagement totally defeated the ban of Croatia at Hegyes, and drove him out of the Banat. On 10 August he took part in the battle of Temesvar, but the might of the united armies of Austria and Russia was too great.

The surrender of Görgey on 13 August brought the war to a close, and Guyon, with Kossuth, Bem, and others escaped into Turkey, where they were afforded protection by the sultan, in spite of demands for their extradition by Austria and Russia on 16 September 1849. Guyon for some time resided at Konia in Karamania. In 1852 he entered the service of the Turkish government, and was sent to Damascus, with the rank of lieutenant-general on the staff and the title of khourschid pasha, the first Christian to obtain the rank of pasha and a Turkish military command without being obliged to change his religion. In November 1853 he joined the army in Anatolia, and reached Kars shortly after the Turkish forces had been defeated at Soobaltan. Here he was named chief of the staff and president of the military commission, with authority to remodel the army. The jealousy and internal rivalry of colleagues, however, prevented him from doing very much. At the battle of Kurekdere, on 16 August 1855, he fought with his accustomed bravery and skill. His plan of battle was admirable, but it was defeated by the ineptitude of the Turkish commanders, who nevertheless blamed him; he was placed on half pay and denied further employment. Guyon was eminently a man of action, courage, and daring, and had he been put at the head of a detached corps would undoubtedly have rendered better service to the Turks. The fact that he was both a foreigner and a Christian prevented his effective advancement.

Guyon died from a sudden attack of cholera, after less than twenty-four hours' illness, at Scutari, Turkey, on 12 October 1856, and was later buried in the English ground at Haydon pasha cemetery, Constantinople. His wife, the Baroness Spleny, was for some time kept a prisoner by the Austrians at Pressburg, but after obtaining her liberty lived in retirement in Damascus.

G. C. Boase, *rev.* James Falkner

**Sources** *ILN* (15 Nov 1856), 489 · *The Times* (29 Oct 1856) · *GM*, 3rd ser., 1 (1856), 780 · E. A. Kinglake, *The patriot and the hero General Guyon* (1856) · E. H. Nolan, *The illustrated history of the war against Russia*, 2 vols. (1855–7) · Boase, *Mod. Eng. biog.*
**Likenesses** G. Stodart, stipple (after daguerreotype), NPG · portrait, repro. in Nolan, *Illustrated history of the war*, vol. 1, p. 294 · portrait, repro. in Kinglake, *The patriot and the hero*

**Guyse, John** (*bap.* 1677, *d.* 1761), Independent minister, was baptized at St Albans Abbey on 11 July 1677, the son of John and Elizabeth Guyse. He was educated for the ministry at the academies of the Revd Thomas Goodwin at Pinner and the Revd John Payne at Saffron Walden, and began to preach at the age of nineteen. He sometimes assisted William Haworth (*d.* 1703), then minister of a congregation of dissenters in Hertford, and succeeded him in the charge on 27 September 1705. His ministry in Hertford was distinguished by the vigour of his attacks upon Arianism, particularly his sermons *Jesus Christ God-Man*, published in 1719 at the time of the Salters' Hall controversy. In 1727 he was invited to become senior minister of a London congregation which had been formed by a secession from Miles Lane, Cannon Street, and had established itself in New Broad Street.

Guyse played a leading part among London dissenters as a frequent lecturer and member of trusts and committees. From about 1728 he preached the Coward lecture on Fridays at Little St Helen's, and from 1734 the Merchants' lecture on Tuesdays at Pinners' Hall. Two Coward lectures, which he published in 1729 under the title *Christ the Son of God*, were attacked by Samuel Chandler in *A Letter to the Rev. John Guyse*. Further published exchanges followed. The chief complaint against Guyse seems to have been the fact that he had accused ministers generally of not preaching Christ. Sharp language was used on both sides and the pamphlet war reflected the growing and keenly felt differences between conservative Calvinism and Arianism. The two ministers were afterwards reconciled. Guyse received the degree of DD from Aberdeen in 1732. He was an active member of the King's Head Society, which was formed by the more conservative ministers for the purpose of assisting young men to obtain academic training for the ministry. He collaborated with Isaac Watts to introduce Jonathan Edwards's *Narrative of the Conversion of many Hundred Souls in Northampton* (1737). He published a number of sermons and commentaries, of which his *Exposition of the New Testament in the Form of a Paraphrase* (1739–52) was the best-known. Orme, however, considered it 'a heavy work … the notes do not throw much light on the text', and 'far inferior' to Doddridge's *Family Expositor* (Allibone, *Dict.*, 751). By contrast, his *Holy Spirit* was much admired. Philip Doddridge invited Guyse to be a visiting examiner at his Northampton academy and left him a guinea for a ring in his will.

In his old age Guyse became lame and blind, but his blindness was thought to have improved his sermons by compelling him to preach without notes. It was said that one of his congregation told him she wished he had become blind twenty years earlier. He was probably married, and his only son, William Guyse, was his assistant at New Broad Street from 1728 until his death in 1758. Guyse himself died in London on 22 November 1761 and was buried in Bunhill Fields.

EDWIN CANNAN, *rev.* STEPHEN C. ORCHARD

**Sources** J. Conder, *The peaceful end of the perfect upright man recommended to consideration; in a sermon occasioned by the death of … Dr John Guyse* • [J. Toulmin], 'Brief memoir of the Revd John Guyse DD', *Protestant Dissenter's Magazine*, 3 (1796), 441–6 • W. Urwick, *Nonconformity in Hertfordshire* (1884), 542, 705 • G. F. Nuttall, 'Philip Doddridge, John Guyse and their expositors', *Essays presented to J. van der Berg* (1987) • *IGI*

**Likenesses** oils, 1630–40, New College, London • J. Faber junior, mezzotint, 1734 (after R. van Bleeck), BM, NPG • portrait, DWL

**Guyton, Mrs Etherington**. *See* Worboise, Emma Jane (1825–1887).

**Gwalchmai ap Meilyr** (*fl.* 1132–1180). *See under* Gogynfeirdd (*act.* *c.*1080–1285).

**Gwallawg** [Gwallog] (*fl.* 572x9–585x92), king in Britain, is said to have been the son of a certain Llaenog. He was one of four British kings from what is now southern Scotland and northern England named in the *Historia Brittonum* (composed in 829–30) as fighting against Hussa, king of Bernicia (*r.* 585–92). In the Harleian genealogies, a collection made in the mid-tenth century, his pedigree attached him to the Coeling, descendants of Coel Godebog, to whom the greatest of those British kings, *Urien of Rheged, also belonged. Urien's fatal expedition, during which he besieged the Bernicians on the island of Lindisfarne, seems, however, to be attached to the reign of Theodric, who ruled from 572 to 579. Again, two poems in praise of Gwallawg, described as judge, probably meaning ruler, of Elmet (in west Yorkshire), are ascribed to Taliesin; but the latter's *floruit* is synchronized with the earlier reign of Ida, 547–55. The two poems have some claim to be authentic sixth-century compositions; unfortunately they remain too obscure to add much to our knowledge of Gwallawg's career, other than that he fought several successful battles and had political connections across much of northern and north-western Britain.

T. M. CHARLES-EDWARDS

**Sources** Nennius, *'British history' and 'The Welsh annals'*, ed. and trans. J. Morris (1980), *Historia Brittonum* • *The poetry of Taliesin*, ed. J. E. Caerwyn Williams (1968) • *Canu Taliesin*, ed. I. Williams (1960)

**Gwallter Mechain**. *See* Davies, Walter (1761–1849).

**Gwalther, Rudolf** (1519–1586), theologian, was born on 2 October 1519 in Zürich, Switzerland, the son of Andreas Gwalther (*d.* 1519), master builder in that city, and Adelheid Hartfelder. His father was killed by a falling beam, causing his mother to give birth in the seventh month of her pregnancy. Mother and child were taken in by friends, and the city paid for the nine-year-old Gwalther to be sent to the school at Kappel. When he was twelve Gwalther was taken into the house of Heinrich Bullinger, the chief protestant minister in Zürich; a talented student, at seventeen he produced a prose translation of Homer's *Iliad*. In 1536 Bullinger had taken in an ailing student from England, Nicholas Partridge, who soon became good friends with Gwalther. At the beginning of 1537 Bullinger wished to contact Thomas Cranmer, and he sent a text to the archbishop by the hand of Partridge. Gwalther was chosen to accompany Partridge to England, and the two set off in January. Gwalther's literary account of his journey to England, *Ephimerides peregrinationis*, has survived, and provides an important record of whom he met during his two-month stay. Many of the young men he came to know in England, such as Richard Master, John Parkhurst, Owen Oglethorpe, and Richard Turner, were to remain lifelong friends, some taking refuge in Zürich and Basel during the Marian persecutions. John Parkhurst lived in Gwalther's house in Zürich from 1554 to 1558.

Gwalther's journey was extremely important in establishing personal links between Zürich and the English reformers, and Cranmer entrusted him with a letter to

Bullinger. Following Gwalther's return he himself studied at Basel, Strasbourg, Lausanne, and Marburg between 1538 and 1541, while students from Zürich began travelling to Oxford to study. Gwalther's own son Rudolf took his master's degree in Oxford in 1573. In Zürich, Gwalther became minister at St Peter's Church following Leo Jud's death. He attended the Colloquy of Regensburg between Catholics and protestants in 1541. In the same year he married Regula, Zwingli's daughter, who had also been living in Bullinger's house. When she died in 1565, he married Anna, daughter of Thomas Blarer. Gwalther was a prolific writer and scholar: he translated Zwingli's German writings into Latin, and wrote an apology for the Swiss reformer's life. He was also a dramatist and poet; his comedy *Nabal comoedia sacra* (1549) was performed in Zürich in 1570, and two of his hymns appeared in the hymnbook compiled by his contemporary Ambrosius Blarer. Gwalther's most important literary contribution was his enormous collections of sermons, many of which were translated into English in the sixteenth century. The most sensational among them was his set of five sermons entitled *Der Endtchrist* (1546) based on Matthew 24, a blistering attack on the papacy which nearly caused a religious war in the Swiss confederation, and which was quickly translated into most European languages; an English translation by John Olde was printed in Emden in 1556.

Gwalther's continued interest in Britain was reflected in the dedication to Edward VI of his homilies on the first epistle of John and to the young James VI of Scotland of his homilies on Galatians. In both of his dedications Gwalther showed how well informed he was about the Reformations in these two countries. In Scotland he was in contact with George Buchanan, tutor to the young king, and it was Buchanan who suggested that the Galatians homilies might be dedicated to James. Gwalther was named by Bullinger as his successor to the post of chief minister in Zürich following the latter's death in 1575. In that capacity he continued to defend Zwingli's theology, though he was also instrumental in building the wider Reformed European community. He was the best-travelled of the Zürich divines, and his close personal ties to reformers throughout Europe did much to retain Zürich's status as a centre of the Reformed church, despite the ascendancy of Geneva in theological matters. Gwalther died in Zürich on Christmas day 1586 following a stroke, and was buried alongside the other reformers in the cemetery next to the Grossmünster.

BRUCE GORDON

**Sources** P. Boesch, 'Rudolf Gwalthers Reise nach England im Jahr 1537', *Zwingliana*, 8 (1947), 433–71 · H. Kressner, *Schweizer Ursprünge des anglikanischen Staatskirchentums* (1953) · B. Gordon, 'Zurich and the Scottish Reformation: Rudolf Gwalther's homilies on Galatians of 1576', *Humanism and reform: the church in Europe, England, and Scotland, 1400–1643*, ed. J. Kirk (1991), 207–20 · H. J. Hillerbrand, ed., *Oxford encyclopaedia of the Reformation*, 4 vols. (1996), vol. 2

**Archives** Staatsarchiv Zürich · Zentralbibliothek Zürich, Simler collection

**Likenesses** H. Meyer, portrait, 16th cent., Staatsbibliothek, Winterthur, Switzerland

**Gwatkin, Frank Trelawny Arthur Ashton-** (1889–1976), diplomatist, was born on 14 April 1889 at Laurel Lodge, Twickenham, the son of the Revd Walter Henry Trelawny Ashton-Gwatkin, curate of Holy Trinity Church, Twickenham, and his wife, Frances Lilian, *née* Ashton. He was educated at Eton College, where he was an oppidan, and at Balliol College, Oxford, where he won the Newdigate prize for a poem on Michelangelo. He was a gifted undergraduate with literary flair and a broad interest in the classics, but left Balliol in 1909, after only two years, without completing a degree. In January 1913 he entered the British consular service and in February he was appointed a student interpreter in Japan, based in Yokohama. While there he met and, on 1 April 1915, married Nancy Violet (*d.* 1953), a ballet dancer, daughter of William James Butler, of Melbourne. There were no children of the marriage.

In April 1918 Ashton-Gwatkin was appointed attaché with responsibility for Japanese affairs in Singapore and, following home leave in 1919, he was temporarily employed in the Foreign Office's political intelligence department. In January 1921 he took advantage of recent reforms to transfer from the consular service to the then administratively separate Foreign Office, with the rank of second secretary. Noted for his intelligence, charm, and considerable pertinacity, he was for nearly nine years a member of the office's Far Eastern department. As a specialist in Japanese affairs, he was attached to the suite of Japan's Crown Prince Hirohito when he visited England in May 1921, and three years later his services were honoured with the award of the order of Sacred Treasure (fourth class). He was also a member of the British delegation to the Washington conference of 1921–2, which dealt with naval disarmament and the future security of the Far East. Although too junior to influence policy, he was suspicious of Japanese designs in east Asia, and was personally opposed to the renewal of the Anglo-Japanese alliance which, as a result of the conference, was replaced in 1922 by a four-power consultative pact. He was promoted first secretary in April 1924. Meanwhile, writing under the pseudonym John Paris, he published a novel, *Kimono* (1921), whose comments on Japanese civilization and social mores caused affront in official circles in Japan, and made most unlikely any subsequent posting to the Far East. Other novels followed on an Oriental theme: *Sayonara-Goodbye* (1924), *Banzai* (1925), *The Island beyond Japan* (1929), and *Matsu* (1932). In 1926 his poem 'A Japanese Don Juan: Narihira at the Temple' was published by Collins.

Ashton-Gwatkin probably found solace in his literary work from the daily drudgery of the Foreign Office. But the worsening global economic climate and the slide into depression in the early 1930s offered him the opportunity to put his long-standing interest in commercial diplomacy to practical effect. After a brief but testing spell as acting counsellor in the British embassy in Moscow, from December 1929 to April 1930, he joined the Foreign Office's Western department, and there gave enthusiastic support to Sir Victor Wellesley's proposals for the establishment within the office of an economic intelligence department. These, despite Treasury and Board of Trade resistance, were approved in February 1932 and, following his attendance as an observer at the Imperial (economic) Conference at Ottawa that summer, Ashton-Gwatkin was appointed head of the newly formed economic relations section. In this capacity he acted as economic adviser to the foreign secretary, and was increasingly involved in the affairs of central Europe and the pursuit by successive British governments of a *modus vivendi* with Germany. He accompanied Lord Runciman, the president of the Board of Trade, on his mediatory mission to Czechoslovakia in July 1938, and he participated both in the Munich conference in September and in the subsequent ambassadorial conference at Berlin which oversaw the transfer of the Sudetenland to Germany. Believing that there was little that could be done to prevent Germany becoming the metropolis of central Europe, he hoped that the Munich settlement would, with the assistance of German enterprise and organization, encourage the economic regeneration of the poorer countries of eastern and south-eastern Europe. He was appointed CMG in 1933 and CB in 1939.

Soon after the outbreak of war in September 1939 Ashton-Gwatkin and his staff were seconded to the Ministry of Economic Warfare. Until the fall of France much of his time was devoted to fostering Anglo-French economic co-operation. He returned to the Foreign Office in September 1940 as acting assistant under-secretary and principal establishment officer, a post to which in December 1940 he restored the title, then in abeyance, of chief clerk, and which he used to promote radical changes in the administration of Britain's overseas relations. He was largely responsible for preparing the white paper which Anthony Eden, the foreign secretary, laid before parliament in February 1943, outlining measures which were later to become known as the Eden reforms. These provided for the amalgamation of the Foreign Office, the diplomatic service, the commercial diplomatic service, and the consular service into a single foreign service, with posts and careers organized on a system of grades. Ashton-Gwatkin's own career came to a successful conclusion when in July 1944 he was appointed senior inspector of HM diplomatic missions with the rank of minister, a position which he held until his retirement in December 1947.

On leaving the Foreign Office Ashton-Gwatkin joined the Royal Institute of International Affairs as associate director of studies. There, under the supervision of Arnold Toynbee, he edited and contributed to the institute's *Survey of International Affairs* for the years 1939–46. He also lectured widely: four of his lectures, delivered at Syracuse University and devoted to the evolution and reorganization of Britain's overseas representation, were published as *The British Foreign Service* (1950). A foundation member of the council of the re-established Japan Society of London, he renewed his links with the Far East, visiting Japan in 1974 for Emperor Hirohito's golden wedding anniversary. He died on 29 January 1976 at St Richard's Hospital, Chichester, of a pulmonary embolism. KEITH HAMILTON

**Sources** I. Nish, '"In one day have I lived many lives": Frank Ashton-Gwatkin, novelist and diplomat', *Britain and Japan: biographical portraits*, ed. I. Nish, 1 (1994) · *The Times* (31 Jan 1976) · D. E. Kaiser, *Economic diplomacy and the origins of the Second World War: Germany, Britain, France and Eastern Europe* (Princeton, 1980) · C. Pearl, *Morrison of Peking* (1967) · N. Rose, *Vansittart: study of a diplomat* (1978) · *The correspondence of G. E. Morrison*, ed. H.-M. Lo, 2: *1912–20* (1978) · *The memoirs of Lord Gladwyn* (1972) · *WWW, 1971–80* · *FO List* · b. cert. · m. cert. · d. cert. · d. cert. [Nancy Violet Ashton-Gwatkin, wife]

**Archives** Mitchell L., NSW, letters to G. E. Morrison · PRO, FO 371 · PRO, papers of chief clerk's dept, FO 366 · U. Warwick Mod. RC, corresp. with A. P. Young

**Likenesses** photograph, Foreign Office, London

**Wealth at death** £201,168: probate, 18 March 1976, *CGPLA Eng. & Wales*

**Gwatkin, Henry Melvill** (1844–1916), historian and theologian, was born at Barrow upon Soar, Leicestershire, on 30 July 1844, the second son of the Revd Richard Gwatkin (*b.* 1791) and his wife, Ann Middleton. He attended St John's College, Cambridge, with a scholarship in 1863, after seven years at Shrewsbury School. In 1867 he took three first classes, as thirty-fifth wrangler, ninth classic, and third in the moral sciences tripos—an achievement to which he added in 1868, when he was placed alone in the first class in the theological tripos. In the same year he was elected to a fellowship at St John's. In 1874 the college appointed him to a new lectureship in theology. On 10 June of the same year he married Lucy de Lisle Brock, daughter of the Revd Thomas Brock, vicar of St John's, Guernsey, with whom he had two sons and a daughter.

Between 1874 and 1891 Gwatkin lectured in the faculties of theology and history, and was instrumental in establishing ecclesiastical history in Cambridge as a subject worthy of serious attention. In 1891 he was elected Creighton's successor as Dixie professor of ecclesiastical history, a post to which Creighton had narrowly beaten him in 1884. He took orders, and held the chair, with the attached fellowship at Emmanuel College, for the rest of his life. In 1903 he was Gifford lecturer in the University of Edinburgh.

Gwatkin published seven solid, if unexciting, historical works, of which the most notable are *Studies of Arianism* (1882) and *Early Church History* (1909), the latter based on his Gifford lectures. He was editor of (and a contributor to) the Cambridge Medieval History (1911), and was active in promoting ideas about the value of ecclesiastical history and the best means of teaching it (in, for instance, his *The Meaning of Ecclesiastical History*, 1891). Late in life Gwatkin became a leading radical theologian: his wife edited his sermons (*The Sacrifice of Thankfulness*, 1917), and his famous anti-German pro-war tract *Britain's Case Against Germany* (1917) became a *cause célèbre*. Gwatkin also gained an international reputation for his papers on the radulae of snails; his collection of radulae was presented to the British Museum (Natural History).

A childhood attack of scarlet fever left Gwatkin's hearing seriously impaired, which in turn contributed to inarticulacy in speech. His sight deteriorated rapidly, a deterioration brought about, it was said, through the strain imposed by prolonged and intensive reading. These

Henry Melvill Gwatkin (1844–1916), by James Russell & Sons

defects, which made direct and elaborate personal communication difficult, gave rise to a public persona that shunned polite conversation, and was rather blunt and dogmatic in formal committee and debate. Never fully at home with college life, he nevertheless was a popular teacher and preacher in Cambridge. He died at his home, 8 Scroope Terrace, Cambridge, on 14 November 1916, of a seizure, probably the result of a street accident the previous August. His wife survived him. PETER R. H. SLEE

**Sources** P. Slee, 'The H. M. Gwatkin papers', *Transactions of the Cambridge Bibliographical Society*, 8 (1981–5), 274–83 · F. Stubbings, *Forty nine lives* (1983), 37–8 · E. M. Gwatkin, *The Gwatkins of Herefordshire* (1914) · *Cambridge Review* (22 Nov 1916) · *Cambridge Review* (29 Nov 1916) · Venn, *Alum. Cant.* · *DNB* · *CGPLA Eng. & Wales* (1917)

**Archives** Emmanuel College, Cambridge, corresp. and papers | BL, corresp. with Sir Sydney Cockerell, Add. MS 52717 · CUL, corresp. with Lord Acton · King's Cam., letters to Oscar Browning · NL Scot., corresp. with publishers

**Likenesses** J. Russell & Sons, photograph, Emmanuel College, Cambridge [*see illus.*] · photographs, Emmanuel College, Cambridge

**Wealth at death** £13,757 16s. 11d.: probate, 19 Jan 1917, *CGPLA Eng. & Wales*

**Gwavas, William** (1676–1741/2), Cornish language scholar, was born on 6 December 1676 at Huntingfield Hall, Suffolk, and baptized on 1 January 1677 at Huntingfield church. He came from an old Cornish family originally from Gwavas in Sithney. He was the eldest child (of eleven in total) of William Gwavas (*c*.1638–1684x95) and Anne (*b*. *c*.1652, *d*. in or after 1711), daughter of William Chester of East Haddon, Northamptonshire. Like his father and grandfather on the Gwavas side, he became a barrister of the Middle Temple, purchasing 4 Brick Court there as his chambers. He retired to Penzance shortly before he married Elizabeth (*bap*. 1685, *d*. 1752), daughter and heir of Christopher Harris of St Ives, Cornwall, merchant, on 29 April 1717. They had two daughters, Elizabeth (1719–1791) who married William Veale, and Anne (1723–1797) who married the Revd Thomas Carlyon. Their son, William, died aged four months in 1727. As Gwavas recounts in an autobiographical piece (Gatley MSS), the family's Cornish property was heavily in debt at his father's death because of thirteen lawsuits, but he paid off the creditors and redeemed the mortgage on the rectory of Paul. He spent much time involved in a chancery suit over the right of the rector of Paul to the tithes of fish landed at Mousehole and Newlyn in that parish. The suit had started in 1680, was revived in 1725, and went before the House of Lords early in 1730, with victory going to Gwavas over the local fishermen. After a period of obedience while William was alive, the fishermen again resisted the tithe and the dispute with his heirs continued until 1830 when the tithe was abolished.

Gwavas was an assiduous collector of Cornish language information and kept up an important correspondence on, and to an extent in, Cornish with other enthusiasts such as John Keigwin, John and Thomas Boson, and most importantly Thomas Tonkin. Much of the Gwavas–Tonkin correspondence, mainly dating from 1733 to 1736, survives in two manuscripts, one in the British Library and one in the library of the Diputación Foral de Bizkaia in Bilbao in Spain. These show that Tonkin's 'Archaeologia Cornu-Britannica', later to be published in part by William Pryce in a book of the same name, was very much a collaboration between the two of them, although Tonkin was the lead partner. In the Bilbao manuscript is a Cornish vocabulary by Tonkin with Gwavas's corrections and additions, and the letters contain their collaboration in translating the Cornish preface from Edward Lhuyd's 'Archaeologia Britannica' into English. Also in the Bilbao manuscript is Tonkin's 1736 dedication of the vocabulary section of his work to Gwavas where he is fulsome in his praise of the latter for providing much material in Late or Modern Cornish, as it was then spoken in the westernmost parts of Cornwall. Even earlier, in 1733, Tonkin acknowledged him as 'perhaps the only gentleman now living who hath a perfect knowledge of the tongue' (Tonkin, 'Carew's survey', vi). Some of the specimens of Modern Cornish written or collected by Gwavas were published in Pryce and Polwhele, and more recently in various issues of *Old Cornwall*. Gwavas was not a native speaker of Cornish and had learned it from other scholars such as Thomas Boson, John Boson, and Edward Lhuyd.

Gwavas died at Chapel Street, Penzance, and was buried at Paul church on 9 January 1742; his widow was buried there on 9 December 1752. The various Cornish language pieces Gwavas collected from a range of people in the western parts of Cornwall are an invaluable source for the final stage of Cornish as a living language. Within sixty years of his death the language was effectively dead. The twentieth-century revival of Cornish owes an enormous amount to scholars like Gwavas who observed the language's decline and made efforts to record it for posterity. MATTHEW SPRIGGS

**Sources** W. Gwavas, 'Liver ve', Royal Institution of Cornwall, Truro, Gatley MSS • BL, Gwavas MS, Add. MS 28554 • T. Pawlyn, 'The Cornish pilchard fishery in the eighteenth century', *Journal of the Royal Institution of Cornwall*, 3rd ser., 3 (1998), 67–90 • T. Tonkin, 'Bilbao MS', Diputación Foral de Bizkaia, Bilbao, Spain, MS BDV m/s Bnv-69 • H. Jenner, 'The Cornish manuscript in the Provincial Library at Bilbao in Spain', *Journal of the Royal Institution of Cornwall*, 72 (1925), 421–37 • T. Tonkin, 'Archaeologia Cornu-Britannica', 1736, Royal Institution of Cornwall • W. Pryce, *Archaeologia Cornu-Britannica* (1790) • T. Tonkin, The first book of Mr Carew's survey of Cornwall, with large notes and additions, 1733, Diputación Foral de Guipúzcoa, San Sebastián, Spain, MS FDG m/s B-11 • Boase & Courtney, *Bibl. Corn.*, 1.200–01; 3.1213 • O. Padel, *Exhibition of manuscripts and printed books on the Cornish language*, Royal Institution of Cornwall (1975), 2–4 [unpaginated] • W. Borlase, 'Autobiographical notice of William Gwavas, extracted from his common place book, 1710', *Journal of the Royal Institution of Cornwall*, 21 (1879), 176–81 • parish register, Paul, Cornwall RO • H. Jenner, *A handbook of the Cornish language* (1904), 33–46 • F. W. P. Jago, *An English-Cornish dictionary* (1887), vii, xi–xiii • R. Polwhele, *The history of Cornwall*, 7 vols. (1803–8), vol. 5, pp. 35–6 • P. A. S. Pool, *The death of Cornish (1600–1800)* (1982), 16–17 • R. M. Nance, 'The Cornish language in America, 1710', *Old Cornwall*, 1/1 (1925), 37 • R. M. Nance, 'A Cornish letter, 1711', *Old Cornwall*, 1/3 (1926), 23–5 • A. K. Hamilton-Jenkin, 'William Gwavas poetises on Penzance', *Old Cornwall*, 1/4 (1928), 30–31 • R. M. Nance, 'A Cornish letter from John Boson to William Gwavas, 1710', *Old Cornwall*, 1/7 (1928), 24–7 • R. M. Nance, 'Two hitherto unnoticed Cornish pieces', *Old Cornwall*, 1/10 (1929), 22–4 • R. M. Nance, 'Two new-found Cornish scraps', *Old Cornwall*, 1/12 (1930), 29–30 • R. M. Nance, 'A puzzle solved', *Old Cornwall*, 2/1 (1931), 23–4 • R. M. Nance, 'An unprinted Cornish scrap', *Old Cornwall*, 2/3 (1932), 43 • R. M. Nance, 'More Cornish from Gwavas', *Old Cornwall*, 2/12 (1936), 34–6 • E. G. R. Hooper, 'The Cornish of William Gwavas', *Old Cornwall*, 9/11 (1984), 529–30

**Archives** BL, papers, Add. MS 28554 • Penzance Library, MS relating to Newlyn quay • Royal Institution of Cornwall, Truro, lease of tithe, MS HA/8/19 • Royal Institution of Cornwall, Truro, on fishing, MS HA/8/25 | Bodl. Oxf., Richard Carew's *Survey of Cornwall* (1602), notes and poems by William Gwavas interleaved • Cornwall RO, 1708 catalogue of Gwavas's books, MS Dd.CN.3460 • Cornwall RO, William Borlase's 'Memorandums relating to the Cornish tongue', MS Dd.Enys.2000 [contains material from William Gwavas's writings] • Diputación Foral de Bizkaia, Bilbao, Spain, Bonaparte collection, Thomas Tonkin's 'Bilbao MS', MS BDV m/s Bnv-69 • Royal Institution of Cornwall, Truro, George Borlase's MS copy of some Gwavas papers on Cornish • Royal Institution of Cornwall, Truro, Gatley MSS, W. Gwavas, 'Liver ve'

**Likenesses** portrait, *c*.1697–1741, Royal Institution of Cornwall, Truro; repro. in Pool, *Death of Cornish*, 16–17

**Gwenfrewi** [St Gwenfrewi, Winefrith, Winifred] (*fl. c*.**650**), nun, is the patron of Holywell and Gwytherin. Her relics were translated to Shrewsbury in 1138, but even before that date she appears to have had an English as well as a Welsh cult. The form of her name given in Latin texts, even in the strongly Welsh *Vita prima* (*c*.1135), was derived from her Old English name, Winefrith. Tegeingl in Clwyd (Flintshire), where she is said to have been born, under Mercian control in the tenth century, was reconquered by the Welsh shortly before the Norman conquest but subsequently came under the control of the earldom of Chester. It is reasonable to assume that her English name and cult derive from the period of Mercian rule. Her well, Ffynnon Wenfrewi, hence Holywell, is the most important of numerous Welsh cults centred on wells.

The *Vita prima* consists of a life followed by a collection of posthumous miracles, all belonging to the two generations before the date of writing. It has been suggested that the life and the miracles are two different texts, the life being earlier than the miracles. No good reason has been given for this proposal; a good early parallel for the form of the text as its stands (namely life followed by miracles) is the seventh-century life of Fursa.

The life revolves around two relationships with men. The first is with Beuno (*d*. 653/659), the saint of Clynnog Fawr in Caernarvonshire but originally from Powys (as, so the genealogies claim, was Gwenfrewi's mother, Gwenlo). When Gwenfrewi vowed herself to virginity, she was educated by Beuno in the liberal arts (there is no hint that a good clerical education was unusual for nuns). In return, Beuno received land from the estate of her father, Tyfid ab Eiludd, and settled in the valley, Sychnant, where Holywell stands. As well as educating Gwenfrewi, Beuno also said mass for the family: effectively, his church is portrayed as an estate-oratory. The second relationship, which also came to redirect the first, was with a local prince, Caradog ab Alog. He met her when she was fetching things necessary for Sunday mass from her father's house and demanded sexual favours, whereupon Gwenfrewi, under the pretence that she was changing her clothing, fled from the back of the house in the direction of the church. Caradog perceived that he had been tricked, overtook her close to the door of the church, and cut her head from her body with his sword. Where the severed head fell, a spring burst out of the ground; Beuno slew the miscreant Caradog with a curse and rejoined the head to the body, so bringing Gwenfrewi back to life. The life reports Beuno's reaction to the miracle:

> My sister, God has appointed this place for you, and it is right that I should go somewhere else, where God will procure me somewhere to live. But every year, around this day, do this for me: send me a cloak made by your own labour. ('Vita prima', 293)

The gift went presumably to Beuno's chief church at Clynnog Fawr. Gwenfrewi's church at Holywell, the principal cult site of Tegeingl, was thus attached to one of the principal churches within the heartland of Gwynedd, which at the date of the life had recently conquered Tegeingl. The rest of the life contains some interesting variations on familiar themes. Gwenfrewi went on pilgrimage to Rome (not Jerusalem, like David); on her return she summoned a synod at which it was ruled that monks and nuns should no longer live singly but in cenobitic communities. This canon was used to explain why she settled as an abbess of nuns at Gwytherin (a church also associated with St Eleri), and so why there were two places in the twelfth century, and later, attached to the saint, Gwytherin and Holywell. Other explanations can be suggested: first, more generally, a distinction was recognized between a monastic retreat and a major cult site open to lay people; and, second, that Gwytherin might well have been established as a place of refuge when Tegeingl came under Mercian rule in the tenth century.

The miracles are divided into two categories by the hagiographer: those that punished the wicked (oppressors of the weak; plunderers of the church; persons who refused due reverence to the holiness of the well) and those that healed the sick, and they are unsurprisingly located at Holywell not Gwytherin. It is, however, interesting that all the miracles are recent, most being 'in the time of the French', namely when Tegeingl was subject to the earldom of Chester. One miracle, indeed, is included to demonstrate how delighted Gwenfrewi was when the French were expelled from the region by the men of Gwynedd.

The *Vita prima* reflected the cult from the point of view of the Welsh; the *Vita secunda*, by Robert, prior of Shrewsbury, written after Gwenfrewi's relics had been translated to Shrewsbury in 1138, had a different audience in view. Chronologically, there may be no significant difference between the lives; what does distinguish them is authorship and implied readership—Welsh in the one case, Anglo-Norman in the other. It does not appear that Robert had read the *Vita prima*. Whatever the *Vita prima* might imply about Gwenfrewi's political loyalties, the cult continued to flourish at Holywell down to the sixteenth century, attested by the late medieval buildings and a long series of Welsh poems. Holywell came under the control of the nearby abbey of Basingwerk; one of the finest poems, a *cywydd* by Tudur Aled (*d.* 1526), was composed for Thomas Pennant, abbot of Basingwerk, who was responsible for buildings at Holywell. The survey of the honour of Denbigh (1334) shows that Gwytherin was largely held by 'abbots of the lineage of Cynon ap Llywarch': it had become a family monastery.

T. M. CHARLES-EDWARDS

**Sources** P. C. Bartrum, ed., *Early Welsh genealogical tracts* (1966), 70 [*Auchau'r Saint*, 27] • 'Vita prima sancti Wenefredae', *Vitae sanctorum Britanniae et genealogiae*, ed. and trans. A. W. Wade-Evans (1944), 288–309 [Lat. edn, *Acta Sanctorum*, Nov 3/1, pp. 702–8] • Robert, prior of Shrewsbury, *Vita secunda Sanctae Wenefredae* • Welsh vernacular life, Peniarth MS 27, pt 2 [15th cent., perhaps in the hand of Gutun Owain, paper], pp. 91–120 (incomplete) • Welsh vernacular life, NL Wal., Llanstephan MS 34 [16th cent., in hands of Roger Morys of Coed y Talwrn and Thomas ab Ifan of Hendre Forfydd in Edeirnion], pp. 189–250 • A. W. Wade-Evans, ed., 'Hystoria o uuched Beuno', *Vitae sanctorum Britanniae et genealogiae* (1944), 16–22 • F. Morgan and P. Vinogradoff, eds., *The Survey of the Honour of Denbigh, 1334* (1914) • S. Baring-Gould and J. Fisher, *The lives of the British saints*, Honourable Society of Cymmrodorion, Cymmrodorion Record Series, 3 (1911), 185–96 • F. Jones, *The holy wells of Wales* (1954), esp. 49–50 • P. C. Bartrum, *A Welsh classical dictionary: people in history and legend up to about* AD *1000* (1993), 315–16 • E. R. Henken, *The Welsh saints: a study in patterned lives* (1991) • E. R. Henken, *Traditions of the Welsh saints* (1987)

**Gwent, John** (*d.* 1348). *See under* Siôn Cent (*fl.* 1400–1430).

**Gwent, Richard** (*d.* 1543), clergyman and canon lawyer, was the son of a Monmouthshire farmer. He was elected a fellow of All Souls College, Oxford, in 1515 and on 17 December 1518 became a bachelor of civil law, and of canon law on 28 February 1519. On 20 March 1523 he supplicated for doctor of canon law, and proceeded doctor of civil law on 3 April 1525. For a time he was chief moderator of the canon law school at Oxford, and was instituted by the abbess and convent of Godstow to the vicarage of St Giles', Oxford, a benefice which he resigned in April 1524.

From Oxford, Gwent moved to London, where he entered Cardinal Wolsey's service. He was employed in a junior capacity on Queen Katherine of Aragon's behalf at her trial in 1529. On 13 April 1528 he was presented to the rectory of Tangmere, Sussex, and on 31 March 1530 to that of St Leonard, Foster Lane, London, which he resigned to become, on 17 April 1534, rector of St Peter's Westcheap, London. He was admitted to the prebend of Pipa Parva in Lichfield Cathedral on 6 October 1531, but quitted it for Longdon, also in Lichfield, three months later. Having been vicar-general of Coventry and Lichfield diocese, he was appointed chaplain to the king and, on 18 September 1532, dean of the arches and master of the prerogative. He was collated archdeacon of Brecon and prebendary of Llanddewi Aber-arth, both in the diocese of St David's, in 1534, and prebendary of Leighton Ecclesia at Lincoln Cathedral on 6 May 1534. In the course of Archbishop Cranmer's metropolitical visitation in September 1534, Gwent, as his commissary, visited Merton College, Oxford, and altered many of the ancient customs of that house. He was collated to the archdeaconry of London on 19 December 1534. He was appointed rector of Cleve, Gloucestershire, and in 1535 held a prebend at Llandaff Cathedral called Prebend Caer, otherwise known as Doctoris Gwent. His appointments in 1536 were reputedly worth over £200 a year.

Between 1533 and 1535 Gwent was also extensively employed by Cranmer and Thomas Cromwell in enforcing the royal supremacy, being associated with Cranmer in interrogating Elizabeth Barton, the nun of Kent, and with ensuring that the pope's name was duly expunged from the service books. He headed the commission of ecclesiastical lawyers which in 1535–6 drew up a revision of canon law for the English church, although in the end it was never promulgated. Convocation elected Gwent as its prolocutor in 1536, 1540 (after two prolonged sessions of discussion), 1542, and 1543. In 1538–9 he was much preoccupied with searching out Anabaptists, under a commission of 10 October 1538, and also with receiving the surrender of larger monasteries in the west midlands and assigning pensions to their inmates. In July 1540 he was one of those appointed by convocation to determine the validity of Henry VIII's marriage to Anne of Cleves, and in May 1541 was a commissioner in London for prosecutions upon the six articles.

Gwent continued to be amply rewarded with ecclesiastical preferment, and has consequently been described as an 'extreme example of a pluralist' (Brigden, 54). He became archdeacon of Huntingdon on 5 April 1542 and on 12 April 1543 prebendary of Tottenhall in St Paul's Cathedral. He also held the rectories of Walton on the Hill, Lancashire, Newchurch, Kent, and North Wingfield, Derbyshire. To the end of his life he continued to hunt down the heretical and the unorthodox, including heretics in London and Kent, Portuguese Jews, and the Lutheran dean of Exeter.

Gwent's health deteriorated sadly in 1543 and on 21 July that year he made his will, which was proved on 11 February 1544. In it he commended his soul unto 'Almighty God and his holy hands' and made no provision for masses or prayers. He left his best gelding to Thomas Cranmer, noting that the archbishop owed him £40, but his most pressing concern seems to have been that his estate should not be unduly burdened with dilapidations. Gwent died in London and at his own request was buried in the middle of St Paul's Cathedral before the high altar. As 'Richardus Ventanus juridicus' he was eulogized for his virtues and learning in John Leland's 'Encomia'.

GLANMOR WILLIAMS

**Sources** G. Williams, *Welsh Reformation essays* (1967), 75–89 • *LP Henry VIII*, vols. 4–18 • *Fasti Angl.* (Hardy), vols. 1 and 2 • D. Wilkins, *Concilia*, 4 vols. (1737), vol. 3 • *Reg. Oxf.*, vol. 1 • Wood, *Ath. Oxon.*: *Fasti* (1815), 47, 67 • R. Newcourt, *Repertorium ecclesiasticum parochiale Londinense*, 1 (1708), 394, 522 • W. H. Turner, *Records of the city of Oxford, 1509–83* (1800), 52 • A. Wood, *The history and antiquities of the University of Oxford*, ed. J. Gutch, 2 (1796), 63–4 • *Miscellaneous writings and letters of Thomas Cranmer*, ed. J. E. Cox, Parker Society, [18] (1846) • J. Strype, *Ecclesiastic memorials*, 1/1 (1822), 378, 553, 559, 565 • J. Strype, *Memorials of the most reverend father in God Thomas Cranmer*, new edn, 2 vols. (1812) • *DWB* • Emden, *Oxf.*, 4.252 • S. Brigden, *London and the Reformation* (1989)

**Archives** LPL, T. Cranmer registers • PRO, state papers domestic

**Wealth at death** see will, PRO, PROB 11/30, sig. 3

**Gwenwynwyn** (*d.* 1216?), ruler in Wales, was the eldest son of *Owain Cyfeiliog, prince of southern Powys. In 1187 he is first mentioned as joining with his brother Cadwallon in slaying Owain, son of Madog ap Maredudd, by treachery. In 1196 he was engaged in war with Archbishop Hubert Walter and an army of English and north Welsh. His castle of Trallwng Llywelyn (Pool Castle) was besieged and taken by undermining the walls; but the garrison escaped, and before the end of the year Gwenwynwyn again took the castle. In 1197, after the death of the Lord Rhys of Deheubarth, Gwenwynwyn took part in the struggle for power between Maelgwn and Gruffudd ap Rhys, and actively supported Maelgwn. When Maelgwn took Gruffudd prisoner he handed him over to Gwenwynwyn's custody. But Gwenwynwyn transferred him to the English and received the castle of Carreghofa in exchange. Gwenwynwyn next subdued Arwystli on the death of its ruler Owain o'r Brithdir and annexed it to Powys.

The death of Owain Cyfeiliog in 1197 made Gwenwynwyn ruler of the whole of southern Powys. As his father had previously taken the monastic habit at Strata Marcella (Ystrad Marchell), it is likely that he was already the effective ruler. He now formed great plans for restoring to the Welsh their ancient rights, property, and boundaries; he assembled a great army from Powys and Gwynedd in July 1198, and besieged William (III) de Briouze in Painscastle. The siege was relieved by the justiciar Geoffrey fitz Peter, who on 13 August put the Welsh to flight and slew many of them. King John, however, took Gwenwynwyn under his protection in December 1199, and made him grants of land. John's policy appears to have been to maintain control in Wales by playing off Gwenwynwyn and Llywelyn ab Iorwerth of Gwynedd against each other.

In 1202 Llywelyn ab Iorwerth, now ruler of Gwynedd, who, says the *Brut y tywysogyon*, 'though he was a kinsman to him by blood … yet he was a man most hostile to him in deeds', planned a war against Gwenwynwyn, but the clergy patched up a peace between them. In the next year Gwenwynwyn was much occupied in helping Maelgwn in his war against his nephew, Gruffudd ap Rhys. In 1203 William de Briouze again complained that Gwenwynwyn was attacking his lands. Next year Gwenwynwyn received a safe conduct to meet the king at Woodstock, and the result of the interview apparently proving satisfactory, he received back the lands at Ashford in Derbyshire granted to him by John in 1200.

In 1208 Gwenwynwyn tried to take advantage of the fall of William de Briouze by ravaging the lands of Peter Fitzherbert. The king summoned him to Shrewsbury and confiscated his lands which were immediately occupied by Llywelyn ab Iorwerth. He was released after taking oaths of fealty and handing over twenty hostages and in 1210 his lands were restored. In 1211 he followed John on his expedition against Llywelyn, but in the next year he joined Llywelyn in a new war against the king. Innocent III absolved them and the other Welsh princes from their allegiance to the excommunicated king, and they all levied war against him. In 1215 Gwenwynwyn accompanied Llywelyn in his victorious expedition through the south. King John now deprived him of Ashford, which he granted to Brian de Lisle. In 1216, however, Gwenwynwyn made peace with King John, to the great indignation of Llywelyn, to whom he had given hostages and written pledges of loyalty. The prince speedily overran his dominions, took possession of them all, and drove Gwenwynwyn to take refuge in Cheshire. John restored his lands, and thanked him for his help, but he never regained his possessions.

On Gwenwynwyn's death, apparently in 1216, Llywelyn agreed to provide a sufficient sum from their revenues to maintain his family, and to give his widow her reasonable dower, but bargained to hold them until his sons came of age. Brian de Lisle was also required to give to the widow her dower from his lands at Holme and Ashford. Gwenwynwyn's wife was Margaret, daughter of Robert Corbet. Their eldest son was *Gruffudd. Gwenwynwyn had other sons named Owain and Madog. In the days of his prosperity he had been a liberal benefactor to the Cistercians of Strata Marcella. The poet Cynddelw addressed three poems to him. From him southern Powys, over which he had ruled, became known as Powys Wenwynwyn.

T. F. TOUT, *rev.* A. D. CARR

**Sources** T. Jones, ed. and trans., *Brut y tywysogyon, or, The chronicle of the princes: Peniarth MS 20* (1952) • J. Williams ab Ithel, ed., *Annales Cambriae*, Rolls Series, 20 (1860) • J. E. Lloyd, *A history of Wales from the earliest times to the Edwardian conquest*, 3rd edn, 2 vols. (1939); repr. (1988) • G. T. O. Bridgeman, 'The princes of upper Powys', *Montgomeryshire Collections*, 1 (1867–8), 1–103, esp. 11–21 • *Gwaith Cynddelw Brydydd Mawr*, ed. N. A. Jones and A. P. Owen, 1 (1991), 229–49

**Gwilliam, Freda Howitt** (1907–1987), educationist, was born on 29 July 1907 at Feltham, Middlesex, the only daughter of Frederick William Gwilliam, a prison governor, and Kate Elizabeth Howitt. She was educated at Rochester Girls' Grammar School, Kent, at Notting Hill high school, London, and at Girton College, Cambridge, from where she graduated with a BA honours degree in history in 1929 (MA, 1934). She subsequently taught at Falmouth county high school from 1929 to 1931 and the Francis Holland School, London, from 1931 to 1936 before becoming a lecturer at the Bishop Otter Teachers' Training College in 1936 and then principal of the Brighton Training College from 1941 to 1946. In May 1947, aged almost forty and after much soul-searching, she abandoned the security and status of a senior teaching position for the uncertainty of the newly created post of woman educational adviser at the Colonial Office.

During the next twenty-three years (from 1947 to 1970) Freda was to play a unique role in the promotion of education, and in particular teacher training and the education of women and girls, throughout the British colonial empire. From the outset she proved to be an inveterate and indefatigable traveller in an age which largely preceded jet air travel and one of the best-known of the Whitehall advisory staff to numerous directors of education in Britain's far-flung outposts of empire. Her visits provoked mixed feelings from colonial officials, her initial question invariably being 'Now what are you doing for the girls?' Woe betide the director of education who did not have a convincing answer ready to hand. Over the years she was also a constant and invaluable source of inside knowledge to her immediate superior, Sir Christopher Cox. Her many letters to him from abroad were always highly informative and exceedingly frank, and reflected a very close working relationship with him. When not away on tour, Freda spent much of her time recruiting and interviewing prospective female staff for service abroad.

Throughout her life Freda was a staunch Anglican with a strong social conscience which manifested itself in a variety of roles. These included a member of the house of laity and the World Council of Churches, a JP, a youth worker in Battersea in the 1930s and later with the Red Cross Society and the Girls' Training Corps, the chairperson of the executive committee of Voluntary Services Overseas, a council member of the Associated Country Women of the World, and an honorary fellow of the College of Preceptors.

Freda made no claim to academic scholarship—writing reports reduced her to pulp—but she was a popular and frequent lecturer to students in the colonial department of the London Institute of Education in the 1950s. When in London she also regularly attended the monthly meetings of the advisory committee on education in the colonies and served on its numerous subcommittees. She was also deeply involved in the staging of the Cambridge conference on African education in 1952 and the first Commonwealth education conference held at Oxford in 1959. Her services to colonial education were formally acknowledged by her appointment as OBE in 1954 and CBE in 1966, and the award of an honorary DLitt from the New University of Ulster, Coleraine, in 1973.

By the late 1960s Freda was aware that it was time to make way for new blood. To Cox she wrote 'I should go. … I'm the Great Aunt figure—the batterer at doors that are opening ajar—unable to move with the young (why should I—with my life behind me)' (Gwilliam to Cox, 2 May 1968, Cox MSS). Her last major educational assignment was to lead the British delegation to the conference on education in rural areas held at the University of Ghana in March 1970.

Freda Gwilliam never married. She lived out her well-earned but characteristically busy retirement with her late brother's family in the village of Frant in Sussex where she became a much loved and respected figure. Her last major public duty occurred in 1972 when she served as the only woman member of the commission of inquiry led by Lord Pearce, which visited Rhodesia to determine whether the people supported proposals for a settlement of the constitutional crisis. She died unexpectedly at her home, One Ash, Frant, on 14 August 1987, aged eighty. Freda Gwilliam belonged to that breed of tough and tireless ladies who fostered the education of girls across the globe. She was no feminist but she helped many thousands of women in developing countries. She was equally no do-gooder, but she did untold good.

CLIVE WHITEHEAD

**Sources** private information (2004) · PRO, Christopher Cox MSS, CO 1045/1497 · C. Whitehead, 'Miss Freda Gwilliam (1907–1987): a portrait of the "great aunt" of British colonial education', *Journal of Educational Administration and History*, 24 (1992), 145–63 · *The Times* (18 Dec 1961) · *The Times* (18 Aug 1987) · *Times Educational Supplement* (25 Aug 1967) · *CGPLA Eng. & Wales* (1987) · R. Cordon, *Seven years' island hopping* (1996)

**Archives** Bodl. RH, papers | PRO, Sir Christopher Cox MSS

**Likenesses** photograph, repro. in Cordon, *Seven years' island hopping*, frontispiece

**Wealth at death** £5156: probate, 4 Nov 1987, *CGPLA Eng. & Wales*

**Gwilt, Charles Perkins** (1809–1835). *See under* Gwilt, Joseph (1784–1863).

**Gwilt, George** (1746–1809), architect, the younger son of Richard Gwilt, peruke maker, and his wife, Sarah, was born in St Saviour's parish, Southwark, on 9 June 1746. At Mr Crawford's school, Newington Butts, he gained mathematical skills and an acquaintance with classical languages. Apprenticed at the age of fourteen to Moses Waite, a local mason, in 1768 he joined a surveyor, George Silverside, and occasionally acted with one of the Jupps, acquiring a general knowledge of building and designing. From about 1770, acting as Surrey county surveyor (appointed formally in 1803), he built houses of correction at Hangman's Acre (1772) and Kingston (1775); and rebuilt the county bridewell, St George's Fields (1781), and bridges at Leatherhead and Godalming (1782–3). He also designed the county gaol, Horsemonger Lane (1791–8, dem. 1880–92), and the county sessions house, Newington Causeway (1798–9, dem. 1912). Quarter sessions added a gratuity of

£50 in addition to his 5 per cent commission for his efficient bridge-building in 1786. He resigned at Michaelmas, 1804, his integrity and ability over thirty-five years being praised by quarter sessions.

Gwilt's main patron was Henry Thrale, the Southwark brewer and friend of Johnson (whose temper Gwilt objected to); he served Thrale 'with a Fidelity not very common' (copy of letter from Hester Thrale, 2 Dec 1781, in Gwilt). Elected under the Metropolitan Building Act as district surveyor for St George's, Southwark, in 1774, he soon resigned, disliking the manner of enforcing the act. From 1771 to 1801 he was surveyor to the commissioners of sewers in east Surrey. He was master of the Masons' Company in 1790. Pupils included his sons George *Gwilt the younger (1775–1856) and Joseph *Gwilt (1784–1863), and John Shaw (1790).

Gwilt's principal work was the formidable neo-classical range of nine North Quay warehouses for the West India Dock Company, half a mile long, built rapidly in 1800–03, and linked by lower structures in 1804 (largely blitzed in 1940). Gwilt and his elder son, preferred to several leading architects, were appointed architects at 1000 guineas p.a., after an abortive competition in 1799. They devoted their full time to the project. The warehouses' internal structure was conventional timber-framing (cast iron was added in 1812), but the wide windows—which became characteristic of dock architecture—were the first to employ cast-iron security grilles, and copper was used for roofing the shallow-pitched upper slopes. Gwilt resigned from the project in 1804 after a quarrel between his son and an official.

Gwilt married Hannah Trested (*d*. 1821) at St George the Martyr, Southwark, on 6 September 1773. Of their four sons and two daughters, only George and Joseph survived him. Joseph described him as 'a person of irascible temper but … kind hearted, and an excellent father and husband' (Gwilt). He was scrupulous in his religious duties, and his 'extremely evangelical notions' (ibid.) appear to have led him into dissent for a time, but he returned to the Church of England. His health declining, in 1805 Gwilt resigned his remunerative business to his sons. He died of a dropsy on the chest on 9 December 1809 at his home, 18 Union Street, Southwark, one of a group of houses he had built. He was buried in St Saviour's Church, now Southwark Cathedral: his family monument is now on the exterior, on the south side. M. H. PORT

**Sources** J. Gwilt, 'Matters relating to the family of Gwilt', Surrey HC, MS 688/1 • Colvin, *Archs.* • S. Porter, ed., *Poplar, Blackwall and the Isle of Dogs: the parish of All Saints*, [1], Survey of London, 43 (1994), 284–92 • will, PRO, PROB 11 • executor's account book of Gwilt's estate, Surrey HC, MS 4332/1 • D. Cruickshank, 'Gwilt complex', *ArchR*, 185 (1989), 54–61 • *Bankside: the parishes of St Saviour and Christchurch, Southwark*, Survey of London, 22 (1950), 84, pl. 62 • N. Briggs, 'The evolution of the office of county surveyor in Essex, 1700–1816', *Architectural History*, 27 (1984), 297–307, esp. 301

**Wealth at death** over £30,000—disposes of £28,000 in 3 per cent bank annuities, about twenty freehold houses, shares in Imperial Insurance Company, county of Surrey £100 bonds, totalling £2400, and some household property: executor's account book, 23 July 1806, Surrey HC, MS 4332/1

**Gwilt, George, the younger** (1775–1856), architect, was born on 8 May 1775 in Southwark, London, the elder son of George *Gwilt (1746–1809), architect, and his wife, Hannah. The architect Joseph *Gwilt (1784–1863) was his brother. He was articled to his father in 1789 and succeeded him in his architectural practice. He helped his father with the design of the large warehouses built for the West India Dock Company between 1800 and 1803.

Gwilt was best-known for his restoration of Southwark Cathedral, and his work on St Mary-le-Bow, Cheapside, a Wren church. Here he had to take down and rebuild the upper part of the spire (1818–20), and while strengthening the foundations of the church he discovered the remains of the original Norman building. From 1822 to 1825 he supervised the restoration of the choir and tower of Southwark Cathedral, and later (1832–3) he restored the lady chapel. He also rebuilt the first ten almshouses of Cure's College, Southwark.

Gwilt was interested in archaeology, and was elected a fellow of the Society of Antiquaries in 1815. He contributed to *Archaeologia* and the *Vetusta monumenta*. He studied the antiquities of Southwark, and wrote about the remains of Winchester Palace in Southwark in the *Gentleman's Magazine* (1815).

Gwilt was master of the Masons' Company in 1835, 1846, and 1854. He died at his home, 8 Union Street, Southwark, on 27 June 1856, a few weeks after the death of his wife, and was buried on 7 July in the family vault on the south side of the choir of Southwark Cathedral. He had four sons, only one of whom survived him, and four daughters. G. W. BURNET, *rev.* ANNE PIMLOTT BAKER

**Sources** Colvin, *Archs.* • *The Builder*, 14 (1856), 386 • *Dir. Brit. archs.* • d. cert. • *IGI*

**Archives** RIBA BAL, biography file

**Likenesses** lithograph, 1847, RIBA; repro. in J. S. Gwilt, 'Slight memoir of Joseph Gwilt', RIBA drawings collection • lithograph (aged seventy-two), BM • portrait, RIBA BAL, photographic collection

**Gwilt, John Sebastian** (1811–1890). *See under* Gwilt, Joseph (1784–1863).

**Gwilt, Joseph** (1784–1863), architect and writer, son of George *Gwilt the elder (1746–1809) and his wife, Hannah, and younger brother of George *Gwilt the younger, was born in Southwark on 11 January 1784 and baptized on 7 February 1784 at Colliers' Rents Independent congregation, Southwark. Educated at St Paul's School, he entered his father's architectural office in 1799 and in 1800 sent his first exhibit, a design for a villa in Surrey, to the Royal Academy. He was admitted to the Royal Academy Schools in 1801 and won the silver medal in that year for a drawing of St Dunstan-in-the-East. In 1808 Gwilt married Louisa (*d*. 1861), third daughter of Samuel Brandram, a merchant of Lee, with whom he had four sons and three daughters.

Relying heavily on his father's influence, Gwilt soon established his own practice and was extensively employed in south-east London, where his early works included the rebuilding of St Margaret's Church at Lee (1813–14; replaced 1839–41), a floor-cloth manufactory at Newington Causeway, Lambeth (1814), and the approaches to Southwark Bridge (1819). Despite his busy practice, Gwilt found time to travel extensively on the continent; he visited Paris in 1814, Flanders in 1815, Rome in 1816, and Paris once again in 1818 (and on later occasions besides). He had a particular interest in bridges, and designed a five-span timber bridge intended to cross the Wye at Hoarwithy, Herefordshire (exh. RA, 1813; unexecuted); his failure to win the competition for London Bridge led to his penning a polemical tract entitled *The conduct of the corporation of London considered, in respect of the designs submitted to it for rebuilding London Bridge, in a letter to G. H. Sumner, M.P., by an architect* (1823). Of his twenty exhibits at the Royal Academy in the years up to 1830, eight were of a sepulchral nature, including two designs for memorials to Lord Nelson, one of which was an unsuccessful entry for the competition organized in Dublin for a commemorative column. Gwilt also designed funerary monuments: that of Anne Brocas at Banbury, Oxfordshire, of 1824 is jointly signed by Gwilt and the sculptor Henry Hartley. Later works included the Unitarian chapel at Swansea (1845–7), the Byzantine St Thomas's Church at Charlton, Kent (1847–50), its exterior embellished with polychromatic brickwork, and the schoolroom at Oundle, Northamptonshire (1854–5). His largest project was the alteration of Markree Castle, co. Sligo, in 1841–3, undertaken with his second son, John Sebastian Gwilt [*see below*], with whom he worked in partnership in his later years.

Though varied, Gwilt's buildings were limited in number; however, he was extremely active in other fields of his profession. He was appointed surveyor to the commissioners of sewers for Surrey and Kent in 1805, a post he held until 1846, during a period of considerable urban growth. Together with his fellow surveyors Edward I'Anson and John Newman he wrote an influential report on the sewers of Kent and Surrey in 1843: their advocacy of large sewers rather than pipes was of considerable influence upon the country as a whole. Other professional appointments were the surveyorships to the Grocers' and Waxchandlers' companies, and the post of architect to the Imperial Fire Assurance Company. In 1838 he was appointed one of the three assessors of the competition for the rebuilding of the Royal Exchange, London; although invited in 1840 to enter himself after the rejection of the winning entry of C. R. Cockerell, Gwilt, to his credit, declined. He was also frequently employed by the Office of Woods and Forests as a consultant, and was one of the principal architects of the 1855 Metropolitan Building Act, a major piece of legislation that determined the nature of the growth of Victorian London.

Today Gwilt is better known as a writer than as an architect, and is remembered above all for *An Encyclopaedia of Architecture, Historical, Theoretical and Practical*, first published in 1842 and illustrated with drawings by his son J. S. Gwilt. One of the most popular Victorian books on the subject, which drew extensively on French sources, the book's success is attributable to its comprehensiveness and organization: its historical sections are combined with summaries on building legislation and tables of mathematical calculation. It went through numerous editions, Wyatt Papworth being responsible for the revised fifth edition of 1867. Gwilt's earliest published work was *A Treatise on the Equilibrium of Arches* (1811), followed by *Notitia architectonica italiana* (1818) and *Sciography, or, Examples of Shadows, with Rules for their Projection* (1822), the latter work based on C. S. L'Eveille's *Études d'ombres à l'usage des écoles d'architecture* (1812). Gwilt's 1823 paper *An Historical, Descriptive, and Critical Account of the Cathedral Church of St. Paul, London* appeared in the first volume of J. Britton and A. C. Pugin's *Illustrations of the Public Buildings of London* (2 vols., 1825–8). His annotated edition of Sir William Chambers's *Treatise on the Decorative Part of Civil Architecture* began to appear in 1825, and in 1826 his translation of Vitruvius, *The Architecture of M. Vitruvius Pollio* (long the standard edition), was published, as was his *Rudiments of Architecture, Practical and Theoretical*. He twice wrote on the development of Trafalgar Square: *Observations on the Communication of Mr Wilkins Relative to the National Gallery* (1833) and, with his son J. S. Gwilt, *A Project of a National Gallery on the Site of Trafalgar Square* (1838).

Elected a fellow of the Royal Society of Antiquaries in 1815, Gwilt, a man of wide accomplishments, was also a fellow of the Royal Astronomical Society from 1833. Non-architectural works included an article on 'Music' for the *Encyclopaedia metropolitana* (1835) and *Rudiments of the Anglo-Saxon Tongue* (1837): like his elder brother George, he was also a studious antiquary and genealogist. He died at his home, South Hill, Henley-on-Thames, Oxfordshire, on 14 September 1863.

Gwilt's eldest son, **Charles Perkins Gwilt** (1809–1835), antiquary, was born on 4 January 1809 in Westminster and baptized on 10 March 1809 at Christ Church, Southwark, London. He was educated at Westminster School, Christ Church, Oxford (1827–31), and the Middle Temple. He wrote *Notes Relating to Thomas Smith of Campden, and to Henry Smith, Sometime Alderman of London* (1836, posthumously edited by his father), and devoted himself to heraldic and antiquarian pursuits. He died on 22 December 1835. Gwilt's second son, **John Sebastian Gwilt** (1811–1890), architect, also attended Westminster School and subsequently worked with his father. His designs for laying out the Hampstead estate of Sir Thomas Maryon Wilson bt were exhibited at the 1845 Royal Academy but never implemented. His only other exhibit was of Markree Castle in 1843. He died at Hambleden, near Henley-on-Thames, where he lived, on 4 March 1890, aged seventy-nine.

Roger Bowdler

**Sources** Colvin, *Archs.* • *DNB* • *GM*, 3rd ser., 15 (1863), 647ff. • *The Builder*, 21 (1863), 701–3 • D. Watkin, *The life and work of C. R. Cockerell* (1974), 207–9 • J. Lever, ed., *Catalogue of the drawings collection of the Royal Institute of British Architects: G–K* (1973), 78–9 • Foster, *Alum. Oxon.* • *Dir. Brit. archs.* • *IGI* • *Old Westminsters*, 1.407 • *CGPLA Eng. & Wales* (1863) • *CGPLA Eng. & Wales* (1890) [John Sebastian Gwilt] • *The exhibition of the Royal Academy* [exhibition catalogues]

**Archives** Bodl. Oxf., illustrated diaries • Canadian Centre for Architecture, Montreal, earlier diaries • GL, corresp. and papers relating to Royal Exchange • RIBA, photos, drawings, notes; nomination papers • RIBA BAL, corresp. and papers incl. MSS of encyclopaedia of architecture

**Likenesses** A. Robertson, miniature, 1810, NPG · photograph, c.1860, RIBA drawings collection
**Wealth at death** under £14,000: probate, 9 Nov 1863, *CGPLA Eng. & Wales* · £165 17s. 8d.—John Sebastian Gwilt: probate, 1890, *CGPLA Eng. & Wales*

**Gwilym ap Gruffudd** (*d.* 1431). *See under* Tudor family, forebears of (*per. c.*1215–1404).

**Gwilym ap Phylip Brydydd** [*called* y Prydydd Bychan] (*fl.* **1222–1268**), court poet, took his sobriquet from his occupation (*prydydd*, 'poet') and from his relation (*bychan*, 'little, minor') to his father, assumed to be Phylip Brydydd; the two are mentioned together (the son by his baptismal name, Gwilym), in an elegy for Trahaearn Brydydd Mawr by Gwilym Ddu o Arfon, as coming from Ceredigion (Cardiganshire), a fact confirmed by the references to places in his poems (Llannarth, Rhystud Barth, and so on) and the location of the lordship of his chief patron, Maredudd ab Owain. More of his poems have survived than of any other court poet of south Wales: in all, nineteen complete poems and fragments of another two. The earliest seems to be his elegy for Rhys Ieuanc (*d.* 1222), the latest his elegy for Goronwy ab Ednyfed (*d.* 1268). This suggests an exceptionally long poetic career. His patrons were drawn from all parts of Wales, but the majority of them were among the descendants of Rhys ap Gruffudd (*d.* 1197) of Deheubarth. His major sponsor was Maredudd ab Owain of Ceredigion, a great-grandson of Rhys; he was the subject of six of the poet's odes. Y Prydydd Bychan's poems are valuable for the light they throw on the minor princes and their courts, including their developing bureaucracy, in south-west Wales. They are mostly traditional in style, but reflect the increasing popularity of the *englynion* metres and greater awareness of continental culture, including the spread of the Arthurian legend.

J. E. Caerwyn Williams

**Sources** J. Morris-Jones and T. H. Parry-Williams, eds., *Llawysgrif Hendregadredd* (1933) · O. Jones, E. Williams, and W. O. Pughe, eds., *The Myvyrian archaiology of Wales, collected out of ancient manuscripts*, new edn (1870) · *Gwaith Bleddyn Fardd ac eraill o feirdd ail hanner y drydedd ganrif ar ddeg*, ed. R. Andrews and others (1996) · D. Huws, 'Llawysgrif Hendregadredd', *National Library of Wales Journal*, 22 (1981–2), 1–26
**Archives** NL Wales, MS 6680B

**Gwilym ap Tudur** (*d.* after **1401**). *See under* Tudor family, forebears of (*per. c.*1215–1404).

**Gwilym Cadfan**. *See* Jones, William (*bap.* 1726, *d.* 1795).

**Gwilym Ddu o Arfon**. *See* Williams, William (1738–1817).

**Gwin, Robert**. *See* Gwyn, Robert (*c.*1540–1604?).

**Gwinne, Matthew** (1558–1627), physician and playwright, 'descended from an antient family in Wales' (Ward, 260) and probably the eldest son of Edward Gwinne (*d.* 1584), grocer or mercer, was born in London on 16 May 1558. On 28 April 1570 he was entered at Merchant Taylors' School, London (which his brother Robert, born in 1570, also attended). He was elected to a scholarship at St John's College, Oxford, in 1574. He took his BA on 14 May 1578 and his MA on 4 May 1582 and in the same year was appointed a regent master in the university. Gwinne read lectures in music, styling himself *praelector musicae publicus* (his inaugural 'Oratio in laudem musices' survived in manuscript and was published in Ward's *The Lives of the Professors of Gresham College* in 1740) but was allowed to discontinue the lectures because 'the practice of that science was unusual if not useless' (*DNB*), and turned his attention to medicine. He built up a flourishing practice in the city, and at St John's 'probably became medical fellow in 1586 on the resignation of Hutchinson' (Stevenson and Salter, 294). Unusually, Gwinne took both his MB and his DM on the same day, 17 July 1594, the latter 'by virtue of two letters of the chancellor of the university [Lord Buckhurst] for that purpose' (Wood, *Ath. Oxon.*, 2.266). This was because he was 'being designed for an employment of considerable trust' (ibid., 2.415), and in the following year he accompanied the English ambassador, Sir Henry Unton, to France.

In the mean time Gwinne had established himself as one of the university's literary luminaries, playing a central role in its poetic, theatrical, and oratorical activities. In 1583 he took part in the academic disputations for the visit of the Polish aristocrat Albertus Laski, a historically important occasion in which Gwinne's friend John Florio and the controversial Italian philosopher Giordano Bruno were probably also involved. Gwinne seems to have been taken up by Bruno: at about this time Gwinne and Florio accompanied Bruno to the celebrated 'Ash Wednesday supper' in London recorded in Bruno's philosophical dialogue *La cena de le ceneri* (1584), and he may well be the Ermesso who speaks up for Oxford in its sequel, *De la causa, principio e uno* (1584). On 23 September 1592, now proctor of the university, Gwinne took part in another disputation, staged for the queen on her visit to Oxford, 'wherein his wittie handlinge of the matter, and discreete behavior, seemed much to please hir majestie' (Ward, 260). He was a prolific writer of occasional verses in Latin and also in Italian—he was one of the group of young Oxford enthusiasts for Italian culture who came to play an important role in the English Renaissance—and these appeared (the Italian ones signed 'Il Candido', meaning 'the white one' as well as 'the honest one', a Welsh-Italian pun on his surname) in several of the university's presentation volumes, including that on the death of Sir Philip Sidney (*Exequiae illustrissimi equitis, D. Philippi Sidnaei*). Gwinne was clearly an intimate of the Sidney circle and, in terms of breadth of influence, his most important literary work is his edition of *The Countesse of Pembrokes Arcadia* (1590) in association with Fulke Greville. Gwinne co-edited and contributed to the obsequies for Henry, earl of Derby (*Epicedium in obitum H. comitis Derbeiensis*), in 1593. He also wrote memorial inscriptions for St John's College chapel, including tributes to the philosopher and physician John Case, and to his fellow poets John Wicksteed and (to judge from stylistic evidence) Richard Latewar. In addition Gwinne composed dedicatory verses for colleagues' works, notably for the *Ulysses Redux* and the *Meleager* (both 1592) of William Gager, then the most important Anglo-Latin dramatist in either university; for John Case's commentary on Aristotle (*Reflexus … Aristotelis*) in 1596 and his *Lapis philosophicus* in 1599; and for William Vaughan's *The Golden Grove* in 1600.

But it is Gwinne's long friendship and collaboration with Florio, the most influential of Elizabethan translators, which is of most interest to posterity: his commendatory verses preface Florio's *Worlde of Words* (the first Italian dictionary) in 1598 and *Queen Anna's New World of Words, or, Dictionarie of the Italian and English Tongues* in 1611, as well as his great translation of Montaigne in 1603, in the preface to which Florio lamented that 'my onelie dearest and in love-sympathising friend, Maister Doctor Guinne' was not more widely renowned, praised his breadth of interests, and recorded that he had been a major collaborator in the work:

> pitty is it the World knowes not his worth better; for … I [may] truely say of him. *Non so se meglior Oratore e Poeta, o Philosopho e Medico.* So Scholler-like did he undertake what Latine prose; Greeke, Latine, Italian or French Poesie should crosse my way (which as Bugge-beares affrighted my unacquaintance with them) to ridde them all afore mee, and for the most part drawne them from their dennes … for, who but he could have quoted so divers Authors, and noted so severall places? So was hee to mee in this bundle of riddles an understanding Oedipus, in this perilous-crook't passage a monster-quelling Theseus or Hercules.

However, the theatre was perhaps Gwinne's greatest love. Both Merchant Taylors' School (under the influence of its remarkable headmaster, Richard Mulcaster) and its sister college St John's had strong traditions of academic drama, and Gwinne was no doubt energetically involved throughout his Oxford years in the numerous tragedies, comedies, interludes, and 'sportes on twelth night', in both English and Latin, which St John's then mounted. Two of Gwinne's own plays have survived. *Nero*, published in 1603 but never performed, is a massive Senecan tragedy of some 5000 lines and over eighty speaking characters—making it one of the longest plays written in Elizabethan England—which lavishly fulfils its Chorus's promise to the audience of 'murder, revenge, weeping, slaughter, evil'. Its preface is of considerable interest, for in it Gwinne both defends his disregard of classical unity and economy, and mounts a general defence of the drama against its detractors: although he names no names, this was clearly his intervention in the fierce dispute which had begun in Oxford in the 1590s, with his friend Gager leading one side and John Rainolds the other (see *The overthrow of stage-playes, by the way of controversie betwixt D. Gager and D. Rainoldes, wherein all the reasons that can be made for them are notably refuted*, 1629).

Gwinne claimed in the preface to *Nero* that he had no talent for comedy, but when James I and Queen Anne made their state visit to Oxford in August 1605, he tried his hand at it in *Vertumnus, sive, Annus recurrens*, a curious and witty allegorical piece, which presents the four ages of man as analogues of the four seasons and the four humours, includes a memorable chorus of militantly feminist Oxford matrons, and was elaborately staged in Christ Church with a central palm tree hung with twelve 'signs' and 'scena in formam Zodiaci' (a stage-setting in the form of the zodiac; Wake, 112). The fulsome dedication to Prince Henry includes a defence of his use of the tragic trimeter in a comedy and, in response to anonymous detractors, of his right to be taken seriously as a playwright as well as a physician. Gwinne once again took part in the academic disputations—defending the propositions that we imbibe our morals with our mothers' milk and that tobacco is good for the health (he was politic enough to explain his real views on that matter to the king in private at the end of the debate)—as well as in the organization of the elaborate programme of theatrical events. In addition to *Vertumnus* (which sent the king to sleep), he staged a little pageant, *Tres sibyllae*, at the gates of St John's when three undergraduates dressed as sibyls greeted the king and praised him for the length of his lineage and his descent from Banquo, 'the conceipt wherof the Kinge did very much applaude' (Nixon, sig. Br). These were the months in which Shakespeare must have been working on *Macbeth*, and it seems probable that Gwinne's work played a role in its gestation. Since *Tres sibyllae* was not published until 1607, well after *Macbeth* had been completed, it also seems plausible to argue that Shakespeare may have been present at the performance.

Gwinne had in fact been specially brought back from London to help arrange the Oxford progress: in 1597 he had been nominated by the university as the foundation professor of physic at the new Gresham College, and moved to Bishopsgate, although he did not resign his St John's fellowship until 1601. Because he had been 'an auntient fellow and a good ornament of this College'—he had been vice-president and was especially active in building up its new library—he was granted an annuity, and free commons during his stay (Costin, 14). His inaugural lectures in praise of Gresham's foundation, which contain the first known reference to Montaigne by an English writer, were published as *Orationes duae Londini in aedibus Greshamiis* in 1605. He taught at Gresham until 1607, when he unsuccessfully petitioned James I for royal dispensation to marry and still retain his position at the college. Gwinne's lectures were given in English as well as in Latin:

> for as much as the greatest part of the auditory is like to be of such citizens and others, as have small knowledge or none at all of the Latin tongue, and for that every man for his healths sake will desire to have some knowledge in the art of physick. (Ward, vii)

Gwinne rapidly established himself as one of London's most influential physicians, both as a teacher and as a practitioner, 'much esteemed both in the city and at court' (ibid., 264). His court connections had long been strong, at least from the time of his diplomatic mission to France in 1595, and his old schoolmate and fellow St John's man Sir William Paddy—personal physician to James I for his entire reign and four times president of the College of Physicians—was actively advancing his career. Gwinne succeeded Paddy in the politically sensitive and prestigious post of physician to the Tower at the beginning of 1605, and in the same year he was elected as fellow of the College of Physicians. He moved rapidly into key offices: he was appointed registrar and censor in 1608, occupying both posts for many years, and was thus centrally involved in some of the fierce controversies which preoccupied the college, and determined the future shape of the English medical profession in the Jacobean period. On the one hand, as a Latinist and literary scholar, he was well placed to defend traditional Galenic medicine, with its reliance on organic remedies, against the newly fashionable Paracelsians, with their advocacy of chemical ones, and in particular against the swarm of unqualified quacks who were claiming Paracelsus's authority for their potions: Gwinne's only published medical work, *In assertorem chymicae sed verae medicinae desertorem Fra. Anthonium Matthaei, Gwynn philiatri &c. succincta adversaria* (1611), records one of the major battles of that war. In it Gwinne responds to the notorious Francis Anthony's *Medicae chymicae et veri potabilis auri assertio* (1610) and vehemently denies the efficacy of drinkable gold, the superiority of metallic to vegetable and animal medicines, and the existence of a panacea.

On the other hand, Gwinne was also well placed to adjudicate in the demarcation disputes—or to encourage co-operative ventures—between the physicians and the two other main groups of practitioners, the surgeons and the apothecaries. In November 1609, on Paddy's motion, he replaced his friend 'for the redinge of the Anathomyes lectures' for the Barber-Surgeons' Company, and when, in September 1612, the company asked the physicians for 'the weeklie lectures of Surgery on Tewsdaies', Gwinne put himself forward, was appointed, and was allowed a yearly payment of £10. He continued to lecture to the barber-surgeons until the end of his life, although records for 1616 suggest that he had to be encouraged to lecture on what the barber-surgeons wanted to hear. There is a reference in the records to a 'free gift' of £12 paid to him to support his son in taking a BA at Oxford, and on 1 February 1627 the company authorized 'payment for makeing of Mr Doctor Gwins picture'.

Gwinne was also well suited to promote the professionalization of pharmacy, a key development in the emergence of modern scientific medicine, given his own interest in drugs and the fact that Roger Gwinne, the lord admiral's apothecary, may have been his brother. Matthew would actively have supported the king in his pet project (realized in 1617) of separating the apothecaries from the grocers and setting them up as a separate company, and when the king commissioned the College of Physicians to prepare the *Pharmacopoeia Londoniensis* (1618)—the first systematic work of its kind in England and one that, through many editions, was to remain the standard work for centuries—Gwinne was on the committee to see it through the press. The Latin of the preface, with its elaborately euphuistic style and liberal name-dropping from classical literary sources, is in Gwinne's style, and its envoi—'Candido lectori'—looks suspiciously like a pun on his pen-name, 'Il Candido'. When, two years later, the king decided that if he could not stamp out tobacco, he would at least regulate it rigorously, he appointed Gwinne, Paddy, and six others as his garblers (quality-controllers) of the drug, 'that the badd and unwholsome Tobacco maye be severed distinguished and discerned, and yet the good receive noe prejudice'.

It was to be Gwinne's last major public office. He died in October 1627 in Old Fish Street, London. In 1635 Alexander Reid (or Read), his successor as lecturer in surgery, paid tribute in his *Chirurgicall Lectures* to 'Master Doctor Gwyn of famous memorie, who by reason of his not vulgar learning, hath left an eternall memorie in the minds of those who knew him inwardly' (sig. Br). Gwinne was survived by his wife, Susan, with whom he had three sons: Matthew (*b.* 1603), John (*b.* 1608), and Henry (*b.* 1612), all of whom followed him to the Merchant Taylors' School and Oxford. In March 1639 she presented his manuscripts to the company but, like his portrait, they have not survived, and were probably destroyed in the great fire. They perhaps included the 'Book of travels' which Ward lists among his works, and that is a loss, for Gwinne seems to have seen much of the continent in the 1580s and 1590s: St John's actually gave him permission to travel for five years (though the college records show that he was not away continuously). Since it was Sir Francis Walsingham who on 31 October 1587 had personally asked the college to release him for one year to travel 'by my direction' as assistant to Fulke Greville, 'being gone beyond the seas about some special service of her Majesty' (Stevenson and Salter, 265), there is a possibility that he was involved in intelligence work, at least in a supporting role. Intriguingly, Ward also mentions 'Letters concerning Chymical and Magical Secrets', and the Bodleian Library did indeed once possess a manuscript containing works by both Gwinne and John Dee. It may be that he dabbled in hermetism and alchemy—he had after all been one of Giordano Bruno's English friends—and that his Elizabethan youth was more heterodox than his later years in the Jacobean establishment. IAIN WRIGHT

**Sources** R. H. Adams, ed., *Memorial inscriptions in St John's College Oxford* (1996) · J. W. Binns, *Intellectual culture in Elizabethan and Jacobean England: the Latin writings of the age* (1990) · G. Bruno, *La cena de le ceneri* (1584) · G. Clark and A. M. Cooke, *A history of the Royal College of Physicians of London*, 3 vols. (1964–72) · W. C. Costin, *The history of St John's College, Oxford, 1598–1860*, OHS, new ser., 12 (1958) · J. Dobson and R. M. Walker, *Barbers and barber-surgeons of London: a history of the barbers' and barber-surgeons' companies* (1979) · M. de Montaigne, *The essayes, or Morall, politike and millitarie discourses of Lo: Michaell de Montaigne* (1603) · Munk, *Roll* · J. Nichols, *The progresses, processions, and magnificent festivities of King James I, his royal consort, family and court*, 4 vols. (1828) · J. Nichols, *The progresses and processions of Queen Elizabeth*, 3 vols. (1823) · A. Nixon, *Oxfords triumph: in the royall entertainement of his moste excellent maiestie, the queene, and the prince: the 27. of August last, 1605* (1605) · W. H. Stevenson and H. E. Salter, *The early history of St John's College, Oxford*, OHS, new ser., 1 (1939) · I. Wake, *Rex platonicus, sive, De potentissimi principis Iacobi Britanniarum regis, ad illustrissimam Academiam Oxoniensem, adventu Aug. 27. anno. 1605* (1607) · J. Ward, *The lives of the professors of Gresham College* (1740) · Wood, *Ath. Oxon.*, 1st edn · S. Young, *The annals of the barber-surgeons of London* (1890) · W. J. Birkin, 'The fellows of the Royal College of Physicians of London, 1603–1643: a social study', PhD diss., University of North Carolina at Chapel Hill, 1977 · *DNB* · will, PRO, PROB 6/12, fol. 177r

**Gwinnett, Button** (*bap.* 1735, *d.* 1777), revolutionary politician in America, was baptized at St Catherine's Church, Gloucester, on 10 April 1735, the son of the Revd Samuel

Gwinnett (*d.* 1777) and Anne, *née* Emes (*d.* 1767). Following an education in the Gloucester area he went to Bristol, where he was introduced to the world of commerce. Having left England he spent a number of years trading in the British colonies from Newfoundland to Jamaica, earning in the process a reputation of undependability amid rumours of outright dishonesty. On 19 April 1757 he married Ann Bourne (*bap.* 1735, *d.* 1785?), and together they settled in 1765 in Savannah, Georgia. There he opened a store, which failed during the Stamp Act crisis. With borrowed money he bought St Catherine's Island, off the Georgia coast, and set out to become a planter.

Although Gwinnett proved no better at planting, in 1767 he was commissioned justice of the peace in St John's parish. With this his political career began. Two years later he was elected to the Commons house of assembly, where he co-authored a 'Humble address' which protested against the taxing of parishes not represented in the assembly. Because of financial problems he served only one term, and by 1773 he had been forced to put his property up for sale and withdraw from public life. He seems to have played no role in protests over the 'Intolerable Acts' (1774), nor does his name appear among those from his parish who in 1775 challenged men from Savannah and the surrounding Christ Church parish for leadership of the infant whig movement. It seems rather that he was seeking to persuade whigs from rural parishes that they would be better off as allies of a faction, his 'nocturnal Cabal', rather than as members of the more conservative clique controlled by Christ Church. Through this effort he was able to organize an alliance, variously called the country party, the popular party, or the radicals, whose goal was to create and lead a more democratic government. The first indication of the strength of his creation came in early 1776, when Georgia's provincial congress elected Gwinnett as commander of the state's continental battalion. Conservative whigs threatened to leave the congress, so Gwinnett accepted election to the continental congress in Philadelphia, where he arrived on 20 May 1776. The military post went to Lachlan McIntosh, a wealthy South Georgia planter with strong Savannah ties.

In congress Gwinnett served on a number of committees, including one which debated the formation of a confederation of the revolutionary states. He did not speak on the subject of independence prior to 2 July, when he voted in favour of the resolution calling for separation from the mother country. On 4 July he voted to approve the Declaration of Independence, which he signed on 2 August, after which he returned to Georgia, in the hope of appointment as commander of the newly authorized Georgia brigade. Frustrated when McIntosh secured that post, Gwinnett endeavoured to get members of his party elected to the provincial congress; when this succeeded, he was elected as speaker and as chairman of the committee that drew up the state's first constitution. This document empowered Gwinnett's backcountry allies and it signalled the end of the low country's domination of the government. Officers not loyal to his faction were dispensed with, and as many were friends and relatives of McIntosh, the already strained relations between the two men grew worse.

The legislature adjourned in mid-February 1777, leaving government in the hands of the council of safety and its president, Archibald Bulloch. A month later Bulloch died, and Gwinnett was selected to replace him. The only negative vote was cast by George McIntosh, Lachlan McIntosh's brother. Now commander of the state militia, Gwinnett ignored advice from continental officers and launched an invasion of East Florida. Convinced that McIntosh and his allies were working against him, Gwinnett began looking for ways to immobilize his enemies. That opportunity came in mid-March, when he received word from the continental congress to arrest George McIntosh for treason, following the interception of a letter from Patrick Tonyn, governor of East Florida, which suggested that McIntosh had secretly aided the British. General McIntosh immediately rushed to his brother's aid and denounced the arrest as part of a conspiracy against his family. Meanwhile the Florida expedition, as predicted, foundered. With state and continental officials refusing to work together the invasion was abandoned, and Gwinnett returned to Savannah to defend himself.

When the first assembly under the new constitution met in May 1777, Gwinnett was defeated in his bid to be elected governor, but the legislature found his conduct in the Florida expedition to have been legal and proper. Outraged, Lachlan McIntosh publicly denounced Gwinnett as 'a Scoundrell & lying Rascal'. Gwinnett responded with a challenge, and the next morning (16 May 1777) the two men met in a duel outside the city. Both were wounded. McIntosh recovered, but in Gwinnett's case 'a Mortification came on' and three days later he died, in Savannah, where he was buried, probably on 20 May. Eulogized by his political ally Lyman Hall as 'a Whig to excess', Gwinnett made himself many friends and many foes by his passionate devotion to the American cause (and to his own). Although he contributed to the extreme factionalism of the whig movement in Georgia, he also brought that region into the struggle on the whig side and made the revolution a more democratic event.

HARVEY H. JACKSON III

**Sources** C. F. Jenkins, *Button Gwinnett, signer of the Declaration of Independence* (1926) • H. H. Jackson, *Lachlan McIntosh and the politics of revolutionary Georgia* (1979) • H. H. Jackson, 'Button Gwinnett and the rise of the "Western Members": a reappraisal of Georgia's "Whig to excess"', *Atlanta Historical Journal* (summer 1980), 17–30 • H. H. Jackson, '"Whig to excess" or " Scoundrell and lying rascal"? Just who, or what was Button Gwinnett', *American History Illustrated* (Aug 1981), 18–25 • H. H. Jackson, 'Button Gwinnett', *Georgia's signers and the Declaration of Independence* (1981), 37–58 • J. Carson, 'Adventures of the brigantine *Rebecca*: wherein a Quaker ship-owner becomes involved with one B. Gwinnett', *Autograph Collectors Journal* (autumn 1952) • K. H. Thomas, 'Genealogies of the signers', *Georgia's signers and the Declaration of Independence* (1981)

**Archives** Georgia Department of Archives and History, Atlanta, Georgia • Georgia Historical Society, Savannah, Georgia • National Archives, Washington, DC

**Likenesses** J. Theus, oils, Fulton Federal Savings and Loan, Atlanta, Georgia

**Wealth at death** in debt; much of property later sold: Jenkins, *Button Gwinnett*

**Gwinnett, Richard** (1675–1717), playwright, was born on 16 October 1675, the son of George Gwinnett (1647–1724), gentleman, of Shurdington, Gloucestershire. He studied at College School, Gloucester, before matriculating on 1 March 1692, aged sixteen, from Christ Church, Oxford, where he was a pupil of Francis Gastrell. He graduated BA in 1695 and was admitted to the Middle Temple in June 1697. While in London Gwinnett became engaged to the poet Elizabeth *Thomas (1675–1731), but the marriage was postponed for financial reasons. Failing to find a place, Gwinnett retired to his father's estate, where he lived for the remainder of his life. From 1700 to 1716 Gwinnett and Thomas carried on a literary correspondence consisting of letters, poems, and philosophical essays, posthumously published in two volumes (1731–2) under the title *Pylades and Corinna, or, Memoirs of the lives, amours, and writings of R. G. … and Mrs. E. Thomas, junr. … which passed between them during a courtship of above sixteen years*. In addition to the letters, the volumes contain Gwinnett's 'An essay on the mischief of giving fortunes with women in marriage', earlier printed anonymously in Swift's *Miscellanea: the second volume* (1727), and a comedy, *The Country 'Squire, or, A Christmas Gambol*, which was separately published in 1732. The play, which ridicules country manners, was produced in Gloucestershire 'by a select company of neighbours', the author acting the part of Balance (Gwinnett, *Country 'Squire*). In 1716 Gwinnett returned to London to press his suit with Thomas, but the wedding was again deferred owing to the illness of the lady's mother. Early in the following year Gwinnett fell ill with consumption, and he died on 16 April 1717. He left Thomas a legacy of £600, most of which was lost in settling a suit when Gwinnett's family refused to honour the bequest.

Gwinnett's manuscripts were published in circumstances that raise doubts about their authenticity. Edmund Curll compiled *Pylades and Corinna* from the papers of Elizabeth Thomas following her death in 1731, appending a somewhat lurid 'Life of Corinna. Written by herself'. The title-page asserts that that the authenticity of *Pylades and Corinna* is 'Attested By Sir Edward Northey, Knight' though Northey had died in 1723. Material assembled for the second volume included (in addition to letters from Thomas to John Norris of Bemerton and Lady Elizabeth Chudleigh) a testimonial from Samuel Gwinnett, Richard's cousin. The presentation and substance of the letters recounting the philosophical courtship differ little from those of other romances and semi-fictional memoirs published at the time, and *Pylades and Corinna* appears in William H. McBurney's *A Check List of English Prose Fiction, 1700–1739* (1960). More recently, however, T. R. Steiner has found that where facts can be verified 'Thomas proves to be surprisingly reliable about details of her own life' (Steiner, 799n.). The work was reprinted in 1736, though interest in Elizabeth Thomas may have waned, as Curll was still advertising the volumes a decade later. Published in George Wright's *The Four Seasons of the Year* (1787) was 'The Shepherd's Day: in Four Pastoral Dialogues; Imitated from Mr. Gay' attributed to 'the author of the Country Squire'. Although the poems do not appear in *Pylades and Corinna*, they may have been cobbled together from verses originally composed by Richard Gwinnett.

David Hill Radcliffe

**Sources** *Pylades and Corinna, or, Memoirs of the lives, amours, and writings of R. G. … and Mrs. E. Thomas junr.*, 2 vols. (1731–2) • R. Gwinnett, preface, *The country 'squire* (1732) • T. Cibber, 'Elizabeth Thomas', *The lives of the poets of Great Britain and Ireland* (1753) • D. E. Baker, *Biographia dramatica, or, A companion to the playhouse*, rev. I. Reed, new edn, rev. S. Jones, 3 vols. in 4 (1812) • 'Richard Gwinnett', *Port Folio*, new ser., 5 (12 March 1808), 182 • Foster, *Alum. Oxon.* • *DNB* • T. R. Steiner, 'Richard Gwinnett and his "Virtuous Lover", Elizabeth Thomas', *Georgia Historical Quarterly*, 78 (1994), 794–809
**Likenesses** portrait, repro. in *Pylades and Corinna*

**Gwydir**. For this title name *see* Burrell, Peter, first Baron Gwydir (1754–1820) [*see under* White Conduit cricket club (*act. c.*1785–1788)].

**Gwyer, Barbara Elizabeth** (1881–1974), college head, was born at 11 Dorchester Place, Marylebone, London, on 1 January 1881, the only daughter of John Edward Gwyer, secretary to the Provident Clerks' Life Assurance Association, and his wife, Edith, *née* Linford. She was educated at the Grove School, Highgate, Middlesex. From 1900 to 1904 she was a scholar at Lady Margaret Hall, Oxford, where she gained seconds in classical moderations (1902) and in *literae humaniores* (1904). She later graduated BA and MA in 1920, when Oxford degrees were finally opened to women. After completing her studies she spent two years doing secretarial work, after which, from 1906, she was educational organizer for the West Riding county council educational department.

In her two subsequent positions Barbara Gwyer was responsible for women students in their university accommodation, overseeing their pastoral care and physical needs, and ensuring that their place of residence was comfortable and appropriate to the *mores* of the period. Between 1910 and 1916 she was vice-warden of Ashburne Hall, University of Manchester, which had opened in 1900. In 1917 she was appointed warden of University Hall, Leeds, where she worked until 1924. The position of warden was an attractive one for a woman of Barbara Gwyer's level of education:

> After 1900, many of the new generation of university-educated women saw the wardenship of university hostels and halls of residence as a valuable career opening, offering scope for their talents, qualifications and experience. (Dyhouse, 108)

Barbara Gwyer's appointment as principal of St Hugh's College, Oxford (founded in 1886), came at the end of a stormy period for the college following the notorious 'row' between Eleanor Jourdain, principal of the college (1915–24), and a group of women tutors. In the wake of an inquiry by the university chancellor in 1924 which found for the St Hugh's tutors, Miss Jourdain died suddenly of a heart attack, leaving a college in turmoil and in need of sound guidance and leadership. 'At this moment Barbara Gwyer took over and to her the college undoubtedly owes its subsequent recovery' (Thornton, 10). Her 'quiet and healing influence which would allow confidence and trust to grow again' (*The Times*, 19 Feb 1974) was universally

Barbara Elizabeth Gwyer (1881–1974), by Hubert Andrew Freeth

praised. Dedicated and devout, she led the college with firm direction. Women had only recently been admitted to full membership of the university and she was aware of the need for tact. Her long tenure as principal—twenty-two years—helped to lay a firm foundation for the successful future of women's higher education in Oxford. She held the college together during the Second World War, a challenging task in that it was then housed in seven separate sites. In wartime she also represented Oxford University on the southern region tribunal for conscientious objectors.

Barbara Gwyer's capable leadership was appreciated by Elizabeth Wordsworth, founder of St Hugh's and herself a former principal of Lady Margaret Hall. An existing friendship between the two women was deepened during the early years of Barbara Gwyer's principalship, and Miss Wordsworth welcomed the strengthening of a connection with St Hugh's which had been strained under Miss Gwyer's predecessors. Barbara Gwyer eschewed glamour and sophistication, preferring simplicity and dignity. Known to her students as 'the Gwyer', 'she had a magnificent Episcopal presence' (Pitt) and a strong individuality and determination which refused to be swayed by the opinions of others. Her Christian beliefs were deeply held and she described a college as being 'called into being by God … a society in which each member exists in unescapable [*sic*] responsibility to his fellows' (Gwyer, 'Elizabeth Wordsworth', 95). She was also imbued with a unique sense of humour which was appreciated by her students.

Upon her retirement in 1946 Barbara Gwyer was made an honorary fellow of St Hugh's College. Looking back on her career, she described herself as 'the last of the amateur Principals' (Gwyer, 'Report of gaudy', 11). During a lengthy retirement, living in Stokenchurch, Buckinghamshire, she was, variously, a member of Buckinghamshire education committee, chairman of council, St Margaret's House Settlement, Bethnal Green, east London, and a founder of the Institute of Christian Education. Barbara Castle commented in her diary on her return to St Hugh's as an honorary fellow for a dinner in February 1970: 'there was the Gwyer, a frail, gentle figure in a wheelchair—aeons away from the ogre I had known when she was principal' (*Diaries 1964–70*, 766). She died at her home, New Patch, New Road, Stokenchurch, on 16 February 1974.

ANNE KEENE

**Sources** 'Centenary reminiscences', St Hugh's College, Oxford, archive • V. Pitt, 'Recollections from the 1940s', St Hugh's College, Oxford, archive • B. Gwyer, *Exhortations: selected from among those delivered in St Hugh's College chapel, 1925–1935* (1936) • B. Gwyer, 'Elizabeth Wordsworth', *Exhortations: selected from among those delivered in St Hugh's College chapel, 1925–1935* (1936) • *St Hugh's College Chronicle* (1924–46) • B. Gwyer, 'Report of Gaudy, 1946', *St Hugh's College Chronicle*, 19 (1946), 11 • *The Times* (19 Feb 1974) • P. Griffin, ed., *St Hugh's: one hundred years of women's education in Oxford* (1986) • V. M. Brittain, *The women at Oxford: a fragment of history* (1960) • G. Battiscombe, *Reluctant pioneer: a life of Elizabeth Wordsworth* (1978) • A. G. E. Carthew, *The University Women's Club: extracts from fifty years of minutes books, 1886–1936* (1936) • C. Dyhouse, *No distinction of sex? Women in British universities, 1870–1939* (1995) • G. Thornton, *Conversation piece* (1979) • matriculation records, U. Oxf., archives • b. cert. • d. cert.

**Archives** Bodl. Oxf., letters to J. L. Myres • Bodl. RH, corresp. with Margery Perham

**Likenesses** F. Dodd, charcoal drawing, 1936, St Hugh's College, Oxford • H. Lamb, group portrait, oils, 1936 (*Conversation piece*), St Hugh's College, Oxford • M. Coatman, bust, 1976, St Hugh's College, Oxford • H. A. Freeth, pencil drawing, St Hugh's College, Oxford [*see illus.*]

**Wealth at death** £12,376: probate, 10 June 1974, *CGPLA Eng. & Wales*

**Gwyer, Sir Maurice Linford** (1878–1952), lawyer and civil servant, was born in London on 25 April 1878, the eldest son of John Edward Gwyer, public auditor and secretary of the Provident Clerks' Life Assurance Association, and his wife, Edith Linford. His sister, Barbara Elizabeth *Gwyer, was principal of St Hugh's College, Oxford (1924–46). Educated at Westminster School and Christ Church, Oxford, he took a first in classical moderations (1899) and a second in *literae humaniores* (1901). He was elected to a prize fellowship at All Souls in 1902 and took a first in bar finals. Called by the Inner Temple in 1903, he became a pupil of Frank MacKinnon. In 1906 he married Alsina Helen Marion (*d.* 1953), daughter of Sir Henry Charles *Burdett, philanthropist; they had one son and two daughters.

Gwyer's future did not lie in the high-class commercial work for which MacKinnon's chambers were renowned or in the rough and tumble of circuit life. In 1912 Warren Fisher, after an intensive search for the right man, invited Gwyer to join the legal staff of the National Health Insurance Commission and (although tempted to return to the bar after the war) he remained in the public service for the rest of his working life.

In 1919 Gwyer decided (albeit with some reluctance and

perhaps primarily to ensure the financial security of his wife, who had become an invalid, and family) to accept appointment as legal adviser and solicitor to the Ministry of Health. The new ministry (created by statute after a long and fierce Whitehall battle) had wide responsibilities, extending not only to public health but also to housing; and the legislation required to implement the ambitious 'homes for heroes' policies enthusiastically adopted by Christopher Addison was complex, highly technical, and often contentious. Gwyer's clear reasoning and consummate drafting skills enabled him to meet the challenge; and, over a politically turbulent seven-year period, he rendered signal service to no fewer than six ministers.

Gwyer acquired a formidable reputation. In 1926 he was appointed Treasury solicitor (in effect, the head of the government legal service) and his talents were deployed over the whole range of public administration. In 1928 he was plunged into what was politically an extremely sensitive matter. Allegations had been made in the course of litigation suggesting that senior Foreign Office officials had taken advantage of their knowledge to speculate in foreign currencies; and these broadened to suggest that one senior official had manipulated the publication of the so-called Zinoviev letter so as to ensure the defeat of the Labour government in the general election of 1924 and thereby facilitate a spectacularly profitable foreign currency coup. These allegations were examined by a special board of enquiry composed of Gwyer, Fisher, and the auditor-general (Sir Malcolm Ramsay). In less than a month the board carried out a meticulous and detailed examination of the evidence. While the broader charges were demonstrated to lack foundation, the board was satisfied that the admitted transactions should never have been undertaken by a civil servant. Although there had been no breach of trust or betrayal of confidence, the board forcefully asserted the obligation on civil servants so to order their private affairs as to avoid any suspicion of impropriety. The report (mostly written by Gwyer) emphasized the importance of the 'instinct and perception of the individual' as against 'cast-iron formulas'.

After the emotional pressures of this enquiry into failures by civil service colleagues (two of whom lost their jobs as a result) Gwyer may have found it a relief to serve on the royal commission on London squares established because of well-founded fears that the green squares of Bloomsbury and Kensington might be sold for housing development. Although the legal position was obscure and the technical demands correspondingly great, there was little dispute about the merits. Gwyer's most lasting achievement as Treasury solicitor was in connection with the conference on the operation of dominion legislation which drafted what became in 1931 the Statute of Westminster, a title which he suggested. The conference described the proposed legislation in words characteristic of Gwyer as an

> association of constitutional conventions with law … [which] has provided a means of harmonizing relations where a purely legal solution of practical problems was impossible, would have impaired free development, or would have failed to catch the spirit which gives life to institutions.

Gwyer took silk in 1930 and in 1934 was appointed to succeed Sir William Graham-Harrison as first parliamentary counsel to the Treasury. Gwyer's appointment was not at first welcomed by the small group of highly gifted lawyers in the parliamentary counsel office: he had never (one of them recorded) 'drafted an Act of Parliament in his life and was patently too old to learn'. But this initial hostility soon 'melted away in the warmth and charm of Gwyer's personality' (Kent, 51). Gwyer's profound learning—he had edited Sir William Anson's *Law and Custom of the Constitution: Parliament* (1922) and between 1910 and 1923 taken responsibility for four editions of Anson's *Law of Contract*, and he had been lecturer in private international law at Oxford and the first British delegate to the Hague conference on private international law—also won the respect of the counsel, as did his ability to negotiate greatly improved terms of service for them from the Treasury. The most substantial legislative monument of Gwyer's term of office is the Government of India Act of 1935. The act's 478 sections and 16 schedules covered more pages of the statute book than any previous act.

It seems that Gwyer saw himself as presiding over a team of draftsmen, 'only dealing personally with matters of high policy or problems of presentation in the sensitive political areas' (Kent, 51). But in November 1936 Edward VIII's wish to marry Wallis Simpson precipitated a major constitutional crisis. Gwyer played an important part, advising on difficult and unprecedented issues of constitutional law and practice: for example, was the cabinet entitled to advise the king on the propriety of the marriage? What would be the position if the king refused to take any advice offered? What was the position of the dominions (whose consent to legislation affecting the crown was required by the Statute of Westminster)? Gwyer's calm and skilful handling of these vitally important technical issues was an important factor in enabling His Majesty's Declaration of Abdication Act to become law on 11 December 1936—coincidentally shortly after Gwyer's appointment as chief justice of the federal court of India had been announced.

The 1935 Government of India Act had been intended to establish responsible government for both the provinces and for an all-India federation. But the pressures for full independence were such that the provisions for federation never came into effect. For this reason, although Gwyer was duly sworn in on 1 October 1937 and the federal court sat for the first time in the Prince's Chamber, New Delhi, in December, there was at first little business for the court to handle. Cases from the eleven provinces did begin to come to the court; and the *Federal Court Reports* fairly indicate Gwyer's broadly liberal approach. He regarded the court's existence as demonstrating that the Indian nation was 'on the march'; and his assurances that the British people wished to promote the constitutional development of India may have had some impact.

The fact that the chief justice had at first little judicial work allowed him, with encouragement from the viceroy, to take in hand the reform of the University of Delhi; Gwyer was appointed vice-chancellor in 1938. Despite ill health he continued in that office until 1950. He lived in style, and almost from the first his house in Delhi became a place of meeting for a large circle, both British and Indian. He knew everybody and all that was going on. He travelled widely but some of his visits to princely states with which the government was having difficulties caused embarrassment.

Gwyer, a 'man of monumental physical proportions and genial aspect' as one of his colleagues was to describe him, had a distinguished presence (Kent, 51). Good living he enjoyed—and good company; Maurice Gwyer would have been at ease in Dr Johnson's circle. He was by nature tolerant, and sometimes conveyed a misleading impression of indolence. He was certainly ready to see redeeming features, but drew a rigid line between frailty and vice.

Gwyer was appointed CB (1921), KCB (1928), KCSI (1935), and GCIE (1948). He became an honorary student of Christ Church (1937), an honorary DCL of Oxford (1939), LLD of Travancore (1943) and Patna (1944), and DLitt of Delhi (1950). He died at his home, 14 Kepplestone, Eastbourne, Sussex, on 12 October 1952, and was buried at St Marylebone cemetery, East Finchley, on 17 October.

DOUGLAS VEALE, *rev.* S. M. CRETNEY

**Sources** personal knowledge (1971) • private information (1971) • *WWW* • H. S. Kent, *In on the act: memoirs of a lawmaker* (1979) • *The Times* (13 Oct 1952) • *The Times* (18 Oct 1952) • *The Times* (7 Nov 1952) • 'Report of the board of enquiry appointed by the prime minister to investigate certain statements affecting civil servants', *Parl. papers* (1928), 7.515, Cmd 3037 • *Report of the royal commision on London Squares*, md. 3196 (1928) • *Report of the conference on the operation of dominion legislation*, md. 3479 (1929) • M. Gwyer and A. Apodorai, eds., *Speeches and documents on the Indian constitution, 1921* (1957) • *Federal Law Journal of India*, 1–6 (1937–43) • *Federal court reports*, 1–5 • S. M. Cretney, 'The king and the king's proctor', *Law Quarterly Review*, 116 (2000), 583 • S. M. Cretney, *Law, law reform and the family* (1998) • *CGPLA Eng. & Wales* (1953)

**Archives** BL OIOC, corresp., MS Eur. D 714 | Bodl. Oxf., corresp. with his wife, Alsina • Bodl. Oxf., corresp. with Sir Henry Burnett • Bodl. Oxf., letters to R. W. Chapman • Bodl. Oxf., Somervell papers

**Likenesses** W. Stoneman, photograph, 1931, NPG • photograph, repro. in *Federal Law Journal of India*

**Wealth at death** £39,270 1s.: probate, 20 Jan 1953, *CGPLA Eng. & Wales*

**Gwyllt, Ieuan**. *See* Roberts, John (1822–1877).

**Gwyn, David** (*fl.* 1588–1602?), poet and pirate, was doubtless of Welsh extraction, though his origins remain obscure. According to his one work published in 1588, Gwyn was a Spanish prisoner and a galley slave for nearly twelve years; he appears in Richard Topcliffe's notes on 'such as traffic in Spain' (1584?), which mention the 'Ill treatment and probable death of David Gwyn' there (*CSP dom.*, *1581–90*, 220). Motley tells how Gwyn, a prisoner of war, was a slave on the Armada galley *Bazana*, which left Lisbon in 1588. The gallerians, headed by Gwyn, killed the soldiers with daggers, captured the *Bazana*, and took over the *Capitana* galley. However, Gwyn was not on board the *Bazana*, but the *Diana*; slaves could never have made daggers from broken sword-blades; and the story—though touched upon by Hakluyt—is otherwise unknown. Gwyn really did escape from the *Diana* at Bayonne, and from there he made his way to England.

Gwyn is known for *Certaine English Verses Penned by David Gwyn*, printed in London in 1588 by Richard Hudson, a work known in only two copies, in different editions. The three short poems concern, respectively, alleged Portuguese traitors; the Spanish Armada being prepared; and Sir Francis Drake. They have no great merit, though an occasional felicity, such as this from his eulogy on Drake:

O Noble knight, O worthie wight,
O prince of navigation:
In martiall affaires is thy delight,
for countrie[']s preservation.
(p. 8, lines 1–4)

On 23 September 1588 Gwyn was sent to Ireland as 'one that knoweth the men of quality in the Spanish fleet' (*APC*, 16.288), and he appeared in Drogheda, interrogating Armada survivors. Later, one Eustace Hart reported that Gwyn had accused Sir Francis Walsingham of promising to surrender the queen to Spain and that Gwyn had dishonestly handled money and gold chains while in Ireland. On 18 October he was due to be sent back to England for judgment. Gwyn was said to have been imprisoned in 'the Compter' (Morris, 37) as a Catholic recusant, dying there about 1590, but the local parish registers record no such burial.

Gwyn was probably the pirate of that name who, in 1590, captured the *Thomas* of Leith off Yarmouth, Norfolk, and other felonies followed. His ship was said to come from Ratcliff, Middlesex. In 1596 the master of Orkney was robbed by Gwyn, 'an English pirate and fugitive' (*APC*, 25.204). In 1602 an English agent in Scotland told Sir Robert Cecil that 'Quyn [*sic*] or Wyn' (*CSP Scot.*, 13.2.1085) had called on him, hoping to obtain pardon. Thereafter, Gwyn's history is unknown.

JOHN BENNELL

**Sources** J. L. Motley, *History of the United Netherlands*, [new edn], 2 (1869), 447–9 • J. K. Laughton, ed., *State papers relating to the defeat of the Spanish Armada, anno 1588*, 2, Navy RS, 2 (1894), esp. 281–3 • R. Hakluyt, *The principal navigations, voyages, traffiques and discoveries of the English nation*, 4, Hakluyt Society, extra ser., 4 (1904), 210 • *CSP Scot.*, 1588–93, nos. 467, 481, 483, 569; 1597–1603, nos. 881, 1085 • *APC*, 1588, 288; 1590, 373; 1593–6, 204 • *CSP dom.*, 1581–90, 220 • J. Morris, ed., *The troubles of our Catholic forefathers related by themselves*, 3 (1877), 37 • *STC*, 1475–1640 • parish register, London, St Michael Wood Street, 1559–1659, GL, MS 6530 • parish register, London, St Mildred Poultry, 1538–1724, GL, MS 4429/1 • parish register, Southwark, St Saviour, 1571–1610, LMA, microfilm X.097/270

**Gwyn, Eleanor** [Nell] (1651?–1687), actress and royal mistress, was born, according to a contemporary horoscope, on 2 February 1651. Her parentage remains obscure, as does her place of birth. Nell had a sister named Rose and her mother was Helena (*d.* 1679), but her father is unknown. A satire of 1681 claimed that he had died a debtor in an Oxford prison (Lord and others, 2.242–5), while the antiquary Anthony Wood's incomplete pedigree of Nell suggested Dr Gwyn, a canon of Christ Church,

**Eleanor Gwyn** (1651?–1687), by Gerard Valck, *c.*1673 (after Sir Peter Lely, *c.*1670)

Oxford, as her grandfather. In 1688 another writer asserted that Nell's father was a Captain Thomas Gwyn. Contemporary sources have neither confirmed nor disproved these suggestions, while the places claimed for Nell's birth—London, Oxford, or Hereford—rest on tradition rather than evidence.

**The actress** Nell Gwyn's early life is also a matter of speculation: the diarist Samuel Pepys records a story that Nell herself said she was 'brought up in a bawdy-house to fill strong water to the guests' (Pepys, 8.503), while contemporary satire alleges employment both in raking cinders and as a street vendor selling herrings. The first notice of the Gwyns may be in 1663, when a Rose Gwyn, possibly Nell's sister, petitioned Mr Brown, cupbearer to the duke of York, and Mr Killigrew, probably Henry Killigrew, another official to the duke of York, to expedite her release from Newgate gaol, where she had been imprisoned for theft. Rose's petition added that her father had 'lost everything in service to the late King [Charles I]' (*CSP dom.*, *1663–4*, 390, 393). Rose's connection with Mr Killigrew may provide a link with the King's Theatre, of which Henry Killigrew's father, Thomas Killigrew, was the proprietor and where Nell apparently became an orange girl, selling oranges to the theatregoers in 1663 (Lord and others, 2.243).

Nell Gwyn made the transition to the stage about a year later, probably taking bit parts in 1664–5. Traditionally she is said to have been introduced to the stage either by one Robert Duncan, or the well-known actor Charles Hart (*c.*1630–1683), who was also alleged to be her lover. By April 1665 she had come to the attention of Pepys, who, on a visit on 3 April that year to the Duke's Theatre at Lincoln's Inn Fields, noticed 'pretty witty Nell' among the audience (Pepys, 6.73). Pepys saw Nell again on 1 May 1667, standing at her lodgings' door in Drury Lane (off Bridges Street, the site of the King's Theatre), 'in her smock sleeves and bodice … she seemed a mighty pretty creature' (Pepys, 8.193). Contemporary portraits suggest she was of slight build, with fair hair. Pepys first saw Nell on stage on 8 December 1666 and over the next three years observed her acting, finding her outstanding in comic parts but disappointing in serious roles: after seeing her as Mirida in *All Mistaken* he wrote, 'Nell's … mad parts are most excellently done … which makes it a miracle to me to think how ill she do any serious part … just like a fool or changeling; and in a mad part doth beyond imitation almost' (Pepys, 8.91, 594).

**The king's mistress** An affair with Charles Sackville, Lord Buckhurst (1643–1706), interrupted Gwyn's career in July 1667, when Buckhurst promised her £100 a year and she went with him to Epsom, but the arrangement did not last and Nell was back in London in August that year. In the winter of 1667–8 Nell was one of the actresses promoted by the duke of Buckingham as a new mistress for *Charles II (1630–1685), and in January 1668 it was reported that 'the King did send several times for Nelly' (Pepys, 9.19). She may not, however, have become a royal mistress until 1669—at least this was when she became pregnant with her first child by Charles II, and late that year she stopped acting and moved to a house in Lincoln's Inn Fields. The child was a son, born about 14 or 15 May 1670 and christened Charles [*see* Beauclerk, Charles, first duke of St Albans] on 7 June, Buckingham and Buckhurst being two of the godparents (newsletter, 11 June 1670, BL, Add. MS 36916, fol. 183). That summer a house at the east end of Pall Mall was leased for Nell, but she returned to act in *The Siege of Granada* from December 1670 to February 1671 before leaving the stage for good.

In February 1671 Nell Gwyn moved into a much grander house at the fashionable west end of Pall Mall, the freehold being purchased for her by the king in 1677. This house signalled Nell's acknowledgement as a royal mistress; it was on the south side of the Mall and, backing onto St James's Park, was well situated for royal visits. In March 1671 John Evelyn observed a 'very familiar' discourse between the king and Nell, 'she looking out of her garden on a tarrace at the top of the wall, and [the king] standing on the greene walke under it' (Evelyn, 3.573). Nell's second son, James, was born there on 25 December 1671. Nell was also given a pension of £4000 a year from 1674 'during pleasure', increased to £5000 in 1676; £800 a year on Irish revenues in 1677; Burford House at Windsor in September 1680; leases of land in Bestwood Park, Nottinghamshire, by 1681; and a grant of the customs paid on logwood from 1683. In 1675 Nell was apparently appointed to the position of lady of the privy chamber. There is no indication that she ever performed her duties as such and the position was probably purely honorary. Nell may also have aspired to a title, if rumours in 1673 and in 1675 are to be believed. She certainly wanted a title for her elder son, and in 1676 it was reported that she was 'hartily greved' at her lack of success and 'she hath bine so very hie offin of lat uppon this pynt, that she hath beged his [the king's] love for to be gon, but he will by noe manes suffer that' (Thibaudeau, 3.173). Eventually Nell gained her point, and her son Charles was given the surname Beauclerk and created Baron Heddington and earl of Burford on 27 December 1676; his younger brother received the courtesy title Lord Beauclerk on 17 January 1677. Rose Gwyn also benefited from Nell's position: she and her first husband John Cassels were granted a pension of £100 a year in 1672, and this was increased to £200 a year after Rose was widowed in 1674.

Nell Gwyn provided an alternative for the king, one which he clearly found congenial, to the usual formalities of Whitehall. She appears to have positively enjoyed upsetting polite conventions: Sir Francis Fane heard that Nell, thinking that the duchess of Cleveland, a former mistress of the king, was a little cool towards her, 'clapt her on the shoulder, and saide she perceaved that persons of one trade loved not one another', while on another occasion, Mrs Kirk having called her a whore, Nell replied that 'had another done soe shee had not greeved soe much, but to bee called soe by an old notorious whore even before whoreinge was in fashion, that afflicted her' (Fane's commonplace book, fols. 169*v*, 180). Nell was clearly not accepted by all at court. On one occasion she complained to the king that Mary, dowager duchess of Richmond, had said she could 'not abide to converse with Nell and the rest of that gang' (ibid., fol. 179*v*). In contrast to other royal mistresses Nell could be directly attacked for her low birth: she was the mistress 'Who from the dunghill was raised', and her swearing, associated with her low origins, was also satirized (Wilson, *Court Satires*, 33, 98–100). Nell's main rival for the king's affections was his French mistress Louise de Kéroualle, duchess of Portsmouth. Nell clearly relished ridiculing Portsmouth's pretensions, and was well aware of the latter's unpopularity. Once the king was said to have asked Nell what to do to appease parliament, whereupon she answered 'hang up … the French bitch' (Fane's commonplace book, fol. 182*v*). A report reached France that when Portsmouth appeared at court in mourning on the death of the chevalier de Rohan, Nell wore mourning for the cham of Tartary and declared that she was as closely related to him as Portsmouth was to de Rohan. In July 1676 Nell joked that she would have to arm herself against Portsmouth's displeasure at Charles's frequent visits, and in January 1677 she publicly asked the French ambassador for a present from Louis XIV, saying she served Charles better than Portsmouth, and that he slept with her more often. Nell's own position was briefly threatened in June 1678, when Elizabeth, Lady Harvey, wife of Sir Daniel Harvey and sister of the courtier Ralph Montagu, and like the latter an inveterate intriguer, attempted to interest the king in Jenny Middleton, daughter of the court beauty Jane Middleton. Henry Savile wrote of Nell, 'this poor creature is betrayed by her ladyship … [as she] might easily perceive if shee were not too giddy to mistrust a false friend' (*Bath MSS*, 2.132–3). On 20 July 1679 Nell's mother died and was buried in St Martin-in-the-Fields.

**'The protestant whore'** In the late 1670s Nell Gwyn's friendship with men such as the duke of Buckingham and the king's son the duke of Monmouth associated her with the opposition to the lord treasurer, the earl of Danby, and then the duke of York during the crisis over the succession. In 1677, when Buckingham was in the Tower for demanding the dissolution of parliament, Nell was an intermediary for him with the king, and Buckingham was soon released. Later that year entertainments were put on at Nell's house, where Danby's wife was caricatured (perhaps acted by Nell), and Danby himself ridiculed. On 28 September 1678 Danby gave instructions to his wife to make clear his disappointment:

> remember to send to see my Lord Burford without any message to Nelly, and when Mrs. Turner is with you, bid her tell Nelly you wonder she should be your Lord's enemy that has always been so kind to her, but you wonder much more to find her supporting only thouse who are known to be the King's enemies, for in that you are sure she does very ill. (*Buckinghamshire MSS*, 387)

But Nell continued to support her allies: in 1678 Buckingham had permission to lodge with her, and in 1679 she attempted, but failed, to reconcile Monmouth with the king. Whether or not Nell herself ever aspired to promote the 'protestant cause' and the exclusion of the duke of York from the throne, her political associations, in conjunction with her English birth and protestantism, meant that Nell was usually compared favourably with the duchess of Portsmouth in opposition satire, such as that of 1682, *A Dialogue between the Duchess of Portsmouth and Madam Gwin at Parting*, which celebrates both Nell's Britishness

> In my clear veins best British bloud does flow
> Whilst thou like a French tode-stool first did grow

and her relative low cost:

> I neither run in court or city's score,
> I pay my debts, distribute to the poor.

The well-known anecdote of Nell's coach being surrounded by an angry mob who thought she was the duchess of Portsmouth until she put her head out of the window and reassured them with the words, 'Pray good people be silent, I am the Protestant whore', is usually dated to March 1681, when Nell was in Oxford with the court for the short-lived Oxford parliament (Wilson, *Nell Gwyn*, 197). While the story has not been confirmed from any contemporary source, it is from about this date that the epithet 'the protestant whore' is applied to her in contemporary satire. In the 1680s Nell's status as a royal mistress was assured and strengthened by the further elevation of her elder son, who became the duke of St Albans on 10 January 1684. An account of 1688 claimed that but for the king's death Nell herself would soon have been made countess of Greenwich. Nell's letter of 14 April 1684, addressed to Madam Jennings, includes a characteristic reminder to Lady Williams concerning some material Nell wished to buy: 'pray tell my Lady Williams that the King's mistresses are accounted ill paymasters, but she shall have her money the next day after I have the stuff' (Wilson, *Nell Gwyn*, 241). The few letters by Nell in existence, though signed by herself E. G., were all written by others and undoubtedly she could barely write.

After the death of Charles II on 6 February 1685 Nell Gwyn's creditors gained a judgment against her for some £730. However, James II not only ordered the payment of these creditors but continued to pay Nell's pension and in 1687 redeemed a mortgage on Bestwood Park, settling the estate on Nell and her son, lending some colour to Burnet's version of Charles II's deathbed request that his brother continue to support Nell, although whether after recommending his children to James, the king really did conclude with, 'Let not poor Nelly starve', as Burnet heard tell, remains unknown (*Bishop Burnet's History*, 2.473). Nell died at Pall Mall on 14 November 1687, and was buried on 17 November in the church of St Martin-in-the-Fields. Her will was proved on 7 December following, her principal heir being her son the duke of St Albans, his brother James having died in France in 1680. She also left £200 to her sister Rose, now married to one Guy Forster, and £100 to William Cholmley, named as a 'kinsman' in her will, probably the same Cholmley who in October 1678 gained a commission as an ensign in the 1st foot guards and by 1684 had the rank of lieutenant. Confirming her reputation for charity to those in debt, Nell left £100 for debtors in the parish of St Martin, and £20 a year for releasing debtors from prison every Christmas day. She gave £50 to poor Catholics 'for showing my charity to those who differ from me in Religeon' (PRO, PROB 11/389, fol. 246*v*). In July 1688 sentence was passed in favour of a codicil to the will which gave a further £200 to Nell's sister.

Nell Gwyn stands at the head of what was to be a long tradition of liaisons between royalty and actresses. Her humble origins attracted scorn during her lifetime but paradoxically also provided the basis for her popular reputation: her unconventional approach to the court and high-spirited good humour, in conjunction with a reputation for generosity and the contrast she offered to the duchess of Portsmouth, assured her of lasting fame. In Bishop Burnet's opinion Nell was the 'indiscreetest and wildest creature that ever was in court' (*Bishop Burnet's History*, 1.485), while Mme d'Aulnoy (whose anecdotes concerning the English court may have been largely invented but who nevertheless clearly had sources from inside that court) concluded she was one whom 'the King loved more for her wit than the attractions of her person … it was difficult to remain long in her company without sharing her gaiety' (d'Aulnoy, 289). S. M. WYNNE

**Sources** J. H. Wilson, *Nell Gwyn, royal mistress* (1952) • Highfill, Burnim & Langhans, *BDA*, vols. 6–7 • S. Wynne, 'The mistresses of Charles II and Restoration court politics, 1660–1685', PhD diss., U. Cam., 1997 • Pepys, *Diary*, vols. 6–10 • Sir Francis Fane's commonplace book, Shakespeare Birthplace Trust RO, Stratford upon Avon, ER 93/2 • M. C. La Mothe, *Memoirs of the court of England in 1675*, ed. G. D. Gilbert, trans. Mrs W. K. Arthur (1913) • G. de F. Lord and others, eds., *Poems on affairs of state: Augustan satirical verse, 1660–1714*, 7 vols. (1963–75), vols. 1–2 • P. Cunningham, *The story of Nell Gwyn and the sayings of Charles the second*, ed. G. Goodwin (1903) • GEC, *Peerage* • *The life and times of Anthony Wood*, ed. A. Clark, 5 vols., OHS, 19, 21, 26, 30, 40 (1891–1900) • N. Luttrell, *A brief historical relation of state affairs from September 1678 to April 1714*, 1 (1857) • Evelyn, *Diary*, vol. 3 • A. Thibaudeau, ed., *Catalogue of the collection of autograph letters and historical documents, formed between 1865 and 1882 by Alfred Morrison*, [1st ser.], 3 (1883) • *Bishop Burnet's History*, vols. 1–2 • T.C.D., 'The will of Nell Gwyn', *Genealogist's Magazine*, 7 (1935–7), 8–11 • *Letters from the marchioness de Sévigné to her daughter, the countess de Grignan*, 10 vols. (1763–8), vol. 4 • *A dialogue between the duchess of Portsmouth and Madam Gwin at parting* (1682) • *Calendar of the manuscripts of the marquis of Bath preserved at Longleat, Wiltshire*, 5 vols., HMC, 58 (1904–80), vol. 2 • *Seventh report*, HMC, 6 (1879) • *The manuscripts of the earl of Buckinghamshire, the earl of Lindsey … and James Round*, HMC, 38 (1895) • *CSP dom.*, 1663–4 • J. H. Wilson, *Court satires of the Restoration* (1976) • S. Pegge and J. Nichols, *Curialia, or, An historical account of some branches of the royal household*, 5 pts in 3 vols. (1782–1803), vol. 1 • J. N. Dalton, ed., *The manuscripts of St George's Chapel, Windsor Castle* (1957) • Bodl. Oxf., MS Ashmole 423, fol. 103 [Nell Gwyn's horoscope] • newsletter, 11 June 1670, BL, Add. MS 36916, fol. 183 • PRO, PROB 11/389, quire 169, fols. 246*r*–247*v* • BL, Harleian MS 6835, fol. 21 [monumental inscription of Helena Gwyn]

**Likenesses** H. Gascar, line print, *c*.1672–1673, BM, NPG • G. Valck, engraving, *c*.1673 (after P. Lely, *c*.1670), BM, NPG [*see illus.*] • R. Tompson, mezzotint, *c*.1673–1675 (after P. Lely), BM • studio of P. Lely, oils, *c*.1675, NPG • V. Green, mezzotint, pubd 1777 (after P. Lely), BM, NPG • R. Earldom, mezzotint, pubd 1810 (after S. Cooper), BM, NPG • A. de Blois, mezzotint (after P. Lely), BM, NPG • R. Tompson, mezzotint, BM • G. Valck, line print (after S. Cooper), BM

**Gwyn, Francis** (1648/9–1734), politician and government official, is said to have been born at Combe Florey, Somerset, the first son of Edward Gwyn (*d.* before 1667), landowner, and Eleanor, daughter of Sir Francis Popham of Houndstreet, Somerset. The Fraunceis family, to whom Gwyn was related through his mother, owned property at Combe Florey but his father's estate was at Llansanwyr in Glamorgan, where the family had been inconspicuously settled for more than a century before Gwyn's birth. He matriculated from Christ Church, Oxford, on 1 June 1666 aged seventeen, and entered the Middle Temple in 1667 but was never called to the bar.

Gwyn was the first of his family to enter parliament, sitting for Chippenham on the interest of the Pophams from 1673 to 1679. In the election of February 1679 he went down to his borough 'and there bestowed both his money and his time of them, yet he lost the election by thirteen' (*CSP dom.*, 1679–80, 90), and indeed he failed to secure election to any of the parliaments of 1679–81. After his defeat in 1679 Gwyn bought a privy council clerkship and in 1681 took office as under-secretary of state under his cousin Lord Conway; he left in 1683 at the same time as Conway and was appointed to the minor court post of groom of the bedchamber to the king (1683–5). According to one satire he would not regret being:

> turned out of employment.
> Since he finds time to ply women and wine,
> Which will prove a more lasting enjoyment.
> (HoP, *Commons, 1660–90*)

Always important in the west, however, Gwyn held a number of local offices there for most of his career. He was prothonotary and crown clerk for the Brecon circuit from 1677 to 1734; and a JP in Wales and later Devon from 1680 to 1685, and then from 1687 to 1734. He was also a freeman of Portsmouth, chamberlain for Brecon (1681–90), recorder of Totnes (1708–34), and mayor of Christchurch (1719–20).

Returned to parliament again in 1685 for Cardiff Boroughs, Gwyn found that his career prospered under James II. His connections with Ireland had begun with his appointment as one of the Irish revenue commissioners in 1676–81, and in 1685 he was appointed joint secretary to the Treasury with special responsibility for Irish finances by the new lord treasurer, the high tory Laurence Hyde, earl of Rochester. Rochester became one of Gwyn's most important patrons, to the extent that one contemporary later wrote of 'Frank Gwine, Lord Rotchester's Gwine as they call him' (*Wentworth Papers*, 163).

Gwyn did not oppose the revolution; indeed he acted as secretary to the lords who assumed the government after James fled in 1688. In 1689, however, he was a teller in the Convention Parliament for the motion to agree with the House of Lords that the throne was not vacant. During the Christmas recess in 1690, on 18 December, he married a first cousin once removed, Margaret (*d.* 1709), daughter and heir of Edmond *Prideaux, who owned the magnificent mansion of Forde Abbey in Dorset. Gwyn's London address was in Scotland Yard, Westminster, but he retreated every summer to Forde Abbey, eventually inheriting the property in 1702. Gwyn and his wife had four sons and three daughters, and Gwyn's earlier reputation for womanizing gave way to a self-proclaimed contentment with his family. 'You are the father of children', he wrote to the politician Robert Harley on the birth of a son in 1693:

> and can give grains of allowance to those who trouble their friends with news of this kind, but if one should write such a letter to Harry Boyl or such rake hells, they would wonder what the satisfaction a man could take in things of this sort. (*Portland MSS*, 3.543)

Gwyn's shrewdness and pragmatism enabled him to keep on terms with both the ostentatiously high tory Hydes and the uncertain, procrastinating Harley for some twenty-five years after 1690.

Returned for Christchurch on the Hyde interest in 1690, Gwyn sat almost continuously, for a variety of boroughs in the south-west, until 1727: Callington from 1695 to 1698; Totnes from 1699 to 1701; Christchurch again from 1701 to 1710; Totnes again from 1710 to 1715; Christchurch from 1717 to 1722; and finally Wells from 1722 to 1727. With his extensive connections in the west country, he was an active electioneer for the tory party, but it was symptomatic of his deferential character that he was never quite able to establish his own interest: while he may have aspired to taking Edward Seymour's place as head of the tory interest in the area, at the same time he appeared content to remain a client of the Hydes.

In 1696 Gwyn was chosen by parliament as a commissioner for examining the public accounts but was somewhat exasperated by such proceedings, writing to Harley:

> I have of late often admired the Wisdom of the Government of Amsterdam, who when they had built their Stat House ffor their Glory & conveniency and had expended in it more than was ffit ffor Prudent men to doe, burnt their Acc[oun]ts instead of examining taking & stating them. (BL, Portland loan 29/188, fol. 123)

Because of his refusal to sign the compulsory 1696 association pledging to defend the king, he was in fact excluded from attending the accounts commission. His absence deprived the commission of the necessary quorum for it to meet and, coming under enormous pressure (which no doubt partly explains his irritation), he did eventually sign. He opposed the attainder of the Jacobite conspirator Sir John Fenwick, remained suspicious of the war in Europe, and was happy to align himself with the landed interest, writing of himself as one of 'us poor landlords'. He also condemned extravagance, giving vent to his irritation at the antics in 1697 of Sir Edward Seymour, whose progress in the west reminded him of the tsar of Muscovy and was evidently costly enough 'to eat up a Country Gentleman and his Family' (letter of 21 July 1697).

Rochester's appointment as viceroy of Ireland in December 1700 signalled an appointment for Gwyn, who duly became Rochester's chief secretary and a privy councillor in Ireland. After Anne's accession in 1702, however, Gwyn followed his patron into opposition, losing his Irish offices when Rochester resigned in 1703. He continued to campaign for the tories, and his influence in the west country proved useful in 1702 when the whig Thomas Erle decided to stand as a candidate in Dorset, disrupting previous arrangements. Harmony was restored when Erle desisted, no doubt influenced by his reappointment as governor of Portsmouth which Gwyn had ensured. A grateful Erle acknowledged that 'you have acted sincerely and friendly of all sides' (Erle to Gwyn, 10 May 1702, Erle-Drax MSS). True to his principles, Gwyn voted in 1704 for the 'tack', a high tory manoeuvre to suppress occasional conformity. A rapprochement between Rochester and Harley, now earl of Oxford, led to Gwyn being appointed a commissioner of trade (1711–13) and then secretary at war (1713–14).

After the accession of George I Gwyn continued in the Commons, but his parliamentary activity greatly declined. Antiquarianism had long been a delight: in the 1690s he had been a leading patron of the Welsh scholar Edward Lhuyd, and he introduced his fellow MP and antiquary Narcissus Luttrell to Robert Harley. After 1715 this hobby increasingly claimed him. He died on 14 June 1734 at Forde Abbey and was buried in the chapel there. His antiquarian collections survived at Forde Abbey until their dispersal by sale in 1846. COLIN BROOKS

**Sources** *CSP dom.*, *1679–80*, 90; *1683–4*, 161 • B. D. Henning, 'Gwyn, Francis', HoP, *Commons, 1660–90* • B. D. Henning, 'Chippenham', HoP, *Commons, 1660–90*, 1.439–41 • *The manuscripts of his grace the duke of Portland*, 10 vols., HMC, 29 (1891–1931), vols. 1–4 • History of Parliament Trust, London, transcript, Churchill College, Cambridge, Erle-Drax MSS • BL, Althorp MSS, letters of Francis Gwyn and the earl of Nottingham, 27 Aug 1698 and 29 Aug 1698, Halifax papers, box 7 [transcript, History of Parliament Trust, London] • BL, Althorp MSS, letters of Francis Gwyn, 1 June 1697, 21 July 1697, and 9 Aug 1697, Halifax papers, box 4 • BL, letters of Francis Gwyn to Robert Harley, 12 May 1694, 19 Sept 1692, 4 May 1696, 4 Sept 1697, 9 Dec 1700, 9 July 1692, 17 July 1693, Portland loan 19/187; 29/186; 29/188, fols. 123, 193; 29/189, fol. 288; 29/313 • *The parliamentary diary of Sir Richard Cocks, 1698–1702*, ed. D. W. Hayton (1996) •

P. K. Monod, *Jacobitism and the English people, 1688–1788* (1989), 287 • P. Jenkins, 'Francis Gwyn and the birth of the tory party', *Welsh History Review / Cylchgrawn Hanes Cymru*, 11 (1982–3) • *The Wentworth papers, 1705–1739*, ed. J. J. Cartwright (1883) • *DNB* • G. S. Holmes, *British politics in the age of Anne* (1967) • 'Gwyn, Francis', HoP, *Commons, 1690–1715* [draft]
**Archives** Thomas Gilcrease Institute of American History and Art, Tulsa, Oklahoma, papers | BL, letters to second marquess of Halifax • Glamorgan RO, Cardiff, account book as protonotary for Monmouthshire • NL Ire., corresp. with duke of Ormond

**Gwyn, Owen** (*d.* 1633), college head, was the fourth of seven known sons of Gruffith Wynn (*d. c.*1613) of Berth-ddu in Creuddyn, near Llanrwst, Denbighshire, and Maenan, Caernarvonshire, and his wife, Gwen (*d.* in or before 1614), daughter and coheir of Robert Salesbury of Berth-ddu and Caemilwr. His father was a gentleman in the service of William Herbert, first earl of Pembroke. As a nephew of Dr John Gwynne, who endowed fellowships and scholarships there, in 1584 he was admitted as a pensioner to St John's College, Cambridge. He graduated BA in 1588, proceeded MA in 1591, and by 1595 was a fellow of the college. Following the death on 4 December that year of the master, William Whitaker, Gwyn was one of twelve fellows who complained to Lord Burleigh that the presbyterian-inclined Henry Alvey (whom Whitaker had promoted over the heads of others to be president) had packed the college with his supporters in order to secure the mastership for himself. Elizabeth I consequently intervened to nominate two candidates whom she found acceptable, and Richard Clayton, another member of the anti-Alvey faction, was elected.

Having proceeded BD in 1599, Gwyn was in 1600 presented to the rectory of Honington, Suffolk, by Robert Redmayne, former fellow of St John's and then chancellor of Norwich diocese. He was subsequently rector of East Ham, Essex (where the Breame family held the advowson), from 1605 to 1611 and of South Luffenham, Rutland (on the presentation of Thomas Cecil, earl of Exeter), from 1611 to 1633. However, Gwyn's life continued to centre on St John's, of which he served as bursar for four years, and his career was decisively influenced by the arrival at college in 1598 of his cousin John Williams. Bishop Richard Vaughan of Chester, a Caernarvonshire man, commended Gwyn to Williams as a countryman and 'no indiligent tutor' (Hacket, *Scrinia reserata*, 7). William's subsequent rise, first as fellow from 1603, then as a right-hand man of Master Clayton and protégé of Archbishop Richard Bancroft, together with his advocacy and negotiating skills, helped ensure that on Clayton's death in 1612 Gwyn was elected in his place. This was in the face of formidable opposition: although the senior fellows preferred the good-natured and sociable Gwyn, they were in a minority; Thomas Morton, dean of Winchester, 'admirable in piety, humility, and learning' (ibid., 22), was strongly supported.

In 1613 Prince Charles and the elector palatine visited the university, and, through Williams's influence, were entertained at St John's. Trumpets were sounded from its tower, verses written and presented, and a feast prepared. The rewards were portraits of King James and Queen Anne for the college, and an honorary DD for Gwyn. In 1615 the king himself visited. £500 was spent on entertaining him. Gwyn then set his eyes on the vice-chancellorship, and paid court to Bishop Samuel Harsnett of Chichester, the current holder of the office, so that he was made pro-vice-chancellor. When James I returned the same year, Gwyn, in his new position, organized the gathering of scholars to see him and made an oration greatly praising the king and his virtues. Later in 1615 he achieved his ambition; as vice-chancellor he was commended for honest accounting, although his attempt to achieve city status failed.

In June 1621 it was reported that the king, through the prince of Wales's influence, had bestowed on Gwyn the bishopric of St David's, and he responded with great enthusiasm, but did not hasten to thank the king and prince. However, the marquess of Buckingham had his eye on the post for William Laud, and Williams, fearing that otherwise he would lose his deanery of Westminster to Laud, abandoned his old protégé. At the end of the month Laud was nominated. In 1623 Gwyn was promised the bishopric of St Asaph, and then a deanery in default. Neither of these offers came to fruition. He achieved only the archdeaconry of Huntingdon and a prebend at Lincoln, both of which he held from 1622 until his death; a set of his visitation articles as archdeacon survives.

As master of St John's, Gwyn instituted a fund-raising campaign to build a new college library. This led to an anonymous donation ultimately traced to John Williams, by this time lord keeper and bishop of Lincoln, whose superscription adorns the end. The library was finished in 1624. Gwyn resisted efforts by Lucius Carey (later Viscount Falkland) and Bishop Richard Neile, both former St John's men, to under-endow scholarships and fellowships, but finally Williams induced him to compromise by promising extra money. Gwyn faced some difficulties of his own making in running the college. He allowed a good proportion of the property fines and leases to be granted to senior fellows. This led those who did not benefit to appeal first to the earl of Holland, as university chancellor, and then to the bishop of Ely for remedy. The dispute dragged on for years, and was settled only in 1630 after conciliatory efforts by Bishop John Buckeridge. Other difficulties were caused by requests from courtiers for grants of fellowships which were not vacant. Gwyn and the fellows resisted petitioners such as the marquess of Hamilton, only to find them backed by royal command. After James's death the college sent an exasperated letter to Hamilton complaining they had now suffered eight years' financial loss by being compelled to accept a supernumerary fellow, and objecting strongly to continuance of the practice. Charles I went so far as to dispense people for belonging to an ineligible diocese so that they could hold fellowships. In one case, in 1629, the college replied it had no precedent for waiving the conditions attached, but it still had to provide otherwise for the royal candidate. The college also suffered from having fellows seconded by the king to travel abroad on his business while, through a technicality, retaining their emoluments, as in Mr Mason's case. Such impositions cost an appreciable amount, and eroded both the function of the college as a seat of learning, and fellows' patience with the royal prerogative.

Gwyn never married. He died in 1633, probably at St John's, and was buried in the chapel on 5 June. Among the many beneficiaries of his will, dated 3 June, were his brother Edward Winne, who received £50, and his nephews William and Henry Bodarda, both fellows of St John's, who received all his books. The executor and residuary legate was his servant Griffith Gwin.

ELIZABETH ALLEN

**Sources** T. Baker, *History of the college of St John the Evangelist, Cambridge*, ed. J. E. B. Mayor, 1 (1869), 199–203, 210, 479, 481, 488, 491–3, 496, 498, 500–02 • Venn, *Alum. Cant.* • J. E. Griffith, *Pedigrees of Anglesey and Carnarvonshire families* (privately printed, Horncastle, 1914), 184 • *The letters of John Chamberlain*, ed. N. E. McClure, 2 (1939), 382, 392 • H. C. Porter, *Reformation and reaction in Tudor Cambridge* (1958), 187–9, 192–3, 201–4 • H. R. Trevor-Roper, *Archbishop Laud, 1573–1645*, 2nd edn (1962), 56–7 • [J. Ballinger], ed., *Calendar of Wynn (of Gwydir) papers, 1515–1690, in the National Library of Wales* (1926), 4, 8, 78, 102, 150 • B. Dew Roberts, *Mitre and musket* (1938), 14, 16–17, 19 • J. Hacket, *Scrinia reserata: a memorial offer'd to the great deservings of John Williams*, 2 pts (1693), pt.1, pp. 7, 22 • *Cambridgeshire*, Pevsner (1954), 148–9 • Peterborough institution book, Northants. RO, 4, fols. 28*v*, 102*v* • J. Venn and J. A. Venn, eds., *The book of matriculations and degrees … in the University of Cambridge from 1544 to 1659* (1913), 208 • will, CUL, department of manuscripts and university archives, vol. 3, fol. 203*r*–*v* • Norfolk RO, REG/14/20, fol. 286*v*; REG/16/22, fol. 9*r* • K. Fincham, ed., *Visitation articles and injunctions of the early Stuart church*, 2 (1998), 266

**Wealth at death** see will, Cambridge University Archives, wills, vol. 3, fols. 203*r*–203*v*

**Gwyn** [White], **Richard** [St Richard Gwyn] (*c.*1537–1584), martyr and Welsh-language poet, is said in two contemporary accounts of his martyrdom to have been born in Llanidloes, Montgomeryshire, with the surname Gwyn. Knowledge of his life is almost entirely derived from these two accounts—the Holywell MS and *Concertatio ecclesiae catholicae in Anglia* (2nd edn, 1588)—and from the records of his imprisonment and trial.

Richard Gwyn was aged twenty 'before he did frame his mind to like of good letters' (Holywell MS). He went to Oxford, briefly, and then to Cambridge, where, at St John's, he lived by the charity of the college, and chiefly of Dr Bullock, the master. At university he came to be known as White (the English for Gwyn). Dr Bullock refused to take the oath of supremacy in 1558 and went into exile. Gwyn returned to Wales, evidently about 1562, to Maelor, where he served as a schoolteacher for sixteen years, mainly in Overton and Wrexham. Referring to this period, the Holywell MS says that he was 'of the people generally loved for his diligence in teaching and other good partes known to be in him', and that 'he soe profited by his own private study of good literature, that it was wonder to them that knew him before to see in the man soe great ripeness from soe late a beginning', but 'in his latter time he gave his time wholly to the study of divinity'. He married 'a young girl' of Overton, called Catherine. At the time of his death three of their six children survived (one son, William, sought admission to Douai College in 1598).

About 1578, persecuted for his recusancy, Gwyn was forced to go into hiding. In 1580 he was captured. The last four years of his life were spent as a prisoner, though in the summer of 1584 he was at times allowed extraordinary liberties by an indulgent gaoler who later was obliged to be his executioner. His court appearances and his trial are well documented in the records of great sessions in Wales and in the two accounts of his martyrdom as, in the latter, are his torture and the wit he displayed in court. At the autumn sessions at Wrexham in 1584 he was found guilty of high treason by a jury *tales de circumstantibus*, and there on 15 October he was hanged, drawn, and quartered.

Richard Gwyn's poetry was the fruit of his religious conviction. A series of five *carolau* (poems in a simple, popular metre, meant to be sung) is his best-known work. The 'carols' survive in a dozen manuscripts, and there is evidence that a copy of a printed text (dated 1600, no doubt the product of an illicit press) survived until about 1720, though no copy is now known. Much of the exhortation in the five carols, and their plain language and strength of metaphor sounding a new note in Welsh poetry, might be paralleled two decades later in the similar poems of Gwyn's puritan counterpart, Rhys Prichard; but in each of the carols Catholic doctrine also emerges, sometimes forcibly. The carols probably date from Gwyn's last years: the third, which echoes Robert Parsons's *A Brief Discours*, cannot be earlier than 1580, while the last two date from his time of imprisonment. Also attributed to Gwyn in one of the two manuscripts in which it survives is a *cywydd* rejoicing in the murder of William the Silent in 1584; this attribution has been questioned. Richard Gwyn was beatified in 1929 and canonized in 1970, the 'protomartyr of Wales'.

DANIEL HUWS

**Sources** D. A. Thomas, *The Welsh Elizabethan Catholic martyrs* (1971) • T. H. Parry-Williams, ed., *Carolau Richard White* (1931) • Holywell MS, Heythrop College [printed in Thomas, *Catholic martyrs*] • great sessions records, NL Wales, 4/6/1–6, 21/62–66 • automated index to Welsh poetry in manuscript, NL Wales • M. Williams, *Cofrestr o'r holl lyfrau printiedig* (1717) [annotated copy with author's MS addns, Bodl. Oxf.] • 'The carols of Richard White', *Unpublished documents relating to the English martyrs*, ed. J. H. Pollen, 1, 90–99, Catholic RS, 5 (1908) • O. J. Murphy, *Blessed Richard Gwyn* (1955)

**Gwyn** [Wynne, Jones], **Robert** (*c.*1540–1604?), Roman Catholic priest and author, was a native of Llŷn, Caernarvonshire, in the diocese of Bangor, the son of Siôn Wyn ap Thomas Gruffudd of Penyberth, near Pwllheli, and Catrin, daughter of Siôn ap Robert ap Llywelyn of Castellmarch. He may have been educated at Friars' School, Bangor, and was admitted BA at Corpus Christi College, Oxford, on 9 July 1568. He later claimed to have been present at a sermon of John Jewel, the bishop of Salisbury, in London in 1559. His family conformed to the Elizabethan settlement, but he was persuaded by Robert Owen of Plas-du, Caernarvonshire, to enter the English College at Douai in 1571: Gwyn graduated BTh at the University of Douai on 23 December 1575 and was ordained a priest.

Having been tutored at Douai by Thomas Stapleton, Gwyn began his literary career there and wrote long letters to his friends and family entitled 'Nad oes vn Ffydd onyd y wir ffydd' ('There is no faith but the true one') and 'Gwssanaeth y gwŷr newydd' ('The service of the new men'); both survive in the National Library of Wales as MS 155248 entitled 'Lanter Gristnogawl' ('Christian lantern').

After returning to Wales in 1576 Gwyn laboured extensively in Llŷn, Maelor, the Usk valley, Glamorgan, and Monmouthshire. A document in the archives of the English College at Rome says that he 'tam scriptis quam laboribus maximum in afflictissimam patriam auxilium contulit' ('helped his afflicted native land as much through his writings as his actions'); on 18 July 1576 the college diaries note that many devout women in Wales were so inflamed by Gwyn's words that they put to flight the 'heresiarch and pseudo-bishop' Nicholas Robinson, who came to capture their missioner (*Diaries of the English College*, 288, 108). By an instrument dated 24 May 1578 Pope Gregory XIII granted Gwyn a licence to exercise certain episcopal powers, including that of consecrating portable altars.

Gwyn's concern for promulgating the faith did not stop with manuscripts or oral declamation. He attended a meeting of missioners at Uxbridge in October 1580—Edmund Campion and Robert Persons are also said to have been present—where arrangements were made to establish secret printing presses. One such press was set up in a coastal cave near Llandudno in 1586–7, and part of *Y drych Kristnogawl* was produced there. This work, the first Welsh language book to be printed in Wales and certainly the most valuable Welsh Catholic book of the sixteenth century, has been associated with the grammarian Gruffydd Robert, but stylistic characteristics suggest that it may have in fact been written by Gwyn. In 1586 Gwyn was said to have been given sanctuary at Werngochen, near Abergavenny. His life after 1591 appears to be unrecorded, but he is thought to have died in 1604.

Surviving manuscript works by Gwyn are 'Coelio'r saint' ('Believing the saints') and a Welsh translation of Francisco Toledo's *Summa casuum conscientiae*. Gwyn was also responsible for translating the 1596 Catholic work *A Manvall, or, Meditation*. He may have translated Robert Persons's *The First Book of the Christian Exercise* (1581), 'which translation', says Wood, 'was much used and valued, and so consequently did a great deal of good among the Welsh people' (Wood, *Ath. Oxon.*, 1.586); this translation does not survive, but a 1631 translation by John Davies of Mallwyd is said to have been based upon it. However, the attribution to Gwyn of a *cywydd* (short poem of rhyming concatenated couplets of fourteen syllables) written to celebrate the assassination of Prince William of Orange seems very doubtful. As the 'most prolific Welsh writer of the Elizabethan age' Gwyn was described in a 1604 manuscript copy of one of his treatises as 'one of the most cultured persons from Rome to St David's, Menevia' (Stephens, 299; Bowen, *Welsh Recusant Writings*, 29).

THOMPSON COOPER, *rev.* CERI SULLIVAN

**Sources** A. F. Allison and D. M. Rogers, eds., *The contemporary printed literature of the English Counter-Reformation between 1558 and 1640*, 1 (1989) • G. Anstruther, *The seminary priests*, 1 (1969), 140 • T. F. Knox and others, eds., *The first and second diaries of the English College, Douay* (1878), 5, 7, 24, 100, 108, 259, 273–4, 288 • T. M. Chotzen, 'Some sidelights on Cambro-Dutch relations (with special reference to Humphrey Llwyd and Abrahamus Ortelius)', *Transactions of the Honourable Society of Cymmrodorion* (1937), 101–44 • L. Hicks, ed., *Letters and memorials of Father Robert Persons*, Catholic RS, 39 (1942), xxxi • A. Possevino, *Apparatus sacer ad scriptores veteris et novi testamenti*, 2 (Cologne, 1608), 342 • *DWB* • Gillow, *Lit. biog. hist.*, 3.69–70 • W. Rowlands, *Cambrian bibliography / Llyfryddiaeth y Cymry*, ed. D. S. Evans (1869), 93–4 • Wood, *Ath. Oxon.*, new edn • D. A. Bellenger, ed., *English and Welsh priests, 1558–1800* (1984) • R. Gwyn, *Gwssanaeth y gwyr newydd Robet Gwyn (1580)*, ed. G. Bowen (1970) • G. Bowen, *Y drych Kristnogawl* (1996) • G. Bowen, 'Robert Gwyn o Benyberth, awdur Catholig', *Transactions of the Honourable Society of Cymmrodorion*, new ser., 2 (1996), 33–58 • G. Bowen, *Welsh recusant writings* (1999), 28–42 • R. G. Gruffydd, *Argraffwyr cyntaf Cymru* (1972) • M. Stephens, ed., *The new companion to the literature of Wales*, rev. edn (1998) • G. Williams, *Wales and the Reformation* (1997) • *Reg. Oxf.*, 1.271 • private information (2004) [G. Williams]

**Gwynllyw** [St Gwynllyw, Woolloos] (*fl.* **6th cent.**), king of Glywysing, became, after a religious conversion, patron saint and founder of St Woolloos, Newport. His *vita*, probably of the early twelfth century, has a triple function: first, it sets out a model of the good king; second, it is a story of a conversion from worldly power and riches to monastic asceticism, so written as to proclaim the saintly status both of St Gwynllyw and of his wife, St Gwladus; and, third, it is designed to enhance the reputation of St Woolloos. The structure of the life is similar to that of the *Vita prima* of St Gwenfrewi, namely a brief biography followed by miracles, all of which belong to the century before the time of writing, not to the saint's own lifetime. The hagiographer (anonymous) was a literary show-off especially fond of alliteration, but he had a difficult task to perform, namely to rescue St Gwynllyw and St Woolloos from the dangerous proximity, genealogical and topographical, of a more famous saint, Gwynllyw's son, St *Cadog, and in particular from Lifris's *Vita sancti Cadoci*. For Lifris, St Gwynllyw was 'very partial to thieves, and used to instigate them somewhat often to robberies' (Lifris, chap. 1); for the *Vita sancti Gundleii*, Gwynllyw (Gundleius in Latin) was a model king, notably in his willingness to give territories to each of his brothers. For Lifris, Gwynllyw obtained his wife, Gwladus, daughter of *Brychan, king of Brycheiniog, not by paternal consent but by seizure; for the *Vita sancti Gundleii*, on the other hand, Brychan was happy to give his consent. Both lives tell the story of Gwynllyw's death: Lifris's narrative includes a blessing and testament in which Gwynllyw gave rights of burial to Cadog's foundation of Llancarfan throughout the cantref of Gwynllŵg (named after Gwynllyw); the *Vita sancti Gundleii* makes no such admission. The likelihood is, therefore, that the life was written on behalf of the church of St Woolloos, which, unlike Llancarfan, lay within Gwynllŵg. Many details about Gwynllyw were already known from the life of St Cadog, which also mentions his son *Cynidr; Gwynllyw's hagiographer did not need a rich narrative but an effective correction to unwelcome tendencies in the older life.

Gwynllyw belonged to an era of eponymous kings: his father, Glywys, gave his name to Glywysing, the kingdom that preceded Glamorgan; he himself gave his name to one of 'the seven cantrefs of Glywysing', Gwynllŵg, between the Taf and the Usk. His mother, Gwawl, was the daughter of Ceredig ap Cunedda, eponymous king of Ceredigion. Brycheiniog, to the north, was named after his father-in-law, Brychan. The idiom in which his life was cast was not just onomastic, it was also patriarchal, in the sense that it was modelled after the story of Jacob and his sons in the book of Genesis. It may also have served as an answer to a similar story, with the same model, the account of how Cunedda came from the north with his sons and conquered most of Wales. The furthest extent of their claims brought them to the Gower peninsula and to Kidwelly, on the very borders of Glamorgan. The story by which Glywys became a patriarch for the south-east, parallel to Cunedda for most of Wales, confirmed the right of Glamorgan to remain independent of the heirs of Cunedda. There was also, however, a problem internal to Glamorgan: the account of the political divisions of the region in Lifris's life of Cadog is in terms of Glywysing, with its ten subdivisions; for the life of Gwynllyw the issue is the division of Glamorgan, with seven regions or cantrefs. Lifris's account is archaic, in that it is constructed in terms of a long-extinct Glywysing, and centrifugal, in that it gives no priority to any of the sons of Glywys: Glywysing is simply divided and hence acquires its regions. The life of Gwynllyw was careful to change this: not only is it more up to date but it asserts that Gwynllyw succeeded his father as king of all Glywysing, even though he allowed his brothers to rule their cantrefs under his authority. A similar sensitivity to political needs may be apparent in the miracle collection: the fertility of Glamorgan offered a tempting target for powerful kings, whether of Gwynedd or of England, as well as for Scandinavian raiders. What was vital was to defend St Woolloos.

T. M. CHARLES-EDWARDS

**Sources** 'Vita sancti Gundleii', *Vitae sanctorum Britanniae et genealogiae*, ed. A. W. Wade-Evans (1944), 172–93 • Lifris, 'Vita sancti Cadoci', *Vitae sanctorum Britanniae et genealogiae*, ed. and trans. A. M. Wade-Evans (1944), 24–141 • P. C. Bartrum, ed., *Early Welsh genealogical tracts* (1966) • 'Vie de Saint Cadoc par Caradoc de Llancarfan', ed. P. Grosjean, *Analecta Bollandiana*, 60 (1942), 35–67, esp. 45–67 • P. C. Bartrum, *A Welsh classical dictionary: people in history and legend up to about AD 1000* (1993), 355–6 • S. Baring-Gould and J. Fisher, *The lives of the British saints*, 4 vols., Honourable Society of Cymmrodorion, Cymmrodorion Record Series (1907–13) • C. N. L. Brooke, *The church and the Welsh border in the central middle ages* (1986) • E. R. Henken, *Traditions of the Welsh saints* (1987) • E. R. Henken, *The Welsh saints: a study in patterned lives* (1991) • M. Richards, *Welsh administrative and territorial units* (1969)

**Gwynn** [Gwyn, Gwynne], **John** (*bap.* **1713**, *d.* **1786**), architect, was born in Shrewsbury, probably at Coleham, the eldest of the five children of John Gwynn (1667?–1735) and his wife, Elizabeth (*d.* 1758). He was baptized at St Julian's Church, Shrewsbury, on 12 November 1713. He retained links with Shrewsbury throughout his life and when his friend Samuel Johnson visited the town in 1774, he asked Gwynn to show him around. Nothing is known about his early life or education, but 'the Revd Hugh Owen of Shrewsbury claimed that Gwynn left Shrewsbury early in life' (Chambers, 504). According to Joseph Farington, Gwynn 'was originally a Carpenter, and by industrious study acquired knowledge sufficient to become an Architect' (*Farington Diary*, ed. Greig, 180). The architect Robert Mylne scathingly referred to him as 'late of another profession' (Publicus, 22), implying a lack of an architectural education. There is no information about where Gwynn learned his profession and despite consistent affirmation of Gwynn's abilities as an architect he carried out comparatively little work and is better-known for his publications.

Details of Gwynn's early life in London are sparse before he published, in 1749, *An Essay on Design*, which included 'Proposals for erecting a public academy'. This was a subject which Gwynn pursued with vigour to counteract what he considered undue French influence on art. The essay was written partly in response to Abbé Bernard Le Blanc's contemporaneous account of the arts in England in his *Letters on the French and English Nations*, published in 1747. Gwynn believed that 'Art has been in small Estimation unless the Artist was foreign. Our Neighbours have spoken contemptuously of us without reserve' (J. Gwynn, *An Essay on Design*, 1749). He was connected with the St Martin's Lane Academy, which included the artists William Hogarth and Samuel Wale and the architects Isaac Ware and James Paine. In 1755 Gwynn was a member of the committee formed to found a 'Royal Academy of London for the improvement of painting, sculpture and architecture'. He exhibited at the Society of Artists from 1760 until 1767, showing eight architectural drawings including designs for Blackfriars Bridge in 1760 and 1762; he was a director of the Incorporated Society of Artists. As a founder member of the Royal Academy Gwynn exhibited there annually for four years from 1769, when he showed *A Design for the Alteration of an Old Room in Shropshire*.

Gwynn lived at Little Court, Castle Street, Leicester Fields, near St Martin's Lane, where 'Mr Payne [James Paine] built 2 small houses at the end of his garden purposely to accommodate Gwynn and Wale' (Smith, 209). In 1755–8 Gwynn and Wale published measured drawings of St Paul's Cathedral. Farington remarked that his 'industry … and his accuracy in making the Section and taking the measurements … [were] extraordinary & his perseverance equal both' (*Farington Diary*, ed. Greig, 180). When the measurements were nearly completed, 'He had … his pocket picked of the Book which contained them, which He never recovered & had to do the work again' (ibid.). He fell while measuring 'the top of the dome for a section of the Cathedral', but fortunately a 'small projecting piece of lead' broke his fall (Hornor, 21).

Gwynn's *Thoughts on the Coronation of his Present Majesty King George the Third* was published in 1761; in it he advocated a longer route for the coronation procession so that more people might see it in more comfort and safety. He added sagely that the cost of improving the route was 'money spent at home' (p. 8). In a later publication, *London and Westminster Improved* (1776), Gwynn included a 'Discourse on public magnificence', believing that public works would give employment to artists and craftsmen and help to bring wealth to the country. This far-sighted work has been considered 'one of the most remarkable books ever written about the planning and architecture of London' (Summerson, 121) and many of Gwynn's proposals were subsequently executed; it is for this work that Gwynn is best remembered. Dr Johnson, who proved a 'steady friend' and 'wrote several powerful letters concerning his talent and integrity' (Smith, 209), provided a preface for the book.

Gwynn's most prominent architectural works were his bridges. His interest in bridge building dated from 1759, when, with the engineer John Smeaton, he entered the competition for the proposed Blackfriars Bridge. His design was short-listed but Robert Mylne's was chosen, although not without disputes about semicircular and elliptical arches, the former of which were favoured by Gwynn. Dr Johnson was prevailed upon to write in favour of semicircular arches in the *Daily Gazetteer* on 8 and 18 December 1759. In 1762 Gwynn was consulted about the building of the Shrewsbury foundling hospital and his professional connections with the town continued, when, on 18 September 1767, he submitted two designs for the English Bridge (rebuilt 1925–7), formerly the Stone Bridge, over the River Severn at Shrewsbury, one with seven semicircular arches and another with seven elliptical arches. The semicircular design was approved, preparatory work started the following spring, and the first stone was laid in 1769, with an inscription including the words 'Mr. John Gwynn, a native of this Town, being the Architect' (Smith, 209). Shortly afterwards the first stone of Gwynn's fine Atcham Bridge over the River Severn was laid in July 1769. Two other important bridge-building commissions followed; Worcester Bridge in 1771–80 (widened in 1932), followed by Magdalen Bridge at Oxford (1772–90), a job which did not go smoothly. Dr Johnson in 1777 referred to Gwynn's problems over an 'ill-finished job', which may have been Magdalen Bridge. In 1773–4 he designed the Oxford covered market (reconstructed 1839), 'one of the finest modern ones in the country' (Chambers, 504), and the Oxford workhouse (1772–5). Reward came late to Gwynn. In May 1771 the appointment of surveyor to the commissioners of the Oxford Paving Act brought a salary of £150 a year 'for three years certain and for one year more if necessary'. This must have been appreciated as 'Gwynn gets, little: but Wale being employed by Booksellers obtained sufficient for a frugal maintenance for them both' (*Farington Diary*, ed. Greig, 180). When the bridges at Shrewsbury and Oxford were completed Gwynn moved to Worcester. For many of these jobs his assistant and pupil was William Hayward, also from Shrewsbury, who himself became an architect. Other recorded works by Gwynn are a reredos for Bledlow church in Buckinghamshire, designed to accompany Wale's altarpiece, Park Farmhouse at Pitchford, Shropshire, and a house in or near Piccadilly for a person named Deards (*Farington Diary*, ed. Greig, 180).

The only known portrait of Gwynn, now in Shrewsbury Museum, is unfinished and attributed to Johan Zoffany; it captures Gwynn's alert and intelligent character which is borne out by contemporary accounts. James Boswell said that 'Gwynn was a fine lively rattling fellow. Dr. Johnson kept him in subjection but with a kindly authority', although occasionally Gwynn managed to get the better of the conversation (Boswell, 6.69). The Revd Hugh Owen of Shrewsbury confirmed that Johnson 'was fond of Gwynn's lively humour, and odd and sometimes keen sallies'. He remembered Gwynn as 'lively, quick, sarcastic, of quaint appearance and of manner' and described him as one who 'was never largely employed as an architect, though he possessed unquestionable talents and considerable taste … he was poor, but high-spirited, and of unimpeachable integrity' (Chambers, 504). William Shenstone described Gwynn in 1757 as 'very well-bred & ingenious', saying he was most 'agreeable' and that Shenstone 'wish'd for more of his company' (*Letters of William Shenstone*, 465). In December 1783 Gwynn was given the freedom of the city of Worcester, where he died on 27 February 1786. He was buried in the churchyard of St Oswald's Hospital, as directed in his will, in which he left the rents of property in Abbey Foregate, Shrewsbury, to his brother Richard. He left the plates for *London and Westminster Improved* to Charles, his natural son with Ann Sansenil, and left money for the boy's maintenance and education until he was old enough to be apprenticed to a painter, sculptor, or engraver. As a precaution against Charles's early death Gwynn directed that the money go to the Royal Society and the Royal Academy for prizes for an essay promoting 'the happiness of mankind' (will) and other worthy aims; this proved a wise step as Charles died in 1796, aged eighteen, but both societies seem to have turned down the bequest. Boswell confirms that Gwynn was considered 'an architect of considerable celebrity' and Gwynn's obituary in the *Shrewsbury Chronicle* (11 March 1786) compared his 'vast and comprehensive mind in his profession' to that of Sir Christopher Wren. A number of his plans are in the British Library, London.

JULIA IONIDES

**Sources** J. T. Smith, *Nollekens and his times*, 2 (1828) · J. Boswell, *The life of Samuel Johnson*, ed. J. W. Croker, rev. J. Wright, [another edn], 3, 5–6 (1835); repr. (1859) · *The Farington diary*, ed. J. Greig, 1 (1922) · J. L. Hobbs, 'The parentage and ancestry of John Gwyn, the architect', *N&Q*, 207 (1962), 22–4 · *The letters of Samuel Johnson*, ed. R. W. Chapman, 2 (1952); repr. (1984) · J. Chambers, *Biographical illustrations of Worcestershire* (1820) · Colvin, *Archs.* · E. Harris and N. Savage, *British architectural books and writers, 1556–1785* (1990) · T. Hornor, *View of London and surrounding countryside* (1823) · Publicus [R. Mylne], *Observations on bridge building* (1760) [letter to the gentlemen of the committee appointed by the common council of the City of London] · *The letters of William Shenstone*, ed. M. Williams (1939) · D. Whitehead, 'John Gwynn, R.A. and the building of Worcester Bridge, 1769–86', *Transactions of the Worcestershire Archaeological Society*, 3rd ser., 8 (1982), 31–45 · W. Papworth, *The builder* (1864) · *DNB* · *The exhibition of the Royal Academy* (1769–72) [exhibition catalogues] · J. Summerson, *Georgian London* (1945) · W. M. Jaine, 'The building of Magdalen Bridge, 1772–1790', *Oxoniensia*, 36 (1971), 59–71 · M. Graham, 'The building of Oxford covered market', *Oxoniensia*, 44 (1979), 81–91 · C. O. Skilbeck, 'Some notes on Bledlow parish church', *Records of Buckinghamshire*, 12 (1927–33),

142–7 • J. Pye, *Patronage of British art: an historical sketch* (1845) • *Letters of Richard Radcliffe and John James of Queen's College, Oxford, 1755–83*, ed. M. Evans, OHS (1888) • will, PRO, PROB 11/1141, 220
**Archives** LMA, Foundling Hospital MSS, A/FH/DO2
**Likenesses** attrib. J. Zoffany, oils, *c.*1775 (unfinished), Shrewsbury Museum Service • J. Zoffany, group portrait, oils (*Royal academicians, 1772*), Royal Collection • etching, BM • oils, NPG

**Gwynn, John** (1827–1917), biblical scholar and Church of Ireland dean of Derry, the eldest son of the Revd Stephen Gwynn (*d.* 1873), rector of Agherton, Portstewart, co. Londonderry, and his wife, Mary Stevenson, was born at Larne, co. Antrim, on 28 August 1827. He was educated at the Portora Royal School, Enniskillen, co. Fermanagh, and Trinity College, Dublin, which he entered in 1845. He became a scholar there in 1848 and a fellow in 1853. He was warden of St Columba's College, near Dublin, from 1856 to 1864. In 1860 he was admitted to Oxford University *ad eundem* as a doctor of civil law.

For the next eighteen years Gwynn was a clergyman at Ramelton, co. Donegal, having been presented to the benefice of Tullyaughnish by Trinity College, Dublin. He became successively dean of Raphoe, co. Donegal (1873), and rector of Templemore and dean of Derry (1882). He was an excellent classical scholar and in 1883 he returned to Trinity College, Dublin, as Archbishop King's lecturer in divinity, and in 1888 succeeded Dr George Salmon as regius professor, a post which he held until his death. He served the Church of Ireland in the north of Ireland during the difficult period of the disestablishment, and he came to notice in the early days of the general synod as a moderate high-churchman. Academic life provided the true sphere of his activities, and his association with the divinity school of Trinity College, Dublin, for thirty-four years was much to its advantage. He married in 1862 Lucy Josephine (*d.* 3 April 1907), the elder daughter of William Smith *O'Brien, the Irish nationalist, and they had six sons and two daughters. Soon after his marriage he resigned his Trinity College, Dublin, fellowship, having been presented to a college living.

Gwynn claimed that, when aged about fifty, he set himself to the study of Syriac to relieve the tedium of long railway journeys from Donegal to Dublin; and he steadily became a master of the language. Within about ten years he had contributed nearly forty articles to the *Dictionary of Christian Biography*, chiefly concerned with the early Greek and Syriac translators of the Bible; and in 1888 he wrote an erudite essay on the Peshitta version for the *Church Quarterly Review*. An important paper, 'Hippolytus and his heads against Caius', in which these two persons were distinguished from each other, appeared in *Hermathena* (1888); and an article on his discovery that the Syriac *Pericope de adultera* belongs to the Harkleian version was published in the *Transactions* of the Royal Irish Academy (1888). These preliminary studies were crowned by the publication in 1897 of a new Syriac text of the Apocalypse, accompanied by an introductory dissertation and very full and careful notes. Gwynn's researches also included *Remnants of the Later Syriac Versions of the Bible* (1909). He published all that now remains of the sixth-century Philoxenian version, and increased the knowledge of its successor, the Harkleian.

Gwynn's *magnum opus* was his superb edition of the Book of Armagh, an Irish manuscript of the ninth century, containing the whole New Testament in Latin, the life of St Martin of Tours, and some Patrician pieces, in Latin and Irish, of high importance for the history of early Christianity in Ireland. The text had been in the hands of Bishop Reeves who had died too soon to publish it and the task was entrusted to Gwynn by the council of the Royal Irish Academy. Gwynn was permitted to have a deputy for his divinity lectures in order to carry out this important work. He worked on the text for more than twenty years, and when it appeared in 1913 it was at once recognized as a masterly achievement. His infinite patience, his meticulous accuracy, and his sound judgement were notably illustrated by this fine book, which was welcomed by scholars all over Europe. He was elected a member of the Royal Irish Academy in January 1887 and continued his association with it until his death. In the pages of its *Transactions* he published two distinguished articles. He also contributed regularly to *Hermathena* and *Kottabos*, writing over thirteen articles for these publications alone.

Gwynn died at his home, Ashbrook, Howth Road, Clontarf, Dublin, on 2 April 1917. His distinguished career at Trinity College, Dublin, was followed by that of his children: three sons became fellows and one of his daughters became registrar of women students. A man of strong influence, he was reported to be unfailingly courteous and kind. J. H. BERNARD, *rev.* AIDEEN M. IRELAND

**Sources** Burtchaell & Sadleir, *Alum. Dubl.* • Foster, *Alum. Oxon.* • *WWW*, 1929–40 • *Annual Register* (1917) • *The Times* (4 April 1917) • *Irish Times* (4 April 1917) • minute book, 16 March 1918, Royal Irish Acad., 13–16 • Burke, *Peerage* (1909) • J. B. Leslie, *Derry clergy and parishes* (1937), 42–3 • personal knowledge (1927) • d. cert.
**Archives** NL Ire., corresp. with William Smith O'Brien, MS 8656 • Representative Church Body Library, Dublin, corresp., MSS 38, 64, 248, 536, 284 • TCD, notebooks and papers, mostly Syriac, MSS 3796–3803a | PRO NIre., letters to J. Irvine Peacocke, Mic 87
**Likenesses** S. Purser, oils, TCD
**Wealth at death** £2240 13*s.* 0*d.*: probate, 1917, *CGPLA Ire.* • £275: probate, 1917, *CGPLA Eng. & Wales*

**Gwynn, (John) Peter Lucius** (1916–1999), administrator in India and linguist, was born on 22 June 1916 at 37 Hyde Park Mansions, Marylebone, London, the eldest child and only son of John Tudor Gwynn (1881–1956), a member of the Indian Civil Service, and his wife, (Joan) Katharine, youngest daughter of John Dando *Sedding, architect of the magnificent Holy Trinity Church, Sloane Street, London. Gwynn's great-great-grandfather Sir Edward O'Brien, fourth baronet, was a direct descendant of Brian Boru and the O'Brien kings of Munster; his great-grandfather William O'Brien, MP for co. Limerick, was deported to Tasmania for leading the Young Irish insurrection in 1848; his great-great-aunt Harriet Monsell, founder of one of the first Anglican communities of women, the Community of St John Baptist, was later canonized; his paternal grandfather, the Revd John Gwynn, was senior regius professor of divinity at Trinity College, Dublin; and the writer Stephen Lucius Gwynn was his uncle. Gwynn's father retired from the Indian Civil Service in 1922 and went to live with his family in Oxford. Gwynn was educated at the Dragon School, Oxford, and St Columba's, Rathfarnham, where he was senior prefect and won several prizes, including those for mathematics and English. He was remembered at school for his impeccable manners, his intellectual powers, and his speed as a runner. He was also good at rugby and cricket. He won a junior exhibition to Trinity College, Dublin, in 1934, to read classics, thus following in a long line of Gwynn family scholars there. He graduated with first-class honours in 1937 and won a gold medal. He then chose an Indian Civil Service career, following in his father's footsteps, and for his probationary year he was at University College, Oxford, where his interest in Sanskrit earned him an honorary scholarship.

Gwynn began his career in the Indian Civil Service in November 1939 in Madras, as collector, an administrative officer with powers to collect revenue and act as a magistrate. He chose to stay in the service when India gained its independence in 1947; he said that his Irish background ensured that he grew up with a strong feeling of sympathy for the Indian nationalist cause. His decision to stay on was prompted also by his desire to learn a new language. In 1950 he was posted as district collector of West Godavari at Ellore in the Northern Circars, one of twenty-seven districts in the old Madras presidency, where Telugu was the mother tongue of the people. After being transferred briefly to Srikakulam and then to Visakhapatnam, Gwynn moved to Hyderabad as commissioner of the road transportation corporation of Andhra Pradesh. Within a few months he was appointed education secretary to the government of Andhra Pradesh; he spoke of this post as the most gratifying assignment of his career. As education secretary his achievements were diverse and enduring. He was able to transform the Salarjung Museum from a jumble of rare and curious objects into a clearly organized modern museum. He chaired the committee which set up the Telugu Academy, and drew up the proposal to introduce Telugu as the language of administration, higher education, and legislation. He succeeded in framing and pushing through the Andhra Pradesh Compulsory Primary Education Act making education compulsory for children from the age of five to the age of eleven, a provision which included for the first time the tribal areas, which had been neglected for centuries. As a result of this liberal enactment, there were soon scores of graduates employed as teachers and civil servants whose families had never in the entire course of history had the chance of an education.

Gwynn studied Telugu not as part of his official responsibility but out of a deep fascination with the language. He was loved and respected by his colleagues, his superiors, and the people of Andhra Pradesh for his upright character, his subtle sense of humour, and his humane and unassuming nature. He was an educational pioneer, and his plans and specifications for the future of learning at all ages in Andhra Pradesh were many years later still in use. On 27 June 1959 he married, in Calcutta, Patricia Margaret (Peggy), daughter of Andrew Emmanuel Satur, administrator of a tea and coffee estate in the Nilgiris, of an Armenian family that had for centuries prospered in the commercial heart of Madras. They had two sons, John and Robin. Gwynn retired as second member of the board of revenue in 1967; he had the distinction of being the very last British officer to retire from the Indian Civil Service. He returned to England and went to live in Bromley, Kent, serving in the Treasury until 1976.

Though Gwynn was not unfamiliar with the other south Indian languages when posted to West Godavari in 1950, he was at once enchanted by the mellifluous sound of spoken Telugu, which has been described as the Italian of the East. He made the decision then to live in that part of the country for the remainder of his time in the service. A separate state was created for the Telugu-speaking Andhra people in 1953, and in 1956 it became Andhra Pradesh, with Hyderabad as its capital and a present-day population of 80 million. After Hindi, Telugu is the most widely spoken language in the subcontinent. J. B. S. Haldane had argued that it should become the official language of all India because of its precision of grammar and the ease with which it could be learned.

Gwynn determined to master this language, and described it as 'extremely versatile and flexible' (Gwynn, introduction to *A Telugu–English Dictionary*, 1991, xvii), akin to classical Greek in its power to express shades of meaning by using particles and obtaining subtle degrees of emphasis by varying the word order of a sentence. He worked for many years, in collaboration with Professor Bhadriraju Krishnamurti, on the book that eventually became *A Grammar of Modern Telugu* (1985). Gwynn made himself familiar with the whole range of Telugu literature and in the mid-1960s began compiling a vast Telugu word list. He found the existing dictionaries of the language wholly inadequate and devoted twenty-five years to producing his *magnum opus*, *A Telugu–English Dictionary* (1991). This monumental work, written with the assistance of J. Venkateswara Sastry, was designed to present a 'true image of the living language' (ibid.). It contained 28,000 entries and admitted a great many words which had come into use only in the previous hundred years. It covered the technical vocabulary of science, technology, and agriculture, the language of politics and journalism, and the most informal colloquial terms. Gwynn advocated modern reforms of spelling and transliteration, which he incorporated in the dictionary with great practical care. This work of patient unpaid labour and brilliant understanding was the crowning achievement of his life.

Gwynn died of cancer of the pancreas at Bromley Hospital, Bromley, Kent, on 14 September 1999. His funeral took place at St Mary's parish church, Shortlands, Bromley, on 23 September, following which he was cremated at Beckenham, Kent. His ashes were laid to rest, marked with a memorial slab, in the grave of his maternal grandparents in St John the Baptist churchyard, West Wickham, Kent. He was survived by his wife, Peggy, and their two sons. On 14 May 2000 a well-attended memorial service, which brought together colleagues, friends, and relatives from abroad, was held in his grandfather's Holy Trinity Church, London. GUTALA KRISHNAMURTI

**Sources** *The Independent* (17 Nov 1999) • *Irish Times* (30 Nov 1999) • *Andhra Bhoomi* (4 Oct 1999) [Hyderabad] • *Andhra Bhoomi* (11 Oct 1999) [Hyderabad] • *The Hindu* (20 Sept 1999) [Madras] • *Indian Express* (19 Nov 1999) • *Old Columban Society Bulletin*, 55 (May 2000) • *Indo-British Review: A Journal of History*, 23/1 (1981) • personal knowledge (2004) • private information (2004) • b. cert. • d. cert.

**Likenesses** F. Gwynn, crayon drawing, priv. coll. • F. Gwynn, watercolour drawing, priv. coll. • photograph, repro. in *The Independent* • photographs, priv. coll.

**Gwynn, Stephen Lucius** (1864–1950), author and politician, was born on 13 February 1864 at St Columba's College in Rathfarnham, near Dublin, where his father was warden. He was the eldest of the eight children (six sons and two daughters) of John *Gwynn (1827–1917), biblical scholar and Church of Ireland clergyman, and his wife, Lucy Josephine (1840–1907), daughter of the Irish nationalist William Smith *O'Brien. Shortly after Stephen's birth the family moved to Ramelton, co. Donegal, to which parish John Gwynn had been appointed parson; he later became dean of Raphoe (1873) and dean of Derry (1883), before returning to Trinity College, Dublin, where he became regius professor of divinity. Stephen Gwynn's early childhood in Donegal was to shape his later view of rural Ireland. As he wrote in his autobiography: 'My life has been spent largely in an effort to understand Ireland, and that corner of Donegal has been the key to all my study' (Gwynn, 18). He was educated at St Columba's College and at Brasenose College, Oxford, where he was a scholar and was awarded first-class honours in classical moderations in 1884 and *literae humaniores* in 1886. Gwynn returned to Dublin during college holidays, where he met several of the political and literary figures of the day. His brother Edward John Gwynn (1868–1941) became provost of Trinity College, while another brother, Robert Malcolm Gwynn, became senior dean.

In December 1889 Gwynn married his cousin Mary Louisa (*d.* 1941), daughter of the Revd James Gwynn. She later converted to Catholicism, and they had two sons and two daughters, of whom Aubrey Gwynn (1892–1983) became a Jesuit priest and professor of medieval history at University College, Dublin, and Denis Rolleston Gwynn (1893–1971) was professor of modern Irish history at University College, Cork.

After graduating Gwynn spent some time tutoring in France, beginning a lifelong interest in French culture, later expressed in his *In Praise of France* (1927). During the ten years he spent as a schoolmaster (1886–96) he developed an interest in writing. In 1896 he became a writer and journalist in London, concentrating on English themes until he came into contact with the emerging Irish literary revival, serving as secretary of the Irish Literary Society. A long and prolific writing career followed, ranging over a

Stephen Lucius Gwynn (1864–1950), by Sir William Rothenstein, 1915

variety of literary genres. Among his poems was *A Lay of Ossian and Patrick* (1903), concerned with the historical tension between paganism and Christianity in Ireland; a volume of *Collected Poems* was published in 1923. His many biographical subjects included studies of Tennyson (1899), Thomas More (1904), Scott of the Antarctic (1929), Mary Kingsley and Horace Walpole (both 1932), Swift (1933), Oliver Goldsmith (1935), Henry Grattan (1939), Robert Louis Stevenson (1939), Sir Walter Scott (1930), and an important work on the career of John Redmond from the 1890s until his death entitled *John Redmond's Last Years* (1919). This, and the full biography of the former Irish leader later written by Gwynn's son Denis, contributed to later historians' more positive reappraisal of Redmond.

Gwynn also wrote general historical works on Irish and English subjects, making the eighteenth century his particular specialism. He wrote numerous books on travel and topography, mainly upon his own homeland: reviewing *The Fair Hills of Ireland* (1906), the playwright J. M. Synge commended his 'excellent patriotic spirit, kept in check by a scholarly urbanity' (*Manchester Guardian*, 16 Nov 1906). His *Irish Literature and Drama in the English Language* (1936) was a pioneering guide to the topic. Perhaps his most cited remark—and one which captures his ambivalence about the temper of his times—came from another piece of literary criticism: after seeing Yeats's *Cathleen ni Houlihan* he 'went home asking myself if such plays should be produced unless one was prepared to go out to shoot and be shot' (cited in F. Tuohy, *Yeats*, 1976, 129). He also wrote about his other interests—including wine, eighteenth-century painting, and fishing.

Gwynn returned to Ireland in 1904 and entered politics. In a by-election in November 1906 he won a seat for Galway City, which he represented as a nationalist until 1918. He was one of the few Irish party MPs to have close links with the literary revival, was active in the Gaelic League, and helped to found the Dublin publishing house of Maunsel and Company. A supporter of the campaign for a Catholic university, Gwynn served on the Irish University royal commission in 1908. He was involved in a controversy over the demand for Irish as a compulsory subject for matriculation: although a member of the governing body of the Gaelic League, he was opposed to this.

During the debate surrounding the third Home Rule Bill, Gwynn wrote *The Case for Home Rule* (1911) at the request of his party leader, Redmond. On the outbreak of the First World War he strongly supported Redmond's encouragement of Irish nationalists to support the British war effort. Now over fifty, he enlisted in January 1915 as a private in the 7th Leinsters in the 16th (Irish) division, and was made a captain of the 6th Connaught Rangers that July, serving at Messines, the Somme, and elsewhere. He was one of seven Irish nationalist MPs to join up; his brother Charles and his son Denis did likewise. Together with Tom Kettle and William Redmond, Gwynn undertook a recruitment drive for the British army. He collaborated with Kettle on a collection of ballads called *Battle Songs for the Irish Brigade* (1915), contributing 'The Last Brigade, 1914', which Kettle's biographer has termed 'a fervid recruiting appeal in fifteen uninspired stanzas' (Lyons, 276). Later in his life he expressed in verse his appreciation of those Irish who participated in the Second World War, in a poem entitled 'Salute to Valour' (1941). He was made a chevalier of the Légion d'honneur in July 1915.

Returning to Ireland in the spring of 1917, Gwynn participated in the Irish Convention, an attempt chaired by Sir Horace Plunkett to achieve consensus on a home rule settlement for Ireland which would avoid partition. When Redmond died in 1918, Gwynn took over as leader of the moderate nationalists in the convention. He opposed the attempt to impose compulsory military service in Ireland in 1918 but when the government announced that it would not be enforced if Ireland provided 50,000 recruits voluntarily in six months he joined the Irish Recruiting Council to try to meet the demand, encountering intense opposition led by Sinn Féin. In 1918 he formed the Irish Centre Party and stood unsuccessfully as an independent nationalist for Dublin University in the general election at the end of that year. The party subsequently merged with Plunkett's Irish Dominion League, but Gwynn broke with the league over his willingness to accept partition as a temporary compromise. Gwynn's brand of moderate, cultural nationalism was increasingly sidelined by the polarization of opinion brought about by the War of Independence and civil war. He supported the newly emergent nation, but condemned some of the excesses—as in his letter to *The Observer* on 4 February 1923 to protest against burning houses belonging to Free State senators.

From 1919 Gwynn devoted himself to writing, covering political events in the War of Independence in 1919–20 for *The Times* and becoming a weekly correspondent for *The Observer*. Among the substantial works he wrote not hitherto noticed were his *History of Ireland* (1923) and his autobiography, *Experiences of a Literary Man* (1926). In 1940 he was awarded an honorary DLitt from the National University of Ireland and another from the University of Dublin in 1945. In April 1950 the Irish Academy of Letters awarded him the Gregory medal. He died at his co. Dublin home—Temple Hill, Kimmage Road East, Terenure—on 11 June 1950 and was buried at Tallaght cemetery on 12 June.

Gwynn was described as fair, blue-eyed, somewhat taller than average, and 'lean but not thin' (*DNB*). Although he was not ultimately a major literary figure, he nevertheless stood for a humanism and tolerance that were qualities relatively rare in the Ireland of his day; the author J. B. Lyons has called him 'intellectually and physically fearless' (Lyons, 87). CARLA KING

**Sources** S. Gwynn, *Experiences of a literary man* (1926) · *Irish Times* (12 June 1950), 4 · *DNB* · H. Boylan, *A dictionary of Irish biography*, 3rd edn (1998) · R. Hogan, ed., *Dictionary of Irish literature*, 2nd edn (Westport, CT, 1996) · T. Johnstone, *Orange, green and khaki: the story of the Irish regiments in the Great War, 1914–1918* (Dublin, 1992) · J. B. Lyons, *The enigma of Tom Kettle* (Dublin, 1983) · P. Maume, *The long gestation: Irish nationalist life, 1891–1918* (Dublin, 1999) · R. B. McDowell, *The Irish Convention, 1917–18*, Studies in Irish History, 6 (1970) · 'Stephen Gwynn', *Modern Irish lives*, ed. L. McRedmond (Dublin, 1996), 122 · R. Sloan, *William Smith O'Brien and the Young Ireland rebellion* (Dublin, 2000) · *Thom's Irish who's who* (1923) · R. J. Hayes, ed., *Manuscript sources for the history of Irish civilisation*, 2 (Boston, 1965) · www.pgil-eirdata.org/html [Princess Grace Irish Library, Monaco] · will, 1950, NA Ire., wills and admons

**Archives** BL, notes relating to Dilke, Add. MSS 43930–43941 · NL Ire., letters to Gwynn, MS 8600 · NRA, corresp. and literary papers | NA Scot., corresp. with Lord Lothian · NL Ire., F. S. Bourke collection, MS 10, 737 · NL Ire., Irish Convention letters, MS 8380 · NL Ire., Michael MacDonagh MS 1, 439 · NL Ire., letters to John Redmond · NL Ire., Roberts papers, MS 8320 · NRA, priv. coll., letters to Lord Aberdeen · Plunkett Foundation, Long Hanborough, Oxfordshire, corresp. with Sir Horace Plunkett · PRO, corresp. with Lord Midleton, PRO 30/67 · Ransom HRC, corresp. with John Lane · TCD, letters to Thomas Bodkin · TCD, corresp. with J. Dillon · U. Reading L., letters to Bodley Head Ltd

**Likenesses** W. Rothenstein, chalk drawing, 1915, NPG [*see illus.*] · W. Rothenstein, chalk drawing, 1916, Hugh Lane Municipal Gallery of Modern Art, Dublin · photographs, repro. in Gwynn, *Experiences of a literary man*

**Wealth at death** £125: will, NA Ire., wills and admons, 1950

**Gwynne, Howell Arthur** (1865–1950), journalist, was born on 3 September 1865 at Kilvey, near Swansea, the first of the ten children of Richard Gwynne, schoolmaster, and his wife, Charlotte Lloyd. He was educated at Swansea grammar school. In 1892 he worked for *The Times* as a Balkan correspondent. He transferred to Reuters News Agency and reported from Romania in 1893, Asante in 1895, Sudan in 1896, and Greece during the Graeco-Turkish War of 1897. He went to Peking (Beijing) in January 1898, and remained there until May 1899, when he sailed directly to South Africa. He organized Reuters' coverage of the Second South African War, and followed the operations first of Lord Methuen and then of Lord Roberts up to the capture of Pretoria. In 1904 he was appointed foreign director of Reuters, but left immediately to become editor of *The Standard*, the paper bought by C. Arthur Pearson to advocate tariff reform as one means of binding together the British empire. In 1907 he married Edith Douglas, daughter of Thomas Ash Lane, who had at one time owned property in Shanghai; they had no children.

Until becoming editor of *The Standard* Gwynne had not set foot in a newspaper office. Recognizing that, as he put it, 'I knew as much about it as the office cat', he turned for advice to R. D. Blumenfeld, editor of the *Daily Express* (Blumenfeld, 65). Gwynne resigned from *The Standard* in May 1911. On 8 July 1911 he was appointed editor of the *Morning Post*, owned by Lilias, Countess Bathurst, at a salary of £2000 per annum. He owed this appointment to the fall from grace of the previous editor, Fabian Ware, and to the recommendation of Rudyard Kipling—undoubtedly, in terms of Gwynne's career, the most important of the friends and contacts he made in the course of the war in South Africa. Gwynne (nicknamed Taffy in newspaper circles) remained editor of the *Morning Post*, which underwent a change of ownership in 1924, until its absorption into the *Daily Telegraph* in 1937. In terms of twentieth-century British journalism, only Blumenfeld, and J. L. Garvin of the weekly *Observer*, exceeded Gwynne's length of tenure as editors of a single newspaper. He became a Companion of Honour in 1938.

When he was on the point of severing his connection with *The Standard*, Gwynne had written to A. J. Balfour, the leader of the Conservative and Unionist Party, to say that he was looking for 'a paper in which I might do useful work for the party and the Empire' (Wilson, *Rasp of War*, 10). This sufficiently describes the causes Gwynne espoused throughout his professional life. The cause of empire was an absolute—so far as he was concerned no part of it was to be relinquished, or allowed more responsibility for governing itself. This applied equally to Ireland, Egypt, and India. The cause of the Conservative and Unionist Party was more problematic, because it seemed to him to be altogether too inclined to deviate from the true faith, and to consider compromising on such issues as tariff reform and compulsory service. As self-appointed keeper of the flame of Unionism he increasingly identified with the 'die-hard' faction within that party, establishing in 1922 a Die-Hard Fund, which he managed until 1933. His sponsor, Kipling, paid him the somewhat incestuous compliment of describing his own poem of October 1919 'Gods of the Copybook Headings' (as opposed to the gods of the market place) as 'practically a summary of a good many of your leaders' (Wilson, *History and Politics*, 6).

The First World War brought out Gwynne's true political proclivities. Having late in 1915 called for a League of Patriots (or Patriotic League, National League, or War League) he was active in founding the National Party in the summer of 1917, the programme of which was that of the Unionist die-hards, and considered standing for parliament in that connection. Going beyond that position, he had written to Lady Bathurst in June 1916, 'There are times when one feels that a military dictatorship is the only thing for England' (Wilson, *History and Politics*, 107). He went on, early in 1918, to try to mastermind a coup, the successful outcome of which would have been the replacement of the civilian prime minister, David Lloyd George, by the chief of the Imperial General Staff, Field Marshal Sir William Robertson. To accomplish this, he was prepared to put the *Morning Post* at risk, and in this connection he, and his military correspondent, Charles à Court Repington, defied the Press Bureau, were prosecuted, and found guilty at Bow Street magistrates' court (21 February 1918) for violations of the Defence of the Realm Act. Gwynne thus revealed himself as, basically, a soldier in mufti, unreservedly at the disposal of the gods of war.

The First World War also brought out Gwynne's paranoia and antisemitism—his inability to comprehend British reverses, or the treatment of Germany in 1919, unless there existed a 'hidden hand' directing affairs. From this it was but a small step to his accepting as genuine the 'Protocols of the elders of Zion', to his publishing them in the *Morning Post* in July 1920, and in book form, under the title *The Cause of World Unrest*, in August 1920. In 1923, still in this vein, albeit tempered by his campaign against the sale of honours and his presidency of the League of Help for the Devastated Areas in France, which he had set up in 1920, Gwynne published his only novel, *The Will and the Bill*, the plot of which was based on the susceptibility of politicians to hypnosis.

In September 1930, as president of the Institute of Journalists, Gwynne delivered the following address:

> If and when [the Press] attempts to create political parties and so challenge other parties, or even Parliament itself, then it will have to stand violent assaults and attacks … If political affairs be conducted without ability, or if the system under which we govern ourselves becomes unwieldy, top-heavy and unpracticable, the temptation to intervene in some practical manner may be most difficult to resist. If it be not resisted, the newspapers of the country may find themselves involved in a conflict from which they are bound to emerge defeated. For the sake of our profession, therefore, I most earnestly hope that we shall limit our activities to the proper functions of the Press, which are to keep watch and ward, to inform, to advise, and to instruct. To go beyond them would be to invite disaster. (*Journal of the Institute of Journalists*, 18/171)

As many present would have appreciated, this address was very much on the lines of 'Do as I say, not as I do'. Gwynne's 'capacity for manoeuvre' had been remarked upon, by E. T. Raymond, in 1919 (Raymond, 176). There was hardly anyone in public life against whom Gwynne had not intrigued, with a view to advancing what he regarded as the true values. What is more, he continued to do so. In November 1932 his fundamentals of a political philosophy ran to twenty-five points. In July 1936 he reduced them to seven, with the working title 'Seven points of Conservative policy' (Wilson, *History and Politics*, 157). Throughout the 1930s he campaigned publicly and privately, devising a secret code in which to conduct his correspondence, against the policies of British governments as regards the future of the Indian princes.

Gwynne died on 26 June 1950 at his home, Mawbyns, Little Easton, Dunmow, Essex. According to his will, he kept a diary from the outbreak to the end of the Second World War, and hoped that it might be deemed worthy of publication. The fate and whereabouts of this diary are unknown. KEITH WILSON

**Sources** Bodl. Oxf., MSS Gwynne • U. Leeds, Brotherton L., Glenesk-Bathurst MSS • *The rasp of war: the letters of H. A. Gwynne to the Countess Bathurst, 1914–1918*, ed. K. Wilson (1988) • K. M. Wilson, *A study in the history and politics of the Morning Post, 1905–1926* (1990) • R. D. Blumenfeld, 'What is a journalist', *Journalism by some masters of the craft* (1932) • E. T. Raymond, *Uncensored celebrities* (1919) • *CGPLA Eng. & Wales* (1950)

**Archives** BL OIOC, corresp. relating to India, MS Eur. D 1101 • Bodl. Oxf., corresp., diaries, and papers • IWM, corresp. and papers • U. Leeds, Brotherton L., corresp., incl. copy-out letters (*Morning Post*) | BL, corresp. with Arthur James Balfour, Add. MS 49797, *passim* • BL, letters to R. J. Marker, Add. MS 52278 • HLRO, corresp. with Lord Beaverbrook • HLRO, corresp. with Bonar Law • HLRO, corresp. with John St Loe Strachey • Mitchell L., NSW, letters to G. E. Morrison • NL Aus., corresp. with Alfred Deakin • PRO, letters to Lord Kitchener, 30/57, WO 159 • PRO NIre., corresp. with Edward Carson • U. Leeds, Brotherton L., letters to Lilias, Countess Bathurst, as editor of the *Morning Post* • U. Leeds, Brotherton L., letters to Lord Bathurst

**Likenesses** W. Stoneman, photograph, 1938, NPG • B. Partridge, drawing, repro. in *Punch* (11 Sept 1929)

**Wealth at death** £11,351 4*s*. 8*d*.: probate, 26 Aug 1950, *CGPLA Eng. & Wales*

**Gwynne** [Gwyn], **John** (*fl.* **1642–1682**), army officer, was the son of Robert Gwynne, gentleman, of Trelydan, Montgomeryshire, and Catherine, daughter of Oliver Price of Forden, Shropshire. His grandfather Edward Gwynne was a barrister-at-law of Gray's Inn.

Before the civil war Gwynne was a clerk to the officers of the board of greencloth and also assisted the royal princes and the young duke of Buckingham with physical exercises and military drill, at Richmond and Windsor. Gwynne was proud of his athleticism. He joined the royal army on Hounslow Heath on 12 November 1642, enlisting in the regiment of Sir Thomas Salusbury, and was immediately engaged in the attack on Brentford. He was in the garrison of Reading that surrendered on 26 April 1643, and his regiment took part in the capture of Bristol in July. Gwynne was at the siege of Gloucester and the first battle of Newbury in the same year, and the battle of Cropredy Bridge, the campaign in the west country, and the second battle of Newbury in 1644. He then joined the garrison of Devizes, under Sir Charles Lloyd, who had taken over command of Salusbury's regiment in the summer of 1643. Following the surrender of Devizes on 23 September 1645 Gwynne joined the royalist garrison at Faringdon, where he was given command of a company. At some point following the surrender of Faringdon on 24 June 1646 he was offered a major's commission in the parliamentary army, but refused it. He went to London, where he became involved in royalist plots, and in 1648 was made a captain in the earl of Holland's newly raised regiment and was captured at the battle at Kingston upon Thames on 7 July. The chronology of his adventures is not entirely clear, but at some point he was imprisoned in London and was questioned by Thomas Scott. It is likely that it was after the defeat at Kingston that he went to Newcastle, where the mayor expelled him from the town, and into Scotland, eventually returning to London and crossing to the Netherlands.

At Amsterdam in 1649 he enlisted under the earl of Kinnoul and was with his force which landed in the Orkney Islands in September, where it was joined by the marquess of Montrose in the following January. After Montrose's defeat at Carbisdale, Gwynne returned to the Netherlands. He again saw action in Scotland during the Glencairn rebellion in 1654, and he later went back again with supplies, wintering in Caithness before joining the earl of Middleton on the Isle of Skye and returning with him to the Netherlands. He subsequently joined the Royal regiment of guards as a lieutenant under the earl of Rochester and served under the duke of York with the Spanish army in Flanders. He was at the siege of Ardres in August 1657 and the battle of the Dunes on 3 June 1658, where he was taken prisoner when the regiment surrendered. He remained with the regiment in Flanders and experienced considerable hardship.

After the Restoration, Gwynne was a captain in the Royal regiment of guards and later served under the duke of Monmouth, who was his commanding officer when he wrote his memoirs. These seem to have been prepared between 1679 and 1682 and detail his services to Charles I and Charles II, perhaps in support of a request for promotion. Nevertheless, he was critical of the judgement of the royalist commanders at the abortive relief of Reading, the second battle of Newbury, and the defeat at Kingston, and of the failure to attempt to rescue Montrose after Carbisdale. In the early nineteenth century the memoirs came into the possession of the Revd John Graham of Lifford, co. Donegal, who was a correspondent of Sir Walter Scott, who edited them for publication in 1822 as *Military Memoirs of the Great Civil War, being the Military Memoirs of John Gwynne*. They were re-edited by Norman Tucker, whose edition was published in 1967.

STEPHEN PORTER

**Sources** 'The military memoirs', *The civil war*, ed. N. Tucker, Military Memoirs (1967) • N. Tucker, *Royalist officers of north Wales, 1642–1660* (1961), 31 • *CSP dom., 1660–61*, 443

**Gwynne, Sir Rowland** (*c.*1659–1726), politician, was the eldest son of George Gwynne (*c.*1623–1673) of Builth, Radnorshire, an MP under the protectorate and in the 1660 Convention, and his wife, Sybil, only child of Roderick Gwynne of Builth. He attended St John's College, Oxford, matriculating on 16 July 1674, and was entered at Gray's Inn in 1679. In 1681 he was elected a fellow of the Royal Society.

Having barely attained his majority, Gwynne was returned to the first Exclusion Parliament for Radnorshire, and, although a gentleman of the privy chamber and knighted by Charles II in 1680, threw himself with an almost desperate zeal into the cause of exclusion, with the result that in 1683 he went into voluntary exile in the Netherlands, suspected of complicity in the Rye House plot.

Gwynne had married Mary Bassett (*d.* 1722), daughter

and heir of William Bassett of Glamorgan. However, having wasted his own considerable inheritance and his wife's fortune, he stood in need of a greater reward at the revolution than the minor place of treasurer of the chamber, which, aside from various local dignities, was all he received. In 1692 he forfeited even this office when a characteristic political gamble backfired. He laid an information before Queen Mary accusing the lord lieutenant of Ireland, Henry, Viscount Sidney (later earl of Romney), of corruption, but was unable to prove the charge. Deprived of royal favour and hounded from Radnorshire politics by his great rivals the Harleys, he sought out a new patron, Thomas Grey, second earl of Stamford, a new parliamentary seat (first for Brecknockshire and then as Stamford's nominee for Bere Alston), and a new reputation as an energetic House of Commons man.

It was Gwynne who in 1696 proposed the introduction of a loyal association, in response to revelations about the assassination plot, and who in 1698 led the inquiry into clandestine trade with France during the Nine Years' War. By 1701 he was serving as chairman of the influential elections committee, and was even talked of as a possible speaker. In politics he was a thoroughgoing whig, committed to the maintenance of the revolution settlement and the Hanoverian succession. Indeed, he was selected to carry up the Bill of Settlement to the Lords, and in 1702 piloted through parliament a measure to attaint the Pretender. He was thus a particular target for the tories, and according to his own account lost his seat at the 1702 election after a specific campaign against him inspired by the tory leaders. Harassed by creditors and pressed by the Treasury to render his long overdue chamber accounts, he fled to Hanover, where he attempted to ingratiate himself with the electoral family.

In 1706 Gwynne blundered badly once more in permitting his name to be subscribed to a paper written by the philosopher Leibniz in support of moves in England to invite over the Hanoverian heir presumptive to the throne, which was published in the form of an open letter to Lord Stamford. The effect was to alienate both Queen Anne and the Electress Sophia. Gwynne retired to Hamburg, a sad and lonely figure, 'rusting for want of the conversation I was used to' (Gwynne to Robert Harley, 9 Dec 1710, BL, Add. MS 70229), until Queen Anne's death opened the way for him to return to England. Although he sailed over with King George, as some twenty-five years previously he had accompanied the prince of Orange on his voyage to claim the crown, he received only an annuity of £400 from the new monarch, was soon deep in debt again, and ended his days in a debtors' prison.

Mary Gwynne died in 1722, four years before her husband. The couple left no children, and at Sir Rowland Gwynne's death her entailed estate returned to her family. Gwynne himself was able to bequeath only plate and household goods, and to request in his will to be buried under a 'plain black stone' with a simple inscription recording his Christian belief (PROB 11/607, fols. 46*v*–47*r*). Gwynne died 'in the rules of the King's Bench' on 24 January 1726. D. W. Hayton

**Sources** HoP, *Commons, 1660–90*, 2.458–9 • HoP, *Commons, 1690–1715* [draft] • D. R. L. Adams, 'The parliamentary representation of Radnorshire, 1536–1832', MA diss., U. Wales, 1969 • BL, Add. MS 61147, fols. 15–35 • BL, Stowe MS 222, fols. 225, 280, 286–7 • BL, Stowe MS 223, fols. 25–9, 192–9, 426, 444 • *Letters illustrative of the reign of William III from 1696 to 1708 addressed to the duke of Shrewsbury by James Vernon*, ed. G. P. R. James, 3 vols. (1841) • *The parliamentary diary of Sir Richard Cocks, 1698–1702*, ed. D. W. Hayton (1996) • *The Marlborough–Godolphin correspondence*, ed. H. L. Snyder, 3 vols. (1975) • [C. Gildon], *A review of the Princess Sophia's letter … and that of Sir Rowland Gwynne* [1706] • will, PRO, PROB 11/607, sig. 6 • Foster, *Alum. Oxon.* • BL, Add. MS 70229

**Archives** BL, Blenheim MSS, Add. MS 61147 • BL, corresp. with Jean Robethon and the elector of Hanover, Stowe MSS 222, 223, 241, *passim* • BL, Portland MSS • Northants. RO, Isham MSS

**Wealth at death** plate, furniture, clothes, and other household goods: will, PRO, PROB 11/607, sig. 6

**Gwynne, Violet Kate Eglinton**. *See* Woodhouse, Violet Kate Eglinton Gordon (1871–1948).

**Gwynneth** [Gwynedd], **John** (*d.* 1560x63), composer and polemicist, is of uncertain origins. According to Arthur Bulkeley, his contemporary and bishop of Bangor, Gwynneth was the son of Dafydd ap Llewelyn ab Ithel of Castellmarch, Llŷn, Caernarvonshire. Church music gave him the opportunity of advancement. In minor orders as an acolyte when admitted rector of Stuchbury, Northamptonshire, in 1528, he successfully supplicated for the degree of DMus at the University of Oxford in 1531. Gwynneth, who had now been priested, claimed that he had practised the art of music for twelve (or even twenty) years, and that he had composed three five-part and five four-part masses as well as hymns and antiphons. All that certainly survives of his music is the bass part of his four-voice song 'My love mournyth', a meditation on the passion adapted from a popular song and published in Wynkyn de Worde's *XX Songes* of 1530. Thomas Morley credited him as a distinguished musician in his *Plaine and Easie Introduction to Practicall Musicke* of 1597.

The key to comprehending the middle years of Gwynneth's career lies in his close association with the Benedictine abbey of St Albans. In 1522 'John Gwynneth, clerk' was owed £18 by the abbey (*LP Henry VIII*, 3/2, no. 2583), no doubt for his role in the musical life of the house. Cardinal Wolsey had been granted St Albans the previous year, and was eager to recruit musical talent: Gwynneth probably encountered the prestigious composer of masses and votive antiphons, Robert Fayrfax, at the abbey in 1521. Although he did not himself take the tonsure, Gwynneth appears to have lived close to the monks as a secular ecclesiastic; he was described as 'chapelyn' there in 1535. Unusually among England's Benedictine houses, when protestantism and dissolution began to loom in the early 1530s, St Albans fiercely resisted both. Gwynneth, too, rose to the challenge: religious reform imperilled his career as a composer of sung masses as much as his sacred community.

Resistance came in the form of the printing press located in the abbey precincts. In early 1536 Gwynneth used this press and the abbey printer, John Herford, to publish *The Confutacyon of the Fyrst Parte of Frythes Boke*.

Their collaborator was Richard Boreman, spokesman of the St Albans monks opposed to alteration in religion. John Frith's contribution to protestant theology had been to argue, with some wit, that Christ's body was in heaven, and thus could not be in the mass—opinions that had brought him to the stake at Smithfield in the summer of 1533. Frith became a martyr to the evangelical cause, prompting Gwynneth to write three years later to confound those who upheld the injustice of his execution. The tract was cast as a dialogue between Catholicus (an upholder of religion) and Hereticus (a follower of Frith), a literary form to which Gwynneth would return. Frith's interpretation of the eucharist is attacked in the last twelve chapters, more notable for the vigour of their expression than for the sophistication of their thinking: Frith's own scholarship is dismissed as 'a dyrtye dunghyll heepe of camel rakyng whiche few coude come near for it styncke so' (Clark, 307). Gwynneth also supported Boreman's petition of April 1536 for Sir Francis Bryan's help in defending the abbey.

St Albans Abbey finally succumbed to official pressure to close in December 1539; but it did not entirely give up the ghost. Several of its religious and secular clergy acquired livings that had been associated with the abbey, and Gwynneth was numbered among them. Vicar of the St Albans parish of Luton, Bedfordshire, since 1537, Gwynneth was presented to the London rectory of St Peter Westcheap by a former steward of the abbey, Sir Thomas Audley, in 1543. By 1540 he had also become a chaplain to the king, Henry VIII's dislike of protestant heresy having hardened by then. Meanwhile Gwynneth went to law to assert his title to the Caernarvonshire living of Clynnog Fawr. His incumbency of this prosperous collegiate church was worth defending; and Gwynneth spent eight years and 500 marks in so doing, only to find that the Chantries Act of 1545 threatened to take it away from him. He then changed tactics, persuading Stephen Vaughan (who had married Gwynneth's sister) to write to William Paget in January 1546 to seek his protection.

Although he is not known to have resisted the far more sweeping protestant reforms of Edward VI's reign, Gwynneth's continuing sympathy for traditional religion can be read in the rarest and most interesting of his writings, *A Briefe Declaration of the Victory of Quene Marye in her Accession to the Throne*. The substance of a sermon delivered by Gwynneth in Luton church on 23 July 1553, just four days after Mary was proclaimed queen in London, the text was published by the royal printer John Cawood. Only one copy is extant. Gwynneth explains that he is preaching on this topic lest there be some in his congregation who perceive Mary's providential accession less favourably than he does himself. What follows is a remarkable attempt to defend a woman's right to rule England. Gwynneth works outwards from the assumption that, woman being the weaker vessel, it is all the more astonishing that Mary has triumphed against 'the moost myghty powers of the realme', namely the duke of Northumberland, with all the forces and treasure of the crown at his disposal. The overthrow of this 'Tyraunte' is a miracle equivalent to Judith's victory over Holofernes. God has chosen a woman to help mankind escape the captivity of the devil, so that his own power might be more manifest: 'the weaker the meane be wherby god doth any such worke, the more laude and prayse the meane is worthye to have' (J. Gwynneth, *A Briefe Declaration*, sig. Aviir). For Gwynneth, 'the myghtye operation of god' provides a far more plausible explanation for the commons' unity of mind in flocking to Mary's standard than does a putative popular belief in her just title to rule.

Even more intriguing is Gwynneth's choice of royal imagery. He is overt in comparing Mary to the Blessed Virgin: 'suche is the similitude betwene them both women, both maydens, both Maries, both descending of regal progenitours, both persecuted with the malice of men, both delyvered by thonely marvelous worke of God' (J. Gwynneth, *A Briefe Declaration*, sig. Biv). Gwynneth takes the opportunity to protest against the opprobrium into which the mother of God has lately fallen, 'compared in pulpettes to safferne bagges, compared also in ale houses, to leud felowes wives' (ibid., sig. Dir), and lambastes the 'dreamynge inventours' who have dared to cut the Ave Maria from the liturgy.

This was a deft piece of propaganda on behalf of the Marian regime, plainly argued and timely. The same cannot be said for Gwynneth's three further polemical tracts, two of which exhumed his old feud with Frith. *A manifeste detection of the notable falshed of that part of John Frithes boke, whiche he calleth his foundacion*, published by Thomas Berthelet in 1554, stresses the centrality of the eucharist and of Christ's presence in it, and is notable for praising Thomas More and quoting him against Frith. *A Playne Demonstration of John Frithes Lacke of Witte and Learnynge* followed in 1557, and summons Augustine to refute evangelical objections to the mass. Both recall his work with Richard Boreman in 1536, and the timing of Gwynneth's Marian tracts may owe something to Boreman's plans to resurrect St Albans Abbey. Gwynneth's twin disputants Catholicus and Hereticus return to the fray in his *A Declaracion of the State, wherin All Heretikes Dooe Leade their Lives* (1554), the former arguing that to deny one part of the true faith is to deny its whole. The book concludes with a spirited assault on the heretics' strategy of subverting order in the church: 'Where there is no order, there is continual fear, trembling, astonishment, adversitee, or thraldome' (J. Gwynneth, *A Declaracion*, 1554, sig. Nr). Reformers have undermined the sacraments and ancient ceremonies of the church, replacing them with the 'newfangled fassions' of the prayer book and the royal arms. If their sway had lasted a little longer, Gwynneth quips, the communion table would have travelled so far from the chancel into the body of the church that it would have ended up outside the door.

Theology such as this would not have endeared Gwynneth to the royal supremacy of Queen Elizabeth after 1559, and he was duly imprisoned in 1560. By March 1563 he was dead. His defence of the old faith was echoed by his niece, the recusant and priest-harbourer Jane *Wiseman (*d.* 1610). J. P. D. Cooper

**Sources** Emden, *Oxf.*, vol. 4 • *New Grove* • Wood, *Ath. Oxon.*, new edn, 1.246 • *DWB* • *LP Henry VIII* • *ESTC* • J. G. Clark, 'Reformation and reaction at St Albans Abbey, 1530–58', *EngHR*, 115 (2000), 297–328 • W. A. Clebsch, *England's earliest protestants, 1520–1535* (1964) • G. Williams, *Wales and the Reformation* (1997), 139, 160

**Gwyther, John Howard** (1835–1921), banker, was born at Milford in Pembrokeshire, and was educated privately in Ramsgate. He was married and had five children. He started work in the London private bank, Rogers, Olding & Co., aged seventeen. He entered City Bank, which was established by charter in 1855 and, unusually, had both a large British retail base and an international business, and he spent some time in its discount office before going east to join his brother-in-law, a discount broker in Shanghai. He entered Chartered Bank in March 1859, a year after it started business. Consistently one of the largest publicly owned British overseas banks before 1914, it specialized in India and the Far East. First appointed sub-agent and accountant at its Singapore branch, he was transferred to Shanghai in October 1860 as sub-manager. Within a few months, he was promoted to manager, but left in 1863 to become a partner in his brother-in-law's business.

Gwyther rejoined Chartered Bank in 1868. On holiday in England, he was offered the post of secretary to the bank, which he accepted. He was promoted to London sub-manager from January 1869, and in 1871, aged only thirty-five, became manager.

Gwyther was successively London manager (1871–92), director (1887–1904), managing director (1892–6), and chairman (1896–1904) of Chartered Bank during a period of great difficulty for banks working in the East. His time as manager (in which capacity he was the bank's senior executive officer), began soon after the crisis of 1865–6, during which several Eastern banks failed. Chartered Bank's balance sheet did not regain its 1865 level until 1872, and it was unable to pay its shareholders any dividend in 1870 or 1871. Indeed, it was only possible to start rebuilding its reserve in 1874. This was an object lesson for Gwyther. Building up a substantial reserve fund became an integral part of the bank's policy, and by 1904, when Gwyther retired, the reserve had surpassed issued capital for the first time. Moreover, it had been built up entirely by allocations from profits.

It is arguable that the depreciation of silver was even worse for banks than the crisis of 1865–6. Many institutions working in the East foundered on this rock, including the great Oriental Bank Corporation in 1884. That Chartered Bank survived was largely due to the wise measures undertaken by Gwyther; and his ability and knowledge of Eastern conditions enabled him to secure for it much of the business formerly undertaken by the Oriental Bank Corporation.

In the 1870s Gwyther advocated the substitution of gold for silver as the basis of the Indian and other silver currencies. He elucidated his views in a memorandum submitted to the secretary of state for India in March 1876. Rejecting the prevalent idea that the fall in silver was a temporary phenomenon, he believed correctly that the chance of any permanent recovery in its price was remote—demand for the metal was still falling, while supplies continued to increase. This was crucially important for those countries based on silver, particularly India, which badly needed a fixed and stable currency.

By the mid-1880s, Gwyther had embraced bimetallism as the solution to the problems faced by Eastern currencies. Aware of the difficulties faced by companies which traded in the East but were based in the West, he urged Chartered's shareholders in 1887 'to preach bimetallism constantly for without bimetallism the trade of England with silver-using countries can never be profitable and peaceful' (AGM report, 1887, Chartered Bank MSS).

Chartered Bank had already grasped this nettle. In 1885, its overseas branches were told to remit to London their allotted silver capital as favourable opportunities arose. The bank's capital employed in the East was thus halved, and all its assets were revalued in its balance sheet in terms of gold at the current exchange rate. This was a brave decision, largely inspired by Gwyther. Together with a cautious exchange policy, it saved Chartered Bank from the fate of several of its competitors.

Gwyther's prudent direction of Chartered Bank, and his financial knowledge, were much valued in the City. Although Chartered remained his main interest, he also accepted seats on the boards of City Bank, Anglo-Egyptian Bank, and Anglo-Californian Bank. He retired into private life in 1904, aged sixty-nine, having seen Chartered Bank become a great institution. On 21 October 1921, he died at his home, 13 Lancaster Gate, London, of old age.

FRANCES BOSTOCK

**Sources** C. Mackenzie, *Realms of silver: one hundred years of banking in the East* (1954) • *Banker's Magazine* (1909) • *Banker's Magazine*, 112 (1921), 589 • *The Statist*, 98 (July–Dec 1921), 649 • GL, Standard Chartered MSS, Chartered Bank MSS • d. cert.

**Archives** GL, Standard Chartered Bank archive

**Wealth at death** £144,881 4s. 7d.: probate, 22 Nov 1921, *CGPLA Eng. & Wales*

**Gye, Dame Emma**. *See* Albani, Dame Emma (1847–1930).

**Gye, Frederick, the elder** (1781–1869), tea dealer and proprietor of Vauxhall Gardens, was by 1806 a printer in partnership with G. Balne at 7 Union Court, Broad Street, in the City of London, where, having secured the contract for printing state lottery tickets, he made a profitable living. Gye and Balne also printed lottery posters and advertisements for the lottery agent Thomas Bish. This connection was the making of Gye's fortune. On the eve of one of the lotteries Bish prevailed upon Gye to take off his hands a whole ticket left unsold (lottery tickets were usually sold in fractions as small as one-sixteenth to encourage smaller gamblers), and the fortunate Gye drew one of the great prizes—£30,000.

Rather than sit back to a life of ease, Gye invested first in a wine company (the London Wine Company, opened at 44 Southampton Row, Holborn, in 1817), and then in the tea trade, which he took by storm. He opened the London Genuine Tea Company on 5 November 1818 at 23 Ludgate Hill, and made his mark by prominent advertising, which exploited public indignation about the post-war practice of adulteration by unscrupulous tea dealers. Gye was less than scrupulous himself, however, in implying that the established practice of blending inferior with superior teas also amounted to adulteration. The respectable trade was outraged, meetings were held, and counter-advertisements placed, accusing Gye of scurrility, but the publicity kept him in the public eye. Gye's company sold tea in sealed and labelled packages, to guarantee purity, at low prices for amounts as small as quarter of a pound.

Gye achieved further publicity by opening two more branches, at 148 Oxford Street and 8 Charing Cross. At the latter he built a grand saloon which he had luxuriously furnished and decorated with Chinese views and figure subjects painted by Clarkson Stanfield and David Roberts to impress customers. These were mostly country tea dealers whom Gye sought to develop as a team of agents in order to bypass the high-class country grocers whose connections were with the established trade. He claimed to have 500 within a year of starting.

Gye's marketing techniques were not original, having been anticipated in the 1780s but not systematically implemented. Within three years he had achieved an annual turnover of hundreds of thousands of pounds. Imitated by others, he had commenced a pattern which rapidly became the norm—turning the tea trade upside down.

In the 1820s Gye was active in a number of fields. In 1821 he entered into partnership with the musically inclined William Hughes and, together with Thomas Bish, they purchased Vauxhall Gardens from the Tyers family for £28,000. In 1822 he moved the London Wine Company to 141 Fleet Street. In 1826 'Frederick Gye, Esq, of Wood Green, in the County of Middlesex', became member of parliament for the industrially depressed town of Chippenham—an election secured by sending two wagon loads of wool to the principal mill as an earnest of his determination to bring work to the borough. He remained member for Chippenham until 24 July 1830.

Gye's regime at Vauxhall was nothing if not varied and adventurous, with notable attractions presented to the public such as the sword swallower, Ramo Samee, in 1822. In the following year a shadow pantomime, invented by a carpenter in the gardens, was a great success, and nearly 140,000 visitors produced receipts of £29,590. In 1825 Madame Vestris was the hit of the season with her rendering of 'Cherry Ripe', and Gye raised the normal price of 2s. to a gala price of 4s. to take advantage of the demand. In 1827 and 1828, responding to competition from Astley's Amphitheatre, Gye recreated the battle of Waterloo, with horses, foot soldiers, and vivid pyrotechnics. The composer Henry Rowley Bishop was employed as musical director from 1830 to 1833. In this period too Gye invented and introduced some ingenious optical illusions: a basket of fruit which retreated as visitors advanced to touch it, and a living person, springing from nowhere, seen through a telescope on a blank wall.

By the mid-1830s, however, there were signs that Vauxhall was beginning to lose some of its audience, despite the popularity of a 1s. night, attended by 27,000 people in 1833. In 1834 Gye began to open only on three alternate nights a week, taking singers, musicians, fireworks, and lamps to Sydney Gardens in Bath in between. He also permanently reduced the ordinary entry fee to 1s. and in 1836 introduced daytime fêtes, with balloon ascents as the new chief attraction, especially those of Charles Green, who built for the proprietors an unprecedentedly large balloon, the *Royal Vauxhall*. In November 1836 it made a record eighteen-hour voyage to the grand duchy of Nassau, and was renamed the *Royal Nassau*.

Gye's earlier good fortune now began to go into reverse. In 1836 the London Wine Company failed owing to speculation in a port which had proved to be an inferior vintage. At Vauxhall others no doubt felt, with Charles Dickens, that daylight opening made it look tawdry. Certainly Gye was pushing at the boundaries of good taste when he imported 'poses plastiques' from Paris in 1837. Then, in July, a tragedy occurred when Robert Cocking, a landscape painter in his sixties, was killed in attempting to descend in a parachute of his own invention from the *Nassau* balloon. Several wet seasons damaged Gye's attempts to recover. By 1840 he was compelled to sell the Genuine Tea Company to meet his debts on Vauxhall. This was not enough, however, and he was forced to sell the gardens the same year.

Gye retired to Brighton, ruined. His son, Frederick *Gye the younger (1810–1878), who had been expensively educated at foreign universities, and who had enjoyed a grand tour, resented his father's failure and his loss of expectations so much that he resolutely refused to speak to him again. The younger Frederick became renowned as a producer of Italian opera. His sisters, who had been promised dowries of £30,000, held out for titles, failed, and were doomed to penurious spinsterhood. As an old man Gye senior was reduced to cadging opera tickets from the sons of former friends—for he retained a 'passion for the luxuries of life' (Vizetelly, 1.21). He died of influenza at 2 Lansdowne Street, Hove, on 13 February 1869, aged eighty-eight. DOUGLAS A. REID

**Sources** H. Vizetelly, *Glances back through seventy years: autobiographical and other reminiscences*, 2 vols. (1893) · *The Times* (30 Oct 1818) · *The Times* (2–7 Nov 1818) · *The Times* (9 Nov 1818) · *The Times* (20 Nov 1818) · Hoh-Cheung Mui and L. H. Mui, *Shops and shopkeeping in eighteenth century England* (1989) · R. D. Altick, *The shows of London* (1978) · W. W. Wroth, *Cremorne and the later London gardens* (1907) · C. Knight, ed., *London*, 6 vols. (1841–3), vol. 1 · *CGPLA Eng. & Wales* (1869) · Boase, *Mod. Eng. biog.* · *DNB*

**Likenesses** C. Baugniet, lithograph, 1844, BM, NPG

**Wealth at death** under £1000: probate, 2 Aug 1869, *CGPLA Eng. & Wales*

**Gye, Frederick, the younger** (1810–1878), businessman and opera manager, was born at Finchley, Middlesex, the son of Frederick *Gye the elder. He probably had 'a good public school education' in Britain (Edwards, *Lyrical Drama*, 1.15–30) before spending some time at Frankfurt-am-Main, Germany. He assisted his father in the management of Vauxhall Gardens from about 1830 until its enforced sale in 1840. He was already an inventor, interested in lighting and photography, and won a contract to light the new houses of parliament; as a businessman he supplied Covent Garden Theatre with soap, oil, and candles. At an unknown date he married the daughter of his father's partner William Hughes, with whom he had a large family. His father's loss of his businesses left Gye to fend for himself, chiefly as a businessman managing musical and theatrical enterprises. In the mid-1840s he was manager for some of Louis Jullien's Promenade Concert seasons and, again, in 1847–8, for Jullien's ill-planned season of English opera at Drury Lane. He apparently escaped blame for that débâcle, for in February 1848 the new lessee of the Italian Opera House, Covent Garden, Edward Delafield, appointed him director. In the spring of 1849 Delafield fled abroad and, on 14 July, was made bankrupt. Gye, in conjunction with the artists, carried on the remainder of the season as a joint-stock undertaking. In September 1849 he acquired the lease for seven years, using £5000 provided by Colonel Brownlow Knox; he then paid himself £1500 per annum as director.

The basic problem of Italian opera in London—unsubsidized and enjoyed mainly by the rich—was that as a monopoly it could be profitable but was only doubtfully so when two theatres competed. Covent Garden as an Italian opera house had begun in 1847, with the defection of leading artists, especially the singing couple Giulia Grisi and G. M. Mario and the conductor Michael Costa, from Benjamin Lumley's management of Her Majesty's. Theirs was still the dominant influence down to the early 1860s. Until 1852 Gye and Lumley competed (attempting in 1851 to take over each other's theatres); after the destruction of Covent Garden Theatre by fire on 5 March 1856 Lumley came back briefly, to be succeeded as rival by J. H. Mapleson. Only after another fire, this time at Her Majesty's in 1867, did Gye and Mapleson come together for two lucrative though uneasy 'coalition seasons' (1869–70). Those apart, only in the 1870s, when Mapleson, though still active, was artistically and financially weakened, did Covent Garden show more than a marginal profit. This explains the considerable difficulties with which Gye struggled, especially after the fire. Insured for only £8000, he raised at least £150,000 in loans and through the lease of boxes and stalls to rebuild the theatre; this was done (to Edward Barry's design) in under eight months, and the new house opened on 15 May 1858. The burden of debt repayment was further complicated by Knox's claim to be not a creditor but a continuing partner; his chancery suit dragged on from 1861 until, on 8 July 1872, the House of Lords upheld Gye. Meanwhile, the suit prevented Gye from raising capital by selling the lease (as he thought of doing in 1865) while remaining as manager. Probably only his standing as a careful businessman and a gentleman whose word was his bond, together with his connections with Coutts's Bank and a few other long-term backers, saved him from going under.

In the first period of Gye's management the staples were—as always in a theatre where everything, in the fashionable spring–summer season, was done in Italian—the operas of Rossini, Bellini, Donizetti, and especially Verdi, but the presiding deity was Meyerbeer, then at the height of his fame. His works took up thirty per cent of performances between 1849 and 1858; Delafield secured the first London production of *Le Prophète* (1849) soon after the Paris première, and Gye did the same over *L'Africaine* (1865), while *Les Huguenots* reopened Covent Garden after the fire. In keeping in close touch with Meyerbeer and inducing him to come to London, Gye was doing what any shrewd opera manager of the time would have done. That apart, his feeling for what would do well was uncertain. He introduced Gounod to London with *Sapho* (1849) but declined repeatedly to put on *Faust*, so allowing Mapleson to get in first (1863). He brought Berlioz to London for his *Benvenuto Cellini* (1853), which failed only partly because of a hostile cabal. Far less well acquainted with Italian music than Mapleson, Gye put on the British premières of Verdi's *Rigoletto* (1853) and *Don Carlos* (1867) but would not stage *Aida*, which he thought tuneless and ineffective, until 1876, after it had succeeded in Vienna, Madrid, and St Petersburg.

By then, however, Gye could count on the extraordinary soprano Adelina Patti, who dominated the second half of his management as Grisi had the first. From her Covent Garden début in 1861 he oversaw her early engagements until she was able to run her career with a business acumen at least equal to his. He did the same from her arrival in 1872 for Emma Albani, whose talents enabled him from 1875 to put on the more accessible works of Wagner, a composer he disliked—*Lohengrin*, *Tannhäuser*, and *The Flying Dutchman*—even then (as his prospectus stated) only after they had succeeded in Italy; Albani eventually married his son Ernest. Though prosperous for his management, the 1870s were a period of artistic staleness; in 1869 Gye had got rid of the autocratic Costa—by then old-fashioned though still effective—and replaced him with the more mediocre Enrico Bevignani and Augusto Vianesi. His efficient stage manager Augustus Harris died in 1873. After the 1877 season Gye retired, handing over to Ernest (who was briefly joined by another son, Herbert). Still active as an inventor, he patented on 5 November 1878 a new electric light system with which he proposed to illuminate the opera house. On 27 November 1878 he was shot accidentally while a guest at Dytchley Park in Oxfordshire. He died from the effects of the wound on 4 December and was buried at Norwood cemetery on the 9th. Although his knowledge of music was very limited, his business abilities were highly thought of. He was the most businesslike and successful of British nineteenth-century opera managers, but the competition was not great and he did operate in the most prosperous mid-Victorian decades, retiring just as the so-called great depression was beginning to affect some of his patrons. He 'held aloof, save professionally, from journalists and artists' (Bennett, *Forty Years of Music*, 184–5). Berlioz, who thought well of his management, wrote, 'he has a businessman's terseness' (*Correspondance générale*, 305). Highly deferential to the royal family, he was disappointed not to have been knighted like Costa. In his will he left the lease of Covent Garden Theatre and the adjoining Floral Hall to his children.

G. C. Boase, *rev.* John Rosselli

**Sources** G. Dideriksen and M. Ringel, 'Frederick Gye and "the dreadful business of opera management"', *19th Century Music*, 19 (1995), 3–30 • H. Rosenthal, *Two centuries of opera at Covent Garden* (1958) • H. S. Edwards, *The lyrical drama*, 1 (1881), 15–30 • *The Mapleson memoirs: the career of an operatic impresario, 1858–1888*, ed. H. Rosenthal (1966) • J. Bennett, *Forty years of music, 1865–1905* (1908) • *From Mendelssohn to Wagner: being the memoirs of J. W. Davison, forty years the music critic of The Times*, ed. H. Davison (1912) • A. Carse, *The life of Jullien* (1951) • C. L. Gruneisen, *The opera and the press* (1869) • *Correspondance générale: Hector Berlioz*, ed. P. Citron, 4 (Paris, 1983) • G. B. Shaw, *Music in London, 1890–94*, 1 (1932), 1 • *The Times* (6 Dec 1878) • *MT*, 20 (1879), 24 • G. Meyerbeer, *Briefwechsel und Tagebücher*, ed. H. Becker and others, 4 (Berlin, 1985), 474; 5 (1999) • private information (2004)

**Archives** Royal Opera House, Covent Garden, London, diaries

**Likenesses** Count Gleichen, marble statue, Royal Opera House, London • engraving, repro. in Rosenthal, *Two centuries of opera*, 96–7 • portrait, repro. in *Illustrated Sporting and Dramatic News* (24 June 1876) • portrait, repro. in *Illustrated Sporting and Dramatic News* (7 Dec 1878) • portrait, repro. in *The mask* (1868), 97 • print, Harvard TC

**Wealth at death** under £35,000: probate, 16 May 1879, *CGPLA Eng. & Wales*

**Gyles, Althea.** *See* Gyles, Margaret Alethea (1868–1949).

**Gyles, Henry** (*bap.* **1646**, *d.* **1709**), glass painter, was born in Micklegate, York, and baptized there in the church of St Martin-cum-Gregory on 4 March 1646, the fifth of fourteen children of Edmund Gyles (1611–1676), glazier, and his wife, Sarah (*d.* 1686). Gyles presumably learned his father's craft; however, he preferred to be called an artist, having been taught drawing and painting by one Mr Martins. Gyles appears to have been self-taught in the technicalities of painting and firing glass. His friends included the artists Francis Place, William Lodge, and John Lambert, the antiquaries Ralph Thoresby and Miles Gale, the mathematician Thomas Kirke, the zoologist Martin Lister, and the publisher and printseller Pierce Tempest. These and others, known as the 'York virtuosi', met at Gyles's house. They found patrons for him and raised technical matters concerning coloured glass at the Royal Society.

Gyles's earliest known works, the arms of the Merchant Taylors' Company (1662) in their hall at York and the royal arms in Acomb church, York (1663), illustrate the heraldic work for which he was chiefly commissioned and which is seen at its best in Staveley church, Derbyshire (1676), and the library of Trinity College, Cambridge (1690). He also painted sundial windows which are best represented by those incorporating the four seasons (n.d.) at Tong Hall, Bradford, and Nunappleton Hall, near York (1670), now in York City Art Gallery. Following the work of Bernard Dinninckhoff (*fl.* *c.*1585–*c.*1620) at York and the Van Linges at Oxford until the outbreak of civil war in 1642, the art and craft of glass painting had virtually died out.

Gyles revived glass painting in England after the civil wars, along with religious imagery. Of his *Nativity* (1687) in the chapel of University College, Oxford, only fragments remain there, but Gyles's cartoons for the window, after Dürer, survive in York City Art Gallery. He rediscovered pot metal colours, including flashed ruby, for use along with his usual enamel colours and stain in creating this window. A similar combination was used in the window depicting St Cecilia, King David, and an angel choir (1700, after an engraving by Johannes Sadeler (*c.*1589–1593) in the Rijksmuseum, Amsterdam), now in St Helen's Church, Denton in Wharfedale. Many of Gyles's figures, such as *The Virtues* (1690) in Gray's Court, York, were derived from Flemish, Dutch, and German prints acquired for him by Pierce Tempest.

Of Gyles's three sons and two daughters only Rebecca survived him, along with his wife, Hannah (*d.* 1721). He left no known apprentices and died in Micklegate, York, in debt 'without leaving any behind him to transmit to posterity that art' (R. Thoresby, *Diary*, 2.61). He was buried on 25 October 1709 in the church where he had been baptized. Some fifty-eight glass paintings can be attributed to him, together with a self-portrait in crayon in the British Museum. His cartoons for glass together with a trade card with a mezzotint portrait by Francis Place are in York City Art Gallery. TREVOR BRIGHTON

**Sources** J. T. Brighton, 'Henry Gyles, virtuoso and glass painter of York, 1645–1709', *York Historian*, 4 (1984), 1–62 • J. T. Brighton, 'Cartoons for York glass—Henry Gyles', *Preview, City of York Art Gallery Quarterly*, 21 (1968), 772–5 • J. T. Brighton, 'The enamel glass painters of York, 1585–1795', 3 vols., DPhil diss., University of York, 1978 • J. T. Brighton, 'The heraldic window in the Frescheville chapel of Staveley church', *Journal of the Derbyshire Archaeological and Natural History Society*, 80 (1960), 98–104 • J. T. Brighton, 'The painted glass in Gray's Court, York [pts 1–2]', *Yorkshire Archaeological Journal*, 41 (1963–6), 709–25; 42 (1967–70), 61–2 • J. T. Brighton, 'The lost east window by Gyles of York', *University College Record*, 5/5 (1970), 350–60 • J. T. Brighton, '17th century painted glass in Witherslack church', *Transactions of the Cumberland and Westmorland Antiquarian and Archaeological Society*, new ser., 72 (1972), 90–96 • J. T. Brighton, 'The lost Guildhall window, York', *York History*, 3 (1976), 109–17 • J. A. Knowles, 'Henry Gyles, glasspainter of York', *Walpole Society*, 11 (1922–3), 47–72 • J. A. Knowles, *Essays in the history of the York school of glass painting* (1936) • J. A. Knowles, 'Glasspainters of York: the Gyles family', *N&Q*, 12th ser., 9 (1921), 312–15 • will, Borth. Inst., probate registers, vol. 76, fol. 55 • E. Bulmer, ed., *Parish registers of St Martin-cum-Gregory* (1897) • CUL, Add. MS 4024 • [J. Hunter], ed., *Letters of eminent men, addressed to Ralph Thoresby*, 2 vols. (1832)

**Archives** BL, Stowe MS 746, Harley MS 6376 • York Minster Library, minster fabric accounts | Bodl. Oxf., Lister MS 36 • Carlisle Cathedral, dean and chapter library, Machell MS II, fol. 275 • Ripon Minster, fabric accounts and letter, box 3, no. 27 • Trinity Cam., junior bursar's accounts • University College, Oxford, notes in college muniments • W. Yorks. AS, Leeds, Yorkshire Archaeological Society, Thoresby MSS • York City housebooks

**Likenesses** H. Gyles, self-portrait, chalk and watercolour, BM • H. Gyles, self-portrait, crayon, BM • F. Place, mezzotint (after unknown artist), BM, York City Art Gallery • aquatint, BM, NPG • pen-and-ink drawing (after engraving), NPG

**Wealth at death** died in debt: will, Borth. Inst., probate registers, vol. 76, fol. 55

**Gyles, Margaret Alethea** [*known as* Althea Gyles] (**1868–1949**), artist and poet, was born in Kilmurry, co. Cork, Ireland, the daughter of 'mad' George Gyles and his wife, Alithea Emma, daughter of the Hon. and Revd Edward Grey, bishop of Hereford. Her family, from Minehead, Somerset, had settled in Youghal about 1649, and was 'so haughty that their neighbours called them the Royal family' (Yeats, *Autobiographies*, 237).

Severing herself from her family and surviving by 'selling her watch, and then by occasional stories in an [unidentified] Irish paper', Gyles attended an art school in Stephen's Green, Dublin, in the late 1880s. Living in poor accommodation and starving, she was taken by E. J. Dick to live in the 'household', a theosophical commune at 3 Ely Place, which included his wife and George Russell (A. E.). To W. B. Yeats, who joined them in 1891, she seemed 'a strange red-haired girl, all whose thoughts were set upon painting and poetry'. Quarrelling with the Dicks, she returned to 'starvation and misery [which] had a large share in her ritual of worship' (Yeats, *Autobiographies*, 237–8).

At 53 Mountpleasant Square, Dublin, Gyles wrote a never-published novel, 'The woman without a soul' (MS, NL Ire.). Its black magician is loosely based on the mysterious Captain Roberts whose rituals involving animal sacrifice are described in 'The Sorcerers', in Yeats's *The Celtic Twilight* (1893). Late in 1891 or early in 1892 Gyles moved to London where she studied at Pedders, then at the Slade School, financed by one of her Grey relatives. By 1896 she had established herself in her 'studio' at 86 Charlotte Street, Fitzroy Square. Her friends included Lady Colin Campbell, art critic of *The World* (Gyles almost certainly providing the cover design for *A Woman's Walks*, 1903), and the artist Mabel Dearmer of the *Yellow Book* circle. '[S]huddering from her rustic surname', Oscar Wilde urged 'Ah! you must call yourself Althaea Le Gys' (Clifford Bax, ALS, U. Reading L.).

The *Pall Mall Magazine* took Gyles's poem 'Dew-time' in October 1894. It was influenced by A. E., illuminated by Gyles, and was followed by others derivative of Yeats and, from time to time, worked over by him. Her drawing *The Offering of Pan* appeared in *The Commonweal* in June 1896 and her illustration for T. W. Rolleston's *Deirdre: the Feis Ceoil Prize Cantata* in 1897. Gyles was not a member of the Order of the Golden Dawn, but she and Yeats collaborated closely over the cabbalistic iconography of her wrap-around design for *The Secret Rose* (1897), with its Celtic and medieval knotwork inspired by the eleventh-century sacramentary of Fleury attributed to Nivardus of Milan. Yeats analysed her work in 'A symbolic artist and the coming of symbolic art' (*The Dome*, December 1898) and she was accepted again by A. H. Bullen, T. Fisher Unwin, Elkin Mathews, and Hodder and Stoughton, as she and Yeats collaborated on programmes for talismanic designs to his 'total books', *The Wind Among the Reeds* and *Poems* (1899). The spinal design of the latter was used until 1927.

Aleister Crowley claims to have witnessed Yeats, with Gyles, attempting an astral vision of a red and white hawk and deer in his rooms at Woburn Buildings. Crowley told Richard Ellmann in 1946 that when Gyles sought to save herself from his insidious aura, Yeats ordered her to obtain a drop of Crowley's blood so that Yeats might overcome black magic with white. She compromised on a hair from his head and one of his books, which she dropped as she fled when Crowley confronted her with a skeleton in his *sanctum sanctorum*. Yeats used the hair for his invocations, and Crowley wrestled with a 'vampire for ten nights' (McFarlin Library, University of Tulsa, Richard Ellmann papers). Ellmann relates that Gyles then 'gave way entirely to [Crowley's] baleful fascination', but Crowley was perhaps remembering only his fictional characters Count Swanoff (himself), Hypatia Gay (Althea), and Will Bute (Yeats) in his short story 'At the Fork of the Roads', published in *The Equinox* (1909).

In Paris early in May 1899 Gyles agreed to illustrate Wilde's *The Harlot's House* for the publisher, pornographer, and patron of Aubrey Beardsley, Leonard *Smithers (1861–1907). Soon they were caught up in an ostentatious affair. She executed five coloured drawings which Smithers described as 'weirdly powerful and beautiful' and eventually published in the pirate edition in 1904 (Sherard, 342). At the height of her energies, postponing all other work to finish the illustrations for *The Harlot's House*, she was plainly in love with 'so *excellent* a person as Mr Smithers' (Finneran and others, 56). Martin Secker would often see them playing chess in the domino room at the Café Royal. The gold-stamped covers for Ernest Dowson's *Decorations* followed in December 1899, using a stylized rose, which Yeats identified as her 'central symbol', on the white parchment top board, and a pattern of thorns and foliage on the back. Four swirling birds pecking at a heart between a sun and moon surrounded by stars form the top board of John White-Rodyng's *The Night* (1900).

By November 1899 Gyles had deposited her valuable books with W. B. Yeats—he refused Smithers's 'improper Japanese ivories'—before the bailiffs arrived. In mid-September 1900 Arthur Symons found her in bed in a bare room at 15 Granby Place, Hampstead Road, 'without a thing in the place, except five books (one a presentation copy from Oscar Wilde) and one or two fantastic gold ornaments which she used to wear; chloral by her side, and the bed strewn with MSS', wanting to read his article on Ernest Dowson. Dowson had died on 23 February 1900 but she told Symons 'When I meet him I'll tell him about it!' Symons sold her poem 'For a Sepulchre' to the *Saturday Review*. Gyles, recovering in the Hospital for Diseases of the Chest in the City Road, apologized to the bankrupt Smithers for not raising money from her people to save him. Back in Granby Place by Wilde's death on 30 November, she offered Smithers £6 to go to Wilde's funeral. He refused.

Faith Compton Mackenzie portrayed Gyles and her relationship with Smithers in *Tatting* (1957). Gyles appeared as Ariadne Berden who:

> after treating reasonable admirers with prudish contempt, had fallen into the arms of an abominable creature of high intelligence, no morals and the vivid imagination which was perhaps what she had been waiting for … Ariadne lost caste, and when the affair ended after more than a year of heady intoxication, and with a certain amount of inspired work, she collapsed. (F. C. Mackenzie, *Tatting*, 1957, 12)

For Symons, Smithers was 'a drunken brute whom no one could stand' who had 'left her as soon as he had alienated her other friends' (Columbia University, Arthur Symons papers).

By 1902 Gyles was once again ill, but survived to tell untrustworthy 'romantic tales of her night escape from a terrible sanitorium' (Symons, 167). Her productive life as a designer was over. Her cover design for *The Shadowy Waters* (1900) uses only the rose from her rejected frontispiece portrait of Yeats for *The Wind Among the Reeds* (her only surviving original work, now in the British Museum), and while her spinal design from *The Secret Rose* is reused on the 1902 edition of *The Celtic Twilight* it is unclear whether she executed the small gold emblem on the top board (three fletched arrows pointing through a crescent moon). Her front and rear cover designs for *The Wind Among the Reeds* were redrawn when full vellum bindings were produced in 1903, but it is unlikely that she redrew them herself. Yeats refused her spinal designs on several books.

Gyles continued intermittently to publish verse in the *Saturday Review*, the *Candid Friend*, and *The Kensington*, *The Venture*, *The Academy*, *Orpheus*, and *The Vineyard*, organ of the Peasant Art Guild at Haslemere. Her close friend and patron Cecil French, who bought her fine portrait of Yeats, recalled her 'considerable reputation around 1900. She was a most difficult being with noble qualities, who invariably became the despair of those who had helped her.' French also records that her projected collection of verses was 'at one time actually in type (I saw it). She flatly refused to correct the proofs, saying the effort would kill her; nor was anyone else allowed to correct the proofs. The publisher was not pleased' (U. Reading L.). Typescripts of her verses survive in A. H. Bullen's archive in Stratford.

Arthur Symons, however, claimed that he had introduced her to a London publisher who was happy with her verses but rejected the dedication she insisted on: 'To the beautiful memory of Oscar Wilde'. In 1904 Thomas B. Mosher, the pirate publisher, rejected the poems pressed on him on behalf of the 'quite unmanageable and unpractical' author (Symons, 171–2). Her last book cover may well be that of Arthur Humphrey's Wilde anthology, *Sebastian Melmoth* (1905). In March 1907 she was 'comparatively prosperous', writing:

> art notes for Frank Harris, and reviewing novels. She even does an occasional drawing, and has never been known to look upon the world with so little malice. She has quite a group of friends, but changes them completely every six months. (Yeats, 2 March 1907, Berg Collection, NYPL)

Yeats affirms that by 1908 she had ended a love affair by reading Browning to her lover in the middle of the night (Wade, 511). Faith and Compton Mackenzie visited her in Paradise Walk, Chelsea, where she was living in 'an atmosphere of squalid poverty', spending her time 'lying upon a broken-down truckle-bed', an episode which finds its way into *Tatting*, where the room is adorned with a Beardsley 'solitary on the whitewashed wall, a delicious riot of satyrs and fauns' (F. C. Mackenzie, *Tatting*, 1957, 97–8). Compton Mackenzie invited her to Cornwall in May 1908:

> She looked rather like a part of the decorations of a harvest festival which had been caught up unwittingly by one of the congregation and dragged outside. Her large-brimmed black hat was wreathed with poppies; her green silk dress hung upon her … Her cheeks, no doubt once rosy and bloomed with youth, were now pale; her hair, no doubt once autumn-gold, was now dead as a faded rug; her pale blue eyes lacked lustre … In a tiny cottage she was an intolerable nuisance. (Mackenzie, octave 4, 36–9)

In February 1906 Gyles had offered Grant Richards an 'alphabet' which she was designing, 'The alphabet of the wonderful wood', but it was one of many projects never completed (University of Texas, Ransom HRC). Beginning with the letter U, she painted 'an entrancing water-colour of a very white unicorn against a very blue sky, and did no more'. Eleanor Farjeon, who occasionally typed her poems, thought her 'quite exquisitely gifted, as a writer and an artist; with the sort of temperament that stood in her own light', she was 'fascinating and exhausting', and 'filled the air with fantastic talk and anecdotes on the "nineties"'. Her hands were the most beautiful Farjeon had ever seen but 'quite the dirtiest' (letter, U. Reading L.)

In 1914, as John Meade, Gyles published *Letters to Children about Drawing, Painting, and Something More*. She continued to write, paint, drift, be ill, and to gravitate towards small arts and crafts or religious communities (such as the Order of the Holy Mount, Folkestone), supported by increasingly disgruntled patrons including Clifford Bax, who thought her a parasite. Urged by Grant Richards to write her memoirs of the 1890s, she wrote a novel, *Pilgrimage*, in Folkestone about 1919, which Richards rejected in February 1921. The characters include Pascoe, an Irish theosophist, mystic folklorist, and painter (George Russell), and Benador Quested, a dark-eyed mystical poet and animal lover (Yeats) who runs a donkey sanctuary in Devon (MS, U. Reading L.). In January 1924 Richards was still asking her for her memoirs. In the 1930s Eleanor Farjeon had a 'sudden wild letter' from her. She was living in a Brixton basement, in an 'awful state' with a big mongrel dog (U. Reading L.). Her last address was 19 Tredown Road, Lewisham, where she lived in a room empty but for a chaise longue, some bric-à-brac, and the manuscripts now in the University of Reading. She died on 23 January 1949 in a nursing home at 69 Crystal Palace Park Road, Beckenham, Kent, leaving £611 1s. WARWICK GOULD

**Sources** W. B. Yeats, *Autobiographies* (1955) · W. B. Yeats, 'A symbolic artist and the coming of symbolic art', *The Dome* (Dec 1898) · A. Symons, *Selected letters, 1880–1935*, ed. K. Beckson and J. M. Monro (1989) · R. H. Sherard, *The life of Oscar Wilde* (1906) · R. J. Finneran and others, eds., *Letters to W. B. Yeats* (1977) · R. Ellmann, 'Black magic against white: Aleister Crowley versus W. B. Yeats', *Partisan Review* (1948) · K. Beckson, *Arthur Symons: a life* (1987) · J. Adams, *Madder music, stronger wine: the life of Ernest Dowson, poet and decadent* (2000) · J. G. Nelson, *Leonard Smithers, publisher to the decadents* (2000) · C. Mackenzie, *My life and times* (1963–71) · *The letters of W. B. Yeats*, ed. A. Wade (1954)

**Archives** U. Reading L., MSS

**Wealth at death** £611 1s.: administration (limited), 13 April 1949, *CGPLA Eng. & Wales*

**Gyles, Mascal** (1595/6–1652), Church of England clergyman and writer, was born at Lewes, Sussex. He attended Cambridge University, matriculating as a sizar from Pembroke College in Michaelmas term, 1611, and graduating BA early in 1619. On 12 March 1620, aged twenty-four, he was ordained as a deacon in the diocese of London. After serving for a short time as curate of Hamsey, near Lewes, Gyles was instituted in 1621 to the vicarage of Ditchling, also in the archdeaconry of Lewes. He married a wife, Frances, who survived him, together with sons Samuel and Edward, daughters Mercy and Helen, and Frances's two children of a previous marriage. In his will Gyles provided financial inducements for Samuel and Edward to settle in the Americas and Ireland respectively.

Gyles is chiefly remembered for the protracted controversy in which he was involved with Thomas Barton, rector of the nearby parish of Westmeston. On Gyles's own account, 'especially since this Archbishop's time' (since William Laud's elevation in 1633) both biblical texts and canons of the church were being used locally to establish the practice of 'corporal bowing of the knee' whenever the name of Jesus was spoken during services, and he had felt compelled to distribute arguments against this among his own parishioners. Gyles claimed that his chief opponent had refused all offers of conference, and traduced his own views as factious and seditious, so compelling him to commit them to print. His first published salvo appeared about July 1642 under the title *A Treatise Against Superstitious Jesu Worship*, which Barton reprinted in *A Tryall of the Counterscarfe* (preface dated 31 December 1642), the second of two works issued by him on the matter disputed.

The controversy centred upon a religious observance, but was also closely bound up with political divisions. Gyles identified the practice of bowing as part of the superstitious baggage of popery which, by mid-1642, parliament was engaged to root out; his work was dedicated to Sir Anthony Stapley, one of the two members for Sussex in the Short and Long parliaments and later a member of the council of state. In Barton's first work on the subject, *Antiteixisma, or, A Counterscarfe*, he included a preface to the House of Commons, but his opening epistle to Charles I stressed that 'no clouds of horror shall frighten my obedience before God and the King' and recognized 'your majestys supremacy, next under Christ'. His distaste for parliamentarian puritanism is reflected in his references to 'confessor [William] Prynne' and 'father [Henry] Burton', and to these Gyles drew attention in *A Defence*, dated by George Thomason on 8 August 1643, in order to deflect his opponent's accusations of extremism and to identify himself with the authority of parliament. This work seems to have marked the end of the controversy. In 1644 Gyles was succeeded at Ditchling by Nathaniel White. Following his nomination on 1 March 1648 Gyles acted as vicar of Wartling, also in Sussex. He reports in his will of July 1652 that he had 'adventured £50 upon the service of Ireland, if or when the said land shall be declared to be reduced' (PRO, PROB 11/230, fols. 75–6). He died soon afterwards and was buried at Wartling on 14 August. STEPHEN WRIGHT

**Sources** Venn, *Alum. Cant.* • C. H. Cooper and T. Cooper, *N&Q*, 3rd ser., 6 (1864) • PRO, PROB 11/230, fols. 75–6 • G. L. Hennessy, *Chichester diocese clergy lists* (1900) • W. A. Shaw, *A history of the English church during the civil wars and under the Commonwealth, 1640–1660*, 2 vols. (1900) • T. Barton, *Antiteixisma, or, A counterscarfe prepared anno 1642, for the eviction of those zealots that in their works defy all external bowing at the name of Jesus* (1642) • T. Barton, *A tryall of the counterscarfe, made 1642 in answer to a scandalous pamphlet, intituled 'A treatise against superstitious Jesu worship' written by Mascall Giles, vicar of Ditchling, in Sussex* (1642)

**Gyrth, earl of East Anglia** (*d.* 1066), magnate, was one of the younger sons of *Godwine, earl of Wessex (*d.* 1053), and his wife, *Gytha (*fl.* c.1022–1068) [*see under* Godwine], and accompanied his parents to Flanders when the family fled into exile in 1051. Unlike his brothers (*Swein, *Harold, *Tostig, and *Leofwine), Gyrth does not attest the early charters of Edward the Confessor, but he may nevertheless have been older than Leofwine, for he seems to have been promoted before him. The life of King Edward, after recording Harold's succession to Wessex in 1053 and Tostig's elevation to Northumbria in 1055, adds that the king 'did not suffer the younger brother Gyrth … to be left out of the honours, but gave him a shire [Norfolk] at the extremity of eastern England, and promised to increase this … when he had thrown off his boyhood years' (*Life of King Edward*, 33). Norfolk was part of the earldom of East Anglia, held by Ælfgar (*d.* 1062?) from 1053 to 1057, but perhaps Gyrth received it when Ælfgar was exiled in 1055. There are no charters for the years 1055–8, and Gyrth first attests as earl in 1059. By then he held the whole of East Anglia, Ælfgar having succeeded to Mercia on his father's death in 1057. A series of royal writs addressed to Gyrth show that his authority covered East Anglia generally and particularly Norfolk, Suffolk, and also Oxfordshire, which Ælfgar too had held. Cambridgeshire, where Gyrth possessed the large manor of Whittlesford, may also have been part of his earldom. Gyrth seems to have had a close relationship with his brother Tostig, whom he accompanied to Rome in 1061, attending the papal synod held at Easter (15 April) of that year. He also held the large (and probably comital) manor of Kempston in Bedfordshire, which lay within Tostig's earldom. Gyrth's landed wealth can be estimated from Domesday Book. Among the estates probably inherited from his father is the huge manor of Washington in Sussex, the shire from which his family originated, and he and his mother, Gytha, had land at Chaddleworth, Berkshire. Most of his manors, naturally, lay in Norfolk and Suffolk, but even here he is overshadowed by his brother, Earl Harold, who retained some of the comital estates even when he ceased to be earl. Gyrth's standing is shown by the number of men, of varying rank and wealth, who chose to commend themselves to him, not only in the shires of his own earldom (Norfolk, Suffolk, and Cambridgeshire) but also in Berkshire, Bedfordshire, and Hertfordshire.

Gyrth was killed at the battle of Hastings on 14 October 1066; whether he had previously fought at Stamford Bridge on 25 September is uncertain, though men from the eastern shires did take part in that battle. As with Harold himself, Gyrth's name attracted much legendary embroidery. Orderic Vitalis makes him advise Harold against meeting Duke William so soon after the exhausting victory at Stamford Bridge; Gyrth offers to lead the army instead, since 'I have taken no oath and owe nothing to Count William', but Harold angrily refuses (Ordericus Vitalis, *Eccl. hist.*, 2.170–73). The author of the *Carmen de Hastingae proelio* has Gyrth killed in single combat with Duke William himself, but on the Bayeux tapestry the knight who rides Gyrth down as he wields his spear is unnamed. The story was known to Wace, who greatly embellishes Gyrth's role in the Hastings campaign, though he is vague about whether he was actually killed. The thirteenth-century life of Harold maintains that Gyrth, like Harold, survived the battle. It relates that Walter, abbot of Waltham (1184–1201), met him at Henry II's palace of Woodstock, where he dismissed the story that Harold's body rested at Waltham Holy Cross. Gyrth is described as a tall, handsome man, though very old (he would have been at least 150). ANN WILLIAMS

**Sources** *ASC*, s.a. 1051, 1066 [texts C, D, E] • F. Barlow, ed. and trans., *The life of King Edward who rests at Westminster* (1962) • F. E. Harmer, ed., *Anglo-Saxon writs* (1952) • F. Barlow, *Edward the Confessor* (1970) • R. Fleming, *Kings and lords in conquest England* (1991) • P. A. Clarke, *The English nobility under Edward the Confessor* (1994) • A. Williams, 'Land and power in the eleventh century: the estates of Harold Godwineson', *Anglo-Norman Studies*, 3 (1980), 171–87, 230–34 • Ordericus Vitalis, *Eccl. hist.*, vol. 2 • *The Carmen de Hastingae proelio of Guy, bishop of Amiens*, ed. C. Morton and H. Muntz, OMT (1972) • L. Watkiss and M. Chibnall, eds. and trans., *The Waltham chronicle: an account of the discovery of our holy cross at Montacute and its conveyance to Waltham*, OMT (1994) • F. Michel, ed., *Chroniques anglo-normandes: recueil d'extraits et d'écrits relatifs à l'histoire de Normandie et d'Angleterre*, 3 vols. (Rouen, 1836–40) • R. Abels, 'An introduction to the Bedfordshire Domesday', *The Bedfordshire Domesday*, ed. A. Williams (1991–) • D. M. Wilson, ed., *The Bayeux tapestry* (1985) • A. Farley, ed., *Domesday Book*, 2 vols. (1783), 1.28, 59v, 154, 194, 198, 202, 217, 217v; 2.15

**Likenesses** portrait, repro. in Wilson, ed., *Bayeux tapestry*, pl. 68

**Gytha** (*fl. c.*1022–1068). *See under* Godwine, earl of Wessex (*d.* 1053).

**H. A.** (*fl.* 1613), poet, was the author of *The Scourge of Venus*, an erotic narrative poem printed in 1613 and reissued in 1614 and 1620. A. B. Grosart identified him as Henry Austin, from the following remark by Thomas Heywood prefixed to *The Brazen Age* (1613):

> What imperfection soever it have, having a brazen face it cannot blush; much like a pedant about this towne, who, when all trades fail'd, turn'd *pedagogue*, once insinuating with me, borrowed from me certaine translations of *Ovid*, as his three books *De arte amandi*, and two *De remedio amoris* which since, his most brazen face hath most impudently challenged as his own, wherefore I must needs proclaime it as far as *Ham*, where he now keeps schoole, *Hos ego versiculos feci, tulit alter honores*, they were things which out of my juniority and want of judgement, I committed to the view of some private friends, but with no purpose of publishing, or further communicating them. Therfore I wold entreate that *Austin*, for so his name is, to acknowledge his wrong to me in shewing them, & his owne impudence, & ignorance in challenging them. But courteous Reader, I can onely excuse him in this, that this is the *Brazen Age*. (T. Heywood, *The Dramatic Works of Thomas Heywood*, 1874, 3.167–8)

Grosart's identification has not, however, been accepted by subsequent editors. *The Scourge of Venus* is a reworking of the tale of Cinyras from Ovid's *Metamorphoses*, while Heywood is talking about the *Ars amatoria* and the *Remedia amoris*. Heywood's enemy **Austin** (*fl.* 1613) remains a shadowy figure, and there remains no evidence to reveal his first name, or to link him to the otherwise unknown H. A. of *The Scourge of Venus*.

MATTHEW STEGGLE

**Sources** *DNB* • H. A., *The scourge of Venus*, ed. A. B. Grosart (1876) • P. W. Miller, ed., *Seven minor epics of the English Renaissance (1596–1624)* (1967) • A. M. Clark, 'Thomas Heywood's *Art of love* lost and found', *The Library*, 4th ser., 3 (1922–3), 210–22, esp. 212 • T. Heywood, *The brazen age* (1613)

**H. B.** *See* Doyle, John (1797–1868).

**H. D.** *See* Doolittle, Hilda (1886–1961).

**Haag, (Johann) Carl** (1820–1915), watercolour painter, was born on 20 April 1820 at Theaterstrasse 2, Erlangen, Bavaria. His father, a baker and amateur draughtsman, Johann Christoph Wilhelm Haag (1789–1828), would not allow the precocious boy to have drawing lessons, but after Johann's death in 1828 Carl was encouraged by his mother, Joanna Barbara Weber (1789–1866). From 1834 he studied with his uncle, Johann Rudolph Weber, a porcelain painter in Nuremberg. Haag attended the Polytechnic Drawing School there and later the Nuremberg Academy under Albert Reindel, and made book illustrations. In Munich in 1844 Haag painted miniature portraits of distinguished sitters including the duke and duchess Maximilian of Bavaria. He spent five months in Brussels and met the painters Gustaf, Baron Wappers, and Louis Gallait. In London in April 1847 he was much impressed by the English watercolour technique. On visits to Rome in the winter of 1847–8 and again in 1852 and 1856 he made oil studies from which he developed elaborate watercolours, many showing figures in local costumes or landscapes in the Campagna. He evolved his own watercolour technique, using different colours imposed on one another. He never used whites, but scraped out his highlights. He later invented a fixative, of wax and spirit of lavender, to use on his watercolours. In 1848 Haag enrolled at the Royal Academy Schools in London to study anatomy. An accident with a pistol in December 1848 almost cost him the use of his right hand. His thumb was torn off except for two tendons, but was healed by Prescott Hewett, then a skilled medical student. Hewett introduced Haag to his first patron, Colonel Douglas-Pennant (later Lord Penryhn). Between 1849 and 1881 Haag showed eleven pictures (including seven portraits) at the Royal Academy. He gave up painting in oils, and was elected an associate of the New Watercolour Society in 1850 and a member in 1853. There he exhibited 343 pictures in all (portraits were excluded).

In the Tyrol in 1852 Haag chanced to meet Charles, prince of Leiningen, half-brother of Queen Victoria, and Prince Albert's brother, Ernest II, duke of Saxe-Coburg and Gotha (to whom Haag subsequently became *Hofmaler*). He painted a large watercolour of the prince of Leiningen with the duke, on a chamois hunt in the mountains, which they gave to Queen Victoria. In 1853, at her invitation, Haag spent six weeks at Balmoral and painted large watercolours entitled *Morning in the Highlands* and *Evening at Balmoral*. The queen later acquired three of his oriental scenes, including *The Jews at the Wailing Wall*. After the death of the prince consort, Haag returned to Balmoral to

(Johann) Carl Haag (1820–1915), by Cundall, Downes & Co., c.1863

paint mementoes of former happy times. Over twenty works and many studies remain in the Royal Collection.

In 1854 Haag, on a visit to Dalmatia and Montenegro, painted Danilo I, prince of Montenegro. He spent the winter in Venice, returning to England via Dresden. In August 1858 he travelled to Egypt, visiting Germany, Trieste, and Athens *en route*. In Cairo he shared a house with the painter Frederick Goodall and together they saw the pyramids of Giza and Suez. From April 1859 Haag spent some months in Jerusalem, and under Queen Victoria's 'protection' received permission to paint inside the mosque of Oman. He visited Samaria, Galilee, Damascus, Baalbek, and the camp of Aghile Agha, the chief of the Bedouin. In the desert Haag wore Bedouin costume and enjoyed local food. Through Sheikh Medjuel and his wife, the former Jane Digby (Lady Ellenborough), he was permitted to travel and paint at Palmyra. Early in 1860 Haag was working hard in Egypt, Palestine, and Syria, returning to London in April. For the rest of his life he used the material he had collected to paint finished watercolours.

Haag settled in London, became naturalized, in 1860, and on 16 May 1866 married Ida Juliane Margarethe Luise (1832–1911), the daughter of General Büttner, commandant of Lüneburg in Hanover. They had three sons and a daughter. The following year he built an oriental studio in his house in Hampstead, London. In Egypt again in 1873 he was entertained by the khedive through an introduction from Albert Edward, prince of Wales, for whom Haag painted several oriental watercolours. In Haag's later work his figures are usually larger, and wear modern rather than historical dress. In 1903 Haag retired to the Rote Turm at Oberwesel on the Rhine, which he had originally restored in 1863, and where he died on 17 January 1915 in his sleep. He was cremated at Mainz on 21 January, and his ashes are said to have been scattered in the gardens of Rote Turm. Haag's importance as an orientalist is now appreciated; his works are in many galleries including the Victoria and Albert Museum, London, at Bristol, Leeds, and Manchester, at Erlangen and Oberwesel, Germany, and in the Jordan National Gallery (Amman) and the Israel Museum (Jerusalem). DELIA MILLAR

**Sources** family papers and diaries, priv. coll. • C. Oelwein, 'Der Erlanger Maler Carl Haag', *Erlanger Bausteine zur Fränkischen Heimatforschung*, 48 (2000), 7–42 • J. L. Roget, *A history of the 'Old Water-Colour' Society*, 2 (1891), 341–52 • M. P. Jackson, *Introduction to exhibition of Haag's work* (1885) [exhibition catalogue, Goupil Galleries, New Bond Street, London] • F. Wedmore, 'Carl, Haag R. W. S.', *Magazine of Art* (1889), 52–61 • D. Millar, *Queen Victoria's life in the Scottish highlands* (1985) • D. Millar, *The Victorian watercolours and drawings in the collection of her majesty the queen*, 2 vols. (1995), 385–98 • sale catalogue (1982), lots 1–83 [Sothebys, 29 April 1982] • Dreweatt Neate's sale catalogue (2000), lots 1–140 [6 June 2000] • private information (2004) [family]

**Archives** priv. coll., diaries, etc. • Royal Arch.

**Likenesses** Cundall, Downes & Co., photograph, c.1863, NPG [*see illus.*] • drawing, 1889, priv. coll.

**Haak, Theodore** (1605–1690), translator and natural philosopher, was born on 25 July 1605 at Neuhausen, near Worms, where his father, Theodor Haak, held some administrative office; his mother, Maria, was the daughter of Daniel Tossanus, a Huguenot refugee who had become rector of the University of Heidelberg. Haak's own studies at the university were probably disrupted by the Thirty Years' War, and he spent a year in England in 1625–6, first at Oxford, then at Cambridge. On his return to the continent he translated two pious English tracts into German for friends in Cologne. Returning to England in 1628 he studied at Oxford for three years, at Gloucester Hall, where he learned mathematics with Thomas Allen. Although without a degree, he was ordained a deacon, and was then involved in collecting money for protestant clergymen in Germany who had been impoverished by the war. Subsequently he went back to Germany in 1633. It seems that he had an adequate income, as he travelled widely: at first in parts of Germany still held by protestants, and certainly in the Netherlands, where he matriculated at the University of Leiden in 1638, before finally settling in England later that year.

Soon after his arrival Haak became a close friend of Samuel Hartlib, and so was involved in plans to promote Comenius's schemes for a universal digest of all real knowledge. Haak's family connections had given him a good knowledge of French, and in 1639 he began to correspond with Marin Mersenne, who was at the heart of a network of all those interested in recent developments in natural philosophy. There survive (in Haak's copies) at

**Theodore Haak (1605–1690),** by Jonathan Richardson the elder

least eleven of Mersenne's letters to Haak, seeking information on recent books and research carried out in England. Haak sent copies of John Pell's *Idea matheseos*, as a model for a more general reform of natural knowledge, together with Comenius's outline of his programme. Now aware of the group of enthusiasts that met at Mersenne's convent in Paris to discuss such new discoveries, Haak may have been inspired to organize something similar. During the civil war he remained in London, apart from a diplomatic journey to Denmark on parliament's behalf. According to the mathematician John Wallis it was Haak who in 1645 instigated meetings to investigate new theories and experiments in natural philosophy or in medicine. This also encouraged him to write again to Mersenne in 1647–8, to exchange ideas and inform him of scientific news from England. As he declared, it would be better to know less 'que d'en manquer la vraye jouissance, qui gist en la communication' ('than to lose the true pleasure that lies in communication'; Brown, 269).

However active Haak may have been at first, he was soon distracted by work on *The Dutch Annotations upon the Whole Bible*, the original of which had been published in the Netherlands in 1637. The translation, commissioned by the Westminster assembly of divines, dominated his life for some time, for it did not appear until 1657. During the same period he was employed by the council of state as a translator and a source of information through his correspondence. Haak stayed in touch with the elector palatine and throughout his life was always a welcoming friend to German visitors in London. In 1656 he married a widow, Elisabeth Genue (*d.* 1669); she had had a daughter, born in Utrecht, and so may have been Dutch herself.

Soon after the Restoration, Haak was among the founder members of the Royal Society, and was asked to look into such technical matters as oyster fishing. Until quite late in his life he may have attended meetings of the society, although he only occasionally contributed information, usually from correspondents abroad. He did acquire a collection of instruments and curious substances, including phosphorus, and he even invented a phosphorus lamp. On one occasion he demonstrated how a magnet which had apparently lost its powers could be reinforced; the Royal Society's portrait, donated as a memorial to him, shows him with his magnet on the table before him.

Probably in the late 1660s Haak began to translate John Milton's *Paradise Lost* into German. This was the first attempt to do so; a manuscript copy of the first three books only survives, although the first printed German translation, by Ernst von Berge (1682), made use of Haak's version. Having survived his wife by many years, Haak celebrated his eighty-first birthday in style. He died on 5 May 1690 in Bartlett Buildings, off Fetter Lane, London, and was buried three days later in St Andrew's, Holborn. Generally admired as a generous and kind person, he had many friends and no enemies, always looking on the good side of his acquaintance. So he was one of the few who remained friends with Robert Hooke for many years—they met frequently, and played chess together.

A. G. KELLER

**Sources** P. R. Barnett, *Theodore Haak, F.R.S., 1605–1690* (1962) · Wood, *Ath. Oxon.*, new edn · H. Brown, *Scientific organisations in seventeenth century France*, reissue (1967) · T. Birch, *The history of the Royal Society of London*, 4 vols. (1756–7); repr. with introduction by A. R. Hall (1968) · C. Webster, *The great instauration: science, medicine and reform, 1626–1660* (1975) · *The diary of Robert Hooke … 1672–1680*, ed. H. W. Robinson and W. Adams (1935) · *La correspondance de Marin Mersenne*, ed. C. De Waard, 17 vols. (Paris, 1932–88) · *DNB*

**Archives** Bibliothèque Nationale, Paris, Nouvelles Acquisitions Françaises | BL, Pell papers

**Likenesses** J. Richardson the elder, portrait, RS; copy, Bodl. Oxf. [*see illus.*]

**Wealth at death** see Barnett, *Theodore Haak*

**Haast, Sir (John Francis) Julius von** [*formerly* Johann Franz Haast] **(1822–1887)**, geologist and explorer, was born on 1 May 1822 at house no. 320, Bonn (now 1 Bonngasse), Germany, one of the nine children of Mathias Haast (1784–1852), tailor and lottery office keeper, and his wife, Anna Eva Theodora (1788–1853), daughter of Theodor Rüth and his wife, Veronica Haltermann. He adopted the forename Julius from 1859. Haast attended school in Bonn and the Höhere Bürgerschule in Cologne, which he left prematurely in 1838. He never studied at a university, but was probably apprenticed to a merchant. From 1844 he practised different commercial occupations in Frankfurt am Main, spending periods as a self-employed textile-seller, a haulage contractor, and a salesman at a bookseller's. On 26 October 1846 he married, at Frankfurt, Antonie Auguste Caroline Schmitt (1825–1859), daughter of the well-known musician Aloys Schmitt. Later in New Zealand Haast spared no effort in hushing up most of the events of his unsuccessful early life in Europe.

Haast was commissioned by a firm of British shipowners to report on prospects for German emigration to New Zealand, and arrived at Auckland on 21 December 1858. By chance, the following day he met the German geologist Ferdinand Hochstetter (1829–1884), a participant in the Austrian *Novara* expedition. This meeting changed the course of Haast's life. He joined Hochstetter in his eight-month-long explorations and became his zealous pupil. After Hochstetter's return to Europe, Haast was asked by the government of the province of Nelson to explore its western portion; he investigated fully the coalfields at Brunner, discovered a new coalfield at Coalbrookdale, and reported traces of gold in a number of west coast rivers. Haast sent his 'Report of the topographical and geological exploration of the western districts of the Nelson province, New Zealand' to the University of Tübingen in Germany and applied for the degree of doctor of philosophy, which, in part because of Hochstetter's emphatic recommendation, he was awarded in 1862. The following year, on 25 June, he married Mary Dobson (*b.* 1844), daughter of the provincial engineer Edward Dobson.

Haast's geological investigation of the rocks in Canterbury's Port hills in 1860–61 had established the feasibility of constructing a tunnel to connect Christchurch and the port of Lyttelton. In 1861 he was rewarded by being appointed geologist to the Canterbury province; at the same time he became a naturalized British subject. In the same year Haast commenced his ten-year topographical and geological surveys, especially based in the Southern Alps. He named the Franz Josef glacier, predicted artesian water under the Canterbury plains, and collected much botanical information. The results were written up in his book *Geology of the Provinces of Canterbury and Westland, New Zealand*, published in Christchurch in 1879.

Haast's interests ranged far and wide. He reported not only on geology, palaeontology, and geomorphology, but also on recent animals and ethnology. Scientists from many parts of the world showed a special interest in his studies of the extinct, flightless, moa and he sent a number of moa skeletons to European institutions (he was nicknamed 'moa-man'). Interest was also shown in the results of his studies on Quaternary glaciation in New Zealand, although in this field he was obviously influenced by some hypotheses written by his European contemporaries. In all, Haast published some 150 works, many of them printed in Christchurch.

Haast founded the Philosophical Institute of Canterbury in 1862. He was appointed first director of the Canterbury Museum in 1868, and in 1870, together with Bishop H. J. C. Harper, established the Canterbury Collegiate Union to promote the formation of Canterbury College; Haast was subsequently appointed the college's first professor of geology in 1876. He was elected FRS in 1867, received an Austrian knighthood in 1875 (at which time he added 'von' to his name), and was appointed KCMG in 1886. A forceful, ebullient and wholly self-made man, von Haast died of heart disease on 16 August 1887 in Christchurch, where he was buried. Although his publications on geological topics in New Zealand have little relevance to modern geology, he played a large part in the development of the subject, both in Canterbury and in New Zealand generally. WOLFHART LANGER

**Sources** G. vom Rath, 'Denkrede auf Sir Julius Johann Franz', *Sitzungsberichte der Niederrheinischen Gesellschaft für Natur- und Heilkunde zu Bonn* (1880), 217–32 • b. cert., Bonn register office • school report, Historical archive, Cologne, Germany, no. 73, p. 45 • University of Tübingen Archives • H. F. von Haast, *The life and times of Sir Julius von Haast* (1948) • M. Müllerott, 'Haast, Sir Julius Johann Franz Ritter v.', *Neue deutsche Biographie*, ed. Otto, Graf zu Stolberg-Wernigerode (Berlin, 1953–) • J. B. Waterhouse, 'Haast, Johann Franz Julius von', *DSB* • W. Langer, 'Der Bonner Neuseelandforscher Sir Johann Franz Julius von Haast, 1822–1887', *Bonner Geschichtsblätter*, 39 (1992), 273–93 • D. R. Oldroyd, 'Haast's glacial theories and the opinions of his European contemporaries', *Journal of the Royal Society of New Zealand*, 3 (1973), 5–14 • O. Krösche, *Die Moa-Strausse: Neuseelands ausgestorbene Riesenvögel* (1963), 148 • m. cert., Bonn register office, Germany [parents of J. F. J. von Haast] • W. A. S. Sarjeant, *Geologists and the history of geology: an international bibliography from the origins to 1978. Supplement 2, 1985–1993*, 3 vols. (1996) • R. Barton, 'Haast and the moa: reversing the tyranny of distance', *Pacific Science*, 54 (2000), 251–63

**Archives** NL NZ, Turnbull L., notebook; family papers

**Likenesses** photograph, *c.*1863, repro. in von Haast, *Life and times* • Bassano, photograph, 1886, repro. in von Haast, *Life and times* • A. Küppers, marble bust, 1889, Canterbury Museum, Christchurch, New Zealand; repro. in Langer, 'Der Bonner Neuseelandforscher' • R. T. & Co., wood-engraving, NPG; repro. in *ILN* (7 Aug 1886) • four photographs, Geologische Bundesanstalt, Vienna; repro. in Langer, 'Der Bonner Neuseelandforscher' • photograph, University of Bonn Library

**Wealth at death** £2000 and a farm: von Haast, *Life and times*, 342

**Haberkorn, Johann Christoph** (*c.*1720–1776), printer, was probably born in northern Germany. About his family origins and upbringing nothing is known, but by the summer of 1746 he was certainly in London, marrying Sarah Burscoe in St George's, Mayfair, on 7 September of that year. By early 1749 Haberkorn had set up as an independent printer with his partner Johann Nicodemus Gussen and had begun paying rates on a property of the north side of Gerrard Street, Soho.

One of the earliest productions of the Gerrard Street press was a duodecimo edition of Luther's New Testament published early in 1751, but certainly in the press during 1750. This was announced in an advertisement printed in the *Daily Advertiser* shortly before Christmas 1750. It would be printed 'mit neuen Buchstaben und auf fein Papier' ('with new type and on fine paper'; *Daily Advertiser*, 22 Dec 1750, 4). In the preface to the New Testament, Haberkorn and Gussen describe their motive in setting up a German press in London as 'entirely in order to print good, improving works that would promote true Christianity' (p. 4). Certainly most of their early productions are octavo sermons or devotional works by Friedrich Michael Ziegenhagen, preacher at the German court chapel in St James's. In their preface Haberkorn and Gussen also mention various target groups for the sale of this material, including German-speaking schoolchildren, German professionals and tradesmen who had moved to London, charitable persons who would be disposed to buy a number of copies to distribute among the indigent German poor, and German-speaking protestants in the North American colonies.

In the same month as they were announcing the completion of the New Testament Haberkorn and Gussen were arrested:

> on a charge of having printed at Gerrard Street, St. Ann's Parish, Soho, for James Marmaduke, bookseller in St. Martin's Lane, five hundred copies of a book entitled *Morning and night prayers with the litanies and prayers recommended to be said in Catholic families.*

They appear, however, to have recovered quickly from this setback (Mosher, June 1978). Haberkorn's partner is no longer mentioned after 1753, by which time Haberkorn had himself become a widower. On 17 November 1753 he married 'Ann Weston, spinster, a minor', at St George's, Hanover Square, London. Haberkorn now acquired a family: John George Haberkorn was baptized on 1 September 1754 at St Anne's, Soho, and a daughter, Mary Haberkorn, followed him on 5 January 1756 (Chapman, 50).

Having established himself as a specialist for printing with Fraktur types in German with the capability of printing in English books, Haberkorn now quickly expanded into other areas of the market. He appears to have made something of a speciality of programme books, for example, in both French and Italian. In the mid-1750s Haberkorn began to diversify his business further, taking him in quite unexpected directions. In 1754 he was responsible for the letterpress in Thomas Chippendale's *The Gentleman and Cabinet-Maker's Director*, one of the most celebrated productions of its kind in this period. The publication, which includes 160 plates, may have influenced other authors in the field to seek Haberkorn's services. Prominent among them was William Chambers, whose *Designs of Chinese Buildings, Furniture, Dresses and Utensils* of 1757 (sold by the author 'next door to Tom's Coffee-house, Russel-street, Covent-Garden') was the first of a number of his works printed by Haberkorn. As with the Chippendale, Haberkorn's name is omitted from this first edition, but the printer's ornaments are undoubtedly his, and he is named as the printer on the French version that appeared in the same year.

It is known that Haberkorn had lost his second wife by 1758 because, as her executor, he had entered into what was clearly a bitter legal dispute with his mother-in-law by November of that year. He had left Gerrard Street by December 1759, moving to nearby Grafton Street, about half-way down on the south side. When the 'new' John Haberkorn of Grafton Street re-emerges in 1761, the list of the publications printed by him reads very differently from that of ten years earlier: of the titles so far identified, not a single one is in German. In 1762 Haberkorn embarked on probably his most ambitious project to date: the first volume of James 'Athenian' Stuart's and Nicholas Revett's *Antiquities of Athens*, one of the most significant English architectural publications of the period. The engravings are found not only as separate plates but also well integrated with the letterpress. It is remarkable that standard bibliographies of British architectural writers omit any mention of Haberkorn's contribution to the project, although it surely establishes him among the most innovative and sophisticated printers of the period. Haberkorn was clearly pleased with the solution for the title-page for *The Antiquities of Athens* because a similar 'archaic' or 'architectural' quality can be found on the title-page of another large work he printed in 1762: an edition of Boccaccio's *Decamerone* printed for John Nourse.

Mortimer's *Universal Director* of 1763 lists 'Habberkorne, John. Grafton-street, Soho' firmly among the leading tradesmen of London (Maxted, 15). In the same year he took his first recorded apprentice, John Jones, indentured for £10. After 1763, however, no further grand illustrated works are associated with Haberkorn's name; most of the titles known to have been printed by him during the next two years are again devotional works in German. It must be assumed his business was failing by this time; he had certainly stopped paying the rates on the Grafton Street property by May 1766. Not unusually, the chancery case against his in-laws was still in progress in the following year and a document dated 19 June 1767 shows that Haberkorn was by then living in the parish of St George, Southwark, although his name continues to appear in imprints with the Grafton Street address during that year. If the details are unclear, it seems certain that the business was effectively handed over to the German printer and bookseller Carl Heydinger during 1767. Apparently abandoning the chancery case and leaving his children in London, Haberkorn returned to Germany, probably in late 1767 or 1768.

Haberkorn went to Altona, now a part of Hamburg but at that time a separate entity and a dependency of the Danish crown. In 1771 he was married for the third time; his new wife was Gesine Metta Spieringk or Spiering. On 15 May 1772 he was arrested again, for reprinting a pamphlet regarded as favourable to Caroline, queen of Denmark, George III's sister, now disgraced after the fall and execution of her lover Count Struensee. After three years' imprisonment Haberkorn received a pardon on 16 March 1775, but survived only a further eighteen months, dying, probably in Altona, on 8 August 1776.

Haberkorn was an innovative entrepreneur prepared to take risks in response to a rapidly developing market. Unexpectedly, he turns out to have been associated with some of the most ambitious titles printed in London during the century. His printing shop could handle a range of languages, undertaking major projects and producing presswork of the highest quality. His role in Anglo-German cultural exchange during the mid-eighteenth century was clearly significant. GRAHAM JEFCOATE

**Sources** parish poor rate books for St Anne's, Soho, London, Gerrard Street · City Westm. AC, Leicester Fields Ward, A190, A191a, A194 · Copulations-Register, 1766–92, Ev.-Luth. Hauptkirchen Gemeinde in Hamburg-Altona, Anwhang, 70 I b, 1771, No. 6 · Inland Revenue registers, PRO, vol. 23, fol. 222 (1763) · court of chancery, Six Clerks' Office, Pleadings, 1758–1800, PRO, C12/496/29, C12/964/56 · Georg-August-Universität Göttingen, Universitätsarchiv, Theol. 75, 12 March 1765 · H. R. Plomer and others, *A dictionary of the printers and booksellers who were at work in England, Scotland, and Ireland from 1726 to 1775* (1932), 112 · F. J. Mosher, 'John Haberkorn', *Factotum: Newsletter of the XVIIIth-Century Short Title Catalogue*, 1 (March 1978), 4–6; 2 (June 1978), 9 · D. F.

McKenzie, ed., *Stationers' Company apprentices*, [3]: 1701–1800 (1978) • V. A. Berch, 'An additional note on John Haberkorn, printer', *Factotum: Newsletter of the XVIIIth-Century Short Title Catalogue*, 5 (April 1979), 4–5 • V. A. Berch, 'Haberkorniana', *Factotum: Newsletter of the XVIIIth-Century Short Title Catalogue*, 6 (Oct 1979), 5 • I. Maxted, *The London booktrades, 1735–1775: a checklist* (1984) • *Daily Advertiser* (22 Dec 1750) • J. H. Chapman, ed., *The register book of marriages belonging to the parish of St George, Hanover Square*, 1, Harleian Society, 11 (1886)

**Habersham, James** (1713–1775), benefactor and colonial official, was born in June 1713 at Beverley, Yorkshire, the son of James Habersham (*d.* in or after 1736), a dyer and innkeeper, and Elizabeth, *née* Sisson (*d.* 1720). Upon his mother's death, his father apprenticed him, aged seven, to his uncle, Joseph Habersham, a London merchant importing indigo dyes, deerskins, and sugar from the colonies. As a young adult he successfully managed two sugar-refining houses for his uncle, learning as he did the intricacies of bills of credit, insurance, shipping, and warehousing fees within Britain's far-flung empire. After hearing George Whitefield's persuasive and evangelistic message in 1736, Habersham determined to accompany him on a mission to frontier Georgia, despite the objections of his uncle and father.

James Habersham thus came to Georgia not to trade for goods and profit but, instead, to bargain for human souls, to exchange a comfortable life as a London merchant for a more satisfying one as a missionary in Britain's newest province. Whitefield travelled with him on that memorable voyage to Savannah in 1738 to succeed John Wesley. The two forged a friendship and mutual understanding that transcended four decades, a great religious awakening in America partly inspired by Whitefield, and a political revolution.

Whitefield's return to England later in 1738 left Habersham in charge of religious affairs in Savannah and of an orphanage for destitute and needy children throughout the province. Habersham's economical style and personality soon clashed with those of William Stephens, the elderly secretary and locum tenens for the trustees of the Georgia corporation, a philanthropic board that governed the colony for twenty years. Avoiding Stephens's person but not his pen, Habersham soon moved the orphanage, now named Bethesda, 10 miles outside Savannah; it became his home until 1744. There he met and married Mary Bolton (1723/4–1763), a sixteen-year-old student at the orphanage; her father, a Philadelphia merchant, had been converted by Whitefield's evangelical message on one of his 'Great Awakenings' in the middle colonies, and Whitefield performed the ceremony in 1740. They had ten children, three of whom, James, John, and Joseph, survived to adulthood.

A coincidence brought Habersham back to his mercantile roots. First, the trustees' store in Savannah closed, leaving many colonists without a source of supplies. Francis Harris, a former clerk at the store and a friend of the orphanage, took his pay from the trustees in kind and began a small operation in the summer of 1742. At almost the same time Habersham received a generous gift for Bethesda, as a result of Whitefield's preaching, which he

James Habersham (1713–1775), by Jeremiah Theus, 1772?

used to purchase a schooner and a large stock of supplies in Charles Town. Convinced that God had led him back into trade so he could help Bethesda and Georgia survive, Habersham, with Harris as his factor in Savannah, began a fledgeling business that resold dry goods and foodstuffs largely imported from Charles Town. Within a decade Habersham and Harris became the most successful merchants in Georgia, trans-shipping goods from Charles Town and trading directly with London and the West Indies. In 1749 the trustees appointed Habersham to the board of assistants, their official governing body in Georgia.

When the trustees surrendered their charter in 1752 and Georgia became a royal colony, the crown recognized Habersham's economic and political standing by appointing him to the royal council. Thereafter he prospered, as did Georgia. By the time of the revolution he had amassed a considerable fortune, including several plantations and homes, over 6000 acres, and 200 slaves, which enabled him to produce more than 1000 barrels of rice annually. Not surprisingly he named his main plantation 'Silk Hope' after the failed trustee's (i.e. his own) mercantile dream.

The Stamp Act crisis of 1765 not only saddened Habersham but also split him from his family. His 'dearest Mary' died in 1763, and, heartsick, he moved to Savannah to be closer to his sons and their mercantile activities, and to throw himself into the work of governing the growing province. Following Whitefield's evangelistic tack, Habersham sent his sons to Princeton, a 'New Light' Presbyterian college, where they not only learned the classics but also to question some of their father's generation's most cherished beliefs. In 1771 Sir James Wright, the colony's last royal governor, sailed for England. In his place he left James Habersham, a loyal, true, and 'firm friend of government', to preside over the administration and to help quell the 'liberty faction', led partially by Habersham's sons Joseph and John. Tormented by the endless strife between crown and colony, and also between himself and Joseph, and grieved at the death of his wife, Habersham welcomed Wright's return in 1773. Depressed, in poor health, and with the Calvinistic fatalism of someone who knew events were passing him by, he took a passage for the north and then to England. He died at sea, off New Jersey, in August 1775. MILTON READY

**Sources** K. Coleman and C. S. Gurr, eds., *Dictionary of Georgia biography*, 2 vols. (Athens, GA, 1983) • W. C. Smith, 'Georgia gentlemen: the Habershams of eighteenth-century Savannah', PhD diss., University of North Carolina, 1971 • K. Coleman, *Colonial Georgia: a history* (1976) • W. C. Smith, 'The Habershams: the merchant experience in Georgia', *Forty years of diversity: essays on colonial Georgia*, ed. H. Jackson and P. Spalding (1984) • A. D. Candler and others, eds., *The colonial records of the state of Georgia*, 26 vols. in 28 (1904–16); ongoing, with some vols. rev. (1970–) • E. Surrency, 'The life and public career of James Habersham, sr.', MA diss., University of Georgia, 1949 • W. C. Smith, 'Habersham, James', *ANB*
**Archives** Duke U., items • Georgia Historical Society Archives, Savannah, Georgia, family papers
**Likenesses** J. Theus, portrait, 1772?, Telfair Museum of Art, Savannah, Georgia [*see illus.*]

**Habershon, Matthew** (1789–1852), architect, was born into a family that came from Rotherham, Yorkshire. He was the father of the architects William Gilbee Habershon (1818–1892) and Edward Habershon; he also had four daughters. In 1806 he was articled to the architect William Atkinson, with whom he remained for some years as assistant. He began to exhibit at the Royal Academy in 1807, and entered the Royal Academy Schools in 1808; he continued to exhibit there until 1827.

Habershon designed many Gothic churches, including St Peter's, Belper (1824), Bishop Ryder's church, Derby (1838–40), and churches in Winster, Derbyshire (1842), and Kimberworth, Yorkshire (1840–42). He built the town hall (since burnt down), the county courts, and the market in Derby.

Habershon became interested in sixteenth- and seventeenth-century timber-framed houses, and in 1836 published *The Ancient Half-Timbered Houses of England*. He built several half-timbered houses himself, including a farmhouse at Hadzor, near Droitwich (*c*.1830), The Grange, Seacroft, near Leeds (1834), and Aston Sandford rectory, Buckinghamshire (1836–7).

In 1842 Habershon went to Jerusalem on behalf of the London Society for Promoting Christianity among the Jews, to supervise the completion of the Anglican cathedral there; the previous architect, J. W. Johns, had been dismissed. On his way home from the Holy Land in 1843, Habershon had a long interview with the king of Prussia, who had been involved in setting up the bishopric of Jerusalem, and in 1844 the king conferred the great gold medal for science and literature on him in appreciation of *The Ancient Half-Timbered Houses of England*.

Habershon also wrote many theological works, including *A Dissertation on the Prophetic Scriptures* (1834) and *An Historical Exposition of the Prophecies of the Revelation of St. John* (1841). He died on 5 July 1852 at Bonner's Hall, Victoria Park, London, and was buried in Abney Park cemetery.
GORDON GOODWIN, *rev.* ANNE PIMLOTT BAKER

**Sources** Colvin, *Archs.* • *Dir. Brit. archs.* • [W. Papworth], ed., *The dictionary of architecture*, 11 vols. (1853–92) • Redgrave, *Artists* • Boase, *Mod. Eng. biog.* • *The Builder*, 2 (1844), 561

**Habershon, Roy** (1925–1992), police officer, was born at 38 Sylvester Street, Sheffield, on 15 May 1925, the son of William Habershon, table blade cutter, and his wife, Melia, *née* Cocker. Educated at Greystones elementary school, Sheffield, he left at fourteen, and worked in Sheffield railway offices until he joined the RAF in the Second World War. He was with Coastal Command, and served as a sergeant in a Wellington bomber, acting also as wireless operator and rear air gunner in Aden and Tobruk. He joined the Metropolitan Police on 14 October 1946 as a constable. On 7 June 1947 he married Edith Maud (*b.* 1922/3), Post Office telephonist, of Abertillery, and daughter of John Gallier, coalminer; they had one son, David (*b.* 1949).

Habershon was recruited to the CID in 1948, and gained a reputation for integrity and honesty in his various posts, which included several years with the fraud squad. He became detective sergeant (second class) in June 1958, detective sergeant (first class) in June 1960, detective inspector in November 1963, detective chief inspector in February 1966, detective superintendent in November 1967, and detective chief superintendent in June 1969. When the Angry Brigade, a terrorist group, planted two bombs at the home of the secretary of state for employment, Robert Carr, in Barnet on 12 January 1971, Habershon was detective chief superintendent covering the area, having just been moved there after a two-year secondment as assistant director of command courses at Bramshill Police College, Hampshire. Habershon's qualities of leadership were respected, and he took command of the investigation with a small squad which within six months was moved to Scotland Yard and reinforced with officers from special branch and the flying squad. Its team of about forty was placed under the overall control of Commander Ernest Bond, and it became the bomb squad (later the anti-terrorist squad). Forceful, persistent, methodical, and determined in the face of libertarian protest, Habershon conducted extensive enquiries and produced evidence which soon secured the conviction of five members of the Angry Brigade.

The IRA presented a new challenge in March 1973 with their first large-scale attack on London. Habershon's evidence at Winchester crown court helped to ensure the conviction of nine terrorists. Promoted to commander in January 1974, he was appointed MBE and left the bomb squad for a time, but he returned in March 1975 as commander, on the retirement of Robert Huntley, at the time when the dramatic six-day siege of a four-man IRA unit at Balcombe Street in London's West End led ultimately to the unit's capture without loss of life. Harold Wilson, then prime minister, telegrammed Sir Robert Mark, Metropolitan Police commissioner, after the arrests, noting that 'the Metropolitan Police have again demonstrated the very highest levels of skill and patience in bringing an incident of this kind to a successful conclusion. The whole nation is in the force's debt' (*The Guardian*, 13 Dec 1975). The four men were released under the amnesty associated with the peace process in Northern Ireland in April 1999.

The Balcombe Street siege was only one of more than a hundred terrorist incidents which Habershon investigated. By then bespectacled and balding, 'he was variously feared, revered and reviled by those with whom he came into contact' (*Daily Telegraph*, 28 March 1992). He became head of Scotland Yard's serious crimes branch, but felt much less at home in 1976 when unsuccessfully probing the source of a leak about cabinet discussions on child benefit than when hunting earlier for terrorists. Nor did anything come of his enquiry in the same year into the bankrupt Cheshire businessman Jesse Robert Rennie's allegation that Harold Wilson had inspired a policeman's attempt to bribe Rennie into returning letters received from an unnamed MP. Habershon left the senior ranks at Scotland Yard in 1977 to become head of E division, responsible for both CID and uniformed men in north London, including the busy area of Camden Town. He retired in 1980 after earning twenty-three commendations. He then became a director of the firm Control Risks, advising on security.

Roy Habershon was thorough, and liked to do a job well, but he was not keen on the political side of police work, and 'if something needed to be said, then he would say it' (private information). He was good company, with a dry sense of humour, and a good after-dinner speaker. Very much a man's man, he played football and cricket for the Metropolitan Police in his earlier years, and latterly golf. His son recalled him as an easy-going parent, and enjoyed going on fishing expeditions with him. In retirement Habershon took pleasure in his grandchildren and was fond of gardening. He died at his home, 6 Hoe Lane, Ware, Hertfordshire, from cancer on 18 March 1992. He was survived by his wife and son. BRIAN HARRISON

**Sources** G. Carr, *The Angry Brigade: the cause and the case* (1975) • *The Times* (3 April 1992) • *The Independent* (8 April 1992) • *Daily Telegraph* (28 March 1992) • private information (2004) [David Habershon] • b. cert. • m. cert. • d. cert.

**Likenesses** photograph, repro. in *The Times* (20 Dec 1973) • photograph, repro. in *The Times* (3 April 1992) • photograph, repro. in *The Independent* (8 April 1992)

**Wealth at death** £79,254: *The Independent*, 1 Aug 1992

**Habershon, Samuel Osborne** (1825–1889), physician, the son of Joseph James Habershon, an iron-founder, was born in Rotherham, Yorkshire; the family was originally from Lancashire. He was educated at Brampton, near Wath, and then in Ongar, Essex, before beginning to study medicine at about the age of fifteen, in London, with Ebenezar Pye-Smith. He also studied medicine at Guy's Hospital, where he greatly distinguished himself, and gained numerous scholarships at the University of London, where he graduated MB in 1848 and MD in 1851. Habershon assisted the Darby Street ragged school in 1849 and later became its superintendent. On 8 August 1854 he married Grace (*b*. 1820/21), daughter of James Ince, a furrier. He practised from his home, 48 Finsbury Circus, moving later to Wimpole Street and then to Brook Street in Mayfair, London.

At Guy's Hospital Habershon was appointed in succession demonstrator of anatomy and of morbid anatomy, lecturer in pathology, and in 1854 assistant physician. He took charge of the skin department in 1864, and in 1866 he became full physician. He lectured at Guy's on materia medica from 1856 to 1873, and on medicine from 1873 to 1877. Having been a member of the Royal College of Physicians from 1851, and fellow from 1856, he was successively examiner, councillor, and censor, and in 1876 Lumleian lecturer. In 1883 he was Harveian orator, and in 1887 he became vice-president of the college. He was president of the Medical Society of London in 1873. In November 1880, being then senior physician to Guy's, he and John Cooper Forster, the senior surgeon, resigned following a dispute with the hospital's governing body over a new system of nursing care which was being introduced. Habershon died at his home in 70 Brook Street, Mayfair, on 22 August 1889, from a gastric ulcer, leaving one son and three daughters; his wife had died in April of the same year. He was buried in Hampstead cemetery on 27 August.

As a physician Habershon had a high reputation, especially in abdominal diseases. He was the first in England to propose the operation of gastrostomy for stricture of the oesophagus, which Cooper Forster performed on a patient of Habershon's in 1858. He was amiable, high-minded, and deeply religious, holding services for students at his home. He was also one of the founders of the Christian Medical Association, which was founded by medical teachers and practitioners to encourage students of medicine to study the Bible.

Habershon wrote twenty-eight papers published in *Guy's Hospital Reports* between 1855 and 1872, as well as articles in various medical transactions and journals; other works of his include: *Pathological and Practical Observations on Diseases of the Abdomen* (1857), which ran to four editions and was also published in the United States; *On the Injurious Effects of Mercury in … Disease* (1859); *On Diseases of the Stomach* (1866); *On some Diseases of the Liver* (Lettsomian lectures, 1872); and *On the Pathology of the Pneumogastric Nerve* (Lumleian lectures, 1877), which was translated into Italian. G. T. BETTANY, *rev.* KAYE BAGSHAW

**Sources** Munk, *Roll* • *The Lancet* (31 Aug 1889), 445 • *The Lancet* (26 Oct 1889), 880–82 • *The Lancet* (9 Nov 1889), 979 • *BMJ* (31 Aug 1889), 486 • *BMJ* (14 Sept 1889), 627–8 • m. cert.

**Wealth at death** £40,001 13*s*. 5*d*.: probate, 19 Nov 1889, *CGPLA Eng. & Wales*

**Habington, Thomas** (1560–1647), antiquary, was born at Thorpe, near Chertsey, Surrey, on 23 August 1560, the second son of John Habington (1515–1582) and Catherine Wykes (*fl*. *c*.1520–*c*.1580), daughter of John Wykes. At his baptism he was the godson of Elizabeth I, for his father was the cofferer, or treasurer, of the household below stairs. After studies at Lincoln College, Oxford (1576–9), he studied in Paris for over a year, when he became a Catholic. However, two months after he entered the English College at Rheims his parents summoned him home, in March 1581. He followed his elder brother, Edward *Abington (*c.*1553–1586) [*see under* Babington, Anthony], in visiting the court, and both by 1585 were drawn into the circle of Anthony Babington, who was leader of a treasonous intrigue against the queen of which Sir Francis Walsingham, secretary of state, was already aware. In September 1586 Edward Abington was among eight condemned to death, while Thomas was confined to the Tower of London until 1592. There he translated the *De excidio et conquestu Britanniae* of the sixth-century monk, Gildas, whose Latin text was printed in England in 1525 and 1567. Later, in 1638, Habington published it as *The Epistle of Gildas … who Flourished in the Yeere 546*. After his release he retired to Hindlip House near Worcester, which had been acquired by his father in 1563. Here he created a safe haven for an itinerant priest to minister to recusants of the area. At Hindlip Nicholas Owen, a master carpenter, created unique hiding places in case of danger. For fourteen years Edward Oldcorne, a Jesuit, was a frequent visitor and Dorothy Habington, Thomas's sister, became a Catholic under his guidance, as did his wife, Mary Parker (*d.* after 1656). Her parents, Edward, twelfth Lord Morley, and Elizabeth Stanley, and her brother, William, fourth Lord Monteagle, were protestants. In 1604 Habington was part of a group of Catholic gentry who sought the election, as an MP for Worcester, of Sir Edward Harewell, who would support the mitigation of the penal laws, but their candidate failed to win the seat. A year later, on 4 November 1605 (though some contemporaries claimed 5 November; see Wood, *Ath. Oxon.*), Habington's son and heir, William *Habington (1605–1654), poet, was born at Hindlip.

The discovery of the Gunpowder Plot on the following day led to an unexpected crisis for Habington. First, there was a report in Worcester that his wife had written to her brother, Monteagle, the famous letter of warning against entering the parliament house, whereas it is clear that she did not. Then, in January 1606, two Jesuit priests, Oldcorne and Garnet, and two Jesuit brothers, Owen and Ashley, were captured at Hindlip. They had first entered in Habington's absence and were unaware of the proclamation against them or of the betrayal by Littleton, one of the conspirators. Even so, Habington was arrested for sheltering the priests and indicted in London, but was spared by the influence of his brother-in-law, Monteagle. Over the next forty years he studied, parish by parish, the history of the county up to the opening of Elizabeth's reign. By 1647 he had compiled a small folio on Worcester Cathedral and a lengthy manuscript book on the parishes 'of 360 folios or 760 pages with 137 in his own hand' (Habington, iv). After his death on 8 October 1647 he was buried in the family vault in Hindlip parish church.

Unlike those of his fellow antiquaries Dugdale for Warwickshire or Thoroton for Nottinghamshire, Habington's texts were not printed for several decades. During the war his son, William, preserved his manuscripts when Hindlip House was plundered in 1651 by soldiers who stole the money, jewels, and plate of his widowed mother. In 1654 Habington's grandson, also Thomas, inherited Hindlip and some time after the Restoration brought to Oxford Habington's two texts on the cathedral and parishes of Worcestershire to be read by Anthony Wood, who in his *Athenae Oxonienses* eulogized them for 'every leaf is sufficient testimony of his generous and virtuous mind, of his indefatigable industry and infinite reading' (Wood, *Ath. Oxon.*, 3rd edn, 3.223–4). Not until 1717 was the smaller treatise, *The Antiquities of the Cathedral Church of Worcester* finally in print, while in 1781–2 T. R. Nash incorporated excerpts from the manuscript on parishes in his *Collections for the History of Worcestershire*. In 1895 J. Amphlett edited valuable sections of that manuscript in two volumes entitled *A Survey of Worcestershire*, which has remained a standard source for the history of the county.

A. J. LOOMIE

**Sources** *The condition of Catholics under James I: Father Gerard's narrative of the Gunpowder Plot*, ed. J. Morris (1871) • A. Fraser, *The Gunpowder Plot: terror and faith in 1605* (1996) • I. D. Grosvenor, 'Catholics and politics: the Worcestershire election of 1604', *Recusant History*, 14 (1977–8), 149–62, esp. 151–6 • *VCH Worcestershire*, vol. 3 • Wood, *Ath. Oxon.*, new edn, 3.222 • T. Habington, *A survey of Worcestershire*, ed. J. Amphlett, 2 vols., Worcestershire Historical Society (1895–9) • T. F. Knox and others, eds., *The first and second diaries of the English College, Douay* (1878) • T. Nash, *Collections for the history of Worcestershire*, 2nd edn, 2 vols. (1799) • P. Carraman, *Henry Garnet, 1555–1606, and the Gunpowder Plot* (1964) • *DNB* • Gillow, *Lit. biog. hist.*

**Archives** Hagley Hall, Hagley, Worcestershire, antiquarian working MSS | BL, corresp. with Sir Symon Archer, Add. MS 28564 [copies] • Bodl. Oxf., corresp. with Sir Symon Archer • S. Antiquaries, Lond., Worcestershire collections

**Likenesses** T. Habington, engraving, 1638 (after Marshall)

**Habington, William** (1605–1654), poet, the son of Thomas *Habington (1560–1647), antiquary, and Mary, daughter of Edward Parker, twelfth Baron Morley, was born at Hindlip Hall in Worcestershire on 4 November 1605. He had three sisters, Mary, Frances, and Elizabeth, who all married, and a brother, Anthony, who died a bachelor in 1649. Thomas Habington and his brother Edward were punished, by six years' incarceration in the Tower and by execution respectively, for involvement in the Babington conspiracy of 1586, and Thomas was in trouble again in the months following the discovery of the Gunpowder Plot of 1605 for harbouring Jesuit priests at Hindlip Hall.

William Habington was sent abroad by his recusant father to receive a Catholic education, first from the Jesuits at the English College at St Omer between 1618 and 1622 and later in Paris, probably at the Jesuit Collège de Clermont (*Poems*, xix–xxi). A fellow student at St Omer described him as 'ingenious and well learned' and recalled how he had narrowly escaped being recruited into the Jesuit order (Wadsworth, 21–2). On his return from France he continued his studies at home and developed an interest in history from assisting with his father's researches into the antiquities of Worcestershire. By 1629 he was spending much of his time in London, where he lived in his father's house in Holborn.

At this time Habington composed two of his earliest poems, in commendation of Shirley's *The Wedding* and Davenant's *The Tragedy of Albovine*. Habington's acquaintance with the literary wits at the court of Charles I and his courtship of Lucy Herbert, daughter of William Herbert, first Baron Powis, and granddaughter of Henry Percy, eighth earl of Northumberland, resulted in *Castara*, a collection of poetry published anonymously in 1634. Evidence in this volume and in the augmented edition of 1635 indicates that the couple married clandestinely in late February or early March 1633 against the wishes of Lord Powis. During the rest of the 1630s Habington and his wife passed their time between Hindlip, where they were part of a local network of Catholic families, and the court, where Lucy's cousin, the countess of Carlisle, was the reigning beauty and where William associated with the Catholic faction that surrounded Queen Henrietta Maria. An elegy by Habington in the memorial volume *Jonsonus viribus* (1638) suggests that he had become recognized as one of the 'Sons of Ben'. There is no record of the births of Habington's children but there is firm evidence of an eldest son, named Thomas, who inherited Hindlip and died without issue some time after 1684, and a daughter named Catherine, who married Thomas Osborne and had two daughters, Lucy and Eleanor. Single references have been found to another son, George, and a fourth child, named Hurbart in the record of his burial on 2 January 1641.

Habington's connection by marriage with the lord chamberlain, Philip, earl of Pembroke and Montgomery, who was first cousin to Lord Powis, almost gained him a prestigious appointment as the queen's agent at the papal court in 1636. The post eventually went to another candidate but Pembroke's patronage was again significant in the poet's one venture into drama, when he caused *The Queen of Arragon* 'to be acted at court, and afterwards to be published against the author's will' (Wood, *Ath. Oxon.*, 3.224–5). The play was performed twice in April 1640 before the king and queen, at Pembroke's expense, and later by the players at the Blackfriars. A third edition of *Castara* appeared in 1640, adding twenty-two new poems to the 1635 collection; the fruits of what Habington described, in an authorial preface to the poems, as his 'more serious study' were published under the titles *Observations upon Historie* (1640) and *The Historie of Edward the Fourth, King of England* (1641), which was reissued as *Praeces principium, or, The President of Illustrious Princes* in 1659.

In a poem written at the time of the first campaign against the Scottish covenanters in 1639 Habington praised Sir Henry Percy, probably a cousin of his wife, for his 'pure devotion to the King', in whose 'just cause' he was prepared to try 'the hazard of the armie' (*Poems*, 139). He himself bore arms on the royalist side during the civil war, being named among the 'gentlemen of Worcestershire who were in the garrison' when Worcester finally surrendered to the parliamentary forces on 26 July 1646 (Nash, 2, appx, cv). Hindlip Hall was plundered after the fall of Worcester and, upon the death of the poet's father on 8 October 1647, the estate was sequestrated. Habington's last poem, a tribute printed among the commendatory verses in the *Comedies and Tragedies* of Beaumont and Fletcher in 1647, regrets that Fletcher's works should be exposed to 'th' Ages rude affronts' in 'the worst scaene of Time' (*Poems*, 158–9). Habington died on 30 December 1654 at Hindlip Hall and was buried in the family vault in the parish church at Hindlip. It is thought that his wife survived him.

Three prose characters—'A Mistris', 'A Wife', and 'A Holy Man'—announce the dominant themes of each part of *Castara* but the poems of courtship, married love, and religious reflection are interspersed with others addressed to prominent members of the Caroline court, and the second part ends with eight elegies on the death of George Talbot, introduced by the prose character of 'A Friend'. Respected in the seventeenth and nineteenth centuries for what he himself called 'the innocency of a chaste Muse' (*Poems*, 5), Habington has been characterized by his modern editor as 'a Catholic Puritan', whose love poems are often insipid and banal in comparison with his 'best and most mature writing', which is found in the religious poems of part 3 (ibid., xxx, lix). He had modest expectations that the place occupied by his poetry in the 'worlds opinion' would be 'not so high, as to be wondred at, nor so low as to be contemned' (ibid., 7). His own preference for history, however, 'that faithfull preserver of things past, that great instructor of the present', led him to dedicate his labours to King Charles with the hope that his hitherto peaceful reign would continue to provide 'the best example to the future' (W. Habington, *Historie of Edward the Fourth*, 1641, sig. A2*v*). His habit of moralizing has made his historical works 'unread and unreadable today' (*Poems*, xxii), although they retain some interest as expressions of royalist disdain for 'the injustice of all popular election' (W. Habington, *Historie*, 8) and 'the disorder'd voting in the people' (W. Habington, *Observations upon Historie*, 1640, 4–5).

It was when he brought together his activities as poet and historian that Habington produced the work for which he is currently most admired. *The Queen of Arragon* has been commended for the simplicity of its design and the poetic quality of its language (A. Harbage, *Cavalier Drama*, 1936, 123) and for breaking 'the mould of the Cavalier play' by subjecting its 'ideal pretensions' to the test of reality (*Poems*, xxxviii). Read in the context of the Short Parliament of April 1640 it has been rated even more highly as 'a courtly play of real poetic distinction and literary merit', in which the dramatist penetrated 'into the moment of crisis' through which he was living and engaged with 'the contradictions inherent, and finally unresolvable, in the politics of his time' (Butler, 62, 76).

ROBERT WILCHER

**Sources** *The poems of William Habington*, ed. K. Allott (1969) • Wood, *Ath. Oxon.*, new edn, 3.222–5 • T. Nash, *Collections for the history of Worcestershire*, 2 vols. (1781–2) • J. Wadsworth, *The English Spanish pilgrime* (1629), 21–2 • H. C. Combs, 'Habington's *Castara* and the date of his marriage', *Modern Language Notes*, 63 (1948), 182–3 • A. D. Cousins, *The Catholic religious poets from Southwell to Crashaw: a critical* *history* (1991), 115–23 • M. Butler, *Theatre and crisis, 1632–1642* (1984), 62–76

**Wealth at death** Hindlip estate sequestrated in 1647; known to have been in financial difficulties as early as 1640: *Poems of William Habington*, ed. Allott, xlii–xliii

**Hack** [*née* Barton], **Maria** (**1777–1844**), educational writer, was born in Carlisle on 16 February 1777, the eldest child of John Barton (1755–1789) and Maria (or Mary) Done (1752–1784). Both her parents were members of the Society of Friends. The family moved to London shortly before Mrs Barton died in 1784. John Barton then married Elizabeth Horne (1760–1833) of Bankside and Tottenham, Middlesex; after his death in 1789 Maria's stepmother took her to live with her family. At Tottenham, on 17 November 1800, Maria married a currier from Chichester, Stephen Hack (1775–1823), the son of James Hack and his wife, Priscilla Hallyer; they had four sons and six daughters.

Maria Hack's youngest brother, Bernard *Barton (1784–1849), the friend of Charles Lamb and a minor poet, recalled that in his youth his sister had been 'a sort of oracle to me' (*Selections*, xxvii). Her enthusiasm for the education of children extended beyond her own family: in 1812 she published *First Lessons in English Grammar*, and a variety of other educational works for children followed. In *Winter Evenings* (4 vols., 1818), a mother teaches geography through the medium of travellers' tales to her two children, Harry and Lucy; *Grecian Stories* (1819) and *English Stories* (1820–25) follow the same format, providing essentially episodic and anecdotal introductions to Greek and English history. In the preface to *Grecian Stories*, Hack outlined her philosophy as a history textbook writer: believing that lengthy historical narratives full of political detail were unsuitable for children, she aimed to encourage the development of comprehension rather than memory skills. Viewing history as a school of morality, she emphasized the importance of children learning to form correct moral judgements by reflecting on the behaviour of historical figures. Her *English Stories* met with the approval of an anonymous reviewer in the *Quarterly Journal of Education* (1831), who praised her attempt to convey 'beautiful lessons of morality' and her 'entire freedom from all party spirit' (V. E. Chancellor, *History for their Masters: Opinion in the English History Textbook, 1800–1914*, 1970, 9).

However, Maria Hack's best work was probably *Harry Beaufoy, or, The Pupil of Nature* (1821), which reached a third edition in 1830. Largely based on William Paley's *Evidences of Christianity* (1794), it is an ingenious textbook of natural theology, in which a boy's parents encourage him to reason from creation to a benevolent creator: 'the watch must have a watchmaker' (M. Hack, *Harry Beaufoy*, 1821, 183). Divine design is illustrated by reference to diverse natural phenomena, including the circulation of blood in the human anatomy and the workings of the beehive. Other works included *Oriental Fragments* (1828), the contents of which are less alluring than its title, *Geological Sketches and Glimpses of the Ancient Earth* (1832), and *Lectures at Home* (1834), an introduction to optics. Most of Hack's works reached a second edition; *Winter Evenings* and *English Stories* were still appearing in revised editions in the 1870s.

Works such as her *Familiar Illustrations of the Principal Evidences and Design of Christianity* (1824) showed the influence of contemporary evangelicalism on Maria Hack's theological outlook. In the late 1830s she played a minor role in a controversy which arose among the Quakers after the publication of Isaac Crewdson's *A Beacon to the Society of Friends* (1835), in which this Manchester minister argued that the Friends should regard scripture as the ultimate authority. With this downplaying of the role of the inner light as spiritual guide went, for many evangelical Quakers, a call for the sacraments of baptism and communion. Maria Hack sympathized with the movement, and in 1837 she was baptized by Crewdson. Some months later, she resigned from the Society of Friends, publishing a short tract entitled *The Christian Ordinances and the Lord's Supper* (1837). Shortly afterwards, following the example of three of her children and her sister Elizabeth, she joined the Church of England. Not all her relatives were persuadable: her brother Bernard opined that 'a sprinkling, or water-sprinkled, sacrament-taking Quaker is a sort of incongruous medley I can neither classify nor understand' (*Selections*, 49).

In 1841 or 1842 Maria Hack moved from Gloucester to Southampton; she died there at Bevis Hill, on 4 January 1844. Her eldest and youngest sons, John Barton Hack (1805–1884) and Stephen Hack (1816–1894), were among the earliest Quaker settlers in Adelaide, Australia; both subsequently left the Society of Friends. Her daughter, Margaret Emily (1814–1886)—also a textbook writer—married Thomas Gates Darton (1810–1887), from the firm of Darton and Harvey, which had published some of Maria Hack's books. ROSEMARY MITCHELL

**Sources** 'Dictionary of Quaker biography', RS Friends, Lond. [card index] • L. Darton, 'The baptism of Maria Hack, 1837: an episode of the Beacon controversy', *Journal of the Friends' Historical Society*, 46 (1954), 67–77 • C. Fell-Smith, 'Maria Hack', *The Athenaeum* (24 Dec 1892), 889 • *Selections from the poems and letters of Bernard Barton*, ed. L. Barton (1849) • J. Smith, ed., *A descriptive catalogue of Friends' books*, 2 vols. (1867); suppl. (1893) • *The Friend*, 2 (1844), 47 • *GM*, 2nd ser., 21 (1844), 219 • Allibone, *Dict.* • H. Carpenter and M. Prichard, *The Oxford companion to children's literature*, pbk edn (1999), 234

**Hack, William** (*fl.* **1671–1702**), chart maker, was the son of Charles Hack, a Winchester innkeeper. He was apprenticed to Andrew Welch, a cartographer of the Thames, or Drapers' Company, school of chart makers in London for a term of nine years on 25 January 1671. There is no record that Hack was ever made free of the Drapers' Company. The school specialized in the composition of highly stylized manuscript portolan charts. Towards the end of his apprenticeship Hack introduced several innovations in charts prepared for Welch, the most striking of which was the replacement of rhumb lines 'by the rectangular grid of the projectionless plane chart with the quarter compass rose which is perhaps Hack's most individual feature' (Campbell, 94). After leaving Welch, Hack concentrated mainly on the production of paper charts, bound into atlases, offering sequential coverage of large areas of coastline.

In 1682, under conditions of the utmost secrecy, Hack was commissioned by government ministers to copy the book of charts seized by Captain Bartholomew Sharpe off Cape Pasado (modern Ecuador) in June 1681. Hack capitalized on this opportunity by producing an unnecessarily lavish presentation copy for Charles II in what appears to have been a deft suit for royal patronage (BL, Maps K. Mar. VIII.15). Hack also obtained the journals of Sharpe and Basil Ringrose, which were copied and edited under his direction over the course of the next twenty years (copies of these two works are at BL, Sloane MS 46B and 48 respectively). The finished products were among items he presented to his royal patrons, Charles II and James II, and to a select coterie of other sponsors, notably Christopher Monk, second duke of Albemarle, and John, Lord Somers, chancellor of England. Hack is not known to have kept an apprentice, but he was assisted in producing copies of Sharpe's journal by the Jewish linguist Phillip Dassigny.

Hack's prolific output of manuscript charts outstripped that of any other member of the Thames school. A conservative estimate of the total number of charts he personally produced between 1682 and 1702 exceeds 300, although this probably represents a fraction of the true figure. Many of these were multiple copies of the charts deriving from Sharpe's voyage, but he also produced atlases of coastlines in Africa and the Orient. His business premises were 'At the Signe of Great Britain and Ireland' by Wapping New Stairs, London, although from the evidence of several charts dated 1686 he seems to have had a temporary address at Gun Wharf. Towards the end of his career Hack prospered and his interests diversified. In December 1695 he was apparently resident in Mile End Green, having adopted the rank of captain in correspondence with Sir William Trumbull over a scheme to press foreigners into the naval service. In 1699, as 'Capt. William Hacke', he edited and published *A Collection of Original Voyages* printed by James Knapton, printer to the Royal Society. The collection contained an abridged account of Sharpe's voyage and illustrations by Herman Moll.

Hack's activities formed part of the thriving industry which surrounded England's general maritime expansion in the late seventeenth century. Although he was primarily a copyist, his shrewd manipulation of patronage enabled him to remain buoyant throughout the period when manuscript charts were displaced by printed ones, and the influence of his work may even have extended beyond his lifetime. Upon the formation of the South Sea Company in 1711, the directors obtained a copy of Hack's South Sea Waggoner (a book of sea charts known as a waggoner after the first printed atlas of charts by Lucas Sanszoon Waghenaer), containing 131 charts (Hunt. L., HM 265). These charts may have informed the audacious plans for a south sea trade which the directors laid before Robert Harley.

Hack's last map is dated 1702. Nothing is known of his subsequent life or his death. It is not known whether he married or had children. JAMES WILLIAM KELLY

**Sources** A. Campbell, 'The Drapers' Company and its school of seventeenth-century chart-makers', *My head is a map: essays and memoirs in honour of R. V. Tooley*, ed. H. Wallis and S. Tyacke (1973), 81–99 · D. Howse and N. J. W. Thrower, eds., *A buccaneer's atlas: Basil Ringrose's atlas, Basil Ringrose's South Sea waggoner* (Berkeley, CA, 1992), 261–83 · T. R. Smith, 'Manuscript and printed sea charts in seventeenth-century London: the case of the Thames school', *The complete plattmaker: essays on chart, map, and globe making in England in the seventeenth and eighteenth centuries*, ed. N. Thrower (Berkeley, CA, 1978), 45–101 · E. Lynam, 'William Hack and the South Sea buccaneers', *The mapmaker's art: essays on the history of maps* (1953), 101–17 · E. G. R. Taylor, *The mathematical practitioners of Tudor and Stuart England* (1954), 77 · S. Tyacke, *London map-sellers, 1660–1720* (1978), 75 · T. R. Adams, 'William Hack's manuscript atlases of "The Great South Sea of America"', *John Carter Brown Library Annual Report, 1965–6* [Providence, Rhode Island] (1967), 45–52 · W. Hack, letter to Trumbull, 20 Dec 1695, BL, Add. MS 72534 · private information (2004) [Tony Campbell and Rodney Shirley] · W. Hacke, ed., *A collection of original voyages* (1699)

**Hackenschmidt, George** (1877–1968), wrestler and philosopher, was born on 20 July 1877 at Dorpat, Estonia (then part of the Russian empire). Little is known about his parents, other than that his father was a dyer, and despite his Germanic-sounding name, was of Swedish origin. Hackenschmidt trained as an engineer's draughtsman, but excelled in weightlifting, and became Russian champion in 1899. His strength became apparent in 1896, when he reputedly picked up a milkman's horse and carried it around on his shoulders.

However, it was as a wrestler that Hackenschmidt became famous. His first big tournament was in Vienna, in 1898, when he won the amateur heavyweight championship of the world, wrestling in the Graeco-Roman style. He soon established a reputation as one of the strongest and most skilful wrestlers in Europe. In 1900 he turned professional, and until his retirement in 1911, he was never defeated in this style.

In 1902, speaking little English, Hackenschmidt arrived in Britain to advance his career in music-hall wrestling, and met the impresario C. B. Cochran, who became his manager. With Cochran's guidance, he became 'the Russian Lion', and introduced showmanship into his performances, which usually involved allowing local wrestlers to look good for a while before throwing them, or using a paid 'villain' before throwing him. As he fought every challenger, he claimed the championship of the world, since there was no international wrestling body to award titles. Within a year he and Cochran had between them created a music-hall boom in wrestling, with wrestlers arriving in Britain from around the world.

Hackenschmidt's most famous match, which elevated him to hero status, was against Ahmad Madrali, 'the Terrible Turk', at Kensington Olympia, London, on 30 January 1904. With Cochran's flair for publicity the match became the sporting event of the year, although the outcome itself was an anticlimax; Madrali was thrown in forty-four seconds, dislocating his arm in the process.

With his popularity at its zenith, Hackenschmidt toured Britain drawing huge houses wherever he went, wrestling five challengers a night, and defeating them all in twenty minutes. He had now adopted the free or catch-as-catch-can style, which the public favoured over the Graeco-Roman style, and was twice defeated by the American

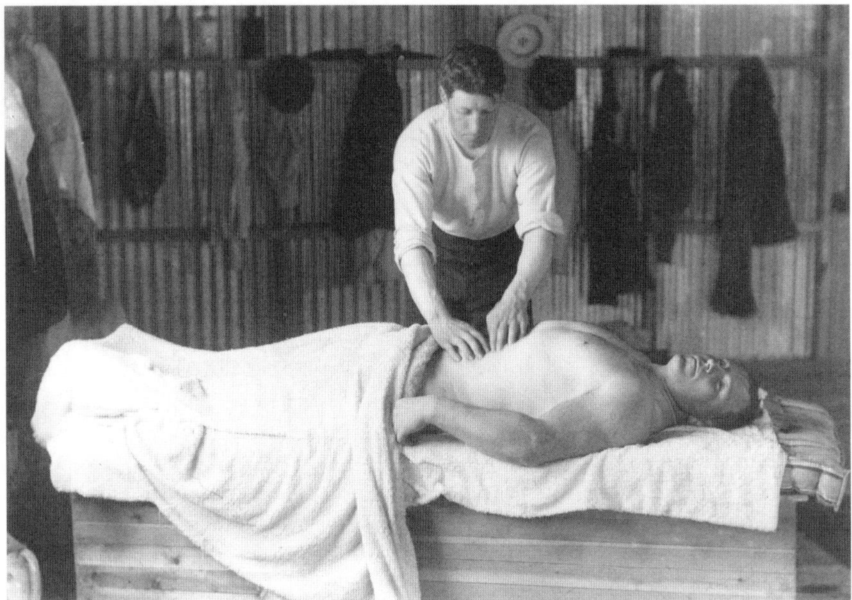

**George Hackenschmidt (1877–1968)**, by unknown photographer, 1926 [undergoing massage during training]

wrestler Frank Gotch, in 1908 and 1911, in Chicago. The latter defeat prompted his retirement.

In 1935 Hackenschmidt published *Man and Cosmic Antagonism to Mind and Spirit*, the first of several books describing his system of personal philosophy, which he formulated while being held by the Germans in an internment camp during the First World War. This influenced many sportsmen, particularly the Australian athletics coach Percy Cerutty.

In 1945 Hackenschmidt came to Britain from France, with his French wife, Rachel Marie Lucienne (*d.* 1987), and settled in West Norwood, south London, where he successfully ran a physical culture school. In 1950 he became a naturalized British subject. He abstained from both alcohol and tobacco, and after his retirement became a strict vegetarian. He died in St Francis Hospital, East Dulwich, London, on 19 February 1968, following a short illness, at the age of ninety. He was buried in Norwood cemetery.

MIKE TRIPP

**Sources** G. Kent, *A pictorial history of wrestling* (1968) · *The Times* (20 Feb 1968) · J. Arlott, ed., *The Oxford companion to sports and games* (1975) · '1000 makers of sport', *Sunday Times* (2 June 1996?–7 July 1996) · A. Oakley, *Blue blood on the mat* (1971) · G. P. Stone, 'Wrestling: the great American passion play', *The sociology of sport: a selection of readings*, ed. E. Dunning (1971), 301–35 · R. Flanagan, *West Norwood cemetery's sportsmen* (1995) · *CGPLA Eng. & Wales* (1968) · d. cert.

**Likenesses** photograph, 1926, Hult. Arch. [*see illus.*] · photographs, repro. in Kent, *Pictorial history*

**Wealth at death** £10,182: probate, 2 July 1968, *CGPLA Eng. & Wales*

**Hacker, Arthur** (1858–1919), painter, was born on 25 September 1858 at 9 Rochester Road, Camden New Town, London, the second son of Edward Hacker (1813–1905), an engraver, and his wife, Sophia Eliza Sidney. He studied at the Royal Academy Schools and with Léon Bonnat in Paris. He began exhibiting at the Royal Academy at the age of twenty and soon attracted public notice. In the early 1880s he visited Paris, Spain, and north Africa, the latter providing the setting for his painting *Pelagia and Philammon*, exhibited at the Grosvenor Gallery, London, in 1887. This and *Christ and the Magdalene* (exh. 1891)—both now in the Walker Art Gallery, Liverpool—established him as a serious painter in the French academic manner. But although female nudes and intense religious subjects were fashionable in the French art world, in Britain such subject matter branded this new associate of the Royal Academy (1893) as un-English.

Hacker's sensuous nudes were couched in tasteful, often classical, allegory—*Daphne* (1895), *The Cloud* (1901, Cartwright Hall, Bradford), and *Leaf Drift* (1903) are examples of this idiom. Certain of his biblical paintings, such as *By the Waters of Babylon* (1888, Rochdale Art Gallery) and *The Annunciation* (1892, Chantrey bequest purchase for the Tate collection)—both in need of restoration—are outstanding works in the academic tradition, while *And there was a Great Cry in Egypt* (1897; ex Fine Art Society) indicates the influence of symbolism. *The Cloister or the World* (1896, Cartwright Hall, Bradford), depicting a nun's choice between the flesh and the spirit, attracted belated attention at the Royal Academy's 1998 exhibition 'Art treasures of England'. To contemporary eyes, some of Hacker's work seems overblown—*The Temptation of Sir Percival* (1894, Leeds City Art Galleries) borders almost on the ridiculous—but a reassessment of his academic achievement is long overdue.

By the time Hacker married another painter, Lilian Price-Edwards (1878/9–1948), the third daughter of Edward Price-Edwards, secretary of Trinity House, on 18 November 1907, the taste of the British public for the olympian heights of high art was on the wane; like other artists, he had already taken to society portraiture. By 1909 he had consciously changed his style of painting in favour of atmospheric and light-imbued pastorals and street scenes in the French post-impressionist manner: he became a full member of the Royal Academy in 1910 with a work in this style, his diploma painting *A Wet Night at Piccadilly Circus* (Royal Academy of Arts). He died, childless, of a heart attack at his home, 178 Cromwell Road, South Kensington, London, on 12 November 1919 and was buried on 17 November at Brookwood cemetery, near Woking, Surrey. He was survived by his wife.

SIMON REYNOLDS

**Sources** A. L. Baldry, 'The paintings of Arthur Hacker', *The Studio*, 56 (1912), 175–83 · *The Times* (14 Nov 1919) · *Daily Telegraph* (14 Nov 1919) · *DNB* · E. Morris, *Victorian and Edwardian paintings in the Walker Art Gallery* (1996), 194–9 · J. Christian, ed., *The last Romantics: the Romantic tradition in British art* (1989), 127–8 [exhibition catalogue, Barbican Art Gallery, London, 9 Feb – 9 April 1989] · Graves, *RA exhibitors* · b. cert. · m. cert.

**Likenesses** S. P. Hall, group portrait, chalk and wash (*The St John's Wood Arts Club, 1895*), NPG · S. P. Hall, group portrait, pencil and chalk study, NPG · J. Russell & Sons, photograph, NPG · photograph, NPG

**Wealth at death** £51,742 12s. od.: probate, 23 Dec 1919, *CGPLA Eng. & Wales*

**Hacker, Francis** (*d.* 1660), parliamentarian army officer and regicide, was the eldest son of Francis Hacker (*d.* 1646) of East Bridgeford and Colston Bassett, Nottinghamshire, and Margaret Whalley (*d.* 1634), daughter of William Whalley of Cotgrave. The dates of his birth and baptism are not known, but on 5 July 1632 he married Isabella Brunts (*b.* 1608?) of East Bridgeford; they had a son, Francis, and a daughter, Anne.

Little is known about Hacker until the first civil war, when his godly zeal drove him to become a firm supporter of the parliamentarian cause, unlike his brothers, Thomas, who died fighting for the king at a skirmish at Colston Bassett in 1643, and Rowland, who was an active commander for the king in Nottinghamshire and lost his hand in his service. During the war Francis gained a reputation as a zealous parliamentarian cavalry commander of the Leicestershire, Nottinghamshire, and Derbyshire horse, seeing active service mainly in Leicestershire. He was appointed a member of that county's militia committee by parliamentary ordinance on 10 July 1644. On 27 November 1643 he was taken prisoner at Melton Mowbray by Gervase Lucas, the royalist governor of Belvoir Castle. A month later parliament ordered that he should be exchanged for Colonel Sands. Subsequently he took Bagworth House and defeated the enemy at Belvoir and in May 1645 he was again taken prisoner when the king captured Leicester. In the recriminations that followed he was blamed for the defeat, but was warmly defended in a pamphlet published by his colleagues on the Leicestershire committee, including his friend Sir Arthur Hesilrige (Lucy Hutchinson called Hacker Hesilrige's 'creature'; Hutchinson, 200). He was commended for his service at Bagworth House and Belvoir. He was also credited with having freely given 'all the prizes that he ever took' to the state and to his soldiers, and with having, while a prisoner at Belvoir, scornfully refused an offer of 'pardon and the command of a regiment of horse to change his side'. 'At the king's taking of Leicester', his fellow committeemen claimed, he 'was so much prized by the enemy as they offered him the command of a choice regiment to serve the king' (*An Examination Examined*, 15). During the second civil war Hacker again raised forces in Leicestershire and on 5 July 1648 he commanded the left wing of the parliamentarian forces at the defeat of the royalists at Willoughby Field in Nottinghamshire.

During the trial of Charles I, Colonel Hacker was one of the officers specially charged with the custody of the king, and he usually commanded the guard of halberdiers which escorted the king to and from Westminster Hall. Sir Thomas Herbert, Charles I's groom of the chamber, later accused Hacker of roughly treating the king, and said that he was dissuaded only by bishops Juxon and Herbert from putting two musketeers constantly in the king's chamber. Hacker and two fellow officers, Colonel Hercules Hunck and Lieutenant-Colonel Robert Phayre, were given the warrant for the king's execution and after a dispute between them about who should sign the order to the executioner Hacker agreed to do so. On 30 January 1649 he was present on the scaffold and supervised the execution [*see also* Regicides].

Hacker faithfully served the Commonwealth and protectorate of Oliver Cromwell as a soldier. The intention that Hacker's regiment should reinforce Cromwell's expeditionary force to Ireland in 1649 was not put into effect, but Hacker and his regiment accompanied Cromwell to Scotland in 1650, before fighting at Musselburgh on 30 July, escorting Scottish prisoners of war to Newcastle after the battle of Dunbar in September, and seizing a royalist ship at Kirkcudbright in January 1651. Later in the year Hacker went south with Cromwell and fought at the battle of Worcester on 3 September 1651, before returning to Scotland to fight with the parliamentarian commander, Colonel Richard Deane, in the highlands in the summer campaign of 1652. He had returned to England by August 1652 when he was one of the 'loyal Cromwellians' who took a petition from army officers to parliament complaining at the slow progress in carrying out reform (Gentles, 419). While Oliver Cromwell lived Hacker was a staunch supporter of the protectorate. He arrested Lord Grey of Groby and Nottinghamshire royalists, seized arms at Newstead Abbey in the spring of 1655, and was employed in the following year to suppress the intrigues of royalists and Fifth Monarchists in Leicestershire and Nottinghamshire. In 1657 his regiment was again in Scotland and early in 1658 it sent a loyal address to Oliver Cromwell after the dissolution of the second protectorate parliament.

Hacker's religious views, though, were much less tolerant than those of Cromwell. On 25 December 1650 Cromwell wrote to Hacker, rebuking him for slightingly describing one of his subalterns as a better preacher than a fighter, and telling him that he expected him and all the chief officers of the army to encourage preaching. In 1654 Hacker and his son-in-law, Clement Needham, arrested the Quaker George Fox at Whetstone in Leicestershire and sent him to London, where he was released by the protector. Shortly before his death Hacker confessed 'that he had formerly born too great a prejudice in his heart towards the good people of God that differed from him in judgment' (*A Compleat Collection of the Lives, Speeches … of those Persons Lately Executed*, 170). But, despite his wife's possible conversion to Quakerism (she was, reported Fox in his *Journal*, 'convinced' when he made a second visit to Whetstone in 1655, and an Isabella Hacker was transported to Jamaica for Quakerism in 1664), Hacker's hostility to people whom he considered religious extremists like Quakers remained undimmed (*Journal of George Fox*, 1.251). In April 1657 his regiment in Scotland was reported free of Quakers.

Hacker's fear of Quakers, together with his friendship with Hesilrige, help to account for his activities in the troubled period between the death of Oliver Cromwell and the restoration of Charles II. By refusing to obey Richard Cromwell's orders to take his regiment from Cheapside to Whitehall in April 1659, Hacker effectively supported the army's dissolution of the new protector's parliament and the end of the protectorate. But from that point onwards he broke ranks with the senior army commanders, Fleetwood and Lambert, whom Hacker considered to be far too friendly to religious extremists. Hesilrige persuaded him to become the first of all the colonels in the army to accept a new commission from the speaker of the restored Long Parliament, and he was among the first to acknowledge the supremacy of the civil power over the army. Early in October 1659 his son-in-law wrote to Fleetwood protesting at the army's petition that demanded that the parliamentarians press ahead with reforms, and Hacker himself clearly approved of parliament's condemnation of it. Although his regiment was among those used by Fleetwood and Lambert to expel parliament on 13 October 1659, Hacker opposed the expulsion and was suspended from his military command, and his regiment was sent under new commanders to the north to join Lambert's forces. At the end of the year he was active with his friends in the midlands, securing Coventry and Leicester for parliament, and in January 1660, after the Long Parliament was again restored, Hacker was again put in command of his regiment. Unfortunately for him, however, as in the previous year, some of his soldiers failed to follow his lead. When General Monck marched south from Scotland, though Hacker gave him his support, part of his regiment mutinied behind Lambert. This is no doubt why, despite Monck's outward show of friendliness towards Hacker in the first weeks after he reached London, Hacker was removed from his command on 25 June. On 5 July he was arrested and sent to the Tower for his part in the execution of Charles I.

The House of Commons did not at first except Hacker from the Act of Indemnity, but during the debates upon it in the Lords the fact came out that the warrant for the execution of the king had been in Hacker's possession. The Lords wanted to use it as evidence against the regicides, and ordered him to produce it. Mrs Hacker was sent to fetch it, and in doing so on 31 July she, perhaps unintentionally, provided a major piece of evidence for the prosecution case against him. On the next day the Lords added Hacker's name to the list of those excepted, and on 13 August the Commons accepted this amendment. At his trial on 15 October Hacker made no serious attempt to defend himself, simply using a defence often used throughout the ages by soldiers accused of war crimes: 'I have no more to say for myself but that I was a soldier, and under command, and what I did was by the commission you have read' (*The Indictment, Arraignment, Tryal … of Thirty-Nine Regicides*, 249). He was sentenced to death, and was hanged on 19 October 1660. His body, instead of being quartered, was given to his friends for burial, and is said to have been interred in the church of St Nicholas Cole Abbey, London, the advowson of which was at one time vested in the Hacker family. He was probably spared the full horrors of a traitor's death because of his brothers' loyalty to the crown. BARRY COWARD

**Sources** C. H. Firth and G. Davies, *The regimental history of Cromwell's army*, 2 vols. (1940) • J. P. Briscoe, *Old Nottinghamshire*, 1st ser. of 2 series (1881) • P. Temple and others, *An examination examined, being a full and moderate answer to Major Innes relation concerning the siege and taking of the town of Leicester* (1645) • L. Hutchinson, *Memoirs of the life of Colonel Hutchinson*, ed. J. Sutherland (1973) • *The memoirs of Edmund Ludlow*, ed. C. H. Firth, 2 vols. (1894) • T. Herbert, *Memoirs of the two last years of the reign of King Charles I*, ed. G. Nicol, 3rd edn (1815) • W. S., *A compleat collection of the lives, speeches … letters and prayers of those persons lately executed* (1661) • *The indictment, arraignment, tryal, and judgment, at large, of thirty-nine regicides* (1913) • A. Woolrych, introduction, in *Complete prose works of John Milton*, ed. D. M. Wolfe, 7, ed. R. W. Ayers (1980), 1–228 • I. Gentles, *The New Model Army in England, Ireland, and Scotland, 1645–1653* (1992) • C. V. Wedgwood, *The trial of Charles I* (1967) • *The journal of George Fox*, ed. N. Penney, 2 vols. (1911) • *JHC*, 7 (1651–9) • *JHC*, 8 (1660–67) • *JHL*, 11 (1660–66) • C. H. Firth and R. S. Rait, eds., *Acts and ordinances of the interregnum, 1642–1660*, 1 (1911) • Z. Grey, *An impartial examination of the fourth volume of Mr Daniel Neal's 'History of the puritans'* (1739) • *The letters and speeches of Oliver Cromwell*, ed. T. Carlyle and S. C. Lomas, 3 vols. (1904), vol. 2 • J. Besse, *A collection of the sufferings of the people called Quakers*, 1 (1753) • G. Davies, *The restoration of Charles II, 1658–1660* (1955) • *IGI*

**Archives** PRO, state papers, domestic | Bodl. Oxf., Thurlow state MSS • Bodl. Oxf., Clarendon state MSS • Worcester College, Oxford, Clarke MSS

**Likenesses** group portrait, line engraving, 1660 (*The regicides executed in 1660*), BM; repro. in W. S., *Rebels no saints, or, A collection of the speeches, private passages, letters, and prayers of those lately executed* (1661)

**Hacket, John** (1592–1670), bishop of Coventry and Lichfield, was born on 1 September 1592 in the Strand, near Essex House, in the parish of St Martin-in-the-Fields, London, the son of Andrew Hacket, a Scot later employed in the household of Prince Henry. After an early education at Westminster School, where he first displayed his facility as a Latinist, he matriculated as a pensioner from Trinity College, Cambridge, on 10 April 1609, graduating BA in 1613. He was elected a fellow of Trinity in 1614, and proceeded MA in 1616, the year he was incorporated at Oxford. He was ordained deacon and priest by John King, bishop of London, in December 1618, and gained the degree of BD in 1623.

John Hacket (1592–1670), by unknown artist

**Early career** As soon as John Williams was appointed lord keeper in 1621 he made Hacket his household chaplain. Williams had been aware of him during his own Cambridge days, and had consulted him in May 1620 about his old school before taking responsibility for its well-being as dean of Westminster. Williams was to prove a generous patron, and Hacket had already been appointed vicar of Trumpington, Cambridgeshire, during 1620. He quickly also became rector of Stoke Hammond, Buckinghamshire, Kirkby Underwood, Lincolnshire (both in 1621), and Barcombe, Sussex (in 1622). He was elected to the prebend of Aylesbury in Lincoln Cathedral in February 1623, just as James I's retirement to Newmarket on the departure of Prince Charles and Buckingham for Spain gave Williams more scope to use his influence while affording Hacket a taste of the cultural ambience of the king's country retreats. When Coloma and Boiscott, respectively ambassadors for Spain and for the Spanish Netherlands, visited Cambridge late in February on their way to meet James, Trinity put on as part of the university's entertainment a provocative comedy, *Loyola*, which Hacket had written in Latin some years earlier, and which Williams confidently assured the college elders would not sit ill with any misgivings they might have about the prince's foolhardy activities in Spain. For their own reasons, Coloma and Boiscott had doubts, too, and after taking advice about its likely drift, declined to attend. A month later, however, James I unexpectedly paid a rare visit to Cambridge from Newmarket to see the play, and subsequently made Hacket his chaplain. As a mark of his rising favour, Hacket was entrusted with the thanksgiving sermon at court on 5 November in both 1623 and 1624, and in one of those years also preached at court on the anniversary of the Gowrie conspiracy (5 August). At Williams's urging, James appointed Hacket in 1624 to two livings with which he was to be long associated: the rectory of St Andrew's, Holborn, then held by the king during the minority of Thomas Wriothesley, earl of Southampton, and the rectory of Cheam in Surrey, vacant on the translation of Richard Senhouse to the bishopric of Carlisle. About this time he married his first wife, Elizabeth (*d.* 1638), daughter of William Stebbing of Earl Soham, Suffolk. This marriage produced Hacket's elder son, Andrew (*b.* *c.*1632), and his other son, Gustavus (who is likely to have been born not long after the death of the Swedish king late in 1632), and probably all four of his daughters, Elizabeth Hutchinson, Marie Davenport, Theophila Dynes, and Anne Lockart.

**Royal chaplain and Calvinist archdeacon, 1625–1642** On Charles's accession in March 1625, Hacket was confirmed as a royal chaplain, although two of John Williams's other clergy, put forward for consideration as new appointments, failed to find favour; and he was not entirely cast into the shadows by Williams's predictable dismissal from the lord keepership in the following October. He took the degree of DD at Cambridge in 1628, and the quality of his preaching was further recognized by his nomination, for the first time, as one of the court's Lenten preachers in 1630. He owed his continued presence in this highly selective list, for all but two of the years to 1640, to the Calvinist preferences of the lord chamberlain, Philip Herbert, earl of Pembroke and Montgomery, who did not allow the necessarily frequent inclusion of an anti-Calvinist like Richard Steward, highly esteemed by the king, to be at the expense of other 'eminent men', such as Hacket, who should not 'be thought … laid aside with disrespect' (PRO, SP 16/183/13). In the event, Hacket was listed more often during the 1630s than Steward. He also regularly waited his month at court, an opportunity that not all the king's chaplains were privileged to have; yet his unswerving, if moderate, Calvinism, was unlikely to attract high favour in the changed circumstances of the new reign, and he belonged to a group of Charles's chaplains who received no substantial royal patronage during the personal rule.

In 1631 Williams appointed Hacket archdeacon of Bedford. On his annual visitations he expounded the liturgy and commended the Book of Sports, but his defence of the term 'table' in preference to 'altar' got him into trouble with William Laud. Hacket became president of Sion College in 1633, but he gained none of the thirty or more deaneries that fell vacant between 1625 and 1640, most of which went to other royal chaplains. He remained too close to his errant master for further advancement, and was liable to be drawn into his restless scheming. While waiting at court late in 1633, he seems to have attempted to set the new clerk of the closet, Matthew Wren, against

Laud, but failed as Wren suspected 'Dr Hacket's foolery … to be a contrivance of Bishop William[s] to breed in him a dislike of the archbishop' (Wren, 49). On occasion, however, he ably defended Williams on doctrinal grounds. When in an opportunist attack on the bishop's views on the holy table, one of the young prebendaries of Westminster, Peter Heylyn, appealed, as was the ceremonialists' fashion, to the liturgical practice of early Christians, Hacket was quick to point to a recent edition of the work cited, the *Liturgy of St John Chrysostom*, which cast serious doubt on the authenticity of its supposed authorship. He also demonstrated how unconvincing it could be to pluck quotations out of context from latter-day authorities of the acknowledged stature of Richard Hooker and Lancelot Andrewes in support of current altar policy.

After Williams was confined to the Tower of London in the late summer of 1637, Hacket visited him regularly until his release in the early days of the Long Parliament, by the way gathering information that he could use in the biographical study of his master, which he had in mind long before it was written. Meanwhile, he busied himself in raising several thousand pounds for badly needed repairs to St Andrew's—money collected so late that it was unspent when the civil war began, and was later appropriated by the parliamentary side. Once convocation reconvened, Hacket was prominent in criticism of the altar-wise position of the holy table, and with fellow Calvinist archdeacons Ralph Brownrig and Richard Holdsworth, mounted a rearguard action against the new canons in the lower house, embarrassing Laud and disturbing Steward's equanimity. Together, the archdeacons spoke with a freedom that Calvinist bishops found it unwise to attempt.

On 15 March 1641 Hacket was appointed to the subcommittee of the Lords' committee on religious innovations, chaired by Williams, where he defended the Book of Common Prayer so ably that his fellows nominated him as their advocate before the Commons to protect deans and chapters against abolition under Dering's Root and Branch Bill. Hacket seemed at first to have succeeded, only for the vote on the bill to be reversed on 15 June 1641. He was elected prebendary of St Paul's on 28 March 1642, and saw John Williams for the last time on his release from the Tower in May 1642, before Williams headed, as primate of the northern province, for York and soon afterwards for his homeland in north Wales.

**Parish clergyman and biographer, 1642–1660** His first wife having died in 1638, on 13 December 1641 Hacket had taken out a licence to marry Frances Bennett (*d.* 1646), widow of Dove Bridgeman, clergyman, a son of John Bridgeman, bishop of Chester. On 25 April 1642 the Commons ordered Hacket to admit Vere Harcourt as lecturer at St Andrew's, Holborn. Imprisoned for refusing to contribute to parliament in November 1642, he paid part of his assessment the next year. Following accusations of superstition, covetousness, sending money to the king and aversion to the Covenant, in October 1643 he was sequestered from St Andrew's. Hacket spent the civil war at his rectory at Cheam, suffering occasional interruptions and indignities, and apparently no longer in touch with Williams; his wife, Frances, died in 1646. At Cheam he used the Book of Common Prayer when he could, but also practised occasional conformity to the new regime often enough to be made a member of the Westminster assembly of divines in 1644, although he did not attend for long.

Hacket's comedy *Loyola* was published for the first time in London in 1648. Williams's death in March 1650 then turned his thoughts to the task he had already set himself, to produce an informed life of the man he had first remarked before writing the play in his earliest days as a student at Cambridge. By the end of 1650 he had taken stock of his sources of information, and apparently concluded that from direct knowledge, his subject's reminiscences, and accounts from witnesses he was well supplied for all but the period between 1642 and 1650 when Williams had returned to his Welsh roots. He sent 'earnest messages' to William Dolben, lawyer to Williams's niece Grace, Lady Wynn, and her family. On 11 December 1650 Dolben passed on his appeal for help over the 'Conway business' to Lady Wynn, having heard that the archbishop had kept copies of important letters. The thinness of the coverage of the Welsh years, apparent when the manuscript was completed on 17 February 1658, suggests that the Wynns had little to offer and that he was no luckier elsewhere. Once finished, the text was not revised before it was published, more than twenty years after Hacket's death, as *Scrinia reserata: a Memorial Offer'd to the Great Deservings of John Williams* in 1693. It provides a study, remarkable in its time, of the life of a public figure not quite of the highest importance, and puts the case for a minister whose perversity, overshadowing the firmness of his Calvinist faith, has encouraged others to vilify him. Although the quality of Hacket's evidence, often a single source, makes his accuracy variable, the biography conveys information and offers insights not readily found elsewhere. Its florid style is, however, no help to the clarity of its exposition, and was not to the taste of all its readers in the 1690s or since. More seriously, the work's credibility is put at risk by Hacket's determination to see Williams in the best possible light, and too often to impute to him motives of a naïvety he would almost certainly have been reluctant to own.

**Restoration bishop, 1661–1670** Hacket became a bishop soon after the Restoration, turning down Gloucester in 1660 before accepting Coventry and Lichfield, vacant since Accepted Frewen's translation to York in October 1660 and already refused by Edmund Calamy and possibly by Richard Baxter. He was consecrated on 22 December 1661, finding his diocese seriously lacking in fabric as well as in faith. His cathedral was almost in ruins; but, as his correspondence with Gilbert Sheldon shows, Hacket pursued the work of fund-raising and rebuilding with such energy and determination that it was possible to dedicate it at Christmas 1669. The occasion was celebrated by three days of sedate feasting. Hacket gave £3500 for the work, and launched an appeal for £20,000, raising at least

£15,000 for the organ, stalls, altar ornaments, and other essentials. All was not well with the management of the cathedral, however, and Hacket, a choleric man, was frequently at odds with the well-connected but obstructive dean, Thomas Wood, his eventual successor; in 1667–8 they fell out to such an extent that they provoked widespread concern in church circles, while pleasing both nonconformists and court gossips by managing to have each other excommunicated in the court of arches.

In autumn 1662 Hacket was among the first post-Restoration bishops to visit his diocese, adapting to local needs the standard articles provided by an episcopal committee. He assured the earl of Clarendon as he set out that he intended to keep a firm grip on Coventry and Shrewsbury, but dealt charitably with two ejected ministers in Coventry in the hope of winning them over to the church, and later offered one of them, Obadiah Grew, a prebend of Lichfield. Thomas Plume, in his memoir of the bishop, believed Hacket persuaded twenty-three presbyterian ministers to submit to reordination, and others were given a period of grace in which to come to terms with the reformed church. He also confirmed 500 in 'troublesome' Coventry (Green, 142). Thereafter Hacket seems to have visited his diocese in stages, sending detailed reports to Sheldon, now his archbishop, in 1665, 1666, and 1668. He used his time effectively. Visiting Shropshire for two weeks in June 1665, he confirmed a total of 5384 people, and preached in eight of its market towns as well as at Stafford on his way home. A sermon delivered at about this time at Lichfield warned, in dramatic fashion, of 'an ocean of ungodliness' threatening all sections of society (Spurr, 277).

Hacket resumed preaching at court in March 1661. In the presence of Charles II and before his own elevation to the episcopal bench, he argued strongly in a sermon, published soon afterwards, for the local autonomy of bishops, especially over the ordination of clergy: 'unless you give some prerogative of power to the bishop in a diocese to examine, order and maintain sound doctrine, you will have so many fashions as there are men and so many faiths as there are parishes' (Spurr, 149). On Whit Sunday 1662 Samuel Pepys, from his pew as clerk of the privy seal in Whitehall chapel, heard Hacket, with the king again present, preaching a more reassuring and 'most excellent' sermon 'upon he that drinketh the water shall never thirst' (Pepys, 3.84). Hacket had attended the meetings in Worcester House in October 1660 and was a commissioner at the Savoy conference in 1661. Towards the end of the Savoy proceedings Baxter's proposals for a draft liturgy which might satisfy both church and presbyterians were referred to him for an opinion, to be delivered within two nights. He found they did too little to bridge the divide, and recommended their rejection, bringing a summary end to early attempts at reconciliation. In the Lords he was no friend of comprehension, praising those 'prudent and religious patriots' in the Commons who consistently voted for suppressing conventicles and nonconformity (Beddard, 170). He was relieved that a further attempt at comprehension in 1667–8 was averted 'by the finger of God … immediately in it' (Sykes, 73).

Hacket took a particular dislike to the moderate presbyterian divine, John Wilkins, partly because of his manoeuvrings over bills for comprehension, but primarily because of what he regarded as the distasteful manner of his preaching. Wilkins's appeal to self-interest as well as to duty in the cause of moral reform put an unseemly emphasis on the 'advantages' of religion to the individual. He also failed to appreciate Wilkins's preference for intelligibility, brevity, and plainness of delivery over the wealth of textual allusions and rhetorical flourishes familiar in a conventional learned sermon, dismissing him as nothing more than 'shallow … both in philosophy and divinity'. He was incensed when Wilkins, on becoming bishop of Chester in November 1668, was for consecutive years included in the Lent list of court preachers, still more so when his sermons were ordered to be printed. 'What a pittiful sermon of his, preached in Lent, is commanded to be printed. Is it because the Court likes no sermons longer than a quarter of an hower?' he asked plaintively of that delivered in 1670 (Shapiro, 72–5, 180). A similar question might have been asked of the critics of *Scrinia reserata*, itself published perhaps a generation too late.

Despite his many duties in his diocese, from superintending building work to sitting regularly in his diocesan court, hearing complainants at his home and preaching almost daily, Hacket did not neglect his responsibilities in the House of Lords. Only once does he seem to have shown reluctance to attend yet another of the nine sessions of the Cavalier Parliament during his episcopate when, in October 1667, he told Sheldon he had hoped instead 'for recuperation from the summer's labours and for health', but all the same 'would prepare for a most distasteful journey' (Sykes, 21, 25). But he went to the eighth session in 1669 with high hopes of strict action against nonconformists and conventiclers. He died, probably at Lichfield, on 28 October 1670, and was buried in Lichfield Cathedral beneath a 'very noble and conspicuous' monument provided by his elder son (Newcourt, 1.182n.).

Hacket drew up his will with his own hand on 9 January 1666, with a codicil added on 31 August 1669, reflecting minor changes in his circumstances. The only landed estate he disposed of were two Suffolk manors, near Earl Soham, which must have come to him on his marriage to Elizabeth Stebbing. They, and the bulk of his goods and chattels, went to his son and sole executor Andrew, a Gray's Inn barrister who became a master in chancery in 1670 and was knighted in 1671. After spending heavily on his cathedral and donating £1200 to Trinity College for the rebuilding of Gerard's Hostel, on the condition that it be known in future as Bishop's Hostel, Hacket had £2000 in hand with which to provide modestly for his immediate family and domestic servants, and to allow £20 for the purchase of plate for Archbishop Sheldon and £2 apiece for rings for clerical friends and relatives and for church court officials. He left his books to the University of Cambridge, with a gift of £100 to Trinity for its college library. To

Thomas Plume, the vicar of East Greenwich and one of the overseers of his will, who had sent him books from London after his removal to Lichfield, he gave £10. He also left him, without comment, two velvet-covered volumes containing the manuscript of his own sermons, which Plume, doubtless already aware of Hacket's intentions, subsequently published as *A Century of Sermons upon Several Remarkable Subjects* (1675), prefaced by a memoir. It provided a fitting memorial to a cleric who, through changing times, had remained firm in his Calvinist faith and a ready preacher in his chosen manner.

BRIAN QUINTRELL

**Sources** Bodl. Oxf., MSS Tanner, esp. vols. 44–8 [for correspondence with G. Sheldon] · PRO, LC 5/132, 134 · will, PRO, PROB 11/334/175 · *CSP dom.*, 1603–70, esp. PRO, SP 16/183/13 · BL, Sloane MS 1710 [correspondence with T. Dillingham, master of Emmanuel College, Cambridge] · J. Hacket, *A century of sermons*, ed. T. Plume (1675) [with memoir]; new edn, ed. M. Walcot (1865) · J. Hacket, *Scrinia reserata: a memorial offer'd to the great deservings of John Williams*, 2 pts (1693) · R. Newcourt, *Repertorium ecclesiasticum parochiale Londinense*, 2 vols. (1708–10) · J. Nichols, ed., *The progresses … of King James I*, 4 vols. (1828), vol. 4 · S. Wren, *Parentalia or memoirs of the family of Wren* (1750) · Pepys, *Diary* · J. L. Chester and G. J. Armytage, eds., *Allegations for marriage licences issued by the bishop of London*, 2, Harleian Society, 26 (1887) · *The letters of John Chamberlain*, ed. N. E. McClure, 2 vols. (1939) · P. E. McCullough, *Sermons at court: politics and religion in Elizabethan and Jacobean preaching* (1998) [incl. CD-ROM] · A. Milton, *Catholic and Reformed: the Roman and protestant churches in English protestant thought, 1600–1640* (1995) · R. C. Bald, *John Donne: a life*, ed. W. Milgate (1970) · N. Tyacke, *Anti-Calvinists: the rise of English Arminianism, c.1590–1640* (1987) · J. Davies, *The Caroline captivity of the church: Charles I and the remoulding of Anglicanism, 1625–1641* (1992) · N. Sykes, *From Sheldon to Secker* (1959) · J. Spurr, *The Restoration Church of England, 1646–1689* (1991) · G. F. Nuttall and O. Chadwick, eds., *From uniformity to unity* (1962) · I. Green, *The re-establishment of the Church of England, 1660–1663* (1978) · R. S. Bosher, *The making of the Restoration settlement: the influence of the Laudians, 1649–1662*, rev. edn (1957) · B. Shapiro, *John Wilkins, 1614–1672* (1969) · A. M. Mimardière, 'Hacket, Sir Andrew', HoP, *Commons, 1660–90* · K. Fincham, ed., *Visitation articles and injunctions of the early Stuart church*, 2 (1998), xxiv · *Walker rev.*, 49 · *DNB* · *Staffordshire*, Pevsner (1974) · R. A. Beddard, 'The Restoration church', *The restored monarchy, 1660–1688*, ed. J. R. Jones (1979), 170 · *VCH Cambridgeshire and the Isle of Ely*, vol. 3

**Archives** Bodl. Oxf., corresp. with Sheldon, etc., and papers

**Likenesses** attrib. V. Ritz, oils, before 1679, Trinity Cam. · W. Faithorne, line engraving, BM, NPG; repro. in Hacket, *A century of sermons* · oils, Trinity Cam. [*see illus.*] · portrait, repro. in Hacket, *A century of sermons*

**Wealth at death** approx. £3000; spent heavily on his cathedral and a hostel at Trinity College, Cambridge, in last years: will, 1669, PRO, PROB 11/334/175

**Hacket, Roger** (1559–1621), Church of England clergyman, was born in the parish of St James Garlickhythe, London, the son of Sir Cuthbert Hacket. In 1573, aged fourteen, he obtained a scholarship at Winchester College. He was admitted as a scholar at New College, Oxford, in 1575, and was elected fellow in 1577, graduating BA on 16 October 1579, MA on 1 June 1583, BTh on 9 July 1590, and DTh on 10 November 1596. On 7 April 1590 he was instituted to the rectory of North Crawley, Buckinghamshire, and held this benefice until his death, being listed as resident there at several intermediate dates. Hacket was a celebrated preacher and at least six of his sermons were published, including one given at Paul's Cross on 14 February 1591.

A conformist who yet displayed sensitivity to puritan scruples, in 1605 Hacket asked of his nonconformist brethren 'should a cross and a surplice thrust you from your needful labours … what is a linen garment?' (Hacket, *Learned Sermon*, 22). A few months later he was appointed by the ecclesiastical authorities to speak at a visitation of the archdeaconry of Buckingham, and in his address he wrote of his sadness at the 'raylings and bitter speakings' against him, and at his having been misrepresented as a 'broacher of popery' in a book by ministers of Lincoln diocese. But since their 'labours have been most fruitful in the work of their God', he sought to persuade them towards conformity (Hacket, *Sermon Principally Entreating*, preface).

Hacket prospered at North Crawley, acquiring Franklin's Farm, Broughton Manor, and other properties in the area. He had been presented to the rectory by the father of John Garbrand, his predecessor, but in 1604 acquired a share in the advowson for himself—and for his descendants. Here, 'having bought in several estates and laid them together, he built the principal house in the whole parish' (*VCH Buckinghamshire*, 4.331). Still under construction at Hacket's death, this was 'a sizeable Elizabethan brick mansion', constructed 'on the E plan with straight gables and transomed windows' (Pevsner, *Buckinghamshire*, 216). The estates, and probably the rectory, then passed to his son, also Roger, later a royalist in the civil war, who in turn seems to have passed them to his own son Thomas, a leading Buckinghamshire tory. Roger Hacket died in 1621 and was buried at North Crawley church on 16 September.

STEPHEN WRIGHT

**Sources** *VCH Buckinghamshire*, 4.331, 337 · R. Hacket, *A sermon needfull for theese times, preached at Paule's Cross* (1591) · R. Hacket, *A sermon principally entreating at the cross in baptism* (1606) · R. Hacket, *A learned sermon handling the question of ceremonies* (1605) · M. McClure, *The St Paul's Cross sermons, 1534–1642* (1958) · C. W. Foster, ed., *The state of the church in the reigns of Elizabeth and James I*, Lincoln RS, 23 (1926) · *Buckinghamshire*, Pevsner (1960) · J. A. Boodle, 'The sepulchral brasses of Buckinghamshire', *Records of Buckinghamshire*, 3 (1870), 16–18, esp. 109–10 · H. A. Handley, 'A Buckinghamshire tory', *Records of Buckinghamshire*, 19 (1971–4), 457–70 · Foster, *Alum. Oxon.*

**Wealth at death** substantial property in North Crawley, Buckinghamshire: *VCH Buckinghamshire*, 4.331, 337

**Hacket, William** (*d.* 1591), prophet, was born in humble circumstances in Oundle, Northamptonshire, of unknown parents. Reputedly illiterate, he was employed as a serving man in the households of Gilbert Hussey, Sir Thomas Tresham, and Sir Charles Morrison successively. Throughout this period he seems to have held Catholic opinions, and in October 1577 was presented before the ecclesiastical court for repeated failure to receive communion. While in the service of Hussey he married Anna Moreton, the widow of a prosperous farmer, whose estate he allegedly soon wasted by idle and riotous living. Given to blaspheming and swearing, he was also renowned for his violent and volatile temper, most notably displayed during a quarrel in which he bit off a schoolmaster's nose and 'did in a most spitefull and divelish outrage eat it up' (Cosin, 4–5). Some time in the 1580s he underwent a religious conversion and became an outspoken advocate of presbyterianism. This coincided with his growing friendship with a recently deprived puritan minister, Giles Wigginton, with whom he entered into partnership in the malt trade. The two also seem to have become leaders of a semi-separatist splinter group verging on a conventicle. In 1589–90 Hacket was cited for having misappropriated the surplice and 'contemptiously in the time of service layd it under his tayle' (Peterborough diocesan records, MS X609/23, fol. 143*v*), and his precisian scruples eventually induced him to forsake his own parish church and resort to the neighbouring village of Stoke Doyle.

Inspired by a series of supernatural revelations and ecstatic experiences, Hacket began to believe that he had a unique prophetic vocation. He claimed to have special gifts of clairvoyance and other miraculous powers, and acquired a considerable reputation as an exorcist and sorcerer. An intense and charismatic figure, whom some women evidently found sexually compelling, the allegation that he had attempted to rape a virgin 'under colour of giving godly counsell' (Cosin, 6) may have been more than a mere vicious slander. In the course of the 1580s he travelled to Lincoln and York, and took on the mantle of John the Baptist, announcing that he had been 'sent thither by God' to prepare the way for Christ's second coming in judgment (ibid., 7). Whipped and banished by civic officials, he continued his itinerant ministry in Hampshire, Hertfordshire, and Northamptonshire. Magistrates in these counties apparently regarded Hacket as a madman, and attributed his 'seditious speaches' against the queen and several leading statesmen 'to some spice of phrenesie' rather than to 'setled and advised malice' (ibid., 8). The harsh correction he received at their hands simply reinforced his belief that he was a persecuted servant of the Lord. At the beginning of the Easter term 1591 he went to London at the suggestion of Wigginton, who appears to have seriously entertained the possibility that Hacket had an 'extraordinary calling'. There he was introduced to Edmund Coppinger and Henry Arthington, two puritan gentlemen with whom he was to form an intimate but fatal alliance. Increasingly convinced of his own immortality, Hacket wrestled with the lions in the Tower of London without being mauled, a feat recorded in the personal 'historie' he later dictated to his devoted disciples.

Obsessed by the plight of Thomas Cartwright and other presbyterian ministers confined in the Fleet, Hacket, Coppinger, and Arthington devised a dangerous scheme to effect Cartwright's release and abolish the institution of episcopacy. This was to be accompanied by a political coup involving the deposition of Elizabeth I and the ejection of Lord Chancellor Christopher Hatton and other privy councillors unsympathetic to the puritan cause. Hacket defaced the queen's coat of arms and pierced a portrait of her with a bodkin 'in the very place, representing her royall heart' (Cosin, 61), an iconoclastic act with overtones of image-magic which would later clinch the government's case that he was guilty of treason. Printed propaganda was dispersed under cover of night to potential participants, and early on the morning of 19 July Coppinger and Arthington went through the streets of London warning of vengeance and preaching repentance. They mounted a cart in Cheapside and announced to the thronging crowd that Hacket, whom they had left in bed in a lodging-house in Broken Wharf, was the long-awaited messiah. The three were arrested later that day and imprisoned in Bridewell.

On 26 July Hacket was tried at the sessions house near Newgate, and, despite attempts by the defence to acquit him on the grounds of insanity, was convicted and condemned to death. The execution took place near Cheapside cross on 28 July, and he died uttering 'execrable blasphemie', denouncing the queen, and calling upon 'mightie Jehovah' to 'send some miracle out of a cloude' to deliver him (Cosin, 71–3). An official account of the affair entitled *Conspiracie, for Pretended Reformation* was prepared by Richard Cosin, and the 'desperate adventures' (Hooker) of the threesome were also discussed in Richard Bancroft's *Daungerous Positions and Proceedings* (1593) and the preface to book 5 of Richard Hooker's *Lawes of Ecclesiastical Politie* (1594) (sig. A4*v*). Intent on disgracing the puritan movement, all three writers exaggerated the loose links between the conspirators and leading presbyterians. In the later seventeenth century Hacket was frequently invoked by Anglican writers in their efforts to brand religious enthusiasm as a species of madness.

Alexandra Walsham

**Sources** R. Cosin, *Conspiracie, for pretended reformation* (1591) • *The manuscripts of Lord Kenyon*, HMC, 35 (1894), 607–9 • Thomas Phelippes to Henry Saintmains (?), 19 July 1591, PRO, state papers domestic, Elizabeth, SP 12/239/93 • *APC*, *1591*, 293, 297, 299–300, 319, 325 • Northants. RO, Peterborough diocesan records, MS 607/9, fol. 40*v* • Northants. RO, Peterborough diocesan records, MS X609/23, fols. 143*v*, 144*v*–146*r* • Northants. RO, Peterborough diocesan records, MS X609/23a, fol. 51*r* • Northants. RO, Peterborough diocesan records, MS X610/25, fol. 19*r* • visitation court book 5, 1574–80, Northants. RO, Peterborough diocesan records, fols. 39*r*, 85*r* • H. Arthington, *The seduction of Arthington by Hacket especiallie* (1592) • [R. Bancroft], *Daungerous positions and proceedings* (1593) • J. Throkmorton, *The defence of Job Throkmorton, against the slaunders of Maister Sutcliffe* (1594) • T. Cartwright, *A brief apologie of Thomas Cartwright* (1596) • R. Hooker, *Of the lawes of ecclesiasticall politie* (1597), bk 5, dedication to Archbishop John Whitgift • J. Stow, *The annales of England … untill this present yeere 1592* (1592), 1288–90 • LPL, Fairhurst MS 2008, fol. 29*r* • A. Walsham, '"Frantick Hacket": prophecy, sorcery, insanity, and the Elizabethan puritan movement', *HJ*, 41 (1998), 27–66 • W. J. Sheils, *The puritans in the diocese of Peterborough, 1558–1610*, Northamptonshire RS, 30 (1979), 136–8

**Hackett, James Thomas** (1805–1876), astrologer, was born in co. Cork, the son of James Hacket. In early life he practised as a surveyor. He also possessed respectable mathematical knowledge, which led him about 1826 to join the Phrenological and Astrological societies. He was secretary of the latter, and the last member, when the discovery of Neptune disrupted the society's activities. In 1836 he published *The student's assistant in astronomy and astrology. … Also a discourse on the harmony of phrenology, astrology, and physiognomy.*

Hackett married, about 1840, Amelia Sophia (*b.* 1818); they had two sons and two daughters. Hackett subsequently became more devout as a Roman Catholic and eschewed astrology. Latterly he was railway correspondent to *The Times*; he had been for many years previously reporter on the staff of *Herapath's Railway and Commercial Journal* to which he contributed some valuable statistical tables. John Herapath, mathematician and founder of various railway journals, left him a legacy of £250. Hackett died of heart failure at his home, Park Villa, Alexandra Road, Friern Barnet, Middlesex, on 13 February 1876.

GORDON GOODWIN, *rev.* ANITA MCCONNELL

**Sources** *The Athenaeum* (15 April 1876), 535–6 · *Herapath's Railway Journal*, no. 518 (6 May 1876) · Boase, *Mod. Eng. biog.* · J. T. Hackett, *The student's assistant in astronomy and astrology* (1836) · d. cert. · census returns, 1881

**Wealth at death** under £200: probate, 9 May 1876, *CGPLA Eng. & Wales*

**Hackett, John Baptist** (*c.*1606–1676), Roman Catholic priest and theologian, was born of a prominent Old English family at Fethard, co. Tipperary. Having entered the Dominican order and made his profession at Cashel he studied in Spain and was ordained deacon and priest at Barcelona in 1630. Later he lectured with distinction in the order's *studia generalia* of Milan, Naples, and Rome and was conferred with its most prestigious theological degree at its general chapter in 1644. He was eagerly sought as theological adviser by several Roman cardinals, including Aemilius Altieri, who, as Pope Clement X (*r.* 1670–76), appointed him his personal theologian. Hackett declined bishoprics and the cardinalate. While regent of studies at Sant' Eustorgio, Milan, he was very influential in strengthening the resolve of Lord Philip Howard (1629–1694), grandson of Thomas Howard, fourteenth earl of Arundel, and a recent convert to Catholicism, in his dramatic decision to join the Dominicans at Cremona in 1645. At this news consternation ensued in the Howard family, who made vigorous representations through diplomatic channels to the most powerful cardinals at the Roman court to prevent Howard's entering the Dominican or any other religious order, or indeed receiving holy orders. Finally the pope himself interviewed Howard and approved both the motivation for his vocation and his aspirations to promote the restoration of Catholicism in England. Howard then proceeded to Santa Maria alla Sanità in Naples, designated in 1644 as a house of formation for English, Irish, and Scottish Dominicans intended for the priestly ministry in their countries. On 29 May 1675, largely at Hackett's urging, he was named a cardinal by Clement X.

Hackett devoted the last years of his life to publishing the fruits of his scholarship in Rome. He published a number of works on Thomistic theology and philosophy: *Controversorium theologicum complectens omnes tractatus totius primae secundae Doctoris Angelici D. Thomae Aquinatis* (Rome, 1654); *Synopsis theologica in tractatum de fide, spe, et charitatis* (Rome, 1659); *Synopsis summulistica* (Rome, 1659); *Synopsis physica* (Rome, 1659); *Synopsis meteorica* (Rome, 1659); *Synopsis philosophiae* (2 vols., Rome, 1662); and *Synopsis universa theologiae scholasticae et moralis in quinque tomos distributa iuxta mentem Doctoris Angelici D. Thomae Aquinatis* (Rome, 1662).

Hackett died on 26 August 1676 at the Dominican convent of Santa Maria sopra Minerva, Rome, and was buried in its church in the common vault of the brethren. Two of his Cashel kinsmen, Pádraigín *Haicéad and Patrick Kearney, also became Dominicans. Haicéad became one of the finest Irish language poets of the seventeenth century. Kearney graduated from the University of Louvain in 1637, and was subsequently appointed a professor and master in theology (1650) in the Irish Dominican College of Louvain.

THOMAS S. R. O'FLYNN

**Sources** T. Burke, *Hibernia Dominicana, sive, Historia Provinciae Hiberniae ordinis praedicatorum* (Cologne, 1762) · B. de Jonghe, *Belgium Dominicanum, sive, Historia Provinciae Germaniae Inferioris Sacri Ordinis FF. Praedicatorum* (Brussels, 1719) · register of ordinations, 1621–41, Archivo Diocesano, Barcelona · T. S. Flynn, *The Irish Dominicans, 1536–1641* (Dublin, 1993) · M. Ní Cheallacháin, ed., *Filíocht Phádraigín Haicéad* (Dublin, 1962) · E. Ó Raghailligh, *A genealogical history of the O'Reillys*, ed. J. Carney (Dublin, 1959)

**Hackett, Sir John Winthrop** (1910–1997), army officer, was born on 5 November 1910 in Perth, Western Australia, the only son and one of five children of Sir (John) Winthrop Hackett (1848–1916), newspaper proprietor and politician, and his wife, Deborah Vernon (1887–1965), daughter of Frederick Slade Drake-Brockman and his wife, Grace Vernon (*née* Bussell). The family was of Norman-Irish origin, descended from a William de Haket who had accompanied King John to Ireland and settled in co. Tipperary. Hackett's father had graduated at Trinity College, Dublin, and emigrated to Sydney in 1875. A lawyer and journalist, he became a wealthy newspaper proprietor in Western Australia, assisted in drafting the commonwealth constitution, and became the first chancellor of the University of Western Australia, an institution he richly endowed with buildings and scholarships. Hackett's mother was not only a leading society hostess and active welfare worker but a metallurgist and mining company director, who explored Australia for mineral resources in a single-seater plane and was instrumental in the development of tantalite and wolfram for industrial purposes. This formidable parentage was a major factor in young Hackett's decision to make his career outside his native country.

Hackett was educated at Geelong grammar school, Melbourne, from 1921 to 1928, and at New College, Oxford (1929–33), which was to elect him to an honorary fellowship in 1972. He gained a second-class degree in *literae humaniores* in 1932, and another in modern history the following year. Dissatisfied with an academic performance that he felt had not done him justice, and pursuing an intellectual interest fired by the career of T. E. Lawrence,

**Sir John Winthrop Hackett** (1910–1997), by Walter Bird, 1966

he began research on Saladin's campaign in northern Syria during the third crusade for a BLitt degree that was eventually awarded in 1945. He never abandoned his academic ambitions: in later life he used to remark, to somewhat sceptical audiences, that his military career was simply the result of 'forty years' absence of mind' (personal knowledge).

Yet even before graduating Hackett had been commissioned, in 1931, into the 8th King's Royal Irish Hussars, a regiment with which he had a close family connection. Having been posted to Egypt, he was seconded in 1937 to the trans-Jordan frontier force, which enabled him to research the subject of his thesis on the ground, and to learn Arabic—he was already fluent in German, French, and Italian—in the intervals of campaigning at the height of the Arab uprising. After the outbreak of the Second World War he fought in the Syrian campaign in 1941, in which he was wounded, and was awarded a Military Cross. While convalescing on the shores of Lake Galilee he met Margaret, widow of Friedrich Grossman and daughter of Joseph Peter Frena of Graz, Austria. The fact that she was an 'enemy alien' did not prevent him from wooing, winning, and marrying her in high style in St George's Cathedral, Jerusalem, on 21 March 1942. They had one daughter, Susan Veronica, and Hackett adopted his wife's two daughters from her first marriage, Bridget and Elizabeth.

After rejoining his regiment in the western desert Hackett was again wounded, and was appointed DSO. For a time he was occupied in organizing the light raiding forces such as the long range desert group and the Special Air Service, which were to play so distinctive a part in the campaign, before being selected, at the age of thirty-three, to raise and command the 4th Parachute brigade. The sequel was to be tragic. After briefly seeing action in Italy in September 1943 the brigade was posted back to the United Kingdom, only to be committed to the disastrous Arnhem operation in September 1944 and destroyed in a matter of hours. As Hackett himself put it, 'I had been its midwife and was now to be its sexton' (Hackett, 9). He himself was gravely wounded but escaped capture, to be hidden and nursed back to health by a friendly Dutch family, and eventually smuggled back to the British lines by the Dutch resistance. His account of his experiences, *I was a Stranger* (1977), was one of the most moving works of literature to emerge from the Second World War. For his exploits at Arnhem he was awarded a bar to his DSO.

After the war Hackett was posted back to the Middle East to command and, sadly, to disband the trans-Jordan frontier force. Typically he chose to spend his leave attending a postgraduate seminar in medieval studies on his wife's home territory at the University of Graz. The rest of his military career was to be spent in Europe, divided between postings in the United Kingdom and Germany, where he commanded 20th armoured brigade in 1954 and 7th armoured division in 1956–8, before becoming commander-in-chief, British army of the Rhine, from 1966 to 1968. To each level of command he brought a quick, iconoclastic intelligence; a reluctance to suffer fools gladly, irrespective of their rank, that did not endear him either to his seniors or to some of his contemporaries; and a deep concern for the welfare of all under his command that made him immensely popular with his juniors—and, no less important, their wives. In Germany he saw his task as being as much political as military, cementing Anglo-German friendship by encouraging links between the units under his command and the people among whom they lived. The command of the British army of the Rhine carried with it a NATO command, that of northern army group, which gave Hackett a degree of independence from his political masters in London that he relished and never hesitated to exploit when he thought it necessary. By the end of his career he was regarded throughout the army with admiration and affection, but his independence of spirit and unpredictability was probably to deny him the final accolade of becoming chief of the general staff.

Hackett was thus able in 1968, at the age of fifty-eight, to take up the academic career after which he had sometimes hankered. His appointment as principal of King's College, London, caused some surprise; but some senior members of the college had known and admired him when he had commanded the Royal Military College of Science between 1958 and 1961, while others hoped that the political skills he had honed in the corridors of Whitehall might be exercised to similar effect in the no less byzantine environment of the University of London. They were not to be disappointed, but Hackett himself did not find that the appointment provided the opportunity for scholarly research for which he had hoped. In addition to his heavy administrative responsibilities he found himself plunged into the thick of the student revolts that were sweeping Europe and the United States between 1967 and 1974. It was a challenge that he welcomed. He soaked himself in subversive literature, outwitted the radicals, astonished the student body by his deep interest in their affairs, and made the headlines by leading a march down Whitehall, immaculate in bowler hat and furled umbrella, demanding higher student grants. At the same time he became much in demand for lectures and media comments on military affairs—a demand that he took relish in satisfying.

These demands absorbed Hackett's time after his retirement in 1975, though he staunchly denied that he had ever retired: he had, as he put it, 'simply withdrawn to a flank and regrouped' (personal knowledge). In 1978 he published a futuristic study, *The Third World War*, which, with its successor, *The Third World War: the Untold Story* (1981), enjoyed worldwide sales. He also published an illustrated edition of the elegant Lees Knowles lectures he had given in Cambridge in 1962, *The Profession of Arms* (1983). But he did not abandon his classical studies: he remained visiting professor in classics at King's College, and became president of both the Classical Association and the English Association. (His insistence on the correct use of the English language had not been the least of the qualities that had intimidated his military staffs.) Further honours were rained on him: he became colonel of his own regiment, the Queen's Royal Irish Hussars, and others, an honorary liveryman of the Worshipful Company of Dyers, a freeman of the City of London, and a deputy lieutenant of Gloucestershire. Honorary doctorates were bestowed on him by the universities of Western Australia, Exeter, and Buckingham. In 1985 he was awarded the Chesney gold medal of the Royal United Services Institution. He was a member of the lord chancellor's committee on reform of the law of contempt (1971–4) and of the disciplinary tribunal of the inns of court and the bar (1972–83).

Hackett looked every inch the professional soldier: short, compact, elegant, with a high colour and clipped moustache. Only his twinkling blue eyes hinted at the spirit of mischief lurking within that orthodox exterior. By the time of his death he had become a national figure, and—in the words of his *Times* obituarist—'probably no man did as much as he to dispel the widely-held British belief that most generals are fools, and ignorant fools at that' (*The Times*, 10 Sept 1997). A portrait of him in uniform by Brenda Bury hangs in the regimental headquarters of the Queen's Royal Hussars, and one in academic robes by Michael Noakes at King's College, London.

In retirement Hackett lived at Coberley Mill, Gloucestershire, indulging in recreations he listed in *Who's Who* as 'fishing, wine, music and the pursuit of exactitude, called by some pedantry', while, in his own words, 'having to do a fair bit of work more appropriate to a middle-aged peasant than to an elderly intellectual' (personal knowledge). He died at Coberley Mill on 9 September 1997 at the age of eighty-seven. His ashes were interred in the Hackett mausoleum at Karrakatta cemetery at Claremont, Perth. He was survived by his wife and two adopted daughters, the daughter of his marriage having predeceased him.

MICHAEL HOWARD

**Sources** personal knowledge (2004) · private information (2004) · *WWW* · *AusDB* · *The Times* (10 Sept 1997) · *The Guardian* (10 Sept 1997) · *The Guardian* (11 Sept 1997) · *Daily Telegraph* (10 Sept 1997) · *The Independent* (11 Sept 1997) · J. W. Hackett, *I was a stranger* (1977) · Burke, *Peerage*

**Archives** King's Lond., Liddell Hart C., papers relating to Arnhem | King's Lond., Liddell Hart C., corresp. with Sir B. H. Liddell Hart | SOUND BL NSA, 'Serendipity', NP2834R C1 · BL NSA, current affairs recordings · BL NSA, performance recordings

**Likenesses** W. Bird, photograph, 1966, NPG [*see illus.*] · H. J. Baker, oils, 1987, NPG · B. Bury, portrait (in uniform), Queen's Royal Hussars Headquarters · M. Noakes, portrait (in academic robes), King's Lond. · photograph, repro. in *The Times* · photograph, repro. in *Daily Telegraph* · photograph, repro. in *The Guardian* (10 Sept 1997) · photograph, repro. in *The Independent*

**Wealth at death** £214,371: probate, 30 Jan 1998, *CGPLA Eng. & Wales*

**Hackett, Maria** (1783–1874), philanthropist, was born in Birmingham on 14 November 1783, the only child of Joseph and Grace Hackett. Her father died when she was four months old, and in October 1787 Grace married Samuel Capper, the son of a Birmingham cloth merchant, and bore him two sons, John and Samuel James. Capper died in 1790, and about the turn of the century Grace and her children moved to London. Here they lived with Capper's unmarried brother George, a provision broker and agent in the City, who had a country home at Snaresbrook, Essex, and a town house at 8 Crosby Square where, by 1809, Maria Hackett was residing.

Maria Hackett, who never married, devoted her time and money (the latter of which was probably inherited from George Capper) to a campaign to improve the living and educational conditions of boy choristers in the cathedrals and other Anglican choral foundations. Her active interest in the welfare of choristers began in 1810, when she enrolled her seven-year-old orphaned cousin Henry Wintle as a chorister at St Paul's Cathedral. The boys were not receiving proper housing, education, or supervision, and were routinely hired out, to the singing master's profit, to perform at public concerts and dinners with little thought for their safety or moral welfare. Maria Hackett undertook a study of documents in the muniment room at St Paul's and in the British Museum to determine the cathedral authorities' responsibilities towards the choristers. In January 1811 she sent the bishop of London a detailed account of her findings. His evasive reply prompted her to write to other cathedral dignitaries, but with no more success. In 1813 she, George Capper, and her half-brothers initiated legal proceedings that had to be abandoned prematurely because of expense. Nevertheless, a court order of August 1814 restored some of the funds that had been diverted from the choir to other purposes.

Maria Hackett continued her letter writing and research, and her efforts began to meet with some success. She published her *Correspondence and evidences respecting the ancient collegiate school attached to St Paul's Cathedral*

(1811–32). Meanwhile her attention was extended to all the choral foundations of England and Wales, resulting in the publication of a *Brief account of cathedral and collegiate schools with an abstract of their statutes and endowments* (1827).

Never an aloof benefactor, Maria Hackett took a personal interest in the choristers, richly deserving her informal title the Choristers' Friend. She often visited the choristers of St Paul's Cathedral, where she worshipped regularly, and brought them treats. For more than fifty years she made autumn visits to other choral foundations, calling on each at least once in three years, noting the names of the choristers in her diary and presenting to each boy a book, a purse, and a new shilling. Her lifelong efforts were crowned at the age of ninety, when she was shown the new St Paul's choir school in Carter Lane.

In 1831 Maria Hackett established the Gresham prize for cathedral composition. A patron of promising musicians, she funded John Stainer's organ studies after he left the St Paul's choir. She was a keen student of London history, publishing in 1816 *A Popular Account of St Paul's Cathedral*, which went through some twenty-one editions by 1833. The manuscript of her unpublished novel, 'Wharfdale, or, A Legend of St Nicholas', is in the Guildhall Library. In 1832 she, her half-brothers, and some friends formed a committee for the preservation and restoration of Crosby Hall, an imposing fifteenth-century structure adjoining her house. It became an important musical and educational venue.

At the time of her death, on 5 November 1874, Maria Hackett was living with her half-brother John and his family at 77 Amhurst Road, Hackney. A devout member of the Church of England, she expired during a communion service held at her bedside. She was buried at Highgate cemetery. In 1877 a cenotaph in her memory was placed in the crypt of St Paul's Cathedral with funds raised by subscription from the nation's cathedral choristers.

William J. Gatens

**Sources** K. I. Garrett, 'Miss Hackett of Crosby Square', *Guildhall Studies in London History*, 1 (1973–5), 150–62 • D. Gedge, 'The redoubtable Miss Hackett', *Musical Opinion*, 108 (1984–5), 441–6; 109 (1986), 11–14, 49–53 • K. I. Garrett, 'Maria Hackett, Crosby Hall and Gresham College', *Guildhall Studies in London History*, 3 (1977–9), 42–54 • K. I. Garrett, 'Selections from the papers of Maria Hackett', *Guildhall Studies in London History*, 2 (1975–7), 23–30 • D. Gedge, 'The Choristers' Friend', *Music Teacher*, 62/12 (1983), 21 • D. Gedge, 'The Choristers' Friend, Maria Hackett and her reforming zeal', *MT*, 132 (1991), 466–70 • S. Nicholson, *Quires and places where they sing* (1932) • K. R. Long, *The music of the English church* (1971) • P. Charlton, *John Stainer and the musical life of Victorian Britain* (1984) • P. Chappell, *Dr S. S. Wesley, 1810–1876: portrait of a Victorian musician* (1977) • d. cert.
**Archives** GL, corresp. and papers • Royal School of Church Music, Dorking, Surrey • St Paul's Cathedral, London, papers relating to St Paul's Cathedral choir | Yale U., Beinecke L., letters to J. G. Nichols, with annotated copies of three of her works
**Likenesses** photograph, 1857, St Paul's Cathedral, London; repro. in Scholes, ed., *Oxford companion to music*, 10th edn (1970)
**Wealth at death** under £300: probate, 24 Dec 1874, *CGPLA Eng. & Wales*

**Hackett, Patrick**. *See* Haicéad, Pádraigín (*d.* 1654).

**Hackett, Sarah** [*formerly* Esther; *known as* Mrs La Tournelle] (**1737/8–1797**), schoolmistress, was born in London in 1737 or 1738. Her parentage is unknown, but there may have been a family connection with the stage, as she later talked incessantly to her pupils about plays, green room gossip, and the private lives of actors and actresses. Having changed her baptismal name of Esther to Sarah, in 1755 she became an assistant to Lydia Bell—described in official documents as her lawful sister but doubtless a half-sister—in Reading Ladies Boarding-School, housed in the old abbey gateway and an adjoining eighteenth-century residence. To strengthen her credentials for teaching French, which were probably weak, as she avoided speaking the language openly, she called herself Mrs La Tournelle; in fact, she never married. She remained in this subordinate post at the school for twenty-seven years.

Lydia, who in 1768 had married the parish organist, William Spencer, died in 1783, and bequeathed the school to Sarah, who then took on as partner and senior teacher Ann Pitts (*b.* *c.*1761, *d.* before 1825), a former parlour boarder. In mid-1785 Jane Austen and her sister Cassandra joined the school, which their cousin, Jane Cooper, had attended since the previous year. They remained there until December 1786. As the staff went off duty in the afternoons and left pupils to their own devices, Jane Austen may have spent this leisure time in reading the popular novels she was to satirize in her juvenilia from 1787 onwards. The writer Mary Martha Butt, later Mrs Sherwood, became a pupil in 1791; her reminiscences provide much information about the school. She was a year senior to Frances Arabella Rowden, subsequently a teacher and poet.

Very plain and stout, Mrs La Tournelle was motherly and full of energy, despite having a cork leg, but was not particularly well organized in her manifold tasks as school matron. She always dressed in an old-fashioned way, wearing a muslin apron, short sleeves, cuffs, and ruffles; for untidy jobs she would don an ancient brown or grey-striped dress. Her wainscoted parlour was hung around with chenille pieces representing tombs and weeping willows. She held morning prayers in the schoolroom, with her niece Mary Brown reading from the Bible, to be instructed in a whisper 'Make haste, make haste!' on the days when the washerwoman was awaited. Socially, although not intellectually, she was on equal terms with Dr Richard Valpy, headmaster of the nearby Reading School for boys. The two principals and selected pupils regularly attended each others' formal parties and similar events.

The school altered dramatically when in 1789 Ann Pitts married Dominique de St Quentin, originally from Alsace and lately of the French embassy in London. St Quentin became a partner in the school and turned out to be an inspired teacher, writing various textbooks and raising the number of pupils from about forty to sixty. However, once the French Revolution broke out he disrupted the school's routine by giving house room to a host of émigrés. He also gambled night after night with Dr Valpy and other Reading notables. Predictably, by 1794 his debts were so great that the school and its assets had to be sold. Mary Butt wrote a historical romance, *The Traditions* (1795), to help pay off those debts, and the St Quentins and Miss Rowden opened a new school in Hans Place, London.

Mrs La Tournelle took herself off to Henley-on-Thames to run a school in Bell Street. She died there of a paralytic seizure on 6 October 1797, in her sixtieth year, and was buried in the town on 10 October. Her will was proved, with assets of under £300, in the prerogative court of Canterbury rather than locally, the executor being her cousin, Thomas Sharp. Jane Austen recalled her caring regime, although not her idiosyncrasies, in a sympathetic portrayal of Mrs Goddard's school in *Emma*.

T. A. B. Corley

**Sources** S. Kelly, ed., *The life of Mrs Sherwood, chiefly autobiographical* (1854) • F. J. H. Darton, ed., *The life and times of Mrs. Sherwood (1775–1851)* (1910) • *GM*, 1st ser., 67 (1797), 983 • [M. M. Butt], *The traditions: a legendary tale* (1795) • *Reading Mercury* (22 Jan 1781) • *Reading Mercury* (10 Feb 1783) • *Reading Mercury* (24 Feb 1794) • *Reading Mercury* (3 March 1794) • *Reading Mercury* (9 Oct 1797) • T. A. B. Corley, 'Jane Austen's schooldays', *Jane Austen Society Report* (1996) • T. A. B. Corley, 'Jane Austen's "real, honest, old-fashioned Boarding-school": Mrs. La Tournelle and Mrs. Goddard', *Women's Writing*, 5 (1998), 113–30 • PRO, PROB 31/713/99 • parish register (burial), Henley-on-Thames, 10 Oct 1797

**Wealth at death** under £300: administration, PRO, PROB 31/713/99

**Hacking, Douglas Hewitt, first Baron Hacking** (1884–1950), politician, was born on 4 August 1884 at his parents' home, Henfield House, Clayton-le-Moors, Lancashire, the son of Joshua Hacking JP (1846–1925), a soap manufacturer, and his wife, Eliza Simpson Boyle (*d.* 1928). He was educated at Giggleswick School and at Manchester University, and on 15 April 1909 he married Margery Allen (*b.* 1887/8), eldest daughter of Harry Hargreaves Bolton JP. They had two sons and a daughter. During the First World War, he served with the East Lancashire regiment in France and was mentioned in dispatches.

With the end of hostilities a political career beckoned as a Conservative politician. Hacking represented the Lancashire seat of Chorley from his election in December 1918 until June 1945. During the 1926 general strike he was civil commissioner for Yorkshire, where he refused to sanction distribution of the *British Gazette* in preference to the *Yorkshire Post*. Although he never secured high office, Hacking held a number of junior posts, first as parliamentary private secretary to Lord Craigavon (1920–21), then as Worthington-Evan's parliamentary private secretary at the War Office before becoming an under-secretary of state at the Home Office (December 1925–November 1927). His tenure at the Home Office meant that among parliamentarians he 'gained a considerable reputation by the brevity and wit of his answers to questions' (*The Times*, 31 July 1950). Considered to be 'a tall, handsome man with a most friendly and pleasant address' some observers were surprised by his failure to advance (Brooks MSS, 4 May 1938). With the advent of the 1931 National Government he once again held a succession of under-secretaryships (Home Office, February 1933–June 1934; War Office, June 1934–November 1935; Dominions Office, November 1935–March 1936), but his career was increasingly being tied to the party machine as vice-chairman of the National Union (1930–33), as chancellor of the Primrose League (1931), and then with his appointment in March 1936 as party chairman, a position he retained until February 1942. In June 1938 he was created a baronet. As chairman, Hacking inaugurated a series of reviews into party organization, including the London organization committee and an examination of the financial obligations incurred by MPs to their local association. These eventually saw fruition in the 1949 Maxwell-Fyfe reforms.

Hacking's reputation suffered because of his association with the policy of appeasement. Yet despite being a firm supporter of Neville Chamberlain he was never subservient. These were characteristics Chamberlain doubtless admired. At the time of the September 1938 Czech crisis Hacking admitted to being 'dubious' about what he saw as Chamberlain's policy of surrender (Headlam MSS, diary, 19 Sept 1938); while in the aftermath he counselled his leader against rushing to the polls, fearing it would alienate the support of the trade unions at a crucial moment in the rearmament programme. When Winston Churchill succeeded Chamberlain as party leader in December 1940, Hacking was persuaded to remain as party chairman, mostly to allay fears of a party split. With foresight he warned his political masters of the need to adjust 'the party's outlook to the radically different trends of thought which prevail now' (Ramsden, *Policy*, 96). Yet his concerns about the need for a Conservative social reform programme met with little response. Despite declaring in 1937 that he would not contest his Chorley seat again, he was obliged by war to remain an MP until 1945. His reward was elevation to the House of Lords in July 1945 as Baron Hacking of Chorley. Outside politics he championed the cause of tourism, and was a founder member in 1928 of the Travel Association of Great Britain. He was also a lay member of the General Medical Council and a governor of Cranleigh School, Surrey. He died in the London Hospital, Whitechapel, on 29 July 1950 and was succeeded in the title by his eldest son, Douglas Eric Hacking. His wife survived him.

N. J. Crowson

**Sources** journals, priv. coll., Collin Brooks MSS • *The Times* (31 July 1950) • *The Times* (14 Sept 1950) • diaries, Durham RO, Cuthbert Headlam MSS, D/He/34 • J. Ramsden, *The age of Balfour and Baldwin, 1902–1940* (1978) • J. A. Ramsden, *The making of conservative party policy* (1980) • N. J. Crowson, *Facing fascism: the conservative party and the European dictators, 1935–1940* (1997) • b. cert. • m. cert. • *WWW* • *CGPLA Eng. & Wales* (1950)

**Archives** Bodl. Oxf., Conservative Party archive | CAC Cam., corresp. with Lord Croft • U. Leeds, Brotherton L., corresp. with Henry Drummond-Wolff

**Likenesses** group portrait, photograph, 1943, Hult. Arch.

**Wealth at death** £92,951 6*s.* 9*d.*: probate, 7 Sept 1950, *CGPLA Eng. & Wales*

**Hacking, Sir John** (1888–1969), electrical engineer, was born on 16 December 1888, at Crawshaw Booth, Burnley, Lancashire, the only son and the eldest of three children of William Edward Hacking, engineer, of Burnley, and his wife, Martha, only daughter of Albert Birtwistle, of Crawshaw Booth. He was educated at Burnley grammar school and Leeds Technical Institute.

Hacking joined the Newcastle upon Tyne Electric Supply Company (NESCo) in 1908 and gained valuable engineering experience in the development of their area supply system, at that time the largest in Britain. His diligence earned him a transfer in 1913 to Merz and McLellan who were responsible for the design and development of the NESCo system. He joined the Merz and McLellan team in Buenos Aires, and stayed there until the electrification of the Central Argentine Railway was completed in 1922. In 1917, in Buenos Aires, Hacking married Janet Stewart, only child of Alexander Stewart Scott, of Newcastle upon Tyne, and his wife, Elizabeth, second daughter of William Davison, of Ovington, Northumberland. They had one son and one daughter.

On Hacking's return in 1923 he was based at the London office, but travelled to supervise projects in South Africa and India. These included the electrification of the Bombay to Baroda and the Great India Peninsular railways.

Hacking was the consultants' supervisor for the Mid-East England area of the national grid. This scheme started in 1929 and was completed by the end of 1932. A technical review paper on transmission and distribution, which he wrote with J. R. Beard, for the *Journal of the Institution of Electrical Engineers* (69, 1931, 739), was based on this experience. In 1933 Hacking began his principal work of technical responsibility for first the national grid and later the national system of the British Electricity Authority (BEA). He was appointed deputy chief engineer to the Central Electricity Board (CEB) in 1933, and chief engineer in 1944. The chief engineer carried responsibility for both the operation of the system and the planning to meet future demand. In wartime these tasks were carried out in spite of bombing, drifting barrage balloons, and shortages of every kind. In 1944 the CEB warned the government that if it continued to stop plans for future construction then there would be a great shortage of electricity after the war. The government held to its policy and absolved the CEB of responsibility. In 1947 Hacking gave a detailed account of the grid in wartime to an audience of the Institution of Electrical Engineers (IEE).

When the electricity supply industry was nationalized in 1947, the CEB and company and local authority undertakings were abolished. The BEA was established to own and operate generating stations and main transmission systems and to sell electricity in bulk to the new area (distribution) boards. Hacking's appointment in 1947 as deputy chairman (operations) of the BEA was welcomed throughout the industry, for he was a well-liked and respected engineer.

Hacking found himself with the serious problem of shortage, especially of power stations, which he had predicted three years earlier. His leadership, based on experience, encouraged BEA's operational, planning, and research engineers and British manufacturing industry to mitigate the shortage, in every way possible, since post-war recovery depended on electricity. He described his experience of that time in a paper read to the South African IEE in 1954, after he had resigned from the BEA. This paper showed Hacking's awareness of the importance of electricity supply in Britain and the contribution to it from technology.

Hacking retired from his deputy chairmanship of the British Electricity Authority in 1953 and returned to Merz and McLellan as a consultant until his final retirement in 1966. He made several overseas tours on his firm's behalf, principally in South Africa, Nigeria, and Australia.

Hacking was a good family man. Although by nature quiet and reserved towards those outside his family, he was friendly and sincere, a considerate and honourable man, on whom his friends knew they could rely. A photograph of 1959 shows a well-built man, still young-looking for his age. In an IEE short film, he described aspects of his career in a modest manner which belied the magnitude of his engineering achievements.

Hacking was knighted in 1949. He served as president of the Electrical Research Association, of the British Electrical Power Convention, and of the IEE in 1951–2, being appointed an honorary member of that institution in 1962. Hacking died at Orpington Hospital, Kent, on 29 September 1969. CECIL T. MELLING, *rev.* ALBERT SNOW

**Sources** *IEE News* (13 Oct 1969) · L. Hannah, *Engineers, managers and politicians* (1982) · J. R. Beard and J. Hacking, 'Transmission and distribution', *Journal of the IEE*, 69 (1931), 739 · J. Hacking and J. D. Peattie, 'The British grid system in wartime', *Journal of the IEE*, 94/2 (1947), 463 · J. Hacking, 'The electricity supply industry in Great Britain', *Transactions of the South African IEE* (1954), 245 · A. Snow, 'The role of electrical power transmission systems in Britain (1875–1948)', PhD diss., Open University, 1995 · A. Snow, 'The first national grid', *Journal of the IEE*, 2/5 (1993) [E.seE] · J. Rowland, *Progress in power* (1960) · L. Hannah, *Electricity before nationalisation* (1979) · J. Hacking, 'Inaugural address as president IEE', *Proceedings of the IEE*, 99/1 (1952), 1

**Archives** Electricity Council Archives, Manchester | FILM Inst. EE, short film of Sir John Hacking talking about his career

**Likenesses** photograph, 1952, repro. in Hacking, 'Inaugural address' · photograph, repro. in Rowland, *Progress in power*

**Wealth at death** £15,146: probate, 23 June 1970, *CGPLA Eng. & Wales*

**Hackman, Alfred** (1811–1874), librarian and Church of England clergyman, was born at Fulham, Middlesex, on 8 April 1811. His father, Thomas Hackman, was the parochial vestry clerk, and his office brought him into connection with the bishop of London, William Howley. Through Howley's influence Hackman matriculated as a servitor of Christ Church, Oxford, on 25 October 1832. He had been educated in France, and had then spent some years as usher in a boarding-school kept by his father. He graduated BA in 1837, and proceeded MA in 1840. Through the influence of Dean Gaisford he obtained a temporary post in the Bodleian Library in 1837, and was then connected with the library for more than thirty-five years. In 1837 he also became chaplain of Christ Church, and curate to the Revd Henry Cary at St Paul's in Walton Street, Oxford. He was appointed by his college vicar of Cowley, near Oxford, in 1839, and was from 1841 to 1873 precentor at Christ Church. From 1844 to 1871 he was vicar of St Paul's, Oxford. Here he exercised a considerable influence as an

Anglo-Catholic preacher, not only on his own parishioners, but also on the undergraduates of the university, who were attracted by his earnestness and vivacity, which were heightened by a habit of oratorical gesticulation said to have been picked up during his stay in France.

Curates attended to Hackman's parish, while his own time was largely occupied by his work in the Bodleian Library. He was responsible for the greater part of the general catalogue of printed books, which came out in 1843, and edited the 1851 supplementary volume. He catalogued the Bodleian's Tanner manuscripts (1860). In 1862 a prohibition on beneficed clergymen becoming library officers was dissolved specifically to allow Hackman to be appointed sub-librarian. This alteration of the statutes was controversial and proceeded only after a 'pamphlet warfare' and the strong urging of the curate, Edward Pusey. A genial man, with a broad mouth and a shock of curly hair, he was accustomed to work sitting on top of a thick volume which, as a result, he forgot to include in the library catalogue. A gradual paralysis induced Hackman to retire from the library and to resign his chaplaincy at Christ Church and his incumbency of St Paul's in 1873. He died, unmarried, in his brother's house at Long Ditton, Surrey, on 18 September 1874. His funeral was held at St Paul's, Oxford, on 23 September 1874 and he was buried in the St Sepulchre's cemetery, Oxford.

W. A. Greenhill, *rev.* Nilanjana Banerji

**Sources** W. D. Macray, *Annals of the Bodleian Library, Oxford*, 2nd edn (1890) · *Oxford University Herald* (26 Sept 1874) · H. H. E. Craster, *History of the Bodleian Library, 1845–1945* (1952)

**Wealth at death** under £200: probate, 13 Sept 1875, *CGPLA Eng. & Wales*

**Hackman, James** (*bap.* **1752**, *d.* **1779**), murderer, was baptized on 13 December 1752 at Holy Trinity Church, Gosport, Hampshire. He was the son of William Hackman, a former naval lieutenant, and his wife, Mary. He was apprenticed to a mercer, and at sixteen possibly became a member of St John's College, Cambridge, although he cannot be traced in the college records. In 1772 he became an ensign in the 68th regiment of foot and was promoted to lieutenant in 1776. As a member of a recruiting party, probably in 1775, he visited the home of John Montagu, the fourth earl of Sandwich, at Hinchingbrooke. There he met Martha *Ray (1742?–1779), a stay maker's daughter. She had been apprenticed to a mantua maker in Clerkenwell when, about 1761, she met the earl, possibly through Mrs Harding, a procurer. She became his mistress, and gave birth to nine children, five of whom survived her, including Basil Montagu. Ray was 'a lady of an elegant person, great sweetness of manners, and of a remarkable judgement and execution in vocal and instrumental music' (*Case and Memoirs of … Hackman*, 2).

The nature of Ray's relationship with Hackman is unclear, although even her supporters believed that they were lovers and had discussed marrying. However, when Hackman's regiment was posted to Ireland the relationship broke down. In 1776 he resigned his commission to

**James Hackman** (*bap.* **1752**, *d.* **1779**), by Robert Laurie, pubd 1779 (after R. Dighton)

enter the church. He was ordained deacon on 24 February 1779, priest four days later, and was instituted to the living of Wiveton, Norfolk, on 1 March, although he probably never went there. Instead he pursued Ray. Eventually, suspecting that she had a new lover, he followed her to the Covent Garden Theatre on 7 April 1779, where she was attending a performance of *Love in a Village*. Having seen her talking to Lord Coleraine, whom he assumed to be her lover, he stormed out of the theatre, obtained two pistols, and waited in the nearby Bedford Coffee House. As Ray emerged Hackman grabbed her cloak and, swinging her around, he put a pistol to her forehead and shot her dead. He turned the other pistol on himself but the ball only grazed his head and so he beat himself with both pistols until restrained. Ray's body and Hackman were taken to the Shakespeare tavern, St James's Street. On being told of Ray's death Lord Sandwich was said to have 'wept exceedingly' (*Morning Post*, 9 April 1779). She was buried on 14 April in the chancel of Elstree parish church, Hertfordshire, although she was later reburied in the cemetery.

Hackman was committed by Sir John Fielding to Tothill Fields bridewell, then tried at the Old Bailey on 16 April, where, in spite of a previous determination to plead guilty, he entered a plea of not guilty because he would not be 'accessory to a second peril of my life' and 'the justice of my country ought to be satisfied by suffering my offence to be proved' (*Old Bailey Sessions Paper*, 209). Defence counsel argued that Hackman was insane and that a love letter to Ray, which was found on him, indicated a lack of premeditation. Hackman read a speech, possibly written by James Boswell, in which he claimed to have intended only suicide, but 'a momentary phrensy overcame me, and induced me to commit the deed I now deplore' (ibid.). Mr Justice Blackstone summed up against Hackman, saying that murder did not require 'a long form of deliberation' and that another letter found on him, to his brother-in-law Frederick Booth, showed 'a coolness and deliberation which no ways accorded with the ideas of insanity' (*The Genuine Life, Trial and Dying Words of the Rev James Hackman*, 17).

Hackman was convicted and, in accordance with the Murder Act of 1752, sentenced to be hanged on 19 April 1779, then dissected in public at Surgeons' Hall. He was described as 5 feet 9 inches, 'very genteely made, and of a most polite Address' (*Public Advertiser*, 12 April 1779). After the trial James Boswell reported to Booth, who could not bear to attend, that Hackman had behaved 'with Decency, Propriety, and in such a Manner as to interest everyone present' (*Public Advertiser*, 19 April 1779). Hackman travelled to Tyburn in a mourning coach, accompanied by a friend, the Revd Moses Porter, curate of Holy Trinity Church, Clapham, the Revd John Villette, the ordinary of Newgate, and Mr Davenport, the sheriff's officer. Boswell may have attended the execution but squashed rumours that he travelled in the coach (*Public Advertiser*, 21 April 1779). At Tyburn Hackman 'behaved with great fortitude; no appearances of fear were to be perceived, but very evident signs of contrition and repentance' (Jesse, 4.85). That same day the earl of Sandwich, who had attracted a good deal of public sympathy as a result of the murder, survived votes of censure in both houses of parliament. Whether Hackman intended to commit suicide in front of Ray, as he claimed, or had planned to kill both Ray and himself was hotly disputed at the time and prompted a row between Dr Johnson and Topham Beauclerk. The case attracted a great deal of attention and inspired Sir Herbert Croft's *Love and Madness* (1780), letters purportedly written by Ray and Hackman. Some blamed Ray as 'a capricious and ungrateful woman' (*Case and Memoirs of … Hackman*, 7th edn, postscript), although more typical was Boswell's view that the case revealed 'the dreadful effects that the passion of Love may produce' (*N&Q*, 3rd ser., 4.232–3).

Philip Rawlings

**Sources** *The case and memoirs of the late Rev. Mr James Hackman* (1779) • *The case and memoirs of Miss M. Ray* (1779) • *The genuine life, trial and dying words of the Rev James Hackman* (1779) • *N&Q*, 3rd ser., 4 (1863), 232–3 • *N&Q*, 4th ser., 3 (1869), 339, 447, 488–9, 514; 4th ser., 4 (1869), 147; 4th ser., 8 (1871), 369 • *N&Q*, 7th ser., 6 (1888), 87, 212; 7 (1889), 172, 296, 392 • *Public Advertiser* (9 April 1779) • *Public Advertiser* (10 April 1779) • *Public Advertiser* (12 April 1779) • *Public Advertiser* (14–21 April 1779) • *Morning Post* (9 April 1779) • *Morning Post* (21 April 1779) • *London Chronicle* (20 April 1779) • *GM*, 1st ser., 49 (1779), 210, 212–13, 320 • *The whole proceedings on the king's commission of the peace* (1778–9) [Old Bailey sessions papers, 14 April 1779] • Boswell, *Life*, 2.383–4 • J. H. Jesse, *George Selwyn and his contemporaries, with memoirs and notes*, new edn, 4 vols. (1882), vol. 4, pp. 58, 83–5 • H. Angelo, *The memoirs of Henry Angelo*, 2 vols. (1904), vol. 1, pp. 376–8, vol. 2, p. 192 • parish register, Holy Trinity, Gosport, 13 Dec 1752 [baptism]

**Likenesses** R. Laurie, mezzotint, pubd 1779 (after R. Dighton), BM, NPG [*see illus.*] • engraving, repro. in *Case and memoirs of the late Rev. Mr James Hackman*

**Hackston** [Halkerstoune], **David, of Rathillet** (*d.* 1680), covenanter, was a son of James Halkerstoune of Hilcairney. He had one sister and a brother, William, minister of Cleish from about 1678 to 1690. He was entered as heir to his father in March 1670 and is described as a 'tall slender man black harid and black vissaged' (NA Scot., JC2/15, fol. 224*r*). Before becoming religiously conscious he confessed to having a rather wayward life. In January 1678 he was listed among the noblemen and heritors of Fife and Kinross who had not signed the bond for public peace, and in the same year was among those heritors in the parish of Kilmany who had not signed the bond against conventicles and disorderly walking. In February 1678 he is listed to be charged with security for having failed to take those bonds.

Hackston was present at the murder of Archbishop Sharp on Magus Muir on 3 May 1679, though he questioned the legality of it and did not take an active part in the murder. He refused to take up the leadership of the group on account of having a disagreement with Sharp and thus being open to accusations of personal revenge. As Sharp was both the primate and a privy councillor, the murder was viewed as a visible attack on both church and state. On 8 May William Carmichael, sheriff-depute of Fife, was empowered 'to secure and put under inventor all the goods and moveables' of Hackston and others suspected of the murder (*Reg. PCS*, 3rd ser., 6.192). Hackston and his brother-in-law, John Balfour of Kinloch, escaped to the west of Scotland.

Hackston was involved in the declaration of Rutherglen, a condemnation of all past violations of the covenants, issued on 29 May 1679, the anniversary of the Restoration. He was a commander at the battle of Drumclog on 1 June, and is described as being among the covenanters' 'best and greatest officers' (*Reg. PCS*, 3rd ser., 6.241). On 22 June 1679 he participated in the battle of Bothwell Bridge, and on 14 August a reward of 10,000 merks, with indemnity, was offered for his apprehension. He joined in the Sanquhar declaration, renouncing allegiance to Charles II on 22 June 1680. At the defeat of the covenanters at Airds Moss on 22 July 1680 Hackston was taken prisoner by Bruce of Earlshall. He was severely wounded and roughly conveyed to Edinburgh, where he was tried before the lords of justiciary and condemned to a cruel and barbarous death. His execution took place on 30 July 1680, and his body was then mutilated and parts displayed in various towns. One of his hands was buried with the heads of two other covenanters in the old churchyard in Cupar, Fife.

Alison G. Muir

**Sources** *State trials*, 10.791–850 • *Reg. PCS*, 3rd ser., 5.640, 647–8, 651; 6.192, 241, 260, 308, 322, 503–11, 524, 559–60; 7.35; 8.403, 624; 10.40, 75 • R. Wodrow, *The history of the sufferings of the Church of Scotland from the Restauration to the revolution*, 2 (1722), 28–33, 141–3 • A. H. Millar, *Fife: pictorial and historical*, 2 vols. (1895), 2.318 • legal and miscellaneous papers, NA Scot., NRAS 3698/845 • trial of Hackston of Rathillet, justiciary records, books of adjournal, 30 July 1680, NA Scot., JC2/15, fols. 214–26 • *CSP dom.*, 1683–4, 115, 187, 287 • J. Buckroyd, *The life of James Sharp, archbishop of St Andrews, 1618–1679* (1987) • *Historical notices of Scotish affairs, selected from the manuscripts of Sir John Lauder of Fountainhall*, ed. D. Laing, 1, Bannatyne Club, 87

(1848), 270 · *APS*, *1670–86*, app. 39, 43, 48, 54, 61, 65, 69 · *Fasti Scot.*, new edn, 5.61

**Archives** NA Scot., legal and other papers | NA Scot., trial of Hackston of Rathillet, 30 July 1680, MS justiciary records, books of adjournal, JC2/15, fols. 214–26

**Wealth at death** all goods were declared forfeit: trial of Hackston of Rathillet, justiciary records, book of adjournal, 30 July 1680, NA Scot., JC2/15, fols. 214–26

**Hackworth, Timothy** (1786–1850), locomotive engineer, was born on 22 December 1786 in Wylam, Northumberland, the eldest of three sons and five daughters of John Hackworth (*d.* 1802), master blacksmith at Wylam colliery, and his wife, Elizabeth Sanderson of Newcastle. He went to Wylam School and at the age of fourteen was apprenticed, initially to his father, who died the following year. He showed a natural aptitude for mechanical construction, and on completing his apprenticeship he was appointed to his late father's post at the colliery. There he was involved in experiments with steam locomotion. In 1812 Hackworth and Jonathan Foster, the colliery enginewright, were responsible for the *Wylam Grasshopper* and in 1813 for the *Wylam Dilly*, two locomotives incorporating novel means of propulsion.

In 1816 Hackworth regretfully left Wylam colliery, because Sunday work offended his Methodist principles, and became foreman blacksmith at the nearby Walbottle colliery. In 1825 he became locomotive superintendent, and also manager and contractor, for the Stockton and Darlington, Britain's first public railway. Its early locomotives were unreliable, and in 1827 the owners' committee authorized Hackworth to build a new one to his own design. The result was the *Royal George*, a marked advance on previous types, which established the effectiveness of the steam locomotive. It had two vertical cylinders with direct rod drive to cast-iron wheels with shrunk-on tyres of wrought iron, the first of their type; most importantly, it pioneered the discharge of exhaust steam through a converging nozzle blast pipe in the chimney, greatly increasing combustion intensity and steam production. It was also the first to use controlled pre-heating of boiler feed-water. Twelve similar locomotives, with further improvements, were built. In 1830 Hackworth built the *Globe*, which had inside cylinders and crank axle, and a boiler with transverse water tubes running through the main flue—a forerunner of the Galloway patent boiler.

In 1840 Hackworth left the Stockton and Darlington Railway to concentrate on his own engineering business, conducted from new workshops at New Shildon, co. Durham, where locomotive, marine, and industrial engines and boilers were built. As well as supplying a number of British railway companies, the firm supplied some of the earliest locomotives for Russia and Canada.

Hackworth was one of the great pioneers of the steam locomotive and the eminent railway engineer D. K. Clark stated in 1855 that no single individual had, up to the year 1830, done so much for the improvement of the locomotive. He had the reputation of a kindly man, much respected by those who worked for him. He was elected to the British Association for the Advancement of Science. His *Sanspareil*, which competed unsuccessfully in the Rainhill locomotive trials of 1829, instituted by the directors of the London and Manchester Railway and won by the *Rocket* of Robert Stephenson, gave excellent service on the Bolton and Leigh Railway until 1844 and subsequently became an exhibit at the Science Museum, London.

In 1813 Hackworth married Jane Golightly, who shared his devout Methodism. They had three sons and six daughters; the eldest son, John Wesley Hackworth (1820–1891), carried on the business after his father's death, which took place from typhus on 7 July 1850 at his home, Soho, Shildon, co. Durham. He is commemorated by the Timothy Hackworth Museum at Shildon.

George W. Carpenter, *rev.*

**Sources** *Wylam and its railway pioneers* (1975) · R. Young, *Timothy Hackworth and the locomotive* (1923) · J. Tomlinson, 'Presidential address', *Institution of Mechanical Engineers: Proceedings* (1890), 27–8 · D. K. Clark, *Railway machinery* (1855) · L. T. C. Rolt, *George and Robert Stephenson* (1960) · E. L. Ahrons, *The British steam railway locomotive, 1825–1925* (1927) · *The Oxford companion to British railway history* (1997) · d. cert.

**Likenesses** silhouette, 1833, repro. in Young, *Timothy Hackworth*

**Hacomblen** [Hacomplaynt], **Robert** (1455/6–1528), college head and composer, is of unknown parentage. The record of his admission in 1469, as a king's scholar, to Eton College, where he spent three years, provides all that is known of his origins: he was thirteen years old and from the parish of St Andrew in London. Hacomblen followed the standard route from Eton to King's College, Cambridge, of which he was a member for more than five decades; his ascent of the college hierarchy culminated in his being provost for the last nineteen years of his life. His association with King's began in 1472, when he was admitted to a scholarship; he was awarded a fellowship in 1475. During the next two decades he served the college in various capacities: as dean in 1482–3, bursar in 1488–9, dean again in 1489–90, and vice-provost in 1492–3; he was junior proctor of the university in 1483–4. He began to accumulate the degrees necessary for an academic career, becoming BA (1475/6), MA (1480), and BTh (1490/91). He also took holy orders: the date of his ordination to the priesthood is unknown, but was probably within a year or two of his ordination as acolyte in King's College chapel on 18 September 1473. In 1492 the college presented him to the vicarage of Prescot, Lancashire, worth some £24 a year, to which he was admitted on 30 August. In 1493 he resigned his college fellowship; there seems to be no further record of him at Cambridge until 1506–7, when he was awarded a doctorate of theology. On 28 June 1509 he was elected provost of King's; he held the office until he died. He was named among the commissioners of the peace for Cambridgeshire in November 1509 and November 1514.

One musical composition by Hacomblen survives: a five-part *Salve regina* ascribed to Hacomplaynt in the Eton choirbook. An inventory of polyphonic music made at King's College in 1529 mentions 'Haycomplaynes Gaude', evidently a setting of *Gaude flore virginali* or *Gaude virgo mater Christi*, but this work is lost. The *Salve regina* is a well-crafted piece whose intricacy and ornateness are striking even by the standards of the Eton repertory as a whole. It incorporates an unidentified cantus firmus, probably a plainchant melody, and also makes fleeting allusion to the *Salve regina* chant itself, for instance at 'et spes nostra' and 'et filium'. Hacomblen's compositional skill seems remarkable for one who was not a professional church musician. Although musical activity at Eton and King's was greatly reduced during most of Edward IV's reign, it recovered during the 1480s, and this may have encouraged his musical interests. A copy of Aristotle's *Ethica Nichomachea* ascribed to him in King's College MS 11, together with an associated commentary which may also be his, are more predictable productions of a late medieval academic.

There is some uncertainty about when Hacomblen died. Various writers have quoted the date as 5 or 8 September or 21 October 1528; it has been claimed that on the last of these dates he signed his will. The latest known document signed by him is dated 24 July 1528; he must have died before 22 September 1528, when the college authorities wrote to inform Cardinal Wolsey that a new provost had been elected and that a new vicar for Prescot was needed. In his will he bequeathed to King's College his 'chieff bookes' and a chalice and paten 'with a schochyn of the 5 woundes', left £33 6*s.* 8*d.* for the celebration of masses of the five wounds of Our Lord, and requested burial in the chantry that he had founded in the college chapel. His devotion to the cult of the five wounds is confirmed by his memorial brass, which shows him in doctor's robes holding a ribbon with the legend 'Vulnera Christe tua: michi dulcis sint medicina' ('May your wounds, O Christ, be sweet medicine to me'). He also gave the college the superb brass lectern that is still in the chapel.

NICK SANDON

**Sources** Emden, *Cam.*, 278 • Cooper, *Ath. Cantab.*, 1.34; 3.90 • W. Sterry, ed., *The Eton College register, 1441–1698* (1943), 152 • *LP Henry VIII*, 1/1, no. 1083; 1/2, p. 1534; 4/2, no. 4765 • J. Caley and J. Hunter, eds., *Valor ecclesiasticus temp. Henrici VIII*, 6 vols., RC (1810–34), vol. 5, p. 220 • *VCH Lancashire*, 3.344 • F. L. Harrison, *Music in medieval Britain*, 2nd edn [1963] • F. L. Harrison, ed., *The Eton choirbook*, 2, Musica Britannica, 11 (1958), 12–17 • F. L. Harrison, 'An English "Caput"', *Music and Letters*, 33 (1952), 203–14

**Archives** Eton, MS 178

**Haddan, Arthur West** (1816–1873), ecclesiastical historian, was born at Woodford in Essex on 31 August 1816, the son of Thomas Haddan, solicitor, and Mary Ann, his wife and second cousin, whose maiden name was also Haddan. Thomas Henry *Haddan was his brother. He received his early education at a private school kept by a Mr Fanning at Finchley, and while there learned Italian out of school hours; he acquired a knowledge of German in later life. In 1834 he entered Brasenose College, Oxford, as a commoner, and in the November of that year stood unsuccessfully for a scholarship at Balliol, but was elected scholar of Trinity on 15 June 1835. He graduated BA in 1837, obtaining a first class in classics and a second in mathematics, proceeded MA in due course, and in 1847 took the degree of BD.

After graduating Haddan applied himself to theology. In 1839 he was elected to the (university) Johnson theological scholarship, and in 1840 to a fellowship at his college. He was deeply affected by the high-church revival at Oxford, and was much influenced by Isaac Williams, the Tractarian poet and theologian, at that time a tutor of Trinity. At Trinity the special effect of the movement was to lead its more distinguished adherents to the study of history in order, in the first instance, to maintain the historical position and claims of the church. From the first Haddan never swerved from his loyalty to the Church of England, or faltered in his defence of its apostolic character. Having been ordained deacon on his fellowship in 1840 by Dr Bagot, bishop of Oxford, he acted in 1841–2 as curate to John Henry Newman at the church of St Mary the Virgin, Oxford. He was ordained priest in 1842, and on being appointed to succeed Williams as classical tutor of his college, resigned his curacy. He was dean of the college for several years from 1841 and was appointed vice-president in 1848. He was pro-proctor to Henry Peter Guillemard when in 1845 the proctors put their veto on the proceedings against Newman. Haddan was not very popular with the younger men at Trinity, except among the scholars: he was reserved in manner, and his devotion to study and his exacting moral standards caused him to view offences in a specially serious light.

For some time after his ordination Haddan was engaged in work for the Library of Anglo-Catholic Theology, for which he published an edition of Thorndike's *Theological Works*. From the date of its first publication in 1846 he wrote much for the *Guardian* newspaper, and he also sent many reviews to the *Christian Remembrancer*. The judgment in the Gorham case in 1850 troubled him, and for a while he doubted whether he could conscientiously accept a benefice. He found complete satisfaction through studying the foundation of the claims of the Church of England. Some of the results of his studies on this subject were afterwards embodied in his book *Apostolical Succession in the Church of England* (1869). In this work, which ran to several editions, besides stating the nature of the doctrine, its importance, and its scriptural basis, he refuted the seventeenth-century 'Nag's Head' story of Matthew Parker's invalid episcopal consecration, which he had already worked out exhaustively, although more briefly, in his edition of Archbishop Bramhall's works for the Anglo-Catholic Library; he ended the work by attempting to prove the validity of Anglican orders.

In 1847 Haddan was one of the secretaries of Gladstone's election committee, and supported him on the three other occasions when he sought election as a member for the university. He acted not so much for political reasons as because he believed that Gladstone was a fitting representative of the university as a scholar and a churchman. On like grounds he supported Lord Derby's election as chancellor in 1852. In 1857 he accepted the small college living of Barton on the Heath in Warwickshire, and left Oxford to reside there with two sisters. He took pleasure in his parochial duties, and fulfilled them conscientiously. He was appointed Bampton lecturer in 1865, and contemplated taking as his subject the value and authority of the creeds. He was, however, forced to resign the appointment owing to ill health.

Haddan's most significant works were those produced in collaboration with William Stubbs. Early in 1869 they brought out the first volume of the great work, *Councils and Ecclesiastical Documents*, founded on the collections of Sir Henry Spelman and David Wilkins. Haddan was mainly responsible for the contents of this volume, and during that and the following year he assisted in the preparation of the third volume; but his health was failing, and the publication of the second volume, which was his responsibility, was delayed. The part of this volume which is devoted to the early Irish church required much research into language as well as history, and occupied him during his last days. At the same time he was writing articles on church organization in the first volume of Smith's *Dictionary of Christian Antiquities*. His other publications include a translation of St Augustine's *De trinitate* (1871), various articles, reviews, a reply to Pattison, and other essays. His university made little recognition of his industry, but in 1870 he was made honorary canon of Worcester. Haddan died a bachelor at Barton on the Heath on 8 February 1873, at the age of fifty-six.

WILLIAM HUNT, *rev.* MYFANWY LLOYD

**Sources** A. P. Forbes, ed., *Remains of the late A. W. Haddan* (1876) · Foster, *Alum. Oxon.* · F. L. Cross, ed., *The Oxford dictionary of the Christian church*, 2nd edn, ed. E. A. Livingstone (1974)

**Archives** Bodl. Oxf., corresp. and papers | BL, corresp. with W. E. Gladstone, Add. MS 44183

**Wealth at death** under £2000: probate, 1 April 1873, *CGPLA Eng. & Wales*

**Haddan, Thomas Henry** (1814–1873), lawyer and newspaper editor, the eldest son of Thomas Haddan, solicitor, of Lime Street Square, London, and Mary Ann, daughter of John Haddan, and brother of Arthur West *Haddan, was born in London. Educated at a private school at Finchley, he matriculated from Brasenose College, Oxford, on 2 July 1833, gained a scholarship there, took a double first in 1837, and graduated BA on 5 May in that year. He was Petrean fellow of Exeter College from 30 June 1837 until 11 January 1843. His essay 'The test of national prosperity considered' won the chancellor's prize in 1838. He gained an Eldon law scholarship in 1840, and a Vinerian fellowship in 1847. He proceeded MA in 1840 and BCL in 1844, and was called to the bar of the Inner Temple on 11 June 1841, practising as an equity draftsman and conveyancer. He was a sound lawyer, and had a steady practice at the bar. He was a member of The Engagement, the secret society of Tractarian laymen founded by T. A. and A. H. D. Acland in 1844. In 1846, at a meeting in Haddan's chambers, 6 New Square, Lincoln's Inn, *The Guardian* newspaper was planned. He was the first editor (though for a brief time) of this weekly newspaper, which so effectively advanced the liberal Tractarian cause. Haddan married, on 3 October 1861, Caroline Elizabeth, youngest daughter of James Bradley, a captain in the Royal Navy; five of their children survived him.

In 1862, at the invitation of the council of the Incorporated Law Society, Haddan delivered a course of lectures on the jurisdiction of the court of chancery. His publications were: *Remarks on Legal Education with Reference to Legal Studies in the University of Oxford* (1848), *The Limited Liability Act with Precedents and Notes* (1855), and *Outlines of Administrative Jurisdiction of the Court of Chancery* (1862). He also wrote an interesting memoir of his brother Arthur, which was printed as the introduction to A. P. Forbes's *Remains of Rev. A. W. Haddan* (1876). Having gone to Vichy to take the waters, Haddan died there suddenly on 5 September 1873, and was buried there the following day; his body was afterwards removed to Highgate cemetery, Middlesex.

G. C. BOASE, *rev.* H. C. G. MATTHEW

**Sources** *Law Times* (20 Sept 1873) · *Law Times* (15 Nov 1873) · *The Guardian* (10 Sept 1873) · C. Matthew, 'Gladstone, evangelicalism and "the Engagement"', *Revival and religion since 1700: essays for John Walsh*, ed. J. Garnett and C. Matthew (1993), 111–26

**Wealth at death** under £12,000: probate, 28 Nov 1873, *CGPLA Eng. & Wales*

**Hadden, James Murray** (*d.* 1817), army officer, is said to have been the son of a Captain John Hadden of the Royal Marines who served at the capture of Belle Isle in 1761. He entered the Royal Military Academy, Woolwich, as a cadet on 2 April 1771 and was commissioned a second lieutenant in the Royal Artillery on 26 January 1774. Following the outbreak of the American War of Independence, Hadden embarked for Quebec on 4 March 1776, arriving there four months later. In October 1776 he commanded a gunboat at the battle of Valcour Island, when the American flotilla on Lake Champlain was largely destroyed.

Hadden joined General Burgoyne's army in 1777 for the campaign in the Hudson Valley. His journal of the subsequent operations, first published in 1884, is one of the best accounts to survive. At the battle of Freeman's Farm, on 19 September, his two-gun artillery detachment, in the most exposed of positions, lost nineteen of its twenty-two men as casualties; he himself received a shot through his cap. But with Burgoyne's surrender at Saratoga, in the following month, Hadden became a prisoner. He was later exchanged and finished the war serving under General Clinton at New York.

Hadden had been promoted lieutenant on 7 July 1779 and was made captain-lieutenant on 7 March 1784. He married Harriet Farrer in London on 15 February 1787; they had two sons. With his captaincy, gazetted on 15 August 1793, Hadden took command of no. 1 company of the 2nd battalion, Royal Artillery, only to be assigned three months later to the command of D troop of the newly raised Royal Horse Artillery. In the same year he was appointed secretary to the master-general of the ordnance, the duke of Richmond. On 4 March 1794 he received his brevet majority, and until September 1796 served as a brigade-major in the southern district in England. He was then promoted brevet lieutenant-colonel (9 April 1797) and on 5 September 1797 was appointed adjutant-general to the forces serving in Portugal under Sir Charles Stuart. In 1801 he became once again secretary to the master-general of the ordnance, relinquishing the post in 1804 when he became surveyor-general of the ordnance. He was promoted colonel on 30 October 1805.

Hadden remained surveyor-general of the ordnance until 3 July 1810, when the new master-general, the earl of Mulgrave, brought in his own man to replace him. He was promoted major-general on 4 June 1811, and died at his home in Harpenden, Hertfordshire, on 28 October 1817. He was survived by his wife. His brother Colonel John Hadden, formerly of the 11th foot and paymaster of the forces in Portugal, predeceased him, on 24 September 1817. ALASTAIR W. MASSIE

**Sources** *Hadden's journal and orderly books: a journal kept in Canada and upon Burgoyne's campaign in 1776 and 1777*, ed. H. Rogers (1884) • *GM*, 1st ser., 66 (1796), 1118 • *GM*, 1st ser., 87/2 (1817), 475 • will, 1817, PRO, PROB 11/1600(21) • W. H. Askwith, ed., *List of officers of the royal regiment of artillery* (1900) • J. E. Portlock, *Memoir of the life of Major-General Colby* (1869) • F. Duncan, *History of the royal regiment of artillery*, 3rd edn, 2 vols. (1879) • *Report on the manuscripts of the late Reginald Rawdon Hastings*, 4 vols., HMC, 78 (1928–47), vol. 3 • *The later correspondence of George III*, ed. A. Aspinall, 5 vols. (1962–70), vol. 5 • *Army List* • *IGI*

**Wealth at death** freehold and copyhold property in Hertfordshire and Middlesex to wife and two sons: will, PRO, PROB 11/1600 (21)

**Haddington**. For this title name *see* Hamilton, Thomas, earl of Melrose and first earl of Haddington (1563–1637); Hamilton, Thomas, second earl of Haddington (1600–1640); Hope, Helen, countess of Haddington (*bap.* 1677, *d.* 1768); Hamilton, Thomas, sixth earl of Haddington (1680–1735); Hamilton, Thomas, seventh earl of Haddington (1720/21–1795) [*see under* Poker Club (*act.* 1762–1784)]; Hamilton, Thomas, ninth earl of Haddington (1780–1858).

**Haddock, Nicholas** (*bap.* **1685**?, *d.* **1746**), naval officer, was the third and youngest son of Sir Richard *Haddock (*c.*1629–1715), naval officer and politician, and his second wife, Elizabeth Hurlestone (1650?–1710), of Rotherhithe, Surrey. He may have been the Nicholas Haddock baptized on 8 November 1685 at St Olave's, Hart Street, London, to parents Richard and Elizabeth.

Haddock entered the navy on 19 May 1699, as a volunteer on the *Portland*, under the command of his kinsman, Captain Edward Whitaker.

In 1702, as midshipman of the *Ranelagh*, Haddock was in the expedition to Cadiz, and at the destruction of the Franco-Spanish fleet at Vigo, in which, as his father wrote, he 'behaved himself with so much bravery and courage that he hath gained the good report of the Duke of Ormonde … and was the first man that boarded one of the galleons' (Thompson, 43). Haddock passed his lieutenant's examination on 29 December 1702 and on 6 January 1703 he was appointed fifth lieutenant on the *St George*. On 10 February 1704 he was lieutenant on the *Association* and on 15 June he became second lieutenant on the *Crown*. On 18 December he was moved and became fourth lieutenant on the *Royal Anne*, and on 27 December 1705 he returned to the *St George* as third lieutenant. In her he was present at the relief of Barcelona under Sir John Leake and the earl of Peterborough, of which operation he wrote an interesting account to his father. In July 1706 he was present at the capture of Alicante, and on 6 April 1707 he was promoted captain of the *Ludlow Castle*. Later that year (30 December), while cruising in the North Sea, he recaptured the *Nightingale*, a small frigate which had been taken by the French a few months before, and fitted out under the command of Thomas Smith, a renegade Englishman, who was now sent to London and duly hanged as a traitor.

Haddock afterwards commanded the *Chatham* in 1710, the *Exeter* in 1715, and the *Shrewsbury* in 1717; and on 14 March 1718 he was appointed to the *Grafton*, which went to the Mediterranean in the fleet under Sir George Byng. The *Grafton* was the leading ship in the action off Cape Passaro, where Haddock, by his brilliant conduct, contributed much to the destruction of the Spanish fleet on 31 July. At some point before 1717 he had married Frances (*d.* 1735), about whom further details are unknown. The couple had one daughter and at least three and possibly five sons. Haddock commissioned the *Torbay* in 1721, and was still in command of her when Sir Charles Wager hoisted his flag in her as commander-in-chief, first in the Baltic in 1726 and then at the relief of Gibraltar in 1727. In 1728 Haddock was again appointed to the *Grafton*, in which, in 1731, he accompanied Wager to the Mediterranean, and in 1732 he was commander-in-chief at the Nore. In March 1734 he was appointed to the *Britannia*, but on 4 May he was promoted rear-admiral of the blue, when he hoisted his flag on the *Namur*, as third in command of the Grand Fleet under Sir John Norris. In the same year he was elected MP for Rochester, which he represented until his death; much of his time as a member of the Commons was spent at sea, and there is no record of his having spoken in debates. In December 1734 he was promoted rear-admiral of the white and on 2 March 1736 he became rear-admiral of the red.

In May 1738 Haddock was appointed commander-in-chief in the Mediterranean; with an Anglo-Spanish war imminent, Haddock's squadron threatened the Spanish coast, and played an important part in the diplomatic events that finally led to the outbreak of hostilities in October. Haddock already had orders to attack Spanish shipping and in the year that followed the receipt of these instructions, in June 1739, he made many rich prizes, including two treasure ships reputed to be worth £2 million. On 11 March 1741 he was promoted vice-admiral of the blue. In December 1740 Britain's war with Spain became entangled in the much broader War of the Austrian Succession. Haddock's command was stretched as he had now to prevent Franco-Spanish forces from attacking Austria's Italian possessions from the sea. During 1741 Spanish forces and transports were being assembled at Barcelona in order to invade Italy, but the Spanish warships needed to convoy this force were concentrated at Cadiz. For most of the year Haddock was able to maintain his position between the warships and the invasion forces, but in December 1741 he was forced to go to Gibraltar to refit, and the Spanish squadron succeeded in slipping out of Cadiz and through the straits. Haddock immediately followed, and on 7 December came up with the Spanish squadron off Cape Gata, but only in time to see it effecting a junction with a large French squadron which had come south from Toulon to meet it. Britain was not then at war with France; but the attitude of the French admiral, Lieutenant-General Claude-Élisée Court de la Bruyère, as well as many previous instances of ill will left no doubt in Haddock's mind that an attack on the Spaniards would be resisted by the whole combined force, to which his own squadron was very inferior. He fell back to Port Mahon, while the combined fleets convoyed the Spanish troops to Italy, and then sailed on to Toulon, where they remained for the next two years. Haddock's health had been severely tried by the anxious service of the two years preceding. The situation was not improved by the severe criticism he received from the duke of Newcastle who held Haddock responsible for the failure to contain the Spanish forces.

On 1 February 1742 Haddock asked to be relieved of his command. The ministry approved, but before news reached him, Haddock's health had collapsed and he had already handed over effective command to Richard Lestock. By the time Haddock arrived back in England, gout and nervous exhaustion made it impossible for him to reply to official letters. Although he never returned to sea, Haddock was appointed vice-admiral of the red in December 1743 and, on 19 June 1744, admiral of the blue. He died on 26 September 1746 and was buried in the churchyard of St Clement's, Leigh, Essex, on 6 October. Some twenty years later a white marble tablet to his memory was put up on the exterior wall of the church; but it was destroyed in 1837 during restoration work.

J. K. LAUGHTON, *rev.* RICHARD HARDING

**Sources** BL, Egerton MS 2528 · BL, Egerton MS 2529 · PRO, SP 42/86 · PRO, ADM 6/7–14 · captain's letters, 1707–33, PRO, ADM 1/1877, 1878, 1879, 1880, 1881 · E. M. Thompson, ed., 'Correspondence of the family of Haddock, 1657–1719', *Camden miscellany, VIII*, CS, new ser., 31 (1883), i–ix, 3–55 · A. J. Dunkin, *The archaeological mine: a collection of nuggets relating to the county of Kent*, 1 (1855), 46–9 · J. Bundock, *Leigh parish church of St Clement* (1978), 55 · burial of N. Haddock, 6 Oct 1746, Essex County Council archives, D/P 284/1/1 [supplied by archivist; their reference 7A/Harding, 15 Sept 1998] · PRO, PROB 11/750, q. 29 · PRO, ADM 107/1, fol. 301 · PRO, ADM 1/2815 · E. Cruickshanks, 'Haddock, Nicholas', HoP, *Commons, 1715–54*

**Archives** BL, official corresp. and papers, Egerton MSS 2528–2529 | Hunt. L., letters to Sir George Pocock

**Likenesses** oils, *c.*1715, NMM · oils, *c.*1742–1743, NMM · J. Faber junior, mezzotint (after T. Gibson), BM, NPG · copper medal, BM

**Haddock, Sir Richard** (*c.*1629–1715), naval officer, was the eldest of the four sons of William Haddock (*c.*1607–1667) and his wife, Anna Goodlad (*c.*1611–1689), of Leigh-on-Sea, Essex. The Haddock family had been mariners since at least 1327, and both Richard's father and grandfather, another Richard (*c.*1581–1660), commanded ships for parliament in the civil wars and afterwards. William Haddock commanded the *Hannibal* against the Dutch in 1653, and the younger Richard served under him at that time. He obtained his own command, the *Dragon*, in 1657, serving in the channel and operations at Dunkirk, and was among the naval officers who signed the oath of allegiance to Charles II in 1660. Following the Restoration Haddock traded in the Mediterranean as master of the *Supply* before returning to the navy in June 1666 as captain of the *Portland*, which he commanded in the attack on

**Sir Richard Haddock** (*c.*1629–1715), by John Closterman, *c.*1689

Dutch shipping at the Vlie. After leaving the *Portland* in October 1667 he returned to the Mediterranean trade as master of the *Bantam*, which he part owned. Haddock married twice. His first wife, Lydia, whom he had married by 1657, was the daughter of John Stevens, mariner, of Leigh. She had died before 1671 when he married Elizabeth Hurlestone (1650?–1710), the daughter of a Rotherhithe mariner.

At the beginning of the Third Anglo-Dutch War Haddock was appointed flag captain to the earl of Sandwich, admiral of the blue, aboard the *Royal James*, and led her brave but doomed resistance to a concerted Dutch attack in the battle of Sole Bay on 28 May 1672. Largely due to Haddock's direction, the *Royal James* freed herself from the attacks of the Dutch flagships *Groot Hollandia* and *Dolfijn*, but, in Haddock's words, while 'the surgeon was cutting off the shattered flesh and tendons of my toe' (Thompson, 19) following a shot from the *Dolfijn*, a fireship succeeded in attacking the *Royal James* and setting her alight. The ship was burned to the waterline and Sandwich drowned, but Haddock escaped. His gallantry earned him substantial amounts of royal bounty money and the king's own cap, which he took from his head to give to Haddock. He commanded the *Lion* over the winter of 1672–3 before becoming flag captain to Prince Rupert for the 1673 campaign, first aboard the *Royal Charles* and then, from 5 to 30 June 1673, aboard the *Sovereign*. The relationship between Haddock and Rupert was stormy, with the prince accusing his captain of cowardice and inconsistent tactics during the battles of Schooneveld (28 May and 4 June 1673). The consequence was Haddock's premature removal from the fleet and appointment as a commissioner of the navy. He was knighted on 3 July 1675 and served as MP for Aldeburgh in the first Exclusion Parliament (1679), voting against exclusion and being labelled 'vile' by Shaftesbury. He returned to the Commons in 1685 as MP for New Shoreham. Haddock was also an elder brother of Trinity House from 1675 onwards, serving as master in 1687–8.

On 2 February 1682 Haddock became controller of the navy, being additionally appointed first commissioner of the victualling in 1683. The reorganization of the Navy Board following the return of Samuel Pepys to the Admiralty led to Haddock's effective demotion to commissioner for the old accounts, a position which he held for the duration of Pepys's 'special commission' to reconstruct the navy, namely from April 1686 to 12 October 1688. Haddock was reinstated as controller on that day and continued to hold the post until his death. He was imprisoned for a fortnight late in 1689 as a consequence of a parliamentary inquiry into alleged corruption in the victualling accounts, and was later removed as first commissioner. Following the disgrace of Arthur Herbert, earl of Torrington, after the battle of Beachy Head in June 1690, it was decided to revert to the precedent of the Dutch wars and appoint a triumvirate of joint admirals. Although he had never held flag rank before, Haddock's experience made him an obvious candidate and he was duly appointed on 6 August in commission with Sir John Ashby and Sir Henry Killigrew, despite the opposition to his elevation from several younger officers who had already held flag rank and also of a number of the Admiralty commissioners, who felt that Haddock had been disparaging towards Britain's Dutch allies. The joint admirals commanded aboard the *Sovereign*, then the *Kent*, for the remainder of the 1690 campaign, concentrating on the recapture of Cork and Kinsale.

Haddock was ashore again by the beginning of 1691, and throughout the French wars he was one of the mainstays of the naval administration. His ability from his own and his family's experiences to recall precedents from the 1640s and even earlier meant that he was often called upon as an 'expert witness' in parliamentary and other enquiries into naval matters, as well as making him a valuable source of information for Pepys. Haddock's increasingly great age meant that some of his duties eventually had to be delegated to others. He died in London on 26 January 1715 and was buried in the family vault at Leigh, after having survived in office every change of government from the Rump Parliament to the accession of the house of Hanover. Although often suspected of retaining the dissenting religious tendencies of his youth, after the Restoration Haddock conformed at least outwardly to the established church.

By his will, dated 13 November 1712, Haddock made bequests to his two surviving sons, Richard, a future controller of the navy, and Nicholas *Haddock (*bap.* 1685?, *d.* 1746), who became admiral of the blue, and to his three daughters, Martha (who married Dennis Lyddall), Lydia, and Elizabeth. Richard, who died in 1751, inherited his father's house in Mile End and property in Soham, Cambridgeshire. Both sons received the gold medals which their father and grandfather William had received from the Commonwealth for good service in the First Anglo-Dutch War, over sixty years earlier. Sir Richard also made bequests to the poor of Trinity House and his home parish of Leigh-on-Sea, at least partly proving Pepys's assertion that his was 'the greatest instance of an estate raised purely from sea service' (Tanner, 69–70). J. D. DAVIES

**Sources** BL, Egerton MS 2521 • E. M. Thompson, ed., 'Correspondence of the family of Haddock, 1657–1719', *Camden miscellany, VIII*, CS, new ser., 31 (1883), i–ix, 3–55 • PRO, ADM MSS • *CSP dom.*, 1653–91 • PRO, PROB 11/544, fols. 199–201 • R. C. Anderson, ed., *Journals and narratives of the Third Dutch War*, Navy RS, 86 (1946) • S. Pepys, *Naval minutes*, ed. J. R. Tanner, Navy RS, 60 (1926) • *Report on the manuscripts of Allan George Finch*, 5 vols., HMC, 71 (1913–2003), vol. 2 • *The manuscripts of the House of Lords*, new ser., 12 vols. (1900–77) • J. M. Collinge, *Navy Board officials, 1660–1832* (1978) • J. Ehrman, *The navy in the war of William III, 1689–1697* (1953) • J. D. Davies, *Gentlemen and tarpaulins: the officers and men of the Restoration navy* (1991)

**Archives** BL, personal, official, and family corresp. and papers, Egerton MSS 2520–2527 • BL, order and warrants, Add. MSS 20085, 22183 | Leics. RO, letters to earl of Nottingham • PRO, ADM MSS

**Likenesses** J. Closterman, oils, *c.*1689, Gov. Art Coll. [*see illus.*] • W. Faithorne junior, mezzotint (after J. Closterman); version, Philips, sale, 29 July 1974

**Wealth at death** house in Mile End; mortgage on an estate at Soham; tenements and fields at Leigh-on-Sea; individual bequests of over £1000, incl. £50 to poor of Trinity House, and £10 to poor of Leigh: will, PRO, PROB 11/544, fols. 199–201

**Haddon, Alfred Cort** (1855–1940), anthropologist, was born in London on 24 May 1855, the second child and elder son of John Haddon (1823–1904), head of a firm of typefounders and printers with a strong Baptist tradition, the family having its origins in farming near Naseby, Northamptonshire. From his mother, Caroline Waterman (1827–1899) of Bristol, who published books for children under the name Caroline Hadley, Haddon gained insight into natural history and skill in drawing and design. His formal education was sporadic. He attended various schools in London including the City of London School in 1866 and Mill Hill School in 1867–8. The family moved a number of times within London from New Barnet to Finchley, Lewisham, and Wimbledon according to the fluctuations in the family business. Though Haddon spent a year in his father's firm after leaving school, his interest was always natural history and his free time was spent collecting specimens and teaching himself zoology. After attending evening classes at King's College, London, he taught zoology and geology at a girls' school in Dover run by his paternal aunts. His father eventually conceded that his son would never be a businessman and in 1875 Haddon entered Christ's College, Cambridge, where his mentors were F. M. Balfour, to whom he dedicated his first book, *An Introduction to the Study of Embryology* (1887), and Michael Foster. In 1878 he obtained a first class in the natural sciences tripos (comparative anatomy), and in 1879 he was given a grant by the university to work for six months at the zoological station at Naples, where he began what was to be a lifelong friendship with Patrick Geddes. On his return from Naples he was appointed curator of the Zoological Museum at Cambridge and a university demonstrator in zoology.

In 1880, with the help of T. H. Huxley and the Cambridge ornithologist Alfred Newton, Haddon was appointed professor of zoology at the Royal College of Science, Dublin, where he also served as assistant naturalist to the Science and Art Museum. On 21 September 1881 he married Fanny Elizabeth (1857–1937), daughter of Thomas Rose, draper, of Bedford. They had a son and two daughters. While doing pioneering field research in the scientific classification of sea anemones around the Irish coasts, he developed an ethnographical interest in western Irish life. In 1888–9, with the aid of grants from the Royal Irish Academy and the Darwin fund of the Royal Society, he went to the Torres Strait to study the marine biology of coral reefs. In addition to biological specimens he collected a large amount of material on the Torres Strait islanders, anxious to record their way of life before contact with Europeans had extinguished native custom. Papers read before the British Association (1889) and at the Royal Institution (1890, published in *Nature*, 30 October) on his return brought him into touch with J. G. Frazer and W. H. Flower and added to his links with T. H. Huxley. Since his work in Dublin occupied only a part of the year, and he was keen to find opportunities to indulge his interest in anthropology, Haddon began lecturing in physical anthropology at Cambridge (1894–8), where he was awarded a DSc degree in 1897. The following year he organized and led the famous Cambridge anthropological expedition of 1898–9 to the Torres Strait and New Guinea. On his way back from Melanesia he spent several months with Charles Hose in Borneo, and made further anthropological observations for comparative purposes. In 1900, on the strength of the scientific results of the expedition, he was appointed university lecturer in ethnology at Cambridge, and in 1901 election into a fellowship at Christ's College permitted him to resign his Dublin chair. That same year he published his popular account of the Torres Strait expedition, *Head-Hunters Black, White and Brown*. Although he had to lecture in London (1904–9) to supplement his income, this enabled him to exercise a valuable influence at the Horniman Museum, where he was deputy curator from 1902 to 1915. His friendships with G. Laurence Gomme, Henry Woodd Nevinson, Edward Clodd, and George Amos Dorsey widened his sphere of influence in Britain and opened the way to a series of visits to the United States. In 1909 he was able to reduce his outside work on appointment to a readership in ethnology at Cambridge and in that year published *The Races of Man and their Distribution*.

In 1910 Haddon completed his *History of Anthropology* and the following year published *The Wanderings of Peoples*. The meeting of the British Association in Australia in 1914 and a grant from the Percy Sladen Trust enabled Haddon to visit the Torres Strait and Papua once more, in the company and with the help of his younger daughter, Kathleen (later Mrs Rishbeth), who published several books on string figures. Returning to Europe, Haddon worked at the scientific reports of the Torres Strait expedition and in 1917 took up educational and welfare work with the British army in France until he was compelled to withdraw by temporary ill health. In 1920 he was appointed deputy curator of the Cambridge University Museum of Archaeology and Ethnology and organized his own Melanesian collections. Under his direction the museum became a primary centre for anthropological study and research.

Haddon was a humanist, teacher, scientific pioneer, and a keen champion of public education. His wit and missionary zeal for his subject were appreciated by his wide circle of colleagues, students, and friends. The Torres Strait expedition of 1898–9 marked an epoch in anthropological research, particularly in the development of field methodology. It is characteristic of Haddon that it brought together a group of distinguished scientists (including the experimental psychologist W. H. R. Rivers), who all kept their affectionate respect for him during their lifetime as did his many friends among the Torres Strait islanders.

Haddon was elected FRS in 1899 and received honorary doctorates of science from the universities of Manchester and Perth (Australia). He was president of section H (anthropology) of the British Association in 1902 and 1905, and in 1902–4 of the Royal Anthropological Institute, which appointed him Huxley memorial lecturer in 1920 and awarded him the first Rivers memorial medal in 1924.

Haddon retired from teaching in 1925 at the age of seventy. To mark the occasion P. A. de Laszlo was commissioned to paint his portrait. Christ's College celebrated his seventieth birthday by a dinner in hall, the first occasion on which women dined in a men's college hall in Cambridge, an appropriate event for a champion of women's education. For his eightieth birthday (1935) he was presented on behalf of many friends with a case containing 10,000 anthropological photographs, most of them from Haddon's own negatives. He subsequently donated the collection to the Cambridge museum, where it now resides. In 1935 he also completed *We Europeans* (with J. Huxley and A. Carr-Saunders) and volume one of the *Reports of the Cambridge Anthropological Expedition to Torres Straits*, of which volumes two to six had appeared between 1901 and 1912. In the next five years he published (with L. Start) *Iban or Sea Dayak Fabrics and their Patterns* (1936), the result of years of study of textile designs, and *Canoes of Oceania* (with J. Hornell, 3 vols., 1936–8), and he completed *Smoking and Tobacco Pipes in New Guinea* (published posthumously in 1946) a few weeks before he died at his home, 3 Cranmer Road, Cambridge, on 20 April 1940. He was cremated at Cambridge.

H. J. FLEURE, *rev.* SANDRA ROUSE

**Sources** A. H. Quiggin, *Haddon the head hunter* (1942) • CUL, Haddon MSS • S. Rouse, 'Ethnology, ethnobiography and institution: A. C. Haddon and anthropology at Cambridge, 1889–1926', PhD diss., U. Cam., 1997 • W. Cruft, *A history of the Haddons of Naseby* (1915) • H. J. Fleure, *Obits. FRS*, 3 (1939–41), 449–65 • A. H. Quiggin and E. S. Fegan, 'Alfred Cort Haddon, 1855–1940', *Man*, 40 (1940), 97–100 • A. Herle and S. Rouse, eds., *Cambridge and the Torres Strait: centenary essays on the 1898 anthropological expedition* (1998) • *The Times*

(22 April 1940) • personal knowledge (1949) • private information (1949)

**Archives** Australian National University, Canberra [microfilm copies] • BLPES, letters to C. G. Seligman relating to Hamitic peoples • CUL, corresp., diaries, and papers • Horniman Museum and Library, corresp. relating to Actinians • U. Cam., Museum of Archaeology and Anthropology, artefacts, corresp., notes, papers, photographs, record cards | BL, corresp. with Macmillans, Add. MS 55158 • Bodl. Oxf., letters to J. L. Myres • NL Aus., Haddon MSS [microfilm copies] • NL Scot., corresp. with Sir Patrick Geddes • U. Oxf., Pitt Rivers Museum, letters to Sir W. B. Spencer | FILM BFI NFTVA, ethnographic film from 1898 Torres Strait expedition | SOUND BL NSA, wax cylinders, phonograph recordings from 1898 Torres Strait expedition

**Likenesses** W. Stoneman, photograph, 1921, NPG • P. A. de Laszlo, oils, 1925, Christ's College, Cambridge • P. A. de Laszlo, oils, 1925, U. Cam., faculty of archaeology and anthropology • photographs, U. Cam., Museum of Archaeology and Anthropology, photographic archives

**Haddon, James** (*b.* *c.*1520, *d.* in or after **1556**), evangelical divine, was the third son of William Haddon of Buckinghamshire and Dorothy, daughter of John Young of Croome d'Abitot, Worcestershire; she later married William Saunders, then Paul Dayrell. James followed his elder brother Walter *Haddon (with whom he was formerly much confused) to Eton College, and, by 1539, to King's College, Cambridge, where he graduated BA in 1541/2 and MA in 1544. In 1546 he became a founding fellow of Trinity College. In or by 1548 he was licensed to preach. He was domestic chaplain to Henry Grey, successively marquess of Dorset and duke of Suffolk. It was from his patron's Leicestershire seat, Bradgate, that in May 1551 Haddon initiated a correspondence with Heinrich Bullinger, introducing himself at the recommendation of John ab Ulmis. In August 1552 Haddon reported enthusiastically to Bullinger on the destruction of images and impending changes to the prayer book and ordinal. But he was dismayed that Suffolk, who had forbidden card-playing to his household, still indulged in this 'unchristian' behaviour among his intimates. It seems that Martin Bucer was also among Haddon's correspondents. Of the English protestant leaders his closest friends were John Parkhurst and John Jewel.

Circumstances would allow Haddon only a few steps towards what promised to be an important public career. On 29 August 1552 he was appointed a canon of Westminster Cathedral. By 29 October he had resigned without installation, having in the same month been named dean of Exeter. To this office he was formally appointed on 8 January 1553 and was installed on 10 July. It is not clear if either of these preferments was the 'certain office in the state' which though 'not very lucrative' he intended to occupy to promote the gospel (Robinson, *Original Letters*, 289). In Lent 1553 he 'most learnedlie oppinit the causes of the bypast plagues' in a sermon at court, warning that 'worse wer to follow, unless repentance suld schortlie be found' (*Works of John Knox*, 3.177). Following Mary's accession he was prominent in the convocation debate of October 1553, with scholarly defence of the reformed eucharistic doctrine. In an exchange with the prolocutor Weston he asked 'Did Eucharistia or sacrament suffer upon the cross for us?' (Dixon, 4.84). In November he was still at large in London, understandably anxious because of the imprisonment of many of his friends.

Haddon joined the exile in 1554, taking a letter for Bullinger written in prison by John Hooper on 23 May; in this Haddon was praised for his 'singular erudition and virtue' and for avoiding 'all desire of those perishing objects which foolish mortals admire' (Robinson, *Original Letters*, 103). Having arrived at Strasbourg by 9 July, he passed the letter on by the hand of Parkhurst. In August 1554, writing again to Bullinger, Haddon advised against the publication of the papers of Lady Jane Grey, Suffolk's daughter, who had been executed following her father's rebellion earlier that year. Jane had been Haddon's pupil, and was now considered a protestant martyr. Her papers had been smuggled from England by John Banks, whom Haddon financed. Haddon's worry was that his own English assets might be confiscated (as by December they were). It is thought that he nevertheless saw to the printing of the papers at Strasbourg during 1554.

Soon after his arrival in Strasbourg, Haddon had been among those chosen to minister to the Frankfurt exile community; but around October he asked 'for divers considerations' to be excused that charge ([Whittingham?], *Brieff Discours*, 16). In April 1555 he wrote that he was no longer engaged in any public work. In December he had the satisfaction of hearing that Gardiner, whom he had once called the 'pest of the state' was dead (Robinson, *Original Letters*, 298). Haddon's last extant letter was written from Frankfurt on 12 March 1556; it is presumed that he died soon afterwards, perhaps of plague. His brother Walter composed an elegant valediction, concluding with the lines

O tempestiva foelicem morte Iacobum
O utinam fratri iungar et ipse meo.
('O James, fortunate in a happy death,
O that I might be united to my brother and he to me.')
(*Poëmata*, 100)

C. S. Knighton

**Sources** W. Sterry, ed., *The Eton College register, 1441–1698* (1943), 152 • C. H. Garrett, *The Marian exiles: a study in the origins of Elizabethan puritanism* (1938), 169–70 • *CSP dom.*, 1547–53, no. 74 • *CPR*, 1550–53, 310, 312, 402 • L. V. Ryan, 'Walter Haddon: Elizabethan Latinist', *Huntington Library Quarterly*, 17 (1953–4), 99–124, esp. 101 • H. Robinson, ed. and trans., *Original letters relative to the English Reformation*, 1, Parker Society, [26] (1846), 103, 279–302, 303–5, 307 • *The examinations and writings of John Philpot*, ed. R. Eden, Parker Society, 5 (1842), 170, 182, 200–01 • R. W. Dixon, *History of the Church of England*, 4 (1891), 67n., 81–5 • J. Strype, *Ecclesiastical memorials*, 2/2 (1822), 274 • *Fasti Angl.* (Hardy), 1.387 • CCC Cam., MS 113, no. 5 • *The works of John Knox*, ed. D. Laing, 6 vols., Wodrow Society, 12 (1846–64) • *The poetry of Walter Haddon*, ed. C. J. Lees (1967), 11, 26, 163–4 • W. Haddon, *Poëmata* (1567), sig. N3v [p. 100] • J. Parkhurst, *Ludicra sive epigrammata iuvenilia* (1573), 160 • [W. Whittingham?], *A brieff discours off the troubles begonne at Franckford* [1574], 13, 16 • M. A. Simpson, *John Knox and the troubles begun at Frankfurt* (1975), 57–8 • *The works of John Jewel*, ed. J. Ayre, 4 vols., Parker Society, 24 (1845–50) • W. P. W. Phillimore, ed., *The visitation of the county of Worcester made in the year 1569*, Harleian Society, 27 (1888), 153 • G. Lipscomb, *The history and antiquities of the county of Buckingham*, 4 vols. (1831–47), vol. 3, p. 32

**Wealth at death** reduced to poverty (by his claim) on seizure of his English assets in December 1554: Robinson, ed. and trans., *Original letters*, 294–6, 297, 307

**Haddon, Walter** (1514/15–1571), civil lawyer, the son of William Haddon and his wife, Dorothy, daughter of John Young of Croome d'Abitot, Worcestershire, and brother of James *Haddon, was born in Buckinghamshire. He was educated at Eton College (*c.*1529–1533) under Richard Cox. In August 1533 he was elected from Eton to King's College, Cambridge, and was a fellow there from 1536 to 1552. He took his BA degree in 1538 at Cambridge, where he excelled as a writer of Latin prose. He became an MA in 1541 and read lectures on civil law for two or three years. In 1549 he was made a doctor of civil law at Cambridge, and he was vice-chancellor of that university in 1549–50.

Haddon was 'one of the great and eminent lights of the reformation in Cambridge under King Edward' (Strype, *Parker*, 2.365–6). With Matthew Parker, then master of Corpus Christi College, he acted as an executor of his friend Martin Bucer, and both men delivered orations at his funeral on 2 March 1551. Later Haddon also wrote a poem in honour of Bucer. Soon afterwards he was dangerously ill, and received a pious consolatory letter from Sir John Cheke (19 March). Two days later he was appointed regius professor of civil law, in accordance with a petition from the university, drawn up by his friend Roger Ascham, and he held the post until the end of September 1552. During a serious illness about this time Cheke asked the king to appoint Haddon to succeed him as provost of King's College, but he recovered and continued in office. When Cheke died in 1557 Haddon wrote his epitaph.

In February 1552, after Bishop Stephen Gardiner, then master of Trinity Hall, refused to comply with the request of the duke of Somerset to amalgamate that college with Clare College, the king appointed Haddon in his place. On 8 April 1552 he, Parker, Ralph Aynsworth, master of Peterhouse, and Thomas Lever, master of St John's, were commissioned to settle a disputed claim to the mastership of Clare. During this time Haddon revised some parts of the draft of the 'Reformatio legum ecclesiasticarum', but his role in this was minor and seems to have been confined to matters of style. He was certainly not the text's author, as various reference works have stated.

In late September 1552 the king and council removed Owen Oglethorpe, president of Magdalen College, Oxford, who was opposed to further religious changes, and Haddon was appointed to succeed him. The fellows petitioned the king against this flagrant breach of the college statutes, but in vain. Finding the council inflexible, Oglethorpe made an amicable arrangement with Haddon and resigned on 27 September. Haddon was admitted president by royal mandate on 10 October 1552, on which occasion Michael Renniger, one of Oglethorpe's strongest opponents, addressed him in a congratulatory oration. The new president

> contrived, during his short and unstatutable career, to sell as many of the precious effects of the chapel as were valued at about a thousand pounds for £52 14*s.* 8*d.*, which sum he is said to have consumed on alterations, as also nearly £120 of the public money. (Ingram, 16n.)

Some libellous verses against the president, affixed to various parts of the college, were attributed to Julius Palmer, who was expelled on the ground of 'popish pranks'. On the other hand, when Bishop Gardiner visited Oxford in October 1553 he found Magdalen to be the most protestant college in the university, which suggests that Haddon had had a major influence on it in a very short time.

On Queen Mary's accession Haddon wrote some Latin verses congratulating her. On 27 August 1553 he prudently obtained a month's leave of absence from the college to attend to urgent private business. The following day letters were received from the queen commanding that all injunctions contrary to the founder's statutes issued since the death of Henry VIII should be abolished. As Haddon had already retired, Oglethorpe was re-elected president on 31 October. Haddon was admitted to the College of Advocates on 5 May 1555, and practised for a time in the court of arches. In the same year he was elected member of parliament for Reigate, probably thanks to the influence of William Howard, Lord Effingham, who was lord of the borough and a friend. He was admitted a member of Gray's Inn in 1557, and was one of the members for Thetford, Norfolk, in the parliament which assembled on 20 January 1558. This seat he owed to Richard Fulmerston, a distant relative and the local agent of the duke of Norfolk. There is no sign that he played an active part in either parliament, and he gave no indication that he was opposed to Mary I's religious policies. In 1557 he translated into Latin a letter to Pope Paul IV from the parliament of England, trying to dissuade him from revoking Cardinal Pole's legatine authority. However, Haddon's personal sympathy with protestantism was displayed in a consolatory Latin poem addressed to the Princess Elizabeth on her afflictions. He was an accomplished master of Latin verse, and his poems were much praised during his lifetime, though posterity has been less kind to him. His modern editor has summed him up as a mediocre poet, but one who is important as a mirror of his age.

On Elizabeth's accession (17 November 1558) Haddon was summoned to attend her at Hatfield; he congratulated her in Latin verse and was immediately constituted one of the masters of the court of requests. He was also made a master of the prerogative court of Canterbury in December 1558. But in spite of his protestant opinions he was an admirer of the learning of Bishop Cuthbert Tunstal and in 1559 he composed the epitaph on his tomb. On 20 June in that year he was appointed one of her majesty's commissioners for the visitation of the University of Cambridge and the college of Eton, and on 18 September 1559 the queen granted him a pension of £50 per annum. In the 1559 parliament he sat for Poole, a seat secured for him by the earl of Bedford, and his efforts succeeded in getting the town incorporated, though not until 23 June 1568. He was on the commission for administering oaths to ecclesiastics (20 October 1559) and was also one of the ecclesiastical commissioners. About the same time he received from his friend Archbishop Parker the office of judge of the prerogative court.

In 1560 a Latin prayer book was prepared under the superintendence of Haddon, who took a former translation by Alexander Alesius as a model. The prayer book was authorized by the queen's letters patent for the use of the colleges in both universities and those of Eton and Winchester. On 22 January 1561 he was one of the royal commissioners appointed to peruse the order of lessons throughout the year, to cause new calendars to be printed, to provide remedies for the decay of churches, and to prescribe some good order for collegiate churches in the use of the Latin service. In December 1561 he was recommended by Bishop Grindal for the provostship of Eton College, but the queen's choice fell upon William Day instead. In June 1562 Haddon and Parker, at the request of the senate, persuaded Sir William Cecil not to resign the chancellorship of the University of Cambridge. In the 1563 parliament Haddon sat for Warwick, probably thanks to the influence of his friend the earl of Warwick. In the second session of the parliament a bill concerning perjury was committed to him (18 February 1566) and on 31 October that year he was appointed to the succession committee. On 5 November 1566 he was one of thirty members summoned to hear the queen's message on her succession.

In 1563 Jerome Osorio da Fonseca, a Portuguese priest, published in French and Latin an epistle to Queen Elizabeth exhorting her to return to the communion of the Catholic church. Haddon, by direction of the government, wrote an answer, which was printed at Paris in 1563 through the agency of Sir Thomas Smith, the English ambassador. Osorio, who had been meanwhile created bishop of Silves, published in 1567 a reply to Haddon, and the latter commenced a rejoinder. It was left unfinished at the time of his death, but was ultimately completed and published by John Foxe. There is extant a satire in verse, known as the *Chorus alternatim canentium*, on the controversy between Haddon and Osorio, attached to a caricature in which Haddon, Bucer, and Peter Martyr Vermigli are represented as dogs drawing a car whereon Osorio is seated in triumph. It is undated and the place of publication is uncertain, though it was probably Antwerp.

In August 1564 Haddon accompanied the queen to Cambridge, and determined the questions in law in the disputations in that faculty held in her presence. On 2 March 1565 the queen granted him the site of the abbey of Wymondham, Norfolk, with its manor and lands. He was later employed at Bruges in 1565 and 1566 with Viscount Montagu and Nicholas Wotton, in negotiations for restoring the ancient commercial relations between England and the Netherlands. In the last years of his life Haddon acquired considerable property in Kent and in 1570 the queen leased him the manor of Hatcham Barnes, which is partly in that county and partly in Surrey. By 28 July 1570 he was suffering from the stone, and a few months later he made his will, leaving £200, his books, and a gold chain to his son. He also left £40 to Christ's Hospital, London, and asked that some gift be made to Peter Osborne and his wife. The rest of his property was to go to his widow.

Haddon's first wife was Margaret, daughter of Sir John Clere of Ormesby, Norfolk; they had two boys and two girls. His son Clere, who drowned in the River Cam shortly after his father's death, mentioned them in a poem he wrote in memory of his father, though it appears that the other three predeceased him as they are not mentioned in his will. On 17 December 1567 Haddon married Anne, daughter of Sir Henry Sutton, who survived him and married Henry Brooke, brother of Lord Cobham, whom she also survived. Haddon died aged fifty-six in London on 21 January 1571, and was interred four days later at Christ Church Greyfriars, where there was a monument to his memory until the great fire in 1666. Its Latin inscription has been preserved in Weever's *Ancient Funerall Monuments*. GERALD BRAY

**Sources** HoP, *Commons, 1509–58* • HoP, *Commons, 1558–1603* • C. J. Lees, *The poetry of Walter Haddon* (1967) • G. D. Squibb, *Doctors' Commons: a history of the College of Advocates and Doctors of Law* (1977) • J. Strype, *The life and acts of Matthew Parker*, new edn, 3 vols. (1821) • J. Strype, *Ecclesiastical memorials*, 3 vols. (1822) • Cooper, *Ath. Cantab.*, 1.299 • *Literary remains of King Edward the Sixth*, ed. J. G. Nichols, 1, Roxburghe Club, 75 (1857), clxi • J. Ingram, *Memorials of Oxford* (1837) • W. K. Clay, *Liturgical service in the reign of Elizabeth* (1847), xxiv • *CSP dom.*, 1552–70 • J. Weever, *Ancient funerall monuments* (1631), 391

**Wealth at death** considerable property and at least £200: PRO, C 142/161/120; will, PRO, PROB 11/53, sig. 7

**Haddow, Sir Alexander** (1907–1976), experimental pathologist in cancer research, was born on 18 January 1907, at Leven, Fife, Scotland, the elder son of William Haddow (1864–1928), miner, later a landlord of a hostelry, and his wife, Margaret Docherty (1870–1922), the daughter of a hawker and coachman. The family lived in Broxburn, Linlithgowshire, and Haddow was educated at Broxburn high school and Broxburn Academy, where he won the dux gold medal. He was a quiet, shy boy, dubbed the Professor by his classmates; he enjoyed solitary pursuits including bird-watching and field botany. He was greatly influenced by Alexander Scott, the family doctor, who cared for him during his serious attack of scarletina at the age of ten and peritonitis following a perforated appendix a year later. In 1922 a double tragedy struck the family. Haddow's twelve-year-old brother, Willie, was killed in an accident, and his mother died in the same year.

Haddow's interest in cancer was aroused by Scott's contacts with the local shale-oil workers who succumbed to skin cancers. Supported by his father Haddow began his medical studies in 1924 at Edinburgh University; he graduated MB ChB in 1929. After serving as house physician and Carnegie research student at Edinburgh Royal Infirmary he worked in general practice in Hull while waiting to take up his appointment as assistant lecturer in bacteriology, helped by a research studentship, under Professor T. J. Mackie. In 1932 he became full lecturer, and Davidson research fellow. He became PhD and MD in 1937 and DSc in 1938.

The turning point in Haddow's career came in 1936 when he joined Ernest Kennaway's pioneering group at

**Sir Alexander Haddow (1907–1976)**, by Godfrey Argent, 1970

the research institute of the Royal Cancer (later the Marsden) Hospital in London. This group had isolated, from coal tar, the first pure chemicals that could cause cancer in experimental animals. While still in Edinburgh Haddow had been collaborating with J. W. Cook, the group's organic chemist. Haddow made two crucial additions to the discovery of chemical carcinogenesis which came to dominate the research effort after he became director of the new Chester Beatty Research Institute in 1946. In the same year he was also appointed professor of experimental pathology in the University of London.

First, Haddow recognized that minor differences in chemical structure between substances that were carcinogenic and those that were not might throw light on the mechanism that transformed normal cells to cancer cells. Second, he discovered that carcinogens, but not closely related non-carcinogens, could retard the growth of tumours induced by chemical carcinogens—the 'Haddow phenomenon'. He inferred a single mechanism responsible for both, namely a specific retarding effect on growth regulation, with malignant transformation arising as an adaptation permitting damaged cells to survive. His aim as director was therefore to explore the nature of these events in depth. He believed, too, that the Haddow phenomenon might be exploited for cancer treatment, and a major programme for testing the growth-inhibiting potential of many compounds was begun. He established liaison with the consultants at the Royal Cancer Hospital with a view to testing the most promising compounds clinically. In five years chlorambucil, melphalan, and busulphan, three of the many compounds synthesized and tested, were indeed found to be clinically effective, though not curative, and nearly fifty years later they were still widely used in the treatment of malignant blood diseases, cancer of the breast and ovary, and other illnesses. In 1970 Haddow felt that encouraging experimental work on the platinum compound cisplatin (cis platin diammine dichloride) justified a clinical trial, and his colleague Dr Eve Wiltshaw soon obtained good results in cancer of the ovary, even when the patients were no longer responding to chlorambucil. Platinum compounds are now used routinely in the treatment of several malignant diseases.

In his role as director Haddow adopted a liberal approach. He assembled a team of experts in every scientific discipline with a bearing on cancer, explained his broad aims, and encouraged each one to develop the work as he or she saw fit without being tied to a rigid programme. Original and unexpected findings were to be followed up even if they seemed to deviate from the proposed enquiry. Some of these proved to be major scientific breakthroughs, such as Jacques Miller's discovery of the function of the thymus, which revolutionized the science of immunology. Miller had been engaged to discover how a virus caused leukaemia in mice. Haddow was fortunate that, for some twenty years, funds were readily available for scientific research, and he could provide his staff with the best available equipment. He established and maintained close contacts with the leading world centres, and the institute quickly acquired an international reputation. Haddow himself published many influential articles in scientific journals.

When the staff assembled to discuss the potential importance of new findings, Haddow would sit silently, smoking his pipe until comment was required. With a few well-chosen words he seized on obscurities, inconsistencies, and fallacies, but was quick to recognize the importance of a finding that had eluded its discoverer, and to suggest ways of redeeming ill-designed experiments. He had a calmly authoritative demeanour and an upright bearing. On first acquaintance he could seem aloof, but he quickly revealed a deep interest and willingness to listen and respond to a potentially promising suggestion. He was deeply concerned with the personal welfare of everyone in the institute and with their families, to whom he gave unstinting support in times of need.

Haddow did not take kindly to the progressive reduction in the funding of scientific research towards the end of his career, and his distress increased when he lost his sight as a result of diabetes. He nevertheless continued, with indomitable courage, to prepare and deliver, with slides, important guest lectures at home and abroad, which were given with his ringing, slightly purring Scottish accent. At this hard time he summed up his philosophy, when asked whether he was looking forward to his transatlantic visit next day, by saying 'I never look forward to anything, I take each day as it comes'. But his warm sense of humour never left him. He had a good singing voice, and could still enjoy music, particularly opera, long after he could no longer paint. In politics he was a Liberal.

Haddow was elected FRS in 1958, and knighted in 1966. He received many international awards, medals, and prizes, including the croix de chevalier de la Légion d'honneur. He gave much advice to the BBC and served on the Press Council, the British Association for World Government, and the Pugwash conferences. He put in a great deal of work for the Royal Institution and for the CIBA Foundation, which promoted valuable scientific contacts between international experts in its residential scientific symposia. He was president of the International Union Against Cancer from 1962 to 1966.

Haddow was twice married. First, in 1932, to Dr Lucia Lindsay Crosbie Black (*d.* 1968), daughter of Captain George Black, of Castle Douglas, Scotland. They had one son, William George (*b.* 1934); his second wife was Feo Standing (*née* Garner), scientific photographer, whom he married in 1969. Haddow died on 21 January 1976 at the General Hospital, Amersham, Buckinghamshire, and was cremated at Chilton crematorium, Amersham. His wife survived him. D. A. G. Galton

**Sources** F. Bergel, *Memoirs FRS*, 23 (1977), 133–91 · *WWW* · personal knowledge (2004) · *DNB* · private information (2004) · E. Wiltshaw, *A history of the Royal Marsden Hospital* (1998)

**Archives** Wellcome L., research notes, corresp., and autobiographical notes | Bodl. Oxf., corresp. with C. D. Darlington · Rice University, Houston, Texas, Woodson Research Center, corresp. with Sir Julian Huxley · Wellcome L., corresp. with Sir Ernst Chain

**Likenesses** G. Argent, photograph, 1970, NPG [*see illus.*] · W. Churcher, photograph, Wellcome L. · photograph, repro. in Bergel, *Memoirs FRS*

**Haddow, Sir (Thomas) Douglas (1913–1986)**, civil servant, was born on 9 February 1913 at Summit Schoolhouse, Crawford, Lanarkshire, the son of George Haddow, the local schoolmaster, and his wife, Helen Jamieson Stewart. He was educated at George Watson's College, Edinburgh, Edinburgh University, where he graduated with a first-class MA (honours) degree in mathematics (1932), and Trinity College, Cambridge, where he held a scholarship and read for the mathematical tripos and graduated as a wrangler in 1934. He took first place in the competition of 1935 for entry into the administrative grade of the civil service, but surprised everyone by electing to serve in the Department of Health for Scotland in Edinburgh rather than one of the more prestigious London departments. He was the first direct entrant from the administrative grade to enter the department, which had previously been staffed with executive-grade officers. On 15 September 1942 he married Margaret Ross Steven Rowat (1913/14–1969), a clerical officer in the Department of Health and the daughter of David Rowat, an Edinburgh master tailor. They had two sons.

In 1941 Haddow became private secretary to Tom Johnston, the secretary of state for Scotland, and learned much from Johnston's assertive approach to defending the Scottish interest in Whitehall and his deep-seated desire to be seen leading Scottish attitudes. In 1943 Haddow was promoted to assistant secretary in the department. He was closely associated with the preparatory work that led to the introduction of the National Health Service in Scotland, which in contrast to England aroused very little criticism from the medical profession. He forestalled potential unrest through his appreciation of the strong relationship between medical education in the four Scottish cities and the financial position of the consultant in teaching hospitals. In 1948 he spent a year in the USA studying the health services as a fellow of the Commonwealth Fund and returned to become the under-secretary responsible for the Scottish hospital services.

During the early 1950s Haddow played a leading role in advising ministers on the methods required to control and reduce hospital costs, largely by the introduction of time and motion studies of labour and the strict control of supplies. He subsequently advised ministers to resist a Treasury attempt to impose a boarding charge for hospital care. Haddow argued that the low income of many families in Scotland would mean the extensive use of a means test, thus raising administrative costs and transferring a significant proportion of the supposed savings to the National Assistance Board. As in the rest of the UK, the charge was not introduced.

In 1956 Haddow became the under-secretary responsible for town and country planning and was immediately involved in the overspill arrangements designed to move a third of Glasgow's overcrowded population into new towns and other settlements across Scotland. By 1958 he saw that the overspill programme could usefully link a public-health issue with the economic regeneration of Scotland in a planned and co-ordinated manner, and he became an advocate for reorganizing the Scottish departments around this task. He devised a plan to create a development department which combined the housing and physical planning functions of the Department of Health with that of the roads, electricity supply, and development area functions of the Scottish home department. However, he failed to convince a somewhat conservative Scottish Office, whose officials opposed it.

In December 1961 the Scottish Council (Development and Industry), SC(DI), an independent body, published a report on the Scottish economy (the Toothill report) which recommended that a Scottish development department should be established and that government regional policy should be aimed at stimulating investment in areas, such as new towns, with the potential to grow. Haddow denied that his office had influenced the report (despite the presence of departmental assessors on the SC(DI) inquiry), but in June 1962, following a reorganization of offices, a development department was finally established, of which he became secretary. After a sustained campaign at official and ministerial level, the government's regional policy was altered in the following year and led to the creation of a fifth Scottish new town at Irvine, where a number of new light industries had been established.

Haddow became permanent under-secretary at the Scottish Office in 1965 and immediately established a regional development division (RDD) of senior officials directly responsible to his office. The group's aim was to maintain close contact with UK economic ministries in London to ensure that the Scottish interest in investment discussion was maintained more directly at official level. The period after 1965 witnessed considerable structural change in the Scottish economy with the run-down and closure of many collieries and Clydeside shipyards. Inevitably this increased unemployment, and Haddow's later career was overshadowed by repeated Scottish Office attempts to prevent closures. Such efforts masked much of the substantial work that Haddow's RDD pursued in attracting overseas investment to the new towns, which by the early 1970s totalled nearly a quarter of Scottish factory space. On his retirement from the civil service in 1973, he was made chairman of the North of Scotland Hydro-Electric Board, combining this with part-time membership of the South of Scotland Electricity Board, an innovative appointment designed to bring the work of the two boards into closer partnership. He was appointed KCB in 1966.

To colleagues, Haddow's approach to administration was distinguished by its energy and directness of style. His forthright manner and speed in reaching a decision often conflicted with civil service traditions, but in the context of the issues besetting post-war Scotland he helped convert a rather cautious office into one prepared to accept challenge, operate at a more strategic level, and take risks. At times this led to bitter argument, but where it affected a younger colleague Haddow usually apologized. Outside the office Haddow's main interest was in golf; his tendency to play in khaki shorts and eat a bowl of rice pudding afterwards was confirmation to many of his single-minded sense of purpose. He died in the Royal Infirmary, Edinburgh, on 26 December 1986 after a short illness.

IAN LEVITT

**Sources** *WW* • *The Times* (31 Dec 1986), 14 • *Glasgow Herald* (29 Dec 1986) • *The Scotsman* (29 Dec 1986) • *Glasgow Herald* (2 Sept 1964) • *The Scotsman* (2 Sept 1964) • I. Levitt, ed., *The Scottish office: depression and reconstruction, 1919–59*, Scottish History Society, 5th ser., 5 (1992) • I. Levitt, 'The origins of the Scottish development department, 1943–62', *Scottish Affairs*, 14 (winter 1996) • I. Levitt, 'Scottish papers submitted to the cabinet, 1917–45: a guide to records held at the Public Record Office and National Archives of Scotland', *Scottish Economic and Social History*, 19/1 (1999) • I. Levitt, 'Scottish air services, 1933–75, and the Scottish new towns, 1943–75: a guide to records at the National Archives of Scotland', *Scottish Archives*, 5 (1999) • I. Levitt, 'Scottish papers submitted to the cabinet, 1945–66: a guide to records held at the Public Record Office and National Archives of Scotland', *Scottish Economic and Social History*, 20/1 (2000) • '"Taking a gamble": the Scottish Office, Whitehall and the Highlands and Islands Development Board, 1965–1967', *Northern Scotland*, 20 (2000) • NA Scot., SOE, 2/34 • private information (2004) [retired Scottish office civil servants] • b. cert. • m. cert. • d. cert.
**Wealth at death** £168,700.12: confirmation, 1 June 1987, *CCI*

**Haden, Sir Francis Seymour** [*pseud.* H. Dean] (**1818–1910**), etcher and surgeon, was born at 62 Sloane Street, London, on 16 September 1818, the son of Charles Thomas Haden (1786–1824), a surgeon at Derbyshire General Infirmary. His mother, Emma, was the daughter of the singer Samuel Harrison, and was herself an excellent musician.

Haden received his general education at Derby School, Christ's Hospital, and University College, London, and continued his professional studies in the medical schools of the Sorbonne, Paris, and Grenoble, where he acted as *prosecteur* in 1839, and, later, lecturer on surgical anatomy at the military hospital. In 1842 he became a member, and in 1857 a fellow, of the Royal College of Surgeons. From 1851 to 1867 he was honorary surgeon to the Department of Science and Art. He had settled in private practice at 62 Sloane Street in 1847, but moved in 1878 to 38 Hertford Street, Mayfair. In addition to his large private practice, he undertook much public work in relation to surgical science, serving on the juries of the international exhibitions of 1851 and 1862, and contributing in this capacity in 1862 an exhaustive report on the operation of ovariotomy. He was consulting surgeon to the Chapel Royal, a vice-president of the Obstetrical Society of London, and one of the principal movers in the foundation of the Royal Hospital for Incurables in 1850. Throughout his life he maintained a vigorous campaign against cremation, advocating a natural 'earth to earth' burial, which he effected by his invention of a papier mâché coffin. He published several pamphlets on the subject: *The Disposal of the Dead*, *A Protest Against Cremation*, *Earth to Earth* (1875), and *Cremation an Incentive to Crime* (2nd edn, 1892). Among his fellow practitioners he was noted for an instinctive power of diagnosis, due largely to a disciplined sense of vision. While a student in Paris he attended art school in the evenings, believing in the importance of the use of drawing for training the hand and eye of the surgeon.

Haden sought relaxation from his professional work of surgeon, which he pursued until 1887, in the art and study of etching. It is for his etched work, although technically that of an amateur, and for his writing on etching that he is best known. Except for a few plates after Turner, and some family portraits after Wright of Derby, his work is entirely original. His etchings are primarily studies of landscape subjects. These works are characterized by their selective use of line and for their ability to convey the sense of a spontaneous sketch from nature. Most of Haden's 235 etchings and mezzotints were executed between 1858 and 1879, also the period of his greatest professional activity. He combined etching trips with his other hobby, angling.

Haden's earliest six plates were etched on a trip to Italy in 1843–4, but there was an interval of fourteen years before he took up etching again in 1857. By that time he had become friends with James Abbott McNeill Whistler, whose half-sister Deborah (Dasha) Delano Whistler (1825–1909) he married on 16 October 1847. The etchings of Whistler and Haden bear traces of a mutual influence which is visible in portraits by both of Lady Haden reading by lamplight, which were done on the same evening in 1858, the year in which Whistler published the thirteen prints of the 'French set'. There is evidence that the two men were working on a joint project to publish etchings of the Thames in 1863, but this was abandoned when they broke off their friendship after a quarrel in 1867.

One half of Haden's etchings were produced in the decade succeeding 1859, sixty-eight being done in the two years 1864–5 alone. He published a portfolio of etchings executed at this period entitled *Études à l'eau-forte* (1864–5), with text by Philippe Burty (taken from the latter's article on Haden in the *Gazette des Beaux-Arts*), published to critical and popular acclaim. Then in 1877, when he was staying at Newton Manor with Sir John Charles Robinson, and afterwards travelling with Robinson in Spain, Haden completed his record number of works for one year, etching thirty-nine plates. In 1879 he etched *The Breaking up of the Agamemnon*, one of his most important compositions and the sign of a move to larger scale exhibition etchings, produced at more infrequent intervals. From 1880 he worked more frequently in mezzotint. His last plate, a sketch of Woodcote Park, done on a pewter plate from the artist's bedroom window, is dated 1901.

Haden was one of the most important spokesmen for etching in nineteenth-century England. His contribution towards the professionalization of the art included the foundation in 1880 of the Society (later the Royal Society) of Painter-Etchers, whose president he remained until his death. The society did much to promote etching as an art through its annual exhibitions. Haden's public service was rewarded in 1894 by a knighthood, and his distinction recognized abroad by honorary membership of the Institut de France in 1905, the Académie des Beaux-Arts, and the Société des Artistes Français; however, it rankled that he was never recognized by the Royal Academy, despite his campaign under the auspices of the Society of Painter-Etchers to gain greater recognition for etchers in both its exhibitions and its membership. He was elected a member of the Athenaeum in 1891. Among the medals awarded him at various times for etching were grands prix at the international exhibitions at Paris in 1889 and 1900. He exhibited etchings in the Royal Academy from 1860 to 1885, using the pseudonym H. Dean in the exhibitions of 1860 to 1864. He also produced a large number of landscape drawings, and received a medal for some exhibited at the International Exhibition in Chicago in 1893. Haden's rhetoric of etching from nature expounded in his writing led to claims believed by many contemporaries that all his plates were executed in one sitting in front of the subject. However, Schneiderman has demonstrated that this was rarely the case, and preparatory studies for many of his etchings are known, and almost all his etchings exist in variant states. The chief collections of his etchings and drawings are in the British Museum, the Victoria and Albert Museum, the Avery collection in the New York Public Library, and the Allbright Art Gallery, Buffalo.

As a critic and writer on art, Haden will be chiefly remembered both as a pioneer of the scientific criticism of Rembrandt's etchings (of which he had a considerable collection) and as a leading writer on etching as an original art form. He was largely responsible for the Rembrandt exhibition at the Burlington Fine Arts Club in 1879, and his introductory remarks to the catalogue began the work of dividing Rembrandt's own work from that of his school. His publications on the essential qualities of etching as an art are arguably more important than his artistic work, and include 'About etching' (*Fine Arts Quarterly Review*, new ser., 1, 1866), *About Etching* (1879), *The Art of the Painter-Etcher* (1890), *The Art of the Painter-Etcher* (1891), 'Mr Seymour Haden on etching' (*Magazine of Art*, 2, 1878–9), and *The Relative Claims of Etching and Engraving to Rank as Fine Arts* (1883). His conception of etching as an art of 'learned omission' in which sparse linearity stood for intellectual thought is pioneering for its time and is both influenced by theories of the sketch in France and relates closely to the theories of the nineteenth-century art critic P. G.

**Sir Francis Seymour Haden** (1818–1910), self-portrait, 1862

Hamerton, who was closely associated with Haden. The writing of the two men reveals a reciprocal influence of ideas. Haden's article 'About etching' (1866) is a pioneering example of art theory in its consideration of the interaction of line and blank paper in the etching and its assignment of an active role in creating the meaning of an art work to the viewer. Haden was also responsible for promoting etching on the lecture circuit, lecturing at the Royal Institution in 1879 and the Society of Arts in 1883, and undertaking a lecture tour of America in 1882–3.

Frederick Keppel described Haden as a well-bred gentleman, but also a proud man who was intolerant of the opinions of others (Keppel, 292–3). After retiring from his London practice in 1887 Haden lived near Alresford, Hampshire, and from 1888 resided at Woodcote Manor, Bramdean, where he died on 1 June 1910, leaving one daughter and three sons. He was buried in Brookwood cemetery, Surrey. His eldest son, Francis Seymour CMG, had a distinguished career in the colonial service in South Africa. A. M. Hind, *rev.* E. Chambers

**Sources** *The Times* (2 June 1910) • R. Schneiderman, *The etchings of Sir Francis Seymour Haden* (1983) • H. N. Harrington, *The etchings of Francis Seymour Haden* (1910) • P. Burty, 'L'oeuvre de M. Francis Seymour Haden', *Gazette des Beaux-Arts*, 17 (1864), 271–87; 356–66 • P. G. Hamerton, 'Mr Seymour Haden's etchings', *Scribners Magazine*, 20 (1880), 586–601 • F. S. Haden, 'About etching', *Fine Arts Quarterly Review*, new ser., 1 (1866), 145–60 • F. S. Haden, 'Mr Seymour Haden on etching', *Magazine of Art*, 2 (1878–9), 188–91, 221–4, 262–4 • F. S. Haden, *The relative claims of etching and engraving to rank as fine arts* (1883) • E. Chambers, 'From chemical process to the aesthetics of omission: etching and the languages of art criticism in nineteenth-century Britain', *Art History*, 20 (1997), 556–74 • F. Keppel, 'The personal qualities of Sir Seymour Haden', *Print Collectors' Quarterly*, 1 (1911), 291–312, 421–42 • F. Newbolt, *The history of the Royal Society of Painter-Etchers and Engravers* (1931) • F. S. Haden, *About etching* (1879) • K. Lochnan, 'The Thames from its source to the sea: an unpublished portfolio by Whistler and Haden', *Studies in the History of Art*, 19 (1987), 29–45 • *CGPLA Eng. & Wales* (1910) • E. C. Beck, 'Sir Francis Seymour Haden', *Annals of Medical History*, new ser., 6 (1934), 475–82 • *The Lancet* (11 June 1910), 1653–5 • *BMJ* (11 June 1910), 1449–50

**Archives** Bankside Gallery, London, Society of Painter-Printmakers' archive, MSS • Bodl. Oxf., corresp. and papers • NYPL, corresp. | BL, letters to C. W. Sherborn, Add. MS 39581 • U. Glas., letters, with documents and artefacts relating to Whistler family

**Likenesses** J. A. M. Whistler, pen-and-ink drawing, *c*.1858–1859, Smithsonian Institution, Washington, DC, Freer Gallery of Art; related lithograph, BM, NPG • J. A. M. Whistler, group portrait, etching, 1859 (*The music room*), U. Glas., McCallum collection • C. W. Cope, chalk, 1860, NPG • F. S. Haden, self-portrait, etching, 1862, BM, NPG [*see illus.*] • L. Flameng, etching, 1875, BM • L. Lacretelle, etching, 1878 • C. W. Sherborn, etching, 1880, BM • A. Legros, mezzotint, 1881, BM • A. Legros, drawing, *c*.1883; formerly in possession of Messrs Keppel, New York • W. Strang, etching, 1883 • G. Robinson, mezzotint, 1887 • H. von Herkomer, two etchings, 1892 • G. P. Jacomb-Hood, oils, 1892, Royal Society of Painter-Etchers, London • W. Rothenstein, pencil drawing, *c*.1897, NPG • W. Rothenstein, print, 1897, BM, NPG • P. Thomas, etching, 1900 • F. Short, mezzotint, 1911 (after G. P. Jacomb-Hood) • G. P. Jacomb-Hood, oils, NPG

**Wealth at death** £32,138 6*s*. 11*d*.: probate, 17 Aug 1910, *CGPLA Eng. & Wales*

**Hadenham, Edmund of** (*supp. fl.* 1307), supposed annalist, is supposed to have written a series of annals about the church of Rochester. He is named as their author by the sixteenth-century Kentish topographer William Lambard (*d.* 1601) in BL, Cotton MS Vespasian A.v, folio 54*r*: 'Ex chronico quodam claustri Roffensi cuius author erat Edmundus de Hadenham qui usque ad finem Edwardi primi hystoriam deduxit'. No other evidence survives for Hadenham's authorship, or, indeed, existence. This manuscript is Lambard's extracts from the annals, which also survive in interpolations in BL, Cotton MS Nero D.ii, although Lambard was probably working from a different copy. The interpolations relate to the period down to 1307, and are followed on folios 203–14 by a brief history of England between then and 1377 in another hand, unrelated to Rochester. Cotton MS Nero D.ii is a version of the *Flores historiarum*, the Rochester material from which has been published by Wharton in *Anglia sacra* (1691) and by H. R. Luard in his edition of *Flores historiarum* (1890). However, J. C. Russell argued in 1936 that John of Renham, prior of Rochester (1262–83 and 1291–4), was the author of part of these annals, basing his argument on the prominence given to the activities and attitude of the prior. M. C. Buck

**Sources** BL, Cotton MS Nero D.ii • BL, Cotton MS Vespasian A.v • [H. Wharton], ed., *Anglia sacra*, 1 (1691), 341–55 • J. C. Russell, 'Dictionary of writers of thirteenth century England', *BIHR*, special suppl., 3 (1936) [whole issue], esp. 27, 72 • H. R. Luard, ed., *Flores historiarum*, 3 vols., Rolls Series, 95 (1890)

**Hadfield, Charles** (1821–1884), journalist, the son of Charles and Anne Hadfield, was born at Glossop, Derbyshire, on 14 October 1821. He was taken to Manchester when only one year old, and was brought up to the trade of a house-painter and decorator. On 24 December 1843 he married Emily Frances, daughter of John Pontey and Mary Ann Kemp.

Educated at the Old Mechanics' Institution in Cooper Street, Hadfield wrote two prize essays, one in 1850, entitled 'The best means of enlarging the usefulness of Mechanics' Institutions' (for which he won money and a silver medal), and the other in 1857, entitled 'Suggestions for improving the homes of the working classes'. He also wrote verses in the *Manchester Times*, and soon turned to journalism. In 1861 he edited a monthly paper in association with trade unions, called *Weekly Wages*, which only ran to five issues. In the same year he accepted an offer from Joseph Cowen MP, to join the staff of the *Newcastle Chronicle* and to act as a lecturer for the Northern Reform Union. On his return to Manchester in January 1862, he became connected with the commercial department of the *Manchester Examiner and Times*. Subsequently he was employed to write for the *Manchester City News*, and he edited that paper from 1865 to 1867, remaining a contributor for two or three years longer. On retiring from the editorship of the *Manchester City News* Hadfield became literary secretary to the mayor of Manchester. Hadfield next moved to Glasgow, where for a short time he was on the staff of the *Glasgow Herald*, and then between 1870 and 1871 took the editorship and management of the *Warrington Examiner* and other papers connected with it, including the *Mid-Cheshire Examiner*. After several years in this position he was presented with a testimonial.

In 1880 Hadfield became editor of the *Salford Weekly News*, in which position he remained to the beginning of 1883. As a journalist his strength lay in his knowledge of, and sympathy with, working-class lives. He contributed from December 1867 to July 1868 to the *Free Lance* (which he helped to launch along with five others, including J. H. Nodal, then editor of the *Manchester City News*), and from July 1868 to October 1871 to *The Sphinx*, two Manchester literary, artistic, and humorous journals. He was a campaigner for the Manchester Fine Art Gallery, and played a part in movements to secure the Saturday half-holiday and to provide public baths and washhouses. After his retirement Hadfield became an invalid, and he died at 3 Chester Road, Stretford, Manchester, on 4 June 1884.

G. C. Boase, *rev.* Joanne Potier

**Sources** *Manchester Guardian* (9 June 1884), 5 • Boase, *Mod. Eng. biog.* • *Momus* (8 Dec 1881), 114 • *Manchester City News* (7 June 1884) • *Manchester City News* (14 June 1884) • D. Griffiths, ed., *The encyclopedia of the British press, 1422–1992* (1992) • C. W. Sutton, *A list of Lancashire authors* (1876), 47

**Likenesses** drawing, 1881 (after W. Percy), repro. in *Momus*

**Hadfield, George** (1763–1826), architect, was born in Florence on 15 September 1763, one of the five children of Charles Hadfield (*d.* 1776) and his wife, Isabella, *née* Pocock (*d.* 1809), who owned and managed three hotels in and around the city, establishments that offered English style comfort to grand tourists for thirty years from the mid-1740s. George Hadfield's eldest sister, Maria *Cosway, and his older brother William were both painters. After Charles Hadfield's death the family returned to London in 1779.

Hadfield entered the Royal Academy Schools in 1781 and gained the gold medal in 1784, the year in which he entered James Wyatt's office. During a visit to Paris in 1789 he met Thomas Jefferson, the friend of his sister Maria (now the wife of Richard Cosway). In 1790 he won the three-year Royal Academy travelling scholarship, vouched for by the flower painter Mary Moser, one of only two women members of the Royal Academy, and returned to Italy, accompanying his sister and going on to Rome. His drawings of the temple of Fortune at Palestrina were much remarked on, and he worked as an architect in Rome and is known to have designed two chimney-pieces for the prince of Wales (but bought by his brother the duke of Sussex). Hadfield became a leading member of the expatriate artist community in Rome, helped by the fact that Italian was his first language. He was back in London by 1794 and exhibited examples of his work at the Royal Academy in 1795. His promising return was marred by a blackball, which barred his election to the Architects' Club. At this time he received, through the recommendation of the American painter John Trumbull, an invitation to superintend the building of the Capitol at Washington, DC.

Hadfield arrived in America in 1795, the year before his fellow architect Benjamin Henry Latrobe, to find himself embroiled in a peculiarly ill-starred project. It was the inexperienced Hadfield's thankless task to work in the midst of continual political and contractual scheming; he also became the victim of the unprofessional conduct of the commissioners. Even George Washington sided against him. In 1798 he was dismissed from his post, without payment for his designs, including those for the executive and treasury offices, which were built only to be badly fire damaged when the British attacked in 1814. Hadfield's bold design displayed little ornament beyond an Ionic portico, still novel in America. Despite this setback, he remained in Washington and gradually built up a practice, while also inventing a brick- and tile-making machine, which he patented in 1800. Having become a naturalized American in 1802—the first such citizen of Washington, DC—he stood for the city council and was elected in 1803, a supporter of Jefferson.

Hadfield received a steady trickle of government jobs, including the city gaol and arsenal, and worked for several leading figures in the new city. In 1802 he designed Arlington House (now overlooking Arlington cemetery) for George Washington Parke Custis, and it is the heavy Greek revival portico, with its unfluted Doric columns, added some years later, that is his best-known surviving work. Latrobe described Hadfield in 1806 as 'ruined in fortune in temper and reputation', prevented from using 'his elegant talent' (*Journals*, 72) to best effect. However he later designed mansions for John Van Ness, mayor of Washington, and Commodore David Porter. On Latrobe's death in 1820, Hadfield found himself admirably placed for the pick of official jobs and that year he began his major work, Washington city hall (now the district of Columbia court house), again employing a stern Greek revival vocabulary. Just before his own death he designed John Van Ness's mausoleum, on the model of the temple of Vesta in Rome, which was later moved to Oak Hill cemetery in Georgetown, DC. Trumbull blamed himself for Hadfield's disappointing career, 'causing the ruin of this most admirable artist and excellent friend'. Had he not induced him to leave London, his connection with the prince regent 'might have procured him the execution of the extensive and splendid works which were committed to Mr. Nash' (*Autobiography of Colonel John Trumbull*, ed. T. Sizer, 1953, 177–8). Hadfield died, unmarried, on 5 February 1826, and was buried in the congressional cemetery, Washington, DC.

Gillian Darley

**Sources** G. L. M. Goodfellow, 'George Hadfield', *ArchR*, 138 (1965), 35–6 • *DAB* • J. Ingamells, ed., *A dictionary of British and Irish travellers in Italy, 1701–1800* (1997) • Colvin, *Archs.* • *The journals of Benjamin Henry Latrobe*, ed. E. C. Carter II, J. C. Van Horne, and L. W. Formwalt, 3 (1980) • R. G. Kennedy, *Architecture: men, women and money (1600–1860)* (1985), 214–21 [many inaccuracies]

**Hadfield, George** (1787–1879), politician, the son of Robert Hadfield, manufacturer, and his wife, Anne, daughter of W. Bennett, was born at Sheffield on 28 December 1787. He served his articles with John Sherwood of Sheffield, and was admitted an attorney in January 1810. In 1814 he married Lydia, daughter of Samuel Pope, of Cheapside, London. For forty-two years he practised in Manchester, in partnership first with James Knight, next with James Grove, and lastly with his son George Hadfield, jun.

Hadfield's prime importance is as a church reformer. An Independent dissenter, he demanded the complete separation of church and state. He was active in the Manchester vestry during 1833–4 in opposing the levying of a church rate. He first came to prominence as the author of *The Manchester Socinian Controversy* (1825) and used his legal knowledge to attack the possession by Unitarians of property originally intended for use by orthodox dissenters. He was active in the legal proceedings begun in 1830 by Independents in Manchester to prove that Lady Hewley's endowment should be applied to the benefit of Trinitarian dissenters, and finally secured a decision in their favour in 1842. The dispute was settled by the Dissenters' Chapels Act of 1844. A letter from him published in the *Baptist Magazine* in 1833 (see N. Gash, *Reaction and Reconstruction in English Politics*, 1965, 67n.) marked him out as one of the more radical dissenters.

Hadfield contested Bradford as a Liberal on 12 January 1835, and was defeated by John Hardy, but he continued his political interests in the 1830s and 1840s through close involvement with the Anti-Corn Law League in Manchester. After retiring from legal practice, he was elected an MP for Sheffield in July 1852, and retained the seat until January 1874. In parliament he was a radical Liberal and spoke frequently in support of measures towards economic, legal, and religious reform. He introduced the act relating to the registration of judgments, gave great help in passing the Common Law Procedure Act of 1854, and was the author of the Qualification for Offices Abolition Act of 1866, which removed religious tests for crown and municipal posts.

Hadfield was a prominent member of the Congregational church. In 1864 he offered £1000 a year for five years on condition that during that time fifty Independent chapels should be built. He afterwards repeated the offer with the same success. In association with Dr Thomas Raffles and William Roley he established the Lancashire Independent college, first at Blackburn and then at Whalley Range, where in 1840 he laid the foundation-stone of the new building and gave £2000 towards the cost of the erection. Hadfield died at his residence in Conyngham Road, Victoria Park, Rusholme, Manchester, on 21 April 1879.

G. C. Boase, *rev.* Matthew Lee

**Sources** J. B. Ridley, 'Hadfield, George', *BDMBR*, vol. 2 · M. Taylor, *The decline of British radicalism, 1847–1860* (1995) · B. L. Manning, *The protestant dissenting deputies* (1952) · *The Times* (22 April 1879) · *Leeds Mercury* (22 April 1879) · *Solicitors' Journal*, 23 (1878–9), 503 · *Law Times* (17 May 1879) · D. Fraser, *Urban politics in Victorian England* (1976) · *CGPLA Eng. & Wales* (1879)
**Archives** Sheff. Arch., journal | BL, letters to W. E. Gladstone
**Wealth at death** under £250,000: probate, 18 June 1879, *CGPLA Eng. & Wales*

**Hadfield, James** (1771/2–1841), assailant of George III, is of unknown parentage. Critically wounded at the battle of Roubaix in 1794, he sustained eight sabre wounds to his head before being captured by the French. After making his way back to England, he fell under the sway of a millenarian cult, becoming convinced that his death at the hands of the state would effect the second coming. Hadfield apparently reasoned that treason—or even attempted treason—would carry mortal punishment, and thus conspired with Bannister Truelock to assassinate George III at Drury Lane Theatre on the evening of 15 May 1800. As the king acknowledged the orchestra's playing of the national anthem, and the audience rose to its feet to welcome him, Hadfield climbed on a seat and fired a horse pistol at the royal box. The assailant's actual intention remains a mystery because when the king, unhurt, insisted on speaking to the soi-disant assassin, Hadfield greeted him by saying, 'God bless your royal highness; I like you very well; you are a good fellow' (Quen, 1221).

Despite such patriotic sentiment Hadfield was placed on trial for high treason, which although doubtless a dire prospect none the less entitled him to certain privileges not accorded the ordinary felon. Chief among these was the right to be represented by counsel, in this case perhaps the most brilliant attorney of his day, Thomas Erskine, the later lord chancellor. Erskine's task was extremely difficult since the common law required a complete derangement for an insanity acquittal: 'lost to all sense … incapable of forming a judgement upon the consequences of the act which he is about to do' (Moran, 499). Hadfield's ability to secure a firearm, place himself at the theatre in such a position to secure the best possible aim, and name the king as his intended target appeared to speak against any appearance of complete madness. Erskine wisely chose to confront directly the traditional criterion of total deprivation of memory and understanding. Could such a person even be capable of committing an act, criminal or otherwise? In place of a total derangement, Erskine asserted that delusion 'unaccompanied by frenzy or raving madness [was] the true character of insanity' (Eigen, 49). Hadfield's particular delusion, according to the attorney, stemmed unambiguously from his millenarian beliefs, even to the point of requiring death by the state. This characterization was reinforced by two surgeons and a physician who supplied a physical basis for the insanity—brain damage due to war wounds—and a mental consequence: Hadfield's belief that he was ordained to die in a manner that paralleled Christ's execution.

Following this unequivocal testimony, Lord Chief Justice Kenyon halted the trial, announcing to the court that the case 'was clearly an acquittal' and that 'the prisoner, for his own sake, and for the sake of society at large, must not be discharged' (Walker, 78). The significance of Hadfield's acquittal in the evolving jurisprudence of criminal intent remains in question because there is no way of knowing whether the court found most persuasive Erskine's deft application of the defendant's delusory ideas to the attempted regicide, or the plain evidence of head trauma manifest in the still detectable sabre wounds to Hadfield's scalp. Nevertheless, Erskine succeeded in introducing the first form of partial insanity into the English criminal trial, challenging the notion that total derangement alone merited an acquittal. The verdict also had a lasting effect on the treatment of future insanity defendants. Prior to this case, defendants acquitted on the grounds of mental derangement were simply released to their families, their parish, or, most often, to no one in particular. Following the Hadfield verdict, parliament hastily passed the Criminal Lunatics Act of 1800, mandating that defendants acquitted on the grounds of insanity must be kept in strict custody until 'His Majesty's pleasure be known'. After Hadfield, the special verdict 'not guilty by reason of insanity' carried automatic and indefinite commitment to some sort of institution: one could be acquitted of a crime and still face life confinement, as Hadfield's experience vividly demonstrates.

Following his acquittal Hadfield remained locked in a cell for most of the remaining forty-one years of his life, an incarceration interrupted only for a short time when he escaped from Bethlem Hospital to be captured in Dover as he was about to flee to France. Subsequently taken to Newgate prison, Hadfield was finally transferred to the newly opened criminal department at Bethlem, where he averred 'the loss of liberty was worse than death' (Moran, 516). He died there of tuberculosis on 23 January 1841 aged sixty-nine.

Although Hadfield's acquittal did not result in a courtroom precedent to rival the 1843 McNaughtan rules, the introduction of delusion into courtroom testimony has had far-reaching, although perhaps not immediately obvious, effects. Erskine's invitation to the jury to broaden its conception of insanity to consider not just the beastly histrionics of raving mania, but the quietly methodical consequence of impelling ideas, blurred the lines separating total from partial insanity. Hadfield saw the world through a lens so profoundly distorted by a ruling delusion that even the act of regicide was not a moral wrong. Indeed, it was a moral duty. In consequence, jurors over the past two centuries have faced the dilemma of assigning criminality to an act that to any sane person would seem an unambiguous legal wrong, but which to the profoundly deluded represented no moral wrongdoing at all.

JOEL PETER EIGEN

**Sources** N. Walker, *Crime and insanity in England*, 1 (1968) • R. Moran, 'The origin of insanity as a special verdict: the trial for treason of James Hadfield, 1800', *Law and Society Review*, 19 (1985), 487–519 • J. P. Eigen, *Witnessing insanity: madness and mad-doctors in the English court* (1995) • J. M. Quen, 'James Hadfield and medical jurisprudence of insanity', *New York State Journal of Medicine*, 69 (1969), 1221–6

**Hadfield, Maria Louisa Catherine Cecilia**. *See* Cosway, Baroness Maria Louisa Catherine Cecilia (1760–1838).

**Hadfield, Matthew Ellison** (1812–1885), architect, was born on 8 September 1812 at Lees Hall, Glossop, Derbyshire, the eldest son of Joseph Hadfield and his wife, Mary, a sister of Michael Ellison, agent to the duke of Norfolk. He was educated at Woolton Grove Academy, Liverpool, and from 1827 to 1831 worked with his uncle Ellison at Sheffield in the Norfolk estate office. In October 1831 he was articled to Messrs Woodhead and Hurst of Doncaster, and after three years went to London as pupil of P. F. Robinson. He married Sarah, daughter of William Frith of Angel Street, Sheffield.

After setting up practice in Sheffield in 1834, Hadfield was in partnership first (1838–58) with J. G. Weightman and was then joined (1850–60) by their pupil George Goldie and later (in 1864) by his own son Charles (1840–1916). Hadfield was a successful church architect and an early Catholic imitator of Pugin, who published the design of Hadfield's St Bede's, Rotherham, in his *The Present State of Ecclesiastical Architecture in England* (1843). However, he was a far less assured designer, and fell back in the composition of his largest church, St John's Roman Catholic Cathedral, Salford (1844–8), on the reproduction of existing medieval models. His earliest churches were neo-classical, such as the Tuscan-style All Saints' Roman Catholic Church, Glossop (1836–8), and he exhibited all the stylistic changes of the Gothic revival, following Pugin's Decorated at St Marie's, Sheffield (1847–50)—said by his son Charles to be his favourite church—and the 'Early French' style at St Hilda's, Whitby (1865–7), while St Joseph's, Wath-on-Dearne, Sheffield (1879), returns to the English Decorated style, first suggested by him in 1870 for an unexecuted church at Lincoln. He designed stations for the new railways, such as the Italianate-style station at Glossop (1847) and the neo-classical Wicker Arches Bridge at Sheffield (1848). His private work for successive dukes of Norfolk, Glossop Hall (1851–2) and The Farm, Sheffield (*c*.1858), does not survive; his work at Arundel Castle, Sussex, for the fourteenth duke was replaced from 1890 by C. A. Buckler. A devout Roman Catholic, Hadfield was prominent in Sheffield philanthropy and politics as Liberal town councillor; he was president of the school of art (1878–80).

Hadfield died on 9 March 1885 at Knowle House, Sheffield, survived by his wife, one son, and three daughters. He was buried in St Michael's Roman Catholic cemetery, Rivelin Glen, Sheffield. Some illustrations of his architectural work are reproduced in *The Builder* (11 April 1885).

RODERICK O'DONNELL

**Sources** Sheffield Central Library, Hadfield MSS • Sheffield Central Library, Caukwell MSS • Sheffield Central Library, Davidson MSS • *150 years of architectural drawings: Hadfield, Caukwell, Davidson: Sheffield, 1834–1984* (1984) • S. Welsh, 'Biographical notes and list of principal works', RIBA BAL [also Sheffield Central Library] • C. Hadfield, *A history of St Marie's Mission and Church, Norfolk Row, Sheffield* (1889) • *DNB* • P. Howell, ed., 'Letters from J. F. Bentley to Charles Hadfield [2 pts]', *Architectural History*, 23 (1980), 95–137; 25 (1982), 65–97 • *IGI* • *CGPLA Eng. & Wales* (1885)

**Archives** Birm. CL, Hardman & Co. archive, letters • priv. coll., diary • Sheffield Central Library, Hadfield MSS | Arundel Castle, West Sussex, letters to fourteenth duke of Norfolk • RIBA, corresp. with Pugin • Sheffield Central Library, Caukwell MSS; Davidson MSS

**Wealth at death** £4689 11*s*. 8*d*.: probate, 30 May 1885, *CGPLA Eng. & Wales*

**Hadfield, Sir Robert Abbott, baronet** (1858–1940), metallurgist and steel maker, was born in the Vestry Hall, Hilltop, Attercliffe, near Sheffield, on 28 November 1858. He was the only son of Robert Hadfield (1832–1888) and his wife, Marianne Abbott, the daughter of an Oxfordshire shire-horse breeder. The Hadfields were an old Derbyshire family and relatives included Sir John Brown, the steel maker, and George Hadfield, the Sheffield MP and master cutler. The elder Robert Hadfield was a rate collector when his son was born, but in 1872 he entered the steel trade by establishing the Hecla works in Attercliffe. With the help of his foundry manager, John Mallaband, Hadfield concentrated on the production of steel castings, then still a novelty in England. Large hydraulic cylinders and steel projectiles, until then only made in France, were among the products, and the foundations of a great armament industry were laid.

Hadfield was educated at Sheffield collegiate school, but declined the chance to go up to Cambridge or Oxford. Intent on joining the family firm, he interested himself in chemistry and metallurgy, receiving some instruction from a local analyst, A. H. Allen. He also began experimenting with steel at the Hecla works, even continuing his trials in a furnace at home. The stage was set in 1882 for Hadfield's discovery of manganese steel, the revolutionary nature of which has long been recognized. This alloy (the first commercial austenitic steel), containing about 1 per cent carbon and 12½ per cent manganese, is essentially soft and non-magnetic: but any attempt to cut or deform the surface makes the alloy intensely hard. Encouraged by this success, Hadfield launched a wide-ranging research programme, in which he rang the changes on hundreds of alloy steel combinations. His work was always patient and systematic; and he often collaborated with physicists interested in the properties of metals. In 1886 he patented another major alloy steel—a low-carbon silicon–iron type—later known simply as silicon steel. William Barrett was to research its unique electrical properties.

Meanwhile, Hadfield took over the growing family business as his father's health failed. In 1888—the year the elder Robert Hadfield died—Hadfields Steel Foundry Company became a limited company with £90,750 in issued capital and nearly 500 workers. Hadfield became both chairman and managing director and he was to exercise absolute control over the company until his death. His dominance stemmed from a large personal shareholding, his control of the board, his autocratic personality, and his phenomenal energy. He regularly worked a sixteen-hour day and was described as the 'hardest working man under the sun' (*The Engineer*, 235). Helped by a loyal board, which included John Mallaband and a string of able metallurgists, Hadfield soon made a commercial success of his discoveries by pioneering the production of manganese and silicon steels. Manganese steel was found to have a wide application in crushing and grinding machinery, in tramway and railway crossings, and wherever resistance to abrasion was required. Silicon steel proved to have exceptionally low magnetic hysteresis, which was found ideal in the production of transformers. Research into the production of sound steel ingots and corrosion resistance also engaged Hadfield and his steadily expanding works laboratory.

Hadfield continued his father's involvement with the armaments industry. Indeed, it was one of his main interests, especially the design and alloy composition of shells. In the arms race before the First World War, Hadfields became the leading British maker of armour-piercing projectiles. Hadfield also incorporated manganese steel and other alloys into cast steel armour-plate for gun shields. As both arms orders and commercial business boomed, Hadfields grew rapidly in the late nineteenth century. In 1897 commercial work was transferred to a major new factory, the East Hecla works, at Tinsley, near Sheffield. Before 1914 (when it was renamed Hadfields Ltd), the firm was the fastest growing steelmaker in Sheffield, reaching its zenith in the First World War. Hadfields by 1918 was the largest employer in the city, with a workforce of over 13,000, its issued capital now £1.9 million.

Hadfield had become one of Sheffield's most prominent steel makers, with a string of public honours (the presidency of the Iron and Steel Institute in 1905, a knighthood in 1908, election as fellow of the Royal Society in 1909, and a baronetcy in 1917). Of slim build and medium height, invariably formally dressed with high starched collar, Hadfield's demeanour was austere. He had a pronounced streak of snobbery and vanity, with a deep-seated craving for honours and recognition. On the other hand, he was an enlightened employer (pioneering the eight-hour working day in 1891), a staunch Liberal, and a generous supporter of scientific research. He also gave away a small fortune (£100,000) to fund the charitable wartime hospital work of his wife, Frances Belt Wickersham (*d.* 1949). She was a well-connected American, whom he had married on 19 September 1894 in Philadelphia.

The Hadfields (who had no children) split their time between their Sheffield country home, Parkhead House, the south of France, and London, where Hadfield was able to chase government ministries for orders and indulge in one of his favourite pastimes—mingling with fellow scientists and businessmen at the technical societies. For many years he rarely missed a council meeting of the Iron and Steel Institute. He had an international standing as a metallurgist, particularly in America which he visited regularly before 1914. He also maintained particularly close connections with his French colleagues. His hospitality contributed much to the success of international scientific meetings held in the UK, especially during his presidency of the Faraday Society from 1914 to 1920. A pioneer of research and development in his own city's industry, he was deeply committed to the furtherance of industrial research world-wide.

The 1920s and 1930s, however, saw the end of his almost unbroken success. Arms orders virtually vanished after 1918, leaving Hadfields' production profile seriously distorted; the firm's technical lead weakened once Hadfield's major alloy patents expired; and the demand for castings began to stagnate in the face of the rapid growth of the newer stainless and heat-resisting steels. In 1921 Hadfield also had a serious operation (probably for a fistula). He recovered, but he and his long-serving fellow directors (who were also ageing like their chairman), never quite recaptured their pre-war momentum.

Under Sir Robert's direction, the firm attempted to diversify in the 1920s by running an automobile factory in the Black Country (Bean Cars) and by opening an American steel castings subsidiary in Ohio. Both ventures proved disastrous. Hadfields was more successful in its traditional lines in steel castings and alloys, but it was only the next upswing in the arms cycle in the late 1930s that rescued the company from the doldrums. Hadfield continued his metallurgical researches in the inter-war period and still lectured and published prolifically. But no more revolutionary alloys resulted and though he published two major monographs on the development of alloy steels and their history—*Metallurgy and its Influence on Modern Progress* (1925) and *Faraday and his Metallurgical Researches* (1931)—they were penned by a man looking to the past rather than the future. Those who knew him at this time found that 'his chief interest appeared to be his abiding fame (already assured by his achievements)' (Headlam-Morley, 12). Like many powerful businessmen—the tool steelmaker Arthur Balfour, Lord Riverdale, is another example—Hadfield continued working far too long and neglected to make any arrangements for a successor.

In late 1937 Hadfield had a complete mental and physical breakdown and he died on 30 September 1940, aged eighty-one, virtually alone at his home, Kenry House, Kingston Hill, in Surrey. He was survived by his wife and left £420,690, with many bequests to scientific and technical institutions. He was buried at Brookwood cemetery in Surrey. C. H. DESCH, *rev.* GEOFFREY TWEEDALE

**Sources** G. Tweedale, *Giants of Sheffield steel* (1986) • G. Tweedale, 'The metallurgist as entrepeneur: the career of Sir Robert Hadfield', *Historical Metallurgy*, 26 (1992) • G. Tweedale, *Steel city: entrepreneurship, strategy, and technology in Sheffield, 1743–1993* (1995) • G. Tweedale, 'Sir Robert Hadfield, FRS (1858–1940), and the discovery of manganese steel', *Notes and Records of the Royal Society*, 40 (1985–6), 63–74 • C. H. Desch, *Obits. FRS*, 3 (1939–41), 647–64 • S. A. Main, 'The Hadfields of Sheffield', *Bulletin of the Institute of Metallurgists*, 8 (Dec 1950) • S. A. Main, 'The contributions of Sir Robert Hadfield to metallurgical science and technology', *The Sorby centennial symposium on the history of metallurgy*, ed. C. S. Smith (1965) • *The Engineer* (11 Oct 1940) • K. Headlam-Morley, *British Steelmaker*, 6 (Nov 1940) • b. cert. • m. cert.

**Archives** Kelham Island Industrial Museum, Sheffield, ephemera, photographs, artefacts • NRA, priv. coll. • RS, papers • Sci. Mus., specimens of his work • Sheff. Arch., corresp. and papers | California Institute of Technology, corresp. with G. E. Hale

**Likenesses** F. May, sketch, 1934, NPG • F. May, gouache drawing, 1935, NPG • F. J. Halnon, bronze bust, Cutlers' Hall, Sheffield • photographs, Sheff. Arch. • portrait, Sheff. Arch.

**Wealth at death** £420,690 2s. 3d.: probate, 12 Feb 1941, *CGPLA Eng. & Wales*

**Hadfield, William** (1806–1887), writer and businessman, is a figure about whose early life nothing is known. During his youth he travelled extensively in Brazil, the River Plate republics, and the islands of the south Atlantic, including the Falklands, where, at an early age, he developed modest commercial activities.

Declared bankrupt on 6 November 1847, due to an execution levied on his goods, Hadfield subsequently devoted most of his time to writing, and the dissemination of commercial information about South America; activities which did much to popularize Latin America with British investors. He was first secretary of the Buenos Ayres Great Southern Railway Company Ltd (1863–7), soon to become the premier British-owned Argentinian line, and a promoter of the South American General Steam Navigation Company.

Hadfield resided in Brazil for several years, later moving to Argentina. While in Brazil, in addition to his association with the railway company, he attempted to establish steamer services on the Paraná, as well as to make links with neighbouring countries, and Europe. He set up the first steamship agency in Buenos Aires when he arrived there in 1852. Later, when the province of Buenos Aires temporarily broke away from the Argentine confederation, he developed contacts with General José de Urquiza, sometime president of the confederation, who was anxious to promote foreign investment in the region.

Hadfield's principal books about South America were *Brazil, the River Plate, and the Falkland Islands, with the Cape Horn Route to Australia* (1854), later revised as *Brazil and the River Plate in 1868, showing the Progress since … his Former Visit in 1853* (1869), and *Brazil and the River Plate, 1870–76* (1877). However, his main literary and commercial endeavours were associated with the *Brazil and River Plate Mail*, subsequently re-titled the *South American Journal*, which he founded in London in 1863 (first issue 7 November), and edited until his death in 1887. This journal published commercial and financial information about the continent, devoting considerable attention to Latin American economic and political affairs, aimed at British investors in Latin American public bonds and British-registered enterprises operating in the region. During its heyday, from the 1890s to the 1920s, the magazine was arguably the most influential publication in the field. In common with similar periodicals, it was frequently accused of being too closely associated with company promoters and financial representatives of Latin American governments to provide unbiased information. Certainly, Hadfield's enthusiasm for South America coloured his commercial judgement, which was often far from dispassionate and disinterested. He died at Ferndale, East Dulwich Grove, Camberwell, London, on 14 August 1887, and was buried at St Peter's, Walthamstow, alongside his wife (about whom nothing is known). COLIN M. LEWIS

**Sources** *Bradshaw's Railway Manual, Shareholders' Guide and Directory* (1863–7) • W. Hadfield, *Brazil, the River Plate and the Falkland Islands* (1854) • W. Hadfield, *Brazil and the River Plate in 1868, showing the progress since … his former visit in 1853* (1869) • *DNB* • V. O. Cutolo, *Nuevo diccionario biografico Argentino* (1971) • Boase, *Mod. Eng. biog.* • d. cert.

**Hadland, Selina** (1838–1919), headmistress, was born on 18 February 1838 at 34 Holborn Hill, London, the daughter of Henry Hadland, a cheesemonger and one-time keeper of the Guildhall, and his wife, Sarah Ann Hadland *née* Matthews. Little is known of her early life and education. In her twenties she taught in private schools in London, moving to Malvernbury, Great Malvern, in 1871, to a school whose headmistress, Miss Cooper, she much admired.

In 1873 Selina Hadland applied for the position of lady principal of the new Milton Mount College, at Milton, Gravesend, Kent, which was being established for the education of the daughters of Congregational ministers, under the leadership of the Revd William Guest (1818–1891) and a committee of management of leading Congregationalists. The term 'college' was used because the new institution was intended for the training of teachers as well as for the education of schoolgirls. Her application was supported by both Newman Hall and C. H. Spurgeon, and she was selected by the governors from fifty-eight candidates. At the opening of the college in May 1873 many of the pioneers of women's education were present, and Emily Davies was among the speakers.

During the following sixteen years as principal Selina Hadland proved herself a pioneer of courage, ability, vigour, foresight, and religious faith. Her courage was shown in her struggle with some of the governors for appropriate authority within the school, at a time when many regarded women as incapable of public management. In these struggles she was well supported by her friends Dorothea Beale and Frances Mary Buss, and by others who were facing the same problems. Her administrative ability was amply demonstrated, not only in her running of the school, but as one of the first nine members of the Association of Headmistresses (of which she was the second vice-president, elected in 1880) and as one of the founders, and first honorary secretary, of the Teachers' Guild. In 1875 the annual conference of the Association of Headmistresses was held at Milton Mount.

By the time Selina Hadland resigned from Milton Mount in 1889, and largely due to her initiative, there was attached to the college not only a training section for teachers but also a high school—the first technical school for girls in England—where the trainee teachers were given practical experience. The school itself had grown, and a new wing had been built to accommodate more pupils. Milton Mount was one of the first girls' schools to have a gymnasium, to gain recognition as a school of art, and to require practical work in every scientific subject. The academic standards had steadily improved, due in part to the many well-qualified teachers who travelled down regularly from London, and almost from the beginning the girls were prepared for the Cambridge local examinations.

Selina Hadland's foresight was demonstrated in her concern for employment and public roles for women of all classes, with a particular emphasis on technical education. She wrote on *Occupations of Women other than Teaching* (1891) and *Technical Education for Girls and Women* (1891). She believed that women should be able to earn their own livelihoods if necessary, and, though reserved about women's suffrage, favoured their participation in local government.

After her resignation, Selina Hadland moved with her sister, Ellen (who had helped her with domestic arrangements at Milton Mount), first to Hampton Hill, Middlesex, then in 1898 to St Leonards, in Sussex. Their home was a centre of generous hospitality for old pupils and others. An inheritance from their father enabled Selina Hadland to offer public service in a variety of fields for another twenty years. In 1893 she and her sister visited the United States and Canada in order to study schools, colleges, and technical institutions, particularly those which had their origin in Congregational traditions, and she subsequently published *Education and Life in the United States* (1895). She served as one of the first governors of the new Battersea Polytechnic, on the committee of the Canning Town Women's Settlement (of which she was one of the founders), as a member of the Kingston board of guardians, and as a manager of a primary school. She was also active in Free Church Sunday schools and on the local Free Church Council. During all this time, she kept in touch with her former pupils, often gathering holiday parties in Switzerland, and paying herself for those unable to afford the cost.

Selina Hadland died on 17 November 1919 at her home, Miltolino, 2 Combermere Road, St Leonards; and her funeral, attended by a large congregation, was held at Christ Church, Westminster Bridge Road, London, four days later, followed by burial in Nunhead cemetery.

ELAINE KAYE

**Sources** *Miltonian News Sheet* (Feb 1920) • S. Hadland, *Annals of Milton Mount College* (c.1915) • minutes of the Committee of Management, Milton Mount College, DWL • annual reports, Milton Mount College, DWL • H. Harwood, *The history of Milton Mount College* (1959) • A. E. Ridley, *Frances Mary Buss and her work for education* (1896) • *Milton Mount Magazine*, 8–14 (1882–8) • *Christian World* (27 Nov 1919), 6 • *Times Educational Supplement* (4 Dec 1919) • b. cert. • d. cert. • *CGPLA Eng. & Wales* (1919)

**Archives** DWL, minutes of the management committee of Milton Mount College; annual reports of Milton Mount College • W. Sussex RO, records of Milton Mount

**Likenesses** photograph, repro. in Harwood, *History of Milton Mount College*, frontispiece

**Wealth at death** £2717 2s. 5d.: probate, 29 Dec 1919, *CGPLA Eng. & Wales*

**Hadley, George** (1685–1768), natural philosopher, was born in London on 12 February 1685, the second son of George Hadley (1649–1729) of East Barnet and his wife, Katherine Fitzjames (1654/5–1712); John *Hadley (1682–1744), natural philosopher, was his elder brother. Hadley entered Pembroke College, Oxford, on 30 May 1700, and on 13 August 1701 became a member of Lincoln's Inn, where his father purchased chambers for him. He was called to the bar on 1 July 1709, but was more interested in mechanical and physical studies than in legal work, being of independent means. He and his brother Henry assisted John Hadley in his improvements to the reflecting telescope, and in the invention of the reflecting or Hadley quadrant, for which John received great acclaim. George Hadley was probably the anonymous author of the pamphlet *A Description of a New Instrument for Taking the Latitude or other Altitudes at Sea* (1734), with a corresponding pamphlet in Latin, on the reflecting quadrant.

Hadley was elected fellow of the Royal Society on 20 February 1735, and on 22 May that year published a short paper in *Philosophical Transactions* (vol. 39, 1735, 58–62), in which he accounted for the regularity and direction of the trade winds. These he ascribed to the heating and lifting of the atmosphere over the seasonal equator causing air to flow from both tropics towards the equator at lower levels. With the earth's rotational velocity increasing towards the equator, this air flow was deflected to give north-east trade winds in the northern hemisphere and south-east trade winds in the southern. Hadley succeeded William Derham as interpreter of the various meteorological diaries sent to the Royal Society from observers mainly in Britain and Scandinavia. He endeavoured to reconcile the different scales then in use and commented on the general patterns that emerged from year to year, noting that barometric tendencies seemed on the whole to agree; twice he published an account and abstract of the results in *Philosophical Transactions*.

Hadley, who was unmarried, left London and lived for a while at East Barnet with a nephew, probably John Hadley's son John, but most of his later years were spent at Flitton, Bedfordshire, where another nephew, Hadley Cox (*d.* 1782), son of his sister Elizabeth, was vicar. Hadley died at Flitton on 28 June 1768, and was buried in the chancel of Flitton church. Cox passed to his own son John Hadley Cox the 'reflecting telescope … being the first of the sort that was ever made, invented by my late uncle, John Hadley, Esq., and made under the direction of his two brothers, George and Henry' (PROB 11/1089/169).

ANITA MCCONNELL

**Sources** S. P. Rigaud, 'Biographical account of John Hadley, esq., VPRS, the inventor of the quadrant, and of his brothers George and Henry', *Nautical Magazine*, 4 (1835), 12–22, 137–46 • F. C. Cass, *East Barnet*, 2 vols. (1885–92), 1.80–82 • W. P. Baildon, ed., *The records of the Honorable Society of Lincoln's Inn: the black books*, 3 (1899), 235 • PRO, PROB 11/1089/169

**Hadley, George** (*d.* 1798), army officer in the East India Company and philologist, was appointed an ensign in the East India Company's Bengal army on 17 November 1762. He sailed for India in the following year, having received permission from the court of directors to take 120 ounces of silver bullion with him, presumably for private trade. He was promoted to lieutenant on 5 February 1764 and to captain on 26 July 1766, a position of command that proved disconcerting to him given that he could neither speak the language of his soldiers nor find any printed aids to acquiring it. *Munshis* were available to instruct him in Persian, but Persian was not the language spoken by his Sepoys. He therefore set about compiling a grammar of Hindustani, the language that prevailed in the army camps and bazaars of north India, where he was posted, and which was commonly referred to by Europeans as 'Moors'. The grammatical basis of Hindustani was the Indo-Aryan language of Hindi (or Hindavi), but under the influence of the Persian-speaking officer and administrative class of the Mughals it had acquired many loan words from Persian and Arabic, and, unlike Hindi, which used the Devanagari alphabet of Sanskrit, it was written in a Perso-Arabic script. When Hadley began to compile his grammar, the European science of philology was in its infancy, and confusion was rife among early orientalists about the origins of the various Indian languages and dialects. Hadley was considerably ahead of contemporary British opinion in identifying Hindustani not as a lesser or vulgar version of Persian, but as a completely different language with its own distinct grammar. He did not, however, trace Hindustani's origins to Hindi, instead postulating that the Tartars had brought it to India.

Hadley originally compiled his grammar and vocabulary for personal use, but a copy he had deposited with a friend found its way to London, where in 1771 W. Flexney published it, in a corrupt and mutilated form and without acknowledgement to Hadley, as *A Short Grammar and Vocabulary of the Moors Language*. On being sent a copy of the pamphlet, Hadley decided to publish a corrected version, and in 1772 the work appeared in London as *Grammatical remarks on the practical and vulgar dialect of the Indostan language, commonly called Moors*. A commercial success, it was reprinted in 1774, 1784, 1790, 1797, and issued in another edition in 1796, 1801, and 1809. In 1776 Hadley published a similar beginner's manual on Persian, entitled *Introductory Grammatical Remarks on the Persian Language*; this did not do as well as its predecessor and was never reprinted. Hadley was modest about his pioneering efforts in Hindustani, but although he made no greater claim than to have elucidated the grammar of the 'corrupt dialect' of 'common Moors', this did not save him from a savaging by later scholars, in particular the self-regarding John Borthwick Gilchrist, who labelled his version of Hindustani as 'viler than English butchered by Negroes in the West, and mangled by Bungalees in the East Indies … as remote from the proper Hindoostanee, as light is from darkness' (Gilchrist, v). Under the weight of such criticism and the expansion of orientalist scholarship Hadley's linguistic initiative was all but forgotten by the mid-nineteenth century.

Little is known of Hadley's life beyond his publications. He did not marry while in India, although an illegitimate daughter, Sarah, was born to him there. She was baptized in Calcutta in October 1771, shortly before Hadley resigned the company's service in December 1771. It is presumed that he then returned to Britain. In 1788 he was named by the printer Thomas Briggs as the compiler of *A New and Complete History of the Town and County of … Kingston-upon-Hull*. There is nothing in the work to associate Hadley or his family with Hull, but the title-page additionally credits him with translating extracts from Joseph Labrosse's seventeenth-century work on Persia, *Gazophylacium linguae Persarum*, and composing 'divers Poetical Pieces'. Hadley died on 10 September 1798 at his residence in Gloucester Street, Queen Square, London.

KATHERINE PRIOR

**Sources** Dodwell [E. Dodwell] and Miles [J. S. Miles], eds., *Alphabetical list of the officers of the Indian army: with the dates of their respective promotion, retirement, resignation, or death … from the year 1760 to the year … 1837* (1838) • court minutes, 1762–3, BL OIOC, B/78, 226,

308 • *GM*, 1st ser., 68 (1798), 816 • ecclesiastical records, Bengal baptisms, 1771, BL OIOC, N/1/2, fol. 210 • J. Gilchrist, *A dictionary of English and Hindoostanee*, pt 1 (1787)

**Hadley, John** (1682–1744), natural philosopher and mathematician, was born on 16 April 1682 in Bloomsbury, London, the second of six children and eldest son of George Hadley (1649–1729) and his wife, Katherine (1654/5–1712). He was baptized at the parish church of St Giles-in-the-Fields, Bloomsbury, on 21 April by the rector, Dr John Sharp (1645–1714), who later became archbishop of York. Hadley's father was a landed gentleman who became deputy lieutenant and in 1691 high sheriff of Hertfordshire, the family's principal estate being at East Barnet in that county, and his mother was the daughter and coheir of Sir John Fitzjames of Leweston in the county of Dorset. Nothing is known of Hadley's education, but he evidently became proficient in mathematics, mechanics, and optics. He has sometimes been confused with an older John Hadley who patented a device for raising and lowering a water wheel in 1693.

On 21 March 1717 Hadley was elected a fellow of the Royal Society, and he took an active part in the society's proceedings for the rest of his life. In 1718 he was asked to comment on an analysis of the orbits of revolving bodies presented to the society by Colin Maclaurin (1698–1746), which is evidence of his mathematical ability, since the subject was complex and involved an understanding of Newton's theories of gravitation. He was elected to the council of the society in 1720 and, except for the years 1721, 1723, and 1725, was re-elected annually. On 12 February 1728 he was sworn in as vice-president, and he appears to have retained this office until his death, as he is normally referred to as VPRS from that date.

The first achievement that made Hadley's name well known beyond the Royal Society was his improvement of the reflecting telescope in 1719–20. The principle of the instrument had already been demonstrated by James Gregory (1638–1675) and Sir Isaac Newton (1642–1727), but neither had succeeded in producing a telescope with any significant advantage over the older refracting type. Assisted by his brothers George *Hadley (1685–1768) and Henry Hadley (1697–1771), Hadley succeeded in making a Newtonian reflector of just over 62 inch focus, with 6 inch mirror and a new kind of stand. It was demonstrated to the Royal Society on 12 January 1721, and on 6 April Hadley reported on the observations he had made with it of Jupiter's satellites and Saturn's ring. Meanwhile Edmond Halley, the astronomer royal, also tried out the reflector and reported in March that it 'Shews the Limbs of the Planets with a greater degree of distinctness than other Sort of Telescopes do, in which particular … it excells even the great Telescope at Wanstead' (RS, classified papers, 8.1.67). Further trials were carried out by James Bradley, a future astronomer royal, and James Pound (1669–1724), who also compared its performance with the society's aerial 123 foot refractor at Wanstead. They concluded that the definition was about equal, though the image was a little less bright, but the reflector, being only just over 6 feet long, was much easier to manipulate and focus. The other great advantage of the reflector as against an aerial telescope was that the closed tube meant it could be used during twilight. Hadley devised a method of polishing the metal mirror that produced a brighter finish and he attempted to give it a parabolic figure to reduce spherical aberration, hence the performance of his reflector surpassed that of Newton's. Subsequently, Hadley succeeded in producing a successful reflector using the slightly different arrangement of mirrors originated by Gregory. Once Hadley had demonstrated that the reflector could be an effective observing instrument it was further developed with his assistance by a number of opticians, notably Edward Scarlett (*d.* 1743) and James Short (1710–1768), and became a standard part of their stock by the middle of the century.

Although Hadley's main concerns were his mathematical and scientific studies and the work of the Royal Society in London, he also took some interest in the local community around the family estates, and in 1720 was elected a governor of Barnet grammar school. At his father's death in January 1729 he inherited the landed property, which enabled him to continue his scholarly pursuits.

The invention for which Hadley was best remembered is the navigational instrument known as the octant, or Hadley's quadrant. With the help of his brothers he made the first octant in 1730, and reported it to the Royal Society on 13 May 1731 in a paper entitled 'Description of a new instrument for taking angles' (*PTRS*, 37, 1731–2, 147–57). He explained that 'The Instrument is designed to be of use where the Motion of the Objects, or any Circumstance Occasioning an unsteadiness in the common Instruments renders the Observations difficult or uncertain' (ibid., 147). By means of two mirrors the images of two objects could be made to appear to coincide and the angle between them read from the scale. The arc of the instrument was one-eighth of a circle, hence the name octant, but, because of the double reflection, 1° on the arc represented 2° between the objects observed, so that the instrument could measure 90° or a quarter of a circle and be called a quadrant. Hadley gave a full mathematical explanation to the society, showing that the invention depended on his appreciation of the optical laws involved. The idea was not entirely original, as Hooke had made a quadrant that incorporated a single mirror to provide a reflected image and Newton had written to Halley with ideas for improving it by using a double reflection, though he seems not to have attempted to put them into practice. There is no evidence, however, that Hadley knew of Newton's proposals, and he was certainly the first to produce a practical instrument. Thomas Godfrey of Philadelphia later claimed the invention, but news of his design did not reach London until 1732, and it is clear that the two men independently arrived at a similar device. The octant was tested on board the yacht *Chatham* in 1732, the observers including James Bradley and Hadley's brother Henry, and was found to be superior to other nautical instruments for measuring angles. Hadley added a refinement in 1734 in the form of a spirit level to make altitude measurements possible when the horizon was obscured. He took out a patent (no. 550) for his instrument in November of that year. A sign that his octant had superseded earlier navigational instruments for measuring the altitudes of the sun and stars for finding latitude at sea came in 1754, when Christ's Hospital ordered that the boys in the mathematical school should be issued with Hadley quadrants rather than the outdated Davis quadrant and forestaff. In 1757 Captain John Campbell enlarged Hadley's octant to a sixth of a circle, so that it could measure up to 120°, thereby creating the sextant.

On 6 June 1734 Hadley married Elizabeth Hodges (*d.* 1752) at the parish church of St George's, Bloomsbury. She was the daughter of Thomas Hodges FRS, attorney-general for Barbados under Queen Anne, and had a personal fortune of £5000. The trustees of the marriage settlement were her younger brother, Colonel John Hodges, and Sir Hans Sloane, who had a town house near Hadley's in Bloomsbury; a letter in the British Library indicates that Hadley's friendship with Sloane went back to at least his earliest days as a fellow of the Royal Society. The Hadleys' only child, John, was born on 21 February 1738. Hadley died at East Barnet on 14 February 1744, and was buried there in the churchyard of St Mary the Virgin on 22 February. His wife was amply provided for in his will, being given the rent from his estates at East Barnet, Edmonton, and Enfield for her lifetime, as well as £100 from annuities. On her death in 1752 all the property passed to their son, who sold off the estates and spent all the proceeds. GLORIA CLIFTON

**Sources** S. P. Rigaud, 'Biographical account of John Hadley, esq., VPRS, the inventor of the quadrant, and of his brothers George and Henry', *Nautical Magazine*, 4 (1835), 12–22, 137–46 · F. C. Cass, *East Barnet*, 2 vols. (1885–92), 1.74–80 · PRO, PROB 11/731/41 · J. Hadley, 'An account of a catadioptrick telescope', *PTRS*, 32 (1722–3), 303–12 · parish register (baptism), 21 April 1682, Bloomsbury, St Giles-in-the-Fields · parish register, Bloomsbury, St George, 6 June 1734, LMA, P82/GEOI/015 [marriage] · monumental inscriptions, East Barnet, St Mary the Virgin, Society of Genealogists, London [microfilm] · index to parish register, St George, Bloomsbury, London, 1737–8, LMA, P82/GEOI/14 [baptism] · W. Bulloch, 'Roll of the fellows of the Royal Society', index, RS · RS, classified papers, 2.16.21; 8.1.67; 8.2.44

**Archives** RS, classified papers · Sci. Mus., reflecting telescope, inv. 1937/601 · Sci. Mus., speculum, inv. 1932/459 | BL, letters, Sloane MSS

**Likenesses** B. Dandridge, oils, NMM · engraving, repro. in Rigaud, 'Biographical account' · lithograph, Sci. Mus.

**Wealth at death** landed estates sold after death for almost £16,000: Rigaud, 'Biographical account'

**Hadley, John** (1731–1764), physician and chemist, was born in London, the eldest son of Ann Hoffman and Henry Hadley. His family included his uncles, John Hadley and George Hadley, both respected instrument makers and natural philosophers in the metropolis. He matriculated at Queens' College, Cambridge, as a pensioner in May 1749, and proceeded to BA in 1753 as fifth wrangler. This achievement in the Senate House examinations helped him to procure a fellowship at Queens' in 1756. When the chair of chemistry fell vacant with the death of John Mickleburgh later in that year, Hadley enlisted the aid of Russell Plumtre, a senior fellow of Queens' and the university's regius professor of physick, to help him secure the professorship.

As professor, Hadley delivered lectures in 1758 and 1759, years in which, he claimed, 'Chemistry is rising in its reputation; and is becoming a very usefull as well as entertaining branch of Natural Philosophy' (J. Hadley, *A Plan of a Course of Chemical Lectures*, 1, 1758, 2). In his lectures he described many technical aspects of the discipline, including a variety of industrial processes; he also enlivened his narration with over five hundred demonstrations. Although the course was intended for undergraduates who had little knowledge of the discipline, the lectures nevertheless evinced Hadley's familiarity with even the most recent developments in the discipline. Whereas his predecessor, Mickleburgh, was influenced considerably by Newton's *œuvre* and, especially, the 'Queries' appended to the *Opticks*, Hadley's lectures were largely based on the work of the continental chemists. Despite his praise for Joseph Black and Stephen Hales, his material relied on scholars such as Becher, Stahl, Boerhaave, and Macquer. And despite his cautionary remarks concerning theories, Hadley's ontology revolved around a core set of 'primary principles', including the principle of inflammability, which he identified as phlogiston.

Although he retained his chemistry chair until his death, Hadley returned to London in order to pursue a career as a physician, taking a post as an assistant physician at St Thomas's Hospital in 1760. Shortly after taking his medical degree in 1763, he was admitted as a fellow of the College of Physicians, and left St Thomas's for a more lucrative position at the Charterhouse. In addition to his chemical enquiries at Cambridge and, later, his duties as a physician, Hadley also became a fellow of the Royal Society in 1758, and the Society's *Philosophical Transactions* of 1764 (1–14) contains his 'Account of a mummy', which he had inspected with Dr Wollaston and the Hunter brothers. In this paper he speculated about the chemical techniques involved in mummification and contended that he had conducted extensive analytical investigations of the mummy in order to comprehend the methods that Egyptians utilized.

Unfortunately, Hadley was unable to enjoy his growing reputation and financial security, for he died of a fever on 5 November 1764, aged only thirty-three. Dr Robert Plumtre, president of Queens', noted that 'He was an ingenious, worthy, and agreeable man, and died much lamented by all who knew him' (*Queens' College Conclusion Book, 1734–87*, 58). He was also remembered as a great friend of Thomas Gray, the poet. KEVIN C. KNOX

**Sources** L. J. M. Coleby, 'John Hadley: fourth professor of chemistry in the University of Cambridge', *Annals of Science*, 8 (1952), 293–301 · Munk, *Roll* · J. Twigg, *A history of Queens' College, Cambridge, 1448–1986* (1987) · Venn, *Alum. Cant.* · *GM*, 1st ser., 84/1 (1814), 427 ·

*Queens' College Conclusion Book*, 1734–87, Queens' College, Cambridge · Cambridge University Grace Book 'K', CUL, fol. 257
**Likenesses** B. Wilson, portrait, 1759, Queens' College, Cambridge · E. Fisher, mezzotint (aged twenty-eight; after B. Wilson), BM

**Hadley, Patrick Arthur Sheldon** (1899–1973), composer and university teacher, was born at 66 Barton Road, Cambridge, on 5 March 1899, the younger of the two sons of William Sheldon Hadley (1859–1927), fellow and later master of Pembroke College, Cambridge, a distinguished classical scholar; his mother was Edith Jane (1874–1940), the daughter of the Revd Robert Foster, chaplain of the Royal Hibernian Military School, Dublin. He was enrolled (though not as a choirboy) at King's College School, Cambridge, in January 1909, moved to St Ronan's in October, and completed his education at Winchester College from 1912 to 1917, when he joined the Royal Field Artillery. His elder brother died of pneumonia while convalescing from war wounds in 1918 and in the final weeks of the war Hadley too was wounded, losing one leg above the knee. This disability had a profound effect, for not only did the false limb give him constant pain: he felt that he had been cheated of his youth and had lost part of his manhood. The compensatory mechanisms were a frequently outrageous and comical exterior, and copious draughts of alcohol.

Hadley attended Pembroke, his father's college, from 1919 to 1922, gaining a MusB in 1922, his MA in 1925, and his MusD in 1938. He studied from 1922 to 1925 at the Royal College of Music, where he was a composition pupil of Vaughan Williams and a conducting pupil of Adrian Boult and Malcolm Sargent. He was awarded the Sullivan prize in composition (1924) and was appointed to the teaching staff in 1925. Up to 1930 he had produced some fifteen compositions, eleven of which are word settings with either piano or chamber ensemble accompaniments, but in 1931 there appeared a major work for chorus, orchestra, and baritone soloist based on the folk-song 'The trees so high'. The first three instrumental movements are built on themes drawn from the contours of the song, and only in the finale does the chorus sing the folk-song complete with its haunting tale.

Hadley's father had died in 1927, and in the 1930s his possessive mother seems to have made a prospective (American) wife unwelcome. Henceforth Paddy, as he was known to friends and students alike, resigned himself to bachelordom, while at the same time indulging in casual affairs. In 1938 he accepted a lectureship in music at Cambridge and became a fellow of Gonville and Caius. Among his duties were looking after the few music students there and stimulating music-making in the form of college concerts (including Gilbert and Sullivan performances) and chapel services. For both purposes he instigated, and continued for twenty-four years, a remarkably high standard of male-voice singing that drew in large numbers of college members regardless of musical ability, arranging standard classical works and folk tunes himself. Because of his disability the office of precentor of Caius was created for him; he directed the music of the chapel services, while an assistant played the organ. During the absence on active service of Boris Ord from 1941 to 1945, Hadley conducted the Cambridge University Musical Society's chorus and orchestra in memorable performances of Bach, Beethoven, Verdi, and Delius, who had been a valued friend until his death in 1934.

Hadley's most significant work was *The Hills*, completed in 1944 and first performed in 1947. Another choral symphony (text by the composer), it is a profound reflection on the death of his parents (his mother had died in 1940). The hills are those in the Peak District where, he knew, his father had proposed, and a love duet and an uproarious wedding feast are included. He was appointed professor of music in 1946, and his unconventional behaviour and reputed consumption of alcohol became legend. As a result his meticulous craftsmanship and acute sensitivity as a composer tended to be overlooked, though the creative process was for him a laborious effort: 'Composing—it's hell' (Todds, 9). He was unusually hospitable and accessible to generations of undergraduates who regularly visited his rooms for his amusing company. He was the personal friend of Adrian Boult, Arnold Bax, Balfour Gardiner, Herbert Howells, Constant Lambert, E. J. Moeran, Alan Rawsthorne, and William Walton, any one of whom might call into his rooms at Caius to seek his advice—to the delight of his students. He was a trustee of the Cambridge Arts Theatre and a co-founder of both the King's Lynn festival and the Noise Abatement Society. In 1962 he retired prematurely, and visits to Ireland, sometimes twice yearly, became an obsession, motor tours always taking in Roscommon, his mother's birthplace near Athlone.

Discouraged by his publisher's rejection of *Connemara*, Hadley composed virtually nothing in his remaining years. He continued to live in the family home, Shallcross, Station Road, Heacham, near King's Lynn, Norfolk, until his death from throat cancer on 17 December 1973. He was buried at Heacham church on 21 December.

ERIC WETHERELL

**Sources** E. Wetherell, *'Paddy': the life and music of Patrick Hadley* (1997) · W. Todds, *Patrick Hadley: a memoir* (1974) · private information (2004) · FM Cam., Music MSS · *DNB* · b. cert. · d. cert. · *The Caian* (1936–74)
**Archives** Oxford University Press, file | King's AC Cam., letters and telegram to G. H. W. Rylands | SOUND BL NSA, performance recordings
**Likenesses** E. Kapp, drawing, 1965, Gon. & Caius Cam.
**Wealth at death** £107,876: probate, 21 March 1974, *CGPLA Eng. & Wales*

**Hadley, William Waite** (1866–1960), newspaper editor, was born at East Haddon, Northamptonshire, on 18 January 1866, one of the ten children of Joseph Hadley and his wife, Elizabeth Waite. Joseph Hadley, a head gardener, was a great reader and a stalwart Congregationalist, activities both taken up by his son. He attended the village school, leaving about the age of twelve or thirteen and working locally, probably in manual labour. He went to night school in Northampton and a part-time master at Rugby School taught him shorthand, essential to a reporter in the days of verbatim note-taking and long printed reports. At the age of fifteen he was apprenticed to the *Northampton Mercury*. He was soon given reporting assignments which took him all over the county. Charles Bradlaugh and Henry Labouchere were then members of parliament for Northampton, a radical borough, and in later life Hadley used often to recount how as a junior reporter he was present at the hustings at the famous by-elections caused by Bradlaugh's refusal to take the oath. He later wrote on their political activities for the journal of the Northamptonshire Record Society. In 1920 he also wrote a short history of the *Mercury* to mark its bicentenary.

In 1887 Hadley joined the editorial staff of the *Rochdale Observer*, and married, in 1889, Emma (*d.* 1952), a schoolteacher, daughter of Joseph Chater, shoe manufacturer, of Northampton. They had three daughters. In 1893 he became editor of the *Rochdale Observer*. His time at the *Observer* was broken by an eight-months' editorship of the *Merthyr Times*. This interlude proved crucial for his later career as it was in Merthyr Tudful that he made friends with the family of John Mathias Berry, two of whose sons were destined to become national newspaper proprietors, and one of them, William, later Viscount Camrose, was, at fourteen, given by Hadley his first employment, on the local paper.

After editing the *Rochdale Observer* for fifteen years, and also taking an active part in local government and education, and in Liberal politics, in Yorkshire, Hadley returned in 1908 to Northampton as managing editor of the *Mercury* group of papers, of which he soon became a director. In 1924, at the age of fifty-eight, as a highly respected provincial newspaper editor and in his native community, he might have been thought to have reached the peak of his career; but in January that year he accepted an invitation to move to London and become parliamentary correspondent of the *Daily Chronicle*. When in 1930 the *Chronicle* was merged with the *Daily News*, he found himself out of work, at the age of sixty-four, competing with much younger men who had spent most of their lives in Fleet Street. However, in a fortunate incident which prompted the saying among fellow journalists that: 'We should all go round patting little boys' heads. On the law of averages it must pay off in the end' (Hobson, Knightley, and Russell, 192), Lord Camrose, then chairman and editor-in-chief of the *Sunday Times*, offered him the assistant editorship, which he took up in 1931. A year later, in 1932, the editor, Leonard Rees, died. Hadley, without ever being formally appointed, simply took over the role, and, as he 'never was told to stop' (ibid.), remained editor of the *Sunday Times* (of which Lord Kemsley became chairman and editor-in-chief after he and his brother divided their press interests in 1937) until his retirement in 1950 at the age of eighty-four.

The *Sunday Times*, under Kemsley, was a Conservative newspaper and Hadley 'put aside his residual Liberalism' and accepted 'with a certain complacency' the politics of his proprietor (Koss, 627). His politics had been gradually moving to the right with the post-war decline of the Liberal Party and his dislike of socialism. He became a friend and supporter of Neville Chamberlain, seeing him weekly when Chamberlain was prime minister. Hadley became, with the support of Kemsley, 'one of the most determined apostles of appeasement' (Hobson, Knightley, and Russell, 192), defending this policy in his book *Munich: before and after*, published in 1944.

Although he was 'not a brilliant or spectacular editor' (Hobson, Knightley, and Russell, 192), Hadley's absolute and unique calm in the frequent uproar of a newspaper office was what was most often noted by his colleagues, along with his modesty and courtesy to staff. As well as being his own chief leader writer until the last few years of his editorship, his contribution to the growing success of the *Sunday Times* was his skilful handling of a gifted team of regular contributors, including Ernest Newman, James Agate, Desmond MacCarthy, and R. C. K. Ensor. A small, exceptionally neat, man he reminded many more of a minor official in local government than the editor of a major newspaper. Hadley died at his home, Innisfree, Bramshott Chase, Hindhead, Surrey, on 16 December 1960. He was cremated at St John's, Woking, on 20 December. H. V. Hodson, *rev.* Marc Brodie

**Sources** *The Times* (17 Dec 1960) · personal knowledge (1971) · private information (1971) · *Northamptonshire Past and Present*, 3 (1960–66), 49–51 · *Sunday Times* (18 Dec 1960) · *Haslemere Herald* (23 Dec 1960) · H. Hobson, P. Knightley, and L. Russell, *The pearl of days: an intimate memoir of the 'Sunday Times', 1822–1972* (1972) · S. E. Koss, *The rise and fall of the political press in Britain*, 2 (1984)

**Archives** BL, corresp. with Albert Mansbridge, Add. MS 65259 · JRL, letters to the *Manchester Guardian*

**Likenesses** photograph, repro. in Hobson, Knightley, and Russell, *Pearl of days*

**Wealth at death** £15,460 7*s.* 0*d.*: probate, 7 March 1961, *CGPLA Eng. & Wales*

**Hadow, Grace Eleanor** (1875–1940), college head and social worker, was born on 9 December 1875 at South Cerney vicarage, near Cirencester, Gloucestershire, the youngest child and fourth daughter of William Elliot Hadow (1826–1906), vicar of South Cerney, and his wife, Mary Lang (*d.* 1917), daughter of Henry Cornish of Tavistock. Grace drew from her family a deep understanding of rural life, and a liveliness of wit and scholarly curiosity—particularly from her elder brother and godfather, Sir William Henry *Hadow, to whom she remained devoted.

Grace Hadow was educated at Brownshill School, near Stroud, and at Truro high school, where she later stayed on as a student teacher, with time of her own for working at languages and literature; she then spent a year in Trier, in Germany, studying music and languages. In October 1900 she went to Somerville College, Oxford, where she soon overcame an early shyness, 'simply pouring herself into college life' (Deneke, 29), and developed skills and interests which remained throughout her life, including her quick wit and charm as a speaker. Both then and later she had the active support and sponsorship of her brother, then a fellow of Worcester College and also a member of Somerville College council.

After gaining first-class honours in English language and literature, in 1903, Hadow held a teaching post at Bryn Mawr, Pennsylvania. In 1906 she was appointed English tutor at Lady Margaret Hall, Oxford, and became lecturer there in 1909. During this period she published *The Oxford Treasury of English Literature*, edited with her brother, W. H. Hadow (3 vols.; 1907–8), and *Chaucer and his Times* (1914). She also edited collections of essays on Addison (1907) and on Goldsmith (1918), and selections of work by Walter Raleigh (1917), and translated (with W. H. Hadow) Litzmann's biography of Clara Schumann, published as *Clara Schumann—an Artist's Life* (1913).

Grace Hadow's interests in social problems and practical solutions, and her flair for organization, quickly became apparent during the First World War. Her life as a scholar was interwoven with practical concerns: her writing was undertaken while looking after her widowed mother; at the same time, she was working with Belgian refugees and helping to develop the Women's Institute in Cirencester and surrounding villages of which she was elected president in 1916. When her mother died, early in 1917, Grace resigned her Lady Margaret Hall lectureship to seek full-time war work, and was recruited to run 'a most unconventional department of Extra Mural Welfare' in the Ministry of Munitions, charged with organizing women's work in the factories, crèches, housing, and lodgings. Following this, she was persuaded by W. G. S. Adams in 1920 to become secretary at Barnett House in Oxford, founded a few years earlier in memory of Canon Barnett of Toynbee Hall.

The key to Grace Hadow's work was her vision of adult education—particularly for women—as a means to citizenship. This combination of self-government and social service was crucial for post-war reconstruction. Barnett House was developing rapidly as a centre for social and economic studies and social-work training, with lectures and debates by eminent academics and public figures on the social and economic issues of the time. It also became a springboard for new organizations such as the National Council of Social Service, based on ideals of 'citizen service', 'the corporate citizen effort to improve social conditions' (*Daily Herald*, 12 May 1919). Grace's vision fitted well in this context, and she was encouraged to pioneer rural adult education development based on Barnett House, fostering village industries, libraries, lectures, and classes on social and economic questions, music, and drama. The Oxfordshire scheme became the prototype for rural community councils nationally. Her aim, in her words, was not simply to take 'folk dancing and travelling cinemas to the villages', but 'to get people to formulate their own demands and tackle problems' and 'to take their own place in local government or voluntary organisation, and future development can be left in their hands' (Campbell, 14). For the same reasons, she remained deeply involved in the development of Women's Institutes and the National Federation of Women's Institutes, of which she was vice-chairman from 1916 until her death.

Grace brought her experience and a wider vision of women's education and civic responsibility to her appointment as principal of the Society of Oxford Home Students in 1929 (she had earlier been unwilling to stand against Margery Fry as principal of Somerville). Links continued between the society and Barnett House, fostered by her and C. V. and Ruth Butler—all three played key roles in both places. She encouraged opportunities for Ruskin College students and for the 'Bodley girls', and suggested a wide range of careers, 'not just teaching', for her graduates. Her organization skills and sympathetic vision were well demonstrated by her Friday lunches for tutors, the personal contact she maintained with students, and the wide support she nurtured in the university and beyond. During her time as principal, the society's academic status increased and new endowments and buildings were secured. She was one of only two women members of the university's hebdomadal council at the time. With a true sense of the links between university life and civic life, she served on bodies such as the university's extra-mural delegacy (in particular the Oxfordshire, Buckinghamshire, and Berkshire committee, which organized adult education in the region), and Oxfordshire's county education committee. She also served on national bodies such as the BBC's advisory council, the adult education committee of the Board of Education, and the National Council of Social Service, as well as fostering hundreds of small village communities throughout England.

The last two years of Grace Hadow's life were taken up by the British Commonwealth conference in Sydney, in the summer of 1938, followed by a lecture tour in the United States that autumn, during which she visited and lectured in twenty-two colleges. She had been granted sabbatical leave for the trip and returned very excited about the international role of women. But she was exhausted, and did not fully recover before the outbreak of war in the autumn of 1939, and the subsequent large-scale evacuation of London schools to Oxford. She caught pneumonia and died at 11 Beaumont Street, Marylebone, London, on 19 January 1940.

Grace Hadow was remembered as one of the best women speakers in England. An assistant secretary of the National Federation of Women's Institutes who knew her just before the war described how:

> her conversation strayed from Chaucer to the art of throwing boomerangs, from water divining to women's emancipation. There seemed in fact no subject in which she was not interested and in which she could not kindle the interest of others. (private information)

She was one of a remarkable generation of women who combined a life of scholarship with public service devoted to education and citizenship, lived with energy, enthusiasm, good humour, and common sense.

TERESA SMITH

**Sources** H. Deneke, *Grace Hadow* (1946) · P. Adams, *Somerville for women: an Oxford college, 1879–1993* (1996) · C. V. Butler, *Barnett House, 1914 to 1964: a record for its friends* (privately printed [Oxford], [1964]) · M. E. Campbell, *The Oxfordshire Rural Community Council: a history of the first fifty years, 1920–1970* (1970), 14 · M. Reeves, *St Anne's College, Oxford—an informal history* (printed by the college, 1979) · *The Ship* [year book of the Society of Oxford Home Students, Old Students' Association] · archives of St Anne's College, Oxford · Barnett House, Oxford · private information (2004) [Dr Marjorie Reeves] · *The Times* (22 Jan 1940) · *Manchester Guardian* (22 Jan 1940) · *Home and Country: the Magazine of the National Federation of Women's*

*Institutes* (22 Jan 1940) · *Oxford Times* (26 Jan 1940) · *Oxford Times* (2 Feb 1940) · *Oxford Magazine* (1 Feb 1940) · private information (2004) [National Federation of Women's Institutes] · *DNB* · *CGPLA Eng. & Wales* (1940)

**Archives** Barnett House, Oxford · St Anne's College, Oxford · Worcester College, Oxford, papers relating to education

**Likenesses** Bassano, photograph, National Federation of Women's Institutes, London · photograph, repro. in Campbell, *Oxfordshire Rural Community Council*, 38

**Wealth at death** £5839 5*s*. 9*d*.: probate, 7 March 1940, *CGPLA Eng. & Wales*

**Hadow, Sir (William) Henry** (1859–1937), educationist and historian of music, was born at Ebrington, Gloucestershire, on 27 December 1859, the eldest son of William Elliot Hadow (1826–1906), curate, afterwards vicar, of Ebrington, and his wife, Mary Lang (*d*. 1917), the second daughter of Henry Cornish, of Tavistock. After more than seven years at Malvern College he went in 1878 to Worcester College, Oxford, of which he was successively scholar, lecturer (1885), fellow, classics tutor (1888), dean (1889), and finally honorary fellow (1909). He obtained a first class in classical moderations (1880) and in *literae humaniores* (1882), and after taking his BA degree studied music in both Germany (at Darmstadt) and back in England with C. H. Lloyd (1884–5). He took the Oxford BMus degree in 1890 (having received the MA in 1885). He lectured in both classics and music, became a proctor for the university (1897), and examined in the final schools of *literae humaniores* (1899–1901), modern languages, and English. He was widely considered a brilliant lecturer, apparently always speaking without notes (in his lectures on Aristotle even without a text).

A significant number of musicians at Worcester College during this period benefited from their contact with Hadow, in particular Percy Buck, who also contributed a great deal to English musical education. Hadow also composed chamber music, wrote and edited songs and hymns, and stimulated the performance of music in Oxford at a time when the art was perhaps undervalued in the university at large. But it was his practical knowledge of music that was most important as the foundation of his critical and historical writings. The two small volumes of *Studies in Modern Music* (1893–5) opened a new era in English music criticism, and while they evince certain Victorian prejudices they remain interesting reading at the end of the twentieth century. For the second volume, Hadow was able to visit both Brahms and Dvořák when compiling his biographical material. By setting music against a background of general culture, he made music criticism more accessible and helped to give music its rightful place in a liberal education. *Sonata Form* (1896, 2nd edn 1912) is ostensibly a textbook, but it is presented in simple terms and in flowing prose typical of Hadow. In 1897 came *A Croatian Composer*, in which the Slavonic origin of Joseph Haydn is asserted (this allegation was also included in his revision of Pohl's article in the second edition of *Grove's Dictionary*, 1904–10). His conclusions were later disproved, but the value of his work on Haydn's melodic style remains. One of his most acclaimed works, *The Viennese Period* (vol. 5 of

Sir (William) Henry Hadow (1859–1937), by Bassano, 1920

the Oxford History of Music, of which he was general editor from 1896), was published in 1904 (2nd edn 1931). Between 1906 and 1908 he joined with his sister Grace Eleanor *Hadow in producing the three volumes of the *Oxford Treasury of English Literature*. As part of his desire to improve the repertory of songs, and in particular national or folk songs in schools, his *Songs of the British Islands* appeared in 1903, the choice of the English material foreshadowing Stanford's *The National Song Book* (1906). In 1906 he published *A Course of Lectures on the History of Instrumental Forms*, and in later years he published short books on *Music* (1924), *Church Music* (1926), *English Music* (1931), and *Richard Wagner* (1934) as well as a volume of *Collected Essays* (1928). He was an enthusiastic admirer of the Tudor music brought to light by Dr Edmund Horace Fellowes and others. 'They call William Byrd the English Palestrina; I shall not rest until Palestrina is called the Italian Byrd!', he once remarked.

In 1909 the direction of Hadow's life changed. He became principal of Armstrong College, Newcastle upon Tyne (part of Durham University), a post which he held until 1919. There he proved himself as able in administration as he had been in scholarship, and from 1916 to 1918 he was vice-chancellor of the University of Durham. In 1918, the year in which he was knighted for his wartime services to education, he was made director of education for the Young Men's Christian Association with the British army on lines of communication in France, and shortly afterwards was appointed assistant director of staff duties (education) at the War Office. Also in 1918, he published

*The Needs of Popular Musical Education*. He was appointed CBE in 1920.

From 1919 to 1930 Hadow was vice-chancellor of the University of Sheffield. The times were difficult, and external duties entailed frequent absences (including lecturing at the Rice Institute of Texas in April 1926), but Hadow was still able to achieve a great deal. He continued to lecture, and during his tenure of office at Sheffield the chair of music was established (1927) and steps were taken towards the institution of degrees in music. F. H. Shera, who went to Sheffield from Malvern, Hadow's own school, became the first, full-time, resident professor in 1928.

The period 1920 to 1934 saw Hadow as a leading influence in national education. During this time he was chairman of the consultative committee of the Board of Education, and under his chairmanship six valuable reports were issued. One of these, *The Education of the Adolescent* (1926), became known as the Hadow report, and remained for many years the standard handbook for teachers and administrators. Hadow's work on this committee and on others was far-reaching in its effects. The place of music on the syllabus was subsequently raised so that it became the equal of other subjects. His breadth of outlook and the range of his knowledge persuaded many who would perhaps have otherwise resisted such changes. Hadow's efforts were responsible for the new interest in the training of the amateur and the development of musical appreciation on a wider scale that can be seen to emerge during this period. Hadow's honorary degrees included a DMus from Oxford (1909), Durham (1910), and Wales (1921); LLD from St Andrews (1923), Liverpool (1925), and Birmingham (1930); and DLitt from Bristol (1925), Leeds (1930), and Sheffield (1930).

In Hadow it is apparent that a brilliant and rapid mind and an exceptional memory were accompanied by great charm and wit. His range as an academic is remarkable enough but perhaps even more striking is how he was able to turn from scholarship to administration with equal success and authority. His influence in various fields was significant for his own and succeeding generations.

When about to retire from Sheffield in 1930, he married a lifelong friend, Edith, the second daughter of Revd Dr John Troutbeck, a former precentor of Westminster Abbey. She died on 15 March 1937, less than a month before him. He died in London, at his home at 13 Belgrave Road, Westminster, on 8 April 1937.

F. H. SHERA, *rev.* DAVID J. GOLBY

**Sources** H. C. Colles, *MT*, 78 (1937), 404–6 • N. Fortune, 'Hadow, William Henry', *New Grove* • H. J. Foss, 'William Henry Hadow', *Music and Letters*, 18 (1937), 236–8 • G. Cox, *A history of music education in England, 1872–1928* (1993) • J. R. Simmons, '"So deft a builder": an account of the life and work of Sir Henry Hadow', PhD diss., University of Sheffield, 1978 • P. A. Scholes, *The mirror of music, 1844–1944: a century of musical life in Britain as reflected in the pages of the Musical Times*, 2 vols. (1947) • *The Times* (10 April 1937)

**Archives** Worcester College, Oxford, diaries, corresp., and MS music | BL, corresp. with Macmillans, Add. MS 55240

**Likenesses** W. Stoneman, two photographs, 1918–31, NPG • Bassano, photograph, 1920, NPG [*see illus.*] • W. Rothenstein, sanguine and black drawing, 1920, University of Sheffield • photograph, repro. in Scholes, *Mirror of music*, vol. 2, p. 652

**Wealth at death** £16,257 16*s*. 11*d*.: probate, 24 May 1937, *CGPLA Eng. & Wales*

**Hadow, James** (1667–1747), Church of Scotland minister and college head, was born on 13 August 1667 in Douglas, Lanarkshire, the son of George Hadow, probably a merchant, and nephew of William Cleland, the covenanting commander. He probably attended Lanark grammar school, but took flight to Utrecht for university study, enrolling there in 1684 and remaining until at least 1688. From Latin disputations he presented in 1685 and 1686, and from accounts of travellers and other sources, a clear picture of his associates among the large number of Scottish and English students and their elders in Utrecht can be gathered. They included Matthew Meade and his son Samuel, John Howe, who tutored students like Hadow in giving disputations, Sir Arthur Thompson (probably an unrecorded son of Sir John Thompson, later Baron Haversham), John Erskine of Carnock, who attended sermons given in Hadow's residence, and Edmund Calamy, who in 1709 in St Andrews called on Hadow, 'my old acquaintance … one of my fellow-students at Utrecht' (Calamy, 1.172, 2.196). William Cleland also enrolled in 1684, and Hadow can scarcely have avoided meeting his future opponent James Hog, who studied and tutored in the Netherlands from 1679 to 1689, quite possibly in Utrecht. The story recorded by John Brown of Whitburn that Hog offended Hadow in the Netherlands is quite plausible. Further study of Hadow's Utrecht associates and professors, including John Best, minister of the English speaking reformed church there from 1655 to 1696, will elucidate Hadow's theological formation.

Last glimpsed at Utrecht about mid-1688 (Calamy arrived in March), Hadow no doubt returned to Scotland with or after William of Orange's return. Ordained to the second charge of Cupar, Fife, before 31 July 1692 he was translated to the first on 30 October 1694, then to the chair of divinity (second master) in St Mary's College, St Andrews, on 5 April 1699, and finally to the principalship on 8 September 1707. Hadow married Isabel (*d.* in or before 1705), daughter of William Tullidelph, principal of St Leonard's College, St Andrews, possibly on 6 July 1697. Their daughter Barbara (*d.* 1767) married Thomas Ayton (1694–1739), minister in Perthshire and Fife. Following Isabel's death Hadow married, in 1705, Margaret Forrester (*d.* 1758); the couple had eight children, including George (1712–1780), professor of Hebrew at St Mary's (1748–80).

Hadow's public career was consumed in ecclesiastical and theological controversy. In 1713 the crown presented Alexander Scrimgeour to the chair of divinity in St Mary's, unaware that he was an Episcopalian layman and so ineligible. Hadow pressed for his removal in the church courts, but Scrimgeour still enjoyed the chair's emoluments on his death in 1731 or 1732. When the published views of the professor of church history, Archibald Campbell, raised the spectre of Pelagianism, Hadow apparently acquiesced, uncharacteristically, in the general assembly's decision merely to issue a general warning (1736).

Against the deists Hadow prepared for publication *Natural Religion Insufficient* (1714), the chief work of Thomas Halyburton, his successor in the chair of divinity. In 1703 he issued anonymously against the toleration of Episcopalians *Remarks upon the Case of the Episcopal Clergy* and *A Survey of the Case of the Episcopal Clergy*. Similarly anonymous, *The Doctrine and Practice of the Church of Scotland anent the Sacrament of Baptism* (1704) rejected the aspersions of the Episcopalian Alexander Sutherland with impressive erudition. When the teachings of John Simson, professor of divinity at Glasgow University, incurred suspicion a second time, Hadow entered the lists against his Arianism. Unlike Thomas Boston, Hadow did not dissent from the general assembly's lax verdict of permanent suspension after Simson recanted in 1729, but he subsequently published, again anonymously, *An Enquiry into Mr Simson's Sentiments about the Trinity* (1730) and *A Vindication of the Learned and Honourable Author of 'The History of the Apostles Creed'* (1731), namely Peter King, whom Simson had maligned.

Hadow's star performance was reserved for the Marrow controversy. He had pursued similar issues in 1711–12 with Alexander Hamilton, minister of Airth, Stirlingshire, over the seeming universalism of his *Short Catechism* (published 1714). Hadow's 1719 sermon to the synod of Fife, *The Record of God and the Duty of Faith Therein Required*, raised the first public alarm at James Hog's 1718 republication of *The Marrow of Modern Divinity* (1646) by Edward Fisher. Hadow kept up a pamphlet war with Hog in *A Review of a Conference betwixt Epaphroditus and Epaphras* (1719), probably drafted the assembly's condemnation of *The Marrow* in 1720, and, amid attempts to repeal it, produced his most ambitious work, *The Antinomianism of the Marrow … Detected* (1722), which Robert Riccaltoun satirically criticized in *The Politick Disputant* (1722). *The Marrow* provoked the first doctrinal division in the post-Reformation Church of Scotland. Victory lay with Hadow's narrower, terminologically insistent Calvinism, but the seeds of secession and later controversy were sown in the 1730s. Hadow proved a magisterial disputant in defence of an insensitive orthodoxy. He died on 4 May 1747 in his college house at St Mary's, St Andrews. D. F. WRIGHT

**Sources** *DNB* • D. C. Lachman, *The Marrow controversy, 1718–1723: an historical and theological analysis* (1988) • C. G. McCrie, 'Studies in Scottish ecclesiastical biography: III, Rev. James Hog of Carnock and Principal Hadow of St. Andrews', *British and Foreign Evangelical Review*, 33 (1884), 669–719 • *Fasti Scot.*, new edn • *Acts of the general assembly of the Church of Scotland, 1638–1842* (1843) • H. R. Sefton, 'St Mary's College, St Andrews, in the eighteenth century', *Records of the Scottish Church History Society*, 24 (1990–92), 161–80 • *DSCHT* • *Journal of the Hon. John Erskine of Carnock*, ed. W. Macleod, Scottish History Society, 14 (1893) • A. L. Hadow, 'Hadow', 1953, BL, 09915.tt.21 [typescript] • E. Calamy, *An historical account of my own life, with some reflections on the times I have lived in, 1671–1731*, ed. J. T. Rutt, 2nd edn, 2 vols. (1830) • *Album studiosorum academiae Rheno-Traiectinae MDCXXXVI–MDCCCLXXXVI: accedunt nomina curatorum et professorum per eadem secula* (Utrecht, 1886), col. 80

**Archives** NL Scot. • U. Edin., New Coll. L. • U. St Andr.

**Likenesses** oils, U. St Andr.

**Hadrian** [Traianus Hadrianus] (**AD 76–138**), Roman emperor, was born on 24 January AD 76 into a senatorial

**Hadrian** (AD **76–138**), bust

family which had its roots at Italica on the lower Guadalquivir near Seville in southern Spain. His father was Publius Aelius Hadrianus Afer, a leading member of the city who had reached the rank of praetor in the senate; he died when Hadrian was ten years old. His mother's name was Domitia Paulina, and his own name until he became emperor was Publius Aelius Hadrianus.

**Birth, early career, and accession as emperor** It is not certain that the future emperor was born at Italica. One tradition speaks of Rome as his birthplace. One of the original settlers at Italica in the third century BC was an ancestor of Hadrian, from Hadria on the east coast of Italy. The emperor-to-be was thus a provincial who possessed an ancient link with Italy, and his interests and policies as emperor owed much to these features in his ancestry. Italica was also the home of Marcus Ulpius Traianus (Trajan), Hadrian's second cousin and predecessor as emperor. Early in his life Hadrian acquired as his guardians Trajan and another prominent citizen of Italica, Acilius Attianus. Much of his youth was passed in Rome where he first developed his deep admiration for Greek culture, another leitmotif of his reign. As a member of a senatorial family, he embarked on the customary career towards the senate, holding posts as a military tribune on the Danube and Upper Rhine between AD 95 and 97, tribune of the people in 105, and the praetorship in 108. But he also enjoyed less usual distinctions. He served on Trajan's staff in Dacia and in the east. When Trajan was adopted by the emperor Nerva as his son and successor, it was Hadrian who carried the congratulations of the Danube legions to him. Hadrian held the command of a legion, exceptionally, before his praetorship and he governed the Danubian frontier province of Pannonia before his election as consul (in 108), again unusually. Eventually, in 117, he was allotted one of the most senior of all provincial commands, the governorship of Syria. These exceptional features in Hadrian's *cursus honorum* naturally spring from the fact that he was Trajan's closest male relative and had married, in AD 100, the emperor's closest female relation, Vibia Sabina. Trajan's adoption of Hadrian on his deathbed in 117 was not therefore wholly unexpected. But gossip in Rome, stemming from suspicious circumstances surrounding the event, hinted at darker purposes, and specifically at the involvement of Trajan's wife, Plotina, on Hadrian's side. The truth did not emerge but it is possible that the adoption was engineered from within palace circles rather than issuing directly from Trajan's own wishes.

On his accession, Hadrian was careful to pay respect to senatorial opinion. His immediate position was secure: he had been acclaimed by the army. But in the early months of the reign a conspiracy involving ex-consuls and other adherents of Trajan was detected and quashed by the execution of four of the alleged ringleaders. Thereafter, Hadrian was not quite able to shake off a reputation for cruelty and his relations with the senate remained uneasy.

Hadrian's views on the extent of the empire and its external relations were made manifest at an early date. Disturbances in Mauretania Tingitana (Morocco) and Britain were promptly suppressed and mounted nomads were prevented from attacking the Danube provinces. But forward movement from existing frontiers was not to be countenanced. It was even reported that he considered abandoning the trans-Danubian province of Dacia, only recently added to the empire by Trajan. External wars were avoided throughout the reign. The concomitant of this strategic policy was the planning of strong frontiers, clearly demarcated and well garrisoned. The classic instance is the great barrier of stone and turf which was constructed across northern Britain from about 122: Hadrian's Wall. Another decisive step was taken in Upper Germany, where a series of frontier works had been under development from about AD 90 onward. Under Hadrian a more coherent frontier was brought into being, consisting of a timber palisade set in front of pre-existing watchtowers and a communication track. In north Africa, too, measures were taken to guard the main routes through the desert fringes, without disrupting the economics of native life.

**Hadrian's Wall** Hadrian's frontier solution in Britain took the form of the most elaborate frontier work of any date in the empire. In the original plan this was to be a stone wall running from Segedunum (Wallsend) on the Tyne to the River Irthing and a rampart of turf and clay from the Irthing to the Solway Firth. At every Roman mile there was to be a fortlet (milecastle) and between each pair of fortlets two evenly spaced towers (turrets). Garrison forts were to lie to the rear, supplying auxiliary units to patrol the frontier and operate beyond it as necessary. Immediately in front of the wall lay a great ditch, while to the rear another ditch and accompanying mounds (the vallum) were designed to close off the frontier to unauthorized personnel. Lateral communication was to be supplied by a road running behind the wall (the military way). The terrain traversed by Hadrian's Wall is diverse. On the eastern and western flanks the ground is low lying. In the centre the volcanic outcrop of the Whin Sill offers a magnificent northward-facing scarp, along the top of which the wall was to run. The exposed western flank on the Cumberland coast was seen as vulnerable and was covered by a series of fortlets and towers, echoing those on the wall itself.

The building of this immense work was begun in the governorship of Hadrian's ally, Aulus Platorius Nepos (122–5), and may well be a direct result of Hadrian's visit to Britain in 122. The coherent structure of the frontier in its first form bears all the hallmarks of a single organizing mind and it is most likely that that mind was Hadrian's own. Its purpose was not in the first instance tactical. A wall 80 miles long is not the most obvious or effective means of defence, particularly for an army trained and habituated to open warfare. Hadrian's Wall defined the limits of the Roman empire in Britain, but it did more. In the words of Hadrian's fourth-century biographer, it separated Romans from barbarians, one of the few recorded statements on the role of Roman frontiers and one which may be traced back to Hadrian's own thought.

The original conception of this frontier, whether or not it sprang fully formed from the emperor's mind, did not come to fruition. Modification was quickly found necessary. In particular, the garrison bases lay too far to the rear and by 125 or 126 forts were being established on the line of the wall itself. The width of the wall was reduced as building proceeded westward, presumably to diminish the scale of the task. The western flank was further protected by a number of outposts north of the wall, perhaps revealing the region from which raiding was expected. These were major changes, and there were to be others, but the wall remained largely Hadrian's in concept and execution. Although raided for its stone in subsequent centuries, considerable sections of the wall remain, and Hadrian's Wall is Britain's most substantial and best-known Roman structure.

The visit of Hadrian to Britain in 122 was followed by a renewed stimulus to urban development as an essential feature of the Romanization of the province. Several cities either built or rebuilt public buildings in Hadrian's reign, including several which lay close to the zone of military control. The splendid inscription set up in 129 by the *civitas* (citizen body) of the Cornovii in dedication of the new forum at their centre of Viroconium (Wroxeter) occurs in precisely the kind of setting that would have caught Hadrian's attention.

The emperor's care for the provinces went far beyond the defence of their frontiers. When his position was wholly secure, in 120–21, he embarked on several years of travel, inspecting provinces and their armies. Of the sixteen years from 117 to 133, more than twelve were devoted to journeys across the empire. Hadrian left his mark where he travelled. In Gaul he ordered and consecrated a temple to Plotina at Nemausus (Nîmes). In Spain he brought together provincial representatives to examine a scheme for troop levies. In Mauretania he directed a military operation of some kind. But most of his travelling was done in the Greek provinces of the east. Here there were no military preoccupations and few of a pressing administrative kind. Hadrian's deep admiration for Greek culture was to find full expression during his long sojourn in Greece and Asia Minor. The city populations there responded to his progress with immense enthusiasm. In a second series of journeys he visited north Africa, inspecting the army and its works. His detailed interest in military training and effectiveness is attested by a remarkable inscription found at Lambaesis, which provides extracts from addresses given to the troops, praising and encouraging them and their commanders. In 129 Hadrian passed through the Levant and visited Jerusalem, ordering that city to be rebuilt as Aelia Capitolina, thereby unwittingly laying the foundations for the great Jewish revolt of 132. Later in the year the emperor's entourage moved into Egypt, where Hadrian's beloved boy Antinous drowned in the Nile. The emperor's reaction was one of uncontrollable grief. Statues of the youth were carved in their thousands and near the scene of the fatality the city of Antinopolis was founded. The cult of the deified Antinous now inaugurated was honoured not only in Egypt but across the empire.

Most of the rest of the reign was spent amid peaceful pleasures in Rome. As well as literature, art, and philosophy, Hadrian was devoted to architecture and spent both time and money on buildings in Rome and Athens. In Rome, the temple of Venus and Roma was completed in his last years. The Pantheon, one of the greatest surviving works of Roman architecture, had been built early in the reign, replacing a building of Marcus Agrippa. But the most characteristic creation of this complex man was the vast private villa which he laid out at Tibur (Tivoli), close to Rome. This was an architectural ensemble which reproduced many of the buildings and places seen and admired by Hadrian on his journeys, among them the Canopus and Serapeum in Egypt, and the Academy, the Stoa Poikile, Lyceum, and Prytaneium in Athens. In Rome itself, on the Tiber bank below the Janiculum Hill, he built his own great mausoleum in the form of a brick drum; it survives as the Castel Sant' Angelo. There his remains were duly laid, after two years of increasing infirmity ended at Baiae (modern Baia, west of Naples) on 10 July 138. It is reported that he died with a valedictory verse to his own soul on his lips. MALCOLM TODD

**Sources** A. R. Birley, *Hadrian: the restless emperor* (1997) • D. Magie, ed. and trans., 'Vita Hadriani', *Scriptores historiae Augustae*, 1 (1921) • *Dio's Roman history*, ed. and trans. E. Cary, 8 (1925), lxix [epitome] • [Eutropius], *Eutropi Breviarium ab urbe condita*, ed. H. Droysen, MGH Auctores Antiquissimi, 2 (Berlin, 1879), 138–40 • H. Mattingly and E. A. Sydenham, eds., *Vespasian to Hadrian* (1926), vol. 2 of *The Roman imperial coinage*, ed. H. Mattingly and others (1923–94) • P. Strack, *Die römische Reichsprägung des zweiten Jahrhunderts*, 2 (1931) • A. Piganiol, *Histoire de Rome*, 5th edn (1962) • A. Garzetti, *From Tiberius to the Antonines* (1974) • E. Nash, *Pictorial dictionary of Rome* (1962) • G. W. Bowersock, *The sophists in the Roman empire* (1969) • B. W. Henderson, *The life and principate of the Emperor Hadrian, AD 76–138* (1923) • D. J. Breeze, *Hadrian's Wall*, 3rd edn (1987) • J. Skinner, *Hadrian's Wall in 1801: observations on the Roman wall*, ed. H. Coombs and P. Coombs (1978)

**Likenesses** bronze head, BM • bust, BM [*see illus.*]

**Wealth at death** very wealthy

**Hadrian** (630x37–709), abbot of St Peter's and St Paul's, Canterbury, was a native of north Africa. The broad outlines of his career are known from Bede's *Historia ecclesiastica* and may be supplemented by incidental references in the corpus of biblical commentaries and glosses which derive from the teaching of Hadrian (and his colleague Archbishop Theodore) at Canterbury.

**African and Italian origins** The exact date of Hadrian's birth is unknown, but apparently fell during the years 630 to 637 (he cannot in any case have been born later than 637, since he must have been at least thirty years old when he was offered the archbishopric of Canterbury by Pope Vitalian in 667). Bede describes Hadrian as an African by birth (*vir natione Afir*) who was equally skilled in Greek and Latin. In combination these remarks imply that Hadrian originated in one of the eastern (Greek-speaking) provinces of Africa; and an observation preserved in the Canterbury biblical commentaries concerning the furnishings of houses in Libya further suggests that Hadrian originated in Libya Cyrenaica, perhaps in one of the cities of the Pentapolis. Hadrian is next recorded (by Bede) as the abbot of a *monasterium Ni[s]idanum* in Campania near Naples. The identity of this monastery has caused difficulty (not least because manuscripts of Bede's *Historia ecclesiastica* give the adjective in the form *Hiridanum*; but the orthographical confusion is easily explained by letter forms of the presumed cursive half-uncial script of the document from which Bede derived his notice), but most scholars now agree that the monastery in question was located on the islet of Nisida in the Bay of Naples, now in the suburbs of Naples and joined to the mainland by a causeway. No trace of the monastery remains; but there is sound evidence that there were numerous other monasteries in the vicinity of Naples, and that, in the sixth century, particularly through the activities of Eugippius and his followers, there was a strong tradition of biblical scholarship. It may be assumed that the young Hadrian arrived in the bilingual community of Naples as a (Greek-speaking) refugee from the Arab invasions of Cyrenaica (which took place in 644–5), devoted himself there to biblical studies, and in due course became abbot of a small monastery on Nisida.

In the mid-seventh century much of southern Italy was under the control of Lombard rulers, with the centre of their dukedom at Benevento; Naples and its environs, however, because they could be defended from the sea by the Byzantine fleet, were independent of Lombard dominion. It was in the attempt to recover the Lombard lands that the Byzantine emperor Constans II (641–68) invaded southern Italy in 662. Although the expedition was largely unsuccessful, Constans II made his base at Naples, where he spent most of 663 and from where he travelled to Rome to meet Pope Vitalian. Perhaps because Greek was his native language, Hadrian may have served as an interpreter for the emperor, and may have accompanied him on his journey to meet the pope; in any case, it is known from Bede that Hadrian was subsequently entrusted with two imperial embassies to Francia, perhaps for the purpose of raising Frankish support for the emperor's struggle against the Lombards. A few years later, in 667, the archbishop-elect of Canterbury (one Wigheard) died in Rome, and Pope Vitalian offered the archbishopric to Hadrian. Hadrian declined the offer, and suggested instead the name of one Andrew (then chaplain of a nunnery in the Naples area), who was deemed too ill to accept. On Hadrian's advice the post was subsequently offered to Theodore, then a monk in Rome, who accepted the appointment, with far-reaching consequences for the English church. The story (as related by Bede) shows that Hadrian was the trusted counsellor of the pope and the Byzantine emperor, then the two most powerful authorities in Christendom.

**Abbot and teacher at Canterbury** One condition of the election of Theodore was that Hadrian should accompany the new archbishop to England. Hadrian and Theodore set off from Rome together on 27 May 668; but when they were passing through Francia, Hadrian was detained by the mayor of the palace, Ebroin, on the suspicion that he was carrying some embassy from the Byzantine emperor to the kings of Britain. Only when the suspicions were proved groundless was Hadrian allowed to pass. He arrived in England in 670, a year later than Theodore. On his arrival he was given the monastery of St Peter and St Paul at Canterbury (it had been a papal condition that Hadrian and his followers be suitably housed in England). Little is known of Hadrian's administrative activity as abbot; but it is noteworthy that he obtained from Pope Agatho (*r.* 678–81) a papal privilege for his monastery, and in other ways assisted Theodore in his administrative duties (soon after their arrival, for example, they visited every part of the archdiocese) and in giving instruction at their school in Canterbury to which, in Bede's words, they 'attracted a crowd of students into whose minds they daily poured the streams of wholesome learning' (Bede, *Hist. eccl.*, 4.2), giving instruction in scripture as well as in metre, astronomy, and computus. A surviving letter from Aldhelm to Hadrian, preserved fragmentarily by William of Malmesbury, shows that Aldhelm was one of these Canterbury students.

It is unfortunate that no writings have been preserved in Hadrian's name. He is frequently cited by name in the corpus of biblical commentaries and glosses which were based on his (and Theodore's) teaching at their Canterbury school, and these citations indicate that Hadrian, like Theodore, was concerned with literal (Antiochene) exposition of the biblical text. Various surviving preconquest manuscripts provide evidence of liturgical books brought to England by Hadrian. Pericope lists preserved in various Northumbrian manuscripts (including the Lindisfarne gospels) pertain to feasts and saints of Naples, and were presumably derived from a (now lost) gospel book of Neapolitan liturgical use brought from Naples by Hadrian; and the feasts of many Campanian saints commemorated in the Old English martyrology and in the calendar of St Willibrord apparently derive from a Campanian sacramentary brought by Hadrian. Hadrian's influence on early Anglo-Saxon liturgy, through the medium of these two lost books, was very considerable.

According to Bede, Hadrian died in the forty-first year after he was sent to England by Pope Vitalian, hence in 709; he would have been between seventy-five and eighty years old at the time. He was buried in his own monastery, where his remains were translated and rehoused in the new buildings there in 1091. Later Anglo-Saxon liturgical calendars record his deposition on 9 January. An unprinted life of Hadrian, probably by the late eleventh-century hagiographer Goscelin, is preserved in two contemporary manuscripts; but the historical information contained in this life is derived wholly from Bede.

MICHAEL LAPIDGE

**Sources** Bede, *Hist. eccl.*, 4.1–2; 5.20 · B. Bischoff and M. Lapidge, *Biblical commentaries from the Canterbury school of Theodore and Hadrian* (1994), 82–132

**Hadrill, (John) Michael Wallace-** (1916–1985), historian, was born at Bromsgrove, Worcestershire, on 29 September 1916, the eldest of the three sons (there were no daughters) of Frederic Wallace-Hadrill, schoolmaster, and his wife, (Tamsin) Norah White, who came from a family of brewers. From 1930 to 1935 he went to Cheltenham College. From there he won a scholarship to Corpus Christi College, Oxford, to read modern history, in which he gained a second class in 1938. During the Second World War he served in intelligence and from 1943 to 1945 he was seconded to MI6.

Returning to Corpus in 1945 and elected a junior research fellow, Wallace-Hadrill could now pursue wholeheartedly the Frankish and Anglo-Saxon studies which became his life's work. In 1947 he was elected to a tutorial fellowship at Merton College and a university lectureship soon followed. In 1950 he married Anne, daughter of Neville Wakefield, schoolmaster; they had two sons.

In 1952 appeared Wallace-Hadrill's first book, *The Barbarian West, 400–1000*, which surveyed in a spirited manner the German peoples' invasions of the disintegrating western empire, not just in terms of occupation, settlement, and power struggles, but more in search of the Goths', Lombards', and Franks' historical self-awareness after they had become Christians. In 1955 he accepted the chair of medieval history at Manchester, where he stayed until 1961, restlessly moving house more than once. The edition of the *Fourth Book of the Chronicle of Fredegar* (1960) was his chief publication during these years, but there were also a number of seminal papers, for example on the Frankish blood feud and the failure of the Visigoths in France. His editing and translation were vigorous, masterly, and full of life. In 1962 appeared *The Long-Haired Kings*, a collection of papers. His study of the Merovingians and the rise of the Arnulfings who replaced them is outstanding in its sensitive use of the foremost historical sources to illuminate the horizons of kings, bishops, and the warrior society they had to try and 'correct'.

The administrative demands of his chair could only be met at the expense of his own scholarly efforts and aims; in 1961, therefore, Wallace-Hadrill gratefully accepted a senior research fellowship, to which his old college, Merton, elected him. Nevertheless in 1965 he took over the onerous editorship of the *English Historical Review*, at first single-handed and from 1967 until 1974 together with his Merton colleague J. M. Roberts. In 1969–70 he gave the Ford lectures, published in 1971: *Early Germanic Kingship in England and on the Continent*. Never before had Anglo-Saxon, Merovingian, and Carolingian history been looked at so closely together, particularly from the angle of the beliefs and rituals that grew up to sustain kings during the crisis-ridden ninth century. In 1974 he was elected Chichele professor of modern history at Oxford in succession to Geoffrey Barraclough and migrated to All Souls College. He had not coveted the post and was almost a reluctant professor but as always performed his duties of office vigorously and twice served as an examiner in the final honour school.

During these years Wallace-Hadrill's *magnum opus*, *The Frankish Church*, took shape, published though it was shortly after his retirement in 1983. Like all his books, it is headed by a clear statement of intent. Those looking for a textbook systematically setting forth every development would look in vain. His chief themes were the spiritual centres where religious life, ideas, personalities, and learning flourished. He was a man of profound and deep-rooted faith and convictions, which can be sensed by his readers in what he wrote about the great missionaries of the seventh and eighth centuries.

Wallace-Hadrill was elected a fellow of the British Academy in 1969 and was made an honorary DLitt in the same year. Both Merton in 1974 and Corpus Christi in 1984 elected him to honorary fellowships, and in 1982 he was appointed CBE. Next year his pupils presented him with a Festschrift and in 1984 he became a corresponding fellow of the Medieval Academy of America. His last years were devoted to a new commentary on Bede's *Ecclesiastical History*, which was nearly completed when he died.

Wallace-Hadrill was a sturdy man with a kindly eye. He hated being telephoned and was laconic in his notes, all written in a memorably fine hand. He was a forceful writer (though sometimes elliptical and allusive); authority seemed to emanate from him and to suit him naturally. His advice was much sought after: he served on the councils of the Royal Historical Society and the British Academy for many years. In a world of doubts and equivocation he conveyed a sense of certainty and direction, with his formidable and incorruptible views and criticism. He could be a hard taskmaster to his researchers, expecting punctual work and measured progress. He was all the same accessible and warm-hearted, with an irresistible and indestructible sense of humour. He knew a great deal about flowers, plants, and gardening. During his last months he was well aware of a heart condition but did not allow it to turn him away from his Bede commentary and accustomed pursuits. He died on 3 November 1985 while working hard in his beloved garden at his home, Reynolds Farm, Cassington, near Oxford. KARL LEYSER, *rev.*

**Sources** *The Times* (7 Nov 1985) • K. Leyser, 'John Michael Wallace Hadrill', *EngHR*, 101 (1986), 561–3 • personal knowledge (1990) • private information (1990)

**Wealth at death** £94,713: probate, 9 April 1986, *CGPLA Eng. & Wales*

**Hædde** [St Hædde, Heddi] (*d.* **705/6**), bishop of Winchester, was the third bishop of that see. His appearance as bishop in the witness list of a charter of 675 alongside his predecessor Leuthere (*d.* 675/6) suggests that Hædde was appointed while Leuthere was still alive. Bede characterized Hædde as 'a good and just man, whose life and teaching as a bishop depended more on his innate love of virtue than what he learned from books' (Bede, *Hist. eccl.*, 5.18). Nevertheless, Hædde was the recipient of a respectful Latin octosyllabic poem from Archbishop Theodore, who consecrated him as bishop in London, and a verse in similar form commemorates the dedication by Hædde of a church or altar to St Paul. Hædde's episcopate coincided with the consolidation of the kingdom of the West Saxons as a result of the conquest of new territory under the kings Cædwalla and Ine and it would appear that as bishop he had a leading role to play in the expanding province. He is named by Ine as an adviser in the compilation of his law-code which contained provisions for enforcing baptism, payment of tithes, and other ecclesiastical measures. In spite of the large size of the West Saxon diocese, which covered the area of what is now Hampshire to Devon, the West Saxons apparently resisted Archbishop Theodore's attempts to divide it, which led to their excommunication in 703 or 704 by Archbishop Berhtwald. A relaxation of restrictions had to be sought the following year so that a meeting to establish peace between the East and West Saxons could be held, for which Hædde, together with Bishop Waldhere of London, had drawn up the terms. Hædde witnessed a number of West Saxon charters during his episcopacy and made a grant of land in what is now Somerset to Glastonbury Abbey. Possibly Hædde had a particular connection with Glastonbury, as William of Malmesbury records that 'Hædde *episcopus*' was one of those whose names he saw commemorated there on a stone 'pyramid'. Hædde was responsible for translating the body of St Birinus from Dorchester to Winchester, and was subsequently to be recognized himself as a saint in Winchester; he died on 7 July in either 705 or 706 and may be presumed to have been buried at Winchester. Pehthelm, who was a monk and deacon with Hædde's successor Aldhelm, told Bede how soil taken from the (unidentified) place where Hædde had died and mixed with water had cured sick men and cattle; so much soil had been removed for this purpose that a sizeable hole had been excavated. BARBARA YORKE

**Sources** Bede, *Hist. eccl.*, 3.7; 4.12; 5.18 • *AS chart.*, S 1249, 51 • P. Chaplais, 'The letter from Bishop Wealdhere of London to Archbishop Berhtwald of Canterbury: the earliest original "letter close" extant in the west', *Medieval scribes, manuscripts and libraries: essays presented to N. R. Ker*, ed. M. B. Parkes and A. G. Watson (1978), 3–23 • H. Edwards, *The charters of the early West Saxon kingdom* (1988) • M. Lapidge, 'Some remnants of Bede's lost *Liber epigrammatum*', *EngHR*, 90 (1975), 798–820, esp. 817–18 • *The early history of Glastonbury: an edition, translation, and study of William of Malmesbury's De antiquitate Glastonie ecclesie*, ed. J. Scott (1981), 84–5

**Hael, Rhydderch**. *See* Mills, Richard (1809–1844).

**Hæsten** [Hásteinn, Hasting] (*fl.* **882–893**), viking leader, makes his first certain appearance in the work of two contemporary Frankish annalists, who independently reported Northmen on the Loire in 882 led by 'A(l)stingus', a Frankish attempt at a name the Norse form of which was probably Hásteinn; he appears as Hæsten in English sources and has sometimes been named, in Anglicized form, as Hasting. The West Frankish king Louis III induced him to quit the Loire for the channel coast. Perhaps active in the ravaging of northern Francia by the 'great army' during the 880s, Hæsten is next named in the annals of St Vaast under 890. He established a base on the Somme at Argœuves, then made a 'treacherous' deal with Rudolf, abbot of St Vaast, 'that he might be able to go freely wherever he wanted' (*Annales Vedastini*, s.a. 890), apparently undertaking to protect St Vaast against other vikings at Noyon; then on 27 December he attacked St Vaast. It is unclear if Hæsten was among those Northmen defeated at the Dyle in 891. The St Vaast annalist reports Hæsten's wintering in 891–2 at Amiens, whence he launched a successful surprise attack on forces led by another West Frankish king, Odo. In autumn 892 famine caused the Northmen to leave Francia for England.

Hæsten, the only viking leader named in the section of the Anglo-Saxon Chronicle devoted to the years 892–6, crossed the channel, evidently bringing wife and sons, 'with 80 ships', and 'made a fort' at Milton Royal in north Kent. A 'great army' came in 250 ships to Appledore, south Kent. In 893 Alfred, adopting a classic tactic, came to terms with the smaller force: Hæsten's two sons were baptized (Hæsten himself had perhaps adopted Christianity in Francia), with Alfred and Ealdorman Æthelred of the Mercians as respective godfathers; Hæsten gave 'hostages and oaths'; Alfred 'made him generous gifts of money'. Hæsten then crossed the Thames to Essex, 'made a fort' at Benfleet, and 'immediately went harrying in that very province which Æthelred, his son's godfather, was in charge of' (*ASC*, s.a. 893 [text A]). He made no further attacks south of the Thames, and Benfleet became a key base.

Meanwhile the Appledore army raided in Wessex, and, wishing to carry booty 'across the Thames into Essex to meet the ships', was beaten at Farnham. The survivors eventually reached Benfleet. Hæsten now went raiding again into Mercia, leaving wife and sons at Benfleet with the 'great army'. The raiders included 'great reinforcements both from East Anglia and from Northumbria', which were now under Danish control. Reaching the Severn they made a fort at Buttington. After 'many weeks' besieged by a combined West Saxon, Mercian, and Welsh force Hæsten's men 'became distressed for lack of food and had devoured most of their horses, the remainder perishing with hunger'. They attempted a break-out, and a fierce battle ensued, in which 'many king's thegns were slain' (*ASC*, s.a. 893 [text A]). Æthelweard, the well-informed author (*c*.980) of a Latin version of the Anglo-Saxon Chronicle, says: 'further effort was seen as foolish by the Danes: they confirmed peace a second time; they did not refuse hostages; they promised to withdraw from that region'. They went back to Benfleet and 'divided out the year's booty' (*Chronicle of Æthelweard*, 50).

Hæsten now met Alfred a second time in 893, for, in Hæsten's absence, a small contingent of West Saxons, augmented by Mercian troops from London, had 'stormed the fortification at Benfleet, captured all that was in it, goods, women and children', and carried all these off to London, along with some ships. Hæsten's second encounter with Alfred thus perhaps occurred at London. Alfred, mindful of their spiritual kinship, 'restored his wife and sons to him' (*ASC*, s.a. 893 [text A]). Hasty repairs to the Benfleet ramparts damaged by the Saxon–Mercian force (Æthelweard mentions the collapse of a rebuilt section) confirm the overriding importance of forts to viking strategy.

Though Hæsten never reappears in the Anglo-Saxon Chronicle, the further Danish efforts of 893–6 may have continued under his leadership. Late in 893 there was another raid into Mercia, again involving forces from East Anglia and Northumbria. After moving to Chester, then Wales, and thence, with their loot, via Northumbria and East Anglia back to Essex, this army went up the Thames and the Lea, where, early in 895, another fort was built, 20 miles above London. When Alfred blocked the Lea, the Danes again escaped westwards, abandoning their ships (and leaving their womenfolk 'for safety in East Anglia'), to Bridgnorth on the Severn, where they overwintered. In summer 896 'the army dispersed, some to East Anglia, some to Northumbria, and those that were moneyless got themselves ships there and sailed south oversea to the Seine' (*ASC*, s.a. 896 [text A]). The annals of St Vaast (s.a. 896), naming a viking leader on the Seine as 'Hundeus', clearly distinguished him from 'Alstingus'. Hæsten probably ended his days moneyed and settled in England with his family.

If the 'Hastingus' mentioned by Regino of Prüm as 'commander of Northmen' active on the Loire in 866, when they slew Robert, count of Anjou, and in 868, when they accepted a peace-offering of 500 cows from the Bretons in return for hostages, is the same Hæsten (and not a kinsman), his uniquely well-documented career spanned three decades. Longevity alone hardly explains why legends later clustered around him. His reputation as an archetypal viking lies behind his legendary appearances in the histories of the dukes of Normandy by Dudo of St Quentin (1015–26) and William of Jumièges (*c*.1070), which take him as far as the town of Luni in north-west Italy, as well as a number of other high-medieval legends of his exploits in north-west France. The genuine Hæsten, in the

890s, applied his continental military and political experience to England in campaigns of dramatic mobility, resourcefulness, and skilful manoeuvre matching Alfred's own. Hæsten's personal journey from raiding to acculturation and settlement typified the viking age.

JANET L. NELSON

**Sources** *ASC*, s.a. 892–6 [text A] · *The chronicle of Æthelweard*, ed. and trans. A. Campbell (1962) · *Alfred the Great: Asser's Life of King Alfred and other contemporary sources*, ed. and trans. S. Keynes and M. Lapidge (1983) · J. L. Nelson, ed. and trans., *The annals of St Bertin* (1991) · 'Annales Vedastini', *Annales Xantenses et Annales Vedastini*, ed. B. von Simson, MGH Scriptores Rerum Germanicarum, [12] (Hanover and Leipzig, 1909) · *Reginonis abbatis Prumiensis chronicon cum continuatione Treverensi*, ed. F. Kurze, MGH Scriptores Rerum Germanicarum, [50] (Hanover, 1890) · C. Clark, 'The narrative mode of the Anglo-Saxon Chronicle', *England before the conquest: studies in primary sources presented to Dorothy Whitelock*, ed. P. Clemoes and K. Hughes (1971), 215–35 · R. Waterhouse, 'The Haesten episode in the Anglo-Saxon Chronicle', *Studia Neophilologica*, 46 (1974), 136–41 · F. Amory, 'The viking Hasting in Franco-Scandinavian legend', *Saints, scholars and heroes: studies in medieval culture in honor of C. W. Jones*, ed. M. H. King and W. M. Stevens, 2 vols. (1979), 2.265–86 · T. Shippey, 'A missing army: some doubts about the Alfredian Chronicle', *In Geardagum* (1982), 4.41–55 · P. H. Sawyer, *The age of the Vikings*, 2nd edn (1971) · P. H. Sawyer, *Kings and vikings* (1982) · S. Coupland and J. L. Nelson, 'The vikings on the continent', *History Today*, 38/12 (1988), 12–19 · A. P. Smyth, *King Alfred the Great* (1995)

**Haffenden** [Wilson-Haffenden], **Elizabeth** (1906–1976), costume designer, was born on 18 April 1906 at Homewood, Hazeldean Road, south Croydon, the daughter of James Wilson-Haffenden, a wholesale draper, and his wife, Edith Maud Carruthers. She attended Croydon School of Art and London's Royal College of Art, then became a commercial artist before moving into theatre costume design during the 1930s, in association with the production designer Laurence Irving. Her experiments with expressionist masks on the 1939 J. B. Priestley play *Johnson over Jordan* were deemed controversial by contemporary critics hostile to German-influenced aesthetics. Haffenden's first job in the film industry was on the 1933 Sound City production *Colonel Blood*, a historical drama set in the seventeenth century, with Laurence Irving and John Bryan, who also had a background in British theatre, as art directors. Haffenden continued to work in theatre until the 1950s, but joined the Gaumont-British film studio at Shepherd's Bush in 1939, and from 1942 to 1949 was in charge of costume design for the associated company Gainsborough. Her connection with Bryan, who, like Haffenden, went on to become a major international figure, continued during the 1940s. They worked together on several Gainsborough productions, including *Fanny by Gas light* (1944) and some of the cycle of melodramas for which Haffenden became renowned: *Love Story* (1944), *The Wicked Lady* (1945), and *Caravan* and *The Magic Bow* (both 1946).

Despite being made on low budgets in wartime austerity conditions, these films were visually splendid and made the most of Haffenden's flamboyant, stylish costumes, particularly in the period romances. Although critics regarded them as potboilers, the Gainsborough melodramas were very popular with female audiences, and the company promoted several of the films on the basis of their costumes, and on Haffenden's fashionable designs. For example, Gainsborough's publicity for *Caravan* credited her with having predicted in 1944 the post-war swing to glamorous, new look-style fashions. Haffenden's designs for the Gainsborough costume cycle were often quite daring. Indeed, it has been argued that she used the luxurious abundance of folds and furls in period dress to put on display, in coded form, an eroticized female sexuality (Harper, 44). Some scenes of *The Wicked Lady* had to be reshot for the US market because the low-cut dresses revealed too much cleavage for American tastes, while in publicity stills for *Caravan*, it is clear that Jean Kent, as Rosal, is not wearing a brassière under her skimpy Gypsy blouse. Such extravagant sexual display was not lost on British audiences tired of austerity and looking forward to a post-war consumer economy.

In the 1950s, after the demise of Gainsborough, Haffenden became resident costume designer for the British arm of Metro-Goldwyn-Mayer, based at Elstree, and worked on historical extravaganzas such as *Beau Brummell* (1954) and *The Adventures of Quentin Durward* (1955). In the late 1950s she became freelance, and from 1959 consistently worked in association with her close friend the Technicolor colour consultant Joan Bridge (*b.* 1919), whom she first met at Gainsborough in 1946. They won academy awards for *Ben-Hur* (1959) and *A Man for All Seasons* (1966), and British Academy of Film and Television Arts (BAFTA) award nominations for *The Amorous Adventures of Moll Flanders* (1965) and *Half a Sixpence* (1967). They also received a BAFTA award for *A Man for All Seasons*. Haffenden's designs for colour films were as dramatic and evocative as those she created for black and white. The costumes had an eye-catching vibrancy and textural richness, and a distinctive visual style that went beyond the demands of character and narrative.

During the 1960s and 1970s Haffenden and Bridge worked on many highly successful productions, including *The Prime of Miss Jean Brodie* (1968), based on Muriel Spark's novel and starring Maggie Smith, *Fiddler on the Roof* (1971), and *The Homecoming* (1973), scripted by Harold Pinter from his own play and directed by Peter Hall. Haffenden started pre-production work with Joan Bridge on *Julia* (1977), but died before production began. Her death brought to an end an illustrious career in theatre and cinema, spanning more than forty years. She died at 20 Devonshire Place, St Marylebone, London, on 29 May 1976.

PAM COOK

**Sources** S. Harper, 'Art direction and costume design', *Gainsborough melodrama*, ed. S. Aspinall and R. Murphy, BFI Dossier, 18 (1983), 40–52 · P. Cook, *Fashioning the nation: costume and identity in British cinema* (1996) · E. Leese, *Costume design in the movies* (1991) · SIFT database, BFI National Library · BFI, Special Collections · stills, posters, and designs, BFI · Theatre Museum, London · personal knowledge (2004) · *CGPLA Eng. & Wales* (1976) · b. cert. · d. cert.

**Archives** FILM BFI NFTVA

**Likenesses** newspaper photograph (with J. Bridge), BFI · photograph (with J. Bridge), BFI, *Ben Hur* (1959) file

**Wealth at death** £15,423: administration with will, 19 Oct 1976, *CGPLA Eng. & Wales*

**Haffkine, Waldemar Mordecai Wolff** [*formerly* Vladimir Aronovitch Chavkin] (**1860–1930**), zoologist and bacteriologist, born Vladimir Aronovich Chavkin in Odessa, Russia, on 15 March 1860, was the son of Aaron and Rosalie Chavkin (*d. c.*1866), members of a Jewish merchant family formerly of Landsberg. Shortly after his mother's death, which occurred when Haffkine was only six, the family moved to Berdyansk, 300 miles from Odessa, where his father found employment as a schoolteacher. After early education at home and at the county school in Berdyansk, in 1872 Haffkine entered the *Gymnasium* at Berdyansk. Here he excelled in both sports and academic subjects, showing a particular aptitude for natural sciences—the subject he later chose to study at Novorossiysk (later Odessa) University from 1879 to 1883. During his time at Odessa, Haffkine came under the formative guidance of the zoologist and pioneer of immunology Ilya Mechnikov, with whom Haffkine was later to collaborate. He also became active in politics, joining a populist-socialist revolutionary organization called Narodnaya Volya ('Will of the people').

Haffkine remained at Odessa until 1888, obtaining a position in the Zoological Museum, but since he refused to be baptized into the Christian faith there was no prospect of his ever obtaining a university professorship in Russia. Indeed, a series of pogroms against Jews in southern Russia—some of which affected Haffkine personally—induced him to emigrate to Switzerland; his mentor, Mechnikov, had left for Paris earlier that year. Haffkine remained in Geneva for one year, where he taught at the university medical school. In 1889 he joined Mechnikov at the Institut Pasteur, though in the junior capacity of assistant librarian. However, he was able here to pursue his interest in the hereditary characteristics of unicellular organisms, and published work on the protozoan *Paramecium* in the *Annals de l'Institut Pasteur.*

While at the institute Haffkine became interested in bacteriological research and particularly in immunization against cholera. In 1892 he published a brief paper in which he demonstrated that immunity could be induced in animals by inoculating them with attenuated cholera bacilli. By July he had conducted successful experiments on human subjects, including himself, thus raising the possibility of preventing one of the most dreaded diseases of the nineteenth century. News of Haffkine's work spread quickly and soon came to the notice of Lord Dufferin, a former viceroy of India. Dufferin wrote to the secretary of state for India requesting that Haffkine be permitted to pursue his studies in what was regarded by many as the 'home' of the disease.

Haffkine arrived in Calcutta in 1893. After injecting himself and four Indian doctors, he was able to induce some villagers in the cholera belt of Bengal to come forward for inoculation. Encouraged by his early success he set off on an expedition through northern India which was to last almost two and a half years. However, he met with far more opposition than he had anticipated, not only from the Indian population, which was often suspicious of Western medicine, but also from the Indian Medical Service (IMS), whose members were dubious about the efficacy of his inoculation (which was then, as now, far from completely effective). Medical scepticism was reinforced by racial prejudice and Haffkine's Jewish-Russian origins made him doubly suspect in the eyes of the Anglo-Indian establishment. While touring the North-Western Provinces Haffkine was denounced by some newspapers as a Russian spy. He found that his only true friend and supporter in India was the health officer of Calcutta, W. J. Simpson, who had achieved almost pariah status in Calcutta through his trenchant criticisms of both the government and the Indian-dominated municipal corporation.

Despite the limited success of mass inoculation in India, Haffkine was persuaded to continue, and tens of thousands were inoculated before his work was interrupted in 1896. But while he received support at the highest level, there remained considerable antipathy towards him and his methods. This became evident when he was called upon to investigate the plague epidemic which swept India following its first appearance in Bombay in the summer of 1896. Haffkine established a plague laboratory at Grant Medical College, Bombay, and began to work on a vaccine to prevent the disease using the same immunological principles which underlay his inoculation against cholera. This time, however, Haffkine found that immunity could be conferred by using killed bacilli, rather than merely attenuated ones—a method which was subsequently to be used by Almroth Wright in his inoculation against typhoid. By December the vaccine was ready, and Haffkine's success in immunizing rats against the disease was published in a scientific paper in the following year. By January 1897 Haffkine was confident enough to test the vaccine on himself, and in the coming months successful trials were conducted in prisons and among Indian volunteers. Advocates of inoculation were also cheered by the report of the Indian plague commission, in 1900, which concluded that Haffkine's inoculation 'can and does exercise an immune effect' and that there had been no sign of any serious side-effects.

However, the report of the plague commission did little to reassure sceptics that the vaccine was safe and effective. Even those who admitted its efficacy warned against relying too heavily on inoculation, and continued to urge more general sanitary reforms. They pointed out, quite reasonably, that it was not feasible to inoculate the entire population of India in time to prevent the spread of the disease. There was also considerable hostility among Indians to the idea of inoculation and initial reservations deepened after November 1902 following a tragic incident in the village of Malkowal in the Punjab, where 19 out of 107 villagers developed tetanus after inoculation and later died. A commission appointed by the government of India found that the vaccine had been infected before the bottles had reached Malkowal, which led many to conclude (rather too readily) that this had occurred at Haffkine's laboratory.

The Malkowal incident left Haffkine a disappointed if not broken man. He left India in 1904 with the controversy still hanging over him, though Simpson—now editor of the *Journal of Tropical Medicine*—and prominent bacteriologists in London had taken up the cudgels on Haffkine's behalf. Firm evidence against Haffkine and the Bombay laboratory was not found, and in 1907 he was invited to return to India. This he did, but cut a solitary and unhappy figure until retiring in 1914. The remainder of his life was spent in Europe, and he lived in Paris until moving to Lausanne, two years before his death. He died there aged seventy on 25 October 1930. Although not by upbringing a religious man, Haffkine had become a devout Orthodox Jew in later life and had contributed generously to the endowment of Jewish schools in eastern Europe. Never fully recognized during his lifetime, his contribution to health care in India was nevertheless memorialized in 1925 when the government of Bombay renamed the plague laboratory as the Haffkine Institute—a name it retained to the end of the century. MARK HARRISON

**Sources** S. A. Waksman, *The brilliant and tragic life of W. M. W. Haffkine* (1964) · M. Harrison, *Public health in British India: Anglo-Indian preventive medicine, 1859–1914* (1994) · I. J. Catanch, 'Plague and the tensions of empire', *Imperial medicine and indigenous societies*, ed. D. Arnold (1988) · D. Arnold, *Colonizing the body: state medicine and epidemic disease in nineteenth-century India* (1993) · G. H. Bornside, 'Waldemar Haffkine's cholera vaccines and the Ferran–Haffkine priority dispute', *Journal of the History of Medicine and Allied Sciences*, 37 (1982), 399–422 · I. Löwy, 'From guinea pigs to man: the development of Haffkine's anticholera vaccine', *Journal of the History of Medicine and Allied Sciences*, 47 (1992), 270–309 · *CGPLA Eng. & Wales* (1931)

**Archives** Hebrew University, Jerusalem · National Archives of India, New Delhi, government of India sanitary and medical records · RS

**Likenesses** photograph, *c*.1890, repro. in Waksman, *Brilliant and tragic life* · photograph, 1894, repro. in W. J. R. Simpson, *Cholera in Calcutta in 1894 and anti-choleraic inoculation* (1894) · photograph, Wellcome L.

**Wealth at death** £170 6*s*. effects in England: administration, 6 Nov 1931, *CGPLA Eng. & Wales*

**Haggard, John** (1794–1856), ecclesiastical lawyer, was born on 2 January 1794 at Bradfield, Hertfordshire, the fourth son of William Henry Haggard (1757–1837), of Bradenham Hall, Norfolk, and Park Street, Westminster, and Frances, only daughter of the Revd Thomas Hans Amyand. John Haggard was the great-uncle of the famous writer and barrister Sir Henry Rider Haggard. He was educated at Westminster School and entered Trinity Hall, Cambridge, as a pensioner on 9 June 1807. He graduated LLB in 1813 and LLD in 1818, and was elected a fellow of his college on 1 December 1815. He held his fellowship until his marriage on 20 July 1820, to Caroline (*c*.1795–1884), daughter of Mark Hodgson of Bromley, Kent. They had seven sons and three daughters.

Haggard was admitted to Lincoln's Inn on 2 November 1814, and on 3 November 1818 he became a fellow of the College of Doctors of Law in London. He was the editor of several volumes on civil and ecclesiastical law, including reports of cases argued in the consistory court of London (2 vols., 1822), in the court of Admiralty (3 vols., 1822–40), in the ecclesiastical courts at Doctors' Commons and in the high court of delegates (4 vols., 1829–32), and in the arches and prerogative courts of Canterbury (1835). In 1836 Haggard was appointed chancellor of Lincoln by his college friend Dr John Kaye, the bishop, and accompanied him on the visitation of his diocese. He was nominated chancellor of Winchester in June 1845, and two years afterwards he became commissary of Surrey in the same diocese. In 1847 he received the appointment of chancellor of Manchester from James Prince Lee, the first bishop of the diocese. He held all four posts up to his death, at Brighton, on 31 October 1856.

G. C. BOASE, *rev.* BETH F. WOOD

**Sources** *GM*, 3rd ser., 1 (1856), 784 · *The Times* (6 Nov 1856), 5 · *Manchester Guardian* (4 Nov 1856), 3 · Boase, *Mod. Eng. biog.* · Burke, *Gen. GB*

**Haggard, Sir (Henry) Rider** (1856–1925), novelist, was born on 22 June 1856 at Wood Farm, West Bradenham, Norfolk, the eighth of the ten children of William Meybohm Rider Haggard (1817–1893), squire and barrister, and his wife, a poet, Ella (*d*. 1889), daughter of Bazett Doveton, of the East India Company. Rider Haggard was educated at Ipswich grammar school and by tutors and crammers. In June 1875, when he was nineteen, his father, learning from *The Times* that an old friend and Norfolk neighbour, Sir Henry Bulwer, had been appointed lieutenant-governor of Natal, offered Sir Henry the services of the son he had early proclaimed 'only fit to be a greengrocer' (*Days of my Life*, 1.5). Bulwer took the boy sight unseen and, before long, Rider found himself managing Bulwer's household in Natal.

Africa stunned, excited, and ripened the youth. Thrust into the maelstrom in which Zulu, Boer, and Briton struggled for superiority, Rider Haggard worked hard, hunted wild game, travelled through jungle and over veld. He made a good impression, and in April 1877, when the British annexed the Transvaal, Haggard, as special commissioner to Theophilus Shepstone, raised the union flag in Church Square, Pretoria. The following year, at the age of twenty-one, he became master and registrar of the high court of the Transvaal, the youngest head of a government department in South Africa.

Before he left for Natal, Haggard had fallen deeply in love with a beautiful young woman he had met at a ball at Richmond: Mary Elizabeth Jackson, daughter of a wealthy Yorkshire farmer. But the elder Haggard had insisted that his impecunious son establish himself before he married and packed him off to South Africa instead. For three years Rider Haggard pined and yearned to return to be united with his love, but in vain. The young woman's patience ran out and she married another. Deeply scarred, Haggard fell into a rash and reckless life, resigned his civil service post, and undertook, with a friend, to raise ostriches. He had an affair with a married woman, Johanna Catherine Ford, who bore his illegitimate daughter, Ethel Rider. In 1879 he returned, unannounced to his father, to England. He met (Mariana) Louisa Margitson (*b*. 1859/60), a schoolfriend of his sister staying at Bradenham Hall, the orphaned daughter of Major John Margitson and heir to Ditchingham House, a small Norfolk estate. Within a week, they were engaged, and they were married

**Sir (Henry) Rider Haggard (1856–1925)**, by George Charles Beresford, 1902

on 11 August 1880. Later that year he returned to South Africa with his wife and a retinue of servants. There he settled down to ostrich farming and their son was born, but the First South African War began, and the trio returned to England in August 1881.

Family responsibilities weighed heavy upon Haggard now, and he entered Lincoln's Inn to read for the bar. While studying in London he also wrote his first book, *Cetywayo and his White Neighbours* (1882; 2nd edn 1888), a denunciation of Britain's South African policies. He paid his publisher £50 to have it published, but only 150 copies were sold in the year that followed. Haggard nevertheless kept on writing because he found reading for the bar a drastic downturn from exhilarating South African adventures.

Haggard actually stumbled upon fiction as a means of expressing himself. While he and his wife were in church one Sunday morning, they noticed sitting near them a 'singularly beautiful and pure-faced young lady' (*Days of my Life*, 1.209) who, they decided, deserved to be the heroine of a novel. Husband and wife each began to write a story about her. Although Mrs Haggard soon gave up, Rider wrote on and completed his first three-decker, *Dawn*. Finding a publisher was not easy, but Hurst and Blackett finally brought it out in 1884. *Dawn* earned mixed reviews and did not sell; but it received sufficient notice to encourage Haggard to return to his writing, where he next produced *The Witch's Head* (1885), a hotchpotch of manners, morals, autobiographical ruminations, and excursions into the grotesque. When the hero is forced to escape from Britain, Haggard sends him to Africa, and, immediately, the piece takes on a brilliance not evident elsewhere. Now writing from the heart, Haggard found his true milieu, and readers were enthralled by this new adventure story set in a strange, uncharted, mesmerizing part of the world.

Haggard was called to the bar, but, once there, found the law stultifying. While his need to earn a living kept him rooted to his profession by day, his hunger for adventure drove him to his desk in the evening. In 1885 one of Rider's brothers asked his opinion of an adventure story that had just been published, *Treasure Island*, and Rider replied recklessly that, though it was certainly a good tale, he himself could write a boy's book just as good. His brother challenged him, and for the next six weeks Rider spent his evenings at his pedestal desk in his Kensington house, trying to win the wager with a tale of African adventure. Cassells, who had published *Treasure Island*, agreed to publish *King Solomon's Mines* (1885), and Haggard was offered a choice of terms: £100 outright for the copyright or a 10 per cent royalty. He was ready to accept the £100, when, in the chief editor's momentary absence from the room, a clerk advised him to take the royalty. Haggard reversed himself and made the right choice. *King Solomon's Mines* met with instant success and transformed his life. The barrister was at once subordinated to the author, and he completed three more works of fiction in the next six months. The third of these, strange, mystifying, and mythological, was *She* (1887), which he wrote in just over six weeks, done, as he put it, 'at white heat, almost without rest … it came faster than my poor aching hand could set it down'. When it was ready, he took it to his recently acquired agent, slammed it down on the table, and proclaimed, 'There is what I shall be remembered by' (*Days of my Life*, 1.245–6). The novel was a *succès fou* and made Haggard and his heroine, Ayesha, household names. He gave up the law and wrote full time, producing at least a book a year until his death.

Now financially secure, Haggard retrieved Ditchingham House from tenants, took up residence, and donned the mantle of gentleman farmer, dividing his time on the one hand between writing his 'romances' (he took to dictating to a typist-secretary while pacing up and down in his study) and, on the other, in steeping himself in farming lore, developing his wife's estate, and conducting agricultural experiments. Three daughters were born during this period. Haggard also travelled widely, in Europe, the Americas, Egypt, the Holy Land, Iceland, and back to South Africa; he took easy inspiration from distant lands and foreign cultures. While he and his wife were travelling in Mexico in 1891, their son, in the charge of the Edmund Gosses in London, died suddenly of a perforated ulcer. The news turned Haggard's world upside down: years before, he had lost his only love; now he had lost his only male progeny. He returned to Ditchingham depressed and guilt-ridden, and lived for years dejected, in deep melancholy.

Still Haggard continued to write, and he tended his gardens and his farms. Slowly, too, he returned to public life. In 1895 he stood for parliament as a Unionist in East Norfolk, but he lost; that same year he was elected to the Athenaeum. He pushed on, eager 'to do something … more practical than the mere invention of romance upon romance' (Cohen, 158). To that end he addressed himself to the desperate state of farming in England and kept a diary for the year 1898, published as *A Farmer's Year* (1899), becoming an agricultural authority and expert on rural affairs. In 1901 and 1902 he travelled throughout England and Wales and wrote articles for the *Daily Express* on agricultural conditions. The result was *Rural England* (2 vols., 1902), a survey that depicted the wretched condition of farming and proposed reforms. Later he went on to publish *A Gardener's Year* (1905) and *Rural Denmark and its Lessons* (1911), a survey of co-operative farming which he held up as a model for England to adopt.

In 1895 Haggard was appointed to a royal commission to examine Salvation Army labour colonies for rehabilitating indigents in the United States. In America he was hailed in the press and lavishly entertained, not least by President Theodore Roosevelt in the White House. But when he returned to England, he, his report, and its recommendations were totally ignored. He none the less went on to serve on the royal commission for coast erosion, but after it had worked for three years the government again ignored its recommendations. Haggard resumed his daily routine of romance-writing. He also wrote a long autobiography which was published after his death as *The Days of my Life* (1926). In 1911 he was summoned to serve on the royal dominions commission, and its work took him around the world on visits to Canada, Newfoundland, South Africa, Australia, and New Zealand. Later he served on the empire settlement committee, to help relocate veterans of the First World War.

Haggard was tall and swarthy, 'a Norseman in looks' (Cohen, 147); he moved easily among the public figures of his time, becoming friendly with politicians and literati alike. A man of his time, he was an imperialist who believed deeply in the superiority of white Britons. He was also a moody fatalist who steeped himself in the occult, in antiquity, in mysticism, Buddhism, anthropology, and archaeology; he more than dabbled in spiritualism, believed in reincarnation, and sought answers to the meaning of life in the world's ancient myths. He shared many of his views with two of his closest friends, Andrew Lang (with whom he wrote *The World's Desire*, 1890) and Rudyard Kipling (who helped him plot some of his romances).

Haggard's reputation rests on his two great *tours de force*, *King Solomon's Mines* and *She*, both of which appeal to successive generations. *King Solomon's Mines* has been filmed three times (1937, 1950, and 1985), and yet none of the versions has adequately captured the adventurous pace or atmosphere of the novel. Likewise, *She* has been adapted for the cinema several times, the 1935 version altering the setting from Africa to the Arctic. Nevertheless, Graham Greene said of this production that 'To an unrepentant Haggard fan it does sometimes seem to catch the thrill as well as the childishness of his invention' (*Halliwell's Film Guide*, ed. J. Walker, 1994, 964). The 1965 remake, however, starring Ursula Andress and Peter Cushing, was critically panned, although it did return the scene of the action to Africa. Of the other more than fifty works of fiction that he wrote, most significant is *Ayesha* (1905), the sequel to *She*; the *Allan Quatermain* series; and his Zulu chronicles, particularly *Nada the Lily* (1892), *Marie* (1912), *Child of Storm* (1913), and *Finished* (1917). Haggard was a gifted story-teller, who drew upon his own experiences and observations to propel his readers out of grey and soggy England, on to adventures in uncharted lands and cultures, but he never achieved the refinements of art. He undervalued his talent and would have preferred to be accepted in the corridors of power.

Although Haggard suffered many tragic turns and disappointments, including waning popularity, his contributions were ultimately rewarded. In 1912 he was knighted, and in 1919 appointed KBE. He continued to write to the end, and to his labours he added a diary, which he kept from July 1914 to the end of his life in 1925, upon which he hoped later to base another book. It is, sadly, the account of a sour old man who sees himself betrayed by fate, a disillusioned imperialist with authoritarian, racist leanings, who ranted against the Jews, communists, bolsheviks, trade unionists, the Irish, and Indian nationalists (the editor of his diaries omits from the published text most of Haggard's harangues).

H. Rider Haggard died in London at 3 Devonshire Terrace, a nursing home, on 14 May 1925; his body was cremated and the ashes buried in the chancel of Ditchingham church. His wife survived him; one of his daughters, L. R. Haggard, published a memoir of him, *The Cloak that I Left*, in 1951. MORTON N. COHEN

**Sources** H. R. Haggard, *The days of my life*, ed. C. J. Longman, 2 vols. (1926) • *The private diaries of Sir H. Rider Haggard*, ed. D. S. Higgins (1980) • H. R. Haggard, diary, 22 vols., Norfolk RO • L. R. Haggard, *The cloak that I left* (1951) • M. N. Cohen, *Rider Haggard: his life and works* (1960); 2nd edn (1968) • M. N. Cohen, ed., *Rudyard Kipling to Rider Haggard: the record of a friendship* (1965) • D. S. Higgins, *Rider Haggard: a biography* (1981) • W. R. Katz, *Rider Haggard and the fiction of empire* (1987) • N. Etherington, *Rider Haggard* (1984) • N. Etherington, ed., *The annotated 'She'* (1991) • d. cert. • m. cert. • *CGPLA Eng. & Wales* (1925) • Burke, *Gen. GB* • H. R. Haggard, *Diary of an African journey*, ed. S. Coan (2000)

**Archives** Col. U., corresp. • Cornell University, Ithaca, New York • CUL, papers relating to employment of ex-servicemen • Dalhousie University, Halifax, Nova Scotia • Hunt. L., corresp. • Norfolk RO, corresp., MS First World War diaries, and papers • Ransom HRC, letters and MSS • Syracuse University, New York | BL, corresp. with Society of Authors, Add. MS 56720 • Bodl. Oxf., corresp. with Lewis Harcourt • HLRO, letters to Herbert Samuel • NL Wales, letters to D. R. Daniel • Norfolk RO, letters to Andrew Uvredale Corbett • Norfolk RO, letters, mainly to Louisa Haggard • Richmond Local Studies Library, London, corresp. with Douglas Sladen • U. Reading L., letters to W. T. Horton • University of Exeter, letters to Sir J. Norman Lockyer

**Likenesses** L. Little, oils, 1886, NPG • J. Pettie, oils, 1889, NPG • M. Greiffenhagen, oils, 1897, Castle Museum, Norwich • G. C.

Beresford, photograph, 1902, NPG [*see illus.*] · G. C. Beresford, photograph, *c.*1902, NPG · M. Greiffenhagen, chalk drawing, 1920, NPG · W. Tittle, lithograph, 1922, NPG · Barraud, photograph, NPG; repro. in *Men and Women of the Day*, 3 (1890) · H. Furniss, pen-and-ink caricatures, NPG · J. Russell & Sons, photographs, NPG · Spy [L. Ward], chromo-lithograph caricature, NPG; repro. in *VF* (21 May 1887) · B. Stone, photograph, Birm. CL · W. Strang, etching, NPG · photograph, NPG

**Wealth at death** £61,725 7*s*. 5*d*.: probate, 28 July 1925, *CGPLA Eng. & Wales*

**Haggart, Alastair Iain Macdonald** (1915–1998), Scottish Episcopal bishop of Edinburgh, was born at 30 Nairn Street, Glasgow, on 10 October 1915, the son of Alexander Macdonald Haggart, a timekeeper, and Janet Mackay. The family had moved from Fort William to Glasgow, where the young Haggart was brought up and educated at Hyndland primary and secondary schools. On leaving school he worked for some years at Burroughs Accounting Machines. Although his Christian life had begun as a member of the Free Church of Scotland, he made a conscious decision as a young man to become an Episcopalian. At the age of twenty-three he began training for the ministry at Coates Hall, the Episcopal theological college in Edinburgh. From there he gained an open exhibition to Hatfield College, Durham, where he graduated BA in 1941 and proceeded MA four years later. The University of Dundee made him an honorary LLD in 1970.

Haggart's clerical ministry initially was very much along traditional lines. He was ordained deacon in 1941 and priest in the following year. A three-year curacy at St Mary's Cathedral in Glasgow was followed by a similar period at St Mary's, Hendon, in London. At St Mary's, Glasgow, he married Margaret Agnes (Peggy) Trundle (1911/12–1979), a shorthand typist, on 14 May 1945. They had two daughters. In 1948 he returned to Scotland to become precentor of St Ninian's Cathedral in Perth, where he remained until he went to his first incumbency, King's Park, Glasgow, in 1951. Eight years later he was appointed provost of St Paul's Cathedral in Dundee, where he exercised an effective and efficient pastoral ministry. His wide gifts were recognized in 1970, when he received a unanimous call from the college of bishops to accept appointment as principal of Edinburgh Theological College. Although he laid no claim to scholarship, he was an avid reader and regarded theological reading as an essential part of the priestly life. He kept very much in touch with the latest developments in theology. Under his leadership, the whole pattern of teaching at the college was reshaped. Formal links were established with New College, the theological faculty in the University of Edinburgh, as a consequence of which Episcopal church ordinands trained alongside candidates for the ministry of the Church of Scotland. He went on to establish a concordat with the advisory council for ministry in the Church of England, under which courses were integrated and became acceptable to all three parties.

Haggart was elected bishop of Edinburgh in 1975 at the age of sixty, when he described himself as 'an old man in a hurry' (*The Times*). Two years later he became primus. In that capacity he clearly recognized and responded to the need for radical reform of many of the structures of the church. He presided over the creation of a general synod which amalgamated the two bodies previously responsible for the governance of the church. The representative church council had been concerned with finance, while a provincial synod had dealt with doctrine. His eight years as primus saw a number of other significant changes. Among these were new patterns of ministry, a fresh approach to pastoral discipline in the matter of the marriage of divorced persons, and the development and introduction of new liturgies.

A committed ecumenist, Haggart soon made his mark in the British Council of Churches. As chairman of the division of ecumenical affairs he was one of those responsible for the change to new ecumenical structures in Britain in which the Roman Catholic church could be full participants. He drafted the introduction to the Swanwick declaration when the churches agreed to ratify the 'Not Strangers but Pilgrims' process. It was later a source of disappointment to him that church life in Britain had failed to sustain that early commitment. He made his presence and influence felt unmistakably in the Anglican consultative council, where he served for a time as vice-chairman. During the pope's visit to Canterbury in 1982 Haggart initiated a dialogue for the discussion of inter-faith marriages.

In 1983 Haggart travelled to Johannesburg as one of the Anglican observers at the trial of Archbishop Desmond Tutu and others. His first wife having died in 1979, on 3 April 1983 he married chief nursing officer Mary Elizabeth Scholes (*b.* 1924). He retired as primus in 1985, but returned to the Anglican stage to act as chaplain to the 1988 Lambeth conference. A lifelong pacifist, he was a member of the Peace Pledge Union and a conscientious objector during the Second World War. More controversially, perhaps, he became an office-bearer in the Voluntary Euthanasia Society of Scotland. Perhaps the most striking impressions made by Haggart on first acquaintance were the admonitory forefinger, which was frequently raised in conversation, and his very distinctive Scottish accent, neither highland nor Lallans. Both combined made for a memorable and effective means of communication. Haggart died on 11 January 1998 in Astley Ainslie Hospital, Edinburgh. His funeral was held on 17 January at St Mary's Cathedral, Edinburgh. His second wife survived him. EDWARD LUSCOMBE

**Sources** *Bonds of affection: proceedings of ACC 6* (1984) [Anglican consultative council] · *Not strangers but pilgrims* (1987) [Swanwick conference] · E. Luscombe, *A seminary of learning* (1994) · *The Times* (15 Jan 1998) · personal knowledge (2004) · D. Bertie, *Scottish Episcopal clergy, 1689–2000* (2000) · *The Guardian* (3 Feb 1998) · *The Scotsman* (14 Jan 1998) · *The Independent* (19 Jan 1998) · *The Daily Telegraph* (14 Jan 1998) · b. cert. · m. certs. · d. cert. · *Yearbook of the Scottish Episcopal Church* (1963) · E. Templeton, ed., *Travelling with resilience: essays for Alastair Haggart* (General Synod Office of the Scottish Episcopal Church, 2002)

**Haggart, David** (1801–1821), thief and murderer, was born at Golden Acre, Cannon Mills, Edinburgh, on 24 June 1801, according to his own account. He was the son of John Haggart, a dog trainer and gamekeeper. He kept the kennels and was sometimes taken as a gillie to work in the highlands for the gentry, who tipped him lavishly. It was to the fact that he early became used to having money to spend that he attributed his downfall, saying 'it was just fate'. He received a good plain education but soon turned to petty theft. In July 1813 he enlisted as a drummer boy in the Norfolk militia, then stationed at Edinburgh Castle, but soon tired of the life, obtained his discharge, and took up an apprenticeship with a firm of millwrights, Cockburn and Baird. On the bankruptcy of the firm he 'plunged into the depth of misery and crime' and became a regular pickpocket at fairs and racecourses around Kendal, Carlisle, and Newcastle, and sometimes as far north as Aberdeen. He lodged in Newcastle with an unsuspecting, respectable woman and her daughters, to whom he was known as John Wilson, and picked pockets on theatre visits with them. In January 1818 he was apprehended after rifling a house near Durham and was thereafter imprisoned six times; four times he broke out of gaol.

On 10 October 1820, in escaping from Dumfries tolbooth, Haggart felled the turnkey, Thomas Morring, with a stone and killed him. He escaped to Ireland and jaunted with two girl companions around counties Fermanagh and Cavan, but was recognized at Clough fair, near Downpatrick, in March 1821 and arrested in Belfast; he escaped to Dublin, but was re-arrested there and arraigned on 28 March. He was brought, heavily ironed with a crippling iron helmet, from Kilmainham to Dumfries. From there he was moved to the Edinburgh gaol, and was tried on 11 June 1821 and found guilty of murder. He was taken to the city's Lock-up-House and was hanged before a large crowd on 18 July 1821. While in gaol he partly wrote and partly dictated an account of his life and crimes, entitled *Life of David Haggart*, which was to be published after his death by George Robertson to raise money for his father and other members of the family. It was said that 'an air of improbability breathes over many of his pages' and he was thought to have followed in the footsteps of Baron Munchausen in making himself out to be worse than he was. His statement that sexual passion was his greatest failing was, however, probably correct. A phrenologist, George Combe, visited him in gaol and sensed some redeeming features, and indeed he seems to have been a merry rogue. John Huston directed a 1969 film for United Artists, *Sinful Davey*, based on Haggart's book, in which John Hurt and other British stars appeared; Haggart's *Life* was reprinted under the same title in 1969.

F. H. GROOME, *rev.* J. GILLILAND

**Sources** D. Haggart, *Sinful Davey*, first published as *Life of David Haggart* in 1821 (1969) · C. Pelham, *The chronicles of crime*, [another edn], 2 vols. (1886) · review, *Edinburgh Magazine and Literary Miscellany*, 88 (1821), 154–6

**Haghe, Charles** (*d.* 1888). *See under* Haghe, Louis (1806–1885).

**Haghe, Louis** (1806–1885), lithographer and watercolour painter, was born in Tournai, Belgium, on 17 March 1806. His father and grandfather both practised as architects in Tournai and it was expected that he would follow suit. As a child he was encouraged to draw in his father's office, and this exposure to an architectural environment may have determined his predilections as an artist. Between the ages of ten and fifteen he was educated in the college at Tournai; he also attended a local drawing academy and was taught watercolour painting by a French exile, the chevalier de la Barrière. This was about the time the relatively new process of lithography was being taken up in various parts of Europe. When the first lithographic press in Tournai was set up by the chevalier de la Barrière and Dewasme, Haghe was employed as an assistant. While still only seventeen he contributed with the chevalier de la Barrière and J. B. De Jonghe to a *Collection des principales vues des Pays-Bas* (1822–3), both as an original draughtsman and as a lithographer working from the drawings of others. While this publication was in production his former teacher returned to France, leaving him to complete the work with De Jonghe and also to instruct a young English visitor named Maxwell in lithography. This chance contact with this otherwise unrecorded person led Haghe to London. Attracted by the prospect of work he travelled to England, where he settled for good around 1823.

**Louis Haghe (1806–1885)**, by unknown engraver, pubd 1885 (after M. J. Ganz)

Haghe is next recorded in 1825, when he lithographed some of the plates for a book for artists, George Simpson's *The Anatomy of the Bones and Muscles* (1825), and two plates for *The Manx Sketch Book*, ed. T. Ashe (1825). In December of the same year he lithographed *Three Views of Hereford* (1826). All the earliest lithographs Haghe drew in England were printed by William Day of 59 Great Queen Street, London. This was the beginning of a connection between artist and printer that lasted until Haghe gave up lithography in 1852 to concentrate on watercolour painting. It is not clear how binding the association was, but by 1833 the style 'Day & Haghe' made its first appearance in directories. By this time the firm had moved to 17 Gate Street, Lincoln's Inn Fields—though Haghe did most of his work from no. 6. He was the senior draughtsman at the press, and William Simpson, who joined the firm just before Haghe left it, claimed that the firm owed its reputation to him (Simpson, 204). In the 1830s Day and Haghe provided the first real competition in Britain to Hullmandel's press, and were appointed successively lithographers to the king and queen. By the time Haghe left the firm he had secured a reputation as one of the finest lithographic draughtsmen in Europe, and Day and Haghe had become the leading printers of pictorial lithographs in Britain.

Haghe does not appear to have been particularly active as a lithographer in the 1820s, though the set of twenty-four vignetted lithographs he produced for J. R. Planché's *Lays and Legends of the Rhine* (1827–9) are among the most delicate and meticulous of early English lithographs. At this stage he may have divided his time between lithography and watercolour painting, as he was elected a member of the New Society (later the Royal Institute) of Painters in Water Colours in 1835. He was the major overseas contributor to Baron Taylor's *Voyages pittoresques et romantiques dans l'ancienne France* (1820–78), for which he made nearly eighty lithographs; the majority were from his own drawings, the remainder after French artists. They were printed mostly by the firm of Day (and Haghe), though some were printed in Paris. Haghe's lithographs for this one publication spanned his whole lithographic career in England. His earliest prints for its Franche Comté volume (1825) may even have been made before any other lithographs he produced in England; by the time his last print for the publication appeared in 1854 he had retired from lithography. Some of his most carefully rendered tonal lithographs are to be found in the early volumes of the *Voyages pittoresques*.

Haghe's later reputation in lithography was mainly as a reproductive draughtsman, though he produced three series of his own architectural interiors and exteriors, *Sketches in Belgium and Germany* (1840, 1845, 1850), in the tinted style of lithography. In this period he came to be associated with publications of tinted lithographs made after other artists, some copies of which were issued coloured by hand. In the 1840s he was the most prolific exponent of this temporarily fashionable style of lithography and was greatly in demand as a reproductive lithographer. The most ambitious of these publications, and the one for which he is best known, is David Roberts's *The Holy Land, Syria, Idumea, Arabia, Egypt & Nubia* (1842–9). With the help of assistants, he was responsible for putting Roberts's drawings on to stone in the tinted style of lithography: there were nearly 250 such images, and all involved at least two stones, many three, and a few even more. The burden of such work must have been demanding, and may even have prompted Haghe's early retirement as a lithographer. Roberts appreciated his skills in interpreting his work, and remarked that he reproduced the views 'with a masterly vigour and boldness which none but a painter like him could have transferred to stone' (Abbey, 341). Ruskin took a different view, and referred to Haghe's lithographs in general as 'conventional, forced, and lifeless' and those for *The Holy Land* as 'a libel on Mr. Roberts' (*Works*, 3.220, 598).

Haghe's last major work in lithography was for G. Fossati's *Aya Sofia, Constantinople* (1852). In the course of the twenty-five years he spent as a lithographic draughtsman he changed his style radically in response to developments in the process and changes in taste. For the first ten years his work is characterized by its carefully laid tones and its confident and stylish handling of the crayon in foregrounds. When he turned to tinted lithography from the late 1830s his crayon work became more open and less tonal, the tint stone serving as an artistic prop for effects in skies and highlights.

After his retirement from lithography, Haghe established a second career as a watercolourist. His favourite subjects, architectural scenes in Belgium and other parts of northern Europe, reflect the nostalgia of the time for the middle ages. In 1853 he visited Rome with Roberts, and between 1864 and 1865 he produced a striking series of thirteen large views of St Peter's, which are in the Victoria and Albert Museum, London. He was president of the New Society of Painters in Water Colours from 1873 to 1884 and exhibited over 200 works there from 1835 until the year of his death. He also produced oil paintings, which he exhibited occasionally at the British Institution. He is represented by original works in several public collections in Britain and abroad, but, perhaps unjustifiably, his conscientiously executed paintings have not attracted as much attention as his lithographs. In 1834 he was awarded a gold medal in Paris for his lithography, in 1847 he was elected an associate member of the Belgian Academy, and later he became a member of the Antwerp Academy; he was also a knight of the order of Leopold I. His output as an artist was all the more remarkable because it was achieved in spite of the handicap of a deformed right hand. His watercolours in the Victoria and Albert Museum are signed 'L. Haghe' and dated. Although his lithographic work was not normally signed, imprints on his original lithographs include 'L. Haghe del' and 'L. Haghe del et lith.' and those on his reproductive work 'L. Haghe lithog.' and 'on stone [zinc] by L. Haghe'. He died at 103 Stockwell Road, Surrey, on 9 March 1885, leaving two sons and a daughter, and was buried in Norwood cemetery. At his death his effects were valued for probate at £16,018.

**Charles Haghe** (*d.* 1888), lithographer, worked as an assistant to his elder brother with Day and Haghe from the early 1830s and continued as a reproductive lithographer with Day for some years after his brother gave up the process. He worked on many publications, the best known being W. Simpson's *The Seat of War in the East* (1855–6). He died on 24 January 1888. MICHAEL TWYMAN

**Sources** [W. Simpson], 'Our contemporaries: Louis Haghe', *Printing Times and Lithographer* (15 Oct 1877), 203–5 · 'British artists, their style and character: no. XLI, Louis Haghe', *Art Journal*, 21 (1859), 13–15 · M. Twyman, *Lithography, 1800–1850* (1970) · J. R. Abbey, *Travel in aquatint and lithography, 1770–1860*, 2 vols. (1956–7) · M. Twyman, *A directory of London lithographic printers, 1800–1850* (1976), 30 · G. Wakeman and G. D. R. Bridson, *A guide to nineteenth-century colour printers* (1975), 30–32 · W. S. Williams, 'On lithography', *Transactions of the Society for the Encouragement of Arts, Manufactures, and Commerce* (1847–8), 226–50 · Mallalieu, *Watercolour artists* · Thieme & Becker, *Allgemeines Lexikon* · Graves, *Artists* · *Library of the Fine Arts*, 1 (1831), 44–58 · *Library of the Fine Arts*, 1 (1831), 201–16 · J. Ballantine, *The life of David Roberts* (1866) · *The works of John Ruskin*, ed. E. T. Cook and A. Wedderburn, library edn, 39 vols. (1903–12) · M. Hardie, *Water-colour painting in Britain*, ed. D. Snelgrove, J. Mayne, and B. Taylor, 3 vols. (1966–8) · *CGPLA Eng. & Wales* (1885) · *DNB*

**Archives** priv. coll., catalogue of the library and collection of the engravings of Louis Haghe • priv. coll., catalogue of the whole of the remaining works of Louis Haghe
**Likenesses** wood-engraving (after photograph by M. J. Ganz), NPG; repro. in *ILN* (28 March 1885) [*see illus.*]
**Wealth at death** £16,018 1*s*. 2*d*.: resworn probate, Aug 1885, *CGPLA Eng. & Wales*

**Hagthorpe, John** (*bap.* 1585, *d.* in or after 1630?), poet, was probably the son of Roland Hagthorpe (*d.* 1593) of Nettlesworth in the parish of Chester-le-Street, co. Durham, and his first wife, Clare, daughter of Sir Ralph Hedworth of Harraton in the same county. He was baptized at Chester-le-Street on 12 February 1585. In his writings he refers to the time when he lived in Scarborough Castle, Yorkshire. He married Judith, daughter of Anthony Wye, who had a lawsuit in 1605 with Elizabeth Saltonstall, mother of Wye Saltonstall, the poet.

In 1607 Hagthorpe sold his manor and estate of Nettlesworth to John Claxton. On 27 February 1608, being then of Whixley, Yorkshire, he surrendered certain copyhold lands in Chester-le-Street to the use of Henry Thompson and his wife, Jane, who was his father's widow. In 1611 licence was granted to Hagthorpe and Judith, his wife, to alienate to Francis Wright the half of Greenbury Grange in the parish of Scorton, near Scarborough. He does not seem to have profited by these transactions for he complained bitterly in the dedication, to James I, of his *Divine Meditations and Elegies* (1622) that he had been impoverished by lawsuits that he had lost. A selection from this tiny volume was presented to the Roxburghe Club in 1817 by Sir S. E. Brydges under the title *Hagthorpe Revived, or, Select Specimens of a Forgotten Poet*. The meditations are laboured but the lyrics 'To Earth', 'To Time', and 'To Death' have much charm. In *Visiones rerum: the Visions of Things, or, Foure Poems* (1623), dedicated to Charles, prince of Wales, he renewed the suit addressed in his former volume to the king. Fearing that he might be compelled by poverty to emigrate with his family to Virginia, he entreated the king to procure for his son a presentation to Charterhouse School.

Hagthorpe may be identical with the Captain John Hagthorpe who, on 22 April 1626, was certified by Robert Hemsworth as a fit person to command 'one of the ships to waft the cloth fleet to the East land' (*CSP dom., 1625–6*, p. 316). This was perhaps a result of his having displayed a specific interest in, and expertise on, seaworthy matters in an eloquently written prose tract, with poetry interspersed, titled *Englands-exchequer, or, A discourse of the sea and navigation, with some things … concerning plantations* (1625); the work was inscribed to the duke of Buckingham. Hagthorpe also wrote laudatory verses prefixed to Captain John Smith's *Sea Grammar* (1627). During 1626 Captain Hagthorpe did good service in protecting the Hull ships bound for the Netherlands against the attacks of the 'Dunkirkers'. He had also taken part in the Cadiz expedition of 1625 and, with four other captains, petitioned Buckingham on 20 September 1626 for payment of the king's gratuity of 100 nobles. A week later he was charged by William Hope, gunner of the *Rose of Woodbridge*, with illegally selling ship's stores, a course he was probably driven to adopt on account of the persistent neglect of the admiralty to furnish him with victuals and beer. Captain Hagthorpe was alive in January 1630, when he presented a petition to the admiralty.

GORDON GOODWIN, *rev.* JOANNA MOODY

**Sources** *The new Cambridge bibliography of English literature*, [2nd edn], 1, ed. G. Watson (1974), 476, 795 • Watt, *Bibl. Brit.*, 1.455 • W. T. Lowndes, *The bibliographer's manual of English literature*, ed. H. G. Bohn, [new edn], 2 (1864), 968 • E. Brydges, *Restituta, or, Titles, extracts, and characters of old books in English literature*, 4 vols. (1814–16), vol. 1, p. 236 • R. Surtees, *The history and antiquities of the county palatine of Durham*, 4 vols. (1816–40) • *CSP dom., 1625–6*, pp. 316, 352, 405, 420, 433, 438; *1629–31*, p. 179 • J. Hunter, 'Chorus vatum Anglicanum', BL, Add. MS 24487 • *ESTC*

**Hague, Bernard** (1893–1960), electrical engineer, was born in Barnsley, Yorkshire, on 7 July 1893, the son of Joseph Hague, a theatrical manager, and his wife, Amy Florence Kitching. He was educated at Eccles grammar school and Rochdale central higher-grade school, and from 1908 until 1910 worked as an apprentice turner and fitter to Carter Brothers, millwrights in Rochdale. In 1911 he became a junior electrical designer with Ferranti, Hollinwood, studying part-time at Rochdale Technical College. He gained an exhibition at the City and Guilds College in London, matriculating in 1912 and entering the second year of the course. Hague gained the degree of BSc in electrical engineering with first-class honours in 1915, and went on to obtain the diploma of Imperial College (1916), the degrees of MSc (1919) and DSc (1927), and fellowship. He worked at the Royal Aircraft Establishment as a lecturer until 1919, when he returned to the college as a lecturer. His talents were recognized by George Howe, professor of electrical engineering at the University of Glasgow, and Hague was invited to become a lecturer in the department in 1923. His PhD thesis, 'Testing of instrument transformers', was accepted three years later, and he quickly acquired a reputation as a superb lecturer and a precise and methodical scholar.

In 1929 Hague went as a visiting lecturer to the Brooklyn Polytechnic Institute, returning to Glasgow the following year to become a senior lecturer. In 1946 he was appointed to the James Watt chair of electrical engineering in succession to his mentor, Howe. He became dean of the faculty of engineering, and served for fifteen years as the president of the Student International Club. Hague was also a member of the council of the Institution of Electrical Engineers, serving as a member of council from 1950 until 1953, and was a founder and director of the Scottish Electrical Training Scheme.

Beyond the confines of his own department and profession Hague made a great impression on the cultural life of the university. An accomplished oboist, he was a mainstay of the university orchestral society, and played in the orchestra. He was a member of the Royal Scottish Academy of Music. His hobbies included working in wood and metal at his home in Hyndland in Glasgow. Latterly he collected and restored musical instruments.

Hague published prolifically in technical journals. His

most influential book was *Electromagnetic Problems in Electrical Engineering*, published in 1929 and reprinted after the Second World War as *The Principles of Electromagnetism Applied to Electrical Machines*. Another well-known textbook, *Alternating Current Bridge Methods*, was first published in 1923 and translated into many languages. He continued to revise the text until his death, and a sixth edition, revised by his colleague, Thomas R. Foord, was published in 1971.

Hague married Muriel Thorne Grose, and they had a daughter, Sheila Thorne Hague. Muriel died in January 1960, and he never fully recovered from the sadness of her loss. He died on 29 September 1960 at Glasgow's Western Infirmary. The University of Glasgow's principal, Sir Hector Hetherington, remembered Hague for

> his expressive face, crowned by the oriflame of his snow white hair, his dress, his handwriting, his craftsman's skill, his love of music and his mastery of his own beloved instrument. He was quiet, even reticent, though easy in conversation, uncontroversial, though firm and clear in judgement, helpful to others, especially to students from overseas, and altogether loyal. (Hetherington, 59)

IAIN F. RUSSELL

**Sources** A. J. S., *Journal of the Institution of Electrical Engineers*, new ser., 6 (1960), 728 • *Galpin Society Journal*, 15 (1962), 92 • C. A. Oakley, *A history of a faculty: engineering at Glasgow University* (1973) • *Glasgow Herald* (1 Oct 1960), 8 • H. Hetherington, 'Hague, Professor Bernard', *College Courant: Journal of the Glasgow University Graduates Association*, 13/25 (1960), 59 • B. Hague, 'The tonal spectra of wind instruments', *Proceedings of the Royal Musical Association*, 73 (1946–7), 67–83 • ICL, archives • U. Lond., archives • d. cert.

**Archives** Hunterian Museum and Art Gallery, Glasgow, collection of musical instruments

**Likenesses** group portrait, photograph, repro. in www.finsysgp.com/macbob/Pictures/MackayAlanLindsay4.html, 31 Jan 2002

**Wealth at death** £21,545 9s.: confirmation, 16 Nov 1960, *CCI*

**Hague, Charles** (1769–1821), university professor, was born on 4 May 1769 at Tadcaster, Yorkshire, the son of Robert Hague. He was taught music and the violin by his elder brother William. In 1779 he moved to Cambridge, where his brother had a music shop, and studied the violin and singing with Antonio Manini and thoroughbass and composition with Pieter Hellendaal. He soon became well known as a violinist, and this led to a friendship with Dr Joseph Jowett, regius professor of civil law. After the death of Manini in 1786, Hague moved to London and studied with Johann Salomon and Benjamin Cooke. On his return to Cambridge he became 'first master of the violin' in succession to Manini, and attracted pupils, among whom was William Crotch. In 1794 he took the degree of MusB from Trinity Hall, for which he composed the anthem 'By the waters of Babylon', which was performed in Great St Mary's Church on 29 June of that year. In 1799 he succeeded John Randall as professor of music, and in 1801 became MusD.

Among his other compositions are two collections of glees, the second published in 1800 under the auspices of the Harmonic Society of Cambridge, and an ode written in 1811 for the installation of the duke of Gloucester as chancellor of the University of Cambridge, to words by William Smyth, professor of modern history. He also helped James Plumptre with the publication of *A Collection of Songs, Moral, Sentimental, Instructive, and Amusing* (1805), and arranged twelve of Haydn's symphonies as quintets for flute and strings (1815).

Hague, who was married on 12 November 1791 to Harriet Hussey of Clapton, died at Cambridge on 18 June 1821. His eldest daughter, Harriet, an accomplished pianist, who published *Six Songs, with an Accompaniment for the Pianoforte* (1814), died in 1816, aged twenty-three.

N. D. F. PEARCE, *rev.* ANNE PIMLOTT BAKER

**Sources** [J. S. Sainsbury], ed., *A dictionary of musicians*, 2 vols. (1824) • *New Grove* • D. Baptie, *Sketches of the English glee composers: historical, biographical and critical (from about 1735–1866)* [1896], 73–4 • *IGI* • *GM*, 1st ser., 81/2 (1811), 37, 157 • *GM*, 1st ser., 61 (1791), 1061 • Venn, *Alum. Cant.*

**Likenesses** A. Cardon, stipple, pubd 1803 (after Gilchrist), BM • G. H. Harlow, oils, *c.*1813, FM Cam. • H. H. Meyer, mezzotint, pubd 1813 (after G. H. Harlow), NPG • T. Uwins, watercolour drawing, BM • print, Harvard TC

**Hague, Samuel** [Sam] (1829/30–1901), minstrel show manager, was born in Sheffield. He was apprenticed to a cutler as a boy, and also appeared as a clog dancer in local theatres. In the early 1840s Hague, with two of his brothers, emigrated to the United States, where he danced in the burgeoning 'blackface minstrel' shows, and formed a partnership with the American minstrel Happy Cal Wagner. At the end of the American Civil War in 1865, Hague took over the management of a group of sixteen African-American minstrel performers in Georgia, touring them successfully in America, before bringing them to Britain in 1866. Billed as the Great American Slave Troupe, Hague's company was the first troupe of black, as opposed to blackface, performers to appear in Britain. Mixing the broad comedy and clowning characteristic of minstrelsy with stylized presentations of scenes from plantation life and the sentimental politics of songs such as 'Emancipation Day', Hague attempted to exploit popular interest in American slavery and emancipation provoked by the civil war. He also hoped to capitalize on the growing popularity of blackface minstrelsy in Britain, combining its entertainment with the voyeuristic appeal of a display of 'former slaves'. The tour began in Liverpool in July 1866 and pursued a punishing provincial schedule through Great Britain and Ireland until 1869. During its course, Hague was faced with criticism of the troupe's inability to reproduce the style of conventional blackface acts. His response was to replace most of the African-American performers with white minstrels, changing what he had advertised as 'the only true representation of negro life on the plantations of America' into a standard minstrel show.

In 1869 Hague leased St James's Hall, Liverpool, and this became the base for his resident minstrel company, and of a second touring company that he founded in the mid-1870s. The troupes were large—up to sixty performers—and Hague gained a reputation for extravagant productions such as his Christmas show in Birmingham in 1879 which lasted five hours and added gymnasts, highland dancers, a dog act, trick cyclists, and a military band to the minstrel show's mixture of song, comedy, and burlesque. In the early 1870s Hague began *Hague's Minstrel and Dramatic Journal*, a monthly magazine. His business survived the destruction by fire of St James's Hall in 1875, a bankruptcy in 1880, and the loss of his touring company's properties (again by fire) in 1887. St James's Hall was sold in 1896, an indication of the general decline in the popularity of minstrel entertainments. However, Hague continued to manage his touring troupe until his death.

Sam Hague's career spans the period of blackface minstrelsy's greatest popularity in Britain and illustrates the entrepreneurial methods that characterized provincial theatrical management during the growth of a British mass-entertainment industry. His original Slave Troupe also illustrates the racial politics of blackface minstrelsy in Britain. Its initial popularity was based upon public sympathy with the cause of emancipation in America, yet when audiences later proved critical Hague quickly abandoned his performers. Later evidence of his unscrupulous management came in the wake of the Fisk Jubilee Singers' successful tour of Britain in 1873. Hague took over the management of another American black choir, the Wilmington Jubilee Singers, which came to England in 1876. He dismissed their black manager, leaving him destitute in England, and set about a wholesale imitation of the Fisk Singers, one of whose members termed him 'a very unprincipled man' after complaining of his theft of their performance and publicity styles (Seroff, 50). Despite such activities, Hague maintained a respectable position in Liverpool and in the wider entertainment industry. The trade magazine *The Era*, for example, reports an elaborate presentation of a jewelled and illuminated address in 1877, marking his achievements as a 'public caterer' (*The Era*, 1 July 1877).

Hague married, but no information is available about his wife. His only son, Sam Hague jun., died in America in 1879. Sam Hague died at his home, Marsfield, Wellington Avenue, Wavertree, Liverpool, on 7 January 1901 at the age of seventy-one. He was buried in Anfield cemetery, Liverpool, on 11 January. SIMON FEATHERSTONE

**Sources** H. Reynolds, *Minstrel memories: the story of the burnt cork minstrelsy in Great Britain from 1836 to 1927* (1928) • R. J. Broadbent, *Annals of the Liverpool stage* (1908) • S. Featherstone, 'The blackface Atlantic: interpreting British minstrelsy', *Journal of Victorian Culture*, 3/2 (1998), 234–51 • D. Seroff, 'The Fisk Jubilee Singers in Britain', *Under the imperial carpet: essays in black history, 1780–1950*, ed. R. Lotz and I. Pegg (1986), 42–52 • 'Presentation to Mr Sam Hague', *The Era* (1 July 1877) • *Liverpool Echo* (8 Jan 1901) • *Liverpool Mercury* (12 Jan 1901) • d. cert.

**Likenesses** photograph, repro. in Reynolds, *Minstrel memories*

**Hague, William** (*c*.1840–1899), architect, was probably born in Cavan Town, co. Cavan, the son of a local builder, also called William Hague, who is otherwise little known, though described in the *Dublin Builder* as 'an old established and highly respectable builder who has executed most of the principal works in his neighbourhood' (1 Sept 1863, 146). The young Hague opened his own offices in Dublin in 1861, though his practice was still based on Roman Catholic commissions from his home county, such as the interesting and quirky church at Butlersbridge of 1861. His ambitions registered in his competition entries, including one for the new Church of Ireland cathedral in Cork, of 1862, eventually won by William Burges. While Hague's early training was probably undertaken with his father, he was quickly accepted by the professional establishment, and was elected as a fellow of the Royal Institute of the Architects of Ireland in 1863; he later acted as auditor to the society. He was elected also to the Royal Society of Antiquaries of Ireland in 1864.

In the same year Hague's burgeoning practice gained prestigious success with the award of the first premium in the open competition, against some thirty other entrants, for the new town hall in Sligo, the foundation-stone of which was laid in 1865. Hague's designs displayed a competent understanding of the Ruskinian inspiration found in Deane and Woodward's work of a decade earlier, though much of the decorative carving originally intended remained unexecuted. The building affirmed his command of this type of civic design, but his forte remained church design, almost wholly for Roman Catholic patrons. Hague worked in a competent Gothic style, much indebted, especially in later years, to the work of Pugin and Ashlin. His reliable professionalism, alongside a dry orthodoxy, secured him wide respect in the Roman Catholic establishment, a position assisted no doubt by his marriage to the daughter of the solicitor Vesey Daly (*d*. 1880), and his service from 1885 as justice of the peace for co. Cavan. Hague's recognition by the Roman Catholic establishment was confirmed with his commission for the design of the new cathedral at Letterkenny, co. Donegal, in 1891. Here he produced an impressive but conventional design, completed after his death with uncommonly good and extensive finishings. His own completion of a number of works by other major Catholic architectural practices, including Pugin and Ashlin, in the years from *c*.1890, reflected further his authoritative position. A number of notable architects were associated with Hague's office, including Harry Allberry (1872–1952), and after his death on 22 March 1899 his wife established with his managing assistant, T. F. McNamara (1867–1947), a partnership that survived as Hague and McNamara until at least 1907. William Hague is buried in Glasnevin cemetery, Dublin, where he is commemorated by a memorial dedicated also to his daughter Kathleen (*d*. 1919) and sister Anne (*d*. 1843). SEÁN O'REILLY

**Sources** A. Jones, Biographical index, Irish Architectural Archive, Dublin • A. Jones, Index of Irish architects, Irish Architectural Archive, Dublin • *North-west Ulster: the counties of Londonderry, Donegal, Fermanagh and Tyrone*, Pevsner (1979) • J. Williams, *A companion guide to architecture in Ireland, 1837–1921* (1994) • *Thom's directory: Dublin* (1861–99) • records, Glasnevin cemetery, AJBI

**Hahn, Kurt Matthias Robert Martin** (1886–1974), educationist, was born in Berlin on 5 June 1886, the second of four sons (there was no daughter) of Oskar Hahn, a businessman in the steel industry, and his wife, Charlotte Landau, who was of Polish origin. After secondary education at the Wilhelmsgymnasium in Berlin he spent two years

**Kurt Matthias Robert Martin Hahn (1886–1974)**, by Howard Coster, 1938

(1904–06) at Christ Church, Oxford, four years (1906–10) at the universities of Berlin, Heidelberg, Freiburg, and Göttingen, and another four years (1910–14) at Oxford, all without taking a degree. He suffered severe sunstroke in 1904 which caused him ill health throughout his life. He had his occipital bone removed in 1907 by Sir Victor Horsley, the noted surgeon.

In the First World War, Hahn was exempted from military service on health grounds. Instead he served first in an intelligence unit of the German foreign ministry and later in the military department of the same ministry. He was active in groups concerned with war aims and the ending of hostilities. In this context he became a collaborator, and for a short time private secretary, of Prince Max of Baden, who was briefly imperial chancellor before the abdication of Kaiser Wilhelm II and whose educational ideas coincided with those of Kurt Hahn. From this collaboration the idea of creating a co-educational boarding-school emerged. It was to be housed in the prince's castle at Salem, a former Cistercian monastery not far from the shore of Lake Constance. The aim of the school was to inculcate in the post-war generation self-discipline, enterprise, physical fitness, skills, craftsmanship, and compassion. At that time Hahn 'tended towards rejection [of the Weimar Republic] … Hahn was a monarchist … as the faithful servant of a German prince for whom monarchy was a matter of course' (Mann).

The link with Prince Max of Baden had significant consequences for the dissemination of Kurt Hahn's ideas on education. Prince Max's son Berthold, the margrave of Baden, married the second sister of Prince Philip of Greece (later duke of Edinburgh) in 1931. This gave her a settled base and enabled her to offer her brother the opportunity to join the new school at Salem. Philip left Cheam preparatory school earlier than usual and joined Salem in September 1933 when he was twelve.

Kurt Hahn's educational philosophy is scattered throughout many speeches and writings. He never wrote a volume setting them out systematically. The seven 'Laws of Salem', which he developed in the early 1920s, comprised the following: give the children opportunities for self-discovery; make them meet with triumph and defeat; give them the opportunity of self-effacement in the common cause; provide periods of silence; train the imagination; allow games an important but not a dominant role; and relieve the children of rich or important parents of the enervating sense of privilege. The 'laws' were not original ideas. Several of them originated in the progressive-school movement of the time. Hahn's gift lay in putting the ideas of other educational reformers together and applying them in a coherent fashion in his own educational environment.

It has been noted that 'By 1930, together with physical fitness, his preoccupation was to train a moral independence devoted to finding "a moral equivalent to war"'—a phrase of William James which Hahn never tired of quoting (Stewart, 320). His school benefited 'by its connections and its twin heredity, on the one hand in the German and English establishments, and on the other in the progressive movement in education' (ibid.) and drew both teachers and pupils from a variety of countries:

> It was and was not of Lietz's *Landerziehungsheim*; it was and was not a relative of the *Wandervögel* movement; it was and was not an English public school; it was and was not like Abbotsholme or Bedales; it was and was not Plato's Athenian Academy transported to Baden. (ibid.)

With Hitler's seizure of power in Germany, Hahn's position, as a Jew, became precarious. He wrote to all former pupils of the school asking them to choose between Salem and the Nazis. This provocation gave the local Nazi party the excuse, on 11 March 1933, to surround the castle and to order the local police to arrest Hahn. No charge appears to have been required other than that he was Jewish and that he was suspected of having contacts with communists and Social Democrats.

Hahn's imprisonment evoked vigorous protests from the parents of the pupils and other supporters of the school. As a result of these and the intervention of Ramsay MacDonald he was released on 16 March 1933, although he was not able to return as headmaster. Pressure by the National Socialist Party drove the school on 20 May to accept the supervision of its administration by the provincial school authorities. Hahn himself attempted to defuse the relationship by withdrawing his critical circular of September 1932, but to no avail. A new headmaster was appointed who enjoyed the confidence of the Nazi authorities.

Hahn emigrated to Britain when the Nazis ousted him from Salem, and later (1938) took out British citizenship. In 1934, supported by British well-wishers such as William Temple (later archbishop of Canterbury), Lord Tweedsmuir (John Buchan, the novelist), and G. M. Trevelyan, the historian, he created a company called British Salem Schools Ltd, which founded Gordonstoun School on the coast of Moray. Many distinctive features of Salem were reproduced there: the emphasis on developing the whole person; the involvement of the school in the local community; physical fitness; fees which took account of ability of parents to pay; and the stretching of pupils in the face of the challenges of the mountains and the sea. He took on all sorts of pupils: the brilliant and the difficult, the swift and the weak. Prince Philip rejoined the school there in 1934 and stayed until the spring of 1939. His experience there formed his view of education, and his three sons, the princes Charles, Andrew, and Edward, received parts of their education at Gordonstoun.

Hahn's ideas flourished during and after the Second World War. Prince Philip also took on board these wider applications of Kurt Hahn's educational ideas. Beginning with the Outward Bound schools in 1941 and leading to the duke of Edinburgh's award scheme launched in 1956, the Trevelyan scholarships in 1958, the Medical Commission for Accident Prevention in 1964, and the Atlantic (later the United World) colleges from 1962, these ideas and institutions developed alongside the formal educational and vocational training systems. Their influence on education in Britain and elsewhere has been considerable, especially in their recognition of the need to develop the whole person and to consider education as a lifelong process.

Hahn, who was baptized into the Church of England in 1945, retired as headmaster of Gordonstoun in 1953. He received honorary doctorates from several universities and was appointed CBE in 1964. He was unmarried. After his retirement he lived mainly at Hermannsberg, near Salem, where he died on 14 December 1974. He was buried at Stefansfeld, Salem. GEORGE WEDELL

**Sources** *DNB* • M. Knoll, *Kurt Hahn: Reform mit Augenmass* (1998) • D. A. Byatt, ed., *Kurt Hahn, 1886–1974, an appreciation of his life and work* (1976) • H. L. Brereton, *Gordonstoun: ancient estate and modern school* (1968) • W. A. C. Stewart, *Progressives and radicals in English education, 1750–1970* (1968) • *The Times* (16 Dec 1774) • G. Mann, *Erinnerungen und Gedanken: eine Jugend in Deutschland* (1986), 117–205 • R. Poensgen, 'Die Schule Schloss Salem im Dritten Reich', *Vierteljahrshefte für Zeitgeschichte*, 1 (1996), 25–54 • private information (2004) [M. Schweitzer, former secretary of Kurt Hahn, 1956–62; H. Poensgen, retired *Wirtschaftsleiter* of Salem; R. Poensgen, former pupil of Salem] • P. Gordon and D. Lawton, *Royal education, past, present and future* (1999) • leaflet produced on the occasion of a meeting of the International Council of the United World Colleges at St Donat's Castle, 12 April 1978

**Archives** Schule Schloss Salem, Germany, Salem Archives • Schule Schloss Salem, Germany, archives • U. Cam., faculty of education, bibliography | Bodl. Oxf., corresp. with Lord Monckton • King's Lond., Liddell Hart C., corresp. with Sir B. H. Liddell Hart • NL Wales, corresp. with Thomas Jones

**Likenesses** H. Coster, photograph, 1938, NPG [*see illus.*] • H. Coster, photographs, NPG • photographs, Hult. Arch.

**Haicéad, Pádraigín** [Patrick Hackett] (*d.* **1654**), Dominican prior of Cashel and Irish-language poet, was the second surviving son of James Hackett FitzPiers and his wife, Margaret Kearney, of Baltarsna in the parish of Ballysheehan, co. Tipperary. Pádraigín ('ín' being a diminutive suffix of endearment) had been a popular Christian name among the Hacketts of the barony of Middlethird since the fourteenth century. It has been suggested on the evidence of poetry he composed for Edmund Butler, third baron of Dunboyne, that as a child Haicéad was fostered with that family at their residence at Kiltinan, near Fethard, co. Tipperary.

Given that his poetry shows Haicéad to have been particularly well acquainted with the mindset and norms of élite Gaelic bardic culture, it is likely that as a young man he frequented the company of the local Ó Con Mhuighe bardic family. And in view of his mixed Gaelic and Anglo-Norman parentage, it may be assumed that he was raised in an Irish-speaking environment where families from both historic ethnic communities melded unselfconsciously in a Gaelic cultural nexus. The mid-fifteenth-century bardic elegy composed for Philip Hackett of Ballysheehan vividly attests to the extent to which this Anglo-Norman family had long become Gaelicized in cultural idiom. Significantly, like many Irishmen of this period, Haicéad was multilingual, being competent in English, French, Latin, and Flemish in addition to Irish.

Concrete details relating to Haicéad's life and career are sparse. He entered the Dominican order some time about 1627 when he was listed as a student at the Dominican convent of Coleraine along with his cousins John Baptist Hackett and Patrick Kearney. It has been proposed that Haicéad in fact studied at the Dominican convent in Limerick at this time and that his documented association with Coleraine may have arisen from a secretarial error or misunderstanding. Passing through southern England in 1628, he proceeded to the Irish Dominican house at Louvain, where he appears still to have been resident in 1630. He spent the greater part of the 1630s on the continent. In 1632 he was at Morlaix in Brittany and in the period 1634–5 his presence was recorded at the Dominican convent of Rennes, while in 1635 he was assigned to the church of St Jacques in Paris.

Haicéad returned to Ireland at some stage in the late 1630s and was appointed prior of the Dominican convent at Cashel, approximately 3 miles from his family's home. The outbreak of the 1641 rising and the subsequent formation of the confederation, uniting both Gaelic and Old English in the government of the greater part of the island between 1642 and 1649, represent both a personal and ideological watershed in his work. He strove actively to advance the interests of the papal nuncio Giovanni Battista Rinuccini, archbishop of Fermo, and when the confederation split in 1646 Haicéad mercilessly satirized those whom he felt had betrayed the nuncio and by extension the Roman Catholic and Irish cause. In the *Commentarius Rinuccinianus*, a contemporary account of the papal nuncio's mission to Ireland based on original documents relating to confederate politics, there are four references dating to 1647 to complaints made to the confederate authorities in Kilkenny that Haicéad, along with other priests of his order, had been encouraging sedition among the troops in Clonmel. By 1651 Haicéad had returned to Louvain, from where he wrote to Rinuccini on 21 April, complaining of the apparent willingness of some Irish bishops to compromise with Ormond, the lord lieutenant, in 1649–50. Notwithstanding such treachery, he assured his correspondent of the determination of the mass of the Irish population to maintain its loyalty to the Roman Catholic faith and of its readiness to withstand the worst depredations of Cromwell's forces. However, Haicéad would not be remembered for his marginal role in the politics of the 1640s. Rather his significance lies in his literary and historical importance as a major Gaelic poet of the seventeenth century. While bearing the undoubted intellectual imprint of his bardic precursors, he is prominent among the ranks of the new early seventeenth-century cadre of non-professional poets who combined bardic and broader cultural influences to redirect the composition of poetry in Irish. His poetic brilliance is exemplified, for instance, in his reinvigoration of the traditional Gaelic elegy, such as 'Druididh suas, a chuaine an chaointe' ('Move aside, Band of Keeners') which he composed in memory of Edmund Butler who died in 1640, and where he succeeded in redeploying bardic conventions and motifs in a manner which is spectacularly passionate and heartfelt. His technical and linguistic skills are evident in the variety of genres he tackled so successfully: love poetry, poems of exile, occasional pieces, political poetry, and of course elegies. The best of this work is characterized by his deeply personal, often fierce and impassioned manipulation of traditional motifs to discuss new themes, especially in the area of politics and sectarian polemics. Haicéad's highly politicized consciousness of Irish nationality, which he linked intimately to profession of the Roman Catholic faith, is brilliantly articulated in political poems such as 'Éirghe mo dhúitche le Dia' ('May my homeland rise for God') and 'Músgail do mhisneach, a Bhanbha' ('Summon your courage, Ireland') composed against the backdrop of political and social upheaval in the 1640s. His unparalleled intellectual audacity and powerful exposition of his political credo invest his work with a cultural and ideological significance which has yet to be exploited by cultural and political historians of seventeenth-century Ireland.

Haicéad appears to have spent the remainder of his life unhappily at Louvain. In 1652 he unsuccessfully sought permission from the head of the Dominican order, John Baptist de Marinis, to return to Ireland to prepare for his proposed role as the Irish delegate to the order's forthcoming general chapter. Relentless in his promotion of the Irish and Roman Catholic causes, he wrote in 1652 of his plans for a book documenting what he perceived to be Ormond's malign intervention in the affairs of the confederacy. It may have been during this phase in his life that he compiled in association with Baothghalach Óg Mac Aodhagáin OFM a now lost work in Latin, *Annals of the Kingdom of Ireland*. Haicéad's final years were beset by a somewhat farcical squabble concerning the rotation of the headship of the Irish Dominican house at Louvain among natives of the four Irish provinces respectively. He was characteristically vehement in his denunciation of the Connaught head of house, William de Burgo, who it was claimed was attempting to fill the college with men from the western province. Having incurred the wrath of de Marinis and de Burgo owing to the harshness of his invective, Haicéad died in November 1654 in advance of the conclusion of the official investigation of the affair. A scholarly, annotated edition of his extant poetry is available in *Filíocht Phádraigín Haicéad*, edited by M. Ní Cheallacháin (1962). MARC CABALL

**Sources** *Filíocht Phádraigín Haicéad*, ed. M. Ní Cheallacháin (Dublin, 1962) · A. Valkenburg, 'Pádraigín an Doiminiceach as Caiseal Mumhan', *Dúchas, 1983–1984–1985* (Dublin, 1986), 21–32 · H. D. Gallwey, ed., 'A Kearney funeral entry of 1641', *Irish Genealogist*, 5/2 (1975), 264–6 · A. Coleman, ed., *The Irish Dominicans of the seventeenth century by Father John O'Heyne, O.P., first published at Louvain in 1706* (1902) · T. S. Flynn, *The Irish Dominicans, 1536–1641* (Dublin, 1993) · B. O'Ferrall and D. O'Connell, *Commentarius Rinuccinianus de sedis apostolicae legatione ad foederatos Hiberniae Catholicos per annos 1645–1649*, ed. J. Kavanagh, 6 vols., IMC (1932–49) · P. F. Moran, ed., *Spicilegium Ossoriense*, 3 vols. (1874–84) · M. Hartnett, trans., *Haicéad* (1993) · J. Carney, ed., *A genealogical history of the O'Reillys* (Dublin, 1959) · N. Canny, 'Pádraigín Haicéad: an sagart agus an file i gcomhthéacs a aimsire', *Dúchus, 1983–1984–1985* (Dublin, 1986), 8–20 · T. Ó Donnchadha, ed., *Saothar filidheachta an athar Pádraigín Haicéad* (1916) · P. de Brún, 'Cnuasach d'fhilíocht Phádraigín Haicéad', *Éigse*, 12 (1967–8), 291–6 · D. Pochin Mould, *The Irish Dominicans: the friars preachers in the history of Catholic Ireland* (Dublin, 1957) · S. Ó Tuama, 'Ceathrúna Phádraigín Haicéad', *Irish Review*, 23 (winter 1998), 1–23

**Archives** Royal Irish Acad. · St Patrick's College, Maynooth · Stonyhurst College, Lancashire · University College, Cork

**Haid, Johann Elias** (1739–1809). *See under* Boydell, John, engravers (*act.* 1760–1804).

**Haid, Johann Gottfried** (1710–1776). *See under* Boydell, John, engravers (*act.* 1760–1804).

**Haie, Nicola de la** (*d.* 1230), landowner, was a daughter and coheir of Richard de la Haie, the hereditary constable of Lincoln Castle and sheriff of Lincolnshire, and his wife, Matilda, the daughter of William de Vernon. She was married twice, first to William, son of Erneis, and second, before 1185, to Gerard de *Canville (*d.* 1214). The office of constable passed through her to each of her husbands, and in August 1189 she and Canville crossed to Barfleur, Normandy, to obtain a charter confirming their inheritance in both England and Normandy from King Richard. This included Lincoln Castle as it had been held by Nicola's father and grandfather. It is likely that the shrievalty of the county of Lincoln was also included in the grant, which cost Canville and Nicola 700 marks.

In 1191 Nicola was besieged with her husband at Lincoln Castle when he quarrelled with William de Longchamp (*d.* 1197), the chancellor and justiciar of England in Richard's absence. In 1194 she fined for the sum of 300 marks with King Richard to marry her daughter, Matilda, according to her will, excepting one of the king's enemies. She continued to account for this debt until 1212, having renegotiated the amount with King John in 1200, and in 1201 she still owed £20, 40 marks, and one palfrey. Nicola enjoyed a cordial relationship with the fickle John. According to a later tradition recorded nearly sixty years after the events, Nicola had met John when he went to Lincoln in 1216. Her husband had recently died, and she went to meet the king leaving the castle by the eastern postern gate with its keys in her hand. She offered them to John saying that she was of great age and unable to continue with the office any longer. John sought her out and said, 'My beloved Nicola, I will that you keep the castle as hitherto, until I shall order otherwise' (*Rotuli hundredorum*, 1.315). The king granted the shrievalty of Lincoln to Nicola and Philip Marc a few hours before his death on 18 October 1216. The ageing widow was besieged at Lincoln by the rebels under the leadership of Louis of France, and she held the castle for the royalists until she was relieved in 1217. One source alleges that she had been entrusted with the castle 'in exchange for money' and that the castle was relieved since it would have been considered 'dishonourable not to help so brave a lady' (*Historical Collections of Walter of Coventry*, 2.237–8). The *Histoire de Guillaume le Maréchal* narrates that, before the attack by the royalist forces, Peter des Roches, bishop of Winchester, penetrated the castle by a secret route and met Nicola to reassure her that the siege would shortly be raised. She was apparently delighted to hear the news, and it seems that her intransigent defence of the castle facilitated a successful attack by the royalists which saw the rout of the rebel forces. The battle at Lincoln on 20 May 1217 was one of two decisive battles that ended the claim of Louis to the throne of England. The ending of the siege was followed by looting and sacrilege. Despite her alleged earlier protestations of age and incompetence, Nicola determinedly held on to the office in the face of repeated attempts by William (II) Longespée, the husband of her granddaughter Idonea and son of the earl of Salisbury, to eject her from it. In 1219 she is recorded as holding dower in Swaton, Lincolnshire, worth £20 annually. Nicola resigned the office of castellan in 1226 and died in Swaton on 20 November 1230.

SUSAN M. JOHNS

**Sources** *Chronicon Richardi Divisensis / The Chronicle of Richard of Devizes*, ed. J. T. Appleby (1963) • 'The "History of William the Marshall" for the years 1216–19', *English historical documents*, 3, ed. H. Rothwell (1975), 81–103, esp. 88–91 • *Memoriale fratris Walteri de Coventria / The historical collections of Walter of Coventry*, ed. W. Stubbs, 2, Rolls Series, 58 (1873) • W. Farrer, *Honors and knights' fees … from the eleventh to the fourteenth century*, 3 vols. (1923–5) • F. Hill, *Medieval Lincoln* (1948) • *Rogeri de Wendover liber qui dicitur flores historiarum*, ed. H. G. Hewlett, 3 vols., Rolls Series, [84] (1886–9) • *Chronica magistri Rogeri de Hovedene*, ed. W. Stubbs, 4 vols., Rolls Series, 51 (1868–71) • J. H. Round, ed., *Ancient charters, royal and private, prior to AD 1200*, PRSoc., 10 (1888) • D. M. Stenton, ed., *The great roll of the pipe for the third and fourth years of the reign of King Richard the First*, PRSoc., new ser., 2 (1926) • H. C. M. Lyte and others, eds., *Liber feodorum: the book of fees*, 3 vols. (1920–31) • [W. Illingworth], ed., *Rotuli hundredorum temp. Hen. III et Edw. I*, RC, 1 (1812) • *Pipe rolls*, 6 Richard I – 14 John

**Haig, Axel Herman** (1835–1921), etcher and architectural draughtsman, was born at Katthammarsvik, on the Swedish island of Gotland, on 10 November 1835, the son of Axel Hägg (1804–1872), a local landowner and timber merchant, and his wife, Anna Margreta Lindström (1807–1891). From 1850 he studied shipbuilding in the government dockyard at Karlskrona, from 1856 he worked in Glasgow with the Clyde shipbuilding firm of Lawrence Hill & Co., and from 1859 he was a pupil in the London office of Ewan Christian, architect to the ecclesiastical commissioners. At the end of this triple apprenticeship, in 1866, he married Sarah May Street (*d.* 1930) and set up in London as an architectural draughtsman. For the next twenty years he was much in demand as a perspectivist, preparing presentation views and competition drawings for leading architects, notably Robert Rowand Anderson, E. W. Godwin, G. E. Street, and, most famously, William Burges. It was Haig, for example, who produced the spectacular watercolour perspectives for Burges's competition design of 1866 for the new law courts. The eventual winner, Street, is said to have remarked: 'I wouldn't mind being beaten by drawings like those' (*The Builder*, 1884, 713).

Haig began to exhibit in his own right at the Royal Academy—watercolour topographical sketches, mostly from Italy, Sicily, Austria, Germany, and Belgium—from 1870 onwards. It was only ten years later that he began to exhibit etchings, firstly at the Dudley Gallery, then at the Society of Painter-Etchers and Engravers (Haig was a founder member in 1880). Between 1880 and 1910 he produced a long series of large-scale etchings, designed not for the collector's portfolio but for framing and hanging as part of a scheme of interior decoration. Starting with *The Vesper Bell* (1879) and *The Morning of the Festival* (1880), the sequence moves on through *Chartres* (1881, 1882), *Mont-St Michel* (1882), *Limburg on the Lahn* (1886), *The Alcázar, Segovia* (1886), and *Pampeluna* (1887), to *Rheims* (1892), *The Legend of the Bells* (1895), *Assisi* (1893), and *Monreale* (1907). All these—and many more in the same vein—sold well. Haig was a regular prize winner at international exhibitions. His printer, Frederick Goulding, was the best in England; his print seller, Robert Dunthorne, knew the upper reaches of the print market on both sides of the Atlantic. Technical mastery; compositional drama; a combination of archaeology, sentiment, and flair: all these turned Haig, in the eyes of the late Victorian public, into a veritable Piranesi of Gothic. And in his native Sweden he earned one more claim to fame: he was the tutor of Anders Zorn (1860–1920), perhaps the greatest of modern etchers.

As an architect, Haig had a practice that was limited mostly to church restoration. Churches at Dalhem (1899–1904) and Ardré (1896–1902) as well as the cathedral at Wisby (1896–1903), all on the island of Gotland, illustrate his ambitions in this field. In his later years an amiable, smiling old man with a fine Viking beard (K. Asplund, *Anders Zorn*, 1921, 16)—Haig spent his summers in Sweden and his winters at Grayshurst, the house he designed for himself at Haslemere in Surrey in 1891. He died at 26 Kent Road, Southsea, Hampshire, on 23 August 1921, and was buried at All Saints', Haslemere, beneath a rock of craggy shape and a runic inscription of his own design. A collection of his etchings is in the department of prints and drawings in the British Museum, London.

J. Mordaunt Crook

**Sources** E. A. Armstrong, *Axel Herman Haig and his work* (1905) • J. M. Crook and C. A. Lennox-Boyd, *Axel Haig and the Victorian vision of the middle ages* (1984) [incl. work list] • M. B. Adams, 'The career and work of Axel Haig', *RIBA Journal*, 28 (1920–21), 582–4 • *CGPLA Eng. & Wales* (1921)

**Archives** NRA, priv. coll., family archives

**Likenesses** photograph, 1898, repro. in Crook and Lennox-Boyd, *Axel Haig* (1984), pl. 2 • photograph, 1905, repro. in Armstrong, *Axel Herman Haig*, vol. 1

**Wealth at death** £2312 4*s*. 2*d*.: probate, 18 Nov 1921, *CGPLA Eng. & Wales*

**Haig, Douglas, first Earl Haig (1861–1928)**, army officer, was born at 24 Charlotte Square, Edinburgh, on 19 June 1861, the fifth son of John Haig (1802–1878) of Cameron Bridge, Fife, and his wife, Rachael Mackerras (*d*. 1879), daughter of Hugh Veitch of Stewartfield, Midlothian. Descended from the younger branch of a Scottish border family of long standing, Haig was the last of eleven children, nine of whom survived infancy. His father had become wealthy as a distiller of whisky. After preparatory schooling at Orwell House, near Edinburgh, and in Warwickshire, Haig was sent to Clifton College in 1875. He entered Brasenose College, Oxford, in 1880. At Oxford he led an active sporting and social life and paid some attention to his studies, gaining a good command of written English (though never becoming fluent with the spoken word) and qualifying for a pass degree, which he never took.

**The young staff officer** Haig had early resolved on a military career, and entered the Royal Military College, Sandhurst, in 1884. There he devoted himself to his work, developed a reputation for being aloof and taciturn, passed out first in his year, and was awarded the Anson memorial sword. He also made good progress as a horseman and polo player (he had played polo at Oxford), both important attributes for a cavalry officer. His interest in golf was to develop later. In 1885 he was commissioned into a fashionable cavalry regiment, the 7th hussars, where his accomplishments at polo proved considerable.

Despite his activities as a sportsman, what marked Haig out in the ensuing years was his devotion to his profession. His regiment had moved to a peaceful part of India known as the 'Sloth Belt', but Haig proved the reverse of slothful. After three years his assiduity in the performance of his duties caused him to be raised to the position of adjutant, promoted captain, and directed to undertake staff work with the headquarters of the Bombay army at Poona. He plainly found this type of activity appropriate to his talents and inclinations, and in 1893 sought to enter the Staff College, Camberley, back in Britain. Briefly his career suffered a setback when his application was rejected on account of colour blindness and a poor performance in the compulsory mathematics examination.

The setback proved only temporary. Haig's cause may have been aided by the royal acquaintanceships enjoyed by his youngest sister, Henrietta, to whom he was devoted. But it was also materially assisted by the attention which his professional activities had secured him from Sir Evelyn Wood, a leading member of the influential 'Wolseley ring' engaged in identifying officers of promise. Haig had come to Wood's notice as a result of a report he had written following attendance at French cavalry manoeuvres. Soon afterwards Haig was appointed aide-de-camp to the inspector-general of cavalry, and reinforced his good standing with Wood by further reports on visits to military manoeuvres on the continent, this time by the German army as well as the French. In 1896 he finally secured entry to the Staff College, by nomination.

**Douglas Haig, first Earl Haig (1861–1928)**, by Walter Stoneman, 1914

A considerable influence on Haig at that institution was the eminent military historian G. F. R. Henderson, who based his tactical exercises on an intense knowledge of important recent conflicts, particularly the American Civil War and the Franco-Prussian War. Haig, as his written papers from the time attest, took good note of Henderson's instruction. Henderson, for his part, soon came to appreciate Haig's potential. He singled him out, among a body of students of whom many would become familiar names in the course of the First World War, as the individual who in time would attain the position of commander-in-chief.

**From the Sudan to South Africa** Henderson's good opinion soon worked to Haig's advantage. Late in 1897 Horatio Kitchener, then sirdar (commander-in-chief) of the Egyptian army, chose to embark on the reconquest of the Sudan, from which Egyptian (and some British) forces had been driven in the 1880s. Kitchener applied to London for a group of special service officers to participate in his largely Egyptian force. Out of many applicants Haig, with the backing of Henderson and Wood, was one of only three chosen. Thereby in 1898 he received his first experience of battle. In the course of the Sudan expedition he distinguished himself by rallying Egyptian cavalry against a surprise attack, and by the effectiveness of the reconnaissance he carried out for the climactic battle of Omdurman. He also, at Sir Evelyn Wood's prompting, sent Wood frank reports concerning the conduct of operations, including pointed criticism of Kitchener himself.

Haig returned to Britain to become a brigade-major at Aldershot. His commander was Major-General John French, with whom he had previously acted as staff officer during cavalry exercises. For a time they became closely associated. (In a curious incident Haig even lent French a considerable sum of money to help him out of some financial difficulties. It is not clear that the loan was ever repaid.) In anticipation of a war breaking out in South Africa, French in June 1899 was appointed commander of a cavalry division then being assembled for dispatch overseas. He chose Haig as his staff officer and in October the two men arrived in Natal, ahead of their division, just as the Boers invaded that colony. They assumed charge of such mounted troops as were already available, and in an encounter largely planned by Haig inflicted defeat on a Boer force.

French and Haig were then directed to Cape Town to take charge of their division, which was in the process of disembarking. They left Ladysmith amid a hail of gunfire in the last train to get away before the Boer trap closed. There followed, in December 1899, a month of disasters for nearly all British units. French's cavalry—again aided by Haig's staff work—provided an exception, holding at bay a numerically superior Boer force.

As reinforcements arrived from Britain early in 1900, and as changes were made in the higher command, the cavalry division was directed to spearhead the relief of Kimberley, which had also been placed under siege. That accomplished, it pursued the Boer force which had been carrying out the siege and cut it off in a successful action at Klip Drift. However, a subsequent operation at Poplar Grove against the principal remaining Boer force did not go so well. The cavalry failed to act with similar dispatch, and Haig's staff work contributed to its shortcomings.

In the ensuing months Mafeking was relieved and the regular Boer forces defeated. Assuming the war to be all but over, the British command broke up the cavalry division along with other units, and instituted a system of mobile columns. Haig was placed in charge of a group of these, so exercising independent command for the first time. The Boers from August 1900 had resorted to guerrilla warfare, and Haig was thereafter engaged in largely ill-rewarded attempts to capture such leading opponents as General Smuts. In May 1902 the Boers abandoned the struggle.

The Second South African War had given Haig the opportunity to establish a reputation as a first-class staff officer, who both influenced the decisions taken by his commander and (more often than not) translated those decisions into effective orders. On his return to Britain late in 1902 he resumed command of his regiment, the 17th lancers. Appearing before the Elgin commission set up to inquire into the conduct of the Second South African War, he not only related his experiences but offered some views on the shape of future wars. Speaking of the role of infantry and artillery he suggested that the latter was 'only likely to be really effective against raw troops', and took the view that the cavalry would be of greater rather than less importance in coming conflicts. Such judgements scarcely proved appropriate to the next great conflict in which Haig would be involved.

**Influential patrons: preparing for war** Among those impressed by Haig's activities in both the Sudan and South Africa was Kitchener, who in 1903 took up the post of commander-in-chief in India. Despite expressions of displeasure among some in the military hierarchy at Haig's lack of seniority, Kitchener appointed him his inspector-general of cavalry, with the rank first of colonel and then of major-general, making him the youngest officer with that rank in either the British or the Indian army. As Kitchener soon became fully involved in a struggle with the viceroy over authority in military matters, Haig was left with responsibility for training the Indian cavalry. One outcome was *Cavalry Studies* (1907), his only published book.

In the summer of 1905 Haig interrupted his tour of duty in India for a spell of leave in Britain. This would have important personal consequences. As a guest of Edward VII at Windsor he met the Hon. Dorothy Maud Vivian (*d.* 1939), daughter of Hussey Crespigny *Vivian, third Baron Vivian; she was a maid of honour to Queen Victoria and then to Queen Alexandra. Two days after their first encounter he proposed marriage and was accepted. They married in the private chapel at Buckingham Palace on 11 July 1905. So began a lifelong partnership which sustained Haig throughout his career and provided him with a family of three daughters and a son. (The latter, born in 1918, was ultimately his successor as the second Earl Haig.) Lady Haig published a memoir of her husband, *The Man I Knew* (1936). Their eldest daughter, Alexandra, was later married to Rear-Admiral C. D. Howard-Johnston and, secondly, to Hugh Trevor-Roper, Lord Dacre, the historian. Their second daughter, Victoria, was married to Brigadier C. A. Montagu-Douglas-Scott, and their third to Gavin Astor. Lady Haig's connection to the court was to prove valuable during the politics of the First World War.

Haig had by the time of his marriage attracted the appreciative attention of Lord Esher, the *éminence grise* of British military affairs. Esher was engaged in revamping the nation's armed forces in the light of their disheartening experiences in South Africa. When in 1905 Lord Haldane, an eminent legal figure, was appointed secretary of state for war in the new Liberal government, Esher persuaded him to bring Haig back to London, first as director of military training and then as director of staff duties. So from 1906 Haig assumed a major role in preparing Britain for participation in a continental war. It was with his considerable assistance that the nation became equipped with a general staff capable of making and implementing large decisions on military matters, acquired a small but highly efficient and well-equipped expeditionary force of regular soldiers capable of early intervention in a Franco-German conflict imperilling Belgium, and established a second-line 'Territorial' army consisting of civilians who voluntarily undertook part-time military training. Haig also aided in establishing the Imperial General Staff, under whose guidance the self-governing dominions modelled both their military establishments and their training procedures on British practices, and so readied themselves to participate alongside Britain's forces in the event of an international war.

In 1909 Haig agreed, though without alacrity, to accept the post of chief of staff in India under Kitchener's successor. His purpose was primarily to develop India's military resources into a force able to serve imperial and not just Indian needs—something which both the secretary of state for India and the viceroy resisted, but which went into effect with the onset of war. In 1909 he was created KCVO and in 1910 promoted lieutenant-general.

In 1911, at Haldane's prompting, Haig returned to Britain and took over the command at Aldershot. Thereby he spent the remaining years of peace in the training of troops. The post was important in that, in the event of overseas conflict, it carried with it the command of the First Army corps. Haig's devotion to his profession, experience of battle, and proven capacity as a staff officer appeared ample preparation for the exercise of leadership in war.

**The opening phase of the war** On 4 August 1914, responding to the German invasion of Belgium, Britain went to war. As chief of one of Britain's only two corps Haig on the following day was invited to attend the first war council summoned by the prime minister. Also present was Sir John French, now elevated to the position of commander-in-chief of the British expeditionary force (BEF). Discussion centred on the destination appropriate for this body. Haig listened with alarm as French spoke in disregard of the pre-war arrangement whereby the BEF would take its place on the left of the French army and act in unison with it in support of Belgium. French proposed taking his force as an independent unit to Antwerp, where it would assist the Belgians in the defence of that city. Haig argued the contrary: that the small BEF, in a conflict between the giant armies of France and Germany, could not afford to operate separately from the French. That view prevailed.

The incident served to strengthen Haig's increasingly doubtful view concerning Sir John French's competence in military matters, an attitude which had been forming since they acted together in South Africa. Nor was he averse to conveying his negative judgements on his commander to George V, who had succeeded to the throne in 1910 and with whom Haig had become well acquainted.

Haig left for France on 15 August, where the two corps of the BEF took up position alongside the French and moved into Belgium. This progress was short-lived. A vastly superior force of Germans (some 200,000 as against the BEF's 75,000) bore down upon them, intent on sweeping through Belgium and proceeding all the way to Paris. With the French on the British right already in retreat, Haig by 24 August was fully occupied in calling on his divisional commanders and brigadiers to cancel plans for the projected forward move, and in arranging for their participation in a general withdrawal. Briefly in the ensuing days Haig lost contact with 2nd corps which was bearing the brunt of the German attack in this sector, and started to show undue signs of alarm. But he quickly recovered his composure, and was soon proposing positive action to aid embattled French forces. These his commander-in-chief refused to countenance.

The retreat of the allied left wing continued, without catastrophe, for thirteen days. Then, on the Marne, the French high command struck out from Paris with a recently assembled fresh army against the German right flank, driving the enemy into retreat. Haig's forces were in good order and able to participate in the pursuit of the Germans. By mid-September he had advanced as far as the River Aisne. But that was the limit of progress. On the ridge overlooking the Aisne the enemy dug trenches and brought in an imposing array of defensive weaponry. Against these obstacles, further advance proved impossible. It was a grim foreshadowing of events to come.

In the ensuing weeks, as the great armies of France and Germany attempted swift movements in an endeavour to outflank each other, the lines of opposing trenches extended ever further north until they reached the coast of Belgium. Thereby the phenomenon of stalemate, first evident on the Aisne, asserted itself along the entire length of the western front. Well-dug entrenchments, protected by barbed wire, occupied by full complements of infantrymen, and disposing of ample quantities of machine-guns and mortars and shrapnel and high-explosive shells, proved able to hold at bay even well-mounted attacks. This was an alarming development, given that victory for either side could only be accomplished by means of fruitful offensives. Haig would spend the next four years seeking to resolve the conundrum of trench stalemate.

Following the rebuff on the Aisne the BEF was transferred back almost to where it had started: to a sector near the coast in that small piece of Belgium still in allied hands. Here Sir John French hoped to launch a cavalry attack which would turn the German flank. Instead for a full month from mid-October the BEF yet again found itself confronting a massive German offensive, this time intended to break through to the sea and occupy the channel ports of Calais and Dunkirk. Haig's corps happened to be placed in a crucial area, occupying the ridges overlooking the old fortress town of Ypres. He spent the key days of battle well forward, observing his troops in action and counselling their commanders. The crisis of this first battle of Ypres was reached on 11 November 1914, when German assaults employing large numbers of troops and much artillery were only just held by Haig's carefully prepared defences. By late in that day he was concluding that, unless well reinforced, his positions would be in serious peril. But the danger passed. While sustaining heavy loss themselves the BEF had managed to inflict on their attackers a measure of slaughter too great for the German command to bear. The offensive closed with Ypres and the channel ports still in allied hands.

**Haig's strategic analysis** Sir John French paid warm tribute to Haig's part in this action and provided appropriate reward. In the last weeks of 1914 the expanding forces of the BEF in France and Belgium were divided into two armies, and Haig was appointed commander of the First Army with the rank of general. This promotion would signal the end of his close involvement in the actual course of battle and his emergence as an active participant in the development of British strategy.

Already Haig had concluded that, certainly as far as Britain's endeavours were concerned, the battle lines of France and Belgium constituted the decisive front in this war. Here the main armies of the principal enemy were concentrated, and here they must be engaged and fought to defeat. From that position, to the war's end, he would not deviate. And though his judgement on this matter would be soon challenged, not least by leading political figures such as David Lloyd George and Winston Churchill, and though ever since it has been a matter of severe dispute, nothing that happened between late 1914 and the end of battle in 1918 showed it to be anything but well founded.

Haig at the same time drew a further conclusion. He argued that stalemate on the western front, imposed by the employment of systems of trenches in alliance with potent defensive weaponry (such as barbed wire and machine-guns and mortars and shrapnel and high-explosive shells), was neither permanent nor irreversible. With the acquisition of fresh recruits supported by imposing quantities of guns and ammunition, he believed, the British and French commands could in time overwhelm the enemy lines. Then, employing cavalry for exploitation, the attacking forces could sweep into open country, unhinge the German system of defence, and drive the enemy from the soil of France and Belgium.

These judgements require careful appraisal. In some respects they were sound enough. Defensive systems were unlikely to prove impregnable if sufficient firepower could be brought against them. But that raised important questions. For example, what quantities of firepower would constitute a sufficiency, and how long would it take for allied industry and neutral suppliers to develop the facilities and the skill to supply them? Again, what developments in the employment of weaponry, both in the training of executants and in improvements of techniques, must occur to render firepower sufficiently effective? And how far would even the successful employment of ample resources go towards neutralizing enemy defences? That is, would suppression ever be total or must it always remain partial?

Haig was certainly correct in his belief that an offensive employing sufficient resources and delivered with appropriate skill could make progress into defended positions. But as single trench lines were replaced by systems of defence in depth, in which successive lines of trenches were supplemented by concrete pillboxes spread in chequerboard fashion to a considerable distance, it ceased to follow that an attack which broke into defended positions would manage to break right through them. Furthermore trenches did not take long to dig, especially under pressure of an offensive. So even as the defenders' forward positions were being overrun, they retained the opportunity to call further trench lines into existence. There remained a further issue: whatever measure of advance an offensive might accomplish, how was success to be exploited? It soon became evident that defensive weaponry had developed such a killing capacity as to render the established means of exploitation, the cavalry, too vulnerable to retain any place in a western front offensive.

Haig proved reluctant to acknowledge the force of some of these negative considerations. So, in the ensuing years, his repeated endeavours to accomplish a compelling breakthrough of the enemy's lines in the west brought heavy loss and much hardship upon his forces, yielded insufficient rewards either in captured territory or enemy casualties, and caused severe damage to his long-term reputation.

**Commanding First Army** As commander of First Army during the course of 1915 Haig directed a succession of offensives against segments of the German front in Belgium and France. These were usually devised as supplements to much larger endeavours by the French. (By contrast Germany in 1915 was for the most part standing on the defensive in the west and directing its assaults against the Russians and the Serbs, with noteworthy success.)

Haig's first attack was made towards the town of Neuve Chapelle which led on to the Aubers Ridge, a rise overlooking the city of Lille. For his purpose he accumulated a considerable quantity of artillery ammunition. This was delivered with careful preparation against the enemy front line. As a result the opening phase of the action on 10 March 1915 went well, securing Neuve Chapelle for the attackers. That, however, proved the limit of their success. Haig soon concluded that, had the initial advance been pressed home without delay, the Aubers Ridge could also have been taken and the cavalry pushed through the gap. He failed to recognize that the enemy had been able at an early stage in the battle to create a fresh line of defences, and that his forces possessed neither the quantities of ammunition, nor the time necessary to register the guns, to overcome this.

Subsequent operations in May and June, directed against more complex German defences, for the most part lacked even the quantities of artillery ammunition required to repeat the modest success of Neuve Chapelle, let alone to accomplish more. There followed in September 1915 the controversial action at Loos. Neither Sir John French nor Haig welcomed this undertaking. It was imposed upon them by the authorities in London, in response to both the parlous circumstances of Russia and the urgings of the French high command. (The latter was proposing simultaneously to launch an even more ambitious offensive.)

The supply of artillery ammunition for the Loos operation was plainly insufficient. So Haig decided to employ poison gas (first introduced to battle by the Germans in the previous April) as a supplement, even though it would require the chance of a favouring wind to render this weapon operative. In the event the early stages of the attack on 25 September went comparatively well. Haig's forces overran the German front lines and pressed on up the imposing Hill 70. But on the far side of the hill they were halted and then driven back by fire from the unbombarded second line of enemy defences.

As it happened, no reserves were close to hand that day to press home the attack. Their positioning was the responsibility of the commander-in-chief. Sir John French had chosen to hold them well back and under his own direction. This conduct was ill-judged, and Haig swiftly became convinced that French's actions had robbed him of the opportunity for a substantial victory; that the Germans were in disorder, that their second line was almost undefended, and that a prompt follow-up attack would have gone right through. Close investigation hardly bears this out. Even had the reserve divisions been placed where Haig wanted them and under his command, they could not have been in a position to attack before the early afternoon of 25 September, by which time German reinforcements had taken up position on the second line. So the British reserves would have been sent forward without significant artillery support across open ground that provided a clear field of fire for enemy machine-gunners and into a warren of uncut barbed wire. The probable consequence of such action became evident on the following day. On the morning of 26 September Haig did indeed send the reserve divisions forward against the German second line after a derisory bombardment that did not dent the enemy machine-guns or the barbed wire. The result was a terrible slaughter, with the survivors of the attacking divisions fleeing in terror and panic.

Despite Haig's unhappy contribution to this debacle, opprobrium for what had gone wrong settled firmly on Sir John French. It was aided by communications to important people in London from Haig and others, bluntly stating French's bungles. The event confirmed misgivings about the commander-in-chief's capacity which had been developing in high quarters since the early weeks of the war, and French was relieved of his post. Haig, whose steady demeanour and capacity as a staff officer were everywhere acknowledged, was appointed his successor. Satisfaction, in political as well as military circles, was widespread.

**Commander-in-chief** From this point to the end of the war Haig was in the chief position to devise and direct the great endeavours of the British army on the western front. Any action he took there, it needs to be added, required the authorization of the British government. Throughout this war the principal civilian authorities of the nation both retained and continued to exercise ultimate authority for choosing the locality and extent of Britain's military operations. Haig, contrary to an oft-expressed view, never sought to question or reverse this established pattern of civil–military relations.

In undertaking a succession of great campaigns between 1916 and 1918 Haig was able to draw much sustenance from his religious beliefs. It was his good fortune during these years to have at his service a preacher congenial to his views. The Revd George Duncan of the Free Church of Scotland came to his attention in 1915. Thereafter Haig was regular in attending Sunday services and recorded in his daily diary the gist of Duncan's sermons. Duncan had the great advantage for Haig that he could turn a biblical text to whatever battlefield situation confronted the commander-in-chief. So after the bloody first fortnight of the Somme campaign in 1916 Haig recorded the following:

> 16 July. Mr Duncan took as his text: 'The Kingdom of Heaven is likened unto treasure hid in a field', which in order to buy 'a man sells all he possesses with joy'. Anything worth having has always to be paid for fully. In this war our object was something very great. The future of the world depends on our success. So we must willingly spend all we have, energy, life, money, everything in fact, without counting the cost. (Haig MSS, *Diary*, NL Scot.)

These must have been comforting words for the architect of the Somme and subsequent campaigns.

During the years of his command of the BEF, from late 1915 to the close of the war in November 1918, along an ever-lengthening stretch of the western front, Haig commanded by far the largest segment of Britain's expanding army and mounting supply of weaponry in what usually proved the principal operations of the allied armies. Already, by the Somme campaign of July to November 1916, he had under his direction five British armies numbering 1.5 million men formed into twelve corps consisting of 38th infantry and five cavalry divisions. The use to which he put these forces, on the Somme and in the two years that followed, has ever since been a subject both of strong praise and unsparing denigration.

Haig's critics have rarely acknowledged the formidable problems which confronted him. He was required—by his political masters, by a vociferous media, and by the determination of the British public—not just to hold the line but to get on and win the war: that is, to carry the struggle to the enemy and drive the invader from the soil of France and Belgium. Yet consequent upon the relative equality of manpower and industrial resources between the two sides, and upon the clear advantages which developments in weaponry had bestowed upon the defender, there was no sure path to victory on offer, and any offensive operation was bound to bring heavy loss of life upon the attacking forces. Nor do Haig's critics usually notice the respects in which he responded positively to the changing face of warfare. For example, he embraced with enthusiasm both new devices of battle, such as tanks and aircraft, and new methods of employing established weaponry, such as striking innovations for increasing the effectiveness of artillery: aerial photography, sound-ranging, and flash-spotting.

Haig's defenders, by contrast, are often loath to acknowledge the inappropriate aspects of his conduct of operations. He proved determined to do more than just wear down the enemy in a succession of limited operations conducted in appropriate weather and within artillery range, thereby providing some measure of protection for his attacking troops, facilitating full use of available weaponry, and keeping casualties within tolerable bounds. Rather, time and again he chose to embark on wide-ranging campaigns with imaginative objectives which happened to lie beyond his—or any other western front commander's—powers of attainment. The charge more usually levelled against Haig, that he could conceive of no operation more creative than battles of attrition designed to wear down his own forces equally with those of the enemy, is entirely wide of the mark. On the western front in this war, attritional battles—but of a sort that would wear down the enemy more severely than one's own side—were the best that could be striven for. Haig was reluctant to recognize this.

As a result of his determination to accomplish great victories Haig too often disregarded key factors such as weather and the condition of the battlefield, placed his objectives beyond the range which his artillery could cover, and incorporated in his schemes a role for cavalry which this arm was helpless to accomplish. These shortcomings, it needs to be stressed, were not at all peculiar to Haig, as is borne out by various ill-starred campaigns by the French in 1915 and 1917, and by the flight into Cloud-cuckoo-land of the German high command in the first half of 1918. But the outcome, too often, was British operations directed towards unrealizable objectives and persisted in long after they had ceased to serve any worthwhile purpose. The consequence was excessive loss of British lives, insubstantial accomplishment, and waning morale.

**The battle of the Somme, 1916** The pros and cons of Haig's proceedings were evident in the first great campaign he conducted, the battle of the Somme (1 July–16 November 1916). Originally conceived as an Anglo-French endeavour in which French forces would make the larger contribution, it became, as the German assault at Verdun from 21 February 1916 drained the armies of France, a predominantly British affair. The opening day of battle, 1 July, proved a catastrophe. At Haig's insistence, and overriding the somewhat muddled proposals of his army commander, he spread his preliminary bombardment over a lengthy front and to a considerable depth. Thereby he intended to subdue the entire enemy defensive system, opening the way for breakthrough and cavalry exploitation. The result was quite otherwise. His limited supplies of artillery failed to put out of action even the German forward defences, and his attacking infantry were devastated. For only meagre capture of territory on one part of the front, the British army suffered greater casualties in action than on any other day in its history. The Somme campaign continued for another five months, eventually costing Haig's armies 400,000 casualties and achieving only an inconsiderable capture of territory still short of his objectives for the first day. These operations demonstrate three aspects of Haig's manner of proceeding which were hardly to the advantage of his troops.

First, Haig was slow to recognize which factors contributed to success in offensive operations and which did not. On 14 July and 25 September on the Somme his army made worthwhile (if hardly major) gains at moderate cost. But Haig failed to take note that both successes had been brought about by the employment of overwhelming quantities of artillery in conditions of fine weather; that his forces had attacked on a front broad enough to protect those in the centre from flanking fire and to deny the enemy the opportunity to concentrate a large volume of artillery against a limited area; and that his objectives had been sufficiently modest to ensure that his attacking forces remained within the protection of their own artillery. As a result of this failure of appreciation, many other operations on the Somme were carried out on narrow fronts of attack, often in indifferent weather, by unsupported units which attracted great concentrations of German artillery and flanking fire.

At times, by contrast, Haig seemed about to recognize what was required to succeed on the battlefield. In August 1916 he even wrote to his army commander on the Somme, General Sir Henry Rawlinson, pointing out that attacks should be delivered on a front broad enough to protect the troops in the centre from flanking fire and to force the enemy to spread his artillery retaliation over a wide area. But this brings us to a second of Haig's command characteristics. When Rawlinson failed to amend his ways in response to Haig's missive, the commander-in-chief did not enforce his will. Throughout the war Haig maintained a hands-off approach to command, allowing Rawlinson in 1916 and General Sir Hubert Gough in 1917 to conduct a series of operations in which he steadily lost confidence. Thus, as against the usual picture of Haig's implementing a dictatorial style of generalship, there appear to have been occasions when he was not interventionist enough.

A third aspect of Haig's exercise of command requires comment. This was his persistent conviction that, under the weight of his assault, the enemy were approaching collapse. His conclusion from this was that his own attacks must be persisted in to the limit of his army's endurance. So, in the aftermath of the disaster of the first day on the Somme, he felt able to claim that the Germans were about to collapse 'perhaps within a week'. This conviction persisted throughout the Somme campaign. By October it was exerting a truly malign influence on operations. The deteriorating weather had by now turned the battlefield into a sea of mud. This rendered almost impossible the traverse of no man's land by the infantry, and made any assistance that the artillery could offer no more than a matter of chance. Yet Haig held to the belief that the German will to resist was about to disintegrate. So the cavalry remained massed for the projected breakthrough.

And operations continued well into November. Only representations by Rawlinson that, at the existing rate of loss, he would not have an army capable of combat in 1917 caused Haig to close down the battle.

At one time the view was widely held that Haig arrived at his erroneous conclusions regarding the imminent collapse of German morale through the incompetence of his chief of intelligence, Brigadier-General John Charteris. The release of Haig's comprehensive diaries throws doubt on this judgement. It appears, rather, that Haig's sanguine temperament disposed him towards these conclusions, and that, if anything, Charteris was influenced by Haig rather than the other way round.

**Messines Ridge; third Ypres; Passchendaele: 1917** By the opening of 1917 Britain had acquired a new prime minister. David Lloyd George had no great regard for Haig. He disliked operations on the western front, distrusted Haig's methods, and deplored heavy casualties among Britain's forces. Yet he possessed no will to remove Haig. This would have curious consequences.

In the first campaigning months of 1917 Haig was required by his political masters to participate in an ill-devised French offensive and to accept subordination to a dubiously equipped French commander. The manner in which this latter aspect was implemented by Lloyd George appeared so devious that it established bad feeling between Britain's high command and political rulers for the remainder of the war. But it had no lasting effect on Haig's position. The resulting French offensive proved a calamity, its commander was sacked, and Haig was swiftly restored to full control of his army. And, ironically, the British aspect of these operations in April bore a positive message. Acting as a supplement to the abortive French offensive, Haig's forces managed by the employment of massed artillery with enhanced expertise to achieve not a breakthrough but two effective advances with limited objectives. The message seemed plain: further vast undertakings, on the lines of the Somme in 1916 and the French endeavour of April–May 1917, would continue ill-rewarded and terribly costly. Attacks for limited purposes could fully employ available weaponry and avoid heavy losses among the attackers.

Haig soon received further evidence that this was the case, in what was intended as the prelude to his planned major campaign for the second half of 1917. Haig was determined to launch a mighty offensive that would carry the British army all the way from the Ypres salient to the coast of Belgium. But as a preliminary he sought to capture the high ground of Messines Ridge overlooking that part of the salient from which his major attack would be delivered. This initial operation, under the command of General Sir Herbert Plumer, was spectacularly successful. A series of mines earlier planted underneath the ridge, in combination with a massive artillery bombardment, enabled his troops to take this objective at moderate cost.

But Haig still hankered after bigger things. So, for all its carping, did the British government. And because Plumer, along with Rawlinson, was thought to be insufficiently ambitious for his preferred type of undertaking, Haig called in a new commander, Sir Hubert Gough, to conduct the main attack. Among other unfortunate consequences, the change-over cost the British a period of seven weeks between the Messines operation and the opening of the campaign proper. That gave the Germans the time required to strengthen their defences in the salient.

The third Ypres campaign was launched on 31 July 1917. Success on the first day was severely constricted not only on account of the enhanced German defences but because Haig once more spread his artillery evenly over the front of attack. Worse soon followed. August was characterized by heavy rain, rendering the artillery ineffective and turning the battlefield into a quagmire. Gough, undeterred, pressed on unavailingly with his attacks. Haig exhibited increasing unease about the progress of the offensive but failed to intervene. Only after a month, with his army exhausted and Gough bereft of ideas, did he finally act. Gough was sidelined and Plumer given the main command.

Before resuming the offensive Plumer required an interval for preparation which was accompanied by the onset of fine weather. Haig concurred. The outcome might have been instructive. In three set-piece battles with strictly limited objectives, Haig's forces moved towards Passchendaele Ridge (the objective for the first day). This seemed to indicate, as had Messines, that the British had now developed a method by which, at least in dry weather, modest amounts of ground could be captured at limited cost to themselves. Haig did not take this to heart. After Plumer's third blow the weather deteriorated. The mud even exceeded in depth that of the last period of the Somme. Nevertheless Haig drove his troops forward until in November a section of the Passchendaele Ridge fell. Only then was the campaign abandoned. As a result of this protracted endeavour Haig's army had again suffered losses heavier than those inflicted on their opponents, had gained no worthwhile objectives, and was clearly lowered in morale. The episode did not redound to Haig's credit.

The termination of the Ypres campaign coincided with Haig's last operation for 1917. On 20 November he delivered an attack towards Cambrai. In addition to the effective employment of massed artillery he was able for the first time to employ tanks in large numbers over suitable campaigning territory. Thereby he secured an impressive early success. But the wearing down of his forces during the Ypres campaign, and the necessity just then to send some of his divisions to assist Britain's imperilled ally Italy, meant that no back-up forces were available at Cambrai even to repel counter-attacks. So the ground captured at the start was soon lost, and 1917 ended in general disappointment.

**1918: Counter-offensive and victory** Haig's occupancy of the western front command seemed imperilled. Public comments by the prime minister suggested a lack of confidence in his operations. And the calling into existence of new inter-allied bodies appeared a proceeding for diminishing his authority. Further, as a result of pressure from the government he was obliged to part with some of his principal advisers, who were deemed to have been more concerned to encourage him in the way he wanted to go than to acquaint him with the realities of the battlefield. Yet in the outcome none of this reflected a serious determination on the part of the government to remove him. Sniping at Haig for what had not been accomplished proved a substitute for seeking a replacement (who might or might not do better) and accepting responsibility for the outcome.

As 1918 dawned Haig still wrote as if the appropriate proceeding was a resumption of the Ypres offensive. He also proved slow to acknowledge the approach of grave peril to his armies on account of dramatic changes on the other side of the front: the collapse of Russia and so the freeing-up of German divisions for a mighty offensive against Haig's drained forces. Yet if these developments would initially gravely menace the British army on the western front, the larger consequence would prove quite different. What emerged was that any tendency on Haig's part towards over-ambition, and any reluctance to embrace the limited offensive, paled into insignificance alongside the leaps into unreality about to be assayed by the military masters of Germany. Haig, in the aftermath, would find himself overseeing sensible operations of large importance.

In the first six months of 1918 the German high command, while keeping far more troops than they could afford on their now-defunct eastern front (for the purpose of appropriating commodities and annexing territory), employed their enhanced army in the west in a huge bid for final victory. The opening stage of that endeavour was directed against an undermanned part of the British front and achieved early successes beyond Haig's worst expectations. But in the longer term the German offensive of March–June 1918 proved entirely counter-productive. Haig under pressure revealed himself a commander of resolve and resource, capable of a succession of countermoves which proved sufficient to the occasion. (The same positive qualities were also being revealed by his political masters.)

On 12 April 1918 Haig issued to the First and Second Armies an order which became famous:

> Every position must be held to the last man: there must be no retirement. With our backs to the wall and believing in the justice of our cause, each one of us must fight on to the end. (Cooper, 2.23)

Overall, the Germans' offensive fell short of securing any strategic gains and left them holding a dangerously extended front with severely reduced forces. By mid-1918, this situation was presenting Haig—even more than it was his French and American allies—with a great opportunity. After allowing his forces time for recuperation and re-equipment, he seized it.

On 8 August 1918, outside the threatened rail centre of Amiens, Haig's Fourth Army delivered a powerful counter-attack employing a great range of weaponry in effective combination. The result was a masterly initial success. Yet again, Haig anticipated that more could be accomplished by pressing on with the attack on the following days than was at all possible. But he did not persist in this misjudgement, as he had done too often in the past. Responding to urgings by his lower-order commanders, and disregarding the directives of the recently appointed allied generalissimo Marshal Foch, he called off the Amiens offensive and set about organizing another set-piece attack on a different part of the front. That produced another notable success, and a further series of well-planned operations.

These events set the pattern for the last hundred days—a period of unrelenting advance by Haig's forces which, before the year was out, would force the enemy to capitulate. To the end, apparently, Haig regarded his operations as a prelude to that great breakthrough offensive for which he had striven so long. Consequently even now he cluttered up his lines of communication with a great force of cavalry intended one day to sweep through a ruptured front into green pastures. But this had ceased to matter. While awaiting larger things Haig's armies were proceeding to deliver against their enemies a succession of thunderclap blows which could not be endured indefinitely. Employing massive fire-power and proceeding only within artillery range, these actions inflicted draining losses on the Germans and drove them from one defended position to another.

The climax came in the second half of September. By this time the enemy had been forced back into the powerful defensive system established early in 1917, the Hindenburg line. The British government, while not actually forbidding Haig to attack it, made it clear that a costly and ill-rewarded offensive might not go unpunished. Haig snorted his disgust to his diary ('What a wretched lot of weaklings we have in high places at the present time!') and went ahead with the operation anyway. In the wake of huge bombardments delivered with the utmost skill his forces first seized the ridge overlooking the German positions (18 September), then smashed their way right through (29 September). The decisive nature of these events escaped even Haig. Time and again he had claimed, without good cause, that the German army was on the verge of collapse. Now in October 1918, with his prediction at last coming true, he retreated from that view and expressed the opinion that the enemy might well fight on into the next year. The German army collapsed anyway.

With Germany's capitulation on 11 November 1918 Haig led his armies to the Rhine. He then returned to Britain, where he took up the post of commander-in-chief of the home forces, which he continued to occupy until January 1921. Honours descended upon him in the aftermath of victory. From the Houses of Parliament he received a vote of thanks and a grant of £100,000. The king created him Earl Haig and conferred on him the Order of Merit. In 1921, as a result of public subscription, he was presented with the ancestral home of the Haig family, Bemersyde House, Berwickshire, and its fishings on the River Tweed.

**After the war** Thereafter Haig worked devotedly in the cause of the soldiers who had served under him. He assisted in the establishment of the Royal British Legion in 1921 and of the Royal British Legion Scotland the same year. These united existing associations of former servicemen in a single body for each country, and Haig became president of both organizations. And he accepted chairmanship of the United Services Fund, formed to administer for the benefit of former soldiers and their families the large profits made during the war by army canteens. At the time these bodies constituted between them the largest benevolent organization ever formed in Britain.

Haig died suddenly of heart failure, at 21 Prince's Gate, London, on 29 January 1928. He was accorded a state funeral in Westminster Abbey, in the course of which thousands of former servicemen turned out voluntarily to line the route. Their action was some indication of the high respect, if not necessarily personal affection, with which he was regarded by large numbers of those who had served under him. He was buried, at his own request, in Dryburgh Abbey, near Bemersyde, Berwickshire, on 7 February. An equestrian statue of him was erected on the Castle Esplanade in Edinburgh, another by his former headquarters at Montreuil, and parliament paid for a fine equestrian statue in Whitehall by A. F. Hardiman. He appears as one of the chief figures in J. S. Sargent's large group portrait of the allied military and political leaders (National Portrait Gallery). The sale of poppies which annually commemorates the war-dead of the United Kingdom supported what for many years was known as the Haig Fund, with the letters 'H.F.' printed on the centre of each poppy.

Since Haig's death the fierce controversy over his conduct of military operations, which had already surfaced during the First World War, has raged unabated.

Robin Prior and Trevor Wilson

**Sources** *The private papers of Douglas Haig, 1914–1919*, ed. R. Blake (1952) · J. Terraine, *Douglas Haig: the educated soldier* (1963) · D. Cooper, *Haig*, 2 vols. (1935) · J. E. Edmonds, ed., *Military operations, France and Belgium*, 14 vols., History of the Great War (1922–48) · J. F. Maurice and M. H. Grant, eds., *History of the war in South Africa, 1899–1902*, 4 vols. (1906–10) · E. K. G. Sixsmith, *Douglas Haig* (1976) · J. H. Boraston, *Sir Douglas Haig's despatches* (1919) · NL Scot., Haig MSS · B. Bond and N. Cave, eds., *Field Marshal Sir Douglas Haig: seventy years on, 1928–1998* (1999) · GEC, *Peerage* · Burke, *Peerage* (1957)

**Archives** NL Scot., corresp., diaries, and papers | BL, account of operations on western front, Add. MS 52460 · BL OIOC, letters to Sir Harcourt Butler, MS Eur. F 116 · Bodl. Oxf., letters to Herbert Asquith · HLRO, corresp. with John St Loe Strachey · IWM, corresp. with Sir Henry Wilson · King's Lond., Liddell Hart C., letters to Sir Launcelot Kiggell · King's Lond., Liddell Hart C., corresp. with Nivelle and Pétain · Lpool RO, corresp. with Lord Derby, 920 DER · NA Scot., corresp. with Philip Kerr, GD 40 · NL Scot., letters to James Curle · NL Scot., letters to G. S. Duncan · NL Scot., letters to Lord Haldane · NRA Scotland, priv. coll., letters to Sir Douglas Baird · NRA Scotland, priv. coll., corresp. with Sir John Ewart · PRO, corresp. with Lord Kitchener, PRO 30/57, WO 159 · U. Warwick Mod. RC, corresp. with W. G. Granet | FILM BFI NFTVA, 'An historic meeting in France', 1917 · BFI NFTVA, 'Sir Douglas Haig in Flanders', Topical Budget, 17 Sept 1917 · BFI NFTVA, 'Earl Haig—the soldier and the man', 1928 · BFI NFTVA, *Timewatch*, BBC2, 3 July 1996 · BFI NFTVA, documentary footage · BFI NFTVA, news footage · IWM FVA, 'Haig and his army commanders', 1918, IWM 132 · IWM FVA, actuality footage · IWM FVA, documentary footage · IWM FVA, news footage · IWM FVA, propaganda film footage (Ministry of Information and War Office Official) | SOUND BL NSA, *Timewatch*, BBC2, 3 July 1996 · IWM SA, oral history interview

**Likenesses** Mrs G. Smith, chalk drawing, 1894, NPG · W. Stoneman, photograph, 1914, NPG [*see illus.*] · J. Russell & Sons, photograph, *c*.1915, NPG · M. Bone, black chalk drawing, 1916, IWM · F. Dodd, charcoal and watercolour drawing, 1917, IWM · W. Orpen, oils, 1917, Brasenose College, Oxford; copy, IWM · Bassano, photograph, *c*.1919, NPG · H. Olivier, oils, 1919, Gov. Art Coll. · J. Guthrie, oils, 1921, Royal and Ancient Golf Club, St Andrews, Fife · J. S. Sargent, group portrait, oils, 1922 (*General officers of World War I, 1914–18*), NPG; oil study, *c*.1922, Scot. NPG · S. J. Solomon, oils, 1922, IWM · G. E. Wade, bronze equestrian statue, 1922, Castle Esplanade, Edinburgh · W. Stoneman, two photographs, 1925, NPG · A. F. Hardiman, bronze equestrian statue, 1937, Whitehall, London · H. Lund, lithograph, IWM · W. McMillan, statue, Clifton College, Bristol

**Wealth at death** £17,599 3*s*. 6*d*.: confirmation, 1 Sept 1928, *CCI*

**Haig, Edward** [Ned] **(1858–1939)**, rugby player, was born at Pleasants in the Scottish borders town of Jedburgh on 7 December 1858, son of Edward Haig, labourer, and Margaret Haig, *née* Waugh. He attended Jedburgh grammar school (1870–75) before going to find work in the neighbouring town of Melrose, where he was taken on by the local butcher Davie Sanderson. Sanderson was a keen rugby player and through him Haig took up the game, making his début for the Melrose club in 1880. He went on to become a regular member of the Melrose first fifteen and made several representative appearances for the South of Scotland. In addition, he was a member of the local cricket, curling, and golf clubs. When his playing career ended he became an active committee man.

Ned Haig is remembered as the originator of seven-a-side rugby. His suggestion of a football tournament was made in 1883, when Melrose Football Club were trying to find a way to raise money to help club finances. He later recalled that 'as it was hopeless to think of having several games in one afternoon with fifteen players on each side, the teams were reduced to seven men' (Allan, 20). The first final, held on 28 April 1883, was contested between Melrose and Galashiels, with Haig in the Melrose starting line-up. This ended in a highly controversial manner when the game ended with neither team having scored. It was agreed by the captains that a further fifteen minutes would be played to decide the tie. Melrose were first to score, with a try by Haig's employer, Sanderson, and left the field claiming the silver cup presented by 'the ladies of Melrose'. The tournament was an immediate commercial success and has been held ever since, with interruptions during the world wars, though the nature of the competition and the prizes awarded were regarded with some suspicion in the early years by rugby's governing body in Scotland, the Scottish Football Union. Sevens rugby has spread round the world, with competitions held at Buenos Aires since 1921, Twickenham (the Middlesex sevens) since 1927, and Hong Kong since 1968.

Haig spent his last years in Dingleton Hospital, Melrose, suffering from mental illness, and died there on 29 March 1939. The border rugby clubs erected a tombstone to commemorate the most famous Scot, with the exception of

Robert the Bruce, to be buried in Melrose. At the Greenyards, home of Melrose Rugby Football Club, stands the impressive Ned Haig bar behind the grandstand, where supporters from all over the world gather annually on the second Saturday of April to watch the game of seven-a-side rugby. WALTER ALLAN

**Sources** W. Allan, *The official history of the Melrose sevens* (1994) • J. Gilbert, *Melrose rugby football club, 1877–1977* (1977)
**Likenesses** photographs, repro. in Allan, *Official history*, pp. 21, 40–41

**Haig, Sir Harry Graham** (1881–1956), administrator in India, was born on 13 April 1881 at 43 Kensington Park Gardens, Kensington, Middlesex, the fourth son of Henry Alexander Haig, merchant, and his wife, Agnes Catherine, *née* Pollock. Educated at Winchester College, he was elected to a scholarship at New College, Oxford, in 1900, took a second in classical moderations in 1902 and a first in *literae humaniores* in 1904. In that year he passed third into the Indian Civil Service and was appointed to its United Provinces cadre, where by 1910–12 he was serving as an under-secretary in its government. During the First World War he was in the Indian army reserve of officers. In 1920 he was appointed a deputy secretary in the finance department of the government of India. In 1921–2 he was secretary of the Indian fiscal commission, and in 1923–4 he was attached to the royal commission on the superior civil services, before serving briefly as private secretary to the viceroy, Lord Reading, in 1925.

In 1926 Haig was appointed secretary of the home department of the government of India, and so began his all but fifteen years' engagement at the highest levels of British government in India with all the forces of Indian nationalism—a record equalled only by Lord Hailey, after whom he may be accounted the most distinguished member of the Indian Civil Service in its final decades. Throughout he was especially notable for his strategic sense and tactical adroitness. As home secretary he consistently argued, aside from one moment of alarm, for a continuance of the largely non-repressive policy that had so successfully stymied Gandhi's non-co-operation movement of 1920–22, while in taking a principal role in mounting the Meerut conspiracy case against India's communist leaders in 1929, he successfully argued against any step that might 'rouse for the Communists any general sympathy among the nationalists or provide the nationalists with … a good rallying cry for an intensive anti-Government agitation' (Haig's Note, 9 Jan 1929, National Archives of India, Home Political file no. 18/XVI/28; Low, *Congress and the Raj*, 166, 192).

In 1930 Haig went to London as adviser to the Indian delegates to the first Indian round-table conference, and in the following year chaired a committee to plan the transformation of the North-West Frontier Province into a full governor's province with a representative legislature. Then early in 1932 he succeeded Sir James Crerar in the key position of home member of the government of India under the viceroy, Lord Willingdon.

Shortly beforehand Gandhi had renewed his major civil disobedience campaign; the government of India had for the first time assumed full-scale emergency powers, and had immediately imprisoned thousands of Congress activists, with Gandhi principal among them. Over the next two years Haig masterminded the actions of the government of India in upholding (and in some respects restoring) British authority in India. It involved what was called its 'dual policy'; 'first and foremost', so Haig averred, 'every effort should be made to reach practical conclusions about the constitution … [but] side by side … we must defeat the menace of civil disobedience' (Haig to Mieville, 13 April 1932, Low, *Britain and Indian Nationalism*, 79). Together with protracted constitutional discussions in London, that involved an adamantine refusal to negotiate further with Gandhi (as Lord Irwin had done in 1931) and a resolute determination to keep the Congress leaders in gaol until their commitment to civil disobedience had withered away. This in turn entailed not only a protracted propaganda duel with Gandhi while he was still their political prisoner, but prolonged telegraphic debates with the cabinet in London. Eventually, however, Haig's tenaciousness, alertness, and readiness to respond to Gandhi's craftiness with some of his own won the day. In due course, at a moment of the government's own choosing, Gandhi was released from gaol (and was subsequently worsted as never before), and by mid-1933 his civil disobedience campaign was no more.

In 1934 Haig became, in succession to Hailey, governor of his old province, the United Provinces. There he very successfully adjusted his style so as to work closely in 1937–9 with an elected Congress government following the institution of full responsible government in the provinces after the constitutional reforms of 1935. Momentarily there was a crisis when the premier, G. B. Pant, resigned over the refusal of the new viceroy, Linlithgow, to permit a wholesale release of some remaining political prisoners, but this was soon overcome, and at the end of Haig's term Pant went out of his way to thank him 'for the courtesy and guidance which we have received from you in the discharge of your office', a tribute which Haig warmly reciprocated (Pant to Haig, 20 Oct 1939, Haig to Pant, 4 Nov 1939, Low, *Britain and Indian Nationalism*, 302). As he left India on retirement, Linlithgow asked him to reflect on his career. 'For many years', Haig characteristically responded,

> I have regarded our position and policy in India as that of fighting a rearguard action. We are deliberately surrendering our power and we ought to do it with good-will; but we must not let the rearguard action turn into a rout. There are times when we have to stand and fight, even though at the end of it we continue to retire. (Haig to Linlithgow, 4 Dec 1939, Low, *Britain and Indian Nationalism*, 343)

No sooner was Haig back in Britain than early in 1940 he was appointed regional commissioner for civil defence for the north-west region, with headquarters in Manchester, where he was much esteemed for being at once 'modest, retiring, possessed of sound judgment and delightful to work with' (*The Times*, 18 June 1956). He was then transferred in 1942 to the southern region with headquarters in Reading, where he served until the end of the war.

On 25 August 1908 Haig had married Violet May (*b.* 1882/3), daughter of Joseph Deas, also of the Indian Civil Service. They had three sons. In 1923 he was made CIE, CSI in 1930, and KCSI in 1933. A keen churchman, he was active as chairman of the Indian Church Aid Association, originally under the presidency of his brother-in-law Bishop Eyre Chatterton, while in later years he played a prominent role in the Royal Institute of International Affairs, presiding at many a Chatham House meeting. He died on 14 June 1956 at his home, Valelands, Oxted, Surrey. He was survived by his wife. D. A. Low

**Sources** *The Times* (18 June 1956) • BL OIOC, Haig MSS, MS Eur. F 115 • D. A. Low, *Britain and Indian nationalism: the imprint of ambiguity, 1929–1942* (1997) • *WWW, 1951–60* • J. B. Wainewright, ed., *Winchester College, 1836–1906: a register* (1907) • D. A. Low, ed., *Congress and the raj: facets of the Indian struggle, 1917–47* (1977), chap. 4 • m. cert. • b. cert.

**Archives** BL OIOC, corresp. and papers, MS Eur. F 115 | BL OIOC, corresp. with Lord Linlithgow, MS Eur. F 125 • National Archives of India, New Delhi, home political files

**Wealth at death** £49,139 15*s.* 11*d.*: probate, 3 Aug 1956, *CGPLA Eng. & Wales*

**Haigh, Arthur Elam** (1855–1905), classical scholar, was born at Leeds on 27 February 1855, the third son, in a family of three sons and two daughters, of Joseph Haigh, chemist, and his wife, Lydia, daughter of Charles James Duncan. He was educated at Leeds grammar school, where he gained nearly every school distinction. In 1874 he matriculated at Corpus Christi College, Oxford, with a scholarship, and began his lifelong career of study and teaching at the university. He took a first class in classical moderations in 1875 and in *literae humaniores* in 1878; he won the two Gaisford prizes for Greek verse (1876) and Greek prose (1877), the Craven scholarship (1879), and the Stanhope prize for an essay entitled 'The political theories of Dante' (1878). He made pungent and witty speeches at the Oxford Union on the Liberal side, and he rowed in the Corpus eight when it was near the head of the river.

On graduating BA in 1878 Haigh was elected to a fellowship at Hertford, which he held until 1886, proceeding MA in 1881. He became classical lecturer at Corpus also in 1878, and for the next twenty-seven years was constantly engaged in teaching at that and other colleges. In 1901 he was admitted fellow of Corpus, and was appointed senior tutor the following year. He was classical moderator in 1888–9, and again in 1897–8. In August 1886 he married Louisa Matilda Forth, daughter of Jeremiah Giles Pilcher JP DL. She predeceased him in July 1904, leaving two sons and a daughter.

Haigh collaborated with T. L. Papillon in an edition of Virgil (1892); he also published *The Attic Theatre* (1889), third edition revised by A. W. Pickard-Cambridge (1907), and *The Tragic Drama of the Greeks* (1896). These works, which gave Haigh a general reputation, exhibited sound scholarship, independent judgement, the faculty of lucid exposition, and a wide range of classical and miscellaneous reading.

In his teaching Haigh laid much stress on verbal accuracy and the need for close textual study. But the limitations of his method were consistent with broad and sympathetic literary interests. He studied English literature with the same fastidious diligence with which he treated the classics, and he was an extremely well-informed critic of the English poets, and of some of the greater writers of Germany, France, and Italy.

Haigh took little part in university business or society, living a quiet family life and cherishing a few close friendships. He died somewhat suddenly at his house, 4 Norham Gardens, Oxford, on 20 December 1905, and was buried in Holywell cemetery. S. J. Low, *rev.* Richard Smail

**Sources** P. A. Hunt, *Corpus Christi College biographical register*, ed. N. A. Flanagan (1988) • A. G. [A. D. Godley], *Oxford Magazine* (24 Jan 1906), 149–50 • *CGPLA Eng. & Wales* (1906)

**Wealth at death** £3297 12*s.* 9*d.*: administration, 27 Jan 1906, *CGPLA Eng. & Wales*

**Haigh, Daniel Henry** (1819–1879), Roman Catholic convert and antiquary, was the son of George Haigh, a calico printer. He was born at Brinscall Hall, Wheelton, near Chorley, Lancashire, on 7 August 1819. Before the age of seventeen he lost both his parents and became head of the family, as the eldest of three brothers who had inherited a large fortune. He spent some time in business at Leeds, but soon decided to take orders in the Church of England. He went to live with the clergy of St Saviour's Church, Leeds, contributing liberally towards various ecclesiastical projects, chiefly the erection of All Saints, York Road, Leeds. When the four clergymen of St Saviour's joined the Roman Catholic church Haigh followed their example, ascribing his conversion to the writings of Bede. He entered St Mary's College, Oscott, on 1 January 1847 and was ordained priest there on 8 April 1848. Immediately he laid the foundation-stone of St Augustine's Church, Erdington, near Birmingham, contributing £15,000 to its building costs and endowment. He lived near this church until 1876, and was popular among the large congregation of Catholics whose poverty he treated with compassion; he even shared his own house with several orphans. He resigned from Erdington in 1877 and went to live at Oscott College, where he died of bronchitis on 10 May 1879, leaving less than £100 as the sole residue of what had once been a large fortune.

Haigh's antiquarian interests included Assyrian lore, Anglo-Saxon antiquities, numismatics, and biblical archaeology, and he was said to have been the chief authority in England on runic literature. The bulk of his work is preserved in the transactions of learned societies, especially in the *Numismatic Chronicle*, *Archaeologia Cantiana*, *Archaeologia Æliana*, *Royal Irish Academy*, *Yorkshire Archaeological Journal*, *Archaeological Journal*, *Transactions of the Lancashire and Cheshire Historic Society*, *British Archaeological Association* (Winchester Congress, 1845), and *Zeitschrift für Ägyptische Sprache und Alterthumskunde*. He also published *An Essay on the Numismatic History of the Ancient*

*Kingdom of the Angles* (1845), *On the Fragments of Crosses Discovered in Leeds in 1838* (1857), *The Conquest of Britain by the Saxons* (1861), and *The Anglo-Saxon Sagas: an Examination of their Value as Aids to History* (1861).

C. W. SUTTON, *rev.* LEO GOOCH

**Sources** Gillow, *Lit. biog. hist.* • *The Tablet* (24 May 1879), 659 • *Yorkshire Archaeological and Topographical Journal*, 6 (1879–80), 53 • C. R. Smith, *Retrospections, social and archaeological*, 3 vols. (1883–91), vol. 2, p. 78 • *Palatine Note-Book*, 1 (1881)

**Wealth at death** under £100: administration, 30 June 1879, *CGPLA Eng. & Wales*

**Haigh, Emily Alice** [*pseud.* Beatrice Hastings] (**1879–1943**), writer and journal editor, was born at Port Elizabeth, Cape Colony. Her exact date of birth and the names of her parents are not known. She was sent to school in Pevensey, Sussex, near Hastings, from which town she may have taken the name she used and was known by, although one source (Fifield) indicates that she married a Mr Hastings in Cape Colony in 1896. She spent some time in France before moving to London, where she began to publish poems, stories, and literary essays in periodicals. Interested in the modern movements of her time—including feminism, women's suffrage, and socialism—Hastings met the editor and social reformer Alfred Richard *Orage (1873–1934) when she attended a lecture he gave on theosophy in 1906.

Hastings and Orage fell in love and began a rather fraught affair which continued until 1914. There was evidently no question of marriage: Orage was already married and, however estranged from his wife, may well have been aware from the start of Hastings's volatile personality. Reputed to be a beauty, Hastings was an independent woman, financially secure, and familiar with the city in ways Orage initially was not. They soon began to live together, not only in London but during the summers at seaside resorts and, as Orage prospered, in several suburban homes. In 1907, when Orage took over as editor of the *New Age*—a periodical which soon championed established as well as new, experimental writers—Hastings joined the editorial staff and became a regular contributor. She published under her own name as well as anonymously and under a variety of pseudonyms (including Beatrice Tina, Alice Morning, Robert à Field, T. K. L., D. Triformis, Edward Stafford, S. Robert West, V. M., G. Whiz, J. Wilson, T. W., A. M. A., and Cynicus). Her submissions were informed and spirited, and ranged from poems and stories to letters, literary articles (over 200), and essays on feminism and social reform. In her autobiography, *The Old 'New Age': Orage—and Others*, published in 1936 as a 42-page pamphlet by a small press, she took credit for discovering or arguing with Orage for the inclusion of such promising young writers as F. S. Flint and Ezra Pound. She worked closely with other members of the staff, among them Huntly Carter, J. M. Kennedy, and A. E. Randall.

By early 1914 Hastings's relationship with Orage had become, according to her autobiography, 'intolerable' (Hastings, 8), and that spring she left London for Paris. She immediately joined the flamboyant circle of artists in Montparnasse that included the Italian modernist painter Amedeo Modigliani (1884–1920), with whom she fell in love. They lived together, first at his flat at 53 rue Montparnasse, then at her cottage at 13 rue Norvins. Their frequently violent affair, fuelled by alcohol and hashish, soured late in 1915; after a brief affair with Jean Cocteau's lover Raymond Radiguet, Hastings left Paris for the south of France. According to June Rose, Hastings served as a 'stimulant, irritant and catalyst' (Rose, 109) for Modigliani's work during this important period in his development, and he depicted Hastings in at least fourteen contemporary paintings and numerous sketches, not only as herself and his lover, but as Sappho and Mme de Pompadour. These pictures reveal Hastings as a compelling and dramatic woman. Clothed, she appears poised, with a small, proud head and long neck, her black hair pinned back in a low bun; nude, she is sometimes dishevelled, her nakedness emphasized by drapery that fails to cover her body. She continued to write for the *New Age* until 1920, contributing essays on pacifism, a sequence of short stories, and 'Impressions of Paris', a series of weekly articles that appeared for eighteen months. After the war she lived in both Paris and the south of France as well as in Switzerland, not returning to London until the early 1930s.

Generally quarrelsome, often drunk and unwell, Hastings squandered a large inheritance and became increasingly difficult and unreliable. Her highly emotional autobiography, which she described at the start as 'Extracts from an Introduction to "Incidents in the Life of the old *New Age*, 1907 to 1916"', a volume 'in preparation' (p. 1), is the only book she published. It is a painful and generally vitriolic account of her betrayal by former literary friends, top among them Orage himself, whom she pillories as a fraud, a bad writer, an incompetent editor, a stupid and grossly ungrateful one-time lover, a 'consummate schemer' (p. 15), and a 'maniac' (p. 29)—an estimate in sharp contrast to the man of grace, charm, generosity, and good sense admired by all of those who wrote about him after his death in 1934.

Orage was not the only figure to receive such harsh and unfair criticism: Hastings portrayed Katherine Mansfield, another contributor to the *New Age*, as a pretentious and twittering would-be 'saint', who 'fouled' the world 'wherever she went', while her writing was 'incredibly vulgar stuff' (p. 28). Hastings similarly accused Richard Aldington, an author Orage encouraged and whose third novel, *All Men are Enemies*, appeared in 1933, of stealing his title from one of her articles, 'Women's worst enemy, woman'; she went on to lambast him as a 'silk-fingered, scratch-nailed, sob-stuffing, eaten-brained curate of the feminine soul' (p. 9).

The effect of Hastings's bitter autobiography is not finally comic, but both deeply disquieting and pathetic. She clearly felt wronged by the world, particularly by the English literary establishment, and above all by Orage himself, yet while she struggled to elicit the reader's sympathy, she demonstrated her own emotional instability and lack of judgement. In his revised edition of *A. R. Orage:*

*a Memoir*, Philip Mairet admits that Hastings's book was embarrassing and outrageous, but refrains through kindness from arguing with her, stressing instead her competence as an editor in the formative years of the *New Age*.

Clearly unhappy and financially pressed, Hastings could in 1936 nevertheless declare proudly in her autobiography, 'I still love the social rebel, and challenge mere man-made laws ... I am still the same crusading, anti-philistine woman I ever was' (p. 9). By the early 1940s, however, Hastings had failed to complete the book-length study she had initially projected, and was living in Worthing as the widow of a pugilist, Lachie Thomson. She made a will in mid-October 1943, leaving 'the whole of my household furniture from beds to tin tacks' to a 'devoted friend', Doris Lillian Green, and her 'Literary Estate' to the British Museum or 'the first Public Library that puts in a claim'. On 31 October 1943 her dead body was discovered in her flat, 4 Bedford Row, Worthing, Sussex. At the inquest the coroner stated that she died as a result of asphyxia from carbon monoxide poisoning due to inhaling coal gas, and her death was officially registered 'as a suicide while mentally unhinged' (d. cert.). It seems likely, as stipulated in her will, that 'no Service whatever' was held and that Hastings was cremated; Green also probably followed Hastings's explicit instructions to throw her ashes 'down a hill, or in a field'. CAROLINE ZILBOORG

**Sources** B. Hastings, *The old 'New Age'—Orage and others* (1936) · P. A. Mairet, *A. R. Orage: a memoir*, rev. edn (New York, 1966) · W. Fifield, *Modigliani: the biography* (1978) · J. Rose, *Modigliani* (1990) · P. Selver, *Orage and the 'New Age' circle: reminiscences and reflections* (1959) · W. Martin, *The 'New Age' under Orage* (New York, 1967) · A. R. Orage, *Orage as critic*, ed. W. Martin (1974) · D. Milburn, *The Deutschlandbild of A. R. Orage and the 'New Age' circle* (1996) · T. H. Gibbons, *Rooms in the Darwin Hotel: studies in English literary criticism and ideas, 1880–1920* (1973) · *New Age* (1906–20) · d. cert. · will

**Likenesses** A. Modigliani, fourteen paintings, 1914–15 · A. Modigliani, sketches and drawings, 1914–15

**Wealth at death** £341 18s. 4d.: probate, 18 Jan 1944, *CGPLA Eng. & Wales*

**Haigh, John George** (1909–1949), murderer, was born at home at 22 King's Road, Stamford, Lincolnshire, on 24 July 1909, to John Robert Haigh (*b. c.*1871), an unemployed electrical engineer, and Emily Haigh (*c.*1869–1955), both natives of Yorkshire and married for eleven years. They were members of the strict religious body the Plymouth Brethren. When Haigh was one year old the family moved to Outwood, Yorkshire, where his father gained employment as an electrician at the nearby colliery. His upbringing was strict, in accordance with the faith of his parents, who affectionately called him Sonnie. The young Haigh soon displayed a musical talent. He attended Wakefield grammar school and was seen as a smart, polite, intelligent boy with a good character and home life. His musical talent won him a scholarship to Wakefield Cathedral at the age of ten. He became a choirboy at the cathedral and later at Leeds parish church. He left school at the age of seventeen and, as he was lazy by nature, forgery and deception became the easy alternatives to work.

The suave, dapper Haigh discovered he could make money to finance his expensive tastes in cars and clothes without having to work too hard. On 6 July 1934 he married Beatrice (Betty) Hamer, a former waitress and model three years his junior, at Bridlington register office. His occupation at this time was given as company director, and both gave their residence as the Alexandra Hotel, Bridlington. His business was fraudulent hire purchase and selling non-existent cars. The marriage did not last long. In November 1934, at Leeds assizes, Haigh received fifteen months' imprisonment for fraud offences, with six offences taken into consideration. He saw his wife only once again. She had borne a daughter while Haigh was in prison and the baby was adopted. Haigh never made a paternity claim and never saw the child.

A life of fraud still seemed the easy option and in November 1937 Haigh was sentenced at Surrey assizes to four years' imprisonment for false pretences with twenty-two offences taken into account. In wartime Haigh became a fire-watcher during the enemy raids on London; however, he was sentenced in June 1941, at the London sessions, to twenty-one months' hard labour for stealing bunks, kitchen and curtain material, and a refrigerator. In Lincoln prison he worked in the tinsmith's shop, where he gained a knowledge of sulphuric acid and its use. In 1944 he moved to Crawley, Sussex, where he lived with a family named Stephens. Ever the dapper, polite, businessman, he wore a small moustache and greased, slicked-back hair. He was always impeccably dressed. He became fond of the Stephenses' attractive teenage daughter Barbara, a friendship which lasted to the end.

Around this time Haigh took a room in the Onslow Court Hotel, South Kensington. The comfortable hotel was favoured by retired elderly ladies and the charming Haigh was a desirable table companion. There Haigh became friendly with a wealthy 69-year-old widow, Mrs Henrietta Helen Olivia Robarts (Olive) Durand-Deacon, who was amenable to business ideas. She was interested in marketing cosmetics. On 18 February 1949 Haigh took her to see his 'factory' in Leopold Road, Crawley. There he shot her and put her body into a 40 gallon drum, which he filled with sulphuric acid, wearing a gas mask, rubber gloves, and apron to protect himself. He took her valuables, including jewellery and a Persian lamb coat. She was reported missing by a friend at the hotel, who was accompanied to the police station by Haigh. He came under suspicion, his criminal record was checked, and he was arrested. Mrs Durand-Deacon's property was traced to where he had sold it, for he had needed the cash to settle debts.

The search of the premises at Crawley was a triumph in forensic medicine for the pathologist Dr Keith Simpson. Remains consisting of a few bone fragments, fat, three gallstones, false teeth, plastic handbag, and a few personal items were recovered. With blood tests on stains found in the 'factory' these were enough to prove he had murdered her, despite the lack of a body. Haigh then confessed to the murders of William McSwann and his parents in 1944–5, and of Dr Archibald Henderson and his wife, Rosalie, in 1948, all for gain. They too had been disposed of in a similar manner. To avoid the hangman's rope his only recourse was a plea of insanity. He told of lurid blood-filled dreams and claimed that he had tapped blood from the necks of his victims and drunk it from a glass. The press gave him the nickname 'the Vampire Killer'. He claimed three more unknown past victims, presumably to enhance his insanity plea.

The trial, which lasted three days, opened at Lewes assizes on 18 July 1949. He was found guilty, and the judge, Mr Justice Humphreys, pronounced sentence of death on Haigh. Executed by Albert Pierrepoint at Wandsworth prison at 9 a.m. on Monday 10 August 1949, he was buried the same day within the precincts of the prison. The 'Acid Bath Murderer', as he was known, left clothing to Madame Tussaud's waxworks to dress his effigy, which remains there to this day. STEWART P. EVANS

**Sources** A. La Bern and W. H. Allen, *Haigh: the mind of a murderer* (1973) · D. Briffett, *The acid bath murders* (1988) · Lord Dunboyne, ed., *Trial of John George Haigh* (1953) · S. Sommerfield, *The authentic story of J. G. Haigh* (1950) · G. Byrne, *John George Haigh* [1950] · S. Jackson, *John George Haigh* (1953) · m. cert. · b. cert. · d. cert.
**Archives** FILM BFI NFTVA, documentary footage
**Likenesses** three photographs, 1949, Hult. Arch.

**Haigh, Mervyn George** (1887–1962), bishop of Winchester, was born in Islington, London, on 14 September 1887, the only son and the second of the three children of William Edward Haigh (*b.* 1850), vicar of Holy Trinity, Islington, and his wife, Janet Middleton (*b.* 1861). He was educated at home before attending a day school at Highbury and then, from 1899, Clifton College. At New College, Oxford (1906–10), he gained second-class honours in moderations and greats, after which he underwent theological training at the bishop's palace in Hereford, under the supervision of Dr Hastings Rashdall. He was ordained deacon at St Paul's Cathedral in 1911 and priested in 1912, then served curacies in East Finchley and Cranley Gardens, Chelsea, before volunteering as an army chaplain (1916). Haigh served in the former German colonial territories in east Africa until the end of the war, particularly in Dodoma, where, in addition to his normal chaplaincy duties, he distinguished himself as an effective counsel for the defence in three courts martial. He ministered, under appalling conditions, to soldiers suffering from a deadly 'Asian flu', before succumbing to malaria and returning to Britain (1919).

Building on his experience as an army chaplain, Haigh taught Reformation and Renaissance history in the Ordination Test School at Knutsford, a training centre for ex-soldiers interested in the ministry, based in a disused prison. Knutsford, the brainchild of P. T. B. (Tubby) Clayton, was a precursor of modern pre-ordination training, and Haigh responded enthusiastically to its ethos: more egalitarian and less academic than traditional theological colleges, and yet still open to theological innovation under the leadership of its principal, F. R. Barry. He also became examining chaplain to the bishop of Llandaff, J. P. Hughes—the beginning of a long and fruitful association with Wales. He was involved in the early 1920s in the committee, led by Percy Dearmer, which produced the innovative (and doctrinally relaxed) *Songs of Praise*, and he was a key contributor to the 'Grey Book', a set of proposals for the revision of the prayer book drawn up by some of the leading liberals in the Church of England. The latter gave him the opportunity to exhibit his considerable flair for liturgy, and the poetic power and ecological sensitivity of a litany preserved in his hand might well have received more thorough recognition:

> Spirit of God, Thou art also the Perfect Artist:
> Thy handiwork is the supreme miracle of beauty:
> Thou didst clothe the grass of the field: the gleam of the buttercups and bluebells is Thy artistry, and the wind that sways them into laughter is Thy breath.
> (Barry, 77–8)

In 1923 Haigh went to University College, Oxford, for a short-lived chaplain fellowship, and in 1924 Archbishop Davidson invited him to succeed George Bell as his chaplain. He found himself writing several of the archbishop's judicious pronouncements and overseeing the proposed revisions to the prayer book. He was instrumental in launching the 'Way of renewal', a scheme designed to make prayer and study the focal point of ruri-decanal chapters. Under Archbishop Cosmo Gordon Lang he was deeply involved in preparations for the 1930 Lambeth conference, and the encyclical letter which ensued, with its assertion that 'there is much in the scientific and philosophical thinking of our time which provides a climate more favourable to faith in God than has existed for generations' (Barry, 107–9), was written by Haigh. During this time Haigh established himself as a spokesman for a broad Anglican liberalism, which had little in common with the extreme modernism and rationalism of Bishop E. W. Barnes of Birmingham.

Late in 1930 Haigh was appointed to the see of Coventry, where he immediately distinguished himself as an imaginative preacher, unafraid to criticize the past role of the church, for example, in trying 'to keep the arts, like the sciences, tied to the apron strings of its own elaborate but inadequate interpretation of life' (Barry, 123). In 1936 he underwent a severe physical breakdown, which almost induced his resignation, but he recovered enough to persevere. He led the diocese through the blitz in 1940, responding to the overnight destruction of the cathedral and four parish churches with an almost proverbial fortitude (it was also he who recognized the potential of the 'cross of nails' devised by A. P. Wales). On 11 December 1940 he spoke publicly on the blitz, arousing considerable controversy with his conviction that:

> If the British Government were to decide that this form of attack will be used against German cities if it continues to be used against ours, it might well be morally justified in coming to that conclusion … we could not desire to inflict on any German city such a general bombardment of women and children and beautiful old buildings as there was in Coventry … But there are still many people among us who seem to think that the methods of warfare to which they have grown accustomed are morally defensible, while refusing as morally impossible for us, in any circumstances or on any conditions, to adopt novel and more terrible forms of warfare when and so long as these are performed against ourselves. These people do not seem to have quite realized what total warfare may require, and if we are not prepared

for that we might have done better not to have begun resisting the Nazi aggression by force. (Barry, 137–8)

Writing privately to Bishop Hensley Henson, Haigh explained that 'Experience & knowledge alike suggest that the Gov't may be minimizing the element of discrimination (as distinct from indiscriminate bombing) … and that it might be well for us … to concentrate more planes on larger targets' (Henson papers, 6 Jan 1941). Despite the widespread criticism of his remarks, they merely defended an attitude that was already covert government policy. The explosion of the two atomic bombs in 1945, which drove many who had criticized area bombing to a position of virtual pacifism, made Haigh's comments about 'total warfare' seem the more prophetic.

In 1942 Haigh was translated to Winchester. At his enthronement he criticized the 'savage and inhuman theologies' of the Barthians (Barry, 123) and vigorously defended the church's right to campaign for social reform. As prelate of the Order of the Garter he was in constant contact with George VI. He was among those considered for the primacy after the death of Archbishop William Temple, but his own poor health, plagued by life-threatening low blood pressure, was already becoming a severe handicap. He resigned in 1952 at the age of sixty-five, but threw himself energetically into exploring the north Welsh countryside, taking rooms in the Golden Lion Hotel in Dolgellau. As county president of the Council for the Preservation of Rural Wales he campaigned to preserve the countryside, despite his increasing incapacity. He lived to see the rebuilding of Coventry Cathedral, and died on 20 May 1962 at Argoed, Dolgellau, shortly before its consecration. He was buried at Winchester Cathedral on 26 May. Bishop Haigh remained unmarried.

GILES C. WATSON

**Sources** F. R. Barry, *Mervyn Haigh* (1964) • A. Wilkinson, *Dissent or conform? War, peace and the English churches, 1900–1945* (1986) • A. Hastings, *A history of British Christianity, 1920–1985* (1986) • R. Lloyd, *The Church of England, 1900–1965* (1966) • *The Times* (21 May 1962) • b. cert. • *CGPLA Eng. & Wales* (1962) • M. Haigh, letter to Bishop Hensley Henson, 6 Jan 1941, Durham Cath. CL, Henson papers, vol. 82 • *WWW* • d. cert.

**Archives** LPL, corresp. | BL, letters to Albert Mansbridge, Add. MSS 65254, 65256 • LPL, corresp. with John Douglas • LPL, corresp. with Edwin James Palmer • LPL, letters to Athelstan Riley

**Likenesses** W. Stoneman, two photographs, 1939–45, NPG • P. Greenham, oils, *c*.1953, Bishop's Palace, Winchester • photograph, NPG • sculpture, Bishop's Palace, Coventry

**Wealth at death** £40,582 8*s*. 4*d*.: probate, 3 Sept 1962, *CGPLA Eng. & Wales*

**Haigh, Thomas** (1769–1808), composer, was born in London and studied composition with Haydn during the latter's first visit to London in 1791–2. From 1793 to 1801 Haigh lived in Manchester, where he probably had family connections, and became known as Thomas Haigh of Manchester. He returned to London in 1801, and died there in April 1808.

Haigh's many compositions show the strong influence of Haydn. They include two sets of piano sonatas and the violin sonatas op. 8 and op. 10, dedicated to his teacher, as well as many other piano sonatas and sonatas for piano accompanied by violin or flute, a piano sonata including an air from *The Beggar's Opera*, op. 28 (*c*.1800), six keyboard concertos (*c*.1783), *A Favourite Symphony* (*c*.1794), and ballads. He arranged many of Haydn's orchestral works for the piano, including symphonies nos. 70 and 81 and the overture *Armida*.

ANNE PIMLOTT BAKER

**Sources** *New Grove* • *DNB*

**Haighton, John** (*c*.1755–1823), surgeon and physiologist, was born in Lancashire. After studying under Joseph Else at St Thomas's Hospital, London, he became a surgeon to the guards, but resigned on being appointed demonstrator of anatomy at St Thomas's, under Henry Cline. He was a skilful surgeon and so promising an anatomist that John Hunter considered letting Haighton assist him in his lectures. Haighton, however, was not so popular with students as his junior, Astley Paston Cooper, whose developing talent and influence hindered his advancement. Consequently Haighton resigned his demonstratorship in 1789 and turned his attention to physiology and to midwifery, lecturing in both at the united hospitals, St Thomas's and Guy's. He was somewhat suspicious, irritable, and argumentative, but a good lecturer on physiology and an excellent obstetric operator. For his physiological experiments, which were certainly ruthless and numerous, he was called the 'Merciless Doctor' by his opponents. When Sir Astley Cooper disputed the result of some of Haighton's experiments, the latter killed a favourite spaniel, on which he had previously operated, in order to prove Sir Astley wrong.

Haighton often presided at the meetings of the Physical Society at Guy's Hospital, was joint editor of *Medical Records and Researches* (1798), and assisted William Saunders in his *Treatise on the Liver* (1793). He wrote several original papers on subjects including vomiting, deafness, and nerves which were published in *Medical Commentaries*, *Memoirs of the Medical Society of London*, *Philosophical Transactions*, and *Medical Records*. He also published full syllabuses of his courses of lectures at various dates. He was awarded the silver medal of the Medical Society of London in 1790 for his paper on deafness, and in 1815 became a fellow of the Royal Society, mainly for his papers on mathematics and astronomy. In later years he suffered from asthma, and his nephew, James Blundell, began to assist him in his lectures in 1814, and took the entire course from 1818. Haighton died on 23 March 1823.

G. T. BETTANY, *rev.* CAROLINE OVERY

**Sources** [Clarke], *The Georgian era: memoirs of the most eminent persons*, 4 vols. (1832–4) • B. B. Cooper, *The life of Sir Astley Cooper*, 1 (1843), 119–28, 197–202, 279 • T. J. Pettigrew, *Medical portrait gallery: biographical memoirs of the most celebrated physicians, surgeons … who have contributed to the advancement of medical science*, 4 vols. in 2 [1838–40] • S. Wilks and G. T. Bettany, *A biographical history of Guy's Hospital* (1892)

**Archives** McGill University, Montreal, Osler Library of the History of Medicine, lecture notes • Wellcome L., lecture notes

**Likenesses** N. Branwhite, stipple, pubd 1801 (after *Institutors of the Medical Society of London* by S. Medley), BM • I. Kennerley, mezzotint, 1818 (after H. Ashby), Wellcome L. • C. Armstrong, line engraving, 1819 (after F. Simonau), Wellcome L.

**Hailes**. For this title name *see* Dalrymple, Sir David, third baronet, Lord Hailes (1726–1792); Hepburn, Patrick George Thomas Buchan-, Baron Hailes (1901–1974).

**Hailey, (William) Malcolm, Baron Hailey** (1872–1969), administrator in India and writer on Africa, was born in Newport Pagnell, Buckinghamshire, on 15 February 1872, the third son of Hammett Hailey (*d.* 1881), a doctor, and his wife, Maria Coelia Clode (*d.* 1911), of a long-established family in the City of London. Malcolm was educated at Merchant Taylors' School, London, and at Corpus Christi College, Oxford, graduating in the first class in 1894. Having been placed third in the Indian Civil Service examinations, he served briefly in Calcutta before being posted in 1895 to the land division of the Punjab secretariat. There, he recalled, he sat at the feet of Septimus S. Thorburn, whose *Musulmans and Moneylenders in the Punjab* (1886) was a classic statement of the conservative, paternalist attitudes characteristic of the Punjab school, which identified with peasants and small landowners, and against urban-educated élites, Hindu moneylenders, and the *laissez-faire* judgments of English courts in enforcing land foreclosures.

**Character and marriage** Always a hard worker, as Hailey grew older he became a classic workaholic. More than 6 feet tall, bald by his thirties, with a hawk nose, and the possessor of a deep bass voice, he was a commanding figure. His hobbies were hiking and fishing. Affable and witty, he loved to escape from official circles and meet ordinary people. But he was also cold and reserved, a man with many acquaintances but few truly intimate friends. His wife, Andreina Alessandra Balzani (*d.* 1939), whom he married in 1896, was the daughter of a Roman count. She was beautiful, athletic, musically talented, and possessed of considerable courage, as for example when she went up in a small aeroplane at Lahore, crashed, and walked away vowing to go up again as soon as possible. But she was a foreigner, and never really fitted into British colonial society. The Haileys had two children; their son Allan (Billy) was killed on active service in the Middle East during the Second World War, and their daughter, Gemma, died as a teenager in 1922 from a burst appendix. For Andreina Hailey, Gemma's death was a traumatic turning point from which she never really recovered. Thereafter she suffered from severe depression, and became an alcoholic; her increasingly eccentric behaviour was commonly thought to have prevented her husband from becoming viceroy. She died in 1939.

**Early career in India** Between 1901 and 1907 Hailey served as the first colonization officer of the Lower Jhelum Canal Colony, Shahpur district. This was one of several large-scale irrigation projects, comparable to ventures in Sudan, the Middle East, and the south-western United States, turning deserts into prosperous, bread-basket communities. Aged twenty-nine at the time of his appointment, he was responsible for surveying, choosing colonists, siting the town that became Sargodha, setting up a seed farm, and countless other things required in

**(William) Malcolm Hailey, Baron Hailey** (1872–1969), by Elliott & Fry

founding a new society. In 1903, halfway through his term, bubonic plague struck the colony, including Hailey himself. The canal colony was his formative experience. There he developed deep feelings of empathy with rural people that would persist through his Indian governorships, resurfacing still later in his advocacy of colonial development in Africa. In 1936, when he was raised to the peerage, he asked to be designated Baron Hailey of Newport Pagnell and Shahpur.

In 1907 Hailey returned to secretariat work, this time in the government of India's finance department. There he demonstrated the qualities that would make him a first-class administrator: an apparently unlimited appetite for work, the ability to handle massive quantities of detail without losing sight of the main points, coolness under pressure, and willingness to delegate. In 1911 he was financial member of the planning committee for the highly complex gathering of Indian notables and their sovereign, the Delhi durbar; it was best known for the decisions of the viceroy, Lord Hardinge, to reverse the controversial partition of Bengal and for moving the capital from Calcutta to Delhi. The durbar assignment, which brought him into direct contact with the viceroy, was Hailey's big break. Lack of seniority and relatively little field experience notwithstanding, Hardinge chose him as the first chief commissioner of the Delhi capital enclave. Hailey served there throughout the First World War, where he was concerned with military recruiting, the rising nationalist demands of Indian politicians, the disastrous influenza epidemic of 1918, and the feuding between the architects Sir Herbert Baker and Sir Edwin Lutyens (who were planning, respectively, the new secretariat and Government House).

**The Amritsar massacre** In 1918 Hailey was disappointed not to succeed Sir Michael O'Dwyer as lieutenant-governor of the Punjab. He considered early retirement and, while awaiting a vacancy, went on temporary duty to the Punjab. During the summer of 1919 he wrote the unsigned report on the administration of martial law following the violence connected with the Rowlatt *satyagraha* and General Reginald Dyer's infamous massacre of unarmed crowds in a walled garden, the Jallianwalla Bagh, in Amritsar. Part of Hailey's report was published, again without attribution, in 1920 as a parliamentary paper. Although it was factual and detached to the point of bloodlessness, he left room for Dyer's only conceivable defence: that he had supposed his troops to be in danger. But the report also provided evidence that would have made such a defence difficult to sustain. In testifying before the Hunter committee Dyer changed his case, asserting that he had acted to produce a moral effect, to forestall another Indian mutiny. Although it provoked violent denunciations in the House of Lords, as well as a substantial defence fund raised by the *Morning Post*, the army council's decision to censure and retire him was allowed to stand. Indian politicians, including M. K. Gandhi, were outraged at the episode, and at the official and unofficial British response. Reflecting on the episode half a century later, Hailey concluded that it had changed the trajectory of Anglo-Indian relations for ever. He also remarked that Dyer might have got away with his actions, if only he had kept his mouth shut.

**Finance member and home member** By the time the report was published in 1920 Hailey had taken his seat on the government bench as finance member, where he remained until 1922, in which year he was appointed KCSI. This was a turbulent period, marked by rapidly fluctuating currencies, to which the British authorities responded with a stubborn and ultimately futile effort to maintain the rupee at a high rate. While India's gold reserves, which had built up appreciably during the war, melted down week by week, Indian critics charged that the high-rupee policy (keeping exports dear and imports cheap) was favourable to British and detrimental to Indian interests, that it constituted a 'drain', if not outright theft. Although Hailey's term as finance member cannot, by any stretch of the imagination, be called a success, the controlling role of the India Office in London was well known, so his own reputation did not suffer unduly.

In 1922 Hailey moved to the Home Office, the most important division of which, the home political department, had the task of responding to the challenge of Indian nationalism. As home member he launched a series of prosecutions which ultimately succeeded in preventing the Indian Communist Party from gaining much strength outside a few strongholds, such as the Bombay cotton-mill workers. He also helped to formulate the government's bumbling, inconsistent, often harsh, response to the reformist Sikhs' campaign to gain control over their shrines (*gurdwaras*) in the Punjab. In the legislative assembly, as leader of the official forces in the system of diarchy under the Government of India Act of 1919, the home member had to fight uphill against a permanent minority. The popularly elected opposition could reject all but the military portion of the budget. (The viceroy could still restore it.) Gaining a reputation as a skilful debater, Hailey came to sympathize with liberals such as the law member, Sir Tej Bahadur Sapru. In his most controversial intervention Hailey argued that the phrases 'responsible government' and 'dominion status', both of which the secretary of state for India, Edwin Montagu, had promised in 1917 in an attempt to ensure Indian loyalty throughout the war, were not the same. Responsible government was a distinct, entirely separate process; although dominion status might be its logical or even inevitable result, it might also be long deferred—and so it proved to be.

**Governor of the Punjab** In 1924 Hailey became governor of the Punjab, which would ordinarily have been the culmination of his career. Two issues dominated his governorship. The first was the concluding phase of the conflict with the reformist party among the Sikhs. During his period as home member, when he had been partly responsible for the provincial government's policy, the Sikh campaign had been militant, determined, and sometimes tragic. By 1924, however, it was already losing its intensity. In a cool, calculating, rational, thoroughly Machiavellian manner, Hailey split his opponents by enabling them to gain control of their *gurdwaras* legally, but refusing to budge if they broke the law. In effect, he solved the Sikh issue for a generation, curbing and controlling, but not annihilating, a community whose role in the army made their importance to the British far outweigh their numbers. The second major issue was likewise both Machiavellian and successful. He manoeuvred to defeat the nationalist boycott of the Simon commission (which had been appointed by parliament to enquire into the working of the 1919 reforms) by encouraging local Muslim politicians to co-operate with the commission, a strategy that would give them an advantage in the Punjab, thereby forcing Hindus to co-operate as well. (In advising the viceroy, Lord Irwin, and the secretary of state, Lord Birkenhead, Hailey was singularly short-sighted; he urged them to make the Simon commission a purely parliamentary body, which served as a pretext for appointing no Indian members.) Hailey hated the violence and what he regarded as the petty nastiness of communalism, which became increasingly prevalent in the 1920s, but he played the communal card skilfully, and without undue remorse.

**Governor of the United Provinces** In 1928, following the unexpected death of Sir Alexander Muddiman, Hailey became governor of the United Provinces (later Uttar Pradesh), regarded as the top position open to a member of the Indian Civil Service. There he remained until his retirement in 1934. The United Provinces were a primary focus of the civil disobedience campaign which Gandhi launched with his famous salt march in the spring of 1930. The climax came in 1931, when the dramatic fall in agricultural prices (part of the great worldwide depression) coincided with a no-rent, no-tax movement to produce something close to an agrarian revolution. The crisis passed, partly because Hailey granted substantial remissions, partly because the Indian National Congress (many of whose influential members were landlords) did not really want a full-scale revolution, and wished to be heard at the forthcoming series of constitutional discussions in London. Like the nationalist leader, Jawaharlal Nehru, Hailey concluded that the landlord (*zamindari*) system was obsolete and doomed. Since the landlords were the only class allies in sight, however, he kept his opinion to himself. Publicly, he exhorted the landlords to organize and defend themselves. By the time he left, three years before Congress's decisive victory in the important provincial elections of 1937, he knew very well that his effort to build a viable landlord party as a bulwark against Congress had failed. During the United Provinces governorship Hailey attended the first round-table conference on constitutional progress (1930–31), and played a very considerable role in framing the Government of India Act of 1935, not least in voicing the priorities of the Indian Civil Service.

**The *African Survey*** After Hailey retired from India in 1934 he shifted the direction of his career. In 1933 he had accepted the directorship of the *African Survey*, sponsored by the Carnegie Corporation, a project the inspiration for which is usually attributed to General Jan C. Smuts, although the true father was the missionary leader Joseph H. Oldham. In 1936 Hailey toured Africa—east, west, and south; French and Belgian as well as British—and then set out to write what was supposed to be a brief report of about 150 pages, setting out the major themes and problems of research. In fact, although he had been writing all his life, he had never written a real book before, and the attempt to produce a short work on a large subject under time pressure created psychological depression so intense it nearly killed him. He actually drafted only one chapter himself, 'Law and Justice'; the rest was composed by staff members (including Lucy Mair, who became a distinguished anthropologist at the London School of Economics) or was farmed out to various specialists. In the autumn of 1937, while in Geneva as British representative to the permanent mandates commission of the League of Nations, he suffered a breakdown and went to the south of France to recuperate. Meanwhile, Frederick Pedler from the Colonial Office took over the editorship of the *African Survey*, and whittled down what he estimated to be at least a million words to a mere 1600 pages. Hailey was unable to work at all until the early summer of 1938, and his contributions during the last year before publication were confined to correcting some of the galley proofs. In the preface to the *Survey* the marquess of Lothian played down Hailey's illness; Pedler's crucial role (knowledge of which would have tarnished the project's claims to objectivity) was covered up entirely. The aim was not so much to save Hailey's reputation as that of the *Survey*.

*An African Survey* was widely acclaimed, frequently consulted, and seldom read. Hailey's position as its director made him the logical successor to another figurehead, Frederick, Baron Lugard, as an official standard-bearer for the British Africanist establishment. He also played a prominent role in the colonial reform movement during and after the Second World War, including a lecture tour of the United States in 1942–3 devoted to attempting to moderate anti-colonial American opinion. The primary motif of this reformist campaign was colonial welfare and development, dedicated to raising African living standards. Here, especially, Lord Hailey of Shahpur returned to the themes of the Punjab school, to his youthful experiences on the Lower Jhelum.

**Africanist** Early in 1940, accompanied by Pedler as his secretary, Hailey toured Africa to report on 'native administration' and political developments. Where was Britain's policy of indirect rule going? How soon was African nationalism likely to mount a real challenge to colonial rule? He was also asked, confidentially, whether differences in the treatment of Africans in Northern and Southern Rhodesia were so irreconcilable as to make the amalgamation of the two colonies impossible. His answers were that indirect rule was going nowhere, that nationalism seemed to be less advanced than he had expected, that it would certainly come, and that Africans should be appointed at every level of the bureaucracy, including the central governments. As for the Rhodesias, he found that the differences were indeed substantial and likely to widen. Ruling out closer union was not within his brief, however, and he hedged. In June 1940, just after the fall of France (as well as other western European states, including Belgium), Hailey and Pedler returned to Africa, this time to the Belgian Congo, charged with negotiating the opening of British markets to its products, and with helping the governor-general, Pierre Ryckmans, keep the territory out of German hands. While there, Hailey crossed the Congo to Brazzaville to meet the leader of the Free French, Charles De Gaulle.

**Last decades** After 1943, although the Colonial Office continued to consult him from time to time, Lord Hailey became increasingly peripheral to official thinking. His reputation, however, which had been deliberately inflated at the time of the *Survey*, was a national and Commonwealth asset, and he continued to speak and write on African issues until the early 1950s. He also served on a wide variety of governing boards, including that of the University of London's School of Oriental and African Studies, and the Rhodes Trust. As he aged, he took to wintering in Natal, and it was there that he wrote his last book, *The Republic of South Africa and the High Commission Territories* (1963), which appeared when he was ninety-one. Hailey died in Putney, London, on 1 June 1969, at the age of ninety-seven. His ashes were placed in the family vault in Simla. Born in the year of Benjamin Disraeli's Crystal Palace speech, which is sometimes cited as the dawn of the new imperialism, having gone out to India five years before Curzon at the high noon of empire, Lord Hailey had lived on beyond its sunset.

**Assessment** By the time of his retirement from India in 1934 Hailey was regarded as the twentieth century's most distinguished Indian civil servant. He was not so much a great Africanist as a great man who devoted his last quarter-century to Africa. Although his African phase is better known, his Indian governorships were actually much more substantial achievements. His entire career, like that of the British empire he served, can be regarded as a series of gradual and reasonably well-prepared retreats, across decades and continents, before the insurgent, ultimately irresistible force of Asian and then African nationalism. By about 1915, when he wrote a note on how to respond to what he called the 'Asian Risorgimento', Hailey already understood the dynamic of colonial nationalism, intellectually if not emotionally. In India he fought the Congress intelligently, shrewdly, rationally, and, on the whole, humanely. Gandhi called him 'one of our best governors'. On such important issues as the salt march in 1930 and the landlord system in the United Provinces, Hailey and Nehru reached strikingly similar conclusions (on which they acted in diametrically opposing ways), and they clearly respected one another. On Hailey's retirement the Allahabad *Leader* praised his courage in going to riot-torn Cawnpore during the heat of May 1931 when he was still recovering from a serious operation. The communal violence of India's partition in 1947, most vicious in the Punjab, shocked and saddened him. Although the member of the House of Lords realized there was no alternative, the Old Punjabi thought Britain had run out on its duty to the ordinary people of India. In Africa, too, where he happened to be on tour in Accra during the important riots of 1948, he noted tersely in his diary: 'Gold Coast a "political situation" not administrative. Government not organized for it. No intelligence department'. That was where he had come in, in India, about 1907. During the next few years decolonization proceeded with what to him seemed imprudent, indecent, and unnecessary haste. Well aware that his faith was going out of style, Lord Hailey remained an imperialist to the end. JOHN W. CELL

**Sources** J. W. Cell, *Hailey: a study in British imperialism, 1872–1969* (1992) · *DNB* · private information (2004) [Philip Mason and Sir Frederick Pedler] · Lord Hailey [W. M. Hailey], *An African survey*, [new edn] (1957) · Lord Hailey, *Native administration and political development in British tropical Africa* [n.d., 1944?]; [new edn], 5 pts (1950–53); repr. in 3 vols. (1979) · *CGPLA Eng. & Wales* (1969)

**Archives** BL OIOC, papers, MS Eur. E 220 · BL OIOC, letters, MS Eur. D 714 · Bodl. Oxf., corresp. relating to the 'Round Table' · Bodl. RH, corresp., journals, and papers; corresp. and papers relating to his survey tours of Africa · National Archives of India, New Delhi · PRO, papers relating to Africa, CO 1018 · Punjab secretariat, Lahore · Uttar Pradesh Archives, Lucknow | BL OIOC, corresp. with Sir John Simon · Bodl. Oxf., letters to P. S. Allen; corresp. with Lionel Curtis; corresp. with Sir Aurel Stein · Bodl. RH, corresp. with Lord Lugard; corresp. with Margery Perham and related papers; corresp. with Sir R. R. Welensky relating to Belgian Congo · Borth. Inst., letters to Lord Halifax · RIBA BAL, corresp. with Herbert Baker relating to New Delhi

**Likenesses** W. Stoneman, two photographs, 1930–45, NPG · J. Gunn, oils, 1954, Royal Institute of International Affairs, Chatham House, London; copy, Bodl. RH · Elliott & Fry, photograph, NPG [*see illus.*] · D. Low, pencil caricature, NPG · G. Philpot, oils, Lawrence Memorial House, Lahore, India · photograph (as governor of the Punjab), Secretariat, Lahore, Anarkali's Tomb

**Wealth at death** £56,934: probate, 16 Oct 1969, *CGPLA Eng. & Wales*

**Hails, William Anthony** (1766–1845), writer, son of William Hails, a shipwright, and his wife, Mary, *née* Elsdon, was born at Newcastle upon Tyne on 24 May 1766. He was a delicate boy, unable to attend school until the age of eleven. His mother taught him his letters—reputedly from an old church prayer book—and his father instructed him in writing and arithmetic. After spending three years at school in Wallsend, where he learnt a smattering of geometry, algebra, and trigonometry, he was bound as an apprentice shipwright at the age of fifteen to Messrs William Hurry of Howden, the foremost shipbuilders on Tyneside. Hails hoped to become a seaman, and in his leisure while an apprentice he studied hydrography and nautical astronomy. His father, a schoolfriend of Charles Hutton, the mathematician, encouraged him in these studies, and by nineteen Hails was considered a local prodigy. In May 1784 John Wesley preached in Howden, and soon afterwards Hails joined the Methodists. He quickly taught himself Latin and Greek, and also studied Hebrew, together with some other oriental languages, to enable him to appraise the various translations of the Bible and criticize the use made by preachers of passages of scripture. In the summer of 1798 he obtained the post of writing-master in a Newcastle boarding-school, and a few years later opened his own school at 11 Westgate Street, in premises originally built by Dr Charles Hutton. On 17 February 1795 he had married Mary Wilde, at St Mary's Church, Gateshead.

Hails wrote several papers for the *Classical Journal*, and contributed to the *Gentleman's Magazine* and *Monthly Magazine*. In 1806 he published a volume of poetry, *Nugae poeticae*, followed later the same year by *An Enquiry Concerning the Invention of the Life Boat*, in which he demonstrated that its true inventor was William Wouldhave, not Henry Greathead. He subsequently wrote letters to the *Classical Journal* on Bible criticism. These were followed by a series of pamphlets on doctrinal matters, including an attack on Unitarianism. Hails was regarded at the time as the leading Hebrew scholar in the north of England. Although his views tended towards Calvinism he continued to be associated with the Methodists, and was for many years a class leader and local preacher. He was also secretary of the Newcastle Benevolent Society for Visiting and Relieving the Sick and Distressed Poor, a charity supported mainly by that denomination. He died at Blenhein Street, Newcastle, on 30 August 1845. C. M. FRASER

**Sources** *DNB* · R. Welford, *Men of mark 'twixt Tyne and Tweed*, 2 (1895), 410–15 · E. Mackenzie, *A descriptive and historical account of the town and county of Newcastle upon Tyne*, 2 vols. (1827), 403–4 · T. Fordyce, *Local records* (1867), 198 · W. Richardson, *History of the parish of Wallsend and Willington* (1923), 399 · J. F. Clarke, *Building ships on the north east coast*, 1: *c*.1640–1914 (1997), 28–9 · J. Latimer, *Local records*,

*or, Historical register of remarkable events which have occurred in Northumberland and Durham ... 1832–57* (1857), 204 • *IGI*
**Likenesses** sketch, repro. in Welford, *Men of mark*, 411

**Hailsham.** For this title name *see* Hogg, Douglas McGarel, first Viscount Hailsham (1872–1950).

**Hailstone, Edward** (1818–1890). *See under* Hailstone, Samuel (1767–1851).

**Hailstone, John** (1759–1847), geologist, born at Hoxton near London on 15 December 1759, was the second son of John Hailstone (1730–1771) of the Bank of England and Elizabeth, *née* Whitaker (1733–1800/01). He was placed at an early age under the care of a maternal uncle at York, and was sent to Beverley School in the East Riding. Samuel *Hailstone was a younger brother. John Hailstone went to Cambridge in 1778, entering first at St Catharine's College, and afterwards at Trinity College, and was second wrangler of his year in 1782. He was elected fellow of Trinity in 1783 and in 1788 became Woodwardian professor of geology, an office which he held for thirty years. In 1792 he published *A Plan of a Course of Lectures* together with a translation of an essay on mineral collections by A. G. Werner, under whom he later studied for some months at Freiburg during a continental tour of 1792–3. On his return he devoted himself to collecting and studying geological specimens, as he was to do always, and he regularly attended and exhibited at the museum where he had 'numerous and frequent visitors' (*Cambridge University Calendar*, 1806, 51). He appears to have given the first lectures at any British university on his subject, but only for a short period. He formed no school and his career was overshadowed by that of Edward Daniel Clarke (1769–1822), for whom a chair of mineralogy was created in Cambridge in 1808 and whose lectures were enthusiastically received. He aspired to the mastership of Trinity in 1798 without success but became well regarded as its bursar.

Hailstone married, at York on 21 May 1818, Mary (1783–1838), daughter of John Telford, and retired to the vicarage of Trumpington, near Cambridge. There he worked zealously for the education of the poor of his parish. He devoted much attention to chemistry and mineralogy, as well as to geology, and for many years kept a meteorological diary. He made useful additions to the Woodwardian Museum, and left manuscript journals of his travels at home and abroad, and much correspondence on geological subjects. The great friendship of Hailstone's life was with his pupil Robert Grosvenor, afterwards marquess of Westminster (1767–1845), who introduced him to the turf, where he made a great deal of money, and who entertained him at Eaton Hall. Hailstone was elected to the Linnean Society in 1800, and to the Royal Society in 1801, and was one of the original members of the Geological Society. He contributed papers to the *Transactions of the Geological Society* (3, 1816, 243–50, on the geology of Cambridgeshire), the *Transactions of the Cambridge Philosophical Society* (1, 1822, 453–8), and the British Association (*Report*, 1834, 569). He died at home in Trumpington on 9 June 1847, in his eighty-eighth year, and was buried in the parish church six days later. The diarist Joseph Romilly recorded without comment a report soon after Hailstone's death that he had fathered four illegitimate children; if he did, they were not provided for in his will. JOHN D. PICKLES

**John Hailstone** (1759–1847), by unknown artist

**Sources** H. T. de la Beche, *Quarterly Journal of the Geological Society*, 5 (1849), xix–xx • *Proceedings of the Linnean Society of London*, 1 (1838–48), 372–3 • J. W. Clark and T. M. Hughes, *The life and letters of the Reverend Adam Sedgwick*, 1 (1890), 152, 155, 195–7 • J. James, *Continuation and additions to the history of Bradford, and its parish* (1866), ix–xi • York Minster Library, Hailstone MSS, album [1696–1871] • *Catalogue of scientific papers*, Royal Society, 3 (1869), 125 • *GM*, 2nd ser., 28 (1847), 328 • *Cambridge University Calendar* (1802–18) • *Romilly's Cambridge diary, 1842–47: selected passages from the diary of the Rev. Joseph Romilly*, ed. M. E. Bury and J. D. Pickles, Cambridgeshire RS, 10 (1994), 239 • M. J. S. Rudwick, 'Hutton and Werner compared: George Greenough's geological tour of Scotland in 1805', *British Journal for the History of Science*, 1 (1962–3), 117–35, esp. 128 • Venn, *Alum. Cant.*
**Archives** CUL, Hailstone family MSS
**Likenesses** oils, Trinity Cam. [*see illus.*] • oils (in old age), Sedgwick Museum of Earth Sciences, Cambridge; repro. in J. W. Goodison, *Catalogue of Cambridge portraits* (1955), pl. xii

**Hailstone, Samuel** (1767–1851), botanist, was born on 25 February 1767 at Hoxton, near London, the third of seven children of John Hailstone (1730–1771) and his wife, Elizabeth (1733–1800/01). The family moved to York, where Samuel's interest in natural history was stimulated by his elder brother, John *Hailstone. In 1783 he became articled to John Hardy, a Bradford solicitor who took him into partnership in 1791. A staunch whig, Hailstone served for ten years from 1794 in the Bradford volunteer corps, denouncing a local physician, George Mossman, for his alleged seditious republicanism. In 1801 he set up his own legal practice which prospered by serving the local canal and iron companies. On 4 April 1808 he married Ann (1780–1833), daughter of Thomas Jones, a Bradford surgeon. Of their eight children, Anne (1811–1834) married William Sharp (1805–1896), the leading local surgeon, in 1833. Hailstone's first son, John (1810–1871), became a Cambridgeshire clergyman and his fifth, Edward Hailstone [*see below*], an antiquary.

Hailstone was prominent in the agitation of 1803 for a Bradford Improvement Act and became a lighting commissioner that year. He was the principal founder in 1808 and 1822 of two short-lived Bradford literary and philosophical societies, and supported the Bradford Mechanics' Institute established in 1832. An ardent collector, he amassed materials relating to Bradford which were used by John James (1811–1867), a Yorkshire antiquary. As an expert on Yorkshire flora, Hailstone contributed to Thomas Whitaker's *History of Craven*. His valuable herbarium was given after his death to the Yorkshire Museum, York. After the deaths of his wife and daughter, Hailstone rented Horton Hall, Bradford, about 1835. He died there on 26 December 1851, and was buried at Boston Spa near Tadcaster on 31 December 1851.

**Edward Hailstone** (1818–1890) was born in Bradford on 17 February 1818. He qualified as a solicitor in 1840 and succeeded to his father's practice, of which he was a sleeping partner. He devoted himself to collecting books, especially about Yorkshire, but did not neglect local and national responsibilities. He was churchwarden at Bradford parish church, where he stopped the supply of beer to the choir on Sunday, promoted the building of St George's Hall, and helped to found the Bradford Festival Choral Society. He was a commissioner for the 1851 exhibition. A lifelong Liberal, he married on 6 June 1855 Sarah Harrietta Lilla, only daughter of William *Ferrand, of St Ives, Bingley, a Conservative MP. She was an authority on lace, which she collected. In 1871 Hailstone moved from Horton to Walton Hall, near Wakefield, where he lived as a recluse, savouring his library, which occupied the whole of the upper floor.

Edward Hailstone suffered repeated attacks of rheumatic fever. He died at Walton Hall on 24 March 1890 and was buried at Crofton, near Wakefield, on 28 March. He was suspicious of public libraries as spoliators of books, and left his unique Yorkshire library of manuscripts and about 10,000 printed works to the dean's library, York Minster. His wife survived him. JACK MORRELL

**Sources** *Bradford Observer* (1 Jan 1852) • *Bradford Observer* (26 March 1890) [Edward Hailstone] • *Bradford Observer* (29 March 1890) [Edward Hailstone] • J. James, *Continuation and additions to the history of Bradford, and its parish* (1866) • J. B. Morrell, 'Wissenschaft in Worstedopolis: public science in Bradford, 1800–1850', *British Journal for the History of Science*, 18 (1985), 1–23 • *Yorkshire Archaeological and Topographical Journal*, 11 (1890–91), 204–7 • W. Cudworth, *Rambles round Horton* (1886) • West Yorkshire Archive Service, Bradford, 11 D 74/2/2/9 • West Yorkshire Archive Service, Bradford, deed box 50, case 3 • parish register, Boston Spa, 31 Dec 1851, Borth. Inst., PR BOS. 72, p. 42 [burial]

**Archives** West Yorkshire Archive Service, Bradford, collection of Bradford documents • York Minster Library, Edward Hailstone collection of Yorkshire, topographical collection

**Wealth at death** sale of two portions of Edward Hailstone's library in 1891 generated £8992 for 5632 items: catalogue of the library of the late Edward Hailstone, London, 1891

**Hailwood, (Stanley) Michael Bailey** (1940–1981), racing motorcyclist, was born in Great Milton, Oxfordshire, on 2 April 1940, the only son and elder child of Stanley William Bailey Hailwood, millionaire businessman and managing director (motor car sales), and his wife, Nellie Bryant. Hailwood was educated at Pangbourne Nautical College, Berkshire. He left after two and a half years. Despite a lack of academic achievements he was a champion boxer and a very accomplished musician on several instruments. Even in his early days he displayed the will to win that made him such a talented competitor. He spent a short time in the family business before his father sent him to work at Triumph motor cycles near Coventry. His first race was at Oulton Park, Cheshire, on 22 April 1957. He finished eleventh in the 125 cc race, riding an Italian MV Augusta machine. With encouragement and financial backing from his father his career blossomed. He won his first race on 10 June 1957 at Blandford Camp, Dorset. He repeated that success many times during his first season and gained more experience racing in South Africa in the winter.

In 1958 Hailwood competed in his first tourist trophy (TT) race in the Isle of Man and finished third in the 250 cc event. At the end of an outstanding year he was British champion in the 125, 250, and 350 cc classes and had won seventy-four races. He was fourth in the world 250 cc championship and sixth in the 350. A year later Hailwood won the first of his seventy-six grand prix victories in the Ulster 125 cc race. In 1961 he captured the first of his nine world titles when he won the 250 cc championship on a Japanese Honda machine. The same year he made history at the TT races by becoming the first rider to win three TT races in one week. At the end of the season he joined the world-famous MV Augusta team and dominated the 500 cc world championship for the next four years. The combination of his ability and the superb Italian machinery proved unbeatable but typically Hailwood was bored at winning so easily. The large Japanese Honda factory had achieved great success in the smaller classes but had not won the blue riband, of the 500 cc class. Hailwood joined Honda in 1966 and won both the 250 and 350 cc world titles for the next two years. The unstable handling of the 500 Honda prevented him retaining his 500 crown.

When Honda quit grand prix racing in 1968 Hailwood switched to car racing. He had already tried to combine the two sports, without having much success on four wheels, although he scored one formula 1 point in 1964. He won the European formula 2 championship in 1972 but never repeated his motor cycle racing successes. He competed in fifty formula 1 grand prix races, and scored a second place in the 1972 Italian grand prix. He was nineteenth in the 1964 world championship, eighteenth in 1971, eighth in 1972, and tenth in 1974. His career came to a premature halt in the 1974 German grand prix at the

(Stanley) Michael Bailey Hailwood (1940–1981), by Bob Aylott, 1968

Nurburgring. He crashed and broke his right leg in three places and could not race cars again. He then retired to New Zealand. In 1978 he made an exceptional comeback when at the age of thirty-eight he decided to return to the Isle of Man to compete in the TT races after an absence of eleven years. In front of record crowds he won the formula 1 race on the Italian Ducati machine. A year later he returned and won his fourteenth TT race, the senior, riding a 500 cc Suzuki. He then felt it was time to retire. He was appointed MBE in 1968 and was awarded the George Medal when he rescued Clay Regazzoni from a blazing car in 1973. Following his TT comeback he was also awarded the prestigious Segrave trophy (1979).

Away from the track Hailwood was a modest, shy person with a great sense of fun. He hated fuss and unwanted attention but was hero-worshipped by thousands of fans throughout the world. On 11 June 1975 he married Pauline Barbara, daughter of Alfred Henry Nash; they had a daughter and a son. Hailwood died on 23 March 1981 in Birmingham Accident Hospital two days after being involved in a traffic accident on the A435 road in Warwickshire. His daughter, Michelle, also died in the crash. Thousands of mourners attended his funeral to honour a man simply known to many as Mike the Bike. His wife survived him.

Nick Harris, *rev.*

**Sources** private information (1990) • personal knowledge (1990) • *The Times* (24 March 1981) • M. Hailwood and T. Macauley, *Hailwood* (1968); new edn (1978) • S. Hailwood, *The Hailwood story: my son Mike* (1966) • T. Macauley, *Mike: the life and times of Mike Hailwood* (1984) • M. Woollett, *Mike Hailwood: a motorcycle racing legend* (2000) • b. cert. • m. cert. • d. cert. • *CGPLA Eng. & Wales* (1981)
**Archives** FILM BFI NFTVA, documentary footage
**Likenesses** R. Dumont, photograph, 1967, repro. in J. Huntington-Whiteley, *The book of British sporting heroes* (1998) • B. Aylott, photograph, 1968, Hult. Arch. [*see illus.*]
**Wealth at death** £141,415: administration with will, 21 July 1981, *CGPLA Eng. & Wales*

**Haime, John** (*bap.* **1708**, *d.* **1784**), soldier and Methodist preacher, was born in Shaftesbury, Dorset, and baptized at Holy Trinity Church in Shaftesbury on 18 February 1708 (though he gave the date of his birth as 1710 in his autobiography), the son of a gardener. He followed his father's occupation for several years, but disliked it; he left to work with his uncle as a button maker, first in Shaftesbury and then in Blandford, Dorset. At this period he suffered from acute religious depression and gave himself up to 'drinking, swearing, card-playing, lewdness' ('Short account of God's dealings', 209). Tired of button making, he was employed by a tanner, and then enlisted in the Queen's regiment of dragoons. On Christmas day 1739 he parted with his wife and children (of whom nothing further is known) to march for Gloucester, and in the course of the following year was at various camps in Hampshire, Oxfordshire, and Wiltshire.

In Highworth, Wiltshire, Haime found among other old books John Bunyan's spiritual autobiography, *Grace Abounding to the Chief of Sinners*: 'I read it with the utmost attention, and found his case nearly resembled my own' ('Short account of God's dealings', 211). The regiment was ordered to march for Scotland, and on the first day he bought *Grace Abounding* from a bookseller in Banbury, Oxfordshire. Bunyan's account clearly influenced Haime's interpretation of his experiences and the autobiography he was to write at John Wesley's request at the end of his life. Throughout this period he was a regular churchgoer, but he found no solace and was often tempted to blaspheme. By the bank of the River Tweed he felt that God had lifted him out of his dungeon, but he had recurrent experiences of despair and release. He was sent by sea from Leith to London with the camp equipage, and at Deptford went to hear the Calvinist Methodist John Cennick, then one of George Whitefield's preachers. After hearing his account Cennick told him the work of the devil was on him, but he was later comforted by reading Cennick's own life. On rejoining the regiment he heard Charles Wesley preach at Brentford, Middlesex, and was much encouraged by speaking to him.

In June 1742 Haime's regiment embarked for Flanders, and in February 1743 began their march from Ghent to Germany. After further alternations of relief and despondency, on 22 April, while walking in the fields, he thought God at last answered his prayer: 'My head was as waters, and my eyes as a fountain of tears. I wept: I sung' ('Short account of God's dealings', 215). At the battle of Dettingen (27 June 1743 NS), in which the British, Hanoverian, and Austrian armies defeated the French, he found his heart filled with love, peace, and joy, and stood the enemy fire for seven hours. In winter quarters at Ghent in

1743–4 he started a meeting for prayer and Bible reading with two fellow soldiers, John Evans and Pitman Stag, and their number soon increased to twelve. John Wesley replied encouragingly to his letter of 2 February 1744 asking for advice (*Journal of John Wesley*, 3.115–16; *Letters*, 2.19). Haime's success as a preacher was remarkable. At camp near Brussels in May 1744 he usually had 1000 hearers. When he settled in any camp he built a tabernacle with two or three rooms; he soon had 300 members in his society and six preachers beside himself, including Evans and William Clements. He often walked 20 to 30 miles a day and preached 35 times in a week. At the battle of Fontenoy (11 May 1745 NS), in which the allies were defeated by the French, several members of the society were killed—Evans lost both his legs and died praising God—though Haime himself was unharmed and went through the battle full of joy. Their bravery was praised in a letter by John Wesley of 26 October 1745, rebuking the troops camped near Newcastle for blasphemy (*Journal of John Wesley*, 3.216–17).

For nearly three years Haime had a full assurance of faith, until on 6 April 1746 he fell instantaneously into despair, the symptoms of which were physical as well as mental: he wept and howled, he partly lost his sight, he thought he was on fire. For seven years he continued to suffer, but he went on preaching and converting others. He returned to England, was discharged from the army, and joined the Methodists as a travelling preacher, sometimes accompanying Wesley. Many thought him 'very unstable', but Wesley assured him that it was good for him to be in the fiery furnace ('Short account of God's dealings', 307–8). He set up a society in his home town of Shaftesbury, and was briefly imprisoned in Dorchester gaol because he would not undertake to give up preaching. He twice went to Ireland as a travelling preacher, still in great distress of mind.

In 1766 Wesley tried to help by sending Haime to live with John Hoskins, a farmer in Cornwall, as a kind of domestic chaplain. Haime's agony increased, until suddenly he felt freed from his bondage. But he could not bear to stay in one place, and went back on circuit. In looking back over his life for Wesley he divided it into twenty years before his conversion, three years of faith, twenty years in the wilderness, and his present deliverance. His account was designed to show that God did not will that any should perish ('Short account of God's dealings', 313). It is important as a detailed record of Methodist practices in the army in the 1740s, as a powerful analysis by a deeply unbalanced man of his own mental suffering, and as a masterpiece in the tradition of the seventeenth-century spiritual autobiography. Haime died on 18 August 1784 at Whitchurch, Hampshire, worn to skin and bone by fever.

Isabel Rivers

**Sources** 'A short account of God's dealings with Mr John Haime', *Arminian Magazine*, 3 (1780), 207–17, 255–73, 307–13 • G. Story, 'A short account of the death of John Haim', *Arminian Magazine*, 8 (1785), 19–20 • *The journal of the Rev. John Wesley*, ed. N. Curnock and others, 8 vols. (1909–16), vols. 3–5 • *The letters of the Rev. John Wesley*, ed. J. Telford, 8 vols. (1931), vols. 2–5, 7 • J. Telford, ed., *Wesley's veterans: lives of early Methodist preachers told by themselves*, 7 vols. (1909–14), vol. 1 • T. Jackson, ed., *The lives of early Methodist preachers*, 3rd edn, 6 vols. (1865–6), vol. 1 • I. Rivers, '"Strangers and pilgrims": sources and patterns of Methodist narrative', *Augustan worlds*, ed. J. C. Hilson and others (1978), 189–203

**Likenesses** engraving, repro. in 'A short account of God's dealings', *Arminian Magazine*, facing p. 207

**Haimendorf, Christoph von Fürer-** (1909–1995), anthropologist, was born in Vienna on 27 July 1909. Members of his family had served the Habsburg dynasty since the year 1273 and one of them had been a famous traveller through Egypt, Palestine, and Arabia in the early sixteenth century. His father was Rudolph von Fürer-Haimendorf (1876–1946), governor of Silesia and an Austrian cabinet minister; his mother was Ida Kurzbauer (1880–1969). The future anthropologist and his brother were brought up in a cultured atmosphere where Christoph developed a passion for the surrogate travel afforded by opera. He was trained in anthropology by Schebesta, Frobenius, and Heine Geldern at the University of Vienna from 1927. He received his doctorate in 1931 and partly inspired by Bronisław Malinowski, whose seminar he attended at the London School of Economics (1935–6), he went to work in Assam among the Nagas of the north-eastern frontier of India. He was helped by the district officer and anthropologist J. P. Mills, with whom he went on a punitive expedition, returning with a number of skulls for the delighted Nagas. Back in London, on 2 April 1938, he married (Edith) Elizabeth Mary (Betty) Barnardo (1911–1987). They had one son.

Haimendorf returned to Austria and then to India for further work on the Nagas, but was promptly interned as an enemy alien when the war broke out. He was confined to Hyderabad but was able to undertake some of his best fieldwork among the Chenchus, Reddis, and Raj Gonds. He was also, curiously, allowed to do fieldwork among the remote Apa Tanis of the Arunachal Pradesh area of Assam. At the end of the war he became adviser to the nizam of Hyderabad and set up various educational and other welfare schemes for tribal peoples. In 1949 he was made reader and then in 1951 professor of anthropology at the School of Oriental and African Studies (SOAS) in London. At SOAS he built up the largest department of anthropology in the country.

In 1953 Haimendorf visited Nepal, thus adding a third area of competence to Assam and Hyderabad. In each area he studied the languages and the culture of between three and six societies. He published ten ethnographic monographs on his fieldwork, including *The Chenchus* (1943), *Reddis of the Bison Hills* (1945), *Raj Gonds of Adilabad* (1948), *Sherpas of Nepal* (1964), and *The Konyak Nagas* (1969). He also published several other volumes of essays and theoretical works, including *Morals and Merit* (1967) and *The Tribes of India: Struggle for Survival* (1982), which drew heavily on his fieldwork. In all, he published over 3650 pages of ethnographic observations describing more than a dozen tribal groups.

The published work is only the surface of Haimendorf's achievement. As well as his meticulous and detailed field notes and diaries, he was one of the few anthropologists of the great inter-war generation in Britain to realize the importance of visual documentation. His collection of black and white photographs extends to over 10,000 separate photographs, capturing memorably many aspects of tribal culture. They were accompanied by an equal number of colour slides, documenting worlds which have since changed beyond recognition. He was also the most prolific of British ethnographic film-makers, starting to film in the 1940s, and shooting over 100 hours of 16 mm film, a number of which were used for television documentaries. He made many hundreds of hours of tape recordings to accompany the films. He assembled extensive collections of artefacts for the anthropology museums at Vienna, Oxford, and Cambridge.

A number of factors help to explain Haimendorf's ability as an ethnographer. There was his curiosity: he was clearly immensely interested in people, in exploring, in wanting to know and understand, and then to move on to a new encounter. There was his aesthetic ability and appreciation of beauty, which lay behind his photography and his delight in the graceful peoples with whom he worked. There was his photographic memory combined with self-discipline which fill his notebooks and diaries with thousands of pages of vivid and insightful comment. There was his obvious sympathy for tribal peoples and their increasingly difficult position. There was his intelligence.

While Haimendorf put forward some exciting ideas, particularly on morality and religion in his Frazer lecture, 'The after life in Indian tribal religions', and his Henry Myers lecture, 'The sense of sin in cross-cultural perspective', his main interest was in understanding and describing how societies work. Haimendorf's great ability to make friends and to manage human relationships, especially in difficult situations, won him the trust of both Europeans and his many non-European co-workers and colleagues. In all this he depended very heavily on his wife, Betty, his co-worker, organizer of his expeditions, and inspiration and herself a notable ethnographer. His autobiography, *Life among Indian Tribes* (1990), with long excerpts from her diaries and a moving account of her death in India, was a tribute to her. He died from bronchopneumonia at St Mary's Hospital, Paddington, London, on 11 June 1995 and was buried in London. His work will stand out as one of the major ethnographic contributions of all time. ALAN MACFARLANE

**Sources** U. Cam., department of social anthropology, Haimendorf MSS · personal knowledge (2004) · private information (2004) · SOAS, Haimendorf MSS · *The Guardian* (29 June 1995) · *Daily Telegraph* (26 June 1995) · *The Times* (June 1995) · *Bulletin of the School of Oriental and African Studies*, 59/3 (1996), 548–51 · *WWW* · m. cert. · d. cert.

**Archives** SOAS, papers, diaries, and field-books | FILM U. Cam., department of social anthropology, some copies of films

**Haimo** [Haymo] (*supp. fl.* **1054**), archdeacon of Canterbury, is said to have fled to France during the Danish invasion and become a monk at St Denis, before returning to England and becoming archdeacon of Canterbury, dying on 2 or 9 October 1054; he has also been named as the author of a number of Latin texts, mainly biblical commentaries. This impressively precise information has, however, extremely tenuous antecedents. There are no contemporary records of any Haimo at Canterbury. Most of the works attributed to him are actually by the ninth-century Haimo of Auxerre, and the first mention (by the fourteenth-century writer Henry Kirkestede) of the supposed archdeacon may indeed be a confusion with his namesake, although the source and nature of Kirkestede's information is not known. To Kirkestede's floruit of 1054 John Bale (1495–1563) added that Haimo was said to have died on 9 October (possibly Haimo of Auxerre's death date); this seems to have been taken by Thomas Tanner as a full death date, 2 October 1054, for which there is no evidence whatever. Most of what has been stated about this probably non-existent figure is thus of modern provenance. PETER DAMIAN-GRINT

**Sources** R. Sharpe, *A handlist of the Latin writers of Great Britain and Ireland before 1540* (1997) · J. Greatrex, *Biographical register of the English cathedral priories of the province of Canterbury* (1997) · P. Collinson, P. N. Ramsay, and M. Sparks, eds., *A history of Canterbury Cathedral* (1995) · *Fasti Angl., 1066–1300*, [Monastic cathedrals] · [H. Wharton], ed., *Anglia sacra*, 2 vols. (1691) · J. Bale, *Illustrium Maioris Britannie scriptorum … summarium* (1548) · N. Brooks, *The early history of the church of Canterbury: Christ Church from 597 to 1066* (1984) · Tanner, *Bibl. Brit.-Hib.*

**Hainault**. For this title name *see* Jacqueline, *suo jure* countess of Hainault, *suo jure* countess of Holland, and *suo jure* countess of Zeeland (1401–1436).

**Haines**. *See also* Haynes.

**Haines, Sir Frederick Paul** (**1819–1909**), army officer, was born on 10 August 1819 at Parsonage Farm, Kirdford, Sussex, the youngest child in the family of three sons and a daughter of Gregory Haines CB (1778–1853), who served with Wellington's commissariat throughout the Peninsular War and at Waterloo, and ended his career as commissary-general for Ireland, and his wife, Harriet (1777–1869), daughter of John Eldridge of Kirdford. His father was descended from a family of prosperous Sussex farmers, of whom the most well known was Richard Haines (*bap.* 1633, *d.* 1685), author of various books on the poor. Frederick Haines was educated at Midhurst School, and in Brussels and Dresden, and at the Royal Military College, Sandhurst. He married Charlotte Jane Sophia, daughter of Colonel Edward Miller of the Madras army, in 1856, and they had three sons. She died in 1880 and Haines did not remarry.

Frederick, following his two elder brothers, entered the army and was commissioned ensign in the 4th (the King's Own) regiment on 21 June 1839. He joined his regiment at Bangalore, in India, where his eldest brother, Gregory, had just married a daughter of Sir Hugh Gough, who commanded the Mysore division. This family connection led in 1844 to the appointment of Haines, who had been promoted lieutenant in 1840, as aide-de-camp to Gough, then commander-in-chief in the East Indies. During the First Anglo-Sikh War he was acting military secretary to the commander-in-chief, and fought at Mudki and at Ferozeshahr, where he was dangerously wounded. Haines's services were rewarded by a captaincy, without payment, in the 10th foot (May 1846), from which he exchanged, in June 1847, into the 21st foot (the Royal Scots Fusiliers). Between 23 May 1846 and 7 May 1849 he served as Lord Gough's military secretary, and was present at the skirmish at Ramnagar, the crossing of the Chenab, and the battles of Chilianwala and Gujrat during the Second Anglo-Sikh War. For his services he was given a brevet majority in June 1849 and a brevet lieutenant-colonelcy in August 1850 in the 21st foot, with which he then briefly served in Scotland and Ireland.

The 21st foot was sent to the Crimea in 1854, and Haines was present at the battles of the Alma and Balaklava. During the battle of Inkerman (5 November 1854) he commanded a small force which defended for six hours the barrier on the post road guarding the approach to the 2nd division camp. Haines was also responsible for sending troops to silence the Russian artillery on Shell Hill, helping to bring the battle to its final crisis. After Inkerman he succeeded to a majority in the 21st foot, and was promoted brevet colonel (28 November 1854) in recognition of his conduct. In April 1855 he was gazetted lieutenant-colonel, unattached, and from June 1855 to January 1856 he was assistant adjutant-general at Aldershot. From June 1856 to June 1860 he acted as military secretary to the commander-in-chief at Madras, Sir Patrick Grant, accompanying him to Calcutta during the interval between the death of General Anson and the arrival of Sir Colin Campbell in the summer of 1857. He served at Madras throughout the Indian mutiny. In October 1859 he was gazetted lieutenant-colonel of the 8th foot, which he commanded from September 1860 to August 1861. After brief periods of service as an acting brigadier-general at Aldershot, as deputy adjutant-general at headquarters in Ireland, and as a brigadier-general in the Curragh, he was promoted major-general (November 1864) and commanded the Mysore division in India from March 1865 to March 1870. On his return from India he became quartermaster-general at headquarters from November 1870 to March 1871, and then from May 1871 to December 1875 was commander-in-chief at Madras, becoming a KCB in 1871 and a lieutenant-general in 1873.

Between April 1876 and April 1881 Haines, who was promoted general on 1 October 1877, was commander-in-chief in India. The Indian government was occupied by difficulties with Russia and with Afghanistan from the beginning of his term of office. When war between England and Russia seemed imminent, in 1876, he strongly opposed a proposal of the viceroy, Lord Lytton, to invade central Asia with a small force of troops. Although he did not oppose Lytton's 'forward policy', regarding the Afghan war as inevitable, he differed entirely from the viceroy's estimate of the number of troops required, and opposed Cavagnari's suggestion to make a surprise attack on Ali Masjid. He believed that the Kurram valley, which was held to be of great strategic value by Lytton and his confidential adviser, Sir George Colley, was a cul-de-sac and useless as a military route to Kabul. The reinforcements which Haines insisted were necessary at the outset of the 1878–9 campaign proved to be essential, and for his general supervision of the war he received the thanks of both houses of parliament and was appointed knight grand cross in the Order of the Star of India in July 1879. He had been made a GCB in 1877, and on the institution of the Order of the Indian Empire in 1878 he became, *ex officio*, CIE.

In the Afghan campaign of 1879–80 Haines again had serious differences with Lord Lytton about the number of troops required, the Kurram route as a line of communication, and the relationship between the commander-in-chief and commanders in the field. His relations with Lytton's successor, Lord Ripon, were more cordial, but his warnings of the danger of an attack on Kandahar by Ayub Khan were disregarded by the viceroy. He unwillingly acquiesced in General Burrows's advance on the Helmand River, and ordered Bombay troops to move up in support. After Burrows was defeated at Maiwand (27 July 1880) Haines suggested that Kandahar should be relieved by a force from Kabul commanded by General Roberts. For his services during the war of 1879–80 Haines again received the thanks of both houses of parliament and was offered a baronetcy, which he declined. The remaining period of his term of command was occupied with discussions regarding the retention of Kandahar and the recommendations of the Indian army commission of 1879, from which he dissented, urging the continuance of three separate presidential armies.

From 1881 until his death Haines lived in London, spending much time at the United Service Club. He represented the British army at the Russian manoeuvres of 1882 and at the German manoeuvres of 1884. Haines was placed on the retired list on 8 April 1886 and was promoted field marshal on 21 May 1890. He was colonel of the Royal Munster Fusiliers from 1874 to 1890, when he became colonel of his old regiment, the Royal Scots Fusiliers. During his retirement Haines took a keen interest in foreign policy, especially central Asian questions, and in military affairs, art, the theatre, and cricket. He died in his London home, 123 Pall Mall, of bronchitis on 11 June 1909 at the age of eighty-nine, and was buried on 16 June in Brompton cemetery. R. S. RAIT, *rev.* T. R. MOREMAN

**Sources** R. S. Rait, *The life of Field-Marshal Sir Frederick Paul Haines* (1911) · *The Times* (14 June 1909) · *Army List* · H. B. Hanna, *The Second Afghan War*, 3 vols. (1899–1910) · Memorandum by his Excellency General Sir Frederick Paul Haines on the report of the special army commission, 1879, 20 March 1880, BL OIOC, L/MIL/17/S/1698 · R. S. Rait, *The life and campaigns of Hugh, first Viscount Gough*, 2 vols. (1903)

**Archives** BL, corresp. relating to Indian mutiny, Add. MS 41488 · NAM, papers and corresp. as commander-in-chief, India | BL, letters to Lord Ripon, Add. MS 43609

**Likenesses** J. Collier, portrait, 1891; at United Service Club, London, 1912 · J. T. C., caricature, chromolithograph, NPG; repro. in *VF* (25 March 1876) · portrait, repro. in Rait, *Life of Field Marshal Sir Frederick Paul Haines*, frontispiece · wood-engraving (after photograph by Shepherd & Bourne of Calcutta), NPG; repro. in *ILN* (4 Jan 1879)

**Wealth at death** £5056 2*s.* 2*d.*: probate, 10 July 1909, *CGPLA Eng. & Wales*

**Haines, Herbert** (1826–1872), antiquary, seventh son of John Haines, surgeon, of Hampstead, and his wife, Jane, was born on 1 September 1826. He was educated at the College School, Gloucester, and matriculated in June 1844 at Exeter College, Oxford, where he graduated BA in 1848 and proceeded MA in 1851. In 1848, while still an undergraduate, he published under the auspices of the Oxford Architectural Society *A Manual for the Study of Monumental Brasses*. In September 1849 he was licensed to the curacy of Delamere in Cheshire; in 1850 he was ordained priest. On 16 January 1851 he married Rosina (*b.* in or before 1830), daughter of Thomas Dugard, at St Pancras. On 22 June 1850 he was appointed by the dean and chapter of Gloucester to the second mastership of his old school, the College School, Gloucester. This office he retained until his death, and on two occasions during vacancies in 1853–4 and in 1871 he acted for some time as headmaster. Nicknamed Badger, Haines was an effective teacher who knew how to make his lessons interesting. A former pupil, Frederic Hannam-Clark, recalled that 'the gentle good nature, combined with perfect strictness and justice, which marked Mr Haines' dealings with the boys, made him pre-eminently the popular master of my time' (Robertson, 113).

In 1854 Haines was appointed chaplain to the Gloucester County Lunatic Asylum, and in 1859 he became also chaplain of the newly opened Barnwood House Asylum, near Gloucester. In 1861 he brought out a much enlarged and improved edition of *Monumental Brasses*. Haines also published a Latin grammar textbook (1855), *A Guide to the Cathedral Church of Gloucester* (1867), which reached a third edition in 1885, and a sermon preached before the University of Oxford (1867). He died, after a very short illness, at his home, Hampden House, Barton Street, Gloucester, on 18 September 1872, and was buried in the Gloucester cemetery. His wife and a number of young children survived him. J. R. Washbourn, *rev.* Brian Frith

**Sources** Crockford (1870) • D. Robertson, *The King's School, Gloucester* (1974), 113–15 • Foster, *Alum. Oxon.* • private information (1890) • personal knowledge (1890) • m. cert. • d. cert. • *CGPLA Eng. & Wales* (1872)
**Likenesses** brass effigy on monument, *c.*1872, Gloucester Cathedral • photograph, repro. in Robertson, *The King's School, Gloucester*, 114–15
**Wealth at death** under £5000: probate, 9 Oct 1872, *CGPLA Eng. & Wales*

**Haines, John Thomas** (1798/9–1843), playwright, from 1823 up to the year of his death supplied the minor theatres of London with a great many plays of the 'blood-and-thunder' type, which were mostly successful, and he occasionally acted in his own pieces. His sea plays gave full scope to the talents of the actor T. P. Cooke; *My Poll and my Partner Joe*, a nautical drama in three acts, produced at the Surrey Theatre on 7 September 1835, yielded a profit of £4000. Haines adapted and arranged from the French of Scribe and St Georges the songs, duets, quartets, recitatives, and choruses in the opera of *Queen for a Day*, which, set to music by Adolphe Adam, was first performed at the Surrey Theatre on 14 June 1841. His works, which also included melodramas and 'domestic dramas' along with lighter entertainments, are now almost wholly forgotten. A letter in verse from Haines to Morris Barnett is in the British Library.

Haines died at Stockwell, Surrey, on 18 May 1843, aged forty-four. He was at that time stage-manager of the English Opera House. Gordon Goodwin, *rev.* John Wells

**Sources** *GM*, 2nd ser., 20 (1843), 103 • d. cert.
**Likenesses** five engravings, Harvard TC

**Haines, Joseph** (*d.* 1701), actor and writer, was the child 'of mean Parents' and also the son of 'Sir Thomas Hayns', according to the sometimes fanciful *Life of the Late Famous Comedian, Jo. Hayns* (Highfill, Burnim & Langhans, *BDA*). He was probably educated at St Martin-in-the-Fields School, London, and may have attended Queen's College, Oxford, as the *Life* suggests. About 1667 Haines joined John Coysh's strolling players in Cambridge and probably moved on to the Hatton Garden Nursery, which trained performers for both London theatres. His first confirmed performance in London was on 7 March 1668 with the King's Company, when Pepys was impressed by his dancing between the acts of Middleton's and Rowley's *Spanish Gypsies*:

> a very silly play, only great variety of dances, and those most excellently done, especially one part by one Hanes, only lately come thither from the Nursery, an understanding fellow, but yet, they say, hath spent £1,000 a-year before he come thither. (Pepys)

Indeed, there are almost more records of Haines's debts than of his theatrical performances, for he had already figured in the lord chamberlain's papers on 1 February 1668 for a debt, pursued by Thomas Jennings. Pepys met Haines on 7 May that year, at the house of the actress Elizabeth *Knipp, who was to become Haines's lover, after a performance of Dekker's and Massinger's *The Virgin Martyr*, in which he may have played. With the King's Company for the 1668–9 season, Haines played Piperollo in Shirley's *The Sisters* and delivered a prologue to Beaumont's and Fletcher's *The Coxcomb*. During this season and the next he was also pursued for considerable sums in debt by at least five individuals.

In July 1670 Haines travelled to France in the train of the duke of Buckingham, and remained with the court of Louis XIV in order to dance in the première of Molière's *Le bourgeois gentilhomme*. On his return to London Haines resurfaced, dancing in Buckingham's *Rehearsal*, where he was introduced within the dialogue at the end of the play. When *Le bourgeois gentilhomme* was adapted by Edward Ravenscroft as *The Citizen Turn'd Gentleman* in 1671, Haines briefly defected to the Duke's Company to play the French tutor and another part, according to Downes. Although Downes also thinks Haines moved because 'having affronted Mr. Hart, he gave him a Discharge and then he came over to our house' (Downes), amends must have been made because the following season Haines was once more with the King's Company, as the guitar-playing Benito, a part written for him in Dryden's *Assignation*. Haines was never a shareholder in the theatre companies, and the lord chamberlain's papers are peppered with his

**Joseph Haines** (*d.* **1701**), by unknown engraver, pubd 1720 [on the stage of Drury Lane Theatre, delivering the epilogue to *The Unhappy Kindness, or, A Fruitless Revenge* by Thomas Scott, 1697]

discharges and renewals. Perhaps summer 1672 was the moment when Haines resorted to playing in a stable at Greenwich, Kent, as a lampoon attributed to him in the *Covent Garden Drollery* implies (Thorn-Drury, 20–25). Records of Haines's roles are patchy for this period and the only other records suggest that in May 1674 he presented the prologue to Lee's *Nero* and designed the induction and gave the prologue to Duffet's farcical *The Mock Tempest*.

During the seasons from 1674 to 1679 Haines played a variety of foolish roles at the King's Company including Sparkish in Wycherley's *Country Wife*, Plausible in his *Plain Dealer*, Roderigo in *Othello*, Visconti in Francis Fane's *Love in the Dark*, Dwindle in John Leanerd's *The Country Innocence*, Harlequin in Ravenscroft's *Scaramouch*, Sir Simon Credulous in William Chamberlayne's *Wits Led by the Nose*, and Whiffler in Edward Howard's *The Man of Newmarket*. Haines was a popular writer and performer of prologues and epilogues, specializing in elaborately dressed characters such as Launce 'in a Red Coat like a Common Soldier' in the prologue to D'Urfey's *Trick for Trick*. The style of his writing and presentation was most often satiric and sometimes got him into trouble, as when Edmund Windham objected to his 'ill & scandalous language and insolent carriage' towards him in October 1675, or when, on 18 June 1677, the lord chamberlain had Haines arrested 'for reciteinge … a Scurrilous and obscoene Epilogue' (Highfill, Burnim & Langhans, *BDA*). Nor was Haines always a pliable company member, if the *Life's* anecdote about his upstaging of Charles Hart is to be credited. Forced to make up one of the crowd of senators in Jonson's *Catiline's Conspiracy*, Haines dressed absurdly and sat smoking on a stool upstage of Charles Hart in the title role, laughing at him until he brought the play to a halt. This anecdote also contains the only reference to the salary Haines was paid, but 50*s.* a week seems an over-estimation of Haines's status to the company, even as a leading prologuer. During this time Haines was being harassed over his debts almost continuously, including one to Hannah Barton, his landlady at Gutter Street, Cheapside, hardly a London address for a gentleman of means.

The King's Company were experiencing considerable management and financial difficulties by 1680 and Haines was one of several defectors, including Cardell Goodman and Mrs Knipp, who gained a warrant to tour to Edinburgh. He wrote about the mixed experience of his stay in Scotland, which seems to have included the miscarriage of a child and death of his lover Mrs Knipp, in a manuscript poem (Haines, 'To Madam Nell Gwin'). This doggerel was a plea to join the more successful Duke's Company, but by the time of Haines's return to London in 1682 the two companies had merged. Haines did contrive to earn a place with the United Company and is first recorded in March 1684 delivering the prologue and playing Bullfinch in Richard Brome's *The Northern Lass*. Records imply that prologues and epilogues were his main fare with the company early on. He had a couple of parts in the summer troupes of 1684 and 1685, most notably as Hazard in D'Urfey's *The Commonwealth of Women*, to which he delivered a characteristic epilogue 'habited like a Whig, Captain of the Scyth-men in the West, a Scythe in his Hand', in a satiric reference to the duke of Monmouth's rebellion. Haines may have been supplementing his income during this period by running a booth at Bartholomew fair, where one year he was in hot water for his droll *The Whore of Babylon, the Devil and the Pope*. He was also writing occasional pieces like his *Satyr Against Brandy* (1683) and may have spent time masquerading as a fortune-teller or astrologer.

In 1685 Haines embarked on another continental excursion, either in the train of Sir William Soames, who was on his way to become ambassador in Constantinople, before his death at sea left Haines stranded in Malta and then Leghorn, or with Lord Castlemaine, on his ambassadorial appointment to Rome. There are multiple anecdotes concerning Haines's exploits abroad, some of which are confirmed by letters from Grand Duke Cosimo III's household about Joseph's dancing at court and his conversion to Catholicism. The story of Haines's conversion was certainly current in London because when he reappeared in London performance records in April 1689, after William III's accession, it was to play Bayes and deliver the prologue to *The Rehearsal* in 'a white Sheet, with a burning Taper in his Hand, upon his Admittance into the House after his Return from the Church of Rome' (Van Lennep, 370). By this stage Haines was married, if a passing reference in the prologue of his fellow actor Mountfort's *The Injur'd Lovers* is to be trusted. Haines is credited with writing the prologue to George Powell's *Alphonso, King of Naples* (1691) and in 1692 with trying a play of his own, *The Fatal Mistake, or, The Plot Spoil'd*, which Gildon thought 'abominable' (Gildon). Although no performance record exists for the play, ballads and prologues elsewhere confirm that Haines was known for his writing as well as performing.

Sparse records remain of Haines's comic roles with the United Company and, after 1695, with Christopher Rich's Patent Company. Significant parts he created included Bully in Thomas Wright's version of *The Female Vertuosos*, Gines de Passamonte in D'Urfey's *Don Quixote*, Knowlittle in Delariviere Manley's *The Lost Lover*, Serringe in Vanbrugh's *The Relapse*, and Tom Errand in Farquhar's *The Constant Couple*. It is perhaps significant that we have very few reflections on Haines's acting ability, although Tony Aston thought Haines was unsurpassed in his creation of Noll Bluffe in Congreve's *The Old Batchelor* (1693) and of Roger in Vanbrugh's *Aesop* (1696) (Aston, 2.323). He was more often noted for playing himself, as in Elkanah Settle's *World in the Moon*, and for his prologues and epilogues, particularly one which he delivered astride a donkey at the end of Thomas Scott's *The Unhappy Kindness*, a rough print of which adorns a volume of Tom Brown's *Works*. Haines's performance of the epilogue to Susanna Centlivre's *The Perjured Husband* in October 1700 was his last recorded appearance on stage.

Haines died on 4 April 1701 at his lodgings in Hart Street, Long Acre, London, and was buried at St Paul's, Covent Garden. His posthumous reputation as a comic satirist on and off stage was established by the prompt publication of the heavily fictionalized *Life*, possibly compiled by his fellow actor Tobias Thomas according to Cameron, although attributed to Tom Brown by contemporaries. Haines also appeared as a correspondent in Tom Brown's *Letters from the Dead*, debating with the arch-reformer Jeremy Collier, and nicknamed Signior Salmatius and Giuseppe Hanesio. The anonymous broadside elegy on his death laments:

> Must *Haines* depart, while *Asses* multiply:
> Could nothing less suffice thy Hungry Jaws,
> Than chief promoter of the players Cause.
> (Robinson, 99)

J. MILLING

**Sources** Highfill, Burnim & Langhans, *BDA* • W. Van Lennep and others, eds., *The London stage, 1660–1800*, pt 1: *1660–1700* (1965) • Pepys, *Diary* • J. Downes, *Roscius Anglicanus*, ed. J. Milhous and R. D. Hume, new edn (1987) • T. Thomas, *The life of the late famous comedian, Jo. Haynes* (1701) • K. M. Cameron, 'Jo Haynes, *Infamis*', *Theatre Notebook*, 24 (1969–70), 56–67 • T. Lucas, *Lives of the gamesters* (1714) • *The works of Mr Thomas Brown*, ed. J. Drake, 5th edn, 5 vols. (1720–21) • G. Thorn-Drury, ed., *Covent Garden drollery: a miscellany of 1672* (1928) • A. Aston, 'A brief supplement to Colley Cibber, esq.: his "Lives of the famous actors and actresses" (1747)', in C. Cibber, *An apology for the life of Mr Colley Cibber*, new edn, ed. R. W. Lowe, 2 (1889), [297]–318 • J. W. Robinson, 'An elegy on the death of Mr Joseph Haynes, 1701', *Theatre Notebook*, 35 (1981), 99 • [C. Gildon], *The lives and characters of the English dramatick poets … first begun by Mr Langbain* [1699] • J. Haines, 'To Madam Nell Gwin', BL, Add. MS 27407, fols. 60–61v • J. Haines, *The fatal mistake, or, The plot spoil'd* (1692)

**Archives** BL, Add. MS 27407, fols. 60–61*v*

**Likenesses** engraving, BL; repro. in Haines, *Fatal mistake* • engraving, repro. in Brown, *Works*, vol. 1 • engraving, Harvard TC; repro. in Brown, *Works*, vol. 2 • line engraving, Mander & Mitchenson Theatre Collection, London; repro. in Brown, *Works*, vol. 5 [*see illus.*]

**Haines, Richard** (*bap.* 1633, *d.* 1685), farmer and pamphleteer, was baptized on 4 or 14 May 1633, the eldest son of Gregory Haines, yeoman farmer of Shere in Surrey and Sullington in Sussex, and his wife, Elizabeth Pollard. He farmed at Sullington, near Horsham, and was the most prominent member of the Horsham Baptist congregation, of which Matthew Caffyn was minister. He styled himself 'gentleman' and his publications show him to have been something of a virtuoso, interested in the state of agriculture, industry, and the national economy. He corresponded with members of the Royal Society, had lodgings in Christ Church parish, Newgate Street, London, and sought support for his projects at court, and in parliament and the City.

In 1672 Haines obtained a patent for a new method of cleaning trefoil so as to improve the seed, and this led to public controversy with Caffyn, who was himself a local farmer, jealous of Haines's influence with local notables, and convinced that patents were unchristian and patentees covetous. Haines published *New Lords, New Laws* (1674) in his own defence, but his excommunication by Caffyn was not finally overturned by the general Baptist assembly until 1680. Also in 1674 Haines published *The prevention of poverty, or, A discourse of the causes of the decay of trade, fall of lands, and want of money throughout the nation*, stressing the importance of the balance of trade and advocating a 25 per cent devaluation of shilling coins in order to stimulate domestic manufactures and discourage imports. In the following years, however, Haines turned his attention to workhouses as a panacea for national ills, after a visit to the Netherlands, where he admired Dutch methods of employing the poor.

In 1677 Haines published *Proposals for building, in every county, a working-alms-house or hospital, as the best expedient to perfect the trade and manufactory of linen cloth*. In 1678 he took out a patent for a simple 'engine' that turned wheels for spinners of flax, and recommended county workhouses to parliament in *Provision for the Poor*. Further publications followed, all aimed at a parliamentary audience: *A Breviat of some Proposals for the Promoting of Industry* (1679), including wool as well as linen manufacture in the workhouse scheme; *A Method of Government for such Publick Working Alms-Houses* (1679), proposing the union of small parishes for workhouse purposes and the election of 'delegates or overseers' by contributing parishes to oversee the new institutions; and finally *England's Weal and Prosperity Proposed* (1681), a summary statement. The Exclusion parliaments found no time to discuss Haines's scheme, but, along with the proposals of Thomas Firmin, whom Haines knew, it influenced later projects for reform of the poor laws.

Haines's last publication was *Aphorisms upon the New Way of Improving Cyder or Making Cyder-Royal* (1684), publicizing his third patent, for a method of doubling the strength of cider and so competing with imported wines and spirits, and including general advice on the management of orchards. His own farming seems not to have been profitable, however, perhaps because of his other activities; he and his heirs sold off over 500 acres in the late seventeenth century. He married Mary Green on 14 December 1654, and had seven children, three of whom (two sons and one daughter) survived infancy. He died in London on 29 May 1685 and was buried at Christ Church Greyfriars.

PAUL SLACK, *rev.*

**Sources** C. R. Haines, *A complete memoir of Richard Haines* (1899) · J. Thirsk, ed., *The agrarian history of England and Wales*, 5/1 (1984) · E. D. Bebb, *Nonconformity and social and economic life, 1660–1880* (1935)

**Haines, Stafford Bettesworth** (1801/2–1860), political agent in Aden, was from a Sussex family, but his place and date of birth are unknown. He was appointed midshipman in the Bombay marine in 1817 and arrived in India in May 1818. Haines made his name as a surveyor in the Persian Gulf, and was appointed assistant surveyor in 1826. In 1829 he went on leave, taking the opportunity in June 1831 to marry Mary Saulez in Alton, Hampshire. They had a daughter and a son, born after his return to India in 1832. After a short period as quarantine master in Bombay in 1832, Haines was appointed to the survey ship *Palinurus* to chart the south coast of Arabia.

In 1833 Haines was instructed to survey the island of Socotra as a possible coaling station for steamships, which had just begun to sail between Britain and India. Following the sultan of Mahra's refusal to sell and British troops' failure to seize Socotra, Haines convinced the government of Bombay that Aden could be made into both a strategic and a great commercial centre.

In 1837 Haines persuaded the sultan of Lahej to sell Aden despite the opposition of his son, who tried to kidnap Haines to thwart the sale. Haines returned to India, but because there was a fear that Mehmet Ali Pasha, governor of Egypt, might seize Aden, Haines returned with 700 troops successfully to storm the town on 19 January 1839. Haines was appointed political agent, and administered Aden from 1839 to 1854, being promoted captain in 1841. His first tasks were to erect fortifications, to intrigue to prevent the Arabs from uniting to expel the intruder, and to use the Jews to set up a highly efficient intelligence network. After he had beaten off three attacks to retake Aden, Haines was able to concentrate on his plans for turning a ramshackle town where 600 people, nearly half of them Jews, lived in squalor into the main entrepôt for Arabia and east Africa. An attempt to bring the imam of the Yemen into alliance was vetoed by India, but he played tribal politics with consummate skill, cheaply keeping the peace with well-placed bribes. At the same time, offering low rents to those who would agree to build in stone, he laid out a town which after seven years had a population of 25,000, served by a free port.

Haines had no friends in high places and his requests for administrative help went unheeded. He was a virtual dictator, but had to write every letter himself and took no leave for fifteen years. When auditors arrived they found a deficit of £28,000, for, in the absence of a bank, Haines had used the Treasury for political and administrative expenses without keeping proper records. He was recalled to Bombay by the East India Company in February 1854 and put on trial for fraud and embezzlement, and, although twice acquitted, he was nevertheless cashiered. No one believed him guilty of financial dishonesty, but the governor, John Elphinstone, demanded restitution of the money. Haines, with an annual salary of £2400, was unable to pay and was consigned to a debtors' prison. He remained there for six years until the new governor of Bombay, Sir George Clerk, took pity on him. He was released on 9 June 1860.

Haines was a strange mixture, a man with a romantic vision for the future of the first conquest of Queen Victoria's reign, a skilful politician among Arabs but not among his fellow countrymen, who was possessed of a sailor's practicality in such matters as building a town but not in administration. He was a formidable man, often devious, but liked by his colleagues and subordinates, energetic, and determined. He was thickset, with a broad forehead, full beard, and very light-coloured, widely set eyes that could be most intimidating. Haines died on 16 June 1860, at Bombay harbour on a ship that was to take him to England, one week after his release from prison.

ROBIN BIDWELL, *rev.*

**Sources** BL OIOC · G. Waterfield, *Sultans of Aden* (1968)

**Haines, William** (1778–1848), engraver and painter, was born at Bedhampton, Hampshire, on 21 June 1778, but moved as an infant with his family to Chichester, Sussex. He was educated at Midhurst grammar school, and while there, in 1793, witnessed the destruction by fire of Cowdray House, a notable sixteenth-century mansion. Two years later he was with the engraver Robert Thew at Northaw, Hertfordshire, where, when proficient, he worked with Edward Scriven and others on an important series of prints illustrating Shakespeare after paintings by British artists for the print publisher John Boydell. In 1800 he sailed to the Cape of Good Hope. At Cape Town and in excursions up country he made numerous drawings, especially of local people. From the Cape he travelled to Philadelphia, where he engraved a number of book illustrations and portraits.

After returning to England in 1805 to work in London, Haines took up miniature painting, and he exhibited at the Royal Academy as a miniature painter from 1808 to 1830. Between 1808 and 1840 he also exhibited at the British Institution, the Society of British Artists, and the Old Watercolour Society. He re-established his connections with Chichester through William Hayley, for whose *Life of George Romney* (1809) he engraved a plate, but, failing to secure a livelihood in Chichester or afterwards in Southampton, he returned to London. There he took up oils but painted portraits mostly in miniature, working from the studio he built at 3 Boyle Street, Savile Row. Many of his sitters were heroes of the Napoleonic wars, especially the Peninsular campaign. A number of his miniatures were reproduced in contemporary accounts such as *The Military Panorama* (1812–14) and C. H. Gifford's *History of the Wars* (1817). His work is mainly known through prints, such as the portrait in oil of the Arctic explorer Sir William Edward Parry, which he published himself. Having succeeded to some property, he retired to East Brixton, where he died on 24 July 1848. A watercolour by Haines of Earl Stanhope, later first chairman of the trustees of the National Portrait Gallery, London, is in the Stanhopes' home at Chevening, Kent.

WILLIAM HAINES, *rev.* KATHERINE COOMBS

**Sources** D. Foskett, *Miniatures: dictionary and guide* (1987) • Graves, *RA exhibitors*

**Haining, Jane Mathison** (1897–1944), Christian missionary and martyr, was born on 6 June 1897 at Lochenhead Farm, Dunscore, Dumfriesshire, the fifth of the six children of Thomas John Haining (1866/7–1922), farmer, and his first wife, Jane Mathison (1865/6–1902), a farmer's daughter. After her mother's early death in childbirth she was nurtured in the strongly evangelical piety of Craig church, Dunscore, formerly Reformed Presbyterian, from 1876 in the Free Church of Scotland and then, after the 1900 church union, the United Free Church.

From the village school Haining gained a scholarship in 1909 to Dumfries Academy, boarding in the new Moat Hostel for Girls. She won numerous prizes, ending up as modern dux. After training at the commercial college of Glasgow's Athenaeum, she became a secretary in J. and P. Coats' thread business in Paisley (1917–27). Her home in Glasgow (50 Forth Street, Pollokshields) was near Queen's Park West United Free Church, where Jane's missionary leanings strengthened during the ministry of Joseph L. Craig (1866–1953) which lasted from 1899 to 1927. After a year's diploma course at the Glasgow College of Domestic Science and temporary posts in Glasgow and Manchester, in 1932 she was appointed matron of the girls' home in the Church of Scotland's Jewish mission in Budapest, founded in 1841.

After training at the women's missionary college (known as St Colm's after 1929) in Edinburgh, Haining left for Budapest on 20 June 1932. There she became fluent in Hungarian with impressive speed. The Scottish school had about 400 pupils, with some fifty boarders in Jane's care. A majority in both categories were Jewish, some orphans or otherwise unwanted. Jane became their substitute mother, starting weekly reunions when old girls returned 'home'. The Christian faith was taught to all, but Hungarian law forbade conversion below eighteen years old. As Hungary moved into the orbit of Hitler's Germany, anti-Jewish measures intensified.

On furlough visits to Scotland (1935, 1939), Jane avoided public speaking. While she was on holiday in Cornwall in 1939 with Margit Prém, headmistress of the higher school, the Second World War broke out. They immediately returned to Budapest and Jane defied the foreign missions committee's instruction to return home in 1940. 'If these children need me in days of sunshine, how much more do they need me in days of darkness' (McDougall, 24). As conditions worsened and communications with Edinburgh failed, Jane arranged for the Hungarian Reformed church to take charge of the mission. The story of its role in sheltering refugees has still to be fully told.

On 19 March 1944 the Germans occupied Hungary. To her sore distress, Jane had to affix the yellow Star of David to her Jewish boarders' clothing. Despite safe conduct from the Swiss legation she was arrested between 4 and 7 April 1944. She admitted all the charges against her (including working among Jews and listening to the BBC), except engaging in political activity. She was detained first in a Gestapo villa, then in Fö utca prison in Buda, before removal to Kistarcsa holding camp, 25 kilometres away, in late April. About 12 May she was loaded on a wagon for Oswiecim (Auschwitz), Poland. On arrival at Auschwitz II she was tattooed as prisoner 79467. Her last letter-card, of 15 July to Margit Prém, was largely concerned with the welfare of the school and its children. She died in Auschwitz in unknown circumstances on 17 July, among almost half a million that month. The death certificate from the German legation in Budapest reached Edinburgh on 17 August: 'Miss Haining, who was arrested on account of justified suspicion of espionage against Germany, died in hospital, July 17th., of cachexia following intestinal catarrh' (McDougall, 31). Her personal effects were returned to the Scottish mission on 22 August. She is believed to have been one of only two or three Scottish women to die in a German extermination camp.

The memory of Jane Haining's sacrificial devotion, especially to Jewish children, is perpetuated by two stained-glass windows in her old church in Glasgow, now Strathbungo Queen's Park, by two plaques in the Scottish mission in Budapest (one from the Jewish community), by her enrolment among the righteous among the nations at Yad Vashem in Jerusalem, and by continuing links between Dunscore, Strathbungo, and Budapest. The Church of Scotland's Jane Haining prize brings two pupils and a teacher from Budapest to Scotland each year. She is honoured as a martyr among Christians in both countries.

D. F. WRIGHT

**Sources** D. McDougall, *Jane Haining, 1897–1944*, rev. I. Alexander (1998) • E. Walker, 'Jane Haining: devotion far from home (1897–1944)', *A legacy of Scots*, ed. C. T. Walker (1988), 242–53 • D. Czech, *Auschwitz chronicle, 1939–1945* (1990) • A. Bereczky, *Hungarian protestantism and the persecution of the Jews* (1945) • Church of Scotland, *Jewish Mission Quarterly* (1944–8) • R. L. Braham, *The politics of genocide: the Hungarian holocaust*, 2nd edn, 2 vols. (1994)
**Archives** Church of Scotland, Edinburgh, department of world mission, letters
**Likenesses** photographs, repro. in McDougall, *Jane Haining*
**Wealth at death** £607 5s. 3d.: confirmation, 20 June 1945, *CCI*

**Haistwell, Edward** (*c*.1658–1709), merchant, was the son of Thomas Haistwell of Orton, Westmorland. An active Quaker, he was at the age of nineteen or twenty employed as an amanuensis by George Fox, the founder of the Society of Friends. During this engagement, lasting from March 1677 to June 1678, he accompanied Fox on missionary journeys through England, Holland, and Germany and kept his employer's journal. William Penn and Robert Barclay also accompanied Fox to the continent and thus Haistwell would at an early age have been well acquainted with many of the emerging leaders of the Quaker movement.

At the end of his service to Fox in 1678, Haistwell became an informal apprentice or clerk to James Claypoole (1634–1687), a Quaker merchant of Scotts Yard,

Bush Lane, in the parish of St Mary Bothaw, London, whose business included the importation of sugar from the West Indies, linen and beer from Germany, wine from Bordeaux, and furs from Hudson's Bay. When Claypoole decided to emigrate to Pennsylvania in 1683, he turned over his premises and his not too large merchant business to Haistwell, who continued Claypoole's activity in the 'open', or unregulated, trades, particularly that to the West Indies. It is likely that the young man received financial help from his father with whom he afterwards had some joint ventures.

The customs records for 1686 (PRO E 190/143/1) show that Haistwell's principal importation was sugar from Barbados, though he also entered ginger from there and Nevis, and much logwood from Jamaica. He also imported wine from the Canaries, wine and brandy from Bordeaux, Brunswick mum (beer) from Bremen, linen from Bremen and Amsterdam, and tallow from Ireland. Some of these imported commodities, particularly linens, were almost certainly intended for re-export in his West Indian trade.

In 1687 Haistwell married Rachel, daughter of Richard Marsh, a merchant of London but originally from Lyme Regis. Marsh was a more important merchant than Haistwell, whose business and affluence began to grow noticeably following this alliance. His grander style of living soon attracted unkind comments from some offended Quakers, and, to mollify them, Haistwell removed the pictures he had recently hung on his walls. His higher status was reinforced when, on 11 February 1692, he was admitted a freeman of the prestigious Grocers' Company. In the 1690s, supported by the greater resources of his father-in-law, Haistwell ventured into the tobacco trade on a large scale, importing from Virginia and Maryland and exporting to the continent—primarily to Rotterdam, but also in some volume to Germany and Spain where his father-in-law also traded (he sometimes acted jointly with his father, Thomas, and with Anthony Haistwell, presumably a kinsman).

Haistwell owned shares in the old East India Company by 1696 and bought more in the following years, but this investment did not constitute a partisan commitment. In 1697 he also acquired shares in the second subscription to the Bank of England and, when Richard Marsh died in 1704, Haistwell's wife, Rachel, inherited from her father over £6000 in additional bank shares. These holdings seem to have brought Haistwell into a co-operative relationship with Gilbert Heathcote and other important directors of the Bank of England. Haistwell subscribed £1000 to the £250,000 loan which several of the bank directors managed for the Habsburg emperor in 1706. In 1698 eight prominent City figures in the Heathcote group, directors of both the bank and the new East India Company, took advantage of Peter the Great's visit to England to obtain from the tsar an exclusive privilege of importing tobacco (formerly banned) into Russia. As none of them had much experience in tobacco, they welcomed the participation in their adventure of Haistwell, now quite familiar with that commodity, who became a manager of the undertaking. This adventure lasted on paper until 1723 but quite early found its privileges unenforceable in Russia and its earnings disappointing. In retrospect, the only lasting achievements of the adventurers were their successes in persuading parliament in 1699 to open the hitherto closed Russia Company and in influencing the ministry to send the first resident English minister to Moscow in 1705.

Haistwell died of fever, intestate, on 4 January 1709 in London and was buried on 7 or 8 January in the Quaker burial-ground, Ratcliff. His post-mortem inventory of 21 January shows that in addition to his fairly large house in Scotts Yard, Haistwell had a smaller suburban residence in Hampstead. Both appeared to be furnished in solid comfort but without pictures or other ostentatious items, except for a coach and chariot, two coach horses, and over £250 worth of silver plate. His business interests then embraced shares in four ships, one chartered to the transport service, one to the East India Company, with two engaged in private trade to the East Indies. He was also partner with Anthony Haistwell in a firm that had large bill-of-exchange operations. On his own, he had an unspecified interest in mines at Tor Bay, Devon, and owned all or part of shipments of tobacco to Alicante and Bilbao and other goods at Barbados, Antigua, Virginia, and Archangel. Besides his part of the Russian Tobacco Company, Edward Haistwell had shares in the Bank of England, the new and old East India companies, and the Blue Paper Company, plus some Million Lottery tickets and exchequer annuities paying £186 p.a. In addition to the loan to the German emperor, he was owed money by sundry persons in England as well as in Barbados, Lisbon, Alicante, Bremen, Königsberg, and Narva.

In 1698 Haistwell had become a fellow of the Royal Society—as a patron rather than as an active scientist. William Penn's records show that Haistwell had been one of the eminent Friends who advanced £100 each to a fund that enabled Penn to buy out the Ford family interest in the Pennsylvania grant. Haistwell had obviously advanced much more to support Penn's undertaking, for his own inventory showed £1000 owed by Penn. Throughout his life, Haistwell remained an active Friend, contributing to the society's work. His most important services were as a member of the meeting for sufferings, a standing committee of the yearly meeting which in 1696 obtained the important parliamentary act permitting Friends to affirm rather than swear to proceedings in civil suits.

Haistwell's loyalty to the Quaker movement was not continued by his only surviving child, Edward (1696–1744). Three years after his father's death, the son was admitted to the Middle Temple on 1 March 1712 and subsequently called to the bar on 23 May 1718. He also continued some of his father's investment interests, eventually becoming a major shareholder in and ultimately a director (1733–42) of the post-Bubble South Sea Company. There is evidence that some of the money owed by the British government to the Russian Tobacco Company (primarily for hemp) was converted after the elder Edward Haistwell's death into shares in the new South Sea Company and thus provided part of the basis of his son's later role in that company. Neither the oaths required of barristers nor the slave-trading activities of the South Sea Company were compatible with the expectations of the Society of Friends. JACOB M. PRICE

**Sources** *The short journal and itinerary journals of George Fox*, ed. N. Penney (1925) · *The journal of George Fox*, rev. edn, ed. J. L. Nickalls (1952) · *James Claypoole's letterbook: London and Philadephia, 1681–1684*, ed. M. Belderston (1967) · *The papers of William Penn*, ed. M. M. Dunn, R. S. Dunn, and others, 5 vols. (1981–7) · J. M. Price, *The tobacco adventure to Russia: enterprise, politics, and diplomacy in the quest for a northern market for English colonial tobacco, 1676–1722* (1961) · PRO, Customs, entries inward, London, 1686, E. 190/143/1 · PRO, Customs, entries outward, London, 1695, E. 190/152 · Inventory of Edward Haistwell, PRO, PROB 5/3824 · 17 Feb 1703, PRO, Adm. 106/572 · Records of Bank of England · Records of East India Co. · H. A. C. Sturgess, ed., *Register of admissions to the Honourable Society of the Middle Temple, from the fifteenth century to the year 1944*, 3 vols. (1949) · South Sea Co., Court Minutes, 1732–60, BL, Add. MS 25, 545 · *GM*, 1st ser., 14 (1744) · N. Luttrell, *A brief historical relation of state affairs from September 1678 to April 1714*, 6 (1857) · T. L. Underwood, 'Edward Haistwell', *Notes and Records of the Royal Society*, 25 (1970), 179–87 · Grocer's Company, register of freemen, 1686–1721, GL, MS 11598

**Wealth at death** see inventory, excl. liabilities, PRO, PROB 5/3824

**Haite, John James** (1808/9–1874), composer, was a prominent member of the Society of British Musicians, which produced several of his works. His published compositions include songs and glees and collections of *Favourite Melodies* arranged as quintets, sextets, and septets (1865). He also wrote a pamphlet entitled *Principles of natural harmony, being a perfect system founded upon the discovery of the true semitonic scale* (1855?), and possibly a cello tutor. However, in the last few years of his life he devoted his attention principally to choral works, and wrote the oratorios *Abraham's Sacrifice* (1871), *The Song of the Year*, and *David and Goliath* (1880), in addition to three masses, two operettas, and shorter choral pieces. Haite died at his home, 154 King Edwards Road, Hackney, London, on 2 October 1874, aged sixty-five. DAVID J. GOLBY

**Sources** *MT*, 16 (1873–5), 686 · Brown & Stratton, *Brit. mus.* · J. D. Brown, *Biographical dictionary of musicians: with a bibliography of English writings on music* (1886) · *Musical Standard*, 7, 290 · d. cert.

**Hake, Alfred Egmont** (1849–1916), author and social philosopher, was born at Guildhall Street, Bury St Edmunds, Suffolk, on 12 October 1849, the fourth son of the physician and poet Thomas Gordon *Hake (1809–1895), and his wife, Lucy Bush. Nothing is known of his education or early life, though through his father, who attended Dante Gabriel Rossetti, he became a friend of the critic and biographer William Michael Rossetti. He seems to have spent time abroad for his first book was a series of vignettes of Parisian types, *Paris Originals* (1878). He moved in London intellectual circles, and was a member of the Savile Club from 1878 to 1895. On 4 December 1879 he married, at Kensington register office, Philippa Mary (*b.* 1860/61), daughter of Alexander Charles Handley, commercial traveller.

Hake came to literary prominence as the author of a popular biography of Major-General Charles George Gordon, to whom he was related: Thomas Gordon Hake's mother was Gordon's aunt. Hake's account, *The Story of Chinese Gordon* (1884), which celebrated Gordon's mysticism and self-sacrifice, went through many editions. Following Gordon's death at Khartoum, Hake rushed out a second volume (1885) together with an edition of Gordon's journals, which remain an important source for studies of Gordon. On the eve of the general election in December 1885, Hake lectured widely on Gordon and on the failure of the Gladstone government to rescue him. In 1886 he edited a short-lived weekly Conservative journal, *The State*, which attacked Gladstone and Irish home rule.

As well as miscellaneous literary work, Hake seems to have become increasingly involved in pressure groups on the fringes of politics. His *Free Trade in Capital* (1889), written with O. E. Wesslau under the auspices of the Free Trade in Capital League, addressed the question of why free trade had not led to universal prosperity, and attributed the economic depression and the resulting social problems of unemployment and sweated labour to the limitations on the issue of bank notes laid down in the Bank Charter Act of 1844. He was a strident critic of collectivist, socialist trends in public policy, and was a defender of individualism and free trade (see A. Egmont Hake and O. E. Wesslau, *The Coming Individualism*, 1895). In the wake of classical British liberalism, he criticized all socialist utopias.

Although not a professional scholar, Hake was an able metaphysician and sociologist. His most important theoretical contribution was an anonymous book, *Regeneration: a Reply to Max Nordau* (1895). Nordau, who was a follower of the Italian psychiatrist and founder of criminal anthropology Cesare Lombroso, had written an epoch-making work entitled *Entartung* (1892–3, English translation as *Degeneration*, 1895). In an almost prophetic mood, Nordau disclosed the growing *anomie* of the European societies. Hake's reply was a fundamental and seminal work, proposing not only a cultural and anthropological interpretation of the sociological problems, but even a philosophy of history and a theodicy. While dehumanization and self-deception were the side effects of the moral and psychological decadence of humankind, Hake argued that moral and religious improvements were the prominent features of Victorian Britain and of the British empire. He criticized Nordau's excessive emphasis on the scope of degeneration, extended to the spheres of religion, literature, and art, and also his Germanocentric standpoint. For Hake perceived the momentous peril of the expansionist and militarist German empire. By contrast, he contended that the 'British race' had brought civilization, education, and economic prosperity. Thus, in Hake's account, General Gordon became a British and Christian hero, who tried to improve the ethical and social conditions of Sudan's people.

Hake denounced Nordau's prescription of authoritarian intervention from above as a solution to social problems, arguing that such repression produced demoralization and conformity. The problem of degeneration was to be solved, in Hake's view, not by authoritarian measures but by the moral and religious improvement of mankind.

He applied evolutionary theory to sociology in the sense applied by Benjamin Kidd, believing that evolution was not a mechanistic system, regulated by chance, but was teleological. Drawing on the tradition of Mill, Herbert Spencer, and T. H. Green, Hake contrasted the English liberal model to the Prussian-German militarism and statolatry. The British empire was the liberal empire *par excellence* and therefore superior to the Habsburg empire, the German, tsarist, and Napoleonic empires.

Hake's personal life remains obscure. His eulogy upon George Borrow, the author and traveller who was one of his father's friends, contains an autobiographical glimpse in its remark that humour 'is given us to neutralize the worst forebodings' (*Macmillan's Magazine*, vol. 45, November 1881). In 1901 he was living as a lodger at 96 Archel Road, Fulham, and subsequently he lived in Kennington Park Road, Lambeth. He died of peripheral neuritis in the City of London Lunatic Asylum, Stone, near Dartford, Kent, on 8 December 1916. CRISTIANO CAMPORESI

**Sources** Allibone, *Dict.* • J. F. Henderson, *The Savile Club, 1862–1923* (1923) • M. W. Taylor, *Man versus the state: Herbert Spencer and late Victorian individualism* (1992) • R. W. Peattie, ed., *Selected letters of William Michael Rossetti* (1990) • *Wellesley index* • L. Goldman, *Science, reform, and politics in Victorian Britain: the Social Science Association, 1857–1886* (2002) • b. cert. • m. cert. • d. cert. • *CGPLA Eng. & Wales* (1920) • census returns, 1881 • census returns, 1901 • E. Baring, *Modern Egypt*, 2 vols. (1908)

**Wealth at death** £100: administration, 1920, *CGPLA Eng. & Wales*

**Hake, Edward** (*fl.* 1564–1604), lawyer and satirist, is of obscure origins. Educated by the Revd John Hopkins, he was a student at Barnard's Inn from 1564 to 1567. He had a room there for some time, and later had a chamber at Gray's Inn. He wrote a poem from Barnard's Inn on the anniversary of Elizabeth's succession on 17 November 1575. There is no evidence that he was called to the bar. He was under-steward at Windsor, Berkshire, for the earl of Leicester by 1576, acting as town recorder in September, a bailiff in 1578, and town clerk in 1579 with a fee of 20s. p.a. In that year he presided over the town's court leet and was its commissioner for musters. He drafted a book of orders with proposals for a new charter in 1582, but nothing came of it in his lifetime (Hake, xxvi). It appears that he reverted to deputy under-steward in 1584, but was elected mayor for 1586–7. When the queen visited Windsor on 10 August 1586 she was received in state by the corporation and addressed by Hake; and on her birthday, 7 September 1586, he delivered an oration in her honour at the Guildhall. He was elected MP for Windsor in the parliament of 1588, when he was again under-steward. Apart from serving on a royal commission on the queen's lands and tenements in 1595 he held no other offices.

Hake wrote much of his poetry in his early years at the inns, between 1564 and 1576. This would place him in that matrix of students who went to the inns more for entertainment and advancement than for a professional career in the high courts. His career as a local office-holder followed in Windsor from 1576 to 1589. Shortly after becoming town clerk and judge of the court leet, he wrote to the new attorney-general, Sir Thomas Egerton, applying for a commission of the peace. Styling himself 'counsellor', he apologized for his 'base form of living', regarding it as no disgrace (Hunt. L., Ellesmere MS 6091). Unfortunately for Hake, Egerton's views on counsellors (failed barristers) as the caterpillars of the kingdom would not have brought him an endorsement. Some time after 1588 Hake returned to the chambers he had rented in Gray's Inn from about 1585. In 1593 he is recorded as making payment for a new gate from his chamber in Fulwood Lane to Holborn.

Hake's verses have been characterized as 'monotonous fourteeners characteristic of the time' (Smith, 215). Lacking polish, Hake apologized for his efforts by stating that his professional duties did not allow him the time to study and write. A puritan, he showed a keen hatred of Roman Catholics throughout his works. Of his ten published tracts from the 1560s to 1604, *Newes out of Powles Churchyarde* (1579) and *A Touchestone for this Time Present* (1574) were the most prominent.

*Newes out of Powles Churche Yarde a Trappe for Syr MONYE*, was entered in the Stationers' register in 1567. No copy of the first edition is known, but it was reprinted in 1579. With a dedicatory verse to the earl of Leicester, Hake confessed that he did not aspire to rank 'amongst the better sort of english Poetes of our tyme'. He states that he has corrected the text of the first edition, and made additions. The preface includes Latin elegies of praise by John Long and Richard Matthew, and an engraving of Leicester's arms with Hake's rhymed inscription beneath. The eight satires take the form of a dialogue between Bertulph and Paul in the aisle of St Paul's Cathedral, London. They denounce clerical and legal abuses, lawyers who obstruct justice and rack-rent their tenants for monetary greed; physicians, apothecaries, and surgeons who work for profit and not for health; merchants who promote vain luxuries rather than useful goods; and the dangers of spendthrifts, bankrupts, bawds, brokers, and usurers. A strong puritan, Hake also warns about the consequences of allowing Sunday sports, profanity, bawds and whores, and irreligious economic and social practices in the cathedral.

*A touchestone for this time present, expresly declaring such ruines, enormaties, and abuses as trouble the Churche of God and our Christian common wealth at this daye. Whereunto is annexed a perfect rule to be observed of all parents and scholemaisters, in the trayning up of their schollers and children in learning* followed in 1574. The first part, dedicated to Hake's friend Edward Godfrey, merchant, brandishes the vices of the clergy, and censures parents for their careless training of children. The second, dedicated to John Harlow, was an abridged metrical rendering of *De pueris statim ac liberaliter instituendis*, containing a series of quaint dialogues on the education of children. Hake says that 'being tied unto solytarinesse in the countrey' he had translated the tract for recreation, and used verse because it was more easily written than prose. Both works display his zest for a classical, Christian education, and close parental supervision.

Hake's most prominent work was the unpublished treatise 'Epieikeia', in three parts. Part 1 was on what is equity, and how it is observed in every law of man. Part 2 was a discussion of equity in the common law, and in English government. Part 3 was on equity in the chancery, and the antiquity of the court and the office of lord keeper. Hake extolled the Elizabethan lord keeper Sir Nicholas Bacon (1558–79) for profundity in judgement and integrity in conscience (Hake, 143). He probably sat in the chancery as a student during Bacon's tenure on the woolsack. The treatise's significance is that it was the only comprehensive description and analysis of equity and the court of chancery prior to the seventeenth-century reforms.

Hake took considerable effort in composing 'Epieikeia' between 1587 and 1591. He corresponded with Sir Julius Caesar, master of requests, for suggestions in 1596–7, promising a similar work on the court of requests. He revised it after Elizabeth's death for presentation to James in 1604. He wrote again to Caesar for suggestions in July 1603, and the work was read by chief justice Sir Edmund Anderson and justice Sir Thomas Walmesley. It was dedicated to his friend Sir Edward Vaughan, deputy officer of the pipe in the exchequer and Hake encouraged him to have the king read it, hoping for advancement. He also sent a copy to Edward Bruce, Lord Kinloss, just appointed master of the rolls, urging him the same. He wrote that he was willing to pay for preferment, and had suffered from 'many shrewde crosses' that hindered him and his wife (BL, Add. MS 12503, fol. 47).

The best parts of 'Epieikeia' were Hake's concept of equity (5–44), and an analysis of chancery as a court and bureaucracy (119–44). Equity, for Hake, was an unwritten moral law, derived from the law of God, containing the sense or 'kernal' of all law (BL, Lansdowne MS 161, fol. 43*v*). Drawing on the early Tudor work of Christopher St German, Hake saw equity not as a set of principles separate from law, but as inherent within the law whether in equitable or common-law remedies. He borrowed heavily from the cases reported by Edmund Plowden, using them for procedural and non-essential parts of law, and not their substantive content. When he revised the work for King James, he inserted the view of chancery as the court of the king's absolute power, exercising his conscience. This was contrary to that of the lord chancellor and his masters, who were developing the law of equity according to rules of law, as well as to most common lawyers and jurists who were fearful of judicial discretion and royal intervention in case law.

The problem was that Hake's work was not relevant to the legal issues of the early seventeenth century; nor were the speakers of the discourse well known at the time. Lovelace was probably Lancelot Lovelace, admitted to Gray's Inn in 1581 and a prominent barrister after 1610 (Hake, xxvi). Elliott was his cousin. The treatise also was not a polished work. Much of the content was pedestrian, pillaging the work of others. While the writing style has been categorized as 'terse' (ibid., xvii), there are often long, cumbersome sentences, awkward and confusing phraseology, and erratic spelling.

Hake does not seem to appear in the historical record after 1604. He refers to a wife, but not children. There is no will, nor an inquisition *post mortem*. LOUIS A. KNAFLA

**Sources** E. Hake, *Epieikeia: a dialogue on equity in three parts*, ed. D. E. C. Yale (1953), v–xxix • C. Edmonds, ed., *Introduction to newes out of Powles churchyarde*; in *Isham reprints* (1872) [discussion of Hake's tracts] • C. Burrow, *Epic romance: Homer to Milton* (1993), 135–9 • T. Warton, *Gesta Romanorum: the history of English poetry*, ed. W. C. Hazlitt, 4 (1871), 203–4 • R. R. Tighe and J. E. Davis, *Annals of Windsor*, 2 vols. (1858) • R. Robinson, *Rewarde of wickednesse* (1574) [praise of Hake] • New Windsor offices, Bodl. Oxf., MS Ashmole 1126, fols. 46–50 • letters to J. Caesar, 1596–1603, BL, Lansdowne MS 161, fols. 42–3, 233, 247 • letter to Caesar, 1603, BL, Add. MS 12503, fol. 47 • Hake's transcription of Christopher Pett's poem, 'Commemoration of the reign of Queen Elizabeth', *c*.1603, BL, Add. MS 30370, fols. 34–46 • Arber, *Regs. Stationers*, 162b • HoP, *Commons, 1558–1603* • W. R. Prest, *The rise of the barristers: a social history of the English bar, 1590–1640* (1986), 192, 237, 319 • L. A. Knafla, *Law and politics in Jacobean England* (1977), 155, 161 • W. J. Jones, *The Elizabethan court of chancery* (1976), 32, 467, 492 • R. Tittler, *Nicholas Bacon: the making of a Tudor statesman* (1976), 73–4, 83 • T. Barrier Clendenin jun., 'The common lawyers in parliament and society: a social and political study of the common lawyers in the first Jacobean parliament', PhD diss., Chapel Hill, 1975, 131–2 • H. D. Smith, *Elizabethan poetry: a study in conventions, meaning, and expression* (1952), 215–16 • J. Nichols, *The progresses and public processions of Queen Elizabeth*, 2 (1823), 460–61 • R. J. Fletcher, ed., *The pension book of Gray's Inn*, 1 (1901), 99 • G. Burgess, *The politics of the ancient constitution: an introduction to English political thought* (1992), 87 • D. E. C. Yale, '"Of no mean authority": some later uses of Bracton', *On the laws and customs of England*, ed. M. S. Arnold, T. H. Green, S. A. Scully, and S. D. White (1981), 387–8 • letter to Egerton, *c*.1580, Hunt. L., Ellesmere MS 6091 • Hake's annotated copy of his 'Epieikeia', BL, Add. MS 35326 • commission, 1595, BL, Lansdowne MS 28, fol. 90

**Archives** BL, commission, Lansdowne MS 28, fol. 90 • BL, letters to J. Caesar, Lansdowne MS 161, fols. 42–3, 233, 247

**Hake, Thomas Gordon** (1809–1895), physician and poet, was born on 10 March 1809 at Leeds, the son of Thomas Bedford Hake (*d*. 1812/13) and his wife, the eldest daughter of Captain William Augustus Gordon and aunt of General Charles *Gordon. Hake grew up in Sidmouth, Devon. His father died when Hake was three years old and after his death his mother stayed on in Devon.

Hake was educated at Christ's Hospital, first at the preparatory school at Hertford (as a boarder), and afterwards in London. Having decided upon a medical career, he studied at Lewes under Thomas Hodson, then at St George's Hospital, and at the universities of Edinburgh and Glasgow, taking his medical degree from Glasgow in 1831. After graduation he travelled for some time in Italy (meeting Trelawney and Landor in Florence) before returning to Brighton, where he was physician to the dispensary from 1833 to 1838. In 1838 he went to Paris for a further year's study. It was probably about this time that he married Lucy Bush, their fourth son being the author and social philosopher Alfred Egmont *Hake.

On his return from Paris in 1839 Hake published *Piromides*, a tragedy on the mysteries of Isis. The following year *Vates, or, The Philosophy of Madness* was published anonymously in four parts, with illustrations by Charles Landseer, and later republished in *Ainsworth's Magazine* as *Valdarno, or, The Ordeal of Art-Worship*. By this time Hake had settled at Bury St Edmunds, where he became friendly with George Borrow and J. W. Donaldson. He spent much of his free time contributing scientific papers to medical journals. In 1853 he gave up his medical practice and travelled in America. On his return he established a home at Roehampton and became physician to the West London Hospital and also private physician to the countess of Ripon, a relative on his mother's side of the family.

It was while at Roehampton that Hake began to write poetry. He published his first collection, *The World's Epitaph*, privately (in an edition of 100 copies) in 1866. Dr R. G. Latham lent his copy to Theodore Watts-Dunton, who in turn showed it to Dante Gabriel Rossetti, already an admirer of *Valdarno*. Hake did not actually meet Rossetti until 1869, but from that time on his association with the family was an important one. Indeed, he is often discussed in terms of his involvement with Rossetti, and the part he played in the events leading up to Rossetti's overdose in 1872. W. M. Rossetti, in the memoir of his brother (included with the two-volume edition of Dante Gabriel Rossetti's *Family Letters*) called Hake 'the earthly Providence of the Rossetti family in those days'.

Hake's role in the events of 1872 was briefly as follows. In June Hake advised that it would be best if Rossetti were removed from the house in Cheyne Walk and offered him shelter at his own house. Rossetti was already suffering delusions and the cab journey from Chelsea to Roehampton was a difficult one. The next day Rossetti was no less troubled and during the night swallowed a bottle of laudanum. As both doctor and poet, Hake was interested in the healing capacity of sleep and dreams, and Rossetti's deep sleep the following morning initially pleased him. Not until late in the afternoon did he raise the alarm, and begin his attempts to revive Rossetti with ammonia, with eventual success. Following this crisis, Hake continued to advise W. M. Rossetti. His son, George Hake, accompanied D. G. Rossetti on his trips out of London and acted as general factotum until, in 1877, the derangement of the patient's mental and physical health rendered the position untenable.

Hake moved from Roehampton to St John's Wood and published a number of poetry collections throughout the 1870s and 1880s. These included *Parables and Tales* (1872), for which D. G. Rossetti provided the cover design; *New Symbols* (1876); *Legends of the Morrow* (1879); and *Maiden Ecstasy* (1880). His final collection of poems was a set of Shakespearian sonnets, *The New Day* (1890). Hake's poems have only rarely appeared in anthologies, and very little criticism has been written about them. Dante Rossetti reviewed *Madeline and other Poems* in *The Academy* in 1871 and *Parables and Tales* in the *Fortnightly Review* in 1873, but Hake appears to have had few other contemporary enthusiasts. Swinburne, to whom Hake sent copies of his later collections, clearly did not share the Rossettis' taste. He wrote to W. M. Rossetti in 1886: 'You will allow me to add that I regret the reproduction of the kindly but not uncritical notices of Dr. Hake's poems (so-called).' Alice Meynell wrote in the preface to her 1894 selection: 'Dr. Hake has a solemn and distinct note … Dr. Hake's expression always implies long intention, deliberate decision. The verse is a consequence long foreseen.' George Saintsbury, writing in his *Short History of English Literature* (1911), described Hake's verse as 'too mystical and difficult'. Oliver Elton, in his 1920 *Survey of English Literature*, found that Hake's 'mystical mode of naturalism is rooted in science, though distinctly alien to the agnostic cult of the time'.

Hake, who wrote nearly all his verse after the age of fifty, now and again produced work of a more striking and accessible quality. 'The Inscrutable', about the visualization of horror and the passage from imagination to reality, and 'The Cripple', a graphic description of nineteenth-century life in the shadow of the poorhouse, are both poems which could be used to support the view that Hake should be remembered for more than his medical advice to the Rossetti family.

Hake's autobiography, *Memoirs of Eighty Years*, which includes many useful reminiscences of the Rossettis, was published in 1892. In it Hake is depicted as a shrewd but not unkindly observer of other men, cheerful rather than congenial, communicative but not garrulous, and with a proud confidence in his own powers. W. M. Rossetti described him as 'a man of more than common height, lithe and straight, with very self-possessed gentle manners, and clear deliberate utterance'. During the last four years of his life Hake was confined to his couch by a fracture of the hip. He died on 11 January 1895 at his brother's home, where he had been living, 59 Acacia Road, St John's Wood, London. One of his sons, Alfred Egmont Hake, wrote a biography of General Gordon and edited his Chinese journals. Another, Thomas Hake, helped to edit the correspondence of Thomas Watts-Dunton.

RICHARD GARNETT, *rev.* MICHAEL THORN

**Sources** T. G. Hake, *Memoirs of eighty years* (1892) · W. M. Rossetti, *Family letters and a memoir of Dante Gabriel Rossetti*, 2 vols. (1895) · *The diary of W. M. Rossetti, 1870–1873*, ed. O. Bornand (1977) · *The Swinburne letters*, ed. C. Y. Lang, 6 vols. (1959–62) · O. Elton, *The survey of English literature, 1830–1880*, 2 (1920) · A. Meynell, preface, in *The poems of Thomas Gordon Hake*, ed. A. Meynell (1894) · T. St E. Hake and A. Compton-Rickett, *The life and letters of Theodore Watts-Dunton*, 2 vols. (1916) · d. cert. · *CGPLA Eng. & Wales* (1895) · J. Hutchinson, ed., *A catalogue of notable Middle Templars: with brief biographical notices* (1902) · Allibone, *Dict.*

**Archives** BL, corresp. and papers, Add. MSS 49461–49470 | Bodl. Oxf., letters to Linda Villain · Union College, New York, Schaffer Library, special collections, letters to Alfred Henry Miles

**Likenesses** W. & A. H. Fry, carte-de-visite, mignonne, NPG

**Wealth at death** £123 19*s.* 3*d.*: administration, 23 March 1895, *CGPLA Eng. & Wales*

**Hakewill, Arthur William** (1808–1856). *See under* Hakewill, James (1778–1843).

**Hakewill, Edward Charles** (1816–1872). *See under* Hakewill, Henry (1771–1830).

**Hakewill, George** (*bap.* 1578, *d.* 1649), Church of England clergyman and author, was baptized on 25 January 1578 at St Mary Arches, Exeter, the third son of John Hakewill (*d.* 1615), merchant of Exeter, and his wife, Thomazin, daughter of John Peryam and his wife, Margaret Horne; he was the younger brother of William *Hakewill (*bap.* 1574, *d.* 1655) and cousin of Thomas Bodley. After early education at Exeter grammar school he matriculated on 15 May

1595 as a commoner of St Alban Hall, Oxford. On 30 June 1596 he was elected to a fellowship at Exeter College, remarkable for one of his age, on account of his skill as a disputant and orator. He graduated BA on 6 July 1599 and proceeded MA on 29 April 1602. From 1604 Hakewill spent four years abroad, principally with Swiss and German Calvinists, including a winter in Heidelberg with David Pareas and Abraham Scultetus, which confirmed his fierce anti-Catholic Calvinism. He was permitted to count eight terms abroad towards his BD, gained on 25 March 1610. He proceeded DD on 2 July 1611, having resigned his fellowship on 30 June.

In August 1611 Hakewill was presented to the rectory of Heanton Punchardon, near Barnstaple, Devon, by Sir Robert Basset, whose wife, Elizabeth Periam, was Hakewill's first cousin. Major court preferment followed in December 1612. When Prince Charles became heir to the throne following his brother's death, Hakewill and Prince Henry's former chaplain Richard Milbourne were appointed chaplains with special orders from the king never to leave the prince and to protect him from any influence of Roman Catholicism. Hakewill performed his duties with zeal. His successful preparation of Charles for examination at his confirmation on Easter Monday 1613 inspired his defence, *The Auncient Ecclesiasticall Practice of Confirmation* (1613).

On 23 June 1615 Hakewill married Mary Ayer or Ayers (*née* Delbridge; 1588–1618), a widow with a daughter, Martha. The couple had two sons, one of whom, John, was later a fellow of Exeter College, Oxford, but their married life was brief. Mary Hakewill was buried at Barnstaple on 5 May 1618.

In 1616 James I appointed Hakewill to refute his former chaplain Benjamin Carier's defence of conversion to Rome. Hakewill's forceful 300-page *Answer to a Treatise Written by Dr Carier* is an epitome of his conformist Calvinism—opposed to any toleration of Rome and convinced of the doctrinal unity with Geneva. Higher preferment seemed guaranteed with his collation on 7 February 1617 to the archdeaconry of Surrey by Bishop James Montagu of Winchester, a leading court patron of progressive protestants, but James's betrayal of his earlier commitment to Calvinist anti-Catholicism in the interest of the Spanish match suddenly put Hakewill at odds with the new pro-Spanish, Arminian powers at court.

Against the advice of Prince Charles's secretary, Sir Thomas Murray, in August 1622 Hakewill wrote a treatise against the Spanish match while negotiations were in progress, and presented it to the prince without the king's knowledge. Upon learning of the tract James swiftly committed both Hakewill and Murray to prison and the leading anti-Calvinist Lancelot Andrewes, who as current bishop of Winchester and dean of the Chapel Royal had jurisdiction over Hakewill as archdeacon of Surrey and as a royal chaplain, was appointed to rebut the tract. Never printed, the tract, with its dedication to the prince, survives in the Bodleian Library (MS Rawlinson D 853). Hakewill never regained a presence at court.

Seven sets of Hakewill's visitation articles for the Surrey archdeaconry survive, all closely based on those of Bishop Andrewes; among his very few alterations, Hakewill insisted on a younger age for compulsory communion (sixteen) and specifically enquired about 'popish recusants' (Fincham, 1.185–6; 2, appx). Otherwise he concentrated on his ministry in north Devon and became a major benefactor to his Oxford college. His private means must have been considerable, for on 11 March 1623 he laid the foundation stone of a new chapel at Exeter College, which he built at a personal cost of £1200. Known until its destruction in 1858 as Hakewill's chapel, it was unique among college chapels for its plan, which included a south aisle like a parish church. Hakewill's arms were ubiquitous in the Renaissance woodwork, fragments of which survive in churches and other buildings associated with the college. It was consecrated on 5 October 1624, the day of Prince Charles's return to England from Spain, and John Prideaux preached the consecration sermon, published with a dedication to Hakewill. To his gift Hakewill added £30 for an annual sermon on the anniversary of the consecration.

Hakewill's prose is lively and forceful. His largest work, *An Apologie … of the Power and Providence of God* (1627), argued against the prevailing view that the created order degenerates over time. A rebuttal by Bishop Godfrey Goodman resulted in the greatly expanded edition of 1635; this was later read with 'great pleasure' by Samuel Pepys (Pepys, *Diary*, 1985, 8.43). James Boswell listed Hakewill among the literary giants of the preceding century who had influenced Dr Samuel Johnson's prose style. However, the argument, popular since the nineteenth century, that the *Apologie* influenced John Milton has been questioned. Hakewill avoided open print debate over Laud's reforms of the church. The *Apologie* confessed to being a 'private exercise' in 'an untrodden path': his intention to write a second volume touching the question of decay in church government was no doubt politically impossible (sigs. C1*r*–1*v*, C5*v*). Publication of a Barnstaple sermon celebrating protestant successes in the Thirty Years' War in 1632, and an edition of works by his fellow Calvinist, kinsman, and neighbour John Downe in 1633 were his muted reminders of a churchmanship now out of favour with archbishop and king. After the collapse of censorship in 1641 he published a defence of sabbath observance and a rejection of Arminian eucharistic theology.

As early as 1630 Hakewill had complained of chronic ill health and was the patient of doctor–astrologer Richard Napier. On the resignation of John Prideaux, Hakewill was elected rector of Exeter College on 23 August 1642, but college records suggest that he was an absentee. He was left unmolested by parliamentary visitors on appeal by Devon MPs and ministers. He died at Heanton Punchardon on 2 April 1649, and was buried in the chancel of his church on 5 April.

Hakewill's will, written on 10 February 1647, with a codicil of 7 February 1648, was proved in May 1649. It makes clear that his sons had predeceased him, John having died at Exeter College some time after proceeding MA in 1637.

The heir and executor was John's cousin, with whom he has often been confused, John Hakewill, son of George Hakewill's brother John of Exeter. To his nephew, George Hakewill left the advowson of Heanton Punchardon and his personal estate, including his library. He also left legacies to his stepdaughter, Martha Matthews, and her husband, Thomas, and appointed his brother-in-law, Martin Blake, overseer; the two men were respectively royalist mayor and rector of Barnstaple. Hakewill asserted his loyalty to the Church of England as it had flourished in the time of 'prudent Queene Elizabeth', and asked that his heart be buried under the communion table or reading desk in his college chapel. This wish was not carried out: the badly broken floor monument to him at Heanton was replaced with a new mural tablet in the chancel's north wall by the rector and fellows of Exeter College in 1891.

P. E. McCULLOUGH

**Sources** C. W. Boase, ed., *Registrum Collegii Exoniensis*, new edn, OHS, 27 (1894) • PRO, PROB 11/208/77 • F. T. Colby, ed., *Visitation of … Devon … 1620* (1872) • J. Chanter, *Life of Martin Blake, D. D.* (1910) • P. E. McCullough, *Sermons at court: politics and religion in Elizabethan and Jacobean preaching* (1998) [incl. CD-ROM] • *Walker rev.* • *Fasti Angl., 1541–1857*, [Canterbury] • E. A. G. Lamborn, 'The woodwork of Hakewill's chapel', *N&Q*, 187 (1944), 137–9 • R. Napier to G. Hakewill, Bodl. Oxf., MSS Ashmole 1492. viii; 1488. ii; 232 • K. Fincham, ed., *Visitation articles and injunctions of the early Stuart church*, 1 (1994), 185–6; 2 (1998), appx

**Archives** Bodl. Oxf., Ashmolean MSS; Ballard MSS; Jones MSS; English Theology MSS; Rawl. MSS • Exeter College, Oxford • PRO, SP 14/122/88

**Likenesses** oils, *c.*1630, Exeter College, Oxford • oils, *c.*1630–1640, Exeter College, Oxford

**Wealth at death** see will, PRO, PROB 11/208/77

**Hakewill** [Hakewell], **Henry** (**1771–1830**), architect, was born on 4 October 1771, the eldest son in the family of eight surviving children of John *Hakewill (1742–1791), landscape and portrait painter, and decorator, and his wife, Anna Maria Cook (1747–1818). He was the brother of James *Hakewill (1778–1843). He was a pupil of John Yenn RA, and was admitted to the Royal Academy Schools in 1790, in which year he was awarded a silver medal for a drawing of the Strand front of Somerset House. He exhibited at the Royal Academy between 1792 and 1809. In his transcription of the registers of the Royal Academy Schools 1768–1830, Sidney Hutchinson noted that some members of the Hakewill family were registered as 'Hakewell', and this has led to both forms of the name being used in reference to members of the Hakewill family. In 1804 Hakewill married Anne Sarah, daughter of the Revd Edward Frith of North Cray, Kent, with whom he had seven children.

In 1809 Hakewill was appointed architect to Rugby School, and designed the Gothic buildings and chapel there between 1818 and 1821. He was also architect to the Radcliffe trustees at Oxford, and to the benchers of the Middle Temple, where he designed the parliament chambers (1822–4). Among the churches built by him were the neo-Norman Wolverton church (1810–13) and St Peter's, Eaton Square (1824–7), a Greek revival church. He also built country houses, including the Greek revival Coedcoch in Denbighshire (1804), Rendlesham House, Suffolk, and Cave Castle, Yorkshire.

Hakewill wrote *An Account of the Roman Villa Discovered at Northleigh, Oxfordshire*, first published in Joseph Skelton's *Antiquities of Oxfordshire* (1823) and reissued separately in 1826.

Hakewill died on 13 March 1830, and was buried at North Cray, Kent.

**John Henry Hakewill** (1810–1880), architect, was born on 12 October 1810, the son of Henry Hakewill, and was articled to his father. He exhibited at the Royal Academy between 1828 and 1879. He began to practise as an architect in 1838, and was in partnership with his brother Edward Charles Hakewill by 1840. He built churches and rectories, mainly in Wiltshire, Suffolk, and Essex, and was the architect of Stowlangtoft Hall, Suffolk, and the hospital at Bury St Edmunds. He was one of the consulting architects of the Church Building Society, and helped to set up the Architects' Benevolent Fund. He was elected FRIBA in 1842. Married to Lucy, he died on 30 August 1880 at his home, 77 Inverness Terrace, Bayswater, London. **Edward Charles Hakewill** (1816–1872), architect, was born on 20 March 1816, son of Henry Hakewill. He was admitted to the Royal Academy Schools, and was articled to Philip Hardwick RA in 1831. His first important work was the church of St John of Jerusalem, south Hackney (1845–8), and other churches he designed included St James's, Clapton, and St Peter's, Thurston, Suffolk. In 1851 he published *The Temple: an Essay on the Ark, the Tabernacle, and the Temple of Jerusalem*. In 1853 he married a widow, Mrs H. Davidson, of Cantry, daughter of W. Monkhouse. He was appointed a metropolitan district surveyor for St Clement Danes and St Mary-le-Strand, and later for the Hanover Square district, but he retired in 1867, and settled in Playford, Suffolk, where he continued to practise, building churches at Stonham Aspal and Grundisburgh, and Wickham Manor. He was elected ARIBA in 1848 and FRIBA in 1854. He died on 9 October 1872 in Playford.

L. H. CUST, *rev.* ANNE PIMLOTT BAKER

**Sources** Colvin, *Archs.* • *Dir. Brit. archs.* • Redgrave, *Artists* • [W. Papworth], ed., *The dictionary of architecture*, 11 vols. (1853–92) • *The Builder*, 30 (1872), 860 • *The Builder*, 39 (1880), 315 • Boase, *Mod. Eng. biog.*

**Archives** RIBA BAL, biography file [Edward Charles Hakewill] • RIBA BAL, drawings collection [Edward Charles Hakewill] • RIBA BAL, genealogical notes [Edward Charles Hakewill] • RIBA BAL, Royal Institute of British Architects nomination papers [Edward Charles Hakewill] • RIBA BAL, biography file [John Henry Hakewill] • RIBA BAL, drawings collection [John Henry Hakewill] • RIBA BAL, genealogical notes [John Henry Hakewill] • RIBA BAL, Royal Institute of British Architects nomination papers [John Henry Hakewill]

**Wealth at death** under £7000—John Henry Hakewill: probate, 18 Sept 1880, *CGPLA Eng. & Wales* • under £4000—Edward Charles Hakewill: probate, 7 Nov 1872, *CGPLA Eng. & Wales*

**Hakewill, Henry James** (**1813–1834**). *See under* Hakewill, James (1778–1843).

**Hakewill, James** (**1778–1843**), architectural draughtsman, was born on 25 November 1778, the second son in the family of eight surviving children of John *Hakewill (1742–

1791), landscape and portrait painter, and decorator, and his wife, Anna Maria Cook (1747–1818). The architect Henry *Hakewill (1771–1830) was his brother. He was trained as an architect and entered the Royal Academy Schools in 1807, from which date he became a regular exhibitor there. The same year he married Marie Catherine, daughter of W. Browne of Green Street, Grosvenor Square, London. She was a portrait painter and frequent exhibitor at the Royal Academy and the Society of Arts. They had four sons, the youngest of whom were Frederick Charles Hakewill, a portrait painter, and Richard Wentworth Hakewill.

James Hakewill is chiefly known for his architectural publications. In 1813 he published *The History of Windsor and its Neighbourhood*, illustrated with engravings from his own drawings. In 1816–17 he travelled in Italy, and on his return published *A Picturesque Tour of Italy* (1818–20), his best-known work, illustrated with plates engraved from watercolours painted by J. M. W. Turner, based on sketches by Hakewill. After a visit to Jamaica, Hakewill published *A Picturesque Tour in the Island of Jamaica* (1825), from his own drawings. Other works included *Plans, sections, and elevations of the abattoirs in Paris, with considerations for their adoption in London* (1828) and *An Attempt to Determine the Exact Character of Elizabethan Architecture* (1835). At the end of his life he worked on drawings for a book on the Rhine, to be a companion volume to *Italy*, but this was not completed.

Hakewill's architectural designs included the Greek doric lodge at Tatton Park, Cheshire (1833–4), and the pump room at Dorton Spa, Buckinghamshire (1834). In 1835 he submitted a design in the competition for the rebuilding of the houses of parliament in a sixteenth-century style based on Longleat House and Hatfield House. Hakewill was also said to be the author of *Caelebs Suited, or, The Stanley Letters* (1812). He died on 28 May 1843 in London, and was buried in Paddington churchyard, Middlesex.

**Arthur William Hakewill** (1808–1856), writer on architecture, was the eldest son of James Hakewill. He was educated by his father, and in 1826 became a pupil of Decimus Burton. He also studied in Paris and travelled in Italy. In 1848 he married Jane Sanders of Northill, Bedfordshire, and in the same year was appointed lecturer to the Architectural Society. Hakewill was best-known as a writer and lecturer. His works include *An Apology for the Architectural Monstrosities of London* (1835), *Plans of Thorpe Hall, Peterborough* (1851), and *Modern Tombs, or, Gleanings from the Cemeteries of London* (1851). He died on 19 June 1856. **Henry James Hakewill** (1813–1834), sculptor, the second son of James Hakewill, was born on 11 April 1813 in St John's Wood, London. He was admitted to the Royal Academy Schools in 1830, and exhibited sculptures at the Royal Academy and at the Society (later Royal Society) of British Artists, Suffolk Street, between 1832 and 1834, including a statue in armour of the time of Richard I (1832), and in 1833 a bas-relief. He also designed a statue of Earl Grey. He died on 13 March 1834. L. H. Cust, *rev.* Anne Pimlott Baker

**Sources** Colvin, *Archs.* • Redgrave, *Artists* • C. Powell, 'Topography, imagination and travel: Turner's relationship with James Hakewill', *Art History*, 5 (1982), 408–25 • Boase, *Mod. Eng. biog.* • [W. Papworth], ed., *The dictionary of architecture*, 11 vols. (1853–92) • *Dir. Brit. archs.* • J. Johnson, ed., *Works exhibited at the Royal Society of British Artists, 1824–1893, and the New English Art Club, 1888–1917*, 2 vols. (1975) • Graves, *RA exhibitors*

**Archives** RIBA BAL, biography file [Arthur William Hakewill] • RIBA BAL, drawings collection [Arthur William Hakewill] • RIBA BAL, MSS [Arthur William Hakewill]

**Hakewill, John** (**1742–1791**), painter and decorator, was born in London on 27 February 1742, the son of William Hakewill and his wife, Mary Dransfield. He was the great-grandson of William Hakewill (*bap.* 1574, *d.* 1655), master of chancery. His father was foreman to James Thornhill the younger, serjeant-painter. Hakewill studied under the book illustrator Samuel Wale, and worked in the duke of Richmond's gallery. In 1763 he gained a premium from the Society of Arts for a landscape drawing, and in 1764 another for a drawing from the antique in the duke's gallery. In 1771 he gained a silver palette for landscape painting. In 1769 he enrolled at the Royal Academy Schools. From 1765 to 1773 he exhibited with the Society of Artists, chiefly portraits, but was already establishing a reputation as a house decorator specializing in the grotesque style, a fashionable adoption of antique and Renaissance ornament. From 1766 to 1775 he worked with Sir William Chambers and John Yenn in decorating the state rooms at Blenheim Palace, Oxfordshire, and he also executed decorative works at Drayton House, Northamptonshire (after 1763), and King's Gate, near Margate, Kent (1771). Established in Broad Street, London, by 1771, he conducted a successful business decorating houses. From the mid-1770s he engaged in property investment, and he undertook some building in London. Hakewill married at St James's, Westminster, on 9 September 1770 Anna Maria Cook (1747–1818). Together, they had fifteen children, eight of whom survived to adulthood. Three sons, Henry *Hakewill, James *Hakewill, and George were architects; Henry and James trained under John Yenn. A daughter Caroline married Charles Smith; their son was Edward James Smith, surveyor to the ecclesiastical commissioners. John Hakewill died on 21 September 1791 at his home in Broad Street, London, and was buried in the family tomb in North Cray churchyard, Kent. Anna Maria Hakewill survived until 1818, and was buried with her husband. L. H. Cust, *rev.* Martin Myrone

**Sources** W. R. Hakewill, 'A history of John Hakewill', 1989, V&A, department of furniture and woodwork • E. Croft-Murray, *Decorative painting in England, 1537–1837*, 2 (1970) • E. Edwards, *Anecdotes of painters* (1808); facs. edn (1970) • PRO, PROB 11/1209 • *IGI*

**Wealth at death** over £1000: will, PRO, PROB 11/1209

**Hakewill, John Henry** (**1810–1880**). *See under* Hakewill, Henry (1771–1830).

**Hakewill, William** (*bap.* **1574**, *d.* **1655**), lawyer and politician, was baptized in the parish of St Mary Arches, Exeter, on 30 October 1574, the eldest son of John Hakewill (*d.* 1615), a merchant, and his wife, Thomazin Peryam, who was a cousin of Sir Thomas Bodley (1545–1613), founder of the Bodleian Library. George *Hakewill (*bap.* 1578, *d.* 1649), Anglican preacher, was a younger brother, and another brother, John, became mayor of Exeter. William began his legal training in Staple Inn, one of the inns of chancery. On 3 August 1598 he became a member of Lincoln's Inn, and he was called to the bar on 26 November 1606. In 1600 or 1601 he entered Exeter College, Oxford, but he apparently left without a degree. He was a member of the first Society of Antiquaries, for which he wrote two papers, both included in Thomas Hearne's *Collection of Curious Discourses*. These were 'The antiquity of the laws of this island', published in the 1720 edition, and 'Of the antiquity of the Christian religion in this island', dated 29 November 1604 and published in the 1771 edition.

**Member of parliament** Hakewill served as member of parliament for three Cornish constituencies, Bossiney (1601), Michell (1604–11), and Tregony (1614 and 1621), and for Amersham in Buckinghamshire (1624 and 1628–9). From the first he was an active speaker on a variety of topics, and on 21 November 1601 he made his mark as an opponent of monopolies, asking 'Is not Bread there? Bread quoth another? This voice seems strange quoth a third. No quoth Mr. Hackwell, but if order be not taken for these, Bread will be there, before the next Parliament' (W. Monson and H. Townsend, *Megalopsychy*, 1682, 239).

A major issue of the session of 1610 was the question of whether the king had the right to lay impositions on merchandise without parliament's agreement, and Hakewill's speech was based on a detailed study of the records. He admitted that he had previously been swayed by the arguments in *Bate's case* (1606), which had supported the king, but had changed his mind in the light of the historical evidence. He presented a formidable case for the view that duties on exports and imports could not be levied without parliament's consent. Twentieth-century commentators have remarked that, while some of his arguments were overstated, his position was substantially correct. The speech was widely circulated in manuscript, and in 1641 it was published, with Hakewill's own corrections and additions, under the title *The Libertie of the Subject Against the Pretended Power of Imposition*.

Hakewill's historical and legal expertise was called into play on a number of topics outside parliament. In 1604–5 he wrote a report, entitled *Aurum reginae*, on 'queen gold', a levy payable to the queen in addition to the sum payable to the king for certain royal favours. He acted as counsel for the barons in a dispute which arose in 1612 as to whether their younger sons should have precedence over the new rank of baronet, in which the barons were successful. He was also one of the executors of the estate of his kinsman Sir Thomas Bodley, and on 28 March 1613, the day after Bodley's funeral, the University of Oxford conferred on him the degree of MA by special grace.

Hakewill was one of the most active committee men in the Addled Parliament of 1614, and was one of those members selected on 12 May to discuss the question of impositions in an intended conference with the Lords. On 26 May he delivered the report from the committee on how to respond to the alleged attack on the Commons by Bishop Neile. As soon as he had dissolved parliament James I confiscated and burnt the notes of those who had been briefed to speak at the meeting on impositions. In spite of this, Hakewill acted as adviser to the court on several issues in the next few years. In 1615 he put forward a suggestion for solving the nation's financial problems by issuing a general pardon on a payment of £5 by each delinquent, but after two months' consideration the idea was dropped. He was consulted in 1616 on the question of whether a legal case could be taken to the court of chancery after judgment at common law. Hakewill's reply survives in the British Library (Lansdowne MS 174). Perhaps in an attempt to secure him to the court interest, he was appointed solicitor-general to the queen in May 1617. In the same month he married Elizabeth (1597/8–1652), daughter of Sir Henry Wodehouse of Waxham, in Norfolk. She was a niece of Bacon, and related by marriage to Sir Robert Killigrew. The marriage was ideally happy, and the puritan divine William Crompton dedicated his sermon *A Wedding Ring* to the couple when it was published in 1632.

In the parliament of 1621 much time was taken up with attacks on monopolies, and the punishment of Bacon and others who had abused their positions. Hakewill, along with William Noy, was given the task of searching for precedents for the Commons to prosecute delinquents against the state as well as those who offended against itself. He was one of six members who put the views of the Commons on prosecuting monopolists to the Lords on 8 March. In December, when the Commons asserted its privileges in the protestation, Hakewill strongly defended the rights of parliament as an integral part of the law, not dependent on the favour of the king. His attitude may be summed up in the sentence 'The privileges of this House are the flowers of the Crown, and we shall never sit here again if they be not maintained' (W. Notestein, F. H. Relf, and H. Simpson, eds., *Commons Debates, 1621*, 1935, 2.533). On the dissolution of parliament Hakewill was one of several members summoned before the council, but unlike Sir Edward Coke, Sir Robert Phelips, and others, was not imprisoned. He had already suffered a short period of custody in the previous August, for alleged complicity in his brother George's treatise against the Spanish marriage.

**Provincial duties** In spite of his west-country origins, Hakewill made his home in Buckinghamshire. By 1619 he was living in the village of Ellesborough, at Chequers, the house which three centuries later became the official country residence of the prime minister. In 1607 he was appointed joint receiver of the revenues of the duchy of Lancaster for Berkshire, Buckinghamshire, and other counties, and he also served as a justice of the peace on the Buckinghamshire bench. About 1633 he acquired the manor of Wyvelsgate, and it was probably at this time that he moved to Wendover. There he is reputed first to have occupied Bucksbridge House, and by 1634 was living at The Hale, which was his home until his death. Through his efforts the parliamentary representation of three Buckinghamshire constituencies, Amersham, Marlow, and Wendover, which had been in abeyance since 1309, was restored in May 1624, Hakewill himself sitting for Amersham in the 1624 parliament. During the session he acted as counsel for Pym in the dispute over his election for Chippenham, and for the earl of Middlesex in his trial before the Lords on various charges of corruption.

Hakewill was not a member of the parliaments of 1625 and 1626, but he continued to play a part in public business. He appeared for the vice-chancellor of the University of Oxford in another election case in 1626, and in 1627 he was appointed to commissions for inquiring into offices which existed in the reign of Queen Elizabeth, and for inquiring into excessive fees.

The most important work of the 1628 parliament was the drafting of the petition of right. Hakewill, representing Amersham, was prominent in the debate, and chaired the committee of the whole house which debated the Lords' proposed amendments. He was also chairman of the committee of privileges, and strongly encouraged a wider franchise in a number of cases where this was in dispute. This was in contrast to his stance in the Chippenham and University of Oxford cases, where he had argued professionally for the franchise to be limited.

Hakewill set down much of his parliamentary expertise in writing, but was in no hurry to rush into print. A treatise written about 1610 and circulated widely in manuscript was printed in 1641, from a corrupt copy, under the title *The Order and Course of Passing Bills in Parliament*. This prompted him to publish the authentic text, with the title *The Manner how Statutes are Enacted by Passing of Bills*. He also published, in 1641, a collection of materials on parliamentary procedure, entitled *The Manner of Holding Parliaments in England*. This included a translation of the manuscript, ascribed to the fourteenth century, known as *Modus tenendi parliamentum*, the title used for later enlarged editions of the work. Other writings by Hakewill which exist in manuscript have been published in modern times with the titles 'The speaker of the House of Commons', edited by C. S. Sims, and 'Speaking in the House of Commons', edited by E. R. Foster.

Apart from his parliamentary career, Hakewill was an active member of Lincoln's Inn, where he had established chambers by 1609. He was appointed a bencher on 12 November 1618 and was Lent reader in 1625. He became keenly involved in the restoration of the chapel, becoming treasurer for the project in 1622. His arms were set up, with those of others, in the west window. In 1633 he was made keeper of the black book, and he was treasurer in 1637–8. He was still contributing to the life of the inn in 1650 when he was temporarily appointed as dean of the chapel and master of the library, and also master of the walks.

Hakewill's interest in building projects was not limited to Lincoln's Inn. In April 1631 he was placed on the renewed commission for the repair of St Paul's Cathedral, and in 1634 he was appointed to a smaller working party. Late in life he was appointed to another official post when in 1647 he was made a master in chancery and nominated to sit with the commissioners of the great seal. He died, probably at The Hale, on 31 October 1655, leaving two sons, William and Robert, and was buried in Wendover church, where a monument was erected to him and his wife, who had died three years previously.

Modern writers have praised Hakewill for his painstaking research and historical integrity. His main achievement was his use of his historical skills to establish the legal foundations for the parliamentary position in the early stages of the contest for power between king and parliament which culminated in the civil war. His writings have become a significant source of parliamentary history. SHEILA DOYLE

**Sources** HoP, *Commons, 1558–1603*, 2.237–8 · W. P. Baildon, ed., *The records of the Honorable Society of Lincoln's Inn: the black books*, 2 (1898) · *CSP dom.*, *1595–7; 1603–23; 1625–8; 1631–5; 1637–8* · E. R. Foster, 'Speaking in the House of Commons', *BIHR*, 43 (1970), 35–55 · C. S. Sims, 'The speaker of the House of Commons, an early seventeenth-century tractate', *American Historical Review*, 45 (1939–40), 90–95 · E. Spencer, 'The life and works of William Hakewill', PhD diss., Washington University (St Louis, Mo), 1933 · W. Notestein, *The House of Commons, 1604–1610* (1971) · T. L. Moir, *The Addled Parliament of 1614* (1958) · R. Zaller, *The parliament of 1621: a study in constitutional conflict* (1971) · C. Russell, *Parliaments and English politics, 1621–1629* (1979) · C. G. C. Tite, *Impeachment and parliamentary judicature in early Stuart England* (1974) · D. Hirst, *The representative of the people?* (1975) · will, PRO, PROB 11/251, sig. 442

**Wealth at death** £450 in legacies, household goods; value of residence not stated: will, PRO, PROB 11/251, sig. 442

**Haking, Sir Richard Cyril Byrne** (1862–1945), army officer, was born on 24 January 1862, probably in Halifax, Yorkshire, son of the Revd Richard Haking, Church of England clergyman, and his wife, Mary Elizabeth (*née* Byrne), daughter of a Brighouse card manufacturer. He was educated at the Royal Military College, Sandhurst, and was commissioned into the 67th foot (later the Hampshire regiment) on 22 January 1881. Having served in Burma (1885–7), he gained his captaincy in 1889. On 28 September 1891 he married Rachel Violette (*b.* 1862/3), daughter of Sir Henry Burford-Hancock, chief justice of Gibraltar; they had no children. After passing through the Staff College, Camberley (1896–7), he became deputy assistant adjutant-general, Cork district (1898–9). He held a staff post in the Second South African War, going on to be a professor (1901–4; lieutenant-colonel 1903) and then deputy assistant adjutant-general (1904–6; colonel 1905) at the Staff College. During this period he established a reputation as a sound tactical thinker, demonstrated in the publication of *Company Training* (1913). Its emphasis on the moral superiority of the strategy of attack reflected the mainstream of army thought, as expressed by Douglas Haig in the 1909 field service regulations. More staff jobs (general staff officer, grade 1, 3rd division, 1906–8; brigadier-general and brigadier-general, general staff, southern command, 1908–11) were followed by the command of 5th infantry brigade (1911), with which he went to France in August 1914.

Effectively uninvolved at Mons, Haking's brigade was important in the forcing of the Petit Morin during the battle of the Marne, and was at the forefront on the Aisne, at which point Haking was wounded (16 September 1914). He returned to France in November, and in December took command of 1st division, as a major-general. The division was involved in heavy fighting in late 1914 and early 1915. In May, at the battle of Aubers Ridge, its attack failed, but the flawed overall plan and lack of artillery support were not of Haking's doing, and the failure did not adversely affect his position. Indeed, he was deemed suitable to take command of the new 11th corps, from August 1915. It was in this capacity that Haking's career has been controversial among historians. The corps' first engagement, at the battle of Loos, was a disaster. On the second day of the battle, two of its divisions were sent to attack an enemy ready and waiting for them. These troops were entirely inexperienced, as well as being exhausted and hungry following an overnight march; after suffering severe casualties they fell back in disorder. Haking escaped censure on this occasion since they were under the command of the commander-in-chief, Sir John French, at the time. He was, in any case, quick to back Haig in the subsequent intrigues against French, and after Haig became commander-in-chief, the security of Haking's position was not in doubt, even though his attempts later in the battle of the Somme to take the German position known as the Hohenzollern Redoubt were also bloody failures.

The next corps operation Haking undertook was no more successful. The attack at Fromelles (19 July 1916) was a First Army initiative intended to capture a limited amount of ground while the Germans' attention was focused on the Somme. In the event, a combination of poor staff work and tactics led to a costly failure, losses being especially heavy in the 5th Australian division. Although the Australian official historian blamed Haking for the affair, fault also lay with the First Army and the Australian division itself. In any case, Haking was nevertheless Haig's favoured candidate for the command of First Army in August 1916, although he was overruled.

The 11th corps took no part in the major battles of 1916–17, which does not argue for much faith in Haking's competence in some circles at general headquarters. The corps was transferred to Italy in November 1917, as part of the force sent under General Plumer to assist the Italians in the aftermath of their defeat at the battle of Caporetto. The 11th corps returned to the western front in March 1918, and was heavily involved in the German attack on the Lys in April. Haking's defensive dispositions served well, and the situation on his left after the rout of the Portuguese corps was contained in consequence. Haking's performance continued to be far more convincing than earlier in the war as his troops carried out the completely successful action at La Becque in June, and undertook the advance to victory under the Fifth Army, entering Lille on 17 October.

After the war Haking was variously chief of the British section of the armistice commission (1918–19), commander of the British military mission to Russia and the Baltic provinces (1919), commander allied troops in the plebiscite area of East Prussia and Danzig (1920), high commissioner of the League of Nations in Danzig (1921–3), and general officer commanding British troops, Egypt (1923–7). He retired with general's rank in 1927, having been appointed CB in 1910, KCB in 1916, KCMG in 1918, and GBE in 1921. Sir Richard Haking died at Mill Cottage, Bulford, Wiltshire, on 9 June 1945. His promise before the First World War was never realized during it, but he undoubtedly showed far more skill with the soldiers of 1918 than with those under his command in 1915–16.

A. SIMPSON

**Sources** J. E. Edmonds, ed., *Military operations, France and Belgium*, 14 vols., History of the Great War (1922–48) · T. Travers, *The killing ground* (1987) · T. Travers, *How the war was won: command and technology in the British army on the western front, 1917–1918* (1992) · A. F. Becke, ed., *Order of battle*, 1, 4 (1934–45) · J. Terraine, *Douglas Haig: the educated soldier* (1963) · J. Terraine, *Mons* (1960) · S. Bidwell and D. Graham, *Firepower* (1982) · *DNB* · *The Times* (11 June 1945) · *WWW* · m. cert. · d. cert. · *CGPLA Eng. & Wales* (1945)

**Archives** PRO, war diary and dispatches, WO144 | IWM, corresp. with Sir Henry Wilson · Lpool RO, corresp. with seventeenth earl of Derby | FILM IWM FVA, news footage

**Likenesses** F. Dodd, charcoal and watercolour, 1917, IWM

**Wealth at death** £5579 12*s*. 1*d*.: probate, 26 Nov 1945, *CGPLA Eng. & Wales*

**Hakluyt, Richard** (1552?–1616), geographer, was one of six children of Richard Hakluyt, of London, member of the Skinners' Company, and his wife, Margery. The Hakluyts were an old Herefordshire family, which in Tudor times believed its name and ancient roots were Welsh in origin. Hakluyt's father died in 1557, his mother soon after, and Hakluyt came under the care of his cousin and namesake, Richard Hakluyt the lawyer (*d*. 1591). Hakluyt was educated at Westminster School (queen's scholar, 1564) and Christ Church, Oxford (BA, 1574; MA, 1577). Ordained priest by late 1580, he was a student (that is, fellow) of Christ Church until 1586, when he obtained a prebend at Bristol Cathedral. From 1583 to 1588 he was chaplain to Sir Edward Stafford, English ambassador in Paris, and from 1590 until 1616 was rector of Wetheringsett and Blockford, Suffolk, a living in the gift of Stafford's wife, Lady Sheffield. In 1602 he was made a prebendary of Westminster Abbey. Hakluyt married, first, Douglas Cavendish, who died in 1597 and with whom he had a son, Edmond, born in 1593; and, second, in 1604, Frances Smith. Hakluyt was buried in Westminster Abbey on 26 November 1616.

Hakluyt is notable as an editor, translator, and encourager of geographical literature and was associated in various ways with the publication of over twenty-five travel books. His single most important work is *The principal navigations, voiages, traffiques and discoveries of the English nation, made by sea or over-land, to the remote and farthest distant quarters of the earth*, a massive collection of voyages, many printed for the first time, ranging from the fourth century to the recent exploits of Elizabethan seamen such as Drake and Cavendish. This appeared in two editions, the first in 1589, the second, much expanded, in three volumes, 1598–1600.

Hakluyt's interest in geography was aroused as a boy when his cousin, the lawyer, who was closely connected with overseas trading circles, responded to his curiosity about 'certeine bookes of cosmographie, with an universall mappe' on his table. Pointing to the 'seas … empires … and territories' on the map, he spoke of 'their speciall commodities, & particular wants, which by the benefit of traffike, & entercourse of merchants, are plentifully supplied', and then directed the young Hakluyt to a Bible and Psalm 107:

> where I read, that they which go downe to the sea in ships, and occupy by the great waters, they see the works of the Lord, and his woonders in the deepe, &c. Which words of the Prophet together with my cousins discourse (things of high and rare delight to my yong nature) tooke in me so deepe an impression, that I constantly resolved, if ever I were preferred to the University … I would by Gods assistance prosecute that knowledge and kinde of literature.

Hakluyt kept this resolution, reading at Oxford 'whatsoever printed or written discoveries and voyages' he found extant 'in Greeke, Latine, Italian, Spanish, Portugall, French, or English' (Taylor, 2.396–7).

At Oxford, and until 1586, Hakluyt received awards from the Clothworkers' Company, whose sometime master, Richard Staper, provided material on the Turkey trade for the *Principal Navigations*. He became known to Sir Francis Walsingham (secretary of state and an associate of Hakluyt the lawyer), Sir Francis Drake, Sir Humphrey Gilbert, Walter Ralegh, and others active in promoting overseas ventures. In 1584 Hakluyt presented the queen with his 'Discourse of western planting', elaborating ambitious colonial projects in North America and written at Ralegh's direction. It is untypical of Hakluyt's work in general, being an extended piece of his own prose and designed for manuscript circulation only, to express the interests of a particular group at court. Much discussed by modern commentators as a pre-eminent Elizabethan colonial tract, the 'Discourse' had no discernible political impact in Hakluyt's time.

The earliest book associated with Hakluyt is John Florio's translation of Jacques Cartier's *Shorte … Narration* of French discoveries in America, published with Hakluyt's assistance in 1580. Hakluyt's own first book, *Divers Voyages Touching the Discoverie of America*, containing useful information for prospective colonization projects, appeared in 1582, coinciding with Gilbert's drive for investors in his North American ventures. It was dedicated to Hakluyt's Christ Church contemporary, Philip Sidney, who remarked to Stafford that he 'was haulf perswaded to enter into the journey of Sir Humphry Gilbert very eagerli; whereunto your Mr Hackluit hath served for a very good trumpet' (Payne, 5). Sidney's friend, the poet-courtier, Edward Dyer, was to be exceptionally important to Hakluyt in encouraging the *Principal Navigations*.

Although Hakluyt contemplated following Gilbert to America, his only travel abroad was to the embassy in Paris. There he met the French royal cosmographer, André Thevet, who lent him René Goulaine de Laudonnière's manuscript *L'Histoire notable de la Floride*, printed in 1586 at Hakluyt's expense and in 1587 in an English translation by Hakluyt. He learned much from Dom Antonio, the exiled claimant to the Portuguese throne. Hakluyt's greatest editorial achievement during these years was his new edition (in the original Latin) of *De orbe novo … decades octo* (1587) by Peter Martyr (Pietro Martire d'Anghiera), used subsequently by Michael Lok in making the first complete English translation, *De Novo Orbe, or the Historie of the West Indies* (1612). Hakluyt dedicated his Peter Martyr to Ralegh, and it was through Hakluyt's intercession that Theodor de Bry published Thomas Harriot's *Briefe … Report* of Ralegh's Virginia colony with illustrations by Ralegh's draughtsman, John White, in 1590.

Hakluyt owed much to Walsingham's support and probably gathered intelligence for him in Paris; the first edition of the *Principal Navigations* was both dedicated to and licensed for publication by him. After Walsingham's death (1590), the patronage of Sir Robert Cecil (secretary of state 1596–1608) was increasingly important to Hakluyt, especially in obtaining ecclesiastical preferment. Volume one of the second edition of the *Principal Navigations* was dedicated to the lord admiral, Lord Howard of Effingham, but the other two were dedicated to Cecil: 'I cannot but acknowledge my selfe much indebted for your favourable letters heretofore written in my behalfe in mine honest causes' (Taylor, 2.462–3). Referring to the demands of 'my profession of divinitie, the care of my family' (ibid., 2.474), Hakluyt also acknowledged the scholarly assistance of his friend, John Pory, whose English edition of Leo Africanus's *Geographical Historie of Africa* appeared with Hakluyt's commendation in 1600; it was dedicated to Cecil, as was Hakluyt's translation of Antonio Galvão's *Discoveries of the World* (1601).

In the early years of the seventeenth century Hakluyt advised the East India Company and invested in the Virginia Company, interests reflected in *The Journall … of Jacob Corneliszen Neck* (1601), translated at Hakluyt's persuasion to assist East Indian voyagers, and *Virginia Richly Valued* (1609), translated by Hakluyt and dedicated to the Virginia Company. In 1606 he received, but did not take up, a dispensation to go to Virginia without surrendering his ecclesiastical appointments in England.

Hakluyt is sometimes seen as an imperial propagandist, but among his motives simple patriotic pride and a desire to add to geographical knowledge need not be discounted. Referring to the projected *Principal Navigations* in 1587, Hakluyt hailed the fortune of the Spanish in having Peter Martyr as chronicler of their deeds overseas and pointed to the need:

> to collect in orderly fashion the maritime records of our own countrymen, now lying scattered and neglected, and … bring them to the light of day in a worthy guise, to the end that posterity … may at last be inspired to seize the opportunity offered to them of playing a worthy part. (Taylor, 2.369)

In the first edition of the *Principal Navigations* he stresses its use of firsthand reports:

> I have referred every voyage to his author: for I am not ignorant of Ptolemies assertion, that *Peregrinationis historia* [the history of travel], and not those wearie volumes bearing the titles of universall cosmographie … most untruly and unprofitablie ramassed and hurled together, is that which must bring us to the certayne and full discoverie of the world.

He includes 'the navigations onely of our owne nation' and excludes voyages 'neere home' or 'neither of search and discoverie of strange coasts, the chiefe subject of this my labour' (Taylor, 2.402–3). (The second edition relaxed these criteria to include naval actions such as the defeat of the Armada.) In its concern to discover an English past the *Principal Navigations* may be associated with the work of William Camden and other antiquarians, although his book's English focus should not distract from Hakluyt's many continental European contacts and intellectual debts. Several hundred copies survive today, suggesting that it was printed in relatively large numbers; contemporary references and provenances indicate a wide circulation, at least among élites.

Hakluyt's successor was Samuel Purchas, whose *Hakluytus Posthumus, or, Purchas his Pilgrimes* (1625) is much indebted to Hakluyt's papers, obtained by Purchas some time after 1616. The *Principal Navigations* continues to be an invaluable source for narratives not otherwise preserved, while Hakluyt's achievement as an editor is commemorated by the Hakluyt Society, founded and named after him in 1846 to publish historic voyages and geographical texts. ANTHONY PAYNE

**Sources** D. B. Quinn, ed., *The Hakluyt handbook*, 2 vols. (1974) • G. B. Parks, *Richard Hakluyt and the English voyages*, 2nd edn (1961) • A. Payne, '"Strange, remote and farre distant countreys": the travel books of Richard Hakluyt', *Journeys through the market: travel, travellers and the book trade*, ed. R. Myers and M. Harris (1999), 1–37 • E. G. R. Taylor, ed., *The original writings and correspondence of the two Richard Hakluyts*, 2 vols. (1935) • P. A. Neville-Sington and A. Payne, 'An interim census of surviving copies of Hakluyt's *Divers voyages* and *Principal navigations*', in A. Payne, *Richard Hakluyt and his books*, Hakluyt Society (1997), 25–76 • R. Helgerson, 'The voyages of a nation', *Forms of nationhood: the Elizabethan writing of England* (1992), 149–91 • G. D. Ramsay, 'Clothworkers, Merchants Adventurers and Richard Hakluyt', *EngHR*, 92 (1977), 504–21 • E. Lynam, ed., *Richard Hakluyt and his successors*, Hakluyt Society, 2nd ser., 93 (1946) • J. Parker, *Books to build an empire: a bibliographical history of English overseas interests to 1620* (1965) • R. C. Bridges and P. E. H. Hair, eds., *Compassing the vaste globe of the earth: studies in the history of the Hakluyt Society, 1846–1996*, Hakluyt Society, 183 (1996) • HoP, *Commons*, 1509–58, 2.273–4

**Hákon Paulsson** [Hákon Pálsson], **earl of Orkney** (*d. c.***1126**). *See under* Magnús Erlendsson, earl of Orkney (1075/6–1116?).

**Halas, John** [*formerly* Janos Halasz] (**1912–1995**), film animator, was born in Budapest, Hungary, on 16 April 1912, the son of Gyozo Halasz (also known as Victor Halasz), journalist, and his wife, Bertha. He was educated in Budapest. At the age of eighteen he moved to Paris, where he studied at the Académie des Beaux-Arts and contributed freelance drawings to various illustrated magazines. He returned home in 1932 and joined the animation studio formed by George Pal. There he did his first animation, making advertising shorts with paper cut-outs. Pal would later develop the different idea of animated puppets, creating 'Puppetoons' at first for Horlicks malted milk advertisements, and eventually moving to Hollywood to produce such award winning features as *Destination Moon*, which would blend live action with puppets. Halas left Pal in 1933 to study modern art at The Studio, a private school of graphic design run by Laszlo Moholy-Nagy and Alexander Bortnyik as a split-off from the famous German group, the Bauhaus. In 1935 he established his own animation studio in Hungary but could not expand beyond making cinema advertisements for cigarettes and alcohol. However, one of his colour cartoons was seen in London, leading to an invitation to come to England to work for British Animated Films, a small company run by photographers Trigg and Denes and financier Weisbach. There, working on the Technicolor cartoon *Music Man*, released in 1938 and directed by Henry Elwis, Halas met his future wife, Joy Batchelor, for the first time.

**Joy Ethel Batchelor** (1914–1991), film animator, was born at 22 Euston Avenue, Watford, Hertfordshire, on 12 May 1914, the daughter of Edward Joseph Batchelor, lithographer, and his wife, Ethel Amy, *née* Herbert. After a course in art and design at the local art college she began to submit her freelance sketches to the *Daily Mirror*, where her work pleased the art editor, Donald Zec. She entered animation working for Champion Films, the company of the Australian cartoonist and producer Denis Connolly. The result, *Robin Hood*, was shown in late 1935 but was not reviewed by the trade or any other press. 'There was no paper work', she recalled, 'we drew directly onto the celluloids with ink' (BECTU tape). In 1936 she saw an advertisement placed in the *Evening Standard* by John Halas, 'Animators wanted'. She applied and got the job.

The first film that Halas and Batchelor made together, *Music Man*, was based on the life of the composer Liszt. 'The design was good, the colour was nice, the script terrible!' Batchelor remembered (BECTU tape). The company went out of business, and Halas and Batchelor went to Hungary together. Prospects were not much better and with war in the offing they returned to England, where Halas drew a few cartoons for the pocket magazine *Lilliput*. On 27 April 1940 they married at the register office in Paddington, London.

In 1940, with the wartime shortage of newsprint, the large advertising agency J. Walter Thompson decided to enter the cinema commercial field. Halas and Batchelor joined the film unit, but also formed their own company, Halas and Batchelor, and in 1941 produced *Carnival in the Clothes Cupboard* for Lux Soap. They also made their first entertainment short, *Pocket Cartoon*. In 1942 the wartime Ministry of Information films division, headed by Jack Beddington, contracted them to make a series of propaganda shorts for cinema release. Produced under the aegis of the documentary makers Realist Films, *Filling the Gap*, sponsored by the Ministry of Agriculture and Fisheries, exhorted cinema-goers to cultivate allotments, while *Dustbin Parade* concluded with the then urgent message 'Mobilize your scrap!' The little company now supported a staff of animators that included Vera Linnecar, Kathleen Murphy, and Wally Crook, with their original music composed by Ernst Meyer and Matyas Seiber. The first British feature-length cartoon film was made by the team in 1945, the sixty-five-minute *Handling Ships*, sponsored by the Admiralty. Using animated drawings and models, this specialized semi-documentary directed by Bob Privett was never seen by the general public. The same applied to their second feature, *Water for Fire Fighting* (1949), sponsored by the fire brigade. Their first successful series starring a regular character, Charley (voiced by comedian Harold Berens), was a run of six sponsored by the peacetime equivalent of the old Ministry of Information, the central office of information. The first was *Charley's New Town* (1947). Finally in 1949 they broke free from governmental sponsorship with *Heave Away my Johnny*, a sing-song short for children's cinema clubs. Advertising films came back with *The Flu-ing Squad* (1951) for Aspro tablets.

Halas's personal devotion to modern art at last found its way onto the animated screen when he produced four shorts known as the Poet and Painter series for the Festival of Britain in 1951. With the combined talents of artists Mervyn Peake and Henry Moore, actors Michael Redgrave and Eric Portman, the series lacked only colour. A year later they made the first British cartoon in three dimensions, Edward Lear's *The Owl and the Pussycat*. In 1954 came the first British feature cartoon proper, produced by the American entrepreneur Louis de Rochemont. This was *Animal Farm*, from the fantastic novel by George Orwell. Although the styling was truly too Disneyesque for most purists, the film was also a *tour de force* for actor Maurice Denham, who supplied all the voices.

Halas and Batchelor entered the new world of television with excitement. First came a series with the ungainly name *Habatales* (1959), then a series about Foo-foo (1960), designed without dialogue for the international market. Paper sculpture was employed for the series *Snip and Snap* (1961), but easily their finest hour came with *Tales of Hoffnung* (1965), a colour series animating the extremely amusing musical cartoons of Gerard Hoffnung, the best of which was *The Hoffnung Symphony Orchestra*. In 1966 Batchelor directed the feature-length adaptation of Gilbert and Sullivan's operetta *Ruddigore*, but frankly without great acclaim. Meanwhile their company had been sold to a television consortium, and although their name appeared on countless television series from *The Lone Ranger* to *Popeye*, these had nothing to do with either partner. Halas's final feature was made for German television, animating the strip-cartoon pioneer Wilhelm Busch and his famous characters *Max und Moritz* (1977).

Continuing to pioneer every advance in animation including computerization, Halas was also the founder and president of the International Animated Film Association and he was appointed OBE in 1972. He was the author of numerous books and articles on animation, including *How to Cartoon* (1959), *Computer Animation* (1974), *Visual Scripting* (1977), and *The Contemporary Animator* (1991). Joy Batchelor died at their home, 6 Holford Road, Hampstead, London, on 14 May 1991, after a long illness. John Halas died, also in London, on 20 January 1995. They were survived by their son and daughter.

As animators and later producers of animated cartoon films, Halas and Batchelor held the record for UK production, having overseen some 2000 films in the genre during half a century in partnership. Together they made every kind of animated film, from official shorts during wartime to cinema and television commercials, three-dimensional experiments, 'art films', series for television, and the first British feature-length cartoons. They were sometimes hailed as the British equivalent of America's Walt Disney. Nevertheless it has rightly been said that 'they remained curiously European in their styling, design, colouring and humour' (*The Independent*, 25 Jan 1995).

Denis Gifford

**Sources** *WWW*, 1991–5 · *The Times* (16 May 1991) [Joy Ethel Batchelor] · *The Times* (13 Feb 1995) · *The Independent* (25 Jan 1995) · b. cert. [Joy Batchelor] · m. cert. · d. cert. [Joy Halas] · BECTU tape, BFI [John Halas] · BECTU tape, BFI [Joy Batchelor]
**Archives** FILM BFI NFTVA | SOUND BFI, BECTU tape interviews
**Likenesses** double portrait, photograph (with Batchelor), repro. in *The Independent* · photograph (Joy Ethel Batchelor), repro. in *The Times* (16 May 1991) · photograph, repro. in *The Times* (13 Feb 1995)
**Wealth at death** £893,914: probate, 24 April 1995, *CGPLA Eng. & Wales* · £116,092—Joy Ethel Batchelor: probate, 22 Nov 1991, *CGPLA Eng. & Wales*

**Halcomb, John** (1790–1852), serjeant-at-law, was the son of John Halcomb of Marlborough, a coach proprietor. He studied law in chambers with the future judges John Patteson and John Taylor Coleridge, and was called to the bar at the Inner Temple in June 1823. He joined the western circuit.

In 1826 Halcomb published *A Report of the Trials … in the Causes of Rowe and Grenfell*, which dealt with legal problems relating to Cornish copper mines; in the same year a second work appeared, *A Practical Measure of Relief from the Present System of the Poor Law*, which was submitted to parliament. Halcomb entered parliament in 1833 as the Conservative member for Dover, having earlier stood several times as the anti-Catholic candidate for the town. On the dissolution in 1835, he unsuccessfully contested the borough of Warwick as a Liberal candidate and lost his seat.

In the following year, drawing on his parliamentary experience (he may well have acted as a parliamentary draftsman), Halcomb published his most significant work, *A Practical Treatise of Passing Private Bills through both Houses of Parliament* (1836). This 362 page manual was intended to instruct lawyers unfamiliar with such work in the business of a parliamentary agent. Considerably longer than the standard work which it superseded, C. T. Ellis's *The Sollicitor's Instructor in Parliament Concerning Estate and Inclosure Bills* (1799), Halcomb's work reflected the great development which standing orders had undergone since 1800.

In 1839 Halcomb was made serjeant-at-law, but his continuing political ambition is said to have damaged his legal career. He died at New Radnor in Wales on 3 November 1852, leaving a widow and four sons.

Francis Watt, *rev.* Joanne Potier

**Sources** *Law Times* (13 Nov 1852), 95 · *WWBMP* · Boase, *Mod. Eng. biog.* · D. L. Rydz, *The parliamentary agents: a history* (1979), 46–7
**Archives** BL, letters to Sir Robert Peel, Add. MSS 40399–40565, *passim* · U. Southampton L., letters to duke of Wellington

**Halcrow, Sir William Thomson** (1883–1958), civil engineer, was born on 4 July 1883 in Sunderland, the only son of John Andrew Halcrow, master seaman in the merchant service, and his wife, Jane Halcrow. After education at

George Watson's College, Edinburgh, and Edinburgh University, he began his engineering career as a pupil to P. W. Meik, the senior partner of Thomas Meik & Sons, a leading firm of consulting engineers in London.

Early in his training Halcrow became an assistant on the Kinlochleven hydroelectric works, thus beginning his connection with a branch of the engineering profession to which he was destined to make considerable contributions. In 1905 he became resident engineer at Pozzuoli, Italy, for the reconstruction of a deep-water pier in reinforced concrete—one of the earliest uses of the material for such a purpose—following which he was engaged as an assistant engineer on the construction of the Loch Leven water-power works, Scotland, before gaining further experience abroad in Italy, Portugal, and Argentina.

In 1910 Halcrow became chief engineer to the contracting firm of Topham, Jones, and Railton, his major work being the construction of the King George V graving dock at Singapore, and in 1913 survey work for the dredging of the approach channel to the Rosyth Dockyard then under construction. During the war he was engaged on several Admiralty projects in Orkney and the Shetlands. At that time he recommended an effective eastern barrier to Scapa Flow, a project only undertaken after the sinking of the aircraft-carrier *Royal Oak* during the Second World War. Afterwards he worked on the construction of the Johore causeway which joined Singapore Island to the mainland of Malaya, and on the design and construction of the port of Beira. In 1921 he resumed his connection with engineering consultancy, becoming a partner with C. S. Meik; the firm was known as C. S. Meik and Halcrow until 1944 when, after his knighthood, it was renamed Sir William Halcrow & Partners. He served as senior partner until his retirement in 1955.

Throughout his career as a consultant, Halcrow's work was highly varied in type and locality. He was joint consulting engineer with Sir Harley Dalrymple-Hay for the London Passenger Transport Board's tube railways, and he carried out the extensions of the Bakerloo Line to Finchley Road and the Northern Line as far as East Finchley. As a consultant under the Reservoirs (Safety Provisions) Act he inspected many dams for water-power companies and advised on canal reservoirs for the railways and Birmingham Canal navigations.

During the Second World War Halcrow's firm designed and constructed deep-level tunnel shelters in London for the Ministry of Home Security. He also acted as head of a group of consulting engineers who designed and constructed ordnance factories and storage depots. He was also associated with the War Office, as a member of the cabinet engineering advisory committee, on the design and construction of the 'Phoenix' units which formed part of Mulberry harbours for the invasion of Europe. In 1944 he was chairman of a panel of engineers appointed to report on the Severn barrage tidal power scheme. In 1950 he advised the New Zealand government on traffic problems in the city of Auckland. In 1951 he was chairman of a panel of engineers reporting on the Kariba Gorge and Kafue River hydro-electric projects in Rhodesia.

Halcrow was president of the engineering section of the British Association in 1947, president of the Smeatonian Society of Civil Engineers (1953), and vice-president of the commission on large dams of the World Power Conference (1955). He held many other appointments, among which were colonel-commandant of the engineer and railway staff corps Royal Engineers (TA), member of the advisory council of the Department of Scientific and Industrial Research, chairman of the Hydraulics Research Board; and member of the executive of the National Physical Laboratory and of the Royal Fine Arts Commission.

Halcrow became a member of council of the Institution of Civil Engineers in 1934, a vice-president in 1943, and was president in 1946–7; in 1930 he received the Telford gold medal for his paper on the Lochaber (water-power) scheme. In 1937–9 he was president of the British section of the Société des Ingénieurs Civils de France, whose gold medal he was awarded in 1939. He was a chevalier of the Légion d'honneur and an officer of the order of the Black Star.

In 1921 Halcrow married Phoebe Mary, daughter of Alfred Henry Roberts, civil engineer; they had one son. Halcrow and his wife eventually separated, and Elizabeth (Bunty), widely known as Lady Halcrow, was his companion for much of the last decade of his life.

A reserved and impersonal man, Halcrow was neat, shrewd, and authoritative. He was an accomplished pianist and organist. His greatest gift was the ability to attract talented engineers to work with him, leading in consequence to the development of a firm of consulting engineers of high international reputation in several areas of civil engineering. He died at his Folkestone home, Milden House, Dixwell Road, on 31 October 1958.

F. A. Whitaker, *rev.* Alan Muir Wood

**Sources** *PICE*, new ser., 12 (1958–9), 233–5 · private information (1971) · personal knowledge (2004) · *CGPLA Eng. & Wales* (1958) · d. cert.

**Archives** Commonwealth War Graves Commission, Maidenhead, papers relating to work for Imperial War Graves Commission

**Likenesses** J. Gunn, oils, 1947, Inst. CE · W. Stoneman, photographs, NPG

**Wealth at death** £140,537 13*s*.: probate, 4 Dec 1958, *CGPLA Eng. & Wales*

**Haldane, Alexander** (1800–1882), newspaper proprietor and barrister, was born in Edinburgh on 15 October 1800, the second of three sons, one of whom died young, and the fifth of nine children of James Alexander *Haldane (1768–1851), pastor and religious writer, and his first wife, Mary (1771–1819), daughter of Major Alexander Joass of Culleonard, Banffshire. His half-brother was the physician Daniel Rutherford *Haldane. He was educated at Edinburgh high school and the University of Edinburgh before moving to London, where he entered the Inner Temple in 1820. In August 1822 he married Emma Corsbie (1800–1867), youngest daughter of Joseph Hardcastle of Hatcham House, Surrey, a merchant and treasurer of the London Missionary Society; they had one son, James Robert Alexander Chinnery-*Haldane, later Episcopalian bishop of Argyll and the Isles, and five daughters.

Haldane's personal convictions and family connections caused him quickly to assume a prominent role on the more extreme wing of Anglican evangelicalism. He was associated with Edward Irving and Henry Drummond and participated in the early prophetic conferences at Albury, but later distanced himself from the movement that was to result in the formation of the Catholic Apostolic church. In 1828 he began to write for the fledgeling *Record* newspaper, and subsequently became its chief proprietor and the dominant influence on editorial policy for half a century. Under his leadership *The Record* was the major public voice of a new school of evangelicals that emerged about 1830. The Recordites, as they were called, followed Haldane in affirming the verbal inspiration of the Bible, attacking liberal theology and Catholicism, maintaining a rigorous sabbatarianism, and staunchly defending the established church. Haldane further contributed to evangelical self-awareness by writing the lives of his father and of his uncle, Robert *Haldane, and describing their careers as itinerant evangelists.

Although never an MP Haldane was keenly interested in politics and was an active force in a variety of parliamentary and ecclesiastical networks. He was a close friend and adviser of Anthony Ashley Cooper, seventh earl of Shaftesbury, and through him, between 1855 and 1865, influenced the church appointments made by the third Viscount Palmerston. A vigorous and intellectually acute controversialist, he worked with great energy to sustain the protestant character of the English church and nation, and hence contributed substantially to the entrenched conservatism of Victorian Anglican evangelicalism. Haldane died at 118 Westbourne Terrace, London, on 19 July 1882 and was buried at Paddington cemetery on 24 July. JOHN WOLFFE, *rev.*

**Sources** A. Haldane, *Memoirs of the lives of Robert Haldane of Airthrey, and of his brother, James Alexander Haldane* (1852) · *The Record* (28 July 1882) · J. A. L. Haldane, *The Haldanes of Gleneagles* (1929) · private information (1993)

**Wealth at death** £7961 19*s*. 11*d*.: probate, 16 Aug 1882, *CGPLA Eng. & Wales*

**Haldane, Archibald Richard Burdon** (1900–1982), lawyer and historian, was born at 55 Melville Street, Edinburgh, on 18 November 1900, the youngest child of Sir William Stowell Haldane (1864–1951), lawyer and landowner, younger brother of Richard Burdon Haldane, Viscount Haldane of Cloan, and Professor John Scott Haldane. His mother was Margaret Edith Stuart Nelson (1870–1943), daughter of Thomas Nelson of Achnacloich. They had three sons and a daughter. His father, besides being an active lawyer in Edinburgh, had built up the estate of Foswell, near Auchterarder, a mixture of farm and rough woodland adjacent to the existing Haldane estate of Cloan, and connections between the two branches were closely maintained. Haldane missed service in the First World War, but his emotional attachment to his eldest brother, Patrick, killed in 1915, meant that the war accentuated his natural inclination to a traditional way of life. He had an old-fashioned education: eleven years at Edinburgh Academy (1906–17), then Winchester College, followed by Balliol College, Oxford (1919–23), where he took a second in modern history, and Edinburgh University, where he gained an LLB (1925), finally entering his father's legal firm, W. and F. Haldane, writers to the signet, in 1925. He became a writer to the signet in 1926 and a partner in the firm in 1927.

Haldane had no particular liking for the law, and definitely disliked litigation, but his firm's status brought it a considerable amount of factorial work. This involved travel and opportunities for getting to know the Scottish countryside—as did his favourite recreation, trout fishing. The Foswell estate of 1100 acres also gave him a base for other outdoor pursuits: shooting, riding to hounds, and country walking. At Oxford he had rowed for his college's first boat. He was a man of medium build with considerable muscle power.

Haldane's most striking characteristic was his willingness to undertake useful tasks. He chaired Edinburgh city's library committee, was a trustee of the National Library of Scotland, and chaired the Scottish branch of the Legal and General Insurance Company. His special area of outside work was for the Trustee Savings Bank structure and he eventually (1944) became chairman of its inspection committee. This position meant meetings in London, which gave him long evening opportunities for research and writing. He had already put in print two memoirs of his fishing experiences with *The Path by the Water* (1944) and *By Many Waters* (1946), to which he later added *By River, Stream and Loch* (1973).

On 12 December 1941 Haldane married Janet Macrae Simpson-Smith (*b*. 1906), a solicitor. For two years (1942–3) they both worked in London as principals in the civil service, he in the Ministry of Production, she in Supply. In 1944 they returned to Scotland, where they had a daughter and a son. Haldane began to use his Oxford historical training. He produced three considerable books, very much in his own mode and well supported by evidence: *The Drove Roads of Scotland* (1952), *New Ways through the Glens* (1962), and *Three Centuries of Scottish Posts* (1971). Edinburgh University gave him a DLitt in 1950.

*The Drove Roads* used Haldane's detailed knowledge of the Scottish valleys and tracks. He had been able to meet some old men who had taken cattle by them on the long journey to market. The book marked a new interest in the history of Scotland after the union. His second was on an important theme, the creation of the parliamentary roads in the Scottish highlands and of the Caledonian Canal—a project which raised funds from Scottish landowners and also from the state. New methods of accounting and of financial security had to be devised. Communications were important in accelerating Scotland's belated economic growth. The third book was a detailed survey of the growth of a public service largely taken for granted today, well documented and elegantly written. The problems of research while Haldane's main work was for the legal partnership were met by special library concessions, probably the result of long-standing goodwill arising from his committee work. His discovery of the Scottish end of the correspondence about the roads was based on his detailed knowledge of legal Edinburgh.

Haldane's work was paralleled by a general revival of public interest in Scottish economic and social history in the 1960s and 1970s. There were government grants for research. The grant-giving bodies encouraged their beneficiaries to relate social history to other social sciences, but Haldane's work stood apart from this trend: he stuck to the techniques and concepts he had acquired at Oxford. His books show that there was still a lot of mileage in the careful handling of records and a detailed knowledge of the physical setting of his stories. Haldane died on 18 October 1982. His wife survived him.

ROSALIND MITCHISON

**Sources** personal knowledge (2004) • private information (2004) [Haldane family] • *WWW, 1981–90* • E. Lemon, ed., *The Balliol College register, 1916–1967*, 4th edn (privately printed, Oxford, 1969) • m. cert.
**Archives** NL Scot., notes and corresp. relating to publications
**Likenesses** A. Davidson-Houston, portrait, *c.*1975, priv. coll.
**Wealth at death** Foswell estate, mixed forestry and farms, 1100 acres: private information

**Haldane** [*née* Franken]**, Charlotte** (1894–1969), writer, was born on 27 April 1894 in Sydenham, south London, the elder daughter of German Jewish immigrants Joseph Franken (*d. c.*1935) and his wife, Mathilde (*c.*1873–*c.*1955), whose father, Julius Saarbach, had migrated from Bavaria to New York in 1848. Joseph Franken left the Rhineland for London at fourteen to become a successful fur dealer. Mathilde Saarbach left New York at nineteen to live in Frankfurt, married Joseph Franken there in July 1893, and returned with him to London.

Charlotte Franken was educated at South Hampstead high school and, after the family moved to Antwerp in 1906, at the Allgemeine Deutsche Schule, where she first experienced overt antisemitism. On their return to London in 1910 her father's business failed and she could not attend Bedford College for Women as planned. With the outbreak of the First World War he was declared an enemy alien, and escaped internment only by fleeing to America. Franken stayed in London, isolated by her German surname. She worked as a secretary and in 1916, under the pseudonym Franklyn, published her first story. On 30 July 1918 at St Marylebone parish church she married John McLeod Burghes (*c.*1894–*c.*1930), a soldier from Purley, whom she supported throughout an increasingly problematic marriage. Their son, Ronald John McLeod Burghes, was born on 27 January 1919 when she was freelancing as Charlotte Burghes. She became a *Daily Express* reporter in 1920, and said she survived as one of the first newswomen on Fleet Street because her father had taught her to drink like a man (Adamson, 30). A prototype of the woman whose way was opened largely because of the social transformations of the war, her articles called for divorce law reform, contraceptive access for women, the right for married women to work, state-subsidized motherhood, and research into children's education.

**Charlotte Haldane (1894–1969)**, by unknown photographer, 1938 [left, with her son Ronnie Burghes, Maria Teresa Gouzalez, and some Basque children]

In 1924 she interviewed the geneticist John Burdon Sanderson *Haldane (1892–1964), and married him on 11 May 1926, after a divorce which quoted Haldane as co-respondent and cost him his readership at Cambridge, in 1925, though he was reinstated in 1926. She left the *Express* staff to freelance from their home at Roebuck House in Old Chesterton, Cambridge, and ran Science News Service, which she had started in 1925 to prepare J. B. S. Haldane's articles for the popular press. Fluent in French and German, she quickly built the service into a much needed international syndicate through which she popularized scientific discoveries.

Haldane's first novel, the dystopia *Man's World* (1926) was a source for Aldous Huxley's *Brave New World*. It was followed by a controversial book on motherhood, and the novels *Brother to Bert* (1930) and *I Bring not Peace* (1932), in which she turned the novelist Malcolm Lowry into her protagonist. Lowry was part of Haldane's Cambridge salon, which included William Empson and other students associated with the journals *Venture* and *Experiment*, scientists, and musicians. In 1932 the Haldanes moved to 16 Park Village East, London, and she quickly published three books, of which the autobiographical *Youth is a Crime* (1934) is the best.

The rise of fascism affected her profoundly: after Hitler became chancellor of Germany she committed herself increasingly to the British Communist Party; when the Spanish Civil War broke out she energetically supported the republicans. She joined the party in 1937 after her son volunteered for the International Brigades. That spring she worked clandestinely in Paris for the British battalion; in London she initiated and became honorary secretary for the Dependants and Wounded Aid Committee. In 1938 she went to Spain as Paul Robeson's guide, to Marseilles to speak at the World Congress Against Fascism, and to China to report for the *Daily Herald*. She then edited *Woman Today* for the British Women's Committee Against War and Fascism.

When Hitler attacked the Soviet Union in June 1941 Haldane became war correspondent for the *Daily Sketch*. She was the only woman on the first British war convoy to Russia, where she joined a group of distinguished American and British journalists. She had visited Russia in 1927 and questioned its political system. A socialist and ardent anti-fascist, she was never a Stalinist and in 1941 her party sympathies were severely challenged by the difference between what she had been led to believe and what she saw. She was so profoundly shocked that she left the party on her return. In *Russian Newsreel* (1942), her account of the Soviet Union at war, she avoided her personal political dilemma, which she discussed only in 1949 in her autobiography, *Truth will out*. The difficulties she experienced after leaving the party included, in November 1945, divorce from J. B. S. Haldane (who joined the party officially when she left and remained a prominent communist into the fifties), and problems getting her court awarded alimony. No vulgar McCarthyite, she none the less spoke bitterly against the party in that book.

In August 1943 a friend secured her a job in the BBC's Eastern Service. In 1951 she wrote the first of nine biographies; the last was published posthumously. She called them potboilers to indicate her financial need, but those about creative, unorthodox women such as Marie d'Agoult (*The Galleyslaves of Love*, 1957) and Celeste Mogador (*Daughter of Paris*, 1961), were among her best books. Nearly blind from macular degeneration and almost penniless, she died of pneumonia on 16 March 1969 at Flat 164, 20 Abbey Road, London. Her body was cremated.

Charlotte Haldane was a talented, versatile writer whose generous use of autobiographical material in her fiction turned personal experience into political discussion. Honest and radical, her novels and journalism form a unique record of the most pressing social movements of the century, especially as they affected women.

JUDITH ADAMSON

**Sources** J. Adamson, *Charlotte Haldane: Woman writer in a man's world* (1998) • C. Haldane, *Truth will out* (1949) • UCL, J. B. S. Haldane MSS • *CGPLA Eng. & Wales* (1969) • private information (2004) [family]

**Archives** BBC WAC, file • MHS Oxf., MSS | Marx Library, London, British Battalion MSS • UCL, J. B. S. Haldane MSS | FILM BFI NFTVA, documentary footage | SOUND BL NSA, 'My husband the professor', M516W BD1 • BL NSA, documentary recording

**Likenesses** photograph, 1938, priv. coll. [*see illus.*] • R. de Maistre, watercolour, 1966, priv. coll.; repro. in Adamson, *Charlotte Haldane* • photographs, repro. in Adamson, *Charlotte Haldane* • photographs, repro. in *Daily Express* (*c*.1922–1926) • photographs, repro. in *Sunday Express* (*c*.1922–1926)

**Wealth at death** £3202: probate, 19 Aug 1969, *CGPLA Eng. & Wales*

**Haldane, Daniel Rutherford** (1824–1887), physician, son of James Alexander *Haldane (1768–1851), Baptist minister and author, and his second wife, Margaret Rutherford (1788–1867), daughter of Professor Daniel *Rutherford (1749–1819), physician and botanist, was born in Edinburgh on 27 March 1824. He was the half-brother of Alexander *Haldane (1800–1882), barrister and newspaper proprietor. Daniel Haldane was educated in Edinburgh, at the high school and then at the university. After graduating MD in 1848 he worked as resident physician at the Edinburgh Royal Infirmary before travelling abroad to study in Vienna and Paris.

On his return Haldane again entered the infirmary, to serve as assistant physician and then as staff physician; when he retired he became consulting physician. For some years he was also pathologist to the infirmary. In addition he lectured on medical jurisprudence, the practice of physic, clinical medicine, and pathology, in the Edinburgh medical school at Surgeons' Hall, where he succeeded Alexander Wood. He had the good fortune to be able to dispense with most private practice and to concentrate on his work at the infirmary and medical school, where he was known as an excellent teacher and was very popular with students.

Haldane was successively secretary and then president of the Royal College of Physicians of Edinburgh, and he represented the college on the General Medical Council on Wood's retirement; he was also its representative on the board of the infirmary managers' committee. In 1865 he published *The Modern Practice of Medicine: a Lecture*. Haldane had a high reputation among his fellow physicians and was 'esteemed for his kindly, unostentatious disposition' (*BMJ*, 854). At the tercentenary of the University of Edinburgh the degree of LLD was conferred upon him. His death, at his house at 22 Charlotte Square, Edinburgh, on 12 April 1887, was caused by a fractured leg—the result of a fall on ice on the previous Christmas day. He was buried on 14 April at Dean cemetery, Edinburgh, and was survived by his wife, Charlotte Elizabeth Lowthrop, and at least one son.

PATRICK WALLIS

**Sources** *BMJ* (16 April 1887), 854 • *The Lancet* (23 April 1887) • *The Scotsman* (13 April 1887) • W. S. Craig, *History of the Royal College of Physicians of Edinburgh* (1976) • *DNB* • parish register (birth), Edinburgh, St Andrews parish, 27 March 1824 • *CCI* (1887)

**Wealth at death** see confirmation, 1887, *CCI*

**Haldane, Elizabeth Sanderson** (1862–1937), public servant and author, was born in Charlotte Square, Edinburgh, on 27 May 1862, the fifth of six children and only daughter of Robert Haldane (1805–1877), writer to the signet, and his second wife, Mary Elizabeth Burdon-Sanderson (1825–1925). The family possessed a residence in Charlotte Square as well as a country seat at Cloan, Auchterarder, Perthshire. Three of her brothers survived to become eminent in later life: Richard Burdon *Haldane, politician and lord chancellor, John Scott *Haldane, physiologist, and William Stowell Haldane, a lawyer. The children were brought up in a strongly Calvinistic but highly cultivated religious atmosphere. Elizabeth was educated mainly at home, where she shared her brothers' tutors, so she could participate in their discussions on philosophy, science, and politics. This experience was undoubtedly important in her intellectual development. She then spent some time from the age of fifteen at a private day school in Edinburgh. But she regarded the instruction she received as 'scrappy' and uncoordinated (Haldane, 60). In the view of the historian Hume Brown, a long-standing friend of the family, Elizabeth possessed a mind more remarkable than those of her distinguished brothers, yet she was denied the education or opportunity that her talents warranted.

After her father died it was understood that Elizabeth Haldane's duty as the daughter was to remain with her mother, and this she did during Mary Elizabeth Haldane's forty-eight years of widowhood. A winter which they spent in Paris in 1877 enabled her to form wider interests and friendships, though life in Auchterarder on their return was more restrictive. Her family connections and opportunities to travel both in Britain and abroad enabled her to overcome these limitations and brought her into contact with many of the leading figures of her day. On a visit to London in 1884 she met Octavia Hill, who encouraged her to establish an organization to tackle the appalling housing conditions in which many families in Edinburgh lived. Her resulting visits to the homes of the Edinburgh poor revealed to her the extent of overcrowding, poor sanitation, and sweated labour and convinced her of the need for state help. This view was reinforced after introductions to Sidney and Beatrice Webb and George Bernard Shaw through her elder brother R. B. Haldane, and through reading Arnold Toynbee and John Ruskin, and the idealist philosophy of T. H. Green and F. H. Bradley. Her own voluntary social work during her regular visits to London included helping to run a club for boys and girls in Lisson Grove, London, founded by Margaret Llewellyn Davies. She attended lectures on first aid and nursing organized by the St Andrews and Red Cross associations, and passed her St John's first-aid examination at the Regent Street Polytechnic in London. In 1890 she helped to found the Scottish Women's Benefit Society, whose members were later admitted to the Ancient Order of Foresters, the pioneers of old-age pensions for women in Scotland (on which she contributed an article to the *National Review* in 1896).

From 1886 onwards Elizabeth Haldane helped in her brother Robert's election campaigns, and this political activity led to her becoming treasurer of the Scottish Women's Liberal Association. She also pursued philosophical and literary work, producing with Frances Simson *The History of Philosophy* (1892), a three-volume translation of Hegel, followed by an account of Hegel's thought, *The Wisdom and Religion of a German Philosopher* (1897). Her *Life of James Ferrier* (1899) was written for the Famous Scots series, and it was followed by a *Life of Descartes* (1905), in recognition of which St Andrews University conferred on her the honorary degree of LLD (1906), and a translation (in collaboration with G. T. T. Ross) entitled *The Philosophical Works of Descartes* (2 vols., 1911–12). She contributed many articles to the *Encyclopaedia of Religion and Ethics* (1908–21), edited by James Hastings.

After 1900 Elizabeth Haldane was increasingly prominent in both voluntary associations and public bodies. In 1903 she was elected a member of the Auchterarder school board, having already founded an institute and library in the town. This brought her into contact with Andrew Carnegie, who in 1913 personally appointed her the first woman trustee of the Carnegie United Kingdom Trust, a position she held until her death. In 1905 she became involved in running a health society in Westminster concerned with infant welfare and maternal mortality. She also gave evidence to the poor-law commission on the administration of Scottish poorhouses, drawing on her own experience of the lack of nursing care provided in them.

As a result of Robert Haldane's membership of the Liberal governments between 1905 and 1914 Elizabeth Haldane spent increasing amounts of time in London, where she regularly attended debates in the House of Commons, watching from the gallery; she was herself a lifelong believer in women's suffrage and supported the constitutional campaigning of the National Union of Women's Suffrage Societies. A manager of the Edinburgh Royal Infirmary, and a council member of the Scottish branch of the British Red Cross Society, she became involved in 1907 in building up the Territorial Forces' nursing service, established as a result of her brother's army reforms, and originated the voluntary aid detachments. In 1909 she became a member of the Scottish universities' committee. Following her studies of friendly societies for women during a visit to Berlin, Lloyd George asked her to become a national insurance commissioner for Scotland, and though she did not feel able to accept a full-time civil service appointment she later joined the advisory committee for insurance in England. In 1912 she was appointed a member of the royal commission on the civil service, chaired by Lord MacDonnell; concerned to protect the interests of women civil servants, she wrote a memorandum of dissent from the recommendations of the majority on the question of women's conditions of employment. As a member of an interdepartmental committee on the outdoor staff appointed under Lloyd George's National Insurance Act she was also concerned to ensure that women received equal pay.

During the First World War, Elizabeth Haldane, who was vice-chair of the territorial nursing service, was mentioned in dispatches and received the Reine Elisabeth medal for work on behalf of Belgian soldiers and housing Belgian refugees, and in 1916 she was the first woman member of the Scottish War Savings Committee. In recognition of her war work she was appointed CH in 1918. Her public career continued with her election as a member of the Perthshire county education authority (1919–22). Following the Sex Disqualification Removal Act (1919) she became the first woman to be appointed a JP in Scotland (1920). Between the wars she continued her voluntary work. Her earlier interests were continued through membership of the National Council for Maternity and Child Welfare, while she promoted the professional interests of nurses as a representative from 1928 on the General Council of Nursing. She instigated the support given by the Carnegie Trust to save the Sadler's Wells Theatre and Ballet, and took a close interest in the Institute of Industrial Psychology, which carried out vocational guidance tests. Her lifelong practical support to her brother continued when he became lord chancellor in 1924; she assisted in his domestic arrangements at his home in Queen Anne's Gate. At her suggestion, the wives of the ministers in the Labour government of 1924 were invited to meet the king and queen informally at tea before taking on their formal duties at court.

Elizabeth Haldane's later writings included *The British Nurse in Peace and War* (1923), *Mary Elizabeth Haldane* (edited, 1925), *George Eliot and her Times* (1927), *Mrs Gaskell and her Friends* (1930), *The Scotland of our Fathers* (1933), and *Scots Gardens in Old Times* (1937). She was a regular contributor to *The Scotsman*. Her reminiscences, *From one Century to another* (1937)—as well as providing an account of her activities and friendships, based in part on diaries—contain her reflections on the changes in the position of women during her lifetime. She valued above all freedom of life, and described the restrictions imposed by the conventions of the Victorian family during her early years. Her own experience, illuminated by a childhood recollection of Flora Stevenson standing for the Edinburgh school board, indicated that the 'greatest advance' dated from the early 1870s, when local bodies such as school boards were instituted on which women could not only vote but serve as members. She regarded this as possibly more important than the eventual concession of the parliamentary franchise (Haldane, 314).

With her homely manner and kindly disposition, Elizabeth Haldane was at ease in all levels of society. If she was known as the Queen of Perthshire, it did not betoken any grandness of manner on her part but rather indicated her deep-seated loyalty to her community. She transcended the upbringing that had simultaneously conferred privileges on her, while yet denying opportunities, by setting her mind and energies to those areas where it was possible for her to succeed. Her friend Ella Christie described the outstanding features of her character as 'love of humanity, courage, and ability, coupled with a clarity of vision, and force which enabled her to overcome any obstacles encountered in her way' (*DNB*). In appearance she was 'of medium height, rather thick set, not exactly good looking, but with a high forehead and an expression of extreme intelligence and benevolence' (ibid.). Another friend, Violet Markham, considered that she had sacrificed her own ambitions to the claims of family obligations during her mother's long widowhood: 'I often wished that her life had been less wholly devoted to the service of others and had belonged more to herself' (Markham, 48). Her public service, which she pursued with few distractions other than a keen interest in curling, was set aside only in the last months of her life when she fell ill, saddened by the deaths of her two brothers. She died at St Margaret's Hospital, Auchterarder, on 24 December 1937 and, after a service at St Andrew's Church, Auchterarder, she was cremated at Warriston crematorium, Edinburgh, on 28 December. LIONEL ALEXANDER RITCHIE

**Sources** *DNB* • E. S. Haldane, *From one century to another* (1937) • *The Times* (28 Dec 1937) • *The Scotsman* (27 Dec 1937) • *Glasgow Herald* (27 Dec 1937) • F. Maurice, *Haldane* (1937–9) • *WWW* • Burke, *Peerage* (1927) • V. Markham, *Friendship's harvest* (1956) • O. Banks, *The biographical dictionary of British feminists*, 2 (1990) • J. Alberti, 'Inside out: Elizabeth Haldane as a women's suffrage survivor in the 1920s and 1930s', *Women's Studies International Forum*, 13 (1990), 117–25
**Archives** NL Scot., corresp. and papers
**Likenesses** photograph, 1895, repro. in Haldane, *From one century to another* • W. Stoneman, photograph, 1921, NPG • photograph, repro. in *The Times*
**Wealth at death** £15,800 3*s*. 11*d*.: confirmation, 23 Feb 1938, *CCI*

**Haldane, James Alexander** (1768–1851), Baptist minister and author, was born on 14 July 1768 at Dundee, the younger and posthumous son of Captain James Haldane (1728–1768) of Airthrey estate, Stirlingshire, and Katherine Duncan (*d.* 1774) of Lundie, Forfarshire. Brought up by his grandmother, Lady Lundie, after his mother's death, he was educated at Dundee grammar school (1777) and the high school of Edinburgh (1777–81) before matriculating at the city's university in 1781. In 1785 he sailed as midshipman aboard the *Duke of Montrose*, an East Indiaman in which the family had a financial interest. During the course of four voyages to the Far East he rose to second officer, and had attained his own command when on 18 September 1793 he married Mary (1771–1819), daughter of Major Alexander Joass of Culleonard, Banffshire. The following March, as captain of the *Melville Castle*, he helped to quell a mutiny within the East India fleet anchored at Spithead, but during the enforced delay and under the influence of David Bogue, Independent minister at Gosport, his thoughts turned increasingly in a religious direction. Shortly before the fleet sailed, he decided to sell his command and quit the sea.

As he became associated with an Edinburgh circle which included the clergymen Walter Buchanan, David Black, and John Erskine and the Grassmarket ironmonger John Campbell, Haldane's impulse towards evangelical religion gained momentum. Following the 1796 general assembly he made a short but significant tour of Perthshire and central Scotland with Charles Simeon (1759–1836), vicar of Holy Trinity Church, Cambridge, during which his companion preached in a number of pulpits. In 1797 Haldane embarked on his own career as an evangelist, initially as a lay preacher, making a tour to the north of Scotland accompanied by two friends. In the course of this journey, publicized afterwards in a printed journal, the men intruded into parishes, made converts, encouraged Sunday schools, and criticized clerical doctrine, creating enemies as well as friends among the clergy of the established church. This initial foray, which extended to the Orkney Isles, led to the founding in Edinburgh in January 1798 of the Society for the Propagation of the Gospel at Home, a body in which James Haldane played a formative and continuing role. Over the next decade, notwithstanding the hostility of leading politicians and churchmen and the wrath of the general assembly, expressed in the 1799 Declaratory Act and Pastoral Admonition, the society supported a stream of lay preachers and catechists, including native Gaelic speakers, on an explicitly undenominational and non-political basis.

On 3 February 1799 Haldane severed his links with the Church of Scotland, accepting ordination as pastor of a newly raised Independent congregation meeting in the former Circus building in Edinburgh. In May 1801 a new tabernacle was opened at the head of Leith Walk, although his pastoral commitment did not prevent him in the early years from engaging in a continuing programme of itinerant preaching tours during the summer months. In keeping with his new role most of his writings before 1810 concentrated upon the biblical model for a reconstituted church. This focus is explicit in the title of his 1805 work, *A view of social worship and ordinances observed by the first Christians, drawn from the sacred scriptures alone; being an attempt to enforce their divine obligation; and to represent the guilt and evil consequences of neglecting them.* His experimental approach to the structure and functioning of the church placed him at variance with established presbyterianism, while his concern to recover apostolic practices such as weekly communion, mutual exhortation, and plurality of elders led to disagreements with his associates. In 1808 his decision to abandon infant baptism for that of believers split the Haldane movement irretrievably. But experimentalism did not incline him to support the later outburst of tongues among the Irvingites, and he was especially critical of the involvement of women in that phenomenon.

Although Haldane's later writings included such larger subjects as the atonement and the epistle to the Galatians, a polemical note was often sounded. In 1829 he attacked Edward Irving's belief in the human fallibility of Christ and two years later he made a thinly veiled contribution to the Row controversy, criticizing the concept of universal pardon. He debated issues such as religious establishment, publishing open letters to Thomas Chalmers in 1818 concerning the proposed increase in the number of churches in Glasgow, in which he suggested that worldliness and professionalism were the hallmarks of an established clergy. Despite his own staunch independency, in 1839 he publicly rebuked John Brown (1784–1858), a prominent United Secession minister and spokesman for voluntarism, for supporting those who refused to pay the Edinburgh annuity tax levied for the maintenance of the established clergy. Haldane argued that non-compliance went against the biblical injunction to be subject to civil government.

Together with his brother, Robert *Haldane (1764–1842), James Haldane was responsible for encouraging the spread of non-confessional Calvinist biblicism linked to congregational church government and lay involvement in Christian ministry. He died at his home, 34 Drummond Place, Edinburgh, on 8 February 1851 and was buried in the West Church cemetery on 14 February. He was survived until 1867 by his second wife, Margaret (1788–1867), daughter of Professor Daniel Rutherford, whom he had married on 23 April 1822, and by eleven of the fifteen children born during the two marriages, including the physician Daniel Rutherford *Haldane.

DERYCK LOVEGROVE

**Sources** A. Haldane, *The lives of Robert Haldane of Airthrey, and of his brother, James Alexander Haldane*, 2nd edn (1852) · J. A. Haldane, *Journal of a tour through the northern counties of Scotland and the Orkney isles, in autumn 1797. Undertaken with a view to promote the knowledge of the gospel of Jesus Christ* (1798) · *An account of the proceedings of the Society for Propagating the Gospel at Home* (1799) · J. A. L. Haldane, *The Haldanes of Gleneagles* (1929) · D. W. Lovegrove, 'Unity and separation: contrasting elements in the thought and practice of Robert and James Alexander Haldane', *Protestant Evangelicalism … essays in honour of W. R. Ward*, ed. K. Robbins, SCH, Subsidia, 7 (1990), 153–77

**Archives** NL Scot. · priv. coll.

**Likenesses** J. Kay, caricature, etching, 1801, NPG · G. Zobal, stipple (aged seventy-seven; after C. Smith), NPG; repro. in Haldane, *Lives*

**Wealth at death** £2340 8*s*. 5*d*.—in Scotland: NA Scot. · £2031 16*s*. 3*d*.—outside Scotland: NA Scot.

**Haldane, James Robert Alexander Chinnery-** (1842–1906), bishop of Argyll and the Isles, was born on 14 August 1842 at Hatcham, Deptford, London, the only son among the six children of Alexander *Haldane (1800–1882), barrister and newspaper proprietor, and his wife, Emma Corsbie, *née* Hardcastle (1800–1867). His father was an Anglican evangelical and had founded *The Record*, while his grandfather James Alexander *Haldane had been a dissenting minister and controversialist. Initially tutored at home, Haldane attended Bury St Edmunds grammar school before going on to Trinity College, Cambridge, in 1861: he graduated LLB in 1865. At university he relished outdoor pursuits, particularly rowing, and was an interested yet unexceptional scholar. On 23 August 1864 he married Anna Elizabeth Frances Margaretta (*d.* 1907), heir of the Revd Sir Nicholas Chinnery, bt, of Flintfield, co. Cork. He added his name to hers as Haldane-Chinnery but in 1878 changed it to Chinnery-Haldane. They had three children, Agnes Elizabeth, who died shortly after birth in 1866, James Broderick, and Patrick Vernon.

Soon after his marriage Haldane-Chinnery returned to Cambridge in preparation for ordination. In 1866 he was ordained deacon (priest in 1867) by Bishop W. K. Hamilton of Salisbury, as curate to the Tractarian John Duncan, vicar of Calne, Wiltshire. The choice of curacy was an indication that Haldane-Chinnery had exchanged his filial evangelicalism for an increasing Anglo-Catholicism. He combined the fervent Christo-centric preaching of evangelicalism with Catholic practice in the sacraments and the liturgy, although a natural scrupulousness in religious matters was prevented from becoming religiosity by his urbane cheerfulness. The death of his in-laws in a railway accident in 1868 caused him to consider ministry in his ancestral country.

The Haldane-Chinnerys moved that year to Edinburgh, where Alexander (as he was known) became curate of All Saints, Edinburgh, in the Scottish Episcopal church. During his highland summer holidays Haldane-Chinnery volunteered for pastoral duties to episcopal congregations. He became incumbent of St Bride's, Nether Lochaber, in 1876, and in 1878 moved into the district. In 1879 he was elected incumbent of St John's, Ballachulish, the remaining centre of traditional highland episcopalianism. He was made dean of the diocese of Argyll and the Isles in 1881, and was elected bishop in 1883, being consecrated on 24 August. In 1884 he was granted an LLM from Cambridge University, and in 1888 a DD.

The most extreme Anglo-Catholic yet to be ordained a bishop of the Scottish Episcopal church, Chinnery-Haldane continued for a while his membership of the Society of the Holy Cross and remained a lifelong member of the Confraternity of the Blessed Sacrament. He had a number of good friends among leading English ritualists, including Alexander Heriot Mackonochie of St Alban the Martyr, Holborn, London. He developed a reputation as an assiduous pastor in his 23-year episcopate, and attempted to learn Gaelic. He used a bicycle to travel around his large diocese: according to family tradition, he was 'physically very strong and could stand a great amount of fatigue' (Haldane, 262). His only publications were a collection of his diocesan charges and a manual of eucharistic devotions for lay communicants. Chinnery-Haldane died on 16 February 1906, possibly from lung cancer, at Alltshellach House, North Ballachulish, Inverness-shire, which he had purchased in 1876. The funeral was held at St Bride's, Nether Lochaber, in which cemetery he was buried on 21 February. The family history recalled him as 'an orthodox Evangelical of the old school', and added that 'there was little of the Puritan about him; he enjoyed a good play, liked to take a hand at cards, and frowned on no amusement that could in any sense be called innocent' (ibid., 263–4). ROWAN STRONG

**Sources** T. I. Ball, *A pastoral bishop: a memoir of Alexander Chinnery-Haldane* (1907) • J. R. A. Chinnery-Haldane, *A charge delivered to the clergy of … Argyll and the Isles* (1883–92) • Venn, *Alum. Cant.* • J. A. L. Haldane, *The Haldanes of Gleneagles* (1929)

**Archives** Argyll and Bute archives, Lochgilphead, Argyll | Archives of the Diocese of Argyll and the Isles, confirmation register; diocesan fund papers

**Likenesses** Russell & Sons, two photographs, 1890–97, repro. in Ball, *Pastoral bishop* • K. Pragnell, photograph, 1902, repro. in Ball, *Pastoral bishop*

**Wealth at death** £3189 11*s.* 9*d.*: confirmation, 21 April 1906, *CCI*

**Haldane, John Burdon Sanderson** (1892–1964), geneticist, was born on 5 November 1892 in Oxford. He was the only son of John Scott *Haldane (1860–1936), physiologist, and his wife, Louisa Kathleen (1863–1961), daughter of Coutts Trotter of Dreghorn; he was named after his great-uncle John Burdon *Sanderson (1828–1905). His younger sister was the writer Naomi *Mitchison (1897–1999). The family home provided a stimulating environment for Haldane's precocious intelligence, and at an early age he was assisting with his father's experiments on the physiology of breathing. Through his father, Haldane also developed

**John Burdon Sanderson Haldane** (1892–1964), by Claude Rogers, 1957

an interest in the philosophical and religious implications of science. However, where his father was idealist (and in general sympathetic to religion), Haldane became associated with the Marxist philosophy of dialectical materialism. His mother held strong views on political matters, being a passionate feminist, a tory, and an imperialist. Haldane was also keen on politics, but unlike his mother he became a socialist and saw imperialism as shackles to be broken. These philosophical and political views were particularly important later in his life, when he was a major figure of the British scientific élite.

Haldane received a broad education, from which he developed an interest in a great variety of subjects. He went to Lynam's School in Oxford, from where he gained a scholarship to Eton. At both schools he suffered from a great deal of bullying, perhaps because of his short temper and intellectual arrogance. However, as he grew up, his large size and aggressiveness meant that he was left well alone. Although he disliked Eton intensely at first, he soon took the measure of the school and became its captain (a position which gave him access to the prestigious Pop society). After Eton he entered New College, Oxford, with a scholarship in mathematics. He obtained first-class honours in mathematical moderations (1912) and then in classics and philosophy (1914).

The First World War broke out two months after Haldane graduated; he served in the 3rd battalion of the Black Watch. He experienced trench warfare and was wounded in France in 1915. After running the Nigg Bombing School (in Ross-shire) from August 1915 to March 1916 he was sent to Mesopotamia, where he was again wounded. He went to India to convalesce, and there he lectured at a bombing school, in Mhow.

In October 1919 Haldane returned to Oxford as a fellow of New College. He did research in physiology and published a number of papers in genetics (the first of which had appeared in 1915 and was on linkage in vertebrates). In 1923 he was appointed reader in biochemistry at Cambridge under F. Gowland Hopkins. In 1925 he was dismissed from his readership at the instigation of the 'Sex Viri' because he had been quoted as co-respondent in a divorce case. Unlike others in the same situation, Haldane appealed against his dismissal, and was reinstated in 1926. Following these events the 'Sex Viri' changed both in name (perhaps to avoid Haldane's proposed translation of 'sex weary') and in content. As a result, university officers were no longer harassed on account of their private lives. In 1926 Haldane married his first wife, Charlotte Burghes, *née* Franken (1894–1969), a journalist who later wrote several books, including two volumes of autobiography [*see* Haldane, Charlotte].

While still holding his readership at Cambridge, Haldane became officer in charge of genetical investigations at the John Innes Horticultural Research Station at Merton, Surrey, in 1927, a position he occupied until 1936. He was elected a fellow of the Royal Society in 1932. He also held the Fullerian professorship of physiology at the Royal Institution from 1930 to 1932. In 1933 he resigned from Cambridge to occupy the chair of genetics, and then of biometry, at University College, London. Between 1941 and 1944 he and his staff were moved out of London to Rothamsted Experimental Station.

Haldane's marriage to Charlotte ended in divorce in 1945. In the same year he married a former student, Helen Spurway (*d.* 1978), who later became a lecturer in his department. Charlotte had one son by her previous marriage, but Haldane had no children by either of his marriages. In 1957, before retirement age, Haldane retired from University College to become a member of the Biometry Research Unit at the Indian Statistical Institute, Calcutta.

Haldane's main contributions to science were theoretical rather than experimental. His greatest achievement was in uniting Darwinian evolution theory with Mendelian genetics. In a series of papers starting in 1924 he used a Mendelian system of heredity to work out, mathematically, the consequences of natural selection. He assigned selective values to genes, and deduced the number of generations required to bring about changes in gene frequency under many alternative assumptions. By developing a quantitative theory of evolution Haldane's work, together with that of R. A. Fisher and Sewall Wright, re-established Darwinian natural selection as the accepted mechanism of evolutionary change. He did much to encourage the development of human genetics, both through his own work and through discussions with others, particularly during his time at University College. He continued working in this field all his life, but made important contributions in many other areas. His early work in biochemistry laid the foundations of a mathematical theory of enzyme action. His other interests ranged from cosmology to animal behaviour and the origin of life.

Haldane's great strengths as a scientist were an ability to reduce complex systems to simple mathematical equations, a wide range of interests that allowed him to see connections missed by others, and a gift for lucid and vivid exposition. He was one of the most effective popularizers of science, and his influence was considerable on scientists and non-scientists alike. His books *Daedalus, or, Science and the Future* (1923), *Possible Worlds* (1927), and *The Inequality of Man* (1932), and his weekly articles in the *Daily Worker* combine original scientific insight, verbal wit, appeal to everyday experience, and radical political and philosophical criticism. The same qualities can also be found in *My Friend Mr Leakey* (1937), a collection of children's stories.

Haldane was less successful as an experimenter. It is significant that his main experimental contributions were to the physiology of diving: he had learned the two principal techniques, the handling of gases and experiments on human subjects (including himself), from his father when a child. The research was carried out between 1939 and 1945 when he was invited to investigate the disaster in the submarine *Thetis* by the Amalgamated Engineering Union and the Electrical Trades Union, many of whose members had died in the accident. He subsequently worked on behalf of the Royal Navy on the physiological effects of gases at high pressures, and undertook physiological work for the Royal Air Force and the Ministry of Aircraft Production.

Haldane worked for the British armed forces at a time when his commitment to communism was becoming stronger. He had embarked very gradually into political activity. When he was a student at Oxford he became a socialist, but a socialist of a rather liberal kind: he was more concerned with attacking religion than the ruling class. His experience of the First World War made him lean further to the left. At the same time, like other scientists of his generation, he developed eugenic views. These views, expressed in *Daedalus*, were closely linked to his interest in human genetics and to his belief in the potential of science to change humanity. Although he became more cautious later on, he retained a lifelong commitment to eugenic ideals.

Haldane's participation in organized political activity increased during the 1930s, in response to the rise of Hitler and to other events. He visited Spain three times during the civil war, and advised the Spanish government about defence against gas attacks and air raids. As a result of this experience he published his book *A.R.P.*, which gave a quantitative estimate of the likely effects of air raids in the coming war. During this period he also became associated with the communist movement, for which he was a frequent and effective speaker, but he did not become a member of the Communist Party until 1942. In 1940 he became chairman of the editorial board of the *Daily Worker*, a post he held until 1950 when the board was disbanded.

In the years immediately after the war Haldane's political position became increasingly untenable as a result of the Lysenko affair (the controversy that resulted from the suppression of Mendelian genetics in the Soviet Union during the 1940s under Trofim Lysenko). It became an acute crisis in 1948, when Lysenko was put in charge of Soviet biology by Stalin and research in human genetics was officially banned. Until the end of his life Haldane maintained that there was some positive content to the science of Lysenko, in particular in its applications to Soviet agriculture. However, he also admitted that much that was said by Lysenko himself and in his support was wrong, and he objected consistently to the possibility of Lamarckian inheritance in man. The contradictions between his public and private views, which became apparent at the time, can also be seen in other scientists whose loyalties were being severely tested by the affair. The interference with scientific research taking place in Russia eventually undermined Haldane's sympathies for the Soviet Union and for the Communist Party, although he was reluctant openly to condemn or criticize their policies. His resignation from the party occurred about 1950, but it was never publicly announced. He later said that he had resigned because of Stalin's interference with science.

Haldane left England for India in 1957. He and his wife became Indian citizens in 1961, and in 1962 he was appointed head of the laboratory of genetics and biometry established by the government of Orissa at Bhubaneswar, where he continued to live until his death from rectal cancer on 1 December 1964. V. M. QUIRKE

**Sources** R. Clark, *J. B. S.: the life and work of J. B. S. Haldane* (1968) · N. W. Pirie, *Memoirs FRS*, 12 (1966), 219–49 · G. Werskey, *The visible college* (1978); repr. (1988) · K. R. Dronamraju, *Haldane: the life and work of J. B. S. Haldane with special reference to India* (1985) · K. R. Dronamraju, *Haldane and modern biology* (1968) · K. R. Dronamraju, *Haldane's Daedalus revisited* (1995) · D. B. Paul, 'A war on two fronts: J. B. S. Haldane and the response to Lysenkoism in Britain', *Journal of the History of Biology*, 16 (1983), 1–37 · L. K. Haldane, *Friends and kindred* (1961)

**Archives** Bodl. Oxf., corresp. relating to Society for the Diffusion of Useful Knowledge · IWM, letters to his sister while serving in the Black Watch · King's AC Cam., letters · NL Scot., corresp., notebooks, and papers; letters to his family, essays, etc.; letters to his sister · UCL, corresp. and papers; further papers incl. letters to his sister | Bodl. Oxf., corresp. with Cyril Darlington · Rice University, Houston, Texas, corresp. with Sir Julian Huxley · U. Oxf., Edward Grey Institute of Field Ornithology, corresp. with David Lack · UCL, corresp. with Lionel Penrose · Wolfson College, Oxford, corresp. with H. B. D. Kettlewell

**Likenesses** O. Edis, photograph, 1925, NPG · group portrait, photograph, 1937, NPG · H. Coster, photographs, 1938, NPG · W. Stoneman, photograph, 1943, NPG · C. Rogers, oils, 1957, UCL [*see illus.*] · pencil sketch, study, BM

**Haldane, John Scott** (1860–1936), physiologist, was born in Edinburgh on 3 May 1860, the fourth, but third surviving, son of Robert Haldane (1805–1877), writer to the signet, of Cloanden (later called Cloan), Auchterarder, Perthshire, and his second wife, Mary Elizabeth (1825–1925), second daughter of Richard Burdon-Sanderson, of West Jesmond and Otterburn Dene, Northumberland. He was a younger brother of Richard Burdon *Haldane, and an elder brother of Elizabeth Sanderson *Haldane and William Stowell Haldane, crown agent for Scotland.

John Scott Haldane (1860–1936), by Philip A. de Laszlo, 1933

**Education, marriage and early career** Haldane was educated at Edinburgh Academy from 1870 to 1876, when he entered the University of Edinburgh, taking a general MA degree in 1879. In the spring of that year he spent three months at the University of Jena, returning to Edinburgh to begin medical studies. He completed his training in 1883, but failed his final MB examination because, he claimed, he had devoted his time to independent reading rather than to course material, and so did not produce the stereotyped answers expected by his examiners. He subsequently sat and passed the conjoint examination of the royal colleges of Physicians and Surgeons of Edinburgh in December 1883, thereby qualifying for medical practice; and in 1885 he successfully resat his final MB examinations.

Haldane's aim had always been to pursue a career in medical research rather than practice. He was encouraged in this by his uncle, John Scott Burdon Sanderson, who in 1882 was appointed Waynflete professor of physiology at Oxford University. In January 1884 Haldane began conducting research in Oxford and London, studying the chemical pathology of fevers under Burdon Sanderson's guidance. No formal appointment being available for him in the Oxford department at that time, Haldane moved on in late 1884 or 1885 to University College, Dundee, where he and the professor of chemistry, Thomas Carnelley, conducted chemical and bacteriological analyses of the air of schools and slum dwellings. Invited by Sir Henry Roscoe to investigate the source and possible effects of the offensive smells that troubled the House of Commons during warm weather, they went on to examine the constituents of sewer air in Dundee and other cities. Their findings indicated that sewer gas was not the serious source of infection that it was widely supposed to be.

In May 1886 Haldane heard that a post would soon become available in Oxford. He spent three months refining his skills in chemical physiology in Salkowski's laboratory in Berlin, and in January 1887 he began work as a demonstrator in the Oxford University department of physiology. He would remain in the department for the next twenty-six years, being promoted to lecturer in 1894 and reader in 1907. He initially found the closed society of the Oxford colleges rather uncongenial, but in 1901 he was elected a fellow of New College. By that time he had become deeply attached to the city, which remained his home until his death. In 1891 he married Louisa Kathleen Trotter (1863–1961), only child of Coutts Trotter of Dreghorn. A son, John Burdon Sanderson *Haldane, was born on 5 November 1892, and a daughter, Naomi [*see* Mitchison, Naomi Mary Margaret], on 1 November 1897. In 1907 the family moved to Cherwell, Linton Road, a rambling house built to their own specifications—including a well-equipped laboratory—on what is now the site of Wolfson College.

**Initial research** Haldane's first researches in the department of physiology revolved around the development of precise and delicate techniques for determining the rate of heat production during normal metabolism, and subsequently for measuring the respiratory exchange. This work earned him the Edinburgh University MD and Ellis prize in 1889. Haldane did not regard this work as an end in itself, but as a means to address practical concerns in public health and hygiene. Late in 1889 with James Lorrain Smith he began investigating the composition and physiological effects of expired air—a project that grew directly out of his Dundee work on the air of dwellings. Over the next four years, Haldane and Lorrain Smith refuted the widely held view that expired air contained potent organic poisons, and showed that while accumulation of carbon dioxide might cause discomfort, it was unlikely under normal conditions to damage health. They concluded that the current enthusiasm among public health experts for higher standards of ventilation was misguided, and that more beneficial effects would be secured by promoting cleanliness and removing potential sources of infection.

**Work on oxygen secretion** Late in 1893 Haldane and Lorrain Smith went to Copenhagen to work for a while in the laboratory of the respiratory physiologist Christian Bohr. Bohr had recently conducted experiments which suggested that oxygen entered the blood from the lungs not by simple mechanical diffusion across the pulmonary epithelium as was widely supposed, but by active secretion. During 1895 Haldane devised a new and more sensitive method for determining the partial pressure of oxygen in arterial blood, with which he and Lorrain Smith went on to generate further evidence in support of the oxygen secretion theory. Other researchers were sceptical, however, and over the next twenty-five years Haldane conducted a lively controversy with August and Marie Krogh of Copenhagen, Joseph Barcroft of Cambridge, and others. In the course of this controversy both sides refined their techniques, modified their theories, and generated important new knowledge about the processes of gas exchange and the chemistry of haemoglobin. Haldane's search for evidence took him, in 1911, to the summit of Pike's Peak in Colorado to investigate the processes of breathing at high altitude; his colleagues on this expedition were C. G. Douglas and Mabel FitzGerald of Oxford, Yandell Henderson of Yale, and E. C. Schneider of Colorado Springs. By the 1920s the controversy was widely held to have been settled in favour of diffusion, though Haldane insisted that the facts still supported a role for secretion during periods of oxygen stress, for instance during hard physical work and at altitude.

**Haldane's philosophical approach** Haldane's interest in oxygen secretion was closely bound up with the philosophical commitments he brought to his scientific research. While still an undergraduate, he had become actively involved in promoting the post-Hegelian idealism that was becoming established in Britain at that time, and that provided the conceptual framework for much political and ethical debate during the final decades of the nineteenth century. In contrast to the reductionist ethics of utilitarianism, philosophical idealists argued that other aspects of reality, including aesthetic and moral qualities, were objectively present to the observing mind. Such a perspective was at odds with the view then gaining ascendancy among professional scientists, who claimed that objective knowledge was confined to causal and mechanical interactions between physical and chemical entities. Haldane looked to physiology for a refutation of this scientific reductionism. Following Kant, he argued that living organisms could be fully understood only in terms of distinct principles of teleological action. Organisms, far from being mechanical arrangements of discrete physical parts, were self-regulating wholes, whose activities were directed towards the continuance of their own existence and identity.

The oxygen secretion theory, which challenged the claim that purely mechanistic processes of diffusion could account for the facts of respiration, provided Haldane with evidence in favour of his preferred philosophical viewpoint. So too did his most celebrated physiological work—the classic series of experiments that he conducted with J. G. Priestley from 1903 to 1904, that led to his pathbreaking demonstration that the breathing rate is regulated by highly sensitive organic responses to changes in the carbon dioxide content of the blood. These latter findings were quickly assimilated to a mechanistic account of biological regulation, but Haldane himself saw them as further evidence that the phenomena of life can only be properly understood from a teleological perspective. He went on to conduct research into a range of other regulatory processes, including the maintenance of pH in the blood, and of fluid balance and temperature in the body as a whole. His work in this area, but especially on the regulation of the breathing rate, is widely remembered as helping to lay the foundations for the concept of homeostasis.

**Practical applications of his work** Important though these findings were in their own right, Haldane was always concerned that they should find some practical application in the sphere of public health. From 1894 his work on the properties of vitiated air led him to an interest in the effects and constitution of the various gases commonly found in coal mines, in particular the suffocating 'black damp'. A series of colliery explosions from 1894 to 1896 enabled him to extend his investigations to include 'fire damp' and 'after damp', and to conclude in an important report to the home secretary that the major cause of death in such disasters was poisoning by carbon monoxide produced by the partial combustion of coal dust. As a result of these investigations, he was able to recommend a variety of measures to improve the safety of coal mines, including the provision of oxygen breathing apparatus to assist in rescuing miners incapacitated by gas, and the use of mice or other small animals to indicate the presence of carbon monoxide.

Thereafter, a large proportion of his time was devoted to work on various aspects of industrial health, not least as a co-founder and co-editor of the *Journal of Hygiene* from 1901. He served on a Board of Trade committee to inquire into the ventilation of tunnels on the Metropolitan Railway, which reported in 1897. Around this time he was appointed one of three metropolitan gas referees responsible for regulating the quality of town gas in London; in 1921 he would become gas referee for the whole of the United Kingdom. Further work for the Home Office came in 1901, when he was appointed to a departmental committee on the ventilation of factories and workshops. Reporting in 1902 and 1907, the committee defended the controversial view that more stringent legislative standards of ventilation would do little to improve the health of workers. Also in 1902 the home secretary asked Haldane to investigate an epidemic of anaemia among Cornish tin miners. He found that the disease was due, not to bad ventilation as the miners themselves argued, but to ankylostomiasis, a parasitic infection usually found in the tropics but which thrived in the hot damp conditions of the mines. He also investigated the causes of 'miner's phthisis' and recommended that water sprays should be used to suppress the siliceous dust caused by blasting and by the pneumatic rock drills that had recently been introduced into the mines. In 1905 or 1906 the Admiralty sought Haldane's advice on the causes, prevention, and treatment of caisson disease—now called the bends—which was hindering the development of deep diving for marine salvage. He suggested that decompression by stages would be more practicable than the continuous decompression then being practised, and with the help of experiments on goats and humans he devised decompression tables that are the basis, with relatively few modifications or corrections, of those in use today. From 1906 to 1911 he was a member of the royal commission on mines, concerned with health and safety matters, and from 1911 to 1912 he served on the royal commission on metalliferous mines and quarries. This work brought him into close contact with coal owners and mining engineers, and thereafter he became increasingly active in promoting and directing research within the industry, notably as director of a laboratory established by the Doncaster Coal Owners' Association in 1912.

**Work in the war and post-war years** In 1913 Frances Gotch, Burdon Sanderson's successor in the Oxford chair of physiology, died suddenly. He was replaced by C. S. Sherrington. Haldane, frustrated at being passed over for the chair, resigned his university readership. He retained his New College fellowship, however, and continued to conduct research in his private laboratory with colleagues from the department of physiology, as well as in the Doncaster Coal Owners' Association laboratory. In April 1915, when the Germans initiated the large-scale use of chemical weapons with a chlorine attack on the Ypres salient, Kitchener asked Haldane to visit the site of the attack, and to advise the War Office on the development of defensive and retaliatory measures. He went on to work on the design of respirators, and subsequently on the medical aspects of war-gas poisoning, and did much to demonstrate the value of oxygen for treating gassed soldiers.

In the years that followed the First World War, Haldane devoted himself chiefly to the advancement of research in the mining industry. From 1917 to 1924 he was a member of the mine rescue apparatus research committee set up by the newly established Department of Scientific and Industrial Research. In 1921 he became a member of the Safety in Mines Research Board, set up under the newly established Miners' Welfare Fund, where he was responsible for initiating and directing research. In the same year the Doncaster Coal Owners' Association laboratory was transferred to Birmingham University, where Haldane was awarded an honorary chair in mining. He was responsible for initiating and supervising research into a wide range of health and safety measures, including the use of stone dusting to minimize the spread of explosions, mine ventilation, illumination at the coal face, and pulmonary diseases caused by the inhalation of dust. His services to the mining industry were recognized when he was elected president of the Institution of Mining Engineers in 1924, a position he held until 1928.

**Character and assessment of his work** A large man, Haldane bore himself with the energetic self confidence he acquired from his upbringing among the Scottish aristocracy, though in later life he became stooped with rheumatism and a heart condition exacerbated by exposure to poisonous gases in the course of his war work. He had great respect for technical skill, as much among the coalminers whom he taught to use his mine safety and gas analysis apparatus as among his co-workers in the laboratory. But committee work tried his patience, and despite his scientific achievements he took little part in the affairs of organizations such as the Royal Society and the Medical

Research Council. The hours he kept were long and late; he usually rose when the rest of the family had breakfasted and frequently remained in his study until well past midnight. Age did not stop him working, and in his seventy-seventh year he undertook a trip to Persia to investigate cases of heat stroke in the oil refineries there. Shortly after his return he was taken ill with pneumonia, and he died at his home, Cherwell, at midnight on 14–15 March 1936. His burial at Golders Green crematorium on 17 March was followed the next day by a smaller service at Gleneagles.

Haldane's research was exceptional for the way it combined the articulation of physiological theory with the pursuit of practical applications. Many of his contemporaries, fighting for professional status and independence in the universities, argued that science was best conducted in academic isolation and purity, and should engage with the wider world only through the subaltern disciplines of applied science. Haldane never accepted such a distinction between pure and applied research, and his own work forcefully repudiated it. It was not just that his physiological studies informed and guided his work in industry; equally, his hygienic investigations were crucial in suggesting topics for physiological research. His work on the regulation of breathing, for instance, grew directly out of his early interest in carbon dioxide as a constituent of vitiated air; while his experience of working in hot deep mines inspired him to study the regulation of body temperature and fluid balance. Whether conducted in the laboratory or in the workplace, his investigations were guided by an overarching interest in how the human organism maintained its functional integrity amid the vagaries of the lived environment. The intensely practical orientation of all his work is perhaps best represented in the various measuring instruments he designed. Of these the most widely used were his haemoglobinometer, his apparatus for the measurement of blood gases, and his apparatus for the accurate and rapid analysis of mixtures of gases. All were remarkably compact, portable, and simple to use, and lent themselves equally well to research in the laboratory and in the most awkward corners of coal mines.

In his later years, Haldane devoted an increasing amount of time to promoting his idealistic interpretation of physiology. He gave the Silliman lectures at Harvard in 1916, and published them a year later in a little book entitled *Organism and Environment as Illustrated by the Physiology of Breathing*. A more physiologically detailed treatment of the same subject appeared in 1922 as *Respiration* (new edn, 1935). In the session of 1927–8 he delivered the Gifford lectures at the University of Glasgow, and in 1930 he was Donnellan lecturer at Dublin University. His philosophical views never became widely accepted by his fellow physiologists, but his contributions to science were highly valued. He was elected a fellow of the Royal Society in 1897, and was awarded the society's royal medal in 1916 and the Copley medal in 1934 in recognition of his discoveries in human physiology and their practical application. He received honorary degrees from many universities, and in 1928 he was appointed CH for his scientific work in connection with industrial disease. STEVE STURDY

**Sources** C. G. Douglas, *Obits. FRS*, 2 (1936–8), 115–39 [incl. bibliography] • S. W. Sturdy, 'A co-ordinated whole: the life and work of John Scott Haldane', PhD diss., U. Edin., 1987 • N. Mitchison, *You may well ask: a memoir, 1920–1940* (1979) • *DNB* • *The Times* (18 March 1936) • *The Times* (19 March 1936)

**Archives** Medical Research Council, London, corresp. • NA Scot., papers • NA Scot., MSS • NL Scot., corresp. and papers • RS • University of British Columbia, Woodward Biomedical Library, corresp. and papers | Australian Academy of Science, Canberra, J. T. Wilson MSS • Bodl. Oxf., Mabel Purefoy FitzGerald MSS • CAC Cam., corresp. with A. V. Hill • NL Scot., letters to Lord Haldane • UCL, Burdon Sanderson MSS

**Likenesses** B. Stone, photograph, 1902, NPG • W. Stoneman, photograph, 1931, NPG • P. A. de Laszlo, oils, 1933, Courtauld Inst. [*see illus.*] • photograph, repro. in Douglas, *Obits. FRS*

**Wealth at death** £54,430 13*s*. 2*d*.: confirmation, 10 June 1936, *CCI*

**Haldane, Patrick** (1683/4–1769), lawyer and politician, was the second son of John Haldane of Gleneagles (1660–1721) and his wife, Mary (*d*. 1685), daughter of David Drummond, third Lord Madderty, and Lady Beatrix Graham. He came from an ancient family, settled at Gleneagles since the fifteenth century. His father, a zealous whig, had represented Perthshire and Dunbartonshire in the parliament of Scotland, and represented Perthshire in the first parliament of Great Britain.

Haldane matriculated at St Andrews University on 22 February 1699, graduated MA on 11 July 1701, and then spent four years reading law in Edinburgh under the eminent lawyer John Spottiswood. In 1705 he became professor of Greek at St Andrews. This appointment was not without difficulty, for though he obtained more votes than his rival for the post he was not selected, and succeeded only after taking the matter to court where the election was annulled. No reason was given for his being supplanted in the first instance, but it appears to have been an early example of the extraordinary unpopularity which he attracted and which was later to blight what was otherwise a most promising career. This first appointment was followed in 1707 by the post of professor of ecclesiastical history.

In 1711 Haldane left St Andrews for the University of Leiden to resume his legal studies, remaining there for about four years. After completing his studies he returned home, and on 18 January 1715 was admitted advocate. The following two years were noteworthy: on 16 February 1715 he was returned as MP to represent (as a whig) the Perth district of burghs, a position he held until 1721; and in November 1715 was appointed a commissioner of the equivalent. In October 1716 he was elected provost of St Andrews, retaining this office until October 1720, and in May 1716 he exchanged his commissioner's post for that of a member of the commission charged with arranging the sale of estates forfeited after the 1715 Jacobite rising. The salary of £1000 per annum was considered enormous, but was scant compensation for the exceptional enmity he incurred from the Jacobites and other prominent landowners connected with the dispossessed families. To the inherently unpopular nature of this post Haldane added a ruthless enthusiasm for his duties, earning himself a lifelong reputation for severity and harshness, and lack of Scottish patriotism. Nor was his unpopularity confined to the Scots; the whig ministry also came to disapprove of his overzealous approach.

In the Commons, Haldane voted consistently with the government, but here too there was ample scope for his ability to attract enmity. His speeches are said to have rendered him obnoxious for most of his life. On one occasion at least his vote seemed calculated to incur hatred: having voted in favour of a petition to allow the wives and widows of forfeited estate owners in England their jointures, he opposed a similar proposal for their Scottish counterparts.

Some time before 1721 Haldane married Margaret (*b.* 1694), daughter of William, fourth Lord Forrester; soon afterwards their son, George, was born, followed by a daughter, Margaret. Domestic happiness, however, was quickly overshadowed by fresh controversy in his career. On the conclusion of the forfeited estates commission's work Haldane had returned to the bar, but, obtaining little work on account of the prejudice against him, put himself forward for a seat on the bench. In December 1721 he succeeded in obtaining the king's nomination to be a judge of the court of session, but this raised a furious outcry from his numerous enemies. The Faculty of Advocates, determined to prevent his appointment, caused the court of session to refuse him admission on a technicality. The House of Lords overruled this decision, whereupon his opponents raised fresh objections, accusing him, *inter alia*, of Jacobitism, bribery, and extortion by threats. The court of session now voted to admit Haldane by eight votes to seven, but two of his supporters were extraordinary (honorary) lords of session and their right to vote was promptly challenged. Again the case was referred to London, where in view of the controversy a reluctant George I withdrew the judgeship nomination for an alternative preferment. Haldane bore with remarkable fortitude this crushing blow, and on 30 May 1724 the promised preferment materialized, in the form of a commissionership of excise in England, which he held until its termination on George II's accession in 1727.

Haldane again returned to the bar, with greater success, acquiring a reputation of being 'not only the best electionmonger, but the best election lawyer of his time' (HoP, *Commons*) and on 5 March 1746 he was appointed joint solicitor-general of Scotland. In 1750, weakened by age, he made an unsuccessful application for a judgeship, pleading that advancing years were diminishing his ability to cope with the rigours of the bar. Further applications also failed, and he retired in 1755, much broken, on a pension.

In retirement Haldane suffered further pain. His wife had died some time before 3 February 1747, and in 1759 he was to bear the sorrow of the death of his son, George, soon to be followed by that of his daughter, Margaret. His grief was heightened by the necessity in 1760 of selling the family estate of Gleneagles, recently inherited from his brother Mungo, to pay his son's and his own debts, in both cases incurred through electioneering expenses. He died on 10 January 1769 at Duddingston manse, Duddingston, Edinburgh, and was buried in the vault of Sir Alexander Dick, bt, at Duddingston cemetery, Edinburgh.

ANDREW M. LANG

**Sources** *Scotland and Scotsmen in the eighteenth century: from the MSS of John Ramsay, esq., of Ochtertyre*, ed. A. Allardyce, 2 vols. (1888) • J. Foster, *Members of parliament, Scotland … 1357–1882*, 2nd edn (privately printed, London, 1882) • F. J. Grant, ed., *The Faculty of Advocates in Scotland, 1532–1943*, Scottish RS, 145 (1944) • J. A. L. Haldane, *The Haldanes of Gleneagles* (1929) • *Members of parliament: return to two orders of the honorable the House of Commons*, House of Commons, 2 vols. (1878) • J. Lauder, ed., *The decisions of the lords of council and session*, 2 vols. (1759–61) • *Scots Magazine*, 31 (1769), 54 • HoP, *Commons, 1715–54* • BL, Hardwicke MSS, Add. MS 35447 • records, U. St Andr. • St Andrews burgh council records, U. St Andr.

**Archives** NL Scot., MSS 3430–3431, 5074–5075, 5351–5352, 6481

**Likenesses** G. Knapton?, oils, repro. in Haldane, *Haldanes of Gleneagles*, following p. 134; priv. coll. [registered with Scot. NPG]

**Haldane, Richard Burdon**, **Viscount Haldane** (**1856–1928**), politician, educationist, and lord chancellor, was born at 17 Charlotte Square, Edinburgh, on 30 July 1856. He was the second son (but first surviving infancy) of Robert Haldane (1805–1877), writer to the signet and a Baptist, and his second wife, Mary Elizabeth (1825–1925), second daughter of Richard Burdon-Sanderson of West Jesmond and Otterburn Dene, Northumberland, and the sister of Sir John Burdon-*Sanderson (1828–1905), the physiologist. The Haldanes of Gleneagles, Perthshire, were a well-known family, with a seat at Cloanden (later Cloan). They were prominent in naval and military life, though Richard's grandfather James Alexander *Haldane (1768–1851) and his great-uncle Robert *Haldane (1764–1842) had given up a naval career to serve the evangelical cause in Scotland. On his mother's side, Richard was great-great-nephew to Lord Eldon, the lord chancellor, and to Lord Stowell, the judge. His maternal grandfather had left the law for country life and the pursuit of religion. Evangelicalism was thus a prominent strain on both sides of the family, though the young Richard did not follow it. Richard Haldane's mother, a centenarian, lived until almost his death, and he wrote to her, normally daily, from 1877 until she died. Richard was close to his younger sister, Elizabeth Sanderson *Haldane (1862–1937) who, like him, never married and who wrote his memoir for the *Dictionary of National Biography*.

**Education and early legal career** Richard Haldane briefly attended an Edinburgh preparatory school and then Edinburgh Academy, which he did not much like ('school was indeed never an interesting period for me'; Haldane, *Autobiography*, 5), but where, influenced by Dr James Clyde, a Stoic, he left behind the strict Calvinism of his family. He enjoyed holidays at Cloan and in Northumbria and acquired a lifelong passion for walking. Aged sixteen, Haldane went to Edinburgh University, studying the classics and philosophy. In the Students' Philosophical Society he formed a lifetime friendship with Andrew Seth (later Andrew Pringle-*Pattison) and absorbed the university's prevalent Hegelianism, which included the influence of J. F. Ferrier (see Haldane's preface to his sister's biography

**Richard Burdon Haldane, Viscount Haldane** (1856–1928), by Lafayette, 1906

of Ferrier, 1899). His Christian faith began to be disturbed. His parents considered sending him to Balliol College, Oxford, where T. H. Green, whose writings powerfully influenced the young Haldane, was a tutor; but they feared the influence of Anglicanism (probably not realizing that it was Christianity not a particular church which was becoming problematic for their son). Professor James Stuart Blackie suggested Göttingen in Germany as an alternative and thither Haldane went in August 1874 to study with Hermann Lötze. There he learned German, philosophy, and geology, and attended duels fought by members of his *Verbindung* (student corps). Göttingen was a formative six months for Haldane and affected in a variety of ways his public career: he returned a convinced idealist, influenced by Berkeley and Fichte, a view of philosophy to which he remained constant, even after it ceased to be fashionable among British philosophers. He also returned a competent German speaker, a very unusual attribute in British political life. Haldane took a first in arts at Edinburgh, winning many of the academic prizes available, including the Bruce of Grangehill prize and the Gray and Ferguson scholarships, all for philosophy. He failed to become doctor in science (in philosophy); his thesis was passed by the philosophers but failed by the professor of botany. Haldane shocked his parents when, having been baptized as an adolescent, he disclaimed his faith as he rose, dripping, from the font. Following his father's death in 1877, he went to London to read for the bar at Lincoln's Inn, working first in William Barber's chambers and then in Lumley Smith's (the latter on the introduction of Farrer *Herschell, a relative on his mother's side). He was called to the bar in 1879 and set up chambers at 5 New Square, Lincoln's Inn. He specialized initially in the rather humdrum matter of conveyancing, and maintained work in this area 'to nearly the end of my time at the Bar' (Haldane, *Autobiography*, 66). Haldane's philosophical turn of mind also led him naturally to jurisprudential cases. In 1882 he was taken on by Horace Davey as a junior, mostly for tribunal and appeal cases before the judicial committee of the privy council or before the House of Lords. Though Haldane's income was initially slow to grow, with Davey it picked up rapidly and he was earning £2000 per annum by the mid-1880s, took silk in 1890, and became a bencher of Lincoln's Inn in 1893. He became a close friend of Edmund Gosse, librarian of the Lords, where Haldane was frequently appearing in cases. During this time, Haldane maintained his philosophical interests. In 1883 with Andrew Seth he published *Essays in Philosophical Criticism* (1883), dedicated to T. H. Green with an introduction by Edward Caird and probably Haldane's most influential philosophical work; in the same year he issued, with J. Kemp, an important translation of Schopenhauer, *The World as Will and Idea*. He maintained his scholarly contacts in Germany, normally making an annual visit, often in the company of his close friend the Scottish historian Peter Hume Brown.

**Moving in politics** Despite his successful career, Haldane was a somewhat gauche young man, who found relations with women outside his family difficult. His view of life as a social and personal journey along a pathway towards progress led him naturally to Liberal politics, an involvement encouraged by his Perthshire neighbour, the whig peer Lord Camperdown. Partly as a result of Camperdown's introduction, Haldane became involved with the Albert Grey Committee before and during the 1880 general election and was its honorary secretary when it became the Eighty Club in 1881, responsible for organizing its many political dinners. Haldane thus found himself at the hinge of metropolitan and regional Liberal affairs, and quickly became well known in the party. He became friendly with H. H. Asquith about 1882 and soon formed a powerful combination with him. With Asquith he organized a Liberal discussion group which used to meet in the Blue Post public house in Cork Street. In 1885 Haldane was elected for East Lothian (Haddingtonshire), easily seeing off a Liberal Unionist in 1886. He was an assiduous MP and was careful to ensure that the mining element in his constituency remained sufficiently Liberal not to oppose him. He held the seat comfortably (except in 1892 when he was close run by the master of Polwarth) until his peerage in 1911.

By 1887 Haldane was helping Gladstone with Irish legislation. As a young MP he worked with Asquith and from 1888 with Sir Edward Grey and R. Munro-Ferguson, to whose sister, (Emma) Valentine, he was briefly engaged in 1890. The Fergusons and the Haldanes had a long-standing family friendship. This was his only recorded romance, which Val Ferguson abruptly terminated; she subsequently lampooned Haldane in *Betsy* (1892), *Music hath Charms* (1894), and *Life Again, Love Again* (1897), before dying insane in 1897. From that time Haldane always played the part of a jovial bachelor, but Beatrice Webb, who knew him very well, noted in 1897 that, despite 'the beaming kindliness of his nature … there is pathos in his personality … he is a restless, lonely man, in his heart still worshipping the woman who jilted him seven years ago' (Webb, *Our Partnership*, 98). The suggestion that he also proposed to Beatrice Webb in 1890 is based on an ambiguous phrase in her diary which is unsupported by other evidence and cannot be regarded as more than highly improbable.

These young Liberals proposed amendments to a variety of Unionist bills and proposed some of their own, especially with respect to land and its tenure, and spoke in favour of land registration; in 1895 Haldane was a member of the select committee on the Land Transfer Bill (Matthew, 10). Haldane was always a supporter of the enfranchisement of women and played a part in sponsoring the annual bill which kept the question before the Commons. He was friendly with both the Webbs from 1890 (Beatrice thought him initially supercilious, 'a successful lawyer, tinged with socialism' (*Diary of Beatrice Webb*, 345)) and acted as a go-between for his group of progressive Liberals and the Fabians. On another front, he organized contacts with his group and Lord Rosebery, consolidated in 1889 in the Articles Club (from its thirty-nine members). Haldane and his group tried to combine progressivism and imperialism. His machinations in attempting to do so soon got him the reputation of an intriguer. In 1892 he was the only member of his group not to be given some sort of political office, and in 1894 Rosebery passed him over for the solicitor-generalship (in 1895 Rosebery sounded him out about the speakership, to which W. C. Gully was elected). Moreover, the Fabians turned away from their Liberal connections, despite intense lobbying by Haldane. Even so, Haldane remained a staunch supporter of Rosebery and saw him, rather improbably, as he wrote in a letter of 11 October 1896, as the leader of 'a revolution in our party' (Matthew, 22).

**Liberal Imperialism** Haldane played a part in the making of the 1894 budget which graduated the death duties and was prominent in its defence in the Commons, and in opposition after 1895 he continued to encourage progressivist developments in the Liberal Party. He developed his views in speeches and in periodical articles, notably 'The Liberal creed' and 'The eight hours question', in the *Contemporary Review* (October 1888 and October 1893), 'The new Liberalism'—the first use of that phrase—in the *Progressive Review* (November 1896), and his preface to L. T. Hobhouse, *The Labour Movement* (1893). He encouraged resumption of relations with the Fabians and worked with the Webbs to found the London School of Economics (1895) and to prepare the University of London Act (1898). He thought the religious disputes which so dominated English education at this time antiquated. Haldane saw education as the vital element in the movement for 'national efficiency' which he helped to promote from the late 1890s and his frustration at its slow advance encouraged him to seek wider associations than the Liberal Party. Thus to the Fabians and the Liberals he attempted to add progressive elements in the Unionist Party. He was a friend of A. J. Balfour (whose home was in his constituency) and shared his taste for philosophical writing. Of all the Liberals involved in the various centrist movements of the 1895–1903 years, Haldane was the most committed. But he remained an active politician within the Liberal Party, supporting the government over the Second South African War and hoping for a split in the Liberal Party which would leave the Liberal Imperialist group in majority control. He was involved in a variety of organizations such as the Liberal Imperialist League and the Scottish National Liberals, and was one of the most energetic proponents of the Liberal League, founded in February 1902 (and was its vice-president 1905–10). He hoped the league would play a constructive, cross-party role in the disputes over A. J. Balfour's 1902 Education Bill, but he soon found himself acting largely on his own in offering support to the government. Haldane pressed on with his attempts to integrate national and imperial thinking on matters of policy (such as making the Lords into an imperial senate, thus solving both the question of imperial integration constitutionally and the domestic problem of the anomaly of the Lords). He liked to believe, as he wrote to Rosebery on 6 October 1902, that 'the sense of the nation is working towards the construction of a great centre party' (Matthew, 145). He was at the centre of the group known as the co-efficients, who sought a bipartisan policy in domestic and imperial questions, almost setting aside the usual conventions of party politics. Chamberlain's tariff reform campaign ruined such attempts at centrism. Haldane's short biography of Adam Smith (1887)—the first in a revival of interest in Smith—showed him a cautious free-trader. In 1903 he and Percy Ashley attempted a dispassionate inquiry, but Haldane concluded that, in contrast to Chamberlain's view, there was no necessary connection between fiscal and constitutional imperial unity and that he should strongly support the free-trade cause (see Haldane's preface to Percy Ashley, *Modern Tariff History* (1904), and Matthew, 166–8). John Buchan attended one of Haldane's meetings at this time and left the hall with two old farmers after hearing Haldane speak on Chinese labour in South Africa: 'Was he for it or against it?', one asked; 'I'm damned if I ken' replied the other (Sommer, 141).

Haldane's position within the progressive movement was also consolidated by his role as counsel for the trade unions in the Taff Vale case. He had always shown an interest in labour law and in 1893 had successfully encouraged Asquith to get Gladstone to appoint Rosebery as conciliator in the coal strike. His attitude to the unions was, however, integrationist, that is, he wished them to be contained by law. He and Asquith worked in detail on such a policy, Haldane's memorandum of April 1905 providing the basis for the Liberal government's bill of 1906, which was, however, substantially amended in committee, when Campbell-Bannerman's undiscussed acceptance of the Labour Party's amendment set aside Haldane's approach and gave the unions freedom from suit for damages (Haldane remained cautious about trade union power and in 1910 'took an extreme anti Trade Union view' on the question of reversing the Osborne judgment (Pease, 218)). Haldane also supported Webbite plans for wide-ranging improvements to welfare, housing, and employment law.

The Taff Vale case, with Haldane appearing for the union, was an important case in the definition of the nature and obligations of associations. It reflected the sort of high-level legal work for which he had become known. In 1897 he had 'gone special' and appeared chiefly before the judicial committee and the House of Lords, often on dominion and Indian constitutional cases, but also in others with a high degree of abstraction. In a very different case from that of Taff Vale, but one also important for its significance for the law of association, Haldane appeared in the Lords for the United Free Church (the product of the union in 1900 between the Free Church and the United Presbyterian church) in the great case in which the remnant of the Free Church (the 'Wee Frees') claimed that they were the true church and thus owned all the property, the new body being unsound on predestination and other elements of Calvinism. Part of the case turned on truth and theological definitions, and this part Haldane won; but the part which turned on trust deeds, he lost, which was, however, of little benefit to the Wee Frees, for Haldane, working with A. J. Balfour and others, had the judgment soon reversed by an act of parliament in a striking demonstration of the subservience of judge-made law to legislative sovereignty. His friend Edmund Gosse described the scene: 'Haldane, bland, tireless, imperturbable, never at a disadvantage, always courteous, always ready, pushes on in a faultless flow of language, turning the whole thing into a supplement of his "Pathway to Reality"' (Sommer, 136).

**Higher education in opposition** Haldane's achievements during his opposition years would have been substantial for a cabinet minister. From an early stage in his public career, he promoted the cause of higher educational expansion, which tended to be neglected by politicians amid the constant, deflecting wrangles about the religious issue in English elementary and secondary education. From the late 1880s Haldane was involved in the reform of Edinburgh University, and from 1890 to 1898 he was on the council of University College, London. In 1896 he was defeated by Balfour of Burleigh for the lord rectorship of Edinburgh University, for which he had been asked by the students to stand. Higher education, Haldane believed, played a vital role in national efficiency because it was both the agent of progress—moral, scientific, and economic—and was the means of social development. His best statement of his objectives was in his collected articles and addresses *Education and Empire* (1902). He was active with Sidney Webb in developing the University of London (then in effect merely an examining board) and he played a part in passing the University of London Commission Bill through the Commons in 1897 and again in 1898 (in the latter year making a memorable speech in its defence) and in engineering a compromise which enabled it to pass. In April 1901 a visit to the Technische Hochschule at Charlottenburg in Germany—'by far the most perfect University I have seen' (Ashby and Anderson, 45)—enthused Haldane to a missionary passion for the development of technical education in London. The result, after a long campaign in partnership with Webb, was the establishment at South Kensington of what became Imperial College. Haldane persuaded the firm of Wernher and Beit to divert funds intended for University College to establish the new institution, and he was aided politically by A. J. Balfour. The final report was submitted in January 1906, just after Haldane took office. Imperial College was the chief tangible achievement of the 'national efficiency' movement, and its success owed much to Haldane.

Haldane also encouraged the development of English civic universities, appearing in April 1902 for University College, Liverpool, in its successful suit to the privy council for separation from the Victoria University. The case set an important precedent (for separate rather than federal university development) and led the way for others to follow the Birmingham–Liverpool model. Balfour made Haldane a privy councillor in 1902 (a most unusual encomium for a politician who had never held office). In 1904 he chaired a committee on university grants, an issue which, once in government, he was able to take forward. His popularity in Scotland was marked by his election in 1905 as lord rector of Edinburgh University (regaining the office for the Liberals after twenty-five years). Haldane's educational plans showed a rare combination of the visionary and the practical, and the ability to work with a wide range of people: academics, industrialists, politicians, and administrators. His educational biographers rightly comment: 'nearly all the schemes he submitted had the credibility of an architect's design which is accompanied by a quantity surveyor's estimate' (Ashby and Anderson, 46). His importance as an all-round reformer in scientific education was marked by his election as a fellow of the Royal Society in 1906.

**Haldane and philosophy** Haldane was not an amateur philosopher, as was A. J. Balfour, yet he was not exactly a professional either. His command of German, his early work on Hegel and Schopenhauer, and his capacity for linking philosophical terms with those of the wider world (a distinction he would have denied), meant that his philosophy was authoritative. Yet in the rapidly increasing professionalization of the discipline, he was clearly not an academic practitioner, even though to political colleagues he often seemed a practical academic. His enthusiastic Hegelianism coincided with the mainstream of British philosophy in the 1890s and to an extent in the 1900s, but he rarely figures in histories of the philosophical trends of those decades, in which Bernard Bosanquet is often seen as the most consistent of the Hegelians. Haldane's most extensive statement of his views was given in *The Pathway to Reality* (2 vols., 1903–4), the Gifford lectures given in the University of St Andrews in 1902–3. Haldane's aim was to account for 'the world as it seems', and to analyse all its phases; if all phases are included, we end by seeing them in their appropriate relationships, higher and lower, and 'by interpretation through the highest we come nearest to a true account of the ultimately real' (Pringle-Pattison, 434). Haldane's lectures show him an articulate and well-read Hegelian. After his early essays and translation, his philosophy was not, however, innovative, and is chiefly interesting as posing the question: to what extent did it influence or condition his approach to practical affairs? Haldane would have seen this as a false distinction: what most people saw as mere 'practical affairs' were inherently the consequence of philosophical belief. Haldane had a grasp of structures and relationships in politics which was very unusual in the English context. He declined to be bound by the usual empirical precedents of history and practice, and tried to see the essential purpose of institutions as they were and as they might be, and in this sense he brought his philosophical precepts directly to bear. He was then able to link this analysis with the practical skills of the political reformer. In that lay his distinctive contribution, one rarely matched in twentieth-century British public life. He was elected a fellow of the British Academy in 1914 (it is odd that he was not invited to be one of the founding fellows in 1902).

**Cabinet minister and army reformer** More than his Liberal Imperialist colleagues, Haldane mistrusted Campbell-Bannerman's ability to lead an energetically reforming Liberal government, and he was the chief architect of the so-called 'Relugas Compact' of 1905 by which the king would persuade Campbell-Bannerman to go to the House of Lords and the 'Limps' (as they were called) would capture what they saw as the chief offices (with Haldane to be lord chancellor). None of the plan worked in detail, but the Limps did well in the offices when Campbell-Bannerman formed his government in December 1905 on A. J. Balfour's resignation. He offered Haldane the attorney-generalship (declined), then the Home Office (declined), and the War Office, the latter being accepted on 8 December, Lord Lucas (Auberon Thomas) being his private secretary at Haldane's request. Haldane took a large cut in income (having earned over £20,000 in his last year at the bar), and moved to 28 Queen Anne's Gate, his London home for the rest of his life. 'We shall now see how Schopenhauer gets on in the Kailyard' was Campbell-Bannermann's pawky comment (Sommer, 152).

Haldane entered the War Office in December 1905 knowing more about the navy than the army. He had advocated a 'scientific' army since the Second South African War, and in 1901 wanted 'a comparatively small Army—one extremely efficacious and capable for foreign service', but not one able to 'compete with the enormous armaments of Europe' (Matthew, 219). But he had not studied military affairs with the attention he had given to the navy or education, though he had regularly visited Woolwich as a member of Lord Rayleigh's committee on propellent explosives (which he had originally himself been asked to chair). In naval matters, he was a 'bluewater' Liberal and opposed Brodrick's army reform proposals on the grounds that it must be assumed that the navy could prevent invasion. The embarrassment to the army of its performance in the Second South African War and the failures of the plans of both Haldane's predecessors—St John Brodrick and H. O. Arnold-Forster—meant that senior army officers felt demoralized: they responded quickly and on the whole enthusiastically to Haldane's careful self-presentation both as an intelligent reformer wanting 'A Hegelian Army' and 'as a young and blushing virgin just united to a bronzed warrior' (both phrases he recalls relating to the army council (Haldane, *Autobiography*, 183–5)). It was at once clear to the generals that any Liberal would be worse for them than Haldane. As a veteran of internecine strife in the Liberal Party during the previous decade, Haldane knew that he had to preserve a delicate balance between the radical wing of his own party and the Unionist opposition. He was aided, however, by the fact that the Unionists' record as military reformers—when reform was generally agreed to be needed—was so poor that their usual playing of the patriotic card could receive shortish shrift. He was in a strong position to maintain the tradition that military reform was best done by a progressive government. His views were collected in *Army Reform and other Addresses* (1907).

Haldane's initial months were vital to his secretaryship. On Lord Esher's advice, he chose Gerald Francis *Ellison as his military private secretary and was inducted by Ellison, during a visit to Cloan in December 1905, into the thinking of army reformers. Grey, shortly afterwards, as foreign secretary, permitted the start of the Anglo-French military conversations which cast such a long shadow over Liberal foreign and defence policy. Haldane's first policy statement was a memorandum on retrenchment (the first of four strategic documents) produced for the army council on 1 January 1906. It offered savings within a £28 million estimate (more generous than the generals had anticipated from the Liberal government) and Haldane from the start energetically effected the maxim that 'economy and efficiency were not incompatible', thus guarding if not securing his radical flank. On 9 January, just after consultation with Haldane, Grey authorized the military conversations: if the die was not cast, the direction of military planning was fenced in. Plans for an expeditionary force, adumbrated since Brodrick, were honed to a force most probably for use in Europe, and probably against Germany. The conversations were secret, even from most members of the cabinet, and Haldane's plans for an expeditionary force had to be presented accordingly. In the course of 1906 the 'continental strategy' became the dominant though not publicly acknowledged ideology of strategic planning in the British army, though this and its consequences were not clear at the time. Haldane's expeditionary force was not solely planned for a European war, but this was soon its chief *raison d'être* and plans for its mobilization for a European war were soon drawn up, chiefly by Henry Wilson and by Douglas Haig (Haldane probably exaggerated the role of the latter in his autobiography (Spiers, 154–9)); these plans were those used, without much alteration, in August 1914. In reply to the question, 'why did the British government between 1906 and 1914 not discuss in public a situation which it understood well by appealing to the nation?', Haldane argued after the war that 'to have done so would have been greatly to increase the difficulty of averting war' (Haldane, *Before the War*, 11).

Haldane presented his plans publicly on 8 March 1906 achieving a 'triumph he would rarely emulate' (Spiers, 57). Some Liberals, led by Seely, called for increased reductions but Haldane, backed by the Unionists, had a majority of 240. The cuts Haldane then made included two battalions of guards; this produced a predictable storm, with the guards reductions being reduced though not abandoned. Haldane's reductions amounted to 16,600 men and £2.6 million while providing for an expeditionary force and an adequate flow of highly trained reserves, facilitated by a return to the Cardwellian principle of seven years with the colours and five with reserve, one of his first changes (Spiers, 62–4, 143).

Together with this change, Haldane made historic changes to the non-professional army, which because of the important status of the yeomanry, the volunteers, and the militia, especially in country life, was a courageous political undertaking: none of the traditional organizations was thought capable of participating effectively in a modern war. In a second memorandum of 1 February 1906, Haldane agreed that 'the basis of our whole military fabric must be the development of the idea of a real national army, formed by the people … It might be styled the Territorial Army' (Spiers, 95). Remnants of the militia and the yeomanry would provide a striking force; the Territorial Force (as it was officially called until 1921) would be partially trained, ready for intensive training when required. This was enacted in the Territorial and Reserve Forces Bill, adumbrated in Haldane's speech on the army estimates of 25 February 1907, and introduced that April. Opposition was less than expected both in the Commons and the Lords, but the measure received royal assent in August 1907 stripped of some of its 'citizenship' elements. One of these was provision for county associations (the name borrowed from Oliver Cromwell) to run the territorials and to fund the cadet corps. The latter was proposed via a committee set up by the previous Unionist government. The committee's main proposal, an Officers' Training Corps (OTC) replacing the existing school and university corps, was none the less launched on 1 April 1908, despite some opposition from Labour and Conservative MPs (for different reasons). Haldane campaigned strenuously for both the territorials and the OTC and gained the important support of Edward VII who gave social status to the territorials. Haldane's reorganization of the nation's reserves was a deft piece of political management; even so, the concessions he had to make to the volunteers on the responsibilities of the territorials—an ambiguous balance between home defence and support for the expeditionary force—later caused difficulties. Within a year there were 9313 officers and 259,463 other ranks in the Territorial Force (Dennis, 17), but this rate was not sustained, and Haldane's view in 1909, expressed in a letter to his mother on 23 June, that his 'great reform of the Army is now complete & an accomplished fact' was not wholly true (ibid.). His hopes that the OTC would act as a catalyst for a greater union between army and society were improbable, but in the OTC (later, in schools, the combined cadet force) he created an organization of profound significance to the ethos of British public school education for much of the twentieth century. By 1914 it had over 27,000 members. The number as yet taking commissions was disappointingly small (Spiers, 141), but its importance as a supply of officers in wartime was incalculable.

Haldane's reforms were partly intended to show that Britain's military needs could be met without conscription, which was increasingly supported by sections of the army and by some Unionists. The conscription lobby, led by Lord Roberts of Kandahar as president from 1905 of the National Service League, had an interest in the failure of the voluntary territorials. Haldane authorized the publication of a memorandum by General Ian Hamilton (later chosen by Asquith to command the army at the Dardanelles): *Compulsory Service: a Study of the Question in the Light of Experience* (1910), with an introduction by Haldane, caused a furore in army circles.

Haldane was bequeathed by Balfour three related organizations, the committee of imperial defence (CID), the army council, and plans for a general staff, none with a clear identity or established authority. Despite his support for it in opposition, Haldane as secretary of state was rather cool about the CID, finding it a problematic forum; he found inter-service co-operation more easily developed at a lower level. He did not use the army council as much as his predecessors, preferring not to meet the generals too often *en masse*, and his qualities best shone in face-to-face discussion. He established the general staff by order in September 1906, and successfully developed it into an Imperial General Staff (IGS) via the Colonial Conference in 1907. Haldane entrusted the development of the IGS to General Douglas *Haig, an important act of patronage, as things turned out. He also strongly encouraged the establishment of a naval equivalent. He had the opportunity to observe German methods at first hand when he conducted what became known as the 'Haldane mission' to Berlin in September 1906. This visit, which included an extensive interview with the Kaiser, briefly improved the tone of relations between Britain and Germany, but was not intended to attempt more than that.

The War Office seemed the natural office to develop the new weapon of air power. But there was considerable military diffidence about exploiting what the Germans at once saw as the military equivalent of the dreadnought. In May 1909, with a press campaign led by Northcliffe already under way and reports of airships, real or phantom, over Britain becoming common, Asquith announced the solution Haldane had prepared: the advisory committee for aeronautics, a joint committee, chaired by Lord Rayleigh (with whom Haldane had worked on the explosives committee) of the War Office, the Admiralty, and the National Physical Laboratory at Teddington. Northcliffe criticized the committee for a lack of practitioners in its membership, but Haldane replied, with some effect and insight, in a letter of 18 May 1909: 'The Naval and Military experts have demonstrated to the

Defence Committee [of the CID] that dirigibles and still more aeroplanes are a very long way off being the slightest practical use in war … The scientific problems are not worked out' (Gollin, 45–6). Haldane's aim was not to create a quick solution to the problem of the supply of planes, but to work out first a sound scientific appraisal of the uses to which flight could be put in war. This became the advisory committee, a very British device, in due course achieved.

Haldane's success at the War Office was extensive and profound. He succeeded to a remarkable degree in taking the army out of politics (the comment of *The Times* on his death, that his secretaryship was 'the most tempestuous and bitterly contested period of his life', was true of the inquest on his secretaryship; it was not the verdict at the time). His reforms gave the Liberals a modernized army without conscription, his financial control protected it from cabinet inquiries, and as E. M. Spiers observes, to the army 'a Secretary of State in a Liberal cabinet who could preserve Estimates in excess of £27 millions and conceal a new departure in Continental planning was a considerable asset' (Spiers, 195). His astute handling of army and CID business in cabinet saw off much of the attempt by the 'economists' (led by Lloyd George and Churchill) for much more sweeping defence retrenchment. Haldane's reforms were thought to have modernized the British army for a possible or even probable war in Europe. They can be seen as an important part of British self-deception as to what that war would involve and they can be seen as in themselves associating Britain prospectively with that war to a greater extent than Haldane and other informed politicians allowed. But in the early months of the First World War, Haldane's army worked more efficiently than any other British army at the start of a major war.

**Haldane and Liberal politics** Haldane's involvement in the War Office, and his concern to shelter his department, meant that he played less of a role in the Liberal government than might have been expected. By 1909 his eyesight had seriously deteriorated and he was badly affected by rheumatism; he was ordered by doctors to take a complete rest. He thus missed much of the drama of the 1909 session. In 1910 he almost lost the sight of one eye through an attack of iritis and the same year he was diagnosed as a diabetic, a condition for which at that time dietary control was the only remedy. Even so, he was a legendary walker and cigar smoker. Despite this ill health, he chaired a demanding royal commission on London University from 1909 until 1913, war then preventing the implementation of its recommendations.

In November 1910 Asquith asked Haldane to become Indian secretary in place of John Morley, with a peerage. Haldane declined, but stated his willingness to move to the Admiralty; he had long favoured establishing a naval general staff and believed he could achieve for the navy the sort of unified purpose on the part of its senior officers which he had been so successful in establishing for the army and which the navy so obviously lacked. Lord Crewe succeeded Morley, but soon fell ill. In March 1911 Haldane accepted a peerage, as Viscount Haldane of Cloan, and took on Crewe's duties as leader of the Liberal peers in the Lords, a vital task in the year of the Parliament Bill. Haldane's views about the poor state of the Admiralty were confirmed by differences of planning for mobilization exposed during the Agadir crisis of July 1911 and especially at a meeting of the CID on 23 August when the Admiralty revealed the extent of its absence of co-ordinated planning. Haldane pressed Asquith for the post of first lord of the Admiralty, which Winston Churchill (until very recently a fierce armament retrencher) also wanted. Asquith procrastinated, and may have been alarmed to discover the extent to which the army's plans committed the British to involvement in a German–French war. He floated the lord chancellorship at Haldane, eventually appointing Churchill to the Admiralty and informing Haldane of the need for the first lord to be in the Commons. Haldane took what was undoubtedly a disappointment with equanimity; but it was the first sign of his place in Asquith's priorities. Haldane was not at this time entitled by the usual rules to sit on the judicial committee, never having held high legal office, but under a clause of the 1833 act, he was placed there by royal nomination. Haldane's peerage was followed by the freedom of two of the cities in his former constituency, Haddington (1911) and Dunbar (1912), and of Edinburgh (1913). He was appointed a knight of the Thistle on 19 May 1913.

The resignation of Balfour as Unionist leader had as much effect on Haldane as any changes in the government. Haldane had worked closely and confidentially with Balfour, using him almost as a member of the government (and thus adumbrating Balfour's wartime role). Bonar Law, Balfour's successor, knew nothing of defence matters, as his early attempts to criticize the government showed, but his move towards a less bipartisan approach were accompanied by strong attacks on Haldane by Leo Maxse in the *National Review*, which linked Haldane's sympathy for German intellectual life with his supposed incompetence as war secretary.

Despite Asquith's unwillingness to make Haldane first lord of the Admiralty, it was Haldane whom the cabinet sent to Berlin in February 1912 (the second 'Haldane mission'), to attempt a compromise on naval expansion. He went as if on an educational inquiry (he was then chairing the royal commission on London University) and with his brother John, an Oxford physiologist, as his secretary. Haldane had no powers to negotiate but was to see if a negotiation was possible. He conducted the discussions mostly in German and returned with some modest prospect of agreement (but premised on a British guarantee of unconditional neutrality) and a copy of the new German law of naval expansion, which greatly alarmed the Admiralty. But the Germans insisted on the unconditional guarantee and subsequent negotiations came to nothing.

**Lord chancellor** In June 1912, in a process of considerable contortion of the sort which Haldane seemed to attract, he succeeded Lord Loreburn as lord chancellor (Heuston, 166ff.), who resigned from ill health (and was to become the senior of the critics of Haldane and Grey's concealment of the military conversations in France). In an obvious sense the lord chancellorship was the natural culmination of Haldane's career. Yet there was another sense in which the Admiralty in 1911 would have been the more natural move. Haldane was cautious about his new post. He left a sharp self-assessment of his legal capacities in his *Autobiography*:

> I never considered that I was equipped by nature for the part of a great judge. It was not that I did not know the law. I knew it pretty thoroughly; I had had a long experience at the Bar of the most difficult and miscellaneous kinds of work; and memory had preserved the bulk of my knowledge, notwithstanding absence for over six years at the War Office. But the judicial temperament of the highest order is a very rare gift. (Haldane, *Autobiography*, 255)

In the view of one of his close colleagues, Lord Dunedin, 'he was thoroughly sound in his judgments. He was, I think, very seldom wrong' (Pringle-Pattison, 443). Haldane's chief contributions to the law came in 1914–15, and particularly in the fields of equity and dominion constitutional law. In equity, Haldane was 'particularly strong … in the uncertain area where the principles of common law and equity overlap' (Heuston, 215), judgments in the cases of *Nocton* v. *Ashburton* in 1914 and *Sinclair* v. *Brougham* being of especial elegance. In dominion law, Haldane presided over the judicial committee of the privy council (JCPC) in every important appeal. He was particularly energetic on Canadian subjects, playing a part in thirty-two judgments between 1912 and 1929 on the validity of Canadian legislation. In 1912 he attended a meeting of the Canadian Bar Association in Montreal, to which he gave a speech entitled 'The higher nationality: a study in law and ethics', reprinted in *The Conduct of Life and other Addresses* (1914).

But Haldane was unable to effect the plans he had suggested in the early 1900s for imperial integration by making the judicial committee of the privy council into an imperial court of appeal, though he did tell their lordships that the judicial committee and the House of Lords should be combined into one supreme imperial court. Nor did he encourage the Lords in his ideas about their becoming an imperial senate or council, the 'Senate House of the Empire', as he had proposed in his article 'The cabinet and the empire' in the *Proceedings of the Royal Colonial Institute* (34, 1903, 325–52). The Parliament Act of 1911 was intended by the Liberal government as a first step towards constitutional reform, but this was not a course to which Haldane was able to give priority, though he had a plan for a ministry of justice and a separation of the judicial from the administrative duties of the lord chancellor. In the area of land law, in which Haldane had been active earlier, his record was ambivalent. On his appointment as lord chancellor he was invited to dine with the Institute, as the conveyancing barristers' association was known, and the conveyancers looked to Haldane to maintain his earlier support for registration of land title—a matter in which the conveyancers had a long-standing dispute with the solicitors. But Haldane set aside Loreburn's plans for registration and, working with Benjamin Cherry, produced a bill much more satisfactory to the solicitors. Introduced in the Lords in 1913 and 1914, it made no further progress at that time. Haldane thus played only a minor role in the Liberals' land campaign in the years before the war.

As speaker of the Lords, Haldane had a heavy burden as Liberal legislation—particularly the third Government of Ireland Bill—made its way through the Lords under the Parliament Act. He was also in effect the War Office spokesman in the Lords. Moreover, in 1911 he became chancellor of the University of Bristol, a position he took seriously, his inaugural address, 'The civic university' (1912) being a notable statement (reproduced in *The Conduct of Life and other Addresses*, 1914). He remained an active member of the CID and tried to take seriously Asquith's suggestion in 1911 that he give 'much needful inspiration and guidance' to Churchill as first lord. He frequently found himself a broker between the Admiralty and other departments.

It was thus not surprising that in August 1914 Asquith (who was acting war secretary) in effect recalled Haldane to his old post, for he, of cabinet ministers, best knew the intended working of the war book which determined the course of British mobilization. Very early on 3 August Asquith wrote a note requesting Haldane to 'put the necessary machinery, messages, etc., in order' for mobilization (Maurice, 1.355). This Haldane took to the War Office, where he assembled the army council and ordered mobilization. He also recommended Kitchener for the War Office. Haldane favoured sending all six divisions of the expeditionary force to France immediately, but others, led by Kitchener and fearful for home defence, prevailed and on 6 August only four divisions were sent. This diminution quickly became a central feature of a press campaign against Haldane, led by the *Daily Express*, which proved lasting and effective. Haldane's refusal to publish a letter he had received from Albert Ballin, the arranger of his visit to Berlin in 1912 and his guest in London in July 1914, was thought to add substance to charges of deception and pro-Germanism. He was not helped by Professor Oncken of Heidelberg stating that Haldane had called Germany 'his spiritual home' (in fact, at a dinner party held by Mrs Humphry Ward in April 1913 for Haldane to meet German professors he had said that Lötze's classroom in Göttingen was his spiritual home (Sommer, 318–19)). In September 1914 Haldane's offer of resignation was declined by Asquith. A further offer was also rejected, but when Asquith formed his coalition government in May 1915, Haldane was dropped and never again held office as a Liberal. The xenophobic campaign against him in the Unionist press was utterly misplaced. No minister bore greater responsibility for Britain's capacity to engage Germany in 1914—almost non-existent when Haldane went to the War Office in December 1905—but Haldane's reputation as an intriguer, his writing of philosophical books, his often opaque statements, the fact that he spoke fluent German (uniquely among the class of executive politicians) made him, in the foetid domestic political atmosphere of the time, an unsurprising target for a frustrated press and party, for whom 'patriotism' had become almost the only card left to play. Asquith and Grey, his closest political friends, could have done more to protect him, but they may have felt the gale too strong to do anything but let Haldane swing in it.

**Out of office but not out of influence** Haldane was made a member of the Order of Merit by George V on his retiral. Asquith, embarrassed, handled the retiral awkwardly, but wrote a fulsome letter of appreciation for a meeting at the National Liberal Club. In his memoirs Haldane stated that he 'was never depressed by even the most violent abuse' (Haldane, *Autobiography*, 287). None the less, he understandably soon began, in April 1916, a retrospective defence, in the form of a 'Memorandum of events between 1906–1915' for private circulation; publication was proscribed by the Foreign Office. In August 1915 the Foreign Office published some of the documents on the Berlin visit of 1912 which it had previously declined to release. Haldane's memorandum formed the basis of his *Before the War* (1920). The Harmsworth Press found other targets and by the end of 1915 Haldane was able to play a part in affairs without jingoistic outrage. The duke of Buccleuch embarrassed the dignity of the House of Lords on 12 July 1916 by directly charging Haldane with 'misleading Great Britain upon the German danger, and misleading Germany upon British policy' (Sommer, 338); their lordships applauded Haldane's dignified reply. Haldane was defended at length by Harold Begbie in *The Vindication of Great Britain* (1916). He returned to legal work in the Lords, and made further educational contacts. With Albert Mansbridge, R. H. Tawney, and others he improved the organization of the Workers' Educational Association and formed the British Institute of Adult Education and he persuaded Sir Ernest Cassell to fund it. Until 1926 Haldane was its president. He chaired a royal commission on the organization of university education in Wales and a Home Office committee on coal conservation. In May 1916 he returned to direct involvement in the course of the war, advising the government on the creation of the Air Ministry. He chaired the education sub-committee of Asquith's reconstruction committee in 1916, and on 12 July 1916 made in the Lords 'perhaps the greatest education speech in his career', advocating a progressive and co-ordinated approach to educational reform (Ashby and Anderson, 135). He also advised the king on constitutional questions such as the possibility of a general election as the Asquith coalition came to its end. Haldane was not offered a post when Lloyd George formed his coalition government in December 1916, but he continued to be active at the fringes of the government, particularly striking up a constructive relationship with H. A. L. Fisher, president of the Board of Education. He advised Fisher during the preparation of the Education Act of 1918, though his own preferred method of organization of English education (through eight or nine provincial educational authorities) only appeared in the bill in shadowy form.

Lloyd George asked Haldane to chair a committee on the machinery of government, which reported in December 1918, one of the very few official attempts to consider the overall purpose, character, and composition of British government; however, it was published during the general election just after the armistice and made little immediate impact. After the war Haldane continued in such activities. He sat on sub-committees of the CID and chaired a committee in 1922 to produce a plan to enable the Church of Scotland to unite with the United Free Church, the church whose interests he had represented against the Wee Frees twenty years earlier.

During the post-war period, Haldane remained active on educational questions, particularly in London and in Scotland (where he was one of the Carnegie trustees). He secured admission of Birkbeck College as a school of London University in 1920. In that year, negotiations which he had had with Fisher, as minister for education, almost came to fruition and the Bloomsbury site north of the British Museum was about to be secured for London University. However, complications arose between the London colleges and the offer lapsed (it was successfully recovered in 1927 by William Beveridge). The London University Act of 1926 drew on the findings of Haldane's royal commission of 1909–13, though these had inevitably lost immediate relevance. Haldane continued to be a frequent speaker at places such as Toynbee Hall, being particularly helpful there with the annual American seminar. He was involved in the establishment of the privy council's committee on scientific and industrial research and was first president of the Institute of Public Administration (1922).

**Haldane's later philosophical writings** By the 1920s Hegelianism in Britain was waning fast, with Haldane almost its last full-blooded exponent. In 1921 he published *The Reign of Relativity*, an investigation of the philosophical implications of Einstein's ideas; the book was planned in 1915 after he ceased to be lord chancellor. In the course of it, he offered a general defence of Hegelianism and attempted a rebuttal of Bertrand Russell's 'New Realism'. The 'Concluding reflections' linked Hegel, Goethe, and Burke. The book ran to three editions in six weeks. On Haldane's invitation Einstein came to visit him in London in June 1921; Haldane chaired Einstein's lecture and gave a dinner party for him at Queen Anne's Gate, at which it became clear that Einstein did not believe that his theory had any implication for morals, but otherwise the visit was a considerable success and introduced Einstein to British cultural life. Haldane also published *The Philosophy of Humanism* in 1922 and *Human Experience* in 1926, the latter a popular philosophical discussion of new ideas in science.

**Post-war politics and return to office** Not surprisingly, Haldane's relations with Asquith cooled after May 1915 or, as Haldane put it in his *Autobiography*, 'With my old friend Asquith, I had long ceased to have much opportunity to talk about politics' (Haldane, *Autobiography*, 309). But he remained on quite close terms with Edward Grey. Haldane was attracted by Lloyd George—despite his view that Lloyd George was 'really an illiterate with an unbalanced mind' (Sommer, 352)—for Haldane liked to get things done. In the Maurice debate in May 1918, Haldane stated in the Lords that there was no alternative to the existing government, even though he thought Lloyd George had been wrong (Maurice, 2.53). Haldane had always found the Liberal Party too compromised by its nonconformist connections to be a constructive force in education, and the educational context in which he now moved was largely Fabian and Labour in political character. He did not, however, formally join any party organization. He acted as go-between with Lloyd George and the Labour leadership (just the sort of covert task he especially enjoyed) during the strikes of 1919–20 and about the personnel of the Sankey commission in the coal industry, to which in due course he gave evidence (reprinted as *The Problem of Coal Nationalization*, 1921, with an introduction by Harold Laski and R. H. Tawney). He stated in the Lords his support for coal nationalization and for the Labour Party's educational policy, and he resisted an attempt by Asquith and Grey to draw him back into Liberal politics, telling them he felt the Liberals had little to offer on education (Maurice, 2.108). This in effect formalized a break already made. In the general election campaign in 1923 he spoke at several meetings for Labour candidates. Haldane expected the Asquithian Liberals to support a Conservative rather than a Labour government and was surprised to find himself wrong. After complex negotiations with Ramsay MacDonald, in which he was offered education, India, or the lord chancellorship (MacDonald hoping to have Sankey as lord chancellor) (ibid., 2.144), Haldane returned to office as lord chancellor in January 1924, with an arrangement that Lord Cave, his predecessor, would carry a fair part of the office's judicial duties to allow Haldane time to chair the CID and bring forward reforms in the machinery of government. In consideration of Cave's help, Haldane allowed him to remain in the lord chancellor's official residence in the House of Lords. Haldane also renounced £4000 of his salary of £10,000.

Haldane was a substantial catch for the first Labour government. He explained the etiquette of cabinet—including the habit of always addressing the prime minister by his office—at its first meeting and used his advantage of unquestioned experience to introduce smoking in cabinet. He was able to help inexperienced Labour MPs deal authoritatively with their civil servants. He found MacDonald 'an excellent President' (Marquand, 310). Haldane was seen as chairman of the CID as long-winded and excessively nostalgic (Heuston, 236). As lord chancellor he began plans for a ministry of justice, but these made little headway. One small but important achievement was the introduction in February 1924 of a government grant for the British Academy (which otherwise had little income) and the obtaining for it of premises at Burlington House; this Haldane negotiated together with A. J. Balfour, the academy's president (Haldane was a member of its council from 1919 until his death).

Haldane sat on a cabinet committee on the Zinoviev letter (now known to have been a forgery), published just before the general election in October 1924. The committee came to no conclusion, having not seen the original of the letter, and the Labour government, already heavily defeated in the country, resigned on 4 November 1924. With it ended Haldane's cabinet career. However, he continued to lead the Labour peers after 1924 (not an extensive duty) and on Baldwin's invitation he continued his membership of the CID, which rather irritated MacDonald. He continued to sit as a law lord, though he released himself from his rule of sitting on every dominion appeal with a constitutional element. His last case was *Medway Oil Co. Ltd* v. *Continental Contractors Ltd*, in which he showed 'no sign of intellectual exhaustion' (Heuston, 237). The Haldane Society for radical lawyers was founded in his memory.

In 1926 Haldane drafted his *Autobiography* (prepared in 1929 for posthumous publication by his sister) and sympathized with the miners during the general strike. In 1927 his memory began to fail slightly, though he was able to pay tribute in the Lords to the memories of Haig and Asquith early in 1928. With his health rapidly declining, he was delighted to hear of his election as chancellor of St Andrews University in June 1928 and his final public address, to the Association of Headmistresses on 9 June, linked the relativity of knowledge to an understanding of Indian thought and showed little signs of failing mental powers. He died at Cloan on 19 August 1928 and was buried at Gleneagles, Perthshire, a large contingent of regular and Territorial Army units attending, with a lament played by the Black Watch pipe band.

**Assessment** Haldane was a strange, exotic figure in British public life, one of the few of our politicians who might have passed for a continental intellectual in politics. His tubby, latterly almost spherical appearance, soft, high-pitched voice, and strange arm gestures when speaking—the cartoonist F. Carruthers Gould drew him as a speaking penguin—reinforced a sense of intellectual oddness. Leo Amery recalled of him that 'in figure, features and demeanour there was something about him of the old-fashioned family butler' (L. S. Amery, *My Political Life*, 1953, 1.277). Haldane relished politics as well as philosophy, and often seemed to relish them too much, hence his reputation as an intriguer, an aspect of his character brilliantly captured in Max Beerbohm's cartoon of 1907, *8.30 p.m. Mr. Haldane Exercising a Ministerial Prerogative* (Ashmolean Museum, Oxford). To an unusual extent his sometimes rather tortuous attempts to link people and solve problems were disinterested; he had little personal ambition, and his behaviour out of office, after the initial shock, was generous. He went to some lengths to try to safeguard his reputation through his later publications, but his writings on the war were, by the standards of Churchill and Lloyd George, restrained and dignified. Haldane's achievements in the areas of education and army reform and a number of others are indisputable, and remarkable by any standard, but there is, even so, a sense of something missing, even before the débâcle of 1915. Haldane was not at all anti-democratic, in the way of many imperialists in the period, but his interests and objectives were for the sorts of changes which the representative governmental system—mired in the problems of the Lords and of Ireland—found hard to give priority. As a result, his achievement carries with it an air of incompleteness, just as much of his report on the future structure of British government still languishes. H. C. G. MATTHEW

**Sources** R. B. Haldane, *An autobiography* (1929) • R. B. Haldane, *Before the war* (1920) • F. B. Maurice, *Haldane*, 2 vols. (1937–9) • D. Sommer, *Haldane of Cloan* (1960) • A. S. Pringle-Pattison, 'Richard Burton Haldane (Viscount Haldane of Cloan), 1856–1928', *PBA*, 14 (1928), 405–44 [with an additional note by Viscount Dunedin] • S. E. Koss, *Lord Haldane, scapegoat for liberalism* (1969) • R. F. V. Heuston, *Lives of the lord chancellors, 1885–1940* (1964) • E. Ashby and M. Anderson, *Portrait of Haldane at work on education* (1974) • E. M. Spiers, *Haldane: an army reformer* (1980) • E. S. Haldane, *From one century to another* (1937) • H. C. G. Matthew, *The liberal imperialists* (1973) • N. d'Ombrain, *War machinery and high policy: defence and administration in peacetime Britain, 1902–1914* (1973) • I. F. W. Beckett and K. Simpson, eds., *A nation in arms: a social study of the British army in the First World War* (1985) • I. Beckett and J. Gooch, eds., *Politicians and defence: studies in the formulation of British defence policy, 1845–1970* (1981) • A. Gollin, 'The mystery of Lord Haldane and early British military aviation', *Albion*, 11 (1979), 46–65 • A. Gollin, *The impact of air power* (1989) • B. Bond, 'R. B. Haldane at the war office, 1905–1912', *Army Quarterly*, 86 (1963), 33–43 • Viscount Wavell and others, 'Haldane centenary essays', *Public Administration*, 35 (autumn 1957) [whole issue] • C. H. Wilson, *Haldane and the machinery of government* (1957) • L. von Reiken, *Haldane: Umriss eines liberalen Imperialisten* (1938) • E. K. Bramstedt, 'Lord Haldane and Germany', *Contemporary Review*, 157 (1940), 583–90 • J. H. Morgan, 'The riddle of Lord Haldane', *Contemporary Review*, 252 (1929), 339–56 • E. Grey, *Viscount Haldane of Cloan, O. M.: the man and his work* (1928) • C. Schuster, 'Lord Haldane as chancellor', *Public Administration*, 6 (1928), 361–4 • A. Offer, *Property and politics, 1870–1914* (1981) • B. Webb, *My apprenticeship* (1926) • B. Webb, *Our partnership* (1948) • *The diary of Beatrice Webb*, ed. N. MacKenzie and J. MacKenzie, 4 vols. (1982–5), vol. 1 • *H. H. Asquith: letters to Venetia Stanley*, ed. M. Brock and E. Brock (1982) • [J. A. Pease], *A liberal chronicle*, ed. C. Hazlehurst and C. Woodland (1994) • D. Marquand, *Ramsay MacDonald* (1977) • *DNB* • P. Dennis, *The Territorial Army, 1906–1940*, Royal Historical Society Studies in History, 51 (1987)

**Archives** NAM, corresp. and papers • NL Scot., corresp. and papers | BL, corresp. with Arthur James Balfour, Add. MS 49724 • BL, letters to Sir Henry Campbell-Bannerman, Add. MS 41218 • BL, corresp. with Lord H. J. Gladstone, Add. MSS 46055–46084 • BL, corresp. with Lord Northcliffe, Add. MS 62155 • BL, letters to George Bernard Shaw, Add. MS 50538 • BL, corresp. with J. A. Spender, Add. MS 46390 • BL OIOC, letters to Lord Reading, MSS Eur. E 238, F 118 • BLPES, letters to the Webbs • Bodl. Oxf., corresp. with Herbert Asquith • Bodl. Oxf., letters to Sir William Harcourt and Lewis Harcourt • Bodl. Oxf., corresp. with Lord Selborne • CAC Cam., letters to W. T. Stead • Cornell University, Ithaca, New York, letter to G. W. Cunningham • CUL, corresp. with Lord Hardinge • HLRO, letters to David Lloyd George • HLRO, Gosse MSS • HLRO, letters to H. Samuel • HLRO, corresp. with John St Loe Strachey • IWM, French MSS • JRL, letters to *Manchester Guardian* • NA Scot., corresp. with G. W. Balfour • NL Ire., letters to A. S. Green • NL Scot., letters to John Buchan • NL Scot., letters to Mrs C. W. Earle • NL Scot., letters to A. C. Fraser • NL Scot., corresp. with Lord Rosebery • NL Wales, corresp. with Thomas Jones • NRA, priv. coll., corresp. with Sir John Ewart • Nuffield Oxf., letters to Lord Mottistone • PRO, corresp. with Lord Kitchener, PRO 30/57, WO 159 • Rutgers University, New Jersey, letters to Sir Edmund Gosse • Sci. Mus., corresp. with Oswald John Silberrad • U. Birm. L., corresp. with Joseph Chamberlain • U. Birm. L., corresp. with W. H. Dawson • U. Leeds, Brotherton L., letters to Sir Edmund Gosse • U. Newcastle, Robinson L., corresp. with Walter Runciman | FILM BFI NFTVA, news footage

**Likenesses** Lafayette, photograph, 1906, V&A [*see illus.*] • M. Beerbohm, cartoon, 1907, AM Oxf. • M. Beerbohm, watercolour caricature, 1912, NPG • A. S. Cope, oils, 1914, Gov. Art Coll. • W. Rothenstein, pencil drawing, 1916, Scot. NPG • P. A. de Laszlo, oils, 1928, NPG • F. C. Gould, pen-and-ink cartoon, NPG • Owl, caricature, NPG; repro. in *VF* (19 March 1913) • B. Partridge, caricature, drawing, NPG; repro. in *Punch* (1 Nov 1926) • Spy [L. Ward], cartoon, repro. in *VF* (13 Feb 1896) • G. F. Watts, oils, Lincoln's Inn, London • G. F. Watts, oils, Scot. NPG • photographs, NPG • photographs, repro. in Maurice, *Haldane* • photographs, repro. in Sommer, *Haldane*

**Wealth at death** £69,334 16s. 4d.: confirmation, 26 Oct 1928, *CCI*

**Haldane, Robert** (1764–1842), theological writer and evangelical patron, was born on 28 February 1764 in Queen Anne Street, Cavendish Square, London, elder son of Captain James Haldane (1728–1768), heir to Airthrey estate, Stirlingshire, and Katherine Duncan (*d.* 1774) of Lundie near Dundee. Brought up by his maternal grandmother and educated at Dundee grammar school (1777) and the high school of Edinburgh, he joined the navy in 1780, serving as midshipman in the *Monarch*, commanded by his uncle, Adam Duncan, and subsequently experiencing action against the French in the *Foudroyant* under Sir John Jervis. With the return of peace in 1783 he resumed civilian life, attending Edinburgh University for two academic sessions. After the customary continental tour he married Katherine Cochrane (1768–1843), daughter of George Oswald of Scotstown, on 24 April 1786 and settled at Airthrey, where their only child, Margaret, was born the following year. About 1795, through various influences, including David Bogue, Independent minister at Gosport, and William Innes, second minister of Stirling, his previously conventional adherence to established religion became noticeably more serious.

This religious change intensified suspicions which Haldane had aroused by a speech to Stirlingshire freeholders in July 1794 opposing the arming of volunteers and the continuance of war with France, and displaying clear sympathies for democratic developments in that country. Though an attraction to the doctrine of human depravity rapidly destroyed Haldane's earlier confidence in the efficacy of political experiments, his emerging evangelicalism led him into activities which, in the heightened tension of the later 1790s, drew from critics accusations of subversive intent towards the establishment. These he attempted to silence in 1800 in his *Address to the public concerning political opinions, and plans lately adopted to promote religion in Scotland*.

Searching for greater usefulness Haldane put the Airthrey estate up for sale, intending with three ordained companions, their families, and a group of catechists to mount a Christian mission to Benares. When the scheme foundered in 1797 on the opposition of the East India Company directorate, his interest turned to Scotland and to the work of the Society for the Propagation of the Gospel at Home, which had been formed in January 1798 by a group of Edinburgh laymen led by his brother, James Alexander *Haldane. The lack of a suitable corps of young men trained for popular itinerant preaching led him to finance a series of academy classes held in Edinburgh, Glasgow, and Dundee between 1799 and 1808 under the tutorship of sympathetic ministers including Greville Ewing, who resigned from the ministry of the Church of Scotland. In

1799 he joined his brother's newly formed Independent congregation in Edinburgh, committing considerable sums to the creation of preaching centres or tabernacles across Scotland based on the Whitefieldite model. However, his autocratic attitudes provoked tensions within the tabernacle network and led in 1809–10 to a vitriolic exchange of pamphlets with Ewing. With a financial involvement reportedly exceeding £70,000 Robert Haldane was a pivotal figure in the popular evangelicalism which developed in Scotland between 1798 and 1810 with its strong lay emphasis, and in the associated growth of Scottish Congregationalism. But his decision in 1808 to follow his brother and adopt Baptist views split the tabernacle congregations and checked the spread of the movement. Retaining his home in Edinburgh, he purchased the estate of Auchingray near Airdrie in 1809.

The following decade saw the publication of the two works on which Haldane's reputation as a theological writer most depend: *The Evidence and Authority of Divine Revelation* (1816) and the *Exposition of the Epistle to the Romans*, which first appeared in a French edition in 1819 and then in revised form in English in 1835–9. The earlier work emphasized the full verbal inspiration of the holy scriptures and moved sharply away from the contemporary preoccupation with natural religion and evidences, with their inherent distrust of revelation and the miraculous. The commentary on Romans began as a series of alternative lectures delivered to protestant seminary students in Geneva between January and June 1817. Haldane commenced the lectures when he discovered a widespread ignorance of the Bible and orthodox doctrine among the *proposants*. His influence at Geneva and later at the protestant seminary at Montauban, evident in his relationships with Frédéric Monod, César Malan, and J. H. Merle d'Aubigné, contributed to the growing mood of dissatisfaction within reformed protestantism and helped to ignite the continental *Réveil*. It also marked his entrance into the field of theological controversy, with pamphlets directed at different times against Professor Chenevière and the Genevan pastors, and August Tholuck of Halle. His influential advocacy of evangelical Calvinism amounted to a restatement of biblical doctrines such as election rather than any return to the articles of seventeenth-century confessionalism.

With his enduring interest in Christian missions and his concern to expose any departure from biblical standards, Haldane displayed a mixture of unitive and divisive tendencies. His combative spirit expressed itself most clearly in the campaign waged from 1824 with fellow members of the Edinburgh auxiliary including Andrew Thomson, the Church of Scotland evangelical leader, against the London committee of the Bible Society over the inclusion of the Apocrypha in Bibles supplied to agents abroad. During the controversy part of his earlier work on revelation was republished and widely sold under the title *The Authenticity and Inspiration of the Holy Scriptures Considered* (1827). His writings, which included tracts supporting the Edinburgh annuity tax and opposing Sunday trains, absorbed most of his declining energies. He died at his Edinburgh home, 6 Randolph Crescent, on 12 December 1842 and was buried in Glasgow Cathedral. His wife died six months later.

DERYCK LOVEGROVE

**Sources** A. Haldane, *The lives of Robert Haldane of Airthrey, and of his brother, James Alexander Haldane*, 2nd edn (1852) • G. Ewing, *Facts and documents respecting the connections which have subsisted between Robert Haldane, Esq. and Greville Ewing, laid before the public, in consequence of letters which the former has addressed to the latter, respecting the tabernacle at Glasgow* (1809) • A. Bost, *Mémoires pouvant servir à l'histoire du réveil religieux des églises protestantes de la Suisse et de la France*, 3 vols. (1854–5) • D. W. Lovegrove, '"The voice of reproach and outrage": the impact of Robert Haldane on French-speaking protestantism', *In divers manners: a St Mary's miscellany*, ed. D. W. D. Shaw (1990), 73–83 • D. W. Lovegrove, 'Unity and separation: contrasting elements in the thought and practice of Robert and James Alexander Haldane', *Protestant Evangelicalism … essays in honour of W. R. Ward*, ed. K. Robbins, SCH, Subsidia, 7 (1990), 153–77 • J. A. L. Haldane, *The Haldanes of Gleneagles* (1929)

**Archives** NL Scot. • priv. coll. | U. Edin. L., Laing MSS

**Wealth at death** £5383 13s. 2d.: NA Scot. (1843)

**Haldane, Robert** (1772–1854), Church of Scotland minister and university teacher, was born on 27 January 1772 at Overton ('the big farm') in the parish of Lecropt, Perthshire, the eldest son of John Haldane, farmer, and his wife, Margaret Kinross. He was educated at a school in Dunblane and at Glasgow University, where he matriculated in 1787, before studying divinity at Edinburgh University. After a conventional period as a private tutor (first with the Robinson family of Leddriegreen House, Strathblane, and then with the household of Colonel Charles Moray of Abercairney, Perthshire), he was licensed by the presbytery of Auchterarder on 5 December 1797, but was not ordained to his first charge, Drumelzier in Peeblesshire, until 19 March 1807 (*Fasti Scot.*, 1.269). This he resigned on 2 October 1809 on his appointment to the chair of mathematics at United College, St Andrews University, made vacant by the death of Nicolas Vilant.

Haldane was a competent mathematician, 'little if anything inferior to Chalmers', according to a nineteenth-century biographer, who also observed that 'it was well known that his mathematical drilling was the most successful ever exhibited in any of our Scottish colleges' (Conolly, 210). With the death of Professor George Hill, the leader of the moderate party in the Church of Scotland, Haldane was made principal of St Mary's College, St Andrews, and primarius professor of theology on 21 September 1820 (*Fasti Scot.*, 7.243), holding the parish church of St Andrews in conjunction, as was usual, because of the poor endowments of the chair (ibid., 5.236). His last years at St Andrews were clouded by conflicts with the reforming (and Free Church) principal of United College, Sir David Brewster, whose vendetta against Haldane, and Haldane's own sturdy defence of his administration and financial management of his college, is documented at length in the *Report of the St. Andrews' University Commissioners* (1845).

'The busy Principal Haldane, who in his day occupied many situations, and displayed a singular aptitude for each' (J. W. Taylor, *Some Historical Antiquities, Chiefly Ecclesiastical, Connected with St. Andrews*, 1859, 87), was described as

**Robert Haldane** (1772–1854), by David Octavius Hill and Robert Adamson

one of the best of men and very kind, 'of unceasing charity …, his heart was entirely in the well-being of his students' (Conolly, 210); 'a most faithful and thorough teacher; it was almost impossible to attend his classes without getting a thorough knowledge of systematic theology' (Gray, 54). On 17 May 1827 Haldane was elected moderator of the general assembly of the Church of Scotland (where he was the first to invite ladies to his official breakfasts); while at the Disruption of May 1843, it was he who was called to take the chair *ad interim* when Dr Welsh, the moderator, walked out. Though ranked as a moderate, his preaching was evangelical enough to retain most of his parishioners within the established kirk at the Disruption.

Haldane was made DD at St Andrews on 14 June 1815, and was elected FRSE on 24 January 1820. His only publication was one pamphlet, on poverty in St Andrews, written in 1841. A bachelor and (at least latterly) 'not very methodical or tidy in his habits' (Gray, 54), he died at St Mary's College on 9 March 1854, aged eighty-two. He was buried in the cathedral cemetery there on 15 March, the funeral sermon being given by his colleague the Very Revd George Buist, the professor of church history; the whole town suspended business for two hours as a mark of respect.

PETER BELL

**Sources** *DNB* • M. F. Conolly, *Eminent men of Fife* (1866) • *Fasti Scot.*, new edn • 'Report of the St Andrews University commissioners, Scotland', *Parl. papers* (1846), 23.119, no. 717 • *University of St. Andrews* (1837), vol. 3 of *Evidence, oral and documentary, taken and received by the commissioners … for visiting the universities of Scotland* • W. H. Gray, *Jottings by the way* (1908) • parish register (baptism), Lecropt, Perthshire, 9/2/1772 • matriculation album, U. Glas., Archives and Business Records Centre

**Archives** U. St Andr., special collections department, letters | NL Scot., corresp. with John Lee • U. Edin., New Coll. L., letters to Thomas Chalmers

**Likenesses** J. W. Gordon, oils, 1841, U. St Andr. • J. Caw, oils, U. St Andr. • D. O. Hill and R. Adamson, photograph, NPG [*see illus.*] • D. O. Hill and R. Adamson, photographs, repro. in S. Stevenson, *David Octavius Hill and Robert Adamson: catalogue of their calotypes taken between 1843 and 1847 in the collection of the Scottish National Portrait Gallery* (1981) • eight photographs, U. St Andr., special collections department, photographic collections

**Haldenston** [Haldenstoun], **James** (*d.* 1443), prior of St Andrews, is said to have been of noble birth, although nothing otherwise is known of his origins. He studied theology, probably in Paris, and obtained a bachelorate by 1412 and a doctorate by 1416. He subsequently taught theology at the newly established University of St Andrews, where he also became dean and acquired a reputation for the pursuit of heretics. In 1439 he was appointed inquisitor, and he has been credited with authorship of tracts against Lollards and heretics, as well as a work on the privileges of his monastic order, none of which survives.

Haldenston's early ecclesiastical career is obscure. He was an Augustinian canon of St Andrews by 1408, and was then involved in protracted and unresolved litigation with William Nory over the office of prior of May. In 1417 Haldenston abandoned his claims to May and was elected prior of St Andrews. He also abandoned the Avignon Pope Benedict XIII, for whom he had previously acted as a penitentiary, and instead received papal confirmation from Martin V on 17 February 1418.

He may have attended the council held at Perth in October 1418 which discussed Scotland's papal allegiance, and he was certainly a member of the embassy which in 1419 informed Pope Martin of Scotland's change of papal obedience. Martin repaid Haldenston's loyalty by appointing him papal nuncio and collector in Scotland in 1419.

Thereafter most of Haldenston's time was devoted to the affairs of the university and the priory. His letter-book, or *Copiale*, sheds a good deal of light on the latter during the years of his priorate. The contemporary chronicler Walter Bower, who seems to have known him well, credits him with putting the priory's estates in good order and with repairing the cathedral and the priory buildings. But allegations made in August 1440, that he had appropriated valuables entrusted to one of the canons for charitable distribution and exiled the canon to England for four months, suggest that his rule could sometimes be heavy-handed. Earlier that year, following the death of Bishop Henry Wardlaw of St Andrews, Haldenston was appointed vicar-general of the vacant see. He died on 18 July 1443 in St Andrews and was buried in St Andrews Cathedral.

DAVID DITCHBURN

**Sources** D. E. R. Watt, *A biographical dictionary of Scottish graduates to AD 1410* (1977), 248–51 • [J. Haldenston], *Copiale prioratus Sanctiandree: the letter-book of James Haldenstone, prior of St Andrews, 1418–1443*, ed. J. H. Baxter, St Andrews University Publications, 31 (1930) • W. Bower, *Scotichronicon*, ed. D. E. R. Watt and others, new edn, 9 vols. (1987–98), vol. 3 • E. R. Lindsay, A. I. Dunlop, and others, eds., *Calendar of Scottish supplications to Rome*, 1–2, Scottish History Society, 3rd ser., 23, 48 (1934–56); 3, Scottish History Society, 4th ser., 7 (1970); 4 (1983) · A. I. Dunlop, ed., *Acta facultatis artium universitatis Sanctiandree, 1413–1588*, 1, Scottish History Society, 3rd ser., 54 (1964) · A. I. Dunlop, *The life and times of James Kennedy, bishop of St Andrews*, St Andrews University Publications, 46 (1950), 414

**Haldimand, Sir Frederick** (1718–1791), army officer and colonial official, was born at Yverdon, Switzerland, the second of four children of François-Louis Haldimand, an administrator in Yverdon, and his wife, Marie-Madeleine de Treytorrens. Haldimand sought a career in the Prussian army, and first saw action at the battles of Mollwitz, Hohenfriedberg, and Kesseldorf during the War of the Austrian Succession. Ever on the alert for promotion, he accepted a position in the regiment of Swiss guards serving in the Dutch army. By 1748 he had risen to the position of first lieutenant. Imperial rivalries and rising tensions in America presented further opportunities. Haldimand was part of a group of foreign officers who transferred to the British army to provide an officer corps for a regiment recruited from the German and Swiss inhabitants of Pennsylvania. In January 1756 Haldimand was promoted to lieutenant-colonel of the 2nd battalion of the Royal Americans (62nd, later the 60th foot). Despite regulations allowing only naturalized officers to serve with British forces in Europe, Haldimand benefited from special legislation which permitted up to fifty non-British officers to hold commissions in units serving in America. Nevertheless, throughout his career he faced discrimination from British officers who resented the presence of foreigners in their ranks.

During the Seven Years' War, Haldimand demonstrated his military proficiency as well as the qualities of diligence and loyalty that characterized his service to the British crown. In 1758 he took part in the failed attack led by General James Abercromby against French forces occupying Fort Carillon near Ticonderoga, New York. In the following year he commanded the troops who successfully repelled an attack by French forces trying to dislodge the British from their partially reconstructed fortifications at Oswego, New York. Haldimand's excellent service record and his command of French made him invaluable to Brigadier Thomas Gage, commander of the British forces in North America. In 1760 he was given the responsibility of liaising with Governor Vaudrieul and François de Lévis to accept the capitulation of Montreal. Later he was appointed military governor for the district of Trois-Rivières. He provided competent administration of the district but was removed in September 1765. A discouraged Haldimand now received permission to travel to Europe with the expectation that further promotion in the military was now at an end. However, before he could return he received news of the death of his fellow officer Henry Bouquet. He was now promoted brigadier-general, and replaced Bouquet as commander of the southern department. In many ways his experience as a military commander in East and West Florida foreshadowed the challenges of his tenure as governor of Quebec. Despite a parsimonious and neglectful Treasury, a careless Colonial Office, and the tumultuous politics of a frontier colony, Haldimand provided a competent administration between April 1769 and his departure in 1773.

Haldimand's steady service to the crown partially overcame the issue of his foreign birth. In May 1772 he received a much deserved promotion to colonel-commandant in the 60th foot, and was raised to the rank of major-general later that year. During this time Thomas Gage called Haldimand to New York, where from June 1773 to May 1774 he served as acting commander-in-chief while Gage visited London. In this capacity Haldimand showed great tact to avoid inflaming American enmity towards Britain's colonial policy. Even so, on Gage's return the British government appointed the less senior and experienced officers William Howe, John Burgoyne, and Henry Clinton as Gage's advisers.

When Haldimand departed for England in August 1775 it seemed as though his career was yet again coming to an end. Nevertheless, he still enjoyed the support of George III and of many powerful politicians. While in London Haldimand had private interviews with, among others, the king and Lord North. As a token of the government's esteem he received the lucrative sinecure of inspector-general of the West Indian forces, and was indemnified £3000 for expenses incurred while he was commander-in-chief.

In 1777 Haldimand was successfully recommended to the king as a replacement for Guy Carleton, the former governor of Quebec. When Haldimand arrived in Quebec to take up his new position on 26 June 1778, he was confronted by a number of serious challenges. The deteriorating military environment in the American colonies compelled him to focus more on his duties as commander-in-chief than his role as governor. France's official entry into the conflict only heightened Haldimand's concern that a renewed campaign against Quebec was all but certain. In these conditions his first priority was to secure the loyalty of the Canadians and the British merchants to defend the colony, and to detain those colonists who were considered a threat to the province's internal security. In order to secure the loyalty of Britain's indigenous allies Haldimand spent huge sums to purchase presents, supplies, and arms. With the cessation of hostilities in April 1783 he feared that the Indian population, which justifiably felt betrayed by the British, might launch attacks on isolated loyalist communities currently being established on the British side of the Great Lakes.

In light of the need to buy the Indians' loyalty, together with supporting 4000 exiled loyalist settlers, Haldimand ignored the Colonial Office's demand for retrenchment. In order to find the means to finance these initiatives Haldimand authorized John Cochrane, son of the earl of Dundonald, and an agent for the well-connected London firm Harley and Drummond, to issue bills of exchange which could be redeemed by their London suppliers from the Treasury. Late in 1782 Haldimand was mortified to discover that Cochrane had issued bills of exchange far in excess of the amounts he had intended. The Cochrane affair resulted in great hardship for the Quebec merchant community, which stepped up their attacks on Haldimand and demanded significant constitutional reforms for the colony. The complaints meant that Haldimand's days as governor were numbered. When he travelled to London in November 1784 he had served for the last time in British America. Yet as before he continued to enjoy the respect of many London policy makers. Indeed, George III demonstrated his recognition of Haldimand's loyal and valuable service by appointing him to the Order of the Bath in September 1785.

Haldimand's final years were spent in the polite company of some of London's finest drawing-rooms. He continued to take an interest in Quebec affairs and lent his influence to colonial officials and administrators. Since he did not have the benefit of inherited wealth he was obliged to husband his financial resources wisely. Anthony Haldimand, his nephew and a successful London banker, helped him invest his savings to live in dignity and comfort. Since leaving Quebec, Haldimand had the leisure to dispose his significant landholdings in Quebec, Pennsylvania, and Florida. He also took a greater interest in his property in Yverdon, Switzerland. It was here that he died in June 1791, after an apoplectic seizure. In his will he left funds for friends from Quebec, certain charities, and his nephews, Anthony and William *Haldimand (1784–1862). K. DAVID MILOBAR

**Sources** BL, Haldimand collection, Add. MSS 21661–21885 · Quebec corresp., PRO, colonial office, 42, vols. 1–84 · *Report on the Canadian archives, 1889–1898* (1890–99) · *The correspondence of Thomas Gage*, ed. C. E. Carter, 2 vols. (1931) · *The journal of Jeffery Amherst*, ed. J. C. Webster (1931) · S. Pargellis, ed., *Military affairs in North America, 1748–1765: selected documents from the Cumberland papers in Windsor Castle* (1936) · N. W. Wallace, *A regimental chronicle* (1879) · G. S. Brown, *The American secretary: the colonial policy of Lord George Germain, 1775–1778* (1963) · *Quebec Gazette* (1764–91) · K. D. Milobar, 'The constitutional development of Quebec from the French régime to the Canada Act of 1791: a British perspective', PhD diss., U. London, 1990 · *The correspondence of King George the Third from 1760 to December 1783*, ed. J. Fortescue, 6 vols. (1927–8) · *Annual Register* (1791)

**Archives** BL, corresp. and papers, Add. MSS 21661–21885, 21892 · PRO, corresp., 30/55 | PRO, corresp. with Jeffrey Amherst, WO 34 · Thomas Gilcrease Institute of American History and Art, Tulsa, Oklahoma, corresp. and papers relating to Indian Affairs · U. Mich., Clements L., corresp. with Thomas Gage

**Likenesses** studio of J. Reynolds, oils, *c*.1778, NPG; repro. in J. C. Webster, ed., *The journal of Jeffrey Amherst* (1931)

**Haldimand, William** (1784–1862), philanthropist, was born in London on 9 September 1784, the son of Anthony Francis Haldimand (1741–1817), a London merchant and the nephew and heir of Sir Frederick *Haldimand. He was one of twelve children, most of whom died young. After receiving a plain English education he entered at the age of sixteen his father's counting-house, where he showed great business sense; when he was twenty-five he became a director of the Bank of England. He was an enthusiastic advocate of the resumption of specie payments, and gave evidence in the parliamentary inquiry which led to the act of 1819. In 1820 he was elected MP for Ipswich, and was re-elected in 1826, but, the return being disputed, he gave up the seat.

In 1828 Haldimand settled permanently at his summer villa, Denantou, near Lausanne. He took a great interest in the cause of Greek independence, sending the insurgents £1000 by his nephew, and guaranteeing Admiral Cochrane £20,000 to prepare a fleet. A visit to Aix-les-Bains for his health resulted in his erecting there in 1829 a hospital for poor patients. The municipality named it after him, but after the annexation of Savoy to France it was styled the Hortense Hospital, although Queen Hortense had merely endowed some beds in it.

Large purchases of French rentes, made with a view of strengthening the new Orléans dynasty, involved Haldimand in considerable losses, but his philanthropic donations still continued. He gave £24,000 for an asylum for blind people at Lausanne, and £3000 towards the cost of an Anglican church at Ouchy. Inclined to radicalism in politics, and to scepticism in religion, he nevertheless exerted himself in favour of the free church in Vaud, threatened with state persecution.

Haldimand died at Denantou on 20 September 1862. He was unmarried, and bequeathed £20,000, the bulk of his remaining property, to the asylum for blind people at Lausanne. In 1857 he had presented a collection of manuscripts to the British Museum, which included Sir Frederick Haldimand's official correspondence.

J. G. ALGER, *rev.* MARK CLEMENT

**Sources** W. de la Rive, *Vie de Haldimand* · A. Hartmann, *Gallerie berühmter Schweizer der Neuzeit*, 2 vols. (1868–71) · Boase, *Mod. Eng. biog.* · *CGPLA Eng. & Wales* (1862)

**Wealth at death** under £40,000: resworn probate, Feb 1865, *CGPLA Eng. & Wales* (1862)

**Haldingham, Richard of**. *See* Holdingham, Richard of (*d.* 1278?).

**Hale, Sir Bernard** (*bap.* 1677, *d.* 1729), judge, was baptized on 18 March 1677 at King's Walden, Hertfordshire, a younger son of William Hale of King's Walden, and his wife, Mary, daughter of Jeremiah Elwes of Roxby, Lincolnshire. His grandfather Rowland had been a member of Gray's Inn and MP for Hertfordshire in the 1670s. Bernard was sent to Eton College, and proceeded to Cambridge as a scholar of Peterhouse in 1695, graduating BA in 1699 and MA in 1702. His scholarship was sufficiently well regarded for him to be elected a fellow of his college, and he remained so during his early years at the bar, until 1715. In the meantime he had been admitted to Gray's Inn in 1696, and called to the bar in 1705, moving to Lincoln's Inn in 1710. His personal accounts show that between 1716 and 1719 his professional fees had reached £160 to £175 a year, augmented by a private income of about £300; and by 1719 he had acquired an office which brought him more than £200 a year.

In June 1722 he went to Ireland as chief baron of the exchequer there, in succession to Sir Jeffrey Gilbert, but in October 1724 he turned down the chief justiceship of the common pleas in Ireland, on the advice of Sir Philip Yorke that it might hinder his return to England. He wrote to Yorke that the offer had given him 'great perplexity', but that his return was 'of all others, of the greatest interest and concern to me ... it is impossible for me to forget England or not to wish to return to it' (BL, Add. MS 35584, fol. 340). The following June he did return, when Gilbert's promotion to be chief baron of the English court of exchequer created a vacancy among the junior barons; he took his seat on 23 October, and was knighted in 1726. In 1724 he had been called to the bench of Gray's Inn, presumably *per incuriam*, but he accepted call to the bench by Lincoln's Inn the following year, remaining a bencher for only a few months before his call to the order of the coif upon becoming an English judge. He died within four years of the latter appointment, on 7 November 1729.

Hale and his wife, Anne, daughter of J. Thoresby of Northamptonshire, had four sons and three daughters, and their descendants were still at King's Walden in Victorian times. Their third son, **Bernard Hale** (*bap.* 1725, *d.* 1798), commanded the 20th foot in the 1760s, was appointed major-general in 1772, lieutenant-governor of Chelsea Hospital in 1773, lieutenant-general of the ordnance in 1777, and a full general in 1793. He married Martha (*d.* 1803), daughter of Richard Rigby of Mistley Hall, Essex, and their only son assumed the surname of Rigby. Hale's fourth son, **John Hale** (*d.* 1806), also served with distinction in the army. After commanding the 17th dragoons in the 1760s he was appointed governor of Londonderry and Culmore forts in 1781, and attained the rank of general at the same time as his brother. He and his wife, Mary, second daughter of William Chaloner of Gisborough, had eleven surviving children. J. H. BAKER

**Sources** Baker, *Serjeants* • Sainty, *Judges* • Foss, *Judges* • Venn, *Alum. Cant.* • R. J. Fletcher, ed., *The pension book of Gray's Inn*, 1 (1901) • W. P. Baildon, ed., *The records of the Honorable Society of Lincoln's Inn: admissions*, 2 vols. (1896) • Hardwicke correspondence, BL, Add. MS 35584, fol. 340 • W. Sterry, ed., *The Eton College register, 1441–1698* (1943) • memorial inscription, parish church, King's Walden, Hertfordshire • *IGI*

**Archives** BL, accounts; memorial, Add. MS 33579, fols. 58, 60, 314–44; Add. MS 35584, fol. 340

**Likenesses** oils, Gray's Inn, London

**Hale, Bernard** (*bap.* **1725**, *d.* **1798**). *See under* Hale, Sir Bernard (*bap.* 1677, *d.* 1729).

**Hale, Cicely Bertha** (**1884–1981**), suffragette and health visitor, was born on 5 September 1884 at 8 Sussex Gardens, Paddington, London, the youngest of the five surviving children of Charles Douglas Bowdich Hale (1850–1927), a general practitioner, and his wife, Bertha Maria, *née* Poole (1840–1937). When Cicely was seven the family moved to a large house in Sussex Place near by. A timid child, she felt inadequate and unloved, and was close only to her protective next sister, Betsy. Taught by their mother, then by governesses, in their late teens the girls were sent to the ladies' department of King's College in Kensington, headed by Lilian Faithfull. They also attended 'the Gym' run by the Misses Bear, where fellow students included several princesses. Because Dr Hale had treated high school girls whose health had allegedly suffered from overwork, he forbade his daughters to undertake more than four hours of classes a day. Despite a broad cultural education, including theatregoing and continental travel, Cicely Hale always felt disadvantaged by her lack of formal schooling. She resented having to wait on her brothers as a child, and in later life she came to resent the way the daughters' education was thought less important than the sons'.

Hale trained as a secretary and, after an uncongenial first post, went in 1908 as assistant to Mary Home in the information department of the Women's Social and Political Union (WSPU), the result of hearing Emmeline and Christabel Pankhurst speak in Hyde Park. There she provided a news-cutting and research service, learned to typeset *The Suffragette*, and, in 1912, took charge of the department. Though she experienced many police raids, she was never arrested. Concern for her father's reputation restrained her militancy, so that she felt guilty at having given less than her colleagues.

After the outbreak of the First World War, Hale continued to typeset *The Suffragette* (renamed *The Britannia*) until 1916 when her father's retirement deprived her of both home and allowance. Her experience in the WSPU greatly boosted her self-confidence. Recognizing that without qualifications she could not obtain interesting work or a reasonable salary, she decided to study for the health visitor's certificate of the Royal Sanitary Institute (training at the Infant Welfare Clinic at Salisbury Street, Marylebone) and the certificate of the Central Midwives' Board (at the General Lying-In Hospital in York Road, Waterloo, and in Camberwell). She partly financed her studies by acting as Dr Christine Murrell's secretary.

After six months at the maternity almoners' office at the London Hospital in Whitechapel, working with Russian and Polish Jewish mothers, Hale returned to the Salisbury Street clinic as health visitor superintendent, a post she held for sixteen years. As a sideline she answered letters from customers of Glaxo Laboratories about their baby products. In 1918 she rented rooms in Ormonde Terrace, facing Primrose Hill, where, in 1920, Ann Campbell moved next door. Campbell, a pioneer policewoman who became chief inspector of the Women's Auxiliary Police Service, shared her life for twenty years. They lived together in a flat in Dorset Square, Marylebone, holidaying abroad every year.

In 1934 Hale moved to a health visitor's post in Littlehampton to be nearer her mother; on her mother's death, in 1937, she returned to London. From the Holland Park flat she shared with Campbell she conducted the 'Baby circle' for the *Woman's Own*, writing a weekly column and answering an enormous correspondence. When war broke out, Hale and Campbell moved to Oxford, where Campbell died in 1941. To fill the gap in her life, Hale wrote *Can I Help you with Baby?*, which went into three editions. She returned to London in 1943, but took a flat in Littlehampton in 1944 and lived there half the week. When a new management took the *Woman's Own* up-market she gave up the 'Baby circle' after nine years and retired to Littlehampton in 1946.

In 1947 Hale met Mary Cuningham Chater (1896–1990), music adviser to the Girl Guides Association, and began a new career. As division secretary to the Arun Valley

Guides, she helped to assemble the International Song Books, ran a Brownie pack, and experienced camping for the first time, acting as camp nurse for three summers. She finally retired in 1968, aged eighty-four. She shared Mary Chater's home in St Winefride's Road, Littlehampton, from 1950 to 1965, when they took adjoining flats on South Terrace. At her death she was living at Kenwith, St Winefride's Road.

After the publication of her memoir *A Good Long Time* (1975), Hale found herself in demand, as one of the few suffragettes still alive, as a speaker in schools, on radio, and on television. In the book she emerges as a person of progressive views, a tolerant, interested observer of society, whose self-esteem, damaged in childhood, had been amply repaired by professional and personal fulfilment. The pages reveal no sense of irony or self-consciousness that her life's work consisted in advising others about things she had not herself experienced, or that she lived with women rather than husband and children.

Cicely Hale died on 28 May 1981 of pneumonia and lung abscesses at 43 Glenville Road, Rustingdon, Sussex, after a 'good long' life of ninety-six years. Her obituary in *The Times* noted that 'Her courage, kindness and enterprise made her a delightful friend and a much loved aunt of numerous nephews and nieces of three generations'.

ROSEMARY AUCHMUTY

**Sources** C. B. Hale, *A good long time: the autobiography of an nonagenarian* (1975) • B. H. Harrison, tape-recorded interview, 6 Nov 1974, Women's Library, London • *The Times* (6 June 1981) • b. cert. • *CGPLA Eng. & Wales* (1981) • will of C. B. Hale • d. cert. • G. Huelin, *King's College, London* (1978) • L. M. Faithfull, *In the house of my pilgrimage* (1924) • J. Lock, *The British policewoman: her story* (1979) • E. Tancred, *Women police, 1914–50* (1951) • *Guiding Magazine* (Nov 1990)
**Likenesses** photographs, repro. in Hale, *A good long time*
**Wealth at death** £3683: probate, 3 July 1981, *CGPLA Eng. & Wales*

**Hale, Horatio Emmons** (1817–1896), anthropologist, born on 3 May 1817, at Newport, New Hampshire, USA, was one of five children of David Hale (*d*. 1822), a prominent lawyer of Newport, and of Sarah Josepha Buell, his wife, who was a journalist and editor and a campaigner for women's rights. After the death of her husband, Sarah Hale made a living from literature. After entering Harvard College in 1833 to study oriental languages and literature, Horatio Hale showed a marked linguistic skill. His first original work appeared the next year, and attracted the attention of the college authorities. It consists of an Algonquian vocabulary, which he gathered from native speakers who were wintering near the college grounds. Three years later, when the United States exploring expedition to the Pacific was organized under Captain Charles Wilkes, Hale was recommended, while still an undergraduate, for the post of ethnologist and philologist. He was appointed on his graduation in 1837. From 1838 to 1842 he was employed in the work of the expedition, visiting South America, Australasia, Polynesia, and north-western America. From this point he returned overland. His report of the expedition, published as *Ethnography and Philology* (1846), was very well received by scholars in the United States and Europe.

Having taken his degree of MA, Hale toured Europe from about 1843 to 1853, and, on his return, studied law in Chicago. In 1854, at Jersey City in the state of New Jersey, he married Margaret, daughter of William Pugh, formerly justice of the peace for the township of Goderich in the county of Huron, Upper Canada. He was admitted to the Illinois bar in 1855. The year after he moved to Canada, and settled at Clinton, Ontario, where his wife's family had a substantial property, the management of which they wanted him to undertake. He continued to reside in Clinton until his death, acting as a conveyancer, estate executor, and insurance agent, and contributing significantly to the development of that newly established town. He devoted much attention to the development of the Ontario school system. He was influential in introducing co-education of the sexes in high schools and collegiate institutes, in increasing the grants to these institutions, in establishing the normal school system, and in improving the methods of examination. He also helped to found a mechanics' institute, of which he became president.

The vicinity of the Canadian reserves on the banks of the Thames and Grand River gave Hale ample opportunity for further investigation into ethnological and linguistic matters. From 1867 to 1877 he worked with a committee of chiefs to establish the history, structure, and rituals of the Six Nations Confederacy. In 1872 he was elected to the American Philosophical Society, to which he presented in December 1879 an important paper on the Tutelo language and on his discovery in 1879 of Mohawk and Onondaga texts of the Iroquois book of rites. In 1883 he published his translation of these manuscripts, with notes and a substantial introduction. In numerous papers he made significant contributions to the study of the Iroquoian family of languages and to the development of scientific anthropology.

In 1884, at its Montreal meeting, Hale reorganized the section of anthropology as an independent department of the British Association for the Advancement of Science. He had already done a similar service for the American association. At the request of the British committee, he undertook the supervision of the anthropological section's work in the Canadian north-west and British Columbia. The reports, which are very elaborate, appeared in the published *Proceedings* from 1885 to 1897. Continuing a member of the committee, he was asked to accept the position of vice-president at the association's meeting in Toronto (1896), but declined on the ground of ill health.

Hale's writings dealing with the more general questions of anthropology are scattered through the *Proceedings* of the British and American associations for the advancement of science, the Anthropological Institute of Great Britain, Royal Society of Canada, Canadian Institute, Toronto; and through periodical publications such as the *Andover Review*, *Popular Science Monthly*, *Journal of American Folklore*, *Science*, and *The Critic*.

Among other learned bodies Hale was fellow of the Royal Society of Canada (1889), president of the American Folk-Lore Society (1893), and an honorary fellow of the

Anthropological Institute of Great Britain, to which he contributed his last papers. He died on 29 December 1896 at Clinton, Ontario, and was buried there.

T. B. BROWNING, *rev.* C. A. CREFFIELD

**Sources** W. N. Fenton, 'Hale, Horatio Emmons', *DCB*, vol. 12 · A. F. Chamberlain, *Journal of American Folklore*, 10 (1897), 60–66 · *The Athenaeum* (30 Jan 1897), 152 · *The Globe* [Toronto] (31 Dec 1896) · *Appletons' Popular Science Monthly*, 51 (1897), 401–10 · C. Wilkes, *Narrative of the United States exploring expedition* (1844) · *Canadian Magazine*, 8 (1897), 449 · *DCB*, vol. 12

**Hale, John** (*d.* 1806). *See under* Hale, Sir Bernard (*bap.* 1677, *d.* 1729).

**Hale, Sir John Rigby** (1923–1999), historian and public servant, was born on 17 September 1923 at Ashford, Kent, the only son and youngest of the three children of Edward Rigby Stephenson Hale, a medical doctor, and his wife, Hilda, *née* Birks. As a boy he was extraordinarily precocious in both reading and writing, and at thirteen he went to Eastbourne College with a scholarship. He won a scholarship to Jesus College, Oxford, in 1941, but postponed taking it up until after the war, spending the intervening years in the merchant navy as a radio operator. He went up to Oxford in 1945, won the Gladstone memorial prize for history in 1947, and graduated with the top first in history in 1948. As an undergraduate he was also heavily involved in the theatre, being secretary of the Oxford University Dramatic Society (1946–7), and making several notable stage appearances in Oxford. In the summer of 1948 he was elected to a fellowship and college tutorship in modern history at Jesus, but postponed taking up the appointment for a year in order to hold a Commonwealth fellowship in the United States.

Hale was a passionate traveller. His years in the merchant navy and in America, followed by many later visits to the USA, nourished an enthusiasm which lasted all his life and coloured much of his writing. His first visit to Italy in 1947 captured his imagination completely, and on his return he studied the Italian Renaissance with Cecilia Ady in his final undergraduate year. From that beginning he went on to become one of the foremost Renaissance historians in Britain. He remained an Oxford don for fifteen years, continuing to play a central role in the university's theatrical life, and editing the *Oxford Magazine* in 1958–9. He married a student, Rosalind Margaret, daughter of Theodore Rowland Williams, a member of the executive council of Jamaica, on 19 July 1952. They had three children, Sophie, Matthew, and Charlotte. The marriage ended in divorce, and on 22 December 1965 he married Sheila MacIvor, an American journalist and travel writer, and daughter of Frederick Hamm, an advertising executive. They had one son, John.

In 1964 Hale accepted the founding chair of history at the new University of Warwick. Over a period of five years he created a history department with a strong emphasis on European and American history, and a syllabus which involved undergraduates in studying abroad both in American universities and in Venice, where he established a Warwick Renaissance programme. In 1969 he left Warwick to take up a visiting professorship at the University of California, Berkeley, and in the following year he was appointed to the chair of Italian at University College, London, after the death of Roberto Weiss. He remained at University College until he retired in 1988, presiding over the Italian department until 1985 and then moving to a personal chair in history.

Hale was a man of extraordinarily wide interests. Among his early books were contributions to the history of travel and colonization, *England and the Italian Renaissance* (1954), *Machiavelli and Renaissance Italy* (1961), and the chapters on war and diplomacy in the first three volumes of the *New Cambridge Modern History* (1957– ). All were distinguished by a fresh and vivid style, and an ability to cut straight to the heart of a subject. By the late 1960s two particular interests had emerged: the first was what he once called 'consensus history', that is, the investigation of popular ideas, attitudes, and perceptions as expressed in literature, letters, and diaries; the second was in Renaissance fortifications, both as indications of changing priorities and preoccupations in war, and as works of art, a subject on which he had lectured in the early 1960s. Literary and visual culture were the sources for some of his best-known books, the stimulating textbook *Renaissance Europe, 1480–1520* (1971), *Artists and Warfare in the Renaissance* (1990), and above all his final book, the monumental *Civilisation of Europe in the Renaissance* (1993). Also in the late 1960s came a growing interest in and commitment to Venice, which led him to make increasing use of archive sources in his work and led to a stream of specialist articles on aspects of Venetian history, mostly associated with war. Many of these were brought together in *Renaissance War Studies* (1983) and woven into the fabric of his book written jointly with Michael Mallett, *The Military Organisation of a Renaissance State: Venice, c.1400–1617* (1984). While it was as a leader of a new generation of military historians that he came to be best-known, his sensitive handling of a wide range of cultural topics, from printing to painting, was also a trade mark.

Apart from being a charismatic teacher and a very productive working historian, Hale also had another career, as a successful and influential cultural administrator. He was for six years chairman of the trustees of the National Gallery (1974–80) at a time of remarkable development for the gallery, and he served on the committees of many other galleries and museums. He chaired the museums and galleries committee working party on museum professional training and career structure, and was largely responsible for its influential report in 1987. He masterminded the *Genius of Venice* exhibition at the Royal Academy in 1983, and was knighted in the following year for his services to scholarship and the arts. In 1977 he had been elected a fellow of the British Academy, and in 1986 he was awarded the academy's Serena medal for distinguished publications in Italian studies.

Hale was an immensely popular figure. Auburn-haired, of medium height, quietly elegant, and a brilliant conversationalist and raconteur, he radiated both enthusiasm and good sense. In an increasingly busy life he always seemed to have time for everyone, though not necessarily at the time appointed. Nothing was more indicative of his own inner toughness and zest for life, and of the strength of his friendships, than the courage with which he faced the effects of a severe stroke in 1992, and the love with which his friends and family supported and encouraged him. The last seven years of his life were as much a triumph as a travail, given that he continued to lead a full life and to communicate, without speech, with his friends. He died peacefully in his sleep at his home, 26 Montpelier Row, Twickenham, of a secondary stroke on 12 August 1999. He was survived by his wife Sheila and his four children. MICHAEL MALLETT

**Sources** M. E. Mallett, *PBA*, 111 (2001), 531–50 • D. S. Chambers, C. H. Clough, and M. E. Mallett, *War, culture and society in Renaissance Venice: essays in honour of John Hale* (1993), ix–xi, xiii–xxiii • *WWW* • *The Times* (13 Aug 1999) • *The Guardian* (13 Aug 1999) • *Daily Telegraph* (16 Aug 1999) • *The Independent* (19 Aug 1999) • private information (2004) • personal knowledge (2004) • m. certs. • d. cert.

**Archives** National Gallery, London, corresp. • UCL, official corresp. and academic papers | Tate collection, corresp. with Lord Clark

**Likenesses** F. Martin, photograph, 1977, repro. in *The Guardian* • photograph, 1977, repro. in *Daily Telegraph* • photograph, 1987, repro. in *The Times* • S. Quill, photograph, repro. in *The Independent*

**Wealth at death** £53,261—gross; £51,261—net: probate, 8 Nov 1999, *CGPLA Eng. & Wales*

**Hale** [*née* Burke; *other married names* Peabody, McLean], **Kathleen** (1887–1958), fund-raiser, was born in London on 24 October 1887, the daughter of Thomas Francis Burke, an official of the London and North-Western Railway Company, and his wife, Georgina, *née* Connolly. Educated in London, she passed the senior examination of the Oxford delegacy for local examinations at the age of fourteen, becoming an Oxford associate of arts, and she later studied at the Sorbonne in Paris. Kathleen Burke was in New York when the First World War broke out, but she rushed back to Britain, where she was appointed secretary to one of the first British commissions to Belgium, helping the refugees flee to Britain before the German advance. After such work was no longer possible she became a secretary in the London office of the Scottish Women's Hospitals for Foreign Service (SWH), the organization founded by Dr Elsie Inglis to send all-women medical units to allied armies in the field. Before spring 1915 she had never made a speech in her life, but when Dr Inglis asked the young woman to take her place as a speaker for the SWH Kathleen Burke proved to have a natural gift for inspiring her audiences to part with money for the cause she pleaded.

In summer 1915 Burke was invited by General Pétain to visit Verdun after it was evacuated, and she was escorted to the trenches, an experience that she wrote up as *The White Road to Verdun* (1916). On a more personal note she advised the SWH treasurer that she had been borrowed by the French Red Cross for

> a special and rather delicate mission to the French Military Authorities. I was obliged to track a French General down and when I found him we had to carry on our 'conversation' in writing owing to the noise of the guns!!! I was lucky enough to be successful … You see I have lived half my life with French Military people and so understand the 'kinks' in their character. (Burke file, SWH collection, Mitchell L., Glas.)

Unfortunately there is nowhere any hint of how or why the daughter of a British railway official came to have such close connections with the French military.

In December 1915 Kathleen Burke shared a platform at Winchester with a rich American woman who knew her uncle well in New York; she tried to persuade Burke to spend some months in America to help raise money for the Serbian cause. Initially, Burke wrote in confidence to the SWH treasurer, 'the offer was a determined attempt to steal me from my present work', but she 'refused to consider the scheme unless I saw a good profit coming to the Hospitals' (Burke file, SWH collection, Mitchell L., Glas.). The SWH committee agreed to her going, and she crossed the Atlantic in February 1916. By early March she had already raised about £3000, and a fortnight later Andrew Carnegie gave her a further £1000. The SWH committee agreed that if she raised £10,000 they would send out a unit called the American unit, and in May she achieved that goal.

Burke's success was so great that, inevitably, she went over to North America a second time, criss-crossing the USA and Canada for months, and raising so much money that she became known as the $1000-a-day girl. At one point she looked so tired that a millionaire friend made her an offer: he would pay the SWH $500 a day for two days if she would 'go down to his country place and stay quietly with his daughter'. Burke raised $1000 by doing nothing: 'I wish some of the other millionaires would follow his example', she wrote (Burke file, SWH collection, Mitchell L., Glas.). At San Francisco, when the mayor heard that, due to some petty bureaucracy, Burke had not been allowed onto the railway station platform to collect her luggage, he had her appointed a 'special policeman'; she said: 'I carry a good five pointed silver star inside my coat. It may be useful someday' (ibid.). She was given the freedom of several American cities and was appointed honorary colonel of the 138th US field artillery in recognition of her work for the American Red Cross. It was estimated that she raised about $4 million for various allied services. She was appointed CBE (1918), chevalier of the Légion d'honneur, and knight of St Sava, Serbia.

In January 1920 Kathleen Burke was in hospital in Santa Barbara in California, USA, 'with a general break down'; she wrote that she was 'threatening to marry one of the California multi-millionaires' (Burke file, SWH collection, Mitchell L., Glas.). Later that year, on 5 April, she did indeed marry company president Frederick Forrest Peabody (1859–1927) of Santa Barbara. In 1929, two years after his death, she married John Reginald McLean, but he died in the same year. Her third marriage, in 1931, was to Girard van Barkaloo Hale (*c.*1884–1958). Born in Denver, Mr Hale studied at the Rochester (New York) School of Art and at the École des Beaux-Arts in Paris, France. He was co-painter of a mural in the Utah State Capitol, Salt Lake City. During the First World War he was a member of the American field ambulance service, attached to the French army, when he received the Croix de Guerre and two citations.

In the spring of 1940 Kathleen Hale returned to France, working with relief units of the American Friends of France. In 1946 the Hales 'adopted' the French village of Maille in Indre-et-Loire, which had been devastated in the Second World War, shipping out supplies for its 400 inhabitants, and its schools, churches, and farms. Kathleen Burke Hale died in Santa Barbara in November 1958, less than a month after her husband. Kathleen Burke's charisma, which induced her audiences to pour such vast amounts of money into allied coffers during the First World War, cannot be captured by the written word, but her warmth, charm, sense of humour, and intelligence are evident in every letter of hers preserved in the SWH collection. LEAH LENEMAN

**Sources** L. Leneman, *In the service of life: the story of Elsie Inglis and the Scottish Women's Hospitals* (1994) • Mitchell L., Glas., Scottish Women's Hospitals collection, Kathleen Burke MSS, tin 27 • *Evening Telegraph* (7 April 1920) • *Daily Mail* (7 April 1920) • *WWW*, 1951–60 • *New York Times* (31 Oct 1958) • *New York Times* (28 Nov 1958) • *Who was who in America*

**Archives** Mitchell L., Glas., Scottish Women's Hospitals collection

**Hale, Kathleen** (1898–2000), artist and writer, was born on 24 May 1898 at her family's holiday house, St Bede's, Broughton, Lanarkshire, the youngest of the three children of Charles Edward Hale (1859–1903), a travelling agent for Chappell pianos, and his wife, Ethel Alice Aylmer (1868–1965), the daughter of Revd T. A. A. Hughes, vicar of Shelf in Yorkshire. She was brought up in Manchester until her father died of tertiary syphilis when she was five, after which her mother took over his job, settling the children with relatives. Hale and her brother stayed with their maternal grandparents in Shelf, moving three years later, after their grandfather's retirement, to Didsbury, Manchester. Eighteen months later, their mother bought a recently built house in Didsbury, where the family was reunited. Hale developed a passion for animals during childhood and kept numerous pets, drawing them with a skill well beyond her years.

At nine, Hale was sent to Manchester High School for Girls, where she was described by the headmistress as 'uneducable and the naughtiest child she had ever had to deal with' (Hale, 26). She did, however, win a scholarship to study art at Reading University College, where she spent two years before escaping to London. She lived at the Baker Street YWCA, got a wartime job painting maps for the Ministry of Food, and was introduced into Bohemian society by Jacob Epstein's favourite model, Meum Stuart.

In 1918 Hale joined the land army, transporting fruit and vegetables from a grower in Barnes to Covent Garden market in a horse and cart. At the end of the war she went to live in Soho and got a job designing book jackets for W. H. Smith. She had an affair with the painter Frank Potter, who was ten years her senior and the first of several older men in her life. When the work with W. H. Smith ran out she moved around London from lodging to lodging, often without enough money to eat properly, taking a number of temporary jobs. At the Studio Club in Lower Regent Street, a favourite haunt, she introduced herself to Augustus John. Appalled that she was spending time doing odd jobs when she should have been painting, John immediately decided to employ her as his secretary. She became part of his circle and once, 'out of curiosity', allowed John to seduce her, but she did not, as he had hoped, become his mistress (Hale, 91). After sixteen months she realized she was still being left too little time to pursue her own career, and so joined Potter in Étaples, where her relationship with him came to a faltering end. She returned to London with a portfolio of drawings, which John encouraged her to exhibit, thus attracting the attention of periodicals and buyers. She worked on murals for the dance-hall at the Wembley Exhibition Centre, for the editor C. K. Ogden, and with Duncan Grant and Vanessa Bell. She lived

**Kathleen Hale (1898–2000)**, by Kurt Hutton, 1949

in Fitzrovia and was a frequent *habituée* of the Cave of Harmony, being one of the first people to become a member of this famous cabaret club when it opened in 1924.

In 1926 Hale entered the London Fever Hospital with suspected diphtheria and fell in love with John McClean, a 66-year-old doctor, who recognized that she was in fact suffering from a fungal infection. Feeling himself too old to marry Hale, McClean suggested she should instead marry his depressive son, Douglas McClean (1896–1967), a bacteriologist. Hale agreed, chiefly because she wanted children. 'I fell in "friendship"—not in love—with Douglas', she recalled; 'this was to grow deeper, and become indestructible' (Hale, 154). Before marrying on 30 April 1926, they lived together for six months, during which period she studied oil painting with Bernard Meninsky at the Central School of Arts and Crafts and moved in Fitzrovian circles.

Douglas McClean and Kathleen Hale were very different, but in its disengaged way the marriage was a success and produced two sons. About 1930 they moved to a former horticultural nursery in the Hertfordshire countryside, which they restored, and it was there at Rabley Willow that Hale started writing and illustrating books about Orlando, the marmalade cat. Bored with reading to her sons the few children's books she admired, Hale decided to make up stories about Orlando (drawn from the family cat but based partly on McClean), his wife, Grace (the sort of domestic paragon Hale would have liked to have been), and their three kittens, Blanche, Pansy, and Tinkle (this last a self-portrait in unruliness). The first book, *Orlando the Marmalade Cat: a Camping Holiday* (1938) was inspired by a spartan excursion she had undertaken with McClean, and was published by *Country Life*. The books were large-format, modelled on Jean de Brunhoff's *Barbar the Elephant* series, and this allowed the illustrations to be full of detail. They were printed by colour lithography, a perfect medium for reproducing Hale's original chalk drawings, but a time-consuming one. When her publisher threatened to cut out all but 'the essentials' for reasons of cost, Hale went to the printers, Cowells of Ipswich, to learn the technically demanding process and subsequently made up all the plates herself, unpaid (Hale, 211). Each book, she reckoned, 'took four to five months of working seven hours a day, seven days a week', but they set new standards for quality in illustrated children's books (ibid., 214).

After a slow start, the Orlando books became hugely popular. There were seventeen in all, the last published in 1972. (Prompted by her lifelong pacifist convictions, she planned a further outing for Orlando, in which he bought and leased a desert to warmongers, allowing the rest of the world to live in peace, but this book was never written.) Most of the stories were inspired by the activities of her own cats (among which were two Orlandos), or by travel, and many of her friends featured in them: Antonia White's husband, Eric Earnshaw-Smith, became the shopkeeper Mr Cattermole, and the painters Cedric Morris and Arthur Lett-Haines were portrayed respectively as a dancing-master and the sinister Katnapper. The bisexual Haines also became Hale's 'rescuer' when, shortly before the Second World War, suffering from painter's block, she was advised by a psychoanalyst to have an extra-marital affair. This, she said, 'shook me out of myself and immensely widened my view of life' (Hale, 239): her marriage was reinforced, her friendship with 'Lett' continued after the relationship ended, and she began working again.

A ballet based on *Orlando's Silver Wedding*, with costumes designed by Hale, was presented at the Festival of Britain in 1951, for which she also designed a large Orlando mural in the schools section. Hale wrote several other illustrated children's books, including *Manda the Jersey Calf* (1952), inspired by a trip to Ireland, and *Henrietta the Faithful Hen* (1943), based on the numerous chickens she had kept since childhood. She also designed, at the author's suggestion, the dust jacket of Evelyn Waugh's *Basil Seal Rides Again* (1963). She always felt, however, that her true vocation was painting, 'the often interrupted mainstream of my life' (Hale, 285). She exhibited infrequently, and usually in shops such as Heal's and Fortnum and Mason. She was essentially a decorative artist, and among her most striking work were some exquisitely crafted sculptures and pictures created (amid much bloodshed) out of tin. Inspired by the mobiles of Alexander Calder, they were figurative, depicting the birds, animals, and fish that had always been an important part of her life.

In 1961, after McClean's retirement, he and Hale moved to Todd House, a cottage in Oxfordshire. Their sons had grown up and left home, but there were still plenty of cats. McClean died in 1967, followed shortly afterwards by the second Orlando. Hale wrote her last book when she was in her nineties. *A Slender Reputation* (1994) is a frank and evocative memoir, its characteristically modest title taken from Cedric Morris's remark: 'Do you mean to tell me, Kathleen, that you have hung your slender reputation on the broad shoulders of a eunuch cat?' (Hale, epigraph).

Hale had exacting standards and stood no nonsense. She had thick hair, bobbed at the age of eighteen and kept short all her life, and this emphasized her strong profile. She was made an OBE in 1976, and wore her usual assortment of eclectic and colourful clothes, mostly bought from second-hand shops, when presented with the award by the queen at Buckingham Palace. She died at Abbots Leigh Nursing Home, Clevedon, Somerset, on 26 January 2000 at the age of 101. She was cremated at Canford Lane cemetery, Bristol, on 4 February and her ashes scattered.

PETER PARKER

**Sources** K. Hale, *A slender reputation* (1994) • *Daily Telegraph* (28 Jan 2000) • *The Times* (28 Jan 2000) • *The Guardian* (28 Jan 2000) • *The Independent* (27 Jan 2000) • *The Scotsman* (2 Feb 2000) • private information (2004) [Peregrine McClean] • d. cert.

**Archives** SOUND NSA, 'Orlando keeps a dog' • NSA, 'Orlando buys a cottage' • NSA, 'Desert island discs'

**Likenesses** K. Hutton, photograph, 1949, Hult. Arch. [*see illus.*] • photograph, repro. in Hale, *Slender reputation*, 267

**Wealth at death** £527,119: probate, 15 June 2000, *CGPLA Eng. & Wales*

**Hale, Sir Mathew** (1609–1676), judge and writer, was born on 1 November 1609 at Alderley, Gloucestershire, only

Sir Mathew Hale (1609–1676), by Robert White, pubd 1676 (after John Michael Wright, c.1670)

child of Robert Hale (1563?–1614), barrister, and Joan Poyntz (1577–1612) of Alderley. He normally signed himself as Mathew Hale; contemporaries in general referred to him as Hales. Hale was inclined to play down his social origins, but he inherited an income of at least £100, probably ultimately derived from his paternal grandfather, a clothier of Wotton under Edge. His father had described himself as 'plebeian' on his matriculation at Oxford's Broadgates Hall; after he went to Lincoln's Inn, a conscientious scruple about the tricks expected of a courtroom advocate restricted him to a mere 'chamber practice', but Robert Hale was prosperous enough to erect a modern house at Alderley, suitable for a minor gentleman. Hale's parents were both dead within five years of his birth, and Hale was educated by one Antony Kingscot, of Kingscot, Gloucestershire, a puritan kinsman on his father's side, in spite of some objections raised by his maternal uncle. A godly education led to matriculation at Magdalen Hall, Oxford (20 October 1626), where his youthful tutor was Obadiah Sedgwick (1599/1600–1658), later a noted presbyterian preacher. In early 1629 Hale may have considered a spell as a soldier in Flanders, where Sedgwick became chaplain to the famous puritan warrior Horace Vere, but in the event he entered Lincoln's Inn on 18 May 1629, where he rapidly acquired some useful contacts. There is a story that his aptitude was spotted by the barrister John Glanville (1586–1641) in the course of a professional consultation (Burnet, 9–10). While Hale was still a student, he was referred to as 'young Noy' because of his closeness to William Noy (*d.* 1634), the former constitutionalist turned loyal attorney-general. Noy had a reputation as a pioneering legal antiquary, and he no doubt shaped Hale's subsequent commitment to the study of medieval manuscripts. At some time in the later 1630s this influence was reinforced by friendship with John Selden (1588–1654), the lawyer, antiquary, and orientalist who was the greatest influence upon Hale's legal and religious thinking.

**Early career** Hale was called to the bar in 1636 after the usual seven years of training. He would no doubt have gained prominence in any circumstances, but his professional progress was much accelerated by England's political troubles. In 1641 he was assigned to the defence of the ship money judge Sir John Bramston. In the course of the next decade he acted for a varied group of political defendants, including the twelve bishops impeached by the Commons, Archbishop Laud himself, the Irish papist rebel Connor McGuire, the duke of Hamilton, and the presbyterian minister Christopher Love. He was later said to have written the very effective speech in Laud's defence delivered by his senior colleague John Herne (*State trials*, 4.577); he certainly found ingenious arguments for Hamilton and Love, with whom he probably had more sympathy. Counsel for the defence in treason trials were in principle selected by the court, so the role in itself reveals nothing about his sympathies, but though he once appeared against the leveller John Lilburne, he never prosecuted royalists.

Although Hale's private papers show that his understanding of the constitution was broadly royalist, he stayed in London in the civil wars and seems to have been respected by all parties. It has usually been thought significant that he later produced some political 'Observations' to accompany his *Life and Death of T. Pomponius Atticus* (a translation from a Latin work by Nepos). These 'Observations' side with Atticus in his decision to adopt a strictly private life in troubled times, largely because they express a confidence that 'factions in a state never long hold their ground' (*Works*, 1.460). At all events, Hale made some compromises; according to Anthony Wood, he took the solemn league and covenant (Wood, *Ath. Oxon.*, 3.1091). From the re-opening of the courts to the protectorate, he had an extensive practice in king's bench; this was presumably the source of £4200 dispensed on land in 1648, the year he was elected a bencher of his inn. His professional activities were unaffected by the regicide and he certainly took the engagement, but the pattern of his subsequent behaviour suggests a pragmatic conservative position. In December 1650 he took part in a public debate on elections for the London corporation, defending an electorate confined to liverymen against supporters of a freeman franchise whose spokesman was the leveller John Wildman. He was the best-known member of the so-called Hale commission to consider law reform that met on a fortnightly basis from January 1652 until some time in late summer. Hale chaired the first two meetings, but thereafter became an irregular attender. The commission's minutes show that his influence was used in a conservative direction: he opposed the innovation of a land register, and even defended benefit of clergy on the grounds that it was 'in the parent's power to breed his child to read' (Cromartie, 71). Hale later not implausibly maintained that he had been deliberately obstructive, on the grounds that 'that which wise and honest men do now desire, they did then industriously decline' (F. Hargrave, *A Collection of Tracts Relative to the Law of England*, 1787, 274).

**Public career, 1654–1660** Cromwell appointed Hale a justice of the court of common pleas in January 1654 as part of a reshuffle of the judges that was apparently meant to reassure conservative opinion. Thereafter Hale's behaviour suggested a qualified support for the protector. In early 1654 Hale is said to have told the council that English fundamental law demanded monarchy. That autumn he sat as a member for Gloucestershire in the first of the protectorate parliaments, where he argued that 'the government should be in the parliament and a single person, limited and restrained as the parliament should think fit' (*Diary of Thomas Burton*, 1.xxxii). There is, however, no evidence that he continued to sit after Cromwell had purged the assembly by asking for an oath of recognition. Hale's subsequent behaviour was confusing; he did not sit in Cromwell's second parliament of 1656–7, but was admired by Major-General Whalley, who never knew 'any at their own cost more willing to serve the present government than he' (Thurloe, 4.686). His biographer Gilbert Burnet says that Hale refused to play a part in the trial of the royalist Penruddock, and that his scruples led him, after a period of hesitation, to stop presiding over criminal cases (Burnet, 40, 45–6), but Burnet had an interest in minimizing the degree of Hale's collaboration. We can be sure, however, that Hale refused to accept any office from Richard and that his exercise of his profession was restricted to chamber practice until the king's return. It was noted that he kept the title serjeant, granted by Oliver.

Hale sat for Oxford University in Richard Cromwell's parliament and for Gloucestershire (again) in the Convention. He seems to have played no significant part in the former, but was one of the leading members of the latter until he was named chief baron of the exchequer in November 1660. Throughout this period he would have been seen by his contemporaries as in a loose sense 'presbyterian'—that is, as someone who was royalist, but favoured the adoption of restrictions upon the power of monarchy and bishops. His personal opinions are known from a private memorandum in which he 'feared the detestation of the latter extreme under which we last smarted … will carry us over to the former extreme' (Williams, 63); he certainly showed a reckless disregard for altering political circumstances by defending the right of the regicide Edmund Ludlow to occupy a seat in parliament (later, however, he sat on the commission that tried the regicides). In Burnet's *History of my Own Time* Hale is said to have argued for a settlement based on the Isle of Wight negotiations of 1648 (*Bishop Burnet's History*, 1.160). Hale's final act as a member of the Commons was to bring in a bill that would enact the compromise church settlement of the Worcester House declaration. One motive for appointing him chief baron was probably to remove him from the house.

**Public career, 1660–1676** Hale was knighted in 1661. After the Restoration, he enjoyed virtually universal reverence but there are signs that royalist Anglicans were suspicious of what they perceived as pro-puritan and anti-government bias. In contrast to his colleague, the peppery Chief Justice Sir John Kelyng, Hale was certainly consistently relaxed when national security was thought to be threatened. In *Tonge's case* (1662) he was one of only two judges to refuse to convict a radical puritan printer; in *Messenger's case* (1668), which arose from an apprentice riot with an anti-government tinge, he was the only judge to oppose the decision to treat the rioters as traitors. In *Hopkin Hugett's case* (1666), in which he was for once a part of the majority, he treated the death of a member of a press-gang as merely manslaughter. Unlike Kelyng, he took a restrictive view of the use of martial law and he disliked the practice of fining juries. King Charles himself believed that 'his servants were sure to be cast on any trial that was heard before him: not that he thought the judge was possibly to be bribed: but that his integrity might be too scrupulous' (*Essays of John Dryden*, 2.69), though Charles, with his usual political astuteness, took care to appear unruffled by such behaviour. The tory historian Roger North made detailed criticisms, but even North admitted that 'when Hales was Chief Baron of the Exchequer, by means of his great learning, even against his inclination, he did the Crown more justice than any others, in that court, had done with all their good will' (North, 61). In May 1671 Charles made Hale the chief justice of king's bench, an appropriate appointment for someone who was writing a great digest of criminal law, but one that necessarily involved him in numerous politically sensitive cases. The government was probably particularly enraged by his reasoning in *Thomas* v. *Sorrell* (1674), a suit about the limits to the prerogative of dispensation, and in *Barnardiston* v. *Soame* (1674), a suit arising from the sheriff's conduct in a bitterly contested by-election. Hale survived an attempt to sack him in December 1672, perhaps on the grounds of refusal to endorse the royal declaration of indulgence, and he eventually retired, pleading ill health, in February 1676. Charles magnanimously insisted on paying him his salary as a pension.

**Judicial conduct** Hale was a dominant figure on the bench for almost twenty years. His style in that capacity was vividly described by his enemy North. He took seriously his educational role and did his best to make the court's proceedings intelligible to students. Although he had no time for oratory and was happy to pause to search for the right word, he sometimes uttered 'sentences heroic' (North,

62). He held and expressed a conventional faith in the prescriptive wisdom of the law, but was prepared to countenance reform, so long as it was guided by the judges. He drafted a number of bills with this in mind, including, it was said, the Statute of Frauds of 1677 (Simpson, 602–4). He also devised the effective 'fire court' that was set up in 1667 by parliamentary statute to assist the rebuilding of London. The court showed a pragmatic willingness to disregard the rights of property owners so as to expedite the work of reconstruction. With equal pragmatism he fostered the exchequer's role as a court of equity. For obvious self-interested reasons, the exchequer had long assisted royal debtors by granting equitable remedies to help them to recover their own debts, but it was only in 1649 that the claim to be a debtor of the state became a legal fiction. Hale let this fiction be, and in so doing he helped to create a national equitable jurisdiction to supplement the court of chancery. He showed a similar freedom from merely legalistic prejudice in his attitude to other legal systems. He was not above defending the encroachments of common lawyers on the church courts and on the Admiralty, but he accepted the legitimacy of non-common-law jurisdictions, even when their activities were demonstrably neither based on statute nor immemorial. In 1670, in *King v. Standish*, he decisively rejected Coke's assertion that the medieval offence of *praemunire* (improperly resorting to a foreign jurisdiction) could be committed by a litigant who made appeal to the lord chancellor.

Hale's personal fame and his authorship of the standard English criminal law textbook have tended to draw disproportionate attention to probably quite commonplace opinions. Thus one of his final judgments, in *R.* v. *Taylor* (1676), established that an act of blasphemy was a common-law offence, but this development was unsurprising, given that the church now lacked an appropriate way to punish such offences. The cautionary words in Hale's textbook about crediting rape accusations were often quoted by judges in the twentieth century; together with his view that wives could not complain of rape, because a wife had 'given up herself in this kind to her husband, which she cannot retract' (M. Hale, *Historia placitorum coronae*, 1.629), they have given him an unfair reputation as a misogynist. The best-known single episode Hale was connected with was undoubtedly the witchcraft trial over which he presided at Bury St Edmunds assizes in 1662. Like many liberal protestants of his time Hale saw the existence of witches as evidence for Christianity, if only as showing the inadequacy of a materialistic atheism. He none the less conducted the proceedings in an admirably scientific spirit. The future chief justice John Kelyng was very sceptical and thought the evidence was insufficient, but he may have been influenced by prejudice against the victims, who were puritan. The court was understandably reluctant to believe that children from three separate families could have colluded to accuse two innocent old women, so the women were duly convicted and executed. An eighteenth-century story claimed that Hale later changed his mind; if so, this would explain the curious fact that none of his subsequent writings makes any reference to the episode, even when first-hand knowledge of occult phenomena was clearly relevant to his purposes.

**Major legal writings** Hale's generation at the inns of court was probably more erudite than those that followed and preceded it. Unlike their post-revolutionary successors, they benefited from a professional culture that integrated 'readings' at the inns (the delivery of lectures about statutes) into the normal pattern of professional advancement; unlike their predecessors, they profited from the steadily rising standard of antiquarian investigation. Like his early mentor Noy, Hale was committed to research in legal manuscripts. He bequeathed his great collection to Lincoln's Inn as 'a treasure worth the having and keeping'; but he wished to confine the fruits of such research to trained professionals, and indeed to fellow members of the inn. It is revealing of his attitudes that he thought the manuscripts were 'a treasure … not fit for every man's view', and the terms of his will forbade their publication (Williams, 347). These attitudes extended to his own professional writings; they delayed, and in consequence muted, the influence of his most important works. His purely professional writings are erudite, clear, and exhaustive in their treatment of an extraordinary range of questions, but only a short essay in praise of common law (a preface to Chief Justice Rolle's *Abridgement*) was printed in his lifetime. He himself produced a manuscript 'Abridgement', the so-called 'Black book of the new law', but it has never been seriously studied.

Aside from his judicial contribution, Hale's influence on the course of legal history has rested upon two substantial achievements: his unfinished *Historia placitorum coronae*, and his *History and Analysis of the Common Laws of England*. Neither was printed for a generation after his death in 1676, although the *History*, at least, was probably quite widely circulated. The *Historia placitorum coronae* was printed in an edition by Sollom Emlyn in 1736 and was the main authority on English criminal law for a century thereafter (it is occasionally confused with a much sketchier notebook on the subject, published in 1678 as *Pleas of the Crown, or, A Methodical Summary of the Principal Matters Relating to that Subject*). Stephen believed that the work displayed 'a depth of thought and comprehensiveness of design which puts it in quite a different category from Coke's *Institutes*' (J. F. Stephen, *A History of the Criminal Law of England*, 1883, 2.211). According to Gilbert Burnet, Hale started it before the regicide, suspending work during the interregnum; he was certainly still adding new material in the months of illness following his retirement. Like the *Historia*, the *History* is a history in the seventeenth-century sense—a comprehensive treatment of its topic, though much of its length is taken up with the story of the law's development. It is notable for a Burkean account of the wisdom of a customary law, and for a temperate defence of the system's continuity across the Norman conquest. The *Analysis* at its conclusion is a complete taxonomy of matters handled by the common law; it was borrowed by William Blackstone with minimal modification and therefore provides the structure of Blackstone's *Commentaries*.

**Other legal/historical treatises** Hale also produced a number of detailed treatments of legal/historical questions, most of them printed in the 1790s by the great antiquarian barrister Francis Hargrave. His intellectual response to the English civil war was to compose three separate drafts of a work about the king's prerogative, which is the nearest thing we have to a statement of the English constitution from a legalistic royalist perspective. Comparison of the first two drafts, composed at some time in the 1640s, with a more polished but unfinished version that dates from some time after 1660, confirms Hale's essential consistency of outlook. If published in the seventeenth century, this work would surely have become the main authority upon the subject, but in spite of some preliminary work by Hargrave, no edition appeared until 1975, by which time it had dwindled to a curiosity. Hale's masterly account accepted the fact of constitutional change (though he believed that English law survived the Norman conquest, he indicated that he thought the Saxon monarchy had been elective). He considered that royal power had been fixed, by statute and by custom, and therefore denied the existence of a residual prerogative that might entitle Charles I to override the laws. He none the less endorsed by implication the royalist position of 1642, partly because the course of English history had shown that kings could be restrained without the use of force.

Hale's other professional essays included discussions of law reform, the customs, the powers of the court of the marches, and the relationship between king's bench and common pleas, but his most elaborate and impressive works concerned the jurisdictions of the Admiralty and of the House of Lords. His treatise on the former almost certainly arose from the vigorous rearguard action conducted in the early 1670s by the civilian Sir Leoline Jenkins. As might have been expected, Hale defended the Admiralty's right to exist while justifying the common law's removal of virtually all its commercial jurisdiction. His treatment of the latter, *The Jurisdiction of the Lords House*, was prompted by the friction between the two houses over *Skinner's case* (1669) and *Shirley* v. *Fagg* (1675)—cases concerned, respectively, with the claim of the peers to original jurisdiction and with their right to entertain appeals from chancery. Hale's subtle and learned argument depended on detecting the operation of a royal council in the precedents brought forward by the Lords. This council (which included the king's judges) was part of the Lords, but was by no means identical with it. He did not believe that the house possessed an intrinsic jurisdiction and he feared the constitutional consequences if such a claim were generally accepted. These works have barely been more influential than the doomed treatise on prerogative, though Hargrave ensured that all except the Admiralty treatise at least became available in print. The pattern of late publication dictating practical irrelevance was completed by an interesting fragment: about 1672 Hale saw a copy of Hobbes's *Dialogue between a Common Lawyer and a Student, of the Common Laws of England* (judges had the responsibility of licensing legal works for publication) and he was stimulated to compose some brief but suggestive 'Reflections' upon its ideas, defending common law's prescriptive wisdom. They have been much admired by recent scholars, but they remained unpublished until 1921.

**Personal characteristics** Hale's standing among his contemporaries was derived from his integrity as much as from his learning, and his integrity was seen as founded upon an attractive mixture of puritan manners and rational religion. Even as lord chief justice his behaviour took lack of pretension to the verge of eccentricity. He favoured cheap, drab clothing, adopted a deliberate manner of speech, and lived with ostentatious modesty at Acton, Middlesex. Unlike his mentor, the gregarious Selden, Hale had no interest at all in sociable eating and drinking. He regretted some youthful visits to the theatre, but his only self-indulgence later in life was an immoderate use of pipe tobacco. It was highly characteristic that when he was knight of the shire he needed to be lent the sword required.

About 1640 Hale married his first wife, Anne Moore (1621–1658?), granddaughter of Sir Francis Moore, the noted Jacobean law reporter, and also Geoffrey Palmer's niece by marriage. There were ten children of this first marriage, of whom six survived to early adult life; Hale's enemies said that he was 'a great cuckold' whose sons died 'in the sink of debauchery' (*Brief Lives*, 1.278; North, 62). On 18 October 1667 his second marriage, to Anne Bishop (*d.* 1694), who was apparently a household servant, embarrassed his friends and much amused his critics. It seems most unlikely, however, that he 'said there was no wisdom below the girdle', as Roger North maliciously alleged, if only because the reported remark was uncharacteristically pithy (North, 62). Together with Hale's attitude to witchcraft and to rape, these oddities have given some support to accusations of misogyny. The accusations seem anachronistic; his dealings with women in fact suggest the rather ponderous kindness that typified his conduct generally. He named his wife as an executor, allowed her to control the upbringing of his orphan grandchildren, and left her books about divinity, so he can hardly have lacked confidence in her capacities; the generous tributes in his will suggest that the marriage was also an emotional success.

All sources uninfected by tory animus agree about Hale's charm of character. About 1646 the barrister John Maynard was asked the difference between a just man and a good one. He replied:

> 'I'll tell you the difference presently: Serjeant Rolle is a just man and Matthew Hale is a good man' … For Serjeant Rolle was just, but by nature penurious … Matthew Hale was not only just, but wonderfully charitable and openhanded, and did not sound a trumpet neither, as the hypocrites do. (*Brief Lives*, 2.203–4)

Hale was not just a charitable man; he took an interest in social problems. *A Discourse Touching Provisions for the Poor* (written in 1659 and posthumously printed) elaborates and costs a detailed scheme for county workhouses. He disapproved of any sport involving killing animals for pleasure, refused to accept the most trivial gifts from litigants before him, and had to overcome his squeamishness when punishing capital crimes.

**Religion** Hale and others would have attributed these virtues to his religion. By his own account he had had a religious conversion at the age of twenty-five or twenty-six (*c.*1635); his hagiographer Burnet says this was a reaction to witnessing a friend collapse in a student drinking session. About 1638 Hale gave an account of his religious views, published by Richard Baxter as *A Discourse of the Knowledge of God and of Ourselves* (1688). The autodidact Baxter was much impressed by the work's scholastic learning, but it is probably most valuable as a statement of the Calvinist position, as understood by a conventional but highly intelligent layman. Hale was close to the learned Calvinist Archbishop Ussher during the interregnum, when the latter had a post as the Lincoln's Inn preacher. Hale defended rule by bishops on pragmatic and secular grounds, but hoped to establish a 'moderate episcopacy' (rule by bishops with assistance from their clergy) along the lines that Ussher advocated; he was therefore disappointed by the rigid Restoration settlement and would have preferred a more inclusive church.

By 1660 Hale had moved to an Arminian theology, but this did not diminish his sympathy with English puritans; he even disliked church music and he sympathized with puritan complaints that apparently innocent ceremonial practice could be the occasion of idolatry. Together with his mode of speech and dress, such attitudes suggested a principled old-fashioned puritanism, but some allowance should be made for an innocent love of singularity. His eccentric insistence on standing up in church for every Bible reading (not just, as the rubric dictated, for the gospel), was not a puritan habit, although it is easy to see that puritans might find the idea appealing. For a number of years he wrote an annual poem in honour of Christmas day, and he was happy to defend the wealth of diocesan bishops as an effective stimulus to learning. He had a conventional terror of antinomianism and saw the fragmentation of English religion during the interregnum as showing the practical wisdom of uniformity. An undiscriminating toleration was sure, in his opinion, to lead to popery or anarchy.

As might have been expected, the libertarian character of Hale's judicial practice became particularly noticeable in cases affecting the treatment of nonconformity. In Exeter in 1664 he refused to treat a silent Quaker meeting as a conventicle, on the grounds that only *seditious* conventicles were outlawed by the wording of the statute. After he moved to Acton, Middlesex, in 1667, he struck up an intimate friendship with his presbyterian neighbour Richard Baxter, another puritan who had rejected the predestinarian rigour of Calvinist doctrine. Although their conversations in general avoided politically treacherous topics, Hale did reveal his deep regret about the Restoration Act of Uniformity. In January 1668 he drew up a draft Comprehension Bill based on negotiations between moderate presbyterians led by Baxter and the lord keeper Sir Orlando Bridgeman, but the militantly Anglican behaviour of the parliament that met in February discouraged its proponents from taking the scheme any further. Baxter exaggerated how far Bridgeman had accepted his proposals, but he did extort the valuable concession that ministers without episcopal orders need not be re-ordained. When Baxter was next arrested, in 1669, Hale probably influenced the court of common pleas, which discovered a number of technical excuses for ordering his release. On at least one other occasion he himself discovered some technical grounds for freeing a dissenter and he rejected urgings to imprison the Quaker George Fox. Hale remained on very friendly terms with Baxter, consulting him about predestination, and left him 40s. as a token of esteem; the will significantly coupled Baxter with the established church's minister at home in Gloucestershire.

**Religious writings** Hale was a fluent writer who liked to do his thinking pen in hand, and some of his religious works were written as a kind of exercise to concentrate his thoughts on Sunday evening (he had a puritan regard for the Sabbath's sanctity). These writings had the clarity and taxonomic flair of his professional output, but the circumstances of their composition encouraged his extreme prolixity. A selection of his short devotional essays, the *Contemplations Moral and Divine*, was published anonymously in 1676 by his son-in-law Edward Stephens, apparently with his tacit acquiescence, and a number of similar writings were subsequently posthumously printed. Hale also wrote apologetic works on a much larger scale, apparently for his private edification, including an unfinished treatise entitled 'De Deo' that extends over five closely written folio volumes. 'De Deo' was shown to Baxter, but is clearly quite unpublishable in its surviving form. Hale took more pains about the presentation of his most celebrated religious treatise, *The Primitive Origination of Mankind, Considered and Examined According to the Light of Nature* (1677), which seems to have been written in the early 1660s, although he had revised it with a view to publication during the period before his death. A German translation was published in 1683. *The Primitive Origination* argues for the creation of the human race by an intelligent agent; its arguments touch on numerous topics, including the impossibility of an infinite succession, the character of time and space, the demographic tendencies of modern England and of ancient Israel, and the unlikelihood of spontaneous generation in anything more complex than a mouse. Hale also composed a number of drafts of a sequel about the 'secondary origination' of the individual soul. As he discusses sexual reproduction and a number of very heterodox ideas, this work was partly composed in a barbarous Latin. It would have concluded by treating of supernatural regeneration.

Hale's writings about Christianity suggest a not unusual drift towards a broadly ethical religion. Perhaps under Selden's influence, he moved from an infralapsarian Calvinism during the 1630s to a basically Arminian position; like many Arminians, he was inclined to cover this shift in doctrine with professions of indifference to theological aridities. By the later 1660s he expected virtuous pagans to be saved. His writings show no interest in ecclesiology or in the nature of the sacraments, and he regarded Roman Catholics as victims of a clerical confidence trick. Most of these views were typical of the non-Laudian divines since known as latitudinarian. Among this varied group Hale is said to have known Tillotson, Stillingfleet, and Barrow (Burnet, 74), though his religious standpoint was probably closest to Tillotson's brand of post-puritan rationalism. After his comprehension scheme of 1668 Hale certainly became a friend of John Wilkins, the bishop of Chester; something of what they might have had in common can be encapsulated by the fact that Wilkins, who had married Cromwell's daughter, was Tillotson's father-in-law.

**Scientific writings** Hale chose to present his works of natural philosophy as a busy professional's hobby, but they reflect the principal concerns of his religious writings and show an impressive level of acquaintance with recent literature. His serious apologetic writings on the origination of mankind lean heavily on scientific detail. In youth (no doubt at Oxford) he had been interested in such questions, but his renewed attention to natural-philosophical enquiry appears to date from about the time of the Restoration. His basic position had certainly been formed when he wrote the *Primitive Origination* in the early 1660s. Hale occasionally performed experiments, particularly with magnets, but he seems to have regarded as his primary role the solution of phenomena presented in the existing literature. Like Newton he disliked hypotheses—the habit, stemming from Descartes, of suggesting mechanistic explanations of all phenomena. His interests therefore centred on those well-known features of the natural world (magnets, plants, animals, and gravity) that seemed most difficult to understand in mechanistic terms. On the other hand, he was distrustful of a naturalistic teleology, exemplified for him by Henry More; both mechanism and teleology excluded God from nature. Drawing upon the thinking of the chemist J. B. van Helmont, Hale tried to avoid both extremes by reference to the concept of a 'ferment'. These active principles within the world were ranged upon a spectrum, running from flames and magnets to the animal (and perhaps the human) soul; they could not themselves be explained except as motions obedient to a divine command.

In his last years Hale ventured to apply this theory in three short publications. The first, *An essay, touching the gravitation and non-gravitation of fluid bodies, and the reasons thereof* (1673), explained the supposed phenomenon that fluid bodies do not gravitate (that water at the bottom of the sea is not significantly pressed upon by water higher up). It was followed by *Difficiles nugae, or, Observations Touching the Torricellian Experiment* (1674; 2nd edn, 1675), a pamphlet concerned with Boyle's claim that the 'spring of the air' (a fluid) holds up the column of mercury within a primitive barometer. A reply by Henry More, *Remarks upon Two Late Ingenious Discourses* (1676), evoked a further pamphlet, *Observations Touching the Principles of Natural Motion* (1677), which discusses rarefaction and condensation, the ability of a given piece of matter to fill a greater or a lesser space. Though he disclaimed appeals to final causes, these writings in practice defended the principles he would have learned at Oxford, and his most significant debts, after Helmont, were to Honoratus Fabri and Francis Linus, two broadly Aristotelian Jesuits. Although the pamphlets were anonymous, their authorship appears to have been well known, a fact that may have helped diminish their impact; respect for the chief justice, by muffling criticism, may also have denied him the attention arising from polemical exchanges. Hale died at Alderley on Christmas day 1676, and was buried in Alderley churchyard, having left instructions that he should not be buried in the church—that being a place for the living, not the dead.

**Posthumous reputation** Hale left a place in national memory as the type of the virtuous lawyer and the incorruptible judge. This image was cemented by Gilbert Burnet's hagiography, *The Life and Death of Sir Matthew Hale* (1682), a book that soon achieved a classic status. The date of this work's composition at a period of royalist reaction made Burnet relatively reticent about his hero's brand of politics. The balance was somewhat redressed by Baxter's remarks in his *Additional Notes on the Life and Death of Sir Matthew Hale* (1682), which stressed Hale's sympathy for the dissenters, and by the account of their friendship in the posthumous *Reliquiae Baxterianae* (1696). There were more critical voices, suspicious of Hale's 'presbyterianism', most notably Anthony Wood in *Athenae Oxonienses* and Roger North in his life of his brother, Lord Guilford, but their snipings have the shrillness of the consciously perverse. During the eighteenth century Hale ceased to be regarded as the property of any particular party. Even Jacobites were anxious to maintain that Hale would have supported their position. Samuel Johnson recommended Burnet's *Life*, and the edition of *Works Moral and Divine* published by Thomas Thirlwall in 1805 contains a dedication to Lord Eldon.

Hale has continuously enjoyed the reverence of lawyers as the greatest Stuart jurist after Coke, and treatments of his place in legal history have virtually always been tinged with piety. In non-professional eyes Hale's reputation has been less consistent. Down to the early nineteenth century, his short religious tracts were recommended as edifying reading, no doubt because the point about these works was not their content but their authorship. Since then, the fact that such a man was also an exemplary protestant Christian has lost apologetic usefulness. During the twentieth century the best-known episode in Hale's career was undoubtedly his role in trying witches. This has usually been treated, given Hale's learning and his character, as a striking indication of the blindness of his age, although a more recent tradition has traced the aberration to his own misogyny. In Arthur Miller's play *The Crucible*, the clerical expert on witchcraft is called Hale.

ALAN CROMARTIE

**Sources** G. Burnet, *The life and death of Sir Matthew Hale* (1682) • J. B. Williams, *Memoirs of the life, character and writings of Sir Matthew Hale* (1835) • A. Cromartie, *Sir Matthew Hale, 1609–76: law religion and natural philosophy* (1995) • R. North, *The life of the Right Honourable Francis*

North, baron of Guilford (1742) · Brief lives, chiefly of contemporaries, set down by John Aubrey, between the years 1669 and 1696, ed. A. Clark, 2 vols. (1898) · R. Baxter, Additional notes on the life and death of Sir Matthew Hale (1682) · Wood, Ath. Oxon., new edn · E. Heward, Matthew Hale (1972) · The works moral and religious of … Matthew Hale, ed. R. Baxter and T. Thirlwall, 2 vols. (1805) · State trials · Diary of Thomas Burton, ed. J. T. Rutt, 4 vols. (1828) · Thurloe, State papers · Essays of John Dryden, ed. W. R. Ker, 2 vols. (1900); repr. (1926) · A. Simpson, A history of the common law of contract: the rise of assumpsit (1975) · DNB · parish register, Alderley, Gloucestershire, 1 Nov 1609 [birth] · Foster, Alum. Oxon. · gravestone, Alderley churchyard, Gloucestershire · IGI

**Archives** BL, treatises, Harley MSS; Add. MSS 18234, 41661 · CUL, history of common law · Glos. RO, corresp. and papers · JRL, history of the pleas of the crown · Lincoln's Inn, London, legal and historical collections · LPL, collected papers, incl. notebook of cases as lord chief justice of the king's bench and antiquarian items · Middle Temple, London, MSS · U. Cal., Los Angeles, William Andrews Clark Memorial Library, cases and opinions, drafts, papers · Yale U., Sterling Memorial Library, papers | Bodl. Oxf., papers relating to role as an executor of John Selden

**Likenesses** J. M. Wright, oils, c.1670, Guildhall Art Gallery, London · oils, c.1670 (after J. M. Wright), NPG · R. White, engraving, pubd 1676 (after J. M. Wright, c.1670), NPG [see illus.] · F. H. Van Hove, line engraving, 1677, BM, NPG; repro. in M. Hale, The primitive origination of mankind (1677)

**Wealth at death** approx. £900 p.a.: will, Williams, Memoirs, 327–58

**Hale, Richard** (1670–1728), physician, was born at Beckenham, Kent, the eldest son of Richard Hale (1649–1703), of New Windsor, Berkshire, and Elizabeth, *née* Church (*b.* 1649). Hale, who came from a rather modest, country gentry background, had two sisters, Elizabeth and Sarah, and three brothers, Henry (1672–1707), John (*d.* 1720), and William. Educated at Trinity College, Oxford, Hale graduated BA (19 May 1693); MA (4 February 1695); MB (11 February 1697); and MD (23 June 1701). After graduation, he practised for several years in Oxford, but he was forced to move to London, as his reputation had begun 'to sink upon Account of his using opiat[e]s too much' (Hearne, 2.130; Bodl. Oxf., MS Rawl. J.4.1, fol. 284). Hale received patronage early in his career from Edward Tyson, the renowned anatomist and physician of the Bridewell and Bethlem hospitals, London, who communicated Hale's first paper, 'The humane alantois' (human foetal membrane), to the Royal Society in 1701. Hale's continued interest in anatomy is further attested by his later contribution to *Philosophical Transactions* (1721) of 'An account of the external maxillar glands'. Partly as a result of this work, Hale was proposed (by Edmond Halley) and elected FRS in 1721. He was elected FRCP in 1716, and served as censor to the college in 1718, 1719, and 1724. He delivered the Harveian oration in 1724; it was notable for his account of the achievements of English doctors, and criticisms of the current fashion among medical men for education on the continent.

Hale's association with Tyson probably helped him succeed the latter on 10 September 1708 as physician to Bridewell and Bethlem, where he served until his death. The connection was further cemented by the marriage of Richard Tyson, Edward Tyson's favourite son, to Hale's

**Richard Hale (1670–1728)**, by Jonathan Richardson the elder

niece, Elizabeth. Hale later supported Richard's successful candidacy for the post of physician to St Bartholomew's Hospital in 1725. Hale's physicianship at Bethlem coincided with the erection of wards for 'incurable lunatics' at the hospital. He attended Bethlem at least once a week, as the governors required him to do. Under his superintendence, admission and discharge procedures seem to have been tightened up, with all applicants being examined a week before admission and a fair number being rejected as unfit. Hale was distinguished posthumously for the mildness of his medical treatment at the hospital, which was said to rely on 'sedating' maniacs with medicine rather than on 'restraining them with chains or bars' (Monro, 22). Hale was 'mechanistic' in his approach to medicine, strongly influenced by the 'iatromathematical' school of medicine, which tended to conceptualize disease and fevers as resulting from obstructions in the glands and other vessels of the body, and to rely heavily on evacuative methods of treatment. However, he published nothing explicitly on insanity.

Hale's post at Bethlem was partly honorary, and carried an annual salary of less than £27, plus a supplementary (discretionary) gratuity of £50. His main residence seems to have been in Lincoln's Inn Fields, a fashionable address for well-to-do professional men. Clearly successful in building up his assets, and social status, he also owned houses in Magpie Alley, and Fenchurch Street, and in Hampstead (the base for his private practice), and inherited or bought considerable country manors and estates, in Essex, Cheshire, and Hexham. Hale was married, but nothing further is known about his wife, Frances.

Like his predecessors, Hale amassed most of his fortune by way of the private practice which his hospital post helped to generate, although, as was customary, he mixed mad doctoring with ordinary general practice. His private practice, however, was drawn under the glare of unsavoury publicity in 1718 through the widely publicized case of Sarah Clerke, whose confinement under Hale's care and subsequent release aroused a heated controversy between her advocates and the brothers who had confined her. This incident has been interpreted by some historians as a clear-cut case of false confinement, and indeed appears to emphasize the ease with which individuals could be certified at the behest of an interested party; however, Hale was one of a number of distinguished medical men who had considered Mrs Clerke insane. Her supporters argued cogently and ultimately successfully that she was merely 'vaporish', or nervous, and that the 'violent' methods employed by Hale were inappropriate. However, the case probably says more about the ambiguous nature of mad doctors' practices at this time, and the social impropriety of using interventionist, 'terrific' tactics in treating patients from the genteel classes (in distinction from the pauper insane), than it does about the peculiar nature of Hale's medical attendance. Towards the end of his career, Hale was also the attending physician concerned in another rather more modest controversy, over the sanity or otherwise of Lady Frances Erskine Mar. Nevertheless, Hale's reputation seems to have emerged from both cases relatively intact. Private attendance of a different order on Mehemet, George I's notorious body servant, earned Hale the offer of a baronetcy, but, apparently sensitive to the rather scandalous aura surrounding the king's favouritism for his Turkish entourage, he prudently declined.

Hale's facial expression, in a contemporary painting of him by Jonathan Richardson, seems to hint at the qualities of frankness, mixed with severity, that contemporaries testify to have characterized his manner. His death from apoplexy at his address in Lincoln's Inn Fields, London, on 28 September 1728 was greeted with numerous expressions of regret from colleagues and friends echoed by his lapidary inscription at New Windsor, where he was buried.

Hale died a wealthy man, leaving 'an Estate of near £100,000' (*Daily Journal*, 28 Sept 1728), and making hefty legacies, including £500 to the library of the College of Physicians, and £500 to the incurables of Bethlem Hospital. JONATHAN ANDREWS

**Sources** will, PRO, PROB 11/625, sig. 291 • J. Andrews, 'A respectable mad doctor? Dr Richard Hale, FRS (1670–1728)', *Notes and Records of the Royal Society*, 44 (1990), 169–203 • J. Andrews, '"In her vapours … [or] indeed her madness"? Mrs Clerke's case: an early eighteenth century psychiatric controversy', *History of Psychiatry*, 1 (1990), 125–43 • Court of Governors minutes, Sept 1708–Oct 1728, Bethlem Royal Hospital • *Remarks and collections of Thomas Hearne*, ed. C. E. Doble and others, 11 vols., OHS, 2, 7, 13, 34, 42–3, 48, 50, 65, 67, 72 (1885–1921), vol. 2, p. 130; vol. 5, pp. 182–5, 222, 316; vol. 8, pp. 372–3 • T. Rawlinson, Bodl. Oxf., MS Rawl. J. 4.1, fol. 284 • T. Rawlinson, Bodl. Oxf., MS Rawl. D. 347, fol. 19 • J. Monro, *Oratio comitiis anniversaris Harveiana memoriae sacris* … 1737 (1737) • Munk, *Roll* • *London Evening-Post* (26–8 Sept 1728) • *Daily Journal* (26–8 Sept 1728) • journal book (copy), 1701, RS, fol. 261 • journal book (copy), 1721, RS, fols. 71–2, 74, 110 • will of Richard Hale (sen.), PRO, PROB 11/471, sig. 60 • will of John Hale, PRO, PROB 11/357, sig. 84 • Foster, *Alum. Oxon.*

**Archives** Bethlem Royal Hospital, Beckenham, Kent, archives

**Likenesses** J. Richardson the elder, oils, 1733, RCP Lond. • J. Richardson the elder, oils, RCP Lond. [*see illus.*] • J. Richardson the elder, oils, Bodl. Oxf.

**Wealth at death** approx. £100,000: *Daily Journal*

**Hale, Sarah Jane** (1851–1920), college head, was born on 15 February 1851 at Burton Latimer, Northamptonshire, the younger daughter of John Hale, a grocer. She became a pupil-teacher at Freeman's endowed school, Wellingborough, before entering Whitelands College, Chelsea, as a queen's scholar in January 1870. From 1874 she became successively headmistress of three elementary schools, in London, Wellingborough, and Leicester, before moving into teacher training in 1877, as the first headmistress of the new St Katherine's College at Tottenham. Here she came to feel the need of a wider education, and in 1885 resigned her post to go to Newnham College, Cambridge, to read for a degree in mental and moral science. In 1888 she gained an honours tripos third class, the first woman elementary schoolteacher to achieve honours at Oxford or Cambridge.

Sarah Hale returned to Tottenham before moving to St Mary's Hall, Cheltenham, as method mistress. Soon after, she was proposed by Joshua Fitch for the vacant principalship of Edge Hill Training College, Liverpool. This was already in the front rank of colleges, and under Miss Hale's leadership continued to grow and to enhance its academic reputation. She settled into her new post and made it her life's work. The vision which had guided her in her own education—the importance of the development of the educated mind—and the acute realization of how lack of opportunity prevented many from developing to their full extent led her to organize schemes for the higher education of her students and to encourage them to continue their education throughout their lives.

At Edge Hill, Sarah Hale had the opportunity to use her gifts of administration and organization. She built up strong links with the University of Liverpool and served on many local bodies, becoming widely known and genuinely respected in Liverpool for her religious, educational, and political work. In 1903 she was the only external member of a committee of HM inspectors established to examine the different methods of education and training for pupil teachers. She successfully guided the college through the war years. Her policies were often in advance of official thinking: she had 'an instinctive realisation both of the needs of the moment and of desirable developments in the future' (*Edge Hill College Magazine*, 1920, 5).

Gracious and dignified, a deeply religious Anglican, Sarah Hale was a woman of unfailing kindness and humour, patience, uncompromising principle, and sound common sense. She had a powerful presence and influence, was an excellent teacher, and inspired respect, loyalty, and love in her students, in whom she took a very real interest and care. She believed fervently in the importance of professionally trained teachers and of the quality of the teaching profession. Her message to her students, however, was a traditional one: that a woman's main career was to be found in marriage and the home, and that as teachers they held responsibility for the future women of England. She was no supporter of women's suffrage, though she did support equal pay for women teachers. Politically a staunch Conservative, she sought to promote in her students a philosophy of patriotism, service, and duty. Her recreation was to be found mainly in travel, usually to Europe and North America.

For the last eleven years of her life Miss Hale suffered from tuberculosis. Due to retire in July 1920, she died suddenly of pneumonia at the college on 1 April that year. Her body was cremated on 6 April and her ashes were buried in her parents' grave in Burton Latimer, near Kettering.

SYLVIA HARROP

**Sources** F. A. Montgomery, *Edge Hill College: a history, 1885–1997* (1997) · *Edge Hill College Magazine* (1892–1920) · *Times Educational Supplement* (29 April 1920) · *Liverpool Daily Post and Mercury* (7 April 1920) · *Liverpool Courier* (8 April 1920) · G. E. Hodgson, 'In memoriam S. J. Hale', *Newnham College Roll Letter* (1921), 77–9 · *WWW* · registers, University of Surrey, Roehampton, London, Whitelands College · vice-chancellor's letter books, U. Lpool · N. Daglish, *Education policy-making in England and Wales: the crucible years, 1895–1911* (1996) · G. Handley, *The College of All Saints* (1978) · J. G. Fitch, *Liverpool Mercury* (28 Jan 1885); pubd separately as *Inaugural proceedings, the Edgehill Training College: address on the office and work of a training college* (1885) · E. B. Challinor, *The story of St Mary's College, Cheltenham* [1978] · T. Kelly, *For advancement of learning: the University of Liverpool, 1881–1981* (1981) · b. cert. · d. cert.

**Likenesses** photograph, 1888 (group), Newnham College, Cambridge · photograph, repro. in *Edge Hill College Magazine* (1920), 4 · photographs, repro. in Montgomery, *Edge Hill College*

**Wealth at death** £3639 9s. 6d.: probate, 19 June 1920, *CGPLA Eng. & Wales*

**Hale, Warren Stormes** (1791–1872), tallow chandler and benefactor, was born on 2 February 1791 at Benington, Hertfordshire, the youngest of eight children of Edward Hale (1754–1791), farmer, and his wife, Edith, *née* Warren (1750–1808). Before he was a year old his father died, and in 1805 Hale was apprenticed to his brother, Ford Hale, a wax chandler in Cannon Street, London. On 6 July 1813 Hale married Sarah Morshead (1790–1865), daughter of Philip Morshead and his wife, Catharina Dulcibella, *née* Pritchett, of Southwark; of their eight children, only one, Samuel, married and had children.

In 1813 Hale set up in business as a tallow chandler at 21 Cateaton (from 1842 Gresham) Street, with additional premises in Bunhill Row in the early 1840s, and subsequently others in Orange Street, Southwark. He became a freeman of the Tallow Chandlers' Company and of the City of London on 6 January and 18 May 1814 respectively, as required by City ordinances. He moved his business from Gresham Street to Queen Street, and his residence to the Vale of Health, Hampstead, about 1853, living at West Heath, Hampstead, by 1858. His business owed its success to his being the first English manufacturer to apply the research of the French chemists Chevreul and Lussac on animal and vegetable fatty acids.

Warren Stormes Hale (1791–1872), by John Robert Dicksee, 1853

Hale became a member of the common council for Coleman Street ward in 1827. In 1833 he was chairman of the City lands committee, the corporation of London's premier committee, which administered the bequest of John Carpenter (*d.* 1442) for the clothing and education of four poor boys. At Hale's instigation the corporation sponsored an act of parliament, passed in 1834, which charged the Carpenter estates for the support of the new City of London School, which was built in Milk Street, Cheapside, and opened on Hale's birthday, 2 February 1837. By tradition, Hale's son Josiah was the first pupil to cross the threshold of the new school on its opening day. The school's curriculum was a liberal one for the period and included French as well as Latin and Greek, together with lectures on chemistry and philosophy. Hale was chairman of the City of London School committee from 1834 to 1869, after which he became president of the City of London School (an otherwise unknown title) and an ordinary member of the committee until his death. During this time, Hale was also the driving force behind the establishment of the mixed City of London Freemen's Orphan School (now the City of London Freemen's School) which opened in Brixton in 1854. He served as a member of the Orphan School committee, 1850–72, and as chairman, 1850–56. Hale's educational achievements were recognized by the foundation, in 1865, of the Warren Stormes Hale scholarship at the City of London School, money for which was raised during his mayoralty in 1864–5.

Hale became deputy of Coleman Street ward in 1850, and alderman of the same ward on 3 October 1856. He was master of the Tallow Chandlers' Company in 1849 and 1861, sheriff of London 1858–9, and lord mayor in 1864–5.

During his mayoralty he continued to raise a fund for the relief of Lancashire operatives who suffered from the cotton famine of 1862–5. He also helped to found the Albert Orphan Asylum, the Asylum of Aged Mariners, and the Alexandra Orphanage.

Hale died on 23 August 1872 at his house, West Heath, Hampstead, and was buried on 30 August in his family vault in Highgate cemetery. VIVIENNE ALDOUS

**Sources** A. B. Beaven, ed., *The aldermen of the City of London, temp. Henry III–[1912]*, 2 vols. (1908–13) · A. E. Douglas-Smith, *The City of London School*, 2nd edn (1965) · P. Boult, 'Warren Stormes Hale', *History of the Tallow Chandlers' Company* · E. Hale, *A year in the life of Warren Stormes Hale, lord mayor of London, 1864–5* (privately printed, 1995?) · parish registers, Therfield and Benington, Herts. ALS · parish registers, St Peter-le-Poer, St Swithin London Stone, St Olave Old Jewry, All Hallows Staining, St Mary Woolnoth, GL, manuscripts section · Tallow Chandlers' Company court minutes, GL, manuscripts section · City Freedom Admission Papers, May 1814, CLRO · Corporation of London Pocket Books, CLRO · Common Hall Minutes, 29 Sept 1865, CLRO · Hustings Book 14, 20 Jan 1868, CLRO · City of London School Register, 1837–1900, CLRO · V. Knight, *The works of art of the Corporation of London* (1986) · J. E. Price, *A descriptive account of the Guildhall of the city of London* (1886) · private information (2004) · trade directories, London, GL · *City Press* (12 Oct 1872) · *City Press* (31 Aug 1872) · *The Times* (24 Aug 1872), 9 · d. cert.

**Likenesses** J. W. Allen, oils, 1841, Guildhall Art Gallery, London · J. R. Dicksee, oils, 1853, Guildhall Art Gallery, London [*see illus.*] · portrait, 1859, Tallow Chandlers' Hall, Dowgate Hill, London · C. Bacon, marble bust, 1866, Guildhall Art Gallery, London · D. Fowler, oils, 1972, Guildhall Art Gallery, London · woodcut, NPG

**Wealth at death** under £5000: probate, 9 Oct 1872, *CGPLA Eng. & Wales*

**Hale, William** (1797–1870), rocket inventor and entrepreneur, was born on 21 October 1797 in Colchester, Essex, the son of Robert Hale, baker, and his wife, Elizabeth, and may have been descended from Sir Matthew Hale, lord chief justice.

Hale's early education is unknown, but his maternal grandfather, William Cole, was a versatile teacher and writer on diverse subjects and may have taught and influenced Hale, though the latter was apparently largely self-educated. In his youth he may possibly have been a sailor. He showed a penchant for mechanics, especially ship-related. In the first half of the nineteenth century there was much experimentation, study, and a search to improve vessel performance, as wooden vessels began to be supplanted by iron ones and steam power supplemented and replaced sails. Hale's first patent for 'Improvements to propelling vessels'—boats—was granted in 1827 for a steam-powered Archimedean screw to suck in water then quickly discharge it sternward, a crude form of jet propulsion, driving the boat forward.

In 1832 Richard Penn read a paper before the Royal Society about Hale's proposed internal-screw vessels, and a clockwork model was demonstrated to the king and queen at Virginia Water. Hale won a gold medal from the Royal Society of Arts in Paris, submitted his invention to the Admiralty, then lost interest in the project. At about the same time he took out varied patents—including for an improved windmill and for 'aerated liquors'—and joined in a partnership to develop ideas for improving gunpowder, but in this he was let down and unsuccessful.

About 1828 Hale married Elizabeth Rouse (*d.* 1846) of Colchester. They had two sons, William jun. (*b.* 1829) and Robert (*b.* 1831)—who both worked with their father on rocket development and production—and two daughters. In 1867 Hale married Mary Wells of Bath.

Hale's primary interest then being in boats and ships, about 1835 he moved to Greenwich to be near the Royal Navy, but in 1839 he returned to Woolwich where rockets, developed by Sir William Congreve, became the chief attractions.

Possibly influenced by rifling in firearms, Hale attempted to improve the performance of Congreve rockets by replacing the stabilizing stick by spin-stabilization: the concept was not new but previously had not been successfully implemented. He gradually evolved this rotation method from about 1843—with his first rocket patent (no. 10008) in January 1844—to 1865, using much money and effort to produce and promote internationally. Meanwhile he developed new manufacturing techniques and improved the hydraulic rocket press. His rocket factory was at Lower Deptford Road, Rotherhithe, London, on the Thames near Woolwich. His rockets ranged in size from 3 pounders to 100 pounders, though the 9 and 24 pounders were most used by the British. Made of iron and later mild steel, like their Congreve predecessors they were propelled by gunpowder and had various explosive and solid warheads. The British military made successive trials of Hale's successively modified rockets, and he complained that they used his rockets on campaign without proper compensation. Hale, his sons, and agents negotiated sales with other states. In 1846 he made his first foreign sale, when the United States bought manufacturing rights for $20,000, and they used the rockets in the Mexican war (1846–8). In 1848 the Hungarian revolutionary government negotiated, unsuccessfully, for rockets. Hale, dissatisfied with his agents overseas, from 1849 travelled on the continent trying to sell his rockets. He failed to persuade the Prussians, but sold to Denmark and Hamburg. In 1850 he demonstrated his rockets to Prince Albert at Osborne, Isle of Wight.

Hale negotiated with Lajos Kossuth, the Hungarian leader, and employed some Hungarian exiles at his Rotherhithe rocket factory. One of them, August Usever—either personally aggrieved or an Austrian agent—informed the police that Hale was manufacturing weapons for Italian and Hungarian revolutionaries. In April 1853 police searched the factory, and Hale was tried at Bow Street police court, London: this 'Rotherhithe case' attracted international media attention. The magistrate dismissed conspiracy, but fined Hale for illegal manufacture and storage of gunpowder near the London city limits, so almost bankrupting him. However, the Crimean War offered new opportunity. In 1854 he went to the British army in Bulgaria and sold them rockets and launchers for £500, then returned to England and manufactured rockets for the British forces. He sold to the USA in 1855, to Austria in 1858, and to Prussia in 1859. In 1863 he published his *Treatise on the Comparative Merits of a Rifle, Gun and Rotary Rocket*, one of the first works on the exterior ballistics of rockets. He also disproved the hypothesis that rockets moved because their exhaust gases pushed against the air, and explained rocket motion in terms of Newton's third law. In 1867 the British government finally purchased Hale's invention for £8000, and so superseded Boxer stick rockets which had recently replaced Congreve rockets. Hale's rockets, though increasingly marginalized by improved artillery, were used by British forces in Abyssinia (1868) and various colonial wars. They were probably last used in Sierra Leone in 1899, and were finally declared obsolete in 1919.

Hale latterly also attempted to develop life-saving rockets, and resumed work on ship propulsion. In 1868 he published his *Treatise on the Mechanical Means by which Vessels are Propelled by Steam Power*, which was poorly received. He died of typhoid on 30 March 1870 at his home, 9 Edith Terrace, Edith Grove, West Brompton, Middlesex, and was buried in the Old Brompton cemetery, London. According to Frank H. Winter, 'Although Hale's improvements did not completely solve the problem of rocket instability … they still represented revolutionary strides in early rocket technology and Hale is thus considered a major pioneer' (Winter, *First Golden Age of Rocketry*, 180). He also anticipated the nineteenth-century machine-gun inventor-entrepreneurs, notably Hiram Maxim, as an international arms merchant. His rockets may be seen at Firepower, the Royal Artillery Museum, Woolwich, London, and at the National Air and Space Museum, Washington, DC.

W. JOHNSON

**Sources** F. H. Winter, *The first golden age of rocketry: Congreve and Hale rockets of the nineteenth century* (1990) • *DSB* • F. H. Winter, 'William Hale: a forgotten British rocket pioneer', *Space Flight*, 15 (1973), 31–3 • C. E. Franklin and W. Johnson, 'William Hale's improvements in rockets', *International Journal of Impact Engineering*, 18/2 (1995), 231–41 • O. F. G. Hogg, *The Royal Arsenal: its background, origin and subsequent history* (1963) • C. E. Franklin, 'The Hale rocket in the British service, part 2: Operations and evaluation', *Journal of the British Interplanetary Society*, 52/7/8 (July–Aug 1999), 259–66 • *Annual Register*, pt 2, pp. 55–6 • J. Scoffern, *Projectile weapons of war, and explosive compounds*, 3rd edn (1858) • *IGI* • d. cert.

**Likenesses** W. Walker, mezzotint, pubd 1850 (after T. A. Woolnoth), BM

**Wealth at death** under £450: probate, 21 May 1870, *CGPLA Eng. & Wales*

**Hale, William Hale** (1795–1870), Church of England clergyman, son of John Hale (*d. c.*1799), a surgeon, of Lynn, Norfolk (possibly of Cornish or Devonian descent), was born on 12 September 1795, probably at Lynn. After the death of his father he became a ward of James Palmer, treasurer of Christ's Hospital, and from 1807 to 1811 went to Charterhouse School. On 9 June 1813 he matriculated at Oriel College, Oxford, and graduated BA in 1817 and MA in 1820, being placed in the second class in classics and mathematics. Ordained in 1819, he served in London as curate to Dr Gaskin at St Benet Gracechurch and from 1821 to Dr Blomfield at St Botolph without Bishopsgate. When Blomfield accepted in 1824 the bishopric of Chester, Hale became chaplain, a position which he retained on the bishop's translation to London in 1828. Hale had married at Croydon, on 13 February 1821, Ann Caroline Coles; they had five sons and three daughters. His wife died on 18 January 1866 at the Charterhouse, and was buried in St Paul's Cathedral.

Hale was preacher at the Charterhouse from 1823 until his appointment to the mastership in February 1842. He was a prebendary of St Paul's Cathedral from 1829, and archdeacon of St Albans from 17 June 1839, but vacated this in favour first of the archdeaconry of Middlesex (in August 1840) and then of London (in November 1842). Between 1846 and 1853 he was also almoner of St Paul's, and from 1847 to 1857 he retained the rich vicarage of St Giles Cripplegate in London.

Hale enjoyed—probably in both senses—a profoundly conservative reputation, assisted by his perception of Disraeli as an ally against the abolition of church rates, an instance (according to A. C. Tait) when 'Dizzy humbugged old Hale' (Machin, 344). But, eccentric, complex, and usually opinionated, he was something more individual than 'a Tory of the old school' (*The Times*, 28 Nov 1870; *The Guardian*, 30 Nov 1870). At Charterhouse, he not only carried through a major rebuilding aimed at greater hygiene, but strove to check ill-disciplined foundationers. Yet he fruitlessly opposed reform of the school, striving to uphold nomination over examination as a condition of entry. Presumably, his antiquarian studies published as *The Early History and Foundation of the Hospital of King James …* (1854) had reconciled him more fully to the former measures than to the latter as being consonant with the founder's intent. Equally, at St Paul's, he pressed through structural innovations such as gas lighting, sought unsuccessfully weekly disciplinary meetings, and (as almoner) tried to divert surplus chapter funds to support the choir.

Hale was considerably involved in the SPCK and (following his mentor Blomfield) the Colonial Bishoprics Fund. He was also a prolific writer of pamphlets arguing for 'extension of the ministry' through judicious use of the offices of suffragan bishop and of subdeacon, which he sought to save from the imputation of Romanism. That he opposed the Union of Benefices Act in 1865—to the extent that a special clause was brought forward to remove from the archdeacon of London the administrative role assigned to his fellows—was due rather to a personal concern about sacrilegious treatment of redundant churches than to lack of concern to improve the urban ministry. The church building commission was another cause close to his heart. His denunciation of the removal of new burials to extramural cemeteries, on the other hand, was an eccentric mixture of a very traditionalist belief in the community of the living with the dead and of a fear of a nonconformist conspiracy against the Anglican parochial system. The latter also led him to invectives against civil registration—'what more subtle scheme could the infidel have designed to unchristianize the country?' (*Remarks on … a Bill for Registering Births*, 1836, 16), and, in due course, to overthrow the monarchy (*The Designs and Constitution of the*

*Society for Liberation of Religion from State Patronage and Control Stated and Explained*, 1861).

Hale—a sympathetic editor of such divines as Lancelot Andrewes, Joseph Hall, and Jeremy Taylor—confessed to having been nearly 'carried away' in youth by Roman theology (*The Doctrine and Government of the Anglican Church under Henry VIII* …, 1869, 34). Remembrance of this may have convinced him that government support for the Maynooth seminary was both potentially suicidal and 'a national sin' (*The Approaching Contest with Romanism Considered*, 1845, 10). Most of the time, however, his battle was with threats perceived from protestant extremes. Hale's remarks in his charge *The Case of Obedience to Rulers in Things Indifferent* (1843) were understood by some as a reinforcement, or aggravation, of the ritualism imputed to Blomfield for his attempts to enforce the wearing of the surplice. At times, Hale's conservatism sounded so old-fashioned as to be quite Tudor (or even medieval, given his researches on the continuity of church discipline across the Reformation). He reacted tellingly to Samuel Wilberforce's support for the pretensions of Robert Gray to autonomous authority as metropolitan in South Africa: 'It is well Queen Elizabeth is not alive; she would have sent the bishop at once to the Tower'. Gray's supporters, he thought, aimed at detaching from the Church of England the colonial bishoprics he had helped to fund and 'dissolving the union between the church and the state' (Tait MS 84, fol. 35), which was the object of his most devoted attachment. Hale died at the master's lodge, Charterhouse, on 27 November 1870, and was buried in St Paul's Cathedral on 3 December.

Hale was a skilled antiquarian, involved in the improvement of both St Paul's Cathedral and Lambeth Palace libraries. More than his many controversial pamphlets and archidiaconal charges, his exceptionally accurate transcriptions of medieval and Tudor documents have stood the test of time—including volumes of documents relating to the foundations of Charterhouse (1854) and Christ's Hospital (1855), volumes for the Camden Society on the medieval properties of St Paul's and of Worcester Cathedral, and *A series of precedents and proceedings … extracted from the act-books of ecclesiastical courts in the diocese of London* (1847; repr. 1973). Here his antique sympathies found a consummation more satisfactory than any possible in Victorian church politics. JULIAN LOCK

**Sources** *DNB* • A. Quick, *Charterhouse: a history of the school* (1990), chap. 6 • G. L. Prestige, *St Paul's in its glory: a candid history of the cathedral, 1831–1911* (1955) • W. R. Matthews and W. M. Atkins, eds., *A history of St Paul's Cathedral and the men associated with it* (1957) • Boase, *Mod. Eng. biog.* • Allibone, *Dict.* • P. Barrett, *Barchester: English cathedral life in the nineteenth century* (1993) • G. I. T. Machin, *Politics and the churches in Great Britain, 1832 to 1868* (1977) • A. M. G. Stephenson, *The first Lambeth conference, 1867* (1967) • LPL, Tait MSS • *The Guardian* (30 Nov 1870) • *The Guardian* (7 Dec 1870) • *The Times* (28 Nov 1870), 10 • *The Record* (30 Nov 1870) • *ILN* (3 Dec 1870) • Foster, *Alum. Oxon.* • private information (2004) • A. Blomfield, *A memoir of Charles James Blomfield, with selections from his correspondence*, 2 (1863)
**Archives** Charterhouse, MSS • LPL, proofs of his *Church government in the colonies*, MS 1383 • St Paul's Cathedral, London | Birmingham Oratory, corresp. with J. H. Newman • BL, Bliss MSS, Add. MSS 34570, 34575, 34577, 34580 • BL, Gladstone MSS, Add. MSS 44360, 44363, 44372, 44391, 44415, 44421, 44527 • BL, Peel MSS, Add. MSS 40501, 40569 • Bodl. Oxf., letters to Benjamin Disraeli, Hughenden deposit 130/1 • LPL, corresp. with Charles Blomfield • LPL, letters to A. Burdett-Coutts, MSS 1377, 1381 • LPL, Lambeth Conference MSS • LPL, corresp. with A. C. Tait
**Likenesses** W. Walker, mezzotint, pubd 1850 (after T. A. Woolnoth), BM • photograph, repro. in *The Church of England photographic portrait gallery* (1859), no. 41
**Wealth at death** under £14,000: probate, 16 Feb 1871, *CGPLA Eng. & Wales*

**Hales, Alexander of** (*c*.1185–1245), Franciscan friar and theologian, was born at Hales (now Halesowen, Worcestershire), from which his name derived, but his academic career was pursued entirely at Paris. After incepting there and teaching as a master of arts in the first decade of the thirteenth century, he turned to theology and incepted as a regent master of theology about the year 1220. His teaching career was interrupted by the 'great dispersal' of the University of Paris lasting from 1229 to 1231, a protest at the savage repression of a student riot by the city authorities. The endorsements of some of the papal letters issued in connection with this event show that Alexander was one of a group of masters who attended the papal curia to plead the case of the scholars and helped to obtain for the university the famous privilege *Parens scientiarum*, granted by Pope Gregory IX (*r*. 1227–41) in 1231.

At some time during the suspension of the university Alexander came to England and obtained a number of benefices. In or about the year 1229 he became a canon of St Paul's, London, and prebendary of Holborn. In 1231 he was appointed a canon of Lichfield and archdeacon of Coventry. A charter from Combe Abbey, Warwickshire, shows that in 1232 he was still in England, attending the chapter of Lichfield, when as archdeacon he arbitrated in a tithe dispute between the abbots of Combe and Leicester. Soon after this he returned to Paris and resumed lecturing. He was still archdeacon of Coventry when, on 25 August 1235, he was commissioned by Henry III to receive the oaths of envoys swearing on the king's behalf to observe a truce between England and France. But at some time between this date and early 1236 he resigned his livings and took the habit of the Friars Minor at Paris. As a friar he continued to teach as a regent master, and thus became the first Franciscan to occupy a chair of theology in the university. Roger Bacon (*d*. 1294) observed that the conversion of such an eminent theologian, who was already an old man, greatly enhanced the standing of the friars at Paris. The impact of his arrival was soon felt throughout the order. Together with his former pupil Jean de La Rochelle and Haymo of Faversham (*d*. 1244) he mobilized opposition to the autocratic regime of Brother Elias, the minister-general, which led in 1239 to the deposition of Elias by Gregory IX. In 1241 Alexander was one of four masters commissioned by the general chapter of Montpellier to investigate and report on doubtful points in the rule of St Francis. He was called to attend the general council at Lyons in 1245, and while there he acted as one of a panel of four theologians deputed by Innocent

IV (*r.* 1243–54) to examine the dossier of evidence submitted by the promoters of the canonization of St Edmund of Abingdon (*d.* 1240). On returning to Paris, he succumbed to an epidemic and died on 21 August 1245.

According to Bacon, Alexander initiated the practice, which became normal in the schools, of using the *Sentences* of Peter Lombard as the authoritative textbook for comment for the purpose of the ordinary lectures in speculative theology. His gloss on the *Sentences* survives in a *reportatio* or authorized copy, as do other collections of *quaestiones* ascribed to him. The so-called *Summa theologica Alexandri*, edited by the Quaracchi fathers between 1924 and 1948, a large-scale work often quoted in the thirteenth century, was only partly his. As Bacon, no lover of Alexander's scholastic method, observed tartly and with some justification, 'it weighs more than a horse and was made by other people' (*Rogeri Bacon opera*, 1.326). In fact, although many of the *quaestiones* in the first three books have been identified as Alexander's, the treatise *De corpore humano* and much of the fourth book was the work of his pupils, Jean de La Rochelle and William of Milton, who succeeded him in the Paris chair.

In many ways the *Summa Alexandri* represents a milestone in Latin theology. It inaugurated a new trend by using, albeit in an eclectic and unsystematic fashion, the whole range of Aristotle's philosophical and scientific works, and the commentaries of Avicenna, in the service of theological speculation. In the organization of its material, which was suggested by the structure of Lombard's *Sentences*, it offered a synthesis of Christian doctrine that served as a model for the later *summae* of Aquinas and others. It also proved a seminal work in its treatment of a number of themes that became a distinctive mark of Franciscan theology, such as the hylomorphic composition of all created beings, the plurality of forms (Alexander attributed both form and 'intellectual matter' to the rational soul), the absolute predestination of Christ, and the role of divine illumination in the process of cognition—a concept derived from Augustine. C. H. LAWRENCE

**Sources** *Magistri Alexandri de Hales 'Glossa in quatuor libros sententiarum Petri Lombardi'*, ed. Fathers of the College of St Bonaventure, 4 vols. (1951–7) [incl. valuable account of Alexander's career, prolegomena, vol. 1] · *Fr. Rogeri Bacon opera quaedam hactenus inedita*, ed. J. S. Brewer, Rolls Series, 15 (1859) · [*Cronica fratris Salimbene de Adam ordinis Minorum*], ed. O. Holder-Egger, MGH Scriptores [folio], 32 (Hanover, 1905–13) · H. Denifle and A. Chatelain, eds., *Chartularium universitatis Parisiensis*, 1 (Paris, 1889) · *CPR*, 1232–47 · BL, Harleian Charter 83A.32 · H. E. Savage, ed., *The great register of Lichfield Cathedral known as Magnum registrum album*, William Salt Archaeological Society, 3rd ser. (1924, [1926]) · F. van Steenberghen, *Aristotle in the West: the origins of Latin Aristotelianism*, trans. L. Johnston, 2nd edn (1970) · *Doctoris irrefragibilis Alexandri de Hales Ordinis Minorum 'Summa theologica'*, ed. Fathers of the College of St Bonaventure, 4 vols. (1924–48) [incl. critical history of the work and its sources, prolegomena, vol. 4] · F. Stegmüller, ed., *Repertorium biblicum medii aevi*, 2 (Madrid, 1950), 67–70 [lists Alexander's Biblical commentaries] · V. Doucet, 'Autour des *Prolegomena ad summam Fratris Alexandri*', *Archivum Franciscanum Historicum*, 43 (1950), 196–200

**Hales, Sir Christopher** (*d.* 1541), judge, was the son of Thomas Hales, eldest son of Henry Hales of Hales Place in Halden, near Tenterden, Kent, and was a kinsman both of John *Hales, baron of the exchequer, and of his son Sir James *Hales, justice of the common pleas. All three attended Gray's Inn, where Christopher is recorded as an ancient in 1516 and became autumn reader in 1524. By the time of his readership he was an established practitioner whose regular clients included the corporation of Canterbury (by 1520), the duke of Buckingham (from 1521), and the Cinque Ports (from 1524). He acquired a home at Hackington, on the outskirts of Canterbury, and represented that city in the parliament of 1523. On 14 August 1525 he was appointed solicitor-general, and in the same year was mentioned as a member of Princess Mary's council in the marches. He was a commissioner to survey Calais and Guînes in 1525 and 1528–9, and became a justice of the peace for Kent in 1526.

Hales was promoted to attorney-general on 3 June 1529, and, being qualified by that office, went the home circuit as a justice of assize between then and 1536. By the mid-1530s he was steward of St Augustine's Abbey and St Gregory's Priory in Canterbury, of Cobham College, of Dover Priory, and of St Radegund's Abbey in Bradsole, Kent, of the bishop of Rochester's lands, and of the bishop of Winchester's manor of Southwark. He married Elizabeth, daughter of John Caunton of London, and sister of Thomas Cromwell's servant Nicholas Caunton. Hales's closeness to Cromwell suited him well as he carried out the heavy duties of a state prosecutor executing government policies during the turbulent years preceding the break with Rome. His first major task as attorney-general, in October 1529, was to prefer the indictment against Cardinal Wolsey for misusing his legatine authority. This was followed by fourteen further prosecutions in 1530–31 which led to the submission of the clergy in 1532. In 1533 Hales was actively engaged in investigating the case of the 'holy nun' Elizabeth Barton; in 1534 he assisted in the prosecution of Lord Dacre of the North for treason and preferred a bill of *praemunire* against Richard Nix, bishop of Norwich; and in 1535 he played a prominent part in the proceedings against Sir Thomas More, Bishop Fisher, and Queen Anne.

On 10 July 1536 Hales succeeded Cromwell as master of the rolls; he was knighted some time between then and 1538. He sat in chancery while Thomas Audley was chancellor, and a story was told of him that:

> He, resting at the side bar in Westminster after the Lord Audley, Lord Chancellor, had gone up to sit, and being sent to that it was not his place *sedente curia*, answered that he wist well enough where his place was. (BL, Lansdowne MS 163, fol. 98*v*)

As master of the rolls Hales also took part in the treason trials of 1538 and 1539. In 1540 he was one of the commissioners for remodelling the foundation of Canterbury Cathedral, ousting the monks and supplying their place with secular clergy. He profited largely from the dissolution of the monasteries, obtaining many grants of monastic land in Kent. Hales died in office on 20 April 1541. He left his house and lands in Hackington to his wife, and was buried there in the parish church of St Stephen.

Although he had been one of the Kentish lawyers whose lands were disgavelled by act of parliament in 1539 (31 Hen. VIII c. 3) he had but one son, John, who died in 1546 aged fourteen, whereupon Hales's three surviving daughters became his coheirs. J. H. Baker

**Sources** HoP, *Commons, 1509–58*, 2.274–5 • Sainty, *King's counsel*, 44, 60 • Sainty, *Judges*, 149 • F. Hull, ed., *A calendar of the white and black books of the Cinque Ports, 1432–1955*, Kent Archaeological Society Records Branch, 19 (1966) • C. Rawcliffe, *The Staffords, earls of Stafford and dukes of Buckingham, 1394–1521*, Cambridge Studies in Medieval Life and Thought, 3rd ser., 11 (1978), 162, 198, 228 • *The reports of Sir John Spelman*, ed. J. H. Baker, 1, SeldS, 93 (1977), 1.54 • *The notebook of Sir John Port*, ed. J. H. Baker, SeldS, 102 (1986), 58, 75 • G. R. Elton, *Policy and police* (1972), 295, 311, 404 • J. Weever, *Antient funeral monuments*, ed. W. Tooke (1767), 58 • precedent book, BL, Hargrave MS 279 • Lincoln's Inn, London, MS misc. 486(1), fol. 17

**Hales, Sir Edward, third baronet and Jacobite earl of Tenterden (1645–1695)**, courtier and Roman Catholic convert, was born on 28 September 1645, the eldest son (of four) of Sir Edward Hales, second baronet (1626–1683/4), of Tunstall Place, Kent, and his wife, Anne (*fl.* 1630–1656), youngest of the four daughters and coheirs of Thomas Wotton, second Baron Wotton. He came from an ancient Kentish family enriched by the law—Sir James Hales (*c.*1500–1554), driven to suicide for enforcing anti-Catholic statutes, was, ironically, a relation. His great-grandfather, Sir Edward Hales, first baronet (*d.* 1654), was a member of the Long Parliament fined £6000 for suspected royalism: his exactions from his royalist debtors to pay this helped create the Kentish resentment against the family which exploded in 1688. His father was the nominal first leader of the Kentish royalist rising of 1648, and was MP for Queenborough from 1661 to 1680.

Edward Hales travelled in France and Italy from 1657 to 1664, and matriculated at the University of Padua in 1664. It was presumably during this period that he became a secret Roman Catholic; after the revolution of 1688 he claimed that one of his tutors (Mr Godliman and Mr Anderton, both converts) secretly converted him when he was twelve (which would avert the penalties for adult apostacy). Obadiah Walker of University College, Oxford, popularly blamed for this, educated several of his relations but not Hales himself, although Hales did grant him a £30 annuity. However, for some years Hales took the oaths and test, being 'but young, and did not much consider the matter of Religion' (Morrice, vol. 2, fol. 631). He married (giving his address as Paulerspury, Northamptonshire, his mother's inheritance, transferred in 1668, sold by 1687) by licence of 12 July 1669, Frances (*c.*1645–1694), daughter and heir of Francis Windebank (who had been gentleman usher to Charles II when prince of Wales, and was the younger son of Sir Francis Windebank, secretary of state to Charles I), an Anglican. They had five sons and seven daughters. In 1675 he bought St Stephen's, a mansion at Hackington near Canterbury, later the family seat, and became a local JP.

In 1679 Hales was elected to the first Exclusion Parliament for Canterbury, and voted against the Exclusion Bill. Re-elected with difficulty, he was attacked in the 1680 session over a 'Popish sermon' (Henning) by his son's tutor, and did not stand again. He was a lord of the Admiralty from February 1679 to May 1684, with £1000 salary. In October 1681 he refused appointment as ambassador to Holland. His father retired in 1681 permanently to France, possibly converted independently to Catholicism, and died there between August 1683 and February 1684.

On 22 June 1685 Hales was commissioned by James II to raise an infantry regiment in Kent. On 11 November 1685 he formally converted to Catholicism. He was among the army officers whom James dispensed from taking the oaths of allegiance or the sacramental test. It was decided to make this a test case of the legality of the dispensing power. In a collusive action, Hales's coachman Arthur Godden sued him at Rochester assizes for the £500 penalty due under the Test Act, and he was convicted on 28 March 1686. He pleaded the dispensation, and the case was removed to the king's bench. After it had been argued there at length on both sides, the lord chief justice, Sir Edward Herbert, after consulting his colleagues, on 21 June 1686 delivered judgment in Hales's favour, declaring the dispensing power to be part of the royal prerogative. James had not waited for the result, and on 9 April 1686 had appointed Hales lieutenant-governor of Dover Castle and Admiralty judge in the Cinque Ports.

Hales's conversion exposed the breakdown of his marriage. He kept his apprehensive wife in a Paris convent for two years from 1686. Several, perhaps all, of his children, however, followed him in turning Catholic.

As so few experienced administrators had converted, James multiplied Hales's duties. From 13 June 1687 he was lieutenant of the Tower of London besides his Dover and army posts. He became a Kentish JP and deputy lieutenant and a Middlesex JP. He bought a fashionable house in Duke Street, Westminster. A private oratory was installed in the Tower for him, and in June 1688 a public Catholic chapel was expected to follow.

Hales had a convert's hatred and distrust of protestants. He had sufficient political sensitivity to disapprove of pointless affronts to them, such as the appointment of Father Edward Petre to the council, but his hostility towards protestantism unsuited him for keeping the peace. When his most famous prisoners at the Tower, the seven bishops, were released before their trial, they refused him his fees, claiming that their detention and his commission were both illegal. Hales then threatened them with harsh treatment on their next imprisonment. After James marched to fight William, Hales mounted mortars upon the Tower with which to bombard London if it rebelled. This obliged James to dismiss him in late November 1688. In Kent his unpopularity went far beyond the inevitable hostility to the military commander in a smuggling county. On 8 December 1688 some Dover inhabitants surprised the castle. The mob wrecked Hales's country mansion and killed his deer.

Hales was thus badly placed, despite his local knowledge, to act as organizer and companion to James II on the king's first flight on the night of 10–11 December 1688. After riding through Kent they boarded the customs hoy prepared for them at Elmley Island (Hales's property) next morning; but a delay to take on ballast enabled local fishermen, smugglers, and sailors to board it that night and carry them prisoners to Faversham on 12 December. Recognition of Hales increased the mob's fury, and James lost his (very slight) chance of escape by refusing to leave him. Hales was committed to Maidstone gaol on 17 December.

In January 1689 Hales and his brother Charles returned to the Tower as prisoners. In October he applied for a writ of habeas corpus; but on 26 October he and Walker were brought before the House of Commons charged with treason as converts. Hales's able defence protected Walker as well. Returned to the Tower, they were bailed on 31 January 1690 and discharged on 2 June, but both were excepted from the Act of Grace in May 1690. Hales's estate was valued at £3000 a year, probably an underestimate. That autumn he crossed to France, landing at Cherbourg on 1 October 1690, and proceeded to James's court at St Germain.

Hales's eldest son, Edward, had been killed fighting for James at the Boyne. Several of his children followed him to France. In 1692 his eldest, favourite daughter, despite his entreaties, became an Augustinian nun at Paris. He later repented having allowed a cleric to persuade him to place two of his other daughters in the harsh order of Poor Clares at Rouen.

Only in private life did Hales show such moderation in his religion. The historian Charles Dodd claimed that his diary, now missing, indicated that at St Germain 'he rather attended his old master as a friend than as a statesman' (Dodd, 3.451). If so, it was misleading. Though receiving no formal office, perhaps to avoid forfeiture, he joined the Catholic cabinet then managing policy, and his dominance over his lightweight colleagues and influence over James swung the court's attitudes towards absolutism and Catholic bigotry—it was the one period for which John Macky's propaganda claims of general hostility towards protestants there were largely true. Hales was interested in Irish affairs, where he dealt with both Richard Talbot, duke of Tyrconnell, and Tyrconnell's enemies. He considered John Drummond, first earl of Melfort, then exiled as ambassador in Rome, the only Jacobite statesman capable of enforcing the policies necessary for a restoration in England and Scotland, and worked for his return. The Williamite exposure in early 1691 of Lord Preston's plot, including the intention to use French pressure to make James follow a protestant policy, provided justification for Hales to have Preston's St Germain allies disgraced. He urged Melfort on his forthcoming return 'to cleanse ye Court of Prots (the likelyest to be Spyes)' (Browne MS, 67).

When Melfort, on returning in December 1691, dissolved the Catholic cabinet and almost monopolized power, Hales, unlike several colleagues, apparently felt not aggrieved but vindicated, as Melfort persuaded the French to launch a full-scale invasion of England. As James waited in Normandy for the French fleet's arrival, he created Hales on 3 May 1692 NS earl of Tenterden, Viscount Tunstall, and Baron Hales of Emley. While waiting to embark with the cavalry at Le Havre, and even after the defeat at La Hogue, Hales prepared for Melfort a detailed scheme for governing a reconquered England. To ensure security, a 30,000 strong Catholic army was to protect the regime. All the chief ministers, the cabinet, the lord lieutenants in the counties with greatly increased authority, and the revenue officials were to be Catholics. The powers of parliament, the law courts, and London and the other corporations were to be drastically reduced. These ideas, though requiring several times the existing number of English Catholics, certainly appealed to one strong side of Melfort's political views; though James's unfinished 'Advice to his son', which he was revising then, showed only a very limited influence.

The defeat at La Hogue drove the Jacobite court away from the idea of restoration by armed intervention alone, leaving Hales isolated. On 2 June 1693 NS James discussed with him and justified the new declaration he had issued making major concessions to protestants. Hales said little, secretly thinking it both sinful and disastrous. On 13 October 1694 NS, having dismissed Melfort, leaving all power with Charles Middleton, second earl of Middleton, the other secretary of state, James aired old grievances against Middleton to Hales, who suggested printing Jacobite absolutist propaganda contradicting Middleton's policies. Dodd's claim that Hales that year sought William's permission to return home arises from the mixing of his papers with those of Henry Browne, secretary of state for England in 1690–91, who did cross back in 1695. Hales died at Paris on 3 November 1695 NS and was buried there in the church of St Sulpice.

Hales's will, which left £500 (not £5000 as stated by the *Dictionary of National Biography*) for Catholic charities, shows that the family remained rich. His second son and successor, Sir John Hales (*d.* 1744), returned outwardly to protestantism. Edward Hasted reported in his *History of Kent* that George I offered Sir John Hales a peerage, but that Sir John insisted on his father's titles and their precedence. Behind this façade of conformity, however, the family remained deeply Catholic for two or three generations, and therefore took no part in politics. The baronetcy became extinct on the death of Sir Edward Hales, sixth baronet, in 1829. PAUL HOPKINS

**Sources** B. D. Henning, 'Hales, Edward II', HoP, *Commons, 1660–90* • M. W. Helms and B. D. Henning, 'Hales, Sir Edward', HoP, *Commons, 1660–90* • Westm. DA, Old Brotherhood papers, vol. 3 • Westm. DA, Browne MSS • *The life of James the Second, king of England*, ed. J. S. Clarke, 2 vols. (1816) • E. S. de Beer, 'The early life of Sir Edward Hales, titular earl of Tenterden', *N&Q*, 170 (1936), 164 • D. Szechi, 'A blueprint for tyranny? Sir Edward Hales and the Catholic Jacobite response to the revolution of 1688', *EngHR*, 116 (2001), 342–67 • *CSP dom., 1685–95* • C. Dodd [H. Tootell], *The church history of England, from the year 1500, to the year 1688*, 3 (1742) • E. Hasted, *The history and topographical survey of the county of Kent*, 2nd edn, 12 vols. (1797–1801); facs. edn (1972) • R. Morrice, 'Ent'ring books' 1–3, DWL, MS Morrice P–R • Turner correspondence, Bodl. Oxf., MS Rawl. letters 98 • *Remarks and collections of Thomas Hearne*, ed. C. E. Doble and others, 11 vols., OHS, 2, 7, 13, 34, 42–3, 48, 50, 65, 67, 72 (1885–1921), vols. 8–9 • will, PRO, PROB 11/500, fols. 345v–348 • Hales papers, Birm. CL, Baker MSS • N. Luttrell, *A brief historical relation of state affairs from September 1678 to April 1714*, 6 vols. (1857) • *Memoirs of the secret services of John Macky*, ed. A. R. (1733) • J. L. Chester and J. Foster, eds., *London marriage licences, 1521–1869* (1887) •

W. A. Shaw, ed., *Calendar of treasury books*, 8, PRO (1923) • P. A. Hopkins, 'Aspects of Jacobite conspiracy in England in the reign of William III', PhD diss., U. Cam., 1981 • GEC, *Baronetage* • R. Beddard, ed., *A kingdom without a king: the journal of the provisional government in the revolution of 1688* (1988) • J. Knatchbull, diary, BL, Add. MS 33923 • Sir David Nairne's journal, MS 14266, fol. 94*v* • J. Macpherson, ed., *Original papers, containing the secret history of Great Britain*, 2 vols. (1775), 1.128–9

**Archives** Canterbury Cathedral, archives, family papers | Birm. CL, Baker MSS • Westm. DA, Browne MSS • Westm. DA, Old Brotherhood MSS

**Likenesses** P. Lely, group portrait, oils, *c.*1656 (with his family), Guildhall, London

**Wealth at death** large estates in Kent, small ones in Yorkshire; gave elder marriageable daughters £3000 portions, younger daughters £2000, and three younger sons £100 annuities plus £1000–£2000 lump sums: will, PRO, PROB 11/500, fols. 345*v*–348

**Hales, Sir James** (*c.*1500–1554), judge, was the eldest son of John *Hales (1469/70–1540?), baron of the exchequer, and his wife, Isabel Harry. He was admitted to Gray's Inn, where his father was a bencher, between 1517 and 1519 and was elected an ancient in 1528. He is mentioned as counsel in the court of requests in 1530 and in the duchy chamber in 1531. In 1532 he became a bencher of his inn and gave his first reading on the recent Statute of Costs (23 Hen. VIII c. 15), which includes the first known lectures on actions on the case. In 1540 he was granted the coif, and gave a third reading, as serjeant-elect, on the Statute of Westminster II c. 45. The following year he became standing counsel to the corporation of Canterbury, and he was also an adviser to Thomas Cranmer. On 4 November 1544 he was appointed one of the king's serjeants, a position which was renewed by Edward VI, who made him a knight of the Bath at the coronation in 1547. On 20 May 1549 he received a patent as one of the justices of the common pleas, an office which he held until his death.

In 1553 Hales incurred the wrath of the duke of Northumberland by refusing to seal the instrument purporting to settle the crown on Lady Jane Grey, stoutly offering 'his head in his hand sooner than be forced to subscribe' (MacCulloch, 200). On the accession of Mary he showed an equally independent spirit in his charge to the grand jury at the Kent assizes by directing that the statutes of Henry VIII and Edward VI against nonconformists remained in force and should not be relaxed in favour of Roman Catholics. Although he was granted a new patent on 4 October 1553, when he went to Westminster Hall two days later to be sworn, Bishop Gardiner, the lord chancellor, refused to administer the oath on the ground that Hales stood not well in her grace's favour by reason of his conduct at the assizes. He was shortly afterwards committed to the king's bench prison, whence he was removed to the Bread Street compter and afterwards to the Fleet, where it was hoped he would recant. In prison he was visited by Dr Day, bishop of Chichester, Sir William Portman, justice of the queen's bench, and others, whose attempts to unsettle his religious beliefs so affected his mind that he attempted to commit suicide by opening his veins with a penknife. This intention was frustrated. He recovered and was released by the queen's command in April 1554, but his mind was still disturbed and he drowned himself by lying face downwards in a shallow stream at Thanington, near Canterbury, on 4 August following. This death was held by the coroner to be a felonious suicide.

Sir James left a widow, Margaret, two sons, Humphrey and Edward (both members of Gray's Inn), and a daughter, Mildred. In 1558 Lady Hales began proceedings against Cyriac Petit to recover an indenture of lease of Graveney Marsh which had been made in 1551 to her husband and herself and limited to commence in 1560 after the determination of a prior lease to her husband alone. She recovered the deed, and in 1561 brought a second action to recover the land itself, on the footing that the lease had now commenced in her by survivorship. The case turned chiefly on the conundrum whether the act of felony, which caused the forfeiture of the first lease, occurred during Sir James's lifetime or after his death, and gave rise to a discussion of the possibility of dividing an instant of time into two parts for legal purposes: 'for every instant is the end of one time and the beginning of another' (*Les commentaries*, 258*v*). Lady Hales was unsuccessful in this suit, it being held by the common pleas in 1562 that the king's title, under which Petit claimed, had priority. The case of *Hales* v. *Petit* became widely known, as a result of Plowden's full report published in 1571, and is often held up as an extreme example of abstract legal reasoning. It is thought to be alluded to by Shakespeare in the gravedigger's speech in *Hamlet*. J. H. Baker

**Sources** Foss, *Judges*, 5.370–74 • *The acts and monuments of John Foxe*, new edn, ed. G. Townsend, 6 (1846), 394–5, 710–16 • D. MacCulloch, 'The *Vita Mariae Angliae Reginae* of Robert Wingfield of Brantham', *Camden miscellany, XXVIII*, CS, 4th ser., 29 (1984), 181–301, esp. 198, 200, 242–3, 246, 248, 292 • BL, Hargrave MS 92, fols. 21–40 • BL, Hargrave MS 253, fols. 62–68*v* • Baker, *Serjeants*, 168, 515 • inquisition post mortem, PRO, C142/102/84 • PRO, REQ 1/5, fol. 89*v* • PRO, DL, DL 5/5, fol. 489*v* • *Les commentaries, ou, Les reportes de Edmunde Plowden* (1571), fols. 253–64 • *Reports from the lost notebooks of Sir James Dyer*, ed. J. H. Baker, 1, SeldS, 109 (1994), 46–8, 72–6 • Sainty, *Judges*, 62 • J. H. Baker and S. F. C. Milsom, eds., *Sources of English legal history: private law to 1750* (1986), 345–51 • E. Hasted, *The history and topographical survey of the county of Kent*, 2–3 (1782–90)

**Hales, John** (1469/70–1540?), judge, was the son of John Hales of Tenterden, Kent, and cousin to Sir Christopher *Hales (*d.* 1541), master of the rolls. He was probably admitted to Gray's Inn about 1490, and was described as a member of the inn when he appeared as counsel in the requests in 1506. Already by 1501 he was steward of the liberties of the priory of Christ Church, Canterbury, and in 1509 he had a residence in that city and another at Nackington. At an unknown date he married Isabel Harry, who predeceased him; they had four sons and a daughter. In 1503 Hales became a justice of the peace for Kent, and the next year he was retained as counsel to Rye corporation. He was elected to represent Canterbury in the parliament of 1512, and he was re-elected in 1515, becoming also standing counsel to the corporation. During his time in parliament, in the autumn of 1514, he became a bencher of Gray's Inn and delivered a reading on chapter 39 of the Statute of Westminster II, concerning the return of writs by sheriffs. A surviving text shows that it was attended by

Chief Justice Fyneux and Sir Thomas Nevill. The subject of his second reading, in 1520, is not recorded.

Hales had by this time caught the attention of those in power, and there is some evidence that his principal patron was Sir Henry Guildford, comptroller of the household. In 1519 he obtained the important and lucrative position of attorney-general to the duchy of Lancaster, though he enjoyed it for only three years until his appointment as third baron of the exchequer on 1 October 1522. This judicial office he held concurrently with that of general surveyor of crown lands, to which he had been appointed the previous year. During his time as a judge he was regularly employed as a member of the king's council responsible for legal matters, and conducted criminal investigations on its behalf. He was promoted to second baron in 1528 but was passed over for chief baron in 1529, when Lyster was appointed. In a deposition of 1 February 1535 Hales's age was given as sixty-five; he retired in Michaelmas term 1539 and probably died the following year. His will is dated 20 July 1540 but the date of probate is missing. At that time he was living at the Dongeon in the suburbs of Canterbury, and he requested burial next to his wife in the church of St Mary Bredin. Hales's eldest son, Sir James *Hales (*c.*1500–1554), became a justice of the common pleas and committed suicide in 1554. The grandson of their third son, Edward, was created a baronet in 1829. Two other baronetcies were conferred on other descendants, but all are extinct. J. H. Baker

**Sources** HoP, *Commons, 1509–58*, 2.275–6 • PRO, REQ 1/3, fol. 252 • Gray's Inn, MS 25, fols. 290–300v • BL, Add. MS 42077, fols. 27, 50 • R. Somerville, *History of the duchy of Lancaster, 1265–1603* (1953), 407, 455 • *The reports of Sir John Spelman*, ed. J. H. Baker, 2, SeldS, 94 (1978), 2.383–4 • PRO, C 24/1 • Foss, *Judges*, 5.184–6

**Hales, John** (1516?–1572), administrator and member of parliament, was the son of Thomas Hales of Halden, Kent, and brother of Christopher, Bartholomew, and Stephen Hales. Brought up in the household of his uncle, Sir Christopher *Hales, attorney-general and master of the rolls, he may have spent some time at Oxford, but was largely a self-taught scholar of Greek, Latin, Hebrew, and the law. By 1535 Hales had come into Thomas Cromwell's service, where he served in the king's bench as keeper of the writs and clerk of the new court of first fruits and tenths (both 1537–40). After the dissolution of the monasteries Hales acquired confiscated ecclesiastical property in Bishopsgate, London (1541), and extensive lands in and around Coventry. He established a free school in St John's Hospital, Coventry, possibly at the request of Henry VIII, after whom it was named. Rather than endow the school, as was the original intention, Hales merely provided an annual stipend until his death, thereby displeasing numerous local officials.

Hales served as clerk of the hanaper (1545–57 and 1559–72) with his friend Sir Ralph Sadler. In 1547, with the accession of Edward VI, Hales became a justice of the peace for Middlesex and Warwickshire, and an MP for Preston, Lancashire. While in parliament he became an outspoken champion of social, economic, and religious reform. He submitted three bills that dealt with regrating, husbandry, and sheep raising, none of which became law. In June 1548 Hales was appointed by Protector Somerset to a six-member commission to investigate enclosure practices in the midland counties. When rioting in support of the commission broke out in Buckinghamshire, Hales was blamed by the earl of Warwick for inciting rebellion. Hales wrote a famous defence of his behaviour where he put the blame squarely on the injustices of the local landlords. With the fall of Somerset in October 1549, Hales was sent to the Tower of London. In 1550 he was freed and both sold and enfeoffed his various properties to his brother Stephen and to Sadler.

On 2 February 1551 Hales obtained a licence to leave England with his friend Sir Richard Morison, the new ambassador to Emperor Charles V. Hales remained first in Brussels with Morison before going to Germany with his brother Christopher. When Mary I ascended the throne in 1553 she sent an agent to Hales, now at the exile community in Frankfurt, to deny him his clerkship of the hanaper; but Hales refused to recognize his jurisdiction, and would not return to England. An assessment of October 1556 indicated that Hales had taken 5000 florins' worth of taxable property with him into exile. His remaining real property in England was confiscated in his absence in 1557. During the 'troubles in Frankfurt', Hales was known for being a peacemaker. He had returned to England by 3 January 1559, just after the accession of Elizabeth I. At that time he presented her with a congratulatory oration. He quickly resumed his duties at the hanaper and sat for Lancaster in parliament (1563–7). The lands he had quitclaimed in 1551 were now returned to him.

Hales soon found himself in trouble, however, when he wrote a book in 1564 in favour of the Grey (Suffolk) title to the crown. Thereby he endorsed the marriage of Lady Katherine Grey and Edward Seymour, earl of Hertford and the late protector's son, whose marriage had been declared illegal; both of them were then in prison. Hales went to the Tower in 1565 for this, but with the help of William Cecil obtained release the following year, although for the next four years he was not to leave his home without a royal licence. He had petitioned for his release from the Tower in order to defend himself against the claims of Francis Kempe, to whom Mary had given the hanaper clerkship during Hales's exile. Sadler turned against Hales in 1571, in an attempt to replace him in the hanaper with his son, Henry Sadler. In spite of these manoeuvres, Hales remained in the office until he died on 28 December 1572. He was buried in the church of St Peter-le-Poer, Broad Street, London. Unmarried, he left most of his estates in Warwickshire, including Hales Place, to his nephew John, son of his brother Christopher.

Hales was sometimes called Club-foot Hales, supposedly because of a walking impairment he received from an accidental, self-inflicted dagger wound to the foot. Until recently most scholars believed him to be the author of the erudite *Discourse of the Commonweal of this Realm of England* (1549), attributed now largely to Sir Thomas Smith. In addition to the writings listed above, Hales wrote a grammar-school text for his free school (*Introductiones ad grammaticum*) and 'Highway to nobility', and published a translation of Plutarch, *Precepts for the Preservation of Health* (1543). BEN LOWE

**Sources** HoP, *Commons, 1509–58* • will, PRO, PROB 11/55, sig. 8 • C. H. Garrett, *The Marian exiles: a study in the origins of Elizabethan puritanism* (1938) • E. Lamond, ed., *A discourse of the commonweal of this realm of England* (1893) • *DNB* • A. J. Slavin, 'Sir Ralph Sadler and Master John Hales at the hanaper: a 16th century struggle for property and profit', *BIHR*, 38 (1965), 31–47 • Wood, *Ath. Oxon.*, new edn, 1.404 • F. L. Colvile, *The worthies of Warwickshire who lived between 1500 and 1800* [1870] • J. Hales, 'An oration of John Hales to the Queen's Majesty and delivered to her by a certain nobleman at her first entrance into her reign', in S. Johnson, *Second five year's struggle against popery and tyranny* (1689), 68–85 • R. Tittler, *Nicholas Bacon: the making of a Tudor statesman* (1976) • M. L. Bush, *The government policy of Protector Somerset* (1975)

**Archives** BL, Lansdowne MS 238

**Likenesses** D. Turner, etching, BM

**Wealth at death** extensive properties in London and Warwickshire: will, PRO, PROB 11/55, sig. 8

**Hales, John** (1584–1656), scholar, was born on 19 April 1584 in Bath, the fourth of the twelve children of John Hales (*bap.* 1549, *d.* 1622), attorney and steward to the Horner family at Mells, of Highchurch in the parish of Hemington, Somerset, and his wife, Bridget (*d.* 1628), daughter of Robert Goldsborough of East Knoyle, Wiltshire, and Cicely Biggs. He was admitted scholar at Corpus Christi College, Oxford, on 16 April 1597, his uncle Augustine Goldsborough having been scholar and fellow of that college. After graduating BA on 9 July 1603, he was recruited by Sir Thomas Bodley, as one 'that writeth faire and finely', to maintain the donations register of gifts to Bodley's new library, opened in 1602, entries which Hales began shortly before the visit of James I to the library in August 1605, and continued until 1609 (*Letters of Sir Thomas Bodley*, 134). In that year he proceeded MA, having already entered holy orders. Meanwhile his reputation as a Greek scholar had gained him a fellowship at Merton College (2 September 1605) under the warden, Sir Henry Savile, Greek scholar, academic politician, and also provost of Eton College. Hales was appointed to the Merton Greek lectureship once held by Bodley, and became closely involved in work towards Savile's edition of the Greek text of St Chrysostom, eventually printed in eight volumes on Savile's own press at Eton (1610–12), one of the great scholarly enterprises of the time, along with the preparation of the Authorized Version of the Bible (1611), work on the Greek text of which was undertaken by Savile and others in the warden's lodgings at Merton.

On 29 March 1613, in Merton College chapel, Hales delivered the Latin funeral oration on Bodley, an appropriately florid but perspicuous tribute to his old patron, in which he recalled his own excitement in 1598, as a youth ('puer') at Corpus Christi, on hearing the news of Bodley's offer to the vice-chancellor to bring back the library to its former use, at his own charge. Hales was admitted fellow of Eton College on 24 May 1613, resigning his Merton fellowship but from 1615 to 1619 holding the regius professorship of Greek in the university. As chaplain to Sir Dudley Carleton, ambassador at The Hague, he reported the proceedings of the Synod of Dort in letters to Carleton from November 1618 to February 1619, later published in Hales's posthumous *Golden Remains* (1659). Of his experience at the synod he was later said to have recalled that 'there, I bid John Calvin good-night' (*Golden Remains*, sig. A4*v*).

By 1619 Hales had withdrawn from all his Oxford pursuits to become what he remained until his death, 'Mr. Hales of Eton'. He combined the office of bursar with his fellowship, both under Savile as provost and under Sir Henry Wotton, provost from 1624 to 1639, with whom his relations were amicable. At some time in the 1630s he became known to Lucius Cary, Lord Falkland, and his circle of friends, notably Edward Hyde, later earl of Clarendon, William Chillingworth, and John Earle. The slight and infrequent but precise references to Hales's presence among men of letters in London in the 1630s give credence to Dryden's anecdote, in his *Essay of Dramatic Poesy* (1668), of Hales defending Shakespeare against all rivals. Neither Bodley nor Savile had much time for 'wits', but their protégé Hales was at home with the moderns as well as with the ancients, and was described by the poet Henry King as 'the best Critick of our later time' (Walton, 15), though nothing of that kind survives from his pen. A hint of what may have been the style of his 'very open and pleasant conversation' (Clarendon, 1.59) is to be found in his epistolary essay 'The method of reading profane history', where in a remarkable passage—a very early and enthusiastic response by an Englishman to his discovery of Dutch genre painting—he recommends this art of 'things of ordinary course' as a model for the writing of history, instead of 'great matters of more note, but less use' (*Golden Remains*, 276; Hales, 1.173–4).

Nothing troubled Hales more, wrote Clarendon, 'than the brawls which were grown from religion … and he thought that pride, and passion, more than conscience, were the cause of all separation from each other's communion' (Clarendon, 1.60). Such was also the position from which Falkland and his friends, notably Chillingworth, opposed claims to infallibility, whether by Rome or Geneva, and urged that all things necessary were contained in a few 'plain places' of scripture, on which all who called themselves Christian could unite. Hales had come to such a view some years before, as is clear from his first published sermon, *Abuses of Hard Places of Scripture* (1617). Inevitably Hales and his like were called Socinians, either loosely or in bitter polemic; indeed, while explicitly denying the Socinian rejection of the doctrine of the Trinity, Hales shared many of the views of Socinian writers, especially in appealing as he did to 'the faculty of reason which is in every one of you, even the meanest that hears me this day' (Hales, 3.156) and perhaps, above all, to the need for toleration. In a larger perspective he can be seen as in the line of Erasmus, of Richard Hooker, and of his contemporary Hugo Grotius, an exile from the Low Countries after the Synod of Dort, whose portrait Hales kept in his study. Hales's appeal to younger men, and which made him 'ever memorable', was derived partly from his belonging to a heroic age of scholarship, associated with Hooker (of Corpus Christi), Bodley, and Savile, partly from the range and ease of his reference from ancients to moderns, and perhaps, too, from his refusal of the role of ecclesiastic though a priest—his being simply 'Mr. Hales', though, as Clarendon put it with pardonable exaggeration, 'one of the greatest scholars in Europe'.

Hales's reputation for learning was not matched by weight of publication. His reticence as a writer was attributed by Clarendon to his being 'very reserved in communicating what he thought himself in those points, in which he differed from what was received' (Clarendon, 1.60), a position more easily maintained in the relative seclusion of Eton than in the confrontational arena of the university. His best-known work, the *Tract Concerning Schisme and Schismaticks*, written about 1636, circulated widely in manuscript, and was printed without his knowledge in 1642. When his works were finally collected, in three small volumes in 1765, they amounted to the oration on Bodley, thirty-three letters to Carleton about the Synod of Dort, eighteen sermons, and some twenty short tracts or epistolary responses to questions put to him by enquirers. The *Tract Concerning Schisme*, unguarded and sceptical in tone in its examination of the church's responsibility for the growth of schism, could not have been relished by Archbishop Laud, who summoned Hales to account for it. At some point Hales wrote to Laud, frankly and eloquently defending his 'pursuit of truth' (Hales, 1.135–44). Their encounter ended amicably, and shortly afterwards, in June 1639, Hales received from Laud his first church preferment, a canonry of Windsor, only to lose it in 1642 on the outbreak of the civil war.

In 1650 Hales was expelled from his Eton fellowship; he had failed to subscribe to the engagement required by the republican government. By 1653 he was living in the household of Lady Salter of Richings Lodge, near Iver, Buckinghamshire, where the poet Andrew Marvell made his acquaintance. Almost twenty years later, quoting at length from Hales's *Tract Concerning Schisme*, Marvell described him as 'one of the clearest heads and best prepared brests in Christendom' (*The Rehearsal Transpros'd*, 1971 edn, 79). Hales sold his valuable library for, it was said, £700—less than it had been worth—from which he was able to assist other clergy in need. In November 1655 he felt compelled to retreat to the house of the widow of a former college servant, Mrs Hannah Dickenson, in Eton town. Here John Aubrey met him, 'sanguine, of a cheerful countenance', wearing not clerical black but a violet-coloured gown, and reading Thomas à Kempis. 'He loved Canarie; but moderately, to refresh his spirits' (*Brief Lives*, 1.279–80). Others, including Izaak Walton, remembered his habit of fasting from Thursday to Saturday.

In his will, dated the day of his death, 19 May 1656, Hales made bequests amounting to £43, with the small residue left to Hannah Dickenson, his executor. He was buried in Eton churchyard on 20 May 1656. His inalienable title, 'the ever memorable', first appeared on the title-page of *Golden Remains*, where in the prefatory matter by John Pearson and Anthony Farindon the recovery of knowledge of Hales began, pursued especially by Walton, Aubrey, and William Fulman, the scattered accounts eventually reaching Anthony Wood in his *Athenae Oxonienses* (1691), and John Walker in his *Sufferings of the Clergy* (1714). Clarendon's character of Hales did not appear in print until 1759. BASIL GREENSLADE

**Sources** J. Hales, *Works*, ed. D. Dalrymple, Lord Hailes, 3 vols. (1765) • J. H. Elson, *John Hales of Eton* (1948) • J. Butt, 'Izaak Walton's collections for Fulman's life of John Hales', *Modern Language Review*, 29 (1934), 267–73 • J. Bevan, 'Izaak Walton's collections for Fulman's life of John Hales: the Walker part', *Bodleian Library Record*, 13 (1988–91), 160–71 • *The life of Edward, earl of Clarendon … written by himself*, new edn, 3 vols. (1827), 1.58–62 • *Brief lives, chiefly of contemporaries, set down by John Aubrey, between the years 1669 and 1696*, ed. A. Clark, 1 (1898), 278–81 • Wood, *Ath. Oxon.*, new edn, 3.409–16 • I. Walton, *The lives of John Donne, Sir Henry Wotton, Richard Hooker, George Herbert, and Robert Sanderson*, [new edn] (1927) • *Letters of Sir Thomas Bodley to Thomas James, first keeper of the Bodleian Library*, ed. G. W. Wheeler (1926) • H. J. McLachlan, *Socinianism in seventeenth-century England* (1951) • H. Trevor-Roper, *Catholics, Anglicans and puritans: seventeenth-century essays* (1987) • J. Suckling, *The works of Sir J. S., containing all his poems, love-verses, songs, letters, and his tragedies and his comedies* (1709) • *The life and letters of Sir Henry Wotton*, ed. L. P. Smith, 2 vols. (1907) • CCC Oxf., MS 306, fols. 71–127 • parish register, St Mary, Hemington, Som. ARS • parish register, East Knoyle, Wilts. & Swindon RO • parish register, Eton, Bucks. RLSS, 20 May 1656 [burial]

**Archives** Bucks. RLSS, parish register, Eton • CCC Oxf., MS 306, fols. 71–127 • Eton, register, 60/3/4, vol. 3, fols. 28, 69–70 • Eton, account books • Som. ARS, parish registers of Bath (St James) and Hemington • Wilts. & Swindon RO, parish register, East Knoyle

**Likenesses** engraving, NPG • line engraving, BM, NPG; repro. in J. Hales, *Tracts* (1716)

**Wealth at death** approx. £50; bequests of £43: will, Hales, *Works*, vol. 1, pp. 203–6; CCC Oxf., MS 306, fol. 86; Eton, register, 60/3/4, vol. 3, fols. 69*v*–70*r*

**Hales, Sir Robert** (*d.* 1381), administrator and prior of the hospital of St John of Jerusalem in England, may have come from a Lincolnshire or Norfolk family. He probably began his career at Rhodes, where he had become preceptor of Sanford and Slebech before August 1358, when he was allowed to leave the convent. Having returned to England, he acted as attorney for the prior of England, John Paveley, in July 1362, but in October 1365 was one of the 100 knights of St John who took part in the crusade of Pierre I of Cyprus which captured Alexandria. By February 1366 he was an associate of the master, Raimond Bérenger, and perhaps also preceptor of Upleden, while in April 1367, Pope Urban V granted him full absolution in the case of his death. He was back in England no later than November 1370, and when Paveley died in 1371, he was nominated as his successor. As prior of England, Hales was summoned to parliament in 1372 and 1373, and between 1375 and 1380, while in June 1373 he was called to the king's service against the French, though the expedition did not materialize.

In June 1374 a serious dispute arose when the master, Robert Juilly, appointed the Scot Robert Mercer to be administrator of the Scottish properties of the order. The appointment was confirmed by Pope Gregory XI in January 1375, but by then Hales, who claimed authority over the Scottish preceptory, had caused Edward III to put a stop on the order's moneys from England that were destined to finance the return of the master to Rhodes and an expedition against the Turks. Although in February 1375 Gregory warned that anyone claiming to have rights in Scotland would be forced to bow to justice, pope and master soon gave in. On 15 October 1375 Juilly and the convent of Rhodes revoked the grant of the Scottish preceptory to Robert Mercer, and reserved the provision of this preceptory to the English prior, while the pope nominated a foreign administrator to take over the Scottish properties of the order for the time being. In December Gregory asked King Edward to lift the arrest on the order's moneys and to allow the English contingent of an expedition planned for 1377, consisting of thirty-eight brethren and thirty-eight serjeants, to leave the country. However, only a few went, and Hales, who also stayed in England, was made admiral of the fleet from the Thames to the west in November 1376, and again in August 1377. In November 1377 Hales went to sea with a fleet led by Thomas of Woodstock, earl of Buckingham, and others. Having endured storms and many other difficulties, they returned without success.

Nevertheless, Hales became increasingly important in English politics. In November 1378 he was appointed to the third of the continual councils which administered the country in the name of the young Richard II; the fact that he was subsequently paid for 238 days' attendance shows that he was among its more active members. In September 1380 he was a member of a commission, headed by John of Gaunt, duke of Lancaster, to deal with breaches of the truce with Scotland. Presumably it was such services that lay behind his appointment, on 1 February 1381, to be treasurer of England. The fact that he himself then lent the government 1000 marks did nothing to relieve Hales of the stigma of association with the third poll tax in four years, even though it had been granted in the previous November, before he took up office. The collection of this extremely unpopular tax led directly to the peasants' revolt, of which Hales was to be one of the principal victims. On 10 June 1381 Temple Cressing and other hospitaller properties in Essex were burnt down, while on 13 June the priory in Clerkenwell was sacked and destroyed, as was its manor at Highbury, which Hales himself had restored and beautified. Like the king and the chancellor, the aged Archbishop Sudbury, Hales fled for safety to the Tower of London. But when Richard went out to meet the peasants at Mile End on 14 June (on his way there he received a complaint against Hales from a London goldsmith, Hugh Farringdon), a company of the rebels was able to enter the Tower. They found Sudbury and Hales in the chapel of St John in the White Tower, dragged them out, and beheaded them on Tower Hill. The fate of Hales's body is unknown. The leaders of the peasants' revolt were killed or executed, but many others were pardoned, and it is not known who was responsible for the death of Hales. In spite of his violent end, in historiography and political poetry he was acclaimed as a most energetic and doughty knight.

JÜRGEN SARNOWSKY

**Sources** National Library of Malta, Valletta, Arch. 48, fols. 34*v*–35*r*, 52*v* • National Library of Malta, Valletta, Arch. 316, fol. 202*r* • National Library of Malta, Valletta, Arch. 319, fols. 171*r*–172*r*, 316*r* • National Library of Malta, Valletta, Arch. 320, fols. 2*v*–3*r*, 32*r*, 41*v*–42*r* • National Library of Malta, Valletta, Arch. 321, fol. 136*r* • National Library of Malta, Valletta, Arch. 322, fol. 110*r* • private information (2004) [Dr Anthony Luttrell, Bath] • *Chancery records* • Rymer, *Foedera*, 3rd edn, 3/3.24–5, 52, 68 • *CEPR letters*, 4.3–4, 110, 135, 140–42, 205 • M. Hayez, ed., *Urbain V (1362–1370): lettres communes analysées d'après les registres dits d'Avignon et du Vatican*, 6 (1980), no. 18493, p. 8 • G. Mollat, ed., *Lettres secrètes et curiales du pape Grégoire XI, 1370–1378*, 2 (Paris, 1963), nos. 3514–22, 3634, 3655, pp. 153–4, 169, 172 • *Thomae Walsingham, quondam monachi S. Albani, historia Anglicana*, ed. H. T. Riley, 2 vols., pt 1 of *Chronica monasterii S. Albani*, Rolls Series, 28 (1863–4), vol. 1, pp. 450, 456–8, 460–62 • G. B. Stow, ed., *Historia vitae et regni Ricardi Secundi* (1977), 49, 63–4 • I. B. Cowan, P. H. R. Mackay, and A. Macquarrie, eds., *The knights of St John in Scotland* (1983) • *Polychronicon Ranulphi Higden monachi Cestrensis*, ed. C. Babington and J. R. Lumby, 9 vols., Rolls Series, 41 (1865–86), vol. 8, pp. 395, 402 (appx) • R. B. Dobson, ed., *The peasants' revolt of 1381*, 2nd edn (1983) • A. Luttrell, 'The hospitallers at Rhodes, 1306–1421', *A history of the crusades*, ed. K. M. Setton and H. W. Hazzard, 3 (1975), 278–313; repr. A. Luttrell, *The hospitallers in Cyprus, Rhodes, Greece, and the West, 1291–1400* (1978) [no. I] • J. Delaville Le Roulx, *Les Hospitaliers à Rhodes, 1310–1421* (Paris, 1913); repr. (1974) • H. Eiden, *'In der Knechtschaft werdet ihr verharren …': Ursachen und Verlauf des englischen Bauernaufstandes von 1381* (Trier, 1995) • E. King, *The knights of St John in the British realm*, 3rd edn (1967) • W. K. R. Bedford and R. Holbeche, *The order of the hospital of St John of Jerusalem being a history of the English hospitallers of St John, their rise and progress* (1902) • Tout, *Admin. hist.*, vol. 3 • N. Saul, *Richard II* (1997) • *Knighton's chronicle, 1337–1396*, ed. and trans. G. H. Martin, OMT (1995) [Lat. orig., *Chronica de eventibus Angliae a tempore regis Edgari usque mortem regis Ricardi Secundi*, with parallel Eng. text]

**Hales, Stephen** (1677–1761), natural philosopher, was born on 17 September 1677 at Beakesbourne in Kent, the tenth child and sixth son of Thomas Hales (1641–1692) and grandson of Sir Robert Hales, first baronet, a descendant of Sir John Hales, baron of the exchequer under Henry VIII. His mother, Mary (1648–1687), was the daughter of Richard Wood of Abbots Langley, Hertfordshire. Following the death of his mother in 1687, father in 1692, and grandfather in 1693, at the age of fifteen Hales became the responsibility of his elder brothers Sir Thomas Hales, second baronet, and Robert Hales, future clerk to the privy council. Having first been taught by a Mr St Clare in Kensington (*c*.1689–93) and then by the Revd Richard Johnson at Orpington (*c*.1693), Hales was placed as pupil to the Revd Mark Hildesley, newly inducted vicar of Murston, a parish to the north of Beakesbourne (1694). Hildesley, as his son the bishop records, soon discovered his 'too improveable genius especially in the philosophical way to be confined to a country parson's institutions', and he was sent to Cambridge (Mann, 713).

**Introduction to science** Hales enrolled at Corpus Christi College, Cambridge, in the Easter term of 1696, and commenced residence in the following Michaelmas term. The college had been attended both by his grandfather and by the family chaplain, Thomas Ventris. Hales evidently found it congenial since he remained in residence for

**Stephen Hales** (1677–1761), studio of Thomas Hudson?, *c.*1759

twelve years. He received his BA degree in the Lent term of 1700, was pre-elected a fellow of Corpus in April 1702, became a fellow in February 1703, and qualified as an MA in the following Easter term. The years of Hales's fellowship, as distinct from his time as an undergraduate, saw considerable scientific activity in the university and college; Hales together with his young friend William Stukeley participated in this. Hales designed a machine, which Stukeley drew, to represent the motion of the planets according to Newton's system. The two perambulated Cambridgeshire in search of Ray's plants; conducted chemical experiments, dissections, and electrical demonstrations; and studied optics, astronomy, and the use of telescopes and microscopes. By the time Hales left Cambridge to begin his career as a parish priest in 1709, his enduring interest in scientific matters was firmly established.

**Ecclesiastical career** A family connection secured Hales's presentation to the perpetual curacy of Teddington in Middlesex, a ministry that he held until his death. He was much involved in local affairs, such as the rebuilding of the parish church and the provision of an adequate water supply for the village. He vacated his fellowship of Corpus in 1718 when he accepted the living of Porlock in Somerset, which he exchanged for that of Farringdon, Hampshire, in 1723. He found time to pay at least one visit to Porlock, and Farringdon became his summer home for many years. On 26 March 1720 he married Mary Newce, daughter of a wealthy Sussex clergyman. She died childless in 1721 and was buried at Teddington. Hales's niece Sarah Margaretta, daughter of Robert Hales, later kept house for him at Teddington and inherited the dwelling and garden, which he purchased in 1739. Hales provided his parishioners with bibles, prayer books, catechisms, and copies of the *Whole Duty of Man*. He imposed public penance at both Teddington and Farringdon for moral lapses. His sermons appear to have been popular, and two were published.

Hales was created a doctor of divinity by Oxford University in 1733, and the peak of his ecclesiastical career was reached with his appointment as chaplain to the princess dowager of Wales in 1751. He is supposed to have declined a canonry at Windsor when this additional honour was offered to him by George II. He was elected proctor by the diocese of Winchester for the convocation of 1754.

**Physiology and other experiments** Hales was elected a fellow of the Royal Society in 1718. His experiments, which he had carried on since his Cambridge years, first came to public notice in the following year, when he read a paper to the society on the effect of the sun's rays on the sap of plants. His book on the same subject, the *Vegetable Staticks* (by 'staticks' he meant functional equilibrium, the measured balance of input and output), was published in 1727, and the results of similar investigations into the arterial systems of animals appeared in 1733 under the title *Haemastaticks*. By this date Hales's interests had become increasingly centred on the practical consequences of scientific research. He undertook experiments on food preservation and ventilation, and published *Philosophical Experiments* (1739), *A Description of Ventilators* (1743), and *A Treatise on Ventilators* (1758), besides numerous shorter works and monographs on related subjects.

Hales's ventilator, designed to draw fresh air into confined spaces, was publicized in the *Gentleman's Magazine* and was described in lectures given in the provinces by Thomas Yeoman, the engineer that made the machine. It was fitted, with successful results, on men-of-war and slave ships, in the House of Commons, the court of king's bench, Drury Lane Theatre, and Newgate prison, and in hospitals, workhouses, and gaols throughout the country. French prisoners of war held in England and English prisoners of war held in France benefited from the invention, which led Hales to say that he hoped none would accuse him of corresponding with the enemy. Showers of fresh air, he demonstrated, could be used in the distillation of sea water and to improve the taste of milk. He contributed to the mid-century debate on the causes of earthquake, in a paper read before the Royal Society in 1750 and reprinted several times.

**Philanthropy and other interests** Hales received the Royal Society's Copley medal for his investigations of the complaint known as 'the stone' in 1739, and in the same year he was appointed by parliament as one of the trustees to examine the remedy proposed by Joanna Stephens. He was a lifelong opponent of the excessive consumption of alcohol, an insistent and fearless publicist of the evils of gin-drinking. Here his scientific work impinged on his public and religious concerns. For the Society for Promoting Christian Knowledge, of which he had been an active corresponding member since 1722, he wrote *A Friendly*

*Admonition to the Drinkers of Brandy and other Distilled Spirituous Liquors* (1734), and sent copies for distribution throughout North America, in particular to the newly established proprietary colony of Georgia, of which he was trustee and common council member from 1732 to 1752. Other organizations that attracted his interest were the Bray Associates, a missionary and educational trust for which he worked during his years of service for the Georgia Trust, and the Society for the Propagation of the Gospel, which he remembered in his will. In 1753 he was elected a foreign associate of the Académie Royale des Sciences, and in the same year he introduced William Shipley, the founder of the Society for the Encouragement of Arts, Manufactures, and Commerce, to lords Folkestone and Romney, two influential peers whose support was essential for its success. Hales became a founding member (1754) and a vice-president (1755) of the society, and was concerned with its affairs to within a year of his death.

Though not formally appointed preceptor to the young prince of Wales as had been rumoured in 1752, Hales guided the botanical studies of the princess, and of her children and Lord Bute. A shrub found in Carolina by Alexander Garden was given the name 'Halesia', and Hales gave drawings of it to Bute and to one of the royal children. In 1758 he helped the princess in planning a hot greenhouse, 120 feet long, to be built in the gardens at Kew.

From his likeness in the National Portrait Gallery (studio of Thomas Hudson, 1759), Hales appears a commanding figure with handsome features, certainly benevolent but clearly a man used to wielding authority over his parishioners and indifferent to those who mocked his scientific observations. In old age he had become a national figure. His work for the colony of Georgia brought him into contact with eminent politicians, religious zealots, sea captains, and American Indians. In his campaign for ventilation he was obliged to argue with hospital governors and naval officers. Yet this varied experience did nothing to alter what Peter Collinson called his 'native innocence and simplicity of manners', or to awaken in him ambition either for honours or preferment (Collinson, 273–8). He received £200 a year for his work as the princess's chaplain, a substantial increase to his income, which was useful to him for such purposes as the enlargement of the church at Teddington but otherwise, it seems, hardly welcomed. He had sufficient means to live simply and comfortably. For health's sake he always began dinner with plain pudding and yet enjoyed the delicacies produced by his syllabub machine, as well as wine, 'Nature's Cordial', preserved in cool cellars. To the young Charles Wesley he seemed, in spite of his position as a common councillor of Georgia, 'a truly pious, humble Christian' (*The Journal of the Revd Charles Wesley*, ed. T. Jackson, 1849, 1.56).

Alexander Pope, who was Hales's friend and neighbour in Middlesex, criticized him for his experiments on animals, but likened him to Mahmet, the king's devoted body servant:

From Peer or Bishop 'tis no easy thing
To draw the man who loves his God, or King:
Alas! I copy (or my draught would fail)
From honest Mah'met or Plain Parson Hale.
(*The Works of Alexander Pope*, ed. J. Wharton, 1797, 3.222)

Gilbert White noted that 'His whole mind seemed replete with experiment which of course gave a tincture and turn to his conversation often somewhat peculiar, but always interesting'. He listed a series of anecdotes to support this view, among which were Hales's concern with the incrustation of ladies' tea-kettles, his advising the use of showers of water to test the salubrity of wells, his directing air-holes to be let in the outer walls of rooms, his imploring young people not to drink their tea scalding hot, his *ad hoc* advice to ferrymen on how to maintain the bottoms of their boats, and his teaching housewives to place inverted teacups in their pies to prevent the syrup from boiling over. 'The last act of benevolence' White saw was in a street in Farringdon, where Hales was busy painting white 'the tops of the foot-path posts, that his neighbours might not be injured by running against them in the dark' ('Correspondence', 52–4).

Hales died at Teddington on 4 January 1761, after what was called a slight illness, having reached the age of eighty-three. He was buried according to his own request under the church tower at St Mary's, Teddington. 'Minister of this parish fifty one years' ran the lettering on his tomb, and there can be little doubt that he left behind him many affectionate memories among his parishioners. A monument in Westminster Abbey, carved by Wilton and paid for by the princess, shows the figures of Religion and Botanical Science supporting a medallion portrait of the dead philosopher, and a Latin inscription links him to Newton.

**A reputation revived** It was the special achievement of Stephen Hales to have combined eminence in science with dedicated service as a parish priest in the Church of England. In three subjects, pneumatic chemistry, vegetable physiology, and animal physiology, Hales devised research techniques, designed experiments, and made discoveries that inspired scientists for nearly a century. By the early 1900s his scientific work was largely forgotten by scientists themselves, though in the emerging discipline of the history of science, notably in the writings of Henry Guerlac, its significance was soon to be re-established. Hales came to be regarded as a major figure in eighteenth-century science, and it was noted that in Britain his reputation was second only to that of Newton, and that every significant figure in pneumatic chemistry acknowledged his work, from Joseph Black, Henry Cavendish, and Joseph Priestley, to Antoine Lavoisier and Humphry Davy. The leading plant physiologists, from Duhamel du Monceau, through Buffon, and thence to von Sachs, had admitted the work of Hales into their considerations. And, for a hundred years, animal physiologists had come to terms with the studies of Hales before proceeding with their own work. It was a record of which any professional scientist of later times would be proud. For an eighteenth-century amateur such as Stephen Hales, incidentally trained in science and devoting major portions of his time to religion, public duties, and public service, it was considered a phenomenal achievement (Allan and Schofield, 139–40). D. G. C. ALLAN

**Sources** D. G. C. Allan and R. E. Schofield, *Stephen Hales: scientist and philanthropist* (1980) • A. E. Clark-Kennedy, *Stephen Hales, D.D., F.R.S.: an eighteenth century biography* (1929) • P. Collinson, 'Memoir of Stephen Hales', *GM*, 1st ser., 34 (1764), 273–8 • *GM*, 1st ser., 69 (1799), 267–8 • M. S. Mann, *GM*, 1st ser., 71 (1801), 712–13 • 'The correspondence of Robert Marsham … and Revd Gilbert White … 1790–1793', ed. H. P. Marsham and Dr Bell, *Transactions of the Norfolk and Norwich Naturalists' Society*, 2 (1874–9), 133–93 • H. Guerlac, 'The continental reputation of Stephen Hales', *Archives Internationales d'Histoire des Sciences*, 4 (1951), 393–404 • I. B. Smith, 'The impact of Stephen Hales on medicine', *Journal of the Royal Society of Medicine*, 86 (1993), 349–52 • J. Harrison, '"The ingenious Mr Yeoman" and some associates', *RSA Journal*, 145 (June 1997), 53–68 • C. H. Wilkie, *The parish register of St Peter's Beakesbourne* (1896) • *N&Q*, 2nd ser., 4 (1857), 407 • GEC, *Baronetage* • J. W. Clay, ed., *The registers of St Paul's Cathedral*, Harleian Society, register section, 26 (1899) • parish register, Teddington, St Mary's, A1/14 • W. Butler, *Memoirs of Mark Hildesley* (1799), 373

**Archives** BL, observations on bills of mortality and parish registers • CCC Cam., MSS • LPL, letters • RCP Lond., letters • RS, papers • RSA, guard books • Sci. Mus., papers relating to ventilators • Society for Promoting Christian Knowledge, London, abstract letter-books • Trinity Cam. • United Society for the Propagation of the Gospel, London, Bray Associates MSS | Berks. RO, Hartley MSS • BL, letters to Thomas Birch • Bodl. Oxf., Bradley MSS • Cleveland Medical Library Association, Ohio, letters to William Lee • Linn. Soc., letters to John Ellis • Norfolk RO, letters to Henry Lee-Warner • U. Edin. L., Alston MSS

**Likenesses** W. Verelst, group portrait, oils, 1734 (*The Georgia Council*), H. F. du Pont Winterthur Museum, Winterthur, Delaware • J. Macardell, mezzotint, *c*.1759 (after T. Hudson), BM, NPG • studio of T. Hudson?, oils, *c*.1759, NPG [*see illus.*] • J. Wilton, medallion on marble monument, 1762, Westminster Abbey, London • etching, 1799, repro. in *GM*, 1st ser., 69 (1799), 9 • J. Hopwood, engraving (after T. Hudson), repro. in R. J. Thornton, *Elementary botanical plates* (1810) • J. Hopwood, engraving (after portrait by Coates), RS

**Wealth at death** copyhold dwelling house at Teddington 'with outhouses, yard and garden'; £270 cash legacies: will, Clark-Kennedy, *Stephen Hales*, 240–42; index to Teddington Manor court rolls (entry for 1764)

**Hales, Thomas of** (*fl. c*.1250), Franciscan friar and ecclesiastical writer, probably came from Hales in Gloucestershire. He was at one time thought to be a Dominican, as manuscripts of some of his works were once in Dominican libraries, but the titles of, and prologues attached to, some of the surviving manuscripts confirm his Franciscan status. A friar called Thomas of Hales was a friend of Adam Marsh (*d*. 1259), and very probably this is the same man. Thomas was long believed to have been a doctor of theology of the Sorbonne at Paris, but in fact nothing is known of his life.

Thomas of Hales was one of a number of Franciscan lyricists of the mid- to late thirteenth century. Several friars from the English province either composed lyrics or translated them into the vernacular. Hales was the author of 'A Luve Ron'—a love rune or love song, which survives in Oxford, Jesus College, MS 29. This comprises twenty-six eight-line stanzas, apparently written at the request of a girl consecrated to God. In it Thomas speaks of the fickle nature of earthly life, encouraging the girl to look to heaven for her true love. The author shows a clear awareness of courtly tradition and writes with the stylized erotic language that is a part of this genre. Thomas of Hales also wrote a *De vita seu genealogia Beatae Virginis Mariae*, which survives in a thirteenth-century copy once in the library of the abbey of St Victor (now University of Basel Library, MS B.VIII. 1., fols. 47vb–57vb), and a number of sermons (Oxford, St John's College, MS 190).

JENNY SWANSON

**Sources** J. Moorman, *History of the Franciscan order* (1968), 271 • C. Brown, ed., *English lyrics of the XIIIth century* (1932), 68 • C. Morris, *Old English miscellany*, EETS, original ser., 49 (1872) • J. V. Fleming, *An introduction to the Franciscan literature of the Middle Ages* (1977), 11, 20, 183 • G. Meyer and M. Burckhardt, *Die mittelalterlichen Handschriften der Universitätsbibliothek Basel*, 1 (Basel, 1960), 828f. • *DNB*

**Archives** Jesus College, Oxford, MS 29 • St John's College, Oxford, MS 190 • University of Basel Library, MS B.VIII.1

**Hales, Thomas** (*c*.1740–1780), playwright and librettist, was born in Gloucestershire, possibly in Gloucester, to a 'distinguished' family, possibly Irish, or of Irish descent. Grétry, his musical collaborator, describes Hales as an Irishman called Hall in England (Grétry, *Réflexions*, 3.261). During the Seven Years' War, Hales served in the British navy and was sent to Jamaica, where he stayed until 1763. In October 1778 he contributed a brief account of his Jamaican experience relating to an aspect of slave legislation in 1761 to Friedrich Melchior Grimm's *Correspondance littéraire* (12.170–71). After military service in Jamaica he settled for a time in Havana in 1763, and thereafter travelled widely in Europe, living for extended periods in Switzerland and Italy. He arrived in Paris about 1770 and was soon in financial difficulties, ruined, according to anecdote, by women and wine. Rapidly acquiring fluency in the French language, he frequented the Café du Caveau, and soon embarked on a literary and musical career to earn his living. The first example of his talent was a short story entitled 'Le roman de mon oncle', published by Grimm in July 1777 in the *Correspondance littéraire* (11.484–9), reprinted in 1863.

Hales first met Grétry about 1775 in the salon of Jean-Baptiste Suard, and through Grétry he met Madame de Montesson. Collaboration with Grétry started soon after Hales had shown the composer his libretto for *Les fausses apparences, ou, L'amant jaloux*, which Grétry did not at first like. Altogether Hales wrote four plays, three of which served as librettos for Grétry's *opéras comiques*. His first work was *Le jugement de Midas*, a three-act prose comedy, completed in 1776, for which Grétry subsequently composed the music. *Le jugement de Midas* was published in Paris in 1778 (two editions), in 1779 (with full score), and in Parma in 1784, and was translated into German in 1781. The play formed the basis of Hales's first joint venture with Grétry and, with the support of the poet Stanislas-Jean Boufflers, the resulting *opéra comique* was first performed on 28 March 1778 under the auspices of Madame de Montesson, to whom it was dedicated, in the duc d'Orléans's *théâtre de cour* at the Palais-Royal. This private performance, in which Madame de Montesson herself participated, attracted a large audience drawn from the highest levels of Parisian society, including bishops, archbishops, and possibly also Voltaire. It was subsequently performed on 27 June and 1 July 1778 at the Comédie-Italienne, and on 3 July at Versailles, where it was well received. From 1778 to 1793 there were eighty performances, with successful revivals until 1824. In a laudatory review Grimm expressed astonishment at Hales's theatrical genius and linguistic ability (*Correspondance*, 12.118–19). Hales probably borrowed his theme from *Midas*, an Irish burletta by Kane O'Hara first performed publicly in 1762 in Dublin, and in London in 1764. However, Hales's polished style, keen wit, and freshness of interpretation set his *Midas* easily apart from O'Hara's version.

*Les fausses apparences, ou, L'amant jaloux*, the most successful and arguably the best of the Hales–Grétry *opéras comiques*, was first performed at the Comédie-Italienne on 23 December 1778, the second Paris performance being on 9 January 1779. It was published in Paris in 1778 (two editions), in 1779 (with full score), and in Parma in 1784. Grimm noted its success (*Correspondance*, 12.198–99), but La Harpe thought its reception over-generous, though declaring it to be a model of good French style (La Harpe, *Lycée, ou, Cours de littérature ancienne et Moderne*, 16 vols., 1798–1808/9, 12.537–8). Both libretto and score went through many changes, and between 1779 and 1788 there were 150 performances. The plot owes something to *The Wonder: a Woman Keeps a Secret* by Susanna Carroll (Mrs Centlivre) (1714), and also possibly something to Nicolas Lagrange's *Les contretemps* (1736). Known usually from the score title simply as *L'amant jaloux*, it was an outstanding success, and was revived at the Opéra-Comique on 18 September 1850 with twenty-four performances.

Hales's third comedy libretto for Grétry was *Les evénements imprévus*, published in Paris in 1779, 1780, and 1781 (with full score). A new edition was printed in Toulouse in 1788. Dedicated to the comte d'Artois, *Les evénements imprévus* was first performed at Versailles on 11 November 1779, and at the Comédie-Italienne on 13 November. Altogether there were 15 performances in November and December and over 300 between 1779 and 1823. The plot was borrowed, according to Grimm (*Correspondance*, 12.341), from an Italian source, still unidentified, *Di peggio in peggio*. It received a mixed reception in the *Mercure de France* (4 Dec 1779, 84–8), but was reported as a success by the *Journal de Paris* (14 Nov 1779) and by Bachaumont on 15 November (Bachaumont, 14.267). Very different from anything that Hales had written previously, the plot reflects the ambience of the last decade of the *ancien régime*, and was written in the Italian theatrical tradition rather than the French. Translated into English during the period 1805–6 by Thomas Holcroft as *Unforeseen Events, a Comic Opera in Three Acts, from the French of M. d'Hèle*, Hales's comedy inspired *The Gay Deceivers* by George Colman the younger, performed at the Haymarket on 12 August 1804 (Kelly, 2.223). A Danish translation by Lars Knudsen appeared in 1785.

Hales's first three works were reprinted in the *Petite bibliothèque des théâtres* (1784) and the *Théâtre de l'Opéra-Comique* (1812, vol. 7), and were listed in the *Suite du répertoire du théâtre français* (Lepeintre-Desroches, 56.85). Little is known of Hales's view of Grétry, although he was reportedly not always pleased with the changes that had to be made to his comedies to accommodate Grétry's music (*Chef-d'œuvres dramatiques Dhele*, 2 vols., 1791, 1.4). Hales's last play was *Gilles ravisseur*, a one-act *comédie parade* written in prose for the actor Volange. Grimm announced the first performance at the Théâtre des Variétés Amusantes in the Foire St Germain on 1 March 1781. It was performed at Versailles on 10 September and in Paris in 1782 and 1783, and published in Paris in 1784 and 1788. Hales collaborated early in 1780 with J. F. Cailhava d'Estendoux on the revisions to Collalto's *Les trois jumeaux vénitiens*, first performed on 7 December 1773.

Hales's reputation survived the French Revolution, and his achievements as a dramatist writing in a foreign language for a difficult hybrid genre continued to be recognized in France well into the nineteenth century. An elusive figure, Hales has received little attention since the mid-nineteenth century, but his achievements as one of Grétry's librettists are now recognized. Contemporaries refer to the cause of his death, which occurred in Paris on 27 December 1780, as being a chest infection, possibly the consequence of an accident incurred during his military service, aggravated by depression caused by the return to Italy of his lover, the actress Mme Bianchi, known as Argentine. Hales left several projects unfinished, including a commission from Marie-Antoinette received during a performance of *L'amant jaloux* at Choisy. There are no known surviving likenesses. Grétry describes Hales as being 5 feet 3 inches tall, thin, fair, blue-eyed, eccentric, laconic, and temperamental, and offers the most detailed personal portrait (Grétry, *Réflexions*, 3.264–5; *Mémoires*, 1.327). Grimm was greatly impressed with Hales's quiet dignity, unaffected manner, and independent spirit (*Correspondance*, 12.497, 16.10). DAVID WILLIAMS

**Sources** A.-E.-M. Grétry, *Réflexions d'un solitaire: manuscrit inédit*, ed. L. Solvay and E. Closson, 4 vols. (1919–22) · A.-E.-M. Grétry, *Mémoires, ou, Essais sur la musique*, 3 vols. (1789), rev. 2nd edn (1797), repr. (1971) · *Correspondance littéraire, philosophique et critique par Grimm, Diderot, Raynal, Meister*, ed. M. Tourneux, 16 vols. (1877–82) · L. Petit de Bachaumont and others, *Mémoires secrets pour servir à l'histoire de la République des lettres en France, depuis 1762 jusqu'à nos jours*, 36 vols. (1777–89) · D. Charlton, *Grétry and the growth of opéra-comique* (1986) · C. D. Brenner, *The Théâtre Italien: its repertory, 1716–1793* (1961) · S. E. M. Van de Weyer, *Lettres sur les Anglais qui ont écrit en français* (1854) · P.-M.-M. Lepeintre-Desroches, *Suite du répertoire du théâtre français*, 81 vols. (1822–3) · M. Kelly, *Reminiscences*, 2nd edn, 2 vols. (1826); repr., R. Fiske, ed. (1975) · D.-J. Garat, *Mémoires historiques sur la vie de M. Suard, sur ses écrits et sur le XVIIIe siècle*, 2 vols. (1820)

**Wealth at death** lacking in fortune: *Correspondance*, ed. Tourneux; Bachaumont and others, *Mémoires*; Grétry, *Réflexions*; Grétry, *Mémoires*

**Hales, William** (1747–1831), Church of Ireland clergyman and scientific writer, born on 8 April 1747, was the son of Samuel Hales, who was for many years curate and preacher at the cathedral church of Cork. He was educated by his maternal uncle, James Kingston, prebendary of Donoughmore, and in 1764 entered Trinity College,

Dublin, where in 1768 he became a fellow, and graduated BA and afterwards DD. As tutor at the college he wore a white wig to avoid confrontations with parents alarmed at his youthful appearance. His numerous pupils are said to have described his lectures as 'pleasant', though he occasionally roused his students from bed by a dose of cold water ('Memoir', 1.323). Hales was also professor of oriental languages in the university. His first published work was *Sonorum doctrina rationalis et experimentalis* (1778), a vindication and confirmation from recent experiments of Newton's theory of sounds. In 1782 he published *De motibus planetarum dissertatio* on the motions of the planets in eccentric orbits, according to the Newtonian theory. Six years later he printed at his own expense *Analysis aequationum*; this was later included by his friend Baron Maseres in his *Scriptores logarithmici*, of which 250 copies were printed. Lagrange sent Hales a complimentary letter from Berlin on the *Analysis*.

In 1788 Hales, who had already taken orders, resigned his professorship for the rectory of Killashandra, co. Cavan, where he lived in retirement for the remainder of his life. In mid-1791 he married Mary, the second daughter of Archdeacon Whitty; they had two sons and two daughters. In 1798 he procured government troops to regain control of the country round Killashandra, following the invasion by French soldiers at Killala. From about 1812 Hales also held the chancellorship of the diocese of Emly. A good parish priest, Hales was 'equally pleasing to the gentry and the lower orders' ('Memoir', 1.325). He rose at six and spent the day in learned studies. Until 1819 he was constantly engaged in writing for publication. His best-known work, *A New Analysis of Chronology*, took twenty years to complete, and was finally published by subscription in three volumes between 1809 and 1812. Hales, noting the great discordance of previous chronologists, 'laid it down as a rule to see with mine own eyes' (letter to Bishop Percy, 6 June 1796), and investigated original sources. Hales's work deals with the chronology of the whole Bible, and gives a portion of the early history of the world. Aside from his work on scientific subjects Hales also published, among other titles, *The Inspector, or, Select Literary Intelligence for the Vulgar* and *Irish Pursuits of Literature* (both 1799), *Methodism Inspected* (1803–5), and *Letters on the Tenets of the Romish Hierarchy* (1813). From about 1820 or earlier he suffered from melancholy, and his mind seems to have become disordered. He died on 30 January 1831.

W. W. WROTH, *rev.* PHILIP CARTER

**Sources** 'Memoir of William Hales DD', *British Magazine and Monthly Register*, 1 (1832) · Nichols, *Illustrations*, 7.786, 8.317, 320, 678
**Archives** Hunt. L., letters to Charles O'Conor
**Likenesses** oils, TCD

**Halévy, Élie** (1870–1937), historian and philosopher, was born on 6 September 1870 at Étretat, Normandy, in France. He was the elder son of Ludovic Halévy (1834–1908), writer and librettist, and his wife, Louise, *née* Bréguet (1847–1930), heir to the industrialist and scientist Louis Bréguet. His younger brother was the critic and contemporary historian Daniel Halévy. Halévy's father was Jewish and his mother protestant; the children were raised as protestants. Brought up in Paris, Halévy was educated at the Lycée Condorcet and at the École Normale Supérieure. He passed the *agrégation* in 1892, but instead of proceeding to an academic career within the state system he accepted Émile Boutmy's offer of a post at the École Libre des Sciences Politiques in Paris. He held a chair there from 1898 until his death, and his teaching was interrupted only by a period of wartime medical service.

Boutmy, himself a distinguished student of British history and institutions, initially invited him to teach the history of British political ideas, and from 1902 Halévy offered this alternately with a course on the history of socialism. These were to remain his chief interests in a remarkably focused career. His private income spared him the quest for academic preferment and enabled him to devote himself to his scholarly writing. He was no recluse: like his brother, he was active in rallying intellectuals to the cause of Dreyfus in 1898, and after the First World War he was offered, but declined, a post in the secretariat of the League of Nations. But he was unwavering in his commitment to his scholarly vocation. On 17 October 1901 Halévy married Florence Noufflard (*c.*1880–1957), daughter of the musicologist Georges Noufflard and his Italian wife, Emilia Landrini. There were no children of the marriage. Florence accompanied him on many of his research trips to Britain, and shared in his scholarly activities to the full.

Halévy was by training a philosopher rather than a historian: his first book was *La théorie platonicienne des sciences* (1896), and together with his former classmates Xavier Léon and Léon Brunschvicg he founded and co-edited the *Revue de Métaphysique et de Morale*. He also assisted in the foundation of the Société Française de Philosophie. Halévy's involvement in both institutions was lifelong. His closest friends were *normalien* philosophers such as Émile Chartier (Alain) and Célestin Bouglé, as well as Brunschvicg and Léon. Yet Halévy made his name not as a philosopher but as a historian of nineteenth-century Britain. He seems to have been launched on this intellectual itinerary by a distaste for philosophies that lacked practical bite, and this led him to the study of Bentham, a philosopher not of the front rank, but who fascinated Halévy as 'le type du philosophe *réformateur*' (*Correspondance*, 179). This interest yielded a remarkable and enduring work of intellectual history, *La formation du radicalisme philosophique* (3 vols., 1901–4), part of which he submitted as his doctoral thesis in 1901; it then led him into mainstream political and general history of Britain in his multi-volume *Histoire du peuple anglais au XIXe siècle*. This work, Halévy's *magnum opus*, remained incomplete: volumes 1–3 (1912–23) dealt with the period 1815–41, and in 1926 and 1932 he published a two-volume epilogue treating the period 1895–1914. He never completed his treatment of the high Victorian period. Nevertheless he made a major and lasting impact upon the study of modern British history. The popularity of the English translations, which first appeared between 1924 and 1934, was confirmed by their publication in paperback by Penguin Books.

Halévy's study of the philosophic radicals was a pioneering work in the history of ideas, and in analytical depth it greatly surpassed Sir Leslie Stephen's contemporaneous work on *The English Utilitarians*. It has never been bettered as a study of Benthamism, although more recent work has suggested a more modest estimate of the Benthamite influence on the nineteenth-century mind. Halévy's interpretation—which was characteristic of his historical method—was structured about a pivotal distinction between two ultimately contradictory strands in Benthamism: the principle of the artificial identification of interests, which underpinned the philosophic radicals' political and legal theory; and the principle of the natural identity of interests, which underlay their economic doctrine. Halévy hinted at the collectivist potential in utilitarianism, and the implications of his work were thus subtly different from those of Dicey's lectures on the shift from individualism to collectivism in public policy.

In his volume *L'Angleterre en 1815*—Halévy's acknowledged masterpiece, which was rejected by the first publisher he approached—he expounded the 'Halévy thesis' that nineteenth-century Britain was saved from revolution by the influence of nonconformist religion, and especially Methodism. His work displayed great historical sensitivity and command of the sources; it also revealed, typically, a deep philosophical purpose. Like Max Weber just a few years before, Halévy was keen to deploy historical investigation as a tool with which to refute historical materialism. The Marxist thesis would suggest that Britain was ripe for revolution in the aftermath of the Napoleonic wars. Britain's avoidance of that fate could hardly be explained by the strength of its political institutions, for the student of Bentham depicted the unreformed British state as a ramshackle chaos. It was ideas—not abstract ideas, but ideas as they acted on the public mind and were altered thereby—that provided the only credible explanation for Britain's political stability in the early phase of the industrial revolution.

The volumes Halévy's fellow countrymen most admired dealt with the period 1895–1914. Here he expounded a remarkably controlled thesis that both predated and surpassed George Dangerfield's more famous interpretation in *The Strange Death of Liberal England* (1936). But these volumes on the pre-war crisis were somewhat detached from the overall conception of Halévy's *History*; they were distinctly more pessimistic, as he traced the erosion of the vigorous liberal consensus of the high Victorian decades. They had more affinity with his inter-war reflections on problems in the interpretation of contemporary history. War and its impact now preoccupied him, and he served on the commission for the publication of French diplomatic documents on the origins of the First World War. He expounded an original thesis on this question in *The World Crisis of 1914–1918: an Interpretation* (1930); and in a paper, 'L'ère des tyrannies', which he delivered to the Société Française de Philosophie in 1936, he considered the relations between socialism and fascism, and traced their convergence to the impact of the war. These works, acute and powerful as they are, show his sympathetic interest in socialism hardening into the hostility of the liberal critic of generic totalitarianism.

Halévy moved easily between French and British intellectual circles, perhaps more easily than any other twentieth-century French academic of the first rank. He spent a good portion of each year in Britain, usually working in the British Museum, and he reviewed for British periodicals. He also had an impressively wide range of British friends, who included H. A. L. Fisher, Graham Wallas, the Webbs, and Bertrand Russell; this circle of friends, mostly to the left of Halévy in politics, reflected his lifelong interest in British political ideas and in the history of socialism. He was awarded the honorary degree of DLitt by the University of Oxford in 1926, and delivered the Rhodes memorial lectures in the same university in 1929. He died suddenly of a heart attack on 21 August 1937, at his home, La Maison Blanche, Sucy-en-Brie (Seine-et-Marne), to the south-east of Paris.

In his lifetime, and for decades afterwards, Halévy and his works were better known in Britain than in France. Later, however, French interest in Halévy revived with the rediscovery of that lost tradition of French liberalism stretching from Constant and Guizot through Tocqueville to Halévy's protégé Raymond Aron. Halévy's work came to be celebrated by the allies of François Furet. The philosopher who turned via the history of ideas to British political history at last became, through his historical work on Britain, an important presence in the intellectual history of France. H. S. JONES

**Sources** *Élie Halévy: correspondance, 1891–1937*, ed. H. Guy-Loë (1996) • M. Chase, *Élie Halévy: an intellectual biography* (1980) • M. Richter, 'A bibliography of signed works by Élie Halévy', *History and Theory*, suppl. 7 (1967), 46–71 • *Élie Halévy: 6 septembre 1870 – août 1937*, École Libre des Sciences Politiques (c.1938) • R. Aron and others, 'Pour le centenaire de Élie Halévy', *Bulletin de la Société Française de Philosophie*, 66 (1971), 1–31 • E. Barker, 'Élie Halévy', *EngHR*, 53 (1938), 79–87 • C. Haugh Smith, 'Élie Halévy (1870–1937)', *Some historians of modern Europe*, ed. B. E. Schmitt (1942), 152–67 • C. C. Gillespie, 'The work of Élie Halévy: a critical appreciation', *Journal of Modern History*, 22 (1950), 232–49

**Archives** priv. coll. | Archives Nationales, Paris, Célestin Bouglé MSS • Bibliothèque Victor Cousin, Paris, Xavier Léon MSS • McMaster University, Hamilton, Ontario, William Ready Division of Archives and Research Collections, Bertrand Russell MSS

**Likenesses** photograph, repro. in École Libre des Sciences Politiques, *Élie Halévy*

**Haley, Sir William John** (1901–1987), broadcasting executive and newspaper editor, was born on 24 May 1901 in St Helier, Jersey, the son of Frank Haley of Bramley, Leeds (who died when Haley was two years old), and Marie Berthe Sangan, a Jersey Frenchwoman. French-speaking until the age of five, he was educated at Victoria College, Jersey, but left school at sixteen and served as a wireless telegraph operator on a tramp ship during the last two years of the First World War. He was inspired to become a journalist, he later said, after reading Philip Gibbs's *The Street of Adventure*, and after a short period at a Jersey weekly, in 1919 he joined *The Times* as a shorthand copy-taker in the foreign news department. There he met Edith Susie Gibbons, secretary to the foreign editor, whom he married in 1921. On his suggestion the newspaper sent

**Sir William John Haley (1901–1987)**, by unknown photographer, 1942 [broadcasting *Tonight's Talk* ('As I see it: truth in the news') on the BBC Home Service on 13 October 1942]

them to Brussels, where Haley successfully reorganized the paper's European news-gathering operation. He also contributed a freelance weekly letter from Brussels to the *Manchester Evening News*, on the strength of which he was offered a job as a reporter in 1922.

**Newspaper editor** Haley, a deeply shy man, was not a success as a reporter and was soon moved to sub-editing, where he excelled. He was promoted to chief sub-editor in 1925, and in 1930 was appointed both managing editor of the *Manchester Evening News* and a director of its parent company, Manchester Guardian and Evening News Ltd. His task was to develop the paper to withstand the increasingly competitive evening newspaper market of the 1930s. As managing editor Haley proved a brilliant newspaper technician with an instinct for popular journalism, and demonstrated the single-minded and austere professionalism that would become his defining characteristic. Reserved in manner, he was forceful, even ruthless, in both business dealings and moral judgements. He led by example, working the longest hours of any of his staff, maintaining a desk in every department, and constantly checking every aspect of production. His own office had no chair, just a standing desk, where he revised proofs and lunched on a bun and a glass of milk. A large man with a resemblance to G. K. Chesterton, he had no social life beyond the office and his young family of four children. He was a non-smoker and almost teetotal, joined no clubs or social organizations, and repelled all attempts at workplace friendships (though he did permit himself twenty minutes of ping-pong each evening—he was office champion—and the occasional game of golf). Despite the considerable financial constraints under which the newspaper operated, Haley ensured the reputation of the *Manchester Evening News* as one of the leading evening papers in the country. He also managed to pursue in print his passionate love of literature (particularly Victorian literature), writing a weekly book review column under the pseudonym Joseph Sell (the name itself a literary allusion, to Borrow). To his fellow journalist A. P. Ryan these books took the place of the comradeship Haley's life lacked.

The Spanish Civil War politicized Haley's editorial journalism. His leader articles for the *Manchester Evening News* became far more hard-hitting, in particular his denunciation of the bombing of Guernica ('the bombs of Guernica may be the forerunners of our doom') and of the Munich agreement, which the *Manchester Evening News* opposed in the strongest moral terms. On the outbreak of the Second World War J. R. Scott, manager of Manchester Guardian and Evening News Ltd, appointed Haley joint managing director, and with his success at the *Evening News* having helped save the *Manchester Guardian* from closure he was made one of the original Scott trustees. From 1939 to 1943 he was also a director of the Press Association and of Reuters. He became a director of the Reuters Trust on its establishment in 1941, and travelled to the USA and Australia on its behalf to negotiate new news-gathering agreements. His success here, where so many had failed before, spread his reputation well beyond Manchester. He was by now, however, suffering from a severely debilitating form of anaemia, as yet undiagnosed. This caused a drastic weight loss that dramatically altered his appearance.

**Wartime broadcasting** In 1943 Haley, after some initial doubts, accepted the newly created post of editor-in-chief at the BBC. The increased importance of broadcasting during the war had placed enormous strain on the relationship between the BBC and the government, and the new post (which ranked barely below that of director-general) was designed specifically to bring high-level journalistic expertise into the corporation as well as to strengthen leadership at the top. Haley's faith in the value of public service broadcasting, and his uncompromising belief that the BBC should provide the best possible of whatever it broadcast, echoed that of the first BBC director-general, John Reith, and Haley brought to the BBC the same single-minded conviction. With his illness now successfully diagnosed and treated, he proved both a successful administrator and a tireless defender of the corporation. His first task as editor-in-chief was to visit the Italian battle front to discuss BBC provision with British servicemen and BBC war correspondents; this led to the launch of the BBC's new General Forces Programme (amalgamating the domestic Forces Programme and the General Overseas Service that had previously provided programmes for servicemen abroad), which both saved the BBC money and, by providing a single forces service for soldiers abroad and their families in Britain, raised morale. The renewed sense of confidence at the BBC in the last part of the war was in no small part due to Haley's decisiveness and clarity of purpose—as well as to the cordial and trusting relationship he developed with the minister of information, Brendan Bracken. In 1944 he was the natural choice to succeed Robert Foot as director-general.

**Director-general of the BBC** After the end of the war Haley reshaped the post-war BBC. His reorganization of the corporation in 1947 was the most wide-ranging since 1933, recentralizing important aspects of its administration and creating a new central board of management, which historians later came to consider one of the most important institutional developments in the BBC's history. He also set his stamp on the corporation's post-war output. No director-general since Reith had believed so forcefully in the cultural importance of broadcasting, but Haley recognized the need to maintain the BBC's wartime popularity even while answering widespread criticism that the wartime BBC had become too populist. To this end he oversaw the redesignation of the two wartime BBC wavelengths as the Light Programme and Home Service, and was the driving force behind the launch in 1946 of the Third Programme, a new service specifically devoted to high culture, music, and the arts. It was Haley who coined the image of the post-war BBC as a cultural pyramid, whereby listeners, attracted first to the populist Light Programme, might progress gradually upwards via the middlebrow Home Service to the summit of the resolutely élitist Third Programme. In many respects the Third Programme was typical of Haley himself. Quixotically highbrow, even on its inception it was looked on by many as a Reithian anachronism at the heart of the BBC's modernization programme. Yet it offered unprecedented scope for innovation and experiment, gave opportunity to a new generation of musicians and literary figures, and made classical music, literature, and the arts available to all who cared to listen. Praised and mocked in equal measure, often attracting only tiny audiences, the Third Programme nevertheless represented an essential facet of the BBC's *raison d'être* as a public service institution: the provision of high culture for its own sake and in disregard of merely commercial imperatives. It survived until 1967, when it was subsumed into BBC Radio 3.

In common with most other BBC executives, Haley considered television (which began re-broadcasting in 1946 after its wartime suspension) as secondary in importance to radio. In part, this was because he recognized television's innately populist appeal and feared that, left unchecked, it would come to dominate the home; however, his relative neglect of the BBC's television service in favour of the 'spoken word' alienated more forward-looking staff members (some of whom—notably Norman Collins—left the BBC to help set up commercial television). Haley fought the creation of commercial television in the early 1950s, fearing it would inexorably undermine broadcasting values and standards. Although his achievements at the BBC were singled out for praise by the Beveridge committee on broadcasting in 1950, when he left the BBC in 1952 he knew that the battle to maintain the BBC's monopoly had been lost.

**Editor of *The Times*** In 1952 Sir William Haley (he had been appointed KCMG in 1946 as well as being appointed to the Légion d'honneur in 1948) succeeded William Casey as editor of *The Times*. Here, as at the BBC in 1943, morale was low. Newsprint was still rationed, and *The Times* in particular struggled to maintain its role as the newspaper of record, hampered in addition by outdated working practices and staff tensions between the 'gentlemen' (specialist commentators) and 'players' (journalists). Although Haley was hardly a revolutionary, over the next fourteen years he changed *The Times* from a moribund national institution into (in the words of Lord Beaverbrook) a 'real newspaper'. He fought successfully to end newsprint rationing, and used the space gained for far wider coverage of the arts and of women's features. He introduced cartoons and a corrections column to the newspaper. He challenged the Oxbridge and public-school tone of much of the paper, and brought in more professional journalists. He presided over the replacement of *The Times*'s Victorian offices with a modern open-plan working environment. In May 1966 he made history by returning news to the front page for the first time in nearly two centuries. However, he continued to devote considerable space to obscure and erudite topics, and resisted any attempt to change the newspaper's long-standing tradition of anonymous journalism, despite the difficulties this caused in retaining some of his best journalists. (It was left to his successor as editor, William Rees-Mogg, to institute this long-overdue change in 1967.) Haley's one personal indulgence was his own renewed weekly literary column, written on his one day off a week under the new pseudonym Oliver Edwards. Its eclecticism attracted a certain amount of derision from the younger literati, but it eloquently expressed his own love of reading.

Meanwhile, Haley sought to break the long-standing perception that *The Times* was the newspaper of the establishment. He sought to distance the paper from Whitehall and the City. He brought a new scepticism and independence to its reporting of government, for example famously publishing a report about the stationing of US Polaris submarines in Scotland, in defiance of the Ministry of Defence and 10 Downing Street. He discouraged sycophancy towards royalty (and always personally referred to the duke of Edinburgh as 'that young man who looks like a soda syphon'). Characteristically, he deplored *The Times*'s (highly successful) advertising campaign 'Top people take *The Times*', and insisted on the inclusion of scientists and engineers as well as bishops, judges, and generals in the advertisements. Above all, he restored a passionate moral tone to *Times* leaders. His editoral philosophy was eloquently summed up in his last speech before his retirement from the paper:

> The truth is that there is a difference between right and wrong … no half-way house between honesty and dishonesty … things which are bad and false and ugly and no amount of argument or specious casuistry will make them good or true or beautiful. It is time that these things were said, and time for the Press to say them.

Haley's leading article on 11 June 1963 at the height of the Profumo affair, 'It is a moral issue', became a historic indictment of the Macmillan government (whom he considered a 'bunch of thugs'). A 'Manchester Liberal' by inclination, he supported the Conservative Party in all elections, but regretted that the Liberal Party was not stronger. His moral outlook shaped his attitude to government policies: he supported the move towards colonial change in Africa, for instance, and (cautiously) endorsed Britain's quest for membership of the EEC.

Throughout his tenure at *The Times* Haley remained the unclubbable, distant, and driven figure he had been at the *Manchester Evening News* and the BBC. He was an exacting taskmaster ('Working fourteen to sixteen hours a day himself, Haley cannot understand why others wilt after twelve hours', said one executive), rarely took holidays, kept a close eye on every part of the newspaper, and could be harshly unforgiving of mistakes, though protective of his staff against unjustified criticism from outside. As before, he discouraged personal relationships with his staff (he never, apparently, addressed any employee by his or her Christian name), and avoided social occasions. He was a wooden public speaker. Yet he inspired fierce loyalties among many of his staff. His relaxations were reading (an estimated three Victorian novels a week) and listening to music. He accumulated many honours, including several honorary degrees, and from 1955 to 1962 was president of the National Book League.

**Late years** In his last years at *The Times* Haley was principally concerned with business matters. In 1965 he became chief executive and director of the Times Publishing Company Ltd, but was unable to resolve the economic crisis that hit the entire newspaper industry in this period and especially *The Times*. At one point he entered into talks with Alistair Hetherington, then editor of *The Guardian*, to consider a merger. However, in 1966 Haley oversaw instead the change of proprietorship from the Astor family to the Thomson organization (owners of the *Sunday Times*), serving as the first chairman of Times Newspapers Ltd in 1967. In 1968–9 he left *The Times* to become editor-in-chief of the *Encyclopaedia Britannica*, based in Chicago, but his plans for the new edition were opposed and the appointment was short-lived. He retired to Jersey, where he acted as the island's commissioner of appeal for income tax (1971–83) and chairman of the Jersey Arts Council (1976–7), and continued to read and to review until a debilitating attack of shingles when he was eighty curtailed this lifelong pleasure. Sir William Haley died in a nursing home in Jersey on 6 September 1987, aged eighty-six, and was buried in Gouray churchyard, Jersey. He was survived by his wife, two sons, and two daughters.

Sir William Haley's contribution to the mass media in twentieth-century Britain was profound. Yet, despite holding two of the most powerful posts in the British media, he was a self-effacing figure whose public profile never matched that of, for instance, John Reith, or C. P. Scott. To most who worked for him Haley remained an enigma: an outstanding modernizer whose inspiration was his uncompromising Victorian conscience; the man who took broadcasting into the second half of the twentieth century but whose passion was the literature of the nineteenth, who left school at sixteen but rose to edit the most celebrated newspaper in the English-speaking world. SIÂN NICHOLAS

**Sources** A. P. Ryan, 'Haley, the great informer', *The Guardian* (8 Sept 1987) • J. Grant, 'Every newsman's editor', *The Times* (8 Sept 1987) • J. Beavan, 'Sir William Haley', *The Independent* (8 Sept 1987) • *The Times* (8 Sept 1987) • *WWW, 1981–90* • A. Briggs, *The BBC: the first fifty years* (1985) • A. Briggs, *The history of broadcasting in the United Kingdom*, 4 vols. (1961–79), vols. 3–4 • H. Carpenter, *The envy of the world: fifty years of the BBC Third Programme and Radio 3, 1946–1996* (1996) • G. R. Balleine, *A biographical dictionary of Jersey*, [1] [1948]

**Archives** BBC WAC • CAC Cam., corresp., diaries, and papers | BLPES, corresp. with Lady Rhys Williams • CUL, corresp. with Sir Samuel Hoare • JRL, letters to the *Manchester Guardian* • King's Lond., Liddell Hart C., corresp. with Sir B. H. Liddell Hart

**Likenesses** photograph, 1942, BBC Picture Archives, London [*see illus.*] • photographs, 1943, Hult. Arch. • J. Epstein, bust, 1958, BBC Broadcasting House, London • photograph, repro. in *The Guardian*

**Hálfdan** [Healfdene] (*d.* **877**), king of the Danes, was the brother of *Ívarr inn Beinlausi (Ívarr the Boneless). The tradition that both were the sons of Ragnarr Lodbrók (Ragnarr Hairy Breeches) is unreliable. Hálfdan and his brother were among the leaders of the 'great army' that arrived in England from Denmark in 865. After wintering in East Anglia from autumn 865, the army moved to York, which it took on 1 November 866. A Northumbrian attempt to retake the city was repelled and the Northumbrian kings Osberht and Ælle killed on 21 March 867. The vikings established Ecgberht as their puppet king in the north before moving, in the autumn of 867, to Nottingham in Mercia. The army returned to York in 868, staying for a year before crossing Mercia to Thetford in East Anglia. At this point they engaged the East Angles, killing their king, Edmund (*d.* 869). Unlike his brother Ívarr, who left England at this time, Hálfdan was not implicated in this deed by later tradition. Hálfdan's army left East Anglia in the autumn or early winter of 870, and invaded Wessex, establishing their base at Reading. The Anglo-Saxon Chronicle, which for this period is a near contemporary West Saxon source, gives a detailed narrative of the ensuing campaign. The vikings fought nine general engagements against the West Saxons, who were led by their king, Æthelred I, who died in April 871, and his brother and successor, Alfred. The most important of these took place on the Berkshire downs, then called Ashdown, in the early months of 871. Hálfdan makes his first appearance in a written source in the chronicle's report of that battle, in which the viking army was drawn up in two divisions: one, opposed by Alfred, was led by *jarls*, the other, which Æthelred engaged, was under the command of 'the heathen kings Bagsecg and Healfdene' (*ASC*, s.a. 871). Bagsecg was slain in the battle. The outcome of Ashdown, and ultimately of all the engagements of 871, was indecisive, despite the arrival at some point of a 'great summer army', probably led by Guthrum, which reinforced Hálfdan's host. In the autumn of 871 the combined army left Reading and wintered in London. Coins minted there at the time bear the name Hálfdan, indicating his status as the army's most prominent leader. From London, in the early autumn of 872, the army was drawn to Northumbria by a revolt against the Danish-appointed puppet king Ecgberht, before it settled for the winter in Mercia, at Torksey on the Trent. The vikings remained there for a year after the Mercians had bought peace from them, until late in 873 they moved to Repton; they drove the Mercian king, Burgred, from his kingdom, establishing in his place Ceolwulf (*fl.* 874–879), who gave them hostages and swore oaths that Mercia should be at their disposal whenever they wanted it. In the following year the viking army divided into two. While Guthrum occupied Cambridge, from where he invaded Wessex again in 875, Hálfdan took his contingent north to a base on the Tyne from which he attacked the Picts and Strathclyde Britons. His army then settled in Northumbria from autumn 875, where they 'proceeded to plough and to support themselves' (*ASC*, s.a. 876). The area occupied seems to have been broadly the old kingdom of Deira, centred on York; the northern part of Northumbria, Bernicia, remained in the hands of English rulers.

Hálfdan himself does not seem to have settled with his followers. The annals of Ulster's record for the year 875 includes the notice that 'Oistín son of Amlaíb, king of the Norsemen, was deceitfully killed by Albann' (*Ann. Ulster*, s.a. 874). Albann was almost certainly Hálfdan, his victim the son of Óláf the White, who had partnered Hálfdan's brother Ívarr in widespread campaigning in Ireland in the 850s and early 860s. Hálfdan may, therefore, have been attempting to reclaim the inheritance of his brother, who had died in Ireland in 873. If so, the killing of Oistín (Eysteinn) was not decisive. Hálfdan may have returned to Northumbria to complete the settlement of his warriors, but he appeared again in Ireland in 877. The annals of Ulster record a skirmish at Strangford Lough in that year, between the *Finngenti* and the *Dubgennti*, meaning literally the 'Fair Heathens' and the 'Dark Heathens', and referring to the Norwegians and the Danes respectively. Hálfdan, the king of the Danes, was slain there.

MARIOS COSTAMBEYS

**Sources** *ASC*, s.a. 871, 876 • *Ann. Ulster* • A. P. Smyth, *Scandinavian kings in the British Isles, 850–880* (1977) • F. M. Stenton, *Anglo-Saxon England*, 3rd edn (1971) • *Alfred the Great: Asser's Life of King Alfred and other contemporary sources*, ed. and trans. S. Keynes and M. Lapidge (1983)

**Halford, Frank Bernard** (1894–1955), aero-engine designer, was born in Nottingham on 7 March 1894, the son of Harry Baker Halford, estate agent, surveyor, and sometime sheriff of Nottingham, and his wife, Ethel Grundy. He was educated at Felsted School and Nottingham University College; he emerged without academic qualifications, yet for forty years he was one of the world's great aircraft engine designers. At the age of nineteen he learnt to fly at Brooklands and became an instructor at the Bristol School of Flying. Early in 1914 he entered the aeronautical inspection directorate of the War Office as an engine examiner: there he was able to study aero-engines, which became his lifelong interest.

Halford joined the Royal Flying Corps on the outbreak of war in 1914, but was recalled from France in 1915 to redesign the Beardmore Company's Austro-Daimler engine to give greater power. It was used extensively in the DH 4 aeroplane, one of the outstanding bombers of the time. Later, in production form known as the Puma, it was recognized as a significant contribution to engine progress by a young man still in his early twenties. At this time he came to know the designer Geoffrey De Havilland.

In 1916 Halford met Harry Ricardo, a brilliant engine designer, from whom he gained much experience. At the close of the war he joined Ricardo and spent two and a half years in the United States negotiating the licensing agreements for Ricardo's patents, including those for superchargers, returning to England to help in the development of the Ricardo–Triumph motorcycle engine, which won many racing records in 1921–2. He designed the Halford engine, which raced at Brooklands about this time at 108 m.p.h. Halford also raced in the Isle of Man, riding his own machine. He designed a small short-stroke, high-r.p.m. auto engine, later the intellectual basis of the Sabre aero-engine.

In 1923 Halford became a designer, working on his own with one assistant, J. L. P. Brodie, who was to remain with him all Halford's life. In 1924–7 Halford worked for the Aircraft Disposal Company to modernize the large number of wartime aero-engines. Halford's foresight was quite exceptional. From the company's engine, the Airdisco, he produced the 60 hp Cirrus engine for the De Havilland light aeroplane, the Moth. Flown in February 1925, the Moth was the first practical private aeroplane; its production proved to be a turning point in Halford's career and a significant milestone in British aircraft and engine progress. Halford had seized his opportunities brilliantly, making full use of obsolete war material. It was rightly declared that he had a feeling for engines comparable with that of a stock farmer for animals, bringing to his aid an intuitive talent which years of engineering training might not have provided. The Cirrus engine was remarkable for its silence; it made the Moth one of the quietest aircraft in flight. Both the engine and the plane heralded a revolution in flying, and became in demand all over the world. Halford had that genius for basic engine design which enabled increasing power to be obtained with little modification.

In 1928 Halford produced the Gipsy engine, following the demand for still more power for light aircraft; in various modifications it reached such power and reliability that light aeroplanes made aeronautical history on the long air routes—England to Australia, to South Africa, and the crossing of the north and south Atlantic—remarkable tributes to the reliability of the Halford engines. In its inverted form the Gipsy powered the De Havilland Comet aeroplane in 1934 to win the England–Australia race, for which, in the following year, Halford was awarded the silver medal of the Royal Aeronautical Society. In 1939 a Gipsy engine energized a 50 foot diameter alternator coil which was fitted under the fuselage of the Wellington bomber to destroy the magnetic mines sown round the British coasts by Germany in the Second World War. The Gipsy was still in use in the sixties and the Cirrus in the fifties.

Halford became responsible for the designs of the Rapier and Sabre series of engines for the Napier Company, of which he became the technical director in 1935. The Rapier, a 16-cylinder engine of 400 horsepower, was fitted to a number of aircraft, including the seaplane part of the Mayo Composite, the first aeroplane to fly the Atlantic from east to west carrying a commercial load. From

1940 the Sabre, with 24 cylinders, at the time the most powerful piston engine in operation in the air, developing 3000 horsepower, was fitted to Hawker Typhoons. From 1941 to 1943 Halford was developing De Havilland propellers.

In 1941, at the request of the British government, Halford entered the field of jet propulsion. He followed closely Frank Whittle's pioneer work and in just 295 days he designed the Goblin, with a 3000 lb thrust, for the Gloster Meteor, the first British jet aircraft to enter RAF service. A more powerful version of the Goblin, the Ghost, was designed in 1945 and fitted to the Vampire to fly at the then record height of 59,446 feet in 1948. From 1941 Halford also served on the highly secret committee advising the ministers of aircraft production on engine, aircraft, and other aviation problems.

In 1935 Halford had become the technical director of the Napier engine company, a position he relinquished in 1944 to become the technical director of the newly formed De Havilland Engine Company. In the following year he was appointed a director of the parent De Havilland Aircraft Company.

At the end of the war, Halford was leading a powerful engine design team. He never hesitated to give those he led full credit for their share in engine developments and his team led the way in developing the ever-increasing jet propulsion power. In 1953 appeared the Gyron, giving a thrust of 15,000 lb, doubled a few years later. Much of the development carried out after his death was due to his guidance for supersonic flight. The Sprite rocket motor and the larger Spectre only became known a few days after his death, when the veil of secrecy was raised.

In 1927 Halford was elected a fellow of the Royal Aeronautical Society; he was its president in 1951–2, and in addition to its silver medal, received its gold medal in 1950. In 1946 he read a paper on jet propulsion before the Royal Society of Arts, for which he was awarded its silver medal. In 1948 he was appointed CBE.

In 1920 he married Monica Bevan, of Hove; they had a daughter. The marriage was dissolved in 1932. In 1939 he married Marjorie Moore. He died on 16 April 1955 at his home, Monkbarns, Sandy Lane, Northwood, Middlesex.

J. L. PRITCHARD, *rev.* ROBIN HIGHAM

**Sources** *The Times* (22 April 1955) • R. Higham and P. Masefield, 'Halford, Frank Bernard', *DBB* • *The Aeroplane* (22 April 1955) • *Flight* (22 April 1955) • F. R. Banks, *I kept no diary: 60 years with marine diesels, automobile and aero engines* (1978) • A. J. Jackson, *De Havilland aircraft since 1909* (1978) • H. Smith, *Aircraft piston engines* (1986) • C. M. Sharp, *DH: a history of De Havilland*, rev. edn (1982) • C. H. Wilson and W. Reader, *Men and machines: a history of D. Napier and Son, Engineers, Ltd, 1808–1958* (1958) • d. cert. • D. R. Taylor, *Boxkite to jet: the remarkable career of Frank B. Halford* (1999)

**Likenesses** F. Eastman, print, 1957, Royal Air Force Museum, Hendon • photograph, repro. in J. P. Brodie, *Journal of the Royal Aeronautical Society*, 63/580 (April 1859), 193 • photograph, British Aerospace Aircraft Group, Hatfield • photographs, repro. in D. R. Taylor, *Boxkite to jet* (1999)

**Wealth at death** £153,866 2s. 11d.: probate, 4 July 1955, *CGPLA Eng. & Wales*

**Halford** [*formerly* Hyam], **Frederic Michael** (1844–1914), angler and writer on fly-fishing, was born at Spring Hill, Birmingham, on 13 April 1844, one of the five children of Samuel Hyam, clothier, and his wife, Phoebe, *née* Levy. The Hyams were a Jewish family, originally from Germany, and were pioneers in the mass production of ready-made clothes. Frederic was educated at University College School, London, and entered the family business. On 10 January 1872 he married Florence St Losky (1849/50–1907), with whom he had one child, named Ernest.

Halford's main preoccupation from childhood lay in fishing. At first he pursued the coarse fish and trout of the Thames, and even tried sea-fishing. But increasingly he became fascinated with fly-fishing. Beginning on the River Wandle—then a notable trout stream, but long since engulfed by the growth of Greater London—he migrated in 1877 to the River Test in Hampshire. By this time he had changed his name to Halford, as had the other members of the family firm.

Halford was to spend the rest of his life fishing and writing about the famous and exclusive chalk streams of southern England. In the course of the next decade his name came to be associated with the cult of the dry fly. Halford did not invent dry-fly-fishing: it had been practised for some years in several parts of England. But techniques were still primitive and haphazard, equipment was defective, and there was little guidance in books. It was Halford's achievement to pull together the many practices and ideas, to systematize them, and to add a number of new elements.

It was fortunate for Halford that his arrival in Hampshire coincided with great changes in fly-fishing. Anglers were becoming more numerous, and it was no longer so easy to catch trout by the older and cruder methods worked out in earlier centuries. New technology was at hand: split-cane rods of great power and durability were being developed, and the new heavy oil-dressed silk lines enabled anglers to be independent of the wind. Also, membership of the Houghton Fly-Fishing Club gave Halford access to the help and advice of a remarkable group of forward-thinking men. These included Francis Francis, the angling editor of *The Field* and author of several fishing books; H. S. Hall, developer of the eyed hook; and, most importantly, George Selwyn Marryat, the most skilful fly-fisherman of his generation. Halford attached himself to Marryat, and soon proposed a joint collaboration from which a book or books might result. Strangely, although willing to give generous help, Marryat declined to couple his name with Halford's in any publication, or indeed to publish anything substantial himself, thus giving rise to one of the unsolved mysteries of fly-fishing history.

Altogether Halford wrote seven books, as well as numerous pieces for *The Field* under the pseudonym of Detached Badger, but his best work is in the first two books: *Floating Flies and How to Dress Them* (1886), a monograph rationalizing the dressings of flies already available, and *Dry-Fly Fishing in Theory and Practice* (1889), a book of wider scope which describes the methods of the chalk-stream angler.

In 1889 Halford withdrew from the family business, having accumulated enough capital to live comfortably, and resolved to devote the rest of his life to the solution of fly-fishing problems. Ironically, his most original work had now been done. In 1893, with three colleagues, he rented a stretch of the River Kennet at Ramsbury, Wiltshire, where his ideas on river management were tested. The experiment was not satisfactory and was abandoned in 1896, although Halford derived another book from it: *Making a Fishery* (1895). In 1897 he published *Dry Fly Entomology*, a book not regarded then or now as of much practical use to anglers. In 1905 he secured his own piece of fishing, at Mottisfont, on the lower Test. Here he lived for a large part of each trout season, engaged a keeper, fished, and entertained his friends. His autobiography had been published in 1903, and two more books followed: *Modern Development of the Dry Fly* (1910) and *The Dry-Fly Man's Handbook* (1913). The former is Halford's final statement on artificial flies, a retreat into a super-purist position of 'exact imitation'. The latter was (according to Halford) intended to present the latest information on tackle, tactics, entomology, and fishery management, but it may really have been written in part as a riposte to G. E. M. Skues's forward-looking book *Minor Tactics of the Chalk Stream* (1910). Skues's view was that the dry-fly-only code had become too rigid, and that there was a place on chalk streams for the sunk fly, a view which challenged Halford's most cherished beliefs.

Halford died rather suddenly of pneumonia on 5 March 1914 while returning on ship from his customary winter retreat in north Africa. The funeral was at Willesden Jewish cemetery on 8 March. His reputation survived for some years, then suffered an eclipse. In recent years there has emerged a more just appreciation of his crucial role in establishing a major part of the modern system of chalk-stream practice. TONY HAYTER

**Sources** F. M. Halford, *An angler's autobiography* (1903) • F. M. Halford, 'Angling diaries', 6 vols. 1879–1913, priv. coll. • scrapbook of obituaries, priv. coll. • scrapbook of reviews and notices of Halford's books, priv. coll. • W. Senior, 'Halford and his contemporaries', *Lines in pleasant places* [1920] • G. E. M. Skues, *Salmon and Trout Magazine*, 54 (Jan 1929) • J. W. Hills, *A history of fly-fishing for trout* (1921) • b. cert. • d. cert. [Florence Halford] • *WW* • *Daily Telegraph* (7 March 1914) • *The Times* (9 March 1914) • T. Hayter, *F. M. Halford and the dry-fly revolution* (2002)

**Archives** priv. coll., MSS | Fly Fishers' Club, 69 Brook Street, London, photographs and memorabilia

**Likenesses** J. H. Amshewitz, portrait, 1907, priv. coll. • photographs, Fly Fishers' Club Library, 69 Brook Street, London

**Halford** [*formerly* Vaughan], **Sir Henry**, **first baronet** (**1766–1844**), physician, born at Leicester on 2 October 1766, was the second son of James Vaughan, a successful physician of Leicester, and Hester, daughter of John Smalley (who had married a daughter of Sir Richard Halford). James Vaughan devoted his whole income to educating his seven sons, of whom Sir John *Vaughan (1769–1839) became baron of the exchequer, Peter Vaughan (*d.* 1825) became warden of Merton College, Oxford, and Sir Charles Richard *Vaughan (1774–1849), became a diplomatist. The sixth son, Edward Thomas Vaughan (1772–1829), was father of Charles John *Vaughan (1816–1897), headmaster, and dean of Llandaff. Henry was educated at Rugby School before matriculating in 1781 at Christ

**Sir Henry Halford, first baronet (1766–1844)**, by Sir Thomas Lawrence, *c.*1825

Church, Oxford, where he graduated BA in 1788, MB in 1790, and DM in 1791.

After studying some time at Edinburgh, Vaughan settled in London, having borrowed £1000 on his own security. His good manners and learning soon made him friends, and he was elected physician to the Middlesex Hospital in 1793, and fellow of the Royal College of Physicians in 1794, having been appointed physician-extraordinary to George III in the previous year. On 31 March 1796 he married Elizabeth Barbara (*d.* 1833), the third daughter of Lord St John of Bletso, and by 1800 his practice had so greatly increased that he gave up his hospital appointment. He inherited a large property on the death of Lady Denbigh, widow of his mother's cousin Sir Charles Halford, seventh baronet, and consequently changed his name from Vaughan to Halford by act of parliament in 1809. George III, who had a strong liking for him, created him a baronet in the same year, and he subsequently attended George IV, William IV, and Queen Victoria. He became FRS in 1810 as a reward for being a 'zealous promoter of the Objects of Science' (Lawrence, 281).

For many years after Matthew Baillie's death Halford was indisputably at the head of the medical profession in London. He was president of the Royal College of Physicians from 1820 until his death, an unbroken tenure which was by no means favourable to reform and progress, though he was largely instrumental in securing the transfer of the college in 1825 from Warwick Lane to Pall Mall East. He was made KCH on this occasion and GCH by William IV. However, he opposed the physical examination of patients, knew little of pathology, and disliked innovation. As stated in *The Lancet*: 'He is all tact and nothing else. He is ignorant of the modern discoveries in pathology and never employs the modern instruments of diagnosis; he has never written a line that is worthy of perusal on any scientific subject' (Whitefield, 64). Halford's success stemmed mainly from his elegant manners and social connections. His chief publications were first given as addresses to the Royal College of Physicians, on subjects such as 'The climacteric disease', 'Tic douloureux', 'Shakspeare's test of insanity' (*Hamlet*, III.iv), 'The influence of some of the diseases of the body of the mind', 'Gout', and 'The deaths of some illustrious persons of antiquity'.

Halford is described by J. F. Clarke in his *Autobiographical Recollections* as vain, cringing to superiors, and haughty to inferiors. James Wardrop, surgeon to George IV, termed him 'the eel-backed baronet'. Lord Grey considered him to be 'the damndest conceited fellow in the world' (Whitefield, 64). Some charges of unprofessional conduct are made against him by Clarke, who further states that when Charles I's coffin was opened in 1813 Halford obtained a portion of the fourth cervical vertebra, which had been cut through by the axe, and used to show it at his dinner table as a curiosity. This may be held to be confirmed by Halford's minute description of this bone in his *Account of what Appeared on Opening the Coffin of King Charles I* (1813).

Halford died at his house in Curzon Street, Mayfair, on 9 March 1844, and was buried in the parish church of Wistow, Leicestershire, where a monument was erected to his memory. He left one son, Henry (1797–1868), who succeeded to the title, and one daughter.

G. T. Bettany, *rev.* Michael Bevan

**Sources** Munk, *Roll* • Foster, *Alum. Oxon.* • S. C. Lawrence, *Charitable knowledge: hospital pupils and practitioners in eighteenth-century London* (1996) • J. F. Clarke, *Autobiographical recollections of the medical profession* (1874) • Burke, *Peerage* (1857) • A. Whitefield, 'The gentle queen', *Journal of the Royal College of Physicians of London*, 20 (1986), 63–6

**Archives** Bucks. RLSS • Leics. RO, extensive corresp. and papers • LPL, letters and papers relating to George III • RCP Lond., notes on lectures and cases, account and appointment books | All Souls Oxf., letters to Sir C. R. Vaughan • BL, corresp. with Sir Robert Peel, Add. MSS 40309–40509 • CUL, letters and reports to Spencer Perceval • Niedersächsisches Hauptstaatsarchiv Hannover, Hanover, letters to duke of Cumberland

**Likenesses** W. Beechy, oils, 1811, NPG • T. Lawrence, oils, *c.*1825, RCP Lond. [*see illus.*] • F. Chantrey, marble bust, 1826, RCP Lond. • C. Turner, mezzotint, pubd 1830 (after T. Lawrence), BM • F. Chantrey, model (for his marble bust, 1826), AM Oxf. • J. Cochran, stipple (after H. Room), BM, NPG, Wellcome L.; repro. in T. J. Pettigrew, *Medical portrait gallery: biographical memoirs of the most celebrated physicians, surgeons … who have contributed to the advancement of medical science* (1838–40) • J. Cochran, two coloured engravings (after H. Room), Wellcome L.

**Halford, Sir Henry St John, third baronet** (1828–1897), rifleman, born at Maidwell, Northamptonshire, on 9 August 1828, was the son of Sir Henry Halford, second baronet (1797–1868), MP for South Leicestershire from 1832 to 1857, and his wife, Barbara (*d.* 1869), daughter of his uncle Sir John Vaughan (1769–1839). The physician Sir Henry *Halford, first baronet, was his grandfather. Henry St John Halford was educated at Market Bosworth grammar school from 1835 and then Eton College from 1840 to 1845. He matriculated as a commoner of Merton College, Oxford, on 26 November 1846, and graduated BA in 1849. In 1853 he married Elizabeth Ursula, daughter of John Bagshawe. At his father's death on 22 May 1868 he succeeded to the baronetcy, thereafter living at the family seat, Wistow Hall, Leicestershire.

Halford took an active part in the public business of his county, Leicestershire. In 1872 he held the office of high sheriff. In 1876 he was elected deputy chairman of quarter sessions, and in 1883 chairman. This office he held until his death. On the formation of the Leicestershire county council in 1889 he was elected chairman, and he held the office until 1893, when ill health compelled him to resign. Professedly a 'tory' rather than a Conservative, he rejected invitations to stand for parliament.

It was, however, in connection with rifle-shooting and the volunteer movement that Sir Henry was best known. At the beginning of the movement in 1860 he took command of a company of the Leicestershire Volunteers. In 1862 he became colonel of the battalion but in 1891 reverted to the position of honorary colonel. In 1886 he received the order of CB.

In the first rifle match between England and Scotland for the Elcho shield in 1862, Sir Henry shot for England, and made the highest score, as he did again in 1872. In all, he shot for the Elcho shield twenty times up to 1893. His principal individual successes at the National Rifle Association meetings at Wimbledon and Bisley were the Albert prize in 1862 and 1893, the Duke of Cambridge prize and the Association cup in 1871, the Dudley in 1893, and the Cambridge long-range cup in 1864, using the newly invented Metford rifle.

In 1877 Sir Henry acted as captain of a team of eight riflemen chosen from England, Ireland, and Scotland who went to the United States to shoot a match at long distances against eight representative American marksmen. The latter won. In 1882 and 1883 he led teams of twelve British volunteers in matches with service rifles against the national guard of America. The British won, thanks to their adoption of Metford rifles and conversion to the American Fulton back position for shooting. Halford now used it invariably; he also found he could only achieve good scores with a pipe in his mouth.

In 1880 Halford was appointed a member of the government small arms committee. The introduction of the Lee-Metford rifle as the British service arm was due to the report of that committee, Halford having substantially assisted its inventor, William Ellis Metford. Halford had great knowledge, both theoretical and practical, of gunnery and gunmaking, and maintained a sophisticated ordnance workshop at Wistow Hall. In 1888 he published *The Art of Shooting with the Rifle* (reprinted 1984, 1990).

Halford died at Wistow Hall on 4 January 1897 after a long illness—despite heart trouble, he had insisted on shooting (and had won) at Cambridge the previous spring. He was buried at Newton Harcourt. His wife survived him but he died childless, and was succeeded to the baronetcy by his brother the Revd John Frederick Halford. The baronetcy became extinct at his brother's death less than four months later. The National Rifle Association instituted a memorial challenge cup for Sir Henry Halford.

J. A. DOYLE, *rev.* JULIAN LOCK

**Sources** W. J. Freer, 'Memoir', *Transactions of the Leicestershire Architectural and Archaeological Society*, 8 (1899), 291–303 • *The Times* (5 Jan 1897) • Boase, *Mod. Eng. biog.* • S. Cornfield, *The Queen's Prize: the story of the National Rifle Association* (1987) • Burke, *Peerage* • E. Lodge, *Peerage, baronetage, knightage and companionage of the British empire*, 81st edn, 3 vols. (1912) • *CGPLA Eng. & Wales* (1897) • *WWW*, 1897–1915 [Rev. Sir John Frederick Halford]
**Archives** Leics. RO, Halford family and estate MSS
**Likenesses** J. Collier, oils, 1897, Leicester town hall • photograph (with wife), repro. in Cornfield, *Queen's Prize*, following p. 32 • portrait, repro. in *Strand Magazine* (Nov 1893), 496, 531–42 • portrait, repro. in *ILN* (12 April 1884), 349 • portrait, repro. in *ILN* (9 Jan 1897), 42
**Wealth at death** £6938 17*s.* 6*d.*: probate, 4 Aug 1897, *CGPLA Eng. & Wales*

**Halfpenny, Joseph** (1748–1811), topographical engraver and watercolour painter, was born on 9 October 1748 at Bishopthorpe, Yorkshire, where his father, Thomas Halfpenny, was gardener to the archbishop. He was apprenticed to a house-painter in York, where he lived in the parish of St Michael-le-Belfrey by the minster. By 1786 he had established himself as a drawing-master, and his practical skills and antiquarian knowledge commended him to John Carr, the architect, who employed him as clerk of works during the restoration of the minster in the early 1790s. Halfpenny was responsible for the sensitive repair of many of the decorative features in the minster, and he made careful drawings of much of the medieval detail. These drawings, which were often taken from the scaffolding erected for the restoration, were engraved by him and formed the basis of his *Gothic Ornaments in the Cathedral Church of York*, which he published in twenty parts to subscribers between 1795 and 1800. The series, which comprised 175 details of ornament and four general views of the interior and chapter house, established his reputation and has subsequently been used as an important source for details lost or damaged by the minster fire of 1829. The engravings were reprinted in a single volume in 1807, and a second edition was published in 1831 shortly after the fire. A number of the original drawings and watercolours survive in the York City Art Gallery, including one, which was not engraved for publication, showing the scaffolding and restoration work in progress.

Halfpenny went on to record other medieval details in York buildings and published another volume of engravings in 1807, *Fragmenta vetusta, or, The Remains of Ancient Buildings in York*, in which he recorded a number of the parish churches as well as secular monuments such as the walls and bars of the city and its guildhall. The high quality of his work led to employment as an engraver for other architectural writers. Five further views of York churches were published posthumously by his daughters in 1816 and 1817, and his work continues to be a valuable source for architectural historians. Halfpenny was also a competent watercolour painter who produced a number of views of the Yorkshire dales and of the scenery of the Lake District, following sketching tours undertaken in the early 1790s, and some of these survive in the collection at York City Art Gallery, as well as single items in London, at the British and the Victoria and Albert museums. He married Jane Atkinson of Bishopthorpe, who may have been a member of the family of builder-architects associated with Carr, on 24 March 1772, and they had two daughters. After her death he married Frances-Maria Barrett on 12 July 1786, with whom he lived in Gillygate, just beyond the city walls, until his death there on 11 July 1811, when his profession was given as drawing-master. He was buried two days later in St Olave's churchyard, close to the abbey ruins which he had recorded.

BERTHA PORTER, *rev.* WILLIAM JOSEPH SHEILS

**Sources** J. Halfpenny, *Gothic ornaments in the cathedral church of York* (1795–1800) • J. Halfpenny, *Fragmenta vetusta, or, The remains of ancient buildings in York* (1807) • R. Green, H. Murray, and others, *York through the eyes of the artist* (1990) • F. Mee and B. M. Wilson, *The medieval parish churches of York: the pictorial evidence* (1998) • *Bishopthorpe parish registers*, Yorkshire Parish Register Society, 150 (1986) • parish registers, St Olave, York • W. Hargrove, *History of York* (1818)
**Archives** Yale U., Beinecke L., letters to Richard Cough relating to his plan to publish *Fragmenta vetusta*

**Halfpenny, William** [*pseud.* Michael Hoare] (*d.* 1755), architect and writer on architecture, was the author of *The Builder's Pocket-Companion* (1728), which he published under the pseudonym Michael Hoare. The identity of his alias was revealed in Batty Langley's *Ancient Masonry* (1736). Although Halfpenny's origins remain obscure, his earliest recorded work, an unexecuted design of 1723 for Holy Trinity Church, Leeds, and the dedication of his first book, *Practical Architecture* (1724), to Thomas Frankland, eldest son of Sir Thomas Frankland of Thirsk, Yorkshire, suggest that he was a Yorkshireman, possibly a kinsman of Nicholas Halfpenny, gardener and mathematician.

By 1725 Halfpenny was established as a carpenter in Richmond in Surrey, where he found numerous local craftsmen, including several carpenters to Frederick, prince of Wales, to subscribe to his second book, *The Art of Sound Building* (1725). But he never found as much encouragement for his architectural designs as he did for his architectural books. He was in the Bristol area in search of work in 1731, when he published *Perspective Made Easy*, demonstrated by views of Bristol and Bath and including an important prospect of the buildings on the north side of Queen's Square, Bath, before they were demolished. From there he went to Ireland, where he built a horse barracks at Hillsborough, co. Down, for the first Viscount Hillsborough in 1732. However, he failed to raise any interest in his scheme of 1739 for a classical church to replace Waterford Cathedral.

On returning to Bristol, Halfpenny submitted designs for the new exchange in 1739–40 and for adding wings to the infirmary in 1742, neither of which was accepted. John Cossins of Redland Court, Bristol, employed him in 1742 to supervise the completion of Redland Chapel, which was probably designed by the architect of Cossins's house, John Strahan, who had recently died: the altarpiece, made in 1742, is all that is known to have been designed by Halfpenny himself. His only other documented works are the Coopers' Hall, King Street, Bristol, erected in 1743–4, and a Chinese bridge at Croome Court, Worcestershire, which he illustrated in his last book, *Improvements in Architecture and Carpentry* (1754).

Several buildings in Bristol and south Gloucestershire have been attributed to Halfpenny on the basis of stylistic affinities with his popular pattern book designs: Clifton Court, Clifton Green, Bristol, for Martha Dandervall (*c.*1742–3); 40 Prince Street, Bristol (1740; dem.), and the assembly room, Prince Street, Bristol (1754–5; dem.); Stout's Hill, Uley, Gloucestershire, for Timothy Gyde, and the orangery at Frampton Court, Gloucestershire for Richard Clutterbuck (both *c.*1750), in the Gothic style; and Upton House, Tetbury, Gloucestershire, for Thomas Cripps (1752).

It should be noted, however, that by 1748 Halfpenny had moved from Bristol to London, where he published *A Perspective View of the Sunk Pier and the Two Adjoining Arches at Westminster* (one folio sheet, 1748)—proposing a remedy for the failure—and *Arithmetic and Measurement* (1748), his first new book for seventeen years. The two distinct periods of Halfpenny's publishing activity are focused on quite different aspects of building practice. Convenient tables of the proportions of the orders converted from modules to feet and inches and easy methods of drawing the geometry of arches and buildings in perspective were dispensed to ordinary builders in *Practical Architecture* (1724), *The Art of Sound Building* (1725) and its popular octavo version, entitled *The Builder's Pocket-Companion* (1728), *Magnum in parvo* (1728), and *Perspective Made Easy* (1731). These quasi-mathematical subjects, though now rarely associated with Halfpenny's name, were a deep-seated interest of his which persisted into the 1750s in *Arithmetic and Measurement* (1748), *Andrea Palladio's First Book of Architecture* (1751)—a misleadingly titled treatise on perspective which was deceptively reissued in 1757 as the work of J. Miller, esquire—and *Geometry, Theoretical and Practical* (1752).

The main matter of Halfpenny's prolific outpouring after 1748 consists of designs for small country houses, parsonages, farmhouses, and garden ornaments in the Chinese, Gothic, and rustic styles. These eminently affordable pattern books, complete with dimensions and estimates, were expressly intended to enable 'workmen at a distance from the Metropolis' (*Chinese and Gothic Architecture Properly Ornamented*, 1752, preface) to erect all manner of rural buildings in a wide variety of materials and in all the latest fashions at little cost. Though often bordering on the ridiculous, his pattern books for chinoiserie in the form of garden furniture, temples, bridges, and other follies were the first of their kind and were enormously successful; far more so than his more ambitious houses in a 'decorated' Vanbrughian or bastardized Palladian style published in *The New and Compleat System of Architecture* (1749). The latter was his first pattern book; the others include: *Rural Architecture in the Chinese Taste* (1752, 1755), *Twelve Beautiful Designs for Farm-Houses* (1750, 1759, 1774), *Useful Architecture* (1752, 1755, 1760), and *The Country Gentleman's Pocket Companion* (1753, 1756). *The Modern Builder's Assistant* (1757), containing designs by Halfpenny, Robert Morris, and Thomas Lightoler, is a compilation of unused plates brought together by the publisher Robert Sayer.

Often working in collaboration with his son John, Halfpenny's productivity in the last six years of his life was remarkable. Not a year passed without a new book or a new edition of an earlier one, occasionally under a new title. Although his whimsical Chinese and Gothic inventions earned him a name, they evidently did not earn him a fortune: he died in debt in 1755. EILEEN HARRIS

**Sources** Colvin, *Archs.*, 446–8 · E. Harris and N. Savage, *British architectural books and writers, 1556–1785* (1990), 218–28 · admon, PRO, PROB 6/131, fol. 195*v*

**Wealth at death** in debt at death

**Halhed, Nathaniel Brassey** (1751–1830), orientalist, was born on 25 May 1751 in the City of London and baptized in St Peter-le-Poer, the first of the five children of William Halhed (1722–1786), a merchant, and his first wife, Frances (1722–1783), daughter of the late John Caswall, MP for Leominster. His father, from a merchant family of Banbury, conducted business in Angel Court, Throgmorton Street, and resided in Clapham for most of his career, and was a director of the Bank of England from 1767. Halhed (pronounced Hal-ed) was educated at Harrow School, where he distinguished himself in Greek and Latin composition. The first in his family to enter university, he matriculated at Christ Church, Oxford. A brilliant but inconsistent student who boasted of his neglect of hall and chapel, he engaged with his Harrow friend the future playwright Richard Brinsley Sheridan in literary schemes which are the subject of an extensive correspondence. They led to an anonymous publication of bawdy imitations, billed as translations, of *The Love Letters of Aristaenetus* (preface signed H[alhed] S[heridan], 1771; further edns, 1773; repr. in Kelly, *Erotica*, 1854, 1883, 431–96) and an unpublished farce, 'Jupiter', renamed 'Ixion' (in Halhed's hand with corrections by Sheridan, preserved as Sheridan's; BL, Add. MS 25935). This partnership, in which Halhed provided groundwork which Sheridan edited, ended in 1771—with some tension over their rival affections for Elizabeth Linley, whom Sheridan later married—when William Halhed withdrew his spendthrift, debauched son from Oxford and procured him an East India Company writership.

Halhed's fame rests on the productions of the years 1772–8, which he spent in Bengal, where his superior education and knowledge of Persian, acquired in Oxford at the example of his friend William Jones and perfected in Cossimbazar, attracted the governor's notice. Warren Hastings chose him to translate the crowning piece of his orientalist policy, a code of laws commissioned from a committee of pandits which was to serve as a basis for the administration of civil justice to Hindus. Halhed's translation of a Persian abstract of the Sanskrit text was rushed to London in instalments to stave off the feared imposition of British laws on the company's Indian subjects, and, at Hastings's request, was published by the East India Company to much attention (*A Code of Gentoo Laws*, 1776; further edns, 1777, 1781; French and German trans., 1778). Its learned preface describing Sanskrit, claiming a high antiquity for Hindu civilization, and challenging biblical chronology elicited enthusiasm with some, but condemnation from others such as the Revd George Costard, whose published *Letter* (1778) Halhed answered on his passage home in an unpublished letter (1779) (Rocher, *Orientalism*, 290–312). This reply was remarkable for its reasoned anticipation of Jones's famed declaration of the kinship of Sanskrit with Greek and Latin, which he probably shared with Jones. Halhed also produced the first English grammar of Bengali (1778; repr., 1969, 1980), modelled after Jones's Persian grammar, which Europeans culled for observations on Sanskrit and which is famous in Bengal for its first British use of Bengali fonts: Charles Wilkins, whom Halhed inspired to study Sanskrit, and blacksmith Panchanan cut the fonts at Hastings's request, founding what became the East India Company Press in Bengal. These achievements earned Halhed the governor's favour, and hostility from his antagonists. When his appointment as commissary-general was rescinded, he returned home on grounds of ill health, bringing a Bengal-born Dutch wife, (Helena) Louisa Ribaut (*bap.* 1757, *d.* 1831), stepdaughter of J. M. Ross, Dutch director for Bengal, through whom Halhed and others remitted money to Europe.

In London, Halhed became a pamphleteer with an anonymous *Narrative* defending Hastings's Maratha policy (1779) and letters under the pseudonym Detector opposing the reports of the House of Commons select committee, Fox's East India Bill, and Burke's charges against Hastings (1782–3). After his return to Bengal in 1784 with a coveted appointment to the first vacancy on the committee of revenue, he joined Hastings in Benares. Hastings was preparing to leave India, but obtained for Halhed a London agency for the nawab of Oudh. Though enthused by the *Bhagavad Gita*, which Wilkins was translating, he had no time for scholarship in the seven months of his second and last stay in India. Back in London, living grandly at 31 Harley Street, he was part of a group that helped Hastings respond to his accusers before the Commons, drafting the answer to the Benares charge, parts of which Hastings had to disown later in the trial before the Lords in which Halhed testified. A bitter opponent of the Foxites, Halhed became MP for Lymington in 1791 after withdrawing from a contest in Leicester, and published the truculent anonymous *Imitations of Some of the Epigrams of Martial* (1793–4). Lavish spending and losses in French *assignats* made him seek unsuccessfully another assignment in Bengal and forced a move to 17 Pall Mall.

Halhed's reputation was ruined when, in 1795, he published testimonies to the divine inspiration of self-proclaimed prophet Richard Brothers (collected in *The Whole of the Testimonies to the Authenticity of the Prophecies and Mission of Richard Brothers; Two Letters to Lord Loughborough*) and stood up in parliament to oppose Brothers's conviction as a criminal lunatic, in motions that failed to be seconded. In the rising Indophobia of the 1790s some blamed his enthusiasm on oriental mysticism, yet his manuscripts which the British Museum acquired in 1795–6 (BL, Add. MSS 5569–5662, some published by Hindley, 1807, 1809), one of which, on the Upanishads, he was preparing for publication, show that in the 1780s and 1790s he increasingly imposed on Hindu texts allegorical confirmations of the Bible, a practice he decried in the 1770s. Brothers's lack of education and incapacity to perpetrate textual fraud convinced him of the authenticity of prophecies he checked against the Bible, while bitterness with political events made the time appear ripe for the millennium. In 1804 he put like faith in the millenarian Joanna Southcott's prophecies, but, a recluse from 1796 to 1808, he limited himself to manuscript comparisons of Hindu, Graeco-Roman, and biblical texts. Only in 1814 did he release an opinion supporting her marriage when, shortly before her death, she announced herself pregnant with a divine child.

Want forced Halhed out of reclusion and ended his refusal to write. In 1809 he was appointed a civil secretary with the East India Company. Persian manuscripts in the company's library in the care of his old coadjutor Charles Wilkins prompted comments on the *Mahabharata* (now in the Asiatic Society, Calcutta) and Tipu Sultan's dreams of persisting gnostic character. His new residence at 20 Charles Street became a London *pied-à-terre* for Hastings, with whom he resumed a steady correspondence and exchange of verses. True to Hastings's orientalist policy, he penned in 1813 an unpublished paper opposing company chairman Charles Grant's proposal to send missionaries to India. Increasing deafness and Hastings's death prompted his retirement in 1819. A claim against his French banker in 1814 may have succeeded, since his estate was valued at £18,000 when he died, childless and intestate, at his home in West Square, Southwark, on 18 February 1830. He was buried in the family tomb in the churchyard of St Peter's Church, Petersham, Surrey.

Path-breaking in the 1770s, Halhed's scholarship was overtaken by new paradigms after Wilkins unlocked Sanskrit in 1785, while, missing in Britain the instruction of Indian pandits and the intellectual ferment of Jones's Asiatic Society, Halhed remained dependent on Persian intermediaries. His later allegorical interpretations harked back to the 1760s. He was prickly in character, and recklessly supportive of those (like Hastings and Brothers) in whose purposes he believed. Likenesses at twenty, at forty-four, and in late life show him sharp-featured, prematurely bald, and of slight build. ROSANE ROCHER

**Sources** R. Rocher, *Orientalism, poetry and the millennium: the checkered life of Nathaniel Brassey Halhed, 1751–1830* (1983) • 'Sketch of the life of N. B. Halhed', *Register of the Times*, 4 (1795), 330 • 'Warren Hastings in slippers: unpublished letters of Warren Hastings', ed. [J. Grant], *Calcutta Review*, 26 (1856), 59–141 • priv. coll. • R. Rocher, 'Nathaniel Brassey Halhed, Sir William Jones, and comparative Indo-European linguistics', *Recherches de linguistique: hommages à Maurice Leroy*, ed. J. Bingen and others (1980), 173–80 • R. Rocher, 'Nathaniel Brassey Halhed's collection of oriental manuscripts', *Annals of Oriental Research*, Silver Jubilee vol. (1975), 1–10 • R. Rocher, 'Nathaniel Brassey Halhed on the Upaniṣads (1787)', *Annals of the*

*Bhandarkar Oriental Research Institute*, Diamond Jubilee vol. (1977–8), 279–89 • J. H. Hindley, ed., *Extracts, epitomes, and translations, from Asiatick authors* (1807) • [J. H. Hindley], ed. and trans., *Antient Indian literature* (1809) • W. K. Kelly, ed., *Erotica* (1854); repr. (1883) • Foster, *Alum. Oxon.* • *GM*, 1st ser., 56 (1786), 909 • *Ladies' Magazine*, 1 (1751), 112

**Archives** Asiatic Society, Calcutta, extracts, translations, etc. from the *Mahabharata*, Persian copy, MS E/48 • BL, 'Ixion', a play by Halhed, with corrections by Richard Brinsley Sheridan, Add. MS 25935 • BL, Oriental MSS, translations and notes, Add. MSS 5569–5662 • BL OIOC, 'Translation of a pootee or compilation of the ordinations of the pundits', MSS Eur.B.11–12 • priv. coll., poems and MSS | University of Minnesota, Minneapolis, Ames Library of South Asia, W. Hastings, MS 17

**Likenesses** portrait, 1771, repro. in W. F. Rae, *Sheridan: a biography* (1896) • White, stipple, pubd 1795 (after I. Cruikshank), BM, NPG; repro. in *Register of the Times*, 4 (1795) • N. B. Halhed?, self-portrait?, drawing, *c*.1815, priv. coll.

**Wealth at death** £18,000: administration, PRO, PROB 6/206, fol. 92

**Haliburton family** (*per. c*.1375–*c*.1500), nobility of Dirleton, enjoyed a brief period of power as servants to the Scottish crown, especially before 1450. The first prominent family member was **Sir Walter Haliburton** (*c*.1375–1446?), the eldest son of probably Sir John Haliburton (*fl.* 1378–1402) and his spouse, Margaret Cameron. Although Sir Walter had no known public career before his father's death, he was permitted to marry Isobel, daughter of Robert Stewart, duke of Albany (*d.* 1420), and widow of Alexander Leslie, earl of Ross (*d.* 1402), probably shortly after the latter's death. (The Walter Haliburton who *c*.1403 married Mary, daughter of Archibald, third earl of Douglas (*d.* 1400), and widow of David Stewart, duke of Rothesay (*d.* 1402), seems to have been a different man.) Despite this apparently advantageous marriage Haliburton made only sporadic appearances at court in the next thirty-five years (perhaps becoming more frequent as time passed). He was present at the battle of Long Hermiston Moor (14 February 1406) at which Sir David Fleming, a guardian of Prince James, heir to the throne, was killed. The evidence does not make it clear if he was a companion of Fleming or of James Douglas of Balvenie, who ambushed him.

A usually reliable contemporary chronicle states that Haliburton was knighted at the coronation of James I in May 1424, but he was a hostage in England for the ransom demanded for the king in 1424–5. It would seem significant that he is not styled as a knight in any other document until after the coronation of James II in March 1437. As Albany's son-in-law he was in fact unlikely to have found favour with James I, and advancement came only after the king's murder in 1437. He was created treasurer by June 1438, a post he held for about two years. This elevation reflects the power of a patron—probably Archibald, fifth earl of Douglas (*d.* 1439)—and undoubtedly also the depletion of the Scottish nobility following the deaths or forfeitures of many nobles in the previous fourteen years.

The Haliburton family held land in Edinburghshire, Berwickshire, Perthshire, and Angus, but the main estate became Dirleton in Haddingtonshire, where there was considerable building work in the fifteenth century on the very imposing castle (which may have caused the mortgaging of part of the estate). Sir Walter, whose income in 1424 was estimated at 800 merks, also founded Dirleton collegiate church. He died certainly after July 1444, and probably in late 1446. His spouse, Isobel, is thought to have been the mother of his four sons and one daughter, although he may have had at least one further son. One possible son of his, **Mark Haliburton** (*d. c*.1456), briefly entered the limelight *c*.1449 as a result of association with the eighth and ninth earls of Douglas. Although apparently a layman, Haliburton was secretary to the latter. He escaped at first the forfeiture of the earl and his associates in 1455 through a display of loyalty to James II, and began to develop a career at court, even being rewarded with land forfeited by Douglas; but for some unknown reason he was himself forfeited, and perhaps executed, *c*.1456.

It is possible that before his death Sir Walter Haliburton assumed (simultaneously with some other Scottish landed families) a peerage title, but the evidence is uncertain. It is more likely that it was his eldest son, **John Haliburton** (*c*.1405–*c*.1454), who became the first Lord Haliburton, shortly after his father's death. He was sheriff of Berwick by 1448, a post probably inherited from his father, whom he did not long outlive. He married Janet, daughter of William Seton and sister of George, Lord Seton (*d.* 1478). She was the mother of at least four of Haliburton's six sons. All but one—George, third lord (*c*.1435–1492)—of the next four lords Haliburton were short-lived and the family went into eclipse, appearances at court being confined to attendance at parliament. They had little authority independent of their principal patron, the earl of Douglas, and after 1455 the Haliburtons mainly confined themselves to local affairs.

Alan R. Borthwick

**Sources** J. M. Thomson and others, eds., *Registrum magni sigilli regum Scotorum / The register of the great seal of Scotland*, 11 vols. (1882–1914), vols. 1, 2 • G. Burnett and others, eds., *The exchequer rolls of Scotland*, 23 vols. (1878–1908) • *APS*, *1424–1567* • [T. Thomson] and others, eds., *The acts of the lords of council in civil causes, 1478–1503*, 3 vols. (1839–1993) • various collections of manuscript estate and other papers in archive offices and in private hands in Scotland and England • *CDS*, vol. 4 • *RotS*, vol. 2 • W. Bower, *Scotichronicon*, ed. D. E. R. Watt and others, new edn, 9 vols. (1987–98), vol. 8 • *Scots peerage*, vol. 4 • F. McGurk, ed., *Calendar of papal letters to Scotland of Benedict XIII of Avignon, 1394–1419*, Scottish History Society, 4th ser., 13 (1976) • Melrose charters, NA Scot., GD55/559 • M. Brown, *The Black Douglases: war and lordship in late medieval Scotland, 1300–1455* (1998) • A. Grant, 'Acts of lordship: the records of Archibald, fourth earl of Douglas', *Freedom and authority: historical and historiographical essays presented to Grant G. Simpson*, ed. T. Brotherstone and D. Ditchburn (2000) • *The 'Original chronicle' of Andrew of Wyntoun*, ed. F. J. Amours, 6 vols., STS, 1st ser., 50, 53–4, 56–7, 63 (1903–14) • S. I. Boardman, *The early Stewart kings: Robert II and Robert III, 1371–1406* (1996)

**Haliburton, Arthur Lawrence**, **Baron Haliburton** (**1832–1907**), civil servant, third son of Thomas Chandler *Haliburton (1796–1865) and Louisa (*d.* 1841), daughter of Captain Lawrence Neville, was born at Windsor, Nova Scotia, on 26 December 1832. He was educated at King's College there, from which he received in 1899 an honorary

DCL. He was called to the Nova Scotian bar in 1855, but a few months later he received a commission in the commissariat department of the British army, and during the later stages of the Crimean War he served as a civil commissary at the base in Turkey. After the Peace of Paris he was posted to the forces in Canada. In November 1859 he was appointed deputy assistant commissary-general, and transferred to the London headquarters.

In 1869 Haliburton was made assistant director of supplies and transports, resigning his commission in the army and formally entering the civil service. He consolidated and simplified the chaotic arrangements for the transport and travelling allowances of the army at home. In 1872 he was appointed deputy accountant-general in the military department of the government of India, which post he held until 1875. On returning to the War Office he was chairman of a committee which brought about decentralization and substantial economies there. In 1878 he was appointed director of supplies and transport, and he supervised the victualling of the army during eight campaigns, including the Nile expedition of 1884–5. Wolseley testified no army that he had been associated with was so well fed as the troops were then, in circumstances of great difficulty. Haliburton was made CB in February 1880 and KCB in August 1885. On the abolition of the office of civilian director of supplies and transports in 1887 he was placed temporarily on the retired list. After serving on several important public inquiries at home and abroad he became in May 1891 assistant under-secretary for war, and in 1895 permanent under-secretary, which office he held until his retirement by operation of the age limit in 1897. He was made GCB in June 1897, and in June 1898 Baron Haliburton of Windsor in the province of Nova Scotia.

In 1891 Haliburton represented the War Office on the Wantage committee on the terms and conditions of service in the army. His dissentient report contained a strong defence of the principle of the existing short-service system, and effectually neutralized the recommendations for modifying it on which the rest of the committee agreed. In December 1897, after his retirement from the War Office, he conducted a vigorous campaign in *The Times* against Arnold-Forster and others on short versus long service. His letters were reprinted in pamphlet form, as was another series contributed to *The Times* in 1901, 'Army administration in three centuries'. He attempted to explain to the public and to military critics the real nature of Cardwell's reforms and of the army reserve created by them. He was Conservative in politics, and in his later years became a convert to the principle of compulsory military service: a few weeks before his death he published in the *Nineteenth Century* a scheme for universal military training.

On 3 November 1877 Haliburton married, at Upper Norwood, Mariana Emily (1833–1919), daughter of Leo Schuster and widow of Sir William Dickason Clay, second baronet; they had no children. He died at Branksome Towers Hotel, Bournemouth, on 21 April 1907, and was buried on 26 April at Brompton cemetery. Haliburton was considered by his admirers the finest type of civil servant, uniting indefatigable industry with lucidity of expression and breadth of view; his opinion was highly regarded by some officers who were well versed in the problems of military administration.

J. B. Atlay, *rev.* M. G. M. Jones

**Sources** J. B. Atlay, *Lord Haliburton: a memoir of his public services* (1909) • Burke, *Peerage* • private information (1912) • GEC, *Peerage*
**Archives** BL, corresp. with Sir Henry Campbell-Bannerman, Add. MS 41218
**Wealth at death** £2600 15*s*. 6*d*.: probate, 8 May 1907, *CGPLA Eng. & Wales*

**Haliburton, George** (*c*.1616–1665), bishop of Dunkeld, was probably born in Glenisla, Forfarshire, the son of George Haliburton (*d*. *c*.1659), minister there, and his wife, Janet Ogilvie. He graduated MA at King's College, Aberdeen, in 1636. Licensed by Meigle presbytery, during 1640–41 he became an army chaplain, and on 15 November 1642 was admitted to Menmuir. During 1643 he attended the army at Newcastle, and shortly after 10 November that year married Catherine (*d*. 1669), daughter of David *Lindsay (*c*.1575–1639/40), deposed bishop of Edinburgh.

Soon after Haliburton's admission on 1 August 1644 to the collegiate charge of Perth, Montrose defeated the covenanting army at Tibbermore and occupied Perth on 1 September. On 27 November, for saying grace at dinner with the marquess despite his excommunication, Haliburton was deposed by the general assembly. After expressing his remorse he was reponed (reinstated) on 25 May 1645. In 1648 he preached against the king's imprisonment and for the lawfulness of renewing war for the covenant. In 1649 the assembly investigated his alleged sympathy with the engagement and the 'divisive supplication'. He congratulated Charles II on his visit to Perth in 1650. Next year the Cromwellian garrison silenced him for preaching loyalty to Charles. During the 1650s as a resolutioner he was at odds with his colleague and the factious kirk session and town council.

In 1655 Haliburton recanted over the supplication, becoming moderator of the synod. Reappointed moderator in 1658 and 1660 he moved with the episcopalian revival. Presbyterians vilified him for his sermon before parliament on 20 January 1661 condemning the solemn league and covenant. He became a commissioner of visitation of the Aberdeen colleges, and James Sharp, archbishop of St Andrews, recommended him for a bishopric. He was nominated to Dunkeld on 18 January 1662, and on 7 May was consecrated at Holyrood with five others. Although in presbyterian orders he was not reordained. He enacted a strict disciplinary code in his second synod in 1663, deposing nonconformists, including his kinsman George Haliburton, minister of Aberdalgie. On 10 October 1664, in declining health, he resigned the charge of Perth, which he had retained. He died at Perth on 5 April 1665 and was buried in Greyfriars churchyard, Perth, on the 17th.

Tristram Clarke

**Sources** J. Hunter, *The diocese and presbytery of Dunkeld, 1660–1689*, 2 vols. [1915] • *Fasti Scot.*, new edn, vol. 7 • J. Buckroyd, *Church and state* *in Scotland, 1660–1681* (1980) • E. B. Fryde and others, eds., *Handbook of British chronology*, 3rd edn, Royal Historical Society Guides and Handbooks, 2 (1986)

**Haliburton, George** (1635?–1715), bishop of Aberdeen, was perhaps the son of Dr George Haliburton, or of William Haliburton, minister of Collace, Perthshire, and Elizabeth or Elspeth, daughter of Archbishop Gledstanes. He was probably the George Haliburton who matriculated from St Salvator's College, St Andrews, in 1649, and graduated MA on 12 June 1652. He was admitted minister of Coupar Angus between 14 June and 8 November 1659. Conforming to episcopacy in 1662 he became archdeacon of Dunkeld by July 1663 and served as moderator of the presbytery of Meigle from 1667 to 1678. At an unknown date he married Margaret Lammie, who bore two children, and, following her death, on 20 August 1671 he married Agnes Campbell, widow of his kinsman James Halyburton of Pitcur. He received a doctorate of divinity at St Andrews in 1673.

On 16 May 1678 Haliburton was nominated bishop of Brechin, and consecrated on 13 June 1678, retaining the charge of Coupar until 1682. As bishop he was both minister and provost of Brechin, and his slight revenues were augmented with the living of Farnell. On 22 June 1682 he was named as bishop of Aberdeen, where he was translated on 5 July 1682. He immediately enjoined his clergy to liturgical observance of the Lord's prayer and the doxology, and was active against the Quakers. Adam Ferguson's father noted disapprovingly his public singing of psalms in a procession on James VII's birthday in 1687.

On 22 July 1689 Haliburton was deprived of his bishopric and retired to Newtyle parish, Forfarshire, where he assisted the Episcopal minister in the parish church. After the presbytery forcibly possessed it in 1698 he continued services in his own house at Halton, nearby. In 1699 he was granted a pension of £100. He ordained clergy, not necessarily extracting a Jacobite oath from the candidates. It was said that, unlike Bishop Alexander Rose, he would not deny ordination on the grounds of political allegiance, and 'conversed equally with them that complyed and them that did not' (Christ Church, Oxford, Wake MS 19, fol. 189*r*). Indeed, early in 1703 he helped Archbishop John Paterson prepare an address to the queen by some complying clergy, against the wishes of Archbishop Arthur Ross and his nephew Alexander Rose. In 1710 Haliburton moved to Denhead, near Coupar Angus, from where he continued to oversee his diocese. In 1712 he nominated presiding ministers for its four reorganized districts, whose monthly meetings he cautioned should be circumspect. However, in his old age his own discretion was unreliable, so he was kept in ignorance of the secret consecrations of new bishops in 1705, 1709, and 1711. The bishop's last action was courageously to attend, on 9 September 1715, the raising of James Stuart's standard at Fetteresso, which signalled the Jacobite rising. On 29 September he died at his house. TRISTRAM CLARKE

**Sources** J. Hunter, *The diocese and presbytery of Dunkeld, 1660–1689*, 2 vols. [1915] • *Fasti Scot.*, new edn, vols. 7, 8 • R. Keith and J. Spottiswoode, *An historical catalogue of the Scottish bishops, down to the year 1688*, new edn, ed. M. Russel [M. Russell] (1824) • G. Barclay, account of bishop Rose's Jacobitism, 1716, Christ Church Oxf., Wake MS 19, fol. 189*r* • *CSP dom., 1699–1700* • T. Rattray, account of the Scottish Episcopalians after 1689, NA Scot., CH12/12/227 • letter of Bishop Haliburton, 1712, NA Scot., CH12/12/6b • Newtyle kirk session minutes, 1691–1717, NA Scot., CH2/284/1–2 • register of sasines, Forfarshire, 1680–86, NA Scot., RS35/7–8 • biographical notes on Haliburton, *c.*1930, Dundee University, Br.MS.3.DC/99 • acta rectorum, U. St Andr., vol. 3 • E. B. Fryde and others, eds., *Handbook of British chronology*, 3rd edn, Royal Historical Society Guides and Handbooks, 2 (1986) • C. J. R. Armstrong, 'The Kinmuck meeting house: a seventeeth-century scandal?', *Aberdeen University Review*, 45 (1973–4), 369–79
**Likenesses** chalk drawing, Scot. NPG

**Haliburton** [Haleburton; *formerly* Burton], **James** (1788–1862), Egyptologist, was born on 22 September 1788 at Crescent Place, Bloomsbury, London, the fourth of the twelve children of James *Burton (1761–1837), a successful speculative builder, and Elizabeth (1761–1837), daughter of John Westley of Loughton, Essex, and his wife, Mary. His brothers included the architect Decimus *Burton. Although James was christened Haleburton, his family had called itself Burton for at least two generations and he himself used Burton until 1838. He began his education at the age of eight with the Revd Lewis Turner in Hammersmith and then went to Dr Charles Burney's academy in Greenwich. In July 1805 the architect Sir John Soane employed him as an 'improver', a trainee making architectural drawings. After two months he left to study mathematics at Trinity College, Cambridge, under the Revd George Tavel, returning briefly to Sir John Soane's employment during January 1806. According to Tavel he was not a good pupil, having a dilatory nature. On graduation in 1810 he was articled to Mr Rouppel, a solicitor in Lincoln's Inn. In 1811 he met George Bellas Greenough who became his mentor and a go-between when relations with his father proved difficult. In 1819 his father threatened to disinherit him unless he found gainful employment. Greenough recommended him as assistant to Sir Humphry Davy, then employed to develop a method for unrolling papyri in the collection of the king of Naples. Burton failed to arrive in time and forfeited the job. In Italy he met Sir John Gardner Wilkinson. Learning of Wilkinson's plan to visit Egypt he formed the idea of going there himself. Greenough found him a salaried position as mineralogist to the pasha, Mohammed Ali, with the task of finding coal.

Burton arrived in Egypt in April 1822 with his secretary, Charles Humphreys. After meeting the pasha he made a first expedition into the eastern desert. Sensing he was not up to the task, Greenough sent him assistants: Charles Sheffield, a mining engineer, and James Thornton, a chemist. A second journey was made into the desert with Wilkinson in the party. They failed to find coal and Burton was dismissed by the pasha. During these journeys, however, he located the porphyry quarry of the Romans and the site of Myos Hormos on the Red Sea coast. In January 1825 he sailed up the Nile. Reaching ancient Thebes he camped in the Memnonium and studied the surrounding monuments, attempting excavations at Medinet Habu. In

James Haliburton (1788–1862), by unknown photographer, *c.*1855

the Valley of the Kings he recorded the open tombs and was probably the first to enter KV5, tomb of the sons of Rameses II. He continued southwards to Abu Simbel before returning to the temple of Amun-Ra at Karnak and drawing the plan. There he excavated the Granite Sanctuary and found a new king-list which filled gaps in that from Abydos. Returning to Cairo, he prepared plates and printed the *Excerpta hieroglyphica* (4 parts, 1825–8), assisted by Humphreys, Joseph Bonomi, Lord Prudhoe, and Orlando Felix. In 1828 he found the trilingual inscription known as the Caristie stone which subsequently came to be housed in the Louvre.

After years camped in the eastern desert, Burton returned to England, arriving on 24 December 1835, having spent a year in Italy and France. To repay debts he sold his collection of antiquities through Sothebys, who went bankrupt before making payment. The British Museum purchased several items; a mummy and case went to Liverpool Museum. Shunned by his family, Burton survived the remainder of his life on a small allowance and the help of friends including Bonomi and Robert Hay, writing text for *Illustrations of Cairo* (1840) in return. In July 1838 he met by chance Thomas Chandler Haliburton, the Canadian author 'Sam Slick'. Haliburton was in London searching for relatives, as the two branches of the family had lost contact nearly a century before. To remove any doubt, they prepared a genealogy which also indicated a family link with Sir Walter Scott. Soon after, Burton reverted to using the surname given at his birth, spelling it Haliburton. He spent his last years living in Edinburgh, and died at 10 Hamilton Place, Newington, Edinburgh, on 22 February 1862 and was buried at West Dean cemetery. He was survived by Adriana (probably *née* Garofalaki; *c.*1813–1883), a Greek slave purchased for him in Egypt, and referred to as his wife.

Neil M. R. Cooke

**Sources** J. Burton, 'Collectanea Aegyptica', BL, Add. MSS 25613–25675 • UCL, Greenough MSS • letters to Robert Hay, BL, Add. MSS 38094, 38510 • J. Burton [senior], manuscript diary, Hastings Museum • S. Tillett, *Egypt itself: the career of Robert Hay* (1984) • J. Thompson, *Sir Gardner Wilkinson and his circle* (1992) • *The collected letters of Thomas Chandler Haliburton*, ed. R. Davies (1988) • J. M. Baines, *Burton's St Leonards* (1956) • J. Burton [J. Haliburton], ed., *Excerpta hieroglyphica*, 4 pts in 1 (Cairo, 1825–8) • R. Hay and J. Burton, *Illustrations of Cairo* (1840) • N. Cooke, 'Burton and KV5', *Minerva*, 7/3 (May–June 1996) • N. Cooke, 'Burton's mummy', *Minerva*, 7/6 (Nov–Dec 1996)

**Archives** BL, watercolours, Add. MSS 29812–29860 • BM, Egyptian antiquities • V&A, sketchbook | BL, 'Collectanea Aegyptica', Add. MSS 25613–25675, 29812–29860 • BL, letters to Robert Hay, Add. MS 38094 • CUL, letters to Joseph Bonomi • LUL, corresp. with George Greenough, etc. • U. Durham, Oriental Museum, Prudhoe collection of Egyptian antiquities • University of Nova Scotia, Canada, Thomas Chandler Haliburton letters, with genealogy put together by Burton and Haliburton

**Likenesses** portrait, 1829 • silhouette, 1834?, Hastings Museum • lithograph, 1839, NPG • photograph, *c.*1855, Hastings Museum [*see illus.*] • Josephs, miniature (aged eight or nine) • drawing (*On board the boat Egypt, 1828*), V&A, Searight coll. • group portrait, pencil sketch (*Yakoob, el Khasnadar, Dupuy*), V&A, Searight coll. • pencil drawing, V&A, Searight coll.

**Wealth at death** £3680 16*s.* 5*d.*: confirmation, 21 Aug 1863, NA Scot., SC 70/1/117, 630–35

**Haliburton, John, first Lord Haliburton** (*c.*1405–*c.*1454). *See under* Haliburton family (*per. c.*1375–*c.*1500).

**Haliburton, Mark** (*d. c.*1456). *See under* Haliburton family (*per. c.*1375–*c.*1500).

**Haliburton, Thomas Chandler** (1796–1865), politician and writer, was born on 17 December 1796 at Windsor, Nova Scotia, the only child of William Hersey Otis Haliburton (1767–1829), lawyer, MLA, and judge of the inferior court of common pleas, and Lucy Chandler Grant (*d.* 1797). Haliburton described himself as of 'ancient Scottish descent' (BL, Add. MS 28510, fol. 173). In 1803 his father married Susanna Francklin Davis, a widow, daughter of former Nova Scotia lieutenant-governor the Hon. Michael Francklin. Thomas Chandler Haliburton was educated at the Windsor grammar school, and then at the Anglican King's College, Windsor, graduating BA in 1815. A significant family influence came from his New England planter grandfather, William Haliburton (*d.* 1817), a Yankee adventurer and lawyer, and an inveterate scribbler. On 28 May 1816, during a visit to his step-aunt's in Henley-on-Thames, England, Thomas Chandler Haliburton married his first wife, Louisa Neville (*d.* 1841), daughter of Captain Lawrence Neville (*d.* 1811) of the 19th light dragoons. They had a large family of five daughters and three sons, including Arthur Lawrence *Haliburton, a successful civil servant; three other children died young.

Haliburton studied law in the office of his father in Windsor, Nova Scotia, and invested in gypsum mines. He applied to be a notary public in 1819, then moved to Annapolis Royal in 1821 to practise law. On 13 December 1824 he was appointed judge of the probate court at Annapolis. From 1826 to 1829 he represented Annapolis county in the Nova Scotia house of assembly. His reputation for sarcastic oratory in the legislature nearly prevented his being appointed judge of the inferior court of common pleas for the middle division of Nova Scotia after his father's death. The transformation from sarcastic orator to judge astonished his friends who had characterized

**Thomas Chandler Haliburton (1796–1865)**, by Herbert Watkins, 1858

him as the sociable 'Tom Haliday' in 'The Club' papers (which he helped to write) in the columns of *The Novascotian* between 1828 and 1831. His legal career culminated in his appointment to the supreme court bench on 29 March 1841.

Haliburton's publishing career began anonymously with *A General Description of Nova Scotia* (1823), followed by the ambitious *Historical and Statistical Account of Nova Scotia*, published by Joseph Howe in 1829. The *General Description* encouraged immigrants but the *Historical and Statistical Account* described a colony in an advanced state of cultivation without any need for newcomers.

In 1835–6, at the same time as he was building Clifton, an estate of over 30 acres near the centre of Windsor, Nova Scotia, Haliburton began publishing in *The Novascotian* newspaper the humorous work for which he is most famous. *Recollections of Nova Scotia: the Clockmaker, or, The Sayings and Doings of Samuel Slick, of Slickville* details the conversations between Sam Slick, a loquacious Yankee clock pedlar, and an Anglophile squire as they travel through Nova Scotia. Sam Slick's wit immediately appealed to readers. Richard Bentley, the English publisher, successfully reprinted *The Clockmaker* in England, and Haliburton was so flattered that he overlooked Bentley's piracy of the book and travelled to England to offer him a sequel. Slick's catch-phrase 'soft sawdur and human nature' made Haliburton famous. A second series in 1838 was followed by a third in 1840 and two series of *The Attaché, or, Sam Slick in England* (1843–4).

In an attempt to silence the garrulous Sam Slick, Haliburton wrote *The Old Judge, or, Life in a Colony*, published serially in *Fraser's Magazine* in 1846–7, and as a book in 1849. *The Old Judge* is a vivid evocation of colony life and a testament to what V. L. O. Chittick called his 'provincial Toryism'. The narrator is English and a stranger to the province. His guides are old Judge Sandford and his nephew, the young lawyer Mr Barclay. During a winter storm, in an inn at Mount Hope, they encounter homespun Stephen Richardson, a teller of tall tales. Stories like 'Old Judge Beler's Ghost' and 'The Witch of Inky Dell' in *The Old Judge* represent Haliburton's writing at its best.

*Sam Slick's Wise Saws and Modern Instances, or, What He Said, Did, or Invented* (1853) and *Nature and Human Nature* (1855) followed. The *Acadian Recorder* (18 June 1853) accused Haliburton of making 'soup from the bones' of Sam Slick. Haliburton also wrote *The Letter-Bag of the Great Western* (1840), now forgotten, in which he exploited the contemporary phenomenon of the *Great Western* steamship, by indulging his talent for mimicry and dialect in a series of letters from passengers and crew. In response to a request from Henry Colburn, the publisher, for 'any work on America' (*Letters*, 119), he compiled two three-volume collections of American humorous writing, *Traits of American Humour by Native Authors* (1852) and *The Americans at Home, or, Byeways, Backwoods, and Prairies* (1854). His final work, *The Season Ticket* (1860), was serialized in the *Dublin University Magazine* in 1859. As with all his books, Haliburton needed only a flimsy narrative (a journey from London to Southampton by train) to set his characters talking about subjects he himself wished to address.

Politically, Haliburton stood on the extreme right. During his ten-month stay in England, he hastily wrote and published *The Bubbles of Canada* (1839), and when the *Report of the Earl of Durham* appeared, he sent seven letters to *The Times*, subsequently issued by Richard Bentley as *A Reply to the Report of the Earl of Durham*. Such outbursts of political polemic diminished his reputation as a humorist. In 1851 he wrote *Rule and Misrule of the English in America*, much of its second volume reiterating material from *The Bubbles* (1839).

In England, on a visit in 1853, Haliburton met his second wife, a childhood friend of Charles Darwin, Sarah Harriet Hosier Williams, *née* Mostyn Owen (1804–1887), a widow. In August 1856 he resigned his judgeship, sold Clifton, moved to England, remarried on 30 September of that year, and settled at Gordon House, Isleworth. His public profile continued to be high. He published a speech on colonial matters in 1857, advised Richard Bentley, and on 16 June 1858 was awarded an honorary DCL from Oxford University. On 29 April 1859 he became MP for Launceston in Cornwall, a seat in the pocket of the duke of Northumberland. His after-dinner and other speeches regularly appeared in the newspapers.

Haliburton fought two court cases to secure a 'paltry pension' (*Letters*, 243) from the Nova Scotia government. Despite being increasingly afflicted by gout, he crossed the Atlantic in 1860, 1861, and 1864, in his capacity as chairman of the Canada Land and Emigration Company. The town of Haliburton in northern Ontario is named after him. The evidence of his bank account at Coutts &

Co. suggests his income in 1864–5 was over £8000 a year. He died of a stroke at his home, Gordon House, Isleworth, Middlesex, on 27 August 1865 and was buried in Isleworth churchyard on 1 September. His widow died in England in 1887 and was also buried in Isleworth churchyard.

In his era and for many years afterward, Haliburton's humour was widely enjoyed. His use of offensive stereotypes in his caricatures of black people, however, goes well beyond the ethnocentrism of the age, and his portrayal of women is unenlightened. Thomas Adolphus Trollope recalled 'he was large and burly in person, with grey hair, a large ruddy face, a humorous mouth, and bright blue eyes always full of mirth … a delightful companion—for a limited time' (*What I Remember*, 1.359–60). His reputation has never regained the peak it achieved in his lifetime. RICHARD A. DAVIES

**Sources** *The letters of Thomas Chandler Haliburton*, ed. R. A. Davies (1988) • V. L. O. Chittick, *Thomas Chandler Haliburton, 'Sam Slick': a study in provincial Toryism* (1924) • T. C. Haliburton, *The Clockmaker Series One, Two, and Three*, ed. G. L. Parker (1995) • G. E. Clarke, 'White niggers, black slaves: slavery, race and class in T. C. Haliburton's *The Clockmaker*', *Nova Scotia Historical Review*, 14 (1994), 13–40 • *The Thomas Chandler Haliburton symposium*, ed. F. M. Tierney (1984) • S. E. McMullin, *Thomas Chandler Haliburton and his works* (1989) • A. W. H. Eaton, 'Old Boston families, V: the Haliburton family', *New England Historical and Genealogical Register*, 71 (1917), 57–74 • *The Novascotian* • *Acadian Recorder* • m. cert.

**Archives** Acadia University, Wolfville, Nova Scotia, Wilson collection • BL, papers relating to suit v. R. Bentley, Add. MS 46634 • National Archives of Canada • Nova Scotia Public Archives of Halifax | Harvard U., Houghton L., letters to Richard Bentley

**Likenesses** W. Valentine, oils, *c*.1831, Nova Scotia Museum, Halifax • M. Gauci, lithograph, pubd 1839 (after portrait by E. U. Eddis, 1838), BM, NPG • M. Torre, portrait, *c*.1840–1849, National Archives of Canada • plaster bust, *c*.1856–1864, Isleworth Branch Library • H. Watkins, photograph, 1858, NPG [*see illus.*] • Parish & Co., photograph, *c*.1860–1869, Acadia University, Wilson collection • Beatham, oils, Nova Scotia Legislature, Halifax, Nova Scotia • D. J. Pound, stipple and line engraving (after photograph by Mayall), NPG; repro. in D. J. Pound, *The drawing-room portrait gallery of eminent personages* (1860) • lithograph, BM • wood-engraving, repro. in *ILN* (9 Sept 1865)

**Wealth at death** under £6000: probate, 27 Sept 1865, *CGPLA Eng. & Wales*

**Haliburton, Sir Walter** (*c*.1375–1446?). *See under* Haliburton family (*per. c*.1375–*c*.1500).

**Haliday, Alexander Henry** (*c*.1728–1802), physician and politician, son of Samuel *Haliday (1685–1739), the non-subscribing divine, was born at Belfast. He was educated at Glasgow University as a physician, qualifying MA MD in 1751, and he practised in Belfast, where for many years he was an influential public figure.

On 23 December 1770 a group of 1200 farmers calling themselves the 'Hearts of Steel' marched from Templepatrick, co. Antrim, to rescue David Douglas, who had been imprisoned on a charge of maiming cattle. The 'Hearts of Steel' movement was the product of widespread agrarian discontent, and its immediate grievance was related to the eviction of tenants by the Upton family from their Templepatrick estate and their replacement by speculators who had been able to outbid them when leases expired. The farmers approached Belfast's North Gate and surrounded the barrack where Douglas was held. Haliday approached the crowd and was captured while attempting to dissuade them from burning the house of Waddell Cunningham, a shipowner, who was one of the speculators with whom the crowd had a grievance. Haliday was sent to negotiate Douglas's release, but:

> The Doctor had just reached the Barrack on this embassy, passing through an immense multitude consisting of the people from the country intermixed with those of the town, when the gate was thrown open by the military, who fired upon the assailants, killed five persons and wounded nine others. (Bardon, 206)

Haliday's house in Castle Street later became the headquarters of James Caulfeild, earl of Charlemont, on his annual visits to Belfast from 1782 in connection with the volunteer conventions. Haliday's correspondence with Charlemont lasted until the earl's death, and is informative about the politics of the north of Ireland.

Haliday died in Belfast on 28 April 1802, and was buried in Clifton Street cemetery. He left to his wife (an Edmonstone, of Red Hall) 'a legacy of £100 by way of atonement for the many unmerciful scolds I have thrown away upon her at the whist table', and 'the sum of £500 in gratitude for her never having given on any other occasion from her early youth till this hour any just cause to rebuke or complain of her'; he also bequeathed her a further sum of £100 for her goodness in amusing him with 'a game of picket' when his eyesight had decayed. His library, rich in classics, was sold after his death; part of it became the property of the First Presbyterian Church, Belfast. Haliday wrote, but did not publish, a tragedy, on Lucius Junius Brutus, and many satirical verses, some of which appeared in the *Belfast Magazine* in September and October 1810 and in June 1811. In 1844 Haliday's grandson and namesake published anonymously a volume of original hymns.

ALEXANDER GORDON, *rev.* MICHAEL BEVAN

**Sources** G. Benn, *A history of the town of Belfast from the earliest times to the close of the eighteenth century*, 1 (1877), 520, 615, 631, 663; 2 (1880), 35 • J. Bardon, *A history of Ulster* (1992), 206 • *Belfast News-Letter* (30 April 1802) • private information (1890) • W. I. Addison, *A roll of graduates of the University of Glasgow from 31st December 1727 to 31st December 1897* (1898) • D. J. O'Donoghue, *The poets of Ireland: a biographical dictionary with bibliographical particulars*, 1 vol. in 3 pts (1892–3)

**Wealth at death** over £700: *DNB*

**Haliday, Charles** (1789–1866), public health reformer and antiquary, was born at Carrick-on-Suir, co. Tipperary, the second son of William Haliday, an apothecary. In 1809 he was sent by his father to London to work as a clerk in Lubbock's Bank. He returned to Dublin in 1812 on the death of his brother William. William *Haliday (1788–1812) had married the daughter of a Mr Alter, a trader in bark on Arran quay. Alter gave his business to Charles Haliday, and this formed the basis of his fortune. He married Mary Hayes of Mountmellick, Queen's county.

In 1833 Haliday was elected a member of the corporation for improving the harbour of Dublin and superintending the lighthouses on the Irish coasts. Haliday also campaigned for much of his life for the improvement of the living conditions of the Dublin working class. This began during the cholera epidemic of 1832, and he later worked for the provision of clean water and main drainage. When the construction of a railway down the coast threatened free bathing in what was then Kingstown, he ensured that the poor continued to have a bathing place. In 1864 the construction of the new station in Connolly Street included a large viaduct across Westmoreland Street; Haliday gave evidence in London which ensured the protection of the view across the Liffey to the customs house. For many years he was consul for Greece, secretary of the chamber of commerce in Dublin, and director of the Bank of Ireland. In 1834 he moved to Monkstown, co. Dublin, and in 1843 he bought Monkstown Park, which he demolished and rebuilt. The new house had a large library to house his collection of Irish pamphlets and tracts. Among these was the manuscript of the secret service money book which contained details of payments made to informers during the rebellion of 1798, and which was used by R. R. Madden in his work on the United Irishmen. Haliday died at Monkstown Park on 14 September 1866 and was buried in the cemetery at Monkstown. In 1847 he had been elected a member of the Royal Irish Academy, and his work on the early history of Dublin was published posthumously in 1881, edited by J. P. Prendergast. His collection of over 25,000 pamphlets and tracts was presented to the Royal Irish Academy by his widow, who died in 1868. MARIE-LOUISE LEGG

**Sources** G. F. Cuming, 'Charles Haliday: merchant and scholar', *Catholic Bulletin*, 12 (1922), 588–92 • J. P. Prendergast, 'Some notice of the life of Charles Haliday', in C. Haliday, *The Scandinavian kingdom of Dublin*, 2nd edn (1884), iii–cxxiii • A. J. Webb, *A compendium of Irish biography* (1878) • F. G. Hall, *The Bank of Ireland, 1783–1946*, ed. G. O'Brien (1949)

**Archives** Royal Irish Acad.

**Likenesses** C. Smith, oils, 1869, Royal Irish Acad.

**Wealth at death** under £45,000: probate, 4 Oct 1866, *CGPLA Ire.*

**Haliday** [Hollyday], **Samuel** (1685–1739), nonsubscribing Presbyterian minister, was born probably in Omagh, co. Tyrone, where his father, Samuel Haliday (1637–1724), was a Presbyterian minister. Samuel Haliday senior was minister at Convoy, co. Donegal, from 1664, although he was not formally installed until 1676 and left for Omagh (Longfield and Drumraer) in the following year. In 1688 he fled to Scotland, where he was successively minister at Dunscore, Dryfesdale, and New North Church, Edinburgh. In December 1692 he was installed at Ardstraw, co. Tyrone, where he remained until his death.

Like his father, Samuel Haliday was educated at Glasgow University. He matriculated in 1701 and studied under John Loudon, professor of logic and rhetoric. His name is recorded in the register as 'Samuel Hollyday, Scoto-Hibernus'. Following graduation at Glasgow he went to Leiden University to study theology and was admitted there as 'Samuel Halideus, Hibernus' on 19 November 1705. On completion of his studies he defended a thesis on Leviticus 24: 11–16 before Hermann Witsius on 10 July 1706 and was licensed at Rotterdam in that year, on which occasion he subscribed to the Westminster confession.

Up to this date Haliday seems to have shared the rigid Calvinism of his father. However, a further period of travel and study in Switzerland brought him back to Rotterdam 'entirely changed' in the eyes of his former professor (Bruce, 273). In 1708 he chose to be ordained in Geneva 'because the Terms of Church-Communion there, are not narrowed by any human Impositions' (S. Haliday, *Reasons Against the Imposition of Subscription*, 1724, iv). Shortly afterwards he accepted a post as chaplain to Colonel Anstruther's Cameronian regiment and served with it throughout Marlborough's campaigns in Flanders.

In 1712 Haliday was back in Ulster and was recognized by the general synod meeting in Belfast as being eligible to receive a call from any vacant pulpit. The following year the congregation of Plunket Street, Dublin, sought the permission of the synod to call him but, although he at first seemed inclined to accept, ultimately nothing came of this. In fact Haliday spent some years in London, where, according to Reid, he 'appears to have been highly esteemed and well known to the leaders of the Whig party both in and out of the government' (Reid, 3.135). In 1714 he was active in trying to prevent the Schism Act from being extended to Ireland. Four years later he was instrumental in securing an increase in the *regium donum*, and the synod granted him a payment of £30 in recognition of this work.

In 1719 Haliday attended the Salters' Hall conference in London, where English dissenters debated the question of subscription. Shortly afterwards he received a call to the First Presbyterian Congregation of Belfast. At the same time he was accused of being an Arian by the Revd Samuel Dunlop, a fellow Irish minister who had also been present at Salters' Hall. In fact Haliday was not an Arian (although he did not believe that the doctrine of the Trinity was an essential article of belief) and in June 1720 the synod resolved that he had 'sufficiently clear'd his Innocency, and fully vindicated himself from the aspersions of Arianism' (*Records of the General Synod of Ulster*, 1.537).

The question of subscription to the Westminster confession now came to the fore in Ireland. At the 1720 meeting the synod agreed to the 'pacific act', which required ministers to adhere to the Westminster confession, although they were allowed to do so in words of their own choosing, explaining any scruples that they might have. However when Haliday's installation at the First Belfast Congregation took place on 28 July 1720 he refused to subscribe to the confession. Though four members protested, the presbytery went ahead with the installation, but the matter was taken up by the synod of 1721, when ministers were invited to renew their subscription to the confession. Those who refused became known as nonsubscribers and were eventually separated into the presbytery of Antrim in 1725.

After Haliday's installation the disaffected subscribing minority in the First and Second Belfast congregations left to form a Third Congregation. Further controversy arose when Haliday and James Kirkpatrick, minister of the Second Congregation, were prevented from participating in the Third Congregation's communion service; correspondence concerning this event is published with Kirkpatrick's *A Scripture Plea Against a Fatal Rupture and Breach of Christian Communion* (1724). The success of the Third Congregation in raising funds from supporters in Scotland forced the nonsubscribers to publish *A Letter from the Reverend Mrs. Kilpatrick and Halliday, Ministers in Belfast. To a Friend at Glasgow, with Relation to the New Meeting-house in Belfast* (1723).

With Kirkpatrick and John Abernethy, Haliday was one of the leading exponents of nonsubscription. His main work, *Reasons Against the Imposition of Subscription to the Westminster Confession of Faith* (1724), is a powerfully argued pamphlet against subscription that brought forth a number of responses. In turn Haliday replied with *A Letter to the Reverend Mr. Gilbert Kennedy* (1725) and *A Letter to the Reverend Mr. Francis Iredel* (1726). He was also one of the anonymous authors of *A Narrative of the Proceedings of Seven General Synods of the Northern Presbyterians* (1727). He was a gifted preacher whose sermons were mostly delivered extempore; consequently he published only one sermon, *A Sermon Occasioned by the Death of the Reverend Mr. Michael Bruce* (1735). He was described by James Duchal as being 'not capable of a mean or dishonest thing' (Duchal, 44) and was widely respected by colleagues; he supplied testimonials to the synod in 1721 signed by no fewer than ninety-six of the leading theological professors and divines from all over Europe.

The name of Haliday's wife is not recorded except as the widow of Arthur Maxwell. She had a considerable income. With Haliday she had two sons, one of whom, Alexander Henry *Haliday (*c*.1728–1802), became a leading physician in Belfast. Haliday died on 5 March 1739 in his fifty-fourth year, probably at the manse in Rosemary Lane, Belfast, where he had lived since 1720, and was buried at night in St George's churchyard, Belfast, on 7 March. His funeral sermon was delivered by the Revd Thomas Drennan.

A. D. G. Steers

**Sources** J. Duchal, 'Brief memoirs of the life and character of the Reverend Mr. Samuel Haliday', *A sermon on occasion of the much lamented death of the late Reverend Mr. John Abernethy* (1741), 43–7 • *Records of the General Synod of Ulster, from 1691 to 1820*, 3 vols. (1890–98), vols. 1, 2 • *Belfast News-Letter* (6 March 1738) • *Belfast News-Letter* (9 March 1739) • *Belfast News-Letter* (13 March 1739) • W. Bruce, 'The progress of non-subscription to creeds', *Christian Moderator*, 8 (1826), 271–4 • C. Innes, ed., *Munimenta alme Universitatis Glasguensis / Records of the University of Glasgow from its foundation till 1727*, 3, Maitland Club, 72 (1854), 31, 171 • E. Peacock, *Index to English speaking students who have graduated at Leyden University* (1883), 45 • J. Scott Porter, 'History of the First Presbyterian Congregation, Belfast', *Bible Christian*, new ser., 1/11 (1836), 375–80 • J. S. Reid and W. D. Killen, *History of the Presbyterian church in Ireland*, 3 (1853), 134–253 • T. Witherow, *Historical and literary memorials of presbyterianism in Ireland, 1623–1731* (1879), 266–80 • A. Gordon and G. K. Smith, *Historic memorials of the First Presbyterian Church of Belfast* (1887), 12, 56, 112–16 • J. McConnell and others, eds., *Fasti of the Irish Presbyterian church, 1613–1840*, rev. S. G. McConnell, 2 vols. in 12 pts (1935–51) • *Fasti Scot.*, new edn, 1.143; 7.530 • *DNB* • G. Benn, *A history of the town of Belfast from the earliest times to the close of the eighteenth century*, 1 (1877), 406 n. 1

**Wealth at death** £500 left to wife; also £200 p.a. which she possessed as relict of Arthur Maxwell, plus plate, furniture, and leases of fields on road to Shankhill: Benn, *History*, 406 n. 1

**Haliday** [O'Hara], **William** [*pseud.* Edmond O'Connell] (**1788–1812**), grammarian of Irish, was born in Dublin, the son of William Haliday, or Halliday, an apothecary; he was the elder brother of Charles *Haliday. He was trained as a solicitor, and learned Irish from three Munstermen who lived in Dublin, MacFaelchu, O'Connaill, and O'Cathasaigh; yet so despised by the middle-class Irish was the native Gaelic that Haliday assumed the name William O'Hara when he began to take lessons from O'Cathasaigh.

In 1808 Haliday published in Dublin *Uraicecht na Gaedhilge: a Grammar of the Gaelic Language*, under another assumed name, Edmond O'Connell (E.O'C.). In this compilation indebted to Stewart's *Gaelic Grammar* Haliday hails 'the cheering prospect of seeing the remains of our Literature, our Laws, Poetry and History undergo candid and rational investigation' (E.O'C., vii). He was one of the founders in 1807 of the Gaelic Society of Dublin, established for the investigation and revival of ancient Irish literature, and in 1811 published in Dublin the first volume of a text and translation of Keating's *History of Ireland*. He had begun an Irish dictionary when he died, on 26 October 1812, leaving a young widow, the daughter of a Mr Alter. Haliday was an enthusiastic student of Irish literature of the same kind as the lexicographer O'Reilly, who described Haliday as 'a master of the language of his native country' (O'Reilly, Preface, 2). Their work was limited by their imperfect training, but was of service to more scholarly persons and gave enjoyment to the common reader. Norman Moore, *rev.* John D. Haigh

**Sources** E. O'Reilly, preface, *An Irish–English dictionary* (1821), 2 • E. O'C. [W. Haliday], introduction, *Uraicecht na Gaedhilge: a grammar of the Gaelic language* (1808) • A. J. Webb, *A compendium of Irish biography* (1878) • J. O'Donovan, preface, *A grammar of the Irish language* (1845) • *Transactions of the Gaelic Society of Dublin* (1808)

**Halifax**. For this title name *see* Savile, George, first marquess of Halifax (1633–1695); Montagu, Charles, earl of Halifax (1661–1715); Savile, William, second marquess of Halifax (1664/5–1700) [*see under* Savile, George, first marquess of Halifax (1633–1695)]; Dunk, George Montagu, second earl of Halifax (1716–1771); Wood, Charles, first Viscount Halifax (1800–1885); Wood, Charles Lindley, second Viscount Halifax (1839–1934); Wood, Edward Frederick Lindley, first earl of Halifax (1881–1959).

**Halkerston, Peter** (*d. c.*1833), legal writer and antiquary, is said to have received a university education, and to have taken the degree of MA. He studied law, and in 1791 was admitted to the Society of Solicitors to the Supreme Courts of Scotland. For ten years he acted as one of the examiners of that body, and was its honorary librarian from 1808 to 1821. As the first librarian, he worked hard to build up the library from unsatisfactory beginnings, when he found books in poor condition or missing altogether. He was also for some time bailie of the abbey of Holyrood; during his tenure he studied the records of the place, and produced in 1831 *A Treatise on the History, Law, and Privileges of the Palace and Sanctuary of Holyrood House*, at a time when sanctuary was still important for debtors.

Halkerston, who seems to have been a theoretical rather than a practical lawyer, received the honorary degree of LLD, and was also elected an extraordinary member of the Royal Physical Society. His *Compendium or general abridgment of the faculty collection of decisions of the lords of council and session from Feb. 4 1754 to the session of 1817* (1819–20) provided useful indexes and abstracts of the judgments of lords of session who recommended the work to lawyers. His *Analysis of Acts of Parliament* (1827) was thought invaluable at the time, especially to young solicitors. These were his most important works, but others by him also aimed to increase understanding of the law.

Halkerston is thought to have died about 1833. He left a daughter, Elizabeth (*d.* 1885), but nothing more is known of his private life.

FRANCIS WATT, *rev.* ELIZABETH BAIGENT

**Sources** J. B. Barclay, *The S.S.C. story, 1784–1984* (1984) • Watt, *Bibl. Brit.* • private information (2004)

**Halket, George** (*bap.* **1692**, *d.* **1756**), Jacobite songwriter and schoolmaster, son of James Halket, was baptized in Banff on 6 July 1692. He completed his studies at King's College, Aberdeen, 1709–13, but—as was then quite common—did not graduate. In 1714 he was appointed schoolmaster, precentor, and session clerk of Rathen in Aberdeenshire. On 6 March 1718 he married Janet Adamson, probably of the Crawford family, lairds of Rathen. They had three sons and a daughter. Halket was dismissed in 1725 after coming to blows with the minister, James Anderson, during divine service. Rathen lay in a strongly Episcopalian area of the Jacobite north-east, and it took many years for the Presbyterians to dislodge their rivals after the revolution of 1688. Halket's ties were with the leading Episcopalian families of the district, including the Frasers of Philorth and Memsie, and Alexander Moor and his son James, successively Episcopalian ministers of Fraserburgh, until the latter was deposed amid scenes of violent confrontation in which James Anderson had taken a leading part. Halket next started his own school, in the fishing village of Cairnbulg near Fraserburgh, where he taught, apparently with great success, for the following twenty-five years. From 1750 he was employed as a tutor by the Frasers of Memsie and the Inneses of Tyrie.

Only one contemporary publication of George Halket's is recorded: a slim duodecimo volume entitled *Occasional Poems on Several Subjects*, published in Aberdeen in 1727, whose contents include an elegiac pastoral on Alexander Moor, presenting him as a living example of the good shepherd:

> *Armenian* tygers, *Punic* lions, boars
> *Arcadian* fled from *Fraserburgian* shores,
> When *Sandy* kept the flock with watchful eye.
> (p. 21)

Halket's main fame, however, is as a composer of Jacobite songs (including 'Whirry Whigs Awa'', and 'A Dialogue between the Devil and George II', which apparently caused the duke of Cumberland to offer a reward of £100 for the author dead or alive) and the classic love lyric 'Logie o' Buchan', usually reckoned among the dozen or so best lowland Scottish songs:

> O Logie o'Buchan, O Logie the laird,
> They hae taen awa Jamie that delv'd in the yaird,
> Wha played on the pipe an' the viol sae sma';
> They hae taen awa Jamie the flower o' them a'.
> He said, Think na lang, lassie, tho' I gang awa …
> For I'll come and see ye in spite o' them a'.
> (Buchan, 175)

The song was published in Robert Burns's and James Johnson's *Scots Musical Museum* (vol. 4, 1792, no. 358), possibly having been picked up by Burns when visiting the north-east in the summer of 1787. It enjoyed a brisk circulation thereafter in song-slip and chap-book form, and was published by Peter Buchan in *Gleanings of … Scarce Old Ballads* (1825) with a long and detailed note identifying Halket as the composer and giving several particulars about his life and career. Numerous attempts were made in later years, most notably by the folk-song collector Gavin Greig, to establish the historicity of the song and identify real-life parallels for the people in it. But popular song was subject to continuous re-creation, receiving attention from every inventive personality through which it passed. Even after it was printed, the verbal text of 'Logie o' Buchan' took more than a generation to become stable in its modern form, and the tune—achieved by transposing the opening section of Burns and Johnson's air up a third—may have taken as long. The extent of Halket's personal contribution to this process is not known. George Halket died at Memsie House, near Fraserburgh, in 1756 and was buried in the old kirkyard of Fraserburgh at the west end of the aisle. WILLIAM DONALDSON

**Sources** P. Buchan, *Gleanings of Scotch, English, and Irish, scarce old ballads* (1825) • W. Walker, *The bards of Bon-Accord, 1375–1860* (1887) • G. Greig, 'On two Buchan songs', *Transactions of the Buchan Field Club*, 5 (1898–1900), 78–92 • E. B. Lyle and others, eds., *The Greig–Duncan folk song collection*, 4 (1990) • A. Jervise, *Epitaphs and inscriptions from burial grounds and old buildings in the north-east of Scotland*, 2 vols. (1875–9) • R. Burns and others, *The Scots musical museum*, ed. J. Johnson, 6 vols. (1787–1803) • J. B. Pratt, *Buchan*, rev. R. Anderson, 4th edn (1901) • R. Chambers, ed., *The songs of Scotland prior to Burns* (1862) • A. Tayler and H. Tayler, *Jacobites of Aberdeenshire and Banffshire in the rising of 1715* (1934) • A. Fraser, *The Frasers of Philorth*, 3 vols. (1879) • P. J. Anderson, ed., *Roll of alumni in arts of the University and King's College of Aberdeen, 1596–1860* (1900) • G. Eyre-Todd, ed., *Scottish poetry of the eighteenth century*, 2 vols. (1896)

**Halkett** [*née* Murray], **Anne** [Anna], **Lady Halkett** (**1623–1699**), autobiographer, was born in London on 4 January 1623, the youngest daughter of Thomas *Murray (1564–1623), provost of Eton College, and Jane Drummond (*d.* 1647), both of whom claimed descent from families recently ennobled in Scotland. Although her father died when she was three months old her family's court connections ensured her a comfortable childhood. Tutors taught her and her sisters to write, speak French, and play the lute and virginals, and a gentlewoman taught them all kinds of needlework, 'which shows I was not brought up in an idle life' (*Memoirs*, 10), though Anne rated highest of all her religious education 'in the Church of England; where I blese God I had my education and the example of a good mother' (ibid., 11). Her mother was governess to Princess Mary, the princess royal, and Prince Henry, duke of Gloucester, in and after 1642, and Anne herself may have served briefly in 1642 as a lady of the bedchamber to Queen Henrietta Maria. Anne emerges from her later autobiography as deeply pious, but also as a determined, and sometimes stubborn, woman, ready to defy her mother and ignore the opinions of others in her search for love and a husband. In 1644 she met Thomas Howard (*bap.* 1625, *d.* 1678), the eldest son of Edward Howard, Lord Howard of Escrick, and fell in love with him, but both her mother and his father forbade the match, as the Howard family needed to marry into money to restore its fortunes. Anne's insistence on continuing to meet Howard led to bitter quarrels with her mother; news that on 21 July 1646 he had privately married someone else left her devastated.

About the end of 1647, her mother having died that August, Anne met and became intrigued by Colonel Joseph *Bampfield (1622–1685), a royalist agent. Bampfield plotted to help James, duke of York, escape from imprisonment by the parliamentarians, and Anne was enlisted to procure women's clothes for the duke. This she did, and on 20 April 1648 the liberated prince was brought to her to dress him in his disguise, and he 'was very pretty in itt' (*Memoirs*, 25). After this Anne was eager to take part in further royalist intrigues with Bampfield, and he sought to strengthen her trust in him by telling her that his wife was dead, and asking her to marry him. She agreed, but there were stories that his wife was still alive, and rumours of Anne's involvement in York's escape began to circulate, so in September 1649 she left London to stay with friends in the north of England. There she received news that Bampfield had been imprisoned and expected to be executed, that his wife was indeed living, that his loyalty to the royalists was suspect, and that her relationship with him was causing scandal as he was a married man. Under the pressures of shame and guilt combined with defiance of the advice of family and friends she collapsed into serious illness, and concluded that death would be 'extreamely wellcome' (ibid., 33). When she recovered she insisted passionately that Bampfield was innocent—and a widower—in spite of all the evidence to the contrary. A further complication was that her host was attracted to her, and she thus earned the jealousy of her hostess.

Anne therefore moved to Scotland, Bampfield having persuaded the earl of Dunfermline to invite her to stay with him. Arriving in Edinburgh in June 1650 she soon heard that Charles II had landed in the north and she joined the court at Dunfermline—and forced the king to take notice of her when she thought she was receiving insultingly little attention. After the defeat of the Scottish army by Cromwell at Dunbar on 3 September, however, she showed another side of her character. She had long taken an interest in medicine, and when she found many wounded soldiers wandering through Fife, as no provision had been made for their care, she spent several days treating them and encouraging others to help. She then moved north to the Dunfermlines' castle of Fyvie, and the king rewarded her for her care of the wounded by sending her 'fivety pieces' from a purse of gold given to him (*Memoirs*, 56). Such financial assistance, which she had previously sought unsuccessfully, was welcome, for after she had left London she had lost control of property and revenues left to her by her mother.

Anne spent nearly two years at Fyvie, where 'itt was so agreeably that in all my life I never was so long together so truly contented' (*Memoirs*, 58). Her stay was not without incident, however. The indefatigable Bampfield turned up, and she again fell sick through the 'conflict betwixt love and honour' (ibid., 57). She loved him and refused to accept that his wife was still alive, yet honour meant that she could not allow herself to be courted by a man whom others believed was still married. Then late in 1651 English soldiers of the advancing Cromwellian army appeared at Fyvie, beating up the servants and threatening to shoot anyone who did not give them all they wanted. The earl of Dunfermline was away, and the tearful countess begged Anne to confront them—though warning her that they knew there was 'an English woman in the housse' and said that they would 'treat her worse than anyone else'. The 'English whore', as they at first called her, outfaced the soldiers, telling them that, as Englishmen, they should be ashamed of their disgraceful behaviour (ibid., 59). In the months that followed she sometimes argued fiercely on religion and politics with Cromwellian officers, but she won their respect. She continued offering medical care to those that needed it—though the price paid by English soldiers for aid was exhortations to repent their sin of rebellion.

Always anxious to avoid being a burden to others Anne left Fyvie in mid-1652, and in Edinburgh began legal proceedings to recover her property. Yet again Bampfield appeared on the scene, still deep in royalist intrigue, and she was also courted by Sir James Halkett of Pitfirrane, a widower with several children. Early in 1653 she learned for certain that Bampfield's wife was alive. Once she had recovered from the shock she was won over by Halkett's advances, and agreed first to look after his daughters, then to marry him. Wishing first to settle her debts, so as to avoid being a burden on her husband, she went to London, where for the last time she encountered Bampfield. To get rid of him she told him that she was already married to Halkett, and he then disappeared from her life. To herself she excused her little lie by claiming that she had silently inserted 'not' in her statement that she was married.

Anne was in fact still uncertain as to whether or not to marry Halkett, but his persistence, confirmed by his following her to London, won her over, and she at last paid off the creditors who were pressing her (though only with the help of loans from friends). Her marriage took place on 2 March 1656 at her brother-in-law's house at Charlton in Kent, and thereafter she lived with her husband at Pitfirrane in Fife. According to Scottish custom she would have retained her maiden name of Murray, but latterly she signed herself Halkett, and was known as Lady Halkett. Between 1656 and 1661 she gave birth to four children;

only one survived infancy. Following the restoration of the monarchy she visited court (1660–61) to express her joy, and received £500 sterling from the king and a gift of £50 sterling to one of her children from the duke of York, but her delight was outweighed by grief at her son Henry dying 'to teach mee nott to love the world' (*Autobiography*, 110).

Following her husband's death in September 1670 Anne moved to Dunfermline. In 1677–8 she wrote her memoirs. In 1683 she began caring for and teaching the orphan children of local gentry, to add to her income—and doubtless also as an expression of her desire to find practical expression for her piety. She also held a weekly free surgery for the local sick, and her reputation led to her receiving requests for advice and medicines from all over the country. The accession of the duke of York as James II in 1685 brought her a pension of £100 sterling in recognition of her part in his 1648 escape. She died at Dunfermline on 22 April 1699. For two centuries after her death Anne was remembered, if at all, for her religious writings, which eventually ran to twenty-one manuscript volumes (fourteen of which survive). Extracts were published in Edinburgh in 1701, but they make no claim to originality. Her brief *Instructions for youth … for the use of those young noblemen and gentlemen whose education was committed to her care* (1701), for example, consists of conventional notes closely based on the Bible, starting from the standard premise that all youth is 'infected with the contagion of sin' (*Instructions*), and needs cleansing. But her piety was tempered by brisk common sense (washing feet as a charitable act was rendered inappropriate in Scotland by the climate).

However, these tracts are now greatly overshadowed in reputation by her memoirs or autobiography. It is outstanding in its century for the detail in which she records her emotions and depicts her search for love, marriage, and security. Sadly she misses out her childhood, as uninteresting, and if she wrote about her life after her marriage this has been lost. Pages concerning her mother's death, and her reaction on finally accepting that Bampfield's wife was alive, have been torn out of the manuscript, and it may be that she censored her own text, having decided she had written too frankly on these matters and on her marriage. What survives of the text reveals her as courageous and determined, writing to make sense of her life, justifying some of her actions but censuring other ones. Though a staunch Anglican her introspection recalls some puritan memoirs devoted to soul-searching, but her text also shows Anne seeing her life as a drama, with repeated build-ups of suspense in her search for love. Bampfield stars as a hero as ambiguous as any novelist could have invented—is he an honest man, indeed a heroic royalist agent, worthy of love, or a cunning dissembler? Eventually he is revealed and rejected as unworthy. But to the end Anne refuses to denounce him, stressing all his good qualities. By the time she wrote he had long been discredited as having become a double agent, working for Oliver Cromwell, but Anne still bathed him in a romantic aura. Perhaps the memoirs end at the point they do because Anne decided that the security that marriage brought also provided the climax, or the anticlimax, that ended the drama of her life, the part she felt worth recording. David Stevenson

**Sources** *The memoirs of Anne, Lady Halkett and Ann, Lady Fanshawe*, ed. J. Loftis (1979) · *The autobiography of Anne Lady Halkett*, ed. J. G. Nichols (1875) · D. Stevenson, 'A lady and her lovers', *King or covenant: voices from civil war* (1996) · *DNB* · M. Bottrall, *Every man a phoenix: studies in seventeenth-century autobiography* (1958) · L. M. Cumming, 'Anne, Lady Halkett', *Blackwood*, 216 (1924), 654–76 · [S. Couper], *Life of Lady Halkett* (1701) · M. B. Rose, 'Gender, genre, and history: seventeenth-century English women and the art of autobiography', *Women in the middle ages and the Renaissance: literary and historical perspectives*, ed. M. B. Rose (Syracuse, 1986) · W. Shumaker, *English autobiography: its emergence, materials and form* (Berkeley, 1954) · GEC, *Peerage*

**Archives** BL, autobiography, Add. MS 32376 · NL Scot., meditations, MSS 6484–6502 | NA Scot., letters to Sir William Bruce

**Halkett, Sir Colin** (**1774–1856**), army officer, eldest son of Major-General Frederick Godar *Halkett (1727/8–1803), and his wife, Georgina Robina Seton, was born on 7 September 1774, at Venlo, in the Netherlands. His father was at that time a major in the regiment of Gordon of the Scots brigade. Halkett served as an officer in the Dutch foot guards from 1792 to April 1795. On 3 January 1799 he was appointed ensign, 3rd Buffs, which he never joined, resigning his commission in February 1800, when the Dutch levies, which had been serving on the continent under the prince of Orange, were taken into British pay. Halkett became captain in the 2nd Dutch light infantry, commanded by Lieutenant-Colonel T. Sprecher van Bernegg and quartered in Guernsey. These troops never appeared in the *Army List*. They were stationed in the Isle of Wight and the Channel Islands until the peace of Amiens, when they were sent to the Netherlands to be disbanded, the officers receiving special gratuities on discharge.

In August 1803, on the dissolution of the Hanoverian army after the convention of Lauenburg, when many discharged soldiers were looking to Britain for employment, Halkett, described as a major in the Dutch service, which by then he seems to have left, was authorized by the British government to raise a battalion of light infantry in Hanover. Halkett was to be major-commandant, with the promise of a lieutenant-colonelcy should the battalion muster 800 men. As German recruits abounded in England at that time the formation of a German legion, under the duke of Cambridge, was decided on soon after. Recruiting for the independent levies of Baron von der Decken and Major Halkett in Germany then ceased, and these two corps became respectively the 1st and 2nd light battalions of the new King's German Legion. They were dressed as riflemen, and stationed at first in the New Forest and afterwards at Bexhill, Sussex. Halkett was appointed lieutenant-colonel on 17 November 1803.

At the head of the 2nd light battalion Halkett served under Lord Cathcart in the north of Germany in 1805–6, and in Ireland in 1806. After being shipwrecked with part of the battalion off Land's End in May 1807 he served on the Isle of Rügen and in the Copenhagen expedition later that year. He was in Sweden and Portugal during 1808; in Moore's retreat through Spain, when the German light battalions were among the troops that retired on Vigo; and in the Walcheren expedition, where these battalions distinguished themselves. As part of the German light brigade under Charles Alten, Halkett's battalion joined Beresford's army before Badajoz in April 1811, a few days before the fall of Olivença.

Halkett commanded the brigade at the battle of Albuera and, having been appointed brevet colonel on 1 January 1812, was with his battalion at Salamanca and in the operations against Burgos. He led the German light brigade in the ensuing retreat, where he won the approbation of Wellington; in the affair at Venta de Pozo, where the 2nd light battalion was commanded by his brother, Hugh *Halkett; at the bridge of Simancas; and during the succeeding campaigns, including the battle of Vitoria, the occupation of Tolosa, the passage of the Bidassoa, and the battles on the Nive and at Toulouse. He became a major-general on 4 June 1814, and KCB in January 1815. In the Waterloo campaign he commanded a British brigade composed of the 30th, 33rd, 69th, and 73rd regiments, in the 3rd division, which was very heavily engaged at Quatre Bras and Waterloo, where Halkett himself received four severe wounds. Wellington referred to him in a dispatch as 'a very gallant and deserving officer' (*Supplementary Despatches*, 10.752).

Halkett remained in the British army; he was lieutenant-governor of Jersey from July 1821 to August 1830, and commander-in-chief at Bombay from July 1831 to January 1832. He had become a lieutenant-general in July 1830, and was made general in November 1846. Halkett was appointed colonel in succession of the 71st Highland light infantry, 31st and 45th regiments. He was a GCB (December 1847) and GCH (1820) and knight of Dutch, Bavarian, and Portuguese orders, and honorary general in the Hanoverian service. Appointed lieutenant-governor of the Royal Hospital, Chelsea, in 1848, he became governor on the death of Sir George Anson in 1849. Halkett married Letitia (*née* Crickett), widow of Captain Tyler, Royal Artillery, and they had one son and two daughters. He died at the hospital, on 24 September 1856.

H. M. CHICHESTER, *rev.* DAVID GATES

**Sources** Boase, *Mod. Eng. biog.* • *GM*, 3rd ser., 1 (1856), 649 • N. L. Beamish, *History of the king's German legion*, 2 vols. (1832–7) • J. Philippart, ed., *The royal military calendar*, 3rd edn, 3 (1820), 380 • *The dispatches of … the duke of Wellington … from 1799 to 1818*, ed. J. Gurwood, 6: *Peninsula, 1790–1813* (1836), 136, 142 • *The dispatches of … the duke of Wellington … from 1799 to 1818*, ed. J. Gurwood, 8: *Peninsula, 1790–1813* (1837), 147, 150 • *Supplementary despatches (correspondence) and memoranda of Field Marshal Arthur, duke of Wellington*, ed. A. R. Wellesley, second duke of Wellington, 15 vols. (1858–72), vol. 8, pp. 9, 29, 419; vol. 10, pp. 3, 535, 551, 604, 659, 661, 752; vol. 13, p. 670; vol. 14, pp. 203, 209 • C. W. C. Oman, *A history of the Peninsular War*, 6 (1922), 69, 83, 425 • Burke, *Gen. GB* (1914) • A. B. Rodger, *The war of the second coalition: 1798–1801, a strategic commentary* (1964) • D. Gates, *The Spanish ulcer: a history of the Peninsular War* (1986)

**Likenesses** J. W. Pieneman, oils, Wellington Museum, London • W. Salter, group portrait, oil study (*Waterloo banquet at Apsley House*), NPG • W. Salter, group portrait, oils (*Waterloo Banquet at Apsley House*), Wellington Museum, London

**Halkett, Frederick Godar** (1727/8–1803), army officer, was born in the Netherlands, the son of Lieutenant-General Charles Halkett (1683–1758), of the Dutch army, colonel of a regiment of the Scots brigade in the pay of the Netherlands, and his second wife, Anne Le Foucher, a Frenchwoman. He was descended from a distinguished military family: his great-great-grandfather was Sir John Halkett (*d.* 1628), general in the Dutch service; his grandfather Lieutenant-Colonel Edward Halkett (*d.* 1706) served in the Scots brigade during the War of the Spanish Succession; and his half-brother, Colonel Charles Halkett (*d.* 1812), was of the Dutch service and governor of Namur. He became an ensign in the regiment of Gordon on 13 June 1743, and rose through each grade to be lieutenant-colonel of the 2nd battalion of the regiment of Dundas on 5 November 1777.

On 21 October 1771 Halkett married Georgina Robina, daughter of George Robert Seton and Margaret Abercrombie; they had several children, including Colin *Halkett (1774–1856) and Hugh *Halkett (1783–1863). He left the Netherlands for Edinburgh in 1782 after the Dutch, critical of Britain's war with the American colonies, demanded that members of the Scots brigade now recognize the Dutch states general as sovereign and give up their British uniform and colours.

After the outbreak of the French Revolutionary War, Halkett was summoned to The Hague to advise on the military position, but he refused to take any command, though he accepted a commission in the Dutch guards for his son Colin. On his return to Edinburgh he raised one of the battalions of the so-called Scots brigade, a corps which, after service in India and the Peninsula, was disbanded, as the 94th foot, in 1818.

Halkett, whose commission as lieutenant-colonel was dated 5 July 1793, became a brevet colonel in 1795. He retired from active service on account of age soon afterwards. He became a major-general in 1802, and died at 46 George's Street, Edinburgh, on 8 August 1803.

H. M. CHICHESTER, *rev.* ALEXANDER DU TOIT

**Sources** J. Ferguson, *The Scots brigade in Holland*, 3 vols. (1899–1901) • Anderson, *Scot. nat.* • R. Douglas and others, *The baronage of Scotland* (1798) • Burke, *Gen. GB* • *Scots Magazine*, 65 (1803), 671

**Halkett, Sir Hugh** (1783–1863), army officer, second son of Major-General Frederick Godar *Halkett (1727/8–1803) and his wife, Georgina Robina, daughter of George Robert Seton, was born at Musselburgh, near Edinburgh, on 30 August 1783. He was an active boy who loved horses. On 19 April 1794 he was made ensign in his father's battalion of the Scots brigade, then raising, and became lieutenant in 1795. He joined the regiment in 1797, and in 1798 (until when he was on the rolls as on recruiting service) went out to India in charge of a draft of 240 men, arriving after the capture of Seringapatam. He served in India until 1801, when he was invalided home. In 1803 he was nominated senior captain of the light battalion raising in Hanover under his brother, Colin *Halkett, which became the 2nd light battalion of the King's German Legion in British pay, and in which Hugh Halkett became major before he was twenty-two. He served with the battalion in the north of

Germany under Lord Cathcart in 1805–6, in the Isle of Rugen and at the siege of Stralsund in 1807, and in the expedition against Copenhagen later in the year. His promptitude in outpost duty in seizing a Danish redoubt without waiting for orders won the approval of Sir David Baird. Halkett, who was modest in speaking of his own deeds, used to allude to the occurrence in after years as 'the best thing I ever did' (Beamish, 1.116–18). He went with his battalion to Sweden in 1808, and from there to Portugal.

Halkett was in the Corunna retreat, in the Walcheren expedition, and at the siege of Flushing, and in 1811 went to the Peninsula and commanded his battalion at the battle of Albuera. He commanded it again in the following year at the siege of the forts of Salamanca, at the battle of Salamanca, and in the Burgos retreat, where the light brigade, composed of the 1st and 2nd light battalions of the German legion, formed the rear-guard of the army. On 22 October 1812 these battalions distinguished themselves by their gallant repulse of the French cavalry at Venta de Pozo. Halkett was promoted lieutenant-colonel of the 7th line battalion of the legion, then in Sicily.

In April 1813 Halkett, then on leave in England, was sent to north Germany, with some officers and men of the German legion, to assist in organizing the new Hanoverian levies. In command of a brigade of these troops in Count Walmoden's army he distinguished himself at the battle of Göhrde on 16 September 1813, and in the unsuccessful fight with the Danes at Schestedt in December following. On the latter occasion, when a Danish cavalry regiment was attacking a battalion of his brigade, Halkett dashed upon the standard-bearer, seized the standard, and escaped by clearing a quickset hedge with double ditch, over which none of his many pursuers chose to follow. He held command at the sieges of Glückstadt and Harburg in 1814.

In the Waterloo campaign Halkett commanded the 3rd and 4th brigades of the subsidiary force of Hanoverian militia or *Landwehr*, which accompanied the newly organized Hanoverian regular troops (not to be confused with the German legion) into Belgium. On 18 June these brigades were with Clinton's division in the wood to the right of Hougoumont, where, at the close of the day, Halkett distinguished himself by taking prisoner the French general, Pierre J. E. Cambronne, commander of the imperial guard. Halkett rode up to the broken French troops, seized Cambronne, and cantered off with him back to the British line. After the peace the German legion in British pay, in which Halkett was still lieutenant-colonel of the 7th line battalion, was disbanded. Halkett was put on British half pay, which he drew until his death.

Halkett and other legionaries received permanent appointments in the new Hanoverian army. In 1817 he was colonel of the Emden *Landwehr* battalion, linked with the 10th Hanoverian line infantry; in 1818 he became a major-general in the Hanoverian army, and colonel of the 8th or Hoya infantry. The following year he was made colonel of the 4th or Celle infantry, in 1834 lieutenant-general and commander of the 4th infantry brigade, in 1836 commander of a division, and in 1848 general and inspector-general of Hanoverian infantry. He was sent to Osnabrück in 1839, when disturbances were feared following constitutional changes. His tact and popularity rendered repressive measures unnecessary. He was put in command of the 10th army corps of the German confederation assembled for autumn manoeuvres near Lüneburg in 1843, and in 1848 commanded the same army corps in the Prussian-Danish War, under Von Wrangel. Ten years later Halkett sought leave to retire. On the anniversary of Waterloo in 1858 the Hanoverian chambers voted him a life pension equal to the full pay of his rank. He was also made a baron.

Halkett was a CB (June 1815) and GCH (1851), and he had Prussian, Russian, Danish, and Swedish orders and various war medals including the British gold medal. He was described as a bright, active, cheery little man, very popular with all ranks, speaking German very badly with an English accent. He married, on 25 May 1810, Emily Charlotte, daughter of Sir James Bland *Burges, afterwards Lamb, and Anne de Montolieu, Sir James's second wife, and they had four sons and four daughters. Three of his sons were officers in the British army. Halkett died at Hanover after a long illness on 26 July 1863.

H. M. CHICHESTER, *rev.* JAMES LUNT

**Sources** Burke, *Gen. GB* • Burke, *Peerage* • *Army List* • N. L. Beamish, *History of the king's German legion*, 2 vols. (1832–7) • W. F. P. Napier, *History of the war in the Peninsula and in the south of France*, 3 vols. (1878) • E. von dem Knesebeck, *Leben des Freiherrn von Halkett* (1865) • Poten, 'Halkett, Hugh', *Allgemeine deutsche Biographie*, ed. R. von Liliencron and others, 56 vols. (Leipzig, 1875–1912), vol. 10 • *Hof- und Staats-Handbuch für das Königreich Hannover* (1864) [necrology] • C. A. Wilkinson, *Reminiscences of the court of King Ernest I of Hanover* (1886) • Boase, *Mod. Eng. biog.*

**Likenesses** wood-engraving, NPG; repro. in *ILN* (1863)

**Wealth at death** under £1500: administration with will, 20 April 1864, *CGPLA Eng. & Wales*

**Halkett, Samuel** (1814–1871), librarian, was born on 21 June 1814 in the North Back of the Canongate, Edinburgh, where his father, also Samuel, was a brewer; his mother was Euphemia Wallace. Educated at White's English School in Frederick Street, and Smith's classical academy in George Street, Edinburgh, he was apprenticed at the age of fourteen to the firm of Marshall and Aitken, drapers and hosiers. After five years there he moved to the employ of Abernethy and Stewart, merchants, but by 1838 had set up his own drapery business, partnered by a fellow former apprentice, George Harrison (later Sir George, lord provost of Edinburgh from 1882 to 1885). On 9 April 1850, in Edinburgh, he married Caroline Sophia Roland (1823–1883); they had two sons and two daughters.

Despite the long hours necessary to pursue his business, Halkett devoted what leisure time he had to the deep study of languages, not only European but also Middle Eastern and Asian. By his mid-thirties his remarkable linguistic skills, later described in his obituary in *The Athenaeum* as 'simply stupendous', had become internationally well known, and testimonials written by scholars with whom he had dealings secured him in 1848 the vacant position of keeper of the Advocates' Library in Edinburgh. He thus became working head of the largest library in Scotland, a startling departure from his previous career. He continued his linguistic studies until his death, but his professional life was dominated by the desire for a comprehensive printed library catalogue of the 200,000 printed items in the collection. He soon organized the production of a much improved and augmented author catalogue in manuscript, and then used this as a basis for a printed version, which was to include biographical details on authors and very full titles. The printing began in 1860, with volume 1 complete by 1867, but by Halkett's death only entries beginning with the letters 'cast' had been reached in volume 2. The work, totalling seven volumes, was completed on a reduced plan in 1879. Halkett's other professional preoccupations centred upon the complete inadequacy of the library's funds and accommodation, which prevented it from fulfilling what was increasingly seen as a national role. Despite the issuing of an 1868 memorandum by a faculty committee pleading for government help, to which Halkett contributed an appendix, his budget and working conditions did not improve.

Halkett began to compile, as an offshoot of his catalogue work, an index of works produced anonymously or pseudonymously in Britain with authors identified. After his death this material passed to his friend John Laing, librarian of New College, Edinburgh, who greatly increased the entries. The work, in four volumes, *A Dictionary of the Anonymous and Pseudonymous Literature of Great Britain*, was eventually published after Laing's death, between 1882 and 1888, and quickly became a standard reference work with a high reputation for accuracy. An expanded edition in nine volumes appeared between 1926 and 1962. Halkett also wrote three articles, on bibliography, bibliomania, and libraries, for Chambers's *Encyclopaedia* (1860–68).

In April 1871, having been ill with stomach trouble since the beginning of the year, Halkett contracted typhus; he died in Edinburgh on the 20th of that month. He was buried in Warriston cemetery, Edinburgh, on the 22nd. He was mourned as an amiable, modest, and social man, a good administrator, and a great linguist always willing to share his knowledge with others. He was also a talented amateur musician, playing several instruments. His library, mostly relating to his linguistic studies, was sold in over 700 lots at auction in Edinburgh on 23 January 1872.

MURRAY C. T. SIMPSON

**Sources** 'Death of Mr Halkett, keeper of the Advocates' Library', *Edinburgh Evening Courant* (21 April 1871); pubd separately (1871) · W. Black, 'Biographical notices of some eminent Edinburgh librarians', *Third annual meeting of the Library Association* [Edinburgh 1880], ed. E. C. Thomas and C. Welch (1881), 30–48 · *Testimonials in favour of Mr Samuel Halkett* (1848) · *DNB* · *The Athenaeum* (29 April 1871), 528 · P. Cadell and A. Matheson, eds., *For the encouragement of learning: Scotland's National Library, 1689–1989* (1989), 210–12 · parish register (baptisms), Edinburgh, South Leith, 15 July 1814 · register of deaths, Edinburgh, 20 Apr 1871

**Likenesses** watercolour, Scot. NPG

**Wealth at death** £790 10s. od.: confirmation, 31 May 1871, NA Scot., SC 70/1/153/347

**Hall family** (*per.* c.**1650–c.1750**), ironmasters, became involved in the iron trade with the marriage, late in the 1640s, of **Michael Hall** (1623/4–c.1670), a younger son of Richard Hall of Greet, Shropshire. Michael had been educated at Christ Church, Oxford, from where he matriculated aged seventeen in 1641; his wife was **Elizabeth Hall** [*née* Cotton] (*d.* 1679), sister of the ironmaster William *Cotton (*d.* 1675) [*see under* Cotton family]. They had nine children. In 1662 Cotton became partner of the Myddelton family of Chirk Castle in their Denbighshire ironworks and by 1663 Michael Hall was living at Ruabon, where the partnership's blast furnace was situated. He died about 1670, being succeeded as clerk in the ironworks by his eldest son, a second Michael Hall (1654–1684). Elizabeth Hall subsequently had the oversight of the furnace for which, in addition to 'riding charges' incurred for sales of iron and purchase of charcoal, she was paid £30 a year until her death in 1679.

A younger son, **Thomas Hall** (1657–1715), who was born at Tenbury, Worcestershire, on 26 March 1657, operated the furnace at Madeley, Staffordshire, from 1683, probably in conjunction with Norton and Winnington forges. By 1687 he was a partner in the Cheshire ironworks with his cousin William *Cotton (1648/9–1703) [*see under* Cotton family]. During the 1690s he managed this partnership (Lawton furnace, Warmingham and Cranage forges, Cranage slitting mill, and Street plating forge), which from 1696 onwards was closely linked with the Staffordshire works (Mear Heath furnace, Consall, Tib Green, Oakamoor, Chartley, Abbots Bromley, and Cannock forges, with Consall and Rugeley slitting mills), a Foley and Wheeler concern. Hall further cemented his family's industrial links by his marriage in 1697 to Cotton's sister, Joanna (*d.* 1721), though this union left no surviving children.

Hall built a new Cheshire furnace in 1696 at Vale Royal. It smelted haematite ores brought by sea from Furness, so most of its product was tough pig iron. Some of this went to a forge which Hall built in 1699 at Bodfari to supply north Wales. Vale Royal, Lawton, and Mear Heath were three of the largest furnaces of the period, and because the Cheshire partnership now had two large furnaces, it was able to make good the Staffordshire deficit of pig iron with either tough pig from Vale Royal or cold-short pig smelted from local ores at Lawton. This made the amalgamation of the two partnerships in 1707 a logical step. In the Staffordshire works Hall owned a seventh share, and after the death of John Wheeler he also acted as managing director for a short time. But his responsibilities covered a wide area; in Yorkshire after the death of William [ii] Cotton he witnessed a wood agreement of 1704 and the new lease of Colne Bridge forge in 1706, on behalf of Anna Cotton (*d.* 1721), his sister-in-law. Thomas Hall died at The Hermitage, Cranage, on 25 March 1715.

Thomas's younger brother **Edward Hall** (1664–1750) of Cranage was born at Ruabon, Denbighshire, on 14 April 1664. He was briefly a scholar at Brasenose College,

Oxford, in 1684, and he is known to have delivered iron for the use of Sir Thomas Myddelton in 1685. In 1701 he married Anne Frances Maurice (*d.* 1758) in Chester; they had three sons and three daughters. By 1700 his investment of £10,251 made him the largest shareholder in the Cheshire works. Hall's responsibility was Warmingham forge, though in 1706 he transferred to Vale Royal furnace and Bodfari forge. After the amalgamation of the partnerships he had a sixth share in the Cheshire works and a seventh in those of Staffordshire, and he gradually succeeded to the dominating role played by his brother. Already in 1711, along with his cousin Daniel *Cotton (*c.*1660–1723) [*see under* Cotton family], he had established a furnace at Cunsey in Furness, though the company continued to smelt haematite ores in Cheshire, until 1718 at Vale Royal and then at a new furnace built at Oulton in 1719. In 1720 Hall acquired a share in the new Bretton furnace–Kilnhurst forge partnership of his Yorkshire nephew, William Westby *Cotton (*bap.* 1689, *d.* 1749) [*see under* Cotton family]. The same year he built a furnace at Carr Mill, near St Helens, on a thirty-year lease from a Roman Catholic co-religionist, Sir William Gerard of Garswood. This furnace presumably worked in conjunction with Aintree forge, which Hall held in 1727. In Furness he had the Cheshire company's second furnace built at Duddon Bridge in 1736.

Edward Hall cannot have been a Roman Catholic when at Brasenose College, but was described as such when his estates were duly registered in 1723. The ironmasters Thomas Hall and William Hall, who presented silver communion patens to Bodfari and Lawton churches respectively in 1699, were presumably his elder brothers Thomas and William (1659–1700). William resided at Ruthin from 1679 to 1685 and died at Mostyn. In 1708 Thomas presented a double-tiered brass candelabrum to the church at Holmes Chapel, and there he also endowed schools. 'The present Ironmasters of Lawton Furnace' donated a peal of bells to the church at Lawton in 1713. There is, however, no record of similar gifts by Edward Hall himself, who died on 23 September 1750.

Edward's eldest son was **Thomas Hall** (1702–1748) of The Hermitage, Cranage, who was born on 3 June 1702 at Warmingham forge. He possibly attended Peterhouse, Cambridge. He married Elizabeth Bayley (*d.* 1745) of Nantwich in 1738, and they had a son and a daughter. Thomas's will mentions his interest in Bodfari forge; from there he had supplied iron to Ruthin church in 1720. Receipts of iron at the Stour valley forges during the 1730s demonstrate Thomas Hall's involvement at Sowley furnace in Hampshire, and in 1729 in connection with this he, along with Myles Troughton of Beaulieu, took a sixteen-year lease of Viscount Montagu's mines at Lindal and Dalton in Furness. Thomas Hall served as mayor of Chester during the Jacobite rising of 1745, and was apparently of the established church. He died at The Hermitage, Cranage, on 27 June 1748. Edward Hall's youngest son, Maurice (1715–1741), was involved in wood-procurement in south Lancashire in 1741, but also predeceased his father. The second son and executor, Richard Edward Hall (1703–1793), was a Manchester surgeon, so managerial interest in the iron industry passed out of the family.

After the building of the Vale Royal furnace by Thomas Hall in 1696, the Hall family was of major importance for the development of the iron industry in north-west England. The decision of the Cheshire partnership to establish its own mines, furnace, and forge in Furness provoked local ironmasters into forming the Backbarrow company, and suddenly opened up the whole area to the blast furnace. The effective failure of the male line in the Hall family, however, coincided with the major technological and organizational changes within the iron industry which attended the transition from charcoal to coke smelting. Like their cousins and sometime partners, the Cottons, the Halls withdrew from the iron trade after a century of involvement. Their forge at Cranage and the furnaces at Cunsey, Carr Mill, and Lawton are all thought to have been discontinued about 1750.

The Hall family together with the associated kindred families of *Cotton and *Kendall, played a pioneering role in the growth of the iron industry in Britain between the mid-seventeenth and the mid-eighteenth centuries. Members of the family were active in wide-ranging business partnerships which were the leading producers of iron in Staffordshire, Cheshire, and the north-west of England.

BRIAN G. AWTY

**Sources** B. G. Awty, 'Charcoal ironmasters of Cheshire and Lancashire, 1600–1785', *Transactions of the Historic Society of Lancashire and Cheshire*, 109 (1957), 71–124 • A. Fell, *The early iron industry of Furness and district* (1908) • W. M. Myddelton, ed., *Chirk Castle accounts*, 2 vols. (1908–31) • B. L. C. Johnson, 'The Foley partnerships: the iron industry at the end of the charcoal era', *Economic History Review*, 2nd ser., 4 (1951–2), 322–40 • J. P. Earwaker, *History of Sandbach* (1890) • G. Ormerod, *The history of the county palatine and city of Chester*, 2nd edn, ed. T. Helsby, 3 vols. (1882) • I. Edwards, 'The charcoal iron industry of Denbighshire, *c.*1690–1770', *Transactions of the Denbighshire Historical Society*, 10 (1961), 1–49 • P. W. King, 'The Vale Royal Company and its rivals', *Transactions of the Historic Society of Lancashire and Cheshire*, 142 (1992), 1–18 • will, proved, 1748, Ches. & Chester ALSS [Edward Hall] • Foster, *Alum. Oxon.*, 1500–1714 [Michael Hall, Robert Hall] • Venn, *Alum. Cant.* [Thomas Hall, 1702–1748] • J. H. Turner, T. Dickenson, and O. Heywood, eds., *The nonconformist register of baptisms, marriages, and deaths* (1881)

**Hall** [*married name* Hall-Hicks], **Adelaide Louise Estelle** (**1901–1993**), jazz and cabaret singer, was born on 20 October 1901 in Brooklyn, New York, the elder daughter of William Arthur Hall, a piano and singing teacher at the Pratt Institute, New York, of African-American and Dutch descent, and his wife, Elizabeth, *née* Gerard, of African-American and North American Indian descent. Her father died when she was fourteen, and her younger sister, Evelyn, died in the flu epidemic of 1918. A self-taught tap dancer, Hall began her stage career in Noble Sissle's and Eubie Blake's Broadway musical *Shuffle Along* (1921). This was the most successful musical created to date by African Americans, and demonstrated that there was a place for them in commercial musical theatre. In 1924 she married a merchant seaman, Bertram (Bert) Hicks. Born in Trinidad, he was a British subject, educated in London and Edinburgh.

Adelaide Louise Estelle Hall (1901–1993), by Walery, *c.*1930

He gave up the sea to become her manager—a role he kept until his death in 1963. There were no children of the marriage.

Hall enjoyed another success on Broadway in *Runnin' Wild* (1923) and toured Europe in the revue *The Chocolate Kiddies* (1925), with a music score written by Duke Ellington and Jo Trent. Her association with Duke Ellington continued when he encouraged her to become one of the first scat vocalists in jazz. It happened, almost by chance, when she was appearing with Ellington in *Jazzmania* at the Lafayette Theatre in Harlem. Her wordless vocal on 'Creole Love Call', which they subsequently recorded on 26 October 1927, was innovatory as a use of the voice as pure jazz instrument. However, most jazz critics and historians have undervalued her work as a jazz singer or, worse still, ignored her altogether. An exception is Gunther Schuller who, in *The Swing Era: the Development of Jazz, 1930–1945* (1989), described her recording of 'Drop me off in Harlem' as 'totally original … Her singing is rich with delightful, pert inflections and impeccable diction. It virtually transforms [Duke] Ellington's opus into an American art song' (Schuller, 389). Adelaide's association with Duke Ellington continued throughout her career. In 1974 she performed at his memorial service at St Martin-in-the-Fields, London. In 1928 she starred opposite the legendary dancer Bill Bojangles Robinson in another stage hit, *Blackbirds of 1928*—Broadway's longest-running black-cast revue. It was in this musical that she introduced Dorothy Fields's and Jimmy McHugh's standard 'I can't give you anything but love'. In 1931 she visited London for the first time and became one of the first black entertainers to top the bill at the London Palladium. On returning to the United States, she toured extensively using jazz musicians, such as Art Tatum and Joe Turner, as accompanists; in 1934 she headlined at New York's famous Cotton Club, where she introduced 'Ill Wind', written for her by Harold Arlen and Ted Koehler.

After leaving the Cotton Club, Hall settled in Paris with her husband and together they opened their own nightclub, La Grosse Pomme (The Big Apple). While running the club, she performed in cabaret all along the French coast. In 1938 she accepted an offer to appear in *The Sun Never Sets*, a stage production at London's Drury Lane Theatre. After selling La Grosse Pomme, she and her husband made London their permanent home, and opened the Florida Club in Mayfair. Also in 1938 she recorded 'I can't give you anything but love' and 'That Old Feeling' with jazz legend Fats Waller at the HMV Studios in London. Between 1939 and 1945 she made over seventy recordings for Decca. In 1940 she made a brief appearance in the film classic *The Thief of Bagdad*. After losing the Florida Club in an air-raid during the London blitz, she spent the remainder of the war broadcasting for the BBC, touring Britain's music-halls, and entertaining the troops for the Entertainments National Service Association. After the war, she appeared in cabaret and occasional West End musicals, including Cole Porter's *Kiss me, Kate* (1951). In the same year she and her husband opened their third nightclub, the Calypso, in London's Regent Street. Also in 1951, for BBC radio, she made a rare acting appearance with Flora Robson and John Gielgud in *Helena* by Evelyn Waugh and Christopher Sykes. In 1957, after an absence of twenty-seven years, she reappeared on the Broadway musical stage in *Jamaica* with Lena Horne. It ran for over 500 performances.

After the death of her husband in 1963, Hall's career lost direction, and for a while she supported herself by taking boarders into her South Kensington home. By the 1970s her career had reached such a low point that she could be found performing in town halls up and down Britain. There were also occasional guest appearances in pantomimes and revues such as *Dick Whittington* and *The Jolson Minstrel Show*. Things began to look up in 1980 when she returned to New York to take part in *Black Broadway*—a vaudeville-style song-and-dance salute to several surviving black Broadway legends of the 1920s. Five years later, when Francis Ford Coppola's film *The Cotton Club* was released in Britain, the British press discovered they had a real-life Cotton Club legend in their midst. To her delight the release of the film gave Hall an unexpected career boost and she found herself in demand for press interviews, cabaret appearances, and two important television documentaries: *Omnibus: the Cotton Club Comes to the Ritz* (BBC) and *The South Bank Show: the Real Cotton Club* (London Weekend Television). In an interview with Clive Goodman in the *Daily Mail*, she said:

> Look, I'm way past seventy. Before the film, I'd been singing in town halls up and down the country, doing charity shows. People thought I was back in the States, that's how quiet things were. But ever since the movie came out my phone hasn't stopped ringing. It feels good to be a legend—and still living. (*Daily Mail*, 25 May 1985)

She continued performing in her one-woman show until her early nineties, and in 1986 Bruce Crowther and Mike Pinfold assessed her performing style in their book *The Jazz Singers: from Ragtime to the New Wave*:

> She has a light, flexible voice and her sense of style is perfectly balanced with a degree of sophistication and warmth rarely encountered in popular singing. She has the ability to project the feeling of a lyric with great finesse. Not always at ease with a fast tempo, her forte is the slow, meaningful ballad which she invariably portrays with rare skill and sensitivity. (Crowther and Pinfold, 76)

In October 1988 there was a triumphant, sell-out home-coming when Hall made an appearance in her one-woman show at the Weill recital room at New York's Carnegie Hall. Audiences voted her the artiste they most wanted to come back, and she obliged with another appearance in 1992. Meanwhile, in 1989, Adelaide's happy and joyful personality was successfully captured in *Sophisticated Lady*, a Channel 4 television documentary which included reminiscences by the star and excerpts from a concert filmed at the Riverside Studios. Also in 1989 she was given a special award from the BBC's Jazz Society for her 'outstanding contribution to music over the past sixty-two years'. This was followed in 1992 with a gold badge of merit from the British Academy of Songwriters, Composers and Arrangers. In 1991 she celebrated her ninetieth birthday with an all-star tribute at the Queen Elizabeth Hall. She died in London's Charing Cross Hospital on 7 November 1993 and her funeral took place in New York at the cathedral of the Incarnation in Garden City. She was buried with her father, mother, and sister.

STEPHEN BOURNE

**Sources** R. Dunbar, 'American-born entertainer is the darling of London', *Baltimore Afro-American* (27 Feb 1948) • B. Green, 'A timeless voice of Britain's queen of jazz', *Daily Mail* (11 Nov 1993) • F. McHugh, 'Sweet Adelaide sings on', *The Times* (30 Jan 1988) • C. Larkin, *The Guinness who's who of stage musicals* (1994) • S. Bourne, 'The love call', *Wire* (Aug 1988) • A. Woll, *Black musical theatre: from Coontown to dreamgirls* (1989) • B. Crowther and M. Pinfold, *The jazz singers: from ragtime to the new wave* (1986) • H. Rye, 'Visiting firemen: 10 (a) Adelaide Hall, Joe Turner and Francis J. Carter', *Storyville*, 114 (Aug–Sept 1984) • G. Schuller, *The swing era: the development of jazz, 1930–1945* (1989) • C. Ellis, 'Adelaide Hall—the singing blackbird', *Storyville*, 31 (Oct–Nov 1970) • S. Nicholson, *A portrait of Duke Ellington: reminiscing in tempo* (1999) • A. Rose, *Eubie Blake* (1979) • d. cert. • personal knowledge (2004) • S. Bourne, *Sophisticated lady—a celebration of Adelaide Hall* (2001)

**Archives** FILM BFI NFTVA, *Omnibus*, BBC1 • BFI NFTVA, *South Bank show*, LWT • BFI NFTVA, 'Sophisticated lady', Channel 4, 1989 | SOUND BBC WAC • BL NSA, Oral history of jazz in Britain, 13 Dec 1988, T989–T990OYC1 • BL NSA, 'Sweet Adelaide' (4 parts), BBC Radio 4, April 1992, B9187/3

**Likenesses** Walery, photograph, *c*.1930, Hult. Arch. [*see illus.*] • photograph, repro. in *The Times* (8 Nov 1993) • photograph, repro. in *The Independent* (8 Nov 1993)

**Wealth at death** £194,881: probate, 31 Dec 1993, *CGPLA Eng. & Wales*

**Hall** [*née* Scott], **Agnes C.** [*pseud.* Rosalia St Clair] (**1775/6–1846**), writer and translator, was born in Roxburghshire. Little is known of her early life, but about 1796 she married Robert *Hall MD (1763–1824), in Linton, Roxburghshire. She was an industrious and versatile contributor on literary and scientific topics to the encyclopaedias of O. G. Gregory, William Nicholson, and Abraham Rees, and she also displayed her scientific interests in her *Elements of Botany* (1802). In the same year, under the initials A. C. H., she published *Rural Recreations, or, Modern Farmer's Calendar; and Monthly Instructor … by a Farmer*, a practical guide to the implementation of new agricultural methods and tools.

Hall was also a gifted translator, and had a particular interest in travel literature. In 1805 she translated *Voyage to, and Travels through, the Four Principal Islands of the African Seas* from the original work in French by J. B. G. M. Bory de Saint-Vincent, in 1806 M. A. B. Mangourit's *Travels in Hanover*, and in 1807 F. R. J. de Pons's *Travels in South America … during 1801, 1802, 1803, and 1804*. She also published translations of *The Memoirs of the Life and Writing of Victor Alfieri* (2 vols., 1810), and several historical romances by the comtesse de Genlis, including *La duchess de la Vallière (a novel)* (1804). Hall herself also wrote several novels, feeling it necessary to publish them under the pseudonym of Rosalia St Clair, even though they were later described as 'inculcating the purest morals, and the most patriotic and virtuous principles' (*GM*, 98). Among her original fiction was *The First and Last Years of Wedded Life* (1827), a story of Irish life in the reign of George IV, and a historical novel founded on the massacre of Glencoe. *Obstinacy* (1826), a didactic tale for young people, was published under her own name. In her later years, Hall contributed to the *Annual Biography*, the *Westminster Review*, and *Fraser's Magazine*. She died at 5 Charles Street, Clarendon Square, Somerstown, London, on 24 November 1846.

M. CLARE LOUGHLIN-CHOW

**Sources** *GM*, 2nd ser., 27 (1847), 97–8 • J. Britten and G. S. Boulger, *A biographical dictionary of British and Irish botanists* (1893) • *DNB* • *IGI* • d. cert.

**Archives** BL, letters as applicant to the Royal Literary Fund, loan no. 96

**Hall** [*née* Fielding], **Anna Maria** (**1800–1881**), writer, was born on 6 January 1800 in Anne Street, Dublin, the daughter of an obscure Irishman named Fielding and his wife, Sarah Elizabeth, of Swiss Huguenot extraction. Her father died in her infancy and she was raised by her mother and her mother's stepfather, George Carr, in the latter's household at Graige, Bannow, co. Wexford. In 1815 Carr brought mother and daughter to London, where in 1823 Anna Maria met another recent arrival from Wexford, (Samuel) Carter *Hall (1800–1889). The two were married on 20 September 1824 and settled in Chelsea, from where Carter Hall built up a career by bits and pieces as writer and journalist. Failing to start up the family both evidently wanted badly—only one child, Maria Louisa, was born alive, but did not live long—the Halls made a home with Mrs Fielding, who lived with them for thirty years until her death in 1856.

Carter Hall gradually brought Anna Maria into his multifarious enterprises. By 1829 her first book had appeared—reminiscences of her Irish childhood, collected as *Sketches of Irish Character*—and she had taken on her first editorship, that of the *Juvenile Forget-me-Not*, an illustrated annual. There followed in quick succession children's tales (starting with *Chronicles of a School-Room*, 1830), novels (including *The Buccaneer*, 1832, *Marian*, 1839, and *The Whiteboy*, 1845), more Irish tales (*Lights and Shadows of Irish Life*, 1838, includes some of the best known), plays (including *The French Refugee* at the Adelphi, 1836, and her own adaptation of *Marian* at the St James's, 1838), and an endless stream of homiletic essays, tracts, sketches, and stories. She had a hand, too, in many of her husband's works, certainly including a substantial book on Ireland in 1840; a companion volume on Scotland was planned in 1845–6 but never materialized.

Though skilled at all of the popular genres of the booming early Victorian publishing industry—historical, touristic, domestic, moral, melodramatic—Anna Maria's most popular and significant works were Irish in subject matter. Her goal in these Irish writings was to show how character transcended national and sectarian divides and that national improvement could only be achieved by individual moral striving. This general approach she shared with Maria Edgeworth and Lady Morgan, to whom she is often compared (albeit, on artistic grounds, unfavourably). In her eyes, and in those of many sentimental English readers, it made her something of a patriot—she liked to wear a mixture of orange and green ribbons in her hair—but it did little for her popularity in Ireland.

The Halls were at the height of their productivity and, probably, income in the 1840s, when they made their cottage home, The Rosery, Old Brompton, into a meeting-place for writers and artists at the mass end of the market. While Carter Hall was frankly disapproved of by this group, as too tory, self-satisfied, and puritanical, Anna Maria was thought to be altogether more sympathetic. She wrote in her study in absolute silence until 2 p.m. each day, but kept a popular 'at home' on Thursday afternoons and evenings, to which young women flocked for simple hospitality and advice delivered with 'love and candour' (Crosland, 123–4). Lady Bulwer-Lytton laughed at her as a 'red-round-of-beef' (Maas, 209), but others found her plain plumpness and self-effacing manner reassuring. Although she was generally unsympathetic to women's involvement in politics and opposed female suffrage, women were among the chief objects of her active philanthropic life. She had a lifelong interest in women's employment, mounting a petition in 1836 to secure 'reasonable hours' for shop-girls, writing and fund-raising in aid of the Governesses' Benevolent Institution, and concerning herself too with suitable jobs for married women, although she wished them above all to be understanding helpmeets for their husbands. Street musicians, temperance, the Brompton Consumption Hospital, and the Chelsea Hospital (where a ward was named after her) were other favoured causes.

The catholicity of Anna Maria's benevolence recommended her to a wide circle with which she did not necessarily see eye-to-eye on all things. Dickens, who found Carter Hall almost impossible to stomach, was markedly more partial to Anna Maria; in a letter of April 1844, he praised one of her improving tales on the plight of the governess, which had appeared in *Chambers's Journal*, as 'an immense relief to that somewhat cast-iron and utilitarian publication … delicately and beautifully done; with a womanly touch that cannot be mistaken' (*Letters of Charles Dickens*, 110). The more ardent feminists of the 1850s also found her amenable, and she mixed easily with the likes of Eliza Meteyard and Mary Howitt.

In 1849 the Halls moved their centre of operations out of town, to Firfield, a country house near Addlestone in Surrey. There they were less in the maelstrom of London literary life, and Anna Maria devoted more time to gardening and local charities. However, she took on the editing of *Sharpe's London Magazine* for a time (1852–3) and, more durably, the *St James's Magazine* (1861–8), where she published much decent serial fiction. Nor did the flow of writing abate, standards of quantity if not quality being maintained to sustain the couple's country life. By the end of their career, Carter Hall estimated that between them they had produced 545 books. He probably accounted for the majority by number, but Anna Maria's are on balance more memorable, as good illustrations of Victorian popular writing and of prevailing attitudes to gender relations as well as to Ireland.

Disraeli recognized both the Halls' respectability and their financial precariousness by granting Anna Maria a £100 civil-list pension in 1868. Further relief came on the occasion of their fiftieth wedding anniversary in 1874, when 600 subscribers presented them with a £100 annuity and £670 in cash at a meeting chaired by Lord Shaftesbury. The Halls still continued to write, now in a smaller home, Devon Lodge, in East Molesey, Surrey. Anna Maria's last book appeared a few months before her death on 30 January 1881. She was buried on 5 February in Addlestone churchyard, where Carter was also buried eight years later. PETER MANDLER

**Sources** M. Keane, *Mrs S. C. Hall: a literary biography* (1997) · S. C. Hall, *Retrospect of a long life, from 1815 to 1883*, 2 vols. (1883) · J. Newcomer, 'Mr. and Mrs. S. C. Hall: their papers at Iowa', *Books at Iowa* (Nov 1985), 15–23 · B. Sloan, 'Mrs Hall's Ireland', *Éire–Ireland*, 19/3 (1984), 18–30 · Mrs N. Crosland [C. Toulmin], *Landmarks of a literary life, 1820–1892* (1893) · S. J. B. Hale, 'Anna Maria Hall', *Woman's record, or, Sketches of all distinguished women*, 2nd edn (1855), 691–2 · W. Maginn, 'Mrs S. C. Hall', *Fraser's Magazine*, 13 (1836), 718 · 'Our portrait gallery, no. X: Mrs. S. C. Hall', *Dublin University Magazine*, 16 (1840), 146–9 · J. Maas, 'S. C. Hall and the *Art Journal*', *The Connoisseur*, 191 (1976), 206–9 · C. R. Woodring, *Victorian samplers: William and Mary Howitt* (1952) · *The letters of Charles Dickens*, ed. M. House, G. Storey, and others, 4 (1977)

**Archives** University of Iowa, Iowa City

**Likenesses** D. Maclise, lithograph, 1836 (after his drawing, 1836), BM, NPG; repro. in Maginn, 'Mrs. S. C. Hall', frontispiece · C. E. Wagstaff, stipple, 1838 (after J. Hayter), BM, NPG · C. C. Vogel, pencil and chalk drawing, 1850, Staatliche Kunstsammlungen, Dresden · G. de Latre, oils, 1851, NG Ire. · D. Maclise, lithograph, 1873 (after his drawing, 1836), BM, NPG · Robinson & Cherallt, photograph, 1874, repro. in C. W. Mann, 'Memories', *History of Photography*, 3 (1979), 330 · J. Kirkwood, etching (after H. MacManus, *c.*1840), NPG; repro. in 'Our portrait gallery, no. X: Mrs. S. C. Hall' · D. J. Pound, mixed engraving (after photograph by J. and C. Watkins), BM · J. and C. Watkins, double portrait, carte-de-visite (with her husband), NPG · stipple, NPG

**Hall, Anthony** (1679–1723), antiquary, was born at Kirkbride, Cumberland, the eldest son of Henry Hall (*d.* 1717), rector of Kirkbride, and his wife, Jane (*d.* 1720). After some schooling at Carlisle grammar school he matriculated at the Queen's College, Oxford, on 18 November 1698 and graduated BA on 15 December 1701. After his ordination he proceeded MA on 16 June 1704. He was elected fellow of his college on 18 April 1706.

Soon after taking his MA degree Hall began his career as an antiquarian editor by preparing an edition (1709) of John Leland's *Commentarii de scriptoribus Britannicis* from the original manuscript in the Bodleian Library. He undertook this work at the instigation of Edward Thwaites and other fellows of Queen's, and also enjoyed the support of Arthur Charlett, master of University College, and John Hudson, Bodley's librarian. The edition was announced in the *History of the Works of the Learned* in 1705. This caused a considerable stir in Oxford academic circles as the antiquary Thomas Tanner had already been working on an edition of Leland's works since 1694 and Hall had not informed Tanner of his plans. Tanner was much disappointed by this turn of events. Even though Tanner's tendency to procrastinate was well known and much lamented by scholars, many felt that forestalling his work was an injustice to his scholarship. Foremost among them was Hall's rival antiquarian editor, Thomas Hearne. Today, however, Hall's work is still the only edition of Leland's *De scriptoribus*, and it is judged a valuable edition of average quality compared to other historical editions produced at the time. Hearne's criticism, partly based on his collation of the work with the manuscript, was severe. He claimed that there were many faults and omissions of passages in the work. Hearne's comments in his diaries were not always fair as they were coloured by personal enmity and political prejudice. He did not respect Hall, describing him as 'a Man of no Industry, it being common with him to lye abed 'till very near dinner time, and to drink very freely of the strongest liquors' (*Remarks*, 2.171).

Although Hall announced a further edition of English historians in 1709, he did not publish anything until 1719 when his edition of Nicholas Trevet's *Annales sex regum Angliae* came out at the Oxford University Press. Hall edited the work from the Queen's College copy, which he called the 'Glastonbury manuscript', and corrected it from the Merton College copy. Thomas Hog, a later editor of Trevet, used Hall's text and had a better opinion of it than Hearne, who thought his own edition had been thwarted by Hall's supporters at the Bodleian. After Hudson's death in 1719, Hall aspired to succeed his friend as Bodley's librarian but he lost the election to Joseph Bowles. In 1720 Hall published Hudson's edition of Josephus and added a preface. He also contributed the account of Berkshire to Thomas Cox's *Magna Britannia* (1720), but repudiated the description of Cumberland in a postscript to his edition of Trevet's *Annales*.

Hall was instituted rector of Hampton Poyle, Oxfordshire, on 8 April 1720. On 25 May 1721 he married Hudson's widow, Margaret (*bap.* 1686, *d.* 1731), daughter of Sir Robert Harrison (*c.*1647–1716), an alderman and mercer of Oxford, and his wife, Elizabeth. Hall was Margaret's third husband (her first husband may have been Robert Knapp, a barrister). They lived at Garford in Berkshire. On 4 July 1721 Hall accumulated his degrees in divinity. In 1722 he published his final work, *Nicolai Triveti annalium continuatio*, which also included writings by Adam Murimuth, John Boston, and Edmund Bolton. He died at Garford on 4 April 1723 of a dropsy, according to Hearne. He was buried on 6 April at Kingston Bagpuize.

THEODOR HARMSEN

**Sources** A. Hall and A. Charlett, correspondence, Bodl. Oxf., MS Ballard 18, fols. 23–7 · correspondence between Thomas Hearne, Thomas Rawlinson, and Thomas Smith, Bodl. Oxf., MS Rawl. letters 34, 38 · will, 2 Jan 1721/2, Berks. RO · *Remarks and collections of Thomas Hearne*, ed. C. E. Doble and others, 11 vols., OHS, 2, 7, 13, 34, 42–3, 48, 50, 65, 67, 72 (1885–1921) · *F. Nicolai Triveti, de ordine frat. praedicatorum, annales sex regum Angliae*, ed. T. Hog, EHS, 6 (1845); repr. (1964) · M. J. Sommerlad, 'The historical and antiquarian interests of Thomas Tanner', DPhil diss., U. Oxf., 1962, 233–55 · W. Hutchinson, *The history of the county of Cumberland*, 2 (1794), 485 · R. J. Dean, 'Nicolas Trevet, historian', *Medieval learning and literature: essays presented to Richard William Hunt*, ed. J. J. G. Alexander and M. T. Gibson (1976), 328–52 · R. G. [R. Gough], *British topography*, [new edn], 1 (1780), 33–4 · W. D. Macray, *Annals of the Bodleian Library, Oxford*, 2nd edn (1890); facs. edn (1984), 35, 75, 198 · J. R. Magrath, *The Queen's College*, 2 (1921), 116–17 · Wood, *Ath. Oxon.* [John Hudson] · Foster, *Alum. Oxon.* · A. Chalmers, ed., *The general biographical dictionary*, new edn, 17 (1814), 45–6 · 'Hudson, Dr John', *The general biographical dictionary*, ed. A. Chalmers, new edn (1812–17), vol. 18, p. 281 · D. C. Douglas, *English scholars, 1660–1730*, 2nd edn (1951), 162, 177 · H. Carter, *A history of the Oxford University Press*, 1: *To the year 1780* (1975), 236; appx · G. B. Routledge, ed., *Carlisle grammar school memorial register, 1264–1924* (1924) · B. Nightingale, *The ejected of 1662 in Cumberland and Westmorland: their predecessors and successors*, 1 (1911), 598–9 · W. N. Clarke, preface, *Parochial topography of the hundred of Wanting: with other miscellaneous records relating to the county of Berkshire* (1824) [Wantage] · *DNB* · parish register, Kirkbride, Cumberland, Cumbria AS, Carlisle, 1717, 1720 [burial] · parish register, Denchworth, Berkshire, 1721, Berks. RO [marriage]

**Archives** Bodl. Oxf. | Bodl. Oxf., Ballard MSS · Bodl. Oxf., Rawl. MSS, corresp. with Arthur Charlett

**Likenesses** G. Vertue, line engraving, BM; repro. in A. Hall, *Nicolai Triveti annalium continuatio* (1722)

**Wealth at death** wife sole legatee, except for spinet left to stepdaughter: will, Berks. RO

**Hall, Archibald** (1736/7–1778), minister of the Secession church, was born at Marfield, Penicuik, in Edinburghshire. His parents, who were noted for their piety, died in quick succession when Hall was about nine years old. He studied Latin, Greek, and Hebrew at Spittal School, near Penicuik, with the Secession minister and theologian John Brown of Haddington, before reading logic, mathematics, and philosophy at Edinburgh University, and divinity with John Fisher at the Associate Synod seminary, Glasgow. He was licensed to preach in 1758 and was soon afterwards ordained minister of the Associate congregation of Torphichen in Linlithgowshire. In 1765 he moved to London as an Associate minister at the Well Street church. Here Hall pursued an energetic and evangelical ministry. This was also the period in which he produced a number of theological essays characterized by a 'masculine understanding' and 'practical good sense' (M'Kerrow, 874). His first work, *An Humble Attempt to Exhibit a Scriptural View … of the Gospel Church*, appeared in 1769 (second edition in 1795), and was followed four years later with the studies *Church Fellowship* and *An Impartial Survey of the Controversy about the Religious Clause of some Burgess Oaths* (reproduced in McKerrow, 212–14). Hall's *Grace and Holiness* (1777) was later reprinted by another Associate Synod minister, John Brown of Whitburn, in the first volume of *The Evangelical Preacher* (1802), while James Peddie edited Hall's *Treatise on Faith and Influence of the Gospel*. A memoir of the author was provided in his collection of edifying personal letters, *The Life of Faith Exhibited* (1828). While in London, Hall was regularly troubled by an asthmatic illness which hastened his death, unmarried, aged forty-one, on 6 May 1778. He was buried at the Bunhill Fields cemetery.

T. B. JOHNSTONE, *rev.* PHILIP CARTER

**Sources** J. M'Kerrow, *History of the Secession church*, rev. edn (1841) • N. R. Needham, 'Hall, Archibald', *DSCHT* • memoir, A. Hall, *The life of faith exhibited* (1828)

**Hall, Sir Arnold Alexander** (1915–2000), aeronautical engineer, was born at 62 Fitzgerald Road, West Derby, Liverpool, on 23 April 1915, the son of Robert Alexander Hall, upholsterer, and his wife, Ellen Elizabeth, *née* Parkinson. From Alsop high school he gained a scholarship to Clare College, Cambridge, where he took first-class honours in the engineering tripos of 1935, winning with distinction the three chief prizes—for aeronautics, applied mechanics, and heat engines. During this time at Cambridge he began some early collaboration with his fellow engineering student Frank Whittle on the development of turbojet propulsion for aircraft under Sir Bennett Melville-Jones.

From Cambridge, Hall secured a fellowship funded by the London Company of Armourers and Braziers which provided him with a two-year postgraduate appointment in aeronautics. He went on to take up an appointment as a principal scientific officer at the Royal Aircraft Establishment (RAE) at Farnborough in 1938. His original work there included the design of an advanced electronic gunsight. At the same time he was collaborating with Beverley Shenstone and Kenneth Wilkinson of British European Airways, under Peter Masefield, in the early stages of bringing into service the first Rolls-Royce Dart propeller-turbine engines on the Vickers Viscount. Between 1945 and 1951 he was Zaharoff professor of aviation at London University and head of the department of aeronautics at the Imperial College of Science and Technology.

Hall returned to the RAE at Farnborough from 1951 to 1955, when, following the early death of W. G. A. Perring, he was appointed—at the age of thirty-six—to succeed him as director. These were the early days of the first jet-propelled passenger aircraft, the new De Havilland Comet 1, three of which in 1953–4 suffered fatal accidents. As director Hall was charged with establishing the causes of these crashes at a time when they were wholly misunderstood. With his RAE colleague Percy Walker, Hall designed and had constructed a water tank in which a complete Comet fuselage could be immersed and subjected to repeated pressure tests. In due course this established beyond doubt the cause of these accidents: structural fatigue from repeated pressurization. There were two basic reasons: first, cracks extending from sharp angles in window casings, and second, inadequate applications of Redux bondings of structural components. The rebuilt Comets were brought back into service, their metal fatigue problems understood and corrected.

Hall was at once recognized, with Percy Walker, as a brilliant scientist and, with it, as a wise industrial leader of sound common sense, free from the political intrigues of that time. He was elected FRS in 1953 and knighted in 1954. Working closely with Sir Thomas Sopwith, Hall went steadily up the professional ladder, and in 1967 was promoted to chairman of Hawker Siddeley Aircraft. In that capacity he stubbornly and steadily upheld the importance to Britain of a leading role in international aerospace and particularly in the design of advanced wings for major types of civil aircraft. At the same time he opposed the Labour government's desires to reduce the British share in the essentials of aeronautical production. Hall's qualities were now more widely appreciated. Between 1966 and 1985 he held appointments as a director of Lloyds Bank, of Phoenix Assurance (1965–85), of Rolls-Royce Ltd (1979–88), and of ICI (1976–85). He was chairman of the board of trustees of the Science Museum, and received, in 1962, the gold medal of the Royal Aeronautical Society, and in 1963 the Albert medal of the Royal Society of Arts.

In 1966, at the age of seventy-one and in failing health, Hall retired as chairman of the Hawker Siddeley Group but kept in close contact with aeronautical affairs in general. Hall was twice married, first, on 29 November 1946, to Moira (Constance) Dione Rathmell, *née* Sykes (*b.* 1910/11), with whom he had three daughters. After her death in 1966 he married Iola Nealon who brought to the family a stepson and a stepdaughter. Hall died at Wexham Park Hospital, Slough, on 9 January 2000.

PETER G. MASEFIELD

**Sources** A. Tucker, *The Guardian* (11 Jan 2000), 20a–h • *The Times* (11 Jan 2000) • *Daily Telegraph* (11 Jan 2000) • P. Masefield, *The Independent* (14 Jan 2000), 6a–c • b. cert. • m. cert. [Moira Rathmell] • d. cert.
**Archives** CAC Cam., letters to John Lloyd and related papers concerning co-authored biography of W. S. Farrer • Institution of Mechanical Engineers, London, corresp. with Lord Hinton
**Likenesses** two group photographs, 1971–5, Hult. Arch. • photograph, repro. in *The Times*

**Hall, Arthur** (1539–1605), translator and politician, was the only son of Francis Hall, of Grantham, Lincolnshire, deputy surveyor and comptroller of Calais (where Arthur was probably born), and Ursula, daughter of Thomas Sharington. When Francis died he owned lands in and around Calais, Guînes, and La Marque, in Lincolnshire, and also 'one litle Lordshyp' of 'Knoke in Wilteshire', altogether valued at over £200 per annum (Wright, 24, 173). In his will Francis Hall requested that his widow should be given wardship of their son. After his death on 10 June 1552, however, the wardship was acquired by William Cecil, and Arthur Hall's name appears in Cecil's household papers for Wimbledon in 1555. As Hall later wrote, he and Cecil's heir, Thomas, were educated together 'in my Lord your father's house' (Hall, *Iliades*, fol. Aiii); there is no evidence to support the suggestion that he studied at Cambridge.

Although on 12 January 1558, five days after the French capture of Calais, Hall requested an allowance from Cecil to attend the inns of court or to journey to France, he does not appear to have done either. He did, however, draw on his linguistic skill, possibly acquired in his early life in France, to translate into English ten books of Homer's *Iliad* from the French version of Hugues Salel, a copy of which he acquired in 1556. It was a long process which began some time after 1556, was reactivated when, in 1562–3, Roger Ascham and Jasper Heywood 'animated me much, with great entreatie to goe forwarde with my begun enterprise' (Hall, *Iliades*, fol. Aiv), and reached publication stage only in 1581. It was notable as the first English translation of Homer, albeit a free and often inaccurate one. In his dedication to Sir Thomas Cecil, Hall thanked him for his friendship and, through him, praised his father, William Cecil, now Lord Burghley. On 1 January 1559 he had also presented his guardian with new year verses 'from your most obedient pupill and servant' (PRO, SP 12/2/1). Most of Hall's surviving letters, until Burghley's death in 1598, were to his patron and former guardian.

When Hall came of age in 1560 his French lands were lost, but his English property was supplemented by the inheritance of lands from John Hall of Grantham, his father's uncle, in 1552. Thereafter he was, in some ways, the typical country gentleman, acquiring and alienating property and, at various times, in the service of great courtiers such as the earls of Leicester and Sussex. In 1564 he entered the queen's service, a move which, however, was not to his advantage, as he lamented to Burghley in 1591: 'Her Majestyes servant I have been these 26 or 27 yeares' but 'I never receaved any way the benefyt of anything' (PRO, SP 12/238/55). Furthermore, his profligacy ran him into trouble with creditors by 1564 and gave him his first taste of debtors' prison in 1566. This may explain his choice of wife: Mary Dewie (*d.* 1582), a London goldsmith's daughter whom he married about 1566. They had two sons and three daughters, of whom Jane died in her infancy in 1577 and the second son was born 'an idiot' in 1571. The following year Sir Francis Knollys described Arthur Hall's father too as 'somewhat inclined to madness', while some MPs regarded Arthur as 'a rashe head and foole' or even 'a mad man' (Hartley, 1.361, 366).

After the birth of his eldest son, Cecil, in 1567, Hall went on the grand tour, visiting France, (possibly) Spain, Italy, Constantinople, Hungary, and Germany, supplying William Cecil with one or more intelligence reports on the way. He returned to England early in 1569, but in the following year he offended his former guardian when he expressed his annoyance at failing to obtain a wardship. In 1571 he was elected parliamentary burgess for Grantham. It was in parliament that his personality traits, so astutely summed up by Hall himself as if writing about another, were to become familiar to many contemporaries: 'Overweenyng of himselfe … furious when he is contraried, without patience to take tyme to judge or doubte the daunger of the sequele … [and] so implacable if he conceyve an injurie' (Hall, *A Letter*, fol. Aiv). He is recorded only once, as a member of the subsidy committee, in the 1571 parliament. He was re-elected for Grantham in 1572 and it was in each of that parliament's three sessions that he acquired public notoriety. In 1572 parliament was dominated by two related issues: the threat posed by Mary Stuart and the implementation of the fourth duke of Norfolk's death sentence. There was an overwhelming parliamentary demand for harsh action against both. On 12 May, Hall spoke in favour of mercy towards Mary, and three days later extended that to Norfolk too, arguing 'The nature of the lion not to devoure the prostrate' (Hartley, 1.354). His action provoked a Commons debate on members' freedom of speech. Then, on 19 May, he appeared at the bar to answer charges on seven specific points from 'sundry lewd speeches', uttered not only in parliament but also 'abroad' (*JHC*, 1.95–6). At first he professed amazement; then he recalled being so angered by members' interruptions that '[h]e spake he knewe not what'; but finally he submitted, saying that he was 'sorie for it'. The speaker then admonished and dismissed him (Hartley, 1.273, 329–30, 365–6).

Hall spent much of his time and resources in search of pleasure in the ordinaries, bowling alleys, and taverns of London, where his quarrelsome nature led him into a feud with one Melchisedech Mallory. It began when they disagreed while playing dice at a Lothbury ordinary in December 1573. Although, in Hall's words, 'Etna smoked [and] daggers were a drawing', the rest of the company pacified them. The dispute continued, however, with verbal confrontations, 'evil wordes in corners one of another', and in June 1574 a violent affray at Worme's tavern near Fleet Bridge between the antagonists and their followers (Hall, *A Letter*, fols. Bii(v)–Biv). Finally, in November, Hall's servant, Edward Smalley, wounded Mallory in St Paul's Churchyard. Mallory, who was awarded £100 damages in a civil action against Smalley, died on 18 September 1575 before payment was made.

When Mallory's brother Andrew secured Smalley's arrest, the second session of parliament had begun. Hall's feud now provoked another crisis for him, this time about parliamentary privilege, when Smalley claimed immunity from arrest as the servant of a member. The Commons ordered his release on 20 February 1576 but then ordered his committal on suspicion of fraudulently evading a debt. A Commons committee judged Smalley guilty and consigned him to the Tower. Suspicion fell on Hall; a bill was introduced to make him honour the debt, to expel him 'for a wrangler' and thereafter debar him, and he was eventually obliged to pay the £100.

It was one of Hall's self-confessed traits to bear grudges. Between 1576 and 1579 he wrote and had printed a two-part pamphlet: *A Letter Sent by F. A.*, which was a bold, colourful, at times amusing account of the Hall–Mallory affair, and *[A]n Admonition to the Father of F. A.*, which examined the nature of parliament, its antiquity, and the necessary qualities of Commons members. About 100 copies were printed, of which only fourteen were distributed. Nevertheless, it was bound to cause widespread offence: he condemned the partiality of the late Sir Robert Bell, speaker in 1576; and he maligned current members such as William Winter (full of 'choller and melancholie'). Worse still, he impugned the Commons' authority and antiquity and charged its members with drunkenness. He also made the provocative comment about 'the olde father of Rome, a dad whome I have heard some say Mr. Hal doth not hate' (Hall, *A Letter*).

Meanwhile Hall's financial difficulties increased as he paid Smalley's debt and the associated costs. In February 1579 he sought some 'scrapes of her highnes' great liberale bestowed fare' (BL, Lansdowne MS 27, no. 79), and appealed for Burghley's support of his suit to the queen. A year later he sold his mother-in-law's late home in Foster Lane, London. Life was further complicated by a dispute with Bishop Cooper of Lincoln, who made enquiries about the *Letter*; in response, Hall threatened to expose to the queen the bishop's involvement in prophesyings. During 1579 he was several times called before the privy council and enjoined to seek Cooper's good favour. He was also questioned about his pamphlet and rebuked for printing it, but no further action was taken until parliament reassembled in January 1581. The work was then denounced as 'dangerous and lewd' and a Commons committee drew up eight charges against him. When Hall was brought to the bar there was 'some meane reverence by him doon, though not in such humble and lowlye wise as the state of one in that place to be chardged and accused requyred' (BL, Lansdowne MS 31, no. 20). He was fined 500 marks, imprisoned for six months and thereafter until he made a written retraction of the book, and expelled from the Commons for the rest of the session. The house had asserted its right to remove and replace members. From the Tower, Hall wrote letters of complaint to Burghley, but he did not make a full retraction for seven weeks and then, on 2 April 1581, it was to the privy council, because parliament had ended. His written submission, however, was drafted with the assistance of one of those councillors, Burghley.

In 1582 Hall sought royal permission to become 'a yonge student of an old unthrift' in a foreign university (BL, Lansdowne MS 36, no. 74). His wife died in September 1582 and in the same year he inherited substantial property in Lincolnshire. In 1584 he was again returned to parliament for Grantham and on 12 December he was summoned to attend because of continuous absenteeism. Hall was not a member of the 1586–7 parliament, but he claimed arrears of wages from Grantham borough, for his parliamentary service since 1571. When a Commons committee asked him to remit them he was 'very willing to do anything which might be grateful to this House … which [was] well liked of' (D'Ewes, 417–18).

During the 1580s and 1590s Hall's personal circumstances deteriorated. There were frequent local disputes with William Porter (over a schoolmaster), Justice Monson, and Sir Anthony Thorold (with whom there were provocative verbal exchanges and even armed confrontations). Debts increased and creditors were pressing. Then, in 1586, Hall embarked on his tactless, even ludicrous courtship of the widowed Frances, countess of Sussex. She rejected his advances, they openly quarrelled, and Hall went to press with the libel *Hungaryous Hystory*, an account of their relationship, which was quickly suppressed. The queen was offended by Hall's conduct. During 1588–9 he was imprisoned first in the Marshalsea and then in the Fleet. Until Burghley's death in 1598 Hall wrote to him with complaints, charges of unfriendliness and financial neglect, and, more frequently, with thanks for his services, praise, and prayers 'dayly beseching God to kepe and prosper your Lordship' (BL, Lansdowne MS 86, no. 37). In 1591 he even ventured to offer economic advice against grain and beer export licences in a time of dearth. As late as 1597 Burghley intervened with the exchequer on his behalf, over a £400 debt to the crown. Burghley's death in the following year was a blow to Hall who, in 1601, was again in prison, this time for debt. Burghley's son Robert now became the recipient of Hall's petitions, protests, and lamentations. In 1600 he had sent Sir Robert Cecil proposals for the debasement of the Irish coinage. During the enforced leisure of imprisonment he penned for the new monarch, James I, a *Treatise on Transportable Commodities* in 1603 (BL, Royal MS 18A, 74) and, in the following year, advice on the corrupt elections for his first parliament, recommending that the king dissolve it. Hall died, perhaps in prison, on 29 December 1605 and was buried at Grantham on 7 January 1606.

Hall was not a man devoid of talent. He was, however, wayward and, sometimes, his own worst enemy. His defence of Mary Stuart in 1572 suggested sympathy for Roman Catholicism. His reference to the pope and his stated admiration of Cardinal William Peto, both in his two-part tract, must have reinforced suspicions about his religious position. There is, however, no proof that he was or became a Roman Catholic and such references in his text are probably no more than examples of his provocative and mischievous manner. He should not, however, be dismissed as an irresponsible troublemaker. Hall was, after all, the first to translate Homer's *Iliad* into English. His *Letter* and *Admonition* revealed both scholarship and a capacity for racy prose. Furthermore, his record of parliamentary misconduct is significant in the institutional history of the House of Commons. His actions in 1576 and his offending pamphlet both prompted proceedings against him. These established precedents for the Commons' jurisdiction over the privileges of the house and its members, and also the punishment of those members who breached or misused them. MICHAEL A. R. GRAVES

**Sources** H. G. Wright, *The life and works of Arthur Hall of Grantham* (1919) • A. Hall, *A letter sent by F. A. … to his very friende L.B.* [1576] • *JHC*, 1 (1547–1628), 82–137 • T. E. Hartley, ed., *Proceedings in the parliaments of Elizabeth I*, 1 (1981) • Lansdowne MSS, 7, 27, 31, 36, 43, 51, 58, 68, 85, 86, 118, BL • *CSP dom., 1547–90; addenda, 1566–79; 1591–4; 1603–10* • A. H. [A. Hall], trans., *Ten books of Homers 'Iliades', translated out of French* (1581) • *Calendar of the manuscripts of the most hon. the marquis of Salisbury*, 1–12, HMC, 9 (1883–1910) • G. R. Elton, 'Arthur Hall, Lord Burghley, and the antiquity of parliament', *History and imagination: essays in honour of H. R. Trevor-Roper*, ed. H. Lloyd Jones, V. Pearl, and B. Worden (1981), 88–103 • HoP, *Commons, 1558–1603* • G. R. Elton, *The parliament of England, 1559–1581* (1986) • M. A. R. Graves, *Thomas Norton: the parliament man* (1994) • *CPR, 1558–69; 1578–82* • *APC, 1578–80; 1588* • [W. Lambarde], *William Lambarde's Notes on the procedures and privileges of the House of Commons*, ed. P. L. Ward (1977) • Cooper, *Ath. Cantab.*, vol. 2 • S. D'Ewes, ed., *The journals of all the parliaments during the reign of Queen Elizabeth, both of the House of Lords and House of Commons* (1682)

**Archives** BL, address to James I on transportable commodities, Royal MS 18 a lxxiv

**Hall, Arthur Henry** (1876–1949), engineer, was born at Clifton on 17 August 1876, the eldest son and second of the eight children of Henry Sinclair Hall and his wife, Anne Leigh Keturah, daughter of Matthew Knapp, of Little Linford Hall, Buckinghamshire. His father had returned to his old school, Clifton College, as a mathematics teacher and was also in charge of its military side from its inception. He was co-author of the well-known textbooks *Hall and Knight's Algebra*, *Hall and Stevens's Geometry*, and other works. The young Hall entered Trinity Hall, Cambridge, with a scholarship in 1895 after his early education as an exhibitioner at Clifton. He read engineering and took a first in the mechanical sciences tripos in 1898.

Hall next served his five years' engineering apprenticeship with W. Denny Brothers, of Dumbarton, and in 1905 joined the ordnance department of the War Office. In the following year he became an assistant mechanical engineer at Woolwich arsenal, and in 1914 he transferred to the Royal Small Arms Factory, Enfield. On the outbreak of war in 1914 he returned to Woolwich where he remained until 1917, supervising the purchase and installation of the additional plant needed by the arsenal for wartime production. For the next two years he was at the Admiralty directing the production of torpedoes, mines, and other anti-submarine devices. During this period he exhibited a particular talent for arranging the supply in bulk of urgently required stores—with a speed which up to then had been regarded as impossible. From 1919 he was seconded to the Ministry of Munitions, where he was in control of the disposal of various surplus stores.

With the decision to intensify experiment and research on large rigid airships, Hall was next appointed, in 1926, to the Air Ministry, with the post of superintendent of production at Cardington, where the ill-fated R101 was built. He had much to do with obtaining the high dimensional accuracy required in the long girders used, where the tolerances demanded on the overall lengths between the end fittings were of an order not previously realized in such light construction. In view of the disaster which overtook the R101 on her maiden flight to India in 1930 (by which time Hall was already in his next post), it should be recorded that he was of the opinion that she was not sufficiently tested to be allowed to undertake the flight so early in her career.

In 1928 Hall was appointed chief superintendent of the Royal Aircraft Establishment at Farnborough, with a mandate to enforce economy and increase efficiency by centralizing such common services as transport, workshops, and drawing-office staffs. It says much for his personality that a policy necessarily unwelcome to the technical departments was carried out in reasonable harmony. By the middle of his term of office the policy had changed to one of expansion in the air, and the establishment entered upon a period of intensive growth which continued unchecked throughout the subsequent war. Hall's knowledge of men and ability to direct them were invaluable, for he was able to attract the right types and to select for promotion those best equipped to carry additional responsibility. He knew, and conversed intimately with, every man and woman in the establishment. He was a stimulating personality, with a keenly analytical mind and a visual memory of remarkable range and character. He also served throughout as a member of the Aeronautical Research Committee.

After his retirement in 1941 Hall continued for some five years as consultant to the Ministry of Aircraft Production and the English Electric Company. He was appointed CBE in 1918 and CB in 1937. He was a member of the Institution of Mechanical Engineers, a fellow of the Royal Aeronautical Society, and an honorary fellow of the Institute of Aero Sciences of the United States, a distinction rarely accorded outside that country.

With his parentage and qualifications, it is surprising that Hall wrote little of a technical nature. His publications were confined to articles on photography and fly-fishing which, in conjunction with ornithology, were his hobbies. Some of his photographs of gulls on the Embankment were exhibited, and he was a keen and polished exponent of colour photography, delighting in reproducing the type of scenery encountered in his favourite fishing haunts. He married in 1910 Maud Henrietta (*d.* 1953), daughter of Lieutenant-Colonel G. H. Webster. They had three sons, all lost in tragic circumstances, the eldest at the age of seven, and the other two in their twenties. Hall died in St Thomas's Hospital, London, on 10 September 1949. H. L. STEVENS, *rev.* ANITA MCCONNELL

**Sources** W. G. A. Perring, *Nature*, 164 (1949), 603–4 • *The Times* (12 Sept 1949) • J. A. O. Muirhead, ed., *Clifton College register, 1862–1947* (1948) • personal knowledge (1959) • private information (1959) • d. cert.

**Likenesses** photograph, Royal Aircraft Establishment, Farnborough, Hampshire

**Wealth at death** £32,732 3*s.* 2*d.*: probate, 10 Dec 1949, *CGPLA Eng. & Wales*

**Hall, Sir Arthur John** (1866–1951), physician, was born in Sheffield on 27 July 1866, the second son and youngest of the three children of John Hall, a well-known medical practitioner in Sheffield, who had married his cousin, Elizabeth Hall. After Rugby School, Hall was first sent to the Sheffield medical school, which was then a primitive place where some practitioners in their unpaid spare time gave dull and formal instruction in anatomy to a few students apprenticed to doctors in the town. Fortunately Hall's father was persuaded to send him to Gonville and Caius College, Cambridge, and St Bartholomew's Hospital, London. After qualifying in 1889 Hall spent a year assisting his father, but the practice was small and exclusive, and finding himself inadequately employed he decided on a career as a physician. In 1890 he therefore became assistant physician to the Sheffield Royal Hospital (then called the Public Hospital and Dispensary) on the staff of which he spent the rest of his professional life.

Meanwhile the medical school, having surprisingly survived its worst period, had been transferred to new premises close to Firth College and the technical school. Hall was appointed assistant demonstrator in physiology there in 1889, and from then onwards his great resources of energy, intellect, personality, and tact were largely devoted to building up the school. It was soon well established, and was amalgamated with Firth College and the technical school in what became in 1897 the University College of Sheffield. Later it was to grow into the faculty of medicine at the University of Sheffield on the latter's formation in 1905, and by 1920 it was regarded as one of the most advanced medical faculties in Britain.

Although Hall was unquestionably the creator of the modern school of medicine in Sheffield, he had from the first the wisdom to realize that this was not a job for one man working single-handed, and it was his great endeavour to bring to Sheffield some of the most talented physicians he could find: among the first was Christopher Addison; a later appointment was Edward Mellanby. For a time Hall himself was responsible for the teaching in physiology, first as demonstrator and later as part-time professor; but as soon as the school was ready and able to finance a full-time chair Hall resigned to allow such an appointment to be made. He then turned his interests to pathology. First he became demonstrator and curator of the museum (which was largely his own creation); later, in 1899, he became professor, and again resigned when a full-time chair of pathology was established in 1905.

Until his retirement in 1931 Hall was both a practising consultant physician and on the medical staff of the Sheffield Royal Hospital, where he taught clinical medicine in the wards. He was also dean of the medical faculty there from 1911 to 1916 and professor of medicine from 1915 to 1931. Physicians and teachers of medicine of his day were not expected to make their names in research, but Hall's careful and meticulous observations of the two epidemics in Sheffield of encephalitis lethargica, in 1917–18 and 1924, contributed greatly to the knowledge of this disease, and he became an authority of international standing. His book on the subject was published in 1924.

Hall was of commanding appearance and personality, a man to whom one would listen in any company, who took himself seriously but was saved from being pompous by a brilliant wit and a delightful sense of humour. Although he had his critics he nevertheless had the talent of bringing people together and enabling them to work smoothly with one another. He was a good physician and a good teacher, but his great talent was in administration. To his students he was friendly and approachable, but his nickname of 'Lord Arthur' showed that he had their respect as well as their affection and that, while approachable, he was not to be treated as an equal. As a young man he had considerable gifts as an actor and traces of this remained discernible throughout his life; but his main interest outside the medical school was music. He was a talented cellist who regularly played chamber music, and it was one of his great regrets that after his retirement, when he would have had more time, he was unable to enjoy it because of increasing deafness.

Hall was elected FRCP in 1904 and served the college as examiner, councillor, Lumleian lecturer, and finally as senior censor. He was examiner in medicine to Oxford and Cambridge and several other universities, and was a member of the radium commission and of the industrial health research board. During the war of 1914–18 he was placed in charge of the medical division of the 3rd Northern General Hospital. He received an honorary degree of DSc from Sheffield in 1928, was president of the Association of Physicians of Great Britain and Ireland in 1931, and was knighted in 1935.

In 1900 Hall married Hilda Mary (*d.* 1945), daughter of Charles E. Vickers, solicitor, of Sheffield; they had two sons and one daughter. He died in Sheffield on 3 January 1951. PLATT, *rev.*

**Sources** *The Lancet* (13 Jan 1951) · *BMJ* (20 Jan 1951), 140–41 · University of Sheffield · personal knowledge (1971)

**Archives** Medical Research Council, London, corresp. and papers · University of Sheffield, notes and case papers | Wellcome L., letters to Sir Edward Mellanby

**Likenesses** Elliott & Fry, photograph, NPG · E. Moore, oils, University of Sheffield

**Wealth at death** £41,686 0s. 2d.: probate, 13 April 1951, *CGPLA Eng. & Wales*

**Hall** [*née* Waddington], **Augusta**, **Lady Llanover** (**1802–1896**), promoter of the Welsh national revival, was born on 21 March 1802 at Tŷ Uchaf, Llanofer, Monmouthshire, the youngest daughter of Benjamin Waddington (1749–1828), landowner, and of Georgina Mary Ann (1771–1850), daughter of John Port of Ilam, co. Durham, and a great-niece of Mary Granville (Mrs Delany; 1700–1778). Of her five sisters, three died in infancy and another, Emilia, died in 1819 at the age of twenty-five. Her surviving sister, Frances *Bunsen (1791–1876) [*see under* Bunsen, Christian Karl Josias von] married Christian Karl Josias von Bunsen, Baron von Bunsen, Celtic scholar and later Prussian ambassador to Britain. Augusta and her sisters received a wide-ranging education at home under the direction of their accomplished mother. On 4 December 1823 she married Benjamin *Hall (1802–1867) of Aber-carn and Hensol, industrialist and politician, son of Benjamin Hall (1778–1817), the industrialist. She became Lady Hall in 1838,

**Augusta Hall, Lady Llanover (1802–1896),** by Charles Augustus Mornewick, 1862

when her husband was created a baronet; in 1859 he became Baron Llanover of Llanover and Abercarn. Both their sons died young, and their only surviving child, Augusta Charlotte Elizabeth, married John Arthur Edward Jones (Herbert) of Llan-arth Fawr in 1846.

Although Lady Llanover was a talented editor and illustrator, and a well-connected and accomplished hostess within the London parliamentary circle, she is mainly remembered for her contribution as patron of the language, literature, and national institutions of Wales. Her interest in all things Welsh was fostered both by contact with the Welsh-speaking tenants of her father's estate, and through the influence of Lady Coffin Greenly of Titley Court, Herefordshire, a patron of the emerging national literary revival of the time.

It was through Lady Greenly that Augusta Hall met the leading figures of this movement, and became an enthusiastic supporter. A vivacious and resolute personality, her reputation in Wales was established in 1834, when she won first prize for an essay at the Cardiff eisteddfod on the preservation of the language, literature, and traditional dress of Wales, and received the honour of ovate of the national Gorsedd of Bards. She subsequently adopted the pseudonym Gwenynen Gwent ('the bee of Gwent'). In the previous year, the Abergavenny Cymreigyddion Society, a Welsh literary society that was to play a major role in the revival of interest in Welsh and Celtic scholarship, had been established. Augusta Hall and her husband soon became its chief patrons. She also played an active role as patron of the Welsh Manuscripts Society, formed under the auspices of the Cymreigyddion. She built up an extensive library at Llanofer and, in 1853, secured the manuscripts of Edward Williams (Iolo Morganwg), which were transferred to the National Library of Wales in 1916. She assisted and patronized Maria Jane Williams of Aberpergwm in preparing for publication a collection of Welsh airs, and supported Lady Charlotte Guest in her translation of the Mabinogion legends. She was a patron of the Welsh Collegiate Institution at Llandovery, established in 1848, and subscribed to and supported the publication of many Welsh books, including the financing of the first periodical for women in Wales, *Y Gymraes*, in 1850.

Llanover House, completed in 1837, became the centre of a wide cultural circle that encompassed many leading scholars of Wales and Europe. Poets and authors, antiquarians, musicians, prominent clergymen, politicians, diplomats, and members of the royal houses of Europe all spent time at Llanofer. The household was staffed by Welsh-speaking personnel, and the traditional Welsh seasonal celebrations held there became renowned. Llanofer estate was populated almost entirely by Welsh speakers, ensuring the survival of the language in this Anglicized area for another half-century or more. At Aber-carn, the school that Lady Llanover directly supervised taught through the medium of Welsh, and it was there also that she and her husband endowed an Anglican church, which was transferred to the Welsh Calvinistic Methodists in 1862 following the refusal of the vicar to conduct the services in the vernacular. At that time she personally supervised the preparation of a revised version of the Book of Common Prayer for use at the new church. A fervent protestant, she later endowed other Welsh dissenting chapels at Llanofer and Aber-carn. Her interest in the continuation of Welsh traditions led her to employ a resident harpist and to establish a harp manufactory at Llanofer. She was also an ardent supporter of the Welsh woollen industry, which is reflected in her design for a Welsh national costume, the creation of which she is credited with. Her other interest was temperance, and it was owing to her influence that several public houses on the Aber-carn and Llanofer estates were converted into temperance inns.

During the 1860s Lady Llanover published a major work, *The Autobiography and Correspondence of Mrs Delany* (1861–2), and a housekeeping manual, *Good Cookery … and Recipes Communicated by the Hermit of the Cell of St Govan* (1867), which contained her well-known illustrations of Welsh peasant dress. She also illustrated a children's book, *The Paper People*, by Mrs Shaw Lefevre, and, with others, illustrated *The Literary Remains of the Reverend Thomas Price (Carnhuanwc)* (1854–5), edited by her friend Jane Williams (Ysgafell) of Talgarth.

Lady Llanover survived her husband by over twenty-eight years. During her widowhood she spent some time in London and Bath, but lived mainly at Llanofer, where she continued to support Welsh literature and other Welsh causes. In her latter years and afterwards, some commentators ridiculed her rather eccentric zeal for Wales and the Welsh, yet at her death tributes were paid to her long-standing and active role as a leading patron of the Welsh literary and national movement. She died at Llanover House on 17 January 1896 and was buried there six days later. SIAN RHIANNON WILLIAMS

**Sources** M. Fraser, 'The Waddingtons of Llanover, 1791–1805', *National Library of Wales Journal*, 11 (1959–60), 285–329 · M. Fraser, 'Lord Llanover's last years', *National Library of Wales Journal*, 16 (1969–70), 272–92 · M. Fraser, 'Lord and Lady Llanover, 1862–3', *National Library of Wales Journal*, 16 (1969–70), 105–22 · M. Fraser, 'Sir Benjamin Hall is raised to the peerage', *National Library of Wales Journal*, 16 (1969–70), 23–42 · M. Fraser, 'Sir Benjamin Hall in parliament in the 1850s', *National Library of Wales Journal*, 15 (1967–8), 72–88, 113–26, 310–24, 389–404 · M. Fraser, 'Sir Benjamin and Lady Hall at home in the 1850s', *National Library of Wales Journal*, 14 (1965–6), 285–300, 437–50 · M. Fraser, 'Sir Benjamin and Lady Hall in the 1840s', *National Library of Wales Journal*, 14 (1965–6), 35–52, 194–213 · M. Fraser, 'Benjamin Hall, MP for Marylebone, 1837–1839', *National Library of Wales Journal*, 13 (1963–4), 313–28 · M. Fraser, 'Benjamin and Augusta Hall, 1831–1836', *National Library of Wales Journal*, 13 (1963–4), 209–23 · M. Fraser, 'Young Mr and Mrs Hall', *National Library of Wales Journal*, 13 (1963–4), 29–47 · M. Fraser, 'The girlhood of Augusta Waddington', *National Library of Wales Journal*, 12 (1961–2), 305–22 · M. Fraser, 'Benjamin Hall's youth, 1802–1823', *National Library of Wales Journal*, 12 (1961–2), 250–64 · *DWB* · *Cardiff Times* (25 Jan 1896) · *Western Mail* [Cardiff] (18 Jan 1896) · *Western Mail* [Cardiff] (20 Jan 1896) · *Western Mail* [Cardiff] (22 Jan 1896) · *Western Mail* [Cardiff] (24 Jan 1896) · M. E. Thomas, *Afiaith yng Ngwent* (1978) · H. M. Vaughn, *The south Wales squires* (1926) · M. Barnes, ed., *Augustus Hare* (1953) · GEC, *Peerage*

**Archives** NL Wales, corresp. and papers | BL, corresp. with W. E. Gladstone, Add. MSS 44418–44479 · Bodl. Oxf., corresp. with Sir Thomas Phillipps · Bodl. Oxf., corresp. with Sir J. G. Wilkinson · Gwent RO, Cwmbrân, Llanover and Abercarn estate MSS · NL Wales, Aberpergwm letters · NL Wales, Dolaucothi corresp. · NL Wales, Glansevern MSS · NL Wales, letters to Johnes family · NL Wales, Welsh School MSS and records · NL Wales, letters relating to ecclesiastical matters · Yale U., Beinecke L., Osborn collection, corresp. relating to her edition of Delaney's autobiography

**Likenesses** Woodford, portrait, 1817, Llanover Hall, Monmouthshire · portrait, *c*.1823, Llanover Hall, Monmouthshire · G. Gwent, self-portrait, 1837, NL Wales · C. A. Mornewick, portrait, 1862, priv. coll. *[see illus.]*

**Wealth at death** £74,165 6*s*. 8*d*.: probate, 14 July 1896, *CGPLA Eng. & Wales*

**Hall, Basil** (1788–1844), naval officer and author, second son of Sir James *Hall, fourth baronet (1761–1832), of Dunglass, Haddingtonshire, and his wife, Helen (*d*. 12 July 1837), second daughter of Dunbar Douglas, fourth earl of Selkirk, was born on 31 December 1788. He was educated at Edinburgh high school and entered the navy in May 1802, on the *Leander* (50 guns), then fitting for the flag of Sir Andrew Mitchell as commander-in-chief on the North American station. He was present at the *Leander*'s capture of the *Ville de Milan* on 23 February 1805, and continued in the ship until the admiral's death in spring 1806. Sir George Berkeley, who succeeded to the command, shortly afterwards transferred his flag to the *Leopard*, taking Hall and other officers with him.

In March 1808 the *Leopard* returned to England, and Hall, after passing his examination, was promoted on 10 June to lieutenant of the *Invincible*, from which he was very shortly moved at his own request into the *Endymion*, one of the finest British frigates, under the Hon. Thomas Bladen Capel, which in October was sent to Corunna, convoying reinforcements for Sir John Moore. She was afterwards ordered back to assist in re-embarking the troops, and Hall, ashore, saw the battle on 16 January 1809. The *Endymion* was afterwards employed in co-operating with the Spaniards of Galicia, and in independent cruising on the coast of Ireland, and as far south as Madeira, the incidents of which Hall graphically described in his *Fragments of Voyages and Travels* (1st ser., 3; 2nd ser., 1).

In March 1812 he was appointed to the frigate *Volage*, and in her went out to the East Indies, where he was moved into the *Illustrious*, flagship of Sir Samuel Hood, to whom he had been recommended. On 22 February 1814 he was promoted to command the sloop *Victor*, then building at Bombay, which he took to England in the following year. He was then appointed to the brig *Lyra* (10 guns), ordered to China in company with the frigate *Alceste* and Lord Amherst's embassy. Hall's book *Account of a Voyage of Discovery to the West Coast of Corea and the Great Loo-Choo Islands* (1818) describes this commission, his explorations in the little known eastern seas, and his visit to Canton (Guangzhou). His interview with Napoleon, who had known his father as a schoolboy at Brienne, is also recounted in the book, the later editions of which contain more personal narrative.

The *Lyra* reached England in October 1817, and on 5 November Hall was posted to the rank of captain. He seems to have employed the next two years in travelling on the continent. In May 1820 he was appointed to the *Conway*, a 26-gun frigate, for service on the South American station. He sailed from England in August, and on joining the commodore, Sir Thomas Hardy, in the River Plate, was at once sent round to Valparaiso. For the next two years he continued on the west coast of America, his voyage ranging as far north as San Blas, Mexico, where, as at Rio de Janeiro and at the Galápagos, he carried out a series of geophysical pendulum observations, the account of which was published in the *Philosophical Transactions of the Royal Society* (1823, 211–88). He had already, while in China, been elected FRS (28 March 1816). He sailed from San Blas in June 1822, and after touching at Rio de Janeiro returned to England, and was paid off in the spring of 1823. His *Extracts from a Journal Written on the Coasts of Chili, Peru, and Mexico* (2 vols., 1823) had a remarkable success.

Hall had no further service in the navy, and married in 1825 Margaret (*d*. 1876), daughter of Sir John Hunter, consul-general in Spain. They had two daughters and a son, Captain Basil Sidmouth De Ros Hall RN (*d*. 1871). After retiring from the navy, Hall spent his time in private travel or in literary and scientific pursuits at home. Of his travels in North America in 1827–8, he published a three-volume account in 1829, which was translated into French. His frank criticism of American customs provoked indignation in the United States, of which an interesting account appears in Frances Trollope's *Domestic Manners of the Americans* (1831). In September 1831, while living in London, he was able to present to Sir James Graham, then first lord of the Admiralty, the medical recommendation that the novelist Sir Walter Scott spend the winter abroad, and to obtain for Scott a passage to Malta in the frigate *Barham*.

(Hall's account of this is given in his *Fragments of Voyages and Travels*, 3rd ser., 3.282).

Besides his major work, the three-volume *Fragments of Voyages and Travels*, which contains many interesting accounts of the internal state of the navy in the early nineteenth century, Hall also wrote other books and numerous papers; some of the papers were printed in leading scientific publications. In addition to his fellowship of the Royal Society, he was a fellow of the Royal Astronomical, Royal Geographical, and Geological societies.

In 1842 Hall's mind gave way; he was placed in Haslar Hospital, Gosport, Hampshire, and died there on 11 September 1844, his wife surviving him, dying in 1876.

J. K. LAUGHTON, *rev.* ROGER MORRISS

**Sources** B. Hall, *Fragments of voyages and travels*, 9 vols. (1831–3) [3 ser., each in 3 vols.] · J. Marshall, *Royal naval biography*, suppl. 4 (1830), 142–84 · *Journal of the Royal Geographical Society*, 15 (1845), xlii · J. Foster, *The peerage, baronetage, and knightage of the British empire for 1883*, 2 [1883] · D. Gates, *The Spanish ulcer: a history of the Peninsular War* (1986) · R. Muir, *Britain and the defeat of Napoleon, 1807–1815* (1996) · G. S. Graham and R. A. Humphreys, eds., *The navy and South America, 1807–1823*, Navy RS, 104 (1962) · *Abstracts of the Papers Communicated to the Royal Society of London*, 5 (1843–50), 526

**Archives** Hunt. L., letters · NL Scot., letters · NMM, diary | All Souls Oxf., corresp. with Sir Charles Richard Vaughan · BL, letters to Macvey Napier, Add. MSS 34614, 34619–34621, *passim* · Bodl. Oxf., letters to Mary Somerville; corresp. with Sir J. G. Wilkinson [incl. copies], and map of Thebes · Derbys. RO, letters to Sir R. J. Wilmot-Horton · NL Scot., letters to Blackwoods; corresp. with Robert Cadell; corresp. with Archibald Constable · NL Scot., corresp. with Constable and Cadell; letters to Lady Hunter; corresp. with J. G. Lockhart; letters to Sir James Russell · RS, corresp. with Sir John Herschel · U. St Andr. L., corresp. with James Forbes · UCL, letters to G. B. Greenough

**Likenesses** F. Chantrey, pencil drawing, NPG · S. Joseph, marble bust, Pollok House, Glasgow · J. Swaine, line engraving, BM · J. Swaine, stipple and line (pubd 1842; after Bonnor), NPG

**Hall, Benjamin**, Baron Llanover (1802–1867), politician and eponymist of 'Big Ben', was the eldest son of Benjamin Hall (1778–1817), MP and ironmaster, of Hensol Castle, Glamorgan, and his wife, Charlotte, daughter of William Crawshay of Cyfarthfa, Glamorgan. He was born on 8 November 1802 in Upper Brook Street, London, and was educated at Westminster School, where he was admitted in January 1814. On 24 May 1820 he matriculated at Christ Church, Oxford, but left without taking a degree. On 4 December 1823 he married Augusta Waddington [*see* Hall, Augusta (1802–1896)], daughter and coheiress of Benjamin Waddington of Llanofer; they had two sons and a daughter.

At the general election in May 1831 Hall was returned to parliament for Monmouth boroughs as a whig, but he was unseated upon petition in the following July. He was, however, duly elected for the same constituency at the next general election in 1832, and continued to represent it until the dissolution of parliament in July 1837. Hall's first reported speech was delivered during the debate on the address in February 1833. In March 1834 he seconded Divett's motion for the abolition of church rates, and in March 1837 he supported Grote's motion in favour of the ballot. At the general election in July of that year he was

Benjamin Hall, Baron Llanover (1802–1867), by George Zobel (after T. Hurlstone)

returned as a Liberal at the head of the poll for the borough of Marylebone, for which constituency he continued to sit until his peerage in 1859, and on 16 August 1838 was created a baronet. In July 1843 he both spoke and voted in favour of Smith O'Brien's motion for the consideration of the causes of discontent then existing in Ireland. Hall gradually became a frequent debater in the house. He insisted on the right of the Welsh to have the services of the church spoken in their own tongue, and took an active part in the cause of ecclesiastical reform and the abolition of church rates. The speech which he delivered on the Ecclesiastical Commission Bill on 8 July 1850 was afterwards published as a pamphlet (1850). In *A Letter to his Grace the Archbishop of Canterbury on the State of the Church* (1850), and again in a *Letter to the Rev. C. Phillips, M.A.* (1852), he called the attention of the public to the great abuses existing in the management of ecclesiastical property, and in the distribution of church patronage.

Upon the reconstruction of the General Board of Health, in August 1854, Hall was appointed president, and he was sworn a member of the privy council on 14 November in the same year. In July 1855 he became chief commissioner of works (without a seat in the cabinet), an office he held until Palmerston's fall in February 1858. On 16 March 1855 he brought in a bill 'for the better local management of the metropolis', by which the Metropolitan Board of Works was first established (18 & 19 Vict. c. 120). During his tenure of the office of chief commissioner considerable improvements were made in the London parks. He made strenuous efforts to restrain Barry's expenditure on the new Palace of Westminster. In 1856 the bell for its clock tower, with Hall's name inscribed on it, was cast but cracked. The substitute was also defective but worked sufficiently well to be hung in 1858; it was named 'Big Ben' and rings to this day.

On Palmerston's accession to power for the second time Hall was created Baron Llanover of Llanover and Abercarn in the county of Monmouth, on 29 June 1859. He took his seat in the Lords on 4 July following, but never took much part in the debates, and spoke there for the last time in July 1863. On 20 November 1861 he was sworn in as lord lieutenant of Monmouthshire. He died, after a long illness, at his home, 9 Great Stanhope Street, London, on 27 April 1867. His sons having predeceased him, his title became extinct. He was buried at Llanofer churchyard. Lady Llanover, the noted writer on Welsh customs and antiquities, died on 17 January 1896, aged ninety-three.

G. F. R. Barker, *rev.* H. C. G. Matthew

**Sources** GEC, *Peerage* · *Men of the time* (1865) · M. H. Port, ed., *The Houses of Parliament* (1976)

**Archives** Gwent RO, corresp., household, estate, and election papers · NL Wales, corresp. | NL Wales, letters to Johnes family · U. Southampton L., corresp. with Palmerston

**Likenesses** Hurlstone, portrait; formerly in possession of Lady Llanover, 1890 · Ploszczynski, group portrait, lithograph (*Banquet given by the Reformers of Marylebone, 1st Dec 1847*; after C. Compton), BM · G. Zobel, mezzotint (after T. Hurlstone), BM, NPG [*see illus.*] · memorial, Llandaff Cathedral, Cardiff · monument, Llanofer churchyard, Monmouthshire · portrait, repro. in *ILN*, 34 (1859), 429 · woodcut, NPG; repro. in *Illustrated Times* (9 Jan 1858)

**Wealth at death** under £25,000: probate, 16 Sept 1867, *CGPLA Eng. & Wales*

**Hall, Dame Catherine Mary** (1922–1996), nurse, was born in Hollwood Road, Sheffield, Yorkshire, on 19 December 1922, the daughter of Robert Hall (1890–1955), police chief constable at Rotherham, Yorkshire, and his wife, Florence Irene, *née* Turner (1894–1975). She was educated at the Hunmanby Hall School for Girls (a Methodist boarding-school) at Filey, Yorkshire. From there her parents wanted her to train to be a doctor, but her preference was always for nursing. The outbreak of the Second World War cut short the argument, and with young women required to choose between the armed forces, munitions manufacture, nursing, and the land army, the way ahead for Hall was clearly with nursing. She began her general nurse training in 1941 at the Leeds General Infirmary, where she successively became the youngest ward sister at the age of twenty-two, night superintendent, and then at twenty-eight the youngest assistant matron. In 1950 the hospital awarded her its first travelling scholarship and she travelled widely in Canada and the United States, studying North American teaching and administration. Following a year of study in 1953–4 on the Royal College of Nursing's administration programme, she was appointed assistant matron at the Middlesex Hospital, London. Although assistant matrons were seldom involved in bedside care she was known for stopping on her rounds to make a patient comfortable or to tutor an inexperienced nurse.

Hall was so fond of the Middlesex that she was reluctant to take up the post of general secretary at the Royal College of Nursing (RCN) and applied only when it was advertised for a second time. It required pressure from friends and colleagues to encourage her to take the job in which she was to make the central contribution of her life; however, once she realized the job would give her an unrivalled opportunity to change attitudes and misconceptions about the profession, she was persuaded. The RCN of 1957 enjoyed a high standing but suffered from a restricted membership, and Hall inherited a genteel organization for female nurses, dominated by matrons with a background in general nursing. She quickly reformed its structures and brought in lawyers, accountants, and financial advisers, and she appointed some of the first graduate non-nurse administrators. With Hall as general secretary the RCN enjoyed a period of unprecedented growth, with membership leaping from 30,000 to 200,000. In 1960 she supported the campaign which lifted the constitutional ban on male nurses joining the RCN. She believed passionately that the RCN should be representative and in 1969 succeeded in extending the membership to enrolled nurses, and again in 1970 to include student nurses. In 1977 the RCN registered as a trade union, a development which Hall believed was an essential step, directly linked to its role as the UK's professional body for nursing.

In her twenty-five years as general secretary of the RCN, Hall engineered considerable changes in the environment in which nurses worked and a substantial amelioration in their pay and conditions. Yet she was always acutely aware that she had not achieved as much for nurses as she would have liked. Although she remained opposed to nurses taking industrial action in pursuit of pay claims, she had some sympathy for those who did. In 1962 she was drawn into her first serious conflict with the government over nurses' pay, publicly criticizing a salary award of only 2.5 per cent, while stressing that her nurses would never take strike action. This tacit appeal for public support encouraged sympathetic workers across the country to send money to nurses, while others went on strike in support. The move angered the then minister of health, Enoch Powell, who complained that the nurses' methods of controversy 'have caused widespread embarrassment' (*Daily Telegraph*, 29 Aug 1996). Yet the tactics worked and Hall secured an increase of 7.5 per cent for nurses—three times more than the original government offer.

Hall's preoccupations at the RCN went much deeper than pay. Like many nurse reformers, she believed that establishing nursing as a powerful professional group depended on securing a new system of education. In 1964 the RCN reported to the Platt committee on education that nurses in training should have student status, and that schools of nursing should be separate from hospitals. Student status for nursing was not achieved until after Hall had retired, but her work in the 1960s laid the foundations for nursing education for the next thirty years.

Between 1980 and 1985 Hall was the first chair of the nurses' regulatory body, the United Kingdom Central

Council for Nursing, Midwifery and Health Visiting, which established nursing's code of professional conduct. She was the first nurse to serve on the General Medical Council (1979–89), pioneering closer links between doctors and nurses long before it was more common for them to share responsibilities for the care of patients. She also worked hard with the medical profession to set up the joint board of clinical nursing studies, of which she was vice-chair between 1970 and 1980. From 1963 to 1983 she was a member of the World Health Organization's expert advisory panel on nursing, from 1971 to 1974 she was a member of the commission on industrial relations, and from 1975 to 1977 she was a member of the committee of enquiry into the regulation of the medical profession and also of the British Rail board for London and the South-east.

Hall was appointed CBE in 1967 and DBE in 1982, the year in which she retired to Buckfastleigh, Devon. She was awarded an honorary doctorate by City University, London, in 1975, and made a fellow of the Royal College of Nursing in 1976 and an officer sister of the order of St John of Jerusalem in 1977. She remained unmarried, and died of ovarian cancer at the Rowcroft Hospice, Torquay, on 26 August 1996. She had converted to Roman Catholicism in 1946, and her funeral mass was held at Buckfast Abbey, Devon, where she was buried, on 2 September 1996.

CHRISTINE HANCOCK

**Sources** *The Times* (29 Aug 1996) • *Daily Telegraph* (29 Aug 1996) • *The Guardian* (13 Sept 1996) • *The Independent* (2 Sept 1996) • personnel file, Royal College of Nursing Archives, Edinburgh • M. Green, 'Nursing education—"reports are not self-executive"', *Nursing and social change*, ed. M. Baly (1995), 295–310 • Royal College of Nursing Archives, Edinburgh, Catherine Hall MSS, ref. C312 • private information (2004) [M. Green] • *WWW* • b. cert. • baptism cert. • d. cert.

**Archives** Royal College of Nursing Archives, Edinburgh | SOUND Royal College of Nursing archives, Edinburgh, oral history interview, 1987, ref. T15

**Likenesses** oils, Royal College of Nursing, London • photograph, repro. in *The Times* • photograph, repro. in *The Independent* • photograph, repro. in *Daily Telegraph* • photograph, repro. in *The Guardian* • photographs, Royal College of Nursing, Edinburgh • photographs, Royal College of Nursing publishing company picture library, Harrow, London

**Wealth at death** £535,265: probate, 26 Nov 1996, *CGPLA Eng. & Wales*

**Hall, Chambers** (1786–1855), collector of antiquities and works of art, was the son of Captain and Mrs Hall whose portraits by Johan Zoffany are in the Ashmolean Museum, Oxford. His father probably served in the East India marine service. He had two brothers and a sister. Unfortunately little is known of his life. He lived with his brother Thomas at Elmfield Lodge, Southampton, but later moved to a house of his own in London, at 16 Bury Street, St James's, where he lived for the rest of his life.

Both Chambers Hall and his brother Thomas were amateur watercolour painters, and together they made journeys to Europe (albums of their drawings are in the Ashmolean Museum). Hall was a generous patron to the Southampton artist David Charles Read, and also to John Linnell, who made several views of Southampton water on commission, as well as three portrait drawings of Hall, all dated 1835 (now in the Ashmolean), which were part of his later gift to Oxford. Of a painted portrait by Linnell, the *Gentleman's Magazine* said that it failed 'to convey the benevolence of expression which all who knew him must remember' (*GM*, 1856).

There are no records of Hall's collecting, but it occupied him for much of his life. His taste for landscapes may well have been related to his own practice of drawing. Gustav Waagen described him as one of the principal print collectors of the day, and, at the time of his gift to Oxford, Jackson's *Oxford Journal* (7 April 1855) described him as 'well-known for his refined taste and judgement in subjects connected with the arts of design'. In its obituary the *Gentleman's Magazine* described him as 'one of the most intelligent collectors of objects *recherché* in art. With a taste that was catholic, he sought every opportunity of enriching his portfolios or garnishing his walls with the choicest works' (*GM*, 1855, 548).

In February 1854 Hall took a walking tour in the Swiss mountains. On a similar tour in the Pyrenees the following year, he was taken ill. Perhaps aware of his declining health, he decided to give away his collection of works of art. To the British Museum he gave various antiquities, a drawing by Raphael, a large group of watercolours by Thomas Girtin, and etchings by Parmigianino, Annibale Carracci, and Anthony Van Dyck. To the University Galleries (now the Ashmolean), Oxford, Hall gave numerous 'specimens of great variety, but of unequal merit' (*GM*, 1856). These comprised mainly small items; oil sketches by Rubens and Hogarth and others; drawings, which were nearly all of the highest quality, by such artists as Leonardo da Vinci, Dürer, Rubens, Van Dyck, Rembrandt, Claude Lorrain (a large group), and Watteau; and bronzes, both ancient and later. The gift also included paintings by Francesco Guardi, Canaletto, and Constable, as well as a Roman painting from a house in Pompeii.

The reason for Hall's association with Oxford is not known, but he refers to his gift as 'a long cherished desire' (Garlick, 296) in a letter to the Revd Henry Wellesley, scholar, art connoisseur, and principal of New Inn Hall, Oxford. Since the latter played a major role in the acquisition of the Michelangelo and Raphael drawings from Sir Thomas Lawrence's collection for the University Galleries, he may have influenced Hall in his intentions.

Hall died at his home at St James's on 29 August 1855. He was unmarried. The principal beneficiaries of his will were the widow of the painter D. C. Read, her daughter, and Henry Hobman, of Redhill, Surrey.

CHRISTOPHER WHITE

**Sources** G. F. Waagen, *Treasures of art in Great Britain*, 1 (1854), 37 • *GM*, 2nd ser., 44 (1855), 548–9 • *GM*, 2nd ser., 45 (1856), 162 • A. Michaelis, *Ancient marbles in Great Britain*, trans. C. A. M. Fennell (1882), 175, 571 • K. Garlick, 'The Chambers Hall gift', *Apollo*, 117 (1983), 296–301 • C. White, *Ashmolean Museum: Dutch, Flemish and German paintings before 1900* (2000), 1–2 • d. cert.

**Likenesses** J. Linnell, crayon drawing, AM Oxf. • attrib. R. Lucas, wax medallion, AM Oxf.

**Hall, Charles** (*c.*1720–1783), engraver, was born about 1720 and resided for most of his life in London. Having progressed beyond his original role as a writing engraver, he became well known as an antiquarian illustrator, specializing in seals, coins, and medals. He also engraved portraits, most of which were copied from the work of seventeenth-century engravers such as Abraham Hertocks, Wenceslaus Hollar, William Marshall, and Magdalena and Crispin van de Passe. These portraits, mainly of English sitters, are competent representations of the originals from which they are taken and represent Hall's best work. They include portraits of Thomas Howard, second duke of Norfolk, and Henry Fitzalan, earl of Arundel, after Holbein, and an engraving of Bishop William Warburton, after Howe, prefixed to an edition of Warburton's *Works* published in quarto in 1784.

Hall attracted some attention as a religious man in a profession not usually noted for its devotional instincts. He died at his lodgings in Grafton Street, Soho, on 5 February 1783. RICHARD SHARP

**Sources** J. Strutt, *A biographical dictionary, containing an historical account of all the engravers, from the earliest period of the art of engraving to the present time*, 2 vols. (1785–6) • *Engraved Brit. ports.* • Bryan, *Painters*

**Hall, Charles** (1745?–1825?), social and economic theorist, was probably the Carolus Hall, Anglus, who became a student at the University of Leiden on 30 May 1765. He later took the degree of MD, and in 1785 published *The Medical Family Instructor, with an Appendix on Canine Madness*. His experiences as a doctor led him to consider the sufferings of the poor, and his *Effects of Civilisation on the People in European States* appeared in 1805. In this work Hall stressed the importance of inquiry into the condition of the lives of the working classes, for 'to know those particulars with regard to the great mass of the people, is truly to know the state of a nation'. He claimed that the working classes kept only one-eighth of the product of their own labour, and advocated state ownership of the land, as land was the source of all wealth, with individual ownership of the produce of the land. In this he was anticipating later socialist ideals.

By the time this work was published Hall was living in extreme poverty as a result of losing a lawsuit, and soon afterwards he was sent to the Fleet Prison in London, where he refused to accept money from his friends to pay for his release because he felt he had been unfairly treated by the lawcourts, and wanted to die in prison. Hall died there at the age of eighty. ANNE PIMLOTT BAKER

**Sources** J. M. Morgan, *Hampden in the nineteenth century, or, Colloquies on the errors and improvement of society*, 2 vols. in 1 (1834), 20–21 • A. E. Egerton, 'Hall, Charles, M.D.', *Dictionary of political economy*, ed. H. R. I. Palgrave (1894–9) • A. Menger, *Das Recht auf den vollen Arbeitsertrag in geschichtlicher Darstellung* (1886) • E. Peacock, *Index to English speaking students who have graduated at Leyden University* (1883) • *DNB*

**Hall, Sir Charles** (1814–1883), judge, was born on 14 April 1814, the fourth son of John Hall of Manchester and Mary, daughter of John Dobson of Durham. His father sustained heavy losses by a bank failure and did not send him to university, articling him instead to a solicitor in Manchester. In 1835 he entered the Middle Temple, and read for the bar successively with William Taprell, special pleader, James Russell of the chancery bar, and Lewis Duval, a conveyancer. At the end of his year as a pupil he became Duval's principal assistant, and by extraordinary industry contrived to earn from him £700 or £800 a year, though receiving the unusually low proportion of one quarter of the fees received by Duval. In 1837 he married Sarah, daughter of Francis Duval of Exeter, and Lewis Duval's niece. Hall was called to the bar in Michaelmas 1838. Eventually he succeeded to the bulk of Duval's practice, and through his wife to the bulk of his fortune. At some point after his marriage, possibly following Duval's death in 1844, he took up residence in Duval's house, 8 Bayswater Hill, once the London residence of Peter the Great. It remained his home until his death.

During the next twenty years Hall became the recognized leader of the junior chancery bar, and the first authority of his day on real property law. He gradually obtained a large court practice. His pupil-room was always crowded, and from it came the foremost of the succeeding generation of equity lawyers. His best-known cases were the Bridgewater peerage case in the House of Lords in 1853, the Shrewsbury peerage case, and *Allgood* v. *Blake* in the exchequer chamber in 1872. The lord chief baron said of his argument in this last case that it was the most perfect he had ever listened to. He drew several bills for Lord Westbury, including his Registration of Titles Act, and assisted Lord Selborne in drafting the Judicature Act of 1873. Twice Lord Westbury offered him silk; but being without a rival at the chancery bar, and earning £10,000 a year, he refused it. In 1862 he became under-conveyancer and in 1864 conveyancer to the court of chancery, and in 1872 a bencher of his inn.

Hall was raised to the bench in succession to Vice-Chancellor Wickens in November 1873 and knighted. His hard work in this post was held responsible for a stroke he suffered while walking home from court in June 1882. He resigned his judgeship before the ensuing Michaelmas sittings, and died at his Bayswater home on 12 December 1883. He was fond of art and literature, but never played any part in politics. One of his sons, Sir Charles *Hall (1843–1900), became recorder of London.

J. A. HAMILTON, *rev.* CATHERINE PEASE-WATKIN

**Sources** *The Times* (13 Dec 1883) • *Solicitors' Journal*, 28 (1883–4), 136 • *Law Magazine*, 4th ser., 9 (1883–4), 220 • *Law Journal* (15 Dec 1883) • private information (1890) • *CGPLA Eng. & Wales* (1884)
**Likenesses** Lock & Whitfield, woodburytype photograph, 1876, NPG; repro. in T. Cooper, *Men of mark: a gallery of contemporary portraits*, 7 vols. (1876–83)
**Wealth at death** £86,080 10*s*. 10*d*. in UK: probate, 21 Jan 1884, *CGPLA Eng. & Wales*

**Hall, Sir Charles** (1843–1900), judge, was born on 3 August 1843 at Petersburgh House, Bayswater Hill, London, the second son of Vice-Chancellor Sir Charles *Hall (1814–1883) and his wife, Sarah, daughter of Francis Duval, and niece of the eminent conveyancer, Lewis Duval. He was educated at Harrow School and at Trinity College, Cambridge, where he matriculated in Michaelmas 1862, graduated BA in 1866, and proceeded MA in 1870. Admitted student at Lincoln's Inn on 15 November 1862, he was called to the bar there on 17 November 1866, and was admitted on 13 May 1872 *ad eundem* at the Middle Temple, of which he was elected bencher on 7 November 1884. He was a pupil of Sir James Hannen, and had for some years a considerable practice in the court of Admiralty and on the south-eastern circuit.

In November 1877 Hall was appointed attorney-general to the prince of Wales and on 2 June 1881 became QC. In 1890 he was created KCMG in recognition of his services as British representative at the international maritime conference held at Washington during the last quarter of the preceding year. He resigned his office at court on being elected recorder of London on 8 February 1892, but remained until his death on close terms with the prince of Wales. He performed the duties of the recordership with conspicuous efficiency. In 1899 he was sworn of the privy council. From 1885 until his death he was a Conservative MP. He represented the western division of Cambridgeshire from 1885 until 1892, when he was defeated. At a by-election in August 1892 he was returned for the Holborn division of Finsbury. He died unmarried on 9 March 1900 at his home, 2 Mount Street, Berkeley Square, London, and was buried in Kensal Green cemetery.

J. M. RIGG, *rev.* CATHERINE PEASE-WATKIN

**Sources** J. Foster, *Men-at-the-bar: a biographical hand-list of the members of the various inns of court*, 2nd edn (1885) • Venn, *Alum. Cant.* • Burke, *Peerage* • *Law List* (1867) • *Law List* (1885) • *Annual Register* (1889), 47, 50, 63 • *Annual Register* (1892), 9 • *Solicitors' Journal*, 22 (1877–8), 73, 529 • *Solicitors' Journal*, 23 (1877–8), 529 • *Hansard 3* (1886), vols. 302, 308 • *Hansard 4* (1893), vol. 8 • J. Haydn, *The book of dignities: containing rolls of the official personages of the British empire* (1851) • *The Times* (10 March 1900) • *Law Times* (17 March 1900) • *Law Journal* (10 March 1900) • *WWBMP* • *CGPLA Eng. & Wales* (1900)

**Likenesses** J. Collier, oils, 1895, Lincoln's Inn, London • Spy [L. Ward], chromolithograph, cartoon, NPG; repro. in *VF* (14 Feb 1888)

**Wealth at death** £55,874 3*s*. 7*d*.: probate, 3 May 1900, *CGPLA Eng. & Wales*

**Hall, Charles Henry** (1763–1827), dean of Christ Church, Oxford, was the son of Charles Hall DD (1718–1774), dean of Bocking, Essex, and chaplain to Archbishop Secker, and his wife, Elizabeth, daughter of Robert Carsan, a Lambeth surgeon. He was admitted on the foundation at Westminster School in 1775, and was elected thence to Christ Church, Oxford, and matriculated on 3 June 1779. His career began well: he won the chancellor's prize for Latin verse with 'Strages Indica Occidentalis' (1781) and the English essay for 'The use of medals' (1784); he graduated BA in 1783, MA in 1786, BD in 1794, and DD in 1800. From 1792 to 1794 he was tutor and censor of Christ Church; among his pupils was Peter Elmsley. In 1793 he served the office of junior proctor.

On 29 August 1794 Hall married Anna Maria Bridget (*d.* 1852), third daughter of John Byng, fifth Viscount Torrington. He thus vacated his studentship at Christ Church and was presented to the college living of Broughton in Airedale, Yorkshire. In 1798 he was appointed Bampton lecturer and prebendary of Exeter. His Bampton lectures were published as *Fullness of Time* in 1799. He became rector of Kirk Bramwith, Yorkshire, in 1799 on the nomination of his former pupil Lord Hawkesbury (later Lord Liverpool), and from 1807 vicar of Luton, Bedfordshire, a preferment which he held until his death.

As a student of Christ Church, Hall had basked in Dean Jackson's favour, and in 1794 Jackson recommended him to the duke of Portland, then home secretary, for preferment in Ireland, as 'the very man to be brought forward hereafter. He has real learning, and real good qualities' (Bill, 78). In 1799 Hall became a canon of Christ Church, and in 1807, through the influence of Lord Liverpool, regius professor of divinity. Jackson's view of him now changed and he thought Hall's lectures as professor 'sadly sterile and jejune'. Within months of his promotion to the chair, Hall wrote to Liverpool for a bishopric, complaining of Jackson's hostility (Bill, 79). However, mainly through Liverpool's influence (Bill, 126, 233), Hall was in October 1809 'brought forward' to succeed Jackson as dean of Christ Church, thus becoming one of the few former students to achieve this ultimate triumph.

It was the not continuously resident Reginald Heber of All Souls College who made a telling but qualified contrast between Hall's rule and that of his predecessor: Jackson's rule 'was an absolute monarchy of the most ultra-oriental character, whereas [Hall] is as little attended to, to all appearances, as the peishwah of the Mahrattas; the whole ground resting on an oligarchy of tutors' under whom, Heber rightly thought, the college flourished as much as under Jackson ('Reginald Heber', *Reminiscences of Oxford, by Oxford Men*, ed. L. M. Quiller-Couch, 1892, 241). Hall's dependence on an oligarchy became painfully clear in 1817, when he failed to gain the support not only of the canons but also of the censors (and therefore of the common room) when he proposed George Canning as successor to Charles Abbott as MP for the university; such a rebuff was inconceivable under Jackson.

Frederick Oakeley, who resided at Christ Church from 1820, gives more detail: Hall cloaked his inferiority to Jackson by imitating his gait and dress (though there is no pictorial record of these in Hall's case), but Oakeley found Hall's manner 'haughty and overbearing', and had 'no pleasant recollections about him'. Wine parties were frequent and Oakeley found his surroundings and the attitudes of many of his contemporaries with their 'vice and loose conversation' not conducive to his own academic progress. Hall's own son fell into bad company there and had to be sent away without graduating. Under Hall, Christ Church did not fully maintain the high place in the class lists which had been foreshadowed under his predecessor; in the 29 honours examinations of Hall's time, Christ Church obtained 94 firsts, though 21 of these came in his earliest years, when candidates admitted by Jackson were involved. Few men who later distinguished themselves in politics were undergraduates under Hall, though several who proved sound tutors were selected, among whom C. T. Longley, Augustus Short, Charles Dodgson, and W. F. Hook were later to obtain promotion in the church. According to Hook, Hall was not interested in what undergraduates said to him (Bill, 223).

As dean, Hall presided at probably the most historic public function held in Christ Church, the dinner of 15 June 1814 during the visit of the allied sovereigns; he sat between the prince regent and the duke of York, with Lord Grenville (chancellor of the university) and Prince Blücher in adjoining seats. Hall could greet foreign princes and conduct society weddings with appropriate dignity, but all was not well in the deanery itself. In 1824 Lord Liverpool wrote to George IV that twelve or thirteen years earlier (just after he became dean) Hall might have become a bishop (as Hall himself had hoped), but this promotion was impossible because of his 'embarrassed circumstances' (*Letters of George IV*, no. 1139, n. 2); these were explained by an observer in 1827: 'Bailiffs were continually in the House at Oxford' (S. Markham, *A Testimony of her Times*, 1990, 157)—a circumstance which cannot have enhanced Hall's standing among undergraduates richer than himself. Liverpool thought that Hall must be found a prosperous deanery; in 1824 the most suitable one, Durham, fell vacant, and Hall was appointed to it. Three years later, on 16 March 1827, Hall died at Edinburgh, where he had gone on medical advice. A month earlier a writ of sequestration read in Durham Cathedral (in Hall's presence) gave his debts as £35,800.

Hall's career did not fulfil its early promise; he never became a bishop. If it was an amusing chance that he was the only dean of Christ Church to have a brother-in-law nicknamed Poodle, it was by his own (or his wife's) mismanagement that he became the only dean who had bailiffs in the deanery—perhaps they were out of sight when the prince regent stayed there in mid-June 1814.

J. F. A. Mason

**Sources** *Old Westminsters*, 1.412–13 • *GM*, 1st ser., 97/1 (1827), 563 • F. Oakeley, 'Christ Church under Dean Hall', *Reminiscences of Oxford by Oxford men, 1559–1850*, ed. L. M. Quiller-Couch, OHS, 22 (1892), 301–19 • E. G. W. Bill, *Education at Christ Church, Oxford, 1660–1800* (1988) • *A correct account of the visit of … the prince regent and his illustrious guests to the university and city of Oxford in June 1814* (1814) • *The historical register of the University of Oxford … to the end of Trinity term 1900* (1900) • W. R. Ward, *Victorian Oxford* (1965), chaps. 3–4 • *The letters of King George IV, 1812–1830*, ed. A. Aspinall, 3 vols. (1938) • *DNB*

**Archives** BL, corresp. with Lord Grenville, Add. MS 69112 • BL, corresp. with first and second earls of Liverpool, Add. MSS 38225–38321, 38424, 38473–38474, 38574, 38580 • BL, corresp. with Robert Peel, Add. MSS 40257–40360, *passim* • Bodl. Oxf., Petty MSS • Christ Church Oxf. • priv. coll., letters to Lord Lansdowne

**Likenesses** G. S. Newton?, oils, Christ Church Oxf.

**Hall, Chester Moor** (*bap.* 1703, *d.* 1771), lawyer and inventor of an achromatic lens, was baptized on 9 January 1703 at Leigh, Essex, the only son of Jehu Hall (*d.* 1728) and Sarah Moor (*née* Bittridge). Both families were of some antiquity and substance. Hall was admitted as a student at Inner Temple on 5 October 1724 and subsequently practised as a barrister. By 1755 he was a JP for Essex, in which county he held considerable estates, and in 1763 he was made a bencher of Inner Temple. For his fellow benchers he compiled a table to show the daily increase of any sum (such as a rent of chambers) and the annual revenue of Inner Temple over the past twenty years; this was printed in 1771. He is not known to have belonged to any of the learned or polite societies, nor have any of his letters or papers been traced.

The fame of this otherwise obscure man rests on his invention of the achromatic lens; that is, a lens yielding an image free from the fringe of colours inseparable from telescope lenses at that time, which so handicapped accurate observation. What attracted Hall to the subject of optics is unknown, but presumably he did not accept Isaac Newton's assertion that the achromatic lens was an impossibility. Through experiment he reached the broadly correct conclusion that a compound lens made of two types of glass of differing refractive index would correct the chromatism and throw an image largely free from spurious colours. In 1733 he approached Edward Scarlett and the elder James Mann, London opticians, requesting from one a convex lens of crown glass, and from the other a concave lens of dense lead crystal. It so happened that each optician contracted the job to the glass-grinder George Bass, who, realizing that he had been asked to make two lenses which perfectly fitted together and gave a colourless image, discovered that the buyer was Hall.

News of this invention spread round the optical trade and telescopes with the new achromatic lenses were made. Nothing was heard from Hall, however, either during those years or in 1758 when the highly respected optician John Dollond (1706–1761) patented the achromatic lens; nor did any of the craftsmen making such lenses object, until, after Dollond's death, his son Peter Dollond attempted to prosecute those who were infringing the patent he had inherited. The craftsmen then defended themselves, saying that they had been making achromatic telescope lenses since Hall first conceived the idea. The case was heard before Lord Mansfield in the court of common pleas, judgment being given in February 1766. Lord Mansfield, though recognizing Hall as the inventor, found for Dollond, declaring in a phrase which has since passed into patent case law: 'it was not the person who locked up his invention in his scrutoire that ought to profit by such an invention, but he who brought it forth for the benefit of the public' (PRO, CCP judgments, H.6 Geo. III, 626 Middx).

The reasons for Hall's silence during these events are matter for conjecture; a disabling illness seems possible, for he left no will. In later life he resided at New Hall, Sutton, Essex, where he died on 17 March 1771. His library was auctioned in London the following year. Hall never married, his elder sister Martha being his legal heir. At her death in 1782 she left £100 for a monument to be placed in Sutton church where she and her brother were buried. The inscription placed there by his godson William Cockerton described Chester Moor Hall as 'a judicious lawyer, an able mathematician, a polite scholar, a sincere friend and a magistrate of the strictest integrity'.

Anita McConnell

**Sources** Essex RO, D/DGs M37; D/DS 43/5 and 6, 48/6; D/DNe · A. C. Ranyard, 'The inventor of the achromatic telescope', *Astronomical Register*, 19 (1881), 194–201 · A. C. Ranyard, 'Note with respect to the invention of the achromatic telescope', *Monthly Notices of the Royal Astronomical Society*, 46 (1885–6), 460–61 · J. Ramsden, observations on the invention of achromatic telescopes, RS, letters and papers, decade 10, no. 138 · A. L. Humphries, 'History of glass making and the glass trade', *N&Q*, 11th ser., 9 (1914), 312–13 · R. Willach, 'New light on the invention of the achromatic telescope objective', *Notes and Records of the Royal Society*, 50 (1996), 195–210 · R. B. P., 'The invention of the achromatic lens', *N&Q*, 12th ser., 3 (1917), 334–6 · 'Queries respecting Mr Hall's original discovery of achromatic telescopes', *Philosophical Magazine*, new ser., 6 (1829), 233–5 · CCP judgments, PRO, H.6 Geo. III, 626 Middx

**Wealth at death** books; estate tenancies

**Hall, Sir (Alfred) Daniel** (1864–1942), agricultural educationist and researcher, was born on 22 June 1864 at 44 Milnrow Road, Rochdale, Lancashire, the eldest of the five children of Edwin Hall (1835–1918), flannel manufacturer, and his wife, Mary Ann Billett (*d.* 1888), daughter of Alfred Birks, salesman, of Manchester. He was educated first at the Pickles Academy, Elliott Street, Rochdale, and then at Manchester grammar school from 1877 to 1881, in which year, having been elected to a Brackenbury scholarship in natural sciences, he went up to Balliol College, Oxford. He stroked the college eight, debated in the Oxford Union, and obtained a first-class degree in natural science (chemistry) in 1884. He remained in Oxford for a further year, and then became a schoolmaster, first in Scotland, subsequently at Hulme grammar school, Manchester, and finally at King Edward VI School, Birmingham, where he was appointed senior science master in April 1888. On 20 April 1892 he married Mary Louisa (*d.* 1921), daughter of John Brooks, a Birmingham paper manufacturer, and sister of one of his close friends at Oxford. They had two sons.

In the autumn of 1891 Hall decided to move to Surrey to become one of an expanding number of Oxford University extension lecturers. Whatever his reasons for this decision (and they remained obscure even to the biographers who knew him personally) it was crucial, for it brought him into the world of agricultural science and education in which he was to spend the rest of his life. In fact he spent less than three years as an extension lecturer, and most of the lectures he gave were on chemistry in general rather than agricultural chemistry, but his experiences appear to have convinced him that the application of science to agriculture was a worthwhile endeavour. In the spring of 1894 he was appointed the first principal of the newly established South Eastern Agricultural College at Wye in Kent.

This was a period of great expansion in agricultural higher education, when most of the university agricultural departments were founded. Wye became part of London University in 1900, and by 1913 was one of the largest departments of agriculture in the country. Hall learned with his students, for he was hardly an experienced agriculturist when first appointed to Wye. But lecturing, research, and writing, talking to farmers about the research that was necessary to help solve their problems,

Sir (Alfred) Daniel Hall (1864–1942), by Lafayette, 1927

visiting their farms, and extramural lecturing to farmer audiences all combined within a few years to give him a practical expertise, which ensured his credibility with the farming community, in addition to his scientific reputation. He also became an expert gardener, and won prizes at shows with his roses and tulips. In February 1902 he left Wye to become director of the Rothamsted Experimental Station at Harpenden in Hertfordshire.

It was, on the face of it, a surprising move. Hall's new job carried a lower salary than he had earned at Wye, and Rothamsted itself, although possessed of the prestige accorded to the first (and for about fifty years the only) agricultural experimental station in England, was, by the beginning of the twentieth century, lacking money, staff, and direction. Hall appealed unsuccessfully to the Board of Agriculture for funding, but subsequently persuaded a variety of individuals and institutions to provide the resources necessary to increase the staff. He provided the direction necessary by recognizing that Rothamsted could not hope to tackle all aspects of agricultural science, but should identify its strengths and concentrate on soils, plants, and their interrelationships. He also realized that much of the work which had been done at Rothamsted since the 1840s was effectively unavailable to its potential users because it was scattered through a wide range of publications, so one of the first tasks he set himself was to bring it all together in *The Book of the Rothamsted Experiments* (1905). The appearance of the book may have signalled a revival, but Hall probably did more to ensure the survival and later success of Rothamsted by his work with the Development Commission, which began in May 1910.

The commission was a product of Lloyd George's budget of 1909, in which money was provided to stimulate the economic development of rural areas. Hall was appointed—part-time and unpaid—one of the commissioners who would oversee its use, and it was largely due to his influence that a significant proportion of the money was used to establish research institutes to cover investigations into the whole range of the agricultural sciences, from the soil to economics. He had perceived the need to establish institutions which could carry out long-term research without being distracted by the need to show short-term results, and which could offer professional careers to the scientists involved. It might perhaps be argued that Hall was using his influence to advance the interests of his own institution (for Rothamsted was a recipient of Development Commission money) and the concerns of his colleagues, such as R. H. Biffen and T. B. Wood at Cambridge, with whom he had previously collaborated in launching the *Journal of Agricultural Science*. On the other hand, there is no doubt that the Development Act was an effective means of stimulating agricultural research, in which it was widely accepted that Britain was lagging behind comparable countries at that time, and many of the research institutes which it brought into being remained active and productive throughout the twentieth century. Among Hall's numerous activities, this was probably the one which had most long-term influence; from 1912, when he left Rothamsted and became a salaried commissioner, he devoted most of his time to it.

In 1913 Hall published his most enduring book, *A Pilgrimage of British Farming*, a collection of articles originally written for *The Times*, recording journeys made in the summers of 1910 to 1912 with T. B. Wood and E. S. Beaven. His other works included the textbooks *The Soil* (1903), *Fertilisers and Manures* (1909), and *The Feeding of Crops and Stock* (1911), and a pioneering survey, *The Agriculture and Soils of Kent, Surrey and Sussex* (1911), written with E. J. Russell.

The outbreak of war in 1914 meant that short-term problems had to take precedence over the longer perspective of the commission. Hall initially sat on Lord Milner's committee, which investigated ways of increasing domestic food production, but became much more closely involved in agricultural policy after Lloyd George became prime minister at the end of 1916. They knew each other from their joint work on the Development Act. The new president of the Board of Agriculture, Lord Ernle, was an old friend of Hall. Together they determined that Hall should take over as secretary to the board, which he did in June 1917. He remained there until 1927, acting as chief scientific adviser from 1920. Following the death of his first wife he married, on 3 August 1922, Ida Scott Audsley (*b.* 1887/8), daughter of Alfred Beaver, author and journalist.

From 1919 Hall was on the council of the John Innes Horticultural Institution. When the directorship became vacant in 1926 his fellow council members, having failed to find a suitable candidate, appointed Hall to the job. Although he was then nearly sixty-three years old, and neither a geneticist nor a cytologist, he had long experience in the administration of research. He expanded the institution's teaching role, arranged for its affiliation to the University of London, and returned to writing, publishing *The Book of the Tulip* (1929), *The Apple* (with M. B. Crane, 1933), and *The Genus Tulipa* (1940). From 1931 he was also a member of the newly formed Agricultural Research Council. He relinquished both posts in 1939, but with the outbreak of war volunteered to act as principal of Lord Wandsworth College at Long Sutton in Hampshire, a school of which he had been a trustee since 1916. He died at University College Hospital, London, from cancer, on 5 July 1942.

To be the principal of a college, the director of a research station, a senior civil servant, a headmaster, or a prolific author would represent the culmination of a career for many. Hall was all of these, and still found time for an extensive range of leisure pursuits: he took pleasure in music, painting, and literature, collected early Chinese pottery, was devoted to fly-fishing, and was said to have a discriminating palate for French wines. He was almost 6 feet tall and broad-shouldered, with reddish-brown hair and a heavy moustache. Among the distinctions bestowed upon him were a fellowship of the Royal Society (1909), a knighthood (KCB) in 1918, honorary doctorates from the universities of Oxford, Cambridge, and Aberdeen, and an honorary fellowship of Balliol College, Oxford, in 1939. On his seventy-fifth birthday a group of his friends presented him with a book of essays entitled *Agriculture in the Twentieth Century*. PAUL BRASSLEY

**Sources** H. E. Dale, *Daniel Hall, pioneer in scientific agriculture* (1956) · E. J. Russell, *Obits. FRS*, 4 (1942–4), 229–50 · H. V. Taylor, 'Sir Daniel Hall', *Journal of the Royal Horticultural Society*, 67 (1942), 319–21 · R. Olby, 'Social imperialism and state support for agricultural research in Edwardian Britain', *Annals of Science*, 48 (1991), 509–26 · *The Times* (7 July 1942) · *DNB* · b. cert. · m. certs. · d. cert.

**Archives** John Innes Centre, Norwich, corresp. and papers mainly relating to research into tulips, incl. work on *Tulipa* · Rothamsted Experimental Station, Harpenden, corresp. and papers · U. Reading, Rural History Centre, corresp. and papers relating to biography | Bodl. Oxf., corresp. with C. D. Darlington · CUL, corresp. with Charles C. Hurst · HLRO, letters to David Lloyd George · Plunkett Foundation, Long Hanborough, Oxfordshire, corresp. with Sir Horace Plunkett

**Likenesses** W. Stoneman, two photographs, 1921–40, NPG · Lafayette, photograph, 1927, NPG [*see illus.*] · C. Hall, oils, Lord Wandsworth College, Long Sutton, Hampshire · R. Paget, chalk sketch, Athenaeum, London · photograph, repro. in Dale, *Daniel Hall*

**Wealth at death** £15,254 0*s.* 1*d.*: probate, 13 Nov 1942, *CGPLA Eng. & Wales*

**Hall, David** (1683–1756), schoolmaster and Quaker minister, was born on 22 December 1683 at Skipton in Craven, West Riding of Yorkshire, the fourth of the five children of John Hall (*c.*1637–1719), tailor, innkeeper, and Quaker, and his wife, Elizabeth (*c.*1644–1725), daughter of Adam Payteffeild of Skipton. He was brought up within the dissenting network of first-generation Quakers who had experienced persecution. His own parents suffered during the 1680s. With easier times after 1689 his father organized the erection in 1693 of Skipton's Quaker meeting-house.

Smallpox struck in the same year. Hall's two brothers had died in infancy; now his two sisters succumbed to the disease. He himself was incapacitated for five years, and to the end he 'could rarely walk steddily' (*A Collection of Testimonies*, 1760, 328–31). Eventually he resumed at Ermysted's Grammar School, Skipton, and did well.

In 1703, excluded from university by his dissent and unfit for a manual trade, Hall set up a school in his parents' home, which until then had been an inn. It had twelve rooms, with stabling and a smallholding. Here, with the meeting-house near by, he ran a boarding-school for Quaker boys for the next fifty years. Such schools were in demand by Friends. The number of pupils varied from more than forty to fewer than a dozen, 'many Friends from different parts of the nation sending their children' (*A Collection of Testimonies*, 1760), including 'south-country boys' (Hall, *Memoirs*, 11). The annual fee was £8. The school's influence also spread through his young assistants or ushers, four of whom—James Gough, Robert Proud, George Routh, and Abraham Shackleton—became noted Quaker schoolmasters elsewhere. On 24 February 1717 Hall married Mary Storrs (1686–1717), a Quaker from Todmorden; she died during pregnancy on 10 October of that year. His second wife was Ann Foster (*bap.* 1698, *d.* 1736), a Quaker from Rylstone, near Skipton, whom he married on 17 November 1725; the couple had nine children, three of whom reached adulthood.

Hall's vocal ministry in meetings was welcomed as plain and simple. He had a talent for using his intimate Bible knowledge, and from his early thirties he was a recognized minister. In 1736, retaining an apartment in the house, he put the school under the care of George and Elizabeth Routh. Soon after, on 8 July, Ann died. Hall had always travelled widely to Friends' meetings, and there now came five busy years of visiting, counselling, and speaking among Friends in Scotland, Ireland, and many parts of England. As was the custom he liked to be accompanied by a young Friend, maybe a former pupil, for whom it was a fine experience. He doubtless travelled on horseback; certainly his father had kept two riding horses. Other travelling Friends liked to call at the school and to attend the Skipton meeting. Such visits gave strength to the Society of Friends.

A bent for teasing spiced the social morality in Hall's school rules. He wrote playful doggerel celebrating a Quaker anniversary at Preston and a whimsical letter recalling his visit to the London yearly meeting. In a pencil-drawn caricature of Hall a severe mouth is balanced by twinkling eyes.

Hall's published works, written between 1738 and 1753, reveal his perception of the current state of the society. His life bridged what he saw as its inspired simplicity under persecution to its easier times when he felt Friends' conduct often fell short. So his messages spoke of their lifestyle, discussing standards of conduct for their varied roles of parent, employer, trader, servant, and child, and exploring the problems of disownment from membership, mere nominal membership, and marrying out or mixed marriage. Memoirs by him of his own and his father's lives, with most of his printed writings, were published in one volume in 1758, with a second edition in 1799.

After the death of his second wife, Hall married again on 5 November 1740; his third wife was Deborah Atkinson, *née* Story (1705–1767), a Quaker originally coming from Preston Patrick, near Kendal, and the widow of Thomas Atkinson. Hall died at Skipton on 16 September 1756 and his body was interred in the burial-ground adjoining Skipton meeting-house. He was survived by his wife, who now returned to Kendal, where she remained until her death.

RICHARD HARLAND

**Sources** D. Hall, *Some brief memoirs of his life and of his father John Hall [with] divers of his epistles* (1758) • J. Gough, *Memoirs* (1781) • Society of Friends, records, U. Leeds, Brotherton L. • *A collection of testimonies* (1760) • D. Hall, 'Letter to James Wilson', *Journal of the Friends' Historical Society*, 18 (1921), 26–8, 110 • [D. Hall], 'Quaker school rules', *The Friend*, new ser., 48 (1908), 557 • L. J. Stroud, 'The history of Quaker education in England, 1647–1903', MEd diss., University of Leeds, 1944 • W. A. C. Stewart, *Quakers and education* (1953) • R. M. Jones, *The later periods of Quakerism*, 1 (1921) • J. Kendall, ed., *Letters on religious subjects written by divers Friends deceased*, 2 vols. (1805), no. 2, pp. 3–5 [letter by David Hall] • [D. Hall], 'Upon the anniversary held at Preston, 1738', RS Friends, Lond., B 14 • Skipton manorial court rolls, W. Yorks. AS, Leeds, Yorkshire Archaeological Society, DD 121

**Archives** U. Leeds, record of sufferings • U. Leeds, Knaresborough Monthly Meeting's minute books of ministers and elders

**Likenesses** pencil drawing, RS Friends, Lond.

**Wealth at death** school and smallholding premises; no other assets known: W. Yorks. AS, Leeds, Yorkshire Archaeological Society, Skipton manorial court rolls, DD 121

**Hall, Edmund** (*bap.* 1620, *d.* 1687), Church of England clergyman, was baptized on 8 September 1620 at St John Bedwardine, Worcester, a younger son of Richard Hall, clothier, of Worcester, and Elizabeth Bonner. His elder brother was the presbyterian polemicist Thomas *Hall, and like him he was probably educated at King's School, Worcester. On 8 July 1636 he matriculated plebeian from Pembroke College, Oxford, but left with his studies incomplete, taking a commission in the parliamentarian army against the royalists. Like his brother he appears to have been a supporter of the presbyterian party in both church and state. As a soldier he took the solemn league and covenant and rose to the rank of captain.

Hall left the army in 1647 when it began to radicalize and turn against its presbyterian officers, and returned to Pembroke. There he received election to the fellowship and graduated MA on 11 March 1650. Like many presbyterian clergymen he turned his scholarly abilities to criticizing the new military republic. Anthony Wood, the Anglican polemicist and biographer, attributed a number of pamphlets attacking the Commonwealth to Hall. These included *Lazarus's Sores Licked* (1650), an attack on the *de facto* arguments of Lazarus Seaman, the presbyterian master of Peterhouse, Cambridge. Seaman argued that the victory of the republican army over the king and his supporters showed that the republic was the *de facto* authority and that it was the religious duty of Christians to submit to the new government. Hall rubbished this view, countering Seaman's arguments by asserting the divine election of kings and the consequent duty of Christians to deny usurpers political legitimacy. Wood also attributes *Lingua testium* (1651) and *Manus testium movens* (1651), written by the eponymous 'Testis-Mundus Catholicus Scotanglo-Britanicus', to Hall. These pamphlets also asserted the divine election of kings and charged the Commonwealth with the anti-Christian sin of usurpation. The latter pamphlet was a critique of Nathaniel Homes's millenarian justification for the republic. In contrast, Hall's work interpreted 1647 as the moment of the removal of magistracy and ministry by the Beast (Cromwell), whom he expected to fall in 1651, arguing that it was impossible for him to reign above three and a half years; his defeat would then usher in the beginnings of a period of spiritualist millennial rule. Although also in favour of a Stuart restoration, Hall's tracts were written from a moderate presbyterian covenanter position. The reason for the eponymous authorship was that he wrote the pamphlets while in prison at the pleasure of the council of state for his criticism of the government. He was released (perhaps significantly) in 1652 and sought to avoid trouble by returning to Oxford, where according to Wood his antic gestures during sermons before the university prompted laughter among the younger members.

In June 1653 Hall published *A Scriptural Discourse of the Apostasie and the Antichrist*, a commentary on 2 Thessalonians 2. In the introduction he attacked Laud and his bishops for bringing the Church of England nearer to Rome; this, Hall said, unleashed the heretical reaction of the sects. He described himself as a presbyterian but showed he was moderate in that position by commending the 'primitive episcopate' of the Elizabethan church. The main thrust of the work, however, was millenarian. Hall concluded that the conversion of the Jews was a necessary step to the realization of the kingdom of heaven. He criticized the 'mock-saints' of the republic and believed that Charles I was the slain witness talked about in Revelation. Perhaps as a portent of his future conformity, he described himself as 'An obedient Son and Servant to the Church and State of ENGLAND' (introduction).

In 1657 Hall received employment as chaplain to Sir Edmund Bray, a royalist gentleman who owned the estate of Great Rissington in Gloucestershire. Bray attempted to present Hall to the rectory of Great Rissington, but was unsuccessful. Hall conformed at the Restoration and in May 1661 presented a petition to the government to take the rectory of Great Rissington from the incumbent, Lewis Atterbury. The petition was not successful, but he was rewarded for his conformity by obtaining the living of Chipping Norton in Oxfordshire. According to Wood he received a mixed reception as minister, some considering him to be 'a fantastical, and … others … an edifying preacher' (Wood, *Ath. Oxon.*, 4.213). This probably refers to Hall's firm Calvinism, which in the new environment of the Restoration church was less acceptable than before the civil wars. Hall also served as rector of Abington St Nicholas in Berkshire in 1676–86 and achieved his ambition of becoming rector of Great Rissington in 1680. He married soon after his appointment and lived there for the remainder of his life. He died about August 1687 and was buried in the chancel of Great Rissington church.

E. C. VERNON

**Sources** Wood, *Ath. Oxon.*, new edn, 4.212–14 • *CSP dom.*, *1651–60* • *DNB* • *Lazarus's sores licked* (1650) • *Lingua testium* (1651) • *Manus testium movens* (1651) • E. H. [E. Hall], *Hē apostasia ho antichristos, or, A scriptural discourse of the apostasie and the Antichrist* (1653) • *IGI* • Foster, *Alum. Oxon.* • B. W. Ball, *A great expectation: eschatological thought in English protestantism to 1660*, Studies in the History of Christian Thought, 12 (Leiden, 1975)

**Hall, Edna Clarke** [*née* Edna Waugh], **Lady Clarke Hall** (**1879–1979**), painter, was born on 29 June 1879 in Shipbourne, Kent, the tenth of the twelve children of the Revd Benjamin *Waugh (1839–1908), philanthropist and nonconformist minister who founded the National Society for the Prevention of Cruelty to Children (NSPCC), and Sarah Elizabeth (Lilian) Boothroyd. When Edna was two years old the family moved to Southgate, in north London. In 1889 Benjamin Waugh resigned his ministry in order to devote himself full-time to the NSPCC, and the family settled in St Albans, Hertfordshire.

Edna Waugh early showed a precocious talent for drawing. At fourteen she entered the Slade School of Art, London, at the instigation of William Clarke Hall, a family friend. A contemporary and friend of Gwen and Augustus John, Ida Nettleship, Ambrose McEvoy, and Albert Rutherston, she celebrated these friendships in a series of drawings and etchings (now in the National Museum and Gallery of Wales, Cardiff). Her assured and spirited draughtsmanship won her many certificates, prizes, and a Slade scholarship.

On 22 December 1898 Edna married William Clarke Hall (1866–1932), barrister and later magistrate. Beginning married life in Thames Ditton, Surrey, they moved in 1901 to Great House, Upminster Common, Essex, where Edna Clarke Hall lived for the rest of her life. From the beginning tension surfaced in the marriage, particularly between Clarke Hall's artistic ambitions and her husband's domestic expectations. One consequence was that for the next two decades her art became an intensely personal and private activity shared with only a few intimate friends and only occasionally seen in group exhibitions. During this period of personal conflict she found artistic inspiration in Emily Brontë's *Wuthering Heights* (1847), producing a group of powerful drawings and etchings to which she added during periods of emotional crisis. These illustrate her stylistic development—from the early detailed realism of *Catherine and Heathcliffe* (1902, Tate collection) to the bold and summary use of line seen in *The Young Couple* (1924, Ashmolean Museum, Oxford).

Born in 1905 and 1910 respectively, Clarke Hall's two sons, Justin and Denis, became important subjects she painted while unconsciously absorbed in their own pursuits. The resulting portraits show great tenderness but nevertheless avoid sentimentality. Many of these studies were executed in watercolour, her chief medium and one in which she displayed a great diversity in style and content. In many of her portraits, such as that of Katie Gliddon (1912, National Museum and Gallery of Wales, Cardiff), she employed fluid atmospheric washes. In contrast, in her important series of Figures in Landscape the brush was drawn almost dry across the paper in rapid strokes, as in *Girl Leaning on a Gate* (1915, Tate collection). In 1914 she was persuaded by Henry Tonks, her former drawing master, to show her work in a one-woman show at the Chenil Galleries, London, where it was well received. In the *Saturday Review* J. H. Collins Baker described her as a 'sensitive and expressive draughtswoman who reaches a masterly plane' with a sense of colour that was 'individual and instinctive' (14 April 1914).

Ten years elapsed before Clarke Hall exhibited again. In 1919 she suffered a nervous breakdown, though with the help of the psychologist Henry Head she was able to resolve some of the problems of her marriage and develop a new life centred on her art. In 1922 she acquired a studio in South Square, Gray's Inn. Etching and lithography became a new and important part of her work, and in 1924 she held the first of a series of successful exhibitions at the Redfern Gallery, London. After seeing Clarke Hall's *Painting with Poems* in her 1926 show at the Redfern Gallery, the art critic of *The Times* hailed her as 'the most imaginative artist in England' (9 Feb 1926). In the 1920s and 1930s she published several volumes of poetry, some of the earlier poems recalling William Blake's manner of interweaving lines of verse with swirling arabesques of colour or flowing lyrical figures, such as her distinctive series of Poem Pictures, of which three appeared in lithograph versions in *Facets*, published by Elkin, Mathews, and Marrot in 1930. She spent the winter of 1926–7 in Egypt. While that visit formed the focus of her work in her 1930 Redfern Gallery show, the work itself forms a fascinating record of traditional life in the Nile villages.

Edna Clarke Hall's last Redfern exhibition was in 1941, the same year that her London studio, and much of her work, was destroyed during a bombing raid. After this catastrophe her artistic energies gradually ebbed away until she ceased painting in the early 1950s. She lived another twenty-five years, sharing her life with her niece and devoted companion, Mary Fearnley Sander, until her death at the age of 100 on 16 November 1979 at Deal, Kent. Essentially an autobiographical artist, Clarke Hall painted with great sensitivity and understanding the people and places she knew and loved. ALISON THOMAS

**Sources** R. H. Wilenski, *Draughtsmen* (1924) · E. Clarke Hall, 'The heritage of ages', Tate collection · unpubd correspondence, priv. coll. · A. Thomas, *Portraits of women: Gwen John and her forgotten contemporaries* (1994)

**Likenesses** E. C. Hall, self-portrait, watercolour, 1899, Man. City Gall. · A. John, pencil drawing, Carlisle City Art Gallery · A. John, sanguine, Carlisle City Art Gallery

**Wealth at death** £11,727: probate, 11 March 1980, *CGPLA Eng. & Wales*

**Hall, Edward** (1497–1547), lawyer and historian, was born in the parish of St Mildred Poultry, London, the son of John and Katherine Hall. His father, a successful grocer, served as a warden of his company from 1512 to 1513, and several generations of Halls appear before this date in the company records. Edward Hall started his education at Eton College and was admitted to King's College, Cambridge, in 1514; he graduated BA in 1518. By 1521 he had entered Gray's Inn. Subsequently Hall made his living as a lawyer, and he often served in parliament.

**Career in law and parliament** Hall may have been first elected to the House of Commons in 1523; by 1528 he was sufficiently established to be included among 'the nobility, judges and councillors and divers other persons' summoned by Henry VIII to Bridewell Castle to hear the king explain his 'great scruple' in person (Harding, 2.280). In 1529 he was certainly elected to the house to represent the borough of Much Wenlock. Consequently his comments about the work of this, the Reformation Parliament, constitute an eyewitness account, and almost certainly he was among those 'learned in the law' appointed by the Commons to draw up bills concerning the probates of wills, mortuaries, clerical non-residence, and pluralities. Along with Thomas Cromwell and Paul Withypol, he sponsored a bill directed against the abuse of royal protections. In 1533 Hall was promoted to autumn reader at Gray's Inn; moreover, at the king's request he was elected common serjeant of London, in which capacity he helped administer the oath of succession to Londoners. He must have performed his duties well, for on 1 June 1535 Henry VIII wrote again to ask the city for 'our well-beloved subject Edward Hall to be now promoted to the office of under sheriff' (ibid., 2.281). The appointment was made the following day. Thus to all outward appearances Hall was a dutiful and obedient subject, thoroughly loyal to the king; in 1538, however, he was accused of ignoring a notice of royal protection issued against a plaintiff in a lawsuit, suggestive of the independent streak that found expression in his chronicle.

In 1536 Hall was re-elected to represent Wenlock, and in 1539 he was returned again, but his constituency this time is unknown. In 1542 he represented Bridgnorth, Wenlock's neighbouring borough. During the parliament of 1539 he answered a speech attacking the theology of the Act of Six Articles by referring to the authority of 'chronicles' and to the necessity of the subject to submit to the prince in these matters:

> it is the bounden duty of us that be subjects, to be obedient and ready to observe all such things touching our religion, as our prince ... with the consent of the bishops and the rest of the clergy, shall at any time please to set forth for to be observed or believed. (Foxe, 5.505)

In 1542 Hall was appointed a commissioner to mediate between Ludgate prisoners and their creditors, and he witnessed the confession of Anne Askew on 20 March 1545, which resulted in her liberation. He apparently did not participate in the later interrogation that led to her execution in the following year. Perhaps because of his earlier enthusiasm for Henry VIII's role in prescribing religious belief, on 31 March 1547 Hall was named to a commission charged with enforcing the Act of Six Articles, but he is unlikely to have contributed much to its proceedings, for he had died by 25 May following, when his will was proved. The exact date of death is uncertain, but may have been 15 April. He asked to be buried in the former Greyfriars church.

Hall's will, drawn up in the year 1546–7, gives no evidence for either marriage or children, mentioning as family only his brother, William, whom he appoints executor of his estate, and his mother, named as overseer of his will. While his *Chronicle* shows considerable dislike for powerful clerics associated with the 'old religion', for prelates like Cardinal Wolsey and the 'crafty' Cardinal Lorenzo Campeggi, Hall was more probably a moderate protestant—his will states his belief in redemption only through Christ, 'by whose passion and not by my desertes I trust onely to be saved' (Pollard, 'Hall's will', 176)—than a member of a strongly reformist family, as was once thought.

**Hall's *Chronicle*: origin and printing history** Hall's fame rests on his authorship of *The Union of the Two Noble and Illustre Families of Lancaster and York*, covering the history of England from the usurpation of Henry IV to the death of Henry VIII, generally known today as *Hall's Chronicle*. Hall did not complete this work before his death, and he bequeathed it in his will to the publisher and historian Richard Grafton: 'Item I give to Richard Grafton prynter my Cronycle late made trusting that he will set it forward' (Pollard, 'Hall's will', 177). Grafton fulfilled Hall's wishes, but despite his disclaimer in the prefatory letter that he neither 'altered nor added' anything, the final product certainly contains some contributions by Grafton. Since the latter records that Hall 'perfited [perfected] and writ this history no farther than to the four and twenty year of King Henry the Eight [1532]: the rest he left noted in divers and many pamphlets and papers' (*Hall's Chronicle*, vii), the final years must have required some editorial shaping by Grafton. While the chapters indicate a pattern of alternating good and bad kings (thus 'The unquiet time of Henry the Fourth' is succeeded by 'The victorious acts of King Henry V'), it remains uncertain if the titles originated with Grafton or Hall.

The history of this text is exceedingly difficult to untangle 'because of the perplexities in the order of its printing, in the intentions of its publisher, and in the imperfect and/or sophisticated state of many surviving copies' (*STC, 1475–1640*, 557). Grafton began to print the chronicle in 1547, then seems to have stopped at Edward IV's reign in order to enlarge the edition size, which involved reprinting the first set of quires. This edition finally came out in 1548. In 1550 Grafton issued a second edition, sharing the work with Steven Mierdman; it included a new note to the reader from Grafton and tables summarizing the reign of each king. Because of the work's clear protestant sympathies, Mary Tudor issued a proclamation in 1555 calling for the destruction of the *Chronicle* (the last in a long list of protestant works by such authors as Luther, Calvin, and Zwingli), but in 1560, probably in repudiation of Mary's act, John Kingston issued yet another edition, made up of the remaining sheets of the first edition but with new preliminary matter. Many extant copies differ considerably in their components.

**Sources and influence** Hall's text represents an important confluence of humanist and vernacular historical writing. He did not produce a raw chronology of events; rather, he absorbed the lessons of humanist historiography both in giving his history a narrative shape and in concerning himself with political rather than divine causes. In addition to providing him with important source material, Polydore Vergil's *Anglica historia* also taught Hall the need to make a critical evaluation of his sources. The London chronicle tradition—histories written about London from the perspective of the city merchants—also exerted an important influence. For example, Hall pays particular attention to how political developments, especially Henry VIII's enforced loans to pay for his war in France, affected London's merchant class. One of Hall's signal achievements may be the melding of continental historiographical techniques with the London chronicle tradition's concern for local history. His decision to write in English rather than Latin not only shows his desire to reach a local rather than an international audience, but also reflects a growing national pride and a desire to write English history in a way that will match the achievements of historians both classical (for example, Tacitus and Livy) and continental (for example, Froissart and Philippe de Commines).

The earlier parts of Hall's work draw heavily on earlier writings in Latin, French, and English, such as Higden's *Polychronicon*, Fabyan, Monstrelet, Hardyng, and the London chronicles, some of which are cited by name—for instance, a marginal note towards the beginning of the chapter on Richard III records that 'From the beginning of King Edward the fifth [hitherto], is of Sir Thomas More's penning' (*Hall's Chronicle*, 379). But Hall also consulted unnamed sources, several of which are either lost or were private to himself. His information on the fall of Caen in 1450, for example, may have originated with his ancestor Davy Hall, who was captain of Caen at the time. Hall also preserves details drawn from documents now lost, such as the articles and arbitrament between Henry Beaufort and Humphrey of Gloucester in 1426. However, the chapter on Henry VIII is for the most part Hall's own work, and remains a key source for the reign. Hall also exerted considerable influence on subsequent sixteenth-century writers, as an important source for John Stow's chronicles, the *Mirror for Magistrates*, *Holinshed's Chronicles*, and Shakespeare's history plays. His representation of Jeanne d'Arc, for instance, as a 'monster', who would 'do thynges, that other yong maidens bothe abhorred & wer ashamed to do' (ibid., 148), was copied both by Stow and by Shakespeare in *1 Henry VI*.

***Hall's Chronicle*, the Tudor myth, and Henry VIII** The understanding of Hall's work and its relationship to early Tudor political culture has shifted significantly. While earlier commentators emphasized how *Hall's Chronicle* endorsed the Tudor myth of divinely sanctioned dynastic origins and the absolute necessity of order, more recent interpretations have highlighted Hall's scepticism towards the Henrician court's chivalric play-acting, together with his sympathetic portrayal of popular dissent. The extended final chapter covers 'The triumphant reign of Henry the VIII', and much within it does indeed justify Hall's intent to explicate '[w]hat profit, what comfort, what joy succeeded in the realm of England by the union of the forenamed two noble families' (*Hall's Chronicle*, 2). None the less, the full story Hall tells complicates rather than confirms this sentiment. For example, Hall revels in the chivalric splendour accompanying the preparations for the French war:

> To see the lords and gentlemen, so well armed and so richly appareled in clothes of gold, and of silver, and velvets of sundry colors, pounced and embroidered, and all petty captains in satin and damask, of white and green, and yeomen in cloth of the same colors ... it was a pleasure to behold.

But this chivalric glory is severely undercut once this marvellously arrayed troop arrives in Brittany, for nothing turns out as planned. Although Ferdinand promised to supply 'ordinance, horsemen and beasts for carriages', everyone discovers to their mutual surprise that the Spanish king neglected to inform anyone of his intentions:

> The Biscaynes that brought vitaile [food] to the army, said to the soldiers: Sirs you bee arrived her, in trust that the king of Aragon will help you with ordinance and carriages, we hear no preparation that he maketh, nor never sent us word to prepare for your coming, of the which wee marvel much.

Undaunted, the English decide to buy their own, and the 'Biscaynes' to cheat them blind: 'one sir John Stile an Englishman, caused to brought two. C. Mulettes and asses, of such price as the Spaniards gained greatly'. Compounding matters, the animals are useless, for 'when they were put to carry, they would neither bear nor draw, for they were beasts which were not exercised a fore' (ibid., 528).

More seriously, Hall records with considerable sympathy the social unrest caused by Henry VIII's financial exactions to support his invasion of France. In June 1522 Hall describes how the king 'sent to the city of London to borrow xx M. [20,000] pound', but Londoners were not thrilled to be asked to support the king's 'honorable' war. The loan 'sore chafed the citizens', and while the mayor only asks 'men of substance', this move only exacerbates class tensions: 'The poor men were content with this payment and said, let the riche churls pay, for they may well' (*Hall's Chronicle*, 642).

Hall's treatment of the 1539 Act of Six Articles, in particular, demonstrates his use of history to register dissent. Despite his earlier support of the prince's right to mandate religious practice, the enforcement of the act clearly horrified him:

> among the common people it was called the act of six articles, & of some it was named the whip with six strings, and of some other, and that of the most part, it was named the bloody statute, for of truth it so in short time after scourged a great number in the city of London ...

Hall records that its enforcers kept expanding the scope of offence until:

> in fourteen days space there was not a preacher nor other person in the city of name, which had spoken against the supremacy of the Bishop of Rome, but he was wrapped in the six articles, insomuch as they indited and presented of suspicion to the number of five hundred persons and above.

An accusation alone sufficed to ensure a guilty verdict and execution:

> although in the time that these six Articles endured which was eight years and more, they brought many an honest and simple person to their deaths, for such was the rigor of that law, that if two witnesses false or true, had accused any and avouched that they had spoken against the sacrament, there was then no way but death, for it booted not to confess that his faith was contrary, or that he said not as the accusers reported: for they would believe the witnesses ye[a] and sometimes certain of the clergy, when they had no witnesses would procure some, or else they were slandered. (*Hall's Chronicle*, 828)

Hall undoubtedly wrote most of this passage, but he obviously could not have written the clause 'endured ... eight years or more', since the act was repealed four months after his death. This addition suggests that Grafton, notwithstanding his repeated claim to have printed Hall's chronicle 'utterly without addition of mine' (ibid., vii), understood Hall's intentions, agreed with them, and amended the passage accordingly.

**Hall and monarchic authority** Hall's scepticism toward royal authority and the pieties of providential historiography show up in other parts of the chronicle as well. Although Hall begins by asking, 'What mischief hath insurged in realms by intestine division?' (*Hall's Chronicle*, 1), he does not depict the deposition of Richard II as a crime against an anointed monarch which results in God's punishing England with civil war. Instead Hall's treatment of this key moment demonstrates that kingship is a privilege revocable by parliament. First, Hall includes a speech by the archbishop of Canterbury asking Henry Bolingbroke to 'take upon [himself] the high power, governance, and scepter of your native country'. But also, Hall emphasizes how charges are laid 'against [Richard] in the open parliament', how 'it was thought by the most part the King Richard was worthy to be deposed', and therefore how 'instruments authentic and solemn to depose ... were made'. Richard's deposition is orderly, by process of law, and done with the sanction of church and parliament. There is nothing in the act of deposition itself which goes against either religion or law. The blame for the 'unquiet time of king Henry the Fourth'—who, Hall reminds the reader, 'with one voice both of the nobles and commons was published, proclaimed and declared' king—rests with two noblemen, Edmund Mortimer, earl of March, and Richard, earl of Cambridge, because these men 'were with these doings neither pleased nor content' (ibid., 7–13). Aristocratic ambition, in other words, causes the ensuing civil strife, not the orderly deposition of a bad monarch. Nor is it accidental that Hall chose to interpolate Thomas More's *History of King Richard III*, for that text also adopts a critical position towards monarchic authority. More sets up a dichotomy, which Hall follows, between the gullible aristocrats who allow Richard III to thrive and the hard-nosed merchants who do not believe a word Richard says.

Hall's *Chronicle* thus presents a more complex narrative than has been generally allowed, and far from slavishly endorsing the Tudor myth in general and Henry VIII in particular, Hall uses history to criticize both. Henry Ellis edited the only complete modern edition under the title *Hall's Chronicle, containing the History of England during the Reign of Henry IV and the Succeeding Monarchs to the End of the Reign of Henry VIII* (1809); it was reprinted in 1965. Charles Whibley published *Henry VIII*, a separate edition of Hall's concluding chapter, in 1904. Janette Dillon has edited all the descriptions of revels and other scripted events, such as the Field of the Cloth of Gold, in *Performance and Spectacle in 'Hall's Chronicle'* (London, 2002).

PETER C. HERMAN

**Sources** *Hall's chronicle*, ed. H. Ellis (1809); repr. (1965) · A. Harding, 'Hall, Edward', HoP, *Commons*, 1509–58, 2.279–82 · A. F. Pollard, 'The bibliographical history of *Hall's chronicle*', *BIHR*, 10 (1932–3), 12–17 · A. F. Pollard, 'Edward Hall's will and chronicle', *BIHR*, 9 (1931–2), 171–7 · D. Woolf, 'Edward Hall', *Sixteenth-century British nondramatic writers: first series*, ed. D. A. Richardson, DLitB, 132 (1993), 160–65 · P. C. Herman, 'Henrician historiography and the voice of the people: the cases of More and Hall', *Texas Studies in Literature and Language*, 39 (1997), 261–83 · F. J. Levy, *Tudor historical thought* (1967) · M. McKisack, *Medieval history in the Tudor age* (1971) · J. Foxe, *Acts and monuments*, ed. G. H. Townsend, 8 vols. (1843–9), vol. 5, p. 505

**Wealth at death** not wealthy: will, PRO, PROB 11/31, sig. 36; Pollard, 'Edward Hall's will'

**Hall, Edward** (1664–1750). *See under* Hall family (*per. c.*1650–*c.*1750).

**Hall, Sir Edward Marshall** (1858–1927), lawyer, was born on 16 September 1858 at Brighton, the youngest of ten children of Alfred Hall (1812–1897), a well-known doctor, and Julia Elizabeth (*d.* 1889), daughter of James Sebright of Glasgow, an official in the postal service. After two years at Rugby School he became a clerk in a tea merchant's office, which his housemaster thought a suitable occupation for an unpromising pupil. His father thought differently, and sent his son to St John's College, Cambridge, where he matriculated in 1877. Following a year in Paris and a visit to Australia, he took a pass degree in 1883. In the same year he married Ethel (*d.* 1890), daughter of Henry Moon MD, of Brighton. He subsequently married Henriette, daughter of Hans Kroeger, of Altona, Germany, in 1896, with whom he had a daughter, Elna, the following year.

His early marriage made a profession essential, and in accordance with his father's wishes Marshall Hall was admitted to the Inner Temple in 1880 and called to the bar in 1883. He took silk in 1898 and became a bencher in 1910. His previous experience was not altogether wasted. From his father he had acquired a knowledge of medicine; the tea trade had given him some insight into business methods; and a precocious knowledge of the world was to prove very useful in his future career as an advocate. The local connection helped him on the south-eastern circuit and the Sussex sessions, and briefs began to come in.

Marshall Hall's personality was much to his advantage. A handsome man with a commanding presence, he always appealed to the lay client, as solicitors were not slow to appreciate, and he had an instinct for making the most of his qualities. It was eleven years, however, before a real opportunity came. He was retained in a squalid and repulsive murder case, *R.* v. *Hermann*. His client was Marie Hermann, a 43-year-old prostitute. She was tried in 1894 for the murder of an elderly man whose body she hid in a trunk after the killing. Hermann herself had been convinced that she would hang but Marshall Hall's defence of her, including the challenge to the jury at the end of his final speech, 'Gentlemen, on the evidence before you I almost dare you to find a verdict of murder', led to a verdict of manslaughter, despite the presence as prosecutors of C. W. Mathews and Archibald Bodkin, both highly regarded. It was a fine performance by Marshall Hall and attracted both public and professional attention.

Although Marshall Hall never practised regularly in the criminal courts, the publicity which such cases entailed kept him in the public eye, where he remained even in the late twentieth century: in 1989, *Famous Trials of Marshall Hall* was published as a Penguin paperback, and the 'brides in the bath' case, in which he acted for the defence, continued to attract popular attention. His practice rapidly increased, and justified him in taking silk at the early age of thirty-nine. The result was never in doubt. He soon became a fashionable leader in cases where fact rather than law was the predominant issue.

Success introduced Marshall Hall to politics, and in 1900 he was elected Conservative member for the Southport division of Lancashire. He retained the seat until 1906, and represented the East Toxteth division of Liverpool from 1910 to 1916. However, an unfortunate maiden speech, a superficial knowledge of politics, an inability to make speeches in the House of Commons that were as effective as those in court, and a failure to associate himself with any of the major political issues of the day meant that he made no mark in parliament. Professionally, he seemed on the crest of a wave. He was made recorder for Guildford in 1916 and knighted the following year. But a certain irresponsibility and a tendency to quarrel with authority became apparent. In a libel case against the *Daily Mail* in 1901 he procured very large damages by suggesting that an adjournment had been obtained for the purpose of finding out something detrimental to the character of his client, Hettie Chattell, an actress. There was no foundation for this suggestion, and his conduct was severely criticized in the Court of Appeal and a hostile press. His differences with the judges became so marked that his practice was affected and a fine professional income reduced to a mere pittance. It was the major crisis of Marshall Hall's career, but he went on to build up a new and sounder practice.

The brilliant and successful defence in 1907 of Robert Wood, a young artist, in which the accused became the first man to be acquitted of murder after giving evidence on his own behalf, did much to help Marshall Hall. Before long few sensational cases seemed complete without him. Both the prosecution for murder of Frederick Henry Seddon (March 1912) and the 'brides in the bath' case (June 1915) saw him act, albeit unsuccessfully, for the defence.

In the former, he came up against the forensic toxicologist William Willcox and demonstrated his ability to understand and challenge scientific evidence. However, he regarded this case as the 'blackest' of his career. It was one of the few capital cases in which he did not believe in the innocence of his client, who was convicted of murdering an elderly lodger by poisoning her with arsenic. The 'brides in the bath' case was even more sensational. George Joseph Smith faced trial in June 1915 for the murder in July 1912 of his wife, whose body had been found in a bath. There was little direct evidence on which Smith could have been convicted for this crime, but his fate was sealed when Marshall Hall failed to prevent the prosecution from showing 'system', when evidence was presented to the jury that his two subsequent wives had also been found dead in the bath in December 1913 and 1914 respectively.

Marshall Hall's greatest civil triumph was the divorce that he won for John Hugo Russell from his wife, Christabel, in 1923 after two such redoubtable advocates as John Simon and Douglas Hogg had failed. Unable to appear in the second trial, Sir Douglas Hogg said to Russell: 'There is only one man at the bar who might pull it off for you. He might win you a brilliant victory and he might make a terrible mess of it' (Marjoribanks, 427). It was an apt description of Marshall Hall's advocacy, but the brilliant victory came about only to be reversed on appeal upon a point of law in the House of Lords.

For some time before his death Marshall Hall's health had been failing. An attack of pneumonia years before had left him weakened and it became obvious that he was often working under physical disabilities. He carried on, however, securing a victory in court only a few months before his death at his home, 57A Wimpole Street, London, on 24 February 1927. His death was a great shock to the bar, which realized that with all his limitations Marshall Hall had been a unique figure. He enjoyed, perhaps, a greater reputation with the public than with his profession but at his best he was a powerful advocate, and always the kindest and most generous of leaders. His strength lay in his ability to challenge expert witnesses by ensuring that he became sufficiently knowledgeable about the scientific aspects of each case, and in his ability to persuade a jury to believe as strongly as he did that his clients had acted properly, be it in a civil or criminal case. His personality included a passion for showing off, coupled with an attractive simplicity and love of the marvellous, which even his harshest critics found difficult to resist. He was a keen spiritualist and a collector of antique silver. A cartoon of Marshall Hall by 'Spy' appeared in *Vanity Fair* on 24 September 1903. C. BIRON, *rev.* MIKE CLARKE

**Sources** E. Marjoribanks, *The life of Sir Edward Marshall Hall* (1929) · C. Wilson and P. Pitman, *Encyclopaedia of murder* (1964); repr. (1984) · Venn, *Alum. Cant.* · *CGPLA Eng. & Wales* (1927) · d. cert.

**Archives** Wellcome L., letters to Henry Lee

**Likenesses** H. Furniss, pen-and-ink, NPG · London Stereoscopic Co., photograph, NPG · J. Russell & Sons, photograph, NPG · Spy [L. Ward], chromolithograph, caricature, NPG; repro. in *VF* (24 Sept 1903)

**Wealth at death** £110,644 5*s.* 8*d.*: probate, 5 May 1927, *CGPLA Eng. & Wales*

**Hall, Elizabeth** (*d.* 1679). *See under* Hall family (*per. c.*1650–*c.*1750).

**Hall, Elizeus** (1502–1565), prophet, also known by the Christian names Elias, Ellis, and Elisha, was born in Manchester in 1502. The son of a carpenter, between the ages of seven and twenty-seven he was brought up in a house which later belonged to Sir Gilbert Gerard, attorney-general to Elizabeth I. A pious child, he was 'geven to solitarynes abstinence & prayer' ('Declaracon of Elye'). He married and practised the trade of drapery, making as much as £500 per annum during the reign of Edward VI. One night in 1551, while studying his accounts, he heard a voice addressing him as 'Eli, thou carpenters son' and exhorting him to arise and humble himself 'for the daye draweth nere'. Hall then saw a vision of the Five Wounds of Christ which he dismissed as a dream until April 1552 when an angel reappeared to him during a serious illness which confined him to bed. This time the voice told him that he was 'elect and chosen of God to declare and pronounce unto his people his worde', but castigated him for abandoning 'vertuous lyvinge' and wholly giving himself over to worldliness. Lifted from his bed 'as it were in a tufte of fethers with a worlewynde', he visited heaven and hell for the space of two nights and a day, during which he 'was not sene of anye mann in the yearth lyvinge' ('Declaracon of Elye'). He was commissioned to watch and pray for seven years, and then, although illiterate, to write for three and a half, at the end of which he would 'be trobled & falle into persecution' (PRO, SP 12/23/39). As a consequence he began to wear strange clothes and revive the ascetic practices of his youth. This did not prevent him from becoming junior constable of Manchester in 1557. Around 1557–8, 'forsaking all thinges pleasante to the flesshe' and abstaining from fish, meat, and wine, Hall began to write down the visions he had experienced in a 'greate booke', every word of which he wrote while on his knees. It appears that neither this nor a shorter work, which he entitled 'his booke of obedience', is now extant, though a copy of the latter, together with 'The Visions of Elizeus Hall in Metre', was owned by Sir John Parker, son of the archbishop. Both were composed as a result of direct revelation and showed little knowledge of the Bible, in which he freely confessed that he had 'notte moche redde'.

In 1562 Hall travelled from Manchester to London dressed in a garment of camel's hair, in imitation of the prophet Elijah, and proclaimed himself 'a mesenger sente from godde to the Quene & to all princes' (PRO, SP 12/23/39). On 8 June he was interrogated by the earl of Bedford, Lord Clinton, Sir Ambrose Cave, and Sir Richard Sackville. Shortly thereafter he went to see Elizabeth at Greenwich, where he was denounced in a sermon by Bishop James Pilkington of Durham. Three days later he visited Edmund Grindal, bishop of London, to deliver a warning and admonition from God. During his examination by Grindal on 12 June he stated that he had been interrogated by commissioners 'divers tymes' in the preceding year, and said that his divine vocation would shortly come to an end. He was suspected of retaining Catholic opinions about purgatory and transubstantiation, and of failing to receive communion, and, according to Grindal, 'diverse of his speaches' proved that he was 'of the popishe Judgemente in religion' (ibid.). On 26 June Hall was pilloried in Cheapside wearing a gown of grey skins and then committed to Bridewell, where he died in 1565. He had a daughter, who in 1577 was declared 'as notable a curtesan as ever was Lais' (Lansdowne MS 24, no. 81). ALEXANDRA WALSHAM

**Sources** PRO, SP 12/23/39 [Hall's confession] · 'The declaracon of Elye otherwyse called Elys Hall the carptenters sonne of Manchester in the countie of Lancaster … the xviijth of June', Bodl. Oxf., MS Tanner 50, fols. 16v–17v · J. Strype, *Annals of the Reformation and establishment of religion … during Queen Elizabeth's happy reign*, new edn, 1/1 (1824), 433–5; 1/2 (1824), 196 · Recorder Fleetwood to Lord Burghley, 10 Nov 1577, BL, Lansdowne MS 24, no. 81 · Tanner, *Bibl. Brit.-Hib.*, 372 · *The diary of Henry Machyn, citizen and merchant-taylor of London, from AD 1550 to AD 1563*, ed. J. G. Nichols, CS, 42 (1848), 284 · J. Harland, ed., *A volume of court leet records of the manor of Manchester in the sixteenth century*, Chetham Society, 63 (1864), 170

**Wealth at death** *c.*1547–1553 income was £500 per annum

**Hall, Fitzedward** (1825–1901), oriental scholar and philologist, was born at Troy, New York, on 21 March 1825, the eldest of the family of five sons and one daughter of Daniel Hall, a lawyer, and his wife, Anginetta (or Anjinette) Fitch. A younger brother, Benjamin Homer Hall, was a barrister and was city chamberlain of New York (1874–7 and 1884–5). After education in his native town of Walpole, New Hampshire, and Poughkeepsie, New York, Hall took the civil engineer's degree at Troy Rensselaer Polytechnic in 1842. In early life he showed a passion for English words and phrases, an interest which grew and matured in his later years. He formally entered Harvard in 1846, but before beginning his studies there was sent early that year to Calcutta in pursuit of a runaway brother. He never found his brother, but after being wrecked in the Hooghly River in September, and compelled to stay for a time in India, Hall took lessons in Hindustani and Sanskrit, and finally resolved to remain in order to master these and other languages. After three years in Calcutta (where he studied Hindustani, Persian, Bengali, and Sanskrit) and five months at Ghazipur, Hall went to Benares in January 1850. At the government college there Hall was appointed tutor in February 1850 and professor of Sanskrit and English in 1853. He married at Delhi in 1854 Amelia Warde (*d.* 1910), daughter of Arthur Shuldham of the East India Company's service. Of their five children three died young; a son and a daughter survived him. In July 1855 he became inspector of public instruction for the British administrative province of Ajmer-Merwara in Rajputana, and in December 1856 for the central provinces at Saugor. There he served as a rifleman for nine months during the sepoy mutiny. He then spent eighteen months in England, France, and America, revisiting England in 1860 to receive the honorary degree of doctor of civil law from Oxford University. He finally left India in 1862 and settled in London as professor of Sanskrit, Hindustani, and Indian jurisprudence in King's College, and librarian at the India Office. From 1864 until his death he was examiner in Hindustani and Hindi for the civil service commissioners; he was also examiner in Sanskrit in 1880 and in English in 1887.

From his early years in India, Hall devoted himself with exceptional zeal and industry to studying both Indian and English literature and philology. While at Benares he followed the example of the principal of the college, James Robert Ballantyne, in discovering many unknown Sanskrit manuscripts and in editing and translating several Sanskrit and Hindi works. He was the first American to edit a Sanskrit text, namely the Vedanta treatises *Ātmabodha* (with commentary) and *Tattvabodha* (1852). He subsequently edited and published at Calcutta between 1856 and 1865 a number of pioneering editions of Sanskrit texts concerning the Samkhya system of philosophy, astronomy, poetics, and dramaturgy, as well as the prose romance *Vāsavadattā* by Subandhu. These scholarly editions, with their long, detailed, and ground-breaking introductions based on the most meticulous primary research in manuscript sources, as well as the critical examination of published works, appeared in the Bibliotheca Indica series sponsored by the East India Company for the Asiatic Society of Bengal. Hall also produced in 1859 a classified 'Index to the bibliography of Indian philosophical systems', valuable in its time. His numerous Hindi translations and other publications included philosophical and scientific educational works printed in Allahabad and Agra between 1850 and 1855, and he edited J. R. Ballantyne's Hindi grammar (1868) and himself brought out a Hindi reader (1870). Hall's other works on Indian literature and thought included *Lectures on the Nyâya Philosophy* in both Sanskrit and English (1862), and *A Rational Refutation of the Hindu Philosophical Systems, Translated from the Hindi and Sanskrit* (1862). He subsequently re-edited and annotated Horace Hayman Wilson's translations of the *Ṛgvedasaṃhitā* (1866) and of the *Viṣṇupurāṇa* (vols. 1–5, pt 1, 1864–70; vol. 5, pt 2, index, 1877).

While he was librarian at the India Office, Hall directed much of his attention to English literature. Between 1864 and 1869 he edited a number of books for the Early English Text Society, of which he was an original committee member. In 1869 he retired, or was forced to retire, from the India Office and moved to the Hill House, Marlesford, Suffolk. There he divided his time between work on his edition of the *Viṣṇupurāṇa* and his research in English philology. *Recent Exemplifications of False Philology* (1872) contained a pungent criticism of Richard Grant White's *Words and their Uses* (1870). *Modern English* (1873) and *On English Adjectives in -able* (1877) contained much that was new and valuable. From 1878, when Dr (later Sir) James Murray became editor of the *New English Dictionary* (afterwards the *OED*), Hall became a conscientious and enthusiastic contributor of material. 'As a voluntary and gratuitous service to the history of the English language, [he] devoted four hours daily to a critical examination of the proof sheets, and the filling up of deficiencies, whether in the vocabulary or the quotations' (preface to *New English Dictionary*, 1888). During the same period Hall contributed some 2200 words and expressions he had heard and noted in the Suffolk dialect for letters A to M in Professor Wright's *Dialect Dictionary*. He also published many articles in *The Academy*, *The Spectator*, and other periodicals. At his death he left many long lists of quotations for Sir James Murray's use.

Hall's correspondence, particularly after 1869, shows him in an increasingly oversensitive, bitter, and perhaps pathological state of mind in which he quarrelled with colleagues and institutions, but he continued to his last days to support the dictionary project and to argue for the upholding of quality above speed of publication. Many of his own contributions to the dictionary have been of lasting value. Though they never met, Murray came to regard Hall as a close friend and colleague.

Hall died at his home at Marlesford on 1 February 1901. His ashes after cremation were interred in Oakwood cemetery, Troy, New York. There is a brass tablet to Hall's memory in Marlesford church. In 1895 he received an honorary LLD from Harvard, to which during his lifetime he gave over 1000 oriental manuscripts, many of them of great scholarly value, and some printed books. Correspondence from the early years after Hall's return to England from India shows that he wished at that time to present his manuscript collections to Oxford University, but the negotiations foundered over financial and other disagreements. W. B. Owen, *rev.* J. B. Katz

**Sources** W. P. G., memoir, *The Nation* [New York] (14 Feb 1901) · notice, *Modern Language Notes* [Brooklyn] (March 1901) · notice, *The Bookman* [New York], 13 (July 1901), 516 · J. G. Wilson and J. Fiske, eds., *Appleton's cyclopaedia of American biography*, 7 vols. (1887–1900) · *The Times* (15 Feb 1901) · private information (1912) [J. A. H. Murray and R. D. Hall] · S. Winchester, *The surgeon of Crowthorne* (1998), 147ff. · K. M. E. Murray, *Caught in the web of words: James A. H. Murray and the 'Oxford English dictionary'* (1977), 304ff., 375 · D. Pingree, 'The sources of Harvard's Indian manuscripts', Harvard U. · *IGI*

**Archives** BL OIOC, typescripts of corresp., etc. · Bodl. Oxf., letters · Bodl. Oxf., library records, e. 268 · Harvard U., Indian manuscripts, etc., and related papers and letters | Oxford University Press, corresp. with James Murray, etc.

**Likenesses** photograph, 1862, repro. in Murray, *Caught in the web of words* · portrait, 1893, repro. in *Bookman* · photograph of drawing, BL OIOC

**Wealth at death** £399 14*s.* 4*d.*: probate, 8 Aug 1901, *CGPLA Eng. & Wales*

**Hall, Francis Russell** (1788–1866), Church of England clergyman and writer, son of the Revd Samuel Hall, incumbent of St Peter's, Manchester, and his wife, Elizabeth, was born in Manchester on 17 May 1788. He was educated at Manchester grammar school and at St John's College, Cambridge, where he matriculated in 1806 and graduated BA in 1810, MA in 1813, BD in 1820, and DD in 1839. He was a fellow of St John's from 1815 to 1826. From 1826 until his death there on 18 November 1866 he was rector of Fulbourn, near Cambridge. He published some minor poetry, a hymnbook, *Reasons for not Contributing to Circulate the Apocrypha* (1825), *A Letter … on the Present Corrupt State of the University of Cambridge* (1834), and other pamphlets. On 4 January 1853 he married Mary Annie, daughter of G. F. West of Rosoman House, Islington. They had at least three sons. C. W. Sutton, *rev.* H. C. G. Matthew

**Sources** Venn, *Alum. Cant.* · Boase, *Mod. Eng. biog.* · *GM*, 2nd ser., 39 (1853), 306 · *GM*, 4th ser., 3 (1867), 116

**Wealth at death** under £6000: probate, 26 March 1867, *CGPLA Eng. & Wales*

**Hall, George** (*bap.* **1613**, *d.* **1668**), bishop of Chester, was the third son of Joseph *Hall (1574–1656), bishop of Exeter from 1627 to 1641 and of Norwich from 1641 to 1647, and his wife, Elizabeth Winiff (1582/3–1652). George was baptized on 24 August 1613 at Waltham Abbey, Essex, where his father was the rector for many years. He entered Exeter College, Oxford, in 1628, graduated BA in April 1631 and proceeded MA in January 1634 (a degree which was incorporated at Cambridge the following year). From 1632 until his resignation in June 1638 he was a fellow of Exeter College. He became vicar of Menheniot, Cornwall, in October 1637, a prebendary of Exeter Cathedral in December 1639, and archdeacon of Cornwall on the resignation of his eldest brother, Robert, in October 1641. He married Gertrude Meredith (*d.* 1669), daughter of Edward Meredith of Maristow, on 28 June 1641.

During the civil war Hall was sequestered from vicarage, prebend, and archdeaconry and was prevented from keeping a school, but he and his wife both received compensation from parliament. In November 1651 he was chosen as 'minister' at St Bartholomew by the Exchange in London, in spite of opposition from five or six vestrymen who attempted to delay the proceedings in favour of other candidates. On 5 January 1654 the vestry elected Hall as rector, but this was disallowed by the keepers of the great seal, to whom the living belonged. Thereafter he was admitted to the rectory of Berwick, Sussex, and of St Botolph, Aldersgate, London (1654–5). At the Restoration, Hall was created DD and became chaplain to Charles II, then canon of Windsor and archdeacon of Canterbury. He was elected bishop of Chester on 24 April 1662 (consecrated 11 May), serving until his death on 23 August 1668. The oft-repeated story that he was mortally wounded by a knife in his pocket when he fell from his garden mount first appears in Thomas Birch's *Life of … Tillotson* (2nd edn, 1753, 38). He was buried in the chancel of Wigan church, Lancashire.

Hall's position in the Restoration church, like that of many Cromwellian conformists, was ambiguous. On the one hand, he was a pluralist prelate, who resided at the comfortable rectory of Wigan, granted him by Sir Orlando Bridgman, while failing to supervise the routine business of his see, where in his time presentations to livings or subscriptions by clergy were recorded only 'by chance' (bishop's act book, fol. 137). Hall championed conformity to the Anglican liturgy; according to one dissenter 'his letter to the Bp of London was of utmost importance tow[ards] the crossinge of the indulgence' proposed by the king in 1662 (*Diary of the Rev. Henry Newcome*, 119). But Hall also appears to have espoused his father's moderation in devotional matters. During the interregnum he found himself 'ingaged, betweene opposite Parties, which I was to speake unto; the rigid Punctilio-men, both of the right hand, and of the left' (G. Hall, *God's Appearing for the Tribe of Levi*, 1655, sigs. A2v–3). He published a satirical attack on the common Catholic enemy, *The Triumphs of Rome over Despised Protestancie* (1655, repr. 1667). After the Restoration he was a constant preacher in the neighbourhood of Wigan, his sermons regularly attracting the Presbyterian diarist Robert Lowe and his companions. On one such occasion Hall inveighed 'against atheisticalnes' (*Diary of Roger Lowe*, 105), and he did not hesitate to employ the same theme in the House of Lords (G. Hall, *A Fast Sermon Preached … on the Day of Solemn Humiliation for the Continuing Pestilence*, 1666). Hall's marriage was childless. Apart from providing for his widow—who was to survive him only by some seven months—during her lifetime, Hall bequeathed his entire landed estate to Exeter College, leaving £100 for the poor of Waltham Abbey and no legacy at all to his relations. His youngest brother, Samuel, felt aggrieved by this will, bringing suit over it in the court of arches in 1671. JOHN D. RAMSBOTTOM

**Sources** G. Ormerod, *The history of the county palatine and city of Chester*, 2nd edn, ed. T. Helsby, 3 vols. (1882) • Wood, *Ath. Oxon.*, 1st edn • *Walker rev.* • E. Freshfield, ed., *The vestry minute books of the parish of St. Bartholomew Exchange in the City of London, 1567–1676* (privately printed, London, 1890) • *The diary of Roger Lowe*, ed. W. L. Sachse (1938) • W. A. Shaw, *A history of the English church during the civil wars and under the Commonwealth, 1640–1660*, 2 vols. (1900) • *The diary of the Rev. Henry Newcome, from September 30, 1661, to September 29, 1663*, ed. T. Heywood, Chetham Society, 18 (1849) • T. Birch, *The life of the Most Reverend Dr John Tillotson, lord archbishop of Canterbury*, 2nd edn (1753) • J. Spurr, *The Restoration Church of England, 1646–1689* (1991) • J. Houston, ed., *Index of cases in the records of the court of arches*, British RS, 85 (1972) • bishop's act book, Chester, 1576–1686, Ches. & Chester ALSS, EDA1/4 • C. W. Boase, ed., *Registrum Collegii Exoniensis*, new edn, OHS, 27 (1894) • *DNB*

**Likenesses** oils, Exeter College, Oxford • portrait, Emmanuel College, Cambridge

**Wealth at death** landed estate to Exeter College, Oxford; £100 to poor of Waltham Abbey; provision for widow's lifetime; nothing else to relatives: will, PRO, PROB 11/328, sig. 164

**Hall, George** (*bap.* 1753, *d.* 1811), college head and Church of Ireland bishop of Dromore, son of the Revd Mark Hall, was born in Northumberland, and baptized on 14 May 1753 at Earsdon by North Shields, but settled early in life in Ireland. His first employment was as an assistant master in Dr Darby's school near Dublin. He entered Trinity College, Dublin, on 1 November 1770, aged seventeen. Under the tutorship of the Revd Gerald Fitzgerald he soon distinguished himself, and was elected a scholar in 1773; he graduated BA (1775), MA (1778), BD (1786), and DD (1790). He was elected a fellow of the college in 1777, and on 14 May 1790 he was co-opted a senior fellow. In addition he held various offices, including that of Archbishop King's lecturer in divinity (1790–91), regius professor of Greek (1790 and 1795), professor of modern history (1791), and professor of mathematics (1799). He resigned his fellowship in 1800, and on 25 February of that year was presented by his college to the rectory of Ardstraw in the diocese of Derry. In 1806 he returned to Trinity College, having been appointed to the provostship by patent dated 22 January, and held that office until his promotion, on 13 November 1811, to the bishopric of Dromore. He was consecrated in the college chapel on the 17th of the same month, but died, unmarried, on the 23rd in the provost's house, from which he had not had time to remove. He was buried in the college chapel, where a monument was erected by his niece, Margaret Stack. There is a second memorial in the parish church of Ardstraw in Newtownstewart, co. Tyrone.

B. H. BLACKER, *rev.* PHILIP CARTER

**Sources** *GM*, 1st ser., 81/2 (1811), 493, 667 • H. Cotton, *Fasti ecclesiae Hibernicae*, 1–5 (1845–60) • Burtchaell & Sadleir, *Alum. Dubl.* • W. S. Mason, *A statistical account, or, Parochial survey of Ireland*, 1 (1814), 119 • *IGI*

**Archives** TCD, corresp. and papers as provost of Trinity College, Dublin

**Likenesses** W. Coming, oils, TCD

**Hall, George Henry**, **Viscount Hall** (1881–1965), trade unionist and politician, was born at Penrhiw-ceibr, Glamorgan, on 31 December 1881, the son of George and Ann Hall. At the age of twelve, after a basic education at Penrhiw-ceibr elementary school, Hall began work at Penrikyber colliery; he remained a collier until 1911, when he was elected to the position of checkweighman. This was a key post, entailing the recording of the daily output by the workmen, which determined their weekly wages. As with other leaders to emerge from the south Wales coalfield, Hall's position as checkweighman served as a springboard to a full-time trade union career within the South Wales Miners' Federation, in which he became miners' agent for his local area.

Hall's political career had already been launched in 1909 when he was elected as member for the Penrhiw-ceibr ward in local council elections. He remained a member of Mountain Ash town council and its education committee for eighteen years. He had a lasting interest in education, and in later life served as a governor of University College, Cardiff. In 1910 he married Margaret Jones, the marriage lasting until her death in 1941. They had two sons, Leonard and Bruce, the latter killed on active service in the Second World War.

In 1922 Hall defeated C. B. Stanton to win the Aberdâr division of the Merthyr Tudful constituency as a Labour candidate, with a majority of 5217. Hall retained this seat for twenty-four years, and had the distinction of being returned unopposed in 1931 and 1935 when his popularity was at its height as the result of his uncompromising stand against the means test. His work as a constituency MP was always as important to him as the more prominent government duties he later assumed. In particular, he was always keen to encourage new employment opportunities in the area to replace the declining coal industry. He was, for example, able to attract a new cable works to Aberdâr, of which he became a director.

In 1929 Hall began a long association with the Admiralty when Ramsay MacDonald appointed him to the post of civil lord of the Admiralty, which he held until the creation of the National Government in 1931. His next appointment, as a member of the wartime coalition government, was as parliamentary under-secretary of state for the Colonial Office from 1941 to 1942. He only agreed to take this post in return for a promise by Churchill to establish a Royal Ordnance factory at Hirwaun, near Aberdâr, to alleviate continuing unemployment. In 1943 Hall returned to the Admiralty as financial secretary, his major duty being to oversee production during the battle of the Atlantic. Later the same year he moved to the post of parliamentary under-secretary of state for foreign affairs, remaining in this office until the end of the war.

Hall refused the first of two offers of a peerage to mark his wartime achievements. But with the return of a Labour government in 1945, and Hall's successful retention of his seat with a majority of 27,969, Attlee prevailed on him in 1946 to accept the title of Viscount Hall of Cynon Valley and with it the post of first lord of the Admiralty. This was designed to boost Labour representation in the upper house, but the move caused bitterness among die-hard Labour Party activists in Aberdâr. Hall agonized long over the decision before resolving that, for someone who had always considered himself in the mainstream of the Labour Party, loyalty to that party must come above any recriminations over supposed compromise of socialist principles.

In 1947 Hall became deputy leader of the House of Lords, holding both this and his position at the Admiralty until he retired, in poor health, at the general election of 1951. During this period he supervised the transition of the navy to a peacetime footing, ensuring that the service began adapting itself to the new demands of the atomic age. In February 1964 Hall married Alice Martha Walker. He died at Leicester on 8 November 1965, survived by his second wife. KEITH DAVIES

**Sources** R. P. Arnot, *South Wales miners / Glowyr de Cymru: a history of the South Wales Miners' Federation*, [1–2] (1967–75) • *WWW* • *WWBMP*
**Archives** Nuffield Oxf., corresp. and papers • U. Hull, Brynmor Jones L., corresp. and papers
**Likenesses** W. Stoneman, photograph, 1946, NPG
**Wealth at death** £30,659: probate, 10 March 1966, *CGPLA Eng. & Wales*

**Hall, (Oliver) Grahame**. *See* Muncaster, Claude Grahame (1903–1974).

**Hall, Henry** (*d.* 1680), covenanter, was the son of Robert Hall (known as Hobbie Hall), owner of Haugh-Head, in the parish of Eckford, Teviotdale, and had at least one sister. Described as a 'bold brisk man' (Wodrow, 206) he was raised in a covenanting family and was active in the cause of the covenants throughout his life. He opposed the public resolutions of 1650 which, by admitting 'malignants' to the service of the regime, divided the Church of Scotland. As a result he refused to sit under his own minister at Eckford, who complied with the resolutions, and chose rather to hear John Livingstone at Ancram. Later he refused to conform to episcopacy, reintroduced at the Restoration, and his nonconformity forced him to flee to the north of England in 1665.

In 1666 Hall left his place of refuge to join the covenanter uprising then underway in Pentland, but while travelling there was seized and imprisoned in Cessford Castle, near his home. On regaining freedom he went back to Northumberland, but in 1678 was forced to return to Scotland as a result of the pursuit of Scotsmen in the area by Colonel Struther. After his return he spent much time in the company of the covenanter field preachers Richard Cameron and Donald Cargill. With the next uprising he was among the insurgents in the area around Roxburgh, Berwick, and Selkirk. He fought as one of the officers at Drumclog on 1 June 1679 and at Bothwell Bridge on 22 June 1679. On 25 June the privy council identified Hall as a probable instigator of further trouble and authorized his apprehension as a rebel, and on the following day he was identified as one of those to whom subjects were to refuse aid or refuge. Amid these difficulties he fled to the Netherlands.

Hall did not remain abroad long, and returned to Scotland in the spring of 1680. In May and June of that year he kept company with Donald Cargill and they sought refuge in the countryside on both sides of the Forth, particularly around Bo'ness. However, their location was discovered by the curates (conformist clergy) of Bo'ness and Carriden and reported to Captain Middleton, governor of Blackness Castle. On 3 June 1680 Middleton followed them to Queensferry to attempt their arrest. Hall struggled with the soldiers, allowing Cargill to escape, and, though wounded, escaped also. He was helped by a group of local women of whom at least one was later imprisoned for over sixteen weeks, while several other local people were fined for aiding his escape. General Dalziel, alerted to the escape, pursued and seized the now dying Hall, intending to convey him to Edinburgh.

At Hall's capture, a copy of a document known as the Queensferry paper was found on his person. A particularly extreme and, from the government's point of view, threatening document, it upheld the binding obligation of the covenants and renounced the government. It reached the hands of the privy council where it was read 'with horror and amazement' (*Reg. PCS*, 3rd ser., 6.481). Hall died as a result of his wounds on 3 June 1680 and his body was brought to Edinburgh and placed in the Canongate tolbooth where it lay for three days before being buried in secret. As a result of his actions he was branded a traitor and in September 1683 the privy council gave permission for a process of forfaulture to be carried against him. This was carried out by the lords of justiciary in March 1684. Hall was declared to have been guilty of high treason and rebellion, and his goods were pronounced forfeit; his lands of Haugh-Head were granted to Robert Middleton. The forfaultures were rescinded by act of parliament on 4 July 1690. ALISON G. MUIR

**Sources** *Reg. PCS*, 3rd ser., vols. 6–8, 11 • trial of Henry Hall of Haugh-head, March 1684, MS justiciary records, book of adjournal, NA Scot., JC 2/16, 4/3/1684 • R. Wodrow, *The history of the*

*sufferings of the Church of Scotland from the Restoration to the revolution*, ed. R. Burns, 3 (1829), 202–10 · NA Scot., GD 124/1/1173, 16/4/1684 · *APS*, 1689–95, 164–6 · W. H. Carslaw, preface, in J. Howie, *The Scots worthies*, ed. W. H. Carslaw, [new edn] (1870), ix–xv, 417–20 · J. H. Thomson, ed., *A cloud of witnesses* (1871), 511–17 · J. Herdman, ed., *The third statistical account of Scotland*, 28: *The county of Roxburgh* (1992), 95 · NL Scot., Wodrow MS Qto 36 · *Historical notices of Scotish affairs, selected from the manuscripts of Sir John Lauder of Fountainhall*, ed. D. Laing, 1, Bannatyne Club, 87 (1848), 264–5

**Hall, Henry** (*d.* 1713). *See under* Hall, Henry (*c.*1656–1707).

**Hall, Henry** (*c.*1656–1707), musician and poet, was reputedly born in New Windsor, Berkshire, the son of a tailor named Captain James Hall (*bap.* 1616, *d.* 1672), but although this information derives from Anthony Wood, documentary evidence for the assertions is lacking. When young, Hall became a chorister at the Chapel Royal, where he studied under Henry Cooke and Pelham Humfrey. He was a contemporary there of Henry Purcell, and in a verse tribute printed in the latter's posthumous *Orpheus Britannicus* (1.vi) he describes how he and Purcell were jointly taught composition by John Blow:

> Apollo's Harp at once our Souls did strike,
> We learnt together, but not learnt alike,
> Though equal care our Master might bestow,
> Yet only Purcell e'er shall equal Blow:
> For Thou, by Heaven for wondrous things design'd,
> Left'st thy Companion lagging far behind.

Hall left the chapel in 1672 when his voice broke. After temporary employment at Wells Cathedral, he was appointed organist and lay vicar-choral at Exeter Cathedral in August 1674. His first anthems date from this time, notably 'By the waters of Babylon', which achieved wide circulation. Its subject matter, 'a poignant reminder of Charles II's exile' (Spink, 268), is an early indication of its composer's Stuart sympathies.

Hall left Exeter in 1679, with an undischarged debt, but in June that year he became assistant organist at Hereford Cathedral, where he took minor orders and was elected a vicar-choral. He had to wait until 1688 to succeed John Badham as organist, but meanwhile he served the vicars' college in various capacities, and he remained a vicar-choral until his death. He is likely to have married in the mid-1680s, a period that saw the birth of his son Henry [*see below*]. His wife, formerly Catherine Woolmer, died in 1690 aged twenty-one. On 28 October 1696 Hall married Anne Gower; a daughter, born in 1700, lived for only two months.

Hall was a serious composer of church music, esteemed by his contemporaries and successors: by 1683 his anthems were in use at Windsor and Worcester and by 1686 at Lincoln, and 'Hall and Hine'—a pairing of his Te Deum in E♭ with a Jubilate by William Hine of Gloucester—retained its popularity throughout the eighteenth century. Hall has come to be ranked as 'the most distinguished among the lesser composers of Purcell's generation' (*New Grove*, 10.699). Though at times mannered and somewhat restricted in its effects, his work exhibits both harmonic and melodic boldness, and is particularly successful in passages of declamatory writing. His musical tribute to Purcell, the elegy 'Yes, my Aminta', was recorded in 1991.

Flamboyant tendencies in Hall's serious music are mirrored in the spirited nature of his secular songs and poems, of which well over 100 survive. There are drinking songs, love songs, autobiographical verse epistles to friends, many satires—on both national and local events—and numerous occasional poems. Hall evidently found verse-making and songwriting easy, to the extent that a nineteenth-century vicar-choral, William Cooke, believed him to have been too readily distracted from his professional duties:

> Since among his poems several songs are inserted, it is presumed, that in his twofold capacity of poet and musician, he had no difficulty in giving proof of this combination of talent, by carolling those ditties in the Black Lion Club Room, where frequent carousals are spoken of, among his jovial and political associates; compeers of those nightly revelries, which most likely divested his thoughts from the greater duties of his professions, for which education and genius had so abundantly qualified him. (Cooke, 4–5)

Hall was, at the least, humorous and convivial; the drinking, gambling, and womanizing that feature in his verses may partly result from poetic exaggeration.

Many of Hall's songs were printed, beginning in 1685 with 'Haste, Charon, haste', which vilifies Oliver Cromwell. Comparatively little of his other verse was published during his lifetime. Much of it survives, unprinted, in sizeable manuscript anthologies (now at Leeds University and the National Library of Wales) apparently compiled by friends intent on preserving his poetic memory. In terms of content, many of the satires were unpublishable, and can only have circulated privately (those that did get out into professional manuscript miscellanies may not all be his). Although he took the oath of allegiance, his poems reveal him as an unrepentant Jacobite, fiercely attacking William and Mary and urging the return of James II.

Anne's accession changed Hall's attitudes and strengthened his links with London. He wrote fulsomely in praise of the new queen—the ode 'Bless Albion, bless thy stars above' survives in his autograph at Christ Church, Oxford—and he composed songs, sung in the London theatres, celebrating the success of the English forces abroad. The anonymous poem *A Tryal of Skill*, published in 1704, even presents him, though satirically, as a candidate for the 'poetical crown'.

Hall died in Hereford on 30 March 1707 and was buried in the cathedral there the next day. He was succeeded at Hereford by his son **Henry Hall** (*d.* 1713), to whom the *Dictionary of National Biography* attributed the less serious part of his poetical output. Modern scholarship does not support the *Dictionary of National Biography*'s assertion that the court violinist **William Hall** (*d.* 1700) was another son.

Oliver Pickering

**Sources** H. W. Shaw, *The succession of organists of the Chapel Royal and the cathedrals of England and Wales from c.1538* (1991) · I. Spink, *Restoration cathedral music, 1660–1714* (1995) · *New Grove*, 2nd edn · O. Pickering, 'Henry Hall of Hereford's poetical tributes to Henry Purcell', *The Library*, 6th ser., 16 (1994), 18–29 · Hereford Cathedral, college of vicars-choral act book, Michaelmas 1660 to Michaelmas

1717, Hereford Cathedral Library, HCA 7003/1/3 • W. Cooke, 'Biographical memoirs of the custos and vicars admitted into the college of Hereford from 1660 to 1823: Henry Hall', Hereford Cathedral Library, HCA 7003/4/3 • H. Purcell, *Orpheus Britannicus: a collection of the choicest songs compos'd by Mr Henry Purcell*, 2 vols. (1698–1702) • A. Wood, Bodl. Oxf., MS Wood D 19 (4) • S. Bond, ed., *The first hall book of the borough of New Windsor* (1968) • F. T. Havergal, *Monumental inscriptions in the cathedral church of Hereford* (1881) • Hereford Cathedral, dean and chapter act book, III, 1600–1712, Hereford Cathedral Library, HCA 7031/3 • collections of Hall's poetry, U. Leeds, Brotherton L., MSS Lt q 5 and Lt 6 • H. Hall, poetry, NL Wales, Ottley papers • O. Pickering, *The poems and songs attributed to Henry Hall of Hereford* [forthcoming] • disc notes, *Odes on the death of Henry Purcell*, CDA66578 (Hyperion Records, 1992)

**Archives** U. Leeds, Brotherton L., MSS Lt q 5 and Lt 6 | NL Wales, Ottley papers

**Hall, Henry Robert** (1898–1989), dance band leader and radio broadcaster, was born on 2 May 1898 at 23 Bonar Road, Peckham, London, the eldest son in the family of three sons and three daughters of Henry Robert Hall, blacksmith, and his wife, Kate Ellen Smith. Part of his childhood in a poor but happy Salvation Army family in Peckham was spent learning the trumpet. While still at the London county council school in Waller Road, Peckham, he won a scholarship to Trinity College of Music, London, for trumpet, piano, and music theory lessons on Saturday mornings. He left school at fourteen, but his musical education fortunately continued when he was employed at the age of sixteen as a music copyist at the Salvation Army head office in Judd Street, King's Cross. His employer, Richard Slater, worked him hard but helped to develop his talents as player and composer. His 'Sunshine March' was later the basis for his BBC signature tune, 'Here's to the Next Time'.

In December 1916 Hall enlisted in the Royal Field Artillery. His musical prowess was quickly recognized and he spent much time playing at troop concerts. After the war he undertook desultory engagements in the seedier music halls and played a cinema piano to finance advanced piano lessons at the Guildhall School of Music. In 1922 he accepted a Christmas job as relief pianist at the Midland Hotel, Manchester. A Chopin study played at a minute's notice in the hotel cabaret stopped the show, and Arthur Towle, general manager of Midland Hotels, signed up Hall as resident pianist. Within a year he was musical director of the hotel band, within ten he was in charge of the bands in all thirty-two hotels in the LMS railway group, and when the Gleneagles Hotel opened in 1924 Hall persuaded the BBC to broadcast his band on the opening night. This was the start of a broadcasting career which lasted forty years. In 1924 he married Margery (1894–1976), daughter of Robert Brook Harker, commercial traveller. It was a perfect partnership, and they had a son and a daughter. In 1932 Hall succeeded Jack Payne as musical director of the BBC dance orchestra, a move which involved a large cut in salary, but promised enhanced prospects. His was the first programme to be heard from the newly built Broadcasting House, in 1932.

Hall's purist style of music left some listeners lukewarm, but the impeccably played musical arrangements,

**Henry Robert Hall** (1898–1989), by unknown photographer

often made by Hall himself, and his modest way of announcing the items were appealing. The repertory of straight dance tunes interspersed with novelty items such as 'The Teddy Bears' Picnic' soon made the band, broadcasting at teatime and in the evening, enormously popular. In 1934 he had the idea of inviting show business stars to join him and his band in a programme called *Henry Hall's Guest Night*. His introductory words, 'This *is* Henry Hall speaking', became something of a national catchphrase. The show was an instant success and ran for 972 performances over twenty-three years. The first chat show on British radio, it featured stars including Noël Coward, Stan Laurel and Oliver Hardy, Danny Kaye, and Gracie Fields, with whom he always established an immediate rapport. The programme made him a major figure in the golden age of radio.

A royal command performance, a film *Music hath Charms* (1935), and an engagement to conduct the ship's band on the maiden voyage of the *Queen Mary* showed a widening recognition of Hall's star status. By 1937, when many other dance bands were broadcasting, he asked permission to leave the BBC and take his band with him. Sir John Reith granted it and agreed that they would not be replaced. It was said that 40 million people listened to their final broadcast.

Hall now faced a freelance career touring the major variety theatres with his band topping the bill. Fears that the public would not support a wireless star in the theatre were unfounded. 'Sold out' boards were everywhere and Hall was frequently mobbed by the fans. The tours continued during the years of the Second World War, during which Hall also gave troop concerts and guest nights. These strenuous and demanding years culminated in a second royal command performance (1948). After the war Hall began presenting stage shows, notably *Irma la Douce* (1958). He continued to appear regularly on radio and television until 1964, and finally announced his retirement in 1970, when he was appointed CBE.

A tall, dignified man, immaculately dressed, his dark hair brushed down, with a quizzical face and horn-rimmed glasses, Hall had flair and an engagingly hesitant style, which did not conceal a quiet authority inseparable from a lifetime of demanding high standards from himself and those around him. In return he received universal respect and affection. He was a showman completely in tune with the age in which he flourished. Hall died in Eastbourne after a long retirement, on 28 October 1989.

IAN WALLACE, *rev.*

**Sources** H. Hall, *Here's to the next time* (1955) · press books, BBC WAC · *The Times* (30 Oct 1989) · *The Independent* (1 Nov 1989) · personal knowledge (1996) · private information (1996) · b. cert. [Margery Harker] · *CGPLA Eng. & Wales* (1990)
**Archives** SOUND BBC Sound Archives · BL NSA
**Likenesses** photographs, 1932–70, Hult. Arch. · L. E. Ray, watercolour, 1935–45, NPG · photograph, NPG [*see illus.*]
**Wealth at death** £254,634: probate, 9 April 1990, *CGPLA Eng. & Wales*

**Hall, Hubert** (1857–1944), archivist, was born at Hesley Hall, Ecclesfield, Yorkshire, on 27 July 1857, the younger son of Richard Foljambe Hall and his wife, Elizabeth Breese Orridge. He was educated at Shrewsbury School, where he developed a lifelong interest in natural history and fishing. In 1879 he entered the civil service and joined the Public Record Office as a junior clerk. He was promoted senior clerk in 1892 and assistant keeper in 1912. In 1882 he married Edith (*d.* 1889), daughter of James Robinson. They had a son and a daughter, both of whom predeceased their father. In 1895 he married Jane Winifred, daughter of Robert Robert Evans, with whom he had a son. His second wife survived him.

Hall's official work lay in modern departmental records, but he spent his leisure in research on medieval history. His *Introduction to the Study of the Pipe Rolls* (1884) was the third volume in the series published by the Pipe Roll Society, of which his colleague W. D. Selby was treasurer. Hall subsequently published *The Antiquities and Curiosities of the Exchequer* (1891), *The Receipt Roll of the Exchequer for Michaelmas Term xxxi. Henry II, A.D. 1185* (1899), and *The Pipe Roll of the Bishopric of Winchester … 1208–9* (1903). In 1889 he succeeded Selby as editor of the Rolls Series edition of *The Red Book of the Exchequer* (3 vols., 1896). The work was not well conceived, but Hall completed it to the plan laid down, and was abusively criticized by J. H. Round. Hall also wrote two works of popular appeal, *Society in the Elizabethan Age* (1886) and *Court Life under the Plantagenets* (1890), based upon material in the Public Record Office.

Hall served the Royal Historical Society as literary director (1891–1938), honorary secretary (1894–1903), and vice-president (1923–7). His policies greatly enhanced the society's reputation, not least by promoting its succession to the work of the defunct Camden Society (1897). He also took an active part in the work of the Selden Society, of which he was vice-president from 1939 to 1942. He collaborated with Sidney and Beatrice Webb in their history of *English Local Government* (1906–29) and in the foundation in 1895 of the London School of Economics and Political Science. There from 1896 to 1919, and at King's College from 1919 to 1926, as a reader in London University, he taught palaeography, diplomatic, and economic history, and trained many contributors to the Victoria History of the Counties of England. His *Studies in English Official Historical Documents* (1908), with the valuable *Formula Book* (1908–9), and his *Select Bibliography for the Study, Sources and Literature of English Mediaeval Economic History* (1914) were all products of that work. His varied experience made Hall's appointment as secretary (1910–18) of the royal commission on public records an obvious choice, and he was largely responsible for the appendices to its three reports (1912–19). His *British Archives and the Sources for the History of the World War* (1925) was another testimony to his professional skills. In 1931 and 1932 he was invited to the United States, where he supervised the arrangement of British family manuscripts in the Huntington Library, California. He received the honorary degree of LittD from Cambridge University in 1920. Hall died at 42 Magpie Hall Road, Chatham, on his birthday, 27 July 1944, a few days after his house, Cartree, near Walderslade, Kent, had been destroyed by a German flying bomb.

Hall twice suffered disparagement in his long professional career. On the first occasion he withstood Round's vituperative and obsessive attacks on the *Red Book* with notable dignity. The episode was plainly discreditable to Round, and displayed Hall's extraordinary good nature and patience. On the second, he fell into disfavour with Henry Maxwell Lyte, deputy keeper of the public records, who was disappointed in the outcome of the royal commission. Hall himself was not wholly in sympathy with the commission's findings, but Maxwell Lyte believed that Hall could and should have directed them differently, and he may have stayed in office beyond the First World War to debar Hall from the deputy keepership. Both incidents were wounding to Hall, but he rose above them, and they are inconsiderable in comparison with his services to historical scholarship as an archivist, editor, and teacher.

CHARLES JOHNSON, *rev.* G. H. MARTIN

**Sources** J. D. Cantwell, *The Public Record Office, 1838–1958* (1991) · C. Johnson, 'Hubert Hall', *TRHS*, 4th ser., 28 (1946), 1–5 · private information (1959) · personal knowledge (1959) · *CGPLA Eng. & Wales* (1944)
**Archives** CKS, papers · King's AC Cam., notes · PRO, corresp. and papers, PRO44 | King's AC Cam., Browning MSS · LUL, letters to J. H. Round
**Likenesses** two photographs, Royal Historical Society, London

**Wealth at death** £3568 15s. 7d.: probate, 21 Nov 1944, *CGPLA Eng. & Wales*

**Hall, Jacob** (*fl.* 1662–1681), rope dancer and acrobat, became fashionable in London during the 1660s for his daring displays of agility on a tightrope. He performed at Bartholomew fair in Smithfield and other similar meeting places in the city where people from all walks of life would come to see varied and often spectacular entertainments. According to one source, on 22 February 1662 Hall, along with Thomas Cosby and William Fuller, was sworn one of the king's 'vaulters and Dancers on the Rope and other agility of Body' (Highfill, Burnim & Langhans, *BDA*). On 26 March 1667 Hall and Fuller were permitted to set up a rope-dancing booth near the maypole in the Strand. Among Hall's audience at Southwark fair on 21 September 1668 was Samuel Pepys, who was introduced to him at a nearby tavern after the performance. Pepys records asking him 'whether he had ever any mischief by falls in his time; he told me, "Yes, many; but never to the breaking of a limb." He seems a mighty strong man.' After an earlier viewing, at Bartholomew fair itself on 29 August 1668, Pepys had described Hall's 'dancing of the ropes' as 'a thing worth seeing and mightily fallowed'. Thomas Shadwell called Hall 'a most admirable Rope-Dancer' in his *The Sullen Lovers*, first performed in 1668.

Hall, Robert Turner, and John Perin were sued on 20 May 1669 by Sir Henry Herbert, the master of the revels, probably for illegal performance. Hall later tried to set a stage up in Lincoln's Inn Fields too, but was thwarted by local residents who feared the disruption to the area his audiences might bring. But such objections notwithstanding, Hall's city-wide fame continued undimmed. Hall participated in city pageants honouring the lord mayor and is known to have danced in the lord mayor's show on 30 October 1671. About 1673 he performed illegally at Stourbridge fair, Cambridge. There are no references to his performances after 1681. However, Hall was still being mentioned in numerous songs and verses in the 1680s; among these is a verse on Bartholomew fair, in the second edition of *Wit and Drollery* (1682), which includes the lines:

> Tat, tat, tat, tat, tat, says the little penny Trumpet,
> Here's Jacob Hall that does so jump it, jump it.

In 1681 John Dryden, in his epilogue to Nathaniel Lee's *Mithridates*, refers to 'Jacob's Cap'ring Tricks'. Hall's performances are also mentioned in Dr John King's collection of riddles and Robert Wild's *Rome Rhy'med to Death* (1683). In a letter of 4 September 1679 to Sir Robert Southwell, William Blaythwaite describes just having attended one of Hall's performances (*DNB*).

At some time in the late 1660s the famously athletic and attractive Hall (Hercules and Adonis combined, it was said) began a dalliance with the king's open-hearted mistress Barbara Villiers, Lady Castlemaine, who even bestowed on him a pension which he retained for some years.

DANIEL HAHN

**Sources** Highfill, Burnim & Langhans, *BDA* • H. Morley, *Memoirs of Bartholomew fair* (1892) • J. H. Jesse, *Memoirs of the court of England during the reign of the Stuarts including the protectorate* (1857) • *N&Q*, 2nd ser., 7 (1859), 61–2 • A. Hamilton, *Memoirs of the court of Charles II*, ed. W. Scott (1891) • Pepys, *Diary*, 9.293, 313 • *DNB*

**Likenesses** P. de Brune, etching (after J. Van Oost), BM; repro. in Morley, *Memoirs* • oils, Trinity College, Oxford • portrait, repro. in Morley, *Memoirs*

**Hall, James** (*d.* 1612), polar explorer, was born in Hull and was perhaps the son of the Christopher Hall of Hull who was master of the *Gabriel* in Martin Frobisher's voyage to Greenland. James Hall is famous for his four voyages to Greenland. His first voyage was in 1605 as chief pilot on an expedition sent to Greenland by Christian IV of Denmark in order to re-establish communication with the Norse settlers on Greenland. Contact with them had been lost in the fifteenth century shortly before the Norse colony is now known to have died out. Christian's concern was partly because if any Norse settlers survived they would be his subjects and partly because activities by English and Dutch ships in Arctic waters prompted him to reassert Danish interests in the area. The expedition was led by John Cunningham, a Scot, who like Hall had been recommended to Christian IV by James I of England, Christian's brother-in-law. Gosch (1897) suggests that Hall might have been recommended because he had participated in John Davis's second Greenland expedition of 1587 and had gained knowledge of Arctic waters, especially in the Davis Strait, on that voyage. A connection between the two voyages is also suggested by the fact that one of the 1605 expedition's three ships was named *Røde Løve*, showing that it was either Davis's ship, *The Red Lion*, or had been named after it. Lyschander (1608) also suggested that Hall was an experienced voyager who had sailed to Friesland, the mythical island often confused with Greenland, and towards America. The expedition as a whole consisted of three ships: *Trost* (Captain Cunningham, pilot Hall), *Røde Løve* (Captain Godske Lindenov), and *Marekatten* (Captain John Knight). The expedition left Copenhagen on 2 May 1605 and made for Greenland. They reached a point near Kap Farvel (Cape Farewell, Umanarssuaq), naming their landfall Kap Christian. Here disagreement broke out between the Englishmen on the one hand and Lindenov on the other, as a result of which the ships parted company. Hall and Cunningham went north, heading for the Davis Strait, looking for Cape Desolation (Kap Desolation, Nunarssuit). Hall made charts of the coast and reached Itivdleq (66°33′ N) which he named Kong Christians Fjord. At this point Hall and Cunningham split up, agreeing that Hall should explore the coast while Cunningham investigated Itivdleq. Despite being greeted with stones and arrows by suspicious Inuit, Hall reached 67° N and investigated Kangerdluarssuk, which he called Cunningham's Fjord, and Ataneq Fjord at 68°8′ N, which he named Briede Rantzaus Fjord. On 27 July he reached the northernmost point achieved by the expedition, namely the western edge of the large island of Sarquardleq (68°35′ N), which he called Cape Christian Friis. He then turned back and the expedition proceeded home to Denmark.

Another expedition to Greenland left Copenhagen on 27

May 1606 under the command of Lindenov. Hall and Cunningham served again on this voyage, Hall again acting as pilot. Hall wanted to bring home some ore which he had discovered at Kangerdluarssuk, and which he thought might bear silver; the expedition brought back samples, which proved worthless, and four Inuit. (Christopher Hall, who may have been James's father, had also discovered possibly valuable but actually worthless ores on Greenland, so James's interest in ore lends some substance to this possible connection.) In 1607 Hall served in a third Danish expedition, which had the express intention of finding the lost eastern settlement of Norse colonists. This expedition was ill-fated, as it was predicated on the assumption that the eastern settlement was on the eastern coast, whereas it was in fact on the southern coast. The expedition failed as it could not break through the ice on the eastern coast to land. The voyagers thus returned home, arriving in Copenhagen on 25 June 1607 with nothing to show for their efforts.

In 1612 Hall made his last visit to Greenland on an English expedition which was sent to investigate trading possibilities with Greenland. It was financed by Sir James Lancaster, Sir Thomas Smith, Sir Richard Ball, and William Cocken or Cockayne, and Hall himself had a financial stake in it. The expedition comprised two vessels, *Patience* (140 tons) and *Heartsease* (60 tons). Hall was still pursuing his belief that the ores he had found were silver-bearing despite previous analysis which proved that they were not. The ships sailed again to the western coast of Greenland, and from the Godthåb's fjord complex, whose northern arm he named Ball's River, while Ameralik Fjord was named by him Lancaster River, Hall went on to Kangerdluarssuk once again to investigate the supposed silver ore, but again unsuccessfully. On the way back Hall explored the Amerdloq Fjord which he called Ramel's Fjord, but on 22 July 1612 was shot dead by an Inuk's arrow there. He was buried on an island not subsequently identified.

Hall's reports of his voyages became known when Samuel Purchas published them in *Purchas his Pilgrimes* (4 vols., 1625), but characteristically Purchas edited the reports heavily, inserting general information and leaving out some of Hall's own text and, most important, Hall's maps. Since the late nineteenth century a more comprehensive set of accounts of the voyages has been known. Most important is the discovery of a manuscript copy of Hall's report and four maps which he made for Christian IV of Denmark after his 1605 voyage (BL, Royal MS 17a XLVIII). The maps represent the first attempt at anything like accurate depiction of the western coast of Greenland. The maps are Hall's main account of the results of his 1605 voyage, but, having been omitted by Purchas, were first published in 1897 in the Hakluyt Society's record of Hall's voyages. The only account of the voyage of 1606 remains that of Purchas. The only account of the voyage of 1607 is that by C. C. Lyschander, in *Den grønlandske chronica* (1608), which became known to most anglophones only in the nineteenth century. It is an account in verse and is not intended as an objective report of the voyage, but none the less provides the only information there is. The voyage of 1612, originally known from William Baffin's account as edited by Purchas but later complemented by the account of John Gatonby, quartermaster on the expedition, was published by the Hakluyt Society in 1897. These accounts, and particularly Hall's maps, show the importance of Hall's contribution to the exploration of western Greenland. But while modern scholarship has thrown new and significant light on his explorations no more has been discovered of his personal life than was known in the seventeenth century. ELIZABETH BAIGENT

**Sources** C. C. A. Gosch, *Danish Arctic expeditions, 1605–1620*, Hakluyt Society, 96–7 (1897) • F. Gad, *Grønlands historie*, 3 vols. (1969) • C. C. Lyschander, *Den grønlandske chronica* (1608) • H. Ostermann, *Dansk biografisk lexikon*, 5 (1980), 497–8 • *DNB*

**Archives** BL, narrative of Greenland voyage, Royal MS 17a XLVIII

**Hall, James** (1755–1826), Associate Synod minister, was born at Cathcart, near Glasgow, on 5 January 1755. His parents were zealous adherents of the Associate Synod, one of Scotland's dissenting Presbyterian denominations. Hall's father died while he was a child. It was from him that Hall obtained the feu on which was built the meeting-house of Shuttle Street, afterwards Greyfriars, Glasgow, the earliest Secession congregation in the city. Hall's mother presented the seceders of Kirkintilloch with land which she owned there for a meeting-house and manse, and to her James and his brother Robert, afterwards minister of the Secession church in Kelso, owed their early training. After studying in the University of Glasgow, under George Young, George Jardine, and Thomas Reid, Hall proceeded to the theological course under John Brown (1722–1787) of Haddington, the Associate Synod's sole theology tutor. In the spring of 1776 he was licensed to preach by the Associate Presbytery of Glasgow. He scornfully rejected an offer of a good living in the established Church of Scotland, and on 16 April 1777 he was ordained pastor of the Associate Synod congregation at Cumnock, in Ayrshire. A call to the congregation of Wells Street, London, in 1780 was set aside by the synod, which sat as a tribunal on the transfer of ministers from one congregation to another. However, on 15 June 1786 Hall was allowed to move to the congregation of Rose Street, Edinburgh, which had seceded from the Scottish capital's first Associate congregation. In 1800 he declined a call to Manchester.

Hall was an eloquent and popular preacher and minister, and his breadth of mind and polished manners gave him a high standing in Edinburgh society. The meeting-house in Rose Street was regularly filled to overflowing, and a larger church was erected in Broughton Place in 1820–21. In the life of his denomination, Hall was a masterly church-court debater, and a leading advocate of the church's freedom from state patronage in the Old Light/New Light controversy which then agitated Scottish dissenting Presbyterians. His published sermons include *Comfort to the Christian* (1789), *David and Goliath, or, Great Britain and France* (1793), and *The Lord's Voice Crying to the Nations of Europe* (1794). He encouraged Bible and missionary societies, and was chairman of the committee which, on 8

James Hall (1755–1826), by T. Blood, pubd 1814

September 1820, brought together the Associate Synod and the General Associate Synod to form the United Secession church. He received a DD from Columbia College, New York, in 1812. Hall died in Edinburgh on 20 November 1826, and was buried in Edinburgh's new Calton cemetery, in a tomb purchased by the congregation. A commemorative marble tablet was placed in the lobby of the church. JAMES TAIT, *rev.* N. R. NEEDHAM

**Sources** R. Small, *History of the congregations of the United Presbyterian church from 1733 to 1900*, 2 vols. (1904) • N. R. Needham, 'Hall, James', *DSCHT*

**Likenesses** T. Blood, stipple, 1814, BM, NPG; repro. in *Evangelical Magazine*, 22 (1814) [*see illus.*] • plaster medallion (after J. Tassie), Scot. NPG

**Hall, Sir James, of Dunglass, fourth baronet (1761–1832)**, chemist and geologist, was born on 17 January 1761 at Dunglass, East Lothian, the eldest son of Sir John Hall, third baronet (1710/11–1776), and his wife, Magdalen (*d.* 1763), daughter of Sir John Pringle of Stichell and his wife, Magdalen Elliott. Hall's family connections gave him an immediate entrée to scientific circles at home and abroad; his uncle, William Hall, was one of the Scottish intelligentsia and another uncle, Sir John Pringle, was president of the Royal Society of London.

Hall was educated at home until he was sent to school in London at the age of ten. He was at Elim's military academy in Kensington when, at the age of fifteen, he inherited the baronetcy. He spent eighteen months at Christ's College, Cambridge, where he did not take a degree, and some time in France and Geneva. Returning home he enrolled in Edinburgh University, where he attended lectures by John Robison and Joseph Black, and as many balls and other social events as time would allow. It was probably also at this period that he formed the friendship with James Hutton—a close friend of William Hall and of Black—that was to have such an influence on his scientific thinking.

In 1783 Hall sat for Reynolds, who depicted him as a conspicuously romantic young man. The same year he set off on the grand tour, not returning home until the summer of 1786. He went as far east as Berlin and as far south as Sicily, recording the natural history and social customs, the art, and the fashionable gossip of the lands through which he passed. Notably, he visited the mines of Harz; he climbed Vesuvius no fewer than five times; he explored some of Sicily with the French vulcanologist Dolomieu; and, passing through Brienne, he met Napoleon, who was a student at the military academy there. During his months in Paris he was much in company with Lavoisier and was slowly converted to the 'new chemistry' which centred on Lavoisier's ideas about the role of oxygen. Subsequently, in the spring of 1788, he propounded these doctrines at three meetings of the Royal Society of Edinburgh, opposed by Hutton who supported the older, and then almost universally accepted, phlogiston theory. The papers Hall gave remained unpublished but nevertheless these debates helped to change the course of chemical thinking in Scotland.

At 'a fine merry wedding' (J. Hall to William Hall, NA Scot., GD206/II, 300, no. 26) on 9 November 1786, Hall married Lady Helen Douglas (1762–1837), second daughter of Dunbar Douglas, fourth earl of Selkirk, with whom he had three sons and three daughters. 'Unequalled stability and sweetness of disposition' are said to have been among his domestic virtues, while in politics and religion he was 'a declared democrat and avowed atheist' (*The Times*). In his youth he particularly delighted in dancing.

After his marriage most of Hall's life was divided between his estate at Dunglass and his house in Edinburgh, except for March to August 1791 when he was in France observing the political situation in company with his three brothers-in-law, one of whom was Lord Daer, well known as a radical. In the daytime he listened to the debates in the national assembly. The evenings were often passed with Lavoisier and his wife, and other savants. A tour to Clermont gave him a chance to study French agriculture and the volcanic landscape of the Auvergne.

By the end of the 1780s Hall was one of only a handful of people who accepted the new geological theories of James Hutton, who believed that crystalline rocks had cooled from hot liquids generated deep in the earth. This was in direct opposition to Abraham Gottlob Werner (1750–1817) and his leading British disciple, Robert Jameson, professor of natural history at Edinburgh University from 1804 to 1854, who maintained that such rocks had crystallized out from a primeval ocean. Hutton further believed that the heat of the earth consolidated the sediments at the bottom of the ocean and subsequently elevated them to form new land. His theories were based largely on field evidence and the appearance of hand specimens: Hall determined to verify them experimentally in spite of Hutton's view that 'the immensity of natural agents … lies far beyond reach of our imitation' (J. Hall, 'Account', 76).

James Keir and others had noticed that molten glass forms crystals if it is cooled too slowly and Hall realized that crystal formation in rocks also probably depended on the rate of cooling. He therefore heated fifteen different whinstones and lavas in the furnace of an iron foundry, cooled them to glass, remelted them, placed them in a cooler furnace for a length of time, and, after much trial and error, achieved stony, crystalline masses comparable to those at the beginning of the experiment. He published his results in 1799.

Hall next tackled the problem of limestone, which was well known to decompose on heating. He heated 'all calcarious substances; chalk, common limestone, marble, spar and the shells of fish' (J. Hall, 'Account', 95) in sealed gun barrels and other containers, in order to show that if the pressure is sufficiently high no decomposition takes place. After many difficulties and 'above five hundred experiments' (ibid.) between 1798 and 1804, including one in which 'the furnace was blown to pieces' (ibid., 78), he managed to convert the powdered carbonates into limestones or marbles, depending on the degree of heat. He measured the temperature of his furnace with a Wedgwood's pyrometer, then the only method of measuring high temperatures, and achieved temperatures as high as 64 ° on Wedgwood's pyrometric scale; for comparison, the melting point of copper is about 33 °W. He himself designed a thermostat on the well-understood principle of a spring made of two metals which curled or uncurled in response to the radiant heat of the furnace. The thermostat was described by his son Basil.

Hall also demonstrated how folding takes place in sedimentary rocks. He placed layers of clay under weights in a long, thin container, and by pressing them inwards from either end created folds analogous with those widely observed in nature. However, his further suggestion that granite intrusions could cause folding is not now accepted. In another paper in the same volume of the *Transactions of the Royal Society of Edinburgh*, 'On the revolutions of the earth's surface', he took up the ideas of De Saussure and Pallas, suggesting that the earth's surface is reshaped and recycled, not by the ordinary processes of erosion as Hutton believed, but by immense tidal waves. These he attempted to simulate 'with explosions of some pounds of gunpowder under water' (J. Hall, 'Revolutions', 156). Among the phenomena which he sought to explain were erratic boulders and slickensides. In a final paper Hall described attempts to turn sand into sandstone by heating it in brine.

Hall's experimental work, some of which was also published in Nicholson's *Journal of Natural Philosophy*, made a great impact at home and abroad at the same time as John Playfair's *Illustrations of the Huttonian Theory* (1802) was also winning converts. It was by the combined efforts of these two men that Hutton's views gradually prevailed against those of Werner, thus ending a particularly lengthy and acrimonious controversy and bringing about a revolution in geology.

In 1813 Hall published a book on Gothic architecture, which was much noticed in his own day. He suggested that the style had its origins in the interlacing structures of simple wattle buildings. He was elected to the Royal Society of Edinburgh in 1784 and was its president in 1812–20, and was elected FRS in 1806. The member of parliament for Mitchell, in Cornwall, from 1807 to 1812, he was at first a conscientious and independent-minded member but his activities were curtailed by an illness in December 1810. His last two decades were overshadowed by ill health; he died in Edinburgh on 23 June 1832 and was buried at Dunglass collegiate church. He was succeeded by his eldest son, John (1787–1860). His other two sons were Basil *Hall (1788–1844), naval captain and travel writer, and James *Hall (1800–1854), portrait and landscape painter.

JEAN JONES

**Sources** J. Hall, 'Account of a series of experiments, shewing the effects of compression in modifying the action of heat', *Transactions of the Royal Society of Edinburgh*, 6/2 (1812), 71–185; see also *Journal of Natural Philosophy, Chemistry, and the Arts*, 9 (1804), 98–107; 13 (1806), 328–43, 381–405; 14 (1806), 13–22, 196–212, 302–18 · J. Hall, 'On the revolutions of the earth's surface', *Transactions of the Royal Society of Edinburgh*, 7 (1815), 139–210 · NA Scot., Dunglass Muniments, letters of Sir James Hall, GD206/II · J. Hall, *Essay on the origin, history and principles of Gothic architecture* (1813) · B. Hall, 'Notice of a machine for regulating high temperatures, invented by the late Sir James Hall', *Transactions of the Geological Society*, 2nd ser., 3 (1835), 489, 490 · *The Times* (30 June 1832); repr. *The Scotsman* (4 July 1832) · V. A. Eyles, 'The evolution of a chemist: Sir James Hall … and his relations with Joseph Black, Antoine Lavoisier, and other scientists', *Annals of Science*, 19 (1963), 153–82 · J. A. Chaldecott, 'Scientific activities in Paris, 1791', *Annals of Science*, 24 (1968), 21–52 · HoP, *Commons* · Chambers, *Scots.*, rev. T. Thomson (1875) · V. A. Eyles, 'Hall, Sir James', *DSB* · memorial stone for Lady Helen Hall, Dunglass collegiate church · J. Foster, *The peerage, baronetage, and knightage of the British empire for 1883*, 2 vols. [1883]

**Archives** NA Scot., corresp., diaries, and papers · NHM · NL Scot., notes on experiments, letters, and travel journals; notes on perspective · NRA Scotland · U. Edin., department of geology and geophysics | NL Scot., letters to Alexander Marcet

**Likenesses** J. Reynolds, oils, 1783, priv. coll. · A. Kauffman, oils, 1785, Scot. NPG · J. Watson-Gordon, oils, *c.*1820, Royal Society of Edinburgh · P. Park, marble bust, probably Geological Museum, London

**Hall, James** (1800–1854), painter, was born on 6 June 1800, at Dunglass, East Lothian, the third and youngest son of Sir James *Hall of Dunglass, fourth baronet (1761–1832), and his wife, Lady Helen Douglas (1762–1837), daughter of the fourth earl of Selkirk. He was educated at the high school of Edinburgh and at Shrewsbury School. From his father he inherited an enquiring mind, especially in scientific matters: Sir James was a geologist of note, and James shared these interests. But it was in the realm of art that he achieved greatest prominence. Science and art were, however, united in his studies of optics, and in his application of science to the capturing of images for portraits by means of the camera lucida. In 1828 he prepared a paper for the Royal Society of Edinburgh on binocular perspective and its application to various classes of painting. This, through diffidence, he never delivered; but he later published the gist of his argument in two contributions to the *Art Journal* in March and August 1852.

The young Hall was intended for the law. After attending the University of Edinburgh he was admitted to the Faculty of Advocates on 10 July 1821. Although he seems never to have practised at the bar, he remained loyal to the faculty, and in 1850 presented to the Advocates' Library, Edinburgh, the autograph manuscript of Sir Walter Scott's *Waverley*, which he had bought (for a greatly increased price) only six days after it had been sold at auction in London by Archibald Constable's trustees in August 1831. He had intended to bequeath the manuscript, but advanced his donation lest he be tempted to give away more portions of the literary relic. Hall could not have realized that his act of generosity was to lay the foundation of the present-day great Scott collection of the National Library of Scotland.

In July 1821 Hall embarked on a grand tour which is commemorated in a remarkable series of illustrated journals in the National Library of Scotland (MSS 27623–27637). He had taken drawing lessons in Edinburgh from John Francis Williams. His account of a journey which began the very day after he was called to the bar is notable for its approach: on-the-spot recording in appealing sketches of scenes, described in the present tense, in a record of intimacy and immediacy that reflects the whimsical delight of his nature. His travels took him to Paris and through France into Spain; through all the great cities and sites of Italy to Sicily, where he noted geological locations his father had seen in the 1780s; through Switzerland and down the Rhine. Mountains and sublime scenery greatly appealed. Hall travelled abroad on several subsequent occasions, in 1834 corresponding with the painter David Wilkie from Rome. Wilkie, who at his death left a portrait of Hall unfinished, was one of his most admired contemporaries, and he acquired and presented the painter's favourite palette to the National Gallery, where it decorated the plinth of Samuel Joseph's statue of Sir David. He was also on close terms with the artists Sir William Allan and Sir John Watson Gordon, who was in the habit of using Hall's London studio at 40 Brewer Street.

Hall, who studied at the Royal Academy Schools, early enjoyed a reputation for accurate recording of places and events. During the great fire of Edinburgh in 1824 Scott recorded his 'omni-presence', dashing about making sketches among the smouldering ruins (*Letters*, 8.438, 462). These were published as a series of lithographs, a copy of which rare work Scott had at his home, Abbotsford. An equally rare collection is *Fac Similes of Select Etchings & Drawings by the Old Masters*, which may actually be by James Hall rather than Joseph Hall. There is some confusion between the activities and the addresses of this Edinburgh lithographer and those of James, who contributed works to Royal Scottish Academy exhibitions from addresses (The Diorama, Lothian Road, and 33 Howe Street) also said to be those of Joseph Hall. These fine plates do seem to echo James Hall's known taste in Italian painting.

Hall, who spent a memorable hogmanay and new year season in 1824–5 with his brother Captain Basil Hall at Abbotsford, later used camera lucida sketches by Basil (taken in 1830) in making his portrait of Sir Walter. This was to be a posthumous image (completed in 1838), and Basil Hall arranged with Scott that his brother might keep the sketches beside him with a view to executing a finished portrait when Scott was no more: they were, in effect, an investment towards a hoped-for artistic career. Other portraits by Hall, exhibited at the Royal Academy, included those of Wellington and Colonel John Gurwood, the duke's private secretary, whose bust he also commissioned from Joseph. Wellington was Hall's hero. One of the great episodes of his life was the time in 1836 he spent at Walmer Castle, Kent, assisting Thomas Campbell with the completion of his statue of the duke by providing camera lucida sketches in order to perfect details. These sketches formed the basis of Hall's own oil portrait of Wellington. Hall exhibited mainly Scottish and English landscapes at the Royal Academy and the British Institution, to the funds of which he contributed handsomely. He also tried his hand at interpreting the 'real scenery' of Scott's Waverley novels, as did so many of his brother artists. His last picture for the British Institution was of Ashestiel in Selkirkshire, Scott's former Tweedside house, which became the residence of Hall's sister, Lady Russell. Though the law never claimed Hall, politics might have done. He stood unsuccessfully as a Conservative in 1841 and 1842 at Taunton. *The Jotting Book: a Political and Literary Experiment*, published under the pseudonym An Amateur in 1839 and reissued in 1840 under his own name, preserves his political creed. The work offers a very personal commentary on the world of the Reform Bill, the opinions and impressions being those of 'an obscure individual, of probably average intelligence and means of observation' (p. viii), but which, in their modesty and charm, are characteristic of Hall's outlook. Hall died suddenly, after a short illness, at Ashestiel, on 26 October 1854. He was unmarried, a member of the Athenaeum, and materially generous. Though a painter of only modest talent he was, all in all, by no means the least of a family whom Scott characterized as 'inexhaustible in spirits, curiosity and enthusiasm' (*Letters*, 8.462n.). IAIN GORDON BROWN

**Sources** I. G. Brown, 'Intimacy and immediacy: James Hall's journals in Italy and Germany', *Britannia Italia Germania: taste and travel in the nineteenth century*, ed. C. Richardson and G. Smith (2001), 23–42 • I. G. Brown, 'Collecting Scott for Scotland: 1850–2000', *Book Collector*, 49/4 (2000), 502–34 • *Art Journal*, 6 (1854), 364 • J. Hall, *The jotting book: a political and literary experiment* (1839–40) • J. Hall, 'Binocular perspective', *Art Journal* (March 1852), 89–90; (Aug 1852), 245–6 • A. Cunningham, *The life of Sir David Wilkie*, 3 vols. (1843) • *The letters of Sir Walter Scott*, ed. H. J. C. Grierson and others, centenary edn, 12 vols. (1932–79), vol. 8 • H. Smailes, 'Sir Walter Scott in camera', *Bulletin of the Scottish Society for the History of Photography* (spring 1986), 2–5 • H. Smailes, 'Thomas Campbell and the "camera lucida": the Buccleuch statue of the 1st duke of Wellington', *Burlington Magazine*, 124 (Nov 1987), 709–14 • C. B. de Laperriere, ed., *The Royal Scottish Academy exhibitors, 1826–1990*, 4 vols. (1991), vol. 2 • Graves, *RA exhibitors*, vol. 3 • Graves, *Brit. Inst.* • Hall journals, NL Scot., MSS 27623–27637 • NL Scot., Ashestiel MSS 3220, 3231

**Archives** NL Scot., sketch books and travel journals, MSS 27623–27637 | U. Southampton L., letters to first duke of Wellington

**Likenesses** J. Hall, self-portrait, oils, 1834, priv. coll. • D. Wilkie, oils, 1840, repro. in Cunningham, *Life of Wilkie*, 3

**Hall, John** (1529/30–1568/9), surgeon and author, lived and worked in Maidstone, Kent. Nothing is known of his parents or his education. In 1550 Thomas Raynauld printed Hall's *Certayn Chapters Taken out of the Proverbes of Salomon* in metre. According to the title-page Hall's *Proverbes* had lately appeared attributed 'untruely' to Thomas Sternhold; three other editions exhibit slight variations in contents. In January 1554 Hall apparently supported the rebellion proclaimed at Maidstone by Thomas Wyatt the younger (the Wyatts were a local family). Hall was perhaps imprisoned, but soon pardoned (with other local men).

Hall's two principal works were both published by Thomas Marshe in 1565. *The Courte of Vertue* includes reprints of some of his earlier biblical paraphrases, and *A Poesis in Forme of a Visyon* (against necromancy and witchcraft), first published in 1563. Hall's new verses, some with music, sought to counteract *The Courte of Venus*, 'or other bokes of lecherous Ballades'. His verse was influenced by that of the elder Wyatt, some of whose lyrics had appeared in *The Courte of Venus*. Hall dedicated his book to Thomas Cole, archdeacon of Essex (formerly master of Maidstone School, 1549–52?), a radical protestant preacher. Acrostic verses in *The Courte of Vertue* name twelve people involved in local government and commerce at Maidstone, establishing a social context for Hall's verse and its place in middle-class Elizabethan culture.

*A Most Excellent and Learned Woorke of Chirurgerie* (1565) was the first complete English translation of the *Chirurgia parva* by Lanfranc of Milan, with additions by Hall, based on his own experience. These include: his index of diseases and simples; his 'Anatomie', whose full title implies the superiority of his work over that of Thomas Vicary (sergeant-surgeon until 1561, formerly of Maidstone); and 'An historiall expostulation' in which Hall describes his encounters with nine individuals who visited the Maidstone area (1555–64), offering non-professional medical services, some of whom were prosecuted as a result of Hall's interventions. *Chirurgerie* contains strong defences of his profession and his medical publications in the English language, which were devoted 'to the edification and building up of good science, & to the subvertion of all haters and abusers of the same' (Hall, sig. +2*v*). He was concerned above all to instruct apprentice surgeons in the substance, methods, and ethics of their profession.

The combative and didactic qualities of Hall's literary personality are evident in all his publications. However, he was well regarded by physicians and other surgeons. William Cunningham MD of London (reader in anatomy, 1563) wrote verses prefixed to *Chirurgerie* and 'Salutations' to the Company of Barber–Surgeons, in which Hall is styled 'one of your fellowshippe' (but there is no record of his admission to the company). John Yates and Thomas Gale (both officers of the company) also wrote verses to promote Hall's work, as Hall had written prefatory verses for Gale's *Institution* and *Enchiridion of Chirurgerie* both in *Certaine Workes of Chirurgerie* (1563). A manuscript in the Bodleian Library (MS Bodley 178), annotated by Hall, includes his unpublished English translations of two contemporary treatises on the treatment of syphilis, and samples of his correspondence with Cunningham on this new disease. The vehemence of his poetry when moralizing against what he considered literary incitements to lechery may need to be understood in the context of his experience in treating venereal diseases.

In 1566 a John Hall complained (with Roger Hall), apparently to John Foxe, about the 'monster' who, as parish priest, was alleged to have overseen the martyrdom of seven protestants in Maidstone (June 1557) and was still refusing to repent publicly. Hall's will (dated 22 October 1568, during his final illness) was proved on 21 April 1569. All his Latin books were bequeathed to his brother Thomas, a medical student in Oxford. His wife, Anne, was the sole executor and chief beneficiary for life, but the terms of her occupation of his rented house and gardens 'towards the bringinge upp of my children' suggest that she was perhaps not the mother of his young sons, John and Isley, and therefore not his first wife. The overseers and witnesses of the will were his 'cousin' Edmund Hall and John Nicolson, both prominent Maidstone citizens who had been named in *The Courte of Vertue* acrostics. A portrait of him aged thirty-five (dated 1564) is prefixed to his *Chirurgerie*. RIVKAH ZIM

**Sources** *STC, 1475–1640*, nos. 2760, 11529, 12631–3, 15192, 24650 • J. Hall, *A most excellent and learned woorke of chirurgerie* (1565) • will, Canterbury consistory register, 1569, vol. 31, fols. 225*v*–226*r* • R. Zim, 'The Maidstone burghmote and John Hall's *Courte of vertue* (1565)', *N&Q*, 231 (1986), 320–27 • R. Zim, *English metrical psalms: poetry as praise and prayer, 1535–1601* (1987), 125–9, 226, 234 • J. M. Russell, *The history of Maidstone* (1881), 67 • *CPR*, 1554–5, 92 • S. Young, *The annals of the Barber–Surgeons of London: compiled from their records and other sources* (1890) • Bodl. Oxf., MS Bodley 178, fols. 19*r*–36*v* • BL, MS Harley 416, fols. 123*r*–124*v* [letter to Foxe (?)]

**Likenesses** woodcut, repro. in Hall, *Most excellent and learned woorke*

**Wealth at death** Latin books left to brother; wife sole beneficiary for life: will, Canterbury consistory register, 1569, vol. 31, fols. 225*v*–226*r*

**Hall, John** (1574/5?–1635), physician, was one of the eleven children of William Hall (*d.* 1607) of Carlton, Bedfordshire, also a medical practitioner. With his brother he attended Cambridge, gaining an MA in 1597, but no medical qualification has been traced. During the next ten years he seems to have studied abroad, possibly at Montpellier in France, and he certainly knew French. By 1607 Hall had arrived in Stratford upon Avon where on 5 June he married Susanna Shakespeare (*bap.* 1583, *d.* 1649), daughter of William *Shakespeare, the poet gave them 105 acres of land when the wedding was arranged. Their only child, Elizabeth, was baptized on 21 February 1608. In the early sixteenth century there were no other physicians in Stratford, although there were several surgeons, and John Hall attended patients within a 20 mile radius of the town, but also travelled as far as Ludlow and Worcester. He lived in the Shakespeare family home, New Place, which Susanna inherited from her father.

For the years 1611–35 Hall recorded the details of 155 patients he attended, including paupers, tradesmen, clerics, gentry, and the grandest aristocracy. Thus he treated the earl and countess of Northampton, Lady Sandys, Sir Simon Clark, Lady Jenkinson, and Lady Rous, as well as the staff of great households. Hall was a known puritan and at this time the town of Stratford was sharply divided between a strong puritan element and an opposing papist group. He noted that seven of his patients were Catholics, all from famous midland recusant families such as the Winters, Fortescues, and Talbots; in 1606 his wife had been accused of being 'popishly affected'. He also treated the extreme puritan gentry and preachers. Nearly two-thirds of the patients whose cases he noted were females, many with widespread kin connections, but he treated very few children. A number of his patients lived to be very old indeed, including John Thornborough, the bishop of Worcester, who reached the age of ninety; Sir Thomas Beaufou, eighty-six; and Lady Hunks, eighty-five. Hall usually recorded patients' details, including their age, status, place of residence, symptoms, and medications; he selected cases of medical interest and with a successful outcome. During the quarter-century covered by Hall's case notes Stratford experienced some severe epidemics, especially in 1616 and 1625, when typhus, a new disease, decimated the area, and a number of his patients were affected.

Hall's case notes were written in Latin, clearly intended for publication towards the end of his life. His widow sold the manuscript to James Cooke (1614–1688), a civil war surgeon from Warwick, in 1643. Cooke translated the notes into English, with minor amendments, and the first edition of *Select Observations on English Bodies of Eminent Persons in Desperate Diseases* appeared in 1657; two later editions were published in 1679 and in 1683. In the eighteenth century the original case notes were owned by both David Garrick and Edmond Malone, before being bought by the British Museum in 1868. There is no mention in the notes of Hall's treating his father-in-law when Shakespeare was dying in 1616, although Susanna's and Elizabeth's illnesses were recorded in detail. Hall and William Shakespeare seem to have had an amicable relationship, and Hall was one of the executors of the poet's will.

Hall was a significant local figure in Stratford, although always trying to excuse himself from involvement in civic affairs, pleading his medical duties as a reason. After avoiding office as a burgess twice, in 1617 and 1623, he was finally obliged to serve in 1632 but was fined for not attending. He was not a man who shrank from confrontation and he was expelled from the council on one occasion for 'wilful breach of language … and continued disturbances'. He was actively involved in the bitter struggles over appointing incumbents to Holy Trinity Church; he was a churchwarden in 1629 and 1633 and he keenly supported the puritan vicar, Thomas Wilson. He gave an appropriate gift, a carved pulpit, to the parish church in 1629. He was fined rather than accept a knighthood in 1626.

Hall himself was very ill for two months in 1632. He died at Stratford on 25 November 1635, and was buried at Holy Trinity the next day, the parish register noting him as 'medicus peritissimus' ('a most skilful physician'). His tombstone recorded his age as sixty. John Hall had made his will orally only a day before during an epidemic that was afflicting the town, in which two of his neighbours also died. He died a wealthy man, with goods and cash worth some £2000, leaving a house in London to his wife and a house in Acton, Middlesex, as well as Stratford meadowland, to his daughter, Elizabeth; his books and papers he bequeathed to Elizabeth's husband, Thomas *Nash (*bap.* 1593, *d.* 1647), a local lawyer. JOAN LANE

**Sources** J. Lane, *John Hall and his patients: the medical practice of Shakespeare's son-in-law* (1997) · S. Schoenbaum, *William Shakespeare: a documentary life* (1975) · B. R. Lewis, *The Shakespeare documents* (1941), 587–99 · E. I. Fripp, *Shakespeare, man and artist* (1938) · A. Hughes, *Politics, society and civil war in Warwickshire, 1620–1660* (1987) · parish registers, Holy Trinity Church, Stratford upon Avon · I. Gray, 'Shakespeare's son-in-law'

**Archives** BL, Latin case notes, Egerton MS 2065

**Wealth at death** approx. £2000—three houses, meadowland, and books: will, PRO, PROB 11/172, sig. 115

**Hall, John** (*bap.* 1627, *d.* 1656), poet and writer, was baptized on 20 August 1627 in Durham, the first of the seven children of Michael Hall (1615?–1655), of Consett and Framwellgate, and Elizabeth (*d.* 1677), daughter of John Gyll, of the city of Durham. Hall was educated at Durham School and intended for Cambridge in 1640, but was delayed by the troubles of the time. After six years of private reading, during which he studied languages and history as well as the classics, he went to St John's College, Cambridge, where he was admitted, as a pensioner or commoner, on 26 February 1646. Encouraged by his tutor John Pawson, Hall published *Horae vacivae, or, Essays* (1646), dedicated to John Arrowsmith, master of St John's. It was accompanied by commendatory verses by his particular friend Thomas Stanley, and by James Shirley, William Hammond, Henry More, and others; a preface, dated 12 June, by Pawson; and an engraved frontispiece by William Marshall. The precocious essays, much influenced by Bacon, created a stir, and were admired in print by James Howell (*Epistolae Ho-Elianae*). During this year Hall became the friend and patron of his earliest biographer, John Davies of Kidwelly, and began a correspondence with Samuel Hartlib and Samuel Worsley, on whose behalf he communicated with other members of the university, including Ralph Cudworth. In return Hartlib put Hall in touch with Robert Boyle and John Milton (Hall held a lifelong admiration for Milton and his works; there is no evidence that Milton reciprocated). By the time of the publication of *Poems* (published 1647, dated 1646), Hall was a celebrity.

Hall was soon translated into a fellow-commoner but remained dissatisfied with Cambridge and left it in May 1647 for Gray's Inn, where he was admitted on 7 June. Between May and August he wooed and won a Hertfordshire woman. Hall had been financially pinched throughout his life, and he married her despite her lack of fortune; this turned his family against the match, and, according to his friend and biographer, 'This raised a feud between the Families; that, a discontent between the new-married; and that, a distance: so that she became in a manner a widdow soon after the Nuptials' (Davies, sig. b3*r*). She wrote to him with passion and eloquence; he denied her, claiming that parental rigour offered an indefeasible barrier. This wife is almost certainly the Rebecca Hall who was actually widowed in 1656 and inherited his goods.

The engraving of the nineteen-year-old Hall accompanying *Horae vacivae* shows a long-faced youth in a neo-Roman pose. He was 'somewhat above the ordinary stature' (Davies, sig. b7*v*). In his youth he broke a leg and consequently walked little, and over the years his disinclination to any kind of physical exertion resulted in 'pursinesse and fatnesse', resulting in 1650–51 in his seeking to suppress his appetite by swallowing pebbles. Davies admitted 'He was very carelesse of ornament, impatient of those dresses and effeminacy which some study so much, looking on a Barber as a tedious Torment' (ibid., sig. b8*r*). Hall was accused of being similarly careless of religion, and his friend and biographer took pains to stress his sermon attendance to dispel these charges of atheism and 'absolute alienation from the Nationall Beleef' (ibid., sig. A2*v*). Little evidence of orthodox Christian faith can be found in his writings, though there are numerous elements of mysticism, and it may well be that he was partly estranged from the church.

During this period Hall was primarily engaged in writing and translating literary works; his choice of texts for translation was consistently interesting and imaginative. Hartlib requested, among other works, a translation of a utopian fiction by Johann Christian Andreae, which Hall published under the name of *A Modell of a Christian Society* (1647). Hall also began to compose a utopia in the form of a romance, entitled 'Leucenia', but which was loaned to a friend and lost before completed. The same year he edited from manuscript and published *In aliquot sacrae paginae loca lectiones ex autoris autographo manu-scripto fideliter transcriptae* by Robert Hegge (another Durham man), and wrote, under the pseudo-initials N. LL., *A true account and character of the times, historically and politically drawne by a gentleman to give satisfaction to his friend in the countrey*, published in 1647. This polemical pamphlet combined royalist sympathies—shared by many of Hall's friends—with an interest in classical political theory that would soon result in republicanism; Davies suggested that Hall's experiences at Cambridge had already 'raised in him those aversions to *Monarchy*' (Davies, sig. b*v*).

These sentiments were disclosed in the spring of 1648, when Hall founded a weekly newsbook entitled *Mercurius Britanicus*, borrowing the former title and idiosyncratic orthography of the journalist and pamphleteer Marchamont Nedham—they may have been acquaintances by this time—who had recently deserted parliamentarianism for the royalist cause. Hall's *Britanicus*, written in a bright style, combining news, redargution of the royalist newsbooks (the abrasive manner and literary affectations of which Hall emulated) that flourished during the second civil war, with echoes of Milton, interest theory, and a radical public spirit. He praised and defended the astrologer William Lilly, whom he had scorned in *A True Account*, and Lilly's royalist rival George Wharton suggested that Lilly had sponsored Hall (*Elencticus*, 27, 31 May 1648, 205–6). While at Gray's Inn, Hall continued to pursue his literary ambitions through commendatory verses—one to Richard Lovelace's *Lucasta* (1649), others to James Shirley and Richard Brome—and an educational treatise in the spirit of Milton and Hartlib, *An Humble Motion to the Parliament of England Concerning the Advancement of Learning* (1649). These efforts drew him into the purview of Gualter Frost and the council of state: on 14 May 1649 he was employed, with a pension of £100 per annum, 'for answering pamphlets against the commonwealth' (*CSP dom., 1649–50*, 139).

Hall offered good service to the Commonwealth. In 1650 he attended Cromwell on his Scottish expedition, which duty resulted in *The Grounds and Reasons of Monarchy* (1651), Hall's most sophisticated political analysis, combined with a dry history of the disturbances in hereditary succession to the Scottish throne. John Toland would later include this in his edition of *The Oceana of James Harrington, and his other Works* (1700). On 19 September 1649 Hall was appointed to assist the attorney-general in prosecuting the charge against John Lilburne. Unlike his colleague Milton, Hall was not fussy in accepting commissions, and he wrote works to confute William Prynne, Christopher Love, John Streater, and probably a number of others, including Lilburne, under cover of anonymity. Some have suggested that Hall was involved in editing *Mercurius Politicus* with Marchamont Nedham, not improbable in itself though contemporary affirmation can only be found in hostile Restoration pamphlets. One of Hall's publications, an edition of a 1624 anti-Dutch treatise, *A true relation of the unjust, cruel, and barbarous proceedings against the English, at Amboyna in the East-Indies* (1651), to which he contributed a new preface, provoked a complaint from the Dutch ambassadors that the work was inflammatory, which went unheeded by the parliament. His most distinguished literary work of this period was his *Peri ypsous, or, Dionysius Longinus of the Height of Eloquence* (1652), a translation of the pseudo-Longinus treatise on the sublime, with a dedication to Bulstrode Whitelocke associating sublime eloquence with the exercise of government, and thus with the needs of the Commonwealth.

On the political changes of 1653 Hall proved himself flexible, defending the dissolution of the Long Parliament in *A Letter Written to a Gentleman in the Country* (1653), and the introduction of the protectorate in *Confusion Confounded, or, A Firm Way of Settlement Settled and Confirmed* (1654). The payment of Hall's salary was irregular and on 10 May 1654 he petitioned Cromwell for its continuance, alleging that he had 'been a constant servant of the several Councils, being brought in by your Highness, and always discharged my duty' (*CSP dom., 1654*, 163). His request was granted, but on 17 April 1655 the financial troubles of the republic caused his salary to be permanently removed. His final extant work for the Commonwealth was a translation of William Drummond's history of Scotland (1655); a partner volume to this, an edition of Drummond's poems, was edited by Milton's nephew Edward Phillips the following year.

About Easter 1655, having been sick for some time, Hall

left St Martin-in-the-Fields, London, and travelled into Hertfordshire and to St Albans and convalesced under the hospitality of friends, before returning to London and thence in July to his father's house in Durham. In September that same year his father died. Hall died, of unknown causes probably related to his extended illness, in Durham on 1 August 1656, not yet twenty-nine. Rebecca inherited his 'goods chattels & debts' (will, PRO, PROB 6/32, fol. 254*v*), though contemporary references to Hall's penury suggest that these amounted to little.

In his writings Hall deliberately explored a diversity of literary forms and genres, from lyric and romance to paradox and essay, through translation, pamphlet, and history. More works were left incomplete and unpublished at the time of his death, including a translation of Procopius, a chemical poem in Spenserian stanzas, and a translation of a Neoplatonic work, *Hierocles upon the Golden Verses of Pythagoras*, which appeared posthumously in 1657, accompanied by Davies's biography. Possessed of a powerful memory, Hall worked at great speed: he was reported to have translated a whole canto of Edward Benlowes's *Theophila* (1652) into Latin in a day; and to have half-completed his translation of Michael Maier, *Lusus serius, or, Serious passe-time: a philosophical discourse concerning the superiority of creatures under man* (1654), 'in one afternoon, over a glasse of wine in a Tavern' (Davies, sig. b6*r*). According to Davies, Thomas Hobbes praised Hall: 'Had not his debauches & intemperance diverted him from the more serious studies, he had made an extraordinary person; for no man had ever done so great things at his age' (ibid., sig. A*r*). JOAD RAYMOND

**Sources** J. Davies, 'Preface', *Hierocles*, trans. J. Hall (1657) • Wood, *Ath. Oxon.*, new edn, 2.457–60 • R. Surtees, *The history and antiquities of the county palatine of Durham*, 4 vols. (1816–40) • *CSP dom.*, 1649–50; 1654 • J. Pendleton, 'The prose works of John Hall of Durham', BLitt diss., U. Oxf., 1934 • G. H. Turnbull, 'John Hall's letters to Samuel Hartlib', *Review of English Studies*, new ser., 4 (1953), 221–33 • University of Sheffield, Hartlib papers • J. Hall, 'A method of history', Bodl. Oxf., MS Rawl. D. 152 • will, PRO, PROB, 6/32, fol. 254*v* • J. Foster, *The register of admissions to Gray's Inn, 1521–1889, together with the register of marriages in Gray's Inn chapel, 1695–1754* (privately printed, London, 1889) • D. Norbrook, *Writing the English republic: poetry, rhetoric and politics, 1627–1660* (1999) • J. Raymond, 'John Hall's *A method of history*: a book lost and found (with transcription)', *English Literary Renaissance*, 28 (1998), 267–98
**Archives** University of Sheffield, Hartlib MSS
**Likenesses** W. Marshall, engraving, repro. in J. Hall, *Horae vacivae, or, Essays* (1646), frontispiece • W. Marshall, line engraving, NPG; repro. in *The works of Joseph Hall*, 1 (1647)

**Hall, John** (1633–1710), bishop of Bristol and college head, was born at the vicarage in Bromsgrove, Worcestershire, on 29 January 1633, the son of John Hall (*b.* 1598/9), vicar there, and his wife, Anne, and grew up in a predominantly puritan ambience. One uncle, Edmund *Hall (*bap.* 1620, *d.* 1687), theologically Calvinist, fought in the parliamentarian army before becoming a fellow of Pembroke College, Oxford, and later conformed as rector of Great Rissington, Gloucestershire. Another uncle, Thomas *Hall (1610–1665), as a presbyterian, was, however, ejected from

**John Hall** (1633–1710), by Thomas Forster, 1699

his living in 1662, while Hall's brother-in-law, John Spilsbury, presbyterian minister of Bromsgrove, resigned at the Restoration; they always remained on close terms.

Hall was educated at Merchant Taylors' School, which he entered in June 1644. After an initial spell at Wadham College, Oxford (1648), he matriculated at Pembroke College, Oxford, as a scholar in 1650, and was taught by his uncle Edmund. He became a fellow in 1650 and graduated BA in 1651, proceeding MA in 1653. He received presbyterian ordination in 1655. After the Restoration, Bishop Robert Skinner of Oxford initiated a continuing, urgent, and intensive strategy of ordinations to replenish the Anglican ministry; as part of this on 31 March 1661 he conferred Anglican orders on twenty-two men as deacon and priest at the same ceremony. One of these was Hall. Reportedly to conciliate the puritans Charles II later made him one of his chaplains. Already popular in the college, he was elected master of Pembroke on 1 December 1664, aged only thirty-one. Archbishop Sheldon, suspecting his presbyterian provenance, unsuccessfully tried to block the election. As the mastership was inadequately endowed Hall was also presented to the neighbouring college living of St Aldates, which he held *in commendam* until his death, and to a prebend at St Paul's. After proceeding BD in 1666 and DD in 1669, academic promotion followed. Calvinism was still widespread in the Restoration church and the divinity faculty elected him in March 1676 Lady Margaret professor of divinity, to which post was attached a Worcester Cathedral prebend. It was then that he became noted as a leading Anglican divine.

With his strongly puritan background Hall was inevitably open to suspicion, even criticism, especially in the highly charged atmosphere after the Popish Plot (1678), when he was temporarily thrown off balance. On 5 November 1678 he preached at St Mary's 'sharply and bitterly against the papists' (*Life and Times of Anthony Wood*, 2.422). Anthony Wood noted him as a 'malapert presbyterian since this plot, nothing of malapertness before' (ibid., 2.428), while some regarded him as the leading whig in Oxford. Certainly in August 1681 he was prepared to risk hostility by visiting and praying in Oxford Castle with the whig pamphleteer Stephen College, 'the protestant joiner', condemned for treason and waiting to be hanged, drawn, and quartered. Hall, however, worked to redeem himself; he was determined not to fall into the trap of faction, and thus endanger the new, fragile, and therefore temporary consensus between high-churchmen and Calvinists within the Anglican church; for him the chief bogeys were Rome and Socinianism. In July 1683, after the discovery of the Rye House plot, Hall personally presented the king with the university's loyal address of congratulations on his escape from assassination. Nevertheless, when he preached the coronation sermon at St Mary's, Oxford, on 23 April 1685, he fearlessly told the crowded congregation not to 'hearken in the least after popery' (ibid., 3.187)—innocuous enough at the time—but he riskily followed it with his hope that God 'would open (the king's) eyes to see the light' of the Reformation; James had already clearly rejected it (Beddard, 910).

Sheldon had distrusted Hall earlier because of his late entry into Anglican orders and his thoroughgoing presbyterian connections in family and friendship circles. In 1689, however, the national situation changed. The new king, William III, himself a Calvinist, favoured Hall as one of the few theologically sympathetic divines, while for his part, as a member of the commission on the prayer book, Hall actively co-operated with the new government's policy for comprehension of moderate dissenters. Indeed, Hall was the only Oxford don who remained working on the commission after William Jane and Henry Aldrich had ostentatiously walked out in opposition to any reform of the liturgy. In July 1689 William contemplated appointing him to the see of Worcester, and in 1691 to Hereford, but preferred him to Bristol, a bishopric so poor that holders usually needed another preferment. As Hall, however, was clearly devoted to his Pembroke life, Tillotson granted him dispensation specifically to hold the mastership of the college and the St Aldates living *in commendam* with the see. On 30 August 1691 he consecrated him and Richard Kidder bishops in Bow church, London; Gilbert Burnet and Edward Stillingfleet were co-consecrators. Paucity of Bristol diocesan sources precludes any serious study of his tenure there, but contemporaries reported, not necessarily reliably, that he was rarely present. Noble noted: 'His merit as a scholar and as a pious divine obtained him his mitre; but he was more known in than out of Oxford where he long presided as a faithful and munificent head of a college' (Noble, 2.102). Certainly no political prelate he attended the House of Lords less regularly than many colleagues, but, even so, in most years of William's reign he attended on at least fifteen occasions, sometimes more. After 1702, with his royal patron dead, his attendances were rare.

Theologically Hall was an old-style 'thorough-paced calvinist' (*Remarks*, 2.343), 'unadulterated, iconoclastic, sabbatarian' (Beddard, 833); even the nonconformist Edmund Calamy reported that he 'brought all the catechism of the Westminster assembly out of the catechism of the Church of England' (Tyacke, 612). Nevertheless, ecclesiastically, like some of his Calvinistic Oxford colleagues, he favoured the established church and its liturgy, working within it to attack both Rome and Socinianism. Nor would he, Calvinistic as he was, have any truck with increasingly prevalent latitudinarianism.

Hall was a skilled preacher and lecturer. At St Aldates he was much 'frequented for his edifying way of preaching by the precise people and scholars of Oxford' (Wood, *Ath. Oxon.*, 4.900). The scholarly nonconformists Calamy and Thomas Gilbert highly approved of his catechizing there each Sunday evening. Calamy reported: 'I never heard Mr. Gilbert applaud anyone more than the bishop' (Macleane, 270). Even Thomas Hearne, naturally vilifying him as 'one of the rebel bishops … and defender of the republican doctrines', acknowledged him to have been 'a learned divine, a good preacher, and his lectures, while professor, were looked upon by the best judges as excellent in their kind' (*Remarks*, 3.50, 2.343). In general most considered him a good man, 'esteemed for his godliness by pious people' (Stoughton, 5.223); one contemporary reported that everyone acknowledged 'that the whole business of his life is to feed that flock over which the Holy Ghost has made him overseer' (Dunton, 445), presumably, however, at Pembroke College rather than Bristol. His attendance on the condemned Stephen College also attests to Hall's 'pastoral heart'.

When Archbishop John Tillotson died in 1694 William III seriously considered Hall, together with Jonathan Trelawny, for succession to Canterbury. Latitudinarians reportedly favoured Hall, but in the end William, wisely perhaps, followed Tillotson's own choice and chose the less controversial Thomas Tenison.

At Pembroke, where as master he mostly resided, Hall was apparently often in dispute with the fellows, and was once criticized for allowing the dissenting Gilbert to read to his scholars. More important, however, he was a substantial builder, responsible for construction of the gate tower and the north and east sides of the old quadrangle. With far-sighted care and single-hearted determination he supervised the planning and financing of the development. After its completion in the 1690s he brought his scheme to conclusion with a large, elegant master's lodging, for which he personally met almost the whole expense. In the last year of his life, and presumably before his death, a library was built over the old hall. Proud of the achievement, he commissioned at his own expense an engraving of the completed work. He was also one of the major personal donors to the rebuilt All Saints' Church.

Hall died in the master's lodgings on 4 February 1710 and was buried at Bromsgrove church, where a monument was erected in his memory. Before his death he not only gave his books to the newly constructed college library, he also made provision in 1708 for a charity to clothe the poor of Bromsgrove and to distribute bibles to certain Worcestershire towns. Dying a bachelor, Hall's principal heir was his nephew, John Spilsbury, a dissenting minister of Kidderminster to whom he bequeathed substantial estates in Worcestershire, from which Hall's charities were funded. WILLIAM MARSHALL

**Sources** D. Macleane, *A history of Pembroke College, Oxford*, OHS, 33 (1897) • N. Tyacke, 'Religious controversy', *Hist. U. Oxf.* 4: *17th-cent. Oxf.*, 569–620 • R. A. Beddard, 'Restoration Oxford and the making of the protestant establishment', *Hist. U. Oxf.* 4: *17th-cent. Oxf.*, 803–62 • G. V. Bennett, 'Loyalist Oxford and the revolution', *Hist. U. Oxf.* 5: *18th-cent. Oxf.*, 9–30 • G. V. Bennett and J. D. Walsh, eds., *Essays in modern English church history: in memory of Norman Sykes* (1966) • will, PRO, PROB 11/514, sig. 78 • *Calamy rev.* • C. J. Abbey, *The English church and its bishops, 1700–1800*, 2 vols. (1887) • *VCH Worcestershire*, vol. 2 • Foster, *Alum. Oxon.* • *Fasti Angl.* (Hardy), vols. 1, 3 • C. J. Robinson, ed., *A register of the scholars admitted into Merchant Taylors' School, from AD 1562 to 1874*, 2 vols. (1882–3) • Oxford episcopal register, Oxfordshire Archives, Oxf. dioc. d.106, fol. 5 • Tillotson's archiepiscopal register, 1691–4, LPL • *JHL*, 15–19 (1691–1714) • letters of dispensation, Bristol RO, 35530/1/b • *CSP dom.*, *1691–2* • J. Stoughton, *History of religion in England from the opening of the Long Parliament to the end of the eighteenth century*, 6 vols. (1881) • Wood, *Ath. Oxon.*, new edn • *Remarks and collections of Thomas Hearne*, ed. C. E. Doble and others, 2, OHS, 7 (1886) • *Remarks and collections of Thomas Hearne*, ed. C. E. Doble and others, 3, OHS, 13 (1889) • J. Granger, *A biographical history of England, from Egbert the Great to the revolution*, 2nd edn, 4 vols. (1775) • *A biographical history of England, from the revolution to the end of George I's reign: being a continuation of the Rev. J. Granger's work*, ed. M. Noble, 2 (1806) • N. Luttrell, *A brief historical relation of state affairs from September 1678 to April 1714*, 6 vols. (1857) • J. Dunton, *The life and errors of John Dunton … written by himself* (1705) • 'Catalogue of books given by the Rt. Revd. John, Lord Bishop of Bristol 1709', Pembroke College, Oxford, MS 45/1/1 • *The life and times of Anthony Wood*, ed. A. Clark, 5 vols., OHS, 19, 21, 26, 30, 40 (1891–1900)

**Archives** Pembroke College, Oxford, 'Catalogue of books given by the Rt Revd John, Lord Bishop of Bristol 1709', MS 45/1/1 • Pembroke College, Oxford, corresp. and papers, 60/4 • Yale U., Beinecke L., letters

**Likenesses** T. Forster, miniature, 1699, Bristol City Museum and Art Gallery [*see illus.*] • T. Trotter, line engraving, pubd 1796, BM, NPG • oils, Pembroke College, Oxford

**Wealth at death** substantial estates at Hanbury and Stoke Prior in Worcestershire: will, PRO, PROB 11/514, sig. 78

**Hall, John** (*d.* **1707**), Church of England clergyman, came from Shropshire; the names of his parents are unknown. He was admitted sizar at Trinity College, Cambridge, on 29 May 1652. He was elected a scholar in 1655, graduated BA in 1656, was appointed a fellow of his college in 1658, and proceeded MA in 1659 and BD in 1666. Hall was collated on 11 March 1664 to the rectory of Hanwell, Middlesex. On 11 July 1664 he was made prebendary of Islington in the church of St Paul, and on 20 February 1666 was appointed the rector of St Christopher-le-Stocks, London. On 21 March 1667 he exchanged the prebend of Islington for that of Holywell (Finsbury). It was probably about this time that he married his wife, Hannah (*d.* 1691), with whom he had many children, though few seem to have survived to adulthood. He was made first assistant at Sion College, London, in 1672 and junior dean in 1679, and held the office of president from 1694. Hall contributed to the building of Sion College and St Paul's Cathedral. He was the father of John Hall (*bap.* 1678), also of Trinity College and ordained deacon at Lincoln in 1701. Hall died towards the end of 1707, surviving his wife by sixteen years, and was buried at St Christopher-le-Stocks on 19 December 1707.

Hall was best known as the author of *Jacobs Ladder, or, The Devout Souls Ascention to Heaven* (1676?; no copy of the first edition survives, but the second, enlarged, edition was certainly published in 1676), a compilation of private, family, and occasional devotions that went through many editions well into the eighteenth century. The book included prayers commemorating the plague of 1665 and the great fire of 1666, as well as a number of prayers thanking God for the nation's deliverance from popery during the reign of Mary I, in 1588, and in 1605. The daily devotions that Hall drew up for individuals and families also contained regular prayers for the safety of Charles II and James, duke of York. However, the text of the 1692 edition was changed to give thanks to William III for delivering the nation from popery and French tyranny.

An earlier work, *Grace Leading unto Glory* (1652), has sometimes been ascribed to a (presumably somewhat precocious) John Hall, because of the coincidence that the author, J. H., happens to use the phrase 'Jacob's ladder' in its dedicatory preface (sig. A4*r*). EDWARD VALLANCE

**Sources** Venn, *Alum. Cant.* • E. Freshfield, ed., *The register book of the parish of St Christopher le Stocks*, 3 vols. in 1 (1882) • E. H. Pearce, ed., *Sion College and library* (1913), 345 • *N&Q*, 3rd ser., 6 (1864), 37

**Hall, John** [Jack] (**1674x7–1707**), thief, was born in Bishop's Head Court, off Gray's Inn Lane in the parish of St Andrew's, Holborn, Middlesex, the son of Anthony Hall, cobbler, and his wife, Rebecca. Just before his execution in December 1707 Hall gave his age as thirty-two, suggesting that he was born in 1674 or 1675. However, the parish register of St Andrew's, Holborn, records that he was baptized there on 18 January 1677. A pamphlet life published at the time of his death describes his parents' circumstances as 'very mean … his Mother at this time carrying a Basket in Brook's-Market, and living upon the Alms of the Parish' (Lorrane, 2). Hall, who did not learn to read and write, became a chimney sweep, and lived all or most of his life in the parish of his birth, interrupted by periods of service in the navy from about 1692 onwards. According to the pamphlet account, he was married at the age of twenty-four to 'an Oyster-wench'. The records of St Andrew's, Holborn, suggest that he may have married earlier: its registers record on two occasions in the 1690s the baptism of a son of John Hall and his wife, Mary: Samuel in January 1694 and Matthias in March 1694. At the latter date Hall was noted as living in Smith's Court in Holborn. A tax assessment made in 1695 for the portion of the parish that lay in the City records the household of John Hall, his wife, Mary, and daughter, Mary. When in 1699 he lay in the New Prison in Clerkenwell for his involvement in a riot, Hall pleaded his case for release by claiming that he had a wife great with child and a family ready to starve.

Hall became notorious as a prolific thief, specializing in street robbery and in housebreaking. The pamphlet life described how he would cut boxes and bags from off coaches and horses' backs, and told how on one occasion Hall and his accomplices dogged a wagon all the way from Knightsbridge to the City, unable to rob it because the wagon master and his son were riding behind it. Finally Hall snatched the child and ran off; while the father and the driver chased after him Hall's accomplices plundered the wagon. Rather more prosaically, in November 1698 a fellow criminal, Walter Griffin, in the course of informing against several of his confederates, told how Hall and Philip Clark had stolen a hat from a gentleman in the street some three months earlier. It was as a burglar that Hall was finally convicted.

The pamphlet account reported that Hall's crimes often brought him to Newgate, and that service at sea and in the army was the price he paid for his crimes (Hall himself, interviewed by the ordinary—prison chaplain—of Newgate, spoke only of having served in the navy). In the last three years of his life, he himself owned, 'he had committed a great many Robberies, some of them very considerable, in and about London' (Lorrain).

What sealed Jack Hall's notoriety seems to have been not the frequency of his crimes alone, but the betrayals of the last year of his life. On 5 November 1706 he and his confederate Arthur Chambers were committed to Newgate to await trial for breaking into the house of William Green in Westminster and for wounding a constable. Chambers was another figure with a long criminal record. He had already been pardoned once after turning informer and helping send to the gallows his accomplice Moll Raby, and was believed by the authorities to have been involved in the murder of a constable at Bartholomew Fair in 1702. Hall now saved his own neck by testifying against Chambers in part of a flurry of prosecutions between December 1706 and February 1707 that saw one small group of criminals—Hall, Richard Low, Stephen Bunce (or Bunch), and James Hackett—providing the evidence to hang a rather larger number of their confederates—Chambers, William Nutting, Richard Morris, Luke Matthews, James Gardner, Thomas Bell, Thomas Arnold, Richard Fitch, and John Goodwin alias Plump. It is certain, from the names of witnesses scrawled on the backs of indictments, only that Hall testified in court against the first two, though it is also likely in pre-trial examinations that he would have been expected more broadly to name names and specify particular crimes. Bunce in one such examination admitted one offence of his own, and listed others committed by his associates, confirming that Hall, Hackett, and Chambers had robbed Green's house.

Hall was never tried for that crime, and in January 1707 he was released on bail. Within the year he had followed Chambers and the others to Tyburn. On the night of 25 November 1707 he and Richard Low were arrested; Bunce got away but was later caught. Their capture was sufficiently newsworthy for a broadside to be rushed out the next day, its title a witness to the impact of the trials of the preceding twelve months on their reputations, *A full and true account of the apprehending and taking of Jack Hall, the chimney-sweeper, and Richard Low, for shooting a constable near Grays-Inn-Lane on Monday last; together with one Stephen Bunch who made his escape; being three most notorious house-breakers and robbers; being the three persons who by their evidence have hang'd nine or ten of their companions within this 12 months*. The broadside's highly coloured account of the three men as openly challenging authority is more significant as a piece of myth making than as a reliable account of their capture. It told of how the three men dauntlessly confronted the constable and watch of Clerkenwell on three nights, 'they being arm'd with Pistols, and desperate Rogues, not caring what Mischief they did'. After wounding a constable on one night they were finally overwhelmed by a reinforced watch the next night in a house on Clerkenwell Green. According to the pamphlet life, here probably more reliable, between one and two in the morning of 25 November Hall and his confederates robbed the house of Captain John Guyon in Stepney. About 4 a.m. a boy named Briggs saw them dividing up the spoils in the Green Man in Billingsgate. Asked how he could distinguish the thieves one from another, he replied 'That when they spoke aloud, they call'd one another Brother Stitch, but when they spoke softly, they call'd one another by their proper names' (Lorrane, 5). They agreed to meet again at the Two Fighting Cocks in Bunhill Fields between 5 and 6 a.m., where Briggs's father gathered a group of men and after a chase through the streets caught them.

Hall, Bunce, and Low were convicted at the Old Bailey for the burglary of Guyon's house and sentenced to hang. Awaiting execution the three men were interviewed by the ordinary of Newgate, Paul Lorrain. 'That what they had done before they were made evidences against Arthur Chambers … was very well known', they conceded, 'That for what they had done since, it was not very considerable'. They had never fired a pistol with intent to kill, only 'to secure themselves from being taken'. In bizarre testimony to the swirl of rumour around Hall's name, Lorrain asked Hall, 'Whether (as 'twas reported by some) he had made a Contract with the Prince of Darkness, for a set time to act his Villanies in; he answered, *He never did, nor said any such thing*' (Lorrain). Hall was indeed duly penitent, confessing

> That he was much addicted to Idleness and gaming, which two Vices brought him to the commission of others, particularly that of Robbing at such a rate as he did; and, That when of late he had some Thoughts of leaving off of Thieving, he found his inclinations were still that way. (Lorrain)

Hall was hanged at Tyburn on 17 December 1707, alongside Low, Bunce, and three other men: 'I never saw so many Condemn'd Offenders, at once, behave themselves with more Decency than these did', Lorrain recorded. On the gallows Hall told the crowd 'That he had been very wicked, and done much Mischief; but he hop'd God had forgiven him; and he desir'd all Persons to take Warning by him, and pray for him' (Lorrain).

Hall's death provided Grub Street with good copy, and they gave a rather different picture from that provided by the ordinary. The pamphlet life, *The ordinary's account of the life, birth, death and parentage of John Hall, Richard Lewis, Stephen Bunch*, stole the name of the official account from which it was partly cribbed, evidently also drawing on court testimonies as well as its own inventions. Here the chimney sweep was credited with being 'very ambitious of obtaining the Title of the King of Thieves' (Lorrane, 7). The *Memoirs of the right villainous Jack Hall, penn'd from his mouth some time before his death*, published in 1708 and reaching its fourth edition by 1714, was actually no such thing, using the saleability of his name to top and tail a highly generalized parody of the conventions of the true-life crime genre. Its concluding epitaph ironically celebrated his bravado:

At last thy Roguish Reign is ended,
And thou (deservedly) Suspended;
Where art thou now, thou Reprobate,
Who jested at a Future State,
And said, the Place the Devils kept,
Was Sooty, wanted to be Swept?
(*Memoirs*, 29)

Hall's name carried enough force to find its way into cartoon, helped no doubt by the iconographic distinctiveness of his occupation: in 1724 Hogarth's attack on the current fashions of the theatre, *A Just View of the British Stage*, showed a theatre manager dangling a puppet to demonstrate 'Scaramouch Jack Hall the Chimney-Sweeper's Escape from Newgate through the Privy'.

However, Hall's memory was most powerfully preserved in song. The ballad *Jack Hall* was probably contemporary with his death, but broadside and oral transmission gave it a remarkably long life, and indeed it is first visible as a song which Francis Place remembered as having heard in his youth in the 1780s. It was reprinted as a broadside in the 1820s, 1830s, and 1840s, while the powerful performance of the singer W. G. Ross, who renamed it *Sam Hall*, gave it a further lease of life which took it across the Atlantic. In the early twentieth century Cecil Sharp collected four versions of the song in the west country. The ballad's strong metre and tune powerfully underpinned the words given to the chimney sweep. His occupation provided a somewhat sinister image at the heart of the ballad which complemented his sardonic defiance in the face of the gallows, celebrating Jack Hall not as the model penitent of Lorrain's account but as the archetype of the condemned man who 'died game':

My name it is Jack Hall, chimney sweep, chimney sweep,
My name it is Jack Hall, chimney sweep,
My name it is Jack Hall,
And I rob both great and small,
But my life must pay for all,
When I die, when I die
But my life must pay for all,
When I die.
…
The ladder and the rope went up and down, up and down,
The ladder and the rope went up and down,
Oh! the ladder and the rope,
My collar bone they broke,
And a devil a word I spoke coming down,
And a devil a word I spoke
Coming down.
(*Jack Hall*, Bodl. Oxf., Ballad collection, Harding B 15, 145a)

TIM WALES

**Sources** P. Lorrain, *The ordinary of Newgate his account of the behaviour, confessions and last speeches of the malefactors that were executed at Tyburn on Wednesday, Dec 17, 1707* (1707) [the authentic broadside ordinary's account] · P. Lorrane, *The ordinary's account of the life, birth, death and parentage of John Hall, Richard Lewis, Stephen Bunch* (1707) [a fake: a pamphlet purporting to be the ordinary's account] · *A full and true account of the apprehending and taking of Jack Hall, the chimney-sweeper, and Richard Low, for shooting a constable near Grays-Inn-Lane on Monday last* (1707) · Middlesex gaol delivery rolls, December 1706, January 1707, February 1707, December 1707, LMA, MJ/SR/2082, 2085, 2087, 2102 · information of Walter Griffin, 10 Nov 1698, LMA, MJ/SP/1698/December/28 · petition of John Hall, 1699, LMA, MJ/SP/1699/December/1 · examination of Stephen Bunce, LMA, MJ/SP/1706/December/1706 · examinations of Letticia Browne and others, May 1702, LMA, MJ/SP/1702/July/50–53 · *Memoirs of the right villainous Jack Hall*, 4th edn (1714) · V. A. C. Gatrell, *The hanging tree: execution and the English people, 1770–1868* (1994) · B. H. Bronson, 'Samuel Hall's family tree', in B. H. Bronson, *Ballad as song* (1969), 18–36 · *Jack Hall*, Bodl. Oxf., Ballad collection, Harding B 15, 145a [between 1833 and 1851] · parish register, Holborn, St Andrew's, 1676–1704, GL, MS 6667/5, 6 · 'Inhabitants of London, 1695', typescript, 4 vols., 1937–8, GL

**Hall, John** (1739–1797), history and portrait engraver, was born in Wivenhoe, near Colchester, Essex, on 21 December 1739. He was a pupil with William Wynne Ryland of the French immigrant engraver Simon François Ravenet and first found work at Sir Theodore Janssen's Chelsea porcelain manufactory. In 1756 and 1761 he won prizes from the Society for the Encouragement of Arts, Manufactures, and Commerce, the second being for a print of Andromache after a painting by Guido Reni in the possession of the art dealer and royal librarian Richard Dalton. Hall became a fellow of the Society of Artists in 1765 and was elected a director in 1768, 1769, and 1771. In 1769 and 1770 he exhibited two historical scenes after Benjamin West, *Pyrrhus when a Child, Brought before Glaucias* and *Venus and Adonis*, and he then engraved and exhibited the king's painting of Timon of Athens by Nathaniel Dance (1771). His links with painters favoured at court and with the king gave Hall the opportunity of joining the Royal Academy but his pupil Abraham Raimbach records that he 'invariably spurned' the diploma of associate engraver, 'considering, as did Woollett and Strange, that it was injurious to the profession, and degrading to the individual' (*Memoirs and Recollections*, 19).

Hall shared with William Woollett the job of engraving Benjamin West's history paintings, producing *Penn's Treaty with the Indians* and the *Battle of the Boyne* as companions to prints by Woollett, and he succeeded Woollett in the post of history engraver to the king after Woollett's death in 1785. He lived in Berwick Street, Soho, from 1764 to 1768 or 1769. About the latter date he married Mary de Gilles and moved to Great Cheyne Walk in Chelsea. Four children, George William, Charlotte Sophia, Stephen Theodore, and John Edward, were baptized between 1770 and 1775. In 1776 the family moved back to Berwick Street where they lived until Hall's death. He took as apprentices Charles Wood in 1767, Joseph Thornthwaite in 1769, and

**John Hall** (1739–1797), by Gilbert Stuart, 1785

Burnet Reading in 1770. His studio handled the plates for Bell's *British Theatre* with scenes by Hall and portraits of actors in character by Thornthwaite and Reading. He also engraved a number of significant portraits, including Reynolds's of Richard Brinsley Sheridan. Raimbach described him somewhat condescendingly as 'not of first rate powers' but exercising 'very respectable abilities' (*Memoirs and Recollections*, 5). He was 'gentlemanly in his habits and connexions and somewhat disposed to extravagance in dress' (ibid., 6). The portrait of him by Gilbert Stuart, which used to hang in Boydell's shop, is now in the National Portrait Gallery. Hall did perhaps lack the flair to be considered great rather than good, but he was professionally successful. His son George William Hall (1770–1843) became master of Pembroke College, Oxford. One daughter, Mary, was the second wife of Stephen Storace the composer; another, Julia, married the poet Rann Kennedy.

On Christmas day 1796 Ozias Humphry, a personal friend, called on Farington to tell him that 'Hall, the Engraver, has a dropsy at the Heart; that he may live some weeks or months but cannot recover' (Farington, *Diary*, 730). It turned out to be months. On 24 March 1797 William Byrne told Farington that 'Hall, the engraver, is dying.—A complication of disorders' (ibid., 806). He died in Berwick Street, Soho, on 7 April 1797 and was buried in St Mary's churchyard, Paddington.

TIMOTHY CLAYTON

**Sources** *Memoirs and recollections of the late Abraham Raimbach*, ed. M. T. S. Raimbach (1843) • Farington, *Diary* • Graves, *Soc. Artists*, 103 • I. Maxted, *The London book trades, 1700–1777* (1979) • sale of John Hall's goods, 1 July 1799, BM, department of prints and drawings, print room, A.1.1 • T. Mortimer, *The universal director* (1763) • *A register of the premiums and bounties given by the society instituted at London for the encouragement of arts, manufactures, and commerce from the original institution in the year 1754, to the year 1776 inclusive* (1778) • T. Clayton, *The English print, 1688–1802* (1997) • PRO, PROB 11/1289, sig. 245

**Likenesses** G. Stuart, oils, 1785, NPG [*see illus.*] • P. Sandby, sketches, *c*.1790, BM • attrib. W. Lawranson, pastel drawing, NPG • Mrs D. Turner, etching (after O. Humphrey), BM • plaster medallion (after J. Tassie), Scot. NPG

**Hall, Sir John** (1795–1866), military surgeon, the son of John Hall and his wife, Isabel (*née* Fothergill), was born at Little Beck, Westmorland. After leaving Appleby grammar school he studied medicine at Guy's and St Thomas's hospitals in London. In June 1815 he entered the Army Medical Service as hospital assistant and joined the forces fighting against Napoleon in Flanders.

In 1817, after a year on half pay in England, Hall sailed for Jamaica; he arrived at Port Royal in the wake of a terrible hurricane in January 1818. During his nine years in Jamaica, he encountered further disasters in the form of two severe epidemics of yellow fever, in 1819 and 1825, which claimed many victims among the British garrison. Hall himself almost died from the disease. However, his hard work in the first of these epidemics earned him a promotion to the rank of assistant surgeon in 1822, and a reputation as a courageous and efficient officer.

Hall returned to England in 1827, only to be recalled to Jamaica in 1829, where he remained for another three years. Afterwards he served in England, in Ireland (from 1835 to 1836), and in Spain and Gibraltar (until 1839), after which he returned to the West Indies in 1841. In 1844 he left the West Indies for Dublin, where he took medical charge of military recruiting. In the same year he was promoted to deputy inspector-general of hospitals and made a fellow of the Royal College of Surgeons of England. He took his MD at St Andrews University in 1845.

Hall's next active service was in South Africa during the Cape frontier wars of 1847 and 1851, as principal medical officer. Between these engagements Hall was employed at various medical institutions in Cape Town, where in 1848 he met and married Lucy Campbell, daughter of Henry Hackshaw and widow of Duncan Sutherland of St Vincent, West Indies. In 1851 Hall travelled with his wife to Bombay, where he was attached to the presidency garrison and undertook important reforms in medical statistics and barrack accommodation. He remained in Bombay until 1854, when he was ordered to take charge of medical services in the war against Russia. He served in the Crimea from June 1854 to July 1856, and was present at many engagements. He was mentioned in dispatches, made KCB and officer of the Légion d'honneur, and received the third class of the Turkish order of the Mejidiye.

Hall's writings were published in two pamphlets, in 1857 and 1858; these defended the army medical officers in the Crimea from the criticisms made of them by Florence Nightingale and in the report of the sanitary commission which was sent out to investigate conditions in the field. Hall contended that the insanitary state of the army had been largely remedied before the commission got to work, that the members of the latter accomplished little, and that what little they accomplished was effected with an amount of difficulty that should have taught them more consideration for the army medical officers, who were less fortunately situated and who were hampered by the exigencies and discipline of the service.

The Crimean War was the zenith of Hall's long and varied career, and in January 1857 he retired from military service. His intention had been to return to India, there to write a medical history of the Crimean campaign, but a stroke left him partially paralysed. Afterwards Hall gave up hope of accomplishing such a task, and he spent the remainder of his life touring Europe. He ended his days in Italy, at Pisa in Tuscany, where he died of heart failure on 17 January 1866. He was buried in the English protestant cemetery, Leghorn. He was survived by his wife and two daughters, Lucy and Alice—the latter being a musician and linguist of great ability.

Hall never reached the pinnacle of the military medical hierarchy—the post of director-general of Army Medical Services—but he is better known than many who did. He was held in the highest regard by contemporaries in Britain and overseas, and achieved considerable fame for his work in the Crimean War. He was known as a hard worker and a strict disciplinarian, but his subordinates were highly appreciative of his ability and courage.

MARK HARRISON

**Sources** S. M. Mitra, *The life and letters of Sir John Hall* (1911) • *The Lancet* (27 Jan 1866) • *GM*, 4th ser., 1 (1866), 444 • V. G. Plarr, *Plarr's Lives of the fellows of the Royal College of Surgeons of England*, rev. D'A. Power, 1 (1930), 487–8 • Wellcome L., Hall MSS, RAMC 397
**Archives** BL, corresp. relating to nursing service • Wellcome L., letter-book, incl. diary entries, and memoranda • Wellcome L., corresp., diaries, and papers | NAM, corresp. with Lord Raglan • NAM, letters to Sir William Codrington
**Likenesses** photograph, repro. in Mitra, *Life and letters of Sir John Hall*, frontispiece
**Wealth at death** under £6000: probate, 26 March 1866, *CGPLA Eng. & Wales*

**Hall, Sir John** (1824–1907), premier of New Zealand, born at Hull, probably on 18 December 1824, was the third son of George Hall, a shipowner, of Hull and of Elloughton, Yorkshire, and his wife, Grace Williamson. After attending a dissenting academy, at the age of ten he went abroad to finish his education in Germany, Switzerland, and Paris. From 1840 to 1843 he worked in a merchant's office in London, and then entered the secretary's department of the London General Post Office. He soon became private secretary to the secretary of the Post Office, and he served as a volunteer in the Honourable Artillery Company and as a special constable during the Chartist riots of 1848.

In 1852, frustrated at his lack of opportunities in England and attracted by the ideas of the Canterbury Association, Hall emigrated to Lyttelton, New Zealand. With his two brothers, who arrived soon afterwards, he bought sheep-runs to form the Terrace station near Canterbury. He soon entered politics, sitting on the Canterbury provincial council from 1853 to 1860 and from 1863 to 1873. He held executive office and used his position to promote the interests of pastoralists like himself as well as to advocate transport developments.

In addition Hall was resident magistrate for Lyttelton, sheriff, and commissioner of police (27 November 1856), a resident magistrate for the colony (27 April 1857), and a justice of the peace (May 1857). From December 1858 to July 1863 he was a resident magistrate for Christchurch, and from January 1862 to 15 June 1863 first mayor of Christchurch. He was also the first chairman of Selwyn county council, and chairman (in 1869) of the Westland provincial council. In June 1863 he was commissioner of the Canterbury wastelands board.

From 1855 to 1859 Hall was a member of the house of representatives under responsible government, and in 1856 acted briefly as colonial secretary. In 1860 he visited England, where on 3 April 1861 in Hull he married Rose Anne (*d.* 1900), the daughter of William Dryden, of Hull; they had three sons and one daughter. After their return from England in 1862 Hall was called to the legislative council (4 July). He resigned in February 1866, but was re-elected to the lower house for Heathcote, a seat he held until 1872. He was a member of the executive council under Edward Stafford's ministry (24 August 1866 – 28 June 1869), postmaster-general (24 August 1866 – 5 February 1869), and electric telegraph commissioner (12 October 1866 – 5 February 1869). In 1872 he became leader of the legislative council and colonial secretary in the Waterhouse cabinet.

From 1873 to 1876 Hall was in England for health reasons. He returned in 1876 and that year he was briefly a member of the executive council, without portfolio, under Harry Atkinson.

As a prominent Anglican, Hall strongly opposed the Education Act of 1877, which established secular education. Having withdrawn from the upper house, he was elected for Selwyn in 1879. He then found himself leader of the opposition, and early in October he carried a hostile motion against Sir George Grey, the premier. On 10 October he formed a ministry, and he remained premier until 1882. The period was exceptionally acrimonious. Hall maintained unity by implementing Grey's reforms of triennial parliaments elected by universal male suffrage, but introduced measures to bolster rural influence. He survived the Parihaka crisis by enacting repressive measures against the Maori. However, his ministry is remembered mostly for its prudently financed steady development. Ill health compelled Hall's retirement in 1882, and that year he was made a KCMG.

Hall was in England from 1883 to 1887, but returned to New Zealand to serve as a member of the house of representatives from 1887 to 1894, though he refused office on health grounds. In 1890 he represented New Zealand at Melbourne, at the first conference on Australasian federation. Although he was becoming increasingly conservative, in 1893 he introduced into the ministry's electoral bill an amendment conferring the vote on women, a reform which he had always actively supported, not least as he thought women's votes would strengthen conservative interests and because his wife was active in the suffrage movement. It was passed into law on the eve of the general election. In addition to serving in colonial, provincial, and, in 1906, Christchurch municipal politics, Hall was active in the Church of England in its religious and educational activities. On 25 October 1906 he fell ill, and on 25 June 1907 he died, at Park Terrace, Christchurch. He was buried in the family vault in Hororata cemetery. Hall was the leading conservative politician of nineteenth-century New Zealand. He used his influence to preserve the interests of landholding families against what he saw as the rising tide of radicalism.

A. B. WHITE, *rev.* ELIZABETH BAIGENT

**Sources** W. J. Gardner, 'Hall, John (1824–1907)', *DNZB*, vol. 1 • *New Zealand Times* (3 July 1907) • *Canterbury Times* [Christchurch, New Zealand] (3 July 1907) • *Auckland Star* (3 July 1907) • W. Gisborne, *New Zealand rulers and statesmen, 1840–1885* (1886)
**Archives** BL, corresp. with Lord Stanmore, Add. MS 49206
**Likenesses** portrait, repro. in *Canterbury Times* • portrait, repro. in Gisborne, *New Zealand rulers*
**Wealth at death** estate seemingly worth £95,000 in 1891: Gardner, 'Hall, John'

**Hall, John Vine** (1774–1860), religious writer, was born on 14 March 1774 at Diss. His father had been a man of property, but had lost it. At eleven 'little Jack' was apprenticed to a schoolmaster who, he recounted, 'taught me to write the law-hands, and, by way of making the most of me, hired me to the then clerk of the peace' (Hall, 3). In January 1786 he became errand-boy to a bookseller in Maidstone, and rose to be the chief assistant. In 1801, tempted by higher pay, he became clerk and traveller to a Maidstone wine merchant. At this time Vine Hall began a long career of alcohol addiction. He also embraced atheism. In 1802 a friend lent him Porteus's *Evidences of Christianity*, and his views changed. In February 1804 he bought a bookseller's shop at Worcester, and on 26 August 1806 married Mary Teverill. In 1812 he had a powerful religious experience and became a Methodist. His alcohol problem continued to cost him dearly until he became (in 1818) a total abstainer and an ardent advocate of teetotalism.

In April 1814 Vine Hall returned to Maidstone, having purchased the bookshop where he had begun work twenty-eight years before. Here he joined Week Street Independent Church in 1818 and began visiting the prisoners in the county gaol, especially those sentenced to death. In 1821 Vine Hall conceived the idea of writing *The Sinner's Friend*, the first edition of which consisted of selections from the German pietist Karl Heinrich von Bogatzky's *Golden Treasury*, with a short introduction by himself. In subsequent editions he gradually substituted pages from his own pen for those taken from Bogatzky, until in the end the work was entirely his own, excepting one extract. *The Sinner's Friend* was a highly successful religious tract, eventually sixty-four pages in length, populist and sensational in style, with a strong emphasis upon evangelical conversion, justification by faith alone, and the torments which awaited the impenitent. It was translated into thirty languages, and nearly 3 million copies were sold.

In 1850 Vine Hall retired, and in 1854 went to reside at Heath Cottage, Junction Road, Kentish Town. He became an elder at the Congregational Surrey Chapel, where his son, (Christopher) Newman *Hall, was minister. He died on 22 September 1860 at Heath Cottage, and was buried in Abney Park cemetery on 26 September.

THOMAS HAMILTON, *rev.* I. T. FOSTER

**Sources** J. Vine Hall, *The author of 'The sinner's friend': an autobiography*, ed. N. Hall (1865) • Allibone, *Dict.* • Boase, *Mod. Eng. biog.* • private information (2004) • D. Bank and A. Esposito, eds., *British biographical index*, 4 vols. (1990)
**Likenesses** portrait, repro. in Hall, ed., *Author of 'The sinner's friend': an autobiography*, frontispiece
**Wealth at death** under £4000: probate, 4 Oct 1860, *CGPLA Eng. & Wales*

**Hall, Joseph** (1574–1656), bishop of Norwich, religious writer, and satirist, was born on 1 July 1574 at Bristow Park, Ashby-de-la-Zouch, the son of John Hall (*d.* 1608) and his wife, Winifred Bambridge. In *Observations of some Specialities of Divine Providence in the Life of Joseph Hall* (1647), the first of two autobiographical tracts, Hall states that he was one of twelve children and that his father, who was an 'officer' of Henry Hastings, third earl of Huntingdon and president of the council of the north, 'had the government' of Ashby-de-la-Zouch; other sources suggest that he was employed as the town bailiff. Hall's mother, whom he regarded as 'a woman of rare Sanctity', was greatly influenced by the teachings of Anthony Gilby, the incumbent of Ashby and a leading puritan controversialist. Although Hall was later to reject Gilby's views on church governance, he adhered to Calvinist theology throughout his life. He attended the grammar school at Ashby-de-la-Zouch which was superintended by Gilby and served by a succession of radical protestant masters; among the most illustrious of his contemporaries was William Bradshaw, the future author of *English Puritanisme* (1605). Hall's sister Barbara (*b.* 1578) later married the school's famous headmaster John Brinsley.

**Cambridge and early works** Hall's intellectual distinction was evident from an early age but, lacking funds to send him to university, his father arranged to have him privately tutored by William Pelsett (or Pelsant), the rector of Market Bosworth. However, thanks to the intervention of Nathaniel Gilby, Anthony Gilby's son, Hall matriculated in 1589 at Emmanuel College, Cambridge, where Gilby held a fellowship. Hall was accompanied to the university not only by Bradshaw but also by his schoolfriend Hugh Cholmley 'who, as we had been partners of one lesson from our Cradle, so were we now for many years partners of one Bed' ('Observations', 7). Owing to his father's 'weariness of expense', he was briefly recalled home in 1591 with the intention of teaching at his old school, but he returned to Cambridge when an uncle, Edmund Sleigh of Derby, undertook to pay half of his costs. He graduated BA in 1593 but then found his aspirations to a fellowship blocked by the presence of Nathaniel Gilby, his tutor,

**Joseph Hall** (1574–1656), by John Payne, 1628

since the college statutes permitted the election of only one fellow per county. In order to open up a vacancy for Hall the earl of Huntingdon offered Gilby a lucrative household chaplaincy but died shortly after he had accepted it, leaving him without a position. Hall appealed to the master, Lawrence Chadderton, to have Gilby reinstated but 'answer was made me, that the place was pronounced void' (ibid., 10). After an 'exquisite' examination, Hall was duly elected in Gilby's place in 1595, defeating William Bradshaw.

Hall proceeded MA in 1596 and was subsequently elected to the university lectureship in rhetoric for two successive years, becoming celebrated for defending the proposition 'mundus senescit' (Fuller, *Worthies*, 129–30). During these years he appears to have written some pastoral poetry which is no longer extant, but in 1596 he contributed his first published verse to the memorial volume for William Whitaker, Chadderton's brother-in-law. He came to public notice the following year with the publication of *Virgidemiarum*, the first collection of formal verse satires on the Latin model to be published in England. The three books of 'Tooth-Lesse Satyrs' which appeared in 1597 were followed in 1598 by a further three books of socially trenchant 'Byting Satyres'. These works involved Hall in a bitter dispute with John Marston who accused him of pasting a satiric epigram into all of the copies of *The Metamorphosis of Pigmalions Image* 'that came to the Stationers at Cambridge' (A. Davenport, ed., *The Poems of Joseph Hall*, 1949, xxix). In 1599, when the archbishop of Canterbury and the bishop of London attempted to ban the publication of satire, the *Virgidemiarum* appeared on the list of prohibited materials which were ordered to be called in and burned in Stationers' Hall. For reasons that remain unclear they were subsequently reprieved, yet they were never reprinted during Hall's lifetime and are notable by their absence from the various editions of his collected works. During the Smectymnuuan controversy John Milton sought to embarrass Hall by recalling his authorship of the *Virgidemiarum* and the anonymously published *Mundus alter et idem* (1605), which takes the form of a dystopian journey to the Antipodes and was eventually to serve as one of Swift's models for *Gulliver's Travels*. The *Mundus* appears to have been written during Hall's time at Cambridge, but may have been revised as late as 1603. It was translated into English by John Healey in 1609 as *A Discovery of a New World*. Hall's reputation as a literary innovator, particularly in the satiric vein, was confirmed by the publication in 1608 of his *Characters of Vertues and Vices* which introduced the Theophrastan character to English literature and greatly influenced the work of Thomas Overbury and John Earle. His conspicuous adoption of a Senecan prose style in this and other early works led to his being dubbed 'the English Seneca' although, as he explained in *Heaven upon Earth* (1606), his adoption of the fashionable vogue for neo-Stoicism was entirely subordinate to the promotion of distinctively Christian ethics.

**Clergyman and poet, 1601–1607** Shortly after his ordination at Colchester on 14 December 1600 Hall was offered the headship of Peter Blundell's new school at Tiverton but, believing that his destiny lay in the ministry, he declined the offer in favour of Hugh Cholmley. Instead, on 2 December 1601 he accepted the rectory of Hawstead in Suffolk from Anne, Lady Drury, the wife of Sir Robert Drury and granddaughter of Lord Keeper Bacon. Hall found himself much impeded in the discharge of his new duties by 'a witty and bold Atheist, one Mr *Lilly*' who exercised considerable influence over Sir Robert ('Observations', 13). The culprit was William Lyly, brother-in-law of the poet John Donne whose friendship with Hall probably dates from his Hawstead years. Hall later contributed prefatory verses to *An Anatomie of the World* (1611) and *The Second Anniversary* (1612), written by Donne to commemorate the untimely death of Elizabeth Drury, the daughter of Hall's former patron.

In 1603, the year that he proceeded BD, Hall married Elizabeth Winniff (1582/3–1652), daughter of George Winniff of Brettenham in Suffolk, with whom he had six sons and two daughters. His attitude towards his children is revealed in an anecdote recounted in *The Balme of Gilead* (1646):

> I remember a great man coming to my house at *Waltham*, and seeing all of my children standing in the order of their age, and stature, said, These are they that make rich men poor; but he straight received this answer, Nay, my Lord, these are

> they that make a poor man rich, for there is not one of these whom we would part with for all your wealth. (p. 269)

In 1605 Hall visited the Netherlands with Sir Edmund Bacon, Lady Drury's brother, and, at some considerable risk to himself and his party, availed himself of the opportunity to enter into theological discussion with members of the Jesuit order including Father William Baldwin, vice-prefect of the English mission at Brussels. That same year there appeared his first collection of *Meditations and Vowes, Divine and Morall* which, together with the highly influential *Arte of Divine Meditation* (1606), served to introduce continental contemplative methods to an English protestant readership and strongly influenced the development of English religious verse. These publications were complemented by the *Contemplations on Principall Passages of the Holy Storie* (1612–34) which appeared in successive instalments in the various collected editions of Hall's works. While the *Contemplations* are largely devotional in nature, Hall exploited perceived biblical parallels to comment upon contemporary political situations and, in particular, to express his opposition to the proposed Spanish match.

**Controversialist and courtier, 1607–1627** In 1607, following a dispute with Sir Robert Drury over his stipend in which he complained that he was 'forced to write books to buy books' ('Observations', 24), Hall left Hawstead and accepted the donative of Waltham Holy Cross in Essex from Lady Denny, the wife of Sir Edward Denny, later earl of Norwich. About the same time he was also appointed chaplain to the court of Prince Henry and continued to serve in that capacity until the prince's death in 1612, preaching the farewell sermon on the dissolution of the royal household on new year's day 1613. As the publication of his *Epistles* (1608–11) bears witness, Hall's introduction to court life greatly widened the circle of his acquaintance and brought him to the attention of James I whose accession he had celebrated with *The King's Prophecie, or, Weeping Joy* (1603). He was accordingly invited to deliver his first sermon at Paul's Cross, 'Pharisaisme and Christianity', in 1608 and thereafter emerged as one of the most noted, and imitated, preachers of the century. His forty-six extant sermons cover the entire duration of his public career from 1608 until his retirement but represent only a small fraction of his homiletic canon.

Hall proceeded DD in 1610, two years later, at the instigation of his cousin Samuel Burton, archdeacon of Gloucester, and became a prebend of the collegiate church of Wolverhampton in order to conduct the legal battle for the recovery of its income from Sir Walter Leveson, who held its estates in perpetual fee-farm. After a lengthy period of litigation, and the discovery of manifest fraud on the opposing side, the suit ended in victory, but Hall immediately resigned his prebend in favour of a minister 'who should constantly reside there' ('Observations', 31). In 1616 he was sent to France to accompany the embassy of Viscount Doncaster, later earl of Carlisle, but was 'surprised with a miserable distemper of body, which ended in a *Diarrhoea Biliosa*, not without some beginnings and further threats of a Dysentery' (ibid.). He made his way home with great difficulty and found he had been appointed dean of Worcester in his absence.

Despite his continuing indisposition, Hall was ordered to accompany the king to Scotland in 1617 in an attempt to impose prelacy on the kirk. The unusually warm welcome that he received in Edinburgh bred suspicion among other members of the English delegation (including William Laud, who had travelled north as chaplain to Bishop Richard Neile), and he judged it wise to request permission to leave. Upon the king's return he was summoned to court to account for his allegedly 'over plausible Demeanure and doctrine to that already prejudicate people', and by way of satisfaction wrote a defence of the five articles of Perth ('Observations', 34). In 1618 he was chosen as one of the English delegates to the Synod of Dort at which, despite renewed attacks of serious illness, he delivered a Latin sermon. He was eventually forced to retire to The Hague in order to receive medical attention in the house of the English ambassador, Dudley Carleton. Upon his departure from the Netherlands he was awarded the 'rich Medall of Gold' displaying 'the portraicture of the Synod' which is now held at Emmanuel College, Cambridge. Choosing to remain at Waltham, he refused the bishopric of Gloucester in 1624, but was consecrated bishop of Exeter on 23 December 1627.

**Bishop of Exeter** During his years at Waltham, Hall had frequently engaged in religious controversy, attacking Roman Catholicism in *The Peace of Rome* (1609) and the Brownist sect in *A Common Apology of the Church of England* (1610). He also upheld clerical marriage against the objections of the Jesuit Edward Coffin in *The Honor of the Married Clergy* (1620). His *Via media* (1626) represents an attempt to arbitrate in the mounting dispute between Calvinists and Arminians occasioned by the writings of Richard Mountague. By representing the Anglican church as an ideal mean between the extremes of radical nonconformity and Roman Catholicism, he sought to formulate a compromise position which might accommodate both factions. In the event, however, the work fell victim to official censorship and was suppressed until after his death. Even less well received was *The Olde Religion* (1628) which offended radical protestant opinion by asserting that the Church of Rome remained 'a true visible Church' despite its perceived corruption (p. 7). Hall suspected that his elevation to the see of Exeter had given rise to fears that 'preferment had changed my note, and taught mee to speake more plausible language concerning the Roman Church, then I either did, or ought' (*Olde Religion*, 3rd edn, 1630, 189–90). He was forced to issue an apology entitled *The Reconciler* (1629) with supporting testimonies from Thomas Morton, John Davenant, Gilbert Primrose, and John Prideaux, and to append an 'advertisement' to the second edition of *The Olde Religion* (1628) in which he maintained that Rome was 'a true visible Church, in respect of outward profession of Christianity' but 'an heriticall, Apostaticall, Anti-christian Synagogue in respect of doctrine and practice'. At this moment of crisis Hugh Cholmley, now Hall's chaplain, came to his aid with *The State of the now-Romane Church* (1629), recalling 'the old innocent familiarity, which almost from the cradle hath beene betweene us' (sig. A5r). Further support was provided by Robert Butterfield in *Maschil: a Treatise … Touching the State of the Church of Rome* (1629). For those who remained sceptical, Hall reasserted his anti-papal credentials in *An Answer to Pope Urban his Inurbanitie* (1629), an open letter to Urban VIII. So far as inter-protestant controversy was concerned, Hall recommended tolerance in matters indifferent and anticipated some aspects of the latitudinarian movement in recognizing an allowable 'latitude' of doctrinal diversity within the church (*Pax terris*, 1648, 28; *Susurrium cum Deo*, 1651, 61). He frequently urged protestant controversialists to unite in opposition to Rome as the common enemy, and supported English intervention in the Palatinate on anti-Catholic grounds.

While bishop of Exeter, Hall claimed to have 'not one Minister professedly opposite to the anciently received orders (for I was never guilty of urging any new Impositions) of the Church in that large Diocess' ('Observations', 42). The claim was somewhat disingenuous in that it related solely to matters of church government rather than to doctrine. Hall defined 'puritanisme' in purely formal terms as 'a refractory opposition to the ceremonies, rites and customes of the church' and rejected the suggestion that its more 'subtile' practitioners hid their 'unquiet and pestilent humours' under 'the colour of a full outward conformity'. Outward conformity was all that Hall required. 'I have no dore nor window into mens hearts', he asserted, 'these I must leave to theyr maker' (Fincham and Lake, 880). Such attitudes, not surprisingly, rendered him highly suspect to the Laudian party. 'Some that sate at the sterne of the Church', he asserts, 'had me in great Jelousie for too much favour to Puritanisme' ('Observations', 41). Complaints of his 'too much Indulgence to persons disaffected' (McCabe, 16–17) were common, spies were sent into the diocese, and he was openly threatened by the lawyer Richard Kilvert, Laud's principal agent in the downfall of Archbishop John Williams. 'The billowes went so high', he records:

> that I was three severall times upon my knee to his Majesty, to answer these great Criminations … under how dark a Cloud I was hereupon, I was so sensible, that I plainly told the Lord Archbishop of Canterbury, that rather then I would be obnoxious to those slanderous tongues of his misinformers, I would cast up my rochet.
> ('Observations', 42)

Hall's use of personal patronage during his time as bishop of Exeter often led to charges of nepotism, and with some justification. His eldest son, Robert (1605–1667), became canon of Exeter (1629) and archdeacon of Cornwall (1633); his second son, Joseph (1607–1669), acted as cathedral registrar; his third son, George *Hall (*bap.* 1613, *d.* 1668), the future bishop of Chester, gained a prebend at Exeter in 1639 and two years later succeeded his brother as archdeacon of Cornwall; and his fourth son, Samuel (1616–1674), served for a time as subdean.

**Defender of the church** In 1639, following the repudiation of the episcopal system by George Graham, former bishop of Orkney, Hall suggested the calling of a general synod to discuss the deepening crisis, but was prevailed upon by Laud to undertake a defence of episcopacy with the proviso that the archbishop himself should approve the text before publication. Their subsequent correspondence indicates their fundamental difference in outlook. Hall was disposed to take a conciliatory line and admits to 'some mitigation in stating the cause, which I confess to have purposely used out of a desire to hold as good terms with our neighbour churches abroad as I safely might' (*Works*, 10.541). He was far less eager than Laud to insist that episcopacy constituted a separate 'order' rather than merely a distinct 'degree' of the priesthood, and agreed to the amendment with reluctance. When finally published in 1641, with considerable alterations by Laud and Matthew Wren, *Episcopacie by Divine Right* occasioned a storm of protest and severely damaged Hall's reputation among anti-Arminians. The theological 'moderation' by which he set such store was now increasingly perceived as political trimming, and he was widely seen to have betrayed the cause he was formerly accused of covertly supporting.

In 1640, following the imposition of the so-called 'et cetera oath' by convocation—an oath which he accepted in principle but refused 'to tender to any one Minister of my Diocess' ('Observations', 43)—Hall defended the church in the House of Lords and publicly in *An Humble Remonstrance to the High Court of Parliament* (1640). The latter evoked an immediate reply from five puritan ministers (Stephen Marshall, Edmund Calamy, Thomas Young, Matthew Newcomen, and William Spurstowe) writing under the collective pseudonym of 'Smectymnuus', composed of their initials. Exploiting Hall's ambivalent ecclesiastical stance, and his strained relationship with Laud, they identified him as one of those who had 'been labouring these twelve yeeres to get off the name of Puritan, and yet it will not doe, and because of this have been printed *Tantum non in Episcopatu Puritani* ["Puritans in all but episcopacy"]' (*A Vindication of the Answer to the Humble Remonstrance*, 1641, 204). Hall's *Defence of the Humble Remonstrance* (1641) attracted the attention of John Milton who viciously attacked both his beliefs and his character in his *Animadversions upon the Remonstrants Defence Against Smectymnuus* (1641). Following the publication of an anonymous, and equally scurrilous, reply, Milton returned to the attack in *An Apology Against a Pamphlet Call'd a Modest Confutation of a Sclanderous and Scurrilous Libell, Entituled 'Animadversions upon the Remonstrants Defense Against Smectymnuus'* (1642) which contains the most savage condemnation of Hall's life and works ever to appear in print.

A graphic account of subsequent events is provided in Hall's second autobiographical tract, *Bishop Hall's Hard Measure* (1647). As the political situation worsened, Hall agreed to sit on the Lords' committee on religion (March 1641) but strongly protested on 1 May against the attempt to deprive the bishops of their representation in parliament. Preliminary articles of impeachment were drawn up against him and twelve other bishops in July, but he was nevertheless translated to the see of Norwich in November in succession to Richard Mountague, in an attempt to pacify mounting opposition by displaying

Laud's willingness to promote non-Arminians. Intimidated by the London mob from attending the winter session of parliament—he recalls hearing the crowd crying out 'No Bishops, No Bishops' from his lodgings ('Hard measure', 47)—Hall joined the archbishop of York in drafting a petition to the king requesting:

> that since we were legally call'd by his Majesties writ to give our Attendance in Parliament, we might be secured in the performance of our Duty and Service against those Dangers that threatned us; and withall to protest against any such Acts as should be made during the time of our forced Absence. (ibid., 48)

A draft copy of the petition was sent prematurely from the Lords to the Commons, where it was widely regarded as treasonable, 'some comparing, yea, preferring it to the Powder-plot' (ibid., 49). Together with a number of other signatories, Hall was committed to the Tower where he remained, apart from one brief period of bail, from early January 1642 until the following May. While incarcerated he issued a strong defence of his position in *A Letter Lately Sent by a Reverend Bishop from the Tower to a Private Friend* (1642). As the charge of high treason proved increasingly difficult to sustain, the prisoners were eventually judged guilty of a *praemunire* and had their estates confiscated, although a sum of £400 per annum was awarded for their maintenance.

**Bishop of Norwich and final years** Upon his release from the Tower, Hall proceeded to Norwich where, initially at least, he received a surprisingly friendly reception. However, under the terms of the Act for the Sequestration of the Property of Malignants (April 1643), in which he was mentioned by name, the revenues from all of his properties were confiscated, and the annual allowance agreed by parliament was withheld. The sequestrators were merciless in their rigour 'not leaving so much as a dozen Trenchers, or my Children's pictures out of their curious Inventory' ('Hard measure', 57). Even Hall's personal library was distrained, but was secured for his use by loyal members of his congregation. His wife was compelled to appeal for the payment of the 'fifth' portion of the sequestered income commonly allowed to the dependants of 'malignants', but the assessment of the episcopal revenues was made in such a confused manner that the relevant sum proved impossible to calculate. In the meantime both the cathedral and the bishop's private chapel were besieged by iconoclasts. On being informed that the windows were 'full of images, which were very offensive' he replied that 'they were the Pictures of some antient and worthy bishops, as St. *Ambrose*, St *Austin*, &c'. 'It was answered me', he records, 'that they were so many popes'. In an attempt to save as much of the stained glass as possible, he ordered the heads to be removed 'since I knew the bodies could not offend' (ibid., 62). But worse was to come:

> in a kind of Sacrilegious and profane procession, all the Organ pipes, Vestments, both Copes and Surplices, together with the leaden crosse, which had been newly sawne down from over the Green-Yard Pulpit, and the Service books and singing books that could be had, were carried to the fire in the publick Market place; a leud wretch walking before the Train, in his Cope trailing in the dirt, with a Service book in his hand imitating in an impious scorne the tune, and usurping the words of the Letany used formerly in the Church. (ibid., 63)

Hall was finally driven out of the bishop's palace about 1647 at the insistence of the future regicide Miles Corbett, and eventually took a house in the village of Higham where he continued to perform his clerical duties, and even to ordain candidates for the Anglican ministry, among the most prominent being Simon Patrick, later bishop of Ely. During his final years Hall suffered greatly from ill health, particularly strangury, but enjoyed the care of his personal physician, the essayist Sir Thomas Browne, as is evident from the latter's works. Hall was prolific in his retirement, producing a series of highly popular contemplative and devotional tracts, among the most important of which were *Resolutions and Decisions of Divers Practicall Cases of Conscience* (1649), a popular casuistical handbook, *The Revelation Unrevealed* (1649), directed against the millenarian prophecies of John Archer, and the informative soteriological treatise *The Invisible World* (1652). Despite the suspicion in which he was held by the authorities, his devotional works continued to be licensed for the press and were often published with a personal recommendation from the licenser, John Downame.

Hall survived his wife by four years and died at Higham on 8 September 1656. In his will, dated from 21 July 1654 to 7 September 1656, he indicated that he did not wish to be buried within a church, for 'I do not hould Gods house a meete Repositorie for the Dead Body of the Greatest Saints' (PRO, PROB 11/258, fols. 160–62). He bequeathed land in Devon, Essex, and elsewhere to his sons, and the gold medal given to him by the states of the Netherlands to mark his participation in the Synod of Dort to his eldest grandson, as yet unborn. His youngest son and executor, Samuel, received the trunk containing his sermons, tracts, and letters to foreign divines. Hall was buried at Higham. In the funeral sermon, *Israel Agchithanes: Death's Alarum*, John Whitefoote, rector of Higham, captured the essence of Hall's ambiguous ecclesiastical reputation when he asserted that 'all men honoured the *Doctor*, though some loved not the *Bishop*' (p. 66). Hall's reputation remained high for two centuries after his death. His satires were admired by Alexander Pope, and he was among the favourite authors of Laurence Sterne. Three editions of his *Complete Works* were issued during the nineteenth century and he was the subject of a novel by Emma Marshall, *Winifrede's Journal of her Life at Exeter and Norwich in the Days of Bishop Hall* (1892). RICHARD A. MCCABE

**Sources** J. Hall, 'Observations of some specialities of divine providence in the life of Joseph Hall', *The shaking of the olive-tree: the remaining works of the incomparable prelate Joseph Hall* (1660) · J. Hall, 'Bishop Hall's hard measure', *The shaking of the olive-tree: the remaining works of the incomparable prelate Joseph Hall* (1660) · Fuller, *Worthies* · *The works of the Right Reverend Joseph Hall*, ed. P. Wynter, 10 vols. (1863) · R. A. McCabe, *Joseph Hall: a study in satire and meditation* (1982) · G. Lewis, *A life of Joseph Hall* (1886) · J. M. Wands, 'The early printing history of Joseph Hall's *Mundus alter et idem*', *Publications of the Bibliographical Society of America*, 74 (1980), 1–12 · C. Cross, *The puritan earl: the life of Henry Hastings, third earl of Huntingdon* (1966) · F. S. Teager, 'Patronage of Joseph Hall and John Donne', *Philological Quarterly*, 15 (1936), 408–13 · T. F. Kinloch, *The life and works of Joseph*

*Hall* (1951) · *Complete prose works of John Milton*, ed. D. Wolfe, 8 vols. in 10 (1953–82) · *The works of the most reverend father in God, William Laud*, ed. J. Bliss and W. Scott, 7 vols. (1847–60) · K. Fincham and P. Lake, 'Popularity, prelacy and puritanism in the 1630s: Joseph Hall explains himself', *EngHR*, 111 (1996), 856–81 · P. Lake, 'The moderate and ironic case for religious war: Joseph Hall's *Via media* in context', *Political culture and cultural politics in early modern England*, ed. S. P. Amussen and M. Kishlansky (1995), 55–83 · will, PRO, PROB 11/258, fols. 160–62 · J. Whitefoote, *Israel Agchithanes: Death's alarum, or, The presage of approaching death* (1656)

**Archives** Folger, commonplace book · Harvard U., Houghton L., 'Henochisme' | Hatfield House, Hertfordshire, Hatfield MSS

**Likenesses** J. Payne, engraving, 1628, NPG [*see illus.*] · mezzotint, pubd 1825 (after unknown artist), NPG · W. Faithorne, line engraving, BM, NPG; repro. in J. Whitefoote, *Israel Agchithanes: Death's alarum, or, The presage of approaching death* (1656) · W. Marshall, line engraving, BM, NPG; repro. in J. Hall, *Resolutions and decisions of divers practicall cases of conscience*, 2nd edn (1650) · P. D. Zetter, line engraving, BM, NPG; repro. in J. J. Boissard, *Bibliotheca chalcographica* (Frankfurt, 1650) · engraving, repro. in J. Hall, *Susurrium cum Deo*, 2nd edn (1651) · oils, Emmanuel College, Cambridge

**Wealth at death** property sequestered in 1643: will, PRO, PROB 11/258, fols. 160–62

**Hall, Marguerite Antonia Radclyffe-** [*pseud.* Radclyffe Hall] (**1880–1943**), novelist, was born on 12 August 1880 at Sunny Lawn, West Cliff, Bournemouth, the second child of Radclyffe (Rat) Radclyffe-Hall (1846–1898) and Mary Jane Sager, *née* Diehl (1854–1945), an American widow from Philadelphia. By her own account, Radclyffe Hall's childhood was not a happy one. Her elder sister Florence's death in infancy left her an only child and her parents divorced acrimoniously when she was three. She rarely saw her father thereafter and was unloved by her volatile mother, who remarried in 1890. Her mother's third husband was Alberto Visetti (*d.* 1928), a professor of singing at the Royal College of Music. Despite showing a precocious musical talent, she received scant encouragement from her stepfather (though he did, it seems, make sexual advances towards her). Her education was fitful and she remained a chronic bad speller all her life. Governesses and fashionable day schools were followed by a brief stint at King's College, London (there is no record of any degree), then a year in Dresden. At twenty-one she inherited a considerable legacy left in trust by her grandfather Charles Radclyffe-Hall (*d.* 1879), who had made a fortune treating tuberculosis patients in Torquay, Devon.

Without the need to earn a living, Radclyffe Hall was well into her forties before she took up writing seriously. She claimed to be a 'congenital invert' and is best known today for her novel *The Well of Loneliness*, a serious if sentimental treatment of lesbianism which was the occasion of great controversy when it was published in 1928. Home Office papers released on 27 November 1997 reveal the furore into which Whitehall was thrown over the possible general release of the novel. The work was described to Jonathan Cape by a government official as 'inherently obscene … it supports a depraved practice [and] is gravely detrimental to the public interest' (*The Guardian*, 28 Nov 1997, 8). Cape felt it prudent to withdraw the novel, and it was subsequently banned in England, with proofs intended for a publisher in France seized in October 1928. This led to the order of the chief magistrate, Sir Chartres Biron, that all copies be destroyed, and that literary merit presented no grounds for defence. Despite protests from literary figures such as Virginia Woolf, Leonard Woolf, and John Buchan, Biron's judgement was upheld by a Court of Appeal.

*The Well of Loneliness* was, in fact, the fifth of seven novels written by Radclyffe Hall, the others being *The Forge* (1924), *The Unlit Lamp* (1924), *A Saturday Life* (1925), *Adam's Breed* (1926), *The Master of the House* (1932), and *The Sixth Beatitude* (1936). A volume of short stories, *Miss Ogilvie Finds Herself*, was published in 1934. All these works, traditionalist in style but exhibiting an impressive psychological grasp, reflect in varying degrees her deep sense of being a social outsider and, increasingly, demonstrate her preoccupation with a search for spiritual self-knowledge through suffering and denial. *Adam's Breed*, a best-seller which also won two prestigious literary prizes, the Femina Vie Heureuse and James Tait Black (only E. M. Forster's *A Passage to India* had previously achieved this 'double'), marked the peak of her career. Some of her best writing has a descriptive power which owed much to her early experiments with lyric poetry. Between 1906 and 1915 five slim volumes of her poems were published, many being set to music by popular composers of the day. The best-known was 'The Blind Ploughman'.

Despite a modern resurgence of interest in Radclyffe Hall, she does not fit easily into the stereotype of the gay or feminist pioneer. A staunch Roman Catholic after her conversion in 1912, her instincts, political and temperamental, remained deeply conservative. (By the late 1930s, indeed, she was expressing protofascist and antisemitic views.) Believing herself a man trapped in a woman's body, she liked to be called John, assumed a male pseudonym (her father's name, significantly), and cultivated a strikingly masculine appearance, sporting cropped hair, monocles, bow-ties, smoking jackets, and pipes. A woman's best place, she proclaimed, was in the home.

And yet Radclyffe Hall's campaigning stand on behalf of homosexuals was undeniably courageous. Moreover, her most important relationships were with notably independent-minded women. Her first partner, Mabel Veronica Batten (*c*.1856–1916), a well-known lieder singer and society beauty, exercised an educating influence, introducing the future novelist to a highly sophisticated coterie of professional women (many of them lesbians), and her first real taste of artistic and intellectual life. After Mabel's death, Hall sought to contact her through a medium and became a lifelong adherent of spiritualism. Una Elena Troubridge (1887–1963), a talented sculptor and translator, and Mabel Batten's cousin, set up house with Hall in 1918, becoming at once 'wife', amanuensis, and soulmate. The couple stayed together for the rest of Hall's life, braving an acrimonious separation from Una's husband (who was an admiral), winning a lawsuit for slander in 1920 (Hall was called 'a grossly immoral woman'), and surviving a tortuous nine-year relationship between Hall and a Russian nurse, Eugenia Souline, in the 1930s.

In her heyday in the 1920s Hall was a conspicuous figure

at writers' gatherings (she was a leading member of PEN and the Writers' Club), at theatrical first nights, and in the society of many well-known authors, actors, and artists. She moved restlessly between a succession of homes in London, Sussex, Paris, and Florence, and mixed with a diverse cosmopolitan circle which included E. F. Benson, Noël Coward, Colette, Gabriele d'Annunzio, Romaine Brooks, and Natalie Barney. The 1930s heralded a progressive decline in both her literary output and her reputation. Plans to live permanently in Italy were forestalled by the onset of another world war. Ill health dogged her last years and she died of cancer of the colon on 7 October 1943 at her London flat, 502 Hood House, Dolphin Square, Pimlico. She was buried in Highgate cemetery, Middlesex. *The Well of Loneliness* was finally republished without a stir in 1949. In 1974 the BBC broadcast it on the radio on *Book at Bedtime*. MICHAEL BAKER

**Sources** M. Baker, *Our three selves: a life of Radclyffe Hall* (1985) · U. Troubridge, *The life and death of Radclyffe Hall* (1961) · C. Stillman Franks, *Beyond the well of loneliness* (1982) · S. Cline, *Radclyffe Hall: a woman called John* (1997) · L. Dickson, *Radclyffe Hall at the well of loneliness: a sapphic chronicle* (1975) · R. Ormrod, *Una Troubridge: the friend of Radclyffe Hall* (1984) · b. cert. · d. cert.

**Archives** LUL, letters · Ransom HRC · Richmond Local Studies Library, London, corresp. · Society for Psychical Research, London | A. M. Heath & Co., London [literary agents] · NA Canada, Lovat Dickson collection · priv. coll., Audrie Atcheson MSS · priv. coll., Cara Lancaster collection · priv. coll., Ariadne Nicolaeff MSS · priv. coll., Alessandro Rossi-Lemeni collection · Ransom HRC, Morris Ernst collection · U. Birm., letters to Evgeniya Soulina · UCL, letters to Arnold Bennett

**Likenesses** K. Amyat, oils, 1885, priv. coll. · C. Buchel, oils, 1918, NPG · photographs, 1920–33, Hult. Arch. · photographs, 1923–33, Hult. Arch. · Pax, cartoon, 1927, repro. in *The Popular Pictorial* [British Library] · B. Egan, brush and ink cartoon, 1928, priv. coll. · H. Coster, photographs, 1930–39, NPG · A. Atcheson, photographs, 1934, priv. coll. · G. Hines, portrait, 1937, Michael Parkin Gallery, London · cartoon, repro. in *T.P.'s Weekly* (20 Feb 1926) · photographs, Ransom HRC

**Wealth at death** £118,015 19s. od.: probate, 19 Nov 1943, *CGPLA Eng. & Wales*

**Hall, Marie Pauline** (1884–1956), violinist, was born on 8 April 1884 at 15 Victoria Street, Newcastle upon Tyne, the daughter of Edward Felix Handley Hall and his wife, Helen Parsons. She was born into a musical family. Her father was a harpist in the Carl Rosa Opera Orchestra and hoped that she would learn that instrument. He first taught her but she wanted to learn the violin, so from an early age had lessons from a local teacher, Hildegarde Werner, and soon became a very good player. Together with her father, her uncle and brother (violins), and sister (harp) she played in the homes of music lovers in her home town, Malvern, and also in Bristol. Émile Sauret heard her play when she was aged nine, but her parents did not follow up his advice to send her to the Royal Academy of Music in London. She continued her studies locally, and over the next few years was under various well-known teachers.

Elgar had heard her and gave her some lessons at Malvern in the summer of 1894, and he sent her to A. E. D. F. Wilhelmj in London where she studied under him for three months in 1896, and in 1898 she studied under Max Mossel at the Midland Institute in Birmingham. In 1899 she won a scholarship to the Royal Academy of Music against forty competitors but the poor financial state of her family prevented her from taking it up. However, the music scholar Edmund Fellowes was a great help to her: he took some friends to hear her play at a concert which had been arranged at All Saints Hall and they were so impressed that they began a campaign to raise funds to enable her to receive a good training. In 1900 Johann Kruse gave her free lessons in London. Also she was helped by the wealthy English music patron and amateur composer P. Napier Miles. Then in 1901 she played for Jan Kubelík and he advised her to study under his old teacher Otakar Ševčík at the Prague Conservatory. She went there in September. Ševčík thought her very talented and she made excellent progress. Her professional début was made at a concert in Prague in 1902 and was an immediate success, as was her performance in Vienna in January 1903. Her studies under Ševčík ended in 1903 and she began touring with great success.

Edmund Fellowes, when comparing Hall with other violinists in his memoirs, cited tributes from *The Times* and other papers. One reviewer commented that

> Miss Hall is the only female violinist who has essayed the Paganini Concerto in D in public. This she played with a technical skill so consummate that it seemed as if it were just as easy to play octaves on the violin as on the piano. (Fellowes, 80)

According to another, 'If Kubelík has not been actually out-Kubelíked, he must look to it on pain of being outshone by Miss Marie Hall as a virtuoso, while her musical temperament and equipment are far more sympathetic and responsive than his' (ibid.). It was observed that 'Her technique is flawless, but besides this she has at her command a fund of real musical feeling which she exhibited in Beethoven's Kreutzer Sonata and especially in Bach's Chaconne' (ibid.). In 1903 she played the Tchaikovsky violin concerto and Wieniawski's 'Faust' fantasia under Henry Wood with the Queen's Hall Orchestra: a critic observed that 'This wonderful girl gave a performance of Wieniawski's "Faust" Fantasia that was notable for brilliant execution, fire, and decision. She was recalled nine times after this exploit amid a scene of enthusiasm rarely witnessed in a concert-room' (ibid.). There was a remarkable occasion on 22 January 1904 at St James's Hall when she performed the Mendelssohn, Beethoven, and Tchaikovsky violin concertos in succession with the Queen's Hall Orchestra under Henry Wood. Marie Hall toured all over the world with enormous success, and made her début in America on 8 November 1905 with the New York Symphony Orchestra under Walter Damrosch. She was in Australia in 1907 and India in 1913. She appeared with the Queen's Hall Orchestra again on 1 January 1909, when she performed the Tchaikovsky concerto.

On 27 January 1911 Marie Hall married her manager, Edward Baring. They settled in Cheltenham and had a daughter. After her marriage, although she cut down on her appearances, she also introduced new violin works, including *The Lark Ascending* by Vaughan Williams (composed for and dedicated to her in 1914), which she premièred in London on 14 June 1921 with the British Symphony Orchestra under Adrian Boult. Other new music she performed was by Rutland Boughton, Gordon Bryan, and Percy Sherwood. Her appearances continued until 1955 with her daughter, Pauline, as accompanist. She played on a 1709 Stradivarius which was named after her.

Regarded as one of the finest violinists of her time, Marie Hall had a beautiful tone and fine musicianship. Sir Henry Wood wrote that 'In my mind's eye I can still see that frail, delicate girl coming on to the platform and can hear her faultless intonation and pure technique' (Wood, 204). She made many recordings on the HMV and Gramophone and Typewriter labels. These included a shortened version of the Elgar violin concerto in 1916, N. Paganini's *Moto perpetuo*, J. J. Raff's *Cavatina*, Sarasate's *Jota aragonesa*, op. 27, and C. Sinding's romance no. 1, op. 79. She died on 11 November 1956 at the General Hospital, Cheltenham.

JEAN M. HAIG-WHITELEY

**Sources** Grove, *Dict. mus.* (1954); suppl. (1961), 200 · E. H. Fellowes, *Memoirs of an amateur musician* (1946) · H. Wood, *My life of music* (1938) · J. Creighton, *Discopaedia of the violin* (Toronto, 1974) · *Baker's biographical dictionary of musicians*, rev. N. Slonimsky, 7th edn (1984) · *New Grove*, vol. 8 · *CGPLA Eng. & Wales* (1957)
**Archives** BL, music collections, letters to Mrs R. Jacomb-Hood and family, Add. MS 58439
**Likenesses** photograph, repro. in A. Bachmann, *An encyclopedia of the violin* (1966), 363, no. 5 on pl. 67
**Wealth at death** £18,952 13*s*. 10*d*.: probate, 3 Jan 1957, *CGPLA Eng. & Wales*

**Hall, Marshall** (1790–1857), physician and neurophysiologist, was born at Basford, near Nottingham, on 18 February 1790, the fourth son and sixth of eight children of Robert *Hall (1754–1827), a cotton manufacturer and bleacher, and his wife, Ann. His eldest brother, Samuel *Hall, was a prolific inventor. Their father, Robert Hall, had a knowledgeable interest in chemistry and its application to his own industrial concerns, and was also one of the first to use chlorine for bleaching on a large scale; he received a prize from the Society of Arts for the invention of a new crane. He was a Wesleyan and it was said that during the Luddite disturbances he received assurance that no harm would come to him. His wife outlived him to be eighty-four years old.

Marshall Hall was stockily built and below medium height, due, his mother thought, to a childhood illness. He attended the academy of the Revd J. Blanchard in Nottingham where his curriculum included French, but not Latin, in which he was later self-taught. He left school at fourteen and after a year's private study was placed with a successful chemist at Newark, probably with a view to becoming an apothecary. But Hall was ambitious and liked neither his position nor his prospects. Having worked hard at Latin he entered as a medical student the University of Edinburgh in October 1809, determined to become a physician and, if possible, chief physician to the monarch.

Hall was an extremely diligent student, spending many hours in the dissection room and on reading but few on social activities, which he regarded as a waste of time. However, he did come to love wine and fast horse-riding. Hall was elected senior president of the student Royal Medical Society of Edinburgh for the session 1811–12, the year of his graduation, and the year in which he was appointed physician's clerk—resident house physician—to Andrew Duncan and Thomas Spens in the Edinburgh Royal Infirmary. During his clerkship Hall gave an informal course of lectures on diagnosis—the identification of diseases—based on careful observation of symptoms made at the bedside in the infirmary. These lectures formed the basis of *On Diagnosis* (1817), in which Hall, addressing young physicians, presented his nosology of diseases. As a student, he also published in the *Journal of Natural Philosophy, Chemistry and the Arts*, and in 1818 was elected a fellow of the Royal Society of Edinburgh.

Hall resigned his clerkship and left Edinburgh prematurely in 1814, probably fearing that the competition for posts there was too great. He travelled on the continent visiting a number of medical schools. According to his wife's sometimes unreliable record, Hall walked alone over the 600 miles from Paris to Göttingen. Hall returned to England in November 1816 and although he had contemplated practising in the thriving city of Bristol, he spent six months in Bridgewater before moving to Nottingham, where he established himself in the fashionable High Pavement area. Here, despite the competition, he built up a good practice and in 1825 was elected physician (unpaid) to the Nottingham General Hospital. However, Hall left hurriedly the following year, perhaps hoping to join former Edinburgh contemporaries, such as Robert Grant, who were to obtain posts in the University of London, soon to be called University College, London, established in 1828. In London, Hall lived first at 15 Keppel Street, Russell Square, with his friend William Burnside, partner of Robert Benton Seeley, the publisher. On 11 November 1829 Hall married Charlotte (1800/01–1884), daughter of Valentine Green, a Leicestershire landowner, and in September 1830 the couple moved to 14 Manchester Square, where they lived for twenty years and where their only son, also named Marshall, was born in 1831. Hall jun. eventually became a barrister, but was more interested in geology and marine biology than the law. Hall's family took up their last London abode in 1850 at 38 Grosvenor Street, which they left on Hall's retirement in 1852. There followed a part professional, part social fifteen-month tour of the United States, Canada, and Cuba. Hall loved travelling and throughout most of his career spent up to two months annually on the continent, especially in France, where he included M. S. P. Flourens and P. C. A. Louis among his long-standing friends.

Hall showed great skill in dissection and as an experimenter. His wife maintained a veritable menagerie of animals in one room of their house, for his experimental work. Much of this was carried out at night after a light supper, although no doubt Hall maintained his stocky form with snacks always available at a side table. His experiments were written up late at night or while he was in his carriage travelling to appointments. Hall was the object of attacks by anti-vivisectionists. Many of these attacks came from fellow professionals who feared the impact on the supremacy of anatomy in medical education and practice of Hall's drive to promote experimental medicine, that is, physiology.

During his time in Nottingham and his early years in London, Hall's publications included articles and books on chemistry and disorders in women and children. These include an unattributed work on child-rearing, *Eupaedia, or, Letters to a Mother on the Watchful Care of her Infant* ([1831]), and two on diseases affecting women at different stages in their life cycle: *On the Mimoses* (1818) and *Commentaries on some of the More Important of the Diseases of Females, in Three Parts* (1827), which contains attractive portraits by H. Adlard showing selected symptoms of female diseases. During this period, and with the aim of gaining a fellowship of the Royal Society, Hall also turned his attention to the circulatory system and questioned the current widespread therapeutic use of bloodletting. His experimental investigations led to his proposals for distinguishing between inflammation, where bloodletting was appropriate, and bowel irritation or exhaustion, where it was not, and to rational rules for using bloodletting as a therapy, contained in *Researches Principally Relative to the Morbid and Curative Effects of Loss of Blood* (1830). Between 1831 and 1847 Hall submitted seven papers to the Royal Society detailing his investigations. The four submitted in 1831 and 1832 dealt with the capillary system, the effect of temperature on metabolism in amphibia, and the relationship between respiration and irritability and its application to hibernation. Only the two on respiration and hibernation were published in *Philosophical Transactions*, and were followed by Hall's election to a fellowship of the Royal Society on 5 April 1832. For his first paper, 'On the anatomy and physiology of the minute and capillary vessels' (RS archives, 1831, AP.15, 32, 6), Hall, who was dissatisfied with the standard of microscopes available, had used a Dolland achromatic microscope. He examined a range of lung, mesentery, and skin tissue to investigate two key contemporary concepts concerning whether or not capillaries were true vessels—he believed they were—and whether or not they were contractile—he believed they were not. He was correct in both cases. Hall's rejected papers were published as *A Critical and Experimental Essay on the Circulation of the Blood* (1831). In the introduction to the book, Hall proposed a code of ethics for carrying out research using live animals. He also called for the establishment of a physiological institute which was realized only in 1876, when the Physiological Society was founded.

The year of Hall's Royal Society fellowship also saw his first pronouncements, at the Zoological Society on 25 November 1832, on what he regarded as the area of his major contributions to science, namely the nervous system and in particular the concept of reflex action. In 1833, 1837, and 1847, Hall submitted three substantial memoirs on the nervous system to the Royal Society. Only the first, 'On the reflex function of the medulla oblongata and spinalis' (*Philosophical Transactions*, 123, 2, 1833, 635–65), was published. During an investigation of newt lung tissue in a decapitated animal, Hall had noticed that touching the skin provoked muscular movements in the limbs. This observation set in train a series of experiments on stimulation of the skin of a range of animals decapitated or even cut across the spinal cord into four sections, including an isolated tail. Hall found that, provided a portion of the spinal cord remained intact, isolated sections of the body were capable of responding to stimulation. Hall discovered that though this observation had been made by others, none had attempted to explain the phenomenon or to unite a disparate collection of movements in animals as reflex actions. He came to postulate both a special principle or property, and special anatomical tracts, within the nervous system which were responsible for reflex action, and formed what he called the excito-motory system. These notions were later rejected. But Hall's work, in which for a time Hall regarded Johannes Müller as a rival, contributed substantially to the mechanistic explanation of reflex action. It also provoked lively discussion on the notion of a spinal soul to explain what appeared to be purposive responses in decapitated creatures, and provided a foundation for the work of Hall's intellectual successor in the field, Sir Charles Sherrington. Hall was quick to react to criticism and his work involved him in a number of controversies. The most significant of these was the unjust charge against him, of plagiarizing his ideas on reflex action from the Czech G. Prochaska.

Following the rejection of Hall's 1837 memoir by the Royal Society, which he published along with the memoir of 1833 as *Memoirs on the Nervous System* (1837), Hall in an open letter begged the council to appoint a commission to witness his experiments before dismissing his work completely. Furthermore, if offered funding he volunteered to withdraw from his practice for a while and devote himself entirely to further research on the nervous system. Two years later he even sought the help of the president, Sir John F. W. Herschel, to secure publication of his work in *Philosophical Transactions* (RS, letters between M. Hall and J. F. W. Herschel, 1839–40, HS.9.199.204). This approach was also unsuccessful and Hall resolved to shun the society in future. In 1847 he broke his resolve and submitted another paper, 'Researches into the effects of certain physical and chemical agents on the nervous system' (RS archives, MS M. Hall, 1847, AP.29.5–6). This paper on nerve function detailed Hall's investigations on electrophysiology, a subject for which the physiological committee of the Royal Society lacked appropriate referees. This paper too was rejected.

Once again Hall protested, this time in a privately printed, but open, letter to the president, the earl of Rosse, about the treatment of his paper. There followed Hall's appointments to council in 1850 and as a referee of papers a year later. He never received any of the Royal Society medals, although he had been recommended to council in 1842 for the Copley medal but was unsuccessful.

Hall also initially resented his treatment within the Royal College of Physicians, which he, as an Edinburgh graduate, criticized heavily for offering him only a licentiateship rather than a fellowship. The fellowship was eventually awarded in 1841 and a year later he delivered the Goulstonian lecture, published as *On the Mutual Relations between Anatomy, Physiology, Pathology and Therapeutics and the Practice of Medicine* (1842). He later delivered the Croonian lectures, on the nervous system, in 1850, 1851, and 1852; these were published as *Synopsis of the Spinal System* (1852).

The British Medical Association, founded in 1836, had appointed Hall as one of its earliest vice-presidents. He delivered its 1840 annual oration, entitled 'Medicine, its divisions, its rewards and its reforms'.

Hall had never held a hospital appointment in London, although through his reputation for treating nervous diseases he became visiting physician to the Moorcroft House Asylum near Uxbridge. During the 1830s he undertook a strenuous programme of part-time lecturing in a number of private medical schools, including the Aldersgate Street and Webb Street schools and Sydenham College. In 1839 voice failure—clergyman's throat—interrupted this work, although he was lecturing in St Thomas's Hospital medical school from 1842 to 1846, where he attracted larger classes than a friend and colleague, Thomas Hodgkin (1798–1860), who was relieved of his post. In 1839 Hall had, unsuccessfully, applied for a chair in the Institutes of Medicine, just vacated by John Elliotson, at University College, London. Hall never joined any religious group but he accused the college of religious discrimination against him.

From time to time Hall had criticized what he saw as injustice to the underprivileged. He had warned against the possible injurious effects on health of open railway carriages and had spoken out against flogging, following the death of a soldier flogged for drunkenness at Hounslow barracks in 1846. On his return from the United States, where he had visited Indian reservations, Hall wrote on slavery: *The Two-Fold Slavery of the United States* was published in 1854.

Towards the end of his life, Hall suggested some practical and socially useful applications of his research on reflex action. These included recommendations on resuscitation for cases of drowning and stillbirths, which were taken up by the Royal Humane Society, the forerunner of the Lifeboat Association. He also devised a most sensitive 'strychnoscope', using frog nerve–muscle tissue, for the detection of strychnine in cases of suspected poisoning, and he put forward a proposal, involving development along the River Thames, for dealing jointly with the transport and sewage problems of central London.

Over the years Hall had received honours in many countries and was elected corresponding member of the French Institute in 1855. His books were translated into a number of languages, including German, Dutch, Italian, and French, in which language he himself also published *Aperçu du système spinal* in 1855. During 1857 Hall's earlier throat condition, diagnosed post-mortem as probably cancer, worsened. He worked until the end, and died at 37 King's Road, Brighton, Sussex, on 11 August 1857. He was buried on 19 August 1857 in the general cemetery, Nottingham.

The Medical and Chirurgical Society, which became the Royal Medical Society, devoted a room to Hall's memory and organized the Marshall Hall Fund, set up in 1873. A prize was offered every five years for the best published research on the anatomy, physiology, or pathology of the nervous system recorded in English during the previous half decade. The prizewinners included Hughlings Jackson (1878), David Ferrier (1883), and W. H. Gaskell (1888).

DIANA E. MANUEL

**Sources** D. E. Manuel, *Marshall Hall (1790–1857): science and medicine in early Victorian society* (1996) • D. E. Manuel, 'Marshall Hall (1790–1857): his life and work with special reference to his investigations in neurophysiology', PhD diss., U. Lond., 1979 • [C. Hall], *Memoirs of Marshall Hall* (1861) • *DNB* • J. F. Clarke, *Autobiographical recollections of the medical profession* (1874) • A. B. Granville, *The Royal Society in the XIXth century* (1836) • P. Macleod and P. Collins, eds., *The parliament of science: the British Association for the Advancement of Science, 1831–1981* (1981) • E. M. Little, *History of the British Medical Association, 1832–1932* [1932] • W. F. Bynum, *Science and the practice of medicine in the nineteenth century* (1994) • Munk, *Roll*

**Archives** RS • U. Edin. • UCL

**Likenesses** J. Holl, stipple, 1839 (after J. Z. Bell), Wellcome L. • J. Luntley, pastels, 1856, Wellcome L. • J. Z. Bell, portrait, repro. in T. J. Pettigrew, 'Marshall Hall', *Medical portrait gallery*, 4 (1840), frontispiece • J. Z. Bell, portrait (after Pettigrew), repro. in F. Fearing, *Reflex action* (1930), facing p. 123 • Mayall, daguerreotype, repro. in *The Lancet*, 2 (27 July 1850), 121 • drawing (in youth), repro. in J. Tillotson, *Our untitled nobility* • engraving (after photograph by J. B. Hunt), repro. in Hall, *Memoirs*, frontispiece

**Hall, Michael** (1623/4–*c*.1670). *See under* Hall family (*per. c*.1650–*c*.1750).

**Hall, (Christopher) Newman** (1816–1902), Congregational minister, born at Maidstone on 22 May 1816, was the son of John Vine *Hall (1774–1860), proprietor of the *Maidstone Journal*, and Mary, daughter of James Teverill of Worcester. Educated at Rochester and at Totteridge, he entered his father's printing house at fourteen, working successively as compositor, reader, and reporter. In 1837 he went to Highbury College, Middlesex, to train for the Congregational ministry, and read widely in a variety of subjects—theology, Greek, philosophy, and natural science. In 1840 the charter of London University was extended to Highbury and other colleges. Hall took advantage of this to obtain a degree, graduating BA with first-class honours in 1841. In 1842 he was ordained pastor of Albion Church, Hull. There he gathered a large congregation, was in demand as a preacher, and in 1844 issued his first publication, a sermon entitled *Christian Union*. His tract *Come to Jesus*, issued in 1848, made his name widely known. Over 4 million copies in some forty languages or dialects were circulated during the author's life.

In 1854 Hall became minister of Surrey Chapel, Blackfriars, the scene of Rowland Hill's labours. His success was pronounced. As a mental discipline, he read at London University for the degree of LLB, which, with a law scholarship, he obtained in 1856. During the American Civil War he was conspicuous for his advocacy of the northern cause, and in 1866 he was appointed chairman of the Congregational Union. He was warmly welcomed on visiting

**Christopher Newman Hall** (1816–1902), by Lock & Whitfield, pubd 1877

Canada and the United States in 1867, was made DD of Amherst College, and afterwards declined the offer of a pastorate in Chicago. Hall was the means of bringing W. E. Gladstone, with whom he became well acquainted and exchanged much correspondence, into conference on several occasions in the 1860s with representative nonconformists. This was partly to obtain Gladstone's political advocacy of dissenting claims, and Gladstone showed himself willing to conform with this to a considerable extent. During the controversy attending the Education Act of 1870 Hall sought to effect a reconciliation between W. E. Forster, the minister in charge of the measure, and nonconformist members of the Birmingham Education League, who distrusted Forster's policy. But in this he was unsuccessful, and the educational policy favoured by most dissenters after 1870 was not in line with his own views. Throughout his career Hall sought to promote closer relations between the established church and dissent. He was also relatively tolerant of Roman Catholicism, but was against Irish home rule from 1886, even though this meant opposing Gladstone's policy. In 1876 the congregation of Surrey Chapel moved to Christ Church, Westminster Bridge Road, built, mainly through Hall's exertions and with American contributions, at a cost of £64,000.

Hall was a forceful and fluent preacher, a man of wide sympathies, artistic feeling, and evangelical fervour. For many years his work was done amid circumstances of great trial. He married, on 14 April 1846, Charlotte, daughter of Dr Gordon of Hull. They separated in 1870. Litigation followed. Hall filed and withdrew a petition for divorce in 1873, but was successful in a second suit, which he initiated in 1879, when a counter-charge of adultery against him was withdrawn. Gladstone helped him indirectly to strengthen his defence by putting in a word for him with his counsel, Sir Henry James QC, a Liberal MP and former attorney-general. A decree nisi (obtained on 8 August 1879) was made absolute on 17 February 1880. On 29 March 1880 he married Harriet Mary Margaret, eldest daughter of Edward Knipe, of Water Newton, Huntingdonshire, who survived him. There were no children of either marriage. In 1892 Hall resigned his pastorate, and in the same year received the degree of DD from Edinburgh University. He died from paralysis at Vine House, Hampstead Square, London, on 18 February 1902, and was buried at Abney Park cemetery.

Hall published at least forty-three tracts, also speeches, collections of hymns, and other religious works. These included *The Spiritual Claims of Teetotalism* (1846); *Dissent and the Papal Bull: No Intolerance—a Response to the Cry of 'No Popery'* (1850); *Congregationalism for Christ* (1855); *The Assassination of Abraham Lincoln: a Lecture* (n.d.); *Hymns for Christian Worship* (1867); and *Napoleon III: a Sermon* (1873). He also edited his father's autobiography in 1865 and published his own in 1898. A. R. Buckland, *rev.* Ian Machin

**Sources** N. Hall, *Newman Hall: an autobiography* (1898) · G. I. T. Machin, 'Gladstone and nonconformity in the 1860s: the formation of an alliance', *HJ*, 17 (1974), 347–64 · G. I. T. Machin, *Politics and the churches in Great Britain, 1832 to 1868* (1977) · D. W. Bebbington, *The nonconformist conscience: chapel and politics, 1870–1914* (1982) · G. I. T. Machin, *Politics and the churches in Great Britain, 1869 to 1921* (1987) · T. W. Reid, *Life of the Right Honourable William Edward Forster*, 1 (1888), 539–42 · *The Times* (9 Aug 1879) · *The Times* (18 Feb 1880) · *The Times* (30 Dec 1890) · *The Times* (19 Feb 1902), 4 · Gladstone, *Diaries* · T. Larsen, 'Sex, lies and Victorians: the case of Newman Hall's divorce', *Journal of the United Reformed Church History Society*, 6 (1997), 589–96 · A. Peel, *The Congregational two hundred, 1530–1948* (1948)

**Archives** BL, corresp. with W. E. Gladstone, Add. MS 44188

**Likenesses** Lock & Whitfield, photograph, pubd 1877, NPG [*see illus.*] · E. O. Ford, terracotta bust, exh. RA 1878 · E. O. Ford, bronze bust, exh. RA 1885 · Barraud, photograph, 1890, NPG · J. Cochran, stipple (after G. Sayer), NPG · J. & C. Watkins, carte-de-visite, NPG · Maull & Polyblank, carte-de-visite, NPG · D. J. Pound, stipple and line engraving (after photograph by J. & C. Watkins), BM, NPG · oils, Congregational Centre, Castle Gate, Nottingham · portraits, DWL

**Wealth at death** £15,290 15*s.* 3*d.*: probate, 6 May 1902, *CGPLA Eng. & Wales*

**Hall, Peter** (1803–1849), Church of England clergyman and topographer, was born on 31 December 1803, the third son of James Hall of St George's, Bloomsbury, London. At the age of thirteen he was sent to Winchester College, where he was educated on the foundation, and thence proceeded to Brasenose College, Oxford, matriculating on 15 January 1822. He graduated BA on 1 December 1825 and MA on 21 January 1830. In 1828 he was ordained and became curate of St Edmund's, Salisbury, where he remained until 1833. He gave an account of his dismissal from this curacy in the preface to 'The church and the world', a sermon preached at St Thomas's, Salisbury, on 21 April 1833. In September 1834 he was instituted to the rectory of Milston-cum-Brigmerston, Wiltshire, but was soon obliged to abandon residence by the ill health of his wife. He was for a short time curate of St Luke's, Chelsea, and afterwards, in May 1836, became minister of Tavistock Chapel, Drury Lane. In June 1841 he undertook the charge of Long Acre episcopal chapel, in the parish of St Martin-in-the-Fields. In 1843 he became minister of St Thomas's Chapel, Walcot, Bath. He was also for some time travelling secretary to the Reformation Society.

His obituarist described Hall as having been particularly active and zealous in both his ministry and his writing. Hall wrote prolifically from 1824 until immediately before his death. His best works were topographical descriptions of parts of Hampshire, Wiltshire, and Dorset, but even these have not endured. Hall was also a prolific editor of the works of others. Most works were religious in character and were judged of modest value even in his own lifetime. Exceptions were his English edition of *The Harmony of Protestant Confessions* (1841), his *Reliquiae liturgicae* (5 vols., 1847), and *Fragmenta liturgica* (7 vols., 1848), which all received some commendation.

Hall claimed descent from Joseph Hall (1574–1656), bishop of Exeter and Norwich, and produced editions of his works entitled *The Works of Joseph Hall* (12 vols., 1837–9) and *Satires and other Poems, by Joseph Hall, D.D.* (1838). The former was an improvement on the first complete edition (1808, under the editorship of Josiah Pratt), but was itself soon superseded.

Hall's health deteriorated and he went to Great Malvern in the summer of 1849, leaving his family at Bath. His treatment there brought no relief, however, and 'in a paroxysm of delerium he inflicted a wound upon himself' (*GM*, 543) which ultimately led to his death.

Hall died at Great Malvern, Worcestershire, on 10 September 1849, leaving a widow and three daughters. His library was sold between 27 May and 4 June 1850.

GORDON GOODWIN, *rev.* ELIZABETH BAIGENT

**Sources** *GM*, 2nd ser., 32 (1849), 542–3 · Foster, *Alum. Oxon.* · Allibone, *Dict.*

**Hall, Peter Andrew** (1936–1996), folklorist and musicologist, was born on 28 June 1936 at 285 Harrow Road, Paddington, London, the son of Thomas Temple Hall, corporal in the Coldstream Guards, and Marion Coghill Smith. His parents married shortly after his birth. After an upbringing in Aberdeen and Newcastle, Hall entered Aberdeen University in 1955 to read first medicine and then, after national service, science. He after entered the teaching profession, first as an uncertified teacher, though he graduated BEd from Aberdeen University in 1972. He spent a professional lifetime in the region as a dedicated, stimulating, and popular teacher of physics, standing down only weeks before his death. On 17 February 1959 he married a fellow student, Marion Harvey Maclennan (*b.* 1939); they had a daughter and a son. She was later to become an obstetrician and gynaecologist of international repute.

Hall and his wife shared a love of music, and with the advent of the folk-song revival in the early 1960s his obsession with playing in jazz bands was transmuted into a consuming interest in folk-song and folklore. The north-east

**Peter Andrew Hall (1936–1996)**, by unknown photographer

of Scotland had been known to scholars for hundreds of years as one of the richest areas in the world for its vibrant tradition of folk-song. Francis Child of Harvard searched there successfully for the great balladry of Britain in the nineteenth century; at the beginning of the twentieth the region produced the 3100 songs of the *Greig–Duncan Folk Song Collection*. In the 1960s the area was still rich in song and performers, including the travellers, of whom Jeannie Robertson became a famous example. Hall rapidly became an expert on folk-song and traditional culture and an experienced collector. A founder member of the influential Aberdeen Folk Song Club in 1962, he established a group, the Gaugers, to perform the rich north-east material in 1967, bringing out *Beware of the Aberdonian* in 1976; they were in the process of completing a series of commercial recordings for Aberdeen City Library at the time of his death.

Hall tape-recorded more than 600 items of folk-song and folk-tale from tramps and travellers, farmworkers, and folk in general in Aberdeen, Aberdeenshire, Banffshire, and the west of Ireland. Many of these were later used in commercial recordings and in radio and television broadcasts. He was a spirited singer and able musician (having exchanged the jazz trumpet for the concertina and melodeon), and performed on radio and television and at concerts and festivals throughout Britain, France, Germany, and Belgium. He was as much in demand as a superb musicologist (who could also wear his scholarship lightly) to write record notes, produce broadcasts, and judge in competitions, especially of the Traditional Music and Song Association of Scotland. He wrote articles, both scholarly and popular, and was the first editor (later musical editor) of the folk revival magazine *Chapbook*, from 1964 to 1969. Supervised by the eminent sociologist Ian Carter, he gained an MLitt degree from Aberdeen University in 1985 for his thesis 'Folk songs of north east farm servants in the nineteenth century', the 'bothy ballads'. It remains the classic work on the subject, but he was too modest to publish, preferring to distil much of its content into an authoritative introduction to volume three of the *Greig–Duncan Folk Song Collection*, which he co-edited in 1987. He collaborated with Norman Buchan MP to produce the thoroughly researched and influential *The Scottish Folksinger* in 1973 (reprinted in 1986). In 1995 he was invited to be consultant to the Edinburgh International Festival for a unique and highly acclaimed series of twenty-one concerts of songs from the north-east of Scotland, based on the *Greig–Duncan* collection.

Bearded and stockily built, this deeply modest man was a committed socialist and humanist. An *uomo universale*, Hall was a scientist who loved the arts, a scholar who loved hill walking, a devotee of both classical and folk music, and a talented photographer whose work was exhibited in Aberdeen Art Gallery. A sympathetic and loyal friend, he was kindly and generous (especially with his research findings), and a humorous and fascinating conversationalist who gave very careful thought to any question asked of him. He was as much in demand for talks to local associations and continuing education groups as for international conferences, where he was renowned for his clarity, humour, musical illustrations, and startling originality. Having committed all too little of his encyclopaedic knowledge and extensive findings to print in his lifetime, he worked on his researches until the very end, concerned that he was leaving so much unfinished by nature of the sudden onset and rapidity of his illness. He died of prostatic cancer in Aberdeen Royal Infirmary on 5 December 1996 and was cremated following a humanist service at Aberdeen crematorium on 10 December. He was survived by his wife and two children. IAN A. OLSON

**Sources** *The Herald* (7 Dec 1996) • *The Scotsman* (9 Dec 1996) • *The Times* (14 Dec 1996) • I. A. Olson, 'Peter Andrew Hall', *Folklore*, 108 (1997), 104 • b. cert. • personal knowledge (2004) • private information (2004)

**Archives** U. Edin., School of Scottish Studies | SOUND Cecil Sharp House, London, Vaughan Williams Memorial Library • U. Aberdeen • U. Edin., School of Scottish Studies

**Likenesses** photograph, News International Syndication, London [*see illus.*] • photograph, repro. in *The Scotsman* • photograph, repro. in *The Times*

**Wealth at death** £23,806.71: confirmation, 4 March 1997, NA Scot., SC/CO 987/114

**Hall, Philip** (1904–1982), mathematician, was born on 11 April 1904 in Hampstead, the natural son of George Hall and Mary Laura Sayers, dressmaker, of Hampstead, daughter of Joseph Sayers, gardener, of Balcombe. George Hall disappeared from his life soon afterwards and Philip was brought up by his mother. He was educated at Christ's Hospital and, as a scholar (1922–5) and senior scholar (1925–6), at King's College, Cambridge. He was in the first class in part one (1923) and a wrangler in part two (1925) of the mathematical tripos. In 1927 he was elected to a fellowship at King's, which he held for the rest of his life. He was appointed university lecturer in 1933. From 1941 to 1945 he worked at the Government Code and Cypher School at Bletchley Park, first on Italian ciphers and later on the Japanese diplomatic ciphers. He was reader in algebra at Cambridge from 1949 and Sadleirian professor of pure mathematics from 1953 until 1967, when he elected to retire.

While still an undergraduate Hall began to study the works on group theory of William Burnside, whom he never met but who was the greatest influence on his ways of thinking. In *A Note on Soluble Groups* (1928), he proved a result as important for the theory of finite soluble groups as Sylow's theorem of 1872 is for finite groups in general, that if $G$ is a soluble group of order $mn$, where $m$ and $n$ are coprime, then every subgroup of $G$ whose order divides $m$ is contained in some subgroup of order $m$, and these subgroups of order $m$ are all conjugate in $G$. Ten years later he characterized soluble groups by such arithmetic properties, and went on to develop a general theory of finite soluble groups. Hall's most influential pre-war paper was *A Contribution to the Theory of Groups of Prime-Power Order* (1934), in which he discovered many features which underlie the structure of the most general $p$-group, initiated the theory of regular $p$-groups, laid down the basic laws of the commutator calculus, and revealed one of the links connecting the study of groups with that of Lie rings. In 1935 he proved a fundamental combinatorial result known as the marriage theorem, which became part of mathematical folklore.

Between 1940 and 1954 Hall published no mathematics. His work in the mid-1950s on theorems like Sylow's and, in collaboration with Graham Higman, on the $p$-lengths of $p$-soluble groups was indispensable for the great achievements in finite group theory of the 1960s. He also studied combinatorial questions arising from the appearance of partitions in different parts of group theory and invented an important and elegant algebra of partitions. He made many contributions to the theory of infinite groups. Of seminal importance was his systematic investigation between 1954 and 1961 of certain finiteness conditions in soluble groups, which, for example, initiated the representation theory of polycyclic groups. In 1959 he constructed a universal locally finite simple group and in 1963 a non-strictly simple group, and in 1974 he proved very general theorems about embedding groups in simple groups.

Both through his own work and through that of his students, to whom he was always most generous with his ideas, Hall exercised a profound influence on English mathematics, which was felt throughout the mathematical world.

He had unusually wide interests in both the sciences and the humanities, with an encyclopaedic knowledge and prodigious memory. For many years when doing mathematics he would smoke one cigarette after another, but, to test his will, used, from time to time and for predetermined periods, to give them up. Hall was unmarried and for much of his life lived alone, always studious and caring nothing for hot water or central heating. He had little liking for large gatherings or formal occasions, but behind his shyness lay a particularly friendly disposition, and when he was with friends he was the best company in the world. He had an extensive but discriminating love of poetry, which he spoke beautifully, not only in English. He enjoyed music and art, flowers, and country walks. He was gentle, amused, kind, and the soul of integrity.

Hall was elected FRS in 1942 and received the Sylvester medal in 1961. He was president of the London Mathematical Society (1955–7) and was awarded both the senior Berwick prize (1958) and the De Morgan medal and Larmor prize (1965). He had honorary doctorates from Tübingen (1963) and Warwick (1977). From 1976 he was an honorary fellow of Jesus College, Cambridge. Hall died at Addenbrooke's Hospital, Trumpington Street, Cambridge, on 30 December 1982 and his ashes were interred in his mother's grave in Impington churchyard near Cambridge. He left half his residuary estate to the National Trust. J. E. ROSEBLADE, *rev.*

**Sources** J. A. Green, J. E. Roseblade, and J. G. Thompson, *Memoirs FRS*, 30 (1984), 251–79 · personal knowledge (1990) · *WWW* · *CGPLA Eng. & Wales* (1983) · d. cert.

**Likenesses** photograph, repro. in Green, Roseblade, and Thompson, *Memoirs FRS*

**Wealth at death** £158,600: probate, 18 April 1983, *CGPLA Eng. & Wales*

**Hall, Sir (William) Reginald** (1870–1943), naval officer and intelligence officer, was born at The Close, Salisbury, on 28 June 1870, the second child and elder son of Lieutenant William Henry Hall RN of Ross, Herefordshire, and his wife, Caroline Elizabeth, daughter of the Revd Henry Thomas Armfield, vicar of Salisbury Cathedral. Hall entered HMS *Britannia* as a naval cadet in 1884, and was commissioned as a lieutenant in 1890. In 1894 he married Ethel Wooton (*d.* 1932), daughter of Sir William de Wiveleslie *Abney, a prominent scientist. They had one daughter and two sons, both of whom followed their father into the navy. As befitted the grandson of a clergyman, Hall remained a devout churchman throughout his life.

An instinctive seaman, Hall excelled in his chosen specialism of gunnery, and was promoted to commander in 1901. Although a strong disciplinarian, he understood the pressures of life on the lower deck and he built a reputation as an innovative and humane officer. He introduced considerable improvements in the living environment of the sailors under his charge, thereby earning the disapproval of some navy traditionalists. Such carping meant nothing to Hall, a determined and forthright man whose mannerism of frequent blinking earned him the enduring nickname 'Blinker'; it is said that the trait, in combination with bushy eyebrows, a piercing stare, and conspicuous false teeth, worked wonders in negotiations, confrontations, and interrogations.

After two years in a staff job in the Admiralty, Hall reached the pinnacle of his seagoing career with his appointment as captain of the new battlecruiser *Queen Mary* in 1913, and he seemed set fair to complete his navy days as a seagoing officer. He saw action at the battle of the Heligoland Bight in August 1914, but in October was recalled to the Admiralty to become director of the intelligence division. This move not only altered his career; it also probably saved his life, as his old ship blew up when hit at the battle of Jutland in 1916, a casualty of the inadequacies of Britain's pre-war naval architects.

**Sir (William) Reginald Hall (1870–1943)**, by Walter Stoneman, 1917

There was little in Hall's professional formation to indicate any special aptitude for intelligence work, although his father had been the first head of naval intelligence in 1884. He was, however, an exceptional organizer and leader, and he was always willing to act on his own initiative. Furthermore, Hall inherited an organization geared entirely towards the acquisition of intelligence on maritime affairs for supply to the naval staff; he was greatly to expand its interests and activities. The First World War was the first conflict in which intelligence tools such as code-breaking, direction finding and traffic analysis, and aerial photography were widely used. The effectiveness of the machinery to manage the analysis and dissemination of such intelligence lagged far behind the technical capabilities for its collection. Although Hall's name is indelibly associated with the code-breaking department Room 40 (named after its location in the Admiralty), his relations with its founder, Sir Alfred Ewing, were poor, and it was only when Ewing retired at the end of 1916 that Hall was able to reorganize and develop the office into an effective intelligence centre for both naval and diplomatic purposes. There were also difficulties with the chief of the naval staff, Sir Henry Oliver. Hall regarded him as incompetent, a judgement borne out particularly in the mishandling of decodes during the battle of Jutland; Oliver saw Hall as an overweening menace who attempted to interfere in operational matters. This tension meant that excellent intelligence from decodes was sometimes not exploited to the maximum, much to the frustration of Hall and his staff.

Despite his conventional naval background, Blinker Hall appreciated the unusual talents required to break, translate, and analyse codes and ciphers, and he readily accepted and worked with the strange congeries of dons, clergymen, and other civilians, including women, needed to run Room 40. He had the confidence of his staff, as they had his. By the time of the armistice, Room 40 had become a sophisticated intelligence bureau capable of decrypting and putting in context a wide variety of enemy and neutral military and diplomatic traffic. Crucially, it built up considerable expertise on German U-boat operations, and became an invaluable aid to anti-submarine activities. It also passed on much useful information based on decodes of diplomatic and consular traffic, although the flow of material was subject to Hall's idiosyncratic selection of what he thought other departments needed to know, and when they should be told.

Hall believed in hunting the enemy wherever he might be. Using attachés, reserve officers, and civilians, he ran agents in a number of countries, including Mexico, the United States, Morocco, and Spain. On the credit side, naval intelligence was successful in clandestine operations to disrupt German communications and to thwart intrigues and espionage in Mexico and elsewhere, and in combination with other agencies did much to hamper German sabotage efforts in the United States. Hall arranged for the capture of the German saboteur Von Rintelin at Ramsgate, *en route* from the United States to Holland. In a further coup in 1916 he seized incriminating papers from the baggage of the German military attaché in Washington, DC, Frans von Papen, and from these Hall was able to supply the United States government with further evidence of German sabotage operations. On the other hand, the drawbacks inherent in his penchant for independent action can be seen in an early essay in intelligence gathering. This was the voyage of the yacht *Sayonara* under a United States flag along the west coast of Ireland in search of evidence of German activity in the winter of 1914; its only fruits were a flood of scare stories which reached London about the mysterious activities of a craft which most people assumed to be on a German spying mission. Hall forged a close partnership with the Scotland Yard assistant commissioner in charge of the special branch, Sir Basil Thomson, a kindred spirit with whom he collaborated against German activities and, after the Russian Revolution, in battling Bolshevism at home and abroad. By contrast, little is known of his dealings with either the Security Service, MI5, or the Secret Intelligence Service, MI6, despite the potential for overlap and conflict between the various clandestine agencies.

Hall's single greatest coup was his handling of the Zimmerman telegram of 16 January 1917, a decrypted communication sent from Berlin to the German embassy in Washington, DC, for onward transmission to the German ambassador to Mexico. This disclosed Germany's intention to resume unrestricted submarine warfare in the Atlantic, and her plan to secure Mexican co-operation in the war through promising the restoration of territories ceded to the United States in the mid-nineteenth century. Hall's problem was how to bring this into the public domain without disclosing its true source—or, more correctly, sources, as it had been sent by a number of routes—and the means by which it had been obtained, to either the Americans or to the Germans, and without letting the Foreign Office queer the pitch. Hall consequently kept the telegram to himself for almost a fortnight before informing the foreign secretary, and he told the United States embassy about it only on 19 February (taking care naturally to conceal the sensitive fact that Britain was reading United States diplomatic traffic).

Hall contrived an elaborate series of ruses, whereby the impression was sustained that the telegram had originally been obtained by agents in Mexico. The eventual publication of the telegram in the United States, and German confirmation of its authenticity, had a profound effect on American opinion, reinforcing the mood for joining the war on the allied side while concealing the original British source of the decode. Hall used similar tactics to expose German intrigue in South America while preserving the secret of Room 40's successes. However, another attempt in 1918 to have the United States government publish a selection of elderly decodes, this time as evidence of a supposed 'German plot' for a second Irish rising, went awry when the Americans refused to help.

Hall had mixed success in exploiting good intelligence on Ireland. In 1916 decodes disclosing the plans hatched in the United States between German diplomats and Irish separatists for a rebellion led to the interception by the navy of a German arms ship and to the capture of the renegade Sir Roger Casement in co. Kerry upon landing from a U-boat. However, the Dublin Castle authorities were not briefed about the nature and limits of the navy's intelligence on the plot, and assumed that London had penetrated to the Irish roots of the conspiracy and had matters under control. They were consequently slow to act, and were caught unprepared when the rebels struck. This was a catastrophe for British policy in Ireland, and Hall must shoulder some of the blame as the man in early possession of intelligence which should have been sufficient to nip the rebellion in the bud.

Hall was an easier chief than he was a colleague or subordinate. He was directly involved in the intrigues surrounding the departure of Lord Fisher as first sea lord in 1915, and the independence of mind and action which he displayed at the Admiralty antagonized some in Whitehall. This may explain why, although greatly exercised by the need for a powerful unitary peacetime intelligence system to defend the empire and to counter the new spectre of Bolshevism at home and abroad, the end of the war saw his retirement with the rank of rear-admiral and a KCMG. He had been appointed CB in 1915 and promoted rear-admiral in 1917. Oxford created him an honorary DCL in 1919, and Cambridge an LLD in 1920, and he was advanced to vice-admiral (retired) in 1923 and admiral in 1926.

Elected as Conservative member for the West Derby division of Liverpool in December 1918, in March 1923 Hall became principal agent in party headquarters. He stood down after losing his seat in the December 1923 election which saw the advent of Labour to office under Ramsay MacDonald, a development Hall regarded as a mortal threat to Britain. He was instrumental in the intrigues surrounding the publication by the *Daily Mail*, at Conservative Party prompting, of the 'Zinoviev letter' during the October 1924 general election campaign, an affair calculated to destroy Labour's chances by portraying it as soft on Bolshevism. While its impact on the election is debatable, this plot undoubtedly involved the use of intelligence channels to discredit the government, and Hall stands indicted for his participation. He was returned to the Commons as member for Eastbourne in 1925, but made little impact and retired in 1929.

Blinker Hall was an intelligence chief of daring and initiative. He understood the importance of getting intelligence in a form appropriate to those taking the decisions in naval operations, and once he took control of Room 40 he secured this through skilful reorganization and management. He was an inspiration to the next generation of Admiralty men such as John Godfrey who were to fight the intelligence war against Hitler. Doubts about his reputation arise in three respects: his propensity to take unilateral initiatives on foot of diplomatic and political intelligence produced by Room 40; his frequent disinclination to place intelligence in the hands of those departments best placed to judge it; and his involvement while a post-war politician in anti-government intrigues drawing on his old intelligence connections. Like many able intelligence officers, he sometimes succumbed to the professional temptation of manipulating good intelligence in order to influence the decisions and actions of the government which he served. He died on 22 October 1943 at Claridges Hotel, Brook Street, London.

EUNAN O'HALPIN

**Sources** P. Beesly, *Room 40: British naval intelligence, 1914–18* (1982) · C. Andrew, *Secret service: the making of the British intelligence community* (1985) · E. O'Halpin, *The decline of the union: British government in Ireland, 1892–1920* (1987) · W. M. James, *The eyes of the navy* (1955) · CAC Cam., Hall papers · *CGPLA Eng. & Wales* (1944) · *DNB*

**Archives** CAC Cam., papers and corresp. | CAC Cam., corresp. with H. A. Williamson · PRO, Room 40 papers, HW 7

**Likenesses** F. Dodd, charcoal and watercolour drawing, 1917, IWM · W. Stoneman, photographs, 1917, NPG [*see illus.*] · K. Kennet, bust, *c*.1926, Royal Naval College, Dartmouth

**Wealth at death** £65,558 16*s*. 6*d*.: probate, 7 April 1944, *CGPLA Eng. & Wales*

**Hall, Reginald** (1931–1994), endocrinologist, was born on 1 October 1931 at Montpellier, Belmont, co. Durham, the only child of Reginald Peacock Hall (1899–1969), head postmaster, and his wife, Maggie Watson Wilson (1901–1980), daughter of William Wilson, miner. He was educated at Alderman Wraith Grammar School, Spennymoor (1943–8), Berwick upon Tweed grammar school (1948–50) and King's College, University of Durham, where he graduated BSc with first-class honours in physiology (1953), MBBS with first-class honours (1956), and MD (1963). On 6 August 1955 he married Joan Scott Patterson (1933–1959), student teacher, daughter of John Derry Patterson, lorry driver. They had one daughter, Susan Margaret (*b*. 1958). Six months after Susan's birth, Joan Hall died of a brain tumour. Hall then married, on 11 June 1960, Molly Hill (*b*. 1932), daughter of Clifford Vincent Hill, electrical engineer, and herself a doctor. They had four children: Amanda Mary (*b*. 1962), twins John Reginald and Andrew James (*b*. 1963), and Stephanie Claire (*b*. 1966).

Hall won numerous prizes while an undergraduate and many honours in his subsequent career in academic medicine. He undertook postgraduate clinical training mainly in Newcastle upon Tyne, then spent a formative year as a Harkness fellow at Harvard University and the Massachusetts General Hospital (1960–61), where he developed further his particular interest in autoimmune thyroid disease. He returned to Newcastle as first assistant in the department of medicine (1962–4), Wellcome senior research fellow (1964–7), and honorary consultant physician (1966–9), before being awarded a personal chair as professor of medicine in 1970. He was elected FRCP the same year. The next decade was a very productive research period in the broad field of endocrinology, and Hall was widely acknowledged to be the leading expert in the UK. His research interests included clinical and physiological studies of the hypothalamic releasing hormones, the epidemiology of thyroid diseases, and the mechanisms underlying autoimmune thyroid disease, particularly Graves' disease. He attracted research fellows from within the UK and around the world, whom he guided and befriended. All responded to his warmth and enthusiasm and the generous hospitality offered by the Halls at their home, which was open to friends and colleagues of all colours and creeds.

Hall moved to Cardiff in 1980, when he was appointed professor of medicine and head of department at the University of Wales College of Medicine. His dynamism, intellectual rigour, and personality enabled him to establish a unit at Cardiff with an international reputation in a remarkably short period of time. He took with him from Newcastle a number of bright young colleagues, and others joined him from further afield. Many of them went on to distinguish themselves in chairs of medicine in the UK and elsewhere. The 1980s in Cardiff were as productive for Hall as the previous decade had been in Newcastle. The research teams under his leadership were at the forefront in the fields of endocrine immunology, neuroendocrinology, thyrotrophin receptors, regulation of synthesis of thyroid antibodies, and other aspects of autoimmune thyroid disease, as well as the study of thyroid disease in pregnancy and the post-partum period. Hall's achievements during this time were all the more remarkable because he developed a rare illness, primary amyloidosis, which became apparent soon after he moved to Cardiff. This led to his having a heart transplant performed by Magdi Yacoub in 1984. He was able to give, in the *British Medical*

*Journal*, an extraordinarily dispassionate account of his illness through the succeeding nine and a half years of his survival with the disease.

Hall was a prolific writer, publishing more than 400 scientific papers and contributing to many textbooks. He was president of the endocrine section of the Royal Society of Medicine (1974–6), president of the Thyroid Club (1978–84), and chairman of the speciality advisory committee for endocrinology and diabetes of the Joint Committee for Higher Medical Training (1979–84). He was an honorary member of the Association of American Physicians, the British Diabetic Association, and the European Thyroid Association, of which he was a very active member. He was appointed CBE in 1989 for his services to medicine. He retired that year at the age of fifty-eight because of the chronic fatigue associated with his illness. He nevertheless remained intellectually alert and continued to entertain friends and colleagues at home. With typical enthusiasm and application he mastered culinary skills as well as continuing his lifelong interest in bryophytes. He received an honorary MD from the University of Wales in recognition of his services to academic medicine. Complications related to the amyloidosis eventually overtook him and he died at the University Hospital of Wales, Cardiff, on 20 July 1994; he was cremated at Cardiff on 29 July. He was survived by his wife, Molly, and his five children.

Hall made many contributions to medicine and characteristically pushed others ahead to become leaders of the profession in their turn, both in clinical and academic fields. A tribute paid by Professor David London, then registrar of the Royal College of Physicians and a fellow endocrinologist, embraces the essence of the man:

> He was one of the seminal endocrinologists of his generation. A force in medicine and a towering intellect … [a] living example … of the true and good doctor. A truth and a goodness that were given to the many who passed through his life. A generosity of spirit and concern for others that is the real religio medici and above all the dispassionate clinical curiosity and wonderment with which he chronicled his own long mortal illness, full of vicissitudes, with a courage of Homeric proportions. Many are honoured. He was loved. (London, 27)

W. MICHAEL G. TUNBRIDGE

**Sources** R. Hall and others, *BMJ* (29 Oct 1994), 1135–7 · D. London, *Royal College of Physicians of London Commentary*, 128 (Sept–Oct 1994), 27 · *The Times* (3 Aug 1994) · Munk, *Roll* · *WWW, 1991–5* · personal knowledge (2004) · private information (2004) [Molly Hall, Sheila Taylor] · b. cert. · m. certs. · d. cert.
**Likenesses** portrait, priv. coll.
**Wealth at death** £97,140: probate, 14 March 1995, *CGPLA Eng. & Wales*

**Hall, Reginald Holland** [Harry] (1873–1930), ancient historian and archaeologist, was born Reginald Holland at 39 Birkbeck Road, Islington, London, on 30 September 1873. The name of his mother was recorded as Emma Holland, who was later married to Sydney Prior *Hall (1842–1922), portrait painter and artist to *The Graphic*; the name of the father was not registered. In later sources he was recorded as the couple's only child. Sydney Hall's father was Harry Hall of Newmarket, a painter of racehorses. He entered Merchant Taylors' School, London, in 1886, and proceeded to St John's College, Oxford, in 1891 with an open scholarship in modern history. As a boy he had shown an interest in antiquity—apparently influenced by his aunt K. M. Hall, a naturalist and museum curator—especially the histories of Persia and Egypt, and he ran a private museum, addressing fund-raising letters to his relatives. He offered the history and language of ancient Egypt as a special subject in *literae humaniores*, in which he gained a second class in 1895.

Hall then joined the staff of the British Museum, where in 1896 he was appointed an assistant in the department of Egyptian and Assyrian antiquities. Here he gained that familiarity with Near Eastern antiquities which, along with an inherited artistic taste, made him a leading authority on the date, style, and authenticity of any object that came from the Near East. As part of his duties in the department he produced three of the official catalogues: *Coptic and Greek Texts of the Christian Period* (1905), *Egyptian Scarabs* (1913), and *Hieroglyphic Texts from Egyptian Stelae*, volumes 2–7 (1912–25). His first publication, however, had been *The Oldest Civilization of Greece* (1901), the first attempt made to harmonize the new discoveries by Heinrich Schliemann, Arthur Evans, and others with what had previously been known of the Aegean area. Coming from one whose studies might reasonably have been confined to Egypt and Mesopotamia, this work was a revelation, and together with the later *Aegean Archaeology* (1915) it established its author as a kind of chief liaison officer between the studies of these three widely separated areas, a position which he occupied unchallenged until his death. His primary interest lay not in their archaeology for its own sake but in their history and art, as was shown by his best-known work, *The Ancient History of the Near East* (1913; 7th edn, 1927), a standard university textbook for many years.

The trustees of the museum believed in the advisability of fieldwork for their younger staff, and in the winter of 1903–4 Hall was allowed to assist Edouard Naville in his excavations for the Egypt Exploration Fund (later Society) at Deir al-Bahri. He proved so valuable that he was released again in the two following winters for the same work, and collaborated with Naville on parts 1 and 3 of the excavation report, *The XIth Dynasty Temple at Deir el-Bahari* (1907–13). In 1910 he took part in Naville's excavations for the same society at Abydos, and returned there in 1925.

During the First World War, Hall was employed first in the military section of the press bureau, from 1916 in the intelligence department of the War Office (where his long-held interests in British and German military history proved very helpful), and from 1918 on political service in Mesopotamia, where he held the rank of captain. For his war service he was mentioned in dispatches and made MBE. In 1918 he was sent to Iraq by the British Museum with a mandate to protect the antiquities there from damage and to take advantage of any opportunity for profitable excavation. In 1919 he directed the British Museum excavations at Tell al-Muqayyar (Ur of the Chaldees) and the nearby Abu Shahrain (Eridu), and discovered a new site at Tell al-ʿUbayd. The results were described in *Ur Excavations* (vol. 1, 1927), the official account he co-authored with C. L. Woolley, and *A Season's Work at Ur*, a more amusing personal account which appeared in 1930, shortly after Hall's death, and reveals more of his character.

Hall could now speak of the Near East with an authority based on experience that few equalled. In 1919 he was made assistant keeper in the department of Egyptian and Assyrian antiquities, and in 1924 keeper. From this time onward his main concern was with the collections in his charge, in the arrangement of which his artistic eye and his ability to understand and sympathize with the popular as well as the academic aspect of a museum stood him in good stead. During these years he also produced many valuable articles on Egypt, Babylonia, and the Aegean; the Rhind lectures on *The Civilization of Greece in the Bronze Age*, which he delivered at Edinburgh in 1923, were published in that year and reissued with new material in 1928.

Hall was an influential member of the councils of many archaeological societies, in particular of the Royal Asiatic Society, the Egypt Exploration Society, and the Society for the Promotion of Hellenic Studies; he was chairman of the Palestine Exploration Fund (from 1922) and a vice-president of the Society of Antiquaries (1929), of whose Cocked Hat Club he was a popular member. On all these bodies he was valued not only for the soundness of his judgement but also for the energy with which he would enter into and push forward any scheme he believed in. He received an honorary DLitt from Oxford in 1920, and was elected a fellow of the British Academy in 1926. But the honour he appreciated most was his election in 1929 to an honorary fellowship at his own college, St John's. He often represented the British Museum or the government at international academic conferences, and his last illness followed such a trip to Belgium and Germany.

Hall died, unmarried, at his home, 22 King Henry's Road, Hampstead, London, on 13 October 1930. He was cremated at Golders Green on 15 October. He was remembered for his 'boyish' character, which combined infectious enthusiasm with cheerful warm-heartedness, although it could give rise to impatience, especially with superstitious 'Egyptomania' or hampering bureaucracy. He was a vigorous oarsman, swimmer, and walker, and enjoyed travel, especially to Greece, Crete, and Norway; outside his subject his main interest was in the art of the sixteenth to nineteenth centuries, especially Dutch ship paintings. T. E. Peet, *rev.* R. S. Simpson

**Sources** personal knowledge (1937) · R. C. Thompson, *PBA*, 16 (1930), 475–85 · H. Last, *Journal of Egyptian Archaeology*, 17 (1931), 111–16 · *The Times* (14 Oct 1930), 16 · *The Times* (16 Oct 1930), 17 · b. cert. · *CGPLA Eng. & Wales* (1930) · W. R. Dawson and E. P. Uphill, *Who was who in Egyptology*, 3rd edn, rev. M. L. Bierbrier (1995) · *Antiquaries Journal*, 11 (1931), 73–4 · *Palestine Exploration Quarterly* (1931), 1, 9–11 · *WWW* · Mrs E. P. Hart, ed., *Merchant Taylors' School register, 1561–1934*, 2 vols. (1936) · W. Baker, ed., *Merchant Taylors' School register, 1871–1900* (1907) · E. S. Craig and W. M. Gibson, eds., *Oxford University roll of service*, 3rd edn (1920)

**Archives** BM, corresp. | Egypt Exploration Society, corresp. with Egypt Exploration Society

**Likenesses** photograph, *c.*1930, repro. in *ILN* (18 Oct 1930) · Russell, photograph, repro. in *Journal of Egyptian Archaeology* · photograph, repro. in *Palestine Exploration Quarterly*, facing p. 9 · photograph, BM

**Wealth at death** £5226 1*s.* 5*d.*: resworn probate, 28 Nov 1930, *CGPLA Eng. & Wales*

**Hall, Richard** (*c.*1537–1604), Roman Catholic priest and author, was educated at Cambridge; he matriculated at Clare College in November 1552, moved to Christ's College and graduated BA in 1555–6, and was a fellow of Pembroke College in 1556; he proceeded MA in 1559. He matriculated at Louvain on 17 November 1561, and received his degree of STD there or in Rome. He was ordained deacon in 1565 and priest by 8 February 1570. According to Venn there were two Richard Halls, both Catholic exiles and both alumni of Cambridge, whose lives were conflated in the article on Hall in the *Dictionary of National Biography*. Most of the references in Dodd are to a Mr Hall who came from England on 5 June 1577 rather than Dr Hall.

At one time Hall was believed to have written the earliest life of John Fisher. The *Dictionary of National Biography* credits him with being intimate with the leading Catholics of Queen Mary's reign, including Bishop Stephen Gardiner, and attributes the material in the Fisher biography to them. Hall did not write the biography of Fisher, whose authorship is unknown, although he did translate it into Latin. Hall was also responsible for the editing and publishing in Latin of John Fisher's *Tractus de orando Deum* (written in 1521) at Douai in 1576. For a time he was a professor of scripture at the Benedictine monastery of St Rictrude at Marchiennes, near Douai, and served a term as regent there. Dodd reports that he joined the faculty at Douai on 14 December 1576. He then began to expound on holy scripture in place of Richard Bristow between January and 13 June 1577. He was a visitator of the college on 12 August 1577. But, in all, Hall's labours at the English College seem to have been overestimated by Gillow. He was never mentioned in the correspondence of William, Cardinal Allen, or his successor Richard Barrett.

Hall became a canon of St Géri at Cambrai because he had a reputation as a good debater in both English and French, because of his learning and zeal, and because he was a strict moralist. In addition to his translation of Fisher's life, his written works include a defence of monastic custom (*De proprietate et vestiario monachorum*, 1585), a work on conscience (*De quinque partita conscientia*, 1598), a piece against the religious diversity of the Spanish Netherlands, later Belgium (*Opuscula quaedam his temporibus per necessaria causis tumultum Belgicorum*, 1581), and a defence of royal and episcopal authority (*Tractatus pro defensione regiae et episcopalis auctoritatis contra rebelles horum temporum*, 1584). Later he became a resident canon of St Omer and an official of the diocese there. He retained those two positions until his death on 26 February 1604. He was buried in the cathedral of St Omer on the south side of the rood screen with a short inscription to his memory. Fuller notes that at his death he was much lamented. John J. LaRocca

**Sources** G. Anstruther, *The seminary priests*, 1 (1969) · *DNB* · A. F. Allison and D. M. Rogers, eds., *The contemporary printed literature of the English Counter-Reformation between 1558 and 1640*, 1 (1989) · E. E. Reynolds, *St. John Fisher* (1955) · T. Fuller, *The church history of Britain*, ed. J. Nichols, 3rd edn, 3 (1842) · J. Lewis, *The life of Dr. John Fisher, bishop of Rochester in the reign of Henry VIII* (1855) · Venn, *Alum. Cant.* · E. Surtz, *The works and days of John Fisher: an introduction to the position of St. John Fisher … in the English Renaissance and Reformation* (1967)

**Hall, Robert** (1753–1836). *See under* Hall, Samuel Carter (1800–1889).

**Hall, Robert** (1754–1827), cotton manufacturer and bleacher, was born on 25 February 1754, in Nottingham, the third son of Robert Hall (1706–1781), mercer, bleacher, and thread merchant. His father being already a prosperous merchant and manufacturer, young Robert enjoyed a liberal education. The principal influence on his life was the Wesleyan Methodism that he espoused from the age of seventeen, which encouraged a love of order and punctuality in all his affairs. Robert Hall and his wife, Ann, married in 1781: they had eight children, among whom were Samuel *Hall (*bap.* 1782, *d.* 1863), engineer and inventor, and Marshall *Hall (1790–1857), the physician.

The elder Robert Hall had a thread mill for bleaching and preparing linen for the hosiery industry in Nottingham from 1754. Land was also acquired at Basford, 2 miles out of the town, probably for bleaching by natural sunlight, and presently the family took up residence at The Firs, which they built there in 1752 and which they extended in subsequent years. It was on the River Leen in this area that the younger Robert Hall built an Arkwright-type cotton mill in 1787.

The introduction of the Arkwright system led to a greatly increased output of cotton and made the traditional process of bleaching by sunlight even more of a bottleneck to production than it had always been. Robert Hall loved scientific research and experiments, and he corresponded with Dr Joseph Priestley and Dr William Henry after making a close study of the works of Black, Scheele, Lavoisier, Berthollet, and other eminent chemists of the day. In 1792 or 1793 he discovered the bleaching properties of a fluid made by passing chlorine into a well-agitated mixture of lime and water, and built a plant which reduced the textile bleaching process from a month to two days. The process was disclosed only to his partners and workmen, so that his achievement came to light only in a court case, *Tennant* v. *Slater* (king's bench, 1802), in which the system registered in patents of Charles Tennant of Glasgow was shown to have been in widespread use in the 1790s and first employed by Hall.

Robert Hall was well thought of by his contemporaries. 'His unaffected piety, benevolence of character, and sweetness of temper endeared him in a peculiar manner to all who knew him. He possessed a refined mind, genial manners, and a very handsome countenance, beaming with kindness and intelligence' (*Memoirs*, 3). When the Kilhamites or Methodist New Connexion broke away from the Wesleyans in 1797 he was one of the leaders of this democratic sect and was twice secretary of its annual conference. In the Luddite period (1810–12) he is said to have received an assurance that his property would be safe. He died on 6 August 1827 at Nottingham.

S. D. Chapman

**Sources** S. Woodhouse, 'Memoir of Robert Hall', *New Methodist Magazine* (Jan–Feb 1828) · [C. Hall], *Memoirs of Marshall Hall* (1861) · F. M. Wilkins-Jones, 'The Firs, Old Basford: relic of an eighteenth century textile complex', *Nottinghamshire Historian*, 18 (winter 1976), 5–8 · W. Felkin, *A history of the machine-wrought hosiery and lace manufactures* (1867), 300–01 · A. Clow and N. L. Clow, *The chemical revolution* (1952), 191–3 · R. C. Swift, *Lively people: Methodism in Nottingham, 1740–1979* (1982), 33–6 · G. Packer, ed., *Centenary of the Methodist New Connexion* (1897), 96

**Likenesses** portrait, repro. in Packer, ed., *Centenary of the Methodist New Connexion*

**Hall, Robert** (1763–1824), military surgeon, was born at Haughhead, Roxburghshire. He was descended from the ancient Border family of the Halls of Newbiggin, and was great-grandson of Henry Hall of Haughhead (*d.* 1680), the covenanter.

Following his education at school in Jedburgh, Hall attended medical classes at Edinburgh University. After three years' practice in Newcastle, he became a surgeon in the navy, and served several years on the Jamaica station, and for some time was surgeon's first mate on the *Ruby*.

On his return Hall received an MD from Edinburgh, and took up practice at Jedburgh. He then went to London and occupied himself in the translation, compilation, and editing of a number of medical works. He translated L. Spallanzani's work on the circulation, and Guyton de Morveau's work, which he published as *Means of Purifying Infected Air*, in 1802. In the same year he also produced a revised edition of Martin Clare's *Treatise on the Motion of Fluids*.

In March 1814 Hall was appointed assistant surgeon to the forces, and became surgeon to the forces in May 1816. He retired on half pay on 11 April 1817.

At some point in his career, Hall served as a medical officer during the fitting out of an expedition to the Niger, but a fall, combined with the harsh climatic conditions, caused him to be invalided home.

Hall's wife, the writer Agnes C. *Hall (1775/6–1846), was also born in Roxburghshire. She survived his death, which occurred early in 1824, at Chelsea, London.

Charles Creighton, *rev.* Claire E. J. Herrick

**Sources** A. Peterkin and W. Johnston, *Commissioned officers in the medical services of the British army, 1660–1960*, 1 (1968), 252 · *GM*, 1st ser., 94/1 (1824), 283 · [Clarke], *The Georgian era: memoirs of the most eminent persons*, 2 (1833), 585 · J. Gorton, *A general biographical dictionary*, 3 vols. (1841) · H. J. Rose, *A new general biographical dictionary*, ed. H. J. Rose and T. Wright, 12 vols. (1848)

**Hall, Robert** (1764–1831), Baptist minister, was born at Arnesby in Leicestershire on 2 May 1764, the youngest of fourteen children of Robert Hall (1728–1791), Arnesby's much respected Baptist minister, and his wife, Jane (*née* Catchaside). Hall was a sickly baby and slow to develop, but became a precocious child, writing hymns at seven, devouring theological works by Jonathan Edwards and

**Robert Hall (1764–1831)**, by J. Flowers, *c.*1820

others at nine, and inviting his brothers and sisters to hear him preach. In 1770, after attending local dame-schools, he became a day scholar and then a weekly boarder at a Mr Simmons's school in Wigston, but by the age of eleven had allegedly outstripped his tutor. On the advice of Baptist friends in Kettering he spent eighteen months at Dr Ryland's academy in Northampton, where a sermon preached by a Mr Robins of Daventry inspired a lasting love of composition. Returning home, he was taught by his father. On 6 September 1778 he was baptized as a believer at Arnesby, and in October, when still only fourteen, he went as a Ward scholar to the Bristol Baptist college. In August 1780 the Arnesby church set him apart for the Baptist ministry.

In 1781 Hall progressed, under the terms of his scholarship, to King's College, Aberdeen, where he became a prize student and formed a lifelong friendship with James Mackintosh. Graduating MA in March 1785 he returned to Bristol, having agreed in December 1783 to become assistant to Caleb Evans, minister at Broadmead Baptist Church. From August 1785 he was also classical tutor at the Bristol Baptist college. Hall was popular with the students and his preaching drew crowds, but some, including well-wishers, began to question his orthodoxy. His love of speculative conversation, his open admiration for Joseph Priestley, his 'advanced' views on some theological points, and a tendency to make rash remarks fuelled their suspicions. Discomfited by these fears, disappointed also in love, Hall agreed to fill the pulpit at St Andrew's Street, Cambridge, left vacant by the death of Robert Robinson, for a month from September 1790. In December he agreed to stay six months longer, and in July 1791 he formally accepted the Cambridge pastorate. Faction fighting at Broadmead and a personal breach with Evans marred his closing weeks in Bristol.

During his time at Cambridge, Hall modified some of his views in an orthodox direction, but from the outset he could speak his mind, for the Cambridge church prided itself on its tolerance and freedom of enquiry. During his pastorate there of over fourteen years, Hall reinvigorated a congregation that had dwindled and fragmented, bringing it new spiritual depth. He visited widely, showing special concern for the church's poorer members, and encouraged house groups for reading, religious conversation, and prayer. A reluctant author, he nevertheless became widely known and admired for two pamphlets putting the case for civil and religious freedom, *Christianity Consistent with a Love of Freedom* (1791) and *Apology for the Freedom of the Press and for General Liberty* (1793). In 1795 he attacked Charles Simeon for preaching a political sermon and circulating an 'inflammatory prayer' supporting the cause of refugees from the French Revolution. Three extremely topical published sermons made a name for Hall. The first of these, *Modern Infidelity* (1800), was widely regarded as his best work, and gave rise to controversy in Cambridge. There followed *Reflections on War* (1802) and *The Sentiments Proper to the Present Crisis* (1803).

Above all, Hall became known while in Cambridge for his electrifying preaching. To begin with, newcomers often wondered how he had earned his reputation for, while he cut an impressive figure, his voice was weak from childhood illness and he faltered a great deal. Once in his stride, however, his eloquence, intensity, intellect, and clarity of thought, coupled with his quick-fire delivery, transfixed his congregation. 'It is impossible', recalled the *Baptist Magazine* in 1832, 'to describe the impression which many of his most powerful sermons produced, the glow, the rapture, the delight with which they were heard'. Growing numbers of university students, several of whom went on to positions of influence, were among the crowds who flocked to listen.

From childhood Hall suffered from almost constant and severe back pain caused by stones in his kidney, leading him, in later life, to depend very heavily on laudanum—but to this was added, in November 1804, a serious mental breakdown. The Cambridge church gave him a life annuity backed by a capital sum, and for a time he resumed his pastoral duties, but a further breakdown in November 1805 led to his resigning the pastorate in March 1806 on medical advice. Recuperating in Leicestershire, he began occasional village preaching. He also preached at Harvey Lane in Leicester, and in October 1807 became minister there. On 25 March 1808 he married Eliza Smith, formerly cook for Thomas Edmonds, Baptist minister at Clipstone. The couple had three daughters and two sons, one son dying in infancy.

The Harvey Lane Church was smaller and less refined

than St Andrew's Street, but under Hall—and despite his continuing ill health and spiritual self-doubt—the congregation grew. Admirers made detours to hear sermons less polished but more personal than before, and the chapel was twice enlarged. Quarterly days of prayer and fasting were introduced. While never at ease on the public platform, Hall was more active than before in public life, interesting himself especially in the formation and progress of the Leicester Auxiliary Bible Society. He wrote an appeal on behalf of the new Baptist academy in Stepney, and preached and wrote on behalf of the Baptist Missionary Society. In 1815 he published *On Terms of Communion*, prompting a lengthy pamphlet controversy with Joseph Kinghorn of Norwich. During these exchanges Hall argued strongly that there was no basis in scripture, or in the practice of the early church, for Baptists to deny communion to Christian coworkers, whose sincerity was not in doubt, simply because they believed in infant baptism, although he was never able to persuade the Harvey Lane church fully to accept his position. In 1817 he was awarded an honorary DD by Marischal College, Aberdeen, but he never used the title. Among several important publications, his sermon in 1817 on the death of Princess Charlotte again showed his talent for touching the popular nerve, running to sixteen editions in ten years. In 1819 and 1821 Hall used his pen anonymously on behalf of the local framework knitters' friendly relief society. In 1823 he wrote an anti-slavery address.

In April 1826, after much heart-searching, Hall left Leicester for Bristol, having accepted a unanimous invitation to return to Broadmead as pastor. His preaching, as ever, drew crowds, but before long deteriorating health meant that he could walk only with difficulty. The onset of heart disease aggravated his condition and led him, in the summer of 1830, to spend some time away from Bristol. Hall preached at Broadmead for the last time on 6 February 1831, and after a series of attacks died in Bristol of heart failure on 21 February. His body was interred at Broadmead, but was later moved to Bristol's Arnos Vale cemetery. His wife survived him.

Hall's character was many sided. He was forgetful but dignified; humble and childlike but a brilliant conversationalist; pious but intensely superstitious; artless but with a sharp wit and ready supply of pithy phrases which he used to puncture arrogance and conceit. His significance partly lies in the radicalism of his early publications, against the flow of dissenting political quietism induced by the French Revolution (although he came to regret some of his rather acid early forays into politics). Above all, however, it lies in the reputation he established as perhaps the greatest pulpit orator of his time. With admirers including William Wilberforce, Lord Brougham, Sydney Smith, and several Anglican bishops, and accolades in well-known periodicals, Hall's oratory and writings did much to enhance the Baptists' standing. (He was rumoured, indeed, to have been offered high preferment within the Church of England.) His works, including letters, circular letters, memoirs, sermon outlines, notes made by others of his sermons, and contributions to the *Eclectic Review*, were published in six volumes, with a memoir, by his friend and admirer Olinthus Gregory.

ROSEMARY CHADWICK

**Sources** J. Foster and J. Macintosh, *The works of Robert Hall, AM: with a brief memoir of his life, by Dr Gregory; and observations on his character as a preacher, by J. Foster*, ed. O. Gregory, 6 vols. (1832) • A. H. Macleod, 'The Life and Teaching of Robert Hall, 1764–1831', MLitt diss., U. Durham, 1957 • *Baptist Magazine*, 24 (1832), 89ff. • review, *QR*, 48 (1832), 100–32 • J. W. Morris, *Biographical recollections of the Rev. Robert Hall* (1833) • J. Greene, *Reminiscences of the Rev. Robert Hall … and sketches of his sermons preached at Cambridge prior to 1806* (1832) • J. M. Chandler, *An authentic account of the last illness and death of the late Rev. Robert Hall* (1831) • R. Robinson, *Church book: St Andrew's Street Baptist Church, Cambridge, 1720–1832* (1991) • J. H. Y. Briggs, *The English Baptists of the 19th century* (1994) • *Modern memorials: Leicester* (1875) • *EdinR*, 72 (1840–41), 66–98, esp. 81 • R. H. Warren, *The Hall family* (1910) • M. Walker, *Baptists at the table* (1992)

**Archives** Bristol Baptist College, letters • NRA, priv. coll., letters to John Ryland • Regent's Park College, Oxford

**Likenesses** Ridley, stipple, pubd 1810 (after Branwhite), NPG • T. R. Poole, wax medallion, 1814, NPG • J. Flowers, portrait, *c.*1820, Leicester Museum [*see illus.*] • R. J. Lane, lithograph, pubd 1850 (after E. Eden), NPG • J. B. Philip, statue, De Montfort Square, Leicester • mezzotint (after J. Flowers), BM • stipple (for *New Evangelical Magazine*), NPG

**Wealth at death** £3000—value of goods, chattels, and credits granted to widow: administration

**Hall, Robert** (1817–1882), naval officer, was born at Kingston in Upper Canada, where his father, Captain Sir Robert Hall RN commanded the naval squadron on the Great Lakes. He entered the navy on 27 May 1833, and did his early service largely in the flagships of his father's old friends. On 28 November 1843 he was made lieutenant, and, after serving in the frigate *Grampus* on the Pacific station from 1845 to 1848, and on the west coast of Africa, was promoted commander on 6 September 1852. In 1853 he served as commander of the *Agamemnon*, one of the earliest screw line-of-battle ships; in 1854 he commanded the paddle sloop *Stromboli* in the Baltic, sailing in her to the Mediterranean and the Black Sea; in May and June 1855 (as acting captain of the *Gladiator*) he took part in the expedition to Kerch and the Sea of Azov, under the command of Captain Lyons. After Lyons's death Hall was promoted captain of the *Miranda*, which he brought home and paid off in 1857. From 1859 to 1863 he commanded the *Termagant* in the Pacific, and on his return to England was appointed private secretary to the duke of Somerset, then first lord of the Admiralty. This was an important and influential salaried post requiring knowledge and tact. In March 1866 he was appointed superintendent of Pembroke dockyard, where he introduced an effective system of accounting. He remained there until March 1871. In June 1869 he was made a CB. In May 1872 he became naval secretary to the Admiralty. This was a new post created as part of George Goschen's reform of the Admiralty, to assist with the routine of the office. In November 1877 the office of permanent secretary was abolished and the duties merged with those of the naval secretary. In 1882, the situation was reversed. While at the Admiralty Hall served as a naval aide-de-camp. Under the 1870 retirement regulations, after ten years' service ashore, Hall was promoted to the rank of retired rear admiral on 30 April 1873, and to retired vice-admiral on 21 March 1878.

Hall served as naval secretary until the post was abolished in May 1882, when he resigned; but one week afterwards, the new permanent secretary was sent to Ireland as under-secretary, and Hall replaced him. He had barely done so when he died suddenly of heart disease at his home, 28 Craven Hill Gardens, Hyde Park, London, on 11 June 1882. He was survived by his widow, Teresa Bridget, daughter of Thomas Tunstall.

J. K. LAUGHTON, *rev.* ANDREW LAMBERT

**Sources** R. V. Hamilton, *Naval administration* (1896) • J. H. Briggs, *Naval administrations, 1827 to 1892: the experience of 65 years*, ed. Lady Briggs (1897) • N. A. M. Rodger, *The admiralty* (1979) • J. C. Sainty, ed., *Admiralty officials, 1660–1870* (1975) • *The Times* (14 June 1882) • K. Bourne, *Britain and the balance of power in North America, 1815–1908* (1967) • Boase, *Mod. Eng. biog.* • Kelly, *Handbk* (1879) • *CGPLA Eng. & Wales* (1882)

**Wealth at death** £10,027 11*s.* 1*d.*: administration with will, 6 July 1882, *CGPLA Eng. & Wales*

**Hall, Robert Lowe**, **Baron Roberthall** (**1901–1988**), economist, was born on 6 March 1901 in Tenterfield, New South Wales, Australia, the second of the three sons (the eldest of whom was killed in action in 1917 in the First World War) and third of the five children of Edgar Hall, lecturer at the University of Sydney and later a mining engineer, who had emigrated to Australia, and his wife, Rose Helen, daughter of Archibald Kennedy Cullen, of Undercliffe Station, New South Wales. His parents moved to Silverspur in Queensland when he was a baby and, after attending the local school there, he won a state scholarship to the grammar school in Ipswich, near Brisbane. He studied civil engineering at the University of Queensland in Brisbane, graduating BEng in 1922 and going the following year to Magdalen College, Oxford, as a Rhodes scholar. He obtained first-class honours in philosophy, politics, and economics (1926) and was appointed to a college lectureship at Trinity College, Oxford. He was a fellow of Trinity from 1927 to 1950 and of Nuffield College, Oxford, from 1938 to 1947 (visiting fellow in 1961–4).

In the 1930s Hall became a prominent member of the Economists' Research Group, joining some younger Oxford dons who were sceptical of current economic doctrine, and undertook empirical research on how business actually behaved—for example, in fixing prices or reacting to price signals. His contribution to this research included an article in 1939, 'Price theory and business behaviour', written in collaboration with the American Charles J. Hitch, which first introduced the idea of the kinked demand curve. (The article was reprinted in *Oxford Studies in the Price Mechanism*, 1951, edited by Thomas Wilson and Philip Andrews.)

On the outbreak of the Second World War in 1939 Hall joined the Ministry of Supply (raw materials department) and, after America's entry into the war, served for two years in 1942–4 with the British raw materials mission in Washington, DC. In 1947 he succeeded James Meade as director of the economic section of the Cabinet Office, having meanwhile divided his time between Oxford and the Board of Trade, and continued as director for nearly fourteen years until April 1961. He was in charge of the only substantial group of professional economists in Whitehall, and although he was not given the title of economic adviser to the government until 1953, when he moved to the Treasury, that accurately describes his role. He retained this post until 1961, serving under eight chancellors of the exchequer and exercising more influence on economic policy than any other official. Among the matters in which he took a prominent part were the devaluation of 1949, rearmament in 1950–51, the Robot proposal to float the pound in 1952, the introduction of the investment allowance in 1953, the credit squeeze which began in 1955, and the Treasury's evidence to the committee of 1957–9 chaired by Cyril Radcliffe. During his years in the economic section he kept a diary, contrary to the rules; it provides both a picture of the writer and a unique insight into the way in which economic policy took shape in the post-war years.

On leaving the Treasury, Hall returned to Oxford and in 1964 was elected principal of Hertford College, spending much of his three years there as a member of the commission of inquiry into Oxford University (1964–6), chaired by Baron Franks. He continued to maintain contact with Whitehall, for a short time as an adviser to the Ministry of Transport, and for six years as a member of the Commonwealth Economic Committee (1961–7). He also accepted two business appointments, one as an advisory director of Unilever (1961–71), and the second, at the invitation of Baron Plowden, as adviser to Tube Investments (1961–76). He took an active interest in the National Institute of Economic and Social Research, whose role as economic commentators and forecasters he had earlier done much to encourage, and served as chairman of the executive committee from 1962 to 1970.

In 1969 Hall was made a life baron and changed his name by deed poll to become Lord Roberthall. For the next two decades he was an active member of the House of Lords, latterly as a member of the Social Democratic Party. He spoke in debates and served on many standing committees, taking the chair of a select committee on commodity prices in 1976–7. He received many honours. Appointed CB in 1950 and KCMG in 1954, he was an honorary fellow of both Trinity College (1958) and Hertford College (1969), Oxford, and was created an honorary DSc at the University of Queensland. He was president of the Royal Economic Society in 1958–60 and of the Society of Business Economists from 1968 to 1973. Earlier he had been chairman of an international group of experts at the Organization of European Economic Co-operation (OEEC) which was the forerunner of working party 3 of the OECD. He delivered the Sidney Ball lecture in Oxford in 1954 and the Rede lecture in Cambridge in 1962 ('Planning', 1962).

Hall was not at his best as a theoretician and published relatively little: several articles and two books, of which the more substantial is *The Economic System in a Social State* (1937), based on lectures delivered in 1934. As is clear from his diaries, his gifts were those of a highly successful economic adviser. He had a remarkable feel for the state of the economy and could outdo his staff as a forecaster. He was outstanding as a draftsman, but a man of few words in committee. He was a realist, endowed with great common sense, appreciating the limits of what was feasible, and a good judge of men. He took great pains over recruitment of staff and initiated a scheme for borrowing economists from their universities for a two-year spell. His unaffected modesty, good humour, and thoughtfulness won him the affection, as his abilities won the respect, of his colleagues.

Hall married twice. His first marriage in 1932 was to (Laura) Margaret Linfoot (*d.* 1995), daughter of George Edward Linfoot, musician, of Nottingham. She became a well-known economist in her own right and a fellow of Somerville College, Oxford. They had two daughters. When the marriage was dissolved in 1968 he married Perilla Thyme, daughter of Sir Richard Vynne *Southwell, aeronautical engineer, and the former wife of Patrick Horace Nowell-Smith, philosopher and fellow of Trinity College, Oxford. The two spent much of the next twenty years in their house, Quarry, Trenance, near Newquay in north Cornwall. Hall was a passionate gardener, working on his Oxford allotment at weekends even when in the Treasury and winning prizes with his sweetcorn from the Treasury Horticultural Society. After a stroke in 1987 Lord Roberthall never fully recovered; he died by his Cornwall garden next to the sea at Quarry on 17 September 1988. He was survived by his second wife.

ALEC CAIRNCROSS, *rev.*

**Sources** *The Robert Hall diaries, 1947–1953*, ed. A. Cairncross (1989) • *The Robert Hall diaries, 1954–1961*, ed. A. Cairncross (1991) • personal knowledge (1996) • *The Times* (19 Sept 1988) • *CGPLA Eng. & Wales* (1988)

**Wealth at death** £164,309: probate, 1988, *CGPLA Eng. & Wales*

**Hall, Ronald Owen** (1895–1975), bishop of Hong Kong, was born on 22 July 1895 at 7 St Thomas Square, Newcastle upon Tyne, the second of nine children of Cecil Gallopine Hall (1868–1938), curate of St Andrew's, Newcastle, and his wife, Constance Gertrude (1868–1936), daughter of the Revd Henry Berners Upcher and his wife, Lucy. Three of his brothers became priests or missionaries; another, Sir Noel Hall, was principal of Brasenose College, Oxford, and his sister Faith was headmistress of St Hilda's School, Ootacamund, India.

Hall was educated at the Royal Grammar School, Newcastle upon Tyne, and at Bromsgrove School before serving in the First World War in the Northumberland Fusiliers, becoming the youngest brigade major in the army with an MC and bar. He then took a shortened degree course as a scholar of Brasenose College, Oxford, and studied at Cuddesdon College before being ordained deacon in 1920 and priest in 1922. On 24 April 1923 he married a distant relative, Nora Kathleen Suckling-Baron (1897–1982); they had two sons and one daughter. After serving as missionary secretary of the Student Christian Movement from 1921 to 1925, he spent a year with the Young Men's Christian Association in China, working under T. Z. Koo, who became one of his heroes. From 1926 to 1932 he was vicar of St Luke's, Newcastle, where he felt a burning sympathy with the unemployed and their families in the depression of 1931, in which he initiated housing and food distribution schemes.

In 1932 Hall was appointed bishop of Hong Kong and until 1951 of southern China also. He early made clear his attitude that foreigners exercised too much authority and that in differences of opinion between European and Chinese he would back the Chinese. In a remarkable book, *The Art of the Missionary* (1942), he advised anyone who aspired to be a missionary in China to sell his books on religion and make friends with Chinese artists to learn the secrets of the saints (pp. 9–12). His criticisms of the administration from the cathedral pulpit caused the governor to describe him as the Pink Bishop.

When the Japanese took Hong Kong in December 1941, Hall happened to be attending a conference in the USA. On his return he lived in parts of his diocese still under Chinese control. It was then that the incident occurred which made him notorious. In 1944, after informing William Temple, archbishop of Canterbury, he ordained as priest a deaconess, Florence Li Tim Oi, in order that the congregation of Macau (Macao), which was cut off from the mainland, should be able to continue to receive the sacrament. Temple seems not to have been wholly unsympathetic (Paton, 130–35), but on his sudden death his successor, Fisher, accused Hall of obstinately refusing the advice of his friends to suspend the woman, and successfully called on the Chinese house of bishops, who were heavily dependent on outside aid after the war, to repudiate his action. Hall's own diocesan synod supported him and appealed to the Lambeth conference of 1948 to allow the experiment. The conference refused: Florence Li Tim Oi gave up her priestly function but not her indelible holy orders. The precedent was to be of great importance in the long battle within the Anglican church on the ordination of women. Ironically, Hall was not primarily interested in feminism; coming from a Tractarian background his motivation had been the supreme importance of enabling his flock to receive the sacrament from a priest, not a layman.

After the war Hall, who was always a disciple of F. D. Maurice, worked ceaselessly for social justice in his diocese, particularly through voluntary agencies. In partnership with the government he established church schools on the new housing estates and was a principal architect of the Chinese University which, unlike the existing Hong Kong University, used Cantonese, not English, as the medium of instruction. He encouraged trade unions and looked forward to a situation in which his diocese would be entirely staffed by Chinese priests, many of them self-supporting.

Hall's expressed views on politics appeared to some impetuous. In 1943 he described the Chinese nationalist leader Chiang Kai-shek in a pamphlet as 'a man of God whose achievements are tremendous' (*China's Fight*, 20). When however the Kuomintang's corruption and defeat became evident he referred in a further pamphlet to 'the splendid efforts of the People's Republic of China' (*Hong Kong: what of the Church?*, 11). Strong sympathy for the aspirations of Asia and its poor was not altogether unusual in a contemporary colonial ecclesiastic, but Hall's writing on other questions was also striking. He maintained that international commerce was the handmaid of the kingdom of God, and that there was no better school of charity than the bar of a public house. In a fashionably ecumenical age he declared that a divided church helped rather than hindered the spread of Christianity. He delighted that politicians no longer felt easy in claiming that God was on their side, and said that God preferred enjoying people to improving them (Hall, *Hong Kong: what of the Church?*, 11; *Family*, 25; *Art*, 49). His principal hobby was to breed Anglo-Nubian goats whose milk, unlike that of cows, could be digested by the Chinese. Some admirers felt that his charismatic qualities might very profitably have been exercised in an English diocese, but his alienation of the establishment in ordaining a woman precluded such a move. In 1966, on retirement, he became CMG.

A handsome, attractive, but somewhat shy man with a keen sense of humour, Hall preferred to work through an inspired choice of assistants rather than by setting up committees. Occasionally peremptory, he was quick and humble in apologizing. Deeply, though informally, devout, he was widely revered as a saint. He retired in 1966 to Lewknor, Oxfordshire, where he played a modest but helpful part in church and village life until his final illness, dying on 22 April 1975 at the Radcliffe Infirmary, Oxford. He was cremated at St Margaret's, Lewknor, Oxfordshire, three days later. His wife survived him.

RICHARD SYMONDS

**Sources** D. M. Paton, *'R. O.': the life and times of Bishop Hall of Hongkong* (1985) • R. O. Hall, *The art of the missionary* (1942) • R. O. Hall, *A family in the making* (1925) • R. O. Hall, *New church order: the future of the world wide episcopal church* (1942) [27th Hale Memorial Sermon] • R. O. Hall, *Hong Kong: what of the church?* (1952) • R. O. Hall, *China's fight for freedom* (1943) • R. O. Hall, *China and Britain* (1947) • private information (2004) [Canon Christopher Hill, son] • *WWW* • *CGPLA Eng. & Wales* (1975) • b. cert.

**Likenesses** photographs, repro. in Paton, *'R. O.'* • photographs, priv. coll.

**Wealth at death** £214,818: probate, 4 Nov 1975, *CGPLA Eng. & Wales*

**Hall, Samuel** [*called* the Sherwood Forest Patriarch] (**1769–1852**), agriculturist, was born on 9 April 1769 in Forest Lane, Sutton in Ashfield, Nottinghamshire, the second son of Samuel Hall and his wife, Dorothy Wilcock. He was apprenticed to Timothy Broadhurst, a cousin in the cobbling trade in Nottingham, but ran away to London before serving his time. While singing in a church in Holborn, he was struck with the impropriety of vocal praise, and, after a period of uncertainty, joined the Quakers. He fully adopted their distinctive practices of dress and speech, although by his marriage out of the pale, he ceased to belong to the society. He became a confidential servant to a Westminster leather merchant until, after seven years, he returned to Sutton in Ashfield and set up in business for himself. He married Eleanor Spencer, a Derbyshire shepherdess and dairymaid, the widow of another Quaker convert, James Bacon; among their children was Spencer Timothy *Hall. A financial speculation led to his ruin, and although he was the inventor of a machine for sowing, manuring, and pressing turnip seed in one operation, it was patented by a rival and he derived no financial benefit from his work. He published several tracts on religious subjects, the most important of which was *A few remarks, among which are reasons why the Quakers suffer loss rather than serve in the army* (1797). He also produced a treatise on the cultivation of turnips, and, after his wife's death, wrote an address to his children in which he set out his religious opinions. He died at his home, Brookside Cottage, Sutton in Ashfield, on 20 August 1852.

K. D. REYNOLDS

**Sources** S. T. Hall, *Biographical sketches of remarkable people* (1873), 211–28 • *GM*, 2nd ser., 38 (1852), 435 • Boase, *Mod. Eng. biog.* • J. Smith, ed., *A descriptive catalogue of Friends' books*, 1 (1867), 907

**Hall, Samuel** (*bap.* **1782**, *d.* **1863**), cotton spinner and engineer, was baptized on 17 March 1782 at Basford, Nottinghamshire, the second son of Robert *Hall (1754–1827), cotton manufacturer and bleacher, and his wife, Ann. Marshall *Hall, the physiologist, was his younger brother. In 1813 Robert and Samuel Hall filed a patent for the improvement of knitting frame machinery, and thereafter the younger man, trading as S. Hall & Co. of Basford, filed patents for improving textile machinery, thread making, and the manufacture of starch. His method of 'gassing' lace, set out in his patents of 1817 and 1823, consisted in passing the fabric rapidly through a row of gas flames, which removed all the loose fibres without damaging the lace. The process brought a considerable benefit to the Nottingham lace trade and much wealth to Hall, which he then dissipated in his later inventions.

From 1824 Hall was concerned with improving the performance and fuel consumption of steam engines. He installed the first two in his own factory and a third at another Nottingham works. A sequence of patents covered various modifications, the most novel being those in which the lubricating oil and the water which condensed the steam were both recycled. Such a closed cooling system had potential value for marine engines, where recycled fresh water could replace the corrosive salt water normally used to condense the steam. By 1834 Hall's condensers were fitted to the engines of the steam packet *Prince Llewelyn*, and Hall was able to publish testimonies from engineers and ships' captains as to the advantages of his system, together with a list of those engine builders who had taken licences for his improvements (*Mechanics' Magazine*, 22, 1834–5, 84–5). In 1837 two 180 hp Hall engines were installed in HMS *Hercules* and gave satisfactory results on a test run from London to Gravesend. By this time Hall was describing himself as 'civil engineer of Basford', though he also had business addresses in London. In 1842, however, Sir Edward Parry reported on behalf of the Admiralty that six of Hall's condensers had been fitted in steam packets and that they had given two to six years' service but had then been taken out, because they were difficult to keep in order due to the complexity of their construction.

Hall, described as 'formerly of Basford', filed his last patent in 1851. It related to the manufacture of starches and gums. He died on 21 November 1863 in very reduced circumstances at 6 Morgan Street, Tredegar Square, Bow, east London. ANITA MCCONNELL

**Sources** *Mechanics' Magazine*, 18 (1833), 65–8, 86–90, 156–7, 183–6, 271–2, 324–7, 440–42 • *Mechanics' Magazine*, 19 (1833), 20–22, 182–3, 256 • *Mechanics' Magazine*, 21 (1834), 48 • *Mechanics' Magazine*, 22 (1834–5), 82–6, 260–61, 278–9, 329–30, 376–7 • *Mechanics' Magazine*, 22 (1834–5), 329–30, 376–7 • *Mechanics' Magazine*, 23 (1835), 368, 459–60, 464 • *Mechanics' Magazine*, 37 (1842), 333, 471–2 • *Nautical Magazine*, 6 (1837), 330–31, 485 • *VCH Nottinghamshire*, 2.360–61 • R. Hall and S. Hall, 'Experiments on stoving cotton goods with sulphur', *Quarterly Journal of Science and Arts*, 4 (1818), 196–9 • *Mining Journal* (10 Sept 1842) • *DNB* • d. cert.

**Hall, Samuel Carter** (1800–1889), journal editor and writer, was born at Geneva barracks, co. Wexford, on 9 May 1800, the fourth of twelve children of Ann, *née* Kent, and **Robert Hall** (1753–1836). The father, a Devon man, had purchased a commission as ensign in the 72nd regiment in 1780, served in Gilbraltar, and then settled for a time at the manor house of Topsham, near Exeter, where on 6 April 1790 he married Ann Kent. In 1794 he raised a new regiment, the Devon and Cornwall fencibles, with which he served in Ireland, garrisoning Cork, until 1802. In that year (or possibly earlier) he returned to Topsham with his growing family; his son Samuel Carter's first memory was of the illuminations there after the battle of Trafalgar in October 1805. The eldest son, Revis, was killed at the battle of Albuera in May 1811, allegedly inspiring Samuel Carter's first literary effusion, an elegiac poem. By then the family had gone back to Ireland, Robert importing some of his Cornish troopers to help him exploit the copper mines he leased as a speculation. These speculations came a cropper, partly it was said as a result of sharp dealing by the absentee owner, Lord Audley, and his steward, which gave Samuel Carter a lifelong distaste for the Irish social system and its moral and economic effects. Subsequently the family was maintained by a business in Cork run by Ann Hall. Robert Hall died at Chelsea on 10 January 1836.

Samuel Carter Hall's early interests lay in the arts, of all kinds. On youthful visits to London he saw Kemble act Coriolanus and bought books from William Godwin's shop. He met the painter Daniel Maclise in Cork in 1820. Having set out for London to make his fortune in 1822, he immediately fell into the right company: the author Eyre Evans Crowe introduced him to Ugo Foscolo, the exiled Italian poet, and young Hall was engaged as the latter's secretary. Tempted by Foscolo's life of indolence and libertinism, Hall later testified that he was 'saved' by an Irishwoman, Anna Maria Fielding (1800–1881) [*see* Hall, Anna Maria], daughter of Sarah Elizabeth Fielding and her husband, whose name is unknown. Hall met Anna Maria Fielding in 1823 and they married in London on 20 September 1824. The young couple settled in Chelsea, suffered through several failed pregnancies (only one child, Maria Louisa, lived briefly), and scrambled to support themselves on Samuel Carter Hall's Grub Street earnings. On 3 July 1824 he was entered as a student of the Inner Temple, but he was not called to the bar until 30 April 1841, and never practised.

The variety of Hall's early activities was dazzling. After leaving Foscolo's employment, he worked for a time on behalf of Sir Robert Wilson's attempt to raise an Anglo-Spanish legion against France; reported parliamentary debates for a number of journals, including the *British Press*, to which the young Charles Dickens was then offering 'penny-a-line' police news; edited and wrote every word of the *Literary Observer* for six months in 1823; from 1826 edited *The Amulet*, an annual that offered the usual dose of sub-romantic poetry, stories, and woodcuts to (in this case) a Christian audience; edited the monthly *Spirit and Manners of the Age* (in 1826) and the *British Magazine* for Westley and Davis (who also took over *The Amulet* from 1830); and deputized for the editor of the ultra-tory *Morning Journal* in 1829–30. At the peak of this frenzy, in 1830, he collated a 400-page *History of France* from 100 volumes of sources in three weeks for Henry Colburn's Juvenile Library, after which he understandably suffered a brief nervous collapse. Soon enough he was back at his post, editing a Peelite newspaper, *The Town*, writing leaders for the Wesleyan paper *The Watchman*, and, most substantially, serving under Thomas Campbell as sub-editor of the famous literary paper the *New Monthly Magazine*.

From 1826 Samuel Carter's mother-in-law, Mrs Fielding, came to live with the Halls, an added burden, but one met to some degree by the launch in 1829 of Anna Maria's literary career. She was soon occupied in much the same range of writing and editing projects as her husband (including her own annual); thereafter the two acted as a partnership, and it is often difficult to discern from whose pen writings under his name actually issued. At this point in his career Hall, despite his financial insecurities, also had a busy extra-professional life in a number of spheres. He hung about on the fringe of Coleridge's circle in Highgate; otherwise, his friends were mostly less exalted scribblers, actors, and engravers all serving the newly burgeoning mass market. With other 'working authors' he was a member of the Literary Union, which later split to form the Garrick Club. In 1828 he was among the founders of the Society of Noviomagus, an antiquarian dining club (of which he was president, 1855–81).

Life at the *New Monthly Magazine*—of which Hall was alternately sub-editor and editor from 1830—provided some kind of stability, but this was badly shattered when Colburn finally preferred Theodore Hook (whom Hall had himself hired as a writer) as editor in 1836. Hall predicted that Hook's 'unseemly and mischievous high-Tory politics' (Hall, 1.318) would spell disaster, but such was his financial situation that he accepted from Hook the consolation prize of the sub-editorship of *John Bull* in 1837. He did this despite his disapproval of *John Bull*'s frivolous, libellous character, perhaps because at the same time Westley and Davis's bankruptcy brought *The Amulet's* run to an end and left him paying some of the firm's bad debts. Other short-term expedients included the editorship of

*The Britannia* (of which he also disapproved, as it was funded by a distiller).

Far more congenial was the offer, at the end of 1838, of the editorship of a new magazine, *The Art-Union*, to be funded by Charles Landseer RA and published by Hodgson and Graves, producers of art prints. The first issue appeared on 15 February 1839 at 8*d*.; 750 were printed. This was the turning point in Hall's career. The *Art Journal* (the title adopted in 1849) would prove to be the pioneer of fine-art journalism in Britain. In a number of ways it helped to stabilize the shaky position of the art world in a period when old canons and patronage networks were collapsing. Hall worked to expose the roaring trade in faked old masters, thus reducing that market but also making it more respectable. At the same time he championed the cause of modern British artists, both in painting and in sculpture. For this he earned the gratitude not only of artists but also of leading critics such as Ruskin. He campaigned tirelessly to expand and uplift the audience for art by publicizing exhibitions and collections open to the public, by publishing a great deal of criticism (much by his assistant editor James Dafforne), and eventually by printing in the magazine high-quality engravings of great works of art (notably, from 1848, the whole of the Vernon collection).

The magazine was also a popular success. Benefiting at first from the publicity attendant upon the appointment in 1841 of the Fine Arts Commission and the competitions it organized for the decoration of the new houses of parliament, as well as from a general interest in art-manufactures (which he supported), Hall kept the *Art Journal* on the qui vive, constantly expanding the range of contents, and the number and quality of illustrations, as early as 1846 experimenting in photographic illustration, using prints supplied by Fox Talbot. By then its circulation had reached 7000, to Hall's profit, as he had bought up the title from the publishers after its first year for £200. An over-ambitious Great Exhibition number in 1851 proved a financial disaster, however, and Hall was forced to sell his interest and accept a salary as editor. Under his aegis, the *Art Journal* remained virtually in sole possession of its field for decades, until the appearance of the *Magazine of Art* in 1878.

The first decade of the *Art Journal* was Hall's heyday. He was able to yoke his new-found influence in the art world to some of his earlier preoccupations. *The Book of British Ballads* (1842) allied selections from popular balladry to engraved illustrations which he commissioned from some of the premier artists of his day, among them Richard Dadd, W. P. Frith, Richard Redgrave, and John Gilbert. *The Baronial Halls, Picturesque Edifices, and Ancient Churches of England* (1845–6) applied a similar treatment to antiquarian subjects, mostly stately homes, in the Romantic style popularized by Joseph Nash. *Ireland, its Scenery, Character, etc.* (with Anna Maria, 1840) was also well-illustrated and had a good reception as a mixed travelogue and social commentary. Hall extended his pre-existing commitment to projects of moral uplift. As early as 1835 he had been recruited by John Lilwall into the movement for early closing of shops on Saturday, to liberate shopworkers for self-improvement. For a few years Lilwall and Hall laboured alone and unnoticed, holding meetings such as one later recalled by Hall in a smoke-filled room in Whitechapel, 'a miserable hole under a railway, the roll of trains over which necessitated frequent pauses in the proceedings' (Hall, 434–6). Partly owing to his new influence, the movement gathered steam in the 1840s—an Early Closing Association was founded in 1843 and a climax of respectability was reached with a great public meeting at Exeter Hall in 1856. At the same time he was active in the temperance movement, in fundraising for the Consumption Hospital, Brompton (which he helped to found in 1840), and for the Chelsea Hospital (recruiting his friend Jenny Lind to sing in its support), and in aid of indigent governesses, army and navy pensioners (he assisted in the establishment of the Corps of Commissionaires), and Florence Nightingale's nursing crusades.

These were also the years when the Halls lived at The Rosery, their cottage in Old Brompton in London, which became faintly notorious among actors, writers, and artists for Thursday 'at-homes' and other generally teetotal entertainments. Bohemian opinion was frankly divided about the Halls, especially about Samuel Carter: artists were grateful for his patronage; women were drawn by his tall and handsome bearing; and all admired his genuine concern for the moral condition of the poor and oppressed. But his smooth self-righteousness, his conspicuous puritanism, and (for some) his Peelite politics were sources of irritation. He was guyed as Shirt-Collar Hall; The Rosery became The Prosery or The Roguery. W. J. Linton complained of his 'small talk and smaller Marsala' (Linton, 74). As far afield as south Wales, an *Art Journal* salesman sneered to a subscriber, 'She does it all. Hall himself is an umbug' (Purnell, *The Athenaeum*, 375–6). Charles Dickens seems to have been more aggravated than most. Hall is generally regarded as the model for Pecksniff in *Martin Chuzzlewit*, and certainly Dickens is recorded as fuming, after one particularly flowery and (he felt) hypocritical speech, at 'the snivelling insolence of it, the concentrated essence of Snobbery in it, the dirty Pecksniffianity that pervaded it, and the Philoprogullododgeitiveness wherein it was steeped' (*Letters of Charles Dickens*, 8.161).

Hall retrenched his activities somewhat after 1849, when he bought a country home, Firfield, near Addlestone, in Surrey. Both Halls lavished money and attention on its flower-filled conservatory, its collection of painting and statuary, and on hospitality for visiting celebrities (who were invariably required to plant a fir tree in the grounds). The *Art Journal* remained Samuel Carter's central preoccupation. His most substantial work of later years, the two-volume *Stately Homes of England* (1874–7, co-authored with his friend Llewellynn Jewitt), originated in articles written for the magazine: artistic and historical accounts of stately homes open to the public.

By this date retirement was possibly desired but made impossible by financial circumstances. The difficulty was eased by Anna Maria's receipt in 1868 of a £100 pension from Disraeli, and even more by a munificent golden wedding gift to the couple of £1600, in an annuity and cash, presented by 600 subscribers at a public meeting presided over by Lord Shaftesbury. Yet it was surely money worries that persuaded Hall, as late as 1878, to take on for a year the editorship of *Social Notes*, a weekly floated by the Marquess Townshend to advocate social and moral reform. It was a painful move, as it embroiled him in lengthy litigation with a disgruntled sub-editor. Finally, after the receipt of two further pensions (£150 from Disraeli and £300 from Virtue, the *Art Journal's* publisher), he was able to retire in December 1880. Almost immediately he lost Anna Maria, on 30 January 1881. They had already moved from Firfield to Devon Lodge in nearby East Moulsey, and now he returned to London. He occupied himself in writing temperance tales and memoirs, and in complaints about moral decline, but also in cheerful marvelling at the pace of social change until his death on 16 March 1889 at 24 Stanford Road, Kensington; he was buried a week later at Addlestone, beside Anna Maria. None of his works long survived him; even the *Art Journal* was quickly superseded by rivals such as the *Magazine of Art*. And yet his life as a whole stands as a model of Victorian energy and uprightness, and his work as editor and *animateur* did much to popularize art and literature and thus to support the mass market for high culture so characteristic of the middle third of the nineteenth century. PETER MANDLER

**Sources** S. C. Hall, *Retrospect of a long life, from 1815 to 1883*, 2 vols. (1883) · J. Maas, 'S. C. Hall and the *Art Journal*', *The Connoisseur*, 191 (1976), 206–9 · D. N. Mancoff, 'Samuel Carter Hall: publisher as promoter of the high arts', *Victorian Periodicals Review*, 24 (1991), 11–21 · J. Newcomer, 'Mr. and Mrs. S. C. Hall: their papers at Iowa', *Books at Iowa*, 43 (Nov 1985), 15–23 · W. H. Goss, *The life and death of Llewellyn Jewitt* (1889) · A. Wilsher, 'Hall of fame', *History of Photography*, 3 (1979), 133–4 · T. Purnell, 'Mr. S. C. Hall', *The Athenaeum* (23 March 1889), 375–6 · W. J. Linton, *Memories* (1895) · *The letters of Charles Dickens*, ed. M. House, G. Storey, and others, 8 (1995)

**Archives** Hist. Soc. Penn., papers · Hunt. L., letters · Knox College, Galesburg, Illinois, personal and professional corresp. · NL Scot., corresp. and poem · University of Iowa Libraries, Iowa City, special collections, corresp. and papers · Wolverhampton Archives and Local Studies, letters | BL, letters to G. Hall, Add. MS 45883 · National Gallery Libraries and Archives, letters to Ralph Nicholson Wornum · U. Aberdeen, special libraries and archives, letters to Peter Buchan relating to his literary work, enclosing proofs and MS poems with testimonial for same

**Likenesses** H. B. Burlowe, marble bust, 1834, Bethnal Green Museum, London · C. C. Vogel, pencil and chalk drawing, 1850, Staatliche Kunstsammlungen, Dresden · Robinson & Cherallt, photograph, Sept 1874, repro. in C. W. Mann, 'Memories', *History of Photography*, 3 (1979), 330 · F. Joubert, carte-de-visite, NPG · D. J. Pound, stipple (after photograph by Mayall), BM, NPG; repro. in D. J. Pound, ed., *The drawing room portrait gallery of eminent personages* (1861) · L. Stocks, engraving (after drawing by P. De La Roche, 1847), repro. in Hall, *Retrospect*, vol. 1, frontispiece · J. and C. Watkins, carte-de-visite (with his wife), NPG

**Wealth at death** £500 14*s*. 2*d*.: probate, 10 May 1889, *CGPLA Eng. & Wales*

**Hall, Selina** (1781/2–1853). *See under* Hall, Sidney (1788/9?–1831).

**Hall, Sidney** (1788/9?–1831), map maker and engraver, was probably born in 1788 or 1789. Nothing is known of the circumstance of his birth, parentage, education, or early life, although the terms of his will suggest that he had a brother and a sister.

Hall first appears in 1814 in partnership with Michael Thomson, an obscure map maker and engraver under whom he may have trained. By 1816 Hall had taken over Thomson's premises in Bury Street, Bloomsbury, London, where he was to remain throughout his career. His early work included maps of London produced for Samuel Leigh in 1818 and 1819, and a set of miniature county maps for the same publisher's *Leigh's New Pocket Atlas, of England and Wales* in 1820. By 1821 Hall was already utilizing the new steel-engraving plates manufactured by Jacob Perkins's process. The hardness of these plates enabled engravers to achieve much greater density of detail without loss of clarity, and Hall was almost certainly the first map maker to realize the potential of this development. Among much fine work he is remembered in particular for the fifty-three folio maps, produced from 1827, for his *A New General Atlas* of 1830. This atlas was of such detail as to require the separate publication of a closely printed 360-page index of place names in 1831. Equally impressive were the maps produced between 1828 and 1830 for *An Historical Atlas* by Edward Quin. These maps show considerable technical virtuosity, with dark clouds (produced by aquatint) rolling back to reveal the world as known to Western civilization at different periods. The finished work is a striking piece of nineteenth-century design and a significant contribution to the development of the historical atlas.

Hall's last work was a set of quarto English county maps for the publishers Chapman and Hall. These maps were used in a variety of publications and could also be bought individually, folded to pocket size, and 'mounted in a case'. Periodically revised to include new information, and later photo-mechanically enlarged, they remained in print for the next half-century. Hall died before the set was completed and it is noticeable that counties from the latter part of the alphabetical sequence are signed not in his usual form 'Sid[y]. Hall' but with the plainer 'S. Hall'. This was the style adopted by his widow, **Selina Hall** (1781/2–1853), who continued the business, seemingly without a pause, until her death. Many maps of this period simply signed S. Hall are undoubtedly her work, or work done under her direction, although it was her husband's name that continued to appear on the title-pages of atlases as well as in contemporary directories. Her work is highly competent and may be characterized as slightly looser and more open in appearance than that of Sidney Hall.

Selina Price and Sidney Hall had married on 25 August 1821 at St George's, Bloomsbury. The bride came originally from Radnorshire, Wales. The marriage was childless. Of Sidney Hall's character and disposition no record is found. His circle of acquaintance is likewise unknown, although one of the executors of his will was the London surgeon Sidney Van Butchell, whose forename perhaps suggests a family connection. George Shillibeer was a near neighbour in Bury Street and presumably an acquaintance at just the period that Shillibeer planned the first London omnibus routes.

Sidney Hall died on 18 February 1831, his age being given as forty-two, and was buried at St George's, Bloomsbury, on the 27th of that month. His will provided for his wife's security in slightly varying terms, depending on her continuance of the business. The sale of a copyhold estate in Richmond, Surrey, provided legacies for nephews and a niece. There was £100 for a brother and £50 for his wife's nephew to pay an apprenticeship fee. On the death of Selina Hall in November 1853 the Bury Street premises passed to that same nephew, Edward Weller (1819–1884), who himself became a map maker of considerable repute, and whom Selina may have trained. The family connection was maintained in the naming of his son, Francis Sidney Weller, also a map maker of some note.

LAURENCE WORMS

**Sources** *British Museum catalogue of printed maps, charts and plans*, 7 (1967), 168–72 • will of Sidney Hall, PRO, 1226/1259/94 • will of Selina Hall, PRO, 1226/1998/18 • parish registers, St George, Bloomsbury, LMA • B. Hunnisett, *An illustrated dictionary of British steel engravers*, new edn (1989) • d. cert. [Selina Hall]

**Archives** BL, Map Library

**Wealth at death** under £400; incl. £150 bequeathed to brother and wife's nephew; left wife unspecified assets, apparently large enough to purchase annuity of £100 p.a.: will, PRO, 1226/1259/94

**Hall, Spencer** (1806–1875), librarian, was born in Ireland; William Hall, of the publishers Chapman and Hall, was his brother. He was articled to John Booth, bookseller, of Duke Street, Portman Square, London. He lived briefly in Germany and afterwards worked for Hodges and Smith of Dublin. He was appointed librarian of the Athenaeum in 1833, on the recommendation of his relative Magrath, who had succeeded Faraday as the first secretary of the club. The club had only occupied its new house in Pall Mall for three years, so Hall was responsible for much of the early organization of the library; under his management it gradually became one of the best collections of reference books in London. Hall's knowledge of books and general literature was extensive and he was always ready with advice. He issued a pamphlet on the classification of the library in 1838, followed three years later by a letter to John Murray suggesting an edition of Shakespeare with literary criticisms. His other publications in the *Archaeological Journal*, the *Proceedings of the Society of Antiquaries of London*, the *Art Journal*, and other periodicals were mainly antiquarian articles. He was elected a fellow of the Society of Antiquaries of London on 13 May 1858. Hall retired after forty-two years' service, owing to failing health, in May 1875, when he was elected an honorary member of the club and voted a pension. He lived in Maida Vale, Paddington, but died on 21 August 1875 at 1 Revesby Place, Tunbridge Wells. His own library was sold at Sothebys on 26 June 1876.

H. R. TEDDER, *rev.* BERNARD NURSE

**Sources** H. Ward, *History of the Athenaeum, 1824–1925* (1926) • *The Athenaeum* (11 Sept 1875), 338 • *Proceedings of the Society of Antiquaries of London*, 2nd ser., 7 (1876–8), 11–12 • *Transactions of the Conference of Librarians, 1877* (1878)

**Archives** Bodl. Oxf., corresp. with Sir Thomas Phillipps • Derbys. RO, corresp. with J. J. Briggs

**Wealth at death** under £4000: resworn probate, Dec 1876, *CGPLA Eng. & Wales*

**Hall, Spencer Timothy** (1812–1885), writer and mesmerist, was born on 16 December 1812 in a cottage near the village of Sutton in Ashfield in Sherwood Forest, Nottinghamshire, the son of Samuel *Hall (1769–1852), a Quaker cobbler and agriculturist, and Eleanor Spencer, a Derbyshire shepherd and dairymaid. He received some education from his father. At seven years of age he wound cotton for stocking makers, and at eleven began weaving stockings himself.

After reading the life of Benjamin Franklin, Hall resolved to become a printer. In January 1829 he went to Nottingham and bound himself apprentice typesetter at the office of *The Mercury* newspaper. About this time he first began writing poetry, and by 1832 he was contributing verse to *The Mirror*, the *Metropolitan Magazine*, and other periodicals. His work gained him an introduction to the Howitts and other members of Nottingham's literary circles. He also helped to found a scientific institution in the town, at which he read essays.

In 1836 Hall's apprenticeship came to an end, and he returned to Sutton in Ashfield, where he started his own printing and bookselling business, and printed a monthly periodical called the *Sherwood Magazine*, in which he published his work under the name of 'The Sherwood Forester'. He also served as village postmaster. In May 1839 he accepted the post of superintendent in the printing establishment of Messrs Hargrove at York. In 1841 he published a volume of prose and verse descriptive of his birthplace called *The Forester's Offering*, which he set up in type himself, the greater portion without manuscript. The book earned Hall an invitation from James Montgomery to Sheffield, where he became co-editor of *The Iris* newspaper and governor of the Hollis Hospital. He wrote a volume of prose sketches entitled *Rambles in the Country* for *The Iris*; it was reissued in an enlarged form in 1853 as *The Peak and the Plain*. As the result of a visit to Ireland in the famine years he published *Life and Death in Ireland as Witnessed in 1849* (1850).

As well as pursuing his literary career, Hall was also keenly interested in a number of popular scientific movements. He was the first honorary secretary of the Sheffield Phrenological Society and later an honorary member of the Phrenological Society of Glasgow. In 1841 he learned about mesmerism from watching some spectacular demonstrations by a Frenchman named Lafontaine, who was touring northern England. Hall then taught himself mesmerism and began to make his own tours of the country, giving public demonstrations, offering tutelage and therapy, and selling copies of a journal he founded in 1843, *The Phreno-Magnet, or, Mirror of Nature*. He saw himself as a spokesman for the common man, and he argued that scientific knowledge should not be restricted to professionals. Hall claimed that the forces of nature were readily accessible to the senses, and therefore apprehensible, in principle, to everyone. In 1845, after lecturing throughout

Britain, Hall wrote that in no 'rank' of society 'have I ever seen a more intense ... interest evinced in mesmerism, than by some of the large popular audiences in the manufacturing districts' and felt that the 'common people' were as entitled to its benefits as 'the class to which several writers would have mesmerism confined!' (Hall, *Mesmeric Experiences*, 1845).

Hall's most illustrious patient was Harriet Martineau, whom, it seems, he cured of an apparently hopeless disease of the uterus. Martineau was first diagnosed in 1839; after over five years of suffering, she was introduced to mesmerism by her brother-in-law, who had been impressed by one of Hall's lectures in Newcastle. 'Everything that medical skill and family care could do for me had been tried, without any avail', Martineau wrote in her *Autobiography* (1877), 'Now that a new experiment was proposed to me ... I had nothing to do but try it'. About 1852 Hall became a homoeopathic doctor, and published *Homoeopathy: a Testimony* (1852). He was particularly interested in hydropathy and was at one time head of an establishment near Windermere. Since he was never legally qualified, however, his practice did not flourish, and the final years of his life were spent in poverty, although a few months before his death he received a grant of £100 from the government. He was also granted the honorary degrees of MA and PhD from Tübingen.

After living for some time at Derby, Hall settled in 1866 at Plumgarths, near Kendal; in 1870 or 1871 he moved to Burnley, in 1880 to Lytham, and soon afterwards to Blackpool. He was married twice: his first wife, Sarah, died only nine months after their wedding; his second marriage produced several children, to whom he was extremely devoted. He died at Blackpool on 26 April 1885, and was buried in the cemetery there on 29 April.

GORDON GOODWIN, *rev.* STEPHANIE L. BARCZEWSKI

**Sources** S. T. Hall, 'The Sherwood Forester', *Chambers' Edinburgh Journal*, 11 (1842), 6–7 • *Manchester Weekly Times* (2 May 1885) • *Glasgow Examiner* (5 Oct 1844) • *Blackpool Herald* (1 May 1885) • *Blackpool Gazette* (1 May 1885) • *Blackpool Times* (29 April–6 May 1885) • *The Academy* (9 May 1885), 329 • A. Winter, 'Mesmerism and popular culture in early Victorian England', *History of Science*, 32 (1994), 317–43 • [H. Martineau], *Harriet Martineau's autobiography*, ed. M. W. Chapman, 2 (1877)

**Wealth at death** died in relative poverty, though given grant of £100 from government shortly before death

**Hall, (William) Stephen Richard King-**, **Baron King-Hall** (**1893–1966**), writer and broadcaster, was born at Blackheath, London, on 21 January 1893, the eldest of the three children and the only son of Admiral Sir George Fowler King-Hall (1850–1939), and his wife, Olga Felicia (*d.* 1950), daughter of Richard John Charles Rivers Ker, of the diplomatic service, and MP for Downpatrick. She came of an Ulster family with not only diplomatic but also literary associations. His grandfather (Sir William King *Hall, who distinguished himself during the Second Anglo-Chinese War) and uncle were also admirals. His father, a liberally minded man, held religious convictions of an evangelical cast. He was also a lifelong teetotaller, as was his son. After

**(William) Stephen Richard King-Hall, Baron King-Hall (1893–1966)**, by Howard Coster, 1932

early schooling at Lausanne, Switzerland, King-Hall was educated at the Royal Naval College at Osborne and Dartmouth. He was in action at Jutland in the *Southampton*, the 'little ship' of his naval affections. After the war he wrote the first Admiralty manual on cruiser tactics. On 15 April 1919 he married (Amelia) Kathleen (*d.* 1963), daughter of Francis Spencer, an associate of Cecil Rhodes. He had met his wife in Cape Town as a midshipman. They had three daughters.

Having been awarded the gold medal of the Royal United Service Institution in 1919, King-Hall went on to serve in the training and staff duties department of the Admiralty. In 1920–21 he passed through the Royal Naval Staff College, afterwards proceeding as a torpedo lieutenant to the China squadron, until the end of 1923. In 1924 he was appointed for one year to the Army Staff College, Camberley, as a student instructor, and from 1926 to 1927 he was intelligence officer to Sir Roger Keyes in the Mediterranean Fleet. In 1928 he was promoted commander, and called to work on the naval staff.

Though King-Hall's feeling for the navy was deep, he had early confided to his family his impatience with some of its traditional practices. He shared his generation's revulsion from war. Though never a pacifist, he pinned hopes on disarmament. He had, moreover, long cultivated the talents that would make him a publicist. He wrote much for the press under a pseudonym. On the China station he had produced his first book under his own name, *Western Civilization and the Far East* (1924). *Imperial Defence*

(1926) attracted a preface by Viscount Haldane. Meanwhile his verve had overflowed in the improvisation of ships' entertainments with results that would prove fruitful in the theatre.

In 1929 King-Hall resigned from the service to take a research post in the Royal Institute of International Affairs at Chatham House. His slender finances, now supporting a family, were transformed by the success of a naval comedy, *The Middle Watch* (1929), produced in collaboration with John Hay Beith (Ian Hay), which ran for two years, and was to be five times filmed. He was now poised to become one of the most popular interpreters of current events of his generation.

As organizer of discussions at the institute King-Hall met authorities in many fields, including J. M. Keynes whose respect he gained, and whose influence became apparent in his work. He made no claims as an original thinker, but saw himself as a mediator, whose information would be 'respected by the expert, and acceptable to the general reader'. His strongly held opinions, sometimes simplistic, at other times lit by genuine insight, were those of a liberal internationalist, who was early alert to the rising menace of fascism. His independence was patent. The press had forfeited much public confidence, and an audience lay ready. From 1930 until 1937 he broadcast a talk on current affairs every Friday in the BBC *Children's Hour*. His directness and warmth (not without an occasional breeze from the quarter-deck), combined with his rare gift for reducing complexities to simple language, enthralled not only the children but many adults, including such diverse personalities as Lloyd George, the duke of Westminster, and Lord Perry, chairman of Ford Motor Company Ltd.

By 1935, when King-Hall left the staff of Chatham House, he was not only a radio celebrity, but a widely published journalist, in demand as a lecturer at home and abroad, a name in the theatre, and a prolific author. (His books would eventually total forty.) In 1934–5 he published *Our Own Times*, a voluminous contemporary history, which went through four editions. An invitation to the board of the United Kingdom Provident Institution gave him practical insight into insurance and investment. In 1936 came his most characteristic venture. Single-handed, save for family and a few friends, and with no capital, he undertook to post a weekly letter, the *King-Hall News Letter*, to subscribers. At first there were 600. In three years there were 60,000. The *King-Hall News Letter* became, without advertisement revenue, a self-financing institution. His touch remained personal, but always with an eye to world horizons. Again and again he returned to the need for preparedness to meet the threat of Hitler. On the eve of war he contrived to infiltrate a German version to individuals in the Reich, provoking a vehement reaction from Goebbels and Hitler himself.

In October 1939 King-Hall entered the House of Commons as National Labour member for Ormskirk, unopposed under the wartime truce. This climax to long-cherished parliamentary ambitions proved hollow. He could endure the yoke of no party, even the loosely associated National Labour remnant soon becoming too constrictive. He resigned from it in February 1942 but continued to sit in the house as an independent. He vented his wartime energies in administrative and propaganda work, combining his duties as an MP with honorary appointments, first as director of factory defence in the Ministry of Aircraft Production and then as director of the fuel economy campaign in the Ministry of Fuel and Power. His foundation of the Hansard Society in 1944 attested his devotion to parliament as an institution. He lost his seat to Harold Wilson in 1945, and failed as independent candidate at Bridgwater in 1950.

Meanwhile King-Hall's appeal as a publicist had declined somewhat from its pre-war peak. He appeared on television, but it was too late for him to match there his earlier success on radio. Fashions in journalism had changed. Yet his personal following remained considerable. When, in 1959, rising costs threatened the *News Letter*, pressure from subscribers persuaded him to continue it, though at less frequent intervals. His flow of books was unabated. In them he argued strenuously for European union. Quick to seize the implications of the atom bomb, he put a reasoned case for unilateral nuclear disarmament by Britain, though he never countenanced agitation by unconstitutional means.

Though many good things lie scattered in his writings, King-Hall left no memorial commensurate with his dispersed talents. He saw himself primarily as an educator and former of opinion. As such he remains a distinctive figure, unlikely to be overlooked by students of his time. He was a companion of infectious vitality. In appearance he realized the traditional idea of the sailor: short and sturdy, with a merry eye and a pugnacious chin.

King-Hall was knighted in 1954, and in January 1966 he received a life peerage. His last years were overshadowed by the death of his wife. He died in the Westminster Hospital, London, on 2 June 1966. E. R. THOMPSON, *rev.*

**Sources** *The Times* (3 June 1966) · private information (1981) · Burke, *Peerage* (1967) · *CGPLA Eng. & Wales* (1966)

**Archives** King's Lond., Liddell Hart C., papers · NRA, papers | Bodl. Oxf., corresp. with Lionel Curtis · King's Lond., Liddell Hart C., corresp. with Sir B. H. Liddell Hart | FILM BFI NFTVA, performance footage

**Likenesses** H. Coster, photographs, 1932, NPG [*see illus.*] · W. Stoneman, photograph, 1944, NPG · D. Low, pencil caricature, NPG

**Wealth at death** £21,225: probate, 6 Oct 1966, *CGPLA Eng. & Wales*

**Hall, Sydney Prior** (1842–1922), artist, was born at All Saints, Newmarket, Suffolk, on 18 October 1842, the eldest son of Harry (Henry) Hall (*c.*1814–1882), artist, of Newmarket, who painted racehorses and other sporting subjects, and his wife, Ellen Ann Payne. He was educated at Merchant Taylors' School, London, and at Pembroke College, Oxford, where he held a scholarship and in 1865 gained a first class in *literae humaniores*. He also attended the Royal Academy Schools in London. 'A gifted draughtsman able to capture natural attitudes and postures with great skill' (Stewart and Cutten, 226), Hall produced a series of 100 'Oxford sketches' (1864–6) illustrating topical events in the life of the university. The caricatures, which circulated in photographic copies, displayed 'a keen sense of the outlook and prejudices' of the primarily undergraduate audience (Brock and Curthoys, xxi).

Although he was a talented painter in oils and in watercolours, it was as an illustrator that Hall became best-known. With the likes of Luke Fildes and Hubert von Herkomer, he was one of the principal contributors to William Luson Thomas's illustrated weekly *The Graphic*, which became renowned for its pictorial coverage of world events. Hall was special artist of *The Graphic* during the Franco-Prussian War (1870–71): his drawings of Paris during the German siege and the commune were dispatched to London by balloon post. A selection of his work from France was published in *Sketches from an Artist's Portfolio* (1875), which was dedicated 'by special permission' to the prince of Wales.

Hall first met the prince of Wales during a bear-hunt in Russia in February 1874, which he sketched, and after summoning up the courage to approach the prince he was peremptorily cut short: 'Hush! for God's sake; we expect the bear' (Hall, *Sketches*, 30). The prince later invited Hall to join his suite on his voyage to India in 1875–6; many of the resulting Indian sketches are now at Osborne on the Isle of Wight. Hall also accompanied the marquess of Lorne when he went to Canada as governor-general in 1879. He returned in 1881, as special artist of *The Graphic*, accompanying the marquess on a journey to the north-west territories to promote settlement of the country and raise capital for the completion of the Canadian Pacific Railway. 'To the Great North-West with the Marquis of Lorne', illustrated with over 100 drawings, ran in *The Graphic* from August 1881 to February 1882.

Hall's domestic arrangements were unconventional: for much of the 1870s he lived out of wedlock with Emma Dinah (1846/7–1894), daughter of John Holland, cellarman, at 39 Birkbeck Road, Islington, London. On 30 September 1873 a son was born, Reginald Holland (Harry) *Hall, later assistant keeper of Egyptian and Assyrian antiquities at the British Museum. The couple later married at Islington register office, on 14 January 1877, when they were living at 3 Pyrland Villas, Calverley Grove. With Arthur Hughes, Hall illustrated an edition of *Tom Brown's School-Days* (1882), and he was the sole illustrator of an edition of the sequel, *Tom Brown at Oxford* (1886). He also produced a large number of life studies of public figures, many made in parliament and the law courts, and he was 'a penetrating observer' of the notable legal encounters of the day (Hogarth, 66). 'His biggest triumph was a chronicle of over two hundred brilliant off-the-cuff pencil drawings of the Parnell Commission' (1888–9), which appeared as a fifty-page special number of *The Graphic* (ibid.).

Among Hall's many pencil drawings in the National Portrait Gallery are studies of Charles Bradlaugh, John Bright, Joseph Chamberlain, Michael Davitt, William Ewart Gladstone, Charles Stewart Parnell, and Oscar Wilde. There are also a number of his oil paintings in the gallery, including *The Duke and Duchess of Teck Receiving Officers of the Indian Contingent, 1882* (1883), *The Three Daughters of King Edward VII and Queen Alexandra* (1883), and a study of Joseph Chamberlain and Arthur James Balfour (*c.*1895), depicted on the benches of the House of Commons. Hall exhibited at the Royal Academy from 1875: his works included portraits of Indian officers, a portrait of the prince of Wales at Baroda, *The Marriage of HRH the Duke of Connaught KG*, and *Mr Gladstone Playing his Evening Game of Backgammon*. His sensitive oil study of an Oxford viva voce, *We Pause for a Reply*, was originally given the title *Dominus illuminatio mea* when exhibited at the Royal Academy in 1895. Hall also exhibited fourteen works at the Grosvenor Gallery. A watercolour of the progress of the Education Bill in the House of Lords was reproduced in *The Graphic* of 13 December 1902. Hall is pictured in the group portrait *Primrose Hill School* (1893), by an unknown artist, alongside, among others, Sir Ernest Albert Waterlow and Arthur Hopkins.

In 1901 Hall was a member of the suite of the duke and duchess of York, and special artist of *The Graphic*, on board HMS *Ophir*. He was created MVO that year. After the death of his first wife he married second, on 4 August 1906, Mary Lightbody (1851–1929), the daughter of James Gow, painter. The artist Andrew Carrick Gow (1848–1920) was her brother. Mary Gow too was a painter, mostly producing figures and genre in watercolours, and she exhibited widely, principally at Suffolk Street, where she sent eighteen works between 1869 and 1880. She was represented at the Royal Academy from 1873, and her *Marie-Antoinette* was purchased under the Chantrey bequest in 1908. She was elected a member of the Institute of Painters in Water Colours in 1875. Sydney Prior Hall died at his London home, 36 Grove End Road, St John's Wood, on 15 December 1922. He was survived by his wife. MARK POTTLE

**Sources** G. M. Waters, *Dictionary of British artists, working 1900–1950* (1975) • B. Stewart and M. Cutten, *The dictionary of portrait painters in Britain up to 1920* (1997) • Wood, *Vic. painters*, 3rd edn • J. Johnson and A. Greutzner, *The dictionary of British artists, 1880–1940* (1976), vol. 5 of *Dictionary of British art* • P. Hogarth, *The artist as reporter* (1986) • *WWW* • S. P. Hall, *Sketches from an artist's portfolio* (1875) • S. P. Hall, *Oxford caricatures* [n.d.] • www.npg.org.uk [National Portrait Gallery], March 2002 • b. cert. • m. certs. • d. cert. • b. cert. [Harry Reginald Hall, son] • will • M. G. Brock and M. C. Curthoys, eds., *The history of the university of Oxford*, 7: *Nineteenth-century Oxford*, 2 (2000) • A. Bott, *Our fathers (1870–1900)* [n.d.]

**Likenesses** group portrait, oils, 1893 (*The Primrose Hill school*) • engraving (after portrait, 1895), NPG

**Wealth at death** £1700 10s.: probate, 1 Feb 1923, *CGPLA Eng. & Wales*

**Hall, Thomas** (1610–1665), clergyman and ejected minister, was born on 22 July 1610, the second son of the clothier Richard Hall and his wife, Elizabeth (*née* Bonner), in the parish of St Andrew's, Worcester. His younger brother was Edmund *Hall. He was educated at King's School, Worcester, under the famous schoolmaster Henry Bright (*d.* 1626), of whose brutality he was critical in a manuscript biography (written in the third person by himself or another) which is an important source of information on him. Hall entered Balliol College, Oxford, in 1624 but migrated to the newly founded Pembroke College. There he was a pupil of Thomas Lushington, later a Socinian and at that time a 'starke staring Arminian' (DWL, 'Life', fol. 16). He graduated BA in February 1629.

Later in 1629 Hall became master of the grammar school at King's Norton (then in Worcestershire, now a part of Birmingham), and he remained in this post until 1662. The 'Life' says that he fought against the 'lewd custom' of 'barring out' the master, at the cost of some personal injury. He took over the school when it was at a low ebb, and made it highly successful (Vaughan, 'Former grammar school', 29; 'Life', fol. 17). King's Norton lay in the large parish of Bromsgrove, whose vicar was Thomas's brother, John. In 1632 Thomas Hall became curate at Wythall, and in 1635 at Moseley, both chapelries within Bromsgrove. At Moseley he was under the protection of the Grevis or Graves family of Moseley Hall. The 'Life' says that Moseley was the place 'which of all places … he loved the most' ('Life', fol. 44). In 1640 he became curate of King's Norton and took over a 'rude and ignorant people' who soon became 'in the general tractable and teachable' (ibid., fol. 53).

In August 1650 Hall engaged in a debate with five unordained 'mechanick' preachers (one of whom was Samuel Oates, Titus's father) at Henley in Arden, Warwickshire. This led to the publication of his first major work, *The Pulpit Guarded* (1651), followed in 1652 by *The Font Guarded*, a defence of infant baptism. Both works are written in a highly polemical style, influenced perhaps by the Martin Marprelate tracts. His works are an amalgam of populist and erudite writing, combining, say, mock trials with vigorous and punning Latin diatribes. This dual character extended even to the titles of his works, which regularly had Latin or Greek alternatives to the English titles. One example is *Comarum akosmia: the Loathsomenesse of Long Haire* (1654), his attack on the fashion for wearing the hair long; Hall himself was described by his memorialist as 'a man of middle stature, his hair blackish, which he wore very short, scarce to cover his ears; his face pale and somewhat long' (Moore, 44). Another is *Chiliastomastix redivivus: … a Confutation of the Millenarian Opinion* (1657), an attack on a 'jejune, empty peece' ('Life', fol. 8) by Dr Nathaniel Holmes.

At King's Norton, Hall was on the cusp of Worcestershire and Warwickshire. Though he had been born in Worcestershire and held a Worcestershire parish, in ecclesiastical affairs he gravitated increasingly to the neighbouring county. His disciple Richard Moore wrote in 1675 that Hall was in the early 1630s 'a diligent attender of the learned Lectures of sundry Orthodox Divines at Birmingham' (Moore, 75), and implies that his presbyterianism dated from this period. In 1648 he signed the testimony of Warwickshire ministers in favour of the solemn league and covenant, and added the words 'Lect(urer) at Birmingham' to a printed copy now in Birmingham Central Library. In the preface to *The Font Guarded* he praised the citizens of Birmingham for the soundness and orthodoxy of their religious views.

When the Kenilworth classis of ministers was set up in Warwickshire, probably in December 1654, Hall chose to join this organization rather than the Worcestershire Association begun in 1652. His *Apologia pro ministerio evangelico* (1658), which also has a Greek title meaning 'the salt of the earth', is dedicated to twenty named brethren of the classis. The companion volume, so to speak, to the *Apologia* is Hall's 1660 work *The Beauty of Magistracy*, in which he stressed the interdependence of magistracy and ministry, and recalled (in the preface) the 'visible Reformation' which had occurred in King's Norton while Colonel Richard Grevis was an 'active, prudent pious Justice' there, and was assisted by Hall himself.

Thomas Hall seems to have made every effort to back the Cromwellian settlement in church and state, and a passage in the 'Life', later crossed out, speaks of Oliver the protector with considerable warmth and considerable regret ('Life', fol. 11). In 1658 Hall saw England as possibly on the verge of becoming another 'Canaan' (T. Hall, *Samaria's Downfall*, 1658, 51–2). Three years later he 'lookt upon it as a very good time to dye in' ('Life', fol. 82), his dreams shattered by Oliver's death, the anarchy of 1659–60, and the Restoration. The work of Thomas Hall which most vividly conveys his feelings about the harm done by the Restoration of May 1660 is *Funebria Florae, the Downfall of May Games* (1660), an attack on popular revels and superstitions, and especially on maypoles. This work, which has a typically hybrid title, is written in the manner of Hall's publications of 1651–2, and includes a mock trial of Flora, the personification of revelry. It helps to explain why Hall could not conform but was ejected from the living of King's Norton.

Hall lived in great poverty after his ejection but continued to serve his 'people', as he called them. And his house at King's Norton remained to the end of his life a kind of puritan seminary for young ministers, to whom he gave guidance and ministerial training. Some, such as William Fincher, Joseph Cooper, and Samuel Shaw, he regularly referred to (as for example in his will) as his 'sons'. He died at King's Norton, unmarried, on 13 April 1665, having chosen to be buried there, in the churchyard, among 'the meanest' of his flock in an unmarked grave. He was 'a lover of books and learning' ('Life', fol. 211). He left a library to the parish of King's Norton and another set of books to the town of Birmingham. In 1892 the King's Norton Library was transferred to Birmingham Reference Library, and now forms the Thomas Hall library held by Birmingham Central Library. Hall was a dedicated minister, a successful teacher, a passionate (and at times acerbic) controversialist, a man who fought all his life against popular revels and pastimes, and a man who could inspire devotion in pupils, fellow ministers, and parishioners. C. D. Gilbert

**Sources** A. Hughes, 'Popular presbyterianism in the 1640s and 1650s: the cases of Thomas Edwards and Thomas Hall', *England's long Reformation, 1500–1800*, ed. N. Tyacke (1998), 235–59 · 'A briefe narrative of the life and death of Mr Thomas Hall', DWL, Baxter treatises, 9.293–9 [photostat in Birm. CL, no. 467148] · F. J. Powicke, 'New light on an old English presbyterian and bookman', *Bulletin of the John Rylands University Library*, 8 (1924), 166–90 · A. Hughes, *Godly reformation and its opponents in Warwickshire, 1640–1662*, Dugdale Society, 35 (1993) · W. S. Brassington, *Transactions of* *the Birmingham and Midland Institute, Archaeological Section*, 14 (1887), 10ff • J. E. Vaughan, 'The former grammar school of King's Norton', *Transactions of the Worcestershire Archaeological Society*, new ser., 37 (1960), 27–32 • J. E. Vaughan, 'John Hall of Bromsgrove: a biographical note', *Transactions of the Worcestershire Archaeological Society*, new ser., 38 (1961), 20–24 • C. D. Gilbert, 'Magistracy and ministry in Cromwellian England: the case of King's Norton, Worcestershire', *Midland History*, 23 (1998), 71–83 • D. Thomas, 'Thomas Hall', MA diss., U. Birm., 1997 • J. E. Vaughan, 'The Hall manuscript', MA diss., Bristol University, 1960 • H. Goodger, *King's Norton* (1990) • *Calamy rev.* • M. Craze, *King's School, Worcester* (1972) • R. Moore, *A pearl in an oyster shell*, 2 pts (1674–5), 'together with a character of Mr. Thomas Hall' [incl. *Abel redivivus, or, The dead speaker*] • B. W. Ball, *A great expectation: eschatological thought in English protestantism to 1660* (1975), 72–5

**Wealth at death** see will, 'A briefe narrative'

**Hall, Thomas** (1657–1715). *See under* Hall family (*per.* *c.*1650–*c.*1750).

**Hall, Thomas** (1659/60–1719), Roman Catholic priest, born in London, was the son of Thomas Hall, a cook, and his wife, Elizabeth Hawkins. They resided for some time in Ivy Lane, near St Paul's Cathedral; Thomas Hall's brother was William *Hall, prior of the Carthusians at Nieuwpoort. The family were notorious recusants whose house was often searched for harbouring priests. Hall entered the English College at Lisbon with his brother on 10 March 1674; after studying philosophy and theology he was ordained deacon in 1683; but, not old enough to be ordained priest, he returned to England and then went to St Gregory's, Paris, to study divinity and to take his degrees. After about six years he was admitted STB.

In December 1688 Hall became professor of philosophy in the English College at Douai, where on 24 September 1689 he was ordained priest. He returned to Paris on 21 August 1690 and was created DD on 27 April 1694. He was then summoned by Mathias Watkinson, president of the English College, Lisbon, to become vice-president and theology lecturer, but was unsatisfactory, and in 1696 was recalled by Bishop Leyburn to England. He finally retired to Paris, and died there on 6 November 1719. Dodd describes him as a person of extraordinary natural parts and an eloquent preacher.

Hall left four works in manuscript: 'A treatise of prayer'; 'Spondani annales', a translation; 'The catechism of Grenoble', a translation; and 'A collection of lives of the saints', a translation, left incomplete.

Thompson Cooper, *rev.* G. Bradley

**Sources** G. Anstruther, *The seminary priests*, 3 (1976), 89–90 • D. A. Bellenger, ed., *English and Welsh priests, 1558–1800* (1984), 67 • Gillow, *Lit. biog. hist.*, 3.95 • T. F. Knox and others, eds., *The first and second diaries of the English College, Douay* (1878), 83 • M. Sharratt, ed., *Lisbon College register, 1628–1813*, Catholic RS, 72 (1991), 74 • E. H. Burton, ed., 'The register book of St Gregory's College, Paris, 1667–1786', *Miscellanea, XI*, Catholic RS, 19 (1917), 93–160, esp. 107–12

**Archives** Ushaw College, Durham, Lisbon Archives

**Hall, Thomas** (1702–1748). *See under* Hall family (*per.* *c.*1650–*c.*1750).

**Hall, Timothy** (*bap.* 1639, *d.* 1690), bishop of Oxford, was baptized on 17 March 1639 at St Katharine by the Tower, London, the son of Thomas Hall and his wife, Judith. Thomas, a woodturner and householder of St Katharine's, owned property in the area. Timothy matriculated at Pembroke College, Oxford, on 12 December 1654, when the college was under presbyterian influence. Here he was taught by the blind puritan preacher Thomas Cheseman. He graduated BA on 15 January 1658 and on 1 May following married Sara Rouls of Twickenham. He obtained the livings of Southam, Warwickshire, and Norwood, Middlesex, and was admitted vicar of Hayes, Middlesex, on 13 April 1659. He was ejected from these benefices after the Restoration, but on 11 January 1668, having complied with and signed the Thirty-Nine Articles, he was presented to the small living of Horsenden, Buckinghamshire. He became perpetual curate of Prince's Risborough in 1669 and vicar of Bledlow in 1674, both also in Buckinghamshire. He relinquished all of these positions in 1677 for the City living of All Hallows, Staining. In 1685 he was appointed curate of Hackney and in 1688 lecturer there. He seems to have acted as a broker for the king's mistress, the duchess of Portsmouth, in the sale of pardons, and appears to have obtained a regular grant of arms.

Hall's notoriety comes largely from his having promoted James II's declaration of indulgence for liberty of conscience in 1687 in contrast to the overwhelming refusal of the clergy, both in London and nationwide, to read it from their pulpits—although the eighteenth-century antiquary Daniel Lysons claimed that Hall did not read it himself but 'gave half a Crown to another (the Parish Clerk, I think) to do it' (Lysons, 2.500). The death of Samuel Parker on 10 March 1688 left the see of Oxford vacant; when the king got round to filling the bishopric at the end of July his choice was Hall, who was elected under the royal *congé d'élire* on 18 August and consecrated at Lambeth on 7 October. However, in the atmosphere of increasingly overt hostility at Oxford to James's policies, the canons of Christ Church refused the academically ill-qualified Hall installation and consequent admission to the temporalities, while the university refused to grant him the degree of doctor of divinity, despite Hall having a royal mandamus. He was snubbed by the university hierarchy and openly mocked by many who addressed him as 'doctor' or 'sir'. At the revolution he at first refused to take the oaths of allegiance to William and Mary, but he conformed on 17 January and thereby kept his title. He died on 9 April 1690 at Homerton, apparently in poverty, and was buried at St John's Church, Hackney, four days later.

Lysons alleged that Hall had converted to Catholicism (Lysons, 2.500). However, Gilbert Burnet's judgement that he was 'half a Presbyterian' seems far more accurate (Macleane, 309). His two printed sermons indicate, at the very least, sympathy with presbyterianism. In 1684 he published a funeral sermon for Robert Huntington, a former parliamentarian major who resigned his commission in 1648 in protest at the proceedings against the king. Hall's only other printed work, a sermon on Leviticus 19: 17, given at Mercer's Chapel on 13 January 1689, called on his congregation to show 'special preferment' to 'spiritual neighbours' (meaning protestant dissenters) (Hall, *Sermon Preached at Mercers-Chapel*, 4). Hall was described by White

Kennett as 'one of the meanest and most obscure of the city divines, who had no merit but that of reading the king's declaration' (Kennett, 3.491).

EDWARD VALLANCE

**Sources** D. Macleane, *A history of Pembroke College, Oxford*, OHS, 33 (1897), 251, 309, 310 · *Calamy rev.*, 243 · A. W. Hughes Clarke and R. H. D'Elboux, eds., *The registers of St Katharine by the Tower, London*, 2, Harleian Society, register section, 76 (1946), 75–81 · T. Hall, *A sermon preached at St Botolphs Aldersgate* (1684) · T. Hall, *A sermon preached at Mercers-Chapel* (1689) · D. Lysons, *The environs of London*, 2 (1795), 500 · [W. Kennett, J. Hughes, and J. Strype], eds., *A complete history of England: with the lives of all the kings and queens thereof*, 3 (1706), 491 · Foster, *Alum. Oxon.* · *Hist. U. Oxf.* 4: *17th-cent. Oxf.*, 947 · *Fasti Angl.*, 1541–1857, [Bristol]

**Wealth at death** 'hopeless poverty': *DNB*

**Hall, Virginia** (1906–1982). *See under* Women agents on active service in France (*act.* 1942–1945).

**Hall, Westley** (1711–1776), dissenter, was born at Salisbury on 17 March 1711. His father, Thomas, was a clothier and his mother, Margaret, was the daughter of Thomas Westley, rector of Imber, near Warminster. Her brother, Robert Westley, became lord mayor of London and was knighted in 1744. The Halls were in comfortable circumstances. Westley inherited Hornington Manor from his father and a house at Fisherton, near Salisbury, from his mother. He received his early education from his mother's brother, Thomas Westley, who was rector of Berkeley, near Frome, and he matriculated as a gentleman commoner at Lincoln College, Oxford, on 26 January 1731. At his entry he presented the college with two silver sauce boats, and at his departure he gave the college's rector, Euseby Isham, 'who was always kind to me', a copy of Raphael's cartoons.

Hall became a pupil of John Wesley, who recalled later that he had been 'holy and unblamable in all manner of conversation', and he was an assiduous attender at the Holy Club, making so favourable an impression on Wesley that he was invited to his home at Epworth. He became secretly engaged to Wesley's elder sister, Martha (Patty; 1710–1791), whom he had met when she was staying with her uncle, Matthew, in London. A few months later, however, he proposed to her younger sister, Keziah, and gained the family's consent to the marriage. When Martha revealed her engagement, he abandoned Keziah and married Martha in 1735. His action was strongly condemned by John Wesley's brothers, Charles and Samuel, who described him as a 'smooth-tongued hypocrite'. More immediately John reconciled himself to the marriage, which was highly praised in verses in the *Gentleman's Magazine* for September 1735. For a time Keziah resided with the Halls, later becoming a pupil teacher at Lincoln and dying young—her death hastened, according to John, by the treatment she had received from Westley Hall.

Hall, who had left Oxford in 1734 without a degree, was made deacon and priest by the bishop of London with a view to his becoming chaplain at Savannah in the newly established colony of Georgia in succession to Samuel Quincy. He joined the Wesleys and other members of the intended expedition at Gravesend in 1735 but (in spite of having expended £100 on clothing and furniture), partly because of objections from his family, he opted out, informing James Edward Oglethorpe that he had been offered a living by an uncle. He became a curate at Wootton Rivers in Wiltshire, moving to his mother's house at Fisherton, Salisbury, in 1735, where in 1737 he was joined by Wesley's widowed mother, Susanna, who then described him as a 'man of extraordinary piety and love to souls'. In 1739 the household moved to London, where Hall became actively engaged in promoting the youthful Methodist society, preaching against the Moravian doctrine of 'stillness' and urging the expulsion of two members of the society for failing to adhere to the principles of the Church of England. Within a year he had himself adopted Moravian tenets, converting Susanna Wesley to the 'witness of the Spirit' and strongly criticizing John Wesley's management of the society as well as his religious teaching.

In 1743 'poor Moravianized Mr Hall', as Charles Wesley called him, returned to Salisbury, where he set up a religious society which he urged John and Charles to join, but his views were to become increasingly extreme, moving from Moravianism to deism, repudiating the sacraments, denying the resurrection, and preaching and practising polygamy. His wife, whom he treated with little consideration, remained loyal to the Church of England. 'You are', John Wesley wrote to him on 18 August 1743, 'a weak, injudicious, fickle, irresolute man, deeply enthusiastic and highly opinionated. You need a tutor now more than when you first came to Oxford' (*Letters, 1740–55*, in *Works of John Wesley*, 26.103). In a strongly worded letter of 22 December 1747 Wesley remonstrated with Hall for his heterodox religious teaching and immoral manner of life, listing some of his many affairs.

Hall was, however, to persist in his eccentric opinions, in 1750–51 seeking to disturb Charles Wesley's prayer meetings at Bristol, for which Charles was to criticize him in his *Funeral Hymns* (no. 11). Shortly afterwards, accompanied by his mistress, he moved to the West Indies, visiting Essequibo in Guiana and Barbados, where in 1758 his mistress apparently saved his life when some black people entered his house and tried to slit his throat by hurling a pewter tankard at the miscreant's head.

On his return to England Hall took clerical duty and became reconciled to his wife; John Wesley commented to his brother Charles, 'Is it right that my sister, Patty, should suffer Mr Hall to live with her? I almost scruple giving her the sacrament, seeing he does not pretend to renounce Betty Rogers [the seamstress whom Hall had seduced]' (26 Dec 1761, *Letters*, ed. Telford, 4.166). Nevertheless John and Charles took over the responsibility for the maintenance and education of the Halls' eldest son, Westley, but the boy died from smallpox at the age of fourteen, much mourned by Charles in his *Funeral Hymns* (no. 10): 'unspotted from the world, and pure and saved and sanctified by grace'. His father, with characteristic ineptitude, had addressed a tract to the boy entitled *The Art of Happiness, or, The Right Use of Reason*, in which he strongly criticized orthodox religious teaching. In all Hall had apparently twelve sons and daughters, of whom at least two were illegitimate, of whom only three were still living in 1774. After suffering much ill health, Hall died at Bristol on 3 January 1776. John Wesley was too late to visit him but helped at his burial service, commenting in his journal: 'God had given him deep repentance. Such another monument of divine mercy, considering how low he had fallen, and from what height of holiness, I have not seen, no, not in seventy years' (*Works of John Wesley*, 22.479–80). Hall was a plausible and charismatic figure, especially where women were concerned, but of a very unstable character. His wife, Martha, survived him, dying on 12 July 1791. She was buried in the ground attached to the New Chapel in the City Road, London. VIVIAN H. H. GREEN

**Sources** *The works of John Wesley*, [another edn], 18–23, ed. F. Baker and others (1988–95) · *The works of John Wesley*, 25, ed. F. Baker (1980) · *The works of John Wesley*, [another edn], 26, ed. F. Baker and others (1982) · *The journal of the Rev. John Wesley*, ed. N. Curnock and others, 8 vols. (1909–16) · *The letters of the Rev. John Wesley*, ed. J. Telford, 8 vols. (1931) · J. Wesley and C. Wesley, *Funeral hymns* (1759) · *The journal of the Rev. Charles Wesley*, ed. T. Jackson, 2 vols. [1849] · *Diary of an Oxford Methodist: Benjamin Ingham, 1733–1734*, ed. R. P. Heitzenrater (1985) · *Proceedings of the Wesley Historical Society*, 5 (1906), 146–57 · *Proceedings of the Wesley Historical Society*, 22 (1939–40), 28–31 · L. Tyerman, *The early Methodists* (1873) · M. Edwards, *Family circle: a study of the Epworth household in relation to John and Charles Wesley* (1949)

**Hall, William** (*d.* 1700). *See under* Hall, Henry (*c*.1656–1707).

**Hall, William** (1655–1718), Carthusian monk, was born in London. His father, perhaps named Thomas, was a pastry maker in Ivy Lane near St Paul's Cathedral, and his younger brother was Thomas *Hall, a secular priest. Both brothers studied at the English College in Lisbon. After ordination William was sent back on the English mission and became a royal chaplain and preacher-in-ordinary to James II. A sermon which Hall preached before the queen dowager on 9 May 1686 was published in the same year. A further sermon is recorded by Wood on the occasion of James II's visit to Oxford in September 1687, when, on 4 September, Hall preached in the newly constituted Catholic chapel in the Canterbury quadrangle of Christ Church. Wood records that this sermon 'was applauded and admired by all in the chapell, which was very full, and [by those] without that heard him' (Wood, *Ath. Oxon.*, 1.cix). Indeed, Hall was held by the king to be the best Catholic preacher in England. He appears also to be the author of *A Sermon Preached … on Advent Sunday …*, before the king, published in Dublin in 1689.

Some time after the revolution of 1688 Hall visited James II in exile at St Germain before entering the charterhouse of Sheen Anglorum at Nieuwpoort in the Southern Netherlands, making his profession on 19 April 1693. He was soon entrusted with the office of novice master, but in 1695 he was transferred with his novices to the charterhouse of Brussels, as the community of Sheen Anglorum was too small to allow the complete observance of the rule. In 1696 the five monks of Sheen Anglorum elected him as prior. In 1697 his agent in England, Valentine Baily, was able to remit about £1000 sterling, which had been collected to relieve the poverty of the community. These funds were spent on a new high altar, black and white marble paving, and oak choir stalls in the monastic church, and on the construction of the little cloister. In 1699 the Carthusian general chapter accepted Hall's resignation as prior and he was transferred to the charterhouse of Hérinnes, near Enghien, also in Flanders. In 1702–3 he was vicar at the charterhouse of Bruges and in 1715 vicar at Sheen Anglorum, when the community again elected him prior. His resignation was once more accepted by the Carthusian general chapter in 1718, when he was nominated procurator of Sheen Anglorum. He died there on 6 November 1718, and was buried in its cemetery. JAMES HOGG

**Sources** W. Hall, 'A sermon preached before her majesty the queen dowager, in her chapel, at Somerset House, upon … May 9, 1686', *A select collection of Catholick sermons*, 2 (1741), 183 · J. Long, 'Notitia Cartusianorum Anglorum', Bibliothèque Royale, Brussels, MS Inv. no. 555–6, cat. no. 4530, fols. 200, 228, 236 · Wood, *Ath. Oxon.*, new edn, 1.cix, cxii; 4.450, 548 · Gillow, *Lit. biog. hist.*, 3.16 · P. Bastin, 'Chartreuse de Nieuport, Jésus-de-Bethléem, province de Teutonie', *c*.1920, Grande Chartreuse Archives, MA A.5.167a · J. de Grauwe, 'Chartreuse de Sheen Anglorum à Nieuport', *Monasticon belge*, 3/4 (1955), 1231–62 · J. de Grauwe, *Prosopographia Cartusiana Belgica (1314–1796)*, Analecta Cartusiana, 28 (1976), 129 · J. de Grauwe, *Histoire de la chartreuse de Sheen Anglorum au continent, Bruges, Louvain, Malienes, Nieuport (1559–1783)*, Analecta Cartusiana, 48 (1984), 101, 104, 107, 155, 162 · J. de Grauwe, *Historia Cartusiana Belgica*, Analecta Cartusiana, 51 (1985), 243–52 · J. Hogg, 'William Hall', *Dictionnaire d'histoire et de géographie ecclésiastiques*, 23 (Paris, 1990), 158–9 · *DNB* [Thomas Hall] · J. de Grauwe and F. Timmermans, *Prosopographia Cartusiana Belgica renovata (1314–1796)* (1999), 445

**Hall, William** (1748–1825), poet and antiquary, was born on 1 June 1748 at Willow Booth, a small island in the fen district of Lincolnshire near Hickington Ease, in the parish of South Kyme. His parents were very poor, his ancestors being fen slodgers on his father's side. Hall went to school for six months in Brothertoft. At a very early age Hall married a girl named Susanna Holmes, and became a gozzard, or keeper and breeder of geese. But the floods swept away his flock, which was appropriated by his neighbours, and after much wandering he settled in Marshland in Norfolk, where he gained for some time a living as an auctioneer and 'cow-leech', while his wife practised midwifery and phlebotomy. One of his poems tells that it was here that his arm broke on account of rheumatic throbbing, whereupon he moved to Lynn and commenced business as a dealer in old books in Ferry Street. 'The Antiquarian Library', as he called his shop, did fairly well, though he was obliged to sell, as opportunity offered, many other things besides books.

Hall published a considerable number of strange rough rhymes, dealing with the fens, fen life, and the difficulties of his calling. Low-Fen-Bill Hall, as he sometimes styled himself, had a perception of his own faults, which he describes when mentioning John Taylor, the 'water poet', 'who near two centuries ago wrote much such nonsense as I do'. But his verse is not without a certain Hudibrastic force, and it frequently contains graphic touches descriptive of modes of fen life now passed away. He published at Lynn *A sketch of local history, being a chain of incidents relating to the state of the fens from the earliest accounts to the present time* (1812) and *Reflections upon Times, and Times, and Times! or, A More than Sixty Years' Tour of the Mind* (1816; a second part was published in 1818). Hall died in 1825.

FRANCIS WATT, *rev.* REBECCA MILLS

**Sources** *Sketches of obscure poets* (1833), 156–77 · *IGI*

**Hall, William** (1800/01–1847), bookseller and publisher, emerged from an obscure past to become a partner with Edward *Chapman (1804–1880) in 1830 in a bookselling and publishing business housed in narrow premises at 186 Strand, London. Chapman and Hall's first enterprises, usually joint ventures with other firms, were, in the words of John Forster, 'ingenious rather than important' (Forster, 1.87), being modest periodicals and factual compendia. By 1835 they were expanding into illustrated fiction and magazines issued weekly or monthly; such periodicity encouraged customers to return to the shop on a regular basis and recycled the firm's capital often. In December 1835 the comic artist Robert Seymour, who was doing other work for Chapman and Hall, proposed to them a monthly serial spoofing Cockney sportsmen. He had prepared some initial drawings and needed a writer to produce accompanying letterpress. A few weeks later Charles Whitehead, just hired to edit a monthly, *Library of Fiction*, which the firm launched in April 1836, was asked by the proprietors if he knew the real name of Boz, who had recently contributed lively sketches to the *Monthly Magazine* for which Whitehead had formerly worked. He did; it was Charles Dickens. William Hall then paid a visit to Dickens in his Furnival's Inn chambers on 10 February 1836. Dickens immediately recognized him as 'the person from whose hands' he had bought in December 1833 a copy of his first story, just published in the *Monthly*. Both hailed this as 'a good omen' (preface to the Cheap Edition, *Pickwick Papers*). Dickens listened to Hall's proposal and agreed to it in principle, though in fact he made many alterations from the first, and after Seymour's suicide in April took control of the venture. The result, *Pickwick Papers*, grew into an unprecedented success, both because of its exuberant humour and sympathy and because its serial issue at 1*s*. per month put upwards of 40,000 copies into circulation, some £2000 into Dickens's pockets, and made about £14,000 for his publishers.

Hall, a brisk businessman who inspired respectful awe in the clerks, paid most attention to the commercial aspects of the firm. It proved most generous to Dickens, buying out competitors who could not keep up with his accelerating popularity and price, and capitalizing on the mode of serialization both in monthly parts (reissuing the previously published *Sketches by Boz* in twenty 1*s*. parts from November 1837 to June 1839 and the newly composed *Nicholas Nickleby* in the same format from April 1838 to October 1839) and, at Dickens's request, in weekly numbers (*Master Humphrey's Clock*, containing *The Old Curiosity Shop* and *Barnaby Rudge*, from 4 April 1840 to 4 December 1841). During these heady days 'the best of booksellers past, present, or to come' (*Letters of Charles Dickens*, 1.601–2) gave many celebratory dinners and gifts. Dickens attended Hall's marriage, an event he fictionalized for *Sketches of Young Couples* which Chapman and Hall published in 1840. There Mr Chirrup (Hall) is described as having the smartness and 'the brisk, quick manner of a small bird' (Waugh, 6). The Halls resided at Norwood, where they hosted pleasant, playful evenings. Hall's younger brother Spencer *Hall (1806–1875), a skilled bibliographer and librarian of the Athenaeum from 1833 until his death, took a 'kind interest' in Dickens's election to the club in 1838 (*Letters of Charles Dickens*, 1.399, n.5).

Dickens's friend the lawyer John Forster became literary adviser to Chapman and Hall by 1837. In addition to supervising Dickens's publication arrangements, he edited the *Foreign Quarterly Review* after the firm bought it late in 1841, and he brought other authors to the Strand, notably Thomas Carlyle. But in the early 1840s the firm was still largely dependent on Dickens, so when in August 1841 Dickens asked for a year's retirement, with advances to be set against future works, Hall and Chapman were troubled. They agreed reluctantly: Chapman was 'very manly', Dickens judged, while Hall, 'with his pocketfull of figures and estimates' (*Letters of Charles Dickens*, 2.366) seemed feeble though well-intentioned. However, instead of taking the rest he said he required, Dickens took off for America on a lecture tour. At his return he wrote up his travel notes and letters into *American Notes* (October 1842). Though the book went through four editions before the end of the year, it was not considered by Dickens or his publishers notably successful. The serial novel that Dickens commenced immediately afterwards, *Martin Chuzzlewit* (January 1843–July 1844), fell victim both to a downturn in the economy and to the four-year hiatus since Dickens's last monthly. When it became clear that the profits from *Chuzzlewit* would not pay off the advances, in June 1843 Hall hinted that it might be necessary to invoke a clause in the agreement of 7 September 1841 reducing by £50 the £200 monthly stipend Dickens received for writing each instalment. Dickens was so irritated he could not write. 'I am bent upon paying Chapman and Hall *down*', he told Forster. 'And when I have done that, Mr. Hall shall have a piece of my mind' (ibid., 3.517). First he tried to work off the balance by publishing a short holiday gift, *A Christmas Carol* (19 December 1843). He insisted that Chapman and Hall take nothing but a commission on sales, but then he spent so much on binding and hand-coloured illustrations that, at the retail price of 5*s*. he specified, there was very little in the way of profit to divide in spring 1844. Dickens severed relations. However, he believed that Chapman and Hall understood the business of serial publishing better than the printers, Bradbury and Evans, whom he asked to be his new publishers. Moreover, Chapman and Hall owned a share in most of his copyrights. Consequently Dickens continued to receive accounts from, and plan republications with, the firm, which co-published *The Chimes* (16 December 1844) and was considered though not chosen by a nervous Dickens as publisher for *Dombey and Son* (October 1846–April 1848).

Hall fell ill suddenly and died at the firm's office at 186

Strand, London, on Sunday, 7 March 1847, aged forty-six. Dickens, having ascertained from Chapman that his presence at the funeral would be acceptable, attended the burial at Highgate cemetery 'to pay that last mark of respect'. Hall 'had a good little wife, if ever a man had,' he wrote afterwards to H. K. Browne, who did not attend; the 'accounts of her tending of him at the last, are deeply affecting' (*Letters of Charles Dickens*, 5.36).

ROBERT L. PATTEN

**Sources** A. Waugh, *A hundred years of publishing* (1930) • *The letters of Charles Dickens*, ed. M. House, G. Storey, and others, 12 vols. (1965–2002) • J. Forster, *The life of Charles Dickens*, 3 vols. (1872–4) • R. L. Patten, *Charles Dickens and his publishers* (1978) • J. D. Vann, 'Chapman and Hall', *British literary publishing houses, 1820–1880*, ed. P. J. Anderson and J. Rose, DLitB, 106 (1991), 95–109 • S. M. Ellis, *William Harrison Ainsworth and his friends*, 2 vols. (1911) • *The George Eliot letters*, ed. G. S. Haight, 9 vols. (1954–78) • L. Stevenson, *Dr. Quicksilver* (1939) • *The letters and private papers of William Makepeace Thackeray*, ed. G. N. Ray, 4 vols. (1945–6) [with 2 vol. suppl., ed. E. F. Harden (1994)] • A. Trollope, *An autobiography*, ed. B. A. Booth (1947) • J. A. Sutherland, *Victorian novelists and publishers* (1976) • J. Sutherland, *Victorian fiction: writers, publishers, readers* (1995) • English literature and history including the Charles Dickens archive (1999), L09209 [sale catalogue, Sothebys, London, 15 July 1999] • K. J. Fielding, 'Charles Whitehead and Charles Dickens', *Review of English Studies*, new ser., 3 (1952), 141–54 • *The Times* (20 Feb 1880) • *DNB* • d. cert.

**Archives** Associated Book Publishers, Andover, archives • Methuen office, London | BL, Dickens legal MSS

**Likenesses** G. Cruikshank, etching, repro. in C. Dickens, *Sketches by Boz* (1836)

**Hall, William** (1827–1904), sailor, the first black man to be awarded the Victoria Cross, was born on 28 April 1827 at Horton's Bluff, Nova Scotia. He was the son of slaves who were being transported from west Africa to America when they were intercepted by a British warship during the Anglo-American War of 1812–14 and liberated at Halifax, Nova Scotia. His father was assisted to make a living as a smallholder in Hants county, and adopted the name Hall from his benefactor.

Hall was educated locally at Avonport and first went to sea as a deckhand on various ships before entering the Royal Navy on 10 February 1852. He joined the *Rodney* at Halifax, Nova Scotia, as able seaman. He served with this ship until 30 January 1856, taking part in the Crimean War, for which he received the Crimea medal with clasp and the Turkish medal. He was paid off to the *Victoria* for a short period, but reportedly deserted and forfeited all his previous time served, bounty, medals, and personal effects left on board.

However, when the steam frigate *Shannon* was commissioning for service in Asia, Hall was able to join her as able seaman in October 1856. The *Shannon* was conveying troops to China when the Indian mutiny broke out in May 1857, and a naval brigade was assembled by Captain William Peel VC and diverted to India. They were towed 1000 kilometres up the River Ganges from Calcutta to Cawnpore, where they witnessed the aftermath of terrible atrocities committed by the rebels on British women and children.

Determined to avenge, the British troops under Sir Colin Campbell marched on Lucknow, where a British force was besieged in the residency by a large rebel army. They had to fight their way through the city, assaulting heavily manned masonry fortifications. On 16 November 1857 the naval brigade reached the Shah Najaf mosque, a domed building situated in a garden enclosed by a high loopholed wall. Hall went forward with the 24-pounder naval guns brought up close to the mosque, and the gun crews kept up a steady fire in an attempt to breach the walls, while a hail of musket balls and grenades from the mutineers inside caused heavy casualties. Hall and Lieutenant Young, in command of the gun crews were, after a time, the only survivors, all the rest having been killed or wounded, and between them they loaded and served the last gun. Eventually the walls were breached, the Shah Najaf was taken, and the residency was relieved. For his conspicuous bravery at Lucknow, Hall was awarded the Victoria Cross, gazetted on 1 February 1859. Having been appointed captain of the foretop in July 1859, and after joining the *Donegal* in June 1859, he received the VC from Rear-Admiral Charles Talbot at a special parade on board ship at Queenstown, Ireland, on 28 October 1859, the first non-white and the first Canadian sailor to receive the VC. He had also received the Indian mutiny medal with clasp.

Hall left the *Donegal* in June 1862, and while serving with the *Canopus* in February 1866 a controversy concerning his date of birth prevented him from signing on for ten years' continuous service. The Admiralty eventually cleared up the matter in 1869 and his service was backdated to 1866. At the time he was serving in the *Bellerophon*, and he finished his career as petty officer in the *Peterel*, leaving the navy in June 1876, having served twenty-four years. He settled at Hantsport, Nova Scotia, where he farmed a smallholding. He remained unmarried and lived with his two spinster sisters. His main recreation was shooting crows. He died at his home on 25 August 1904, aged seventy-seven, and he was buried at Brooklyn cemetery, Hantsport, where an obelisk was erected over the grave. His VC and other medals were deposited in the Nova Scotia Museum.

JAMES W. BANCROFT

**Sources** Lummis file (Hall), Military Historical Society • Lummis file (Hall), NAM • VC files (Hall), IWM • *LondG* (1 Feb 1859) • *Chronicle-Herald* [Halifax, Nova Scotia] (23 Feb 1996)

**Archives** IWM, VC files | NAM, Lummis files

**Likenesses** photographs, Military Historical Society, Lummis file (Hall) • photographs, NAM, Lummis file (Hall)

**Hall, William Edward** (1835–1894), writer on international law, was born at Leatherhead, Surrey, on 22 August 1835, the only child of William Hall, a descendant of a junior branch of the Halls of Dunglass, and his wife, Charlotte, daughter of William Cotton. His father was physician to the king of Hanover, and subsequently to the British legation at Naples, and much of Hall's childhood was spent on the continent, where perhaps he first developed his interest in art and modern languages. He matriculated from University College, Oxford, on 1 December 1852 and graduated BA in 1856 with a first-class degree in the recently instituted school of law and modern history.

In 1859 he graduated MA and gained the chancellor's prize for an English essay.

Hall was called to the bar at Lincoln's Inn in 1861, but took no great interest in law as a profession, lacking the patience necessary for the steady pursuit of a career as a lawyer. His energies were thrown rather into foreign travel, sport, and the study of history, art, languages, botany, and strategy. He was an enthusiastic climber and member of the Alpine Club, making several first ascents, notably that of the Lyskamm, and contributing both articles and drawings to the *Alpine Journal*. He was also a contributor to the *Contemporary Review*, the *Cornhill Magazine*, and the *Fortnightly Review*. In 1864 he was under fire during the defence of Sonderborg by the Danes, as he was also, twenty years later, during some of the operations in the neighbourhood of Suakin, Sudan. In his early days at the bar he visited South America to collect evidence on behalf of the Tichborne claimant, Arthur Orton, and in later years travelled in northern Scandinavia, Norway, Egypt, Bulgaria, India, Burma, and Japan. From these expeditions, undertaken partly for pleasure and sport, but also with a view to acquiring information on social, political, and especially on military questions, Hall never failed to bring home competent watercolour sketches as well as additions to what became a valuable collection of Greek vases, Arab weapons, Etruscan urns, Japanese sculptures, and other antiquities. These he was able to arrange to advantage in the fine old Elizabethan mansion which he occupied in the 1870s at Llanfihangel, Monmouthshire, and at another fine old house, Coker Court, near Yeovil, Somerset, where he moved in the 1880s. Hall was married twice: first in 1866 to Imogen Emily, daughter of the physicist and judge Sir William Robert *Grove; and second, after her death in 1886, in 1891 to Alice Constance, youngest daughter of Colonel Arthur Charles Hill of Court of Hill, Shropshire. He had no children.

Although eclectic in his interests, Hall was a strenuous and methodical writer. In an early pamphlet he anticipated much that was later said about the defects of the British army, and advocated a scheme of compulsory military service. He had at one time amassed materials and formed plans for ambitious treatises upon such topics as the history of civilization and the history of the British colonies, but was at length led, almost by accident, to concentrate his efforts on international law. *The Rights and Duties of Neutrals*, published in 1874, was followed in 1880 by Hall's *magnum opus*, *International Law*. This was extremely well regarded and found success even among continental jurists, to whom as a rule Hall's adherence to what they called '*l'école historico-pratique*' was distasteful. It reached a fourth edition in 1895.

Hall was elected in 1875 associate, and in 1882 member, of the Institut de Droit International. Nor were his merits overlooked by his own government. From 1871 to 1877 he made inquiries and drew up reports for the education office and for the Board of Trade; he delivered several courses of lectures at the Royal Naval College at Greenwich, and he was selected to be one of the British arbitrators under the convention of 1891 for the settlement of the conflicting claims of Great Britain and France with reference to the Newfoundland fisheries. His death took place quite suddenly at Coker Court on 30 November 1894, depriving his friends of a charming companion, and legal science of an able exponent.

T. E. HOLLAND, *rev.* CATHERINE PEASE-WATKIN

**Sources** *Alpine Journal*, 1 (1863), 92–3, 141, 209 • *Alpine Journal*, 3, 200 • W. E. Hall, 'The Straits of Magellan and the Andes of central Chile', *Alpine Journal*, 4 (1869), 327–36 • W. E. Hall, 'The fatal accident on the Lyskamm', *Alpine Journal*, 5 (1870), 23–32 • W. E. Hall, 'Across Lapland', *Alpine Journal*, 7 (1875), 169–79 • A. J. Butler, 'In memoriam: William Edward Hall', *Alpine Journal*, 17 (1895), 443–4 • *Peaks, Passes and Glaciers*, 2nd ser., 1 (1862), 383–96 • T. E. Holland, 'In memoriam, W. E. Hall', *Law Quarterly Review*, 11 (1895), 113–17 • private information (1901)

**Wealth at death** £28,419 17*s.* 7*d.*: resworn probate, July 1896, *CGPLA Eng. & Wales*

**Hall, William George Glenvil** (1887–1962), politician, was born at Spearmarsh Villa, Almeley, Herefordshire, on 4 April 1887, the eldest of the five children of William George Hall, who undertook pastoral work for the home mission of the Society of Friends, and his wife, Elizabeth Holl, of New Radnor, Radnorshire. His family had been yeoman farmers in the district for several generations. Both of Hall's parents were devout Quakers, and he was educated at the Friends' school, Saffron Walden.

Hall left school at fifteen and was employed as a clerk in branches of Barclays Bank, gaining a qualification from the Institute of Bankers. His work in the Pall Mall branch showed him the affluence of London's West End; his social conscience soon led him to social work in the East End. He went to live at Toynbee Hall, encouraged the Boy Scout movement in Hoxton and Whitechapel, and lectured at Toynbee Hall on economic and social history. He was also a tutor for the Workers' Educational Association. The encounter with East End poverty shaped his politics; in 1905 he joined the Independent Labour Party (ILP). Within the London left the ILP was relatively weak, but its ethical socialism appealed to Hall. Until 1914 he was an active party member and served for a while as treasurer of the ILP's London and southern division.

Despite his Quaker background and ILP membership, Hall enlisted for military service at the outbreak of war. He served for two years as a private in the Queen's Westminster rifles, and in 1916 he was commissioned in the East Kent regiment (the Buffs). Later he served with the tank corps. He was wounded and mentioned in dispatches. After retiring with the rank of captain, he wrote a history of the battalion, *The Green Triangle* (1920). During 1919 to 1920 he was a member of the executive of the National Union of Ex-Servicemen.

The post-war ambitions of the Labour Party produced a significant expansion of its organization. An accounts department was formed, and in November 1919 Hall was appointed to head this. He remained a party employee for the next twenty years. In 1921 he married Rachel Ida (*d.* 1950), daughter of the Revd Robert Bury Sanderson, a Church of England clergyman, and a direct descendant of Bishop Sanderson, a chaplain to Charles I. They had a son and a daughter.

Hall's first parliamentary contests were at the Isle of Ely in 1922 and at Bromley in 1923. Both were hopeless from the Labour standpoint, but in the general election of 1924 Hall made a considerable impact at Portsmouth Central. The marquess of Tavistock took the chair at one of Hall's meetings, saying that he had been impressed by Hall's personality and thought that he was the kind of person needed in parliament. In the 1920s Labour Party strategists sought to extend the party's appeal beyond its core working-class support. Both Hall's ethical seriousness and his military record facilitated this strategy. His first Portsmouth campaign ended with Labour rising from third to second place; in 1929 he became Portsmouth's first Labour member and parliamentary private secretary to F. W. Pethick Lawrence, the financial secretary to the treasury.

As a back-bencher in the parliament of 1929 Hall was an assiduous advocate of his constituents' concerns, mastering among other issues the complexities of naval life. As the government's economic difficulties intensified, Hall remained one of the loyal majority within the Parliamentary Labour Party. In August 1931 his opposition to the National Government was combined with private sympathy for MacDonald: 'I understand the difficult circumstances in which you have been placed and the reasons which have led you to take the course you have' (W. G. Hall to MacDonald, 31 Aug 1931, PRO, MacDonald papers, 30/69, file 1315). Having lost his Portsmouth seat in the general election of 1931, Hall returned to full-time party employment. He was also called to the bar by Gray's Inn in 1933, and after his return to the Commons in 1939 he joined the chambers of Sir Valentine Holmes.

Hall contested Norwich unsuccessfully in November 1935, but in July 1939 he was successful in one of the last by-elections before the outbreak of war. His new seat, Colne Valley in the West Riding, had an ethical socialist tradition that was at one with Hall's own politics. His style could appeal also to some of the constituency's radical Liberals, and he retained the seat at five post-war elections (1945–59).

Hall was rarely involved in the factionalism of the extra-parliamentary party but in the spring of 1943 he became a factor in the complex bargaining over trade union votes that characterized Labour Party conferences. The post of party treasurer had become vacant because of the death of the incumbent, and Hall was nominated for the post by the Miners' Federation of Great Britain. This union's vote gave Hall a strong base, but apart from the steelworkers further support was sparse. Instead, the effective contest lay between Arthur Greenwood and Herbert Morrison. Greenwood headed the first ballot on a minority vote and attempts to hold a further ballot without Hall were unsuccessful. He had sterilized the miners' vote, which could well have gone in his absence decisively for Morrison; his involvement in the episode was characteristically non-adversarial.

With the formation of the post-war Labour government Hall became financial secretary to the treasury, serving under Hugh Dalton and Sir Stafford Cripps. He carried much of the burden of defending the detail of finance bills in all-night sessions. His good humour and tact contrasted with Dalton's ebullience and Cripps's rather forbidding public style. These years were the culmination of Hall's politics, marked by decency and loyal service to his party. He remained very much outside the making of key economic decisions; he was not involved in the discussions over devaluation in 1949. His ministerial role was an extension of his work as a party official—detail, not broad agendas. When Dalton unsuccessfully lobbied Attlee to promote Hall, his recommended post was appropriately as minister of pensions. Beyond his departmental brief, Hall participated in several gatherings; the final assembly of the League of Nations and the Paris peace conference in 1946, and as the British representative at the United Nations assembly on three occasions (1945, 1946, and 1948). In 1950, 1951, and 1952 he attended the consultative assembly of the Council of Europe at Strasbourg. He was also an effective speaker at party gatherings, presenting the government's case and insisting that its achievements represented a unique revolution by consent. Yet he eventually felt that this achievement needed a more thorough ethical transformation. 'I sometimes wonder today whether workers are not spoiled. I am not sure if we have not travelled too far too quickly' (*Huddersfield Examiner*, 3 May 1950).

After the general election of 1950, Hall was not re-appointed to the government; instead he became chairman of the Parliamentary Labour Party (PLP). Over the next eighteen months his qualities were severely tested. The government's small majority increased the stress on back-benchers, and the Bevanite resignations of April 1951 were the prelude to some acrimonious PLP meetings. In the election of October 1951 Hall faced his most serious challenge in Colne Valley. A local Conservative-Liberal pact led to a straight fight between Hall and the Liberal, Lady Violet Bonham-Carter. Some local Liberals seem to have preferred Hall, and he secured a majority of over 2000. With Labour in opposition, Hall was elected regularly to the opposition front bench. In an increasingly factionalized party he was often viewed as a non-factional party loyalist, although in the spring of 1955 that loyalism meant that he supported those who tried unsuccessfully to withdraw the whip from Aneurin Bevan. He did not stand for the front bench after Labour's election defeat in 1955, but remained an active back-bencher. He made several journeys in connection with the Commonwealth Parliamentary Association. From 1952 he was a member of the BBC advisory council. As an advocate of temperance (in 1959 he was president of the United Kingdom Alliance) he strongly opposed the liberalization of the licensing laws in 1960.

An unostentatious and loyal advocate of Labour Party policy, Hall evinced neither the culture of trade unionism nor the socialist zeal of the Labour left; but his appeals to decency and reason linked the party to a broader radical tradition. Described as 'tall and romantically good-looking in his youth', he 'retained to the end of his life his ascetic good looks and the spare figure and light step of a young man' (*DNB*). He died at 16 Hillsleigh Road, Kensington, London, on 13 October 1962, and was cremated at Putney Vale crematorium on 18 October.

DAVID HOWELL

**Sources** *DNB* • *The Times* (15 Oct 1962) • *The Labour who's who* (1927) • press cuttings, People's History Museum, Manchester • H. Dalton, *The fateful years: memoirs, 1931–1945* (1957) • H. Dalton, *High tide and after: memoirs, 1945–1960* (1962) • *The political diary of Hugh Dalton, 1918–1940, 1945–1960*, ed. B. Pimlott (1986) • *The Second World War diary of Hugh Dalton, 1940–1945*, ed. B. Pimlott (1986) • B. Donoughue and G. W. Jones, *Herbert Morrison: portrait of a politician* (1973) • *The diary of Hugh Gaitskell, 1945–1956*, ed. P. M. Williams (1983) • *Daring to hope: the diaries and letters of Violet Bonham Carter*, ed. M. Pottle (2000) • *Labour party conference report* (1920), p. 11 • b. cert. • *CGPLA Eng. & Wales* (1963)

**Archives** PRO, MacDonald papers, 30/69 [for Hall response to 1931 split, file 1315]

**Likenesses** T. Binney-Gibbs, oils, 1932, priv. coll.

**Wealth at death** £9846 5*s*. 4*d*.: probate, 20 Feb 1963, *CGPLA Eng. & Wales*

**Hall, Sir William Hutcheon** (1797?–1878), naval officer, son of William Hall and his wife, Mary, *née* Hutcheon, entered the navy in October 1811 on the *Warrior*, under the Hon. George Byng, and for the rest of the war served continuously in her in the North Sea and the Baltic. In November 1815 he was appointed to the sloop *Lyra* with Commander Basil Hall, and served in her during her voyage to China with Lord Amherst's embassy. Shortly after his return to England in November 1817, Hall was appointed to the frigate *Iphigenia*, carrying the broad pennant of Sir Robert Mends on the west coast of Africa, and from her was promoted master of the sloop *Morgiana* (18 guns). He served actively on the West Indian, the Mediterranean, and the home stations until 1836; then, after studying steam engines at Glasgow and on steamers trading to Ireland, he went to the United States, and was employed on steamboats on the Hudson and Delaware.

In 1839 John Laird, the Birkenhead shipbuilder and advocate of iron ships, built, in secrecy, on speculation, the first iron warship, the paddle-steamer *Nemesis*. Laird, as owner, appointed Hall to command her, and in 1840 sent her as a private armed steamer to the First Opium War. Her voyage out was the longest yet by a steam-assisted vessel, and she reached China in January 1841. She served with the East India Company's Bengal marine (that is, navy), and was bought by the company in 1841. She had a prominent, successful, and well-publicized role in the war, including assisting at the capture of Chuenpe (Chuanbi) Fort on the Canton River in January 1841.

Hall, by his energy and his skilful handling of the *Nemesis*, won mention in dispatches and the commendation of the naval officers under whom he served. Consequently, an order in council permitted his promotion to lieutenant (the commission was dated back to 8 June 1841); another order in council sanctioned his time on the *Nemesis* as though on a queen's ship; and on 10 June 1843 he was promoted commander. The *Nemesis* was paid off at Calcutta, and Hall returned overland. His report had considerable influence on the Admiralty decision to use iron ships from 1844 or 1845. Partly to distinguish him from Sir William King Hall, with whom he was sometimes confused, Hall became known in the navy as 'Nemesis' Hall. He invented iron bilge tanks for ships, adopted by the navy, and 'Hall's patent anchor'.

On 1 July 1843 Hall was appointed to the royal steam yacht *Victoria and Albert*, from which, on 22 October 1844, he was advanced to post rank. He served in Ireland in 1847 during the famine, and in 1848 against the attempted uprising, and then until 1850 commanded the steam paddle frigate *Dragon* in the Mediterranean. On 28 October 1849, when Sir William Parker brought the fleet to Besika Bay to show support to the Turks against the demands of Austria and Russia on the Hungarian refugees, Hall was sent with the news to the British minister at Constantinople. In 1847 Hall was elected a fellow of the Royal Society. On the outbreak of the Russian war, unable to obtain command of a vessel corresponding to his seniority, he accepted the *Hecla*, a small paddle-steamer, in which he served in the Baltic in 1854. In June 1854 the *Hecla* and two other ships under Hall's command, on his initiative, bombarded the Bomarsmund fortifications, but caused little damage. In 1855 in the Baltic he commanded the blockship *Blenheim*, in which he was present at the successful bombardment of Sveaborg (August 1855), and in July was made a CB. He had no further service, but became rear-admiral in 1863, was made a KCB in 1867, was advanced to vice-admiral on the retired list in 1869, and became an admiral in 1875.

On 30 April 1845 Hall married the Hon. Hilare Caroline Byng, third daughter of his first captain, Viscount Torrington; they had one daughter, married in 1879 to Captain C. D. Lucas RN, who, as a mate in the *Hecla*, had won the Victoria Cross by throwing a lighted shell overboard, before Bomarsmund, on 21 June 1854.

Hall was instrumental in establishing sailors' homes and in attempting to improve their social conditions. He published two pamphlets, *Sailors' Homes, their Origin and Progress* (1852; enlarged edn, 1854) and *Our National Defences* (1876); the latter contains autobiographical notes. He died at his residence, 48 Phillimore Gardens, Kensington, London, of 'apoplexy' on 25 June 1878, and was buried at Mereworth, Kent, on 29 June. His wife survived him.

J. K. LAUGHTON, *rev.* ROGER T. STEARN

**Sources** *The Times* (27 June 1878) • O'Byrne, *Naval biog. dict.* • B. Greenhill and A. Giffard, *Steam, politics and patronage: the transformation of the Royal Navy, 1815–1854* (1994) • *Proceedings* [Royal Geographical Society], new ser., 1 (1879), 214–16 • W. D. Bernard, *Narrative of the voyages and services of the Nemesis from 1840 to 1843* (1844) • A. Phillimore, *The life of Admiral of the Fleet Sir William Parker*, 3 (1880) • S. Lane-Poole, *The life of … Stratford Canning*, 2 (1888) • *Dod's Peerage* (1878) • R. Gardiner and A. Lambert, eds., *Steam, steel and shellfire: the steam warship, 1815–1905* (1992) • A. D. Lambert, *The Crimean War: British grand strategy, 1853–56* (1990) • E. Holt, *The opium wars in China* (1964)

**Archives** NMM, diary and papers • U. Birm. L., journal of naval service as master on HMS *Morgiana* off west coast of Africa | BL, letters and reports, mainly to Sir Charles Napier, Add. MSS 40024, 40030, 40033, 40042–40044

**Likenesses** wood-engraving, NPG; repro. in *ILN*, 25 (1854), 641–2

**Wealth at death** under £6000: probate, 27 July 1878, *CGPLA Eng. & Wales*

**Hall, Sir William King** (**1816–1886**), naval officer, son of Dr James Hall RN (*d.* 1869), and his wife, Frances, daughter of Lieutenant Miller RN, was born in London on 11 March 1816. He entered the navy in September 1829 and, after serving in Burma and off the coast of Spain during the First Carlist War (1836–9), was mate of the *Benbow*, under Captain Houston Stewart, off the coast of Syria and at the bombardment of Acre in 1840. On 28 July 1841 he was promoted lieutenant of the *Britannia*, flagship of Sir John Acworth Ommanney, commander-in-chief in the Mediterranean, and commanded by Captain Michael Seymour. From September 1841 to 1844 Hall was a lieutenant of the *Indus*, also in the Mediterranean; and from 1845 to 1848 was again with Captain Seymour in the *Vindictive*, flagship of Sir Francis William Austen on the North American station. On her paying off, Hall, as her first lieutenant, was promoted commander in March 1848, and from 1849 to 1851 was in charge of the coastguard in the Isles of Scilly. In July 1851 he was appointed to the *Styx*, which he commanded at the Cape of Good Hope during the Cape Frontier War (1852–3), and on 6 June 1853 was advanced to post rank.

In the Crimean War in 1854 Hall commanded the paddle-steamer *Bulldog* in the Baltic, on board which, at the capture of Bomarsund in August 1854, the commander-in-chief, Sir Charles Napier, hoisted his flag. In 1855, again in the Baltic, Hall commanded the *Exmouth* (90 guns) as flag-captain to Sir Michael Seymour, and on 3 July was made a CB. In the following year he was appointed to the *Calcutta* (84 guns), Seymour's flagship, going out to China as commander-in-chief. The *Calcutta* had scarcely arrived at Hong Kong when the Second Opium War broke out, and through the operations of 1856–8 Hall was virtually the captain of the fleet, in which capacity his energy and zeal repeatedly elicited the admiral's warm praise. The *Calcutta* returned to England in August 1859, and Hall was immediately sent out to take command of the *Indus* as flag-captain to Sir Houston Stewart on the North American station.

From July 1860 to December 1861 Hall was employed as captain of the steam reserve at Plymouth, and during 1862 was captain of the coastguard at Falmouth. From April 1863 to April 1865 he was captain of the steam reserve at Sheerness, and afterwards as superintendent of the dockyard there until his promotion to rear-admiral on 17 March 1869. On 20 May 1871 he was made a KCB. From 1871 to 1875 he was superintendent of the Devonport dockyards; he became a vice-admiral on 30 July 1875, was commander-in-chief at the Nore from 1877 to 1879, and was promoted admiral on 2 August 1879. Hall was twice married. He first married, on 20 June 1848, Louisa (*d.* 29 June 1875), daughter of James Forman of Coldstream. They had several sons, including (the eldest) Admiral Sir George Fowler King-Hall (1850–1939), father of William Stephen Richard King-*Hall (1893–1966), and Admiral Sir Herbert Goodenough King-Hall (1862–1936). No details are known about Hall's marriage to his second wife.

Throughout his career Hall showed himself deeply impressed by religious feeling; while in command of seagoing ships, in the absence of a chaplain, he conducted the church service himself and preached original sermons. From the time of his service at Sheerness he promoted temperance among seamen and became a prominent advocate of total abstinence. He was also widely associated with various naval charities and many other branches of charitable or religious organizations. He died suddenly of apoplexy at 38 Jermyn Street, St James's, London, on 29 July 1886.

J. K. Laughton, *rev.* Roger Morriss

**Sources** O'Byrne, *Naval biog. dict.* · *Navy List* · *The Times* (30 July 1886) · personal knowledge (1890) · private information (1890) · A. D. Lambert, *The Crimean War: British grand strategy, 1853–56* (1990) · E. Holt, *The opium wars in China* (1964) · G. S. Graham, *The China station: war and diplomacy, 1830–1860* (1978) · Boase, *Mod. Eng. biog.* · Burke, *Peerage* (1879) · Kelly, *Handbk* (1879) · *CGPLA Eng. & Wales* (1886)

**Archives** Harrowby Manuscript Trust, Sandan Hall, Staffordshire, letters to Admiral Ryder · Northants. RO, letters to Revd H. Bradford

**Likenesses** woodcut, NPG; repro. in *British Workman* (Sept 1877)

**Wealth at death** £4486 11*s.* 9*d.*: probate, 23 Aug 1886, *CGPLA Eng. & Wales*

**Hallahan, Margaret Mary** [*name in religion* Margaret of the Mother of God] (**1802–1868**), Roman Catholic nun, was born in London on 23 January 1802, the only daughter of working-class Irish parents, Edmund Hallahan and his wife, Catherine, *née* O'Connor. Orphaned at the age of eleven she spent three years in the orphanage attached to the Catholic mission at Somers Town, London, before going into domestic service.

In 1823 Hallahan was placed with the family of Dr Morgan, a court physician. She remained with the family after Morgan's death, first with his son and then for twenty years with his married daughter. In 1829 she went with her mistress to live in Bruges, and absorbed the Catholic culture of the country. Here Hallahan made her initial trial of the religious life, spending six months as a lay sister at the English convent of Augustinian canonesses. Coming under the direction of a Dominican friar she was eventually received into the third order secular in 1834, making her profession the following year.

In 1842 Hallahan returned to England to teach in the school attached to the Catholic mission in Coventry. By 1844 she had attracted a group of local textile workers to assist her and transformed them into a community of Dominican sisters. The superior of the mission, William Bernard Ullathorne, although a Benedictine, gave support to the group and encouraged them to follow him to Bristol when he was appointed vicar apostolic of the western district. The community settled in Clifton in 1846, and in 1851 branch houses were opened at Bridgwater and at Longton, Staffordshire; both were short-lived. In 1853 the latter foundation was transferred to Stone, also in Staffordshire, and St Dominic's Convent, Stone, became the mother house of the congregation. The constitutions of the community, officially known as the sisters of the Third Order of St Dominic of the English Congregation of St Catherine

Margaret Mary Hallahan (1802–1868), by unknown engraver

of Siena, were approved by Rome in 1855. The sisters were placed under the immediate jurisdiction of the master of the Dominican order who nominated Ullathorne, bishop of Birmingham since 1850, as his delegate.

Further foundations were made at Stoke-on-Trent (1857), Leicester (1860, but given up the following year), St Marychurch, Torquay (1865), and Bow, London (1866). In several of these locations Mother Margaret's administrative ability was revealed in the erection of conventual buildings and churches of architectural note; those at Stone, Stoke, and St Marychurch were designed by Charles Hansom. This ability was further displayed in the establishment of diverse works: schools for the poor and middle classes, orphanages, and hospitals for incurables.

Despite her own humble origin Hallahan's personal magnetism attracted to the congregation many women of considerable calibre who aided her in strengthening its liturgical and intellectual life. Among these were her two immediate successors as superior, Imelda Poole and Francis Raphael Drane, as well as members of England's most prominent Catholic families: Howard, Petre, Blount, and Berkeley, and four nieces of Bishop Ullathorne.

Hallahan was a forceful personality, highly intuitive and often impulsive. She exerted profound influence not only over the members of her community but particularly over Ullathorne, who was deeply convinced of her sanctity and kept a detailed memoir of her spiritual life. However, she had difficulties with Bishop Clifford of Clifton, and it was disagreements with the Dominican friars which led to the closing of the Leicester foundation. Hallahan could be stubborn, as is shown by her consistent refusal to accept any form of public funding for her works, on the grounds that this would undermine their Catholic character. Her introduction of such public displays of Catholicism as Marian and Corpus Christi processions into the timid post-emancipation world of English Catholicism drew criticism as much from co-religionists as from protestants. Such controversies, combined with the undoubted sincerity of her charitable endeavours, brought her into the public eye.

Despite her imposing physical stature, a spinal injury as a young woman and a life of extreme asceticism undermined Hallahan's health. After a long and painful illness she died at Stone on 11 May 1868 and was interred in the choir of the conventual church on 13 May. The cause for Margaret Hallahan's beatification was begun in 1936.

Anselm Nye

**Sources** F. T. Drane, *Life of Mother Margaret Mary Hallahan*, 2nd edn (1929) · *Articles for the informative process of the beatification and canonisation of the Servant of God Sister Margaret of the Mother of God* (1936) · S. M. C., *Steward of souls* (1952) · *The conventual third order of St Dominic and its development in England, by a Dominican of Stone* (1923) · M. C. Boulding and M. B. Pearce, *Mother Margaret Hallahan in Staffordshire* (c.1968) · Archives, English Dominican Sisters, St Dominic's Convent, Stone, Staffordshire · S. Hancock, 'From hagiography to history', *Recusant History*, 23 (1996–7), 341–71

**Archives** St Dominic's Convent, Stone, Staffordshire, archives of the English Dominican Sisters

**Likenesses** engraving, St Dominic's Convent, Stone, Staffordshire [*see illus.*] · group photograph (with group of sisters), St Dominic's Convent, Stone, Staffordshire · watercolour, St Dominic's Convent, Stone, Staffordshire

**Wealth at death** £20: probate, 31 Aug 1868, *CGPLA Eng. & Wales*

**Hallam, Arthur Henry** (1811–1833). *See under* Hallam, Henry (1777–1859).

**Hallam, Henry** (1777–1859), historian, born on 9 July 1777 at Windsor, was the only son of John Hallam (*d.* 1812), canon of Windsor (from 1775) and dean of Bristol (1781–1800), and his wife, Eleanor (*d.* 1826), sister (some sources say daughter) of William Hayward Roberts, the provost of Eton College (1781–1791). Hallam came from a family with a strong Lincolnshire connection. His grandfather served twice as mayor of Boston and his father attended the Boston grammar school before moving on to Eton, King's College, Cambridge, and a career in the Church of England. Over the years the family acquired property in the villages around Boston, which Hallam inherited on his father's death in 1812.

**Education** As a child Hallam demonstrated a precocious interest in literature, and wrote poetry at an early age. From 1790 to 1794 he attended Eton College, where he was known for his studious demeanour, and in 1795 he matriculated from Christ Church, Oxford. He was tutored by a student of Christ Church, William Wood, under whose guidance he read extensively in the Greek and Roman classics. While at the university Hallam became friends with Lord Webb Seymour, a younger son of the tenth duke of Somerset, and Peter Elmsley, the future Camden professor of ancient history. Hallam left Oxford in 1798, graduated BA in 1799, MA in 1832, and DCL in 1848. In 1858

Henry Hallam (1777–1859), by George Richmond, 1843

Christ Church made him an honorary student in recognition of his work as a historian. He was among the first in the university to be elected to this position.

**Lawyer and whig** Hallam's first choice of career was the law. He was admitted to Lincoln's Inn in 1798, but for unknown reasons chose to move to the Inner Temple, which called him to the bar in 1802. He practised for a number of years as a barrister on the Oxford circuit. He tired of the legal profession, however, and accepted in 1806 a commissionership of stamps, a sinecure with light duties which he held until 1826. It was at this time that Hallam began his association with many leading whig politicians. He had received his position at the stamp office through their patronage and, possibly at the instigation of Elmsley and Seymour, he began to contribute to the whig *Edinburgh Review*. Between 1805 and 1809 he wrote nine articles on a variety of literary and political topics, including one on the Catholic question, in which he argued the case for emancipation (*Edinburgh Review*, 8, 1806, 311–26). Perhaps his most notorious contribution was a review of Richard Payne Knight's *Principles of Taste* (*Edinburgh Review*, 7, 1806, 295–328). Hallam's failure in the article to recognize some verses by Pindar prompted Byron to quip, 'classic HALLAM, much renowned for Greek' (*Complete Poetical Works*, 1.245). Hallam's connection with the review lapsed after 1809, perhaps because he disapproved of its democratic tone, perhaps because he was now too busy with his own historical research. He did not resume the connection until many years later, when he reviewed historical works by John Lingard and Francis Palgrave in 1831 and 1832.

Though he never sat in parliament, Hallam always took an interest in political questions. He became associated with the whigs at a time when a number of professional men like himself had joined the party and were encouraging it to take a more active stand on reform. Hallam shared this commitment to reform but tempered it with moderation. He once described his whiggism as a belief in a 'well-ordered liberty', where order would prevent anarchy and liberty would prevent tyranny (Horner, 2.263). He advocated the repeal of the Test and Corporation Acts, which would grant political equality to dissenters, and Catholic emancipation. He supported the reform of the Irish church, hoping to make it meet the religious needs of the Irish nation, and he advocated the abolition of West Indian slavery and the slave trade. On the issue of parliamentary reform, however, Hallam was at odds with his party. While he was prepared to accept small adjustments to the constitution, he was unwilling to endorse a measure as sweeping as the first Reform Act, which the whigs carried in 1832. Hallam, distrusting democracy, feared the Reform Act would eliminate the aristocratic influence that he valued as a stabilizing force in the House of Commons.

**Historical writings** By 1809 Hallam had set to work on the historical scholarship for which he is best-known. His *View of the State of Europe during the Middle Ages* (2 vols., 1818) surveyed the political development of the principal west European countries, paying particular attention to England's Anglo-Saxon and Norman constitutions. In an effort to bring his book up to date with current scholarship he published a set of *Supplemental Notes* (1848), which were incorporated into later editions. His next work, *The constitutional history of England from the accession of Henry VII to the death of George II* (2 vols., 1827), continued the discussion of England's political development, and appended to it a brief consideration of events in Scotland and Ireland. Hallam terminated his narrative at the accession of George III because he was unwilling to stir up political passions that were rooted in the recent past. Although these works must be recognized as serious scholarship, they can also be read for their contribution to the ideological debates of the 1810s and 1820s. In his histories Hallam endorsed the moderate whiggism that derived from the revolution of 1688, while he rejected both the radical heritage of the Commonwealth and the tory defence of the Stuarts often associated with David Hume, whose *History of England*, despite its shortcomings, remained the standard authority. He championed the mixed constitution that had emerged out of the middle ages and survived the vicissitudes of the Stuarts, reaching near perfection after 1688. Hallam paid particular attention to religious issues, which was not surprising given their importance in early nineteenth-century politics. He deplored the persecution of Catholic and protestant dissent during the reigns of the Tudors and Stuarts, and he supported the Erastianism of the church–state relationship, which he considered a guarantee against religious persecution. As a historian

Hallam displayed a Burkean appreciation of the continuities in English history that was consistent with his distrust of unnecessary innovation. For much of the nineteenth century his books remained standard authorities, going through numerous editions and earning respect for their sober judgments. Hallam's final work, his *Introduction to the literature of Europe in the fifteenth, sixteenth, and seventeenth centuries* (4 vols., 1837–9), one of the most extensive works of literary history to appear during the early Victorian period, was comprehensive in its treatment and adhered to a neo-classical standard of taste.

Though Hallam's reputation rests on his work as a historian, he made other contributions to Victorian intellectual life. Given the breadth of his interests, he was an obvious participant in the learned societies and literary clubs of the day. He became a fellow of the Society of Antiquaries in 1801, and held the office of vice-president from 1824 to 1851; he was also elected a fellow of the Royal Society in 1821. He helped found London University, and sat on its council from 1828 to 1831, as well as being a founder member of the Statistical Society, and serving as its treasurer from 1834 to 1840. During the 1830s he also worked with the sixth record commission, appointed in 1831 to organize the national records, and he assisted the Society for the Diffusion of Useful Knowledge, an organization dedicated to popular education. In 1837 he was elected a trustee of the British Museum. He was a member of the royal commission on the fine arts established in 1841 to oversee the interior decoration of the new houses of parliament. Hallam was an honorary member of the Royal Academy, a vice-president of the Archaeological Institute of Great Britain and Ireland, president from 1845 to 1849 of the Royal Society of Literature, and a member of the Geological Society. He belonged to three literary clubs: the Roxburghe, the Athenaeum, and The Club.

**Family and character** Hallam's family brought him both happiness and sorrow. In January 1807 he married Julia Maria Elton (1783–1840), daughter of the Revd Sir Abraham Elton, baronet, of Clevedon Court, Somerset. Married for thirty-three years, they had eleven children, but only four of their progeny reached adulthood and only one outlived Hallam himself. The family travelled frequently on the continent, visiting many of the countries of western Europe. It was in 1833, during a stay in Vienna, that tragedy first struck. After a walk about the city, Hallam returned to his hotel to find his eldest and favourite son, Arthur Henry, lying dead on a sofa. One of Arthur's closest friends, Alfred Tennyson, commemorated the loss in the poem *In Memoriam*. After Arthur's death misfortune continued to plague Hallam's family: his daughter Eleanor died in 1837 and his wife in 1840. Hallam now bestowed his affections on his only surviving son, Henry Fitzmaurice, who was destined to repeat his brother's tragedy. In 1850, just months after the publication of Tennyson's poem had awakened old memories, Henry Fitzmaurice joined his father for an excursion on the continent. He, too, took ill and died. 'There is now nothing to fill the gap, nothing to take off from the solitude of my last days', Hallam wrote to Samuel Rogers later that year (Clayden, 2.379). He was survived by his remaining daughter, Julia.

Throughout this period Hallam frequented whig society. He was a regular guest at Holland House and Bowood, the Wiltshire estate of the third marquess of Lansdowne. He was known for the depth of his learning and his conversation, though he never achieved the brilliance of Macaulay, with whom he was often compared. As a young man he had the reputation of being a pedant—at Holland House he was dubbed the 'bore contradictor'—though in later years acquaintances stressed his broad erudition and gentle manner. On meeting him in 1847, the American George Bancroft reported that

> Hallam has a countenance, so full of benevolence, mildly radiant with a most gentle and kindly expression, that he wins very rapidly on those that see him. … His good judgment shows itself as much in conversation as in his books; and his mind takes the widest range. (*Correspondence of … Prescott*, 625)

Hallam died on 21 January 1859 at Pickhurst Manor, near Bromley, Kent, the home of his daughter Julia, who had married John Farnaby Cator. Hallam had suffered a paralytic seizure in 1854, from which he had never fully recovered. He was buried one week later at Clevedon, alongside the other members of his family.

**Arthur Henry Hallam** (1811–1833), poet and essayist, was born at Bedford Place, London, on 1 February 1811. He was a thoughtful child, and took an early interest in serious literature. From 1822 to 1827 he attended Eton College, where he participated in the debating society and was known as the school's best poet. His letters from the period, many of them to his friend W. E. Gladstone, sparkle with whiggish views on past and present politics. Hallam 'messed' with Gladstone, though they were in different houses, and their youthful friendship was, at least for the future prime minister, exceptionally rewarding. Hallam introduced Gladstone to whigs and whiggish views—an important influence on the young tory evangelical. After leaving Eton in July 1827 Hallam travelled with his parents on the continent, where he spent eight months in Italy and fell under the spell of Italian culture. During his stay in Rome he became infatuated with Anna Wintour, the English beauty who inspired eleven of his poems. On returning to England, Arthur entered Trinity College, Cambridge, in October 1828 and became the pupil of William Whewell. He found the study of mathematics uncongenial, however, and turned his attention to metaphysics and modern poetry. He participated in the debates at the Cambridge Union, and once spoke in favour of Wordsworth as a greater poet than Byron. In 1829 he was elected a member of the Cambridge Apostles and he drew most of his friends from among their number. Although he cared little for university honours, he won in 1831 prizes for a declamation vindicating the independents in the English civil war and for an essay on the philosophy of Cicero. In January 1832 he received his BA and left Cambridge.

The most momentous of Arthur's friendships was formed with Alfred Tennyson while the two men were students at Cambridge. A love of poetry drew them together. While at Cambridge they planned to publish jointly some of their poems, but abandoned the project when Henry Hallam objected to it. As a result, Arthur's *Poems* (1830) was privately printed and distributed. While visiting the Tennysons in 1830, Arthur met and fell in love with Alfred's sister Emily, to whom he later became engaged, despite Henry Hallam's reservations. In the summer of 1830 Arthur and Alfred put their liberal politics into practice by travelling to the Pyrenees in a futile effort to aid the Spanish rebellion against Ferdinand VII.

After Cambridge, Arthur resided with his family in London. He was admitted to the Inner Temple in February 1832 and began to prepare for the bar, a career that his father had chosen for him. During the summer of 1833, he travelled with his father on the continent, visiting the Alps and the Danube. While in Vienna he died suddenly of a ruptured aneurysm at Zur Goldenen Birne, Landstrasse 63, on 15 September. He was buried at Clevedon church, Somerset, on 3 January 1834. Shortly after his death some of Arthur's friends, deciding that his compositions deserved wider recognition, persuaded Henry Hallam to publish a selection of his son's prose and verse and to write an accompanying memoir. Henry Hallam proved a heavy-handed editor, expunging from the record Arthur's infatuation with Anna Wintour, his engagement to Emily Tennyson, and his adventures in Spain. A more complete edition of *The Writings of Arthur Hallam*, edited by T. H. V. Motter, appeared in 1943. Today Arthur Hallam is still best-known for his association with Tennyson and as the inspiration for *In Memoriam*, though some now recognize his own talent as a poet and critic.

**Henry Fitzmaurice Hallam** (1824–1850) was born on 31 August 1824. He was named after his godfather, the third marquess of Lansdowne. According to friends he was reserved, thoughtful, and exhibited a 'sweetness of temper' (Maine and Lushington, 54). From 1836 to 1841 he attended Eton College, where he was known for his intellect and broad learning. He participated in Eton's debating club and competed for the Newcastle scholarship, in which he won the medal or second prize. In October 1842 he entered Trinity College, Cambridge, where he was tutored by John Heath and W. H. Thompson. At Cambridge he obtained a Trinity scholarship in 1844 and won first prize for a declamation on the influence of religion on art. He helped to found a historical debating club as an alternative to the Cambridge Union, belonged to the Apostles, and once spoke persuasively at the union in favour of endowing the Catholic seminary at Maynooth. He graduated BA in January 1846, having obtained a first in the classical tripos and the second chancellor's medal. He left the university in December 1846 after failing to win a fellowship; his MA followed in 1849. On leaving Cambridge, he moved to London and began preparing himself for a career in the law. He was called to the bar in 1850 and joined the midland circuit that summer. He died on 25 October 1850 at Siena, Italy, while travelling with his family. He was buried on 23 December 1850 at Clevedon church, Somerset. TIMOTHY LANG

**Sources** *DNB* · T. Lang, 'Henry Hallam and early nineteenth-century whiggism', *The Victorians and the Stuart heritage* (1995), 23–52 · P. Clark, *Henry Hallam* (1982) · *The letters of Arthur Henry Hallam*, ed. J. Kolb (1981) · *Remains in verse and prose of Arthur Henry Hallam*, ed. H. Hallam (1863) · H. S. Maine and F. Lushington, 'Memoir of Henry Fitzmaurice Hallam', *Remains in verse and prose of Arthur Henry Hallam*, ed. H. Hallam (1863), 53–68 · *The complete poetical works: Lord Byron*, ed. J. J. McGann, 1 (1980), 227–64 · *Memoirs and correspondence of Francis Horner, MP*, ed. L. Horner, 2nd edn, 2 vols. (1853) · P. W. Clayden, *Rogers and his contemporaries*, 2 vols. (1889) · *The correspondence of William Hickling Prescott, 1833–1847*, ed. R. Wolcott (1925) · *The writings of Arthur Hallam*, ed. T. H. V. Motter (1943) · P. Thompson, *The history and antiquities of Boston* (1856) · *The 'Pope' of Holland House: selections from the correspondence of John Whishaw and his friends, 1813–1840*, ed. Lady Seymour (1906) · G. Ramsden, *Correspondence of two brothers: Edward Adolphus, eleventh duke of Somerset and Lord Webb Seymour* (1906) · H. Holland, *Recollections of past life* (1872) · L. Sanders, *The Holland House circle* (1908) · P. B. M. Blaas, *Continuity and anachronism* (1978) · Gladstone, *Diaries* · H. C. G. Matthew, *Gladstone*, 2 vols. (1986–95); repr. in 1 vol. as *Gladstone, 1809–1898* (1997) · Eton, archives · archives, Christ Church Oxf.

**Archives** Bodl. Oxf., letters · Christ Church Oxf., papers · Trinity Cam., commonplace books, household accounts, letters, and notes for publications · UCL, letters to Society for the Diffusion of Useful Knowledge | BL, corresp. with W. E. Gladstone, Add. MSS 44353–44373, *passim* · BL, corresp. with Sir Robert Peel, Add. MSS 40495–40599, *passim* · CKS, corresp. with Lord Stanhope · GS Lond., letters to Sir R. I. Munchison · NRA Scotland, priv. coll., letters to John Swinton · Tennyson Research Centre, Lincoln · Trinity Cam., letters to William Whewell · Wellesley College, Massachusetts, love letters to Emily Tennyson

**Likenesses** W. Beechey, oils, 1795, Eton · T. Phillips, oils, 1835, Clevedon Court, Somerset; repro. in H. Ward, *History of the Athenaeum, 1824–1925* (1926) · G. Richmond, chalk drawing, 1843, NPG [*see illus.*] · R. C. Lucas, wax medallion, 1851, NPG · W. Theed, statue, 1863, St Paul's Cathedral, London; related bust, 1864, Royal Collection · G. P. Harding, pencil (after T. Phillips), NPG · attrib. G. S. Newton, chalk drawing, NPG · J. Partridge, group portrait, oils (*The Fine Arts Commissioners, 1846*), NPG · J. Spedding, sketch, repro. in Kolb, ed., *Letters*

**Wealth at death** under £60,000: probate, 18 Feb 1859, *CGPLA Eng. & Wales*

**Hallam, Henry Fitzmaurice** (1824–1850). *See under* Hallam, Henry (1777–1859).

**Hallam, Isabella**. *See* Mattocks, Isabella (1746–1826).

**Hallam, John** (*c.*1495–1537), rebel, is of unknown parentage and education. A yeoman of Calkeld in Watton in the East Riding of Yorkshire, Hallam led the commons of the Yorkshire wolds during the Pilgrimage of Grace. Already an adult in 1524 and assessed for the subsidy at £5, by 1536 he held lands rented at £3 15*s.* 2*d.* in the three parishes of Lowthorpe, Ruston Parva, and Kilnwick near Great Driffield, of which he occupied only a windmill and land leased from Watton Priory in the fields of Kilnwick. This mill explains Hallam's complaint during the Pilgrimage that Robert Holgate, prior of Watton, insisted on payment in cash rather than kind. His other grievance, eviction from a farm, could refer to granges at Watton itself (£14) or Calkeld (£39 3*s.* 4*d.*). As Hallam was also tenant of the

Great Wold and a close at Settrington let to Sir Francis Bigod, his fellow rebel leader, he was a substantial yeoman.

In 1536 Henry VIII's government acted to curtail the celebration of holy days. When on Sunday 8 October the parish priest at Kilnwick failed to announce the forthcoming St Wilfrid's day, by custom marked on 12 October, Hallam objected and the congregation determined on observance nevertheless. On 11 October he visited the house in Beverley where insurrection had been plotted three days previously, learned of the religious objectives of the Lincolnshire rebellion, read the proclamation, and swore the pilgrims' oath. He then raised the commons from Hutton Cranswick to Great Driffield and joined the Stapleton host that captured Hull. Deserted by three gentlemen who had been elected as captains of the commons, Hallam became sole captain of 230 men, the smallest contingent in the smallest host. He divided the proceeds from stolen flocks of sheep and a royal ship among his men. But his motivation was not solely economic; Hallam was a traditional Catholic and politically conservative. His letter of 19 November to the royal council demanded that the Christian faith be kept and the church preserved from the royal supremacy, the laws maintained as at Henry's accession, and that Cromwell, Cranmer, and Audley be ousted as evil councillors. He collected rhymes lampooning Cromwell, even believing the rumour that Henry VIII might name Cromwell as his heir. Failing acceptance of his terms, he threatened the council that he and his men would fight to the death. He extorted information by wringing a captive's beard and dismissed the prior of Watton, replacing him with another man. Hallam was both a dominant personality and an effective articulator of popular feeling.

In December 1536 the pilgrims received assurances from the king and disbanded. Hallam preferred acceptance of their petitions to a pardon—as a loyal subject, he had done nothing requiring a pardon—and wanted the promises fulfilled at a York parliament. By 26 December he was doubting the king's faith, and plotted seizing Hull with the Holderness ringleader William Nicholson. A series of meetings with Sir Francis Bigod confirmed his doubts. On 9 January 1537, when Robert Aske reassured a Beverley audience, Hallam demanded why clerical taxes were being levied ahead of parliament. Although Aske could not satisfactorily reply, Hallam was initially pacified, but was then persuaded by Bigod that the king intended to garrison Hull and Scarborough to repress the commons and that it was imperative to seize them first. Bigod was to attack Scarborough, while Hallam agreed to take Hull. On 16 January, disguised as farmers under cover of market day, Hallam and a score of friends sought to capture Hull. He relied for manpower on Holderness, but failed to notify Nicholson in time. This time he was out of tune with public opinion; the Hull commons did not share his qualms. Recognized and attacked by aldermen Knollys and Eland, Hallam could have escaped but engaged in swordplay, was wounded, and captured. Bigod's projected counter-attack came to nothing. Hallam made a full confession on 24 January and was executed by hanging, probably in Hull, by the end of the month. His widow, Janice Hallam (perhaps *née* Sharp) of Lowthorpe, died in 1541; of their five children, two sons were then of age.

MICHAEL HICKS

**Sources** M. Bush, *The Pilgrimage of Grace: a study of the rebel armies of October 1536* (1996) · M. H. Dodds and R. Dodds, *The Pilgrimage of Grace, 1536–1537, and the Exeter conspiracy, 1538*, 2 vols. (1915) · *LP Henry VIII*, vol. 12 · John Hallam's confession, PRO, E36/119 · Dugdale, *Monasticon*, new edn · PRO, SC6/Hen.VIII/4383 · R. W. Hoyle, 'Thomas Master's narrative of the Pilgrimage of Grace', *Northern History*, 21 (1985), 53–79 · M. L. Bush and D. Bowes, *A study of the post-pardon revolts of December 1536 to March 1537 and their effects* (1999) · probate register II, Borth. Inst., fol. 597

**Hallam, Lewis** (1714?–1756?), actor and theatre manager, was the son of the actor, singer, and dancer Thomas Hallam (*d.* 1735) and his wife, whose name is unknown. Thomas, who was killed by the hot-tempered Charles Macklin when he dared to try on Macklin's wig in Macklin's dressing room at the Drury Lane Theatre, acted at the Smock Alley Theatre in Dublin from at least 1707 until 1724; it may be that his son Lewis was born in Dublin. One of Lewis's brothers was an admiral; the other three brothers and a sister were performers. **William Hallam** (1712?–1758?), Lewis's elder and most theatrically significant brother, was a strolling player in the British provinces and acted in Dublin. He also ran a booth at Bartholomew fair in London, and acted at Covent Garden, the Haymarket, and Lincoln's Inn Fields theatres before opening in 1740 his own playhouse, the New Wells (a 'drinking theatre', at which singing, tumbling, rope-dancing, and pantomimes were performed) in Lemon Street in Goodman's Fields. William Hallam, although apparently a mediocre performer, enjoyed a modest success by offering variety entertainments so that he and his company would not violate the Licensing Act of 1737, which restricted 'legitimate' drama in London to the two patent houses, Drury Lane and Covent Garden. Although he did begin to present 'legitimate' plays in 1744, he remained technically within the law by advertising his entertainment as a 'concert' in two parts, the first part to be followed by a play, offered, according to the advertisement, at no charge to the audience.

**The prospect of America** Lewis Hallam, who gained experience with his family acting in the British provinces, later performed at London's fairs (and perhaps at the minor theatres, including the Haymarket) before working with William's company at the New Wells from 1745 until 1748, and again in 1750. Lewis was possibly a somewhat more accomplished performer than William, but he was clearly unable to achieve success on the London stage.

The Hallam brothers apparently saw that their best chance for theatrical success was to lead a troupe to America, where few professional actors had ventured. They had almost surely heard of—and were perhaps inspired by—the success of John Moody, an Irish actor who had recruited English performers to form a spectacularly successful repertory company in the West Indies. In October

1750 the Hallams dispatched Robert Upton, an actor, to the colonies as an advance scout for the London company. Meanwhile, William's ruse to circumvent the Licensing Act eventually stimulated a grievance, and in 1751, after complaints had been filed, the lord chamberlain closed the Wells in Lemon Street, causing William to seek another method of securing his livelihood in the theatre.

William and Lewis patiently awaited word from Upton. The brothers agreed that Lewis would accompany the troupe to America and William would remain in London. The profits from their colonial company, to be known as the London Company of Comedians, would be divided equally between them. Months passed, however, with no word from Upton. As Lewis later complained, 'On his arrival Upton found … that sett of pretenders with whom he joined and, unhappily for us, quite neglected the business he was sent about from England. For we never heard of him after' (Hornblow, 1.67). The group in question was a short-lived, evidently barely competent acting company, 'composed of stage-struck tradesmen and their wives' (Rankin, 42), headed by Walter Murray and Thomas Kean; Upton later formed his own troupe, which, like the Murray–Kean company, did not last long. The performances of both companies were probably on the most amateurish level. Indeed, until the arrival of the London Company of Comedians, theatrical presentations in America were almost certainly inept, as attested by the failure of the early companies to find audiences loyal and numerous enough to ensure their theatrical survival.

After waiting to hear from Upton for more than a year, the Hallams determined to delay no longer. The troupe, consisting of William and Lewis Hallam (who was to play comic roles and serious old men), the latter's wife, **Sarah Hallam** [*known as* Mrs Lewis Hallam] (*d.* 1774)—her maiden name is unknown but her first name is given in the baptismal record of her daughter Isabella—who was to play female leads, William Rigby, who was assigned the male leads, and nine other adults, plus three of Hallam's four children, sailed for the colonies in early May 1752, on the *Charming Sally*. Hallam's daughter Isabella remained behind to live with her aunt; she later became famous as Isabella *Mattocks (1746–1826), a leading performer at Covent Garden. Aboard ship, the actors rehearsed on the quarterdeck when the weather permitted.

**The colonial stage** The Hallams' company arrived in Yorktown, Virginia, on 2 June and travelled by land to Williamsburg. On 12 June Lewis Hallam placed an advertisement in the *Virginia Gazette*, announcing that his:

> select company of Comedians, [with] Scenes, Cloaths and Decorations … all entirely new, extremely rich, and finished in the highest Taste, the Scenes being painted by the best Hands in London … the company being perfected in all the best Plays, Opera's, Farces, and Pantomimes

was ready to perform. The colonial governor initially disapproved Hallam's application to present plays, for the now disbanded Murray–Kean troupe's rowdy behaviour in Williamsburg had inflamed opposition to all theatrical endeavours. Hallam persisted, however, running his advertisement on two more occasions. One of the troupe's actors advertised that he would offer violin lessons to the inhabitants of Williamsburg and surrounding towns, perhaps helping to persuade the governor of the good character of the Hallam company. At any rate, the governor eventually agreed to grant Hallam a licence. Hallam purchased a building in Williamsburg that Murray and Kean had used to present their plays and refurbished it. The theatre opened on 15 September 1752 with Lord Lansdowne's *The Jew of Venice*, which Hallam billed as *The Merchant of Venice*, 'Written by Shakespear', adding that this was 'the first play performed in America by a regular company of [British] comedians' (Highfill, Burnim & Langhans, *BDA*). Mrs Hallam appeared as Portia, Patrick Malone played Shylock, Rigby was featured as Bassanio, while Lewis Hallam performed the comparatively small role of Launcelot. Playing a servant to Portia was twelve-year-old **Lewis Hallam the younger** (1740–1808), who eventually became one of the leading performers in America, but on this occasion, never having acted before, burst into tears and ran off the stage. Still, the production, given by experienced professional actors—albeit actors who had found only modest success in the competitive theatrical environment of London—was undoubtedly the finest yet seen in America, and it inaugurated an eleven-month stay in Williamsburg, during which the company played three nights a week to large houses. Although several of the actors wound up in debtors' prison and had to be bailed out by Hallam, the first engagement of the London Company could reasonably be described as successful. From Williamsburg Hallam led the company to New York, where they opened on 17 September 1753.

The Hallam brothers' agreement to split whatever profits their company might bring held until 1754, when William, evidently in dire financial straits, sold his interest in the company to Lewis and returned to London. He played at Bartholomew fair and received a benefit at Sadler's Wells in 1756 before he died, presumably in 1758.

From 1753 to 1755 the London Company of Comedians, led by Lewis Hallam, played in New York, where it once again had to overcome opposition based on the misbehaviour of the Murray–Kean troupe; in Philadelphia, where religious opposition to the theatre was particularly strong; and in Charles Town, South Carolina. Hallam built new theatres in New York and Charles Town and remodelled a warehouse into 'the New Theatre in Water-Street' in Philadelphia. In February 1755 the Hallams repaired to Jamaica, perhaps hoping to duplicate John Moody's success. Moody had earlier sailed to England to join David Garrick's company at Drury Lane, but the core of his organization was still intact, now led by **David Douglass** (*d.* 1789), an actor originally recruited from England by Moody. Douglass, who was preparing to return to England to enlist new actors, realized that the arrival of Hallam's troupe made his trip unnecessary. Instead, he and Hallam joined forces.

**Douglass and the younger Hallam** Lewis Hallam died of yellow fever shortly after this time (the exact date is unknown), but the combined company remained united under Douglass's leadership. Still, the credit for having established the first fully professional theatre in colonial America belongs to Lewis Hallam the elder and to his brother William.

In 1758 Douglass married Lewis Hallam's widow and led the troupe back to the colonies. Lewis Hallam the younger, then eighteen, became the company's leading actor, often appearing opposite his mother, on several occasions playing Romeo to her Juliet. William Dunlap, the first historian of the American theatre, described the mature Hallam as 'of middle stature or above' (another account says he was 5 feet 7 inches), 'thin, straight, and well taught as a dancer and fencer' (Dunlap, 1.155). In later years he vied with several others for the title of America's foremost actor. Rivals included John Palmer, who began performing with the London Company in 1759 and later became a leading actor in London. Another was John Henry, like Palmer an actor from England, who joined the company in 1767, and was generally recognized as more gifted than Hallam; he soon began to play many of the leading roles for the American Company, beginning a feud with the younger Hallam that was to last for nearly thirty years.

However, Hallam had his loyal adherents. Alexander Graydon, who expressed early scepticism about Hallam's abilities, later said:

> He was … at Philadelphia, as much the soul of the Southwark Theatre, as ever Garrick was of Drury lane; and if, as Doctor Johnson allows, popularity in matters of taste is unquestionable evidence of merit, we cannot withhold a considerable portion of it from Mr. Hallam, notwithstanding his faults. (Graydon, 87–8)

Douglass and his company invariably faced hostility—economic, religious, political, or moral—to the theatre wherever they played in colonial America, but they shrewdly wore down the opposition by behaving irreproachably offstage, offering performances for charity, and deleting any potentially offensive scenes or lines from the plays they performed. Furthermore, Douglass continued the tradition established by Lewis Hallam the elder of building theatres (or converting existing buildings into playhouses) at many stops, for colonial America lacked theatre structures. Douglass's company offered the first professional production of an American play, Thomas Godfrey's *The Prince of Parthia*, in 1767, and produced Shakespeare's plays (albeit generally in their eighteenth-century versions) and new British plays (Goldsmith's *She Stoops to Conquer* was given in 1773, the same year it had its first performance in London).

Despite the rigours of offering performances where, in many cases, plays had never been seen before, the company appeared in cities and small towns in New York, Pennsylvania, Rhode Island, Virginia, South Carolina, Maryland, and elsewhere, winning influential adherents such as George Washington. Despite periodic defections from the company, Douglass persisted, succeeding more often than not. The company's once-tenuous reputation had improved so greatly by 1761 that the governor and council of Virginia gave Douglass the following letter of reference:

> The company of comedians under the direction of David Douglass has performed in this colony for near twelvemonth; during which time they have made it their constant practice to behave with prudence and discretion in their private character, and to use their utmost endeavours to give general satisfaction in their public capacity. We have therefore thought proper to recommend them as a company whose behaviour merits the favour of the public and who are capable of entertaining a sensible and polite audience. (*Newport Mercury*, 11 Aug 1761)

Perhaps Douglass's shrewdest stroke was to rename his troupe the American Company of Comedians in 1763, thereby attracting American audiences by aligning his company with the colonists in their struggle against Great Britain. While for the most part the company's personnel continued to come from England (Douglass made periodic trips there to recruit new actors and seek out new plays), a few American-born performers also joined the troupe.

Mrs Douglass (the former Mrs Hallam) died in Philadelphia in 1774 of 'a hurt received in the theatre', according to a contemporary report (Rankin, 187). Later that year the Continental Congress passed a resolution condemning all theatrical performances and other 'diversions' until the conflict against the British was resolved. The American Company, preparing to begin a new season, recognized that attempting to defy the congress's direct order would be futile; it immediately closed its theatres and set sail for the British West Indies, where it remained for the next ten years, but under new leadership. Douglass soon retired from the stage, founded the *Jamaica Mercury and Kingston Advertiser* (later called the *New Royal Gazette*), and amassed a considerable fortune. He died in 1789.

Lewis Hallam the younger returned to England in 1775 and gave one performance (and endured a merciless review in the *Morning Post*) as Hamlet at Covent Garden. By 1779 he was again in Jamaica, where he acted under the direction of John Henry, who had taken over the management of the American Company after Douglass's retirement. In 1785 Henry took his troupe to Maryland, then New York. Meanwhile, Hallam, in conjunction with a Mr Allen, had assembled 'a feeble company' (Seilhamer, 2.165) that played in Philadelphia and New York.

**The Old American Company** In New York in 1785, Henry recommended to Hallam that their companies join forces, to which Hallam agreed. Their troupe, now known as the Old American Company, dominated the American theatre until 1792, when one of their actors, Thomas Wignell, formed his own company in Philadelphia.

During the years of its dominance, the Old American Company performed principally in New York and Philadelphia. According to the nineteenth-century historian George O. Seilhamer, the company under the joint leadership of Hallam and Henry:

> was superior to any that had as yet been seen in America. … The pieces produced [by the company] would have been creditable to any of the London theatres. New productions followed each other in rapid succession, and for the first time in the history of the American stage successful plays had what might be called a run. This was notably the case with the 'School for Scandal' and 'The Poor Soldier,' the former being played seven and the latter eighteen times

> during the season. … The long exile of ten years in [Jamaica] had kept the organization together, strengthened it by the addition of new members, and enabled it to keep pace with dramatic progress in England. (Seilhamer, 2.177–9)

The Old American Company was plagued with managerial disputes, no doubt because Henry and Hallam were equally duplicitous. In 1794 Henry was displaced by John Hodgkinson, who, motivated by ambition and an intense dislike for Hallam, began taking all the best roles for himself and his wife, permitting Hallam and his second wife, the former Eliza Tuke, only roles of lesser importance. Mrs Hallam cannot be said to have been blameless, however, as she not infrequently arrived at the theatre in a drunken state. On one occasion, in 1795, she was unable to complete a performance. According to William Dunlap, 'Mr. Hallam attributed the very strange exhibition to opium. The audience were shocked and disgusted' (Dunlap, 1.266).

Two years later in New York, having been deprived of all her roles by Hodgkinson and Dunlap (who had joined Hallam and Hodgkinson in the management of the Old American Company in 1796), Mrs Hallam burst onto the stage during a performance, joined by her husband. She announced that Hodgkinson had engaged in a plot to deprive her of her livelihood. Hallam supported her, and, despite Hodgkinson's appeal to the audience, a near-riot ensued. Later that year Hodgkinson published a pamphlet, *Narrative of his Connection with the Old American Company*, which consisted almost entirely of his account of his grievances against the Hallams.

On 25 May 1797 Hallam quit as co-manager, selling his interest to Dunlap and Hodgkinson, but remained with the company as a salaried actor, as did Mrs Hallam. In 1806, however, Thomas Abthorpe Cooper, the new manager of the company, refused to renew Hallam's contract. Hallam, the last survivor in the group of actors who went to America as members of the London Company of Comedians, died in Philadelphia on 1 November 1808.

Hallam had two children by his first wife, Sarah, a young Jamaican girl he married when he was about eighteen (in or before 1758). Sarah Hallam, who seems to have appeared on stage only once, separated from her husband at some time around 1763. Perhaps as early as 1770, but surely by 1775, she was running a dancing-school in Williamsburg. Lewis and Sarah's son Mirvan (whose date of birth is unknown) became an actor and played in his father's company in 1793. His abilities seem to have been small, for he never became anything but a minor actor. Lewis D. Hallam, the other son of Lewis and Sarah, was a medical student when he died at the age of nineteen in 1780.

JARED BROWN

**Sources** W. Dunlap, *History of the American theatre*, 2nd edn, ed. J. Hodgkinson, 3 vols. in 1 (1963) • H. F. Rankin, *The theater in colonial America* (1960) • Highfill, Burnim & Langhans, *BDA* • G. O. Seilhamer, *History of the American theatre*, 3 vols. [1888–91]; repr. (1969) • A. Hornblow, *A history of the theatre in America*, 1 (1919); repr. (1965) • G. Hughes, *A history of the American theatre, 1700–1950* (1951) • A. Graydon, *Memoirs of his own time*, ed. J. S. Littell (1846); repr. (1969) • parish register, Middlesex, St Mary Whitechapel, 25 May 1746 [baptism; I. Hallam] • private information (2004) [O. Baldwin; T. Wilson]

**Likenesses** G. V. Neist, print (Mrs Lewis Hallam), Harvard TC; repro. in Highfill, Burnim & Langhans, *BDA*, vol. 7, p. 38 • engraving, miniature (Lewis Hallam the younger), Players Club; repro. in Highfill, Burnim & Langhans, *BDA*, vol. 7, p. 39

**Hallam, Mrs Lewis** (*d.* 1774). *See under* Hallam, Lewis (1714?–1756?).

**Hallam, Lewis, the younger** (1740–1808). *See under* Hallam, Lewis (1714?–1756?).

**Hallam, Robert**. *See* Hallum, Robert (*d.* 1417).

**Hallam, William** (1712?–1758?). *See under* Hallam, Lewis (1714?–1756?).

**Hallé, Sir Charles** [*formerly* Carl Halle] (1819–1895), conductor and pianist, was born on 11 April 1819 in Hagen, Westphalia. He was the son of a church organist and concert director, Friedrich Halle, and his wife, Caroline Branschedt. He had his first piano lessons at the age of three and soon showed extraordinary talent, giving a public performance when he was four of a sonatina composed by his father. When he was eleven he deputized for his father and conducted all the operas (at least ten) during the annual visit of a touring company. They included Mozart's *Die Zauberflöte* and Weber's *Der Freischütz*. In 1835 Halle went to Darmstadt to study with Johann Christian Rinck and Gottfried Weber and the following year moved on to Paris with the intention of taking piano lessons from Friedrich Kalkbrenner. But Kalkbrenner sent him to George Osborne.

With his good looks and personal charm, Halle was soon in demand as a pianist in the fashionable salons. There he met and mixed with the astonishing galaxy of artists living and working in the French capital, not only musicians such as the impoverished Richard Wagner and Chopin, Liszt, Thalberg, Paganini, and Cherubini, but the literary figures Alfred de Musset, Alphonse de Lamartine, and George Sand, and the painter Ingres. Above all, he made friends with Hector Berlioz, attending the first performances of several of his works and studying his conducting methods. Halle was the first pianist to perform all the Beethoven sonatas in Paris and he established a series of chamber concerts, then comparatively rare events, with the violinist Delphin Alard and the cellist Auguste Franchomme.

Halle's first visit to England—where he later added an acute accent to his surname—was an eight-week sojourn in London in 1843. Invited by the Philharmonic Society to play at one of its concerts provided he performed a concerto by one of its directors, he refused. In 1848 the revolution in Paris caused him to escape to Britain with his wife, Désirée Smith de Rilieu (*d.* 1866), whom he had married in 1841. They had two children by this date, and later seven more. He performed Beethoven's 'Emperor' concerto at Covent Garden and gave a solo recital. But competition in the capital was fierce because so many of Hallé's Parisian colleagues were also in London. He was invited to settle in

**Sir Charles Hallé** (1819–1895), by George Frederic Watts, *c.*1870

Bath, but while considering the offer he received a letter from a Manchester calico printer, Hermann Leo, informing him that Manchester was 'quite ripe to be taken in hand' and that Leo considered him 'the fittest man to stir the dormant taste for the art' (Hallé, *Autobiography*, 146). Leo, who was the leading patron of music in Manchester, had heard Hallé play when he had been in Paris on business. Hallé accepted the offer and visited Manchester in September 1848 to play the 'Emperor' concerto. Hallé's comment on the Gentlemen's Concerts orchestra was, 'I was fresh from the Concerts du Conservatoire, from Hector Berlioz's orchestra, and I seriously thought of packing up and leaving Manchester so that I might not have to endure a second of these wretched performances. But when I hinted at this, my friends gave me to understand that I was expected to change all this' (ibid., 122–3).

Hallé's first contribution to Mancunian musical life was to found a series of chamber concerts. In November 1849 he was appointed conductor of the Gentlemen's Concerts, which had been established about 1770, with carte blanche to re-form the orchestra. This he duly did; he also formed a choral society and in 1854–5 tried unsuccessfully to establish opera in Manchester. In addition he gave piano recitals. In 1857 Manchester staged a great Arts Treasures Exhibition and Hallé was empowered to enlarge the orchestra. The exhibition coincided with the reconstruction of the Free Trade Hall, where Hallé conducted large-scale works for which there had hitherto been neither suitable venue nor adequate performers. Rather than let this orchestra disperse, he decided to establish his own concerts. On 30 January 1858 the Hallé Concerts were instituted, eventually amounting to more than twenty each winter season.

Hallé now proved himself to be one of the outstanding musical educators of the public. The programmes of his concerts steadily increased in quality and he lost no opportunity to introduce as soon as possible the works of contemporary composers—Wagner, Brahms, Liszt, Dvořák, Tchaikovsky, Parry, Stanford, and many others. In particular he championed the music of Berlioz, giving the first English performances of the *Symphonie fantastique*, *La damnation de Faust*, and *L'enfance du Christ*. He attracted the leading soloists of the day to Manchester and, with his continental contacts, was always able to recruit excellent players for his orchestra.

Hallé also conducted regularly in Edinburgh, Bristol, Liverpool, and London and gave annual piano recitals in the capital. He was a celebrated teacher, his pupils including the princess of Wales (later Queen Alexandra). In 1893 he became the first principal of the Royal Manchester College of Music, which opened in October that year as a result of an initiative taken four years earlier to mark Hallé's seventieth birthday. In July 1888, shortly after he had been knighted, he married the violinist Wilma Norman-Neruda (1838?–1911) [*see* Hallé, Wilma]. With her he toured Australia in 1890 and 1891 and South Africa in 1895.

Hallé's piano playing was, from all accounts, classically correct and scrupulous in its adherence to the composer's score. His temperament was not that of the flamboyant virtuoso either as pianist or conductor, but we can judge from Bernard Shaw's reviews that he had trained a superb orchestra and could persuade it to give remarkable performances of a wide range of composers. He died from a cerebral haemorrhage at his home (now demolished) in Greenheys Lane, Manchester, on 25 October 1895. He was buried on 29 October in the Roman Catholic cemetery at Weaste, Salford. His Manchester concerts, continued by three businessmen and then by a society, were his private property.

With August Manns at the Crystal Palace and, later, Henry Wood at the Promenade Concerts, Hallé was one of the great musical educators of the British public. He transformed his orchestral programmes from a miscellany into virtually the symphony concert of today through a gradual educatory process. Working with most of the same players year after year, he obtained well-rehearsed performances (as Shaw's criticisms of London concerts in the 1890s testify). He also showed that high standards and a strong musical tradition can be established in a provincial city, thereby setting a pattern not only for Manchester, where several illustrious conductors have been content to work with the Hallé Orchestra for long periods, but also elsewhere. MICHAEL KENNEDY

**Sources** C. E. Hallé and M. Hallé, eds., *Life and letters of Sir Charles Hallé* (1896) • *The autobiography of Charles Hallé, with correspondence*

*and diaries*, ed. M. Kennedy (1972) • M. Kennedy, *The Hallé tradition: a century of music* (1960) • C. Rigby, *Sir Charles Hallé* (1952)

**Archives** NRA, priv. coll., letters to J. M. Wood • Royal Northern College of Music, Manchester, letters mainly to Stanley Withers

**Likenesses** V. Moltez, oils, 1850, Hallé Concerts Society, Manchester • Duval, drawing, 1859, Forsyth Bros., Manchester • G. F. Watts, oils, *c.*1870, NPG [*see illus.*] • photograph, 1880?, Forsyth Bros., Manchester • photograph, *c.*1888, Hult. Arch. • Barraud, photograph, 1889, NPG • C. Baugniet, group portrait, lithograph (*The Musical Union, 1851*), NPG • Elliott & Fry, cartes-de-visite, NPG • E. O. Ford, marble bust, Man. City Gall. • bust, Manchester town hall • carte-de-visite, NPG • death mask, Watts Gallery, Compton, Surrey

**Wealth at death** £8459 17*s.* 1*d.*: probate, 30 Dec 1895, *CGPLA Eng. & Wales*

**Halle, John** (*d.* 1479), merchant, was possibly the son of Thomas Halle of Salisbury, who was a member of the city's corporation from 1437 to 1442, during which time he served as custodian of the mace and as mayor's serjeant. John Halle, a mercer and member of the staple, appears in Salisbury's ledger as early as 1421. By 1445 he was a member of the common council, and in the same year was appointed an assessor; he was made an auditor in 1447 and rose to the select council in the same year. Subsequently he served as constable of the city, overseer of the city's wealth, alderman, arbitrator, and delegate of the corporation. He represented Salisbury in four parliaments between 1453 and 1461, and was elected mayor of the city in 1451, 1456, 1464, and 1465. Directly involved in attempts to augment the liberties of the city from 1455 onwards, in 1465 he represented the corporation before the king in its dispute with Richard Beauchamp, bishop of Salisbury (*d.* 1481). In presenting the city's petition Halle showed himself 'right seditious, hasty, willful and of full unworthy disposition' (Salisbury ledger B, fol. 77*r*), which resulted in his imprisonment in London. The corporation refused four royal orders to elect a new mayor, though he was replaced as a delegate after the last order. Halle, then released, was re-elected mayor for the fourth time.

By 1469, Edward IV had confirmed episcopal authority over Salisbury, which may explain Halle's actions in 1470. In September of that year Halle, in his capacity as the mayor's deputy, received 40 marks to raise forty men—who were to be under his own command—on behalf of the earl of Warwick, now in rebellion against Edward IV. It may be doubted if he did so, since on Easter Sunday (14 April) 1471 the earl of Somerset, acting in the name of Henry VI, presented letters under the great seal authorizing him to raise soldiers in Salisbury. The corporation, on Halle's advice, complied, and also ordered that the money levied earlier be paid to King Henry. But within a month the Lancastrian cause was ruined and Somerset was dead. The men of Salisbury were probably able to buy their way back into King Edward's favour. Nevertheless, by 1472 the corporation had relinquished its claims to greater liberty from episcopal control; Halle witnessed the mayor's oath to the bishop. Despite his earlier animosity towards the bishop, Halle repeatedly represented the corporation in negotiations with Beauchamp between 1474 and 1478. He continued to be a merchant of the staple, and wellnigh dominated the wool trade of Salisbury Plain. Styled 'esquire' by 1476, Halle acquired considerable wealth and property, and ranked as the second largest landholder in Salisbury. Some time after 1455 he built a residence, now 15 New Canal, the hall of which was restored in the early twentieth century as the foyer to a cinema. Its stained glass and chimney-piece bear Halle's merchant mark and arms. At his death, on 14 October 1479, he held property in Salisbury and at Shipton Bellinger, Hampshire. With his wife, Joan, he had two surviving children. Their son William was attainted in 1483 for taking part in Buckingham's unsuccessful rebellion, but had that sentence reversed in 1485. William's daughter married Thomas Wriothesley (*d.* 1534), Garter king of arms under Henry VII. John Halle's daughter, Chrystian, married Sir Thomas Hungerford, son of Sir Edmund Hungerford and grandson of Walter, first Baron Hungerford of Hungerford (*d.* 1449).

David R. Carr

**Sources** Salisbury municipal corporation, ledger B, WRO G23/1/2 • D. R. Carr, ed., The first general entry book of the city of Salisbury, 1387–1452, Wilts RS, 54 (2001) • *Liber niger*, WRO D/1/5 • deeds of Trinity Hospital, Salisbury, WRO 1446 • E. Duke, *Prolusiones historicae, or, Essays illustrative of the Halle of John Halle, citizen and merchant, of Salisbury* (1837) • R. Benson and H. Hatcher, *The history of modern Wiltshire*, ed. R. C. Hoare, 6 (1843) • F. Street, 'The relations of the bishops and citizens of Salisbury (New Sarum) between 1225 and 1612', *Wiltshire Archaeological and Natural History Magazine*, 39 (1915–17), 185–257, 319–67 • B. F. Collier, 'John Halle, merchant and mayor of Salisbury', *Journal of the British Archaeological Association*, new ser., 14 (1908), 221–42 • *The ancient and historical monuments in the city of Salisbury*, Royal Commission on Historical Monuments (England), 1 (1980) • *VCH Wiltshire*, vol. 6 • E. R. Nevill, 'Salisbury in 1455', *Wiltshire Archaeological and Natural History Magazine*, 37 (1911–12), 66–91 • J. S. Davies, ed., *The Tropenell cartulary, being the contents of an old Wiltshire muniment chest*, 2 vols. (1908) • W. P. Baildon, ed., *Select cases in chancery*, AD *1364 to 1471*, SeldS, 10 (1896)

**Wealth at death** probably substantial: Salisbury municipal corporation, ledgers A and B; *Liber niger*; Baildon, ed., *Selected cases*

**Hallé** [*other married name* Norman-Neruda], **Wilma** [*née* Vilemína Maria Franziška Nerudová], **Lady Hallé** (1838?–1911), violinist, was born on 21 March, probably in 1838 rather than in 1839 as is often stated. She was the third child and second daughter of the ten children of Josef Neruda (1807–1875), organist of Brno Cathedral, Moravia, from 1832 to 1845 and from 1852 to 1875, and his wife, Frantiska Mertová. Her brothers Viktor (1835–1852) and František (1843–1915) were cellists and her sisters Amálie (1834–1890) and Marie (1840–1922) were a pianist and violinist respectively. Wilma learned to play the violin almost as soon as she could walk. Her first teacher was her father, followed by Baruch von Infeld in Brno and Leopold Jansa in Vienna, where, when she was seven, she played a sonata by J. S. Bach. This led to a family tour of north Germany and other parts of Europe. Wilma first visited England as a child prodigy in 1849, playing at the Princess Theatre, London, on 30 April and at a Philharmonic Society concert on 11 June, when she was soloist in a concerto by Charles de Bériot. Between these engagements she went on tour, playing in Manchester at one of the Gentlemen's Concerts just nine months before her future second husband, Charles *Hallé (1819–1895), became their conductor.

Wilma Hallé, Lady Hallé (1838?–1911), by Barraud, pubd 1889

On 27 January 1864 Wilma, a Roman Catholic, married the Swedish conductor and composer (Fredrik Vilhelm) Ludwig Norman (1831–1885) in St Thomas's Church in Brno, after which she performed under the name Wilma Norman-Neruda. The couple had one son, who was killed mountaineering in the Dolomites on 11 September 1898, and the marriage ended in separation in 1869. From 1867 to 1870 Wilma was professor of violin at Stockholm Conservatory. After a twenty-year absence she returned to London in 1869, and played first violin in string quartets at the Monday Popular Concerts and appeared twice at the Philharmonic Society in concertos by Henri Vieuxtemps and Pierre Rode. So popular did she become that she returned annually, taking part regularly in sonata recitals with Hallé as pianist and frequently playing concertos at Hans Richter's London concerts after 1877 as well as at Hallé's Manchester concerts.

On 26 July 1888 Wilma married the recently knighted Hallé. Together they toured Australia in 1890 and 1891 and South Africa in 1895. Hallé died a few months after this last tour. The prince of Wales headed a committee which raised a fund for his widow's benefit and presented her with the title-deeds of a mansion at Asolo, Italy. She settled in Berlin in 1900 to teach at the Stern Conservatory but continued to visit England every year, playing at Henry J. Wood's concerts and at Hallé concerts in Manchester, where Hans Richter had succeeded her husband. In 1901 she was appointed violinist to Queen Alexandra. Among her last performances in Britain were those with the Hallé Orchestra in Manchester in November 1907 and at the London memorial concert for Joseph Joachim on 25 January 1908.

After 1876 Lady Hallé played on a Stradivari of 1709 which had belonged to her fellow countryman Heinrich Ernst (1814–1865). She had a wide concerto repertory. Those who heard her interpretation of Mendelssohn's E minor regarded it as unsurpassable. She was of striking appearance, and her platform manner was graceful. Her tone was as powerful as that of any male violinist and her interpretations were, it is said, touched with genius. She died at 62 Motzstrasse, Schöneberg, Berlin, on 15 April 1911 from pneumonia. MICHAEL KENNEDY

**Sources** *New Grove* • M. Kennedy, *The Hallé tradition: a century of music* (1960) • *The autobiography of Charles Hallé, with correspondence and diaries*, ed. M. Kennedy (1972) • *The Times* (17 April 1911) • M. B. Foster, *History of the Philharmonic Society of London: 1813–1912* (1912) • *Československý hudební slovník* (1963)
**Likenesses** Barraud, photograph, pubd 1889, NPG [*see illus.*]
**Wealth at death** £192 0s. 8*d*.: probate, 2 Oct 1911, *CGPLA Eng. & Wales*

**Hallett, John Hughes-** (1901–1972), naval officer, was born in Ealing, London, on 1 December 1901, the second of three sons (there were no daughters) of Colonel (James) Wyndham Hughes-Hallett, Indian Staff Corps, and his second wife, Clementine Mary Loch. There were also two sons and a daughter from his father's first marriage. Educated at Bedford School and the Royal Naval College at Osborne and Dartmouth, and for a year after the First World War at Gonville and Caius College, Cambridge, he saw war service in the battle cruiser *Lion* in 1918. As a lieutenant he entered the torpedo branch, gaining the Ogilvie prize for his year. The branch was responsible for torpedoes, mines, and the electrical installations of ships, and his ingenuity was to bring him numerous expressions of their lordships' appreciation for his inventions.

As torpedo officer of the carrier *Courageous* in 1933–5 Jock Hughes-Hallett helped to design a night deck-landing system and produced plans for a gliding torpedo which was to be dropped from aircraft. The latter was ahead of its time—even though the Admiralty rejected it. He then learned to fly. The most interesting feature of his next job, which was at the Admiralty in 1935–7 as a commander, was to act as the secretary to the Anglo-German naval conference of June 1935.

At the start of the Second World War Hughes-Hallett was executive officer of the cruiser *Devonshire* which took part in the Norwegian campaign, after which he was mentioned in dispatches. On promotion to captain in June 1940, he was sent to the local defence division of the naval staff which was responsible for preparations against invasion. Here his energy and ingenuity were invaluable and he produced many ideas for defending the ports and beaches. He also found time to give useful service as chairman of a low-cover radar committee, which planned the use of this new invention. He was again mentioned in dispatches in March 1941, an unusual honour for an officer based ashore.

In December 1941, mainly at the request of Lord Louis Mountbatten, Hughes-Hallett was made naval adviser to combined operations where he was extremely successful in helping to build up the organization. He assisted in the planning of the St Nazaire raid and was the naval commander of the Dieppe raid in August 1942, when his landing-craft carried out their task with skill. Losses were heavy and, although many lessons for the future were learned, the raid was a failure. Hughes-Hallett would have preferred not to land on the main beach, but he was overruled by his military colleagues. He was appointed to the DSO (1942). As commander, Force J, he played an outstanding role in developing the techniques of amphibious warfare. Based mainly on the Isle of Wight, the force became very large: as a junior captain, serving in the rank of commodore, first class, Hughes-Hallett was in charge of 15,000 service personnel. He was lent for three months in the summer of 1942 to the organization preparing for the invasion of France, and was responsible for the initial naval plan for operation Overlord in 1944. It is generally acknowledged that he played the major role in conceiving the idea of the artificial harbours off the beaches and he used to recount that he thought of sinking old ships to form a breakwater when at morning service in Westminster Abbey.

As it was deemed necessary for his career for him to go to sea Hughes-Hallett was appointed to command the cruiser *Jamaica*, thus missing the invasion. The ship took part in the battle off the North Cape when the *Scharnhorst* was sunk in December 1943, and Hughes-Hallett was mentioned in dispatches. As captain he demanded a high standard of efficiency and was ruthless in obtaining it; he was respected rather than loved. In September 1945 he was appointed CB for his services to amphibious warfare and in the *Jamaica*. After the war he commanded the torpedo school at HMS *Vernon* where he made far-reaching changes to adapt to new techniques. He was then for a year captain of the carrier *Illustrious*, a post in which his pilot's licence was of assistance. Promoted to rear-admiral in June 1950, he was appointed vice-controller of the navy, where his technical flair was useful. His last job in the navy was as commander, heavy squadron, Home Fleet (1952–3), during which time he was made a vice-admiral.

A man of high ideals, Hughes-Hallett came to the conclusion that he wanted to serve his country in politics and he resigned in September 1954, finding a safe Conservative seat at a by-election at Croydon East, which became Croydon North-East in 1955. He found politics puzzling and was irritated by the delays and compromises necessary in a democratic institution. As a back-bencher he served on the public accounts committee and on the select committee on the estimates, and between 1958 and 1960 he was a British representative to the consultative assembly of the Council of Europe at Strasbourg and also to the assembly of the Western European Union in Paris. Here his experience of defence matters proved useful. After the Suez débâcle of 1956 he did much to promote a permanent United Nations peace force, but without success.

In April 1961 Hughes-Hallett was promoted to the post of third parliamentary secretary at the Ministry of Transport, with responsibility for shipping and shipbuilding. He introduced some far-reaching measures, some of which were considered interventionist by many of his colleagues. His minister, A. E. Marples, and he formed a strong team. He was well liked in politics, having become less abrupt and more approachable, and he was known for a pungent wit. He was conscientious in looking after his constituents. The reasons for his leaving politics in 1964 are difficult to discern. Perhaps he was disappointed in his progress. He chose a bad moment to retire as pensions for MPs were introduced shortly afterwards.

Hughes-Hallett was a consultant director to the British Shipping Council (1964–9) and he acquired several honorary tasks, among them membership of the Council of Advanced Motorists. An ardent and fast car driver, he also used a bicycle all his life. He was unmarried. His last years were clouded by a fear of penury, caused mainly by a dispute with the Admiralty over the size of his pension about which he had been misinformed before he retired. He died at Slindon, Sussex, on 5 April 1972.

PETER GRETTON, *rev.*

**Sources** *The Times* (6 April 1972) • *WWW* • S. W. Roskill, *The war at sea, 1939–1945*, 3 vols. in 4 (1954–61) • personal knowledge (1986) • private information (1986) • *CGPLA Eng. & Wales* (1972)
**Archives** IWM | FILM IWM FVA, actuality footage
**Wealth at death** £21,355: probate, 30 May 1972, *CGPLA Eng. & Wales*

**Hallett, Joseph** (**I**) (*bap.* **1620**, *d.* **1689**), clergyman and ejected minister, was baptized at Bridport, Dorset, on 21 May 1620, the son of Roger Hallett. He did not attend university, but apparently learned Hebrew and Greek by his own efforts. He had married his first wife, Mary, by 1649, but she died two years later and was buried at Bridport on 25 April 1651. Their daughters, Susannah and Deborah, baptized in the town in 1649 and 1650, seem not to have survived him. In 1652 Hallett was called to the ministry at the sequestered rectory of Hinton St George, Somerset, and was ordained to this charge on 28 October 1652 at St Thomas's Church, Salisbury, by Philip Pynckney and five other ministers of the classis of Sarum. Hallett married a second wife, Elizabeth, who survived him, together with three sons, of whom the eldest was Joseph (II) *Hallett (1656–1722), and three daughters. On 23 April 1656 he was admitted to the rectory of Chiselborough with West Chinnock, Somerset, sequestered from Thomas Gauler. Hallett held it until the time of the Restoration, when Gauler was restored.

After his ejection in 1660 Hallett returned to Bridport for a time, before moving to Bradpole, Dorset, where he kept a conventicle. He was licensed as a presbyterian preacher at Exeter on 22 May 1672, but the following June was imprisoned there for preaching to some 200 persons in the house of one Palmer. On 24 April 1680 Bishop Thomas Lamplugh wrote to Archbishop Sancroft that 'the meetinghouse lately erected [in Exeter] was presented this Sessions, and is now put down. One Hallet, a very pernicious fellow, who used to preach there, doth abscond, they searched his house for him last Wednesday, but could not find him' (*Calamy rev.*, 243). Hallett and his wife, Elizabeth, were presented by the churchwardens of St Mary's, Exeter, on 16 June 1683, for not receiving the sacrament. Between 1673 and 1687 he was fined a total of £120 for preaching at Exeter, and in 1685 he was one of the ministers imprisoned there. In 1687 Hallett refused to read James II's declaration of indulgence in public, but it provided the legal basis for a new meeting-house for Exeter presbyterians—James's Meeting—at which he became the first minister.

Hallett's health was badly affected by his imprisonments. He began to suffer fits, which affected his mental state and even seized him in the pulpit. He died on 14 March 1689, and was buried on 18 March at St Mary Major, Exeter. The funeral sermon was preached by his colleague George Trosse. His eldest son, Joseph, continued Hallett's work in Exeter.

ALEXANDER GORDON, *rev.* STEPHEN WRIGHT

**Sources** *Calamy rev.* • J. Murch, *A history of the Presbyterian and General Baptist churches in the west of England* (1835) • *The nonconformist's memorial … originally written by … Edmund Calamy*, ed. S. Palmer, [3rd edn], 3 (1803), 183–4 • C. Whiting, *Studies in English puritanism* (1931)

**Hallett, Joseph (II)** (1656–1722), Presbyterian minister and tutor, was born on 4 November 1656, probably in Somerset or Dorset, the eldest son of Joseph (I) *Hallett (*bap.* 1620, *d.* 1689), nonconformist minister, and his wife, Elizabeth. He was perhaps educated for the ministry by his father, who was a good Greek and Hebrew scholar, and was ordained secretly in 1683 but in July 1685 he resumed his studies and matriculated at Leiden University. He became his father's assistant at James's Meeting, Exeter, in 1687, the year the meeting-house was built. After his father's death two years later he continued as assistant to George Trosse (1631–1713), who succeeded his father. On Trosse's death in 1713 he became pastor, with James Peirce (1674–1726) from Newbury as his colleague. On 16 April 1688 he married Anna Poole (*d.* 1722); they had three sons and three daughters.

From about 1690 Hallett conducted an important academy at Exeter which prepared students for the nonconformist ministry but was also open to laymen. The account provided by John Fox (1693–1763), the biographer of Devon dissent, who was a student from 1708, indicates that the normal ministerial course lasted three years and covered theology, classics, and Hebrew. The names of more than thirty students are known. They included James Foster (1697–1753), the celebrated preacher; John Huxham FRS (*c.*1692–1768), who later studied at Leiden under Boerhaave and became a noted physician in Plymouth; and Hallett's own sons Joseph (III) *Hallett (*bap.* 1691, *d.* 1744), a leading biblical critic, and William (*bap.* July 1693), who also studied at Leiden (matriculating in 1713) and became a physician. The future lord chancellor, Peter King (1669–1734), the son of a Presbyterian grocer and a cousin of John Locke, is said to have been one of the earliest students. The academy appears to have closed in 1719 or 1720 as a result of the loss of support from the Exeter assembly of ministers following the Exeter controversy.

The controversy, which destroyed unity among the Devon ministers, originated in Hallett's academy. According to Fox, Hallett's son Joseph introduced Arian opinions into his father's academy and in 1710, while still a student, held a secret correspondence with William Whiston (1667–1752). A small group of former students met with great caution, but eventually the indiscretion of one, Hubert Stogdon (1692–1728), led to their opinions becoming public in November 1716. Alarmed at the apparent heterodoxy of the younger ministers, the orthodox party demanded a public declaration of belief in the Trinity at the Exeter assembly of dissenting ministers in September 1718. Hallett complied, but in scriptural terms, rejecting the suggested form of words. In March 1719 Hallett and Peirce were barred from the Presbyterian meeting-houses in Exeter by the trustees on refusing to make an orthodox declaration on the Trinity. They held meetings in a private house until the following year when their supporters built the Mint Meeting, appointing them joint minister. In May 1719 the Exeter assembly called for a subscription from its members. Hallett led the list of eighteen ministers who declined and seceded.

Hallett published a funeral sermon for George Trosse, to which he added an edition of Trosse's celebrated *Life* (1713) from the original manuscript. His most substantial work was *Christ's Ascension into Heaven* (1693). He also wrote an anti-Quaker tract, *Twenty Seven Queries*, which only survives in his opponents' reply, John Gannacliff and Joseph Nott's *Gospel Truth Scripturally Asserted* (1692). From internal evidence he appears to have been the author of the anonymous *Belief of the Subordination of the Son of God* (1719, commonly attributed to his son) in answer to his orthodox opponents in the Exeter controversy. Hallett died in November 1722. His son Joseph succeeded him as Peirce's colleague at the Mint Meeting.

DAVID L. WYKES

**Sources** 'Memoirs of himself, by Mr John Fox … with biographical sketches of some of his contemporaries; and some unpublished letters [pt 1]', *Monthly Repository*, 16 (1821), 129–35, esp. 130–31 • minute book A, Exeter assembly, 1655–9, Devon RO, 3542D M 1/1 [includes list of students educated by Joseph Hallett (1656–1722), published in 'Memorial by Mr Manning of dissenting academies in the west of England', *Monthly Repository*, 13 (1818), 89] • A. Brockett, ed., *The Exeter assembly: the minutes of the assemblies of the United Brethren of Devon and Cornwall, 1691–1717*, Devon and Cornwall RS, new ser., 6 (1963) • A. Gordon, ed., *Freedom after ejection: a review (1690–1692) of presbyterian and congregational nonconformity in England and Wales* (1917), 30, 277 • *Calamy rev.*, 243 • W. P. Courtney, 'Devon and Cornish students at Leyden', *Western Antiquary*, 5 (1884–5), 253 • J. Murch, *A history of the Presbyterian and General Baptist churches in the west of England* (1835), 386ff. • documents and memoranda relating to early nonconformist academies collected by the late Joshua Wilson, esq., of Tunbridge Wells, vol. 4, DWL, New College collection, L54/4/67–68; list of students published in 'Early nonconformist academies: Exeter', *Transactions of the Congregational Historical Society*, 5 (1911–12), 155–7 • 'An account of the dissenting academies from the Restoration of Charles the Second', DWL, MS 24.59, fols. 81*r*–82*r* • 'Collectanea Hunteriana: vol. VIII, being memoirs to serve for a history of protestant dissent', BL, Add. MS 24442, fol. 91*v* • H. McLachlan, *English education under the*

*Test Acts: being the history of the nonconformist academies, 1662–1820* (1931), 109–14 • R. Thomas, 'The non-subscription controversy amongst dissenters in 1719: the Salters' Hall debate', *Journal of Ecclesiastical History*, 4 (1953), 162–86 • A. Brockett, *Nonconformity in Exeter, 1650–1875* (1962), 48, 67, 79ff., 235 • F. J. Powicke, 'Arianism and the Exeter assembly', *Transactions of the Congregational Historical Society*, 7 (1916–18), 41 • J. Evans, 'List of dissenting congregations and ministers in England and Wales, 1715–1729', DWL, MS 38.4, 27 • J. L. Gibbs, ed., *The registers of Clyst St. George, co. Devon, 1565–1812*, Parish Register Society, 25 (1899) • *DNB*

**Hallett** [Hallet], **Joseph (III)** (*bap.* **1691**, *d.* **1744**), Presbyterian minister and biblical scholar, was baptized on 2 September 1691 at Exeter, the eldest son of Joseph (II) *Hallett (1656–1722), Presbyterian minister and tutor, and his wife, Anna Poole (*d.* 1722). He was educated at his father's academy in Exeter, where, according to his fellow student John Fox (1693–1763), he introduced Arian opinions and held a secret correspondence with William Whiston (1667–1752), the controversial theologian and scholar, in 1710 while still a student. Whiston recalled that after his *Directions for the Study of Divinity* was published in 1709, he received a letter from Hallett who asked him not to reply direct, for 'if it were known that he kept correspondence with me, he should be ruined' (Whiston, *Memoirs*, 127). Whiston clearly thought he was corresponding with the father. Fox was lent a number of books by Hallett on the Trinity after the class had been lectured on the subject, and as a result could never afterwards accept the orthodox position. A small group of students met with great caution, but eventually the indiscretion of one, Hubert Stogdon, led to the Exeter controversy, resulting in the ejection from the Presbyterian James's Meeting of Hallett's father and his colleague James Peirce on a charge of Arianism.

Hallett is generally considered to have been an assistant tutor in his father's academy, but according to James Manning, a later minister, Hallett gave his father 'some assistance in the last two or three years of its existence, but was not considered as a tutor' (Manning, 89). The academy appears to have closed following the Exeter controversy, in 1719 or 1720, as a result of the loss of support from the Exeter assembly of ministers. Hallett was admitted as a candidate for the ministry by the Exeter assembly of ministers on 6 May, qualified under the Toleration Act on 14 July 1713, and was ordained on 19 October 1715, when his thesis was entitled 'An s. scriptura sit divinitus inspirata'. As a student he was described as a very 'serious, and thinking young man', who 'read most of any in the house. He had a good judgment and memory, and was very well versed in divinity, morality and such kind of things … He turned out afterwards a popular preacher, learned and laborious'. Fox believed he had a very exalted view of the ministry and the apostolic succession, and a great propensity to rule and management ('Memoirs of himself', 131, cf. 134).

The son and grandson of nonconformist ministers, the third Joseph Hallett was the most considerable of the three. His *Free and Impartial Study of the Holy Scriptures* (3 vols., 1729–36), a series of critical notes on the Old and New testaments, demonstrated his biblical scholarship. He sought to identify discrepancies in the Hebrew text by comparison with the Greek, Latin, and other translations: 'there is scarcely a conjectural emendation of the Hebrew text proposed by him which was not afterwards found by Dr [Benjamin] Kennicott in one manuscript or other to have been an ancient reading' (Murch, 402n.). The work provoked a fierce dispute with the orthodox party in Exeter. John Enty complained that it 'plainly saps the foundation of a great part of natural religion' (Enty, *Preservative*, v). Hallett attempted to steer a middle course between Arianism and orthodoxy. He also published a supplement (1733–7) to the second edition of Peirce's *Paraphrase … to the Hebrews* (1725–7). A number of other controversial works, including *The Unity of God* (1720) and *A Reply to Dr Waterland* (1720), were, according to Enty, generally said and believed to be by Hallett (Enty, *Defense*, 4). Many of the works attributed to Hallett were published anonymously, and at least one, the *Belief of the Subordination of the Son of God* (1719), appears from internal evidence to be by his father. On his father's death in 1722 he became Peirce's colleague at the Mint Meeting, Exeter, built by the secessionists in 1719, where he remained until his death on 2 April 1744. His wife, Frances Hallett, survived him.

DAVID L. WYKES

**Sources** 'Memoirs of himself, by Mr John Fox … with biographical sketches of some of his contemporaries; and some unpublished letters', *Monthly Repository*, 16 (1821), 129–35, 193–200, 257–62, 270–76, 325–31, 441–6, 505–7, 569–74, 633–5, 697–8, 721–7 • 'The Fox memoirs: worthies of Devon', *Report and Transactions of the Devonshire Association*, 28 (July 1896), 110–73, at 131, 135–6, 144–8, 159–62 [printed from a copy of Fox's original manuscript destroyed in Plymouth Library through enemy action] • A. Brockett, *Nonconformity in Exeter, 1650–1875* (1962) • A. Brockett, ed., *The Exeter assembly: the minutes of the assemblies of the United Brethren of Devon and Cornwall, 1691–1717*, Devon and Cornwall RS, new ser., 6 (1963) • J. Murch, *A history of the Presbyterian and General Baptist churches in the west of England* (1835), 388–9, 401–2 • J. Manning, 'Memorial by Mr Manning of dissenting academies in the west of England', *Monthly Repository*, 1st ser., 13 (1818), 89 • W. Whiston, *Sermons and essays upon several subjects* (1709) • W. Whiston, *Memoirs of the life and writings of William Whiston*, 2nd edn (1753) • J. Enty, *A preservative against several abuses and corruptions of reveal'd religion: containing remarks on a late book of Mr Joseph Hallet, jun' intitled, 'A collection of notes', &c.* (1730) • J. Enty, *A defense of a late pamphlet, entitled, 'A preservative &c.', In answer to an abusive letter of Mr Joseph Hallet, jun.* (1730) • preaching licence from Exeter Assembly, 1713, Devon RO, 3542D • certificate of registration under Toleration Act, 14 July 1713, Devon RO, 3542D • H. McLachlan, *English education under the Test Acts: being the history of the nonconformist academies, 1662–1820* (1931), 112–14 • H. McLachlan, *The Unitarian movement in the religious life of England: its contribution to thought and learning, 1700–1900* (1934), 26–7 • register of baptisms and burials, Exeter, St George's Meeting, PRO, RG 4/965, 2 Sept 1691 • DWL, MS 24.21 • J. Peirce, funeral sermon, *Practical Preacher*, 3 (1722), 217–43 [Sermon XI] [Anna Hallett]

**Archives** DWL, essays and papers

**Hallett, Sir Maurice Garnier** (1883–1969), colonial governor, was born on 28 October 1883 at Priors Hardwick, Warwickshire, the younger of the two sons (there was also one daughter) of the Revd John Thomas Hallett (1830–1915), vicar of Priors Hardwick, and Caroline Maria (1841–1915), daughter of the Revd Canon Charles Pilkington. Maurice Hallett joined Winchester College in 1896 on a school exhibition, and matriculated as an exhibitioner at

New College, Oxford, in 1902. He obtained second-class honours in classical moderations (1904) and *literae humaniores* (1906). His BA was conferred in May 1907.

Hallett arrived in India on 25 November 1907 and started his first Indian Civil Service posting in Bengal as assistant magistrate and collector. Like many of his generation, he was promoted quickly. By 1912 he was posted to Bihar and Orissa, a province with which he was associated for most of his career in British India. Between 1913 and 1915 he served as under-secretary to government in the political, appointment, and education departments, at the end of which he became a joint magistrate and collector. On 21 November 1914 he married Gladys Constance Mabel, the daughter of Harley Cyril Veasey.

Within five years Hallett became a magistrate and collector. Such responsibility carried with it new challenges in 1920, the year in which Gandhi launched his non-co-operation movement against the British imperial governor, and a new constitution inaugurated a scheme of dyarchy in the provinces which gave considerable power over local affairs to elected members of the provincial legislature and also altered the relationship between Indian politicians and colonial bureaucracy. As early as 1917, in connection with Gandhi's movement on behalf of cultivators in the Champaran district of Bihar, the 'level-headed' Hallett had been named as a possible candidate for a posting in this politically sensitive region. That official opinion was to earn Hallett the description 'Indianized civilian'. In 1922 he was made secretary to government in the local self-government department, a post that tested his adaptability in the new provincial context in which Indian ministers held portfolios. In these years two sons were born: Stephen (1918–1944), who died in action during the Second World War, and Robin (*b.* 1926), who by the 1950s had become a leading historian of the African continent.

Between April 1927 and June 1930, the period in which an all-white parliamentary commission of inquiry into the working of the constitution provoked Congress's declaration of complete independence and Gandhi's civil disobedience movement, Hallett was officiating chief secretary to the government of Bihar, with a short spell as officiating commissioner of Bhagalpur in 1929. In 1932 he moved to Delhi, having been made secretary, government of India, home department, and by 1936 had become a member of the council of state. Despite these central government postings, Hallett maintained his connection with Bihari affairs: in January 1934 he toured the areas worst affected by the terrible Bihar earthquake.

It was as governor of Bihar (1937–9) and the United Provinces (UP) (1939–45) that Maurice Hallett was able to demonstrate 'resilience of mind', a quality with which one character sketch compared him to earlier governors—Harcourt Butler and Malcolm Hailey (J. N. Sarin, 'Sir Maurice Hallett: a character sketch', April 1943, Hallett collection, MS Eur. E 251, box 63). Like Butler, Hallett was committed to the building of conservative alliances, while attempting to widen social contacts with Indian politicians. Under the 1935 constitution the 1937 elections brought Congress ministries into power in Bihar and UP. British administrators had to build new partnerships with Indian ministers within a system that still sanctioned repression. Friendship and political conflict coexisted. The Halletts instituted the opening of Government House gardens to three Indian clubs for garden parties, although one commentator warned Lady Hallett that 'she is wasting her valuable Lama Tea on idlers' and anti-Congress flatterers (*The Leader* (Allahabad), 3 May 1937). In January 1940 both K. M. Katju and G. B. Pant, former ministers of UP, claimed they had looked forward to working with the new UP governor, had Congress ministers not resigned in protest against the involvement of India in the war without consultation. On 23 January 1940 Hallett also visited for tea Anand Bhavan, the home of the Congress-left leader Jawaharlal Nehru.

By March 1940 animosity had deepened between governor and Congress. Hallett insisted that provincial governments be granted additional powers against persons acting in a manner prejudicial to the war effort, particularly members of Congress. The remark made in a speech by Hallett, in September 1940, that 'those who are not for us are against us' was still a catchphrase of the nationalist papers in May 1942 (*National Herald*), and certain press organs were to be intermittently closed by the UP government as the war progressed. During the Quit India movement of 1942 Hallett was a strong advocate for action against Congress, describing Gandhi himself as 'cunning as a cartload of monkeys' (Hallett collection, MS Eur. E 251, box 38). Between 1942 and 1945 'liberal' and nationalist opinion described Hallett's UP as 'the most autocratic' government and the finest example of a 'police raj' (*The Leader*, 8 June 1945).

But these were war years. In 1942 Japan lurked on the doorstep of Bengal, and the raj faced the most serious internal revolt of recent Indian history. By contrast, the 'Bihari' Hallett of 1937 had spearheaded official attempts to persuade Congress to form ministries, helping to initiate and sustain Congress power within the administrative framework of British India. This initial entrenchment of power contributed to Congress's subsequent electoral success and its championing of a strong central government between 1945 and 1947. The price of a strong-centred India was the eventual acceptance by Congress of partition and the creation of Pakistan. Yet it also helped to maintain Congress power right up to the late 1980s.

If Indian responses to Hallett were mixed, his contribution to empire and national defence was appreciated in London. In 1930 he was made a CIE, and by 1934 CSI. At the beginning of his governorship of Bihar he was made a KCSI and by 1943, as well as holding a knighthood of St John, was made a GCIE. Sir Maurice Hallett retired to St Giles' Hill, Winchester, and died in Beneweeke Nursing Home on 30 May 1969. WILLIAM GOULD

**Sources** BL OIOC, Hallett MSS, MS Eur. E. 251, boxes 38, 57–8, 63 · BL OIOC, Linlithgow MSS, MS Eur. F 125, box 103 · BL OIOC, Haig MSS, L/PJ/5/264 [microfilm] · M. S. Leigh, ed., *Winchester College 1884–1934: a register* (1940), 196 · *The India Office and Burma list*, 55th edn (1945), 212 · U. Cam., Centre of South Asian Studies, Allanson

MSS, box II · B. B. Misra and A. P. Jha, eds., *Select documents on Mahatma Gandhi's movement in Champaran* (Patna, 1963), 457 · *New Thought* [Allahabad] (1 March 1940) · *The Leader* [Allahabad] (3 May 1937) · *The Leader* [Allahabad] (8 June 1945) · *National Herald* (24 May 1945) · memorial inscriptions, Bishops Tachbrook, Warwickshire, Warks. CRO · b. cert. · d. cert.

**Archives** BL OIOC, corresp. and papers, MS Eur. E 251 | BL OIOC, Haig MSS, L/PJ/5/264 · BL OIOC, corresp. with Sir H. G. Haig, MS Eur. F 115 · BL OIOC, corresp. with Lord Linlithgow, MS Eur. F 125

**Likenesses** photographs, 1937–45, BL OIOC · photograph (with maharaja of Darbhanga), BL OIOC

**Wealth at death** £38,033: probate, 1969, *CGPLA Eng. & Wales*

**Halley, Edmond** (1656–1742), astronomer, was born probably on 29 October 1656 at Haggerston in the parish of St Leonard, Shoreditch, a country suburb of London, the eldest of the three children of Edmond Halley (*d.* 1684), a freeman of London, and his first wife, Anne (1628?–1672). The parish records of St Leonard's for that period are missing and the date of Halley's birth cannot be confirmed. His father was a rich soap boiler, a member of the Salters' Company, highly regarded in the City, and a yeoman warder of the Tower of London—to avoid parish duties in the trained bands. Halley's grandfather Humphrey (*d.* 1672) was prominent in the City and had been an alderman. The Halley family may have come from Derbyshire; there were also relatives and other connections in Peterborough and Alconbury near Huntingdon. Almost nothing is known of Halley's mother; even her maiden name, probably Robinson, is unsure. After she had died in 1672, Halley's father married before 1684 as his second wife a woman known only as Joanne. Halley's paternal grandparents and his parents were buried in St Margaret's, Barking, in Essex.

**Early years, 1666–1677** When Halley was a young man, after the great fire of 1666, his father lived in Winchester Street, between London Wall and Broad Street, and owned substantial property there. Among their neighbours in that wealthy district were some who would influence Halley's career. Robert Hooke lived nearby in Gresham College in Broad Street, where the Royal Society had its rooms; two cousins of Samuel Pepys lived in Winchester Street, as did his friend the immensely wealthy merchant James Houblon. Sir Gilbert Roberts, the uncle of Halley's schoolfriend Robert Nelson, was nearby, and so were the Leithullier family, who had property in Barking and owned the East Indiaman on which Halley later took passage to St Helena.

Halley went to St Paul's School, but can have attended for only a very few years, for the school was burnt in the great fire when Halley was not quite ten and reopened only two years before he went up to Queen's College, Oxford, in 1673. The headmaster in his final year was Thomas Gale, later dean of York. Halley is said to have been captain of the school in that year, at the age of fifteen. He began astronomical and magnetic observations at school, and continued them at Oxford in association with a fellow undergraduate, Charles Boucher. When Boucher left England for Jamaica, Halley opened a correspondence with John Flamsteed, whom Charles II was shortly to appoint his 'astronomical observator'. Halley

Edmond Halley (1656–1742), attrib. Isaac Whood, *c*.1720

was already known to Christopher Wren, Jonas Moore, and Thomas Street, as well as to Hooke, and was of the party that viewed the site at Greenwich where the royal observatory was to be built. Halley was observing with Flamsteed before the observatory was completed and continued to do so from time to time until about 1684. Through Flamsteed's correspondence he became known to distinguished astronomers abroad, particularly Johann Hevelius in Danzig and Jean Dominique (Giandomenico) Cassini in Paris. He wrote his first three scientific papers while an undergraduate.

**Travel overseas** Halley left Oxford without taking a degree, as about half the undergraduates did in those days. He had a particular reason—he was going to St Helena to determine the positions of stars in the southern hemisphere, and wished to be there in time for the forthcoming transit of Mercury across the sun in October 1677, so that he might derive the distance of the sun in the way James Gregory had earlier suggested. Charles II supported him, as did Sir Joseph Williamson, a secretary of state and former provost of Queen's. The East India Company offered to assist him; Sir Jonas Moore and Cassini among others gave him advice. He did not fully achieve his aims because the skies were very cloudy, and Flamsteed criticized his procedures. He published his results soon after his return in 1678 as his *Catalogus stellarum australium* (1679), shortly afterwards translated into French. It gave him, at the age of twenty-two, a European reputation and led to his election to the Royal Society and to the award of the MA degree of Oxford by command of the king. Halley was the first to use the new instruments then becoming available, with telescopic sights, eyepiece micrometers, and better divided scales. With these, and reliable pendulum clocks, he was able to establish positions of stars in either hemisphere. Flamsteed and Cassini were preparing to use similar instruments in the north but had not done so when Halley returned from St Helena. Halley's catalogue remained the only one for southern stars for many years, and, although Flamsteed justly criticized him for haste and lax procedures, Flamsteed himself had the catalogue revised and reprinted in his posthumous *Historia coelestis Britannica* of 1725. Halley observed the transit of Mercury successfully, but observers in the north had poor conditions, and so he could make no firm estimate of the distance of the sun. Much later he showed how to find the distance of the sun from transits of Venus, which took James Cook to Tahiti and the exploration of the Pacific after Halley's death.

In 1679 Halley went to Danzig seeking to resolve an acrimonious dispute between Hevelius and Robert Hooke over the use of telescopic sights in the measurement of positions of celestial objects. Hevelius distrusted them; Hooke advocated them strongly. Halley observed with Hevelius and his colleagues, including Hevelius's wife, Elizabeth, from 16 May to 8 July 1679, using both Hevelius's instruments and Halley's small quadrant with telescopic sights. Halley deplored Hevelius's adherence to obsolete methods but recognized the consistency of his observations. There were obviously large systematic differences between the instruments. The visit was agreeable and back in England Halley bought a silk gown and petticoat for Elizabeth; he corresponded with Hevelius for a few years afterwards.

Halley left England at the end of 1680 in company with his schoolfriend Robert Nelson to spend a year in France and Italy. On their way to Paris in December they saw the brilliant comet that had first appeared in November. Halley met Cassini, then director of the Paris observatory, and observed the comet with him. They spent five months in Paris and their journey to Rome took them from August to October. They saw the new Canal du Midi then nearly finished, they visited Montpellier, and Halley observed a lunar eclipse with Père Gallet in Avignon, where his visit is commemorated by the rue Halley. In Rome he would have met astronomers who had observed the comet in November 1680; they were of the circle of Queen Kristina of Sweden, and he may have met the queen herself, for she had observed an earlier comet with Cassini and had offered a prize for a calculation of the orbit of the comet of 1680. Halley discussed many astronomical subjects in the course of his tour; it is likely that comets were a principal topic, for their orbits were of great contemporary interest. Shortly after his return to England early in 1682, Halley met Newton, probably for the first time, and gave him an account of observations of the comet. Newton later discussed its orbit in considerable detail in book 3 of the *Principia*.

**London scientific life** Halley married Mary Tooke (1658–1736) in April 1682. She came of a notable family of lawyers and had inherited property. Three of their children survived beyond childhood: Edmond (1698–1740), who was a naval surgeon, Margaret (1685–1743), who remained unmarried, and Katherine (1688–1765), who married twice. They first lived at Islington, where Halley set up the instruments he had taken to St Helena and observed the moon assiduously for almost two years. In later years they lived in the City of London, in Golden Lion Court, off Aldersgate Street, and later still in Bridgewater Street, Barbican.

In April 1684 Halley's father was found dead on the shore at Stroud in Kent, probably murdered, possibly on account of having been in the Tower as a yeoman warder the day the earl of Essex was found dead there in 1683, and knowing too much of the circumstances—so at least contemporary pamphlets asserted. He had made no will, and Halley became involved in chancery actions with his stepmother. These apparently never came to trial; the parties divided the elder Halley's personal estate of some £4000 about equally. Halley then had an income in excess of £150 per annum from his share. He was active in the Royal Society in those years, in the meetings and in publications. He was a councillor for one period, then was appointed the salaried clerk; as such he brought out the *Philosophical Transactions* as publisher. About 1686 his friendship with Flamsteed turned sour, for reasons that are not wholly clear, and Flamsteed was ever after hostile to him.

**Halley and Newton** Some three months before his father's death, in January 1684, Halley, Robert Hooke, and Christopher Wren, in conversation after a meeting of the Royal Society, asked themselves what the orbits of the planets would be under an inverse square law of attraction to the sun. They could not answer the question, and in August Halley called on Newton in Cambridge and put the problem to him. The delay from January to August is most probably a result of Halley's being involved in the legal matters consequent on his father's death, and he may have been in the neighbourhood of Cambridge in the late summer to deal with business connected with the estate. Halley's question led Newton to take up anew his earlier studies of orbits under an inverse square law attraction, and to go on to write the *Philosophiae naturalis principia mathematica* (1687). Halley saw it through the press, and, although it had the imprimatur of the Royal Society, he paid for the printing and received the proceeds of sales. He composed an effusive Latin ode as a preface, distributed presentation copies, and wrote a review. The *Principia* is one of the most influential works of mathematical science ever written, and has set the agenda for theoretical physics from that day onwards. Halley contributed nothing to its composition. Although he was very impressed by it, he was clearly surprised by each new development as Newton unfolded it, and probably did not fully understand it at the time. None the less, his part in bringing it before the world is arguably his greatest contribution to natural philosophy, as he himself realized when he claimed to be 'the Ulysses that produced that Achilles'. He later made far-reaching applications of some of its results.

In the decade from 1679 to 1689 Halley published many papers on a range of topics, among them his first discussion of the cause of the magnetic declination and how it changed, based on an extensive collection of worldwide data. He drew up a synoptic chart of the trade winds, the first time any such meteorological chart had been produced.

**Marine charts and public service, 1689–1703** The *Principia* was published about a year and a half before William of Orange invaded England at the end of 1688, and for part of that time Halley was working at sea around the coast of the Thames estuary, possibly surveying the approaches. How Halley came by his experience of seamanship is unknown, but he may have learned something on the long voyages on East Indiamen to and from St Helena. He was certainly at sea in the spring of 1689, for that summer he presented to the Royal Society a chart of the Thames approaches, and remarks he had made at earlier meetings of the society indicate that he was familiar with the coast, even while Samuel Pepys was preparing the navy to resist William's invasion. Almost no record remains of those activities. They may have been confidential and may raise questions about his relations with James II and William III. There can be little doubt that he was close to the Stuart courts. Charles II had given support to his expedition to St Helena. Sir Jonas Moore, to whom Halley owed much, had long before been tutor to James II as duke of York. When the *Principia* was published Halley presented a copy to James, who, as a distinguished admiral, might have been interested in the explanation of the tides. Halley also knew Pepys well. He later enjoyed the confidence of William and Anne. It seems probable that he was willing to serve the navy under whoever held the throne and that, as James had valued his services, so would William and Anne.

When the *Guynie*, a frigate of the Royal African Company, was lost in April 1691 off Pagham, near Chichester, with a cargo of gold and ivory, the court of the company asked Halley to attempt salvage. He improved the design of the diving bell, and devised a diving suit with its air supplied by a tube from a bell so that a man could work outside a bell. He was disappointed of the Savilian chair of astronomy at Oxford, to which David Gregory was elected in 1691, but Newton, now warden of the Royal Mint, arranged for him to be deputy controller of the country mint at Chester, one of a number set up to assist with the great silver recoinage. He served there from the summer of 1696 to the spring of 1698, a time that was made difficult and unpleasant for him by quarrels between other officers.

In the last decade of the century Halley wrote many papers on a wide range of topics for the *Philosophical Transactions* of the Royal Society: on mathematics, on the rainbow, on optics, on thermometers and their graduation, and on barometers. He studied the bills of mortality of the city of Breslau and constructed tables of life expectancy, forerunners of modern actuarial methods. His study of the observations of the medieval Islamic astronomer al-Batani led him to propose that the moon was speeding up in her orbit around the earth, as has since been amply confirmed. He discussed the account of the landing of Julius Caesar in Britain in relation to the tides in the channel and fixed the site accordingly.

His most influential work at this time was to calculate the orbits of twenty-four comets, and to argue that the comet of 1682 had an elliptical orbit with a period of seventy-five or seventy-six years. Like Newton, he realized that the attractions of Jupiter and Saturn made it difficult to predict the time of the return. After his death French astronomers recovered the comet in 1759, as predicted by the theoretical work of A. C. Clairaut and the numerical calculations of Lalande and Mme Lepaute. Their success in the recovery of what has become known as Halley's comet was widely seen as a forceful confirmation of Newtonian mechanics.

**Charting terrestrial magnetism** On 20 October 1698 Halley set sail in command of the pink *Paramore* to observe the magnetic declination over the Atlantic Ocean. The *Paramore* was specially built for him as a ship of the Royal Navy, and Halley ranked as a captain RN. His first cruise, to June 1699, was bedevilled by difficulties with his officers, and his lieutenant Edward Harrison was court-martialled on their return. Halley retained the confidence of the Admiralty, and his second cruise from September 1699 to September 1700 was successful. He went south as far as 52° into the ice field north of the site of the modern Halley Bay Geophysical Observatory and was in considerable danger, as he was later from a storm off the coast of Africa. He produced his results as a chart of the magnetic variation over the Atlantic shown by isogonic lines, known at the time as 'Halleyan' lines. It was the first time anyone had published such a representation and was a great advance in cartography. His results remain important for the study of the long-term behaviour of the earth's magnetism. The next year, 1701, Halley took the *Paramore* to sea from June to September to survey tides in the English Channel. His results and the chart on which he showed them were again a great advance on anything done before, and retained their value for almost a century and a half.

The War of Spanish Succession broke out shortly after the channel cruise, and at the end of 1702 Halley was sent by Queen Anne and her ministers to survey harbours on the Adriatic that might be used by an English fleet should one be sent there to support the Austrian empire in the Blenheim campaign. He surveyed harbours from Trieste to Seng and selected Bakar, just south of Rijeka, as a very suitable base. He set out the positions of batteries to defend it, and on a second visit in the autumn of 1703 saw them built. As a naval captain, the equivalent of a colonel and seen as the queen's personal representative, he gained golden opinions and the favour of the emperor. Every account, however otherwise misleading, mentions the valuable diamond ring that the emperor presented to Halley from his own finger. On the way between London and Vienna, Halley met Leibniz and the future George I at Hanover.

**Savilian professor at Oxford** John Wallis, the Savilian professor of geometry at Oxford, died as Halley was on his way back from his second Adriatic visit at the end of 1703.

The secretary of state, the earl of Nottingham, to whom Halley sent his reports on his Adriatic missions, was an elector to the Savilian chairs, and Halley was elected. The university press had a programme to publish editions of the Greek geometers, and some, including Euclid, had already been issued. The *Conics* of the great Greek geometer Apollonius of Perga was still to be done. David Gregory had made a start, but was held up for certain manuscripts. Halley joined Gregory, but Gregory died in 1708, relatively young, and the edition is essentially Halley's. The original text of *Conics* was in eight books. A Greek text (edited from the original of Apollonius) survives for only the first four books, and an Arabic version of books 5 to 7 is preserved in manuscript in the Bodleian Library and elsewhere. The eighth book is entirely lost but there are references to it in Greek and Islamic texts. Halley edited the Greek and Arabic texts, revised the translations into Latin, and printed his edition of the Greek opposite his Latin translation for the first four books, and his Latin alone for books 5 to 7. He also printed a Latin version of the eighth book that he had recovered from allusions by Greek and Islamic commentators. Although other manuscripts, Greek and Arabic, have since turned up, Halley's edition has stood the test of time and is still highly regarded, although his reconstruction of the final book probably does not well represent what Apollonius wrote. He also published an edition of minor works of Apollonius and of a work of Menelaos.

Gregory left another work unfinished at his death. Newton had long pressed for Flamsteed's results from Greenwich to be published, and at last in 1704 he obtained funds from Prince George of Denmark to do so. He arranged for referees, his nominees, to be appointed to oversee the work, essentially excluding Flamsteed, and they asked Gregory to prepare the material for the press. When he died he had printed the observations to 1689 but not the later ones, nor the catalogue of star positions. Gregory died at about the same time as Prince George, and things rested, but then Queen Anne appointed the president (Newton) and other fellows of the Royal Society, Halley among them, as visitors to the observatory, to Flamsteed's intense annoyance. The visitors had funds to continue the publication and Halley was asked to take over. He made considerable changes to the catalogue as Flamsteed had drawn it up, altering the descriptions of stars and including many that Flamsteed did not have in his first catalogue. Halley's version was published in 1712 and Flamsteed's relations with him and Newton, already bad, became far worse. Some thirteen years later, after the accession of George I, Flamsteed was able to recover his material. When he died before it could be published, his former assistants, Crosthwait and Sharp, saw that it was done as he had wished. Flamsteed had included the catalogues of his predecessors to show where he stood in the history of astronomy, and Halley's southern catalogue of fifty years before was one of them, but revised by Abraham Sharp to take account of the positions of stars in Flamsteed's catalogue, all without acknowledging Halley as the original author.

Halley's third major undertaking at Oxford consisted of his tables of the positions of the sun, the planets, and the moon, covering many centuries second by second. The tables of the moon represent Newton's lunar theory as he presented it in the second edition of the *Principia*. They were set in print before 1720 but not published, for the preparatory explanation had not been printed when Halley was appointed astronomer royal, and he hoped to get more observations of the moon with which to compare the tables.

In 1715 there was to be a total eclipse of the sun, the first to be seen in London for hundreds of years. Halley drew up a map of the zone of totality and organized systematic observations throughout the country, the first time any such thing had been done. He himself observed the corona in London. The records of the edge of totality were used in 1988 to show that there had been no detectable change in the diameter of the sun from 1715 to 1988. The eclipse was a notable social occasion. Newton, as president of the Royal Society, entertained distinguished foreign visitors, with his elegant niece Catherine Barton, the 'pretty witty Kitty', as hostess; she greatly impressed the guests from overseas.

**Astronomer royal** Halley was appointed second astronomer royal in 1721, at the age of sixty-nine. He found that Flamsteed's widow had removed all her late husband's apparatus from the observatory, but none the less he began, in remarkably confident hope, to observe the moon over the eighteen years of the saronic cycle, the period after which the circumstances of eclipses repeat. He had identified the importance and utility of the cycle more than fifty years earlier, before the *Principia* was thought of. He did complete a cycle but died before he could publish his results. His colleague John Bevis brought them out afterwards and included with them Halley's final very thorough studies on comets. Halley's observations and some of his calculations survive in his papers (now in the university library in Cambridge) and they include a few of his comparisons between his observations and those of Flamsteed thirty-six years (two saronic intervals) earlier. Over a hundred more are to be found for about five years from 1726, and they show that Halley and Flamsteed were observing with uncertainties of about 1 minute of arc, Flamsteed being rather the more consistent. The observations at the interval of two saronic periods are strongly correlated, confirming Halley's expectations. The standard deviation of the difference from Halley's tables is about 2 minutes of arc. Halley claimed as much in a paper of 1731, but it is not clear how he could do so when the theory of errors and the analysis of variance had not been thought of.

**Character and beliefs** The *Biographia Britannica* describes Halley as slightly above middle height, slender, of fair complexion, and sprightly and vivacious. His letters and the comments of others show that he was genial, affable, and sociable, but could at the same time make very sharp comments on the failings of others who should have known better. He seems to have been modest and did not seek honours. He got on well with most people, Flamsteed notably apart. At sea, and constructing fortifications on the Adriatic, he was forceful and effective in managing men. He met and impressed persons of high rank, including Tsar Peter the Great, the emperor of Austria, George I, and several English ambassadors.

In his own lifetime Halley was spoken of as an atheist or irreligious. The evidence for that is thin indeed. Atheism was a term of abuse by many people, not an accurate assessment of someone's beliefs. Clearly he took the oaths required by the Test Acts when he became Savilian professor and to that extent was a member of the established church. So far as may be gathered from his own very few offhand remarks, he was a latitudinarian, rather like Archbishop John Tillotson (who respected him) or Edward Stillingfleet, bishop of Worcester. At the same time his belief was not uncritical and he seems to have accepted, like St Augustine, that revelation and natural philosophy should not be contradictory. He was a lifelong friend of 'the Pious' Robert Nelson, who became a nonjuror after 1689, and he was also on good terms with Pepys and other well-known nonjurors.

Halley is sometimes spoken of as a tory in politics, but again it is difficult to characterize him so sharply. He was certainly close to Charles II and James II, but he was also close to some members of the Kit-Cat Club, the dining club of supporters of the revolution settlement of 1689. He worked with the earl of Nottingham and George Stepney when on the Adriatic. He was a friend of Sir Samuel Garth, one of a number of influential medical men of his acquaintance, including Sir Hans Sloane and Richard Mead (physician to Newton and Halley), but perhaps the most interesting was the satirist John Arbuthnott, the inventor of 'John Bull', with whom Halley was closely involved over the publication of Flamsteed's results. Arbuthnott was a friend of Jonathan Swift and of Catherine Barton, to whom Kit-Cat Club toasting verses were written, and he collaborated with Pepusch and Handel.

**Natural philosopher** Halley was not a philosopher. He did not, for instance, discuss the Epicurean philosophy of Democritus as propounded by Gassendi and much debated in Europe at the time. Instead, accepting the atomic theory of matter that it involved, he estimated in a matter-of-fact, empirical manner the maximum size of gold atoms from the amount of gold on silver-gilt wire. Three hundred years later the same principle would be used to estimate the size of molecules in monolayers on water. In that and other instances he explored the numerical implications of hypotheses and followed the precept of Robert Boyle, that science should be able to predict what is as yet unknown from what is now observed.

Halley made two predictions of events that should occur when he was dead, which have had great effects on the knowledge and understanding of the natural world, the return of 'his' comet, which gave the death blow to Cartesian natural philosophy, and the observation of the transit of Venus in 1769, which led to Cook's voyages of discovery.

Halley ranged widely in his enquiries: demography, classical scholarship, many topics in what is now called geophysics, the discovery of proper motions of stars, a lifelong devotion to the problem of the longitude, and the motion of the moon. His most notable contributions to natural philosophy were his grasp of the natural world as extended in time and space and his application of the rational principles of Newton's *Principia* to its study. He collected observations widely for his charts of the trade winds and the magnetic variation, and he applied his classical scholarship to reveal changes in the world in historical times. In interpreting his observations he often showed a physical insight far in advance of his time. Thus in his discussion of the earth's magnetic field he understood that there must be relative motions in the earth to account for the change in the variation and also that local differences of variation must come from shallow sources. Centuries would pass before any more fundamental understanding of the earth's magnetism was achieved. Halley's realization that the moon was speeding up also had to wait for centuries before it was fully elucidated.

**Last years** Halley was never seriously ill apart from a fever he caught on his second cruise in the Atlantic and a paralysis of his right hand that developed in 1738. He was able to observe the moon until the end of 1739, although not so assiduously as in earlier years. He went up regularly from Greenwich to London to meetings of the Royal Society.

Halley died peacefully at Greenwich on 14 January 1742 and was buried on 20 January next to his wife in the church of St Margaret's, Lee, Kent, close to the observatory. His daughters set up a memorial with an inscription that was erected at the observatory. On the occasion of the return of 'his' comet in 1987, a commemorative plaque was placed in the cloisters of Westminster Abbey.

ALAN COOK

**Sources** *Correspondence and papers of Edmond Halley*, ed. E. F. McPike (1932) • *Biographia Britannica, or, The lives of the most eminent persons who have flourished in Great Britain and Ireland*, 4 (1757), 2494–520 • N. J. W. Thrower, *The three voyages of Edmond Halley in the 'Paramore'* (1981) • A. Cook, *Edmond Halley: charting the heavens and the seas* (1997) • *The correspondence of John Flamsteed, the first astronomer royal*, ed. E. G. Forbes and others, 1 (1995) • *The correspondence of Isaac Newton*, ed. H. W. Turnbull and others, 2–6 (1960–76) • *The diary of Robert Hooke … 1672–1680*, ed. H. W. Robinson and W. Adams (1935) • 'The diary of Robert Hooke', *Early science in Oxford*, ed. R. T. Gunther, 10: *The life and work of Robert Hooke, part 4* (1935), 69–265 • *Remarks and collections of Thomas Hearne*, ed. C. E. Doble and others, 11 vols., OHS, 2, 7, 13, 34, 42–3, 48, 50, 65, 67, 72 (1885–1921) • *The correspondence of Henry Oldenburg*, ed. and trans. A. R. Hall and M. B. Hall, 11–13 (1977–86) • E. Halley, *Catalogus stellarum australium* (1679) • J. Hevelius, *Annus climactericus* (1680) • J. Flamsteed, *Historia coelestis Britannica*, 3 vols. (1725) • A. Armitage, *Edmond Halley* (1966) • C. Ronan, *Edmond Halley: genius in eclipse* (1970)

**Archives** BL, journals, Add. MS 30368 • BL, papers relating to Saturn and to tides, Sloane MSS 1030, 1782 • CUL, Greenwich Royal Observatory Archives, Newton papers • CUL, observations and papers • Magd. Cam., navigation papers • NRA, priv. coll., corresp. and lectures • PRO, state papers, foreign, and admiralty papers • RS, corresp. and papers; journal books and council minutes | Archivio di Stato, Venice, Senato, Dispacci Germania • BL, letters to Sir Hans Sloane, Sloane MSS • BL, Stepney MSS • Bodl. Oxf., Rigaud MSS • CUL, corresp. with Sir Isaac Newton • King's AC Cam., letters to Sir Isaac Newton • PRO, letters to J. Burchett, ADM1 • Steiermärkische Staatsarchiv, Graz

**Likenesses** T. Murray, oils, *c.*1687, RS • G. Kneller, oils, after 1700, NMM • T. Murray, oils, 1713, Bodl. Oxf. • T. Murray, oils, 1713, Queen's College, Oxford • attrib. M. Dahl, oils, *c.*1720, RS • attrib. I. Whood, oils, *c.*1720, NPG [*see illus.*] • G. White, mezzotint, *c.*1721 (after G. Kneller), BM, NPG • J. Faber, mezzotint, 1722 (after T. Murray), BM • R. Phillips, oils, 1722, NPG • J. A. Dassier, copper medal, BM • F. Kyte, mezzotint, BM
**Wealth at death** approx. £150 p.a. from Savilian professorship; £100 as astronomer royal; probably £150 from father's personal estate and half pay as post-captain RN

**Halley** [Hally], **Robert** (1796–1876), Congregational minister and writer, was the eldest of four children of Robert Hally and his wife, Ann (*née* Bellows), and was born at Blackheath, Kent, on 13 August 1796. Here Hally senior was a nurseryman and a deacon of Butt Lane Independent Chapel. Educated at Maze Hill School, Greenwich, Robert studied at Homerton College under John Pye Smith between 1816 and 1821. He accepted a call to St Neots Independent Church in May 1822, and was ordained and inducted on 11 June of the same year. This was a poor living and he was forced to take in students which proved to be the beginning of his career as an educator. He married in March 1823 Rebekah (*d.* 1865), daughter of James Jacob, timber merchant, of Deptford: they had three sons and three daughters. Robert and Jacob John followed their father into the ministry; Ebenezer became a surgeon.

In July 1825 Halley was appointed to the classical post at the new Highbury Congregational college where he excelled as a tutor for the next thirteen years. He became a director of the London Missionary Society and secretary of the Nonconformist Ministers' Anti-Slavery Society, supporting moral crusades such as this while eschewing party politics. In 1835 he was one of the promoters of the London City Mission. He was drawn into the Lady Hewley Charity dispute, producing a pamphlet in 1834 criticizing the Unitarian Charles Wellbeloved's *Improved Version of the Scriptures*, which won him an unsolicited Princeton DD. In 1839 he succeeded Dr Robert McAll at Mosley Street Chapel, Manchester. In this city he acquired his reputation as a brilliant platform speaker and an inspiring lecturer, particularly to young men. He could be controversial: his plea for indiscriminate baptism in the Congregational lecture for 1843 drew sharp criticism from many quarters, including his former tutor, Pye Smith; as chairman of the Congregational Union the same year he pleaded eloquently for the autonomy of the local church. As the 'hungry forties' drew to a close (he had intervened personally in a threatened bread riot in 1842 and quietened the mob) he inspired his congregation to relocate to new and elaborate premises in Cavendish Street. By 1856 he was one of the leaders of Manchester Congregationalism and was appointed a member of the subcommittee to investigate the Samuel Davidson affair. Later that year, on the death of John Harris, Halley was appointed classical tutor at New College, London. Here he was a guiding influence on a new generation of Congregational students. He was several times pressed to become editor of the *Eclectic Review*, but always declined. He lost heavily in the bank crisis of 1866 but was rescued by his friends.

In 1869 Halley produced his best-known work, *Lancashire, its Puritanism and Nonconformity*, based on a series of lectures given to the young men of Cavendish Chapel. This two-volume work is generally considered one of the best of the regional histories inspired by the bicentenary celebrations in 1862 of the Ejection. Certainly it is not dry as dust, but vivid and imaginative, perhaps overly so. He also wrote *The Prosperity of Churches Promoted by Social Prayer* (1831), *The Sinfulness of Colonial Slavery* (1833), a two-volume work on the sacraments (1844–51), a memoir of Thomas Goodwin prefixed to *Goodwin's Works* (1861), two bicentenary lectures of 1862, published as *The Design and Effects of the Act of Uniformity and the Book of Sports*, and numerous articles for the *Eclectic Review*.

Halley retired finally in 1872 to Clapton. He preached regularly and for a few months was acting principal of Spring Hill College, Birmingham. His last days were spent at his son Robert's home at Batworth Park, Arundel, Sussex. He preached for the last time on 25 June 1876 and died on 18 August of the same year. He was buried in Abney Park cemetery. Halley combined deep intellectual interests with a warm and sensitive approach to others, an attachment to evangelical Christianity with a real catholicity of spirit; he exercised combativeness without rancour, disagreeing with many but making enemies of none. ALEXANDER GORDON, *rev.* IAN SELLERS

**Sources** *A short biography of Robert Halley together with a selection of his sermons*, ed. R. Halley (1879) • *Congregational Year Book* (1877) • T. T. James, *Cavendish Street Chapel, Manchester* (1948) • A. Peel, *The Congregational two hundred, 1530–1948* (1948) • *CGPLA Eng. & Wales* (1877)
**Archives** DWL, corresp. and papers
**Likenesses** Cook, stipple, pubd 1832 (after J. R. M. Wildman), NPG • portrait, repro. in Halley, *Short biography of Robert Halley* • print (after photograph by Elliott & Fry), DWL
**Wealth at death** £9000: resworn probate, May 1877, *CGPLA Eng. & Wales*

**Halliburton, William Dobinson** (1860–1931), physiologist and biochemist, was born in London on 21 June 1860, the only son of Thomas Halliburton, a Yorkshireman, of Upper Norwood, and his wife, Mary Homan. He was educated privately and at University College School, London, and subsequently at University College, London; he graduated BSc in 1879, before he transferred to study medicine at University College Hospital, qualifying MRCS, LRCP and MB in 1883, and MD with gold medal in 1884.

In 1883 Halliburton became Sharpey scholar and later assistant to E. A. Sharpey-Schafer at University College. He received the science research medal in 1885 and subsequently went to Vienna for a short period. In 1886 Halliburton married Ann, daughter of James Dawes; they had no children.

In 1890 Halliburton succeeded Gerald Yeo as professor of physiology at King's College, London, where he remained until his resignation owing to ill health in 1923. He worked with a large number of brilliant investigators, notably F. W. Mott, W. E. Dixon, F. S. Locke, Thomas Gregor Brodie, Charles James Martin, and Otto Rosenheim. Almost every young biochemist of note of that time studied under him, including his great friends, Frederick Gowland Hopkins and Jack Drummond. He also became associated with David Ferrier, a physician at King's College Hospital. At King's College he played a very important part, not only in the development of his department, which was rebuilt under his direction, but also in the college, where he was dean of the medical faculty for many years.

Halliburton was a founding influence on the discipline of biochemistry in Great Britain, a fact acknowledged by Gowland Hopkins. Under the guidance of Schäfer (as Sharpey-Schafer was then known), Halliburton began his physiological career by familiarizing himself with heat fractionation, a new technique for protein separation. Such techniques brought old physiological issues within the ambit of newer chemical ones. Separation techniques gave a fresh impetus to the investigation of protein composition and heterogeneity.

In 1887 Halliburton published a major paper on muscle proteins that secured his reputation not only in Britain, but on the continent as well. In a series of further papers he attempted to apply the same techniques to other animal tissues. He tried to assess the relationship between the functions of different organs and the various proteins found in the cells of each tissue. With Frederick Mott, Halliburton carried out research into the chemical pathology of the nervous system. He showed that choline was produced in true nerve degeneration but not in functional mental illness such as neurasthenia, depression, and hysteria.

Halliburton's textbook, *Chemical Physiology and Pathology* (1891), was an important work of the time. He also wrote *Essentials of Chemical Physiology* (1893), which reached its eleventh edition in 1922. Halliburton's *Biochemistry of Muscle and Nerve* (1904) contains a list of forty scientific papers of his on which that book is based. However, his best-known book was *Physiology*, which became a standard medical student textbook of its day, Halliburton having taken over W. S. Kirke's *Handbook* (1st edn, 1848), in 1896; he prepared a further nineteen editions before his death. Under Robert John Stewart McDowall, who succeeded him at King's College, the book became *McDowall's Handbook of Physiology*.

In 1916 Halliburton was asked by the Physiological Society to edit *Physiological Abstracts*, which the society had decided to inaugurate; during his editorship of the first seven volumes the journal became firmly established and a periodical of international importance. He also played an important part in the foundation of the Biochemical Society in 1911.

Halliburton was elected FRS in 1891, being a member of the council on two occasions. He received the honorary degree of LLD from the universities of Aberdeen and Toronto. He was elected FRCP in 1892 and was awarded the Baly medal in 1911; he gave the Goulstonian lecture (1893), the Croonian lecture (1901), and the Oliver-Sharpey lecture (1907), to the Royal College of Physicians.

An attack of polio when he was very young left Halliburton's right arm paralysed, and this doubtless played a part in the course of his career, probably ruling out active clinical medicine. He was also financially independent. Halliburton was a good organizer and displayed sound all-round judgement. Although he appeared serious, those who knew him described him as approachable with a good sense of humour.

Halliburton's role in the growth of British biochemistry was obviously both important, and at the same time transitional. From an institutional perspective he recruited a number of talented people to the new science. He was elected as the first honorary member of the Biochemical Society in 1923. Within his own work he moved cautiously from physiology into the newer unexplored area of biochemistry, but returned to physiology for his overall perspective on the new science. He died at Southern Hay West, Exeter, on 21 May 1931. A tablet to his memory was placed in the laboratory which bears his name at King's College, and an eponymous lecture is organized annually by the physiology department there.

R. J. S. McDowall, *rev.* Neil Morgan

**Sources** N. D. Morgan, 'William Dobinson Halliburton, FRS (1860–1931): pioneer of British biochemistry?', *Notes and Records of the Royal Society*, 38 (1983–4), 129–45 · R. J. S. McDowall, *BMJ* (30 May 1931), 957–8 · F. G. Hopkins, *BMJ* (30 May 1931), 1006 · *The Lancet* (6 June 1931), 1263–4 · J. A. H., *Biochemical Journal*, 26 (1932), 269–71 · private information (1949) · personal knowledge (1949) · *CGPLA Eng. & Wales* (1931) · W. J. O'Connor, *British physiologists, 1885–1914* (1991)

**Archives** Wellcome L., notebooks | RS, archives · Wellcome L., L. C. Wooldridge MSS

**Likenesses** J. Russell & Sons, photograph, *c*.1915, NPG · photograph, *c*.1920, Wellcome L.

**Wealth at death** £36,754 3*s*. 6*d*.: probate, 24 July 1931, *CGPLA Eng. & Wales*

**Halliday, Sir Andrew** (1782–1839), physician, was born at Copsewood, in the parish of Dalton, Dumfries, on 17 March 1782, the son of Thomas Halliday and Margaret Porteous, of Denbie. He was at first educated for the presbyterian ministry, but preferred medicine and graduated MD at Edinburgh on 24 June 1806 with a thesis entitled 'De pneumatosi', which he later published.

Halliday then travelled for a time in Russia, and on his return settled in practice at Halesowen, Shropshire. However, soon afterwards he joined the army as a surgeon and served in the Iberian peninsula with the Portuguese army during the Napoleonic wars; in 1811 he was contemplating a history of the war (*Dispatches of … the Duke of Wellington*, 137–8, 150). He afterwards entered the British service, and was present at the assault of Bergen op Zoom and at Waterloo.

Halliday later became domestic physician to the duke of Clarence (afterwards William IV), and travelled on the continent with him. He became a licentiate of the Royal College of Physicians of Edinburgh in November 1817 and of the Royal College of Physicians, London, on 22 December 1819. He was knighted by George IV in 1821 and in August 1827 he was elected a fellow of the Royal College of Physicians of Edinburgh. He was given the post of inspector of hospitals in the West Indies in 1833, but his health broke down and in 1837 he retired to his native town.

Halliday, who was married, died at Huntingdon Lodge, Dumfries, on 7 September 1839. He was survived by his wife. His writings include *Remarks on the Present State of Lunatic Asylums in Ireland* (1808), *A general view of the present state of lunatics and lunatic asylums in Great Britain and Ireland and in some other kingdoms* (1828), and *The West Indies: the Nature and Physical History of the Windward and Leeward Colonies* (1837). He also contributed obituaries to the *Gentleman's Magazine*.

NORMAN MOORE, *rev.* PATRICK WALLIS

**Sources** *GM*, 2nd ser., 13 (1840), 93–4 • Munk, *Roll* • *Nomina eorum, qui gradum medicinae doctoris in academia Jacobi sexti Scotorum regis, quae Edinburgi est, adepti sunt, ab anno 1705 ad annum 1845*, University of Edinburgh (1846) • *The dispatches of … the duke of Wellington … from 1799 to 1818*, ed. J. Gurwood, 13 vols. in 12 (1834–9) • W. McDowall, *History of the burgh of Dumfries* (1867) • parish register (birth), 17 March 1782, Dalton, Dumfries

**Archives** BL, corresp. with Sir Robert Peel, Add. MSS 40263–40368, *passim* • Hants. RO, letters to Charles Broughton relating to health of duchess of Clarence

**Halliday, Andrew** [*formerly* Andrew Halliday Duff] (**1830–1877**), essayist and playwright, was born early in 1830 at The Grange, Marnoch, Banffshire, the son of William Duff (1790/91–1844), minister, of Grange, Banffshire, from 1821 to 1844, and his wife, Mary Steinson. He was educated at Marischal College, Aberdeen and in 1849 went to London, where he was for some time connected with the *Morning Chronicle*, *The Leader*, the *People's Journal*, and other periodicals. He soon became known as a writer and discarded the surname of Duff.

In 1851 Halliday wrote an article, 'Beggars', for Henry Mayhew's *London Labour and the London Poor*. He also wrote for William Thackeray's *Cornhill Magazine* and was a regular contributor to Charles Dickens's *All the Year Round*. From 1861 on he wrote a series of essays for *All the Year Round*, afterwards collected into volumes entitled *Everyday Papers* (2 vols., 1864), *Sunnyside Papers* (1866), and *Town and Country Sketches* (1866). 'My account with her majesty', his article about the Post Office Savings Bank in *All the Year Round*, was reprinted by the order of the postmaster-general, and more than half a million copies were circulated. As one of the founders and the president of the Savage Club in 1857, he naturally took an interest in dramatic writing, and on Boxing night 1858, in conjunction with Frederick Lawrence, he produced at the Strand Theatre a burlesque, *Kenilworth*, which ran for more than 100 nights and was followed by a travesty of *Romeo and Juliet*. In partnership with William Brough he then wrote *Pretty Horsebreaker*, *Census*, *Area Belle*, and several other farces. He was the author of the domestic dramas *Daddy Gray*, *Loving Cup*, *Checkmate*, and *Love's Dream*, pieces produced with much success by Pattie Oliver at the Royalty Theatre. The new Vaudeville Theatre in London opened on 16 April 1870 with Halliday's *For Love or Money*. He also was the writer of a series of dramas adapted from the works of well-known authors, such as *Little Em'ly* (Olympic Theatre, 9 October 1869); *Amy Robsart* (Drury Lane, 24 September 1870); *Nell* (Olympic Theatre, 19 November 1870); *Notre Dame* (Adelphi Theatre, 10 April 1871); *Rebecca* (Drury Lane, 23 September 1871); *The Lady of the Lake* (Drury Lane, 21 September 1872); and *Heart's Delight*, founded on Dickens's *Dombey and Son* (Globe Theatre, 17 December 1873). He possessed a remarkable talent for bringing out the salient points of a novel, and his adaptations were successful where others failed; Dickens warmly praised the construction of *Little Em'ly*. From 1873 Halliday suffered from softening of the brain. He died at his home, 74 St Augustine's Road, Camden Town, London, on 10 April 1877, survived by his wife (whose name is not known), and was buried in Highgate cemetery on the 14th. Notable among his other printed works were popular farces written in conjunction with William Brough, such as *Colleen Bawn Settled at Last*, *Going to the Dogs*, and *Upstairs and Downstairs*; a novel, *The Great City* (1867); and his edition of *The Savage Club Papers* (2 vols., 1867–8).

G. C. BOASE, *rev.* NILANJANA BANERJI

**Sources** *ILN* (14 April 1877) • *ILN* (21 April 1877) • *Illustrated Sporting and Dramatic News* (21 April 1877), 105–6 • *The Era* (15 April 1877), 12 • *The Theatre*, 1 (1877), 140–41 • *Illustrated Review* (4 Feb 1874), 81–2 • R. Inglis, *The dramatic writers of Scotland* (1868), 49, 132 • Irving, *Scots.* • F. Waddy, *Cartoon portraits and biographical sketches of men of the day* (1873), 88–9

**Archives** BL, letters, as sponsor, to the Royal Literary Fund, loan no. 96

**Likenesses** Bertin of Brighton, carte-de-visite, NPG • Elliott & Fry, carte-de-visite, NPG • London Stereoscopic Co., carte-de-visite, NPG • portrait, repro. in *Illustrated Review*, 82 • wood-engraving (after photograph by London Stereoscopic Co.), NPG; repro. in *ILN* (21 April 1877) • woodcut, Harvard TC; repro. in *Entr'Acte*, 21 (21 April 1877)

**Wealth at death** under £4000: administration with will, April 1878, *CGPLA Eng. & Wales*

**Halliday, Edward Irvine** (1902–1984), painter, was born on 7 October 1902 at Garston, Liverpool, the second son of James Halliday (*b.* 1870) and his wife, Violet (1870–1940), daughter of Edward Irvine, of Orkney. James Halliday was a successful businessman. He expected his sons to follow in his footsteps and initially gave Edward's interest in art little encouragement. A combination of a determined nature and early success enabled the aspiring artist to pursue his chosen career. Edward was educated at the Liverpool Institute, Liverpool College, the City School of Art, Liverpool (1920–23), and the Royal College of Art, London (1923–5). A travel scholarship awarded in 1922 enabled him to attend life classes at the Académie Colarossi in Paris. He won the Rome scholarship in decorative painting in 1925 and spent three years studying and working on commissions in Rome. Between 1927 and 1931 Halliday made a number of decorative paintings for Liverpool patrons including panels for the Johnson Bros. Co. and the SS *Hilary*. Sir Benjamin Johnson gave him a second commission for three large panels depicting myths of the goddess Athena for the library of the Athenaeum, Liverpool (1928–30; *in situ*). These early murals demonstrate the classical basis of his academic training but also have a strangely dream-like atmosphere and complex narrative that is personal to Halliday. The intellectualism of these works contrasts with the direct and natural style of portrait painting he was developing in the same period.

While in Rome Halliday had met the classical scholar and archaeologist Dorothy Lucy Hatswell (1900–1986), the only daughter of Robert Hatswell MBE, a senior staff officer in the General Post Office. They married in 1928 and settled in London. Dorothy was a constant and loyal support to Edward throughout his career. They had a son, Stephen, born in 1933, and a daughter, Charlotte, born in 1935.

Over the next decade Halliday established himself as a portrait painter exhibiting regularly at the Royal Academy from 1929 when he made his début with a painting of *Lord Darling* (1928). The majority of commissions came by word of mouth. He achieved considerable success due not only to his talent in capturing a likeness but to his real interest in people and his lively and entertaining conversation. Where a commission did not require a formal setting Halliday preferred to paint his subjects in their typical surroundings. Above all, he relished an opportunity to paint a conversation piece. His studies of undergraduates at Worcester College, Oxford (exh. RA, 1938; Worcester College, Oxford), and state rooms at Chatsworth housing a girl's dormitory in wartime (exh. RA, 1941), still at Chatsworth, are among his most successful in this genre.

In the early 1930s Halliday turned his hand to interior design which gave him fresh opportunities for mural painting. He obtained several commissions, including a major scheme for the interior of the restaurant, bars, and sports facilities at Dolphin Square, Pimlico, completed in 1938 (architect Gordon Jeeves FRIBA). Halliday designed everything, from the crockery and carpets to the lighting, on an appropriately maritime theme. There were five murals in the scheme; they have all been destroyed except two which remain in the poolside bar. Beside the swimming pool Halliday painted a 90 foot-long decorative map of the Thames embellished with topical characters past and present. These murals confirmed Halliday's move away from the classicism of his early panels towards a more popular and humorous style echoing the contemporary revival of interest in naïve or folk art.

Halliday was a gifted public speaker and on the strength of this was invited to participate in two early arts series for radio: *Artists at Work* in 1932 and *Design in Modern Life* in 1934. His lively contributions led to further radio and television work providing commentaries on a variety of events, among them the opening of parliament and launch of the *Queen Mary*. In April 1939 he made a pioneering live television broadcast from varnishing day at the Royal Academy which attracted considerable interest by allowing public access to a previously exclusive event. After the war he returned to broadcasting and was for some years in the 1950s the voice behind the BBC Television *Newsreel*.

At the outbreak of the Second World War Halliday joined the Royal Air Force in Bomber Command. He began work in air traffic control but was then seconded for special duties with the Foreign Office working in the 'black propaganda' team led by D. Sefton Delmer. When he was demobbed Halliday shared the common and discouraging experience of having to 'start again'. In 1948 he received a commission from the Drapers' Company for a portrait of Princess Elizabeth (Drapers' Company, London). This picture not only re-established Halliday's name but proved to be the first of many royal portrait commissions. In 1952 he painted *Conversation Piece, Clarence House* of the queen and her family (Royal Collection) creating an unusually informal glimpse of royalty. Portraits of other members of the royal family followed, among them the queen mother, the Earl and Countess Mountbatten, and the prince of Wales.

Over the next decades Halliday's portrait commissions included a wide range of distinguished public figures: Sir Winston Churchill, Sir Edmund Hillary, Lord Denning, Lord Widgery, Sir Louis Gluckstein, the bishop of London, Robert Stopford, Lord Hunt, Sir Frank Whittle, Sir Malcolm Sargent, Leon Goossens, Beryl Grey, Gladys Cooper, Wally Hammond, Brian Johnston, and Ben Travers. He also painted several foreign heads of state: Jawaharlal Nehru, Nnamdi Azikiwe, Kenneth Kaunda, Forbes Burnham, and King Olaf of Norway. Some of these portraits went into private collections; many were for official purposes. His sitters came from all walks of life and frequently became his close friends.

Meanwhile Halliday gave his time freely to several arts societies because he felt he had been more fortunate than many of his contemporaries. In 1958 he was co-founder of the Federation of British Artists, from 1970 to 1975 he was president of the Royal Society of Portrait Painters, and between 1956 and 1973 he was president of the Royal Society of British Artists. He also gave his time generously to the Artists' League of Great Britain and the Artists' General Benevolent Institution, serving on the latter's council from the early 1950s and as chairman from 1965 to 1981. Halliday presided over the monthly meetings with fairness and skill, letting each have his say, and smoothing over controversy with some sensible compromise or piece of well-timed wit. He was a great raconteur and a witty after-dinner speaker. These talents and his natural sociability led him, at various times, to be a member of the Savage Club, the Garrick, and the Athenaeum, as well as chairman of the Arts and Chelsea Arts. He became an associate of the Royal College of Art (1925), a member of the Royal Society of British Artists (1942), a member of the Royal Society of Portrait Painters (1952), and fellow of the Royal Society of Arts (1970). He was appointed CBE in 1973.

In spare moments Halliday sometimes painted self-portraits, making at least twelve in all. These read not as the product of deep introspection, more as a record or appraisal of the different stages in a long and varied career. The 'props' and settings in the self-portraits variously relate to his studies in Paris and Rome, his work in interior design, the war years in the RAF, broadcasting, and family life. In all of these he applied the same principles that he used in portraits of others: to give an appropriate context for his subject, to avoid overt flattery or prettiness, and to convey an understanding of personality coupled with a true and dignified likeness. He died at his London home, 62 Hamilton Terrace, St John's Wood, on 2 February 1984.

GEORGE BUTLER, *rev.* ANN COMPTON

**Sources** D. P. Bliss, 'Edward Halliday', *Studio*, 465 (Dec 1931), 378–82 • S. Casson, ed., *Artists at work* (1933) • A. Compton, *Edward Halliday: art for life, 1925–39* (1997) • priv. coll. • private information (2004)

**Likenesses** E. I. Halliday, self-portrait, 1922–3, priv. coll. • E. I. Halliday, self-portrait, 1927 • E. I. Halliday, self-portrait, 1927–8, priv. coll. • E. I. Halliday, self-portrait, 1937, priv. coll. • E. I. Halliday, self-portrait, 1945, priv. coll. • E. I. Halliday, self-portrait, 1946, priv. coll. • E. I. Halliday, self-portrait, 1947, priv. coll. • E. I. Halliday, self-portrait, 1950, priv. coll. • E. I. Halliday, self-portrait, 1950–59, Liverpool College • E. I. Halliday, self-portrait, oils, 1952, NPG • E. I. Halliday, self-portrait, *c*.1955–1965 • E. I. Halliday, self-portrait, 1958, priv. coll.

**Wealth at death** £381,556: probate, 20 Dec 1984, *CGPLA Eng. & Wales*

**Halliday, Sir Frederick James** (1806–1901), administrator in India, son of Thomas Halliday, was born on Christmas day 1806 in Ewell, Surrey. Educated at Rugby School and at East India College, Haileybury, he opted for the Bengal civil service in 1824, at the age of eighteen. He received his first assignment on 8 June 1825 as assistant to the registrar of the supreme court, and by 1836 was secretary to the board of revenue. On 25 December 1834 he married Eliza Barbara (*d*. 1886), daughter of General Paul Macgregor of the East India Company's army; they had at least two sons and two daughters. In 1849 he was appointed home secretary to the government of India. Even while on furlough in England between July 1852 and November 1853 Halliday was summoned to give testimonies sixteen times during parliamentary debates on the renewal of the East India Company's charter. He sat on the supreme council from December 1853 to April 1854. In recognition of his rich administrative experience, Halliday was made lieutenant-governor of Bengal on 1 May 1854, the first to be appointed as Bengal had previously been directly administered by the governor-general. Contemporary British public opinion in India hoped that Halliday's administration would 'excite in the public mind no ordinary expectation, as to the prosecution of continued improvements in the internal administration of Bengal'. Much to the satisfaction of his patrons, Halliday's tenure in the high office was eventful in strengthening the raj.

Halliday's lieutenant-governorship had its first test during the 1855 Santal uprising, which he suppressed with remarkable dexterity. In 1856 he enacted the Calcutta Municipal Act for 'assessment and collection of municipal rates and taxes' which placed additional burdens on the city's inhabitants. The Bengal police was reorganized and the working of criminal courts monitored. A military police force was raised which proved its worth by curbing disturbances among the Kuki tribes and indigo peasants. Realizing that speedy communication was the *sine qua non* for effective administration, Halliday planned a network of highways linking Calcutta to Darjeeling, Jessore, and Cuttack. The Grand Trunk Road from Calcutta to Karamnasa was almost completed under his administration, and police pickets were placed to ensure safety for commercial traffic. Considerable progress was made in the construction of the East India Railway. To have some personal impression of rural administration, Halliday undertook extensive tours during which he held durbars to display the power of the British raj.

Bengal was not the nerve-centre of the famous 1857 uprising, although the first shots were fired by sepoys from Barrackpore, one of the cantonments in the Bengal presidency. But Halliday worked closely with the governor-general, Lord Canning, to counter the first 'national' challenge to British authority in India. He persuaded Canning to replace the sepoys by British soldiers as guards in Government House, and to create the Calcutta volunteer guards and the Bengal yeomanry cavalry to allay feelings of insecurity among Calcutta's European community following the uprising. In June 1857 a panicky Lord Canning also enacted the Press Act—possibly on Halliday's advice—to check the circulation of 'inflammatory publications'.

Halliday shared the evangelical and utilitarian commitment to modernize and 'reform' Indian society by eradicating customs such as suttee, thuggee, and female infanticide, which were repugnant to Western sensitivities. He subscribed to the liberal idea of a 'just rule over India' based on the efficacy of English character and law. Halliday thus implemented with great earnestness Charles Wood's 1854 education dispatch which advocated English as a medium of instruction in higher education. He created the office of director of public instruction for Bengal in 1855 and promoted Calcutta's Presidency College as an ideal institution. An act of 1857 incorporated Calcutta University on the model of London University. Halliday also enforced the Anti-Sati Act with missionary zeal, and legislated to facilitate the remarriage of Hindu widows. He supported a missionary campaign against *Charak* puja, a Hindu festival which involved swinging on trees and the piercing of arms and tongues by heated spikes. One of Halliday's last administrative measures was the Land Act of 1859, which restricted the landlords' power to enhance rents in specified cases, granted occupancy rights to tenants of twelve years standing, and stipulated rules concerning land sales for revenue arrears. Although apparently pro-tenant, in reality it provided the moneylenders with a better security for realizing their loans.

Halliday symbolized the spirit of nineteenth-century imperialism. Not unnaturally, he considered the 1857 rebels 'thieves and plunderers by taste and profession'. His contributions to the protection and consolidation of British rule in Bengal—once considered the 'most backward of great provinces of India'—was acknowledged by both the East India Company (February 1858) and the British parliament (March 1858). In his minute of 2 July 1859, Lord Canning acclaimed Halliday's 'watchfulness and sound judgement … [in checking] the spread of [the 1857] rebellion in Bengal'. In replying to the farewell address, Halliday himself hoped, on a note of remarkable self-confidence, that his 'name [would be] coupled hereafter with some improvements [in the British administration of Bengal]'. Halliday relinquished the lieutenant-governorship on 1 May 1859 and was created KCB the following year. On 30 September 1868 he was appointed a member of the Council of India. When he resigned from this council in 1886 his salaried public service had extended over sixty-one years.

During his administrative career in Bengal Halliday often differed with members of the government of India, which made even his patron, Lord Dalhousie, remark: '[Halliday] has so managed that … he has not in Bengal a single influential friend but myself' (*DNB*). An unfortunate experience was a controversy which embroiled him with William Tayler, commissioner of Patna, in Bihar, in the last years of his administration, and which lasted for some thirty years. Relations between the two men had been strained for some time, and when in 1857 Tayler failed to recognize the threat posed to Patna by the Dinapore sepoys and fanatic Wahabis and withdrew some officers from outlying stations without Halliday's concurrence, Halliday removed him from office. When Halliday appointed a Muslim as deputy commissioner in Patna, the Europeans objected strenuously, made Canning's sanction of the appointment one of their grounds for petitioning for his recall, and rallied to Tayler's support. The British government, however, consistently supported Canning and Halliday, and Tayler was left with no option but to resign in March 1859. He refused to let the matter drop, and continued to agitate for redress, without satisfaction, until his death in 1892; in 1880 he published *Fact versus falsehood, being a brief summary of Mr Tayler's refutation in reply to the memorandum to the House of Commons by Sir Frederick Halliday.*

Preoccupation with administration did not deter Halliday from pursuing his childhood interest in music. An accomplished contrabass player, he participated in public concerts even when he was lieutenant-governor, earning for himself the nickname Big Fiddle. Back in England, he regularly attended concerts of serious music. Halliday's family continued the Indian connections, his sons Frederick Mytton and George Thomas serving respectively the Bengal civil service and Bengal cavalry. His grandson Sir Frederick Loch Halliday became Calcutta police commissioner. Halliday died in London on 22 October 1901, at his residence, 21 Bolton Gardens, South Kensington, and was buried at Brompton cemetery. SURANJAN DAS

**Sources** C. E. Buckland, *Bengal under the lieutenant-governors*, 2nd edn, 1 (1902); repr. (1976) • C. E. Buckland, *Dictionary of Indian biography* (1906); repr. (Varanasi, 1971) • *Hansard* 3 (1879–80); (1888) • *The Times* (24 Oct 1901) • F. J. Halliday, *Minute on the mutinies as they affected the lower provinces under the Government* (1858) • F. J. Halliday, *Minute on the state of the police and of criminal justice in the lower provinces of Bengal* (1857) • D. Kumar, ed., *The Cambridge economic history of India*, 2 (1983), 105–9 • Burke, *Peerage* (1889) • *CGPLA Eng. & Wales* (1901) • *DNB*
**Archives** BL OIOC | W. Yorks. AS, Leeds, letters to Lord Canning
**Wealth at death** £37,567 0s. 8d.: resworn probate, April 1902, *CGPLA Eng. & Wales* (1901)

**Halliday, John Menzies** (1909–1988), jurist, was born on 29 November 1909 at Ard-darach, Rothesay, Isle of Bute, the son of John Menzies Halliday, a timber merchant, and his wife, Annie Robertson Hume Campbell. He was educated at Glasgow high school and then at the University of Glasgow, from which he graduated MA and LLB (with distinction). The LLB course was then part-time, the student being concurrently an apprentice in a solicitor's office. That meant university classes in the early morning and early evening, with a full office day in between. After qualifying as a solicitor, Halliday became a partner in the Glasgow firm Bishop, Milne, and Boyd; in the 1940s he was engaged as an arbiter in disputes between coal owners and the National Coal Board. On 14 June 1940 Halliday married; he and his wife, Margaret Barclay Smith, adopted three sons.

Halliday's abilities as a conveyancer were recognized by his alma mater in his appointment to the part-time chair of conveyancing in 1955, a post which he occupied with distinction until 1979. As a part-time academic, he was unusual in that he managed to contribute a considerable amount to legal literature; this was particularly important because there were few full-time academic lawyers in Scotland until the 1960s. He contributed to three editions of *An Outline of Estate Duty in Scotland* (1962, 1964, 1967) and wrote numerous articles on a wide variety of conveyancing topics; in all his writings he displayed not only a sound grasp of the law, but also an authoritative knowledge of practice.

In 1965 Halliday was appointed a part-time Scottish law commissioner, a post which he held until June 1974. During that period he contributed to discussion papers and reports on topics ranging from divorce, exemption clauses in contracts, prescription and limitation of actions, floating charges and receivers, to damages for injuries causing death. He was also influential in reforming the law on personal bankruptcy which culminated in the Bankruptcy (Scotland) Act 1985. He also chaired a committee which was charged with examining the law on securities over heritable (real) property, and reported in 1966. Its recommendations were reflected in an act in 1970 which fundamentally altered the law in this area, by attempting to achieve a balance between the interests of debtors and creditors. Halliday wrote an authoritative commentary on the act, *The Conveyancing & Feudal Reform (Scotland) Act 1970* (1970, 1977). He was appointed CBE in 1971, and in the same year an LLD from the University of Edinburgh. Other aspects of his committee's proposals were enacted in the Land Tenure Reform (Scotland) Act 1974, on which he also published an excellent commentary (1974). He played a significant part in introducing land registration in Scotland, which gives a state-guaranteed title to a property.

While occupying the chair, Halliday had an extensive opinion practice. Some of his opinions were edited and published in 1992—he challenged the editor to find a publisher who would publish two sheets of foolscap—but the more work of this kind he did, the more he became aware that the existing works on conveyancing were either of some antiquity, or not comprehensive or inaccurate. He therefore set about remedying these deficiencies. The result was his four-volume work *Conveyancing Law and Practice* (1985, 1986, 1987, 1990), published under the auspices of the Scottish Universities' Law Institute, probably the most prestigious form of publication in Scots law. Three volumes were published during his lifetime, and by the time of his death, he had all but completed the fourth. This work was an instant success, and a second edition was subsequently produced by a partner in Halliday's firm, now Bishop and Robertson Chalmers.

Halliday's efforts with his students and in his writings were always to ensure the highest possible standards in lawyers and in those aspiring to be lawyers; the council of the Law Society of Scotland, recognizing his immense contribution, conferred on him in 1979 the first honorary membership, an accolade that very few have ever had. Those who knew Halliday, in whatever capacity, were charmed by his pawky sense of humour, his sound practical advice, and his obvious industry and enthusiasm. It was often said that he devoted one half of his time to the university, a further half to the firm, yet another half to his family and home life, and the final half to his other loves in life, high among which was golf. He took immense pride in being made an honorary member of a golf club which had to acquire a new site, following the acquisition of the original club by what is now Glasgow airport. He was never too busy to see anyone—student, colleague, or client—and many solicitors in Glasgow and elsewhere benefited from his assistance in dealing with their problems. Much of his efforts in these activities went unsung. Halliday died on 4 April 1988 at the Western Infirmary, Glasgow. His wife survived him.

Jack Halliday was a humble man who listened with patience and was full of common sense. It is that which practitioners looked for in him, along with his extensive knowledge. His writings are still frequently cited in court and approved, but in the days when there were fewer cases on conveyancing than there are now, Jack's opinions were regarded as a court decision.

DOUGLAS J. CUSINE

**Sources** J. A. M. Inglis, *Scots Law Times: News* (1988), 115 • *Scottish Law Commission Reports*, 4–37 (1965–74) • b. cert. • d. cert. • *Glasgow Herald* (6 April 1988)

**Halliday, Sir Lewis Stratford Tollemache** (1870–1966), marine officer, was born on 14 May 1870 at Mechstead, Northampton, the son of Stratford Charles Halliday, a lieutenant in the Royal Artillery, and his wife, Annie Louisa Robinson. He was commissioned in the Royal Marine light infantry (RMLI) on 1 September 1889, and attended a course for RMLI lieutenants at the Royal Naval College, Greenwich (1889–90). As a marine officer he served at sea, abroad, at the three RMLI divisions at home (Plymouth, Portsmouth, and Chatham) and at the depot, Deal.

Halliday was serving on the *Orlando* in China when the Boxer uprising broke out in 1900. He and his marines joined others in defending the foreign legations in Peking (Beijing). According to Halliday's subsequent Victoria Cross citation, amid growing violence he was slightly wounded. Then on 24 June, with the legation area under enemy attack, he led twenty marines through a hole in the west wall on a mission to force adversaries away from adjacent buildings. Personally leading his men, Halliday encountered five Boxers, all armed with rifles. One shot him through the shoulder and lung, whereupon Halliday killed three with his pistol. He then turned over command of the patrol to his senior non-commissioned officer and returned without help to the hospital for medical aid. On the day when allied forces relieved the siege of Peking (15 August) he wrote in his diary, 'Thank God! and I don't think a day too soon.' For his actions the British minister Sir Claude Macdonald recommended Halliday for the Victoria Cross—which was conferred on 25 July 1901. In 1965 an American film, *Fifty-Five Days in Peking*, starring Charlton Heston, was loosely based on the Boxer uprising.

Just before his death Halliday said that the citation for his Victoria Cross was in error. Rather than leading twenty marines against the Boxers, he had led six. Also he noted that though he killed four, the fifth escaped because the last shell in his pistol misfired. Halliday also stated that he was just doing his duty under orders, as anyone would have done. The Ministry of Defence declined to change his citation, stating that it was based on the best available information at the time from sources in China. Halliday continued to be an officer of exceptional ability in his later career, and his subsequent promotions reflected this. In 1903–4 he once more attended the Royal Naval College, Greenwich, and he graduated from the Army Staff College, Camberley, in 1906. Between 1908 and 1912 he was on the staff of the Royal Military College, Sandhurst, and between 1912 and 1914 he served as a lecturer at the Royal Naval College, Greenwich. When the First World War began he was GSO2 in Malta, and later (November 1914 to 10 June 1917) he was GSO1, headquarters, southern army home defence; 39th division in France (until illness associated with his service in China led to his return to Britain); and then the Canadian training division and Bramshott, respectively. Halliday finished the war as assistant director, plans division, of the Admiralty, and in 1919 was a member of the British Admiralty delegation to the Paris peace conference. In the 1920s he rose in rank with diverse duties until assuming the leadership of his corps. He was adjutant-general of the Royal Marines from 1928, retiring in 1930 when he was appointed KCB. He served in 1925 as aide-de-camp to George V and as gentleman usher to the sword of state (1933–45). From 1936 to 1950 he was deputy lieutenant of the county of Devon.

Halliday was twice married. On 9 April 1908 he married Florence Clara Budgen, daughter of Brigadier-General W. T. Budgen. They had one son, but Florence died in 1909. His second marriage, to Violet Victoria Blake, daughter of Major Victor Blake, took place on 15 November 1916. They had a son and a daughter; his second wife died in 1949.

General Halliday's diverse career included traditional assignments at sea, colonial constabulary duty, service in the First World War and at the Paris peace conference, and finally work as head of his service in the inter-war years. Significantly Halliday represents the ability of marines to work with all the services; he noted that in his career he had served ten years each with the marines corps, the navy, and the army, and had made lifelong friends in all three. Just before his death he identified a non-marine assignment, his four years at Sandhurst as a company commander, Royal Military College, as the most interesting period of service. Yet he also played an important role in the transformation of the Royal Marines. As he stated, his corps, always a 'spearhead' of the armed forces, had evolved from sharpshooters aboard ship and landing parties to an organization able to defend naval bases and provide commandos in the Second World War and afterwards.

Halliday died at Dorking General Hospital on 9 March 1966. At the time of his death he was the oldest living recipient of the Victoria Cross. His medals were put on display in the Royal Marines Museum, Eastney, Hampshire.

DONALD F. BITTNER

**Sources** official record of service, PRO, ADM 196/62, pp. 221, 222 • L. S. T. Halliday, 'The siege of Peking' (30 May – 24 June 1900), *Globe and Laurel*, 8/73 (Nov 1901), 124–5 [pubd diary] • Victoria Cross citation, Royal Marines Museum, Eastney barracks, Southsea, Hampshire • *Globe and Laurel*, 8/63 (Jan 1901), 1 • Sandpiper, 'The bronze cross', *Globe and Laurel*, 64/4 (Aug 1956), 145–6 • *Globe and Laurel*, 74/4 (Aug 1965), 243 • 'Boxer rising hero queries his citation', *Portsmouth Evening News* (6 Sept 1965) [formerly in Royal Marines Museum, archives 9/2/H1] • 'V.C.s citation was "Wildly incorrect": general amends it after 65 years' [in unnamed newspaper] [n.d.] [formerly in Royal Marines Museum, archives 9/2/H1] • *Daily Telegraph* (11 March 1966) • 'The rising in China', *Globe and Laurel*, 7/57 (July 1900), 89–90; 7/59 (Sept 1900), 99; 7/60 (Oct 1900), 113–14; 7/61 (Nov 1900), 123–6 • 'The siege of the Peking legations', *Globe and Laurel*, 7/61 (Nov 1900), 130–31 [from *The Times*] • 'The Peking legations', *Globe and Laurel*, 7/62 (Dec 1900), 137–8 [from *Daily Malta Chronicle*] • 'The fighting in China: Peking relief expedition', *Globe and Laurel*, 8/63 (Jan 1901), 89–90 [extracts from *Army and Navy Gazette*] • M. P. H., 'The relief of Pekin', *Globe and Laurel*, 8/66 (April 1901), 43–4 • 'Royal marines legation guard, Pekin', *Globe and Laurel*, 9/70 (Aug 1901), 100–01 [photo] • 'Pictured together: the star of *55 days at Peking*—and the star of the siege itself', *Daily Mail* (3 April 1963) [formerly in Royal Marines Museum, Eastney, archives 9/2/H] • 'Just one boxer escaped', *Daily Express* (25 March 1963) [formerly in Royal Marines Museum, Eastney, archives 9/2/H] • *The Times* (6 April 1927); (7 April 1927); (28 Sept 1927); (14 Dec 1927); (1 Jan 1930); (1 Oct 1930); (4 Oct 1930); (18 Oct 1930) • *Globe and Laurel*, 74/2 (April 1966), 85, 128 • *The Times* (11 March 1966) • *Daily Telegraph* (11 March 1966) • *WWW, 1961–70* • H. E. Blumberg, *Britain's sea soldiers: a record of the royal marines during the war, 1914–1919* (1927) • C. Field, *Britain's sea soldiers: a history of the royal marines and their predecessors*, 2 vols. (1924) • b. cert. • d. cert.

**Archives** Royal Marines Museum, Eastney barracks, Southsea, Hampshire

**Likenesses** W. Stoneman, photograph, 1947, NPG • W. G. Goldsmith, oils, Royal Marines Museum, Eastney barracks, Southsea, Hampshire • group portrait, photograph (Pekin Legation Guard), repro. in *Globe and Laurel*, 9/70 (Aug 1901), 100–01 • photograph (in old age), repro. in *The Times* • photograph (in old age), repro. in *Daily Telegraph* • photographs, Royal Marines Museum, Eastney barracks, Southsea, Hampshire, photographic archive • photographs, repro. in *Globe and Laurel*, 74/2 (April 1966), 128

**Wealth at death** £4272: probate, 18 May 1966, *CGPLA Eng. & Wales*

**Halliday, Michael Frederick** (1822–1869), painter, was baptized on 18 May 1822 at Epsom, Surrey, the son of Michael Halliday, a captain in the Royal Navy, and his wife, Jane Hester Slack. From 1839 until his death he was a clerk in the parliament office of the House of Lords. An amateur artist, in 1853 he exhibited at the Royal Academy a view, *Moel Shabod, from the Capel Curig Road*. In 1856 he showed *The Measure for the Wedding Ring* (ex Sothebys, 19 October 1971) and two scenes of the Crimean War; *The Measure* attracted much notice and was engraved. Other works also appeared in Royal Academy exhibitions: in 1857 *The Sale of a Heart*; in 1858 *The Blind Basket-Maker with his First Child* (ex Sothebys, 30 March 1994); in 1864 *A Bird in the Hand*; and in 1866 *Roma vivente e Roma morta*. He also contributed an etching of *The Plea of the Midsummer Fairies* to the edition of Thomas Hood's *Poems* published by the Junior Etching Club in 1858.

Halliday's work as an artist shows a strong Pre-Raphaelite influence; he was tutored by his friend John Everett Millais, and he was also on close terms with William Holman Hunt. From 1854 he went hunting with Millais and the *Punch* draughtsman John Leech, and Leech used him as the model for the diminutive hunting hero in his series 'The Adventures of Tom Noddy'. Halliday was also an enthusiastic volunteer, a first-rate rifle shot, and one of the first English eight who competed for the Elcho shield at Wimbledon in 1862. He died after a short illness at his home, 30 Thurloe Place, South Kensington, London, on 1 June 1869 and was buried at Brompton cemetery, London.

L. H. CUST, *rev.* MALCOLM WARNER

**Sources** *The Athenaeum* (12 June 1869), 804 • *Art Journal*, 31 (1869), 272 • Redgrave, *Artists*, 2nd edn, 193 • D. Holman Hunt, *My grandfather: his wives and loves* (1969) • J. G. Millais, *The life and letters of Sir John Everett Millais*, 2 vols. (1899) • S. Houfe, *John Leech and the Victorian scene* (1984) • Wood, *Vic. painters*, 3rd edn, 219 • *Victorian painters* (1994), 90 [Sothebys sales catalogue, 30 March 1994] • *The exhibition of the Royal Academy* (1853–66) [exhibition catalogues] • *IGI* • d. cert.

**Archives** JRL, letters to Holman Hunt

**Likenesses** J. E. Millais, drawing, 1853, repro. in M. Lutyens and M. Warner, eds., *Rainy days at Brig o'Turk: the Highland sketchbooks of John Everett Millais, 1853* (1983), 83, no. 44; priv. coll.

**Wealth at death** £3000: administration, 24 July 1869, *CGPLA Eng. & Wales*

**Halliday, Thomas** (1835–1919), trade unionist, was born on 18 July 1835 at Prestolee near Bolton in Lancashire, the son of a coalminer who was killed in an accident when Thomas was only two years of age. His mother, who had been born in Wales, worked in a textile mill following her husband's death.

Halliday's working life started at the age of eight, and he toiled in the coal industry in various parts of the north of England until August 1863, when he became the full-time agent of the newly created Farnworth and District Miners' Union. Together with William Pickard from Ince in Lancashire, Halliday struggled to build up support for mining unionism in the Lancashire coalfield. Trade unionism in the Lancashire coalfield had briefly flourished in the 1840s, when the systematic use of localized strike action supported by neighbouring union branches had led to some improvements in wages and conditions. But the later years of that decade saw unionism decline, and revival was delayed by bitter local rivalries and the absence of solidarity engendered by the social and geographical exclusivity of mining communities in other coalfields. In Lancashire miners tended to live among workers in other trades, and were more vulnerable to the importation of migrant, especially Irish and Welsh, labour.

The two men became leading figures in the Miners' National Association, with Pickard as treasurer and Halliday as vice-president. This organization was dominated by the strategy and personality of its president, Alexander Macdonald, who tended to favour redress of grievances and improvement of conditions through parliamentary action, conciliation, and collaboration with employers. It was a policy which was not without its critics who advocated a more confrontational strategy, and in 1864 this led to schism in the ranks of mining trade unionism when critics of Macdonald withdrew from the national association and established the Practical Miners' Association which pursued a more aggressive industrial policy. This breakaway organization collapsed within two years, and during these disputes Pickard and Halliday remained loyal to Macdonald. The Miners' National Association was, in effect, a loose confederation of local unions which provided Macdonald with a platform from which to lobby parliament and the government for reforms in the conditions of employment in the coal industry. Halliday was among those who felt the need for an organization which could also co-ordinate industrial action, offer financial aid to members in disputes with employers, and organize sympathetic action if necessary.

Although relations with Macdonald never deteriorated into deep personal hostility, Halliday led a new challenge to Macdonald's supremacy within mining trade unionism in the late 1860s. It was the difficulties encountered by Halliday in trying to organize the miners of Lancashire, where the systematic use of strike-breakers, and female and child labour, made effective trade unionism very difficult, that convinced him that only a genuinely amalgamated national union of coalminers would result in significant improvement in wages and conditions. By July 1869 Halliday and Pickard had created the Amalgamated Association of Miners. Macdonald addressed a conference called to discuss the proposed new body; differences over strategy, however, prevented him from supporting the new organization which was formally launched the following month, with Halliday as its president.

Although the Amalgamated Association soon attracted support in Lancashire and some other parts of England, it was in the rapidly expanding but largely un-unionized coalfield of south Wales that the amalgamated miners' union was to have its greatest impact and leave a profound legacy. Until 1870 there had been only sporadic and spontaneous forms of organization among the colliers of south Wales, with no permanent coalfield-wide or even district bodies to co-ordinate activities. Halliday and his amalgamated union provided the catalyst for the creation of effective trade union organization in the south Wales coalfield. Under the amalgamated union a structure emerged, based on lodges organized into district committees, each with its own full-time agent, which was to characterize south Wales mining trade unionism for sixty years. Halliday enjoyed considerable initial success, with two large and successful disputes in 1871 and 1873. With a weakening market for coal, and concerted action by the coal owners, however, the period after 1874 was one of rapid decline for the Amalgamated Association. A strike early in 1875 against major wage reductions in the south Wales coalfield bankrupted Halliday's union, and it never recovered from the effects of this dispute. There was also growing hostility to the lack of rank-and-file control over the executive of the Amalgamated Association, which led to a series of secessions by district miners' associations. In south Wales, the 1875 strike resulted in the creation of a sliding scale for wages administered by a conciliation board, and subsequently coalmining trade unionism in south Wales, where it existed, operated on a highly sectionalized, valley-based, district system until the creation of the South Wales Miners' Federation in 1898. Attempts in 1877 by Halliday to revive the Amalgamated Association failed. Halliday served briefly as the secretary of a reunited Miners' National Association, but by the late 1870s Halliday's career as a national leader of the miners was over and he slipped into an obscurity from which he never re-emerged.

Halliday left no written records, and details of his personality and private life are very sparse. It is not known whether he was married. He must have possessed inspirational qualities; he certainly had a profound impact on rising miners' leaders in south Wales such as William Abraham (Mabon). It is a reflection of the dramatic impact he had on many Welsh miners, that Halliday was put forward as a Liberal candidate for Merthyr Tudful in the general election of 1874. He gained nearly 5000 votes, but proved unable to break the hold of the sitting members for that overwhelmingly working-class borough.

For Halliday the Merthyr Tudful election was the high-water mark of his career. From 1880 he disappears from the annals of the British labour movement, thereafter he seems to have eked out an existence as a small businessman trading in the accessories of employment in the coal industry of south Wales. Halliday died in Cardiff on 24 November 1919. RICHARD LEWIS

**Sources** J. Saville, 'Halliday, Thomas', *DLB*, vol. 3 • R. Challinor, *The Lancashire and Cheshire miners* (1972) • E. W. Evans, *The miners of south Wales* (1961) • E. W. Evans, *Mabon: William Abraham, 1842–1922* (1959) • S. J. Webb and B. P. Webb, *The history of trade unionism*, new edn (1907) • I. G. Jones, 'The Merthyr of Henry Richard', *Merthyr politics: the making of a tradition*, ed. G. Williams (1966)

**Hallifax, Samuel** (1733–1790), bishop of St Asaph, was born in Mansfield, Nottinghamshire, on 8 or 18 January 1733, the eldest son of Robert Hallifax, apothecary, and his wife, Hannah, the daughter of Samuel Jebb, a maltster of that town. His younger brother was Robert Hallifax MD (1735–1810), physician to George, prince of Wales, afterwards George IV; Samuel Jebb (1693/4–1772) was his uncle, and Sir Richard Jebb (1729–1787) and John Jebb (1736–1786) were his first cousins. He was educated at Mansfield School and at Jesus College, Cambridge, where he was admitted sizar on 21 October 1749, matriculated in 1750, and proceeded BA in 1754 and MA in 1757. He was a fellow of Jesus from 1756 to 1760 and held the offices of

**Samuel Hallifax (1733–1790)**, by unknown artist, *c.*1770–80

praelector, dean, tutor, steward, and rental bursar. His study of law took him to Trinity Hall, where he was fellow from 1760 to 1775, taking the degree of LLD in 1764. He was made deacon by Matthias Mawson, bishop of Ely, on 21 September 1755, and was ordained priest on 6 March 1757.

Hallifax was an ambitious man, eager for preferment in university and church, with powerful friends and patrons. The deputy of William Ridlington, he hoped to succeed him as regius professor of civil law. When in 1764 Ridlington sought the mastership of Trinity Hall and the high steward of the university, the duke of Newcastle, supported another candidate, Dr Wynne, Hallifax wrote a series of sycophantic letters trying to avoid upsetting either. The following year he secured the rectory of Cheddington, Buckinghamshire, although Cambridge remained his principal residence, and in 1767 he applied unsuccessfully to become chaplain to the archbishop of Canterbury, explaining that, while his situation at Trinity Hall was 'a very desirable one', because he had 'suffered greatly in my Health & Spirits on account of the variety of business I am burthened with at College, I should be very happy to procure an honourable dismission from my Residence there' (BL, Add. MS 35638, fol. 131*v*). In 1768 he alienated his first cousin John Jebb, whose hopes of the Arabic chair were dashed by Hallifax's appointment to it. Jebb's friends questioned Hallifax's motives, regretting that he who was 'so well assured of succeeding soon to the chair of civil law, (the immediate line in which he was engaged) should impatiently seize the passing offer of the arabic professorship' (*Works … of John Jebb*, 1.21–2) and suggesting his sole motive was 'to keep out Dr Jebb' (Barker, 2.384). But ambition and greed motivated Hallifax more than personal malice. Unknown to Jebb and his friends, Hallifax had first approached Newcastle over the Arabic chair four years earlier when he heard that the elderly professor Leonard Chappelow was 'very ill and thought to be in danger', at the same time assuring Edward Simpson he had 'made it my endeavours to qualify myself for that office' (BL, Add. MS 32958, fols. 285, 355). When in January 1768 Chappelow finally died, Hallifax assured his patron Charles Yorke that 'many years before I came to Trinity Hall, I had thoughts of trying to succeed him' (BL, Add. MS 35640, fol. 239). The chair won, he treated it as a sinecure for two years, holding it jointly with the position of lord almoner's reader in Arabic. He resigned both when he became regius professor of civil law in 1770, the same year in which he was appointed master of the faculties at Doctors' Commons. He remained regius professor of civil law until 1782.

Hallifax was more active as law professor. His *Analysis of the Roman Civil Law, Compared with the Laws of England* (1774) was based on his lectures and remained a basis of bachelor of law courses at Cambridge into the 1850s. But he was not a natural teacher. Sir Egerton Brydges, who attended his lectures, described him as 'a mild, courteous little man … not only of no force, but even languid' (*The Autobiography*, 2 vols., 1834, 1.59). Another student, Philip Yorke, complained: 'He reads his lectures from manuscript, but with such rapidity that it is impossible to take down notes' (BL, Add. MS 35377, fol. 131*r*). Escape from Cambridge remained a theme of his applications for preferment. In 1771 he sought the archdeaconry of Lincoln, although this would be no financial advantage, because:

> I wish much to have an honourable dismission from the burden of taking Pupils, and to reside in the University, with full leisure to attend on the duties of my professorship, and to finish the plan of Lectures I have not yet been able to complete. (BL, Add. MS 35610, fol. 12*v*)

As a preacher, Hallifax modelled himself on Samuel Ogden, whose sermons he published and whose homiletic style he defended. Gilbert Wakefield described him as 'a passionate admirer and close imitator' (*Memoirs*, 2 vols., ed. J. T. Rutt and A. Wainewright, 1804, 1.96) of Ogden, whom he succeeded as preacher at the Round House; Henry Gunning observed at the latter that he affected his predecessor's 'tone and manner of delivery, but did not succeed in attracting so numerous a congregation' (*Reminiscences*, 2 vols., 1854, 1.240). William Beloe described him as 'an admirable scholar, and … a very considerable man, of great abilities and profound learning' (*The Sexagenarian*, 2 vols., 1817, 1.60). The high quality of his scholarship was perhaps most evident in his masterly introduction to his edition of Joseph Butler's *The Analogy of Religion* (1736), which Hallifax published in 1788. A high-churchman in the style of his contemporary Samuel Horsley, he attacked both Roman Catholics and protestants in the defence of Anglican orthodoxy.

In a sermon of 1769 in which he also condemned the

French freethinkers Bayle and Rousseau, Hallifax denounced the seventeenth-century English protestants who 'rejected all rites and ceremonies' and sought 'the abolition of order and subscription in the church' (*Sermon … Preached before the Hon. House of Commons*, 1769, 11–12). Two years later he was a bitter opponent of the Feathers tavern petitioners, defending the Test Acts and opposing the abolition of subscription to the Thirty-Nine Articles for Cambridge graduands. Letters in the newspapers signed 'Erasmus' were attributed to him and alienated his cousin John Jebb and his friends, but the more hostile comments in his three sermons on the topic were omitted in the published version in 1772. In these powerfully argued homilies, his bitterest barbs were directed at the Socinians. He identified the theological principles at stake precisely: 'the Holy Trinity, the Divinity of the Son and Spirit, the antecedent state of Christ, the nature and efficacy of the Sacrifice of his death' (*Three Sermons Preached before the University of Cambridge*, 1772, i). He argued that those who believed that Christ was God incarnate had 'very different sentiments of piety and gratitude' from one who 'conceives of Christ as a mere man, who, after teaching religion to an ignorant and wicked world, lost his life in the cause of virtue' (ibid., iii), and this would effect their political, social, and moral behaviour. The formidable quality of this erudite defence of orthodox Christianity was evidenced by the number of vituperative responses, including a substantial letter by Samuel Blackall and a series of letters in the *London Chronicle* (1772–4), signed 'Priscilla' and written by Ann Jebb.

Hallifax's appointment as a royal chaplain in 1774 provided him with a platform from which to seek higher office in the church. The next year he received a DD by royal mandate, gave up his fellowship, and, in October, married Catherine, the second daughter of Dr William *Cooke (1711–1797), provost of King's College, Cambridge, and dean of Ely, and the sister of William *Cooke (*bap.* 1749, *d.* 1824) [*see under* Cooke, William] and Edward *Cooke (*bap.* 1755, *d.* 1820). They had seven children, one of whom died in a scalding accident in a brewhouse in 1782. Hallifax gave up the rectorship of Cheddington in 1777, but in 1778 was preferred to be rector of Warsop, Nottinghamshire, near his Mansfield birthplace, and he retained this rectorship until his death. On 1 September 1781 he was nominated as bishop of Gloucester, and he was consecrated on 28 October. As bishop, he was involved (with Sir George Onesiphorus Paul) in distributing the sums left by George III for the relief of debtors and the poor following the visit of the royal family to Gloucestershire in summer 1788, and he wrote a report for the king describing the process. On 15 March 1789 George III wrote to William Pitt the younger requesting that Hallifax be informed of his nomination to the see of St Asaph; the nomination was formally made on 20 March 1789, and he was elected on 4 April.

A theological dispute initiated soon after Hallifax's marriage endured throughout the rest of his career and was prolonged beyond his death. In his Warburton lectures of 1776 he mounted an attack on the claims of Roman Catholicism, arguing that 'the Apostasy of Papal Rome is indeed foretold in the sacred oracles' (*Twelve Sermons on the Prophecies Concerning the Christian Church*, 1776, 334) and traced how 'the Papal usurpations were carried to their utmost length, and true religion was obscured and well nigh lost amidst the prevailing interests of vice and superstition' (ibid., 363–4). But, while hostile to Rome, Hallifax defended some practices generally associated with Catholicism. In 1786 he reprinted Joseph Butler's 1751 *Charge to the Clergy of Durham*, which had hitherto been considered too sympathetic to Roman Catholic ideas for republication. Hallifax wrote a preface, considerably longer than the *Charge*, defending 'the Importance of External Religion' (*A Charge Deliver'd to the Clergy … of Durham*, 2nd edn, 1786, i) and denying that the *Charge* represented Butler 'as inclined to Popery, and as dying in the communion of the Church of Rome' (ibid., iii).

This was precisely the accusation levelled against Hallifax himself in 1818 by John Milner, the Roman Catholic bishop of Castabala and vicar apostolic of the midland district, in *The End of Religious Controversy*. Milner claimed that many Anglican clergy vocal against Rome, as Hallifax had been in his Warburton lectures, in fact embraced the Catholic faith on their deathbeds, and that Hallifax was 'probably' one of these (Milner, 77 n. 2). Later he described how a bishop, 'a late Warburton-lecturer' (certainly Hallifax) 'on his death-bed refused the proffered ministry of the primate, and expressed a great wish to die a Catholic. When urged to satisfy his conscience, he exclaimed: *What then will become of my lady and my children?*' (ibid., 224 n. 3, 326). This unsubstantiated claim led Samuel Parr, so critical of Hallifax's treatment of Jebb, to leap to his defence. In *A Letter to Dr Milner* (1825) Parr marshalled Hallifax's protestant credentials—his 'most intimate and confidential friendship with Bishop Hurd' (Parr, 31), his frequent access to 'the sagacious and contemplative recluse, Bishop Law' (ibid.)—and concluded that such a deathbed conversion was most unlikely. Hallifax died on 5 March 1790 at his Westminster home in Dartmouth Street, of a fever and stone in his bladder. He was buried alongside his son in the chancel of Warsop church within 5 miles of his birthplace. ROBERT HOLE

**Sources** Nichols, *Lit. anecdotes*, vols. 5, 6, 8, 9 • P. Searby, *A history of the University of Cambridge*, 3: 1750–1870, ed. C. N. L. Brooke and others (1997) • S. Hallifax, correspondence with the duke of Newcastle, BL, Add. MS 32939, fol. 426; Add. MS 32958, fols. 64, 285, 355; Add. MS 32959, fols. 148, 227, 369; Add. MS 32973, fol. 323; Add. MS 32988, fols. 19, 79 • S. Hallifax, letters to C. Yorke, BL, Add. MS 35637, fol. 222; Add. MS 35638, fols. 131, 140, 144; Add. MS 35640, fols. 239, 319 328 • S. Hallifax, letters to the second Lord Hardwicke, BL, Add. MS 35610, fols. 12, 347; Add. MS 35657, fol. 294; Add. MS 35681, fols. 63, 266 • E. H. Barker, ed., *Parriana, or, Notices of the Rev. Samuel Parr*, 2 vols. (1828–9) • *The works, theological, medical, political and miscellaneous of John Jebb with memoirs of the life of the author*, ed. J. Disney, 3 vols. (1787) • J. Milner, *The end of religious controversy*, 5th edn (1824) • S. Parr, *A letter to the Rev. Dr. Milner* (1825) • *GM*, 1st ser., 60 (1790), 281 • Venn, *Alum. Cant.* • *DNB* • *The later correspondence of George III*, ed. A. Aspinall, 5 vols. (1962–70), vol. 1, pp. 393–4, 401 • *Fasti Angl., 1541–1857*, [Bristol], 43 • *Fasti Angl.* (Hardy), 1.79, 441–2; 3.658, 661, 662

**Archives** BL, letters to the second Lord Hardwicke, Add. MS 35610, fols. 12, 347, Add. MS 35657, fol. 294, Add. MS 35681, fols. 63, 266 • BL, corresp. with the duke of Newcastle, Add. MS 32939, fol. 426, Add. MS 32958, fols. 64, 285, 355, Add. MS 32959, fols. 148, 369, Add. MS 32973, fol. 323, Add. MS 32988, fols. 19, 79 • BL, letters to C. Yorke, Add. MS 35637, fol. 222, Add. MS 35638, fols. 131, 140, 144, Add. MS 35640, fols. 239, 319, 328
**Likenesses** oils, c.1770–1780, Trinity Hall, Cambridge [*see illus.*]

**Hallifax, Sir Thomas** (1722–1789), mayor of London, was baptized at Barnsley on 23 February 1722, the third son of John Hallifax, a clockmaker of Barnsley, and his wife, Anne, daughter of George Archdale of Pilley, near Barnsley. He was educated at Barnsley and was apprenticed to a grocer there, but he left this employment before his indentures had expired and moved to London. There he became a clerk in the banking house of John Martin & Co. and enjoyed rapid promotion to become chief clerk and ultimately, in 1753, to join with the banker Joseph Vere and the City merchant Richard Glyn to found the banking firm of Vere, Glyn, and Hallifax. In the same year he was awarded the freedom of the City of London and was admitted on 27 September to the Goldsmiths' Company. On 27 April 1762 he married, at Ewell, Penelope (*d.* 1762), daughter of Richard Thomson of Lincoln's Inn, but she died on 6 December of that year. He later married, on 1 November 1772, Margaret (1749–1777), daughter of John Saville, linen draper of Clay Hill, Enfield, Middlesex, and with her had two sons, Thomas (*b.* 1774) and Savile (*b.* 1777).

Hallifax was elected alderman of Aldersgate ward in the City of London on 26 November 1766 and was sworn into office on 9 December of that year. From June 1768 to June 1769 he served as sheriff, and in this capacity acted as a returning officer for three of the four Middlesex elections involving John Wilkes, whose election he upheld despite government attempts to invalidate the return. In 1771 and 1772 he stood unsuccessfully as a ministerial candidate for lord mayor, the second time in opposition to Wilkes. He eventually succeeded in being elected as mayor on 29 September 1776. He had been knighted on 5 February 1773. During his term in office as lord mayor Hallifax supported efforts to improve the navigation of the Thames and opposed the operation of press-gangs in the city on the grounds that they interfered with the rights of the citizens. Nevertheless, he issued orders to the city marshals to search the public houses throughout the city and take into custody all suspected criminals and send them into service in the army and navy. 'In endeavouring to secure safety to the persons of his fellow citizens from the rapacious violence of a lawless banditti he gained the thanks and approbation of the city' (Wilkinson, 179).

After his term as lord mayor Hallifax attempted to enter parliament. He was proposed in October 1779 as a parliamentary candidate for Middlesex but his candidature received no backing. He was returned to the House of Commons on 29 December 1780 as member of parliament for Coventry following a bitterly contested election but was unseated on petition on 27 February 1781. He was finally returned unopposed on 31 March 1784 as the member for Aylesbury and continued to represent that constituency until his death. A supporter of the Pitt ministry, Hallifax played little part in parliamentary affairs and is not recorded as having spoken in debate.

During the latter years of his life Hallifax resided at Gordon House, Enfield. He had become a very rich man with a personal fortune estimated to have been in excess of £100,000. However, he appears not to have been noted for his generosity. According to one memoir of him, he refused to give to a group of Enfield parishioners who were collecting for the poor of the parish. He died intestate after four days' illness, aged sixty-six, on 7 February 1789 at his apartment above the banking house in Birchin Lane, London, and was buried on 17 February in Enfield churchyard in the family vault of the Savilles, where his second wife had been buried in November 1777.

CHARLES WELCH, *rev.* M. J. MERCER

**Sources** M. M. Drummond, 'Hallifax, Sir Thomas', HoP, *Commons, 1754–90* • J. Wilkinson, *Worthies, families and celebrities of Barnsley and the district* [1883], 165–86 • *GM*, 1st ser., 46 (1776), 529; 1st ser., 59 (1789), 183–4 • F. G. Hilton Price, *A handbook of London bankers* (1890–91), 57–9, 66ff. • *City biography: containing anecdotes and memoirs of … the aldermen and other conspicuous personages of the corporation and City of London*, 2nd edn (1800) • *IGI*
**Likenesses** Miller, portrait, 1782, Guildhall, London
**Wealth at death** est. over £ 100,000: *GM*, 59, 183–4

**Hallifax, William** (1655–1721/2), Church of England clergyman, was born at Springthorpe, Lincolnshire, on 15 August, and baptized on 24 September 1655, the son of the Revd John Hallifax and his wife, Elizabeth. On 20 February 1670 he entered Brasenose College, Oxford, as a servitor, but was admitted a scholar of Corpus Christi College, Oxford, in April 1674, where he became a fellow in December 1682. He graduated BA in 1675, proceeding MA in 1678, BD in 1687, and DD in 1695.

In 1685 Hallifax published *The Elements of Euclid Explained*, a translation of Father Claud Francis Millet de Chales's work. On 18 January 1688 he was elected as chaplain of the Levant Company in Aleppo and remained there until 27 November 1695. In 1691 he visited Palmyra (biblical Tadmor). He copied transcriptions, which were published in 1695 in the Royal Society's *Philosophical Transactions* (19.83–110), along with sketches by his companions.

The high-church Thomas Hearne described Hallifax as being of a puritanical stamp (*Remarks*, 1.221). Hallifax himself in his will declared his devotion to the Church of England 'esteeming it to Approach the nearest to the primitive Church of Christ of any that is now in the world' (PROB 11/583, fol. 216*r*). That appeal to the ideal of a primitive church reflects perhaps a response to the impact of German pietism, whose influence had spread across protestant Europe from its centre at Halle, and indeed Hallifax left to his old college 'my Hallian Bible in folio' (PROB 11/583, fol. 216*v*). Paul Foley, speaker of the House of Commons from 1695 to 1698 (and an important member of the Harley–Foley connection of old puritan families in the south-west midlands who became country whigs under William III) appointed him as his chaplain in 1695. On 8

June 1698 the customary address was made by the house requesting the king to confer some dignity upon their chaplain, 'yet 'twas his Fortune to get nothing', reported Hearne (*Remarks*, 1.221). Instead he was presented to the richly endowed living of Oldswinford, Worcestershire, by Paul Foley's brother, Thomas Foley of Witley Court, on 17 August 1699. Subsequently, from 18 July 1713, he held it in plurality with the rectory of Salwarpe in the same county. In 1700 he built a new rectory at Oldswinford.

Hallifax married Ann Hill at St Michael's, Stoke Prior, Worcestershire, on 24 March 1701. Though at the time of his death the family portraits of his first wife were still in his home, by then he was married again, this time to Mary, probably the sister of another clergyman, George Martin. A son, William, was buried at Salwarpe on 11 April 1721. Hallifax was buried on 4 January 1722, having left instruction that he wished to be buried under a plain stone at Salwarpe. His bequests to Corpus Christi College, Oxford, also included a manuscript Koran and a Persian version of part of the Psalms of David, a silver-gilt basin bought in Aleppo, and a collection of coins and medals.

DONALD GRAY

**Sources** parish register, Springthorpe, Lincs. Arch. [baptism] · parish register, Salwarpe, Worcs. RO [burial] · Foster, *Alum. Oxon.* · Wood, *Ath. Oxon.*, new edn, 4.620 · [C. B. Heberden], ed., *Brasenose College register, 1509–1909*, 1, OHS, 55 (1909) · J. B. Pearson, *A biographical sketch of the chaplains to the Levant Company, maintained at Constantinople, Aleppo and Smyrna, 1611–1706* (1883), 18, 24, 58 · *Remarks and collections of Thomas Hearne*, ed. C. E. Doble and others, 1, OHS, 2 (1885), 221 · N. Perry, *The story of St Mary's Church and the parish of Oldswinford* (1990?) · PRO, PROB 11/583, sig. 28 · E. Sinker, *Salwarpe* (1918) · D. Gray, *Chaplain to Mr Speaker: the religious life of the House of Commons* (1991) · T. Nash, *Collections for the history of Worcestershire*, 2nd edn, 2 (1799), 212, 214, 339 · *DNB* · *JHC*, 12 (1697–9), 302

**Hallinan, Hazel Hunkins** (1890–1982), campaigner for women's rights, was born on 6 June 1890 at Aspen, Colorado, in the United States, the only daughter of Lewis Hunkins, civil war veteran, jeweller, and watchmaker, and Ann Whittingham, an English emigrée. Hazel Hunkins was brought up in Billings, Montana. She later reflected that it was an early experience at the Episcopalian Church Sunday school which had provided her with her first awareness of gender difference. She recalled listening to a reading of Genesis and her dejection at the information that 'it only took a rib to make me while Adam was made in the image of God'. She later concluded that 'In circumstances such as these little girls have from time immensurable been given a sense of inferiority' (SPG/HHH/M23 Fawcett Library). However, there was nothing inferior about Hunkins's scholastic achievements: she graduated from Vassar College in 1913 with an excellent degree in chemistry. She went on to lecture chemistry to freshmen at the University of Missouri for three years, with special reference to agricultural economics, and began her master's degree in chemistry. Prejudice at the university denied her promotion, despite her having higher qualifications than her male colleagues. Her professional ambitions were thwarted and her studies interrupted by traditional social expectations which compelled her to return home to nurse her critically ill mother. To relieve the tedium of this restricted domestic life she applied for a chemistry teaching post at Billings high school but was informed that only men would be considered for the post. However, she accepted a botany and geography position. Her experience of female subordination was endorsed when she attempted to gain employment as an industrial chemist. Her applications to chemistry laboratories throughout the country resulted in over 200 rejections: in every case the explanation offered was that they did not employ female chemists. She was twenty-six years old and desperate to make her contribution to society and be independent.

Such accumulated frustration was to find release when in the summer of 1916 Hunkins met Anna Louise Rowe, a member of the National Woman's Party (NWP), who was in Billings to establish NWP branches across Montana at the behest of the party's leader, Alice Paul. Hunkins's life as a political activist began with her organizing Billings's own NWP branch, becoming Montana state chair of the National Woman's Party, travelling around the state speaking at public meetings. But when the Democratic Party blocked the proposed equality legislation for women, NWP members concentrated all efforts on picketing the White House in Washington. Hunkins joined them. The women were subjected to physical violence and verbal abuse from crowds and police alike, while they stood silently holding their banners. To the horror of her family, from June 1917 Hunkins served several gaol sentences and took part in prison hunger strikes. She and her fellow women protesters claimed that as American citizens they were being held by their government as political prisoners.

It was soon after her final release from prison that Hunkins met Charles Thomas Hallinan (*d.* 1971) at a pacifist meeting where he was a speaker. Hunkins went to England in July 1920 to carry out research on the co-operative movement for the American Railway Brotherhood, and Charles Hallinan travelled there in November as the financial editor of United Press International. Hunkins and Hallinan then lived together in London and had four children. At the end of the 1920s they married. In this same spirit of independence Hunkins Hallinan adamantly declared that 'I have never in my life called myself Mrs Charles Hallinan. I have always had my own name' (Spender, 25).

During the course of her research on the co-operative movement, Hunkins Hallinan attended lectures at the London School of Economics to improve her knowledge of political and economic issues and was a member of the 1917 Club and attended Fabian socials. In London, she re-established her commitment to women's rights by joining the Six Point Group (SPG) in 1922. The SPG was a nonparty political group formed in 1921 by Lady Rhondda (Margaret Haig) and its membership consisted of former militant suffragettes who were interested in practical action for social, economic, and political equality for women. During the 1920s and 1930s Hunkins Hallinan's friends numbered many of the leading feminists of the day including Crystal Eastman, Dora Russell, and Vera Brittain.

Hunkins Hallinan had various full- and part-time posts which utilized her economic and research experience. In London she became a sub-editor of the *Statesman's Yearbook* and was society correspondent of the *Chicago Tribune* for fourteen years. Having been the SPG's honorary secretary for some time, during the 1950s Hunkins Hallinan became its chair and was prominent in the key campaigns of the period relating to women's employment rights, particularly equal pay and promotion rights. Her concern was not restricted to professional women, but included married women who were trying to combine work with family responsibilities. She was also a member of the Married Women's Association, although her perception of those family responsibilities was likely to have been somewhat limited by her class (she had sons at Oxford and Gordonstoun). By 1917 she was a member of the all-party parliamentary equal rights group which did much valuable groundwork for the anti-discrimination legislation of the 1970s. Birth control and abortion rights were also major interests and she worked with the Abortion Law Reform Association from the end of the 1960s.

Hunkins Hallinan had great admiration for the vitality of the new women's liberation movement. She had sustained her links with America through visits and speaking trips, but in 1973 she bridged the divide between the first and second waves of the women's movement by contacting the recently established National Organization for Women (NOW) in America. In a letter to NOW she declared that her twenty years as chairman of the SPG meant that 'My very modest distinction is that I am the only American woman who has achieved the chairmanship of a national organisation (British) without having climbed to that office through marriage to an English title!' (SPG:M19 Fawcett Library). It should be remembered, however, that by 1971 the SPG's membership had fallen to a modest 122. In 1977 Hunkins Hallinan marched with the NOW demonstration in Washington in support of the Equal Rights Amendment (first proposed in 1923 by her friend Alice Paul, at whose 1977 memorial day service she delivered the address) and was guest of honour at the White House when President Carter signed a women's equality day proclamation.

The early professional rebuffs Hunkins Hallinan experienced undoubtedly contributed to what her son Mark described as 'a very forceful personality'. Her friend of fifty years Muriel Gray pointed out the contrast between her being 'tremendously courageous and very gutsy' and her 'very small, feminine and pretty' appearance. An SPG colleague recalled that 'She was a most energetic person and very determined. If she wanted to do a thing, she carried it through' (*Ham & High*). Although she wrote numerous articles for magazines and newspapers, as well as a children's history of the United States, her most significant publishing contribution was to edit *In her Own Right*, a 1968 SPG book on the successes and remaining problems of women's emancipation.

Hazel Hunkins Hallinan died, aged ninety-one, of respiratory failure at her home, 15B Belsize Park Gardens in north London on 17 May 1982. Her body was returned to Billings, Montana, for burial next to her parents and husband. CHERYL LAW

**Sources** M. Barrett, 'One woman's war', *She* (April 1968), 98 • *Sunday Times* (21 Sept 1969) • *The Times* (20 May 1982) • Women's Library, London, SPG/HHH/M7–M11;M19–23; SPG/HHH/N1–2, Six Point Group • *Ham & High* (28 May 1982) • D. Spender, *There's always been a women's movement this century* (1983) • d. cert. • K. Cullen-Dupont, *The encyclopedia of women's history in America* (1996) • O. Banks, *The biographical dictionary of British feminists*, 1 (1985) • *New York Times* (19 May 1982) • *Washington Post* (24 Aug 1977)

**Archives** Harvard U., Radcliffe Institute for Advanced Study • Women's Library, London

**Likenesses** photograph, repro. in Barrett, 'One woman's war' • photograph, repro. in *Sunday Times* • photographs, repro. in Spender, *There's always been a women's movement this century*

**Wealth at death** £131,100—in England and Wales: probate, 4 June 1982, *CGPLA Eng. & Wales*

**Halliwell, Henry** (1765–1835), classical scholar, son of William Halliwell, master of Burnley grammar school and incumbent of Holme, and his wife, Mary Holgate, was born at Burnley, Lancashire, on 25 August 1765. He was educated at his father's school and at Manchester grammar school (1780–83) before matriculating in 1783 at Brasenose College, Oxford, where he was nominated Hulmean exhibitioner in 1787, and graduated BA in 1786, MA in 1789, and BD in 1803. In 1790 he became fellow, and in 1796 dean and Hebrew lecturer of his college. He was an assistant chaplain of the Manchester collegiate church in 1794, and was presented to the very valuable living of Clayton-cum-Keymer, near Ditchling, Sussex, in 1803, when he resigned all his college offices. From a peculiarity in his gait he was known at Oxford as 'Dr Toe', and he was the subject of an epigram by Bishop Heber on his being jilted by a lady who married her footman. He was also the central object of a satire, entitled 'The Whippiad', by Heber, published in *Blackwood's Magazine* (54, 1843, 100–06). He was one of the scholars who assisted the Falconers in their edition of Strabo in 1807 [*see* Falconer, Thomas (1771–1839)], and he appears to have made an English translation of that work, which was not published. After his marriage on 6 September 1808 to Elizabeth Carlile (*d.* 1837) of Sunnyhill, near Bolton, he lived at Clayton, where he was long remembered as 'a hospitable parish priest of the old high church type', and as a singularly humane and benevolent man. Halliwell collected a good library and a large wine cellar. Shortly after his death more than a hundred dozen bottles of port were advertised for sale at his rectory. He was a short, stout, florid man of pronounced views and a strong opponent of Catholic emancipation. He refused to drink the loyal toast after the Act of Toleration of 1829. He died at his rectory on 15 January 1835, aged sixty-nine, and was buried in Clayton churchyard on the 20th. C. W. SUTTON, *rev.* RICHARD SMAIL

**Sources** J. F. Smith, ed., *The admission register of the Manchester School, with some notes of the more distinguished scholars*, 2, Chetham Society, 73 (1868), 247–9 • *N&Q*, 7 (1853), 393

**Wealth at death** £800 p.a. from living

**Halliwell, James Orchard**. *See* Phillipps, James Orchard Halliwell- (1820–1889).

**Halliwell, (Robert James) Leslie** (1929–1989), film buyer and encyclopaedist, was born on 23 February 1929 in Bolton, Lancashire, the youngest child by thirteen years and only son in the family of three children of James Halliwell, cotton spinner, of Bolton, and his wife, Lily Haslam. He won a scholarship to Bolton School, and after national service in the Royal Army Education Corps he went to St Catharine's College, Cambridge, where he gained a second class (division 1) in both parts of the English tripos (1951 and 1952).

Leslie Halliwell saw his first film at the age of four, and he spent his childhood going to the cinema, usually in the company of his mother. He claimed that at one time there were forty-seven cinemas within 5 miles of the centre of Bolton, and that he visited them all. At Cambridge, where he was editor of *Varsity*, he ran the university film society, and his first job after graduating was working as a journalist on *Picturegoer*. At the end of 1952 he took on the job of running two cinemas in Cambridge. In 1956 he became a trainee publicity executive for the Rank Organization in London, moving in 1958 to Southern Television as a film buyer, and in 1959 he joined Granada Television as a film researcher, where he devised the *Cinema* series before moving to buy films for Granada from other companies. In 1959 he married Ruth Porter, who had one son and one daughter from her previous marriage. She was the daughter of Samuel Edward Turner, clerk and Baptist minister, of Nottingham. The Halliwells had one son.

In 1968 Halliwell became film buyer for the whole independent television network (ITV), and in 1982 Jeremy Isaacs, head of the new television channel Channel 4, asked him to buy American films for Channel 4 as well. Isaacs described him as 'much more than a film buyer. Leslie Halliwell was a film buff, a walking encyclopaedia.' He visited Hollywood twice a year to search in the film libraries. At Channel 4 he was able to help schedule programmes, and he compiled very successful series such as *The British at War*, which he introduced himself. While he continued to buy for the other ITV companies, he earmarked interesting discoveries as 'obvious Channel 4 material', and his seasons of 'golden oldies', neglected films from the 1930s and 1940s, were very popular.

Halliwell was best-known for his reference books. *The Filmgoer's Companion*, the first comprehensive reference book of the cinema ever published, appeared in 1965, and revised editions appeared regularly thereafter. The first edition of *Halliwell's Film Guide*, with synopses and comments on 8000 films, came out in 1977. Revised annually, it had grown to 16,000 entries by the time of the seventh edition in 1988. *Halliwell's Teleguide* (later, with Philip Purser, *Halliwell's Television Companion*) was first published in 1979.

As well as compiling works of reference, Halliwell wrote about the cinema in such books as *The Clapperboard Book of the Cinema* (with G. Murray, 1975) and *Mountain of Dreams: the Golden Years of Paramount* (1965). In *Halliwell's Hundred* (1982) and its successor *Halliwell's Harvest* (1986) he considered some of his favourite films, claiming not that they were the greatest films ever made, or serious works of art, but that they all demonstrated an ability to entertain. In *The Dead that Walk* (1986) he wrote about horror films, with essays on films about Dracula, Frankenstein, and mummies, in which he argued that *Bride of Frankenstein* (1935) was the best horror film ever released. He also wrote a history of comedy, *Double Take and Fade Away* (1987). In the 1980s he published three books of short stories, wrote his autobiography, and also a novel, *Return to Shangri-La* (1987), a sequel to one of his favourite films, *Lost Horizon* (1937). After his retirement from ITV in 1986 he wrote a weekly television column in the *Daily Mail*.

Halliwell's work was directed at the general public, the middlebrow audience which went to the cinema for entertainment, and not at 'the egghead student of film culture who shuns commercial entertainments in favour of middle-European or Oriental masterpieces which never got further than the National Film Theatre' (L. Halliwell, 'Introduction', *The Filmgoer's Companion*, 1965). While he did not ignore foreign films, they did not appeal to him. Brought up in the 1930s and 1940s, he always regarded these years as the golden age of the cinema, the age when films were made in the studio in black and white. He liked very little that was produced after 1950, and lamented the demise of the old studio crafts and film techniques. He found modern films crude and violent, and the language offensive, and he felt that the wit and style of the early movies were lacking. He dedicated *Halliwell's Harvest* to the proposition that art should not be despised because it is popular.

Halliwell's most distinctive physical feature was his very long chin, which he later covered with a beard. He died of cancer on 21 January 1989 in the Princess Alice Hospice, Esher, Surrey. At a memorial meeting at the National Film Theatre excerpts from some of his favourite films were shown, including *Citizen Kane* (1941), which he regarded as the greatest film ever made.

ANNE PIMLOTT BAKER, *rev.*

**Sources** *The Times* (23 Jan 1989) • L. Halliwell, *Seats in all parts: half a lifetime at the movies* (1985) • *The Independent* (23 Jan 1989) • *The Independent* (19 April 1989) • *WW*

**Likenesses** photograph, *c.*1980, Hult. Arch. • photograph, repro. in *The Times* • photograph (as young man), repro. in Halliwell, *Seats in all parts*

**Halloran** [O'Halloran], **Lawrence Hynes** (1766–1831), Church of England clergyman and writer, was apparently a native of Ireland (*GM*, 101.476). He became master of an academy at Alphington, near Exeter, where one of his pupils was the future master of the rolls Lord Gifford. Here he published *Odes, Poems, and Translations* (1790), and *Poems on Various Occasions* (1791), which included an 'Ode on the Proposed Visit of their Majesties to the City of Exeter'. In 1799 he installed himself in a vicarage in the curacy of Elm. When the bishop refused to license him as curate he set up a rival congregation and interrupted church services. It became clear that he had not been ordained, and he was finally arrested for debt and made to leave the area.

While living there, he published 'Lachrymae Hibernicae, or, The Genius of Erin's Complaint, a Ballad' which attacked Lord Hardwicke's role in the Irish union.

A few years later Halloran became chaplain in the Royal Navy. He published a charity sermon for 19 December 1797, in celebration of the naval victories. He was chaplain on board the *Britannia*, the vessel which carried the flag of Admiral the earl of Northesk, third in command at the battle of Trafalgar. During the battle itself Halloran, who had a very loud and clear voice, stood beside the commander and repeated the word of command through a speaking-trumpet after him. He soon published *A sermon on occasion of the victory off Trafalgar, delivered on board HMS Britannia at sea, 3 November 1805*, and 'The Battle of Trafalgar, a Poem' (1806).

Next Halloran was appointed rector of the public grammar school, Cape Town, and chaplain to the forces in South Africa. Here in 1810 a duel took place between two officers and at their court martial Halloran supported the accused parties and wrote their defence. As a result of his intervention Lieutenant-General the Hon. H. G. Grey ordered him to move to the remote outpost of Simonstown. Rather than do this he resigned his chaplaincy and took revenge by publishing a satire, *Cap-Abilities, or, South African Characteristics*, in 1811. At this the governor of the colony, the earl of Caledon, brought a suit against him. He was found guilty, sentenced to pay costs, and banished from the colony.

Halloran returned to England, where, preaching and teaching, he went back to his old ways, declaring himself a doctor in divinity. He introduced himself at Bath to the Revd Richard Warner. Warner described him as of 'striking but not prepossessing appearance' (2.292), but nevertheless employed him for some time until he heard rumours that he was an impostor. Asked for proof of his qualifications, Halloran could only produce papers for deacon's orders; evidence of his ordination as a priest and doctoral degree had (he said) been mislaid by a maidservant. They were never produced, and Halloran left Bath soon afterwards. Warner tells of how, two years later, he was found to be 'playing the same game, under a borrowed name' in Gloucestershire (2.296). He fled before being denounced as an impostor.

In 1818 Halloran was charged at the Old Bailey with forging a frank on a letter addressed to the rector whose church he was serving, 'by which the revenue was defrauded of 10*d*.'. At his trial he 'persisted in pleading guilty, because, he said, the only person who could establish his innocence was dead' and he observed that 'the charge would not have been brought against him, but for a subsequent quarrel with his Rector' (*GM*, 88.462). He was sentenced to seven years' transportation. The reporter, who called him, apparently without suspicion, 'a Doctor of Divinity', added that 'he has a large family' (ibid.), although no further information has been traced about his wife or children. He subsequently established a school at Sydney, New South Wales, which was very successful. He died in Sydney on 8 March 1831.

Besides the works noted, Halloran also wrote *The Female Volunteer* (a drama under the name of 'Philo-Nauticus') (1801) and 'Stanzas of Affectionate Regard to the Memory of Capt. Dawson of the Piedmontaise' (1812).

FRANCIS WATT, *rev.* S. C. BUSHELL

**Sources** *GM*, 1st ser., 101/2 (1831), 476–7 • *GM*, 1st ser., 88/2 (1818), 462 • R. Warner, *Literary recollections*, 2 vols. (1830), vol 2, pp. 292–8 • [J. Watkins and F. Shoberl], *A biographical dictionary of the living authors of Great Britain and Ireland* (1816) • D. Owen, 'James Yorke', *Report of the Society of the Friends of St George's and the descendants of the knights of the Garter*, 4/9 (1967–8), 379–80 • J. S. Crone, *A concise dictionary of Irish biography*, rev. edn (1937), 86

**Hallowell, Benjamin**. *See* Carew, Sir Benjamin Hallowell (1760–1834).

**Hallowes** [*née* Brailly], **Odette Marie Céline** (1912–1995), special operations officer and member of the FANY, was born on 28 April 1912 in Amiens, northern France, the only daughter in the family of three children of Gaston Brailly (*c*.1880–1918), banker, and his wife, Yvonne, *née* Quennchen (*c*.1880–1960). Her father, a sergeant in the French 52nd infantry, was killed at Verdun in October 1918. Her paternal grandfather would regularly take her to visit her father's grave and say 'In twenty years there will be another war … and you will have to do your duty as your father did' (private information). Odette was educated at the Convent of Ste Thérèse in Amiens and privately. In 1931 she married an Englishman engaged in the hotel trade, Roy Patrick Sansom (*c*.1911–1957). A daughter, Françoise, was born in 1932. In 1933 they moved to Britain, where Lili (*b*. 1934) and Marianne (*b*. 1936) were born. At the outbreak of war Roy Sansom was called up and Odette moved with her daughters to Somerset. In the early spring of 1942 she responded to a radio appeal for photographs of France. She was invited for interview at the War Office, where Selwyn Jepson, impressed by her strength of character, invited her to join the Special Operations Executive (SOE), set up in 1940 in response to Winston Churchill's directive to 'set Europe ablaze' by the training and supplying of local resistance groups in all zones of war.

Odette joined the First Aid Nursing Yeomanry (FANY), as did most female SOE agents, and was trained in self-defence, Morse code, map reading, shooting, and how to resist interrogation. In November 1942, leaving her daughters in school, carefully dressed in French clothes, with new French fillings in her teeth, and carrying forged French papers, she was landed by small boat near Cassis. Code-named Lise, she was to cross to occupied France to join a resistance circuit in Auxerre. She was met by Peter Morland Churchill (*d*. 1972), code-named Raoul. On 11 November, in response to the allied invasion of north Africa, the Nazis invaded Vichy France. Churchill persuaded SOE in London to allow Odette to stay as his courier, first in Cannes, before moving to St Jorioz, near Annecy, in February 1943, together with Adolphe Rabinovitch ('Arnaud'), their radio operator. On 16 April, betrayed by a double agent, Odette and Churchill were arrested, Rabinovitch escaped. He was captured on another mission and was executed at Rawicz in 1944. Odette, silent in the face of very harsh treatment by the

**Odette Marie Céline Hallowes (1912–1995)**, by unknown photographer

Gestapo, including months of solitary confinement, protected Rabinovitch, her French colleagues, and Francis Cammaerts ('Roger'), newly arrived in France, who was to run one of the most successful circuits of the war. She also protected Churchill by persuading the Germans that he was related to Winston Churchill.

Odette was condemned to death on two counts, as a Frenchwoman guilty of crimes under German law and as a British spy. 'You must take your pick, gentlemen. I can only die once.' In May 1944 she was sent to Germany, where she ended up in Ravensbrück camp, north of Berlin. There she was again kept in solitary confinement for some months, close to the punishment block, where she was an unseen witness to the brutality of the prison regime: the beatings, the executions, the rumble of carts taking the previous night's dead to the nearby crematorium. Suffering from tuberculosis, she was eventually moved to the camp hospital, and survived execution orders issued by Berlin in early 1945. Fellow SOE agents Violette Szabo and Denise Bloch of FANY, and Lilian Rolfe and Cecily LeFort of the Women's Auxiliary Air Force (WAAF), were murdered. In April the camp commander, Fritz Sühren, still believing Odette to be a Churchill, tried to save his own skin by driving her to the American lines. On arrival she denounced him. She gave evidence against him and several of the camp staff at the Nüremberg trials. Sühren was hanged. Odette was made MBE in 1945, and in August 1946 she was the first woman to be awarded the George Cross. In 1949 a book by Jerrad Tickell, *Odette*, appeared, followed by a film of the same name. Odette co-operated with both projects, not for her own glory but from a sense of responsibility to her murdered colleagues: 'My comrades, who did far more and suffered more profoundly, are not here to speak. Because of this I speak for them' (*The Independent*, 17 March 1995).

Odette was divorced from Roy Sansom in 1946 and on 15 February 1947 she married Peter Churchill. Churchill, the son of William Algernon Churchill, consular official, was by then a captain in the intelligence corps. He was later a writer and estate agent. They divorced in 1955 and on 6 January the following year Odette married Geoffrey Macleod Hallowes (*b.* 1918), wine and spirit shipper, son of Edward Price Hallowes, wine and spirit shipper. Geoffrey Hallowes had served with SOE in France as a Jedburgh.

Odette was a petite, light-haired woman, vividly attractive and always immaculately dressed, whose air of fragility belied her great inner strength. It is a measure of the fame she achieved that she was known simply as 'Odette GC'. She became a vice-president of the FANY in 1967. She was a prominent member of the Victoria Cross and George Cross Association, a founder vice-president of the Woman of the Year luncheon, vice-president of the Military Medallist League, an honorary member of St Dunstan's Ex-Prisoner-of-War Association, and president of 282 air cadet squadron. She died on 13 March 1995 at her home, Rosedale, 8 Eriswell Road, Walton-on-Thames, Surrey, of cardiac arrest following broncho-pneumonia, and was buried at Burvale cemetery, Walton-on-Thames. She was survived by her husband, Geoffrey Hallowes, and the three daughters of her first marriage. She is commemorated on the FANY war memorial at St Paul's Church, Knightsbridge, London, where the names of the dead SOE women agents are listed and where she laid a wreath on remembrance Sunday every year. On her plaque is written: 'Here she laid violets, transforming into service the pain of her survival'. Her medals are in the Imperial War Museum, London. LYNETTE BEARDWOOD

**Sources** Duke of York's Headquarters, London, First Aid Nursing Yeomanry (PRVC) archives · Special Operations Executive (SOE) archives · J. Tickell, *Odette* (1949) · C. Sanders, *Odette Churchill* (1989) · *WWW*, *1991–5* · *The Times* (17 March 1995) · *The Independent* (17 March 1995) · personal knowledge (2004) · private information (2004) [Geoffrey Hallowes] · m. certs. [Peter Churchill, Geoffrey Hallowes]

**Archives** IWM | Women's Transport Service (FANY), Duke of York's Headquarters, London | SOUND IWM

**Likenesses** photograph, 1947, priv. coll. · two photographs, 1947–8, First Aid Nursing Yeomanry (Princess Royal's Volunteer Corps) · photograph, repro. in *The Independent* · photograph, repro. in *The Independent* · photograph, repro. in *The Times* · photograph, IWM [*see illus.*] · photographs, Hult. Arch.

**Hallpike, Charles Skinner** (1900–1979), neuro-otologist, was born on 19 July 1900 in Murree, India, the son of Frank Robert Hallpike (1870–1934), a jeweller, and Rosamund Helen, *née* Skinner (1873–1946), granddaughter of James Skinner (1778–1841), founder of Skinner's Horse light cavalry regiment. Educated at St Paul's School, London, he entered Guy's Hospital medical school, London, in 1919 with an arts scholarship, and was awarded the Beany prize in pathology; he qualified MRCS LRCP in 1924 and graduated MB BS in 1926. He became MRCP in 1926 (FRCP, 1945) and the FRCS in 1931. The experience gained as house surgeon to the aural department at Guy's stimulated Hallpike's interest in the ear and subsequently led him in 1929 to become the Bernhard Baron research fellow in the newly opened Ferens Institute of Otology at the Middlesex Hospital, London. Two travelling scholarships (the Duveen travelling studentship of the University of London, 1930, and the Rockefeller travelling fellowship, 1931) took him to the United States, Canada, and Europe. His visit to Karl Wittmaack's laboratory in Hamburg led him to establish the first temporal bone microscopy unit in the UK, at the Ferens Institute; from there, with Hugh Cairns, he first described in 1938 the histopathology of Ménière's disease (*Journal of Laryngology and Otology*, 53, 1938, 625–55) which was to establish Hallpike's international reputation. From 1937 to 1940 he was Fullerton research fellow of the Royal Society. On 18 July 1935 he married Barbara Lee Anderson (*b.* 1901), daughter of Charles Torr Anderson, a brewer; they had two sons, one of whom became a neurologist, and a daughter, Janet, who died in 1966.

Hallpike developed Perthes' disease in early childhood, and this disability debarred him from service in the Second World War. Instead he became a member of the scientific staff of the Medical Research Council (MRC), the flying personnel research committee of the Air Ministry (1938–1955) and the military research committee. He advised on noise prevention, missile effects, and the development of body armour. In 1940 he was appointed assistant aural surgeon, and in 1944, with the support of Dr E. A. Carmichael and Sir Edward Mellanby, aural physician and director of the MRC otological research unit at the National Hospital for Nervous Diseases, Queen Square, London. Here he worked on the development of the Medresco hearing aid; the 'peep show' technique for measuring deafness in young children whereby the child was conditioned to respond to auditory stimuli and was rewarded with an illuminated picture seen within a darkened box; and the definition of a number of pathological entities previously classified collectively as aural vertigo. With E. Fitzgerald in 1942 he described the bithermal caloric test in which they compared the 20 second irrigation of water, at 7 °C above and below body temperature, into the external auditory meatus in a supine subject, with the head raised by 30°, in order to bring the lateral semicircular canal into the vertical plane. The duration of the resulting nystagmus was measured and compared. The technique not only allowed identification of the affected ear in unilateral vestibular damage (canal paresis), but also was able to show directional preponderance, which is seen in unilateral lesions of the vestibular nuclei and central connections. This was an important new finding (*Brain*, 65, 1125–37). In 1948, with his colleagues Margaret Dix and Derrick Hood, Hallpike demonstrated that loudness recruitment, a phenomenon whereby the loudness of sounds presented to the affected ear increases more rapidly with increasing sound intensity than in the normal ear, was due to damage to the nerve endings in the cochlea (*Proceedings of the Royal Society of Medicine*, 41, 516–26). Hallpike's team established the international reputation of British neuro-otology. Hallpike was also ENT consultant to University College Hospital, London, from 1948 to 1952, and on his retirement in 1965 he returned to the Ferens Institute as director of research until 1968.

Hallpike's classical education and knowledge of languages, in particular German, contributed to his success as a researcher and innovator. He published 241 papers and was an inveterate inventor, using his knowledge of precision engineering. His inventions ranged from a rotating chair for vestibular testing via an apparatus for sectioning the temporal bone, to a monocular ear microscope. (The latter was apparently adapted by poultry farmers for sexing day-old chicks.) He was a perfectionist, and a man of the highest integrity, dogged and determined, loyal and kind-hearted. He inspired dedication and loyalty in his successful research team. This success was won only by the sheer determination of Hallpike to convince his clinical colleagues that the science of neuro-otology was an integral part of clinical neurology. The distinction, rare for an otologist, of being elected fellow of the Royal Society (1956) was acknowledged by the then senior physician with the words: 'Well, Charles, I suppose we will need to take you seriously now.' He was the first audiological physician in the UK at a time when this specialism was not formally recognized. His physical disability, which necessitated the use of crutches, did not deter him from competitive sport: as an expert rifle shot he captained the Public Schools' Veterans' team at Bisley and won many individual trophies. He played the violin and taught himself the piano, enjoyed a game of billiards, and in retirement grew prize-winning roses.

Hallpike won the Gamble (1934, 1947) and Dalby (1941, 1958) prizes of the Royal Society of Medicine, the Bárány medal (University of Uppsala) in 1958 and the Guyot medal (University of Groningen) in 1959. He was appointed CBE in 1958. A joint founder of the Bárány Society in 1960, Hallpike gave his last address to a meeting of the society in London in 1977. He was president of the section of otology of the Royal Society of Medicine in 1965 (Hughling Jackson lectureship and medal, 1967) and a member of the Collegium Oto-rhino-laryngologicum Amicitiae Sacrum (Shambaugh prizewinner, 1955). Hallpike died of pneumonia following a stroke on 26 September 1979 at the South Western Hospital, Southampton; he was cremated at Boscombe, Hampshire. His wife survived him. NEIL WEIR

**Sources** E. H. Cornelius and S. F. Taylor, *Lives of the fellows of the Royal College of Surgeons of England, 1974–1982* (1988) • D. Whitteridge and P. A. Merton, *Memoirs FRS*, 30 (1984), 283–95 • *BMJ* (1 Dec 1979), 1444 • *The Lancet* (13 Oct 1979), 805 • *Journal of Laryngology and Otology*, 94 (1980), 801–4 • Munk, *Roll* • m. cert. • private information (2004) • *CGPLA Eng. & Wales* (1979)

**Archives** National Hospital for Neurology and Neurosurgery, London, Hallpike Room | Wellcome L., letters to Sir Edward Mellanby

**Likenesses** Tunbridge, photograph, 1956, priv. coll.

**Wealth at death** £59,799: probate, 15 Oct 1979, *CGPLA Eng. & Wales*

**Halls, Arthur Norman** [Michael] (1915–1970), civil servant, was born at 39 Crouch Hill, Islington, London, on 6 October 1915, the son of Sidney Edward John Halls, a milk carrier, and his wife, Clara Olive Marlow. He was educated at the Stationers' Company School. Of medium build, with black, crinkly hair and black-rimmed spectacles, he entered customs and excise in 1936, meanwhile studying for an LLB as an evening student at King's College, London. He moved to the Inland Revenue as an assistant inspector in 1939, where he returned after the war. On 10 May 1941 he married Marjorie Florence Claysmith (*b.* 1918/19), who later worked in the Lord Chancellor's Department. A pre-war Territorial Army officer in the Royal Artillery, Halls rose to lieutenant-colonel, was at Dunkirk and Normandy, and was made an MBE (military) in 1945. He became a member of the Army and Navy Club, and spent much of his leisure time with contemporary and younger territorials, in particular to administer welfare funds for those in need.

Michael Halls—as he preferred to be known—entered the administrative class of the civil service in 1947, as an assistant principal in the Board of Trade. In 1948 the permanent secretary, John Henry Woods, prophesied that he would eventually become principal private secretary at 10 Downing Street. From 1948 until 1950 he was private secretary to Harold Wilson, the president of the Board of Trade. During the 1950s he had administrative responsibility for the decentralization of the motor car industry to Scotland, Wales, and Merseyside, and then became assistant secretary dealing with East–West trade. In 1965 he was appointed under-secretary in charge of the distribution of industry division. He was allegedly unpopular within the Board of Trade, and seen as an over-promoted sycophant, but it was recorded in an additional note by 'H. W.', appended to his *Times* obituary, that in his particular fields, Halls 'was acknowledged as one of the greatest authorities in the Government service' (*The Times*, 4 April 1970).

H. W. was Harold Wilson, who 'had sung [Hall's] praises continually from the days … at the Board of Trade' (Williams, 136), and after the general election of 1966 Halls became principal private secretary at 10 Downing Street. Senior officials in Whitehall felt that he was not big enough for the job, but Wilson explained to Sir Lawrence Helsby, the head of the civil service, that the appointment was not an 'intellectual accolade [but] the means of ensuring that my office will work'. 'No. 10', Wilson insisted, was 'an office, not a Government Department' (Ziegler, 214). Halls showed his commitment to the prime minister when Marcia Williams, Wilson's personal political secretary, complained of the Conservative attitudes of the secretaries in 10 Downing Street; Halls made their lives a misery until some of them sought a transfer (Haines, 167). But this belied his characteristic warmth, generosity, and courtesy.

Halls told colleagues how much he enjoyed working for Wilson. R. H. S. Crossman wrote that he

> went in with Harold and was completely his man. He was also naturally attuned to Harold, with the same inhibitions, the same limitations of taste. Harold doesn't really like literature or art, the theatre or the opera. He prefers golf and the telly and the Cup Final and if he hadn't been a civil servant in the war he would have been a Territorial. They are both of the educated petty bourgeoisie. (Crossman, *Diaries*, 3.906)

Both smoked a pipe. These cultural similarities were even reflected in government policy; Barbara Castle wrote that part of Wilson's passion for the Fulton report on the civil service, published in 1968, was that 'he said the classics boys have always been against him and that he prefers the earthy, elementary school types like Michael Halls' (Hennessy, *Whitehall*, 200). Indeed, when Helsby said that appointing Halls would be improper use of prime ministerial patronage, Wilson replied that any patronage which did exist had to be exercised by him, and not by 'a small, self-perpetuating oligarchy of Permanent Secretaries' (Ziegler, 213). This conflict offers a significant background to attempts to modernize the civil service—and, arguably, shows why such attempts failed.

Halls himself may have been influenced by this clash, as civil service reform became his main preoccupation. He became part of the 'inner circle' working on the proposals, with Lord Armstrong, head of the civil service, and Lord Crowther-Hunt. Eventually, however, Halls criticized submissions from the Civil Service Department as insufficiently radical, and had to report to Wilson that Fulton was losing steam, thus demonstrating that even if 10 Downing Street can be both an office and a policy-making department, its policy-making powers then were more limited than they had become at the turn of the twenty-first century. On the day of Halls's death, the prime minister's box contained the last of his reports on civil service reform.

Hall was a loyal civil servant, and perhaps too loyal to Wilson. Said to be a slow reader of official papers and 'befuddled by complex issues' (Ziegler, 214), he was overwhelmed by the work and 'to make up, so it was said, for his difficulty in coping, he worked long hours' (Pimlott, 519). He died in London at Lewisham Hospital on 3 April 1970 after a coronary thrombosis; his funeral took place at St Mark's, Plumstead, five days later. Wilson later wrote that neither his obituary nor his address at the memorial service to Halls, held at St Margaret's, Westminster, on 29 April 1970, could 'begin to assess [Halls's] dedicated contribution to the civil service and to me personally' (Wilson, 974).

Halls's widow, Marjorie, sued the state for £50,000, claiming that his 'death was partly due to the tantrums [he] had to put up with' (Pimlott, 646); she also felt that 'concealing [Marcia Williams's children] and other matters concerned with them had contributed' (Dorril and Ramsay, 250). In 1974 her claims were finally rejected. Wilson put it that Halls's 'unremitting devotion to work, at all hours of the day and night … critically contributed. He died a few weeks before he was due to be posted to a still more challenging post' (Wilson, 684).

DANIEL CREWE

**Sources** H. W., *The Times* (4 April 1970); see also (9 April 1970), (29–30 April 1970) · *WWW*, *1961–70* · P. Hennessy, *Whitehall* (1989) ·

M. Williams, *Inside number 10* (1972) • H. Wilson, *The labour government, 1964–1970* (1971) • P. Hennessy, *The prime minister* (2000) • J. Haines, *The politics of power* (1977) • private information (2004) • R. H. S. Crossman, *The diaries of a cabinet minister*, 3 vols. (1975–7) • B. Pimlott, *Harold Wilson* (1992) • S. Dorril and R. Ramsay, *Smear!* (1991) • A. Morgan, *Harold Wilson* (1992) • P. Kellner and Lord Crowther-Hunt, *The civil servants* (1980) • J. Garrett, *Managing the civil service* (1980) • B. Headey, *British cabinet ministers* (1974) • *CGPLA Eng. & Wales* (1970) • m. cert. • b. cert. • d. cert. • P. Ziegler, *Wilson: the authorised life of Lord Wilson of Rievaulx* (1993)

**Wealth at death** £15,451: probate, 9 July 1970, *CGPLA Eng. & Wales*

**Halls, John James** (1776–1853), painter, was born at Romford, Essex, and baptized there on 16 May 1776, the eldest of the six children of James Halls and his wife, Amelia Garnett (*d.* 1813). In the 1780s the family moved to Colchester. Halls, says Farington, 'practised drawing and painting from a Child', and was taught by 'Sturt of Colchester' (Farington, *Diary*, 4.1216). Aged fifteen, he exhibited a landscape at the Royal Academy. At the end of 1798 he settled as a professional artist in London. In September 1802 Halls went to Paris with Henry Fuseli RA and Joseph Farington RA for six weeks, to study the collections brought together by Napoleon. Fuseli remarked of him that he 'sees, observes, says little, laughs more' (J. Knowles, ed., *The Life and Writings of Henry Fuseli*, 3 vols., 1831, 1.253). Between 1798 and 1827, he exhibited annually at the academy, less frequently at the British Institution, mainly portraits, but with the occasional history painting, such as *Fingal Assaulting the Spirit of Loda* (1798), *Lot's Wife* (1802), *Hero and Leander* (1808), and *Danae* (1811). *Christ Raising the Daughter of Jairus* (Museum Resource Centre, Colchester Museums) won a premium of 200 guineas when it was exhibited at the British Institution in 1813, the committee being 'all struck with it as one of the greatest efforts that has been made in England, not for a young artist, but for any artist' (Halls, 1.369). Perhaps his most successful effort was *A Witch—'but in a Sieve I'll thither Sail'—from Macbeth*, which was engraved in mezzotint in 1807 by Charles Turner, as was also his *Charles Kean as Richard III* (exh. RA, 1815). His portrait of Lord Denman (exh. RA, 1819) hangs in the National Portrait Gallery, London. On 2 December 1819 Halls married Maria Anne (*bap.* 1795, *d.* 1877), daughter of Baker John *Sellon, serjeant-at-law.

In 1813 Halls completed a stained glass window for Lichfield Cathedral, a commission obtained through his close friend the famous explorer in Abyssinia and British consul in Egypt, Henry Salt FRS. In 1834, in fulfilment of a youthful pact with Salt that the survivor should write the other's biography, he published *The Life and Correspondence of Henry Salt*. He had already, in 1831, completed and published Salt's unfinished editing of *The Life and Adventures of Nathaniel Pearce*. He had moved to Hampstead in the 1830s, and he died there at his home, Ivy Cottage, Lower Heath, on 22 July 1853, of a long-standing kidney disease.

L. H. Cust, *rev.* Peta Rée

**Sources** J. J. Halls, *The life and correspondence of Henry Salt*, 2nd edn, 2 vols. (1834) • Graves, *RA exhibitors* • Graves, *Artists* • *IGI* • census returns for Hampstead, 1851 • *GM*, 2nd ser., 40 (1853), 323 • d. cert.

**Hallum** [Hallam], **Robert** (*d.* 1417), bishop of Salisbury, was born probably in the 1360s.

**Family and early career** Hallum's origins are obscure: he has been associated with the Hallum family of Warrington, Lancashire (a connection reinforced by a bequest to the church there), but the link is unconfirmed. If the Kentish lands that later passed to his heirs were part of his own inheritance, this might suggest an alternative area of origin. The family was presumably armigerous: arms of sable, a cross engrailed ermine, in dexter chief a crescent argent, have been ascribed to him. His will names a brother, Richard, and gives a Thomas Hallum (elsewhere described as *domicellus*) as a residuary heir. Other kin can be identified, although the precise relationships are not stated. These include Alice Kirby, whose first husband was Sir Thomas Stonor. In 1422 Gilbert Hallum, clerk, was described as Robert Hallum's cousin and heir, having inherited from him properties at Horton Kirby and elsewhere in Kent: he is presumably the Gilbert Hallum whom the bishop appointed a prebendary of Salisbury.

Hallum was educated at Oxford, being described as a master by October 1387, and becoming a bachelor of both laws by March 1400 and doctor of canon law in 1403. In that year he was appointed chancellor of the university, a post he held until 1406. In January 1406 he was named as a JP for Oxford, in his capacity as chancellor of the university.

The earliest benefice that Hallum is known to have held was the wardenship of the free chapel of St Lawrence, at Halling, Kent, which he exchanged in March 1388 for a prebend in Exeter Cathedral. The Rochester episcopal registers no longer survive to indicate when he acquired the post. He later held a succession of other appointments, from rectories to prebends. Notable were prebends at Chichester, Salisbury, and York, and the archdeaconry of Canterbury (7 April 1400). His involvement with ecclesiastical administration centred on Canterbury diocese. Referred to as a 'familiar clerk' of Archbishop William Courtenay in the autumn of 1386, he had already accompanied the latter on a visitation of Exeter diocese in April 1384, and acted as his principal registrar from June 1389 to March 1394. Courtenay named him as an executor of his will in 1396 (also leaving him his copy of the *Decretals* and a *Sext*): the task of administration lingered for some years, and included involvement in the confirmation of Courtenay's collegiate foundation at Maidstone in Kent. In 1399 Hallum became an auditor of causes in the court of Canterbury, a post abandoned when he was appointed chancellor for Archbishop Thomas Arundel (*d.* 1414) by April 1400. That post he still held in June 1406.

The archdeaconry of Canterbury gave Hallum a role not merely within the diocese, but in the province at large. Indeed, his main concern may have been on the wider stage: in July 1401 he received papal permission to hold archidiaconal visitations by proxy, and receive procurations in cash. Nevertheless, concern with the prerogatives of his archdeaconry is shown by the complaint that he made to Arundel at some point in the early 1400s, possibly about 1404, against the bishop of St Asaph, who had been enthroned without regard to the traditional rights of the archdeacon of Canterbury (exercised in person or by proxy) to perform that ceremony. The context for this complaint is as obscure as its dating: John Trevor had actually held the see since 1395, so the protest seems unduly tardy, unless somehow connected with Trevor's defection to Owain GlynDŵr's revolt against Henry IV. Hallum's administrative experience was further enhanced with appointments in connection with the *sede vacante* governance of the see of Rochester in March 1400 (when he was formally nominated as vicar-general and official) and from April to May 1404. In October 1402 he was appointed prolocutor for the lower clergy in convocation.

Robert Hallum's career was very firmly ecclesiastical. Although he is named as a king's clerk in May 1400, there is no other sign of involvement in secular administration (the Robert Halom who appears as deputy collector of Irish customs in 1391 was probably someone else). Nevertheless, he was not beneath royal notice, as the mention of him as king's clerk occurs in the appointment to the commission to oversee the affairs of Bermondsey Priory, dilapidated by misrule. The commission was still overseeing the priory in 1410, and Hallum was still a member.

**The archbishopric of York** Hallum's extensive ecclesiastical and university activity was bound to bring rewards, although the first attempt to secure a bishopric for him (at London in 1404, after the death of Robert Braybrooke, with the support of Archbishop Arundel) was checked by Henry IV's equally unsuccessful support for Thomas Langley. His second proposed promotion, to the archbishopric of York in 1406, was at the instigation of Pope Gregory XII (of the Roman line during the contemporary schism in the papacy), who presumably noticed him as a result of activities at the curia. (Precisely when he went to Rome is unclear: he may have left in 1404, or possibly not until 1406.) Hallum's provision to York on 14 May 1406 (after the quashing of the election of Henry IV's candidate, again Thomas Langley) was the response of Pope Innocent VII to the execution of Archbishop Richard Scrope in the preceding year, but it proved ineffective as Henry IV opposed the appointment.

Hallum's own role in this manoeuvre is obscure: he can be seen as a papal puppet, or as the tool of forces opposing Henry IV in England. It is not impossible that he simply seized an opportunity to promote himself, catching everyone in England unawares. The period of Hallum's nominal tenure of York must have been a lean time, since although prevented from acquiring York, his prebends and other benefices were treated as vacant by both the papacy and the crown. Hallum evidently considered himself the legitimate holder of York, and used the archiepiscopal title, although he continued to seal documents with his archidiaconal seal until May 1408. The seriousness of his intended promotion is also attested by his episcopal ordination by Pope Innocent. (Although the consecration is usually ascribed to Gregory XII in Siena, after the later translation to Salisbury, Hallum dated a letter of November 1406 in the first year of his consecration.)

**Bishop of Salisbury** Despite his use of the title, Hallum was destined not to become *de facto* archbishop. Henry IV wanted York for his own latest candidate, Henry Bowet (*d.* 1423), and on 7 October 1407, while still at the curia, and as part of a small-scale shuffle among the English bishoprics, Hallum was translated to Salisbury, replacing Nicholas Bubwith (*d.* 1424). Royal approval was confirmed with the grant of temporalities on 1 December. His profession of obedience to Canterbury was offered on 28 March 1408, with spiritualities being released on the same date. He was enthroned on 10 September following, and thereafter held the bishopric until his death. Contemporaries alleged that his move from York was tinged with simony, Gregory XII appointing Bowet to please Henry IV and in return for payment, despite having promised Hallum that he would not be removed from York; but there is no supporting evidence for this. Nevertheless, Hallum's experiences at Rome when 'archbishop' may have induced a sense of anti-curial bitterness, and have been suggested as the reason for the hostility to cardinals that marks some of his later activities (although reportedly it was the cardinals who opposed his demotion from York, a stance which becomes more understandable if he had actually been consecrated).

The register of his tenure of Salisbury reveals Hallum as a competent and efficient, if undynamic, administrator, confronting the difficulties that were the norm for the contemporary church, including occasional outbreaks of Lollardy. His episcopal status at Salisbury carried with it all the temporal responsibilities of the office, including seigneurial oversight of Salisbury town itself. Unlike some of his precursors and successors Hallum seemingly maintained good relations with the townspeople. In 1412 he granted licence for the town guild to acquire lands to the value of £40 a year, as part of the process whereby the burgesses established a corporate identity. He was remembered as a major benefactor throughout the fifteenth century on the town's bede roll. He apparently remained aloof from the factionalism of the last years of Henry IV's reign, although he attended parliaments regularly when he was in the country, apart from the session of April–May 1410, and appears occasionally in the royal council.

**Conciliar envoy and royal councillor** The appointment to Salisbury did not prove to be consignment to a backwater: it was as bishop of Salisbury that Hallum became most active internationally, through his participation in the councils of Pisa (1409) and Constance (1414–18) which eventually reunited the divided Western church. He was appointed as an envoy for the Canterbury province to Pisa in January 1409, reaching that city on 24 April. On 30 April he preached to the assembly, declaring the determination of Henry IV and the English church to work for union by all possible means. The continuation of his links with Oxford University was demonstrated when he presented to the council the lengthy programme for reform contained in Richard Ullerston's *Petitiones quoad reformationem ecclesie militantis*—a work that had originally been dedicated to him. Although he does not appear as a particularly prominent actor in the events at Pisa, on 10 May he assisted Simon de Cramaud in the promulgation of decrees asserting the council's competence to act on the schism, and withdrawing obedience from the then rival pontiffs, Benedict XIII (*r.* 1394–1423) and Gregory XII.

Back from Pisa by 15 October 1409, Hallum reverted to his role as diocesan and national church figure. In March 1410 he was among the imposing group assembled for the heresy trial of John Badby. On 6 June 1411 Pope John XXIII (*r.* 1410–15, successor to Alexander V elected at Pisa) nominated Hallum to the cardinalate. At the time this would have required a move to the curia, something Henry IV apparently did not desire. Royal intervention quashed the promotion, whether to Hallum's relief or chagrin is impossible to determine. The king (or possibly Prince Henry and his supporters, who then controlled the government) alleged that he could not spare Hallum from governmental duties, and it may be that about this time he was more active politically: the scant evidence of his role in the royal council appears at this period. In 1412 the bishop was active in the revival of the campaign for the canonization of his predecessor, St Osmund (although that did not reach a successful conclusion at this point). He also seems to have promoted the use of Sarum as the liturgical standard in the province of Canterbury. In 1413 he received a commission from Pope John to visit and oversee the nunneries of Nuneaton and Amesbury, of the order of Fontevrault, which because of distance and Anglo-French wars could not be visited by the abbess of Fontevrault herself.

**The Council of Constance** On 20 October 1414 Hallum was once again called upon to represent the Canterbury province and now the English crown too, at a general council, at Constance. He reached the city on 21 January 1415. There he was deeply involved in the search for ecclesiastical reunification and church reform, opposing Pope John XXIII to his face, acting as leader of the English nation, and preaching to the assembly on a number of occasions. Once the council had forced John XXIII from the scene (in March 1415) and taken to itself the task of reorganizing the church, Hallum became identified as one of the small coterie who worked with the emperor-elect, Sigismund, against the ambitions of the cardinals—so much so that in August 1417 the cardinals demanded that Hallum be removed from the reform commission because of his notorious hostility to them. The conciliar diarist Guillaume Fillastre placed the bishop of Salisbury among the gang of four who were said to dominate proceedings at Constance, whom he identified by the acronym MARS, formed from the initial letters of their sees—Hallum was the 'S', the others being Bartolomeo Capra, archbishop of Milan, Jean Mauroux, patriarch of Antioch, and Johann Wallenrode, archbishop of Riga. Hallum delivered several notable speeches and sermons to the council, among them the welcoming address on Sigismund's return from foreign negotiations on 27 January 1417.

Texts survive of Hallum's sermons delivered on 15 January and 8 December 1415. He was a member of the committee set up to investigate charges against Benedict XIII (the then pope of the Avignon line), which eventually led to that pontiff's formal deposition. He was also one of the panel of four general judges appointed in March 1415 to settle cases within the council. In June 1417 allegations that on the basis of that judicial authority he had been party to the issue of a commission that would lead to the arrest of cardinals opposing Sigismund resulted in a considerable furore, although Hallum denied knowledge of the document.

Hallum's work for ecclesiastical reunion and reform accompanied diplomatic activity on behalf of Henry V; but he did not live to see the council achieve its goal. On 23 August 1417 he made his will, in Gottlieben Castle near Constance, and died there on 4 September. Two months later the council elected Martin V (*r.* 1417–31) as pope of a church effectively reunified. Hallum was buried on 5 September in Constance Cathedral, at the foot of the steps leading to the high altar. His impressive memorial brass is still there. His exequies were performed on 13 September, the eulogy being delivered by Richard Flemming (*d.* 1431), in the presence of Sigismund and numerous important members of the council. His death may have been opportune: Fleming's oration signalled a marked change in official English policy with regard to the council, so making it appear that Hallum had been a somewhat intransigent adherent to the line previously taken by English delegates, which was one of insistence on church reform before the election of a new pope.

**Bequests and reputation** Hallum's will is mainly a list of personal bequests and arrangements for the payment of his household until they return to England. He left copes to Salisbury Cathedral, with two books, seeking celebrations for himself, his parents, archbishops Courtenay and Arundel, and his friends Nicholas Braybrook and John Godewyk. His lands, after the deaths of those who received a life interest, were to be sold or incorporated as a chantry, to support scholars. (This may not have been implemented: there is no evidence that a chantry was established, and some at least of his lands remained within the family.) According to the inventory, priests were provided out of the estate for one year each at Daresbury, Cheshire, and Warrington, which also received a vestment and a contribution to its fabric fund. The will was proved in Constance on 10 September, although Hallum's affairs were not tidied up in England until late 1419.

Despite his busyness, Hallum leaves few indicators of his personality or personal life. He seems to have been capable of real friendship, using his patronage over prebends at Salisbury to promote old Oxford colleagues. No works by him are known, although he was co-sponsor with Nicholas Bubwith of a Latin version of Dante's *Divina commedia*, prepared by Giovanni di Serravalle during the course of the Council of Constance. Cardinal Fillastre, writing his journal at Constance and on the receiving end of Hallum's opposition, considered him arrogant. In contrast to that criticism, his self-image may be reflected in his own version of his episcopal title: in correspondence he frequently called himself not bishop of Salisbury, but 'ecclesie Sarum servus humilis et minister'—'humble servant and minister of the church of Salisbury'.

R. N. SWANSON

**Sources** *The register of Robert Hallum, bishop of Salisbury, 1407–17*, ed. J. M. Horn, CYS, 72 (1982) • I. J. Churchill, *Canterbury administration: the administrative machinery of the archbishopric of Canterbury*, 2 vols. (1933) • R. G. Davies, 'After the execution of Archbishop Scrope: Henry IV, the papacy, and the English episcopate, 1405–8', *Bulletin of the John Rylands University Library*, 59 (1976–7), 40–74 • J. Vincke, 'Acta concilii Pisani', *Römische Quartalschrift*, 46 (1938), 81–331 • H. von der Hardt, *Magnum oecumenicum Constantiense concilium*, 6 vols. (1697–1700) • *CPR* • *CEPR letters*, vols. 4–7 • E. F. Jacob, *Essays in the conciliar epoch*, 3rd edn (1963), chap. 4 • *The episcopal register of Robert Rede*, ed. C. Deedes, 1; Sussex RS, 8 (1908) • R. Pearsall, 'Account of the memorial brass of Bishop Hallum in the cathedral church of Constance', *Archaeologia*, 30 (1844), 430–37 • R. Griffin, 'The heraldry in the cloisters of the cathedral church of Christ at Canterbury', *Archaeologia*, 66 (1915), 447–568

**Archives** Wilts. & Swindon RO, episcopal register

**Likenesses** tomb brass, 15th cent., Constance Cathedral, Germany; repro. in Horn, ed., *Register*, frontispiece • seal, BL; Birch, *Seals*, 2206

**Wealth at death** £572 18s. 0d.—excl. lands: Horn, ed., *The register of Robert Hallum*, 247–8

**Halpen, John Edmond** (*b.* 1764?). *See under* Halpen, Patrick (*fl.* 1757–1786).

**Halpen** [Halpin], **Patrick** (*fl.* **1757–1786**), engraver, was a native of Ireland and trained in the Dublin Society's School. His work consisted largely of engraving frontispieces and vignettes for the Dublin booksellers; the Dublin Society awarded him prizes of 2 guineas in 1760 and 1763. In 1757 he engraved a reduction in one sheet of Rocque's four-sheet map of the city and suburbs of Dublin, followed by two smaller maps of the city, a plan of the Lying-in Hospital and its new gardens (1764), and the elevation of Government House (1767). He produced an admirable engraved portrait of Dr Charles Lucas, after T. Hickey, in 1771. He worked in Blackamoor Yard, off Anglesey Street, then from 1775 at Temple Bar. From 1778 to 1786 he was the only native line engraver in Dublin.

**John Edmond Halpen** (*b.* 1764?), miniature painter, born probably in 1764 (Strickland), was the son of Patrick Halpen and his wife, Eleanor. He was a pupil of F. R. West and J. J. Barralet in the Dublin Society's School and exhibited copies of their drawings at the Society of Artists in Ireland in 1780. Sent by his father to study in London, he was encouraged by Charles Macklin to indulge his desire to go on the stage, but in deference to his father's objections he returned to Dublin as a miniature painter. His appearance on stage in 1790 at the Crow Street Theatre, Dublin, was not a success. He returned once more to London, where he married Rebecca Woodriff at St Marylebone on 29 July 1794. His later life is unknown.

L. H. CUST, *rev.* ANITA MCCONNELL

**Sources** W. G. Strickland, *A dictionary of Irish artists*, 1 (1913), 424–5 • J. T. Gilbert, *A history of the city of Dublin*, 3 vols. (1859), 2.332; 3.369 [repr. 1972] • parish register, London, St Marylebone, 29 July 1794, LMA [marriage, John Edmond Halpen]

**Halpin, Charles Graham**. *See* Halpine, Charles Graham (1829–1868).

**Halpin, Nicholas John** (**1790–1850**), journalist and literary critic, was born on 18 October 1790 at Portarlington, Queen's county, the son of William Halpin. After studying at Trinity College, Dublin, where he graduated BA in 1815, he took orders in the Church of Ireland, but he spent most of his time writing controversial and critical works and was for many years editor of the *Evening Mail*, the main protestant newspaper in Dublin. In 1817 he married Anne *née* Grehan; they had four daughters and three sons, including the journalist Charles Graham *Halpine (1829–1868), who wrote under the pseudonym of Miles O'Reilly.

After successfully publishing *An university prize poem, on his majesty King George the Third having completed the fiftieth year of his reign* in 1811, Halpin published a number of polemical pamphlets in support of the Church of Ireland, including *Tithes No Tax* (1823), *The Impossibility of Transubstantiation* and *No Chimaera, or, The Lay Reformation in Ireland* (1828). He also published a number of critical essays on the works of Shakespeare, including *Oberon's Vision in the 'Midsummer Night's Dream'* (1843), *Bridal Runaway: an Essay on Juliet's Soliloquy*, (1845), and *The dramatic unities of Shakespeare, in a letter addressed to the editor of 'Blackwood's Edinburgh Magazine'* (1849), and *Observations on Certain Passages in the Life of Edmund Spenser* (1850). He died on 22 November 1850, in Dublin.

FRANCIS WATT, *rev.* DAVID HUDDLESTON

**Sources** *GM*, 2nd ser., 36 (1851), 212 • Burtchaell & Sadleir, *Alum. Dubl.* • [J. H. Todd], ed., *A catalogue of graduates who have proceeded to degrees in the University of Dublin, from the earliest recorded commencements to … December 16, 1868* (1869), 245

**Halpine** [Halpin], **Charles Graham** (**1829–1868**), journalist and author, was born at Oldcastle, co. Meath, Ireland, on 20 November 1829, the son of the Revd Nicholas John *Halpin (1790–1850), and his wife, Anne Grehan. He was educated at Trinity College, Dublin, until 1846, originally for the medical profession, but he preferred the law, and in his leisure wrote for the press. The sudden death of his father and his own early marriage forced him to adopt journalism as a profession.

In 1851 Halpine emigrated to America and settled in Boston, where he became assistant editor of the *Boston Post* and, with Benjamin P. Shillaber, started an unsuccessful humorous journal called the *Carpet Bag*. He afterwards lived in Washington, where he acted as correspondent for the *New York Times*. After moving to New York he was employed on the *New York Herald*, and in a few months established links with several periodicals, producing many ephemeral publications. He next became associate editor of the *New York Times*, acting also as Nicaraguan correspondent during William Walker's filibustering expedition of 1855–6. In 1857 he became principal editor and part proprietor of the New York *Leader*, which under his management rapidly increased in circulation.

At the beginning of the civil war in April 1861 Halpine

enlisted in the 69th New York infantry, in which he was soon elected a lieutenant, and served for three months. He was then transferred to General David Hunter's staff as assistant adjutant-general with the rank of major, and soon after went with that officer to Missouri to relieve General John Charles Fremont. He accompanied Hunter to Hilton Head, and while there wrote a series of burlesque poems in the assumed character of an Irish private. Several of them were contributed to the *New York Herald* in 1862 under the pseudonym of Miles O'Reilly, and with additional articles were published as *Life and adventures, songs, services, and speeches of Private Miles O'Reilly, 47th regiment New York volunteers* (1864) and *Baked meats of the funeral, a collection of essays, poems, speeches, and banquets, by Private Miles O'Reilly, late of the 47th regiment New York volunteer infantry* (1866). Halpine was subsequently assistant adjutant-general on General Henry W. Halleck's staff with the rank of colonel in 1862, and accompanied Hunter on his expedition to the Shenandoah valley in the spring of 1864.

On his return to New York, Halpine resigned his commission in consequence of his bad eyesight, receiving the brevet of brigadier-general of volunteers. He then made New York his home, and resuming his journalistic career became editor, and later proprietor, of *The Citizen*, a newspaper issued by the citizens' association to advocate reforms in the civil administration of New York city. In 1867 he was elected registrar of the county of New York by a coalition of republicans and democrats. Overwork brought on insomnia; he resorted to opiates, and his death in New York city on 3 August 1868 was caused by an overdose of chloroform.

G. C. BOASE, *rev.* NILANJANA BANERJI

**Sources** F. S. Drake, *Dictionary of American biography, including men of the time* (1872), esp. suppl. • *DAB* • J. G. Wilson and J. Fiske, eds., *Appleton's cyclopaedia of American biography*, 7 vols. (1887–1900) • Allibone, *Dict.* • *The poetical works of Charles G. Halpine*, ed. R. B. Roosevelt (1869) [with memoir by ed.] • M. H. Smith, *Sunshine and shade in New York* (1868)

**Likenesses** F. Halpin, engraving, repro. in Roosevelt, ed., *The poetical works of Charles G. Halpine*, frontispiece

**Hals, William** (1654–1737?), antiquary, was born at Tresawen, Merther, Cornwall, the second son of James Hals of Fentongollan and Anne, daughter and coheir of John Martin of Hurston, Devon. His father, a younger son of Sir Nicholas *Halse (*d.* 1636), served at La Rochelle in 1628, and afterwards in the West Indies, where, according to his son, he was governor of Montserrat; he held Tresawen by lease from his mother.

Nothing is known of Hals's education. Although his publishers claimed he was a 'perfect master of the Cornish and very well vers'd in the British and Saxon, as well as the Learned Languages' (Hals, printed wrapper), his etymology is poor. His surviving manuscripts include a translation of Keigwin's 'Mount Calvary' (BL, Add. MS 28554, fols. 51–8). He began researching the history of Cornwall about 1685 and pursued his interest for the rest of his life. The manuscript of his 'Parochial history of Cornwall' (BL, Add. MS 29762) has the appearance of a working copy and, although described as nearly completed at his death, it seems unlikely that he would ever have published the work. According to his own account in his history, his first two wives belonged respectively to the families of Evans of Landrinis in Wales and Carveth of Pewansand; nothing else is known of them. In 1714 he married Jane Courtney (*b.* 1672) of Tremeer; they had no children, and his wife died some time before 1736. Hals died, probably in 1737, at Tregury, St Wenn, of which he owned the rectorial tithes.

Hals's manuscripts passed to William Halse (*d.* 1775) of Truro, who about 1750 arranged for the *Compleat History of Cornwall* to be published by Andrew Brice of Exeter in weekly sixpenny numbers of four sheets. This appears to have been a financial rather than a scholarly venture. The publishers began with the second part of the work, a parochial history taken directly from the manuscript, alleging that the introduction awaited 'considerable additions … by a very great hand'. Hals's 'History of St. Michael's Mount' and 'Dictionary of the Cornish language' were also intended as part of the final work. It seems that the venture was not a financial success and only seventy-two parishes (Advent to Helston) appeared. The suspension of the work was said to have been due to the scurrilous anecdotes it contained, although Lysons blamed the inaccuracies and 'tedious' legends of saints. Its scholarly apparatus was deficient by contemporary standards and it lacked the extensive genealogies and lavish illustrations of a work such as Dugdale's *The History and Antiquities of the County of Warwick* which might have encouraged the Cornish gentry to subscribe. In style the work resembles the county histories of the early seventeenth century, in which Cornwall was amply represented by Richard Carew's *Survey of Cornwall*. It is likely that the majority of gentry families already possessed a copy of Carew or of John Norden's *Topographical and Historical Description of Cornwall* (1728), and felt little inclination to subscribe to the new work. Hals's manuscript was, however, incorporated into the nineteenth-century parochial histories of Cornwall produced by Davies Gilbert and Joshua Polsue.

JAN BROADWAY

**Sources** W. Hals, *Compleat history of Cornwall* (1750) • J. Walker, 'Cornwall', *A guide to English county histories*, ed. C. R. J. Currie and C. P. Lewis (1997), 87–9 • Boase & Courtney, *Bibl. Corn.*, 1.204, 3.1214 • D. Gilbert, *The parochial history of Cornwall: founded on the manuscript histories of Mr Hals and Mr Tonkin*, 4 vols. (1838) • J. Polsue, *A complete parochial history of the county of Cornwall*, 4 vols. (1867–72) • R. Polwhele, *The history of Cornwall*, 7 vols. (1803–8); repr. with additions (1816), vol. 5, p. 203 • D. Lysons and S. Lysons, *Magna Britannia: being a concise topographical account of the several counties of Great Britain*, 3 (1814), cv, 2

**Halsall** [Hassall], **Edward** (*c.*1627–1686), royalist army officer and assassin, was probably born in Lancashire, the younger son of Thomas Halsall of Melling and his first wife, whose identity is unknown. The Halsall family was prominent in Lancashire, although Edward's early life remains obscure. Little is known about him until his emergence as a colonel or major in the royalist army during the 1640s. His fame springs, however, from his role in the murder of Anthony Ascham, a diplomat sent by the republican government in England to the court in Spain in June 1650. Halsall may have been part of the retinue of the royalist envoys to Spain, Edward Hyde, earl of Clarendon, and Francis, Lord Cottington. When Halsall and the other assassins were arrested Hyde protested at their treatment and endeavoured to provide for their maintenance in prison. After a protracted diplomatic dispute concerning the fate of the murderers, and the execution of one of them, Halsall was evidently released in the spring of 1654. He immediately returned to England, where he was reportedly involved in plots to kill Oliver Cromwell later in the year. In addition, he hatched a plan to organize a royalist rising in Liverpool, which was thwarted only by the arrival of Cromwellian troops from Ireland. Halsall spent much of the remainder of the 1650s in Europe with the duke of Gloucester, and at the Restoration became an equerry to the queen, Catherine of Braganza, as well as securing other minor official posts and receiving minor royal grants. He appears to have died in 1686, while living in his native Lancashire, and left a son and four daughters, although the identity of his wife remains unknown.

**James Halsall** [Hassall] (*d.* 1692), royalist army officer and conspirator, Edward's half-brother, was the son of Thomas Halsall by his second marriage, to Margery Maghull. He also served in the royalist army during the 1640s, when he was styled major, and like his brother became active in organizing royalist plots during the 1650s. During 1653 he was in England in order to collect money on behalf of the king, and in early 1655 he was among those anxious to encourage the Sealed Knot to become more active against Cromwell. Later in 1655 he returned to the continent with Lord Wilmot, but when he journeyed to England later in the year was arrested after being betrayed by one of his servants, who was probably an agent of John Thurloe. Halsall's arrest caused consternation among his fellow royalists because of the fear of similar acts of treachery by other colleagues. Following his interrogation, in which he outlined his part in royalist plots, Halsall was imprisoned in the Tower, and although Edward Sexby planned to orchestrate an escape, Halsall told the marquess of Ormond that he expected to be executed. He was certainly kept close prisoner, but his correspondence, intercepted by the government, revealed that he harboured some hope of securing release through a promise to take no further part in plots against the government. Halsall was eventually released, against the wishes of Thurloe, in February 1659, after the issue of a writ of habeas corpus, and promptly returned to the service of Charles II and to active plotting. He was re-arrested in August 1659, although he was subsequently able to engage in negotiations with disgruntled former parliamentarians such as Sir Edward Harley. Released from prison upon the Restoration, Halsall, like his brother, became a minor courtier. He served as cup-bearer to the king, scoutmaster-general of the army, and undertook intelligence work, partly with Aphra Behn. Pepys described him as 'a great creature of the Duke of Albermarle's' (Pepys, 7.177). During the late 1660s and 1670s he returned to military service as captain of a company stationed at Portsmouth, and subsequently on the Isle of Wight. Halsall died, possibly unmarried, in 1692, when the bulk of his estate was left to the children of Edward Halsall.

J. T. PEACEY

**Sources** P. R. Newman, *Royalist officers in England and Wales, 1642–1660: a biographical dictionary* (1981) • D. Underdown, *Royalist conspiracy in England, 1649–1660* (1960) • *Calendar of the Clarendon state papers preserved in the Bodleian Library*, 2: 1649–1654, ed. W. D. Macray (1869); 3: 1655–1657, ed. W. D. Macray (1876); 4: 1657–1660, ed. F. J. Routledge (1932) • Thurloe, *State papers*, vols. 2–4 • *CSP dom.*, 1655–80 • W. A. Shaw, ed., *Calendar of treasury books*, 1–7, PRO (1904–16) • *The Nicholas papers*, ed. G. F. Warner, 3, CS, new ser., 57 (1897) • W. Dugdale, *The visitation of the county palatine of Lancaster, made in the year 1664–5*, ed. F. R. Raines, 2, Chetham Society, 85 (1872), 2.129 • [E. S. de Beer], 'A list of the department of the lord chamberlain of the household, autumn 1663', *BIHR*, 19 (1941–3), 16 • B. G. Blackwood, *The Lancashire gentry and the great rebellion, 1640–60*, Chetham Society, 3rd ser., 25 (1978) • *Seventh report*, HMC, 6 (1879), 145 • Pepys, *Diary*, vol. 7

**Halsall, James** (*d.* **1692**). *See under* Halsall, Edward (*c.*1627–1686).

**Halsbury**. For this title name *see* Giffard, Hardinge Stanley, first earl of Halsbury (1823–1921); Giffard, John Anthony Hardinge, third earl of Halsbury (1908–2000).

**Halse, Sir Nicholas** (*d.* **1636**), projector, was one of the seven children of John Halse of Kenedon and Efford, Devon, and his second wife, Joane, daughter of William Tothill, an alderman of Exeter; John Halse had also had five children with his first wife. His family appear to have been prosperous and well-established landowners, so Nicholas Halse may have inherited money.

By 1596 Halse owned some property in west Cornwall. In or before this year, he married Grace (*d.* 1662), daughter of Sir John Arundel, of Tolverne, and his wife, Anne, daughter of Thomas Godolphin. This marriage connected him to a number of prominent Cornish gentry families. The Halses appear to have had at least fourteen children, several of whom became or married soldiers or naval officers. One grandson became a rich landowner in Jamaica. Another grandson, William Hals, wrote a manuscript entitled *History of Cornwall*, an unreliable work which states that Nicholas Halse's property was very extensive, and also that he held a position in the household of Henry, prince of Wales, and was for many years the governor of Pendennis Castle (BL, Add. MS 29762, fol. 183ff.). Although some or all of these statements may be false, the knighthood which Halse received in 1605 indicates that he was then regarded as a gentleman of some standing.

Towards the end of Halse's life, matters were different. When, about 1633, Halse supported the claim of a Cornish woman named Anne Maddock that a gentleman called Richard Luckin had entered into a contract of marriage with her, his reliability was impugned on the grounds that he and Maddock's mother lived as man and wife, that their supposed marriage had been bigamous, that he 'doth shift from place to place and is much indebted … much decayed in his estate' (*CSP dom.*, XLV. cclvi. 2), that he had been imprisoned for debt, and that he had been defaulting on debts since about 1611.

In the final years of his life, Halse was much concerned with an invention and a variety of projects, perhaps in the hope of raising money. His invention was a kind of combined kiln and kitchen range, 'for the dryinge of mault and hops w[th] seacole, turffe, or any other fewell, w[th]out touching of smoake, and very usefull for baking, boyling, roasting, starchinge, and dryinge of lynnen, all at one and the same tyme and w[th] one fyre' (*Titles of Patents*, no. 85). After it was patented on 23 July 1635, Halse and his assigns petitioned several times for the suppression of rival designs. A debate as to the relative priority of Halse's device and these rivals arose, but appears to have lapsed before the end of the decade, perhaps because the invention was found to be impractical or unprofitable.

Halse wrote a number of addresses to Charles I, suggesting projects by which the royal revenues might be enhanced; several of the projects were to be underwritten with profits from the kilns, or from the use of 'Mundicke, & Sinder Tinne' (copper pyrites and an unidentified west-country mineral) as the material for a debased coinage. The increased consumption of fish was to be enforced by law, and the building of a fishing fleet was to be encouraged by loans from the treasury; the Dutch were to be charged £4 million for their use of English harbours in the past, and another £200,000 a year in the future, and were to deliver part of their territory into English keeping as a gesture of good will; iron was to be mined and smelted in the New World and shipped to England; and the king of Spain was to pay the English £2 million a year to govern the Low Countries and to protect his colonial fleets.

When Halse died in London at the end of 1636, his will was proved by Anne Maddock. The drafts of his projects were gathered from 'scattered & torne papers .. irregulare & vnperfect', and they were transcribed and edited into an ornate octavo manuscript presented to the king as a new year's gift by Francis Stewart, son of the earl of Bothwell, with the title, *Great Britains Treasure; Environing this famous Ile, with brazen walls invincible, maintained with great gaine, by forces invisible … recovered & painefully recollected out of the old papers & fragments of that worthy and lately deceased knight, your Ma[ts] faithfull & ingenuous servant Sir Nicholas Halse* (BL, Egerton MS 1140, fol. 61 and title-page).

JOHN CONSIDINE

**Sources** *CSP dom.* • W. Hals, 'History of Cornwall', 18th cent., BL, Add. MS 29762 • F. Stewart, ed., 'Great Britains treasure', 1637, BL, Egerton MS 1140 • B. Woodcroft, *Titles of patents of invention, chronologically arranged from March 2, 1617 … to October 1, 1852* (1854) • J. H. Rowe, 'Hals of Cornwall', 1924, BL, Add. MS 41178, fols. 130v–131r • F. Godolphin, Letter, Sept 1596, BL, Add. MS 34224, fol. 22 • J. L. Vivian, ed., *The visitations of the county of Devon, comprising the herald's visitations of 1531, 1564, and 1620* (privately printed, Exeter, [1895]) • J. Matthews and G. F. Matthews, eds., *Abstracts of probate acts in the prerogative court of Canterbury*, 2 (1903–4) • J. H. L. Archer, *Monumental inscriptions: British West Indies* (1875) • J. L. Vivian, ed., *The visitations of Cornwall, comprising the herald's visitations of 1530, 1573, and 1620* (1887) • W. A. Shaw, *The knights of England*, 2 (1906) • record of will, proved 19 Nov 1636

**Halsey, John** (1663?–1709?), privateer turned pirate, came from Boston, Massachusetts. Nothing is known about his parents or his early life. As commander of the brigantine *Charles* he received a commission from Governor Samuel Cranston of Rhode Island on 7 November 1704 to cruise against the French on the Newfoundland Banks. After seizing a French vessel he proceeded to the Canaries where he plundered a Spanish ship. By early 1706, equipped with another commission, from Governor Joseph Dudley of Massachusetts, Halsey was in the Red Sea. He fell in with a Dutch vessel of 60 guns outbound from Mocha, and they sailed in company for a week. Halsey was determined to turn pirate but he was also resolved not to attack European shipping, and this scruple caused resentment among those who eyed their consort greedily. Halsey's crew mutinied and tried to seize the Dutchman but in a fleeting engagement the pirates lost their nerve. The attempt was abandoned, and Halsey was reinstated commander.

Halsey now made for the Nicobar Islands where he seized a Bengali vessel, the *Buffalo*, commanded by Captain Buckley. The *Buffalo* was anchored at Car Nicobar and Halsey cruised offshore. A sloop commanded by Captain Collins was also taken, with two English mates, at which point the pirates divided over whether or not to return to the West Indies. Some went on board the *Buffalo* and sailed for Madagascar while Halsey and others made for the Strait of Malacca. Here the *Charles* was chased off by the *Albemarle*, an East Indiaman, and Halsey called a council in which the decision was taken to sail to Madagascar and recruit. On arrival Halsey encountered the *Buffalo* and also the *Dorothy* (Captain Thomas White). After repairs the pirates, augmented by White and some of his men, made for the Strait of Bab al-Mandab in the Red Sea. Here Halsey was galled because his ship lay becalmed among twenty-five vessels from Mocha and Jiddah which managed to row away from him.

A few days later Halsey captured a grab and gained intelligence of several vessels which were about to leave Mocha. This convoy sailed under the protection of Captain Samuel Jago, commander of the *Bombay Merchant*, who was commissioned by the East India Company to deter pirates from interrupting trade in the region. On 7 August 1707 five ships sailed from Mocha, bound for Bombay. Halsey pounced on the convoy, and his opening salvo caused Jago to abandon his charges completely. The pirates then boarded the *Rising Eagle* and killed her commander, Captain Chamberlain, before pursuing the *Essex*. Having been informed that the *Essex* was from Jiddah, and laden with riches, Halsey immediately hoisted the bloody flag to indicate he would give no quarter. The *Essex* struck without a fight which ensured that her captain, Thomas Punt, and some English passengers were treated civilly. Halsey's men rummaged the *Essex* and carried away treasure worth £40,000 which they added to £10,000 taken out of the *Rising Eagle*, before proceeding to Madagascar, via Calicut, where the booty was shared out.

Early in 1708 Halsey traded with the *Greyhound*, a vessel sent to Madagascar by the governor of Madras to treat with the pirates for dry goods seized in the *Essex*. Shortly afterwards the *Neptune*, a Scottish vessel commanded by Captain James Miller, arrived selling great quantities of liquor. The *Greyhound*'s merchants, nettled by this trade, incited the pirates to seize the *Neptune* whereupon

Halsey's men bettered this advice by seizing both vessels. Not long after these events Halsey contracted a fever and died, almost certainly in 1709. He was buried with great solemnity and according to the rites of the Church of England. His coffin was draped with a ship's jack, upon which were placed a sword and pistol. Minute guns were fired forty-six times, commemorating every year of his life, and volleys of small arms followed. According to one source, Halsey 'was brave in his Person, courteous to all his Prisoners, lived beloved, and died regretted by his own people' (Johnson, 2.117). In truth he seems to have been less bloody than many contemporary pirates. Halsey's grave was dug in a garden of water melons, fenced off to prevent the body being rooted up by wild hogs.

James William Kelly

**Sources** PRO, Cal SPC, 1704–5, pp. 314, 445, 592, 663 · deposition of Paul Dudley dated 15 Aug 1705 concerning the granting of a privateer's commission to Capt. John Halsey, PRO, CO. 5:1263, no. 57 XXVI · letter from T. Pitt, Madras, 12 Sept 1707, BL, Add. MS 22850 · letter from Thomas Pitt to Elihu Yale, Madras, 3 Oct 1707, BL, Add. MS 22860, fol. 71 · Misc. letters received, 1701–9, BL, EIO. E1/1, p. 193 · C. Johnson, *A general history of the pyrates*, 4th edn (1726), 114–17 · R. Drury, *Madagascar, or, Robert Drury's journal* (1729), 435–6, 440 · S. Charles Hill, *Notes on piracy in eastern waters* (Bombay, 1923), 135, 138–40 · S. Charles Hill, 'Episodes of piracy in the eastern seas, 1519 to 1851', *Indian Antiquary*, 48–9 (1919–20), 93–5 · A. W. Secord, *Robert Drury's journal and other studies* (1961), 34–5 · D. Defoe, *A general history of the pyrates*, ed. M. Schonhorn (1972)

**Sir Lionel Halsey (1872–1949)**, by Walter Stoneman, 1917

**Halsey, Sir Lionel** (1872–1949), naval officer, was born on 26 February 1872 in London, the fourth of the seven sons in the ten children of Thomas Frederick Halsey (1839–1927), who became first baronet, of Gaddesden, Hertfordshire, and his wife, Mary Julia (*d.* 1922), daughter of Frederick Octavius Wells, of the Bengal civil service. After education at Stubbington House, Fareham, Hampshire, he entered the Royal Naval College, Dartmouth, as a naval cadet in January 1885, and after serving on various stations was sent to the royal yacht in July 1893 and promoted lieutenant in August. He then served in the Mediterranean and on the North America and West Indies station, afterwards joining the *Powerful*. He was landed with his captain, Hedworth Lambton (later Sir Hedworth Meux), and took part in the defence of Ladysmith during the Second South African War, in charge of a battery of naval 4·7 inch guns. For this service he was mentioned in dispatches, awarded the South Africa medal with Ladysmith clasp, and specially promoted commander on 1 January 1901. He served as commander in the cruiser *Diana* in the Mediterranean until June 1902 and then from November 1902 for two years in the *Good Hope*, Sir Wilmot Fawkes's flagship in the 1st cruiser squadron. On 24 January 1905 Halsey married Morwenna (*d.* 1959), younger daughter of Major Bevil Granville, of Wellesbourne Hall, Warwickshire. They had two daughters. Also in January 1905 Halsey was appointed naval member of the Admiralty committee which administered the new Royal Naval Volunteer Reserve Force; after being promoted captain in June he rejoined his old ship *Powerful* in August as flag captain to Fawkes as commander-in-chief, Australia, and in 1908 returned with him to Devonport to remain as flag captain there until April 1911.

Halsey then commanded the *Donegal*, 4th cruiser squadron, until September 1912 when he was selected to command the new battle cruiser *New Zealand*, built at the cost of the New Zealand government, on her cruise round the world to 'show the flag'. Halsey gave speeches at the ports visited and the cruise was a great public relations success. In 1913 he was appointed CMG.

In January 1915 Halsey was mentioned in dispatches for services in the Dogger Bank action. In June he left the *New Zealand* for the *Iron Duke* on joining the staff of Sir John Jellicoe as captain of the fleet with the rank of commodore first class. Jellicoe highly praised Halsey's efficiency, in dispatches following the battle of Jutland. Halsey was appointed CB in 1916.

On 4 December 1916 when Jellicoe joined the Board of Admiralty as first sea lord he brought Halsey with him as fourth sea lord. In May 1917, when Sir Eric Geddes at Lloyd George's request was appointed to the Admiralty board with the revived title of controller, Halsey was made third sea lord. Geddes became first lord in July, and assigned responsibility for managing the *matériel* of the navy to the controller for 'design and production' and to the third sea lord for 'requirements of design'. Halsey, who had been promoted rear-admiral in April 1917 (having until then retained the rank of commodore first class), remained on the board until June 1918, but 'had long been anxious to get back to the sea' (Marder, 5.6). The Australian government had placed its naval ships at the disposal of the

Admiralty and in September 1918 Halsey was lent to that government to take command of the second battle-cruiser squadron of the Grand Fleet in the battle cruiser *Australia* as his flagship. In this capacity he was present at the surrender of the German fleet at Scapa Flow. He came on shore in March 1919 and was employed as president of Admiralty committees on officers' pay and on the position of accountant officers, which recommended long overdue increases and reforms. From August 1919 he was largely engaged in commanding the *Renown* as chief of staff to the prince of Wales for his tour of Canada and the United States, and then from February until November 1920 to Australia, New Zealand, and the West Indies and other colonies.

At the end of this cruise Halsey's career moved completely in the direction of the court, and he was appointed comptroller and treasurer to the prince of Wales, a member of the council of the duchy of Cornwall, and in 1921 extra equerry to the prince. He was placed on the retired list of the navy on 1 November 1922, having been promoted vice-admiral on 5 July 1921. He was promoted admiral on the retired list in October 1926. Halsey remained on the prince's personal staff until 1936, when, as the new king, Edward VIII dismissed him. This was a result, Bryan and Murphy have claimed, of Halsey's 'unwillingness to connive at making Wallis Simpson Queen of England' (Bryan and Murphy, 183). Halsey, as financial manager, had also warned of the demands on royal funds from Edward's lifestyle in this period. After Edward's abdication in 1937 Halsey was appointed extra equerry to George VI.

In the navy Halsey was 'one of the most popular officers of his day' (Marder, 2.17). The vessels he commanded were regarded by contemporaries as all 'happy ships', and his charm and outgoing nature were mentioned by most who knew him. Marder suggests that Halsey 'might have gone to the very top after the war' if he had not taken up the court appointment (Marder, 2.17). He was appointed KCMG (1918), GCMG (1925), KCVO (1919), GCVO (1920), and KCIE (1922). He received several foreign decorations. Halsey was also a prominent freemason. He died at his home, Mount Pleasant, Old Warden, Biggleswade, Bedfordshire, on 26 October 1949 and was buried at Old Warden parish church on 29 October.

V. W. BADDELEY, *rev.* MARC BRODIE

**Sources** *The Times* (27 Oct 1949) · *The Times* (31 Oct 1949) · Burke, *Peerage* · A. J. Marder, *From the Dreadnought to Scapa Flow: the Royal Navy in the Fisher era, 1904–1919*, 5 vols. (1961–70) · J. Bryan and C. J. V. Murphy, *The Windsor story* (1979) · *WWW* · *CGPLA Eng. & Wales* (1949) · private information (1959) · personal knowledge (1959)

**Archives** Herts. ALS, family corresp. | NL Aus., corresp. with Viscount Novar · NMM, letters to David Beatty | FILM IWM FVA, actuality footage · IWM FVA, documentary footage · IWM FVA, news footage

**Likenesses** W. Stoneman, photograph, 1917, NPG [*see illus.*] · O. Birley, oils, Halsey Masonic Hall, Watford · F. Dodd, two charcoal and watercolour drawings, IWM

**Wealth at death** £10,800 5*s*. 9*d*.: probate, 17 Dec 1949, *CGPLA Eng. & Wales*

**Halstead** [Tarlo], **(Lambert) Beverly** (1933–1991), palaeontologist, was born in Pendleton, Lancashire, on 13 June 1933, the son of Lambert Halstead (1907–1983), painter and decorator, and his wife, Elizabeth (Betty), *née* Waring (1911–1991), railway clerk. He was brought up in circumstances of social isolation. His mother was the dominant parent; she believed in treating children without overt affection and as young adults. Moreover, she was an atheist and practising communist, at a time when such views were anathema to Lancashire country folk. His father was a talented artist and a much gentler person, without such strong views. When, during the Second World War, Betty met Maurice Tarlo, a young solicitor who shared her ideals, she abandoned her husband and moved south to Eastbourne, Sussex, to live with him, soon marrying him and insisting that her son adopt the surname Tarlo. Halstead's upbringing was thus harsh, forcing him to be independent and a loner. However, he did gain from his mother a capacity for intellectual exploration and the courage to endure unpopularity when standing up for his beliefs. This did not endear him to the headmaster of Lewes grammar school; the report on him was so adverse that he had trouble in finding a university place. However, its virulence intrigued Professor Leslie Moore of the University of Sheffield, where Halstead was admitted as an honours student in geology—fortunately, since Halstead's interest was in palaeontology, a discipline in which (exceptionally at that time) Sheffield excelled. Upon finding plesiosaur bones during a field excursion on the Yorkshire coast, Halstead determined to specialize on fossil vertebrates. A fellow student, John R. L. Allen, became his close friend; they were soon undertaking joint researches on the Old Red Sandstone strata of the Welsh borderland. By that time Halstead was not only a prominent member of the student Communist Society, but also contributing notes on rocks and fossils to the *Daily Worker*. His political sympathies facilitated a visit in 1955 to Poland, during which he contrived to visit classic Devonian fish localities, making discoveries that culminated in two massive monographs published in *Palaeontologica Polonica* in 1964 and 1965. However, he was not impressed by Poland's social climate—a first stirring of the doubts that caused him to abandon the Communist Party, following the Soviet invasion of Hungary in 1956.

Upon gaining his honours degree Halstead moved to London, to study Jurassic pliosaurs at University College. He elected to present, for his doctorate, a group of published papers instead of a thesis—a permissible alternative, but unpopular with his departmental superiors; their hostility delayed until 1959 the award of his PhD but before then Halstead had gained a three-year research fellowship at the British Museum (Natural History) and resumed research on Palaeozoic fishes. His studies of fossil teeth next earned him a Nuffield research fellowship, enabling researches at the Royal Dental Hospital and the Nuffield Orthopaedic Centre in Oxford. A series of important papers on Palaeozoic fishes and their dentition culminated in two books, *The Pattern of Vertebrate Evolution* (1969) and *Vertebrate Hard Tissues* (1974).

Halstead's early papers were published under the name L. B. Tarlo, but he had never become close to his stepfather. By 1965 he was styling himself L. B. Halstead Tarlo and by 1968, he had reassumed his born name, L. B. Halstead. He had also, on 27 November 1957, married a dentistry student, Beryl Joan Morris (*b.* 1920/21), daughter of Rex Alfred Shalson, musician, and a divorcée with two daughters from her earlier marriage. In 1963 they moved to Reading University where Halstead had gained a joint appointment in the departments of geology and zoology—a congenial move, since John Allen was already there. Halstead proved an excellent and inspiring teacher, beloved by his students and very supportive of them. These were years of high scientific productivity, with visits to Estonia and Russia to study fossil fishes (1961) and writings on such diverse topics as Triassic reptiles and protomammals, a supposed Eocene whale, and amino-acids in Oligocene tortoiseshell. His personal life proved less satisfactory. After some years of increasing marital strife he and Beryl separated, but the divorce proved long and costly; it was not achieved until 1975.

Halstead's restlessness caused him to travel to Nigeria in 1967 at the time of its civil war. Undeterred by an episode of arrest and interrogation, he conceived a liking for its people. He went also to Tunisia (1968) and then to Rhodesia and South Africa (1969), where his defiance of racial prejudices brought both admiration and problems. Desiring to develop co-operative researches between Reading and the University of the Witwatersrand, he returned again to South Africa in 1970, but was instantly expelled as a political subversive. Predictably, this made him a hero among black Africans. A second, brief visit to Nigeria (1970) was the prelude to a three-year appointment as head of zoology at the University of Ife (1971–4), during which he also spent three months at the Punjab University, Chandigarh, India. At both universities he strove to develop low-budget research projects—in Nigeria on the ecology of lizards and fruit-bats and, in India, on the geology of the Siwalik Hills. An expedition into the Sokoto region, north-western Nigeria, brought the discovery of a new fossil crocodile (*Sokotosuchus*).

Halstead had met in 1970 a talented medical illustrator, Jennifer Anne (Jenny) Middleton (*b.* 1941/2), daughter of Wilfred Middleton, a surveyor. They collaborated on a book on the functional and artistic significance and folklore of bones, *Bare Bones* (1972) and, when she joined him at Ile-Ife, on a series of dissection guides for students. They were married on 23 May 1975, after Halstead's return to Reading: their son and only child, Thomas Atlay James, was born on 2 September 1980. Endeavouring to alleviate the straitened circumstances resulting from divorce and remarriage, Halstead began to write books on palaeontology for a general audience, often illustrated by Jenny. They included *The Evolution and Ecology of the Dinosaurs* (1973), *Fossil Hunting* (1977), *The Evolution of the Mammals* (1978), *Hunting the Past* (1982), and four fictionalized biographies of extinct creatures for children. He also contributed to a number of compilative volumes, such as *Elsevier's Animal Encyclopaedia* (1972) and Hallam's *Atlas of Palaeobiogeography* (1973).

Eager for further discoveries, Halstead conducted an international palaeontological expedition to Nigeria in mid-December 1977 with fourteen members (including his wife). Upon arrival in Sokoto, however, they were arrested by the military governor and sent in custody to Lagos. Though soon released and permitted to proceed, the expedition fell apart. Not until late January 1978 did its residual three members—Halstead, Jenny, and Cyril Walker—return to Sokoto where, with belated official assistance, significant discoveries of fossil turtles were made. A journey to China in 1979 resulted not only in the discovery of a new group of Palaeozoic fishes (galeaspids), but also of mineral replicas of their internal anatomy. In 1983, against Jenny's advice, Halstead went again to Nigeria, on official invitation. All went well until he was leaving but then, between air terminal and plane, he was arrested by the security police and sent to prison in Lagos. Though he was released after a week it was a frightening ordeal which aged him considerably. His appearance—slim and intense, with black hair and fiery eyes—had always been mephistophelean; henceforward, with hair prematurely white and lessened energy, he seemed more like an elder satanic statesman.

Yet Halstead's concerns did not diminish; rather, they diversified. He became an increasingly vocal opponent of creationism, engaging in a much-publicized debate with the creationist Duane Gish and writing many critical articles. A visit to Japan in 1984 caused him to challenge the equally erroneous concepts of Kinji Imanishi, in a book published only in Japanese (1988). He opposed the concept of a catastrophic cause for dinosaur extinction and castigated Fred Hoyle's idea that life on earth had an extraterrestrial origin. He was also a participant, always outspoken and courageous, in many other controversies: the efficacy of underground nuclear testing; cladistics as a means for determining evolutionary relationships; the administrative and scientific structure of the Natural History Museum; the concept of 'test-tube' nuclear fusion; the Piltdown hoax; the dangers of AIDS; and, more lightheartedly, the reality of the Loch Ness monster.

Other professional activities continued apace. Halstead was editor for seven years of the *Nigerian Field*, co-editor of *Palaeontology* for five years, and a highly innovative editor of *Modern Geology* from 1983 until his death. He addressed many national and international meetings and was a proud member of London's Athenaeum. His enthusiasm for informing the public at large about geology made him a vigorous and enterprising member of the Geologists' Association and the British Association for the Advancement of Science. At one of its meetings, in 1985, he encountered a psychologist from the University of Bath, Helen Haste; he travelled with her to Canada and the United States in 1987 and shared his latter years with her, although he never completely severed his relationship with his wife, Jenny, and son, Tom. The physical stresses of that North American visit perhaps hastened the onset of cancer of the bladder, shortly after their return to England. Though Halstead's recovery was slow, he was soon involved in fresh controversies. His vigorous advocacy of the abandonment of thesis-writing as a PhD qualification and of the Thatcher government's plans for 'rationalizing' geology departments outraged his Reading colleagues. There was also a confrontation with that university's vice-chancellor, whose actions Halstead had criticized; his formal apology was manifestly insincere. Consequently, when the teaching function of Reading's geology department was eliminated, Halstead lost his academic base. Thereafter, he commuted between Reading, Bath, and London, where he had gained an honorary research position at Imperial College, writing articles on the train.

Halstead's career should have attained its apogee in 1991. He was president of the Geologists' Association and president-elect of section C (geology) of the British Association. He was to be a principal speaker at a special session at the Plymouth meeting, to commemorate the sesquicentennial of Richard Owen's first recognition of the dinosaurs. Instead, driving to Bath on the evening of 30 April 1991, he died in a motor accident caused by the error of a lorry driver.

Halstead's researches transformed understanding of Palaeozoic fishes and of the environment of the earliest vertebrates. His popular writings and lectures on palaeontology and evolution brought scientific enlightenment to many, while his willingness to challenge dogmas stimulated thought among students and public alike. His published bibliography lists 414 publications. The many tributes paid to him at his funeral on 9 May 1991 showed how he had surmounted all the controversies and become widely beloved. WILLIAM A. S. SARJEANT

**Sources** W. A. S. Sarjeant, 'Lambert Beverly Halstead (1933–1991): his life, his discoveries and his controversies', *Modern Geology*, 18/1 (1993), 5–60 [republished in W. A. S. Sarjeant, ed., *Vertebrate fossils and the evolution of scientific concepts: a tribute to Beverly Halstead* (1995), 1–58] • L. F. Dietz and W. A. S. Sarjeant, 'L. B. Halstead: a bibliography of his published writings', *Modern Geology*, 18/1 (1993), 61–83 [republished in W. A. S. Sarjeant, ed., *Vertebrate fossils and the evolution of scientific concepts: a tribute to Beverly Halstead* (1995), 59–80] • Z. Kielan-Jaworowska, 'Remembrance of L. B. Halstead in Poland', *Modern Geology*, 18/1 (1993), 83–7 [republished in W. A. S. Sarjeant, ed., *Vertebrate fossils and the evolution of scientific concepts: a tribute to Beverly Halstead* (1995), 81–5] • P. Janvier and A. Blieck, 'L. B. Halstead and the heterostracan controversy', *Modern Geology*, 18/1 (1993), 89–105 [republished in W. A. S. Sarjeant, ed., *Vertebrate fossils and the evolution of scientific concepts: a tribute to Beverly Halstead* (1995), 103–21] • J. R. L. Allen, 'Bev Halstead: an appreciation', *Palaeontology Newsletter*, 11 (1991) • P. A. Hill, 'Lambert Beverly Halstead', *Outcrop* [Journal of the West Sussex Geological Society], 6 (1991), 22–4 • *The Independent* (3 May 1991) • *The Times* (9 May 1991) • P. Worsley, 'Beverly Halstead (1933–1991)', *Quaternary Newsletter* (July 1991), 42–4 • J. A. Mackenzie, 'L. B. Halstead—a tribute', *Nigerian Field*, 48 (1983), 1–2 • personal knowledge (2004) • private information (2004) • m. certs.

**Archives** priv. coll.

**Likenesses** C. Orr, etching, priv. coll. • portrait, repro. in Sarjeant, ed., *Vertebrate fossils and the evolution of scientific concepts* (1995) • portrait, repro. in *The Independent*

**Wealth at death** £125,837: probate, 14 Oct 1991, *CGPLA Eng. & Wales*

**Halsted** [*married name* Atthill], **Caroline Amelia** (1803/4–1848), historian and author, was the daughter of John Halsted, a captain in the Royal Navy. She published her first work, *The Little Botanist, or, Steps to the Attainment of Botanical Knowledge*, in 1835. This was followed by *Investigations in a Boudoir* (1836), an unusual textbook in which a mother and her daughter conduct a domestic 'grand tour' of their living room, investigating the origins and nature of the everyday objects around them. In 1839 Halsted turned to biography, publishing a *Life of Margaret Beaufort*, the mother of Henry VII. This work won her the Gresham commemoration prize for 1839, and was favourably reviewed in the *Gentleman's Magazine*, where she was viewed as a worthy successor to Lucy Aikin. The reviewer commented that the biography was written with 'care, research, and ability' and was 'far superior to some of the late histories by female hands' (*Gentleman's Magazine*, 2nd ser., 12, 1839, 515). Later historians praised the biography for its recognition of Margaret Beaufort's political role and capacity, an aspect of her life neglected in preceding accounts, which had concentrated on her virtues as a patroness of religion and learning.

Halsted's next work was *Obligations of Literature to the Mothers of England* (1840), in which she enlarged upon a favourite theme, the importance of women's educative influence within the home for the development of English culture. This was awarded the Gresham commemoration prize for 1840. Her most significant work, however, was her *Life of Richard III*, a passionate defence of the character of the last Plantagenet king. Published in two bulky volumes in 1844, it was thoroughly researched and exhaustively argued. Building on the revisionist work of Sir George Buck, Horace Walpole, and Sharon Turner, the biography was based on a thorough knowledge of primary sources, and was the first account to make extensive use of Harleian MS 433, a register of Richard III's grants and writs. The portrait drawn of Richard as a *preux chevalier* was undeniably a romanticized one, but her rebuttal of many of the traditional charges levelled against the king—including the murders of Henry VI, Edward, prince of Wales, and George, duke of Clarence—was cogently argued. Examining the deaths of the princes in the tower, she decided that Richard's guilt was not proven. Many of her conclusions, including her recognition of the importance of Richard's authority in the north of England, have been confirmed by modern research. Contemporary reviewers were generally favourable: the critic of *The Athenaeum* gave her 'great credit for her laborious attempt to vindicate Richard's character', commenting on the 'patient care with which she has sought out, and marshalled her authorities' (*Athenaeum*, 10 August 1844, 731). The *Gentleman's Magazine* was more critical, accusing her of 'an inclination for fine and sentimental writing' and of paying too much deference to contemporary writers whose scholarship was inferior to her own (*Gentleman's Magazine*, 2nd ser., 22, 1844, 273).

On 8 June 1847, at Walmer in Kent, Caroline Halsted became the third wife of William Atthill (1807–1884), subdean and canon of Middleham in Yorkshire, a collegiate church founded by Richard III. Their relationship seems to have begun in a scholarly exchange, when she lent some manuscripts to Atthill, who was editing *Documents Relating to the Foundation and Antiquities of the Collegiate Church of Middleham* (1847) for the Camden Society. She did not long survive the marriage, however, dying on 2 July 1848 at Middleham, aged forty-four. Continuing interest in the life and reign of Richard III means that fellow Ricardians keep Caroline Halsted's memory fresh; her *Richard III* was reprinted in 1977 by Alan Sutton.

ROSEMARY MITCHELL

**Sources** Allibone, *Dict.* • m. cert. • d. cert. • Burke, *Gen. GB* • Walford, *County families* • *The Athenaeum* (3 Aug 1844), 707–8 • *The Athenaeum* (10 Aug 1844), 728–31 • *GM*, 2nd ser., 12 (1839), 515 • *GM*, 2nd ser., 22 (1844), 273–7 • M. K. Jones and M. G. Underwood, *The king's mother: Lady Margaret Beaufort, countess of Richmond and Derby* (1992), 8–10 • P. M. Kendall, *Richard the third* (1955), 429 • J. Potter, *Good King Richard? an account of Richard III and his reputation* (1983), 197–201 • W. Atthill, *Documents relating to the foundation and antiquities of the collegiate church of Middleham*, CS, 38 (1847), xxvii

**Halswelle, Keeley** (1832–1891), book illustrator and painter, was born on 23 April 1832 at Richmond, Surrey, the son of David Halswelle and Elizabeth Spence. He was educated in London and Edinburgh, and while still young contributed drawings to the *Illustrated London News*. Much of his early career was spent in book illustration. In 1856 some work for Robert Chambers's *Illustrated Shakespeare* took him back to Edinburgh, where he became principal illustrator for the publishing company of William Nelson, who became his good friend. Among other books illustrated by Halswelle were collections of poetry by Byron, Scott, and Wordsworth, and *The Knight of the Silver Shield* (1885). On 18 June 1861, in Edinburgh, he married Maria (*b.* 1834/5), daughter of James Browne, advocate, and Isabella Stewart.

Many of Halswelle's early paintings were scenes of fishing life at Newhaven. In 1857 he exhibited at the Royal Scottish Academy and in 1866 he was elected an associate. In 1868 he visited Rome for the first time and in the following year he moved to Italy, where he stayed for a number of years. Italian subjects dominated his work for a considerable time; typical titles at the Royal Academy were *Contadine in St Peter's Rome* and *A Roman Fruit Girl*. The *Roba di Roma*, exhibited at Burlington House, gained a £50 prize at Manchester, but his most popular work of this period, possibly because of its subject, was *Non angli sed angeli*, painted in 1877 and engraved in the *Art Journal* in 1890. Halswelle's large canvases of Italian peasantry and market traders nevertheless attracted only limited recognition. Besides the triviality of the themes and the conventionality with which Halswelle treated them the lack of attention paid to them reflected 'the profound weariness felt by the British public for *contadini* and all connected with them' (*The Athenaeum*).

In the late 1870s Halswelle abandoned figure and genre painting for landscape. He afterwards painted almost exclusively highland scenery and views of the River Thames. He was elected a member of the Institute of Painters in Oils in 1882 and in the following year exhibited eighty-two small oil paintings of the Thames at Agnews galleries, in Old Bond Street. These were the product of six summers spent on a houseboat. Reviewing the exhibition *The Times*'s critic praised Halswelle's draughtsmanship, sense of colour, and composition, while lamenting 'an imperfect mastery of all the more delicate secrets of atmosphere and aerial distance' (*The Times*, 4 Dec 1883). Among the works exhibited was *Trees at Mapledurham after a Storm*, 'which in the minuteness and patience of the work recalls the achievements of the early pre-Raphaelites' (ibid.). Another exceptional work from this period was an oil painting of the Thames above Maidenhead, which was included in Henry Tate's gift to the nation. In 1883 *Six Years in a House-Boat*, a book of plates with commentary, was published to favourable reviews.

Halswelle exhibited thirty-six works at the Royal Academy between 1862 and 1891, and over a hundred works at the Royal Scottish Academy from 1857. He was also represented at the Grosvenor Gallery, the New Gallery, the Society of Artists, Suffolk Street, and the Liverpool Academy. In his later years he lived at Stoner House, Steep, near Petersfield, where he was a ruling councillor of the Primrose League. He died suddenly, of pneumonia, at the Hotel de Lille d'Albion in Paris on 12 April 1891 and was buried at Steep on 20 April. He was survived by his second wife, Helen Marianna Elizabeth, daughter of Major-General N. J. Gordon, whom he married on 27 March 1873, and two sons. His remaining paintings were sold at Christies in June 1891. Commenting on the studio sale *The Times* observed that Halswelle's large landscapes were 'far too conventional' but that his smaller works, whether in oil or watercolour, were 'fresh, spontaneous and charming' (*The Times*, 11 June 1891).

ERNEST RADFORD, *rev.* MARK POTTLE

**Sources** 'The works of KH', *Art Journal* (1879), 49 • *DNB* • *Magazine of Art*, 4.406 • *Men of the time* (1872) • *Annual Register* (1891), 159 • Wood, *Vic. painters*, 2nd edn • Mallalieu, *Watercolour artists* • S. Houfe, *The dictionary of 19th century British book illustrators and caricaturists*, rev. edn (1996) • *The Times* (4 Dec 1883) • *The Times* (14 April 1891) • *The Times* (21 April 1891) • *The Times* (11 June 1891) • E. Morris and E. Roberts, *The Liverpool Academy and other exhibitions of contemporary art in Liverpool, 1774–1867* (1998) • *The Athenaeum* (1891), 512 • K. Halswelle, *Six years in a house-boat: a series of eighty pictures of Thames scenery* (1883) • *IGI* • m. certs.

**Likenesses** R. T. & Co., wood-engraving, NPG; repro. in *ILN* (18 April 1891)

**Wealth at death** £37,988 6*s.* 1*d.*: resworn probate, 13 Oct 1892, *CGPLA Eng. & Wales*

**Halswelle, Wyndham** (1882–1915), athlete, was born on 30 May 1882 at 4 Albemarle Street, Piccadilly, London, the second son of Keeley *Halswelle (1832–1891), an artist known for his genre and landscape paintings, and his second wife, Helen Marianna Elizabeth, *née* Gordon. He was educated at Charterhouse School and the Royal Military College, Sandhurst, and enjoyed a notable athletic career at both institutions. In 1901 he was commissioned into the Highland light infantry and he served in South Africa in 1902. There his athletic ability was noticed by Jimmy Curran, a former professional athlete and later coach. After the Highland light infantry returned to Edinburgh from the Second South African War, Curran persuaded Halswelle to apply himself seriously to running. Halswelle afterwards made rapid progress and in his first year of serious competition, 1904, he won the army 880 yards title (he retained the title in 1905 and 1906). In 1905 he moved down to the quarter-mile and won both the Scottish and the Amateur Athletic Association (AAA) titles.

In 1906, at the 'interim' Olympic games in Athens, Halswelle won medals in the 400 metres and 800 metres. After his return from the games he swept the board of the sprint events at the Scottish championships by winning the 100, 220, 440, and 880 yards on the same afternoon, an extraordinary feat. Two weeks later he retained his 440 yards title at the AAA championships in a personal best time of 48.8 seconds. At the Scottish championships next year he retained his 100 and 220 yards titles, but broke down during the 440 yards race and did not compete again that summer. He showed that the injury was behind him in 1908, the Olympic year, by setting a world record of 31.2 seconds for the 300 yards. Within a fortnight he also set a British record for the 440 yards of 48.4 seconds (which was to survive for twenty-six years). These two brilliant performances were an important confidence-builder in the run up to the Olympic games in London, where a strong 400 metre field assembled. There was fine running in all four heats of the semi-finals, each of which was run in under 50 seconds. Halswelle recorded the fastest time and, having set a new Olympic record in the second round, was the favourite for the final on 23 July 1908.

The three other finalists—W. C. Robbins, T. C. Carpenter, and J. B. Taylor—were all American, and the race reflected the intense competition between the British and American track teams at the London games. The final was not run in lanes and 'consequently something of a free-for-all developed', with Halswelle being baulked by Robbins in the first 50 metres (Watman, 43). Coming to the 300 metres mark Robbins led from Carpenter by about a yard, with Halswelle well placed to strike off the final bend, as he had done in the earlier rounds. But as Halswelle made his move to pass Carpenter in the straight the American began to run wide, forcing him to within 18 inches of the outside of the track. Halswelle later recalled:

> Carpenter's elbow undoubtedly touched my chest, for as I moved outwards to pass him he did likewise, keeping his right arm in front of me. In this manner he bored me across quite two-thirds of the track, and entirely stopped my running. (ibid., 43)

The interference appeared so obvious to the judges that they broke the tape while the race was still being run and declared the result void. That evening they disqualified Carpenter and ordered the race to be rerun in lanes (or 'strings' as they were then known) two days later.

It seemed to *The Times* that the American tactics were part of 'a definite and carefully thought-out plan' which in America would have been considered part and parcel of the race, but which in Britain was 'contrary alike to the rules that govern sport and to our notions of what is fair play' (*The Times*, 24 July 1908). Robbins and Taylor boycotted the final in protest at Carpenter's disqualification and Halswelle was left with a 'walkover' to the Olympic title. He made known his reluctance to run in such circumstances, but the AAA gave him no option. He received a warm reception from the capacity White City crowd during his 50.2 second lap. The controversy, though, continued, and at its annual convention the American Amateur Athletic Union later refused to recognize Carpenter's disqualification, so strongly did its members feel about the verdict of the British judges. The episode soured Halswelle's own attitude to the sport and after a farewell appearance at Glasgow Rangers sports later that year he effectively retired from the track. He afterwards concentrated on his army career. Halswelle, who apparently never married, was killed by a sniper at Neuve Chapelle in France, on 31 March 1915, while serving as a captain with the 1st battalion of the Highland light infantry.

MARK POTTLE

**Sources** I. Buchanan, *British Olympians: a hundred years of gold medallists* (1991) • *The Times* (23 July 1908) • *The Times* (24 July 1908) • *The Times* (27 July 1908) • *The Times* (10 Aug 1908) • M. Watman, *History of British athletics* (1968) • R. L. Quercetani, *A world history of track and field athletics, 1864–1964* (1964) • Lord Killanin and J. Rodda, eds., *The Olympic games: 80 years of people, events and records* (1976) • *Charterhouse School register, 1872–1910* (1911), vol. 2 • *Charterhouse School register, 1872–1931* (1932), vol. 1 • b. cert. • *CGPLA Eng. & Wales* (1915)

**Likenesses** photographs, 1908, Hult. Arch.

**Wealth at death** £12,636 7*s*. 3*d*.: administration, 10 Sept 1915, *CGPLA Eng. & Wales*

**Halsworth, Daniel** (1557/8–*c*.1596), Roman Catholic priest, was presumably born in Lancashire. Having received his schooling at Blackburn grammar school under Lawrence Yates he left England to enrol at the English College, Douai, then located at Rheims, where he arrived on 22 June 1580. Barely a month later he was sent to Rome to continue his studies at the English College where he matriculated, aged twenty-two, on 9 September 1580. Six months later, on 26 May 1581, he signed the oath that committed him to return to the English mission. Halsworth was priested in the chapel of the English College by Thomas Goldwell, the Marian bishop of St Asaph, on 20 November 1583. He was still in Rome in September 1586 when, as a student affiliated to the Society of Jesus, he added his name to a petition against removing the Jesuits from the direction of the English College.

Sent to raise funds for Douai College, Halsworth left Italy with the intention of travelling to England to work as one of the many clandestine Catholic priests there, but was advised by William Allen to return to Italy instead. Back in Italy he joined the household of the duke of Savoy at Turin in May 1587, for whom he certainly was still working until 1591 when, during a visit to Rome, he visited the hospice of the English College in the company of a 'Savoyard'. Halsworth later entered the service of the archbishop of Milan, Cardinal Borromeo, the nephew of Charles Borromeo.

In a register of alumni compiled by Douai College, Halsworth is listed as a doctor of theology. Pits, his contemporary at the English College in Rome, confirms that Halsworth held a doctorate in theology and adds that he also graduated to the degree of doctor of ecclesiastical and civil law at an unspecified Italian university. In his first publication he is described as 'hailing from Turin University' (Halsworth, colophon). Halsworth's written work reflects the early aptitude for classical languages and logic that was noted on his arrival at Rome. It centres on elucidating or translating classical Latin works. As an exiled Englishman 'far from home, without possessions, parents, acquaintances, friends, and every other commodity' (ibid., 12), Halsworth clearly identified with the lot of the exiled heroes of antiquity. A fervent defender of the Catholicity of the church, in his dedication of Virgil's *Bucolica* to William Allen he laments the fall of England to protestantism: 'All have turned heretic. They were invaded and have been devastated' (ibid., 12). It is thought that Halsworth died in Rome about 1596. J. ANDREAS LÖWE

**Sources** D. Halsworth, *Virgilii Maronis bucolica* (1591) • Archivio di Vicariato di Roma, *Libri ordinationum* • *CSP dom.*, 1591–4, p. 151, no. 105, ii • J. Pits, *Relationum historicarum de rebus Anglicis*, ed. [W. Bishop] (Paris, 1619), 794ff. • Tanner, *Bibl. Brit.-Hib.*, 372 • C. Dodd [H. Tootell], *The church history of England, from the year 1500, to the year 1688*, 2 (1739), 90 • H. Foley, ed., *Records of the English province of the Society of Jesus*, 6 (1880), 116, 507, 564 • T. F. Knox and others, eds., *The first and second diaries of the English College, Douay* (1878), 167–8, 375 • Gillow, *Lit. biog. hist.*, 3.103 • W. Kelly, ed., *Liber ruber venerabilis collegii Anglorum de urbe*, 1, Catholic RS, 37 (1940), 21–2 • G. Anstruther, *The seminary priests*, 1 (1969), 170

**Halton, Immanuel** (1628–1699), astronomer, was born on 21 April 1628 at Greenthwaite Hall, Greystoke, Cumberland, the eldest of the ten children of Miles Halton (1599–1652) and his wife, Dorothy, *née* Wybergh (1608–1697). Miles Halton was steward of the Greystoke estates of the Catholic Howard family and, in later years, sheriff of Cumberland. Immanuel Halton was educated at Blencow grammar school, Cumberland, and was admitted to Gray's Inn in 1647. During this time he began to take an interest in astronomy: he made the calculations for and constructed indoor reflecting sundials.

On leaving Gray's Inn, Halton was employed by Henry Howard, who in 1677 succeeded his brother as sixth duke of Norfolk. Halton transacted the latter's business and financial affairs in the Netherlands for several years, and on returning to England he acted as auditor of Howard's household. On 13 February 1660 he married Mary, the daughter of John Newton of Oakerthorpe, Derbyshire; six of their nine children survived him. On his marriage Howard granted Halton rights and lands in Derbyshire, comprising one-third of the manor of Shirland and one-third of his lands in the parishes of Shirland, Morton, and South Wingfield. Before 1666 Halton took his family to live at Wingfield Manor, an impressive but dilapidated house built in the fifteenth century, which he repaired and converted. During the 1670s and 1680s he was employed surveying the Derbyshire estates of the then duke and reorganizing the family's leases and rentals.

Halton continued to pursue the mathematical aspects of astronomy—he made no telescopic observations—and, hearing of the similar activities of the youthful John Flamsteed, called on him in Derby in 1666. They established a warm friendship; Halton guided Flamsteed, lent him important new books, among them Riccioli's *Almagestum* (1651) and Kepler's *Tabulae Rudolphinae* (1627), and translated an essay by Kinkhuysen for him, as 'Moon-wiser'. They corresponded and met over the next ten years, discussing the solutions to mathematical problems and comparing their respective observations of the decade's several solar eclipses. In 1675, when Flamsteed moved to Greenwich as the first astronomer royal, he passed Halton's observations of the eclipse of 23 June 1675 to the Royal Society. Their correspondence lapsed thereafter, but at Halton's death Flamsteed expressed an interest in acquiring some of the former's books.

Towards the end of his service with Norfolk, who died in 1684, Halton may have been caught up in the Popish Plot. The court became increasingly anti-Catholic and Howard went to live in the Netherlands in 1678, at which time he gave Halton further land at South Wingfield and Oakerthorpe, together with Wingfield Manor. Halton's later years were spent, as the inscription on his tomb relates, 'in the studies of music and the mathematics, in which noble sciences he attained a great perfection'. He erected the sundials still in place at Wingfield Manor. After composing his will Halton was moved to change it, 'being much provoked to anger by the late ill action and carriage of my daughter Dorothy', cutting off all legacies, perhaps consequent on her marriage to a Mr Oates, if he was a relative of Titus Oates. Halton died on 31 October 1699 at Wingfield Manor, and was buried two days later in the churchyard at South Wingfield. ANITA MCCONNELL

**Sources** J. B. Robinson, *Historical sketch of the ancient manor of South Wingfield* (1872), 12 • H. T. Wake, 'The Halton family of Cumberland and Derbyshire', *N&Q*, 6th ser., 3 (1881), 44–5 • F. Baily, *An account of the Revd John Flamsteed, the first astronomer-royal* (1835) • S. P. Rigaud and S. J. Rigaud, eds., *Correspondence of scientific men of the seventeenth century*, 2 (1841), 160 • J. Foster, *The register of admissions to Gray's Inn, 1521–1889, together with the register of marriages in Gray's Inn chapel, 1695–1754* (privately printed, London, 1889), 243 • R. Simpson, *A collection of fragments illustrative of the history and antiquities of Derby*, 2 vols. (1826), 2.586–7 • P. M. Barber, 'Immanuel Hilton, the astronomer', *Journal of the British Astronomical Association*, 106 (1996), 22–8 • *The Reliquary*, 5 (1864), 57 • will, 3 April 1700, Lichfield Joint RO, LJRO/B/C/11

**Halton** [Halghton], **John** (*d.* 1324), bishop of Carlisle, was of unknown, but almost certainly northern, origins. He was a student at Oxford, an experience of which he retained affectionate memories, probably before becoming a canon of Carlisle Cathedral priory. He rose to become cellarer of that house, and is recorded as defending its interests in Inglewood Forest, probably in the late 1280s. Following the death of Bishop Irton on 1 March 1292, Halton was one of two canons sent to obtain royal permission to elect a successor. On 23 April he was himself chosen bishop of Carlisle. The king's consent was given on 23 May, and the temporalities were restored on 18 June. Halton was consecrated by the bishop of Durham on 14

September, and enthroned some time after 13 January following. The delay in his enthronement was the result of his becoming engaged in affairs north of the border. Recorded in Scotland on the king's service on 15 October 1292, he was present at Berwick when the Great Cause was decided in John Balliol's favour on 17 November, and was subsequently on good terms with the new king of Scots, who in 1294 addressed Halton as 'his most trusted friend' (Thompson, 1.8).

That friendship is likely to have developed as a result of Halton's being appointed to succeed Bishop Irton as principal collector in Scotland of the crusading tenth imposed by Nicholas IV in 1291 on all the churches of Britain. Between 1292 and 1295 he spent long periods in Scotland, being principally based at Kelso and Jedburgh. He was methodical in his approach to his task, appointing a subcollector for every diocese except St Andrews, which had two. The assessment was considerably higher than that for previous papal taxes, and delays and evasion were commonplace, but considerable amounts were none the less collected; in 1301 his proctor was able to show that of the £15,847 4*s*. 10*d*. for which Halton accepted responsibility, sums totalling £13,562 11*s*. 1¾*d*. had been accounted for to the pope's representatives. It was generally understood that the money from the tenth was intended for Edward I. Halton might also be called upon to serve his king in Scotland more overtly. On 12 October 1295, as Anglo-Scottish relations became increasingly strained, and the Scots entered into negotiations with France, the bishop of Carlisle and the abbot of Newminster were instructed to receive Berwick, Roxburgh, and Jedburgh castles from the Scottish king, to be restored only when England's war with France was over. Such policies made Halton's position ever more difficult. Hitherto he seems to have spent relatively little time in his diocese, but the outbreak of Anglo-Scottish hostilities in 1296 brought him home, and largely kept him there.

There were attacks on Carlisle in 1296 and 1297. Edward I seems to have been impressed by the administrative skills that Halton showed in Scotland, for on 13 October 1297 he appointed him keeper of Carlisle Castle, an office he retained perhaps until May 1304. The bishop would later claim to have spent £100 from the issues of taxation to keep soldiers in the city when William Wallace attacked it in November 1297, at a time when 'there was no other warden within the castle and city than himself' (*CDS*, 3, no. 628). He also carried out substantial works on the castle, spending about £100 per annum on its defence. Cumberland was continually exposed to Scottish raids, and Halton was among those who suffered from their effects, which in February 1301 justified the appropriation of Dalston church to his see, and in November caused him to petition for a reassessment of papal taxation on the diocese. But in the years round 1300 English military successes saved north-west England from the worst effects of the war; in 1298 they enabled Edward to grant forfeited Scottish estates, mostly in Roxburghshire, to Halton, and they also allowed the bishop to devote himself to conventional national and diocesan business.

As well as attending a number of parliaments, Halton attended to the well-being of his cathedral city by securing a grant of pontage for the bridge over the River Eden in January 1300, and obtained a gift of royal timber to repair the bridge a year later. In 1300 he conducted a primary visitation of the cathedral priory, and severely censured the prior, who eventually resigned. In 1302 he tightened his control over the administration of the diocese, by depriving its only archdeacon of judicial authority. Ordinations were held with increasing regularity, with five being recorded in 1305, six in 1306, and five in 1307. In 1306 Halton petitioned for a gift of land between the castle and the city in Carlisle, so that he could build houses on it. In 1307 he was litigating over claims to rights of common at Blackhall, just outside the city. No doubt it was at his prompting that in the same year the archbishop of York granted an indulgence to those who contributed to the restoration of Carlisle Cathedral, badly damaged by fire in 1292 (a further indulgence was granted in 1318).

In 1305 Halton was once more appointed a collector of a papal subsidy in Scotland. But the rebellion and coronation of Robert Bruce in 1306, followed by the death of Edward I in 1307, made this an impossible task. Halton was summoned to Edward II's coronation early in 1308, but thereafter was again usually in his diocese, for as long as increasingly deep and destructive Scottish raids permitted him to stay in north-west England. On 30 May 1311 he was present in York Minster for the consecration of Richard Kellaw as bishop of Durham, while by November he was in France, attending the general council of the church held at Vienne. But on 20 February 1313 he was ordered to stay in the north, 'for the security of the same against the Scots' (*CClR, 1307–1313*, 568), and he contributed to the ransom paid by Cumberland that year to be spared devastation. In April 1314 confusion resulting from conflicting appointments to the command in Carlisle were temporarily resolved by Halton's being designated to the 'superior custody' of the defences. During the same month he was forced to make an agreement with the Scottish king's brother, Edward Bruce, whereby the episcopal manors of Rose (where Bruce had established his headquarters) and Linstock would be spared destruction if Halton could secure the release of two Scottish prisoners. The bishop does not appear to have achieved this, for on 4 July he appointed a vicar-general and withdrew to his manor of Horncastle in Lincolnshire, on the grounds that he could no longer safely live in his diocese; he later reported that all his muniments had been burnt by the Scots. Halton stayed at Horncastle for over two years, only returning to his diocese in October 1316. He remained there for six months, but by May 1317 he was back in Lincolnshire, and although he is recorded at Durham and York during the next two years, he cannot be shown to have been at Carlisle again until 6 August 1319.

In the light of the havoc wrought in his diocese Halton's absences are easily understood. A reassessment of ecclesiastical revenues in 1318 found that the temporalities of the see, valued at £126 7*s*. 7*d*. in 1291, were now worth only

£20. In 1318 a petition to the pope secured the appropriation of Horncastle church to his see, on the now familiar grounds of Scottish devastation. None the less he continued to play a part in national affairs. On 9 August 1318 he became a member of the standing council established under the treaty of Leake between Edward II and Thomas of Lancaster, and shortly afterwards he was summoned with twenty men to an abortive Scottish campaign. And in the following summer he was back in his diocese, encouraged by royal grants of fawns for the park and pickerels for the ponds at Rose. On 22 December 1319 he conducted an ordination in Carlisle Cathedral, his first there for two and a half years. At the beginning of 1320 a two-year truce came into effect. In both 1320 and 1321 Halton was appointed to commissions empowered to treat with the Scots for a lasting peace; but nothing came of their efforts, and when Halton asked for reimbursement of his expenses, he was refused, on the grounds that 'since he went for the common good of the king, the realm and his own bishopric, and did not go far out of the latter, he must bear his own expenses' (*CDS*, 3, no. 743). Perhaps the rejection of his petition inclined him to sympathy with Lancaster, for he attended the assembly convened by the earl at Sherburn in Elmet on 28 June 1321, though he took no part in the confrontation with Edward II and the Despensers that followed it.

The ending of the truce was followed by further Scottish attacks on the north of England. Early in July 1322 King Robert himself directed the burning of Rose. Halton was not in his diocese at the time, and by 7 July he was back in safety at Horncastle. His health was probably failing by now, for on 3 November 1322 he excused himself from attending parliament on the grounds of old age and infirmity. He made similar excuses on 17 February 1324, and in the meantime remained in Lincolnshire. But another Anglo-Scottish truce ultimately made it possible for him to struggle north again. On 9 June 1324 he conducted ordinations at Stanwix, and it was at Rose that he died, on 1 November following. His will does not survive, though he is known to have made one—it contained the bequest of a gold or silver cup to his diocesan official. It is likely that he was buried in Carlisle Cathedral, but no monument remains. Although Halton was himself a graduate, and generous in granting licences to study in the schools, he had no reputation as a theologian or preacher. Rather he was an ecclesiastical man of affairs, and it is appropriate that his lasting memorial should be his register, the first to survive for the see of Carlisle, recording his faltering but dogged efforts to maintain the administration of his diocese in very difficult times.

HENRY SUMMERSON

**Sources** *The register of John de Halton, bishop of Carlisle, AD 1292–1324*, ed. W. N. Thompson, 2 vols., CYS, 12–13 (1913) • *Chancery records* • *RotS*, vol. 1 • *CDS*, vols. 2–3 • Rymer, *Foedera*, new edn, 1/2, 2/1 • F. Palgrave, ed., *The parliamentary writs and writs of military summons*, 2 vols. in 4 (1827–34), vols. 1/2, 2/3 • *CEPR letters*, 2.184 • *RotP*, vol. 1 • *The register of Thomas of Corbridge, lord archbishop of York, 1300–1304*, 2, ed. A. H. Thompson, SurtS, 141 (1928), 150–53 • *The register of William Greenfield, lord archbishop of York, 1306–1315*, ed. W. Brown and A. H. Thompson, 5, SurtS, 153 (1940), 95–7 • *The register of William Melton, archbishop of York, 1317–1340*, 1, ed. R. M. T. Hill, CYS, 70 (1970), 85 • H. R. Luard, ed., *Flores historiarum*, 3 vols., Rolls Series, 95 (1890), vol. 3, pp. 197–8 • *Fasti Angl., 1300–1541*, [York], 97 • H. Summerson, *Medieval Carlisle: the city and the borders from the late eleventh to the mid-sixteenth century*, 2 vols., Cumberland and Westmorland Antiquarian and Archaeological Society, extra ser., 25 (1993) • J. Wilson, *Rose Castle* (1912) • C. M. L. Bouch, *Prelates and people of the lake counties: a history of the diocese of Carlisle, 1133–1933* (1948) • R. K. Rose, 'The bishops and diocese of Carlisle: church and society in the Anglo-Scottish border, 1292–1395', PhD diss., U. Glas., 1984 • M. J. Kennedy, 'John Halton, bishop of Carlisle, 1292–1324', *Transactions of the Cumberland and Westmorland Antiquarian and Archaeological Society*, new ser., 73 (1973), 94–110 • Emden, *Oxf.* • J. Stevenson, ed., *Chronicon de Lanercost, 1201–1346*, Bannatyne Club, 65 (1839), 253

**Halton, Timothy** (*bap.* 1633, *d.* 1704), college head, second son of Miles Halton (1599–1652) of Greenthwaite Hall, high sheriff of Cumberland, and his wife, Dorothy (1608–1697), daughter of William Wybergh, and younger brother of Immanuel *Halton, was baptized at Greystoke, Cumberland, on 19 September 1633. After education at Blencow grammar school, on 9 March 1649 he entered Queen's College, Oxford, where his tutor was Thomas Smith, later bishop of Carlisle, and he established lifelong friendships with, among others, Joseph Williamson, later secretary of state, and Thomas Lamplugh, later archbishop of York. The latter, writing to Williamson in 1655, spoke of this group as 'our fraternity' and as 'Cronyes' (PRO, SP 18/97, fol. 201*r*). Halton graduated BA on 17 February 1653 and proceeded MA on 21 June 1655, achieving a fellowship in April 1657. Surviving correspondence between the friends during the mid-1650s suggests a factious fellowship, the 'fraternity' ever critical of Thomas Barlow, who became provost of Queen's in 1658.

By March 1661 Halton had had offers of chaplaincies from Bishop William Lucy of St David's and from the queen of Bohemia at The Hague. He refused the latter, while accepting as much patronage from the bishop, whose son he had tutored, as was consistent with his fellowship. Subsequently he spent time in Wales, representing St David's at convocation in 1661 and becoming a prebendary in 1662. He proceeded BD at Oxford on 30 April 1662. Having received the archdeaconry of Brecon on 8 February 1672, backed by Williamson, Halton manoeuvred against Barlow and in 1673 was secured from interference by a royal dispensation to keep his fellowship despite excessive income.

During 1673 and 1674 Halton accompanied Williamson and Sir Leoline Jenkins as chaplain on their embassy to Cologne. He became DD on 27 June 1674 and, by Williamson's interest, archdeacon of Oxford on 10 July 1675 in succession to Barlow. In this post he collaborated with Bishop John Fell against dissenters. Following Barlow's elevation as bishop of Lincoln in 1675 and his subsequent resignation from Queen's, Halton was unanimously elected provost on 7 April 1677, Williamson being 'the cheif means of his election' (*Life and Times of Anthony Wood*, 2.438). He came to be regarded as a stern disciplinarian, a generous, convivial companion, and a sound man of business. He received the college rectory of Weyhill, Hampshire, in 1679. Enjoying the confidence of bishops John Fell,

Thomas Lamplugh, and Henry Compton (another Queen's man), Halton was nominated vice-chancellor in 1679, 1680, and again in 1681 by the chancellor, James, duke of Ormond, and was in office during the 1681 third Exclusion Parliament. Halton appeared a loyal high-churchman but, despite efforts by friends, failed to advance.

Urged by Bishop Compton and by Jenkins (who declared it the desire of James II) Halton reluctantly accepted the vice-chancellorship again for the year 1685/6. In 1685 he forbade bookshops to sell the life of Christ published by the Catholic Obadiah Walker. In 1686, however, he restrained anti-Catholic preachers for fear of reaction by the commission for ecclesiastical affairs. He obtained a convenient college rectory, Charlton-on-Otmoor, Oxfordshire, on 29 December 1685 after it was resigned by Lamplugh.

After the revolution of 1688, in which Halton acquiesced sufficiently to gain the enmity of Thomas Hearne, who suggests he was a drinker and vindictive towards political opponents, Halton focused on college and parochial affairs. Between 1692 and 1696, following a 1691 bequest of books from Bishop Barlow and probably guided architecturally by Dean Henry Aldrich of Christ Church, he built the college a magnificent library, contributing £2000 himself and securing other funding to meet the cost of £5247. He improved the provost's lodgings, purchased houses in the High Street, and added buildings to the college. He built a spacious parsonage at Charlton and bought land which he left to his successors subject to an annual payment of £3 to the poor of three Oxford parishes.

Halton died, unmarried, on 21 July 1704, probably at Queen's College, and was buried in the chapel there. He left £50 per annum to the college to fund purchases of livings, and bequeathed 500 books to the library.

A. J. Hegarty

**Sources** Bodl. Oxf., MS Rawl. D. 923, fols. 233r–234v • J. R. Magrath, *The Queen's College*, 2 (1921), 63–76 • R. H. Hodgkin, *Six centuries of an Oxford college: a history of the Queen's College, 1340–1940* (1949), 127–30 • R. A. Beddard, 'Tory Oxford', *Hist. U. Oxf.* 4: *17th-cent. Oxf.*, 863–906 • R. A. Beddard, 'James II and the Catholic challenge', *Hist. U. Oxf.* 4: *17th-cent. Oxf.*, 907–54 • PRO, SP: 18/97, 201r; 18/123, 124r–125r; 18/129, 140r–v; 29/32, 138r; 29/34, 164r; 29/316, 244r • *Fasti Angl.* (Hardy), 1.312; 2.516 • 'The Halton family of Cumberland and Derbyshire', *N&Q*, 6th ser., 3 (1881), 44–5 • *Remarks and collections of Thomas Hearne*, ed. C. E. Doble and others, 11 vols., OHS, 2, 7, 13, 34, 42–3, 48, 50, 65, 67, 72 (1885–1921), vol. 1, pp. 77, 83–4, 306; vol. 2, pp. 63, 69, 109, 224–5; vol. 3, p. 288 • Foster, *Alum. Oxon.* • *The life and times of Anthony Wood*, ed. A. Clark, 2, OHS, 21 (1892), 438

**Archives** Queen's College, Oxford, corresp. and papers incl. notebook and sermons

**Likenesses** M. Burghers, line engraving, BM, NPG • J. Maubert, oils, Queen's College, Oxford; two copies, Queen's College, Oxford

**Wealth at death** left funds on tithes at Llan-faes, Wales, to buy livings; 500 volumes to college library; 8 acres leased, adjoining rectory garden at Charlton-on-Otmoor, to successors in living, providing they paid £3 p.a. to poor of Oxford: will, proved 1 Sept 1704, PRO, PROB 11/478, sig. 184; Magrath, *Queen's College*, vol. 2, p. 72; Bodl. Oxf., MS Rawl. D. 923, fols. 233r–234v

**Halyburton, Andrew** (*d.* 1506), merchant and administrator, was probably a native of Edinburgh, where he owned a tenement on the north side of the High Street. Nothing is known of his family except that he had at least two sisters. By 1493 he had been appointed conservator of the privileges of the Scottish nation in the lands of the archduke of Flanders, comprising Flanders, Brabant, Holland, and Zealand. His ledger survives, recording his transactions in the post from that year until 1506. It shows that he was back in Scotland in April 1495, but otherwise he usually appears to have been in the Netherlands. Perhaps he came to be regarded as insufficiently accountable to his clients, for in 1504 it was decreed that the conservator should return to Scotland once a year, either in person or through a representative, to answer to any complaints against him. Halyburton's usual overseas base was probably Middelburg, but he may have moved to Antwerp before he died, and he was also active at Bruges, Veere, and Brussels.

Halyburton's ledger records that he was himself active in trade, selling wool on his own account and on behalf of his sister, and buying goods for retail. But it also shows that he was principally engaged in oiling the wheels of Scottish commerce in the Low Countries, by taking delivery of exported goods and selling them on behalf of their owners, who included William Scheves, archbishop of St Andrews, his successor James Stewart (second son of James III and also duke of Ross), William Elphinstone, bishop of Aberdeen, the abbot of Holyrood, and numerous Edinburgh and Aberdeen merchants. Those exports were entirely primary wares—wool, sheepskins, hides, fish, meat, on one occasion pearls. The money raised by their sale was very often employed to buy luxury goods for shipping back to Scotland. Spices and wine feature prominently in the ledger, and Halyburton also supplied clothes, cushions, featherbeds, church vestments and plate, books, signet rings, 1000 floor tiles for the archdeacon of St Andrews, tombstones for Scheves and James Stewart, and gunpowder for Elphinstone; he had the latter's clock repaired as well. In every case Halyburton noted the prices of goods sold and his expenditure on goods bought, in transactions complicated by the wide variety of currencies circulating in the Netherlands: he handled the money of England, France, and Scotland, Spanish reals, Hungarian ducats, 'hedis of Myllain', and gulden from the Rhineland, Ghent, Utrecht, and Denmark. He several times recorded transferring money to Rome, usually through the 'Cornellis Altanite' bank (most likely a branch of the Altoviti), sometimes to aid the purposes of Scheves and Elphinstone, but also to obtain marriage dispensations.

As conservator Halyburton was a crown official. It was in that capacity that from 1504 he was required to do justice in disputes between Scottish merchants overseas. When in 1506 James IV intervened to promote Scottish interests in the Netherlands, he referred the relevant authorities to Halyburton as his own agent, declaring that he would 'look on a wrong done to Andrew as an insult to himself' (*Letters of James the Fourth*, 24–5). It may have been as the king's agent that in 1497 the duke of Ross twice employed him to send letters to Margaret, duchess of Burgundy, on the second occasion 'quhit ros lettrys' (Halyburton, 215)—possibly a reference to the white wax of the quarter seal, but more likely relating to the duchess's Yorkism and support for Perkin Warbeck. Halyburton dealt in works of art, sometimes for private individuals, as when in 1496 he provided John Penycuik with an image of St Thomas of Canterbury, but also for the royal court. In 1504 or 1505 the king asked him to send him a painter, and Halyburton secured the services of one 'Piers the painter' (perhaps Peerken Bovelant), who worked for King James from 1505 to 1508. He was well placed to make such provision, for his wife, Cornelia, was the daughter of the Ghent artist Sander Bening and a kinswoman of Hugo van der Goes. Halyburton died in 1506; a successor was appointed to his conservatorship on 31 December 1507. His heir was his son Thomas. HENRY SUMMERSON

**Sources** *Ledger of Andrew Halyburton*, ed. C. Innes (1867) · M. Livingstone, D. Hay Fleming, and others, eds., *Registrum secreti sigilli regum Scotorum / The register of the privy seal of Scotland*, 1 (1908) · *The letters of James the Fourth, 1505–1513*, ed. R. L. Mackie and R. K. Hannay, 3rd ser., Scottish History Society, 45 (1953) · J. B. Paul, ed., *Compota thesaurariorum regum Scotorum / Accounts of the lord high treasurer of Scotland*, 3 (1901) · *Protocol book of John Foular, 1503–1513*, ed. W. MacLeod, 1/1 (1940); Scottish RS, 72 · L. Campbell, 'Scottish patrons and Netherlandish painters in the fifteenth and sixteenth centuries', *Scotland and the Low Countries, 1124–1994*, ed. G. G. Simpson (1996), 89–103 · M. P. Rooseboom, *The Scottish staple in the Netherlands* (1910) · D. Ditchburn, *Scotland and Europe: the medieval kingdom and its contacts with Christendom*, 1 (2000)

**Halyburton, George** (1627/8–1682). *See under* Halyburton, Thomas (1674–1712).

**Halyburton, James** (1518–1589), provost of Dundee and religious reformer, was the son of George Halyburton of Pitcur, a barony in the parish of Kettins, Angus. He entered the University of St Andrews in 1537 and graduated MA in March 1539. His brother Andrew, who had inherited the estate of Pitcur, died about this time naming James as guardian to his son and heir, George. James was therefore known as tutor of Pitcur. In 1540 James V granted him and his betrothed, Margaret Rossy, a charter of lands in the Carse of Gowrie. He was probably enrolled as a Dundee burgess about that time but the revision of the list of burgesses undertaken in 1582 while he was provost has no record of his entry. From 1554 to 1581 he was the commissioner for the burgh of Dundee at almost all Scotland's conventions and parliaments, including the Reformation Parliament of 1560, which effectively abolished papal supremacy in the country. In 1567 he was appointed one of the lords of the articles, the committee which prepared legislation for the full parliament. Though often present at meetings of the privy council in the 1570s, Halyburton officially became a member only in March 1582. He was a regular and active attender at meetings of the general assembly of the Church of Scotland until the year before his death. When in 1581 the assembly nominated agents to set up presbyteries throughout the country, he was one of those responsible for Angus. He acted as one of the king's commissioners to the assembly in 1582 and 1583.

Halyburton first gained a national reputation in the late 1540s. Broughty Castle near Dundee had been captured by English forces in September 1547, and when the major part of the Scottish forces withdrew temporarily he was left in command of the cavalry to continue the siege. His force of local men assisted in the assault in February 1550 when French forces sent to assist the regent, Mary of Guise, recaptured the castle. He was appointed keeper of Liddesdale by Mary in 1556. Soon after his arrival there the Grahams took him prisoner and held him in a keep near the border, intending to move him into England at the first opportunity. However, the nearby Scottish and French forces, informed of his whereabouts, stormed the keep during the night and rescued him.

Despite his energy in the struggle against the English invasions, rewarded by a pension of £500, Halyburton's religious sympathies were not those of the regent. During his years at St Andrews University, John Winram, later a prominent protestant theologian, was sub-provost while religious reform was openly discussed at St Leonard's College. Though Halyburton enrolled at St Salvator's he must have heard and sympathized with the arguments for the new doctrines. By October 1550 he was provost of Dundee, a burgh whose trading contacts with European ports had early brought knowledge of and undoubted sympathy for reforming ideas. As the regent became less lenient towards dissent, the town council and the provost became more recalcitrant and demonstrated their enthusiasm for religious reform. They supported Thomas McGibbon, the schoolmaster of the burgh school, who openly discussed the new doctrines with his pupils. In the spring of 1559 the regent ordered the provost to arrest Paul Methven, a local man, believed to have been a baker by trade but by the mid-1550s a leading protestant preacher. Far from being obedient and arranging for Methven to appear at Stirling in May to answer charges against him, the provost quietly advised Methven to flee the town.

From late in 1557 opposition to the religious policies of Mary of Guise and dislike of her dependence on French advisers and forces began to coalesce round the lords of the congregation, a group of prominent reformers who came to hope for support from Elizabeth of England. In 1559 Provost Halyburton joined this group, and thereafter general recognition of his probity and ability meant that he was never far from the centre of religious and governmental circles, supporting religious reform and pro-English policies. He was a trusted adviser of Lord James Stewart, later earl of Moray, and was one of the few summoned to confer with him and the earl of Argyll in St Andrews in June 1559 as to what action should be taken to establish the reformed religion, since it had become obvious that the regent had no intention of supporting change. When the lords of the congregation took up arms against Mary of Guise in 1559, Halyburton led a force from Angus and Dundee into Fife and was responsible for picking a site at Cupar Muir which gave the army of the congregation such an advantage that the advance of the government army was halted. After Perth was occupied by the forces of the reformers, Halyburton and his brother, Captain Alexander Halyburton, tried in vain to stop the sacking of the abbey of Scone. Later in the year a contingent of Halyburton's men, under his leadership, took part in defending Edinburgh. In October Halyburton was left in charge of ordnance and foot to contain the French force holding Leith, while the other leaders with the cavalry somewhat surprisingly attended a twelve-hour religious service, according to John Knox. His force was surprised at dinner and retreated, leaving the ordnance to the French. In early November Alexander was killed in another attack on Leith. Master James lived to fight another day, and was one of the Scottish commissioners sent to Berwick to negotiate assistance from England, especially to obtain forces to help free Leith from the French.

In 1563 Queen Mary awarded Halyburton a pension after he showed that he had been given one by her late mother for earlier services, particularly against the English. He was appointed to help administer the Act of Oblivion of 1563 which decided who should be pardoned for rebellion against the regent. Unsurprisingly he fell out of favour by taking part in the chaseabout raid of 1565, the earl of Moray's rebellion against the queen's marriage to Lord Darnley. Like Moray he fled to England, thereby escaping imprisonment, but he was forfeited and put to the horn. During a visit to Dundee the queen replaced him as provost by the earl of Crawford, but reconciliation with the monarch soon followed. On 2 March 1566 at Newcastle, Moray and Halyburton were among signatories of a bond promising to support Darnley in his claim to the matrimonial throne. As a result of the subsequent murder of David Riccio, Halyburton's forfeiture was revoked; he once again became provost of Dundee.

Halyburton was involved in Mary's downfall in 1567, and was one of the ten commissioners who accepted her abdication in favour of her son on 24 July. He was present at James VI's coronation at Stirling on 29 July, and subsequently fought at Langside where Mary was defeated on 13 May 1568. Thereafter he was sent to suppress the queen's Gordon supporters, and to capture Kinnaird Castle from John Carnegie. He was active in the civil war between the Marian and the king's parties in the following years. In 1571, while leading an attack on Edinburgh on horseback, he became separated from his force of infantry and was captured by the queen's party. Imprisoned in the castle he was to have been hanged the following morning, but was spared by a combination of the intercession of leading burgesses and Lord Lindsay's threat to treat likewise a number of Mary's supporters from Fife whom he had taken prisoner.

After the assassination of the earl of Moray on 23 January 1570, Halyburton became an adviser to the earl of Morton, who was chosen regent in 1572. He was one of Morton's three representatives in the negotiations to settle his quarrel with the earls of Argyll and Atholl in October 1578. In that year, too, he was one of those appointed by parliament to try to settle the affairs of the kirk. In 1579 he was a member of the commission set up by the privy council to investigate the problem of poor relief. Later this commission was given the additional duty of investigating the affairs of St Andrews University. George Buchanan was another member, both he and Halyburton signing the commission's report. On 1 April 1588 Halyburton was once again a member of a commission appointed to examine the university's affairs and to report on 17 May, previous enquiries and reports not having been acted on because of the unsettled state of the country. On 4 December 1579 Halyburton was made commendator of Pittenweem as a reward for services which had left him heavily in debt, even though he had previously been awarded a number of pensions from church lands. He did not support Morton's removal from power at the end of 1580, but his was a minority view and he was present when Morton was condemned for his supposed involvement in the death of Darnley.

In 1580 and in February 1582 Halyburton was sent to the borders to be justice at the trial of border surnames, inhabitants of Teviotdale and Liddesdale charged with crimes of theft and violence. His appointment to the privy council in March may well have been a reward for his services there, though it was to his constant care for the king's interests since his coronation that this was attributed. He was also a mediator in the feud between the Gordons and Forbeses in 1580. In August 1582 James VI was captured by the Ruthven raiders to remove him from the influence of his French cousin Esmé Stewart, duke of Lennox. Though Halyburton must have sympathized with the raiders' aims, since Lennox was suspected of Catholic and Marian leanings, he seems to have joined the raiders only after the event. After the king regained his freedom in June 1583 Halyburton continued for a time to attend privy council meetings, but he had to resign the commendatorship of Pittenweem in July. It was then given to Sir William Stewart who had helped the king to escape the Ruthven raiders. James also instructed Dundee town council to elect the earl of Crawford as their provost but they persisted in returning Halyburton.

Halyburton seems, indeed, to have retained the loyalty of the town and to have carried out his local duties to the satisfaction of its burgesses despite being so deeply involved in affairs of state. He regularly presided over the burgh's courts and could be seen defending the town's interests in parliament and privy council. When he died in February 1589 the council paid for his funeral and erected a monument to him in the parish church of St Mary's, where he was buried. It was lost in the fire of 1841 which destroyed the church. Margaret Rossy, Halyburton's presumed first wife, had died before 19 April 1564, when he married Grizel Meldrum, widow of Sir James Learmonth of Clatto, who was provost of St Andrews for many years. He is not known to have had any children.

ANNETTE M. SMITH

**Sources** Dundee burgh records, Dundee City Archives, Dundee • *Reg. PCS*, 1st ser. • *APS*, 1424–1592 • M. D. Young, ed., *The parliaments of Scotland: burgh and shire commissioners*, 2 vols. (1992–3) • J. M. Thomson and others, eds., *Registrum magni sigilli regum Scotorum / The register of the great seal of Scotland*, 11 vols. (1882–1914) • *John Knox's History of the Reformation in Scotland*, ed. W. C. Dickinson, 2 vols. (1949) • T. Thomson, ed., *Acts and proceedings of the general assemblies of the*

*Kirk of Scotland*, 3 pts, Bannatyne Club, 81 (1839–45) • A. I. Dunlop, ed., *Acta facultatis artium universitatis Sanctiandree, 1413–1588*, 2 vols., Scottish History Society, 3rd ser., 54–5 (1964) • A. Maxwell, *The history of old Dundee* (1884) • A. Maxwell, *Old Dundee* (1891) • calendar of charters, register of deeds, NA Scot. [Grizel Meldrum] • A. H. Millar, *Roll of eminent burgesses of Dundee* (1887) • J. B. A. T. Teulet, ed., *Relations politiques de la France et de l'Espagne avec l'Écosse au XVIème siècle: papiers d'état, pièces et documents inédits*, new edn, 5 vols. (Paris, 1862) • C. Rogers, *Monuments and monumental inscriptions in Scotland*, 2 vols. (1871–2) • J. B. Paul and C. T. McInnes, eds., *Compota thesaurariorum regum Scotorum / Accounts of the lord high treasurer of Scotland*, 6–13 (1905–78) • F. D. Bardgett, *Scotland reformed: the Reformation in Angus and the Mearns* (1989)

**Halyburton, Thomas** (1674–1712), Church of Scotland minister and theologian, was born on 25 December 1674 at Dupplin, Perthshire. His father, **George Halyburton** (1627/8–1682), Church of Scotland minister and a member of the family of Haliburton of Pitcur, Forfarshire, graduated from St Andrews University in 1652 and was licensed as a minister by the presbytery of Glasgow in November 1656. He was ordained as colleague to the valetudinarian Andrew Playfair, minister of Aberdalgie and Dupplin, Perthshire, on 6 August 1657, appearing in Perth presbytery minutes as George Halyburton the younger, to distinguish him from a close relative and volatile royalist, George Halyburton the elder (1617–1665), minister at Perth, who after the Restoration was briefly bishop of Dunkeld and deposed his kinsman for nonconformity. George the younger remained in the parish, where he was sheltered by a relative of the earl of Kinnoull and subsequently ministered to his episcopalian successor, Mungo Wemyss, when the latter was dying in 1667:

> This poor man lived in great trouble, and seemed to die in despair; for when he took his death-bed, first he sent for Mr Haliburton, and craved him pardon for entring into his church contrare to the will of God; then he desired him to pray for him, which Mr Haliburton did very heartily, but to small purpose, alace! for his horror continued, because of his perjury, even to the last. (Kirkton, 111)

A royal proclamation of March 1676 led to an act of the privy council on 25 April imposing swingeing penalties for nonconformity. George Halyburton was cited on 3 August for keeping conventicles, and was outlawed. He died in October 1682.

George Halyburton's wife was Margaret (*b.* *c.*1629), daughter of Andrew Playfair and Margaret Oliphant. Of their eleven children only two—Thomas and an older sister, Janet (*d.* 1702), who married another minister, Patrick Couper (1660–1740)—survived childhood. In May 1685 the widowed Margaret Halyburton moved with her remaining family to Rotterdam, where Couper had recently been ordained and retained connections. Thomas was later sent back to live with relatives in Perth. He briefly returned to Rotterdam in the spring of 1687 and for a few months attended Latin classes at Erasmus's school. In August his mother moved back to Scotland and he himself went to school in Perth for three or four years, and then to the school of Gavin Weir at Edinburgh. In November 1692 he entered Edinburgh University, where his regent was Alexander Cunningham and where Thomas Aikenhead was a classmate. Here the first signs of a debilitating immobility (probably rheumatoid arthritis) began to show. Next session he was transferred for health reasons to St Leonard's College, St Andrews, where he studied under Thomas Taylor and graduated MA on 24 July 1696. His mother blocked his ambitions to return to the continent for additional study.

Halyburton began to have religious doubts about the age of fifteen, and attempts to dispel them through his philosophical studies left him dissatisfied. Having nevertheless contemplated following his father and brother-in-law (now at Pittenweem) into the ministry, and being deeply influenced by the preaching of Thomas Forrester (*d.* 1706) at St Andrews, he accepted employment as private chaplain in the household of Margaret Wemyss, countess of Wemyss (1659–1705); his college principal, William Tullidelph, had been recently minister of Wemyss. Isolated from close friends or colleagues, Halyburton was out of his element among the aristocracy and unequipped for the open debate on theological issues that was soon to confront him. When challenged to answer the arguments of the deists he found insufficient consolation in the reasoning of their opponents, and became psychologically and physically ill in the effort to reconcile his intellectual condition with the requirements of his post. Early in 1698 he underwent a conversion, by which he came to view faith and philosophy as antithetical and to reject any attempt to found the convictions of the heart upon the deliverances of the head as a diabolical temptation. Despite his self-doubts he sufficiently impressed his hearers by his bearing and scholarship to be sought as a potential tutor, and within two years of leaving college he was approached by the presbytery of Kirkcaldy to undertake trials for the ministry. Though lacking theological training he was entered on trials in March 1699 and licensed on 22 June. By November he had calls from three parishes, William Wishart the elder being particularly solicitous to attract him as a colleague to South Leith. Wishart was under obligations to the countess for her intervention when his own position was threatened, and he was probably the 'minister from Edinburgh' who as a close friend attended Halyburton on his deathbed.

Halyburton accepted the call to Ceres in Fife, judging that it offered the best opportunity to improve his training. On 1 May 1700 he was ordained and on 23 January 1701 he married Janet, daughter and heir of David Watson, a heritor in the parish of St Andrews. He owned an acre of land in St Andrews and, through his wife, acquired an interest in other property there, the income from which they made over to the university. They had four daughters and two sons, of whom the eldest daughter, Margaret, married Wishart's elder son, William (*c.*1692–1753). Kirk session records show Halyburton to have been a diligent and humane pastor and a conciliator. His stipend was £800 Scots but he had occasion to complain of the condition of the manse and the inadequate provision of 'foggage', or winter grazing (Cupar presbytery minutes, 11 January and 1 February 1709). By 1708 his health had broken; he demurred when offered the chair of divinity at

St Mary's College, St Andrews, in 1710, and the Cupar presbytery, which he had long been too ill to attend, avoided releasing him. The queen's commission was nevertheless issued on 1 April and the synod of Fife ruled in favour of his translation. He devoted his inaugural lecture in May 1711 to criticizing the insinuations against the Christian revelation that he found in Archibald Pitcairne's clandestine *Epistola Archimedis* (*c.*1706). Pitcairne, a leading physician and deistic episcopalian with a penchant for baiting the Presbyterian establishment, had adopted the persona of Archimedes to argue that the susceptibility of the world to mathematical description proved a unitary deity but that only the common beliefs of different religions had any probability of being true; he thought that their distinguishing doctrines were imposed on an ignorant public by self-promoting leaders and wonder-workers. To Halyburton this ignored the transparency, as he considered it, of the biblical record and the biblical message. His lecture was posthumously printed in 1714. Otherwise, as a fluent Latinist he probably lectured extempore, having had no opportunity for systematic reading or writing after his health failed.

Halyburton's principal writings, all posthumously published, date from his time at Ceres. They were reprinted under a succession of editors until well into the nineteenth century. Although their primary appeal is to a conservative evangelical readership they have a literary eloquence uncharacteristic of their time and place. His spiritual *Memoirs*, covering the period up to the date of his ordination, published by his widow with extracts from a subsequent diary and an account of his dying discourse, first appeared in 1715 and attracted a preface by Isaac Watts in editions after 1718; John Wesley and George Whitefield added their own forematter to an abridgement published in 1739. These and later editors all accept at face value Halyburton's self-condemning interpretation of his mental turmoil and the spiritual analysis of his physical illness. *The Great Concern of Salvation*, published in 1717, with its graphic depiction of fire and brimstone, is a powerful exposition of the orthodox view of sin and redemption, and was again promoted by Watts. Of wider interest, however, are two separate works central to the eighteenth-century debate on rational religion, which since 1714 have always appeared together. *Natural Religion Insufficient and Revealed Necessary to Man's Happiness* criticizes views that Halyburton claimed to find in Herbert of Cherbury, Charles Blount, and deist pamphleteers of the late seventeenth century, views that he considered to be fuelled by a too philosophical approach to theology among some English divines. Halyburton works within a broadly Lockean theory of knowledge, and with generally sympathetic reference to Locke's *Reasonableness of Christianity*, to show that natural reason cannot adequately demonstrate the nature of deity or of human duty, or the reality of and the preconditions for an afterlife. In *An Essay Concerning the Reason of Faith*, however, he distances himself from Locke, whom he now associates with Jean Le Clerc and other 'rationalists' for demanding that faith founded in revelation be based upon a critical appraisal of the historical signs that validate it. Halyburton sees this, on the contrary, as undermining all ground of certainty in religion, and he raises questions about the internal logic of Locke's position that have continued to linger. Thomas Halyburton died at St Andrews on 23 September 1712 and was buried in the cathedral graveyard.

M. A. Stewart

**Sources** T. Halyburton, *Memoirs* (1715) [incl. anonymous 'Short account of the Rev. Thomas Halyburton'] • legal deeds relating to Thomas Halyburton and Janet Watson, U. St Andr. L. • Glasgow, Perth, Kirkcaldy, and Cupar presbytery minutes, NA Scot. • Synod of Fife minutes, NA Scot. • J. Kirkton, *A history of the Church of Scotland, 1660–1679*, ed. R. Stewart (1992) • R. Wodrow, *The history of the sufferings of the Church of Scotland from the Restoration to the revolution*, ed. R. Burns, 2 (1836), chap. 11 • *Fasti Scot.*, new edn, vols. 4–5 • W. Fraser, *Memorials of the family of Wemyss of Wemyss*, 3 vols. (1888) • W. K. Rutherford and A. C. Rutherford, *Genealogical history of the Halliburton family*, rev edn, 2 vols. (1972)

**Likenesses** J. Scott, engraving (after unknown artist), repro. in R. Burns, ed., *The works of the Rev. Thomas Halyburton* (1835)

**Ham, Elizabeth** (1783–1859), poet and writer, was born on 30 November 1783 in the village of North Perrott, Somerset, on the border with Dorset, the third of the seven children of Thomas Ham, a yeoman farmer and brewer, and his slightly older wife, Elizabeth, who was also, perhaps, of rather higher social standing. Some eighteen months later, at the time of her mother's next pregnancy, Elizabeth lived with various relatives in the neighbourhood and was taken home from time to time. Her own family came together later at Dorchester, Weymouth, and several villages between the two towns and to the west of them. Elizabeth had spells of schooling near home and, for a short time, at an unsatisfactory boarding-school at Tiverton in Devon. Part of her youth coincided with George III's summer visits to Weymouth during the wars with Napoleon when troops and seamen thronged the towns, and for Elizabeth life became a round of plays, balls, parties, fireworks, regattas, and reviews.

Elizabeth's father decided to move to Ireland and on 3 November 1804 he and Elizabeth set out for Milford Haven in Wales and from there by boat to Waterford. Their first winter in Ireland was spent in Carlow, and in March 1805 the family began a roundabout journey taking them to Kilkenny, Tipperary, Limerick, Ennis, Galway, Castlebar, and eventually Ballina in co. Mayo. There Thomas Ham hoped to make his fortune from cheap grain, and set up malting businesses to supply a brewery in Guernsey. Elizabeth deliberately recorded her impressions of the state of Irish society at the time, including the conditions of the Irish poor, whom she none the less admired. However, party-going and dancing among the soldiery still formed a main part of her life. At Ballina she fell in love with a junior officer who, it would seem, acted in bad faith. She never married, later remarking that we 'live a large portion of our lives between fifteen and twenty-five' (Ham, *Elizabeth Ham by Herself*, 61). Her recollections of her time in Ireland are characterized by a late eighteenth-century appreciation of the sublime and picturesque.

Thomas Ham's fortunes did not mend and in 1809 Elizabeth returned to Wessex and to the realization that she no longer had a settled home. She also discovered, to her distress, that her accent had been affected by her years in Ireland. She flitted from relative to relative, serving as housekeeper, maid, or nurse as required, and without payment. She visited Guernsey again (a previous family visit had occurred before she moved to Ireland), by which time she was writing verse. Despite a long romantic interest in Napoleon, she took a leading part in the many peace celebrations in 1814 which were taking place from Blandford in eastern Dorset to Yeovil and East Coker in southern Somerset. Later she taught in a small school in Fordington, near Dorchester.

It was in Yeovil that Elizabeth turned to Unitarianism. Eventually, about 1820, she became the governess to the household of the poet and patron Charles Elton—then also a Unitarian—of Clifton, Bristol, where she was, at last, treated as one of a large family of 'gentlefolks'. *An Infant's Grammar* (1820?) was published, and Elton helped her with a long narrative poem which appeared anonymously in 1824 as *Elgiva, or, The Monks*, the latter displaying a wide reading on her part.

After the 1820s details of Elizabeth's life are few. The last of the Elton children was born in 1825 and it is difficult to tell how long she stayed on as governess. She had a piece published anonymously in *The Remembrance*, an annual, in 1831, and allusions to Dickens and Thackeray show that she kept abreast of the times in her reading. In 1837 she was in Bath, and was in Brislington, near Bristol, in 1844. In 1845 she recalled her Irish experiences in the romance *The Ford Family in Ireland*. She referred to the thunder of Louis Jullien's quadrille band, which she could have heard in Bristol or Bath in 1850, and she was still living in Brislington in 1851 as housekeeper for a lady of property.

At the age of sixty-six Elizabeth began writing her recollections; she had not kept diaries and some of her dates must therefore be accepted with caution. She was still working at it in 1852, by which time she had covered the years up to about 1825. An abridgement of her recollections was published in 1945 as *Elizabeth Ham by herself, 1783–1820*. Her imaginative power strongly evokes a sense of her time and yet also describes events and people from a matter-of-fact Victorian perspective. The autobiography combines propriety with engaging frankness. Elizabeth Ham died of heart disease in Brislington, at Wick House, the home of her employer, on 1 March 1859.

BERNARD JONES

**Sources** *Elizabeth Ham by herself, 1783–1820*, ed. E. Gillett (1945) · M. Nathan, *The annals of West Coker* (1957) · [E. Ham], *Elgiva, or, The monks: an historical poem with some minor pieces* (1824) · [E. Ham], 'Mabel', *The Remembrance*, ed. T. Roscoe (1831) · [E. Ham], *The Ford family in Ireland* (1845) · d. cert. · personal information (2004) · parish register (birth and baptism), North Perrott, Somerset, 1783–4

**Wealth at death** under £1500: probate, 25 March 1859, *CGPLA Eng. & Wales*

**Hambleden**. For this title name *see* Smith, (William) Frederick Danvers, second Viscount Hambleden (1868–1928).

**Hambledon cricket club** (*act. c.*1750–*c.*1796), named for the village of Hambledon, near Portsmouth in Hampshire, affords the earliest major documented source for the administration, membership, and activities of a game which had been played in England for over a century. Its first recorded match was in 1756 against Dartford and its oldest surviving player, William Beldham (1766–1862) [*see below*], told the cricket historian James Pycroft that he believed the club had existed in 1750 on Broadhalfpenny Down. Beldham probably meant a team in the parish. The actual word 'club' is not found being used until 1761. Various reasons may be offered to suggest why cricket flourished so much in an obscure village in the south of England. A local clergyman, Charles Powlett (1728–1809), according to Beldham, supplied much of the enthusiasm and leadership. Equally important, the chalk downlands of unenclosed pasture, closely cropped by sheep, offered ideal conditions for playing. Hambledon itself was near enough to London to provide a country retreat for some 150 members over the years, who were either aristocrats, soldiers, clergymen, or gentry; those who actually played the game were either yeomen or of peasant stock—Charles Bennett, fourth earl of Tankerville (1743–1822), was the exception as a 'given' player and not a member. **Richard Nyren** (1734–1797), publican, baker, and cricketer, was the intermediary who, as captain, secretary, groundsman, and landlord of the Bat and Ball, steered the club through its greatest years. As a player, he scored 98 against Surrey in 1775. The detailed club accounts show him buying claret for the members, settling Farmer Garrett's bill for 10 guineas for the use of the ground, and paying the players. He, together with the shoemaker William Barber (1734–1805)—a useful bowler—set up tents at matches offering the ladies as much ease 'as if they were in their own dressing room' (Ashley-Cooper, 163).

Richard's son, John *Nyren (1764–1837), in *The Young Cricketer's Tutor and Cricketers of my Time* (1833), provided vivid and evocative character sketches of the Hambledon players whose performances were later recorded in Arthur Haygarth's *Scores and Biographies* (1862–1925). **John Small** (1737–1826), shoemaker and gamekeeper, in 1775 three times avoided being bowled out when the ball passed between the two stumps without striking them; the bowler's frustration led to the introduction of the third stump. A more upright style of batting followed, to which Small adapted and for which he began to make and sell suitable bats. Against Surrey at Broadhalfpenny Down in 1775 he made 136 and he was a pioneer of the quick single. Noah Mann (1756–1789), who was also a shoemaker, travelled 20 miles from North Chapel to play, fielding extra longstop besides being a very hard hitter. He died after a day's shooting, when he fell asleep by the fireside and his clothes ignited.

Nyren has immortalized 'those anointed clod-stumpers' (Nyren, 96)—Tom Walker (1762–1831) and his brother Harry (1760–1805). Nicknamed 'Old Everlasting', for his lengthy stay at the wicket, Tom made several centuries at Lord's in the post-Hambledon era but half an hour of Harry's batting was worth an afternoon of Tom's.

James Aylward (1741–1827) made runs for Hambledon including the club's highest individual score, of 167 against England at Sevenoaks in 1777. In 1779 Sir Horatio *Mann employed him as his bailiff and he played for Kent, later becoming (1784) an innkeeper at Bridge, near Canterbury. **David Harris** (1754–1803), potter, was Hambledon's finest bowler. Bringing the ball from under his arm by a twist, he achieved length, lift, and leg-spin. Many of his wickets were secured by catches, for which the bowlers got no credit on the score-sheet. In old age, troubled by gout, Harris would rest on an armchair between deliveries. He linked 'man to man in bonds of fellowship by good works' (Nyren, 106), as did John Wells (1759–1835), a baker, who possessed those 'qualities which render man useful to society as well as happy in himself' (ibid., 101). In a rare match in which the fledgeling MCC combined with the failing Hambledon, he made 63 against England at Lord's in 1792. His brother-in-law, **William Beldham** (1766–1862), a yeoman and later a victualler at Tilford, near Farnham, was the only Hambledon player to be photographed. Nyren called him 'the best batter of his own or, perhaps, of any age' (ibid., 105), and he earned the nickname Silver Billy. His 94 for Hambledon at Lord's in 1789 and 144 for MCC there three years later symbolized the changing loyalties, as did the roles of the ninth earl of Winchilsea (1752–1826) as president of Hambledon and as a founder member of MCC. A man of considerable energy, blessed with good health throughout his life, Beldham was twice married.

There were other luminaries among the sixty or so players who represented Hambledon. Tom Sueter (1750–1827) was a wicket-keeper and one of the first batsmen to come out to meet the ball. Like many of his colleagues he had a fine singing voice, and a stone in the tower of Hambledon church records his work as a surveyor, while his great-grandson became both an admiral and a member of parliament. George Leer (1749–1812), carpenter, sang counter-tenor to Sueter's tenor and, in a short career, was famed as a longstop before becoming a brewer. Both he and Sueter were tested by the fast bowling of Thomas Brett (1747–1809), builder, and William Hogsflesh (1744–1818). In the 1780s Edward Stevens (1735–1819) played for Hambledon as a 'given man'. He was invariably referred to as Lumpy, used as a surname and possibly derived from his having eaten a whole apple pie at a Hambledon dinner. He played with Hambledon in their first match on their new ground on Windmill Down in 1782. Lumpy may have been 'a bit of a smuggler' (Haygarth, 99) in his young days.

With the departure of Richard Nyren in 1791, 'the head and right arm were gone' (Nyren, 64), as his son remembered, but the signs of decline had already become evident some years earlier. The club minutes noted a drop in the attendance of members and an increase in unpaid subscriptions. War with France made its claims on service members, the subscription lists for 1793 showing that three of them had gone to sea. More significant, however, was the burgeoning growth of London. Hambledon's members found it more convenient and more fashionable to belong to the *White Conduit cricket club and its successor, the new club at Marylebone which Thomas Lord had been managing since 1787. At the same time, Hambledon's players—cricket's first professionals—were making their own way to London, taking lodgings, and seeking new patrons to recompense them for their skills. The last club minutes were in 1796, as was the last match at Windmill Down, and henceforth there would be no

**Hambledon cricket club** (*act.* **c.1750–c.1796**), by George Shepheard, *c.*1795 [*Twelve Cricketers in Characteristic Attitudes*; including William Beldham, David Harris, Lord Frederick Beauclerk, Charles Lennox, later fourth duke of Richmond, Tom Walker, and Edward Bligh]

more 'high feasting ... with Little Hambledon pitted against all England' (ibid., 79).

Although the French wars and the rise of the MCC diminished the status of Hambledon, the club did survive the end to its activities in 1796. Account books resumed in 1808 and 'have all the marks of being part of a series, not the first record of a new or refounded club' (Underdown, 184). After 1812 Hambledon were playing with some frequency and there still existed a membership of gentry. 1825 has some claims to be seen as an alternative date for the demise of this eighteenth-century club.

GERALD M. D. HOWAT

**Sources** J. Nyren, *The young cricketer's tutor* (1833) • D. Underdown, *Start of play: cricket and culture in eighteenth-century England* (2000) • J. Goulstone, *Hambledon: the men and the myths* (2001) • F. S. Ashley-Cooper, *Hambledon cricket chronicle, 1772–1796* (1924) • A. Haygarth, *Arthur Haygarth's cricket scores and biographies*, 15 vols. (1862–1925), vol. 1 • J. Pycroft, *The cricket field* (1851) • H. Bentley, *A correct account of all the cricket matches from 1786–1822* (1823); facs. edn (1997) • R. D. Knight, *Hambledon's cricket glory*, 28 vols. (1975–2001) • J. Arlott, ed., *From Hambledon to Lord's* (1948) • E. V. Lucas, *The Hambledon men* (1907) • J. Goldsmith, *Hambledon: biography of a village* (1994) • P. Bailey, P. Thorn, and P. Wynne-Thomas, *Who's who of cricketers* (1984) • C. Martin-Jenkins, ed., *World cricketers: a biographical dictionary* (1996) • T. Harris, ed., *Popular culture in England, c. 1500–1850* (1995)

**Archives** Hants. RO, account book; minutes, accounts, subscription, books, score books, fixture lists, corresp. | CKS, Sackville MSS

**Likenesses** G. Shepheard, watercolour drawing, *c.*1795, Lord's, London, MCC collection [*see illus.*] • S. Woodforde, oils, *c.*1810 • G. Shepheard, photograph, *c.*1862 (William Beldham in old age), Lord's, London, MCC collection • G. Shepheard, portrait, *c.*1862 (William Beldham in old age), Lord's, London, MCC collection

**Hambourg, Mark** (1879–1960), pianist, was born in Boguchar, southern Russia, on 31 May 1879, the eldest son of Michael Hambourg, a professor of music and head of the conservatory at Voronezh, and of his wife, Catherine Herzovna, a professional singer. Two of his younger brothers were musical: Jan, a violinist, and Boris, a cellist. Mark received his first piano lessons from a devoted aunt; when on his fifth birthday he played some of Czerny's exercises, his father was so delighted that he decided that the boy's musical education should begin in a systematic way. A public appearance at the age of seven so impressed his father that he felt his son should have the best tuition available; he therefore obtained an appointment as a professor at the Moscow conservatory, uprooting himself and his family from the provincial surroundings of Voronezh. Mark proved such a remarkable pupil that he learned all of Bach's forty-eight preludes and fugues (*The Well-Tempered Clavier*) before the age of eight. Almost immediately afterwards, in 1888, he appeared with the Philharmonic Society of Moscow in the Hall of the Great Nobles, and at another concert before the Grand Duke Constantine.

Persuaded to try his fortunes in England, and being by nature an adventurer, Professor Hambourg arrived in London with Mark in 1889. Unable to speak a word of English, father and son had some initial struggles, but eventually a Russian friend introduced them to Daniel Mayer, a concert agent who had just presented Paderewski to the British public. Paderewski so eulogized Mark's playing that Mayer decided to present him as an infant prodigy. His début persuaded another agent, Nathaniel Vert, to offer him a three-year contract. After the first of his recitals, at the age of eleven, he was booked to appear in almost every provincial concert hall. The professor now sent for his family to join him in London, and as he had established himself as a teacher of the piano it was Mark's mother who chaperoned her son on his tours. Mark played to many famous people at this time, including Hans Richter, who was particularly impressed. Eventually with the generous financial help of Paderewski and Felix Moscheles, a son of Ignatz Moscheles, a celebrated pianist, Mark was sent to Vienna at the age of twelve and a half, for three years' study under Professor Leschetizky. One of Mark's fellow students was Artur Schnabel, who said that it was always Mark whom the master selected to demonstrate to the class in the weekly exhibitions. Schnabel envied him as the master's favourite pupil but admitted his rival's precocity.

At fifteen Hambourg played at a Berlin Philharmonic concert conducted by Weingartner. In 1894 he received his first paid engagement in Vienna and won the Liszt scholarship of 500 marks; in 1895 he made his début as a full-grown pianist at the Vienna Philharmonic symphony concert conducted by Richter, who had continued to be a great friend. Other engagements followed, and he returned to London to embark, at sixteen, on the first of many world tours. He made his American début with the Boston Symphony Orchestra and then toured the United States to California. When Hambourg, who had been naturalized in 1896, returned to England, the Second South African War was at its height and the musical world somewhat disorganized. He deputized for Busoni, an intimate friend; he gave a series of concerts with Ysaÿe; and played pianoforte concertos at the newly organized Queen's Hall Promenade Concerts with Henry Wood, then at the outset of his career.

Tour after tour followed: the United States, Australia, New Zealand, South Africa, the Middle East, Poland, Russia, engagements in Brussels, Berlin, and Salzburg, where he played with Jacques Thibaud. Hambourg's concert activities easily outnumbered those of any of his contemporary colleagues. However, this over-strenuous early career 'possibly contributed to an eventual decline in the quality of his playing' (Dawes, 62). In 1907 he married Dorothea Frances, daughter of Lord Muir Mackenzie [*see* Mackenzie, Kenneth Augustus Muir], and they had four daughters, one of whom, Michal, became an accomplished pianist.

In 1909 Hambourg made the first of a long series of gramophone records for the Gramophone Company Ltd (HMV). The 'Moonlight' sonata was the first title issued; it might almost be called his signature tune, since it was a best-seller and usually found a place in the hundreds of recitals he gave up and down the country. This and a certain likeness to the Beethoven of our imagination, coupled with a platform manner which endeared him to the masses, made him one of England's most popular recitalists.

Mark Hambourg had a lifelong love of chamber music, which he played with his brothers in a trio in his earlier days, and in middle age he was a concerto player of authority and distinction. He will be remembered, however, chiefly as a recitalist, and in that capacity he appealed to a wider section of the public than did anyone of his own day and age. Short in height, with a leonine head, a powerful frame, a phenomenal technique, and a genial personality, he commanded the attention of any audience. As a pianist he had the power to astonish; as a man he had a dynamic and lovable personality which won for him the admiration of a wide section of the general public. He was the last in a long line of highly individualistic virtuoso pianists who might not so readily have pleased the pundits of a later age more concerned with the literal treatment of music than with its individual and personal artistic conception.

Hambourg played for the last time in public on 2 March 1955 for a Henry Wood birthday memorial concert at the Royal Albert Hall, when he performed Tchaikovsky's piano concerto no. 1. His own musical compositions included *Variations on a Theme by Paganini*, 'Volkslied', and 'Espièglerie'. He died at 6 Drosier Road, Cambridge, on 26 August 1960; his wife survived him.

GEORGE BAKER, *rev.*

**Sources** M. Hambourg, *From piano to forte* (1931) [autobiography] · M. Hambourg, *The eighth octave* (1951) [autobiography] · F. Dawes, 'Hambourg, Mark', *New Grove*, 8.62 · F. W. Gaisberg, *Music on record* (1946) · personal knowledge (1971) · G. Moore, *Am I too loud?* (1962) · H. C. Schonberg, *The great pianists* (1963) · A. Schnabel, *My life and music* (1970) · *CGPLA Eng. & Wales* (1960)
**Archives** SOUND BL NSA, performance recordings
**Likenesses** A. Toft, bronze bust, 1904, Royal College of Music · J. Russell & Sons, photograph, *c.*1917, NPG · O. Birley, portrait, priv. coll. · Spy [L. Ward], lithograph caricature, NPG; repro. in *VF* (29 April 1908) · photograph, NPG · photograph, postcard, NPG
**Wealth at death** £2096 18*s.* 8*d.*: probate, 15 Nov 1960, *CGPLA Eng. & Wales*

**Hambro, Baron Carl Joachim** (1807–1877), merchant banker, was born at Copenhagen into a Jewish-Danish merchant family. He was the only child of Joseph Hambro (1780–1848), merchant and banker, and his wife, Marianne von Halle (1786–1838), daughter of Copenhagen merchant WulfLevin von Halle. His grandfather was Calmer Joachim Hambro (1747–1806), born in Rendsburg in the duchy of Holstein and raised in Hamburg, who had moved to Copenhagen in 1778. Calmer's first wife, Thobe Levi (1756–1820), was the daughter of a Danish merchant, Isach Joseph Levi (1710–1779). The family had lost goods and money in a fire in Copenhagen in 1795, but as Jews they were not yet allowed to own real estate in Denmark. In 1800 Joseph Hambro joined his father as partner in the business, which was renamed C. J. Hambro & Son; the name was to survive until 1920.

Hambro's mother was prone to depression, and this strained his parents' marriage. In 1814, though their only child, he was sent to live with Professor Johannes Reinhardt, founder of the Danish Zoological Museum, and his wife, Nicoline, and their four children. On 3 October 1822, influenced by his foster parents, he was baptized and confirmed into the Christian religion at Trinitatis Church, Rundetarn, Copenhagen. On leaving school in 1824, he worked at Le Havre, Antwerp, Bremen, and then in North America, in order to learn the languages there.

Hambro returned to Copenhagen in 1829 and joined C. J. Hambro & Son. His father, Joseph Hambro, had built the business into an international trading and finance house, and it had arranged Danish government loans from 1821 to 1827. In the process Joseph had become an ally and adviser of the Danish finance minister, Johan Sigismund von Mosting. His firm was also banker to the king of Denmark. In 1831 it financed the building of the first steam mill in Denmark, at the Bodenhoffs Plads on Christianshavns Kanal, Copenhagen, for grinding corn and shelling rice; a hard-tack bakery and a preserving factory were also established on the same site. However, Carl Joachim Hambro took very little interest in the management of this project and preferred to work as a banker.

In 1832 Hambro moved to England and set up a merchant house in London. He married Caroline Gostenhofer (1810–1852), a merchant's daughter, on 12 December 1833, and the couple returned to Denmark in 1834, leaving the London business in the hands of juniors. Their first son was born in that year at the family's house in Oregaard, North Zealand; another son and a daughter were also born in Denmark. Between 1834 and 1838 Hambro, living at Kronprinsessegade, Copenhagen, tried to act as 'right hand' to his father. However, his 'oversensitive and egocentric nature' (Bramsen and Wain, 209) made him unsuitable for the role; and matters were made worse by Joseph Hambro's lack of confidence in his son. In 1838 they quarrelled and he left Denmark for good; he settled in London in the autumn, with £50,000 capital from his father. He also gave up his post as American consul in Denmark, which he had held since 1834.

In 1839 Hambro opened the bank of C. J. Hambro & Son at 70 Old Broad Street, London, but he was immediately overwhelmed by the financial crisis of 1839, and his health collapsed. His father joined him in London in 1840 and rescued the business; he led it during his son's illness, and afterwards, until 1847. Carl Hambro's fourth child, Everard Alexander *Hambro (1842–1925), was born in London on 11 April 1842.

Joseph Hambro died on 3 October 1848 in London, where his assets were now largely concentrated; he left £300,000 to his son, who subsequently prospered in London and Copenhagen in the 1850s through the issue of government loans. The company fared even better than Barings and Rothschilds in such deals: it made a profit of £40,000 from just one transaction connected with a war loan to Denmark in 1850. As recompense for facilitating the funds at a desperate moment, in 1851 King Frederik VII of Denmark bestowed a barony on Hambro, even though the 1849 Danish constitution had in principle abolished such honours. More importantly, it apparently restored Hambro's confidence in himself as a merchant banker.

On 8 March 1852 Hambro's wife, Caroline, died, and this brought on a severe and long-lasting depression. It continued until 1861, when Hambro married Eliza Greathead, *née* Turner (*d.* 1919), a nurse and the widow of a British official in India; she had nursed Hambro in hospital in 1860. Despite his illness, in May 1852 Hambro bought the estate of Milton Abbey, Dorset, from the sixth earl of Portarlington: it comprised 8000 acres, including four villages. In 1862 he employed the architect George Gilbert Scott to restore and rebuild Milton Abbey, which was adjacent to Milton Hall; the work lasted three years and cost £50,000. During that time Hambro bought Gifford House on the edge of Putney Heath, and was happier there than at Milton Hall, where he had been overwhelmed by loneliness.

Hambro's skill and drive were in the business of international finance, in particular with Scandinavia, where the bank financed railways in Zealand and helped to fund the Danish war against Bismarck in 1864. His greatest loan was in support of the Sardinian statesman Camillo Cavour, a driving force in the unification of Italy. C. J. Hambro & Son offered a £4 million loan to the kingdom of Sardinia in May 1851. Notwithstanding an attempt by the Rothschild houses to deflate the market price of the so-called Anglo-Sardinian bonds, the transaction was a success and Hambros emerged in profit on the deal in 1852. For Hambro's steadfastness, an admiring Cavour gave him Sardinia's order of St Mauritius; Hambro continued to support Cavour in the latter's strategy between 1859 and 1861, which led to the emergence of Victor Emmanuel II as king of Italy. Hambro's colleagues subsequently called him 'the kingmaker', and he played an equally significant role in the affairs of the emerging Greek nation. In particular he provided valuable support for the Danish Prince Vilhelm, who was crowned as King George I of Greece in 1863.

Hambro was a major public benefactor in his native country. He gave £6000 to the city of Copenhagen for the building of the first public hot-water baths—the Hambro Public Baths, which opened in Borgergade in 1864. He subsequently funded further public baths, which were built in 1870 in Kobmagergade, next to Trinity Church. He also wrote a history of Denmark and published an illustrated version shortly before he died. In his later years, Hambro's sight failed. He died at his home at Milton Abbey, Dorset, on 17 November 1877 and was buried in the churchyard there.

As Hambro's biographers point out, 'to overcome not only a change of parents but also of religion and nationality is to expect much of such a vulnerable temperament' (Bramsen and Wain, 283). However, he was the founder of C. J. Hambro & Son in the City of London, and was for many years a highly influential international financier and merchant banker, with entrepreneurial instincts and steady nerves. ANDREW ST GEORGE

**Sources** O. Bendix, *Hambros Bank Ltd, 1839–1939* (1939) • B. Bramsen and K. Wain, *The Hambros, 1779–1979* (1979) • J. Clapham, *The Bank of England: a history*, 2 vols. (1944) • H. Clay, *Lord Norman* (1957) • P. Ferris, *The City* (1960) • C. J. Hambro, *Far og son* (1948) • P. Mathias, *The first industrial nation* (1969) • A. St George, *JOH* (1992) [biography of Jocelyn Hambro] • *CGPLA Eng. & Wales* (1877) • d. cert.

**Archives** GL, archives of C. J. Hambro & Son, Hambros

**Wealth at death** under £500,000: probate, 6 Dec 1877, *CGPLA Eng. & Wales*

**Hambro, Sir Charles Jocelyn** (1897–1963), merchant banker, was born on 3 October 1897 at 70 Prince's Gate, London, into a banking family of Danish origin, which had settled in Dorset and the City in the first half of the nineteenth century. He was the elder son of Sir Eric Hambro (1872–1947), who was Conservative MP for the Wimbledon division of Surrey in 1900–07 and a partner in C. J. Hambro & Son, the family firm; his grandfather Sir Everard Alexander *Hambro was a director of the Bank of England. His mother, Sybil Emily Martin Smith (*d.* 1942), was the daughter of Martin Ridley Smith of Warren House, Hayes, Kent, and his wife, Cecilia, daughter of Henry Stuart (1808–1880), of Montfort, Isle of Bute, a descendant of George III's prime minister John Stuart, third earl of Bute. In 1929 Hambro's parents were divorced and his father at once remarried. He had a younger brother and two sisters.

Hambro was at Eton College from 1910 to 1915; he was in the cricket team in 1914 and its captain in 1915, when he took seven wickets for six runs against Winchester College. He went straight from school to Sandhurst, and by the end of the year was an ensign in the Coldstream Guards. He survived two years on the western front, receiving the Military Cross for conspicuous bravery in action. On demobilization in 1919 Hambro married Pamela (1899/1900–1932), daughter of John Dupuis Cobbold DL, an Ipswich brewer, and his wife, Lady Evelyn, daughter of Charles Adolphus Murray, seventh earl of Dunmore; the couple had a son and three daughters.

Hambro went for a period of training to the Guaranty Trust Company in New York, where he and his wife lived with Harry Morgan, son of J. P. Morgan Jr. He then joined the family firm, of which he soon became secretary. He played an important part in its merger with the British Bank of Northern Commerce, which had been founded by, among others, the Stockholm banker Knut Wallenberg. The merger led to the establishment of Hambros Bank in 1921. In 1928, when only thirty, Hambro was elected a director of the Bank of England, and for a spell in 1932–3 he put all other work aside in order to establish, under the direction of Montagu C. Norman, the bank's exchange control division, to deal with some of the consequences of the ending of the gold standard. In 1937 Hambro was offered the chance of succeeding Norman as governor of the Bank of England. He refused, in part because he was suffering from cancer of the tongue. An operation and radium treatment nevertheless allowed him to lead an extremely active life thereafter.

Hambro's commanding presence—he stood 6 feet 3 inches tall—and driving personality were backed by equal strength of character, loyalty, and charm. His wife died from pneumonia in 1932, and in 1936 he remarried. His second wife was Dorothy Helen, daughter of Alexander Mackay of Oban, whose first husband had been Marcus Wallenberg. The couple had a daughter.

Hambro made a notable impact in several spheres of work, particularly on the Great Western Railway, the most successful of the four great British railway companies. He became a director of it in 1928, and deputy chairman in 1934. From 1940 to 1945 he was nominally chairman, but war work took up much of his time.

On the outbreak of war with Germany in 1939, at the invitation of the government minister Ronald Cross, Hambro joined the Ministry of Economic Warfare. In August 1940 Cross's successor Hugh Dalton brought Hambro into the new secret service he was forming under the ministry's cover, the Special Operations Executive (SOE). SOE's purpose was to stimulate resistance in enemy-occupied territory, and Hambro's vigour, energy, and originality were invaluable to it. He began in charge of Scandinavia, and visited Sweden in November 1940. There he arranged for some highly successful smuggling of ball-bearings, and for some sabotage in Swedish harbours, which provoked difficulties with the Swedes. He also, through the anti-Nazi journalist Ebbe Munck, initiated contacts with resistance-minded Danes, which bore useful fruit in the summer of 1944. Dalton thought highly of his Scandinavian work, and Hambro was created KBE in 1941.

From December 1940 to November 1941 Hambro added to his responsibilities the oversight of SOE's nascent French, Belgian, Dutch, and German sections, and from November 1941 for five months he was deputy head of the whole organization, in the rank of squadron leader, Royal Air Force. (Rank in SOE meant little.) He initiated an important development in January 1942, when he persuaded the Norwegians to help form an Anglo-Norwegian planning committee, from which several highly successful small operations derived, particularly the destruction on 27–8 February 1943 of the heavy-water plant at Vemork near Rjukan. When a further stock of heavy water was destroyed, in a separate operation, on its way to Germany, the Germans' search for an atomic bomb was utterly dislocated.

By that time Hambro had become the executive chief of SOE and promoted to air commodore. Dalton's successor, the third earl of Selborne, had appointed him in April 1942 to succeed Frank Nelson after Nelson's health had given way—on the ground that a man who could run the Great Western Railway could run anything. An early and important task for Hambro was to arrange with Colonel William Donovan, his American opposite number, who visited London in June 1942, for co-operation between SOE and the American office of strategic services. Occasional rivalries should not obscure a great deal of close and rewarding interchange.

Hambro's multifarious acquaintances in the business world were often useful to SOE. During his seventeen months of leadership, this small but lively service was transformed from a body still struggling to establish its worth into a recognized, and often highly efficient, military tool. Hambro could not claim undue credit for this development, much of which arose from the general political and military course of the war, and some of it from the excellent work of his predecessor, Nelson, and from technicalities too abstruse even for him. A well-placed observer described him in retrospect as 'always the gentleman, among the professionals'; he was certainly not a professional in the secret-service world.

Hambro and Selborne could not agree over a protracted dispute about control over SOE by the commander-in-chief, Middle East; and early in September 1943 Hambro had to resign. Another weighty post was soon found for him. He spent the last eighteen months of the war in Washington as head of the British raw materials mission: this was cover for supervising the exchange of information between the United Kingdom and the USA which led to the first man-made nuclear explosions in July and August 1945. It was he above all who persuaded the Belgians to re-start mining operations in the Congo, thus providing the essential raw material.

Hambro then returned to the City, and in conjunction with his nephew, Jocelyn Olaf Hambro, worked to increase British exports, particularly to the USA, through the Hambro Trading Corporation. Supported by his uncle (Ronald) Olaf *Hambro, the third chairman of Hambros Bank, he re-established the foreign exchange department. Hambro was also prominent in the acrimonious takeover battle for British Aluminium in 1959–60. Although he failed to prevent the takeover, being out-manoeuvred by the redoubtable Sir Siegmund Warburg, Hambro learned important lessons from the affair—not least about the importance of good public relations and the need to brief the financial press during controversial share-dealing operations.

Hambro became chairman of Hambros Bank following the death of his uncle in 1961. Under his direction the business diversified, through the Union Corporation, into mining, among other interests. Hambro supported several charitable trusts, worked himself harder than he worked his subordinates, and escaped whenever he could to Dixton Manor near Cheltenham to shoot. He died from cancer and cardiac failure on 28 August 1963 at his London home, 72 North Gate, Regent's Park. He was survived by his second wife. Hambro died at the height of his powers and reputation, having had a notable career as merchant banker and wartime soldier. M. R. D. Foot, *rev.*

**Sources** R. Bramsen and K. Wain, *The Hambros, 1779–1979* (1979) · *The Times* (16 July 1915) · *The Times* (29 Aug 1963) · *The Times* (31 Aug 1963) · *The Times* (2 Sept 1963) · *The Times* (3 Sept 1963) · M. R. D. Foot, *SOE in France: an account of the work of the British Special Operations Executive in France, 1940–1944* (1966) · M. R. D. Foot, *Resistance* (1976) · B. Sweet-Escott, *Baker Street irregular* (1965) · A. St George, *JOH* (1992) [biography of Jocelyn Hambro] · b. cert. · m. cert. [Pamela Cobbold] · d. cert. · *CGPLA Eng. & Wales* (1963) · M. Goring, *Britain and atomic energy 1939–1945* (1964)

**Archives** GL, family MSS | PRO, Special Operations Executive papers, HS

**Likenesses** photograph, *c.*1939–1945, Special Forces Club, London

**Wealth at death** £179,918 8s. 8d.: probate, 6 Dec 1963, *CGPLA Eng. & Wales*

**Hambro, Sir Everard Alexander** (1842–1925), merchant banker and philanthropist, was born at Bransbury House, Willesden, in London, on 11 April 1842, the youngest of the three sons and one daughter of Baron Carl Joachim *Hambro (1807–1877), merchant banker, and his wife, Caroline Gostenhofer (1810–1852). By 1839 Carl Joachim had returned from Denmark and founded in London the family firm of C. J. Hambro & Son, which quickly emerged as a leading merchant bank.

Everard (nicknamed Evy) was the brother of Charles Joseph Theophilus Hambro (1834–1891), MP for Weymouth (1868–74) and Dorset South (1886–91), and of Percival Lewis Hambro (1836–1885). He was educated at J. P. Clover's school, Roehampton, and Trinity College, Cambridge. On 23 October 1863 he married (Gertrude) Mary Stuart (1848–1905), the daughter of Martin Ridley Smith of Warren House, Hayes, Kent, and Celia, daughter of Henry Stuart (1808–1880), of Montfort, Isle of Bute, who was a descendant of George III's prime minister, John Stuart, third earl of Bute. The couple settled at 70 Prince's Gate, London; they also rented Mount Clare, Richmond Park, and in 1874 joined his father, Carl Joachim Hambro, at Gifford House, Putney Heath, where J. P. Morgan was his neighbour. They became close friends and collaborators in business.

In 1864 Hambro joined C. J. Hambro & Son. In 1869 he became one of the bank's four partners, and on the death of his father in 1877 he became senior partner of the bank. He held 75 per cent of the bank's capital of £650,000. In 1878 his earnings from the bank were £52,000, and they rose to £150,000 in 1886. By 1890 the bank's capital had grown to £1.3 million; it was one of London's largest and most prestigious houses.

During the 1870s and for the next thirty years, Hambro gave time and money to good causes. In 1873 he bought a house at Roehampton and started an orphanage which he supported until 1879; it became known as the Hambro Orphanage for Girls, and was finally given to the Church of England's Children's Society (Waifs and Strays) in 1909. He played a major part in the foundation of the Royal National Pension Fund for Nurses in 1886. He became KCVO in 1908.

In 1879 Hambro was elected to the court of the Bank of England. Here he was instrumental in proposed reforms to the important Bank of England committee of treasury—which he joined in 1910—and the committee of daily waiting; the passage of his reforms set junior and senior members of the court at odds. His unpopularity with former governors of the bank assured that he would not be elected governor or deputy governor. Henry Gibbs, a former governor, described Hambro's resolutions of 1 February 1894 as 'being antagonistic unlike anything he had known in his forty-one years at the Bank' (Bramsen and Wain, 334).

Hambro was an assertive and imposing man. He greatly increased his private reserves and those of the bank by expanding its finance of international trade, especially between North and South America, by the syndication of railroad loans, and through bullion dealing. In financing international trade he worked closely with the New York banks Phelps, Stokes & Co., Drexel, Morgan & Co., and Heidelbach and Ickelheimer & Co. Although he handled issues for corporate entities in the 1870s and 1880s, the bank's business in foreign loans was of vital importance. Hambro issued loans for the governments of Sweden, Norway, Denmark, Greece, Russia, and Italy. Prominent among his supporters in this work were the houses of Hoskier in France, Tietgen in Denmark, and Morgan in America. His chief ally in London was E. C. Baring (later Lord Revelstoke) of Baring Brothers & Co.

In 1881–2, with Barings, Hambro issued an enormous loan of £29 million for the Italian government, in competition with Baron Alphonse de Rothschild (1827–1905) in Paris. Throughout difficult and fluctuating international markets, Hambro remained steady and reported a profit of 1.14 per cent for his syndicate of banks—or £350,000. This issue broke the Rothschild monopoly of Italian government loans, and confirmed Hambro as one of the greatest international bankers of his generation. However the issue had come within a whisker of failure, which would have ruined both banks.

In 1890 Hambro repaid the support of Revelstoke by playing a leading role in the rescue of Barings at the time of the Baring crisis. Early on he was important in bringing together Barings and the Bank of England while his firm subscribed handsomely to the Bank Guarantee Fund, which underwrote Baring's rescue. Yet Hambros had also been underwriter of the flotation of the Buenos Aires Water Supply and Drainage Company Ltd, the failed transaction which had laid Barings low.

The profits of C. J. Hambro & Son fell sharply, in line with a City slump, in 1890. Hambro sought peace at the Villa Espoir, Biarritz, where he played golf. In 1892 he suffered a bout of ill health which kept him from business. He convalesced at the Scottish estate, Gannochy, near Brechin, in Forfarshire, which he had rented from the earl of Dalhousie, and at Hayes Place, Kent, where he kept a herd of pedigree Guernsey cows. In the mid-1890s, Hambro returned to the City and raised foreign loans for the Scandinavian countries and arranged project finance in South Africa and the Americas.

Hambro and his wife Mary had eight children. One died at birth; two, Hermione and Maurice, died in childhood. Five survived: Charles Eric Hambro KBE (1872–1947), Harold Everard Hambro CBE (1876–1952), Angus Valdemar Hambro (1883–1957), Violet Mary Hambro MBE (1884–1965), and (Ronald) Olaf *Hambro (1885–1961). In June 1900 Hambro bought the Milton Abbey estate from his nephew, Henry Charles (Harry) Hambro (1869–1933). In June 1905 Mary died at the age of fifty-seven. Hambro retreated to Milton Abbey and developed his interest in shooting: a royal shooting party in December 1909 consisted of forty-six beaters, thirty-one gamekeepers and loaders, and ten guns, who in three days shot 1300 pheasants.

At seventy Hambro married Ebba, younger daughter of

C. Beresford Whyte of Leitrim, a woman in her early twenties whom he had met at Biarritz. Hambro was a handsome and charismatic man. A contemporary records, 'Cast like a heroic mould on a colossal scale, one of the handsomest men even at 68 … a giant not only in stature, but in character, in ability, in talents' (Bramsen and Wain, 348). During the First World War Hambro returned to work in the City and closely associated himself and the bank with Scandinavian trade relations, acting as the British government agent for the purchase of Norwegian kroner in 1916. In 1920 he became first chairman of the bank created by the unification of C. J. Hambro & Son and the British Bank of Northern Commerce Ltd, backed by leading Scandinavian capitalists anxious to diversify to London. It was known as Hambros Bank of Northern Commerce Ltd, in 1921 abbreviated to Hambros Bank Ltd, and he was chairman until his death.

Sir Everard Hambro died at Hayes Place, Kent, on 26 February 1925. He had led the bank for forty-eight years, and had presided over changes in the City and as a director of the Bank of England. The meeting of the court in March 1925 reads:

> The Court desire to place on record their high appreciation of his conspicuous abilities and wide knowledge of affairs which, throughout this long period, have always been at the service of the Bank. They also wish to express their feelings of personal regard for one who, by his unvarying kindliness and courtesy and by his personal charm has won the esteem and affection of every member of the Court. (Bramsen and Wain, 376)

ANDREW ST GEORGE

**Sources** O. Bendix, *Hambros Bank Ltd, 1839–1939* (1939) • K. M. Wain, 'Hambro, Sir Everard Alexander', *DBB* • B. Bramsen and K. Wain, *The Hambros, 1779–1979* (1979) • J. Clapham, *The Bank of England: a history*, 2 vols. (1944) • H. Clay, *Lord Norman* (1957) • P. L. Cottrell, *Industrial finance, 1830–1914: the finance and organization of English manufacturing industry* (1980) • R. Davis, *The English Rothschilds* (1983) • P. Ferris, *The City* (1960) • C. J. Hambro, *Far og son* (1948) • D. Kynaston, *The City of London*, 4 vols. (1994–2001) • P. Mathias, *The first industrial nation* (1969) • b. cert. • d. cert. • *CGPLA Eng. & Wales* (1925)

**Archives** GL, business and family corresp.

**Wealth at death** £2,323,710 14*s*. 5*d*.: probate, 9 April 1925, *CGPLA Eng. & Wales*

**Hambro, Jocelyn Olaf** (1919–1994), merchant banker, was born on 7 March 1919 at 39 Upper Brook Street, London, the oldest of the three sons of (Ronald) Olaf *Hambro (1885–1961), also a merchant banker, and his wife, Winifred Emily Martin Smith (1886–1932), the fifth daughter of Martin Ridley Smith, of the banking house of Smith, Payne, and Smith. His parents lived in Upper Brook Street and then Upper Grosvenor Street in London, and at Kidbrooke Park, Sussex. From 1928 the family spent time at Glendoe on Loch Ness, where Hambro's mother was killed in a boating accident on 28 August 1932. In 1928 he had been sent to Summerfields, Oxford, and in 1932 he began at Eton College. At Eton he was a capable student and developed his taste for horse-racing, at one time becoming the school bookmaker. In 1936 he went to Heidelberg to study languages. While there he had a brush with the Gestapo, after the family butler sent a consignment of rancid butter in response to Hermann Goering's claim that the German people wanted 'guns not butter'. In 1937 Hambro went to Trinity College, Cambridge, but his education was cut short by the outbreak of the Second World War. He joined the Coldstream Guards in 1939, going to Pirbright for training, and became part of the 4th battalion (part of the 30th guards brigade); subsequent training on Salisbury Plain and Bellerby Moor prepared the battalion for action in Normandy. Major Hambro, in command of 1 squadron, landed on Red Beach on 20 July. He was awarded the Military Cross for action at Hill 309, Caumont. On 12 August he was wounded by a shell which fell on the headquarters of 8th brigade. Both his legs were severely damaged: the right was saved, but the left was amputated above the knee. He recovered at Birmingham and Roehampton.

In 1945 Hambro joined Hambros Bank in Bishopsgate and was sent to America to promote British exports. After a spell with Brown Brothers Harriman in New York he travelled extensively selling franchises for MG cars, and in 1947 set up the Hambro Automotive Corporation; sales grew from £61,000 to £90 million by 1960. He became managing director of Hambros Bank Ltd in 1947, and served as chairman from 1965 to 1972. He was chairman of Hambros Ltd from 1970 to 1983, and president from 1983 to 1986. Throughout the 1950s he gathered expertise in loans, flotations, and public offerings. In 1959 the bank faced a crisis of identity as Hambros lost the fight with S. G. Warburg for British Aluminium in the 'aluminium war' which set the 'gentlemen' merchant bankers against the new 'players'. Hambro learned from this, and aggressively developed the bank's investment and corporate finance capacity. He initiated the Eurobond and Eurodollar market with a Eurodollar bond for Norges Kommunalbank in January 1963. The market grew, with Hambros, S. G. Warburg, and N. M. Rothschild as leaders. The bank's European connections were crucial; apart from its strength in Scandinavia, it made the first *offerta publica* in Italy and formed the first consortium bank in London in 1968. Hambro's greatest success was the formation of Hambro Life, a unit-based life assurance company, in 1970. He collaborated with Mark Weinberg and his team from Abbey Life to make a company which grew from assets of £1 million in 1970 to £335 million in 1975. The bank's share was sold off later to cover losses in Norwegian shipping loans after the oil crisis of the early 1970s; the Hambro Life investment probably saved the bank.

In an era of increasing specialization, Hambro managed to be a diverse merchant banker: he developed the bank's direct investment and venture capital divisions; and he maintained interests in diamond and bullion broking through I. Hennig & Co. and Mocatta and Goldsmid, in mining through his directorship of Charter Consolidated, and in insurance through his directorship of Phoenix Assurance (1952–77) and his chairmanship (1978–85). In 1986, after fourteen years as chairman and president of Hambros plc, Hambro and his three sons left to set up the investment house of J. O. Hambro.

In business Hambro was a calm, discreet man, with a dry wit. He welcomed new ideas and fitted them to old traditions. He had capacity and vision to take risks and explore new forms of investment. His achievement was to steer Hambros Bank from its essentially nineteenth-century heritage into the era of City deregulation in the 1980s. As the sixth chairman of the bank, he everywhere stressed the qualities germane to his business: 'Merchant bankers aren't supposed to be conventional bankers; merchant bankers are supposed to be risk takers, as opposed to joint stock [clearing] bankers who rarely take a risk and still manage to lose money', he once said (*The Independent*, 24 June 1994). His style mixed the entrepreneurial with the conservative and he had the ability to work with specialists in many areas.

Hambro was married three times. His first wife, whom he married on 28 March 1942, was (Anne) Sylvia (1920/21–1972), the daughter of Rowland Huntley Muir, a member of Lloyds. There were three sons of the marriage: Rupert Nicholas (*b.* 1943), Richard Alexander (*b.* 1946), and James Daryl (*b.* 1949). Hambro's second wife, whom he married on 23 February 1976, was (Margaret) Elisabeth (*d.* 1983), the daughter of Captain Frederick Bradshaw McConnel, of the Gordon Highlanders, and the widow of George Victor Robert John Innes-Ker, ninth duke of Roxburghe. Hambro married, third, on 28 January 1988, Margaret Anne (*b.* 1933/4), the daughter of Charles Michael Stratton, a game farmer, and the divorced wife of Richard Archibald Fortescue, seventh Earl Fortescue. There were no children of the second and third marriages.

Hambro was a keen shot and a keen breeder of horses, at which he had some success, most notably with Cyrus, Sammy Davis, and Archbishop, in the 1950s and 1960s. He bred horses at Redenham Park, Andover, and at Waverton Stud, Gloucestershire. In public life he was a supporter of several charities, including Henry Smith's charity, of which he was chairman from 1978 to 1990. He also supported the Cancer Relief Macmillan Fund and the Britta Dolan Memorial Cancer Fund (his first and second wives had both died of cancer). Elisabeth was president of the Cancer Relief Macmillan Fund for twenty-five years. With her, Hambro established the National Cancer Day Society in 1967 and the Hambro Businessman of the Year lunch in 1969, to benefit Cancer Research, Imperial Cancer Research, the Marie Curie Cancer Care, and the Cancer Relief Macmillan Fund. He died at the John Radcliffe Hospital, Oxford, on 19 June 1994 of a fractured skull, following an accident. He was survived by his third wife and the three sons of his first marriage. ANDREW ST GEORGE

**Sources** A. St George, *JOH* (1992) [biography of Jocelyn Hambro] · B. Bramsen and K. Wain, *The Hambros, 1779–1979* (1979) · *The Times* (22 June 1994) · *The Independent* (24 June 1994) · Hambros plc, London, Hambro Archives · personal knowledge (2004) · private information (2004) [Hambro family] · *WWW*, 1991–5 · m. certs. · d. cert. · Burke, *Peerage*

**Archives** Hambros plc, London, Hambro archives

**Likenesses** photograph, repro. in *The Times* · photograph, repro. in *The Independent*

**Wealth at death** £2,807,343: probate, 8 Dec 1994, *CGPLA Eng. & Wales*

**Hambro, (Ronald) Olaf** (1885–1961), merchant banker, was born on 1 December 1885 at Hayes Place, Hayes, Kent, the youngest of seven children of Sir Everard Alexander *Hambro (1842–1925), merchant banker, and his wife, Gertrude Mary Stuart (1848–1905). His father was senior partner of the family merchant bank, C. J. Hambro & Son. He was educated at Eton College and Trinity College, Cambridge, and in 1909 he joined the family bank at 70 Old Broad Street, London. In 1915 Hambro joined the Coldstream Guards, received a commission, and served near Percy at Arras. He was twice mentioned in dispatches. On 17 February 1917 he married Winifred Martin Smith (1886–1932), daughter of his father's close friend Martin Ridley Smith of the old-established banking house of Smith, Payne, and Smith. The couple had three sons.

In 1920 C. J. Hambro & Son amalgamated with the British Bank of Northern Commerce Ltd to form Hambros Bank of Northern Commerce on 31 October (in August 1921 the name was changed to Hambros Bank Ltd). In 1929 Hambro, with his elder brothers Sir Eric Hambro (1872–1947) and Harry Hambro (1869–1933), established the Hambro Trust Ltd to preserve the family's future interests in the bank, in which the Hambro family retained a controlling shareholding. In March 1932 Olaf Hambro became the third chairman of Hambros Bank on the retirement of Sir Eric Hambro, who had been chairman since 1925. On 28 August 1932 Olaf's wife, Winifred, tragically died in an accident on Loch Ness; he never remarried.

During the depression the bank was badly affected: in 1933 its value had slumped to £21 million, only two-thirds of that at the end of the 1920s. At a time of extreme economic difficulty, Hambro showed remarkable tenacity and skill, despite restricted new issues for overseas borrowers, formerly a major source of the bank's income. Instead, Hambro steered his bank towards a compensating relationship with British industry which was new for the City of London, issuing securities for such firms as John Brown & Co., owners of the Clydebank shipyard, and also the Consett Iron Company of co. Durham, in 1935 and 1936. In the 1930s Hambro was greatly aided by his nephew, Charles Jocelyn *Hambro, in foreign exchange matters.

Between 1939 and 1945 Hambro guided the bank through a decline in new issues and fostered a growth in finance of inland goods. After the war he was responsible for the bank's aggressive export initiative, which even included selling MG cars in the United States. In 1945 he was responsible for the foundation of the Issuing Houses Association, a group of London banks and finance houses eager to promote foreign bond issues in London. Hambro expanded and diversified the bank's operations into diamond broking in the late 1940s: this involved advancing credit to Amsterdam diamond traders, secured on their precious stones. In the 1950s it moved into bullion dealing.

The increasing involvement of Hambros Bank in corporate finance was demonstrated in 1958–9, when it was involved in the acrimonious and much publicized takeover battle waged against its client British Aluminium. It was the last encounter between the 'gentlemen' (in the form of a consortium of merchant banks led by Hambros) and the 'players' (represented by S. G. Warburg & Co.). In 1959 victory fell to Warburgs after aggressive tactics, including the courting of the financial press. It proved to be only a temporary set-back, and after 1959 Hambro and his son Jocelyn Olaf *Hambro, who in due course became chairman after him, made the bank leaner, more competitive, and more enterprising. Hambro was one of the first merchant bankers in London to recognize the value of good public and press relations.

Olaf Hambro's greatest loves were his houses and gardens. In 1921 he had bought Kidbrooke Park, a house on the edge of the Ashdown Forest in Sussex; and Queen Mary visited there for tea on 5 June 1934. In 1938 he moved to Linton Park, in Kent, and restored the house and gardens to their original condition by demolishing additions and undoing alterations. After the war he bought Logan House on the Rhinns of Galloway in Scotland and performed the same architectural rejuvenation. *Country Life* in 1954 called the recovery of the Georgian heart of Logan House 'an architectural miracle' (Bramsen and Wain, 392). Everywhere Hambro pursued a keen interest in gardening; the subtropical gardens at Logan provided the right environment for his species of rhododendrons (Chinese and Himalayan varieties) and were visited by more than 2000 people annually in the 1950s. Hambro was a punctilious and precise man; he smoked a pipe, and insisted on a special tobacco blend from Robert Lewis in St James's, London. He died on 25 April 1961 at the London Clinic, 20 Devonshire Place, London.

Something of an autocrat, Hambro excelled at making key business decisions, and then leaving others to work out the details. He had preserved the status of the bank through the economic slump of the 1930s, he had expanded the business aggressively in the 1940s and 1950s, and he left the bank apt and ready for expansion in the burgeoning Eurodollar market of the 1960s. His importance lay in his bridging the Victorian era of the City of London, the golden Edwardian period of the bank, the harsh recession of the 1920s and 1930s, and the new commercial spirit of the 1950s. He was a fine, technical merchant banker. ANDREW ST GEORGE

**Sources** O. Bendix, *Hambros Bank Ltd, 1839–1939* (1939) • B. Bramsen and K. Wain, *The Hambros, 1779–1979* (1979) • H. Clay, *Lord Norman* (1957) • P. L. Cottrell, *Industrial finance, 1830–1914: the finance and organization of English manufacturing industry* (1980) • R. Davis, *The English Rothschilds* (1983) • P. Ferris, *The City* (1960) • W. L. Fraser, *All to the good* (1963) • A. Gibson-Watt, *An undistinguished life* (1990) • GL, Hambros Bank MSS • GL, Hambros family MSS • L. E. Jones, *Georgian afternoon* (1958) • A. St George, *JOH* (1992) [biography of Jocelyn Hambro] • R. S. Sayers, *The Bank of England, 1891–1944*, 3 vols. (1976) • *CGPLA Eng. & Wales* (1961) • b. cert.

**Archives** GL, Hambro family MSS

**Likenesses** E. Halliday, portrait, *c.*1955, priv. coll.; repro. in Bramsen and Wain, *The Hambros*, 390

**Wealth at death** £97,735 17*s.* 11*d.*: probate, 11 Sept 1961, *CGPLA Eng. & Wales*

**Hambury, Sir Henry** (*b.* in or before **1271**, *d. c.***1350**), justice, seems to have come from Hanbury, near Tutbury, in Staffordshire. It was in Hanbury parish church that he established a chantry towards the end of his life and the pattern of his early appointments as an attorney and of his later judicial appointments also points to origins in this area. His earliest recorded employment was as an attorney in the common bench, specializing in cases from this part of the west midlands between 1292 and 1300. By 1308 he had become one of the small group of serjeants practising in the Chester county court, and he continued acting there until 1317. He was also one of the serjeants of the common bench. His first judicial commissions came in 1315–16. Some, if not all, of these were granted at the request of Thomas of Lancaster, the lord of Tutbury, and he obtained a pardon for adherence to the earl in 1318. He was given a number of further judicial commissions in 1322–4.

In April 1324 Hambury was appointed chief justice of the justiciar's bench (the Irish equivalent of the court of king's bench) but did not take up his post in Ireland until September. In January 1325 he transferred to the Dublin bench as one of its junior justices. In March of the same year he became its chief justice and held that post until May 1327. From May to July 1327 he again acted as chief justice of the justiciar's court. Hambury then returned to England where he received a number of individual judicial commissions from October 1327 onwards. In May 1328 he was appointed to the assize commission for five west midland counties but was superseded in March 1329, perhaps for his involvement in Henry of Lancaster's rebellion against the Mortimer regime. He must have made his peace with that regime, since in late December 1329 he became a junior justice of the English court of king's bench, but he remained a justice of the court for no more than a year. During part of this time he was also on the assize commission for the same five west midland counties as before and (with but a short break) he still executed his office as an assize justice until July 1332. He was knighted by 1333 and continued to be appointed to judicial commissions until 1342.

In 1330 Hambury acquired lands in Derbyshire jointly with his wife, Isabel; the chantry chapel he established at Hanbury in 1345 was for the benefit of her soul as well as his own. He also established a chantry at Tutbury in 1340 for the soul of the murdered Edward II. The John Hambury whom he appointed as his attorney while in Ireland in 1323 and 1324 was probably a relative and may have been his son. Both men served in the 1330s on judicial commissions into poaching in the parks of the earl of Lancaster and in 1334 both acted as forest eyre justices for the earl—Henry in Lancashire, John in Yorkshire. Hambury is not heard of after the founding of his chantry in Hanbury, and he probably died about 1350. PAUL BRAND

**Sources** *Chancery records* • common bench plea rolls, PRO, CP 40 • Chester palatine plea rolls, PRO, CHES 29 • H. G. Richardson and G. O. Sayles, *The administration of Ireland, 1172–1377* (1963) • F. M. Maitland and others, eds., *Year books of Edward II*, 26 vols. in 28, SeldS (1903–69)

**Hamel, Gustav Wilhelm** (**1889–1914**), aviator, was born on 25 June 1889, the only son in a family of four children of

Dr Gustav Hugo Hamel (1861–1922) and his wife, Caroline Magdalena Elisa (1864/5–1960), a German-speaking Dane from Schleswig-Holstein. His father had been born in Hamburg and educated in Sweden and Switzerland, where he took his medical degree; he moved to London and built up a wide medical practice. One of his patients was Edward VII, and Dr Hamel was appointed MVO for medical services rendered to the king on the occasion of his visit to Hamburg in 1901. Edward VII was a regular visitor to the doctor's Grosvenor Square home, often after his daily ride, but Mrs Hamel, who retained her strong German accent all her life, would refuse to allow him to bring his terrier Caesar upstairs to the family drawing room. She died aged ninety-five at Robert Adam Street, London, in February 1960.

Hamel was educated at Westminster School from 1901 to 1907. Although his parents hoped he would take up medicine, Gustav was attracted to motor racing and enthusiastically followed the sport across Europe for two years. He made his first ascent in a balloon in the summer of 1909, flying from London to Peterborough. Attracted to the pioneering flights of the French aviators, by autumn 1910 he had become a pupil at the Blériot flying ground at Issy-les-Molineaux, France; he moved to Pau when the aviators went south for the winter in search of more favourable weather conditions. On his first flight, he was observed by M. Blériot, who remarked that he had never seen so apt a pupil.

Hamel obtained his brevet de l'Aero Club de France on 3 February 1911, certificate no. 358, flying a Morane monoplane. On 14 February, following his test flight on a Blériot monoplane, Hamel acquired his Royal Aero Club 'ticket', no. 64. He subsequently transported his own 50 hp Gnôme Blériot from France to Britain and in March won first prize in a cross-country race from Hendon to Brooklands. He made his first flight to Brighton in April 1911, and landed on the lawns beside the seafront at Hove. From then until his untimely death, his flights were extensively reported in the national press. At Hendon on 11 May 1911 he was invited to demonstrate the military potential of aircraft in time of war before the parliamentary committee concerned with aerial defence. He flew to Farnborough and back carrying military dispatches, performing far faster than any cavalryman and out of reach of gunfire from the ground by arriving back over Hendon at 4000 feet.

Following the coronation of George V, and on the suggestion of Sir Walter Windham, permission was given by the postmaster-general for the first British aerial postal service. Hamel piloted a Blériot on the inaugural flight from Hendon to Windsor Castle on 9 September 1911, in adverse weather conditions. Mail flights continued for ten days and raised funds to endow the 'coronation aerial post bed' at the King Edward Hospital, Windsor.

Hamel made his first cross-channel flight from Boulogne to Wembley Park on 12 October 1911, ferrying a Blériot from the Hardelot factory. On 2 April 1912 he flew from London to Paris in a two-seater Blériot monoplane with Miss Trehawke Davies, the first female passenger to be carried by air across the channel. They were entertained to lunch by Blériot and then flew on to Paris. She was to make a total of eight channel crossings with Hamel; he made twenty-one. By Good Friday he was back at Hendon, having achieved a new height record of 6000 feet. He competed in the first aerial Derby, an 81 mile anticlockwise circuit of London, again with Miss Davies as passenger, but after being declared the winner he was subsequently disqualified for a technicality and the race was awarded to his friend Thomas Sopwith. On 12 June he flew to Ranelagh and, watched by the king and queen, gave exhibition flights over the polo grounds before landing and being received at the royal pavilion.

Many and varied were Hamel's exhibition locations, from demonstrations at local flower shows to meetings held on racecourses. Enormous crowds flocked to the venues, and in his Blériot, Hamel was able to land and take off from almost any open space. At each site local photographers produced sets of postcards depicting Hamel with his aircraft surrounded by the crowds, and the card sales proved extremely profitable.

Early in 1913 Miss Davies purchased her own two-seater

**Gustav Wilhelm Hamel (1889–1914)**, by unknown photographer

Blériot and engaged Hamel as one of her aerial chauffeurs. He was extremely good-looking and debonair, and he possessed an engaging personality. To him flocked not only society's young ladies, but many of their mothers also. There was great competition to be photographed in his company and to obtain passenger flights at £5 for a few minutes in the air. So many flew with him that he was called 'the society flyer' and he was especially popular with people in the theatre, who discovered it was good publicity to be photographed in his company.

In April 1913 Hamel flew Frank Dupree, staff journalist on *The Standard*, to Cologne in four hours and fifteen minutes, and they were very well received by German officers. The departure from Dover had been kept secret from the rest of the press so that the flight preparations and take-off could be filmed. The flight was sponsored by *The Standard* and the imperial air fleet committee, with the intention of bringing to public notice Britain's need of a great imperial air fleet. The organizing committee felt that the Royal Navy's dreadnought programme overshadowed the country's lack of aircraft capable of military service in time of war. When Hamel arrived back at Charing Cross Station he was loudly cheered and carried shoulder high from the train to a motor car. The film was shown at the Scala Theatre. Hamel won the second aerial Derby in September 1913, coping in flight with a faulty petrol tap that vibrated loose and threw fuel over his face while he struggled to keep his finger over the leak for more than 30 miles.

By January 1914 a great new aviation stunt, 'looping the loop', had been brought to Britain by Adolphe Pegoud from France, and immediately it caught the public's attention. On 2 January Gladys Cooper (1888–1971) was already strapped into Hamel's two-seater at Hendon and was about to be taken up for her first loop when Miss Davies, having learned that Hamel was to loop, rose from her sick-bed against doctor's orders, arrived at the aerodrome, and requested Miss Cooper to let her fly instead. Reluctantly she agreed, but was most disappointed on returning to London to see the evening papers proclaiming Miss Davies as the first woman to loop the loop. A special 'upside-down dinner', when all the courses were reversed, was held at the Royal Automobile Club to honour Hamel and the other looping exponent, B. C. Hucks. At the dinner Charles Coburn entertained guests by singing a verse of 'Two lovely black eyes' while standing on his head. In early February 1914 Hamel was twice invited to lunch at Windsor Castle, and on the second occasion he performed fourteen loops. At the end of the month he flew to Worcester, being invited to join the countess of Dudley's house party at Witley Court, which included Lady Diana Manners. Hamel flew Lady Dudley over Worcester racecourse, performing a sequence of five loops. At Hendon on 12 March Hamel joined with Hucks in a display of looping and upside-down flying. Hamel's monoplane was painted jet black with large white circles on the tops of the wings, so that it could be clearly observed when the plane was inverted.

About this time Hamel took Marconi for several flights, during which they experimented with transmitting wireless messages on behalf of the naval and military authorities. Hamel's book, *Flying: some Practical Experiences*, co-written with the journalist and pilot C. C. Turner, was published in 1914. In May the same year Winston Churchill, first lord of the Admiralty, invited Hamel to be his guest on the Admiralty yacht *Enchantress*, off Sheerness. Churchill had been learning to fly with naval pilots since early in 1912, and acknowledged that Hamel was further ahead in the art of flying than any of the naval officers: 'If ever there was a man born to fly, three parts a bird and the rest genius, it was Hamel' (Churchill, 184). As well as demonstration flights for naval personnel, Hamel also took Churchill up in his plane.

Very early on the morning of Saturday 23 May 1914 Hamel set off from Villacoublay aerodrome near Paris to deliver a new racing Morane-Saulnier monoplane direct to Hendon, where he was to take part in the third aerial derby that afternoon. When he reached Hardelot weather conditions were still not favourable for the channel crossing. He set off for Hendon just after noon, but his plane crashed and he was drowned mid-channel. The race was abandoned because of bad weather and the shocking news that Hamel was missing in the channel. Extensive searches were made by the Royal Navy, but these were finally called off and the Admiralty issued its own special tribute to him. The manner of his death caused great distress, and the family received many condolences, including one from Buckingham Palace. Duff Cooper penned a poem 'In Memoriam' and sent it to Lady Diana Manners (later his wife, but then a very close friend of Hamel) and a slightly altered version was published in *The Times* on 29 May. Further poems and tributes appeared widely in the national press and in aeronautical and motor journals. A memorial service was held at the Grosvenor Chapel, London. French aviators paid tribute to him as 'le Garros anglais'. Hamel was unmarried at the time of his death.

SYLVIA ADAMS

**Sources** *The Elizabethan* [magazine of Westminster School] (March–May 1907); (May–Oct 1911); (June 1912); (March 1914); (May 1914); (July 1914) · *Flight* (1910–14) · *The Aeroplane* (1910–14) · *The Aero* [London] (1911–13) · *L'Aérophile* (15 June 1914) · M. Gilbert, *Winston S. Churchill*, 3: *1914–1916* (1971) · W. S. Churchill, *Thoughts and adventures* (1932) · D. Cooper, *Old men forget: the autobiography of Duff Cooper* (New York, 1954) · G. Hamel and C. C. Turner, *Flying: some practical experiences* (1914) · *The Times* (29 May 1914) · *The Times* (25 June 1914) · *The Times* (13 Jan 1915) · *Daily Mail* (11 July 1914)

**Archives** FILM BFI NFTVA, newsreel coverage of first aerial post, 1911, and later flying exhibitions

**Likenesses** bust, Royal Air Force Museum, Hendon · caricature, repro. in *VF* · photograph, priv. coll. [*see illus.*] · photographs, repro. in *Flight* (1911–14) · photographs, repro. in *The Aeroplane* (1911–14) · photographs, repro. in *The Aero* (1911–14)

**Wealth at death** £2226 18*s*. 10*d*.: administration, 22 Sept 1914, *CGPLA Eng. & Wales*

**Hamer, Robert James** (1911–1963), film director, was born on 31 March 1911 (along with his twin sister, Barbara) at 24 Chester Road, Kidderminster, Worcestershire, the son of Owen Dylmer Hamer, a bank clerk, and his wife, Annie Grace Brickell. Both his parents survived him. He was educated at Rossell School in Lancashire, where he showed himself to be intellectually outstanding and won a scholarship to Corpus Christi College, Cambridge. He had intended to join the Treasury as an economist or mathematician but achieved only a third-class degree. Hamer later light-heartedly blamed 'the proximity of Newmarket Heath to Cambridge and the existence in Cambridge of five cinemas changing programmes twice weekly' ('Biography of Robert Hamer') for his disappointing performance. He also spent much of his time writing poetry and contributing to revues, but he suffered a more serious disruption to his studies when he was sent down for having a homosexual affair with another student (Drazin, *Finest Years*, 72).

**Ealing Studios** Hamer began his career in films in 1934 as a 'number boy' and cutting-room assistant at the Gaumont-British Studios in Shepherd's Bush. A year later he joined London Films, which was expanding rapidly after the success of Alexander Korda's *The Private Life of Henry VIII* (1933). Korda attracted a number of European film-makers to Britain, including Erich Pommer, the producer of German films such as *The Cabinet of Dr Caligari* and *Metropolis*. When Pommer formed a production company with Charles Laughton—Mayflower Pictures—to make prestigious films designed for the international market, he asked Hamer to edit *Vessel of Wrath* (1938) and *Jamaica Inn* (1939).

Soon after *Jamaica Inn* was completed Pommer and Laughton left for Hollywood and Mayflower's operations were suspended. As war approached, Hamer joined the General Post Office film unit alongside Alberto Cavalcanti, whose earlier work with the French avant-garde Hamer much admired. In 1940 Cavalcanti was recruited by Ealing Studios and he was soon joined by Hamer. After editing *Turned out Nice Again* (1941), *Ships with Wings* (1941), and *The Foreman Went to France* (1942) Hamer worked as associate producer on *My Learned Friend* (1943), *San Demetrio London* (1943), and *Fiddlers Three* (1944). He also gained some experience in directing by taking over from Charles Frend when he fell ill on *San Demetrio London* and re-shooting sequences for *Fiddlers Three* when Harry Watt, an outdoor realist director, failed to adjust to the demands of a musical comedy set in ancient Rome and starring Tommy Trinder.

In 1945 Hamer directed one of the episodes of the omnibus horror film *Dead of Night*. His contribution, 'The Haunted Mirror', though less praised at the time than Cavalcanti's 'The Ventriloquist's Dummy', has come to be seen as a clever allegory of sexual repression, and the disturbing presence of mirrors became a recurring motif in Hamer's films. A similar fascination with the dark side of life is apparent in *Pink String and Sealing Wax* (1946), Hamer's first feature film, where a Victorian chemist's son, in rebellion against his father's heavy-handed patriarchal domination, strays into the rougher areas of Brighton and is lured into a murder plot by a glamorous barmaid. Hamer was happy to admit that 'he enjoyed the melodrama but never felt happy with the domestic charm' ('Biography of Robert Hamer'). And it is the sequences in the film set in the world of the sensuous and alluring barmaid (Googie Withers, who had played a major role in 'The Haunted Mirror'), which are the most impressive.

Hamer's next film, *It always Rains on Sunday* (1947), was an adaptation of a topical low-life novel by Arthur La Bern. Again it starred Googie Withers as a woman trapped in an unsatisfying marriage, though here the melodrama and the domestic detail are more carefully integrated. Much of the film was shot at Ealing Studios, but it manages to capture a real feeling of East End London and the film is memorable both for its authenticity in depicting life in a cramped working-class household and for the long, atmospheric sequence where the escaped convict is hunted down at night, trapped among shunting freight trains in a railway marshalling yard. Though the critic of *The Observer* dismissed it as 'a dreary round of squalor', other critics praised the film for its realism, and it was a popular success.

***Kind Hearts and Coronets*** Hamer shifted back in time for *Kind Hearts and Coronets* (1949), a black comedy about the poor relation of a noble family who is so stung by the snobbish insensitivity of his rich cousins that he determines to eliminate all who stand between himself and the dukedom. Daringly, Hamer cast Alec Guinness to play all eight of the aristocratic victims, and Dennis Price gave a masterly performance as the suavely vengeful murderer. On its initial release the film was only modestly successful and received respectful rather than ecstatic reviews, but it was one of few British films of the period to be warmly received in France and the USA. By 1959 Hamer was complaining that:

> It's flattering to make a picture which becomes a classic within ten years; it's not so flattering, however, when people get the impression it's the *only* picture you've ever made. … That picture has become a sort of yardstick for everything else I've done. Friends, especially friends, look at my other films and say 'good, brilliant, superb' but not, of course, so 'good, brilliant, superb' as *Kind Hearts and Coronets*. (Vincent, 27)

The comedy of *Kind Hearts and Coronets* is of a much blacker shade than any other Ealing comedy and pessimism haunts Hamer's best films. The darkness of his vision made it difficult for him to find projects which fitted in with the cosy ethos of Ealing Studios. *Soho Melodrama*, a script he developed with Mark Benney, an ex-burglar who had become a successful reporter and novelist, was rejected because of censorship problems. Hamer's idea of casting Margaret Lockwood as Edith Thompson, who had been hanged in 1937 when her lover was found guilty of murdering her husband, was abandoned when the censors proved hostile. Another Hamer project, a dramatization of Richard Mason's novel *The Shadow and the Peak* (1949), which would have had Vivien Leigh in the starring role, was held back by Balcon as too expensive and too erotic (it was eventually filmed as *Passionate Summer*, with Virginia McKenna). In 1949 Hamer took leave from Ealing to make *The Spider and the Fly* for his old company Mayflower, now run by Aubrey Baring and Maxwell Setton. With a solid script by Robert Westerby and good performances from Eric Portman, Guy Rolfe, and Nadia Gray, it is an intelligent and interesting film, but, in contrast to the films emerging from Ealing, it shares the mood and the visual style of the bleakest of American *films noir*.

Hamer was still under contract to Ealing and returned to make *His Excellency* (1951), with Eric Portman as a working-class trade union leader appointed governor of a British colony with a large naval base (very like Malta or Gibraltar). Freda Bruce Lockhart, who interviewed Hamer late in 1951, when the film was being completed, discerned that it was a task 'for which he had little heart', and the film is unconvincing and carelessly plotted. Hamer told his interviewer that he regarded Ealing 'rather as if it were a family co-operative than an employer' and praised 'Sir Michael Balcon's wisdom in giving the members of his team a free hand, subject to rational safeguards' (Bruce Lockhart, 74–5). But he found it impossible to agree with Balcon on a mutually acceptable project and left Ealing for good.

**Later films** Hamer's first film on leaving Ealing—*The Long Memory* (1952), produced by Hugh Stewart, who had co-edited *St Martin's Lane* (1938) with Hamer—harks back to the French poetic realism of the 1930s. John Mills plays a convict released after serving twelve years in prison for a murder he did not commit and determined on vengeance against those responsible. Visually it is an extraordinary film, shot extensively on location around the Thames estuary and ending with the wounded hero chased from Tower Bridge to the mudflats beyond Gravesend by the man he is supposed to have murdered. He is saved (physically) by a canny old tramp and (emotionally) by a European refugee who has lost everything in the war. Happiness—or rather the chance to live without hurting or being hurt—is possible here but only among a community of outcasts.

Hamer was still a highly respected film director and his next film, *Father Brown* (1954), starring Alec Guinness as G. K. Chesterton's detective-priest, was well received by critics and public alike. He followed it with *To Paris with Love* (1955), a light comedy. But frivolity and Technicolor did not suit Hamer and the film springs to life only in the moment of pathos when the middle-aged widower (Guinness again) realizes that his plan to marry a vivacious young French woman is an impossible pipe dream. Much better tuned to Hamer's sensibilities was his adaptation of Turgenev's *A Month in the Country* (1955) for the television company Rediffusion, an intimate drama where bored, unhappy people yearn for, but are never able to achieve, happiness in love. Even within the confines of television production of a stage play, Hamer maintains visual interest and the performances he evokes from his cast—Margaret Leighton, Michael Gough, Laurence Harvey, and Geoffrey Keen—are superb.

Twice in *A Month in the Country* the despairing suitor Ratikin quotes Swinburne's lines 'I can't think how things can be as dreadful as they are. I suppose if I live through this I shall live to see them become worse.' They had a prophetic relevance to Hamer's own life. About 1935 he had married Joan Holt, an aspiring actress, whose brother Seth Holt worked as an editor and director at Ealing. The marriage broke up in the 1950s and Hamer began a relationship with Pamela Wilcox, daughter of the producer-director Herbert Wilcox, with whom he lived until six weeks before his death. She charts their joint decline into alcoholism in her autobiography, *Between Hell and Charing Cross*. Hamer's close friend the Ealing scriptwriter Diana Morgan thought that 'probably he would have been happier to live as a homosexual' (Drazin, *Finest Years*, 73). Apart from the fact that before homosexuality was legalized in 1967 this would have courted legal prosecution, Hamer appeared not to attach much weight to happiness. A script for an unmade film, *For Each the Other*, contained the lines by Hamer that:

> People think they have some right to be happy, and are doubly unhappy because they are not. It is only when they come to accept that the natural human salary is one of unhappiness, and that interims of happiness come as a bonus and must be hungrily seized and savoured, that they have a chance of coming out anywhere near even in the unequal contest with fate. (Kemp, 78)

**Final years** It was not until 1958 that Hamer returned to the cinema. At Michael Balcon's suggestion he was taken on to direct an adaptation of Daphne du Maurier's *The Scapegoat* (1957). This was a big-budget production backed by MGM and its story of a bored Englishman tricked into assuming the life of his aristocratic French *doppelgänger* (with Guinness in both parts), seemed ideal for Hamer. The first half of the film is intriguing and atmospheric, but it then becomes increasingly haphazard and disjointed and makes poor use of the talents of its three leading actresses: Bette Davis, Irene Worth, and Pamela Brown. This seems to have been more the fault of MGM, who would have preferred George Cukor or Vincente Minnelli as director and insisted on drastically recutting the film, than of Hamer, who stuck to his promise not to drink while he was directing the film.

Hamer's disappointment at the mangling of a film which would have restored his reputation seems to have destroyed any desire to reform his life. On his next and last film, *School for Scoundrels* (1960), drink got the better of him and he was replaced by Cyril Frankel after collapsing on the set. It would be unfair to attribute only the good sequences to Hamer, but it is appropriate that the first half of the film, where the hero played by Ian Carmichael is an incompetent failure at life, is much more satisfying and convincing than the second half, where, with the help of a course in 'lifemanship', he learns how to manipulate the world to his advantage. This was something Hamer himself conspicuously failed to do. He was declared bankrupt in November 1961 and although he completed and sold a script (*Down among the Dead Men*) and worked for a few weeks rewriting David Niven's dialogue for *55 Days in Peking* (1963), he was unable to overcome his addiction to alcohol and died of pneumonia on 4 December 1963 at St Thomas's Hospital, Lambeth, London. He was buried at Llandegley church, Radnorshire. Hamer's contribution to British cinema is a significant one, most obviously for the wit and charm of *Kind Hearts and Coronets* and *Father Brown*, but equally for the impressive poetic realism of *It always*

*Rains on Sunday* and *The Long Memory*, which showed he had the emotional range, the humanity, and the visual imagination to have been one of the world's great film-makers. ROBERT MURPHY

**Sources** M. Balcon, *Michael Balcon presents … a lifetime in films* (1969) • C. Barr, *Ealing Studios* (1977) • M. Benney [Henry Ernest Degras], *Almost a gentleman* (1966) • 'Biography of Robert Hamer', Ealing Studios publicity statement, BFI [library microfiche for Robert Hamer] • C. Drazin, *The finest years: British cinema of the 1940s* (1998) • C. Drazin, 'Robert Hamer', *London Magazine* (June/July 1995) • P. Kemp, 'The long shadow: Robert Hamer after Ealing', *Film Comment* (May–June 1995), 71–8 • F. Bruce Lockhart, 'Interview with Hamer', *Sight and Sound*, 21 (1951–2), 74–5 • J. McCallum, *Life with Googie* (1979) • J. Vincent, 'Hamer's potted lifemanship', *Films and Filming* (July 1959), 27 • P. Wilcox, *Between Hell and Charing Cross* (1977) • b. cert. • d. cert. • *CGPLA Eng. & Wales* (1964)
**Archives** BFI, Michael Balcon special collection • BFI, Robert Hamer special collection
**Likenesses** photographs, BFI, Robert Hamer special collection
**Wealth at death** £1100: administration, limited, 1964, *CGPLA Eng. & Wales* (1964)

**Hamerton, Atkins** (*bap.* 1804, *d.* 1857), army officer and first British consul in Zanzibar, was baptized on 29 April 1804 in St Thomas's Church, Marlborough Street, Dublin, the son of Edward Hamerton, clerk of ships' entries at the port of Dublin, and his wife, Elizabeth, *née* Atkins. The parish then housed many sailors and dockers. Hamerton's family was Anglican and he was educated by the Revd John Fea, curate-assistant of St Thomas's. In January 1825 he was selected for the Bombay infantry, and he went on to serve with the 15th Bombay native infantry. In India he showed an aptitude for languages, qualifying as a Hindustani interpreter in May 1831 and later acquiring proficiency in Persian. Also in 1831 he stood trial and was admonished for being a second at a duel in which Lieutenant Montgomery was killed. In May 1838 he was appointed interpreter to a field detachment of his regiment proceeding to the Gulf, where the detachment was then stationed (at Kharaq).

The growing prominence of Buraimi convinced the British authorities that a reconnaissance of the oasis was desirable; Hamerton was sent and, arriving in January 1840, was the first European to see it. In April, while in Muscat, he was appointed agent of the East India Company in the dominions of Sayyid Saʿid bin Sultan al-Busaʿidi, whose rule extended from Muscat to Zanzibar and the Swahili coast. The Sayyid, worried about French activity on the east coast, sailed in December 1840 for Zanzibar to investigate. Hamerton followed, arriving in Zanzibar in May 1841, and was appointed British consul. He was responsible to both the Foreign Office and the Bombay government. His appointment resulted from British concerns with French activity, British-Indian commercial interests, and suppression of the slave trade. He was backed by British naval supremacy in the Indian Ocean. He recognized Saʿid's difficult position with the slave trade—and also that slaves in Zanzibar were generally well treated—and advised the British government to be cautious against the Arab slave trade, warning that more drastic measures, as demanded by abolitionists in Britain, could be counter-productive and could cost Saʿid his throne if not his life.

At Zanzibar, Saʿid generously offered a rent-free property on the sea front for the consulate. In August 1841 Hamerton paid a short visit to Mombasa to investigate matters relating to the slave trade. Before long relations between ruler and agent were less than harmonious, Hamerton making no effort to establish a discreet and subtle influence. Even had Hamerton been more diplomatic in his negotiations, the British policies would have made him unpopular—especially the constant pressure against the slave trade. This, together with the personality of the British consul, contributed to increasing British influence over Sayyid Saʿid. In 1845 Hamerton negotiated with Saʿid the latter's acceptance of a treaty (signed on 2 October 1845, to become effective in 1847) banning the export of slaves from Africa to Saʿid's possessions in the Gulf and enabling British warships to enforce it. Although this became known as the Hamerton treaty it was the product of Lord Aberdeen and the Foreign Office. On paper a major blow against the slave trade, in fact it was initially largely ineffective as Saʿid was unwilling and unable to enforce it and the British lacked sufficient available warships. Hamerton—a forthright, irritable, impatient man and given to drink—tended to treat the ruler and his subjects as inferiors. When Saʿid's envoy Ali bin Nasir al-Busaʿidi went to England in 1842 he complained about Hamerton, who was reprimanded by the Foreign Office. Aberdeen ordered Hamerton's removal in 1845, but shortly afterwards Aberdeen was succeeded by Palmerston and Hamerton remained in post.

In January 1844 Johann Ludwig Krapf, a German missionary for the Church Missionary Society, made his first visit to Zanzibar, where he was 'hospitably received' by Hamerton (Krapf, 121), and was presented by the latter to Saʿid. In April 1851 Hamerton sailed for Muscat and Bombay and returned to Zanzibar in February 1853. In October 1856 Sayyid Saʿid, after a visit to Muscat, set sail for Zanzibar but died at sea on 19 October. Saʿid's death was followed by rivalry among his sons for succession to his various domains. At Zanzibar, Barghash tried to seize power, but Hamerton intervened and helped to ensure the succession of Sayyid Majid, whom Saʿid had nominated, and supported him against his enemies. In December 1856 the explorers Richard Francis Burton and John Hanning Speke arrived at Zanzibar. Burton visited the British consulate almost immediately, to find Lieutenant-Colonel Hamerton a sick man, with his hair and beard 'prematurely snow-white' (Burton, *Zanzibar*, 1.35). The two men got on well together (unlike Burton and Christopher Palmer Rigby, Hamerton's successor), though the relationship between Speke and Hamerton was less close. Burton persuaded Hamerton to accompany the expedition as far as the mainland and in June 1857 they set sail in his highness's yacht *Artémise*, 'the consul's yacht'. After the expedition had disembarked the yacht returned home; Hamerton died aboard, reportedly of dysentery and liver condition, within sight of Zanzibar on 5 July 1857. He was buried at Chapwani (French Island, subsequently Grave Island). P. J. L. Frankl

**Sources** C. S. Nicholls, *The Swahili coast* (1971) • R. H. Crofton, *The old consulate at Zanzibar* (1935) • R. Burton, *Zanzibar: city, island and coast*, 2 vols. (1872) • J. L. Krapf, *Travels* (1860) • A. Hamerton, 'Brief notes', *Selections from the records of the Bombay government*, 24 (1856), 235–45 • *Bombay Gazette* (20 Aug 1857) • J. B. Kelly, *Britain and the Persian Gulf, 1795–1880* (1968) • R. C. Howell, *The Royal Navy and the slave trade* (1987) • R. Oliver and G. Mathew, *History of East Africa*, 1 (1963) • BL OIOC, IOR, L/mil/9/156 • clerk of ships' entries, port of Dublin • R. Burton, *Lake regions*, 1 (1860), 66 • C. E. B. Russell, *General Rigby* (1935), 81 • parish register, Dublin, Marlborough Street, St Thomas's [parents' marriage], 6 Dec 1788

**Archives** PRO, Foreign Office, slave trade papers, FO 84 (Slave Trade) • Zanzibar National Archives, British consular records

**Wealth at death** Rs 6000; and estate

**Hamerton** [*formerly* Hammerton], **Philip Gilbert** (1834–1894), artist and essayist, was born on 10 September 1834 at Laneside, near Shaw, near Oldham in Lancashire; he changed the spelling of his name in 1854. His father, John Hammerton, a solicitor, married Anne, orphan daughter of Philip Cocker, a cotton manufacturer, in 1833: she survived her son's birth by only a few days. He was brought up by aunts in Burnley, and educated at Burnley and Doncaster grammar schools. In 1844 his father, an alcoholic, died. He was prepared for Oxford by a clergyman, but Hamerton never attended university because he did not feel drawn to conventional academic study, and was reluctant to sign the Thirty-Nine Articles. Although never well off, he had sufficient funds to be able to follow his favourite pursuits, 'deciding to try and be a painter, and to try to be an author, and seeing what came of both attempts' (Hamerton, *Autobiography*, 113). He remained active as a practitioner in many visual media, especially etching (on which he published a *Handbook* in 1871), throughout his life.

Hamerton dated his interest in modern painting from a visit to London in 1851 and, especially, to seeing Millais's work at the Royal Academy—an enthusiasm which his purchase of the first volume of Ruskin's *Modern Painters* confirmed, although he later repudiated Ruskin's view that art could be learned from nature. He briefly held a commission in the Royal Lancashire militia (1853–4, first as lieutenant, and then captain), studied painting in London in 1853 with the competent but unadventurous topographical artist John Petit, and travelled and painted in the Scottish highlands. In 1855 Hamerton went to study painting in Paris, and the work of Constant Troyon in particular, as well as that of Charles Daubigny and Charles Jacque, did much to change his early taste for detailed topographical painting and the Pre-Raphaelites. In 1858 he married the lively and intelligent Eugénie Gindriez (*b. c.*1839), the daughter of a republican former prefect: her continuation of Hamerton's *Autobiography*, chronicling both personal and professional events in his life after their marriage in some detail, provides the most sustained information available about Hamerton's life. They had three children: Stephen, Richard (whose suicide in 1888 greatly saddened his parents), and Mary. Just after the marriage, the couple went to live on the isolated small island of Innistrynich on Loch Awe, Argyll. Financial difficulties (including the financial responsibility which Hamerton took on towards his wife's family after her father's death) led them to move in 1861 to France, where they lived first at Sens, then near Autun. His detailed observations of French rural life appear in *Round my House* (1876), and his knowledge of French society also informs *Modern Frenchmen* (1878) and *French and English* (1890): he felt he had a role to play as a mediator between the two countries. The last few years of his life were spent at Boulogne-sur-Seine.

Hamerton began writing freelance articles for the *Historic Times* when he was about fifteen—cobbled together, he freely admitted, from publicly available information. The publication of his first, highly successful, art book, *A Painter's Camp in the Highlands* (1862), with its combination of anecdote, description, and artistic generalizations, led to his being invited to contribute to the *Fine Arts Quarterly Review*, and his first piece was an elaborate criticism of the 1863 Paris Salon. Subsequently he also wrote for the *Cornhill* and *Macmillan's* magazines, and published in the United States in the *International Review* and *Atlantic Monthly*. In 1866 he succeeded F. T. Palgrave as art critic on the *Saturday Review*, but he resigned in 1868 because he was suffering from a stress-induced nervous condition which made travelling very difficult. He did, however, continue to write on contemporary art, not only for the *Saturday Review*, but also for *The Globe* and the *Pall Mall Gazette*. To the end of his life he remained interested in and enthusiastic about new artistic developments. French criticism, which he called 'the most discriminating and the most accurate in the world' (Hamerton, *Autobiography*, 201), informed his authoritative style. His article 'Art criticism', which he published in the *Cornhill Magazine* in September 1863, in listing all the desirable qualities of an art critic, outlines his rigorous standards: a critic, he maintained, should 'make himself as thoroughly informed as his time and opportunities will allow about everything concerning the Fine Arts' (p. 340), something which he extended not just to the history and practice of art, but to historical and classical knowledge, landscape, and literature. His ideal, clearly, was the leisured gentleman critic. In 1869 Hamerton launched *The Portfolio* (its English administration delegated to Richmond Seeley), an innovative publication in terms of the many different forms of reproduction it employed, including etching on India paper and autotype photography. Its aim was to present

> Works of Art of various kinds, but always such as are likely to interest a cultivated public; and to accompany them with literature by writers of proved ability, superior to mere letter press, and more readable than pure criticism and cataloguing. (advertisement, *The Bookseller*, 4 Jan 1870, 35)

It was one of the first English periodicals to introduce reproductions of pen drawings, including, in its first two years, works by George Frederic Watts, Edward Burne-Jones, H. S. Marks, P. H. Calderon, and John Everett Millais. Hamerton was thus responsible for an important diffusion of graphic art forms in England during the last three decades of the nineteenth century in a periodical which, despite retailing at £2s. 6d., carried considerable influence. Additionally he made sure that *The Portfolio* carried technical information which would be valuable to the practising artist. In 1893 the periodical—at the instigation of Seeley and the publisher, Macmillan—underwent a change of direction, each number being devoted to a single artist. Hamerton contributed the first of these, 'The Etchings of Rembrandt'. His artistic monographs, including *The Graphic Arts* (1882), *Landscape in Art* (1883), and *Man in Art* (1883), were largely derived from his *Portfolio* contributions.

In addition to his art criticism, for which he is best remembered, Hamerton wrote two novels, *Wenderholme* (1869), a novel of provincial Lancashire, indebted in its style to the earlier work of George Eliot, and, published under the pseudonym Adolphus Segrave, *Marmorne* (1878), a more sensational story of romantic rivalry between brothers. His volumes of essays—*The Intellectual Life* (1873), *Human Intercourse* (1882), and *The Quest of Happiness* (1897)—were strongly influenced by Ralph Emerson, to whose memory the second of these volumes is dedicated (despite Hamerton's never having met him): he especially revered the American's 'two doctrines of reliance on the compensation of Nature, and of a self-respectful reliance on our own individuality' (Hamerton, *Human Intercourse*, vi). Hamerton's essays were popular on both sides of the Atlantic, and a collected edition of his works was published in Boston in 1882. In the same year he was made an *officier d'Académie*—an academic honour—and in 1894 received the degree of LLD from Aberdeen University.

Hamerton's friends testified to his geniality, straightforwardness, and kindliness, and to his tall, impressive figure. Yet he never enjoyed good health and suffered from a number of nervous complaints. He died from heart disease at his home, Villa Clematis, Boulogne-sur-Seine, on 4 November 1894. KATE FLINT

**Sources** P. G. Hamerton, *An autobiography and memoir* (1897) · M. Betham-Edwards, *Anglo-French reminiscences* (1900) · K. Flint, 'The English critical response to contemporary painting', DPhil diss., U. Oxf., 1985 · *The Times* (7 Nov 1894) · P. G. Hamerton, 'Art criticism', *Cornhill Magazine*, 8 (Sept 1863), 334–43 · H. James, 'An English critic of French painting', in H. James, *The painter's eye: notes and essays on the pictorial arts*, ed. J. L. Sweeney (1956), 33–42 [originally published in *North American Review* in April 1868, as unsigned review of Hamerton's *Contemporary French painters*] · W. B. Scott, *Autobiographical notes* (1892) · Boase, *Mod. Eng. biog.* · Allibone, *Dict.*
**Archives** U. Glas. | BL, corresp. with Macmillans, Add. MS 55225 · National Gallery, London, corresp. with Ralph Nicholson Wornum · NL Scot., letters to William Blackwood & Sons
**Likenesses** Elliott & Fry, photograph, repro. in *Scribner's Magazine* (Feb 1895) · A. H. Palmer, photograph, repro. in Hamerton, *Autobiography* · engraving, repro. in *ILN* (10 Nov 1894) · etching, repro. in *Portfolio papers* (1888) · photograph, repro. in *Magazine of Art* (1895) · woodcut (after photograph), BM

**Hamey, Baldwin, the elder** (1568–1640), physician, a descendant of the crusader Odo de Hame who took part in the siege of Acre in 1190, was born in Bruges in 1568 into a Dutch Reformed church family, which, in the wake of the city's surrender to the forces of Alexander Farnese in May 1584, emigrated to Leiden. Hamey matriculated at the University of Leiden on 28 April 1586 and received his MD on 6 July 1592 with a thesis on dysentery. He became a protégé of the professor of medicine, Johannes Heurnius, with whom he kept up a regular correspondence for years. It was thanks to Heurnius that Hamey was appointed physician to the tsar of Russia in 1594, upon the latter's request to the university to provide him with a court physician. Increasingly worried about the political uncertainties in Russia, Hamey eventually resigned his post in 1597 and left for London where he initially lived with Susanna Demaistres, the aunt of his future wife, Sarah Oeils (1575–1638), whom he married in 1599. By the time their first-born, Baldwin *Hamey the younger (1600–1676), was baptized in the Dutch Reformed church in London in May 1600 Hamey had acquired a house at 40 Sydon Lane in Tower ward and had begun his medical practice without a licence from the College of Physicians. Initially Hamey appears to have held high hopes of becoming personal physician to the earl of Essex. These hopes, however, came to nothing with the execution of the earl in February 1601. Instead Hamey was forced to sustain his family from his unlicensed practice, primarily among the reformed immigrant population of London. Among his patients seem to have been the Dutch ambassador to London, Sir Noel de Caron, and the Anglo-Dutch poet-merchant Jacob Cool, also known as Ortelianus. Being naturally cautious and conservative in outlook Hamey was deeply hostile to anything which smacked of quackery, dangerous novelty, or disrespect for traditional Galenic medicine. Accordingly he sought to obtain a licence from the College of Physicians as early as February 1602, but failed. Despite this disappointment he continued his practice and five years later the College of Physicians warned him to abstain from practice. Another two years passed and in the summer of 1609 Hamey made another unsuccessful attempt to be licensed by the college. Following this attempt the College of Physicians intervened against him and he was fined £5 for unlicensed practice. While paying off his fine in instalments during the autumn of 1609 Hamey eventually managed to pass the examinations required by the college and on 12 January 1610 he was finally made a licentiate.

Hamey's conservative natural philosophy and medicine are strongly in evidence in his correspondence with Johannes Heurnius's son Otto, who had succeeded his father as professor of medicine at the University of Leiden upon the latter's death in 1601. In these letters Hamey makes evident his hostility to astrology and Paracelsianism in particular.

Together with his friend the physician Raphael Thorius, Hamey belonged to a group of reformed immigrant humanists and poets who were centred around the Dutch Reformed community in London, especially its minister, Simon Ruytinck, and Jacob Cool. In 1622 both Hamey and his son Baldwin contributed poems to the commemorative volume, *Epicedia in orbitum*, for Simon Ruytinck. Similarly Hamey wrote an obituary poem for Raphael Thorius upon the latter's death during the epidemic of 1625. Like most of his friends from this circle Hamey belonged to a broadminded, eirenic Calvinism, whose adherents agonized over the religious split in the United Provinces between counter-remonstrants and remonstrants which became so prominent after the Synod of Dort in 1618.

Hamey's medical practice seems to have been successful although he appears to have charged only moderate fees. He was certainly comfortably off when he died at his home in London on 10 November 1640 and left money and possessions in his will to the value of more than £4000. Among his legacies were £20 for a silver drinking cup to the College of Physicians and donations to the poor of his local parish and the poor of the Dutch church in London. However, there are some indications that Hamey may have been struggling financially at least during the first couple of decades of the seventeenth century. This would explain why in 1614 he tried to get his son Baldwin accepted as an alumnus of the Dutch Reformed church in London to study theology and later to be able to serve the reformed communities in England as a minister, offering the proviso that he would reimburse the church should young Baldwin abandon his theological studies for another subject.

Hamey was buried with his wife in the church of All Hallows Barking, near the Tower of London, on 12 November. Their three surviving children erected a monument (now destroyed) in the church to their memory. The eldest son, Baldwin, became a physician and president of the College of Physicians, the second son, Jeremy, became a merchant, while the daughter, Elizabeth, married Andrew Palmer of Roydon in Essex. The Palmers' descendants owned the portraits of Sarah and Baldwin Hamey the elder, which Hamey had commissioned Cornelius Johnson to paint. OLE PETER GRELL

**Sources** J. J. Keevil, *Hamey the stranger* (1952) • O. P. Grell, *Calvinist exiles in Tudor and Stuart England* (1996) • letters, University of Leiden, Western MSS collection • B. Hamey, 'Bustorum aliquot reliquiae ...', RCP Lond. • R. Palmer, 'The life of the eminent Dr Baldwin Hamey', 1733, RCP Lond. • G. du Rieu, ed., *Album studiosorum academiae Lugduno Batavae, MDLXXV–MDCCCLXXV: accedunt nomina curatorum et professorum per eadem secula* (The Hague, 1875)

**Archives** GL • RCP Lond., corresp. and papers • University of Leiden

**Likenesses** oils, 1633, RCP Lond. • line engraving (after W. Stukeley), Wellcome L.

**Wealth at death** £4123 19*s*. 4*d*.: will and inventory, Keevil, *Hamey*

**Hamey, Baldwin, the younger** (1600–1676), physician, eldest son of Baldwin *Hamey MD (1568–1640) and his wife, Sarah (1575–1638), daughter of Peter and Anne Oeils, was born in London on 24 April 1600, and, after schooling in London, entered the University of Leiden as a student of philosophy in May 1617. He visited Oxford for a time in 1621, attended a few public lectures, and studied in the Bodleian Library there. Disappointed with the standard of medical education in Oxford, Hamey was apprenticed to his father during the winter of 1622–3. In August 1625 he returned to Leiden, where he graduated MD on 12 August 1626, writing a thesis 'De angina'. After a brief spell at

**Baldwin Hamey the younger** (1600–1676), by Matthew Snelling, *c*.1674

home he then visited the universities of Paris, Montpellier, and Padua, and after travels in Germany, France, and Italy, was incorporated DM at Oxford on 4 February 1630. Before setting out on these travels Hamey had spent the night at Hastings. Here he dined with the mayor, and was to sail next morning, but the mayor had dreamed that Hamey should not be allowed to travel and accordingly set a guard at the inn, which prevented his sailing with sixty other passengers, who were all lost in a storm which arose less than an hour after the ship sailed.

Hamey was admitted a fellow of the College of Physicians of London on 10 January 1634, was eight times censor from 1640 to 1654, was registrar in 1646 and 1650 to 1654, and treasurer 1664–6. In 1648 he delivered the Goulstonian lectures. On 3 May 1627 he had married Anna de Pettin (1596/7–1660) of Rotterdam, and settled in the parish of St Clement, Eastcheap, London. Simeon Fox helped him to build a successful practice. John Pearson's sermons on the creed were preached in the parish church, and he became one of Hamey's friends. During the civil war Hamey considered leaving London, but an attack of inflammation of the lungs changed his intention. During his convalescence a parliamentary general consulted him, and, delighted with his promise of cure, handed him a bag of gold. Hamey thought the fee too great and handed it back; whereupon the general took a handful of gold pieces from the bag, put them into the physician's pocket, and left. Hamey handed his fee of thirty-six broad pieces to his wife. She was pleased and told him how, during his illness, she had paid that very sum to a state exaction rather than trouble him with discussion of the matter.

Hamey took this incident to be an omen against migration, remained in London, and soon had many patients from the parliament side.

Despite being a royalist Hamey complied with the times so far as to go and hear the preachings of the sectaries, but used to take with him either an octavo Aldine Virgil in vellum, or a duodecimo Aristophanes in red leather with clasps. His fellow worshippers took them for Bible and Greek Testament, and lost in their study he avoided the annoyance of the sermon. Hamey acquired a collection of Stuart relics which included a diamond ring of Charles I bearing the royal arms, bought for £500, and several times sent gifts to Charles II. The ring he gave to Charles II at the Restoration. The king offered Hamey a knighthood, but he declined the honour. He retired from practice in 1666 and went to live at Chelsea, where he died on 14 May 1676. He was buried four days later in the chancel of the parish church there, St Luke's, wrapped in linen, without coffin, and 10 feet deep, and with no monument but a black marble slab bearing his name, the date of his death, and the sentence: 'When the breath goeth out of a man he returneth unto his earth.' In 1717 his great-nephew raised a monument to his memory. Both monuments have since been destroyed.

Hamey had no children, and as he had a good inheritance as well as a lucrative practice he was always well off, and used his wealth with generosity throughout life. When only thirty-three he paid the expenses of the education at school and at Oxford of a deserving scholar, John Sigismund Clewer. He gave £100 towards the repairs of St Paul's Cathedral, and also contributed liberally to the fabrics of All Hallows Barking, of St Clement, Eastcheap, and of St Luke's, Chelsea. He also gave a great bell to Chelsea church with the inscription, 'Baldwinus Hamey Philevangelicus Medicus Divo Lucae medico evangelico, D.D.D.'. He was still more generous to the College of Physicians, and became its largest benefactor. He gave a large sum towards its rebuilding after the fire of 1666, and wainscoted the dining-room with carved Spanish oak, some of which, with his arms, is preserved in the present college. In 1672 he gave the college an estate near Great Ongar in Essex. The rents of this, among other objects, were to pay annual sums to the physicians of St Bartholomew's provided that hospital accepted the nominees of the College of Physicians. On a vacancy the college was informed of it by letter and made a nomination which was rejected by the hospital, while the senior assistant physician was appointed. Thus the physicians of St Bartholomew's never received Hamey's benefaction; but to make up to them the hospital paid each 100 guineas a year, so that, circuitously, his good wish was carried out.

Hamey's thesis was his only printed work, but several of his manuscripts were deposited in the Royal College of Physicians. *Bustorum aliquot reliquiae ab anno 1628, qui mihi primus fuit conducti seorsim a parentibus non inauspicato hospitii* begins with an account of Theodore Goulston and then gives biographies of fifty-three other physicians, contemporaries of Hamey. Besides the original there is a beautiful copy of this manuscript, and another copy exists in the British Library. *Universa medicina* is a folio book of notes on medicine; other works deposited were 'Goulstonian lectures' and 'Notes on Aristophanes'. After Hamey's death Adam Littleton edited in 1693 his *Dissertatio epistolaris de juramento medicorum qui orkos Hippokratous dicitur*. On his journey to the continent he kept a 'Journal of his own travels in the most pure Latin'. He also produced his *Liber amicorum*, 'wherein many of the most Eminent men there, did him the honor with some ingenious Motto of Elegance and taste, to Register their Names, as well as their great Value and Esteem for him' (Keevil, *Stranger's Son*, 23).

NORMAN MOORE, *rev.* MICHAEL BEVAN

**Sources** J. J. Keevil, *The stranger's son* (1953) · Munk, *Roll* · J. J. Keevil, *Hamey the stranger* (1952)

**Archives** RCP Lond., corresp. and MSS

**Likenesses** oils, *c.*1638 (after portrait by A. Van Dyck), Bodl. Oxf. · M.? Snelling, oils, *c.*1674, RCP Lond. [*see illus.*] · E. Pierce, marble bust, *c.*1675, RCP Lond. · line engraving, 1793 (after W. Stukeley), Wellcome L.

**Hamilton**. For this title name *see* individual entries under Hamilton; *see also* Cunningham, Anna, marchioness of Hamilton (*d.* 1647); Campbell, Elizabeth, duchess of Argyll and *suo jure* Baroness Hamilton of Hameldon.

**Hamilton family** (*per.* **1295–1479**), landowners and administrators, is of uncertain origins. A now lost account of the family, supposedly written *c.*1450 (which in its reported form does not inspire much confidence), claims that the first Hamilton to arrive in Scotland was Sir Gilbert, the eldest son of the earl of Southampton, who fled England *c.*1308 after being responsible for the death of one of the Despensers, favourites of Edward II. He was much favoured by Robert I on his arrival in Scotland, to the extent that he married Robert's sister's daughter, Isobel Randolph. Later accounts consider that the family's descent was from the earls of Leicester, but concur in the tale of the flight from England. A recent English origin for the family seems most likely.

Although the parentage of **Sir Walter fitz Gilbert** (*d.* in or before 1346), the earliest undoubted ancestor of the Hamiltons, is uncertain, he first appears on 10 January 1295 as a witness to a charter granted by James, fifth steward of Scotland, in the company of other landholders of Renfrewshire. A close relation of Walter, John Fitzgilbert, also had links with the Stewarts, serving Walter, sixth steward of Scotland, as bailie of Bute; the Bannatyne or Bute mazer, an ornamental drinking bowl, is thought to have been made for John soon after Bannockburn. Walter's name (as Wauter fiz Gilbert de Hameldone) is found on the Ragman rolls, a list of those Scottish freeholders recorded as swearing fealty to King Edward I at Berwick on 28 August 1296. He remained loyal to Edward during the wars with Scotland, briefly holding land in Fife from him, and was captain of the garrison of Bothwell Castle, Lanarkshire, until the battle of Bannockburn in 1314. But when the earl of Hereford with a band of English cavalry sought shelter at Bothwell after the battle fitz Gilbert performed a volte-face, imprisoned them, and surrendered the castle and his erstwhile allies to a Scottish force. The ransom later demanded for Hereford included the return of King Robert's wife. In March 1315, as a reward for this, fitz Gilbert received from the king a grant of the lands of Machan in Lanarkshire, forfeited by John Comyn. Later he also had a grant of the barony of Cadzow (now in Hamilton, Lanarkshire), and in July 1323 various lands in Linlithgowshire. Further testimony to his continuing favour is shown by his temporary commission as a justiciary of Lanark in 1321 and by his being knighted by 1323. He may have fought at Halidon Hill (1333), but escaped from the disastrous Scottish defeat. Fitz Gilbert appears to have died by 1346. He married twice. His first spouse was Helen (surname unknown), while his second, whom he had married by March 1315, was Mary Gordon (*d.* in or after 1323), perhaps the daughter of Sir Adam Gordon of Gordon. They had at least one and possibly two sons.

**Sir David fitz Walter** (*d.* 1375x8) was their elder (or perhaps only) son. He was present at the battle of Nevilles Cross (1346), where he was made prisoner. Because of his status he was entrusted to the archbishop of York, with orders that he was not to be delivered up without a mandate from Edward III. He was eventually liberated, apparently for a heavy ransom, and had been knighted by June 1361. In December 1368 he obtained a charter from King David II referring to a grant of the barony of Cadzow made to his father by Robert I, now confirmed with the addition of the lands of Eddlewood. As a baron he attended the parliaments of 27 March 1371 and 4 April 1373, when the succession to the crown was settled on John, earl of Carrick, and his successors. The name of fitz Walter's wife is not certain, though she may have been a daughter of an earl of Ross. He is known certainly to have had two sons, and may have had two others and a daughter. He was alive in November 1375, but had died by October 1378.

**David Hamilton of Cadzow** (*d.* 1381x8), fitz Walter's eldest son, was perhaps the first head of the family to employ the Hamilton surname. Little is recorded about him, and he died between October 1381 and November 1388. By October 1378 he had married Janet (*fl.* 1378–1422), daughter of Sir William Keith of Galston (who remarried after his death). They had a daughter and at least four sons, of whom **Sir John Hamilton of Cadzow** (*d.* 1402?) was the eldest. He was knighted by November 1388, when he married Jacoba (*fl.* 1388–1410), daughter of Sir James Douglas of Dalkeith; she survived him and married again. The couple had three sons. Hamilton engaged in raids into England, hence the orders given in 1396 (when he was imprisoned at Norwich for violating the Anglo-Scottish truce) and 1398 that he (and others) should be released from captivity in England. Indeed, it is likely that he was killed at the battle of Hamildon Hill on 14 September 1402.

Hamilton's eldest son was **James Hamilton of Cadzow** (*b.* *c.*1388, *d.* in or before 1436). He was in captivity in Lincolnshire in 1413 (the cause not known), but must have been able to negotiate a release. He served as a hostage (valued at 500 marks) for the ransom demanded for James I after the king's return from England in 1424. He may have gone back to Scotland *c.*1426, but as there is no further record of him it is also possible that he died while being held in the Tower of London. He was certainly dead by October 1436. He had married Janet (*b.* *c.*1395, *d.* after 1422), daughter of Sir Alexander *Livingston of Callendar, by October 1422. She may have been his second wife, but no other is on record, and her death date is unknown. Hamilton had five sons and three daughters; it is not clear which spouse was their mother.

**James Hamilton**, first Lord Hamilton (*c.*1410–1479), the eldest son, had been knighted by July 1439. Although his family had no known history of direct support for the earls of Douglas, major landowners in Lanarkshire, in 1441 he married Euphemia (*b.* in or after 1406, *d.* 1468), daughter of Patrick Graham, earl of Strathearn, and widow of Archibald, fifth earl of Douglas (*d.* 1439). (He had previously been affianced to a Janet Maxwell, a marriage perhaps never completed.) This union tied him firmly to the Douglases. His support for them brought further reward. On 3 July 1445 he was one of the first beneficiaries of moves by the greater barons in Scotland to adopt distinct titles: he was granted a hereditary lordship of parliament in a crown charter by which all his lands and baronies were erected into a lordship called Hamilton.

Hamilton evidently continued to associate himself with the Douglases, most notably when he joined the eighth earl in a pilgrimage to Rome in 1450 for the jubilee year; but as the court was dominated by the Livingston interest to mid-1449, and then to 1454 by the Crichtons, he was seldom close to James II. This divided loyalty cast him into the political wilderness after the king killed the eighth earl of Douglas in Stirling in February 1452. In the following month Hamilton was with James, the ninth earl, when the latter ravaged Stirling, and when parliament met in June he and others fixed a letter on the parliament house door renouncing their allegiance to the king. Although an accord between James II and Douglas was reached in August and further sealed in January 1453, the two parties were not fully at ease. Hamilton briefly acted as the king's ambassador, but may have used his ambassadorial duties as the occasion for intrigue with the Yorkists in England.

James II, probably planning a strike against the Douglases in any event, moved swiftly against Douglas and his allies in March 1455. Hamilton had been unable to obtain succour from England and when besieged in Abercorn Castle surrendered after observing that Douglas's courage was fading; he was imprisoned in Roslin Castle. He was not detained long, as the king (no doubt again seeking firm supporters at the climax of the defeat and disgrace of the Douglases) had him released and confirmed him in his tenure of his lands. In addition, he was granted the sheriffdom of Lanarkshire in July 1455 (previously held by the earl of Douglas) and in 1457 some land in Renfrewshire forfeited by the earl. In the following years Hamilton occasionally acted as a witness of crown charters and as ambassador. In 1457 he entered into a bond of manrent with George Douglas, earl of Angus, which obliged him to counsel and support Angus whenever required. The bond demonstrates how Angus's grant of the lordship of Douglas after the forfeiture of the ninth earl had led to his assertion of authority over former Douglas vassals; it also points to Hamilton's status among the nobility.

On the death of James II in 1460 Hamilton briefly became a regular at court, but his star seems to have waned along with that of his uncle James, Lord Livingston (who had played a prominent role in securing his submission to James II in 1455). Hamilton's first wife died between 1 August and 1 November 1468. They had at least a daughter, Elizabeth, who married David, earl of Crawford (created duke of Montrose in 1488).

About 1472 Hamilton began to appear as a witness of crown charters with great regularity. Although no more than a member of the king's daily council, a mark of his enhanced standing at court was his marriage about 1474 to Mary Stewart (1451–1488), the king's sister. She was the former spouse of Thomas Boyd, disgraced earl of Arran (*d.* *c.*1474). This significant alliance would secure for Hamilton's descendants an important role at court, on which they fully capitalized, not least because it made successive Hamiltons heirs presumptive to the throne. The couple had at least one son, James *Hamilton, second Lord Hamilton and later earl of Arran, and a daughter, Elizabeth, who married Matthew Stewart, earl of Lennox. Mary Stewart is thought to have died in mid-1488. Hamilton died on 6 November 1479 and was probably buried in Hamilton kirk. He also had several illegitimate children, including at least four sons, three of them with one Janet Calderwood.

By the mid-fifteenth century the Hamilton family held significant estates in Lanarkshire and Linlithgowshire, as well as land in Kirkcudbrightshire, Roxburghshire, and Renfrewshire. The first lord obtained the erection of Hamilton as a burgh of barony, possibly by 1465 and certainly by 1474, and began to feu out property there. Like many of his contemporaries, he undertook the erection of a collegiate church (at Hamilton), for which the pope's approval was obtained while he was in Rome in 1450. He also endowed a chapel and hospital in the parish of Shotts, because of its distance from Bothwell parish church. In January 1460 he made a grant of land in Glasgow to that city's newly founded university, on condition that the masters and students offered daily prayers for himself, his family, and even his unrequited benefactors. More unusual interests included reclaiming land from the sea, made at great cost near his lands at Kinneil, Linlithgowshire, and investigations into fining lead, both undertaken by the 1460s.

By 1479 the Hamiltons had certainly found a niche at court, particularly through the marriage with the king's sister. As the second Lord Hamilton was only a few years old when he succeeded, there was no guarantee that his position on attaining his majority would be secure; but when he did, the father's uncertain loyalty before 1455 clearly counted for less than the son's being a cousin of King James IV. ALAN R. BORTHWICK

**Sources** Lennoxlove, Hamilton muniments • J. M. Thomson and others, eds., *Registrum magni sigilli regum Scotorum / The register of the great seal of Scotland*, 11 vols. (1882–1914), esp. vols. 1–2 • *APS*, esp. 1424–1567 • *CDS*, vols. 1–4 • *RotS*, vols. 1–2 • various collections of manuscript estate and other papers in archive offices and in private hands in Scotland and England • G. Burnett and others, eds., *The exchequer rolls of Scotland*, 23 vols. (1878–1908) • *The Asloan manuscript*, ed. W. A. Craigie, 2 vols., STS, new ser., 14, 16 (1923–5) • J. Anderson, *Historical and genealogical memoirs of the house of Hamilton* (1825) • *CEPR letters*, vols. 10–11, 13 • C. Innes, ed., *Registrum episcopatus Glasguensis*, 2 vols., Maitland Club, 61 (1843) • *Descriptions of the sheriffdoms of Lanark and Renfrew, compiled about MDCCX, by William Hamilton of Wishaw*, ed. J. Dillon and J. Fullarton, Maitland Club, 12 (1831) • A. I. Dunlop, ed., *Calendar of Scottish supplications to Rome*, 4: 1433–1447, ed. D. MacLauchlan (1983) • *Scots peerage*, 4.340–55 • *The manuscripts of the marquess of Abergavenny, Lord Braye, G. F. Luttrell*, HMC, 15 (1887) [Luttrell MSS at Dunster Castle] • R. Douglas, *The peerage of Scotland*, 2nd edn, ed. J. P. Wood, 1 (1813) • A. L. Brown and M. Moss, *The University of Glasgow, 1451–1996* (1996) • M. Brown, *The Black Douglases: war and lordship in late medieval Scotland, 1300–1455* (1998) • T. Dickson, ed., *Compota thesaurariorum regum Scotorum / Accounts of the lord high treasurer of Scotland*, 1 (1877), 69 • Home muniments, The Hirsel, box 3, bundle 16 • Morton muniments, NA Scot., GD 150/55

**Archives** Lennoxlove, Hamilton muniments

**Hamilton, Alexander** (*b.* before **1688**, *d.* in or after **1733**), East India Company servant and writer, is described in contemporary sources as a 'Scotchman', but they contain no reference to his birth, family connections, or death. The little we know of him is primarily gleaned from his important *A New Account of the East Indies* (1727). In 1688, 'very young', Hamilton went to sea to satisfy the demands of a 'rambling Mind' and because he had 'a Fortune too narrow' to allow him to travel like a gentleman. The details of his early maritime career are unknown beyond his observation that he spent his 'younger Days … visiting most of the maratim Kingdoms of *Europe*, and some parts of *Barbary*' before travelling to Jamaica (Hamilton, xxvi). After returning to England Hamilton set out for India, departing in April 1688 on the *Shrewsbury* as an extra hand, arriving in Bombay in November 1688. Soon after his arrival he was pressed into the East India Company's service against the sidi of Janjira. Given the command of an 8 ton privateer, Hamilton acquitted himself well, capturing eight prizes for the company. By 1690 he had moved north to Surat, one of the most important ports in the Indian Ocean. Here he gained considerable experience in Asian trade, initially in the service of the private trader George Bowcher. After sailing to Karwar and Amoy (Xiamen) under the command of Bowcher's son-in-law George Yeoman, Hamilton returned to Surat, whence he launched his first independent venture in 1694, sailing to Achin and Malacca in a vessel leased from a local Muslim trader. This marked the beginning of a long career in the 'country trade', as Hamilton leased or captained a variety of ships that traversed the Indian Ocean and beyond, reaching as far west as Jiddah, as far north as Amoy, and as far east as Java. Although the records of his movements are patchy, there is no doubt that this was an adventurous life. Along with fifty other Britons he was imprisoned by the governor of Surat in 1695 after a local ship was captured by a European pirate. He played a key role in this crisis as he circulated a plan for an armed uprising by the prisoners. As a result he was interrogated by the East India Company council in Surat, in whose presence he displayed his fondness for 'rude expressions'. Over the next two decades he undertook a host of journeys, repulsing the attentions of Indian pirates, protecting his cargo from Baluchi robbers, blockading ports, or seizing the cargo of Chinese junks. These feats gained him a reputation for courage and resourcefulness, leading to his appointment as the commander of the company's Bombay marine force in June 1717. Although he subsequently acquitted himself well in the relief of the Karwar factory, he became embroiled in conflict with the company and resigned his position in January 1718. Hamilton returned to private trade, travelling to Cambodia and Ayuthaya, and spending much time in the Persian Gulf. Finally, in late 1723 or in 1724, Hamilton returned to Britain, probably settling in Scotland. Over 'two long winters' he worked on his narrative, which, dedicated to James, duke of Hamilton, was printed in Edinburgh by John Mosman in 1727. Although the *Gentleman's Magazine* records the death of a Captain Alexander Hamilton in October 1732, our subject appears in East India Company directors' minutes in June 1733 (BL OIOC, B162, 368). While his death and much of his life remain unclear, his *New Account of the East Indies* is particularly significant as a detailed picture of British involvement in the cosmopolitan world of Asian trade. Reprinted in 1744, his two-volume account was published in a new edition in 1930 with an introduction by Sir William Foster. TONY BALLANTYNE

**Sources** *DNB* • A. Hamilton, *A new account of the East Indies*, 2 vols. (1727); new edn, ed. W. Foster (1930) • C. Downing, *A history of the Indian wars*, ed. W. Foster (1924) • P. Spear, *The nabobs: a study of the social life of the English in eighteenth-century India* (1963) • *Alexander Hamilton: a Scottish sea captain in southeast Asia, 1689–1723*, ed. M. Smithies (1997)

**Hamilton, Alexander** (1712–1756), physician and writer on American life, was born on 26 September 1712 in Edinburgh, the twelfth of fourteen children of William *Hamilton (1669–1732), professor of divinity at Edinburgh University, and his wife, Mary (*c*.1675–1760), daughter of John Robertson, a Glasgow merchant, and his wife, Mary. Alexander, called Sandy, probably attended the Edinburgh high school from 1721 to 1725, and at thirteen matriculated at the University of Edinburgh, where he came under the influence of the historian Charles Mackie. He received his MA degree in 1729.

Shortly afterwards Hamilton served a brief apprenticeship in the shop of the apothecary-surgeon David Knox, and then longer apprenticeships with Robert Eliot and Alexander Monro while attending the latter's anatomy lectures at the university. In 1734 he joined with classmates William Cumming, George Cleghorn, Archibald Taylor, and James Kennedy to form a student medical society that eventually developed into the Royal Medical Society of Scotland. He received his medical degree in 1737 after defending his thesis on bones, *De morbis ossium*. He lived in a garret room at the Society of Brewers' property owned by his widowed sister Jean Cleghorn, and acted as mentor for her son William, a future professor of moral philosophy at Edinburgh.

Hamilton left Scotland in late 1738 for the American colonies. He settled in Annapolis, Maryland, near his elder brother John, another Edinburgh-trained physician. There he established an active medical practice but became more widely known for his travel diary of 1744, published in 1948 as *Gentleman's Progress: the Itinerarium of Dr. Alexander Hamilton*, one of the most extensively quoted sources on life in the colonies.

In 1745 Hamilton organized a social club, the Tuesday Club of Annapolis, in imitation of the Edinburgh Whin Bush Club and other improving societies of his home city. With his encouragement, club members composed and performed musical works. They wrote poetry and satirical essays on a variety of social, political, and religious themes reminiscent of Scottish literary endeavours. Hamilton kept the minutes of the group from its organization until 1756 and, under the name Loquacious Scribble, wrote a history of the club that satirized both Edinburgh and American social and political life. The history included much of the poetry written by the members and many of his humorous essays, as well as fragments of the music composed by himself, another Scot Alexander Malcolm, Thomas Bacon, and several others. Hamilton illustrated these works with pen-and-ink sketches of scenes from the club's activities and caricatures of the members, including several of his own face.

In 1747 Hamilton married Margaret Dulany (*c*.1732–1791), the daughter of one of the richest men in Maryland, Daniel Dulany the elder, and his wife, Rebecca. Her dowry brought opportunities to purchase more than 1000 acres of rural land in the colony, and town lots in Annapolis both for their home and to be leased out for rental income.

Hamilton was a regular contributor to the Annapolis newspaper the *Maryland Gazette*, writing satirical literary and social commentaries under a variety of pseudonyms. He also published a pamphlet, *A Defence of Dr. Thomson's Discourse on the Preparation of the Body for the Small Pox* (Philadelphia, 1751), supporting the right of a fellow Scot, Adam Thomson, to publish a medical treatise, which advocated innovative methods, without the approval of the Philadelphian medical establishment. Hamilton also maintained a regular correspondence with family and associates in Scotland. In a letter to his brother Gavin in Edinburgh, he defended as heroic Colonel Sir Peter Halket's behaviour during the defeat of Major-General Edward Braddock's forces by the French near Fort Duquesne, western Pennsylvania, in 1755. Halket, who questioned Braddock's battle plans, was killed leading his regiment (44th foot).

Hamilton died on 11 May 1756 in Annapolis, where he was buried. He had no children, and left his entire estate, estimated to be worth about £750 sterling, to his wife. ELAINE G. BRESLAW

**Sources** E. G. Breslaw, ed., *Records of the Tuesday Club of Annapolis, 1745–1756* (1988) • J. B. Talley, *Secular music of colonial Maryland, the Tuesday Club, 1745–56* (1988) • A. Hamilton, *The history of the ancient and honorable Tuesday Club*, ed. R. Micklus (1990) • *Gentleman's progress: the itinerarium of Dr. Alexander Hamilton, 1744*, ed.

C. Bridenbaugh (1948); repr. (1992) • R. Micklus, *Comic genius of Dr. Alexander Hamilton* (1990) • J. A. L. Lemay, *Men of letters in colonial Maryland* (Knoxville, Tenn., 1972) • E. G. Breslaw, 'A perilous climb to social eminence: Dr. Alexander Hamilton and his creditors', *Maryland Historical Magazine*, 92 (1997), 433–55 • E. G. Breslaw, 'A dismal tragedy: Drs. Alexander and John Hamilton comment on Braddock's defeat', *Maryland Historical Magazine*, 75 (1980), 118–44 • R. B. Davis, *Intellectual life in the colonial south*, 3 vols. (1978) • A. C. Land, *The Dulanys of Maryland: a biographical study of Daniel Dulany, the elder (1685–1753) and Daniel Dulany, the younger (1722–1797)* (Baltimore, MD, 1955); repr. (1968) • W. Somerville, *The Tuesday Club of Annapolis (1745–1756) as cultural performance* (1996) • parish register, co. of Edinburgh, 1708–14, NA Scot. • *Fasti Scot.* • St Anne's parish vestry, minutes, 1749–52 • Anne Arundel county testamentary records, Annapolis, Maryland

**Archives** L. Cong., Peter Force MSS, series 8D • Maryland Historical Society, Baltimore, Dulany MSS • NL Scot., Halkett of Pitfirrane MSS • U. Edin., New Coll. L., Thomas of Banchory MSS [vols. 2 and 4] | NA Scot., parochial register, co. of Edinburgh • U. Edin., Laing MSS II; C. Mackie MSS • U. Edin. L., special collections division, A. Munro primus, record book of students • Anne Arundel county court judgments [Annapolis, Maryland]

**Likenesses** A. Hamilton, self-portrait, sketch, Johns Hopkins University, Baltimore • A. Hamilton, self-portrait, sketch, Maryland Historical Society, Baltimore, Dulany MSS • A. Hamilton, self-portraits, sketches, repro. in Breslaw, ed., *Records of the Tuesday Club*

**Wealth at death** approx. £750; about 1018 acres of rural land; four and a half town lots in Annapolis: Anne Arundel county testamentary records, 1753–7, liber 36, fol. 310; Anne Arundel county deeds, 1747, RB#1, 2.

**Hamilton, Alexander** (*bap.* **1739**, *d.* **1802**), physician and obstetrician, was baptized on 19 February 1739 at Fordoun, Kincardineshire, the son of Alexander Hamilton, a retired army surgeon. In 1758 he became assistant to John Straiton, surgeon, of Edinburgh; on his master's death in 1762 he became a member of the Edinburgh College of Surgeons, and settled in practice in Edinburgh. After gaining an MD he became a licentiate, and subsequently a fellow, of the Royal College of Physicians of Edinburgh. In 1772 he was elected physician to the Edinburgh Royal Infirmary. In 1777, as deacon of the Edinburgh College of Surgeons, he made a strenuous effort to establish a chair of surgery in the university, but failed, owing to the opposition of Monro secundus. After lecturing on midwifery with success for some years, he was in 1780 appointed joint professor of midwifery in the University of Edinburgh with Dr Thomas Young, and sole professor in 1783 on Young's death. In 1791 he was instrumental in establishing the Lying-in Hospital. In 1792 Hamilton became embroiled in a dispute over the publication of a controversial pamphlet on the study of medicine in Edinburgh University. Published under a pseudonym, the pamphlet was attributed to Hamilton by his rival Dr James Gregory. Hamilton denied the charge, and he was eventually exonerated by the university senate.

Hamilton was a successful practitioner and writer on midwifery. He was the author of a number of treatises on the theory and practice of midwifery and on the treatment of the diseases of women and infants.

Hamilton had two sons, Henry Parr *Hamilton and James *Hamilton. In 1800 he resigned his professorship and he was succeeded by his son James. He died on 23 May 1802. G. T. Bettany, *rev.* Ornella Moscucci

**Sources** W. Anderson, *The Scottish nation*, 2 (1886), 446 • A. R. Simpson, 'History of the chair of midwifery and the diseases of women and children in the University of Edinburgh', *Edinburgh Medical Journal*, 28 (1882–3), 481–98 • J. Kay, *A series of original portraits and caricature etchings … with biographical sketches and illustrative anecdotes*, ed. [H. Paton and others], 2 vols. in 4 (1837–8) • J. Gairdner, 'A history of the medical profession in Edinburgh', *Edinburgh Medical Journal*, 8 (1862–3), 700 • A. Grant, *The story of the University of Edinburgh during its first three hundred years*, 2 vols. (1884) • *IGI*

**Archives** BL, notes taken from his lectures on midwifery, Add. MSS 45919–45920

**Likenesses** J. Kay, etching, 1786, BM, NPG, Wellcome L. • H. Raeburn, oils, *c.*1800, Breamore House, Hampshire

**Hamilton, Alexander** (1757–1804), politician in the United States of America, was born on 11 January 1757 in Nevis, British West Indies, the second of two illegitimate sons of James Hamilton (*c.*1718–1799), itinerant trader, and Rachel Faucett Lavien (*c.*1729–1768). His father deserted the family when Hamilton was eight, and his mother died three years later. He was apprenticed to a mercantile firm and, being precociously gifted in commerce, was soon placed in charge of the business. When he was fifteen he was sent by a Presbyterian minister to study in America at Francis Barber's Elizabethtown Academy, New Jersey. After a year in the preparatory school he was admitted to the College of New Jersey at Princeton, but when the president refused to let him set his own pace, he went instead to King's College in New York in 1774.

That placed Hamilton in a beehive of radical activity. He did not neglect his studies, but he was increasingly drawn into the struggle between the American colonies and Britain. During the winter of 1774–5 he attracted attention by publishing two fiery tracts, *A Full Vindication* and *The Farmer Refuted*. He then organized an artillery company and won a commission as captain in the continental army. Bold in the extreme, he repeatedly saw action throughout 1776.

His prowess as a warrior was exceeded by his administrative skills, and after refusing offers from other generals he accepted the position as aide-de-camp to George Washington. He became Washington's right arm and served with him (as a lieutenant-colonel) until February 1781. Then he sought a field command, obtaining it in July. In October he won the glory he craved, leading a successful attack on a crucial redoubt in the decisive American victory at the battle of Yorktown.

**Early career** Hamilton's military service deepened his nationalism even as it taught him contempt for the corruption and weakness of congress. He also grew disillusioned with his adopted countrymen, whom he characterized as indolent, provincial, and oligarchic. Sensing that both national authority and American society could be reformed and energized by a system of public finance, he spent much of his time studying that arcane subject.

On 14 December 1780 Hamilton had married Elizabeth (*c.*1757–1854), daughter of the wealthy New York aristocrat Philip Schuyler, but he declined to accept monetary support from his father-in-law. After the battle of Yorktown

**Alexander Hamilton (1757–1804),** by John Trumbull, 1792

he resigned his commission, devoted ten months to the study of law, and passed the rigorous New York bar examination. During his study, he wrote a book—a compilation of legal tracts—and memorized it. This book was later published and became a standard manual for aspiring attorneys.

After a brief and unproductive period of service in congress as a delegate for New York appointed in 1782, Hamilton returned to New York to take up his law practice and rapidly rose to the top of his profession. His most important early case, *Rutgers* v. *Waddington* (1784), is often but inaccurately cited as a precedent for the doctrine of judicial review. Flourishing as his law practice was, he sought a public career. His 'ruling passion' was hunger for fame—immortality in the form of the grateful remembrance of posterity. By 1786 he knew how to win his fame: as minister of the nation's finances, provided that the nation could create a government with finances to administer.

Hamilton was instrumental in bringing such a government into being. He was appointed as a New York delegate to the Annapolis interstate commercial convention in 1786. There he joined James Madison and John Dickinson in calling for a general convention to meet in Philadelphia to address the exigencies of the union of states. That call did not evoke an immediate response. But early in 1787 an armed rebellion (Shays's rebellion) erupted in the back-country of Massachusetts, and a desperate congress endorsed the convention call. Twelve states voted to send delegates, and despite Governor George Clinton's anti-nationalist stance, Hamilton was chosen as one of New York's three delegates. He attended the convention only part-time and was of minor influence in it. His one major speech, on 18 June 1787, was an analysis of the nature of man, society, and government. He ended by proposing a strong central government—though he did not, as was later charged, propose a monarchy. The speech raised the general philosophical level of the debate, but did nothing more.

Hamilton would have preferred a higher-toned government, but he cared little for forms and was determined to sign and support whatever the convention produced. In support of ratification he co-wrote the series of eighty-five essays signed 'Publius', which is widely known as *The Federalist* and generally regarded as the greatest commentary on the constitution. John Jay wrote five essays; James Madison is credited with twenty-nine, and Hamilton with fifty-one. Though the two main authors complemented one another, differences between them are obvious. Hamilton self-confidently emphasized the need for 'energy', particularly in the executive; Madison entrusted power hesitantly and stressed the checks and restraints in the document. Madison characterized the system as partly national, partly federal; Hamilton disliked the federal features. His conception was that each level of government was sovereign as to matters within its purview.

*The Federalist* was written primarily to influence the election of delegates to New York's ratifying constitutional convention, and to that end it failed. Opponents of the constitution (anti-federalists) dominated; Jay and Hamilton were among the minority. The convention did, however, ultimately ratify the constitution due to various political manipulations.

**Minister of finance** Once New York ratified the federal constitution Hamilton became eligible to serve in the new government. In 1789 congress created the treasury department, and Washington, as president and head of state, asked Hamilton to be its head. On 21 September, two days before adjourning, the house of representatives directed Hamilton to present a plan for support of the public credit—which had long since disappeared—at its next meeting in January 1790. This command meant that the treasury, unlike the other executive departments, would be responsible to the lower house of the legislature as well as to the president. That suited Hamilton, for it facilitated the implementation of his design for the government and for American society. Establishing public credit was important to him for its own sake and also as a means to broader ends. The constitution did not preclude the development of something like the British ministerial system, in which the first lord of the treasury could be the 'prime' minister; Hamilton's having one foot in the house and the other in the executive branch might make that development possible.

The companion piece in Hamilton's design was to reshape society. He believed that Americans 'labour less now than any civilized nation of Europe', and that habits of industry were 'essential to the health and vigor' of a people (Hamilton, 2.635). Americans, he believed, had few incentives to work hard, for earning a subsistence was easy whereas improving one's social standing was difficult. Status came primarily from the ownership of (usually inherited) landed estates, and Hamilton abhorred inherited status. (He was an active participant in New York's anti-slavery movement.) To transform the existing order, Hamilton proposed to erect fiscal machinery so convenient and necessary to the conduct of daily economic activity that money would become the measure of all things. Bourgeois values would then be embraced, oligarchies would fall, and the best men would rise to the top.

The opening steps of Hamilton's fiscal plans were taken in his 'first report on the public credit', presented to congress in January 1790. Unlike many members of congress, who wanted to pay off the debts rapidly, Hamilton chose to 'fund' them. Accordingly he asked congress to provide semi-permanent appropriations for interest payments on the federal and state debts. Redemption of the principal would be at the government's discretion, but no more than 2 per cent of the total could be retired annually. New government securities were issued to retire the old certificates of debt, and to stabilize them and maintain their market value a 'sinking fund' would be created, financed by the profits from the post office.

Congress readily enacted the funding and sinking fund proposals, but the assumption of the state debts faced opposition. Several states had retired most of their debts, and they were averse to paying added taxes to benefit those states that had not. Among these was Virginia, and James Madison—a leader in the lower house—headed the opposition to assumption. It was defeated in the house of representatives by two votes, whereupon a political deal was struck. The Virginians were eager to locate the permanent national capital on the Potomac. Secretary of State Thomas Jefferson and his friend Madison held a dinner party for Hamilton at which he agreed to find northern votes for the Potomac site (now Washington, DC) and they would find votes for assuming the state debts. The funding and assumption plan became law in August 1790.

When congress reconvened in December Hamilton presented a 'second report on the public credit', proposing to create a national bank. The treasury needed a reliable source of short-term credit, and experience showed that the three existing banks in America were not trustworthy. Moreover, Hamilton wanted to use the bank's notes as a basis for currency. He asked congress to grant a twenty-year charter to a private corporation, the Bank of the United States. It would have $10 million in capital stock, one-fifth of which would be subscribed by the federal government using funds borrowed from the bank itself. Private purchases of the stock were payable one-quarter in gold or silver and the rest in government securities. Because the bank could earn tremendous profits the price of its stock would soar, which would raise the price of government securities since they were interchangeable.

Congressional response was favourable, but an obstacle arose: during the debates Madison objected that chartering a corporation would exceed the congressional powers itemized in the constitution. The bill was passed, but Madison's objections so upset Washington that he asked Jefferson and Attorney-General Edmund Randolph for advisory opinions before signing the bill into law. They held that the bill was unconstitutional. Washington then requested Hamilton's opinion. He responded with the now classic formulation of the doctrine of implied powers and 'loose construction' (Hamilton, 8.63–134). Pointing to the constitutional clause giving congress power 'to make all Laws which shall be necessary and proper for carrying into Execution' the enumerated powers, Hamilton insisted that Randolph and Jefferson had interpreted the word 'necessary' as if the words 'absolutely' or 'indispensably' preceded it. Besides, he continued, Jefferson had confused means with ends. The bank was merely a means of carrying out legitimate, enumerated functions. And, 'If the end be clearly comprehended within any of the specified powers', he said, and 'if the measure have an obvious relation to that end, and is not forbidden by any particular provision of the constitution—it may safely be deemed to come within the compass of the national authority' (ibid., 8.107). Washington signed the bill on 25 February 1791.

Despite their differences Hamilton and Jefferson were still friendly, but a break was soon to come. At a casual dinner in April, during conversation among Vice-President John Adams, Jefferson, and Hamilton, Adams declared that if the British constitution were purged of corruption and if representation in the House of Commons were reformed, 'it would be the most perfect constitution ever devised by the wit of man'. This statement upset Jefferson, but he was appalled by Hamilton's response. 'Purge it of its corruption', Hamilton said, paraphrasing David Hume, 'and give to its popular branch equality of representation, and it would become an *impractable* government: as it stands at present, with all its supposed defects, it is the most perfect government which ever existed' (McDonald, *Hamilton*, 214). Connecting Hamilton's comment to his policies, Jefferson became convinced that Hamilton was trying to erect an American variation of the British system.

Thereafter Jefferson saw every Hamiltonian action as a subversion of the constitution. Jefferson shared his discovery with Washington, who belittled it. He then turned to Madison, who did believe him, and the two began organizing an opposition political party, which they styled 'republican', pointedly suggesting that Hamilton was a monarchist.

Soon issues arising from the French Revolution widened the rift. When the revolution had begun Hamilton was excited, for like most Americans he believed that Louis XVI would voluntarily turn France into a constitutional monarchy. But by the winter of 1792–3 France had proclaimed itself a republic, beheaded the king, and set out to liberate Europe. These developments, in Hamilton's view, portended serious trouble. The United States was bound to France by perpetual treaties of commerce and alliance signed in 1778. America was not obliged to join France in an offensive war, for the alliance pertained only to defensive wars, but Hamilton believed that if America were not strictly neutral it could be dragged into the conflict. The infant nation could not chance a war with France's enemy, Britain, for Britain and the USA remained major trading partners and war would drastically cut the import revenues that supported Hamilton's financial system. The problem became urgent after the arrival in April 1793 of Citizen Edmond Genet. In response to his activities Hamilton urged Washington to issue a neutrality proclamation and suspend the 1778 treaties. Washington issued the proclamation but took no action concerning the treaties.

By then a fresh peril had arisen—from the British side. Under secret orders British naval commanders seized several hundred American vessels for neutrality violations. The popular cries for war were intensified by news that the British were inciting American Indians in the North-west Territory of the USA and were arming a slave rebellion in Hispaniola. Hamilton recommended preparing for war as a precondition for negotiating a peace. A provisional army was authorized, Chief Justice John Jay was sent to Britain to negotiate, and in 1795 Jay returned with a treaty. To defend the treaty against a vigorous republican attack, Hamilton wrote thirty-eight newspaper articles signed 'Camillus'.

**Post-treasury career** Hamilton officially left the cabinet on 31 January 1795 and returned to his long-neglected private business. He became one of a handful of lawyers who were creating a new law of contracts based on market forces and pioneering (through cases, not legislation) a market-driven law of commercial paper and marine insurance. His retirement from public affairs, however, was not complete. The president and cabinet officers repeatedly asked for his advice. He wrote Washington's seventh annual message to congress, and in 1796 he composed much of Washington's famous 'Farewell Address'. In addition he found it necessary to defend his previous work as secretary of the treasury. He was publicly charged with having paid blackmail to a confidence man, James Reynolds, to cover department irregularities. Fearing that if the charges were believed the integrity of the financial system would be shaken, he published a lengthy pamphlet detailing an amorous affair he had had with Reynolds's wife, Maria, that had occasioned the blackmail payments.

In 1798 another call to service sounded. Relations with France had further deteriorated, and amid preparations for war President Adams asked Washington to serve as commander-in-chief. Washington agreed, provided that he would go on active duty only if an invasion occurred and that Hamilton be named his second-in-command. Adams grudgingly accepted but, mistrusting and envying Hamilton, he immediately lost his appetite for war. The quasi-war with France (1798–1800) was a period of frustration for Hamilton; his efforts to organize the army were hampered by the war department's incompetence and by the president's obstruction.

In 1800 Hamilton attempted to defeat Adams's bid for re-election. But when republicans Jefferson and Aaron Burr tied for the lead in the electoral college, the final choice fell upon the house of representatives. Regarding Burr as an embryonic Caesar, Hamilton threw his support behind Jefferson. Jefferson's election in turn marked the end of Hamilton's public career. Hamilton founded a newspaper to act as a responsible critic of the administration, but mainly he stuck to practising law.

Hamilton's last major case had an enduring impact. A newspaper printer, Harry Croswell, was prosecuted for libel for publishing a report that Jefferson had paid a writer to smear Washington and Adams. The statement was true, but truth was not a defence under the common law, and he was convicted. On appeal Croswell employed Hamilton as counsel. Hamilton contended that truth, if not used 'wantonly', must be a defence. Otherwise 'you must for ever remain ignorant of what your rulers do … I never did think the truth was a crime … for my soul has ever abhorred the thought, that a free man dared not speak the truth' (McDonald, *Hamilton*, 359). The court was divided; therefore the conviction was not overturned. But state legislators had heard Hamilton's argument and found it persuasive. The following year they enacted a law making truth a defence.

During the New York gubernatorial election of 1804 Hamilton and his newspaper were fierce critics of Aaron Burr's candidacy. A few weeks after his defeat Burr demanded an explanation for unspecified remarks. Unsatisfied with the response, Burr met Hamilton at the duelling ground in Weehawken, New Jersey—the same place where Hamilton's eldest son had been killed three years earlier in a duel. Burr shot Hamilton through the liver. He died at the home of William Bayard, 80–82 Jane Street, New York city, shortly afterwards, on 12 July 1804, after receiving communion from Benjamin Moore, the Episcopalian bishop of New York (the Revd John Mason, a Presbyterian minister, had refused Hamilton). He was buried two days later in the graveyard of Trinity Church in Manhattan. His affairs were in disarray, and friends had to raise money to discharge his debts and support his wife and seven children. Elizabeth lived on for fifty years, and died on 9 November 1854.

For a century and more after his death Hamilton's niche in the pantheon of American founders seemed secure. But then, during the great depression of the 1930s, Hamilton came to be seen as the founder not of a thriving capitalistic economic system but of a wicked plutocracy. Only since the 1980s has he returned to grace among historians. FORREST McDONALD

**Sources** F. McDonald, *Alexander Hamilton: a biography* (1979) • *The papers of Alexander Hamilton*, ed. H. C. Syrett and others, 26 vols. (New York, 1961–79) • J. Goebel, ed., *The law practice of Alexander Hamilton*, 2 vols. (New York, 1964–9) • R. Brookhiser, *Alexander Hamilton: American* (1999) • B. Mitchell, *Alexander Hamilton*, 2 vols. (1957–62) • J. C. Miller, *Alexander Hamilton: portrait in paradox* [1959] • J. E. Cooke, *Alexander Hamilton* (1982) • G. Stourzh, *Alexander Hamilton and the idea of republican government* (Stanford, CA, 1970) • G. L. Lycan, *Alexander Hamilton and American foreign policy: a design for greatness* (Norman, OK, [1970]) • F. McDonald, *The presidency of*

*George Washington* (Lawrence, KS, 1974) • K.-F. Walling, *Republican empire: Alexander Hamilton on war and free government* (Lawrence, KS, 1999) • M. J. Frisch, *Alexander Hamilton and the political order* (1991)

**Likenesses** A. Chappel, engraving, *c.*1790 (after oils), NYPL • C. W. Peale, oils, *c.*1791, Independence National Historical Park Collection, Philadelphia, Pennsylvania • J. Trumbull, oils, 1792, Yale U. Art Gallery • J. Trumbull, oils, 1792, Donaldson, Lufkin, and Jenrette Collection of Americana, New York [*see illus.*] • J. Trumbull, oils, 1792, National Gallery of Art, Washington, DC • G. Ceracchi, marble bust, 1794, NYPL • W. Rollinson, engraving, *c.*1794–*c.*1804 (after wash drawing by A. Robertson), Museum of the City of New York • R. Ball Hughes, statue, 1831, Museum of the City of New York

**Wealth at death** $80,500, incl. real estate $74,150, personal property $3850, fees due $2500; debts owed $54,722: *Papers of Alexander Hamilton*, ed. Syrett and others, 26.283–90, 305–6

**Hamilton, Alexander** (1762–1824), orientalist, was born on 3 October 1762 in New (or Middle) Greenock, Renfrewshire, the first of many children, six of whom reached adult age, of William Hamilton (*bap.* 1722), merchant, and Jean Donald (*b.* 1740). His father, a cadet son of the laird of Grange, Stevenston, Ayrshire, a junior branch of the ducal family, became an import–export merchant, dealing primarily in tobacco, on marrying into the prominent Donald merchant family of Greenock and Glasgow. It was apparently at the Greenock grammar school that Hamilton acquired what he assessed with characteristic modesty as 'a tolerable knowledge of Latin' and 'a slender knowledge of Greek' (*EdinR*, 13, 1809, 371). He was also trained in accounting towards a trading profession. When his father's business began to fail, he and two brothers were successively sent out as cadets in the Bengal army, from which all sought release. Arrived in Calcutta in 1783, he later described his activities to his American first cousin and namesake as 'in consequence of some genius for acquiring languages [having] officiated as Persian and Bengal Interpreter to the Governmt' (*Papers*, ed. Syrett, 21.197). However, his primary avocation was Sanskrit scholarship, for which he sought dispensation from military duty; he resigned the service in 1790, judging by his later assets probably to engage in private trade as well as scholarly pursuits. He was an assiduous member of the Asiatic Society from 1787, but contributed no essay to its publications. From his marriage to a Bengali woman, of whom nothing is known, came a son, William, whom he took home in 1795.

Back in Greenock, where Hamilton helped his father wind up a bankrupt business and secured from his American cousin a mariner brother's appointment as a lieutenant in the US navy, his activities were entirely scholarly. They included research in the British Museum and contributions to the *Monthly Review* which embraced foreign and general literature, travel, and Scottish affairs, besides Indian politics and orientalist scholarship. Moving to Edinburgh in 1798, he attended Alexander Fraser Tytler's lectures on the history of civilizations, engaged with other scholars such as Dugald Stewart, and contributed to the *Asiatic Annual Register* from its inception in 1800. As one of the young whigs who founded the *Edinburgh Review*, his reviewing experience was as valuable as his collaborative spirit, intellectual breadth, and encyclopaedic oriental learning, while his dedication to Sanskrit scholarship earned him the nicknames Sanscrit Hamilton and the Pundit.

Hamilton's reputation as the most profound Sanskrit scholar yet to return from India followed him to Paris in 1802 when the peace of Amiens allowed him to visit the richest European collection of Sanskrit manuscripts. Detained at the resumption of hostilities, the intervention of French scholars and a personal appeal from his American cousin to Talleyrand obtained for him leave to remain in Paris where he compiled the first informed catalogue of Sanskrit manuscripts in the French imperial library, published in 1807 under his name and that of their keeper, Louis Matthieu Langlès. In contrast to the rising Indophobia in Britain, he was pressed to teach Sanskrit to fellow scholars: the senator Volney, Claude Fauriel, Gottfried Hagemann, and, most important, Friedrich Schlegel, in whose house he lived and whose epoch-making *Ueber die Sprache und Weisheit der Indier* (1808) stemmed from Hamilton's teaching of Sanskrit and comparative philology. Hamilton also was the likely conduit for the influence of Adam Smith's structural–historical classification of languages on Schlegel's linguistic typology.

Hamilton was released from France at the intervention of leading orientalist Silvestre de Sacy so that he could assume the position of first professor of Hindu literature and of the history of Asia at the establishment founded in 1806 by the East India Company that became Haileybury College. His appointment was at the recommendation of Charles Wilkins, a fellow Sanskritist member of the Asiatic Society. They collaborated on Wilkins's *Grammar of the Sanskrita Language* (1808) and Hamilton's edition of the *Hitopadeśa* (1810), the first edition of a Sanskrit text outside India; *Grammatical Analysis of the Sanskrita Hitopadeśa* (1810–11); and *Terms of Sanskrit Grammar* (1814). Intended as textbooks for the college, these works were also sought by scholars. Hamilton's teaching of Sanskrit, Bengali, and occasionally Marathi, was a first in Europe. He was on easy terms with the East India Company chairman Charles Grant, who supported his requests for textbooks and his representations to the governor-general of India in the tug-of-war between the company's colleges at Haileybury and Fort William, and upheld his exclusive admission of outstanding students to Sanskrit classes. Uniquely versed in both Persian and accounting methods, he concurrently served as Persian translator to the company's Carnatic commissioners. He resumed writing for the *Edinburgh Review* but declined contributing to a supplement to the sixth edition of the *Encyclopaedia Britannica*. Elected a fellow of the Royal Society in 1807, Hamilton was consulted by German scholars Othmar Frank and Franz Bopp, the founder of modern comparative linguistics, and was elected in 1815 a corresponding member of the Bavarian Academy. He retired from Haileybury in 1818 and moved to his London *pied-à-terre* at 11 Albany Buildings, Piccadilly; he was a founding member of the Royal Asiatic Society. He spent his last days at Magazines, Liscard, near Birkenhead, Cheshire, the home of his sister Elizabeth, wife of Thomas

Twemlow, a merchant in Liverpool where his son was an attorney. He died at Magazines on 30 December 1824. A rotund, affable, frugal, and serviceable man who shunned the limelight, he was well liked.

Hamilton's legacy is one of personal influence more than publication. However substantial his reviews—all anonymous—in the *Monthly Review*, *Asiatic Annual Register*, and *Edinburgh Review*, their impact is hard to assess. Even though his *Hitopadeśa* constituted the first edition of a Sanskrit text in Europe, his textbooks for Haileybury College had a limited distribution. A manuscript Sanskrit–English dictionary offered for sale after his death may now be lost. But, to the many future company servants to whom he taught Bengali and the chosen few he instructed in Sanskrit, he imparted respect for India's high tradition, while his tutoring of Schlegel and other aficionados, his catalogue of Sanskrit manuscripts in Paris, and his support of Frank and Bopp in London opened to continental scholars the knowledge of Sanskrit and comparative linguistics of Calcutta's Asiatic Society. Celebrated on the continent as the introducer of Sanskrit, he despaired of eliciting a like interest in Britain. A geographical dictionary of Asia with Lawrence Dundas Campbell, editor of the *Asiatic Annual Register*, announced in the *Register* for 1802 and consistent with his interest in ancient geography, was never published but apparently formed a basis for works by a younger brother.

This brother was **Walter Hamilton** (*bap.* 1774, *d.* 1828), baptized in Old (or Wester) Greenock on 6 March 1774, fifth of the children of William Hamilton and Jean Donald who survived infancy. He joined Alexander in India in 1791 as a cadet in the Bengal army but promptly resigned the service to engage in private trade. On his return to Britain in 1801 he became a merchant in Liverpool and maintained a residence in London where he conducted research in the East India Company library and, along with Alexander, was a founding member of the Royal Asiatic Society. His *East India Gazetteer* (1815, 2nd edn, 2 vols., 1828; repr., 1984), rearranged into a *Geographical, Statistical, and Historical Description of Hindostan, and the Adjacent Countries* (2 vols., 1820; repr., 1971), was a *vade mecum* for company servants and, as the first gazetteer of India, inaugurated a type of work that had many followers. Although close, the brothers could disagree, Walter apparently correcting in his *Description* (1.96) Alexander's claim that Indian merchants had been 'from time immemorial, in possession of the method of book-keeping by double entry' (*Monthly Review*, 26, 1798, 129), a suggestion which sparked a recent debate among historians of accounting about a possible Indian origin for this system. Like Alexander's, Walter's life ended at their sister's home in Liscard, on 25 September 1828. ROSANE ROCHER

**Sources** R. Rocher, *Alexander Hamilton (1762–1824): a chapter in the early history of Sanskrit philology* (1968) • R. Rocher, 'New data for the biography of the orientalist Alexander Hamilton', *Journal of the American Oriental Society*, 90 (1970), 423–48 • R. Rocher and M. E. Scorgie, 'A family empire: the Alexander Hamilton cousins, 1750–1830', *Journal of Imperial and Commonwealth History*, 23 (1995), 189–210 • R. W. Chambers and F. Norman, 'Alexander Hamilton and the beginnings of comparative philology', *Studies in English philology: a miscellany in honor of Frederick Klaeber*, ed. K. Malone and M. B. Ruud (1929), 457–66 • F. Plank, 'What Friedrich Schlegel could have learned from Alexander ("Sanscrit") Hamilton besides Sanskrit', *Lingua e Stile*, 22 (1987), 367–84 • M. E. Scorgie, 'Indian imitation or invention of cash-book and algebraic double-entry', *Abacus*, 16 (1990), 63–70 • records of East India Company college, BL OIOC, IOR J/1/19, 21–33, 2/1-3 • *The papers of Alexander Hamilton*, ed. H. C. Syrett, 27 vols. (1961–87) [the papers of the American Alexander Hamilton] • *Wellesley index* • E. Windisch, *Geschichte der Sanskrit-Philologie und Indischen Altertumskunde*, 2 vols. (1917–20) • R. Schwab, *La renaissance orientale* (1950); trans. G. Patterson-Black and V. Reinking (1984) • S. B. Chaudhuri, *History of the gazetteers of India* (1964) • *GM*, 1st ser., 95/1 (1825), 189

**Wealth at death** approx. £19,000: PRO, PROB 11/1694, 184-5; IR 26/1044, 36 • under £9000—Walter Hamilton: PRO, PROB 11/1746, 290–91; IR 26/1167, 5, 193

**Hamilton, Alexander Douglas-, tenth duke of Hamilton and seventh duke of Brandon (1767–1852)**, aristocrat, was born on 3 October 1767 in St James's Square, London, the elder son of Archibald (1740–1819), the ninth duke, and Lady Harriet Stewart (*d.* 1788), fifth daughter of Alexander, sixth earl of Galloway. The marquess of Douglas (as he was known until 1819) was educated at Harrow School and Christ Church, Oxford. His earlier years were spent in Italy, where he acquired a taste for the fine arts. In 1801 he returned home, and in the following year was appointed colonel of the Lanarkshire militia and lord lieutenant of the county. He was whig MP for Lancaster, 1802–6, and made his maiden speech on 22 March 1804 against an alteration in the Militia Bill proposed by Pitt. In 1806 he was sent as ambassador to the court of St Petersburg, and was sworn of the privy council. In the same year he was summoned to the House of Lords by writ, in his father's barony of Dutton. Recalled on the change of ministry in 1807, he remained in the interior of Russia and Poland until October 1808 on account of his infatuation with an 'old battered beauty', the Polish Countess Potocka (GEC, *Peerage*). He married, on 26 April 1810, his cousin-german, Susan Euphemia Beckford (1786–1859), second daughter of William *Beckford, and Lady Margaret Gordon, daughter of Charles, fourth earl of Aboyne. They had two children, William Alexander Anthony Archibald Douglas-*Hamilton, and Lady Susan Harriet Catherine *Opdebeck, married first in 1832 to Lord Lincoln, afterwards duke of Newcastle, from whom she was divorced in 1850.

Douglas succeeded his father on 16 February 1819, as tenth duke of Hamilton in the peerage of Scotland. He was also duke of Brandon in the peerage of Great Britain and duke of Châtelherault in the peerage of France, and was appointed a knight of the Garter in 1836. He was hereditary keeper of Holyroodhouse. He took no prominent part in the debates of the House of Lords. He was lord high steward at the coronations of William IV and Queen Victoria. He was a trustee of the British Museum, vice-president of the Royal Institution for the Encouragement of the Fine Arts in Scotland, FRS, and FSA. He died at his house, 12 Portman Square, London, on 18 August 1852.

The chief characteristic of the duke—at least in his later days—was his intense family pride. He firmly believed that as the descendant of the regent Arran he was the true heir to the throne of Scotland. For the same reason he was buried with 'oriental' pomp (and a Presbyterian service), after the body had been embalmed, in an Egyptian sarcophagus, which was deposited in a colossal mausoleum erected near Hamilton Palace, in Lanarkshire. He showed intelligence in the improvement of his estates, and taste in the large collection of pictures and objects of virtu with which he adorned Hamilton Palace. This collection, which included the famous *Laughing Boy* of Leonardo da Vinci and other gems of art, together with a valuable collection of old books and manuscripts, part of which was made by Beckford, was auctioned by Sothebys in July 1882. L. C. SANDERS, *rev.* K. D. REYNOLDS

**Sources** GEC, *Peerage* • V. Surtees, *A Beckford inheritance: the Lady Lincoln scandal* (1977) • *GM*, 2nd ser., 38 (1852), 424
**Archives** NA Scot., papers • NRA Scotland, priv. coll., corresp. and papers | BL, corresp. with second earl of Liverpool, Add. MSS 38256–38296, *passim* • BL, Add. MSS 38296–48256, *passim* • Bodl. Oxf., Beckford MSS • NL Scot., corresp., incl. with Lord Rutherfurd • NRA Scotland, priv. coll., letters relating to James Skene's application for preferment • priv. coll., corresp. with Robert Brown • U. Durham L., letters to Charles, second Earl Grey • U. Edin. L., letters to David Laing • U. Nott. L., Newcastle MSS • U. Nott. L., letters to fourth duke of Newcastle and Lord Lincoln
**Likenesses** J. Reynolds, oils, 1782, NG Scot. • T. Gainsborough, oils, 1786, Waddesdon Manor, Buckinghamshire • J. Gillray, etching, pubd 1803, NPG • J. Doyle, chalk drawing, 1851, BM • G. Hayter, group portrait, oils (*The trial of Queen Caroline 1820*), NPG • D. Macnee, oils, Lennoxlove, Haddington, East Lothian • W. Maddox, oils, Brodick Castle, Isle of Arran • D. Wilkie, group portrait, oils (*The entrance of George IV at Holyroodhouse*), Scot. NPG • attrib. D. Wilkie, sketch, Lennoxlove, Haddington, East Lothian • pencil drawing, Scot. NPG • portrait, Royal Collection

**Hamilton, Andrew** (*d.* 1691?), Church of Ireland clergyman, was of unknown parents. The Hamiltons were a cluster of interrelated and influential protestant Scots-Irish settler families in the Enniskillen area from the 1630s onwards. Dozens of Hamiltons were active in the locality, at least six being members of the local clergy, and so the identification of Andrew's parents can be little more than supposition. The memory of the rebellion of the Gaelic Irish in 1641 certainly scarred his consciousness, and he grew up as a stalwart protestant who firmly believed himself to be part of a beleaguered and constantly threatened minority. It appears likely that he was trained in the law—graduating MA at an unknown date and from an unknown university—before being admitted to the Church of Ireland as a clergyman on 7 August 1661. A man of considerable wealth and local influence, he was collated as rector to the unified parishes of Kilskerry and Mageracross on 4 April 1666, and it seems more than likely that these offices were within the gift of his own family group. He viewed the appointment of the earl of Tyrconnell—as first marshal, and then lord deputy of Ireland—with a mixture of fear and disdain, and complained bitterly of the free quartering of a popish army upon loyal protestants. However, the flight of James II in December 1688 caught him entirely by surprise, and he wrote that initially neither he nor any of his neighbours knew what had befallen the exiled king. Some said that he retired 'to a monastery, some to Rome, and some [said he was] dead, as every man's fancy led him' (*Actions of Enniskillen-Men*, xiii).

Believing that the Irish protestants now faced robbery, extortion, and massacre by their Catholic fellow countrymen, Hamilton was quick to take up arms and enrolled on 9 December 1688 in an association for the defence of the protestant religion in Enniskillen. At his own cost he raised a troop of horse and a company of foot, and spent January 1689 drilling his men and procuring a motley array of arms and equipment for them. In April 1689 he was sent to the Lough of Derry in an attempt to secure vital munitions from a flotilla of English supply vessels that were believed to have anchored there. Unfortunately, they had set sail for home shortly before his arrival, and Hamilton was captured on his return journey by a party of Jacobite horse. Taken to the siege lines before Derry, he attempted to save 'a poor old woman [of] at least seventy years' who had been accused of attempting to bewitch the troopers' horses. Robbed and beaten, she survived upwards of twenty shots fired at her by the pickets, but was at last run to ground and shot down at point-blank range. Enraged, Hamilton was at pains to point out the groundless nature of the charges brought against her and roundly condemned this 'unnatural piece of cruelty' (*Actions of Enniskillen-Men*, 22, 23).

The amnesty offered by James II in 1689, allowing 'all men that pleased [to have] the liberty to go to their former dwellings' (*Actions of Enniskillen-Men*, 2), enabled Hamilton to argue successfully for his early release and—having procured a pass for his safe conduct—he slipped back to Enniskillen through enemy lines. However, before leaving the Jacobite camp he was able to smuggle a message inside the city walls, advising the garrison of Derry that they should treat any report of the fall of Enniskillen as being false, unless it was signed by his or the governor's hand. His later actions in recruiting soldiers and carrying off horses as mounts for Williamite cavalry, for which he was attainted for treason by James II's parliament in Dublin, appear to have earned him the particular enmity of James Fitzjames, duke of Berwick. During a raid on 4 July 1689 Berwick sought to seize Hamilton and to burn his property as a grim warning to other militant protestant landowners. Luckily, Hamilton had heard of the approach of the strong Jacobite force, and with his own troop of horse drew off, in advance of Berwick's arrival, towards Ballyshannon. Cheated of his quarry Berwick allegedly remarked that: 'if they had got himself [Hamilton] they would have made him meat for their hawks' (ibid., 40). The Jacobite soldiers contented themselves with plundering and firing Hamilton's home—together with his properties in ten separate villages—before driving off 'above a thousand cows, two hundred horses and mares, and about two thousand sheep' taken from Hamilton and his tenants (ibid., 81–2).

Hamilton was present at the battle of Newton Butler on

31 July 1689, when the Enniskillen men inflicted a crushing defeat upon local Jacobite forces under Justin MacCarthy, and—as the pressure upon their city eased—he was chosen to give an account of the proceedings for the defence of Ulster to the new king and queen. He was received by William and Mary at Hampton Court Palace on 12 October 1689, and read out to them the 'Humble address of the governor, officers [and] clergy … of Enniskillen'. Thereafter, he appears to have remained in London, writing and publishing his seminal account of the defence of Enniskillen (*A True Relation of the Actions of the Inniskilling-Men*, 1690, reprinted twice as *The Actions of the Enniskillen-Men*, 1813, 1864), and seeking redress for the crippling financial losses that he had incurred during the Irish war. On 30 April 1690 a royal warrant granted him the house and lands forfeited by Cuconacht More McGuire, a prominent Jacobite commander. However, the promise that they would yield not more than £20 per annum, and that they were now lying waste as a result of the fighting, was probably of little comfort to a man who had once owned large estates and drew a private income of more than £400 a year. The deanery of Kilmore—newly vacated by the death of the incumbent, Edward Dixey—had been set aside for Hamilton, but there is no evidence that he ever took up this lucrative and prestigious appointment. He appears to have been still alive in the spring and summer of 1691, for his former comrade-in-arms Captain William McCarmick wrote that he published his own account of the war out of 'very great esteem' for Hamilton, and that he sought only to correct those things that 'hath slipt' from his memory (McCarmick, 1). Thereafter he disappears from the records; he was succeeded in his benefices by James Kirkwood and probably died in late 1691, possibly without having returned to Ulster from his lodgings in the city of London. JOHN CALLOW

**Sources** A. Hamilton, *The actions of the Enniskillen-men* (1813) [repr. 1864] • H. Cotton, *Fasti ecclesiae Hibernicae*, 3 (1849) • A. Hamilton, *A true relation of the actions of the Inniskilling-men* (1690) • *CSP dom.*, 1689–90 • W. H. Bradshaw, *Enniskillen long ago* (1878) • W. McCarmick, *A farther impartial account of the actions of the Inniskilling-men* (1691) • J. G. Simms, *Jacobite Ireland, 1685–91* (1969) • W. King, *The state of the protestants of Ireland under the late King James's government* (1691) • J. Ware, *The history and antiquities of Ireland … with the history of the writers of Ireland*, ed. W. Harris (1764)

**Hamilton, Andrew** (*c.*1676–1741), politician and lawyer in America, was born in Scotland and migrated to Accomac county, Virginia, about 1698. Hamilton possibly served as an indentured servant to Captain Isaac Foxcroft, and later became sole executor of the Foxcroft estate after the death of his former master's widow. From this time Hamilton began an extensive programme of land acquisition which benefited from his marriage on 6 March 1706 to Anne Preeson, *née* Brown (*d.* 1736), who brought him a further 631 acres; by the time of his death, his holdings totalled over 19,000 acres in Virginia, Maryland, New Jersey, Delaware, and Pennsylvania. The couple's youngest child was James *Hamilton (*c.*1710–1783).

In 1700 Hamilton had begun a legal practice whose success prompted his move to Kent county, Maryland, in 1708. Here he met James Logan, secretary to the Pennsylvania proprietor, William Penn, who informed the proprietor of Hamilton's abilities as a lawyer at a time of increasing tension over a border dispute between Pennsylvania and Maryland whose territorial claims were led by its recently reinstated proprietor, Benedict Leonard Calvert, fourth Baron Baltimore. Through Penn's influence Hamilton spent 1713 at Gray's Inn, London, where he qualified for the English bar before returning to sit briefly in the Maryland assembly and then moving to Philadelphia. In 1717 he was appointed attorney-general of Pennsylvania and from 1720 he served on the colony's provincial council.

Hamilton spent 1725 and 1726 in England, where he was able to secure the Penns' interest in the ongoing boundary dispute with Maryland, and further ingratiated himself with the family by mediating during a domestic disagreement involving William Penn's grandson, Springett. Following his return to Pennsylvania, Hamilton gained considerable influence in diplomatic and legal resolutions between the colony and London. In 1727 he became, as recorder, a prominent member of Pennsylvania's common council, and was elected to the assemblies both of that colony and to that of the lower counties of Delaware. Concerned about the effects of especially German immigration on colonial society, Hamilton now contributed to a bill to safeguard the 'Englishness' of the colony by placing duties upon an immigrant's arrival.

Hamilton's most celebrated case was his defence of John Peter Zenger in 1735. Zenger, the publisher of the *New York Weekly Journal*, had been charged with seditious libel by William Cosby, governor of New York, and had suffered the dismissal of his first defence team for challenging the right of James Delancey, the chief justice, to preside at the trial. Hamilton's appearance unsettled the prosecution, who were forced to observe an unorthodox defence in which he first asserted the truthfulness of Zenger's material. Hamilton next urged the jury to go beyond its expected role in English law—determining the facts in this case concerning the origin of Zenger's published work—and to undertake the judiciary's responsibility of passing a verdict on the defendant. Notwithstanding Delancey's call to ignore this request, the jury, swayed by Hamilton's appeal to the cause of liberty and a free press, adjudged Zenger not guilty, upon which the defendant was acquitted. Despite failing to alter the law of seditious libel, Hamilton's stand was important for influencing a later generation of American lawyers and politicians determined to defend colonial freedoms against what they came to see as an increasingly arbitrary national government.

Returning triumphant to Philadelphia after the Zenger case, Hamilton became judge of the vice-admiralty court in 1737. By then the colonies' most respected lawyer, Hamilton's fame should not obscure his reputation for sharp business practice and avarice, especially during the late

1710s and 1720s, by which time he had acquired his extensive landholdings. Satirical attacks on Hamilton from this period include *The life and character of a strange he-monster, lately arriv'd in London from an English colony in America*, published in London in 1726. Ill health forced Hamilton to retire from his political career in 1739 and he died in Philadelphia on 4 August 1741. He left a sizeable estate including eight slaves and a gold box he had received from the corporation of New York in recognition of his defence in the Zenger case. MARY K. GEITER

**Sources** B. A. Konkle, *The life of Andrew Hamilton, 1676–1741* (1972) • W. H. Loyd, 'Andrew Hamilton', *Great American lawyers*, ed. W. D. Lewis, 8 vols. (1907–9) • J. F. Fisher, 'Andrew Hamilton, esq. of Pennsylvania', *Pennsylvania Magazine of History and Biography*, 16 (1892) • F. C. Nix, 'Andrew Hamilton's early years in the American colonies', *William and Mary Quarterly*, 3rd ser., 21 (1964), 390–407 • R. B. Morris, *Fair trial* (1952) • L. Rutherfurd, *John Peter Zenger: his press, his trial and a bibliography of Zenger imprints* (1904) • L. R. Schuyler, *The liberty of the press in the American colonies before the Revolutionary War* (1905) • E. J. McManus, 'Hamilton, Andrew', *ANB*

**Wealth at death** substantial, incl. eight slaves

**Hamilton, Anne**, *suo jure* **duchess of Hamilton** (1632–1716), noblewoman, was the second of six children of James *Hamilton, third marquess and later first duke of Hamilton (1606–1649), and his wife, Mary *Hamilton (1612/13?–1638) [*see under* Hamilton, James, first duke of Hamilton], daughter of William *Feilding, first earl of Denbigh (*d.* 1643), and his wife, Susan Villiers. Born on 16 January 1632 at Wallingford House, Whitehall, London, Anne was named after her grandmother Anna *Cunningham, marchioness of Hamilton (*d.* 1647). Her father was in Germany, fighting in the protestant armies during the Thirty Years' War, but Charles I arranged her baptism and acted as godfather, for the marquess was his close friend and leading Scottish adviser. Her elder sister died soon after Lady Anne's birth but, after her father's return to London, another sister, Susanna, and three brothers were born in quick succession. Too frequent childbearing damaged their mother's health and she died in 1638 after a long illness. The marquess was anxious for his children, who were all 'both weak and sickly' (*Denbigh MSS*, 5.60) and decided to move them to the healthier air of Chelsea, where he built a new mansion house, but by April 1640 all three little boys were dead, leaving Lady Anne, by right, as her father's heir. However, in times of civil war the marquess considered that such a prominent family needed a man at its head and so he arranged that when he died his younger brother William Hamilton, earl of Lanark, would inherit his titles and estates. In an attempt to bring the influential marquess of Argyll over to the king's side, Hamilton entered into negotiations to marry his elder daughter to Lord Lorne, Argyll's heir. In the end the political differences between the two men were insuperable, and the match fell through. Hamilton then sent Anne north to live with his mother in Scotland.

Reluctantly parting from her sister, who stayed behind with Lady Denbigh, in 1642 Lady Anne made the long journey north to Hamilton Palace in Lanarkshire, and settled down to a very different way of life. Her grandmother the dowager marchioness was a plain, vigorous lady of much

**Anne Hamilton,** ***suo jure*** **duchess of Hamilton** (1632–1716), by Sir Godfrey Kneller, 1679

good sense and firm presbyterian convictions. She had been tirelessly running the family estates ever since her marriage and as well as employing masters to give her granddaughter an education appropriate to an aristocratic young lady, she let her see every aspect of administering the vast Hamilton possessions. Lady Anne remained at Hamilton after her grandmother's death in 1647, and was still there when she received the news of the execution of her father (by this time duke of Hamilton) at Whitehall on 9 March 1649. Her uncle, now the second duke, had managed to escape to the continent and from there he wrote affectionate letters to Anne, urging her to stay at Hamilton Palace and take charge there. He also made his will, leaving everything to her instead of to his own eldest daughter. In 1651 he went back to Scotland with the young Charles II and marched south with him to defeat at the battle of Worcester, where he was mortally wounded. At the age of nineteen Anne became duchess of Hamilton and Châtelherault, marchioness of Clydesdale, countess of Arran and Cambridge, and Lady Aven, Polmont, Machanshire, and Innerdale, with estates stretching from the island of Arran, across Lanarkshire into Linlithgowshire.

The duchess was nominally Scotland's greatest heir, but her father and uncle had contracted enormous debts during the civil war and the Hamilton estates had been confiscated and handed over to various officers in Cromwell's army. In the summer of 1651 she sought shelter on Arran with her sister and the second duke's daughters, then she moved to a little house in the woods near Hamilton Palace.

Her troubles multiplied when her father's second cousin the earl of Abercorn claimed that her estates were entailed on the male line and were rightfully his. On 29 April 1656, however, she gained a valuable ally when she married William Douglas [*see* Hamilton, William, third duke of Hamilton (1634–1694)] in Corstorphine church, near Edinburgh.

In some ways this was an unlikely match, for the earl was a younger son of the Roman Catholic first marquess of Douglas, and her uncle's will had expressly forbidden Anne to marry anyone not of 'the true Protestant religion' (NA Scot., Register of Testaments, Edinburgh, 28 Sept 1652). However, according to Gilbert Burnet, who knew the family well, she had fallen in love with the handsome earl and he was willing to disclaim any Catholic sympathies in order to marry her. His quick temper and imperious manner might annoy his political rivals, but he had a good financial brain and after fighting off Lord Abercorn's claims, he and the duchess set about gathering together the money needed to pay off the fines on their estates. By selling personal possessions they raised the £7000 necessary to reclaim Hamilton Palace, and after the Restoration Charles II paid Anne more than £25,000 sterling which his father had owed hers. She regained her inheritance, and at her special request the king created her husband duke of Hamilton for life.

Duchess Anne was undeniably plain, with a large nose and mouth and a receding chin, but early on her husband told her, 'when I see the ways of others and thinks on you, I cannot but acknowledg[e] myself most happie in so verteus a parson' (NA Scot., Hamilton correspondence, CI8154). They were to enjoy an affectionate working partnership for almost forty years. While the duke represented the family in public life, the duchess gave birth to their thirteen children (among them George *Hamilton and Katherine *Hamilton) and ran the estates. By the late 1680s they were able to begin an ambitious scheme for completely rebuilding Hamilton Palace. The work was still going on when the duke died after a stroke in 1694. The duchess, usually self-contained, admitted to one of her sons, 'My teares … are but too frequent both in the night as well as day' (NA Scot., Hamilton correspondence, CI6659). Everywhere she looked, she said, she saw the results of her husband's industry, and she bitterly regretted that their eldest son was unlikely to leave such a legacy.

James *Hamilton, fourth duke of Hamilton (1658–1712), had been a constant disappointment to his parents, with his refusal to settle down in Scotland and his dissolute way of life. Because Duchess Anne held the estates in her own right, he did not become duke on his father's death. After his second marriage, in 1698, he persuaded his mother to resign her dukedom for a regrant in his favour, but, to his chagrin, she made sure that he received only the title of fourth duke and not any of the properties. He already had a mountain of debt and she well knew that he would soon dissipate his carefully restored inheritance. She had agreed that he might have the title of duke so that he could represent the house of Hamilton in parliament. She was very much against the union of the Scottish and English parliaments, and she looked to him to lead the opposition. His interests were divided, however, for his wife had large estates in the south, and not only did he attend the house drunk, but he also sent excuses when any decisive behaviour was expected of him. After 1707 he spent all his time in the south, finally dying in a duel in London in 1712.

Duchess Anne sat silent in her room for weeks afterwards, overwhelmed by the terrible tragedy of his wasted life, but she knew that once again everything depended on her. At the age of eighty she set about paying her son's debts and bringing up his children, for their mother took little interest in them. Moreover, she continued her efforts to improve her estates. She had introduced coalmining and a thriving salt industry to the island of Arran, providing a ferry, sending a travelling preacher, a doctor, and a schoolmaster, and establishing a harbour at Lamlash. She rebuilt the church at Strathaven, in Lanarkshire, and funded a new schoolhouse and a waulkmill. She granted the little burgh of Bo'ness, Linlithgowshire, its founding charter. Under her patronage it became a thriving port. In Hamilton itself she rebuilt the school, schoolhouse, and almshouse, set up a woollen manufactory, and endowed bursaries in memory of her husband. She was still busy with estate business in the autumn of 1716, but then she suffered a brief illness and died peacefully, in her own bedchamber at Hamilton Palace, on 17 October. As she had wished, she was laid in a simple coffin made of wood from her estates, and buried beside her husband in Hamilton parish church. ROSALIND K. MARSHALL

**Sources** R. K. Marshall, *The days of Duchess Anne* (1973) • R. K. Marshall, 'The house of Hamilton in its Anglo-Scottish setting in the seventeenth century', PhD diss., U. Edin., 1970 [incl. a 5-vol. calendar of the duke of Hamilton's archives] • R. K. Marshall, 'Conscience and costume in seventeenth-century Scotland', *Costume: The Journal of the Costume Society*, 6 (1972), 32–5 • R. K. Marshall, 'The furnishings of Hamilton Palace in the seventeenth century', *Review of Scottish Culture*, 3 (1987), 13–22 • *Bishop Burnet's History of his own time*, new edn, 2 vols. (1838) • G. Hamilton, *The house of Hamilton* (1933) • *Scots peerage*, vol. 4 • *Report on the manuscripts of the earl of Denbigh, part V*, HMC, 68 (1911), 60 • register of testaments, Edinburgh, 28 Sept 1652, NA Scot. • Hamilton corresp., NA Scot., CI6659, CI8154

**Archives** Hamilton archives, Lennoxlove, East Lothian • NA Scot., archives | Blair Castle, Perthshire, Atholl Muniments, letters • NA Scot., Dalhousie Muniments, letters • NA Scot., Yester MSS, letters

**Likenesses** D. Scougall, oils, *c*.1661, Brodick Castle, Garden and Country Park, Isle of Arran • G. Kneller, oils, 1679, Lennoxlove House, Haddington, East Lothian [*see illus.*]

**Hamilton, Lady Anne** (1766–1846), courtier, eldest daughter of Archibald Hamilton, ninth duke of Hamilton and sixth of Brandon (1740–1819), and Lady Harriet Stewart (*d.* 1788), daughter of the sixth earl of Galloway, was born on 16 March 1766. In 1810 she inherited £10,000 from the fourth duke of Queensberry, which she made over in its entirety to her brother, Lord Archibald *Hamilton, despite being far from affluent herself. She became a lady-in-waiting to Caroline, princess of Wales, in 1814, but did not accompany her when she left England in the same year, and hence was not implicated in the scandals arising from Caroline's continental sojourn. When Caroline returned to England to claim her place as queen in 1820, Lady Anne met her in Montbard, Flanders, and they returned to London together. The queen then took up residence with her for a short time in Portman Street. Lady Anne continued to be seen in public with the queen until Caroline's death in 1821, accompanying her on her failed attempt to be present at the coronation. She accompanied Caroline's body to Brunswick and attended its interment.

Lady Anne then returned to private life, during which period a woman, referred to in Lady Anne's letters as 'S. W.' (and who has been identified by some as Olivia Wilmot Serres), gained her confidence and access to her papers. A book, entitled *A secret history of the court of England from the accession of George III to the death of George IV*, was published under her name in 1832, without, she claimed, either her knowledge or her sanction. Lady Anne's life was so complicated by this publication that she retired to France for some time. She returned to England, and died, unmarried, on 10 October 1846 at her home in White Lion Street, Islington, London; she was buried in Kensal Green cemetery. Her appearance was described by Creevey: 'She is full six feet high, and bears a striking resemblance to one of Lord Derby's great red deer' (Smith, 71). A friend and associate, Robert Fellowes, wrote that she was 'one of those to whom misfortune cannot teach caution and whom experience cannot make wise. She was perpetually victimized by her extraordinary credulity on the one side, and her ardent, but inconsiderate benevolence on the other' (*GM*, 1846). K. D. Reynolds

**Sources** *GM*, 2nd ser., 26 (1846), 552, 661 • Ward, *Men of the reign* • E. A. Smith, *A queen on trial: the affair of Queen Caroline* (1993)
**Archives** Bodl. Oxf., corresp., mainly with William Beckford
**Likenesses** stipple, 1820, BM, NPG • attrib. T. Gainsborough, oils, Detroit Institute of Arts • G. Hayter, group portrait, oils (*The trial of Queen Caroline, 1820*), NPG • J. Lonsdale, oils, V&A • oils, NG Ire.

**Hamilton, Anthony** [Antoine], **Count Hamilton in the French nobility** (**1644/5?–1719**), courtier and author, was the third of the six sons of Sir George *Hamilton, first baronet (*d.* 1679) [*see under* Hamilton, James, first earl of Abercorn], and grandson of James *Hamilton, first earl of Abercorn (1575–1618). His mother was Mary Butler, third daughter of Walter, Viscount Thurles, eldest son of Walter, eleventh earl of Ormond. He was probably born at Roscrea, co. Tipperary, in 1644 or 1645. He spent his early years in France, where his family, which was Catholic, settled in 1651. After the Restoration they moved to England and were given new lands in Ireland.

Anthony Hamilton's eldest brother, James, who was a protestant, was groom of the bedchamber to Charles II, and colonel of a regiment of foot; he died of wounds received in a naval engagement with the Dutch on 6 June 1679, and was buried in Westminster Abbey, where a monument was erected to his memory by the duke of Ormond; his eldest son was James Hamilton, sixth earl of Abercorn. The second brother, George, was a page to Charles II during his exile, and after the Restoration was an officer of the Horse Guards until 1667, when he was

**Anthony Hamilton, Count Hamilton in the French nobility** (**1644/5?–1719**), by Alexis-Simon Belle

cashiered for refusing to take the oath of supremacy; he then entered French service with a troop of Catholic ex-soldiers who were enrolled in the bodyguard of Louis XIV, and known as the 'gens d'armes anglais'. He was made a count and maréchal-de-camp, and was killed at the battle of Saverne in 1676; he married Frances Jennings, afterwards duchess of Tyrconnell, and they had three daughters. These two brothers are frequently mentioned in Anthony Hamilton's work, the *Mémoires*. Thomas, the fourth brother, was in the navy and is said to have died in New England. Richard *Hamilton, the fifth son, was a senior Jacobite officer. John, the sixth, was a brigadier in the service of James II, and was killed at the battle of Aughrim in 1691. Anthony Hamilton also had three sisters, of whom the eldest was Elizabeth *Hamilton, Countess de Gramont.

Anthony Hamilton joined his brother George in France in 1667, and was given a captain's commission in the French army. In 1671 he and his younger brother Richard joined a regiment of foot which George raised in Ireland for the service of Louis XIV. They served in the Franco-Dutch War of 1672–8. In 1678, having inherited the title of count from his brother, Anthony left France. After an unsuccessful attempt at farming in Ireland, he fled to England to avoid his creditors, then resumed his military career in France. During this period he appeared alongside the dauphin as a zephyr in Lully's ballet *Le triomphe de l'amour*, which was given twenty-nine performances in the Château de St Germain-en-Laye in January and February 1681. He returned to Ireland as lieutenant-colonel of Sir Thomas Newcomen's regiment of foot in 1685 and was appointed governor of Limerick. He was the first governor of the town to attend mass publicly in thirty-five years. At the end of the following year he was sworn of the Irish privy council, and promoted to the rank of colonel in February 1687. He was also granted a pension of £200 per annum, charged on the Irish establishment. He benefited also from the favour and patronage of his sister-in-law's second husband, the earl of Tyrconnell.

After the revolution of 1688 Hamilton took part in the war in Ireland. He was promoted brigadier, then major-general in July 1689. He commanded the dragoons, under Lord Mountcashel, at the siege of Enniskillen, and in the battle of Newtownbutler on 31 July 1689 was wounded in the leg at the beginning of the action, in which his regiment suffered severe losses. He was subsequently court-martialled for having fled in panic from the battlefield, but acquitted. With his brothers Richard and John, he fought at the battle of the Boyne on 1 July 1690, where Richard was wounded and captured. Anthony and John went to Limerick and endured the siege, and all three brothers were outlawed in 1691. He does not appear to have been present at the battle of Aughrim, when John was killed. After the fall of Limerick in 1691 Hamilton left Ireland for France and joined the court of James II in exile at St Germain-en-Laye. The French ambassador in Ireland maintained that he had never merited his promotion to the rank of major-general, and he never resumed his military career.

Hamilton was given a generous pension by James II of 2000 livres per annum (later reduced to 1320 livres in 1703, increasing to 2200 livres by 1717), but he never had a post in the royal household, whereas his brother Richard was appointed master of the robes in 1696. Unlike many Jacobites, he spoke and wrote French fluently and moved freely between the English court at St Germain and the French court at Versailles. He also had a considerable family circle, which included his brother Richard, his sister Elizabeth and her husband the Count de Gramont, their elder daughter, Claude-Charlotte, who married Henry, first earl of Stafford in 1694, and their younger daughter, Marie-Elisabeth, who later became abbess of Poussay in Lorraine. The countess (now duchess) of Tyrconnell was also at St Germain with Lady Kingsland, one of her daughters by George Hamilton.

At the exiled court Hamilton was on particularly good terms with James FitzJames, first duke of Berwick, natural son of James II, his second wife, Anne (*née* Bulkeley), and her three sisters, Charlotte (Viscountess Clare), Henrietta, and Laura (both unmarried), and many of his letters to them have survived. In 1701 Hamilton accompanied Berwick on his mission to Rome to obtain the support of the new pope, Clement XI, for the Jacobite cause, and it was perhaps at this time that his portrait was painted, probably by François de Troy. At the French court Hamilton frequented the circle of the duke and duchess of Maine, particularly after 1700, when the latter first occupied the Château de Sceaux. By 1701 Hamilton had become increasingly preoccupied with the writing of poetry and various prose works for his friends. With the exception of the celebrated *Mémoires de la vie du comte de Grammont*, none of them was published during his lifetime.

In May 1703 Louis XIV gave Hamilton's sister the use during her lifetime of a house near Meudon called Les Moulineaux. In the five years until her death in June 1708 it was much frequented and became the centre of Hamilton's social world. The Countess de Gramont wished to rename her house Pontalie, and this was the inspiration for the first of Hamilton's 'contes', entitled *Le bélier*. Its aim was to furnish a romantic etymology for the new name, the principal incident being a contest between a prince and a giant for the daughter of a druid. Hamilton produced several other 'contes', including *L'histoire de fleur d'épine*, satirizing the popular imitations of the *Arabian Nights Entertainments*, which Hamilton described as 'plus Arabe qu'en Arabie', and two which were unfinished, *Les quatre Facardins* and *Zénéyde*. The first three were published in Paris in 1730, the fourth the following year in a collection entitled *Œuvres mêlées en prose et en vers*. Most of the poems, which seem to have been written during the years 1699 to 1709, are addressed to various 'nymphes de Saint-Germain'. These nymphs included Princess Louise Marie Stuart, Berwick's sister-in-law the duchess of Albemarle, and the daughters of some of Hamilton's Jacobite friends (Bevil Skelton, Robert Strickland, John Stafford, Lord Melfort, and Lord Middleton). Hamilton also included passages of verse in his prose letters, some of which were later published in *Œuvres mêlées en prose et en vers*. They include some charming descriptions of life at the court of St Germain during the years 1702–10.

Hamilton's decision to write the memoirs of his brother-in-law Philibert, Count de Gramont, was originally taken in 1704, while the two men were at Séméac in Gascogne, two years before Gramont's death in January 1707. The work was planned in three parts, but only the first two were ever published. It is not known if the third part was written, although it is promised in all five extant manuscript copies. The first two parts were circulating in manuscript by May 1712, when the duchesse d'Orléans sent a copy to the dowager electress of Hanover, and they were published anonymously and without authorization the following year allegedly at 'Cologne', though probably really at Rouen.

The first part of the memoirs contains an entertaining account of Gramont's early life in France, but the work's fame largely rests on the second part. This is concerned with Gramont's life at the court of Charles II between 1662 and 1664, and is based on Hamilton's own experiences as well as the recollections of his friend. It provides a detailed and invaluable description both of the Restoration court and of its leading courtiers, concentrating on their various intrigues and love affairs. It ends when 'the Chevalier de Grammont, as the reward of a constancy he had never before known and which he never afterwards practised … was at last blessed with the possession' of Hamilton's sister Elizabeth, whom he married and took back with him to France.

The book was greeted with considerable critical acclaim

on account of its brilliance and vivacity. An English translation was published in London in 1714. But it was resented by many at St Germain. Among other things it described in some detail the amorous adventures of James II while duke of York with the future countess of Erroll (governess of the prince of Wales at St Germain), with Hamilton's sister-in-law the future duchess of Tyrconnell (lady of the bedchamber to Mary of Modena at St Germain), and with Arabella Churchill (mother of the duke of Berwick). Berwick himself commented to James III (James Stuart) in May 1713: 'I wonder M. Anthony Hamilton will still be rambling, his age and infirmitys should induce him to be quiet some where with his friends' (*Stuart Papers*, 1. 267).

By then the circle of Hamilton's family and friends had been greatly reduced. The Gramonts were both dead, the duchess of Tyrconnell and her daughter had returned to Ireland, and his brother Richard had followed James III (James Francis Edward Stuart) and most of his courtiers to Bar-le-Duc in Lorraine. Hamilton concentrated on producing a free paraphrase in French alexandrines of Pope's *Essay on Criticism*, which had been published in London in 1711. He sent a copy to the poet, which Pope very handsomely acknowledged in October 1713. Around the same time Hamilton sat for a portrait by Alexis-Simon Belle, which is now at Lennoxlove.

In his last years Hamilton turned increasingly to his niece Lady Stafford, and through her he carried on a correspondence with her friend Lady Mary Wortley Montagu. He continued to live in the Château de St Germain, where he had an apartment, and where he was looked after in his last years by Mrs Lockhart, the widow of a fellow Jacobite. In 1714 or 1715 he wrote a set of verses entitled *Sur l'usage de la vie dans la vieillesse*, which has been praised for its style, justness, and purity of sentiment. In *Réflexions* he turned his mind in old age entirely to religion and said an eternal farewell to poetry. His brother Richard, meanwhile, retired to live with Lady Stafford's sister at Poussay, where he died in December 1717. Anthony Hamilton died unmarried at the age of seventy-four at St Germain on 21 April 1719 (not 1720 as stated in many biographies) and was buried the following day in the parish church.

Hamilton's four 'contes' had a considerable influence in eighteenth-century France, particularly on Claude Crébillon ('fils'), who married Lady Stafford's niece Henrietta and regarded himself as Hamilton's literary heir. Hamilton's manuscripts, which included the continuation of *Les quatre Facardins* and possibly also the third part of the *Mémoires de la vie du comte de Grammont*, remained in the Château de St Germain, where they were all burned by another of Lady Stafford's nieces (Mary Plowden) at the end of 1754. Some works, however, had been copied. Two more 'contes' were included in the collected edition of 1776, and two other short works in the collected edition of 1812. EDWARD CORP

**Sources** Royal Arch., Stuart papers • *Calendar of the Stuart papers belonging to his majesty the king, preserved at Windsor Castle*, 7 vols., HMC, 56 (1902–23) • A. Feinsilber and E. Corp, 'Crébillon fils et Marie-Henriette Stafford: histoire anglaise. Avec une lettre inédite', *Revue d'Histoire Littéraire de la France*, 96 (1996), 21–44 • *Mémoires de Saint-Simon*, ed. L. de Boislisle, L. Lecestre, and J. de Boislisle, new edn, 45 vols. (1879–1930) • *Mémoires du marquis de Sourches sur le règne de Louis XIV*, 13 vols. (Paris, 1882–93) • E. Black, ed., *Kings in conflict: Ireland in the 1690s* (1990) [exhibition catalogue, Ulster Museum, Belfast, 11 April – 2 Sept 1990] • A. Hamilton, *Œuvres* (1812–29)

**Likenesses** F. De Troy?, oils, *c.*1700; copy, NPG • A.-S. Belle, oils, Lennoxlove, East Lothian [*see illus.*] • E. Fressard, line engraving, BM, NPG • W. N. Gardiner, stipple, BM, NPG; repro. in A. Hamilton, *Mémoires du comte de Grammont*, new edn (1794)

**Hamilton, Archibald** (*d.* 1593), Roman Catholic controversialist, belonged to the family of James Hamilton of Orbiston, parson of Carrington in Edinburghshire. He and his brother Robert went to France in 1548 with James Hamilton, later third earl of Arran, son of the governor of Scotland. In 1553 both brothers entered St Mary's College, St Andrews, at a mature age, but Archibald was a year later in graduating, almost certainly because of a return to France as minister to the family's protestant household at Châtelhérault. In 1558 he was appointed a regent of St Andrews and taught rhetoric. In 1567 he was released for a year to serve the former governor (now duke of Châtelhérault as well as earl of Arran) and 'administered to him the Lord's Table' (Durkan, 'George Hay's *Oration*', 104), but was never a minister in Scotland.

According to Thomas Smeaton, his polemical opponent, Hamilton was an atheist about this time, and he acknowledged having written a satire attacking papal primacy. When John Knox preached in St Andrews in 1571 accusing the Hamiltons collectively of having assassinated the regent Moray, Archibald refused to attend the town's kirk. The appearance two years later of James Tyrie's *Refutation* of arguments by Knox helped to persuade Hamilton of the Roman Catholic case. The Apostate, as he became known, left for Paris soon after November 1576, and his Latin treatise *On the Confusion of the Calvinist Sect in Scotland* appeared the following summer. Smeaton replied two years later, and in 1581 Hamilton came back with *Against the Scurrilous Response of the Ministers of Scotland*. Now a priest and soon a doctor of the Sorbonne, in 1584 he was one of twenty Scots priests around Paris who appealed to Rome for funds as 'now in exile and desirous to return to their country even at the risk of their lives' (Forbes-Leith, 196). But civil war broke out again in France in that year, and Hamilton withdrew to Rome. His learning, which extended to a command of Hebrew, secured for him the friendship of leading figures there and employment as a librarian in the Vatican, where he died in 1593 in the apartments assigned to him by Gregory XIII (*r.* 1572–85). ALASDAIR ROBERTS

**Sources** J. Durkan, 'George Hay's *Oration* at the purging of King's College, Aberdeen, in 1569: commentary', *Northern Scotland*, 6 (1984–5), 97–112 • J. Durkan, 'James, third earl of Arran: the hidden years', *SHR*, 65 (1986), 154–66, esp. 162n • D. McRoberts, ed., *Essays on the Scottish Reformation, 1513–1625* (1962) • W. Forbes-Leith, ed., *Narratives of Scottish Catholics under Mary Stuart and James VI* (1885) • A. Bellesheim, *History of the Catholic Church in Scotland*, ed. and trans. D. O. H. Blair, 3 (1889) • M. Taylor, 'The conflicting doctrines of the Scottish Reformation', *Essays on the Scottish Reformation, 1513–1625*, ed. D. McRoberts (1962), 245–73 • W. J. Anderson, 'Narratives of the

Scottish Reformation, pt 2: Thomas Innes on Catholicism in Scotland, 1560–1653', *Innes Review*, 7 (1956), 112–21

**Hamilton, Archibald** (*c*.1578–1658/9), Church of Ireland archbishop of Cashel and Emly, was the son of Claud Hamilton of Cochno (*d*. 1611?) of Dunbartonshire, Scotland, and his wife, Margaret Betoun, the daughter of Robert Betoun of Creich. He had three brothers and one sister, of which only one, Claud, outlived him. Very little is known of his early life. In 1598 he matriculated at Glasgow University, and he obtained his MA degree the following year. He spent several years teaching at the university, initially as a master in 1602–3, as a regent from 1605 to 1612, and finally as a doctor of divinity in 1617. He had already become the minister for the parish of Paisley in 1610, and also became a member of the general assembly that year. He built a manse, which no longer survives, in 1612 for the ministers of the first charge of the abbey church. During this time he married his first wife, of whom little is known other than that her initials, A. L., were apparently carved above the manse entrance. She may have been Alison Hay, sometime nurse to Queen Elizabeth of Bohemia; an Alison Hay had been married to Alexander Livingston of Terrintirren, Stirlingshire. Between 1619 and 1622 Hamilton was a member of the court of high commission.

By 1621 Hamilton had approached King James VI requesting an appointment to a bishopric, which the king subsequently promised him in Ireland. Alexander Seton, first earl of Dunfermline, then intervened on Hamilton's behalf suggesting that the archbishopric of Cashel would be suitable. However, a see was not forthcoming until 8 March 1623, when he was appointed bishop of Killala and Achonry; the dioceses had been united the previous year. On 20 April 1630 Hamilton was translated to the archbishopric of Cashel and Emly on the death of the previous archbishop, Malcolm Hamilton. Hamilton found that much of the archdiocese's property had been alienated under Malcolm's predecessor, Meiler Magrath, and petitioned Thomas Wentworth, lord deputy of Ireland from 1631, to redress the situation. Magrath's transfers of property were legally valid, and Hamilton regained the land only following a special letter of instruction from Charles I.

Hamilton's assiduous defence of his rights raised the suspicion of William Laud, archbishop of Canterbury, who warned Wentworth that he might prove as independent a spirit as Magrath. Soon afterwards Laud found that Hamilton had 'upon his own authority, commanded a fast once a week for eight weeks together throughout his province' (*DNB*) and that, despite the restoration of the temporalities of Cashel, he was in the possession of sixteen vicarages. Hamilton was summoned to Dublin to account for his conduct, but said he was unable to travel following an acute attack of sciatica. Laud commented to Wentworth, 'Do you not think it would lame any man to carry sixteen vicarages? But surely the burden will help him to a sciatica in his conscience sooner than in his hips' (ibid.). In 1637 Elizabeth, queen of Bohemia, interceded on his behalf, commending his wife as a loyal subject. Hamilton sought, through his friends, a share in the plantations in Ormond or co. Clare, but it was ruled that he already had as much property as he deserved.

In 1632 Hamilton had inherited the estate of Bellonie from his brother Matthew. It is unknown when he married his second wife, Anna Balfour, described in the *Fasti ecclesiae Scoticanae* (8.242) as the daughter of Balfour of Burleigh (not, as stated in the *Dictionary of National Biography*, the daughter of Elizabeth MacDowall, Elizabeth of Bohemia's nursemaid, who was married to James Haig of Bemersyde).

The names of four of Hamilton's children have survived. James was the eldest son, to whom Hamilton bequeathed all his Irish property in 1641. John matriculated at the University of Glasgow in 1631, and his brother Malcolm matriculated there in 1633. Thomas, a fourth son, studied at Trinity College, Dublin, in 1639–40. During the Irish civil war Hamilton and his family were forced to flee Cashel, being initially sheltered by some friendly Catholic neighbours before leaving Ireland and losing goods and property worth £9000 in the process. Hamilton remained Church of Ireland archbishop of Cashel and Emly until his death, but never returned to Ireland. He obtained a recommendation to Charles I from the Scottish cleric John Durie, but as the king himself was engaged in three civil wars he probably found little comfort at the Stuart court. Hamilton then also petitioned William II, prince of Orange, relating that he had received help from a certain George Rataller, implying that Hamilton had already made contacts in the Netherlands. He was employed as a professor of theology there in 1644, but soon moved to Sweden. Some of his sons made their fortunes in Swedish society and became members of the nobility there. Hamilton is believed to have died either in Uppsala in 1658 or in Stockholm in 1659, aged eighty. He was buried in Uppsala Cathedral. A. N. L. GROSJEAN

**Sources** *Fasti Scot.*, 2/1 • *Fasti Scot.*, new edn, 3.162; 7.530; 8.242 • J. Lodge, *The peerage of Ireland*, rev. M. Archdall, rev. edn, 7 vols. (1789) • G. Hamilton, *The history of the house of Hamilton* (1933) • J. Maidment, ed., *Letters and state papers during the reign of King James the Sixth*, Abbotsford Club, 13 (1838) • S. Murdoch, 'Northern exposure: Irishmen and Scandinavia in the seventeenth century', *History Ireland*, 6/3 (1998), 5–6 • A. Grosjean, 'Scots and the Swedish state: diplomacy, military service and ennoblement, 1611–1660', PhD diss., U. Aberdeen, 1998 • John Durie to Samuel Hartlib, 3 December 1643, University of Sheffield, Hartlib papers, 3/1/16A–16B • J. A. Worp, *De Briefwisseling van Constantijn Huygens*, pt 3: *1640–44* (The Hague, 1914) • *DNB* • E. B. Fryde and others, eds., *Handbook of British chronology*, 3rd edn, Royal Historical Society Guides and Handbooks, 2 (1986) • private information (2004) [A. Murray] • F. Werner and J. H. Schröder, *Upsala Domkyrka med dess märkvärdigheter* (Stockholm, 1826), 20

**Archives** Riksarkivet, Stockholm, Pergaments breven och Johan Casimirs arkiv; Stegeborgssamlingen – letter of Archbishop Hamilton, dated Norrköpping September 1648 • Riksarkivet, Stockholm, Carl Gustafs arkiv; Stegeborgssamlingen – undated letter of Archbishop Hamilton • Riksarkivet, Stockholm, Ericsbergsarkivet, autografsamlingen, vol. 269, letter of Archbishop Hamilton to Gabriel de la Gardie • Riksarkivet, Stockholm, Axel Okenstiernas brefvexling, E619

**Wealth at death** left goods and property valued at £9000 in Ireland in 1641: *DNB*

**Hamilton, Archibald** (1719–1793), printer and publisher, was born in Edinburgh. He went to London in 1736 following the Porteous riots, 'in which he was in some degree implicated', according to John Nichols (Nichols, *Lit. anecdotes*, 3.398). Nothing is known of his parents or wife, but he had two children, Archibald and Sarah. He was made free of the Stationers' Company by redemption on 6 June 1749. His address at that time was New Street, Shoe Lane, in the parish of St Bride. By 1752 he was employed as principal manager at William Strahan's printing office in New Street, Fetter Lane.

Hamilton set up in business for himself, probably early in 1756. In a letter of 11 September 1756, Strahan recalled the conditions of Hamilton's employment as his manager:

> He had saved about £300 in my Service; for I gave him 30 Shillings a Week, and allowed him to keep allways three or four Apprentices; so that one way or other his Place was worth above £200 a Year, which most people think he was a fool to quitt. (W. Strahan to D. Hall, 11 Sept 1756, David Hall MSS)

Hamilton was less a fool than expected, for he soon became a prominent printer in his own right.

The occasion for Hamilton's departure was a quarrel between Strahan and the bookseller James Rivington; Strahan broke with Rivington and refused to finish printing for him the lucrative first edition of Tobias Smollett's *Complete History of England*. Strahan commented that 'when Mr. Hamilton saw [this], he thought it a good Opportunity to begin for himself, as he found Rivington was willing to give it him' (W. Strahan to D. Hall, 11 Sept 1756, David Hall MSS). Hamilton set up his printing house in Chancery Lane; press figures reveal that by 1760 he had at least eight presses, and between 1749 and 1789 he bound twenty-four apprentices, one of whom was his son, Archibald, freed on 8 June 1762. By 1763 he had moved his printing office to 4 Falcon Court, Fleet Street, where the business remained until 1794. Around 1766 his son set up business in James Bettenham's former printing office, which was near St John's Gate.

Although never a reviewer himself, the elder Hamilton was both a projector, with his friend the novelist Tobias Smollett, and printer of the *Critical Review*, which was first published on 1 March 1756. In 1758 he became its publisher, and in 1763 he took over chief proprietorship and managing editorship from Smollett, a position he held until about 1791. Besides his work with the *Critical Review*, Hamilton printed Smollett's *British Magazine, or, Monthly Repository for Gentlemen and Ladies*, begun in January 1760. In 1769 Smollett named Hamilton as an executor of his will.

By 1770 Hamilton was a leading periodical printer and publisher. In 1774 father and son each possessed a one-sixth share in the *Lady's Magazine* and the *Town and Country Magazine*, the latter being published by the younger Hamilton. He died on 6 October 1792, predeceasing his father by a few months and leaving several children: two sons, Archibald and Samuel, were printers who inherited both their father's and grandfather's businesses.

A physical description of Hamilton is preserved in Cuthbert Shaw's satirical poem *The Race* (1766):

> Foremost, the spite of hell upon his face,
> Stood the Thersites of the Critic Race,
> Tremendous Hamilton! of giant strength,
> With Crab-tree staff full twice two yards in length.
> (Knapp, 331)

He was apparently a convivial man. Samuel Foote's contemptuous pun on his intellectual attainments—'I grant you he reads a great many proofs but they are no great proofs of his reading' (Whitridge, 29n.)—is countered by John Nichols's reminiscence of George Steevens's regularly calling at 'the literary conversational lounge at Archibald Hamilton's' (Nichols, *Illustrations*, 5.428). Hamilton's daughter, Sarah, remembered meeting Smollett, Oliver Goldsmith, Samuel Johnson, and David Garrick in her father's house.

In his later years, Hamilton was a partner with William Jackson in the Oxford University Press. He died on 9 March 1793 at his London residence in Bedford Row; he also owned a villa at Ash in Hampshire, near Farnham. His will was proved on 17 April 1793. Hamilton's obituary in the *Gentleman's Magazine* praised him 'as a valuable contributor to the literary interests of his time, and as a man whose social qualities, well-informed mind, and communicative disposition, had endeared him to a numerous circle of friends'. BARBARA LANING FITZPATRICK

**Sources** Nichols, *Lit. anecdotes*, vol. 3 • W. Strahan to D. [Hall], 11 Sept 1756, American Philosophical Society, Philadelphia, David Hall MSS • L. M. Knapp, 'Appendix D', *Tobias Smollett: doctor of men and manners* (1949) • D. F. McKenzie, ed., *Stationers' Company apprentices*, [3]: 1701–1800 (1978) • I. Maxted, *The London book trades, 1775–1800: a preliminary checklist of members* (1977) • *GM*, 1st ser., 63 (1793), 285 • J. G. Basker, *Tobias Smollett: critic and journalist* (1988) • D. Roper, *Reviewing before the 'Edinburgh', 1788–1802* (1978) • H. R. Plomer and others, *A dictionary of the printers and booksellers who were at work in England, Scotland, and Ireland from 1726 to 1775* (1932) • records, Stationers' Company, entry book of copies, 1774–86 • Nichols, *Illustrations*, vol. 5 • A. Whitridge, *Tobias Smollett: a study of his miscellaneous works* (Brooklyn, NY, 1925) • *British Magazine, or, Monthly Repository for Gentlemen and Ladies*, 1 (1760) • *Critical Review*, 1 (1756)

**Wealth at death** not poor: will, PRO, PROB 11/1231, sig. 205

**Hamilton, Lord Archibald** (1770–1827), politician, born on 6 March 1770, was the second son of Archibald, ninth duke of Hamilton and sixth duke of Brandon (1740–1819), and his wife, Lady Harriet Stewart (*d*. 1788), fifth daughter of the sixth earl of Galloway. He was the brother of Alexander Douglas-*Hamilton, tenth duke of Hamilton, and of Lady Anne *Hamilton. He was educated at Eton College (from 1785) and at Christ Church, Oxford, where he matriculated on 23 April 1788 and graduated BA in 1792 and MA in 1795. On 14 October 1790 he was admitted a student of Lincoln's Inn, and was called to the bar in Hilary term 1799. He was very deaf, a marked handicap for a barrister, and soon tried to leave the northern circuit on which he briefly practised; on 7 November 1808 he took his name off the books of Lincoln's Inn. At the general election in 1802 he was returned unopposed for Lanarkshire, and continued to sit for that constituency until his death.

Hamilton quickly became an active supporter of the Foxite opposition, and took a frequent part in the debates, speaking on a wide range of subjects. He had a grandee whig's contempt for both Pitt and Addington. He was a strong advocate of political reform and a determined opponent of every kind of injustice and abuse. In 1804 he published *Thoughts on the Formation of the Late and Present Administrations*, in which he contended that Addington's and Pitt's second administration was formed 'upon principles fundamentally opposite to the spirit of the constitution and subversive of its dearest interests'. Fox thought the pamphlet 'excellent'. Hamilton was active in the impeachment of Lord Melville in 1805, drawing up the terms of condemnation. But when his whig friends were back in office, 1806–7, he proved an awkward supporter, declining office himself and objecting to many of the government's actions. On 25 April 1809 he brought forward his resolution of censure upon Lord Castlereagh for corrupt disposal of his patronage as president of the Board of Control. The resolution was lost by a majority of forty-nine. He remained active in the Commons, telling for the whigs and supporting, somewhat spasmodically, Catholic emancipation and parliamentary reform. On 7 May 1819 his motion for referring the petitions from the royal burghs of Scotland to a select committee was carried against the government by 149 to 144. When, however, in February 1822, after enumerating the abuses which the reports of the three committees of 1819, 1820, and 1821 had disclosed, he moved that the house should in committee consider the state of the royal burghs, he was defeated. Like his sister, Lady Anne, he was a strong supporter of Queen Caroline. Hamilton spoke for the last time in the house on 5 December 1826, when he called attention to the great distress which was then prevailing among the Lanarkshire weavers (he had taken a considerable interest in Robert Owen's community at New Lanark).

Hamilton never married. An early liaison with his cousin Lady Augusta Murray produced a son, and he then had a liaison with Lady Oxford. In 1810 the duke of Queensberry deprived him of a promised legacy of £10,000, but his sister, Lady Anne, compensated him to the same amount. He died on 28 August 1827, in the Upper Mall, Hammersmith, Middlesex, and was buried in the mausoleum at Hamilton Palace, Lanarkshire, in Scotland.

Hamilton was one of those Holland House whigs who did not seek office and who declined it when offered, and whose political philosophy combined radicalism and aristocracy. His chief theme was the corruption of the constitution by royal patronage, and he was one of the last of the whigs to rest a political career on that eighteenth-century critique. G. F. R. Barker, *rev.* H. C. G. Matthew

**Sources** HoP, *Commons* • *GM*, 1st ser., 97/2 (1827), 462

**Archives** priv. coll. | BL, corresp. with Lord and Lady Holland, Add. MS 51570 • Bodl. Oxf., Beckford MSS • NA Scot., Stewart-Mackenzie MSS

**Likenesses** T. Gainsborough, oils, 1786, Waddesdon Manor, Buckinghamshire

**Hamilton, Charles, styled count of Arran (1691–1754)**, collector of manuscripts, was born on 30 March 1691 at Cleveland House, Westminster, the illegitimate son of Lady Barbara Fitzroy (1672–1737) and James *Hamilton, then earl of Arran but later fourth duke of Hamilton and first duke of Brandon (1658–1712). His mother was the youngest illegitimate daughter of Barbara *Palmer (*née* Villiers), duchess of Cleveland, and reputedly Charles II, though her father may have been John Churchill, first duke of Marlborough. At the time of Hamilton's birth Arran was imprisoned in the Tower of London. Queen Mary and Arran's father, William Douglas, third duke of Hamilton, were so incensed on discovering the affair that they made it a condition of Arran's release that Lady Barbara should retire abroad. She duly entered the nunnery of the Hôtel Dieu at Pontoise later that year, taking the name Sister Benedicta; she became prioress and died there on 6 May 1737.

Hamilton was brought up at Chiswick by his maternal grandmother, the duchess of Cleveland. Following his father's marriage in 1698 to his second wife, Elizabeth Gerard, Hamilton was sent to the exiled Jacobite court at St Germain in France. Styled the count of Arran, he was put under the care of Charles Middleton, the earl of Middleton, then secretary to James II. He has been confused with Colonel John Hamilton (*d.* 1716), his father's second in his fatal duel with Charles Mohun, fourth Lord Mohun, in November 1712. Charles Hamilton was not present but when Mohun's second, General George Maccartney, was suspected of giving the duke the *coup de grâce* and fled to Antwerp, Hamilton sent him a challenge, which was declined.

Hamilton finally settled in Switzerland where he occupied himself with classical studies and the pursuit of alchemy. In 1737 he married Antoinette Courtney of Archambaud; their only son, Charles (1738–1800), was born in Edinburgh on 16 July 1738. Hamilton died in Paris on 13 August 1754 and was buried in Montmartre. While in France he had collected some historical materials, principally Middleton's correspondence, which he bequeathed to his son, who published them as *Transactions during the Reign of Queen Anne, from the Union to the Death of that Princess* (1790). This overtly tory account portrays Anne as a timid, hesitant monarch easily swayed by the machinations of Bolingbroke and Marlborough; Marlborough is explicitly accused of arranging the duke of Hamilton's assassination. Hamilton's son also published *The Patriot* (1784), a translation of Metastasio's tragedy, and has been confused with the orientalist Charles Hamilton (1752–1792).

Francis Watt, *rev.* R. D. E. Eagles

**Sources** C. Hamilton, *Transactions during the reign of Queen Anne* (1790), preface • GEC, *Peerage* • R. K. Marshall, *The days of Duchess Anne* (1973) • D. Defoe, *A strict enquiry into the circumstance of a late duel* (1713) • *The lives and characters of James duke of Hamilton and Charles, Lord Mohun; who were unfortunately kill'd by each other in Hyde Park* (1712) • R. K. Marshall, 'The house of Hamilton in its Anglo-Scottish setting in the seventeenth century', PhD diss., U. Edin., 1970 [incl. a 5-vol. calendar of the duke of Hamilton's archives] • J. Anderson,

*Historical and genealogical memoirs of the house of Hamilton* (1825) • W. Anderson, *The Scottish nation* (1890)
**Archives** Lennoxlove, East Lothian, papers

**Hamilton, Charles, Lord Binning** (1697–1732), landowner, was the elder son of Thomas *Hamilton, sixth earl of Haddington (1680–1735), and his wife and cousin, Helen Hope (1677–1768), only daughter of John Hope of Hopetoun (1650–1682). Few details of Charles's early life survive, but his father, an enthusiastic planter, noted that the boy was designing walks in Binning Wood when he was only ten. During the Jacobite rising of 1715 father and son fought together on the Hanoverian side, and Charles's bravery at the battle of Sheriffmuir drew much praise. Three years later, he was made knight marshal of Scotland, with an annual pension of £400 sterling.

Much valued by his friends for his gentleness and wit, Charles liked to amuse them with humorous poems. About 1720 he married Rachel (1696–1773), younger daughter of the redoubtable Lady Grisell *Baillie and her husband, George Baillie. He and Rachel had five sons and three daughters. In 1722 he was elected MP for St Germains, Cornwall, and he subsequently became a commissioner for trade, but in 1731 he fell seriously ill with tuberculosis and was advised to go to Italy for the sake of his health. As well as taking his wife with him, he insisted that her mother go too. Lady Grisell nursed him devotedly, but he died in Naples on 27 December 1732, leaving everything to Rachel, whom he made his executor. His friend the poet William Hamilton of Bangour wrote a fine elegy on his death, praising him as 'knowing, humble, friendly, great, humane'. ROSALIND K. MARSHALL

**Sources** W. Fraser, *Memorials of the earls of Haddington*, 2 vols. (1889), vol. 1, pp. 264–70 • Edinburgh register of testaments, testament of Charles, Lord Binning, registered 11/6/1734, NA Scot., CC8/8/96 • *Scots peerage*, vol. 4 • *A catalogue of the royal and noble authors of England, Scotland and Ireland … by the late Horatio Walpole*, ed. T. Park, 5 vols. (1806) • R. Douglas, *The peerage of Scotland*, 2nd edn, ed. J. P. Wood, 2 vols. (1813) • Anderson, *Scot. nat.* • J. Ritson, *Scottish songs*, ed. J. Alexander, 2nd edn (1869)
**Likenesses** I. Gerimia, stipple, pubd 1806, NPG • W. Aikman, oils, priv. coll. • attrib. W. Aikman, oils, priv. coll. • B. Arlaud, miniature, priv. coll. • A. Belucci, oils, priv. coll. • J. de Medina, oils (as a baby), priv. coll. • W. Prewett, miniature (after A. Belucci), priv. coll. • J. Richardson, oils, priv. coll. • bust (after death mask?), priv. coll. • portrait, engraving, Scot. NPG • stipple, BM, NPG; repro. in *A catalogue of royal and noble authors of England, Scotland and Ireland* • watercolour, Scot. NPG

**Hamilton, Charles** (*bap.* **1704**, *d.* **1786**), landscape gardener, was baptized on 13 November 1704 in Dublin, the fourteenth child and youngest of the nine sons of James *Hamilton, sixth earl of Abercorn (*c.*1661–1734), and his wife, Elizabeth (1667/8–1754), daughter of Sir Robert Reading, first baronet, of Dublin. He was educated at Westminster School and Christ Church, Oxford (BA, 1723), where he formed a lifelong friendship with Henry Fox (later first Baron Holland), to whose social, financial, and vocational backing his career owed much. Next, making the grand tour to Rome, he became inspired by the landscape paintings of Claude Lorrain, Nicolas Poussin, and Salvator Rosa. In 1727 he became MP for Strabane in the Irish parliament.

In 1732, on a second visit to Rome with Henry and Stephen Fox, Hamilton's portrait was painted by Antonio David (*c.*1680–*c.*1738). The portrait shows him fashionably dressed, holding a gun, with an attendant, dogs, and a brace of partridges—he was highly rated as a shot. In Rome he acquired antique sculpture, including busts of Roman emperors and a 7 feet tall *Bacchus*, later to adorn his property at Painshill.

In 1734 Hamilton's father died, and, needing an income, in 1738 he gained a position in the household of Frederick, prince of Wales, through the influence of his sister Lady Archibald Hamilton, the prince's mistress. He was MP for Truro (1741–7) and receiver-general in Minorca (1743–57). He was dismissed by the prince of Wales in 1747, and the loss of Minorca in 1756 cost him his receivership. Henry Fox secured a secret service pension for him of £1200 a year as compensation.

By 1737 Hamilton had begun to acquire over 200 acres of what was regarded as desolate heathland sloping down to the River Mole, near Cobham in Surrey, which he turned into the ornamental Painshill Park. He used his varied talents as a soil improver, a collector and grower of newly available exotic trees and shrubs, and an impresario of entertaining devices—ranging from a water wheel pump to a grotto, a hermitage, and rare sculptures and follies, ingeniously placed—to create a series of agreeable surprises on a tour revealing successive aspects of nature presented in terms of art. He created a 30 acre lake and planted two vineyards.

Hamilton was recognized by his contemporaries as having contributed decisively to the emergence of the new naturalistic style of English landscape, and his guidance was sought by his friends for such outstanding creations as Stourhead, Bowood, Hagley, and Holland Park. It was a time when converging philosophical, political, scientific, and economic influences inspired a number of English landowners to transform their estates into prosperous miniature centres for civilized living. To fulfil the process, however, they needed to integrate nature with inspired landscape design in terms consistent with practical land management, silviculture, and land forms which could be changed only within strict limits. By his talents, dedication, social connections, and ability to get quick and exciting results within narrow constraints of money and manpower, Hamilton devised the right model at the right moment. However, in 1773 he was forced to sell Painshill in order to repay a loan from Henry Fox.

Hamilton was married three times. Nothing is known of his first wife, whom he married *c.*1730, but they had two daughters. In 1772 he married Agnes, daughter of Dr David Cockburn of Ayr, and they had one daughter. After Agnes's death later that same year Hamilton moved to Bath, then in its social heyday, where a benign-looking portrait shows him at seventy, grasping a book entitled *Views of Painshill*. In 1774 he married Frances Calvert. Hamilton died on 11 September 1786 in Bath and was buried at Bath Abbey.

Neglect, culminating in damage and destruction, almost destroyed Painshill, until Elmbridge borough council acquired most of it for the Painshill Park Trust, which revived Hamilton's original designs through a vigorous programme of renewal. MAX NICHOLSON, *rev.*

**Sources** M. Hadfield, *A history of British gardening*, rev. edn (1969) · HoP, *Commons, 1715–54*, vol. 2 · B. Kitz and N. Kitz, *Pains Hill Park: Hamilton and his picturesque landscape* (privately printed, Cobham, 1984) · Baronscourt archives, Tyrone, Charles Hamilton papers · J. Ingamells, ed., *A dictionary of British and Irish travellers in Italy, 1701–1800* (1997) · GEC, *Peerage*

**Archives** Baronscourt archives, Tyrone

**Likenesses** A. David, oils, 1732

**Hamilton, Charles** (1752/3–1792), orientalist, was born in Belfast, the only son of Charles Hamilton (*d.* 1759), a merchant from an established but impoverished Scottish family, and Katherine, *née* Mackay (*d.* 1767), of Dublin. His sister was the writer on education Elizabeth *Hamilton (1756?–1816), with whom Charles enjoyed a close relationship. Hamilton worked for two years in the office of a Dublin merchant before he obtained a cadetship on the East India Company's establishment at Bengal and moved to India in 1776. He gained his first commission on 24 October of that year, and was promoted lieutenant on 10 July 1778.

A student of oriental languages, Hamilton was one of the first members of the Asiatic Society of Bengal. During an expedition against the Rohillas of Afghanistan he obtained a collection of Persian manuscripts from which he wrote his *Historical relation of the origin, progress, and final dissolution of the government of the Rohilla Afgans in the northern provinces of Hindostan* (1787). In the year before its publication Hamilton gained permission to return home for five years in order to translate from the Persian the *Hedaya* (published in 1791 as *Hedaya, or, Guide*), a commentary on Muslim laws, for which task he had been selected by the governor-general and council of Bengal.

Hamilton was subsequently appointed resident at the court of the grand vizier of Oudh. He was preparing to leave England when he was taken ill with consumption and died, aged thirty-nine, at Hampstead on 14 March 1792. He was buried at Bunhill Fields, and a monument was erected in Belfast by his sisters. Elizabeth Hamilton, who had been living with her brother since 1790, drew on correspondence from when Charles was in India for her first novel, *Letters of a Hindoo Rajah* (1796). A second edition of Charles Hamilton's *Hedaya* with a preface by Standish Grove Grady appeared in 1870.

GORDON GOODWIN, *rev.* PHILIP CARTER

**Sources** *Memoirs of the late Mrs. Elizabeth Hamilton*, ed. Miss Benger [E. O. Benger], 2 vols. (1818), vol. 1 · J. Thaddeus, 'Hamilton, Elizabeth', *A dictionary of British and American women writers, 1660–1800*, ed. J. Todd (1984)

**Hamilton, Sir Charles, second baronet** (1767–1849), naval officer, born on 6 July 1767, was the eldest son of Captain Sir John Hamilton RN, first baronet (1726–1784) of Trebinshwn, Brecknockshire, and his wife, Cassandra Agnes (*d.* 26 October 1826), third daughter of Edward Chamberlayne of Maugersbury, Gloucestershire; they had two sons, Charles and Edward *Hamilton. John was a grandson of Sir William Hamilton of Chelston, brother of James Hamilton, sixth earl of Abercorn, and was created baronet in 1776 for his gallant conduct during the siege of Quebec in 1775. In 1776 Charles was entered on the books of the *Hector*, then commanded by his father, and in 1777 entered the Royal Naval Academy at Portsmouth, from which in 1779 he was again appointed to the *Hector* and in her went out to the Jamaica station. He was made lieutenant in the sloop *Tobago* on 20 October 1781. On the death of his father on 24 January 1784 he succeeded to the baronetcy. In 1789 he was promoted commander of the sloop *Scorpion* and was advanced to post rank on 22 November 1790.

Early in 1793 Hamilton was appointed to the frigate *Dido* (28 guns), which, after a summer in the North Sea and on the coast of Norway, was sent to the Mediterranean, where, in the spring of the following year, he served at the sieges of Bastia, Calvi, and San Fiorenzo, and in the capture of a martello tower at Girolata. In July he was moved into the *San Fiorenzo* (36 guns), one of the captured frigates, and shortly after into the *Romney* (50 guns), in which he returned to England. He then commissioned the *Melpomène* (38 guns), which he commanded for upwards of seven years; he served in the operations on the coast of the Netherlands in 1799; as senior officer on the coast of Africa, and at the capture of Goree (Senegal) in 1800, when he dressed the crews of the merchantmen under his charge in red shirts, to bluff the enemy into thinking that they were troop transports; and in the West Indies, where he also carried out the duties of commissioner at Antigua until July 1802. He was MP for Dungannon in 1801–2, returned (as a stopgap) by the first Viscount Northland, and again from 1803 to 1806, when he supported the government; and for the venal borough of Honiton from 1807 to 1812, when he also largely supported the government. While an MP he was still serving actively afloat.

On 19 April 1803 Hamilton married Henrietta Martha (*d.* 10 March 1857), only daughter of George Drummond, banker, of Charing Cross, London, and Stanmore, Middlesex, a cousin of Viscount Strathallan. They had one son, Charles John James Hamilton.

In November 1803 the elder Hamilton was appointed to the *Illustrious* (74 guns) in the Channel Fleet, and afterwards to the *Téméraire* (98 guns) and *Tonnant* (80 guns). On 1 August 1810 he was promoted rear-admiral, and hoisted his flag on board the frigate *Thisbe*, as commander-in-chief in the Thames, a post which he held until his promotion to vice-admiral on 4 June 1814. From 1818 to 1824 he was governor and commander-in-chief at Newfoundland, attained admiral on 22 July 1830, and was made a KCB on 29 January 1833. He died at his residence, Iping, near Midhurst, Sussex, on 14 September 1849, and was succeeded to the baronetcy by his son.

J. K. LAUGHTON, *rev.* ROGER MORRISS

**Sources** J. Marshall, *Royal naval biography*, 1/1 (1823), 411–20 · O'Byrne, *Naval biog. dict.* · *GM*, 1st ser., 54 (1784), 150 · *GM*, 2nd ser., 33 (1850), 315 · D. R. Fisher, 'Hamilton, Sir Charles, 2nd bt (1767–1849)', HoP, *Commons* · Burke, *Peerage* (1959) · A. B. Rodger, *The war of the second coalition: 1798–1801, a strategic commentary* (1964) · R. Muir, *Britain and the defeat of Napoleon, 1807–1815* (1996)

**Archives** Bodl. Oxf., corresp. with Joseph Foster Barnham

**Likenesses** W. Beechey, oils, c.1800, NMM

**Hamilton, Charles Harold St John** [*pseud.* Frank Richards] (**1876–1961**), children's author, was born on 8 August 1876 at 15 Oak Street, Ealing, London, the sixth in a family of five brothers and three sisters. His birth certificate states that his father, John Hamilton (1838–1884), who married Mary Ann Hannah Trinder (1847–1912), was a carpenter. In fact, John Hamilton was a journalist, and sometime bookseller and stationer, of unstable temperament who enjoyed confusing officialdom. A heavy drinker, he died from tuberculosis when Charles was seven, after which the family moved house frequently. Hamilton attended various church and private day schools in the west London area and acquired a good knowledge of Latin and French, along with an enduring passion for the classics.

By his own account Hamilton received his first cheque for a short adventure story at the age of seventeen from Dowling Maitland, a literary agent who cut later payments from 5 guineas to £4 on finding that his contributor was a stripling. Hamilton then concentrated his efforts on boys' papers, notably those of Trapps, Holmes & Co. and Pearsons, and never had difficulty in getting his work accepted. In 1907 the Amalgamated Press started a boys' paper, *The Gem*, following it in 1908 with *The Magnet*, and Hamilton turned out 'long, complete' school stories for these weeklies for more than thirty years. He still found time to write elsewhere, under almost thirty pseudonyms, and maintained an annual output of one and a half million words. Once, when pressed, he wrote 18,000 words in a day. In *The Gem*, as Martin Clifford, he wrote about a school called St Jim's, which had originally appeared in *Pluck*, featuring Tom Merry and his friends, known as the Terrible Three of the Shell. Hamilton's favourite came to be *The Magnet* in which, as Frank Richards, he wrote about Greyfriars School and its Famous Five of the Remove, who included Harry Wharton, Frank Nugent (a self-portrait), and the 'dusky nabob' Hurree Jamset Ram Singh who, progressively for 1908, was on equal terms with his British schoolmates. The most famous Greyfriars character, however, was Billy Bunter, the Fat Owl, the boastful, snobbish, obtuse, prevaricating tuck-hunter forever waiting for a postal order which never came. Bunter became a legend in the lifetime of his creator, who liked to recall that an editor to whom he had outlined the character as early as in 1899 had failed to 'see much' in him. As well as writing school stories, from 1908 to 1940 Hamilton wrote pseudonymous tales for a wide range of boys' weeklies on detective and adventure themes. Until the First World War he spent a lot of time travelling on the continent, settling in Kent in 1914, first at Hawkinge, and then at Kingsgate-on-Sea.

Paper shortages of the Second World War put an end to *The Gem* in 1939 and *The Magnet* in 1940. Their circulation had been ailing under strong competition from the D. C. Thomson boys' papers. For Hamilton this was a hard blow. Although he had earned upwards of £2500 a year, a substantial income for those days, he had spent freely and

**Charles Harold St John Hamilton (1876–1961)**, by unknown photographer

helped to sustain the casinos of Europe. However, in the mid-1940s his talents were again in demand and Billy Bunter began to appear between hard covers. Thirty-nine Bunter titles were published, first by Charles Skilton and later by Cassell. From 1952 Hamilton wrote Greyfriars scripts for television, Bunter's role being played by Gerald Campion. Bunter Christmas shows were also staged regularly in London.

Hamilton's autobiography, published in 1952, was written in the third person, as by Frank Richards, under which name his evasive entry appeared in *Who's Who*. His eyesight had deteriorated but he continued to write with the aid of a heavily inked purple typewriter ribbon. Always diffident, he became reclusive, receiving only rare visitors at his Kingsgate home, and generally dressed in black skull-cap, dressing-gown, and with trousers cycle-clipped against the cold.

George Orwell criticized Hamilton's school stories on the grounds that they were escapist, nurtured snobbishness, and represented foreigners as funny. The mentality, Orwell complained, was that of 'a rather exceptionally stupid member of the Navy League in the year 1910' (Orwell, *Horizon*, March 1940). He conceded, however, that Bunter was a 'first-rate' character. Replying, Hamilton maintained (*Horizon*, May 1940) that the aristocratic virtues were worth preserving and that foreigners *were* funny. He made no apology for excluding sex from his stories which, after all, were designed for children. At all times he was alert to defend his work from condescension and misrepresentation. He was aware that many parents would have preferred their children to read 'quality' magazines such as the *Boy's Own Paper*, but he was proud of giving harmless pleasure to several generations of children. His never-ageing characters were compounds of iconoclasm and responsible manliness; even the bounders had redeeming streaks. Hamilton was little influenced by earlier writers on school life, avoiding the ferocities of the Jack Harkaway stories and the *Angst* of *Eric, or, Little by Little*. A suggestion by Orwell which rankled was that, since not all the stories under his pen-names could have been written by one man, they had been couched in a style easily copied, with standardized ejaculations like 'Yarooh'. Hamilton always resented the use of 'his' pseudonyms by stand-in writers, and in fact few of these substitutes could emulate his richly allusive style. However, he rarely failed to bring his characters to vigorous life. Hamilton was the equal of P. G. Wodehouse in giving a high-flown or hackneyed simile a comic flavour. What was savoured uncritically by the child could later be applauded by the adult for its technical accomplishment and flexibility of mood. He appears to have created at least thirty schools. As Owen Conquest he founded Rookwood with Jimmy Silver & Co. in the *Boys' Friend*; he launched Bessie Bunter of Cliff House School in the 1919 *Magnet* and, as Hilda Richards, contributed the first six stories of her to *The School Friend* in the same year; and as Ralph Redway he wrote many Wild West tales. Under his *Gem* name of Martin Clifford he penned a fanciful account of Frank Richards's schooldays at a backwoods school in Canada. His editors joined in the game of laying false trails. Many of his contemporaries who wrote for the juvenile market were astonishingly prolific, but it is unlikely that anyone exceeded Hamilton's lifetime output, which has been put at the equivalent of nearly a thousand full-length novels.

Hamilton, who never married, died in his sleep from a cerebral haemorrhage at his home, Rose Lawn, 131 Percy Avenue, Kingsgate-on-Sea, Kent, on Christmas eve 1961, and was cremated in January 1962 at Charing crematorium, Kent. E. S. TURNER, *rev.* MARY CADOGAN

**Sources** F. Richards [C. Hamilton], *The autobiography of Frank Richards* (1952) • W. O. G. Lofts and D. J. Adley, *The world of Frank Richards* (1975) • M. Cadogan, *Frank Richards: the chap behind the chums* (1988) • B. Doyle, *Who's who of boys' writers and illustrators* (1964) • J. Wernham and M. Cadogan, *The Greyfriars characters* (privately printed, Maidstone, 1976), vol. 2 of *The Charles Hamilton companion* (1972–90) • J. Wernham and M. Cadogan, *Collectors' digest: the first fifty years* (1996), vol. 8 of J. Wernham and M. Cadogan, *The Charles Hamilton companion* (1996) [privately printed, Maidstone] • E. S. Turner, *Boys will be boys* (1948) • private information (2004) • *CGPLA Eng. & Wales* (1962)

**Archives** Charles Hamilton Museum, Maidstone, Kent • priv. coll.

**Likenesses** photographs, Charles Hamilton Museum, Maidstone, Kent [*see illus.*] • photographs, priv. coll.

**Wealth at death** £11,462 12*s.* 9*d.*: probate, 15 June 1962, *CGPLA Eng. & Wales*

**Hamilton** [*née* Hammill], **(Mary) Cicely** (1872–1952), writer and campaigner for women's rights, was born on 15 June 1872 at 15 Sussex Gardens, Paddington, London, the eldest of four children of an Irish mother, Maude Mary, *née* Piers, and an Anglo-Scottish father, Denzil Hammill. Cicely Hammill was educated privately at St Leonard's boarding-school in Malvern and at Bad Homburg, a small spa town in Germany. She worked as a student teacher in the midlands and then as an actress touring the country for some ten years, changing her name to Hamilton when she first went on the stage.

Hamilton joined the suffragettes of the Pankhursts' Women's Social and Political Union and wrote the words anonymously for the WSPU anthem, 'The March of the

**(Mary) Cicely Hamilton (1872–1952)**, by Lena Connell

Women'. She also worked for Charlotte Despard's Women's Freedom League and edited their paper, *The Vote*. Hamilton became a popular and effective public speaker for the women's suffrage campaign. The *Common Cause* of 13 April 1911 wrote that she 'dramatised for us the revolt of the idealistic woman against compulsory self-sacrifice. Her wit and her beauty and her beautiful dress all contributed to the impression that a woman is a thing of great value' (p. 5).

As well as suffrage, the great passion of Hamilton's early years was the theatre, where she experienced prejudice against women actors and playwrights at first hand. Her first stage play, *Diana of Dobson's* (1908), was produced at the Kingsway Theatre by one of London's first actress-managers, the suffragette Lena Ashwell. The heroine, Diana, is a shop assistant who wagers that a wealthy suitor who proposes to her is incapable of earning his own living for six months. In the same year Hamilton founded the Women Writers' Suffrage League with the writer Bessie Hatton, and the Actresses' Franchise League with the actress Elizabeth Robins. *How the Vote was Won* (1909), a one-act comedy, was co-authored with her close friend Christabel Marshall who wrote under the name of Christopher St John. The play is a modern version of *Lysistrata* set at the time of a women's general strike and ridicules the notion of coverture whereby English law assumed a woman to come under the protection of her nearest male relative. The drawing-room of Horace Cole, a clerk of modest means, is invaded by a series of distant, and hitherto economically self-sufficient, female relatives, each intent on persuading Horace to support her.

Hamilton's strongly-held convictions about women and economics were developed in her treatise *Marriage as a Trade* (1909), a robustly forthright, witty, and uncompromising outburst of indignation against the Edwardian family and the tyranny of marriage which women were often compelled to enter because it was the only trade for which they had received any training. In 1910 Hamilton was invited by the actress Edy Craig to write *A Pageant of Great Women*. The pageant, enthusiastically performed by women in London and in venues across the country, demonstrated the capacity to exercise leadership and featured fifty-two great women including Joan of Arc. Some parts were played by very well-known actresses including Ellen Terry. The other plays Hamilton published were *Jack and Jill and a Friend* (1911); *The Cutting Knot* (1911), which was turned into a novel as *A Matter of Money* (1916); a nativity play, *The Child in Flanders*, performed in 1917 and published later; *The Brave and the Fair* (1920); *The Old Adam*, also performed as *The Human Factor* (1926); and a play for children, *The Beggar Prince* (1936).

*Just to Get Married* (1911) was her first novel, and explored the duplicitous behaviour of women desperate to get married. The heroine Georgina Vicary who has consented to a marriage of convenience comes to admire her suitor and marries for love. *Just to Get Married* was turned into a play. During the First World War Hamilton served with the Scottish women's ambulance unit and as an administrator in a military hospital outside Paris and from 1917 to 1919 she was a member of a repertory company organized by her friend Lena Ashwell which provided wartime entertainment for the troops. *Senlis* (1916) is a tribute to a small town which had been treated with great brutality by the Germans. Hamilton's experiences of the war made her disillusioned with the idea that human progress was inevitable, and she came to dislike what she termed as 'the herd instinct' and became impatient with some of the more liberal ideals of her youth. *William: an Englishman* (1919) won the Femina Vie Heureuse prize. William, an idealistic socialist, and Griselda, an altruistic young suffragette, find themselves accidentally caught up in the outbreak of the First World War during their honeymoon in the Ardennes. When Griselda is brutally raped and murdered William comes to see his earlier beliefs as naïve in the extreme and is converted to wholehearted support of the war effort. *Theodore Savage* (1922) is a curious dystopian novel which is set at the end of civilization and again illustrates the human potential for destructive behaviour.

Hamilton's commitment to equality did not waver. In 1919 she became press officer for the International Suffrage Conference in Geneva. She supported herself as a journalist writing for newspapers including the *Yorkshire Post* and the *Manchester Guardian*, served on the editorial committee of *The Englishwoman*, and became a director of Lady Rhondda's feminist journal *Time and Tide*, through which she met Winifred Holtby. She also became a close friend of Lilian Baylis with whom she wrote a history of the Old Vic (1926). In the 1920s she was an early and active member of the Six Point Group which campaigned for the rights of children, widows, and unmarried mothers, equal guardianship, and equal pay in teaching and the civil service. She was also an impassioned advocate of birth control and a supporter of abortion law reform.

In 1931 Hamilton published *Full Stop*, an extraordinary novel which contained only one character and was concerned with the spiritual crisis of a politician who knows that he is nearing his death. Throughout the 1930s Hamilton travelled widely and published a series of commentaries on her impressions of Austria, France, Germany, Ireland, Italy, Russia, and Sweden, and nearer to home, England and Scotland. Her autobiography, *Life Errant* (1935), was critical of her belief in the perfectibility of human beings in her early career although not of her commitment to feminism or of her decision to remain a spinster. She was awarded a civil-list pension for services to literature in 1938. *Lament for Democracy* (1940), published at a moment when the Second World War fared badly for the allies, was pessimistic about the fragility of democracy when faced with the threat of totalitarianism. Hamilton worked as the editor of the press bulletin of the British League for European Freedom from 1945 to 1952. She died from heart failure, after a long illness, on 5 December 1952 at her home, 44 Glebe Place, Chelsea, London.

MAROULA JOANNOU

**Sources** C. Hamilton, *Life errant* (1935) • L. Whitelaw, *The life and rebellious times of Cicely Hamilton, actress, writer, suffragist* (1990) • J. Holledge, *Innocent flowers: women in the Edwardian theatre* (1981) • S. Stowell, *A stage of their own: feminist playwrights of the suffrage era* (1992) • V. Gardner and S. Rutherford, eds., *The new woman and her sisters: feminism and theatre, 1850–1914* (1992) • d. cert. • *CGPLA Eng. & Wales* (1953)

**Archives** NRA, priv. coll., corresp. and literary papers • Ransom HRC, letters | BL, corresp. with League of Dramatists, Add. MSS 63396 • Hull Central Library, Winifred Holtby collection

**Likenesses** E. Kapp, drawing, 1931, U. Birm. • L. Connell, photograph, NPG [*see illus.*] • T. Lowinsky, oils, Graves Art Gallery, Sheffield

**Wealth at death** £976 3*s.* 0*d.*: probate, 24 Jan 1953, *CGPLA Eng. & Wales*

**Hamilton, Claud** [*known as* Lord Claud Hamilton], **first Lord Paisley (1546?–1621)**, nobleman and conspirator, was born probably in 1546, the fifth and youngest son of James *Hamilton, second earl of Arran and first duke of Châtelherault (*d.* 1575), and his wife, Margaret, eldest daughter of James Douglas, third earl of Morton. He was made commendator of Paisley as a child when in 1553 his uncle James Hamilton resigned the position in order to become archbishop of St Andrews. In 1567 he received the very valuable temporalities of the abbey, which was to provide him with his principal residence, Paisley Place. Although never in holy orders he acquired as he grew up a number of other ecclesiastical benefices: dean of the college of Dunbar, canon of Glasgow, and prebendary of Cambuslang. The Hamiltons tended towards Catholicism, in the main, and Lord Claud was probably brought up in the old religion, but displayed no really strong support for it until later in his life. In March 1560, at the age of fourteen, he was sent to England as one of the hostages for the fulfilment of the treaty of Berwick. He was lodged in Newcastle until February 1562, when he was allowed to return home.

**The civil war in Scotland, 1568–1573** A significant thread running through Lord Claud's life was his loyalty to the cause of Mary, queen of Scots. The Hamiltons formed the core of Mary's support after the murder of Darnley in 1567, and Lord Claud played a leading part in the plot to secure Mary's escape from Lochleven in 1568. He met her with fifty horse after she had crossed the Firth of Forth and accompanied her first to Niddry Castle and then to Hamilton. At the battle of Langside (13 May 1568) which followed her escape, according to one account he led Mary's vanguard of 2000 men. Defeated at Langside, Mary fled into England to escape the regent, Moray, and Lord Claud accompanied her and stayed with her for a time at Carlisle.

Scotland slithered into civil war after Mary's flight, and the Hamiltons, partly out of self-interest but also out of loyalty to the queen, formed the main opposition to the 'king's men', or supporters of the infant James VI under a succession of pro-English regents. Lord Claud played a prominent part in the struggle. In 1568 the Hamiltons had been declared forfeit by parliament, and their lands, which included Hamilton Castle and also the abbey of Paisley, were given to Lord Sempill. On 24 October 1568 Lord Claud surprised and recovered Hamilton Castle, and he was among the conspirators who enabled James Hamilton of Bothwellhaugh to assassinate the regent Moray at Linlithgow on 23 January 1570. He took advantage of a truce early in 1571 to launch an attack on Paisley, and defeated Sempill's men there. The regent Lennox, however, forced the Hamilton garrison to return Paisley by cutting off their water supply. Lord Claud played an important part in the defence of Edinburgh Castle in the spring of 1571, but on 16 June he was defeated at Leith by the earl of Morton. On 3 September 1571 the Hamiltons seized Lennox in the 'surprise of Stirling'. Lord Claud led his men through the town with the cry 'Ane Hamilton, God and the Queen. Think on the bishop of St Andrews' (Metcalfe, *History of Paisley*, 148), a phrase referring to Claud's benefactor and uncle, who had recently been executed by the regent. In the ensuing skirmish Lennox was shot by his captors, and Captain Calder, who fired the shot, said he did so on the orders of Lord Claud. The latter and the other leading Hamiltons were denounced as traitors on 3 July 1572. However, under the pacification of Perth of 23 February 1573, which largely ended the war, Claud and many of his relatives were pardoned. He was able after some delay to oust Sempill from his lands in Paisley.

In this interval of peace Lord Claud married, on 1 August 1574, Margaret (*d.* 1616), only daughter of George Seton, sixth Lord Seton. They had nine children, three of whom died in infancy. Their eldest surviving son, James *Hamilton, was made earl of Abercorn in 1606, and is the ancestor of the dukes of Abercorn, who head the house of Hamilton. Lord Claud is also known to have had two illegitimate children.

**Banishment to England, 1579–1584** The Hamiltons had in effect lost the civil war in Scotland, although they were too powerful to be completely defeated. The pacification of Perth had been intended only as a temporary measure, to last until the infant James VI was of age. In 1579 the whole quarrel began again, largely because the regent Morton was fearful that if he did not act his position would be threatened. Taking advantage therefore of the technical majority of the king, Morton and the council on 30 April 1579 revived the old acts against the Hamiltons, their most prominent crimes being the assassination of two regents. Instructions were given for the immediate seizure of their lands. This took Lord Claud at Paisley and his brother Lord John *Hamilton at Hamilton Castle by surprise, but they were able to escape.

Lord Claud spent the next eight years attempting to recover his position in Scotland. He worked with his brother John in this endeavour, although as time went on the two seemed to disagree about strategy. Lord Claud was involved in negotiations at various times in these years of his banishment with Scotland, England, France, and Spain, and also with the exiled Queen Mary. Eventually he succeeded in recovering his influence in Scotland.

Following the declaration of outlawry in 1579, Lord Claud 'conveyed himself quietly to sic pairt as no man knows' (Moysie, 21), hiding at first in Scotland. He then crossed into England, where he was received by Sir John Forster, and travelled on to London to lobby Elizabeth and her ministers for support. He asked Elizabeth to mediate on behalf of the family with James and his advisers. This she did, immediately after Lord Claud's arrival in England, sending Nicholas Arrington to Scotland to plead his cause. Elizabeth's sympathy was motivated by the fact that the eldest Hamilton brother, James, was in effect heir-presumptive to the as yet childless James VI. Moreover the Hamiltons were important figures in Scotland, and despite Lord Claud's attachment to Queen Mary there were good reasons for Elizabeth to keep a foot in their camp. The English also wanted to see that Scotland remained as far as possible at peace. Elizabeth maintained her sympathetic support for Lord Claud for some considerable time, even in the face of evidence that he was negotiating with her enemies behind her back. For much of the time between 1579 and 1584 Lord Claud and his brother John were in England, staying largely at Widdrington in Northumberland.

While they waited in exile, the see-saw of Scottish politics rocked backwards and forwards, sometimes in favour of the Hamiltons and sometimes against. The rise to prominence of Esmé Stewart, duke of Lennox, and of Captain James Stewart at the court of James threatened the Hamiltons, since Esmé came from a great rival family, that of the Lennox Stewarts, and also because James Stewart was made earl of Arran, a title of the Hamiltons, nominally held by Lord Claud's eldest brother James *Hamilton, who had been declared insane. The Ruthven raid in

1582 benefited the Hamiltons since it dislodged Lennox and Arran, but by June 1583 James VI had escaped from the raiders and Arran was firmly ensconced as favourite. Elizabeth I and the Hamiltons had a common interest in opposing Arran, and in 1584 the queen encouraged Lord Claud and his brother to go to the Scottish borders to support the former Ruthven raiders in their counter-attack on James VI's new adviser. In April 1584 he was present at the capture of Stirling Castle. Things then went badly, however, and the earl of Gowrie, head of the anti-Arran conspiracy, was taken prisoner. As a result the Hamilton brothers retreated again into England, although this time for a brief stay. In November 1584, having been promised a safe conduct by the king, Lord Claud returned to Scotland, but was banished to the north on the advice of Arran. Here he stayed with the earl of Huntly, until on 6 April 1585 he was ordered to leave the country.

**Foreign conspiracies and the recovery of royal favour, 1585–1590** When exiled in 1585 Lord Claud went to France, and found a warm welcome from the French government, which saw him as a way of re-establishing influence in Scotland. While he was in Paris, news reached him that Arran had at last been overthrown and he was now recalled to Scotland by James VI. He left Paris much in debt, but with 500 crowns for his journey from the king of France, and he carried with him a letter to James VI from Henri III. When he arrived at James's court he had a successful interview with the young king. Moysie says that Lord Claud was 'a man well lykit of be the king for his wit, and obedience in coming and going at the king's command, and for reveling of certane interpryses of the lordis at thair being in Ingland' (Moysie, 56).

It is at this point in his life that Lord Claud is said to have fully accepted Catholicism, and he was seen at this stage by the English as attempting to revive the fortunes of the Catholic party in Scotland. He had been in contact with the strongly Catholic Guise family when he had been in Paris. He was also communicating, as best he could, with the imprisoned Queen Mary, and while in Paris he had also been in touch with Charles Paget, Mary's agent. In May 1586 Mary wrote to Paget urging him to instruct Lord Claud, now back in Scotland, to secure Scottish support for the Babington plot, which aimed to bring about a combined Spanish and Guisard invasion of England, an insurrection by English Catholics, and an attempt to release Mary from prison and depose Elizabeth. Mary also wanted him to organize a *coup d'état* in her favour in Scotland which would seize the king and install Lord Claud as regent. Paget was instructed by Mary to hint to Lord Claud that if James VI died childless she would name him as her heir.

Lord Claud also entered into correspondence with Spain in connection with these schemes. His intention presumably was to use the Armada campaign, which it was well known was being prepared, to strengthen the Catholic party in Scotland. On 15 May 1586 he sent Robert Bruce to Philip II with letters from himself and also from the earls of Huntly and Morton, urging the Spanish king to support a project for releasing the king of Scots from the captivity of the protestant faction and for establishing the Catholic religion in Scotland. These plans received a significant setback with the execution of Mary, queen of Scots, early in 1587. Lord Claud had urged James VI to press Elizabeth to spare the life of his imprisoned mother, but James took little interest in her cause. Despite these differences, he and the king remained on good terms and on 29 July 1587, as a mark of royal favour, he received the title of Lord Paisley when the abbey's lands were made into a temporal lordship. After Mary's execution Lord Claud pressed the case for a Spanish invasion even harder. There were also reports that he was plotting to have his brother assassinated, in order to establish his own claim to the throne. Even after the defeat of the Spanish Armada in 1588 he continued to correspond with the duke of Parma, and in February 1589 the Scottish government received copies of these letters, which had been intercepted by the English. He was placed in Edinburgh Castle, having voluntarily surrendered himself. He seems to have still been in prison early in 1590, but was released shortly afterwards, apparently because it was feared that he and his Catholic associates would use their imprisonment to seize control of the prison.

**Madness and death, 1590–1621** This imprisonment marks a turning point in Lord Claud's life, and after his release he retired into private life. The English ambassador, Bowes, reported that, like his eldest brother, the earl of Arran, he was suffering from some form of mental illness. On 28 November 1590 Bowes reported that Lord Claud had recovered his sanity, and in the following month that his name was linked with the recently discovered witches of North Berwick. On 16 December 1591, according to Bowes, Hamilton was 'beastly mad' again (*CSP Scot.*, 1589–93, 560). In 1598 he executed letters of factory and commission passing his public duties over to his son, the master of Paisley. Lord Claud lived in retirement for over twenty years, dying in 1621, and was buried in Paisley Abbey.

That Lord Claud had survived his eventful life at all, even if at the expense of his sanity, represents a considerable personal triumph. It was his pliability, courage, and wit which enabled him to do so. From another point of view, as a disenchanted English observer put it in 1586, he was 'ambitious, cruel and dissembling' (*CSP Scot.*, 1586–9, 168). With his death the era of Scottish over-mighty subjects was perhaps at an end, but at least the house of Hamilton had retained much of its wealth and prestige, although under Stewart royal government.

PETER HOLMES

**Sources** *DNB* · G. Hamilton, *A history of the house of Hamilton* (1933) · *CSP Scot.*, 1569–1603 · *CSP Scot. ser.*, 1509–1603 · *Lettres, instructions et mémoires de Marie Stuart, reine d'Écosse*, ed. A. Labanoff, 7 vols. (1852), vol. 5, p. 176; vol. 6, pp. 312 ff., 358 ff., 400 ff.; vol. 7, p. 184 · GEC, *Peerage*, new edn, 10.289–92 · *Scots peerage* · W. M. Metcalfe, *A history of Paisley* (1909), 147–53, 193–4 · W. M. Metcalfe, *The lordship of Paisley* (1912), ix–xiv, 76–87 · A. R. Howell, *Paisley Abbey* (1929), 28, 32, 74, 116, 135 · *The memoirs of Sir James Melville of Halhill*, ed. G. Donaldson (1969), 71, 76–7, 91–8 · C. Nau, *The history of Mary Stewart*, ed. J. Stevenson (1883) · *Calendar of the manuscripts of the most hon. the marquis of Salisbury*, 3, HMC, 9 (1889), 72–3, 92–3, 121, 127, 132, 135, 153–4, 173, 175, 194, 204, 244–5, 250, 307, 318, 352, 390 ·

D. Moysie, *Memoirs of the affairs of Scotland, 1577–1603*, ed. J. Dennistoun, Bannatyne Club, 39 (1830)
**Likenesses** E. Harding, stipple, BM, NPG; repro. in J. Adolphus, *The British cabinet*, 2 vols. (1799–1800)

**Hamilton, Cuthbert Francis** (1884–1958). *See under* Vorticists (*act.* 1914–1919).

**Hamilton, David, of Cadzow** (*d.* 1381x8). *See under* Hamilton family (*per.* 1295–1479).

**Hamilton, Sir David** (1663–1721), man-midwife and physician, was born in Lanarkshire, the tenth and youngest son of James Hamilton, laird of Boggs and Dalzell, and his third wife, Isobell. He matriculated at the University of Leiden on 30 October 1683, leaving there between 1685 and 1686 to graduate MD of the University of Rheims on 23 February 1686 with a dissertation 'De passione hysteria'. He was admitted a licentiate of the Royal College of Physicians in 1688 and soon established a flourishing practice, chiefly as an accoucheur. On 18 July 1689 he married Mary, daughter of Major Philip Starkie, but she died childless shortly afterwards on 21 December 1691. He remarried on 26 September 1694, but although this union to Elizabeth, daughter of Sir Thomas Lane, lord mayor of London, 1694–5, brought him two sons, it was unhappy from the start and the couple separated in 1713, with Hamilton publicly airing his allegations of her persistent infidelity.

Hamilton's career, by contrast with his private life, was conspicuously successful. In 1703 he was elected fellow of the Royal College of Physicians, appointed third physician-in-ordinary to Queen Anne, and knighted. He was subsequently appointed second physician to the queen (1712) but his medical titles did not convey how valuable he had become to the queen as confidant, go-between, and counsellor. His private practice continued to prosper, allowing him to accumulate substantial wealth, according to a rival some £80,000, which he allegedly lost in the South Sea Bubble. He was elected fellow of the Royal Society in April 1708.

Hamilton was appointed physician to Caroline, princess of Wales, in 1714, but his fortunes waned after the death of the queen, not least because he apparently had difficulty in convincing the royal household that he was an accomplished general physician, as well as a notable man-midwife. His health also seems to have declined and he died on 28 August 1721, probably in London, and was buried on 6 September in the south chancel of St Katharine Coleman, Fenchurch Street, London, with his first wife.

Hamilton was a devout dissenting Christian and wrote two religious works (1697 and 1701) as well as one medical work (1710), which was for a time the standard text on military fever; but by far his most enduring work was his diary, which he kept from December 1709 until the death of Queen Anne. In it he recorded in some detail the events of the queen's last years, observed from within the royal household. Intended by Hamilton for publication, the diary did not in fact appear until 1975, by which time it existed only as a copy, which is evidently considerably shorter than the original. Hamilton was, if anything, a whig, but his politics were not strident, and his relative neutrality combined with his closeness to the queen gave him the ear of many. His diary is thus an intriguing insight into the final years of Queen Anne's reign.

ELIZABETH BAIGENT

**Sources** *The diary of Sir David Hamilton, 1709–1714*, ed. P. Roberts (1975) · Munk, *Roll* · A. Wilson, *The making of man-midwifery: childbirth in England, 1660–1770* (1995), 56, 83, 87, 113
**Archives** Herts. ALS, letters to Countess Cowper
**Wealth at death** see *Diary*, ed. Roberts, xxii, xxiv

**Hamilton, David** (1768–1843), architect, was born in Glasgow on 11 May 1768 and baptized there on 14 May, the son of Lesmahagow-born mason William Hamilton and Helen Liddel. He is described in his obituary as self-taught, but copies of unpublished Adam projects in Hamilton's portfolio imply some connection with the office of Robert and James Adam, possibly as clerk of works, and his early designs show strong Adam influence. An architect by the time of his marriage to Magdalene Marshall in 1794, he was probably responsible for completing Adam's Mauldslie, Lanarkshire, and for the erection of James Adam's Professors' Lodgings (1795), after the latter's death. By 1801, when he won the competition for Denburn Bridge, Aberdeen, he had already designed several villas, country houses, and probably (on stylistic grounds) the city block 52–60 Wilson Street, Glasgow. Hamilton had his own marble yard, used predominantly the same stone quarry (implying an interest in it), and became deacon convenor of the Glasgow Incorporation of Masons in 1808.

Hamilton's urban works in Glasgow were of the highest significance and include the delicate French-inspired Hutcheson's Hospital (1802), Glasgow's Theatre Royal (1803), Monteith Row (1812), the tolbooth (1813), the remodelling of St Enoch's Church (1827), the Royal Exchange (also 1827), Royal Exchange Square (1830), and advice on the layout, the bridge, lodge, and the Egyptian vaults in the necropolis (1833–7). He also designed the refined town steeple, Falkirk (1813–14), Irvine Academy (1814–16), and the elegantly steepled town buildings, Port Glasgow (1815–16).

Of the eleven competitions he entered Hamilton won five and was premiated in two more. The remaining entries formed part of the corpus of twelve abortive designs. His competition entries comprised: the Hunterian Museum, Glasgow; the justiciary courts, Glasgow; Denburn bridge, Aberdeen; the Theatre Royal, Glasgow; the Wellington Memorial, Dublin; Lochnaw Castle, Wigtownshire; Airth parish church, Stirlingshire; St Enoch's, Glasgow; the Royal Exchange, Glasgow; the houses of parliament, London (for which he won the third prize of £500); and Donaldson's Hospital, Edinburgh (for which he also won third prize).

Hamilton's networking was excellent: he had a close relationship with Dr James Cleland, Glasgow's superintendent and master of works, resulting from his work on the Nelson monument of 1806, the rebuilding of Glasgow's tolbooth in 1813, the Cleland testimonial building of 1835, and the pavilion for Sir Robert Peel's rectorial banquet of 1837. Hamilton had earlier lost Crawford priory

David Hamilton (1768–1843), by Augustin Edouart

(1809–10) through client dissatisfaction with his dilatoriness as architect and Cleland's as builder. A drop in commissions between 1821 and 1832 may be explained by his absorption in the enormous, monumental, austere Hamilton Palace from 1816 (dem.)—an 'almost Ruritanian episode where he acted as resident court architect to the princely Duke of Hamilton' (I. Gow, 'David Rhind, the master of mercantile ornament', in *The Architectural Outsiders*, ed. R. Brown and K. Downes, 1985, 153). It was by far the most magnificent country house in Scotland. Although his pupil Thomas Gildard remembered how 'this grand old architect knew how to deport himself in the society of Dukes and Earls' (Gildard, 106), particularly Eglinton and Hamilton, he was more at home with Glasgow lord provosts. Castle House, Dunoon, was built for Provost Ewing in 1823–4 and the splendidly flamboyant Castle Toward, Cowal, for Kirkman Finlay in 1821—two buildings that he considered among his best. A number of projects in north Glasgow and Stirlingshire may have derived from the influence of the extended Stirling clan. These included extensions to: Airth Castle, Falkirk, for T. G. Stirling (1807–10); Cadder House, east Dunbartonshire (1817), for Charles Stirling; Larbert House, Falkirk (1822–5), for Sir Gilbert Stirling; and extensions to Keir, Stirlingshire (1829–31), for Archibald Stirling.

Larger buildings in romantic settings were addressed in a castellated picturesque style—such as Hafton (1816), Crawford (1809–10), and Castle Toward (1820–21), the most splendid—or in the Romanesque—exemplified by Lennox Castle (1837–41), which contemporaries considered his most accomplished. Smaller ones were realized in 'lodge architecture'—gables with finials, spikiness, and hoodmoulds, as in Mosesfield (1838) and Gallowflatt (1834). 'Scottish' architecture appears only in his House of Commons submission and in the remarkably thoroughgoing Dunlop House (1831–4).

In 1809 Hamilton announced plans to move office to Edinburgh, 'for the greater convenience of clients', but did not do so. His two promising architect sons William and David died on the same day in 1821, and his daughter in 1829. The drawing office was eventually relocated to the house fronting the marble works at 235 Buchanan Street, on which he borrowed money in 1831 (perhaps to finance speculation in Royal Exchange Square) and which he had to sell by auction four years later (although he remained in occupation). There were clear financial difficulties, and his estate of just under £650 was surprisingly small. A very popular man, he figured affectionately as 'Mr Column' in Leonard Smith's 'Northern sketches' in 1810, and was awarded a public dinner and presentation of £500 in a gold box in 1840. Dr John Strang, the mover behind the Glasgow necropolis, called him 'a gifted and tasteful individual … like most men of genius, he possessed great modesty, and kind and convivial habits endeared himself to a large circle of attached friends who valued his talents and bewailed his loss' (Strang, 567–8). Gildard recalled 'a man of most impressive presence, frank and kindly in manner' (Gildard MS, Mitchell Library, Glasgow).

Possibly showing the influence of the continental tour made by his son James in 1839, Hamilton's stylistically innovative later buildings—mostly banks and the Western Club, Glasgow—were plainer but much more heavily modelled and authoritative, presaging the dominant style of mid-nineteenth-century Glasgow. He died of a stroke on 5 December 1843 and was survived by his wife. His influence lived on in the work of his pupils Charles Wilson and J. T. Rochead, his son James, and his son-in-law James Smith. Described at his death as the 'father of architecture in the west of Scotland', Hamilton was the preferred designer of the cotton-manufacturing entrepreneurs of Glasgow, for whom he designed many suburban or country villas and country houses, some churches, and their principal civic monuments. An extraordinary number of other unattributed pre-1840 houses in Ayrshire and the Clyde valley display details implying the hand of Hamilton. They are exceptionally comfortable, well lit, and gracious houses in a spare understated classical style, particularly horizontal in proportion; the modelling is simple, with particular motifs of corner pilasters, sometimes hollowed, and twin-columned porches with flattened fanlights. Of over 130 projects attributable to him, the largest group is in central Glasgow, closely followed by those (mainly houses) throughout Ayrshire: four in Ayr and seven likely villas in Largs. CHARLES MCKEAN

**Sources** Colvin, *Archs.* • *David Hamilton: architectural drawings* (1995) [exhibition catalogue, Hunterian Art Gallery, University of Glasgow, 29 April – 24 June 1995] • A. Aiken, 'The David Hamilton collection', 4 vols., Mitchell L., Glas. • T. Gildard, 'An old Glasgow architect', *Transactions of the Philosophical Society of Glasgow*, 26 (1894–5), 97–106 • T. Gildard, 'Recollections and reflections', Mitchell L., Glas., MS B 214963 • T. Annan, J. O. Mitchell, and others, *The old country houses of the old Glasgow gentry* (1870) • A. MacKechnie, ed.,

*David Hamilton, architect* (1993) • D. Watters, 'David Hamilton's Lennox Castle', *Architectural Heritage*, 5 (1995), 51–65 • register of Sasines, NA Scot. • NA Scot., sheriff court records, commissariat of Glasgow [inventory], SC 36/48/31, 725 • private information (2004) [Ranald MacInnes; David Walker] • National Monuments Record of Scotland, index • A. Gomme and D. Walker, *Architecture of Glasgow* (1968) • M. C. Davis, *The castles and mansions of Ayrshire* (1991) • M. Davis, 'The villas of Scotland's western seaboard', *The Georgian villa*, ed. D. Arnold (1996), 130–44 • I. Gow, *Scottish houses and gardens* (1997) • [W. Papworth], ed., *The dictionary of architecture*, 11 vols. (1853–92) • D. Paterson, 'Glasgow and its buildings', *Quarterly Journal of the Royal Incorporation of Architects in Scotland*, 11/32 (1930), 108–15 • *The Builder*, 1 (1843), 537–8 • *Edinburgh*, Pevsner (1984) • C. McKean, ed., *Illustrated architectural guides to Scotland* (1982–) • G. Stamp and S. McKinstry, eds., *'Greek' Thomson* (1994) • J. Strang, *Glasgow and its clubs* (1856) • *View of the Merchant's House of Glasgow* (1886), 362, 382 • b. cert.

**Archives** NA Scot. • U. Glas., MSS | priv. coll. • PRO, works 29 entry for houses of parliament

**Likenesses** A. Edouart, silhouette, Scot. NPG [*see illus.*] • D. MacNee, portrait • Saxon, portrait • plaster bust (after bust by Patric Park, *c*.1840), Royal Incorporation of Architects in Scotland, Edinburgh

**Wealth at death** £644 18*s*. 3*d*.; also marble works and home in Buchanan Street: NA Scot., SC 36/48/31, 725

**Hamilton, David James** (1849–1909), pathologist, born on 6 March 1849 at Falkirk, was the third child and second son of the nine children of George Hamilton MD, practitioner in that town, and his wife, Mary Wyse, daughter of a naval surgeon. He studied medicine at Edinburgh, at both the Royal College of Surgeons and the university, where his interest in pathology was aroused by Professor William Rutherford Sanders.

After qualifying in 1870 Hamilton was appointed house-surgeon to the Edinburgh Infirmary, and then became resident medical officer at Chalmers Hospital, Edinburgh. Thereafter he worked for two years at the Northern Hospital, Liverpool, where he had full control of the pathology department. In 1874 he was awarded the triennial Astley Cooper prize of £300 for his pathological researches on diseases and injuries of the spinal cord. This enabled him to spend two years studying pathology in Vienna, Munich, Strasbourg, and Paris.

In 1876 Hamilton returned to Edinburgh and was appointed administrator of pathology at the university. He was also pathologist to the Royal Infirmary.

Hamilton was twice married. First in 1880, to Elizabeth Griffith, daughter of Thomas Griffith, then in 1894 to Catherine Wilson (*d*. 1908), daughter of John Wilson. There were two sons and one daughter of the first marriage. In 1882, while also an extramural teacher in Edinburgh, he was appointed to the chair of pathology newly founded by Sir William James Erasmus Wilson at Aberdeen. Combining this position with an appointment as pathologist to Aberdeen Royal Infirmary, Hamilton established a new school of pathology at Aberdeen with a European reputation.

An enthusiastic and inspiring teacher, with a strong personality and great powers of organization, Hamilton was the first to introduce the practical teaching of bacteriology into general class-work. He was deeply interested in the practical application of pathology, and he initiated the bacteriological diagnosis of diphtheria and typhoid fever in the north of Scotland as well as the examination of water by bacteriological methods. He also took an interest in the diseases of animals, especially those in sheep known as 'braxy' and 'louping ill'. He was chairman of the departmental committee on this question appointed by the Board of Agriculture in 1901, which presented its report in 1906, and he discovered the bacillus of 'louping ill'. Hamilton wrote widely on all branches of pathology, with a particular interest in the nervous system, tuberculosis and other diseases of the lungs, and the healing of wounds. His *Textbook of Pathology* (2 vols., 1889–94) was recognized by contemporaries as a standard work.

In 1908 Hamilton resigned his position due to ill health. He was a member of many medical societies and was elected FRS (Edinburgh) and, in 1908, FRS (London). The University of Edinburgh conferred on him an honorary degree, and following its quatercentenary the University of Aberdeen dedicated to him William Bulloch's *Studies in Pathology* (1906). Hamilton died on 19 February 1909 at Aberdeen and was buried there.

H. D. Rolleston, *rev.* Claire E. J. Herrick

**Sources** *Edinburgh Medical Journal*, 3rd ser., 2 (1909), 264–8 • *Journal of Pathology and Bacteriology*, 13 (1908–9), 500–07 • J. T. C., *PRS*, 81B (1909), i–v • *BMJ* (6 March 1909), 631–3 • *The Lancet* (6 March 1909), 730–31 • private information (1912) • C. Pennington, *The modernisation of medical teaching at Aberdeen in the nineteenth century* (1994), 47–54

**Archives** RS • Wellcome L., lecture notes

**Likenesses** photograph, Wellcome L.

**Hamilton, Sir (Charles) Denis** (1918–1988), newspaper editor, was born on 6 December 1918 in South Shields, co. Durham, the elder son (there were no daughters) of Charles Hamilton, engineer, and his wife, Helena Trafford. He left Middlesbrough high school at seventeen, became a reporter on the local *Evening Gazette*, and as a territorial in 1938 got a commission in the Durham light infantry. In 1939 he married Olive, younger daughter of Thomas Hedley Wanless, farmer. They had four sons, of whom one, Nigel, became a writer.

In September 1939 part of the Territorial Army was embodied and Hamilton soon found himself in France. He was one of the few officers in his battalion who got back from Dunkirk. In 1940 he became a captain and in 1942 a major during a spell in Iceland. In 1944 he was promoted to lieutenant-colonel and commanded the 11th battalion, Durham light infantry, in the Normandy invasion. After the breakthrough in Normandy, Hamilton was posted to the 7th battalion of the duke of Wellington's and led them in an inspired defensive action near Nijmegen, Holland, which won him a place in military history and the DSO (1944). General Montgomery wanted him to remain in the regular army after the end of the war. However, Hamilton went back to provincial journalism and within a few weeks J. G. Berry, first Viscount Kemsley, summoned him to London to be his personal assistant; he held this post until 1950. Now he was at the centre of the Kemsley newspaper empire and was soon exercising influence. The brigadier, as the staff called him (he had ended the war as an acting brigadier), still looked a soldier with his discreet suits, polished shoes, slim, tall figure, and military moustache. If he never failed to find a military analogy to illustrate a newspaper problem, at least he never barked out his commands. He spoke quietly and could be disconcertingly silent when it was his turn to say something. Kemsley made him editorial director in 1950—when he was thirty-one—whereupon he improved the organization and created a training scheme that became the model for a national scheme; he remained in this post until 1967.

Turning his attention to the *Sunday Times*, edited by Henry Hodson, Hamilton believed that new readers would be attracted if they were given plenty to read every Sunday—the 'big read'. He persuaded his wartime friend Viscount Montgomery to let him serialize extracts from his memoirs, with the result that the circulation was increased by 100,000 copies over fourteen weeks; the new readers stayed. (Montgomery's life was later written by Hamilton's son, Nigel.) In 1959 Kemsley sold his newspaper group to Roy Thomson, a Canadian who had acquired *The Scotsman* and Scottish commercial television. Two years later Thomson made Hamilton editor of the *Sunday Times* and the paper became remarkably successful. Within six years it increased its sales by half a million copies. Hamilton, who did not himself write for the paper, recruited ardent young people and pioneered a bulky Sunday paper in separate sections, which included business news and a colour magazine. His 'Insight' team of investigative journalists had outstanding successes. Thomson was a model proprietor, giving editors the widest freedom and in turn Hamilton delegated great responsibility to his assistants.

When Thomson acquired *The Times* in 1967, he made Hamilton editor-in-chief of both that and the *Sunday Times* and chief executive of Times Newspapers. Hamilton appointed as editors William Rees-Mogg for *The Times* and Harold Evans for the *Sunday Times*. He behaved very much as a constitutional monarch, guiding, encouraging, and occasionally warning both men. A successful promotion drive for *The Times* had to be dropped, for it was too costly to earn the expected profits. Difficulties multiplied in the late 1970s. Both *The Times* and the *Sunday Times* were suffering severe losses because militant Unionists, who resented wage restraint and feared the advent of new technology, were hampering production. Roy Thomson, who had died, was succeeded by his son Kenneth, who wanted to know from his Canadian base what the strengthened hierarchy in London was going to do about the dispute. In the end it was decided, despite the reluctance of Hamilton and another director, to stop the presses, in the hope that this would bring the unions to their senses. It did not and the costly stoppage lasted almost a year (1979). Shortly after publication was resumed, the journalists decided to strike. This was the last straw for Hamilton, who advised Thomson to sell for what he could get. The only bidder who looked likely to preserve the precious heritage and to stand up to the unions was the Australian Rupert Murdoch, who acquired Times Newspapers Ltd in 1980.

Hamilton did not stay long after the take-over, resigning as chairman in 1981, and concentrated on his chairmanship of the expanding Reuters (1979–85). A trustee of the British Museum from 1969, he jointly sponsored the great 'Tutankhamun' (1972) and 'Treasures of China' (1973) exhibitions. He was an active trustee of the Henry Moore Foundation from 1980 and was president of the International Press Institute (1978–83), the worldwide protector of press freedom. He was president or chairman of many other institutions. Towards the end of his life, he struggled with the help of his son Nigel to produce a slim but valuable book of memoirs, *Editor-in-Chief* (1989). Appointed TD in 1975 and knighted in 1976, he had honorary degrees from Southampton (1975), City University (1977), and Newcastle upon Tyne (1979).

Hamilton died of cancer, after a long illness, on 7 April 1988 at his home, 78A Ashley Gardens, Thirleby Road, Victoria, London. JOHN BEAVAN, *rev.*

**Sources** D. Hamilton, *Editor-in-chief* (1989) · E. Jacobs, *Stop press* (1980) · H. Evans, *Good times, bad times* (1983) · personal knowledge (1996) · *CGPLA Eng. & Wales* (1988)
**Wealth at death** £225,830: probate, 20 Sept 1988, *CGPLA Eng. & Wales*

**Hamilton, Douglas Douglas-, fourteenth duke of Hamilton and eleventh duke of Brandon** (1903–1973), boxer, aviator, and politician, was born on 3 February 1903, the eldest of the seven children of Alfred Douglas-Hamilton, thirteenth duke of Hamilton (1862–1940), and his wife, Nina Mary Benita Douglas-*Hamilton, *née* Poore (1878–1951), anti-vivisectionist. He was educated at Eton College and at Balliol College, Oxford (1921–5), but took no degree. Then styled marquess of Douglas and Clydesdale, he was 5 feet 7 inches in height and possessed of exceptional strength. At Oxford he formed a close friendship with Eddie Eagan, the American Rhodes scholar who was the Olympic light heavyweight boxing champion, and Clydesdale succeeded Eagan as captain of the Oxford boxing team. Eagan described Clydesdale as having 'the broad shoulders and deft balance of a natural fighter', and together they went on a world boxing tour, taking on all comers. The tour was chronicled in Eagan's enthusiastic, if effusive, book *Fighting for Fun* (1932). Clydesdale reached the semi-finals of the British middleweight amateur championships and won the Scottish middleweight championship; in Scotland his prowess resulted in the sobriquet the Boxing Marquis.

Clydesdale joined the Royal Auxiliary Air Force in 1927 and was rapidly promoted, becoming squadron leader of 602 (City of Glasgow) squadron in 1931. In 1933 he was chosen to be chief pilot of the Houston Mount Everest flight expedition, and on 3 April 1933 was the first man to fly over Everest; he was followed by Flight Lieutenant David McIntyre, both in experimental Westland aircraft. This feat represented a decisive leap forward in aviation development and technology. Clydesdale and McIntyre recounted their experiences in *The Pilot's Book of Everest* (1936). Clydesdale was granted the freedom of Hamilton

**Douglas Douglas-Hamilton, fourteenth duke of Hamilton and eleventh duke of Brandon (1903–1973),** by Bassano, 1945

in 1933 and made a fellow of the Royal Geographical Society; in 1935 he was awarded the Air Force Cross. The Everest expedition gave Clydesdale and McIntyre the standing as professional flying instructors that they needed to start a flying school at Prestwick, after which they founded Scottish Aviation to build aircraft. More than sixty years and several mergers later, it constituted the Scottish division of British Aerospace. On 2 December 1937 Clydesdale married Lady Elizabeth Ivy Percy (*b.* 1916), elder daughter of Alan Ian *Percy, eighth duke of Northumberland. They had five sons.

Having unsuccessfully contested Govan in 1929 Clydesdale was elected MP for East Renfrewshire as a Conservative in 1930, and retained the seat until he succeeded to the dukedom in 1940. He spoke in the House of Commons on RAF and Scottish matters, and travelled with other MPs to Russia, Italy, and Germany. His visit to the Berlin Olympic games in 1936 was to have repercussions: while there, he met not only Goering and Milch, in charge of the Luftwaffe, but also Professor Albrecht Haushofer, a personal adviser to Rudolf Hess, and special adviser on foreign affairs to Hitler and Ribbentrop. From the outbreak of war in 1939, Clydesdale served full time with the RAF. He was a sector commander of 11 group, Fighter Command, and was mentioned in dispatches for service during the battle for France in 1940. During the battle of Britain he was station commander for the Turnhouse air sector in Scotland. He succeeded his father as fourteenth duke of Hamilton and hereditary keeper of Holyroodhouse in 1940, and in the same year became lord steward of the royal household, a position he retained until 1964.

Unbeknown to the new duke, in the autumn of 1940 Haushofer had told Hess that Hamilton 'had access, at all times, to all important persons in London, even to Churchill and the King'. Hess, who had conceived of the idea of negotiating a peace settlement between Britain and Germany, asked Haushofer to write to Hamilton, a letter which received no reply. On 10 May 1941, the same evening that the House of Commons was bombed, Hess parachuted into Scotland, gave a false name, and asked to see the duke of Hamilton, whom he had never met before. On 11 May Hess admitted to Hamilton that he was on a 'personal unauthorised mission', but claimed that he knew what Hitler's peace terms would be. Hamilton at once flew south to report to the prime minister, who was then at Ditchley Park. Churchill found Hamilton's report hard to believe, saying, 'Well, Hess or no Hess, I am going to see the Marx Brothers'. However, later that night he had a long interview with Hamilton, and Hess was identified and treated as a prisoner of war. Later in 1941 Hamilton was promoted to group captain, in command of the Air Training Corps in Scotland. He was made honorary air commodore, and in 1946 was appointed GCVO.

Hamilton, who became president of the British Airline Pilots Association in 1937, was president of the Air League of the British Empire from 1959 to 1968. He was also associated with the Air Cadet Council and the Guild of Air Pilots and Air Navigators. In 1963 prime minister Harold Wilson appointed him to chair a committee on civil aviation pilot training; his recommendations were implemented. He was active as an elder of the Church of Scotland, serving as lord high commissioner to the general assembly in 1953, 1954, 1955, and 1958. He had a lifelong interest in young people, and was president of the Boys' Brigade in Scotland, and in promoting sport, presiding over the National Advisory Council on Physical Training (Scotland) and the Scottish Amateur Boxing Association. He had many business interests, and was president of the Building Societies Association (1961–5). From 1948 until his death he was chancellor of St Andrews University, and his last major act was to go to North America in 1972 to raise more than £1 million of funds for the university. He died in Edinburgh on 30 March 1973, and was succeeded by his eldest son. His ashes were scattered from the air beside Lennoxlove Politicians Walk on the fortieth anniversary of his flight over Everest.

A devoted Scot, the duke of Hamilton 'cared very much about everything to do with Scotland, both in the preservation of her past tradition and continuing identity, but more especially in the building of her future as a meaningful country in the modern world' (*The Times*); his creation of the aviation industry in Scotland was his single most important contribution. SELKIRK OF DOUGLAS

**Sources** Lennoxlove Archives, Lennoxlove, Haddington, East Lothian, Hamilton MSS · Burke, *Peerage* (1967) · *WWW* · *The Times* (2 April 1973) · E. Eagan, *Fighting for fun* (1932) · J. Douglas-Hamilton, *Roof of the world* (1983) · J. Douglas-Hamilton, *Motive for a*

*mission* (1971) • J. Douglas-Hamilton, *The truth about Rudolf Hess* (1993) • I. Elliott, ed., *The Balliol College register, 1900–1950*, 3rd edn (privately printed, Oxford, 1953)

**Archives** Lennoxlove Museum, Haddington, East Lothian • NA Scot., corresp. and papers; corresp. and papers relating to Rudolf Hess and Anglo-German relations [copies] • NRA Scotland, priv. coll., corresp. and MSS • NRA Scotland, priv. coll., corresp. and MSS relating to Rudolf Hess and Anglo-German relations • Lennoxlove, Haddington, East Lothian | FILM BFI NFTVA, documentary footage • BFI NFTVA, news footage • Rank Organization, 'Wings over Everest' | SOUND BBC WAC

**Likenesses** Bassano, photograph, 1945, NPG [*see illus.*] • A. Goudie, portrait, Lennoxlove, Haddington, East Lothian • O. Kokoschka, double portrait (with his wife), Scottish Gallery of Modern Art, Edinburgh • photographs, IWM • photographs, Hult. Arch. • photographs, Times Picture Library • photographs, Hult. Arch.

**Wealth at death** £945,787.16: confirmation, 6 Aug 1973, *CCI* • £1,075,623.99: additional and corrective inventory, 30 July 1976, *CCI* • £1,134,673.40: second additional and corrective inventory, 9 Aug 1976, *CCI*

**Hamilton, Edith Henrietta** (1865–1944). *See under* Fowler, Ellen Thorneycroft (1860–1929).

**Hamilton, Sir Edward, first baronet** (1772–1851), naval officer, son of Sir John Hamilton, first baronet (*d.* 24 January 1784) of The Mount, Middlesex, and his wife, Cassandra Agnes (*d.* 26 October 1826), daughter of Edward Chamberlayne, was born on 12 March 1772. He was the younger brother of Admiral Sir Charles *Hamilton. He reportedly served on the *Hector* with his father in the West Indies from 1779 to 1781. He was then sent to school at Guildford, Surrey, and in 1787 re-entered the navy on the *Standard* with Captain Chamberlayne. On 9 June 1793 he was promoted lieutenant of the *Dido* with his brother, and in 1794 was at the siege of Bastia and the capture of the Girolata Fort. In July 1794 he was appointed to the *Victory*, then Lord Hood's flagship in the Mediterranean, and continued in her, with Rear-Admiral Man, and afterwards with Sir John Jervis, until promoted to command the fireship *Comet* on 11 February 1796, in which he was shortly afterwards sent to the West Indies. On 3 June 1797 he was advanced to post rank and appointed to the *Surprise* (32 guns), a small frigate, formerly the French corvette *Unité*. In her he was employed on convoy service to Newfoundland, and in July 1798 to Jamaica, where he was placed under the orders of Sir Hyde Parker, and is said during the next eighteen months to have taken or destroyed upwards of eighty privateers, armed vessels, and merchant ships, the net proceeds of which, counting only those brought in, amounted to £200,000.

In October 1799 Hamilton was sent off Puerto Cabello, Venezuela, to watch for the Spanish frigate *Hermione*, expected shortly to sail from that port. The *Hermione* had been a British frigate, but on 22 September 1797 had been seized by her crew, who, after murdering their officers, had taken the ship into La Guaira. There they handed her over to the Spaniards, who fitted her out with 44 guns and a complement of nearly 400 men. A proportion of the mutineers had been since captured and hanged, but every officer on the station felt that the presence of the *Hermione* under the Spanish flag was an insult to the navy and to England. The *Surprise* anchored off Puerto Cabello on 21 October, and, finding the *Hermione* moored inside with no apparent intention of stirring, while the *Surprise*'s provisions were running low, Hamilton resolved to cut her out. The *Surprise*'s boats attacked in the dark, very early on the morning of 25 October, and, despite fire from the *Hermione* and two large coastal batteries, the attackers, led by Hamilton, boarded and captured the *Hermione*, and towed her away. The Spaniards lost 119 killed and 97 wounded, the British only 12 men wounded, which was the more extraordinary as the ship was not taken by surprise. Hamilton, however, was severely wounded. The stock of a musket had been broken over his head, he had various flesh wounds in both legs, and a severe contusion of the loins, the effects of which he felt through the rest of his life. But the achievement was outstanding. The king awarded him a knighthood on 1 February 1800, and the naval gold medal; the Jamaican house of assembly voted him a sword valued at 300 guineas; and the City of London conferred on him the freedom of the City in a gold box worth 50 guineas, presented at a dinner at the Mansion House on 25 October 1800, the anniversary of the exploit.

Returning home in the Jamaica packet in April 1800 to recuperate, Hamilton was captured by a French privateer and taken to France. At Paris he is said to have been questioned by Napoleon; he was exchanged very shortly afterwards, and on his return to England was appointed (23 October) to the *Trent* (36 guns). He refused a pension of £300 a year offered by the Admiralty in consideration of his wounds, thinking it would be made an excuse for not employing him again. In 1801 he was engaged in the blockade of the northern coast of France; but on 22 January 1802, while the ship was lying at Spithead, he was tried by court martial for seizing up in the main rigging the gunner and his mates, who, he alleged, had grossly disobeyed his orders. Possibly the blow to his head had affected his brain; the evidence was clear that the men's offence was trivial, and their punishment excessive and illegal. Hamilton was dismissed from the service, but was specially reinstated in the following June.

On 1 November 1804 Hamilton married Frances (*d.* 27 March 1840), daughter of John Macnamara of Llangoed Castle, Brecon; they had two sons and two daughters. In June 1806 he was appointed to the royal yacht *Mary*; he commanded it, and its successor, the royal yacht *Prince Regent*, until 1819. On 2 January 1815 he was made a KCB, and he was created a baronet on 20 October 1818. He became rear-admiral on 19 July 1821, vice-admiral on 10 January 1837, and admiral on 9 November 1846. He died at 17 Cumberland Terrace, Regent's Park, London, on 21 March 1851. His eldest son, John James Edward, having died in 1847, he was succeeded as baronet by his grandson, Edward Archibald.

J. K. LAUGHTON, *rev.* ANDREW LAMBERT

**Sources** D. Syrett and R. L. DiNardo, *The commissioned sea officers of the Royal Navy, 1660–1815*, rev. edn, Occasional Publications of the Navy RS, 1 (1994) • D. Pope, *The black ship* (1963) • J. Marshall, *Royal* *naval biography*, 4/2 (1835) · O'Byrne, *Naval biog. dict.* · Burke, *Peerage* · Boase, *Mod. Eng. biog.* · J. Ralfe, *The naval biography of Great Britain*, 4 (1828) · *Colburn's United Service Magazine*, 1 (1851), 648

**Likenesses** W. Ridley, stipple, 1801 (after W. Thompson), BM, NPG

**Hamilton, Sir Edward Walter** [Eddy] (**1847–1908**), civil servant and diarist, universally known as Eddy, was born on 7 July 1847 at Salisbury, the eldest son of Walter Kerr *Hamilton (1808–1869), bishop of Salisbury, and Isabel Elizabeth, daughter of Francis Lear, dean of Salisbury. He had six sisters and two brothers. Following in his father's footsteps, he entered Eton College in 1860 and Christ Church, Oxford, in 1866. Traditional academic subjects interested him little, and the only degree he took from Oxford was a BMus in 1867; music was to be a lifelong interest. On the nomination of his father's close friend W. E. Gladstone, then the prime minister, he became a junior clerk at the Treasury in January 1870, thus beginning a 37-year connection with that department. In 1872 Robert Lowe, the chancellor of the exchequer, chose him to serve as a second private secretary, and after Lowe's resignation he became briefly (1873–4) a member of Gladstone's secretariat in Downing Street. In both situations he showed a marked aptitude for the work of a private secretary.

With the formation of Gladstone's second government in 1880 Hamilton rejoined the secretariat in Downing Street, becoming the principal private secretary in 1882. When the government fell in the summer of 1885 he was created CB and returned to the Treasury as principal clerk of the finance division. In spite of his close links with Gladstone and with Lord Rosebery, who had been his closest friend since their days at Eton, he became the valued and trusted adviser to a succession of Unionist as well as Liberal chancellors, playing an important role in the shaping of each budget. He assisted Goschen in his complex work on the debt in 1888–9, described in his *Conversion and Redemption* (1890) which, he noted, excited 'the curiosity of the evangelical world' (*Diary*, 8 March 1890). Most chancellors found his annual minute summarizing the budget proposals invaluable; Goschen thought his presentation of the budget in 1891 was a failure because a bout of pneumonia had prevented Hamilton from playing his usual role in its preparation. In 1892 he became the assistant financial secretary of the Treasury and in 1894, on Rosebery's nomination, he was created KCB. Finally in 1902 he came to share the top position as financial secretary of the Treasury with Sir George Murray as administrative secretary, a novel arrangement made necessary by his deteriorating physical condition.

In 1889 Hamilton began to experience increasingly severe symptoms of vascular disease. In 1890 Charcot diagnosed the condition as 'clodification of the arteries of the leg' (*Diary*, 7 Dec 1890). A lifelong bachelor, he had by 1885 come to be much in demand at great houses in London and in the country, but his health forced him to curtail both his professional and social activities. Music continued to be a major interest. He found special pleasure in the compositions of his cousin Hubert Parry and in the operas of Richard Wagner. Several of his own compositions for piano and for voice were published over the years. He tried to remain active in the affairs of the Royal College of Music, in the founding of which he had played a role.

**Sir Edward Walter Hamilton (1847–1908)**, by Cyril Flower, Baron Battersea

Hamilton was aware that the qualities that suited him so well to be a private secretary and Treasury official—diligence, accuracy, discretion, tact, and above all an ability to write clear summaries of complex questions—did not include unusual powers of intellect. Indeed he himself thought that 'the reason why I am clear is that I must explain things clearly in order to make them intelligible to myself' (*Diary*, 28 April 1891).

The same qualities that distinguished Hamilton's professional life are fully exhibited in his diary, which he began when he joined the Downing Street staff in the spring of 1880. Carefully written in full sentences and paragraphs, it contains a detailed account of the political activities taking place around him. He continued writing his diary until 1906. Its fifty-four volumes are deposited in the British Library. Gladstone and Rosebery are the leading figures in it, but everyone of any prominence in politics finds a place.

The last decade of Hamilton's life had a few rewards. His sketch *Mr Gladstone: a Monograph*, published in 1898, was well received. He became the auditor of the civil list in 1902, was awarded the GCB in 1906, and in 1908 was named a privy councillor. But in the main these were melancholy years. His physical condition steadily worsened. The fiscal principles of economy and free trade to which he was devoted came under increasingly severe attack. He had to give up his diary in 1906 because his handwriting was illegible, and in October 1907 he had to resign his post at the Treasury. He died on 2 September 1908 at the Hotel Metropole, Brighton, and was buried in the town.

DUDLEY W. R. BAHLMAN

**Sources** *The diary of Sir Edward Walter Hamilton, 1880–1885*, ed. D. W. R. Bahlman, 2 vols. (1972) • *The diary of Sir Edward Walter Hamilton, 1885–1906*, ed. D. W. R. Bahlman (1993) • Lord Kilbracken [J. A. Godley], *Reminiscences of Lord Kilbracken* (1931) • G. G. Leveson-Gower, *Years of content, 1858–1886* (1940) • Gladstone, *Diaries*

**Archives** BL, corresp. and diaries, Add. MSS 48599–48699 • PRO, financial papers, T168/5–99 | BL, letters to Sir C. Dilke, Add. MSS 43875, 43912–43914, 43916, 43919 • BL, corresp. with Viscount Gladstone, Add. MS 45990 • BL, corresp. with W. E. Gladstone, Add. MSS 44189–44191 • BL, corresp. with General Sir H. F. Ponsonby, Add. MS 45725 • BLPES, letters to Lord Welby • Bodl. Oxf., letters to H. H. Asquith • Bodl. Oxf., corresp. with Sir William Harcourt, and Lewis Harcourt • Bodl. Oxf., letters to Lord Lovelace • LPL, letters to W. E. Gladstone • NL Scot., corresp., incl. with Lord Rosebery • St Deiniol's Library, Hawarden, corresp. with H. N. Gladstone, H. D. Seymour, and others

**Likenesses** C. Flower, Baron Battersea, photograph, NPG [*see illus.*] • photograph (after da Costa), NPG; 1908 original destroyed • sketch, NPG

**Wealth at death** £14,893 0s. 11*d*.: resworn probate, 23 Oct 1908, *CGPLA Eng. & Wales*

**Hamilton, Elizabeth**, **Countess de Gramont** [*called* La Belle Hamilton] (**1641–1708**), courtier, was the eldest daughter of Sir George *Hamilton, first baronet (*d*. 1679) [*see under* Hamilton, James, first earl of Abercorn], and granddaughter of James *Hamilton, first earl of Abercorn (1575–1618). Her mother was Mary Butler (*d*. 1680), third daughter of Walter, Viscount Thurles, eldest son of Walter, eleventh earl of Ormond. James Butler, first duke of Ormond, was her uncle. She was probably born in Ireland in 1641, but educated at Port-Royal-des-Champs in France, where her family, which was Catholic, settled in 1651. They returned to England after the Restoration.

Elizabeth Hamilton was one of the most beautiful and vivacious ladies at the court of Charles II and is described by her brother Anthony *Hamilton in his *Mémoires de la vie du comte de Grammont* as of unrivalled beauty and intelligence. After refusing several other suitors, she married Philibert, Count de Gramont (1621–1707), probably at the end of 1663. Gramont, born in 1621, had been banished from France in 1662 and was a leading spirit in all the diversions of the court. Elizabeth's brother Anthony became his close friend, and Anthony describes the course of Gramont's courtship of his sister in the *Mémoires*.

In November 1664 the Count de Gramont was allowed to return to France, where thenceforth the count and countess mainly lived. However, they paid frequent visits to the English court, where they enjoyed the favour of Charles II. In 1688 Gramont went as a special envoy from Louis XIV to congratulate James II on the birth of the prince of Wales.

At the French court the Countess de Gramont was

**Elizabeth Hamilton, Countess de Gramont** [La Belle Hamilton] (**1641–1708**), by Sir Peter Lely, *c*.1663 [as St Catherine]

appointed a 'dame du palais' to Queen Marie-Thérèse, but after the queen's death in 1683 does not seem to have had a post in the royal household. The following year Fénelon became her spiritual director, and the letters that he wrote her were later included in his published correspondence.

The position of the Countess de Gramont at the French court was greatly enhanced by the arrival of James II and Mary of Modena after the revolution of 1688. As a bilingual French courtier with an English background who had known James II and many of his leading courtiers since her youth she had a considerable social advantage, and was frequently invited to join the two royal families when the exiled Stuarts visited Louis XIV at Versailles, Marly, and Trianon. Her brothers Anthony and Richard *Hamilton both lived at the English court at St Germain-en-Laye, so she acquired a unique position during the regular exchanges between the two courts. On some occasions she was the only French lady below the rank of princess to be invited to join the royal families. The duc de Saint-Simon noted that all the French courtiers treated her with distinction and that even the king's ministers took her opinions into account.

Louis XIV was particularly keen on the Countess de Gramont who had kept her natural beauty and had 'the air of a queen' (*Mémoires de Saint-Simon*, 16.73). In May 1703 the king gave her the use during her lifetime of a house near Meudon called Les Moulineaux. She renamed it Pontalie and quickly made it an important social centre for both her French and her Jacobite friends. When the 85-year-old Count de Gramont died in January 1707 she asked to be allowed to retire from court, but Louis XIV would not let her. Madame de Maintenon confided to a friend that if she herself were to die then the Countess de Gramont might well take her place and marry Louis XIV. But in fact the Count and Countess de Gramont had been very much closer to each other than many of their friends suspected, and Elizabeth never really recovered from her husband's death. It was soon noted that the countess had become unrecognizable, and had lost both her ready wit and her 'English courage' (*Mémoires de Saint-Simon*, 16.73n). She died in Paris on 3 June 1708, shortly after the failure of the Franco-Jacobite attempt to invade Scotland, in which her brother Richard had participated.

The Count and Countess de Gramont had two daughters, Claude-Charlotte (*b. c.*1665) and Marie-Elisabeth (*b.* 1667). They both served as maids of honour to the dauphine until her death in 1690. Claude-Charlotte married Henry, first earl of Stafford, in Paris in April 1694, but separated from him in December 1695. Marie-Elisabeth was elected abbess of Poussay (in Lorraine) in January 1695.

The publication in 1713 of the *Mémoires de la vie du comte de Grammont* made the countess famous and preserved the memory of 'La Belle Hamilton'. But by concentrating on Elizabeth Hamilton's early life at the court of Charles II it also caused generations of historians to neglect the true importance of this intelligent and beautiful woman. For about eighteen years she played a major role in sustaining the amicable relations between the Bourbon and Stuart courts, and thus helped encourage Louis XIV to continue his political support for the Jacobite cause in the years up to her death in 1708. EDWARD CORP

**Sources** *Mémoires de Saint-Simon*, ed. A. de Boislisle and L. Lecestre, new edn, 16 (1902), 16.70–75 • *Journal du marquis de Dangeau*, ed. E. Soulié and others, 19 vols. (Paris, 1854–60), vols. 2–12 • *Mémoires du marquis de Sourches sur le règne de Louis XIV*, 13 vols. (Paris, 1882–93), esp. vol. 8 • A. Hamilton, *Mémoires de la vie du comte de Grammont* (Cologne, 1713) • *DNB*

**Likenesses** P. Lely, oils, *c.*1663, Royal Collection [*see illus.*] • J. G. Eccardt, oils (after P. Lely, *c.*1663), NPG • P. Lely, oils, Althorp House, Northamptonshire • oils (copy of portrait by P. Lely, *c.*1663), Royal Collection

**Hamilton, Elizabeth, duchess of Hamilton and Brandon.** *See* Campbell, Elizabeth, duchess of Argyll and *suo jure* Baroness Hamilton of Hameldon (*bap.* 1733, *d.* 1790).

**Hamilton, Elizabeth** (1756?–1816), novelist and essayist, was born in Belfast, probably on 25 July 1756, though the date is often given as 1758. She was the third and youngest child of Charles Hamilton (*d.* 1759), a Scottish merchant, and his wife, Katherine Mackay (*d.* 1767). In 1762, her widowed mother having found herself incapable of raising all her three children, Hamilton was sent to live with a Mrs Marshall (*d.* 1780), her paternal aunt, who lived with her husband near Stirling, and, after 1772, at Ingram's Crook, near Bannockburn. In a fragmentary autobiography written late in her life and published in Elizabeth Benger's biography of her, Elizabeth Hamilton recalls that her uncle, a prosperous farmer, was thought socially

**Elizabeth Hamilton (1756?–1816),** by Sir Henry Raeburn

beneath her aunt. Hamilton, who was devoted to her uncle, uses the story to mock the social pretensions of impoverished gentry. She received her formal education at a day school she attended at Stirling for four or five years from about the age of eight, and she later recalled her childhood and schooldays fondly, writing that she had never 'met with any thing at all resembling the way in which we lived, except the description given by Rousseau of Wolmar's farm' (Benger, 1.42). Yet however happy her childhood, Hamilton was not exempt from the pressures faced by intellectual girls in the late eighteenth century. Mrs Marshall was apparently disturbed by her niece's intellectual interests, and Hamilton recalls hiding her copy of Lord Kames's *Elements of Criticism* in her chair to prevent visitors from seeing what she was reading. Despite her separation from her family—she returned to Belfast only once during her mother's lifetime—Hamilton remained close to her siblings, particularly her brother Charles *Hamilton (1752/3–1792), an orientalist, who had gone to India with the East India Company in 1772. Her correspondence with him indicates that he raised the possibility of her joining him there, but instead she settled with him in London between 1788 and 1791 while he was on leave in England to translate the *Hedaya*, the Islamic code of laws. Devastated by his sudden death from tuberculosis in 1792, Hamilton turned to her sister Katherine, by then a widow, with whom she spent much of the rest of her life.

Charles Hamilton's death sparked his sister's literary career. Although Elizabeth Hamilton had published an essay in Henry Mackenzie's periodical *The Lounger* in 1785, her first major work, *Translations of the Letters of a Hindoo Rajah* (1796), was written at least in part as a tribute to her brother. The novel, a satire of contemporary British society in the style of Montesquieu's *Persian Letters*, was moderately successful, and Hamilton followed it up four years later with her *Memoirs of Modern Philosophers* (1800), an even more popular satirical attack on what she perceived as the excesses of contemporary radical thought. Yet even though Hamilton was sceptical about the claims of freethinkers such as William Godwin (whom she mocks in both books, despite careful disclaimers that she intended no particular targets), she was no reactionary and was willing to praise aspects of the work of Mary Wollstonecraft, whose ideas about female education were in some respects very similar to Hamilton's. Education was one of Hamilton's major interests, and she explored the subject in a range of fictional and non-fictional writing, often in very ambitious ways. Her *Letters on Education* (1801), republished in a second edition as *Letters on the Elementary Principles of Education* (1801; 4th edn 1808), offers detailed theoretical explorations of how children learn, and owes at least as much to the philosophical theories of John Locke as it does to the era's standard conduct-book advice on girls' education. An anonymous tribute (probably by Maria Edgeworth) proclaimed that in her educational writing Hamilton had 'thrown open to all classes of readers those metaphysical discoveries or observations which had been confined chiefly to the learned' (*GM*, 86/2 1816, 624). This interest in making complex ideas accessible to a wide audience also shapes some of Hamilton's less theoretical work. For example, the *Life of Agrippina, Wife of Germanicus* (1804), a lightly fictionalized biography, attempts to use the techniques of fiction to interest young women readers in questions of ethics and morality raised by historical studies, and *Letters Addressed to the Daughter of a Nobleman* (1806) attempts to explain ethical principles in terms comprehensible to a young child. Hamilton's greatest literary success, however, was *The Cottagers of Glenburnie* (1808), which features the reformation of slothful highland villagers by the good sense and sanitary habits of a retired servant who comes to board with her distant cousins. Although Hamilton's contemporaries seemed to find the exuberant fecklessness of the central village characters thoroughly amusing, the novel's decidedly punitive morality does set it apart from Hamilton's earlier, generally more tolerant, fiction.

In the decade following her brother's death, Elizabeth Hamilton lived in various places in England, including Hadleigh, in Suffolk, and Bath—where she went for her health—but she spent most of her later years in Edinburgh, where she settled in 1804. She first went there after service as governess to Lady Elizabeth Lucan, the nobleman's daughter to whom she addressed her book of 1806 on education; she had relinquished the post after only six months, deciding that the constraints of private employment were uncongenial to her. Once settled in Scotland she cultivated a number of literary friendships, including that of Sir Walter Scott, who paid a polite tribute to her work at the end of *Waverley*, and Maria Edgeworth, whom she met during a visit by Edgeworth to Edinburgh and whom she later visited in turn in Ireland. The reforming interests that mark Hamilton's writing also led her to participate energetically in charitable work in Edinburgh, work that included activities on behalf of a house of industry established to help indigent women. She spent the last few years of her life in failing health, and in May 1816 she travelled from Edinburgh to Harrogate to try to overcome the effects of a winter of illness and depression. She died there on 23 July 1816 and was buried in Harrogate church, leaving, in the words of one friend, 'a blank not easily filled' (Grant, 2.129) in Edinburgh literary circles. PAM PERKINS

**Sources** *Memoirs of the late Mrs. Elizabeth Hamilton*, ed. Miss Benger [E. O. Benger], 2 vols. (1818) • J. P. Grant, ed., *Memoir and correspondence of Mrs Grant of Laggan*, 2 vols. (1845) • [M. Edgeworth?], 'Character and writings of Mrs Elizabeth Hamilton', *GM*, 1st ser., 86/2 (1816), 188, 623–4 • *DNB*

**Archives** BL, corresp., Add. MSS 33964, fol. 359; 18204, fol. 96 • NL Scot., corresp.

**Likenesses** J. Hopwood, stipple, pubd 1815 (after G. Clint), BM, NPG; repro. in *Ladies' Monthly Magazine* (1815) • J. Hopwood junior, stipple, pubd 1823, BM • J. Hopwood junior, stipple, pubd 1825, NPG • H. Raeburn, oils, Scot. NPG [*see illus.*]

**Hamilton, Elizabeth, duchess of Hamilton** (1757–1837). *See under* White Conduit cricket club (*act. c.*1785–1788).

**Hamilton, Elizabeth** (1840–1882), philosopher and educationist, was born in Edinburgh, the only daughter and fourth child of Sir William *Hamilton of Preston, bt (1788–1856), philosopher and professor of logic and metaphysics at Edinburgh University 1836–56, and his cousin and wife, Janet (*d.* 1877), the only daughter of Hubert Marshall, merchant, Glasgow. Sir William Hamilton had a major stroke in July 1844 which left him suffering from paralysis, but he was still able to encourage his children in their studies and join in their games: he probably taught Elizabeth, who was educated at home.

Elizabeth Hamilton was among the fifty women who in 1867 established the Edinburgh Ladies Education Association (subsequently the Edinburgh Association for the Higher Education of Women) led by Mary Crudelius, who became its secretary. The objective of the association was the advancement of the higher education of women by the establishment of university-standard classes for women, taught by university professors. In its first year classes were offered only in English literature, but by 1873 subject choice had increased to include mathematics, moral philosophy, chemistry, physiology, botany, and biblical criticism. By 1874 a university certificate in arts for women had also been established. Elizabeth Hamilton was elected to the executive committee of the association in 1867 and remained on that influential body until her resignation in 1879. Having carried out the secretary's duties intermittently after 1871 during Mary Crudelius's periods of ill health, she was appointed secretary in her own right in 1877 and continued in post for the next two years. As secretary she managed the day-to-day operations of the association, reporting on events, producing the prospectus, advertising classes, and ensuring the smooth running of the classes, examinations, bursary applications, and the library, as well as campaigning for the ultimate goal of the association, an equal university education for women. She herself took advantage of the association's educational opportunities, taking twelve classes between 1867 and 1877, consisting of Latin, Greek, moral philosophy, education, English literature, mental philosophy and logic, and experimental physics.

Elizabeth Hamilton lived in the family home at 16 Great King Street, Edinburgh, until her mother's death in 1877, after which she lived with her brother Hubert Hamilton at 7 North Manor Place, Edinburgh. She wrote the memoir of her father for the *Encyclopaedia Britannica* (9th edn), which her obituarist said gave an inadequate idea of her mental resources, which were such that if she had lived longer 'she might have taken no inconsiderable place in Scottish Philosophy, and among the women … who have reached eminence as metaphysicians' (*The Scotsman*, 8 March 1882). After her resignation as secretary of the association she went to Germany to begin the work of translating Rudolf Hermann Lotze's *Microcosmus* (1885). The translation was completed and co-authored by E. E. Constance Jones after Elizabeth Hamilton's death on 2 March 1882 at 30 Northampton Park, Canonbury, London, the residence of her younger brother, Thomas Hamilton, surgeon at the Holloway and North Islington Dispensary. She was buried on 7 March beside her father in St John's burying-ground, Princes Street, Edinburgh. LESLEY M. RICHMOND

**Sources** class registers, 1867–92, U. Edin. L., special collections division, Edinburgh Association for the Higher Education of Women, GEN 1877/1/2.1.2 · reports and calendars, 1868–79, U. Edin. L., special collections division, Edinburgh Association for the Higher Education of Women, GEN 1877/1 · corresp., U. Edin. L., special collections division, Edinburgh Association for the Higher Education of Women, GEN 1877/20 · M. M. Crudelius, *A memoir of Mrs Crudelius*, ed. K. Burton (privately printed, Edinburgh, 1879) · J. Veitch, *Memoir of Sir William Hamilton, Bart* (1869) · *The Scotsman* (8 March 1882) · *Englishwoman's Review*, 13 (1882), 139

**Archives** U. Edin. L., special collections division, Edinburgh Association for the Higher Education of Women, GEN 1877

**Wealth at death** £7196 15*s*. 4*d*.: confirmation, 5 May 1882, *CCI* · £100: eik additional inventory, 12 Nov 1897, *CCI*

**Hamilton, Eliza Mary** (**1807–1851**), poet, was born in Dublin on 4 April 1807, the daughter of Archibald Hamilton (*d.* 1820), solicitor, and his wife, Sarah Hutton (*d.* 1817). The third of five children, she was largely raised by narrowly pious relatives of her mother—none of the children saw much of their parents—in a Moravian settlement near Balinderry in Northern Ireland, returning to live in Dublin and attend school only in 1822. Her uncle James Hamilton, who educated her brother from the age of three, saw early signs of genius in her but did not have resources to undertake her tutelage, so she was educated mainly at home.

Eliza's one brother was William Rowan *Hamilton (1805–1865), a brilliant linguist and mathematical genius who in 1827 was appointed Andrews professor of astronomy at Dublin University and astronomer royal of Ireland. He was also a gifted versifier who none the less came to admit that his sister Eliza was the poet, encouraging her to show her work to his friend Wordsworth, who not only upheld his judgement but offered valuable criticism and advice in a series of letters and, later, interviews, when Eliza travelled with William to Rydal Mount in the summer of 1830. All of the Hamilton siblings were gifted, and the four eldest formed their own 'Honourable Society' as well as (in 1826) a literary society with friends, the Disneys and Stanleys. Eliza and William each fell in love with a Disney sister: Eliza enjoyed a 'romantic friendship' with Anne Disney.

Eliza, along with her sisters Grace and Sydney (none of whom married), was encouraged by her brother to help him in the running of his observatory at Dunsink, just outside Dublin, where they moved with him in October 1827 (they left on his marriage in 1833). Although she successfully resisted his efforts to turn her into a fully-fledged astronomer, she was virtually unique as a woman poet of the Romantic period with an acute understanding of astronomical principles. This is reflected in some of her verse dealing in complex ways with the moon and the planets, as well as in other (unpublished) work criticizing an over-rationalist approach to astronomy. Eliza herself was deeply religious, with a strong mystical bent, influenced by the Calvinism of her childhood. She even contemplated becoming a missionary, although she supported non-denominational primary education and opposed abolition of the Irish language in schools. From 1835 to 1837 she travelled with two friends to Malta, Smyrna, and Constantinople where other friends were missionaries and spent almost a year there before reluctantly returning to Ireland at the urgent behest of her family after plague had broken out in the region.

Eliza had begun to publish poems in the *Dublin Literary Gazette* in 1830 as Z. Y., then was taken up as a contributor by the *Dublin University Magazine*, where she published most of her subsequent poetry (as E. M. H.). Her one published volume appeared under her full name in June 1838, entitled simply *Poems*. Her poetry is unusual in its focus on philosophical as well as aesthetic and religious concerns. Her work, all published in Dublin, did not reach a wide audience, nor did she move in literary circles, although she did meet Maria Edgeworth and Felicia Hemans through her brother. She became ill in 1846 and eventually died on 14 May 1851; she was buried in St Mary's churchyard, Dublin, with her sister Grace and their parents. Her journal, apart from a few passages, such as a description of Wordsworth's visit to Dunsink in August 1829 (Graves, 1.311–14), was destroyed at her death by William. VIRGINIA H. BLAIN

**Sources** R. P. Graves, *Life of Sir William Rowan Hamilton*, 3 vols. (1882–9) [repr. 1975] · *The letters of William and Dorothy Wordsworth*, ed. E. De Selincourt, 2nd edn, rev. C. L. Shaver, M. Moorman, and A. G. Hill, 8 vols. (1967–93) · T. L. Hankins, *Sir William Rowan Hamilton* (1980) · letters, TCD

**Archives** TCD, corresp.

**Hamilton** [*née* Lyon], **Emma, Lady Hamilton** (*bap.* **1765**, *d.* **1815**), social celebrity and artist's model, was born at Ness, Cheshire, and baptized nearby at Great Neston on 12

Emma Hamilton, Lady Hamilton (*bap.* 1765, *d.* 1815), by George Romney, 1782–6

May 1765. One month later her father, Henry Lyon, an illiterate blacksmith, died and she was thereafter brought up by her mother, Mary Lyon (*née* Kidd), a woman of strong and ambitious character. The child was baptized Emy, but after several variations the name settled as Emma.

**Childhood and early lovers** Mary Lyon and her daughter moved to the Kidds' family home at Hawarden in Flintshire, and it was there that, more than a dozen years later, Emma became an under-nursemaid to the family of a local surgeon, Honoratus Thomas. On a visit to London—probably in 1778—Mary Lyon found work for her daughter as a nursemaid to the children of Dr Richard Budd in Chatham Place near Blackfriars Bridge. Emma then worked as a housemaid for Dr Thomas Linley, a musical and theatrical impresario; it was probably at that time that Emma began to sing, and she might well have become an actress. She was a vivacious, beautiful girl with wide-set eyes, a heart-shaped face, and a straight nose—looks made fashionable by the vogue for classical-revival art. After the Linley family had been been overwhelmed by the death of two of their children Emma was said to have drifted away and into the *demi-monde* of the capital, although there is no reliable evidence to support reports that she was involved in prostitution. She was also said to have worked for a Dr James Graham as a scantily dressed attendant in his Temple of Health, a bogus medical establishment in the Adelphi, where infertile couples paid to use a 'celestial bed'. Her brush with the *demi-monde* may have given her the good-humoured, guilt-free amorality that marked her character.

The first confirmation of what she was to call her 'giddy ways' came in 1781, when a rich young blade, Sir Harry Fetherstonhaugh, invited her to his country mansion, Uppark in Sussex. His mother was at the house so his young mistress was housed nearby at Rosemary Cottage. She entered into fast living with zest and is said to have become a bold horsewoman and to have danced naked on the dining-room table. Later that year she became pregnant, probably by Fetherstonhaugh, and a daughter—known as Little Emma—was born on 12 March 1782.

But Fetherstonhaugh tired of her, and when one of his friends, the Hon. Charles Francis *Greville (1749–1809), was attracted to her she moved to his house at Paddington. Throughout her life she cheerfully made the best of whatever came her way. She settled into Greville's modest household with her mother, who now assumed the more distinguished name of 'Mrs Cadogan', while Emma used the surname Hart. Greville was charmed by Emma as 'naturally elegant'; not only was she 'a clean and comfortable woman' as a mistress (Morrison, 1.101), but as his hostess she was also 'the fair tea-maker of Edgware Row' (Sichel, 68). Charles Greville was a connoisseur of the arts and through him Emma met George Romney, who was also charmed, becoming the first of many artists to be enchanted by her beauty and poise; others included Reynolds, Lawrence, Hoppner, and Angelica Kauffmann.

**Meeting Sir William Hamilton** Proud as he was of his mistress, Greville was in financial trouble and hoped to marry an heiress once he had discarded Emma. Then the possibility occurred to him of achieving the latter and himself becoming an heir. In 1784 Sir William *Hamilton (1731–1803), his maternal uncle, was visiting London from Naples, where he had been British ambassador to the kingdom of the Two Sicilies for twenty years. A childless widower, a connoisseur, and a discreet voluptuary, he was instantly attracted by the beauty of Emma Hart. Greville suggested to his uncle that he should take Emma 'under his protection' in Naples and that in return he (Greville) should become his uncle's heir. Hamilton agreed, but since Emma was clearly still in love with Greville it was arranged that she and her mother would visit Naples for a holiday. Emma arrived in Naples in April 1786, but while enjoying her stay at Hamilton's embassy in the Palazzo Sessa, she realized that she was not expected to return to London; she was aghast, writing first bewildered then pathetic or furious letters to Greville. However, she became beguiled by life in Naples, where her beauty was rapturously admired and where Hamilton introduced her to Neapolitan society and to his love of works of art and antiquities and his enthusiasm for gardens and volcanoes. She learned to speak Italian and French, her voice was trained, and she performed what became known as her 'Attitudes', posing in classical robes in imitation of the figures on the antique Greek vases Sir William collected, while he acted as master of ceremonies. Goethe, visiting Naples, described her as 'a young English girl … with a beautiful face and perfect figure' and her 'Attitudes' as 'like nothing you ever saw before in your life' (J. W. Goethe, *Italian Journey* (1786–1788), trans. W. H. Auden and E. Meyer 1970, 199).

Hamilton was a charming, kindly man and almost inevitably in November or December 1786 she became his mistress. In September 1791, while visiting London, they were married in Marylebone parish church; she signed the register as Amy Lyon. Back in Naples and known at court as 'Miladi', she was useful to her husband in diplomatic scheming. However, because of her past life, she was the subject of much inventive scandal—including a supposed lesbian relationship with the queen—none of which was supported by evidence. She was beginning to lose her looks. Their friend Sir Gilbert Elliot described her: 'Her person is nothing short of monstrous for its enormity and is growing every day .... She tries hard to think size advantageous to her beauty but is not easy about it. Her face is beautiful' (*Life and Letters of Sir Gilbert Elliot, First Earl of Minto*, ed. countess of Minto, 3 vols., 1874, 2.364).

**With Nelson in Naples** Lady Hamilton first met Captain Horatio *Nelson (1758–1805) in September 1793, when Admiral Lord Hood, the commander-in-chief in the Mediterranean, sent him on a diplomatic mission to Naples to seek troop reinforcements for the beleaguered allied garrison of Toulon. He at once took to Hamilton and was charmed by Emma. She was still a flirt and a spark of mutual attraction passed between them and was reflected in a brief correspondence. However, after the successful completion of his mission and his rejoining the fleet, Nelson indulged, a year later, in a brief affair with an Italian opera singer at Leghorn. He had been introduced to fast living by his friend Prince William Henry (later William IV) in the West Indies, and was unhappy in his marriage (he had, like many naval officers entering the Mediterranean, left his marriage vows at Gibraltar). When Emma Hamilton again met Nelson he was the hero of his country and of all enemies of the French. His victory at the battle of Abu Qir Bay in August 1798 had saved the kingdom of the Two Sicilies from immediate French invasion, and when he arrived in Naples on 22 September he received a tumultuous welcome.

Emma Hamilton's appeal for Nelson was presumably not entirely sexual, though she was well trained in the amorous arts. She was motherly—and he still missed his strong-willed mother, who had died when he was nine—and she employed a fanciful sense of humour which reminded him of his father, the gentle Norfolk rector. When Nelson was rewarded for his victory with a barony rather than the expected earldom, Emma wrote to him, 'If I was King of England, I would make you the most noble, puissant Duke Nelson, Marquis Nile, Earl Alexandria, Viscount Pyramid, Baron Crocodile and Prince Victory that posterity might have you in all forms' (BL, Add. MS 34989). She flattered him with high theatricality. When she and her husband came on board his flagship off Naples, he described the scene in a letter to his wife: 'Up flew her ladyship and exclaiming, *Oh, God, is it possible!*, fell into my arm more dead than alive. Tears, however, soon put matters to rights' (*Dispatches and Letters*, 3.125). His hostess pampered Nelson, giving lavish parties in his honour; she also nursed him, for he was suffering both from a head wound and from nervous exhaustion. And she radiated sexual appeal. Meanwhile Nelson and Sir William had taken to each other, the latter introducing his new friend to Ferdinand IV and Queen Maria Carolina (sister of the executed Marie Antoinette), who showered him with compliments and honours. He met the political hierarchy and Hamilton's amusing and intelligent, if sometimes louche, friends.

After the king's rash march on Rome and his repulse by the French, the liberal revolution broke out in Naples at the end of 1798. Nelson rescued the royal family and the Hamiltons and ferried them to Sicily. The escaping ships sailed in one of the worst storms Nelson could remember. The refugees were overwhelmed with fear and seasickness, but Emma was at her best. While Sir William prepared to shoot himself rather than drown, his wife sat up all night nursing one of the young Neapolitan princes, who had gone into convulsions and who died in her arms. In that storm, the mutual attraction between Nelson and Emma was strengthened by his respect for her resolution. The affair was probably consummated either in Palermo or, perhaps, on Nelson's flagship, the *Foudroyant*, when the Hamiltons sailed in her for a cruise off Malta, then still held by the French. Nelson, besotted with Emma, sat up late with her at the card tables, drinking champagne, seeming to condone her loud and vulgar manners and causing concern among his officers.

When the counter-offensive against the Neapolitan rebels was successful and Nelson's squadron returned to Naples the Hamiltons followed with the king. Nelson and Emma were at their worst, disregarding pleas for clemency from captured radicals, some of them liberal intellectuals who had been their friends. Emma seemed pitiless as the vengeful monarch began wholesale executions. Acting as a go-between for Queen Maria Carolina, who was in Palermo, she remained on Nelson's flagship, dealing with royal correspondence, ignoring pleas from imprisoned friends ashore, and playing the harp after dinner. 'Our dear Lady', wrote Nelson to Mrs Cadogan, 'has her time so much taken up with excuses from rebels, Jacobins and fools that she is most heartily tired' (Morrison, 2.408). So in thrall was Nelson that he disregarded orders from his commander-in-chief, Admiral Lord Keith, to meet a French threat to Minorca, maintaining, 'I have no scruple in deciding to save the kingdom of Naples and risk Minorca' (*Dispatches and Letters*, 3.415). After several such disobediences Lord Spencer, the first lord of the Admiralty, ordered him home because 'you will be more likely to recover your health and strength in England than in an inactive situation in a foreign Court' (ibid., 4.242).

**Bearing Nelson's children** In July 1800 Nelson struck his flag in the Mediterranean and returned home with the Hamiltons, travelling via Vienna and some of the minor courts of Europe. An observer noted:

> She leads him about like a keeper with a bear. ... It is plain that Lord Nelson thinks of nothing but Lady Hamilton. ... She puffs the incense full in his face but he receives it with pleasure and snuffs it up very cordially. (R. C. Trench, *Remains of the Late Mrs Richard Trench*, 1862, 105–12)

The *tria juncta in uno*, as they called themselves, arrived in

London on 9 November 1800 for a tense meeting with Lady Nelson at a London hotel. At the end of the year Nelson left his wife's lodgings, their marriage finally ended, and joined the Hamiltons, moving with them to a rented house at 23 Piccadilly. Thereafter the trio were ostracized by the court and polite society. The caricatures, notably by Gillray, showed Nelson as a seducer, Sir William as an elderly cuckold, and his wife as an obese nymphomaniac.

Emma was then pregnant by Nelson. He had to take up his new appointment as second-in-command of an expedition to the Baltic and was frantic with jealousy on leaving Emma, particularly as he imagined the prince of Wales had amorous designs upon her. At the end of January 1801 Emma gave birth to twins, one of whom is believed to have died and may have been stillborn. The survivor was named Horatia; she was given the surname Thompson, the name used by Nelson in his early correspondence with Emma. A third child is believed to have been born to Emma at the end of 1803, or early in 1804, and named Little Emma by Nelson, and to have died shortly after birth.

**Life at Merton Place** On his return in June 1801 Nelson was given command of anti-invasion forces on the south-east coast; this responsibility ended with the signing of the treaty of Amiens in March 1802. He had asked Emma to buy a country house for him near London, where he could be host to the Hamiltons and be visited by his infant 'god-daughter' Horatia. Emma purchased Merton Place near Wimbledon and furnished it as a Nelsonian shrine, of which Lord Minto wrote: 'The whole house, staircase and all, are covered with nothing but pictures of her and him, of all sizes and sorts, and representations of his naval actions, coats of arms, pieces of plate in his honour' (*Life and Letters of Sir Gilbert Elliot, First Earl of Minto*, ed. countess of Minto, 3 vols., 1874, 3.242). Emma's taste was never good and she entertained lavishly and vulgarly at Nelson's house where she was acknowledged hostess, for, as Nelson had put it, 'You are to be … Lady Paramount of all the territories and waters of Merton' (Morrison, 2.172–3).

In the summer of 1802 the trio set out on a visit to Sir William's estate in Pembrokeshire which developed into a triumphant provincial tour for Nelson. When opportunity offered, Emma sang patriotic songs with verses added in praise of the nation's hero and herself led the applause when he appeared. Finally, that same year (the exact date of the letter is unknown—only the year, 1802), the complaisant Hamilton, who had hitherto given no sign of awareness, let alone criticism, of the scandal that was public knowledge, complained. 'Unfortunately our tastes as to the manner of living are very different', he began a long letter, gently rebuking her because 'the whole attention of my wife is given to Lord N.' (Morrison, 2.197). Hamilton died on 6 April 1803.

Emma had hoped that Nelson would leave the navy and use his seat in the House of Lords to enter politics. But he was not a success in politics and despised politicians, so he was relieved when war with France was resumed and he was appointed commander-in-chief in the Mediterranean, sailing in May 1803. During Nelson's long absence Emma managed Merton Place and brought up Horatia, ready for a joyous reunion in August 1805. His few weeks at home were busy with visits to the Admiralty and Whitehall for it was clear that he should soon have an opportunity to intercept the combined French and Spanish fleets. He and Emma were as much in love as ever, and before he left they received holy communion together and exchanged rings in what he considered a marriage in the eyes of God. She made no attempt to keep him at home and liked to boast that he had responded admiringly, 'Brave Emma! Good Emma! If there were more Emmas there would be more Nelsons' (J. Harrison, *The Life of the Rt. Hon. Viscount Nelson*, 2, 1806, 458–9). He left Merton Place on 13 September 1805, and five weeks later was killed in the battle of Trafalgar. Emma was stricken by the news but was aware of the high, operatic drama, playing the tragedienne with gusto. When Nelson's last letters were delivered to her she wrote upon the last of them, 'Oh miserable, wretched Emma. Oh glorious and happy Nelson' (BL, Egerton MS 1614, fol. 125).

**Decline and death** Shortly before he died Nelson had said, 'I leave Emma Lady Hamilton … as a legacy to my King and Country' (W. Beatty, *Authentic Narrative of the Death of Lord Nelson*, 1807, 17). His hopes were not realized. Although Emma received a legacy of £2000, an annuity of £500, and the freehold of Merton Place under Nelson's will, which should have kept her in modest comfort for life, she was soon in debt and showed no sign of restraining her extravagance. Several friends rallied to her aid with gifts, loans, and financial advice but it was never enough and in 1813 she was arrested for debt and consigned to the king's bench debtors' prison in Southwark, although allowed to live with Horatia on parole in nearby lodgings. Her pleas to the prince regent, stressing Nelson's last wishes and her own diplomatic services in Naples, went unheeded. But she did find a friend in an Alderman Joshua Smith, who helped her to extract more of her annuity from Nelson's brother, Earl Nelson. This enabled her to escape, in July 1814, and sail with her daughter to Calais. There she lived in two upper rooms at 27 rue Française. Tended by Horatia, she remained in bed much of the time finding solace in the bottle; indeed Horatia later said that 'she took little interest in anything but the indulgence of her unfortunate habit' (Horatia Nelson to John Paget, 1874, NMM, Nelson-Ward MS 9594/2). She was visited by the local priest—and may have been received into the Roman Catholic church—but otherwise was alone with her daughter and with her memories. On 15 January 1815 she died—probably from a liver disease; she was buried on 21 January in the graveyard of the church of St Pierre, Calais. Her body was reinterred during the rebuilding of Calais. The house where she died was destroyed during the Second World War. In 1994 a memorial to her was set up on the site of her initial burial, in what is now the Parc Richelieu in the centre of Calais.

Horatia was taken home to England by the British consul at Calais and given into the care of Nelson's sister and brother-in-law, Kate and George Matcham, and later lodged with his sister Susanna's family, the Boltons, in Burnham Market, Norfolk, where she married the curate,

Philip Ward, and became the mother of a large family. She knew that Nelson had been her father but, despite strong evidence that Lady Hamilton was her mother, refused to acknowledge her as such throughout her long life.

**Posthumous reputation** Emma Hamilton was more than a colourful character and a foil to the greatest naval commander and popular hero in the long war with revolutionary and Napoleonic France. She inspired Nelson and, if her influence was at times baleful, as at Naples in 1799, she played her part in confirming his sense of destiny, which lifted his conduct as a commander and a national figure to great heights at the climax of his life that ended at his victory at Trafalgar.

For the rest of the nineteenth century Emma Hamilton remained a somewhat shadowy, scandalous figure, often kept in the background of the Nelson legend. Until 1905 Nelson's biographers were reluctant to give her her due, treating her either as an embarrassing irrelevance or as a platonic friend of their subject. This distortion was due in part to Victorian reticence; to the scurrilous *Memoirs of Lady Hamilton*, published anonymously after her death in 1815, which went through several editions during the century; and to her daughter Horatia's reluctance to accept the identity of her mother.

In 1888 John Jeaffreson produced a two-volume biography, *Lady Hamilton and Lord Nelson*, based on the correspondence collected by Alfred Morrison, which was the first attempt to put the relationship into perspective. It was not until the centenary of Trafalgar that Walter Sichel published his admirably researched biography, *Emma, Lady Hamilton*, which has yet to be surpassed. Since then Lady Hamilton has had several good biographers—notably Mollie Hardwick (*Emma, Lady Hamilton*, 1969), Hugh Tours (*Life and Letters of Emma Hamilton*, 1963), and Flora Fraser (*Beloved Emma*, 1986)—who have generally seen her as an important foil and stimulant to the genius of Nelson and a forceful character in her own right. Also, her involvement with Nelson became a celebrated love story and the subject of historical novels, plays, and films. Her national importance was reflected in the wartime film *Lady Hamilton* (1941), in which she was played by Vivien Leigh against Laurence Olivier's Nelson.

TOM POCOCK

**Sources** *The Hamilton and Nelson papers*, ed. A. Morrison, 2 vols. (privately printed, London, 1893–4) · *Memoirs of Lady Hamilton* (1815) · B. Fothergill, *Sir William Hamilton* (1969) · F. Fraser, *Beloved Emma* (1986) · W. Sichel, *Emma, Lady Hamilton* (1905) · E. C. Knight, *Autobiography of Miss Cornelia Knight: with extracts from her journals and anecdote books*, ed. [J. W. Kaye], 2 vols. (1861) · *Nelson's letters to his wife and other documents, 1785–1831*, ed. G. P. B. Naish, Navy RS, 100 (1958) · *The letters of Lord Nelson to Lady Hamilton*, 2 vols. (1814) · H. Tours, *Life and letters of Emma Hamilton* (1963) · J. Russell, *Nelson and the Hamiltons* (1969) · H. M. M. Acton, *The Bourbons of Naples, 1734–1825* (1956); repr. (1959) · *The dispatches and letters of Vice-Admiral Lord Viscount Nelson*, ed. N. H. Nicolas, 7 vols. (1844–6) · T. J. Pettigrew, *Memoirs of the life of Vice-Admiral Lord Viscount Nelson*, 2 vols. (1849) · L. Edwards, 'Horatio Nelson and Lady Hamilton's twins', *Mariner's Mirror*, 86 (2000), 313–15

**Archives** BL, Egerton MSS, corresp. and papers, 1614–1623 · NMM, corresp. | BL, letters to Alexander Davison, Add. MS 40739 · BL, corresp. with Nelson family, Add. MS 34989 · Monmouth Museum, Nelson MSS · NMM, corresp. with Alexander Davison · NMM, corresp. with C. F. Greville · NMM, letters to Earl and Countess Nelson · NMM, corresp. with Nelson family · NMM, Nelson-Ward MSS · Royal Naval Museum, Portsmouth, Nelson MSS

**Likenesses** G. Romney, oils, 1782, Frick Collection, New York · G. Romney, oils, *c.*1782, Tate collection · G. Romney, oils, 1782–4, NMM · G. Romney, oils, 1782–6, NPG [*see illus.*] · G. Romney, two portraits, oils, 1782–6, Kenwood House, London · G. Romney, oils, *c.*1783, Hunt. L. · G. Hamilton, oils, 1786, Burghley House, Northamptonshire · G. Romney, oils, *c.*1786, NPG · G. Romney, two portraits, oils, *c.*1786, Tate collection · T. Lawrence, pencil drawing, 1791, BM · A. Kauffmann, oils, 1796, V&A · J. Gillray, caricature, coloured etching, pubd 1801, BM · R. Cosway, pencil and watercolour drawing, NPG · J. Hoppner, portrait · V. Le Brun, oils, Lady Lever Art Gallery, Port Sunlight · J. Nollekens, marble bust, AM Oxf. · J. Opie, portrait · F. Rehberg, drawings, BM · J. Rising, oils (after J. Reynolds, *c.*1784), Waddesdon Manor, Buckinghamshire · G. Romney, oils, Waddesdon Manor, Buckinghamshire · T. Rowlandson, etching, BM

**Wealth at death** 15 francs; plus clothes valued at 200 francs: Pettigrew, *Memoirs*, 2.636

**Hamilton, Esther**. *See* Bland, Esther (*d.* 1787).

**Hamilton, Eugene Jacob Lee-** (1845–1907), poet and novelist, was born in London on 6 January 1845, the son of Captain James Lee-Hamilton (*d.* 1852) and his wife, Matilda Abadam (1815–1896), the daughter of Edward Hamlin Adams. As a child Eugene lived with his widowed mother and her brother William Abadam at the Château de Biranos, near Pau, until Abadam's death about 1854, when his mother took him to Paris. There in 1855 she married her second husband, Eugene's tutor Henry Ferguson Paget, an engineer, whose active sympathy with the Warsaw uprising of 1848 had compelled him to leave his employment in Poland. They had a daughter Violet *Paget (1856–1935), who wrote under the name Vernon Lee.

Eugene was educated in France and Germany, partly at school and partly by tutors at home. In 1864 he entered Oriel College, Oxford; he gained a Taylorian scholarship for 'French with German' in that year, but left the university in 1866 without a degree. In July 1869 he was nominated an attaché, and was employed for some months in the Foreign Office. He was appointed to the embassy at Paris under Lord Lyons on 21 February 1870. He was with the embassy at Tours, Bordeaux, and Versailles during the Franco-Prussian War. In 1871 he acted as secretary to Sir Alexander Cockburn at Geneva to settle the claims of the United States of breaches of neutrality during the American Civil War, concerning the ship *Alabama*. He suffered in health from the pressure of work.

In January 1873 Lee-Hamilton was promoted to third secretary, and transferred to the legation at Lisbon under Sir Charles Murray on 10 February. He was unemployed from 1 January to 8 September 1875, when he resigned on account of a severe illness. He had been an accomplished skater and dancer, but for twenty years he was almost completely paralysed, and had to lie on his back. He lived at Florence, cared for by his mother and his half-sister, and spent the summers at Siena or Bagni di Lucca. His intellectual powers were dampened but not destroyed by his physical disablement. When his health allowed, he was able to indulge his gifts as conversationalist, and his room became one of the centres of intellectual cosmopolitan society in Florence. His visitors included Edith Wharton, Paul Bourget, and Henry James. One of Lee-Hamilton's anecdotes about Captain Silsbee's efforts to extricate some of Byron's papers from Claire Clairmont provided the inspiration for James's *The Aspern Papers*.

In time, too, Lee-Hamilton was able to compose and to dictate fragments of verse, and poetry was his consolation throughout his long illness. His earliest volume, *Poems and Transcripts*, appeared in 1878, followed by *Gods, Saints, and Men* (1880), *The New Medusa and Other Poems* (1882), and *Apollo and Marsyas and Other Poems* (1884). Most of *The Sonnets of the Wingless Hours* (1894), his most characteristic production, were written between 1880 and 1888. He excelled in the sonnet form, the technique of which he had a perfect mastery, and the dramatic impersonal *Imaginary Sonnets* (1888) and the autobiographical *Sonnets of the Wingless Hours* (1894) rank with the best of their kind.

Under the direction of Dr Erb of Heidelberg, his health improved after 1893. He achieved a full recovery in 1896 after his mother's death. Later that year he visited England, Canada, and the United States, where he stayed with Edith Wharton at her house in Rhode Island. He returned a 'new man', and on 21 July 1898 he married the novelist Annie E. Holdsworth (*b*. *c*.1857), whom he had met in Florence in 1897. They settled in a villa between Florence and Fiesole. A volume of verse, entitled *Forest Notes*, in which both husband and wife collaborated, appeared in 1899.

Lee-Hamilton also wrote *The Fountain of Youth*, a fantastic tragedy in verse (1891); two novels, *The lord of the dark red star, being the story of the supernatural influences in the life of an Italian despot of the 13th century* (1903) and *The Romance of the Fountain* (1905); and a metrical translation of Dante's *Inferno* (1898). In 1903 he made a selection from his poems for the Canterbury Poets series, for which William Sharp wrote a preface.

In 1900 the Lee-Hamiltons moved to the Villa Benedettini, San Gervasio, where in 1903 a daughter, Persis Margaret, was born. The child died in 1904, and the father's grief is recorded in *Mimma Bella*, a series of elegiac sonnets some of which were published in the *Fortnightly Review* in November 1907. The depression culminated in a paralytic stroke, from which Lee-Hamilton died on 7 September 1907 at the Villa Pierotti, Bagni di Lucca; he was buried in the Allori cemetery, the 'new' protestant cemetery outside the Porta Romana, Florence, near his mother and child. The full text of *Mimma Bella* was published posthumously with a preface by his widow in 1909.

Elizabeth Lee, *rev*. Catherine Maxwell

**Sources** P. Gunn, *Vernon Lee: Violet Paget, 1856–1935* (1964) • *The Times* (11 Sept 1907) • W. Sharp, introduction, in *Dramatic sonnets, poems, and ballads: selections from the poems of Eugene Lee-Hamilton* (1903) • *FO List* (1876) • Madame Duclaux, 'In casa Paget: a retrospect. In memoriam Eugène Lee-Hamilton', *Country Life* (28 Dec 1907), 935–7 • H. T. Lyons, 'A publishing history of the writings of Eugene Lee-Hamilton', *Papers of the Bibliographical Society of America*, 51 (1957), 141–59 • A. Lee-Hamilton, 'Introduction', in E. Lee-Hamilton, *Mimma Bella* (1909) • E. Wharton, *A backward glance* (1934), 130–32

**Archives** Colby College, Waterville, Maine, Miller Library, corresp. and MSS | Bodl. Oxf., MS Toynbee d. 15

**Likenesses** photographs, *c*.1865–*c*.1900, Colby College, Waterville, Maine, Miller Library; repro. in Gunn, *Vernon Lee*, facing pp. 37, 149 • S. Haweis, oils (during last illness) • death mask

**Hamilton, Frances**. *See* Talbot, Frances (1648–1731).

**Hamilton** [*formerly* Buchanan], **Francis, of Buchanan** (**1762–1829**), East India Company surgeon and botanist, third son of Thomas Buchanan of Spittal of Glenshee and his wife, Elizabeth Hamilton, heiress of Bardowie, was born at Branziet, Perthshire, on 15 February 1762. He graduated MA from Glasgow in 1779 and MD from Edinburgh in 1783, and in 1784, hoping to establish himself as a botanist, he joined the East India Company's service as a medical officer. To his disappointment, he had to serve as a ship's surgeon for ten years before finally obtaining a land post in Bengal as an assistant surgeon in 1794.

In 1795 he accompanied Captain Michael Symes on Britain's first political mission to Ava and put together a sizeable Burmese herbarium. This he subsequently presented to the company in the hope of gaining scientific recognition and more elevated employment. In 1800 Lord Wellesley appointed him to survey the newly conquered kingdom of Mysore, a posting which enabled him to collect a vast number of new botanical specimens. At the same time his survey, in both its portrayal of Tipu Sultan as a rapacious tyrant and its inventory of Mysore's natural wealth, vindicated Wellesley's controversial conquest, thereby earning Buchanan the governor-general's continued affection. A rambling, unedited version of the survey was published in three volumes in 1807, entitled *A Journey from Madras, through the Countries of Mysore, Canara and Malabar*.

In 1802 Buchanan joined the British embassy to Katmandu and began assembling a Nepalese herbarium. In 1804 Wellesley made him both his personal physician and director of the Natural History Project of India, an ambitious scheme to classify and illustrate all the birds and animals of south Asia. But Wellesley's rift with the court of directors doomed the project from the start and with it the prospects of his favourites; hence when he sailed for London in August 1805 Buchanan went with him, abandoning the menagerie at Barrackpore to the parsimony of the new regime.

Back in London Buchanan was made a fellow of the Royal Society on 1 May 1806. In 1807 he was promoted to surgeon and dispatched to conduct a topographical survey of Bengal, a project which dominated the remainder of his life in India. As in Mysore, Buchanan moulded the survey to suit his botanical interests, but at the same time collected voluminous social, economic, and archaeological information on the districts he toured, albeit often patchy in quality and depth.

In November 1814 Buchanan was finally appointed superintendent of the botanic garden at Calcutta, a post he had long coveted, but by then he was ready to retire. He left India in early 1815, embittered by Lord Moira's confiscation of 750 of his drawings. His disappointments continued in London, where his gift to the court of directors of his entire natural history collection went largely unremarked. He had planned in retirement to edit his Bengal survey reports, but in the wake of his falling-out with the company he concentrated instead on writing up his natural history manuscripts, publishing in 1819 *The Kingdom of Nepal* and *Genealogies of the Hindus*, followed in 1822 by *Fishes Found in the River Ganges*. In later life he compiled systematic commentaries on the pre-Linnaean classics of south Asian botany by Rheede and Rumphius, four parts of which were published by the Linnean Society. The Bengal survey, which had cost £30,000, languished unnoticed in East India House until 1838, when R. M. Martin published a harshly edited version in three volumes, entitled *The History, Antiquities, Topography, and Statistics of Eastern India*.

In 1818, upon the death of his elder brother John, Buchanan succeeded to his mother's estate and took her name of Hamilton in place of Buchanan. In 1826 he became deputy lieutenant of Perthshire and established his claim as chief of clan Buchanan. He married late in life and had a son. He died at Leny, Perthshire, on 15 June 1829. KATHERINE PRIOR

**Sources** M. Vicziany, 'Imperialism, botany, and statistics in early nineteenth-century India: the surveys of Francis Buchanan (1762–1829)', *Modern Asian Studies*, 20 (1986), 625–60 • J. J. Higginbotham, *Men whom India has known: biographies of eminent Indian characters*, 2nd edn (1874) • Chambers, *Scots.* (1835) • W. I. Addison, ed., *The matriculation albums of the University of Glasgow from 1728 to 1858* (1913) • G. R. Kaye and E. H. Johnston, eds., *Catalogue of manuscripts in European languages belonging to the library of the India Office*, 2/2: *Minor collections and miscellaneous manuscripts* (1937) • D. Prain, 'A sketch of the life of Francis Hamilton (once Buchanan), some time superintendent of the honourable company's botanic gardens at Calcutta', *Annals of the Royal Botanic Garden of Calcutta*, 10/2 (1905), i–lxxv • H. Beveridge, 'The Buchanan records', *Calcutta Review*, 99 (1894), 1–17 • *Claim of Dr. Francis Buchanan, Buchanan of Spittal* (1826) • D. G. Crawford, ed., *Roll of the Indian Medical Service, 1615–1930* (1930) • Desmond, *Botanists*

**Archives** BL, descriptions of fish, Add. MSS 9882, 19296 • BL OIOC, papers • Linn. Soc., papers • NA Scot., corresp. and papers • NHM, catalogue of plants • NRA Scotland, priv. coll. • RBG Kew • U. Edin. L., papers | Linn. Soc., letters to Sir James E. Smith • NHM, letters to William Roxburgh • NL Scot., corresp. with Constable & Co.

**Wealth at death** in 1818, when inherited mother's estate from brother, it carried debts of £15,000 which were cleared in lifetime

**Hamilton, Sir Frederick Hew George Dalrymple-** (**1890–1974**), naval officer, was born in London on 27 March 1890, the younger son and youngest of three children (the middle child, a daughter, died two months after he was born) of Colonel the Hon. North de Coigny Dalrymple (1853–1906), Scots Guards, second son of the tenth earl of Stair, and sometime aide-de-camp to the duke of Connaught. His mother was Marcia Kathleen Anne (*d.* 1907), daughter of the Hon. Sir Adolphus Frederick Octavius Liddell. The name Hamilton was added in 1896, when Colonel Dalrymple inherited the house and property of Bargany in Ayrshire. George V, who as Prince George had stood sponsor to the future admiral, nominated him for a cadetship in the Royal Navy, which he entered in 1905. An early appointment on completion of training was to HM yacht *Victoria and Albert* as sub-lieutenant. In August 1914 he joined the cruiser *Cumberland*, seeing action in charge of armed boats in the Cameroon River. Thereafter he served throughout the war in destroyers, gaining command in 1917. In September 1918 he married Gwendolen (1890–1974), third daughter of Sir Cuthbert Edgar Peek, second baronet, of Rousden, Devon, and his wife, the Hon. Augusta Louisa Brodrick, daughter of the eighth Viscount Midleton. She died in November 1974. They had two daughters and a son, Captain North Edward Frederick Dalrymple-Hamilton, of the Royal Navy, of Bargany.

Between the wars Dalrymple-Hamilton served in the battle cruiser *Renown* with the prince of Wales on board for his visit to the emperor of Japan in 1922; again in the *Victoria and Albert*; in the plans division of the naval staff; in the cruiser *Effingham* on the East India station; and as commander of the Royal Naval barracks, Devonport. Promoted captain in 1931, he commanded the fourth destroyer flotilla in the Mediterranean and was then selected to command the Royal Naval College, Dartmouth, which he joined early in 1937. It was an ideal choice. Considerate, but always firm, though with a light touch, he inspired great devotion in the staff and created a good atmosphere, exemplifying to the cadets personal qualities of the highest order. A visit by George VI and Queen Elizabeth to the college in July 1939 was, despite the portents, a particularly happy occasion for Dalrymple-Hamilton as he had known them both since their childhood.

In November 1939 Dalrymple-Hamilton took command of the battleship *Rodney*, where his close interest in his officers and men, and his fine ship handling, won him universal liking and respect. The crucial test came in May 1941, during the *Bismarck* chase. The *Rodney* found herself operating independently to cover the possible courses of the still formidable German battleship towards the French coast. Ignoring contradictory instructions in a confused situation and using his own judgement Dalrymple-Hamilton skilfully brought his ship to the support of the *King George V* in the final gun action which sank the *Bismarck*. For this he was appointed CB (1941). Promotion to rear-admiral followed quickly, and appointment as admiral in charge of Iceland command. Here his care for the hard-pressed escort crews, and his excellent relations with the Americans, newly allied, ensured the most effective use of this vital base. In 1942 he became naval secretary to the first lord of the Admiralty.

Early in 1944 Dalrymple-Hamilton was given command of the 10th cruiser squadron, promoted to vice-admiral, and made second in command of the Home Fleet. In tactical command of north Russian convoy operations, with his cruisers in the bombardment force at the Normandy landings, and in sweeping the Bay of Biscay clear of German surface warships, he was conspicuously successful. An important innovation was his use of an escort carrier as flagship in a convoy support force, so that he could make the best use of his aircraft. In January 1945 he was created KCB and appointed vice-admiral, Malta, where for a time he was acting governor. In 1946 he became flag officer Scotland and Northern Ireland and in January 1948 was promoted admiral.

In the following September, Dalrymple-Hamilton went to Washington, DC, as admiral, British joint services mission, where he served until his retirement in 1950. In this, as in all his previous shore appointments including Iceland, Dalrymple-Hamilton was most ably supported, despite her almost total blindness, by his wife.

Dalrymple-Hamilton was an elder of Inch parish church, lieutenant in the Royal Company of Archers, HM body guard for Scotland, deputy lieutenant for Wigtownshire, and a member of many public and charitable bodies. He died on 26 December 1974 at Biggart Hospital in Prestwick, Ayrshire. IAN MCGEOCH, *rev.*

**Sources** *The Times* (30 Dec 1974) • S. W. Roskill, *The war at sea, 1939–1945*, 3 vols. in 4 (1954–61) • private information (1986) • personal knowledge (1986) • *WWW* • Burke, *Peerage* (1980) • *CCI* (1975)
**Archives** FILM IWM FVA, actuality footage
**Likenesses** W. Stoneman, photograph, 1942, NPG
**Wealth at death** £110,493.96: confirmation, 29 April 1975, *CCI*

**Hamilton, Gavin** (*c*.1561–1612), bishop of Galloway, was the third son of the sixteen children of John Hamilton of Orbieston (*d*. 1568), a descendant of Sir James Hamilton of Cadzow, and his wife, Janet (*d*. 1584), daughter of John Hamilton of Haggs (*d*. before 1553). His father was killed in 1568 at the battle of Langside, fighting alongside the other Hamiltons in the army of Mary, queen of Scots, and after that the head of the family probably took an interest in him. Certainly he was later sent to St Andrews University, where John Hamilton, first marquess of Hamilton, was chancellor, graduating MA in 1584. When he married Alison (*d*. after 1644), eldest daughter of James Hamilton of Bothwellhaugh, he was described as 'servand to the marquis of Hamilton' (Hamilton, 479) and may have been his chaplain.

In 1590 Gavin was appointed to the second charge in Hamilton, Lanarkshire, moving to nearby Bothwell in 1594. On 3 May 1604 he granted a feu charter of the lands of Orbieston and the kirklands of Bothwell to his brother John Hamilton of Orbieston, reserving the cure of the church and 4 acres of glebe for himself. That same year he was appointed to the first charge at Hamilton. He attended the general assembly of the Church of Scotland from 1595 to 1612, and became one of the superintendents. In 1597 he was nominated to a standing commission chosen to confer with James VI on ecclesiastical matters. Supporting the monarch's controversial plans to reintroduce episcopacy he was made bishop of Galloway on 3 March 1605 and in 1606 dean of the Chapel Royal at Stirling, commendator of Whithorn, and abbot of Dundrennan and Glenluce. He also remained minister of Hamilton until 1608. He was present on the scaffold when George Sprott was executed on 12 August 1608 for complicity in the Gowrie conspiracy and bore witness to his confession.

In June 1610 John Spottiswoode, archbishop of Glasgow, and Andrew Lamb, bishop of Brechin, set off for London, followed soon afterwards by Hamilton. Whatever the king's orders, only existing bishops could mediate spiritual power to other bishops and so all three were consecrated in the chapel at London House on 21 October 1610, according to the English rite. 'Gifts were bestowed and glooves were distributed in token of the solemnization of the marriage betwixt the bishops and their kirks', David Calderwood reported (Calderwood, 7.150). After they returned to Scotland, Hamilton took part in the consecration of the other Scottish bishops on 24 February 1611. He died a year later, in February 1612, aged about fifty-one, leaving assets of £22,298, which made him one of the wealthiest Scottish bishops. 'He was', Bishop Robert Keith would later observe, 'an excellent good man' (Keith, 280).

ROSALIND K. MARSHALL

**Sources** G. Hamilton, *The house of Hamilton* (1933), 478–9, 642 • *Fasti Scot.*, new edn, 3.230, 258–62 • R. Keith and J. Spottiswoode, *An historical catalogue of the Scottish bishops, down to the year 1688*, new edn, ed. M. Russel [M. Russell] (1824), 280 • Hamilton testaments, 16 June 1612, NA Scot., CC 10/5/2 • J. Spottiswood, *The history of the Church of Scotland*, ed. M. Napier and M. Russell, 3, Bannatyne Club, 93 (1850), 208–9 • D. Calderwood, *The history of the Kirk of Scotland*, ed. T. Thomson and D. Laing, 8 vols., Wodrow Society, 7 (1842–9), vol. 7, p. 150 • *DNB* • D. G. Mullan, *Episcopacy in Scotland: the history of an idea, 1560–1638* (1986), 104, 113, 128 • C. Rogers, *History of the Chapel Royal in Scotland* (1882), pp. cxi–cxii and n.
**Wealth at death** £22,298: Rogers, *History*, cxi–cxii and n.; Mullan, *Episcopacy*, 128; Hamilton register of testaments, 16 June 1612, NA Scot., CC 10/5/2

**Hamilton, Gavin** (1704–1767), bookseller and paper maker, was born on 11 February 1704 at Cramond, near Edinburgh, the third son and one of the sixteen children of the Revd William *Hamilton (1669–1732) and Mary (*bap*. 1676, *d*. 1760), daughter of John Robertson, a Glasgow merchant. Having grown up at Edinburgh University, where his father was professor of divinity from 1709 and briefly principal (from 1730), he became a central figure in the town's publishing trade and hence a significant contributor to, and promoter of, the Edinburgh Enlightenment.

Initially, however, Hamilton had worked as a cloth merchant in place of his elder brother William, who died in 1722. In 1729 he probably attended Adam Watt's humanity (Latin) class at Edinburgh University, and later that year set up as a bookseller. Soon afterwards he entered local politics, and sat as a member of Edinburgh town council (1732–45), sometimes holding the office of bailie. In this capacity he supervised, on 11 April 1736, the hanging of Andrew Wilson, at which the city guard under Captain John Porteous fired on the crowd, killing six. At the subsequent riot in September, Hamilton was nearly killed by a blow from an axe when masked men broke into the town's gaol aiming to murder Porteous. As first bailie under Lord Provost Archibald Stewart during the Jacobite rising of 1745, Hamilton visited the Stuart camp at Colinton, and was threatened by Charles Edward Stuart over the availability of the town's arms.

Hamilton was politically sympathetic to the whigs, his professional and political interests driven by the goal of improvement. In addition to his role on the town council he was a treasurer of the Royal Infirmary, Edinburgh; a manager of the Edinburgh Society for the Encouragement of Arts, Sciences, Manufactures, and Agriculture (he entered his own books and papers for prizes); a director of the Society in Scotland for the Propagation of Christian Knowledge; and a commissioner for the improvement of the town's streets, often paying from his own purse for old properties to be cleared. Other ventures included the revival of the town's assembly rooms as a site of the polite and modest sociability so easily practised by Hamilton himself.

The success of Hamilton's career as a bookseller owed much to his marriage, on 24 March 1732, to Helen (1709–1793), daughter of John Balfour, merchant of Pilrig. Thereafter Hamilton recruited his brother-in-law John *Balfour (1715–1795) as a clerk and established the firm of Hamilton and Balfour in 1739, despite Helen's concern that they would not be compatible on account of Balfour's fiery temper. In fact theirs quickly became the town's leading publishing firm, and their shop on the High Street a haunt of the Edinburgh literati. In December 1749 they signed a printing partnership with Patrick *Neill (1725–1789), and four years later they became printers to the university. From the following year they leased Bogsmill paper mill on the Water of Leith, near Colinton, and adopted a monogram HB sided with the initials J and G as their watermark.

The company was both highly productive and innovative. Between 1750 and 1762 it produced 340 titles, including works by Swift, Pope, and Bishop Burnet; medical and scientific studies by Francis Home and Robert Whytt; modern Scottish literature, including verse by the blind poet Thomas Blacklock and John Home's *The Tragedy of Douglas* (1757); and work by leading Scottish intellectuals, among them Adam Ferguson, William Robertson, and David Hume, whose first volume of his *History of Great Britain* appeared in 1754. Works in translation included studies by Voltaire, Montesquieu, and Rollin, while a strong reputation for classical literature, including works by Sallust, Livy, and Plutarch, owed much to their 1743 edition of Virgil, which has been seen as heralding a golden age of the Scottish press (Gaskell, 102). Alongside these titles there appeared a journal, the *Edinburgh Review* (1755–6), and an eight-page newspaper, the *Edinburgh Chronicle* (1759–61). In addition to its support of Scottish literature the firm was also a prominent opponent of the copyright prosecution brought by London booksellers between 1743 and 1749, when Scots' nationalistic appeals found favour in the court of session. Hamilton was also the first bookseller to offer substantial copy money to Scottish authors under an Edinburgh imprint, but, lacking London distribution, this pro-Scottish ambition was eventually thwarted. More successful was the firm's export of books to the American colonies (two of Hamilton's brothers, both physicians, lived in Maryland), principally through the Philadelphian distributor David Hall.

In 1762 Hamilton broke with John Balfour, telling their mutual friend William Strahan:

> at the last stage of parting he behaved very civily to me and we parted amicably, nay had he treat me with one sixth part of the civility during the course of the contract I should not have thought of it. (16 Aug 1762, NL Scot., Acc. 10832)

Hamilton retained Bogsmill paper mill, which he ran until suffering a stroke in autumn 1766. He died on 1 January 1767, aged sixty-two, at his home, Millbank House, Bogsmill, and was buried at Colinton kirk on 7 January. He left little money, and his property was shared between his wife, who died in August 1793, and their children: John (1740–1792), a London merchant; Louisa (1733–1793); Anne (1738–1787); Elizabeth (1749–*c*.1842), who published a brief biographical sketch of her father in 1840; and Robert *Hamilton, later professor of mathematics at Aberdeen University. WARREN MCDOUGALL

**Sources** W. McDougall, 'Gavin Hamilton, John Balfour and Patrick Neill: a study of publishing in Edinburgh in the 18th century', PhD diss., U. Edin., 1974 · [E. Hamilton], *Short memoir of Gavin Hamilton, publisher and bookseller in Edinburgh in the eighteenth century* (1840) · B. Balfour-Melville, *The Balfours of Pilrig* (1907) · W. McDougall, 'Gavin Hamilton, bookseller in Edinburgh', *British Journal for Eighteenth-Century Studies*, 1 (1978), 1–19 · W. McDougall, 'Copyright litigation in the court of session, 1738–1749', *Edinburgh Bibliographical Society Transactions*, 5/5 (1971–87), 2–31 · W. McDougall, 'A catalogue of Hamilton, Balfour and Neill publications, 1750–1762', *Spreading the word: the distribution networks of print, 1550–1850*, ed. R. Myers and M. Harris (1998), 187–232 · W. McDougall, 'Scottish books for America in the mid-18th century', *Spreading the word: the distribution networks of print, 1550–1850*, ed. R. Myers and M. Harris (1998), 21–46 · G. Hamilton to A. Fletcher, lord justice clerk, 1745–6, NL Scot., Fletcher of Saltoun MSS, MS 16608, fol. 155; MS 16614, fol. 124; MS 16625, fols. 47–55, 172 · G. Hamilton to W. Strahan, 16 Aug 1762, NL Scot., Acc. 10832 · P. Gaskell, 'Printing the classics in the eighteenth century', *Book Collector*, 1 (1952), 98–111 · bap. reg. Scot. · *Fasti Scot.*, 1.146 · college matriculation roll, U. Edin., 173 · J. Gilhooly, *A directory of Edinburgh in 1752* (1988), 24 · bur. reg. Scot.

**Archives** Maryland Historical Society, Baltimore, Dulaney MSS, letters of Dr Alexander Hamilton and Hamilton family · NL Scot., Fletcher of Saltoun MSS, letters and accounts · U. Edin., New Coll. L., Thomson of Banchory MSS, letters to his children and Hamilton related letters, MSS Tho 1 and Tho 2

**Likenesses** photograph, exh. 1939, Scot. NPG · W. Mosman, oils, repro. in Balfour-Melville, *Balfours of Pilrig*, photographic reproduction; priv. coll.

**Wealth at death** small: Balfour-Melville, *The Balfours of Pilrig*, 266

**Hamilton, Gavin** (1723–1798), painter, archaeologist, and dealer, was born at Murdieston House in the parish of Bertram Shotts, Lanarkshire, second son of Alexander Hamilton (*d.* 1768) of Murdieston, laird of Inverdovat (now Tayfield), Fife, who had inherited Murdieston from his great-uncle Alexander Inglis. Hamilton's parents married in 1719: his mother, Margaret (*d.* 1742), was the eldest daughter of Alexander Stewart of Torrance in the parish of East Kilbride, Lanarkshire. As befitted a young man of his class, he matriculated in humanities at Glasgow University in 1738 where he studied, a contemporary of Adam Smith, until about 1742. He became proficient in classical literature and history, his enthusiasm for the antique doubtless influenced by Professor Francis Hutcheson's advocacy of the superiority of ancient Greek civilization.

It is not known what drew this well-bred 'man of good sense and genteel education' (James Irvine, 10 Feb 1781), but in 1744 Hamilton travelled to Rome with Lord Hyndeford and studied portrait painting there under

Agostino Masucci, president of the Accademia di San Luca. As early as 1748, on a visit to Portici, Hamilton stated that 'the antique triumphed over the modern, both in painting and in sculpture' (Irwin and Irwin, 92), and in April that year travelled with Matthew Brettingham, James 'Athenian' Stuart, and Nicolas Revett to Naples and the ruins at Herculaneum and Pompeii which deeply affected Hamilton's career. He lodged with Stuart and Revett at strada Felice 77 from 1748 to 1750, when the parish register of Sant' Andrea delle Frate lists Hamilton as a protestant. They tried to raise money in 1749 for a visit to Greece, later funded by James Dawkins; Hamilton did not accompany them for some reason when they left for Greece in 1750. Their findings were later published in the hugely influential *Antiquities of Athens* (Society of Dilettante, 4 vols., 1762–1816).

Hamilton had returned to London by July 1751 and made his living as a portraitist, painting his distant relatives, the sixth duke and duchess of Hamilton (priv. coll., and version Scot. NPG), the duchess's sister, Maria, countess of Coventry (priv. coll.). In 1753 Hamilton joined artists led by Francis Hayman in campaigning for a national academy, but the duke of Hamilton's ledger states that Hamilton was in Paris by 15 December 1753 (Hamilton Archives, HA 621–4, priv. coll.). He then perhaps painted the portrait of a kinsman and translator of Homer, in France as a Jacobite exile, *William Hamilton of Bangour* (Scot. NPG), portrayed in antique dress: a similar treatment to that used in Hamilton's *General Sir John Guise as a Roman General* (priv. coll.).

Despite success in portraiture, Hamilton continued 'thinking of fine pictures and fine Compositions' an 'indulgence … very natural to a Man who has been so long in Italy' (Stuart). In 1755 he proposed a work 'representing some great and heroick subject' to the marquess of Tweedale, noting 'there can be no true magnificence without the assistance of either painting or sculpture' (Yester papers). He was back in Rome in 1756 with a pupil, John Day, in the year he won the commission of his first Homeric subject, *Paris and Helen*, from Sir Nathaniel Curzon (not completed until 1759; Kedleston Hall, Derbyshire), notably a year before the publication of Caylus's influential *Tableaux tirés d'Homère* (1757). The Curzon connection led to his portrait of Curzon's sister-in-law, *Juliana Dawkins as Ceres* (Kedleston Hall) and her husband Henry's commission of the enormous *Dawkins and Wood Discovering Palmyra* (1758; NG Scot.), Hamilton's only contemporary scene, but one which renders its protagonists as ancient heroes in classical garb.

When Robert Adam dined with Hamilton in 1757 they talked of 'arts and sciences, of Greece and the Grecian Islands' (Fleming, 230). What Hamilton later described as 'le sublime idee del incomparabile Homero' (Ingamells, no. 13) provided the scheme for six large paintings, some 3 metres high by 4 wide, finished over a number of years and sold to different patrons but intended from the outset as a historic cycle. These were *Andromache Weeping over the Body of Hector* painted for Charles Compton, later seventh earl of Northampton (1758–61; exh. Society of Artists, 1762; des. Gordonstoun, 1943; modello, NG Scot.); *Achilles Mourning the Death of Patroclus*, for James Grant of Grant (1760–63; exh. 1765, Society of Artists, NG Scot.); *Achilles Dragging the Body of Hector from his Chariot*, for Lord Tavistock but later sold to the second earl of Ossory on the former's death in a riding accident in 1767 (1762–5); *The Anger of Achilles for the Loss of Briseis*, painted for the second Viscount Palmerston (1765–8; exh. RA, 1770, priv. coll.); *Priam Pleading with Achilles for the Body of Hector*, for Luke Gardiner, lost (1771–5; modello (?), Tate collection); *Hector's Farewell to Andromache* for the eighth duke of Hamilton (1775–7; on loan to the Hunterian Museum, Glasgow). (Hamilton also painted the young duke's portrait (Scot. NPG) at the same period.) All but the last of these Homeric subjects were engraved by Domenico Cunego between 1764 and 1778 at Hamilton's instruction, cannily preserving the cycle as a set of prints and simultaneously augmenting both his wealth and his international reputation. The first *Andromache* was praised for its Grecian form and restraint by the critic Johann Joachim Winckelmann (to whom Hamilton had been introduced in 1755 by the artist Anton Raphael Mengs). His style was much influenced by the classical antiquities he saw and also by the work of Nicolas Poussin and the Bolognese artists Guido Reni and Guercino, though his painting was criticized for dull and livid colouring.

Hamilton also drew upon Roman history with *Brutus Avenging the Death of Lucretia*, for Lord Hope (1763; Theatre Royal, Drury Lane, London, and version, Yale U. CBA), which was to influence Jacques-Louis David and Henry Fuseli, and painted *Agrippina Weeping over the Ashes of Germanicus*, for Lord Ossory (exh. RA, 1770; lost), and *Agrippina Landing at Brundisium*, for Lord Spencer (exh. RA, 1772; Tate collection). A number of works represented gods and goddesses: *Diana and Endymion* (priv. coll.), *Venus and Adonis* (exh. Free Society of Artists, 1770; lost), *Apollo and Artemis* (Art Gallery and Museum, Glasgow), and *Hygaea* (exh. RA, 1788; priv. coll.). He painted a *Coriolanus* for Alderman Boydell's *Shakspeare Gallery* (1791; lost) and Boydell also presented Hamilton's *Apollo at the Castalian Fountain* to the City of London in 1793 (1782; exh. Boydell's Shakspeare Gallery, London, 1783; Guildhall Art Gallery, des. 1941). His only foray into modern history was *Mary Queen of Scots Resigning her Crown*, for James Boswell (1765–75; exh. RA, 1776; Hunterian Art Gallery, Glasgow University), but this was not well received. However, he did paint two subjects from Milton, *Il Penseroso* and *L'Allegro* (for William Weddell, engraved by Cunego, 1768; lost), and also offered the pendants *Love* and *Friendship* (lost) to the earl of Shelburne in 1779.

Hamilton was a friend of Sir William Hamilton, a distant kinsman, to whom he sold the pendants *Painting* and *Poetry* (Palazzo Sessa inventory, now lost, engraved by R. Morghen, 1779 and 1780) as well as a *Sleeping Venus and Cupid with Lyre* (auctioned at Sir William's sale, 27 March 1801, lot 59, lost; see Jenkins and Sloan, cat. no. 172). Sir William also bought old masters from Hamilton, including a Giordano and Palma Giovane (ibid., 85, 87–8, 274).

His friendship with Sir William led to Hamilton accompanying Emma Hart and her mother from London to Geneva in spring 1786. He had been in London partly to sell his Leonardo (the *Virgin of the Rocks*; National Gallery, London) and perhaps to organize his financial affairs (for in 1783 he inherited a considerable estate from his elder brother). Hamilton painted Emma as *Hebe* (versions priv. coll. and Stamford University, Connecticut) and also as a *Sibyl* inspired by Guercino (formerly Ince-Blundell collection; ex Christies, London, 12 April 1991, lots 32 and 33, priv. coll.), an artist whose work he had also copied.

In 1784 Hamilton completed the *Stanza Elena e Paride*, begun in 1782 in the Villa Borghese (reported in the *Giornale delle Belle Arti*, Rome, 1784, 5): a decorative scheme of eight paintings from the *Iliad* (four still *in situ*, one lost, and three now in the Museo di Roma), designed in conjunction with sculpture and reliefs relating to Paris and Helen by Agostino Penna and Vincenzo Pacetti. His last known picture was the large *Diana and her Nymphs* (1793; priv. coll.) but his painting production dwindled in his later years which were taken over primarily by his dealing activities. More successful than any other British history painter in Rome, Hamilton also used his studio to deal in old-master pictures and antique sculpture. He had an excellent eye and a reputation for honesty. In 1773 he published a folio *Scola Italica picturae* (with plates forming vol. 22, pl. 972–1011, of the collected works of G. B. Piranesi and F. Piranesi). The plates, engraved by various commissioned artists from Hamilton's own drawings, illustrate Italian painting from Leonardo da Vinci to the Caracci, many either owned by Hamilton or sold by him, such as Raphael's *Ansidei Madonna* and *St John the Baptist*, Dosso Dossi's *Adoration of the Kings*, and Guido Reni's *St Jerome* (all now in the National Gallery, London). However significant his coups in picture dealing undoubtedly were, it was as a seller of antiquities that he was most renowned. Charles Townley's collection of classical sculpture now at the British Museum was in part inspired by Hamilton's advice that 'in spite of the sneers of a tasteless age … the most valuable acquisition that a man of refined taste can make, is a peice of fine Greek Sculptour' (Smith, 309; see too A. Wilton and I. Bignamini, eds., *The Grand Tour: the Lure of Italy in the Eighteenth Century*, 1996, exhibition catalogue, Tate Gallery, London, 250, 257–68). Hamilton was Townley's regular agent and provided him with many outstanding Roman examples, while Townley put up some of the money towards excavation costs.

Hamilton's excavations in Italy provided statues, busts, and reliefs for the Museo Pio-Clementino as well as for a list of British clients which reads like a who's who of the eighteenth-century grand tour. His natural instinct was matched by good luck in making discoveries. He began excavation in 1769 at Hadrian's villa below Tivoli, unearthing some sixty marbles. In 1771 he found many statues while excavating on the Via Appia in the 'tenuta del Colombaro'. He also dug at Prima Porta and in the country round the Alban mountains. He discovered some fine marbles (including the *Cupid* in the Townley collection) at Castel di Guido, but his digs in the marshland around Ostia were discontinued owing to malaria. Hamilton excavated the villa of Antoninus Pius at Monte Cagnolo near Civita Lavinia (modern Lanuvio) from 1772 until at least 1777–8, finding a number of sculptures, including two pairs of dogs, one now in the Vatican Museum, Rome, the other bought by Townley (see *Ancient Marbles in the British Museum*, pl. 45, x, frontispiece, pl. 25, 26). Between 1792 and 1794 Hamilton excavated at Pantan de' Griffi, an estate belonging to Prince Marcantonio (IV) Borghese, where he found the ancient town of Gabii on the Via Prenestina, unearthing a number of statues including the *Diane de Gabie* (Louvre, Paris), which became part of the prince's collection (a sketch of Hamilton leading grand tourists around the site in 1793 by Giuseppe Cades is in the National Gallery of Scotland).

The excavations at Hadrian's villa were undertaken by Hamilton with James Byres and also Thomas Jenkins, with whom Hamilton often collaborated on sales. Though G. B. Visconti, papal commissioner of antiquities, spoke highly of his careful diligence, Hamilton did indulge in some creative 'restoration', often abetted by his friend the sculptor Pacetti, transforming, for example, a *Discobolus* sold to Lord Lansdowne (priv. coll.) and underhandedly shipping the *Townley Venus* out in two halves to avoid unwelcome papal interest. William, second earl of Shelburne, afterwards first marquess of Lansdowne, purchased much from Hamilton's excavations between 1770 and 1780. In a letter of 18 January 1772 Hamilton said that he meant to make the Shelburne House collection, including the *Wounded Amazon* (Metropolitan Museum, New York) found in 1771, famous throughout the world. James Smith-Barry of Marbury Hall, Cheshire, also bought from Hamilton, including an *Antinous* for £1000, the highest recorded price for any antiquity sent from Rome to Britain in the eighteenth century. Thomas Mansel-Talbot, Lyde Brown, and the second Lord Egremont of Petworth also acquired sculptures from him. One of the most famous of Hamilton's finds, the massive *Warwick Vase*, is now in the Burrell collection, Glasgow.

Through his own art, picture dealing, and archaeological finds, Hamilton was a central figure in the artistic life of Rome in the latter half of the eighteenth century and a key influence on the formation of neo-classical taste in Europe. Though little known in his native land, he gained recognition in Italy, being elected to the Accademia di San Luca on 11 January 1761, and to the Accademia Clementina, Bologna, on 29 May 1766. John Aikman wrote in 1767 that 'all the young students apply to him for Direction and Instruction in their studies. He is a sweet-blooded gentleman, and being the most renowned of all the history painters of this age is highly respected in Rome' (Ingamells, 448). He was described by Henry Fuseli as a man 'admitted to being genial even by his detractors' (Pilkington, 226) and encouraged young artists such as David Allan (who was told Hamilton was the 'unsolicited friend of every deserving young artist' by Lord Cathcart; Gordon, 18) and his countrymen, Alexander and James Runciman. The combination of classical subjects portrayed in what was perceived to be a classical manner had significant influence upon artists such as the French painter Jacques-Louis David and in 1779 Hamilton's advice to the young Antonio Canova to take up the restrained neo-classical style secured the sculptor's success. Hamilton died at Rome on 4 January 1798, praised by Pacetti, then head of the Accademia di San Luca, as a worthy and honourable man. Unmarried and childless, Hamilton was succeeded in his Scottish estates by his younger brother, General James Inglis Hamilton (*d.* 1803).

JULIA LLOYD WILLIAMS

**Sources** J. Anderson, 'Biographical sketches of eminent Scottish artists: Gavin Hamilton', *The Bee*, 18 (10 July 1793) [first biography of Hamilton, then still alive] • D. Irwin, 'Gavin Hamilton: painter, archaeologist, dealer', *Art Bulletin*, 44 (1962), 87–102 • J. Ingamells, ed., *A dictionary of British and Irish travellers in Italy, 1701–1800* (1997), 447–50 • D. Irwin and F. Irwin, *Scottish painters at home and abroad, 1700–1900* (1975), 40–50 [Hamilton as portraitist] and 101–4 [Hamilton and neo-classicism] • *Letters of Gavin Hamilton edited from the manuscripts at Lansdowne House*, ed. E. Fitzmaurice (1879) • A. H. Smith, 'Gavin Hamilton's letters to Charles Townley', *Journal of Hellenic Studies*, 20 (1901), 306–21 • L. M. Errington, 'Gavin Hamilton's sentimental *Iliad*', *Burlington Magazine*, 120 (1978), 11–13 • S. Q. Hutton, 'A historical painter: Gavin Hamilton in 1755', *Burlington Magazine*, 120 (1978), 87–102 • R. Rosenblum, 'Gavin Hamilton's *Brutus* and its aftermath', *Burlington Magazine*, 3 (1961), 8–16 [Hamilton's influence on European artists, incl. Fuseli and David] • C. Pace, 'Gavin Hamilton's *Wood and Dawkins discovering Palmyra*: the dilettante as hero', *Art History*, 4/3 (1981), 271–90 • J. Lloyd Williams, *Gavin Hamilton*, Scottish Masters series (1994) • I. Jenkins and K. Sloan, *Vases and volcanoes* (1996) [exhibition catalogue, BM, London] • G. Hamilton, *Scola Italica picturae* (Rome, 1773) • G. B. Piranesi, *Vasi e candelabri* (Rome, 1778) • E. K. Waterhouse, 'The British contribution to the neo-classical style in painting', *PBA*, 40 (1954), 57–74 [first re-evaluation of Hamilton's importance to neo-classicism in Eng.] • R. Rosenblum, *Transformations in late eighteenth century art* (Princeton, 1969); 3rd edn (1974) • J. Fleming, *Robert Adam and his circle in Edinburgh and Rome* (1962) • C. A. Hutton, 'Travels of Palmyra Wood in 1750–51', *Journal of Hellenic Studies*, 47 (1927), 108–28 • D. Macmillan, *Scottish art, 1460–1990* (1990) • D. Irwin, *English neo-classical art* (1966), 113–18 • A. T. F. Michaelis, *Ancient marbles in Great Britain* (1882) • C. C. Vermeule and D. von Bothmer, 'Notes on a new edition of Michaelis', *American Journal of Archaeology*, 59 (1955), 129–50; 60 (1956), 321–50; 62 (1959), 139–66 and 329–48 • M. Pilkington, *A dictionary of painters: from the revival of the art to the present period*, ed. H. Fuseli, new edn (1805) • R. Douglas, *The baronage of Scotland*, 1 (1798) • T. C. Gordon, *David Allan* (1951), 18 • J. Irvine, MS letter, 10 Feb 1781, BM, Add. MS 36493, fol. 128In. • A. Stuart, letter, 2 July 1751, NL Scot., MS 8250, fols. 1–2v • parish registers, Archives of San Giovanni in Laterano, Rome, State delle Anime • NL Scot., Yester Ac. 4862, box 98 • John Aikman to John Forbes, 29 Aug 1767, priv. coll., Forbes MSS • Gavin Hamilton's letters to second Viscount Palmerston, PRO

**Archives** BL, letters to Countess Spencer • NRA, priv. coll., corresp. with Lord Shelburne, first marquess of Lansdowne • Paul Mellon Centre for Studies in British Art, London, Brinsley Ford archive, MS notes

**Likenesses** G. Hamilton, self-portrait, pencil drawing, 1767, Scot. NPG • O. Humphry, pencil, 1777, Scot. NPG • C. Hewetson, marble bust, 1784, Hunterian Museum and Art Gallery, Glasgow • A. Skirving, pastels, 1788–9, Scot. NPG • A. R. Mengs, oils; Christies, 6 July 1978, lot 49 • R. Scott, stipple (after A. Skirving), BM, NPG; repro. in *The Bee*, 16 (1793)

**Hamilton, Gavin** (1751–1805), landowner, was born in Mauchline, Ayrshire, the youngest of five sons of John Hamilton of Kype, an attorney, and Jacobina Young, his first wife. Hamilton worked in his father's law office. Like his parents Hamilton was unconcerned with social niceties, a quality that endeared him to Burns. He himself, his relatives, and his employees played important roles in the poet's life.

The two men became acquainted as freemasons. In 1784 Hamilton offered Robert and Gilbert Burns the sublease of Mossgiel Farm, 118 acres in Mauchline parish which Hamilton had recently leased from the earl of Loudoun, stocking it as a dairy farm. The generous offer promised a fresh start for the struggling brothers after years of litigation between their dying father and the landlord at Lochlie Farm. But the £90 rent for Mossgiel proved difficult to extract from the soggy clay soil. Robert's name was soon removed from the lease, but Gilbert continued as Hamilton's subtenant until 1797, borrowing perhaps half the profits of his brother's poems in his struggle to make Mossgiel pay. In 1788 Hamilton wrote to Burns asking him to serve as guarantor for a further loan; the poet's reluctant refusal ended the friendship.

In Burns's 'Holy Willie's Prayer', Hamilton is vilified by the bigoted speaker ('he drinks, and swears, and plays at cartes') but defended by the poet as one of the 'most truly respectable characters in the country' (*Poems and Songs*, 1.74, 77). Hamilton's dispute with the Mauchline kirk session began in 1778 when it ordered him to rectify a shortfall of some £7 in the poor tax for Mauchline, collected by Hamilton since 1775. Hamilton replied, with increasing heat as the quarrel escalated, that poorer parishioners had simply been unable to pay the stent, or property tax. The real source of the kirk session's pursuit of Hamilton seems to have been his defiance of parish authority and discipline: a man of impulsive charity rather than ostentatious piety, his irregular attendance at worship was the more provocative as his house and legal office abutted the churchyard. He appealed against and overturned every censure the Mauchline kirk session attempted to impose.

Gavin Hamilton was, according to Gilbert Burns, the first to urge his brother Robert to publish (*Works*, 1.76). He arranged forty of the subscriptions to the first, Kilmarnock, edition of Burns's *Poems* (1786), which was dedicated to him, and took four copies of the Edinburgh edition that appeared in 1787. It was Hamilton, in his capacity as a lawyer, who drew up the papers by which Burns acknowledged paternity of his first daughter, Elizabeth, and it was in Hamilton's office that Burns and Jean Armour solemnized their marriage. Burns probably met his crony John Richmond through Hamilton, who employed him as a law clerk in 1784–5. Margaret Campbell, Burns's 'Highland Mary', was nursemaid to Hamilton's son Alexander (*b.* 1785). Hamilton's half-sister Charlotte was a friend and flirt of Burns, and Burns unsuccessfully courted Margaret Chalmers, the daughter of Hamilton's stepmother's sister.

Hamilton was married to Helen Kennedy, with whom he had eight children, although further details of his family are unknown. He died on 5 February 1805 at Mauchline and was buried in the churchyard there.

CAROL MCGUIRK

**Sources** *DNB* • *The poems and songs of Robert Burns*, ed. J. Kinsley, 3 vols. (1968) • *The letters of Robert Burns*, ed. J. de Lancey Ferguson, 2nd edn, ed. G. Ross Roy, 2 vols. (1985) • *The works of Robert Burns*, 2nd edn, ed. J. Currie, 4 vols. (1801) • C. Carswell, *The life of Robert Burns* (1930) • J. A. Mackay, *R. B.: a biography of Robert Burns* (1992) • M. Lindsay, *The Burns encyclopedia*, 3rd edn (1980) • D. Wright, *Robert Burns and his masonic circle* (1929)

**Hamilton, Gavin George**, **second Baron Hamilton of Dalzell** (**1872–1952**), horse-racing administrator, was born on 29 June 1872 at Garscube House, Newkilpatrick, Dalziel, near Motherwell, Lanarkshire, the second of the four sons and the fifth of the eight children of John Glencairn Carter Hamilton, first Baron Hamilton of Dalzell (1829–1900), landowner and MP, and his wife, Lady Emily (1840–1882), daughter of David Leslie-Melville, eighth earl of Leven and seventh earl of Melville. His family, whose seat was Dalzell House, Dalziel, had been prominent landowners in Lanarkshire for several centuries and his father, a Gladstonian Liberal, was raised to the peerage in 1886.

Educated at Eton and the Royal Military College, Sandhurst, Hamilton was a regular soldier until 1898 and later served in the Second South African War and in France in the First World War, during which he rose to the rank of major in the Scots Guards and was awarded the Military Cross. Having inherited the barony in 1900, he became a knight of the Thistle in 1909 and a lord in waiting to Edward VII and George V, and remained a friend of the latter after leaving the court in 1911 on being cited as co-respondent in his future wife's undefended divorce case. On 24 July 1912 he married Sybil Mary (1867–1933), daughter of Lieutenant-General Sir Frederick Marshall and formerly wife of William Lawson, later third Baron Burnham.

Though a racehorse owner on only a small scale, Hamilton proved the outstanding turf administrator of his time, with a progressive outlook and reforming zeal which marked him out among the members of the Jockey Club. Even before his election to horse-racing's conservative governing body in 1908 he was responsible for a policy of racecourse stewards' initiating post-race inquiries rather than waiting for an objection to be lodged, and in 1919 he was the principal author of a report, subsequently ignored, which suggested that facilities for racegoers could be improved by using the savings resulting from possible racecourse mergers.

Hamilton was the senior steward of the Jockey Club for three terms of twelve months each and during the second of them, in 1927–8, he set about realizing his ambition of making betting contribute financially to horse-racing. He chaired a Jockey Club committee which recommended the introduction of the totalizator ('tote'), a pool betting service whose profits, unlike those of bookmakers, would be used to the benefit of the sport, as in many other countries. The enabling legislation, the Racecourse Betting Act 1928, was introduced as a private member's bill in the House of Commons by Ralph Glyn (later first Baron Glyn), but Hamilton was its driving spirit and he helped to outmanoeuvre strong lobbying from an unlikely alliance of bookmakers, who feared competition, and moralists, in particular the church, which opposed all gambling as a social evil. However, during the bill's stormy passage through the Commons many concessions had to be made and the original intention that the tote should be run by the Jockey Club had to be abandoned.

The tote started operations in July 1929, managed by the Racecourse Betting Control Board (later the Horserace Totalisator Board), a statutory body of which Hamilton was a member until 1949. The tote overcame considerable teething problems, and though it did not gain as big a share of the betting market as he had hoped, it did eventually prove a significant source of revenue for the sport.

The father of the tote also introduced Jockey Club rules requiring all horses to run on their merits and banning dead heats from being run off in a decider. From 1934 to 1945 Hamilton was the king's representative at Ascot racecourse, where he effected many improvements. He was lord lieutenant of Lanarkshire from 1938 until his death, revived Lanark and Hamilton Park racecourses, and ran a model dairy farm on his 2500 acre Dalzell estate.

Gavin Hamilton, a man of austere appearance and of few words, was a practical visionary. Always seeking ways to benefit the sport he loved, he possessed both the foresight to identify the tote as a potential new source of revenue and the drive to bring about its creation. Few men have left such a lasting legacy to the sporting world. He died on 23 June 1952 at Dalzell House and was buried there three days later. He had no children and was succeeded in the barony by his nephew, John d'Henin Hamilton (1911–1990).

JOHN RANDALL

**Sources** *Bloodstock Breeders' Review* (1952) • *The Scotsman* (24 June 1952) • *Sporting Life* (25 June 1952) • *The Times* (24 June 1952) • A. E. T. Watson, 'Sportsmen of mark: Lord Hamilton of Dalzell', *Badminton Magazine*, 27 (Sept 1908), 237–47 • J. Fairfax-Blakeborough, *History of horse racing in Scotland* (1973) • E. Moorhouse, 'The racing year', *Bloodstock Breeders' Review* (1927) • E. Moorhouse, 'The racing year', *Bloodstock Breeders' Review* (1928) • E. Moorhouse, 'The racing year', *Bloodstock Breeders' Review* (1929) • Lord Hamilton of Dalzell [G. G. Hamilton], 'The tote', *Flat racing*, ed. Earl of Harewood [H. G. C. Lascelles] and P. E. Ricketts (1940), 378–94 • W. Vamplew, *The turf: a social and economic history of horse racing* (1976) • R. Mortimer, *The Jockey Club* (1958) • Burke, *Peerage* (1970) • *WWW* • *Racing Calendar* • b. cert. • d. cert.

**Wealth at death** £103,286 9*s*. 3*d*.: confirmation, 1 Dec 1952, *CCI*

**Hamilton, Gawen** (**1697?–1737**), painter, was born near Hamilton, Lanarkshire, of unidentified parents. He studied under William Wilson, an obscure bird painter (later an auctioneer). By the mid-1720s Hamilton was in London, painting single portraits (the few now known include *Revd Thomas Pocock*, chaplain of Greenwich Hospital, engraved by John Faber junior, 1726), living in lodgings off the Strand, and figuring (convivially) in the Marshalsea prison diary of the composer, trumpeter, and flautist John Baptist Grano (MS, Bodl. Oxf., excerpts published by Ginger).

By the early 1730s Hamilton was specializing in the comparatively new genre of the conversation piece, working on a fairly small scale and rapidly gaining more renown than he had ever gained for single portraits. Vertue described his pictures as 'small figures from the life in their habits and dress of the Times. well disposed gracefull and natural easy actions … Suteable to persons of distinction' (Vertue, *Note books*, 3.81). Most of them depict families at home, with detailed attention to furniture, objects, and, recurringly, framed pictures (possibly of Hamilton's own design) hanging on the walls. Vertue particularly praised Hamilton's *John Wootton and his Family* of 1736 for its 'likeness' of Wootton; Hamilton tended to portray types rather than individuals. Vertue's praise for Hamilton's pictures ('equal to any I have seen of Hogarth': ibid., 3.71, see also p. 81) must be weighed against his pique at Hogarth's rising fame. Hamilton combined geniality with decorum in his groups; but, unlike Hogarth, rarely turned a critical eye on the polite society he depicted. Other family groups include *Thomas Wentworth, Earl of Strafford, and his Family* (1732; National Gallery of Canada, Ottawa; replica, priv. coll.), *Edward Harley, 3rd Earl of Oxford and his Family* (1736?; priv. coll.), and *The Du Cane and Boehm Family Group* of *c*.1734–1735 (Tate collection), in which sixteen living members of intermarried banking families (plus three, recently dead, 'framed' on the walls) turn towards the spectator, less in 'conversation' than in a complacent chorus.

Hamilton's best-known work, *A Conversation of Virtuosis … at the Kings Armes (a Club of Artists)* (1735; NPG), depicts thirteen painters, sculptors, and friends meeting decorously in a Bond Street tavern; among them are Bernard Baron, Charles Bridgman, Michael Dahl, James Gibbs, William Kent, John Michael Rysbrack, John Wootton, George Vertue, and Hamilton himself. Painted 'to promote the Interest of Mr. Hamilton' (Vertue, *Note books*, 3.71–2), then raffled among subscribing sitters, the picture is less a document of a particular artistic association than a fundraiser for Hamilton himself.

Hamilton was among the 'five foot men or less' noted by Vertue (including Hogarth, Samuel Scott, 'Mr Zinke Enameller', and Vertue himself) as none the less 'Elevated … in Art' (Vertue, *Note books*, 3.61). He was a member of the informal Rose and Crown dining club of artists; having dined with them on St Luke's night 1737 (18 October), he caught a feverish cold from which he died ten days later (28 October 1737), in his lodgings near St Paul's, Covent Garden, aged 'near forty' (Vertue, *Note books*, 3.81). He was buried in St Paul's churchyard, Covent Garden.

JUDY EGERTON

**Sources** Vertue, *Note books*, 3.3–5, 48, 61, 71, 81 • H. Finberg, 'Gawen Hamilton', *Walpole Society*, 6 (1917–18), 51–8 • J. Ginger, 'New light on Gawen Hamilton: artists, musicians and the debtors' prison', *Apollo*, 136 (1992), 146–60 • J. Kerslake, *National Portrait Gallery: early Georgian portraits*, 1 (1977), 340–42 • S. Sitwell, *Conversation pieces* (1936), 18, 70, 71, 73, pl. 74, 75, 82 • I. Bignamini, 'George Vertue, art historian, and art institutions in London, 1689–1768', *Walpole Society*, 54 (1988), 1–148, 57, no. 35 • Waterhouse, *18c painters*, 157

**Likenesses** G. Hamilton, group portrait, oils, 1735 (including self, *A conversation of virtuosis*), NPG • G. Hamilton, group portrait, oils (including self, *Elegant company playing cards*), Tate collection

**Hamilton, Gawen William Rowan** (1783–1834). *See under* Rowan, Archibald Hamilton (1751–1834).

**Hamilton, Sir George, first baronet** (*c*.1608–1679). *See under* Hamilton, James, first earl of Abercorn (1575–1618).

**Hamilton, George, first earl of Orkney** (*bap.* 1666, *d.* 1737), army officer, was the fifth son of William Douglas [*see* Hamilton, William, third duke of Hamilton (1634–1694)], and his wife, Anne *Hamilton, *suo jure* duchess of Hamilton (1632–1716). He was born at Hamilton Palace, Lanarkshire, Scotland, and baptized there on 6 February 1666. Under the tutelage of his uncle Lord Dunbarton his education focused upon military affairs, and by the age of eighteen he held a commission as captain in the Royal Scots, the 1st regiment of foot, the British army's premier infantry regiment. The same year he departed for a continental tour, and consequently he did not participate in the battle of Sedgemoor in 1685. In 1690 he received the colonelcy of an Irish regiment of foot. Active at the battle of the Boyne and wounded at the siege of Aughrim the same year, Hamilton became colonel of the 7th foot (Royal Fusiliers) on 23 January 1692. Displays of bravery at Steenkerke shortly thereafter brought him the colonelcy of the Royal Scots, which he retained for the next four decades. Further service in Flanders saw him fight at Landen; after suffering a wound at the siege of Namur in 1695 he was promoted brigadier-general. On 3 January 1696 he was ennobled with the Scottish titles of earl of Orkney, Viscount Kirkwall, and Lord Dechmont.

Following the renewal of hostilities during Queen Anne's reign, Orkney rose to the rank of major-general on 9 March 1702 and lieutenant-general on 1 January 1704. In an age inevitably overshadowed by the duke of Marlborough's reputation he has escaped significant recognition as a military commander. None the less, he was a remarkable subordinate general in his own right. Courageous, indomitable, and tenacious, this stoic and often almost humorously laconic Scot endured deprivations with his regiment and seldom failed to achieve the tasks assigned him; indeed, his achievements often exceeded others' wildest expectations. One of Marlborough's most able lieutenants and wing commanders, he missed not a single major battle or siege in either the Nine Years' War or the War of the Spanish Succession. It is perhaps in the latter conflict, as a British general counted among Marlborough's handful of reliable subordinates, that his most noteworthy service occurred. Orkney played a critical role in all four of Marlborough's major victories against the French, as well as significant action in numerous sieges undertaken in the Low Countries. His letters from the field provide some of the most vivid extant descriptions of battles fought between 1704 and 1712, and military historians have not yet fully availed themselves of many of these. At Blenheim, Orkney attacked the village churchyard with eight battalions of foot and, through sheer bluff and a deceptive self-confidence, tricked a superior French force into surrendering. His timely efforts in 1705 ensured the allied army rescued the besieged town of Liège. At Ramillies in 1706 he achieved notoriety in commanding a dangerous infantry advance through a marsh to assault fortified positions. Secretly designed as a diversionary assault on the French left, his attack was more successful than Marlborough had anticipated or intended, and, when he viewed the time right to launch the primary assault in the French centre, Orkney's troops had gained so much initiative that several couriers were required to procure his withdrawal. Tersely protesting that it 'vexed him to retire' (Cra'ster, 315), Orkney proceeded to command his forces' withdrawal in an orderly fashion under heavy enemy fire and rejoined the main assault. At the battle's conclusion he led the allied cavalry in a relentless twilight pursuit of retreating enemy forces. Orkney was one of three major-generals commanding detachments at the siege of Menin in the summer of 1706, and his letters leave intricately detailed accounts of these operations. After the battle of Oudenarde in 1708 he voted for an immediate march upon Paris, thereby demonstrating what is rightly recognized as one of few occasions where he challenged his superior's judgement. At Malplaquet in 1709 he led fifteen infantry battalions in an assault on fortified positions in the French centre, capturing them with minimal losses in this, a battle that provoked severe criticism for its high casualty rate. Other major engagements in which Orkney participated included the sieges of Douai (1710) and Bouchain (1711). He was promoted general of the foot in 1711, and the same year issued a set of revised regulations for British foot regiments in Flanders. He was also present under the duke of Ormond's command when British forces were forced to detach from the allied camp upon the issuing of the notorious 'restraining orders' of 1712.

Orkney's active military service concluded with the cessation of hostilities in 1712. His long military career had not, however, inordinately hindered his enjoyment of a rewarding family life. On 25 November 1695 he married his distant cousin Elizabeth *Villiers (*c.*1657–1733), the daughter of Sir Edward Villiers and the sister of the first earl of Jersey. Possibly the mistress of William III until 1694, Lady Orkney was widely acknowledged as one of the most intelligent and engaging women of her time. Swift, whom she befriended about 1712, variously described her as the 'wisest woman' he had ever met and, on another occasion, a 'squinting dragon' (Swift, 456). By 1727 observers at George II's coronation were less flattering. Lady Mary Wortley Montagu's acerbic characterization told of ageing Lady Orkney's 'mixture of fat and wrinkle', the 'inestimable roll of her eyes', and 'grey hairs which by good fortune stood directly upright' (Trench, 137).

Despite contemporary speculation about Orkney's motivations for the marriage, such as the desire to curry royal favour by extricating a mistress from court following Queen Mary's death, this seemingly rather mismatched couple apparently enjoyed a happy and mutually beneficial conjugal union. Lady Orkney had received a grant of the confiscated Irish estates of James II, but, allowing for overvaluation, conversion from the Irish pound, and encumbrances of several thousand pounds, Lord and Lady Orkney's total annual income was probably somewhere in the region of £6000 per annum, not an overly spectacular amount for a courtier of his stature. This circumstance probably contributed to his interest in maintaining crown sinecures and his consequent relative political moderation. Of the three daughters born to the couple, the eldest, Anne, inherited the title and married William O'Brien, earl of Inchiquin, in 1720. The second daughter, Frances [*see* Saunderson, Frances Lumley-], married Thomas, earl of Scarbrough. Henrietta, the youngest, was married on 9 May 1728 to John, Lord Boyle (after 1731 fifth earl of Orrery and after 1753 earl of Cork). She died in Cork in 1732. This marriage initially proved problematic. Orkney and his wife intensely disliked the fourth earl of Orrery's retention of a low-born live-in mistress, and Henrietta was forbidden to visit her new father-in-law; the ensuing family quarrel so enraged Orrery that he bequeathed most of his impressive library and scientific instruments to his Oxford alma mater instead of his only son. This prejudice was rather ironic, considering Lady Orkney's own chequered past, yet Orkney fiercely defended her honour. Contemporaries recalled an occasion in Will's Coffee House when he became infuriated by another patron's 'Railing ag[st] men who married whores & King's mistresses' (BL, Add. MS 47128, fol. 48).

As a statesman, Orkney is more properly classified as an influential spectator than as a vigorous and proactive political leader. Oratorical eloquence was not one of his traits, as this admittedly courageous 'well shaped black man' was supposedly rendered timid in public affairs by 'reason of a Hesitation in his Speech' (*Memoirs of the Secret Services*, 162). Swift remarked on Orkney's integrity and amiable nature, and a fellow officer was quick to affirm his sincerity but added that he was 'modest and shy to meddle' (*Portland MSS*, 4.266). In parliament Orkney was naturally protective of the rights and privileges of Scottish peers after the passage of the Act of Union in 1707. He was elected among the first group of sixteen representative peers in February 1707 and sat with every subsequent group thereafter until his death. Along with his elected status in the Lords, Orkney had been made a knight of the Thistle in 1704, and while in the field he participated in ceremonies for other recipients of the order, such as Lord Stair in 1710. He was sworn of the privy council in 1710 and was reappointed when George I took the throne in 1714. Although Orkney generally avoided partisan squabbles and animosity, his significance in the politico-military struggles during the last few years of Queen Anne's reign should not be minimized. He was sometimes utilized by ministries under both Anne and George I to counter aspirations of powerful Scottish generals such as John Campbell, second duke of Argyll, one of many ambitious court figures who exerted themselves to undermine Marlborough's political authority. By the same token, when the tide of court favour began to turn against Marlborough in 1710, even Orkney, who was late in returning to the field, was perhaps unjustly accused of failing to evince the same devotion to duty displayed by other general officers. Even if it is justified in this instance, such criticism pales in comparison to the brazenly overt insubordination of other British generals with tory inclinations, which was apparent even to Dutch observers from the years 1709–11. Moreover, Lady Orkney frequented the court during Anne's reign, and according to Swift exercised considerable influence—yet another factor that made Lord Orkney's support worth cultivating.

Whether Orkney's inclinations towards support of the Hanoverians were motivated solely out of self-interest is unclear; if so, they did not, as was the case with many of his contemporaries, preclude him from associations with well-known Jacobites, such as the exiled Thomas Bruce, second earl of Ailesbury, whom Orkney fêted at a dinner in Flanders in 1705. Orkney's religious views are another matter of some ambiguity. His letters are flavoured intermittently with tinges of Calvinism and belief in providential predestination, yet his political allegiance suggests more lukewarm adherence for the Anglican church. Whatever the case, his moderate stance and court allegiance paid handsome dividends in the form of several appointments which he enjoyed throughout his later years. Although he never visited America, a patent was issued for him as governor of Virginia in 1710, and he retained this post until 1737. He was also appointed lord lieutenant of Lanarkshire in 1711. In 1714 he became a gentleman of the bedchamber to George I, as well as governor of Edinburgh Castle, a post he also held until his death. The sole exception to his political aloofness occurred during the summer of 1716, when animosity between George I and his son sparked the dismissals of Argyll and several other Scottish peers in the royal households. In Orkney's case this dismissal was only temporary, and in 1721 he was reckoned to receive a pension amounting to £2000 per annum. His career culminated with his appointment on 12 January 1736, mere days before the same honour was bestowed on Argyll, as field marshal of his majesty's forces.

Following the end of his active military service, Orkney seems to have spent most of his time living in England. He and Lady Orkney resided primarily in London and at Cliveden, a country estate near the village of Taplow, Buckinghamshire, which was purchased in 1696. Convenient to the capital, situated on a bluff overlooking the Thames valley, adorned with Flemish tapestries commemorating Marlborough's victories in which Orkney had played such a prominent role, Cliveden was the scene of the Orkneys' entertainment of George I in 1724 and George II and his family in 1729. Orkney died at his London house in Albemarle Street on 29 January 1737 and was buried at Cliveden in the spartan funeral ceremony he had requested. Lady Orkney had predeceased him in 1733.

LAWRENCE B. SMITH

**Sources** C. Dalton, ed., *George the First's army, 1714–1727*, 2 (1912), 35–8 • Duke of Hamilton and G. Hamilton, first earl of Orkney, correspondence with Charles, second earl of Selkirk, 1703–36, NL Scot., Hamilton and Orkney MSS 1032–3 • H. H. E. Chaster, ed., 'Letters of the first Lord Orkney during Marlborough's campaigns', *EngHR*, 19 (1904), 307–21 • GEC, *Peerage* • J. C. Leask and H. M. McCance, eds., *The regimental records of the royal Scots* (1915) • dukes of Hamilton, family and estate MSS, NA Scot., GD 406 • Orkney letters, BL, Blenheim MSS, Add. MS 61162, fols. 89–113 • *DNB* • C. Dalton, ed., *English army lists and commission registers, 1661–1714*, 6 vols. (1892–1904) • *The Marlborough–Godolphin correspondence*, ed. H. L. Snyder, 3 vols. (1975) • C. T. Atkinson, *Marlborough and the rise of the British army* (1921) • J. Swift, *Journal to Stella*, ed. H. Williams, 2 vols. (1948) • N. Luttrell, *A brief historical relation of state affairs from September 1678 to April 1714*, 6 vols. (1857) • NL Scot., Newhailes MS Acc. 7228, nos. 530–32, Accession 7228, #530–32 • G. M. Trevelyan, *England under Queen Anne*, 3 vols. (1930–34) • W. Robertson, *Proceedings relating to the peerage of Scotland, from January 16, 1707 to April 29, 1788* (1790) • F. Taylor, *The wars of Marlborough, 1702–1709*, 2 vols. (1913) • W. Coxe, *Memoirs of the duke of Marlborough, with his original correspondence*, rev. J. Wade, 3rd edn, 3 vols. (1847–8) • camp journal of the allied army, BL, Add. MS 61404 • *The manuscripts of his grace the duke of Portland*, 10 vols., HMC, 29 (1891–1931), vol. 10 • J. C. R. Childs, *The Nine Years' War and the British army, 1688–1697: the operations in the Low Countries* (1991) • D. Chandler, *Marlborough as military commander* (1973) • S. H. F. Johnston, ed., 'Letters of Samuel Noyes, chaplain of the royal Scots, 1703–4', *Journal of the Society of Historical Research*, 37 (1959), 33–40, 67–71, 125–35, 145–52 • P. Verney, *The battle of Blenheim* (1976) • C. C. Trench, *George II* (1973) • BL, Add. MS 47128, fol. 48 • *Memoirs of the secret services of John Macky*, ed. A. R. (1733)

**Archives** NA Scot., dukes of Hamilton, family and estate MSS • NL Scot., Hamilton and Orkney MSS | NL Scot., letters to Lord Selkirk • Northumbd RO, Newcastle upon Tyne, Craster MSS, corresp. • NRA Scotland, priv. coll., letters to his mother and nephew

**Likenesses** G. Kneller, oils, *c.*1704, Lennoxlove, Haddington, East Lothian • D. Paton, plumbago miniature, *c.*1710, Scot. NPG • M. Maingaud, oils, *c.*1730, NAM • J. Houbraken, line engraving, 1746 (after M. Maingaud), BM, NPG; repro. in Birch, *Heads* (1746) • oils, Scot. NPG

**Hamilton, George** (1783–1830), Church of Ireland clergyman, was born in Armagh, the fourth son of Hugh *Hamilton (1729–1805) (then dean of Armagh and later bishop of Ossory), and Isabella, the daughter of Hans Widman Wood of Rossmead, co. Westmeath. He was educated at Trinity College, Dublin, from 10 June 1799 and graduated BA in 1804 and MA in 1821. He was married twice, first to Sophia, daughter of George Kiernan of Dublin. They had two daughters, Sophia and Isabella, who died unmarried. His second wife, Frances, daughter of Rear-Admiral Sir Chichester Fortescue, Ulster king of arms, outlived him and then married the Revd George Reade.

In 1809 Hamilton became rector of Killermogh in the diocese of Ossory, where he remained for the rest of his life. He was a conscientious parish priest and an early promoter of religious societies in the Church of Ireland. He was also a zealous apologist for his denomination. Burke's *Landed Gentry* describes him as the 'author of several controversial pamphlets', and his obituaries make clear his hostility to Roman Catholics in Ireland. The following quotation is reasonably mild, yet representative of comments about him generally: 'The Jews, & his Roman Catholic countrymen, were objects upon which … his heart rested … he lost no opportunity of presenting to them the unadulterated truth contained in the Bible … uninfluenced by the … sophistry of Priests and Rabbies'.

Besides some separate sermons and papers in religious periodicals, Hamilton published a large number of tracts and pamphlets, the titles of which describe their content. The following are representative: 'A letter to the Rev. Peter Roe, M.A., November 1813, with papers on apostolick practice and ecclesiastical establishments' (printed in *The Evil of Separation from the Church of England Considered*, 2nd edn,

1817); *A letter to Rabbi Herschell, showing that the resurrection is as credible a fact as the exodus, and that the tract called 'Toldoth', giving the Jewish account of the resurrection, is no more worthy of credit than Tacitus's History of the Jews* (printed in or before 1824); *Tracts upon some Leading Errors of the Church of Rome* (1824); and *The scripture authority of the Christian sabbath vindicated against Roman Catholics and separatists* (anonymous, 1828).

As well as engaging in religious controversy Hamilton attempted scholarly writing, his interest centring on the canon, with attempts to reconcile the various ancient versions in their original languages. For example, in 1813 he produced *A general introduction to the study of the Hebrew scriptures, with a critical history of the Greek and Latin versions, of the Samaritan Pentateuch, and of the Chaldee paraphrases*. Hamilton died on 10 August 1830 and was buried in the churchyard of Killermogh.

B. H. Blacker, *rev.* Gerald Law

**Sources** *Christian Examiner and Church of Ireland Magazine*, 10 (1830), 721–2 • P. Roe, 'Thoughts on the death of the Rev. G. H.', in S. Madden, *Memoir of the life of the late Rev. Peter Roe* (Dublin, 1842), 451–61 • Burke, *Gen. GB* • *Irish Ecclesiastical Gazette* (May 1876), 153 • C. Otway, *Scenes in the rotunda, Dublin* • McGhee, *Life and death of the Kiernan family* (1865)

**Hamilton, George Alexander** (1802–1871), politician, was born at Tyrella, co. Down, on 29 August 1802. He was elder son of the Revd George Hamilton of Hampton Hall, co. Dublin, who died in March 1833, and his wife, Anna, *née* Pepper, the daughter of Thomas Pepper of Ballygarth Castle, co. Meath. His grandfather George Hamilton (*d.* 1793), who was a baron of the exchequer from 1776 to 1793, was a nephew of Hugh *Hamilton, bishop of Ossory. He was educated at Rugby School from 1814, and at Trinity College, Oxford, from 15 December 1818 to 1822, when he took his BA degree. He was created DCL on 9 June 1853. Soon after leaving university he settled at his father's estate and began to take a part in the public political meetings in Dublin. He stood for election to represent county Dublin in 1826, 1830, and 1832 and Dublin city in 1835 and 1837. His only success in either of these constituencies was in 1835 when, together with a Conservative colleague, he unseated Daniel O'Connell and a Liberal-repeal colleague on petition. On 1 May 1835 he married Amelia Fancourt, the daughter of Joshua Uhthoff of Bath. In 1843 he was returned unopposed for Dublin University on the occasion of a vacancy created by the appointment of J. D. Jackson to be judge of common pleas.

Throughout Hamilton's career he was active in Conservative and protestant causes including the Conservative Society formed in Dublin in 1832 and the Lay Association for the Protection of Church Property, of which he became the honorary secretary in 1834. In parliament he presented the petition of the celebrated protestant meeting of 14 January 1837, which gave rise to much discussion and subsequently to the earl of Roden's committee of inquiry. As MP for Dublin University he particularly interested himself in matters related to education. He held the financial secretaryship of the Treasury under Lord Derby's administration from March 1852 to January 1853, and again on the return of the Conservatives to power from March 1858 to January 1859. At this latter date he was appointed assistant secretary of the Treasury. The effectiveness of his quiet campaign to extend the powers of his office was recognized in 1867 by the change of the title to 'permanent secretary'. He was a central figure in civil service reform along lines envisaged by his more controversial predecessor Sir Charles Trevelyan. Although the title 'head of the civil service' does not seem to have been introduced at this time, there was some justice to Hamilton's claim, upon his retirement in 1870, to have presided over that institution. He was sworn of the privy council on 7 August 1869, and in the following year was named one of the commissioners of the church temporalities in Ireland. He was a magistrate and deputy lieutenant for the county of Dublin, and was made an LLD of Dublin University. He took an amateur interest in local antiquities: his memorandum of some excavations which he conducted in the 1840s appeared in the *Proceedings of the Royal Irish Academy*. He died at Clarinda Park, Kingstown, co. Dublin, on 17 September 1871.

G. C. Boase, *rev.* David W. Miller

**Sources** M. Wright, *Treasury control of the civil service, 1854–1874* (1969) • 'Parliamentary portraits, Mr George Alexander Hamilton, MP for Dublin University, joint secretary to the treasury', *ILN* (11 Dec 1852), 517–18 • *ILN* (23 Sept 1871), 283 • *The Times* (20 Sept 1871), 6 • B. M. Walker, ed., *Parliamentary election results in Ireland, 1801–1922* (1978), 211–12, 271–2, 274 • J. C. Sainty, ed., *Treasury officials, 1660–1870* (1972), 131 • Burke, *Gen. Ire.* (1904), 244–5 • C. R. Wilson, *Chapters from my official life*, ed. E. MacAlister (1916), 37–8

**Archives** PRO, letter-books, T168 • TCD, corresp. | BL, corresp. with W. E. Gladstone, Add. MS 44192 • BL, corresp. with Sir Robert Peel, Add. MSS 40504–40570 • Bodl. Oxf., letters to Benjamin Disraeli • Bucks. RLSS, corresp. with first Baron Cottesloe • Lpool RO, letters to fourteenth earl of Derby • Som. ARS, letters to Sir William Jolliffe

**Likenesses** J. Posselwhite, stipple (after W. J. Newton), BM, NPG • portrait, repro. in *Portraits of eminent conservatives*, 2nd ser. (1846) • wood-engraving, NPG; repro. in *ILN* (11 Dec 1852), 517

**Wealth at death** under £8000: probate, 2 Dec 1871, *CGPLA Ire.*

**Hamilton, Lord George Francis** (1845–1927), politician, was born on 17 December 1845 in Brighton, the third son of thirteen children of James *Hamilton, the first duke of Abercorn (1811–1885), Irish landowner, and his wife, Lady Louisa Jane (1812–1905), second daughter of John Russell, sixth duke of Bedford [*see under* Russell, John, first Earl Russell]. This branch of the Hamiltons was an Ulster Conservative family with Scottish antecedents, by this time mainly based in England. An election opponent in 1874 called Lord George 'an Irish gentleman' and he often described himself similarly, but he founded his political career on London, and for most of his life lived in Portman Square. He was educated at Harrow School, and remained a devoted Harrovian, serving as chairman of governors in 1913–24. He joined the rifle brigade in 1864 and served for four years abroad, partly with Garnet Wolseley in Canada.

**Tory politics** In 1868 Hamilton exchanged from the rifle brigade into the Coldstreams, and was settling into a career of more fashionable soldiering when an invitation to contest Middlesex changed his direction. The unexpected

**Lord George Francis Hamilton (1845–1927)**, by London Stereoscopic Co.

invitation was accepted only when repeated by Disraeli with the words 'all right, little David, go in and kill Goliath'. Hamilton could fight a full contest only because caustic remarks about his family by the Liberal MP, Henry Labouchere, persuaded Abercorn to pay the bills; three Middlesex contests had by 1880 cost over £30,000. If Middlesex was, in Hamilton's words, 'notoriously radical', a seat Conservatives rarely even contested, it was also a county in which railways had transformed the electorate, so that 'I was merely the mouthpiece of that transformation, but I got the whole credit of the victory'. His defeat of Labouchere was the harbinger of Conservative success in the burgeoning metropolitan suburbs. When re-elected by over five thousand votes in 1874, Hamilton proclaimed that 'the great majority of the electors of Middlesex were and are Conservative'. He easily held the seat in adverse circumstances in 1880, and the eight constituencies into which Middlesex was then divided all elected Conservatives in 1885. Hamilton was returned for Ealing and held it until retirement in 1905.

Thirty-seven years representing the suburbs made Hamilton one of the parliamentary Conservatives best informed about middle-class voters, and a spokesman for advanced electoral methods. In 1872 he chaired the Conservative National Union conference when it met in London, urging better two-way communications between constituency organizations and parliamentary leaders. He was chairman of the Middlesex Ratepayers' Association in 1884, and subsequently of the London Municipal Society. As a freemason, he was Middlesex provincial grand master, 1892–1924, and Middlesex brought him close to W. H. Smith, whose Westminster victory in 1868 paralleled Hamilton's own and for whom he made his first political speech; they became friends and political allies.

In 1871 Hamilton married Maud (*d.* 14 April 1938), younger daughter of the third earl of Harewood; since she was also one of thirteen children, this did not improve Hamilton's finances, but it was a marriage which lasted until his death and produced three sons; the dukes of Abercorn continued to support his career. He established himself in the Commons as a critic of Gladstone, whom he regarded as dishonest and unscrupulous. He had some successes—for example, with a motion on the *Alabama* treaty in 1873—but was still considered too young to be taken seriously; in 1868 Disraeli had thought he looked eighteen rather than twenty-two, while the hecklers' cry in Middlesex had been 'Milk for the baby!'.

Geordie Hamilton was soon a Disraeli favourite, and Hamilton remembered Disraeli as 'more like an elder relative than a political chief'. He impressed others too, and when the Conservatives regained office in 1874, Derby wanted him at the Foreign Office, a post he evaded by pleading inadequate French. Disraeli made him under-secretary for India, informing him that this required knowledge neither of Hindustani nor of Persian. He spoke for the government on India in the Commons since the secretary of state, Salisbury, was in the Lords. Of his first ministerial statement, Disraeli told the queen that Hamilton had

> greatly distinguished himself … Both sides of the House were delighted with him; with his thorough knowledge of the subject; his fine voice; his calmness, dignity and grace. He spoke for exactly an hour. Mr. Disraeli has rarely witnessed so great a success—and what is better, a promise of greater. (*The Times*)

He contemplated promoting Hamilton to Irish chief secretary in 1875, and made him chairman for the government's annual dinner; Disraeli enjoyed both 'the perpetual flow of wit, and playful humour and grace' in his speech, and the cheek with which he presented the premier with the wooden spoon as the government's worst performer. Derby more sceptically noted that Hamilton 'succeeds in every speech he makes, but seems to want ambition' (Shannon). Hamilton had no great difficulties in Indian debates, which rarely attracted a full house, but met criticism for investing money in Indian railways, rather than tackling food shortages directly, a stance vindicated, however, in select committee.

The 1878 reshuffle provided Hamilton with a sideways move to vice-president of the council, in effect minister of education, though he had difficulties with the lord president, Richmond, when he said so. Beaconsfield gave support when education spending came under Treasury fire, but Hamilton still found it difficult to retain his budget. Without that restraint he could have carried the final measure that made elementary education compulsory, but had to leave this to his Liberal successor. He found education 'terribly meticulous and dull' and was frustrated in a subordinate post under an undistinguished superior. This period was the origin of his low opinion of local government, reinforced when chairman of the London school board in 1894–5, which he was to bring to the poor-law inquiry in 1905.

In opposition, youth, aristocratic connections, and progressive ideas made him a likely supporter of the Fourth Party, but he was deterred by loyalty to Northcote, and by suspicion of Lord Randolph Churchill, whom he regarded as unprincipled; Hamilton's connection with middle-class voters made him unsympathetic to Churchill's tory democracy, which he thought 'too fast'. His personal credo was limited in its application to current domestic politics; he tritely defined Conservatism for an 1880 audience as aiming 'to establish such a state of things in this country, that the great majority of people shall be happy and shall be contented', and revealingly added that 'so long as the Conservatives are in office, the good we do must be measured not merely by the legislation we achieve but by what we stop', a limited horizon that would not have inspired tory democrats. Hamilton was in any case a supporter of his former chief, Salisbury, and established a connection with Salisbury's nephew Balfour, obtaining his support in 1883 for a Commons motion calling for Irish land purchase. Hamilton's proposal, anathema to the family's Ulster interests, was accepted by the house though both front benches had initially resisted; he argued that the 1881 Land Act had transformed the land situation and that unionists must produce policies within its scope; his autobiography records with wry amusement the 'Ashbourne' Land Act of 1885 which carried this idea into party orthodoxy. Hamilton remained opposed to home rule as such, which would bring 'ruin in every sense of the word to those who, like myself, are Anglo-Irish'; one of his doubts about Churchill was his unreliability over Ireland.

**Naval reform** Although getting on well with Churchill in office from 1885 and initially supporting his retrenchment campaign, Hamilton did not join him in resignation, for, as he told Salisbury, 'the duty of every member of your Cabinet was to try to keep the party together'. Hamilton's attention was anyway dominated by external affairs, as it would be for the rest of his life. In 1885 Salisbury offered the War Office, which Hamilton jibbed at, for an ex-regular subaltern would be far too junior to overrule the formidable duke of Cambridge on army reform. W. H. Smith took on the army, and Hamilton got 'the blue ribbon of office', the Admiralty. He proved a determined naval reformer, immediately replacing all the service members of the Board of Admiralty with more radical men. Over seven years, interrupted only by five months of Liberal government, Hamilton strove to modernize the navy. Initially, shipbuilding was slowed, so that ships could be finished and armed more quickly, while better audit ensured that for the first time in years projects were completed within budget. A naval intelligence department was created, the number of torpedoes was quadrupled, and new quick-firing guns introduced. The fleet was reorganized into squadrons, and annual exercises begun. The Naval Defence Act of 1889 regulated future expansion, and linked building to a defined strategic objective—the duty to contain threats from any two enemies; this was Admiralty policy for the next two generations. Equally significant, Hamilton's electioneering experience demonstrated the need to maintain public support for higher naval expenditure, achieved, for example, through a popular demonstration of naval power in the Solent during the 1887 jubilee. *The Times* concluded that 'in seven years the fleet was entirely reconstituted and the foundations were laid for an essential expansion', and the *Morning Post* that 'it was due to him that the two-power standard was adopted'. In opposition after 1892, Hamilton defended his achievement. Since he had enshrined naval expansion in legislation and generated public support, he had made it difficult for Gladstone to economize; in 1893–4 this dilemma, exacerbated by Hamilton's own Commons motions and his speeches around the country, prompted Gladstone's final retirement.

**India** From 1895 Hamilton was secretary of state for India, a post he held for a record eight years. He was a diligent defender of the independence of Indian government, even against the cabinet, but was able, when Lord Elgin was viceroy, discreetly to steer Indian policy from London. From 1899, when Curzon succeeded Elgin, relations deteriorated, and Hamilton could not prevent the feud between viceroy and Kitchener as army commander. He was an architect in 1897 of the garrisoning of Chitral which led to an expensive campaign in Waziristan, but while there was criticism of this, a party majority in the Commons gave steady support. He facilitated the contingents of the Indian army which helped to stave off British defeat in the early months of the Second South African War, and was privately critical of the poor preparation of Britain's own forces. He remained an admirer of Indian arms, and his final public duty in 1917 was to chair the Mesopotamia commission, charged with investigating the defeats of the Indian army. He undertook this task in the hope of restoring the reputation of an admired institution; the report provoked the resignation of his successor as secretary of state but had only limited impact in a Britain more interested in battles to come.

Hamilton believed that long involvement with India dulled his appetite for domestic politics; platform appearances became fewer and knowledge of the issues more remote; in 1890 Salisbury contemplated offering him the exchequer, but by 1903 Balfour wrote that 'his opinion on financial subjects carries weight neither in the Cabinet, the House, nor the country'. On foreign policy he remained fully involved, joining ministers demanding closer relations with Germany in 1898, and in 1900 pressing Salisbury to give up the Foreign Office to encourage that policy. It was largely determination to defend Indian economic interests and his awareness of international implications that brought about his resignation from Balfour's government in 1903 in opposition to tariff reform; he explained his reasons in a speech to his constituents (*The Times*, 23 Oct 1903). On the back benches he again became a public campaigner, but would have no truck with free-traders who wanted an alliance with Liberals, 'even for temporary purposes … I have fought too long and consistently against Radical doctrine to be able now to alter my attitude'. Retirement from the Commons in 1905 owed something to his being no longer in step with his constituents on the central issue of the day.

**Other activities** Hamilton was still only sixty, and continued to lead an active life, first as a generous-minded chairman of the royal commission on the poor law, 1905–9, though even the majority report signed by Hamilton and other moderate members proved too advanced for implementation. Within the commission, Beatrice Webb thought Hamilton 'an attractive grand seigneur' with 'exceptional personal charm and social tact' (Rempel). He made few public appearances after 1905, but was captain of Deal Castle until 1923. He remained throughout his life an outdoor man; he still played cricket in his fifties, having earlier been MCC president, and cycled until at least 1911; he continued to be a keen walker almost until his death. He published in 1916 and 1922 two discreet volumes of autobiography. He died at 17 Montagu Street, London, on 22 September 1927.

The *Times* obituarist (23 Sept 1927) highlighted the 'great work he did at the Admiralty' and his 'long and able tenure of the Indian Office', but felt that 'he held fast to a tradition too austere to be popular; his own political imagination was not inflamed, and he had neither the will nor the power to inflame the imagination of others'. John Morley had found that at the India Office he was remembered as an outstanding minister. These are among many indications that he was a gifted administrator with a strong sense of duty and of loyalty to party, but limited political gifts. Hamilton was always good company, if no great orator—a man unexpectedly and misleadingly catapulted into popular electoral politics.

JOHN RAMSDEN

**Sources** G. Hamilton, *Parliamentary reminiscences and reflections*, 2 vols. (1916–22) • G. Hamilton, *The present position of the conservative party* (1880) • *The Times* (23 Sept 1927) • *Morning Post* (23 Sept 1927) • R. Shannon, *The age of Disraeli, 1868–1881: the rise of tory democracy* (1992) • R. A. Rempel, *Unionists divided: Arthur Balfour, Joseph Chamberlain, and the unionist free traders* (1972)

**Archives** BL OIOC, corresp. and papers relating to India, MSS Eur C 125–126, D 508–510, F 123 | BL, corresp. with Arthur James Balfour, Add. MS 48778, *passim* • BL OIOC, corresp. with Lord Ampthill, MS Eur. E 233 • BL OIOC, letters to Sir Owen Tudor Burne • BL OIOC, corresp. with Lord Elgin, MS Eur. F 84 • BL OIOC, letters to Arthur Godley, MS Eur. F 102 • BL OIOC, corresp. with Lord Wenlock • Bodl. Oxf., corresp. with Sir Henry Burnett • CAC Cam., corresp. with Lord Randolph Churchill • CKS, letters to Aretas Akers-Douglas • CUL, corresp. with Lord Hardinge • Glos. RO, corresp. with Sir Michael Hicks Beach • Hants. RO, letters to Arthur Bower Forwood • Hatfield House, Hertfordshire, Salisbury MSS • HLRO, corresp. with John St Loe Strachey • NA Scot., corresp. with G. W. Balfour • NL Scot., letters to Sir Charles Dalrymple • PRO, letters to Lord Kitchener, PRO 30/57; WO 159 • U. Birm., corresp. with Joseph Chamberlain

**Likenesses** Lock & Whitfield, woodburytype photograph, 1876, NPG; repro. in T. Cooper, *Men of mark: a gallery of contemporary portraits* (1876) • W. Stoneman, photograph, 1920, NPG • London Stereoscopic Co., photograph, NPG [*see illus.*] • J. D. MacDonald, oils, Plymouth Hospital, Admiralty • Russell & Sons, photograph, NPG; repro. in *Our conservative and unionist statesmen* • Spy [L. Ward], chromolithograph caricature, NPG; repro. in *VF* (5 April 1879)

**Wealth at death** £53,568 15s. 5d.: probate, 17 Nov 1927, *CGPLA Eng. & Wales*

**Hamilton, George Nigel Douglas-, tenth earl of Selkirk (1906–1994)**, politician and diplomatist, was born on 4 January 1906 at Merley, Wimborne, Dorset, the second of four sons and third of seven children of Alfred Douglas Douglas-Hamilton, thirteenth duke of Hamilton (1862–1940), and his wife, Nina Mary Benita (*d.* 1951), third daughter of Major Robert Poore. His elder brother was Douglas Douglas-*Hamilton, fourteenth duke of Hamilton (1903–1973). He was educated at Eton College and Balliol College, Oxford, graduating with a third in politics, philosophy, and economics in 1928. He then studied at Edinburgh, Paris, Bonn, and Vienna universities; he graduated LLB from Edinburgh University in 1933, and was admitted to the Faculty of Advocates in 1935. Thereafter he practised at the Scottish bar. He became a QC in 1959. When he was not appearing in court he was looking after the Murrayfield Boys' Brigade, was acting as Conservative councillor for the Murrayfield and Haymarket ward of the city of Edinburgh (he was commissioner of the General Board of Control in Scotland, 1936–9, and commissioner for special areas in Scotland, 1937–9, and became a noted authority on housing and employment), and was an officer with 603 (city of Edinburgh) squadron. By 1934 he had become commanding officer of the Edinburgh squadron, and it was no coincidence that it received the Esher trophy, awarded to the squadron in the Royal Auxiliary Air Force at the greatest peak of readiness.

When the war came in 1939, Douglas-Hamilton, like all three of his brothers, served in the air force. Geordie, as he was known, became the chief intelligence office of Fighter Command, and personal assistant to Lord Dowding, its commander-in-chief. In Kenya he put together plans for the annihilation of the German task force operating off Ceylon, which had been supporting U-boat activity. His promotion to group captain was rapid and he was awarded the Air Force Cross and the air efficiency award, was appointed OBE (1941), and was mentioned in dispatches twice. In 1944, flying a Wellington bomber across the Bay of Biscay on the way to Morocco, he was attacked by five Junker 88 fighter bombers, and took evasive action. After having his windscreen shot away by cannon fire, he disappeared into cloud. His professionalism, skill, and coolness under fire on that day would give him fifty more years of fulfilled life. Years later he learned that four of the German aircraft, each carrying four men, failed to return. He self-deprecatingly suggested that one of his sergeants had shot down one and that the other three ran out of fuel. His youngest brother, Lord David Douglas-Hamilton, was killed in action in 1944.

By a decree of the Lyon court of 11 May 1945, confirmed on 11 September 1945, it was adjudged that Lord George

Douglas-Hamilton had succeeded his father (ninth earl of Selkirk, as well as thirteenth duke of Hamilton) on the latter's death, on 16 March 1940, as tenth earl of Selkirk. His earldom was unusual, coming to him as the result of a novodamus in Latin signed by James II of England and VII of Scotland in 1688. It enabled him to sit and participate actively in the House of Lords, alongside his elder brother, who in 1940 had succeeded as the fourteenth duke of Hamilton. On 6 August 1949 Selkirk married Audrey Durell (Wendy) Drummond-Sale-Barker (*d.* 1994), only daughter of Maurice Drummond-Sale-Barker. She, like her husband, was a skilful aviator, and was a close friend of Amy Johnson; she had served throughout the war in the Air Transport Auxiliary, delivering Spitfires to forward airfields. She was also captain of the British women's ski team in the mid-1930s and reputed to be the best female skier of her generation. There were no children of the marriage, but Selkirk gave wise, thoughtful, and far-sighted advice to his many nephews and nieces.

Selkirk's ministerial career started in November 1951 when Winston Churchill appointed him lord-in-waiting and government whip in the House of Lords. He became paymaster-general in November 1953. Anthony Eden promoted him to the cabinet in December 1955, as chancellor of the duchy of Lancaster. Publicly he loyally supported the Suez venture, although privately he was sceptical. Under Harold Macmillan, he served as first lord of the Admiralty, from January 1957 to October 1959, giving strong leadership to the navy with Lord Mountbatten in the wake of the Suez fiasco. He was sworn of the privy council in 1955 and appointed GCMG in 1959.

In October 1959 Selkirk was appointed UK commissioner for Singapore and commissioner-general for south-east Asia. His appointment came at a sensitive time in the region; announcing it, Harold Macmillan underscored his belief in Selkirk's personal qualities. While in south-east Asia he had to smooth the path of Singapore during the process of transition to self-government, and to ensure good relations between the Chinese, the Malays, the Tamils, and the Europeans. His *Times* obituarist wrote: 'that he acquitted himself well and showed at the same time toughness and a shrewd ability in negotiation was universally acknowledged' (*The Times*, 26 Nov 1994). The prime minister of Singapore, Lee Kuan Yew, described him as a 'convivial and a practical man' who was 'supportive, effective and friendly'. 'I had always thought him a simple country gentleman', he said. 'I did not know that he is also a very skilful diplomat' (ibid.). While he was there he resisted calls from the USA to involve British forces in Laos, Cambodia, and Vietnam, and the British government did not deviate from that view. He was promoted GBE in 1963.

After his retirement from government service in 1963, Selkirk took an active part in the work of the House of Lords, and was president of the Association of Independent Unionist Peers from 1967 to 1979. His attempts to improve bills were not always welcomed by chief whips, but his arguments were cogently expressed and were always taken seriously. He was chairman of the Conservative Commonwealth Council from 1965 to 1972, president of the Royal Society for Asian Affairs from 1966 to 1976, and chairman of the Victoria League from 1971 to 1977. He also devoted much time to family activities, and in particular to strengthening links with Canada. His ancestor Thomas Douglas, fifth earl of Selkirk, had committed his fortune taking to Canada highlanders who had been dispossessed in the clearances. Red River settlement, started by them, became the city of Winnipeg, and Selkirk's visits to Canada caused him to be made an honorary chief of the First Nation Saulteaux, and an honorary citizen of Winnipeg and of Selkirk, Manitoba. He also provided funding for a white Scottish granite memorial to be inscribed to mark the spot in Teba, Spain, where his ancestor Lord James Douglas was killed, carrying the heart of King Robert the Bruce to the Holy Land. When word spread that this might put Teba on the tourist map, 5000 citizens of the town turned out to support the official unveiling of the memorial. Selkirk achieved the great honour in his own country of being appointed a knight of the Order of the Thistle in 1976.

Selkirk had a large circle of close friends and he was an extremely good conversationalist across a wide range of subjects. A man of modesty, courtesy, kindliness, and courage, he achieved considerable distinction in a long and varied life of public service. He died on 24 November 1994 at Poole Hospital, Poole, Dorset, and was buried on 1 December in the churchyard at Berwick St John, Wiltshire. His wife died on 21 December 1994, and a memorial service was held for them both at St Columba's Church of Scotland, Pont Street, London, on 22 February 1995. Selkirk's nephew James Alexander Douglas-Hamilton (*b.* 1942), second son of the fourteenth duke of Hamilton and younger brother of the fifteenth duke of Hamilton, succeeded him briefly as the eleventh earl of Selkirk for four and a half days, before disclaiming his hereditary title. He was Conservative MP for Edinburgh West from 1974 to 1997, minister and subsequently minister of state at the Scottish Office from 1987 to 1997, and a member of the Scottish parliament after 1999. He was made a life peer, as Baron Selkirk of Douglas, in 1997.

SELKIRK OF DOUGLAS

**Sources** *The Times* (26 Nov 1994) • *The Times* (23 Feb 1995) • *The Independent* (1 Dec 1994) • *WWW, 1991–5* • Burke, *Peerage* • personal knowledge (2004) • private information (2004) • d. cert.

**Archives** Lennoxlove, Haddington, East Lothian • NRA Scotland, priv. coll., corresp. and papers • PRO, corresp. relating to south-east Asia, FO 800/897 | FILM British Empire and Commonwealth Museum, Bristol

**Likenesses** photograph, repro. in *The Times* (26 Nov 1994) • photograph, repro. in *The Independent*

**Wealth at death** £1,299,624: probate, 1995

**Hamilton, Gustavus, first Viscount Boyne** (1642–1723), army officer, was the third son of Sir Frederick Hamilton (*c.*1590–1647) of Manorhamilton, co. Leitrim, a younger son of Lord Paisley, who had served in the Swedish army and the wars in Ireland, and his wife, Sidney, daughter and heir of Sir John Vaughan, governor of Londonderry. He matriculated from Trinity College, Dublin, in 1661, but

Gustavus Hamilton, first Viscount Boyne (1642–1723), by unknown artist

joined the army, serving from 1672 to 1676 as a captain in France in Sir George Hamilton's regiment. While attending the duke of Ormond, chancellor of Oxford, he was made DCL of that university in 1677.

From 1678 Hamilton was listed as a captain in the Irish army, and as major of Lord Mountjoy's regiment of foot from 1685. He survived Tyrconnell's purge of protestants from the Irish army, but changed allegiance after the revolution and was attainted by the Jacobite parliament in 1689. In March of that year he beat off the initial attack of the Jacobite army on Coleraine, of which he was governor, but when the enemy used boats to cross the Bann and threaten his rear, he withdrew his small garrison to Londonderry. He seems then to have gone to England, where on 1 June he was given command of a new regiment, afterwards the 20th foot, whose first colonel, Sir Robert Peyton, had died, and whose formation he successfully completed. He commanded his regiment in the war in Ireland in 1690–91, taking part in the major engagements at the Boyne, Limerick, and Aughrim, and especially distinguishing himself at the siege of Athlone, where on 30 June 1691 he led the grenadiers across the river in the hazardous assault that gained the town for the Williamites. He was promoted brigadier-general in 1696, serving in 1702 with the discreditable expedition to Cadiz and the redeeming attack on the Spanish treasure fleet at Vigo, for which Queen Anne presented him with a considerable quantity of plate. In 1704 he was made a major-general.

For his good service in the war in Ireland, Hamilton was appointed to the sinecures of vice-admiral of Ulster and governor of Athlone, and granted 3500 acres of confiscated land in co. Meath, where he built Stackallan House (*c*.1716). He was MP for co. Donegal in the parliaments of 1692–3, 1695–9, and 1703–13, and for Strabane in 1713–14. He was a member of the Irish privy council under William III, Anne, and George I. In 1715 he was created Baron Hamilton of Stackallan and in 1717 Viscount Boyne. He married Elizabeth (*d*. 1721), second daughter of Sir Henry Brooke of Brookeborough, co. Fermanagh, and his second wife, Anne, daughter of Sir George St George, baronet. They had three sons, Frederick (*d*. 1715), Gustavus (*d*. 1735), and Henry (1692–1743), and a daughter, Elizabeth, who married Charles Lambert of Painstown, co. Meath. Hamilton died at Stackallan on 16 September 1723 in his eighty-fourth year, and was buried there. Since Hamilton had been predeceased by his eldest son, his grandson, Gustavus (1710–46), succeeded to his title and estate.

T. F. Henderson, *rev.* Harman Murtagh

**Sources** GEC, *Peerage*, new edn, vol. 2 • J. Lodge, *The peerage of Ireland*, rev. M. Archdall, rev. edn, 5 (1789), 172–81 • C. Dalton, ed., *Irish army lists, 1661–1685* (privately printed, London, 1907) • C. Dalton, ed., *English army lists and commission registers, 1661–1714*, 3 (1896), 6, 65, 283, 413 • H. Murtagh and M. O'Dwyer, eds., *Athlone besieged: eye-witness and other contemporary accounts of the sieges of Athlone, 1690 and 1691* (Athlone, 1991) • K. Ferguson, 'The organisation of King William's army in Ireland, 1689–92', *Irish Sword*, 18 (1990–92), 62–79 • J. G. Simms, *The Williamite confiscation in Ireland, 1690–1703* (1956), 90 • J. C. R. Childs, *Nobles, gentlemen and the profession of arms in Restoration Britain, 1660–1688: a biographical dictionary of British army officers on foreign service* (1987), 107 • J. G. Simms, *Jacobite Ireland, 1685–91* (1969), 57 • M. Bence-Jones, *Ireland* (1978), vol. 1 of *Burke's guide to country houses* (1978–81), 264 • D. Mac An Ghallóglaigh, 'Sir Frederick Hamilton', *Breifne*, 3/9 (1966), 55–99

**Archives** TCD, corresp. with William King

**Likenesses** oils, priv. coll. [*see illus.*]

**Wealth at death** 3500 acres of land in co. Meath: Simms, *Williamite confiscation*

**Hamilton, Hamish** [*formerly* James; Jamie] (**1900–1988**), publisher, was born James Hamilton on 15 November 1900 in Indianapolis, USA, the only child of James Neilson Hamilton, businessman, and his wife, Alice van Valkenburg. He spent his childhood in Scotland. He was educated at Rugby School and Gonville and Caius College, Cambridge, initially reading medicine but changing to modern and medieval languages, in which he obtained a second class in part one (1921), and finally to law, in which he gained a third (1922). He travelled in the USA in 1922–3 and was called to the bar (Inner Temple) in 1925. In the following year he became London manager for the American publishing company of Harper & Brothers, and in 1931 founded his own publishing company, Hamish Hamilton Ltd. In 1929 he married the actress Jean Forbes-Robertson, daughter of Sir Johnston Forbes-*Robertson, actor. This marriage was dissolved in 1933 and in 1940 he married Yvonne (*d*. 1993), daughter of Giorgio Pallavicino, soldier. They had one son, Alastair, an academic and writer, who was to hold various posts at the universities of Amsterdam, Leiden, and Urbino.

His American background and family connections enabled Hamilton to present to the British reading public a series of distinguished writers from the other side of the

Atlantic, ranging from political and economic commentators such as Walter Lippmann, John Gunther, and John Kenneth Galbraith, to novelists such as J. D. Salinger, Truman Capote, and William Styron. His tastes were eclectic, and commercial. A list which included writers of the variety of Sir Denis Brogan, Nancy Mitford, Alan Moorehead, A. J. P. Taylor, Angela Thirkell, Eric Partridge, Richard Crossman, Georges Simenon, Raymond Chandler, James Thurber, Albert Camus, and Jean-Paul Sartre, as well as a number of *New Yorker* contributors (John Hersey, Charles Addams, Rachel Carson), was far from humdrum. He was not, perhaps, a great innovative publisher, and he was not wholly interested in the financial aspects of the business, but he was prepared, in an age when such things were still possible, to back his fancy. Over the years, he built up an extraordinary collection of acquaintances in the worlds of academe, politics, music, the theatre, and above all society. Though he had a surprisingly small coterie of close friends, he appeared to know everyone, however slightly.

This ability to draw so many disparate people into his circle stood Hamilton and his country in good stead during the Second World War. After a brief period in the army (he served in Holland and France during 1940), he was seconded in 1941 to the American division of the Ministry of Information, where he remained until the end of the war. During this period he was able to maintain his publishing company, when other publishers experienced great difficulty in obtaining essential paper for their books. After the war Hamish Hamilton Ltd continued to flourish independently until it was bought by the Thomson Organization in 1965. Hamilton, however, remained as managing director until 1972, and chairman until 1981. Between that date and his death, he was president of the company.

Hamish Hamilton (he was actually baptized James, and was almost universally known as Jamie, although later he changed his name by deed poll to Hamish) was a considerable sportsman in his youth. He was spare stroke of the Cambridge eight in 1921, stroke in the winning boat in the Grand Challenge Cup at Henley in 1927 and 1928, and rowed in the Olympics at Amsterdam in 1928, winning a silver medal. He played squash, skied, executed famously daring dives into the Mediterranean, and flew flimsy planes; in middle age he took up golf. In appearance he resembled a boxer, with a craggy face dominated by a broken nose. He was of medium height, and was noted for the cut of his suits and the high polish of his handmade shoes. But, though he had the friendship of a great many beautiful women, he was no extrovert. In the bar of the Garrick Club, or in the company of friends who could coax him out of his Scottish dourness, he flourished; with others he was reserved and curiously lacking in social graces. He entertained frequently, but his dinner parties were highly formal occasions, gatherings of public figures *en grande tenue*, many of whom he hoped would contribute books to his publishing list. Inevitably, he was accused of snobbery, a criticism which contained more than a germ of truth, but which caused him disproportionate pain. Without his publishing partner, Roger Machell, and his second wife, Yvonne, both his public and his private lives would have been considerably less successful. Unlike Machell, he was not a real publisher, certainly not a man who appreciated new trends in writing; and, without his wife, who was born to be a hostess, invitations to parties at their house in Hamilton Terrace in St John's Wood, London, would have been less sought after.

Hamish Hamilton had an exceptionally low threshold of boredom. He hated meetings and committees, though he was honorary secretary of the Kinsmen Trust from 1942 to 1956, a governor of the Old Vic for thirty years from 1945, a member of the council of the English-Speaking Union, and a governor of the British Institute in Florence. He also founded the Kathleen Ferrier memorial scholarships. None of these activities, however, was at the core of the publishing industry, and his refusal to serve on bodies such as the Publishers' Association was thought to have been the main reason why, unlike other publishers no more distinguished, he never received the knighthood he so much desired. Instead, he had to be content with being made a chevalier of the Légion d'honneur, in 1953, and a *grande ufficiale* of Italy's order of merit, in 1976.

Hamilton died of cancer, asthma, and emphysema on 24 May 1988 in the Hospital of St John and St Elizabeth in St John's Wood, London.

Christopher Sinclair-Stevenson, *rev.*

**Sources** *The Independent* (26 May 1988) • *The Times* (26 May 1988) • personal knowledge (1996) • private information (1996)
**Archives** Bodl. Oxf., letters to Jack Lambert • Bodl. Oxf., corresp. with R. B. Montgomery • CAC Cam., letters to Sir W. J. Haley • Harvard University, near Florence, Italy, Center for Italian Renaissance Studies, letters to Bernard Berenson • Tate collection, corresp. with Lord Clark • U. Warwick Mod. RC, corresp. with Sir Victor Gollancz
**Likenesses** photographs, 1957–71, Hult. Arch.

**Hamilton, Henry Parr** (1794–1880), dean of Salisbury, was born at Blandfield, Midlothian, on 3 April 1794, the son of Alexander *Hamilton (*bap.* 1739, *d.* 1802), professor of midwifery at Edinburgh University. James *Hamilton the younger was his brother. Educated at Edinburgh University under Dr Baird he was admitted in 1811 at Trinity College, Cambridge, where he graduated BA as ninth wrangler in 1816, was elected to a fellowship in 1818, and proceeded MA in 1819. He was well regarded by William Whewell and Adam Sedgwick, and wrote two mathematical textbooks, *The Principles of Analytical Geometry* (1826) and *An Analytical System of Conic Sections* (1828; 5th edn, 1843). He was elected FRS on 17 January 1828 and was also FRS (Edinburgh) (1822), FRAS, and FGS.

Hamilton became curate of Arrington and Orwell, Cambridgeshire, in 1825. The marquess of Ailesbury presented him to the rectory of Wath, near Ripon, Yorkshire, in 1830. He combined this with a personal chaplaincy to the duke of Sussex (1831) and the perpetual curacy of St Mary the Great, Cambridge (1833), a living in the gift of his college. On 31 October 1833 he married Ellen, daughter of Thomas Mason FSA, of Copt Hewick, Yorkshire, with whom he had one daughter. In 1844 he resigned his Cambridge living in order to reside permanently at Wath, becoming rural dean in 1847. He took a special interest in the church's contribution to primary education, delivering a sermon on the subject in 1840. His *Practical Remarks on Popular Education* (1847) pointed to the inadequate provision of elementary education in England. He advocated additional state support for the existing school societies, an enlarged curriculum, more attention to the teaching of girls (since educated mothers were likely to ensure that their own children were literate), and improvements in the training, status, and stipends of teachers. He favoured opening the schools of the National Society to the children of dissenters.

On 17 April 1850 Hamilton was appointed to the deanery of Salisbury, which he held until his death. He was a generous contributor to the restoration of the cathedral and a keen supporter of the diocesan board of education. Hamilton died at the deanery, The Close, Salisbury, on 7 February 1880. GORDON GOODWIN, *rev.* M. C. CURTHOYS

**Sources** *Guardian* (11 Feb 1880) · *Guardian* (18 Feb 1880) · Boase, *Mod. Eng. biog.* · Venn, *Alum. Cant.* · *GM*, 1st ser., 103/2 (1833), 362
**Wealth at death** under £14,000: probate, 17 March 1880, *CGPLA Eng. & Wales*

**Hamilton, Sir Horace Perkins** (1880–1971), civil servant, was born at 34 Hardinge Road, Ashford, Kent, on 20 November 1880, the only son of Horace Hamilton, a solicitor's clerk and later clerk to the East Ashford board of poor law guardians, and his wife, Elizabeth Kitching. His grandparents on his father's side were Scots, but had moved to the home counties in the mid-nineteenth century. Hamilton was educated at Tonbridge School and Hertford College, Oxford, where he gained seconds in mathematical moderations (1901) and modern history (1903).

In 1904 Hamilton entered the Board of Inland Revenue as a third-class clerk in the estate duty department, where he formed a close association and friendship with Warren Fisher, who was then an upper-division clerk. Fisher, who had attended Hertford College a year ahead of Hamilton, became an important patron. In 1912 Hamilton was transferred to the Treasury as a second-division clerk and later that year was recommended to Lloyd George, then chancellor of the exchequer, as his principal private secretary. He held this position to successive chancellors until promoted to deputy chairman of the Board of Inland Revenue in 1918, on Fisher's appointment as chairman. During this period he married, on 11 December 1915, Amy (1884/5–1970), the daughter of Sydney Turner Klein, a merchant, traveller, and writer, whose family firm was heavily engaged in import produce; they had one son and two daughters.

Hamilton's close involvement with the wartime budgets and knowledge of financial matters had greatly enhanced his position within Whitehall. He was appointed CB in 1918, and in 1919 he became the chairman of the board of customs and excise, shortly after Fisher was appointed permanent secretary of the Treasury. Between 1920 and 1925 Hamilton served on the select committee on principles and methods of promotion within the civil service, designed to help realize Fisher's plan for a united service with a common *esprit de corps*; outside his work for the board of customs he was generally preoccupied with matters involving the restructuring of the civil service to enable the permanent secretaries to manage and co-ordinate departmental business more effectively. Like Fisher, Hamilton believed that it was important for senior civil servants to adopt more informal methods of doing business with other departments, encouraging personal discussion and semi-official correspondence ahead of ministerial contact. He received a knighthood in 1921.

In 1927 Hamilton was appointed permanent under-secretary at the Board of Trade and became heavily involved in matters affecting empire and Commonwealth economic co-operation. After 1931 he took a leading role in advising the government on the issue of tariff reform and imperial trade preference. Much of this work reduced the impact of foreign 'dumping' and gave home producers greater security to invest in more modern methods of production.

During the late 1920s the government agreed a reform of Scottish administration, then based on a system of relatively independent Edinburgh-based boards and a small parliamentary 'Scottish' office in London. This looked out of place with the system of Whitehall administration after 1916. In addition, Scottish comment was becoming less comfortable with its apparent lack of influence on regional matters (Scottish unemployment stood at twice the English level) and with the perceived threat to the continuing ability of the Scottish departments and boards to maintain an element of devolved responsibility in social policy. After a series of ill-starred appointments from within Scottish administration, Fisher persuaded Hamilton to accept the post of Scottish Office permanent under-secretary in 1937, largely on the basis that the Gilmour committee on Scottish administration was likely to report on the need to reorganize the Scottish boards and departments on more traditional Whitehall lines, 'co-ordinated' and managed by the permanent under-secretary. Fisher's criterion in recommending such appointments was on the basis of fitness for the job, and his search for the right man covered the whole civil service. In this case Fisher wanted a man who would convince Scottish (and particularly commercial) opinion that its voice would be heard more effectively in Whitehall, but at the same time ensure that nationalist pressures could be constrained by an integrated Scottish administration which on the one hand would enlarge its responsibility for Scottish affairs, but on the other work very much within the Union. Hamilton retained the same salary as at the Board of Trade, which was a grade higher than previous Scottish permanent under-secretaries and signalled, perhaps more than any other change, that the Scottish 'voice' held a significant degree of seniority within the civil service.

The full implementation of the Gilmour reforms was hindered by the outbreak of war in 1939, but by 1942 the Scottish Office's authority within Whitehall had steadily increased. Hamilton's ability to 'have words' within Whitehall gradually encouraged the younger group of Scottish civil servants to press more strongly for the

Scottish interest to be heard at a much earlier stage of policy consideration. For instance, in matters affecting the control of pacifism and the anti-war Scottish nationalist movement, the Home Office, technically responsible for domestic security, acknowledged that Scottish officials were better equipped to deal with the reactions of Scottish institutions and the press than English-based London civil servants. Similarly the newly formed ministry of planning accepted that it was more appropriate for the Scottish Office to deal with UK planning matters in Scotland, particularly if they affected issues such as the sewerage systems of burghs like Clydebank, Pittenweem, and Ardrossan. Elsewhere, Scottish officials took steps to ensure that the Scottish Office would be 'closely associated' with the Board of Trade in its administration of the Distribution of Industry Act of 1945, a move designed to ensure that Scottish officials could actively encourage English industries seeking to expand to move north. In the highlands, the Scottish Office also secured the administration of the newly established Hydro-Electric Board from the Ministry of Fuel and Power.

Hamilton was very much a product of the reformed civil service after 1918: careful and diplomatic in public, but determined to maintain the primacy of his senior position, especially when dealing with other departments in Whitehall. Scottish officials acknowledged his experience, but he never engendered the warmth of appreciation of some of his predecessors and offended a considerable number by indicating that he would not move to Edinburgh on his appointment. In return he remained rather aloof from the predominately Scottish (university) educated officials and found it difficult to recommend a successor from within the Scottish Office.

Following retirement from the Scottish Office in 1946, Hamilton served on a number of government and official committees. These included reviews of the government's regional organization (1947), the remuneration of dentists (1947–8) and consultants (1948–50), and the inquiry into Scottish financial and trade statistics (1950–52). He was a member of the Commonwealth Economic Committee from 1947 to 1963 and chairman from 1947 to 1949. He died at his home, Heath Hall, Bishop's Avenue, Finchley, London, on 15 September 1971. IAN LEVITT

**Sources** *WW* • *The Times* (16 Sept 1971) • b. cert. • m. cert. • d. cert. • *Glasgow Herald* (8 May 1937) • *The Scotsman* (8 May 1937); (3 Jan 1946) • D. Milne, *The Scottish office* (1957) • I. Levitt, ed., *The Scottish office: depression and reconstruction, 1919–59*, Scottish History Society, 5th ser., 5 (1992) • I. Levitt, 'The Scottish secretary, the treasury and the Scottish grant equivalent, 1888–1970', *Scottish Affairs*, 28 (1999) • I. Levitt, 'Scottish papers submitted to the cabinet, 1917–45: a guide to records held at the Public Record Office and National Archives of Scotland', *Scottish Economic and Social History*, 19/1 (1999) • I. Levitt, 'Scottish papers presented to the British cabinet, 1917–66: their archival and historical significance', *Scottish Archives*, 6 (2000), 37–47 • PRO, BT 13/131; DO 222/18; T 1/11477; T 160/1388; T 162/398; T 162/418; T 172/7661; T 222/120; T 268/18; T 275/233–35 • NA Scot., SOE 2/25 • private information (2004) [retired Scottish office civil servants]

**Wealth at death** £87,837: probate, 1 Feb 1972, *CGPLA Eng. & Wales*

**Hamilton, Hugh** [Hugo], **first Baron Hamilton of Glenawly** (*c.*1607–1678), army officer in the Swedish service, was the second son of Malcolm Hamilton (*d.* 1629), archbishop of Cashel and Emly, and his first wife, Mary, daughter of Robert Wilkie of Sauchtonhill. His paternal grandfather was Archibald Hamilton of Dalserf, Lanarkshire. Although Hamilton was born in Ireland both his parents were Scottish and he was known to speak Scots.

Little is known of his early life, but like many younger sons of the time Hamilton travelled to Sweden in 1624 to enlist in the Swedish army: in 1661 he recalled how he was 'one third brother who went abroad 32 [*sic*] years ago to seek fortune in the wars' (*CSP Ire., 1660–62*, 186). In 1630 and 1631 he served as a lieutenant-colonel in John Seaton's and George Cunningham's regiments respectively during the opening phase of Sweden's engagement in the Thirty Years' War. In 1632 Hamilton became a full colonel of a recruited regiment from the British Isles; and in April 1637, in a move typical of the Scottish network in Sweden, he married Margaret Forratt (Margaretha Forath; *d.* 1653), the widow of another Scot in Swedish service, Sir James Spens of Wormiston. Already in 1638 the Swedish Riksråd (state council) noted Hamilton as a good soldier with an excellent service record. He subsequently became the colonel of two conscripted regiments from Ingermanland and Riga, and then remained in Swedish-held Livonia until 1645. His information on the Danish–Norwegian king Christian IV's plans to increase his navy proved vital for the success of the Swedish campaign against Denmark that year.

Hamilton's career advances continued as he became the colonel of another conscripted regiment from Uppland and acted as the commandant in 1646 of a Swedish garrison in Greifswald, on the Baltic coast. In 1648 he was listed among nobles of the third class. The Swedish state marshal, Svante Sparre, instigated the process to make him a baron in 1649, citing his military merits and his land holdings in Sweden. In 1654 he was naturalized and introduced into the Swedish house of nobility as Baron Hamilton of Deserf (a corruption of Dalserf), as was also his half-brother Louis, who had joined him in Sweden in 1645. Hamilton became baron of Ljung and lord of Slefringe in Åtvid parish, Östergötland. That year he was instrumental in obtaining ennoblement for another Scot, Colonel William Barclay. Hamilton's integration into Swedish society was demonstrated by his service as a royal guard at Karl X's wedding, and his regular participation in Swedish political debates from 1654 to 1657. During Swedo-Danish hostilities in 1657 Hamilton was commissioned to undertake the defence of Värmland.

At some point after the death of his first wife in 1653 Hamilton married Jacomina (presumably his second wife), about whom nothing more is known. After 11 May 1659 he married another Scottish woman, Susan Balfour (*d.* 1687), presumably his third wife, the daughter of Sir William *Balfour of Pitcullo; their—and Hamilton's only—son was William, born in 1660 or 1661. Hamilton returned to Ireland, where he held an estate worth £750 per annum, in January 1661, apparently at the request of

Charles II. He was willing to surrender his Swedish estate to be created Baron Hamilton of Glenawly, co. Fermanagh, in March 1661, and was introduced to the House of Lords in June (the barony had been held previously by a branch of the Balfour kin of his wife before their branch became extinct in 1636).

Hamilton settled on the estate of his elder brother Archibald at Ballygally, co. Tyrone. About 1669–70 he returned to Sweden in pursuit of money owing to him from the sale of his estates in Uppland, claiming to be penniless. In 1678 he gave the interest of £20 per annum in perpetuity to the parish of Erigilkeroy, to be disbursed annually by the rector and churchwardens.

Hamilton died in April 1678. His son, William, succeeded to the title but was killed in an accident in February 1681, when the peerage became extinct. Hugh Hamilton's widow married Henry Mervyn of Trillick, co. Dublin, and died in Dublin on 11 December 1687.

A. N. L. Grosjean

**Sources** S. Murdoch and A. Grosjean, 'Scotland, Scandinavia and Northern Europe, 1580–1707', www.abdn.ac.uk/ssne/ • G. Elgenstierna, *Den introducerade svenska adelns ättartavlor, med tillägg och rättelser*, 9 vols. (Stockholm, 1925–36), vol. 6 • G. Hamilton, *A history of the house of Hamilton* (1933) • GEC, *Peerage*, new edn • S. Bergh and B. Taube, eds., *Sveriges ridderskaps och adels riksdags protokoll*, 4–6 (Stockholm, 1871–7) • military muster rolls, Krigsarkivet, Stockholm, MR 1642–1651 • *Sveriges krig, 1611–1632*, Generalstaben, 6 vols. (Stockholm, 1936 9) • L. W. Munthe, *Kongliga fortifikationens historia II* (Stockholm, 1906) • *CSP Ire.*, 1660–62 • J. Lodge, *The peerage of Ireland*, rev. M. Archdall, rev. edn, 2 (1789)

**Wealth at death** gave interest of £20 p.a. in perpetuity to parish of Erigilkeroy: *DNB* • estate worth £750 in 1661: *CSP dom.*

**Hamilton, Hugh**, Baron Hamilton in the Swedish nobility **(1655–1724)**, army officer in the Swedish service, was born on 20 May 1655 at Monea Castle, Ireland, the younger son of Captain John Hamilton (*d.* 1696) of Ballygally, co. Tyrone, and his wife, Jean, the daughter of James Somerville. His father was the second of the three sons of Malcolm Hamilton (*d.* 1629), archbishop of Cashel and Emly: John's two brothers served in the Swedish army and were ennobled there. Hugh saw military service in England before being summoned to Sweden in 1681 by his elder brother, Malcolm *Hamilton, who already led the Älvsborg regiment. Hugh became ensign (30 July 1681) and then captain (20 October 1685) in that regiment. In Göteborg on 2 November 1687 he married Anna Margareta Henriksdotter (*d.* 1722), the daughter of Henrik Arvidsson, a wealthy merchant and councillor of that city, and his wife, Anna (Annika) Jakobsdotter Lindsay. He transferred to the Life Guards on 18 March 1689 and went with them to the west coast. On 12 April 1689 he was ennobled in Sweden and adopted the title Friherr (Baron) Hamilton af Hageby, though he was not introduced into the house of nobility until 1693, and this has led to some confusion over dates in English sources.

In 1690 Hamilton received permission from the king to travel abroad to learn skills which would subsequently be useful in the Swedish service. To this end he returned to England and enlisted in William III's army and saw action in Ireland against James II's troops and in Flanders in 1691. He then returned to Sweden and was promoted major in the Västgöta-Dals regiment in 1698.

In 1703 Hamilton was ordered to raise a reserve regiment in Småland. This was a demanding task, but in only a few months he had raised 900 men, with whom he was ordered the following year to Stockholm to do garrison duty. In 1709 he went with the regiment to Malmö, where he was praised for his work in defending the city, the provincial capital, which that year was attacked by the Danes. Hamilton distinguished himself in the battle of Hälsingborg on 28 February 1710, in which he commanded front-line troops in the victorious Swedish army. In the autumn he was promoted major-general.

Having returned to the castle at Malmö, Hamilton became involved in a fight and was condemned to death in February 1711 for having breached the ban on duelling. The matter was referred to the government, which in April 1711 declared both parties equally to blame and substituted fines as punishment. In 1713 even the fine was waived for Hamilton, who in the course of the trial was described as one of the army's best officers and who afterwards claimed he could not afford to pay the fine.

After his release from his long arrest Hamilton returned to Göteborg and served for one year as the highest official in the county, energetically improving its defences. In 1715 there was some discussion that he be sent to Scotland to join the Jacobite rising, but the plan was forbidden by the king. Instead in 1716 he fought in the Norwegian campaign, having earlier reconnoitred the Swedish-Norwegian boundary, and was that year promoted lieutenant-general and landshövding (county governor) in Västernorrland. He was particularly active, travelling throughout his large region holding landsting (county assemblies) and looking after the many Finnish refugees there. He greatly improved the region's defences, notably by erecting fortifications at Gävle, which prevented the Russians from razing the town in 1719. That year he was promoted field marshal. He was again active in warding off Russian attacks on the Norrland coast in 1721, but had mixed success with his slender resources.

Hamilton died on 17 January 1724 in Stockholm and was buried in Lommaryd church, Jönköping. He had eight sons, many of whom entered the French military service. One son, Gustaf David Hamilton (1699–1788), was created grev (count) in Sweden in 1751.

Elizabeth Baigent

**Sources** A. Åberg, 'Hamilton, Hugo', *Svenskt biografiskt lexikon*, ed. E. Grill, 18 (1969–71), 92–4 • B. Burke, *A genealogical history of the dormant, abeyant, forfeited and extinct peerages of the British empire*, new edn (1883)

**Likenesses** oils, repro. in *Svenskt biografiskt lexikon*, vol. 18, p. 93

**Hamilton, Hugh (1729–1805)**, Church of Ireland bishop of Ossory and author, was born at Knock, co. Dublin, on 26 March 1729, the eldest son of Alexander Hamilton, politician, and Isabella Maxwell. He was descended on his father's side from a Scottish family who had settled in Ireland in the early seventeenth century; the architect Sir James Hamilton of Finnart (*d.* 1540) was an ancestor. He entered Trinity College, Dublin, on 17 November 1742 under the tutorship of the Revd Thomas McDonnell, and graduated BA (1747), MA (1750), BD (1759), and DD (1762). In 1751 he was elected a fellow of the college, having been unsuccessful in the previous year. In 1759 he was appointed Erasmus Smith's professor of natural philosophy at Dublin; at about this date he was also elected a fellow of the Royal Society and a member of the Royal Irish Academy.

Hamilton resigned his fellowship in 1764, and was presented by Trinity College to the rectory of Kilmacrenan in the diocese of Raphoe; in 1767 he resigned this preferment and was collated to the vicarage of St Anne's, Dublin, which benefice he exchanged in April 1768 for the deanery of Armagh.

In 1772 he married Isabella, eldest daughter of Hans Widman Wood of Rossmead, co. Westmeath, and Frances, the twin sister of Edward, earl of Kingston; the couple had two daughters and five sons, including George *Hamilton (1783–1830), Church of Ireland clergyman. On 20 January 1796 Hamilton was promoted to the bishopric of Clonfert and Kilmacduagh; and by patent dated 24 January 1799 he was translated to Ossory. He died at Kilkenny on 1 December 1805 and was buried in his cathedral of St Canice in that city, where there is a monument inscribed to his memory.

Hamilton was the author of several learned treatises, including *De sectionibus conicis tractatus geometricus* (1758), *Philosophical Essays on Vapours* (1767), *Four Introductory Lectures on Natural Philosophy* (1774), and *An Essay on the Existence and Attributes of the Supreme Being* (1784). His principal works were collected and republished, with a memoir and portrait, by his eldest son, Alexander Hamilton, in two octavo volumes (1809).

B. H. BLACKER, *rev.* PHILIP CARTER

**Sources** H. Cotton, *Fasti ecclesiae Hibernicae*, 1–2 (1845–8) • Burtchaell & Sadleir, *Alum. Dubl.* • *GM*, 1st ser., 75 (1805), 1176
**Likenesses** W. Evans, stipple, pubd 1807 (after G. Stuart), BM, NPG • W. Cuming, oils (after G. Stuart), TCD

**Hamilton, Hugh Douglas** (1739–1808), portrait and subject painter, was born in Dublin, the son of a wig maker in Crow Street. He entered the Dublin Society School of Drawing about 1750 and studied under Robert West and James Mannin. He was a pupil there for some eight years, winning three premiums for the best drawings of 1756. In that same year he was a fellow student of the future dramatist John O'Keeffe, who later wrote that Hamilton 'was remarkable for choosing, when drawing the human figure, the most foreshortened view, consequently the most difficult' (O'Keeffe, 12). Hamilton probably left West's academy in the late 1750s and soon set up a flourishing business as a portraitist in pastels. These portraits were usually small but as the years advanced he enlarged his compositions to a rectangular shape, thus allowing for a full-length figure and background. By the early 1760s Hamilton had moved to London and in 1764 was awarded a premium by the Society of Arts for an oil painting, *Priam and Hercules Lamenting over the Corpse of Hector*.

Portraiture continued to be Hamilton's main output, which he exhibited at the Society of Artists throughout

Hugh Douglas Hamilton (1739–1808), self-portrait

the 1770s. In time, he received commissions from the royal family and such grandees as the duke of Northumberland. In 1779 economic security allowed him to move to Italy with his wife, Mary (*c.*1736–1789), and daughter, Harriott. He stayed in Italy until 1792, where he lived mainly in Rome but also spent time in Florence, 1783–85, Venice, 1784, and Naples, 1788. He painted an extensive number of pastel portraits, in both oval and rectangular frames, of British and Irish grand tourists, including resident *émigrés* such as Prince Charles Edward Stuart and his family (1785–8, National Portrait Gallery, London, and Scottish National Portrait Gallery, Edinburgh), and long-term residents such as the fourth earl of Bristol (*c.*1786, Ickworth, Suffolk). While in Rome, Hamilton developed a close friendship with fellow artists such as John Flaxman and especially Antonio Canova, solidifying his relationship with the latter by including him in a superb large-scale pastel (1788–9, V&A) where he stands with another artist, Henry Tresham, next to an early model of Canova's celebrated *Cupid and Psyche* (Louvre, Paris).

A few years earlier in 1783, Hamilton made one of his first known attempts at a large-scale subject picture in oils, *Diana and Endymion* (1783, priv. coll.). Strongly influenced by the then current neo-classical style, this painting has much in common with the antique style of Roman painting of the 1780s. At the same time Hamilton was purchasing a representative collection of old master prints and pictures. Part of this collection was sold by Christies in 1811. One item in the collection, the first volumes of *L'antichità d'Ercolano*, a lavish collection of fine engravings illustrating the discoveries made during the excavations around Naples earlier in the century, greatly influenced Hamilton's few attempts at historical oil paintings during these years. These influences found their most considered application in the oil painting *Cupid and Psyche in the Nuptial Bower* (1792–3, National Gallery of Ireland, Dublin).

During his thirteen years in Italy Hamilton was successful and sociable, yet he stayed clear of factions and, as his fellow Irishman, the sculptor, Christopher Hewetson, affirmed in a letter of 1792, '[he] belongs to no party yet [has his] share of business' (BL, MS 36496). Hamilton also penetrated the Italian establishment, being elected to the Accademia del Disegno in Florence in 1784 and painting a pastel self-portrait for Maria Louisa Bourbon, queen regent of Tuscany, who in 1805 bequeathed it to the Uffizi Gallery where it has since been hung on the Corridorio Vesariano (1785, Uffizi Gallery, Florence).

While in Italy, Hamilton had received commissions from a number of Irish grand tourists and on his return to Ireland in 1792 he renewed his acquaintance with prominent families such as the wealthy bankers La Touche, producing series of pastel portraits for their various homes in Wicklow and Dublin. Similar commissions followed for the duke of Leinster at Carton, co. Kildare. Hamilton had been reluctant to leave Italy but political events made it a sensible decision. His regret on leaving Rome and his many friends is articulated in a number of letters written to Canova between 1794 and 1802, which also describe his activities and refer to the artistic stagnation and unenlightened patronage to be found in Dublin at the turn of the eighteenth century. Yet Hamilton was never short of work. He complained to Canova of the large number of portraits that he had to complete, most of which were in the more time-consuming medium of oil. By far the best portraitist working in Dublin in the 1790s, he received the best commissions: at the end of the decade Hamilton's Dublin studio in Clare Street became a fashionable place to visit. William Drennan, a principal founder of the United Irishmen, commented on the range of portraits being produced by Hamilton in November 1797: a large canvas of the reactionary charity preacher Walter Blake Kirwan, three of the liberal earl of Moira, as well as paintings of radicals such as Lord Edward FitzGerald, his wife Lady Pamela, and Arthur O'Connor (Chart, 264). The portrait of FitzGerald (1797–8, National Gallery of Ireland, Dublin) is a conventional three-quarter-length, but on the death of the rebel leader, Hamilton's image soon became the source for iconic images of a romantic, nationalist hero.

Between 1800 and 1804 Hamilton exhibited in Dublin with great success at the Society of Artists of Ireland exhibitions. Among his first exhibits in 1800 was his *Cupid and Psyche*, which was much admired, while a year later he showed his most successful late portrait, a full length of the melancholic Lieutenant Richard Mansergh St George, who had recently been brutally murdered (1796–8, National Gallery of Ireland, Dublin). The artist painted little after 1804, concentrating his time on a newly developed interest in science. Hamilton died at his home in Lower Mount Street, Dublin, on 10 February 1808. Some of Hamilton's late portraits were finished by his daughter, Harriott. FINTAN CULLEN

**Sources** F. Cullen, 'The oil portraits of Hugh Douglas Hamilton', *Walpole Society*, 50 (1984), 165–208 • F. Cullen, 'Hugh Douglas Hamilton in Rome, 1779–92', *Apollo*, 115 (1982), 86–91 • F. Cullen, 'Hugh Douglas Hamilton's letters to Canova', *Irish Arts Review*, 1/2 (1984), 31–5 • J. Ingamells, ed., *A dictionary of British and Irish travellers in Italy, 1701–1800* (1997) • A. Crookshank and the Knight of Glin [D. Fitzgerald], *The watercolours of Ireland: works on paper in pencil, pastel and paint, c.1600–1914* (1994), 66–72 • J. O'Keeffe, *Recollections of the life of John O'Keeffe, written by himself*, 2 vols. (1826) • *The Drennan letters*, ed. D. A. Chart (1931) • W. G. Strickland, *A dictionary of Irish artists*, 1 (1913), 427–45 • Dublin Society, minute book, 30 May 1754, Royal Dublin Society Library • F. Cullen, *Visual politics: the representation of Ireland, 1750–1930* (1997) • N. Figgis, 'Irish portrait and subject painters in Rome, 1750–1800', *GPA Irish Arts Review Yearbook*, 5 (1988), 125–36 • Biblioteca Civica, Bassano del Grappa, Veneto, Italy, MSS Canoviani • Hamilton to Cumberland, BL, Cumberland MSS, MS 36496, fol. 333 • *A catalogue of the valuable collection of engravings … the genuine property of … Hugh Hamilton … London* (1811) • *IGI*

**Archives** Biblioteca Civica, Bassano del Grappa, Veneto, Italy, letters to Antonio Canova • BL, Cumberland MS 36496

**Likenesses** G. Chinnery, oils, Royal Hibernian Academy, Dublin • H. D. Hamilton, self-portrait, pastels, Uffizi Gallery, Florence [*see illus.*]

**Hamilton, Iain Ellis** (1922–2000), composer, was born at 22 Woodburn Road, Glasgow, on 6 June 1922, the son of James Hamilton, engineer's draughtsman, and Catherine Smail Ellis. The family moved to London when he was seven, and he was educated at Mill Hill School. He then followed his father into the profession of engineering, being apprenticed to Handley Page: he studied music in his spare time. He was thus a late starter when at twenty-five, having won a scholarship, he entered the Royal Academy of Music. He studied composition with William Alwyn and the piano with Harold Craxton, while also pursuing a BMus course at London University. His op. 1, a set of variations for string orchestra, was composed in 1948, as were his first string quartet and his first symphony. Prizes and awards (and with them recognition) then came very quickly: the Dove prize at the academy, the Clements memorial prize for his first string quartet, the Edwin Evans memorial prize for his *Nocturnes for Clarinet and Piano*, the Royal Philharmonic Society prize for his clarinet concerto, and the Koussevitsky Foundation award for his second symphony.

A steady flow of works continued throughout the early 1950s—a violin concerto, an overture, *Bartholomew Fair*, a set of symphonic variations. Chamber music included a viola sonata, a piano sonata, and a piano trio, the last of these commissioned by the Dartington summer school of music and first performed there in August 1956 with Sir William Glock at the piano. A group of vocal works included a Burns cantata and *The Fray of Suport* for chorus, a barbaric *tour de force* well worth revival. A vocal and orchestral piece, *The Bermudas*, set three texts ending with Marvell's poem: its tranced evocation of marine distance makes it memorable. One of the happier episodes of Hamilton's later years was the performance in 1993 of this piece in the Bermudas themselves in their capital—Hamilton.

Until his last years Hamilton was always very aware of the public role of the composer and the responsibilities which arose from it: during the 1950s he was an extremely active presence on the London musical scene. He was chairman of the Composers' Guild, which much later on (in 1974) presented him with the Ralph Vaughan Williams award as composer of the year. He was also chairman of the music section of the Institute of Contemporary Arts, and a member of the BBC's music advisory panel. He did much work for the Society for the Promotion of New Music in its encouragement of young composers. These were also the years when Hamilton found his vocation as a teacher. For several years he taught at Morley College and for London University's extra-mural department. When he lectured his animated style and rapid rate of delivery exactly displayed the mercurial aspect of his character—which otherwise, although always energetic and decisive, tended to be somewhat austere and reserved, almost puritanically so. As a private teacher he was conscientious and encouraging, patient and wise, always eager to instil professional standards of behaviour in his pupils.

By the late 1950s the generation of newly established British composers such as Peter Racine Fricker and Hamilton himself realized that an even younger generation had been captivated by the new sounds and ideas coming out of Darmstadt and Donaueschingen, Cologne and Paris. Hamilton too began to study Webern: the result was immediate and radical. With the sonata for chamber orchestra and the cello sonata (both 1958) and the *Nocturnal* for eleven solo voices (1959) Hamilton suddenly aligned himself with the continental avant-garde of the day. A major collision with a disconcerted public came when the *Sinfonia for Two Orchestras* was performed at the Edinburgh Festival of 1959. The rest of his compositional career, with a few innovatory exceptions, was marked by a gradual retreat from this extreme position.

In 1961 Hamilton went to live in New York and thence commuted regularly to North Carolina, where he taught at Duke University: he was professor of music there during the year 1966–7. In 1962 he was resident composer at Tanglewood; he also acted as visiting composer to the University of Alabama and various other institutions. Visits to the West Indies in the mid-1960s added a Caribbean flavour to his musical interests. He continued to return to Britain for a few months every year, and in 1971–2 held the Cramb lectureship at Glasgow University.

From childhood Hamilton had been enthralled by the theatre, and in his fifties he turned to the writing of opera, usually adopting his own libretto from a pre-existing literary source. This was the case, for instance, with *Agamemnon* and *The Royal Hunt of the Sun*, both written in 1967–9. *The Royal Hunt of the Sun*, indeed, became the best-known of his operas after its production at the London Coliseum in 1977. *The Catiline Conspiracy* (after Ben Jonson; 1972–3) awoke interest because of its apparent relevance to contemporary political events on both sides of the Atlantic, as the governments of Edward Heath and Richard Nixon came to a close. *Anna Karenina* was performed by the English National Opera in 1978, and later had a revival. Some subsequent operas still awaited performance at the time of Hamilton's death.

After his return to England in 1981—precipitated by the tragically sudden death of a close companion—Hamilton continued to write as prolifically as before, in a style increasingly euphonious and romantic in character, inhabiting an altogether more ingratiating sound-world than earlier in his career. Shelley was a particular literary touchstone; otherwise his texts were often taken from French sources: Chateaubriand, Baudelaire, Rimbaud. The full late Romantic panoply of the vocal and orchestral work *Prometheus* (1986) is a good example of his later music.

But the tides of interest and of fashion had turned, and Hamilton's music, old or new, was now to be heard only rarely. The BBC, once the champion of new music in Britain, neglected him and offered only a token celebration of his seventieth birthday in 1992. In his personal life a process of withdrawal from even those who had been intimate friends made him an increasingly isolated figure. Many late scores remained unperformed in his lifetime. The circumstances of his last days saddened all those who remembered his quirky high spirits and vitality, his sharp intelligence, his keen sense of the ridiculous, his integrity, and his wisdom and generosity as adviser, teacher, and friend. He died on 21 July 2000 in the Cromwell Hospital, Kensington, London. HUGH WOOD

**Sources** *New Grove*, 2nd edn • personal knowledge (2004) • *The Scotsman* (31 July 2000) • *The Guardian* (3 Aug 2000) • *The Independent* (27 July 2000) • *The Times* (10 Aug 2000) • *Daily Telegraph* (27 July 2000) • b. cert. • d. cert.

**Likenesses** photograph, repro. in *The Scotsman* • photograph, repro. in *The Guardian* • photograph, repro. in *The Independent* • photograph, repro. in *The Times* • photograph, repro. in *Daily Telegraph*

**Hamilton, Sir Ian Standish Monteith** (1853–1947), army officer, was born on 16 January 1853 on the island of Corfu, then under British occupation, the eldest son of Christian Monteith Hamilton (*d.* 1885), a captain (later lieutenant-colonel) of the 92nd Gordon Highlanders. His mother, Maria Corinna Vereker (1826–1856), was one of five daughters of John Prendergast Vereker, third Viscount Gort. Hamilton never knew his mother, who died of consumption when he was only three. As a result he was raised in the home of his paternal grandparents in Hafton, Argyllshire. The household was dominated by his aunt Camilla who supervised his early education and taught him the proper Presbyterian conventions.

**Education** At the age of ten Hamilton was sent to a fashionable and expensive private school at Cheam. It was his first real contact with the outside world. Having been shielded for the previous seven years by a solicitous aunt and servants, he now found himself bullied and beaten by larger boys and subject to the harsh, often cruel, discipline of a sanctimonious headmaster, the Revd R. S. Tabor. It was an unhappy time for Hamilton and he worked and played without enthusiasm. In 1867 he was sent to Wellington College, where he enjoyed the social scene, but here too showed no scholastic promise.

Hamilton had always intended to follow in his father's

**Sir Ian Standish Monteith Hamilton** (1853–1947), by John Singer Sargent, 1898

footsteps and, as he neared the end of his time at Wellington, he set his sights on obtaining an army commission. All his friends and relatives, including his own father, rated his chances very low. Hamilton thought otherwise and in August 1870, after six months with a reputable 'crammer', took the examination and was placed at 76 among a list of 392 successful candidates. Given an opportunity to study abroad he elected to go to Germany, where he was tutored by I. S. Drammers, a retired general living in Dresden. During his six-month stay (1870–71) in Dresden, he studied the language and military tactics, and gained valuable insight into the German character and German training methods. Back in England he enrolled in a special twelve-month course at the Royal Military College, Sandhurst. Since he was more interested in horseback riding and hunting, it is not surprising that his academic record was undistinguished.

**Early career in India** Hamilton would have preferred his father's old regiment but, as there was no immediate vacancy, he was gazetted to the 12th Suffolk regiment, stationed at Athlone. He remained in Ireland for eighteen months, carrying out routine regimental duties before joining the 92nd Gordon Highlanders in India. Many of the senior officers in the Gordons had served with his father, who had been a popular commanding officer before his retirement a few years before. Whether it was the maturing process or the desire to gain his father's respect, Hamilton became quite serious about his profession. He threw himself fully into everything he undertook, determined as he was to excel and push forward his career. He possessed remarkable qualities. There were few officers in the British army who could match his acute intelligence and formidable gift of expression. Indifferent to personal danger, alert, charming, and witty, he did not evade tough assignments or hard decisions. His skeletal appearance belied his strength and stamina, enabling him to endure privations better than most of his fellow officers. He was typically enough an avid sportsman, but his departure from army convention was reflected in his love of painting and keen appreciation of music and poetry.

During the early months in India Hamilton spent the greater part of the day on the parade ground. Whenever he could arrange a leave he would set out for the hills in search of big game. In between his social and professional commitments he studied Hindustani, which he perfected by speaking to Indian soldiers whenever possible. On returning from England, where he took a course at the musketry school at Hythe, he was appointed musketry instructor of his regiment. Hamilton was convinced that infantry training needed to be revised; that the bayonet and the squares formed to repulse cavalry would prove disastrous against concentrated fire from modern weapons. From every quarter Hamilton encountered prejudice from those who clung to traditional methods. Nevertheless he pursued his own course, sweating, pleading, and even paying for practice cartridges out of his own slender purse. His superiors began to take notice when the returns showed that the regiment's musketry efficiency was the best in India.

**Active service** Hamilton received his first experience of active service in 1879 during the Second Anglo-Afghan War when his regiment was with Sir Frederick Roberts in the march to Kabul. In July, while recuperating from a bad attack of malaria, Hamilton took part in the rescue of survivors of a British outpost overrun by a party of Afghans. In pursuit of the enemy, Hamilton, still in a weakened condition, became separated from his companions. By an odd coincidence it was he who found the raiders. From behind the huge trunk of a tree he held them at bay with his revolver, until his comrades, attracted by the firing, arrived and put them to flight. It was a minor skirmish but Roberts heard about it and sent for Hamilton. He offered Hamilton a glass of sherry and asked him to relate the details of what had occurred. Hamilton later considered this incident the turning point in his career as it brought him into personal contact with his future benefactor. In his first campaign Hamilton received the medal with two clasps and was twice mentioned in the dispatches.

After the Second Anglo-Afghan War the Gordons were on their way to England when at Cawnpore, on 6 January 1881, they received orders to go instead to South Africa where the Boers in the Transvaal had revolted against British rule. Hamilton and three companies of his battalion formed part of the small British force which was decisively defeated at Majuba Hill in February 1881. During the action Hamilton's left wrist was shattered (an injury which left the fingers in his hand shrivelled and unbendable) and he was struck in the back of the head, either by a spent bullet or a small piece of flying rock. After being found unconscious and bleeding by the Boers, who thought he was dying, he was released. Hamilton never swerved from the conviction that a bayonet attack would have saved the day for the British.

Invalided home, Hamilton was given a hero's welcome and invited to dine with Queen Victoria at Osborne. He was recommended for the Victoria Cross but that unique honour was denied on the grounds that he was too young. Before long Hamilton was hard at work in preparation for the Staff College examination. Several days before the examination he received an offer to become aide-de-camp to Sir Frederick Roberts, currently commander-in-chief at Madras. Hamilton accepted the post and, as a newly promoted captain, returned in June 1882 to India, where he would spend the next decade in close association with Roberts.

**Return to India** In October 1884 Hamilton was granted a six-month leave and, with Roberts's blessing, sailed for Egypt in the hope of gaining employment with the Gordon relief expedition. After arriving in the Suez he took the train to Cairo where he learned, to his surprise, that the 1st battalion of his regiment was assembling in Egypt as part of the relief force. He managed, by a combination of persistence and good fortune, to attach himself to the unit and saw action in the now forgotten battle of Kirbekan. Although the expedition failed in its mission, it earned for Hamilton a mention in the dispatches, a medal with two clasps and the Khedive's star, and the rank of brevet major.

Early in 1886 Hamilton resumed his duties as aide-de-camp to Roberts, now commander-in-chief in India, and several months later he met and fell in love with Jean Miller Muir (1861–1941), the engaging and attractive daughter of Sir John Muir, a successful Glasgow businessman. Their marriage was delayed when in November Hamilton went to Burma with his chief, who was charged with pacifying the country after its annexation to Britain. The task was accomplished faster than expected and by early February 1887 Roberts and Hamilton were able to leave Burma. Hamilton was again acknowledged in the dispatches and he received a medal and clasp and a brevet lieutenant-colonelcy. Shortly after his return to India, on 22 February 1887 in St Paul's Cathedral, Calcutta, Hamilton married Jean Muir, who was to be his faithful companion for the next fifty-four years of his life.

It was now apparent that, barring some unforeseen catastrophe, the 35-year-old Hamilton was destined to rise to high rank. In 1890 he was appointed assistant adjutant-general (AAG) for musketry, Bengal, and in the next two and a half years he played an important role in developing a new system that simulated battlefield conditions. The improvement in the firing efficiency of his charges was so dramatic that the new system was extended to British troops. Rewarded with a promotion in 1891, he became the youngest colonel in the army.

Roberts sailed home in April 1893 and was succeeded by Sir George White, who appointed Hamilton his military secretary. In 1895 Hamilton proposed to spend his summer leave in England when General Stedman, who commanded the lines of communications of the Chitral relief expedition, asked him to serve on his staff as AAG and assistant quartermaster-general (AQMG). Hamilton leaped at the opportunity, eager as he was to gain experience in an area in which he was deficient. During the operations Stedman was thrown heavily from his horse and nearly died. While he was recuperating in hospital Hamilton was temporarily put in command. As things were winding down in Chitral he returned to Simla in September as AQMG. He was, as usual, mentioned in the dispatches, and was appointed CB.

In the late summer of 1897 Hamilton was in England on leave when Afridi tribesmen raided frontier forts south of the Khyber Pass, an action which provoked the British government into sending a strong expedition, under Sir William Lockhart, through the mountains to Tirah, the heart of their country. Excited at the prospects of active service, Hamilton cut short his leave and boarded a ship for Aden where he learned, to his delight, that he had been given command of a brigade. On the way good fortune deserted Hamilton. A veiled woman suddenly stepped in front of his horse which shied, slipped, rolled on him, and broke his leg. The bone was improperly set, leaving the injured leg slightly shorter than the other. By the time he was fit enough to rejoin his column the fighting was over.

**The Second South African War** In April 1898, after a quarter of a century of almost continuous service in India, Hamilton returned to England. He turned down an opportunity to become quartermaster-general of the Indian army to accept command of the musketry school at Hythe. He ran the school brilliantly, putting into practice many of the ideas he had long advocated. But his stay at Hythe was brief.

As the dispute with the Boer republics deepened in the summer of 1899, Britain, unprepared for a full-scale war, began pouring troops into South Africa. Sir George White, appointed to command the British contingent in Natal, took Hamilton with him as his AAG when he left England on 13 September. A fortnight after the Second South African War broke out Hamilton, commanding a brigade with the temporary rank of major-general, rode with a British force sent to eject the Boers from their strongly held position at Elandslaagte. The fighting was furious but the British surged forwards over the final crest. Suddenly a group of Boers, hidden near farm buildings, opened a murderous fire and the British recoiled and fell back in confusion. Instantly Hamilton galloped up the slope and was instrumental in stemming the panic and rallying the men. The British reformed and charged, clearing the summit for a second time. The Victoria Cross had never previously been given to a general who led his men personally in battle, and when Hamilton was recommended for the award it was deemed undesirable to establish a precedent.

During the siege of Ladysmith, Hamilton showed the same courage and resourcefulness in defending Platrand Ridge which held the key to the whole southern defences. The ridge was dominated by a hill at either end, Caesar's camp on the east and Wagon Hill on the west. The Boers planned a simultaneous attack against both hills on 6 January 1900. After creeping up undetected they struck at about 3 a.m., initiating a fierce battle that lasted all day and into the evening.

Hamilton was at Caesar's camp when he was awakened by the noise of the firing. Having secured Caesar's camp he went over to Wagon Hill where the situation would remain critical for many hours. Fighting at close quarters, Hamilton came practically face-to-face with the Boer leader, C. J. De Villiers. Shots were exchanged. De Villiers was killed by one of Hamilton's officers but the Boers fought on until dark when a British counter-attack drove them back.

After the relief of Ladysmith, Lord Roberts, who had been sent out to command all the British forces in South Africa, summoned Hamilton to Bloemfontein and gave him command of a division of mounted infantry with the rank of lieutenant-general. Hamilton had long been critical of the old theories of mounted warfare, which he considered no longer relevant on the modern battlefield. His tactical theories worked brilliantly as he used the horse as an instrument of mobility rather than of shock attack. Hamilton took part in Roberts's successful march to Pretoria and was heavily engaged in breaking the resistance of the enemy's main forces at Diamond Hill, which ensured that the city would not be retaken. For his efforts Hamilton was appointed KCB and made a major-general.

Believing that the war was over, Roberts left his former chief of staff, General Herbert Kitchener, to complete such mopping up operations as were necessary. He returned to England in December 1900 to succeed Lord Wolseley as commander-in-chief at the War Office, accompanied by Hamilton, who had agreed to serve as his military secretary. But the war in South Africa dragged on as the Boers resorted to guerrilla tactics, harassing British armies and occasionally inflicting local defeats on them. Kitchener was depressed and losing touch with field operations because of a crushing workload—a situation which prompted Roberts to offer to send him a senior officer as his chief of staff. Accepting the suggestion, Kitchener chose Hamilton, who found himself back in Pretoria on 29 November 1901.

Hamilton was Kitchener's chief of staff in name only for he was rarely, if ever, asked to formulate plans or transmit orders. Kitchener, who delegated as little as possible to subordinates, acted as his own chief of staff and used Hamilton as circumstances might dictate. During the first week in April 1902 Hamilton was sent to manage sweeping operations in western Transvaal, where the absence of a central authority was impeding the work of hunting down the Boer fighters. Hamilton personally directed the last great drive which destroyed a large Boer unit and helped bring an end to the conflict. He left South Africa a substantive lieutenant-general, having enhanced his reputation when so many established officers had lost theirs. He resumed his duties as military secretary at the War Office and nine months later, in April 1903, became quartermaster-general.

**Between the wars** Hamilton's restless spirit made it impossible for him to be content with a sedentary post for any length of time. On the outbreak of the Russo-Japanese War in 1904 he leaped at the opportunity to serve as senior British officer attached to the Japanese army. From the very beginning he formed a high opinion of the Japanese army, confident that it would defeat the Russian army whenever they met on roughly equal terms. Hamilton met and developed friendly relations with a number of Japanese generals, and this enabled him to gain access to classified information and see things in the war zone that were off limits to other foreign observers. He kept a diary in which he described his experiences and reported and analysed the battles. The memoir was later published as *A Staff Officer's Scrapbook* (1912) and excited wide interest in Britain. There were several anecdotes, one in particular about a pock-marked Japanese general, which incurred the disapprobation of some, including the king, as an abuse of hospitality and exceeding the limits of professional etiquette.

After an absence of fourteen months Hamilton returned to England in April 1905 to take over the southern command with headquarters at Salisbury Plain. The Hamiltons moved into Tidworth House, the official residence, a spacious two-storey stone mansion built in the classical style. There, with no financial worries, the Hamiltons entertained frequently, becoming renowned for their warm hospitality and lavish parties.

Hamilton was anxious to apply his experiences in South Africa and Manchuria to the British forces under his command. He co-ordinated the different arms in manoeuvres, placed special emphasis on indirect artillery fire and the timing of barrages to coincide with the infantry assault, and, as might be expected, made musketry practice a large part of the training. It is interesting to note that on two occasions he conducted staff exercises in combined operations against opposed landings. Both were deemed successful, at least on paper. The results would be different in 1915 when, under conditions of war, he directed a combined enterprise that was infinitely more difficult and much larger in scope.

In 1907 Hamilton, aged fifty-four, was elevated to the rank of full general. He was appointed adjutant-general (AG) in 1909 and the following year advanced to GCB. It was as AG that Hamilton unwisely became involved in the highly charged controversy over national military service which was being championed by his former mentor, Lord Roberts. The Liberal government, which was committed to paring down military expenditures in order to subsidize social programmes, was adamantly opposed to a large conscript army. In response to a request by the secretary for war, Richard Haldane, Hamilton produced a memorandum in which he argued that a voluntary, rather than a compulsory, system was better suited to Britain's far-flung imperial interests. Britain's insularity and sea power precluded the need for a large defensive army that conscription would provide. Instead Britain required for overseas purposes a highly trained professional army. This required long-term service of six or seven years which could only be achieved through voluntary service. Hamilton's memorandum, to which Haldane contributed an introduction, was published under the title *Compulsory Service* in April 1910 and instantly created a sensation. The affair endeared Hamilton to the Liberals but damaged his reputation in the army. Many surrounding Roberts considered it a treacherous defection and never forgave him, but, in truth, Hamilton had never pronounced himself in favour of compulsion. Having been caught off guard, Roberts produced a stinging reply in *Fallacies and Facts*, which appeared in March 1911. Roberts was evidently hurt by the action of Hamilton whom he regarded as his protégé, but the old general was not one to hold grudges and their friendship survived the ordeal.

Before the controversy died down Hamilton sailed for Malta to take over the Mediterranean command in succession to the duke of Connaught. The post had initially been offered to Kitchener who turned it down (he likened it to the fifth wheel in a coach) in the higher expectation of succeeding to the viceroyalty of India. Then Haldane had approached Hamilton and, in order to make the offer more attractive, combined the appointment with that of inspector-general of overseas forces. During his four-year tenure Hamilton visited every garrison in the empire and South Africa and, at the invitation of dominion prime ministers, performed similar tours of inspection in Canada, Australia, and New Zealand.

**Outbreak of the First World War** Hamilton was back in England in mid-July 1914 and was appointed aide-de-camp to the king. In the flurry of the opening war in early August 1914, Kitchener was appointed secretary for war and Hamilton was given command of the Central Force which was responsible for the defence of the kingdom. Hamilton's office was in the Horse Guards and practically every day he saw Kitchener, with whom he worked on happy and intimate terms. In November 1914 Kitchener considered sending Hamilton to France to replace Sir John French, the temperamental commander of the British expeditionary force (BEF). But the French commander, General Joffre, persuaded him not to do so, claiming that John French's relations with the French were cordial.

Hamilton's hopes for a field command dimmed with each passing month. Although approaching sixty-two at the close of 1914, there was no evidence of a decline in his physical and mental powers. His record of active service and administrative experience could not be matched by any other senior serving soldiers in the British army. Sooner or later his chance was bound to come. It did, in March 1915, under rather unusual circumstances.

**The Gallipoli campaign** At the start of 1915 Winston Churchill, the first lord of the Admiralty, persuaded the cabinet to send a fleet to force a passage through the Dardanelles with the object of compelling Turkey's surrender and bringing aid to beleaguered Serbia and Russia. As preparations were under way the War Office, under heavy political pressure, consented to send troops to assist the fleet. Kitchener, influenced by Asquith, the prime minister, selected Hamilton to command the military force and broke the happy news to him in an interview on 12 March. Kitchener explained that the Admiralty was confident that its ships could get through the waterway unaided, in which case he thought it likely that Constantinople would surrender. He expected the army's role to be limited to landing parties to destroy any hidden guns that might impede progress and to the occupation of Constantinople. But he made it clear that if the navy encountered unforeseen obstacles Hamilton was to throw his full force into clearing the way. 'Having entered on the project of forcing the Straits', Kitchener remarked, 'there can be no idea of abandoning the scheme'. Kitchener's parting words—the memory of which would haunt Hamilton for the rest of his life—indicated how crucial he considered the operation: 'If the fleet gets through, Constantinople will fall of itself and you will have won, not a battle, but the war' (Hamilton, *Gallipoli Diary*, 1.2–16). Hamilton, who seemed to be gliding into dignified retirement, saw his career unexpectedly revitalized and he was naturally exultant.

Hamilton arrived off the Dardanelles on 17 March, one day before the navy attacked the Turkish forts guarding the entrance to the narrows. From the deck of a ship Hamilton witnessed the unsuccessful attack which was broken off when a row of hidden mines sank three battleships and disabled three more. Although shaken by the fleet's losses and unaware of the cause, the naval commander, Admiral De Robeck, planned to try again after refitting. Hamilton, however, had concluded that the fleet could not get through without the army's help and he so informed Kitchener. Given the assessment of the commander on the spot, Kitchener had no option but to sanction a land campaign which he had so desperately sought to avoid. On 22 April Hamilton and De Robeck met to discuss plans. When De Robeck realized that Hamilton was eager to take the initiative he abandoned plans to renew the attack. In hindsight it would appear that Hamilton's views were influenced by the expectations of a swift and easy victory. The performance of the Turks in the Balkan wars and in the first six months of the First World War, had given rise to the assumption that they would not offer serious resistance.

Hamilton and his small staff began preparations in the face of formidable problems. Naval intelligence could give no accurate information concerning the disposition of Turkish forces. There was a severe shortage of vital equipment, guns, and ammunition. No accurate maps of the Gallipoli peninsula were available. There were few good landing spots and the terrain in the Peninsula was precipitous. The element of surprise had been forfeited. To make matters worse, transports had been loaded without consideration for the tactical requirements of a landing. Four weeks were lost in Alexandria while supplies and equipment were unloaded and reloaded. General Liman von Sanders, who commanded the Turks, used the lull following the naval attack to good effect. He fortified defensive positions, brought in heavy reinforcements, and distributed his men in centrally located areas where they could react fairly quickly to any landings.

The odds were stacked against Hamilton but there remained an outside chance that a well-executed amphibious operation might succeed. Apart from feints and demonstrations, Hamilton's plan called for five landings around Cape Helles at the southern end of the Peninsula, while further north, just above the jutting promontory of Gaba Tepe, a supporting attack was to push inland to the heights of Mal Tepe, thereby cutting off the Turkish defenders in the south. The plan was bold and imaginative but it was beyond the ability of Hamilton's inexperienced troops to carry it out. An equally serious miscalculation was the meagre attention given to logistical support. Hamilton was so sharply focused on getting his men ashore before the mass arrival of the Turks that he gave insufficient thought to the action that would follow.

The operation started on 25 April. The Anzacs in the north brushed aside the small parties of defenders but because they had been put ashore in the wrong place the tangled gullies and ridges slowed down their advance inland. This enabled the local Turkish commander—the then unknown Colonel Mustafa Kemal—to reinforce the area quickly, and in a series of counter-attacks he drove the invaders back to their bridgehead. At Cape Helles three of the landings, although virtually uncontested, failed to press ahead. The British divisional commander was unable to exercise effective control because of poor communications and the lower level officers lacked the initiative to order their men to seize the high ground. Hamilton was on board the *Queen Elizabeth* and could see what was going on, but he chose not to intervene. When the British attacked on succeeding days they made only minimal gains against the defenders who had been reinforced in the interim. Hamilton called off the attack on 8 May after it was apparent that his troops were spent and could no longer advance. British and colonial troops had suffered 20,000 casualties, out of a total of 70,000, in securing a tenuous grip on Turkish soil. Hamilton called for more men and ammunition to which Kitchener acceded.

Hamilton's plan for a second major assault, like the first, was brilliant in theory, but complex and dangerous. The idea was to make a landing at Suvla Bay to draw the Turkish defenders away from the Anzac beachhead, from which the main attack would be launched. Reinforced by British and Indian troops, the Anzacs would break out of their position and attempt to reach the heights of Sari Bahr ridge, which dominated the Turkish forts at the narrows. The operation was badly bungled. Sir Frederick Stopford, an elderly officer with no experience of field command, was placed in charge of the supporting attack at Suvla Bay. His landing on 6 August surprised the Turks but he dallied and wasted invaluable time, instead of immediately ordering the seizure of the surrounding heights. His men were left to relax and enjoy themselves on shore. Peering through spy glasses from a nearby hill, a German officer thought, and later remarked, that the scene 'looked like a boy's scout picnic in progress'. Stopford, supervising the operation from the deck of a ship, did not come ashore with his staff until the afternoon of 8 May, when the opportunity had passed. The whole of Hamilton's plan was ruined and none of the objectives was gained or held. Hamilton admitted to Kitchener on 17 August that his 'coup had so far' failed, but he was anxious to try again if provided with adequate men and munitions (Cassar, *Asquith*, 128). The cabinet, however, had lost faith in his leadership and in October he was recalled.

**Assessment** After a career of unbroken success Hamilton had failed in the ultimate test of his capacity. No one would deny that he was dogged with misfortune at practically every turn or that he faced an enormous challenge, but it must also be added that he had failed to capitalize on his chances. Outwardly he possessed all the qualifications of a great commander. He had personal charm, integrity, more experience of war than any of his contemporaries, intellectual detachment, and physical courage. His flaws were not as visible but they proved fatal. He lacked mental toughness, basic common sense, and sufficient ruthlessness to dismiss an incompetent subordinate. He underestimated the enemy, a cardinal sin in war, and his excessive optimism frequently crossed into the realm of wishful thinking. While it was theoretically sound to refrain from interfering in field operations once in progress, it was unwise to adhere to that principle when subordinates were unproven or inadequate. The plain truth was that throughout the Gallipoli campaign he never acted like a commander-in-chief.

Despite his offers to serve in any capacity Hamilton was never employed in active service again. He was appointed lieutenant of the Tower of London in 1918 and created GCMG the following year. After retiring from the army in 1920 he took a keen interest in the work of the British Legion. He was in great demand as a speaker for veteran organizations and he attended many reunion dinners with his old regiments, including the Gordon Highlanders, of which he had been a colonel for many years. From 1932 to 1935 he was lord rector of Edinburgh University. In his leisure time he put his fluent pen to work and wrote many books, among which was *Gallipoli Diary*, a record of his experience and a revealing self-portrait. Although he remained convinced that history would vindicate his conduct of the operations at Gallipoli he never sought to defend himself in public or to reply to the harsh, often shrill, judgements of armchair strategists.

For many years the Hamiltons had no interest in starting a family but after the war Lady Hamilton changed her mind and they adopted two children, a boy and later a girl. Little is known about the girl, who appears to have caused the Hamiltons a good deal of grief. The boy, Harry, grew into a fine young man, went to Sandhurst, and was commissioned in the Scots Guards. He was a great source of comfort to the Hamiltons in their old age but was killed in action in north Africa in 1941. Hamilton died in London on 12 October 1947 at the age of ninety-four, and was buried in Doune, Perthshire, next to his wife who had preceded him in death by six years. GEORGE H. CASSAR

**Sources** I. B. Hamilton, *The happy warrior: a life of General Sir Ian Hamilton* (1966) · I. Hamilton, *When I was a boy* (1939) · I. Hamilton, *Listening for the drums* (1944) · R. R. James, *Gallipoli* (1965) · C. F. Aspinall-Oglander, ed., *Military operations: Gallipoli*, 2 vols., History of the Great War (1929–32) · I. Hamilton, *Gallipoli diary*, 1 (1920), 2–16 · M. Hickey, *Gallipoli* (1995) · *DNB* · *The Times* (13 Oct 1947) · L. S. Amery, ed., *The Times history of the war in South Africa*, 7 vols. (1900–09), vols. 2, 5 · J. Selby, *The Boer War: a study in cowardice and courage* (1969) · B. Farwell, *The great Anglo-Boer war* (New York, 1976) · T. Pakenham, *The Boer War* (1979) · R. Kruger, *Good-bye Dolly Gray: the story of the Boer War* (1959) · G. Arthur, *Life of Lord Kitchener*, 2, 3 (1920) · P. Magnus, *Kitchener: portrait of an imperialist* (New York, 1959) · D. James, *Lord Roberts* (1954) · A. J. Marder, *From the Dreadnought to Scapa Flow: the Royal Navy in the Fisher era, 1904–1919*, 5 vols. (1961–70), vol. 2 · L. von Sanders, *Five years in Turkey* (1927) · W. S. Churchill, *Ian Hamilton's march* (1900) · I. Hamilton, *A staff officer's scrapbook* (1912) · S. E. Koss, *Lord Haldane: scapegoat for liberalism* (1969) · G. H. Cassar, *Kitchener: architect of victory* (1977) · G. H. Cassar, *Asquith as war leader* (1994) · I. Hamilton, *Jean: a memoir* (1942) · O. Ransford, *The battle of Majuba Hill* (1967) · *CGPLA Eng. & Wales* (1947)

**Archives** King's Lond., Liddell Hart C., MSS · Sheff. Arch., letters relating to West Yorkshire regiment · Wellcome L., report on Japanese medical arrangements | BL, corresp. with Lord Keyes · Bodl. Oxf., corresp. with Herbert Asquith; corresp. with Lewis Harcourt · CAC Cam., corresp. with Sir John De Robeck · HLRO, corresp. with Sir John St Loe Strachey · King's Lond., Liddell Hart C., corresp. with Sir B. H. Liddell Hart; corresp. with John North, and papers · NAM, letters to Spenser Wilkinson · NL Scot., corresp. with Lord Haldane; letters and cards to William Will · NRA Scotland, priv. coll., corresp. with Sir John Ewart · PRO, corresp. with Lord Kitchener, PRO 30/57; WO 159 · Trinity Cam., letters to Sir Henry Babington Smith | FILM BFI NFTVA, documentary footage · BFI NFTVA, news footage · BFI NFTVA, propaganda film footage · IWM FVA, documentary footage | SOUND BL NSA, documentary recordings · IWM SA, oral history interview

**Likenesses** J. S. Sargent, oils, 1898, Tate collection [*see illus.*] · I. Sheldon-Williams, pencil and watercolour drawing, 1900, NPG · W. Rothenstein, two pencil drawings, 1916, IWM, NPG · W. Stoneman, photograph, 1917, NPG · S. de Strobl, bust, exh. RA 1933, NAM · J. S. Sargent, Scot. NPG · Spy [L. Ward], caricature, watercolour study, NPG; repro. in *VF* (2 May 1901)

**Wealth at death** £98,055 12*s*. 11*d*.: probate, 12 Dec 1947, *CGPLA Eng. & Wales*

**Hamilton, James, of Cadzow** (*b*. *c*.1388, *d*. in or before 1436). *See under* Hamilton family (*per*. 1295–1479).

**Hamilton, James, first Lord Hamilton** (*c*.1410–1479). *See under* Hamilton family (*per*. 1295–1479).

**Hamilton, James, first earl of Arran** (1475?–1529), magnate, was the only son of James *Hamilton, first Lord Hamilton (*c*.1410–1479), and Princess Mary (*c*.1450–*c*.1488), daughter of *James II, king of Scots, and his queen, *Mary of Gueldres. He became head of the house of Hamilton following his father's death on 6 November 1479, inheriting a network of lands and influence which the family had been gradually extending since the late thirteenth century. The marriage of his parents in 1474 effectively raised the Hamiltons from inferior rank to a place in the nobility, and, more importantly, it gave them the claim, in the event of the failure of the male line, to the crown of Scotland itself.

**Early advancement** Nothing is known of Hamilton's early years and education, but between 1481 and 1500 he is mentioned several times in the exchequer rolls in the context of sasines of lands in Lanarkshire, Linlithgowshire, Ayrshire, and Renfrewshire, the counties in which the family's strengths lay. In 1489 James IV formally invested him as sheriff of Lanark, an office previously held by his father. He appears to have been close to the king, who was his first cousin: in 1501 James gave him the ward and relief duties of some of his lands, while the treasurer's accounts record several gifts (mainly of animals) made by Hamilton to the king.

On 8 August 1503 Hamilton was present at James's marriage to Margaret Tudor at Holyrood. The king had provided him with 16 ells of white damask flowered with gold for his wedding clothes, at a total cost of £76. On the same day he was created earl of Arran, though the formal grant was not made until three days later, on 11 August, when it was recorded that the lands and earldom were being bestowed *propter propinquitatem sanguinis* ('for his nearness of blood') and for his services, labours, and expenses, at the time of the royal marriage (Paul and Thomson, 2.582).

In May 1504 Arran was given command, under a special commission, of a naval expedition to quell a rising in the Scottish isles. Two years earlier, between April and August 1502, he had commanded a fleet sent to assist the Scottish king's uncle, King Hans of Denmark, to defeat a rebellion by the Swedes. Arran's role as a naval commander, which was unusual among the nobility, shows him giving active support to James IV's policy of developing an effective Scottish fleet.

**Marital problems and family policy** In November 1504 Arran was granted a divorce from his wife, Elizabeth Home (*c*.1477–1544), daughter of Alexander, second Lord Home. The couple had been married for about fourteen years; she was called his spouse in a crown charter of 28 April 1490. The sentence of divorce was granted on the grounds of her previous marriage to Thomas Hay, son and heir of John, Lord Hay of Yester. Hay had apparently gone abroad and was believed to be dead, but he was definitely alive and in Scotland on 20 June 1491, when he was served heir to his father. However, as he did die shortly afterwards, it was only asserted by the depositions of witnesses that he had appeared before a notary to object, stating that Elizabeth Home was his lawful wife. As she could only have been about twelve or thirteen years old at the time of her marriage to Hamilton, it is unlikely that her marriage to Hay was anything more than a child marriage, if, indeed, they had ever been married at all.

In September 1507 Arran was sent as James IV's ambassador to France. On his return journey, early in the following year, he was detained briefly in England on the orders of Henry VII, who was suspicious of a renewal of the Franco-Scottish alliance. Arran appears to have kept a stud of horses at Kinneil, to which the king paid a visit in July 1508. Certainly he was a competent horseman, achieving success in various tournaments, and in 1508 he 'gat the degrie that day givin to him be the judgeis and harrauldis of the best archer athir in horseback or on fut that was in Scotland at that tyme' (Mackay, 1.243).

On 11 March 1510 the sentence of divorce against Elizabeth Home was repeated, implying that Arran had continued to live with her since 1504. While no reason other than her previous marriage to Hay was given in either 1504 or 1510, it is likely that Elizabeth was divorced because the couple had no children. Arran had fathered several illegitimate children by this time and it may be that he desired an heir (though there seems to have been no real urgency as he did not remarry until 1516). However, the lack of a legitimate heir presented no real impediment to the descent of the Hamilton estates. On 17 January 1513 all Arran's lands and baronies were incorporated into one free barony of Hamilton to be held in entail for his legitimate heirs, or, if none, then for James *Hamilton of Finnart (his eldest illegitimate son, born of his liaison with Marion Boyd of Bonshaw), Sir Patrick Hamilton of Kincavil, John *Hamilton (1510/11–1571) (his illegitimate brothers), Sir James Hamilton of Sillertounhill, William Hamilton of Cander, and Gavin Hamilton of Orbiston, and their heirs successively. By a further charter given on 20 January, considering that Arran had no legitimate heirs and desiring to preserve the royal blood in the earl's ancient and honourable house, the king granted him, failing legitimate heirs, as heirs in entail in spite of their illegitimacy, Sir James Hamilton of Finnart, Sir Patrick Hamilton of Kincavil, and John Hamilton of Broomhill, and, to all intents and purposes, legitimated them to succeed in proper order.

This action typified the policy of the house of Hamilton which ensured that no one was alienated from the family nexus. Since the early fourteenth century a powerful and cohesive network of influence had been established whereby all members of the family were provided for, whether heir or younger son, legitimate or illegitimate, male or female. By the early sixteenth century the Hamiltons had become one of the most influential families in Scotland, partly owing to the marriage with Princess Mary, and partly owing to the structure of the family itself which was based upon an extensive loyalty to kin and name, bound by a complicated system of temporal and ecclesiastical wealth, property, and positions, and strengthened by advantageous marriage alliances at every level of society. In addition the family always gave strong support to the king, which proved mutually advantageous, in that the king was assured of loyalty in return for land, offices, and influence.

**Relations with Albany** In July 1513, when Scotland was under pressure to support France against England, Arran was again entrusted with the command of the Scottish fleet. His subsequent actions have been criticized, though it is unlikely that he would have disobeyed orders. Instead of sailing south, the fleet sailed north round the coast of Scotland and attacked Carrickfergus, the chief English stronghold in Ulster. In many ways the manoeuvre was a logical consequence of James IV's recently negotiated treaty with O'Donnel of Tyrconnel, one of the chiefs of Ulster. However, the fleet then returned to Ayr, presumably to take on supplies, and it finally arrived in France in September 1513, too late to be of any effective assistance, for the Scottish army was defeated at Flodden on 9 September.

When Arran returned to Scotland in November he was accompanied by Antoine d'Arces, seigneur de la Bastie sur Melans, the agent of John Stewart, sixth duke of Albany, the son of James III's brother Alexander and, after the infant James V and his baby brother, closest in line to the crown. Even at this early date overtures had been made to Albany to assume the governorship of Scotland. Under the terms of James IV's will, his queen, Margaret Tudor, had been appointed guardian of her sons for as long as she remained a widow, but in August 1514 she played into the hands of Albany's supporters by marrying Archibald Douglas, sixth earl of Angus. In August 1514 the council renewed its request to Albany and he arrived in Scotland on 16 May 1515.

For the first few months of Albany's governorship, the relationship with Arran was unsettled. Arran supported a rebellion by Alexander, third Lord Home, brother of his first wife, and others, in an attempt to deliver the young king from Albany's custody. Albany acted immediately, however, and marched west to besiege Arran's stronghold of Hamilton. He soon had the rebellion under control, and then showed clemency to win support by pardoning the rebels.

Arran has been described as incompetent and indecisive (though his main detractor was George Buchanan, not one of the family's supporters). It was a criticism levelled at the Hamilton family in general, but in the ups and downs of sixteenth-century politics the preservation of oneself and one's family took priority over other considerations. Assured of Albany's support Arran took 'ane new respitt' (Lesley, 106) in March 1516 and for the remainder of the young king's minority he was loyal in his support of the governor. Following the death of James V's baby brother Alexander in 1516, Albany became next in the line of succession and was formally declared second person of the realm by parliament in November that year. James V's nearest kinsman after Albany was Arran himself and it was not in the latter's best interests to distance himself from this proximity to the crown.

It is possible that his position as third in line to the throne made Arran reconsider his lack of a truly legitimate heir, for banns of marriage having been published on 2, 9, and 11 November 1516 he married Janet Beaton, daughter of Sir David Beaton of Creich, niece of James Beaton, archbishop of Glasgow, and widow of Sir Robert Livingstone of Easter Wemyss, who had been killed at Flodden. They married before 23 November, when they had a joint charter of the lands of Kinneil. Janet died about 1522, leaving their three children: Helen (who married

Archibald Campbell, fourth earl of Argyll), James *Hamilton (who succeeded his father as second earl of Arran and later became duke of Châtelherault and governor of Scotland during the minority of Mary, queen of Scots), and Gavin. However, continuing concern over the legality of Arran's divorce from his first wife cast doubt on the legitimacy of the children of the second, and this uncertainty dictated both his own actions and those of the Hamilton family in general, particularly later in the sixteenth century when they were heirs presumptive to the crown.

Arran was one of a council of regency appointed to govern Scotland during Albany's absence in France from 1517 to 1521. During this time he strengthened his position, particularly following the murder of the president of the council of regency, Antoine d'Arces, seigneur de la Bastie, when he gained the appointments of lieutenant of the Merse and Lothian, and provost of Edinburgh. This increase in power, which effectively established him as head of affairs, aroused the jealousy of the earl of Angus and provoked several outbreaks of violence between rival factions of Douglases and Hamiltons, culminating in the street fight known as Cleanse the Causeway on 30 April 1520. Arran and his followers were driven from Edinburgh and Sir Patrick Hamilton of Kincavil, Arran's half-brother, was killed. However, Arran regained control of Edinburgh on 19 January 1521, when the town bound itself to him in manrent service.

**The end of the minority** When Albany again returned to France in May 1524, Arran, realizing that the young king, now aged twelve, would soon be able to rule in his own right, allied with Margaret Tudor (now separated from the earl of Angus) and declared that the king's minority was at an end. James V was brought from Stirling to Edinburgh and on 26 July 1524 was publicly invested by Arran with the crown, sceptre, and sword of state. But whoever controlled the king controlled Scotland and factions again began to emerge. In July 1525 parliament devised a rotation system whereby the earls of Angus, Arran, Lennox, and Argyll would share responsibility for the young king. Angus, however, failed to hand over James V to Arran at the end of the first quarter in November 1525, in effect staging a *coup d'état* which ensured that every office in the administration would now be controlled by Douglases.

James V legally attained his majority in 1526, but in order to remain close to the king Arran still had no alternative but to come to terms with Angus. At Linlithgow on 4 September 1526 Arran and his 'part-takers, there assembled for the preservation and defence of the King's person' (Pitcairn, 1.134), repulsed an attempt by John Stewart, third earl of Lennox, to seize the king. Lennox was killed and Arran was found weeping over his body, lamenting him as 'The wyssist man the stoutest man the hardiest man that ever was bred in Scotland' (Mackay, 1.320). A dramatic scene—but Lennox was Arran's nephew, and Arran's eldest illegitimate son, Sir James Hamilton of Finnart, was suspected of killing him. The defence of the king against the ambitions of the Lennox Stewarts had given the Hamiltons an opportunity for self-preservation. The rivalry between these two increasingly influential families must have been fuelled by the continuing uncertainty over Arran's divorce from his first wife. If his divorce and remarriage were unlawful, then the next in line to the crown was Lennox, the son of Arran's sister Elizabeth and Matthew Stewart, second earl of Lennox. The removal of the third earl of Lennox, leaving a young son as head of the family, could thus have been intended to ensure that the Lennox Stewarts would not be an effective force in Scottish politics in the foreseeable future. The ward of the earldom of Lennox, during the minority of the fourth earl, was initially distributed equally between Angus and Arran, before both halves were made over to Andrew Stewart, Lord Avondale; but the Hamiltons retained an interest in the Lennox estates, for Avondale's wife Margaret was one of Arran's illegitimate daughters.

Arran was present in parliament in Edinburgh in May 1528 when James V finally assumed royal authority, and he remained close to the king as a chief adviser and lord of council, regularly witnessing royal charters. Following the session of the lords of council at Edinburgh on 20 July 1528, he left for the west to deal with an uprising on the island of Arran, part of a long-standing dispute with the Stewarts of Bute over possession of the island. For the rest of the year he was active in affairs of state. On 5 September the Douglases were declared guilty of treason and forfeited, and on 16 November Arran received the lordship of Bothwell, part of the confiscated Angus estates. On 14 December 1528, aware of the potential benefits of Anglo-Scottish peace and friendship, he signed the treaty of Berwick, which established a five-year truce. He continued to witness charters until January 1529.

On 25 March 1529 a ceremony took place whereby Arran resigned land to Sir James Hamilton of Finnart, who, *ut filius obediens* ('as an obedient son'), then returned it—a symbolic resignation of all right to his father's estates (*Hamilton MSS*, 217). While the ceremony demonstrated the mutual trust between father and son, it also served as a public acknowledgement that the rights and interests of Arran's heir, who was still a minor, would be safeguarded. The following day, 26 March 1529, Arran made his will, appointing Finnart as his executor and as tutor to his heir. He had died at Kinneil before 31 March, when Finnart was granted the ward of the earldom; he was buried at the collegiate church at Hamilton in Lanarkshire.

Arran was undoubtedly a key figure during the minority of James V. He also consolidated the strength of the house of Hamilton, and his numerous children, legitimate and illegitimate, added to the family's lands and offices. His legacy became apparent in the ensuing years when his sons held office as heads of state and church, and the family played a prominent role in national affairs throughout the Reformation period. ELAINE FINNIE GREIG

**Sources** *The manuscripts of the duke of Hamilton*, HMC, 21 (1887) • J. M. Thomson and others, eds., *Registrum magni sigilli regum Scotorum / The register of the great seal of Scotland*, 11 vols. (1882–1914), vols. 1–2 • T. Dickson and J. B. Paul, eds., *Compota thesaurariorum regum Scotorum / Accounts of the lord high treasurer of Scotland*, 1–5 (1877–1903) • *The historie and cronicles of Scotland … by Robert Lindesay of Pitscottie*, ed. A. J. G. Mackay, 1, STS, 42 (1899) • J. Lesley, *The history* *of Scotland*, ed. T. Thomson, Bannatyne Club, 38 (1830) • G. Buchanan, *The history of Scotland*, trans. J. Aikman, 4 vols. (1827–9) • E. Finnie, 'The house of Hamilton: patronage, politics and the church in the Reformation period', *Innes Review*, 36 (1985), 3–28 • G. Hamilton, *A history of the house of Hamilton* (1933) • R. Pitcairn, ed., *Ancient criminal trials in Scotland*, 1, Bannatyne Club, 42 (1833) • N. Macdougall, *James IV* (1989) • W. K. Emond, 'The minority of James V, 1513–1528', PhD diss., U. St Andr., 1988 • J. Cameron, *James V: the personal rule, 1528–1542*, ed. N. Macdougall (1998) • *The manuscripts of S. H. Le Fleming*, HMC, 25 (1890) • A. Theiner, *Vetera monumenta Hibernorum et Scotorum historiam illustrantia* (Rome, 1864) • C. Innes, ed., *Registrum episcopatus Glasguensis*, 2 vols., Bannatyne Club, 75 (1843)

**Archives** NA Scot., misc. papers

**Wealth at death** approx. £11,700 Scots; plus 520 cows; also utensils and household goods: will, 26 March 1529, *Hamilton manuscripts*, 52–3

**Hamilton, Sir James, of Finnart** (*c*.1495–1540), administrator and architect, was the illegitimate firstborn son of Lord James *Hamilton (1475?–1529), subsequently first earl of Arran, and his mistress Marion Boyd of Bonshaw. Granted the lands of Finnart in 1507, he had court connections from an early age, being knighted in 1511. Accepted in 1513 as his father's heir failing legitimate heirs, in 1516 he fought for his father against the Angus Douglases at the battle of Kittycrosshill and was taken to Edinburgh Castle afterwards as a hostage for Arran's 'good rewle'. In 1517, by now of age, he was probably one of the heirs of Scottish nobles who accompanied the duke of Albany, governor of Scotland, to Amboise, where he could have met the elderly Leonardo da Vinci. He also acted as ambassador to and from the French court following the murder by the Homes of Albany's agent, Antoine de la Bastie, in September that year. But he continued to be very closely associated with Arran, and as the man with 'most stroke' about the earl played a prominent part in the skirmish known as Cleanse the Causeway, on 30 April 1520, when the Douglases drove the Hamiltons out of Edinburgh. Finnart and his father escaped across the Nor' Loch marshes on the back of a collier's pony. When Albany returned in 1521 the pendulum swung back, and Finnart received the forfeited lands of Cambusnethan, Lanarkshire, where he may have rebuilt the house. Thereafter he became prominent at the court of the queen dowager and the young James V, and was one of the leaders of the army which threatened northern England late in 1523.

In 1525 the earl of Angus took control of King James, initiating a period of great danger for Angus's Hamilton rivals, who retreated to their Clydeside fastnesses, where Sir James probably built the fortress of Cadzow (or Fairholm), a cliffside castle with three wards and certain parallels with Chinon. But in the following year the Douglases, unable to destroy the Hamiltons, beckoned them into an unlikely alliance, which Finnart may have engineered. To judge by its consequences, this was a duplicitous move. At first Finnart led the joint force which on 4 September 1526 defeated John Stewart, third earl of Lennox, at Linlithgow, as he tried to rescue the young king from the Douglases, and is said to have himself killed Lennox. The charge is given strength by the fact that the latter, a cousin of the king, was Arran's closest rival for the position of heir to the throne; in the following year, moreover, a Lennox dependant tried to murder Finnart at Holyrood. But when in 1528 the king escaped from the Douglases, Finnart took part in the siege of Angus's castle of Tantallon, and although he was thought by the besieged to be interceding with the king on their behalf, in fact he seems to have been inciting the king against them. His advancement in 1528 to be master sewer and master of the king's stables (accompanied by substantial grants of money and land) would thus have constituted a reward for loyalty to the crown against Angus. At the same time his promotion underlined the extent to which the Hamiltons had overtaken the Douglases. His father died in 1529, leaving an heir aged nine or ten, and Finnart was granted the ward of the earldom of Arran on 31 March, making him the effective head of his powerful family. He seems to have exploited his position to the full, steadily augmenting his estate at the expense of his half-brother and also of others—he became notorious for his 'conquishing' of lands. Some time earlier he had married Margaret, heiress of Sir Robert Livingstone of Easter Wemyss, with whom he had a son and two daughters, and who outlived him; he was also the father of at least ten illegitimate children, born of liaisons with at least three recorded mistresses, Marion Stewart, Elizabeth Murray, and Elizabeth Elphinstone.

Finnart was an important royal servant during the following decade. Between 1530 and 1533 he became a member of the secret council and an occasional judge, especially in criminal cases. Also in 1533 he was captain of the 'prickers' against the English. But Finnart possessed creative as well as practical talents—an aspect of his personality underlined by his appointment in 1534 to be master of the works at Linlithgow Palace—and may well have been Scotland's first major architect. After the capture of Tantallon Castle in 1528 he may have helped to refortify it. In 1530 he had begun to build a country house for himself at Craignethan, near Lanark: an outstanding, geometrically proportioned house set within double, rectangular-towered courtyards; the principal chamber, uniquely set on the ground floor, is an approximate double cube. The first caponier (a defensive device of Italian origin) in Scotland, and perhaps in the British Isles, crouches in the ditch between the two courts. Although little evidence now survives, he is likely to have carried out work at the principal Hamilton residences of Kinneil and Hamilton. He remodelled Linlithgow Palace for the king in fashionable style, and subsequently undertook works at Blackness (the state prison) and Boghouse of Crawfordjohn. The square-towered courtyards of Craignethan and the manor house at Greenock (the original Finnart seat) were echoed at properties belonging to his allies and friends, notably Blairquhan and Drumlanrig. He may also have been involved in the conversion of the chapter house at Balmerino for the ailing Queen Madeleine, and in the erection of new royal lodgings, later called the Prior's House, at St Andrews, both in 1537. His masterpiece, however, was the sculpture-encrusted palace begun in 1538 within the fortifications at Stirling Castle. This had parallel sequences of apartments for the king and queen, formally proportioned, enfolding a courtyard with a fountain; it may have had an unfinished west-facing gallery. Finnart paid for this great building substantially from his own well-filled pockets. In September 1539 he was appointed 'maister of werk principale to our soverane lord of all his werkis within his realme', with the exceptionally large annual fee of £200 (*Registrum secreti sigilli*, 1529–42, no. 3145).

His wealth and influence had made Finnart a power in Scotland. By now he held the baronies of Ochiltree (granted 1531), Avendale (1534), and Kilmarnock (1535, in exchange for Crawfordjohn, granted 1534), and land held by him, his allies, or his dependants stretched almost uninterruptedly from Edinburgh to the south-west tip of Ayrshire. There were even suspicions that the Hamiltons, supported by Archbishop James Beaton and Cardinal David Beaton (their cousins by marriage), were seeking to replace the Stewarts on the throne. By mid-1540, however, King James had a legitimate male heir and the second earl of Arran had attained his majority. The latter may well have resented Finnart's plundering of his estates. With enemies in high places Finnart was vulnerable, and late in July he was arrested on charges of treason; he was tried and convicted on 16 August, and executed the same day. There may have been some personal element behind the king's dramatic severance of relations with a leading household servant, though its nature remains elusive. Religion, too, may have been a factor in Finnart's downfall: his own views seem to have been conservative, but he was condemned by an assize made up largely of reformers. Formally, however, he was accused of having plotted with members of the Douglas family to murder the king early in 1529, and of having fired a missile at the king from the campanile of Linlithgow, using a weapon of his own devising. Given the dynastic rivalries of the Douglases and Hamiltons, the first charge was almost certainly invention. That the second event occurred seems likely enough—an experiment or invention of Finnart's that went wrong, providing a greedy king with an excuse for action against its deviser. After Finnart's death James became the richer by some £5000 Scots, while the barony of Avendale was worth £370 per annum.

Hamilton's standing at court is hard to define, but there are clues in English sources: a letter to Thomas Cromwell associated him with plans to seize the town of Berwick in 1536 or 1537, and in October 1540 Sir William Eure reported to Henry VIII that Cardinal Beaton 'is not so much in favour since the execution of Sir James Hamilton for treason' (*LP Henry VIII*, 17, no. 120). That Beaton's power at court might have depended to some degree upon Sir James Hamilton of Finnart gives some measure of the latter's standing. His buildings survive as a monument to Renaissance ambition as well as taste.

CHARLES MCKEAN

**Sources** J. B. Paul, ed., *Compota thesaurariorum regum Scotorum / Accounts of the lord high treasurer of Scotland*, 4–7 (1902–7) • R. K. Hannay, ed., *Acts of the lords of council in public affairs, 1501–1554* (1932) • *APS, 1424–1567* • *Scots peerage*, vol. 4 • J. Bain, ed., *The Hamilton papers: letters and papers illustrating the political relations of England and Scotland in the XVIth century*, 2 vols., Scottish RO, 12 (1890–92) • J. Cameron, 'Sir James Hamilton of Finnart' in 'Crown magnate relations in the personal rule of James V', PhD diss., U. Edin. • I. Campbell, 'Linlithgow's "Princely palace"', *Architectural Heritage*, 5 (1995), 1–20 • I. B. Cowan and D. Shaw, eds., *The Renaissance and Reformation in Scotland: essays in honour of Gordon Donaldson* (1983) • J. Dunbar, *The historic architecture of Scotland* (1966) • T. Thomson, ed., *A diurnal of remarkable occurrents that have passed within the country of Scotland*, Bannatyne Club, 43 (1833) • C. Edington, *Court and culture in Renaissance Scotland: Sir David Lindsay of the Mount* (1994) • G. Burnett and others, eds., *The exchequer rolls of Scotland*, 23 vols. (1878–1908), vols. 13–17 • R. Fawcett, *The architectural history of Scotland, 1371–1560* (1994) • R. Fawcett, *Stirling Castle* (1995) • M. Glendinning, R. MacInnes, and A. MacKechnie, *A history of Scottish architecture* (1996) • J. H. Williams, ed., *Stewart style, 1513–1542* (1998) • J. Cameron, *James V: the personal rule, 1528–1542*, ed. N. Macdougall (1998) • NA Scot., GD 237/262/3 • NA Scot., RH/6/1121B • D. Hume of Godscroft, *A history of the houses of Douglas and Angus* (1648) • R. K. Hannay and D. Hay, eds., *Letters of James V* (1954) • *LP Henry VIII*, vols. 2, 4, 6, 15–16 • R. Lindsay of Pitscottie, *A history of the Stuart kings of Scotland* (1778) • S. Mapstone and J. Wood, eds., *The rose and the thistle* (1998) • I. MacIvor, 'Sir James Hamilton of Finnart and the palace at Stirling Castle', 1992 [unpubd] • I. MacIvor, 'Craignethan Castle, Lanarkshire', *Ancient monuments and their interpretation: essays presented to A. J. Taylor*, ed. M. R. Apted, R. Gilyard-Beer, and A. D. Saunders (1977), 239–61 • C. McKean, 'Finnart's Platt', *Architectural Heritage*, 2 (1991) • C. McKean, 'Sir James Hamilton of Finnart—a Renaissance courtier architect', *Architectural History*, 42 (1999), 141–72 • C. McKean, 'Hamilton of Finnart', *History Today*, 43/1 (1993), 42–7 • C. McKean, *Sir James Hamilton of Finnart*, Thomas Ross prize dissertation, RIAS Library • C. McKean, 'The palace at Edinburgh Castle', *Book of the Old Edinburgh Club* (1998) • C. McKean, 'Craignethan—the castle of the bastard of Arran', *Proceedings of the Society of Antiquaries of Scotland*, 125 (1995), 1069–90 • H. Paton, ed., *Accounts of the masters of works*, 1: 1529–1615 (1957) • R. Pitcairn, ed., *Ancient criminal trials in Scotland*, 1, Bannatyne Club, 42 (1833), pt 1 • J. M. Thomson and others, eds., *Registrum magni sigilli regum Scotorum / The register of the great seal of Scotland*, 11 vols. (1882–1914), vols. 2–3 • M. Livingstone, D. Hay Fleming, and others, eds., *Registrum secreti sigilli regum Scotorum / The register of the privy seal of Scotland*, 1–2 (1908–21) • *An inventory of the ancient and historical monuments of the city of Edinburgh, with the thirteenth report of the commission*, Royal Commission on the Ancient and Historical Monuments in Scotland (1951) • M. H. B. Sanderson, *Cardinal of Scotland: David Beaton, c.1494–1546* (1986)

**Wealth at death** over £5000 Scots: Cameron, *James V*, 202

**Hamilton, James, second earl of Arran, and duke of Châtelherault in the French nobility** (*c.*1519–1575), magnate and governor of Scotland, was born at Hamilton, Lanarkshire, the eldest son of James *Hamilton, first earl of Arran (1475?–1529), and his second wife, Janet Beaton (*d.* *c.*1522). His grandfather James *Hamilton, first Lord Hamilton [*see under* Hamilton family], had married Mary Stewart, a sister of James III. This union was the bedrock for Arran's potentially exalted dynastic pretensions, since it made him heir presumptive to the Scottish throne for much of his life, and these in turn guided his policy throughout his political career. However, as the validity of his father's divorce from his first wife was disputed, there were doubts expressed as to his legitimacy, although not seriously after 1543. In fact, the first earl of Arran's marriage to Lady Elizabeth Home was invalid because her husband was still alive at the time. The decree of divorce

**James Hamilton, second earl of Arran, and duke of Châtelherault in the French nobility** (*c.*1519–1575), attrib. Arnold Bronckorst, 1578

between Arran and her was properly granted on 11 March 1510 and he was free to marry *ab initio*.

Aged about ten when his father died in 1529, the second earl of Arran was placed under the care of his half-brother Sir James *Hamilton of Finnart, who certainly exploited his guardianship. The vast Hamilton estates were concentrated in Lanarkshire, Linlithgowshire, Renfrewshire, and Ayrshire, with important outliers in Kirkcudbrightshire and Roxburghshire, and also included the Isle of Arran with its imposing castle of Brodick. Finnart held the ward of the earldom until July 1539, but there are signs that by 1537 Arran was chaffing under his control, and when the earl at last attained his majority, late in 1539 or early in 1540, he was quick to turn on his former guardian. Arran was one of the lords on the assize which convicted Finnart of treason on 16 August 1540. A month later he had charters under the great seal, confirming him in possession of his earldom. This may well reflect the fact that he was now a married man with a growing family. Before 23 September 1532 Arran had married Lady Margaret (*d.* in or after 1579), eldest daughter of James Douglas, earl of Morton. They had five sons: James *Hamilton, third earl of Arran (1537/8?–1609), Gavin (*d.* in or before 1547), John *Hamilton, first marquess of Hamilton (1539/40–1604), David (*d.* 1611), and Claud *Hamilton, first Lord Paisley (1546?–1621); and four daughters: Barbara, who married James Fleming, fourth Lord Fleming, Margaret, who married Alexander Gordon, Lord Gordon, Anne, who married Gordon's brother George Gordon, fifth earl of Huntly, and Jane or Jean (*c.*1535–1596), who married Hugh Montgomery, third earl of Eglinton.

**Governor and tutor** The young Arran lived as a nobleman should. Although most of his income was in kind, he was able to maintain a large number of domestic servants and an enormous stable of mounts. Ignorant of most foreign languages, he could nevertheless read Reformation literature and write. He ate and drank well, and enjoyed the hunt, cards, music, and gambling. In his teens he became very close to James V, and accompanied the king when he went in search of a French bride in 1536, and again during James's expedition to the western isles in 1540. However, his moment came with the death of James V on 14 December 1542. In a series of overlapping declarations (22 December 1542, 3 January 1543, and, in parliament, 12 March 1543) Arran was created governor of the realm and tutor to the infant Mary, queen of Scots. He was also recognized as second person of the realm, or heir presumptive, and never lost an opportunity to have this status enunciated. Becoming governor and tutor transformed Arran from a powerful noble into a near king. He controlled both the great and the privy seals, and Scotland's fiscal apparatus. He could call parliament at his will, chair and direct the privy council, instruct ambassadors and make treaties, and issue pardons and appointments. Arran moved into the royal palaces and became the focus of the royal court, carrying the crown at Mary's coronation on 9 September 1543. He took control of the crown's artillery train and arsenal, and the navy; he could call armies into being and headed no fewer than twenty-one hosts during the next six years. Arran sustained his political position through numerous contracts with his fellow nobles, such as bonds of manrent, as well as kindly acts, such as attending baptisms. He was generous and hospitable, keeping a comfortable table and a lavish cellar. Moreover he was lavish in distributing alms (he was especially affected by the wounded from Pinkie in 1547), rewards, gratuities, and gifts.

From the start Arran signalled a massive break with the policies of James V. Four acts manifested this. On 27 January 1543 Arran dramatically stripped Cardinal David Beaton of his post of chancellor. Second he announced his own, startling, adoption of the protestant faith. The 'assured lords', who had been captured by the English after the battle of Solway Moss in November 1542, and were well known to be sworn to Henry VIII, were given a warm welcome home. The forfeitures of a number of nobles loathed by James V were voided. Last, Arran also welcomed the English ambassador, Sir Ralph Sadler, and made explicit his support for proposals that Mary should make an English marriage.

The first three months of Arran's regency were spent preparing for parliament, where he intended to establish his position and his reforms. That parliament, held between 12 and 17 March 1542, was one of the best attended in recent times and it enacted a highly important sequence of measures. Perhaps its most important act was the reduction of the forfeiture of the sixth earl of Angus, the latter's brother George Douglas of Pittendriech, and their kinsman John Lyon, seventh Lord Glamis, for thereby Arran signalled his decisive break with James V's policies and the return to a more aristocratic polity. Patrick Hepburn, third earl of Bothwell, and

Matthew Stewart, thirteenth earl of Lennox, were also allowed home. Donald Dubh MacDonald, claimant to the lordship of the Isles, was released from his thirty-year captivity in Edinburgh Castle by Arran's express command. When parliament decided upon the composition of the privy council and the lords of the articles, here too the nobility was strongly represented.

**Protestantism and the English alliance** The most notable component of this period in Arran's governorship was his public, even ostentatious, conversion to protestantism. Exactly what form his faith took, whether Lutheran, English evangelical, or an individual blend, is not clear, but his actions were remarkable. Two lapsed friars (Thomas Guilliame and John Rough) became his court chaplains, both of them rock-solid protestants. Arran told Sadler that for the past five years he had regarded the pope as no more than a bishop, 'and that a very evil bishop' (*LP Henry VIII*, 18/1, no. 324). In his first parliament he saw onto the statute book (despite heated opposition) permission for the Bible to be read (although not disputed) in the vernacular. He wrote within weeks of taking up office that he sought 'to reform the state of the kirk here, set forth God's word and profit the common weal'. Even more revealing is the deliberate manner in which he advanced and rewarded men he must have known held reformed opinions (as many of them confirmed by their actions in later years). These included Dr Michael Durham, James V's physician (who was given a jewelled knife on the king's death), Durham's brother Henry, the king's apothecary, a noted Edinburgh member of a privy kirk, and James Henryson, who was made conservator of the Scottish privileges in the Low Countries.

Linked to Arran's aligning himself with protestantism was his acceptance of the proposed marriage of Queen Mary to Prince Edward, heir of Henry VIII. The scheme was revolutionary, for although there had been numerous English marriages in the past, none had so clearly implied a dynastic union of the two monarchies and their realms. The negotiating position hammered out for this, the longest act in the entire parliament, was carefully crafted and did everything it could to protect Scotland's sovereignty and government. The ambassadors sent to London were thus given little room for manoeuvre; moreover any variance that resulted from their discussions would have to be ratified by yet another parliament after their return. In the event, the treaties of Greenwich, concluded on 1 July 1543, were remarkably successful in safeguarding Scottish interests, not least in keeping Queen Mary out of English hands until she was ten. In the whole package of measures with which Arran commenced his 'reign', his role in organizing an acceptable treaty with England was arguably his most striking achievement.

Arran was a great talker and Sadler's dispatches groan under the weight of their conversations. The governor had to talk with a range of people from fishwives (who sometimes threw stones at him), through the nobility, to the queen dowager, Mary of Guise. He quickly earned a reputation for inconsistency. Perhaps Arran was genuinely devious and duplicitous, but this was his first experience of power: it could have been the case that he did not know what he wanted to do and so he said to his listeners what he hoped they wanted to hear. Although he havered, his hesitations may sometimes have covered periods of adjustment to changing situations. Two arrivals in Scotland seem likely to have triggered off such changes. One was that of the governor's clever half-brother John *Hamilton, abbot of Paisley and a firm Catholic, who returned from France to work with Arran in the conviction that the latter's embracing protestantism was contrary to their family's long-term interests. The other was Matthew Stewart, fourth earl of Lennox, who came to Scotland as French ambassador, but who also had a strong claim to be the second person of the realm, and whose apparent closeness to the queen dowager greatly worried Arran.

Arran had been helped in his reforms by a seemingly solid block of supporters of the English alliance, including the assured lords and others who had protestant leanings. With their support, Arran had been able to oust Beaton and ride roughshod over the clergy in parliament. By the summer, however, most of these men had retired to their estates, while in the country at large there were growing doubts both about the English treaty and about the governor's religious policy. Against this background it was easier for the Francophile Beaton, who had been released from confinement in April, to stage a counter-attack. At Linlithgow on 24 July the cardinal mustered a formidable coalition to oppose the English marriage: four earls, eight lords, twenty-three named lairds, and a clutch of clerics.

Arran moved with dispatch, mustering the crown's artillery and transporting it up the Forth in ships while calling out his supporters from as far away as Aberdeen. But he was still outnumbered and he handled the artillery poorly (as he did in all of his engagements). On 25 August the Greenwich treaties, ostensibly guaranteeing Mary's marriage to Edward, were ratified in the gardens of Holyrood. But by this time Arran was slowly losing the initiative. He had begun to give way on the religious front, prohibiting the circulation of heretical literature, and he faced the possibility of French intervention. Even before the treaties were ratified it was noted that 'he begynneth a lytell to droupe' (Sanderson, 168). There was growing hostility in Scotland towards England, and Henry VIII gave little help. Finally Arran gave way to the growing pressure. Early in September he left Edinburgh and met Beaton in Stirling, where at the Franciscan convent he announced his return to the Catholic church as an ally of the cardinal on the 8th. His young son James Hamilton was placed in Beaton's household, effectively as a hostage, though certainly an exalted one—Beaton was reported to favour his marrying Mary, a hope his father came to share. Mary was herself crowned queen of Scots on the day after Arran's reconciliation with the cardinal, which was reinforced in November when the two men went on a judicial progress to Dundee, a hotbed of protestantism, where heretics were executed.

**Rupture with England** Implicit in their reconciliation was the renunciation of the treaties of Greenwich. Henry VIII provided justification for the rupture when he failed to ratify the treaties, which were formally denounced by the Scottish parliament on 11 December. That this might happen may have been a possibility Arran kept in mind from the first. Early in July Sir William Parr reported that the governor had declared in council that:

> Ye know the King of England is a mighty prince, and we not able nor of power to resist his puissance, and for that cause I think and take it best, by fair words and promises, with the concluding of this peace, to defer and put over the danger that might otherwise fall upon us; and in the mean time the young Queen may chance to die, or other chance may happen whereby Scotland may be relieved and more able to resist England. (*LP Henry VIII* 18/1, no. 827)

The cynicism Arran showed on this occasion went with a more overt patriotism later, for when Henry opened hostilities the governor let it be known that he would rule 'to the honour of this realme aganis all thame that wald everte the samin' (Merriman, 136). All was grist to the all-important mill, remaining in office. At the end of a fraught year, Arran had achieved that end.

In the aftermath of the December parliament Arran had to face two more rebellions, by the earls of Angus and Lennox, who had the support of Anglophile and protestant interests. Predictable consequences of Arran's volte-face, the rebellions were swiftly and adroitly mastered—Lennox was driven into exile, while Angus was eventually won over to the governor's side. Equally predictable but much more spectacular was Henry VIII's response to the renunciation of the Greenwich agreement. As early as November, Henry had issued a formal declaration of war and almost immediately English raiding parties swept across the border and Scottish ships at sea were plundered. But these were mere pinpricks compared with what the king had in mind as appropriate retribution for Arran's 'falsidity'. Edward Seymour, earl of Hertford, was put in charge of one of the largest military forces ever to descend upon Scotland. Hertford led it with verve, transporting his infantry by water in order to fall upon Scotland from the North Sea. A mounted force then came up the coast from Berwick to join him, and in May 1544 this combined army rampaged about Edinburgh (although the castle baulked it) and its surrounding countryside. This remarkable amphibious assault did not (as is often alleged) catch Arran unawares. He was in Edinburgh when it appeared; he had trenched about Leith, armed and fortified it, and had called about him a host. Though clearly overawed by the English force, the Scottish defenders did no mean job in resisting, especially the garrison and artillery of Edinburgh Castle, which Arran had refortified. Afterwards he found Holyrood Abbey sacked (its lectern would only be returned in 1998) and half of the town mauled, but otherwise the realm suffered little of consequence. As the English army retired, yet more devastation was laid on Haddingtonshire and Berwickshire.

Arran's reputation took a severe battering, and although Beaton remained loyal there were almost immediate calls for his resignation. At a meeting of the estates in June the attacks on him became so vitriolic that Arran walked out. He was accused of weakness, inept generalship, and pusillanimity. In June and July 1544 an opposition grouping clustered about the queen dowager, demanding that she supplant Arran. Mary of Guise was emboldened to write to Henry VIII as if she headed the government, and to call a parliament in her daughter's name. But Arran, probably advised by Beaton, managed to face her down, and by the start of 1545 he had lanced her 'rebellion' by admitting her onto the council.

The same year witnessed the final reconciliation of Angus to Arran's regime. Angus's lands and possessions had suffered from a series of English raids, and much was made at the time of the desecration of his ancestor's tombs at Melrose. Now he and Arran joined forces in Teviotdale to oppose a massive English raiding party under Sir Ralph Eure and Brian Laiton. Angus was placed in command by Arran and effected a devastating annihilation of the English force at the battle of Ancrum Moor (27 February 1545), a triumph which gained attention in Paris and deeply humiliated Henry VIII. Arran may well have wept over the bodies of the English commanders, described as two 'fell, cruel men', but they were surely tears of joy. His battlefield embrace of Angus, now 'a true Scotsman again', was clearly genuine and the old warrior was richly rewarded by the governor, who used his vice-regal power to grant Angus's bastard son £1000 p.a. from the revenues of Arbroath Abbey. Thereafter, Angus was a loyal and purposeful member of Arran's regime. With Ancrum Moor under his belt, Arran set about putting the country on a permanent war footing in order to resist constant English incursions. He also acted against England's 'assured' allies, funded bands of trained horsemen to protect the Merse and Teviotdale, and set up a network of warning beacons. Most striking of all, he invited a French force to Scotland, both to protect that realm and to create a diversion which would help the French to recapture Boulogne, taken by Henry VIII in the previous year. The Franco-Scottish army won no great victories, but it effectively shadowed Hertford's invasion in September and rendered its accomplishment derisory.

**Lennox, Beaton, and the battle of Pinkie** There was an international context to the Anglo-Scottish war of the mid-1540s, in that England was also at war with Scotland's ally France. The Scots, fearful of being left to face their powerful neighbour unaided, were determined to win comprehension in any Anglo-French treaty. Consequently Scotland was included in the treaty of Camp of 6 June 1546 as France's allies, 'against whom England shall not move war without new occasion' (*LP Henry VIII*, 20/1, no. 1014). At first Arran and his council were by no means pleased by the ambiguities of the terms, but later the Scots exploited them to their own advantage. Camp also gave Arran a breathing space of fifteen months, something he needed, for in May 1546 two thunderclaps assailed him. First the earl of Lennox, in England since 1544, invaded Scotland by sea and took possession of Dumbarton Castle. However, Arran, who was by now well practised in the art of containing revolt, moved with resolution and success. He besieged the castle until Lennox took fright and fled. Then he used his control of patronage to good effect. Lennox had brought with him his brother Robert Stewart, bishop-elect of Caithness. On 16 July Robert submitted to the governor, who now won him over by returning to him all his ecclesiastical benefices, including the bishopric of Caithness, which he had lost two years earlier. Henceforth Robert Stewart devoted himself to the administration of his diocese and gave no further trouble to Arran's government.

The second shock was still more momentous. On 29 May 1546 Beaton was murdered and his castle of St Andrews occupied and held against Arran's regime by the killers, several of whom were radical protestants. Arran's military response was remarkably innovative, dividing the kingdom into quarters and calling up troops from each of them in rotation, but he found St Andrews a harder nut to crack than Dumbarton. Ayrshire miners drove a mine under the walls only to be thwarted by the counter-mine of the defenders. His artillery, too, was no match for the walls of the hold, which Beaton had recently refashioned, and from August to December Arran laboured in vain to take the castle. His desperation doubtless intensified by the fact that his eldest son, Beaton's hostage since 1543, was inside the castle, Arran even persuaded the clergy in parliament that the killers should receive a remission if the pope could be persuaded to absolve them. This ploy, too, failed, and at Christmas Arran dissolved his army and retired to his estates, simply leaving the problem unresolved. But at some point—it is not known exactly when—he again called on the French to aid him.

In July 1547 Arran led an army to the west march and laid siege to Langholm, a Maxwell fortress which in English hands had become a thorn in Scottish flesh. It fell on the 17th, and no sooner was that accomplished than a small French army effected the recapture of St Andrews, where the garrison surrendered on either 30 or 31 July. Important though these developments were, they paled into insignificance compared with the English invasion led by Edward Seymour, now duke of Somerset, which culminated in the battle of Pinkie on 10 September. Thanks to efficient intelligence Arran was very well prepared for battle: an enormous host was assembled a few miles east of Edinburgh on the north bank of the Esk, and Musselburgh was fortified by a massive field entrenchment which included a seaward-facing earth wall. But Arran made the tactical error of leaving his defences to attack the English, and was then taken at a disadvantage by the enemy's superior cavalry and guns. Lacking both mobility and matching firepower, the Scottish army broke up, and may have lost 10,000 men. Somerset did not exploit his victory by capturing, or even burning, Edinburgh. Instead he adopted the policy of setting up permanent garrisons at strategic points in the Scottish lowlands, in order to control the countryside. So entrenched were they in up-to-date Italian-style fortifications that Arran was quite helpless to reduce them, and so a winter war ensued.

**Alliance with France** The political effects of Pinkie were as important as the military ones, for the Scots now accepted a French royal marriage for Queen Mary. Arran ensured that he was amply rewarded for his agreement to this, securing a French duchy, that of Châtelherault in Poitou, worth 10,000 livres tournois per annum (about £5000 Scots), the promise of a French marriage for his son, who was received into the court of Henri II, and a handsome palace in Paris. He also won the command of a large regiment of *gens d'armes* which was staffed almost entirely by Scottish immigrants. Moreover he was confirmed in his position as governor, with access to crown revenues until Mary's majority (her 'perfect age'), which meant four full years in post once peace came.

Collaboration with the French was never going to be easy. Arran's government made massive preparation for the troops before they arrived, organizing food supplies, accommodation, transport, and support services. When the army disembarked at Leith harbour Arran gave a lavish welcome to its leaders and then marched with them to Haddington, accompanied by a large contingent of Scottish nobles and soldiers. He had always insisted firmly that no compact for the French marriage would be concluded, nor would the queen be allowed to go to France, until an effective French siege force was in place, complete with its artillery, before the walls of the newly constructed English fortification at Haddington. A parliament held at Haddington Abbey on 6 July ratified the marriage contract. The French then settled down to a daily battering of the bastions and walls. But scant success attended their efforts; some observers maintained that it was stronger in September than it had been in July. Meanwhile Queen Mary had sailed to France on 29 July 1547; Arran's son had sailed earlier.

With no success in the field and autumn coming in, the armies pulled stakes and retired for the winter to Edinburgh and Leith, where trouble promptly erupted in September. So many foreign soldiers crammed into one of the most densely packed urban spaces in Europe were bound to rub against one another, and their friction tested Arran's skills of command to their limit. A riot broke out in which the captain of the castle, James Hamilton of Stonehouse, was slain. In the hope of restoring good relations with their hosts the entire French force shortly afterwards made a night-time excursion against Haddington, hoping to take it by surprise. The attempted coup almost came off, but the English woke up and beat off the attack, and the army returned to Edinburgh in disgrace. Arran, who had been informed that the town had been captured, and rode furiously to share in the victory, instead encountered the retreat. Irate beyond words, he refused to speak to the French commander for days. But the year 1549 saw the arrival of fresh French troops, and the English were forced to lie low, the more so because the French built a number of forts to hem them in. The English position steadily deteriorated, weakened further by the risings which broke out in several parts of the country in the summer, and then by the fall of Somerset in October. The new regime, which soon came to be headed by John Dudley, earl of Warwick, was only too glad to cut its losses, and first by the Anglo-French treaty of Boulogne (24 March 1550), in which the Scots were comprehended, and then by the Anglo-Scottish treaty of Norham (10 June 1551), withdrew its troops from Scotland.

**Loss of office** Happy to have peace at last, Châtelherault (as he was now known, his eldest son having been invested with the earldom of Arran) requested the French to station 1000 troops in Scotland, and set about trying to remedy the effects of a long and highly destructive war. In particular, he mounted a series of raids described as judicial progresses, though how far they administered justice is uncertain—it was sneeringly remarked at the time, perhaps with truth, that it was the wealth of the accused that determined the governor's sentences. Work began on rebuilding Edinburgh, Dundee, Haddington, and other areas left in ruins. Dundee, which was truly roofless, was exempted from taxes or military service. A silver coinage (the first in the reign) was issued, decorated with cinquefoils, the Hamilton emblem. Trade with the Low Countries and France recommenced and piracy was suppressed. The remaining English fortifications were demolished. Châtelherault now had leisure to attend to his estates and in particular to the building of Kinneil, with superb interior decorations.

Châtelherault was less secure than he seemed, however. The French troops which garrisoned Dunbar, Blackness, Broughty, and Inchkeith were effectively out of his control, while the French resident ambassador in Scotland, Henri D'Oysel, was an authority in his own right, to the extent of undermining the governor's freedom of action. It was noticed that when Châtelherault held a justice ayre at Jedburgh early in 1551, D'Oysel and a force of French soldiers went with him, and a year later D'Oysel was also involved in the division of the so-called 'debatable land', disputed territory on the Anglo-Scottish west march. The duke's reliance on his brother John was probably reflected in the attention his government gave to ecclesiastical issues in the early 1550s. Then in 1552 Mary of Guise returned from an extended visit to France, and began to intrigue to supplant Châtelherault. Her manoeuvres may have been welcomed in Scotland; they were certainly in accordance with French policy. The decisive factors in bringing Châtelherault's regime to an end were the death of Edward VI in 1553, followed by Mary Tudor's proposed marriage to Philip, infante of Spain, in the following year. For the Habsburgs to control England posed a grave threat to France; Henri II therefore wanted to exert a tighter control over Scotland.

In December 1553 the *parlement* of Paris pronounced Mary to be of age. The governor quietly acquiesced; probably Châtelherault was mentally, emotionally, and physically exhausted. Early in the following year he negotiated the surrender of his authority to Mary of Guise, on the best possible terms for himself. He replaced D'Oysel as lieutenant-general of Scotland; he was comprehensively exonerated from any malfeasance in his disbursal of the crown's funds; his position as second person of the realm was confirmed; and it was made explicit that he had admitted Mary of Guise to the regency before the queen's majority (which was to have been in December 1554, at the age of twelve). Châtelherault formally laid down his governorship on 12 April 1554, and returned home. He had not retired completely from public life, receiving summonses to parliaments and a number of commissions of justiciary, one of which, covering the whole earldom of Arran, was to last during the queen's pleasure, but for the most part seems to have been contented to lead the life of a wealthy aristocrat.

**The Reformation and Mary's return** Châtelherault came out of his relative seclusion in 1559, with the emergence of the reformist movement of the lords of the congregation. He may have reverted to protestantism himself, but his motives more certainly included his persisting desire to secure his, and his family's, position with regard to the throne. At first he stood by Mary of Guise, if without great enthusiasm, in part because she had persuaded him (according to John Knox) that the reformers threatened his title to the crown. What seems to have led to his changing sides was less religious conviction than the garrisoning of Leith by French soldiers in September. Now that Mary, queen of Scots, was successively wife to the French dauphin and queen of France, there was a danger that the Hamilton claim would simply be set aside in the interests of French policy. This risk was exploited by the reformers and their English allies, and their hand was strengthened when the duke's eldest son, who had been virtually a hostage in France, escaped to England in the summer. There were proposals that he should marry Queen Elizabeth, so bolstering his claim to succeed Queen Mary if the latter failed to return from France. Arran returned to Scotland, and on 19 September his father joined the congregation. Châtelherault led the reformers when they occupied Edinburgh a month later. His commitment to their cause remained somewhat provisional, however, and when they lost ground in the last months of the year he is said to have offered to change sides again. Only English intervention kept him true to the congregation, not least by underwriting his interest in the Scottish succession. It is significant that it was as 'James duke of Châtelherault, Earl of Arran, Lord Hamilton, second person of the realm of Scotland, and apparent [heir] to the Crown' that he proclaimed the treaty of Berwick, drawn up on 27 February 1560 (*Knox's History*, 1.302).

Yet again Châtelherault's hopes of the succession were disappointed. On 19 August 1561 Queen Mary returned to Scotland. She named the duke to her council, but though he attempted to negotiate her marriage to his son, nothing came of this save James's insanity, to his father's great distress. Men expressed pity 'to see the old man's tears trickling from his cheeks as it had been a child beaten' (Donaldson, *All the Queen's Men*, 69). Châtelherault's attendance at court became patchy, but he remained alert on behalf of his family. The return to Scotland in 1564 of the fourth earl of Lennox, his nearest rival for the position of heir presumptive, and the marriage of Lennox's elder son, Henry, Lord Darnley, to the queen in 1565 posed a serious threat to his dynastic interests, and made him an unlikely ally of James Stewart, earl of Moray, in the latter's revolt against the Darnley marriage in the latter year. The so-called chaseabout raid was a fiasco, and although the duke was able to call out an impressive number of kinsmen and retainers he and Moray were forced to flee to England. At the end of the year Châtelherault told Elizabeth that the price of his pardon had included 'five yeris exile furth of my native cuntre' (*CSP Scot.*, *1563–9*, 242). He withdrew to France, where he sued for the restoration of his duchy, confiscated at the time of his son's flight in 1560, and was bought off with a pension of 4000 francs and a fine collection of plates.

**Last years and death** Following the enforced abdication of Mary, Châtelherault once more stood close to the Scottish succession, and a 'protest for the Duke's title' was made at the coronation of James VI on 29 July 1567 (*CSP Scot.*, *1563–9*, 370). But he remained loyal to James's mother, and soon after her flight to England in the following year Mary drew up an instrument 'giving all her interest "of the governance" of Scotland to the duke of "Shatilleroe" until her return' (ibid., 457). But Regent Moray objected to the duke's claims, both to the succession and to the government, and in any case Châtelherault only returned to London in October 1568, and to Scotland early the following year. On 28 February 1569, however, Mary proclaimed him her lieutenant there, along with the earls of Huntly and Argyll. But Moray was too strong, and the duke was soon taken into custody. The murder of Moray on 23 January 1570, a deed plotted by Archbishop John Hamilton and carried out by James Hamilton of Bothwellhaugh, led to accusations that Châtelherault had himself been implicated. But he obtained his freedom later in the year, and took his place at the head of the queen's party. In April he was the first signatory to a letter inviting Elizabeth to intervene, but by July he was in contact with France and Spain, endeavouring to obtain their armed backing for Mary's cause. At the end of the year he was put to the horn, and on 28 August 1571 his name headed a list of forfeitures. In the same year heavy English raids into southern Scotland in support of the king's party brought a mauling for the Hamiltons: Kinneil, Hamilton, and Cadzow were all torched. It was only on 23 February 1573, when he subscribed the pacification of Perth, that Châtelherault accepted James VI as rightful monarch. Thereafter he returned to his patrimonial possessions and set about rebuilding them. Kinneil was restored to its former glories, and Châtelherault died there on 22 January 1575.

From John Knox—for whom he was 'the inconstant Governor' (*Knox's History*, 1.49)—to the present day, Châtelherault has been chided by historians as weak, ineffectual, avaricious, and inconsistent. It is undeniable that he often altered his mind and political stance, though he could have justified at least some of his changes of course by reference to the violent political currents that often beset him, many of them totally out of his control. In the 1540s he defended Scottish interests to the best of his diplomatic abilities, and also showed some military skills, while he was realistic in accepting French support in 1547 and in surrendering the regency to Mary of Guise in 1554. If he never forgot his own and his family's dynastic aspirations, he was also often mindful of his country's needs. There may have been more than rhetoric, an attempt to sweeten the pill that he was obliged to swallow when he relinquished office, in the praise bestowed upon him in parliament in April 1554, as 'ane noble and mychtie prince', who at great danger to himself had saved 'our soveranis maist noble persoun fra the cruell enrisfull persute of the king and counsell of Ingland And hes left free the haill realme' (*APS*, *1424–1567*, 603–4).

MARCUS MERRIMAN

**Sources** *Scots peerage*, 4.366–8 • GEC, *Peerage*, 1.221–2 • *APS*, *1424–1567* • *CSP Scot.*, *1547–81* • *LP Henry VIII*, vols. 18–21 • J. H. Burton and D. Masson, eds., *The register of the privy council of Scotland*, 1st ser., 14 vols. (1877–98), vols. 1–7 • G. Burnett and others, eds., *The exchequer rolls of Scotland*, 23 vols. (1878–1908), vols. 16–20 • *John Knox's History of the Reformation in Scotland*, ed. W. C. Dickinson, 2 vols. (1949) • J. B. Paul and C. T. McInnes, eds., *Compota thesaurariorum regum Scotorum / Accounts of the lord high treasurer of Scotland*, 6–13 (1905–78) • M. Merriman, *The rough wooings: Mary queen of Scots, 1542–1551* (2000) • J. Cameron, *James V: the personal rule, 1528–1542*, ed. N. Macdougall (1998) • G. Donaldson, *Scotland, James V–James VII* (1965) • G. Donaldson, *All the queen's men* (1983) • R. Marshall, *Mary of Guise* (1977) • M. H. B. Sanderson, *Cardinal of Scotland: David Beaton, c.1494–1546* (1986) • T. I. Rae, *The administration of the Scottish frontier, 1513–1603* (1966)

**Archives** BL, corresp, etc., Add. MSS 32649–32653, 33591–33592, *passim* • NA Scot., papers | BL, Royal MSS, letters and papers

**Likenesses** attrib. A. Bronckorst, portrait, 1578, Lennoxlove House, East Lothian [*see illus.*] • W. Holl, stipple, pubd 1819 (after C. Ketel), BM, NPG • portrait, priv. coll.

**Hamilton, James, of Bothwellhaugh** (*d.* 1581x5), assassin, was the eldest son of David Hamilton, 'good man' of Bothwellhaugh (*d.* 1563), who was descended from the Hamiltons of Orbiston, Lanarkshire. His mother was Janet Hamilton (*d.* in or before 1539), the natural daughter of the first earl of Arran. He was therefore the nephew of the two leading members of the magnate family of Hamilton: James, duke of Châtelherault, and John, archbishop of St Andrews. His father remarried in 1539; his new wife was Christian Shaw and she is often given as his mother, but there is good evidence to the contrary. He himself married Isabel Sinclair (*d.* in or after 1598), coheir of Woodhouselee, about 1560. On 13 May 1568, like others of his family, he fought at the battle of Langside on the side of Mary, queen of Scots, against the earl of Moray, the half-brother of Mary, who had usurped the government of Scotland and become regent. Mary's forces were defeated and Hamilton was taken prisoner and sentenced to death. He was, however, released, although his lands remained forfeit.

On 23 January 1570 Bothwellhaugh assassinated the Regent Moray. He was part of a group involved in the murder, which had strong support from the whole Hamilton family. Moray was tricked into leaving Edinburgh and, after an abortive journey, was returning thither when he stayed the night at Linlithgow. Bothwellhaugh waited for him in a house belonging to his uncle the archbishop of St Andrews which was four doors away from where Moray slept. He had been supplied with a rifled carbine by John Hamilton, abbot of Arbroath. Everything had been carefully prepared for the murder. The floor of the upstairs room where Bothwellhaugh hid had been covered with a mattress to muffle his footsteps, and the walls had been draped with black curtains to conceal his shadow. He hid on a curtained balcony and shot the regent with a bullet of tempered steel as he rode out in the morning along the narrow street. Bothwellhaugh had prepared for his escape by removing the keystone in the arch of the garden gate at the back of the house so he could ride out on horseback. He raced off to Hamilton Castle, pursued by the regent's men; when his spurs and whip failed he used his dagger to urge on his horse, which leapt a very wide pond and so escaped.

Bothwellhaugh's motives for the attack are a subject of controversy. His family was certainly hostile towards the regent, and acted to some degree out of loyalty to the exiled Queen Mary, as well as out of dynastic self-interest. After the assassination Bothwellhaugh wrote to Mary from the hiding place abroad to which he had fled: 'I have lost my wife and bairns and all I had to live on for Her Majesty's service' (*Salisbury MSS*, 1.482). A romantic legend gives him a personal motive for antagonism to Moray. The story is that his wife had been dispossessed from her inheritance at Woodhouselee by her uncle Sir James Bellenden, who was given Moray's support. Bellenden took advantage of Bothwellhaugh's arrest after Langside to evict his wife, who died of grief and indeed exposure after being cast naked out of her home. The fact is, however, that Isabel Hamilton outlived her husband, although there is certainly some truth in the story of the feud over land. The main factor precipitating the assassination was the imprisonment in the previous April of the duke of Châtelherault, Bothwellhaugh's uncle, by the regent. Given Hamilton's later career it is possible that he also adopted the role of assassin simply because he enjoyed it.

Far from strengthening the Hamiltons, the murder led to a backlash against them in Scotland, and Bothwellhaugh was forced to leave the country. Queen Mary, however, expressed satisfaction that she had been avenged, and offered to pay him a pension when she had funds available. In his exile Bothwellhaugh moved between Paris and Brussels, often in the company of his brother John, who had also been involved in the assassination, and is reported on occasion in Spain. In 1573 he was excepted from the pacification of Perth, when many of the rest of his family made their peace with the new Jacobean regime. While in exile his name was linked to two more assassination plots: first, in 1571 he was mentioned as being involved in an attempt on the life of Admiral Coligny, the French Huguenot leader, although there is evidence that he refused to be associated with this affair; second, he and his brother were mentioned between 1573 and 1577 as being implicated in efforts to kill William, prince of Orange. In 1576 he was in prison in Brussels, probably as a result of his involvement in the wars in the Netherlands, but his associate Colonel Balfour negotiated his exchange for some prisoners in Spanish hands. It is possible that he returned to Scotland: in 1575 and 1579 there were reports that he was in the country. In 1579 he was summoned by James VI to answer accusations of treason, but failed to appear. He is last heard of in April 1581, when he was sighted in Paris. He was certainly dead by 1585 when a statute restored his heir to the lands in Bothwellhaugh. There is a tradition that he lies buried in the churchyard at Monkton, which may be accurate if the supposition that he was able to return to Scotland during his years of outlawry is true. PETER HOLMES

**Sources** *DNB* • G. Hamilton, *A history of the house of Hamilton* (1933), 173–4, 176–7 • *N&Q*, 3rd ser., 11 (1867), 453–4, 502–3 • *N&Q*, 4th ser., 12 (1873), 406 • *N&Q*, 5th ser., 12 (1879), 386, 512 • J. A. Froude, *History of England*, new edn, 12 vols. (1893), vol. 9, pp. 194–209 • E. Finnie, 'The house of Hamilton: patronage, politics and the church in the Reformation period', *Innes Review*, 36 (1985), 3–28 • M. Lee, jun., *James Stewart, earl of Moray* (1953), chap. 12 • *Lettres, instructions et mémoires de Marie Stuart, reine d'Écosse*, ed. A. Labanoff, 7 vols. (1852), vol. 3, pp. 354–5 • C. T. McInnes, ed., *Compota thesaurariorum regum Scotorum / Accounts of the lord high treasurer of Scotland*, 12 (1970), 379; 13 (1978), 54, 278 • *Reg. PCS*, 1st ser., 1.452–3; 2.155, 158, 334; 3.147–8, 171, 352 • *CSP Scot.*, 1569–71, 96–7; 1571–4, pp. 202, 363, 437; 1574–81, pp. 337, 376 • *Calendar of the manuscripts of the most hon. the marquis of Salisbury*, 1, HMC, 9 (1883), 482 • *CSP for.*, 1575–7, 1094, 1097, 1113, 1174, 1448; 1577–78, 664; 1579–80, 234, 507, 520–21; 1581–2, 19, 125 • [T. Thomson], ed., *The historie and life of King James the Sext*, Bannatyne Club, 13 (1825), 26–7, 47, 116 • 'The diary of Robert Birrel … 1532 … to 1605', *Fragments of Scottish history* (1798), 18 • *The correspondence of Robert Bowes, of Aske, esquire, the ambassador of Queen Elizabeth in the court of Scotland*, ed. [J. Stevenson], SurtS, 14 (1842), 49

**Hamilton, James, third earl of Arran** (1537/8?–1609), magnate, was the eldest of the eight children of James *Hamilton, second earl of Arran, later duke of Châtelherault (*d.* 1575), and his wife, Margaret, eldest daughter of James Douglas, third earl of Morton. His father not only became regent of Scotland in 1542, with the title of lord governor, but was also, until the birth of the future James VI in 1566, heir presumptive to the Scottish throne by virtue of his descent from James II. As a result, Arran's own heir, James, master of Hamilton, was of considerable dynastic importance and during the negotiations for Henry VIII's son, Edward, to marry Mary, queen of Scots, in 1543, it was proposed that the master of Hamilton should become the husband of Henry's younger daughter, Elizabeth. Soon afterwards, however, Cardinal David Beaton, archbishop of St Andrews, encouraged the lord governor to think that Mary, queen of Scots, could be married to the master of Hamilton instead of to Prince Edward. The lord governor promptly repudiated the treaties of Greenwich which he had recently signed with England, did public penance for having veered towards protestantism, and handed over his son to the cardinal as a hostage for his good faith. The boy was taken to Beaton's castle at St Andrews and was still there when, on 29 May 1546, Beaton was murdered by a group of protestants who seized the castle and made the master their hostage.

Arran prepared to besiege the castle and the Scottish parliament, fearing that Beaton's murderers would hand the younger James Hamilton over to the English, on 14 August 1546 passed an act depriving him of all right of succession to the throne until he was free. On 31 July 1547 the castle finally fell to the French and the master was released. He did not, however, remain with his family for long. Henri II of France announced that he could only consider helping the Scots against the English if Arran's eldest son were sent to him as a hostage and the master sailed to France in the summer of 1548, shortly before the arrival there of Mary, queen of Scots. Henri promised to find a suitable French bride for Hamilton, saw to it that he was educated in an appropriate manner, and gave him command of a troop of men-at-arms in the Scots guard. The lord governor had by this time accepted the French dukedom of Châtelherault as a *douceur* for agreeing to the marriage of Queen Mary and the dauphin and, in consequence of his father's new title, the master was in 1550 put in possession of the earldom of Arran and lordship of Hamilton.

Arran apparently enjoyed his military life and in 1557 his men distinguished themselves during the unsuccessful defence of St Quentin against the imperial army. Meanwhile his father pressed for his marriage. Henri II had originally offered the elder daughter of the duc de Montpensier, later indicating that he could choose from four royal ladies, but by 1554 all four were either married or promised elsewhere. In 1557 Châtelherault agreed to Arran marrying Mademoiselle de Bouillon, Henri's own illegitimate daughter by Diane de Poitiers, but by January 1559 she too was said to be unavailable. Arran's declared protestantism had rendered him unacceptable.

It is not known when Arran converted to the reformed church, but it is perhaps not irrelevant that during part of his time in St Andrews Castle John Knox had been living there too. The Venetian ambassador was of the opinion that Arran declared himself a protestant out of pique when Queen Mary married the dauphin in 1558, having 'persuaded himself that the queen of Scotland was to be no one else's wife' (Hannay, 263), but, be that as it may, Knox for one never questioned the sincerity of Arran's convictions. In February 1559 Arran established a protestant congregation at Châtelherault, bringing a pastor from Poitiers. Henri II, increasingly concerned, urged him to come to court. When Queen Mary fell seriously ill in June 1559, Henri realized how close to the Scottish throne Arran was, and ordered him to be brought in, dead or alive, but by the time the royal messengers arrived, Arran had vanished.

Convinced that the Guise uncles of Mary, queen of Scots, intended to have him arrested and executed, Arran was hiding in a wood near Châtelherault. Ten days later, with the help of the English ambassador, Sir Nicholas Throckmorton, he escaped to Switzerland, almost certainly saw Calvin in Geneva, moved on to Antwerp, and finally crossed to England disguised as a merchant. Taken to Hampton Court by Thomas Randolph, he had an 'accidental' meeting with Elizabeth I in the palace gardens. No one knows what passed between them, but Elizabeth may have hinted that she might be willing to consider him as a husband.

Arran then set off for Scotland. The English had been told that the quickest way of attaching Châtelherault to their interest once more was to send his son to him and, sure enough, after a day in Arran's company, the duke changed sides yet again. Arran rode to Stirling, brought the leading lords of the congregation to Hamilton to see his father, and then went with a force of 700–800 horsemen to Fife, where he and Lord James Stewart engaged in the task of preventing the French soldiers of Mary of Guise from capturing St Andrews Castle. Shortly afterwards, Elizabeth I sent a messenger north with £1000 for the protestants, but the man was intercepted by the earl of Bothwell, who took the money for Mary of Guise. Arran retaliated by seizing Bothwell's title deeds and valuables from Crichton Castle, so beginning a bitter feud between the two men.

Some felt that Arran was too reckless, while others complained that he kept too much to himself, and in April 1560 he was forced to retire to rest in his father's lodgings in the palace of Holyroodhouse. He was then reportedly not yet twenty-three years old, and that autumn the reformers once more suggested him as a husband for Elizabeth I, but on 8 December she declined the offer. At almost exactly the same time, on 5 December, François II, the husband of Queen Mary, died and Arran rejoiced in the thought that he could now marry her himself. Elizabeth I favoured the idea, believing that it would be a means of ending French influence in Scotland, the Hamiltons naturally supported the plan, but Lord James Stewart and William Maitland of Lethington disagreed and Mary herself viewed Arran with dislike.

When Mary returned to Scotland in August 1561, she allowed the protestants freedom of worship but insisted on her right to her own Roman Catholic services. Arran protested publicly and refused to come to court as long as mass was said there, but his obsession with Mary was a common talking point and there were rumours that he planned to kidnap her. That winter Arran's feud with Bothwell reached new heights when Bothwell raided a house occupied by Arran's mistress, Alison Craik. Knox effected a temporary reconciliation between the two men but less than a week later Arran arrived at Knox's lodgings in tears, and poured out a garbled tale. His father and Bothwell planned to kill Lord James and Maitland of Lethington, he said, carry off the queen to the Hamilton fortress of Dumbarton, and marry her to Arran, all in an attempt to incriminate him. Knox could see that he was mentally ill, and tried to calm him, but Arran insisted on sending a message to the queen asking what he should do.

Mary's reply fell into Châtelherault's hands and a violent scene between father and son ensued. Arran escaped from his father's castle of Kinneil down a rope of sheets and was brought to the royal court in St Andrews, talking wildly of witches and demons and claiming to be the husband of Queen Mary. He was, as Thomas Randolph had recently said, 'drowned in dreams' (*CSP Scot.*, 1547–63, 609). The queen herself questioned him in an attempt to get at the truth of the matter, but he remained incoherent on the subject although he was able to talk sensibly about anything else. Declared insane, he was imprisoned in Edinburgh Castle for the next four years. In 1566 he was released into the care of his mother and kept latterly at

Craignethan Castle. Forfeited along with his brothers in 1579 for their support of Queen Mary, he lost his earldom to his cousin's son, Captain James Stewart, in 1581. In 1585 the forfeiture of the Hamiltons was repealed, and in 1586 Arran's resignation of his title was reduced by the court of session. His younger brother John *Hamilton was treated as head of the house of Hamilton after their father's death in 1575, but Arran's signature, pathetically wavering and disjointed, was still required on family charters. Early in 1609 he signed his name one last time, with sudden savage force, scoring it through with his pen. By the end of March he was dead. ROSALIND K. MARSHALL

**Sources** R. K. Hannay, 'The earl of Arran and Queen Mary', *SHR*, 18 (1920–21), 258–76 • J. Durkan, 'James, third earl of Arran: the hidden years', *SHR*, 65 (1986), 154–66 • M. Wood, 'The imprisonment of the earl of Arran', *SHR*, 24 (1926–7), 116–22 • *Scots peerage*, 4.368 • GEC, *Peerage*, new edn, 1.222; 6.256 • R. Douglas, *The peerage of Scotland*, 2nd edn, ed. J. P. Wood, 1 (1813), 701–2 • *CSP Scot.*, 1547–63 • *Lettres, instructions et mémoires de Marie Stuart, reine d'Écosse*, ed. A. Labanoff, 7 vols. (1844), vol. 2, pp. 12–13 • W. Forbes-Leith, *The Scots men-at-arms and life-guards in France*, 1 (1882), 189–93 • *Foreign correspondence with Marie de Lorraine, queen of Scotland: from the originals in the Balcarres papers*, ed. M. Wood, 2: 1548–1557, Scottish History Society, 3rd ser., 7 (1925), 205–6 • Lennoxlove, East Lothian, Hamilton archives

**Archives** Lennoxlove, East Lothian, Hamilton archives

**Likenesses** P. van Gunst, line engraving, 1707 (after A. van der Werff), BM, NPG; repro. in I. de Larrey, *Histoire d'Angleterre* (1697) • chalk drawing, Bibliothèque Nationale, Paris, BN76, C77744 • miniature

James Hamilton, first Viscount Claneboye (*c.*1560–1644), by unknown artist, 1628

**Hamilton, James, first Viscount Claneboye** (*c.*1560–1644), planter in Ulster, was the eldest son of Hans Hamilton (1535/6–1608), vicar of Dunlop in the Cunningham district of Ayrshire, Scotland, and Jonet, daughter of James Denham, laird of West Shield, Ayrshire. He was probably educated at the University of St Andrews, where a James Hamilton graduated BA in 1584 and MA in 1585. Acquiring a reputation as 'one of the greatest scholars and hopeful wits in his time' (Lowry, 4), in 1587 he and James Fullerton became schoolmasters in Dublin (where one pupil was the future archbishop James Ussher); they also acted as agents and informants for James VI of Scotland. On the establishment of Trinity College, Dublin, Hamilton was in 1592 appointed as one of its fellows and was bursar in 1598. He was in London intermittently from August 1600 as agent for James VI (and the duke of Lennox) in connection with the negotiations for James's succession to the English throne. While there he was an advocate for the employment of Scots in the war in Ireland, sent an account of Essex's rebellion to Scotland, and also made useful contacts.

With James's succession and the end of the Nine Years' War in Ireland, Hamilton secured extensive property there, mainly in Ulster; he had returned to Dublin by June 1605 and was at Bangor, co. Down, by March 1606. His principal grant, formalized in November 1605, was of the lordship of upper or southern Clandeboye and the Great Ards in co. Down, but on condition that it be divided between himself, Conn O'Neill, its lord, who had revolted in 1601, and Hugh Montgomery, another Scot also favoured by the king but less influential, who had procured O'Neill's escape from imprisonment in Carrickfergus in 1604 with such an arrangement in expectation. Hamilton also acquired property by purchase or assignment at this time, much of it in co. Antrim, including recently dissolved monastic possessions in both Down and Antrim, and also part of St Mary's Abbey in Dublin, through patents authorized from London in November 1603 to John Wakeman, a Gloucestershire landowner and merchant who was linked to the former lord deputy, Charles Blount, eighth Baron Mountjoy and earl of Devonshire, and in December 1604 to Thomas Irelande of London, a contact man for Scots there, who had both made payments either to the crown or on its behalf. Much of this land was transferred to the newly appointed lord deputy, Chichester, and other English military men (anxious about future security if so much was bestowed upon 'the Scot' (*CSP Ire.*, 1603–6, 195, 295) and also ambitious to secure property in Ireland themselves), but Hamilton retained part of the River Bann and its fishery, acquired from Wakeman in 1606, and also the Foyle fishery. He established a partnership for their commercial exploitation, which included his brother Gawen, a Glasgow merchant who drowned in the Bann, and Thomas Roche of London, but was obliged to surrender these in June 1610, with compensation, to enhance the co. Londonderry plantation. He had been knighted by the king at Royston on 14 November 1609, and he sold a pension, awarded earlier, about this time.

Although not himself a direct beneficiary in the formal plantation in Ulster in 1610, Hamilton held for a time the estate granted to the Scottish Lord Aubigny in the barony of Clankee, co. Cavan. He also briefly had an interest in the estate granted to Trinity College, Dublin, under that plantation, in the procurement of which he had been influential. His energies were from now mainly concentrated on his large co. Down estate which was extended by his acquisition of the lands of the Old English John White of the Dufferin in 1610, and where there were over 1700 settlers by about 1630. At Bangor, where he had built a house and repaired the church, a new town of eighty houses had been established by 1611, and he had other building works under way. He placed 'learned and pious ministers out of Scotland' (Lowry, 33–4) in the parishes of his estate, established schools, and employed schoolmasters. In 1625 and 1626 he commissioned the cartographer Thomas Raven to make maps of the estate. However, he became involved in a lengthy and somewhat destabilizing dispute with Sir Hugh Montgomery over the demarcation of their respective lands and those of Conn O'Neill, which was arbitrated in 1614 and 1615 by the earl of Abercorn.

In 1621, some time after Chichester had been replaced as lord deputy, an inquiry was ordered from Westminster to resolve these disputes. This was carried out by inquisition in October 1623 (at a time when the Irish finances in general were under scrutiny), and Hamilton was eventually granted a new patent of his estate in co. Down in April 1629, which also overturned an effort by Sir William Smith to secure possession deriving from the attempted Elizabethan plantation there in 1571. Hamilton had already been ennobled as Viscount Claneboye in May 1622, and had acquired a share in the farm of the Irish customs in 1623. He was also a privy councillor. Earlier, he had been elected a member for co. Down to parliament in 1613 on the recommendation of the lord deputy to the sheriff, and was a strong supporter of monarchical rights during its proceedings.

Although he made a donation to Glasgow University and erected a monument to his father, and a school, at Dunlop in Scotland, Hamilton was probably not deeply influenced by the rise of the covenanting movement there, and, necessarily cautious under Wentworth's Irish administration when he again had 'much ado to keep himself' (Lowry, 29), in 1639 he took the black oath against it. In the same year his rights over Bangor as a port were questioned by the attorney-general in Dublin, and he and Viscount Montgomery were obliged to surrender an area of church land to Archbishop Ussher. Later, in April 1641, Daniel O'Neill, Conn's son, submitted a petition to the English House of Lords seeking recovery of land against himself and Montgomery. After the outbreak of the 1641 rising Hamilton was one of those given commissions by the king in November 1641 as colonels to raise new troops in Ulster to combat it, but he died, aged about eighty-four, on 24 January 1644 while its outcome was still uncertain.

Hamilton's first wife, Alice Penicook (sometimes, seemingly erroneously, called Penelope Cooke), was with him in Edinburgh in 1602. He divorced his second wife, Ursula (*d.* 1625), sixth daughter of Edward, Lord Brabazon of Ardee, about 1615 in order to marry Jane (*d.* 1661), the mother of his son. She was the daughter of Sir John Philips of Picton Castle, Pembrokeshire, and niece of Chichester's wife, Lettice, herself daughter of Lord Deputy Sir John Perrot. Hamilton was buried in the church at Bangor. He was succeeded by his only son, James, whom he had sent on a European tour for education in 1633. Opportunistic, enterprising, tenacious, and able, the elder James Hamilton had been one of the more successful lowland Scots to secure advancement in Ireland in the reign of James VI and I. R. J. HUNTER

**Sources** T. K. Lowry, ed., *The Hamilton manuscripts* (1867) • M. Perceval-Maxwell, *The Scottish migration to Ulster in the reign of James I* (1973); repr. (1990) • J. C. Erck, ed., *A repertory of the inrolments on the patent rolls of chancery in Ireland commencing with the reign of James I* (1846), 2–3, 28, 189, 194–201, 244–6, 264 • *Calendar of the Irish patent rolls of James I* (before 1830) • *CSP Ire.*, 1598–1600; 1625–47 • Cecil papers 92/21, Hatfield House • *Calendar of the manuscripts of the most hon. the marquis of Salisbury*, 24 vols., HMC, 9 (1883–1976), vols. 10–12, 14–15 • T. W. Moody and J. G. Simms, eds., *The bishopric of Derry and the Irish Society of London, 1602–1705*, 2 vols., IMC (1968–83), vol. 1, pp. 43–53 • J. Shedden-Dobie, 'The church of Dunlop', *Archaeological and historical collections relating to the counties of Ayr and Wigton*, 4 (1884), 26–46 • D. A. Chart, 'The break-up of the estate of Con O'Neill, Castlereagh, County Down, temp. James I', *Proceedings of the Royal Irish Academy*, 48/C3 (1942) • T. M. Healy, *Stolen waters: a page in the conquest of Ulster* (1913) • *Fourth report*, HMC, 3 (1874)

**Archives** Hatfield House, Cecil papers • HMC, Salisbury (Cecil) MSS

**Likenesses** portrait, 1628, Castle Ward, co. Down [*see illus.*]

**Wealth at death** his estate must have been about 50,000 acres; income pa: £1,200 at a fairly early stage, it seems (Lowry, p. 10, though the document is defective); R. G. Gillespie, *Colonial Ulster* (Cork, 1985), p. 232 suggests £4,904 as 'landed wealth' c. 1635; this may be intended to mean income

**Hamilton, James, first earl of Abercorn** (1575–1618), courtier and administrator, was the eldest son of Claud *Hamilton, first Lord Paisley (1546?–1621), and his wife, Margaret Seton (*d.* 1616), daughter of George, fifth Lord Seton. His links by blood and marriage to many of the most powerful nobles in Scotland provided a foundation on which, by his own ability and energy, he built a successful career in politics and land acquisition. In 1598 his father retired from public life and obtained for his son a commission to act for him. Hamilton was then appointed a privy councillor and a gentleman of the chamber, and from 1601 attended council meetings regularly; he was reappointed in 1610, when the membership was cut by more than half. He attended several parliaments and conventions of estates. In 1604 he was a member of the lords of the articles at the parliament that created a commission to negotiate a union with England, and was himself one of the commissioners nominated. On 5 April 1603 he was raised to the peerage as Lord Abercorn, and on 10 July 1606 he was created earl of Abercorn. A protestant in religion, he served the kirk as a member of the 1610 general assembly.

As early as 1597 Hamilton was acting as sheriff of Linlithgowshire, and he was made hereditary sheriff in 1600, a position which he surrendered in 1613. The lands of

Abercorn from which his title was taken also lay in Linlithgowshire, but his residence was usually maintained in the western shire of Renfrew where the family seat of Paisley lay. This westward orientation helps to explain his expansion into Ireland. On 28 April 1608 the privy council ordered Abercorn, in the absence of his kinsman the young second marquess of Hamilton, to defend the Isle of Arran against an expected Irish invasion. On 6 February 1609 he was named to a commission to impose 'civilitie, oure obedyence, and trew religioun' on the Hebrides (*Reg. PCS*, 1607–10, 743). By April 1610 he had been chosen as one of the chief Scottish undertakers in the proposed plantation of Ulster. His initial stake amounted to 3000 acres in the barony of Strabane in co. Tyrone and he soon acquired 3000 more. Abercorn began to shuttle back and forth between his Scottish and Irish lands. He became involved in public affairs in Ireland, and was summoned to the Irish parliament of 1613, though he did not attend. His greatest energy was directed to developing his estates. He built a castle, schoolhouse, and church, and brought in almost one hundred householders. His royal connections also helped: in 1611 King James ordered twenty-five men from the Irish army to help him with his plantation, and on 4 February 1612 the Scottish privy council confirmed a royal warrant allowing Abercorn to impress any ship he wanted to take him, to sail to and from Ireland. On 24 August 1614 the council acknowledged that he had met all the requirements for his 6000 acres. Some time before 1603 he had married Marion Boyd, daughter of Thomas, fifth Lord Boyd; they had five sons and four daughters. She died on 26 August 1632. Abercorn himself died in Monkton parish, Ayrshire, on 23 March 1618 and was buried in Paisley church on 29 April. His eldest son, James, succeeded as second earl of Abercorn.

His fourth son, **Sir George Hamilton**, first baronet (*c*.1608–1679), soldier and landowner, was raised, along with his siblings, by his uncle, Sir George Hamilton of Greenlaw, who converted them to Roman Catholicism. He acquired his father's estate of Donalong, and added other properties throughout his career. Some time before 5 June 1634 he was made a baronet, but of which country is not known. In 1641 he accompanied King Charles to Scotland, but he returned to Ireland soon after. During the Irish wars he served King Charles loyally, in association with his brother-in-law, James Butler, twelfth earl and first duke of Ormond. He was receiver-general of Ireland from 1646 to 1652. In 1649 he was made governor of Nenagh Castle, but in 1651 he retired to France. At the Restoration, Hamilton was one of the minority of royalists who were well compensated for their losses. An act was passed restoring Sir George to his full estates, and in 1662 he was granted all the penalties and forfeitures that the crown might receive through the violation of acts of parliament concerning agricultural practices. On 2 June 1629 Sir George had married Mary Butler (*d*. 1680), daughter of Thomas, Viscount Thurles, and sister of James, duke of Ormond. They had six sons and three daughters, who included Anthony (Comte Antoine) *Hamilton, Elizabeth *Hamilton, Countess de Gramont, and Richard *Hamilton, who became a leading Jacobite. Sir George Hamilton died in 1679. MICHAEL WASSER

**Sources** *Scots peerage*, 1.46–56 · *Reg. PCS*, 1st ser., vols. 5–11 · M. Perceval-Maxwell, *The Scottish migration to Ulster in the reign of James I* (1973) · *CSP Ire.*, *1603–25* · G. Hamilton, *A history of the house of Hamilton* (1933) · *APS*, 1593–1625 · D. Calderwood, *The history of the Kirk of Scotland*, ed. T. Thomson and D. Laing, 8 vols., Wodrow Society, 7 (1842–9), vols. 6–7 · A. Hamilton, *Memoirs of Count Grammont*, new edn, 2 vols. (1811)

**Wealth at death** £8323 6*s*. 5*d*. Scots; plus estate: Perceval-Maxwell, *The Scottish migration*, 107

**Hamilton, James, second marquess of Hamilton** (1589–1625), courtier, was the son of John *Hamilton, first marquess of Hamilton (1539/40–1604), and Margaret (*c*.1545–1625), daughter of John *Lyon, seventh Lord Glamis, and widow of Gilbert Kennedy, fourth earl of Cassillis. All that is known of his education is that he was brought up with Thomas Eglisham (later physician and poet), whose father was the best friend of his father. He was married, by a contract of 30 January 1603, to Lady Anne (Anna) *Cunningham (*d*. 1647), daughter of James Cunningham, seventh earl of Glencairn. His family connections with, and loyalty to, the Stuart dynasty brought him a string of honours and offices. He succeeded his father as marquess in 1604, and his uncle as earl of Arran and sheriff of Lanarkshire in 1604 or 1609. The lands of the abbey of Arbroath were confirmed in his possession in 1608, and he became a privy councillor in Scotland and in England in 1613 and 1617 respectively. An English peerage, as earl of Cambridge, was granted in 1619. In 1618–19 there was talk that he might be appointed treasurer or chamberlain of Scotland, but in the end the offices he attained were confined to the court: he was appointed a gentleman of the bedchamber in 1621 and lord steward of the household in 1624. His nomination as king's commissioner to the Scottish parliament of 1621 was the result both of direct royal favour and of his friendship with the king's favourite, the duke of Buckingham, for he was 'neither active in nor knowledgeable about Scottish affairs' (Lee, 181), though he had accompanied James on his visit to the country in 1617. However, Hamilton was successful in overseeing parliament's acceptance of the king's reforms of worship (the five articles of Perth), and was rewarded with the keepership of the palace of Holyroodhouse. Thereafter he was rather more active in public affairs in both Scotland and England, favour compensating for the lack of experience, and perhaps of application, of this 'young, charming womaniser' (Lee, 213). He acted as a commissioner in negotiations for the marriage of Prince Charles and the Spanish infanta, and was appointed to receive her on her arrival in England in May 1623. However, the plan for the 'Spanish match' collapsed, with Hamilton abstaining from the privy council vote to accept or reject the Spanish terms of January 1624. Though he was made a knight of the Garter in April 1623, thoughts of creating him a duke were abandoned.

Hamilton died at Whitehall of fever on 2 March 1625, a few weeks before King James. Rumours that he had been poisoned, and that he died a Roman Catholic, were denied, the latter denial being supported by the argument that he was 'more subjecte to his pleasors and the companye of wemen then to preests' (*Mar and Kellie MSS*, 1.225). His body was taken back to Scotland, and he was buried on 2 September at Hamilton. His reputation was much better than that of most Scottish court favourites, and John Chamberlain claimed that he was 'held the gallantest gentleman of both nations' and 'the flower of that [Scots] nation' (*DNB*). John Donne evidently had a high regard for him, even if his statement that 'If you had commanded me to have waited upon his body to Scotland, and preached there his Funerall sermon, I should have embraced that obligation' perhaps owes more to respect for his correspondent, Sir Robert Kerr, than for Hamilton. However, he wrote 'An Hymne to the Saints, and to the Marquesse Hamylton' to commemorate him (*Correspondence*, 2.512–13).

His wife survived him, gaining fame for herself by raising a troop of horse in the first bishops' war in support of the covenanters. She was reported as riding at the head of the troop, armed with pistol and dagger, threatening to kill their son James *Hamilton, the third marquess, who commanded the fleet Charles I had sent to the Firth of Forth to overawe the covenanters, if he dared to land. Their younger son William *Hamilton later became a notable politician. DAVID STEVENSON

**Sources** *DNB* · GEC, *Peerage* · *Scots peerage* · *The historical works of Sir James Balfour*, ed. J. Haig, 4 vols. (1824–5) · M. Lee, *Government by pen: Scotland under James VI and I* (1980) · *The manuscripts of the duke of Hamilton*, HMC, 21 (1887) · *Report on the manuscripts of the earl of Mar and Kellie*, HMC, 60 (1904) · *Correspondence of Sir Robert Kerr, first earl of Ancram, and his son William, third earl of Lothian*, ed. D. Laing, 2 vols., Roxburghe Club, 100 (1875)

**Archives** NA Scot., Hamilton MSS

**Likenesses** M. Droeshout, line engraving, 1623, BM, V&A · D. Mytens, oils, Royal Collection · D. Mytens, oils, Lennoxlove, Haddington, East Lothian · D. Mytens, oils, Scot. NPG · R. Vaughan, line engraving, BM, NPG

**Hamilton, James, first duke of Hamilton** (1606–1649), politician, was born at Hamilton, Lanarkshire, on 19 June 1606, the eldest son of James *Hamilton, second marquess of Hamilton and first earl of Cambridge (1589–1625), and Lady Anna *Cunningham (*d.* 1647), fourth daughter of James Cunningham, seventh earl of Glencairn (1580–1630). Styled earl of Arran from 1609, he spent his childhood in the extensive family estates in Scotland, largely at Hamilton Palace. Little is known of his early life, although his extremely able and deeply Calvinist mother, Anna Cunningham, who ran the massive Hamilton estates in the absence of her husband in London from 1616, probably had a strong formative influence on him.

**Early career** Summoned by his father, Arran arrived in London on 12 December 1620, accompanied by his governor, Mr James Baillie, about six personal servants, including Sir John Hamilton of Lettrick and Sir John Hamilton of Grange, a few pages, and five footmen. The first thing he did on his arrival was to go to Westminster Abbey. Over the next six months he was gradually introduced at court: his accounts for this important period show that

James Hamilton, first duke of Hamilton (1606–1649), by Daniel Mytens, 1629

increasing amounts of money were spent on clothes such as ruffs, leghose, silks, velvet, and gold lace, as he became more visible at Whitehall. He regularly played tennis, attended plays, bought books, viewed the lions in the Tower, visited the parliament, and was present at the jousts for accession day on 24 March 1621. In July 1621 he went up to Exeter College, Oxford, to continue his education, but he returned to court on 14 December and failed to take a degree. The termination of his education had a grave effect on his spelling, grammar, and handwriting, which was appalling, anarchic even, throughout his life. On 16 June 1622, just short of his sixteenth birthday, Arran married, in the presence of King James, Lady Mary [**Mary Hamilton** (1612/13?–1638)], daughter of William *Feilding, Viscount Feilding (*c.*1587–1643), soon to be created earl of Denbigh, and his wife, Susan Villiers (*d.* *c.*1655). Although Mary's uncle was the marquess of Buckingham, it was an uneven match for the heir of the premier noble family in Scotland to marry into a little-known Warwickshire family, and Arran resented it for the rest of his life, even alluding to it in his last letter to his brother, a few hours before his death. The marriage was yet another example of the power Buckingham wielded in all aspects of court life and patronage, but since the bride was only about nine years old, the union could not be consummated immediately.

Arran accompanied Prince Charles and the duke of Buckingham on their trip to Madrid in 1623 to woo the Infanta Maria, in the company of his father-in-law, Denbigh. The origins of his close friendship with Prince Charles can be traced to this trip and, following their return to court in October, Arran was made a gentleman of the bedchamber to the prince in January 1624. However, this key breakthrough in Arran's career may also have been part of a compensation package for his humble marriage, as Buckingham had become the unassailable favourite of both the elderly James and his young heir to the throne. The death of Arran's father from a fever at Whitehall on 2 March 1625 brought him at eighteen the titles of third marquess of Hamilton and second earl of Cambridge. In May that year Charles married Henrietta Maria, sister of Louis XIII of France, and Hamilton was part of Buckingham's magnificent cavalcade that travelled to Paris to escort the new king's bride home. He also accompanied Buckingham to the Netherlands in October, together with the earl of Holland, Sir Henry Mildmay, and Sir George Goring, to solicit an alliance against Spain. In London, Hamilton led the Scottish contingent, along with the fourth duke of Lennox, at James's funeral on 7 May 1625, and carried the sword at Charles's English coronation on 2 February 1626. He took the oath of allegiance on 23 June 1625. The young marquess was also a diligent attender at the English parliament, from May 1625 to June 1626. Sitting in the House of Lords as earl of Cambridge, he was present at seventy-four out of 112 meetings.

A few days after the dissolution of the English parliament in June 1626, Hamilton retired from court, owing to crippling debts of over £31,000 sterling left by his father, a continued dissatisfaction with his lowly marriage and the consequent friction this created with Buckingham, and, finally, a growing unhappiness with the king's revocation scheme in Scotland. In February 1627 Hamilton was made a member of the commission for surrenders and teinds, the body set up to implement the king's revocation, but he rarely attended and resisted surrendering his ecclesiastical patrimony back to the crown. He was sworn of the Scottish privy council on 3 April 1627, though he attended only about a dozen times between April 1627 and February 1628. In a dramatic bid to avoid his creditors, and the consequences of the king's revocation, Hamilton went into self-imposed exile on 11 February 1628 on his island of Arran, off the Ayrshire coast. As well as playing something of the feudal lord for the seven months that he was on the island, Hamilton occupied himself in hunting and fishing, and fitting out and equipping a number of privateers to be used against French shipping around the Scottish coast.

The assassination of Buckingham on 23 August 1628 ended Hamilton's exile on Arran and by late October he was back at court, being sworn into Buckingham's vacated office of master of the horse to the king on 12 November. If the court gossips are to be believed—and in this case they probably should be—he was given Buckingham's old post on condition that he consummated his marriage with his wife, to whom he had been married for over six years; the appointment provided a feast of crude puns for the court wags at the expense of the young master of the horse. The Hamiltons were duly reconciled, and from February 1631 had six children in as many years. The eldest, Henrietta Mary, died soon after the birth of the second, Anne *Hamilton (1632–1716); Susanna (1633–1694) was followed by three sons who all died young, Charles (1634–1640), James (1635–1639), and William (1636–1638). Hamilton also had a daughter Mary, probably with one Euphemia Hamilton; known as Mistress Mary, she was brought up at Hamilton Palace and later married Sir Thomas Hay of Park.

**The protestant cause in Europe** Between January and March 1629 Hamilton attended fifteen out of twenty-three meetings of the English parliament, and probably supported continuing the war with Spain, but following its dissolution did not settle at court for long. On 30 May 1630 he agreed articles with the king of Sweden, Gustavus Adolphus, to take a voluntary force of 6000 men to fight in Germany. While Gustavus had a broad vision of defeating Habsburg and imperial forces there and then marching on Vienna, Hamilton was more concerned with assisting in the recapture of the Upper and Lower Palatinate for Charles I's sister Elizabeth and brother-in-law Frederick, elector Palatine and king of Bohemia, who had been evicted from their territories following the battle of the White Mountain in November 1620. It was agreed that Charles I would finance the initial recruitment and launch of Hamilton's army, and Gustavus would take over responsibility for its maintenance and the supply of reinforcements when it was on the continent. It is fairly certain that Gustavus viewed Hamilton's little army as a snare to draw the over-cautious Charles into a full public commitment to the European war against the Habsburgs.

Hamilton's recruitment of the force of 6000 was accomplished with some difficulty, and in the latter stages London was scoured for vagrants and masterless men to make up the quota. Charles financed the expedition, providing in total about £43,000 sterling which was enough to levy, launch, and maintain the force for the first few months. But after Hamilton sailed for Germany, Charles's financial commitment was at an end, and Gustavus, as the articles stated, was to take over. The army was composed of 5000 English and 1000 Scots, organized into four regiments, with a somewhat larger proportion of Scottish officers, including several members of the Hamilton family.

In the early summer of 1631 Hamilton returned to court from Scotland, after finalizing his preparations for the campaign, to be faced with accusations that he intended to use his army to seize the crown of Scotland. The accuser was James Stewart, Lord Ochiltree, whose family were hereditary enemies of the Hamiltons, Ochiltree's father, Captain James Stewart of Bothwellmuir, having temporarily seized the Hamilton estates in 1581. Charles refused to give credence to the allegations, even insisting that his Scottish favourite spent the night alone with him in his bedchamber when Hamilton first arrived back at court. Ochiltree was subsequently sent to Scotland and found guilty of leasing-making, and was confined to perpetual imprisonment. David Ramsay and Donald Mackay, first Lord Reay, whose loose-tongued tittle-tattle had raised the rumours in the first place, were tried in a high court of chivalry, where trial by combat was awarded after insufficient evidence was found, but as he wrote to Hamilton on 8 May 1632, the king eventually decided not to allow the men to fight. Although Hamilton was exonerated from all involvement in the affair, rumours and accusations linking his name to the Scottish crown, to which his family had the next claim after the royal Stuarts, dogged him throughout his career.

Hamilton landed with his army near Wolgast in Pomerania on 31 July 1631, and he was instructed by the king of Sweden to march along the River Oder towards Silesia to conjoin with auxiliary forces under the command of General Sir Alexander Leslie, later earl of Leven. In the next few weeks he relieved the siege of Crossen, took the city of Gubin, and refortified Frankfurt an der Oder. In September his army lay before Custrin, in an attempt to secure the strategic areas against the 22,000-strong Silesian army, and additionally to facilitate Gustavus's retreat, although this proved unnecessary since Gustavus defeated Tilly's imperial army at the battle of Breitenfeld (or Leipzig) on 17 September. By the time Hamilton left Custrin on 15 October his army had been decimated by plague, famine, and sickness. Being forced to leave his sick soldiers behind, and deploying a further 1000 in garrisoning the towns they had taken, Hamilton approached Magdeburg with only 1500 of his original army. He combined his forces with those of General John Baner and lay before Magdeburg, but they were obliged to break off the siege following the arrival of Field Marshal Pappenheim on 4 January 1632. Hamilton desired a battle with Pappenheim, but was overruled by Baner, who was following strict orders from Gustavus not to engage the enemy, and the young marquess subsequently retired to winter quarters in Halberstadt in disgust, his involvement in the Thirty Years' War at an end. For the rest of the year increasingly desultory talks were held with Gustavus Adolphus, Charles's agent Sir Henry Vane, and Hamilton to increase the British king's involvement in Germany, and to find a role for Hamilton. Charles would not be drawn into a full-scale commitment in continental Europe, even if it meant the marginalization of the Palatine family in Gustavus's plans and on 24 September 1632 he ordered Hamilton to return to Britain.

Hamilton continued his association with Sweden, the exiled Palatine family, and various military matters for the rest of his career. He became an unofficial representative for Sweden at the British court, and was the principal broker for matters relating to Elizabeth, electress Palatine, and her son Charles Lewis. These two interests merged in 1637 when he sponsored two marriage alliances, the first between the prince elector, Charles Lewis, and Queen Kristina of Sweden, daughter of the late Gustavus Adolphus, and the second between the palsgrave of Sweden and Charles Lewis's sister. The grand anti-Habsburg alliance, of which these marriages would form a part, petered out towards the end of 1637 and Hamilton's efforts came to nothing. At the same time he was involved, together with Charles Lewis, Sir Thomas Roe, and others, in a plan to set up a West Indies company, on the Dutch model, to promote economic warfare with Spain, but the plan also collapsed on the failure of the grand anti-Habsburg alliance.

**England, 1632–1640** Hamilton finally settled into life at court on his return from Germany and strengthened his position, while enjoying his fair share of the king's bounty. His two main offices were master of the horse and gentleman of the bedchamber to the king. The former was the third highest office in the court and conferred on the holder the right to have a place at the king's side on most public occasions, as well as providing a pension and about 200 staff. The office-holder was also responsible for licensing the import and export of horses, and in 1635 Hamilton secured a patent to license hackney carriages in London. As a gentleman of the bedchamber he had the right of unrivalled proximity to the king. In June 1630 Hamilton was made steward of Hampton Court, which gave him the fees and patronage of one of the largest royal residences in England. He was elected a knight of the Garter in October 1630. He was also made keeper of Portsmouth, which brought further revenue and the right to nominate one of the town's two members of parliament, a nomination he bestowed on his younger brother William *Hamilton, first earl of Lanark and second duke of Hamilton (1616–1651), for the Short Parliament of April–May 1640.

Hamilton was sworn of the English privy council on 8 March 1633. Between 1633 and 1642 he attended 245 out of a total of 1058 meetings of the council, roughly one in four, probably sitting in council when the king was present, when an issue relating to his own personal or political interests was on the agenda, or those of his clients and collaborators. In November 1637 he was appointed to a committee formed to regulate the royal household, and about the same time attempted to bring the disgraced former lord treasurer of England, Lionel Cranfield, first earl of Middlesex, back into the administration, mainly to improve financial management. Hamilton never sat on any of the five main privy council standing committees, not even the committee for foreign affairs, an area in which he had a deep and abiding interest: his strongly anti-Spanish views may have precluded his appointment. The advance of the Scottish troubles, however, prompted the creation of two privy council committees to which Hamilton was appointed, the committee for arms in November 1639 and the council of war in January 1640. Hamilton sponsored the bridge appointments to the privy council in early 1641, which brought into government some of the king's parliamentary opponents, including the earls of Bedford and Essex, Viscount Saye and Sele, and Viscount Mandeville.

As well as the revenue that accrued from his court offices, Hamilton pursued a number of commercial activities. With the earls of Pembroke and Holland in October 1637 he secured a grant of the whole of Newfoundland. With Thomas Horth he developed interests in the Newcastle coal and salt trade, and in the supply of oil to the Scottish soap manufacturers. He was, in a similar way, the patron of Sir Robert Heath, and they worked on various projects together, including measures to curb abuses in the silk trade (1631) and regulating alehouses (1634), as well as establishing stakes in salt works on Tyneside (also with Thomas Horth) and a massive lead mine complex in Derbyshire. Together with Archbishop William Laud, in October 1637 Hamilton secured Heath the position of king's sergeant. Hamilton had further links with members of the English legal fraternity, including Sir Edward Littleton, solicitor-general between 1634 and 1640, and was responsible for the appointment in 1640 of Littleton's successor as solicitor-general, Oliver St John. With his plethora of interests in licensing and restrictive practices on commercial companies, seen most clearly in his £4000 per annum fees from the Vintners' Company in 1638, Hamilton was one of the principal monopolists in England when the Long Parliament convened in November 1640.

Although Hamilton's power base was in the king's court he enjoyed some influence in the queen's circle, mainly through his mother-in-law, the countess of Denbigh, and, until her death from consumption at Wallingford House, London, on 10 May 1638, through his wife. Both women were ladies of the queen's bedchamber, and the latter had a close relationship with Henrietta Maria. As a Scot, Hamilton was naturally pro-French and was also heavily involved in the recruitment of soldiers for service in France throughout his career. He sought to protect the interests of his brother-in-law Basil *Feilding, Baron Feilding of Newnham Paddox, later second earl of Denbigh, who was ambassador-extraordinary to Venice and the princes of Italy between 1634 and 1639. During this period Hamilton's sphere of influence extended there too, and he usually circumvented the English secretary responsible for Italy, Sir John Coke (1563–1644), and read his brother-in-law's dispatches directly to the king and discussed policy towards Italy with Charles. This finally resulted in Hamilton securing Coke's dismissal in 1639, and having him replaced the following year by his own nominee, Sir Henry Vane the elder (1589–1655).

Feilding's residence in Italy also allowed Hamilton to supply his passion for art collecting, and over this period he purchased over 400 pieces, mostly through acquiring the entire collections of Bartolomeo della Nave, the Procurator Priuli, and Nicolas Renieri. His most notable acquisition was the St Margaret by Raphael from the Priuli collection. His accounts show that he paid about £3400 sterling for the three collections. Such was his obsession with the acquisition of visual art that he had formed a plan to visit Italy by 1637, but this was spoilt by the outbreak of the troubles in Scotland. Hamilton additionally inherited a collection of paintings from his father, the second marquess, and he acquired more while campaigning in Germany. Like the other members of the coterie of art collectors at court, Hamilton swapped, gifted, and sometimes sold paintings to Charles. His total collection of paintings, marbles, and other works of art may have approached 1000 pieces. An inventory of under a half of his collection in 1649 listed, *inter alia*, thirty-six paintings by Titian, twenty-four by Palma Giovane, eighteen by Palma Vecchio, twelve by Veronese, nine by Tintoretto, and others by Raphael, Correggio, Giorgione, and Leonardo. Thus, his collection of the Venetian school exceeded in both number and quality that of the late duke of Buckingham.

Hamilton initially occupied about twenty rooms at Whitehall, as master of the horse, and then rented Wallingford House from the dowager duchess of Buckingham about 1636. He also had accommodation at Hampton Court, which he used to house part of his picture collection. He was granted, on 23 June 1638, the manor of Chelsea together with the mansion of Chelsea House, which was being extensively rebuilt and galleries created for his works of art, under the supervision of Sir John Danvers, when the civil wars intervened.

**Scotland and Ireland, 1632–1640** Although Hamilton was mostly resident in England between 1620 and 1640, he did not sever any of his kinship or family ties in Scotland; an act for his naturalization was not framed until the beginning of the Long Parliament, and was never passed. While in England, he retained a Scottish household and most of his men of business were also Scots. He was one of the biggest landowners in Scotland and drew most of his traditional forms of revenue and political allegiance from his native country. An inventory of the land he owned in Scotland, drawn up in 1640, listed the principal holdings as the earldom of Arran, the lordship and baronies of Hamilton, Aven (or Kinneil), Arbroath, Evendale, Lesmahagow, Crawfordjohn, Polmont, Carriden, Kettilston, Kilbryde, Bothwell and Bothwellmuir, Monkland, Stenhouse, Machanshire, Cambuslang, and Carmanock. All his Scottish estates were managed by his mother, Anna Cunningham, the dowager marchioness.

After his return from Germany in late 1632 Hamilton became one of Charles's chief advisers in secular Scottish affairs, but he was excluded from matters concerning Scottish ecclesiastical policy, that being the sole responsibility of the king, Archbishop Laud, and a few Scottish bishops. Hamilton was a great patron at court for his fellow countrymen. The Scottish master of requests, Sir James Galloway, wrote to Hamilton on 16 April 1632, lamenting his inability to get business done at court during the marquess's absence in Germany. Requests for Hamilton's assistance to secure royal patronage came from all political and religious hues of Scottish society. In 1633 John Campbell sought the patent which eventually made him first earl of Loudoun, while in 1635 George Gordon, first marquess of Huntly, asked Hamilton to explain to the king why he had to exact summary justice on one of his rivals in the highlands. In much the same way, the Calvinist lord advocate of Scotland Sir Thomas Hope of Craighall and the Catholic lord high constable of Scotland William Hay, tenth earl of Erroll, both petitioned Hamilton to secure their arrears of pension.

One of Hamilton's first acts on returning from Germany was to collude in the fall, in 1633, of Charles I's chief Scottish minister, William Graham, seventh earl of Menteith, president of the privy council and justice-general of Scotland. Menteith's removal led to the rise of Hamilton and of John Stewart, first earl of Traquair, treasurer-depute from 1630 and lord high treasurer from 1636, as the two most important secular ministers in the Scottish administration; their partnership was a key element in the operation of government in the 1630s. They worked together on a range of issues, from the civil disorder problem in Aberdeen in 1635–6 to the English breaches of the Anglo-Scottish salt agreement in 1637. The two noblemen also formed a formidable double act in the early stages of the Scottish troubles from 1637, pursuing a policy of damage limitation to the Scottish crown.

Hamilton's position as the most important Scot at court was underlined when the king visited Scotland in the summer of 1633 for his coronation. Hamilton, with the help of Traquair, brokered the scramble for honours that were to be issued as part of the celebrations, and he rarely left the king's side during Charles's stay in his native kingdom. In the state entry into Edinburgh on 15 June 1633 Hamilton, symbolically, rode just behind the king, with the Scottish contingent in front of them and the English behind. He was named one of the lords of articles and was made collector-general of the taxations granted in the coronation parliament in that year. The grant of the taxation further guaranteed Hamilton's financial security, and was to be used to pay the £40,000 sterling in compensation he had agreed for surrendering his wine tack back to the crown. His responsibility for the taxations additionally gave him a prominent place in the administration of the Scottish exchequer, which contributed to the political eclipse, in late 1634, of George Hay, first earl of Kinnoull, lord high chancellor of Scotland.

Hamilton sought opportunities for influence and wealth in all of Charles I's dominions, and turned his attention to Ireland in 1635. A feature of this campaign between 1635 and 1641 was the bitter animus that developed between Hamilton and the lord deputy of Ireland, Thomas Wentworth, Viscount Wentworth, later first earl of Strafford. Hamilton made three attempts to acquire a stake in the country, all of which failed. First, he tried in 1635 to secure a large portion of the projected plantation in Connaught which would be managed by his younger brother William Hamilton. Second, in 1637 he procured a grant of lands and royal fishing around the bays of Killelagh and Strangford in co. Down, but these were found to have been granted already to Wentworth's ally Thomas Cromwell, Viscount Lecale. Finally, in 1637 Hamilton led a consortium that bid for the lucrative lands and customs of Londonderry taken from the London corporation in a Star Chamber trial a few years earlier. The consortium probably offered the crown in excess of £10,000 sterling per annum to run the customs operation, but the initiative was stymied in the face of Wentworth's fierce opposition and the need for Hamilton to turn his full attention to the Scottish troubles in 1638. The bitterness between the two men continued after the calling of the Long Parliament in England in November 1640, and Hamilton, like most other Scots at the time, probably welcomed the act of attainder and execution of the anti-Scottish lord deputy of Ireland on 12 May 1641. Nevertheless, no convincing evidence has been found linking Hamilton to the fall of Strafford, and he reaffirmed his innocence to the charge during his speech before his own execution.

**The troubles and the wars of the three kingdoms, 1637–1646** Hamilton was appointed royal commissioner to resolve the Scottish troubles in April 1638, well over a year after the riots in and around Edinburgh that had followed the introduction of the infamous canons and prayer book. By the time he arrived in Edinburgh on 9 June he faced a stubborn and well-organized resistance movement. The magnitude of Hamilton's task was brought home to him by the complete failure of over 100 of his kinsmen and clients to obey his summons to meet him at Dalkeith on 5 June. Having had no part in the formulation or introduction of the religious measures that caused the national covenant, and being himself deeply anti-episcopal, he understood more than most the reasons for the covenanters' determined stance. The attempt to find a negotiated settlement was undermined by the military preparations on both sides. On 20 June Hamilton told Charles that the situation was so grave that he could not see how the king could impose his will on Scotland 'uith out the haserdding of your 3 Crounes' (NA Scot., GD 406/1/327/1–2).

Twice Hamilton returned to court during the summer in an attempt to get the king to relax his harsh conditions, mainly for the surrender of the covenants before he would consider any of the covenanters' demands, and to persuade Charles to allow a general assembly and parliament. Following the second of these visits, Hamilton returned to Edinburgh on 17 September with a set of proposals that swept away the recent ecclesiastical innovations and permitted a general assembly and parliament. Despite valiant attempts to gather a party for the king, the elections to the Glasgow assembly unanimously favoured supporters of the covenant, and Hamilton dissolved it on 28 November, one week after it convened. The assembly sat on in spite of the commissioner's dissolution and reformed the Scottish church over the next three weeks, their most significant act being the abjuration of episcopacy. The commissioner left Edinburgh towards the end of the year in a mood that can best be described by the sentiment expressed in his letter of 27 September:

> Joy I have lytill heere, for lytill confort can I have in being abhorred be my frends and kin[d]red, haitted by my Natione in generall, railled at in the streettis, exclaymed aga[i]nst in

> the pulpits, and that in no other termes then that faggots is alreddie prepaired in hell for me. (NA Scot., GD 406/1/565)

The military phase of Hamilton's commissionership in 1639 was as miserable a failure as his diplomatic one the year before. He was appointed general of the king's forces in Scotland in April 1639 by Charles's 'absolute command'. Increasingly, however, he pursued two objectives: to secure a moderate negotiated settlement, and to look to his own preservation. Hamilton played a large part in the mobilization for the first bishops' war, and sailed up the Firth of Forth on 1 May in command of a naval flotilla carrying a force of 5000 poorly trained men. Within a week he was advising Charles, who was heading towards the border, to find some way of 'paching itt up' with the covenanters (NA Scot., GD 406/1/10548). His humiliation was completed by his mother, Anna Cunningham, who arrived at Leith at the head of her own troop of horse, brandishing pistols loaded with specially made silver bullets that she intended to use on her son, should he step onto Scottish soil. A battle was avoided and Hamilton arrived at Berwick on 7 June to participate in the peace negotiations, but he quickly adopted a lower profile, working behind the scenes and drafting papers for the king. This culminated in his resignation as royal commissioner on 8 July, mainly to avoid returning to Edinburgh to face the hostile crowds and to preside over a parliament that would confirm the abolition of episcopacy. For the remainder of his time at Berwick, Hamilton, with Charles's approval, ingratiated himself with the covenanters in order to discover their plans for the future government of Scotland. Although Hamilton participated in the preparations for the second bishops' war, he carved out a role for himself as confidential secretary to the king on sensitive Scottish matters, which smoothed a path for his brother William, now earl of Lanark, to be appointed secretary of state for Scotland in March 1640 on the death of William Alexander, first earl of Stirling.

Hamilton sat in the Short Parliament in April–May 1640 as earl of Cambridge. He secured the release of John Campbell, Lord Loudoun, who had been imprisoned by Charles in April, and concluded a secret pact with him to pursue the ends of peace and to avert a second war. The Scottish invasion of England in August 1640, and the calling of the Long Parliament in November, brought Charles's efforts to impose his will on his northern kingdom to an abrupt halt. Hamilton adopted a conciliatory role in the Long Parliament, and was voted onto over a dozen committees, as well as being appointed on more than fourteen occasions to delegations of the upper house to the king. He sponsored the bridge appointments to the English privy council, secured Oliver St John's appointment as solicitor-general and considered marriage to the daughter of Francis Russell, fourth earl of Bedford. By the summer of 1641 Hamilton was on intimate terms with some of the king's most powerful opponents in the English parliament. In a similar way, when he arrived in Scotland with Charles in August 1641, Hamilton cemented his political alliance with the covenanter leader Archibald Campbell, eighth earl of Argyll. Hamilton's motives were now being questioned by a number of Scots around the king, whose suspicions were fuelled by James Graham, fifth earl of Montrose, who boasted from his prison cell in Edinburgh Castle that he had proof that Argyll and Hamilton were traitors. From this familiar miasma around the king grew the plot to assassinate the two noblemen known as 'the incident', to which Charles almost certainly gave his approval. Argyll, Hamilton, and Lanark fled the capital on 12 October, returning on 1 November only after the Scottish parliament, not Charles, guaranteed their safety.

Remarkably, Hamilton returned to England with the king in November, yet he found his position increasingly untenable and, like many of his contemporaries, he succumbed to an illness, whether real or imagined, as the country slid into civil war. After spending a month at York with the king and subscribing to pay for sixty horse for the royalist army, he returned to Scotland on 1 July 1642. The alliance between Hamilton and Argyll was fractured when they took opposite sides in the debates on whether Scotland should offer military support to the English parliament. Hamilton's position as the chief agent of royalist policy in Scotland was reaffirmed when he was created duke of Hamilton on 12 April 1643. That summer the increasingly bitter contest on whether to intervene in England was carried from the privy council into the convention of estates, where Argyll was backed by the barons and burghs and Hamilton by the noble estate. Hamilton and the other supporters of the king walked out of the convention on 26 June, and the solemn league and covenant was agreed at the beginning of August. Hamilton and Lanark fled to the king at Oxford to avoid subscribing the league and covenant and were arrested the moment they arrived in the city on Saturday 16 December. A charge of treason was levelled at Hamilton by Montrose and his circle, who were at Oxford and had offered Charles a slash and burn military policy in Scotland as an alternative to Hamilton's timorous diplomacy. He was stripped of his court offices and Prince Rupert replaced him as master of the horse. The duke spent the period from January 1644 to April 1646 as a prisoner in Pendennis Castle in Cornwall, but was never brought to trial.

**The engagement and fall, 1646–1649** Hamilton was released from prison by the victorious forces of the parliamentary general Sir Thomas Fairfax on 15 April 1646 after a confinement of two years and four months. He made his way to London, and in June took the solemn league and covenant and the negative oath. He also made known his intention to live in retirement. Nevertheless, he was persuaded to alter his resolution by the king, the marquess of Argyll, and his brother Lanark. He arrived at Newcastle on 28 July and added his voice to the growing calls for Charles to accept the Newcastle propositions. The resumption of Hamilton's amity with Charles, however fragile, led to a flow of gifts and he was made heritable keeper of Holyroodhouse, palace, gardens, orchards, and bowling greens on 8 August. In October, he received the office of the sheriffdom of Lanark. On 29 January 1647 Charles signed an account stating that Hamilton had lent him £22,853 sterling between 1639 and 1640. The king's refusal to accept the Newcastle propositions moved Hamilton in September to declare his intention to retire abroad, telling Charles that he would not be a witness to his destruction. Hamilton was again persuaded to return to public life by his increasingly assertive and influential brother Lanark, and by the king's personal request.

Hamilton's attendance at the sixth session of the first triennial parliament (3 November 1646 to 20 March 1647) restored the customary party division across the estates led by the duke and Argyll. Hamilton's party wished to keep the Scottish army intact until the fate of the king had been decided, while Argyll wanted the army disbanded and the uncovenanted king surrendered to the English parliament. Argyll won on both counts, following a series of bitter debates and desperate attempts to get Charles to accept the covenant. Before the parliament dissolved, however, the Hamilton brothers had scalded the consciences of those who had abandoned Charles at Newcastle to such an extent that it was agreed that the king might not have to take the covenant himself, but rather only to confirm it as a law. Hamilton also secured the support of half of the members of the committee of estates that governed Scotland until the convening of the second triennial parliament in March 1648.

The abduction of the king by Cornet George Joyce on 4 June ignited royalism in Scotland. None the less, Hamilton was instructed by Charles to resist any attempts by the Scots to intervene in England, until the king saw the outcome of his promising relationship with the independent army. By the end of the year Charles turned again to the Scots, and Hamilton's brother Lanark, together with Lauderdale and Loudoun, signed the engagement with the king on 26 December 1647 at Carisbrooke Castle on the Isle of Wight. The majority of the Scottish parliament that sat down on 2 March 1648 accepted the engagement. Yet Argyll and the Scottish church refused to give their support, until Charles took the league and covenant and fully embraced presbyterian church government.

On 4 May the parliament ordered a levy of nearly 30,000 foot and 3000 horse. A fraction of that number marched into England on 8 July, under the command of Hamilton. The army dallied in the north of England for weeks until reinforcements and supplies came from Scotland. When Oliver Cromwell surprised the engagement forces at Preston on 18 August Hamilton had fatally allowed his cavalry to ride ahead to Wigan, while his auxiliary army under Sir George Monro was about a dozen miles to the north. A small English force of 3000 foot and 600 horse under Sir Marmaduke Langdale engaged Cromwell's army on a sodden, hedge-enclosed Preston Moor, while Hamilton was persuaded by his overbearing lieutenant-general, James Livingstone, first earl of Callander, to take the Scottish foot off the moor and over the River Ribble. Hamilton and his own life guard, together with a small body of Scottish horse, supported Langdale on the moor and later charged the Cromwellian horse to allow Langdale's forces to retreat. A dismal night march in atrocious weather reduced the Scottish foot to half its number. The duke made a last stand at Winwick after linking up with the Scottish horse. After several hours of fighting, the Scots broke and retreated in disarray. Hamilton agreed articles of surrender with Major-General John Lambert at Uttoxeter on 22 August, having been defeated by an army less than half the size of his own. Cromwell estimated that he had 10,000 prisoners by the end of the campaign. News of Hamilton's defeat quickly spread, leading to the disintegration of the engagement regime in Scotland and the collapse of the royalist risings in England.

Hamilton was taken from Uttoxeter to Ashby-de-la-Zouch, where he arrived on 28 August. The English parliament voted a ransom of £100,000 on him, though this was repealed towards the end of the year, probably following Pride's Purge in early December. Hamilton had a brief meeting with Charles at Windsor Castle, where the duke had been conveyed about 11 December, and they exchanged a few words. He escaped from Windsor Castle after Charles's execution on 30 January 1649, but was captured within a few hours, after failing to follow the instructions of his devoted servant Andrew Cole. A second high court of justice was raised on 6 February and he was charged with treason under his English title, earl of Cambridge. Despite lodging a special plea that he was employed by the Scottish parliament, that he was not an Englishman, and that articles of surrender protected his life, he was found guilty of treason and beheaded in Palace Yard, Whitehall, on 9 March 1649. His body was conveyed to Scotland by sea and he was buried in the parish church at Hamilton on 1 May. He was aged forty-two. While his English title became extinct, the duchy of Hamilton passed first to his brother Lanark, and then by special remainder to his elder surviving daughter, Anne.

**Reputation** Derided and respected in equal measure by his contemporaries, Hamilton was one of the most important Scots of the first half of the seventeenth century. His birth, three years after the union of the crowns in 1603, meant that he was exposed to the opportunities and hazards presented by the closer relationship between Scotland, England, Ireland, and Wales. His career stands as a testament to the huge potential of the regal union and a telling example of one who was crushed by the forces unleashed by the wars in Charles's British dominions. As a nascent Briton, with interests in all three kingdoms, he was as vulnerable as Charles. He was tried, condemned, and executed by the same authority that dispatched the king a mere five weeks before.

On the scaffold Hamilton declared that his religion was of the established church of Scotland, but that he 'was not of a rigid opinion' (*The Several Speeches of Duke Hamilton Earl of Cambridge, Henry Earl of Holland, and Arthur, Lord Capel*, 1649, 3), and this statement could be taken as a motto for his life. Although he possessed strong and deeply held views, he was a politician to his fingertips. To Hamilton 'rigid' meant adhering to a view or policy that circumstances had rendered unviable, impracticable, or destructive to the health of the state. He exemplified a political code best described as the politics of the possible. This increasingly distanced him from Charles, whose 'rigid' opinions on episcopacy and covenant scarcely altered during the civil wars. At each stage of the crisis of the three kingdoms, Hamilton possessed enough insight to see what would be required to achieve settlement. He told the king in June 1638 that his rigid stance could result in the loss of his three crowns, and this demonstrates remarkable vision in a man lampooned as craven and irresolute. His oscillation between king and covenant in Scotland, and king and parliament in England, was more a desperate attempt to find the middle ground and to preserve himself than vacillation and weakness, of which he stood accused by many of his contemporaries. Yet he was on many occasions indecisive to the point where he became physically ill, but it was often when faced with insurmountable problems such as Charles abandoning London in 1642. Neither could it be said that he was an accomplished military commander, where the need for a ruthless streak and strong leadership, such as that possessed by Gustavus Adolphus and Cromwell, was often a prerequisite for success.

There is no standard view of Hamilton from contemporaries. Edward Hyde, first earl of Clarendon, described him as duplicitous and self-serving, while Robert Baillie admired him as one of Scotland's 'great men' (*Letters and Journals of Robert Baillie*, 2.383). Marchamont Nedham, a hack journalist of the English Commonwealth, saw Hamilton's every public action as a ploy to seize the Scottish crown. The Revd George Garrard, one of Viscount Wentworth's correspondents, condemned Hamilton as selfish and tenacious when there was the glimmer of personal profit to be acquired. In the summer of 1643 Sir Robert Poyntz reflected the impression of a number of observers of Hamilton and his great rival the earl of Montrose thus: 'Montrose … is a generous spirit, but hes not so good an head-piece as Hamilton' (Bodl. Oxf., Carte MSS, v, 366–367). Sir Phillip Warwick's pen-portrait, looking back to what Hamilton was like in the 1630s, is probably as accurate a contemporary picture as can be retrieved:

> [Hamilton] had a large proportion of his Majestie's favour and confidence, and knew very dextrously, how to manage both, and to accompany the King in his hard chases of the stagg, and in the toilsom pleasure of a racket: by which last he often filled his own, and emptied his Master's purse; and tho' he carried it very modestly and warily, yet he had a strong influence upon the greatest affairs at Court, especially when they related unto his own Country … Hamilton was the polar or northern starr. (Warwick, 104–5)

Hamilton also polarized the opinion of his two biographers. His first biographer, Gilbert Burnet, was motivated by a desire to remedy the prevailing view of his time that the duke had been a 'foul and base' character imbued with 'ingratitude and treachery', which Burnet believed to be 'the greatest injustice in the world' (Burnet, ix). Hilary L. Rubinstein, writing 300 years after Burnet, cast Hamilton as 'the arch-apostle of compromise' compelled by 'vague prejudices or self-interest' who in the final analysis was 'the most disastrous adviser a monarch ever had' (H. L. Rubinstein, *Captain Luckless*, 1976, 174). In comparison with his more frank and direct younger brother, however, contemporaries too were agreed that Hamilton was reserved and subtle. JOHN J. SCALLY

**Sources** Morton MSS, 1583–1662, NL Scot., MSS 78–80; correspondence and papers of the dukes of Hamilton, 1627–1809, MSS 1031–2 · Grantham, Lincolnshire, Tollemache MSS · Traquair House, Innerleithen, Peeblesshire, Traquair MSS · NA Scot., Hamilton MSS, correspondence, MS GD 406/1 · NA Scot., Hamilton MSS, financial papers, MSS GD 406/2/F1, F2 · NA Scot., Hamilton MSS, legal papers, GD 406/2/L1, L2 · NA Scot., Hamilton MSS, state papers, MSS GD 406/2/M1 and 406/2/M9 · Hamilton red books (original royal letters and holograph), NA Scot. · Lennoxlove, East Lothian, Hamilton MSS, esp. account books for earl of Arran, 1620, F1/25/books 1–17, and 'An inventory of the writs and evidents belonging to my Lord Marquis of Hamilton, earle of Arran and Cambridge, Lord Aven, Arbroath and Innerdale, 1640' [in the possession of the duke of Hamilton] · Warks. CRO, Feilding of Newnham Paddox papers, CR 2017/C1, C2, C5, C7, C72, R12 · G. Burnet, *The memoirs of the lives and actions of James and William dukes of Hamilton and Castle-Herald* (1677); repr. (1852) · *CSP dom.*, 1625–49 · [J. Hamilton, duke of Hamilton], *The Hamilton papers: being selections from original letters … relating to … 1638–1650*, ed. S. R. Gardiner, CS, new ser., 27 (1880) · S. R. Gardiner, ed., 'Hamilton papers: addenda', *Camden miscellany, IX*, CS, new ser., 53 (1892) · *The manuscripts of the duke of Hamilton*, HMC, 21 (1887) · J. H. McMaster and M. Wood, eds., *Supplementary report on the manuscripts of his grace the duke of Hamilton*, HMC, 21 (1932) · *Report on the manuscripts of the earl of Mar and Kellie*, HMC, 60 (1904) · H. Paton, ed., *Supplementary report on the manuscripts of the earl of Mar and Kellie*, HMC, 60 (1930) · *The letters and journals of Robert Baillie*, ed. D. Laing, 3 vols. (1841–2) · *The letters of John Chamberlain*, ed. N. E. McClure, 2 vols. (1939) · R. Monro, *Monro his expedition with the worthy Scots regiment (called Mac-Keyes regiment) levied in August 1626* (1637) · *APS* · *JHL* · *Reg. PCS*, 2nd ser. · P. Warwick, *Memoirs of the reign of King Charles I* (1702) · R. Marshall, *The days of Duchess Anne* (1973) · audited account by Justinian Povey, NA Scot., GD 406/2/F1/138

**Archives** NA Scot., MSS · NL Scot., papers and letters · NRA, priv. coll., political and diplomatic corresp. and papers · priv. coll., MSS | NRA, priv. coll., corresp. to first earl of Traquair · Warks. CRO, letters to Lord Feilding

**Likenesses** D. Mytens, oils, 1629, Scot. NPG [*see illus.*] · attrib. A. Van Dyck, oils, *c.*1635, Lennoxlove · A. Van Dyck, oils, 1640, Vaduz Castle, collections of the prince of Liechtenstein · oils, 1640 (after A. Van Dyck), Scot. NPG · A. Van Dyck, oils, before 1649, Lennoxlove · R. White, engraving (after A. Van Dyck), repro. in Burnet, *Memoirs*, frontispiece · oils (after D. Mytens), Scot. NPG

**Wealth at death** estate in considerable debt on death; was owed £22,853 by the king: audited account by Justinian Povey, NA Scot., GD 406/2/F1/138

**Hamilton, James** (*d.* 1666), Church of Scotland minister, was the second son of Gawen Hamilton, merchant and landowner, and Helen Dunlop; he was the grandson of Hans Hamilton, vicar of Dunlop, Scotland. His father drowned when he was young but he received a good education at Glasgow University from his uncle Archibald Hamilton. Impressed by his learning and ability, another uncle, James Hamilton, Viscount Claneboye, took him to Ireland to manage his large estates in co. Down. During the 1620s James became influenced by Robert Blair, a local minister of strongly Presbyterian views, and decided to become a clergyman. He was ordained on 22 November 1625, and Claneboye installed him as minister at Ballywalter, co. Down.

In 1634 Hamilton attended the clerical convocation of

the Church of Ireland in Dublin, which overturned the articles of the church of 1615 and endorsed a hard-line episcopalian stance. Such developments made it increasingly difficult for Hamilton and other Presbyterians to conform to the state church. Matters came to a head in July 1636 when Henry Leslie, bishop of Down and Connor, required his clergy to subscribe to the five canons of the 1634 clerical convocation. Five ministers, including Hamilton, refused to comply, at which Leslie challenged them to a public debate at Belfast on 11 August. Hamilton acted as the dissenters' representative at the disputation with Leslie, which occurred before a large gathering of local notables and ranged widely over a number of doctrinal issues. Both men delighted in the arcane technicalities of theology and the debate was conducted in good spirit. However, under pressure from John Bramhall, bishop of Derry, Leslie abruptly adjourned proceedings and on 12 August deposed the five ministers from their posts. Disillusioned, Hamilton and 140 other Presbyterians set sail for America on 9 September 1636, but were driven back by storms and decided to remain in Ireland. However, in 1637 the five deposed ministers fled to Scotland after the government ordered their arrest. Hamilton became minister at Dumfries near Nidsdale, where he preached against the crown's attempts to introduce the Anglican rite into Scotland. In 1638 he was chosen as a member of the general assembly of the Presbyterian kirk in Glasgow, despite the protests of the Scottish bishops.

By summer 1642 the Irish rising had transformed the situation in Ireland beyond all recognition and the general assembly of the Scottish kirk sent Hamilton and Blair to Ulster to oversee the establishment of Presbyterianism there. From September to December 1642 they toured co. Antrim and co. Down preaching, receiving people into the faith, and imposing penance on repentant episcopalians. After they had returned to Scotland, on 27 March 1644 the general assembly of the kirk authorized Hamilton and three other ministers to tender the covenant in Ulster. During his sojourn in Ulster, Hamilton remained mostly in his old parish at Ballywalter, having by that time married Elizabeth, daughter of David Watson, minister of Killeavy, near Newry. On his return journey to Scotland a frigate, commanded by the Gaelic Catholic leader Alasdair MacColla, captured his ship on 3 July 1644. Hoping to secure the release of his father Coll Ciotach through an exchange of prisoners, Alasdair imprisoned Hamilton and seven others in Mingary Castle on the island of Ardnamurchan. The kirk was amenable, but the marquess of Argyll, captor of Coll Ciotach and mortal enemy to the MacDonnells, was not. Argyll's forces unsuccessfully besieged Mingary Castle from 8 August to 6 October 1644, during which time Hamilton and his fellow prisoners suffered terribly, being all but deprived of food and water. Even after the siege was raised conditions within the prison were clearly poor, and John Weir, a Presbyterian minister, and Hamilton's father-in-law both died in confinement during the course of 1644–5. Meanwhile, the kirk was making increasingly frantic efforts to arrange Hamilton's release, which bore fruit on 29 April 1645 when he was exchanged for two of Alasdair's kinsmen.

Hamilton returned to Dumfries and soon afterwards received a posting in Edinburgh. In 1651 he became chaplain to Charles II, before being captured by Cromwellian forces that August at Elliot, Forfarshire, and imprisoned in the Tower of London. He was released early in 1653 and returned to Edinburgh. Following the restoration of the monarchy in 1660 Hamilton was deprived of his ministry and moved to Inveresk. He died at Edinburgh on 10 March 1666. With his wife he is said to have had fifteen children, all of whom died in infancy except a son, Archibald, who became an important minister in the Presbyterian church in Ireland, and three daughters. TERRY CLAVIN

**Sources** W. Hamilton, *The Hamilton MSS* (1867), 11, 43, 74–9 • J. S. Reid and W. D. Killen, *History of the Presbyterian church in Ireland* (1866), 190, 195–201, 224–6, 375–82, 386–7, 391, 438–9, 459–65, 523–42, 555–60 • D. Stevenson, *Alisdair McColla and the highland problem* (1980), 108–9, 114, 124, 138–40, 195–6 • P. Adair, *A true narrative* (1896), 12, 16, 42–6, 58, 95–101, 102, 117–18 • R. Blair, *Memoirs of Robert Blair* (1844), 68, 130 • J. McBride, *A sample of jet black prelatic calumny* (1649) • J. B. Leslie, *Biographical succession lists of the clergy of the diocese of Down* (1936), 93 • *CSP dom.*, 1651–2, 48, 515; 1652–3, 158, 161

**Hamilton, James** (1610–1674), bishop of Galloway, was born in August 1610, and baptized on 30 September at Canongate, Edinburgh, the second son of nine children of Sir James Hamilton, of Broomhill (*d.* before 1647), and his wife, Margaret, daughter of William Hamilton of Udston. He was educated at Glasgow University, graduating MA in 1628. On 26 August 1635 he married Margaret (1619/20–1667), only daughter of Alexander Thomson, minister of St Giles, Edinburgh. They had seven sons and seven daughters. Hamilton was ordained minister of Cambusnethan in Hamilton presbytery in December 1635 by Archbishop Patrick Lindsay of Glasgow. He was deposed for contumacy on 14 April 1639, in effect for signing the petition of the bishops and their adherents against the assembly of 1638, but following his repentance he was reappointed by the general assembly on 28 August 1639. The committee to whom his case was referred reported that 'he was a young man of good behaviour, and well beloved of his parish, and guilty of nothing directly but the subscribing of the declinature' (*DNB*). Perhaps to avoid future suspicion he became a loyal adherent of the winning side. As Gilbert Burnet wrote:

> he was always believed episcopal. Yet he had so far complied in the time of the covenant, that he affected a peculiar expression of his counterfeit zeal for their cause, to secure himself from suspicion; when he gave the sacrament, he excommunicated all that were not true to the covenant. (*Bishop Burnet's History*, 1.241)

In June 1648, when the duke of Hamilton was given a regiment of horse by the king and parliament, he requested James Hamilton to become its chaplain. The latter was thus committed to the engagers. Following the Restoration Hamilton's views became clear. He was one of a number of preachers in early 1661 who preached the king's authority and the church's right to tithes. When it became evident later in 1661 that even the more moderate of the presbyterians, the resolutioners, would decline to become bishops, Hamilton was summoned to London on 14 August 1661, and presented to the see of Galloway on 14 November 1661. In a controversial move he was consecrated in Westminster Abbey on 15 December. The bishops returned to Scotland, entering Edinburgh 'with great pomp' on 8 April 1662 (*Diary of Mr John Lamont*, 145). Hamilton held regular synods at Wigtown or Kirkcudbright. His wife predeceased him on 16 April 1667. In 1669 his elder brother John, who had been created first Lord Belhaven in 1647, made over to him the estate at Broomhill. Hamilton died on 14 August 1674, being succeeded in the property by his son James, an advocate, who died shortly afterwards.

G. W. Sprott, *rev.* Stuart Handley

**Sources** *Fasti Scot.*, new edn, 7.346–7 • J. Birnie, *Account of the families of Birnie and Hamilton of Broomhill* (1838), 48–63 • J. Buckroyd, *Church and state in Scotland, 1660–1681* (1980) • *IGI* • A. Sympson, *The register of the synod of Galloway from October 1664 to April 1671* (1856) • I. B. Cowan, *The Scottish covenanters, 1660–1688* (1976) • *Bishop Burnet's History of his own time*, new edn, 1 (1838), 241–2 • GEC, *Baronetage* • *Report of the Laing manuscripts*, 1, HMC, 72 (1914), 271–2 • *The diary of Mr John Lamont of Newton, 1649–1671*, ed. G. R. Kinloch, Maitland Club, 7 (1830), 145 • *The life of Mr Robert Blair … containing his autobiography*, ed. T. M'Crie, Wodrow Society, 11 (1848), 378, 394

**Hamilton, James** (*c.*1640–*c.*1720), painter, is said to have been born in Scotland; the date of his birth is estimated from that of his eldest son. The latter was born in Brussels about 1664, and it has been suggested that James Hamilton was a fervent royalist who disapproved of the protectorate, and who left Britain to escape Cromwell's government. If so, the restoration of the monarchy seems not to have tempted him back to his homeland, since he is thought to have stayed in Brussels, where he is said to have died about 1720. Only one work can securely be attributed to the artist: a still life of four game birds and a hunter's bag in the National Gallery of Scotland in Edinburgh, signed and dated 1695. By the standards of contemporary Flemish still life it is very amateurish. Hamilton's three sons, all painters, spent their lives working in Germany and Austria, where they took on the name de Hamilton. **Philipp Ferdinand de Hamilton** (*c.*1664–1750) was appointed court painter at Vienna in 1705, a post he held until his death. In some sources, including the *Dictionary of National Biography*, his first names are given in reverse order. He specialized in game pieces, hunting and animal scenes. **Johann Georg** [John George] **de Hamilton** (1672–1737) was also made a court painter at Vienna, in 1718, after a career in Berlin. He specialized mainly in horse painting, although he also produced game pieces, like his eldest brother. **Karl Wilhelm** [Charles William] **de Hamilton** (*c.*1668–1754) worked at Baden-Baden, before becoming court painter at Augsburg. His speciality was painting scenes of reptiles and insects on forest floors, a genre developed by Otto Marseus van Schrieck in the 1650s. Another de Hamilton, Franz, was possibly James's brother. Like Karl Wilhelm, he painted forest floors, as well as *trompe-l'œil* pictures, game pieces, and animal scenes. He worked in Cleve, Potsdam, Hanover, and Munich between 1661 and 1695. Lionel Cust noted in the *Dictionary of National Biography* that James Hamilton has been erroneously associated with the family of Hamilton of Inderdovat (now Tayfield), Fife, and afterwards of Murdieston, Lanarkshire.

L. H. Cust, *rev.* Paul Taylor

**Sources** Thieme & Becker, *Allgemeines Lexikon* • T. Crombie, 'Scotsmen at the court of the Habsburgs: the de Hamilton family of painters', *The Connoisseur*, 145 (1960), 225–7 • S. A. Sullivan, 'Hamilton, Philipp Ferdinand de', *The dictionary of art*, ed. J. Turner (1996) • artist's file, archive material, Courtauld Inst., Witt Library

**Hamilton, James, fourth duke of Hamilton and first duke of Brandon** (1658–1712), nobleman, was born in Hamilton Palace on 11 April 1658 and baptized that same day. His father was William Douglas [*see* Hamilton, William, third duke of Hamilton (1634–1694)], and his mother was Anne *Hamilton (1632–1716), third duchess of Hamilton in her own right, daughter of James *Hamilton, first duke of Hamilton, and his wife, Lady Mary Feilding, whose father was William, first earl of Denbigh.

**Birth and upbringing** Called after his maternal grandfather, James, like his twelve brothers and sisters, took his mother's surname, for the second duke of Hamilton's entail stipulated that her husband and children were to 'take on, use and weir the name and armes of the house of Hamilton' (Notes by third duke on the second duke's entail, Hamilton archives at Lennoxlove, RH 55/32/4; also 1693 memorandum for the fourth duke, RH 89/36/21).

As the eldest son James Hamilton bore the title of earl of Arran, and his birth was particularly significant, coming as it did after all the traumas suffered by the family during the civil wars. Since their marriage in 1656, Duchess Anne and her husband had worked painstakingly to retrieve her inheritance, a process completed after the Restoration in 1660. Their ambitious plans for the future centred on their heir, and the duchess was doubly attached to her first-born son because, small, dark and swarthy, he bore a close resemblance to her dead father. The duke and duchess gave careful thought to Arran's upbringing. Following the accepted practice of the Scottish peerage they decided to send him to the local school at Hamilton when he was about six. They also appointed John Bannantyne of Corehouse to be his governor. When he was eleven they anxiously consulted Sir Robert Moray as to what they should do next. In the end, however, they ignored Moray's advice that they should keep the boy at home with his governor, and instead they sent him to the grammar school in Glasgow, where he and Bannantyne lodged with Gilbert Burnet, at that time professor of theology in the university there. In 1671 Arran entered Glasgow University to read Greek and Latin, French, theology, geography, and logic. He had a singing-master, attended a dancing-school, and also learned to handle pike and musket. Both Burnet and Bannantyne complained that, high-spirited and thoroughly spoilt, he persistently wasted his time in low-born company, spent too much money, and lied to cover up his misdemeanours. 'Pray consider', his mother wrote to him in her usual forthright manner, 'what credit it will be to you that after four years being at the college you come from it a dunce' (NA Scot., GD 406/C1/5878).

In spite of their misgivings, the duke and duchess then

James Hamilton, fourth duke of Hamilton and first duke of Brandon (1658–1712), by Jacob Ferdinand Voet, 1678

sent Arran off on the grand tour. Whatever his deficiencies, the future head of the house of Hamilton must lack no advantage. After sailing to La Rochelle at the end of October 1675 the earl, his governor, and a page travelled first to Angers, where Arran made the most of his new found freedom. Bannantyne had to send home regular accounts of expenditure and when the duke of Hamilton read how much his son was spending on balls, masquerades, unnecessary clothes, and tennis he was furious. He replaced Bannantyne with James Forbes, who he hoped would be stricter, and wrote to warn Arran that if he did not regulate his expenditure better, 'your abode abroad will not be long, for it was to improve you in useful breeding you was sent there, and not to follow vanity and folly' (NA Scot., GD 406/C1/5878). Forbes escorted Arran to Blois, where they spent a few weeks before moving to Paris. After some carefully planned sightseeing the earl was enrolled in Monsieur Faubert's academy in the rue St Marguerite, off the faubourg St Germain. He passed the winter of 1676–7 there, and when Arran was presented at court Forbes was able to report with satisfaction that Louis XIV actually smiled at the earl, 'which it is not very common to that king to do' (NA Scot., GD 406/5993). A few days before term ended on 4 May 1677 an unexpected letter came from the duke, instructing Forbes to take his charge to Italy.

Not many Scots on the grand tour went as far as Rome, in part because of the expense, in part because of presbyterian disapproval, but it was fashionable in English aristocratic circles and so Arran must have the opportunity. After a summer spent in Bourges they set off for Turin, where Arran was welcomed by the duke and duchess of Savoy, who treated him like a son. Travelling by way of Venice and Florence he and Forbes reached Rome on 20 February 1678. Arran visited all the antiquities, made friends with Philip Howard, known as Cardinal Norfolk, and sat for his portrait to Ferdinand Voet. He had by now developed a passion for paintings which was to remain with him for the rest of his life.

It was more than two years since Arran had left home; the duke of Hamilton had already spent more than £1200 sterling on his son's travels, and he decided that it was high time that his heir came home, found a sensible Scottish wife, and settled down to produce a family. Reluctantly the earl returned to Paris, crossed the channel in the yacht *Merlin* and made his way to London, where his father was waiting. Although at first the duke reported that 'he carys himself discreetly and I use him as a comarade' he was soon telling his wife that their son had neglected his studies abroad, wasted his time in bad company, and 'as for his sincerity, I fear he retains too much of the way he had when he was a child'. Worst of all, the earl made it clear that returning to settle down in Scotland was, as his father remarked wryly, 'much the same to him as to go to the gallies' (NA Scot., GD 406/C1/8130).

**Life at court** After a fleeting visit to Hamilton Palace at the end of the year Arran hurried back to court where Charles II, on 25 January 1679, obligingly made his presence necessary by appointing him to be a gentleman of the bedchamber. Free at last from the oversight of father and governor Arran ran up huge debts, fought in duels, and engaged in numerous affairs, fathering at least three illegitimate children, James Abercrombie and Katherine and Mary Ruthven. In response to repeated parental urgings he also entered into marriage negotiations with a long series of aristocratic English ladies, but always withdrew before any contract could be finalized. In 1683 he was overjoyed when Charles II sent him to France as ambassador-extraordinary to congratulate Louis XIV on the birth of his son, Philippe, duc d'Anjou, and instead of returning home when his mission was over he stayed on. In the spring of 1684 he was made one of the French king's three aides-de-camp, along with the dauphin and the duc de Gramont, and told Lord Dartmouth proudly that this was 'an honour that no stranger ever had but myself' (*Dartmouth MSS*, 1.115–16). He also boasted that he had 'in prospect one of the finest ladies in France with a million' (ibid.).

Arran accompanied Louis XIV on two campaigns and when not on duty lived at Versailles in an apartment lent to him by the duc de Bouillon, swimming each day with the dauphin and walking with the king. He would probably have remained there indefinitely, but on 6 February 1685 Charles II died, and he was recalled to London. As a close friend of the new king, James VII and II, he was in July 1686 given command of a regiment of horse in the force raised to suppress the duke of Monmouth's rebellion. Two years later James made him a knight of the newly revived Order of the Thistle. The earl's financial problems were by now, however, acute. His debts amounted to some £10,000 sterling, and his father had long since told him bluntly, 'untill you marry and thereby you bring in a portion [dowry] to the family, I will nether medle in your transactions nor concern myself in your debts' (NA Scot., GD 406/C1/7068).

**Marriage** Arran's old friend and patron Robert Spencer, third earl of Sunderland, at this point came to the rescue by suggesting that the earl marry his eldest daughter, Lady Anne Spencer (1667/8–1690). Sunderland had his own reasons for suggesting the match. As James II turned increasingly to his Roman Catholic favourites Sunderland's power had been slipping away. The king was, however, relying on the duke of Hamilton in his dealings with Scotland and so Sunderland believed that he would retrieve his own position if he could form an alliance with the duke. The main difficulty lay in Arran's reluctance to commit himself to matrimony. Attractive and intelligent Lady Anne might be, but the earl did not want a wife. When, however, Sunderland suggested that they could work together to extract the best possible financial terms from the duke of Hamilton asking, for example, for a clause binding the duke to pay his son's debts, Arran was immediately won over.

On his arrival in London the duke of Hamilton was none too pleased to discover that negotiations had begun without his knowledge, but he was so relieved that Arran was actually considering a suitable bride that he gave his approval and set about scrutinizing the proposed conditions for the contract. He discussed the details with his wife, who remained at Hamilton, confiding to her that their son was 'in as much perplexety of thinking to be maried as I have been in fears not to be married to you' (NA Scot., GD 406/C1/7755). Although he was affronted by many of Arran's demands, the dowry of £10,000 sterling, which he would control, reconciled him to these difficulties and the contract was finalized at last. During the ceremonial signing, on 5 January 1687, the duke noticed that Lady Anne 'seamed in some concern … which I thought no wonder of, for she cannot but know his wildness and she is not twenty till nixt summer' (NA Scot., GD 406/C1/7806). He went across to speak some encouraging words to her, for he liked her, and felt that if anyone could reclaim his son from his unfortunate way of life, it would be Lady Anne. She still looked very grave when the bishop of Rochester conducted the marriage in the dining-room of her father's lodgings at Whitehall on 10 January 1688, a wedding described by the diarist John Evelyn as being of 'extraordinary splendour' (*The Diary of John Evelyn*, ed. W. Bray, 2 vols., 1966, 2.273). However, against all expectation, she was won over by her husband's charm and fell deeply in love with him. Their first child, a daughter whom they named Anne, was born in London on 18 January 1689, only to die less than a month later.

That was the least of the couple's problems, for on 5 November 1688 William of Orange had landed in England. Arran had accompanied James VII and II to Salisbury and remained loyally by his side until his embarkation for France. The earl then returned to Whitehall, where he was shown into the new monarch's presence and greeted him defiantly, saying that he came by the command of the king his master. William promptly sent him to the Tower of London. Later claims that the third duke had advised the king to do so were based on a comment in Swift's *Memoirs of Captain Crichton* (*Works*, 12.75) and could have been true. His father may have seen this as the only way of restraining his heir from further folly but, on the other hand, it is unlikely that he would have sought such a public humiliation for the family.

Although Arran was released on a technicality when he was about to be tried in April 1689, he made no secret of his Jacobite sympathies and was incarcerated in the Tower again a few weeks later on suspicion of conspiring with the French court. It was almost a year before his father managed to negotiate his release, whereupon the earl promptly announced that he would rather stay in prison than face his irate creditors. The duke eventually managed to have him smuggled out one Sunday morning when no one was about, and Arran rode at once for Scotland, his heavily pregnant wife and his exasperated father following behind in a coach.

Arran and his countess went to live at Kinneil Castle in Linlithgowshire, which was small, but conveniently near Edinburgh. It seemed that, at last, he would be content to settle in Scotland, but all future plans were shattered when Lady Arran gave birth to a second daughter, Mary, but died soon afterwards of puerperal fever. Genuinely distraught, the earl left the baby with his mother and returned to London, where he began an affair with Charles II's illegitimate daughter, Lady Barbara Fitzroy. Nine months later she had his son, whom they named Charles *Hamilton (1691–1754). Arran also seems to have sought solace in a more unexpected quarter. When Patrick Home later gave a public oration on the earl in the College of Edinburgh, he recalled Arran's diligent researches in libraries after the death of his wife. The earl had made volumes of notes on Scottish history, which, said Home, 'wee hope will transmitt his fame to posterity' (NA Scot., GD 406/C1/5902). He had apparently inherited his father's fascination with historical research.

Unwelcome at court and still in financial difficulties, Arran was forced to spend 1691–2 at Kinneil, but by 1693 he was back in London once more. The death of his father in 1694 made no difference to his position, for the family titles and estates remained with his mother, and so he spent much of his time in a renewed pursuit of wealthy heiresses. All his relatives were urging him to remarry and produce an heir, and Duchess Anne now held out the inducement that, if he did take a suitable wife, she would resign her titles to him. She would, of course, remain duchess of Hamilton and she would keep entire control of her estates, but he would have the title of fourth duke of Hamilton and he would be able to represent the family in the Scottish parliament. Thus encouraged, Arran began making serious approaches to Elizabeth Gerard (*c*.1682–1744), the only child and heir of the late Digby, fifth Baron Gerard. Elizabeth was just thirteen when she came to his attention and he was nearing forty, but she was very rich, having inherited extensive properties in Lancashire and Staffordshire. Negotiations dragged on for more than three years but on 9 July 1698 Duchess Anne resigned her titles. The next day William III and II created her eldest son fourth duke of Hamilton; by 16 July 1698 the marriage contract had been signed and the wedding took place on 17 July at Bushy Park. Among James's and Elizabeth's seven children was Lady Susanna *Keck, political manager.

**Fourth duke of Hamilton** The new duke of Hamilton sat in the Scottish parliament for the first time on 21 May 1700, and spoke in an important debate on the Darien scheme. His mother had been the first person to subscribe to the company trading to Africa and the Indies, investing £3000. The Scots blamed William III and II and the English for its subsequent disastrous failure, and the duke earned great popularity by his apparently patriotic stance. In 1702 Queen Anne succeeded William, and when negotiations began for a union of the Scottish and English parliaments the duke led the opposition. He spoke and voted against every article of the treaty of union, moving friend and foe alike to tears with his eloquence, but whenever any really decisive action was required of him he suffered a series of illnesses which seem to have been either diplomatic or psychosomatic. 'Everie one is sparring ether to speak or writ of your brother Hamilton to me', his mother told her eldest daughter, Katherine, on 7 September 1705, adding three days later, 'itt passes my comprehension to find out a tolerable face for his actings this session of parliament and I am so ashamd on his behalfe that I know nither what to say or how to look' (Atholl MS 45 V 119, 120).

Hamilton's supporters were bitterly disappointed by his erratic behaviour, which was occasioned not only by his awareness that his wife had brought him extensive estates in the south, but by his belief that if James VII and II were restored, he himself could become an acceptably protestant king of Scots because of his Stewart ancestry. When he went so far as to draw up a protest in the name of his mother and himself, declaring that the treaty of union should in no way prejudice their right to the crown of Scotland, not only Duchess Anne but the entire family were mortified. She refused to sign, telling him that the petition would do no good and would 'only expose me to be laughed at' (NA Scot., GD 406/C1/9744).

Hamilton seemed at first to support Cunningham of Eckatt's plan for an armed rising of the western shires, but suddenly sent a message to all those involved announcing a postponement and the scheme fell through. He then summoned the country gentlemen to Edinburgh to petition the queen for a new parliament and abruptly decided that unless their address insisted on a Hanoverian succession he could have nothing to do with it; in the ensuing arguments that plan also collapsed. When the twenty-second article of the treaty was being debated it was expected that the marquess of Annandale would move for the settlement of the Hanoverian succession. Everyone assumed that the motion would be defeated, and the duke told his friends that when that happened he would enter a protest and they would all walk out. On the day, however, he first refused to go to parliament at all, claiming that he had toothache, and then, although he was eventually persuaded to attend, he declined to present the counter-resolution. Torn between his old loyalties to the house of Stewart, his desire to please Queen Anne, and his personal ambitions, he felt unable to do anything in case he made the wrong decision.

After the Act of Union was passed Hamilton remained in Scotland until the autumn of 1707, complaining that he could not afford to live anywhere else and hinting that his mother should invite him to stay permanently at Hamilton Palace. He nagged her until she gave him £8000 sterling and then, leaving his two sons and three surviving daughters with her, to be brought up at her expense, he departed with his petulant young wife for the south. During the Jacobite invasion of Scotland in January 1708 he was arrested on his English estates, but he was soon released after he promised to support the whigs in the election of the Scottish representative peers. He himself became a representative peer that summer, and moved to London, renting a large house in St James's Square. He never visited Scotland again.

On the impeachment of Dr Sacheverell, Hamilton abandoned the whigs and was rewarded by the incoming tory administration with the lord lieutenancy of Lancashire. Still preoccupied with his claim to the throne, he was very conscious that Queen Anne's children had all died, and he seems to have decided to ingratiate himself with her in the hope of being recognized as her heir. In 1709 he astonished his friends by calling his third son Anne in her honour. In December 1710 he became a privy councillor and on 11 September 1711 was created a peer of Great Britain with the titles of duke of Brandon and Baron Dutton. There then ensued a long wrangle over whether a Scottish representative peer could sit in parliament by virtue of having been made a peer of Great Britain, and he never actually did so. He was also embroiled in a complicated lawsuit with his wife's family. One of the clauses in his marriage contract with Elizabeth had stated that he would pay her mother £10,000 for her expenses in bringing up his wife. He failed to hand over the money and Lady Gerard sued him. When she died, leaving her daughter only 5s. and a diamond necklace, Lady Gerard's brother Charles, second earl of Macclesfield, continued the legal proceedings, eventually passing on the Gerard claims to his own heir Charles, fourth Baron Mohun. By 1711 Hamilton was insisting that Mohun owed him £43,979 12*s*. 7*d*., the alleged profits from the Gerard estates during Elizabeth's minority together with the value of her parents' personal property.

In autumn 1712 Queen Anne appointed Hamilton to be her ambassador to France, and on 26 October conferred upon him the Order of the Garter. This alarmed the whigs, who feared that he was being sent to negotiate the succession of Prince James Francis Edward Stuart to the British throne, but instead of carrying out his plans and going to Paris at once, Hamilton delayed his departure at the last moment and on 13 November encountered Lord Mohun at the law courts. Mohun was drunk, they quarrelled violently, and the following day Mohun sent him a message challenging him to a duel. The duke accepted. Accompanied by his illegitimate son, seventeen-year-old Charles Hamilton, he left his St James's Square house between seven and eight o'clock on the morning of 15 November 1712. He and Mohun met in Hyde Park. The duke had been involved in many duels in the past but he was fifty-four now, stout and out of condition, and his opponent was a much younger man with an unsavoury reputation for violence. The signal was given. Fighting with his sword in his left hand, for he was ambidextrous, the duke wounded Mohun fatally in the chest. Even as Mohun fell dying he managed to slash at his adversary's unprotected right arm, severing an artery. The duke staggered away, collapsed against a tree, and died there a few moments later. His furious friends declared that the fatal blow had been struck, not by Mohun himself, but by his second, General George MacCartney. Excited pamphleteers elaborated on the murder theory, MacCartney fled, sightseers flocked to Hyde Park to carry away as macabre souvenirs fragments of the tree where the duke had died, and Thackeray later used the duel in his novel *Henry Esmond*. The death of the duke was no mere fiction, of course, but a dreadful reality for his family. His widow shed not a single tear but stormed and raged against her dead husband as well as against Mohun and MacCartney, while Duchess Anne sat motionless in her chair in Hamilton Palace, overwhelmed by the tragedy of her son's wasted life. Hamilton was buried in Hamilton parish church. MacCartney was eventually tried for murder and acquitted, but there is little doubt that he had played a sinister part in the whole affair, fanning the flames of Mohun's hatred of Hamilton.

Lively and engaging, a lover of fine art, and an enthusiastic Francophile, James Hamilton might have had a very different career had he not been weighed down by his devoted parents' demands on him. It was their tragedy and his that, unable to live up to their expectations, he took refuge in subterfuge and evasion, told people whatever they wanted to hear, and was all too easily led into an extravagant and profligate way of life by his self-seeking friends. Swift thought him 'a worthy good-natured person, very generous but of a middle understanding', Macky described him as 'brave in person, with a rough air of boldness; of good sense, very forward and hot for what he undertakes, ambitious and haughty, a violent enemy, supposed to have thoughts towards the crown of England' (*Works*, 17.252), and Gilbert Burnet remarked, 'I am sorry I cannot say so much good of him as I could wish, and I had too much kindness for him to say any evil without necessity' (*Bishop Burnet's History*, 6.130). 'He has ben', Duchess Anne had said sadly, 'many a sore hart both to his father and me' (Atholl MS 45, V, 122).

ROSALIND K. MARSHALL

**Sources** correspondence, NA Scot., Hamilton archives, GD 406 • accounts, memoranda, inventories, etc., Lennoxlove, East Lothian, Hamilton archives • R. K. Marshall, 'The house of Hamilton in its Anglo-Scottish setting in the seventeenth century', PhD diss., U. Edin., 1970 [incl. a 5-vol. calendar of the duke of Hamilton's archives] • R. K. Marshall, *The days of Duchess Anne* (1973) • V. Stater, *High life, low morals: the duel that shook Stuart society* (1999) • R. K. Marshall, '"Scarce a finer seat in Scotland": Kinneil Castle and the 4th duke of Hamilton', *Scottish country houses, 1600–1914*, ed. I. Gow and A. Rowan (1995), 35–42 • the duke of Atholl's archives, Blair Castle, Perthshire, Atholl muniments • *The examiner's account of a duel fought by the duke of Hamilton and my Lord Mohun* (1712) • C. Innes, ed., *Munimenta alme Universitatis Glasguensis / Records of the University of Glasgow from its foundation till 1727*, 3, Maitland Club, 72 (1854), 465 • J. S. Gibson, *Playing the Scottish card: the Franco-Jacobite invasion of 1708* (1988) • *The manuscripts of the earl of Dartmouth*, 3 vols., HMC, 20 (1887–96), vol. 1, pp. 115–16 • *The works of Jonathan Swift*, ed. W. Scott, 2nd edn, 12 (1824), 75; 17 (1824), 252 • *Bishop Burnet's History* • *Scots peerage*

**Archives** Hamilton archives, Lennoxlove, East Lothian, MSS, account books • NA Scot., corresp. • NL Scot., letters and papers • NRA Scotland, priv. coll., corresp. | Blair Castle, Perthshire, Atholl MSS • NA Scot., Edinburgh register of testaments, 16 June 1722 • NA Scot., letters to duke of Montrose • NL Scot., corresp. with the first and second marquesses of Tweeddale

**Likenesses** J. F. Voet, oils, 1678, priv. coll. [*see illus.*] • D. Paton, miniature, 1693, priv. coll. • J. B. Medina, oils, 1703, Royal College of Surgeons, Edinburgh • G. Kneller, oils, priv. coll. • P. Mignard, oils (James Hamilton, the fourth duke?), priv. coll. • W. Wissing?, oils, Hardwick Hall, Derbyshire • oils (after G. Kneller), Scot. NPG

**Wealth at death** £19,612 Scots: will, 16 June 1722, NA Scot., Edinburgh register of testaments

**Hamilton, James, sixth earl of Abercorn** (*c*.1661–1734), soldier and politician, was the eldest son of James Hamilton (*d*. 1673) and Elizabeth (*c*.1637–1709), daughter of John *Colepeper, Baron Colepeper (*bap*. 1600, *d*. 1660); his grandfather was Sir George *Hamilton (*d*. 1679) [*see under* Colepeper, John], the fourth son of the first earl of Abercorn. Following his father's death during a naval engagement in 1673, Hamilton appears to have attended Westminster School until he was appointed a groom of the bedchamber on 18 April 1680; the office had once been held by his father, and Hamilton retained it until the death of Charles II. According to a letter from the bride's father to the earl of Arran, Hamilton married Elizabeth (*c*.1668–1754), only daughter and heir of Sir Robert Reading, first baronet, of Dublin on 21 January 1684, although the marriage licence was dated the 24th. Reading observed that Hamilton had a warrant as Lord Bellamont, but that it would not be executed until 'some further matter be done for him' (*Ormonde MSS*, 7.183).

Hamilton embarked on an army career, serving as a colonel under James II, but he joined William of Orange in 1688, and played a significant role in supplying Londonderry, under siege from Jacobite forces, in 1689. Several of his family were on opposite sides in this conflict, and the fourth earl of Abercorn was killed at the battle of the Boyne and his lands forfeit to the crown. The fifth earl, his brother, the protestant Charles Hamilton, had his attainder reversed and received the lands from the crown in 1691. James Hamilton served as an Irish MP in 1692 and 1695 for County Tyrone, being described as a whig or 'country party' man (Malcolmson, 46). He succeeded Charles as sixth earl of Abercorn in Scotland and Baron Strabane in Ireland in June 1701, and was created Baron Mountcastle, co. Tyrone, and Viscount Strabane in September of that year.

Hamilton was an Irish privy councillor, and present in Dublin between 1701 and 1703. He took his seat in the Irish House of Lords on 21 September 1703. In 1704 he was in

London, pestering Robert Harley for an introduction for his son to the court of Hanover. On 3 October Hamilton took his seat in the Scottish House of Lords, and although he did not vote in the division on 4 November 1706 on the first article of the treaty of union between England and Scotland, he did vote in favour of ratifying the treaty on 16 January 1707. He appears to have moved into the tory camp in 1707–9, for in the Irish parliament in 1709 he was a thorn in the side of the ministry. In 1710 he was in London, possibly hoping for an Irish office through the agency of Jonathan Swift, and he seems to have been a tory during the ministry of Robert Harley, though one with a strong Hanoverian bias. In 1712–13 the peace negotiations with France saw Abercorn keen to press his claim to the French dukedom of Châtelherault, or to receive compensation for not blocking the claim of the dukes of Hamilton. He was active in the 1713 general election, supporting the tory interest in co. Tyrone but the whigs in co. Donegal, because they were his kinsmen. He again attended the Irish privy council in 1714–15.

In 1720 Abercorn was among the backers of a Bank of Ireland, a proposal which fell foul of the Irish House of Commons in the wake of the South Sea débâcle. Abercorn appears to have been a defender of William Wood's patent to coin copper coins in Ireland, as Swift believed him to be the author of at least one tract on the matter. In his declining years Abercorn seems to have settled in London, where he was consulted by Lord Egmont on such matters as the rights of precedence for Irish peers in England, the Irish linen manufacture, and the Georgia corporation.

Abercorn died in London on 28 November 1734, aged seventy-three, and was buried on 3 December in Westminster Abbey. Upon hearing the news Lord Egmont confided to his diary that 'he was a man of great honour, and of as much public spirit as I ever was acquainted with, but passionate and of no great depth of understanding, yet very passable with mankind by reason of his virtues' (*Egmont Diary*, 2.135).

Hamilton was survived by three of his nine sons, the youngest of whom, Charles *Hamilton, was a notable landscape gardener, and by five daughters. He was succeeded as seventh earl of Abercorn by his son **James Hamilton** (1686–1744), born on 22 March 1686, and styled from 1701 Lord Paisley. He married, between 26 March and 28 April 1711, Anne (1690–1776), daughter of John Plumer of Blakesweare, Hertfordshire. A fellow of the Royal Society from 10 November 1715, he published *Calculations and Tables Relating to the Attractive Power of Loadstones* (1729), and translated a work by Pepusch on harmony. He was made a privy councillor in England on 20 July 1738 and in Ireland on 26 September 1739. He died in Cavendish Square, London, on 11 January 1744, and was buried on 16 January with his father. STUART HANDLEY

**Sources** *Scots peerage*, 1.53–8 • J. L. Chester, ed., *The marriage, baptismal, and burial registers of the collegiate church or abbey of St Peter, Westminster*, Harleian Society, 10 (1876), 180, 342, 386 • *Old Westminsters*, 1.417 • J. C. Sainty and R. Bucholz, eds., *Officials of the royal household, 1660–1837*, 1: *Department of the lord chamberlain and associated offices* (1997), 115 • Walpole, *Corr.*, 42.88–90 • *Manuscripts of the earl of Egmont: diary of Viscount Percival, afterwards first earl of Egmont*, 3 vols., HMC, 63 (1920–23), vol. 1, pp. 103, 412, 458; vol. 2, pp. 115, 135 • *The manuscripts of the marquis of Ormonde*, [old ser.], 3 vols., HMC, 36 (1895–1909), vol. 2, pp. 461–83 • *Calendar of the manuscripts of the marquess of Ormonde*, new ser., 8 vols., HMC, 36 (1902–20), vol. 7, p. 183 • J. Swift, *Journal to Stella*, ed. H. Williams, 2 vols. (1948); repr. (1974) • *The letters of Joseph Addison*, ed. W. Graham (1941) • A. Malcolmson, 'The politics of "Natural Right": the Abercorn family and Strabane borough, 1692–1800', *Historical Studies*, 10 (1977) • P. W. J. Riley, *The Union of England and Scotland* (1978), 330 • R. E. Burns, *Irish parliamentary politics in the eighteenth century*, 1 (1989), 77, 120–29 • GEC, *Peerage*

**Archives** PRO NIre., Abercorn MSS • PRO NIre., corresp. and papers | TCD, corresp. with William King

**Likenesses** Harding, stipple, 1800, BM, NPG; repro. in J. Adolphus, *The British cabinet*, 2 vols. (1799–1800)

**Hamilton, James, seventh earl of Abercorn (1686–1744).** *See under* Hamilton, James, sixth earl of Abercorn (*c*.1661–1734).

**Hamilton, James** (*c*.**1710–1783**), colonial governor, was born at Henberry plantation in Kent county, Maryland, the youngest child of Andrew *Hamilton (*c*.1676–1741) and his wife, Anne Brown, *née* Preeson (*d*. 1736). His father was a Scottish immigrant and his mother the daughter of a wealthy Maryland Quaker planter. About 1715–16 the family moved to Philadelphia; there and perhaps in England James received his education. He began practising law in Philadelphia in the early 1730s.

In 1734 Hamilton joined his father, the speaker, in the Pennsylvania assembly, as representative of Lancaster county. The Hamiltons were nominal Anglicans, supported by those of that denomination and by Presbyterians. They supported the aims of the Penn proprietors. In 1739 they retired and the opposition Quaker party, revitalized by financial and defence controversies, took control of the house and prevented James Hamilton's re-election in 1740–42. In the 1742 Philadelphia election riot he had a brief scuffle with Quaker leader Israel Pemberton jun. at the polling place. In 1745 he was appointed to the provincial council.

The Penns commissioned Hamilton governor of Pennsylvania in 1748, hoping that as a native he would be well received. At first he successfully compromised with the assembly on desired legislation. However, by 1750 he and the house had clashed over its challenges to executive authority. In February 1752 the assembly reopened the continually vexing matter of paper money, but Hamilton rejected its first proposed emission, and refused to compromise. He was bound by secret proprietary instructions not to assent to any paper money or excise bill unless the governor was accorded a veto over appropriation of the proceeds. Because he felt trapped between proprietary orders and an assembly that threatened to become completely unco-operative, in February 1753 he announced to Thomas Penn that he would resign. The proprietors temporarily voided their instruction in March, and Hamilton approved a £20,000 emission. In November 1753 the proprietors reinstated their instruction, and Hamilton was compelled to reject all further paper money issues, including an August 1754 appropriation for arms and ammunition for frontier defence to counter French incursions in western Pennsylvania.

After he was replaced in October 1754, Hamilton continued to serve on the council and to advise his successors. Thomas Penn reappointed him governor in July 1759, and permitted him to approve bills taxing the proprietary estates. The assembly would still not agree to let the governor share in the appropriation of money raised, nor grant the proprietary estates the lowest possible tax assessment. Even Indian war in June 1763 did not shake the determination of the house to insist on its conditions. Despite his failure to work out a compromise, Hamilton fared better with the assembly on this occasion than he had in 1748–54. In October 1763 he was succeeded by proprietor John Penn.

Hamilton largely retired from activity, partly because the proprietors would not adopt his conciliatory views. Although he was senior member of the council, his attendance was sporadic. He served as interim governor on two occasions, in 1771 and 1773.

During the pre-revolutionary disputes with Britain, Hamilton criticized British taxation and favoured compromise. He opposed intercolonial organization for resistance, and probably advised rejection of the June 1774 petition of Philadelphia inhabitants to call the assembly to consider colonial unity; he also advocated that the assembly in February 1775 petition the king separately from the continental congress. He ceased council attendance and quit political life after June 1775. During the revolution he remained in Pennsylvania; the new state government only briefly harassed him for supposed loyalist views. After the war Hamilton complained that he lost much of his estate because of hyperinflation, heavy taxation, and uncollectable debts, but he also acknowledged that his wealth ranked high among Americans. He died at Bush Hill, near Philadelphia, on 13 August 1783, and was buried at Bush Hill two days later. An old acquaintance estimated his estate, which included substantial landholdings, household goods, bonds, and cash, at £150,000. Hamilton never married, and his goods now passed to his nieces and nephews. BENJAMIN H. NEWCOMB

**Sources** C. W. Horle and others, eds., *Lawmaking and legislators in Pennsylvania: a biographical dictionary*, [2 vols.] (Philadelphia, 1991–), vol. 2 • J. H. Hutson, *Pennsylvania politics, 1746–1770: the movement for royal government and its consequences* (1972) • J. H. Peeling, 'Hamilton, James', *DAB* • E. J. McManus, 'Hamilton, Andrew', *ANB* • F. C. Nix, 'Andrew Hamilton's early years in the American colonies', *William and Mary Quarterly*, 21 (1964), 390–407 • J. W. Jordan, ed., *Colonial and revolutionary families of Pennsylvania* (New York, 1911); repr. (Baltimore, MD, 1978), vol. 1, pp. 319–24 • B. H. Newcomb, *Political partisanship in the American middle colonies, 1700–1776* (1995) • J. J. Kelley, *Pennsylvania: the colonial years, 1681–1776* (1980) • G. Mackinney and C. F. Hoban, eds., *Votes and proceedings of the house of representatives of the province of Pennsylvania*, 8 vols. (1754–76), vols. 3–6 [Oct 1726 – June 1776] • *The papers of Benjamin Franklin*, 3–5, ed. L. W. Labaree and W. J. Bell (1961–2); 8–10, ed. L. W. Labaree (1965–6) • J. E. Illick, *Colonial Pennsylvania: a history* (1976) • *Minutes of the provincial council of Pennsylvania* (1851–3) • A. Tully, *William Penn's legacy: politics and social structure in provincial Pennsylvania, 1726–1755* (1977)

**Archives** Hist. Soc. Penn., letter-book; MSS • Hist. Soc. Penn., official corresp.

**Likenesses** B. West, oils, Independence National Historical Park, Philadelphia

**Wealth at death** £150,000: Horle and others, eds., *Lawmaking and legislators*

**Hamilton, James, eighth earl of Abercorn (1712–1789)**, politician and landowner, eldest son of James *Hamilton, seventh earl of Abercorn (1686–1744) [*see under* Hamilton, James, sixth earl of Abercorn], and Anne (1690–1776), daughter of Colonel John Plumer of Blakesweare, Hertfordshire, was born on 22 October 1712 at Queen Square, St George the Martyr, Holborn, London. He matriculated from Christ Church, Oxford, in 1729. He was summoned to the House of Lords in Ireland as Baron Mountcastle on 23 March 1736, and succeeded his father as earl of Abercorn and Viscount Strabane in 1744. In 1761 and subsequent general elections, concluding with that of 1784, he was chosen as one of the sixteen Scottish representative peers.

In 1745 Abercorn purchased the Duddingston estate, outside Edinburgh, from the third duke of Argyll, where Sir William Chambers built a mansion for him in the 1760s. At Paisley, in Renfrewshire, the family's former property which he reacquired in 1764 from the eighth earl of Dundonald, he built the Place of Paisley, and then laid out a new town in the 1770s. He also had a seat at Witham, Essex, where he entertained Queen Charlotte in September 1761. Although an absentee landlord, he was later to build one of Ireland's most important neo-classical houses at Baronscourt, Newtownstewart, co. Tyrone. His surviving correspondence reveals a sympathetic, practical, and flexible approach to the problems of estate administration. He was a man of deeds rather than words. Horace Walpole nicknamed him 'his taciturnity, the Earl'. In spite of the bad press, however, he emerges as a man of succinctness rather than mere taciturnity. His letters to his own agents bristle with good sense, and are often pithy and even amusing.

Abercorn's advancement to the British viscountcy of Hamilton in 1786, with remainder to his nephew and heir, John James Hamilton, was in part a response to his own services and standing in Scottish public life. He was a patron of the arts, a builder, and the consolidator of the family's property and influence. He died, unmarried, at Boroughbridge, Yorkshire, on 9 October 1789, and was buried about three weeks later in the abbey of Paisley, in a vault beneath St Mirren's Chapel. He was succeeded by his nephew John James Hamilton, afterwards first marquess of Abercorn. DAVID HUDDLESTON

**Sources** GEC, *Peerage*, new edn • M. B. Hamilton, 'The later earls of Abercorn and Capt. the Hon. John Hamilton R.N.', PRO NIre., D 2152/1 • A. P. W. Malcomson, 'The Abercorn papers', PRO NIre., D 623 • *Scots peerage* • *GM*, 1st ser., 59 (1789), 961 • *The letters of Horace Walpole, earl of Orford*, ed. P. Cunningham, 9 vols. (1857–9) • Foster, *Alum. Oxon.*

**Archives** PRO NIre., corresp. and MSS

**Likenesses** T. Gainsborough, oils, 1778, Alte Pinakothek, Munich

**Wealth at death** more than £200,000 plus landed estates: *GM*

**Hamilton, James** (*bap.* 1740, *d.* 1827), physician and Methodist preacher, was baptized at Dunbar on 26 November 1740, which was possibly also the day of his birth, the fourth of six children of James Hamilton (1696–1768), surgeon, bailie, and kirk elder, and his first wife, Margaret, *née* Alston (1710?–1747). After his apprenticeship in medicine Hamilton served in the Royal Navy from 1759 to 1763 as a surgeon's first mate on the *Isis*, a fourth-rate ship of fifty guns. Here he became a Methodist. Invalided out of the navy he returned to medical practice in Dunbar, where he joined the Methodist Society, to which the kirk was then hostile, and on 13 October 1764 he married Frances Coats (*d.* 1779). He became a local preacher, a trustee of the new chapel, and John Wesley's adviser on Methodism in Scotland.

Elected a town councillor in 1770, Hamilton was given many responsibilities, including setting up a fire service, repairing the harbour, auditing the accounts, and fixing the rates. In 1778 he organized the town's defences against the threat of an American and French attack, and led its opposition to the proposed repeal of the laws inhibiting Roman Catholicism. His fellow councillors repeatedly failed to elect him bailie, probably on account of his Methodism. Frances died in 1779 leaving five children. Ill and depressed, James left the council.

In 1771, sponsored by John Rutherford and John Gregory, Hamilton had been awarded MD from Aberdeen, and in 1780 was elected a fellow of the Royal College of Physicians of Edinburgh. Wesley said 'None can advise you as to your body better than Dr Hamilton' (*Letters*, 6.241).

On 18 January 1785 Hamilton married Ann Annett (*bap.* 1763, *d.* 1788), from a Methodist farming family in Alnwick, and moved to Halhill Farm near Dunbar. Here he was the first in the country to grow and disseminate the Swedish turnip. But these were not years of financial success. He was pursued for debts inherited at his father's death and in 1788 his second wife died leaving him two more children. He left in 1789 for England, where he preached at the Methodist conference in Leeds, the first local preacher to do so. He pleaded, without success, for Methodism to remain a religious society.

At Leeds on 31 August 1791 Hamilton married Mary Iveson (1758/9–1828), the daughter of a prosperous cloth merchant. Thus his fortunes revived, and he was able to run a free clinic in the chapel vestry. Many Leeds Methodists wished to have worship in 'church hours', to which Hamilton was opposed, and there was ill feeling. He moved to London in 1795, becoming physician to the London Dispensary established for the poor, among whom James found lasting repute. From 1797 he served as a governor of the Scottish corporation, which assisted needy Scots in London with money and medical care.

Having accepted Methodism's becoming a church, as a revered elder statesman Hamilton pushed for adequate pensions for the itinerant preachers. He was a founder member of the Wesleyan Missionary Society. As a preacher and healer, his catholic spirit gained him widespread respect. He died at his London home, Artillery Place, Finsbury Square, on 21 April 1827, and was buried at City Road Chapel, London. His wife died in October of the following year.

MARGARET BATTY

**Sources** Dunbar kirk session records, NA Scot., B/18/48 • Dunbar town council minutes, NA Scot., B/18/13/22.5 and 6 • records of East Lothian and Merse Whale Fishing Company, known as the Greenland Company, NA Scot., B/18/42/4 • PRO, ADM 36/5875 • letters of James Hamilton, JRL, Methodist Archives and Research Centre • minutes of the quarterly meetings, Royal College of Physicians of Edinburgh • *Wesleyan Methodist Magazine*, 50 (1827), 359 • H. Moore, 'Memoir of James Hamilton, M.D.', *Wesleyan Methodist Magazine*, 52 (1829), 435–40, 507–12 • *Wesleyan Methodist Magazine*, 51 (1828), 863 • *The journal of the Rev. John Wesley*, ed. N. Curnock and others, 8 vols. (1909–16); repr. (1938) • *The letters of the Rev. John Wesley*, ed. J. Telford, 8 vols. (1931) • L. Tyerman, *The life and times of the Rev. John Wesley*, 4th edn, 3 vols. (1878) • *The letters of John Pawson*, ed. J. C. Bowmer and J. A. Vickers, 3 vols. (1994–5) • J. D. Comrie, *History of Scottish medicine*, 2nd edn, 2 vols. (1932) • *Transactions of the East Lothian Antiquarian and Naturalist Society* • J. Martine, *Reminiscences and notices of ten parishes in the county of Haddington*, ed. E. J. Wilson (1894) • A. Highmore, *Pietas Londiniensis: the history, design and present state in or near London* (1810) • M. Batty, *James Hamilton MD*, World Methodist Historical Society (1998) • parish register, baptism, Dunbar, Scottish Register House, 26 Nov 1740 • parish register, marriage, Dunbar, 29 June 1734, 13 Oct 1764 • parish register, deaths, Dunbar, 8 March 1779 [Frances Hamilton] • parish register, baptism, Alnwick, 3 Nov 1763 [Ann Hamilton] • parish register, marriage, Alnwick, 18 Jan 1785 • parish register, baptism, St Peter's, Leeds, 26 April 1759 [Mary Iveson] • parish register, marriage, St Peter's, Leeds, 31 Aug 1791 • memorial tablet, City Road Chapel, London

**Archives** JRL, Methodist Archives and Research Centre, letters, PLP 48. 45. 3–4 | Royal College of Physicians of Edinburgh, letters of application

**Likenesses** J. Kay, group portrait, etching, 1790, repro. in J. Kay, *A series of original portraits and caricature etchings*, new edn, 1 (1877), 277 • W. Ridley, engraving, repro. in *Arminian Magazine* (June 1794), frontispiece

**Wealth at death** £3100; plus two houses in Finsbury Square: will, 1826, Chancery Square

**Hamilton, James, senior** (1749–1835), physician, was born in Edinburgh, the son of Robert Hamilton (*d.* 1787), professor of divinity at the University of Edinburgh, and Jane (*née* Hay). He was educated at Edinburgh high school before studying medicine in Edinburgh and on the continent. Hamilton became a physician because he found it difficult to watch, let alone carry out, operations. He became a licentiate of the Royal College of Physicians of Edinburgh in 1771 and a fellow the following year. Hamilton was awarded an MD in 1771, though it is not clear by whom. From about 1773 he was physician to the Royal Infirmary and other Edinburgh hospitals, as well as to George Heriot's School. This was in addition to his private practice. It was said that Hamilton knew neither practical anatomy nor pathology, and some complained that he never explained what he was doing on the wards, though he was very kind to children and the poor. His *Observations on the Utility and Administration of Purgative Medicines* (1805; 8th edn, 1826; numerous foreign editions), became a best-seller: 'Never was any [publication] more cordially received by the profession' (*The Lancet*, 1, 1835, 382), though some thought Hamilton's passion for purgatives absurd. It was still considered a classic in 1850.

Hamilton was noted for his jokes and sense of fun, his

passion for fresh air and walking, and his mild eccentricities. He adopted old-fashioned manners and dress, being said to be the last to wear a three-cornered cocked hat. He became a fellow of the Royal Society of Edinburgh in 1783. He had a family by a 'privately contracted' marriage (*London Medical Gazette*), acknowledged only late in his life. He lived in St Andrew's Square, Edinburgh, next door to his younger namesake, James Hamilton (*d.* 1839), an obstetrician; they had 'Senior' and 'Junior' on their respective front doors. He died at his home on 27 October 1835.

G. T. BETTANY, *rev.* JEAN LOUDON

**Sources** *The Lancet* (5 Dec 1835), 381–3 · 'Biographical sketch of Marshall Hall', *The Lancet* (13 July 1850), 120–28, esp. 123 · *London Medical Gazette*, 17 (1835), 181 · F. Boot, 'Memoir of the life and medical opinions of John Armstrong MD, formerly physician to the Fever Institute of London', *British and Foreign Medical Review*, 1 (1836), 34–70, esp. 37–8, 68–9 · *British and Foreign Medical Review*, 1 (1836), 308 [notice of death] · *GM*, 2nd ser., 5 (1836), 102 · W. Newbigging, *Harveian oration for 1838 read at … Harveian Society of Edinburgh* (1838) · J. Kay, *A series of original portraits and caricature etchings … with biographical sketches and illustrative anecdotes*, ed. [H. Paton and others], 2 (1838), 79–81 · B. B. Cooper, *The life of Sir Astley Cooper*, 1 (1843), 164–5 · F. Bennet and M. Melrose, *Index of fellows of the Royal Society of Edinburgh: elected November 1783 – July 1883*, ed. H. Frew, rev. edn (1984)

**Archives** Royal College of Physicians of Edinburgh, corresp.

**Likenesses** etching, 1789?, repro. in J. Kay, *A series of original portraits*, 2 (1838), facing p. 80 · C. Turner, coloured mezzotint, pubd 1813 (after H. Raeburn), BM, NPG, Wellcome L. · J. Burnet, line engraving, 1816 (after H. Raeburn), Wellcome L. · T. Gaugain, mezzotint, 1825 (after J. Watson), Wellcome L. · W. Dyce, oils, 1832, Scot. NPG · A. Edouart, silhouette, Scot. NPG · J. Kay, caricature, etching, BM · portrait, Edinburgh Royal Infirmary · portrait, George Heriot's School, Edinburgh · soft-ground etching, Wellcome L.

**Wealth at death** believed wealthy: *London Medical Gazette*

**Hamilton, James, junior** (**1767–1839**), obstetrician, was one of the two sons of Alexander *Hamilton (*bap.* 1739, *d.* 1802). At the age of twenty-one Hamilton joined his father in his practice and was trained by him as his successor. A graduate of Edinburgh University, Hamilton was fellow of both the College of Surgeons and the Royal College of Physicians of Edinburgh. From 1798 to 1800 he helped his father in his duties as professor of midwifery and on his father's retirement in 1800 he succeeded him in the chair of midwifery. In 1815 Hamilton made an attempt to get midwifery recognized as a compulsory subject in the medical curriculum but he failed, owing to the opposition of Dr James Gregory and others. In 1824 Hamilton sought to achieve his aims through the town council, but he was reprimanded by the senate. This soured the relations between the town council and the senate, which were already under strain. Finally a royal commission was established in 1827 to investigate the matter. The question of the teaching of midwifery was settled in Hamilton's favour in 1830, and in 1832 he got the resolutions censuring him annulled.

Hamilton had a harsh voice and a broad Scottish accent, but he was a powerful and acute lecturer. Thanks to his great experience he had amassed a wealth of original observations and he attracted large classes, despite the fact that during most of his career his subject was not a course requirement. He supported the Lying-in Hospital largely at his expense and he had great influence over his patients. Physically Hamilton was far from remarkable. Short in stature and deceptively frail-looking, he had a quick, nervous step, a slight stoop, and downward look.

Hamilton had a reputation as a harsh judge of others. Sir Robert Christison called him a 'snarling, unfair, unfeeling critic' (*DNB*). Hamilton's fiery and uncompromising character made him many enemies. His quarrels with Andrew Duncan the elder and Thomas Charles Hope ended up in the law courts. In 1792 he became involved in a controversy over the publication of a pamphlet entitled *A Guide for Gentlemen Studying Medicine at the University of Edinburgh*, in which he and his father were praised and other professors were censured. The pamphlet had been published under the pseudonym J. Johnstone, esq., but James Gregory alleged that Alexander Hamilton was its author. Hamilton senior denied the charge, and he was exonerated by the senate. Gregory then accused James Hamilton of writing it. Hamilton's reply so angered Gregory that he thrashed him. Hamilton brought an action against Gregory and was awarded £100 damages.

Hamilton was the author of several works on midwifery. He also published numerous articles in medical journals, and controversial pamphlets. He died on 21 November 1839.

G. T. BETTANY, *rev.* ORNELLA MOSCUCCI

**Sources** *The life of Sir Robert Christison, bart, edited by his sons*, 2 vols. (1885–6), 1.86–8, 320, 321, 334–40 · A. Grant, *The story of the University of Edinburgh during its first three hundred years*, 2 vols. (1884) · J. Kay, *A series of original portraits and caricature etchings … with biographical sketches and illustrative anecdotes*, ed. [H. Paton and others], 2 vols. in 4 (1837–8), vol. 1, pp. 340–41

**Archives** BL, notes taken from lectures on midwifery given by him and his father, Add. MSS 45919–45920 · Royal College of Physicians of Edinburgh, corresp. and papers · U. Edin., shorthand notes taken from his lectures on midwifery

**Likenesses** portrait, repro. in Kay, *Series of original portraits*

**Hamilton, James** (**1769–1829**), teacher of languages, is thought to have been born at Dublin, where he was taught for four years at a school kept by Beatty and Mulhall, two Jesuit priests. For about three years before the revolution he was in business in France. In 1798 he was established as a merchant in Hamburg, where he had bought a house in the Neuen Burg, and applied for instruction in German to General D'Angeli, a French émigré. D'Angeli, without using a grammar, translated for him word for word a German book of anecdotes, parsing as he proceeded, and after about twelve lessons Hamilton found that he could read any easy German book. Beatty and Mulhall had had a somewhat similar system. Hamilton already knew Latin and some Greek, and was well read in French and English. He then moved to Paris, where, in conjunction with the banking house of Karcher & Co., he did considerable business with England during the peace of Amiens. When this ended he was 'detained', and his business in Hamburg and Paris was ruined.

As a result Hamilton went to New York in October 1815, intending to become a farmer and manufacturer of potash, but at the last moment changed his mind and determined to teach languages there on the principle of

D'Angeli. His plan, he says, was 'to teach instead of ordering to learn'. He began at once with a word-for-word translation, and left instruction in grammar until a later stage. His first pupils were three clergymen and Van Ness, judge of the district court, and his whole time was soon occupied in teaching. His pupils, numbering about seventy in his first year, read French easily in twenty-four lessons of four hours each. His charge was a dollar a lesson. In September 1816 he went to Philadelphia, where he gave his first lecture on the 'Hamiltonian System', and printed his first reading-book, chapters 1 to 3 of St John's gospel, in French, with an interlinear and analytical translation. Later several books claiming to follow his system were published without his authority, but did not, as he complained, make a teacher and a dictionary superfluous. Hamilton published many books with literal and interlinear English translations, including *The Gospels of St. Matthew and St. John* in Greek; a Latin *St. John's Gospel* and *Aesop's Fables*; another *St. John's Gospel*, this time in French, which ran to nine editions; Campe's *Robinson Crusoe* (in German); and a final *St. John's Gospel*, in Italian.

In 1817 Hamilton left Philadelphia for Baltimore, where his wife and daughters taught with him. The professors at Baltimore College ridiculed him in a play called *The New Mode of Teaching*, acted by their pupils. Hamilton went to the play, and then published it in a newspaper with his own comments. The college, he says, was soon without a pupil, while the Hamiltonian school at Baltimore had more than 160 pupils and 20 teachers. He was obliged by ill health and financial difficulties to leave the school to his teachers, and went on to Washington, and then to Boston, where he could obtain only four pupils. A professor at Harvard University attacked him as a charlatan, but a committee examined and approved his four pupils, and he soon had 200. Hamilton also taught teachers as well as pupils at the colleges of Schenectady, Princeton, Yale, Hartford, and Middlebury (Vermont). In 1822 he went to Montreal, and then to Quebec. At Montreal he instructed the gaoler, and successfully taught reading to eight ignorant English prisoners there (see Hamilton, 13, 14).

In July 1823 Hamilton went to London, where in eighteen months he had more than 600 pupils learning different languages, and seven teachers. He left his school to the teachers, and afterwards taught his system in Liverpool, Manchester, Edinburgh, Dublin, Belfast, and at least twenty other places. In London he taught at his house, 25 Cecil Street, Strand, and then in Gower Street, usually adults only. His best classes were those numbering from 50 to 100 pupils. From the middle of May to 16 November 1825 he had ten relatively uneducated parish-school boys to live in his house. At the end of this period they passed a fair examination in translating Latin (the gospel of St John and Caesar's *Commentaries*), and also in French and Italian. The expenses of this experiment were partly paid for by John Smith MP.

Hamilton's system and his plan of advertising (on which by 1826 he had spent more than £1000) were much attacked by schoolmasters and others, among them M. Santagnello, a professor of Italian. He deplored Hamilton's dismissal of other methods, questioned his claims regarding mixed-ability groups, and exposed gross errors in his teaching of Italian pronunciation and in his Italian translations (Santagnello, Introduction). A witty and detailed defence of Hamilton's system by Sydney Smith (a stranger to him) appeared in the *Edinburgh Review* for June 1826 (reprinted in *Essays by Sydney Smith*). Linking him with Locke, Smith found Hamilton's basic practice of beginning with an interlineal, literal translation more rapid, economical, and humane than the traditional grind through grammar and dictionary. Others who wrote on his system were Alberte, Donato (1827), Hartnell (1823), Schwarz (1838), Tafel, and Wurm. Hamilton died at Dublin, where he had gone to lecture, on 16 September 1829.

W. W. Wroth, *rev.* John D. Haigh

**Sources** J. Hamilton, *History, principles, practice, and results … of the Hamiltonian system* (1829) • *GM*, 1st ser., 99/2 (1829), 477 • S. Smith, 'Hamilton's method of teaching languages', *EdinR*, 44 (1826); repr. in *Essays*, ed. S. Smith [1828], 466–80 • M. Santagnello, *An impartial examination of the Hamiltonian system* (1827) • *BL cat.*, 138.393 • [S. B. L. P.], *The conversational method of teaching languages …, or, The systems of Hamilton and Jacotot improved* (1832)

**Hamilton, James, first duke of Abercorn** (1811–1885), landowner and politician, eldest son of James, Viscount Hamilton (*d.* 1814), and his wife, Harriet, daughter of the Hon. John Douglas, was born on 21 January 1811 in Seamore Place, Mayfair, Westminster. He succeeded as second marquess of Abercorn in 1818, on the death of his grandfather John James, first marquess. For some years he was under the care of his guardian, George Hamilton *Gordon, fourth earl of Aberdeen, who married Abercorn's mother in 1815. Abercorn was educated at Harrow School and at Christ Church, Oxford. He married on 25 October 1832 Lady Louisa Jane Russell (1812–1905), second daughter of John *Russell, sixth duke of Bedford, with whom he had six sons and seven daughters. All seven of his daughters married peers.

In the House of Lords, Hamilton voted against the Reform Bill of 1832. His maiden speech was not made until 1842, when he moved the address to the queen. In 1844 he was created a knight of the Garter. From 1846 to 1859 he held the office of groom of the stole to the prince consort. He was an active, considerate, and popular landlord on his very extensive Ulster estates, and kept the rents of his smaller tenants stable from 1837 to 1867.

In June 1866 Abercorn was appointed lord lieutenant of Ireland by Lord Derby, a post which he retained after Derby's resignation in February 1868. He adopted a firm policy against both Fenian and Orange agitation. In April 1868 at St Patrick's Cathedral the lord lieutenant presided at the installation of the prince of Wales as a knight of the Order of St Patrick. Abercorn resigned with the rest of Disraeli's ministry in November 1868, having been raised to the dukedom of Abercorn in the Irish peerage on 10 August 1868.

In the 1870s Abercorn chaired the informal meetings of Irish peers which gave effective organization to the Conservative Party in Ireland. Upon Disraeli's return to office

**James Hamilton, first duke of Abercorn** (1811–1885), by Bassano

in 1874, Abercorn again accepted the lord lieutenancy of Ireland. On the death of the duke of Leinster in 1874 he became grand master of the Irish freemasons, and he was also appointed lord lieutenant of Donegal. Abercorn's anxiety to place within the reach of Roman Catholic children the advantages of intermediate and university education was partly met by the Intermediate Education Act (1878) and the Royal University Act (1879). Abercorn was named first chancellor of the Royal University. In December 1876 he resigned the viceroyalty on account of his wife's health. In 1878 he went to Rome to present the Order of the Garter to King Umberto. He occasionally spoke in the House of Lords, and moved several important amendments to the Irish Land Bill of 1881, some of which were accepted by the government. At the opening of the session of 1883 he severely criticized the policy of the Liberal government.

The duke unsuccessfully claimed the dukedom of Châtelherault in France as heir male of the house of Hamilton. The duke was major-general of the royal archers, the queen's bodyguard of Scotland, a governor of Harrow, a privy councillor, and honorary DCL of Oxford and LLD of Cambridge. He died at Baronscourt, co. Tyrone, on 31 October 1885, and was buried there. He was succeeded in the dukedom by his eldest son, James *Hamilton, marquess of Hamilton. G. B. Smith, *rev.* Peter Gray

**Sources** K. T. Hoppen, *Elections, politics, and society in Ireland, 1832–1885* (1984) • F. S. L. Lyons, *Ireland since the famine* (1971) • *Annual Register* (1885) • *The Times* (2 Nov 1885) • *Freeman's Journal* [Dublin] (2 Nov 1885)

**Archives** PRO NIre., corresp. and papers | Bodl. Oxf., letters to Lord Beaconsfield • Glos. RO, letters to Sir Michael Hicks Beach • Herts. ALS, letters to Grimston family • Lpool RO, letters to fourteenth earl of Derby

**Likenesses** C. Silvy, carte-de-visite, 1861, NPG • F. Sargent, pencil drawing, 1870–80, NPG • Maclure & Macdonald, lithograph, 1877, NPG • S. C. Smith, oils, exh. 1877, Dublin Castle • Ape [C. Pellegrini], cartoon, repro. in *VF* (7 Nov 1885) • Ape [C. Pellegrini], cartoon chromolithograph, NPG; repro. in *VF* (25 Sept 1869) • Bassano, photograph, NPG [*see illus.*] • G. Cook, stipple and line engraving (after a photograph by A. Bassano), NPG • Lock & Whitfield, photograph, NPG • engraving, repro. in *Dublin University Magazine* (1874)

**Wealth at death** £144,784 15*s*. 10*d*. in UK: probate, 27 Feb 1886, *CGPLA Eng. & Wales* • £62,730 4*s*. 8*d*. in Ireland: English probate sealed in Ireland, 12 March 1886, *CGPLA Ire.*

**Hamilton, James** (1814–1867), Presbyterian minister, was born at Lonend, Paisley, Renfrewshire, on 27 November 1814, the eldest of six children of William *Hamilton (1780–1835), parish minister of Strathblane, Stirlingshire, and his wife, Jane King (*d*. 1855). He was educated privately and at Glasgow University, which he entered in 1828 and where he graduated MA in 1835. After his father's death his family settled in Edinburgh, where he attended the university classes of Thomas Chalmers and David Welsh. Licensed by the presbytery of Edinburgh in October 1838, Hamilton was briefly a missionary in the Rose Street district of St George's parish, Edinburgh, under Robert Smith Candlish, before he became an assistant in the parish of Abernyte, Perthshire, in February 1839. While there he became acquainted with the circle of evangelical ministers which included Robert Murray McCheyne, Andrew Bonar, and William Chalmers Burns.

On 21 January 1841 Hamilton was ordained minister of the Roxburgh church, Edinburgh. His ministry there had scarcely begun before he was approached to go to the National Scotch Church, Regent Square, London, to which he was inducted on 25 July 1841. At the Disruption of 1843 Hamilton and his congregation sided with the Free Church, a decision which put their property in jeopardy. The debt which the building bore made it safe from any claim from the established church, but it was not until 1860 that a way was found to regularize the congregation's position.

Presbyterian churches in London had difficulty in attracting and retaining ministers, but Hamilton found metropolitan life congenial, and his situation allowed him to pursue his extensive literary interests. From an early age he had aspired to write, and once settled in London he did so incessantly, aided by the extensive library which he inherited from his father. John Angell James described him as 'the Macaulay of Evangelical Literature' (Brown, 543). After his death his *Works* (1869–73) appeared in six volumes. At various times Hamilton also edited the *Presbyterian Messenger*, *Evangelical Christendom*, and *Excelsior*, a monthly magazine with a predetermined life of three years. His *Memoir and Remains of the Rev James D Burns M.A. of Hampstead* appeared posthumously. He also wrote for the *North British Review* and the *British and Foreign Evangelical Review*. His interest in botany was demonstrated in the articles which he contributed to Fairbairn's *Imperial Bible Dictionary*. The great work which he projected was a life of

Erasmus, to which end he learned Dutch in his few spare moments. Hamilton also served as convener of the foreign mission committee of the English presbyterian synod and was prominent in the preparation of the *Book of Psalms and Hymns*.

Never robust in health, Hamilton paid the first of a number of visits to German spas in 1846. He married, on 5 January 1847, Anne Hovenden Moore (*d.* 1886), with whom he had four daughters and two sons. In 1848 he received the degree of DD from the College of New Jersey. Hamilton's ministry at Regent Square was considered successful, though he lacked the voice and manner of a popular preacher. This was due in part to a fragile constitution, but his biographer conceded that 'his poetic temperament, and enthusiasm for nature, gave a tinge to his preaching, which now and then became a stumbling-block in the way of the more prosaic sort of Christians' (Arnot, 141). He became ill in the summer of 1867, died at his home, 48 Euston Square, London, on 24 November, and was buried in Highgate cemetery on 29 November.

LIONEL ALEXANDER RITCHIE

**Sources** W. Arnot, *Life of James Hamilton DD FLS* (1870) · R. Naismith, *Memoir of Rev. James Hamilton* [1896] · J. Hair, *Regent Square: eighty years of a London congregation* (1898) · *Fasti Scot.* · J. Julian, ed., *A dictionary of hymnology* (1892), 482 · *DNB* · *DSCHT* · T. Brown, *Annals of the Disruption*, new edn (1893)

**Likenesses** C. Baugniet, lithograph, BM, NPG · G. B. Shaw, stipple (after H. Anelay), NPG · medallion on monument; formerly in Regent Square church; probably destroyed, 1944 · photograph, repro. in Arnot, *Life*, facing frontispiece · portrait, repro. in Naismith, *Memoir*, facing frontispiece

**Wealth at death** £442 10s. 9*d.*: NA Scot., SC 70/1/137. p. 747 · under £8000—in England: probate, 11 Feb 1868, *CGPLA Eng. & Wales*

**Hamilton, James, second duke of Abercorn** (1838–1913), politician, was born at Brighton on 24 August 1838, the eldest son of James *Hamilton, second marquess and later first duke of Abercorn (1811–1885), and his first wife, Lady Louisa Jane Russell (1812–1905), second daughter of John, sixth duke of Bedford [*see* Russell, John]. He was educated at Harrow School and Christ Church, Oxford where he matriculated in 1857. In 1860, as viscount of Hamilton, he was elected Conservative MP for county Donegal, where part of the family estates lay (the seat was at Barons Court in co. Tyrone). The tradition of the Hamilton family was strongly tory despite their connection with the house of Russell. Five of the brothers sat in parliament, but, unlike the others, Hamilton took no active part in debates and held no ministerial position. He was, however, well connected: he accompanied his friend the prince of Wales to Russia in 1866; he was lord of the bedchamber to the prince from 1866 to 1886, and was groom of the stole from 1886 to 1901, when he was appointed as a special envoy, charged with bringing the news of Edward VII's accession to the courts of northern Europe. On 7 January 1869 he married Lady Mary Anna Curzon-Howe (1848–1929), daughter of Richard William Renn, the first Earl Howe. She was a lady-in-waiting to Queen Alexandra, and she and her husband had a family of seven sons and two

James Hamilton, second duke of Abercorn (1838–1913), by Mayall & Co.

daughters. In the general election of 1880, at the beginning of the Land League campaign, Hamilton lost his seat for county Donegal. In 1885 his father's death raised him to the dukedom; and in 1885–6 he was influential in forging a distinctive unionist political alliance, especially within parliament and his north-western home territory.

The new duke of Abercorn became the official figurehead of the Irish landlord class throughout the later phases of the land war. In 1888 he was president of the Irish Landowners' Convention and in 1892 he received the garter—as much as a mark of Lord Salisbury's sympathy for the Irish landed interest as of the queen's favour. He was arguably the senior Irish Conservative in the House of Lords, and as such was a prominent advocate of the loyalist interest. He chaired the Ulster Unionist convention of June 1892, and in 1893 presided at a great Unionist demonstration held in the Albert Hall in protest at the second Home Rule Bill. The affairs of his own territory interested him greatly, and when the Irish Local Government Act was passed (in 1898), he was elected to the Tyrone county council, and ultimately to its chair. Land purchase, though principally a Unionist initiative, initially left him cold, but he was surprised by the generosity of Wyndham's land act (1903) and was one of the first major landlords to sell to his tenants. Even with the abatement of serious land agitation, he continued to oppose home rule, and in 1905 he became first president of the Ulster Unionist council. Failing health meant that he was at the sidelines of the great Unionist campaign against the third Home Rule Bill, but he was able to make a last public appearance in Londonderry during Sir Edward Carson's campaign tour of 1912. He was too ill to join the other luminaries of the Ulster Unionist movement in publicly signing the solemn league and covenant; and on 3 January 1913 he died of pneumonia at home at Hampden House, 61 Green Street, Mayfair. He was buried at Barons Court on 7 January, and was succeeded by his eldest son, James, marquess of Hamilton, who had represented Londonderry City since 1900. His elevation caused a by-election which resulted in the loss of the seat to a home-ruler: this ended the lengthy Irish electoral career of the Hamilton family.

At root a great Irish landed magnate, the duke was concerned with the rights of the Irish landed interest and (as a natural consequence) with the maintenance of the union. Outside Ireland his main interest lay with the British South Africa Company, where he had a large shareholding, and where he became president after the resignation of Cecil Rhodes. If the duke epitomized landed Unionism, then he also illustrated—on a typically grand scale—the increasing disinvestment and disengagement of landlords from Irish affairs. ALVIN JACKSON

**Sources** PRO NIre., Abercorn MSS • private information (2004) [A. P. W. Malcomson] • A. Jackson, *The Ulster party* (1989) • D. C. Savage, 'The origins of the Ulster unionist party, 1885–6', *Irish Historical Studies*, 12 (1960–61), 185–208 • *DNB* • E. Hamilton, *Old days and new* (1923) • Lord F. Hamilton, *The days before yesterday* [1920] • GEC, *Peerage* • *Thom's directory* (1911) • *WW* (1903)

**Archives** Derbys. RO, papers relating to South Africa Company • PRO NIre., corresp. and papers, D623, T2541 | HLRO, corresp. with fifth Earl Cadogan • PRO NIre., letters to W. E. Bell

**Likenesses** E. Landseer, pencil drawing, 1843, Shugborough, Staffordshire • C. Laurie, line engraving, NPG • J. Massé, pastel drawing, Shugborough, Staffordshire • Mayall & Co., photograph, NPG [*see illus.*] • W. F. Osborne, oils, Masonic Hall, Dublin • photographs, PRO NIre., Abercorn MSS

**Wealth at death** £363,789 6*s*.: probate, 26 June 1913, *CGPLA Ire.* • £15,356 13*s*. 9*d*. in Ireland: probate, 15 Aug 1913, *CGPLA Ire.*

**Hamilton, James Alexander** (1785–1845), music theorist and compiler of instruction books, was born in London, the son of a dealer in old books, and was largely self-educated. He studied the books in his father's shop and acquired a knowledge of languages and particularly of music, sufficient not only to translate and edit important foreign publications such as Cherubini's *Counterpoint and Fugue* and treatises by Campagnoli, Czerny, Dussek, Vierling, Baillot, Rode, and others, but also to write and compile numerous useful instruction books and other works on musical theory and practice, many of which passed through a large number of editions. The best known of these is *Hamilton's Modern Instructions for the Piano Forte*, which reached its thirteenth edition in 1849, and is reported to have sold as many as 1728 editions by its fiftieth year. Hamilton's other publications included a *Catechism of the Violin* (c.1840, 19th edn 1889), *A Standard Tutor, for the Organ* (1842), *Sacred Harmony, a Collection of Three Hundred and Fifty Standard Psalm and Hymn Tunes, Ancient and Modern* (1843), *Method for the Double-Bass* (c.1845), and some posthumous editions, including *Hamilton's Modern Instructions for Singing* (1853), a sonatina for flute and piano (1896), and *Hamilton's Instructions for the American Organ and Harmonium* (1899).

Hamilton, although evidently industrious, appears to have been neither temperate nor provident. Edward Heron-Allen describes how 'he sold to the publishers, for a few pounds, the copyrights of a large quantity of musical works, which … might have kept him in affluence' (*De fidiculis bibliographia*, 1.143–4). Consequently he lived in difficulties and died in London on 2 August 1845, in extreme poverty. L. M. MIDDLETON, *rev.* DAVID J. GOLBY

**Sources** W. H. Husk, 'Hamilton, James Alexander', Grove, *Dict. mus.* (1954) • E. Heron-Allen, *De fidiculis bibliographia, being an attempt towards a bibliography of the violin and all other instruments played with a bow*, 2 vols. (1890–94) • *MT*, 1 (1844–5), 123

**Wealth at death** he died in abject poverty: Heron-Allen, *De fidiculis bibliographia*, 1.144

**Hamilton, James Archibald** (1748–1815), astronomer, was born in or near Athlone, co. Westmeath, Ireland, the son of Colonel Gustavus Hamilton and his wife, Jane Givardot. He attended the Royal School in Armagh, and entered Trinity College, Dublin, in 1764 (BA 1769). There he became actively interested in natural philosophy and astronomy. He began a career in the church in 1776 as rector of Kildress in the diocese of Armagh, and during this appointment set up an observatory in Cookstown, co. Tyrone, where his equipment included a transit instrument, two clocks—for solar and sidereal time—and an achromatic telescope. He was a member of the Royal Irish Academy and corresponded with the astronomer royal, Nevile Maskelyne, who presented Hamilton's observations of the transit of Mercury of 1782 to the Royal Society.

In February 1784 Hamilton resigned Kildress and was briefly rector of Dunbin, before his appointment in March as treasurer of Armagh Cathedral and rector of Creggan. In the same year he took BD and DD degrees at Trinity College. The patronage of Archbishop Richard Robinson, third Baron Rokeby, and Robinson's ambitions for improving Armagh, gave Hamilton an unexpected opportunity to pursue his interests in astronomy and natural philosophy, as he was able to influence the primate's initiative to found an observatory. By 1789, with the help and advice of Maskelyne, Hamilton was involved in negotiations with the leading London instrument maker Edward Troughton for the provision of a substantial equatorial instrument for a permanent observatory at Armagh, and on 31 July 1790, again with support from Maskelyne, he was appointed astronomer and keeper of the newly founded observatory and museum, an appointment ratified by the governors on 24 August. In March of the same year he had exchanged the office of treasurer for that of prebendary of Tynan, and exchanged this in turn for the prebendary of Mullabrack in December. Further evidence of the primate's favour is Hamilton's close involvement on his behalf over the next few years with the arrangements for setting up and endowing the observatory; during this period Hamilton was often resident in Bath, where Robinson generally remained in his final years.

Hamilton's first recorded observation at Armagh was on

18 July 1793, using a transit instrument, but after Robinson's death in October 1794 no further commissions were placed and Hamilton had to make the most of the instruments acquired. In addition to the Troughton equatorial, these included a 42 inch achromatic refractor by Dollond on an equatorial stand, a 10 foot Newtonian reflector by William Herschel, two regulator clocks by Thomas Earnshaw, a third clock by John Crosthwaite of Dublin, and a transit instrument by a local clockmaker, James Waugh. There were also instruments of natural philosophy, such as an air pump and an electrical machine, in keeping with the 'museum' aspect of the new institution, and Hamilton published a design for a new form of mountain barometer.

Hamilton struggled, without real success, to make the observatory's principal instrument, the Troughton equatorial, perform consistently, while he felt the lack of a first-class meridian instrument. The observing records show that he generally worked with the equatorial, leaving the transit observations to an assistant, who from February 1799 was the Presbyterian minister Robert Hogg. Together they established a routine of observational work that was steady and commendable, but scarcely innovative in practical astronomy. Hamilton's major contribution was the founding and equipping of the observatory; later he simply maintained a programme of work that kept it alive.

Hamilton married Jane Bunbury, and, although the wedding date is not recorded, their daughter Harriet was of an age to marry in 1797. A second daughter, Jane, was married in 1800. The summit of Hamilton's career in the church came in September 1804, when he was appointed dean of Cloyne. Hamilton died at the observatory on 21 November 1815, the occasion being noted in the transit book by his assistant Hogg. J. A. BENNETT

**Sources** J. A. Bennett, *Church, state, and astronomy in Ireland: 200 years of Armagh observatory* (1990) • Burtchaell & Sadleir, *Alum. Dubl.*, 2nd edn • J. B. Leslie, *Armagh clergy and parishes* (1911) • W. W. Webb, notes, Armagh observatory, MS M115 • H. Cotton, *Fasti ecclesiae Hibernicae*, 6 vols. (1845–78) • P. A. Wayman, *Dunsink observatory, 1785–1985: a bicentennial history* (1987) • T. R. Robinson, 'On correcting observations made with equatorial instruments', *Transactions of the Royal Irish Academy*, 15: Science (1825–8), 3–19 • C. A. Webster, 'Dean Hamilton of Cloyne', *Journal of the Cork Historical and Archaeological Society*, 2nd ser., 14 (1908), 92–3

**Archives** Armagh observatory | Armagh observatory, corresp. with Nevil Maskelyne

**Hamilton** [*née* Thomson], **Janet** (1795–1873), poet and essayist, was born near Carshill, Shotts, Lanarkshire, on 14 October 1795, the daughter of James Thomson, a shoemaker, and his wife, Mary Brownlee (*c.*1769–1852), a tambourer and descendant of covenanters. She spent most of her life in Langloan, near Coatbridge, where her parents moved when she was seven. Her mother taught her to read (but not to write), and the little girl read *Paradise Lost* and Allan Ramsay's *Poems* at eight. She later remarked that she 'could scarcely remember the time when her love of books was not her ruling passion' (Hamilton, *Poems, Essays, and Sketches*, 16). At nine, she too began to work as a tambourer, an occupation she followed until she began to lose her sight in the 1850s. At thirteen, she married the 25-year-old John Hamilton (1783/4–1878) in February 1809, and he later transcribed for her about twenty religious poems she composed in her head in her late teens. She seems to have set aside such endeavours for several decades after the birth of her third child, and the family Bible recorded the birth of ten children in all. Seven, at least—five boys and two girls—lived into adulthood.

At about fifty, Hamilton taught herself to write, and began shortly thereafter to contribute essays advocating temperance, women's education, and workers' self-improvement to the supplement of working-class writings published in conjunction with *Cassell's Working Man's Friend*. As she gradually lost her sight, she continued to dictate her poems in the late 1850s and 1860s to her eldest surviving son, James, and she published *Poems and Essays* (1863), *Poems of Purpose and Sketches in Prose of Scottish Peasant Life and Character in Auld Langsyne* and *Sketches of Local Scenes and Characters* (1865), and *Poems and Ballads* (1868). A memorial volume of *Poems, Essays, and Sketches* also appeared in two editions after her death (1880, 1885).

Fluent in standard English as well as her beloved Scots, Hamilton ardently supported European independence movements, and was an admirer of W. E. Gladstone. Of the 'United Kingdom', she also observed that

> It's England's meteor flag that burns
> Abune oor battle plains;
> Oor victories, baith by sea an' lan',
> It's England aye that gains,

and she pointedly apologized in 'A Plea for the Doric' for her 'Parnassian' efforts 'to busk oot my sang wi' the prood Southron tongue.' During her lifetime, Coatbridge had evolved into one of the most squalid iron-smelting centres in the British Isles, and she penned brilliantly sarcastic poetic descriptions of its filth, noise, greed, and despair in 'Oor Location', 'Our Local Scenery', and *Rhymes for the Times: IV—1865*. The quiet village environs of her youth lived on only in her 'ballads of memorie' and other retrospective poems.

Hamilton was initially suspicious of middle-class women's causes, but argued passionately that working-class mothers have a duty to teach their children (*Working Man's Friend*), decried the pervasive male bias of working-men's schools and colleges and the 'spirit of predominance and exclusiveness which, with a few exceptions, has met [working-class women] at every turn' ('Address to Working-Women', 1863), and remarked that a tambourer such as herself

> [w]ould have shoes on her feet, and dress for church,
> Had she a third of your pay.

Many of her vigorous denunciations of alcoholism—influenced, perhaps, by the ardour of her cousin William

> Wow, man! he hates and bans the bottle,
> An whaur Wull gangs, there gangs teetotal.
> (Young, 21)

—focused concretely on violence inflicted on children, wives, and aged parents; particular passages also suggest that she may have had some of her sons or close relatives in mind ('Intemperance and the moral law').

In Hamilton's more lyrical 'ballads of memorie', such as *Grannie's Tale: a Ballad of Memorie*, *Grannie's Crack Aboot the Famine in Auld Scotlan' in 1739–40*, and *Grannie Visited at Blackhill, Shotts, July, 1805*, aged storytellers recalled striking visions and other quasi-epiphanic events, and paid tribute to ancestors' steadfastness and resilience. In other poems, Hamilton personified Scotland as a grannie ('Auld Mither Scotland'), and sent her two thousand fellows at an 'annual supper given to the poor old women in City Hall, Glasgow' a message of hope and solidarity from 'the aul' blin' grannie that sings to ye noo!' (*The Feast of the Mutches*)

An unapologetic working-class Scottish survivor of the industrial revolution, Hamilton was grimly inured to urban dislocation and industrial blight, and she clearly benefited from middle-class anthologists' and newspaper editors' interests in 'people's literature'. This upright elderly woman's satires and defences of vernacular usage and oral history also deployed an impressively original array of poetic forms and linguistic registers, and her fiercely independent poems and essays flashed with compassionate retrospection and 'grandmotherly' wit.

Towards the end of her life, Hamilton's poems drew wide praise—an *Athenaeum* reviewer of her first volume, for example, called it 'a book that ennobles life, and enriches our common humanity' (June 1863)—and Queen Victoria gave her a civil-list pension in 1868. Visitors to the blind old woman often commented on her humour, wit, skill at ballad-recitation, and love of intellectual conversation. She died in Langloan after three years confined to her bed on 30 October 1873, and was buried on 4 November in Old Monkland cemetery, Coatbridge. Hundreds of mourners came from Glasgow and nearby towns to her funeral in Langloan, and memorial tributes and poetic imitations witnessed her influence on a generation of Scottish dialect and working-class poets. FLORENCE S. BOOS

**Sources** J. Hamilton, *Poems, essays, and sketches*, ed. [J. Hamilton] (1880) [incl. introductory essays by George Gilfillian and Alexander Wallace] · J. Hamilton, *Poems and essays of a miscellaneous character* (1863) [incl. introductory autobiographical sketch] · J. Young, *Pictures in prose and verse, or, Personal recollections of the late Janet Hamilton* (1877) · J. Wright, *Janet Hamilton* (1889) · D. H. Edwards, *One hundred modern Scottish poets, with biographical and critical notices*, 1 (1880) · *Glasgow Herald* (1 Nov 1873) · *Glasgow Herald* (5 Nov 1873) · family bible, Summerlee Heritage Trust

**Likenesses** portrait, repro. in Hamilton, *Poems, essays, and sketches*, frontispiece

**Hamilton, Johann Georg de** (1672–1737). *See under* Hamilton, James (*c.*1640–*c.*1720).

**Hamilton, Sir John, of Cadzow** (*d.* 1402?). *See under* Hamilton family (*per.* 1295–1479).

**Hamilton, John** (1510/11–1571), Roman Catholic archbishop of St Andrews, was an illegitimate son of James *Hamilton, first earl of Arran (1475?–1529). His mother, whose surname was Boyd, came from a well-respected Ayrshire family.

**Family background** John Hamilton was throughout his life a man of the Roman Catholic church. A child oblate at the Tironensian house of Kilwinning, in May 1525, aged fourteen, he was provided to the abbacy of Paisley (a Cluniac house), to be held *in commendam* until he was twenty-five. In the following year Clement VII appointed the provost of Hamilton collegiate church to manage the temporalities until John was twenty-one. In 1528 Hamilton entered St Leonard's College, St Andrews, and he studied there until 1535 when he attended parliament for the first time. The following spring he became abbot of Paisley, though not yet quite twenty-five years old. At some point he formed a lasting liaison with Grizzel Sempill (*d.* 1575), the daughter of his friend Robert, master of Sempill. She had previously been the wife of James Hamilton of Stanehouse, but they had separated and her husband subsequently remarried. She had six children with John Hamilton, two of whom, John and William, were legitimated on 22 January 1547 and 24 September 1548 respectively.

Hamilton owed his political importance to his membership of the foremost family in Scotland in the mid-sixteenth century, second only to the Stewarts themselves. His half-brother James *Hamilton, second earl of Arran, was next in line to the throne and wielded considerable power, largely because of the deaths in infancy of both the sons of James V. In June 1541 Hamilton was in France (where he was said to have protestant leanings), sent away by the king, who was mourning the recent death of Prince James and feared that the Hamiltons were growing too powerful. At the death of James V on 14 December 1542 only his infant daughter Mary stood between the Hamiltons and the Scottish throne. Arran was made regent and was keen to ally himself with Henry VIII, in order to enjoy English support against the queen dowager, Mary of Guise, the wealth of the Guise family, and the might of France. Bishop Lesley suggests that John Hamilton was at university in Paris, but his age makes this unlikely. He was not at the French court, and he may even have been negotiating with the English on his brother's behalf. Whatever his activities in France, when Hamilton was sent for by the regent it was in the expectation that he would come back to Scotland ready to champion the protestant cause and the diplomatic policies of Henry VIII.

**Involvement in politics** Arran had strong protestant sympathies and he used his position as regent to promote a preaching tour by two friars who were sympathetic to the new doctrines. He also had Cardinal David Beaton, archbishop of St Andrews, imprisoned on grounds both political and religious. He was chancellor of the realm, favoured the French alliance, and championed Catholic orthodoxy. Hamilton's return seems to have changed the configuration of Scottish politics. He went at once to see the imprisoned cardinal after which a stop was placed on the activities of Arran's two protestant preachers, Thomas Williams (or Guilliame) and John Rough. An act against heretical writings was promulgated. Hamilton also reminded Arran of family loyalties, moving him away from his pro-English advisers. In 1543 Beaton was reinstated as chancellor, and along with the dowager became a member of council. As part of this change in the balance of power Hamilton became keeper of the privy seal and treasurer of the kingdom. Henry VIII soon realized that the earl of Lennox, who also had claims to the succession, and his other Scots allies were not going to prevail, and he planned attack under the earl of Hertford. Two marriage plans for Mary were now in contention: the English hoped to wed her to Henry's son Edward, while the Hamiltons hoped to marry Mary to Arran's son, thus securing the succession for themselves.

John Hamilton's usefulness to the French-Catholic cause did not go unrewarded. George Crichton, bishop of Dunkeld, died at the beginning of 1544, and on 20 January Hamilton was admitted to the temporality of the see and presented to the pope, who was asked by the government to permit him to put off monastic habit and wear the episcopal one. In spite of opposition from Robert Crichton, the late bishop's nephew, the petition was successful, and on 17 December Hamilton was provided to the see, though still only in minor orders. Having taken his seat on the privy council in 1545 as bishop-elect, he was consecrated on 22 August 1546. He retained Paisley until 5 December 1553 when he resigned his abbacy while reserving to himself for life the fruits and the administration. In the meantime he remained active in public affairs. He besieged Tantallon Castle in April 1544, and was made an extraordinary senator of the college of justice on 5 November following. On 20 June 1546 he was legitimated. The disastrous Scottish defeat at the battle of Pinkie, on 10 September 1547, which thoroughly discredited the Hamilton-led regime, did not prevent John Hamilton's continued ascent in the ranks of the church. The primatial see of St Andrews had been vacant since the murder of Cardinal Beaton on 29 May 1546, and on 28 November 1547 Hamilton was translated thither, though he did not obtain effective possession until June 1549. Meanwhile he remained active militarily; in April 1548 he led French troops in an attack on Broughty Ferry.

**Church reform** Before Hamilton was fully in possession of his see a provincial church synod was held at Linlithgow in 1548, followed by another in Edinburgh in 1549. The invading English armies had brought vernacular scriptures with them, and the protestantism unleashed by Arran in 1543 had proved difficult to bring under control when government policy on religion changed. The execution of George Wishart in 1546 and the capture of the killers of Beaton in St Andrews Castle in July 1547 had gone a long way to calming the situation, but it was none the less felt that reform, of the clergy and the church, was required, both as an end in itself and to strengthen the Catholic cause against the protestants. A policy of reform also went hand in hand with a desire for the extermination of heresy, and the pursuit of heretics continued with the trial and execution of Adam Wallace in 1550.

The provincial councils summoned by Hamilton represent one of the most significant achievements of his episcopate. Intended simultaneously to bring the Scottish church into line behind his leadership, to deal with perceived abuses, and to counter the threat from protestantism, they were modelled on continental practice—for instance, on a council held at Cologne in 1536. Following the meeting of 1549 another council was held at St Andrews in 1552. In the latter year there appeared the text known as 'Hamilton's catechism', in fact the work of the English Dominican Richard Marshall, an exile from England who had been present at the 1549 council. As an exposition of Catholic doctrine it is a fascinating document that sheds light on Hamilton's ecclesiastical policy. Much has been made, for instance, of the catechism's silence on papal authority. The archbishop seems himself to have believed consistently in the hierarchical structure of the church as something ordained by God, but as a politician first and foremost he appreciated that for the catechism to attract the widest possible support it would have to leave some things unsaid. He oversaw the production of the catechism, and also that of a smaller pamphlet setting out the creed which was known as the 'Twopenny faith'. He also completed the foundation of St Mary's College at St Andrews and gave several books to its library.

By 5 March 1554 Hamilton had resigned as treasurer. He received a discharge for his arrears in office, more than £31,000 Scots, from Mary of Guise, who became queen regent on 12 April. Now out of the political limelight, Hamilton gave his attention principally to religious matters, visiting churches in disrepair from the wars of the 1540s, and pursuing writers of sacrilegious verse and religious iconoclasts. In 1557 he learnt that the earl of Argyll had appointed the protestant John Douglas as his private chaplain. Hamilton demanded Douglas's dismissal and offered to send a more appropriate instructor in religion if Argyll needed one. In 1558, when the regent was in France for her daughter's wedding, Walter Mylne was tried and executed at St Andrews for heresy, an unpopular decision for which Hamilton received some of the blame. Another provincial council was held in 1559, and Hamilton preached at Holyrood, where he confessed to being somewhat unused to such a task. The protestant reformers had now gathered sufficient force, and there was also enough anti-French sentiment for religious tensions to escalate into political conflict. The ailing regent could not control the situation, and on 6 July 1560 the treaty of Edinburgh led to the withdrawal of both French and English troops from Scotland. Hamilton met with Jean de Monluc, bishop of Valence, one of the commissioners who negotiated the treaty, and set forth the demands of the churchmen, the issue of religion not having been discussed. These demands were not met, and in August the Reformation Parliament assembled, with the archbishop in attendance. Arran's desire for his brother's conformity to protestantism found no corresponding zeal in John Hamilton. The latter accepted a need for reforms but did not assent to the evangelical confession of faith. He dissented from an act stating that any feu or tack granted after 6 March 1559 was to be treated as invalid.

**Supporter of Mary** The death of François II and the return of Mary to Scotland did not bring the hoped-for restoration of Catholicism. Nicholas de Gouda, a visiting Jesuit who arrived on 5 July 1562, despaired of religion in Scotland and particularly of the prelates, none of whom were prepared to lead a counter-reformation. Mary did not ratify the Reformation Parliament but she did devise a method of maintaining the reformed church without entirely dispossessing the old churchmen. Hamilton professed to be placed in straitened circumstances by this system of thirds of benefices, whereby prelates kept two-thirds of their livings and the crown took one-third, and even offered the crown money to be able to keep his patrimony. He seemed content to keep his office and his head and yet to try to continue as before. He celebrated mass at Easter 1562, but in 1563 was imprisoned in Edinburgh Castle for hearing confession and assisting at mass in Paisley. He only served two months' imprisonment before Mary ordered his release. In 1564 he distributed ashes on Ash Wednesday, and dissented along with the bishops of Moray and Dunkeld when parliament enacted that no one should celebrate mass outside the royal household.

As Mary grew in confidence in her role as the Roman Catholic monarch in a protestant country, Archbishop Hamilton began to regain power and influence. On 17 December 1566 he baptized the infant Prince James by Catholic rites and returned to the privy council, and by the 23rd he had had his consistorial jurisdiction restored to him. This was possibly in order to facilitate the annulment of the marriage of Mary and Darnley, though the latter's murder shortly afterwards rendered this unnecessary. Hamilton had acted as if he had consistorial rights previously, and he used this power again somewhat dubiously on 3 May 1567 to pronounce the divorce of James Hepburn, earl of Bothwell, and Lady Jane Gordon. He then attended Mary's marriage to Bothwell, even though it was conducted by protestant rites. On 29 June 1567 he signed the bond for the queen's liberty and was a consistent Marian thereafter. Yet he was unable to prevent Mary being forced to abdicate and the earl of Moray becoming regent. He was present on 29 July 1567 when James VI was crowned, having stipulated that the coronation should not prejudice the title of James Hamilton, duke of Châtelherault, and his heirs if the king died without issue.

**Disaster and death** Moray returned to Scotland from France on 11 August to head a new protestant regime. The Hamiltons had no prospects of favour under his regency, and their open opposition became war when on 2 May 1568 Mary escaped from Lochleven to Hamilton and was shielded by the archbishop. This stroke of good fortune turned to defeat at Langside on the 13th. Personal and political loss combined, for two of Hamilton's sons were killed and his hopes of regaining power lost. He advised Mary not to go to England but she ignored him. He was declared a traitor and put to the horn (outlawed). The sentence entailed the loss of his income from his ecclesiastical benefices, further weakening his family's cause and perhaps adding a personal dimension to the archbishop's resentment against the regent. On 23 January 1570 Moray was murdered by James Hamilton of Bothwellhaugh, John Hamilton's nephew, who took aim from his uncle's house in Linlithgow. The archbishop's retreat to Dumbarton Castle did not save him, and on 2 April 1571 he was captured by the earl of Lennox, now regent. He demanded a trial and was given one, at which he appears to have admitted his involvement in the murder of Moray, though not that of Darnley. On 6 April 1571 he was hanged in the market place at Stirling. The death of this old man was as stormy and violent as his life had been. His dedication to his church, his episcopal office, and his family was deeply connected in his mind to his love of his country. That his fellow Scots judged differently is also not to be doubted. Twice in his life he came close to achieving his goal of a Hamilton dynasty which would succeed the Stewarts, and twice he was foiled by the tenacious grip upon life of two Stewart infants, mother and son. JANET P. FOGGIE

**Sources** J. Herkless and R. K. Hannay, *The archbishops of St Andrews*, 5 (1915) • J. Dowden, *The bishops of Scotland … prior to the Reformation*, ed. J. M. Thomson (1912) • M. Merriman, *The rough wooings: Mary queen of Scots, 1542–1551* (2000) • *The works of John Knox*, ed. D. Laing, 6 vols., Wodrow Society, 12 (1846–64) • J. Durham and A. Ross, *Early Scottish libraries* (1961) • G. Donaldson, *Scotland: James V–James VII* (1987) • D. Calderwood, *The history of the Kirk of Scotland*, ed. T. Thomson and D. Laing, 8 vols., Wodrow Society, 7 (1842–9) • T. Thomson, ed., *A diurnal of remarkable occurrents that have passed within the country of Scotland*, Bannatyne Club, 43 (1833) • J. D. Marwick, ed., *Extracts from the records of the burgh of Edinburgh, AD 1557–1571*, [3], Scottish Burgh RS, 4 (1875) • M. Dilworth, *Scottish monasteries in the late middle ages* (1995) • *Scots peerage*, 4.362–3; 7.545–7 • J. K. Cameron, '"Catholic reform" in Germany and in the pre-1560 church in Scotland', *Records of the Scottish Church History Society*, 20 (1978–80), 105–17

**Hamilton, John, first marquess of Hamilton** (1539/40–1604), magnate, was the third son of James *Hamilton, second earl of Arran, later duke of Châtelherault (*c*.1519–1575), and his wife, Margaret, eldest daughter of James Douglas, third earl of Morton. In early childhood he received the commendam of the abbey of Inchaffray, Perthshire, but resigned it to become, on 4 September 1551, commendator of the much wealthier abbey of Arbroath, Forfarshire. That same year he was sent to Paris, with his tutor, Patrick Buchanan, who had previously been employed to teach the illegitimate sons of James V. Lord John returned home in 1555, and first appears in the public records on 10 May 1560 when, along with his father, his elder brother James *Hamilton, now third earl of Arran, and other leading members of the protestant nobility, he signed the ratification of the treaty of Berwick by which Elizabeth I promised to help the Scottish protestants against the French. Lord John likewise signed a parliamentary proposal that Arran should marry Elizabeth. Arran's subsequent mental breakdown culminating in wild claims of a Hamilton plot to carry off Mary, queen of Scots, left the family under something of a cloud, but Lord John was in attendance at court by March 1563 and high in the favour of the Scottish queen.

**Supporter of Mary, queen of Scots** In 1564 Lord John was given permission to visit Italy for two years. Tantalizingly, nothing seems to be known of his presumably private travels there, but he was back in Edinburgh on 10 February 1567 when Lord Darnley was murdered at Kirk o' Field. The duke of Châtelherault's large mansion, Hamilton House, stood in the same square as Darnley's lodging, and on the night of the murder a light was seen burning in one of its windows, but there was never any suggestion that Lord John was implicated in the murder. He was probably with the queen and the rest of her court that evening. It is not impossible, of course, that he knew about the assassination plan beforehand. Two months later he was a member of the court of assize that acquitted the fourth earl of Bothwell of Darnley's murder.

One of Queen Mary's staunchest supporters, despite his protestantism, Lord John assisted her against her rebellious lords that summer and was marching towards Carberry Hill with his nephew George Gordon, sixth earl of Huntly, on 15 June 1567 to bring reinforcements to her when he heard that she had surrendered to her opponents. He declined to attend the general assembly held in Edinburgh ten days later, and during Mary's imprisonment in Lochleven Castle was rumoured to be plotting with Huntly to rescue her. After Mary's forced abdication on 24 July 1567 he stayed away from the coronation of her infant son, James VI, in Stirling, and early in 1568 travelled to England, apparently seeking support for her. Elizabeth I, suspicious of the motives of the Hamiltons because their descent from a daughter of James II brought them close to the Scottish throne, gave him no encouragement, and he moved on to France. He seems to have been still abroad when Mary escaped from Lochleven in May 1568 and went to Hamilton to rally her adherents. There was talk that the Hamiltons planned to marry her to Lord John, but in the event she was defeated at Langside, fled to England, and the Hamiltons were forfeited by the Scottish parliament for supporting her.

James Stewart, earl of Moray, had become regent for James VI in 1567, and the Hamiltons, seeking revenge for their forfeiture, were closely involved when Moray was assassinated at Linlithgow on 23 January 1570, shot by James Hamilton of Bothwellhaugh who then escaped to the continent. Matthew Stewart, thirteenth earl of Lennox, the Hamiltons' hereditary enemy, was chosen to be the next regent, but the following year he was shot in the back during a skirmish at Stirling Castle and died a few hours later. Lord John was reported to have been present during the incident.

At this time Lord John was still very much a younger son of the family, but his importance increased considerably when his father died in 1575. Because of the insanity of his only surviving elder brother, the earl of Arran, Lord John became in effect the head of the house of Hamilton and heir to the Scottish throne. There was obviously a pressing need for him to marry and have sons, and so on 30 December 1577 at Maybole he signed a marriage contract with Margaret Lyon, only daughter of the eighth Lord Glamis and widow of Gilbert Kennedy, fourth earl of Cassillis, who had fought for Queen Mary at Langside and died in 1576. Cassillis was a cousin of the then regent, James Douglas, fourth earl of Morton, and his widow's marriage to Lord John served an additional purpose. The Douglases and the Hamiltons had been engaged in a lengthy feud which had worsened with the murder of Moray, whose mother had been a Douglas. Moray's half-brother, Sir William Douglas of Lochleven, persevered with the feud after other members of his family had made up their differences with the Hamiltons, and when he heard reports in 1576 that Lord John was bringing James Hamilton of Bothwellhaugh home from France, he vowed vengeance, gathered a small army, and twice tried to attack and capture Lord John. Refusing to give an undertaking to keep the peace, he was for a time imprisoned in Edinburgh Castle. Lord John's marriage to Margaret Lyon was therefore seen, in part at least, as an act of reconciliation, and dynastic considerations were satisfied when they had two sons and a daughter. His eldest son and heir, James *Hamilton, was born in 1589.

**Exile** In 1579 Morton declared that Lord John and his younger brother Lord Claud *Hamilton had been implicated in the murders of Moray and Lennox. As a result they were included in the general act of forfeiture of that year, and a commission was issued for their arrest and the seizure of their lands. Lord John fled to England disguised as a seaman and then managed to cross to France, where he found refuge with the exiled James Beaton, archbishop of Glasgow, Queen Mary's agent in Paris. Meanwhile, Morton's forces besieged and captured Hamilton Palace and Draffen Castle, another Hamilton property, and James VI granted the commendatorship of Arbroath to his new favourite, Esmé Stewart, soon to become first duke of Lennox. Henri III of France promised Lord John a pension of 400 livres a month, but it was never paid, possibly because of Lord John's refusal to convert to Roman Catholicism despite the inducements held out to him by the Guise relatives of Queen Mary. He was unpopular with them as a result, but the number of French letters among the small amount of his surviving correspondence bears witness to the friendships he formed with men like King Henri of Navarre during his years in France.

In 1581 Lord John learned that Captain James Stewart, son of his cousin Andrew, second Lord Ochiltree, had been appointed legal guardian of his brother Arran, who was forced to resign his title. On 22 April James VI made Stewart, now his favourite, earl of Arran instead. All Lord John's hopes of a return to Scotland were apparently dashed and he wrote to his wife from Paris on 28 August 1581, urging her to join him before winter came. She had presumably been sending him money from Scotland. When he heard eventually that Elizabeth I wished the new earl of Arran to be dislodged from his position of ever-increasing power, he decided to rely upon her help to reclaim the Hamilton lands and titles, and travelled to the north of England to meet his younger brother Claud. Their attempt in April 1584 to overthrow Arran, who was virtually ruling Scotland, was unsuccessful but the latter, who was much hated by the Scottish nobility, was nevertheless finally ousted the following year.

One of the friends Lord John had made in France was the adventurer and double agent Patrick, master of Gray. While acting for Queen Mary, Gray managed to ingratiate himself with Elizabeth I and he advised her to encourage Hamilton and the other exiled lords to return to Scotland, thereby preventing any attempt by Arran to regain power. On Elizabeth's urging Lord John was reconciled with his former enemy Archibald Douglas, eighth earl of Angus, and in company with John Erskine, eighteenth earl of Mar, and the other banished lords, raised an army, marched rapidly into Scotland, and arrived at Stirling Castle, where the king and court were. By the time they got there, Arran had fled. On 4 November 1585 the banished lords were admitted to James VI's presence and fell on their knees before him. According to one account Lord John, speaking for all of them, begged for his majesty's love and favour, and received a warmer welcome than he might have expected. James apparently greeted him enthusiastically as his mother's faithful servant, saying that he had been the most wronged of all the exiles, and from that moment Lord John's fortunes were transformed.

**The king's friend** On 10 December 1585 Lord John was appointed to the new privy council established that same day, while later that month parliament, meeting at Linlithgow, gave him back his family estates and made him custodian of his brother the third earl of Arran, whose title was also restored. On 1 November 1586 Lord John became captain of Dumbarton Castle for life, and on 4 February 1587 he was made justiciary and lord lieutenant of the western marches during the king's pleasure. Four days later Queen Mary was executed at Fotheringhay, and Lord John received a sapphire ring which she had taken from her finger shortly before her execution. It came to him with a message from her, asking that it be kept in his family forever as a token of her gratitude for their devotion to her and sufferings in her cause. The ring, with a seventeenth-century inscription on the back of the bezel relating its history, is still preserved in the duke of Hamilton's collection at Lennoxlove, Haddingtonshire.

Mary's death strengthened Lord John's position as heir apparent to the Scottish throne, but in spite of that James VI did not view him with suspicion and the two men were close friends. When his old ally the master of Gray was convicted of treason in May 1587, Lord John knelt before the king and the privy council and successfully begged for Gray's life to be spared. Although his Roman Catholic brother Lord Claud Hamilton plotted a Spanish invasion of Scotland after Queen Mary's execution, Lord John took no part. Indeed, the conspirators planned to assassinate him so that his followers would join with Lord Claud.

On 9 July 1588 parliament erected Arbroath Abbey into a temporal lordship for Lord John, and it was he who was chosen that same year to head the embassy sent to Denmark to negotiate the marriage of James VI with Anne of Denmark. He was given £20,000 Scots out of taxation for his expenses and when James, with uncharacteristic daring, decided to sail to Denmark to fetch his bride in person, Lord John was made lieutenant of the realm in his absence. He had a council of his own to advise on military affairs and received a congratulatory letter from Elizabeth I, indicating that she would be ready and willing to help if he found himself in difficulties on the borders. In the event the country remained at peace and James returned safely with his bride. At Anne of Denmark's subsequent coronation in the abbey of Holyrood, Lord John carried the sword of state and, along with the duke of Lennox and two presbyterian ministers, placed the crown on her head. He was godfather at the baptism of the royal couple's first daughter, Elizabeth, at Holyrood on 13 October 1596.

In the early 1590s Lord John was much occupied rebuilding his principal residence at Hamilton, which had been severely damaged when his father's enemy, Robert, third Lord Sempill, set fire to it in 1570. Lord John seems to have been responsible for the sturdy, three-storey building with a central quadrangle and a tower at each corner which can be seen in several late seventeenth-century views of the palace. The king frequently visited him there, and teased him about being too busy building to attend to hunting. James VI soothed Lord John's feelings more than once with his pawky humour. There had been the time when Lord John felt that he was no longer enjoying free access to the king, and complained bitterly. James, who was more than thirty years younger than Lord John, had placated him by telling him that 'it ill became the heir apparent to be angry with the auld laird'. Again, on 10 January 1593 Lord John was present when the lords met in the little kirk of Edinburgh and passed resolutions for removing all Roman Catholics from crown offices. Speaking about it to him afterwards, the king talked of the necessity of allowing freedom of conscience. 'Sir, then we are all gone, then we are all gone, then we are all gone!' Lord John exclaimed in agitation. 'If there were no more to withstand, I will withstand!' James VI merely smiled and, seeing some servants approaching, said calmly, 'My lord, I did this to try your mind' (Calderwood, 5.269).

In May 1594 Lord John was chosen as one of the lords of the articles, the parliamentary committee responsible for preparing legislation. That same year his Roman Catholic nephew the earl of Huntly, already forfeited on suspicion of having plotted a Spanish invasion, refused to submit to the reformed church. Lord John commanded the vanguard of the royal army when James VI marched against Huntly and his ally Francis Hay, ninth earl of Erroll, and sat on the jury that found Huntly guilty of high treason. Huntly escaped the death penalty, however, by agreeing to go abroad. When an anti-Catholic riot broke out in Edinburgh on 17 December 1597, Robert Bruce and the other leading presbyterian ministers tried to persuade Lord John to act as their leader, but he refused and passed on their letter to the king.

**Elevation and death** In December 1597 James asked Lord John to give up Dumbarton Castle, assuring him that this was no sign of disgrace, and indeed he remained high in the royal favour. On 15 April 1599, two days after attending the baptism of the king's second daughter, Princess Margaret, he was created marquess of Hamilton, earl of Arran (although his elder brother was still alive), and Lord Evan, at a lavish ceremony in the king's great chamber at Holyrood. Huntly, recently returned and reconciled with the king, also received a marquessate at the same ceremony.

In March 1604, now in his sixty-fifth year, Hamilton fell seriously ill. He made his will on 31 March, recalling his constant affection to the king's service, and wrote a last letter to James VI, recommending his 'dear and only [surviving] son to his majesty's kind patronage and care' (*Townshend MSS*, 68). On 12 April he died at Hamilton Palace, and was buried in April or May in the family vault in Hamilton parish church. A magnificent gilded monument was erected in his memory, possibly constructed from the alabaster he himself had imported a few years earlier. Both church and monument have long since gone, but in the late seventeenth century the third duchess of Hamilton's secretary copied the inscription on the monument. It records his death and continues with an elegy beginning:

> Here rests, within this tomb, of truth th'unmatched zeal
> The father and the faithfull friend of kirk and commonweell
> In storm and calm to doe his king's command
> Peace the parent, child of Mars, chief glorie of the land.
> (Hamilton archives, 439/19)

While the eulogy on the monument was something of an exaggeration, T. F. Henderson in the *Dictionary of National Biography* erred on the side of severity when he characterized Hamilton as 'indolent and unambitious'. Cosmopolitan, sophisticated, and fond of luxurious display the first marquess of Hamilton certainly was, but he was also vigorous in his support of Mary, queen of Scots, single-minded in his determination to win back his family's estates, and both loyal and energetic in the service of his friend James VI. ROSALIND K. MARSHALL

**Sources** Lennoxlove, East Lothian, Hamilton archives • NA Scot., Hamilton muniments, GD 406 [ex Lennoxlove] • *Scots peerage*, 4.371–2 • D. Harris Willson, *James VI and I* (1963) • Edinburgh register of testaments, NA Scot., CC 8/8/44, 30 June 1608 • J. Durkan, 'James, third earl of Arran: the hidden years', *SHR*, 65 (1986), 154–66, esp. 156–7 • *The manuscripts of the Marquess Townshend*, HMC, 19 (1887), 63–8 • R. Douglas, *The peerage of Scotland*, 2nd edn, ed. J. P. Wood, 1 (1813), 702–3 • GEC, *Peerage*, new edn, 6.257–8 • D. Stevenson, *Scotland's last royal wedding* (1997), 103–7, 114, 139, 141–3, 148 • *DNB* • D. Calderwood, *The history of the Kirk of Scotland*, ed. T. Thomson and D. Laing, 8 vols., Wodrow Society, 7 (1842–9)

**Archives** Lennoxlove, East Lothian, Hamilton archives, charters, corresp., and financial papers • NA Scot., corresp. (ex Lennoxlove), GD 406 • NA Scot., Edinburgh register of testaments, CC 8/8/44, 30 June 1608

**Wealth at death** £4446 in debt; excl. properties: 1608, Edinburgh register of testaments, NA Scot., CC 8/8/44

**Hamilton, John** (*c*.**1547–1610/11**), Roman Catholic controversialist, was the son of Thomas Hamilton of Orchatfield, Linlithgowshire, and brother of Sir Thomas Hamilton, Lord Priestfield, who became the father of Thomas *Hamilton, first earl of Haddington. As such he belonged to the Marian or queen's party in Scotland's civil war. Hamilton, who held the ecclesiastical living of Dunbar in Haddingtonshire, was linked to Mary Stuart in the *Historie and Life of James the Sext*:

> In 1570 the king of Spain being daily solicited by her orator, Mr John Hamilton, persoun of Dunbar, sent commandment to his viceroy in the Low Countries, the Duc of Alva, to send sik supplie as he sould think expedient in Scotland to the queen's lieutenant. (Thomson, 60)

John Hamilton 'sometime persoun of Dunbar' appeared next to Thomas Hamilton 'sometime of Priestfield' in a list of rebels dated 10 July 1572, and having remained 'beyond sea' he was later denounced again with other 'declarit traitors'. Hamilton went to Paris in 1573 and became a professor of philosophy in the Collège de Navarre. In 1576 he was appointed tutor to Cardinal Bourbon, and soon after to the future Cardinal François de Joyeuse. He was tonsured as a priest at Paris on 18 February 1581, and was subsequently described by a French contemporary as 'a man of resolution and of learning, as everyone knows' (*Mémoires-journaux*, 5.173).

A fierce and partly physical dispute about prayer before images, initiated by a visiting Scot, William Fowler, took place in 1581 in front of Hamilton's students. This led (by way of a letter to the protestant ministers in Scotland challenging them to a conference) to the appearance in that year of *Ane Catholik and Facile Traictise … to Confirme the Real and Corporell Praesence of Chrystis Pretious Bodie and Blude*. The book was dedicated to Queen Mary, but appended to it were twenty-four 'catholic conclusions' dedicated to her son King James, implying that both reigned. Along with his kinsman Archibald Hamilton, John Hamilton was one of the twenty exiled priests who were prepared to return to Scotland, 'offering their bodies to the fire' (Law, xliv) in Hamilton's phrase, if they were unable to convict their opponents of heresy. Instead he was chosen rector of the University of Paris on 17 October 1584 and presented to a local living on the recommendation of students of the 'German nation'. The title, disputed before the *parlement* of Paris because Hamilton was a foreigner, received legal confirmation. He was then only a student in theology; he did not become a master until 1586.

Hamilton was a prominent member of the Catholic league during the period of Paris's resistance to Henri IV. He contributed a preface in March 1590 to *Remonstrance faicte en l'assemblée générale des colonels, cappitaines, lieutenans & enseignes de la ville de Paris*, and when Henri besieged Paris later that year he acted as 'drill sergeant to a regiment of 1300 ecclesiastics' (Law, xlv). Representing one of the sixteen districts of Paris, he was party to the French crown's being offered to Philip II of Spain. The sixteen condemned to death the president of the Paris *parlement* and two of the city magistrates. When one of these failed to appear Hamilton dragged him from sick bed to execution chamber. He was reported to have said mass and to have baptized an infant in church without removing his armour. It was also alleged that on the day of Henri's entry to Paris, 22 March 1593, Hamilton was arrested with weapon in hand attempting to renew the civil war, but 'the most authentic accounts of the proceedings make no mention of any such incident' (Bellesheim, 407 n.). Hamilton escaped the fate of other executed leaders by fleeing to Brussels, though he was condemned to be broken on the wheel and the sentence was carried out on his effigy.

In 1600, when Hamilton was a doctor of theology in Louvain, the privy council licensed the printing of a book there 'to confirm the catholics of his land and to refute heresies' (Algemeen Rijksarchief Brussel, papieren van staat en audientie, 1398/7), but without imprint as it was to be distributed clandestinely. *A Facile Traictise*, which was dedicated to James VI, deals with the marks of the 'true church' and its seven sacraments. It shows Hamilton to have been an excellent stylist, and as expressive when his subject was Christian humility and charity as when he was writing in more forceful vein. He reached Scotland later that year with copies of his treatise, and at about the same time as the Jesuit John Hay, who had been present at the start of the dispute with Fowler. A letter attributed variously to Alexander Macquhirrie and to Robert Abercrombie, superior of the Jesuit mission to Scotland, describes Hamilton as 'a strong worker in the Lord's vineyard though he seeks to injure us' (Jesuit Archives, Rome, Angl. 42, fols. 151–6); this was a reference to a quarrel with the Jesuits while Hamilton was rector of the University of Paris. In 1601 an act was passed forbidding anyone to receive Hamilton and Hay, but Hamilton eluded capture for several years, operating as a priest in different parts of the country. His immunity from arrest owed something to the fact that his nephew, the earl of Haddington, was near the head of the justiciary of Scotland under the earl of Dunfermline, King James's 'popish chancellor'. Andrew Melville, the presbyterian leader, accused the two earls of protecting Hamilton.

Hamilton was finally captured in 1608 at Brechin in the home of Lord Ogilvie. Dark and stormy conditions might have enabled Hamilton to escape, 'but the old man, characteristically seizing a weapon, made preparations to resist' (Law, xlvii). On 30 August Sir Alexander Hay requested the lieutenant of the Tower of London to receive Hamilton and another priest who were being sent to England by the earl of Dunbar. King James VI and I refused to allow a capital sentence, though George Con (the Scottish priest and papal ambassador) reported that Hamilton's death (which took place either in 1610 or early in 1611) was widely believed to have been caused by poison. Andrew Melville, a fellow prisoner in the Tower, had held friendly discussions with Hamilton, but failed to convert him to the reformed religion. ALASDAIR ROBERTS

**Sources** T. G. Law, *Catholic tractates of the sixteenth century, 1573–1600*, STS, 45 (1901) • W. Forbes-Leith, *Pre-Reformation scholars in the XVIth century* (1915) • A. Bellesheim, *History of the Catholic Church in Scotland*, ed. and trans. D. O. H. Blair, 3 (1889) • [T. Thomson], ed., *The historie and life of King James the Sext*, Bannatyne Club, 13 (1825) • J. H. Burton, *The Scot abroad*, 2 vols. (1864) • 'Algemeen Rijksarchief Brussel, papieren van staat en audientie, 1398/7', Nationaal Archief, The Hague • M. Lee, 'King James's popish chancellor', *The Renaissance and Reformation in Scotland: essays in honour of Gordon Donaldson*, ed. I. B. Cowan and D. Shaw (1983), 170–82 • M. B. H. Anderson, 'Edinburgh merchants in society, 1570–1603', in I. B. Cowan and D. Shaw, *The Renaissance and Reformation in Scotland: essays in honour of Gordon Donaldson* (1983), 183–99 • *Mémoires-journaux de Pierre de l'Estoile*, ed. G. Brunet and others, 11 vols. (1875–83), vol. 5, p. 173 • Jesuit Archives, Rome, Angl. 42, fols. 151–6

**Hamilton, Sir John, first Lord Bargany** (*d.* **1658**). *See under* Hamilton, John, second Lord Bargany (*c.*1640–1693).

**Hamilton, John, second Lord Bargany** (*c.*1640–1693), nobleman and accused traitor, was the elder son among the seven children of **Sir John Hamilton**, later first Lord Bargany (*d.* 1658), and his wife, Lady Jean (*d.* 1669), second daughter of William Douglas, first marquess of Douglas. Sir John, one of the ten children of Sir John Hamilton (*d.* *c.*1638) of Lettrick (a natural son of John *Hamilton, first marquess of Hamilton), and his wife, Jean Campbell, married Lady Jean in 1632, and was created a peer on 16 November 1641. He served the covenanting regime in parliament and locally in Ayrshire, but in 1648 accompanied James, first duke of Hamilton, in the engagement campaign, commanding an infantry regiment, and was captured. Remaining an active royalist thereafter, he joined Charles II in the Netherlands, returned to Scotland with him, and was captured again with the committee of estates at Alyth in 1651, and again briefly imprisoned in England. His estate was forfeited by the 1654 Act of Indemnity and he had to pay £2000 sterling to recover it. It was probably he who suggested that his kinswoman Anne, duchess of Hamilton, marry his brother-in-law William Douglas, earl of Selkirk (later third duke of Hamilton), a match which ultimately restored the Hamilton fortunes. He died in April 1658.

John Hamilton, second Lord Bargany, was served heir to his father on 17 October 1662. Details of his early life and education are unknown. He married first, by a contract dated 23 August 1662, Lady Mary (*d.* 1670), second daughter of William Cunningham, ninth earl of Glencairn, lord chancellor of Scotland. They had three sons (two of whom predeceased him) and a daughter. Bargany petitioned in vain for partial repayment of his father's fine, or a share of the fines on former Cromwellians; the resulting financial problems made him permanently penny-pinching and litigious. His family, like the ducal house of Hamilton, was divided religiously along gender lines: several of his sisters supported presbyterianism—two allegedly died partly from shock after soldiers hunting covenanters threatened the married one's children—while he, like his uncle the third duke, was more a conformist in religion and politics. In 1666 he led the Carrick gentry to fight against the covenanters at Rullion Green.

Bargany married second, in September 1677, Lady Alice, daughter of Henry Moore, first earl of Drogheda, and widow of Henry Hamilton, second earl of Clanbrassill, evidently for her ill-gotten gains under her first husband's will. In his lifetime, her then lover, Lord Berkeley the lord lieutenant, had in 1671 sponsored her unsuccessful attempt to become Charles II's mistress. Sir John Dalrymple younger of Stair, to whom Bargany was selling Castle Kennedy, Wigtownshire, attempted, for a rebate, to have him created (Irish) earl of Clanbrassill, but he was absent when his new wife died at Dublin on Christmas day 1677, and was denied his inherited claims (and even the £3000 sterling he had advanced to pay her debts) when his Irish deeds were lost.

In 1678 Bargany followed his uncle in constitutional opposition, refusing the bond against conventicles and opposing Lauderdale in the convention of estates. However, he personally helped demolish a presbyterian meeting-house, and during the Bothwell Bridge rising sheltered the local episcopalian minister in Bargany Castle despite rebel threats.

Bargany blamed what followed on an Ayrshire neighbour, James Crawfuird (or Crawford) of Ardmillan, who with his two sons exploited the anti-covenanting laws for personal enrichment, releasing captured rebels for bribes, and extorting money, bonds, and even labour services from innocent local inhabitants. Allegedly fearing that Bargany might denounce him for sheltering the rebel Thomas Cunningham of Montgrenan, Ardmillan persuaded Montgrenan and others to swear to false accusations of treason against Bargany. The most serious were that he had corresponded with John Welsh, the covenanting leader, and had induced various persons to join the Bothwell Bridge rising, that in 1675–6 he had tried to organize the assassination of Lauderdale, and (an afterthought) that he had praised Archbishop Sharp's murder. To encourage government ministers to support the accusation, a treason charge against the duke of Hamilton was linked to it. The privy council had Bargany arrested on 7 November 1679 and committed incommunicado to Blackness Castle, while Ardmillan was left free to 'discover' witnesses on his estates, including his indebted chamberlain and resentful presbyterian tenants. However, the duke of York's intervention gained Bargany a speedy trial. According to Montgrenan (self-confessedly perjured), Lauderdale's brother Charles Maitland, Lord Halton (later third earl of Lauderdale), and Dalrymple (who owed Bargany purchase money for Castle Kennedy, and in January 1680 obtained from Ardmillan other, mortgaged, Bargany lands) promised the witnesses rewards for their false testimony. In contrast, Lord Advocate Sir George Mackenzie, though taking every legal advantage and nominating a biased jury, urged the witnesses to speak the truth, and afterwards wrote to Bargany excusing himself as having only obeyed royal orders. Bargany was brought to the justiciary bar on 3 March 1680, but the trial was postponed to 16 March and then to 14 June. On his petition, and the king's consequent letter of 11 May, the council on 3 June gave orders to bail him on 50,000 merks security. After his release he heard Montgrenan's confession of how he had been suborned.

Bargany petitioned the parliament in full session in June 1681 to examine the evidence on the perjuries and subornation. Although the charges against Halton and Dalrymple created a sensation there, his own main aim was to prosecute the defiant Ardmillan. He was ready to produce his evidence on 28 July, but York intervened to prevent inquiry. Bargany drafted a narrative intended for publication (NA Scot., RH 4/57/1/63). When Ardmillan and his family, under cover of a grant of November 1682 from the privy council of a commission against the region's covenanters, resumed their extortions on a still larger scale, on Mackenzie's instructions Bargany systematically documented their misdeeds, and their arrest was ordered in August 1684. Ardmillan and one son absconded, though the council eventually acquitted the other. Bargany in effect took Ardmillan's place, being appointed on 30 December 1684 convener of the new Ayrshire committee which enforced the harsh punishments of the 'killing time'; he took part in this, though he was not accused, unlike so many involved, of exceeding the laws.

In December 1684 Bargany's mistress Sophia Johnstone (daughter of the ruined royalist laird of Laverocklaw), whose son James he had acknowledged but totally failed to provide for, sued him in the Edinburgh commissary court for seduction under promise of marriage. He had the case transferred to the more favourable council, produced evidence that she had organized witnesses to swear falsely that they had overheard a promise, and counterattacked by accusing her and her brother, a druggist's apprentice, of threatening to murder him unless he married her. At the bar, 'she was much transported with passion against my lord, calling him a false villain' (*Historical Notices*, ed. Laing, 2.579–80).

Bargany heartily supported the 1688 revolution (not least because the Ardmillan family became Jacobites), and in spring 1689 raised an infantry regiment in King William's service. It consisted largely of Irish protestant refugees, and Bargany offered in early 1690 to lead it in William's Irish campaign. Instead it was merged into Colonel Richard Cunningham's regiment. Bargany died on 15 May 1693 at Edinburgh, and was buried at Ballantrae, Ayrshire. His elder son, John, master of Bargany (through whose daughter the estates eventually passed to the Dalrymple family), predeceased him in 1690; his younger son, William, who had served in his regiment, succeeded him as third Lord Bargany.

It is usually assumed that the 1679 accusations against Bargany, though false, yet reflected his religious standpoint. In reality, two of his prosecutors, Ardmillan the younger and Dalrymple, had stronger presbyterian links than he—which emphasizes the ambiguity of the affair, and of the regime which spawned it. PAUL HOPKINS

**Sources** NA Scot., Bargany MSS, GD 109; RH 4/57/1 · H. H. Dalrymple, *A short account of the Hamiltons of Bargany* (1897) · *Scots peerage* · GEC, *Peerage* · R. Wodrow, *The history of the sufferings of the Church of Scotland from the Restoration to the revolution*, ed. R. Burns, 4 vols. (1828–30) · *Reg. PCS*, 3rd ser. · *Historical notices of Scotish affairs, selected from the manuscripts of Sir John Lauder of Fountainhall*, ed. D. Laing, 2 vols., Bannatyne Club, 87 (1848) · J. Paterson, *History of the county of Ayr: with a genealogical account of the families of Ayrshire*, 2 vols. (1847–52) · BL, Lauderdale MSS, Add. MS 23122, fol. 229 · BL, Lauderdale MSS, Add. MS 23245, fols. 73, 75, 86*v* · BL, Lauderdale MSS, Add. MS 23246, fols. 1, 5–6, 47 · *APS*, *1670–95* · Historical Manuscripts Commission, London, Tollemache MSS, 3 vols., catalogue no. 23003, vol. 2 · *Bishop Burnet's History* · R. K. Marshall, *The days of Duchess Anne* (1973) · J. H. Wilson, *Nell Gwyn, royal mistress* (1952)

**Archives** NA Scot., GD 109 · NA Scot., RH 4/57/1 [copies]

**Likenesses** circle of C. Jonson, oils (John Hamilton, first Lord Bargany), priv. coll.; copy by pupil of C. Jonson, priv. coll. · engraving (probably John Hamilton, second Lord Bargany), Scot. NPG

**Wealth at death** significant estates in Carrick and other parts of Ayrshire and Renfrewshire; but heavy debts (including expenses from rebuilding house and raising a regiment): NA Scot., Bargany MSS, GD 109

**Hamilton, John**, **second Lord Belhaven and Stenton** **(1656–1708)**, politician, was born in Edinburgh on 5 July 1656, the eldest son of Robert Hamilton, Lord Presmennan (*d.* 1695), one of the judges of the court of session, and Marion, eldest daughter of John Denholm of

**John Hamilton, second Lord Belhaven and Stenton** (**1656–1708**), by Sir John Baptiste de Medina (after Sir Godfrey Kneller)

Muirhouse. Known as John Hamilton of Biel, in 1674 he married Margaret (*d.* 1717), daughter of Sir Robert Hamilton of Selverton Hill and granddaughter of John Hamilton, first Lord Belhaven and Stenton; they had two sons. In 1675 Belhaven secured a settlement of his title on his granddaughter's husband, and following the former's death, four years later, Hamilton of Biel became second Lord Belhaven and Stenton.

Belhaven appears to have had a fiery temper. On 8 March 1681 the privy council ordered him to stay in his lodgings on discovering that he had arranged a duel with the laird of Ruchlaw. He first caused political controversy in the 1681 Scottish parliament in which James, duke of York, was high commissioner. On 28 July he subscribed a declaration by the clergy and nobility acknowledging that it was unlawful to take up arms against the king under any circumstances but during the parliamentary debate on the controversial Test Act, Belhaven stated that 'he did not see ane Ane Act brought in to secure our Protestant religion against a Popish or phanaticall successor to the Croun' (*Historical Notices*, 1.307–8). As a result of this, he was committed to Edinburgh Castle by parliamentary vote on 29 August and the king's advocate, Sir George Mackenzie, declared that there was matter for an accusation of treason against Belhaven. He was allowed to take his place again in parliament on 6 September, but only after he had craved the pardon of the duke of York and of parliament. Belhaven did so on his knees in front of the bar, acknowledged that he had been justly imprisoned, and retracted the 'rash and unadvised expressions uttered by him' (*APS*, 8.247).

Belhaven attended the 1685 and 1686 parliaments, serving in the former as a commissioner of supply for Haddingtonshire. He was among the Scottish nobles who proceeded to London late in 1688 and who in January 1689 invited William of Orange to assume the government of Scotland and call a convention of estates. He was a member of that convention, subscribing both to the act of 16 March which declared its legality and to its letter to William of 23 March thanking him for his administration of Scotland to date. He was appointed a commissioner for ordering the militia in Haddingtonshire and served as one of the two noble members of the committee to the politically sensitive task of overseeing the election of new magistrates in Edinburgh. Evidently a trusted member of the new regime, on 13 April he was appointed captain of the troop of horse in Haddingtonshire in place of Andrew Fletcher of Saltoun, and on 23 April was named captain of a troop of horse for Lanarkshire and parts of Stirling and Clackmannanshire; in May he was ordered to deploy a troop in Perthshire. On 27 April he was appointed as one of the commissioners of supply for Haddingtonshire.

Belhaven attended the first session of the full parliament, which met from 5 June to 2 August 1689, but he was simultaneously involved in military action against the Jacobites. On 27 July he commanded the Haddingtonshire troop of horse at the battle of Killiecrankie, when he was reported to have acted 'very bravely' (Balfour Melville, 1.187). In August his regiment was active in the north-east of Scotland. A letter from King William appointing Belhaven a privy councillor arrived on 10 January 1690 and four days later he joined a committee for securing the peace of the country, with particular reference to the highlands. On 19 January he was named a commissioner for exercising the office of clerk register, and on 30 January he joined a committee for subscribing proclamations and commissions. During the second session of the Williamite parliament from 15 April to 22 July 1690 he served on the committee for contraverted elections, as a commissioner of supply for Haddingtonshire and as a commissioner for exercising the office of clerk register. As a privy councillor, acting with Sir Archibald Murray of Blackbarony, he examined two prisoners in Edinburgh, and continuing on the new privy council named on 23 June, examined one John Muir who was accused of child murder and addressed the supply of the forces and garrisons in the Mearns. Belhaven is not recorded in the rolls of the third session of the Williamite parliament (3–7 September 1690) but remained active on the privy council during 1691 on committees responsible for military matters. On 29 May he was named captain of the militia horse in Haddingtonshire. The importance of his political and military profile over the previous two years was recognized by the privy council on 26 October 1691 when he was sent to London to present King William with its letter congratulating the king on his safe return from military campaigning. Belhaven was to be paid £300 sterling (£3600 Scots) to cover his expenses for this journey.

Belhaven was active in the parliamentary sessions of 1693, 1695, 1696, 1698, and 1700. In 1693 he was one of the farmers of the poll tax in Scotland and between September 1695 and March 1697 was also one of the farmers of the excise. In the context of the dire economic condition of Scotland, Belhaven was the president of the parliamentary committee for trade which drew up the act passed on 26 June 1695 for the Company of Scotland Trading to Africa and the Indies. He was then a member of the council-general and court of directors which issued stock and decided on the rules and constitution of the company. On 10 September 1696 he subscribed the Association in defence of King William and on the same day he was appointed as a member of the committee for the security of the kingdom and the committee for contraverted elections.

A leading supporter of the Darien project, Belhaven subscribed £1000 to the cause. About this time he became a vocal critic of William's administration of Scotland, his political outlook significantly affected by external interference in the project and the failure of William to defend it. On 10 January 1701 Belhaven spoke in parliament not only defending the integrity of Scotland in pursuing the Darien project, but also strongly criticizing the kingdom's subordinate place in British foreign policy at the peace of Ryswick, despite the fact that Scottish money and manpower had been used in the Nine Years' War (1689–97). On 14 January he voted in favour of a formal act, as opposed to a parliamentary address, to William over the Darien crisis and on 28 January 1701 he voted against a continuation of the armed forces until December 1702.

Belhaven was continued as a privy councillor with the accession of Queen Anne and in the 1703 parliamentary session (6 May to 16 September) he was a strong supporter of the Act of Security. His fiery temper asserted itself early in the session when he clashed with Sir Alexander Ogilvie of Forglen, the MP for the burgh of Banff and a relation of the lord chancellor, Seafield. During the debate over a disputed election of the shire commissioners for Orkney 'some hott words' passed between them and they 'went out together with a design to have fought' (Hume Brown, 2), but the parliament doors were not open. Tempers flared again, Belhaven kicked Forglen, and Forglen hit back in retaliation. This caused mayhem and parliament was adjourned. Reconciliation was achieved through the respective family efforts of Seafield for Forglen and James Douglas, fourth duke of Hamilton, for Belhaven, and on 30 June Belhaven and Forglen jointly petitioned High Commissioner Queensberry and parliament, apologizing for their 'unbecoming expressions and other undutifull behaviour in the house' (*APS*, 11.65–6). An act was passed in their favour which allowed them to return to their seats.

On 13 September 1703 Belhaven adhered to the Tweeddale protestation against the act allowing the importation of French wines and brandy as this was dishonourable to Queen Anne, but he was also accused of being involved in the notorious 'Scots plot' with plans for a Jacobite restoration. During the 1704 parliamentary session (6 July to 28 August) he was employed by Sidney, first earl of Godolphin, to act as an intermediary to try and persuade the duke of Hamilton to vote for the Hanoverian succession. In August, Belhaven was appointed as one of the Scottish Treasury commissioners, although he was removed from office in 1705 and thereafter became a leading opponent of the government and the union project. In April that year he was included in a list of 'the severall persons that are for raiseing in rebellion in Scotland' for the restoration of James VIII and III (James Francis Edward Stuart) (Hume Brown, 196). On 21 July 1705 he made a parliamentary speech in support of a resolution protesting against the nomination of a successor to Queen Anne to the Scottish crown without limitations of its regal authority, and on 1 September he subscribed the protestation of John Murray, first duke of Atholl, against approving the act for a treaty with England.

Belhaven was a vocal opponent of the treaty of union as it passed through the Scottish parliament. On 2 November 1706 he delivered his famous 'Mother Caledonia' anti-Union speech, an emotional and impassioned survey of the Scottish past, mocked and ridiculed by his political contemporaries. Patrick Hume, first earl of Marchmont, scathingly commented, 'Behold, he dreamed, but lo! when he awoke, he found it a dream' (quoted in Hume Brown, 100n.). Seafield wrote to Godolphin from Edinburgh on 3 November commenting that 'My Lord Belhaven had a speech contrived to incense the common people; it had no great influence in the House' (ibid.). From 4 November 1706 Belhaven voted consistently against the articles of the treaty of union and on 12 November he voted against the act for security of the true protestant religion and government of the Church of Scotland, having registered an official protestation that it was:

> no valid security to the Church of Scotland as it is now established by law in case of an incorporating Union and that the Church of Scotland can have no real and solid security by any manner of Union by which the Claim of Right is unhinged, our Parliament incorporated and our distinct Sovereignty and Independency intirely abolished. (*APS*, 11.320)

On 6 January 1707 Belhaven voted in favour of article twenty-one of the treaty which preserved the rights and privileges of the Scottish royal burghs in the post-Union period but on 16 January he voted against ratifying the treaty itself.

Belhaven's opposition continued in the immediate post-Union period. In 1708 he was imprisoned at Edinburgh and in April was brought into custody in London on suspicion of backing an attempted French invasion. He was examined by the English privy council and admitted to bail, but he died shortly afterwards in London on 21 June 1708 from inflammation of the brain. According to John Macky, Belhaven loved to 'make long speeches in Parliament, and hath the vanity to print them' (*Memoirs of the Secret Services*, 236). Macky also described him as a 'rough, fat, black noisy Man, more like a Butcher than a Lord' (ibid.). The Jacobite George Lockhart referred to Belhaven's parliamentary role in glowing terms, stating that 'he affected long, premeditated harrangues, wherein, having a prodigious memory, he used to be very full in citing such passages of history as made for what he advanced, driving parallels betwixt preceeding and present times' (*'Scotland's Ruine'*, 84); he was 'a well-accomplished gentleman in most kinds of learning, well acquainted with the constitution of this kingdom' (ibid.).

JOHN R. YOUNG

**Sources** *APS*, 1670–1707 · *Reg. PCS*, 3rd ser., vols. 7–15 · *Letters relating to Scotland in the reign of Queen Anne by James Ogilvy, first earl of Seafield and others*, ed. P. Hume Brown, Scottish History Society, 2nd ser., 11 (1915) · *'Scotland's ruine': Lockhart of Carnwath's memoirs of the union*, ed. D. Szechi, Association of Scottish Literary Studies, 25 (1995) · J. Grant, ed., *Seafield correspondence: from 1685 to 1708*, Scottish History Society, new ser., 3 (1912) · E. W. M. Balfour-Melville, ed., *An account of the proceedings of the estates in Scotland, 1689–1690*, 1, Scottish History Society, 3rd ser., 46 (1954) · *Scots peerage* · *Memoirs of the secret services of John Macky*, ed. A. R. (1733) · *A speech in parliament on the 10th day of January 1701, by the Lord Belhaven, on the affair of the Indian and African Company and its colony of Caledonia* (1701) · *Lord Belhaven's speech in parliament, the second day of November 1706 on the subject-matter of an union betwixt the two kingdoms of Scotland and England* (1706) · *Historical notices of Scotish affairs, selected from the manuscripts of Sir John Lauder of Fountainhall*, ed. D. Laing, 1, Bannatyne Club, 87 (1848) · G. Brunton and D. Haig, *An historical account of the senators of the college of justice, from its institution in MDXXXII* (1832) · J. Prebble, *Darien: the Scottish dream of empire* (2000) · P. W. J. Riley, *The union of England and Scotland* (1978)
**Archives** NA Scot., letters to Lord Godolphin · NA Scot., letters to laird of Lamington
**Likenesses** J. B. de Medina, oils (after G. Kneller), Scot. NPG [*see illus.*] · oils (after G. Kneller), Scot. NPG · oils, Lennoxlove House, East Lothian · portrait, repro. in J. Pinkerton, *The Scottish gallery, or, Portraits of eminent persons of Scotland* (1799)

**Hamilton, John** (*d.* **1755**), naval officer, second son of James *Hamilton, seventh earl of Abercorn (1686–1744) [*see under* Hamilton, James, sixth earl of Abercorn], and Anne Plumer (1690–1776), was promoted lieutenant on 4 March 1736. In December 1736 he was serving on the *Louisa*, which was wrecked while escorting George II from Hanover; afterwards he served in the *Norfolk* and the *Namur*, before being promoted captain of the *Deal Castle* on 19 February 1741.

In January 1742 Hamilton was appointed to the *Kinsale* (40 guns) and in January 1743 to the *Augusta* (60 guns), which he commanded until the peace in 1748, the ship being stationed for the most part on the south coast of Ireland for the protection of trade. In November 1749 he married Harriot (*d.* 1769), daughter of James *Craggs (1686–1721), diplomatist and politician, and widow of Richard Eliot of Port Eliot.

Hamilton was appointed to the *Lancaster* in February 1755, and during that year commanded her in the channel and the Bay of Biscay. On 13 December he returned to Spithead, and on 18 December he was on his way ashore when his boat struck on the tail of what later became known as Hamilton shoal. The boat was upset and Hamilton, with the greater part of his boat's crew, was drowned.

Hamilton was a man of rare humour, which bubbles up in many of his official letters to the Admiralty; these are also full of outspoken comment on contemporary naval administration. Hamilton and his wife, Harriot, had a daughter, Anne, and a son, John James (afterwards ninth earl and first marquess of Abercorn). Harriot also had several children from her first marriage, including Edward *Eliot, first Baron Eliot.

J. K. LAUGHTON, *rev.* ROGER MORRISS

**Sources** J. Charnock, ed., *Biographia navalis*, 5 (1797), 92 · GEC, *Peerage* · passing certificate record, PRO, ADM 107/3
**Archives** PRO NIre., corresp. and papers | Port Eliot, letters to Edward Eliot
**Likenesses** S. W. Reynolds, mezzotint, pubd 1823 (after J. Reynolds), BM

**Hamilton, John** (*fl.* **1766–1787**), landscape painter and engraver, was born in Dublin but moved to London early in life. A member of the Society of Artists, he subscribed to its roll-declaration in 1766. In 1767 he contributed a moonlight view to their exhibition, and continued to exhibit landscapes and views of Wales and the northwest of England up to 1777. In 1772 he was elected a fellow of the society, in 1773 he was director, and *c*.1775 vice-president. In the print room at the British Museum there is a watercolour drawing by him of Tyburn during the execution of Guest, a banker's clerk, on 14 October 1767. Hamilton was a close friend of the antiquary Francis Grose and etched with good effect the plates to Grose's *Ancient Armour and Weapons*, published in 1786. He managed the estates of the portrait painter John Astley (1720–1787), also a friend, who left him an annuity of £300. Late in life Hamilton married a widow of property with whom he lived in London. He is said to have lived to a very advanced age.

L. H. CUST, *rev.* DEBORAH GRAHAM-VERNON

**Sources** Redgrave, *Artists* · Dodd, MS 'History of British engravers', BL, Add. MS 33401 · exhibition catalogues (1767–77) [Society of Artists] · Waterhouse, *18c painters* · W. G. Strickland, *A dictionary of Irish artists*, 2 vols. (1913); repr. with introduction by T. J. Snoddy (1989)

**Hamilton, Sir John**, **first baronet** (**1755–1835**), army officer, was born on 4 August 1755, the son of James Hamilton of Woodbrook and Strabane, co. Tyrone, and his wife, Elinor, daughter of Robert Stewart of Stewart Hall, co. Tyrone, and Margaret Edwards; his mother was the sister of Andrew Stewart-Moore, first Earl Castle Stewart. In 1771 he was appointed to a Bengal cadetship and became ensign of the Bengal native infantry on 2 March 1773, lieutenant on 22 March 1778, and captain on 15 October 1781. He participated in the conquest of Cooch Behar (1772–3), was present at the capture of Lahar (1780), and commanded a sepoy battalion at the escalade of Gwalior (1780) during the First Anglo-Maratha War (1778–82). He fought in the campaign against the raja of Benares and the capture of Bijaigarh (1781). In 1788 he transferred to the king's service and was commissioned on 1 November as a captain in the newly raised 76th foot, of which he formed two companies in Calcutta. The regiment was first under fire in the capture of Bangalore (7 March 1791) during the campaign against Tipu Sultan. On 1 March 1794 he became brevet major. Two months later on 1 May he married Emily Sophia Monck (*d.* 1856), daughter of George Paul Monck and his wife, Lady Araminta Beresford, sixth daughter of Marcus Beresford, first earl of Tyrone. They had five daughters and one son, John James Hamilton, second baronet (1802–1876).

On 23 December 1795 Hamilton was appointed lieutenant-colonel of the 81st foot, which he commanded in the capture of San Domingo in December 1796. He accompanied the 81st to the Cape in 1798, remaining there as quartermaster-general until August 1803, and resumed command of the 81st until he was appointed brigadier on the staff in Ireland in July 1804. He was made brevet colonel on 29 October 1802, major-general on 25 October 1809, and was appointed inspector-general of the Portuguese infantry between August 1809 and April 1814, commanding the Portuguese division from 16 December 1809 to 22 March 1813. At Albuera on 12 May 1811 his division 'evinced the utmost steadiness and courage' (Halliday, 138) and returned to the investment of Badajoz, being 'particularly mentioned' (ibid., 142) in the attacks on 6 and 9 June. His defence of Alba de Tormes against Marshal Soult in November 1812 was commemorated by an augmentation to his arms on 25 April 1815. In 1813 he was appointed a knight grand cross of the Portuguese order of the Tower and the Sword and was knighted by the prince regent on 15 July 1813. He rejoined the army from sick leave and commanded his old division at the Nivelle on 10 November 1813. He was colonel of the 2nd Ceylon regiment from 13 January 1813 to its disbandment, and became a lieutenant-general on 4 June 1814 and governor of Duncannon Fort in the same year. He was created baronet on 21 December 1814 and appointed colonel of the 69th foot on 15 March 1823. He died at Tunbridge Wells on 24 December 1835; his body was interred in Kensal Green new cemetery. His widow died on 5 January 1856.

H. M. CHICHESTER, *rev.* PETER B. BOYDEN

**Sources** V. C. P. Hodson, *List of officers of the Bengal army, 1758–1834*, 2 (1928) • J. Philippart, ed., *The royal military calendar*, 3rd edn, 2 (1820) • A. Halliday, *Observations of the present state of the Portuguese army* (1811) • F. R. Hayden, *Historical record of the 76th 'Hindoostan' regiment* (c.1908) • [S. Rogers], *Loyauté m'oblige: historical record of the eighty-first regiment* (1872) • copy of warrant for augmentation of Hamilton's arms, NAM, 1968-07-125-153 • GEC, *Baronetage* • Burke, *Peerage* (1859) • *GM*, 2nd ser., 5 (1836), 315 • death duty register, 1836, PRO, IR26/1419

**Likenesses** F. Deleu, line engraving, 1823 (after D. Wilkie), BM; repro. in S. Grace, *Memoirs of the family of Grace* (1823)

**Wealth at death** £64,358 17s. 1d.: PRO, death duty registers, IR 26/1419 • estate was sworn at under £30,000

**Hamilton, John** (1761–1814), songwriter, ran a music-selling and publishing business at 24 North Bridge Street, Edinburgh, and was also a music teacher. As a songwriter, he contributed to *The Scots Musical Museum*, a collection of songs edited and published by James Johnson in Edinburgh (1787–1803), in which his pieces included 'Bright the moon aboon yon mountain' and 'Tell me, Jessy, tell me why', and he helped Walter Scott compile his *Minstrelsy of the Scottish Border* (1802). Among his most popular songs were 'Up in the mornin' early' and 'Miss Forbes's Farewell to Banff'. In some respects his most remarkable contribution to Scottish verse was his addition to Robert Burns's 'Of a' the airts'. His two verses were usually sung as an integral part of the song, and many people assumed they had been written by Burns himself. Hamilton's publications included *A Collection of 24 Scots Songs*, *A Complete Repository of Old and New Scotch Strathspeys, Reels, and Jigs*, and *The Caledonian Museum*, a collection of ancient and modern Scots tunes arranged for flute or violin, in three volumes (all undated).

Hamilton married one of his pupils, 'connected with an ancient family' (Stenhouse, 537). He died on 23 September 1814 in Edinburgh, after a long illness.

T. W. BAYNE, *rev.* ANNE PIMLOTT BAKER

**Sources** W. Stenhouse, *Illustrations of the lyric poetry and music of Scotland* (1853) • D. Baptie, ed., *Musical Scotland, past and present: being a dictionary of Scottish musicians from about 1400 till the present time* (1894) • Brown & Stratton, *Brit. mus.*

**Hamilton, John Andrew**, **Viscount Sumner** (1859–1934), barrister and judge, was born on 3 February 1859 at 47 Rumford Street, Chorlton upon Medlock, Lancashire, the second son and third of the seven children of Andrew Hamilton, a Scots-born iron merchant of Manchester, and Frances, daughter of Joseph Sumner of Sharston, Cheshire.

**Education and early legal career** Hamilton was educated at the Manchester grammar school (1870–77) under its high master, F. W. Walker, becoming captain of the school. In 1877 he won a classical scholarship to Balliol College, Oxford, where he gained first-class honours in classical moderations (1879) and *literae humaniores* (1881), and the Newdigate prize for English verse. Both at school and university he showed 'an addiction to debating societies'. He became president of the Oxford Union in 1882. He was a fellow of Magdalen College from 1882 to 1889. Called to the bar of the Inner Temple in 1883, he joined a set of chambers in Manchester, but unable to find sufficient work on the northern circuit, he returned to London to the chambers of his pupil master, J. C. Bigham. He had a long wait before making any headway at the bar. It was five years before his annual earnings exceeded £100. There were times when he went hungry, and at one stage he contemplated abandoning the law. His meagre earnings were supplemented by his Magdalen fellowship, by university extension lectures, and by writing; he published a life of Daniel O'Connell (1888), and wrote entries, mainly on English judges, for the *Dictionary of National Biography*, to which he was among the first, most prolific, and most distinguished contributors, writing for all but five of the sixty-three main volumes published between 1885 and 1900, and for the supplement of 1927—288 memoirs in all. His articles reflect a sharp and decisive mind. In 1892 he married Maude Margaret Todd, second daughter of the Revd John Todd of Forest Hill, near Sydenham, where she was headmistress of a flourishing girls' school, Tudor Hall, founded by her mother. It was here that he began married life.

By this time Hamilton's prospects had at last improved. He was rapidly developing a large practice in the commercial court, where he was in regular competition with T. E. (later Lord Justice) Scrutton. He established a reputation as an advocate of great thoroughness, quickness of mind, and forcefulness of expression. These gifts were enhanced

**John Andrew Hamilton, Viscount Sumner** (1859–1934), by Sir William Orpen, 1919

by his physical presence—he was tall and well built—and by a natural gravity and 'an incisive imperiousness of manner'. He became head of chambers in 1897 when Bigham was raised to the bench. In 1901 he took silk. Though he practised only in commercial law, he deprecated a popular impression that he knew all there was to know about marine insurance, and nothing else. 'Neither', he said, 'is true'. His wife gave up the school, and they moved to Streatham and later to 25 Gloucester Square, north of Hyde Park. In 1908 he purchased Ibstone House in Buckinghamshire, a country seat with extensive grounds. There were no children of the marriage.

In 1908 Hamilton was appointed under the Education Act of 1902 as arbitrator to conduct a public inquiry into complaints about the running of a Church of England school in Swansea. The Board of Education appealed repeatedly against his findings, but these were upheld by every court up to and including the House of Lords. In 1909 Lord Chancellor Loreburn appointed him a judge of the King's Bench Division, where his powerful intellect at once stamped itself in a succession of memorable extempore judgments. He assumed on the bench an attitude that was frigid, aloof, and intimidating, set off by his heavy-jowled, tight-lipped physiognomy and cold stare. His understanding of the law proved both profound and wide-ranging. None of his rulings was reversed. His decision in *Baker* v. *Courage & Co.* (1910) particularly impressed the judiciary. In 1912, only three and a half years after his appointment to the bench, the lord chancellor, Haldane, promoted him to the Court of Appeal, and he was sworn of the privy council. Twelve months later, in October 1913, under the Appellate Jurisdiction Act of 1913, which increased the number of law lords from four to six, Haldane appointed him a lord of appeal in ordinary at the early age of fifty-four. There being several peers named Hamilton, he took his mother's surname in choosing the title Baron Sumner.

**The law lord** From 1914 until his retirement in 1930 there were few important rulings of the upper house that did not bear Sumner's imprint. During the First World War, he took a leading part in hearing appeals from the prize court to the judicial committee of the privy council. After the death of Lord Parker of Waddington in 1918, he usually presided, adapting prize law—essentially unchanged since the Napoleonic wars—to twentieth-century conditions. His judgments in general display 'a vice-like grip of legal principle', a mastery of case law, and an exposition of the resulting principles couched in lucid and compelling language: a taut concision of phrase, a cumulative pressure of logic which seemed to dispel all doubt, a robust éclat, and a lapidary, indeed adamantine, stamp of finality. 'A judge', he insisted, 'must bring down his fist with a thump.' His emphasis on the need for certainty, particularly in commercial law—'rights', he said, 'ought not to be left in suspense'—was also reflected in his insistence on the authority of precedent and his refusal to allow that decisions of the House of Lords could be altered except by the legislature. If a rule of law exists, he declared, 'time cannot abolish it, nor disfavour make it obsolete' ([1917], Appeal Court Reports, 454). 'It is not for us', he stressed, 'to dispute settled law.' His judicial reasoning, thus dominated by an iron logic, was seldom tinged by human sympathies, which he dismissed as legally irrelevant, especially in cases involving workmen's compensation. Lord Robert Cecil noted of him that 'some very able lawyers can be very cruel men' (Lentin, *Guilt at Versailles*, 113). A sardonic wit enlivened and illuminated his rulings. In *Weld-Blundell* v. *Stephens* (1920), a libel case, he observed that 'few things are more certain than the repetition of a calumny confidentially communicated'. In *Bowman* v. *Secular Society* (1917) he boldly rejected the time-honoured dictum that 'Christianity is part of the law of England' and that to deny scripture is unlawful. Such a proposition, he pointed out, 'imperils copyright in most books on geology'.

Contemporaries such as lords Hewart, Buckmaster, Carson, and MacKinnon hailed Sumner as 'perhaps the greatest lawyer of his generation'. Later observers were less awestruck. Lords Goddard and Devlin felt that the clarity of his dicta was sometimes eclipsed by the dazzling burnish of his style. Lord Scarman rated him as 'a highly professional commercial lawyer' of wit and penetration, but no more. Lord Denning held Thomas Scrutton to be the greater lawyer. Lord Roskill, on the other hand, perceived in Sumner a pioneer who 'saw and was one of the first in this century to see the need for continuous evolution and the process of change in the common law' (Roskill, 254). His contributions to the law, varied and important, bear out this verdict. They include the duty of care to child trespassers in *Latham* v. *Johnson* (1913), the classic dictum on voluntary confessions in *Ibrahim* v. *R.* (1914), on implied terms in *Produce Brokers Company Ltd* v. *Olympia Oil and Cake Company Ltd* (1916), on blasphemy in *Bowman* v. *Secular Society* (1917) (part of which was reproduced by Sir Arthur Quiller-Couch in *The Oxford Book of English Prose*), on the doctrine of frustration in *Bank Line Ltd* v. *Arthur Capel & Co.* (1919), on the relationship between statute and prerogative in *Attorney-General* v. *De Keyser's Royal Hotel* (1920), and on secret trusts in *Blackwell* v. *Blackwell* (1929).

**Judgments and political interests** Sumner's decisiveness and self-assurance were extraordinary. He told Harold Laski that 'discussion in the Court of Appeal was for him a waste of time: he had made up his mind when he read the brief' (Howe, 1040). 'Completely deaf to external opinion', he had no qualms at 'being in a minority of one and insisting that you are right all the same'. He maintained a particularly eloquent and impenitent dissent in *Rodriguez* v. *Speyer Bros.* (1919), where he denied that an enemy alien has any right to sue. His equally robust dissenting judgment in *Russell* v. *Russell* (1924), on admissible evidence in divorce, anticipated a statutory reform of 1949. In *Elder Demster & Co.* v. *Patterson Zochonis & Co.* (1924), a controversial case concerning privity of contract and third-party rights, Sumner, at first in a minority, forced a re-argument by threatening to resign, and then produced a unanimous ruling.

From his youth, Sumner nurtured political interests and ambitions. An aggressive radical at the Union, he championed Irish home rule and attacked the House of Lords. But his early years of struggle appear to have soured his outlook. His initial Liberalism evaporated, transforming itself into its opposite, and he became an outspoken and passionate Conservative on those and most other issues. This side of his character surfaced quite abruptly. Though always a keen and caustic commentator on men and politics, as the last of his pupils, John Buchan (later Lord Tweedsmuir), recalled, he was not known to hold strong political views until about 1917, when he became closely associated with the fourth marquess of Salisbury and the 'die-hard' wing of the Unionist Party.

In 1919 Sumner was appointed to serve on the reparations commission at the Paris peace conference, with Lord Cunliffe and the Australian prime minister, W. M. Hughes. He and Cunliffe were dubbed the 'Heavenly Twins' because of the astronomical sums which they insisted should be demanded of Germany, variously four, five, six, or more times the amount proposed by J. M. Keynes for the Treasury. Against the plain wording of the pre-armistice agreement between Germany and the allies, which confined liability to injury to civilians and damage to their property, he endorsed the claim of the prime minister, Lloyd George, that the allies had an 'absolute right to demand the whole cost of the war'. When this contention was rejected by President Wilson, he argued that Germany must repay the cost of allied military pensions, an argument which, though the president found it 'very legalistic', was eventually accepted. He set his face against an immediate lump sum settlement, dismissing a German counter-offer as 'arrogant' and 'unacceptable'. He persuaded Lloyd George not to prejudice British interests by underestimating Germany's capacity, 'for it will certainly fall short of her liability', or to write off arrears by agreeing to any deadline for repayment. A final sum would be assessed later, and payment would be supervised by an inter-allied reparations commission for which Sumner devised the constitution.

Sumner's speeches in the House of Lords were trenchant and controversial. He was no respecter of persons, including some of his fellow peers and law lords. In 1920 he championed the cause of General Dyer, censured by the House of Commons after the massacre at Amritsar, and in 1922 he vehemently attacked the treaty which created the Irish Free State. He defended his right to speak out on these and other burning issues, and saw no conflict between this and his duty in the privy council to determine appeals from the empire and Irish courts. He had already provoked charges of partisanship by an *obiter* remark in the Irish case of Clifford and O'Sullivan (1921). Undeterred, he held out for the constitutional right and even the duty of law lords to speak their minds on any topic in the House of Lords. Convention, however, was against him and his view was convincingly rebutted by the lord chancellor, Lord Birkenhead. Sumner and Carson were the last of that breed at a time when it had come to be accepted that the only place for a politically minded law lord was on the woolsack.

**Later career** H. H. Asquith had indeed considered Sumner for the woolsack on Haldane's resignation in 1915. With the fall of the Lloyd George coalition in October 1922, Lord Salisbury, as a key mover in the return of a Conservative administration, pressed the new prime minister, Bonar Law, to appoint Sumner, rather than Cave, as lord chancellor. Six months earlier Sumner had proclaimed his political allegiance by signing the 'Diehard manifesto' in *The Times*. 'He is an abler man and I believe a better lawyer', Salisbury wrote to Bonar Law in October 1922, 'and on other grounds I should greatly prefer him' (Bonar Law papers, 109/2/32). Salisbury's influence, however, proved unavailing, and Cave was appointed instead. Sumner took his failure hard. Nor did his chances improve under Baldwin, to whom his intemperate toryism was anathema and who confirmed Cave's appointment in 1923. It was at Cave's instigation, however, and with some reluctance on Baldwin's part, that Sumner was made a viscount in the new year honours of 1927. When Cave fell ill and resigned in 1928, Baldwin moved quickly to replace him by Sir Douglas Hogg (Lord Hailsham), stressing that he 'would not have [Sumner] in the Cabinet'. It was this action which led to Neville Chamberlain's becoming Baldwin's heir apparent and eventually prime minister.

Throughout the 1920s Sumner continued to agitate in the 'die-hard' cause. He lambasted the general strike and trade unions, he castigated Lord Haldane, now Labour lord chancellor, for defending them, he denounced relations with Soviet Russia, the 'flapper' vote, and moves towards independence for India. He was particularly zealous in the cause of House of Lords reform, convinced that a second chamber was essential to stave off radical measures under socialist rule. In 1930 he unexpectedly resigned from the bench at the age of seventy-one, comparatively early for a law lord, because of heart trouble. He immediately embarked, however, on a fresh surge of activity on the joint parliamentary committee on House of Lords reform; and as president of the newly founded Indian Empire Society from 1930, and its successor, the India Defence League, from 1932, he campaigned vigorously against the discussions which led eventually to the Government of India Act of 1935.

Sumner's official public service included chairing the working classes' cost of living committee, the British and foreign legal procedure committee, and the committee of inquiry to investigate the British Cellulose and Chemical Manufacturing Company Ltd ('the dope scandal') in 1918; the royal commission on compensation for suffering and damage by enemy action (1921) and the House of Lords committee on abeyances (1926). He was appointed GCB in 1920 for his services at the Peace Conference. He was standing counsel to the University of Oxford from 1906 to 1909 and was elected an honorary fellow of Magdalen College in 1909. He became a bencher of the Inner Temple in the same year and was treasurer in 1930. He held honorary doctorates from the universities of Oxford, Cambridge, Edinburgh, and Manchester. He was president of the Selden Society in 1920 and 1921. He was a member of the Athenaeum (1909) and the Carlton Club (1929), but made little use of either, dining more often at Grillions or 'The Club', to which he was elected in 1914, and at the Inner Temple, where his conversation and astringent humour were much relished. He was in demand as a public speaker.

Sumner had a formidable presence and a volcanic temper, easily roused. He was cutting, acerbic, cynical, and contemptuous, characteristics well captured in two remarkable portraits of 1919 by Sir William Orpen and Augustus John respectively. A later portrait by Sir Oswald Birley, in the Inner Temple, is also said to bring out, with photographic verisimilitude, what Lord Goddard called his 'benevolent malevolence'. 'He certainly did not wear his heart upon his sleeve,' wrote Lord Buckmaster, 'but fastened it in a burglar-proof safe; and woe betide the man who fumbled at the lock' (Heuston, 307). 'That grim old judge' with his awesome scowl was essentially a disappointed man, highly sensitive, and conscious of outstanding abilities denied full scope.

Sumner was well read, a classical scholar and linguist, a collector of landscapes and still lifes, with a taste for classical music. He showed an interest in the improvement of his estate at Ibstone, and was an avid reader of *Country Life*. He and Lady Sumner travelled regularly to France and Italy and he was a convivial member of the Union Club at Rome. He died suddenly from a heart attack in the Grosvenor Hotel, London, on 24 May 1934, and was cremated at Golders Green. His ashes were buried in the parish churchyard of St Nicholas at Ibstone, where he had worshipped. A. LENTIN

**Sources** *The Times* (26 May 1934) · *The Times* (29 May 1934) · *The Times* (31 May 1934) · *The Times* (9 June 1934) · *DNB* · A. Lentin, 'Lord Sumner, 1859–1934: acerbic master of law and language', *Law Society's Gazette* (27 June 1984), 1852–4 · E. DeW. Howe, ed., *Holmes–Laski letters: the correspondence of Mr Justice Holmes and Harold J. Laski, 1916–1935* (1953) · A. Lentin, *Guilt at Versailles: Lloyd George and the prehistory of appeasement* (1985) · HLRO, Bonar Law MSS · BL, Cave MSS · A. Fitzroy, *Memoirs*, 2 [1925] · R. F. V. Heuston, *Lives of the lord chancellors, 1885–1940* (1964) · Lord Roskill, 'Law lords, reactionaries or reformers', *Current Legal Problems*, 37 (1984), 247–58 · R. Stevens, *Law and politics: the House of Lords as a judicial body, 1800–1976* (1979) · private information (2004) · b. cert.

**Archives** priv. coll. | Bodl. Oxf., Selborne MSS (second earl of Selborne) · Hatfield House, Hertfordshire, Salisbury MSS (fourth marquess of Salisbury) · HLRO, corresp. with David Lloyd George · NA Scot., corresp. with Philip Kerr · PRO, Foreign Office MSS, FO 608

**Likenesses** group portrait, photograph, *c.*1882, Oxford Union · photograph, *c.*1882, Magd. Oxf. · photographs, 1910–30, priv. coll. · A. John, oils, 1919, priv. coll. · W. Orpen, oils, 1919, NPG [*see illus.*] · A. Savage, pen-and-ink drawing, *c.*1920, priv. coll. · photographs, *c.*1927, priv. coll. · O. Birley, oils, 1931, Inner Temple, London · photograph, repro. in *ILN* (1920–27)

**Wealth at death** £36,374 9*s.* 3*d.*: resworn probate, 1934, *CGPLA Eng. & Wales*

**Hamilton, Karl Wilhelm de** (*c.*1668–1754). *See under* Hamilton, James (*c.*1640–*c.*1720).

**Hamilton, Katherine, duchess of Atholl** (1662–1707), noblewoman, was born at Hamilton Palace, Lanarkshire, and baptized at Hamilton on 24 October 1662, the eldest surviving daughter and fifth of thirteen children of William *Hamilton, duke of Hamilton (1634–1694), and his wife, Anne *Hamilton, duchess of Hamilton in her own right (1632–1716). Lady Katherine Hamilton was educated at home, learning to read, write an elegant italic hand, and keep accounts as well as being taught singing and dancing. Tall, dark-haired, and reserved, she was extremely eligible, and when she was twenty John Murray, first marquess of Atholl, approached her parents with the suggestion that she should marry his eldest son, John, Lord Murray (1660–1724) [*see* Murray, John, first duke of Atholl].

Sir George Lockhart acted as intermediary, praising Lord Murray as 'a verie sober and acoomplished youth' (NA Scot., Hamilton archives, GD 406, C1/6083). The duke was doubtful, for he knew all about Atholl's chaotic finances, but the marriage contract was eventually signed on 4 April 1683. Katherine would take with her a dowry of 40,000 merks Scots (£2222 sterling) on the understanding that Atholl would use the money to pay off the debts on his Balquhidder and Huntingtower estates, which would form the jointure lands. The wedding was celebrated on 24 April 1683 with week-long feasting, and Katherine settled down with her husband at Falkland in Fife.

Atholl's subsequent failure to pay off the debts on the jointure lands led to endless family quarrels, and by 1700 Katherine had decided that her parents-in-law were 'the most unraisonable unjust people that I believe is on the earth' (NA Scot., Hamilton archives, GD 406, C1/7960). However, she and her husband were deeply in love with each other. In an early letter he speaks fondly of her feeding him his breakfast while he writes, and Katherine was his ardent partisan in public as well as in private, keeping him within the Hamilton sphere of influence and making sure that he remained a presbyterian amid his own episcopalian relatives. In 1696 Murray became secretary of state for Scotland and was made earl of Tullibardine. During his visits to London, Katherine was his principal source of political intelligence, enlisting support for him whenever he found himself in difficulties. In August 1698, when he and his brothers were placed under house arrest after allegedly beating up the laird of Balnagoun, she persuaded her brother, Charles Hamilton, second earl of Selkirk, to intercede with William III, and Tullibardine was acquitted and released.

With her father-in-law's death in May 1703, Katherine became marchioness of Atholl, and in June 1703, when her husband was created a duke, duchess of Atholl. Like her mother she was a strong supporter of the Darien scheme and an equally vehement opponent of union with England, but when not running the estates during the duke's absence and bringing up their thirteen children (who included the Jacobite campaigner William *Murray, marquess of Tullibardine; James *Murray, later second duke of Atholl; and the Jacobite commanders Lord Charles *Murray and Lord George *Murray), she was preoccupied with spiritual matters. A staunch presbyterian, she kept a religious diary, copied biblical quotations into a book she called her treasury, and observed the sabbath so strictly that even her devoted husband complained that 'there was not one minut of the day that she did not imploy either in hearing sermons, reading or writing concerning religion' (NA Scot., Hamilton archives, GD 406, C1/6045).

In January 1707 Katherine was taken ill during a visit to her mother. Her husband set off on 10 January to visit her with two of their sons, but 2 miles short of Hamilton they were met by a doctor who broke the news that she had died between midnight and 1 a.m. that morning. Shocked, the duke flung himself on the ground, 'where I do not remember what I said or did' (Atholl, 2.69) until the weeping of the boys roused him. Katherine was buried in Hamilton parish church on 17 January 1707 in a simple coffin made of wood from the Hamilton estates.

ROSALIND K. MARSHALL

**Sources** R. K. Marshall, 'The house of Hamilton in its Anglo-Scottish setting in the seventeenth century', PhD diss., U. Edin., 1970 [incl. a 5-vol. calendar of the duke of Hamilton's archives] • R. K. Marshall, *The days of Duchess Anne* (1973) [2000] • Lennoxlove, East Lothian, Hamilton archives, F1 • NA Scot., Hamilton archives, GD 406, C1 • Blair Castle, Perthshire, Atholl muniments, boxes 29, 45 • R. K. Marshall, 'Three Scottish brides', *Costume: the Journal of the Costume Society*, 8 (1974), 41–5 • K. von den Steinem, 'In search of the antecedents of women's political activities in early eighteenth-century Scotland: the daughters of Anne, duchess of Hamilton', *Women in Scotland, c.1100–c.1750*, ed. E. Ewan and M. M. Meikle (1999), 112–22, esp. 113–15 • J. J. H. H. Stewart-Murray, seventh duke of Atholl, *Chronicles of the Atholl and Tullibardine families*, 5 vols. (privately printed, Edinburgh, 1908), vol. 1, p. 502; vol. 2, p. 69 • Hamilton old parish register, General Register Office for Scotland, Edinburgh, 1

**Archives** Blair Castle, Perthshire, Atholl muniments, boxes 29, 45 • Lennoxlove, East Lothian, Hamilton archives • NA Scot., family archives, GD 406, C1

**Hamilton, Lillias Anna** (1858–1925), physician and writer, was born on 7 February 1858 at Tomabil station, New South Wales, Australia, the eldest of four daughters and the third of the eight children of Hugh Hamilton (1822–1900), a farmer from Ayrshire, Scotland, and his wife, Margaret Clunes, *née* Innes (1829–1909), daughter of George Innes of Yarrow, New South Wales.

Little is known about Lillias's childhood except that she was two when the family left Australia and settled, nominally, in Ayr, Scotland. The Hamiltons continued to travel extensively and it was not until they finally moved to Cheltenham in 1874, where Lillias attended the Ladies' College for four years, that she received a real education. Travelling and a brief spell as a teacher followed, but neither satisfied her craving for independence and in 1883, defying family opposition and convention, she began training as a nurse at the Liverpool workhouse infirmary. She took another pioneering step in 1886 when she decided to become a doctor, enrolling at the London School of Medicine for Women. Coincidental to her obtaining her LRCP and LRCS (Edinburgh) in 1890 she met Colonel Joubert of the Indian Medical Service who introduced her to the opportunity of working abroad. In contrast to the prejudice against female physicians practising at home, there was a desperate need for female doctors in India, where religious custom and practice deprived many women of proper medical care. Displaying her characteristic spirit of adventure, Lillias hurriedly acquired her MD in Brussels and undaunted by the prospect of working in a foreign country, promptly left for Calcutta.

With introductions from Colonel Joubert, but without a government appointment or the support and protection of any missionary or philanthropic society—unlike the few other foreign women doctors in the country—Lillias established a successful private medical practice, and for a period held the post of medical officer at the Lady Dufferin Zenana (women's) Hospital in Calcutta. Her career altered dramatically in spring 1894 when she moved to Kabul, Afghanistan. This was prompted by poor health and an insatiable appetite for adventure, for Lillias had already been invited by the amir, who paid her expenses, to spend six months in Kabul showing his queen how English ladies amused themselves. The visit actually lasted for nearly three years, for after she successfully treated the amir in October 1894, Lillias became his personal physician.

Geopolitically Afghanistan was of great significance to Britain, for it acted as a buffer between India and Russia. It was also an inhospitable place for a European, especially a woman, to be. The British government refused to afford Lillias any protection—considering her conduct foolhardy—but she did alert them, certainly on one occasion,

**Lillias Anna Hamilton** (1858–1925), by James Peter Quinn, 1924

through Salter Pyne, their secret news-gatherer in Kabul, to potential hostilities. Although her published writings—she was a prolific journalist and author of two books of fiction—gave the impression that she agreed with the official view of the amir's rule (generously described as severe but just), her unpublished work, 'The power that walks in darkness', presented a different picture, in which she expressed her serious reservations about his often muddled reforms and his 'iron rule'. Even with the amir's protection, she often feared for her life, knowing that a loss of favour or wrong move could result in her execution. She was also the envy of the amir's wives, so had a personal food-taster to ensure she was not poisoned by them. In terms of her medical work, Lillias made a significant impact on the health of the Afghan population. Not only did she establish a hospital in Kabul, but she was also responsible for introducing vaccination into the country.

By late 1896 the strain of working in Afghanistan, allied with the constant danger, became too much for Lillias, and she fled the country. Once home in England she diverted her attention to the plight of homeless women, co-founding the Victoria Women's Settlement in Liverpool in 1897. Her interest in this project quickly waned, and she returned to private practice, setting up a nursing home in London. After two trips to the Transvaal, where she and a brother established a farm, Lillias gave up active medical practice, and travelled again. But in 1908 she applied for and was accepted as warden of Studley College, Warwick (established in 1898 to train women for careers in agriculture and horticulture). Her tenure lasted until her retirement in 1924, interrupted for a brief period in 1915 when she volunteered her medical services to the Wounded Allies Relief Committee, and ran a hospital in Podgoritza, Montenegro. During this period she was also an active member of the Women's Freedom League (founded in 1907, to obtain votes for women under thirty).

Lillias's complex personality meant that she was not universally popular, being variously described as brilliant, ambitious, interesting, humorous, assertive, domineering, and unpredictable. She expected to be treated with deference, but was often disappointed, and not infrequently came into conflict with those in authority. Her appearance became more eccentric in later life, making her the object of ridicule among some of her students at Studley College. Some even speculated that she possessed supernatural powers, acquired from spending too long in the 'mystical' East. Besides being a highly accomplished photographer and talented needlewoman, Lillias enjoyed music, painting, and the theatre. She never married. Lillias Hamilton died on 6 January 1925 at the Queen Victoria Memorial Hospital, Nice, France, and was buried in the English cemetery there on the Saturday after her death.

SUSAN L. COHEN

**Sources** Wellcome L., Lillias Hamilton MSS, PP/HAM · C. L. C. Hamilton, 'Lillias Hamilton', *Cornhill Magazine*, [3rd] ser., 58 (1925), 538–48 · *The Cheltenham Ladies' College Guild leaflet*, 84 (1925), 53–4 · J. Lee, 'Abd al-Rahman Khanand the Maraz ul-Muluk', *Journal of the Royal Asiatic Society of Great Britain and Ireland*, 3rd ser., 1 (1991), 209–40 · J. Chapman, *Quest for Dion Fortune* (1993) · *Magazine of the London (Royal Free Hospital) School of Medicine for Women* (March 1925), 41–3 · *The Times* (9 Jan 1925) · *Women's Employment* (16 Jan 1925) · J. Gordon, *The luck of thirteen: wanderings and flight through Montenegro and Serbia* (1916) · *Cheltenham Ladies' College Magazine* (1891–1911) · women's service records for First World War, PRO · personal knowledge (2004) · press cuttings collection, archives of the Royal Free Hospital, London · *Magazine of the Studley College Guild* (April 1925), 442 · *CGPLA Eng. & Wales* (1925)

**Archives** Cheltenham Ladies' College, corresp. · Wellcome L., MSS | Cheltenham Ladies' College, letters of Miss Beale, college magazines

**Likenesses** J. P. Quinn, oils, 1924, Wellcome L. [*see illus.*] · portraits, Wellcome L., Lillias Hamilton MSS

**Wealth at death** £5047 10*s*. 6*d*.: resworn probate, 28 April 1925, *CGPLA Eng. & Wales*

**Hamilton, Malcolm**, **Baron Hamilton in the Swedish nobility** (1635–1699), army officer in the Swedish service, was born in Ireland on 18 April 1635, the eldest of four sons of Captain John Hamilton (*d*. 1696) and his wife, Jean or Janet Somerville of Connethon, and grandson of Malcolm Hamilton (*d*. 1629), of Dalserf, Scotland, who was consecrated archbishop of Cashel in 1623. On the advice of his father's brother Hugh Hamilton, later first Baron Hamilton of Glenawley, who had served in the Swedish army, Malcolm Hamilton entered Swedish service in 1654 as a pikeman in Queen Kristina's life guards, and in 1655 joined the Dalecarlia regiment of foot as an ensign. In 1656 he became a captain in Colonel Mortagne's regiment, taking part in Karl X's assault on Copenhagen in February 1659. He was promoted to major on 12 February 1659, in 'recognition of the gallantry he showed on that occasion' (Rudelius, 101). In December 1659 he transferred to the Kalmar regiment of foot with the rank of major, and served as adjutant-general with the Swedish army in Norway. In 1664 he was naturalized as a Swedish nobleman. In 1667 he was appointed lieutenant-colonel of the Älvsborg regiment of foot, Göteborg, remaining with this regiment for the rest of his life.

In October 1675, during Sweden's war with Brandenburg, Hamilton commanded a detachment of one company and 100 Germans in defence of Buxtehude, but the town's citizens and the German troops under his command mutinied and forced him to surrender. Soon afterwards he was also obliged to surrender Bremervörde and was imprisoned, but later released by exchange of prisoners. Following renewed war with Denmark the Älvsborg regiment was ordered back to Sweden from Pomerania in November 1677, some of the regiment being lost at sea. In 1678 he was appointed colonel of his regiment. From 1679 until the accession of Karl XII in 1697 Sweden was occupied with the reforms instituted by Karl XI, and Hamilton was engaged in the country's massive military retrenchment. At war with Russia in Finland in 1689 he led his regiment with distinction at the battle of Kaipais. In a letter to Karl XI later this year he regretted that 'because of illness I cannot be present to troop in our old colours', adding that 'these are indeed the very colours which have often faced your royal majesty's enemies both at home and abroad and … none of which have been delivered up to the enemy, though often in peril, or been lost by other means, save one, which with its whole company was buried at sea in their bed of honour' (Bondestam, 198).

In 1661 Hamilton had married Catherine (1637–1709), widow of Colonel David Sinclair, who fell at the battle of Warsaw in 1656, and daughter of Scottish-born Johan (John) or Hans Maclean, then the richest merchant and banker in Göteborg, who had been ennobled in Sweden under the name Makeléer in 1649. By inheritance through this marriage he became the proprietor of Hageby, Hökälla, and Råda, all in Västergötland. In 1693 Hamilton and his youngest brother Hugh *Hamilton (1655–1724) were introduced into the Swedish house of nobles as barons Hamilton af Hageby. Malcolm Hamilton was ill and bedridden for the last fifteen months of his life, but eight months before his death was appointed major-general and governor of Väster-Norrland province. He died on 19 January 1699 in Stockholm and was buried on 8 August in Gustavi Church, Göteborg. Malcolm and Catherine had five children surviving to adulthood, notably Hugo Johan (1688–1748), who became a field marshal in 1734 and bought Boo Manor, Närke province, since then the hereditary seat of the barons Hamilton af Hageby. Hamilton is described as a 'colourful personality' (Bondestam, 210), who served longer with the Älvsborg regiment (thirty-one years) than any other regimental commander, and was also its longest-serving colonel (twenty years). Many members of the Hamilton family, all descended from either Malcolm Hamilton or his brother Hugh, have since played prominent roles in Swedish life.

Charles Harrison Wallace

**Sources** T. Bondestam, ed., *En bok om I.15: kungl. Älvsborgs regemente, 1624–1974* (1974) • F. Rudelius, *Kalmar regementes personhistoria, 1623–1927* (1952) • E. Flodström, *Dalregementets personhistoria*, 1: *1542–1699* (Falun, 1984) • A. Pihlström, *Kungl. Dalregementets historia*, 6 vols. (1902–38), vols. 1–2 • Hamilton family, *De svenska ätterna Hamilton: en släktkrönika* (Stockholm, 1936) • J. Hamilton, *De svenska ätterna Hamilton: historiska och genealogiska data* (Stockholm, 1995) • G. Hamilton, *A history of the house of Hamilton* (1933) • P. Sörensson, *Generalfälttygmästaren Hugo Hamilton* (1915) • H. E. Uddgren, *Karolinen Hugo Johan Hamilton, en lefnadsteckning* (1916) • G. Elgenstierna, *Svenska adelns ättartavlor* (1927), pt 3, 1.5 • G. Anrep, *Svenska adelns ättartavlor* (1861–4), pt 2 • J. Berg and B. Lagercrantz, *Scots in Sweden* (1962)

**Likenesses** oils, 1682, Boo Manor, Närke, Sweden • R. Silvius, oils (after portrait, 1682), Älvsborg Regiment, Göteborg, Sweden

**Hamilton, Lady Mary.** *See* Walker, Lady Mary (1736–1822).

**Hamilton, Mary, marchioness of Hamilton (1612/13?–1638).** *See under* Hamilton, James, first duke of Hamilton (1606–1649).

**Hamilton, Mary** [Charles] (*fl.* **1746**), sexual impostor, was the daughter of William and Mary Hamilton. She was born in Somerset and subsequently moved with her family to Forfarshire, Scotland. When she was about fourteen years old she left home and returned to England, dressed in her brother's clothes. From that time forward she appears to have lived as a man.

Hamilton served an apprenticeship of two to three years with a mountebank physician Edward Green, in Northumberland, and then spent another year in the service of Dr Finly Green before setting up practice as a quack doctor for herself. On the move once more, she went first to Devon; in May 1746 she settled in Wells, in Somerset, where she was known as Charles Hamilton. On 16 July 1746 she married Mary Price, the niece of Hamilton's landlady, Mary Creed. The couple travelled around Somerset for two months, during which time Price discovered that she had been deceived. Hamilton was arrested on 13 September 1746 and committed to the Shepton Mallet house of correction by the justices of the peace for the town and corporation of Glastonbury to await trial at the next quarter sessions.

At the trial, held on 7 October 1746, the prosecution claimed that Price was not the first woman Mary Hamilton had tricked into marriage and that she had in fact married a total of fourteen women. The charge on which Hamilton was to be tried caused the magistrates some confusion. Lesbianism was not a criminal offence and polygamy did not apply to marriages between women. A letter requesting advice, attributed to Hamilton's legal counsel, indicated that the 'principal Inhabitants' of Glastonbury desired that the 'woman imposter … be punished in the severest manner' available to the quarter sessions (Baker, 220). Hamilton, who had been committed to the house of correction as a vagrant, was eventually tried under a clause of the Vagrancy Act of 1744 (17 Geo. II c. 5) for deceiving and imposing on his majesty's subjects. Convicted as a 'notorious uncommon cheat' (*GM*, 612), she was sentenced to be whipped at three-weekly intervals in four market towns—Taunton, Glastonbury, Wells, and Shepton Mallet—and imprisoned for six months. According to a local newspaper—her arrest and trial were briefly noted in the *Bath Journal* (22, 29 September, 3 November), whose account was picked up by the *Daily Advertiser* (7 November), the *St. James's Evening Post* (8 November), and the *Ipswich Journal* (15 November)—she became something of a celebrity in the house of correction, where she appeared 'very gay, with Perriwig, Ruffles and Breeches' (Baker, 221). After her release from prison Mary Hamilton disappeared from the public record.

Little is known of Hamilton's true history before her marriage to Price. An anonymous pamphlet account of her story, *The Female Husband, or, The Surprising History of Mrs. Mary, alias Mr. George [sic] Hamilton*, was published on 12 November 1746 and claimed to be 'taken from her own Mouth since her Confinement' (title page). In this account Mary Price is Hamilton's third wife; details of two previous marriages are also provided. The pamphlet was subsequently identified as the work of Henry Fielding, who appears to have had no actual contact with his subject, instead basing his history loosely on the newspaper reports of her arrest and trial. Literary scholars have tended largely either to ignore *The Female Husband* or to dismiss it as a piece of hack journalism, a potboiler written hastily for money. Sheridan Baker's painstaking comparison of Fielding's narrative with the court record established that the gap between the two is wide indeed: of the pamphlet's twenty-three pages, twenty are 'pure fiction' and fiction is 'not altogether lacking' in the remaining three (Baker, 219). In Fielding's version of events, Hamilton—whose birthplace he assigns as the 'Isle of *Man*' (Fielding, 2; emphasis in the original)—is seduced to both lesbianism and Methodism by a neighbour with whom she subsequently elopes. His prurient account of Hamilton's history is typical of criminal biography of the period. The averred purpose of publication is to deter others from committing the 'foul and unnatural crimes' committed by his 'heroine in iniquity' (ibid., 23, 2). But the account is replete with salacious detail and hints of 'transactions not fit to be mention'd' (ibid., 3). In the late twentieth century both the real Mary Hamilton and Fielding's fictionalized 'poor female bridegroom' (ibid., 12) have attracted the attention of those interested in the history of sexuality, cross-dressing, and lesbianism.

ALLYSON N. MAY

**Sources** S. Baker, 'Henry Fielding's *The female husband*: fact and fiction', *Proceedings of the Modern Language Association of America*, 74 (1959), 213–24 · *GM*, 1st ser., 16 (1746), 612 · A. Knapp and W. Baldwin, *The Newgate calendar, or, Malefactors' bloody register*, ed. B. Laurie, new edn (1932), 377–8 · [H. Fielding], *The female husband* (1746) · T. Castle, 'Matters not fit to be mentioned: Fielding's *The female husband*', *ELH: a Journal of English Literary History*, 49 (1982), 602–23 · R. Norton, *Mother Clap's molly house: the gay subculture in England, 1700–1830* (1992)

**Archives** Som. ARS, Somerset quarter sessions rolls, ref. nos. 314.6(53), 314.7(3), 314.7(5), 314.7(6)

**Hamilton** [*married name* Dickenson], **Mary** (**1756–1816**), courtier and diarist, was the only child of Charles Hamilton (1721–1771), soldier, son of Lord Archibald Hamilton and grandson of the third duke of Hamilton, and his wife, Mary Catherine (*d.* 1778), daughter of Colonel Dufresne, aide-de-camp to Lord Archibald Hamilton. Her father fought as a volunteer in the service of Empress Elizabeth of Russia, and lived in Scotland before settling near Northampton in 1764, in a house he renamed Hamilton House. From an early age she showed an interest in literature, and when she told her guardian, Lord Napier, that she wanted to learn Latin and Greek, he told her to keep this a secret, 'as a Lady's being learned is commonly looked on as a great fault, even by the learned' (Hamilton, 17, August 1772). Mary Hamilton gave similar advice after meeting a highly accomplished young woman at dinner: she was afraid that her education would make women afraid of her and men shun her, and none would associate with her except 'college pedants, rigid philosophers, or pretended femmes-savantes' (Hamilton, 217, 10 July 1784). As well as reading avidly, she kept a diary, and corresponded regularly with her many friends.

After the death of her father Mary Hamilton and her mother lived on in Northamptonshire until 1775, when they moved to London, but in June 1777 she was asked to come to court by Queen Charlotte, who was looking for a third lady to help with the young princesses. Encouraged by her mother Mary Hamilton agreed, and remained at court until November 1782, spending the summers at Kew and Windsor, and the winters in St James's Palace in London. She found the work tiring, in constant attendance on the princesses or sitting with the queen, and attending celebrations such as royal birthday parties. For several months in 1779 the sixteen-year-old prince of Wales became infatuated with her, until he transferred his affections to an actress: although she did not encourage him, she continued to take an interest in him long after she left court. She became ill in 1780, exhausted by the long evenings waiting on the royal family, and, resenting her lack of freedom, tried to retire from court in 1781, but it was nearly two years before the queen would let her go.

When she moved out of her apartment in St James's Palace in January 1783, Mary Hamilton settled at 27 Clarges Street, Piccadilly, with two friends, the misses Clarke, and enjoyed the company of a circle of literary friends which included Hannah More, Fanny Burney, Mrs Delany, and Mrs Garrick. She dined frequently at the houses of Sir Joshua Reynolds and Horace Walpole. She also met Dr Johnson. She sat in Mrs Garrick's box at the Adelphi to watch the actress Mrs Siddons, and went to concerts, including the Handel celebrations and performance of *Messiah* in Westminster Abbey, given by 513 musicians, in the presence of the royal family (5 June 1784).

John Dickenson (*d.* 1842), only son of John Dickenson of Birch Hall, near Manchester, whom Mary had met when he visited Hamilton House while at boarding-school in Northamptonshire, first proposed marriage in 1780, but she turned him down. When he approached her again in June 1784, confessing he had been in love with her since he was fifteen, she accepted him. They were married on 13 June 1785, settling in Taxal, near Chapel-en-le-Frith, Derbyshire, although they continued to visit London, and to keep in touch with all her London friends. Their only child, Louisa, was born in 1787: she married Major-General Sir William Anson, first baronet, in 1815.

Scandal touched the family when Mary's uncle, Sir William Hamilton, envoy at the court of Naples from 1764 to 1800, a widower since 1782, took up with Emma Hart (later the mistress of Lord Nelson), whom he married in 1791, after living with her in Naples for several years. Mary had been very fond of her uncle, but she felt unable to see him when he returned to London in 1800.

The Dickensons sold the house in Taxal in 1793, and settled in Leighton House, Leighton Buzzard, Bedfordshire, in 1797. In 1811 they moved to 32 Devonshire Place, London. Mary Hamilton died there on 25 May 1816. Extracts from her letters and diaries (the latter beginning on 30 July 1776) were edited and published by two of her great-grandchildren, Elizabeth and Florence Anson, in 1925. The diaries appear to have finished about the time of Mary's marriage, but she remained an active correspondent until the end of her life. The letters and diaries provide a valuable source for the life of the court and London society in the eighteenth century. ANNE PIMLOTT BAKER

**Sources** *Mary Hamilton, afterwards Mrs John Dickenson, at court and at home: from letters and diaries, 1756 to 1816*, ed. E. Anson and F. Anson (1925) • H. Blodgett, *Centuries of female days: Englishwomen's private diaries* (1989) • *GM*, 1st ser., 86/1 (1816), 568

**Archives** priv. coll.

**Likenesses** Miss Boyle, drawing, 1781, repro. in Anson and Anson, eds., *Mary Hamilton*, facing p. 322 • Saunders, miniature, 1784, repro. in Anson and Anson, eds., *Mary Hamilton*, frontispiece • D. Orme, group portrait, oils, 1797 (with husband and daughter), repro. in Anson and Anson, eds., *Mary Hamilton*, facing p. 216

**Hamilton** [*née* Adamson]**, Mary Agnes** (1882–1966), politician and broadcaster, was born on 8 July 1882, at 60 Parsonage Road, Withington, Manchester, the eldest of six children of Robert *Adamson (1852–1902), a Scot, professor of logic at Owens College (later part of Manchester University) and subsequently at the universities of Aberdeen and Glasgow, and his wife, Margaret, *née* Duncan, teacher of botany at Manchester High School for Girls before her marriage in 1881. She attended Aberdeen Girls' High School and Glasgow Girls' High School before going to the University of Kiel in 1901 for seven months to learn German. That same year she went up to Newnham College, Cambridge, as Mathilde Blind scholar. She read classics for two years, then economics as the major element of the history tripos. She was awarded first-class honours in 1904. She became intensely interested in politics and her training in the college 'Political' (debating society) together with her strong, low-pitched voice made her a powerful speaker. She complained that Newnham's career advice was 'teach or nothing', so in January 1905 she became assistant to the history professor at University College of South Wales, Cardiff. She married a colleague, Charles J. Hamilton, on 12 September 1905 but the marriage was not a success and they separated. She took up

Mary Agnes Hamilton (1882–1966), by Peggy Smith, 1930

journalism to earn a living, joining *The Economist* in 1913, where her main interests were women's suffrage and reform of the poor law. She published two books on Greece and Rome and two novels before 1914.

In 1914 Mary Agnes Hamilton, a pacifist and admirer of Ramsay MacDonald, joined the Independent Labour Party (ILP) and was an original member of the pacifist Union of Democratic Control (UDC), formed the same year. Even though she could not accept the Marxist doctrine of the ILP, she helped draw up its constitution. In 1916 she joined *Common Sense* as assistant editor, also writing for the monthly *War and Peace*. She joined the 1917 Club, a group of Liberals of the UDC variety and the Labour left who shared similar pacifist feelings. She became part of Lady Ottoline Morell's anti-war group and moved in the literary circle which included the Woolfs, the Huxleys, D. H. Lawrence, and Lytton Strachey. Her novel *Dead Yesterday* (1916) described the dilemma faced by British intellectuals at the outbreak of war. By 1918 she was a well-known journalist and speaker. In the 1920s she became, at MacDonald's instigation, assistant editor of the ILP's *New Labour Leader*, to curb the left-wing tendencies of its editor, H. N. Brailsford; the experiment was not a success. During this period, together with novels, she wrote biographies of Ramsay MacDonald, Margaret Bondfield, and Mary Macarthur.

Mary Agnes Hamilton stood unsuccessfully for parliament in the 1923 general election as Labour candidate for Rochester and Chatham. She was then adopted by Blackburn, where she found herself more in sympathy with the trade unionists than with the intellectuals of the Labour Party, but she lost in the 1924 election. Between 1924 and

1929 she sat on the Balfour committee on trade and industry and signed its minority report. She also served on the royal commission on the civil service (1929–31).

In 1929 Mary Agnes Hamilton won one of the two seats for Blackburn, obtaining the highest number of votes of any Labour woman candidate. She quickly made her mark in the House of Commons with notable speeches and impressive professionalism (and always wearing red shoes in the house). She became parliamentary private secretary to the postmaster-general, Clement Attlee, who acknowledged her help in his autobiography and wrote to *The Times* upon her death that she was 'one of the ablest women who entered the House of Commons'. In 1929 she presented the first *The Week in Westminster* for the BBC, a radio programme designed to teach women about politics. She was appointed one of two women delegates to the League of Nations in Geneva, where she was a great success, in committee and socially. She became an admirer of Arthur Henderson, Labour foreign secretary, later writing his biography (1938). She also became a friend of Hugh Dalton, future chancellor of the exchequer, one of the other delegates. She fully supported the league's search for peace and collective security.

In the Commons Mary Agnes Hamilton increasingly attacked the Labour Party for failing to remedy the unemployment problem. She did not join the National Government in August 1931 and was elected to the Labour Party parliamentary executive. She sat on the front bench and wound up the speech on the budget for the opposition. After losing her seat in the 1931 general election, she never returned to Westminster and her political activities during the 1930s and 1940s were confined to lecturing and broadcasting. She came out in support of League of Nations sanctions, backed by force, against Italy in 1935; and by 1943 Dalton wrote in his diary that she was now 'quite anti-German as opposed to her attitude in World War One'. She broadcast regularly on the BBC on many topics, including new novels, and was a member of *The Brains Trust*. She was a governor of the BBC (1933–7) and alderman of the county of London (1937–40). In 1940 she joined the civil service as a temporary, and became head of the United States section in the Ministry of Information. She was rewarded by being made a CBE in 1949. She remained in the civil service until 1952.

Molly Hamilton (as she was generally known) made many trips and lecture tours to the United States, the first before the First World War, and by 1930 had a feel for the country and many friends there. In 1941 she travelled for the Ministry of Reconstruction expounding the Beveridge proposals. After the war she maintained her close connections with the USA through the English Speaking Union, to whose journal she contributed many articles. She wrote two autobiographical books, *Remembering my Good Friends* (1944) and *Uphill All the Way* (1953), an account of the achievements of a remarkable career woman and a study of her changing political and spiritual beliefs. She moved from humanism to partial acceptance of Christianity. During her latter years she disappeared from the public eye because of ill health but continued to write. She died at 28 Kenilworth Road, Ealing, London, on 10 February 1966 and was buried at Golders Green.

Janet E. Grenier

**Sources** M. Cole, 'Hamilton, Mary Agnes', *DLB*, vol. 5 · M. A. Hamilton, *Remembering my good friends* (1944) · M. A. Hamilton, *Uphill all the way* (1953) · Newnham College, Cambridge, register [entry for 1901] · M. Corbet, *Newnham College Roll Letter* (1967), 54, 55 · *The Times* (11 Feb 1966) · *Daily Telegraph* (11 Feb 1966) · *The Guardian* (12 Feb 1966) · *The Times* (18 Feb 1966) [appreciations by Earl Attlee and P. H. G. B. (former head of British information services in USA)] · 'Mrs. Hamilton's post', *Daily Herald* (31 July 1924) · 'Woman with honours', *Daily Herald* (26 June 1929) · P. Brookes, *Women at Westminster: an account of women in the British parliament, 1918–1966* (1967) · 'Labour women candidates: Mary Hamilton', *Labour Woman* (July 1928) · M. A. Hamilton, 'Our work at Geneva', *Labour Woman* (Aug 1929) · M. A. Hamilton, 'Laying the foundations', *Labour Woman* (Dec 1929) · M. A. Hamilton, 'Chances of disarmament', *Labour Woman* (Jan 1931) · M. A. Hamilton, 'Some impressions of the United States', *Labour Woman* (May 1933) · J. Robins, 'A week in Westminster is a long time', *The Independent* (2 Nov 1999) · Hugh Dalton, diary, BLPES, Dalton MSS, entry 12 May 1943 · C. R. Attlee, *As it happened* (1954), 84 · d. cert. · b. cert.

**Likenesses** Barratt's Photo Press Ltd, portraits, 1929, repro. in Brookes, *Women at Westminster* · photograph, 1929, Hult. Arch.; repro. in Robins, 'A week in Westminster is a long time' · P. Smith, drawing, 1930, University of Bradford, department of peace studies [*see illus.*] · photograph, Women's Library, London

**Hamilton** [*formerly* Himmelschein], **Max** (**1912–1988**), psychiatrist, was born on 9 February 1912 at Offenbach, near Frankfurt, Germany, the son of Jewish parents, Heinrich Himmelschein, a metal manufacturer, and his wife, Sarah, *née* Kleinberg. When Max was three the family emigrated to England and settled in the impoverished East End of London. He was educated at the Central Foundation School, Cowper Street, famous at that time for the number of highly successful first-generation immigrant boys, mainly Jewish, who were educated there. He went on to study medicine at University College Hospital, London, and after qualifying chose to return to the social and economic deprivation of the East End, as a general practitioner.

At the onset of the Second World War, having changed his name to Hamilton, he volunteered, and served from 1939 to 1946 in the Royal Air Force, as a medical officer. Towards the end of the war, having decided that psychiatry must be his vocation, he found the time and energy, while still serving, to pass part 1 of the diploma of psychological medicine (DPM). On 27 August 1933, while still a student, he had married Sybil Ruth, the nineteen-year-old daughter of David Josephs, a merchant, but the marriage did not last. Hamilton obtained a divorce, and on 27 December 1947 married Doreen Margaret (*b.* 1913/14), daughter of Montague Henry Moody, chartered accountant.

After demobilization, according to plan Hamilton began his clinical psychiatric training at the Maudsley Hospital, London, the mecca of British psychiatry, but very soon found his path blocked by the unsympathetic views of his superiors. In a letter to a colleague, H. Rollin, written on 18 February 1987, he described his ignominious exit from the Maudsley and other frustrations which, had he been less determined, would have put paid to his ambitions. 'I did not take up an interest in Psychiatry until late in the War,' he wrote; 'I tried to get into an RAF mental hospital and succeeded in getting an interview with Sir Charles Symonds … he decided that I was unsuitable for Psychiatry! So also did Sir Aubrey Lewis.' (Symonds was at the time an air vice-marshal and head of neuropsychiatry to the RAF medical services; Lewis was professor of psychiatry in the University of London, located at the Maudsley Hospital.) 'In 1946 I was the only Maudsley registrar who did not have his six-monthly appointment renewed. He [Lewis] never apologised' (personal knowledge).

Undaunted Hamilton decided on a different tack, and pursued a parallel interest—clinical psychology. He returned to University College Hospital and worked for the next four years under the eagle eye of Sir Cyril Burt, father of British clinical psychology; he at least was one of the first to recognize Hamilton's worth as a mathematician, statistician, and innovative research worker. Then he switched back to psychiatry; he took a registrarship at King's College Hospital, London, under the eminent psychiatrist Dennis Hill, who was two years his junior. The next step—typical of Hamilton—was to move backwards and accept a post as a senior medical officer at Springfield Hospital, in south-west London—a run-of-the-mill lunatic asylum. For a would-be professor of psychiatry this might be considered retrogressive, but Hamilton was prepared to dirty his hands at the coalface of psychiatry for the sake of the wealth of raw clinical material available to him.

In 1953, after this most serpentine and foolhardy route, Hamilton took the first definitive step on the academic ladder: he was appointed lecturer in psychiatry at the University of Leeds. This job gave him enough free time to concentrate on research, particularly into the field of the depressive disorders, and to begin formulating his rating scale, which, when completed, emerged as his *magnum opus*: the 'Hamilton rating scale for depression'. This scientifically validated scale assists with three elements: the diagnosis of depression, its severity, and progress made in response to treatment. (He subsequently produced a scale for anxiety.) The depression scale has become the international standard and has been translated into innumerable languages; it established Hamilton as an innovator and a researcher of world class.

Hamilton also made a prolific contribution to scientific literature. He wrote six books, on clinical psychiatry, psychosomatics, and research methodology. Again in keeping with his polymathic expertise, he published innumerable papers in corresponding journals and was editor-in-charge of the abnormal psychology section of the Penguin Science of Behaviour series. At forty-five, however, and in search of new academic pastures, he gambled again. He resigned his lectureship and took a research job at Leeds University before accepting an appointment as a visiting scientist at the National Institute of Mental Health, Bethesda, Maryland, USA. After a year (1959–60) he returned to Leeds, as a member of the external staff of the Medical Research Council. In 1963 the incumbent of the chair of psychiatry at Leeds, G. R. Hargreaves, died. In spite of Hamilton's idiosyncrasies and erratic career the powers that be had the wit to appoint him to the vacant Nuffield chair of psychiatry.

Hamilton's tenure as professor coincided with the expansion of the Leeds Medical School and its department of psychiatry. His conviction that psychiatry could not be taught to the exclusion of social studies led to the establishment of courses, jointly with his department and the department of adult education and extra-mural studies, leading to academic qualifications. These courses ceased because of university financial stringencies but in 1965 a joint course in clinical psychology and psychiatry leading to an MSc was established, and thrives into the twenty-first century. This enterprise has trained a tenth of the clinical psychologists practising in Britain. In appreciation the university established the annual Max Hamilton prize for the best dissertation submitted in clinical psychiatry for the degree award.

Towards the end of his life Hamilton was showered with honours. He was founding president of the British Psychopharmacology Association, managing editor of the journal *Psychopharmacology*, and honorary fellow of the Royal College of Psychiatrists. He was honoured in America, as witness his election to an honorary professorship at two universities and the award, in 1980, of the Paul Hoch prize for distinguished psychiatric research. In addition he was elected to honorary membership of learned societies in Belgium and Turkey.

However, in the light of his hurtful rebuff at the hands of the Maudsley moguls way back in 1946, Hamilton must have tasted a degree of bitter-sweet pleasure when, in 1988, he was invited to give the annual Maudsley lecture—the most prestigious award available in British psychiatry. This was to be presented in October 1988, and to be intriguingly entitled 'Mathematical model and clinical judgement'. Tragically Hamilton was cheated of his triumph by the 'last enemy': he died, prematurely, on 6 August 1988, while on holiday at Hemsby Beach Chalet Centre, Great Yarmouth.

Max Hamilton, renowned as a one-off 'character', succeeded, despite the best efforts of the British establishment, in becoming a world-famed psychiatrist. But he was far more than that: he proved himself to be a scholar and leader of distinction in the fields of mathematics, statistics, psychometry, and pharmacology and an expert in the methodology of clinical trials. As a teacher he was inspired, and if the occasion demanded he could deliver his lecture in German or French. He never courted popularity, however, and in certain quarters in Britain he was positively disliked—in all probability because of his bluntness and caustic wit; in America, where he spent a good deal of his time post-retirement, he was revered. Politically he was decidedly left-of-centre; he espoused the underdog and the oppressed. He enjoyed debate—the more heated the better—particularly if he was defending a minority opinion. And yet despite his sharp tongue, he had a soft centre. To his friends he was generous and steadfast. And, perhaps incongruously, he loved flowers, especially orchids and narcissi, which he grew himself at home in Leeds. He was survived by his wife, Doreen, their son and two daughters, and two sons from his first marriage. HENRY R. ROLLIN

**Sources** personal knowledge (2004) · private information (2004) · biographical details of fellows of the Royal College of Psychiatrists · *The Times* (17 Aug 1988) · Munk, *Roll* · *BMJ* (8 Oct 1988), 297, 914–15 · *The Lancet*, 2 (1988), 582 · *Journal of the Royal College of Psychiatrists*, 13/1 (Jan 1989) · *Bulletin of the Royal College of Psychiatrists*, 6/12 · m. certs. · d. cert.
**Likenesses** photograph, repro. in *The Lancet*, 582
**Wealth at death** £239,389: probate, 28 July 1989, *CGPLA Eng. & Wales*

**Hamilton, Nina Mary Benita Douglas-** [*née* Nina Mary Benita Poore], **duchess of Hamilton and Brandon** (**1878–1951**), animal welfare activist, was born at Old Lodge, Nether Wallop, Hampshire, on 13 May 1878, the third daughter of Major Robert Poore (1834–1918), landowner, and his wife, Juliana Benita, daughter of Admiral Armar Lowry-Corry. In 1901 Nina married Alfred Douglas-Hamilton, thirteenth duke of Hamilton and tenth duke of Brandon (1862–1940); they had seven children, including Douglas Douglas-*Hamilton.

Born into an old Wiltshire family, Nina inherited a strong sense of duty and devoted her life to those around her, in particular to her disabled husband, to their children, to their estates' employees, and to the relief and prevention of animal suffering. Brought up an Anglican, she nevertheless wanted her whole family to worship in the Church of Scotland, because it was the church of the local people. Her father's care for the welfare of the people was her great pride, and she kept a lifelong memory of his experiment at Winterslow in which he sought to return to the agricultural labourers the independence they had lost over a century earlier. Her contributions to their welfare were made so discreetly that few apart from the recipients knew of them. Some gifts, however, were too generous to be concealed. One such was the gift in 1910 to Bo'ness town council of a completely equipped and furnished nurses' home, the maintenance of which the duchess made her entire responsibility.

The duchess was more generally known for her concern for animals. She and her husband held that only by companionship with animals can children be taught to develop that nobility of character which will make them champions of the weak, whether of the human race or of their fellow creatures. Through her love of wildlife she developed a deep concern to prevent cruelty to domestic animals. This impulse widened to include those easily forgotten creatures she saw to be suffering for human convenience and pleasure.

In 1920 Nina had met the redoubtable reformer Emilia Augusta Louise Lind-af-Hageby, through whom she developed an interest in spiritualism. Lind (as most knew her) and the duchess teamed to campaign forcefully against vivisection and for more humane slaughtering methods. With Leisa Schartau and the Hon. Stephen Coleridge they brought the first mass campaigns of this movement to London. Through the Animal Defence and Anti-Vivisection Society, founded by Lind in 1906, and of which the duchess became chair in 1917, demonstrations and international congresses were held in England. During the First World War the society set up three veterinary hospitals for horses and campaigned against transportation of live animals, chicken batteries, fur-trapping, bloodsports, cruelty to performing animals, racing, the exploitation of pitponies, and the use of animals in war. Respect for the society owed much to the duchess's gracious but uncompromising advocacy of political change, conducted with humour and restraint.

In 1939 the duchess founded the Ferne Animal Sanctuary at her home near Shaftesbury, Dorset, prompted by the concern she and her husband felt for the well-being of animals whose owners would be leaving for war service. Not only animals, but children from the East End of London were made welcome at Ferne. She also wrote and compiled an illustrated book, *Chronicles of Ferne* (1951).

Nina's convictions about medical research prompted her refusal to be operated on for a non-malignant throat condition, or to take the antibiotics prescribed for the pneumonia that eventually developed. She died at her house, Lynsted, St Edmund's Terrace, London, on 12 January 1951. The funeral service was in Salisbury Cathedral and the burial was at Berwick St John, near Shaftesbury. JON WYNNE-TYSON

**Sources** Burke, *Peerage* · E. Westacott, *A century of vivisection and anti-vivisection* (1949) · C. Niven, *History of the Humane Movement* (1967) · R. D. Ryder, *Animal revolution: changing attitudes towards speciesism* (1989) · *The Times* (13 Jan 1951) · *The Times* (23 Nov 1951) · personal knowledge (2004) · b. cert. · private information (2004)
**Likenesses** oils, priv. coll. · photograph, priv. coll.
**Wealth at death** £115,017 16*s*. 10*d*.: probate, 28 July 1951, *CGPLA Eng. & Wales*

**Hamilton, Patrick** (**1504?–1528**), theologian and protestant martyr, was a younger son of Sir Patrick Hamilton of Kincavel in Linlithgowshire and Stanehouse in Lanarkshire, a bastard son (legitimized in 1513) of Sir James Hamilton of Cadzow, the first Lord Hamilton. His mother was Katherine Stewart, daughter of Alexander, third duke of Albany, the second son of James II and brother of James III. The third wife of his father's brother, James, second Lord Hamilton and first earl of Arran, was Janet, daughter of Sir David Beaton of Creich, brother of the James Beaton who subsequently became archbishop of St Andrews. Patrick Hamilton was probably born in 1504 (François Lambert records that he was about twenty-three in 1527) either at Kincavel or Stanehouse. He registered himself at the University of Paris as 'Patricius Hamelto, Glassguensis, nobilis', which might suggest that Stanehouse was his place of birth, but later registered at Marburg University as 'a Litgovien, Scotus', which would suggest he saw Kincavel as his home. He had an elder brother, James, and a sister, Katherine.

Hamilton was probably educated at the grammar school in Linlithgow. As a younger son he was destined for the church, and after the death of Andrew Stewart, bishop of

Caithness, in 1517, became titular abbot of Fearn in Ross-shire. The abbey had been founded during the reign of Alexander III, and the church, completed by William, seventh earl of Ross (*d.* 1372), was then a handsome building of about 120 feet in length. In either 1517 or 1518 the young Patrick Hamilton went to the University of Paris, where his name was entered in a register of the MAs of the university for 1520. It is not known to which college he was attached, but it was possibly the Scots College, or the Collège de Montaigu, where John Mair still taught until he moved to Glasgow in 1518. Erasmus had left Paris over a decade before, but there is no doubt that his dislike of scholasticism and instinct to study the original sources had left their mark. Luther's theology was also being discussed and his writings were burned by a decree of the Sorbonne in 1521. Alexander Alesius, one of the Augustinian canons of St Andrews, and a pupil of Mair, supplies the most personal contemporary account of Hamilton, describing him as 'a man of excellent learning and very acute mind, and all for recalling philosophy to its sources—to Aristotle and Plato—and for utterly banishing sophistry from the schools' (Alesius, fol. 164*v*). Alesius also records that Hamilton studied in Louvain as well as Paris. No record of his registration has been discovered there, but if Alesius is right it is just possible that Hamilton there met Erasmus, who was at the court of Charles V in Brussels in 1516 and did not move to Basel until 1521.

The precise date of Hamilton's return to Scotland is not known but he was incorporated into the University of St Andrews on 9 June 1523, the same day as John Mair, who had been brought to St Andrews from Glasgow by James Beaton when he became archbishop of St Andrews earlier that year. Although only about nineteen, Hamilton had had the opportunity to acquire a firsthand acquaintance with Luther's work and the issues involved. Yet it may be suggested that he most probably returned to Scotland as an Erasmian humanist rather than a Lutheran.

Hamilton (styled 'abbas de Ferne') was admitted into the faculty of arts at St Andrews on 3 October 1524 and seems to have thrown himself into the life of the university. His academic and personal brilliance was recognized. According to Alesius he composed a mass for nine voices for the office beginning 'Benedicant dominum omnes angeli eius', and himself acted as precentor when it was performed in the cathedral. This and his advancement in the university suggest that he had not yet broken with the structures of the Roman church. He may have been ordained to the priesthood at this stage. John Frith, in the preface to his translation of 'Patrick's places' (published in the enlarged edition of John Foxe's *Actes and Monuments*, London, 1570, 1109–10), tells us that Hamilton, 'to testifie the truth, sought all meanes, & tooke upo him priesthode (even as Paul circumcised Timothye, to wynne the weake Jewes), that he might be admitted to preach the pure word of God'. Contrary evidence is that James Beaton's summons to him in 1527, to present himself in St Andrews, implies that he was without authority to preach ('propria auctoritate et temeraria presumptione predictationis officium … acceptare ausus est'—'on his own authority and with foolhardy presumption he had the audacity to take up the preacher's office'; Mitchell, 289).

The years 1525 and 1526 were particularly unsettled in Scotland, with varying factions vying to influence the young James V. An act of parliament of 1525 forbade the importing and distribution of the works of Luther. The act was reinforced two years later, but contemporary evidence (a report by Cardinal Wolsey's spy, John Hackett, in February 1527) indicates that despite the act large numbers of heretical books were imported to Edinburgh and St Andrews. Unfortunately, available sources give no indication as to which of Luther's works these were. William Tyndale's translation of the New Testament was published in Worms in 1526 and quickly imported to England and Scotland. It was during this period that Patrick Hamilton passed from Erasmian humanism to active sympathy for Luther, thus provoking James Beaton to initiate an inquiry into him in Lent 1527.

Rather than face the inquiry, Hamilton fled to Germany. With him went two friends (Gilbert Wynram of Lothian and John Hamilton of Linlithgow) and a servant. Although Knox in his *History* implies that Hamilton visited Wittenberg and met Luther and Melanchthon, there is no documentary evidence that he registered there. That summer the plague was rife in Wittenberg, and Hamilton and his friends enrolled at the new Lutheran University of Marburg at the end of May. There he met François Lambert of Avignon, the head of the theological faculty. A warm friendship developed between them, and with Lambert's encouragement Hamilton was the first in the new university to publish a set of theses for public debate. These theses were subsequently translated from Latin into English by John Frith and inserted as 'Patrick's places' into both John Knox's *History of the Reformation* and John Foxe's *Actes and Monuments*.

'Patrick's places' are important for showing the stage to which Hamilton's thought had developed. It has often been assumed that, in the freedom of Marburg and under the tutelage of Lambert, Hamilton's thinking suddenly crystallized. It now appears likely, however, that Hamilton arrived in Marburg already equipped with a knowledge of Lutheran theology and that his quickly composed theses were a distillation of a personal commonplace book he had put together in St Andrews. The theses were directly and explicitly biblical. Emphasis was laid on human powerlessness under sin and utter dependence upon God's grace. The old law commands what, humanly speaking, is impossible; the gospel proclaims that Christ, who is accessible through faith, bore our sins and is himself our righteousness. Consequently no work can make us righteous; whoever thinks to be saved by works denies that Christ is our saviour. Literary analysis suggests that, especially in his treatment of faith, charity, and works, Hamilton was following the argument of Luther's tract, *Of the Liberty of a Christian Man* (1520), and Melanchthon's *Loci communes* (1521). This in turn makes it possible to appreciate the pivotal role that Hamilton had in the focusing and application of Lutheran theology in Scotland.

Hamilton remained in Marburg for not more than six

months. He returned, most probably to the family estate of Kincavel near Linlithgow, which following the death of their father in the Cleanse the Causeway skirmish in Edinburgh in 1520 had now been inherited by his brother, Sir James Hamilton. From the fact that they were subsequently called to account for their beliefs, it is evident that he convinced both his brother and his sister Katherine. At this time, according to Alesius, he married, though the name of his wife has not been preserved. A daughter, Isobel, was born after his death. He devoted himself to preaching around Linlithgow, and James Beaton quickly became aware of his return and impact. He issued a summons against him, the *Citatio Patricii Hamilton*, addressed to the dean of the Lothians and concerned specifically with Hamilton's preaching in Linlithgowshire.

Hamilton duly returned to St Andrews around the middle of January 1528, and presented himself for examination. There is evidence that he may have been accompanied by his brother. The conference lasted several days and at first, according to Knox, Beaton and his doctors appeared conciliatory, even acknowledging that many matters in the church required reformation. Hamilton was allowed his freedom and permitted to teach openly in the university for the best part of a month. This may have been so that he would incriminate himself still further, though Alesius notes that Beaton himself wished to allow him an opportunity to escape. Hamilton spent the time in public and private debate. Alesius, though sent to try to confute him, found himself convinced by Hamilton. A Dominican friar, Alexander Campbell, apparently agreeing with Hamilton in private, subsequently became his public accuser.

Hamilton was eventually recalled to answer a series of charges. From these, eye-witnesses point to seven as being 'the very Articles for the which he suffered' (Foxe, 1108). These central charges included Hamilton's contentions concerning free will, original sin, grace, good works, and the interrelation of faith, hope, and love. Literary analysis points to striking parallels between the heresy charges and Luther's *Assertio omnium articulorum* of 1520–21, suggesting that that work was now circulating in St Andrews. Robert Lindsay of Pitscottie provides a graphic account of how Alexander Campbell pressed his accusations upon Hamilton. Other charges emerged: that Hamilton disbelieved in purgatory and the mediation of the saints. Hamilton responded by appealing to the authority of scripture and the sole mediation of Christ: he had passed beyond what could be contained in debate and mounted a fundamental challenge to the existing religious institutions. Inevitably, Campbell summed up: 'my lordis ze heir he denyis the institutiouns of hallie kirk and the authorietie of our hollie father the pape. I neid nocht to accuse him no more' (Pitscottie, 310).

Sentence was pronounced and Hamilton was almost immediately taken to the stake, which was set up outside St Salvator's College, at a spot marked today by the letters PH. The execution, which took place on 29 February 1528, was slow and horrific. Alesius says that he was more roasted than burned ('ustulatus magis quam combustus'; Lorimer, 238). Knox records how the gunpowder, used as a firelighter, scorched Hamilton, but failed to set the wood alight. Pitscottie records how a baker, called Myrtoun, ran and brought an armful of straw. Hamilton suffered for some six hours.

Hamilton's death was a turning point. His courage, brilliance, and gentleness provided an inspiration and model. Famously, Knox records the remark of one John Lindsey to Beaton:

> My Lord, yf ye burne any mo, except ye follow my counsall, ye will utterlye destroy your selves. Yf ye will burne thame, lett thame be brunt in how [deep] sellarris; for the reik of Maister Patrik Hammyltoun hes infected as many as it blew upoun. (Knox, *History*, ed. Laing, 1.42)

At a theological level, examination of Hamilton's writings and trial enable us better to understand the transition in Scotland from an early protestant piety which was essentially biblical and Christocentric, emphasizing preaching and reform of clerical abuse, to a form which realized the wider implications of justification by faith alone and so posed a real threat to the institutions of the Roman church. IAIN TORRANCE

**Sources** A. Alesius, *Primus liber Psalmorum iuxta Hebraeorum et divi Hieronymi Supputationem, expositus ab Alexandro Alesio* (1554) · J. Knox, *History of the Reformation in Scotland*, vols. 1–2 of *The works of John Knox*, ed. D. Laing, Wodrow Society, 12 (1846–8) · J. Foxe, *The first volume of the ecclesiasticall history contayning the actes and monumentes of thynges passed*, new edn (1570) · R. Lindsay of Pitscottie, *The history and chronicles of Scotland* (1724) · A. F. Mitchell, *The Scottish Reformation* (1900), appx B, 'Citatio Patricii Hamilton' · P. Lorimer, *Precursors of Knox* (1857) · G. Wiedermann, 'Martin Luther versus John Fisher: some ideas concerning the debate on Lutheran theology at the University of St Andrews, 1525–30', *Records of the Scottish Church History Society*, 22 (1984–6), 13–34 · R. Haas, 'Franz Lambert und Patrick Hamilton in ihrer Bedeutung für die evangelische Bewegung auf den Britischen Inseln', doctoral diss., Marburg University, 1973 · D. Calderwood, *The true history of the Church of Scotland, from the beginning of the Reformation, unto the end of the reigne of King James VI* (1678) · register, University of Paris, *c*.1520 · register, University of Louvain, *c*.1520–1525 · register, *c*.1523, U. St Andr. · register, University of Marburg, *c*.1527

**Hamilton, (Anthony Walter) Patrick (1904–1962)**, novelist and playwright, was born on 17 March 1904 at Dale House, Hassocks, Sussex, the third of the three children of Walter Bernard Hamilton (1863–1930), writer and non-practising barrister, and his second wife, Ellen Adèle Day, *née* Hockley (1861–1934), writer. Patrick Hamilton's earliest years were spent at 12 First Avenue, Hove, Sussex (now commemorated by a plaque), where his family lived from 1908 until the First World War. His parents' unhappy marriage together with the rigidly regulated social codes of Edwardian middle-class life left the young boy overwrought and introverted. The material privileges of his early years were gradually eroded from a position with servants and nannies to one where his mother had to run the household herself in the early 1920s. His father's alcoholism and mismanagement of an inherited fortune meant that the family spent the war years in boarding-houses in Chiswick and Hove, and Patrick Hamilton's education was patchy and interrupted: Holland House School, Hove (1912–18), Colet Court, Hammersmith (1915), and

(**Anthony Walter) Patrick Hamilton (1904–1962)**, by Elliott & Fry, 1948

Westminster School, London (1918–19). About his fifteenth birthday Hamilton was removed from school by his mother when he contracted Spanish influenza. Apart from a brief, unsuccessful attempt to prepare for his matriculation at a London crammer in 1919, this was the end of Hamilton's formal education. An indefatigable autodidact from then on, he remained conservative in his literary tastes, detesting fictional experimentation in general and modernism in particular, attacking its exponents in his dystopian novel, *Impromptu in Moribundia* (1939).

Both his parents were minor novelists and Hamilton resisted his father's desire that he train for some profession, wishing to pursue his early vocation as a writer. After a series of poorly paid jobs, including those of assistant stage manager, small-part actor (under the stage name Patrick Henderson), and clerk, Hamilton became a full-time writer in 1923, financed by his mother, sister (Lalla), and brother (Bruce). His first novel, *Monday Morning*, was completed when he was only nineteen and published in 1925 by Constable, whose editor, the writer Michael Sadleir, became a long-term friend and mentor. Constable published the twelve novels and seven stage and radio plays which Hamilton wrote over the following three decades. The early books *Craven House* (1926) and *Twopence Coloured* (1928) were well received, and Hamilton was for a short time lionized in 1929 when his 'shocker', the stage play *Rope*, was a West End hit. *The Midnight Bell* also came out in that year, and was the first of three books—including *The Siege of Pleasure* (1932) and *The Plains of Cement* (1934)—which were subsequently published as a trilogy under the title *Twenty Thousand Streets under the Sky* (1935).

The settings and focus of these and most of Hamilton's works were the boarding-houses, pubs, and brothels of inter-war London and Brighton, populated by 'the lost, failed and forgotten' (French, 1). Hamilton later wrote:

> what I was trying to present was a 'black' social history of my times. There were so many 'white' portraits of the twenties and thirties that I wanted to show the other side of the picture. After all, those were the decades in which Hitler rose to power. No one that I read was writing anything about him and the evil he represented. (French, 275)

With his 'bat's wing ear' for dialogue (Cockburn, x) and coruscating wit, Hamilton was the observer and habitué of the kind of society he described in his fiction and his work has been compared to that of Dickens, Gissing, and Orwell. By the late 1920s he was smoking and drinking heavily and regularly and had conceived an infatuation for a prostitute which he depicted in *The Midnight Bell*.

A slight man, bespectacled and expensively dressed, Hamilton cut an elegant figure until in 1932, at the height of his literary success, he was hit by a drunk driver and suffered multiple injuries which resulted in a withered left arm, a limp, and scars on his nose and forehead; his radio play *To the Public Danger* (1939) was commissioned by the road safety campaign. The accident heightened his long-standing shyness. Despite the critical acclaim of his fiction and the financial success of *Rope* and his second play, *Gaslight* (1938), Hamilton was never part of any literary group, preferring the company of family and friends. Early on he compartmentalized his life into his friendships with Sadleir and other writers, his Soho acquaintances, his close relationship with his mother and sister until their respective deaths in 1934 and 1951, and his lifelong intimacy with his brother (also a novelist). Intensely fond of cricket and golf, Hamilton had a great many interests, but his main passion was his work. On 6 August 1930 he married Lois Marie Martin (1900/01–1975), yet Hamilton's attitude to women was based on an unhappy mixture of infatuation and misogyny. Intimate relationships were reserved for men. One way in which his writing differed from Dickens's was that Hamilton never wrote love stories. Nor do his characters belong to families; rather they are lonely men and women who are sympathetically portrayed in their unhappy and somehow inevitable solitariness. Nowhere is this more true than in his highly successful novel *Hangover Square* (1941), whose bleak subject is described in its full title: *Hangover Square, or, The Man with Two Minds: a Story of Darkest Earl's Court in the Year 1939*.

By the time he was writing *Hangover Square*, Hamilton had become intellectually committed to Marxist communism, which he championed with an almost religious fervour. Unfit for active service in the Second World War, he did work for the Entertainments National Service Association, as well as being a firewatcher during air raids. He continued to write plays, including *This is Impossible* (1941) and *The Duke in Darkness* (1943), but neither achieved the success of *Gaslight*, which was filmed in America as *Angel Street* (1942) and, more famously, *Rope*, the basis of Alfred

Hitchcock's 1948 screen version. Unfortunately this was one of Hitchcock's weaker productions and Hamilton was disappointed at the loss of the taut atmosphere of his stage original.

More successful was Hamilton's novel *The Slaves of Solitude* (1947), which led John Betjeman to describe him as one of 'the best English novelists' (Jones, 283). In 1948 Hamilton began an affair with the novelist Lady Ursula (La) Winifred Stewart, *née* Chetwynd-Talbot (1907/8–1966), daughter of Viscount Ingestre. She had changed her surname by deed poll to Hamilton before their marriage on 10 April 1954, a year after Patrick Hamilton's divorce from Lois Martin in 1953. Yet Hamilton's life was no less turbulent and he was looked after by La and Lois in turn as his health continued to deteriorate because of alcoholism. His final three novels were *The West Pier* (1951)—'the best novel written about Brighton' (Graham Greene, in Jones, 310); *Mr Stimpson and Mr Gorse* (1953), which was adapted for the television series *The Charmer*; and *Unknown Assailant* (1955). Together they form *The Gorse Trilogy* and explore the criminal mind, a subject which had long fascinated Hamilton.

Hamilton's final seven years were dominated by his alcoholism and what one doctor diagnosed as menopausal melancholia. In despair he underwent electroconvulsive therapy in 1956. It brought relief but seems to have eradicated his desire and ability to write except for an autobiographical piece, 'Memoirs of a Heavy Drinking Man' (never published), in which he considered how far his alcoholism might be a genetic condition (his sister had also been an alcoholic). Increasingly impaired by regular drinking although suffering from cirrhosis of the liver, Patrick Hamilton died on 23 September 1962 at his home, 3 Martincross, North Street, Sheringham, Norfolk. His body was cremated on 26 September and his ashes scattered on the Blakeney Flats.

Only since his death has Patrick Hamilton's work received its due critical recognition, with republications introduced by J. B. Priestley and Michael Holroyd. He has been the subject of several biographies.

NATHALIE BLONDEL

**Sources** S. French, *Patrick Hamilton: a life* (1993) · N. Jones, *Through a glass darkly: the life of Patrick Hamilton* (1991) · B. Hamilton, *The light went out: a biography of Patrick Hamilton* (1972) · C. Cockburn, 'Introduction', in P. Hamilton, *The slaves of solitude* (1982) · D. Lessing, *The Times* (26 June 1968) · M. Holroyd, 'Introduction', in P. Hamilton, *Twenty thousand streets under the sky* (1987) · J. B. Priestley, 'Introduction', in P. Hamilton, *Twenty thousand streets under the sky* (1943) · J. B. Priestley, 'Introduction', in P. Hamilton, *Hangover Square* (1974) · B. McKenna, 'Confessions of a heavy-drinking Marxist: addiction in the work of Patrick Hamilton', *Beyond the pleasure dome: writing and addiction from the Romantics*, ed. S. Vice, M. Campbell, and T. Armstrong (1994), 231–44 · private information (2004) · m. certs. · *CGPLA Eng. & Wales* (1962)

**Archives** BBC WAC | BL, corresp. with Society of Authors, Add. MS 63261 · Constable publishers, London, Constable archives · NRA, priv. coll., Sean French MSS · NRA, priv. coll., Nigel Jones MSS · Temple University, Philadelphia, Constable MSS

**Likenesses** Elliott & Fry, photograph, 1948, NPG [*see illus.*] · photographs, repro. in French, *Patrick Hamilton* · photographs, repro. in Jones, *Through a glass darkly*

**Wealth at death** £6344 17*s*. 0*d*.: probate, 24 Dec 1962, *CGPLA Eng. & Wales*

**Hamilton, Philipp Ferdinand de** (*c.*1664–1750). *See under* Hamilton, James (*c.*1640–*c.*1720).

**Hamilton, Richard** (*d.* 1717), Jacobite army officer, was the fifth son of Sir George *Hamilton, first baronet (*d.* 1679) [*see under* Hamilton, James, first earl of Abercorn (1575–1618)], the receiver-general of the revenue for Ireland, and his wife, Mary Butler (*d.* 1680), sister of James Butler, first duke of Ormond. Born in Ireland, he was taken to France as an infant, where he was brought up until the Restoration, when his family moved to Whitehall. His brother George raised a regiment for service in France in 1671 in which both Richard and another brother, Anthony *Hamilton (1644/5?–1719), took commissions. In 1678 he replaced Thomas Dongan as the regiment's colonel, and when later that year the regiment was disbanded he was given a French regiment, which he commanded for over six years. He was popular at the French court, and in 1681 danced before Louis XIV as a zephyr in Quinault's ballet *Le triomphe de l'amour* at St Germain-en-Laye. In March 1685 he left the French service after an argument with the minister of war over the state of his regiment. Shortly before leaving France he and the marquis d'Alincourt were found with drawn swords in the palace gardens. They claimed that they were protecting themselves against four ruffians, but it was generally believed that they were fighting one another for the affections of the princess de Conti, Louis XIV's recently widowed daughter.

Hamilton returned to England with a sense of having been ill-treated by the French. He was made a colonel of dragoons on the Irish establishment by James II on 20 June 1685, and in April 1686 he was promoted to brigadier, making him (after the earl of Tyrconnell and Justin MacCarthy) the third most senior member of the Irish army. In the next month he was appointed to the privy council of Ireland. He failed to get on with the earl of Clarendon, the lord lieutenant, but was nevertheless given the colonelcy of an English cavalry regiment in 1687. At the revolution he was in England, where he was promoted to major-general on 12 November 1688 by James.

After James fled to France, the new government in London hoped that Tyrconnell could be persuaded to give up power in Ireland rather than face a war. Hamilton was chosen for this mission and released on parole to return in three weeks if he was unsuccessful. 'He was a Papist, but thought to be a man of honour, and had certainly great credit with the Earl of Tyrconnel' (*Abridgement of Burnet's History*, 291). On landing at Ringsend in January 1689 Hamilton went straight to a tavern, where he 'broke out into loud laughter, saying he could not forbear it, thinking how finely he had shammed the Prince of Orange' (*House of Lords MSS, 1689–90*, 189). The effect of his arrival was immediate: 'The Papists lit bonfires when Dick Hamilton came over; they said he was worth ten thousand men' (ibid., 141). Tyrconnell promoted him to lieutenant-general and sent him with an army to suppress the rebellion in the north. On 14 March 1689 he scattered a rebel force at Dromore and marched on Coleraine. Here he was checked by Gustavus Hamilton on 27 March, but once his troops crossed the Bann in boats at Portglenone on 7 April, Coleraine was evacuated and he advanced on Londonderry. At the same time King James marched north with a force commanded by Marshal Conrad Rosen, an experienced officer seconded from the French army. At the battle of the Fords (15 April) Rosen and Hamilton made separate attacks on Lundy's positions on the rivers Finn and Foyle and forced his troops back to the city. Despite the king's arrival, Londonderry refused to surrender, and on 20 April James and Rosen left for Dublin, leaving the marquis de Maumont in command. On the next day Maumont was killed in a sally led by Adam Murray and Hamilton took sole control of the siege operations. After the humiliating failure of his two attacks on Windmill Hill (6 May and 4 June) he concentrated his efforts on starving the garrison into submission. He raised the siege on 1 August 1689 after three supply ships reached the city. The French blamed the failure of the siege on Hamilton. They considered him to be incompetent, hostile to them, and wholly inexperienced in siege warfare.

Hamilton was nevertheless highly regarded by both Tyrconnell and King James. He commanded under Tyrconnell the right wing of the Irish army at the battle of the Boyne (1 July 1690), in which he acted with great bravery. He was left at Oldbridge to direct the fighting against the main part of King William's army. Once his infantry gave way, he led three desperate cavalry charges, in the last of which he was wounded and captured. He was brought before King William, who asked him whether he thought the Irish would fight any more.

> Yes, (said he) an't please Your Majesty, upon my Honour I believe they will, for they have a great Body of Horse still. The King look'd a little aside at him when he named his Honour, and repeated it once or twice, *Your Honour*: Intimating (as he always says a great deal in a few Words) that what the other affirmed upon his Honour was not to be believed since he had forfeited that before in his siding with my Lord *Tyrconnel*. (Story, 84)

Hamilton was kept a prisoner in Dublin until January 1691, when he was brought to Chester Castle. In January 1692 he was taken to the Tower, where his release was agreed and he was exchanged for Lord Mountjoy in April that year. He travelled to Versailles to thank Louis and took his place under Marshal Bellefonds in King James's invasion force in Normandy. The invasion plans were dashed after the destruction of the French fleet at the battle of La Hogue (19–24 May 1692).

Hamilton thereafter attached himself to the exiled Jacobite court. In 1696 he became James's master of the robes and in expectation of another invasion attempt was given the empty title of lieutenant-general of King James's forces in England. He kept both his military rank and appointment to the royal household after the death of James II, and sailed with the invasion fleet on the abortive attempt on Scotland in March 1708. On his return he accompanied James Stuart, the Pretender, to the war in Flanders, having been given strict instructions by Mary of Modena 'not to quit the king one step in a day of action and also to tell him frankly and positively what is fitt for him to do' (Clark, 296). In this capacity he was present at the battle of Oudenarde (11 July 1708) and in the campaigns of the next two years.

In 1713 Hamilton was dismissed from the service of the Pretender after plotting to take over from Lord Middleton as secretary of state. Such was his disgrace that he was kept out of the royal presence and forbidden to move from St Germain without the king's permission. In the last year of his life he found himself in such poverty that he went to live with his niece, the abbess of the convent of St Marie, Poussay. He adopted a life of piety and died at the convent in his late sixties, a bachelor, in December 1717.

PIERS WAUCHOPE

**Sources** R. Clark, *Anthony Hamilton* (1921) • G. Story, *An impartial history of the wars of Ireland* (1693) • *The manuscripts of the House of Lords*, 4 vols., HMC, 17 (1887–94), vol. 2 • *An abridgement of Bishop Burnet's History of his own times*, ed. T. Stackhouse (1906) • *Journal du marquis de Dangeau*, ed. E. Soulié and others, 19 vols. (Paris, 1854–60) • *The correspondence of Henry Hyde, earl of Clarendon, and of his brother Laurence Hyde, earl of Rochester*, ed. S. W. Singer, 2 vols. (1828) • J. T. Gilbert, ed., *A Jacobite narrative of the war in Ireland, 1688–1691* (1892); facs. edn (1971) • C. D. Milligan, *History of the siege of Londonderry, 1689* (1951)

**Hamilton, Sir Richard Vesey** (1829–1912), naval officer, was born at Sandwich, Kent, on 28 May 1829, the younger son of the Revd John Vesey Hamilton, vicar of St Mary's, Sandwich, and his wife, Frances Agnes Malone. He was educated at the Royal Naval School, Camberwell, Surrey, and entered the Royal Navy in 1843, sailing in the *Virago* to the Mediterranean. In 1850 he volunteered for one of the Admiralty's expeditions to search for the Arctic explorer Sir John Franklin, serving as mate in the *Assistance* (Captain Erasmus Ommanney); on his return he was promoted lieutenant in 1851. He volunteered for the next expedition and was appointed to the *Resolute* (Captain Henry Kellett). In charge of a sledge he was absent from the base for fifty-four days, traversed 663 miles, and discovered the northern end of Melville Island. He reached England in 1854 and served with the Baltic fleet from January 1855 to February 1856 in the steam sloop *Desperate*. He was then appointed to command the gunboat *Haughty*, and was sent to China, where he played a brilliant part in the battle of Fatshan (Foshan) Creek on 1 June 1857, for which he was promoted commander and belatedly, in 1875, received the CB.

From 1858 to 1862 Hamilton commanded the *Hydra* in the north Atlantic. In 1862 he was promoted post captain, and in the same year he married Julia Frances Delmé (*d.* 1897), daughter of Vice-Admiral James Arthur Murray, and great-granddaughter of John, third duke of Atholl. They had two sons and two daughters. Hamilton served in the north Atlantic until 1868, then from 1868 onwards in home waters. In 1875 he was appointed captain-superintendent of Pembroke Dock, where he remained until promoted to his flag in 1877. In 1878 he became director of naval ordnance, and from 1880 to 1883 commanded off the coast of Ireland. After promotion to vice-admiral in 1884, he returned the following year to the China station as commander-in-chief. In 1886 he took his fleet into Vladivostok harbour, through a thick fog. His unexpected appearance inside a major Russian naval base had a powerful effect on the Russians.

At Queen Victoria's jubilee in 1887 Hamilton was promoted admiral and created KCB. On his return from China in 1888 he was appointed to the committee of three admirals whose report in November 1888 on the inadequacy of the fleet for war prepared the way for the Naval Defence Act of 1889 and marked a turning point in naval policy. He was also heavily involved in the design of the new Royal Sovereign class battleships. At the close of 1888 he joined the Admiralty board as second sea lord, and, on the retirement of Baron Hood of Avalon a few months later, became first sea lord, a post he held from 1889 to 1891. Much of Hamilton's time in office was occupied with completion of the Naval Defence Act shipbuilding programme. However, the most important transaction during his term of office was the cession of Heligoland to Germany. He protested against this, but the cabinet, before consulting him, had committed itself too far to draw back. In 1891 he became admiral president of the Royal Naval College, Greenwich, where he served until 1894; in 1895 he received the GCB and was put on the retired list.

During his retirement Hamilton was an active member of the Navy League and devoted himself to naval history. In 1896 he published a pioneer study, *Naval Administration*, and between 1898 and 1903 edited for the Navy Records Society the *Letters and Papers of Admiral Sir Thomas Byam Martin*. He died on 17 September 1912 at his house, Elms, at Chalfont St Peter, near Uxbridge, and was buried at Eltham, London.

Hamilton was an intelligent officer of wide experience. His service at the Admiralty, in a period when the naval estimates were rising rapidly, demonstrated the points so forcefully made in the 'Three Admirals' Report', that national and imperial security depended upon an adequate battle fleet.

G. A. R. CALLENDER, *rev.* ANDREW LAMBERT

**Sources** G. Hamilton, *Parliamentary reminiscences and reflections*, 2: 1886–1906 (1922) · A. J. Marder, *The anatomy of British sea power*, American edn (1940) · J. B. Hattendorf and others, eds., *British naval documents, 1204–1960*, Navy RS, 131 (1993) · private information (1927) · F. T. Jane, *The imperial Russian navy* (1904) · *CGPLA Eng. & Wales* (1912)

**Archives** NMM, corresp. and papers

**Likenesses** oils, after 1895, NMM

**Wealth at death** £2516 6*s.* 5*d.*: probate, 18 Oct 1912, *CGPLA Eng. & Wales*

**Hamilton, Richard Winter** (1794–1848), Congregational minister, was born at Pentonville, London, on 6 July 1794. He was the son of the Revd Frederick Hamilton of Brighton, and his wife, Martha, daughter of the Revd Richard Winter. At the age of nine he was sent to a preparatory school in Hammersmith and later to Newport Academy, Isle of Wight. From his thirteenth to his sixteenth year he attended Mill Hill grammar school. A pious youth, in 1810 he entered Hoxton Academy to study for the ministry. He began to preach early, and when only nineteen delivered the anniversary oration at the Hoxton College chapel. In January 1815 he was chosen to be minister of Albion Independent Chapel, Leeds, where he became a popular preacher. On 21 May 1816 he married Rachel, daughter of Michael Thackeray of Leeds, but she died shortly afterwards.

Hamilton's sermons on French protestants (1816) and the death of Princess Charlotte (1817) attracted a good deal of attention. He was an original member, and sometime president, of the Leeds Philosophical and Literary Society (established 1821), to which he presented several papers, including 'An essay on craniology' in December 1825. A selection of these papers was published as *Nugae literariae* in 1841. In 1828 he made a tour on behalf of the Irish branch of the London Missionary Society, and spoke and wrote in favour of Catholic emancipation. In 1829 he officiated at a special celebration at the Independent church of Hamburg, and in 1833 published a volume of sermons directed against deists and Unitarians. The following year he published *Pastoral Appeals*, on devotion. On 16 December 1834 he married Harriet, daughter of John Robson of Sutton Hall, Yorkshire. In 1838 Hamilton published a volume entitled *Prayers and Thanksgivings*, and in 1841 won a prize of 50 guineas for an essay on Christian missions, published the following year as *Missions: their Authority, Scope and Encouragement*, and in 1843 toured Scotland for the London Missionary Society. He later won a prize of 100 guineas, offered by a citizen of Manchester, for an essay on education, published as *The Institutions of Popular Education* (1845). In 1844 he was made LLD by Glasgow University and DD by a university in New York city. In 1847 he was elected chairman of the Congregational Union of England and Wales. Shortly afterwards he formed part of a deputation to the government to oppose proposed grants of public money to education. The following winter he published *Horae et vindiciae sabbaticae, or, Familiar Disquisitions on the Revealed Sabbath*. Hamilton died at 9 East Baraile, Leeds, on 17 July 1848.

Hamilton was a man of real ability, and at his death one of the most prominent men in his denomination. He was unfortunate in his biographer, W. H. Stowell, whose work was 'welcomed with a general disappointment'.

G. B. SMITH, *rev.* J. M. V. QUINN

**Sources** W. H. Stowell, *Life of Richard Winter Hamilton* (1850) · *Eclectic Review*, 5th ser., 4 (1852) · *The Congregationalist*, 1 (Jan 1872) · d. cert.

**Likenesses** Blood, stipple, pubd 1826 (after J. R. Wildman), NPG · C. Turner, mezzotint, pubd 1836 (after C. Schwanfelder), BM, NPG · C. Baugniet, lithograph, BM, NPG

**Hamilton, Robert** (*d.* 1581), Church of Scotland minister, was the seventh son of Gavin Hamilton of Orbiston, Lanarkshire, and his wife, Marion Wallace. He studied at the University of St Andrews in the early 1550s, and by 1559 was working with John Knox and the protestant lords of the congregation. At the beginning of August that year he and Knox conferred with Sir James Croft in Berwick Castle in the hope of securing assistance from the English government for the congregation, but none was then forthcoming. On 20 December 1560 the general assembly declared Hamilton qualified for the ministry. With Knox, John Row, and George Hay, he met at the house of Sir James McGill, clerk register, in early November 1561, to argue for the right of subjects to suppress the idolatry of their sovereign (that is, Queen Mary's hearing of mass), but the ministers were opposed by a number of leading laymen, including the earl of Morton and Lord James Stewart. At the general assembly of December 1563 Hamilton and others came to Knox's defence, recalling that at the Reformation he had been commissioned to convene the brethren if the church was threatened. Hamilton was apparently in some kind of trouble himself by late 1565, for on 26 December Knox and three superintendents issued a testimonial on his and Robert Campbell's behalf, declaring:

> causes of treasoun ar laid to the charge of innocent men, thare substances ar spoiled, and thare lives ar sought, because thei have travaled for mantenance of vertu and suppressing of ydolatrie, of which nomber, these our brethern … haith bene tuo chief men. (*Works of John Knox*, 6.430)

By 4 September 1566 Hamilton had succeeded Christopher Goodman as minister of St Andrews. On that date Hamilton was one of fourteen ministers who wrote to Theodore Beza endorsing the second Helvetic confession, excepting only its provisions for the celebration of the holy days associated with Christ's life. He attended the general assemblies of June 1567, July 1568, July 1569, March 1572 (when he was moderator), March 1573, and April, June, and October 1576, and served on committees to hear complaints and requests, revise the superintendents' visitation schedules (July 1568), review visitation records (April 1576), and discuss policy (autumn 1576). In July 1569 he was a member of the assembly's delegation that presented articles dealing with clerical maintenance, the appointment of superintendents, and a protest against pluralism to the regent and nobles.

In the political upheavals of the early 1570s Hamilton came under pressure from both sides. In July 1570 he was denounced by James Carmichael, schoolmaster in St Andrews, for failing to condemn the assassins of the earl of Moray. In the civil strife of 1571 he remained neutral, though his kinsmen were among those supporters of Queen Mary who seized control of Edinburgh in April; however, he was criticized for his neutralism by students of St Leonard's College, St Andrews, who supported the king's forces. Yet when Knox attacked the Hamiltons and Sir William Kirkaldy for backing Mary's cause, Hamilton is alleged to have accused him of being himself as much a murderer as any Hamilton for having discussed with Moray plans to murder the earl of Darnley. Knox wrote to Hamilton in November denying the charge, and he also asked Archbishop John Douglas and John Rutherford to urge Hamilton to render satisfaction. Although Hamilton denied Knox's charge, a meeting of the two men accomplished nothing. Richard Bannatyne, Knox's secretary, wrote scathingly of Hamilton's altered preaching, contrasting his willingness to reprove Mary and her court while she was on the throne with his reticence to speak out after the Hamiltons embraced the queen's cause. Hamilton's election as moderator of the general assembly on 6 March 1572 seems not to have been achieved without opposition, 'for thingis went not as the most godly and upricht desyred' (Bannatyne, 227); James Melville regarded him as evil-minded because of his opposition to Knox and 'the guid cause' (*Autobiography and Diary*, 26). Contemporary comments on his sermons suggest that he had sought to rise above the partisan strife by addressing general spiritual concerns.

In August 1574 the general assembly ordered Hamilton and his elders and deacons to respond to allegations that they had tolerated Robin Hood plays during a fast ordered by the assembly as well as secular plays on the sabbath, and had failed to hold exercises for ministers and elders to study scripture. Appearing before the Edinburgh session on 24 February 1575, Hamilton declared he had known nothing of the fast, that he had asked the magistrates to ban the Robin Hood plays, and that he and his elders were too busy to convene exercises. Accused also of not preaching on Friday and Sunday afternoons, he averred that he was only following Goodman's practice.

On 17 January 1575 Hamilton had accepted appointment as principal of St Mary's College, St Andrews, which he also served as a regent (master), and where, owing to reforms in 1574, he did some lecturing on Hebrew. In April 1576, however, the general assembly, whose approval to accept the provostship Hamilton had not sought, objected to his holding two positions, and in October it ordered him to resign the provostship because it impeded the performance of his ministerial duties. He refused, even after a meeting with James Martin, master of St Salvator's, but was finally deprived of his provostship, probably on 13 December 1579 and certainly by 17 June 1580. He later proceeded against his successor, Andrew Melville, for arrears of salary, prompting the latter to appeal to parliamentary commissioners for relief. The case, unresolved at the time of Hamilton's death in Edinburgh on 16 April 1581, was continued by his widow and children. At an unrecorded date he had married Elizabeth (or Elspeth), daughter of John Traill the younger of Magask. They had four children, Robert, James, Thomas, and Helen, who married Robert Hamilton (*d.* *c.*1595), minister of Kennoway, Fife. After Hamilton's death, Elizabeth married Thomas Buchanan, minister of Ceres, Fife, and nephew of the historian George Buchanan. She died on 9 December 1595.

RICHARD L. GREAVES

**Sources** *Fasti Scot.*, new edn, 5.131, 231; 7.417, 438; 8.468 • D. E. R. Watt, ed., *Fasti ecclesiae Scoticanae medii aevi ad annum 1638*, [2nd edn], Scottish RS, new ser., 1 (1969), 382 • T. Thomson, ed., *Acts and proceedings of the general assemblies of the Kirk of Scotland*, 3 pts, Bannatyne Club, 81 (1839–45) • *John Knox's History of the Reformation in Scotland*, ed. W. C. Dickinson, 2 vols. (1949), vol. 1, pp. 148, 294–5; vol. 2, p. 23 • *The works of John Knox*, ed. D. Laing, 6 vols., Bannatyne Club, 112 (1846–64), vol. 6, pp. 429–30, 629–30 • R. Bannatyne, *Memoriales of transactions in Scotland, 1569–1573*, ed. [R. Pitcairn], Bannatyne Club, 51 (1836), 227, 256, 258 • M. F. Graham, *The uses of reform: 'Godly discipline' and popular behavior in Scotland and beyond, 1560–1610* (1996) • *The autobiography and diary of Mr James Melvill*, ed. R. Pitcairn, Wodrow Society (1842), 26, 33, 122–3 • H. Robinson, ed. and trans., *The Zurich letters, comprising the correspondence of several English bishops and others with some of the Helvetian reformers, during the early part of the reign of Queen Elizabeth*, 2, Parker Society, 8 (1845), 362–5 •

T. M'Crie, *The life of Andrew Melville*, 2nd edn, 1 (1824), 167–8 • D. Calderwood, *The true history of the Church of Scotland, from the beginning of the Reformation, unto the end of the reigne of King James VI* (1678), 29, 59, 75 • J. Kirk, *Patterns of reform: continuity and change in the Reformation kirk* (1989) • J. Durkan, 'Education: the laying of fresh foundations', *Humanism in Renaissance Scotland*, ed. J. MacQueen (1990), 123–60 • J. Ridley, *John Knox* (1968)

**Hamilton, Sir Robert, of Preston, second baronet (1650–1701)**, covenanter, was the younger son of Sir Thomas Hamilton of Preston and Fingalton (*d.* 1672) and his second wife, Anne, daughter of Sir James Hamilton of Preston. Sir Thomas had fought for Charles II at Dunbar and Worcester. Robert's brother William (*b.* *c.*1645) was created a baronet of Nova Scotia on 5 November 1673. Robert Hamilton studied at the University of Glasgow under Gilbert Burnet, whose sister was Hamilton's stepmother. A zealous covenanter and initially a follower of the preacher John Welsh, he took up arms against royalist troops commanded by Captain William Carstairs when they attempted to repress field conventicles in the latter half of 1677. For this action the Scottish privy council denounced him as a rebel on 15 March 1678 and declared his property forfeit. On 1 September the same year his uncompromising stance was manifest when he and a group of armed supporters attempted to prevent Matthew Selkirk, minister at Crichton and a supporter of the royal indulgence for moderate presbyterians, from preaching at Monkland, near Glasgow.

According to a correspondent of the duke of Lauderdale, Hamilton was believed to be in command of sixty covenanter horse in late March 1679 when they and approximately 300 foot repulsed royalist troops attempting to disperse a field conventicle near Lesmahagow, Lanarkshire. In the ensuing two months Hamilton and the preachers Donald Cargill and John King, chaplain to Lord Cardross's wife, gathered adherents. Among them was the small party of assassins, including David Hackston of Rathillet and his brother-in-law John Balfour of Kinloch, who had murdered James Sharp, archbishop of St Andrews, on 3 May. After deciding on 25 May to mount an insurrection, Hamilton, Hackston, Cargill, and others drafted a manifesto proclaiming their allegiance to the national covenant and the solemn league and covenant, and condemning episcopacy, royal supremacy in the church, and the policy of indulging ministers who compromised. On 29 May Hamilton and approximately eighty armed men affixed the declaration to the market cross at Rutherglen, near Glasgow, and burnt copies of offensive statutes in retaliation for the government's incinerating of the covenants. Only the presence of royalist forces in Glasgow prevented Hamilton and his adherents from similar action in that city.

Intending to hold a field conventicle on 1 June near Loudoun Hill, east of Darvel, Ayrshire, the covenanters marched eastward. When royalist forces under John Graham of Claverhouse caught up with them, they found that Hamilton and his officers now had some 1400 or 1500 men in arms. In the ensuing battle at Drumclog the covenanters forced the royalists to retreat to Glasgow. That night the countess of Loudoun provided hospitality to the rebel leaders, and Hamilton apparently conferred privately with the earl. The following day the covenanters, despite having no artillery, twice tried to capture Glasgow, failing both times. Nevertheless, several thousand more men flocked to their army in the following weeks, among them the ministers John Welsh and John Blackader. Whatever slim opportunity the covenanters had to succeed was lost as internal dissension mounted. Of the two major factions, Hamilton led the smaller, more extreme group that included Hackston, Balfour, Cargill, and the minister Thomas Douglass. These men rejected the king, the indulgence, and any clergy who accepted it. A moderate faction headed by Welsh defended Charles II, proposed a hearing for indulged ministers, and wanted parliament or a general assembly to resolve all disputed issues. Suspicious of those who proposed to give indulged clergy an opportunity to defend themselves, Hamilton and his allies, who dominated the rebel council of war, attempted unsuccessfully to prohibit moderate ministers from preaching to their forces. Hamilton was also opposed by the minister Gabriel Semple, who accused him of being willing to incite his men to mutiny unless his wishes were explicitly followed.

The covenanters feuded as well over the wording of another manifesto, particularly the provisions concerning the king and the indulged clergy. Hamilton and his supporters wanted to observe a day of humiliation before publishing the declaration, but Welsh persuaded them to settle for a statement in the manifesto acknowledging the church's sins and the need for its members to undertake their Christian responsibilities. To preclude further debate, Welsh and his allies left quietly for Glasgow to have the new manifesto printed and affixed to the market cross. In Hamilton's judgement, this perfidious act further damaged relations between the factions, nearly leading to a complete rupture by 18 June. His adherents, he observed, believed it was their 'duty to appear against all the defections of the times, and not to lay down arms (if the Lord prospered us) till our Lord were redressed of all the affronts done to him' (Ure, 470). As the duke of Monmouth's troops advanced against them, the covenanters closed ranks, and on 21 June sought a safe conduct for their representatives to present a list of grievances to the duke. This petition was published as a broadside bearing Hamilton's name and the heading *For the Right Noble and Potent Prince James Duke of Bucclengh* [*sic*]. Their manifesto, known as the Hamilton declaration because of the town where it was composed, called for adherence to the covenants, a free parliament, and a free general assembly to prevent popery and extirpate prelacy. The declaration was presented to Monmouth on 22 June, but he insisted that they lay down their weapons in return for leniency. When the duke's demand was reported to Hamilton, he laughed, saying 'and hang next' (Ure, 477). In the ensuing battle at Bothwell Bridge, Hamilton was reportedly among the first to flee. A royal proclamation subsequently ordered his apprehension, but he escaped to the Netherlands.

As an exile Hamilton spent most of his time in the Netherlands, though he visited Geneva and the Palatinate. The English government failed in its efforts to have him extradited. Beginning in August 1682 he joined his brother-in-law Alexander Gordon of Earlston as an agent for the radical covenanters known as the United Societies, seeking financial support, a place for them to emigrate, and provisions to train young men for the ministry at the University of Groningen. On 11 January 1683 the Scottish privy council instructed the lord advocate to charge Hamilton with treason for participating in the Bothwell Bridge rebellion and harbouring the assassins of Archbishop Sharp, and on 2 April 1683 the justiciary court gave him and other fugitives in Rotterdam sixty days to appear or be pronounced guilty *in absentia*. When Gordon was arrested on 1 June the government learned of Hamilton's involvement with the United Societies. He continued to serve them, receiving a new commission in August 1683. According to Robert Smith, an apprehended rebel, Hamilton had planned to go back to Scotland with weapons in the autumn or winter of 1683–4, but he changed his mind when some of his fellow exiles returned to the Netherlands after finding conditions in Scotland too dangerous to stay.

Because of his social status, Hamilton was exempted from the general pardon issued by James II shortly after his accession to the throne. In 1686 his relations with the United Societies deteriorated, partly because of poor relations with William Brackel, minister of Leeuwarden and a friend of the covenanters. In October the societies wrote to Hamilton, accusing him of criticizing the Hamilton declaration despite having approved it, signing the petition to Monmouth, and failing to account for substantial sums of money from the Dutch to print the testimonies of persecuted covenanters and aid their cause in Scotland. His response failed to satisfy the less extreme faction in the societies, but he remained close to the zealots. The minister James Renwick wrote to him in January 1687 concerning the societies' dealings with David Houston, a radical presbyterian minister in Ireland. According to the diarist Narcissus Luttrell, an attempt was mistakenly made to seize or assassinate Hamilton in March 1688 on Burnet's behalf.

After the revolution of 1688 Hamilton's attainder was reversed and he returned to Scotland, where he succeeded to the baronetcy following his brother's death. However, he opted not to claim the entailed portion of the family estate because this would require recognizing sovereigns who had not taken the covenant. He continued to support the more extreme faction in the societies, opposing those who formed the Cameronian regiment. Suspected of having written the revolutionary Sanquhar declaration in August 1692, he was apprehended at Earlston, Kirkcudbright, the following month and imprisoned at Edinburgh and then Haddington. Examined by the privy council, he still refused to acknowledge the authority of William and Mary, but he was nevertheless released on 15 May 1693. He never married. On 20 October 1701 he died at Bo'ness, where he was then living, and the baronetcy devolved on his relative Sir Robert Hamilton of Airdrie. His death was marked by the publication of *The believers farewel to the world, or, An elegias on the death of that much honoured gentleman Sir R. H.* (1701). RICHARD L. GREAVES

**Sources** *Reg. PCS*, 3rd ser., 5.393–5; 6.241, 260; 8.20–21, 403 · Burke, *Peerage* (1967), 1149 · J. Ure, 'Narrative of the rising suppressed at Bothwell Bridge', in W. Veitch and G. Brysson, *Memoirs of Mr. William Veitch, and George Brysson, written by themselves*, ed. T. M'Crie (1825) · Bodl. Oxf., MS Carte 45, fols. 484*r*–485*r*, 496*r*–496*v*, 514*r*–515*r* · M. Shields, *Faithful contendings displayed* (1780) · R. Wodrow, *The history of the sufferings of the Church of Scotland from the Restoration to the revolution*, ed. R. Burns, 2 (1829), 501; 3 (1829), 51, 66–7. 90–99, 106–7; 4 (1830), 392–3 · U. Edin. L., MS Dcl. 16, no. 24 · U. Edin. L., MS La. III.344, vol. 2, fols. 60*r*–67*v*; MS La. III. 350, no. 209(2) · *Historical notices of Scotish affairs, selected from the manuscripts of Sir John Lauder of Fountainhall*, ed. D. Laing, 2 vols., Bannatyne Club, 87 (1848), 434, 621–2 · [T. Sprat], *Copies of the informations and original papers relating to the proof of the horrid conspiracy against the late king, his present majesty and the government*, 3rd edn (1685) · *Memoirs of Rev. John Blackader*, ed. A. Crichton (1823) · R. L. Greaves, *Secrets of the kingdom: British radicals from the Popish Plot to the revolution of 1688–89* (1992) · *Report of the Laing manuscripts*, 1, HMC, 72 (1914), 433–4 · N. Luttrell, *A brief historical relation of state affairs from September 1678 to April 1714*, 1 (1857), 433 · *State trials*, 10.743–7; 11.48–9, 57, 59 · *CSP dom.*, 1695, 166 · BL, Add. MS 23243, fol. 34*r*–34*v*; MS 23244, fols. 6*r*, 47*r* · *DNB*

**Archives** BL, Add. MSS 23243–23244 · Bodl. Oxf., MS Carte 45 · U. Edin. L., MSS La. III.344 and 350 · U. Edin. L., MS Dcl. 16, no. 24

**Hamilton, Robert** (1721–1793), physician, born in Edinburgh on 6 December 1721, was the son of James Hamilton. He was educated at the Edinburgh high school, and was apprenticed to William Edmonston, surgeon-apothecary of Leith; he also attended medical lectures. In 1741 he entered the navy as a surgeon's mate, and remained in the service until 1748, occasionally attending the lectures of William Hunter and William Smellie in London. Having settled at King's Lynn, Norfolk, he acquired a good practice and remained there until 1758, when he rejoined the navy briefly, leaving in September the same year owing to ill health. In 1762 Hamilton was appointed agent for the Office for Sick and Hurt Seamen, and he returned to practise in King's Lynn. He received his medical diploma from St Andrews in May 1766, and became a fellow of the Royal College of Physicians, Edinburgh, in 1774. He enjoyed artistic and scientific pursuits and was a member of several learned societies. Hamilton published papers on a variety of subjects, including mumps and gout; some of these were published in the *Transactions of the Royal Society of Edinburgh* (1790), and in the *Philosophical Transactions of the Royal Society* (1776). He was elected a fellow of the Royal Society of Edinburgh in 1783.

Hamilton married a Miss Hawkins and they had four sons and four daughters. He died at King's Lynn on 9 November 1793. He should not be confused with a contemporary of the same name who practised in Ipswich, Suffolk. CHARLES CREIGHTON, *rev.* KAYE BAGSHAW

**Sources** R. Hamilton, *Observations on the marsh remittent fever, … with memoir of the author's life* (1801) · *GM*, 1st ser., 63 (1793), 1060 ·

F. Bennet and M. Melrose, *Index of fellows of the Royal Society of Edinburgh: elected November 1783 – July 1883*, ed. H. Frew, rev. edn (1984)
**Likenesses** A. Edouart, silhouette, Scot. NPG

**Hamilton, Robert** (1743–1829), political economist and mathematician, was born in Edinburgh on 11 June 1743, the eighth son of Gavin *Hamilton (1704–1767), bookseller and publisher, and his wife, Helen Balfour. His grandfather Dr William *Hamilton (1669–1732) had been professor of divinity and principal in Edinburgh University. His working life began as a clerk with Hogg & Son, bankers, during which period he, with other literary and political enthusiasts, formed the Speculative Society. In 1766 he was a candidate for the mathematical chair at Marischal College, Aberdeen, and though he was unsuccessful the judges were impressed by his ability. He next became a partner in a paper mill established by his father. In 1769 he was appointed rector of the Perth Academy, and in 1771 married Anne Mitchell (*d.* *c.*1778) of Ladath. Three of their children survived him.

Hamilton's *Introduction to Merchandise* (1777) was the first of a number of practical treatises. In 1779 he was appointed to the chair of natural philosophy in Aberdeen University, but the following year exchanged duties with Patrick Copland, the professor of mathematics, to their mutual satisfaction, until Copland retired in 1817, when Hamilton was appointed to the mathematical chair. In 1782 he married a Miss Morison of Elsick: there were no children of this union. He published in 1790 *Reflections on Peace and War*, expressing his pacific and philanthropic feelings, and in 1800 *Heads of a Course of Mathematics*.

Hamilton's chief work was *Inquiry concerning the rise and progress, the reduction and present state, and the management of the national debt of Great Britain and Ireland* (1813); enlarged editions were issued in 1814 and 1818. This book commanded attention from its bold attacks on prevailing views of national finance, as well as from its philosophic tone. It demonstrated, with much sound reasoning combined with a great body of well-marshalled historical and statistical facts, that the creation of a sinking fund, as favoured by Pitt, would increase, rather than decrease, the national debt.

Hamilton took an active role in college affairs and maintained a wide correspondence with British statesmen. Lumbago had impressed a permanent stoop on his stance; this, and his permanent air of abstraction, made him a figure of fun to his younger students, but he was unperturbed by this, and remained in good humour. After completing nearly half a century of teaching, he died on 14 July 1829 in Aberdeen. His last work, the *Progress of Society*, was published posthumously in 1830.

R. E. Anderson, *rev.* Anita McConnell

**Sources** Chambers, *Scots.* (1835) • Irving, *Scots.* • J. R. McCulloch, ed., *A select collection of scarce and valuable tracts, and other publications, on the national debt and the sinking fund* (1857), xv–xvi
**Likenesses** W. Holl, engraving, repro. in Chambers, *Scots.*, facing p. 221 • W. Holl, stipple, BM, NPG; repro. in Chambers, *Scots.*

**Hamilton, Robert** (1749–1830), army physician, was born at Coleraine, co. Londonderry. In 1780 he was awarded his MD degree at Edinburgh, his thesis being entitled 'De nicotianae viribus in medicina', and on 27 July the same year he gained a warrant as surgeon's mate of the 10th foot. He first practised medicine at Dorchester, and thereafter, while serving as a surgeon's mate, at Luton. In 1784 he became a member of the Royal College of Physicians, and about the time he left the 10th foot (1 May 1785) he established a practice in Ipswich. He returned to the service briefly in 1795 as physician to the forces in the West Indies, but failing eyesight, in the wake of a rheumatic affliction, forced him to resign, and he was soon blind—although perhaps not totally, for in 1830 he signed his will, quite legibly, in two places. Despite his handicap, he continued to practise medicine until his death.

Before blindness intervened Hamilton contributed significantly to medical literature. By far his most important work was the two-volume *Duties of a Regimental Surgeon Considered*. First published in 1787, then revised and republished in 1794, this was the first treatise to deal systematically with the day-to-day responsibilities of regimental medical personnel, and as such it inspired an adaptation and partial translation by E. B. G. Hebenstreit, *Handbuch der militairischen Arzneikunde für Feldärzte und Wundärzte* (3 vols. in 2, 1790). Hamilton also used his treatise as a vehicle to discuss how medical officers should behave, what they should study, and how they should treat their patients; he commented too on a range of matters that seemed to him to relate to the health or the quality of treatment of the soldiery. No work of the period reveals as much of the nature of Army Medical Services, and none reveals more of the circumstances in which soldiers lived.

Among Hamilton's other medical writings were works on the treatment of influenza, rabies, and those rescued from drowning. He appears also to have produced a study based on vital statistics of Suffolk, but although its forthcoming publication was announced in 1800 it remained unpublished. In accounting for disease and proposing treatment, Hamilton was more a pragmatist than a rationalist. While he accepted the need for phlebotomy and opium in therapy, he criticized the casual use of either.

Politically, Hamilton was an ardent reformer, notable for his support of civil and religious liberty. His humanitarian orientation is reflected in two non-medical writings, on the welfare of soldiers' sick wives and the abolition of the slave trade.

On 23 December 1825 Hamilton married Margaret Bloomfield. Whether he had been married previously is unknown. His wife predeceased him, but in his will he reserved a small bequest to cover the expenses of her son, Hugh Holland Bloomfield, during his minority. Hamilton also provided for his 'reputed Son', Theodore Goodrich Fitzrobert. The son of a widow, Sarah Goodrich, Fitzrobert was reported in the will to be a minor lodging with Hamilton (Suffolk RO, MS 1c/aa1/251/42). Hamilton died at Ipswich on 29 May 1830.

Charles Creighton, *rev.* Paul E. Kopperman

**Sources** returns for 10th foot, PRO, War Office, 27/53 & 27/53–2 • Suffolk RO, MS 1c/aa1/251/42 • *IGI* • Munk, *Roll* • W. Johnston, *Roll of commissioned officers in the medical services of the British army … 20 June 1727 to 23 June 1898*, ed. H. A. L. Howell (1917), 91

**Wealth at death** see will, Suffolk RO, MS 1c/aa1/251/42

**Hamilton, Robert** (1763–1831), lawyer, was born on 19 April 1763, the fourth son of Alexander Hamilton (*d.* 1790) of Gilkerscleugh near Crawfordjohn, Lanarkshire, agricultural authority, and his wife, Helen *née* MacQueen. He was one of eleven children, descendants of Sir James Hamilton of Fynnart, natural son of the first earl of Arran. Little is known of his early life, although contemporaries state that he had an early career in the army, and fought in the battle of Bunker Hill in 1775. Given that he would have been twelve years of age at the time, this seems unlikely, but he is said to have given on his deathbed the sword that he carried there to Sir Walter Scott. Robert Hamilton became an advocate on 15 July 1788, and on 2 August 1796 was appointed regius professor of public law and the law of nature and nations at the University of Edinburgh. He never lectured, but held this post until his death and successfully petitioned parliament for an additional annuity of £200. He was sheriff of Lanark from 1797 until 1822, when he became a principal clerk of session. Hamilton was counsel for William Hamilton of Wishart in his successful bid for the title of Lord Belhaven in 1799. He also represented Miss Lennox of Woodhead in her failed claim to the earldom of Essex. On 27 December 1805 in Peebles, he married Janet Hamilton Anderson (*c.*1785–1871), daughter of John Anderson of Winterfield, whose wife, *née* Dalrymple, daughter of Lord Westhall, a lord of session, had been Sir Walter Scott's childhood sweetheart.

Hamilton is principally remembered through Scott. He supplied Scott with stanzas sixteen to twenty of the ballad 'Sir Patrick Spens' (*Minstrelsy of the Scottish Border*, 1.215–28), and, in omitting to reveal his source, caused speculation that he had written them himself. Family and others, however, defended the additions as genuine, asserting that Hamilton, 'both in outward appearance and in reality, was an "unpoetical" sort of person' and 'about the last man in Scotland to countenance a practical joke' (Maidment, 30–33). Alexander Campbell 'noted down' the unusual tune from Hamilton's singing for *Albyn's Anthology*.

Scott sailed with the commissioners of the northern lights, including Hamilton, around Scotland in 1814. 'Our Lord High Admiral Hamilton' (Lockhart, 3.182) is mentioned frequently in Scott's diary for his gout-defying 'good humour' (ibid., 157) and as a gourmand. On 11 August, dinner ruined by a flood in the galley, Scott noted that Hamilton's 'despair for himself and the public might edify a patriot' (ibid., 182). When Hamilton rebuked the party for killing, in his opinion, inedible cormorants, Scott recorded that he 'will listen to no subordinate authority and rules by the Almanach des Gourmands' (ibid., 216–17).

Hamilton's gout placed a burden on Scott when he became a fellow principal clerk of session. Scott suspected malingering, noting that 'he has a happy tendency that way whenever the fit is like to be most vexatious to other folks'. Dreading a visit from a cursing Hamilton and his praying wife, Scott swears 'I will fire the house and roast them like pratties' (*Letters of Sir Walter Scott*, 9.212–13). Hamilton died, childless, in Edinburgh on 13 December 1831.

Bonnie Shannon McMullen

**Sources** J. Anderson, *Historical and genealogical memoirs of the house of Hamilton* (1825) • F. J. Grant, ed., *The Faculty of Advocates in Scotland, 1532–1943*, Scottish RS, 145 (1944) • J. G. Lockhart, *Memoirs of the life of Sir Walter Scott*, 7 vols. (1837–8) • *The letters of Sir Walter Scott*, ed. H. J. C. Grierson and others, centenary edn, 12 vols. (1932–79) • *The journal of Sir Walter Scott*, ed. W. E. K. Anderson (1972) • *Sir Walter Scott's Minstrelsy of the Scottish border*, ed. T. F. Henderson, 1 (1902) • A. Grant, *The story of the University of Edinburgh during its first three hundred years*, 2 vols. (1884) • J. Maidment, 'Scotish [sic] ballad controversy', *N&Q*, 2nd ser., 9 (1860), 118–19 • J. Maidment, 'Scotish [sic] ballad controversy', *N&Q*, 2nd ser., 10 (1860), 30–33 • D. Glen, *Splendid Lanarkshire, past and present: a rediscovery and anthology* (1997) • A. Campbell, ed., *Albyn's anthology, or, A select collection of the melodies and local poetry peculiar to Scotland and the Isles*, 2 vols. (1816–18) • W. Scott, *The pirate* (1912) • D. M. Walker, *The Scottish jurists* (1985)

**Hamilton, Sir Robert George Crookshank** (1836–1895), colonial governor, was born on 30 August 1836 at Bressay in the Shetland Islands, the son of Zachary Macaulay Hamilton (*d.* 1876) and his first wife, Anne Irvine, *née* Crookshank (*d. c.*1840). His father, who was the nephew of Zachary Macaulay and the first cousin of Lord Macaulay, was, on 30 August 1833, admitted minister of Bressay in the Shetlands, and in 1864 was made honorary DD of Edinburgh University.

Robert Hamilton was educated at Aberdeen grammar school and at University and King's College, Aberdeen, where he graduated MA in March 1854. In 1855 he moved to London and entered the civil service as a temporary clerk at the War Office. In the same year he was sent to the Crimea as a clerk in the commissariat department. He returned in 1857 and worked in the office of works, and in 1861 he became accountant to the education department. On 18 August 1863 he married Caroline Jane Ball (*d.* 1875), daughter of Frederick Augustus Geary, of Putney. They had three sons and one daughter. In 1868 he published a work on *Bookkeeping*, which ran to at least seven editions by 1899.

In 1869, on Lord Lingen's recommendation, Hamilton was appointed to the demanding post of accountant to the Board of Trade, and in this capacity he successfully reorganized the board's financial department. In 1872 he was appointed assistant secretary and in 1874 secretary of Playfair's civil service inquiry commission; in this capacity he spent some time at Dublin Castle with a view to its reorganization. On 4 July 1877 he married his second wife, Teresa Felicia, second daughter of Major Henry Reynolds of the 58th regiment and his wife, Ann (*née* Cox). They had two sons and one daughter. In 1878, as accountant-general of the navy, he simplified the naval estimates, making them intelligible to the public. In 1879 he was appointed a member of Lord Carnarvon's commission on colonial defences, and in May 1882 he was made permanent secretary to the Admiralty.

On the murder of Thomas Henry Burke that month, Hamilton was lent to the Irish administration and was then made permanent under-secretary and CB in April

**Sir Robert George Crookshank Hamilton (1836–1895)**, by unknown engraver, pubd 1882 (after Lombardi & Co.)

1883. On 12 January 1884 he was created KCB, and the following year he became an honorary LLD of Aberdeen University. While in Ireland he became convinced of the advisability of home rule and urged on Lord Carnarvon the need for conciliation. Before the Liberals returned to office, Gladstone had also been informed of Hamilton's views of the situation in Ireland. When Gladstone settled on home rule as the definitive means for solving the Irish question, he was largely assisted by Hamilton in drawing up the legislation. However, with the defeat of home rule in 1886 Hamilton was regarded with considerable suspicion by the new Conservative ministry. He quickly became the target of a campaign spearheaded by *The Times*, which successfully called for his removal in November 1886.

Early in 1887 Hamilton was appointed governor of Tasmania, and succeeded as under-secretary by Major-General Sir Redvers Buller. He promoted public works, and encouraged federation, presiding over the meeting of the Australian federal council held at Hobart in 1887. The greatest contribution he and his second wife made was to the colony's cultural life. They organized celebrations for the queen's jubilee and helped found the University of Tasmania. Hamilton remained governor until 1893 and on his return was appointed royal commissioner inquiring into the working of the constitution of Dominica. In 1894, on Morley's nomination, he served on the commission to inquire into the financial relations between England and Ireland. In November he became chairman of the board of customs. He died at his home, 31 Redcliffe Square, South Kensington, on 22 April 1895, and was buried in the new cemetery at Richmond, Surrey. His second wife survived him. He was one of the ablest civil servants of his time, and was described by Lord Lingen as 'the most all-round man he knew' (*The Times*, 25 April 1895).

A. F. Pollard, *rev.* David Huddleston

**Sources** *The Times* (23 April 1895) • *The Times* (25 April 1895) • *The Times* (27 April 1895) • R. Refshauge, 'Hamilton, Sir Robert George Crookshank', *AusDB*, vol. 4 • P. J. Anderson, ed., *Officers and graduates of University and King's College, Aberdeen, MVD–MDCCCLX*, New Spalding Club, 11 (1893), 306 • *Fasti Scot.* • L. P. Curtis, *Coercion and conciliation in Ireland* (1963) • J. Loughlin, *Gladstone, home rule and the Ulster question, 1882–1893* (1986) • H. C. G. Matthew, *Gladstone, 1875–1898* (1995) • Boase, *Mod. Eng. biog.* • private information (1901) • *CGPLA Eng. & Wales* (1895)

**Archives** BL, corresp. with Lord Carnarvon, Add. MS 60822 • Bodl. Oxf., letters to Sir Henry Burdett • UCL, corresp. with Edwin Chadwick

**Likenesses** engraving (after photograph by Elliott & Fry), NPG; repro. in *ILN* (27 April 1895), 502 • wood-engraving (after photograph by Lombardi & Co.), NPG; repro. in *ILN* (20 May 1882) [*see illus.*]

**Wealth at death** £5629 19*s.* 10*d.*: resworn probate, Nov 1895, *CGPLA Eng. & Wales*

**Hamilton, Sir Robert North Collie**, sixth baronet (1802–1887), administrator in India, was born on 7 April 1802, eldest son of Sir Frederick Hamilton, fifth baronet (1777–1853), of Silverton Hill, Lanarkshire, and his wife, Eliza Ducarel (*d.* 1841), daughter of John Collie MD, of Calcutta. He was educated at the East India College, Haileybury, and in 1819 obtained a Bengal writership. His first post was that of assistant to the magistrate at Benares, where his father, a Bengal civil servant of long standing, was collector of customs (1816–27) and deputy opium agent (1828–30). After filling other subordinate posts the younger Hamilton was appointed magistrate of the city court of Benares in 1827, and acting collector of customs and judge there in 1829, and in July 1830 became acting secretary in the political department. On 6 October 1831 he married Constantia (*d.* 1842), third daughter of General Sir George Anson. They had three sons and three daughters, the eldest son dying in 1841 at the age of seven, shortly before his mother. In 1834 Hamilton became collector and magistrate at Meerut; in 1836, collector and session judge at Delhi; in 1837 he was appointed commissioner at Agra; and in 1843 he was made secretary to Thomas Campbell Robertson, lieutenant-governor of the North-Western Provinces.

In 1844 Lord Ellenborough appointed Hamilton resident with Holkar, maharaja of Indore; he thus joined the political service, though in an unprestigious region, having been accused by Ellenborough of jobbery in the previous year. During his long tenure of this post he acquired his vast knowledge of central India. He succeeded his father in the family baronetcy in 1853, and was in 1854 made governor-general's agent for central India, retaining his post at Indore. In 1857 he went on home leave, but he had been only six weeks in England when news of the mutiny returned him to India. He reached Calcutta in August 1857. At the request of the governor-general he drew up a plan for the restoration of order in central India, which after discussion with Sir Colin Campbell, then in Calcutta, was adopted. Hamilton, as political officer, accompanied a force of troops under Sir Hugh Rose, which started from Indore on 6 January 1858, and he was present with it in every action fought. When the Central Indian field force, as the army was called, approached Jhansi in March 1858, Hamilton set aside the counter-orders of the governor-general and the commander-in-chief, which would have diverted the force to Chirkaree in Bundelkhand, thus enabling Rose to carry the operations to a successful conclusion. On 20 June 1858 Hamilton entered Gwalior with Sindhia, the maharaja, and remained there until order was restored. For his services in central India, Hamilton received the thanks of parliament, and was made a KCB (civil division). He was a member of the legislative council of India in 1859 and 1860, but was compelled to retire through ill health.

After his return to England, Hamilton served as high sheriff of Warwickshire, of which county he was a magistrate and deputy lieutenant, and unsuccessfully contested South Warwickshire as a Liberal in 1868. He died at his home, Avon Cliffe, Alveston, near Stratford upon Avon, on 30 May 1887. H. M. CHICHESTER, *rev.* PETER PENNER

**Sources** P. Penner, *The patronage bureaucracy in north India* (1986) • PRO, Lord Ellenborough MSS • Burke, *Peerage* • J. W. Kaye, *A history of the Sepoy War in India, 1857–1858*, 3 vols. (1865–80) • G. B. Malleson, *History of the Indian mutiny, 1857–1858: commencing from the close of the second volume of Sir John Kaye's History of the Sepoy War*, 2nd edn, 3 vols. (1878–80) • T. R. E. Holmes, *A history of the Indian mutiny*, 4th edn (1891) • W. K. Stuart, *Reminiscences of a soldier* (1874) • *Annual Register* (1887) • *ILN* (8 Oct 1887) • *CGPLA Eng. & Wales* (1887)
**Archives** Shakespeare Birthplace Trust RO, Stratford upon Avon, inventory of effects at Avon Cliffe | BL OIOC, letters to Lord Elphinstone, MSS Eur. F 87–89 • PRO, Lord Ellenborough MSS
**Likenesses** W. Sharp, lithograph (after F. Hayter), NPG • portrait, Gov. Art Coll.
**Wealth at death** £18,671 11*s*. 10*d*.: probate, 26 Sept 1887, *CGPLA Eng. & Wales*

**Hamilton, Stanley Baines** (1889–1977), civil engineer and historian, was born at 23 London Road, Lowestoft, Suffolk, on 10 August 1889, the son of John Miller Hamilton, a Baptist minister, and his wife, Ellen Josephine Baines. The family moved to Darlington where Hamilton attended Darlington grammar school and Dolham Grange School from 1900 to 1906. In 1907–8 he was at Halifax Technical School, where he was awarded a Carnegie scholarship and an exhibition, enabling him to enter the Royal College of Science, London, in 1908, and graduate BSc in 1910. After war service he worked for a few years with R. Young & Co., civil engineers at Penang, Straits Settlements. In 1924 Hamilton joined the chief structural engineers division of the office of works. He moved to the designs branch of the War Office in 1936, and in 1943 to the Building Research Station of the Department of Scientific and Industrial Research, where, in 1955, he was appointed OBE, retiring in 1959. Hamilton was a member of both the Institution of Civil Engineers and the Institution of Structural Engineers, reaching the office of president of the latter in 1954–5.

Hamilton had a lifelong interest in technical history, in particular of civil and structural engineering. His first historical writings were published in 1931, the year he joined the Newcomen Society, of which he served as president in 1944–5 and 1945–6, and editor of the society's *Bulletin* from 1950 to 1976 and of the *Transactions* from 1951–2 to 1972–3. He contributed biographies to the fifteenth edition of the *Encyclopaedia Britannica*, and chapters to Wolf's *History of Science, Technology and Philosophy* (1935–8) and to the *Oxford History of Technology* (1957–8). He also wrote authoritatively about the need for historical education in the training of engineers and scientists to provide them with a rounded, less narrow education. For his work on the history of science he received the degrees of MSc and PhD from the University of London in 1933 and 1950; he also held the university's teacher's diploma.

Hamilton was a member of a wide range of learned societies, including the British Association, the Royal Society of Arts, the Society for the Protection of Ancient Buildings, and others associated with industrial archaeology. On moving to Croydon about 1925 he became active in several local organizations such as the Croydon Natural History and Scientific Society, of which he was president in 1957–61.

Although born into a religious family, in his later life Hamilton moved to agnosticism and then atheism, and by the end of his life was an active humanist. Hamilton was a tall man and on first acquaintance had the appearance of diffidence, soon dispelled by closer contact. He was a kindly man and was most generous in the help he gave to fellow scholars, especially in his editing of papers. His wife, Christina Bruce McFarlane (*b.* 1886) from St Mary Cray in Kent, died on 1 October 1974. Hamilton died on 17 March 1977 at Mayday Hospital, Croydon, Surrey. They left a daughter and two sons. A. P. WOOLRICH

**Sources** R. A. Buchanan, D. Smith, and J. G. James, 'In memoriam Stanley Baines Hamilton, 1889–1977', *Transactions* [Newcomen Society], 51 (1979–80), 1–10 [incl. list of publications] • P. W. Sowen, *Croydon Natural History and Scientific Society Proceeedings*, 16 (1979), 205–9 • private information (2004) • b. cert. • d. cert. [Christina Bruce Hamilton] • d. cert.
**Archives** Croydon Natural History Society Library
**Likenesses** portrait, repro. in Buchanan, Smith, and James, 'In memoriam' • portrait, repro. in Sowen, *Croydon Natural History and Scientific Society Proceedings*
**Wealth at death** £31,028: probate, 6 May 1977, *CGPLA Eng. & Wales*

**Hamilton, Thomas, earl of Melrose and first earl of Haddington** (1563–1637), lawyer and politician, was the eldest son of Thomas Hamilton of Priestfield (*fl.* 1547–1610) and his first wife, Elizabeth Heriot (*fl.* 1558–1563).

**Education and early career** Hamilton was educated at the high school of Edinburgh, and between 1581 and 1587 at the University of Paris, of which his uncle John *Hamilton (*c.*1547–1610/11), scholar and Catholic priest, became rector in 1584. A presbyterian traducer referred to him in 1597 as 'Mr Thomas Hammiltoun, brought up in Parise with that apostat, Mr Johne Hammiltoun, and men say the dregs of stinking Roman professioun sticke fast to his ribbes' (Calderwood, 5.549). But whatever views Hamilton may have acquired in Paris, the vagueness of this denunciation is itself evidence that in Scotland he maintained a formal and correct profession of protestantism. Details of his studies are unknown but must have included law—perhaps canon law, as civil law was not officially taught in Paris.

After returning to Scotland, Hamilton was admitted advocate on 1 November 1587, and practised for some years. He married Margaret Borthwick (*d.* 1596), daughter of a neighbouring laird, about 1588. On 5 June 1592 he was

**Thomas Hamilton, earl of Melrose and first earl of Haddington** (1563–1637), after Adam de Colone, 1624

appointed to a parliamentary committee to prepare a new printed edition of the acts of parliament; two of his colleagues were John Lindsay and John Skene, with whom he was associated for some time. On 9 November 1592 he was promoted to be an ordinary lord of session—one of the fifteen permanent, salaried judges of the court of session. He adopted the style Hamilton of Drumcairn from an estate he possessed in Perthshire. He now had a secure status, retaining his seat on the bench until 1626. However, he clearly had hopes of further promotion. On 14 June 1593 he attended a meeting of the privy council, although he did not become a regular councillor until 1596. On 21 July 1593 he became a member of the queen's financial council, along with five others who later emerged as the nucleus of the Octavians. The creation of this group can be seen to have retrospective significance although at the time it was not a major job.

This was a turbulent period in Scottish politics, and it is not clear to whom Hamilton owed his advancement. He was only distantly related to the head of his surname, Lord John Hamilton, but the connection was clear and might well have elicited patronage from Lord Hamilton's powerful ally the chancellor, John Maitland of Thirlestane. Thomas Hamilton is less likely to have been connected to Maitland's enemies, a loose coalition around the duke of Lennox and Queen Anne. Anne's council was established in 1593 as part of a political settlement with Maitland, but there is no record of how nominations were made to it. Hamilton's later career would at any rate indicate that he was not a strong party man.

**Octavian** On 9 January 1596 Hamilton became one of the Octavians, a group of eight reforming financial administrators appointed as joint commissioners of a new permanent exchequer, with full powers over the collection and disbursement of royal revenues. It is hard to identify Hamilton's contribution to the Octavians' work, because they presented themselves as a team with joint responsibility for their actions. However, their collective impact was vast. They soon began to carve up the offices of state among themselves, and Hamilton was one of the first to acquire one, becoming lord advocate on 31 January 1596.

Hamilton was one of the four Octavians accused by the radical leaders of the church of advising the king to conciliate the Catholic lords. This illustrates the political prominence that he had by then attained. There is no direct evidence that he was a closet Catholic, but he had certainly shown determination to uphold the rights of the crown over the church. In a *cause célèbre* on 30 November, Hamilton as lord advocate prosecuted David Black, one of the radical ministers, before the privy council, whereupon the council declared itself competent to judge him despite his claim that only the church could do so. Hamilton was one of the named targets of an uprising in Edinburgh on 17–19 December which aimed to topple the entire regime. The uprising was initially threatening but collapsed for lack of noble support. On 7 January 1597 the Octavians resigned, but they were reappointed on 17 January to an enlarged exchequer commission that continued for another eighteen months. Hamilton as lord advocate prosecuted the leaders of the uprising. A line was drawn under the Octavian episode when the permanent exchequer, which had been their distinctive governmental agency, was abolished on 29 June 1598.

Hamilton was involved in one noteworthy episode in the later Octavian period. A widower since December 1596, in May 1597 he married his second wife, Margaret (*d.* 1609), sister of the goldsmith and financier Thomas *Foulis (*c.*1560–1628), who had acted as a banker and financial manager to the crown in the pre-Octavian years. The Octavians had attempted to sideline Foulis, though they could not ignore the king's sizeable debts to him. Foulis's influence was reviving in 1597, and in May he also became customs collector. Hamilton's alliance with him seems to have been a bid for advancement—and the sequel indicates division in the Octavian ranks. In December, after lengthy negotiations, Foulis emerged as the sole manager of all royal finances, with treasurer and comptroller binding themselves to ratify all his actions. But after only three weeks, in January 1598, Foulis came crashing down in a contrived royal bankruptcy engineered by another Octavian, John Lindsay of Balcarres. For Hamilton, a supporter of Foulis, the experience probably left scars. Although he had owed his advancement to his financial expertise, the remainder of Hamilton's public career was spent largely in law and administration, avoiding direct responsibility for the royal finances.

**Lord advocate** As lord advocate Hamilton had as his chief responsibility the prosecution of serious crimes in the court of justiciary. He held the office during a formative period: during the 1580s the lord advocate had become a public prosecutor, often prosecuting alongside an injured party, and even alone if the latter declined to act; this enhanced the lord advocate's role. Traditionally two men had shared the duties of the post, and Hamilton initially followed this pattern; he replaced one of the existing advocates, David MacGill of Cranstoun Riddel, while the other, William Hart of Livielands, continued in office alongside him. However, Hart left office at some point in 1597 and thereafter Hamilton was the sole lord advocate. This gave him increased status. Unlike his predecessors, he did not always act personally, but appointed a series of deputes who came to form an embryonic judicial department. Hamilton prosecuted numerous cases in person, but left routine ones to his deputes.

Public prosecution was important because the authorities were increasingly pursuing a variety of offences which might not have a traditional injured party to act as prosecutor. These included adultery, incest, witchcraft, hearing of mass, harbouring Jesuits, usury, and forestalling of markets. Most of these were also ecclesiastical offences which presbyteries were increasingly trying to prosecute. The ultimate ecclesiastical sanction was excommunication, while several of the secular crimes carried the death penalty. Hamilton saw clearly that this could lead to a conflict of jurisdiction. Should a conviction in a church court lead to automatic criminal conviction, as many in the church argued? And what of the presbyteries' demand that defenders testify on oath, which was against the practice of the criminal courts in that it appeared to force defenders to incriminate themselves? Guided by Hamilton, the privy council in the late 1590s and 1600s brought a series of test cases that restricted ecclesiastical jurisdiction and asserted the primacy of the criminal courts. As Hamilton's notes put it in one witchcraft case, witchcraft might be idolatry and heresy, seemingly ecclesiastical offences, but 'the kirk … have onlie power to try what is idolatrie or heresie, and the tryell wha is ane idolater or heretik is onlie competent to the criminall juge and to the assyse' (*Reg. PCS*, 14.612).

At this time Hamilton compiled an extensive collection of copies of official records for his own use. Some of these related to the events of his own day. In excerpting privy council decisions he made occasional notes of debates, of great value to the historian. He also compiled law reports from decisions of the court of session, and transcribed many older historical and legal documents.

In May 1603, shortly after King James's departure for England, Queen Anne attempted to seize her son, Prince Henry, from the custody of the earl of Mar at Stirling. Hamilton was one of those who took her part, apparently to the king's displeasure. However, matters were soon patched up, and in the aftermath (about July) Hamilton was knighted. He was included in the large Scottish delegation appointed to negotiate with the English on closer Anglo-Scottish union in 1604 and was one of a handful of more important Scots summoned for preliminary discussions at Whitehall in late August. The full commission met between 20 October and 6 December and produced agreement on a range of minor issues. Hamilton was one of the Scottish spokesmen in the main discussions, and also served on a subcommittee to collate hostile laws for repeal.

In January 1606 Hamilton helped the earl of Dunbar to organize the trial for treason of six dissident presbyterian ministers who had staged an unauthorized general assembly the previous July. Hamilton prepared the prosecution case while Dunbar fixed the assize. But the ministers' cause was popular; even an assize containing several of Dunbar's relatives proved reluctant to convict until Hamilton had threatened them with prosecution for wilful error if they did not. After conviction the ministers were banished, and Hamilton helped to produce a pamphlet justifying the proceedings. However, his distaste for the business, and his belief that a damaging acquittal had only narrowly been averted, led him to urge the king not to hold any more such trials. Eight more presbyterians thus escaped prosecution for treason. They were instead summoned to Hampton Court in September 1606 and interrogated at length by the king and others in the hope either of obtaining their submission to royal authority or of procuring grounds for their further punishment. Hamilton played a leading role, and had several sharp exchanges with the presbyterians. No agreement was reached, and the presbyterians were banished or placed under house arrest.

When Dunbar and Archbishop John Spottiswoode launched an unsuccessful intrigue against Chancellor Alexander Seton, earl of Dunfermline, in the spring of 1606, Hamilton remained neutral. It seems that he was still at this date a second-rank politician whose allegiance was not crucial. Possibly, though, he deliberately avoided committing himself.

It was about this time that silver was discovered on Hamilton's estates at Hilderstone in Linlithgowshire. He probably knew of it already on 26 June 1606, when he obtained a lease of all minerals on his lands in the sheriffdom; in early 1607 a flurry of leases and feus followed that explicitly granted him rights over gold and silver (regarded as royal prerogatives). On 25 March 1607 he was also appointed master of the metals. Excitement at court was intense, English and Scottish mining experts converged on Hilderstone, and in August Hamilton judged it prudent to surrender his rights to the crown. The English lord treasurer, Robert Cecil, earl of Salisbury, poured resources into the mine, but disappointment followed: 'Untill the same redd-mettle [ore] came unto 12 faddomes deepe, it remained still good; from thence unto 30 fathome deepe it proved nought: the property thereof was quite changed miraculously in goodnes, it was worth litle or nothing' (Atkinson, 50). Still, there was some activity at the mine as late as 1627.

Hamilton was an efficient public prosecutor in several cases of special interest to King James, including those of Margaret Hartside, the queen's servant, charged with divulging royal secrets and stealing jewels (1607–8), George Sprott, allegedly connected with the so-called

Gowrie conspiracy (1609), Lord Balmerino, a former fellow Octavian, accused of having written treasonably to the pope (1609), Lord Maxwell, accused of the murder of the laird of Johnstone (1609), and the Muirs of Auchindrain, accused of various murders (1610–11). From 1611 to 1613 he also served on an eight-man financial commission dubbed the 'New Octavians'.

Promotion now followed. The clerk register, Sir John Skene, a former fellow Octavian, wished to resign in favour of his son Sir James. He sent his son to London with a letter of resignation, with instructions to use it only if the king would agree to the succession. However, Sir James was persuaded to give in the resignation and to accept a less lucrative post as an ordinary lord of session instead, to the frustration of his father. The new clerk register was Hamilton, and it seems likely that Hamilton persuaded the king to refuse the son's succession to the post. Spottiswoode narrated the episode with sympathy for the Skenes, but since he himself was next year to be instrumental in organizing a campaign against the heritability of government office, the king's position seems defensible. Hamilton received his new post on 21 April 1612, and on 24 July exchanged it for that of secretary, currently held by Sir Alexander Hay. Then, in a temporary weakening of Dunfermline's hold on the chancellorship, rumour named Hamilton as one of the candidates likely to succeed him. This did not happen, but his fifteen-year period as secretary was influential. This is noteworthy because the chief traditional responsibility of the secretary was diplomacy, now curtailed by the union of crowns.

**'The fourteenth bishop of this kingdom'** While curbing the jurisdiction of presbyteries, the king had also been nominating bishops to all thirteen dioceses and extending their powers, and a parliament was summoned for October 1612 to ratify this. In August Archbishop George Gledstanes wrote to the king that he, Archbishop Spottiswoode, and Hamilton were working together—and explicitly working against Dunfermline. He acknowledged the king's instructions to him and to Hamilton 'for advysing anent our affairs to be handeled in this approaching parliament', and reported that 'we have made choyse of those things which ar most necessarie, and have omitted those articles which might seame to cary invy or suspition, or which your majestie, by your royall authoritie, might performe be your self'. This reflects Hamilton's long-standing concern with the prerogative. Gledstanes praised Hamilton highly—'wyse, fast, and secret'—and called him 'my good Lord Secretar, the fourtenth bischop of this kingdome' (Laing, 1.294–5). The parliament duly passed the episcopalian programme, and Hamilton compiled detailed notes on its proceedings.

Hamilton's second wife had died on 31 May 1609. In September 1613 he married Julian Kerr (*d.* 1637), sister of the royal favourite Robert *Carr (Kerr), recently created earl of Somerset, and widow of Sir Patrick Home of Polwarth, master of the household. Hamilton now had a court connection second to none. On 19 November he was created Lord Binning. As secretary he was active in all aspects of the administration, though at this period the government spent more time reacting to events (such as highland uprisings) than shaping them. Somerset's downfall in 1615 did not threaten Binning, since Somerset's successor, the future duke of Buckingham, acted in alliance with the marquess of Hamilton, son of his old patron Lord John. On 15 June 1616 Binning became lord president of the court of session, an office requiring regular personal attendance in court, which he held concurrently with that of secretary.

When King James visited Scotland in 1617 Binning was one of those councillors who took communion kneeling, in the English form, at Whitsun (though others refused). He was discreet enough not to give his wife the task of presenting James with a petition in favour of his disgraced favourite Somerset; that role was taken by Somerset's other sister, Anne, Lady Balmerino. Binning may well have entertained James at his Cowgate mansion, and it is then that tradition states the king to have nicknamed him Tam o' the Cowgate. The tradition, however, lacks contemporary warrant, and must be regarded as doubtful in view of the copious evidence for other nicknames bestowed by James.

On 28 November 1617 Binning was joint royal commissioner at the general assembly where the five articles, new ceremonies in church worship, were proposed and rejected. This does not seem to have discouraged the king from appointing him again, as commissioner to the notorious assembly at Perth of 25 August 1618. He was a prominent member of the governmental team that forced the five articles through the assembly, but afterwards begged the king not to employ him again in this capacity. This does not seem to have harmed his career, and on 20 March 1619 he was created earl of Melrose. He remained a staunch supporter of the royal prerogative over the church, which in practice kept him allied with the bishops against their rival, Chancellor Dunfermline. When the king wanted a dissident minister punished by the privy council in 1620, Dunfermline objected that:

> it was not their part to judge in kirk maters: the bishopes have a Hie Commission of their owne to try these things. Secretarie Hammiltoun said, 'Will ye reasoun, whether his majestie must be obeyed or not?' Chancelour Setoun answered, 'We may reason, whether we sall be the bishops' hangmen or not.' So the mater was referred to the bishops. (Calderwood, 7.450)

A parliament was summoned in August 1621 to vote money for royal diplomacy and to ratify the five articles of Perth. Melrose was probably the main author of an innovative and controversial proposal to tax annual rents (interest payments and annuities), hitting the commercial classes. This and the five articles faced vociferous opposition. Melrose took a leading role in managing the parliament, rallying government voters and browbeating the opposition. The royal programme was passed by a modest majority, but the victory was hollow since it was already clear that the five articles were too unpopular to be implemented in full. Melrose reported annually to James on the progress in Edinburgh of the most controversial article, kneeling at the Easter communion; his reports advised patience and stressed the difficulties of enforcing conformity.

Melrose now formed a prudent alliance with the earl of Mar, the treasurer, from whom he had hitherto kept his distance as Mar was a critic of the bishops. His eldest son, Thomas, married Mar's daughter by contract of 27 February 1622. Melrose aided Mar in trying unsuccessfully to restrain royal generosity to the marquess of Hamilton. Chancellor Dunfermline died in June 1622, and was succeeded by Sir George Hay, clerk register. Melrose acquired the clerk registership for his brother John Hamilton of Magdalens. However, he was in a good position to become chancellor himself—yet Spottiswoode wrote at the time that Melrose had peremptorily denied wanting the job. Possibly the strains of public life were already telling on him.

Melrose acquired a large fortune, both through royal grants and (presumably) through gifts from clients. He lent out money at interest, but put most of his efforts into amassing a landed estate, making his purchases with a sharp eye to profitability. His landed acquisitions, widely scattered over southern Scotland, have been detailed by Sir William Fraser (Fraser, 1.160–66); they formed the single largest new estate of the period. He consolidated his aristocratic position through family alliances. Melrose had ten children from his first two marriages, almost all of whom married into the Scottish peerage between 1610 and 1622.

**Career under Charles I** The process of becoming a landed aristocrat, and the alliance with Mar, detached Melrose's political interests from the bishops. This placed him at a disadvantage in the shake-up of the personnel of government that followed the accession of the strongly episcopalian Charles I. He had also been one of the councillors who had frustrated Charles's plans for his landed estate as prince of Scotland in 1624, believing them to be illegal.

Melrose visited the court in London with the other councillors in the spring of 1625, and was well received. At some point after this he was nominated by Charles as president of the privy council, but he concurred with, and perhaps encouraged, the council's decision on 4 November that such a post was unnecessary and that the precedence conferred on it would be objectionable to the nobility. It also became clear that year that the king wished to separate the membership of the privy council and the court of session, in order to give himself and his own advisers more power over both bodies. This would force Melrose to surrender one of his two offices of state.

However, the main issue of the new reign proved to be Charles's revocation, containing sweeping claims to former church and crown land. Melrose supervised the earliest stage, the drawing up of a revocation for the principality of Scotland in May 1625, but the scheme soon grew to vast proportions. The bishops welcomed it, but it stirred up widespread distrust among the nobility, and Melrose identified strongly with this. He obstructed the revocation as far as he could, covertly advising the opposition and urging the king to call a parliament to discuss the scheme. The leading Scottish councillors visited the English court in January 1626 and had extended discussions with Charles. Melrose took a prominent part in criticizing the king's schemes, and his disaffection from the main line of royal policy was now clear.

On the separation of the personnel of privy council and court of session, Melrose was forced to resign as lord president on 15 February 1626, being succeeded by Sir James Skene whom he had outmanoeuvred in 1612. Further demotion followed. According to Sir John Scot of Scotstarvet, Melrose:

> being at court, was challenged by his majesty, that he refused to be president of the council, which the king would have him accept, and for that cause the king took from him the signet, and gave it to Sir William Alexander, master of requests. (Scot of Scotstarvet, 74)

Alexander's initial appointment, on 8 March, was as joint secretary with Melrose, the latter retaining office for another nineteen months; but Alexander was at court, with the king's ear.

Melrose's last important contribution to public business was as a member of the commission for surrenders and teinds (tithes), established in early 1627 to implement the revocation. He fought the bishops' claims and delayed the process—which was, indeed, formidably complex. In June he played an active part in maximizing the value of the compensation to be paid by the crown for surrendered teinds.

On 17 August 1627 Melrose was created earl of Haddington, described in the patent as 'a more worthy title than that of earl of Melrose' (*Scots peerage*, 4.311). Scotstarvet reflected the public view that he sought the change 'not choosing to have his title from a kirk-living' (Scot of Scotstarvet, 74); Melrose was an abbey that might well fall under the revocation. Haddington himself remained tight-lipped about the change, and it is possible that Charles had asked him to make it. Soon afterwards, on 18 October, he was obliged to resign his joint secretaryship, receiving instead a lesser office as keeper of the privy seal. Thereafter Haddington withdrew from the main current of public affairs. In January 1631 he wrote philosophically to the earl of Annandale, another relic of the previous reign:

> The half of the lordis [of session] with whom I have scarce familiar acquentance, much lesse any credit, are placed there since I was thoght fit to be displaced, which some hes contrived to be a disgrace to me, but I take it for a singular favour to me from God and my gracious maister wherby I ame releeved from that toyle which my age and decayed bodie could not have sustained. (Fraser, 1.177)

He continued by reflecting on the 'perpetuall tourmoiles' suffered by the leading politicians. He was not completely retired, since he continued to be appointed to some official commissions until 1634, but he made little discernible impact. He died in Edinburgh on 29 May 1637 and was succeeded by his son Thomas *Hamilton.

The hostile Scotstarvet characterized Haddington as 'very learned, but of a choleric constitution' (Scot of Scotstarvet, 74). This fits with what is known from other sources, but his 'choleric' side was combined with caution, and even distaste for the 'perpetuall tourmoiles' brought by political strife. A more ambitious man in Hamilton's position might well have achieved the chancellorship in 1622—but might have lived to regret it. Another view of him is expressed by an epitaph recorded by Sir James Balfour (Brunton and Haig, 224–5):

> Heir layes a Lord quho quhill he stood
> Had matchless bein had he beene —
> This epitaph's a sylable short,
> And ye may adde a sylable too it;
> Bot quhat gt syllable doeth importe
> My defuncte Lord could never doe it.

JULIAN GOODARE

**Sources** W. Fraser, *Memorials of the earls of Haddington*, 2 vols. (1889) • *Reg. PCS*, 1st ser. • *Reg. PCS*, 2nd ser. • *State papers and miscellaneous correspondence of Thomas, earl of Melros*, ed. J. Maidment, 2 vols., Abbotsford Club, 9 (1837) • *Original letters relating to the ecclesiastical affairs of Scotland: chiefly written by … King James the Sixth*, ed. D. Laing, 2 vols., Bannatyne Club, 92 (1851) • M. Lee, *Government by pen: Scotland under James VI and I* (Urbana, Ill., 1980) • M. Lee, *The road to revolution: Scotland under Charles I, 1625–1637* (Urbana, Ill., 1985) • *Scots peerage* • D. Calderwood, *The history of the Kirk of Scotland*, ed. T. Thomson and D. Laing, 8 vols., Wodrow Society, 7 (1842–9) • J. Scot, *The staggering state of Scottish statesmen from 1550 to 1650*, ed. C. Rogers (1872) • M. Lee, ed., 'An unpublished letter of Thomas Hamilton, earl of Melrose', *SHR*, 58 (1979), 175–8 • S. Atkinson, *The discoverie and historie of the gold mynes in Scotland*, ed. G. L. Meason, Bannatyne Club (1825) • G. Brunton and D. Haig, *An historical account of the senators of the college of justice, from its institution in MDXXXII* (1836)

**Archives** NL Scot., corresp. • NL Scot., historical and legal MSS, Adv. MSS 34.2.2, 22.1.14, 34.2.16, 34.3.11 • NL Scot., session decisions and practicks, Adv. MSS 22.3.4, 24.2.1, 6.2.7 • NRA Scotland, priv. coll., corresp. and papers | NA Scot., letters to Sir Robert Kerr • NL Scot., letters to seventh earl of Menteith

**Likenesses** oils (after A. de Colone, 1624), Scot. NPG [*see illus.*] • oils, Mellerstain House, Scottish Borders

**Wealth at death** £43,052 12*s*. 2*d*. Scots excl. land: testament, Fraser, *Memorials*, 2.310

**Hamilton, Thomas**, **second earl of Haddington** (**1600–1640**), nobleman, was born on 25 May 1600, the eldest son of Thomas *Hamilton, Lord Binning (1563–1637), who was subsequently created earl of Melrose (a title later changed to Haddington), and his second wife, Margaret Foulis (*d.* 1609), daughter of James Foulis of Colinton. He obtained a licence to travel abroad in July 1615 'as he shall thinke moste fitte for his instruction in literature, language, and custome of diuers nations' (Fraser, 1.189), but he had returned by 1621. By a contract dated 27 February 1622 he married Catherine (*d.* 1635), daughter of John Erskine, earl of Mar, a union of the children of two of James VI's most powerful Scottish officials. He was sworn of the Scottish privy council on 7 November 1633. On his father's death, on 29 May 1637, he not only inherited the earldom of Haddington but estates which made him one of the richest of the Scottish nobility. In the early stages of the revolt of the covenanters against Charles I he supported the king, signing the 'king's covenant' with the rest of the privy council of 22 September 1638, but his loyalty became increasingly strained. On 17 September 1638 the marquess of Hamilton had reported to Charles that Haddington 'in a most hartie maner hes offered lyfe, fortoun, as he is able to make for the accomplishing your endes' (*Hamilton Papers*, ed. S. R. Gardiner, 1880, 24), but within a few weeks doubt had crept into Hamilton's assessment. Haddington 'has too much of the humour of these times, but he will never ask what your quarrel is' (Fraser, 1.194). Such unquestioning obedience snapped in November. When Hamilton on behalf of the king tried unsuccessfully to dissolve the general assembly which was reforming the Scottish church, Haddington at first supported him, but then swung round to supporting the defiant assembly.

Haddington's first wife having died on 5 February 1635, he married Jean (*d.* 1655), daughter of the royalist George Gordon, marquess of Huntly, on 14 January 1640. During that year he continued to assert his underlying loyalty to the king, but in the second bishops' war of 1640, when the covenanters' army invaded England (with his brother Sir Alexander Hamilton serving as general of artillery), he assumed command of forces left to defend the south-east of Scotland from attack. On 29 August he drove off an attempt by the garrison of Berwick to capture a magazine near Coldstream. He then returned to his headquarters at Dunglass Castle, and on 30 August he celebrated news of the victory won over the English at Newburn. But, 'Having dyned very jovially' (Gordon, 3.261), he was killed by a huge explosion of gunpowder stored in the castle. Two of the earl's half-brothers, a number of gentlemen and officers, and many servants were also killed, the death toll being about seventy, with many more injured. It was rumoured that the earl's page Edward Paris, 'ane Inglysh Villaine' (*Letters and Journals of Robert Baillie*, 1.258), had been enraged by his master's jeers about English cowardice, and had set off the explosion in a suicidal gesture of national pride. Paris had held the only key to the vault in which the powder was stored, and all that was found of his body was 'ane arm holding ane iron spoune in his hand' (*Historical Works of Balfour*, 2.396), which was regarded as suspicious. 'This sadd accident was variously consterd by such as heard it, according as they loved or hated the Covenanters partye' (Gordon, 3.263).

Haddington, who was buried at his seat, Tyninghame, on 1 September, was typical of many Scots who avoided as long as possible making the painful decision of which side to support as his society disintegrated into civil war, but his only claim to individual attention is his spectacular death.

DAVID STEVENSON

**Sources** *DNB* • GEC, *Peerage* • *Scots peerage* • W. Fraser, *Memorials of the earls of Haddington*, 2 vols. (1889) • J. Spalding, *Memorialls of the trubles in Scotland and in England*, AD 1624 – AD 1645, ed. J. Stuart, 2 vols., Spalding Club, [21, 23] (1850–51) • *The letters and journals of Robert Baillie*, ed. D. Laing, 3 vols. (1841–2) • J. Gordon, *History of Scots affairs from 1637–1641*, ed. J. Robertson and G. Grub, 3 vols., Spalding Club, 1, 3, 5 (1841) • *The historical works of Sir James Balfour*, ed. J. Haig, 4 vols. (1824–5)

**Likenesses** oils (after A. Vandyck), Lennoxlove, East Lothian

**Hamilton, Thomas**, **sixth earl of Haddington** (**1680–1735**), politician and forester, was born on 29 August 1680 at Tyninghame, Haddingtonshire, the second son of Charles, fifth earl of Haddington (1650–1685), landowner, and his wife, Lady Margaret Leslie (*d.* 1700), eldest daughter of John, duke of Rothes, lord high chancellor of Scotland. After his father's death in 1685, while Hamilton was

**Thomas Hamilton, sixth earl of Haddington** (1680–1735), by William Aikman, 1718

in infancy, he was trained up in whig principles by his uncle Adam Cockburn of Ormiston. By an agreement made on the occasion of his father's marriage, Thomas's elder brother, John, succeeded to the earldom of Rothes, and he to the earldom of Haddington; on 25 February 1687 he received a new patent of the earldom with the former precedency. In 1696 he married his cousin Helen *Hope (*bap.* 1677, *d.* 1768), daughter of John Hope of Hopetoun and sister of Charles, first earl of Hopetoun. They had four children: Charles *Hamilton, Lord Binning (1697–1732); John Hamilton; Lady Margaret Hamilton; and Lady Christian Hamilton, mother of Sir David Dalrymple, Lord Hailes.

From about 1700, together with his brother the earl of Rothes, Haddington was one of the leaders of the party termed the squadrone, who by finally declaring for union with England had great influence in overcoming the opposition to it. He became a steady supporter of the Hanoverians, and during the Jacobite rising of 1715 was wounded at the battle of Sheriffmuir, having a horse shot under him. His rewards in 1716 were the post of lord lieutenant of the county of Haddington, the Order of the Thistle, and election as one of sixteen representative peers of Scotland in the House of Lords; he was re-elected in 1722 and 1727. George Lockhart, a Jacobite political opponent, says: 'he [was] much affected and his talent lay in a buffoon sort of wit and raillery', and describes him as 'hot, proud, vain, and ambitious' (Lockhart, 112–13). The buffoon wit is evident in his pornographic verse, some of which was published posthumously and anonymously in *Forty Select Poems on Several Occasions* (1753) and other collections.

In his youth, by his own account, Haddington pursued a passion for dogs, horses, and London life (the magnet for many Scottish nobles of the day), until his wife converted him to the pleasures (once shared by his father) of planting and enclosing the family estate of Tyninghame. Thirty years later he boasted of having 'more thriving Trees of my own Raising than I believe any one Man ever Planted in his Life Time'. The claim is made in the posthumously published *Short Treatise on Forest Trees* (1756), reprinted as *Treatise on the Manner of Raising Forest Trees* (1761). The latter was, according to M. L. Anderson, 'an admirable scientific production' ('Introduction' to T. Hamilton, *Forest Trees*, ed. M. L. Anderson, 1953, xli) still having practical value in the 1950s, and 'in respect of many of the fundamentals of forestry … sound and reliable' (ibid., ix). It combines the fruits of decades of experimentation with a prose of simple clarity.

Haddington was burlesqued for his strong Hanoverian or English sympathies in a painting by Aikman and in a Jacobite poem, but praised in Hamilton's *Faithful Few* (1734) for integrity amid the venality of Walpole's administration—

> Thine is the Honour to retire unbought,
> and persevere in Virtue's sacred Ways.

Haddington died on 28 November 1735 at New Hailes, near Edinburgh, and was probably buried at Tyninghame. He was survived by his wife, who died in Edinburgh on 19 April 1768, and was succeeded in the peerage by his grandson Thomas *Hamilton (1720/21–1795) [*see under* Poker Club], eldest son of Charles, Lord Binning.

T. F. HENDERSON, *rev.* DAVID MOODY

**Sources** W. Fraser, *Memorials of the earls of Haddington*, 2 vols. (1889) · NA Scot., CC 8/8/98; CC 8/8/121/1 · P. W. J. Riley, *The Union of England and Scotland* (1978) · GEC, *Peerage* · R. Mitchison, *Lordship to patronage: Scotland, 1603–1745* (1983) · *Mellerstain, Gordon, Berwickshire* (1994) · G. Lockhart, *The Lockhart papers*, 1 (1817), 112–13

**Archives** priv. coll., letters and papers | NA Scot., corresp. with earl of Marchmont · NA Scot., letters to duke of Montrose

**Likenesses** G. Kneller, portrait, 1708, Mellerstain, Gordon, Berwickshire · W. Aikman, portrait, 1718, priv. coll. [*see illus.*] · stipple, pubd 1800, NPG · J. Medina, oils, Scot. NPG · J. Smith, mezzotint (after W. Aikman), BM

**Hamilton, Thomas, seventh earl of Haddington** (**1720/21–1795**). *See under* Poker Club (*act.* 1762–1784).

**Hamilton, Thomas, ninth earl of Haddington** (**1780–1858**), politician, was the only son of Thomas, eighth earl of Haddington, and his wife, Lady Sophia Hope, third daughter of John, second earl of Hopetoun; he was born in Edinburgh on 21 June 1780 and baptized in St Giles's Cathedral on 3 July. Until he succeeded his father in 1828 he was known as Lord Binning, and nicknamed 'Binny'. He was educated at Edinburgh University and afterwards at Christ Church, Oxford, where he matriculated on 24 October 1798, and graduated BA in 1801 and MA in 1815. On 13 November 1802 he married Lady Maria Parker, heir of the fourth earl of Macclesfield. They had no surviving children. As the eldest son of a Scottish peer, Binning had to seek his political fortune outside that country. His allegiance to George Canning within the Pittites made finding a safe seat hard. He felt himself the 'hereditary friend of Canning' (Fraser, 1.356). At the general election in July 1802 he was returned to parliament for St Germans, Cornwall, in the Pittite interest and he became a steward of the Pitt Club (HoP, *Commons*). He did not stand in 1806 but was elected at a by-election in January 1807 for Cockermouth, and at the general election in May of that year for Callington, which he held until 1812. He served as one of the commissioners for the Indian Board of Control from 17 July to 13 November 1809 and again from 7 September 1814 to 7 February 1822. He was sworn of the privy council in July 1814 and in December that year was elected at a by-election for Michell in Cornwall. From June 1818 until June 1826 he represented Rochester. In 1822 he declined Canning's offer of the foreign under-secretaryship (HoP, *Commons*). At the general election of that year he was returned for Yarmouth but on 24 July 1827, on Canning's accession to the premiership, Binning was created Baron Melros of Tyninghame, in the peerage of the United Kingdom, and took his seat in the House of Lords on 29 January 1828.

Melros succeeded his father as ninth earl of Haddington on 17 March 1828 and was one of the 'waverers', voting against the Reform Bill in 1831 and for it in 1832. He was lord lieutenant of Ireland in Sir Robert Peel's administration of 1834–5. In September 1841, on the formation of Peel's second administration, Haddington declined the governor-generalship of India and was appointed first lord of the Admiralty (with a seat in the cabinet), a post which he held until January 1846, when he succeeded the duke of Buccleuch as lord privy seal. After the Peel government's defeat in June 1846 Haddington did not again hold office, and took but little part in the debates. In 1843 he received £30,674 1*s*. 8*d*. in compensation for the surrender of the hereditary office of keeper of Holyrood Park, conferred upon Thomas, sixth earl of Haddington, by charter dated 23 January 1691 (6 & 7 Vict. c. 64). He was elected FRS in 1844 and was an elder brother of Trinity House from that year. He became a knight of the Thistle in 1853.

Haddington was not a man of any great ability but he had a remarkable appetite for politics. Greville harshly commented on his refusal of the governor-generalship:

> It is a curious circumstance that a man so unimportant, so destitute not only of shining but of plausible qualities, without interest or influence, should by a mere combination of accidental circumstances have had at his disposal three of the greatest and most important offices under the crown, having actually occupied two of them and rejected the greatest and most brilliant of all. (*Greville Memoirs*, 2.46)

Haddington was 'slight in body' and had 'a clear penetrating voice, tinged with burr' (Fraser, 1.358). In later life he was affected by spasms. He died at Tyninghame, one of the family seats, on 1 December 1858 and was buried there on 9 December. His widow died on 11 February 1861 at 43 Berkeley Square, London, and was buried with her husband. H. C. G. MATTHEW

**Sources** HoP, *Commons* • *The Greville memoirs, 1814–1860*, ed. L. Strachey and R. Fulford, 8 vols. (1938) • *GM*, 1st ser., 72 (1802), 1064 • *GM*, 1st ser., 98/1 (1828), 363 • *GM*, 3rd ser., 6 (1859), 92 • *GM*, 3rd ser., 10 (1861), 354 • W. Fraser, *Memorials of the earls of Haddington*, 2 vols. (1889)

**Archives** NA Scot., corresp. and papers • NRA, priv. coll., corresp. and papers | BL, corresp. with Lord Aberdeen, Add. MSS 43229–43230 • BL, corresp. with William Huskisson, Add. MSS 38739–38757 • BL, letters to Lord Liverpool, Add. MSS 38248–38291, 38411, 38573–38576 • BL, corresp. with Sir Robert Peel, Add. MSS 40327, 40456–40458 • BL OIOC, Cochrane MSS • BL OIOC, Hope-Scott MSS • BL OIOC, Lee MSS • BL OIOC, letters to Lord Tweeddale • Flintshire RO, Hawarden, corresp. with Sir John Gladstone • Lpool RO, letters to Lord Stanley • NL Scot., corresp. with Sir Thomas Cochrane • NL Scot., corresp. with J. R. Hope-Scott • NL Scot., corresp. with John Lee • NMM, letters to Sir William Parker • NRA, letters to Sir Thomas Fellowes • PRO, corresp. with Lord Granville, PRO 30/29 • Sheff. Arch., letters to Lord Wharncliffe • Surrey HC, corresp. with Henry Goulburn • U. Southampton L., letters to first duke of Wellington

**Likenesses** J. Brown, stipple (after R. McInnes), BM, NPG

**Hamilton, Thomas** (1784–1858), architect, was born on 11 January 1784 in Glasgow, the son of Thomas Hamilton, mason and builder (1758?–1824), and his wife, Jean Stevenson, whom he had married in Edinburgh. Hamilton senior moved to the capital in 1790, preceded by his brother John (1761?–1812), and both became successful as speculative builders in the New Town; they also worked for the city in repairing St Giles's Church, Greyfriars, and University College. Hamilton attended the Royal High School in 1795–1801 and then served 'a regular apprenticeship as an operative carpenter with my father, and afterwards acted as my father's assistant', as he recorded in his *Attestations Referred to in a Letter to the Lord Provost of Edinburgh* (Youngson, 293). In this, printed in 1819 as part of his unsuccessful bid to become superintendent of public works, Hamilton also stated that he had 'conducted some extensive buildings' for his uncle. When, in 1816, he submitted drawings for the completion of Robert Adam's scheme for the university, Hamilton styled himself 'architect'.

**Early works** Hamilton was the principal beneficiary of his uncle's will, which enabled him to marry at St Andrew's Church, Edinburgh, Ann Richardson Dickson (1790–1850x59) on 6 October 1813. They had five sons and two daughters. He became a burgess of Edinburgh in 1819. Hamilton also seems to have indulged in building speculation, a risky business which resulted in his father's bankruptcy in 1822. His earliest significant commission was for the Norwich Union Insurance Company's offices at 32 Princes Street, Edinburgh (1820; dem.), one of the first buildings which heralded the transformation of the character of the street from domestic to commercial. A later commercial building, at 93 George Street (1833), had external cast-iron columns at first-floor level, and an interest in new building methods is suggested by Hamilton's design for 70 feet high cones at the Alloa bottle works.

Although commercial commissions sustained him throughout his career, Hamilton's ambitions were civic and monumental. He claimed 'acquaintance with all the most eminent authors' on architecture (Colvin, *Archs.*, 453) and his accomplishment at reinterpreting Greek precedents in a city which was attempting to manifest in stone its intellectual reputation as the 'Athens of the north' was encouraged by seeing the watercolours of

**Thomas Hamilton** (1784–1858), by William Nicholson

buildings in Italy, Sicily, and Greece by the landscape painter Hugh 'Grecian' Williams which were exhibited in Edinburgh in 1822 and 1826.

Public renown came in 1818, when Hamilton won the competition for the Burns monument at Alloway, Ayrshire (1820–23). Based on the engravings of the Choragic monument of Lysicrates published in the *Antiquities of Athens* by J. Stuart and N. Revett (1762), this is an open circular temple raised on a massive rusticated basement, triangular in plan, skilfully placed in a romantic rural setting. Hamilton declined the £20 premium 'as the honour … would be recompense more than adequate to his humble exertions' (Hughes, 101). Such devotion to the growing cult of the Scots poet was rewarded by the commission for a second Burns monument. This more elaborate circular temple, intended to house a statue of the poet by John Flaxman, was raised on the edge of Calton Hill in Edinburgh (1830–32) and now enhances the setting of the architect's supreme masterpiece and the finest monument of the Greek revival in Scotland, the new Royal High School (1826–9).

**Major works** The high school was one of several old institutions affected by the social decline of Edinburgh Old Town and the consequent desire to rebuild elsewhere. Hamilton had reported on several sites and prepared a design for the west side of St James's Square in 1824, but the following year a better location was found on the south flank of Calton Hill, then being enhanced as Edinburgh's Acropolis. Hamilton responded with brilliance to this magnificent site, raising a dramatic composition of cubic masses above the basement wall with its flanking skewed pavilions placed on the curve of Regent Road, culminating in the central high hexastyle Doric portico. The design was based on the Theseion and the Propylaea in Athens and, as Joe Rock has written:

> The building's success lies in its solution to the central problem of the Greek Revival, that of adapting the windowless Greek temple to modern use. The central hall of the High School is lit by windows high on the wall of the main 'temple', providing a cross lighting for the coffered ceiling and yet completely invisible from the front. (Rock, 23)

Success also came from Hamilton's skill in treating classical forms picturesquely, and he had earlier quoted William Stark's opinion that 'there is in a bending alignment of streets much beauty. Public buildings break upon the eye at the most favourable point of view. Showing at once a front and a flank' (Fisher, *Scottish Pioneers*, 39). For Alexander 'Greek' Thomson of Glasgow—who, like Hamilton, never travelled abroad to see Greek prototypes at first hand—the high school together with St George's Hall in Liverpool by H. L. Elmes were 'unquestionably the two finest buildings in the kingdom' (Stamp, 76).

The high school was opened with much ceremony in 1829. Unfortunately, three years later Hamilton was involved in an acrimonious public correspondence with Provost John Learmonth over its cost and, despite his considerable reputation and manifest ability, he was denied the opportunity of designing another major public building in Edinburgh. His magnificent but expensive design for building the Scottish Academy and National Gallery of Scotland as parallel colonnaded ranges either side of the road on the Mound was rejected in 1849 in favour of that by the austere and fastidious W. H. Playfair, who wrote how 'I fear Hamilton who is full of intrigue and vulgar taste' (Gow, 17). The cruelly disappointed architect sent his design to the 1855 Universal Exhibition in Paris, at which he was awarded a gold medal.

Hamilton did, however, contribute much to the architectural distinction of Edinburgh. He designed the Hopetoun Rooms in Queen Street (1824; dem. 1967), which C. R. Cockerell thought 'admirably disposed' (Harris, 15), and the Orphan Hospital at the Dean Bridge (1831–3; now the Dean Gallery of the National Galleries of Scotland), a vigorous and surprisingly baroque composition with prominent arched chimneystacks surely inspired by Vanbrugh. His last important building, the Royal College of Physicians (1844–6), was his most delicate and sophisticated, with the flat, straight wall plane of the terraces of Queen Street broken by a portico supporting a projecting first-floor aedicule flanked with figures by Alexander Handyside Ritchie.

Hamilton was much concerned with town planning throughout his life and had published an anonymous article in the *Scots Magazine* in 1817 showing how the decline of the Old Town might be reversed. Following the passing of the Edinburgh Improvement Act in 1827 he served as architect to the improvement commissioners until finally resigning in 1834 after the over ambitious city had become bankrupt amid much acrimony. With William Burn he had proposed in 1824 a 'south approach' and a 'west approach' to the Old Town, the former being executed as the George IV Bridge and the latter as Johnston Terrace over the King's Bridge flanked by obelisks. Hamilton's proposal for a straight approach from the Mound terminated by a John Knox Church in the Lawnmarket was, however, abandoned in 1831. In that year Hamilton designed a temporary pavilion of timber and canvas for a dinner seating 1900 in honour of Earl Grey which was erected in the grounds of the high school in under a fortnight. He delivered a paper on its construction to the new Institute of British Architects, of which he was a founding fellow.

**Works outside Edinburgh** Hamilton worked outside Edinburgh. He designed the new assembly rooms in Ayr (1828–31), which incorporated a new Tolbooth Tower with an unusually tall spire elegantly incorporated into a classical conception on the familiar theme of the church steeple designs of James Gibbs; he was also responsible for the Wallace Tower in the same town (1830–32). In Glasgow he designed the Knox monument at the summit of the necropolis (1825), a large but squat Doric column whose proportions are marred by the grotesque scale of the superincumbent figure of John Knox by Robert Forrest. Unlike Burn and Playfair, Hamilton did not design many country houses but he was responsible for several remarkable villas on the outskirts of Edinburgh, notably Falcon Hall (*c*.1830; dem.), Arthur Lodge (1830; attributed), and those in Claremont Park, Leith (after 1827). He also designed schools in Kinghorn, Fife (1829), and Pultneytown, Caithness (1835).

**Church commissions** Alyth parish church, Perthshire (1839), is an unremarkable building in the Norman style. Although Hamilton's greatest love was for the Greek, like many of his contemporaries he was obliged to use other styles for church commissions. Several are Gothic, such as the Episcopal chapel in Dunfermline (1842), and after the Disruption of 1843 he supplied designs for a number of Free Church congregations and 'was in constant demand as an arbiter of taste—a fact we may find surprising today, in view of his obvious difficulties with the Gothic style', as Joe Rock observed with justice (Rock, 2). Hamilton was responsible for Free churches in Musselburgh (1843), Linlithgow (1844), and Dunbar (1850) and, in Edinburgh, the new North Free Church closing the vista down George IV Bridge (1846–8), the Roxburgh Free Church in Hill Square (1846), and St John's or Dr Guthrie's Free Church (now St Columba's, 1843–5). All are dismal creations when compared with contemporary churches in England, or even with the Tolbooth Church in Edinburgh by Gillespie Graham and A. W. N. Pugin, eventually built on the site proposed in 1829 for Hamilton's John Knox Church design; this last was to have had an openwork spire based on that of Antwerp Cathedral, an idea he revived for his 1846 project for a Knox memorial church which would have abutted and embraced Knox's house in the High Street.

**Later years** With his second son, Peter (1817–1861), Hamilton restored John Knox's house in 1853; earlier they had restored, or rebuilt, South Leith parish church (1847–8) following Peter Hamilton's return from teaching drawing at King Edward VII School, Birmingham, in 1847. His other known pupils were John Henderson (1804–1862) and Patrick Wilson. Hamilton was one of the original founders of the Royal Scottish Academy in 1826 and acted as its treasurer until 1829. For a number of years he declined to exhibit his drawings at the academy's annual exhibition owing to internal disagreements, but in 1845 he was requested to attend council meetings and was elected treasurer again the following year. Following the rejection of his design for the new building on the Mound commissioned by the academy, Hamilton resigned as treasurer on the grounds of ill health, but he attended council meetings until his death. In 1850 he published his *Letter to Lord John Russell, M.P., … on the present crisis relative to the fine arts in Scotland*, in which he set out his proposals for the 'architectural adornment of the Mound'.

Hamilton died at his home at 9 Howe Street, Edinburgh, on 24 February 1858 after a short illness. He was buried in his uncle's lair in the Calton cemetery close to the obelisk to the memory of the political martyrs of 1793 raised in 1844–5 to his design; a bronze memorial plaque was set up there in 1929. Friends and admirers subscribed 100 guineas to purchase the watercolour perspective of the high school executed with David Roberts and presented it to the Royal Scottish Academy in 1859. One obituary described Hamilton as a man of the 'highest integrity and independence of character' (Hughes, 115) and Bertha Porter recorded that 'he was greatly esteemed in his business relations, and beloved for his kindly disposition and cultivated mind' (*DNB*). If he was less successful than Burn or his rival Playfair, this was possibly owing to 'taciturnity and bashfulness, the result in great measure of a constitutional deafness' according to one contemporary (Youngson, 296). Hamilton's will suggests that his financial affairs were in some confusion in his last years and that he was in dispute with some of his children.

A portrait of Hamilton by William Nicholson (1781–1844) is at the Royal Scottish Academy and *Modern Athenians* (1882), by W. S. Douglas and B. W. Crombie, contained a caricature by Crombie. A calotype portrait of the 1840s of an elderly man by David Octavius Hill and Robert Adamson in the Scottish National Portrait Gallery possibly depicts Hamilton (Rock, plate 1). 'It is of course the Royal High School by which this half-deaf, solitary genius will always be remembered', as J. Mordaunt Crook has written (*The Greek Revival*, 1972, 105) and it is a fitting tribute to Thomas Hamilton that, a century and a half after it was built, his noble monument on Calton Hill was widely considered in Scotland to be the most suitable home for the Scottish parliament. GAVIN STAMP

**Sources** J. Rock, *Thomas Hamilton, architect, 1784–1858* (1984) [exhibition catalogue] • private information (2004) [Joe Rock] • I. Fisher, 'Thomas Hamilton of Edinburgh, architect and town planner (1784–1858)', BA diss., U. Oxf., 1965 [copy in National Monuments Record of Scotland, Edinburgh] • I. Fisher, 'Thomas Hamilton', *Scottish pioneers of the Greek revival* (1984) • *DNB* • Colvin, *Archs.* • D. Walker, 'The development of Thomson's style: the Scottish background', *'Greek' Thomson*, ed. G. Stamp and S. McKinstry (1994) • A. J. Youngson, *The making of classical Edinburgh* (1966) • *Edinburgh*, Pevsner (1984) • T. H. Hughes, 'Great Scottish architects of the past, no. 7: Thomas Hamilton', *Quarterly of the Incorporation of Architects in Scotland*, 20 (winter 1926), 101–15 • I. Gow, 'The northern Athenian temple of the arts', in I. Gow and T. Clifford, *The National Gallery of Scotland* (1988) • G. Stamp, ed., *The* *light of truth and beauty* (1999) · J. Harris, 'C. R. Cockerell's *Ichnographica domestica*', *Architectural History*, 14 (1971), 5–29 · b. cert. · m. cert. · *CGPLA Eng. & Wales* (1858) · *Currie Blackwood's Magazine*, 66/90 (July 1894), 128 · will, NA Scot., SC 70/4/59, pp. 315–16

**Likenesses** D. O. Hill and R. Adamson, calotype, 1840–49 (Thomas Hamilton?), Scot. NPG · W. Nicholson, oils, Royal Scot. Acad. [*see illus.*]

**Wealth at death** £631 2*s*. 2*d*.: confirmation, 4 Aug 1858, NA Scot., SC 70/1/98, 451–4

**Hamilton, Thomas** (1789–1842), novelist and travel writer, was born in Glasgow, the second son of William *Hamilton (1758–1790), professor of anatomy and botany at Glasgow University, and his wife, Elizabeth (*d*. 1827), daughter of William Stirling, a Glasgow merchant. He was the younger brother of William Stirling *Hamilton (1788–1856), the philosopher. Following preliminary education in Glasgow, he was assigned to a series of private tutors between 1801 and 1803. In November 1803 he entered Glasgow University, where he studied for three years, proving himself to be an able, if not diligent, student. During his college years he became friends with Michael Scott (1789–1833), author of *Tom Cringle's Log* (1836).

Hamilton worked for a time in Glasgow and Liverpool, but showed no aptitude for business. His bent was towards a military career, and in 1810 he obtained a commission in the 29th regiment. He had two spells of active service in the Peninsula, on one occasion receiving a serious wound in the thigh from a musket bullet. He also served in Nova Scotia and New Brunswick, before being sent with his regiment to France as part of the army of occupation. About 1818 he retired from the army on half pay, and settled in Edinburgh, where he fell in with J. G. Lockhart and the circle of writers associated with *Blackwood's Magazine*.

On 14 November 1820 Hamilton married Anne Montgomery (*d*. 1829), the daughter of Archibald Montgomery Campbell, and spent several summers with his wife at Lockhart's cottage near Abbotsford, where they made the acquaintance of Sir Walter Scott. In 1827 Hamilton published the novel *Cyril Thornton*, which contains fictionalized accounts of his early life in Glasgow and his military experiences; it went through three editions in his lifetime. In 1829 he published *Annals of the Peninsular Campaign*. In the same year he travelled to Italy, and at the end of the year his wife died, and was buried in Florence.

Following his return to Scotland, Hamilton proceeded to visit America, bringing back materials for a book. His genially satirical *Men and Manners in America* (1833) was a popular success, and was translated into French and German. On 15 February 1834 he was married a second time, to Maria Frances Geslip (*d*. 1875), the daughter and coheir of François Joseph Louis de Latour of Madras, and widow of Sir Robert Townsend Farquhar (1776–1830), the former governor of Mauritius. They settled at Elleray, Westmorland, where they became friends with William Wordsworth. While visiting Florence with his wife, Hamilton suffered a paralytic seizure, and died in Pisa of a second attack on 7 December 1842. He was buried in Florence, beside his first wife.

T. W. Bayne, *rev.* Douglas Brown

**Sources** J. F. Waller, ed., *The imperial dictionary of universal biography*, 3 vols. (1857–63) · *Blackwood*, 53 (1843), 280 · [J. G. Lockhart], *Peter's letters to his kinsfolk*, 2nd edn, 3 (1819), 140 · J. Veitch, *Memoir of Sir William Hamilton, bart.* (1869) · J. C. Corson, *Notes and index to Sir Herbert Grierson's edition of the letters of Sir Walter Scott* (1979) · *The letters of William and Dorothy Wordsworth*, ed. E. De Selincourt, 2nd edn, rev. C. L. Shaver, M. Moorman, and A. G. Hill, 8 vols. (1967–93), vols. 5–7

**Likenesses** J. Watson-Gordon, oils, Scot. NPG

**Hamilton, Thomas Watt** (1952–1996), mass murderer, was born at the Maternity Hospital, Glasgow, on 10 May 1952, the only child of Thomas Watt (*b*. 1929), bus driver, and his wife, Agnes Graham, *née* Hamilton (*b*. 1931), box maker and later hotel worker. His parents separated during his infancy, and his mother returned to live with her adoptive parents, Catherine and James Hamilton. The Hamiltons reared the baby as their own, and only when Thomas was a teenager did he learn that Agnes Watt was his natural mother. He continued, however, to treat her as a sister. The family moved to Stirling, where he was educated, first at the Territorial School (1961–3) and then at Riverside secondary school. After obtaining a firearms certificate in 1977 he joined the Stirling rifle and pistol club and became a crack shot, but he was never popular with fellow club members.

During the early 1970s Hamilton opened a do-it-yourself shop, Woodcraft, in Stirling, but it failed after a few years. Thereafter he made his living by buying and selling cameras. His mounting business difficulties he blamed on a whispering campaign against him. Distrust of him began when in 1974 his assistant scout leader's warrant was withdrawn after an outing to Aviemore, during which he left eight boys to sleep in the back of a freezing van. Hamilton next started a succession of boys' clubs in Dunblane, Alva, Bishopbriggs, Tullibody, and Dunfermline. In 1981 he was dismissed from the Boys' Brigade after complaints about a summer camp he had attended. In 1983 the Labour MP George Robertson watched a meeting of the Dunblane Rovers, a boys' club run by Hamilton from the gymnasium of Dunblane high school. 'There was a large number of small boys in shorts, stripped to the waist, being bossed around by two or three middle-aged men swaggering around in a very militaristic way', Robertson recalled; he was reminded of the Hitler Youth. As a result of Robertson's concerns Hamilton was temporarily banned from using school premises for the Dunblane Rovers in 1983. This episode began Hamilton's grievances against the people of Dunblane and the local authorities; the rejection in 1988 of his application to rejoin the Boy Scout movement added certain scout leaders to his list of enemies. In long correspondence with the Conservative MP Michael Forsyth and in pamphlets circulated in Dunblane, Hamilton 'argued his case with the tenacity of a terrier' (*The Times*, 19 June 1996).

After complaints from a mother, the police in 1989 investigated Hamilton's conduct of a summer camp for children, and in 1990–91 they investigated photographs he had taken of boys. No grounds for prosecution were found in either instance. Fife regional council, which had rented school gymnasia to him since 1986, terminated this practice in 1992 after complaints about his video filming of boys. His camera work was suggestive rather than obscene. There were several police inquiries about Hamilton in 1993–4. Lothian police cautioned him in 1994 after he was caught in a compromising situation with a youth in Edinburgh. He became consumed by resentment, and was especially distressed that only one Dunblane boy had attended his summer camp at Loch Lomond in 1995, compared with seventy in 1983. Believing that his reputation had been unfairly sullied he prepared to revenge himself on his detractors at Dunblane. These preparations may have begun as early as two years before his death.

On 12 March 1996 Hamilton posted to the BBC copies of seven letters he had written since 1993 complaining that he had been slurred as a sexual pervert by the Scout Association; the last in this series he had addressed a few days earlier to the queen. Shortly after 9.20 a.m. on 13 March 1996 Hamilton burst into the gymnasium of Dunblane primary school, where twenty-nine pupils aged five and six were gathering for a physical education lesson. Producing four automatic weapons he opened fire, killing fifteen children and their teacher, Gwen Mayor; a sixteenth child died in hospital and thirteen children were wounded. After shooting every child he could see, Hamilton at about 9.35 a.m. turned a pistol on himself.

This massacre of little children caused grief and shock throughout Britain. A day of mourning, with a minute's silence, was declared on 17 March. Lord Cullen, a lord of session, was appointed to chair a tribunal of inquiry. The shootings at Dunblane resulted in amendments in 1996–7 to the Firearms Act, outlawing handguns exceeding .22 calibre, and more than 160,000 handguns were surrendered by their owners at a cost in compensation of about £200 million. The gymnasium where the shootings occurred was demolished, and in its place was created a memorial garden to the dead.

RICHARD DAVENPORT-HINES

**Sources** *The Times* (14–16 March 1996) • *Sunday Times* (17 March 1996) • *The Times* (31 May 1996) • *The Times* (19 June 1996) • b. cert. • d. cert.

**Hamilton, Walter** (*bap.* **1774**, *d.* **1828**). *See under* Hamilton, Alexander (1762–1824).

**Hamilton, Walter** (**1908–1988**), headmaster and college head, was born on 10 February 1908, the only child of Walter George Hamilton, tea trader in the City of London, and his wife, Caroline Mary Stiff, schoolmistress. His paternal grandfather was treasurer of the National Union of Teachers, and one of his great-grandfathers a Scottish rope maker. His mother taught him devotedly at home until he was nine; his father was absent in France throughout the First World War. In 1919 Hamilton went on a scholarship to Catford grammar school and in 1926 won a major scholarship to Trinity College, Cambridge. He was placed in the first class of parts one and two of the classical tripos (1927 and 1929), winning a Craven scholarship, the Porson prize, and the Chancellor's classical medal. In 1931 he was elected to a prize fellowship of Trinity. Two years later, encouraged by friends but in a temporary capacity, he went to Eton College, mainly to share the classics teaching of the headmaster's division. He fell on his feet and stayed thirteen years. In 1937 he was made master-in-college of the seventy king's scholars.

This was the inspired appointment of Hamilton's career. He brought a keen intelligence and perception to his task and six years at Trinity had done his wit no harm. Now his shy but amusing and distinctive personality blossomed. The boys were drawn to his strikingly low voice and lugubrious manner, and, bright and competitive (and often difficult!) though they were, he disarmed them with a trust and equality which conveyed a sense that he and they depended on one another. Shared experience of wartime conditions became a further strength; they enjoyed his usually relaxed regime, accepted his strong moral convictions, and knew that beneath the surface he had much in reserve. He was also cleverer than any of them. For himself, the years at Eton were among his busiest; he felt at home there, and thrived on the school's easy and civilized style. He made many friends, and in later life no honour gave him more pleasure than his appointment as a fellow (1972–81).

In 1946, in need of change, Hamilton returned to Trinity as fellow, university lecturer, and tutor (the latter two from 1947). While there, a number of headmasterships were offered to him but not until 1950 did he feel able to accept one, that of Westminster. In the following year he married Jane Elizabeth (*b.* 1931), daughter of Sir (Robert) John Formby Burrows, solicitor and president of the Law Society (1964–5), and his wife, Mary Hewlett, *née* Salmon; they had three sons and a daughter. The marriage was one of lasting happiness. At Westminster School, home again after wartime evacuation, Hamilton at first seemed withdrawn, even angular. But soon he was the man for the hour. Buildings were restored and reorganized, the number of boys doubled, and his key appointments to the staff prospered. The school developed a disciplined and new momentum and its learning and scholarship were transformed. Yet Dean's Yard was no place to bring up a family of small children and after seven years, in 1957, he accepted the headmastership of Rugby School. By now he was an illustrious figure and it was the first time Westminster had lost its headmaster to another school.

An Old Rugbeian wrote, 'This is the first time they have appointed the right man since Thomas Arnold'. Hamilton seemed to the staff larger than life. With quick and warmly compelling rapport he brought them on. As for the boys, he was again a housemaster (with the assistance of tutors) to seventy of them. He was shrewd and wise, and always ready to listen. He would look, often twinkling, over his half-moon spectacles, puffing gently at his pipe, and the boys would feel they were understood. Unless in difficulty, no one at Rugby was allowed to take himself too seriously, and Hamilton's own witticisms became legendary. The absurd delighted him, pretension he abhorred, and dishonesty aroused fierce anger. He was physically a large man and on formal occasions he presented a solemn appearance, which his tone of voice could dispel or emphasize. He was master of the spoken as well as the written word. Some had hoped he would make considerable changes in the school and he did make some. But he was not given to change for change's sake, preferring to make well-tried procedures work well. Given the increasingly questioning climate of the time, Hamilton knew where he stood—in the liberal but nevertheless firm tradition. Humanity was king and the school's academic record of his time was acclaimed. Meanwhile his influence had spread wide, especially in the schools belonging to the Headmasters' Conference and the Governing Bodies Association. He was chairman of the first for four years (1955, 1956, 1965, and 1966) and of the second from 1969 to 1974. These were years of ideological and political threat to selective education and to independent schools. Hamilton strongly opposed the hostile proposals as being untried, probably disastrous academically, and anyway financially unrealistic.

In 1967 Hamilton was invited back to Cambridge as master of Magdalene. He enjoyed presiding over a college of traditional tendencies. But he disliked complacency and, when student unrest impinged, his skill as chairman of the committee of senior and junior members helped to restore undergraduate goodwill. He warmed more to undergraduates than dons, and regretted that preoccupation with research had come to replace scholarship as he knew it, and that publication was deemed more significant than distinguished teaching. His years as master were difficult ones for universities and colleges, but when he retired in 1978 he left Magdalene strengthened academically and financially on surer ground. He served for five years on the council of the Senate (1969–74) and frequently acted as the vice-chancellor's deputy, notably as chairman of the university examinations syndicate. He was an honorary fellow of Magdalene from 1978. He published for Penguin Books *A New Translation of Plato's Symposium* (1951), Plato's *Gorgias* (1960), Plato's *Phaedrus and Letters VII and VIII* (1973), and (with A. F. Wallace-Hadrill) *Ammianus Marcellinus* (1986). He was a fellow of the Royal Society of Literature (1957) and an honorary DLitt of Durham University (1958). Hamilton deeply loved the Scottish highlands, where he spent most of his holidays. There he was never happier, nor more relaxed and adventurous, with his family and friends. He died on 8 February 1988 in Cambridge where he had lived in his final years at 6 Hedgerley Close. In 2002 his daughter Caroline Hamilton was part of the first all-female expedition to reach both the north and south poles on foot.

A. R. Donald Wright, *rev.*

**Sources** A. R. D. Wright, ed., *Walter Hamilton: a portrait* (1991) • personal knowledge (1996) • private information (1996) • *The Independent* (12 Feb 1988) • *Daily Telegraph* (10 Feb 1988) • *The Times* (10 Feb 1988) • *Sunday Telegraph* (14 Feb 1988) • *Cambridge Evening News* (Feb 1988)

**Archives** Eton • Magd. Cam. • priv. coll. • Rugby School, Warwickshire • Shrewsbury School • St Dunstan's College, Catford • Westminster School, London

**Likenesses** D. Hill, oils, 1986, Magd. Cam. • portrait, Westminster School • portrait, Rugby School

**Hamilton, Walter Kerr** (1808–1869), bishop of Salisbury, born in London on 16 November 1808 and baptized in April 1809, was the elder son of Anthony Hamilton, archdeacon of Taunton and prebendary of Lichfield. His mother was Charity Graeme, third daughter of Sir Walter *Farquhar, bt, physician to the prince regent. William Richard *Hamilton was his uncle. Hamilton's early childhood was passed at Loughton in Essex, of which parish his father was rector. After spending some years at a private school, Durham House in Chelsea, he was sent to Eton College in January 1822, where he remained for four years. There he was taught by Edward Hawtrey and became the friend for life of W. E. Gladstone, James Hope (later James Hope-Scott), and George Selwyn. He was a noted oarsman and cricketer. He was in youth a moderate evangelical. In January 1826 he went as a private pupil to Thomas Arnold of Rugby, then at Laleham, and here it was that (as he says) he first learned what work meant. Morally and intellectually Hamilton was deeply influenced by Arnold, but did not adopt his tutor's theological views. In January 1827 Hamilton matriculated from Christ Church, Oxford, and in December 1827 was nominated to a studentship by Frederick Barnes, the subdean. Parental pressure prevented him rowing in the first boat race. In Michaelmas term 1830 he obtained a first class in *literae humaniores* with Joseph Anstice, Henry W. Wilberforce, and H. E. Manning.

In 1830 Hamilton spent the long vacation on retreat with Gladstone at Cuddesdon, assisting the latter in his choice of career. Hamilton spent 1831 in Christ Church deciding on his own career. At Easter 1832 he was elected to an open fellowship at Merton; in the summer of the same year he went abroad, and passed the winter at Rome, where he was introduced by Arnold to Bunsen, the Prussian ambassador, whom he impressed very favourably. On his return to England early in 1833, he settled at Merton College, Oxford. Among his colleagues there were Edward Denison, afterwards bishop of Salisbury, and H. E. Manning, and he joined in an endeavour to breathe into the life of the college a more earnest, religious, and moral spirit. On Trinity Sunday, 2 June 1833, he was ordained deacon, and priest on 22 December of the same year. He was college tutor for a time, and lost no opportunity of making himself closely acquainted with the undergraduates. Gladstone unsuccessfully encouraged him to move to Edinburgh to work with E. B. Ramsay. At Michaelmas 1833 he became curate of Wolvercote, near Oxford, and took the advice of his cousin, W. F. *Hook, on running a parish. At Michaelmas in the following year he became curate to Edward Denison, vicar of St Peter-in-the-East, Oxford. When in 1837 Denison became bishop of Salisbury, Hamilton was, on the nomination of Merton College and R. D. Hampden, appointed his successor. This post he held until 1841. He was an indefatigable parish priest, and an earnest evangelical preacher. He played a part in the established church's music with his *Psalms and Hymns*

**Walter Kerr Hamilton (1808–1869)**, by Francis Holl, pubd 1862 (after George Richmond, 1858)

(1838), written with his Austrian organist, Alexander Reinangle, and *Collection of Psalms and Hymns* (1840). He also published morning and evening services (1846). These interests reflect the evolution of his theology. After about 1836 he came under the influence of the Oxford Movement. He continued a high-churchman to the end of his life, and is generally associated with the Tractarians, though he was not a thoroughgoingly active partisan: he sought to make their revival generally acceptable in the Church of England.

In 1837 Hamilton was made examining chaplain to his friend the bishop of Salisbury, and in 1841 left Oxford with some reluctance to become a canon in Salisbury Cathedral. At Salisbury he threw himself into the duties of his new position with characteristic energy. As precentor from 1843 he endeavoured to raise the tone of the daily service in the cathedral and he greatly improved the choir. His regular wearing of the cassock revived its use (Bridge, 'The nineteenth-century', 139). A visit to the continent in 1849 encouraged him to make the cathedral more accessible to the public, with extra services (mostly conducted by himself). He restored and refitted the cathedral's muniment room. He thought that constant residence should be enforced upon the canons as well as upon the dean, and accordingly declined the rectory of Loughton which was offered him at his father's death in 1851 (his mother subsequently lived with the Hamilton family in Salisbury). In 1853 he published a pamphlet on cathedral reform, which he reprinted, together with a 'Pastoral letter', in 1855, when bishop of the diocese. When cholera broke out in 1849, Hamilton at once joined his diocesan in visiting the sufferers, but had soon to go abroad for his health. On 9 January 1845 he married Isabel Elizabeth (*d.* 1886), daughter of Francis Lear, dean of Salisbury; they had ten children (five sons, five daughters), two of whom died young.

In March 1854, on the death of Bishop Denison, Hamilton was appointed to succeed him. On his deathbed Denison dictated a message to the prime minister, Lord Aberdeen, strongly recommending Hamilton as his successor. The see was, however, first offered to Charles Blunt, who refused it. Thereupon it was offered to Hamilton, who, after an interval of painful deliberation, was persuaded to accept it by Gladstone, on what was, in the view of the latter, 'a new & auspicious day for the Church of England!' (Gladstone, *Diaries*, 19 March 1854). Manning later alleged that Hamilton was on the brink of converting to Rome—hence Gladstone's energy and delight (Purcell, 531–2). Queen Victoria ineffectively demurred to what was seen as a provocatively high-church nomination (dubbed by Gladstone the 'sin of Sarum'). It was in fact an enlightened appointment, giving a significant section of the church representation at the episcopal level. The national implications of Hamilton's views were less than expected by both supporters and opponents, for his dedication to Salisbury meant that he played a lesser part on the national scene than had been anticipated.

Hamilton was consecrated by Archbishop Sumner on 14 May 1854 at Lambeth. Hamilton continued all his predecessor's episcopal reforms, and improved upon them. He increased the number of confirmations and raised the standard in his ordinations, both of theological attainments and also of spiritual preparation. The idea of establishing at Salisbury a theological college had been suggested to him by his predecessor in 1841; but it was not until twenty years afterwards that the plan was carried out. Until his death he always took the greatest interest in its welfare. He was never absent from Salisbury except upon diocesan business, or for a short holiday in the late autumn of the year, and very seldom appeared in the House of Lords. When at home he almost always attended the daily services in the cathedral, and his life was marked by great regularity and incessant occupation to a late hour of the night. Hamilton was 'an indefatigable preacher' (Liddon, *Hamilton*, 68). He continued to encourage popular use of the cathedral, and in 1861 preached the first sermon heard in the nave for eighty years. He prevented the dean and canons from holding any other preferments so as to encourage their regular attendance in the cathedral. His lifestyle was simple: he soon gave up his episcopal carriage, and he spent little on the palace, though he asphalted the ground floor for the benefit of the servants.

In the administration of his diocese Hamilton secured the respect and affection both of the clergy and the laity, even of those who differed from his decided high-church opinions. He delivered episcopal charges in 1855, 1858, 1861, 1864, and 1867, all of which were published. The last of these excited much attention on account of the fearless clearness with which he asserted the doctrines of the real presence in the holy communion, of the eucharistic sacrifice, and of priestly absolution. He was the more outspoken on these subjects because he had been accused of holding doctrines to which he dared not give public utterance. The support in the charge of 1864 for clergy retreats led to outrage. The charge of 1867 was the subject of a discussion in the House of Lords, where Lord Portman presented a condemnatory petition. Hamilton never expressed or felt any bitterness towards his opponents. It is, however, probable that the anxiety caused by the opposition to this charge, added to his strenuous episcopal work, shortened his life. The first symptoms of heart disease showed themselves early in 1868. He continued his duties until October in that year and voted against the Irish Church Suspensory Bill. However, in convocation he defended Gladstone's motives in proposing disestablishment for the church in Ireland. After spending seven months in London, Hamilton returned to Salisbury on 29 July, and died three days afterwards in his palace, on 1 August 1869, his wife surviving him. He was buried in Salisbury Cathedral. Hamilton was a tall, portly man, with a pleasant, open countenance and winning manners. After his death, the Gladstonian connection continued, as his son Edward Walter *Hamilton became one of Gladstone's secretaries in 1870.

W. A. GREENHILL, *rev.* H. C. G. MATTHEW

**Sources** H. P. Liddon, *Walter Kerr Hamilton, bishop of Salisbury* (1890) • H. P. Liddon, *Life in death* (1869) • A. E. Bridge, 'Walter Kerr Hamilton: the making of a Tractarian bishop, 1808–1854', MLitt diss., U. Oxf., 1988 • A. E. Bridge, 'The nineteenth-century revivication of Salisbury Cathedral, 1841–1854', *Close encounters*, ed. D. Marcombe and C. S. Knighton (1991) • Gladstone, *Diaries* • E. S. Purcell, *Life of Cardinal Manning*, 2 vols. (1895) • D. W. R. Bahlman, 'The queen, Mr Gladstone, and church patronage', *Victorian Studies*, 3 (1959–60), 349–80 • *The diary of Sir Edward Walter Hamilton, 1880–1885*, ed. D. W. R. Bahlman, 2 vols. (1972) • G. White, *The cathedral church of Salisbury* (1911) • D. H. Robertson, *Sarum Close: a history of the life and education of the cathedral choristers for 700 years* (1938)

**Archives** Pusey Oxf., corresp., diaries, logbooks • Salisbury Cathedral, official letter-books • Wilts. & Swindon RO, family and personal papers | BL, corresp. with W. E. Gladstone, Add. MS 44183 • Bodl. Oxf., corresp. with Samuel Wilberforce • LPL, corresp. with A. C. Tait • Pusey Oxf., letters to H. P. Liddon

**Likenesses** G. Richmond, oils, 1858, bishop's palace, Salisbury • F. Holl, stipple, pubd 1862 (after G. Richmond, 1858), BM, NPG [*see illus.*] • Mayall, carte-de-visite, NPG

**Wealth at death** under £14,000: probate, 4 Sept 1869, *CGPLA Eng. & Wales*

**Hamilton, William** (*d.* 1307), dean of York and administrator, originated from Hambleton in Brayton parish, near Selby in Yorkshire. Son of Adam Hamilton and his wife, Alice, he may have received his schooling at Selby Abbey, and had become a chancery clerk by 1265. He received judicial commissions which included presiding with Reynold de Grey over a dispute among lords of the Welsh marches in 1278, holding pleas of the forest in Hampshire and Wiltshire a year later, and hearing assizes with Grey (justice of Chester) in 1295. Having served as the 'king's vice-chancellor' while the chancellor, Robert Burnell, was abroad (1286–9), Hamilton (executor of Burnell's will) was expected to succeed him as both bishop and chancellor in 1292, but was content to serve as lieutenant to Walter Langton (*d.* 1321), taking charge of the great seal during his absences (from March to August 1297 and from February to June 1299). Although Langton was followed by William Greenfield (*d.* 1315), the latter's resignation in December 1304 left a vacancy at the head of chancery to which Hamilton was nominated. He received the great seal on 16 January 1305. As the king's principal clerk and Edward I's confidant (*secretarius*) Hamilton was an influential figure in royal administration. He was closely involved with Scottish affairs, and, with the administration frequently based in the north, he was probably responsible for the recruitment of many able Yorkshiremen into chancery.

Following his appointment as a canon of York, with the prebend of Warthill, in 1287, Hamilton became archdeacon of York in 1288 and by 1290 was precentor of Beverley. In 1298 his local roots secured him the deanery in the face of fierce competition from Cardinal Francisco Gaetani, nephew of Pope Boniface VIII (*r.* 1294–1303). In 1305 Edward I urged Hamilton to use his influence both as head of the chapter at York and as chancellor to find a profitable preferment for the king's godson.

In 1280 Hamilton was given a house in York which had belonged to the notorious moneylender, Aaron the Jew (*d.* 1268). From 1285 he was himself engaged in moneylending enterprises (sometimes with his brother Adam), manipulating conveyances of land and realizing considerable profits. In addition to a number of Yorkshire livings, he possessed a third of the lordship and mines of Taddington, Prestklare, and Over Haddon in Derbyshire in 1287, and was given the rich manor of Great Baddow in Essex, forfeited by Robert Bruce when the latter seized the Scottish throne in 1306.

Hamilton died on 20 April 1307 while staying at Fountains Abbey. Buried in the south transept of York Minster, prayers for the souls of his parents, himself, and successive deans were said in the chantry he had founded five years earlier in Brayton. He was also remembered in the chantries for two priests endowed by him in the minster, and in a chapel at Pateley Bridge endowed by his executor, John Markenfield, in 1321.

A. J. MUSSON

**Sources** *Chancery records* • Tout, *Admin. hist.*, vols. 2, 6 • J. R. Walbran, ed., *Memorials of the abbey of St Mary of Fountains*, 1, SurtS, 42 (1863) • *The register of John le Romeyn … 1286–1296*, ed. W. Brown, 1, SurtS, 123 (1913) • *The register of William Greenfield, lord archbishop of York, 1306–1315*, ed. W. Brown and A. H. Thompson, 1, SurtS, 145 (1931) • *The register of William Greenfield, lord archbishop of York, 1306–1315*, ed. W. Brown and A. H. Thompson, 2, SurtS, 149 (1934) • J. L. Grassi, 'Royal clerks from the archdiocese of York in the fourteenth century', *Northern History*, 5 (1970), 12–33 • R. H. Bowers, 'From rolls to riches: king's clerks and moneylending in thirteenth century England', *Speculum*, 58 (1983), 60–71 • J. A. R. Bickford and M. E. Bickford, 'The rectors of Kirkella', *Kirkella Parish Magazine* (1990), 28–33 • F. M. Powicke and C. R. Cheney, eds., *Councils and synods with other documents relating to the English church, 1205–1313*, 2 vols. (1964) • J. Raine, ed., *The fabric rolls of York Minster*, SurtS, 35 (1859), 277

**Hamilton, William, second duke of Hamilton (1616–1651)**, politician, was born at Hamilton, Lanarkshire, on 14 December 1616, the second son of James *Hamilton, second marquess of Hamilton and first earl of Cambridge (1589–1625), and Lady Anna *Cunningham (*d.* 1647), fourth daughter of James Cunningham, sixth earl of Glencairn (1580–1631). He was eight when his father died on 2

**William Hamilton, second duke of Hamilton (1616–1651)**, by Adriaen Hanneman, 1650

March 1625 and his brother James *Hamilton, third marquess and later first duke of Hamilton (1606–1649), ten years his senior, decided on most matters relating to his education and career until about 1640.

**Education, early career, and secretary of state for Scotland, 1630–1640** Lord William Hamilton, as he was then known, entered the University of Glasgow about March 1630. He may also have been tutored by Robert Baillie, with whom he formed a lasting attachment. In March 1633 he travelled to France, in the company of his governor Henry Maule, to complete his education. His two-year stay there was paid for by the sale of armaments, including over 1000 pistols, from the army that had fought under his brother in Germany in 1631–2. Having left France in May 1635, he spent some months travelling around England and Scotland. His brother wrote to Thomas Wentworth, Viscount Wentworth, on 7 October 1635 seeking on Lord William's behalf a large portion of the projected plantation of Connaught, but the lord deputy resisted this and nothing came of the plan.

Lord William eventually settled in London with his brother, probably in the spring of 1636. He had chambers at his brother's principal residence in the city, Wallingford House, his own coach, and servants and spent a large amount of money on clothes, particularly masquing suits. His brother applied to their mother, Anna Cunningham, to contribute towards Lord William's fortune but was offered only £20,000 Scots since the dowager marchioness had a very low view of the superficial pleasures of the court. An opening at court came in early 1637 with the establishment of young Prince Charles's household, and Lord William was made master of the horse. In the absence of a secure fortune, he married on 26 May 1638 at St Anne Blackfriars, London, Elizabeth (1620–1659), one of the daughters and future coheirs of James Maxwell, later earl of Dirleton (*d.* 1650), who had secured a place as gentleman in James VI and I's bedchamber through the influence of Lord William's father. The bridegroom may have received a dowry of £10,000 sterling and Scottish lands from his father-in-law, and a royal pension of 4000 English merks per annum followed a month after his marriage. The same year there was a plan to make him earl of Roseberrie, but although the king signed the patent, he then deliberately tore it in disgust at the covenanting activities of Lord William's mother; the patent survives, signed by Charles, though undated, with a 6-inch tear running through the centre of his signature (NA Scot., GD 406/1/6598). Lord William was finally created, on 31 March 1639, earl of Lanark, and Lord Machanshire and Polmont. A year later, following the death of William Alexander, first earl of Stirling, Lanark was on 15 March made secretary of state for Scotland at court, a position that was secured for him by his brother, with the additional support of Queen Henrietta Maria. Lanark's former governor Henry Maule was made keeper of the king's signet and his secretary was John Squire. Shortly afterwards Lanark was made sole secretary of state for Scotland, but probably continued to stay with his brother at Wallingford House, underlining the influence the elder brother had over his protégé. Again through the patronage of Hamilton, who was keeper of Portsmouth, he sat in the Short Parliament of April–May 1640 as one of the two MPs for the town. He was sworn a privy councillor in England on 10 June 1640, but he attended only eight out of 133 meetings in 1640, sixteen out of thirty-seven in 1641, and one out of five in 1642.

**The civil wars, 1640–1646** Lanark was present at the negotiations that culminated in the treaty of Ripon of 1640 and the convening of the Long Parliament on 3 November 1640. Many papers in his hand have survived, yet, again, there is no sense, at this stage in his career at least, that he was anything more than his brother's willing instrument and the amanuensis for the commissioners present at the meetings in the summer of 1640. Lanark was with Charles when he arrived in Edinburgh on 14 August 1641. During the king's visit he had his place as secretary of state for Scotland confirmed in the Scottish parliament and he was appointed to the newly constituted privy council in Scotland on 18 November of that year. By the end of September his brother's alliance with the covenanter leader Archibald Campbell, eighth earl and first marquess of Argyll (1598–1661), had created a welter of ill-feeling among royalists in Edinburgh, and a plot to assassinate Hamilton and Argyll, known as the 'incident', was hatched. On 11 October, after being warned of the plot by General Sir Alexander Leslie, Lanark fled Edinburgh with his brother and Argyll, returning on 1 November under the protection of parliament. Lanark penned an authoritative narrative of the events that preceded the plot and drafted most of the papers that led to a reconciliation (NA Scot., GD 406/1/1440, 'Relation of the incident', 22 October 1641). It is about this time that Lanark was becoming a target for those seeking patronage, but the correspondents usually used him as a means of securing the marquess of Hamilton's support.

Lanark was involved in the unsuccessful attempt, initiated by his brother Hamilton, in September 1642 to invite Queen Henrietta Maria to Scotland to mediate a peace in England. From December 1642 to August 1643 Lanark and his brother tried to spoil the plans for the Scots to intervene in the English civil war on the side of the English parliament. Lanark was at the centre of this bruising contest in the privy council, then in the convention of estates. He returned to Edinburgh from court in Oxford on 15 May carrying the king's declaration condemning the English parliament's attempts to draw Scotland into the war in England, which the brothers persuaded the privy council to publish on 1 June. Yet this success was short-lived and the convention of estates that met towards the end of the month agreed, on 26 June, to ignore the king's instructions not to discuss the war in England. Lanark, his brother, and their supporters left the convention in protest and the solemn league and covenant was agreed in August.

Lanark and Hamilton fled to Oxford to avoid signing the covenant and were arrested on the king's orders when they entered the city on 16 December 1643. With the aid of his page Robert Kennedy, Lanark escaped the night before he was to be sent as a prisoner to Ludlow Castle in Wales, and he submitted himself to the Scottish commissioners in London. Within a few months he was back in Edinburgh, and welcomed into the inner circle of the covenanting regime. His old tutor, Robert Baillie, even gave up his chamber and bed to the repentant young earl when he arrived in the capital. On 16 April Lanark took the solemn league and covenant and the convention of estates immediately reversed the act of 12 October 1643 stripping him of his estate and public office, declaring him 'ane good patriot and covenanter' (*APS*, 6.i, 89). Contemporaries noted Lanark's conversion, one observing that he 'acted afterwards so vigorously in the cause, that ere long he was preferred to be a ruling elder' (*Memoirs of Henry Guthry*, 151). Between 1644 and 1646 Lanark had one of the highest attendance records at the convention and committee of estates and the parliament, and was appointed to numerous influential committees. In a single month—June 1644—he was appointed to the committee to consider peace proposals and the committee concerning the Scottish army in Ireland, and was a member of the delegation that met the Swedish commissioner. In July 1644 the parliament confirmed his position as sole secretary of state for Scotland against the claims of Sir James Galloway, master of requests, and Sir Robert Spottiswood, who had been exercising the office at court following Lanark's arrest. He was also a commander in the army raised against James Graham, first marquess of Montrose (1612–1650), being sent into the west of Scotland to levy more recruits shortly before the covenanters were defeated at the battle of Kilsyth on 15 August 1645.

Lanark was in the delegation that was sent by the committee of estates to meet the king when he arrived at Newcastle with the Scottish army on 13 May 1646. Although they told Charles that they would not 'suerve' from their 'Covenant and treaties with oure Brethrene in England' (NA Scot., GD 406/1/1961), Lanark quickly reconciled with the king and played a leading role in trying to improve Charles's relationship with his Scottish subjects. Within a few days the Scottish secretary was dispatching letters at the king's behest, one of the first being a request to the houses of parliament and the Scottish commissioners in London to send north propositions for peace. Yet the reconciliation with the king did not stop Lanark regularly urging Charles to accept the covenant, and to sign the Newcastle propositions tendered by the two parliaments. As well as drafting correspondence and papers over the ensuing months, Lanark supervised a large-scale distribution of gifts and honours to the Scottish political élite. He also wrote to his brother Hamilton, who was in London after being released from over two years in prison, and persuaded him to change his mind about retiring from politics. Hamilton arrived at Newcastle on 28 July 1646 and henceforward the brothers forged a formidable double-act, with Lanark playing an increasingly important part in the relationship. This was strikingly illustrated when Hamilton decided, once more, to retire from public life, for not only did Lanark persuade him to change his mind again, he also held the growing Hamilton party together while his brother brooded at Hamilton Palace in September 1646. From then on, Lanark was the link between the Hamilton party and the king in England, all correspondence and papers being addressed to him.

**The engagement, 1647–1650** The sixth session of the first triennial parliament that lasted from 3 November 1646 to 20 March 1647 voted on 16 January 1647 to hand the king over to the English parliament. Lanark and Hamilton, and a few of their supporters, opposed the vote but the majority of the parliament refused to aid the uncovenanted king. However, the Scots' attitude was dramatically altered by the abduction of the king by Cornet George Joyce on 4 June 1647, who took him to the independent-dominated army. As the situation in England deteriorated further, two new commissioners, one each representing the Argyll and Hamilton parties, were sent south: Lanark for his brother, and John Campbell, first earl of Loudoun, for his kinsman Argyll. Lanark was given a free hand to negotiate all matters with the king, while Loudoun was only to concern himself with issues relating to the English parliament. Lanark and Loudoun joined John Maitland, second earl of Lauderdale, in London on 11 October. The dynamic between the three noblemen who signed the engagement at the end of the year was a key factor over the ensuing weeks, and Lanark enjoyed a dominant role. He had considerable influence over Lauderdale and these two combined to get Loudoun to follow their lead. All correspondence between Charles and the Scottish commissioners went through Lanark, and he penned most of the answers to the king and to the English parliament. In the first meeting with the king at Hampton Court they offered him a Scottish army to restore him in England if he signed an agreement that they had drawn up. Once presented with the terms in writing, however, Charles scraped out the clause relating to religion, and this became the main sticking point in the negotiations.

It was Lanark and Lauderdale who carried news of a leveller plot to assassinate the king. Instead of going to Berwick, as he had agreed with Lanark and Lauderdale, Charles escaped from Hampton Court and arrived at Carisbrooke Castle on the Isle of Wight on 11 November. Lanark and the other commissioners published *The answer of the commissioners of the kingdome of Scotland … upon the new propositions of peace* (1647), their protest to the *Four Bills* drawn up by the English parliament, in which there was no mention of covenant or presbyterianism, and then travelled to the Isle of Wight, ostensibly to protest in person when the *Four Bills* was presented to the king by the English commissioners, but hoping to overcome the impediments to agreeing a treaty with Charles. Instead of accepting the English parliament's peace proposals, Lanark stood over the king as he signed the engagement on 26 December 1647. The engagement did not bind Charles to take the covenant, nor did it compel him to use his power to establish presbyterianism in his kingdoms, even for the trial period of three years.

The religious terms fell far short of what the kirk desired and they rejected the engagement, despite the Scottish parliament approving it shortly after it met on 2 March 1648. Lanark, working from his base in the palace of Holyroodhouse, co-ordinated the engagement and his surviving papers demonstrate that he was the organizational anchor of the three-kingdom strategy that allowed his brother to march into England on 8 July at the head of a Scottish army. He was also the main draftsman of the engagement documents published during 1648. After his brother's defeat at the battle of Preston on 17 August and subsequent surrender at Uttoxeter five days later, Lanark presided over the disintegration of the engagement regime in Scotland. He commanded a small force that had been left in Scotland when the main army marched into England, and he linked up at Haddington with the remnants of Hamilton's army that had fled from Preston. Although he initially opposed the forces raised against him in the west of Scotland (the so-called Whiggamore raid), he was prevailed upon to agree terms of surrender at Stirling on 26 September. Lanark and Lauderdale escaped abroad to Prince Charles in the Netherlands at the end of January 1649, following the Act of Classes that deprived them of all public offices. A rumour that they were to be arrested and handed over to the English parliament as incendiaries was an additional spur to the two fugitives. Lanark became by special remainder second duke of Hamilton and third earl of Cambridge on the execution of his brother in London on 9 March 1649. He was nominated a knight of the Garter on 12 January 1650, but was never installed due to the court being in exile.

**Exile, Worcester, and death** At The Hague, Hamilton allied with the other exiled engagers and urged Charles II to comply with the kirk party, return to Scotland, and take the covenant. The treaty of Breda finally sealed an agreement between Charles and the kirk party, and Hamilton arrived in Scotland with the king on 24 June 1650. By a combination of the Act of Classes and the hostility of Argyll, Hamilton was removed from the king and forced to withdraw to his island of Arran, off the west coast of Scotland, from where he regularly pleaded to have his banishment lifted. The rout of the Scottish army by Oliver Cromwell at Dunbar on 3 September 1650 weakened the kirk party's hold and Hamilton was allowed to participate in public affairs towards the end of January 1651, after making a public repentance. He raised 100 horse on his estates in Hamilton and Clydesdale and harried the occupying forces in the area. A further sequence of military defeats forced Charles to march into England with the remainder of his army at the end of July. Hamilton accompanied the king, with the few hundred horse he had managed to raise, though he viewed the strategy as a last desperate throw of the dice. Cromwell eventually caught up with the army and defeated it at Worcester on 3 September. Hamilton displayed considerable personal courage during the fighting, and even lost the sword presented to him by the king of France while in the thick of battle. He was wounded just below the knee by a musket shot that shattered the bone. Conflicting advice, first from the king's surgeon, then from Cromwell's, meant that the leg was not amputated and following complications or infection the duke died on 12 September. He was thirty-four. His servants were not permitted to return his body to Hamilton, so he was buried in Worcester Cathedral.

A sequence of philosophical reflections and religious meditations that he wrote in the final year of his life demonstrates that Hamilton had become deeply religious, after a youth in which he had enjoyed the usual excesses of the court (NA Scot., GD 406/2/M2/11–13). His will, written at The Hague on 21 March 1650, adopts a similarly confessional line, being liberally sprinkled with scriptural references, which stands in contrast to his brother's will written a few years before. Of his six children, James, Lord Polmont, and Diana had died in infancy, leaving four daughters, Anne, Elisabeth, Mary, and Margaret. His wife survived him, dying on 2 September 1659, but it was Hamilton's niece Anne *Hamilton (1632–1716), eldest daughter of the first duke, who was named as his executor and to whom the titles were to pass, according to the special remainder. Burnet captured his temperament very well, when he wrote that 'his discourse was short, but nervous, witty, and full of stings, when he had a mind to reflect on others; but he was soon heated, and kept his fire pretty long' (Burnet, 532). Burnet also compared the two brothers at length, commenting, for example, that:

> the elder's converse was smoother, but more reserved; the younger, as he was the brisker, so he was the more frank, and was no less beloved: and in fine, the elder spoke more gracefully, but the other had the better pen.

Also unable to resist the temptation to compare the

brothers, Sir Phillip Warwick described them as 'both of some hard visage: the elder of a neater shape, and gracefuller motion, than his Brother' though the elder brother 'loved to gain his point rather by some serpentine winding, than by a direct path: which was very contrary to the nature of his younger Brother' (Warwick, 103–4).

JOHN J. SCALLY

**Sources** Grantham, Lincolnshire, Tollemache MSS · NA Scot., Hamilton MSS, GD 406/1; GD 406/2/F1, F2; GD 406/2/M1; GD 406/2/M9 · NA Scot., Hamilton red books (original royal letters and holograph) · Lennoxlove, East Lothian, Hamilton MSS [in possession of the duke of Hamilton] · *The answer of the commissioners of the kingdome of Scotland, to both houses of parliament, upon the new propositions of peace, and the foure bills to be sent to his majestie* (1647) · G. Burnet, *The memoires of the lives and actions of James and William, dukes of Hamilton and Castleherald* (1677) · *CSP dom.*, 1625–49 · [J. Hamilton, duke of Hamilton], *The Hamilton papers: being selections from original letters … relating to … 1638–1650*, ed. S. R. Gardiner, CS, new ser., 27 (1880) · S. R. Gardiner, ed., 'Hamilton papers: addenda', *Camden miscellany, IX*, CS, new ser., 53 (1892) · *The manuscripts of the duke of Hamilton*, HMC, 21 (1887) · J. H. McMaster and M. Wood, eds., *Supplementary report on the manuscripts of his grace the duke of Hamilton*, HMC, 21 (1932) · *The letters and journals of Robert Baillie*, ed. D. Laing, 3 vols. (1841–2) · *APS* · *Reg. PCS*, 2nd ser. · P. Warwick, *Memoirs of the reign of King Charles I* (1702) · *The memoirs of Henry Guthry, late bishop*, 2nd edn (1747) · audited account by Justinian Povey, NA Scot., GD 406/2/F1/138

**Archives** NA Scot., papers · NL Scot., letters · priv. coll., Hamilton MSS

**Likenesses** C. Johnson, double portrait, oils, 1649 (with John, first duke of Lauderdale), Lennoxlove, East Lothian; replica, Ham House, Richmond upon Thames, London · A. Hanneman, oils, 1650, Royal Collection [*see illus.*] · R. Dunkarton, mezzotint, pubd 1815 (after unknown artist), BM, NPG · A. Hanneman, oils, second version, NPG · R. White, engraving (after unknown original), repro. in Burnet, *Memoires*, 416 · oils (after C. Johnson), Scot. NPG

**Wealth at death** estate in considerable debt; was owed £22,853 by king: audited account by Justinian Povey, NA Scot., GD 406/2/F1/138

**Hamilton, William** (1630x36–1724), historical topographer, is thought to have been born in Wishaw, Lanarkshire, the third son of William Hamilton of Wishaw (*d.* 1636), landowner, and Beatrix, daughter of James Douglas of Morton; his grandfather John Hamilton of Udston was descended from Thomas, younger brother of James, first Lord Hamilton. In 1660 he married his first cousin, Anne Hamilton (*d.* 1671), daughter of John Hamilton of Udston; they had six sons and a daughter. Although he was the third son in a large family, he ultimately succeeded to the estate of Wishaw in 1666, as his elder brothers died childless. He married his second wife, Mary Erskine (*fl.* 1676–1694), eldest daughter of Sir Charles Erskine, on 31 August 1676; the marriage produced five sons and six daughters.

Hamilton was given a legal training and from 1662 was a writer to the signet in Edinburgh. He was admitted as a notary public in 1681. He seems to have enjoyed a high reputation among his contemporaries as an antiquary and genealogist. He is referred to by George Crawfurd, the historian of Renfrewshire, as 'that fam'd antiquary, William Hamilton of Wishaw', and Alexander Nisbet acknowledges his obligations to him in the production of his *System of Heraldry* (1722).

The only work that Hamilton left is a manuscript *Account of the Shyres of Renfrew and Lanark*, kept in the National Library of Scotland. The date of this manuscript is variously given as 1696 and 1710. Nisbet states that he saw it in 1722, while Crawfurd alludes to it in the preface to his work published in 1710. Though largely used by these two writers, the work remained in manuscript until 1832, when it was published as one of the volumes of the Maitland Club edited by William Motherwell. In his preface Motherwell acknowledges his inability to supply information about the author, but quotes from a manuscript then in the possession of James Maidment, which showed that Hamilton's work was regarded as authoritative. The volume consists of brief topographical descriptions of the principal castles and mansions in Renfrewshire and Lanarkshire, with much valuable genealogical information regarding the leading local families, including his own.

Hamilton died in 1724 aged between eighty-eight and ninety-three. He was succeeded by his grandson, also named William, son of Robert from Hamilton's first marriage to Anne Hamilton.

A. H. MILLAR, *rev.* ALEXANDER DU TOIT

**Sources** G. Hamilton, *History of the house of Hamilton* (1933) · *Scots peerage* · R. Douglas and others, *The baronage of Scotland* (1798) · W. Hamilton, *Description of the sheriffdom of Lanark and Renfrew* (1828) · P. Brown, *Historical sketches of the parish of Cambusnethan* (1859)

**Archives** BL, Add. MSS | NL Scot., Ruddiman collection · NL Scot., Stuart Stevenson MSS

**Wealth at death** approx. £900–£1000 p.a.: Hamilton, *History*

**Hamilton** [*formerly* Douglas], **William, third duke of Hamilton** (1634–1694), nobleman, was born on 24 December 1634, probably at Douglas Castle, Lanarkshire, the principal residence of his father. He was the fourth son of William *Douglas, first marquess of Douglas (1589–1660), and the first by his second marriage, to Lady Mary (*d.* 1674), daughter of George Gordon, first marquess of Huntly.

**Childhood and marriage** Douglas's parents, both Roman Catholics, were in constant trouble with the Church of Scotland, not only for their non-attendance at services but also because they made no attempt to give young William and his two younger brothers a protestant education. The local presbytery investigated and, after questioning the family chaplain, wanted to take the children away from their parents, but the marquess refused to give them up. For a short time he sent them to Glasgow grammar school, and in 1644 he offered to send them to board with the minister of Douglas. Perhaps as a reward for this apparent compliance, on 4 August 1646, aged eleven, William was created earl of Selkirk, Lord Daer, and Lord Shortcleuch. Not long afterwards, however, his father sent him to Paris so that he could be brought up as a Catholic.

When the presbytery found out the marquess was charged with keeping his son in France and failing to provide a tutor for him. This was certainly true, for Selkirk had been sent abroad without any companion, either governor or servant. However, his grandfather had lived in exile in the

**William Hamilton** [Douglas], **third duke of Hamilton** (1634–1694), by Sir Godfrey Kneller, *c.*1682–4

French capital and his father had spent some time there, so presumably he was not entirely without friends. Douglas told the presbytery that it was impossible for him to recall the boy to Scotland and it is not known when exactly Selkirk returned. He was definitely back by 1655, when negotiations were in hand for him to marry Scotland's greatest heiress. The Douglas lands in Lanarkshire lay both to the north and to the south of the Hamilton estates, at that time the property of Anne *Hamilton (1632–1716), third duchess of Hamilton in her own right. At twenty-three, she was just two years older than Selkirk, and in many ways it was a most appropriate match. There was, however, one great difficulty in the way, and that was the earl's Catholicism, no mere matter of form. Twenty years later his brother Lord James Douglas was to tell him, 'I pray God that he [their brother George] and you and all our family were good Catholics as our ancestors have been' (NA Scot., GD406/C1/11743).

For her part, not only had Duchess Anne been brought up by her covenanting grandmother to hold strictly presbyterian views, but also the entail made by her uncle, William, second duke of Hamilton, had stipulated that if she did not marry a nobleman of the name of Hamilton, then her husband must be 'a nobleman of any other name, of the reformed Protestant religion and of untainted loyalty and fidelity to the king'. Moreover, if the chosen husband began to fall away from his support of either church or king, he would lose all his rights over the estates. According to a note in the 1857 edition of Burnet's *History*, Selkirk 'was a very handsome man and, having gained the affections of the youthful duchess, to obtain her wide domains he consented to embrace the Protestant religion' (*Burnet's History*, 1.71n.).

Whatever his motives, Selkirk was undoubtedly determined to marry Anne and he persevered with the negotiations for three years. Just when everything seemed to have been agreed, his father changed his mind about the lands to be settled on the duchess by way of jointure. Deploring the delay, the earl took the initiative and had his own lawyers draw up a document settling the previously promised annuity on her. He then sent her the deed with a little note, declaring that 'if it wer more, I wold thinke it all to little for Your Grace, for I confess I can not expres the sence and hie estime I have of your Grace's deservings' (NA Scot., GD406/10749). Finally everything was in order and on 28 April 1656 the earl wrote on a small piece of paper, 'I do hereby declaire in the presence of God and as I shall answer at the great day of judgment, that I am not a papist nor does never resolve to be one' (NA Scot., GD406/C1/10750). The following day he and the duchess were married in Corstorphine church, just outside Edinburgh, and it was presumably then that Selkirk changed his name to Hamilton, in accordance with yet another condition of Duke William's entail. The first of his and Duchess Anne's thirteen children, a daughter, Mary, was born a year and a day later. Among the other children was George *Hamilton, first earl of Orkney.

At least there were no complications with the other condition in the second duke's entail, for Selkirk was an active royalist. After William, ninth earl of Glencairn, obtained a commission from Charles II in 1653 as commander-in-chief in Scotland, landed in the highlands, and raised a force of some 5000 men, Selkirk was one of those who joined him. The First Anglo-Dutch War ended in April 1654, any possibility of continental help evaporated, and on 3 May General Monck issued a pass for Selkirk, his servants, horses, and arms to go to Dalkeith 'to treat for his lordship's coming in' (NA Scot., GD406/C1/2591). Selkirk duly capitulated.

**Public career** According to Gilbert Burnet, when the duke first married 'he then pass'd for a soft man, who minded nothing but the recovery of that family from the great debts under which it was sinking, till it was raised up again by his great management' (*Burnet's History*, 1.71), and he took little part in public life during his first few years as Duchess Anne's husband. Although in theory Anne's inheritance was a very rich one, the reality was rather different. All her estates had been sequestrated by the Cromwellian government because of her family's support of Charles I, heavy fines had to be paid before any of her properties could be reclaimed, her father had lent large sums of money to the king, and she was virtually penniless. Fortunately, Hamilton possessed considerable business acumen and the family archives dating from that period bear evidence of his meticulous attention to detail in the form of the many annotations in his handwriting. He had little time for anything else, although there was one alarming incident in September 1659 when he refused to sign 'the Engagement' (NA Scot., Ailsa Muniments, GD25/9/30), tendered by General Monck to those who had earlier given bonds for their peaceable living, pledging them not to act for the exiled Charles II. As a result he was imprisoned in Douglas Castle, now in the hands of the Cromwellians. The duchess hastily enlisted the support of her powerful friends, however, and by the beginning of November William was home again.

With the Restoration of 1660, the Hamilton family fortunes were dramatically improved and at the duchess's special request Charles II on 20 September 1660 created her husband duke of Hamilton, marquess of Clydesdale, earl of Arran, Lanark, and Selkirk, and Lord Aven, Machanshire, Polmont, and Daer for life. The third duke of Hamilton sat in parliament for the first time in 1661 and was made a member of the Scottish privy council, but even so he was still spending most of the time working hard with the duchess to put their finances on a sound footing. From 1661 to 1669 he attended only 149 of a possible 330 meetings of the council. It was not until the 1670s that he began to play a really prominent part in public affairs. Charles II was governing Scotland through his secretary of state John Maitland, first duke of Lauderdale, an old friend of both the first and second dukes of Hamilton. Lauderdale's rule was, however, becoming ever more unpopular, in part because of corruption, in part because of his repressive measures against the covenanters. Guided by Duchess Anne, Hamilton took a strongly presbyterian line and his relationship with Lauderdale deteriorated sharply. In 1672 several members of the Scottish nobility, including William Douglas, third earl of Queensberry, and John Leslie, seventh earl of Rothes, urged him to take on the role of leader of the opposition to the government.

When parliament opened that year, Hamilton opposed the granting of supplies for the latest Anglo-Dutch war, moving that the state of the nation be considered first and grievances redressed. Lauderdale responded by adjourning parliament, and so the opposition politicians dispatched Hamilton and William Crichton, earl of Dumfries, to court to complain that Lauderdale and his brother Charles Maitland of Hatton, the lord treasurer, had accumulated all the profitable public offices for themselves and their friends. Because Hamilton refused to set down their grievances on paper, for fear of being accused of treason, the king sent the group away, removed all of them except Hamilton from the privy council, and dissolved parliament. The duke lost his place on the council in 1676 as a result of a further disagreement.

By now the government's ecclesiastical policies were reaching a new crisis, and in July 1678 a convention of estates voted the sum of £1.8 million Scots, mainly to suppress the growing number of conventicles. Because of the difficulties of raising the sum and fears that local militia would refuse to act against the conventiclers, Lauderdale quartered a force known as 'the highland host' on the western shires, arousing great opposition. After the defeat of the covenanters by the duke of Monmouth at the battle of Bothwell Bridge on 22 June 1679, Duchess Anne allowed the fleeing rebels to shelter on her estates while the duke, who had learned that writs of law burrows were to be issued against him, had already hurried to court with fourteen other noblemen and fifty country gentlemen to complain again about Lauderdale's rule. The king declined to receive them, and because they once more refused to put their grievances in writing, they were sent away.

Lauderdale finally fell from power two years later and after that policy in Scotland was directed at ensuring that the Roman Catholic James, duke of York, would be accepted as king on the death of Charles II. When James was made commissioner to the Scottish parliament in 1681, presbyterian statesmen looked to Hamilton to oppose the appointment on the grounds that it was illegal but, always conscious of the second duke's requirement that Duchess Anne's husband support the monarchy, he refused and voted for the act settling the succession. As a result, he was rewarded with the Order of the Garter, filling the vacancy left by Lauderdale.

When James VII and II succeeded in 1685, Hamilton was restored to his place on the Scottish privy council and made commissioner to the Treasury. In March 1686 he became an extraordinary lord of session and in October 1687 was given a place on the English privy council. He was in London when news came that William of Orange had landed, and those other Scottish privy councillors then at court sought his advice as to what should be done. The duke urged them to remain loyal to James, but as early as 1674 he had been suspected of corresponding with the prince of Orange, and his presbyterian stance meant that he privately viewed William's arrival with relief. As soon as Hamilton heard that James had fled for France he went to Sion House, where William was staying, and received a warm welcome. The new king and queen looked to Hamilton to settle affairs in Scotland and he was made president of the convention of estates which met in Edinburgh on 14 March 1689 to declare the throne vacant and proclaim William and Mary. He became commissioner when the convention was transformed into a parliament, and served in that capacity again in April 1693, living in almost viceregal state in his Holyroodhouse apartments for the duration of the parliament.

**Estate improvement** The duke and duchess had by this time embarked on an ambitious programme of expansion. They began by adding an elegant, five-storey wing to Kinneil, their tower house above the River Forth near Bo'ness in Linlithgowshire, and then turned their attention to Hamilton Palace. This was a great period of building and improvement, and they were determined not to be left behind. The palace was a late sixteenth-century structure, with four ranges surrounding a quadrangle, and a clutter of office houses at the back. The duke had seen the fine palaces of France during his boyhood, he made a point of visiting English country houses on his way to and from court, and he purchased books on architecture. As early as 1678 he had plans for a new palace drawn up in London, telling his wife: 'I shall make you a fine house in paper which will be some charges, yet I thinke well bestowed, to have such a thing by us againest wee be able to build itt' (NA Scot., GD406/C1/8147). In the end, however, he selected the Scottish architect James Smith to undertake the work, paying him £14 on 30 March 1682 for drawing drafts.

These were not the final plans for the new palace, for its design evolved as the work progressed. In essence, the scheme was to demolish three ranges, leaving only the north front standing, for it contained all the principal rooms. Two entirely new wings would then be built on the site of the former east and west ranges, the new main entrance would be from the courtyard sheltered by the two new wings, and the entire building would now face south instead of north. It was not, of course, possible to demolish everything at once, because the household of more than 200 people had to go on living in the palace, and in any case it would have been far too expensive to do it all at the same time. Work began in 1684 and was not in fact completed for almost twenty years, but in the meantime the duke took the opportunity of buying expensive new furniture and furnishings every time he went to London on business, shipping them home by way of Leith.

Like many of his contemporaries, Hamilton was also an enthusiastic planter and a keen gardener. He planted elders, ash, alders, and avenues of limes in the parkland surrounding the palace and edged the gravel walks with thorns. Purchasing seeds in both Edinburgh and London, he gave particular attention to the huge kitchen garden where he grew everything from French cucumbers to Italian celery and Dutch parsnips. He had special hotbeds for asparagus as well as frames for bringing on melons, gourds, and tender herbs. Extending the brick walls, he grew peaches, apricots, and cherries against them, importing grafts from the Netherlands. He also laid out a new bowling green.

All this work came to an abrupt halt in the spring of 1694. Returning home from his annual winter stay at court, Hamilton suffered a stroke on the coach journey north and lost the use of his left leg. He insisted on continuing, and when his wife heard the news she set off in a coach to meet him, with several eminent doctors and the minister of Hamilton. They were reunited just north of the Scottish border, and managed to get as far as Edinburgh, but the duke was sinking rapidly and he died about half past five on the morning of 18 April in his apartments in the palace of Holyroodhouse. His body was embalmed a few hours later, and on 24 May, as the guns of Edinburgh Castle fired a salute, his funeral procession left for Hamilton. He was buried with suitable pomp in the parish church, five of his surviving six sons walking behind his coffin. James Smith designed a huge and impressive monument, and in December 1694 the duchess authorized the purchase of black and white marble from the Netherlands for it. Placed above the vault where the duke was buried, it remained there until Hamilton church was demolished, when it was removed to St Bride's Church, near Bothwell.

According to Gilbert Burnet, the third duke of Hamilton:

> wanted all sort of polishing. … His temper was boisterous, neither fit to submit nor to govern. He was mutinous when out of power and imperious in it. He wrote well but spoke ill; for his judgement when calm was better than his imagination … a narrow and selfish temper brought such an habitual meanness on him that he was not capable of designing or undertaking great things. (*Burnet's History*, 1.71)

The fact that Burnet's patron in later years was none other than the duke of Lauderdale no doubt accounts for this somewhat jaundiced assessment. Irritable the duke might be, and heavy-handed in his dealings with others, particularly his own eldest son, James *Hamilton, earl of Arran (1658–1712), but his transformation of the Hamilton estates was little short of remarkable. Whatever his reason for marrying Duchess Anne, and in spite of infidelity to her, which resulted in his having an illegitimate daughter, they were a devoted couple, brought all the closer by the 'turmoilings' they had endured together. Amid her great grief for him, the duchess completed all her husband's unfinished improvements at Hamilton Palace. On 24 April 1696, referring to the second anniversary of his death, she told their daughter Katherine: 'That day … I shall not forget while I live, and now I am writing where he used to do it, and everything I see is marks of his industry. I fear his son will not leave such behind him' (Atholl MSS, Blair Castle, 29 I 8, 166). ROSALIND K. MARSHALL

**Sources** R. K. Marshall, 'The house of Hamilton in its Anglo-Scottish setting in the seventeenth century', PhD diss., U. Edin., 1970 [incl. a 5-vol. calendar of the duke of Hamilton's archives] · R. K. Marshall, *The days of Duchess Anne* (1973) · correspondence, NA Scot., Hamilton archives, GD 406 · household accounts and other papers, Lennoxlove, East Lothian, Hamilton archives · W. Fraser, ed., *The Douglas book*, 4 vols. (1885), vol. 2, pp. 412, 430 · *Bishop Burnet's History of his own time*, new edn (1857) · C. Lindsay [earl of Balcarres], *Memoirs touching the revolution in Scotland*, ed. A. W. C. Lindsay [earl of Crawford and Balcarres], Bannatyne Club (1841), 20–25 · *Reg. PCS*, 3rd ser., 15.xvi–xvii · *The diary of Andrew Hay of Craignathan, 1659–60*, ed. A. G. Reid, Scottish History Society, 39 (1901), 147 · C. Rogers, *Social life in Scotland from early to recent times* (1884) · *Scots peerage*

**Archives** Hamilton archives, Lennoxlove, East Lothian, papers · NA Scot., corresp. and papers · NL Scot., corresp. and papers · NRA Scotland, priv. coll., corresp. and papers | BL, letters to duke of Lauderdale and Charles II, Add. MSS 23114–23135 · Blair Castle, Perthshire, duke of Atholl's archives · Buckminster Park, Grantham, Lincolnshire, corresp. with duke of Lauderdale · NRA, priv. coll., letters to duke of Queensberry

**Likenesses** G. Kneller, oils, 1682, priv. coll. · G. Kneller, oils, *c*.1682–1684, Lennoxlove, East Lothian [*see illus.*] · D. Paton, miniature, 1693 (after S. Cooper), Lennoxlove, East Lothian · G. Kneller, oils, priv. coll.; on loan to Scot. NPG

**Hamilton, William, of Gilbertfield** (*c*.1665–1751), poet, was born at Ladyland, near Kilwinning, Ayrshire, the second son of Captain William Hamilton and his wife, Janet, daughter of John Brisbane of Brisbane; as his parents were married in 1662, his birth is approximately dated 1665. The family was a branch of the Hamiltons of Torrance, Lanarkshire, who were descended from Thomas, third son of Sir John Hamilton, lord of Cadzow, who was grandfather of James, first Lord Hamilton. As the second son of a military man—his father had fallen in battle against the French—Hamilton entered the army and, having seen service on the continent, returned with the rank of lieutenant. Thereafter he lived on half pay as a country gentleman, with leisure for field sports and to devote considerable attention to literature. Hamilton formed a close intimacy with Allan Ramsay, who informed him, in one of 'Seven familiar epistles which passed between Lieutenant Hamilton and the author', that he is indebted to certain of his lyrics for poetic inspiration and stimulus. Hamilton's contributions to this correspondence (which extended over three months in 1719, were probably published separately that year, and were included the following year in an edition of Ramsay's *Poems*) are playfully forcible in expression and are marked by very considerable metrical skill. The stanza employed is that which Burns afterwards favoured as an epistolary medium. Burns, in his 'Epistle to William Simpson', no doubt thinking of these 'Familiar epistles', names Ramsay, Gilbertfield, and Fergusson as those in whose company he should desire 'to speel the braes of fame'. Hamilton's other notable poems are the elegy on his dog, 'Bonny Heck', which appeared in James Watson's *Choice Collection* (1706) and which inspired, along with Robert Sempill's 'The life and death of Habbie Simpson', the eighteenth-century tradition of mock elegies in Scots by Ramsay, Burns, and others; and 'Willie was a wanton wag', which first appeared in volume 2 of *Tea-Table Miscellany*, the work that Hamilton helped Ramsay to collect and to edit. 'Willie was a wanton wag' appeared over the initials W. W., which probably represent Hamilton's sobriquet Wanton Willy, used by himself and Ramsay in the 'Familiar epistles'. For dashing and effective verisimilitude, sparkling drollery, and vivacity of movement, this lyric holds a celebrated place in Scottish song.

In 1722 Hamilton abridged and modernized Blind Harry's *Wallace* which went through at least twenty-three editions until 1859. He adapted the work to suit early eighteenth-century Presbyterian sensibilities so that, for instance, in visionary episodes Dame Fortune replaces the Blessed Virgin Mary of Blind Harry's tale, and King Fergus (the legendary first king of Scotland) replaces Andrew, Scotland's patron saint. Hamilton's version was admired by Byron, Keats, Wordsworth, and Burns. Burns wrote to Dr John Moore on 2 August 1787: 'The story of Wallace poured a tide of Scotish prejudice in my veins which will boil along these till the flood-gates of life shut in eternal rest' (*Letters*, 1.136). After living many years at Gilbertfield, on the north side of Dechmont Hill, near Cambuslang, Lanarkshire—the 'Dychmont' of John Struthers's poem—Hamilton changed to Latrick (or Letterick) on the south side of Dechmont Hill; he died there on 24 May 1751.

T. W. BAYNE, *rev.* GERARD CARRUTHERS

**Sources** *The works of Allan Ramsay*, ed. A. Kinghorn and A. Law, 4, STS, 4th ser., 6 (1970) • Anderson, *Scot. nat.* • J. G. Wilson, ed., *The poets and poetry of Scotland*, 2 (1877) • W. Hamilton, *Blind Harry's Wallace* (1998) [with introduction by E. King] • T. F. Henderson, *Scottish vernacular literature: a succinct history*, 3rd edn (1910) • H. Walker, *Three centuries of Scottish literature*, 2 (1893) • D. Irving, *The history of Scottish poetry*, ed. J. A. Carlyle (1861) • A. Campbell, *An introduction to the history of poetry in Scotland*, 2 pts in 1 (1798–9) • J. McIntosh, *The poets of Ayrshire* (1910) • *The letters of Robert Burns*, ed. J. de Lancey Ferguson, 2nd edn, ed. G. Ross Roy, 2 vols. (1985)

**Hamilton, William** (1669–1732), Church of Scotland minister and university professor, was the second son of Gavin Hamilton of Airdrie (1614–1675) and Jane, daughter of Robert Montgomerie of Hessilhead. After graduating MA from Edinburgh University in August 1686 he probably studied in the Netherlands before being ordained to Cramond, near Edinburgh, on 26 September 1694. On 25 February 1696 he married Mary (1676–1760), only daughter of Rebecca Ferriar and John Robertson, a merchant in Glasgow; they had nine sons and four daughters, including Gavin *Hamilton (1704–1767), a prominent Edinburgh bookseller and magistrate, Alexander *Hamilton (1712–1756), a physician and writer on American life, and Robert (1707–1787), who occupied the Edinburgh divinity chair from 1754 until his death and was twice elected moderator of the general assembly, in 1754 and 1760.

On 17 August 1709 Hamilton was elected professor of divinity at Edinburgh, demitted his parish charge, and took up his new position on 21 September. Following the death of Principal William Carstares in 1715 leadership of the church fell to Hamilton and William Mitchell, who were both sent to represent its grievances at court in 1717. For the next decade they were rarely absent from the church courts or important ecclesiastical committees, and Hamilton was chosen moderator of the general assembly five times (1712, 1716, 1720, 1727, and 1730). After Mitchell died in 1727 Hamilton continued to dominate, thanks to a transfer of political allegiance from the squadrone to the ascendant Argathelian interest. The move was partly prompted by financial necessity. After he was denied a parish charge to supplement his professor's salary, provision for his large family had depended, since 1713, upon the additional post of king's almoner. When the new regime removed this office in 1726 Hamilton decided to change sides and was rewarded with a royal chaplaincy the following year. On 16 February 1730 he was promoted to principal, and on 23 March 1732 was also called to West St Giles parish in Edinburgh, where he was admitted on 8 August.

Although his father and one of his brothers had suffered in the covenanting cause, Hamilton consistently sought to move the church away from the harshness of those times, towards a more liberal outlook. The policy was successful, and left a lasting impression on many former students who became prominent figures in the church, including William Leechman and James Oswald, who from him learned 'moderation and a liberal manner of thinking upon all subjects' (*Letters concerning the present state of the Church of Scotland*, 1767, no. 6), though it aroused suspicion in some quarters as to his orthodoxy. His response was to remain personally reticent on matters of doctrinal controversy, while urging leniency towards those of less discretion, such as John Glas and John Simson. Students were warned against inflexible adherence to traditional dogmas, but discouraged from following the fashion for preaching mere discourses on morality. Although his publications were limited to one sermon in 1732, his academic abilities won him wide and genuine respect, and his influence was crucial in helping the kirk to advance from the bitterness of the seventeenth century into the era of the Enlightenment.

Hamilton's contacts with government convinced him that the church was endangered by public displays of intransigence. He therefore used his influence at the general assembly of 1730 to smother recording of dissents, and the following year diverted a campaign to petition the king against lay patronage into the issue of procedure when settlements fell to presbyteries *jure devoluto*. Although no enthusiast for presentations by patrons, he believed it unrealistic to exclude heritors (landowners) from ministerial selection, and worked to pass legislation at the general assembly of 1732 that strengthened the heritors' role in that process, while rejecting all protests by an evangelical wing that had grown increasingly alarmed by the church's policies. For once, however, his acumen failed him. Instead of pacifying the church as he had hoped, his manoeuvres had the opposite effect, and set in train the events which led to the secession of 1733.

Hamilton died in Edinburgh on 12 November 1732 of 'a long and dangerous indisposition' (19 Oct 1732, NA Scot., GD18/5296). LAURENCE A. B. WHITLEY

**Sources** *The correspondence of the Rev. Robert Wodrow*, ed. T. M'Crie, 3 vols., Wodrow Society, [3] (1842–3) · R. Wodrow, *Analecta, or, Materials for a history of remarkable providences, mostly relating to Scotch ministers and Christians*, ed. [M. Leishman], 4 vols., Maitland Club, 60 (1842–3) · registers of the presbytery of Edinburgh, 1709–36, NA Scot., CH 2/121/7–CH 2/121/13 · Saltoun MSS, 1726–32, NL Scot., MSS 16533–16551 · *Fasti Scot.*, new edn, 1.146 · m. reg. Scot. · bur. reg. Scot. · G. Hamilton, *A history of the house of Hamilton* (1933) · R. B. Sher, *Church and university in the Scottish Enlightenment: the moderate literati of Edinburgh* (1985) · H. Sefton, '"Neu-lights and preachers legall": some observations on the beginnings of "moderatism" in the Church of Scotland', *Church, politics and society: Scotland, 1408–1929*, ed. N. MacDougal (1983) · J. Warrick, *The moderators of the Church of Scotland from 1690 to 1740* (1913)

**Likenesses** line drawing, U. Edin., New Coll. L.

**Hamilton, William** (*d.* 1729), Church of Ireland clergyman and author, was the brother of Andrew Hamilton, who held the archdeaconry of Raphoe from 1690 to 1754. He was educated at Trinity College, Dublin, and graduated BA (1691), MA (1696), and LLB (1700). Three of his sons—James, Henry, and Andrew—were later educated at the same university, though details of their mother are unknown.

Having taken holy orders Hamilton was collated, on 24 December 1700, to the archdeaconry of Armagh (to which the rectory of Carnteel, co. Tyrone, was then attached), where he remained for the rest of his life. In 1703 he published *The Exemplary Life and Character of James Bonnell, Esq.*, which reached a fourth edition in 1718. His *Sermon on the Death of Queen Anne* appeared in 1714; this was followed, in 1723, by his *Sermon Preached at Armagh on 5 Nov. 1722* and, in 1725, by the *Sermon before the House of Commons on 5 Nov. 1725*. Hamilton also edited *The Harmony of the Holy Gospels Digested into one History* (1705). He died in 1729.

B. H. BLACKER, *rev.* PHILIP CARTER

**Sources** H. Cotton, *Fasti ecclesiae Hibernicae*, 2 (1848) · Burtchaell & Sadleir, *Alum. Dubl.*

**Archives** NL Ire., letters to James Bonnell · TCD, corresp. with William King

**Hamilton, William, of Bangour** (1704–1754), poet and Jacobite army officer, was born in 1704, after 25 March, at Bangour, Linlithgowshire, the second son of James Hamilton of Bangour, advocate, who died in 1706, leaving an estate of £10,000 Scots (£800), and Elizabeth Hamilton (*c.*1675–1742), who was also a landowner in her own right. His parents were first cousins.

On 6 April 1711 Hamilton's mother married Sir Hew Dalrymple, lord president, who had been a strong unionist and one of the commissioners. Hamilton was brought up in the strongly whig atmosphere of his stepfather's house at Bristo Street and on his North Berwick estates. He appears to have been educated privately and at the University of Edinburgh (1716–20), where he produced his earliest known verse, a translation of the final third of book x of the *Aeneid*, the Mezentius episode, which was Jacobite code for bad and unjust kingship. Hamilton may have been admitted advocate, but there is conflicting evidence on this point. He certainly led the existence of a young man about town without any particular calling, though his evident gift for friendship made him some influential contacts, including Allan Ramsay, to whose 1723 *Tea-Table Miscellany* Hamilton contributed. In the same year the London *Hive* published 'To a Lady who Ridiculed the Author's Loves'. In 1726 Hamilton contributed a long address to the countess of Eglinton to the second edition of Ramsay's *Gentle Shepherd*, a play with Jacobite overtones. In 1727 he contributed to the *New Miscellany of Scots Songs*, and in 1730 his place in the new *Tea-Table Miscellany* included 'The Braes of Yarrow', the poem for which he is best remembered. He played a significant role at this time in the vernacular revival's absorption of folk forms into high Scottish literary culture: 'half of the poems Hamilton wrote between 1720 and 1730 presuppose a musical setting' (Pittock, 173–4).

In the 1720s Hamilton was a member of the Rankinian Club, headed by the Jacobite Thomas Ruddiman and an episcopalian priest. Presbyterian members of Edinburgh society were apparently drawn into its disputes with the aim of promoting the cause of the Stuarts. In the 1730s Hamilton's poem 'The Speech of Randolph' echoed the patriotism of Ramsay's earlier 'Vision' in its alignment of the struggles of 'godlike Wallace' and 'Great Bruce' with anti-Union Jacobitism: Hamilton planned a larger *Bruce* in which 'the Saxons or English' would be 'identified as the common enemy' (Bushnell, 45). Yet Hamilton was far from a fanatic and he readily made friends from different political backgrounds, even though Boswell opined that 'in the latter part of his life he was good for nothing till enlivened by a Bottle' (ibid., 39). By the late 1720s or early 1730s Hamilton had become friends with David Hume; in a letter of 1737 to Lord Kames that enclosed 'Reasonings concerning miracles', Hume asked that 'Reasonings' be shown to no-one else but Hamilton. Besides Hume, Hamilton also became friends with Kames, Adam Smith, George Keith, Earl Marischal, and James Thomson, whose *Seasons* was influential on his work.

**William Hamilton of Bangour (1704–1754)**, by Gavin Hamilton

In 1739 Hamilton was advised to travel abroad, possibly owing to consumption, and he went on tour for two years. While in Rome in 1740 he was admiring the Capitol when a young man placed his hand on Hamilton's shoulder and asked, 'Mr Hamilton, whether do you like this prospect or the one from North Berwick Law best' (Bushnell, 61; *Scotland and Scotsmen*, 1.26 ff.). The young man was Prince Charles and, while at Rome, Hamilton became his friend and possibly the confirmed friend also of Lord Elcho and his fellow poet John Roy Stewart.

In 1741 Hamilton returned to Edinburgh, where the following year he wrote an elegy on the death of the Jacobite Basil Hamilton so politicized that three-quarters of it remained unpublished for a century. On 6 March 1743 he married Catherine or Kathleen Hall (*d.* 1745), the daughter of Sir James Hall of Dunglass, baronet; their son James was born that year or in 1744, and their second child does not seem to have survived infancy. On 17 September 1745 Hamilton joined Charles at the palace of Holyroodhouse; at Prestonpans four days later he may have served either in the prince's bodyguard or in the Perthshire horse. Subsequently he became a gentleman volunteer in Lord Elcho's lifeguards, later being granted the rank of captain. In fact, he seems to have spent much of his time on secondment to the prince's household as 'official propagandist' (Bushnell, 73), in which capacity he composed his famous classical ode on Prestonpans. His wife died on 29 October (allegedly of sorrow over his Jacobitism, according to whig propaganda), but although grieved, Hamilton continued in the Jacobite rising of 1745. At Falkirk he is said to have hidden in a hollow tree, and after Culloden he was variously shielded by a minister's family, on the run with John Roy Stewart ('For God's sake, think of *Willy Hamilton*', Hume wrote on 23 May; Bushnell, 77), and in hiding in Edinburgh, before taking ship and landing in Göteborg on 16 September 1746. Thence he made his way into France, where a promised grant of 1500 livres from Louis XV remained unpaid: France was thus confirmed as the 'proud *Gallia*, Faithless Friend' of Hamilton's poignant version of Psalm 137, which was published in broadside form that year (Bushnell, 84).

Hamilton went to Rouen, where he was in company with Andrew Lumisden and others, eventually receiving 600 livres from the French authorities in 1749. Hamilton intended to prepare a history of the rising and was in correspondence with Lord George Murray, but the positive activities of his friends (including Adam Smith's publication of his poems) and the lack of specific action against him by government allowed him to think of coming home, which he did in early 1750, stopping briefly en route in Cambridge. The same year he succeeded to the Bangour estates on the death of his brother John. In July 1752 he married the teenage Elizabeth Dalrymple of Cranston (1733–1779), but due to continuing poor health he had to return the following year to France. He died at Lyons, probably of consumption, on 25 March 1754, and his body was returned to Scotland and buried on 23 August in the chapel of Holyroodhouse, Edinburgh.

Hamilton was undoubtedly a man with an attractive, though probably weak, personality: his friends spoke of him 'in the language of affection, mingled with regret' (*Scotland and Scotsmen*, 1.30). As a poet he was placed by the *Caledonian Mercury* on a par with Dryden, and by the *Monthly Review*, somewhat less charitably, with Thomas Parnell. His influential friends did a great deal to promote his reputation and he was widely anthologized. His reputation began to diminish in the early to mid-nineteenth century, and by 1900 it rested, as it still does, only on what Wordsworth called 'the exquisite ballad of Hamilton' (*DNB*), 'The Braes of Yarrow', although 'Gladsmuir' and one or two other political pieces are illuminating for the cultural historian of Scotland.

While he was in exile Hamilton's *Poems on Several Occasions* was published anonymously under the editorship of Adam Smith by the Foulis Press, Glasgow, in 1748 and 1749. A second edition was published under the author's name in 1758, and the best text was published at Edinburgh in 1760, with a preface and engraving (taken from Gavin Hamilton's portrait) by Sir Robert Strange. This went through several editions before the production of the major nineteenth-century text *The Poems and Songs of William Hamilton of Bangour* by James Paterson (1850).

MURRAY G. H. PITTOCK

**Sources** N. S. Bushnell, *William Hamilton of Bangour* (1957) • C. Craig, ed., *The history of Scottish literature*, 2: *1660–1800*, ed. A. Hook (1987) • M. G. H. Pittock, *Poetry and Jacobite politics in eighteenth-century Britain and Ireland* (1994) • *Scotland and Scotsmen in the eighteenth century: from the MSS of John Ramsay, esq., of Ochtertyre*, ed. A. Allardyce, 2 vols. (1888) • Chambers, *Scots.*, rev. T. Thomson (1875) • *DNB* • Irving, *Scots.*

**Archives** NA Scot., Abercairney MSS • NA Scot., corresp. with Lord Kames

**Likenesses** Descames, portrait, repro. in *Archaeologia Scotica* • G. Hamilton, oils, Scot. NPG [*see illus.*] • W. Miller, portrait (after G. Hamilton), Oxenford Castle; repro. in Bushnell, *William Hamilton* • R. Strange, engraving (after G. Hamilton) • line engraving, NPG • portrait, repro. in *Transactions of the Antiquarian Society of Scotland*, 3

**Hamilton, Sir William** (1731–1803), diplomatist and art collector, was born, according to the baptismal register, on 12 January 1731, either in London or at Park Place, a family residence near Remenham, Berkshire. He was baptized at St Martin-in-the-Fields, London, on 27 January, the fourth and youngest son of Lord Archibald Hamilton (1673–1754), a lord commissioner of the Admiralty, and Lady Jane Hamilton (*d.* 1752), the daughter of James Hamilton, sixth earl of Abercorn. His mother was from 1736 to 1745 mistress of the robes to Augusta, princess of Wales, and almost certainly became the mistress of Frederick, prince of Wales; William grew up with Frederick's son, the future George III, who later referred to William Hamilton as his foster brother.

**Education, early career, and marriage** In 1739 Hamilton entered Westminster School, where he met and became lifelong friends with Frederick Hervey, later fourth earl of Bristol, and David Murray, later second earl of Mansfield. The Hamiltons, despite their Scottish background, were very much a metropolitan family and had established a residence in London, having sold Park Place in 1738 to the prince of Wales. After leaving school about 1746 Hamilton was commissioned ensign in the 3rd regiment of foot guards in January 1747. He served in the Netherlands under the duke of Cumberland and then acted as aide-de-camp to General Henry Seymour Conway, who purchased Park Place after the death of Frederick in 1751. The next five years (1751–6) were spent as equerry to the young prince of Wales, George, and in 1753 Hamilton was promoted lieutenant. He left the army in May 1758, after having survived a near miss under enemy fire.

On 26 January 1758 Hamilton married Catherine (1738–1782), the daughter of John Barlow (*d.* 1739), MP and landowner, of Slebech, Pembrokeshire, and his second wife, Ann Skrine (*d.* 1770). He later wrote that he had 'married (something against my inclination) a virtuous, good-tempered woman with a little independent fortune' (W. Hamilton to C. F. Greville, 12 Sept 1780; Morrison, 1.62), but the marriage seemed entirely acceptable and proved to be 'a lasting comfort' (ibid.) to Hamilton. Catherine was educated, retiring, and of delicate health; she probably suffered from asthma. As far as is known they had no children, although it has been suggested by one of Hamilton's biographers, Brian Fothergill, that in Naples they adopted a local girl named Cecilia, who died in 1775.

Catherine shared Hamilton's great interest in music: he was an accomplished violinist, having studied, while in the army, under Felice de Giardini. She was such an excellent harpsichordist that Leopold Mozart, when visiting the Hamiltons in Naples in May 1770, complimented her on playing with unusual sensitivity. She was considered

Sir William Hamilton (1731–1803), by David Allan, 1775

fairly wealthy, and on her mother's death in 1770 she inherited rental properties in Pembrokeshire, including coal-bearing sites. Land tax records, leases, and mortgages suggest that the gross annual income from this property was between £1000 and £1600 in 1789. There is evidence that as early as August 1772 Hamilton had encumbered the estates with mortgage debt, which rose to £9000 by 1791 and to £13,000 by 1794.

**Parliament and diplomacy** In 1761 Hamilton entered parliament as MP for Midhurst, Sussex; he supported the king's party led by Lord Bute but kept a low profile in the Commons. Appointed equerry to the new king, George III, Hamilton instead set his sights on a diplomatic career. In April 1763 he applied for the post of envoy-extraordinary to the Spanish court at Naples, should a vacancy arise, which it did later that year. He argued that the warm climate of Naples would benefit his wife's health, and in August 1764 he was appointed, having agreed to give up his seat in the Commons. The Hamiltons arrived in Naples in November 1764 to find the city recovering from the effects of famine and plague. Despite these terrible natural disasters, Naples, then the third largest city in Europe, continued to enjoy a golden age of art, architecture, science, literature, and music. The king of Naples since 1759 was the third son of Charles III of Spain, Ferdinand IV (1751–1825), who came of age in 1767 and the following year married Maria Carolina (1752–1814), an elder sister of Marie Antoinette.

Hamilton's diplomatic duties seem to have occupied little of his time or thought. They consisted mainly of monitoring the activities in Italy of exiled British supporters of the Stuarts; attending to the furtherance of a balance of trade very much in Britain's favour (partly due to a long-standing treaty with Spain); reporting on the shifts of policy between Spain and Naples which could affect Britain's interest; and later, during the war with France, doing what he could to keep Naples unallied to France. The rest of his energy and time was spent in and around Naples, collecting art and living as agreeably as possible, whether at court, at the opera, or at one of the several homes maintained by the Hamiltons. As well as the Villa Sessa, a spacious leased residence, still extant, in the Pizzofalcone district of Naples, they were able to chose between the Villa Angelici at Portici, to the south of Naples, near Vesuvius; a 'capannina', or little cabin, near the royal palace at Caserta; and a 'casino', a little house north of Naples, near Posilippo, which was later known as Villa Emma. They had a steady stream of foreign visitors, as calling upon the Hamiltons became *de rigueur* for anyone of taste or refinement or importance visiting Naples.

**The collector** Hamilton had begun to collect art and antiquities, mainly pictures, bronzes, and terracottas, before he left London for Naples. Indeed, his extravagant purchases meant he had to sell a collection of pictures, on which he 'doted', in February 1761 because he could not 'bear to be dunned' (W. Hamilton to C. F. Greville, 12 Sept 1780). In January 1765 he parted with more of his paintings, which were sold in London, yet his arrival in Naples encouraged him to collect on a grand scale. He occasionally acquired large parts of collections built up by others, such as the items from Prince Porcinari's collection of ancient vases that he bought in 1766 and correctly identified as Greek rather than Etruscan. He also collected vases that had been unearthed in recent archaeological excavations and often witnessed the opening of the tombs himself, for example at Capua, Nola, and Trebbia. Although keen to acquire for his collection the artefacts left as grave goods, Hamilton showed a genuine interest in their context and commissioned sketches of the sepulchres and tombs with the grave goods *in situ*.

There had been British collector-diplomatists before Hamilton, notably Joseph Smith, British consul in Venice, and Hamilton's own predecessor in Naples, Sir James Gray, yet Hamilton far surpassed them in the scope and size of his collections and, most importantly, in his success in publicizing them in Britain and on the continent. Every notable visitor became a walking advertisement for the magnificence and variety of his collection, which he knowingly promoted by referring to it as being in his 'lumber room' (W. Hamilton to C. F. Greville, 18 April 1769). In addition, he advertised his archaeological interests by commissioning a series of fine colour-illustrated books, a process that took several years and resulted in one of the most influential art publications of the eighteenth century, the *Antiquités étrusques, grecques et romaines* (4 vols., dated 1766–7, but actually published 1767–76). With text written by Pierre François Hugues (who styled himself Baron d'Hancarville), this work was an artistic and bibliophilic advance over a royally sponsored project, *Le antichita di Ercolano esposte* (*Le pitture antiche d'Ercolano e contorni*; 8 vols., 1757–92). Although duped by Hugues, who ran off with the engraved plates for the illustrations, Hamilton achieved his aim with this costly project, for the *Antiquités étrusques, grecques et romaines* spread the vogue throughout Europe for the 'antique' in furnishings, porcelain, wall coverings, and interior decoration in general. Within barely a year of the publication of the first volume Josiah Wedgwood had opened his pottery works, Etruria, in Staffordshire, and thrown six black basalt 'first day vases' based on vases in Hamilton's publication. Countless other subsequent Wedgwood articles and designs were inspired by the work.

When Hamilton and his wife returned to London on leave in August 1771, he negotiated for his collection of vases to be bought for the nation. According to tradition, this 'first collection' was purchased for the British Museum in 1772, for £8400, out of funds authorized by act of parliament. There seems to be no evidence for this sale, although the story was known to Horace Walpole, who refers to it in one of his 'books of materials' but mentions the sum of £8000. In 1772 Hamilton was made a knight of the Bath and elected a fellow of the Society of Antiquaries; he and his wife arrived back in Naples early in 1773, after travelling via Vienna, Venice, Florence, and Rome. Believing that he had exhausted the supply of fine Greek vases, Hamilton did not resume collecting until 1789, when he began amassing what would become his second collection of vases. This collection was fully described in *Collection of Engravings from Ancient Vases* (4 vols., 1791–5), edited with illustrations by Johann Heinrich Wilhelm Tischbein, director of the Naples art academy. Far less expensive than the *Antiquités*, the volumes of these vase engravings, which were soon republished in various affordable editions, had considerable influence on public taste and on artists such as John Flaxman and Henry Fuseli.

Hamilton was never a rich man. He received a basic allowance of £5 a day as envoy-extraordinary, which was raised to £8 when he was promoted minister plenipotentiary in 1767, but, even when amplified by other official allowances, this failed to finance the costs of his diplomatic duties and hospitality. He certainly regarded the objects he collected as an investment, even though he protested, somewhat too much, that he would 'hate to be looked upon as a dealer' (W. Hamilton to C. F. Greville, 21 Sept 1790). His desire to collect was compulsive: as he admitted to his nephew, 'it is impossible for me to be without an object, whilst I can command a farthing' (W. Hamilton to C. F. Greville, 6 June 1790). He was often heavily in debt or being dunned by creditors; indeed, many of his art works were sold or had to be sold before his death. On learning that Hamilton had been posted to Naples, Horace Walpole astutely predicted in 1764: 'He is picture mad and will ruin himself in virtu land' (Walpole, *Corr.*, 22.243).

Somehow, presumably with some astute dealing, trading, and bargaining along the way, Hamilton acquired some 350 paintings, including works by Titian, Rubens, Carracci, Canaletto, Tintoretto, Reynolds, Romney, Holbein, Mengs, Hackert, Van Dyck, Lorrain, Velázquez, Solimena, Kauffman, and Vigée le Brun; more than 1000

Greek vases, including amphora, hydria, oinochoe, krater, and pelike forms; 175 terracottas; 300 pieces of ancient glass; more than 600 bronzes; and thousands of other items, such as coins, cameos, intaglios, gems, statuary, jewellery, and erotic curiosa, as well as a valuable book collection and various pieces of scientific apparatus. His most famous acquisitions were the Hamilton vase, a red-figured volute fourth-century Greek krater attributed to the 'Baltimore painter' and believed to have been discovered at Bari; the marble Warwick vase (Burrell collection, Glasgow), excavated from Hadrian's Villa and named after his nephew George Greville, second earl of Warwick, who acquired it after the British Museum declined to buy it for the high price of £500; and the Portland vase (BM), which was formerly part of the Barberini collection and was sold by Hamilton in 1784 to Margaret Cavendish Bentinck, second duchess of Portland. Hamilton was elected to the Society of Dilettanti in 1777 and is at the centre of one of the two group portraits of the society painted by Sir Joshua Reynolds that year.

**Volcanoes** While stationed at Naples, Hamilton developed a great interest in volcanoes, earning a contemporary European reputation as 'the modern Pliny' and the 'professor of earthquakes'. 'I am mad on the subject of volcanoes', he wrote to Greville on 3 March 1778. He was also interested in chemistry and owned and operated electrical equipment, incorporating some of the latest innovations suggested by Benjamin Franklin. (At the time, volcanic activity and atmospheric electricity were thought to be connected.) Vesuvius erupted several times during Hamilton's years in Naples, especially in 1767, 1779, and 1794, and on each occasion he made careful observations. Elected a fellow of the Royal Society in 1766, he submitted to the society many observations and drawings of active volcanoes, which were published in the *Philosophical Transactions* over the period 1767 to 1795. Among his subjects were volcanic eruptions, volcanic soil, and electrical thunderstorms. In 1767 and 1770 he shipped a large number of volcanic rock, ash, and lava specimens from Vesuvius to London; some survive at the Natural History Museum, Kensington. He made more than sixty-five ascents of the crater of Vesuvius, often accompanied by celebrated grand tourists, such as his schoolfriend Hervey. He employed an elderly monk, Antonio Piaggio, to make a regular log of the volcano's daily activities; the eight-volume log covers the period 1779–94 and survives at the Royal Society in London. Hamilton himself made various drawings of Vesuvius before its eruption in 1767. These are among the earliest attempts to record systematically the changing shape of the summit of a volcano about to erupt. In June 1769 Hamilton ascended Mount Etna on Sicily with Lord Fortrose and from the summit watched the sun rise over the island. The following year he was awarded the Copley medal by the Royal Society for one of his papers on vulcanology.

Hamilton used telescopes and thermometers to make field observations, collected rock and soil samples, held discussions with local inhabitants, and assessed historical sources, communicating his findings in notes and drawings to the scientific community. In 1769 Rudolph Erich Raspe sought Hamilton's support for his general theory of the volcanic origin of prismatic basalt. Hamilton responded with a paper of his own that supported Raspe's theory and was published in the *Philosophical Transactions*. He argued for the igneous origin of crystalline rocks such as basalt, which in turn suggested widespread volcanic activity over geological time.

In 1776 Hamilton published his major work on vulcanology (with text in both English and French), *Campi phlegraei: Observations on the Volcanoes of the Two Sicilies*; it included more than fifty spectacular hand-coloured gouache illustrations by Pietro Fabris of eruptions, lightning, and other natural phenomena. This publication did a great deal to make volcanoes—the 'fields of fire' alluded to in the title—a popular subject in art and poetry and to cause a visit to Vesuvius to be a necessary stage on the grand tour. One of the most impressive images in *Campi phlegraei* (plate 38) shows Hamilton conducting the king and queen of Naples alongside the violently erupting volcano, recording their visit of 1771. Hamilton relished such dangerous encounters, even though his friend the earl of Bristol had been severely burned by a volcanic rock on one such guided tour. This was indeed a most challenging way to avoid the ennui that Hamilton dreaded.

**Transition** On 25 August 1782 Catherine Hamilton died, 'carried off by a putrid fever' (Constantine, 110), at the Villa Angelici. She had been in failing health since the previous summer and by the spring of 1782 knew she was dying; Hamilton referred to her 'tatter'd constitution' (ibid., 111) in a letter to his nephew in May 1782. Her body was embalmed and sent by ship to her home of Slebech, where it was buried at the church on 22 February 1783. Hamilton, as he confessed himself to his sister, was grief-struck: 'In spite of all my Philosophy I am quite unhinged by the cruel separation from an amiable and true friend' (ibid., 115). He decided to take leave and, while waiting for London to grant permission, he toured the region of Calabria and Messina that had been devastated by earthquakes in February 1783; his account for the Royal Society of the after-effects of the cataclysmic earthquakes, which had killed some 40,000 people, has been judged 'his best and most characteristic piece of writing' (ibid., 119). Departing Naples on 27 May 1783, he travelled home via Innsbruck and Dresden and arrived in London in August. Soon afterwards he met the young woman who was living with his nephew Greville, then known as Emma Hart, but whose real name was Emma Lyon (1765–1815) [*see* Hamilton, Emma, Lady Hamilton], whom he visited frequently during his thirteen-month stay in England. He commissioned both Sir Joshua Reynolds and George Romney to paint Emma as a bacchante and sat for his own portrait to Romney. Hamilton left London in September 1784 and reached Naples early in November.

Encouraged by Greville, who was keen to replace his mistress with a wealthy wife, Hamilton offered his protection and separate accommodation in his house to Emma during a proposed trip to Naples while Greville was away in Scotland. Ostensibly visiting Naples in order to improve herself, Emma fully expected her stay to be temporary and arrived in Naples on 26 April 1786, chaperoned by her mother, Mary Cadogan. Greville coolly recommended Emma to Hamilton as 'a modern piece of *virtu*' (letter to Hamilton, 10 March 1785), but it is unclear whether the nephew traded his cast-off mistress for the uncle's promise to make him his heir. Whatever his intentions were, Hamilton soon found himself smitten with Emma's alluring beauty, and a week after her arrival informed her that Greville was not planning to take her back. Hamilton tutored her in her celebrated 'attitudes', in which she posed as various classical figures, draped in antique costume; he even devised a black-lined niche for her to stand in, so that the effect imitated the figures on his vases and cameos. She was certainly his mistress by early 1787, though they continued to keep up appearances by living in separate apartments at his houses; rumours none the less circulated that they had secretly married. Until Nelson came into the picture, Hamilton may well have considered Emma, with her singing and her highly theatrical attitudes, to be no less welcome a divertissement for his guests than Catherine had been at her keyboard. Hamilton must have been very proud of his much admired final possession—his animated statue, his singing Galatea; Goethe tellingly described her as a 'Gegenstand' (object) to which Hamilton's whole soul was devoted (*Italienische Reise*, 16 March 1787).

**New projects** About 1781 Hamilton learned of what he believed was a surviving cult of Priapus in Isernia province (then in Abruzzo), north of Naples. After travelling to the region himself in May 1785, he described the cult in a letter to his friend Richard Payne Knight, who printed it together with his own treatise as the controversial *Account of the Remains of the Worship of Priapus* (1786). The frank description and unusually explicit illustrations of the phallic simulacra offered *ex voto* by the wives of sterile men that were discovered at Isernia ensured that the book, originally intended for private circulation only, gained considerable notoriety. Initially the anti-Catholic implications of the cult may have intrigued Hamilton even more than the anthropological ones; in a similar vein he had often expressed dismay at the local Neapolitan belief that an image of the city's patron saint, St Januarius (San Gennaro), could quell the flames of Vesuvius.

In 1785 Hamilton was appointed by Ferdinand and Maria Carolina superintendent of the design and layout of the gardens at the royal palace at Caserta. He worked closely with John Andrew Graefer, a protégé of Hamilton's friend the botanist Joseph Banks, to plan and plant the gardens that became known as Il Giardino Inglese. Graefer, who was a disciple of William Kent and Philip Miller, and a gardener and nurseryman recommended by Banks travelled from England and started work in August 1786.

One consequence of Hamilton's decision to make Greville his heir was the development of Milford Haven as a port. As early as 1787 Hamilton, in writing of the Milford Haven area, predicted to Greville that the port and the town of Hubbertson, which were part of his wife's estates, would 'one day … be as great as Portsmouth and Plymouth' (letter to C. F. Greville, 16 Feb 1787). In 1790, with help from Greville, Hamilton secured a private act in parliament entitling him and his heirs 'to make quays, docks, piers and establish a market' on these estates (30 Geo. III, c. 55). Although the development was mainly carried out under Greville, Hamilton may fairly be considered a founding father of the port of Milford Haven.

**The final statue** The exact course of events that led to Hamilton's marrying Emma on 6 September 1791 at St Marylebone, London, is unclear. Horace Walpole probably got close to Hamilton's motives when he commented 'Sir William Hamilton has actually married his gallery of statues' (letter to Mary Berry, 11 Sept 1791; Walpole, *Corr.*, 11.349). His bride's dubious moral reputation was such that she was not to be received at court, nor be allowed the title of ambassadress. The Hamiltons travelled to Paris, where Emma was received by Marie Antoinette, and this, in turn, ensured her acceptance at the Neapolitan court by Maria Carolina. Hamilton's final nine years in Naples were the most turbulent and controversial of his career, for both personal and political reasons. The execution of the king and queen of France and the ensuing war between Britain and France meant that Naples acquired a new strategic importance to Britain because of its position in the Mediterranean and because of the implacable anti-French hostility of Ferdinand and Maria Carolina, whose closest relations, Louis and Marie Antoinette, had been murdered by the French revolutionaries. Hamilton repeatedly fell ill due to the stress of monitoring Jacobin activities in Naples and Rome and his own money worries; to raise funds, he tried to sell his second collection of vases and attempted to gain assurances about his pension from the government in London, without success. When the ship carrying much of his second collection of vases sank off the Scilly Isles in August 1798, Hamilton was devastated; by contrast, when a few months later his wife began an affair with Horatio *Nelson, hero of the battle of Nile, he seemed to accept the situation with stoicism and perhaps even indifference. Following Ferdinand's failed military campaign south of Rome, the French army invaded Naples in January 1799 and propped up the revolutionary government that had seized power. The Hamiltons, together with the king and queen, had been rescued late in December by Nelson and taken to the royal summer palace at Palermo in Sicily.

The recapture of Naples in June 1799 was followed by savage reprisals by Ferdinand and Maria Carolina, who ignored the terms of surrender agreed between their general, Ruffo, and the Jacobin rebels, and insisted on the execution of those implicated in the brief revolutionary regime. Even though some of his former friends were allowed no clemency, Hamilton washed his hands of the situation, thereby compromising his neutrality as British representative in Naples. Dismayed at his acquiescence in the brutal aftermath of the revolution, and exasperated by his diplomatic impotence, the British government decided to recall Hamilton from Naples early in 1800.

Reluctant to depart, he was unco-operative in handing over to the new minister, Arthur Paget, who arrived in April 1800. After a tortuous journey home through mainland Europe with his wife, by now heavily pregnant with Nelson's child, and her lover, he reached London in November. Stories and anecdotes about the scandalous *ménage à trois* had preceded him, and he found himself shunned by the king and queen and mocked as a cuckold in newspapers and caricatures. His final years were characterized by declining health and by increasingly desperate attempts to secure the pension that he thought due to him. For most of this time, the *trio juncta in uno* (a reference to the motto of the Order of the Bath, which included both Hamilton and Nelson) lived together, whether at Emma and Nelson's retreat, Merton Place (dubbed Paradise Merton), or in London, or on their trip to Milford Haven in 1802.

Sir William Hamilton died in London on 6 April 1803, at his leased house at 23 Piccadilly, with Emma and Nelson at his side; he was buried beside Catherine at Slebech church on 19 April. In his will and codicil, last amended on 31 March 1803, he left the bulk of his estate to Greville and bequeathed Emma £800 and a further annual allowance of £800; to Nelson he left the portrait of Emma by Elizabeth Vigée le Brun.

**Assessment** In an age in which every Briton of note considered the grand tour, however brief, to be part of a refined education, Hamilton may be taken as a supreme example of that type: his grand tour lasted thirty-five years. One senses in him a curiosity which was wide-ranging but not profound, and a desire for things prized for their beauty, rarity, fame, value, or notoriety; these he always regarded as 'things', to be possessed, displayed, or disposed of, with an emotional detachment that was inherent in his defensive, stoical, detached personality. In appearance Hamilton was 'tall and meagre, with a dark complexion, a very aquiline nose' (Wraxall, 139), according to his friend Sir Nathaniel Wraxall, who commented that Hamilton reminded him of Rolando in Le Sage's *Gil Blas*, the captain of a group of high-minded banditti, who expressed the philosophy that 'all men like to seize what belongs to others and … high class people borrow, but do not repay' (chap. 5). Objects and people alike were collectible to Hamilton, interesting for their own sake but valued mainly as a means of avoiding ennui and of securing his own fame. As one enthusiasm faded, he had to form another, for, as he wrote himself, 'the whole art of going through life tolerably in my opinion is to keep oneself eager about anything' (letter to Sir Joseph Banks, 3 May 1785). Hamilton's art collecting and his coterie of celebrity friendships brought him enjoyment and prestige, but they went hand in hand with a commercial, self-promotional marketing strategy that he successfully pioneered, namely to couple selected art of the past with reproduction techniques of the industrial revolution and thereby provide art to the masses. His insight was to understand that art could be good business and that fashion led from above could be a viable commercial aesthetic. That he never took such matters over-seriously is suggested by the fact that he owned a pet monkey, Jack, which he trained to hop from one art piece to another, inspecting with a magnifying glass, in the mode of an overzealous collector. GEOFFREY V. MORSON

**Sources** I. Jenkins and others, *Vases and volcanoes: Sir William Hamilton and his collection* (1996) • D. Constantine, *Fields of fire: a life of Sir William Hamilton* (2001) • C. Knight, *Hamilton a Napoli: cultura, svaghi, civiltà di una grande capitale europea* (Naples, 1990) • L. Burn, ed., 'Sir William Hamilton, collector and connoisseur', *Journal of the History of Collections*, 9 (1997), 187–303 • 'The Portland vase', *Journal of Glass Studies* [Corning, NY], 32 (1990), 1–264 • N. Penzer, 'The Warwick vase', *Apollo*, 62 (1955), 183–8; 63 (1956), 18–22, 71–5 • J. Ingamells, ed., *A dictionary of British and Irish travellers in Italy, 1701–1800* (1997), 453–60 • B. Fothergill, *Sir William Hamilton: envoy extraordinary* (1969) • A. Morrison, *Catalogue of the collection of autograph letters and historical documents formed between 1865 and 1882 by A. Morrison: the Hamilton and Nelson papers* (privately printed, London, 1893–4) • *Catalogue of a select part of the … collection of pictures of Sir William Hamilton* (1801) [sale catalogue, Christies, 27–28 March, 17–18 April 1801] • *Catalogue of the very choice and extremely valuable library of books, etc. … of the late Sir William Hamilton* (1809) [sale catalogue, Christies, 8–10 June 1809] • S. Schulze, ed., *Goethe und die Kunst* (1994) [exhibition catalogue, Schirn Kunsthalle, Frankfurt am Main, 1994] • M. M. Drummond, 'Hamilton, William', HoP, *Commons, 1754–90* • Haverfordwest Public Library, Pembrokeshire • N. W. Wraxall, *Historical memoirs of my own time*, ed. R. Askham (1904) [with introduction and notes by R. Askham]

**Archives** BL, corresp. and letter-books, Egerton MSS 1621–1622, 2634–2641 • BL, corresp. and papers, Add. MSS 37077, 39793, 40714–40716, 41197–41200, 42069–42070, 51315 • Bodl. Oxf., corresp. and papers • Boston PL, corresp. • Haverfordwest Public Library, Milford Haven, estate records • NL Wales, corresp. and papers relating to his Pembrokeshire estate • NMM, corresp. | BL, corresp. with Sir Joseph Banks, Add. MS 34048 • BL, corresp. with Charles Greville, Add. MS 60391k • BL, letters to Lord Grenville, Add. MS 59031 • BL, letters to Sir Robert Keith, Add. MSS 35504–35543, *passim* • BL, corresp. with Lord Nelson, Add. MSS 34903–34916, *passim* • BL, letters to Lord Spencer and Lady Spencer, pp. 4, 10 • Bodl. Oxf., corresp. with William Beckford • Bodl. Oxf., corresp. with James Bland Burges • Hunt. L., corresp. with Charles Greville • NHM, volcanic rock specimens • NL Scot., letters to Sir Thomas Graham • NMM, letters to Lady Hamilton • NMM, corresp. with Lord Hood • NRA, priv. coll., letters to Lord Cathcart • Warks. CRO, letters and accounts • Wilts. & Swindon RO, corresp. with earl of Pembroke

**Likenesses** J. Reynolds, oils, *c*.1760–1769, Toledo Museum of Art, Toledo, Ohio; repro. in I. Jenkins and others, *Vases and volcanoes*, fig. 38 • D. Allan, double portrait, oil on copper, 1770 (with Catherine Hamilton), Blair Castle, Perthshire; repro. in I. Jenkins and others, *Vases and volcanoes*, no. 129 • J. Fenn, etching, 1770–1779?, repro. in Walpole, *Corr.*, 35 (1973), facing p. 403 • J. Reynolds, oils, 1771, NPG; repro. in I. Jenkins and others, *Vases and volcanoes*, no. 51 • Wedgwood and Bentley, black basalt plaque, *c*.1772, Birmingham Museum of Art, Alabama, Beeson Collection; repro. in I. Jenkins and others, *Vases and volcanoes*, fig. 76 • D. Allan, oils, 1775, NPG [*see illus.*] • group portrait, oils, 1777 (after J. Reynolds), BM; repro. in I. Jenkins and others, *Vases and volcanoes*, no. 52 (a) • Wedgwood and Bentley, jasperware plaque, 1779, BM; repro. in I. Jenkins and others, *Vases and volcanoes*, no. 37 • G. Romney, oils, *c*.1783, National Gallery of Art, Washington, DC; repro. in I. Jenkins and others, *Vases and volcanoes*, no. 8 • D. V. Denon, chalk drawing, *c*.1784, priv. coll.; repro. in I. Jenkins and others, *Vases and volcanoes*, no. 15 • H. D. Hamilton, black chalk drawing, *c*.1789, Castle Howard, North Yorkshire; repro. in I. Jenkins and others, *Vases and volcanoes*, fig. 98 • H. D. Hamilton, oils, *c*.1789, Hamilton Collection, Lennoxlove, East Lothian; repro. in I. Jenkins and others, *Vases and volcanoes*, no.

163 [catalogue] • G. Morghen, engraving, *c.*1790 (after H. D. Hamilton), BM; repro. in I. Jenkins and others, *Vases and volcanoes*, no. 185 • W. H. Craft, miniature, *c.*1799 (after painting by C. Grignion), AM Oxf.; repro. in R. Walker, *Miniatures: a selection of miniatures in the Ashmolean Museum* (1997), p. 64 • J. Gillray, caricature, etching, 1801, BM; repro. in I. Jenkins and others, *Vases and volcanoes*, nos. 190(a) and 190(b) • F. Rega, chalcedony intaglio, NMM; repro. in I. Jenkins and others, *Vases and volcanoes*, fig. 55

**Wealth at death** estates in Wales (heavily in debt) and some art; plus various other debts; he may have been worth £10,000 'on paper'; in equity he may have been legally insolvent: will, 1803, Milford Haven estate records (1772–1810); Morrison, *Catalogue*

**Hamilton, William** (1751–1801), history and decorative painter, was born at Chelsea, Middlesex, the son of William Hamilton, a Scottish-born clerk of works in the offices of the architect Robert Adam, and his wife, Sarah. Hamilton was baptized at the church of St Martin-in-the-Fields, Westminster, on 21 June 1751. The painter and sculptor Maria *Bell, Lady Bell, was his sister. Through the support of Robert Adam, he was in Italy *c.*1766–1768 and studied in Rome under the painter Antonio Zucchi. He is said by Farington to have courted Angelica Kauffman there (Farington, *Diary*, 3.938, 8 Dec 1797). Although on his return to England he trained as an architectural draughtsman, it was as a painter that he registered at the Royal Academy Schools on 14 February 1769.

Hamilton was first employed, by Adam, as a decorative painter. At Kedleston, Derbyshire, *c.*1765–70, he painted part of the ceiling in the dining parlour and overdoor panels in the saloon in the manner of Zucchi. Also for Adam, at Highcliffe, Hampshire, he painted arabesque decorations at some time after 1773. An entry in the Adam accounts at Drummonds Bank records two payments to William Hamilton junior in 1773. At Dalton Hall, Yorkshire, he was commissioned to paint a large room with a series of subjects from Virgil's *Pastorals*; however, the death of his patron, Sir Charles Hotham, prevented their completion.

Hamilton exhibited at the Royal Academy for the first time in 1774, sending four works including *King Edgar's First Interview with Elfrida*, and soon established himself as a history and portrait painter. Between 1780 and 1789 he exhibited mainly portraits, and many of his sitters were connected with the theatre. When painting one of his five portraits of his friend the actress Mrs Siddons in October 1782, a stream of carriages was said to have made its way to the artist's door at 63 Dean Street, Soho, London. In 1784 he was elected an associate of the Royal Academy and in 1789 a full academician; his diploma piece was *Vertumnus and Pomona*. After this date his works often represented subjects from poetry, history, or scripture. Among the best were *The Woman of Samaria* and *The Queen of Sheba Entertained at a Banquet by King Solomon*, the latter being a design for a window executed by Francis Eginton for the great dining-room at Arundel Castle, Sussex. It was exhibited at the Royal Academy in 1790, and engraved by James Caldwall. In 1799 he sent to the Royal Academy *Moses Receiving the Law upon Mount Sinai*, and in 1801 *The Elevation of the Brazen Serpent in the Wilderness*, two of a series executed for the gallery at Fonthill Abbey. He also decorated the drawers of two cabinets for the Turkish Room in collaboration with Robert Smirke. Other decorative works included the panels of Lord Fitzgibbon's state coach (V&A), for which he received 500 or 600 guineas, and in 1793 the decoration of a satinwood cabinet designed by Sir William Chambers and made by Shakelton and Seddon for Carlos IV of Spain.

Hamilton was much employed by the proprietors of a number of print galleries. He painted scenes from *Much Ado about Nothing*, *Love's Labour's Lost*, *As You Like It*, *Twelfth Night*, *The Winter's Tale*, and *Cymbeline*, for Boydell's Shakspeare Gallery, but he failed to catch either the spirit of the dramatist or the character of the times. However, he gained more popularity by his small pictures of rural scenes, and the designs which he made for Robert Bowyer's *History of England*, displayed in his gallery in Pall Mall, London, Thomas Macklin's Bible and *British Poets*, and Du Roveray's editions of Milton's *Paradise Lost* and Gray's and Goldsmith's *Poems*. His best designs were those for Thomson's *Seasons* (1797), in collaboration with Henry Fuseli, engraved by Bartolozzi and P. W. Tomkins. His drawings are tasteful and rich in colour, but, like his pictures, are somewhat theatrical in style.

Hamilton produced a number of other, more ephemeral works. For the Great Room or rotunda at Vauxhall Gardens, Vauxhall, Surrey, he painted a transparency of George, prince of Wales, as St George in 1785. His transparencies celebrating the recovery of George III were displayed in London at Soho Square and in front of the Bank of England on 24 April 1789; both were later engraved by Bartolozzi and one of the Tomkins family. He was also responsible for the design of the invitations (engraved by Bartolozzi) to the Mansion House ball in the City in 1790 and 1791.

Hamilton was married to the daughter of a Mr Aylward, a resident of Bath, and they had at least one son and a daughter; the former was intended for a career as an engineer in the East India service, the latter was placed with a mantua maker in Gerrard Street, London. Latterly at least the marriage was not happy, for, according to Farington, the Hamiltons were 'on very bad terms' by September 1797, possibly owing to difficult financial circumstances (Farington, *Diary*, 3.896, 23 Sept 1797). Hamilton died of a fever at his home, 63 Dean Street, Soho, London, on 2 December 1801 and was buried in St Anne's Church, Soho. His widow inherited £11,000 on her father's death a year later but forfeited about half of it to her children when she remarried a few years later. There are sketchbooks in the Victoria and Albert Museum, London, and the Huntington Library, California; the National Portrait Gallery, London, has a number of Hamilton's works.

R. E. Graves, *rev.* Deborah Graham-Vernon

**Sources** E. Croft-Murray, *Decorative painting in England, 1537–1837*, 2 (1970) • A. T. Spanton, 'William Hamilton RA', *The Connoisseur*, 21/81 (May 1908), 37–43 • E. Edwards, *Anecdotes of painters* (1808); facs. edn (1970) • Farington, *Diary* • W. Sandby, *The history of the Royal Academy of Arts*, 2 vols. (1862) • J. Ingamells, ed., *A dictionary of British and Irish travellers in Italy, 1701–1800* (1997) • H. Hammelmann, *Book illustrators in eighteenth-century England*, ed. T. S. R. Boase (1975) • A. A. Tait, *Robert Adam: drawings and imagination* (1993)

**Likenesses** G. Dance, drawing, 1793, RA • H. Singleton, group portrait, oils (*The Royal Academicians*, 1793), RA

**Hamilton, William** (1755–1797), naturalist and political activist, was born at Londonderry on 16 December 1755, the son of John Hamilton (1725–1780), merchant and sea captain, and Elizabeth, daughter of Archibald Hope. He received his early education under the Revd John Torrens of the diocesan school, Londonderry, and entered Trinity College, Dublin, in 1771. He graduated BA in 1776 and MA in 1779, the year in which he was elected fellow. He later graduated BD (1787) and DD (1794).

In 1780 Hamilton married Sarah, daughter of Chamberlain Walker, rector of Rosconnel and Abbeyleix. They had thirteen children, of whom eight survived their father. In 1786 he published his enduring work, *Letters concerning the northern coast of the county of Antrim … wherein is stated a plain and impartial VIEW of the VOLCANIC THEORY of the BASALTES*, an attractively written amalgam of natural history, country life, and folk-lore. The work was translated into German and French and succeeded by two more editions (one posthumous). In 1790 he was presented to the college living of Clondavaddog in co. Donegal, diocese of Raphoe, an appointment deplored by McDowell and Webb in their history of Trinity College as causing a loss to Irish scholarship. However, his early writings suggest that Donegal attracted him; soon there followed the appointment as magistrate which led to his death.

During his years at university Hamilton took part in the deliberations of the new learned societies which came together in the Royal Irish Academy, of which he became a member; he was also a non-resident member of the Royal Society of Edinburgh. It was during this period that his scholarship flourished. He undertook journeys in remote parts of Ireland which informed many of his writings, such as the 'Account of experiments made to determine the temperature of the earth's surface in the kingdom of Ireland in the year 1788'; one reading of the thermometer was made by him in Inishcoo, off Burtonport, in the isolation of the Rosses of Donegal. His later 'Memoir on the climate of Ireland' (1797), largely a discussion of the causes of environmental change on the north-western coast brought about by blowing sands, was reproduced in journals at London and, in French, at Geneva.

In 1792/3 Hamilton published a commentary on the French Revolution, *Letters on the Principles of the French Democracy*, in which he showed himself a supporter of the *status quo* and lamented 'the infatuation of those Dissenting Protestants … who have been misled by that very nation, which … they should despise and detest'. He became a close correspondent of Edward Cooke at Dublin Castle, warning him of the situation in the north-west of Ireland, where Hamilton had identified a district, extending for 18 miles from Londonderry, as a nest of United Irishmen daily awaiting a French invasion. He administered the oath of allegiance freely, caused activists to be pressed into the navy, and exhorted his fellow magistrates to greater activity against the agitators. Shortly after repelling an assault on his rectory Hamilton was murdered, on 2 March 1797, only 8 miles from Londonderry, when he was attacked by a band of United Irishmen while taking refuge from a storm at Sharon rectory, the home of a friend; after a shot killed his hostess the terrified occupants of the house thrust Hamilton out, whereupon he was dispatched.

In consequence of Hamilton's assassination, counteractivity by the authorities increased, some men quietly emigrated, and the neighbourhood of the murder was pacified by yeomanry. The Irish House of Commons voted Hamilton's widow a pension of £700, to be divided between the surviving children at her death. Hamilton's tombstone in the graveyard adjoining St Columb's Cathedral, Londonderry, and a centenary commemorative tablet within the building, are marred by errors in dates.

C. W. P. Mac Arthur

**Sources** W. Hamilton, *Letters concerning the northern coast of the county of Antrim* (1786); [3rd edn] (1822) [3rd edn incl. biographical sketch] • W. Hamilton, 'An account of experiments made to determine the temperature of the earth's surface in the kingdom of Ireland in the year 1788', *Transactions of the Royal Irish Academy*, 2: Science (1787–8), 143–56 • W. Hamilton, *Letters on the principles of the French democracy, and their application and influence on the constitution and happiness of Britain and Ireland* (1792) • W. Hamilton, 'Memoir on the climate of Ireland', *Transactions of the Royal Irish Academy*, 6: Science (1793–7), 27–55 • F. L. Gailey, 'The Sharon murder', *Donegal Annual*, 3/3 (1957), 8–16 • *Dublin Evening Post* (17 Sept 1797) • E. Andrews, 'The Rev. William Hamilton, D.D.', *Ulster Journal of Archaeology*, new ser., 6 (1900), 247–8 • Burtchaell & Sadleir, *Alum. Dubl.*, 2nd edn • R. B. McDowell and D. A. Webb, *Trinity College, Dublin, 1592–1952: an academic history* (1982) • C. W. P. Mac Arthur, 'Mineralogical and geological travellers in Donegal, 1787–1812', *Donegal Annual*, 39 (1987), 39–57 • *Belfast News-Letter* (13 March 1797) • J. B. Leslie, *Raphoe clergy and parishes* (1940) • G. Hamilton, *A history of the house of Hamilton* (1933)

**Archives** NA Ire., Rebellion MSS, letters, RP620

**Likenesses** silhouette, repro. in Hamilton, *Letters concerning the northern coast*

**Wealth at death** Irish House of Commons voted pension to widow, suggesting she was not well-off; parish not rich, with *c.*£300 p.a. tithe-rent, 1835; capital perhaps depleted by advancing £1400 towards new rectory

**Hamilton, William** (1758–1790), surgeon and man-midwife, born at Glasgow on 31 July 1758, was the son of Thomas Hamilton (1728–1782), professor of anatomy and botany, and Isabel Anderson, daughter of a former professor of church history. From the grammar school he went to Glasgow University in 1770 and graduated BA in 1775 and MA in 1776. He studied medicine for two years at Edinburgh under Joseph Black and William Cullen, and afterwards in London, under William Hunter, who took him into his house and put him in charge of his dissecting room. Hunter wrote to Thomas Hamilton that:

> Your son has been doing everything you could wish, and from his own behaviour has profited more for the time than any young man I ever knew. From being a favourite with everybody, he has commanded every opportunity for improvement that this great town afforded during his stay here; for everybody has been eager to oblige and encourage him. I can depend so much upon him, in every way, that if any opportunity should offer for serving him, whatever may be in my power I shall consider as doing as a real pleasure to myself. (Geyer-Kordesch and Macdonald, 224)

In 1780 he returned to Glasgow, and conducted his invalid

father's anatomical class. Next year he was appointed, on the recommendation of William Hunter, to his father's chair. On the death of the latter, in 1782, he succeeded to a large surgical practice, to which he added obstetrics. He was in constant request as a consultant, his anatomical knowledge and obstetric skill being highly valued by his colleagues and old pupils. Hamilton instructed his students that they:

> must see that the knowledge of the actions of the body in a state of health can be the only key to the actions in a state of Disease. Unless we know the natural [state] we can never know the deviation from it. Our anatomical knowledge besides assisting us in determining the seat of the disease is likewise of use in explaining the cure. In almost all diseases the powers of the body attempt to restore themselves to a state of health, in many the cure is entirely effected by them. These efforts must be understood by the Physicians, that they may aid them when too weak and that he may be on his guard not to counteract them when properly exerted. (ibid., 228)

Hamilton married, in October 1783, Elizabeth (*d.* 1827), daughter of William Stirling (1717–1777), a Glasgow merchant. His wife was 'an accomplished lady, connected with several opulent families in Glasgow and its neighbourhood. From these connections his practice, already extensive, was very considerably increased' (ibid., 268); they had two sons, Sir William *Hamilton (1788–1856) and Thomas *Hamilton (1789–1842). In 1783 Hamilton was elected a fellow of the Royal Society of Edinburgh.

Hamilton is credited with smooth manners towards patients, with benevolence to the poor, and with circumspection in public affairs. He kept notes of his cases, intending to write a system of surgery. He died in Glasgow on 13 March 1790 after an illness brought on by overwork. He published nothing, but his biographer preserved four specimens of his accurate method (on treatment of *inversio uteri*, on dislocations of the shoulder, on hydrothorax, and on a form of hernia).

CHARLES CREIGHTON, *rev.* MICHAEL BEVAN

**Sources** R. Cleghorn, *Transactions of the Royal Society of Edinburgh*, 4/1 (1798), 35–63 • W. I. Addison, *A roll of graduates of the University of Glasgow from 31st December 1727 to 31st December 1897* (1898) • W. I. Addison, ed., *The matriculation albums of the University of Glasgow from 1728 to 1858* (1913) • F. Bennet and M. Melrose, *Index of fellows of the Royal Society of Edinburgh: elected November 1783 – July 1883*, ed. H. Frew, rev. edn (1984) • Irving, *Scots.* • *GM*, 1st ser., 60 (1790), 282 • J. Geyer-Kordesch and F. Macdonald, *Physicians and surgeons in Glasgow: the history of the Royal College of Physicians and Surgeons of Glasgow* (1999)
**Archives** U. Edin. L., lecture notes • U. Glas. L., corresp. [copies] • U. Glas. L., botanical papers

**Hamilton, William** (1780–1835), Church of Scotland minister and religious writer, was born on 4 February 1780 at Longridge, in the parish of Stonehouse, Lanarkshire, the son of James H. Hamilton (*b.* 1738), a farmer, and Mary Hamilton, the eldest daughter of Andrew Hamilton and Janet Craig of Colenhill, Avondale, Lanarkshire (Hamilton, 1.1). Hamilton was educated in arts and theology at the University of Edinburgh, and licensed to preach on 4 December 1804. Following service as an assistant at Broughton in Tweedale, Peeblesshire (1805–6), and New Kilpatrick, Dunbartonshire, he was ordained to St Andrew's Chapel-of-Ease, Dundee, on 23 December 1807. Less than two years later, on 14 September 1809, he was translated to Strathblane, Stirlingshire, where he carried on a distinguished ministry for the remainder of his life. He married Jane King of Paisley on 19 January 1813, and had six children with her.

Hamilton was a scholarly man, a keen evangelical churchman, and an excellent pastor. His sympathy with liberal political views and popular movements caused controversy in some quarters. He was an ardent temperance reformer, when such a cause was not popular among the clergy, a friend of missions, and a supporter of Sunday schools and of Bible and tract societies. He established a parochial library, delivered popular lectures on topics of science and philosophy to his parishioners, and instituted and personally managed a savings bank. As a churchman he was strongly opposed to the patronage system as 'a millstone about the neck of the Church of Scotland', moving, in the general assembly of 1834, an unsuccessful resolution against it (Hamilton, 1.53).

A prolific writer, Hamilton produced over twenty works on a variety of doctrinal, devotional, and anti-patronage themes, including *The Establishment of the Law by the Gospel* (1820), *A Defence of the Scriptural Doctrine Concerning the Second Coming* (1828), and *An Essay on the Assurance of Salvation* (1830). His scholarly work was recognized by St Andrews University in 1824 when he was awarded the DD degree.

Hamilton died suddenly at Strathblane on 16 April 1835, and was buried there on 24 April. He was survived by his wife, who died on 5 April 1855. Two sons, James and William, became ministers, and a daughter, Jane, married James Walker, a noted Free Church minister. James *Hamilton also edited the *Life and Remains of the Late Rev. William Hamilton* (2 vols.), the first volume of which was an autobiography and memoir.

DONALD C. SMITH

**Sources** *Fasti Scot.* • J. Hamilton, ed., *Life and remains of the late Rev. William Hamilton*, 2 vols. (1836) • *DNB*
**Archives** U. Edin., New Coll. L., letters to Thomas Chalmers
**Likenesses** Holl, drawing, repro. in Hamilton, ed., *Life and remains*, 1, frontispiece
**Wealth at death** £1356 13*s.* 1*d.*

**Hamilton, William Alexander Anthony Archibald Douglas-, eleventh duke of Hamilton and eighth duke of Brandon** (1811–1863), aristocrat, was the only son of Alexander Douglas-*Hamilton, the tenth duke (1767–1852), and Susan Euphemia Beckford (1786–1859). He was born on 19 February 1811, at Grosvenor Place, London, and was known as marquess of Douglas until he succeeded to his father's several titles and estates in 1852. He was educated at Eton College and at Christ Church, Oxford. He was knight marischal of Scotland, colonel of the Lanarkshire militia, lord lieutenant of that county, deputy lieutenant of the county of Bute, major-commandant of the Glasgow yeomanry from 1849 to 1857, and grand master of the society of freemasons. On 23 February 1843 he married the Princess Marie Amélie (1818–1888), youngest daughter of Karl Ludwig Friedrich, grand duke of Baden, and his wife, Stephanie de Beauharnais, and a cousin of Napoleon

III. They had a son and a daughter. After his marriage he lived chiefly in Paris and Baden Baden, and was frequently a guest at the Tuileries, taking very little interest in British politics. He died on 15 July 1863 from the effects of a fall after a supper at the Maison Dorée, boulevard des Italiens, Paris. He inherited the pride for which his family was noted, and was described by the lord chancellor, Lord Brougham, as 'Very Duke of Very Duke' (GEC, *Peerage*).

L. C. Sanders, *rev.* K. D. Reynolds

**Sources** GEC, *Peerage* • *The letters of Queen Victoria*, ed. A. C. Benson and Lord Esher [R. B. Brett], 3 vols., 1st ser. (1907), vol. 1, p. 549 • *Dearest mama: letters between Queen Victoria and the crown princess of Prussia, 1861–1864*, ed. R. Fulford (1968) • *GM*, 3rd ser., 15 (1863), 237
**Archives** NRA, priv. coll., corresp. and papers | Bodl. Oxf., corresp. with William Beckford and with his parents • Mitchell L., Glas., Strathclyde Regional Archives, corresp. with John Strang
**Likenesses** J. Hayter, chalk drawing, 1835, Brodick Castle, Garden and Country Park, Isle of Arran • F. Palizzi, group portrait, oils, 1848, Brodick Castle, Garden and Country Park, Isle of Arran • W. Holl, mixed engraving, pubd 1864, BM • attrib. R. Buckner, oils, Brodick Castle, Garden and Country Park, Isle of Arran • R. Buckner, portraits, Brodick Castle, Garden and Country Park, Isle of Arran • T. Lawrence, chalk drawing, Lennoxlove, Haddington, East Lothian • group portrait, oils, Brodick Castle, Garden and Country Park, Isle of Arran • oils, Brodick Castle, Garden and Country Park, Isle of Arran
**Wealth at death** under £140,000: administration, 20 Jan 1864, *CGPLA Eng. & Wales*

**Hamilton, William Donald** (1936–2000), biologist, was born on 1 August 1936 at the Anglo-American Hospital, Cairo, Egypt, one of the five children (three sons and two daughters) of Archibald Milne Hamilton (*d.* 1972), a captain in the Royal Engineers, and Bettina Matraves, *née* Collier, a doctor. His parents were natives of New Zealand, but had settled near Sevenoaks, Kent, England, by the time they raised their family. Hamilton went to Tonbridge School and then to St John's College, Cambridge, where he studied biology and maths. After national service (1955–7), Hamilton was appointed to a lectureship at Imperial College, London, in 1964, based at the college's field station at Silwood Park, near Windsor. He was not a successful lecturer. Indeed his lectures later become notorious among biologists: he might forget to turn up, or he might turn up and mumble inaudibly into the blackboard. During the 1960s he was concerned with the evolution of senescence and with the evolution of the sex ratio. Hamilton identified a major assumption of the standard theory of the sex ratio (which explains why sex ratios are usually 50:50). He found various arthropods that do not satisfy the assumption, and can be predicted to have sex ratios biased away from 50:50. The sex ratio paper is important both for introducing game theory into evolutionary biology and also for showing how sex ratio can be used to test quantitative predictions. Both game theory and quantitative research on sex ratio have since grown into major areas of biology.

**The study of altruistic behaviour** Hamilton worked for his PhD, gained in 1968, while variously attached to the London School of Economics and the Galton Laboratory, University College, London. The fruits of his research were published in scientific journals from 1963 to 1967 and they revolutionized a large area of biology. His study concerned the evolution of co-operative, or 'altruistic', behaviour. Altruistic behaviour poses a problem for Darwin's theory of evolution by natural selection. Natural selection favours behaviour that increases the number of offspring produced by the individual performing the behaviour. Yet some animals seem to behave in such a way as to benefit other individuals, at the cost of their own survival and reproduction. The extreme examples are the sterile casts of ants and other insects, in which certain individuals devote their whole lives to enhancing the reproduction of other individuals.

In the 1950s and 1960s, in so far as there was an explanation for altruistic behaviour at all, it was that natural selection works for the good of the species. Altruistic behaviour could then evolve, because it benefited the species as a whole if not the individual who was behaving altruistically. Hamilton proposed another solution. Altruistic behaviour can evolve when genes are shared between the donor and the recipient of the altruism. If an individual helps its sibling in some hour of need, the improved survival of the recipient can genetically more than make up for the reduced survival of the altruist. Hamilton derived an exact condition for natural selection to favour altruism. The benefit to the recipient multiplied by the chance that a gene is shared between donor and recipient must exceed the cost to the altruist. Cost and benefit are measured in terms of number of offspring produced. Benefit is symbolized by $b$, cost by $c$, and the chance of sharing a gene by $r$ (standing for 'relatedness'). The condition for natural selection to favour altruism is $rb > c$. This inequality is called Hamilton's rule and is part of the language of biology. Hamilton's rule makes sense of a huge range of altruistic behaviour patterns in all forms of life, from bacteria to plants and sessile sea animals, as well as ants, monkeys, and humans. The rule has inspired a large number of empirical scientific studies, which aim to test whether the rule correctly predicts when animals do and do not behave altruistically.

Hamilton's rule also has deep consequences for understanding evolution. No principle of the 'good of the species' is required to explain altruism. Instead altruism evolves by selection for selfish genes within a species. Hamilton's work ultimately toppled, or substantially helped to topple, the view that things evolve for the good of the species. In the late 1960s and early 1970s biologists generally came to accept that natural selection works for the good of the individual, or of the genes within an individual. Hamilton was partly responsible for this shift in view.

Hamilton's work on altruism contains a number of characteristic features. He picked a big problem, and began with an idea without knowing in advance whether it would work. He developed that idea in rigorous mathematical form, in a paper (1964) that most biologists found hard to read. He also read the literature on altruism in many forms of life, and carefully thought through how his theory could explain all the available observations. The combined result was the two-part paper 'The genetical evolution of altruistic behaviour', published in 1964 in the *Journal of Theoretical Biology*. It is one of the great papers of biology.

But at the time Hamilton found it difficult to interest his fellow biologists in his work, and to get it published. He had failed to interest any potential PhD supervisors in the basic problem. They seem to have feared that it had something to do with eugenics. He did the work alone—in libraries, in his bed-sitting room, even on the platform of Waterloo railway station. He had no desk in a university department. When he submitted the work for publication, the referees were hostile, and it came out only after a delay and in dismembered form. The main influence of the paper on biology did not begin until some five or ten years later.

In 1967 Hamilton married Christine Friess, the daughter of a Lutheran pastor; they had three daughters. In later years Hamilton moved on to a second relationship, with the Italian writer Luisa Bozzi. He left Imperial College when appointed to a professorship at the University of Michigan, Ann Arbor, USA, in 1978. He stayed there for six years until appointed to a Royal Society research professorship, which he held at Oxford University from 1984 until his death.

**The study of the evolution of sex** Hamilton's work moved on from altruism in the early 1970s. He did return to it, in a major paper on reciprocity (1981) which he wrote with the political scientist Robert Axelrod. Reciprocity is a second theory of altruism, and can evolve in the absence of genetic relatedness between altruist and recipient. However, by 1980 Hamilton's interest had moved on to another big, unsolved problem: the evolution of sex.

The existence of sex had, by the mid-1970s, been identified as the outstanding unsolved problem in evolution. Sex had, like altruism, once been thought to exist for the good of the species, but that style of explanation was no longer accepted. Sexual reproduction is expensive compared with its alternative—asexual (or clonal) reproduction in biological language, virgin birth in informal language. With sexual reproduction, it takes two parents to make an offspring; with asexual reproduction it takes one parent to make an offspring. For this basic reason asexual forms can be expected to reproduce at about twice the rate of equivalent sexual forms. Natural selection ought to favour asexual over sexual reproduction, yet many life forms reproduce sexually.

Hamilton thought that the solution might lie in the relations between hosts and their parasites. Parasites cause infectious disease in their hosts. Hosts defend themselves, over evolutionary time, by evolving genetic resistance to their parasites, but parasites evolve back, evolving counter-resistance mechanisms. One way hosts can keep ahead of their rapidly evolving parasites is by mixing the genetic defences of two individuals. An individual that clones itself produces offspring all genetically identical to itself. A parasite may soon evolve its way round their defences, and consume all the offspring. An individual that reproduces sexually produces offspring with a range of genetic defences. Some of the offspring may survive no matter what penetration mechanisms the parasites possess.

Hamilton began by showing that the theory works (that is, it can explain the existence of sex) in some special cases. By 1990 he had shown that it can work in quite general conditions. He also expanded the theory to explain mate choice, suggesting that individuals pick partners on the basis of health. Hamilton's 'parasitic' theory of sex was one of the main theories of sex, but the problem remained unsolved into the beginning of the twenty-first century. Biologists failed to perform definitive tests of Hamilton's theory, and it remained in limbo. The theory inspired much research, however. Some subcomponents of the theory, for instance his theory of mate choice, became widely accepted.

When Hamilton began thinking about sex, it was an academic problem within evolutionary theory. By the 1990s the cloning of human beings had become technologically almost possible, and the need for an understanding of why sex exists had become more urgent. Hamilton came to hold a bleak view of the human future. He feared that medical technologies would increasingly be used to tamper with our evolutionary heritage, and lead to genetically vulnerable and medically dependent future generations.

Hamilton published his ideas in technical papers, and made no attempt to popularize them. Only a small number of students saw that he was a genius, sought him out, and were led to do exceptional research with him. But behind the uncharismatic social surface lay a man with a taste for adventure. As a child he almost blew himself up with explosives. As an adult he went on rough field trips to many corners of the globe, but particularly to Brazil which he visited repeatedly from 1964 onwards. He liked to sleep in the open, he fought back at Brazilian muggers, and he entertained dubious theories that compounded the risks he ran: he held that Amazonian caymans and piranhas are not dangerous (their reputations being just a local superstition); he also held that he was immune from malaria, a notion that helped to kill him. The streets of Oxford were lit up in the 1980s and 1990s by a fearless, even crazy, white-haired bicyclist. It was Professor W. D. Hamilton FRS, cycling in from Wytham at high speed or travelling between libraries. He explained that the bicycle had belonged to his brother, who had died in a climbing accident at the age of eighteen. Whenever Hamilton mounted that bicycle, the spirit of his dead brother entered him. Less courageous travellers were, like Hamilton's scientific colleagues, left far behind muttering that he lived, as he thought, dangerously.

Elected a fellow of the Royal Society in 1980, and the recipient of many prizes and awards, Hamilton was ferociously anti-establishment, a fact that partly explains why he had difficulty in publishing his work, and why he was an occasional thorn in the side of administrative colleagues. He stood up for the underdog, and would champion an idea if he thought it had been ruled out without proper testing. In the 1990s it was suggested that HIV, the virus that causes AIDS, might have originated in the health campaign against polio in Africa. The theory was condemned, but with little good scientific reason in Hamilton's opinion. Hamilton duly defended it, saying that it deserved to be properly tested. He went on two field trips to Africa to collect material to test it. During the second he succumbed to malaria, and the complications that followed led to his death in the Middlesex Hospital, London, on 7 March 2000. He was buried at Wytham church, near Oxford. MARK RIDLEY

**Sources** W. D. Hamilton, *Narrow roads of gene land*, 2 vols. (1996–2001) · personal knowledge (2004) · W. D. Hamilton, curriculum vitae, U. Oxf., department of zoology · *WW* · b. cert. · d. cert.
**Archives** BL, papers | Bodl. Oxf., corresp. with T. R. E. Southwood

**Hamilton, William Gerard** [*called* Single-Speech Hamilton] (**1729–1796**), politician, was born on 28 January 1729, the eldest surviving son of William Hamilton (*d.* 1754), a barrister of Lincoln's Inn, and his first wife, Helen, daughter of David Hay of Woodcockdale, Linlithgowshire. He was educated at Harrow School from 1742 to 1745 and at Oriel College, Oxford. He went to study law at Lincoln's Inn, but he had little inclination to follow the legal profession, and on the death of his father he embarked on a political career. In 1754 he was elected as MP for Petersfield, and he eventually became a follower of Henry Fox. On 13 November 1755 in the debate on the address he made his celebrated maiden speech. Horace Walpole commented: 'His figure is advantageous, his voice strong and clear, his manner spirited, and the whole an ease of an established speaker' (*Letters*, 2.484). Indeed such was his success on this occasion, and apparent lack of distinction afterwards, that he acquired the rather misleading sobriquet 'Single-Speech'.

Hamilton spoke impressively in the house again in 1756, and in April of that year Fox secured his appointment to the Board of Trade under Lord Halifax. When Halifax became Irish viceroy in 1761, Hamilton resigned his office to become his chief secretary. Lord Charlemont remarked that Halifax's administration 'was rendered more formidable' and 'certainly more entertaining, by the parliamentary abilities of his secretary' (*Charlemont MSS*, 1.18). Edmund Burke accompanied Hamilton as his private secretary, but in 1765 the two quarrelled over the terms of their engagement, seen as a 'settled servitude' according to an irate Burke, who described Hamilton as 'an infamous scoundrel' (Ayling, 19–20).

Hamilton was intensely ambitious, and he embarked on a scheme in Ireland to form a party under his leadership. But although the British government was engaged in a struggle for control in Ireland with local power brokers, the so-called parliamentary undertakers, Hamilton's primary motivation was personal gain. When Lord Northumberland became viceroy, Hamilton secured his continuation as chief secretary, against established practice. He had a high opinion of his own abilities and influence, arguing that 'nothing I think is more probable than that my being secretary will be imposed as a condition upon any one who applies for the lord lieutenancy'. He later claimed that 'by my own personal friends I obtained the government both for Lord Halifax and Lord Northumberland' (*Beaufort MSS*, 233, 252). Political reality, however, was somewhat different, and the Irish undertakers, particularly Primate Stone, responded to Hamilton's intriguing by giving him a lesson in who actually controlled the Irish parliament. A humiliated Hamilton resorted to voting with the opposition, later admitting that he had been 'abused in every company in Dublin' (*Eighth Report*, HMC, 190). But despite his eventual dismissal he left Ireland with the prized sinecure of chancellor of the exchequer, worth £2000 a year.

Hamilton remained an MP at Westminster and involved himself in party politics, but the remainder of his political life was spent in back-bench silence. He became attached to Lord Temple, voting against the repeal of the Stamp Act and opposing the Chatham ministry on the land tax and the Nullum Tempus Bill. Though the attribution has been since discounted, Hamilton was widely believed to have been the politician responsible for the *Letters of Junius*. Walpole was sceptical of Hamilton's denials, claiming that 'his truth was not renowned' (Smith, 3.lxii). Throughout the American War of Independence he was constant in his opposition to government policy and gravitated towards the Chathamites. On American taxation, he wrote, 'I think you have no right to tax them, and that every measure built upon this supposed right stands upon a rotten foundation, and must consequently tumble down, perhaps on the heads of the workmen' (*Correspondence of William Pitt*, 3.203). In 1782 Shelburne offered him the post of secretary at war. He refused, preferring a pension of £2000 a year in exchange for his sinecure. Parliamentary lists show him to have been a supporter of Fox in March 1783, of Pitt a year later, and in opposition again on the regency question in 1788. His inconstancy exasperated patrons, but he was able to remain in parliament until 1796. 'My attachment to nobody', Hamilton boasted, 'lays open to me the society of everybody' (BL, Add. MS 34418, fol. 174).

Hamilton was a prominent figure in London's literary set, and was a close friend of Samuel Johnson. They co-wrote a pamphlet on the corn laws, and Johnson was alleged to have written Hamilton's famous maiden speech. Johnson clearly valued Hamilton's conversation. He famously remarked: 'I am very unwilling to be left alone, Sir, and therefore I go with my company down the first pair of stairs, in some hopes that they may perhaps, return again. I go with you, Sir, as far as the street door' (*Boswell's Life of Johnson*, 346). Hamilton's contemporaries regarded him as gifted but unscrupulous. Fanny Burney wrote that he:

> is extremely tall and handsome, has an air of haughty and fashionable superiority, is intelligent, dry, sarcastic and clever. I should have received much pleasure from his conversational powers had I not previously been prejudiced against him by hearing that he is infinitely artful, double, and crafty. (*Early Journals and Letters*, 3.429)

This was certainly the story of his political life. Although he was talented and well connected, his natural indolence, independent mind, and eagerness to keep well with all parties prevented him from forging a ministerial career. Hamilton, who never married, died on 16 July 1796 in Upper Brook Street, London. He was buried on 22 July in St Martin-in-the-Fields. MARTYN J. POWELL

**Sources** *DNB* • J. Brooke, 'Hamilton, William Gerard', HoP, *Commons, 1754–90* • *The manuscripts of the duke of Beaufort … the earl of Donoughmore*, HMC, 27 (1891) • *The Grenville papers: being the correspondence of Richard Grenville … and … George Grenville*, ed. W. J. Smith, 4 vols. (1852–3) • *Eighth report*, 1, HMC, 7 (1907–9) • *Correspondence of William Pitt, earl of Chatham*, ed. W. S. Taylor and J. H. Pringle, 4 vols. (1838–40) • C. C. O'Brien, *The great melody* (1992) • S. Ayling, *Edmund Burke: his life and opinions* (1988) • *The manuscripts and correspondence of James, first earl of Charlemont*, 1, HMC, 28 (1891) • *Boswell's Life of Johnson*, ed. R. W. Chapman, rev. J. D. Fleeman, new edn (1906); repr. (1976) • *The early journals and letters of Fanny Burney*, ed. L. E. Troide, 3: *The Streatham years, part 1, 1778–1779* (1994) • *The letters of Horace Walpole, earl of Orford*, ed. P. Cunningham, 9 vols. (1857–9)
**Archives** Derbys. RO, letters to Sir Robert Wilmot • Hunt. L., letters to Lord Pery • PRO NIre., Emly (Pery) MSS • TCD, Donoughmore MSS, corresp. with J. Hely-Hutchinson
**Likenesses** W. Evans, stipple (after portrait by J. R. Smith), BM, NPG; repro. in W. G. Hamilton, *Parliamentary logick* (1808) • J. R. Smith, portrait; formerly in the Stowe collection, 1890

**Hamilton, William John** (1805–1867), geologist, was born in London on 5 July 1805, the eldest son of William Richard Hamilton (1777–1859), diplomatist and antiquary, and his wife, Juliana, daughter of John Udny. He was educated at Charterhouse School (from 1817 to 1822) and at the University of Göttingen (in 1824 and 1825), paying special attention to modern languages and history. In 1827 he was appointed attaché to the legation at Madrid, and in 1829 was transferred to Paris. He returned to London shortly afterwards and acted for some time as précis writer to Lord Aberdeen at the Foreign Office. At his father's request Roderick Murchison gave Hamilton some practical instruction in geology, and in 1831 he became a fellow of the Geological Society (he was one of the society's secretaries from 1832 to 1854). On 26 April 1832 Hamilton married Martin (*d.* 1833), daughter of John Trotter of Dyrham Park, Hertfordshire. The couple had a son, William.

Murchison introduced Hamilton to Hugh Strickland, and in 1835 the pair set off on a journey to the eastern Mediterranean. After visiting the Ionian Islands, the Bosphorus, and the volcanic region of the Katakekaumene, Strickland was compelled to return home, but Hamilton proceeded alone on an adventurous journey on horseback into Armenia, through the whole length of Asia Minor, and back to Smyrna. He made careful topographical observations and kept a full diary of geological and archaeological notes. On his return he was elected president of the Royal Geographical Society for 1837, an office which he also held in 1841, 1842, and 1847. He was elected the Conservative MP for Newport on the Isle of Wight, a constituency he served from 1841 to 1847. On 26 July 1838 he married Margaret Frances Florence (*d.* 1885), daughter of Henry Dillon-Lee, thirteenth Viscount Dillon, with whom he had three sons and four daughters, all of whom survived him; the eldest daughter, Victoria Henrietta, married James Graham Goodenough, a naval officer.

Having earlier communicated various details of his eastern Mediterranean journey to the *Transactions* and *Proceedings* of the Geological Society, Hamilton, in 1842, issued a complete narrative in two volumes, illustrated with drawings by himself, entitled *Researches in Asia Minor, Pontus, and Armenia, with some account of their antiquities and geology*. This painstaking work received the commendation of Humboldt, and its author was awarded the founder's medal of the Royal Geographical Society in 1843. In 1844 he read to the Geological Society a lengthy paper on the rocks and minerals of central Tuscany, and in 1848 an account of the agate-quarries of Oberstein. Hamilton was also interested in Tertiary deposits (he studied recent Mollusca to help understand fossils found in them) and in 1854 and 1855 he prepared two elaborate papers on the geology of the Mayence basin and of the Hesse district. He was elected president of the Geological Society in 1854, having long been one of the most active members of its council. With characteristic care his two anniversary addresses were a complete digest of almost all geological research published during the two years. He subsequently made various excursions in France and Belgium with Prestwich and other fellows of the society, and in 1865 was re-elected president.

Though of athletic build, Hamilton's strength was undermined by an internal complaint; he resigned in 1866, and went abroad for a year. He returned to England only shortly before his death, which took place at his home, 23 Chesham Place, London, on 27 June 1867. Urbane and an astute businessman, he had acted as director and chairman of the Great Indian Peninsula Railway from 1849 until his death.

G. S. BOULGER, *rev.* JOHN C. THACKRAY

**Sources** R. I. Murchison, *Journal of the Royal Geographical Society*, 38 (1868), cxxxiv–cxxxvii • W. W. Smyth, *Quarterly Journal of the Geological Society*, 24 (1868), xxix–xxxiii • Burke, *Peerage* (1970) [Belhaven] • W. Jardine, *Memoirs of Hugh Edwin Strickland* (1858), xxviii–clvi • *Geological Magazine*, 4 (1867), 383–4 • *GM*, 4th ser., 4 (1867), 392–3 • *Proceedings of the Royal Geological Society*, 24 (1868), xxix • *IGI*
**Archives** RGS, letters, reports, observation files
**Likenesses** photograph, *c.*1860, GS Lond.
**Wealth at death** under £14,000: resworn probate, Jan 1870, *CGPLA Eng. & Wales* (1867)

**Hamilton, William Richard** (1777–1859), antiquary and diplomatist, born in London on 9 January 1777, was the son of Anthony Hamilton (1739–1812), archdeacon of Colchester, and Anne, daughter of Richard Terrick, bishop of London. The family were descended from the Hamiltons of Wishaw, Lanarkshire. After studying at Harrow School, where he was accidentally lamed for life, Hamilton was admitted to St John's College, Cambridge, where he matriculated in 1795, but ill health prevented him from graduating. In 1799 he went to Constantinople as attaché to Lord Elgin's embassy, and in 1802 he became private secretary. He returned to London in 1803, and was found a place in the Foreign Office as private secretary (April–July 1804) to his cousin Lord Harrowby. On 3 September 1804 he married Juliana, daughter of John Udny of Aberdeen,

**William Richard Hamilton** (1777–1859), by Richard James Lane, 1854 (after Henry Wyndham Phillips)

with when he had six sons and a daughter. After Harrowby left office, Hamilton became précis writer to Lord Mulgrave (July 1804–March 1806). In October 1809 he was appointed under-secretary by Lord Bathurst and he retained that office until ill health forced him to give up his duties in January 1822. He went to Naples to recover his health, serving there as minister from February 1822 to December 1824, when he retired on a pension.

Hamilton's otherwise unremarkable diplomatic career would be of little note but for the extraordinary events that took place during Elgin's mission to Constantinople. The earl frequently entrusted Hamilton with important business, and in 1801 sent him on a diplomatic mission to Egypt following the French evacuation after the battle of Alexandria. Hamilton discovered that the French, contrary to treaty, had stealthily shipped out the famous trilingual Rosetta stone. With an escort of soldiers, and in spite of the danger of fever, he rowed out to the French transport and insisted on carrying off the precious monument. It was also Hamilton who collected together the Parthenon (or 'Elgin') marbles, and in 1802 superintended their removal. When the vessel containing some of the principal groups sank at Cerigo, Hamilton set divers to work and recovered the whole cargo.

In 1815 it was on Hamilton's initiative that the second treaty of Paris contained provisions for the restoration to Italy of the works of art taken away during the Napoleonic era. In 1809 he published *Aegyptiaca, or, Some account of the antient and modern state of Egypt, accompanied with etchings from drawings taken on the spot by Charles Hayes*, the first volume of a projected larger work, which was, however, never carried out. The *Aegyptiaca* shows considerable research; but the most important of its contents is Hamilton's transcript of the 'Greek copy of the decree on the Rosetta stone', with a translation in English. His comment, at the end of chapter 2, is that 'hitherto all attempts to decypher the hieroglyphic or Coptic inscriptions have proved fruitless'. In 1811 Hamilton published a *Memoir on the Subject of the Earl of Elgin's Pursuits in Greece*. In 1833 he was actively employed as one of the founders of the Royal Geographical Society. He also took great interest in the Royal Institution and the Royal Society of Literature. In 1838 he was appointed one of the trustees of the British Museum, an office he retained until 1858. Hamilton died on 11 July 1859 at his home, 12 Bolton Row, Piccadilly, London, in his eighty-second year.

R. E. ANDERSON, *rev.* R. A. JONES

**Sources** *The Times* (27 July 1859) • *FO List* (1859), 133 • J. M. Collinge, ed., *Office-holders in modern Britain*, 8: *Foreign office officials, 1782–1870* (1979) • C. R. Middleton, *The administration of British foreign policy, 1782–1846* (1977) • Venn, *Alum. Cant.* • Chambers, *Scots.* (1835) • *CGPLA Eng. & Wales* (1859) • Burke, *Peerage*

**Archives** BL, corresp. as trustee of British Museum, Add. MS 50132 | BL, corresp. with Lord Aberdeen, Add. MSS 43074, 43238–43243, *passim* • BL, corresp. with Sir William A'Court, Add. MSS 41513–41523 • BL, corresp. with Sir Robert Gordon, Add. MSS 43213, 43217 • BL, corresp. with Lord Melbourne, Add. MS 60420 • BL, letters to Sir Roderick Murchison, Add. MS 46126 • BL, letters to Sir Anthony Panizzi, Add. MSS 36715–36719 • BL, corresp. with Sir Robert Peel, Add. MSS 40198–40603, *passim* • Bodl. Oxf., corresp. with Sir Thomas Phillipps • NL Scot., letters to Lord Stuart De Rothesay • RIBA BAL, corresp. with C. R. Cockerell • U. Nott. L., letters to Lord William Bentinck, etc.

**Likenesses** R. J. Lane, lithograph, 1854 (after H. W. Phillips), BM, NPG [*see illus.*] • C. Baugniet, lithograph, BM, NPG • D. Hardy, oils (after T. Phillips), Brooks's Club, London, Society of Dilettanti

**Wealth at death** under £25,000: probate, 28 July 1859, *CGPLA Eng. & Wales*

**Hamilton, Sir William Rowan** (1805–1865), mathematician, was born at midnight between 3 and 4 August 1805 in Dominick Street, Dublin, the fourth of nine children of Archibald Hamilton (1778–1819), a solicitor, and his wife, Sarah (1780–1817), from the Dublin family of Hutton. He had four sisters who survived infancy, one older than himself, and no brothers. Before he was three years old his parents sent their son to be raised by a curate uncle, James Hamilton, possibly because of the family's financial difficulties. He attended the Church of Ireland diocesan school in Trim, co. Meath, run by his uncle. Both school and home were in Talbot's Castle overlooking the River Boyne where the young Hamilton enjoyed swimming. James Hamilton, a classics graduate of Trinity College, Dublin, soon recognized his nephew's intellectual capabilities and found him a quick and willing learner of Hebrew, Latin, and Greek; by the age of ten he had also gained a facility in Persian, Arabic, Sanskrit, Chaldee, Syriac, Hindustani, Malay, Marathi, and Bengali, as well as the modern European languages. Against a background of political–religious tensions and the agrarian agitation that grew out of the extreme poverty of farm workers, William Hamilton personally enjoyed a comfortable youth in Trim, upon which he looked back with fondness in later life.

**Sir William Rowan Hamilton** (1805–1865), by unknown photographer, *c.*1845 [with his son William Edwin Hamilton]

Hamilton appears to have been largely self-taught in mathematics. His interest in the subject lagged somewhat behind that in languages, however, and it was not surprising that he was outmatched in 1818 when put against Zerah Colburn, the 'American Calculating Boy' and a year older than Hamilton, at a performance in Dublin. On Colburn's return to Dublin in 1820 Hamilton was better prepared and, what was more important, was given the chance to discuss techniques with him. He took notes at the time on what he learned of Colburn's methods and appears to have been more interested in why they worked than in duplicating them.

**Undergraduate life** His uncle guided Hamilton towards entrance in July 1823 into Trinity College, Dublin, with spectacularly high results on the entrance and prize examinations. Tutored by Charles Boyton, a fellow of Trinity and friend of the family, Hamilton began studying the mathematical texts used at the college. He benefited from recent curriculum reforms that, while keeping Isaac Newton's *Principia mathematica* (1687) at the core, took advantage of the progress made since Newton, especially in France by Pierre Simon Laplace, Joseph Louis Lagrange, Siméon Denis Poisson, and Sylvestre François Lacroix. Throughout his stay at Trinity he achieved the highest standing at every examination in classics and mathematics that he took, but even with the time spent preparing for term and prize examinations, which involved largely rote memorization, Hamilton kept up his swimming and gymnastics. He is described as being broad-chested and medium-sized with light blue eyes and dark brown hair, and always cheerful and alert. He also found time to pursue his favourite creative activities, original mathematical researches and composition of poetry. Some of his most important later mathematical ideas, for example those on the theory of rays, stem from this time. His poetry has not proven as memorable as his mathematics but he always maintained that the two endeavours share the same creative source.

Hamilton recorded his feelings in poetry when his love for the sister of college friends, Catherine Disney, was rejected. Awkwardness and shyness had prevented him from expressing himself directly to her though there were signs that she reciprocated his feelings. In any case, her family appears to have discouraged any advances from him and she became engaged to someone else in 1825. After their respective marriages, he made efforts to keep within her circle by, for example, acting as tutor to her children. Hamilton himself seemed to wish to make this lost love of his life public knowledge since he published his poem about it in the *Dublin Literary Gazette and National Magazine* in 1830 and showed it to anyone he thought likely to be sympathetic. There may be some correlation between this episode and Hamilton's periods of creativity and depression, but the evidence is sufficiently indirect that no biographer can do more than speculate on any causal relation.

**Astronomer royal** During his college years Hamilton prepared for the competitive examinations leading to a fellowship that would allow him to stay on as a teacher at the college. However, before he had the chance to take them, he was appointed Andrews professor of astronomy in June 1827, which entailed his appointment as astronomer royal of Ireland and director of the Dunsink observatory, 5 miles from Dublin. Boyton was largely responsible for emphasizing Hamilton's work in geometrical optics and organizing the support for his appointment to this prestigious position. Though Hamilton had been a visitor at the observatory, greatly impressing the astronomer royal, John Brinkley, with his mathematical work, Brinkley himself made clear his strong doubts about Hamilton's experience, ability, and willingness to carry out the required duties. The post indeed included the day-to-day management of the observatory at Dunsink and ostensibly required making astronomical observations, an activity for which Hamilton showed neither enthusiasm nor great skill. Nevertheless, it provided him with more time for research than the teaching fellowship would have done. It also meant that his four sisters could live with him at the observatory and this proved to be a key to his making a success of this life for they assisted not only in the management of the household, but in making observations and maintaining the astronomical records.

On 9 April 1833 Hamilton married Helen Maria Bayly (1804–1869) from Nenagh in co. Tipperary. There were none of the poetic signs of passion in this relationship that marked Hamilton's earlier love, and descriptions of Helen are sparse. Her arrival displaced the sisters to some extent and signalled a less well-managed household.

Friends, and his first biographer, R. P. Graves, in particular, who were concerned with Hamilton's excessive drinking in the 1840s and with a general change into a less cheerful personality, tended to feel that Helen, if not a direct cause, was at least not taking proper care of him. Nevertheless Hamilton's devotion to her comes across very clearly in letters to her when their travels separated them, and especially in his concern whenever she suffered from one of the incapacitating illnesses that plagued her throughout her life. In spite of doubtful health she bore two sons and a daughter.

Hamilton as astronomer royal made no significant direct contributions to astronomy. Instead his reputation from the beginning rested on his genius for devising general and abstract mathematical theories that his contemporaries recognized as of the highest calibre from an aesthetic, if not from a utilitarian, viewpoint. Hamilton's earliest work in 1824 at the age of eighteen, on the theory of systems of light rays, established him as a major contributor to the mainstream of the mathematics of his time. (Mathematics had not yet experienced the bifurcation into the separate spheres of pure and applied that characterized it in the twentieth century.) Though it has not been of such lasting importance as much of his other work, the experimental verification of his prediction of conical refraction of light was regarded in 1833 as spectacularly brilliant science and earned him the royal medal of the Royal Society of London and a knighthood from the lord lieutenant of Ireland in 1835. Hamilton was elected to the presidency of the Royal Irish Academy in November 1837 and conscientiously performed the burdensome administrative duties of the post until 1846. The academy particularly valued his ability to settle the sometimes contentious disputes between members.

**Hamilton's mathematics** Modern historians and philosophers have often and deeply investigated how much philosophy and poetry was essentially involved in the creation, presentation, and justification of Hamilton's mathematics, especially of his contention that algebra was properly the science of pure time. It remains, however, an open and intriguing question. What is clear is that Hamilton claimed that mathematics was akin to poetry, sought advice from his friend William Wordsworth, supported the causes of Samuel Taylor Coleridge, and cited Immanuel Kant in his work. In 1834 he expressed one pervasive, if less poetical, theme of his general methods in dynamics:

> [E]ven if it should be thought that no practical facility is gained, yet an intellectual pleasure may result from the reduction of the most complex and, probably, of all researches respecting the forces and motions of body, to the study of one characteristic function, the unfolding of one central relation. (Hamilton, 2.105)

Though the reductions he obtained were not always as simple or unified as he sought, Hamilton's results made radical progress over similar efforts in the past. Rays of light refracted through a crystal, for example, had long been known to follow a path that minimized the time taken for the light to pass from a point on one side of the refracting surface to a point on the other. Hamilton established a more general principle of least action that is described by what are now referred to as the Hamilton canonical equations of motion, a system of first-order partial differential equations involving a single function, the Hamiltonian. A German contemporary, Carl G. J. Jacobi, extended Hamilton's work on the equations of motion and gave them the generalized form in which they have become most useful. Most of the laws of physics involving gravitation, optics, dynamics, and electricity can be expressed in terms of a maximizing or minimizing of the Hamiltonian. This work originated in Hamilton's idea that optical phenomena could be explained in an analogous fashion to mechanical phenomena, an idea that Erwin Schrödinger and others extended in the 1920s to cover the wave–particle duality theory in quantum mechanics. Hamilton himself could not have anticipated the newer mechanics without the physical evidence that came only after Albert Einstein's work in the first decades of the twentieth century. The unity of form that Hamiltonian mechanics brought to physics has inspired its use as a framework in other fields such as control theory and system theory.

In the realm of algebra, Hamilton's invention of quaternions produced one of the most famous moments in mathematical history: a revelatory experience of the key algebraic relationships that came to him on 16 October 1843. Several years after the centenary of this discovery a commemorative plaque was placed at De Valera's suggestion near the spot on the footpath under the Brougham Bridge in Dublin where the solution came to him. Hamilton had long been working on how to represent rotations in space in the same way that rotations in the two-dimensional plane are represented by the multiplication of complex numbers. What he jotted down in his notebook on that day were the multiplication rules for the four base units, $i$, $j$, $k$, and 1, for a new number system, the quaternions: $i^2 = j^2 = k^2 = ijk = -1$. Hamilton's detailed description of the circumstances and of the justification of his discovery has provided substantial material for sociological and philosophical case studies in mathematical discovery. Mathematically it marked a milestone in the development of modern algebra and he spent most of the rest of his life publicizing its implications. He published 109 papers on quaternions alone and, in 1853, a large compilation, *Lectures on Quaternions*. On his death he left incomplete another, even larger treatise, *Elements of Quaternions*, which one of his sons saw through the press in 1866. His quaternionic followers did not regard his writing style as the best for an elementary introduction and thus, to make up for this, Charles Jasper Joly, his successor as astronomer royal, edited a second, enlarged edition, of the *Elements*, published in two volumes in 1899 and 1901.

Hamilton and his followers had hopes that the quaternion would be the standard notation for representing position and motion in space. Hamilton demonstrated at length the advantages of quaternions over the older notations in mechanics, not least the advantage of compactness that enabled a single-line equation, for example, to replace the three or more lines of equations that were used in the standard eighteenth-century works in mechanics of Lagrange and Laplace. The rise of an alternative, vector notation, especially as expounded by the American mathematical physicist Josiah Willard Gibbs, led to a rivalry about the turn of the twentieth century between advocates of the two systems. For two decades the International Association for Promoting the Study of Quaternions and Allied Systems of Mathematics carried on a vigorous but losing campaign through its publications. Though the more versatile vectors won out over quaternions by the 1920s as the generally preferred notation, this was rather a case of Hamilton's discovery not finding its niche than a sign of its ultimate failure, as some feared at the time. The four quaternion components seemed a natural way to express the four-dimensional space–time continuum of relativity theory in the 1920s, but the main contribution quaternions have made is through their decisive influence on the development of a new branch of mathematics in the late nineteenth century, linear algebra.

After bringing forth quaternions Hamilton returned to an earlier interest in the geometry of polyhedra. At first he regarded it as a largely recreational activity and indeed he created for commercial sale the 'Icosian game' based on his work. In the game a player attempts to trace a one-way path connecting a group of cities on a map without repetition and returning to its starting point. To find such paths, now called Hamiltonian cycles, that connect a collection of points, remains a challenging and important problem in computational mathematics.

**Other interests** Hamilton took an interest in Irish politics, usually defending the tory views of his uncle James when his Liberal father provoked him into good-natured argument. He remained a political Conservative, a supporter of the British monarchy, and in favour of Irish and British union throughout his life, but at the same time he insisted on Ireland as a separate culture from England. Throughout the religious contentions of Hamilton's time, as the Catholic church rose in influence, he remained a staunch member of the Church of Ireland and adhered fairly constantly to its evangelical wing, though for a time in the 1840s he was attracted by the transcendentalism of the Oxford Movement.

In the summer of 1865 Hamilton suffered severe attacks of gout and on 2 September died at his home in Dunsink from what doctors described as complications arising from the attacks. The funeral and the procession to the burial at Mount Jerome cemetery, Dublin, on 7 September, were attended by members of Trinity College in academic regalia and members of the Royal Irish Academy. Though Hamilton was often the executor for the estates of other members of the Hamilton family he did not excel at these tasks and never gained any appreciable wealth himself. Friends helped his family overcome financial difficulties in his last years. Hamilton's civil-list pension of £200 was divided equally between his wife and daughter.

Though acknowledging that both Hamilton's grandmothers were Scottish, Graves maintained that Hamilton was of Irish descent. An extensive debate took place in journals in 1891 between Graves and the Scottish physicist P. G. Tait, a close colleague of Hamilton, who maintained that Hamilton's paternal grandfather, William Hamilton, went to Dublin from Scotland. Though Tait insisted on defining Hamilton as Scottish in his article for the *Encyclopaedia Britannica*, there is no documentary evidence to refute or support the family tradition that their branch of Hamiltons first moved to Ireland from Scotland at the time of James I; a century after Hamilton's most active years, he was unequivocally claimed by Ireland. In 1939 De Valera, a student of mathematics as well as the person chiefly responsible for Ireland's independence from England, invoked Hamilton's name in arguing for the founding of the Institute for Advanced Studies in Dublin as someone who was 'known wherever there is a mathematical physicist or theoretical physicist. This is the country of Hamilton, a country of great mathematicians' (Synge, 645). ALBERT C. LEWIS

**Sources** T. L. Hankins, *Sir William Rowan Hamilton* (1980) • R. P. Graves, *Life of Sir William Rowan Hamilton*, 3 vols. (1882–9) • W. R. Hamilton, *The mathematical papers*, ed. A. W. Conway, J. L. Synge, A. J. McConnell, H. Halberstam, and R. E. Ingram, 3 vols. (1931–67) • M. J. Crowe, *A history of vector analysis: the evolution of the idea of a vectorial system*, 2nd edn (1985) • S. O'Donnell, *William Rowan Hamilton: portrait of a prodigy* (1983) • J. L. Synge, *Memoirs FRS*, 22 (1976), 635–53 [obit. of E. de Valera]

**Archives** TCD, corresp. and papers | BL, corresp. with Sir Robert Peel, Add. MSS 40535, 40547, 40599 • CUL, letters to Lord Kelvin • RS, letters to Sir John Lubbock • Trinity Cam., letters to William Whewell • University of Limerick Library, corresp. with Lord Dunraven

**Likenesses** T. Kirk, bust, before 1830, TCD • T. Kirk, marble bust, 1830, Dunraven-Limerick Estates Co. • T. Farrell, miniature bust, 1833, repro. in Graves, *Life* • photograph, *c.*1845 (with his son W. E. Hamilton), TCD [*see illus.*] • S. Purser, portrait, 1862 (after photograph, 1857), Royal Irish Acad. • J. H. Foley, marble bust, 1867 (after T. Kirk), TCD • C. Grey, etching, repro. in *Dublin University Magazine*, 19 (1842), facing p. 94 • J. Kirkwood, lithograph (after C. Grey), NPG

**Wealth at death** £4000: probate, 30 Oct 1865, *CGPLA Eng. & Wales*

**Hamilton, Sir William Stirling**, baronet (1788–1856), philosopher, was born on 8 March 1788 in the College of Glasgow, the son of William *Hamilton (1758–1790), professor of anatomy in the University of Glasgow, and Elizabeth, *née* Stirling (*d.* 1827), the daughter of a Glasgow merchant. Thomas *Hamilton (1789–1842) was his brother. His father died in 1790, of a long drawn-out illness brought on by overwork, leaving his widow to bring up Hamilton and his brother. Elizabeth Hamilton was entirely equal to the task; there is no evidence that the family ever felt either financial anxiety or the absence of a father's hand.

**Education and legal career** William was energetic and precociously intelligent; he attended schools in both Scotland and England, among them the Glasgow grammar school at the age of nine, and the University of Glasgow's junior classes in Greek and Latin at twelve. Before he was eighteen, he was taking the senior classes in logic and moral philosophy at the university. In 1806–7 he studied

**Sir William Stirling Hamilton, baronet (1788–1856)**, by James Charles Armytage, pubd 1869 (after James Archer)

medicine in Edinburgh, and in 1807 gained a Snell exhibition to study at Balliol College, Oxford. Snell exhibitioners, of whom Adam Smith is the most famous, brought to Balliol from their native Scotland an intellectual energy and ambition that was not yet common in the college. They also inspired a degree of ambivalence in their southern fellows, who admired the talents of their Scottish colleagues but did not wish to see the college fall into their hands.

As an undergraduate, Hamilton was largely left to his own devices; his subsequent contempt for the Oxford tutorial system was no doubt partly inspired by the neglect he suffered from his own tutor, as well as from his belief that the Scottish universities had been right to abandon the 'regenting' system centuries earlier. His voracious appetite for work stood him in good stead, and although he had less literary flair than some of his contemporaries, he 'sent up'—that is, offered himself for examination in—an astonishing number of classical texts; they were said to be at least four times as many as any other student presented. He was awarded a first class in *literae humaniores* in the Michaelmas term of 1810; according to his biographer John Veitch, the examiners were so astonished at his erudition that they kept a list of what they had examined him on. He graduated BA in 1811 and proceeded MA in 1814. At that time the Oxford colleges offered more fellowships than there were holders of first-class degrees to fill them; none the less, Hamilton was not elected to one. His fellow Scot and close friend J. G. Lockhart thought that this was the result of prejudice against the Scots, and suggested that 'no Scots need apply' might be added to the advertisement of a fellowship. One can imagine other explanations; on the personal side, Hamilton was aggressive and opinionated in discussion, and in a university that took the literary qualities of the classics more seriously than their philosophical qualities, his erudition may have seemed more awkward than attractive.

Although he had intended to become a physician, and had done some work in medicine during his time at Oxford, Hamilton abandoned the idea after graduation, and in 1813 was admitted as an advocate at the Edinburgh bar. He remained in Edinburgh for the rest of his life, his mother moving there to be with him from 1815 onwards. He did not develop a large or prosperous practice as an advocate; he enjoyed reading historical cases, but had no great talent for public speaking, and was apparently not sufficiently interested in the minute details on which legal success depends. Perhaps his greatest triumph came in 1816, when he persuaded an Edinburgh court that he was 'heir male in general' to Sir Robert Hamilton of Preston. The object of so doing was to establish his claim to the baronetcy that had been granted to the elder brother of Sir Robert. Sir William Hamilton had been created a baronet of Nova Scotia in 1673, the title to descend to his 'heirs-male in general'. Thereafter, Hamilton styled himself Sir William Hamilton of Preston and Fingalton, baronet. It may have been at this point and it was certainly after 1807 that he abandoned Stirling as a component of his name. His politics were perhaps an even greater obstacle to a successful career than were his antiquarian tastes. He was a whig at a time of the tory ascendancy, and could therefore look to none of the usual forms of preferment open to lawyers. In 1832, however, he was appointed to a minor office, 'the solicitorship of the teinds'.

**Academic appointment** In any case, Hamilton's interests lay in philosophy and the history of philosophy, and he soon began to be well known in literary circles. In spite of his politics, however, he did not form any connection with the *Edinburgh Review* in its heyday under Francis Jeffrey's editorship. In 1817 he visited Germany on behalf of the Faculty of Advocates, and he did so again in 1820 on legal business. It was after this that he systematically learned German and joined an Edinburgh society that subscribed to German periodicals. On the death of Thomas Brown (1778–1820) he stood for the professorship of moral philosophy at the University of Edinburgh. He was supported by the other, and more distinguished, professor of philosophy at Edinburgh, Dugald Stewart, as well as by Jeffrey. His opponent was John Wilson, and the election turned on frankly political considerations; the appointment to professorships at the University of Edinburgh lay at that time with the town council, a body of notorious touchiness on political and theological matters. Hamilton refused to canvass, and ignored hints that it would be politic to announce that he was not active in whig politics. He lost by twenty-one votes to eleven, but did not begrudge his friend's victory, and did not moderate his expressions of distaste for the system whereby professors were appointed by town councillors and for political reasons.

Hamilton was elected a year later to a professorship of 'civil history', for which a rather different electoral system was involved; the Faculty of Advocates nominated two candidates for the council to elect. Hamilton and the previous occupant of the chair, William Fraser Tytler, were duly elected. The chair paid poorly and eventually paid nothing; initially the salary was £100 per annum, the income to pay which was secured on a local duty on beer, but this figure declined to nothing over several years. Initially Hamilton had a reasonable audience, but that, too, dropped away, and when the salary ceased, he stopped lecturing.

During the second half of the 1820s, when phrenology was in vogue, Hamilton spent much of his spare time engaged in anatomical research that, as he thought, thoroughly discredited phrenology. He gave papers to the Royal Society of Edinburgh in 1826 and 1827 on the subject, and kept up a vigorous controversy with George Combe, the leading phrenologist of the day.

Hamilton's mother died in January 1827. He had been devoted to her, and she to him; the shock of her death was evidently considerable. Fourteen months later, however, he married his cousin Janet Marshall (*d.* 1877), daughter of Hubert Marshall. She had lived in the household with Mrs Hamilton and her son for the previous ten years; as Lady Hamilton she evidently saved her husband from a lonely and disorganized existence. She managed the household, acted as his amanuensis, and gently pressed him to finish some of the innumerable projects that he embarked on but had great difficulty in bringing to completion. The couple had a daughter, Elizabeth *Hamilton, who contributed the article on her father to the *Encyclopaedia Britannica*, and three sons of whom the eldest succeeded his father in the baronetcy. Lady Hamilton's greatest service to her husband came some sixteen years after their marriage, when Hamilton had a stroke that enfeebled him for the last dozen years of his life. She supported him unflaggingly through what would otherwise have been a desperate time.

**The *Edinburgh Review*** Hamilton first came to notice as a philosopher in 1829, when he was prevailed upon by Macvey Napier to write an essay on the French philosopher Victor Cousin. Napier had succeeded Jeffrey as editor of the *Edinburgh Review* early in 1829, and very much wanted Hamilton to raise the intellectual level of the *Review*. Jeffrey, on the other hand, thought the idea of recruiting Hamilton preposterous, and denounced the article when it appeared as 'the most unreadable thing that ever appeared in the review' (M. Napier, *Selections from the Correspondence of … Macvey Napier*, 1879, 79). The importance of Hamilton's essay, however, did not lie in its literary qualities or lack of them. Rather, it marked the first time that a British writer of acknowledged philosophical capacity had embarked on a serious discussion of the philosophy of Kant and of the work of his interpreters and successors such as Cousin. It was thoroughly critical of Cousin's attachment to the absolute idealism of Kant's successors, and long after the event it retains a certain interest as evidence of the way German idealism struck philosophically informed British readers. Coleridge and Carlyle had already done something to make their British readers aware of the existence of German idealism, but not in the context of what later generations would have thought of as the central philosophical issues of logic, metaphysics, and the theory of knowledge. As a literary and intellectual event in Hamilton's own career, the essay on Victor Cousin made something of a spluttering start; it was delivered late, it was twice as long as the editor had hoped, and it was pitched at a level far above that of most of the readers of the *Review*. The essay was received rapturously by Victor Cousin himself, even though the criticism of his views was as uninhibited as Hamilton's criticism usually was. Over the next several years Hamilton contributed several more essays to the *Review*, on 'The philosophy of the conditioned', 'Perception', and 'Logic'. These articles at once made Hamilton's reputation. Many were translated into French and German, and they achieved a wide readership in America. He also published in the *Review* a splendid attack on the collegiate arrangements of the University of Oxford. The last took the form of five articles published between June 1831 and January 1835 (reprinted in his *Discussions*, 1852; 2nd edn, 1853; with a preface of further comment on Oxford reform). True to his enthusiasm for German philosophy, Hamilton thought that the German university provided a model of a community of scholars and researchers in a way the somnolent colleges of Oxford could not: Oxford was 'of all academical institutions at once the most imperfect and the most perfectible' (*Edinburgh Review*, 52, June 1831, 384).

Characteristically, Hamilton's assault upon the state of intellectual life in Oxford took the form of an elaborate historical account of the way in which the colleges of Oxford had arrogated to themselves the powers that had once belonged to the university. A simpler argument would have contented itself, as the earlier assault by the *Edinburgh Review* on Oxford had done, with pointing out the deficiencies of Oxford education; its inaccessibility to dissenters, Catholics, and Jews; and the gap between its scholarly aspirations and those of universities in Germany. This last was a slightly dangerous argument; by the time Hamilton came to criticize Oxford, the German universities were well known for sheltering unorthodox biblical critics such as Ludwig Feuerbach and David Strauss. To criticize the home of conservative Anglicanism from the perspective of Jena or Bonn or Berlin was likely to strengthen the determination of the defenders of the old order. Hamilton favoured the admission of dissenters to the ancient universities, of course, and put his weight behind one of the many abortive attempts at reform that preceded the abolition of religious tests a decade and a half after his death.

**Professor of logic and metaphysics** In 1836 Hamilton's political allegiances again came into question when David Ritchie resigned from the Edinburgh chair of logic and metaphysics, and Hamilton stood as a candidate for the vacant professorship. He was attacked for obscurity, pedantry, and religious unorthodoxy. However, he was energetically recommended by Cousin, Jeffrey, and Wilson, and was elected by eighteen votes to fourteen on 15 July 1836. He gave his inaugural lecture on 21 November 1836, and thereafter gave two courses of lectures a year, one on psychology and philosophy, and the other on logic. His lecturing habits were not calculated to improve his temper or sustain good health. He deferred the preparation of his text until the night before the lecture, and would frequently go to bed at dawn, leaving his wife to get the text ready for delivery. His strikingly handsome appearance, and an air of dignity and earnestness, made him an impressive lecturer, but reports on his lectures suggest that students were more puzzled than enlightened by them. Students with a real passion for philosophy, however, enjoyed them and a surprising number went on to become philosophers, including J. F. Ferrier and T. S. Baynes. With almost all his students he appears to have had very friendly relations; he was genuinely interested in pedagogical issues, and was evidently fond of the company of young people. Whatever his shortcomings as a lecturer, he was an effective interlocutor in small groups. He experimented with an honours examination, and with ways of giving students a more active role in their instruction. His relations with the university were not smooth, however; he quarrelled with his employers about his right to charge an extra fee for an advanced lecture course, and later quarrelled again over the conduct of examinations. His active career was sadly brief. In 1844 he had a paralytic stroke, with no warning symptoms. It did not affect his ability to think or do philosophy, but it affected his eyesight, and left him with slurred speech and difficulty in walking. After a short break, he was able to supervise the courses that he had earlier given, but he worked at a much diminished pace.

The work for which Hamilton was best-known in his own day was his edition of *The Works of Thomas Reid* (1846). The publication process was as acrimonious as many of Hamilton's professional dealings turned out to be. He was approached by the Edinburgh bookseller William Tait, with a proposal for an edition of Reid; it is clear that what was wanted was an edition of Reid's work with a short preface by Hamilton. Hamilton took offence at the financial arrangements proposed by Tait; since Hamilton intended to produce an edition in which his own notes and commentary occupied as much space as Reid's original work, it is easy to see that he might have thought himself underpaid, while Tait might equally have thought it unjust to expect him to pay for erudition he did not want. In the end, Hamilton published the edition in a somewhat incomplete form and at his own expense, and one of his admirers, H. L. Mansel, made a tidier production of it after Hamilton's death. Together with the volume of *Discussions* (1852) that collected his contributions to the *Edinburgh Review*, the 'Dissertations' that Hamilton attached to the edition were during his lifetime the most adequate expression of his philosophical views. His edition of Dugald Stewart's *Works* appeared in 1853, but in the autumn of that year he suffered a bad fall, followed by a severe illness in the winter. He became steadily feebler, and died at his home in Great King Street, Edinburgh, on 6 May 1856. Lady Hamilton survived him by twenty-one years.

In spite of his irritability and his pugnaciousness in controversy, Hamilton was extraordinarily happy in his domestic life. His energy and high spirits made him a good friend to his children, and the ponderousness of his literary style was strikingly at odds with his enjoyment of light literature, fairy tales, and Gothic novels. He was mechanically adept, and to his taste for anatomy he added the hobby of bookbinding, appropriately enough for the owner of a library of some 10,000 volumes—which was purchased after his death for presentation to the University of Glasgow. His own philosophical writings had an unfortunate fate, partly in their being scattered among his notes to Reid, but also because his habit of writing up his lectures at the last minute meant that it was only in 1859 that his *Lectures on Metaphysics* made a posthumous appearance, to be followed in 1861 by his *Lectures on Logic*. Since they represented hastily written drafts for oral delivery, and had hardly been touched after Hamilton prepared them soon after his election to his chair in 1836, Hamilton's admirers thought them inferior to the *Discussions* and the 'Dissertations' on Reid.

**Evaluation** Hamilton was best-known as the originator of 'the philosophy of the conditioned', a philosophical perspective that combined, or in the eyes of critics inevitably failed to combine, the insights of Thomas Reid with those of Immanuel Kant. What Hamilton wished to argue was defensible enough: that human beings do perceive an external world, do have knowledge of an objective reality, but do not and cannot have any acquaintance with the Absolute or with 'things in themselves'. He sided with Reid against David Hume in order to repudiate scepticism; and he sided with Kant against Schelling and other absolute idealists who claimed that knowledge of the Absolute was to be had. The mixture was unstable inasmuch as Kant had absorbed Hume's scepticism and had attempted to transcend it in its own terms, while Reid had resisted 'the way of ideas' from the outset. Similarly, Hamilton went far beyond Reid in insisting on what he termed 'the relativity of knowledge', a thesis that at its weakest meant only that human beings experience the world as they do because they have the physical and psychological constitutions they happen to have, but at its strongest came closer to the Kantian claim that we have knowledge only of phenomena, which are the manifestation to us of a noumenal world beyond our knowledge or even of our understanding. Yet Hamilton did not go so far as to accept Kant's own conclusions, either on this, or on the conclusions to be drawn from the famous 'antinomies of reason'. Kant had argued that we are irresistibly drawn to believe both that space and time are infinite and that they are finite; and from this he had concluded that space and time were 'forms of intuition', or ways in which the human mind organized its experience. This has never been an easy view to understand, but one natural interpretation is that it simply makes no sense to ask what space and time are 'really' like. Hamilton, in contrast, concluded that we were impelled by a mental necessity to choose one horn of the dilemma and thus to believe that space and time are infinite.

Underlying Hamilton's misuse of Kant was a religious motivation that was subsequently brought out more clearly by James McCosh and H. L. Mansel. In essence Hamilton held that even though the human mind lost itself in contradiction when addressing such issues as free will, immortality, and the existence of God, it was compelled to believe that we possess free will, that the soul is immortal, and that God exists. It was this defence of the supposed necessity of belief that drove John Stuart Mill to assail Hamilton's every last error in his *Examination of Sir William Hamilton's Philosophy* (1865); and it was McCosh and Mansel's sense that conceding victory to Mill would concede victory to materialism and agnosticism that drove them to respond, as Mill put it, with the fury of men fighting *pro aris et focis*. McCosh, in fact, was a whole-hearted defender of intuitionism, but only a half-hearted defender of Hamilton, as his discussion in *Scottish Philosophy* shows. McCosh wished that Hamilton had remained a disciple of Thomas Reid, and had not confused the issue by involving himself with Kant.

Many philosophers at the close of the twentieth century recall Hamilton precisely because of Mill's savage and devastating attack on his philosophical views, but Mill's *Examination* is one of his least-read works: modern readers confine their attention to Mill's phenomenalist account of the external world and his views on the nature of personal identity. His victim's writings are read not at all. In the middle of the nineteenth century, however, Hamilton was, with Mill, one of a very small handful of British philosophers that a European philosopher might have read. In the latter half of the century he had a posthumous career, in part as the result of the writings of James McCosh and mostly in the United States, where his work remained the basis of the intuitionism taught in many colleges until students' mounting sense that intuitionism appealed to their professors because of its comforting moral and religious qualities rather than for any intellectual credibility irreparably damaged its standing. Hamilton's name is today best remembered by historians of formal logic, and perhaps by them alone. He was one of a handful of thinkers who more or less simultaneously announced their discovery of 'the quantification of the predicate'. It was an old observation that Aristotelian logic could not show that syllogisms of the form [*most cats howl; most cats are furry: so some creatures are both furry and howl*] were valid. Hamilton offered a way to prove the validity of such arguments by elaborately reformulating the premises; in the process he reorganized the traditional Aristotelian scheme for showing the validity of syllogisms, an innovation on which he prided himself a good deal. But he had missed the tide. The work of Augustus De Morgan, George Boole, and John Venn, of whom the two last were much younger than Hamilton, advanced the analysis of sets and classes in ways of which Hamilton had no inkling. Hamilton denounced De Morgan as a plagiarist, a charge that was preposterous and would have been wounding to anyone with a less equable nature than De Morgan. He took some pleasure in the assaults of his critic, knowing no doubt that his own work was incomparably more important in the eyes of mathematicians and logicians. Hamilton suffered the worst of all fates; critics such as Mill and McCosh, who were as committed as he to the traditional logic, thought his innovations a waste of time and an unnecessary complication, while the true innovators in the discipline moved on and ignored his work.

When John Stuart Mill published his *Examination of Sir William Hamilton's Philosophy* in 1865, an enthusiastic reviewer, Mark Pattison, commented

> The effect of Mr. Mill's review is the absolute annihilation of all Sir W. Hamilton's doctrines, opinions, of all he has written or taught. Nor of himself only, but all his followers, pupils, copyists, are involved in the common ruin. The whole fabric of the Hamiltonian philosophy is not only demolished, but its very stones are ground to powder. Where once stood Sebastopol bidding proud defiance to rival systems is now a coast barren and blue: sandheaps behind and sandhills before. (*The Reader*, 20 May 1865, 562)

In spite of the pious efforts of Hamilton's biographer John Veitch and the ferocious counter-attacks of Mansel and McCosh, Pattison's verdict is not far from the truth. Hamilton's reputation as a philosopher is unlikely to revive; his ponderous and pedantic literary style deters the casual reader, while his attempt to marry the insights of Thomas Reid with those of Immanuel Kant carries no more conviction with philosophers late in the twentieth century than it did with commentators in the nineteenth. As a minor figure in the cultural, educational, and philosophical history of Britain, and by extension the United States, he remains, however, perennially interesting. Perhaps we should not mourn Hamilton's fate. Even in his own day, and even in the eyes of friendly commentators, his passion for overloading his philosophical essays with antiquarian references seemed astonishing. That he should himself have become interesting only to philosophers of essentially antiquarian tastes is no more than historical justice. A. RYAN

**Sources** A. Ryan, introduction, in J. S. Mill, *An examination of Sir William Hamilton's philosophy*, ed. J. M. Robson (1979), vol. 9 of *The collected works of John Stuart Mill*, ed. J. M. Robson and others (1963–91) · J. Veitch, *Memoir of Sir William Hamilton, bart.* (1869) · S. W. Rasmussen, *The philosophy of Sir William Hamilton: a study* (1925) · *DNB* · Foster, *Alum. Oxon.* · Burke, *Peerage* (1879) · *Hist. U. Oxf.* 6: *19th-cent. Oxf.*

**Archives** NL Scot., lecture notes · U. Edin. L., lecture notes · U. Glas. L., MSS collection | BL, corresp. with William Wordsworth, RP307 [copies] · Cornell University, Ithaca, New York, corresp. with William Wordsworth · NL Scot., letters, probably to John Cairns · NL Scot., corresp. with John Combe · NL Scot., corresp. with John Lee · U. Edin. L., letters to David Ramsey Hay · U. Edin. L., letters to David Laing

**Likenesses** H. J. Stewart, watercolour, 1845, Scot. NPG · J. C. Armytage, engraving (after J. Archer), repro. in Veitch, *Memoir*, frontispiece [*see illus.*] · J. Ballantyne, oils, Scot. NPG · W. Brodie, bust, U. Edin.

**Wealth at death** £4549 11*s.* 4*d.*: confirmation, NA Scot. (1856)

**Hamley, Edward** (*bap.* 1764, *d.* 1834), poet, the elder son of the Revd Thomas Hamley (*d.* 1766) of St Columb, Cornwall, and his wife, Mary, was baptized at St Columb Major on 25 October 1764. He matriculated from New College, Oxford, on 6 November 1783 and took his BCL degree on 6 December 1791. He was elected a fellow of his college on 5 November 1785, and then spent some time in Italy. In 1789 he published *Sonnets* anonymously. While residing in the Inner Temple, London, he published in 1795 a volume entitled *Poems of Various Kinds*. At this period he was in correspondence with Samuel Parr. He is often credited with the anonymously printed *Translations, Chiefly from the Italian of Petrarch and Metastasio*, which was actually the work of Thomas Le Mesurier, who acknowledged it as his in 1799 in *Poems, Chiefly Sonnets, by the Author of Translations from the Italian of Petrarch, Metastasio, and Zappi*. In 1795 Hamley wrote seventeen sonnets, which were later published in the *Poetical Register and Repository of Fugitive Poetry* at intervals between 1805 and 1809. He became rector of Cusop, Herefordshire, in 1805, and of Stanton St John, Oxfordshire, in 1806, and held both benefices until his death. He died, unmarried, at Stanton on 7 December 1834. G. C. BOASE, *rev.* REBECCA MILLS

**Sources** *IGI* · administration, PRO, PROB 6/210, fol. 164 · Foster, *Alum. Oxon.* · [J. Watkins and F. Shoberl], *A biographical dictionary of the living authors of Great Britain and Ireland* (1816) · *The clerical guide, or, Ecclesiastical directory* (1817), 52, 235 · Boase & Courtney, *Bibl. Corn.*, 1.206; 3.1215 · [D. Rivers], *Literary memoirs of living authors of Great Britain*, 1 (1798), 236 · *The works of Samuel Parr … with memoirs of his life and writings*, ed. J. Johnstone, 8 vols. (1828), vol. 8, p. 185 · Watt, *Bibl. Brit.*, 1.462

**Wealth at death** £1000 given to niece: administration, PRO, PROB 6/210, fol. 164

**Hamley, Sir Edward Bruce** (1824–1893), army officer and military writer, born at Bodmin, Cornwall, on 27 April 1824, was the fourth and youngest son of Vice-Admiral William Hamley (1786–1866) and his wife, Barbara, daughter of Charles Ogilvy of Lerwick, Shetland. William George Hamley was his elder brother. His father's family had been settled in Cornwall since the conquest, but their lands, which filled a page of Domesday Book, had passed from them.

**Education and character** Hamley apparently owed his literary ability to his mother. Educated at Bodmin grammar school, under the Revd L. J. Boor, he obtained a cadetship at the Royal Military Academy, Woolwich, on 19 November 1840, and was commissioned second-lieutenant, Royal Artillery, on 11 January 1843 and lieutenant on 15 September. Christopher North and Marshal Saxe were then favourite authors of his.

Hamley served a year in Ireland, then nearly four in Canada, devoting himself to reading and field sports. He had a notable love of animals, especially cats. Back in England he served at Tynemouth and Carlisle. He had to live on his pay, and having incurred debts he turned to writing to pay them off. His earliest papers, 'Snow pictures' and 'The peace campaigns of Ensign Faunce', appeared in *Fraser's Magazine* (1849–50). He was promoted second-captain on 12 May 1850, and joined his new battery at Gibraltar,

**Sir Edward Bruce Hamley (1824–1893)**, by unknown photographer

where he read much literature—Scott's novels were his favourites—and continued writing. A lady who knew him well there stated:

> He was very thin and angular, and looked much taller than he was … He came to the Rock with the reputation of being very clever, satirical, and given to drawing caricatures. … Most people stood in awe of him, owing to his silent ways and stiff manner, and from his taking but little part in things around him, and never taking the trouble to talk except to a few … He had a most tender heart behind his stiff manner, and many were the kind acts he did to the wives and children of his company. (Shand, 1.63–4)

His connection with *Blackwood's Magazine*, to which his eldest brother, William (a Royal Engineers officer), was already a contributor, began in 1851. His novel, *Lady Lee's Widowhood*, appeared in 1853, and was soon republished with drawings by himself, showing his artistic talent. A prolific writer, he published many and varied books and articles.

**The Crimean war** In March 1854 Colonel Richard Dacres, who commanded the artillery at Gibraltar, was given the command of the batteries of the 1st division in the army sent to Turkey. Hamley went with him as adjutant, and served throughout the war in the Crimea. At the Alma his horse was struck by a cannon-shot. At Inkerman his horse was killed, and he narrowly escaped being made prisoner. He had brought up three guns, and had placed them on the fore-ridge with a boldness and skill which seem to have attracted Todleben's notice. On the death of General Strangways, at Inkerman, the command of the artillery passed to Dacres; Hamley was his aide-de-camp until April

1856. He was mentioned in dispatches, was made brevet major on 12 December 1854 and brevet lieutenant-colonel on 2 November 1855, received a Légion d'honneur (fifth class) and a Mejidiye (fifth class), and was belatedly made a CB on 13 March 1867. He sent *Blackwood's* a series of letters from the Crimea, republished as *The Story of the Campaign of Sebastopol* (1855), vividly portraying the siege. In this, and in his 1856 *Blackwood's* article 'Lessons from the war', he defended the army against its 'ill-informed and ill-judging' civilian critics, alleging that its shortcomings resulted from politicians starving it of money and auxiliary services, and he rejected the accusations of incompetent command in the Crimea.

On his return home Hamley was quartered at Leith, and became a friend of John Blackwood. Through Blackwood he formed many literary friendships: with Aytoun, Warren, Bulwer Lytton, Thackeray, and others. 'He hated fools, he had no tolerance for presumption, and he could never endure self-complacent bores' (Shand, 1.122), but with men he liked he was a genial companion and brilliant talker. He hated music at dinner because it spoilt conversation. He edited the first series of *Tales from Blackwood* (from 1858), which included two of his Gibraltar tales.

Early in 1859 Hamley was appointed professor of military history at the new Staff College at Sandhurst, and remained there six years. His task was to explain military campaigns and their lessons. He was a competent lecturer, though a pedant. Evelyn Wood, one of his students, wrote that 'Colonel Hamley expected his pupils to accept his deductions as well as his facts, and did not encourage original research' (Wood, 215).

**The military historian** From his lectures Hamley wrote his great work *The Operations of War Explained and Illustrated* (1866). Strongly influenced by Jomini, Hamley was primarily concerned with strategy, and believed his subject could be rationally analysed and constant valid principles derived, from which could be deduced lessons for the future. Based on Jomini's rationale of operations and Archduke Charles's geographical analysis, Hamley's book clearly and didactically demonstrated the principles of strategy through descriptions of modern military campaigns, 'representative operations'. Concentrating largely on Marlburian, Frederician, and Napoleonic warfare, he showed little insight into the significance of tactical development in the most important recent war, the American Civil War: his idea of the modern battle was still essentially Napoleonic. As Jay Luvaas has commented, 'Hamley's approach was better calculated to reaffirm established truths than to discover new ones' (Luvaas, 141). Nevertheless *Operations of War* was a remarkable success and established Hamley's reputation as Britain's leading authority on military thought. It was adopted as a Staff College textbook, and in 1870 the second edition as a West Point textbook. The book was intended not only for military men. J. F. Maurice claimed that by it Hamley did 'more than any other Englishman to make known to English officers the value of a methodical treatment of the study of campaigns' (Maurice, *War*, 9). In 1872 Hamley published the third, revised edition, including the Austro-Prussian and Franco-Prussian wars, and advocating a separate corps of mounted riflemen. Five editions were published in his lifetime. However in the 1890s there was a reaction against the book and it was criticized by Spenser Wilkinson and by G. F. R. Henderson, who in 1898 (in the *Journal of the Royal United Service Institution*) alleged it was schematic and ignored the spirit of war, the commander's intentions, moral forces, and the effects of secrecy, rapidity, and surprise. After Hamley's death two more editions, revised by others, were published. The seventh and last (1923), revised by Sir George Aston, attempted to incorporate the lessons of the First World War. Aston claimed Hamley's book had 'stood the supreme test of the Great War'. However, the war, as Azar Gat has written, 'made the Napoleonic strategic model largely irrelevant and marked the final eclipse of both Jomini and Hamley' (Gat, 16).

Kinglake's *War in the Crimea* volumes 3 and 4 were reviewed anonymously by Hamley in the *Edinburgh Review* (October 1868), as he found more fault with them than would have suited Blackwood, their publisher. He became colonel in the army on 2 November 1863, and regimental lieutenant-colonel on 19 March 1864. The latter promotion sent him from Sandhurst to Dover; but on 1 April 1866 he was made a member of the council of military education, and for the next four years he lived in London, at the Albany and the Athenaeum. In 1869 he was made a member of the Literary Society, a small, select dining club. His love of animals was expressed in an article, 'Our poor relations' (*Blackwood's*, May 1870, 107.531–53), afterwards republished with illustrations by Ernest Griset.

The council of military education was dissolved on 31 March 1870. From July 1870 to December 1877 Hamley was commandant of the Staff College, probably his happiest period. He gave the college increased distinction and raised its status in the army. He infused a new spirit, making the course more thorough, outdoor, and practical, putting stress on riding, and carrying out extended reconnaissances. He took great care over the students and their work. He could not endure opposition, and expected subordinates and students to accept his views without question. Somewhat reserved, with little sense of humour, he did not suffer fools gladly. He was more prone to blame than praise, but did not stint praise when it was well earned.

**Later military career** Hamley became regimental colonel on 29 March 1873 and major-general on 1 October 1877 (antedated to 17 May 1869). A distinguished service pension was granted him on 20 December 1879. In March 1879 he was appointed British commissioner for the delimitation of Bulgaria, on the death of Colonel Robert Home. Hamley met with some hostility from the Eastern Roumelians, who wanted to be included in Bulgaria, and much obstruction from his Russian colleague; but his tact and judgement were praised by Lord Salisbury. He returned to England in October, and was made KCMG on 12 January 1880. He was similarly employed on the Armenian frontier in the summer of 1880, and on the new Greek frontier in the summer of 1881, receiving the thanks of the Foreign Office. The sultan promoted him to the Mejidiye (second class) in 1880, but he had to decline the order of the Saviour, offered by the king of Greece in 1881.

On 10 May 1882 Hamley became lieutenant-general, and in July he was offered the command of a division in the expedition under Sir Garnet Wolseley to Egypt [*see also* Wolseley ring (*act.* 1873–1890)]. He gladly accepted, eager to show he was no mere theorist. He embarked on 4 August, and landed at Alexandria on the 15th. Wolseley quickly came to strongly dislike his two infantry divisional commanders, Hamley and Lieutenant-General G. H. S. Willis, whom he considered had 'an overweening opinion of their own importance' (Lehmann, 303), and relations soon became strained. 'If I call myself a strategist, I ought to behave as such' (Luvaas, 155), Hamley had remarked some years before, and in that spirit he submitted to Wolseley a plan of operations based on a landing in Abu Qir Bay. Wolseley deliberately led him to believe that he was going to use it. He endorsed it, and set Hamley and his two brigadiers (Archibald Alison and Evelyn Wood) to operational planning based on it. When Wolseley put to sea with the 1st division on 19 August Hamley, given sealed orders, was left behind with his 2nd division, and found next morning that the true plan, an advance from Isma'iliyyah, had been concealed from him as from nearly every one else. Wolseley wrote to his wife of his deception of Hamley and his brigadiers, 'It is very amusing' (Maurice and Arthur, 149). Hamley, however, was bitter, convinced Wolseley had deliberately slighted him. He was further aggrieved that when he followed the rest of the force to Isma'iliyyah he had to leave one of his two brigades at Alexandria; and it was only after he protested that two battalions were assigned to him for the battle of Tell al-Kebir, as a provisional 2nd brigade.

That battle (13 September) afforded little scope for a general of division. Hamley accompanied the Highland brigade, to which fell the heaviest fighting, and was convinced that he and his troops had won the battle. When he found that Wolseley did not officially recognize this and gave no special praise to him, and that the only unit, the Royal Irish, specially mentioned was from the other division, Hamley was incensed. He wrote a report on the field, and supplemented it by another at Cairo; neither was published. Orders were received on 7 October that the two divisions should be broken up, and Hamley returned to England, further aggrieved at his recall. He was made KCB on 18 November, was included in the thanks of parliament, and received the Osmanieh (second class). He had been mentioned in dispatches. He saw the duke of Cambridge and Hugh Childers (then war minister) and corresponded with Wolseley, but failed to obtain the redress he wanted. Finally, to counter what he considered unwarranted suppression, he published his version, 'The second division at Tel-el-Kebir', in the *Nineteenth Century* (December 1882), claiming his command bore the brunt of the fighting and had the heaviest casualties. This provoked Wolseleyite replies and controversy, which revived in 1895 with Alexander Shand's biography of Hamley. In his last years Hamley continued bitterly critical of Wolseley.

Probably because he had offended Wolseley and the Wolseleyites, Hamley had no further official employment. However, he was widely considered ill-used, and Tennyson linked his name with the 'Charge of the heavy brigade' in 1883. He was Conservative MP for Birkenhead from 1885 to 1892. When Salisbury formed his government in July 1886 Hamley wanted to be surveyor-general of the ordnance, but was disappointed. While supporting the government he candidly criticized official shortcomings, and took a weighty part in discussions on Indian and United Kingdom defence. He championed the volunteers, speaking repeatedly on their behalf, advocating increased expenditure and improved training, and the construction of defensive works around London. He believed there was a real danger of war and invasion, and the volunteers would be crucial. He lectured on Indian defence at the United Service Institution in 1878 and 1884, and in April 1885 gave a lecture there, 'Volunteers in time of need', advocating an increased capitation grant for their field equipment. He published articles on defence in the *Nineteenth Century*, collected in book form as *National Defence* (1899). He became a colonel-commandant of the Royal Artillery on 7 December 1886, and accepted the honorary colonelcy of the 2nd Middlesex artillery volunteers on 5 November 1887. At this time he would have been placed on the retired list in consequence of non-employment, but in deference to public opinion (see *Punch*, 24 Sept 1887) he was specially retained on the active list as a supernumerary until 30 July 1890, when he became general. In 1890 he wrote his masterly one-volume *War in the Crimea*, essentially repeating the views in his 1855 *Blackwood's* letters.

After suffering much for several years from bronchial disorder, exacerbated by London smoke and fogs, Hamley died at 40 Porchester Terrace, Bayswater, London, on 12 August 1893, and was buried in Brompton cemetery, London. He had never married, but after the death of his brother Charles in 1863 had virtually adopted the latter's only daughter, Barbara. Hamley was tall and slightly built. From the 1870s, contrary to army regulations, he wore with uniform a full beard. He was reserved and not always conciliatory, 'nothing of a courtier, and much of a critic' (Shand, 1.xlviii). Allegedly he was autocratic, and of a violent and vindictive temper. The *Athenaeum* obituary claimed he was

> A singularly able man, and highly accomplished, with wide knowledge, wide sympathies, and strong opinions of his own, he would probably have attained higher fame if he had been less versatile. … He was an excellent draughtsman; although essentially self-centred, an admirable actor; he was a skilful sportsman, and a man who could defy fatigue, and who seemed to like hardships.

He wrote for both the army and the civilian public. According to Jay Luvaas, 'there is something enigmatic about Hamley; despite his obvious popularity and success he was in many respects—probably most in his own estimation—a partial failure' (Luvaas, 164). Nevertheless he was probably the most renowned British military writer of the nineteenth century, and among the most influential. E. M. LLOYD, *rev.* ROGER T. STEARN

**Sources** A. I. Shand, *The life of General Sir Edward Bruce Hamley*, 2 vols. (1895) • J. Luvaas, *The education of an army: British military thought, 1815–1940*, new edn (1965) • B. Bond, *The Victorian army and the Staff College, 1854–1914* (1972) • A. Gat, *The development of military thought: the nineteenth century* (1992) • *The Times* (15 Aug 1893) • Mrs Oliphant, *William Blackwood and his sons* (1897), vol. 2 of *Annals of a publishing house* (1897–8) • Mrs G. Porter, *John Blackwood* (1898), vol. 3 of *Annals of a publishing house* (1897–8) • A. W. Kinglake, *The invasion of the Crimea*, [new edn], 9 vols. (1877–88) • J. F. Maurice, *Military history of the campaign of 1882 in Egypt* (1887) • F. Maurice, 'Sir E. Hamley and Lord Wolseley [2 pts]', *United Service Magazine*, 3rd ser., 11 (1895), 414–34, 439–63 • *Contemporary Review*, 68 (Aug 1895) • E. Wood, *From midshipman to field marshal*, 2 vols. (1906) • Lord Sydenham of Combe [G. S. Clarke], *My working life* (1927) • I. F. W. Beckett, *Riflemen form: a study of the rifle volunteer movement, 1859–1908* (1982) • E. M. Spiers, *The late Victorian army, 1868–1902* (1992) • *The Athenaeum* (19 Aug 1893), 261–2 • J. F. Maurice, *War* (1891) • J. H. Lehmann, *All Sir Garnet: a biography of Field-Marshal Lord Wolseley* (1964) • F. Maurice and G. Arthur, *The life of Lord Wolseley* (1924) • B. Bond, ed., *Victorian military campaigns* (1967) • W. S. Hamer, *The British army: civil–military relations, 1885–1905* (1970)

**Archives** NL Scot., corresp. with Blackwoods, articles • Yale U., Beinecke L., letters to Frederick Locker-Lampson

**Likenesses** J. W. Gordon, oils, *c*.1856, Staff College, Camberley • Ape [C. Pellegrini], chromolithograph, NPG; repro. in *VF* (2 April 1887) • chromolithograph, BM • photograph, NPG [*see illus.*] • portraits, repro. in Shand, *Life of General Sir Edward Bruce Hamley* • wood-engraving, NPG; repro. in *ILN* (12 Aug 1882)

**Wealth at death** £6528 1*s*. 11*d*.: probate, 8 Sept 1893, *CGPLA Eng. & Wales*

**Hamlyn, Emma Warburton** (1860–1941), benefactor, born at 4 Abbey Crescent, Torbay Road, Torquay, on 5 November 1860, was the only child of William Bussell Hamlyn (1836–1919) and his wife, Emma Gorsuch Warburton (*d*. 1913). She claimed descent from an old Devon family mentioned in the Domesday Book, but her immediate forebears were of modest social status. Her father, born in Torquay, began as a law clerk and was admitted a solicitor in 1877. He practised on his own in Newton Abbot and Torquay. A Methodist and political Liberal, he was a respected and cultivated but retiring figure who became a justice of the peace and a member of the influential Devonshire Association. Her mother also came from Torquay.

During her father's lifetime Emma travelled extensively in Europe and the Mediterranean and become interested in the relation between the law and the culture of the countries she visited. This explains the otherwise mysterious reference to ethnology in her will. She never married and was not active in Methodist circles. When her father died she inherited his estate. She seems not to have travelled afterwards, but with her wide interests, which included literature, music, and art, remained quietly in the family home at Ilsham, known as Widecombe Cottage, receiving visitors, some of them from abroad, and reading widely until her death at the age of eighty.

In 1939 Emma Hamlyn made a will leaving the residue of her estate, which in the end amounted to some £15,000, to her executors on trust. The trustees were to apply the income

> in the furtherance by lectures or otherwise among the Common People of this Country of the knowledge of the Comparative Jurisprudence and the Ethnology of the Chief European countries including our own and the circumstances of the growth of such jurisprudence to the intent that the Common People of our Country may realise the privileges which in law and custom they enjoy in comparison with other European Peoples and realising and appreciating such privileges may recognize the responsibilities and obligations attaching to them.
> (C. Palley, *United Kingdom and Human Rights*, 1991, xi)

The phrasing was her own and, though pressed by her solicitors, who thought it unduly vague, she resisted all attempts to have it altered. The trust was held to be valid and the court of chancery in 1948 approved a scheme for its administration.

Largely through the energy of Professor Murray, principal of the University College of the South West, a series of annual lectures was set up in 1949. The first Hamlyn lectures, published as *Freedom under the Law*, were delivered by Mr Justice (later Lord) Denning in that year and were widely acclaimed. Despite the meagre resources of the trust, a series of eminent judges, professors, and practitioners have been eager to follow his example. Almost overnight the Hamlyn lectures became the most prestigious series of law lectures in Britain, though not every lecturer has felt able to share the patriotic, indeed triumphalist, spirit of the bequest.

A cousin described Emma Hamlyn as an Edwardian lady, autocratic and intellectual, who wore long dresses and large, dark hats, with semi-herbaceous borders for trimming. Widely read and a good pianist, she was comfortably off but not rich. Her conviction that comparative study would confirm the superiority of the law of England (which was clearly the country she had in mind rather than, as the court of chancery held, the United Kingdom) represents a strand in English thought that her bequest has done much to uphold. No drawing or photograph of this very private person has been traced. She died at her home, Widecombe Cottage, Barrington Road, Torquay, on 1 September 1941. TONY HONORÉ

**Sources** C. Stebbings, 'The Hamlyn legacy', in C. Palley, *The United Kingdom and human rights* (1991), xiii–xx • A. L. Diamond, in Lord Hailsham of St Marylebone [Q. Hogg], *Hamlyn revisited* (1983), xi–xii • *CGPLA Eng. & Wales* (1941)

**Wealth at death** £19,521 10*s*. 9*d*.: probate, 12 Nov 1941, *CGPLA Eng. & Wales*

**Hammersley, James Astbury** (1818–1867), landscape painter, was born at Burslem, Staffordshire, the son of John Hammersley and his wife, Frances. He was baptized on 8 November 1818 at Hanley, Staffordshire. He was a pupil of the landscape painter James Baker Pyne (1800–1870). He lived near Newcastle under Lyme and then in the late 1840s in Nottingham, where he was teacher in the local government school of design. Hammersley served as headmaster of the Manchester School of Design from May 1849 until 31 December 1862. Having taken an active part in its formation, he was elected the first president of the Manchester Academy of Fine Arts on 28 May 1857, ending his term on 30 December 1861. Hammersley exhibited three paintings at the Royal Academy from 1846 to 1848, and from 1842 until 1858 showed three works at the British Institution and ten at the Society of British Artists. He was best known for views in Wales and Cheshire, and in the 1850s exhibited a number of scenes in the Swiss Alps. *Mountain and Clouds—a Scene from the Top of Loughrigg, Westmoreland* of 1850, a view which he painted frequently, was given by the artist to the Royal Manchester Institution in 1851 (transferred to the Manchester City Art Gallery in 1882). It is characteristic of his style, marked by the influence of J. M. W. Turner (1775–1851). About 1848 Prince Albert commissioned him to travel to Germany to paint the prince's birthplace, the castle of Rosenau, and also *Drachenfels, from Bonn*, a panoramic view on the Rhine of the Siebengebirge, or Seven Mountains, seen from the garden of the Hotel Royal, near where Albert attended university. The latter was engraved by R. Brandard for *The Royal Gallery*, volume 4. In 1850 Hammersley delivered an address at Nottingham, later published, 'Preparations on the continent for the Great Exhibition of 1851, and the condition of the continental schools of art'. An article entitled 'Exhibition of art treasures of the United Kingdom' was published in the *Manchester Papers* in 1856 in advance of the Manchester Art Treasures exhibition of 1857. He was chairman of the exhibition of local art in Peel Park, Manchester, that ran concurrently with the Art Treasures exhibition. Hammersley died at 163 Bury New Road, Cheetham, Manchester, on 11 March 1867, and was buried at St John's Church, Higher Broughton, Manchester. JASON ROSENFELD

**Sources** Wood, *Vic. painters*, 3rd edn • *DNB* • S. C. Hall, ed., *The Royal Gallery of Art, ancient and modern*, 4 (1859) • *Concise catalogue of British paintings*, Man. City Gall., 1 (1976) • J. Johnson, ed., *Works exhibited at the Royal Society of British Artists, 1824–1893, and the New English Art Club, 1888–1917*, 2 vols. (1975) • Graves, *RA exhibitors*, vol. 3 • Redgrave, *Artists* • S. H. Pavière, *A dictionary of Victorian landscape painters* (1968) • M. H. Grant, *A dictionary of British landscape painters, from the 16th century to the early 20th century* (1952) • archive material, Courtauld Inst., Witt Library • *IGI* • d. cert.

**Hammerton, Sir John Alexander** (1871–1949), author and editor of reference works, was born in Alexandria, Dunbartonshire, on 27 February 1871, the second in a family of two sons and one daughter of James Hammerton (1832/3–1874/5), clog maker of Oldham, and his second wife, Janet (*b.* 1841/2), shopwoman, daughter of Alexander Lang, mason. His father died when he was aged three, and the family, then living in Manchester, returned to the home of their maternal grandmother in Scotland. He attended first the Freeland School, Glasgow, and then Alexander's endowed school in the same city. As the breadwinner in the family, he left school at fourteen, and for the next four years he was apprenticed as a sculptor and tomb-cutter to the firm of stonemasons J. & G. Mossman. During this time he attended evening classes at the City School and at Glasgow University. He was known to his friends as Sandy.

The most successful creator of large-scale works of reference that Britain has known, Hammerton began his journalistic career in 1889 as a reporter on the Scottish temperance paper *The Reformer*. His light, humorous sketches began to appear regularly in London newspapers and in periodicals such as *Punch*. A succession of posts in journalism took him to Bolton, Blackpool, Nottingham, and Birmingham. While working in Blackpool, he married, on 3 January 1895, Rhoda (1871/2–1948), daughter of Colin Gibb Lawrence, of Glasgow. In 1900 he settled in London, where his lively, robust style of writing caught the eye of the founder of modern popular journalism, Alfred Harmsworth. In 1905 Hammerton was invited to join Harmsworth's Amalgamated Press, then the largest periodical-publishing empire in the world, and for the next seventeen years his employer's energetic and 'radium-like personality', as described by Hammerton, provided him with the background to his life's work. Of the more than ten million bound editions that bear his name as editor or author, he was proudest of the fortnightly *Harmsworth's Universal Encyclopedia* (1920–22) which, under the slogan of 'a penny a day's subscription', sold twelve million copies throughout the English-speaking world and was translated into six languages, including Japanese.

Sir John Alexander Hammerton (1871–1949), by Howard Coster, 1945

In 1911–13 Hammerton lived in Buenos Aires, where he edited *El diccionario encyclopédico Hispano-Americano*. He also wrote under pseudonyms, most notably a novel, *The Call of the Town* (1904), light reminiscences, and biographies of, among others, Arthur Mee and Sir J. M. Barrie. Despite the shortage of paper and the requisitioning of most commercial photographic glass negatives for the war effort, he was never happier, as he recounts in his autobiography, *Books and Myself* (1944), than during those days in the First World War when he worked late into the night to the background of a pavement barrel-organ in the Farringdon Road, alert to imminent air attacks on the city.

Hammerton's formative influence as a boy had been John Cassell's *Popular Educator*, first published in 1852. In 1934 he was able to consummate, in his own words, 'one of the romances of modern publishing', by revising and reissuing the work under the new title *Practical Knowledge for All*, which was, in turn, to become the most familiar series of educational books in millions of homes for a new generation.

To Hammerton's gifts of communication must also be attributed that most popular of all gestures of the twentieth century: the 'V' sign. In late 1940 he reported in the *War Illustrated* his sighting of a 'V' for victory sign apparently blazed by a Hawker Hurricane in the sky over the village of Firle in Sussex. Within months the sign had replaced the customary 'thumbs-up' and had been adopted throughout beleaguered Europe as a symbol of defiance to Nazism.

A lifelong enthusiast of the stage, Hammerton first fell under the spell of music-hall as a boy in Glasgow; from then on he attended performances of all the great variety artists of the day, and for a brief spell managed his own theatre company in Eastbourne. In 1926 he settled near Eastbourne, where he became a familiar sight driving at speed in his superb Lagonda through the Sussex lanes.

Hammerton was knighted in 1932 and was subsequently made a fellow of the Royal Society of Arts and of the Royal Society of Edinburgh. After his first wife's death in 1948 he married on 12 February 1949 his long-time friend and collaborator, the actress and journalist (Kate) Janet Maitland (*b.* 1878/9), daughter of Charles Dallas Alexander, of independent means, and widow of the actor Lauderdale Maitland. He died on 12 May 1949 at the Mayfair Hotel in Westminster, London.

BRIDGET HADAWAY, *rev.*

**Sources** J. A. Hammerton, *Books and myself* (1944) • J. A. Hammerton, *With Northcliffe in Fleet Street* (1932) • R. Pound and G. Harmsworth, *Northcliffe* (1959) • b. cert. • m. certs. • d. cert. • *CGPLA Eng. & Wales* (1949)
**Archives** U. Birm., letters to W. H. Dawson | FILM BFI NFTVA, performance footage
**Likenesses** H. Coster, photograph, 1945, NPG [*see illus.*]
**Wealth at death** £108,088 2*s.* 9*d.*: probate, 14 Oct 1949, *CGPLA Eng. & Wales*

**Hammett, James** (1811–1891). *See under* Tolpuddle Martyrs (*act.* 1834–*c.*1845).

**Hammick, Sir Stephen Love, first baronet** (1777–1867), surgeon, the eldest son of Stephen Hammick, surgeon and alderman of Plymouth, and Elizabeth Margaret, only child of John Love, surgeon, of Plymouth Dock, was born on 28 February 1777 in Plymouth. He began his medical studies under his father at the Royal Naval Hospital, Plymouth, in 1792, and the following year was appointed assistant surgeon there. In 1799 he went to London, and on 7 February of the following year he married Frances (*d.* 1829), the only daughter of Peter Turquand, a merchant of London, and his wife, Eliza. They had two sons and a daughter.

After studying for a few months at St George's Hospital, Hammick became a member of the Company of Surgeons on 3 October 1799. He then returned to Plymouth, and was elected full surgeon to the Royal Naval Hospital in 1803. Although the rules of the hospital forbade him from taking private patients, he frequently gave opinions in difficult cases, and thereby made many influential friends, among whom were Lord and Lady Holland. He was surgeon-extraordinary to George IV, as prince of Wales, prince regent, and king. In 1829 Hammick moved to Cavendish Square, London, and was soon appointed surgeon-extraordinary to the household of William IV. His practice as a surgeon in London was small but lucrative. Hammick was an original member of the senate of the University of London, and was for some years an examiner in surgery there. On 25 July 1834 he was made a baronet, and in 1843 he was appointed an honorary fellow of the Royal College of Surgeons.

Among Hammick's published works were two essays, 'The practice of Dr. Leach in low fever' and 'On the treatment of syphilis by nitrous acid', in Thomas Beddoes's *Contributions to Physical and Medical Knowledge* (1799); and he published many of the lectures he delivered at the Royal Naval Hospital, as *Practical Remarks on Amputations, Fractures, and Strictures of the Urethra* (1830), a book based on wide experience and valued in its day. While at Plymouth Hammick had also formed a useful collection of preparations, particularly rich in specimens of injuries and diseases of the bones, which he presented to the Royal College of Surgeons.

Hammick died at his home, 17 The Crescent, Plymouth, on 15 June 1867 and was succeeded in the baronetcy by his second son, the Revd St Vincent Love Hammick (1806–1888). His eldest son, Stephen Love Hammick (1804–1839) MD, author of *Practical and Experimental Chemistry Adopted to Arts and Manufactures* (1838), was one of the Radcliffe travelling fellows of the University of Oxford.

GORDON GOODWIN, *rev.* JEFFREY S. REZNICK

**Sources** *The Lancet* (22 June 1867), 783–4 • Foster, *Alum. Oxon.* • Burke, *Peerage* • *GM*, 4th ser., 4 (1867), 243–4 • *London Medical Directory* (1846), 67–8 • *CGPLA Eng. & Wales* (1867)
**Archives** U. Durham, archives and special collections, letters to Henry George, third Earl Grey
**Wealth at death** under £35,000: probate, 15 July 1867, *CGPLA Eng. & Wales*

**Hammond**. *See also* Hamond.

**Hammond, Anthony** (1668–1738), politician, was born on 1 September 1668, the eldest son of Anthony Hammond (1641–1680), a country gentleman, and his wife, Amy Browne (*d.* 1693). His paternal grandfather, Anthony Hammond of St Alban's Court, Kent, was the elder brother of William Hammond. In August 1694 he married Jane (*d.*

1749), the daughter of Sir Walter Clarges, bt. Charles Hopkins dedicated a poem to him on the occasion of his marriage, lamenting that it took him away from friends such as himself, Congreve, Moyle, Southerne, and Wycherley. Hammond had thus commenced a career as a poet before he entered politics (some of his poems, such as an 'Ode on Solitude', previously published anonymously, he identified in *A New Miscellany of Original Poems*, published in 1720). Their second son, James *Hammond, was also a politician and poet.

Hammond's father's estate was at Somersham Place in Huntingdonshire, for which county he was returned as a knight of the shire in 1695. He fought a duel with Lord William Pawlet in January 1698 over the merits of an election petition for Cambridgeshire. In the general election of 1698 he was returned for Cambridge University, and following his election he received the degree of MA from the university and was elected a fellow of the Royal Society (November 1698). In an anonymous tract, *Considerations upon the Choice of a Speaker of the House of Commons in the Approaching Session*, he urged members not to vote for Sir Edward Seymour, whom he described as an 'old prostitute of the exploded parliament of Charles the second's reign', but to support a country candidate against the court, presumably Paul Foley. In the event Sir Thomas Littleton, a nominee of the whig junto, was elected. Hammond sat for the university again in the next parliament, returned in January 1701. Following the electoral campaign of the New East India Company, which was accused of corruption when the session began, he wrote *Considerations upon Corrupt Elections of Members to Serve in Parliament* (1701). Up to this point his political stance was that of a country politician, and his country credentials were recognized when he was appointed as a commissioner for stating the public accounts in June 1701. Although his lifelong friendship with the republican Walter Moyle, contracted in 1690, suggests that he was not unsympathetic to country whig views, he was himself a country tory, and was 'known for his noisy tory eloquence' (*Reliquiae*, 2.290). During 1701, indeed, he achieved notoriety as one of three leading tories who were discovered at the Blew Posts tavern in the company of Monsieur Poussin, a French envoy who had been ordered by the government to leave England. The Poussineers, as they were called, were named in a black list of tories drawn up by the whigs for the general election of December 1701.

Hammond stood once more at Cambridge but was defeated. After Anne's accession in 1702 he became a commissioner of the navy and was returned to parliament from Huntingdon in July. This gravitation towards the court doubtless stemmed from his self-confessed 'ambition' and 'regard for the main chance'. It also led to his politics seeming inconsistent. As he himself observed,

> in public affairs he is naturally moderate, something uncertain in his opinions, from which two causes he has been thought to be of both sides or sometimes of one and sometimes of the other, tho' as to the Jacobites in his heart he never was inclined to them. (Bodl. Oxf., MS Rawl. D. 174, fol. 87)

He did not stand for parliament in 1705, but in 1708 was returned on the court interest at New Shoreham. However, the new whig-dominated parliament decided by a majority of eighteen that his office as a commissioner of the navy serving in the outports was incompatible with membership of the Commons according to the place clause in the Regency Act of 1706, and he had to vacate his seat.

In 1711 Hammond was appointed deputy paymaster of the British forces serving in Spain. His conduct was criticized by the duke of Argyll but defended by the paymaster James Brydges. He was out of England from 3 July 1711 until 25 January 1717, except for a short visit 'during the time of the Rebellion in 1715' (Bodl. Oxf., MS Rawl. A. 245, fol. 74). According to Thomas Hearne, Hammond was 'said to have attempted the life of the chevalier on his Scotch embarcation' (*Reliquiae*, 2.290). In 1721 he published *A modest apology occasion'd by the late unhappy turn of affairs with relation to publick credit*. This urged restraint and justice in opposition to writers such as Thomas Gordon and John Trenchard, who, in *Cato's Letters*, were calling for the trial and executions of those responsible for the South Sea Bubble. He even defended Walpole's handling of the national finances, claiming that in 1721 the revenues 'fell into the channel in which they have ever since so happily and quietly continued' (*The National Debt as it Stood at Michaelmas 1730 Stated and Explained*, 1731, 7). By then his own finances were in so deplorable a state that he had voluntarily entered king's bench as a prisoner for debt and, as Hearne caustically put it, 'prostituter of his pen for bread' (*Reliquiae*, 2.290). He died there in 1738. W. A. Speck

**Sources** *DNB* · N. Luttrell, *A brief historical relation of state affairs from September 1678 to April 1714*, 6 vols. (1857) · *Reliquiae Hearnianae: the remains of Thomas Hearne*, ed. P. Bliss, 2nd edn, 3 vols. (1869) · Bodl. Oxf., MSS Rawl. A. 245, fol. 68; D. 174, fol. 87 · *A full and true relation of a horrid and detestable conspiracy* [1701] · *A vindication of Dr Charles Davenant, Anthony Hammond and John Tredenham* (1701)

**Archives** BL, pocket book, Add. MS 22584 | Bodl. Oxf., MSS Rawl. A.245, D.174, D.1202

**Wealth at death** debtor in king's bench prison: *Reliquae Hearnianae*, ed. Bliss · debtor in Fleet prison: *DNB*

**Hammond** [*formerly* Ewbanke], **Anthony** (1758–1838), legal writer and barrister, was born on 30 September 1758 at Richmond, Yorkshire, son of John Ewbanke (*d.* 1789) and his wife, Jane Hammond (1724–1803). In 1773, in accordance with the will of his great-uncle Peter Hammond and as a condition of inheriting his estate at Spennithorne, Yorkshire, Anthony took the surname of Hammond. He matriculated from Trinity College, Cambridge, in 1776 but did not graduate. He was admitted to Lincoln's Inn on 9 April 1777. Hammond initially practised as a special pleader at the Inner Temple and was later called to the bar in 1827. He married at Richmond, on 21 October 1790, Jane (*d.* 1835), daughter of John Close, clerk of assize for the northern circuit and bencher of Lincoln's Inn. They had eight children.

Hammond quit practice as a special pleader in 1819 because of ill health, but it was his (at first) secondary career as a writer on the law that was to prove more significant. By this time he had published several pedestrian, highly technical works on pleading and practice. These were: *The Law of Nisi prius* (1816), *Parties to Actions* (1817), and *Principles of Pleading* (1819). Later works included *Reports in Equity* (1821), *Analytical Digest to the Term Reports and Others* (1824), and *Practice and Proceedings in Parliament* (1825). Hammond's more general interest in the law's form was first demonstrated with the publication of his *Scheme of a digest of the laws of England, with introductory essays on the science of natural jurisprudence* (1820), which set out a utilitarian based reformist treatment of the principles of criminal responsibility and punishment. More significantly, in 1823 Hammond published *The Criminal Code, Including a Digest, Consolidation and Collection of Statutes* illustrating how the criminal law might be consolidated into a more accessible state. The digest on forgery incorporated in his 1823 *Criminal Code* formed the draft code digest appended to the radical 1824 report of the Commons select committee appointed to consider the expediency of consolidating and amending English criminal law. Hammond spent the subsequent five years preaching statutory consolidation and the highly contentious Benthamite cause of comprehensive codification of the common law.

Hammond's campaign was linked to Robert Peel's gradualist consolidation programme of criminal law statutes carried out between 1825 and the early 1830s. Through a combination of Hammond's assertive self-promotion and Stephen Lushington's active support, Peel agreed to Hammond's assisting Home Office draftsmen in the production of draft consolidation legislation. From the arrangement's inception friction between the parties was evident. This followed Hammond's conception of his role as being far more extensive than that intended by Peel. In 1826 Hammond published a comprehensive, highly discursive, criminal code of forgery, grandly styled as 'printed by direction of the Right Honourable Robert Peel, Secretary of State for the Home Office Department, as (amongst the purposes) the Basis of the Consolidation and Amendment of the Criminal Law'. Rather than consolidatory measures previously promised Peel, Hammond's forgery code was a full-blooded critique of the forgery laws with a code digest 'reducing the Common or Unwritten law to Writing and bringing the Criminal Jurisprudence of this Country, Common and Statutory into a Single Law'. The mismatch between Peel's modest consolidation aims and Hammond's ambitious codifying strategy produced a public rebuke of Hammond by Peel in February 1827, appearing in *The Globe*, 9 February 1827, and *The Times*, 10 February 1827, with Peel emphatically denying Hammond's claimed authority to draft codification measures combining statute and common law. In addition to his forgery code of 1826 Hammond published codes on coining (1825), burglary (1826), and larceny (1828 and 1829). His final published work in this area, *On the Reduction to Writing of the Criminal Law* (1829), contained a slashing attack on the legal profession's perceived inertia and self-interested obstructionism in relation to law reform. Hammond's enormous industry in producing criminal codes resulted in no obvious influence on Peel's gradualist consolidation legislation. Hammond's work is best viewed as a distinctive element in the law reform movement leading to Lord Chancellor Brougham's 1833 appointment of the criminal law commissioners charged with considering the expediency of what amounted to codifying all sources of the criminal law.

Hammond died on 27 January 1838 at Richmond; he was also senior deputy lieutenant of the North Riding of Yorkshire. K. J. M. SMITH

**Sources** BL, Peel MSS, Add. MSS 40380, fol. 198; 40383, fols. 17–19; 40384, fols. 102–4; 40389, fols. 15–18; 40392, fol. 170 • PRO, HO 84/2, letters, 2 Feb and 3 Nov 1825; 43/34, letters, 2 Jan–9 Jan, 8 Feb–27 Feb • PRO, T 38/15, fol. 112; 16, fols. 67, 477; 17, fol. 45; T 28, 18, fol. 112 • K. J. M. Smith, 'Anthony Hammond "Mr Surface": Peel's persistent codifier', *Journal of Legal History*, 20 (1999), 24–44 • Burke, *Gen. GB* (1849), 3.146 • Venn, *Alum. Cant.* • *Clarke's New Law List* (1829), 28 • *GM*, 2nd ser., 9 (1838), 334 • 'Select committee on … the criminal law of England', *Parl. papers* (1824), 4.41, no. 205 • W. W. Rouse Ball and J. A. Venn, eds., *Admissions to Trinity College, Cambridge*, 3 (1911), 249

**Archives** BL, Peel MSS, Add. MSS 40380, fol. 198; 40383, fols. 17–19; 40384, fols. 102–4; 40389, fols. 15–18, 40392; fol. 170 • PRO, HO 84/2, HO 43/34 • PRO, T 38/15, T 38/16, T 38/17, T 28/18

**Hammond, (Lucy) Barbara** (1873–1961). *See under* Hammond, (John) Lawrence Le Breton (1872–1949).

**Hammond, Edmund**, Baron Hammond (1802–1890), diplomatist, was born on 25 June 1802 at Spring Gardens, London, the third and youngest son of George *Hammond (1763–1853), diplomatist, from Kirk Ella in the East Riding of Yorkshire, and his wife, Margaret Allen (*d.* 1838), daughter of Andrew Allen, attorney-general of Pennsylvania, USA. He was educated at Eton College (1812–15) and Harrow (1816) and matriculated at University College, Oxford, in 1820. He graduated with a third in classics in 1823. Subsequently he proceeded MA in 1826 and retained his college connections until 1846, first as a scholar and then as a fellow. On 3 January 1846 he married Mary Frances (1815–1888), daughter of Lord Robert Kerr, fourth son of the fifth marquess of Lothian. They had three daughters. The family residence was at 25 Eaton Place, London.

Hammond's father, a career diplomat who had been the first British minister accredited to the USA, was a close personal and political friend of George Canning and served him as under-secretary in the Foreign Office. Canning's patronage was extended to the youngest son and Edmund was appointed to a clerkship in the Foreign Office in April 1824, transferring from the Privy Council Office, where he had been a clerk since October 1823. He subsequently spent his entire working life in the Foreign Office, retiring after nearly fifty years' service. During this time his extraordinary energy and determination took him to the top of his profession, where, as permanent under-secretary from 1854 to 1873, he came to personify the Victorian Foreign Office. His appointment as permanent under-secretary in 1854, however, owed more to Lord Clarendon's failure to persuade his brother-in-law Sir George Cornewall Lewis to accept the position than to Hammond's merits. It was equally fortuitous that successive foreign secretaries after Lord Palmerston all sat in the House of Lords, so that the other under-secretary was

**Edmund Hammond, Baron Hammond** (1802–1890), by Henry Weekes, 1874

required to be a politician who could represent the Foreign Office in the House of Commons. Thus in Hammond's time the convention was established that the permanent under-secretary should be appointed from within the ranks of the profession, should retain his position irrespective of changes in government, and should be the head of the Foreign Office.

The unique and peculiar position that the Foreign Office came to occupy in Victorian public administration (where it became known as 'a study in resistance') owed much to Hammond's intractable and unyielding conservatism. As head of the Foreign Office, he became its spokesman and sternly resisted the tides of administrative reform that washed up against his department after the publication of the Northcote–Trevelyan report. In dismissing the distinction between intellectual and mechanical work that lay at the heart of the Northcote–Trevelyan reforms, Hammond explained to the civil service commissioners that all the Foreign Office required from a candidate for a clerkship was that he should 'be able to write a good bold hand, forming each letter distinctly' (Jones, 45). Hammond believed in keeping the Foreign Office distinct from the diplomatic service. He had no good opinion of the younger diplomats: 'neither the public nor the office gain by making it a profession', he once said to Henry Layard (Jones, 108), and he would have liked to retain the older system of unpaid voluntary service.

As permanent under-secretary, Hammond controlled the work of four of the five political divisions of the Foreign Office. He established a particularly close relationship with the Turkish department, which also managed affairs with Russia and was regarded as the most important division in the office. He also maintained a close and personal control of the Far Eastern business of the American department. The French and Spanish divisions were also his, which left only the German department to the parliamentary under-secretary. For this work Hammond was paid a salary of £2000 per annum, which was supplemented by £500 for the administration of the Foreign Secret Service Fund. He was not a policy maker, however; his duty was 'to advise and recommend' to the secretary of state 'what he thought should be done' (Anderson, 100). He was never a partner with his secretary of state and while his advice may have carried some weight with Lord Clarendon and Lord Granville, it carried less with Lord John Russell. His most significant contribution to the execution of British foreign policy lay in the extensive private correspondence he maintained with British representatives abroad. The story often told against Hammond that, two weeks before the outbreak of the Franco-Prussian War, he told Lord Granville that the world had never been so profoundly at peace can be safely laid to rest, for Hammond specifically excepted the tension between France and Germany from his general remarks.

After his retirement in 1873, Hammond was raised to the peerage as Baron Hammond of Kirkella (22 February 1874). He was the first Foreign Office official to receive such an honour and it caused a number of raised eyebrows, but the honour recognized, rather ironically, that under Hammond the Foreign Office had left behind its early phase of aristocratic amateurism and had become a professional bureaucracy. Hammond died at the Villa Charles, at Menton in the south of France, of paralysis on 29 April 1890, his wife having died two years earlier, on 14 June 1888. He was buried at Old Malden, Surrey.

R. A. JONES

**Sources** M. A. Anderson, 'Edmund Hammond, permanent under-secretary of state for foreign affairs, 1854–1873', PhD diss., U. Lond., 1956 · R. Jones, *The nineteenth-century foreign office: an administrative history* (1971) · C. R. Middleton, *The administration of British foreign policy, 1782–1846* (1977) · E. Hertslet, *Recollections of the old foreign office* (1901) · *The Times* (30 April 1890) · *FO List* (1890), 114–15 · *Foreign Office, diplomatic and consular sketches: reprinted from Vanity Fair* (1883), 19–24 · GEC, *Peerage*

**Archives** NRA, priv. coll., corresp. and papers · PRO, corresp. and papers, FO 391 | BL, corresp. with W. E. Gladstone, Add. MS 44183 · BL, corresp. with Sir A. Layard, Add. MSS 38951–38993 · BL, dispatches from Sir Augustus Paget, Add. MS 51230 · BL, corresp. with Lord Wodehouse, Add. MS 46694 · Bodl. Oxf., Clarendon MSS · Bodl. Oxf., corresp. with Sir John Crampton · Bodl. Oxf., corresp. with Lord Kimberley · Herts. ALS, letters to earl of Lytton · LPL, corresp. with A. C. Tait · Norfolk RO, corresp. with Sir Henry Lytton Bulwer · NRA, priv. coll., letters to John Macpherson-Grant · PRO, corresp. with Stratford Canning, FO 352 · PRO, corresp. with Lord Cowley, FO 519 · PRO, corresp. with second Earl Granville, PRO 30/29 · PRO, corresp. with Lord John Russell, PRO 30/22 · PRO, corresp. with Odo Russell, FO 918 · U. Southampton L., letters to Lord Palmerston

**Likenesses** W. Behnes, bust, 1849, Eton · H. Weekes, marble bust, 1874, Gov. Art Coll. [*see illus.*] · Ape [C. Pellegrini], chromolithograph, NPG; repro. in *VF* (19 June 1895) · photograph (in old age), repro. in Hertslet, *Recollections of the old foreign office*, p. 130 · wood-engraving, NPG; repro. in *ILN* (1 Nov 1873)

**Wealth at death** £62,151 12*s*. 8*d*.: probate, 30 May 1890, *CGPLA Eng. & Wales*

**Hammond, George** (1763–1853), diplomatist, was born at Kirkella, near Hull, Yorkshire, the youngest son of the twelve children of William *Hammond (1727–1793), merchant, and his wife, Ann Bean (*d*. 1785). He was educated at Merton College, Oxford; he matriculated on 6 March 1780 and graduated BA in 1784. In 1783 he was attached to the Paris mission of David Hartley the younger, who completed the peace negotiations between Great Britain, France, and America. In Paris he gained both a knowledge of French and a future career, for after returning to Oxford, where he became a fellow of Merton in 1787 and proceeded MA in 1788, he was appointed secretary to the embassy of Sir Robert Keith at Vienna. Keith, determined to exercise his own patronage, soon arranged for Hammond's removal to Copenhagen in 1790. Six months later Hammond became secretary of embassy in Madrid and then in August 1791 his extremely rapid preferment by the hand of the Grenvilles resulted in his appointment as the first British minister to the United States of America. It was felt that a diplomat associated with the negotiations of 1783 would be the best choice for the post, as the terms for settlement had lain dormant in the intervening eight years, and when David Hartley declined the post it was given to Hammond. Hammond was to be minister-plenipotentiary: his successors were appointed as envoy-extraordinary and minister-plenipotentiary, and it was not until 1893 that ambassadors were exchanged between Britain and America. Hammond took up residence in Philadelphia, where he arrived on 23 October 1791.

The mission was never easy. Anglo-American relations had been treading water for eight years and time had slowly evaporated any goodwill that remained between the imperial power and her revolted former colonies. Loyalists' estates were still confiscated and British troops remained in their frontier posts. Britain's determination to maintain its monopoly of imperial trade prevented commercial negotiations from proceeding and with negotiations deadlocked, personal recriminations soon followed. Hammond was not a conciliatory diplomat and he returned to Britain in 1795 with little to show for his efforts beyond an American wife: he had married, at Philadelphia, on 20 May 1793, Margaret Allen (*d*. 1838), the daughter of Andrew Allen, the attorney-general of Pennsylvania. They had three sons and two daughters. Their son Edmund *Hammond (1802–1890) became permanent under-secretary at the Foreign Office.

On his return to London, Hammond was appointed by Lord Grenville to be one of his under-secretaries at the Foreign Office in the place of George Aust. The second under-secretary was George Canning, who took care of the dispatches associated with the former Southern department while Hammond took those from the former Northern department. There was no distinction between the two under-secretaries in these early days of the Foreign Office, which had only become a separate department of state in 1782, although Hammond, by longevity, became the senior under-secretary. He served at the pleasure of his secretary of state and temporarily retired when the whigs were in power (1806–7). Altogether he served thirteen years as under-secretary, from October 1795 to February 1806 and from March 1807 to October 1809. Canning and Hammond were good friends and shared a similar political outlook: Hammond was closely involved in Canning's high tory literary project *The Anti-Jacobin*, and it was at a dinner party in Hammond's house in Spring Gardens in 1809 that Canning, by now foreign secretary, first suggested the *Quarterly Review*.

Hammond was employed on two special wartime missions, the first in 1796 to Berlin and the second in 1797 to Vienna. After 1815 he was appointed together with David Morier to be a member of the joint commission of arbitration indemnifying British subjects who had lost property during the French Revolutionary Wars. He was more or less permanently living in Paris until 1818 and served on the committee until it was wound up in July 1828. In these years he divided his time between Paris and his country residence at Donnington, Berkshire.

Hammond was a tall, rather portly man, with a self-important manner variously described as pompous, insensitive, combative, petulant, cold, and condescending by American adversaries, though he was regarded more kindly in Britain. Canning's first impression was of 'one of the pleasantest and quietest tempered as well as confessedly one of the ablest men of business in this country' (Hinde, 44); later, Canning remembered with some glee having deliberately rung the bell in the secretary of state's room to summon Hammond when he knew him to be engaged with somebody before whom he wished to appear particularly grand. Hammond died at his London residence, 22 Portland Place, on 22 April 1853, aged ninety. R. A. Jones

**Sources** W. H. Masterton, *Tories and democrats: British diplomats in pre-Jacksonian America* (1985) · S. T. Bindoff and others, eds., *British diplomatic representatives, 1789–1852*, CS, 3rd ser., 50 (1934) · H. Temperley, *The foreign policy of Canning, 1822–1827*, 2nd edn (1966) · D. B. Horn, *The British diplomatic service, 1689–1789* (1961) · *Cambridge history of foreign policy*, 3 vols. (1923–39) · W. Hinde, *George Canning* (1973) · R. Jones, *The nineteenth-century foreign office: an administrative history* (1971) · *DNB* · GEC, *Peerage*

**Archives** NRA, priv. coll., corresp. and papers · PRO, corresp. and papers, FO 95/502, 508–9 | BL, corresp. with Lord Grenville, Add. MS 58939 · BL, corresp. with Sir Arthur Paget, Add. MS 48393 · Bodl. Oxf., corresp. with Sir James Bland Burges · Harrowby Manuscript Trust, Sandon Hall, Staffordshire, corresp. with Lord Harrowby · NL Scot., corresp. with Robert Liston · U. Mich., Clements L., letters to John Simcoe

**Hammond, Henry** (1605–1660), Church of England clergyman and theologian, was born at Chertsey, Surrey, on 18 August 1605, the youngest son of Dr John *Hammond (*c*.1555–1617), Prince Henry's physician, and his wife, Mary (*d*. 1650), daughter of Robert Harrison of London. Through his mother Hammond was closely related to the Temple family and was kin to Dean Alexander Nowell of St Paul's, a celebrated catechism writer, as Hammond too would be.

**Education** Thanks to his father's teaching Hammond entered Eton College already proficient in Greek and Latin and with some elementary knowledge of Hebrew. He became a favourite of the headmaster, his father's friend Matthew Bust, and he was particularly helped in Greek studies by Thomas Allen, one of the fellows. According to his first biographer:

> His sweetness of carriage is very particularly remembered by his contemporaries, who observed that he was never engaged, upon any occasion, into fights or quarrels; as also, that at times allowed for play he would steal from his fellows into places of privacy, there to say his prayers: omens of his future pacific temper and eminent devotion. (Fell, xviii)

Hammond was admitted, aged about thirteen, to Magdalen College, Oxford, and not long afterwards, in 1619, was chosen demy. Having entered so young he did not matriculate until 26 June 1621. During his years at university he generally studied thirteen hours a day, reading over 'all classic authors' (Fell, xx) and systematically indexing each book he read. He graduated BA on 11 December 1622 and proceeded MA on 30 June 1625 (incorporated at Cambridge the following year). On 26 July 1625 he was elected to a Magdalen fellowship, which he held until 1634; at President Langton's funeral in 1626 he delivered one of the two orations. He was admitted praelector in philosophy on 10 February 1629; Bishop Corbet of Oxford ordained him deacon on 31 May and priest on 20 September. Preaching at court in 1633, as substitute for Magdalen's president, Frewen, he so impressed the earl of Leicester that the earl presented him to the rectory of Penshurst, Kent, where he was inducted on 22 August by his old tutor, Thomas Buckner, rector of Chevening.

**At Penshurst and Oxford** Hammond had resolved to marry, but instead made way for 'one of a fairer fortune and higher quality' (Fell, lxvi), who would make the woman in question a better match. His mother kept house for him and his nephew, her grandson William Temple (1628–1699), whom Hammond was educating about 1635–8. Throughout his ten years at Penshurst he was a painstaking preacher and frequent ministrant of the sacraments; also, in a parishioner's words, 'a great releiver of the poore … a carefull instructer and catechizer of youth … a most comfortable visitor of sicke persons … a peacemaker … [and] such a patterne of true christianity, as I never yett saw paralelled by any' (Packer, 21). He maintained contact with Oxford as one of the 'Men of eminent Parts and Faculties' who formed the circle of Lucius Cary, Viscount Falkland, at Great Tew (*Life of Edward, Earl of Clarendon*, 2 vols., 1759, 1.42). He proceeded BD on 28 January 1634 and DD on 7 March 1639.

Bishop Brian Duppa preferred Hammond to the archdeaconry of Chichester, where his name appeared in the act book on 5 January 1642. A member of convocation since 1640, he was nominated to the Westminster assembly of divines on 1 June 1642—the House of Commons withdrawing its veto after representations from the Lords—but like other episcopalians he did not participate. He remained at Penshurst, and 'though the committee of the county summoned him before them, and used those their best arguments of persuasion, threatenings, and reproaches, he still went on in his regular practice' (Fell, xxviii). In May 1643 he published anonymously his first controversial tract, *Of Resisting the Lawfull Magistrate under Colour of Religion*. He was somehow implicated in the Kentish uprising at the end of June and about 25 July took refuge with Buckner at Chevening. Some three weeks later he was on his way to Winchester with his college friend and fellow refugee John Oliver when Oliver received news that he had been chosen president of Magdalen. Hammond agreed to accompany him and stay in his old college, although he initially thought Oxford 'too public a place' and 'too far from his living' (Fell, xxx). Here the Lenten roster for March 1644 reveals that he became a chaplain to the king.

Hammond was persuaded by the provost of Queen's College, Christopher Potter, to publish *A Practical Catechism*, at first anonymously, in 1644 or 1645. This plainly written exposition of theology and morality, developed from the prayer book's short catechism and used to instruct young parishioners at Penshurst, soon became immensely popular. Its emphasis on Christian practice (with auricular confession) and on Christ's dying 'for all the sins of all mankind' inevitably upset proponents of justification by faith and individuals' election. Hammond defended himself first against the Oxford Calvinist Francis Cheynell, then against the Sion College group of London ministers. At the end of July 1645 he responded to the imposition of presbyterian worship by defending the prayer book in *A View of the New Directory*. He had published six theological tracts anonymously over the preceding months; late that year they were reprinted under his name along with *Resisting the Lawfull Magistrate*.

**Chaplain to Charles I** Charles I was impressed by *A Practical Catechism* and later sent a copy from Carisbrooke to his son Henry. At the end of January 1645 Hammond was chaplain to the duke of Richmond and earl of Southampton at the treaty of Uxbridge. He debated there with the parliamentarian Richard Vines and 'dispelled with ease and perfect clearness all the sophisms that had been brought against him' (Fell, xxxiv). At Oxford he was chosen university orator 'but had seldom an opportunity to shew his parts that way' (Wood, *Ath. Oxon.*, 2.246), and the king preferred him to a canonry in Christ Church, where he was installed about 17 March 1645. After Charles had left and Oxford surrendered on 24 June 1646 Hammond was able to pay a brief visit to Penshurst, where he stayed at the earl of Leicester's house. After parliament forbade the university on 2 July to make appointments or grant leases, Hammond as orator composed an appeal to Sir Thomas Fairfax. On 13 October he was elected to the Oxford delegacy that drew up the university's case against the impending parliamentary visitation. In November he defended Falkland's *Discourse of Infallibility* in *A View of some Exceptions Made by a Romanist*; the following April Falkland's widow, Lettice Cary, named him an overseer of her will, which would involve him and Gilbert Sheldon, then warden of All Souls, in the management of an impoverished estate and a spendthrift heir.

On 17 February 1647 the king, detained by parliament at

Holdenby, Northamptonshire, named Hammond among others when he asked unsuccessfully for chaplains. When he passed into the army's custody his request was granted: Hammond and Sheldon waited on him at Royston on 25 June, and Hammond preached before him at Hatfield two days later. Despite parliament's demands for their removal, they remained with the king—Fairfax doubting that they would prejudice the kingdom's peace. On 23 August, Charles arrived at Hampton Court, and there, according to Anthony Wood, Hammond presented to him 'as a penitent convert' his nephew the parliamentary colonel Robert Hammond (Wood, *Ath. Oxon.*, 2.250), although there is no other evidence for this. Robert shortly went to the Isle of Wight as governor, where he became Charles's gaoler at Carisbrooke Castle after the king's misjudged flight of 11 November. Hammond himself was one of the royal chaplains officiating at Carisbrooke for a few weeks until their removal at the end of December.

After returning to Oxford and his Christ Church canonry Hammond was elected subdean and became responsible for running the college—parliament having imprisoned the dean, Samuel Fell. On 27 March 1648 Hammond refused to acknowledge the authority of the visitors, and three days later the London committee voted him out of his canonry and oratorship. Hammond and Sheldon were placed under house arrest, but 'the great resort of persons' to them caused the London committee on 30 May to order their removal to Wallingford Castle, Berkshire (Burrows, 114–15). The governor of Wallingford, Colonel Arthur Evelyn—'though a man of as opposite principles to Church and Churchmen as any of the adverse party'—protested he would entertain them as friends, not prisoners, so they remained in Oxford (Fell, xlv).

**At Clapham, Bedfordshire** The king, having been refused their attendance on grounds that they were under restraint, asked for a copy of Hammond's sermon preached before him the previous St Andrew's day. It was later published as *The Christians Obligations to Peace and Charity* (1649), with nine other sermons and a dedication to Charles dated 16 September 1648. Through the influence of his brother-in-law Sir John Temple, Hammond was moved, after ten weeks' restraint, to the house of his friend Sir Philip Warwick at Clapham, Bedfordshire. 'Here he continued about two yeares, often preaching in the Parish Church, the poverty of the place protecting the Minister in his reading of the Common Prayer and observing the orders of the Church' (William Fulman, Bodl. Oxf., MS Rawl. D. 317A, fol. 4*v*). When the king was tried—with Hammond's brother Thomas as one of his judges—Hammond wrote his *Humble Address*, dated 15 January 1649, which he conveyed to Fairfax and his council of war and later that year defended in *A Vindication*. Hammond's business with printers had taken him to London in the first months of 1649; a year later, however, legislation confining royalists within 5 miles of their homes prevented him from visiting his dying mother.

In March 1650 Hammond responded to the supposed hopelessness of the Church of England's cause by publishing *Of the Reasonableness of the Christian Religion*. This discourse on the uses and limits of reason in matters of faith, published in pocket-sized duodecimo without learned references, anticipated in topic and tone a number of later writers, including John Tillotson and John Locke—but firmly enjoined subjection and non-resistance to the lawful ruler. The crucial question of episcopal government had engaged Hammond since his *Considerations of Present Use* (1644) and, more importantly, *The Power of the Keyes* (1647). In the latter he used, and defended, those epistles of Ignatius that Archbishop James Ussher had authenticated in *Polycarpi et Ignatii epistolae* (1644). As Ussher was disinclined to answer his critics Claude Saumaise and David Blondel he wrote to Hammond on 21 July 1649, asking him 'to publish to the World, in Latin, what you have already written in English' (R. Parr, *Life of Ussher*, 1686, 542). Hammond did so in *Dissertationes quatuor* (1651): the second dissertation deals with Ignatius, others with evidence from the Bible and from sub-apostolic sources.

**At Westwood, Worcestershire** About the end of summer 1650, Hammond was allowed to move to Westwood, Worcestershire, the home of Sir John Packington and his wife, Dorothy. Packington and Hammond were with Charles II at Worcester but after the battle were allowed to retire to Westwood. There Hammond completed *A Paraphrase and Annotations on All the Books of the New Testament* (1653), which he had worked on when restrained at Oxford and Clapham. This 1000-page folio, modelled on the commentaries of Grotius and Ussher, was Hammond's response to the popular demand for English expositions and was later imitated by Richard Baxter among others. Hammond's painstaking composition had begun with a Latin interpretation, in two large manuscript volumes, and a new English translation based on his collation of Greek manuscripts. He took Sheldon's advice, however, and printed the authorized translation, with his own variants in the margin. The paraphrase is printed in a parallel column, and the extensive annotations follow at each chapter's end. Hammond defended his annotations against the Independent John Owen and others in *Deuterai phrontides* (1657). He also defended three times between 1654 and 1657 the orthodoxy of Grotius, whose textual analysis he so admired. His interest in manuscript evidence continued with the scholarly and financial help he gave to Brian Walton for his polyglot Bible (1655–7).

Defeated royalists who fled abroad, disillusioned and impoverished, were pressed to become Roman Catholics. This danger prompted Hammond's tract *Of Schisme* (1653), defending the Church of England against 'the exceptions of the Romanists'—notably those of the Jesuit Edward Knott in his *Infidelity Unmasked* (1652). Hammond's scrutiny of the evidence for papal supremacy—particularly over the original British church—was repeatedly attacked, and he published five replies between 1654 and 1660. Meanwhile the London ministers and the Independent John Owen answered his *Dissertationes* with anti-episcopalian attacks, which he refuted point by point in *A Vindication* and *An Answer* (1654). The presbyterians Daniel

Cawdrey and Henry Jeanes and the Baptist John Tombes were roused, by his *Letter of Resolution to Six Quaeres* (1653), to attack him on church festivals, signing with the cross and paedobaptism; between 1654 and 1657 he replied to each of them. Indeed 'he made himself the common mark of opposition to all parties' (Fell, liv). He also published *Of Fundamentals* in 1654, and it has been suggested that he was the H. H. who translated Blaise Pascal's *Les provinciales* (1657).

Brian Duppa appears to have convened a meeting attended by Hammond at Richmond, Surrey, in August 1653 to discuss use of the prayer book. Hammond probably went there via Boothby Pagnell, Lincolnshire, to discuss questions of God's grace and decrees with Robert Sanderson, whose views were less Arminian than his own. In 1655 he was consulted about Edward Hyde's initiative for the consecration of new bishops. At Westwood he had taken over the functions of family chaplain, preaching constantly from 1652 to 1655, first on the articles of the creed, then on the commandments; so when Cromwell's edict forbidding sequestered clergy to minister was about to come into force he could reassure his congregation, on 23 December 1655, that his sermons had already covered everything needful to be believed or done. His printed response to the edict was *A Paraenesis, or, Seasonable Exhortatory to All True Sons of the Church of England* (1656).

**The prospect of prosperity** Considering that 'the ancient stock of clergymen were by this edict in a manner rendered useless' Hammond 'projected by pensions unto hopeful persons in either University, to maintain a seminary of youth instituted in piety, upon the sober principles and old establishment of the Anglican Church' (Fell, lvii). Some hoped-for subscribers failed him, but he and his friends contributed to the scheme. By September 1657 he was preaching again, but in failing health, afflicted by gout, colic, stone, and cramp. He wrote the letter to the publisher, dated 7 March 1658, which introduced his friend Richard Allestree's *The Whole Duty of Man*. He completed his paraphrase and annotation of the Psalms (published in 1659) and chapters 1–10 of Proverbs (published posthumously in 1683). In May 1659 Allestree returned from Brussels with a paper from Charles II naming new bishops, including Hammond for Worcester. Hammond worried about his imminent responsibilities: 'I must confess I never saw that time in all my life wherein I could so cheerfully say my *Nunc dimittis* as now. Indeed I do dread prosperity, I do really dread it' (Fell, ci).

At the beginning of 1660 Hammond, summoned to London 'to assist in the great work of the composure of breaches in the Church', reflected on ways of doing good in his future diocese, in particular the repair of Worcester Cathedral (Fell, cii). On 4 April he was 'seized by a sharp fit of the stone', of which he died three weeks later, on the night of 25 April, at Westwood. The following evening he was buried in the Packingtons' church nearby at Hampton Lovet, where his monument is on the south side of the chancel. In his will, dated 19 April 1660 and witnessed by John Dolben, who had been with him throughout his last illness, he bequeathed various sums to nephews, godchildren, and several sequestered friends. He left most of his books to Richard Allestree and the residue of his estate to his executor, Humphrey Henchman, for his own relief and for charity. Hammond had always lived abstemiously. He expressed astonishment that, for all his generosity, he could never make himself poor. He died worth £1500.

**Rebuilder of the church** As the bishops largely secluded themselves during the interregnum the defence of the Church of England, in publications and correspondence, was left to a small group of apologists led by Hammond—'the person that during the bad times had maintained the cause of the church in a very singular manner' (*Burnet's History*, 1.314). The new-found confidence of the Restoration church owed much to the theology developed in his writings and to the exemplary character of his life. Despite his dislike of Hammond's 'New Prelatical way' Richard Baxter took his death 'for a very great loss; for his Piety and Wisdom would have hindered much of the Violence which after followed' (*Reliquiae Baxterianae*, 97, 208). John Fell wrote a *Life of Hammond* (1661), an informative and engaging tribute. William Fulman, the carpenter's son from Penshurst whom he had sponsored at Oxford, edited his works (1684) and collected biographical materials, which survive in manuscript. Hammond's far-reaching reinterpretation of the covenant—offered to all but conditional on morality—was persuasively embodied in his *Practical Catechism* and provided the rationale of the English church until the rise of the evangelicals. When asked about Bible commentaries, Samuel Johnson recommended Hammond's *New Testament Paraphrase*. The Tractarians revered him as a Laudian: Nicholas Pocock edited his major works and made good use of his correspondence, but without entirely appreciating his rationalism; Keble wrote 'Hammond's Grave' and associated him with 'Meek, pastoral, quiet souls', but without thinking of his determination and combativeness (Keble, *Miscellaneous Poems*, 1869, 216). HUGH DE QUEHEN

**Sources** J. Fell, 'Life of Hammond', in H. Hammond, *Miscellaneous theological works*, ed. N. Pocock, 1 (1847–50), xvii-cxv • J. W. Packer, *The transformation of Anglicanism, 1643–1660, with special reference to Henry Hammond* (1969) • *Hist. U. Oxf.* 4: *17th-cent. Oxf.* • Wood, *Ath. Oxon.*, 2nd edn • A. Wood, *The history and antiquities of the University of Oxford*, ed. J. Gutch, 2 vols. in 3 pts (1792–6) • J. Walker, *An attempt towards recovering an account of the numbers and sufferings of the clergy of the Church of England*, 2 pts in 1 (1714) • *Walker rev.* • F. Madan, *Oxford books: a bibliography of printed works*, 2–3 (1912–31) • M. Burrows, ed., *The register of the visitors of the University of Oxford, from AD 1647 to AD 1658*, CS, new ser., 29 (1881) • G. C. M. Smith, 'Temple and Hammond families and the related families of Nowell and Knollys', *N&Q*, 151 (1926), 237–9 • G. C. M. Smith, 'Temple and Hammond families and the related family of Harrison', *N&Q*, 151 (1926), 452–3 • M. Toynbee, 'The two Sir John Dingleys, II', *N&Q*, 198 (1953), 478–83 • *Fasti Angl.*, 1541–1857, [Chichester] • *Fasti Angl.*, 1541–1857, [Bristol] • J. Spurr, *The Restoration Church of England, 1646–1689* (1991) • R. S. Bosher, *The making of the Restoration settlement: the influence of the Laudians, 1649–1662* (1951) • *Burnet's History of my own time*, ed. O. Airy, new edn, 2 vols. (1897–1900) • *Reliquiae Baxterianae, or, Mr Richard Baxter's narrative of the most memorable passages of his life and times*, ed. M. Sylvester, 1 vol. in 3 pts (1696) • P. Jansen, *De Blaise Pascal à Henry Hammond* (1954) • Mrs R. Lane Poole, ed., *Catalogue of portraits in the possession of the university, colleges, city and county of Oxford*,

2, OHS, 81 (1926) • will, PRO, PROB 11/301, fols. 41v–42r • Boswell, *Life*

**Archives** BL, Add. MSS • Bodl. Oxf., St Mary's Vicar's library, works [presentation copies] • Christ Church Oxf. | BL, Harley MSS • Bodl. Oxf., Jones MS 45 • Bodl. Oxf., MSS Rawl. • Bodl. Oxf., Tanner MSS • Bodl. Oxf., Corpus Christi College deposit, Fulman MSS • Queen's College, Oxford, corresp. with Bishop Barlow

**Likenesses** oils, *c.*1660–1699, Magd. Oxf. • R. Clamp, mezzotint, 1796 (after S. Harding), repro. in *The Biographical Mirrour*, 2 (1798) • W. Behnes, bust, 1849, Eton

**Wealth at death** £1500: Walker, *Attempt towards recovering*

**Hammond, James** (1710–1742), politician and poet, was born on 22 May 1710; he was the second son of Anthony *Hammond (1668–1738) of Somersham Place, Huntingdonshire, and Jane (1677–1749), daughter of Sir Walter Clarges (1654–1706) and granddaughter of Sir Thomas *Clarges (*d.* 1695). Both parents were wits; Anthony was a politician and spendthrift, but had sufficient foresight to buy for James a commission as ensign, dated 20 March 1713, before the child was three years old. Hammond was admitted to Westminster School in June 1722.

Aged eighteen, Hammond was introduced to Lord Chesterfield by Noel Broxholme MD, who afterwards married Hammond's widowed sister Anne. He and Broxholme were in Chesterfield's embassy at The Hague from 1728, and in 1732 Hammond received a £200 gratuity from the civil list for carrying back to London the Act of Concurrence of the Dutch states general to the treaty of Vienna. In the following year his kinsman Nicholas Hammond of Swaffham, Norfolk, bequeathed him an estate worth £400 p.a. He was now drawn by Chesterfield into the opposition circle centred upon the prince of Wales; he was equerry to the prince from 1733 (salary £300 p.a.) to his death.

'He is said to have divided his life between pleasure and books; in his retirement forgetting the town, and in his gaiety losing the student' (Johnson). Hammond wrote a moving, unsigned prologue for George Lillo's posthumously produced tragedy *Elmerick* (February 1740); the play was dedicated to Hammond's master, Frederick, prince of Wales. Hammond wrote of Lillo: 'Dying he wrote, and dying wish'd to please.'

Hammond was returned as opposition whig MP for Truro, on 13 May 1741, on the recommendation of Chesterfield and in the interest of the prince of Wales, duke of Cornwall. He died on 7 June 1742 at Stowe, the home of Lord Cobham, one of his political mentors. The septuagenarian Erasmus Lewis was sole executor, but he declined to act, and Hammond's mother, the sole beneficiary, administered the estate. By his will (drawn up in Paris in 1730) Hammond's body was to be buried where he died, but this injunction was disregarded.

There is a politically tinged elegy to Hammond in Thomson's *Seasons* (1744: *Winter*, lines 555–71). In 1742 Chesterfield published Hammond's few amatory and complimentary verses as *Love Elegies, Written in the Year 1732*, to which he added a graceful unsigned critical preface. One poem had been published anonymously in *An Elegy to a Young Lady in the Manner of Ovid, with an Answer by a Lady* (1733): the answer is by Lady Mary Wortley Montagu, though wrongly attributed to John, Lord Hervey, in Dodsley's *Collection*, 4 (1755).

Hammond's elegies are avowedly imitations of Tibullus. It was generally believed that most of them were addressed to Miss Catherine (Kitty) Dashwood (*d.* 1779), later a lady of the bedchamber to Queen Charlotte, but contradictory tales were told about her relationship with Hammond. On different occasions Horace Walpole averred that 'Hammond had been in love with her, and then forsaken her' (H. Walpole, *Memoirs of the Reign of King George III*, 1845, 1.71), and that she, 'finding he did not mean marriage, broke off all connection, though much in love with him' (*Bibliographical and Historical Miscellanies*, Philobiblion Society, 11, 1867–8, 17). The countess of Cork (*née* Mary Monckton), a friend of Miss Dashwood, told in old age another story: that she 'had at first accepted, but afterwards rejected him, on [as her contemporaries thought] *prudential* reasons' (J. Hervey, *Memoirs of the Reign of George the Second*, ed. J. W. Croker, 1848, 1.xxx, n. 16).

Hammond's verse was frequently reprinted and was included in most standard collections of English poetry down to the early nineteenth century. Johnson's well-known stricture in *Lives of the English Poets* that Hammond's elegies have 'neither passion, nature, nor manners', and nothing 'but frigid pedantry', was answered in William Beville's *Observations on Dr. Johnson's Life of Hammond* (1782), but time has given its verdict in favour of Johnson.

JAMES SAMBROOK

**Sources** S. Johnson, *Lives of the English poets*, ed. G. B. Hill, [new edn], 3 (1905), 459–60 • R. Shiels, *The lives of the poets of Great Britain and Ireland*, ed. T. Cibber, 5 (1753), 307–9 • W. A. Shaw, ed., *Calendar of treasury books and papers*, 2, PRO (1898), 229 • *N&Q*, 2nd ser., 11 (1861), 493 [quoting Bod. Rawlinson MS A.245] • *GM*, 1st ser., 12 (1742), 330 • *GM*, 1st ser., 49 (1779), 103–4, 205–6 • G. Dyer, 'Life', in *The poetical works of James Hammond, and Lord Hervey* (1818) • Lord Chesterfield [P. D. Stanhope], 'Preface', in J. Hammond, *Love elegies, written in the year 1732* (1742) • M. Maty, 'Memoirs', in *Miscellaneous works of the … earl of Chesterfield*, ed. M. Maty, 2nd edn, 1 (1779) • W. Beville, *Observations on Dr. Johnson's life of Hammond* (1782) • HoP, *Commons, 1715–54* • *The letters of Philip Dormer Stanhope, fourth earl of Chesterfield*, ed. B. Dobrée, 6 vols. (1932) • *Old Westminsters*, 1.418 • D. F. Foxon, ed., *English verse, 1701–1750: a catalogue of separately printed poems with notes on contemporary collected editions*, 2 vols. (1975) • *IGI* • Boswell, *Life* • *DNB*

**Hammond, Dame Joan Hood** (1912–1996), singer, was born on 24 May 1912 in Christchurch, New Zealand, the daughter of Samuel Hood Hammond (*fl.* *c.*1875–1950) and his wife, Hilda May, *née* Blandford (*fl.* *c.*1885–1955). Her parents were British, and when she was a few months old the family moved to Sydney, Australia. She was educated at the Presbyterian Ladies' College, Pymble, New South Wales, where from an early age she showed a natural aptitude for music and for sport. In 1928 she entered the New South Wales Conservatorium of Music to study violin, piano, and singing. She originally intended to be a violinist, but a bicycle accident at the age of twelve had left one arm shorter than the other, so she concentrated on singing. At the same time she played a great deal of golf, and at

**Dame Joan Hood Hammond** (1912–1996), by John Franks, 1959 [rehearsing *Rusalka* by Dvořák at Sadler's Wells Theatre]

the age of seventeen she won the junior state championship.

In 1932 the Williamson Imperial Grand Opera Company gave a season in Australia, visiting Sydney, Melbourne, and other cities. The principal singers were Italian, but the chorus and minor roles were recruited locally. Hammond secured an engagement with the company as a mezzo-soprano, appearing in *Aida*, *Pagliacci*, and *Madama Butterfly*, as Giovanna in *Rigoletto*, and as Siebel in *Faust*. She obtained leave of absence to play in the ladies' state golf championship, which she won. The following year she was runner-up in the Australian open championship. She became golf correspondent for the *Sydney Telegraph*, meanwhile singing whenever and wherever she could, for music clubs, in cinemas, and even in department stores.

Another season of grand opera was presented in Sydney by Sir Benjamin Fuller in 1935. The singer taking the part of Venus in *Tannhäuser* dropped out, and Hammond sang the role at short notice. She also sang Helmwige in *Die Walküre*. A fund of £2000 was raised so that she could travel to Europe to study further. After a final concert in Sydney she sailed on 6 April 1936 in the Norwegian freighter *Dagfred*, arriving in Genoa six weeks later. She went first to Vienna, where she remained a year, though she did not care for her teacher. Then she went to London, where she studied with the Italian tenor Dino Borgioli, an excellent teacher. Now a soprano, she returned to Vienna in 1938 to sing at the Volksoper, as Nedda in *Pagliacci*, in the title role of *Martha*, and as Konstanze in *Die Entführung aus dem Serail*. She made her London début that autumn, giving a recital at the Aeolian Hall and singing in *Messiah* under Sir Thomas Beecham at the Queen's Hall. Early in 1939 she returned to Vienna, to sing Mimi in *La Bohème* and Violetta in *La traviata*, this time at the State Opera. She also prepared the roles of Elisabeth in *Tannhäuser* and Donna Elvira in *Don Giovanni*. Meanwhile the political situation was growing worse by the day. Hammond went back to London in August to sing at a Henry Wood Promenade Concert and did not return to Austria.

After war was declared Hammond volunteered as an ambulance driver, and sang for the BBC and with the Entertainments National Service Association to entertain the troops. In January 1940 she was asked to sing Mimi and Tosca at La Scala. With great difficulty she managed to get to Milan, and even started rehearsals, but Italy was about to enter the war on the side of the Germans, and she had to leave. For two years her operatic career, which had begun with such promise, was in abeyance. However, she was kept extremely busy in the concert hall and the recording studio. Her first recording paired the Bach-Gounod *Ave Maria* and Mendelssohn's 'On wings of song'. This was followed by a number of operatic arias, including 'O my beloved father' from *Gianni Schicchi*. In 1942 Hammond joined the Carl Rosa Opera Company, which had just began to operate again, making her British stage début in Glasgow as Madam Butterfly and touring the country for three years, singing Violetta, Marguerite in *Faust*, Leonora in *Il trovatore*, Mimi, and Tosca, as well as the Marschallin in *Der Rosenkavalier* in concert.

After the war Hammond toured Germany with Sadler's Wells, singing Butterfly, and in 1946 returned to Australia for a four-month concert tour. In 1947 she went back to Vienna to sing Mimi, Tosca, Butterfly, and Violetta. The State Opera was in ruins, and performances were given at the old Theater an der Wien. After a tour of South Africa, in 1948 Hammond made her Covent Garden début as Leonora in *Il trovatore*, and she returned there during the next three seasons as Leonore in *Fidelio*, as Aida, and as Butterfly. She toured the USA in 1949, and also appeared with the New York City Opera as Butterfly, Aida, and Tosca. During the Verdi celebrations in 1951, the fiftieth anniversary of his death, Hammond sang Elisabeth de Valois in *Don Carlos* at Sadler's Wells. She also took part in several performances of the Verdi Requiem, music that she particularly liked.

In the 1950s Hammond travelled widely, touring Scandinavia, east and central Africa, India, the Far East, Canada, the USA, Australia, and the Soviet Union, where she sang Aida and Tatyana in *Eugene Onegin* (in Russian) at Leningrad and Moscow. She also sang Tatyana and Fevronia in Rimsky-Korsakov's *The Invisible City of Kitesh* at Barcelona. One of her most popular recordings was 'O silver moon' from Dvořák's *Rusalka*; perhaps mistakenly, she sang Rusalka in the British stage première of the opera at Sadler's Wells in 1959, which was not a great success. For the Elizabethan Opera Trust in Australia she performed Tosca and two new roles, Desdemona in *Otello* and Strauss's Salome. She broadcast several operas for the BBC, including *La forza del destino*, *Turandot*, Massenet's *Thaïs*, *Guillaume*

*Tell*, and Rimsky-Korsakov's *Mlada*, as well as two contemporary works, Alan Bush's *Wat Tyler* and Dennis ApIvor's *Yerma*.

In November 1965 Hammond suffered a coronary attack and was forced to retire. Her many records continued to sell and in 1969 she was awarded a golden disc for 'O my beloved father', originally used to back Tosca's 'Vissi d'arte'. She published her autobiography, *A Voice, a Life*, in 1970. Having been appointed OBE in 1953, CBE in 1963, and CMG in 1972, she was appointed DBE in 1974. Her home in Australia, together with her golfing trophies and all the souvenirs of her singing career, was destroyed by a bush fire in 1983. Music lovers all over the world sent replacements for her lost treasures. She died at Bowral, New South Wales, on 26 November 1996.

ELIZABETH FORBES

**Sources** J. Hammond, *A voice, a life* (1970) • A. Blyth, 'Hammond, Joan', *The new Grove dictionary of opera*, ed. S. Sadie, 2 (1992) • *WWW* • B. Mackenzie and F. Mackenzie, *Singers of Australia* (1968) • H. Rosenthal, *Sopranos of today* (1956) • H. Rosenthal, *Two centuries of opera at Covent Garden* (1958) • *The Independent* (27 Nov 1996) • *The Times* (28 Nov 1996)

**Archives** SOUND Broadcasting House, Portland Place, London, BBC Music Library

**Likenesses** J. Franks, photograph, 1959, Hult. Arch. [*see illus.*] • photograph, repro. in *The Independent* • photograph, repro. in *The Times*

**Hammond, John** (1542–1589/90), civil lawyer, was the younger son of Thomas Hammond, of Pendleton, near Whalley, Lancashire, and his wife, Beatrice, daughter of John Nowell of Read in the same county and sister of Alexander Nowell, the dean of St Paul's. He was educated at Trinity Hall, Cambridge, graduating LLB in 1561 and subsequently becoming a fellow. In 1569 he proceeded LLD and became an advocate of Doctors' Commons. In 1570 he became commissary of the arches for the deaneries of Shoreham and Croydon; in 1573 commissary to the dean and chapter of St Paul's; a master in chancery in 1574; and chancellor of the diocese of London in 1575.

Hammond was extensively employed in legal work of a varied nature, covering maritime issues, title to property, a dispute as to who was entitled to be chancellor of Coventry and Lichfield, and another between the Stationers' Company and the patentees privileged in printing. In 1578 he was sent, along with Laurence Humphrey and others, to the Diet of Schmalkald. From 1573 he was an active member of the high commission, mild towards conscientious protestants but severe to Catholics. In 1581 he was authorized, along with Thomas Norton, to examine under torture Alexander Briant, and Norton subsequently boasted that the Jesuit had been pulled 'one good foot longer than God ever made him' (*CSP dom., 1581–90*, 48). Later in the same year Hammond and Norton, together with Robert Beale, were instructed by the council to conduct repeated examinations of Edmund Campion, Hammond preparing interrogatories based on Nicholas Sander's *De visibili monarchia* and Bristow's *Book of Motives* designed to draw Campion into admissions of high treason. Subsequently Hammond played the same role in extracting confessions from other Jesuits and seminary priests, and in the pursuit of those who had given them hospitality. His name appears as a principal witness in the official propaganda published soon afterwards, which claimed that those who had been put to death had suffered for high treason, and not for matters of conscience. To a similar end, Hammond prepared at Lord Burghley's request two short discourses, one on the unlawfulness of excommunication of Christian princes, the other on the resistance of Christian princes to excommunication (BL, Add. MS 48063, fol. 6), for use in the preparation of the anonymous *Justitia Britannica*, Burghley's own apologia for government policy.

Hammond was by contrast strongly critical of Whitgift's articles of 1583, arguing that 'such a uniformity as shall be void of difference of opinion there never was, nor never shall be found, but only in ignorance' (BL, Add. MS 48064, fols. 25–9). In the parliament of 1584, in which he sat for the borough of Rye, he was a member of the committee asked to prepare the Commons' petition for ecclesiastical reform, which argued that Whitgift's policy had caused the silencing of able preachers with sensitive consciences, while indulging lazy and ignorant conformists. Hammond sat for West Looe in the parliament of 1586, but does not figure in the published proceedings. Nevertheless, in a memorandum sent to Burghley in the year before he died, he argued strongly against *jure divino* episcopacy. If it had pleased the queen not to have appointed any bishops 'we could not have complained justly of any defect in our church—but since it has pleased her majesty to use them it must be to me, that am a subject, as God's ordinance' (*Salisbury MSS*, 3.367–70).

Hammond was assessed at £20 in lands and fees at Colman Street, London, for the subsidy of 1589. He died between 21 December 1589, when he made his will, and 12 October 1590, when it was proved. His property was left to his wife, Agnes, of whom little is known, and to his son John.

P. O. G. WHITE

**Sources** J. Strype, *Annals of the Reformation and establishment of religion … during Queen Elizabeth's happy reign*, 3rd edn, 4 vols. (1731–5) • J. Strype, *The life and acts of Matthew Parker* (1711) • *APC*, 1580–82, 1586–8 • *CSP dom.*, 1581–90 • *Calendar of the manuscripts of the most hon. the marquis of Salisbury*, 3, HMC, 9 (1889), 367–70, 412 • BL, Add. MSS 48063, fol. 6; 48064, fols. 25–9 • *State trials*, vol. 1 • S. D'Ewes, ed., *The journals of all the parliaments during the reign of Queen Elizabeth, both of the House of Lords and House of Commons* (1682) • Cooper, *Ath. Cantab.*, 2.75 • J. Strype, *The history of the life and acts of … Edmund Grindal* (1710) • HoP, *Commons, 1558–1603* • J. Strype, *The life and acts of … John Whitgift* (1718) • *DNB* • P. Collinson, *The Elizabethan puritan movement* (1967) • C. Read, *Lord Burghley and Queen Elizabeth* (1960)

**Wealth at death** property at Colman Street, London, assessed at £20 in 1589; will mentions 'property in London or Essex'

**Hammond** [Hamond], **John** (*c.*1555–1617), physician, is of unknown birth and parentage, but probably came from a notable family. The legend that he was the son of John Hammond LLD (1542–1589/90), perpetuated in the *Dictionary of National Biography*, Munk, and other sources, was disproved by G. C. Moore Smith in 1926. John Hammond MD may have been a nephew of John Hammond LLD, who is said to have been a son of one of the four sisters of Alexander Nowell (*d.* 1621), dean of St Paul's. John Hammond LLD's will of 1589 was witnessed by Nowell, and by William Hamond (the spelling the physician later preferred), who may have been John Hammond LLD's elder brother, and the father of the physician.

From Eton College, Hammond entered Trinity College, Cambridge, in 1570 as a pensioner. He was a scholar in 1573, BA in 1574, and took his MA in 1577, having been elected a fellow the previous year. He was an MD of Cambridge before he was incorporated DM at Oxford on 30 August 1603. He was elected a fellow of the College of Physicians on 13 May 1608.

Hammond's last will indicates that he married, in 1583, Mary, daughter of Robert Harrison of London, whose youngest son, John, was at Eton with Hammond and their friend William Temple (*d.* 1616). Some time before the Hammonds' fifth son was born, in 1605, they had made their family home on part of the site of the dissolved monastery of Chertsey, Surrey. Hammond had already become physician to James I, and then to Henry, prince of Wales, for which service he is best-known. Hammond attended the prince in his last illness in 1612, and his signature is appended to the original record of the post-mortem examination.

Hammond died in 1617. By a will of 1612 he bequeathed money to found two hospitals and nine scholarships in Cambridge. These bequests are not mentioned in his will of August 1616. Hammond also owned land in Surrey and leases in three counties. From the last will it appears that he was survived by his wife and all but one of their children. Hammond asked to be buried in his own chapel, or those of Trinity or Eton.

The Hammonds had five sons and two daughters. The eldest son was Robert (*d.* 1623), who married Elizabeth, daughter of Sir Francis Knollys of Reading Abbey; their son was Colonel Robert Hammond (1621–1654), Cromwell's governor of the Isle of Wight when King Charles was a prisoner there. Elizabeth's sister Letitia became the second wife of John Hampden. The second son was Thomas *Hammond, parliamentarian lieutenant-general. The other sons were George; Luke, who predeceased his father; and Henry *Hammond, the Anglican divine. Their daughter Jane married Sir John Dingley of Wolverton, Isle of Wight, and had at least three daughters. Mary married her first cousin, the provost's son, Sir John Temple, master of the rolls in Ireland; their son was Sir William Temple, essayist and statesman.

ROGER HUTCHINS

**Sources** G. C. M. Smith, 'Temple and Hammond families and the related families of Nowell and Knollys', *N&Q*, 151 (1926), 237–9 · G. C. M. Smith, 'Temple and Hammond families and the related family of Harrison', *N&Q*, 151 (1926), 452–3 · Munk, *Roll* · Foster, *Alum. Oxon.* · Venn, *Alum. Cant.* · J. R. Bloxam, *A register of the presidents, fellows … of Saint Mary Magdalen College*, 8 vols. (1853–85), vol. 5, pp. 88–100 · *DNB* · will, 19 Aug 1616, PRO, PROB 11/130, sig. 64

**Wealth at death** see will, 19 Aug 1616, PRO, PROB 11/130, sig. 64

**Hammond, Sir John** (1889–1964), physiologist and agricultural scientist, was born on 23 February 1889, at Briston, Norfolk, the eldest child of Burrell Hammond, a tenant farmer, and Janette Louisa Aldis, the daughter of a schoolmaster in East Dereham. He was educated at Gresham's School, Holt, and at Edward VI Middle School, Norwich. In 1907, having failed to gain admission to the Royal Veterinary College, he was advised by T. B. Wood, professor of agriculture at Cambridge (and a Norfolk farmer), to study agriculture. Hammond entered Downing College, Cambridge, where his tutor recommended that he sit the natural sciences tripos; he gained a second-class degree in 1909. The following year he obtained the diploma in agriculture with distinction in all the biological subjects. After a period teaching in the Technical Institute in Chelmsford, he returned to Cambridge to study for an MA under F. H. A. Marshall, focusing in particular on the physiology of reproduction. He also studied bacteriology under G. Smith, and obtained a diploma in public health bacteriology in 1912. In 1914, at the outbreak of the First World War, he enlisted and served as captain and company commander with the British expeditionary force. He was invalided home in 1916 and during the same year, on 1 May, married Frances Mercy (*b.* 1888/9), daughter of John Goulder, a Norfolk farmer. They later had two sons, one of whom, John, became a renowned physiologist.

In 1919 Hammond became a livestock inspector for the Ministry of Agriculture. In the following year he was appointed as physiologist in the Animal Nutrition Institute in Cambridge. However, facilities for his research into the life cycle of farm animals were very limited. Much work had to be with rabbits because farm animals were too expensive for his budget. When this was unworkable Hammond was forced to choose smaller breeds of farm animals to increase the numbers he could afford to keep. The abattoirs and dairies he had visited as livestock inspector were also a significant source of important information for his research. Hammond's ideas and methods are well illustrated in his numerous books, among which are *The Physiology of Reproduction in the Cow* (1927) and *Growth and the Development of Mutton Qualities in the Sheep* (1932).

Hammond's scientific interests were not just agricultural; they extended to problems of general biology. Indeed, he was a founding member of both the Genetical Society and the Society for Experimental Biology. He was also very interested in the practical application of science. He worked with producers to develop standards for carcass assessment which were eventually used internationally. His early interest in artificial insemination led, in 1942, to the formation in Cambridge of one of the country's first centres for artificial insemination of cattle, which became the model for a new system to improve dairy and beef herds. During the Second World War he tested his ideas about practical farming by managing, very successfully, the Downing College estate farms. His expertise in reproductive biology led to him assisting in investigations by the Medical Research Council into human fertility, and he sat on many of the council's committees involved in this area. Nevertheless, many in Cambridge doubted the academic importance of his work, probably because they had reservations about its economic orientation. Thus Hammond's great ambition—to establish a meat research institute in Cambridge—was never realized during his lifetime.

Hammond received, none the less, honorary doctorates from a number of universities, and he was elected foreign member of many academies of agriculture and veterinary science. He became a fellow of the Royal Society in 1933. In 1949 he was appointed CBE, and was knighted in 1960. He was also made a commander of the order of Orange-Nassau (1946) and received a commenda al merito della republica Italiana (1954).

In his spare time Hammond was a keen gardener. He maintained an interest in rowing, having rowed for his college as a student, and was a regular cyclist. He died at the Evelyn Nursing Home, Cambridge, on 25 August 1964. JOSEPH EDWARDS, *rev.* PAOLO PALLADINO

**Sources** W. K. Slater and J. Edwards, *Memoirs FRS*, 11 (1965), 101–13 · A. S. Parkes, *Off-beat biologist* (1985) · *The Times* (26 Aug 1964) · *The Times* (29 Aug 1964) · b. cert. · m. cert. · d. cert. · *CGPLA Eng. & Wales* (1964)
**Archives** NRA, corresp. and papers
**Likenesses** W. Stoneman, two photographs, 1933–45, NPG
**Wealth at death** £24,072: probate, 25 Sept 1964, *CGPLA Eng. & Wales*

**Hammond, (John) Lawrence Le Breton** (1872–1949), historian and journalist, was born on 18 July 1872 at Drighlington, Yorkshire, the second of the eight children of Vavasour Fitz Hammond Hammond (1842–1897), the local rector, and his wife, Caroline (1849–1925). Neither parent was from Yorkshire. Caroline Hammond had grown up in Wimborne, Dorset, where her father, William George Webb, was a maltster. Vavasour Fitz Hammond Hammond was from Jersey, where his father, John Hammond, was bailiff, the highest-ranking civil officer on the island. Drighlington at the time of Hammond's birth was a mere village, but it lay within 5 miles of both Bradford and Leeds, the twin centres of the still-thriving woollen and worsted trades. Politically, Drighlington formed part of the Spen valley division and shared its Liberal commitment. Hammond's father, a keen home-ruler and a member of the Liberal Churchmen's Union, made Gladstone into 'a sort of fourth person of the Trinity' (Weaver, 11), and Hammond himself, from a very early age, felt some confusion over the distinction between God and the Grand Old Man. His earliest memories, he once recalled, were of the early stages of the home-rule struggle. Gladstone's speeches, along with the letters of Joseph Mazzini, the Italian nationalist, and the sermons of F. D. Maurice, the English Christian socialist, made up his earliest serious reading.

From 1886 to 1891 Hammond attended Bradford grammar school where, along with his friend and classmate Sir William Rothenstein, he earned a reputation as a fiery radical. He went up to St John's College, Oxford, in 1891, to read classics with Sidney Ball, the Fabian disciple of T. H.

(John) Lawrence Le Breton Hammond (1872–1949), by Christopher Hall, 1930s?

Green and the recognized leader of university socialism. Ball's was a formative influence; 'I cannot imagine', Hammond later wrote, 'what my Oxford life would have been like without him' (Weaver, 265). But collectivism generally was on the wane among undergraduates in the early 1890s. A Liberal revival was under way in which Hammond, together with his friends J. A. Simon, Francis Hirst, and Hilaire Belloc, played a prominent part. An accomplished debater, Hammond was elected secretary of the Oxford Union in November 1894. This and the presidency of the Palmerston Club distracted him from his studies, and Hammond went down with a disappointing second in Greats in 1895.

Shortly thereafter, he succeeded Tom Ellis, the new chief Liberal whip, as private secretary to Sir John Brunner, co-founder of Brunner, Mond & Co. and Liberal MP for the Cheshire division of Northwich. Hammond's first book was a revision of Brunner's *Education in Cheshire* (1896). In 1897 he contributed to the *Essays in Liberalism by Six Oxford Men* and started writing leaders for the *Leeds Mercury* and the *Liverpool Post*. His life in journalism began in earnest two years later, when he assumed the editorship of *The Speaker*, a weekly alternative to the Liberal Unionist *Spectator*. At a time when imperialism was all the rage, the vital stuff of tabloid sensation, Hammond courageously upheld an older, nationalist tradition. Week in and week out he provided a forum for J. A. Hobson, L. T. Hobhouse, John Morley, James Bryce, and other 'pro-Boers', who opposed the war in South Africa and deplored the army's resort to what Sir Henry Campbell-Bannerman famously called 'methods of barbarism'. With Francis Hirst and Gilbert Murray, the prodigal classicist-cum-liberal internationalist who was to prove a lifelong friend, Hammond at the same time joined in the writing of *Liberalism and the Empire* (1900), a lonely protest in the name of reason against the imperialist excesses of the age.

In 1901 Hammond married (Lucy) Barbara Bradby [**(Lucy) Barbara Hammond** (1873–1961)], the seventh and last child of the Revd Edward Henry Bradby (1826–1893) and his wife, Ellen Johnson (1836–1918). Born on 25 July 1873, Barbara (as she was always called) Hammond had grown up at Haileybury College, where her father, a product of Thomas Arnold's Rugby and Benjamin Jowett's Balliol, was headmaster. When aged ten she had moved with her family to Toynbee Hall, Samuel Barnett's mission settlement in Whitechapel, London, and there been steeped in the late Victorian culture of altruism. After rigorous training in the corporate virtues at Jane Frances Dove's pioneer boarding-school for girls, St Leonard's, at St Andrews, Fife, she followed her sister Dorothy to Oxford, entering Lady Margaret Hall in 1892. Besides meeting Lawrence Hammond she studied with L. T. Hobhouse and was the first woman to earn first-class honours in both classical moderations and Greats. As ardent a Liberal as her husband, she too was a committed 'pro-Boer', a suffragist, and a pillar of the Women's Industrial Council until 1905, when ovarian tuberculosis forced a move from Battersea Park to Hampstead and condemned the Hammonds to childlessness.

It was only on coming down from Oxford in what he later regarded as an appalling state of ignorance that Lawrence Hammond began to read history in any systematic way. His first historical work was an admiring, not to say worshipful, study of *Charles James Fox* (1903). Journalism remained his main occupation until 1907, when he surrendered the editorship of *The Speaker* (henceforth *The Nation*) to H. W. Massingham and became secretary to the civil service commission, a post that evidently (and somewhat scandalously) afforded sufficient leisure for his scholarship. In perfect partnership—hers the research, his the writing, in the main—the Hammonds now entered into an intensive study of the social history of the late eighteenth and early nineteenth centuries. The first fruit of their collaboration was *The Village Labourer* (1911), a passionate indictment of the socially dislocating effects of eighteenth-century enclosure, which long remained the most widely read work of English rural history.

In 1912, after seven years in Hampstead, the Hammonds retreated further from London still, to Oatfield, a farmhouse at Piccotts End near Hemel Hempstead, Hertfordshire. Though handsome and vigorous people—Barbara especially was known for her intensely penetrating blue eyes and her beautifully abundant, copper-red hair—they were never robust, and Oatfield became their sanatorium, a refuge from the miseries and miasmas of the world. Lawrence Hammond's work took him frequently to town, but apart from occasional forays to the Public Record Office, Barbara Hammond avoided it as much as possible, always preferring the quiet of Oatfield, where between paragraphs she pottered about an extensive garden, tended all manner of domestic animals, and brilliantly maintained a caustic correspondence with a wide circle of family members and friends.

At war's outbreak in 1914, Lawrence Hammond, after much political soul-searching, accepted a commission in the Royal Field Artillery. He was an indifferent soldier, however, and in July 1916, on being declared unfit for service overseas, he left the army for Asquith's committee on (later ministry of) reconstruction. Here he joined Vaughan Nash, Edwin Montagu, Beatrice Webb, and others in the work (as Beatrice Webb described it) of 'surveying and unravelling the whole tangle of governmental activities introduced by the war' (Weaver, 132). Barbara Hammond, meanwhile, brought to completion the book that remains 'the classic study of the social and economic conditions of the working people during the industrial revolution' (Clarke, 189): *The Town Labourer* (1917). Appearing when it did, in the gloomy depths of the First World War, this famous indictment of the excessively commercial spirit of one age contributed decisively to the socialist spirit of another. With the publication of *The Skilled Labourer* two years later, the Hammonds completed their famous trilogy—the effect of which was massively to confirm the catastrophic version of the industrial era—and established themselves as the leading social historians of their time.

Lawrence Hammond returned to journalism in 1919 as special correspondent to the Paris peace conference for the *Manchester Guardian*, C. P. Scott's great Liberal daily. Discouraged by the vengeful spirit of the proceedings, he wrote his own J. M. Keynes-like denunciation of the treaty of Versailles, and then turned his mind to Ireland, past and present. In two famous *Nation* supplements of 1921, he exposed both the futility and the barbarity of the Anglo-Irish war and contributed to the change of heart that brought Lloyd George to the negotiating table. Hammond covered the negotiations ending the war for the *Manchester Guardian*, met and admired Michael Collins, and for the next two years conspicuously supported Collins's effort to reconcile Ireland to partition and dominion status.

The labourer trilogy, meanwhile, had led the Hammonds naturally to their interestingly ambivalent life of *Lord Shaftesbury* (1923) and to *The Rise of Modern Industry* (1925), a work of synthesis that R. H. Tawney once described as 'the most instructive and most original introduction to the social and economic aspects of history available in English' (Weaver, 187). But Tawney was a friend and like-minded admirer. In truth, the Hammonds were liberal moralists whose economic arguments were coming under increasingly critical scrutiny in the 1920s by a new generation of more statistically minded historians led by J. H. Clapham. In the first volume of his *Economic History of Modern Britain* (1926), Clapham assailed 'the legend that everything was getting worse for the working man' in the early nineteenth century and in its place made the statistical case for material improvement. This the

Hammonds ultimately begrudgingly conceded, but only after falling back on the more qualitative genealogy of misery that was to inform their last substantial collaborative effort, *The Age of the Chartists* (1930).

In belated tribute to their collaboration, the University of Oxford conferred honorary degrees on both Hammonds simultaneously in 1933. Barbara Hammond was by then at work on her never-to-be-published history of commons preservation, Lawrence Hammond on his magisterial study *Gladstone and the Irish Nation* (1938, reissued with an introduction by M. R. D. Foot, 1964). Conceived and commissioned as a vindication of Gladstone's Irish policy, this great work remains 'the most striking of many works treating aspects of Gladstone's later career' (Matthew, 395); but, appearing as it did in the shadow of the Munich crisis, it found few readers at the time and it remained the least known of Hammond's major works.

At the outbreak of the Second World War in September 1939, the Hammonds let their house at Hemel Hempstead and moved to Manchester, where Lawrence Hammond, now aged sixty-seven, assumed a permanent place on the staff of the *Manchester Guardian*. A lifelong Francophile, he was pained by Vichy, an aberration born of a moment of national bewilderment, he felt, and for four long years he sustained an encouraging series of leaders subsequently published under the suggestive title *Faith in France* (1948). Twice in his life, in 1931 and 1946, Hammond declined honours from his own government, but he proudly accepted appointment to the French Légion d'honneur in 1948. An honorary fellow of St John's College, Oxford, since 1937, he was elected to a fellowship of the British Academy in 1942 and received a second honorary degree of DLitt, from the University of Manchester, in 1944.

The Hammonds returned to Oatfield at the end of the war in 1945. Despite the modest reception accorded *Gladstone and the Irish Nation*, Hammond had not despaired of his romantic notion of bringing the wisdom of Gladstone to bear on his own illiberal age, and in 1946 he began a short life of the Grand Old Man that he did not live to complete. (Eventually completed by M. R. D. Foot, it appeared posthumously as *Gladstone and Liberalism* in 1952.) A longtime sufferer from angina and related maladies, Lawrence Hammond died of heart failure at Oatfield on 7 April 1949. Barbara Hammond survived him, and everyone else she knew, by many years, dying sadly demented at St Paul's Hospital, Hemel Hempstead, on 16 November 1961.

Comparing the collaboration of the Hammonds to that of Sidney and Beatrice Webb at the time of Lawrence Hammond's death, Gilbert Murray noted that the Hammonds were more 'Victorian' in that they based their politics on ethical judgements, not simply on economics or supposed social results. 'They asked first not what would pay but what was true, what was right, and what was humane'. For all his political engagement, moreover, there was in J. L. Hammond especially, Murray said, 'a sort of radiation of personal goodness, of quick sympathy and kindness, combined in a rare way with unswerving integrity and courage', and thus it had been well said of him that 'amid the hottest political controversies, he never made a personal enemy or lost a personal friend' (Weaver, 259–61). STEWART A. WEAVER

**Sources** S. A. Weaver, *The Hammonds: a marriage in history* (1997) • P. Clarke, *Liberals and social democrats* (1978) • H. C. G. Matthew, *Gladstone, 1875–1898* (1995) • *DNB* • A. Ridler, *A Victorian family postbag* (1988) • d. cert. [Lucy Barbara Hammond]

**Archives** Bodl. Oxf., corresp. and papers • Marquette University Memorial Library, Milwaukee, Wisconsin, papers | Bodl. Oxf., letters to Francis Marvin and Edith Marvin; corresp. with Gilbert Murray; letters to Lord Ponsonby; letters to E. J. Thompson • Harvard U., Houghton L., Rothenstein MSS • JRL, letters to the *Manchester Guardian* • JRL, C. P. Scott MSS • U. Birm. L., corresp. with F. B. Young • Worcester College, Oxford, letters to Ruth Dalton

**Likenesses** W. Rothenstein, chalk drawing, 1923, NPG; repro. in R. Rothenstein, ed., *The portrait drawings of William Rothenstein* (1926) • photograph, *c.*1930, repro. in Weaver, *Hammonds* • photograph, *c.*1930 (Lucy Barbara Hammond), repro. in Weaver, *Hammonds* • H. Coster, photographs, *c.*1930–1939, NPG • C. Hall, oils, 1930–1939?, NPG [*see illus.*] • W. Stoneman, photograph, 1945, NPG • W. Rothenstein, oils (Lucy Barbara Hammond), Lady Margaret Hall, Oxford

**Wealth at death** £12,797 2*s.* 5*d.*: probate, 12 Dec 1949, *CGPLA Eng. & Wales* • £25,899 3*s.* 9*d.*—Lucy Barbara Hammond: probate, 22 Feb 1962, *CGPLA Eng. & Wales*

**Hammond, Robert** (1620/21–1654), parliamentarian army officer, was born probably in Chertsey, Surrey, the eldest son of Robert Hammond (*d.* 1623), a country gentleman of Surrey, and his wife, Elizabeth Thorneton. His grandfather Dr John *Hammond (*d.* 1617) was a distinguished court physician. The Hammonds were a divided family during the civil war and interregnum. One of Robert's uncles, Thomas Hammond, was lieutenant-general of the artillery in the New Model Army, and a republican who was one of Charles I's judges (though not actually a signatory of the death warrant); another, Dr Henry Hammond, was a famous Anglican divine and court chaplain who would have obtained a bishopric if he had not died on the eve of the Restoration.

Robert Hammond matriculated at Magdalen Hall, Oxford, in 1636, aged fifteen, but did not graduate. By 1642 he was serving as an ensign in Ireland, fighting to put down the uprising. By 1643 he had returned to England and was captain of the life guard to the earl of Essex, lord general of the parliamentarian army. In 1644 he was promoted major of Edward Massey's regiment. He was abused by a fellow officer who challenged him to a duel; Hammond refused to respond but was then struck by his assailant; a duel then inevitably followed, and Hammond killed his opponent. For this he was temporarily suspended from his command, but after a court martial fully exonerated, having acted solely in self-defence. By 1645 he was the colonel of a foot regiment, and taking an active part in the closing stages of the civil war. Edmund Ludlow states in his *Memoirs* that at the siege of Basing House in October 1645 Hammond, who was related to the earl of Essex, deliberately let himself be captured by the defenders, so that the marquess of Winchester, who was himself connected by marriage to Essex, should be spared when the castle was taken. If this had been so it is scarcely credible that Cromwell would have sent Hammond to report

Basing's capture to parliament, with a strong recommendation that he should be compensated for his losses and sufferings, for which he was awarded £200; moreover Essex had ceased to be commander-in-chief six months before this. Hammond became governor of Exeter in 1646, and then of Gloucester, and that autumn he was a banner-bearer at Essex's funeral. This honour may as easily have arisen from his previous life guard command as from family connection. Hammond had by then married Mary Hampden (*b.* 1630?), youngest daughter of the parliamentarian leader John *Hampden (*d.* 1643), who had had a very close relationship with Essex.

As relations between parliament and army worsened in the spring of 1647 Hammond at first expressed readiness to take his regiment over to serve in Ireland; but when it became clear that most of the officers and men were only prepared to do so on their own terms, he changed his line. Hammond continued to be closely associated with the army's resistance to the presbyterian majority in the House of Commons from May to July. He seems, however, to have grown uneasy about the army's increasingly radical political stance towards both parliament and the king. A convenient way out of this was found when Fairfax, on the advice of Cromwell and other senior officers, appointed him governor of the Isle of Wight on 31 August, this being validated by parliamentary ordinance a week later. At the time this may have seemed a mere formality, but the following year it led to serious doubts—on Hammond's part and more widely—as to whether he was ultimately answerable to the captain-general or to the speakers of the two houses.

None of this would have mattered if Hammond's new post had remained an agreeable backwater, if not quite a sinecure. Some time during the summer he had been introduced to the king by his Anglican uncle and had, like other officers of the army, been flattered and initially attracted by Charles's manner. This led some of the king's closest confidants to believe that Hammond might be won over, even that he was a crypto-royalist in waiting. Thus it was that when the king escaped from Hampton Court on the night of 11–12 November (apparently fearing assassination by the Levellers), mainly on the advice of John Ashburnham Charles ended up on the Hampshire coast; instead of bending every effort to procure a vessel to take him across the channel, as common sense dictated and as his other attendant, Sir John Berkeley, claimed to have advised, his presence was revealed to Hammond, who crossed over to Titchfield, and from 14 November Charles was incarcerated in Carisbrooke Castle on the island. Writing some eighteen years later, the great royalist historian Clarendon blamed Ashburnham for this—as it turned out—fatal outcome. The assertion that, on learning of Hammond's presence downstairs in the house at Titchfield, the king 'brake out in a passionate exclamation, and said "Oh, Jack thou hast undone me"', but then forbade Ashburnham to try to kill Hammond, may be apocryphal, and indicative of the writer's personal preference for Berkeley (Clarendon, *Hist. rebellion*, 4.265). The feeling was evidently mutual. For, on learning of the king's arrival on the coast and his intention of crossing the Solent, Hammond is reported by Berkeley as saying:

> Oh Gentlemen, you have undone me by bringing the king into the island, if—at least—you have brought him; and, if you have not, pray let him not come; for what, between my duty to his majesty, and my gratitude for this fresh obligation of confidence on the one hand, and my observing my trust to the army on the other, I shall be confounded. (Ashburnham, appendix 6, clxxi)

Be that as it may, Hammond proved loyal to parliament and the army. When the king was known to be planning to escape, the conditions of his captivity were tightened; when Charles gave his parole during the renewed negotiations in 1648 they were much loosened again. The many letters which Hammond wrote to Fairfax, the two speakers, and others show his unhappiness with his own role, and his constant shortage of men and money for the supply of the garrison and the king's entourage, but there is no hint of disloyalty. When one of his officers, Edmund Rolfe, was accused of planning to murder the king, Hammond defended him stoutly and helped to get him exonerated. To judge from the two famous letters written to him by Cromwell, and one from Ireton, in November 1648, the army leaders were genuinely worried, not that Hammond was about to turn royalist and let the king escape altogether, but that he would obey the orders of parliament if these conflicted with theirs, as to where Charles was to be taken, when, and by whom. The crunch came at the end of that month, when he received an order from Fairfax recalling him to army headquarters and another from parliament telling him to stay where he was. In the event Hammond was sent up under arrest and the king handed over to other officers, but Hammond was soon released and not proceeded against for disobeying orders. He was awarded an annuity of £500 for his services, though this was later changed to a grant of Irish lands worth £600 per annum.

Hammond took no part in public affairs from January 1649, and we may safely infer that—like Fairfax—he was against the trial and execution of the king. References to him in letters from Cromwell to his friend and erstwhile political ally Lord Wharton in 1650–51 suggest that he regarded Hammond as a backslider, and that Cromwell replied more in sorrow than in anger when Hammond sought employment in Ireland. In 1651 Hammond appealed to Cromwell, by then lord general, for clemency towards the presbyterian conspirator the Revd Christopher Love. With the establishment of the protectorate, and consequent annulment of the engagement (the loyalty oath, eschewing kingship and House of Lords), relations between Cromwell and Hammond were clearly restored. In August 1654 Hammond was appointed to the Irish council at a salary of £1000 per annum, but he became ill with a fever shortly after his arrival and died in Dublin in October. He was later buried there.

In his will Hammond provided generously for his wife and two daughters and an unborn child (another daughter in fact), leaving lands in Buckinghamshire, Berkshire, Surrey, and Ireland; his wife and his brother-in-law Richard *Hampden were made joint executors. The will was proved to Hampden in December 1654 and then again to the widow in March 1655. The Irish lands were presumably forfeited at the Restoration; tracing the descent of landed property through female lines of descent is extraordinarily difficult. Hammond's widow married Sir John Hobart.

Robert Hammond played an important, if unwilling, part in great events for exactly twelve and a half months (from mid-November 1647 to the end of November 1648). Apart from the Essex–Hampden–Cromwell connections there was very little of the religious or political radical about Hammond, and certainly nothing of the republican or regicide. G. E. Aylmer

**Sources** *The Clarke papers*, ed. C. H. Firth, 1–2, CS, new ser., 49, 54 (1891–4) • C. H. Firth and G. Davies, *The regimental history of Cromwell's army*, 2 vols. (1940) • Thomason tracts [BL] • *JHC*, 5–7 (1646–59) • *JHL*, 8–10 (1645–8) • *The writings and speeches of Oliver Cromwell*, ed. W. C. Abbott and C. D. Crane, 4 vols. (1937–47) • H. Cary, ed., *Memorials of the great civil war in England from 1646 to 1652*, 2 vols. (1842) • *The memoirs of Edmund Ludlow*, ed. C. H. Firth, 2 vols. (1894) • Clarendon, *Hist. rebellion* • J. Ashburnham, *A narrative of John Ashburnham …*, 2 vols. (1830) • T. Herbert, *Memoirs of the last two years of King Charles I*, ed. G. Nicol, 4th edn (1839) • Foster, *Alum. Oxon.* • Wood, *Ath. Oxon.*, new edn, 3.500–02 • K. S. Bottigheimer, *English money and Irish land* (1971), appx • wills of Robert Hammond, his father, Robert Hammond, and uncle Thomas Hammond, PRO, PROB 11/; SP24/5; E315/5 • GEC, *Peerage*, 4.614

**Likenesses** G. P. Harding, wash drawing (after C. Johnson), AM Oxf., Sutherland collection

**Wealth at death** lands in Berkshire, Surrey, Buckinghamshire, Ireland; over £800 in legacies: will, PRO

**Hammond, Robert** (1850–1915), electrical engineer, was born on 19 January 1850 at Park Lane, Waltham Cross, Hertfordshire, the son of Robert Hammond, brewer, and his wife, Ann. He was educated at Nunhead grammar school. His first job was in the counting-house of a London cloth merchant, but in 1866 he joined the engineering firm Ullathorne & Co. of Lincoln's Inn Fields. In 1872 he left Ullathorne's for Bryant, Forster & Co., iron merchants, in Newcastle upon Tyne. After a short period with another iron merchant, James Jennings, he established his first engineering company, the partnership of Hammond, Kyle & Co., but this was ruined by a crash in South American securities.

Hammond first became involved in electrical engineering in 1878, when he took it up alongside his continuing iron ore interests. His first lighting installations were of arc lamps, illuminating various iron companies' works in the north east. He soon turned to public and municipal lighting, and was involved in some of the earliest public schemes, including those at Chesterfield and Brighton in 1881, and Hastings and Eastbourne in 1882. He also helped to fund Sebastian de Ferranti's early work on dynamos. A tireless worker, Hammond was responsible for dozens of public lighting installations, as well as several for heavy industry, and schemes in Ireland and Spain. He also set up several 'house-to-house' companies for public electricity supply. However, he often faced financial difficulties, and in 1893 he gave up contracting engineering to concentrate on consulting and expert witness work.

Elected a member of the Institution of Electrical Engineers (IEE) in 1893, Hammond became honorary treasurer in 1902. He was able to apply his varied experiences to bring in reforms that strengthened the IEE's position in relation to the electrical industry. He introduced the IEE's model forms of contract in 1903, which brought a much needed element of standardization to electrical contracting. He was also responsible for introducing the IEE's membership examinations. A colleague said of him that it was just as well that Hammond's engineering knowledge was not subjected to the tests he had introduced. Despite his lack of formal training, he realized that structured, practical training courses were essential to the future of the electrical industry, and to this end he helped to establish one of the first technical colleges, Faraday House, in 1889, after an earlier attempt to found a college in 1883 had failed.

Hammond's capacity for work was almost endless. As a result of touring the country delivering popular lectures on lighting developments, he wrote one of the first popular handbooks on electric light, *The Electric Light in our Homes*, published in 1884. In 1891 he launched a journal, *Lightning*, which aimed to provide information about the electricity industry for users and customers. *Lightning* later became the *Electrical Times*. However, his energy extended beyond the electricity industry. In 1889 he unsuccessfully ran as an MP for the Hallam division of Sheffield, standing as a Liberal free-trader. He was a keen golfer, and wrote two books on bridge and one on whist. He also loved travel, and often combined this with his work, visiting the USA several times to study electric traction systems, and presenting an influential paper in South Africa about electricity development in the Rand. His only son, Robert Whitehead Hammond, born in 1876 from his first marriage, to Elizabeth Whitehead, and also an electrical engineer, was due to take over his father's business, but was killed in the trenches in 1917. His first wife having died, Robert Hammond contracted a second marriage in 1914, to Martha Winifred (*b.* 1876), daughter of Joseph Edwards. Hammond died at his home, 1 Rudall Crescent, Hampstead, on 5 August 1915, and was cremated at Golders Green. Tim Procter

**Sources** *Electrical Times*, 48 (July–Dec 1915), 125–6, 137 • *Electrical Review*, 77 (1915), 207–8 • *Journal of the Institution of Electrical Engineers*, 54 (1916), 679–82 • membership application circular, 1898, Inst. CE • membership application form, 1899, Institution of Mechanical Engineers Archives • A. P. Trotter, 'Reminiscences', Inst. EE, SC MSS 66 • *Institution of Mechanical Engineers: Proceedings* (1915), 802–4 • *PICE*, 201 (1915–16), 393 • R. H. Parsons, *The early days of the power station industry* (1939) • J. F. Wilson, *Ferranti and the British electrical industry, 1864–1930* (1988) • *The Electrician* (6 Aug 1915), 651 • *The Engineer* (13 Aug 1915), 156 • b. cert. [Robert Whitehead Hammond] • d. cert. • b. cert. • *CGPLA Eng. & Wales* (1915) • St Mary's Cheshunt register of baptisms, 1832–50 • St Catherine's House index

**Archives** Museum of Science and Industry, Manchester, Ferranti

Ltd archives, papers relating to Hammond Electric Light and Power Co.
**Likenesses** black and white photograph, Inst. EE, archives · black and white photograph, repro. in *Electrical Times*
**Wealth at death** £7828 7*s.* 2*d.*: probate, 12 Oct 1915, *CGPLA Eng. & Wales*

**Hammond, Samuel** (*d.* 1665), clergyman and ejected minister, was described as a butcher's son of York, though no butcher of that surname can be found among the freemen of the city at an appropriate date. In 1638 he matriculated at King's College, Cambridge, where he was servitor to Samuel Collins, professor of divinity, graduated BA in 1642, and proceeded MA in 1645. He was ordained at Lincoln in 1642 and, through the influence of the earl of Manchester, gained a fellowship at Magdalene College in 1645. Hammond's preaching at St Giles's Church in Cambridge attracted a following within the university and brought him to the attention of Sir Arthur Hesilrige, who took him north as his chaplain and secured him the rectory of Bishopwearmouth, co. Durham, in 1651. That year he married, at Ryton, Margaret, daughter of Justice Ogle of Eglingham, co. Durham. On 5 November 1652 he was chosen to succeed Robert Jenison as preacher and Thursday lecturer at St Nicholas, Newcastle. Hammond was appointed assistant to the commission for the four northern counties in 1654 and on 2 January 1657 he signed the petition to Oliver Cromwell from the congregational churches at Newcastle as teacher of the church at Gateshead on the south bank of the Tyne.

At this time the congregationalist and presbyterian clergy of the area worked closely together, and Hammond had been active in opposing more radical groups. In 1653 he was among those involved in the exposure of Thomas Ramsay, an impostor who claimed to be a Jew called Joseph ben Israel, who had converted to Christianity and been baptized into the Baptist community at Hexham. The account of the fraud was published in 1653 as *The False Jew*, with a dedicatory epistle by Hammond and other Newcastle clergy, and severely damaged the reputation of the emerging Hexham Baptist church and its minister, Thomas Tillam, claiming that its members might have been papal agents. Tillam replied to the charge but the community at Hexham never recovered from the suspicions aroused and Hammond was able to drive a wedge between the Baptists there and their co-religionists in Newcastle, who adopted a less radical stance. The following year Hammond once again joined with fellow Newcastle clergy, this time in an attack on the Quakers following the conversion of Anthony Pearson, secretary to Arthur Hesilrige. Hammond, with others, lent his name to a tract entitled *The Perfect Pharisee under Monkish Holiness*, followed by *A Further Discovery of that Generation of Men called Quakers*, in which the doctrines of the Quakers were likened to those of the Catholics, especially in the matter of the covenant of works. The clergy were supported by the civic authorities in this campaign and matters went quiet until 1657 when further advance among Quakers in the town occasioned a fresh attack, and a new pamphlet from Hammond, *The Quakers House Built upon Sand* (1658).

In November 1659 Hammond was entrusted with a mission to General George Monck, and he remained in Newcastle at the Restoration. He felt unable to subscribe to the articles in 1662, however, and was ejected from his living, sailing to Hamburg on 16 July 1662, to be followed by his wife and children. His connections at Newcastle had secured for him a post as minister to the society of English merchants in the town, but his position was undermined by Lord Chancellor Edward Hyde, who refused to renew the charter of the society if they retained Hammond's services, and forbade him to preach. Hammond moved first to Stockholm and then to Danzig, where his predecessor at Newcastle, Robert Jenison, had also spent some time in the 1640s. He returned to England in 1665, where he settled briefly at Hackney, Middlesex, among some merchants he had known while living abroad, preaching occasionally in his own house. He died there on 10 December 1665, being survived by his wife, Margaret, with whom he had two surviving sons and one daughter.

William Joseph Sheils

**Sources** R. Howell, *Puritans and radicals in north England: essays on the English revolution* (1984) · *Calamy rev.*, 245 · R. Howell, *Newcastle upon Tyne and the puritan revolution: a study of the civil war in north England* (1967) · Venn, *Alum. Cant.*
**Archives** Queen's College, Oxford, reasons for turning Arminian

**Hammond, Thomas** (*c.*1600–1658), parliamentarian army officer and regicide, was the third son among the five children of Dr John *Hammond (*c.*1555–1617), physician to the royal household under James I, and his wife, Mary (or Marie) Harrison. Thomas's eldest brother, Robert, was the father of Lieutenant-Colonel Robert (Robin) *Hammond, Charles I's gaoler in the Isle of Wight during 1647–8, and Oliver Cromwell's cousin through the Hampden family. His youngest brother was the eminent Anglican divine Henry *Hammond. His only sister, Mary (or Marie), married Sir John, father of the more famous Sir William Temple. The family had a country seat at Chertsey in Surrey, and by the time of his death in 1617 Hammond's father was clearly a wealthy man, giving generously to charity as well as providing for his widow and children, Thomas's share being a lease worth £40 per annum and a legacy of £200.

Nothing certain is known of Hammond's career from then until the eve of the civil war, but he must have seen military service in the continental wars, either in the Netherlands or Germany, since he was a trained gunnery officer before 1642. Why he took the side of parliament against the king must remain surmise, unless explained by family connections and/or religious commitment. Evidence of his radicalism is found in 1644 when, as lieutenant-general of the ordnance in the army of the eastern association, he testified against his own commander-in-chief, Edward Montagu, second earl of Manchester, in the latter's celebrated clash with his lieutenant-general of horse, Oliver Cromwell. It is not surprising that Hammond was appointed to the corresponding post in the New Model Army from the spring of 1645.

Hammond was among the politically active officers of 1647–9, serving on the small standing committee to which Sir Thomas Fairfax handed over control of issuing all commissions, and acting as a spokesman for the high command in their successive dealings with the parliament, the king, and the radicals in the army itself (the agitators and their Leveller allies). He was named to the high court of justice in January 1649, attending no fewer than fourteen of its sittings, including the occasion on which judgment was given against the king; he did not, however, sign the death warrant, though there is no corroborative evidence for the statement that he positively refused to do so, and in 1660–61 he was clearly regarded—albeit posthumously—as having been a regicide [*see also* Regicides].

Hammond did not go on the Irish expedition of 1649, but remained on active service; unlike Fairfax he took part in the pre-emptive invasion of Scotland the following year. Like Cromwell, he fell seriously ill in that country and his health appears to have been permanently shattered. Hammond retired from his military position in the course of 1651–2, but continued to be much preoccupied with the pay arrears due to himself and the other personnel of the artillery train from his years of service. He received a grant of Irish lands, having been an 'adventurer' for £200 back in 1642. The artillery men received grants of former crown lands in Middlesex and Surrey in settlement of their arrears; his own share was the royal manor of Byfleet, only 4 miles from his family's seat in Chertsey. He had already acquired, in 1647–8, some previously episcopal lands in settlement of earlier debts owing to him on the public faith.

Hammond had a brush with the Commonwealth's accounts committee in 1651, but protested that he had accounted fully and properly for all the sums which he had received in all the three armies in which he had served; he pointed out that his account from July 1649 onwards was with the army in Scotland, where by this time George Monck had succeeded him as lieutenant-general of the ordnance. He was still acting as a trustee for the officers and men of the artillery train when additional compensation was voted out of crown lands in the act of 1652; a misleading reference from May of that year has led some authorities to assume that Hammond was dead by then.

Hammond was clearly in very poor health when he made his will in 1657, and he died in 1658, not long before the protector, his old colleague and then commander. The liberal if optimistic provisions for his family made in his will (proved 27 April 1658) were all destroyed by the events of 1660. The former church and crown lands which he had acquired were automatically forfeit; the residue of his property was confiscated by his retrospective attainder as a regicide. His widow, Martha, and seven surviving children must have had to make their own ways in the world, unless they received help from their in-laws, the Temple family, after whom one of Hammond's sons was named. His famous Anglican brother had died on the eve of the Restoration. G. E. AYLMER, *rev.*

**Sources** *The Clarke papers*, ed. C. H. Firth, 4 vols., CS, new ser., 49, 54, 61–2 (1891–1901) · G. E. Aylmer, *The state's servants: the civil service of the English republic, 1649–1660* (1973) · A. W. MacIntosh, 'The numbers of the English regicides', *History*, new ser., 67 (1982) · *VCH Surrey*, 4.231; 3.401 · L. R. Stevens, 'Notes on Byfleet manor and the manor house', *Surrey Archaeological Collections*, 45 (1937), 48–73 · will, PRO, PROB 11/130, sig. 64 [of John Hammond] · will, PRO, PROB 11/239, sig. 438 [of Robert Hammond] · will, PRO, PROB 11/276, sig. 217 [of Thomas Hammond]

**Hammond, Walter Reginald** (1903–1965), cricketer, was born on 19 June 1903 in the royal garrison at Dover Castle, the only child of Corporal (later Major) William Walter Hammond (1879–1918) and his wife, (Charlotte) Marion Crisp (1879–1970), of Buckland, near Dover. His father, son of a builder in Hampstead, had joined the Royal Garrison of Artillery in 1897 and, commissioned in the First World War, fell at Amiens. The son's early childhood was spent on service stations in China and Malta and when war broke out in 1914 he went to Portsmouth grammar school, before moving to Cirencester grammar school in Gloucestershire only days before his father's death. At that country school, where he was a boarder, he dominated in all sports. An average of 57.84 (the next highest was 7.86) for the first eleven, in 1920, led to his being offered a contract with Gloucestershire. At school he had already shown a detachment from fame and a remoteness which would be the hallmarks of his character. As a teenager, with the county, he was asked to supper by a girlfriend, a dancer at the Bristol Hippodrome. His mother and the great Victorian actress Marie Lloyd were there. Marion Hammond, whom he held in both awe and affection, remained an influence on him all his life. Marie Lloyd told the young dancer: 'All that boy of yours wants to do is to hit a cricket ball as hard as he can'. The description was apt.

Success did not come immediately, nor was Hammond helped by the MCC ruling, in 1922, that he had not qualified for Gloucestershire by birth or residence. Lord Harris, doyen of Kent cricket and aware of Hammond's Dover birthplace, had seen him bat at Lord's at the start of the season and had been instrumental in challenging his eligibility. For the rest of that summer season Hammond could not play in the county championship but he marked his return to the side in 1923, duly qualified, with 110 and 92 against Surrey. Two years later, in making 250 against Lancashire, he caught the eye of the press and of the influential Sir Pelham Warner, whose friendship he retained throughout his life. Hammond's performance against the Lancashire attack, which included the formidably fast Ted McDonald, led Neville Cardus to write: 'to be present at the rise of a star in the sky and to know it is going to be glorious is a moment thrilling indeed' (*Manchester Guardian*, 20 Aug 1925).

Between 1921 and 1924 Hammond played soccer spasmodically for Bristol Rovers, a third division club. He had shown talent but the football world was more proletarian than he cared for. Despite his 250 against Lancashire, his

**Walter Reginald Hammond** (1903–1965), by Paul Laib

career batting average was as yet only 28.71; nevertheless, his abundant cricket potential took him to the West Indies with MCC in 1925–6 and he made another double century in the opening representative match against the West Indies (not yet of test status). But on that tour he acquired an infection, attributed at the time to a mosquito bite but certainly some form of blood poisoning. Untreated, in a pre-antibiotic age, he came home by ship with his life in danger.

Hammond announced his return to cricket in 1927—thirteen months after his illness—by making 1000 runs in May, the first player to do so since W. G. Grace (in 1895). A season which brought him almost 3000 runs led naturally to his selection for the MCC tour of South Africa. Not until he visited Australia in 1928–9, however, did he fulfil the highest expectations. With 905 runs (average 113.12) in the tests against the Australians, including four centuries, two of which were double ones, he had crossed the threshold of greatness. Ironically, that season saw the début of Don Bradman, whose figures, in every Anglo-Australian series in the 1930s, eclipsed those of Hammond.

In 1929, on his return from Australia, Hammond married Dorothy (*c.*1905–*c.*1964), daughter of Joseph Barker Lister, a Bradford textile merchant. The union brought him some financial security but little happiness. Dorothy tried harder than he to make the marriage work but too many factors militated against it. Early on, they both realized their lack of common interests. Soon the Lister family fortunes failed in the depression; Dorothy Hammond was reluctant to have children and her husband became involved with other women.

Despite some failures, notably in averaging only 20.25 against the 1934 Australians, Hammond was the natural successor to Jack Hobbs in England's batting for the ten years until the Second World War. In the aftermath of the 'bodyline' bowling tour of 1932–3 he crossed the Tasman Sea to score 227 and 336 not out in the two tests against New Zealand. In the triple century there was just the hint of pride in achieving what Bradman had done on several occasions. Hammond himself commented that his only previous triple century had been at Cirencester against schoolboys. His 231 at Sydney in 1936–7 was outclassed by his 240 at Lord's, also against Australia, in 1938. By then Hammond had become the England captain (he was appointed in that year), fulfilling the ambition of a man who had always preferred the social milieu of the amateurs to the artisan realms of the professionals. Not only did he far outshine his Gloucestershire colleagues on the field; he distanced himself from them—as a grammar schoolboy, the son of an officer—in accent, dress, and way of life. Through his friendship with men such as Beverley Lyon, the county captain, he also aspired to the public school and Oxbridge ethos which they represented. The decision to turn amateur at the start of the 1938 season was a necessary prelude to the captaincy and was made possible by the offer of a directorship with the Bristol tyre firm, Marsham.

The artistry of Hammond's 240 at Lord's, in his second test as captain, won the unqualified admiration of his contemporaries and the press. *The Times* called it 'a display of batting which can seldom have been surpassed' (*The Times*, 25 June 1938). Never again, as events turned out, would he exercise such unrelenting authority and display such captivating elegance. His captaincy that season was commended by no less a critic than Lord Hawke. Hammond took MCC to South Africa in the winter. He proved a sound strategist on the tour and averaged 87.00. Against the West Indies, in the final test (August 1939), just before the Second World War broke out, he and the young Len Hutton, making a century apiece, left English cricket with something to savour. Hutton would say of Hammond that 'he was in a class of his own; the finest batsman that I played with or against' (Howat, xv).

Of Hammond's many outstanding contributions to Gloucestershire's cricket, one week at the Cheltenham festival in 1928, when in two matches he made 360 runs, took sixteen wickets and held eleven catches, may be highlighted. Ten years later he hit seven centuries in eight successive innings for the county, making 1082 runs with an average of 180.33. His 'failure' was an 86. Modest and dismissive as he was of such personal success, he was reluctant to commend it in others. Journeymen county players—youngsters looking for encouragement or old campaigners for some endorsement—looked in vain. The tales are legion: a fine catch by a fellow fielder in the slips acclaimed by all except Hammond; a nervous débutant making a fifty ignored both before and after the event.

None of this made him a good 'team' man or a great county captain (in 1939), despite setting a 'fashion in enterprising cricket' (*Wisden*, 1940, 303). Two of his three biographers have searched for an explanation and, to some extent, found it in his shyness.

Hammond's batting embraced power, grace, timing, and footwork and a cover drive which was captured forever in a famous photograph taken at Sydney in 1928 by Herbert Fishwick. As a young man, he had been a ferocious hooker, a stroke which he scarcely played in later years. Only the Australian Bill O'Reilly, bowling to his legs, could contain him at his best. He bowled more for England than for Gloucestershire and mostly early in his career. His medium-paced outswingers were good enough to open the bowling in four tests against South Africa in 1927–8, but he became a reluctant performer, whose 732 first-class wickets (average 30.58) might well have been exceeded. During his poor batting spell against the 1934 Australians, the press unanimously argued he was worth his place as a bowler and fielder alone. In the slips, erect, watchful, tigerish, he was without peer in securing 819 catches.

During the Second World War Hammond served in the Royal Air Force, and reached the rank of squadron leader. He organized cricket in Cairo during the North African campaign. Leave took him to Durban, where he renewed a friendship made during the MCC tour of 1938–9 with Sybil Doreen Ness-Harvey (1922–1983), a former Natal beauty queen whom he would marry in 1947. He was back in England to play in many of the representative matches staged in 1944 and 1945. For England against the dominions at Lord's in 1945 he made a century in each innings. In wartime conditions many servicemen saw and testified to a lighter, more generous side to his character.

Hammond topped the national batting averages, for the eighth successive year, in the first post-war season, his 84.90 well ahead of the younger generation of players. He was the logical and indisputable choice as MCC's captain in Australia in 1946–7, but as the tour progressed he again became the remote figure which critics were all to ready to label him. He was under physical stress, with fibrositis, and under mental strain as his wife's divorce petition was reported in the Australian press, while he also worried about Sybil Ness-Harvey living in England. They married immediately on his return. England was by far the weaker side and he seemed to lose the dynamism to lead and the determination to win. His opposite number, Bradman, felt he 'did not display the leadership and tact which international captains are required to do' (Howat, 46). Others thought differently: Hammond's own team defended him, and the Australian journalist Clif Cary signalled him out for his diplomacy and unselfishness.

Hammond made his final test appearance at the end of that tour, scoring 79 against New Zealand to take him to 7249 runs (average 58.45) in his eighty-five test matches. After the tour he played only two more first-class matches, to give him career figures of 50,551 runs (average 56.10), with 167 centuries, 36 of them double centuries.

In 1951 Hammond moved to South Africa, where he and Sybil brought up their three children. He worked for a car firm in Durban and in 1959 became the first sports administrator to be appointed by Natal University. Contrary to the view which prevailed in England for so long, that he was little more than 'the man who cut the grass', he carried major budget and executive responsibilities. Professor Owen Horwood, who had been instrumental in his appointment, believed that what he did for the university sport was immeasurable. After surviving a car accident in 1960 (in which he was left for dead), Hammond scored his last century in 1961. 'The Hammond cover drive, once the joy of cricket the world over, was still there', reported the *Natal Daily News* (Howat, 133).

The South African years, which allowed Hammond his anonymity and gave him a happy family life, were paradoxically the best ones. When he died of a heart attack, at his home, 21 Park Lane, Kloof, Natal, on 1 July 1965 he still had great plans for his work at Natal University. A man who had given pleasure to thousands had at last secured some for himself. He had enriched cricket with his grace but in the craftsmanship of relationships he had showed human frailty. He was a great public figure but a very private person. He was cremated at Moore Road crematorium, Durban, on 6 July 1965. GERALD M. D. HOWAT

**Sources** G. Howat, *Walter Hammond* (1984) • R. Mason, *Walter Hammond* (1962) • D. Foot, *Wally Hammond* (1996) • W. R. Hammond, *Cricket my destiny* (1946) • W. R. Hammond, *Cricket my world* (1948) • *Wisden* (1928) • *Wisden* (1966) • *The Times* (2 July 1965) • *The Cricketer* (Aug 1965) • E. Blunden, *After the bombing and other short poems* (1949) • D. Lodge, *The test match career of Walter Hammond* (1990) • private information (2004) [Carolyn Kemp, daughter]
**Archives** FILM BFI NFTVA, documentary footage • BFI NFTVA, news footage • BFI NFTVA, sports footage | SOUND BBC WAC
**Likenesses** H. Fishwick, photograph, 1928 (the 'cover drive'), *Sydney Morning Herald*; repro. in Howat, *Walter Hammond* • group photograph, 1936, Hult. Arch. • oils, 1951, Gloucestershire CCC, Bristol • C. Hewitt, photograph, repro. in J. Huntington-Whiteley, *The book of British sporting heroes* (1998), p. 120 • P. Laib, photograph, NPG [*see illus.*] • portraits, Lord's, MCC collection • portraits, repro. in Howat, *Walter Hammond* • portraits, repro. in Mason, *Walter Hammond* • portraits, repro. in Foot, *Wally Hammond*

**Hammond, William** (*b*. 1614), poet, was the third son of Sir William Hammond (1579–1615) of St Albans Court, Kent, and Elizabeth Archer, daughter of Anthony and Margaret Archer. Elizabeth was the granddaughter of Edwin Sandys, archbishop of York, and the niece (on her mother's side) of the poet George Sandys. After her first husband's death she married Walter Balcanqual, dean of Rochester. William had two elder brothers (Anthony, who was the great-grandfather of James Hammond, also a poet, and Edward) and two younger sisters: Mary, who married the author Thomas Stanley, and the youngest, Margaret, who married Henry Sandys.

The only clues to William's life can be gleaned from his fifty or so poems, originally printed in 1655 as *Poems by W. H.*: several are dedicated to Thomas Stanley, others to the death of his brother-in-law Henry Sandys, and yet others to a host of marriages, births, and deaths among

William's friends and relatives. Whether the poems dedicated to 'The cruell mistresse', and 'To his mistresse, desiring him to absent himselfe', were addressed to a real or imaginary mistress remains open to speculation.

Hammond's poems were 'revived' by the champion of minor poets Sir Egerton Brydges in 1816 in an edition of which only a small number of copies (as few as sixty-one, perhaps even forty) were printed. Hammond may have well felt 'Commanded to write verses', as the title of one of his poems proclaims, but there is little sparkle to his verse. Saintsbury argues that Hammond, and other poets of his calibre, are of interest primarily because they provide a measure of the extent to which a particular period and culture were or were not 'poetical' (Saintsbury, 485), and Hammond was lucky to have lived at a time particularly favourable to poetic endeavour. It is not known when Hammond died, but his poem 'Gray haires' suggests that he may have reached a reasonably old age.

ARTEMIS GAUSE-STAMBOULOPOULOU

**Sources** [W. Hammond], *Poems by W. H.* (1655) • S. E. B. [Sir E. Brydges], *Occasional poems &c. &c. William Hammond esq.* (1816) • G. Saintsbury, ed., *Minor poets of the Caroline period*, 3 vols. (1905–21), 2 (1906) • Allibone, *Dict.* • Burke, *Gen. GB* (1937) • *English poetry* (Chadwyck-Healey Ltd, 1995) [CD-ROM; version 4.0] • *DNB*

**Hammond, William** (1727–1793), master mariner and merchant, of Kirk Ella, East Riding of Yorkshire, was the son of Anthony Hammond (1696–1759) and his wife, Mary Hayes. He was accepted as a younger brother of the Hull Trinity House in 1749, eventually becoming an elder brother and three times warden, in 1779, 1785, and 1792. As a representative of the house he regularly attended sessions of the House of Commons during the passage of the Spurn Lights Act of 1766. In November 1771 he sold to the Admiralty two vessels constructed at Whitby which, renamed *Resolution* and *Adventure*, were fitted out for the second great voyage of discovery (1772–5) of Commander (later Captain) James Cook. The two men were reputedly friends and these sturdy cat-built vessels were of a type familiar to Cook from his earliest days at sea, apprenticed to a Whitby shipmaster.

Hammond represented Trinity House, in close co-operation with David Hartley, MP for Hull, during the course of the Hull Dock Act of 1774. As chairman of the Hull Dock Company, Hammond superintended the creation of the town's first enclosed dock, which opened for shipping in 1778. While sheriff of Hull in 1785 he headed a committee set up by the Hull Trinity House to found a navigation school, an establishment which celebrated its bicentenary in 1987.

Hammond married Ann Bean, of York (*d.* 1785). They had twelve children. Hammond died on 26 June 1793 in Kirk Ella and was buried at Welton, near Hull. His son George *Hammond was secretary to David Hartley MP and at twenty-eight became the first British resident minister in Washington, USA (1791–5); he was later under-secretary for foreign affairs. William's grandson Edmund Hammond became Baron Hammond and was appointed an honorary brother of Hull Trinity House, thus renewing the family link with this institution.

ARTHUR G. CREDLAND, *rev.*

**Sources** A. Storey, *Trinity House of Kingston upon Hull*, 2 vols. (1967–9) • D. Thompson, *A history of Hull Trinity House School* (1988) • archives, Whitby Museum • archives, Hull Trinity House
**Archives** Hull Trinity House • Whitby Museum
**Likenesses** oils (as chairman of the Hull Dock Company), Hull Trinity House • oils (as chairman of the Hull Dock Company), Hull Maritime Museum

**Hammond, William John** (1797x9–1848), actor and theatre manager, was born in London between 1797 and 1799. A low comedian and singer, he first played on the London stage as Lopez in John Tobin's *The Honeymoon* in around 1819. In July of that year he was recruited to a newly formed stock company then playing at Walton-on-Thames, and the following September he joined Thomas Trotter's company at the Theatre Royal, Worthing, before going on to John Brunton's company at Brighton. In 1820–21 he alternated between the Haymarket Theatre and Penley's company, which was playing at Worthing, Windsor, and Coventry. After a brief spell at the Olympic, he was engaged by William Macready (father of the tragedian W. C. Macready) as a member of his company at Bristol. Between 1823 and 1826 he played the York circuit under the successive managements of Robert Mansel and Thomas Downe. During these first years of his career on the stage he achieved considerable popularity as Bob Acres in *The Rivals* and as Tony Lumpkin in *She Stoops to Conquer*.

From 1826 to 1829 Hammond and his wife, Jane Matilda, the daughter of Samuel Jerrold and a sister of the playwright Douglas Jerrold, were members of the company playing at the Theatre Royal, Liverpool. In 1829 Hammond entered a partnership to run the Liverpool Pantheon; he reopened it as the Liver Theatre and continued his association with it until 1836. In April 1830 he took over the York circuit, which then included the theatres royal at Hull and York and further theatres at Doncaster, Leeds, and Wakefield. His period of management was brief, but in terms of his reception and the stars he engaged it was second only to that of Tate Wilkinson. Among others, he brought Edmund Kean, Charles Mathews, Frederick Yates, and Madame Vestris to his theatres. None the less he relinquished all but the Doncaster theatre in 1832 when he failed to secure a reduction in his rents. He continued to provide an annual autumn season at Doncaster until 1839, and took on the lease of the Sheffield theatre at £300 a year (exclusive of gas, water, and taxes) from 1833 to 1839.

Meanwhile, and initially in partnership with his brother-in-law Douglas Jerrold, Hammond became the proprietor of the Strand Theatre, London, which had been opened in 1831. Here, from 25 May 1836, he enjoyed his greatest successes, putting on comedies, farces, and burlesques, including *The Pickwickians* and *Sam Weller's Tour*, in both of which he created the part of Sam Weller, and burlesques of *Othello* and *The Lady of Lyons*. Disaster followed when he took on the management of Drury Lane from October 1839. Despite the patronage of Queen Victoria, who made her first public appearance after her marriage at the theatre, Hammond's management ended at the beginning of March 1840, when he was declared bankrupt with debts of £8000.

After more than a year in prison, Hammond sought to revive his fortunes by starring with provincial companies, where he was enthusiastically received in his popular old parts. John Coleman observed that 'He had wigs of all kinds and costumes of every description, but he was always Hammond in another wig and another coat' (Coleman, 1.282). In 1842 he held a brief lease for the Liverpool Theatre Royal, and in 1846 he opened another Liverpool theatre as the Theatre Royal Adelphi. Unsuccessful there, he sailed for America in June 1848, but died in New York on 23 August from dysentery. His effects, put up for auction, included the scarlet frock coat he wore as Tony Lumpkin for his début at Niblo's Theatre, Astor Place, a variety of other costumes, a host of wigs, and the orchestral parts which singers were expected by custom to provide. C. M. P. TAYLOR

**Sources** R. J. Broadbent, *Annals of the Liverpool stage* (1908) • *The Mirror of the Stage, or, New Dramatic Censor*, 2/24 (14 July 1823) • *Actors by Daylight* (1838–9) • C. W. Hatfield, *Historical notes of Doncaster* (1870) • W. Senior, *The old Wakefield theatre* (1894) • S. Rosenfeld, 'The York Theatre', 1948, York Library • E. Stirling, *Old Drury Lane*, 2 vols. (1881) • J. Coleman, *Fifty years of an actor's life*, 2 vols. (1904) • W. B. Jerrold, *The life and remains of Douglas Jerrold* (1859) • Sheffield Theatre and Assembly Rooms cash book, Sheff. Arch. • West Riding Magistrates Quarter Sessions order books, 1830–39 • *Doncaster, Nottingham and Lincoln Gazette* (1830) • *Liverpool Mercury*
**Archives** Theatre Museum, London
**Likenesses** sketch, repro. in *Actors by Daylight* (12 May 1838)

**Hamnett** [*married name* de Bergen], **Nina** (1890–1956), painter and illustrator, was born on 14 February 1890 at 3 Lexden Terrace, Tenby, Pembrokeshire, the eldest of the four children of George Edward Hamnett (*b.* 1864), a captain in the Army Service Corps, and Mary Elizabeth De Blois Archdeacon (1863/4–1947), daughter of Captain William Edwin Archdeacon, a naval officer and cartographer.

Hamnett led a peripatetic childhood, attending the Royal School for Daughters of the Officers of the Army in Bath from 1902 to 1905 and classes at the Portsmouth School of Art in 1903 and the Dublin School of Art in 1905. After her father (by then a lieutenant-colonel) was cashiered in 1906, the family moved to London. Hamnett studied under Sir Alfred Cope at the Pelham School of Art, South Kensington, in 1907, and at the London School of Art from about 1907 to 1910 under Frank Brangwyn, John Swan, William Nicholson, and George Lambert. She first visited Paris in 1912 and in 1914 attended Marie Wassilieff's academy where Fernand Léger taught. In Paris she met the Norwegian dramatist and artist Edgar de Bergen (known as Roald Kristian; *b.* 1893), whom she married in London on 12 October 1914 and with whom she had a child who was born prematurely and died in 1915. Walter Sickert depicted them in *The Little Tea Party* (1916, Tate collection) looking, in Hamnett's words, 'the picture of gloom' (Hooker, 90; Hamnett, *Laughing Torso*, 1932, 82); and when

Nina Hamnett (1890–1956), by Roger Fry, 1917

de Bergen was deported as an alien in 1917, they never saw each other again. Hamnett had a succession of lovers and acquired a taste for boxers and sailors, because, as she said, 'they go away' (Hooker, 233).

A natural rebel, with her tall, boyish figure, short hair, unconventional clothes, and flamboyant behaviour, Hamnett rapidly became a well-known bohemian personality. A self-appointed artistic ambassador between London and Paris, friends and mentors included Henri Gaudier-Brzeska, Amedeo Modigliani, Walter Sickert, Roger Fry, and Augustus John. She benefited from her first-hand knowledge of the avant-garde in both cities to develop her own individual style and she made a significant contribution to the modern movement in London from about 1915 to 1930. She exhibited widely in solo and group shows, including, in London, those of the Allied Artists' Association, the Friday Club, the Grafton Group, the London Group, the New English Art Club, the National Portrait Society, the Goupil Gallery Salon, and the Leicester Galleries' 'Artists of Fame and Promise', and, in Paris, the Salon d'Automne and the Salon des Indépendants. She did decorative work at Fry's Omega workshops from 1913 to 1919, including painting designs on candlesticks and a mural on the theme of contemporary London life (1916) for the art dealer Arthur Ruck's house at 4 Berkeley Street. She also taught a life-drawing class at the Westminster Technical Institute in 1917–19.

Influenced by Fry and French art, particularly Cézanne, Hamnett painted still lifes, landscapes, and views of rooftops and the backs of houses, concentrating on the underlying formal structure. But she was always more interested in human beings and declared: 'My ambition is to paint psychological portraits that shall represent accurately the spirit of the age' (Gordon-Stables, 112–15). Her sitters included many of the leading artistic personalities of her time: Ossip Zadkine, Sickert, Horace Brodzky, Edith Sitwell, Osbert Sitwell, W. H. Davies, Rupert Doone, and Álvaro Guevara. Her portraits are strong, bold statements of character in which features are simplified and exaggerated to express her concise view of the subject's personality. Fine draughtsmanship, well-defined modelling of forms, and a richly low-toned palette relieved by well-placed details of colour give her portraits in oils an almost sculptural solidity. With her sharp eye for the underlying human comedy, Hamnett was always attracted to people and places with any kind of oddity value. Endlessly fascinated by life around her, she found a rich source of subject matter in cafés and pubs, the circus, the boxing ring, and the park bench.

Hamnett excelled as a draughtswoman. Sickert praised 'the sharp silhouette that her uniform and sensitive line defines with such expressiveness and such startling virtuosity' (Hooker, 116; *Cambridge Magazine*, 8 June 1918, 770–71). The ease and fluidity of her line, and her pared-down simplification of form, had much in common with Gaudier-Brzeska and Modigliani. Her witty pen-and-ink illustrations (1928) to Osbert Sitwell's *The People's Album of London Statues* rank among her best work and display what Augustus John called 'her perfectly original talent which (in the case of her drawings) falls into line with the grand tradition of British humouristics' (Hooker, 187; *Vogue*, April 1928).

From 1920 to 1926 Hamnett was the best-known British woman painter in Paris, a focal point for the large expatriate community, and friendly with Jean Cocteau, Erik Satie, Igor Stravinsky, and the composers known as Les Six. However, her commanding position in the hectic social life of Paris and London took its toll; by the mid-1930s her talent was in decline and she produced little beyond quick portrait sketches. In the 1930s and 1940s she presided over London's Fitzrovia and Soho, ever willing to tell another anecdote in return for the next drink. She had always led a financially precarious life, alleviated somewhat by the generosity of her rich and famous friends, but by the 1950s poverty, drink, and ill health severely restricted her movements. When she died in London on 16 December 1956, after falling from a window and being impaled on the railings below her flat at 164 Westbourne Terrace, Paddington, the coroner delivered a verdict of accidental death, which was hotly debated by her friends. She was cremated at Golders Green crematorium on the 23rd.

Hamnett is immortalized in the work of numerous writers and artists, notably Gaudier-Brzeska's famous 1913 marble torso of her (now in the Tate collection) and Roger Fry's portraits of 1917 (University of Leeds; Courtauld Inst.). Vignettes of her appear in countless memoirs of the period and she wrote two volumes of autobiography, *Laughing Torso* (1932) and *Is she a Lady?* (1956).

DENISE HOOKER

**Sources** D. Hooker, *Nina Hamnett: queen of bohemia* (1986) [incl. illustrations and bibliography] · L. Gordon-Stables, 'Nina Hamnett's psychological portraiture', *Artwork*, 1 (1924–5), 112–15 · W. Sickert, 'Nina Hamnett', *Cambridge Magazine* (8 June 1918), 770–71 · A. John, *Vogue* (April 1928)

**Archives** SOUND BL NSA, BBC Sound Archive, *Café Royal*, broadcast 28 Dec 1955

**Likenesses** H. Gaudier-Brzeska, marble torso, 1913, Tate collection · W. R. Sickert, oils, 1916, Tate collection · R. Fry, oils, 1917, Courtauld Inst. [*see illus.*] · R. Fry, oils, 1917, U. Leeds · double portrait, photograph, 1917 (with Pamela Diamond), King's Cam., Fry MSS · J. Kramer, oils, *c.*1926, priv. coll. · D. Farson, bromide print, 1950–55, NPG · D. Farson, photographs, *c.*1954, repro. in Hooker, *Nina Hamnett* · portraits, repro. in Hooker, *Nina Hamnett*

**Wealth at death** see Hooker, *Nina Hamnett*

**Hamo of Hythe**. *See* Hythe, Hamo (*b. c.*1270, *d.* in or after 1357).

**Hamond, Sir Andrew Snape, first baronet** (1738–1828), naval officer and administrator, was born in Blackheath, Kent, on 17 December 1738, the youngest child and only son of Robert Hamond (1704/5–1775), a shipowner of modest means, and his wife, Susannah Snape. Robert Hamond owned five ships in 1748, but then lost two, and, in his son's words, 'fell into misfortune, from which, with all his industry, he could never entirely extricate himself'. The family moved to Stepney where Hamond received his education.

**Early years** In February 1753 Hamond entered the navy on the sloop *Speedwell* (Captain James Webb), and was engaged in anti-smuggling duties around the Channel Islands. He also visited Sweden at this time. In 1754, when the *Speedwell* was laid up in East Cowes, Hamond learned navigation, and next year, with war threatening, he impressed men from the inbound merchant fleet. He then accompanied Webb to the *Sunderland* (60 guns) and immediately transferred with him to the *St Albans* (80 guns), sailing to the Mediterranean. Back in home waters, he passed his lieutenant's exam on 31 January 1759 (PRO, ADM 107/5, 87) and was made acting lieutenant on the *Albany* (14 guns), commanding the ship when the captain moved on. In June 1759, without his command confirmed, he sailed from Plymouth heavily loaded with masts and spars, as an escort for victuallers to Edward Hawke's blockading fleet off Brest. He did well to come through a storm with his cargo intact and received the thanks of Hawke, who was surprised to find that Hamond had not been confirmed in his command. Lord Howe wrote immediately to the Admiralty and Hamond was made fifth lieutenant of Howe's ship the *Magnanime* (74 guns) on 20 June. He was present at the battle of Quiberon Bay and sailed with Howe for the rest of the war, transferring with him to the *Princess Amelia* (80 guns) in 1762.

In April 1763 Hamond was given command of the cutter *Grace*, cruising in home waters, and he was promoted commander on 20 June 1765. According to Hamond's autobiographical account, when the *Grace*'s commission finished

**Sir Andrew Snape Hamond, first baronet** (1738–1828), by George Henry Phillips, pubd 1830 (after Sir Thomas Lawrence, *c.*1800–05)

in 1764 he went to Normandy to study the French language. In 1767 he was given the sloop *Savage*, cruising off the west coast of Ireland, sailing to Newfoundland on 2 June 1769 and returning the same year. At the time of the Falkland Islands mobilization in 1770 Howe chose Hamond as his flag captain in the *Barfleur* (90 guns), his promotion dating from 7 December 1770. In August 1771 he was appointed to the *Arethusa* (32 guns) and in October he was ordered to North America under Rear-Admiral John Montagu. He arrived in Norfolk after a sickly voyage, and later moved up to Boston, and then cruised against smugglers. He quarrelled badly with Montagu after he had prolonged a stay in Philadelphia with Lord Dunmore, the governor of Virginia, though this affair was eventually smoothed over. Hamond left Providence in May 1773, cruising north towards Prince Edward Island and returning to Boston in early October. He paid off the ship at Spithead on 28 November and then spent a year on half pay at his home on the Isle of Wight.

**American War of Independence: the first five years** In July 1775, with trouble brewing in the North American colonies, Hamond was appointed to the *Roebuck* (44 guns) which, newly launched at Chatham, sailed on 9 September and arrived at Halifax on 31 October. Here he and his crew helped build up the defences. By 16 February 1776 he was at Norfolk, with orders to protect the loyalists in Virginia and to blockade the entrances of Chesapeake and Delaware bays. Together with Lord Dunmore, Hamond seized Tucker's Mill Point in the Elizabeth River to use as a base and a place of refuge for loyalists. Commanding a small squadron of small ships, he pursued a number of American ships off the mouth of the Delaware, with moderate success. Hamond prosecuted the blockade very vigorously, the *Roebuck* going aground in the shallow waters more than once; Joseph Des Barres's chart of Delaware Bay, dated 1 June 1779, attributes the soundings and other information to him. Despite his attempts to reduce the maritime defences of Philadelphia, and despite being attacked by American armed galleys, Hamond was unable to bring the Americans to battle. The successes of the revolutionary army eventually led him, on 5 August 1777, to evacuate Dunmore's forces and the loyalists from Virginia to New York.

Under his old captain and patron, Lord Howe, Hamond then participated in the operations against Philadelphia. On 2 October 1777 he took the fort at Billingsport in the effort to keep the Delaware navigation open. In the next year the *Roebuck* was a valuable ship in Howe's operations against d'Estaing, off Sandy Hook and then later at Newport and Boston. It was Hamond who reconnoitred the French fleet in Boston and urged Howe to attack at once, but the cautious admiral stood off. Hamond returned home in December 1778, and was knighted for his services on 15 January of the following year. At the same time he and Howe were to defend their conduct in the American campaign. On 8 March 1779 he married Anne Graeme (*d.* 1838), daughter of Major Graeme, sometime lieutenant-governor of St Helena.

In June 1779 Hamond sailed again for America in the *Roebuck*, this time under Marriot Arbuthnot. He took a distinguished part in the siege of Charlestown, which fell in early May 1780. Hamond was sent home with dispatches, handing over the *Roebuck* to his nephew, Andrew Snape Douglas. The dispatches contained fulsome praise for Hamond: 'Whether in the great line of service or in the detail of duty, he has been ever ready, forward, and animated', Arbuthnot reported (*Private Papers of … Sandwich*, 3.237).

**Nova Scotia, 1780–1782, and appointments in England** Having briefed the king and Lord Sandwich, Hamond was ready to return to North America, but Sandwich made it clear to Arbuthnot that there was no 74-gun ship to spare for the North American station because of pressure on the Channel Fleet. It was for this reason at least, though there must have been others, that in late 1780 Hamond was offered, and accepted, the posts of resident commissioner of Halifax Dockyard and lieutenant-governor of Nova Scotia. He arrived there in late July 1781 and was sworn in on 31 July. He had to defend the dockyard and the coast against American privateers on several occasions, and to ensure the supply of masts to England. He also built a new naval hospital, operational by the end of 1782. As lieutenant-governor he also had to deal with the first of the influx of loyalists. He then heard unexpectedly from London that John Parr had been appointed the new governor of Nova Scotia by the Shelburne administration, whereupon Hamond resigned on 8 October 1782. He continued to perform his naval duties until January 1783. The Nova Scotia council voted him a grant of 10,000 acres at the mouth of the Kennebecasis River. He returned to England during that year and on 18 December was awarded a baronetcy, presumably as compensation for the loss of his lieutenant-governorship.

Hamond remained on half pay. On 13 April 1785 he was appointed to a board to examine the proposals of the duke of Richmond's Fortifications Bill, as one of ten naval officers and fifteen army officers. The two subsequent bills were defeated in 1786 and Richmond had to give up the idea of a major system of fortifications along the south coast. In 1787 Hamond was appointed commodore of the guardships at Chatham, flying his broad pennant in the *Irresistible* (74 guns), where he remained until 1790. In June 1790 he was appointed to the *Vanguard* (74 guns), a position he held until August 1791, when he went to the *Bedford* (74 guns), and from December he flew the flag of Vice-Admiral Mark Milbank, sailing in the Evolutionary squadron in 1792. He remained in the *Bedford* until January 1793 and was appointed to the *Duke* (98 guns). According to his autobiographical memoir, it was at this point, just before his promotion to flag rank, that he had 'a violent fit of sickness' (A. S. Hamond, 'Autobiography', MSS, University of Virginia).

**Controller at the Navy Board, 1794–1806** Having come ashore for a second time, Hamond rapidly established himself in a political and administrative career. Four years earlier, in February 1789, he had applied to Lord North for a position at the Navy Board. He was now appointed an extra commissioner at the board on 11 February 1793, becoming deputy controller on 7 March 1794, and controller just over six months later on 25 September. Recommended by the Treasury, he was elected MP for Ipswich on 28 May 1796. In the Commons he supported Pitt's administration, subscribing £1500 to the loyalty loan for 1797 and voting for Pitt's assessed taxes in January 1798. He was also sworn in as an elder brother of Trinity House on 3 November 1796, while on 3 March 1797 he was elected a fellow of the Royal Society; among his proposers were William Marsden, Neville Maskeleyne, Gilbert Blane, and Philip Stephens.

Hamond's twelve years at the head of the Navy Board were marked by unprecedented administrative change and political controversy. In August 1796 the recommendations of the commission on fees, pushed by Charles Middleton from the early 1780s, were finally implemented, which, together with formation of the transport board in 1794, brought more order into the business of the Navy Office. Even so, Hamond was still not satisfied, and in this desire for reform he agreed with John Jervis, earl of St Vincent, who was made first lord of the Admiralty in February 1801 and with whom Hamond was later to quarrel publicly.

At first relations were cordial between the Board of Admiralty and the Navy Board, though it is perhaps significant that St Vincent, even before he came to office, wrote to Evan Nepean that 'Sir Andrew Hamond and Sir William Rule [the surveyor] are ignorant men' (*Letters*, 1.13). The visitation of the dockyards in 1802, particularly that of Plymouth, began a long paper war between the two boards. The peace of Amiens gave time for the commission of naval enquiry into abuses in the several naval departments, for which parliamentary approval was gained on 29 December 1802. St Vincent, convinced that there was wholesale corruption in the dockyards and major financial irregularities with timber merchants and contract shipbuilders, caused relations to break down. As Hamond began to defend his board, St Vincent closed all private contact from 2 January 1803. On 16 June Hamond stated in the house that 'it was impossible to go on as things now stood', though he later modified this stance. Matters were brought to a head by the political row over the failed 'stone ships' expedition, a semi-private and ill-conceived project in which some ships were to be loaded with stone and sunk at the entrance to Boulogne harbour. Hamond, on instructions from Lord Hobart, provided the necessary funds, if not financial controls. St Vincent, sick and living in the country, was informed, though he had no information of the cost of the project, but he later denied all knowledge. Hamond proved in the house that he had informed the first lord, but was careful not to make any statement which reflected directly upon St Vincent. However, on 24 May 1805 St Vincent referred to Hamond's 'gross abuse' and hoped for his 'ignominious dismissal'. With the scandal over Lord Melville unfolding, and the prorogation of parliament giving him no chance to clear his name, Hamond resigned and his controller's patent was revoked on 3 March 1806. He withdrew his candidature at Ipswich a few days before the election of 29 October 1806 and retired to Hamond Lodge, near Lynn, Norfolk. Hamond lived here until, aged nearly ninety, he died on 12 September 1828; he is thought to have been buried at Lynn. He was survived by his wife and their two children—Caroline, who married into the Hood family, and Graham Eden *Hamond, who became an admiral of the fleet.

**Assessment** Judgement upon Hamond's administrative achievements is not easy, but in the face of St Vincent's violent attacks, it is difficult not to admire his dignity. Early in his controllership in 1795 Hamond perhaps misjudged the vital hemp, masts, and timber contract with Andrew Lindgren in which, new to office and in great secrecy, he handled a large contract personally without sufficient safeguards, and public money was lost. This was revealed in the twelfth report of the commission of enquiry published on 22 January 1806. To those adherents of St Vincent, then and now, Hamond has been portrayed as a conservative, resisting much-needed reform; but when war was resumed in 1803 it was clear to all that St Vincent's measures had stripped the yards of stores and that shipbuilding and repair were in a disastrous state. Hamond, by contrast, did not lose his popularity within the service or in his declining years. He tried to obtain his flag before he resigned, for which there was precedence for naval officers who served in civil posts. He was unsuccessful, though he received a pension of £2000 a year. He was a vigorous naval officer, who never quite fulfilled his potential. ROGER KNIGHT

**Sources** W. H. Moomar, 'The naval career of Captain Hamond, 1775–1779', PhD diss., University of Virginia, 1955 • D. Syrett, *The Royal Navy in American waters, 1775–1783* (1989) • W. Stokes, 'Hamond, Sir Andrew Snape', HoP, *Commons, 1790–1820* • 'Hamond, Sir Andrew Snape', *DCB*, vol. 6 • R. Morriss, *The royal dockyards during the revolutionary and Napoleonic wars* (1983) • J. M. Collinge, *Navy Board officials, 1660–1832* (1978) • B. Pool, *Navy board contracts, 1660–1832* (1966) • T. H. McGuffie, 'The stone ships expedition against Boulogne, 1804', *EngHR*, 64 (1949), 488–502 • J. S. Tucker, *Memoirs of Admiral the Rt Hon. the earl of St Vincent*, 2 vols. (1844) • *The private papers of John, earl of Sandwich*, ed. G. R. Barnes and J. H. Owen, 4 vols., Navy RS, 69, 71, 75, 78 (1932–8) • *Letters of … the earl of St Vincent, whilst the first lord of the admiralty, 1801–1804*, ed. D. B. Smith, 2 vols., Navy RS, 55, 61 (1922–7) • R. Morriss, ed., *Guide to British naval papers in North America* (1994) • J. R. Breihan, 'The Addington party and the navy in British politics, 1801–1806', *New aspects of naval history*, ed. C. L. Symonds (1981), 163–89 • J. Porter, P. Byrne, and W. Porter, eds., *The parliamentary register, or, History of the proceedings and debates of the House of Commons of Ireland, 1781–1797*, 17 vols. (1784–1801), vol. 14, pp. 33–51

**Archives** CUL, corresp. and papers • Duke U., Perkins L., corresp. • Duke U., Perkins L., papers relating to his time as comptroller • NMM, operational reports, logs, and administrative papers • University of Virginia Library, Charlottesville, corresp., journals, papers, and naval papers | BL, letters to Lord Nelson, Add. MSS 34906–34936, *passim* • BL, letters to Lord Spencer • NA Scot., corresp. with Lord Melville • NMM, corresp. with Lord Barham • U. Nott. L., letters to Lord William Bentinck

**Likenesses** T. Lawrence, oils, 1800–05, priv. coll. • F. Chantrey, bust, *c*.1821, AM Oxf. • G. H. Phillips, mezzotint, pubd 1830 (after T. Lawrence, *c*.1800–1805), BM, NPG [*see illus.*]

**Wealth at death** £39,766, excl. lands left to son: will, 1828, PRO, PROB 11/1745

**Hamond, George** (1619/20–1705), clergyman and ejected minister, was born in 1619 or 1620; his parents and origins are unknown. In 1637 he became a scholar of Trinity College, Dublin, where he graduated BA and attracted the notice of Archbishop Ussher, who thought he would become 'a considerable man'. In 1639 he went to Exeter College, Oxford, where he proceeded MA in 1641. At Oxford he knew Ames Short and felt moved towards ministry. He was ordained at Exeter on 26 October 1645 and immediately became rector of Mamhead, Devon. He married Judith, whom he outlived. Their two sons, William (*bap.* 1648) and George (*bap.* 1652), were baptized there; they also had a daughter, Elizabeth.

In 1648, with seventy-two other Devon ministers, Hamond signed a testimony which supported presbyterianism. Also in 1648 he became curate at the nearby parish of Kenton, Devon, and then in 1654 lecturer and minister of Totnes. While there his son George was killed in an accident. In 1655 Hamond was one of the first members of the Devon association of ministers which sought to encourage uniformity of doctrine, worship, and discipline. He became rector of Bigbury, Devon, in 1658, and then, upon being invited in 1660 to be rector of the joint parish of Holy Trinity and St Peter, Dorchester, on an annual salary of £160, resigned his Devon living and took up his new post in February 1661. He was ejected from Dorchester under the Act of Uniformity, remaining in office until March 1663. He stayed on in Dorchester, where the corporation of that godly stronghold hoped that he would again become rector and, after a successor took over in July 1663, that he would stay as schoolmaster. In 1665 he took the Oxford oath, thus avoiding the consequences of the Five Mile Act. In 1672 he was licensed as a presbyterian teacher for houses in Dorchester. His congregation included leading burgesses.

In 1677 Hamond moved to another stronghold of west-country nonconformity when he was called to be co-minister with the elderly George Newton at Pauls Meeting Presbyterian Church in Taunton, built in 1672. Edmund Calamy describes Hamond as 'a man of great learning, exemplary piety, and an admirable temper; but not valued and esteemed according to his worth' (Calamy, *Abridgement*, 2.258). While ministering at Taunton Hamond also kept a boarding-school, where his most notable pupil was Isaac Gilling, who became secretary to the Exeter assembly. In Dorchester the authorities had been sympathetic towards nonconformists but in Taunton they faced persecution at the hands of the mayor. In 1676 a warrant was issued to close Pauls Meeting but it defiantly remained open. In 1680 Newton and Hamond were presented at the Somerset assizes and ordered to stop their nonconformist activities. Hamond defied the order and busied himself preparing his congregation for a Catholic king by lecturing in people's houses on the dangers and evils of popery. Newton died in 1681 and at the end of July 1683 Pauls Meeting was wrecked by order of the mayor of Taunton. Hamond struggled on alone, keeping the congregation together until he was forced to flee to London in the face of the cruelties which followed the Monmouth rebellion. At least one leading member of Pauls Meeting was hanged and others suffered less severe punishments.

In London, Hamond became colleague to Richard Steel at Armourers' Hall, Coleman Street. He was certified as a minister in 1689. When Steel died on 16 November 1692, Hamond preached his funeral sermon and became sole pastor. He was esteemed by his colleagues in the Happy Union of Presbyterian and Independent ministers, even as co-operation was on the verge of collapse under theological differences. He was asked by them to write *A Discourse of Family Worship* (1694), a work which, with an appendix by the Independent Matthew Barker, looks to be a piece to mark out a common ground, but which in the event was published after the effective collapse of the union. In 1699 he succeeded William Bates as one of the Tuesday lecturers at Salters' Hall. He died in July 1705 but his congregation does not seem to have survived him and was probably extinct by 1704; although he had reached the great age of eighty-five, he retained his lectureship at Salters' Hall until his death. His will, dated 15 May 1699 and proved on 2 August 1705, gives him as living in Cheapside, in the parish of St Matthew, Friday Street. Pauls Meeting continues on its original site in Paul Street as Taunton United Reformed Church. BRIAN W. KIRK

**Sources** *Calamy rev.* • W. Wilson, *The history and antiquities of the dissenting churches and meeting houses in London, Westminster and Southwark*, 4 vols. (1808–14), vol. 2, pp. 457–9 • J. Toulmin, *The history of Taunton, in the county of Somerset*, ed. J. Savage, new edn (1822), 172–3 • Foster, *Alum. Oxon., 1500–1714* [George Hammond] • C. W. Boase, ed., *Registrum Collegii Exoniensis*, new edn, OHS, 27 (1894) • *Walker rev.* • *CSP dom., 1680–85* • J. Murch, *A history of the Presbyterian and General Baptist churches in the west of England* (1835) • C. Surman, index of ministers, DWL • A. Gordon, ed., *Freedom after ejection: a review (1690–1692) of presbyterian and congregational nonconformity in England and Wales* (1917) • D. Underdown, *Fire from heaven: the life of an English town in the seventeenth century* (1992) • E. Calamy, ed., *An abridgement of Mr. Baxter's history of his life and times, with an account of the ministers, &c., who were ejected after the Restauration of King Charles II*, 2nd edn, 2 vols. (1713), vol. 2

**Wealth at death** approx. £20—bequests: *Calamy rev.*

**Hamond, Sir Graham Eden**, **second baronet** (**1779–1862**), naval officer, only son of Sir Andrew Snape *Hamond, first baronet, FRS (1738–1828) and his wife, Anne, daughter and heir of Major Henry Graeme of Hanwell, Middlesex, was born in Newman Street, London, on 30 December 1779, and was entered as a captain's servant on board the *Irresistible* (74 guns) on 3 September 1785. This vessel was commanded by his father, and the son's name was borne on the ship's book until March 1790. In January 1793, while a midshipman on the *Phaeton*, Hamond assisted in the capture of the *Général Dumourier* and other ships, and received his portion of a large sum of prize money. The following year, as midshipman on the *Queen Charlotte* (100 guns), the flagship of Earl Howe, he shared in the victory of 1 June 1794. Promoted lieutenant on 19 October 1796, he served in various ships in the Mediterranean and on the home stations.

Hamond's first sole command was of the sloop *Echo* (18 guns), in which he took part in the blockade of Le Havre in 1798, and also took charge of convoys. He was made post captain on 30 November, and in the following year commanded the *Champion* (24 guns) at the blockade of Malta, where he occasionally served on shore at the siege of Valletta. In the *Blanche* (36 guns) he was present at the battle of Copenhagen on 2 April 1801, and on the Sunday following the action held the prayer book from which Nelson read the prayers of thanksgiving to God. From 21 February to 12 November 1803 Hamond commanded the *Plantagenet* (74 guns), and captured the *Courier de Terre Neuve* and the *Atalante*. In 1804 he took charge of the frigate *Lively* (38 guns), with which he captured, on 5 October, three Spanish frigates laden with treasure and then, on 7 December, another treasure ship, the *San Miguel*. He was present at the capture of Flushing in the *Victorious* (74 guns) in 1809.

After this period Hamond was invalided for some years until 1824, when he conveyed Lord Stuart de Rothesay to Brazil in the *Wellesley* (74 guns). Advanced to the rank of rear-admiral on 27 May 1825, he was ordered to England in the *Spartiate* (74 guns) with the mission of delivering on the way the treaty of separation between Brazil and Portugal to the king of Portugal, who created him a knight commander of the order of the Tower and Sword (which he was not, however, permitted to wear as it was not given for war service). His last posting was to the South American station, where he was commander-in-chief from 16 September 1834 to 17 May 1838. He attained the ranks of vice-admiral on 10 January 1837, admiral on 22 January 1847, and admiral of the fleet on 10 November 1862. He had been gazetted CB on 4 June 1815, and KCB on 13 September 1831. On 12 September 1828, on the death of his father, he had succeeded as the second baronet, and on 5 July 1855 he was made a GCB. He died at his residence, Norton Lodge, Freshwater, Isle of Wight, on 19 December 1862.

On 30 December 1806, Hamond married Elizabeth (*d.* 24 Dec 1872), daughter of John Kimber of Fowey, Cornwall; they had five children. The elder of their two sons, Andrew Snape, succeeded as third baronet, became a vice-admiral, and died on 21 February 1874, having taken the name Graeme-Hamond; the younger, Graham Eden William, became a commander.

G. C. BOASE, *rev.* ROGER MORRISS

**Sources** O'Byrne, *Naval biog. dict.* • *GM*, 3rd ser., 14 (1863), 235 • *The Times* (23 Dec 1862), 10 • A. B. Rodger, *The war of the second coalition: 1798–1801, a strategic commentary* (1964) • R. Muir, *Britain and the defeat of Napoleon, 1807–1815* (1996) • Boase, *Mod. Eng. biog.* • *CGPLA Eng. & Wales* (1863)

**Archives** CUL, commonplace book • Duke U., Perkins L., corresp. and papers • LUL, corresp. relating to domestic employees • NMM, corresp., diaries, and papers • University of Virginia, Charlottesville, letter-books and orders; corresp., etc.

**Likenesses** M. Brown, group portrait, oils, 1794, NMM

**Wealth at death** under £14,000: probate, 20 Feb 1863, *CGPLA Eng. & Wales*

**Hamond, Walter** (*d.* **1648**), surgeon and writer on Madagascar, whose origins are unknown, was apprenticed to Arthur Doughton in the Barber–Surgeons' Company of London, and made free in 1616. His translation of Ambroise Paré's treatise of 1551 as *Method of Treating Wounds Made by Arquebuses and other Firearms* (1617) was dedicated to Doughton and described as intended for students and apprentices of that craft. Hamond was in the service of the East India Company and, in 1630, as surgeon to the *Charles* and the *Jonas* (Captain Weddell), bound for the Far East, spent four months on the island of Madagascar.

On a later voyage Weddell's ship was lost to fire on the way home. Upset by the treatment he received from the company Weddell resigned and accepted command of the fleet of Sir William Courten's (or Courteen's) rival organization; Hamond resigned at the same time and probably followed into Courten's service.

In 1637 King Charles was advised that Madagascar was a convenient place to refresh and repair ships making for the trading stations of the Persian Gulf and the Far East. Early plans to settle a colony came to naught, and Sir Thomas Roe wrote to the queen of Bohemia on 8 May 1637: 'The dream of Madagascar, I think, is vanished' (*CSP dom.*, *1635–7*). However, eventually a warrant under privy signet appointed John Bond as captain-general of an expedition, scheduled to sail in 1639. This scheme was resisted by the East India Company, which regarded the region as its own fiefdom, whereas the Courten Association favoured it.

It was against this background that Hamond, who claimed some knowledge of the island, wrote in 1639 *A paradox, prooving that the inhabitants of the Isle called Madagascar or St Lawrence (in temporall things) are the happiest people in the world. Whereunto is prefixed a briefe and true description of that island, the nature of the climate, and the condition of the inhabitants, and their speciall affection to the English above other nations. With most probable arguments of a hopefull and fit plantation of a colony there, in respect of the fruitfulnesse of the soyle, the benignity of the ayre, and the relieving of our English ships, both to and from the East Indies* (1640). This short treatise, clearly written in support of Courten, offers an absurdly exaggerated prospect of the island, its land in every respect fair and fecund, its climate not merely healthy but positively restorative, its population, while naked and ignorant of civilized ways, yet pleasing in its innocence. In his desire to present Madagascar and its allegedly primitive peoples as a semblance of the Garden of Eden, Hamond's writing can be seen as a precursor of the eighteenth-century salute to the noble savage.

The expedition scheduled for 1639 never left port, but late in 1642 Bond revived interest and was authorized to proceed. The East India Company again objected, and the matter was referred to the House of Commons committee of trade. Early in 1643 Bond was given leave to sail, provided that he did not harm East India Company interests. This decision prompted Hamond to publish a second pamphlet, *Madagascar: the richest and most fruitfull island in the world … dedicated to the Honorable John Bond, governour of the island, whose proceeding is authorised for this expedition, both by the king and parliament*. After many delays the Courten fleet transported 145 men, women, and children, with the necessary equipment to found a settlement. They landed in 1645, but the colony lasted little more than a year: by then eighty of the settlers had died and the rest abandoned the island.

Little is known of Hamond's private life. At his death in May or early June 1648 he left a wife, Marie, to execute his modest estate, but his will provided no clue as to his then residence or desired place of burial. The will indicates that a brother, Henry, and a sister were living at the time of his death. ANITA MCCONNELL

**Sources** A. Grandidier and G. Grandidier, 'Les Anglais à Madagascar au 17e siècle', *Revue de Madagascar* (1903) • W. Foster, 'An English settlement in Madagascar in 1645–6', *EngHR*, 27 (1912), 239–50 • L. B. Wright, 'The noble savage of Madagascar', *Journal of the History of Ideas*, 4/1 (1943), 112–18 • *CSP dom.*, 1635–7 • Barber–Surgeons' Company, freedoms, GL, 5265/1 • will, PRO, PROB 11/204, fol. 295*v*

**Hamont, Matthew** (*d.* **1579**), alleged heretic, was a wheelwright at Hethersett, Norfolk, near Norwich, and was probably of Dutch origin. In the Hethersett parish registers the name is spelt Hamoute, Hammonte, and Hammante. Early in 1579 he was cited before Edmund Freake, bishop of Norwich, charged to have proclaimed the scriptures a fable, the Holy Ghost an invention, and Christ 'a sinful man and an abominable idoll' (Holinshed, 3.1299). He does seem to have rejected the deity of Christ, and his resurrection and ascension, but it may be that the charges were deliberately framed to render his views in language as scandalous as possible. William Burton (*d.* 1616), a minister in Norwich about this time, included him among those Arians 'whose life hath beene most strict amongest men, whose tongues have beene tyred with scripture upon scripture, their knees even hardened in prayer'. Hamont was condemned in the consistory court on 18 April 1579, and placed in the custody of the sheriff of Norwich. At the Guildhall, he was found guilty of seditious and scandalous speeches against the queen and the privy council; the mayor, Sir Robert Wood, ordered that he suffer the loss of both ears. Sentence was carried out on 13 May 1579 on the pillory in Norwich market place. For his heresy, Hamont was sentenced to death; he was burnt in the castle ditch on 20 May. He was one of a succession of Arians burned at Norwich; these also included John Lewes (18 September 1583), Peter Cole, a tanner of Ipswich (1587), and Francis Kett (1589). In 1699 Hamont's views and his fate were the subject of a discussion between John Locke and Philip Limborch. Hamont left a widow, who died in 1625, and a son, Erasmus.

ALEXANDER GORDON, *rev.* STEPHEN WRIGHT

**Sources** R. Holinshed and others, eds., *The third volume of chronicles, beginning at Duke William the Norman*, ed. J. Hooker (1587) • R. Wallace, *Antitrinitarian biography* (1850), vol. 2 • F. Blomefield and C. Parkin, *An essay towards a topographical history of the county of Norfolk*, [2nd edn], 11 vols. (1805–10) • W. Burton, *David's evidence* (1592) • *The correspondence of John Locke*, ed. E. de Beer (1981), vol. 6

**Hampden**. For this title name *see* Trevor, Robert Hampden-, first Viscount Hampden (1706–1783); Trevor, John Hampden-, third Viscount Hampden (1748–1824); Brand, Henry Bouverie William, first Viscount Hampden (1814–1892); Brand, Henry Robert, second Viscount Hampden (1841–1906).

**Hampden**. *See* Hart, Adolphus Mordecai (1814–1879), *under* Hart, Ezekiel (1770–1843).

**Hampden, Augustus Charles Hobart-** [*called* Hobart Pasha] (**1822–1886**), naval officer, was born at Walton on the Wolds, Leicestershire, on 1 April 1822, the third son and fourth child of Augustus Edward Hobart, from August 1878 Hobart-Hampden, sixth earl of Buckinghamshire (1793–1885), and his first wife, Mary (*d.* 1825), daughter of John Williams, king's serjeant, and sister to the judge Sir Edward Vaughan Williams; his eldest brother, Vere Henry *Hobart, achieved prominence as governor of Madras. Augustus went to Dr Mayo's school at Cheam, Surrey, but did not distinguish himself, and in 1835 he entered the Royal Navy, joining the *Rover* (18 guns) at Devonport in February. The *Rover* was paid off at Plymouth in July 1838, and Hobart joined the *Rose* in October, became acting mate in July 1841, and, when paid off in July 1842, passed his examinations at the Naval College and on board the *Excellent* at Portsmouth. He qualified as gunnery mate, and joined the *Dolphin* in the autumn of 1843. His first three ships were all

**Augustus Charles Hobart-Hampden (1822–1886)**, by Lock & Whitfield, pubd 1882

employed off the coast of South America in the suppression of the slave trade. He captured a slaver and took her to Demerara in May 1844. He afterwards returned to England, and was appointed to the royal steam yacht the *Victoria and Albert* (Captain Lord Adolphus Fitz Clarence). In September 1845 he was promoted lieutenant and joined the pioneer screw steam sloop *Rattler* in the Mediterranean, and was transferred in 1847 to the *Bulldog* (Commander Key), where he showed himself 'full of zeal' (W. Parker, *Life*, 3, 1880, 323). In 1848 he married Mary Anne, second daughter of Dr Colquhoun Grant; she died on 13 April 1877.

On the outbreak of the Russian war Hobart served as first lieutenant on the same vessel in the Baltic squadron, and commanded the *Driver* for a fortnight (August 1854) at the capture of Bomarsund and the reconnaissance at Åbo (Turkü). His ship was commended in dispatches, and Hobart's 'ability, zeal, and great exertion' at Åbo were specially mentioned. In 1855 he served aboard the *Duke of Wellington*, Admiral Dundas's flagship, and commanded the mortar boats at the attack on Sveaborg (Helsinki), for which he was again mentioned in dispatches and was promoted commander. Then for six years he left the regular service of the navy and became officer of the coastguard at Dingle, co. Kerry, and subsequently (1858–61) of the guardship at Malta. In 1861 he commanded the gun-vessel *Foxhound* in the Mediterranean, was promoted captain in March 1863, and immediately retired on half pay.

In spite of his family 'interest', Hobart's rise had been very slow, reflecting his lack of discipline and incompatibility with the rules of subordination. He retired in the middle of the American Civil War, and as a staunch southerner, joined some brother officers in running the blockade off North Carolina. His daring and skilful seamanship, the exciting chases and narrow escapes, when Hobart was in his proper element, are described in *Never Caught* (1867), which he wrote under the pseudonym of Captain Roberts, and which is practically reprinted in *Sketches of my Life* (pp. 87–186). American authorities stated that this was substantially accurate (*EdinR*, 337).

In 1867, seeking a new career of adventure, Hobart entered the Turkish service as naval adviser to the sultan, in succession to Admiral Sir Adolphus Slade. His first task was the suppression of the Cretan rebellion by intercepting supplies from Greece. For his successes here he was raised to the rank of full admiral, with the title of pasha (1869). The Turkish fleet was reorganized and improved under his direction, but in the war of 1877 the jealousy of the authorities prevented him, as commander of the Black Sea Fleet, from achieving any notable naval success, though he displayed considerable skill in defeating attacks by Russian torpedoes, a weapon he despised. In 1881 the sultan appointed him mushir or marshal of the empire. Hobart's action against Greece in 1867 breached the Foreign Enlistment Act, so he was struck off the British navy list. Restored to his naval rank in 1874 by Lord Derby's influence, he was again struck off in 1877 for his command of the Black Sea Fleet, but was finally restored in June 1885, with the rank of British vice-admiral. On 5 May 1879 he married Edith Katherine (*d*. 1923), daughter of Herbert Francis Hore of Pole Hore, co. Wexford, who edited his *Sketches*. In 1885 he visited London with a view to forming an offensive alliance between England and Turkey at the time of the Panjdeh incident. In 1886 he went to Italy to recover his health, but died at Milan on 19 June.

Hobart-Hampden's *Sketches of my Life* was published posthumously in 1887. John Laughton, in the *Edinburgh Review* (January 1887, no. 337), demonstrated that he unaccountably confused dates and places, and claimed the exploits of brother officers. Hobart-Hampden was a brave and resourceful junior, but lacked the discipline and reflection for a successful career in the peacetime Royal Navy.

STANLEY LANE-POOLE, *rev.* ANDREW LAMBERT

**Sources** *The Times* (21 June 1886) · GEC, *Peerage*, new edn, vol. 2 · Burke, *Peerage* (1967) · A. C. Hobart-Hampden, *Sketches of my life* (1887) · Boase, *Mod. Eng. biog.* · O'Byrne, *Naval biog. dict.* · [J. Laughton], 'The adventures of Hobart Pasha', *EdinR*, 165 (1887) · A. Lambert, *Battleships in transition: the creation of the steam battlefleet, 1815–1860* (1984) · R. Gardiner and A. Lambert, eds., *Steam, steel and shellfire: the steam warship, 1815–1905* (1992) · *CGPLA Eng. & Wales* (1887)

**Archives** Bucks. RLSS, papers, incl. collected genealogical material, corresp., and travel journal | BL, letters to Sir Austen Layard, Add. MSS 39012–39037

**Likenesses** Lock & Whitfield, photograph, pubd 1882, NPG [*see illus.*]

**Wealth at death** £615—in England: probate, 31 May 1887, *CGPLA Eng. & Wales*

**Hampden, John** (1595–1643), politician, was born about June 1595, the eldest son and heir of William Hampden (1570–1597) of Great Hampden, Buckinghamshire, and his wife, Elizabeth (*d.* 1664), daughter of Sir Henry Cromwell alias Williams of Hinchingbrooke, Huntingdonshire.

**The Hampden inheritance** The Hampdens were a family in which Calvinism was well established long before John was born. Griffith Hampden, his grandfather, knight of the shire and sheriff of Buckinghamshire, left a most verbose autodidact Calvinist will, asserting bluntly that 'I know my soul to be sanctified' (PRO, PROB 11/79/29). Similar sentiments are to be found in the will of Hampden's father. Anne Hampden, John's grandmother, showed a discomfort typical of the late Elizabethan godly in arranging for a funeral sermon, because 'I know that after my death nothing can be available for the health of my soul', and made it clear that her bequests to the poor were made 'not in any superstitious meaning of dole for the dead' (Bucks RO, will file 1594). In terms of worldly status the family were less distinguished than they were for godly devotion. In spite of the fact that John's grandfather had been knight of the shire, and his father, William, MP for East Looe in 1593, his grandfather was not a JP in 1573–4. His father was not a JP in 1594. The Hampdens, though they had an honourable place in county society, were clearly not in the magnate league.

John Hampden entered into his inheritance prematurely, and through wardship. His father fell ill while visiting his cousin and namesake William Hampden of Ennington, Oxfordshire. After a week's illness he died, aged twenty-six, on 2 April 1597, leaving two sons. John was reported by the inquisition post mortem as aged one year and ten months, implying a birth date of about June 1595.

The voluminous documentation arising from this wardship reveals an estate gravely encumbered by debt. William Hampden's will records debts which 'I am constrained to leave more heavily upon my executors than I wolde or with some longer respite shoude have done'. William Hampden of Ennington, a long-standing family friend, accepted the executorship on these terms, but George Croke (the judge who was to give the first judgment for Hampden in the ship-money case) prudently refused to act. The estate was compact, being all within Buckinghamshire except for some lands in Edgware, Middlesex, which were valued at £32 in the inquisition post mortem, and which were leased to a father and son. The family owned the manors of Great Hampden, Great Kimble, and Dunton, and lands in Hughenden. (It would be interesting to know whether Disraeli knew he was occupying property which had once belonged to John Hampden.) The total estate was valued by the inquisition post mortem at £119 5*s.* 4*d.* Sensible historians do not accept valuations taken from inquisitions post mortem, yet even if Robert Cecil's rule of thumb were adopted and the sum multiplied by ten, the result would be an income of only £1190 per annum—just about compatible with John Hampden's position as a JP but not of the quorum. It would make him comfortable, but not rich. Yet even of this sum, only £106 2*s.* descended to John Hampden, and of that, £35 3*s.* 4*d.* was his mother's jointure; since his mother lived until 1664, surviving her son by twenty-one years, he never enjoyed its fruits. The £70 18*s.* 8*d.* which remained to him, even if multiplied by ten, would not have yielded any great income.

Elizabeth Cromwell, Hampden's mother, had brought with her a jointure of £2000, but the condition of the estate on his father's death suggests that this sum was already over-committed. The arrangements reached during the last week of William Hampden's life involved a bewildering series of leases of Hampden property at what were apparently undervaluations allowing the creditor to recoup himself by collecting the entry fines. These, being technically capital gains, did not need to be listed as income. It is also noteworthy, in the light of later events, that such Hampden leases as survive specify that taxes are to be paid, not by the landlord, but by the tenants.

All these arrangements, so laboriously entered into, were then set in abeyance by a furious row and subsequent litigation between William Hampden of Ennington and Elizabeth Hampden, the ward's mother. One side believed that William Hampden of Ennington, the only one who had the money, was to bid for the wardship with the full agreement of the family, including Elizabeth Hampden. Elizabeth Hampden claimed to know nothing of any such arrangements. The likeliest possibility is that she had been told of it but, in her tears, had failed to take it in or remember it. One way or another, this quarrel—together with another with Robert Cecil as master of the wards—gave rise to a series of lawsuits which were still in progress in 1604. They cannot have done the estate any good, especially since Elizabeth Hampden, going to the top of the market, briefed Francis Bacon and Sir Thomas Fleming.

**Early life and political career until 1628** There is little sign in John Hampden's life before 1626 that he was a significant politician in the making. He was educated at Thame School and at Magdalen College, Oxford, from which he matriculated on 30 March 1610. Three years later in 1613 he was listed as a student at the Inner Temple in London. On 24 June 1619 he married Elizabeth, daughter of Edmund Symeon of Pyrton, Oxfordshire. She was a substantial heiress, and this fact has been part of his reputation for wealth. However, since he predeceased his father-in-law, he probably did not inherit any substantial sum from him. In the fifteen years before Elizabeth's death shortly before 26 August 1634, the marriage produced ten children.

Hampden's mother, it seems, may have looked forward to a public career for him. In 1620 she wrote:

> If ever my son will seek for honour, tell him to come to court now, for here is multitudes of Lords a making. I am ambitious of my son's honour, which I wish were now conferred upon him, that he might not come after so many new creations. (G. N. T. Grenville, Baron Nugent, *Some Memorials of John Hampden, his Party, and his Times*, 1832, 1.32)

The context adds nothing to this letter, but the obvious interpretation may well be correct. Hampden's service as member for Grampound, Cornwall, in the parliament of 1621 has left no record to shed any light on his preoccupations at this time. He was not a JP in 1621, and though he was a Buckinghamshire JP in 1625 and 1636, he was never of the quorum. Although he did not sit for parliament in 1624, his part in the efforts, ultimately successful, to restore the Buckinghamshire borough of Wendover to its ancient right to return members suggests a liking for parliamentary service. He duly sat for the borough in 1625 and in the following year, but only his membership of a committee on muster-masters in 1626 has left any record, from which nothing may be learned.

However, his career took a new turn on 26 January 1627, when the commissioners for the forced loan arrived at Aylesbury, Buckinghamshire, to be confronted by John Hampden refusing to pay or to subscribe. He is not to be confused with his uncle Sir Edmund Hampden, who was one of the five knights who fought the test case on the forced loan. It would seem likely that the common factor uniting Hampden and his uncle and other key refusers was their membership of the circle around Richard Knightley, Lord Saye and Sele, and John Preston. Knightley employed John Dod the patriarch, who had been deprived of his Oxfordshire living in 1606, as vicar of his church, which was a peculiar. His trustees, along with Hampden, included Saye, Sir Nathaniel Rich, John Crew, John Pym, and Christopher Sherland. It is almost certainly Knightley who was described by the earl of Clarendon as running 'a kind of classis' in his house, and Hampden's membership of such a classis may have been of great importance. Knightley's son Richard married Hampden's daughter Elizabeth about 1637, and, along with John Crew, Hampden was an overseer of Knightley's will, proved in November 1639. Thus Hampden was one of a circle which was at the very centre both of the refusals of the forced loan and of the genesis of the civil war itself.

In this abrupt swing towards hostility to the king's favourite, the duke of Buckingham, and thereafter to Charles I himself, Hampden was one of many. Unfortunately there were many different reasons for these reactions, and these different reasons led to very different subsequent courses of conduct. Some, like the earls of Arundel and Bristol, were against the duke's moves to war with Spain. Others, like the earl of Holland and possibly Sir John Eliot, were against his subsequent moves to war with France. Some, such as John Pym, were against the moves towards toleration of Roman Catholics which followed the king's marriage with Henrietta Maria. Others again, like John Selden and Sir Robert Phelips, were against the arbitrary taxation which necessarily followed the move to war. Others, like Christopher Sherland and Pym, were against the simultaneous moves away from Calvinist orthodoxy which accompanied the duke's election as chancellor of Cambridge University in 1626. In response to speculation on which of these reasons, or how many of them, moved John Hampden hindsight suggests a very clear answer—but hindsight is a treacherous instrument.

What is clear is that Hampden was under restraint for almost a year for refusing to pay the forced loan, and was set free on 2 January 1628 in the general release which heralded the parliament of 1628. His interventions as the member for Wendover are too few to allow certain deductions about the lessons he had learned. He spoke on a private bill for Lord Gerrard, on which his concerns were purely practical and technical. The same seems to be true of his intervention on De Questier's patents for the posts. On 14 June he very sensibly opposed a proposal that the house, in its final remonstrance, should honour Sir Ranulph Crew, who had been sacked as chief justice for his opposition to the forced loan: 'That he honoured that noble gentleman as much as any, but he held it would be neither helpful to us, nor profitable to him' (Johnson and others, 4.322). Here he passed the test for the professional politician: he is concerned, not merely to testify to his feelings, but to work for the best possible result he can achieve, even at the sacrifice of his desire to testify.

Hampden made two other contributions which are much more clearly significant. On 27 May he was named, along with Sir Nathaniel Rich, Peter Ball, and Francis Rous, to assist John Pym in drawing up a charge against Roger Manwaring. The Manwaring charge seems to have brought together those who believed that alteration of religion and alteration of government were logically interdependent, and a threat of one necessarily carried a risk of the other. Hampden's second contribution, perhaps the most revealing speech of his political career, was in the debate of 5 June 1628. That debate came between the king's unsatisfactory answer to the petition of right of 2 June, and the comparatively satisfactory answer of 7 June. It was a day on which members were perhaps nearer despair than on any other day in the 1620s, and therefore spoke with a freedom they might otherwise have avoided. Hampden, as so rare and brief a speaker, must have created some surprise. One summary of what he said runs:

> Here is 1, an innovation of religion suspected; is it not high time to take it to heart and acquaint his Majesty? 2ly, alteration of government; can you forbear when it goes no less than the subversion of the whole state? 3ly, hemmed in with enemies; is it now a time to be silent, and not to show to his Majesty that a man that has so much power uses none of it to help us? If he be no papist, papists are friends and kindred to him. (Johnson and others, 4.121–2)

Here was a fully fledged conspiracy theory. The law was to be altered, and parliament abolished if need be, in order to remove an obstacle to the reintroduction of popery. It is instructive to see who else spoke in this particular vein—they were Richard Knightley, Christopher Sherland, Sir Nathaniel Rich, and, in an unusually muted vein, John Pym. (One inference could be that the mind behind them was that of John Dod, for whom they were all trustees.) This debate, together with the impeachment of Roger Manwaring which was largely the work of the same men, wove together what was to become the parliamentarian cause; and on this day John Hampden well pronounced 'shibboleth', and placed himself in its inner circle: he never left that inner circle until his death.

**Waiting in the wings, 1629–1634** Hampden knew when to maintain silence as well as when to speak. He had reached a conclusion that took fourteen years to put over to the country at large. In the session of 1629 his only recorded contribution is a call for Sir John Wolstenholme, the customs farmer, to be called in. In a parliamentary session in which nothing useful could be achieved, Hampden refrained from creating needless irritation. During much of the 1630s he again kept quiet. He continued a friendly correspondence with Sir Henry Vane, which stood him in good stead when he represented the English parliament in Edinburgh in the autumn of 1641, and Vane kept him up to date with news. In the metropolitical visitation in Buckinghamshire in 1634 Hampden was presented for holding a muster in Beaconsfield church, and for going sometimes from his parish church. He evidently made a soothing response, and a direction was given that there should be no prosecution without the special direction of Sir Nathaniel Brent. It was also reported that he had made over an impropriation of £120 per annum to the vicar of Great Kimble, who was unconformable, but this too appears to have been allowed to pass. When in 1638 Hampden gave his home living to the godly preacher William Spurstow, one of the team who wrote under the pseudonym of Smectymnuus, he was reverting to family type. It may not be irrelevant that he chose as his new vicar a fellow of St Catharine's College, Cambridge, whose head, Ralph Brownrigg, was married to John Pym's niece. These stories illustrate that for a gentleman of manners, prepared to work in county government and to be courteous at need, the regime of the 1630s was very much less frightening in the short term than it was for people of lower status, or than many feared it might become in the long term.

In Hampden the long-term anxiety was clearly present. In the course of a long and friendly correspondence with Sir John Eliot, imprisoned in the Tower since 1629 for his part in resisting the speaker's command to adjourn the Commons, Hampden sent him a tract dealing with a plan for plantation. Hampden was subsequently one of those involved in the plans for Saybrooke (Connecticut), one of the more promising plans for overseas settlement, and there may be a considerable element of chance in the fact that he did not settle in the New World.

**Ships and Scots, 1634–1640** Ironically the king, rather than Hampden himself, may have done most to determine that he would still be in England in 1640, by selecting Hampden as the subject of the great test case on the legality of ship money, perhaps the most notorious financial expedient of the personal rule. The case was to expose a lacuna left in the law by the extension of the military revolution to naval warfare. It had been normal before the military revolution to regard war as a private enterprise matter. The king conscripted privately owned ships from coastal towns for the duration of a campaign. They recouped themselves by plunder and ransoms, and the ships, if not sunk, returned to their owners at the close of the campaign. In the changed naval world of the 1630s this right to conscript privately owned ships was of no military use to the king. The tonnage, the manoeuvrability, and the manning were all such as to make the ships unsuitable for modern warfare. As a result the English were in danger of losing naval control of the channel and the North Sea to the French and the Dutch. The legal powers surviving from the middle ages were no help in meeting this danger.

In a well-ordered world this disjuncture between naval needs and legal rights would have been met by a new act of parliament, giving the king the right to a regular tax to finance a navy without which he could not defend himself. In 1634 there was no more chance that this would happen than that John Hampden would be made king. Charles's solution to his desire for naval rearmament was to transform the crown's ancient right to commandeer ships from coastal towns into a semi-permanent source of revenue: ship money. First, the supply of a ship was commuted into a money payment. Second, such payments were levied not only on coastal towns but on the nation as a whole. And third, the finances raised were deployed directly for the support of a national navy. The king therefore had to pretend that what was, in fact, a naval tax was an old-fashioned exercise in conscription. This is why ship-money writs did not command payment of money for the navy, but demanded, in the case of Buckinghamshire, a contribution to sending one ship of war to Portsmouth, where it was to serve for six months, after which it would revert to Buckinghamshire. Since this was not in fact what the king wanted, he had continually to cut corners with the procedure. The money levied never went anywhere near Portsmouth, but went to the treasurer of the navy at Deptford, where it became part of general naval funds. What the king said he was doing may have been legal, but this was definitely not legal. It crossed the boundary from conscription into taxation, and the king's opponents seized upon ship money as a major issue.

At first the king had hoped to avoid a court case but he was led to change his mind. When he did, Lord Saye and Sele imagined that he was at the front of the queue as the candidate for the case, having been trying for some time to be taken to court over ship money. However, the king selected Hampden, although it is not known why he chose this comparatively obscure figure instead. One possibility which would be characteristic of Charles's vindictive side is that Hampden's uncle Sir Edmund Hampden had died as a consequence of his imprisonment over the forced loan. If so, Charles had misjudged his man, his purpose, and the likely political consequence of his actions—John Hampden did not retreat from danger until he left the battlefield of Chalgrove suffering from the wounds of which he later died. A second point, far too rarely appreciated by Hampden's purported modern admirers, was that his motive was not to set out on a disruptive campaign of tax refusal: it was to secure a court judgment on the legality of the demand being made upon him. Once he had that judgment, however narrow and however pyrrhic, there is no suggestion of any further refusal to pay on his part. Hampden was campaigning for the principles of rule of law and taxation by consent, not for an arbitrary right to refuse any tax he did not like. The ritual character of what was taking place is shown by the calculated limitation of Hampden's refusal. Following a writ of 1635 he owed ship money in some dozen Buckinghamshire parishes, and paid in most of them save for the sum of 20 shillings (£1) which he owed in the parish of Stoke Mandeville. He paid £8 4*s*. at Great Hampden, but defaulted on a demand for 31*s*. 6*d*. at Great Kimble. That gesture was meant to signal that his concern was neither with the amount he was asked to pay, nor with the political purpose of the tax, but simply with its legality.

The judges treated Hampden's case with a procedure reserved for the most important cases. Instead of being heard in the court of exchequer, where it would normally have been heard, it was referred to the court of exchequer chamber, in which all twelve judges in England took part, and the court of exchequer was to follow the advice it got from the majority of the twelve. The proceedings aroused vast national interest, and Sir Thomas Knyvett complained that though he was up by 'peepe of the day' he was unable to crowd into the courtroom to hear the argument (B. Schofield, ed., *The Knyvett Letters, 1620–1644*, Norfolk RS, 20, 1949, 91). The argument in court continued for most of 1637–8. For the crown the case was argued by Sir John Bankes, attorney-general, and Sir Edward Littleton, solicitor-general. Littleton, ironically, was the man who sat in the chair during most of the debates in the 1628 parliament on the liberty of the subject. He was no mere time-server, and refused to put his seal to the proclamation for the arrest of Hampden and the five members in 1642. On Hampden's side the case was argued by the earl of Bedford's client Oliver St John, an obscure young lawyer who made as big a name out of the case as Hampden did, and by Robert Holborne. Holborne, curiously, was more extreme than St John, yet in religious matters was to be a persistent backer of the bishops against the Long Parliament.

The case was never simple. If, as was assumed by Hampden's supporters throughout, ship money was a tax, then all the arguments about taxation by consent followed with remorseless logic. They never quite accepted that the key issue was whether this was what the case was about. To Sir Robert Berkeley, in particular, it was not about taxation, but about the duty to do military service. Yet of all the great lawyers on the case, only chief justice Bramston and chief baron Davenport thought to use the test of where the money was to be paid as a test of its purpose and therefore of its legality. It was their judgments for Hampden which reduced the king's success to the wafer-thin margin of seven judges to five when the court of exchequer ruled in favour of the crown on 12 June 1638. The victory did the king no good. The earl of Holland, reporting the result to Hamilton in Scotland, said: '[it] occasions a great remisse in the businesse, our people being more enclined to beleeve that those that were against the king were lesse against their owen consciences' (Russell, *Fall*, 11–12). Moreover, by obtaining a judgment against Hampden, Charles did not humiliate him, but turned him into a national hero, who, instead of being a not very important member of his county community, could in the Short and Long parliaments count on election as knight of the shire simply for the asking. He had no more need to rely on the borough of Wendover to get him into parliament. The story illustrates the force of Thomas Wentworth's judgement on the William Prynne case, that 'a prince that loseth the force and example of his punishments, loseth withal the greatest part of his dominion' (Gardiner, *History of England*, 8.352).

From the Hampden verdict onwards, ship-money refusal took off, although the case cannot claim all the credit for this. Three things contributed to the fall in the yield of ship money. One was the case; the second was the diversion of local government resources into the task of raising the militia to fight the Scots in the bishops' wars; and the third was a rise of some 20 per cent in food prices. These things were so nearly simultaneous that the old rule of deducing causation from chronology does not hold. The fact remains that the political winner of the case was Hampden, and he was famous for ever after. To be famous for having annoyed a king who remains in undisturbed possession of the throne, and whom one has no power to fight, is an unenviable position.

Hampden's behaviour in the Short Parliament of April and May 1640 is a good guide to the thinking behind his attack on ship money. That parliament was called in the hope that it would offer the king financial support in a war against the religious opposition of his subjects of his other kingdom of Scotland. To anyone whose opposition to ship money rested straightforwardly on the grounds of law and consent, the possibility of trading the abolition of ship money for financial support to Charles for a war against the Scots had obvious attractions. This is the line for which Sir Francis Seymour worked throughout the parliament. To those who took the more complex line stated by Hampden on 5 June 1628, the conclusion was quite the opposite. In this thesis, the king's purpose in trying to abolish taxation by consent was to create the chance to introduce popery. Unless this purpose were defeated, all concessions on the way were so much appeasement. To these people, the first objective in the Short Parliament had to be to prevent any action against their Scottish co-religionists, even if at the price of allowing ship money to continue. It is this second line which Hampden followed throughout the Short Parliament. Only Scottish victory appeared a likely obstacle to the advance of popery.

On 23 April 1640 Hampden insisted on the importance of religion, fearful that for the first time since 1606 convocation had a commission giving it power to make new canons, and, for good measure, joined in John Pym's attack on military changes. However, his key contribution was to oppose Seymour's motion of 2 May that if they had satisfaction for ship money they should trust the king for the rest. Hampden said they must first settle the issue of freedom of speech, which could be relied upon to take a long time. At the very end of the parliament he insisted on a vote on the legality of ship money before any other proceedings. This was a vote the court could not risk, for if they lost, all their bargaining power would be destroyed. Clarendon is surely right in giving Hampden the credit for preventing any decision from being reached at the end of the parliament. These were not the actions of a man who thought taxation by consent was an isolated problem, but they are entirely consistent with his speech of 5 June 1628. For Hampden the religious and the constitutional issues were never separable. April and May 1640, along with January and February 1642, are probably the most important moments of his parliamentary career. In both, his achievement was to prevent an agreement with the king.

**Negotiating with the king, 1640–1642** But even if Hampden, John Pym, or Pym's stepbrother, Francis Rous, are credited with a belief that Charles I intended to reintroduce popery, the crude and unsophisticated suggestion that Charles was about to enter into the obedience of the see of Rome would not follow. There were people in the country who thought this, but few, if any, sophisticated high-level politicians were among them. Serious politicians might, however, look for the intellectual qualities which were the defining marks of popery, for its essence; those who accepted the essence of popery might then be taken, for objective and practical purposes, as being papists. In the circles in which Hampden and Pym moved two things were commonly taken to be of the essence of popery. The first, and the one Hampden would have heard most often from John Dod, was idolatry—the giving of divine honour to anything other than God was idolatry, and therefore popery. Of this Hampden believed Charles guilty, since he believed that the setting up of altars in churches was idolatry. There is no doubt that Charles did believe in setting up altars in churches, so if Hampden's definition is accepted so also must be his judgment. The other defining mark of popery in the minds of his circle concerned the relationship between works and faith in salvation. It was popery to believe that our salvation was contingent on anything we might do in the future. Man did not precede God in the order of causes which led to salvation. A good protestant was assured of his salvation by God's election, independent of anything he might do or think. By this test too, Charles was a papist. It is this definition of assurance Hampden repeated in his will, though without explicitly asserting the contrary view to be popery. Such a statement could have led to the denial of probate. It cannot be proved from surviving evidence that John Hampden held to this definition of popery. However, his parents and his grandparents did hold to it, and he heard his ally Pym and his favourite ministers repeat it so often that he must at least have viewed it without strong disfavour. In this context, a belief that Charles was a papist should not be taken as a case of dishonesty or misobservation, but as a case of misdefinition, commonly made with great sincerity.

If Charles was objectively papist, inducements by bribe or threat were unlikely to deter him more than temporarily from giving vent to his beliefs. The conversion of Henri IV of France to Catholicism was a recent reminder that the design with which they credited Charles was perfectly possible. To stop it, and especially to do so in a country which in the summer of 1640 was still far from sharing their fears, was going to need physical, and not just moral, force. Since the demilitarization of the English aristocracy no such force was available to Hampden and Pym. In this context the appearance of armed Scottish resistance to Charles's popish tendencies must have appeared little less than providential. The cause of closer union between England and Scotland, with the Scots as guarantors of an English religion they would not need to fear that Charles and Archbishop Laud might again try to force on Scotland, appeared the only way to a stable peace. From a date not later than 28 August 1640, when he and Pym assisted in the drafting of the petition of the twelve peers, calling upon the king to recall parliament, Hampden was part of a Scottish party in English politics. The true date may well be considerably earlier.

This meant that Hampden had to consider Scottish priorities for English politics. For the Scottish covenanters the object was to shift English politics so that Charles would not again have the opportunity to pursue his popish tendencies. The chief difference between Scottish and English constitutional thinking about religion was the far smaller power given to the king in the Church of Scotland. It was even doubtful whether he could claim to enjoy the royal supremacy north of the border. It was this pattern Robert Baillie and his Scottish fellows were eager to see their allies introduce in England. That their allies might then take office to help to implement such a settlement was for the Scots no more than icing on the cake. It was the diminution of the king's religious power which mattered.

Bishops were as much a constitutional as a religious issue. The point of bishops was that the church was governed, not by an elected assembly, but by men appointed by the king. This fact alone was now enough to turn many into their opponents who had previously been prepared to accept them. Whether Hampden was one of these will probably never be known. Early on he persuaded Viscount Falkland to agree to the exclusion of bishops from the House of Lords by the assurance that if this were done nothing further would be attempted against the church. On the other hand, on 27 February 1641, when Edward Hyde, riding an anti-Scottish reaction, challenged Hampden to state his opinion on the future of episcopacy, he came back only with the words that 'we are all of a mind in desiring what is best' (Russell, *Fall*, 198). It was not even a competent evasion. On 27 May any suggestion of evasion had quite disappeared: Hampden said the root and branch bill to abolish episcopacy 'had no fault in it' (Bodl. Oxf., MS Rawl. D 1099, fol. 19b). On 11 June he was involved in the attempt to introduce the bill unexpectedly, and remained committed to it for ever after. It is easy to see why Hyde doubted the sincerity of his assurances to Falkland. Hampden was also involved, in both the Short and the Long parliaments, in championing Peter Smart, the canon of Durham who had accused John Cosin as dean of introducing idolatry. At the beginning of June 1641, when Pym was ill, it was Hampden whom he left in charge of his papers for the impeachment of Laud. The impeachment of the archbishop was another issue on which the Scots were anxious to see rapid progress. Hampden was particularly active, both in trying to disarm recusants and in pressing for progress on the bill against pluralities.

Perhaps Hampden's most important speech in the first session of the Long Parliament was on 15 March 1641, on the queen's desire to be allowed to keep the Catholic Sir John Winter as her secretary, and presumably therefore to allow him to attend mass with her. At this stage the projected settlement between king and parliament was as near concluded as it ever was, and the queen, up to this point, had been helpful. However, her desire to keep her Catholic servants was non-negotiable for her, and therefore for the king also. The issue split the Lords from the Commons in the parliamentary leadership, pitting Bedford and Saye against Hampden and Pym. Hampden's comment on the queen's proposal was simply that 'we sit here to see the laws observed, not broken' (Russell, *Fall*, 267). He repeated the point the next day. If any one thing did more than another to prevent a settlement, it was the opposition of Hampden and Pym to this particular proposal. Without it, there would be no settlement. Hampden had simply put his hatred of popery above his desire for peace. On the other hand, he showed unexpected flexibility on the issue of parliament's attempts to bring the earl of Strafford, one of the king's closest advisers, to justice. The point of the changeover from impeachment to attainder of Strafford was that the attainder bill, by specifying the penalty of death, blocked the royal power of pardon. Hampden on this occasion went out of the house before the vote, and did not return until it was over. A readiness to compromise on civil matters was not matched by any equivalent willingness in religion.

Hampden clearly knew what risk he was taking in thus infuriating the king. On 23 November 1640, after the stabbing of a Westminster JP, he was one of the first to move for the houses to have a guard under their own control. Nearly a year later he was one of those who helped to draft the additional instruction that help to suppress the Irish rising should be conditional on the king's appointing commanders the parliament should have cause to confide in. He was one of the secret committee set to investigate the army plot to use force against parliament revealed in May 1641, and was clearly at all times aware of the danger of a violent royal reaction. On at least one occasion—the alleged plot revealed by Thomas Beale in November 1641—he was prepared to inflame these fears by stories which he must surely have known to be untrue. Thomas Beale, a London tailor, claimed to have overheard 108 Catholics planning to kill one MP each, a number which was either too large or too small to be taken seriously. Then, he said, he was detected. They ran him through with their swords 'in four or five places', and he turned up at the House of Commons without a scratch on him. Henry Cogan reported to Sir John Penington: 'Whether this be a truth or imposture time will resolve' (*CSP dom.*, *1641–3*, 169). Hampden repeated the story as gospel.

As Hampden's fear of the king grew, so did his closeness to the Scots. In the autumn of 1641, when the king was attempting to negotiate a separate peace in Edinburgh, Hampden, alongside Lord Howard of Escrick, Nathaniel Fiennes, Sir Philip Stapleton, and Sir William Armyne, was appointed to a parliamentary committee to attend the king in Edinburgh. From then on he was recognized as one of the Commons' Scottish specialists. After the Scottish parliament appointed commissioners to go to London in November 1641 to negotiate the defence of Ireland, it was Hampden who tried to make good the lord mayor's failures in finding them a house, and when the Scots finally found their own house, it was he who persuaded the Commons to pay for it. It was Hampden who moved to thank the Scots for their supportive declaration on the accusation against the five members, following the king's unsuccessful attempt to arrest Hampden, Pym, Denzil Holles, Sir Arthur Hesilrige, and William Strode on 4 January 1642. It was Hampden, on 22 January, who introduced a proposal for the synod which was near the heart of the Scots' demands for what they wanted if they were to enter into an alliance with the English parliament, and he who urged the payment of the remainder of the money due to the Scots for their brotherly assistance.

This growing attachment to the Scots kept pace with a growing hostility to the king. From 20 December 1641 Hampden was one of the early supporters of the militia ordinance. His reply to the king's attempt to impeach him and the others of the five members was to propose to impeach the attorney-general for obeying the king's command. His most provocative act was his reply to the king's message of 20 January 1642, which was designed to set up a negotiation by asking the parliament to state their uttermost demands. Hampden's reply was that the Tower, the forts, and the 'whole militia' of the kingdom should be put into hands that parliament could confide in, 'that so we may sit in safety' (Russell, *Fall*, 465). It is hard to see how distrust of the king could have been more plainly expressed. Hampden backed this up with a proposal to turn the protestation into an oath of association, to make the taking of it compulsory, and to have the names of all refusers returned to the Commons. It is the interpretation Robert Baillie had hoped he could place on the protestation when it was first made. It looks back to Pym's proposals of 1621, and behind that to the bond of association. Behind that, it is the radical tradition of the community of the realm which looks back to Simon de Montfort and the Song of Lewes.

**Civil war and death** From early 1642 Hampden's record is that of a soldier and a man concerned with preparation for war. He did not live to see his plans for the Scottish alliance come to fruition, but as a parliamentarian colonel seems never to have made a serious mistake. After undertaking to raise a regiment of foot for parliament he and his greencoats saw action in Buckinghamshire and took part in the relief of Coventry in August 1642. Although he then continued with the main body of Essex's army he took little part at the battle of Edgehill on 23 October because he was placed in charge of the artillery train, but it was his men who eventually stopped the charge of Prince Rupert's pursuit. On 12 November, when Prince Rupert's men appeared out of the mist at Brentford and routed the regiments of Holles and Brooke, it was Hampden who rallied the troops and held the line. During the winter of 1642–3 he played his part in holding together both the parliamentary war party and its cause, opposing any moves towards the conclusion of a peace on unsatisfactory terms. After negotiations at Oxford were aborted in spring 1643 Hampden was active in the successful siege of Reading. However, it will never be known whether he had the makings of a soldier comparable to his cousin Oliver Cromwell. As the parliamentarian forces advanced upon Oxford on 18 June 1643, at Chalgrove, he faced a charge from Prince Rupert, was shot in the shoulder, and died of his wounds at Thame six days later on 24 June. He was buried at Great Hampden on the following day.

In his will dated 28 June 1636 with a codicil dated 30 June 1642, Hampden took precautions against most of the complications which had overtaken his own wardship a generation before. He began with an economical but unambiguous statement of his assurance of salvation, and asked for a monument in Great Hampden parish church, where he wished to be buried (subsequently erected by his great-grandson). This was to display the inscription 'In Christo mortuus, per Christum resurrecturus, cum Christo regnaturus' ('Died in Christ, will rise through Christ, will reign with Christ'), with pictures of himself and his wife and 'our ten children'. John, the eldest child, was a captain in his father's regiment at the beginning of the civil war, and died shortly afterwards. Richard *Hampden, his second son, lived on to be a whig politician of some standing during the exclusion period. William, born in 1633, died in 1675. Elizabeth (1622–1643) married Richard Knightley the younger. Hampden's daughter Anne (*b.* 1625) married Sir Robert Pye the younger, son of the auditor of the exchequer; Ruth (1628–1687) married Sir John Trevor the younger; Mary (*bap.* 1630, *d.* 1689?) married Colonel Robert Hammond, and subsequently Sir John Hobart, bt; two other daughters, whose names are unknown, died unmarried; and the name of the tenth child is not known. Neither in the will nor in the codicil is there any mention of Hampden's second wife, Lettice (*d.* 1666), widow of Sir Thomas Vachell of Reading, and daughter of Sir Francis Knollys. She bore him no children, but survived him until 1666.

Hampden's feoffees to uses were Sir Gilbert Gerrard, his mother, his son-in-law Richard Knightley the younger, Edmund Waller, his father-in-law Edmund Symeon, and his heir, Richard Hampden. The executors were his mother and his father-in-law. It is a remarkable example of the younger generation handing back the torch to the old. He provided for annuities of £30 for his younger sons up to the age of sixteen, and of £40 from the age of sixteen to twenty-one. His unmarried daughters were to receive £30 a year until they were provided with portions. The executors were responsible for a charge of £500 per annum which was to rest on the land until six years after his death. They were to raise the sum of £14,000 out of the lands, and to that end were given power to sell, to fell woods, and to make leases for any number of years with or without reservation of rent. This sum was to provide for debts and then for the heir, and any overplus was to be distributed among the younger children. The provisos for sale and leases without rent suggest a doubt whether such a surplus was likely to exist. The executors were unambiguously instructed to bid jointly for the wardship of the body and the lands. Elizabeth Hampden could not henceforth claim again that she was unaware of the provisions for wardship. If Hampden's father's will had contained such a provision, much litigation would have been saved. Hampden's 'trusty and faithful' servant John Baldwin was left £50 and a recommendation to his heir, and his neighbour Thomas Stile was left the responsibility of overseer and £10. The codicil provides that since the main will his daughter Elizabeth had married Richard Knightley the younger with a portion of £2500, and his daughter Anne had married Sir Robert Pye the younger with a portion of £2000 of which £1000 was yet to be paid. The will was proved by the executors in the prerogative court of Canterbury on 28 May 1647, and John Hampden was himself in part to blame for the delay; the abolition of episcopal jurisdiction omitted to provide any alternative jurisdiction for probate—a classic example of the law of unintended consequence in legislation.

**Reputation** John Hampden's refusal to pay ship money, leading in 1637–8 to one of the most famous test cases in English constitutional history, guarantees him lasting fame, and he enjoyed the further distinction of being one of the five members selected along with Lord Mandeville by Charles I for impeachment in 1642. Yet even if these two headline claims to fame were taken away, Hampden would deserve a reputation as one of the key members of the intellectual and political powerhouse which fashioned the parliamentarian cause in the English civil war. He was a politician of no ordinary skill, whose day might have come again in the negotiations for peace after the war was over; he is a man without whom the history of England might have been very different. Yet he did not, perhaps, have the talent of Bedford, Essex, and even Saye for understanding minds different from his own. He was, as Gardiner and Clarendon remarked, neither a particularly frequent nor a particularly eloquent speaker. As a soldier after 1642 he discharged the duties which fell to him with honour and with competence, but by sheer chance never seemed, until the day of his final wound, to be stationed exactly where the fighting was fiercest. The reasons for the reputation are therefore not obvious. Yet there has been unanimous agreement from that day to this that his importance was genuine and earned. From Sir Francis Windebank to Nehemiah Wallington in the seventeenth century, and from Wallace Notestein to Kevin Sharpe in the twentieth century, no one has called it into question.

In any period there are politicians who enjoy reputations their public performance does not obviously warrant. About these people there are three obvious questions to ask. First, are they extremely rich? Second, are they extremely well-connected? Third, do they enjoy exceptional skills of judgement and man management? On the first two tests Hampden has always been reputed to have done well. However, his wealth was a great deal less than it has often been taken to be, and resulted in large measure from the habit in successive generations of his family for leaving large sums of money of which they turned out not to die possessed. John Hampden was not poor, and was far richer than, for example, John Pym. Yet by a yardstick of wealth a man like his cousin Sir Thomas Barrington was probably far his superior. His was not a reputation based on wealth. He was of course well-connected, as most of the parliamentary leaders were. The fact that his mother was a Cromwell, and the perhaps more important fact that she had a town house in Whitehall, put him at the centre of the immense Barrington–Masham–Gerrard–Cromwell connection. This was clearly a source of strength, yet it is not unique, and has limits. He does not appear, for example, among the close private contacts of Pym, Bedford, or Warwick. If he was well-connected, he was not uniquely so, and the reputation must rest on something else.

It would seem that Clarendon was right in putting Hampden's influence down to his skills of man management. As an organizer, a man of affairs, and the person capable of holding a cause together, he was of the highest standard. When in 1640 the twelve peers met at Bedford House in the Strand to draft their petition calling for a parliament, Pym and St John, who may have done most of the drafting, attended because they were Bedford's clients and servants. John Hampden and Bedford's son were the only other commoners present. Vital tasks like writing to Sir John Hotham, governor of Hull, to encourage him to preserve his loyalty in the last weeks before the civil war, fell to Hampden, as did the key task of arranging accommodation for the Scottish commissioners who visited London in January 1642. He was in charge of the timing of the unexpected reintroduction of the bill for root and branch abolition of episcopacy on 11 June 1641. Clarendon is quite right about his ability to read which way a debate was going, and to sum it up to his advantage. These examples certainly seem to portray skills of exceptional judgement and man management, and if indeed Hampden possessed such skills, he deserved his reputation.

CONRAD RUSSELL

**Sources** Clarendon, *Hist. rebellion* • *The life of Edward, earl of Clarendon … written by himself*, 2 vols. (1857) • S. R. Gardiner, *History of England from the accession of James I to the outbreak of the civil war, 1603–1642*, 10 vols. (1883–4) • S. R. Gardiner, *History of England from the accession of James I to the outbreak of the civil war, 1603–1642*, 10 vols. (1901–7), vol. 1 • A. Searle, ed., *Barrington family letters, 1628–1632*, CS, 4th ser., 28 (1983) • R. C. Johnson and others, eds., *Proceedings in parliament, 1628*, 6 vols. (1977–83) • *JHC*, 1–3 (1547–1644) • W. Notestein and F. H. Relf, eds., *Commons debates for 1629* (1921) • E. S. Cope and W. H. Coates, eds., *Proceedings of the Short Parliament of 1640*, CS, 4th ser., 19 (1977) • *The Short Parliament (1640) diary of Sir Thomas Aston*, ed. J. D. Maltby, CS, 4th ser., 35 (1988) • *JHL*, 3–4 (1620–42) • *The journal of Sir Simonds D'Ewes from the first recess of the Long Parliament to the withdrawal of King Charles from London*, ed. W. H. Coates (1942) • W. H. Coates, A. Steele Young, and V. F. Snow, eds., *The private journals of the Long Parliament*, 3 vols. (1982–92) • *The journal of Sir Symonds D'Ewes: from the beginning of the Long Parliament to the opening of the trial of the earl of Strafford*, ed. W. Notestein (1923) • *CSP dom.*, 1626–43 • C. G. Bonsey and J. G. Jenkins, eds., *Ship money papers and Richard Grenville's notebook*, Buckinghamshire RS, 13 (1965) • C. Russell, 'The ship-money judgments of Bramston and Davenport', *EngHR*, 77 (1962), 312–18 • *State trials* • A. Thrush, 'The navy under Charles I, 1625–40', PhD diss., U. Lond., 1991 • C. Russell, *The fall of the British monarchies, 1637–1642* (1991) • R. P. Cust, *The forced loan and English politics, 1626–1628* (1987) • *De jure majestatis, or, Political treatise of government (1628–30), and the letter-book of Sir John Eliot (1625–1632)*, ed. A. B. Grosart (1882) • J. T. Cliffe, *The puritan gentry: the great puritan families of early Stuart England* (1984) • correspondence, Yale U., Beinecke L., Howard of Escrick papers, Osborn shelves • U. Hull, Brynmor Jones L., Hotham papers, DD/HO/1 • W. J. Jones, 'Hampden, William', HoP, *Commons, 1558–1603*, 2.243 • *DNB* • Foster, *Alum. Oxon.* • J. G. Nichols and J. Bruce, eds., *Wills from Doctors' Commons*, CS, old ser., 83 (1863), 99–105 • PRO, PROB 11/89/52 • PRO, C 142/248/39/ C 66/1421; C 193/13/1/10–11; C 193/13/26b • PRO, wards 3/19/1 (depositions); wards 2/109 (evidences) • PRO, E 401/2586/358–359 • PRO, SP 16/276/35 • BL, Harley MS 1622, fol. 6a • BL, Harley MS 163, fol. 663a • BL, Add. MS 31954, p. 17

**Archives** Bodl. Oxf., papers relating to trial • Queen's College, Oxford, papers | U. Hull, Brynmor Jones L., letters to Sir John Hotham • V&A NAL, letters to Sir John Eliot

**Likenesses** J. Houbraken, line engraving, 1740, BM, NPG; repro. in Birch, *Heads* • C. Turner, mezzotint, pubd 1810, BM, NPG

**Wealth at death** will, PRO, PROB 11/89/52 • left lands and substantial bequests to relatives: Nichols and Bruce, eds., *Wills from Doctors' Commons*

**Hampden, John** (*bap.* 1653, *d.* 1696), politician and conspirator, was baptized on 21 March 1653 at St Martin-in-the-Fields, London, the second son of Richard *Hampden (*bap.* 1631, *d.* 1695) MP and his wife, Letitia Paget, daughter of William *Paget, fifth Baron Paget, and his wife, Frances. He was the grandson of the John *Hampden of ship money fame.

**Early life** After studying law at the Middle Temple, Hampden, another pupil, and their tutor, the ejected presbyterian minister Francis Tallents, travelled on the continent from February 1671 to July 1673. Hampden learned Hebrew, Greek, and Latin, later impressing Gilbert Burnet with his erudition. On 5 May 1674 Hampden married Sarah (*d.* 1687), daughter of Thomas *Foley (1617–1677) of Witley Court, Worcestershire [*see under* Foley family], and widow of Essex Knightley of Fawsley, Northamptonshire. They had two children, Richard and Letitia. A friend of Richard Baxter, Foley raised his children in a puritan home; Sarah's three brothers, Thomas, Paul, and Philip, served in parliament and had ties to nonconformist ministers. Hampden's father was also close to Baxter, who took refuge in his house during the great plague. A decade later Hampden and his father contributed money to build Baxter's new meeting-house in Oxendon Street, London.

With his father's support, Hampden stood for Buckinghamshire in the first parliamentary election of 1679, spending £800 to win the seat. He sat on the committee for elections and privileges, opposed the sale of Tangier, and voted for exclusion. He also served as an assessment commissioner for Buckinghamshire, Northamptonshire, and Oxfordshire (1679–80). In the election of August 1679 Hampden retained his seat in an unusual contest. He had given the writ to the under-sheriff, who scheduled the polling for Aylesbury, a bastion of country support. However, the sheriff rescheduled the poll for the loyalist town of Buckingham, giving Hampden and his colleague Thomas Wharton only a day's notice. Using carts and horses, Hampden and Wharton transported their supporters across the county and emerged victorious, partly because of backing from the duke of Buckingham and Lord Paget. Hampden was also an ally of Philip, Lord Wharton, the duke of Monmouth, the earl of Shaftesbury, and Algernon Sidney. By the time Charles opened parliament on 21 October 1680, Hampden was ill. Whether he attended this session is unclear, but the following month he, his wife, and Tallents left for France. While there, Hampden was influenced by Richard Simon's *Histoire critique du Vieux Testament* (1678), a critical and philological analysis that uncovered numerous textual errors and discrepancies. His faith in reformed protestantism shaken, Hampden proclaimed himself a freethinker. From the historian François de Mézeray, Hampden learned how representative French political institutions had succumbed to invasive royal powers. Mézeray exhorted him to venture everything to prevent something similar from happening in England, advice that probably helped motivate Hampden to engage in conspiratorial activity in 1683 and 1687–8. After returning to England he was elected to the Oxford parliament from Wendover, but he participated only briefly, if at all, for in September 1681 he went back to the continent.

Hampden's perspective, like Sidney's and Edmund Ludlow's, was international. As early as 1678–9 he was among the adherents of the country who received subsidies from France. When he learned of the Anglo-Dutch alliance in mid-1680, he expressed concern, noting that William might bring a Dutch army to England. Hampden had contacts with the Huguenots, and through Paul Barillon he was also in touch with the archbishop of Paris, probably as part of his and Sidney's efforts to persuade Louis's government that Catholics would benefit from religious toleration in a restored English republic. Hampden returned to England in September 1682, perhaps fortuitously, for Lord Preston, the English ambassador in Paris, thought he would have been arrested two months later in connection with an alleged Huguenot conspiracy had he remained in France.

**Conspiracy and confession** Hampden now became involved in discussions about a general insurrection aimed at compelling Charles to exclude James from the succession. The first meeting of what Lord Howard of Escrick called the council of six occurred at Hampden's house in Russell Street, London, in January 1683. The other participants in this and subsequent meetings were Monmouth, Sidney, the earl of Essex, and Lord William Russell. The conspirators dispatched the whig attorney Aaron Smith to Scotland to seek an alliance with the earl of Argyll and his supporters, and in April Hampden and his associates agreed to loan Argyll £10,000. The six were divided in their aims, with Hampden, Sidney, and Essex arguing for the re-establishment of a republic, whereas the others were monarchists. Hampden and Sidney finally endorsed the monarchical option in late April.

Following disclosure of the plotting, Hampden was committed to the Tower on 8 or 9 July. He admitted only that Monmouth and probably Russell and Sidney had been at his house, but he professed to have forgotten if Howard had been present. Essex in turn acknowledged that he had often visited Hampden. Only Howard fully confessed, leaving the government without the essential second witness. Hampden's wife joined him in prison, but she quickly became ill and had to petition repeatedly for her release. While prisoners, Hampden and Sidney corresponded about a joint defence strategy, and Sidney also proposed that the two men, if freed, should retire to Gascony. After Hampden unsuccessfully petitioned for pardon and liberty on the basis of ill health, he and Sidney sought writs of habeas corpus in late October. On the 31st Charles told Bedford that Hampden must be released in the absence of a second witness, but he remained in prison, probably because Charles hoped for a confession from Monmouth, the potential second witness. On 28 November, after Hampden pleaded not guilty to a charge of high misdemeanour when he was indicted in king's bench, he was released on bail of £15,000. Persuaded by the earl of Halifax, Monmouth signed a confession, a copy of which was shown to Hampden by Sir James Forbes on 5 December. Aghast, Hampden said he was a dead man, but Monmouth retrieved his confession from Charles the following day. Hampden failed, however, to persuade Monmouth to intercede for Sidney, who went to the scaffold on 7 December. When Hampden was tried on 6 February, the state's only material witness was Howard, since efforts to subpoena Monmouth proved unsuccessful. Found guilty, Hampden was fined a staggering £40,000 on the 12th and imprisoned until he could find sureties. The government seized his estate at Great Hampden, Buckinghamshire (worth £700 p.a.), and his manor at Preston, Northamptonshire. When the duchess of Portsmouth attempted to negotiate his release, she was reportedly told that his enemies 'would rather have him rot in Prison than have the Forty Thousand Pounds' (*JHL*, 14.380). After Monmouth's defeat and Ford, Lord Grey's capture and confession, the state had a second witness to try Hampden for high treason. Moved from king's bench prison to the Tower on 17 October 1685, he was arraigned at the Old Bailey on 30 December. Although he protested the injustice of being tried twice for the same offence, he acknowledged his role in planning a rebellion but insisted he had known nothing of an assassination plot. He would later explain that he had confessed at his friends' urging, knowing his admissions could harm no one. Throwing himself on the king's mercy, he was sentenced to death, but he obtained a pardon on 25 January 1686 after paying £6000 to George Jeffreys and Edward Petre. According to Sir John Bramston, his confession infuriated the whigs, but in view of his frail health he probably had little choice. He would later reflect that it was 'hardly possible for a Man to suffer more' than he did (*JHL*, 14.379). According to Gilbert Burnet, his confession had a lasting, depressive impact on him. A royal warrant restored his estates on 3 February 1686, and on 19 June his attainder was reversed. The following year his wife died on 5 November after childbirth. He later remarried; his new wife was Anne Cornwallis, daughter and coheir of Frederick Cornwallis; they had two children, John and Anne.

When James made overtures to whigs and nonconformists, Hampden displayed no interest, and by December 1687 he was working with William's agent, James Johnston. Against this background, Hampden wrote a confession in April 1688 recanting his religious scepticism and circulated the document among his friends. In early June he told Johnston it was time for William's invasion, though he worried about possible French intervention and the people's reluctance to support the prince given the fate of the Monmouth rebels. Hampden would later depict the invasion as the culmination of the council of six's efforts. Some historians have credited him with chairing the committee appointed in December 1688 to draft an address asking William to assume control of civil and military affairs, but his father almost certainly did this.

**Country whig** Sitting for Wendover in the Convention, Hampden served on sixteen committees. During the debate in the grand committee on the state of the nation, chaired by his father in late January, Hampden insisted on the need to 'declare the Constitution and Rule of the Government' (Grey, 9.36). He supported Lord Falkland's proposal not to fill the throne until the nation's rights had been safeguarded, and he sat on the committee to ascertain which rights required new legislation. Citing the threat to protestantism in the Netherlands and Ireland, he called on William in March to articulate his war plans. The same month he fought unsuccessfully to amend the coronation oath by having a monarch pledge to defend protestantism as well as the Church of England. Nor did he succeed in obtaining wording that would facilitate changes in the church's structure and practice. Hampden chaired a committee to draft a bill for the comprehension of moderate nonconformists in the established church, but this effort failed. When the Toleration Bill faltered, Hampden won William's support by raising £40,000 from London dissenters to loan to the king, but Hampden's attempt to include non-Trinitarians in the bill was unsuccessful. In defending toleration, he argued that 'the Empire of Religion belongs to God; men may be forced and constrained, without other effect than to destroy the Country where it is done, and drip people in Blood' (Grey, 9.252). In April he chaired the committee that drafted an address to William calling for war against France, but the Commons rejected it and appointed another chairman because of its harsh references to Louis's bribery of the court and various MPs in Charles's reign.

During the debate on the Indemnity Bill in June, Hampden recognized the need to heal the nation by pardoning as many as possible, but not royal ministers responsible for shedding innocent blood. In August his motion for an address asking William to remove Halifax was defeated in the Commons. William now wanted 'to be rid of' Hampden by dispatching him as an ambassador to Madrid, but he declined the appointment (Foxcroft, 2.229). Halifax had earlier recommended that Hampden be appointed ambassador to The Hague, but this was unacceptable to William, who questioned Hampden's mental health. In November Hampden testified before the Lords' committee investigating the deaths of whig leaders. Recounting his punishment, he averred that he had been 'as much murdered as any of them, by reason of his Sufferings' (*JHL*, 14.378), but his ineffectual attempt to blame Halifax brought only the latter's derision. Hampden continued his attack in the Commons' grand committee on the state of the nation, where in December he called for the removal from office of Halifax, Nottingham, and Godolphin: 'If we must be ruined again, let it be by new men' (Grey, 9.486–7). In the debate on the bill to reverse Sir Thomas Armstrong's attainder in January 1690, Hampden denounced Sir Robert Sawyer, whom he blamed for Sir Thomas's execution, as a bloodhound and a monster.

Hampden lost his seat in the 1690 election, probably in part owing to a breach with his father, but he remained loyal to his whig principles. His sympathies were thus in keeping with those of other country whigs and out-of-office tories opposed to government corruption and placement, and in favour of triennial bills. In 1691 he condemned the excise in *Some Considerations about the most Proper Way of Raising Money in the Present Conjuncture*. The excise, which he valued at £1,500,000 p.a., was endless, undermining the need for parliaments and unfairly burdening the poor. Even the hearth tax was better, though he preferred to raise money by seizing the lands of Irish rebels, ending lavish pensions to civil and military officials, and levying a land tax. After Hampden criticized the management of public accounts in November 1691, the Lords voted to appoint him a commissioner to examine the accounts two months later, but the accounts bill ultimately failed. In *Some Short Considerations Concerning the State of the Nation* (1692), he echoed some of the main points in Locke's *Two Treatises*. The government was unsettled, Hampden averred, because some people repudiated the principles that justified the 1688 revolution, and he was irate that a secretary of state was licensing works by nonjurors. Turning his attention to Samuel Johnson's *An argument proving that the abrogation of the late King James … was according to the constitution* (1693), Hampden, in *A Letter to Mr. Samuel Johnson* (1693), reiterated his conviction that the throne had been vacant because of James's voluntary abdication. He also argued for a triennial bill as a remedy against corrupt MPs. Hampden's radical whig principles were again evinced in his final tract, *An Enquiry, or, A Discourse between a Yeoman of Kent, and a Knight of the Shire* (1693), a blistering attack that called on William to restore the English constitution. Without annual elections 'we are left as much to the King's Will for a Session of Parliament, as evil Ministers in the late Reigns design'd we should be' (*An Enquiry*, 2).

Hampden's attempt to return to parliament failed in 1696 when he lost the by-election for a seat representing Buckinghamshire, in part because of Wharton's opposition. Despondent, Hampden slit his throat on 10 December and died several days later, leaving his estate to his widow. He was buried at Great Hampden. The coroner's verdict was *non compos mentis*. Signs of mental illness had been apparent since at least February 1689, when John

Verney remarked that many thought him insane; Halifax deemed Hampden 'quite … discomposed' the following month (Foxcroft, 2.204). Hampden also had stomach problems, apparently the result of emotional tension.

Two years after his first wife's death, Hampden had become something of a socialite, 'a great beau [who] dresses and powders [and] courts Lady Monmouth' (*Portland MSS*, 3.442). For such conduct he was the butt of public satire, as in the poem 'The Devil Tavern Club':

From [Richard] Hampden the drunkard and Hampden the beau,
Deliver us Lord in manner also.

The satire in 'Omnia sponte sua reddit justissima tellus' was cruel:

Hampden next, with lean grimace
And ogling eyes, adores her beauteous face.
… Her looks his loose affections can remove
From books and plots, and Lady Monmouths love:
See how the meagre madman grins and gapes
Like hungry fox at distant bunch of grapes!
(Lord, 5.167, 358)

Hampden professed not to have been bothered by critics who variously labelled him an atheist, a Catholic, a Socinian, a republican, and a madman; truth, he thought, was the daughter of time. Indeed, Burnet, whom he called to his deathbed, deemed him witty and vivacious, if also mercurial, and John Evelyn described him in 1693 as a scholar and a fine gentleman. Talented, learned, and keenly interested in affairs of state, Hampden was an outspoken and sometimes acerbic defender of the country and whig political traditions. RICHARD L. GREAVES

**Sources** *State trials*, 9.1053–126; 11.479–94 · A. Grey, ed., *Debates of the House of Commons, from the year 1667 to the year 1694*, 7 (1763), 100; 9 (1763); 10 (1763), 47 · *CSP dom.*, 1680–81, 86, 685; 1683–4, 69, 136, 263; 1686–7, 2, 16, 113, 175–6 · *JHL*, 14 (1685–91), 378–80 · *Seventh report*, HMC, 6 (1879) · *The manuscripts of his grace the duke of Portland*, 10 vols., HMC, 29 (1891–1931), vol. 3, pp. 391–2, 407, 442, 580 · *Report on the manuscripts of the late Reginald Rawdon Hastings*, 4 vols., HMC, 78 (1928–47), vol. 4, pp. 308–9 · R. L. Greaves, *Secrets of the kingdom: British radicals from the Popish Plot to the revolution of 1688–89* (1992) · D. R. Lacey, *Dissent and parliamentary politics in England, 1661–1689* (1969) · J. Scott, *Algernon Sidney and the Restoration crisis, 1677–1683* (1991) · HoP, *Commons, 1660–90* · *The life and letters of Sir George Savile … first marquis of Halifax*, ed. H. C. Foxcroft, 2 vols. (1898) · G. de F. Lord and others, eds., *Poems on affairs of state: Augustan satirical verse, 1660–1714*, 7 vols. (1963–75), vol. 5 · *A letter from a freeholder of Buckinghamshire, to a friend in London, concerning the election of the knights of the said county* (1679) · PRO, PROB 11/435, sig. 251

**Archives** BL, Stowe MS 747 · U. Nott. L., Portland MSS

**Likenesses** oils, c.1690, NPG

**Hampden, Renn Dickson** (1793–1868), bishop of Hereford and theologian, eldest son of Renn Hampden, a colonel of militia in Barbados, and of Frances Raven, his wife, was born in Barbados on Good Friday, 29 March 1793. He was sent to England with his godmother in 1798 to be educated by the Revd M. Rowlandson, vicar of Warminster, Wiltshire. In 1811 he entered Oriel College, Oxford (which his cousin, Nassau Senior, had also attended), as a commoner. In 1813 in the Michaelmas examination he obtained a double first (in classics and mathematics), taking his BA in 1814, in which year he also won the chancellor's Latin essay prize and was elected a fellow of Oriel. In

**Renn Dickson Hampden** (1793–1868), after Sir Daniel Macnee, 1867

his university vacations he was a frequent visitor to Bath where he had friends and relations, one of whom, his cousin Mary (*d.* 1865), the daughter of Edward Lovell, he married on 24 April 1816, the year in which he was also ordained deacon. They had at least four children.

**Early career as a Noetic** At Oriel College, Hampden was taught by the first generation of Noetic theologians, who were active in the intellectual revival of the university and the defence of Anglicanism on the ground of its 'reasonableness'. John Davison was his tutor; Samuel Hinds, later bishop of Norwich and also born in Barbados, was his undergraduate friend; and Thomas Arnold and Richard Whately were his contemporaries as fellows. He never abandoned his Noetic upbringing, whether as a source of controversy in the 1830s and 1840s or as a bulwark of religious orthodoxy in the 1850s and 1860s.

In the 1820s, when church parties had not yet acquired their distinctive forms, the Noetics were accepted as part of a general Anglican renewal and not yet anathematized as liberals by Tractarians and Anglo-Catholics. This was reflected in the catholicity of Hampden's early career: after curacies at Blagdon, Faringdon, and Hungerford, he became curate to the high-church Revd H. H. Norris at Hackney and subsequently (1825–6) editor of the *Christian Remembrancer*, a high-church journal with strong financial links to the West Indian merchants. In this capacity he not only published attacks on Unitarianism and Calvinism, but also Baden Powell's denial of the scriptural basis of Sunday observance, which probably owed its origin to Edward Copleston, the Noetic provost of Oriel.

Hampden's first published work was *An Essay on the Philosophical Evidence of Christianity* (1827), which was inspired by Bishop Joseph Butler's *The Analogy of Religion* (1736) and the desire to explain the full force of its argument, which was notoriously obscure. The importance of Butler's *Analogy*, which was a central Noetic text, was that it used evidence of the divine dispensation in the natural world as an auxiliary evidence of the truth of scriptural revelation. Butler's insight was that the two dispensations were similar in nature, and thus that the existence of difficulties and obscurities in understanding scriptural revelation, being of a similar kind to those encountered in the natural world, was evidence of the truth of scriptural revelation just as the natural world was evidence of a divine creator.

From this it also followed, according to Hampden, that the scriptures were to be understood in the same way as the natural world, namely as a collection of facts. Just as the natural world was to be investigated by inductive science, so the scriptural world was properly the subject of an inductive theology. Both were capable of being submitted to the assent of human reason. However, unlike the natural world, where causes and consequences of phenomena could be observed, such observations of the scriptural world were not possible. Accordingly it was not possible to search for the ultimate principle of scriptural truth. The integrity of individual scriptural facts had to be accepted: it was not possible to look behind them to decide, for example, whether divine predestination or free will was the guiding principle of Christianity.

In 1829 Hampden returned to Oxford from London, swapping Upper Seymour Street for the High. He was appointed an examiner for the BA degree, and survived financially by taking private pupils and through literary pursuits (he contributed articles on Aristotle to the *Encyclopaedia Britannica* and on Aquinas to the *Encyclopaedia metropolitana*) until, through the influence of Edward Hawkins, the newly elected provost of Oriel, he was appointed tutor of his former college. He was elected Bampton lecturer in 1832 and in April 1833 was appointed principal of St Mary Hall by Lord Grenville. This he changed from little more than a comfortable hotel for mature students into a respectable academic establishment, himself giving lectures and restoring the chapel at his own expense.

**As professor of moral philosophy** In 1834 Hampden became professor of moral philosophy at Oxford. In this post he continued the Coplestonian revival of classical learning at Oxford, publishing his introductory lectures in 1835. In these he advocated the application of induction to the study of moral facts as an area of inquiry independent of (but complementary with) religion, albeit that one branch of the study of moral philosophy, namely the study of the 'tendencies' or final causes of human nature, led to natural religion. It followed from his conception of moral philosophy as an inductive study of moral facts that it was not possible to derive from them certain rules of conduct akin to deductions from mathematical theorems. Echoing the work of the philosopher Dugald Stewart, whose work he cited in the text and who influenced the Noetics' conception of scientific inquiry, he asserted that such a degree of certainty was possible only in sciences such as mathematics which were founded on definitions. The basis on which moral conclusions might be derived was analogical only. His chief texts were unsurprisingly Aristotle's *Ethics* and Butler's *Analogy*, his main object of attack William Paley's utilitarianism.

Theologically Hampden's attention switched from a consideration of the inductive nature of scriptural truth to an examination of church doctrine, from a study of the facts of Christianity to human deductions from them. This was anticipated in his *Parochial Sermons* (1828), in which he distinguished between Catholic theologians who looked to the scholastic philosophers for their biblical interpretation and the (to his mind superior) Reformers who simply recorded the facts of Christianity as revealed by scripture. His conception of the nature of theological dogma achieved its fullest and most obscure expression in the Bampton lectures, published as *The Scholastic Philosophy Considered in its Relation to Christian Theology* (1833). In this work he characterized the doctrines of the scholastics, in which he included the work of the early church fathers, as no more than deductive statements infused with human imperfection. Doctrinal statements assumed their form by the successive impressions of historical controversy: they were not themselves repositories of Christian truth but attempts to ensure that particular heresies, incompatible with scriptural fact, did not achieve popular currency. This was as true of the Anglican Nicene and Athanasian creeds as it was of Catholic and dissenting formularies.

Hampden's academic consideration of creeds turned into a political polemic in his 1834 pamphlet *Observations on Religious Dissent*. If dogmatic theology was no more than a series of speculative deductions from the language of scripture to be distinguished from the truths of Christianity, it was an improper application of religious zeal to maintain the formularies of a particular communion by political means. Thus he advocated the admission of dissenters to Oxford University and the abolition of subscription to the Thirty-Nine Articles on matriculation since the university was not the Anglican church, but was only accidentally a society of church members. However, he was against parliament's imposing the admission of dissenters on Oxford. He supported Edward Hawkins's proposal to substitute a declaration of loyalty to the Church of England for subscription. But when this was defeated by convocation in May 1835 he helped Lord Radnor draft a bill for the abolition of subscription which was defeated in the House of Lords on 14 July 1835.

**The 'Hampden controversy', 1836** In view of the direct connection which Hampden drew between his theology and his political attitude to reform, the storm of protest which greeted his appointment by the whig Melbourne government in 1836 as regius professor of divinity was scarcely surprising. It began, famously, as a result of someone noticing Melbourne's frank on the letter to Hampden at the Oxford post office. By the evening of the same day, 8

February 1836, in the absence of any denial from either Hampden or Melbourne, Oxford was convinced that it contained the offer of the regius chair. E. B. Pusey, one of the leading opponents of the admission of dissenters to Oxford, gave a dinner party to discuss what should be done. The ensuing weeks saw a concerted campaign to obtain the withdrawal of the offer. It began with a visit to Downing Street by the archbishops of Canterbury and York to protest at the appointment on 9 February; the next day a meeting was held in the common room of Corpus Christi which resulted in a petition of protest being sent to Archbishop William Howley. That night J. H. Newman sat up composing a pamphlet (*Elucidations of Dr Hampden's Theological Statements*) attacking Hampden's theological views, including the Bampton lectures. In all, upwards of forty-five books and pamphlets were published on the controversy, which lasted throughout March. Despite the petitions the opposition, which consisted of a coalition of a few high-churchmen and evangelicals who genuinely objected to Hampden's theology, together with a more substantial number who opposed his views on dissenters and an even greater number of tories who hoped to embarrass a whig government, was ultimately unsuccessful. Hampden's opponents, however, did succeed in May 1836 in depriving him of his place at a board with responsibility for naming select preachers for the university.

The public significance of the controversy was that it marked the emergence of parties within the Church of England, separating high-churchmen from liberal Anglicans, and bringing to an end the process of Anglican renewal as a collaborative enterprise, from which Hampden himself had benefited in his early career. Privately it resulted in the personal vilification of Hampden; this included the false and politically motivated accusation that the Bampton lectures were substantially the work of Joseph Blanco White, the lapsed Spanish Catholic priest who had converted to Unitarianism in 1835.

Although Hampden suffered the attacks stoically he was ill-equipped to do so, losing both sleep and appetite when composing his inaugural lecture as regius professor. A shy, reserved person with few real friendships, he was happier in his study or playing with children than engaged in public speaking. He was inclined to priggishness (he was known as 'Old Hampden' as an undergraduate) and was much hurt when acquaintances appeared to cut him when walking down the High Street during the controversy; in fact, those who chose to recognize him had to do so in an exaggerated manner lest it be taken for a slight. He lacked the clarity of expression and political acumen of the Oriel Noetic leaders such as Edward Copleston or Edward Hawkins: his speaking voice was dull and grating, his literary style at times convoluted (Copleston said of his first book that it might have been 'more perspicuous and less abstract'), at other times rash. Hawkins, in particular, objected to Hampden's deployment of a theological argument in support of substituting a declaration for subscription at Oxford, insisting that his proposal had no theological motivation.

The effect of the controversy was to silence Hampden intellectually. He published nothing of major significance in the years that followed: only occasional lectures and sermons, and some of his charges as bishop. The only substantial work, *The Fathers of Greek Philosophy* (1862), was a reworking of his articles for the *Encyclopaedia Britannica*. Instead he devoted himself to upholding orthodox Anglicanism. He discouraged the formation of any party around him at Oxford and quietly went about his duties. He took his greatest pleasure from the living at Ewelme, which was attached to his chair, and the time he spent there, able to indulge in his hobby of gardening, was perhaps the happiest of his life. As regius professor, in 1840 he was instrumental in persuading Lord John Russell not to reduce the number of canonries at Christ Church to four, but to six, as part of the reform of cathedral chapters, with the recommendation that they be attached to two new theology professorships. These reforms formed the basis of Oxford's theological faculty as a separate school.

**As bishop of Hereford** In 1847 Lord John Russell offered Hampden the see of Hereford on Thomas Musgrave's translation to the archbishopric of York. In one sense it was 1836 all over again: a campaign was got up to protest at the appointment; meetings of clergy and laity were held; thirteen bishops (only one of whom was a whig appointment) presented an address of remonstrance to the prime minister. But the protest this time was less directed at Hampden's orthodoxy than at the exercise of the royal prerogative over the church. Fifteen of the heads of houses at Oxford sent Hampden an address expressing their satisfaction with his religious beliefs, and Archbishop Howley, who had protested at his appointment as regius, now vouchsafed his satisfaction with Hampden's orthodoxy. This was unsurprising given that by 1845 the Tractarian party at Oxford had begun to disintegrate and Newman, who had led the attack on Hampden's theological opinions in 1836, had converted to Rome.

The initial protest came to nothing: the chapter of Hereford elected Hampden bishop, so removing the need for the crown to appoint him by letters patent, although the dean and one other voted against (twelve prebendaries protested by staying away). At his confirmation in Bow church on 11 January 1848, however, three persons appeared by their proctors as opposers, but amid cries of 'Shame' and 'Mockery' they were denied the right to be heard. They thereupon went to court to obtain an injunction compelling the archbishop of Canterbury to hear their objections. At the trial the attorney-general argued that the archbishop had no choice but to obey the act of parliament and consecrate the bishop. In an evenly divided court on 1 February 1848 judgment was given against the grant of the injunction. But Hampden's consecration had to wait until 26 March due to the death of Archbishop Howley and the appointment of his successor, Bishop Sumner of Chester, one of the few non-whig bishops not to sign the remonstrance against him.

The attacks on Hampden appear to have driven him further to quietism. He chose not to use his episcopal office as a national pulpit, and indeed was reputed never to have spoken in the House of Lords, where he was an irregular attender; instead he busied himself in his diocese or educated himself in his study. He founded a Diocesan Education Society in 1849, encouraged church building, secured the reopening of the cathedral during its restoration (which was not completed until 1863), and worried about the examination of ordinands, which he personally conducted and which was generally considered to be difficult. The modest and retiring bishop who presented himself on his first confirmation tour in 1848 was far from the Oxford heretic created by the popular press.

**Last years and death** Indeed Hampden's orthodoxy became more pronounced. He was a vigorous supporter of a state church: he opposed the revival of convocation and was indignant at the Pope's establishment of a Roman Catholic hierarchy in England, which he regarded as 'an invasion of the Royal Supremacy'. He strongly supported Lord John Russell's *Letter to the Bishop of Durham* (1850) on 'papal agression', which he understandably regarded as a blow against Tractarianism, and he continued to challenge Tractarian doctrines in his charges. Above all he remained true to his Noetic origins, but in the changed circumstances of the 1850s and 1860s used Noetic arguments to uphold rather than challenge scriptural orthodoxy. Nowhere was this more apparent than in his attack on the controversial *Essays and Reviews* (1860), in which his friend Richard Whately also joined. In particular, in his 1862 charge he criticized his former Oxford colleague Baden Powell's essay on the evidences of Christianity and the so-called 'mythical' interpretation of scripture, which asserted the independence of faith from any rational foundation. He regarded the attack on miracles which it contained as but the revival of Hume's scepticism in another form. He sought to refute such scepticism just as Whately had done in 1819 in his *Historic Doubts Relative to Napoleon Bonaparte*, a work which Baden Powell had attacked in his essay: the events narrated in the scriptures were to be believed just as any other matter of history, however improbable the event might have been. The evidence of testimony contained in the Bible was sufficient in itself and ought not to be regarded as irreconcilable with the evidence of accumulated experience or probability. Indeed Hampden, according to Bishop Wilberforce, was one of the most determined to seek the prosecution of *Essays and Reviews* at the meeting of bishops which Archbishop Sumner called in February 1861 to discuss what action the church should take following its publication.

Hampden's wife died in 1865, an event from which he never fully recovered. A year later, at about the time of the anniversary of his wife's death, he suffered what appears to have been a stroke, from which his recuperation was slow. The Trinity ordination of 1866 was the first occasion on which he had had to ask for assistance in performing his episcopal duties. His health never fully rallied thereafter and he died at his home, 107 Eaton Place, London, on 23 April 1868. He was buried at Kensal Green cemetery, next to his wife. RICHARD BRENT

**Sources** H. Hampden, *Some memorials of R. D. Hampden* (1861) • R. Brent, *Liberal Anglican politics: whiggery, religion, and reform, 1830–1841* (1987) • O. Chadwick, *The Victorian church*, 2nd edn, 2 vols. (1970–72) • P. Corsi, *Science and religion: Baden Powell and the Anglican debate, 1800–1860* (1988) • I. Ellis, *Seven against Christ: a study of 'Essays and reviews'* (1980) • T. Mozley, *Reminiscences, chiefly of Oriel College and the Oxford Movement*, 2 vols. (1882) • O. Brose, *Church and parliament* (1959) • H. F. G. Swanston, *Ideas of order* (1976)

**Archives** Oriel College, Oxford, corresp. and papers | LPL, Whately MSS • Oriel College, Hawkins MSS • Oxf. UA

**Likenesses** D. W., chalk drawing, Oriel College, Oxford • W. Hall, engraving (after D. Macnee), repro. in Hampden, *Some memorials*, cover • attrib. H. W. Pickersgill, oils, Christ Church Oxf. • oils (after D. Macnee, 1867), Oriel College, Oxford [*see illus.*] • oils, bishop's palace, Hereford

**Wealth at death** under £45,000: resworn probate, May 1870, *CGPLA Eng. & Wales* (1868)

**Hampden, Richard** (*bap.* 1631, *d.* 1695), politician, was baptized on 13 October 1631, the second but first surviving son of John *Hampden (1595–1643), politician, of Great Hampden, Buckinghamshire, and his wife, Elizabeth (*d.* 1634), daughter of Edmund Symeon of Pyrton, Oxfordshire. He married on 11 March 1652 the Hon. Letitia (*d.* 1714/15), daughter of William *Paget, sixth Baron Paget. They had two sons and one daughter.

Hampden was elected to the second protectorate parliament for Buckinghamshire in 1656 and voted for offering the crown to Cromwell. He was appointed to the protector's 'other house' in 1657, apparently the personal nomination of the lord protector, much to the chagrin of republicans who felt it was to 'secure him to the interest of the new court, and wholly take him off from the thoughts of ever following his father's steps' (Oldys and Park, 487). In the Convention of 1660 he was returned in April for Wendover, a borough which was dominated by his family. He was seen as a friend by Lord Wharton, but he was not an active member, although he did suggest that Richard Baxter, the prominent presbyterian divine, be invited to preach before the house.

Hampden was re-elected for Wendover on 15 April 1661, and was reported to the house on 3 July for failing to receive the sacrament, an indication of his continuing nonconformism. Baxter remained a friend and visitor to Hampden's Buckinghamshire residence. Indeed, it was to Great Hampden that Baxter retreated during the plague of 1665, from whence he referred to Hampden as 'the true heir of his famous father's sincerity, piety and devotedness to God' (Keeble and Nuttall, 2.83). Hampden became more active in parliament following the fall of Clarendon in 1667. On 8 April 1668 he supported a motion for an address that the king should send for persons and consult with them on ways to unite his protestant subjects, and on 7 May 1668 he urged that parliament be dissolved. In 1673 and 1674 he voiced his opposition to the war with the Dutch and the alliance with France. By 1676 Sir Richard Wiseman included Hampden among those members from whom little could be hoped; conversely the earl of Shaftesbury marked him as 'thrice worthy'. The Popish Plot saw Hampden more active still: the French ambassador, Paul Barillon, recognized his parliamentary influence by giving him 500 guineas to help undermine Lord Treasurer Danby.

Hampden was again elected for Wendover on 3 February

1679. He was a prominent exponent of the bill to exclude the duke of York from the succession. On 27 April he moved that York's being a papist and heir to the throne had 'given the greatest countenance and encouragement to the present conspiracies and designs of Papists against the king and the protestant religion' (Grey, 7.150–51). He perceived that Charles II's policy of limitations as an alternative to exclusion would not work once James was king, and justified exclusion as necessary 'if a man be likely to ruin the estate he may be heir to, we disinherit every day' (ibid., 7.243).

Hampden was re-elected for Wendover on 6 August 1679. He moved the second reading of the Exclusion Bill on 4 November 1680, noting that 'the Pope is your king when you have a Popish successor' (Grey, 7.421). He also supported the bill to give toleration to protestant dissenters, and even seemed to support a policy of exclusion plus limitations on the monarchy. Hampden's prestige in Buckinghamshire was now such that for the 1681 election he was able to transfer to the county seat on 2 February (swapping it with his son John). He was active in the week-long Oxford parliament, again supporting exclusion.

In the changed circumstances of 1685 Hampden retreated to his old borough of Wendover, but he was not active. He was restored to local office as a JP and a deputy lieutenant in February 1688, but rather than sympathize with James II's religious policies, he was active in support of William of Orange. Following William's invasion he chaired the committee of members of Charles II's parliament on 27 December 1688 which drew up the address to William inviting him to call a convention and to take over the administration of the government in the interim. Hampden was duly elected to the convention for Wendover in January 1689. He chaired many important committees including that of supply. On 22 January he seconded the motion that William should undertake the government pending the settlement of the crown. He chaired the committee of the whole house on 28 January which debated the 'vacancy' of the throne, and on the following day chaired the committee which set in motion the declaration of rights. He reported on many conferences with the Lords, including several on the vacancy of the throne. He even advised the king to abolish the hearth tax. On 14 February 1689 he was made a privy councillor, and on 9 April he was named a commissioner of the Treasury. He acted as an adviser on the church settlement and helped in the management of the Toleration Bill. Still a whig partisan, he supported the disabling clause in the bill restoring corporations.

Hampden was elected for Buckinghamshire in 1690. On 18 March he became chancellor of the exchequer, and as such was preoccupied with devising financial legislation and getting it through the Commons. Indeed, for the first session he also chaired the committee of the whole house on supply and ways and means. In his speeches Hampden was now concerned to defend the court and to promote measures to support the war with France. However, he remained resolutely opposed to popery, especially a compromise settlement in Ireland, and also keen to defend the right of the Commons against encroachment by the Lords. Hampden remained at the Treasury during the summer of 1690, Queen Mary reporting that 'Mr Hampden is the person who tells such sad stories of the Treasury, which I fear will prove to be too true' (Dalrymple, 3.117). When parliament resumed in October 1690 he appears to have been ill, and during his absence he lost the chairmanship of the financial committees of the house.

Hampden was back to the peak of his activity in the 1691–2 session, in which the accounts of debates compiled by the MP Narcissus Luttrell demonstrate that Hampden contributed to most of the important debates in the Commons. When the king remodelled the Treasury commission in March 1692 Hampden lost a dispute with Sir Edward Seymour, fourth baronet, when he argued unsuccessfully that the office of chancellor ranked above that of a baronet. Nevertheless, he was a key court manager when it came to links with whigs with dissenting connections. The 1692–3 session followed a similar pattern with Hampden again an important advocate for the ministry in the Commons. In 1694 there were reports of his suffering from ill health in January, and in late February he suffered an attack of apoplexy which made him incapable of exercising his office. He was thus omitted from the new Treasury commission issued on 3 May 1694. He did not attend the 1694–5 session, and retired from parliament at the 1695 election.

Hampden died on 15 December 1695 and was buried at Great Hampden on 2 January 1696. He was succeeded by his son, John *Hampden; his other son, Richard, died as a child, and his daughter, Isabella, the wife of Sir William Ellys, second baronet, died in 1686. His wife survived him for almost twenty years. STUART HANDLEY

**Sources** L. Naylor, M. W. Helms, and E. Cruickshanks, 'Hampden, Richard', HoP, *Commons, 1660–90* · 'Hampden, Richard', HoP, *Commons, 1690–1715* [draft] · G. Lipscomb, *The history and antiquities of the county of Buckingham*, 4 vols. (1831–47), vol. 2, pp. 236, 252, 259–61, 288, 293 · A. Grey, ed., *Debates of the House of Commons, from the year 1667 to the year 1694*, 10 vols. (1763) · *The parliamentary diary of Narcissus Luttrell, 1691–1693*, ed. H. Horwitz (1972) · W. Oldys and T. Park, eds., 'A second narrative of the late parliament (so called)', *The Harleian miscellany*, 3 (1809), 470–89 · *Calendar of the correspondence of Richard Baxter*, ed. N. H. Keeble and G. F. Nuttall, 2 (1991), 47, 83 · M. Knights, *Politics and opinion in crisis, 1678–1681* (1994) · L. G. Schwoerer, *The declaration of rights, 1689* (1981) · will, PRO, PROB 11/435, sig. 239 · J. Dalrymple, *Memoirs of Great Britain and Ireland*, 3 vols. (1771–8)

**Wealth at death** see will, PRO, PROB 11/435, sig. 239

**Hamper, William** (1776–1831), antiquary, the only child of Thomas Hamper, a Birmingham brass-founder, and his wife, Elizabeth Tyson, was born at Birmingham on 12 December 1776. Both parents died in 1811 and were buried in the churchyard of King's Norton, Worcestershire. Nothing is known of Hamper's childhood. He apparently began his working life as a commercial traveller for the Birmingham brass-founders James Yates & Co., and became a partner in the firm in 1803; from 1807 he held various public offices in Birmingham.

Hamper began his literary career by contributing poems to the *Gentleman's Magazine*, the first being 'The

Beggar-Boy', which was signed H. D. B., the initial letters of Hamper, Deritend, Birmingham. The best known was 'The Devil's Dike: a Sussex Legend'. From 1804 to 1812 he contributed views and descriptions of English churches and other buildings to the magazine. About the same time he composed and published, as Repmah (an anagram of Hamper), many songs and airs. Elected a fellow of the Society of Antiquaries on 5 April 1821, Hamper was competent in Anglo-Saxon and medieval Latin, and was an accurate facsimilist. Several county historians, including William Bray, Edmund Cartwright, John Nichols, and George Ormerod, acknowledged help from him, and he collaborated with Thomas Sharp in the publication of *Kenilworth Illustrated* (1821). From 1812 Hamper was a close friend and correspondent of John Britton, whom he aided in compiling *The Beauties of England and Wales* and *The Dictionary of the Architecture and Archaeology of the Middle Ages*. He helped to sort and arrange several major collections of family and antiquarian papers in the midlands, including that left by the Staffordshire historian Stebbing Shaw.

Hamper's principal publication and most valuable work was *The Life, Diary, and Correspondence of Sir William Dugdale* (1827); the second part of the appendix, consisting of an index to the manuscript collections of Dugdale, had been issued separately in 1826 in an edition of twelve copies. His *Observations on certain ancient pillars of memorial, called hoar-stones; to which is added, a conjecture on the Croyland inscription*, a thin pamphlet, was published at Birmingham in 1820. The materials which he had collected for an enlarged edition were published in *Archaeologia*. He also edited a volume of *Masques Performed before Queen Elizabeth: from a Coeval Copy* (1820), which he wrongly attributed to George Ferrers, and he printed for private circulation in 1822 *Two copies of verses, on the meeting of King Charles the First and his queen Henrietta-Maria, in the valley of Kineton below Edge-Hill, in Warwickshire, July 13, 1643*, which were preserved in manuscript among Dugdale's papers. Many of Hamper's communications on rings, seals, and runic inscriptions appeared in *Archaeologia*. His name first appears as a contributor to Sir Samuel Egerton Brydges's *Censura literaria* (1805–9) in volume 3, but a communication in volume 2, signed W. H., was probably by him. Notes by him on books are inserted in Thomas Frognall Dibdin's *Bibliomania* (1876), and in his *Bibliographical Decameron* (1817). A list of 141 ways of spelling Birmingham, drawn up by Hamper, appears in the first volume of J. A. Langford's *Century of Birmingham Life* (1868). Some of his letters were published after his death in the *Birmingham Weekly Post*. For many years he collected material for a new edition of Dugdale's *History of Warwickshire*, but the project was never completed.

Hamper married at Ringwood, Hampshire, on 7 November 1803, Jane, youngest daughter of William Sharp of Newport, Isle of Wight. She died on 6 June 1829, leaving three daughters. He died suddenly at Highgate, Birmingham (where he lived), on 3 May 1831, and was buried with his parents in King's Norton churchyard.

Hamper's voluminous antiquarian collections were sold by auction in 1831, after his death, and were dispersed. Much of his correspondence and Warwickshire material was subsequently reassembled and was presented to Birmingham Reference Library. Virtually all of this perished when the library was burnt down in 1879, but the library (now Birmingham Central Library) has subsequently acquired other Hamper manuscripts, including the material he gathered for a history of Aston, his interleaved and annotated copy of William Hutton's *History of Birmingham*, and seven volumes of his correspondence. His copy of the 1765 edition of Dugdale's *Warwickshire*, copiously annotated for his projected new edition, is in the British Library.

W. P. Courtney, *rev.* D. A. Johnson

**Sources** *GM*, 1st ser., 101/1 (1831), 566–9 • *Annual Biography and Obituary*, 16 (1832), 339–46 • B. Ronchetti, 'William Hamper, F. S. A., 1776–1831', *Birmingham and Midland Archaeological Society Transactions and Proceedings*, 68 (1952), 111–20 • private information (1995) • S. Timmins, 'William Hamper, F. S. A., 1776–1831', *Birmingham and Midland Institute Archaeological Section, Transactions, Excursions and Report*, 23 (1898), 1–5 • H. S. Pearson, 'William Hamper', *Birmingham and Midland Archaeological Society Transactions and Proceedings*, 46 (1921), 49–53 • M. W. Greenslade, *The Staffordshire historians*, Staffordshire RS, 4th ser., 11 (1982), 117–22 • J. Britton, *The autobiography of John Britton*, 1 (privately printed, London, 1850), 155–9 • *GM*, 1st ser., 73 (1803), 1085 • *GM*, 1st ser., 99/1 (1829), 574 [obit. of Jane Hamper] • Nichols, *Illustrations*, 8.xliii–iv, 661

**Archives** Birm. CA, collections relating to the parish of Aston; corresp. and collected papers; notebook, incl. additions to Hutton's history of Birmingham and other antiquarian works; topographical account of Dunster • BL, antiquarian transcripts and catalogue of Lord Denbigh's MSS, Add. MSS 18673, 47965 • BL, copiously annotated copy of Dugdale's *Antiquities of Warwickshire* • Bodl. Oxf., corresp. and papers • NMM, naval history collection • Som. ARS, account of the history and antiquities of Dunster | Bodl. Oxf., letters to Francis Douce and related papers • Bodl. Oxf., letters to John Nichols and J. B. Nichols • Bodl. Oxf., papers and letters to Sir Thomas Phillipps • NL Scot., corresp. with Sir Walter Scott • Warks. CRO, notebook and pedigree of the Feilding family

**Likenesses** G. Clarke, bust, 1822, Birm. CL

**Hampson, Frank** (1918–1985), cartoonist, was born in Audenshaw, Manchester, on 21 December 1918, the elder son and eldest of three children of Robert Hampson, a police constable, and his wife, Elsie Light. He was educated at the King George V Grammar School at Southport until 1932 or 1933. He had no formal art training but liked to draw. He was fascinated by American newspaper supplements sent by relatives from Canada, and was particularly inspired by the strip cartoons of Hal Foster, Milton Caniff, and Alex Raymond (whose Rip Kirby had a 'cliff-hanger' every three frames). He learned how to tell a story in pictures, using few words. He left school at fourteen and became a telegraph boy. His father got him admitted to life classes at the local art school. He enrolled at Victoria College of Arts and Science in 1938 and obtained his national diploma in design just before being called up in 1939. Rescued from Dunkirk as a private in the Royal Army Service Corps, he was landed in Normandy as a lieutenant: seeing the doodlebugs he later wrote that 'on the quays of Antwerp you could watch the birth of space travel'.

On 7 February 1944 Hampson married Dorothy Mabel (*b.*

1917/18), a bank clerk, daughter of William Rosser Jackson, surveying engineer. They had one son. After the war he set up home with her in Southport, and with his friend Harold Johns enrolled in 1946 at the Southport School of Arts and Crafts. Their tutor, Raymond Geering, said Hampson was an outstanding draughtsman 'prepared to go to endless trouble to get a thing right'. This was to prove both his strength and his undoing.

Hampson could not have dreamed that his big chance was to come through a local parson, the Revd Marcus Morris, vicar of the affluent parish of St James, Birkdale. Morris felt the Church of England was not publicizing its message effectively. He remodelled his parish magazine, *Anvil*, and in 1948 engaged Hampson to illustrate it. At a conference of diocesan editors, it was agreed to form a society for Christian publicity, called Interim, to syndicate the best Christian writers, produce magazines to appeal to the man in the street, and explore the use of strip cartoon.

Britain was being saturated with American 'horror comics'. On 13 February 1949 Morris published an article, 'Comics that bring horror to the nursery', in the *Sunday Despatch*, saying he wanted to see a popular children's comic with clean and exciting adventures: for example, those of the missionary Sir Wilfred Grenfell of Labrador, and 'the daily dangers St Paul met'.

Hampson, who had become Interim's full-time artist at £8 per week, began work on a dummy with a life of St Paul and a story he himself created, 'Dan Dare, Space Pilot of the Future'. Morris now had something to show to publishers: a magazine with large pages, superb drawing, bright colour, and every kind of adventure designed to appeal to girls and boys of the ages eight to twelve. After numerous refusals, Hulton Press wired: 'Definitely interested do not approach any other publisher.' Thus *Eagle* magazine was launched on 14 April 1950, with Marcus Morris as editor. Hampson worked more than full time with a team chosen by himself, first in The Bakery at Southport, and then in houses in Epsom (to which town he and Morris moved), the last one, Bayford Lodge, having a bedroom floor removed so that photographs could be taken of dressed-up posed models from above or below.

Hampson's perfectionism increased with his skill. He would think out his next episode of 'Dan Dare' during the weekend and do a rough in pencil, and then in ink and colour. These were good enough for any other comic but only the start for Hampson. With the aid of his research and reference sheets, models of space ships, plaster heads of characters, mock-ups of space suits, and a complete deep space station, every frame would be posed and photographed on Monday and Tuesday, and on Wednesday the photos and roughs together were given to the artists, Hampson taking the big opening frame which was dramatic, technologically ingenious, or hilarious. On Friday the artwork had to go to Bemrose of Liverpool's German rotogravure presses which could turn out three and a half copies of *Eagle* a second to supply a million copies six weeks later (because of the time needed for artists to work on the photographic plates in three colours). The team then went home after a week of five thirteen-hour days, but Hampson would spend another weekend of creation, invention, and nodding off over his drawing boards until disturbed by 'them dratted birds'. He was a genius of the genre.

In 1959 Hultons was sold to Odhams Press, who wished to alter 'Dan Dare'. Marcus Morris left as the editor of *Eagle* and its sister papers *Girl*, *Swift*, and *Robin*, and Hampson's studio was disbanded. He himself left in the summer of 1961. Thereafter he undertook small advertising commissions, illustrations for magazines, and the pictures for seven Ladybird books. In 1970 he developed cancer of the trachea. He then became a graphics technician at Ewell Technical College. In 1978 he sat for an Open University degree, which he received in January 1979.

In November 1975, at the biannual Lucca comics convention, the Mecca of strip cartoon enthusiasts, Hampson was awarded the Yellow Kid award and declared 'prestigioso maestro' as the best writer and illustrator of strip cartoons since the end of the Second World War. At the British comics convention, Comics 101, he was presented with the Ally Sloper award as the best British strip cartoon artist. Hampson died on 8 July 1985 at the Cottage Hospital, Epsom. CHAD VARAH, *rev.*

**Sources** A. Crompton, *The man who drew tomorrow* (1985) • S. Morris and J. Hallwood, *Living with Eagles: Marcus Morris, priest and publisher* (1998) • private information (1990) [Marcus Morris] • personal knowledge (1990) • b. cert. • m. cert. • *CGPLA Eng. & Wales* (1985)

**Wealth at death** £58,567: probate, 22 Aug 1985, *CGPLA Eng. & Wales*

**Hampson, John** (1760–*c.*1817), writer, was born in Manchester, son of John Hampson of that town. His parents were Methodists, and both father and son acted as preachers under John Wesley. About 1784 Hampson left the Methodists, matriculated at St Edmund Hall, Oxford, on 13 July 1785, and graduated BA in 1791 and MA in 1792. On taking holy orders in the Church of England he obtained a charge in Sunderland, and about 1801 became rector of that town.

Hampson's most important publication was *Memoirs of the late Rev. John Wesley, AM, with a review of his life and writings, and a history of Methodism from its commencement in 1729 to the present time* (3 vols., 1791). A German translation in two parts, by A. H. Niemeyer, appeared at Halle in 1793. He also wrote *A Blow at the Root of Pretended Calvinism or Real Antinomianism* (1788), *Observations on the present war, the projected invasion, and a decree of the national convention for the emancipation of the slaves in the French colonies* (1794), *The Poetics of Marcus Hieronymus Vida, Bishop of Alba* (1793), and several sermons. Hampson died about 1817.

FRANCIS WATT, *rev.* MARI G. ELLIS

**Sources** Foster, *Alum. Oxon.* • W. T. Lowndes, *The bibliographer's manual of English literature*, ed. H. G. Bohn, [new edn], 6 vols. (1864) • J. S. Simon, *John Wesley the master-builder* (1927), 73, 275 • [J. Watkins and F. Shoberl], *A biographical dictionary of the living authors of Great Britain and Ireland* (1816)

**Likenesses** line engraving, 1785, BM

**Hampson, John.** *See* Simpson, John Frederick Norman Hampson (1901–1955).

**Hampton.** For this title name *see* Pakington, John Somerset, first Baron Hampton (1799–1880).

**Hampton, Christopher** (*c.*1551–1625), Church of Ireland archbishop of Armagh, was born in Calais, the son of a Church of England clergyman, John Hampton of Hampshire. He entered Trinity College, Cambridge, as a scholar in 1570 (BA, 1571–2; MA, 1575; BTh, 1582; DTh, 1598; fellow 1574), became vicar of Chesterton, Cambridge (1585–9), and was by 1606 chaplain to Henry Wriothesley, third earl of Southampton. On three occasions between 1606 and 1609 he preached before King James when he was staying at Beaulieu, diplomatically seizing the opportunity to assert that the power of kings came directly from God and that subjects were bound to obey them, and going on to defend the royal supremacy and the distinction between bishops and priests. He was rewarded with a royal chaplaincy, and was chosen to accompany the king's commissioner to the general assembly in Glasgow in June 1610, where Hampton delivered a typical conformist sermon, attacking presbyterianism and defending episcopacy.

On 21 December 1611 Hampton was nominated to the see of Derry in Ireland, but before he could be consecrated the primatial see fell vacant following the death of Henry Ussher on 2 April 1613. Thanks to the efforts of various patrons, Lord Deputy Chichester, Archbishop Abbot, and, most significantly, the Scottish groom of the king's bedchamber, John Murray, Hampton was nominated as archbishop of Armagh on 16 April 1613. He was consecrated on 8 May in St Patrick's Cathedral in Dublin, the unusual speed necessitated by the imminent meeting of parliament, together with the first Reformation convocation of the Church of Ireland on 18 May. Hampton's role in Ireland was not dissimilar to that he had briefly played in Glasgow: to be an advocate of conformity to the royal will in matters ecclesiastical and civil. Given the rather lax attitudes in the Irish church to discipline and ceremonial, fully exploited by some of its more puritan members, he had his work cut out.

From the very beginning of convocation Hampton ran into opposition, having to correct procedural irregularities and defend the right of Armagh to the primacy against the claims of the archbishop of Dublin. Hampton made public his distaste for puritan complaints over 'ceremonies, things indifferent, and Christian liberty', warning that he and his fellow bishops would spare no effort to ensure conformity 'either by persuasive reasons (which please me best) or by discipline (if the other be refused)' (C. Hampton, *An Inquisition of the True Church*, 1622, sig. A4). Along with Abbot, Hampton was involved in the reform of Trinity College, Dublin, the Irish church's chief seminary, trying to amend its constitution and weed out puritanism. He also began inconclusive proceedings in the early 1620s against 'certain factious and irregular puritans' who had recently settled in Ulster—in fact Scottish presbyterians operating within the Church of Ireland. Hampton considerably extended his disciplinary powers by securing by a royal grant of 10 April 1622 the major prize—previously in secular hands—of the courts of prerogative and faculties. Generally he acted as an important source of information (Hampton visited Abbot in Lambeth in 1616, and corresponded with Buckingham) for the authorities in England about irregularities in the Church of Ireland. Hampton took a hard line against Roman Catholics, identifying them as followers of a false, antichristian church, calling on the civil authorities to expel priests from Ireland, and strongly supporting the enforcement of the anti-recusancy legislation against the ordinary population. At the same time, however, he insisted that the supreme governor had the right to suspend such laws at his discretion—in 1622 he rebuked one of his junior colleagues, James Ussher, the bishop of Meath, for an over-zealous and public insistence that recusants be prosecuted.

Hampton became archbishop at a crucial time in the fortunes of his archdiocese, just as the full impact of the Ulster plantation was being felt. Though the new settlers provided a welcome influx of conformist parishioners, and James I's generous re-endowment of the church ensured a dramatic rise in revenues, constant vigilance was needed to fight off the efforts of unscrupulous settlers to wrest from the church its newly acquired wealth. Hampton himself played a considerable, and generous, part in the construction of an Anglicized church in Armagh. Unmarried, he was able to use his personal income to engage in a building programme. His report to the 1622 commissioners summarized his efforts: he had rebuilt the cathedral church in Armagh, partly destroyed by Shane O'Neill, cast a new 'great bell', constructed a new residence in Drogheda, and repaired the old one in Armagh. As landlord Hampton ensured that Armagh gained full benefit from rising rents by modernizing, and Anglicizing, the system of rent collection, and ensuring that church lands had a high proportion of British settlers. Less creditably, he may also have made some short-term profits by taking high entry fines in return for granting more favourable long-term leases. Nevertheless, by 1622 the total income of the archdiocese from temporalities came to £1935, of which over £871 came from land. Hampton also had national financial responsibilities: on 7 August 1617 he was appointed the first king's almoner, additionally charged with distributing the income from recusant fines. Hampton died on 3 January 1625 in Drogheda, and was buried there in St Peter's Church.

ALAN FORD

**Sources** *The whole works of Sir James Ware concerning Ireland*, ed. and trans. W. Harris, 1 (1739), 97–8 • R. J. Hunter, 'The Ulster plantation in the counties of Armagh and Cavan', PhD diss., University of Dublin, 1969 • *The whole works of … James Ussher*, ed. C. R. Elrington and J. H. Todd, 17 vols. (1847–64), vol. 15, pp. 155–60, 183–4, 199 • visitation of Armagh, 1622, Marsh's Library, Dublin, MS Z3.1.3 [also in TCD, MS 865] • visitation of Armagh, 1622, TCD, MS 865 • C. Hampton, 'Proofs of the precedence of Armagh', TCD, MS 582 • C. Hampton, *Articles given in charge to be inquired upon … in every parish within the province of Armagh* (1623) • D. G. Mullan, *Episcopacy in Scotland: the history of an idea, 1560–1608* (1986), 103 • Venn, *Alum. Cant.* • E. B. Fryde and others, eds., *Handbook of British chronology*, 3rd edn, Royal Historical Society Guides and Handbooks, 2 (1986)

**Archives** TCD, 'Proofs of the precedence of Armagh', MS 582

**Hampton, Elizabeth** [Bess] (*d.* **1661**), conventicle keeper and laundress, was perhaps of a family from Cuddesdon, Oxfordshire. She never married. She lived in Holywell Street, Oxford, round the corner from Wadham College, and on a direct route to Magdalen College, in a tenement leased from Merton College. She is known only in her last years, when she saw puritanism overwhelmed by the surge of triumphalist cavalier Anglicanism at the Restoration.

Elizabeth Hampton's conventicle, one of many which flourished in interregnum Oxford, attracted some very able students: Samuel Parker, James II's time-serving bishop of Oxford; William Assheton, another conformist divine; and the nonconformist minister and autobiographer George Trosse. Of these Trosse alone left any account of a meeting at her house. But it was atypical, hastily called when he quit the university at the Restoration. He described her as 'a very poor but excellent Christian' (*Life*, 87–9).

Hampton died on 30 March 1661 at her home, the ninth tenement of Merton College, in Holywell Street, Oxford, and was buried on 1 April in Holywell cemetery. Her grave was adorned with what is surely a mock-heroic epitaph, apotheosizing her as 'since death / another Queen Elizabeth', ending:

> She needs not us, but dearly miss shall we
> Our shee-professor of divinity.

Anthony Wood noted the inscription, attributed it mischievously to Trosse's mentor, Henry Hickman, fellow of Magdalen during the interregnum, and added sedately 'She was a little old crooked maid, and had conventicles in this parish [Holywell], once or twice a week wherein she sometimes spoke, but mostly her customers of Magd. or Wadham College' (Wood, *Survey of the City*, 3.191).

Later Andrew Marvell used Hampton to lambast that rising star, Samuel Parker, in his *Rehearsal Transpros'd* (1672, 1673), and in the process revealed more about Hampton and her conventicle. As an undergraduate at Wadham, Parker had belonged to a group commonly known as the Grewellers, who fasted and prayed together. 'The Brotherhood' and 'the Sisterhood' met at 'another old Elsibeths, Elizabeth Hampton's' where they heard sermons, prayed, and received the sacrament (Marvell, *Rehearsal*, 181). There Parker was 'brought up at the feet of Elizabeth Hampton'. She would have been shocked that this 'so precious a young man' should now 'stir up persecution' and repudiate all he had been taught: trampling the graces of God's spirit, the observance of the Lord's day, vilifying and mocking the English Bible, and preaching. All this out of self-interest, 'like a *Hog*, to procure yourself *Beans*'. She would surely 'grudge all that Oat-meal you spent her in Grewel, and with the Skillet had boyled over' (Marvell, *Rehearsal*, 287–8). This is slapstick. There is though no suggestion of her preaching (unacceptable in a woman), but rather of teaching and hospitality imbibed together. Marvell has Parker, not Hampton, in his sights.

Marvell probably heard of Elizabeth Hampton when in Oxford attending the 1665 parliament, and perhaps visited Holywell cemetery and saw the epitaph to 'another Queen Elizabeth'. Wood elaborated slightly on Marvell in his biography of Parker in *Athenae Oxonienses*. He also located her house, and described her as a laundress. There is now no mention of her 'speaking' (Wood, *Ath. Oxon.*, 226).

Hampton made her will on 23 February 1661. It was, perhaps wisely, uninformative. It has no preamble; no book, not even a Bible, is mentioned, though an uncontroversial clock went to a kinsman. She left £27, £10 going to her servant, and £10 was put in trust for a kinswoman with an unsatisfactory husband. Only in her choice of executor and witnesses was her nonconformity betrayed. Her executor was 'my loving friend' Matthew Martin, town clerk of Oxford and ally of the presbyterian John Nixon, four times mayor of pre-Restoration Oxford. Martin was forced to resign in 1663. The witnesses to her will were purged from the city council in 1662.

Elizabeth Hampton's life affords a rare example of the possibilities and limitations of the role puritanism could offer a poor but able spinster in a critical period of its history, and reactions to it. MARY PRIOR

**Sources** A. Wood, *Survey of the antiquities of the city of Oxford*, ed. A. Clark, 3, OHS, 37 (1899), 37, 191 • will, Oxon. RO, MS wills Oxon., 32/4/4 • A. Marvell, *The rehearsal transpros'd*, ed. D. I. B. Smith (1971), 181, 287 • Wood, *Ath. Oxon.*, new edn, 4.126, 606 • *The life of the Reverend Mr George Trosse* (1714), 87–9 • M. G. Hobson and H. E. Salter, eds., *Oxford council acts, 1626–1665*, OHS, 95 (1933) • lease book, Merton Oxf., B6.2, 76, 739 • *The poems and letters of Andrew Marvell*, ed. H. Margoliouth, rev. P. Legouis, 3rd edn, 2 (1971), 40–41, 362 • W. Assheton, *A theological discourse of last wills and testaments* (1696), 16–19 • B. Worden, 'Cromwellian Oxford', *Hist. U. Oxf.* 4: *17th-cent. Oxf.*, 733–72 • R. A. Beddard, 'Restoration Oxford and the making of the protestant establishment', *Hist. U. Oxf.* 4: *17th-cent. Oxf.*, 803–62 • parish register, Holywell, 1661, Oxon. RO [burials]

**Archives** Merton Oxf., lease book B6.2, 76, 739 • Oxon. RO, MS wills Oxon. 32/4/4

**Wealth at death** £27; plus chattels: will, Oxon. RO, MS wills Oxon., 32/4/4

**Hampton, James** (*bap.* **1721**, *d.* **1778**), translator and Church of England clergyman, was the son of James Hampton of Bishop's Waltham, Hampshire, where he was baptized on 2 November 1721. In 1733 he entered Winchester College, from where he was elected a scholar of Corpus Christi College, Oxford, and matriculated on 20 July 1739. There is a doubtful story that when Lord Peterborough and Alexander Pope visited Winchester College and gave prizes to the scholars for the best copies of verses on a subject proposed by Pope ('The campaign of Valentia'), Hampton was one of the winners, and obtained a set of Pine's *Horace* (*Works of Alexander Pope*, 8.221–2).

At Oxford, Hampton was equally distinguished for his scholarship and boisterousness. On one occasion he deliberately provoked a quarrel by kicking over a tea-table in the rooms of his old schoolfellow the poet William Collins. He graduated BA (1743) and MA (1747), and took holy orders. As early as 1741 he evinced his liking for the history of Polybius by publishing *A Fragment of the 6th Book, Containing a Dissertation on Government*. This was followed by a translation of the first five books and part of the fragments in two volumes (1756–61), which between that date and 1823 went through at least seven editions. The lord chancellor, Robert Henley, was so pleased with the work that in 1762 he presented Hampton to the wealthy rectory of Moor Monkton, Yorkshire, whereupon Hampton dedicated to Henley the second edition of his work.

Hampton's other publications are *An Essay on Ancient and Modern History* (1746), containing a sketch of Gilbert Burnet as a historian; *A Plain and Easy Account of the Fall of Man* (1750); and *Two Extracts* from the sixth book of Polybius's history (1764). In 1775 he obtained the sinecure rectory of Folkton, Yorkshire, which he held with his other benefice. Hampton died at Knightsbridge, London, apparently unmarried, in June 1778. In his will he left his property to William Graves of the Inner Temple.

GORDON GOODWIN, *rev.* PHILIP CARTER

**Sources** Foster, *Alum. Oxon.* • *GM*, 1st ser., 45 (1775), 103 • *GM*, 1st ser., 51 (1781), 11–12 • *GM*, 1st ser., 72 (1802), 6, 130 • *The works of Alexander Pope*, ed. J. Warton, new edn, 8 (1822), 221–2 • will, PRO, PROB 11/1044, fol. 15*v* • *IGI*

**Hampton, John Stephen** (1806?–1869), surgeon and colonial governor, is shown on his death certificate to have been born in 1810; however the British register of surgeons records his certificate as assistant surgeon in January 1829 at the age of twenty-two, and other details of his birth, parentage, and education have not been found. He gained his medical diploma at Edinburgh in 1828 (suggesting a birth earlier than 1810) and the following January joined the navy as an assistant surgeon. After service in HMS *Sphinx* off Mexico, in May 1832 he was given three months' leave for additional study and obtained a further medical certificate in Edinburgh. He was then posted to Plymouth, where he distinguished himself during the prevailing cholera epidemic and made his first acquaintance with convicts, who were working in the dockyard. He was promoted surgeon in December 1834 and served in HMS *Savage*, *Firebrand*, and *Portland*. Between 1841 and 1845 he was surgeon-superintendent on three convict ships sailing to Australia. In 1845–6 he joined others in criticizing the state of the convicts in Van Diemen's Land, the control and management of them since 1842, and the character and incompetence of the governor, Sir John Eardley-Wilmot. Reconstructing the establishment, W. E. Gladstone, then secretary of state, appointed Hampton as the new controller-general of convicts, a post he took up when he arrived back in Hobart Town on 27 October 1846, with his wife, Mary, *née* Essex (*d.* 1869), whom he had married in 1832, and his twelve-year-old son, George.

A tour inspecting the convict probation stations confirmed Hampton's view that drastic reforms were necessary, and these he set about implementing without waiting for the arrival of the new governor, Sir William Denison. He wanted new buildings, better officers, better classifications, more religious and general instruction, and better supervision to reduce 'unnatural crime'. He immediately replaced many officers and, as the number of convicts declined in the next two years, he was able to close a number of the convict stations near Hobart Town and Launceston. In August 1847 he issued new regulations which emphasized task work; they were later criticized for permitting the men's early release for hard work rather than 'reformation'. As a punishment he preferred solitary confinement to flogging, strongly denying the contemporary (and subsequent) belief that this led to mental instability, and arguing rather that it made the men 'very tractable and easily managed' (report, 29 Oct 1846). In 1848 he visited Norfolk Island. He defended the commandant there, John Price, against reports of personal cruelty and administrative abuses, but he published no detailed refutation of these charges and opposed suggestions that the establishment be closed. However, he did so after a second visit, in 1852, and, though evasive and unconvincing in answering the renewed allegations of brutality and misconduct made by the Roman Catholic bishop Willson, he admitted the place was too far away to superintend properly. Bishop Willson also led protests against Hampton's allegedly harsh treatment of the Irish rebels in Van Diemen's Land, particularly the solitary confinement imposed on their leader William Smith O'Brien, which caused meetings in Dublin and Cork and debate in the House of Commons, and, in 1850, led to a reprimand from Governor Denison.

Though Hampton was in many respects apparently an efficient administrator, in May–June 1855 several officers in the convict department, including himself, were accused in the press of misusing materials and employing convict artisans for their private profit. After an inquiry by the executive council, the governor reported that the 'charges of fraud, peculation and embezzlement were not justified', though it was 'evident that great abuses have existed in the Convict Department in the use of convict labour' and 'the Controller-General cannot be considered altogether free from blame' (to Colonial Office, 16 July 1855). The legislative council, dissatisfied with the 'official' inquiry, took the matter up, and naturally wanted to examine Hampton, even though he was an imperial and not a local official. He refused to appear before it and left the colony in October on sick leave, protesting against the council's 'unlawful and tyrannical proceedings'. He never returned, and is remembered less for the admittedly important reforms he made in his department on his arrival than as an unnecessarily severe and unsympathetic disciplinarian, tainted with corruption—'a cold-hearted and devious opportunist' as Mr Justice Barry put it, writing in 1964 (*The Life and Death of John Price*, 55).

In 1857 Hampton went to Toronto, Canada, on urgent private business, and the following year resigned his Tasmanian post. After returning to England in 1861 he found the duke of Newcastle, then secretary of state, ready to overlook any suggestion of past malpractice and appoint him governor of Western Australia, a colony then receiving about 800 convicts a year sentenced to transportation from the United Kingdom.

Hampton assumed office in Perth in February 1862, and again his reputation is mixed. Intent on imposing stricter discipline on the prisoners, he took personal control of the convict department in December on the departure of the successful long-serving controller-general, Colonel Henderson RE. In 1866 he appointed his son to the position, though the latter already held several government posts. By 1867 more accusations of undue severity had reached the Colonial Office, including excessive flogging (the amount per convict had doubled under Hampton), hard labour in chains, and solitary confinement in dark cells. An office investigation exonerated the governor but disapproved some of his actions, under-secretary Sir Frederic Rogers minuting that 'some allegations of cruelty could be substantiated' (18 Feb 1868, CO, 18/155).

Apart from this Hampton had quarrelled with Bishop Hale over convict chaplains. He had taken little interest in Aboriginal welfare, declaring that up-country he could not provide police protection for either settlers or Aborigines, though the settlers were not to use unnecessary violence except in actual self-defence. On the other hand he greatly benefited the colony by employing the convicts extensively on public works, especially on a new causeway across the Swan River to the north of Perth, a bridge across it at Fremantle, a town hall, supreme court, and government house in Perth, and a summer residence for the governor on Rottnest Island, as well as police stations, court houses, jetties, lighthouses, schools, and an extensive road programme. However, he did not oppose the cessation of transportation in 1868 when the imperial government wanted to stop it and Western Australia seemed to have become self-supporting. He encouraged settlement (without convicts) 1000 miles north-west between the Fortescue and De Grey rivers and at Nickol Bay. He restored the public finances. He recommended the extension of representative government and, pending London's decision, he agreed in 1867 to appoint as his nominees to the legislative council persons who had been elected locally.

Hampton left the colony on 14 November 1868 shortly after the last convict ship had arrived. He died of tuberculosis at 1 East Ascent, St Leonards, Sussex, on 1 December 1869, eight months after his wife. Some of his actions had undoubtedly intensified the popular desire to curb gubernatorial authority in the colony, but his labour policies had benefited it and turned its capital into an attractive little town. But he received no official recognition during his career, and the Western Australian newspapers published no obituaries. A. G. L. Shaw

**Sources** 'Correspondence on convict discipline and transportation', *Parl. papers* (1846), 29.291, no. 36, 29.363, no. 402; (1847), 48.313, no. 811; (1847–8), 52.7, no. 941; (1849), 43.63, no. 1022; (1850), 45.11, no. 1153, 45.155, no. 1285; (1851), 45.265, no. 1418; (1852), 41.183, no. 1517; (1852–3), 82.257, no. 1677; (1854–5), 39.267, no. 1916, 39.503, no. 1988; (1856), 44.395, no. 140; (1863), 39.263, no. 3224; (1864), 40.335, no. 3264; (1867–8), 48.429, no. 482 • *AusDB* • I. Brand, *The convict probation system: Van Diemen's Land, 1839–1854* (1990) • W. A. Townsley, *The struggle for self-government in Tasmania, 1841–46* (1951) • P. J. Boyce, 'A Governor: J. S. Hamilton', *Westralian portraits*, ed. L. Hunt (1979) • C. T. Stannage, ed., *New history of Western Australia* (1981) • A. Hasluck, *Unwilling immigrants* (1959) • P. Hasluck, *Black Australian* (1970) • A. G. L. Shaw, *Convicts and the colonies: a study of penal transportation from Great Britain and Ireland* (1966) • F. K. Crowley, *Australia's western third* (1960) • J. V. Barry, *The life and death of John Price* (1964) • *To solitude confined: the Tasmanian journal of William Smith O'Brien*, ed. R. Davis (1995) • L. Hunt, ed., *Bi-centennial dictionary of Western Australians II: to 1888* (1988)

**Archives** PRO, CO 18/125–159

**Wealth at death** under £16,000: probate, 24 Dec 1869, *CGPLA Eng. & Wales*

**Hamson, Charles John Joseph** [Jack] **(1905–1987)**, jurist, was born in Constantinople on 23 November 1905, the fourth child and elder son in the family of two sons and four daughters of Charles Edward Hamson, vice-consul in the Levant service, and his wife, Thérèse Boudon, whose father was a French architect–engineer engaged in building lighthouses in the Bosphorus. He was at school at Downside, and in 1924 entered Trinity College, Cambridge, as a scholar, and read for the classical tripos, obtaining first classes in both parts one (1925) and two (1927). He then turned to law, first in Cambridge, where he later won the Yorke prize (1932), and obtained the LLB (1934) and LLM (1935), and then at Harvard, as Davison scholar in 1928–9. Despite a visibly bad eye, he fenced at Cambridge, and was captain of the university épée team in 1928.

Hamson began teaching at University College, London, but in 1932 he returned to Cambridge as assistant lecturer, where, the war years apart, he spent the rest of his life as a fellow of Trinity, as university lecturer (1934) and then, by way of *ad hominem* appointment, first reader (1949) and later professor (1953–73) of comparative law. In 1933 he married Isabella, daughter of Duncan Drummond, farmer, of Auchterarder, and his wife, Grace Gardiner; they had one daughter. For twenty years from 1955 to 1974 he edited the *Cambridge Law Journal* with notable success and served on many university administrative bodies. He was chairman of the law faculty from 1954 to 1957 and was elected honorary fellow of St Edmund's House in 1976.

Hamson made no secret of his devotion to Cambridge and to Trinity. He also maintained a façade of English insularity, even to the extent of carrying an umbrella when visiting Persepolis, but the whole of his life belied it. He became an internationally recognized authority on comparative as well as common law and the admired friend of comparative lawyers throughout the world. He was president of the International Academy of Comparative Law from 1966 to 1979, chevalier of the Légion d'honneur, correspondent of the Institut de France, and visiting professor in numerous universities overseas. He held seven honorary degrees from foreign universities and received the extreme compliment of a translation into French of his book on the French *conseil d'état*.

Hamson was called to the bar by Gray's Inn in 1937. Though not a practitioner, he became a bencher in 1956 and, unusually for an academic, treasurer in 1975, when he was also appointed QC. He had a great affection for the inn and earned the admiration and gratitude of all for his work there. It gave him particular pleasure, during his year of office, to call to the bar, and admit to the bench, the prince of Wales.

At the outset of the Second World War, Hamson volunteered for service, sending his wife and young daughter to the United States. Seconded to the Special Operations Executive, he was sent clandestinely to Crete, where ultimately he was captured. In captivity from 1941–5 he resumed his vocation by teaching law to his fellow prisoners, at first without the aid of any books. That, he used to say, meant that he did not have to waste time coping with the 'extravagant opinions of colleagues'. While a prisoner he wrote, perhaps as a means for coming to terms with his condition, a manuscript which is part personal history of the Cretan misadventure, part reminiscence, but in the main an analysis, in philosophical mood, of his understanding of himself and his own state of mind. This remarkable document, which remained virtually unknown until his death, was published by Trinity College in 1989 under the title *Liber in vinculis*.

As a legal writer, Hamson's gift was to go directly to the heart of a question and to deal with it pithily and elegantly. He never indulged in lengthy exposition of a legal subject and his published work appears mainly in the form of articles or shorter notes. He wrote some memorable, even influential, pieces on both common law and comparative law topics, but the volume of his publications is relatively small. It was through his ability to convince others by the spoken word, at national and international gatherings as well as in the classroom, that he made his most important contributions to the law and its development.

Hamson was a great teacher. His knowledge of law was profound, but it was his style of presentation that set him apart. His gift of exposition and his evident delight in his subject made his lectures enthralling; his insistence on principle and his willingness to say things that more timid men might think inappropriate for undergraduate lectures made them memorable. Many of his pupils attained high office. To them he made it clear that the respect due to the dignity of office did not extend to the office holders. But they, along with all the others whom he taught—not least those whom he taught in prison camp—or who came to know him in other ways, held him in affection. His homes saw a stream of visitors to the day he died.

Hamson was not a tall man, but well built and physically strong. He could, at times, look severe, but he had a ready smile. With a high forehead and a slightly beaked nose, no one seeing him even briefly could doubt that behind his visible features there lay a formidable brain. His wife died in 1978, and Hamson returned to live in Trinity. A Roman Catholic, and a deeply religious man, whose religion was tempered by his irrepressible scepticism, he died in college on 14 November 1987. J. A. Jolowicz, *rev.*

**Sources** J. Cann, 'Memoir', in C. J. Hamson, *Liber in vinculis* (1989) · J. A. Jolowicz, *Graya* (1987–8) · personal knowledge (1996) · R. David, 'C. J. Hamson, 1905–1987', *Revue Internationale de Droit Comparé*, 40 (1988), 168–70

**Archives** King's Lond., Liddell Hart C., military papers | Bodl. Oxf., corresp. with A. L. Goodhart

**Likenesses** M. Noakes, dark pastel drawing, 1961, Trinity Cam.

**Wealth at death** £199,599: probate, 27 April 1988, *CGPLA Eng. & Wales*

**Hanboys, John** [J. de Alto Bosco] (*fl.* **1375**), music theorist, was the author of a treatise on music notation, the *Summa*. In the single known source of the treatise, an early fifteenth-century copy that is now BL, Add. MS 8866, the author's name is consistently spelt Hanboys. He has been compellingly equated by Trowell with the music theorist J. de Alto Bosco, who is named in an English motet about musicians that dates from the 1370s, *Sub Arturo plebs*. In the text of the uppermost voice of this composition J. de Alto Bosco is said to unlock with his theory the unprecedented works of the singer and composer J. de Corbe, who is documented in music service to the Black Prince and Edward III from 1347 until at least 1381. Trowell argues the equivalence of the Latin Alto Bosco to Haute Bois, or in medieval orthography Hauboys (Hautboys, Haultboys, Hoboys), as in the name of a pair of small villages in Norfolk (now Great and Little Hautbois). This identification and dating overturn a long-standing antiquarian tradition, beginning with John Bale's *Illustrium maioris Britanniae scriptorum* (1548), in which the subject's name was spelt Hamboys and he was reported to be a later fifteenth-century figure, active *c.*1470 in the reign of Edward IV. Bale may have known the *Summa* from Add. MS 8866 or a related copy, because he errs in his citation of its incipit, quoting from the version of the *Quatuor principalia* that stands before the *Summa* in the British Library manuscript. Further, Bale says Hanboys became a doctor of music after years of study, a claim that cannot be substantiated but which might be an unwarranted elaboration upon the explicit of the *Summa*, in which the author is described as *doctoris musice reverendi* ('venerable teacher of music'). Given the apparent unreliability of Bale, his other statements about Hanboys, including one that he composed a book of songs, must be regarded with scepticism.

The *Summa* takes as its point of departure the *Regule* (1326) of the English music theorist Robert Handlo, about half of which is retained in the course of an exhaustively systematic survey of *ars nova* note forms, rests, and mensurations. In addition to the *Regule*, Hanboys draws upon other works, including the *Ars cantus mensurabilis* (*c.*1280) of Franco of Cologne; he also cites the Englishmen W. de Doncastre, Robertus Trowell, and Robertus de Brunham, and one or more anonymous theorists, as well as apparently drawing upon earlier work of his own. Hanboys's central concern is the expansion of the *gradus* system to a total of eight figures. The discussion ranges across two or three previous generations and four or more mensural systems; the most up-to-date practices of the *moderni* that Hanboys describes are rich in original doctrines. The *Summa* contains, moreover, the primary theoretical references to a number of idiosyncratic English notational practices that appear in numerous music sources. The *Summa* itself may once have been part of a larger treatise: in a brief extract that precedes it in Add. MS 8866 (fol. 64*r*) a cross-reference is given to an otherwise unknown multi-volume work by Hanboys that evidently dealt with plainchant ('ut dicit hanboys libro primo capitulo sexto').

PETER M. LEFFERTS

**Sources** Robertus de Handlo and Johannes Hanboys, *Regule / The rules, and Summa / The summa*, ed. and trans. P. M. Lefferts (1991) • B. Trowell, 'A fourteenth-century ceremonial motet and its composer', *Acta Musicologica*, 29 (1957), 65–75 • R. Bowers, 'Fixed points in the chronology of English fourteenth-century polyphony', *Music and Letters*, 71 (1990), 313–35 • A. Wathey, 'The peace of 1360–1369 and Anglo-French musical relations', *Early Music History*, 9 (1990), 129–74

**Archives** BL, Add. MS 8866

# PICTURE CREDITS

Grigg, Edward William Macleay, first Baron Altrincham (1879–1955)—© National Portrait Gallery, London

Grigg, Sir (Percy) James (1890–1964)—© National Portrait Gallery, London

Grimaldi, Joseph (1778–1837)—Garrick Club / the art archive

Grimond, Joseph, Baron Grimond (1913–1993)—© National Portrait Gallery, London

Grimshaw, William (1708–1763)—© National Portrait Gallery, London

Grimston, Edward (*d.* 1478)—© The National Gallery, London

Grimston, Edward (1507/8–1600)—reproduced by permission of the Earl of Verulam. Photograph: Photographic Survey, Courtauld Institute of Art, London

Grimston, Sir Harbottle, second baronet (1603–1685)—© National Portrait Gallery, London

Grindal, Edmund (1516x20–1583)—The Dean and Chapter of Canterbury, photograph Mike Waterman

Grisewood, Frederick Henry (1888–1972)—© National Portrait Gallery, London

Grisi, Giulia (1810?–1869)—© Royal Academy of Music

Gronow, Rees Howell (1794–1865)—© National Portrait Gallery, London

Grose, Francis (*bap.* 1731, *d.* 1791)—Scottish National Portrait Gallery

Gross, (Imre) Anthony Sandor (1905–1984)—© reserved; Belgrave Gallery, London & St Ives

Grosseteste, Robert (*c.*1170–1253)—The British Library

Grossmith, George (1847–1912)—© National Portrait Gallery, London

Grosvenor, Benjamin (1676–1758)—by permission of Dr Williams's Library

Grosvenor, Hugh Lupus, first duke of Westminster (1825–1899)—by kind permission of His Grace the Duke of Westminster OBE, TD, DL, on behalf of himself and his Trustees

Grosvenor, Richard, first Earl Grosvenor (1731–1802)—private collection; Photograph: Photographic Survey, Courtauld Institute of Art, London

Grosvenor, Robert, first marquess of Westminster (1767–1845)—by kind permission of His Grace the Duke of Westminster OBE, TD, DL, on behalf of himself and his Trustees

Grosvenor, Sir Thomas, third baronet (1655–1700)—by kind permission of His Grace the Duke of Westminster OBE, TD, DL, on behalf of himself and his Trustees

Grote, George (1794–1871)—© National Portrait Gallery, London

Grote, Harriet (1792–1878)—The Royal Bank of Scotland Group Art Collection

Grove, Sir George (1820–1900)—© National Portrait Gallery, London

Grove, Henry (1684–1738)—by permission of Dr Williams's Library

Grove, Robert (*c.*1634–1696)—by permission of the Master and Fellows of St John's College, Cambridge

Grove, Sir William Robert (1811–1896)—© National Portrait Gallery, London

Groves, Sir Charles Barnard (1915–1992)—© News International Newspapers Ltd

Grubb, Sir Kenneth George (1900–1980)—© National Portrait Gallery, London

Gryn, Hugo Gabriel (1930–1996)—© Mark Gerson; collection National Portrait Gallery, London

Gubbins, Sir Colin McVean (1896–1976)—© National Portrait Gallery, London

Guedalla, Philip (1889–1944)—© Estate of Sir William Rothenstein / National Portrait Gallery, London

Guest, Edwin (1800–1880)—reproduced by kind permission of the Master and Fellows of Gonville and Caius College, Cambridge; photograph by Christopher Hurst

Guest, Sir (Josiah) John, first baronet (1785–1852)—© National Portrait Gallery, London

Guildford, Sir Henry (1489–1532)—The Royal Collection © 2004 HM Queen Elizabeth II

Guingand, Sir Francis Wilfred de (1900–1979)—© National Portrait Gallery, London

Guinness, Sir Alec (1914–2000)—© Kenneth Hughes / National Portrait Gallery, London

Guinness, Sir Benjamin Lee, first baronet (1798–1868)—National Museum of Ireland; photograph © National Portrait Gallery, London

Guinness, Edward Cecil, first earl of Iveagh (1847–1927)—© National Portrait Gallery, London

Guinness, Henry Grattan (1835–1910)—© National Portrait Gallery, London

Guinness, Rupert Edward Cecil Lee, second earl of Iveagh (1874–1967)—© National Portrait Gallery, London

Guise, John (1682/3–1765)—Christ Church, Oxford

Gulbenkian, Calouste Sarkis (1869–1955)—by courtesy of the Gulbenkian Museum, Lisbon

Gully, John (1783–1863)—© National Portrait Gallery, London

Gully, William Court, first Viscount Selby (1835–1909)—© National Portrait Gallery, London

Gunn, Sir (Herbert) James (1893–1964)—Estate of the Artist

Gunn, Neil Miller (1891–1973)—Trustees of the National Library of Scotland

Gunn, Ronald Campbell (1808–1881)—Collection Royal Botanic Gardens, Kew; © reserved in the photograph

Gunning, Peter (1614–1684)—by permission of the Master and Fellows of St John's College, Cambridge

Gunther, Robert William Theodore (1869–1940)—© National Portrait Gallery, London

Guppy, (Agnes) Elisabeth (1838–1917)—© National Portrait Gallery, London

Gurney, Edmund (1847–1888)—© National Portrait Gallery, London

Gurney, Sir Goldsworthy (1793–1875)—© National Portrait Gallery, London

Gurney, Ivor Bertie (1890–1937)—© reserved; The British Library; photograph National Portrait Gallery, London

Gurney, Joseph John (1788–1847)—© National Portrait Gallery, London

Gurwood, John (1790–1845)—© National Portrait Gallery, London

Guthrie, Thomas (1803–1873)—© National Portrait Gallery, London

Guthrie, Sir (William) Tyrone (1900–1971)—© Cecil Beaton Archive, Sotheby's; collection National Portrait Gallery, London

Gützlaff, Karl Friedrich August (1803–1851)—© National Portrait Gallery, London

Guy, William Augustus (*bap.* 1810, *d.* 1885)—Wellcome Library, London

Gwatkin, Henry Melvill (1844–1916)—by permission of the Master, Fellows, and Scholars of Emmanuel College in the University of Cambridge

Gwyer, Barbara Elizabeth (1881–1974)—by kind permission of the Principal and Fellows of St Hugh's College, Oxford / Freeth family

Gwyn, Eleanor (1651?–1687)—© National Portrait Gallery, London

Gwynn, Stephen Lucius (1864–1950)—© Estate of Sir William Rothenstein / National Portrait Gallery, London

Haag, (Johann) Carl (1820–1915)—© National Portrait Gallery, London

Haak, Theodore (1605–1690)—© The Royal Society

Habersham, James (1713–1775)—Collection of Telfair Museum of Art, Savannah, Georgia; Bequest of Emma Cheves Wilkins

Hackenschmidt, George (1877–1968)—Getty Images - Hulton Archive

Hacket, John (1592–1670)—The Master and Fellows, Trinity College, Cambridge

Hackett, Sir John Winthrop (1910–1997)—© National Portrait Gallery, London

Hackman, James (*bap.* 1752, *d.* 1779)—© National Portrait Gallery, London

Haddock, Sir Richard (*c.*1629–1715)—MOD Art Collection, London

Haddow, Sir Alexander (1907–1976)—© National Portrait Gallery, London

Haden, Sir Francis Seymour (1818–1910)—© National Portrait Gallery, London

Hadow, Sir (William) Henry (1859–1937)—© National Portrait Gallery, London

Hadrian (AD 76–138)—© Copyright The British Museum

Haggard, Sir (Henry) Rider (1856–1925)—© National Portrait Gallery, London

Haghe, Louis (1806–1885)—© National Portrait Gallery, London

Hahn, Kurt Matthias Robert Martin (1886–1974)—© National Portrait Gallery, London

Haig, Douglas, first Earl Haig (1861–1928)—© National Portrait Gallery, London

Hailey, (William) Malcolm, Baron Hailey (1872–1969)—© National Portrait Gallery, London

Hailstone, John (1759–1847)—The Master and Fellows, Trinity College, Cambridge

Hailwood, (Stanley) Michael Bailey (1940–1981)—Getty Images - Bob Aylott

Haines, Joseph (*d.* 1701)—Mander & Mitchenson Theatre Collection

Haldane, Charlotte (1894–1969)—© reserved; private collection; photograph National Portrait Gallery, London

Haldane, John Burdon Sanderson (1892–1964)—© Estate of Claude Rogers / The College Art Collections, University of London

Haldane, John Scott (1860–1936)—The de László Foundation; Witt Library, Courtauld Institute of Art, London

Haldane, Richard Burdon, Viscount Haldane (1856–1928)—V&A Images, The Victoria and Albert Museum

Haldane, Robert (1772–1854)—© National Portrait Gallery, London

Hale, Kathleen (1898–2000)—Getty Images - Kurt Hutton

Hale, Sir Mathew (1609–1676)—© National Portrait Gallery, London

Hale, Richard (1670–1728)—by permission of the Royal College of Physicians, London

Hale, Warren Stormes (1791–1872)—Guildhall Art Gallery, Corporation of London

Hales, Stephen (1677–1761)—© National Portrait Gallery, London

Haley, Sir William John (1901–1987)—BBC Picture Archives

Halford, Sir Henry, first baronet (1766–1844)—by permission of the Royal College of Physicians, London

Haliburton, James (1788–1862)—Hastings Museum and Art Gallery; Greenhalf Photography

Haliburton, Thomas Chandler (1796–1865)—© National Portrait Gallery, London

Hall, Adelaide Louise Estelle (1901–1993)—Getty Images - Walery

Hall, Augusta, Lady Llanover (1802–1896)—© reserved

Hall, Benjamin, Baron Llanover (1802–1867)—© National Portrait Gallery, London

Hall, Sir (Alfred) Daniel (1864–1942)—© National Portrait Gallery, London

Hall, Henry Robert (1898–1989)—© National Portrait Gallery, London

Hall, James (1755–1826)—© National Portrait Gallery, London

Hall, John (1633–1710)—Bristol Museums and Art Gallery

Hall, John (1739–1797)—© National Portrait Gallery, London

Hall, Joseph (1574–1656)—© National Portrait Gallery, London

Hall, Christopher Newman (1816–1902)—© National Portrait Gallery, London

Hall, Peter Andrew (1936–1996)—© reserved; News International Syndication; photograph National Portrait Gallery, London

Hall, Sir (William) Reginald (1870–1943)—© National Portrait Gallery, London

Hall, Robert (1764–1831)—Leicester Museum, on loan from the Trustees of the Belvoir Street Chapel / Bridgeman Art Library

Hall, (William) Stephen Richard King-, Baron King-Hall (1893–1966)—© National Portrait Gallery, London

Hallahan, Margaret Mary (1802–1868)—English Dominican Congregation, Stone

Hallam, Henry (1777–1859)—© National Portrait Gallery, London

Hallé, Sir Charles (1819–1895)—© National Portrait Gallery, London

Hallé, Wilma, Lady Hallé (1838?–1911)—© National Portrait Gallery, London

Halley, Edmond (1656–1742)—© National Portrait Gallery, London

Hallifax, Samuel (1733–1790)—Collection Trinity Hall, Cambridge; photograph © E. Leigh

Hallowes, Odette Marie Céline (1912–1995)—The Imperial War Museum, London

Halsey, Sir Lionel (1872–1949)—© National Portrait Gallery, London

Hambledon cricket club (*act.* *c.*1750–*c.*1796)—© National Portrait Gallery, London

Hamel, Gustav Wilhelm (1889–1914)—Ken Harman Collection

Hamey, Baldwin, the younger (1600–1676)—by permission of the Royal College of Physicians, London

Hamilton, Alexander (1757–1804)—© reserved

Hamilton, Anne, *suo jure* duchess of Hamilton (1632–1716)—in the collection of Lennoxlove House; photograph courtesy the Scottish National Portrait Gallery

Hamilton, Anthony, Count Hamilton in the French nobility (1644/5?–1719)—in the collection of Lennoxlove House, Haddington

Hamilton, Charles Harold St John (1876–1961)—© reserved

Hamilton, (Mary) Cicely (1872–1952)—© National Portrait Gallery, London

Hamilton, David (1768–1843)—© Scottish National Portrait Gallery

Hamilton, Douglas Douglas-, fourteenth duke of Hamilton and eleventh duke of Brandon (1903–1973)—© National Portrait Gallery, London

Hamilton, Sir Edward Walter (1847–1908)—© National Portrait Gallery, London

Hamilton, Elizabeth, Countess de Gramont [La Belle Hamilton] (1641–1708)—The Royal Collection © 2004 HM Queen Elizabeth II

Hamilton, Elizabeth (1756?–1816)—Scottish National Portrait Gallery

Hamilton, Emma, Lady Hamilton (*bap.* 1765, *d.* 1815)—© National Portrait Gallery, London

Hamilton, Lord George Francis (1845–1927)—© National Portrait Gallery, London

Hamilton, Gustavus, first Viscount Boyne (1642–1723)—© private collection; photograph reproduced with the kind permission of the Trustees of the National Museums & Galleries of Northern Ireland

Hamilton, Hugh Douglas (1739–1808)—© reserved

Hamilton, Sir Ian Standish Monteith (1853–1947)—© Tate, London, 2004

Hamilton, James, second earl of Arran, and duke of Châtelherault in the French nobility (*c.*1519–1575)—in the collection of Lennoxlove House; photograph courtesy the Scottish National Portrait Gallery

Hamilton, James, first Viscount Claneboye (*c.*1560–1644)—Castle Ward, The Bangor Collection (The National Trust). Photograph: Photographic Survey, Courtauld Institute of Art, London

Hamilton, James, first duke of Hamilton (1606–1649)—Scottish National Portrait Gallery

Hamilton, James, fourth duke of Hamilton and first duke of Brandon (1658–1712)—in the collection of Lennoxlove House, Haddington

Hamilton, James, first duke of Abercorn (1811–1885)—© National Portrait Gallery, London

Hamilton, James, second duke of Abercorn (1838–1913)—© National Portrait Gallery, London

Hamilton, John, second Lord Belhaven and Stenton (1656–1708)—Scottish National Portrait Gallery

Hamilton, John Andrew, Viscount Sumner (1859–1934)—© National Portrait Gallery, London

Hamilton, Lillias Anna (1858–1925)—Wellcome Library, London

Hamilton, Mary Agnes (1882–1966)—© reserved; photograph National Portrait Gallery, London

Hamilton, (Anthony Walter) Patrick (1904–1962)—© National Portrait Gallery, London

Hamilton, Sir Robert George Crookshank (1836–1895)—© National Portrait Gallery, London

Hamilton, Thomas, earl of Melrose and first earl of Haddington (1563–1637)—Scottish National Portrait Gallery

Hamilton, Thomas, sixth earl of Haddington (1680–1735)—in the collection of the Earl of Haddington

Hamilton, Thomas (1784–1858)—in the collection of the Royal Scottish Academy

Hamilton, Walter Kerr (1808–1869)—© National Portrait Gallery, London

Hamilton, William, second duke of Hamilton (1616–1651)—The Royal Collection © 2004 HM Queen Elizabeth II

Hamilton [Douglas], William, third duke of Hamilton (1634–1694)—in the collection of Lennoxlove House; photograph courtesy the Scottish National Portrait Gallery

Hamilton, William, of Bangour (1704–1754)—Scottish National Portrait Gallery

Hamilton, Sir William (1731–1803)—© National Portrait Gallery, London

Hamilton, William Richard (1777–1859)—© National Portrait Gallery, London

Hamilton, Sir William Rowan (1805–1865)—© National Portrait Gallery, London

Hamilton, Sir William Stirling, baronet (1788–1856)—© National Portrait Gallery, London

Hamley, Sir Edward Bruce (1824–1893)—© National Portrait Gallery, London

Hammerton, Sir John Alexander (1871–1949)—© National Portrait Gallery, London

Hammond, Edmund, Baron Hammond (1802–1890)—© Crown copyright in photograph: UK Government Art Collection

Hammond, Dame Joan Hood (1912–1996)—Getty Images - Hulton Archive

Hammond, (John) Lawrence Le Breton (1872–1949)—© National Portrait Gallery, London

Hammond, Walter Reginald (1903–1965)—© National Portrait Gallery, London

Hamnett, Nina (1890–1956)—© Estate of Roger Fry; Witt Library, Courtauld Institute of Art, London

Hamond, Sir Andrew Snape, first baronet (1738–1828)—© National Portrait Gallery, London

Hampden, Augustus Charles Hobart-(1822–1886)—© National Portrait Gallery, London

Hampden, Renn Dickson (1793–1868)—courtesy of the Provost and Fellows of Oriel College, Oxford; photograph © Studio Edmark